**THE INTERNATIONAL
DICTIONARY OF FILMS AND
FILMMAKERS**

FILMS

THE INTERNATIONAL DICTIONARY OF FILMS AND FILMMAKERS

FILMS

Editor:
Christopher Lyon

Assistant Editor:
Susan Doll

A Perigee Book

Perigee Books
are published by
The Putnam Publishing Group
200 Madison Avenue
New York, NY 10016

Library of Congress Cataloging in Publication Data

Main entry under title:

The International dictionary of films and filmmakers.

  Contents: v. 1. Films.
  1. Moving-pictures—Plots, themes, etc.
I. Lyon, Christopher, date.   II. Doll,
Susan, date.
PN1997.8.I58   1985   791.43′03   85-6310
ISBN 0-399-51178-4 (v. 1)

Printed in the United States of America
1   2   3   4   5   6   7   8   9   10

CONTENTS

INTRODUCTION

This volume is the first of four in the series *International Dictionary of Films and Filmmakers*. Volumes II-IV are devoted to persons: *Directors/Filmmakers, Actors and Actresses,* and *Writers and Production Artists*. This first volume answers the need for a comprehensive reference source, with bibliographies, on the most widely-studied films. The difficulty in such an enterprise is in choosing, from among the thousands that ought to be included, those films that can be adequately covered in a single volume. In this selection process we have relied on a distinguished advisory board.

The films chosen reflect, to some extent, the individual interests of the advisers and, in a broader sense, current concerns of North American, British, and Western European film scholarship and criticism. The selection criteria suggested to the advisers were oriented toward "film as art," and emphasized formal and technical aspects of film: 1) technical innovation resulting in the enhancement of film's expressive potential; 2) formal innovation in terms of structural techniques or narrative strategies now recognized as contributions to the language of film; 3) generic significance through initiating a genre, being an especially mature or successful example of one, or involving an innovative syntheses of established genres; 4) significance as a prime example of a major filmmaker's characteristic themes, style, or concerns; 5) ideological or cultural significance, a criterion intended as leavening for the first four in that it allowed consideration of films relatively undistinguished in artistic or technical terms which nevertheless retain exceptional interest as social documents or cultural artifacts. We asked advisers to give special consideration to films that illuminate the history of filmmaking as a popular art and industry.

We gratefully acknowledge the assistance of all our advisers and contributors, and wish particularly to thank Maria Racheva in Munich and Vladimír Opěla and his colleagues at the Czechoslovak Film Archives for their considerable help with Eastern European films; John Mraz in Mexico for his work on Cuban and Mexican cinema; and Ib Monty, Director of the Danish Film Museum, for his help with Scandinavian film. We are indebted to Dudley Andrew at the University of Iowa for his advice and assistance on French film; to Anthony Slide and Liam O'Leary who have been most helpful on early films; Jack C. Ellis, chairman of Radio-TV-Film at Northwestern University, for his work on British documentaries; Robin Wood and Roger Manvell who have been extremely generous with their time; P. Adams Sitney and Fred Camper for their help on avant-garde and experimental film; and the many film scholars in the Chicago area that have given their time to this project.

Research for this volume was carried out principally at the University of Chicago where we received the assistance and early support of Professor Gerald Mast. A project of this scope could not have been undertaken without the help of the Computation Center at the University of Chicago and particularly James Lichtenstein, who designed the computerized editing system we have used and provided indispensable advice. We also wish to thank the Film Center of the School of the Art Institute of Chicago and its director Richard Peña; the Film Study Center of the Museum of Modern Art, New York, and especially Ron Magliozzi; Ephraim Katz, author of *The Film Encyclopedia*, for his advice and his hospitality in New York; Frances Thorpe of the British Film Institute who provided assistance at each stage of the project; and Patricia Coward who so efficiently carried out the research for this book done at the BFI.

ADVISERS AND CONTRIBUTORS

Advisers

Andrew, Dudley
Bardarsky, Dimitar
Barnouw, Erik
Bodeen, DeWitt
Brito, Rui Santana
Burgoyne, Robert
Ciment, Michel
Cook, David

Ellis, Jack C.
Everson, William K.
Gomery, Douglas
Kaplan, E. Ann
Katz, Ephraim
Kehr, Dave
Khanna, Satti
MacCann, Richard Dyer

Mast, Gerald
Monty, Ib
O'Leary, Liam
Peña, Richard
Rabinovitz, Lauren
Sitney, P. Adams
Slide, Anthony
Thorpe, Frances

Contributors

Affron, Charles
Affron, Mirella Jona
Andrew, Dudley
Armes, Roy
Bardarsky, Dimitar
Barnouw, Erik
Basinger, Jeanine
Baxter, John
Beck, Sandra L.
Bock, Audie
Bodeen, DeWitt
Bowers, Ronald
Bowles, Stephen E.
Boyajian, Marco Starr
Burton, Julianne
Camper, Fred
Chediak, Nat
Clements, William
Conley, Tom
Cook, David
Cripps, Thomas
Derry, Charles
Dunagan, Clyde Kelly
Dunbar, Robert
Edelman, Rob
Ellis, Jack C.
Elsner-Sommer, Gretchen

Erens, Patricia
Faller, Greg
Farnsworth, Rodney
Feinstein, Howard
Fern, Annette
FitzGerald, Theresa
Fulks, Barry A.
Gomery, Douglas
Gomez, Joseph
Hanson, Patricia King
Hanson, Steve
Harris, Ann
Heck-Rabi, Louise
Henry, Catherine
Hirano, Kyoko
Holdstein, Deborah H.
Johnson, Timothy
Kaminsky, Stuart M.
Kanoff, Joel
Kehr, Dave
Kemp, Philip
Khanna, Satti
Kovacs, Katherine Singer
Leab, Daniel
Lee, Sharon
Limbacher, James L.
Lockhart, Kimball

Lorenz, Janet E.
Lowry, Ed
MacCann, Richard Dyer
Malpazzi, Frances M.
Mancini, Elaine
Manvell, Roger
Marchetti, Gina
Mast, Gerald
McElhaney, Joseph
Merhaut, G.
Merritt, Russell
Michaels, Lloyd
Milicia, Joseph
Monty, Ib
Mraz, John
Murphy, William T.
Narducy, Ray
Nastav, Dennis
O'Leary, Liam
Obalil, Linda J.
Palmer, R. Barton
Peña, Richard
Phillips, Gene D.
Poague, Leland
Polan, Dana B.
Porton, Richard
Rabinovitz, Lauren

Racheva, Maria
Reynolds, Herbert
Robson, Arthur G.
Rubinstein, E.
Saeli, Marie
Salvage, Barbara
Schade, W. Curtis
Seiter, Ellen E.
Selig, Michael
Shochat, Ella

Silet, Charles L.P.
Simmon, Scott
Sitney, P. Adams
Slade, Tony
Slide, Anthony
Small, Edward S.
Smoodin, Eric
Snyder, Thomas
Starr, Cecile
Thompson, Frank

Tomlinson, Doug
Tsiantis, Lee
Tudor, Anthony
Urgošikova, B.
Welsh, James
West, Dennis
White, M.B.
Winning, Robert
Wood, Robin

Translators

Robert Streit —
    Czechoslovakian

Zita Laus —
    Portuguese

Lillian Chorvat —
    Czechoslovakian

Stanley F. Smelhaus —
    Czechoslovakian

THE INTERNATIONAL DICTIONARY OF FILMS AND FILMMAKERS:
FILMS

Man of Marble (see Czlowiek z marmuru)
Man Who Shot Liberty Valance, The
Man with a Movie Camera, The
   (see Chelovek s kino apparatom)
Manhattan
March of Time, The (newsreel series)
María Candelaria
Mark of Zorro, The (1920)
Marriage of Maria Braun, The (see Die
   Ehe der Maria Braun)
M★A★S★H
Mat
Matka Joanna od aniolów
Maxim Trilogy, The
Mean Streets
Medium Cool
Meg ker a nep
Meet Me in St. Louis
Memorias de subdesarollo (Memories of
   Underdevelopment)
Menilmontant
Mephisto
Merry Widow, The (1925)
Meshes of the Afternoon
Metropolis
Million, Le
Miracle of Morgan's Creek, The
Miracolo a Milano (Miracle in Milan)
Mr. Hulot's Holiday(see Les Vacances de
   Monsieur Hulot)
Mr. Smith Goes to Washington
Miss Julie (see Fröken Julie)
Moana
Modern Times
Mörder sind unter uns, Die
Morte a Venezia
Mother (see Mat)
Mother Joan of the Angels
   (see Matka Joanna od aniolów)
Murderers Are Among Us, The (see Die
   Mörder sind unter uns)
Murmur of the Heart
   (see Souffle au coeur)
My Darling Clementine
My Life to Live (see Vivre sa vie)

Naked City, The
Naked Night, The (see Gycklarnas afton)
Naniwa ereji
Nanook of the North
Napoléon
Nashville
Neobychanye priklyucheniya Mistera
   Vesta v strane bolsheviko
Nibelungen, Die (Parts 1 and 2)
Night and Fog (see Nuit et brouillard)
Night at the Opera, A
Night Mail
Night of the Hunter, The
Night on Bald Mountain, A (see
   Une Nuit sur le mont chauve)
Ningen no joken
Ninotchka
Nobi
Noire de…, La
North by Northwest

Nosferatu (1921)
Notte, La
1900 (Novecento)
Now Voyager
Noz w wodzie
Nuit et brouillard
Nuit sur le mont chauve, Une
Nutty Professor, The

O slavnosti a hostech
Obchod na korze
Oktiabr (October)
Old Czech Legends
   (see Staré povĕsti české)
Old Dark House, The
Olvidados, Los
Olympia
On the Town
On the Waterfront
Once There Was a War
   (see Der var engang en krig)
Once Upon a Time in the West
One Way or Another
   (see De cierta manera)
Ordet
Orfeu negro
Orphée (Orpheus)
Osaka Elegy (see Naniwa ereji)
Ossessione
Otro Francisco, El (The Other Francisco)
Ostrě sledované vlaky
8 ½ (Otto e mezzo)
Our Trip to Africa
   (see Unsere Afrikareise)
Ox-Bow Incident, The

Paisá
Pandora's Box (see
   Die Büchse der Pandora)
Parapluies de Cherbourg, Les
Partie de campagne, Une
Passenger, The
   (see Professione: Reporter)
Passion de Jeanne d'Arc, La
Pather Panchali (see Apu Trilogy)
Patton
Peeping Tom
Pépé-le-Moko
Persona
Phantom Chariot, The (see Körkarlen)
Phantom of the Opera, The
Philadelphia Story, The
Pickpocket
Pirosmani
Place in the Sun, A
Playtime
Popiól i diament
Portrait of Teresa (see Retrato de Teresa)
Potemkin (see Bronenosets Potemkin)
Potomok Chingis-Khana
Primary
Primera carga al machete, La
Private Life of Henry VIII, The
Procès, Le
Professione: Reporter
Promised Land, The

(see La Tierra prometida)
Psycho
Public Enemy, The
Pugni in tasca, I
Putyovka v zhizn

Quai des brumes, Le
Quatre Cent Coups, Les

Raiders of the Lost Ark
Rashomon
Rear Window
Rebel Without a Cause
Red and the White, The (see Csillagosak ,
   katonák)
Red Desert, The (see Meg ker a nep)
Red River
Redes, Los
Règle du jeu, La
Report on the Party and the Guests, A (see
   O slavnosti a hostech)
Retour à la raison, Le
Retrato de Teresa
Return of the Jedi, The (see Star Wars)
Rien que les heures
Rififi (see Du Rififi chez les hommes)
Rio Bravo
River, The
Road to Life, The (see Putyovka v zhizn)
Roaring Twenties, The
Rocco e i suoi fratelli
   (Rocco and His Brothers)
Rocky
Rocky Horror Picture Show, The
Roma, città aperta (Rome, Open City)
Ronde, La
Room at the Top
Rosemary's Baby
Rules of the Game (see La Règle du jeu)

Safety Last
Saikaku ichidai onna
Salamandre, Le
Salt of the Earth, The
Salvatore Giuliano
Samma no aji
Sang des bêtes, le
Sang d'un poète, le
Sansho dayu (Sansho the Bailiff)
Saturday Night and Sunday Morning
Sawdust and Tinsel
   (see Gycklarnas afton)
Scarface (1932)
Scarlet Empress, The
Schatten
Sciuscia
Scorpio Rising
Searchers, The
Seppuku
Seven Samurai, The
   (see Shichinin no samurai)
7th Heaven
Seventh Seal, The (see Sjunde inseglet)
Shadows of Forgotten Ancestors (see
   Teni zabytykh predkov)
Shane

À BOUT DE SOUFFLE. Breathless. Production: Impéria Films, Société Nouvelle de Cinèma; black and white, 35mm; running time: 89 mins. Released 16 March 1960, Paris.

Produced by Georges de Beauregard; screenplay by Jean-Luc Godard; from an original treatment by François Truffaut; directed by Jean-Luc Godard; photography by Raoul Coutard; edited by Cécile Decugis with Lila Herman; sound by Jacques Maumont; music by Martial Solal from Mozart's Clarinet Concerto, K.622; artistic and technical advisor: Claude Chabrol.

Filmed 17 August-15 September 1959 in Paris and Marseilles; cost: 400,000 N.F. (about $120,000); Prix Jean Vigo, 1960; Best Direction, Berlin Film Festival, 1960.

Cast: Jean Seberg (*Patricia Franchini*); Jean-Paul Belmondo (*Michel Poiccard, alias Laszlo Kovacs*); Daniel Boulanger (*Police Inspector Vital*); Henri-Jacques Huet (*Antonio Berrutti*); Roger Hanin (*Carl Zombach*); Van Doude (*Journalist Van Doude*); Liliane Robin (*Liliane*); Michel Favre (*Plainclothes inspector*); Jean-Pierre Melville (*Parvulesco*); Claude Mansard (*Used car dealer, Claudius*); Jean Domarchi (*Drunk*); Jean-Luc Godard (*Informer*); André-S. Labarthe, Jean-Louis Richard, and François Mareuil (*Journalists*); Richard Balducci (*Tolmatchoff*); Philippe de Broca; Michael Mourlet; Jean Douchet; Louiguy; Virginie Ullman; Emile Villion; José Bénazéraf; Madame Paul; Raymond Ravanbaz.

Publications:

Scripts—*A bout de souffle* (screenplay plus Truffaut's original scenerio and quotations from reviews) in *L'Avant-Scène du cinéma* (Paris), March 1968; *Fino all'ultimo respiro* in *Cinque film* edited by Gianni Rondolino, Rome 1972; *A bout de souffle* by Jean-Luc Godard, Paris 1974; reviews—by François Truffaut in *Radio-Cinéma-Télévision* (Paris), 1 October 1959; "Petit lexique de la nouvelle vague" by Pierre Billard et al. in *Cinéma 60* (Paris), April 1960; "*A bout de souffle*" by Marcel Martin in *Cinéma 60* (Paris), May 1960; "*A bout de souffle*" by Gene Moskowitz in *Variety* (New York), 4 February 1960; "Cubist Crime" in *Time* (New York), 17 February 1961; "*Breathless*" by Arlene Croce in *Film Quarterly* (Berkeley), spring 1961; review by Bosley Crowther in *The New York Times*, 8 February 1961; review by Gordon Gow in *Films and Filming* (London), August 1961; "Adventures of an Anti-Hero" by Stanley Kauffmann in *The New Republic* (New York), 13 February 1961; review by Robert Hatch in *Nation* (New York), 11 March 1961; books— "The New Wave: Jean-Luc Godard" in *Cinema Eye, Cinema Ear* by John Russell Taylor, New York 1964; "Jean-Luc Godard: *A bout de souffle*" in *Regards neufs sur le cinéma* by Max Egly, Paris 1965; "*A bout de souffle*" in *Le Cinéma, art du XXe siecle* by Howard Lawson, Paris 1965; "*Breathless*" in *70 Years of Cinema* by Peter Cowie, New York 1969; "*Breathless*" in *Dwight MacDonald on Movies* by Dwight MacDonald, Englewood Cliffs, New Jersey 1969; "A bout de souffle" in *The Films of Jean-Luc Godard* by Charles Barr, edited by Ian Cameron, New York 1970; *Cinéma et société moderne: le cinéma de 1968 à 1968: Godard, Antonioni, Resnais, Robbe-Grillet* by Annie Goldmann, Paris 1971; *Jean-Luc Godard: 'Breathless' (1959). Close-up* by Marsha Kinder and Beverle Houston, New York 1972; *The New Wave* by James Monaco, New York 1976; articles— "Un Cinéma des gens de lettres" by Jean Douchet in *Arts* (Paris), no.730, 1959; "Jean-Luc Godard: 'Je ne suis pas à bout de souffle" in *Arts* (Paris), 23 March 1960; "Personality of the Month" in *Films and Filming* (London), October 1960; "Mon Film est un documentaire sur Jean Seberg et J.-P. Belmondo" by Yvonnne Baby in *Le Monde* (Paris), 18 March 1960; "*A bout de souffle*" by Jean de Baroncelli in *Le Monde* (Paris), 18 March 1960; "Films nouveaux: *A Bout de souffle*" by J. Chevallier in *Image et son* (Paris), April 1960; "Views of the New Wave" by Louis Marcorelles in *Sight and Sound* (London), spring 1960; "Jean-Luc Godard" by Luc Mouller in *Cahiers du cinéma* (Paris), April 1960; "Quai des Brumes 1960" by Georges Sadoul in *Les Lettres françaises* (Paris), March/April 1960; "*A bout de souffle*" by Gilbert Salachas in *Téléciné* (Paris), May/June 1960; "Quoi de neuf (suite): *A bout de souffle*" by Louis Seguin in *Positif* (Paris), no.33, 1960; "Movies Abroad: Larcenous Talent" in *Time* (New York), 17 March 1961; "Cinema of Appearance" by Gabriel Pearson and Eric Rhode in *Sight and Sound* (London), autumn 1961; "The Sound Track" by T.M.F. Steen in *Films in Review* (New York), August/September 1961; article by Arlene Croce in *Film Quarterly* (Berkeley), spring 1961; "Entretien avec Jean-Luc Godard" by Jean Collet et al. in *Cahiers du cinéma* (Paris), December 1962; "An Interview with Jean-Luc Godard" by Herbert Feinstein in *Film Quarterly* (Berkeley), spring 1964; "*A bout de souffle*" by Jean-Paul Warren and Raymond Lefebvre in *Image et son: Revue du cinéma* (Paris), September/October 1964; "Son of Bogie" by R. Grenier in *Esquire* (New York), January 1966; "The Verge and After: Film by 1966" by Vernon Young in *Hudson Review* (Nutley, New Jersey), spring 1966; "Review of *Breathless*" by Mel Bochner in *Arts* (New York), May 1968; "The Truth 24 Times a Second" by Raymond Solokov in *Newsweek* (New York), 12 February 1968; "Breathless" by Debbie Burk in *Cinema Texas Program Notes* (Austin, Texas), 15 March 1973; "*A bout de souffle*" by C. Bechtold in *Cinématographe* (Paris), May/June 1975.

* * *

A bout de souffle was the first feature directed by Jean-Luc Godard and one of the films introducing the French New Wave in the late 1950s. Godard had made several short films before *A bout de souffle*, but this feature established the international reputation of the director who is regarded as one of the most important filmmakers of the 1960s.

The film's story is fairly simple. Michel Poiccard (Jean-Paul Belmondo), a small time hood, casually kills a policeman. He goes to Paris to collect some money in order to leave the country, and tries to convince his American girlfriend Patricia Franchini (Jean Seberg) to go with him. She is less interested in accompanying him than she is in playing the role of an American intellectual in Paris. (She hawks the New York *Herald Tribune* on the Champs-Elysées while trying to establish herself as a journalist.) When Michel finally secures the money he needs and is ready to leave the city, Patricia betrays him to the police, and he is shot as he half-heartedly attempts to escape.

This basic sequence of events is the minimal thread of continuity that holds the filmic narrative together. However, causal development and character motivation in the traditional sense are relatively loose. While the film does not reject narrative conventions as a whole, it goes a long way towards weakening the tight-knit structure and explanatory mechanisms affiliated with dominant narrative. The film's visual construction works even more aggressively against conventional film style. It systematically departs from the aesthetic guidelines and rules defined by continuity editing, relying variously on long-take sequences (often shot with hand-held camera) and jump cutting. The free-wheeling, almost casual, use of the camera is typical of the New Wave style. Within individual scenes the systematic use of jump cuts and depiction of rambling, repetitious conversations are a way of testing the limits of narrative film style. It often seems that scenes are conceived to show what can be done with cinema rather than to develop the story in a coherent fashion.

While the film seems to willfully disregard the norms of commercial, studio filmmaking, it consistently refers to and plays with aspects of the American cinema. The main character, Michel, styles himself in the image of Humphrey Bogart. Early in the film he is seen standing by a movie poster admiring his hero's picture; in comparison his own status as a modern "tough guy" is only a weak imitation. The police on Michel's trail are similarly pale shadows of their predecessors in American films; they are bumbling, somewhat comical figures. The character of Patricia, and her portrayal by Seberg, refers to the role Seberg played in Otto Preminger's *Bonjour Tristesse*. There are also scenes constructed to "quote" sequences from American films. In Patricia's bedroom, Michel looks at her through a rolled-up poster. The camera zooms through the poster tube, followed by a cut to a close-up of Michel and Patricia kissing. These shots mimic a scene from Samuel Fuller's *Forty Guns* (with a rifle barrel instead of a poster) described by Godard in a review of the film as a moment of pure cinema.

The film's playfulness extends beyond the inside jokes that refer to other films. The sometimes abrupt shifts in tone, style, and plot development within and between scenes are an investigation of (and challenge to) the medium, based in familiarity with and affection for its history. The opening of the film is instructive in this regard. Michel delivers a rambling monologue as he drives through the French countryside. He is speeding, and a policeman starts to follow him. Michel drives off the road, and when he is followed, shoots the policeman. The murder is casual in manner and lacking in clear motive. It becomes almost a comic version of more serious crime dramas in which murders are fraught with tension and often defined as the act of ruthless or psychotic individuals. Because of his manner, the character of Michel is sometimes seen to exemplify the existentially alienated hero figure often found in New Wave films. Harsher critics condemn him as a character for his amoral, nihilistic behavior. However, this moralising attitude ignores the way in which the character derives from and parodies previous film hoodlums, and the appeal of the character as portrayed by Belmondo.

In various ways the film exemplifies the conjunction of a number of factors contributing to the French New Wave cinema. This includes the use of relatively new cameras (a lightweight Eclair, easily handheld); working with low budgets, which promoted location shooting and stories with contemporary settings; and the use of new personnel, including the star Belmondo and cameraman Raoul Coutard. In addition Godard brought a set of attitudes to filmmaking shared by his fellow New Wave directors, derived from his experience as a film critic in the 1950s. Among these was the belief that the director was the responsible creative individual behind a film, that film should be approached as a mode of personal expression, and a deep admiration for the visual style of many Hollywood films.

Beyond its status as a "New Wave film," *A bout de souffle* begins to define attitudes and concerns which are more fully developed in Godard's subsequent work. A broad range of cultural imagery is an integral part of the film's signifying material. Movie posters, art reproductions, and inserts of magazines and books not only function as elements of mise-en-scène, but also construct an image of contemporary life in terms of cultural collage. In addition the strategy of narrative digression is important, incorporating lengthy scenes to explore issues which do not serve to develop the story per se. In *A bout de souffle* Patricia's taking part in an interview with an author (played by French director Jean-Pierre Melville) functions in this way. Both of these practices testify to an interest in cinema as something more than a narrative medium in the conventional sense. As attention is directed to the ways in which filmic images and sounds create meaning, the very nature of cinematic signification becomes the central question for the director and his audience.

—M.B. White

À NOUS LA LIBERTÉ. Production: Tobis (Paris) and Filmsonor; black and white, 35mm, musical soundtrack with sound effects; running time: 97 mins. Released 31 December 1931.

Produced by Frank Clifford; screenplay by René Clair; directed by René Clair; photography by Georges Périnal; edited by René le Hénaff; sound by Hermann Storr; art direction by Lazare Meerson; music by Georges Auric, music directed by Armand Bernard; costumes designed by René Hubert; assistant director: Albert Valentin. Filmed 1931 in Tobis studios and around Paris.

Cast: Henri Marchand (*Emile*); Raymond Cordy (*Louis*); Rolla France (*Jeanne*); Paul Ollivier (*Paul Imaque, Jeanne's uncle*); Jacques Shelly (*Paul*); André Michaud (*Foreman*); Germaine Aussey (*Maud, Louis's mistress*); Alexandre d'Arcy (*Gigolo*); William Burke (*Leader of the gangsters*); Vincent Hyspa (*Speaker*); Léon Lorin (*Fussy official*).

Publications:

Scripts—"*A Nous la liberté*" by René Clair in *L'Avant-Scène du cinéma* (Paris), November 1968; '*A Nous La Liberté*' and '*Entr'Acte*': Films by René Clair translated and English descriptions by Richard Jacques and Nicola Hayden, New York 1970; books—*René Clair* by G. Viazzi, Milan 1946; *René Clair* by J. Bourgeois, Geneva 1949; *Un Maître du cinéma: René Clair* by Georges Charensol and Roger Régent, Paris 1952; *Tre maestri del cinema* by A. Solmi, Milan 1956; *René Clair, an Index* by Catherine De La Roche, London 1958; *The Great Films: 50 Golden Years of Motion Pictures* by Bosley Crowther, New York 1967; *René Clair* by Barthélemy Amengual, revised edition, Paris 1969; *René Clair* by Jean Mitry, Paris 1969; *Gotta Sing Gotta Dance* by John Kobal, London 1970; *Encountering Directors* by Charles Samuels, New York 1972; *René Clair* by Celia McGerr, Boston 1980; articles—"René Clair and Film Humor" by Harry Potamkin in *Hound and Horn* (New York), October/December 1932; "A Conversation with René Clair" by Bernard Causton in *Sight and Sound* (London), winter 1932-33; "The Films of René Clair" by Louis Jacobs in *New Theatre* (New York), February 1936; issue devoted to Clair, *Bianco e nero* (Rome), August/September 1951; article by Edward Connor and Edward Jablonski in *Films in Review* (New York), November 1954; article by Jerry Tallmer in *The Village Voice* (New York), 16 November 1955; "Cinema's First Immortal" by Charles Ford in *Films in Review* (New York), November 1960; "*A Nous la liberté* ...et la presse" in *L'Avant-Scène du cinéma* (Paris), November 1968; "L'arte del comico in René Clair" by V. Berti in *Bianco e nero* (Rome), March/April 1968; "A Conversation with René Clair" by John Baxter in *Focus on Film* (London), winter 1972; "A nous la liberté" by J. Pym in *Monthly Film Bulletin* (London), October 1977.

*   *   *

The fear of a static theatrical cinema resulting from the invention of the sound film was very soon dissipated by liberators such as Ernst Lubitsch and René Clair. With a concentration on music and movement while maintaining strict control over dialogue the cinema began to move again. Clair, with his first two films, had already established a style, and the cycle of development from which this style emerged is curious in itself. The French comedian Max Linder was a direct influence on Chaplin and the whole slapstick school which in turn inspired the young René Clair. And, as if the process of interchange of ideas seemed determined to go on, Chaplin in *Modern Times* drew inspiration from the assembly line sequence in Clair's *A nous la liberté*.

In this film Clair satirizes the industrial malaise which reduces man to the level of a machine. That satire may seem to weaken the human element but fun and joy take over as Clair falls so much in love with his characters that he passes that affection to the audience. One cannot even harbor a grudge against the villains because they too are ridiculously human. It is not difficult to see how the film failed to measure up to the demands of socially committed critics like Georges Sadoul.

Two companions of a jail-break are the protagonists of this musical comedy. One, played with eccentric sympathy by Raymond Cordy, is clever and successful and quickly rises in the world of industry. The other, played by Henri Marchand, wanders innocently throughout the film, willing to accept the unexpected. Even the joy of his escape from prison arises from a potentially tragic situation. His courtship is as artless as everything else he does.

Employing the talents of the brilliant art director Lazare Meerson, Clair uses the vast industrial complex to its fullest until it becomes a fun palace with plenty of room for chases and horseplay. Even the building is deflated. The joyful and carefree music of Georges Auric carries the film along, while Georges Périnal's camera exploits the large white surfaces of the superfactory and the brightness of the walls.

But it is not the technical excellence of the film which remains in one's mind. It is the puncturing of pomposity, the rejection of dehumanizing technical processes, the statement of essential human values and an appreciation of the incongruities of human existence. It is a far cry from the world of *Le Chapeau de paille d'Italie*, but the child-like delight in the demolition of the pretentious in Clair is common to both films. Not for him the sighs of high romance or the exaggerations of grand opera. His heart is always with ordinary people and their simple predicaments. He sees the world through the eyes of the characters Louis and Emile. Maybe his idea of Utopia is naive and impractical but it is an ideal which has been thought of by many people. In an age of mass regimentation and states it remains a recurring vision.

—Liam O'Leary

À PROPOS DE NICE. On the Subject of Nice. Black and white, 35mm; running time: about 25 mins. Premiered May or June 1930, Paris.

Scenario by Mr. and Mrs. Jean Vigo and Mr. and Mrs. Boris Kaufman; directed by Jean Vigo; photography by Boris Kaufman; edited by Jean Vigo.

Filmed winter 1929-March 1930 in Nice.

Publications:

Books—*Jean Vigo* by Harry Feldman and Joseph Feldman, London, 1951; *Jean Vigo* by Pierre Lherminier, Paris 1953; *Jean Vigo* by Jean Smith, New York 1971; *Jean Vigo* by P.E. Salles Gomes, Los Angeles, 1971; *Jean Vigo* by John M. Smith, New York 1972; *Documentary: A History of Non-Fiction Film* by Erik Barnouw, New York 1974; articles—"Jean Vigo" by Alberto Cavalcanti in *Cinema Quarterly* (Edinburgh, Scotland), winter 1935; "Life and Work of Jean Vigo" by James Agee in *Nation* (New York), 12 July 1947; "The Films of Jean Vigo" by H.G. Weinberg in *Cinema* (Beverly Hills), July 1947; "The Work of Jean Vigo" by George Barbarow in *Politics* 5, winter 1948; article by Barthélemy Amengual in *Positif* (Paris), May 1953; "Portrait of Vigo" by Dudley Shaw Ashton in *Film* (London), December 1955; "An Interview with Boris Kaufman" by Edouard De Laurot and Jonas Mekas in *Film Culture* (New York), summer 1955; "Jean Vigo et ses films" by Bernard Chardère in *Cinéma 55* (Paris), March 1955; issue on Vigo in *Etudes cinématographiques* (Paris), no.51-52, 1966; "*A propos de Nice*" by Claude Beylie in *Ecran* (Paris), July/August 1975; "Jean Vigo's *A propos de Nice*" by S. Liebman in *Millenium* (New York), winter 1977-78; "Towards a Social Cinema" by Jean Vigo in *Millenium* (New York), winter 1977-78; "*A Propos de Nice*" in *Travelling* (Lausanne, Switzerland), summer 1979.

*   *   *

Jean Vigo's reputation as a prodigy of the cinema rests on less than 200 minutes of film. His first venture, a silent documentary 25 minutes long, was *A propos de Nice*, and in it one can see immediately the energy and aptitude of this great talent. But *A propos de Nice* is far more than a biographical curio; it is one of the last films to come out of the fertile era of the French avant-garde and it remains one of the best examples to illustrate the blending of formal and social impulses in that epoch.

Confined to Nice on account of the tuberculosis both he and his wife were to die of, Vigo worked for a small company as assistant cameraman. When his father-in-law presented the young couple with a gift of $250, Jean promptly bought his own Debrie camera. In Paris in the summer of 1929 he haunted the ciné-club showings at the Vieux Colombier and at the Studio des Ursulines. There he met Boris Kaufman, a Russian emigre, brother of Dziga Vertov. Kaufman, already an established cameraman in the kino-eye tradition, was enthusiastic about Vigo's plan to make a film on the city of Nice. During the autumn of 1929 Kaufman and his wife labored over a script with the Vigos. From his work Jean began to save ends of film with which to load the Debrie and by year's end the filming was underway.

Originally planned as a variant of the city symphony, broken into its three movements (sea, land, and sky) *A propos de Nice* was destined to vibrate with more political energy than did *Berlin*, *Rien que les heures*, *Mannahatta*, or any of the other examples of this type. From the first, Vigo insisted that the travelogue approach be avoided. He wanted to pit the boredom of the upper classes at the shore and in the casinos against the struggle for life and death in the city's poorer backstreets.

The clarity of the script was soon abandoned. Unable to shoot "live" in the casinos and happy to follow the lead of their rushes, Vigo and Kaufman concentrated on the strength of particular images rather than on the continuity of a larger design. They were certain that design must emerge in the charged images themselves, which they could juxtapose in editing.

The power of the images derives from two sources, their clear-cut iconographic significance as social documents, and the extreme quality they enjoy as photographs, carefully (though not artfully) composed. Opposition is the ruling logic behind both these sources as they appear in the finished film, so that pictures of hotels, lounging women, wealthy tourists, and fancy roulette tables stand cut against tenements, decrepit children, garbage, and local forms of back-street gambling. In the carnival sequence which ends the film, the bursting power within the city's belly spills out onto the streets of the wealthy and dramatizes a conflict which geography tries to hide.

Formally the film opposes a two-dimensional optical schema, used primarily for the wealthy parts of town, to a tactile, nearly 3-D approach. Airplane shots and the general voyeurism of the "Promenade des Anglais" defines the wealthy as indolent observers of sports, while deep in the town itself everyone including the camera participates in the carnal dance of life, a dance whose eroticism is made explicit toward the film's end.

Entranced by Surrealism (at the premiere of this film Vigo paid homage to Luis Buñuel), the filmmakers used shockcuts with strongly symbolic images, like towering smokestacks and baroque cemeteries. A woman is stripped by a stop-action cut and a man becomes a lobster. Swift tilts topple a grand hotel like an earthquake. As he proclaimed in his address, this was to be a film with a documentary point of view. To him that meant hiding the camera to capture the look of things (Kaufman pushed along on a wheelchair along the Promenade cranking away under his blanket), and then editing what they collected to his own designs.

A propos de Nice is a messy film. Full of experimental techniques and frequently clumsy camerawork, it nevertheless exudes the energy of its creators and blares forth a message about social life. The city is built on indolence and gambling and ultimately on death, as its crazy cemetery announces. But underneath this is an erotic force that comes from the lower class, the force of seething life that one can smell in garbage and that Vigo uses to drive his film. *A propos de Nice* advanced the cinema not because it gave Vigo his start and not because it is a beautifully crafted art film. It remains one of those few examples where the several powers of the medium (as recorder, as organizer, as clarifier of issues, as proselytizer) come together with a strength and ingenuity that are irrepressible. The critics at its premiere in June 1930 were impressed and Vigo's talent was generally recognized from that point on. But the film got little distribution; the age of silent films, even experimental ones like this, was coming to an end. This is too bad. Every director should begin his or her career as Vigo did, with commitment, independence, and a sense of enthusiastic exploration.

—Dudley Andrew

ACCATTONE. Production: Cine del Duca-Arco Film; 35mm; running time: 120 mins. Released 1961.

Produced by Alfredo Bini; screenplay by Pier Paolo Pasolini with dialogue collaboration by Sergio Citti; from the novel *Una vita violenta*; English subtitles by Herman Weinberg; directed by Pier Paolo Pasolini; photography by Tonino Delli Colli; edited by Nino Baragli; sound by Luigi Puri and Manlio Magara; art direction by Flavio Mogherini; music direction by Carlo Rustichelli; asssistant directors: Bernardo Bertolucci and Leopoldo Savona. Filmed 1960-61 in the slums of Rome.

Cast: Franco Citti (*Accatone/Vittorio*); Franca Pasut (*Stella*); Silvana Corsini (*Maddalena*); Paola Guidi (*Ascenza*); Adriana Asti (*Amore*); Renato Capogna (*Renato*); Mario Cipriani

(*Balilla*); Roberto Scaringella (*Cartagine*); Piero Morgia (*Pio*); Umberto Bevilacqua (*The Neapolitan*); Elsa Morante (*Prisoner*); Adele Cambria (*Nannina*); Polidor (*Becchino*); Danilo Alleva (*Iaio*); Luciano Conti (*Il Moicano*); Luciano Gonino (*Piede d'Oro*); Gabriele Baldini (*Intellectual*); Adrianno Mazelli and Mario Castiglione (*Amore's clients*); Dino Frondi and Tommaso Nuevo (*Cartagine's friends*); Romolo Orazi (*Accattone's father-in-law*); Silvio Citti (*Sabino*); Adriana Moneta (*Margheritona*).

Publications:

Reviews—review by Ian Cameron in *Movie* (London), September 1962; "Poet and the Pimp" by Stanley Kauffmann in the *New Republic* (New York), 6 April 1968; review by Andrew Sarris in the *Village Voice* (New York), 6 June 1968; books—*Pasolini on Pasolini: Interviews with Oswald Stack* edited by Oswald Stack, Bloomington, Indiana 1969; *Pier Paolo Pasolini* by Marc Gervais, Paris 1973; *Vita di Pasolini* by Enzo Siciliano, Milan 1978; *Teoria e tecnica del film in Pasolini* by Antonio Bertini, Rome 1979; *L'ossessione e il fantasma: il teatro di Pasolini e Moravia* by Enrico Groppali, Venice 1979; *Pier Paolo Pasolini* by Stephen Snyder, Boston 1980; articles—"Letter from Rome" by William Murray in the *New Yorker*, 21 April 1962; article by Robin Bean in *Films and Filming* (London), 12 September 1962; article by Geoffrey Nowell-Smith in *Sight and Sound* (London), autumn 1962; interview with Pasolini by John Bragin in *Film Culture* (New York), fall 1966; article by Randall Conrad in *Film Quarterly* (Berkeley), winter 1966-67; "Pasolini: Rebellion, Art, and a New Society" by Susan MacDonald in *Screen* (London), May/June 1969; "Pier Paolo Pasolini: Poetry as a Compensation" by John Bragin in *Film Society Review* (New York), no. 5, 6 and 7, 1969; "Pasolini: The Film of Alienation" by Noel Purdon in *Cinema* (London), August 1970; "Pasolini" by Roy Armes in *Films and Filming* (London), June 1971; "*Accattone*" in *Séquences* (Montreal), July 1973; "*Accattone*: Mama Roma" in *Etudes cinématographiques* (Paris), no.109-111, 1976; "Une Critique mythique en voie de development" by J. Magny in *Etudes cinématographiques* (Paris), no.109-111, 1976; "Pier Paolo Pasolini," special issues of *Etudes cinématographiques* (Paris), no.109-111, 1976 and no.112-114, 1976; Pasolini issue of *Cinema* (Zurich), no.2, 1976; "*Accattone*" by M. Gervais in *Wide Angle* (Athens, Ohio), no.4, 1977; "Pummi" by J. Hamalainen in *Filmihullu* (Helsinki, Finland), no.5, 1978; "*Accattone*" by T.L. Téllez in *Contracampo* (Madrid), December 1980.

*   *   *

Himself an alien in Rome, isolated by his regional Friulian upbringing, his homosexuality, and his poverty, the young Pier Paolo Pasolini had felt an instant affinity with the young street kids of the crowded, war-ruined city when he arrived there in the winter of 1949. He quickly developed his taste for sexual rough trade among the *ragazzi* of the city, the sarcastic kids dispossessed and wised-up by post-war greed and the opportunism encouraged by the Marshall Plan. In 1955 Pasolini published his first novel, *Ragazzi di vita*, a picture of life in the shantytowns and among the pimping, petty-thieving boys he now knew well. *Una vita violenta*, four years later, explored the same ground through the brief, violent life of Tommaso, smart enough to sense fitfully the ruin of his future. *Una vita violenta* became the basis of Pasolini's first film, and Tommaso the model for Vittorio, the delinquent his pals call Accattone.

Fellini was to have backed the film but pulled out after Pasolini submitted some test footage in which he had overreached himself in trying to shoot in the style of Dreyer's *Trial of Joan of Arc*. With Italian film heading away from neorealism towards a high style and elaborate production values mirroring the new wealth of the cities, Fellini was also dubious about Pasolini's chosen location, a run-down street in the heart of the Roman slums. Nor had he any reason to believe that Franco Citti could carry the leading role; inexperienced, uncommunicative, Citti was the younger brother of the man who had been Pasolini's adviser on Roman dialect for the script editing work he did on films by Fellini and Mauro Bolognini.

It was Bolognini who, seeing stills from the test footage on Pasolini's desk, understood what he was trying to do and interested producer Alfredo Bini in the project. The result was a film more characteristic of Pasolini's temperament than of Italian cinema. To the music of Bach's *St. Matthew's Passion*, Citti moves around a Rome of decadent religious imagery, crumbling buildings, a city pervaded by a sun-dazed, numbed sense of mortality. Dreams show the *ragazzi* buried half-naked in rubble, an evocative image of the ruin Pasolini saw reflected in both the morality and the architecture of his adopted city. Aiming for "an absolute simplicity of expression", Pasolini in fact achieved a studied stylization that was to become typical of his films. Citti became a star, and *Accattone* established Pasolini as a star himself in yet another field, matching his eminence in poetry, fiction and criticism. Today, with Pasolini dead at the hands of just such a boy as Vittorio, it is difficult to see the film as anything but an ironic signpost to the fate of this mercurial polymath.

—John Baxter

ADAM'S RIB. Production: Metro-Goldwyn-Mayer Pictures Corp.; 1949; black and white, 35mm; running time: 101 mins. Released 1949.

Produced by Lawrence Weingarten; screenplay by Ruth Gordon and Garson Kanin; directed by George Cukor; photography by George J. Folsey; edited by George Boemler; art direction by Cedric Gibbons and William Ferrari; music by Miklos Rozsa.

Filmed at MGM studios.

Cast: Spencer Tracy (*Adam Bonner*); Katherine Hepburn (*Amanda Bonner*); Judy Holliday (*Doris Attinger*); Tom Ewell (*Warren Attinger*); David Wayne (*Kip Lurie*); Jean Hagen (*Beryl Caighn*); Hope Emerson (*Olympia La Pere*); Eve March (*Grace*); Clarence Kolb (*Judge Reiser*); Emerson Treacy (*Jules Frikke*); Polly Moran (*Mrs. McGrath*); Will Wright (*Judge Marcasson*); Elizabeth Flournoy (*Dr. Margaret Brodeigh*).

Publications:

Review—"*Adam's Rib*" by Bosley Crowther in the *New York Times*, 24 December 1949; books—*Hommage à George Cukor* by Henri Langlois and others, Paris 1963; *George Cukor* by Jean Domarchi, Paris 1965; *The Films of Spencer Tracy* by Donald Deschner, New York 1968; *Cukor and Company: The Films of George Cukor and His Collaborators* by Gary Carey, New York 1971; *Tracy and Hepburn* by Garson Kanin, New York 1971;

The Films of Katharine Hepburn by Homer Dickens, New York 1971; *On Cukor* by Gavin Lambert, New York 1972; *Spencer Tracy* by Romano Tozzi, New York 1973; *Katharine Hepburn* by Alvin H. Marill, New York 1973; *George Cukor* by Carlos Clarens, London 1976; *George Cukor* by Gene Phillips, Boston 1982; articles—"Cukor and the Kanins" by Penelope Houston in *Sight and Sound* (London), spring 1955; "Katharine Hepburn" by Romano Tozzi in *Films in Review* (New York), December 1957; "Retrospective Cukor" issue of *Cahiers du cinéma* (Paris), February 1964; "Spencer Tracy" by Romano Tozzi in *Films in Review* (New York), December 1966; "The Most Amicable Combatants" by Penelope Gilliatt in the *New Yorker*, 23 September 1972; "*Adam's Rib*" by Anne Louise Lynch in *Magill's Survey of Cinema: Vol. 1* edited by Frank N. Magill, Englewood Cliffs, New Jersey 1980.

*   *   *

Adam's Rib represents a climax in the evolution of the classic Hollywood screwball comedy. In the 1930s, screwball comedies united antagonistic couples whose clashes revolved around egos, class conflicts, and attitudes about money and values. In the 1940s, screwball comedies replaced these conflicts with ones that revolved around egos and career-marriage decisions. In such films as *His Girl Friday*, *Woman of the Year*, *Take A Letter, Darling*, and *They All Kissed the Bride*, the comic crises hinged on the heroines' decisions regarding their professional careers and domestic roles. In 1949, George Cukor's *Adam's Rib* took the familiar marriage-career crisis formula of the screwball comedy to its logical conclusion—a comic study of sex role stereotyping and the invalidity of narrowly defined sex roles.

The film reunited Katharine Hepburn and Spencer Tracy, who had previously teamed on *Woman of the Year*, *Keeper of the Flame*, *Without Love*, and *State of the Union*, and whose successful on-screen romances seemed to radiate some of the genuine love and affection of their off-screen relationship. The film also features a brilliant screenplay by the husband-wife team Garson Kanin and Ruth Gordon. All the principals—director, stars, and writers—had proven track records, and in a financially bad year for Hollywood, their combined box-office appeal led to the three-way teaming on a film project that otherwise might not have been possible.

The movie is about Adam and Amanda Bonner, husband and wife lawyers who find themselves on opposite sides of a courtroom case. The legal case in question concerns a woman (Judy Holliday) who has shot her adulterous husband (Tom Ewell). Defense attorney Amanda Bonner views her case as a woman's rights issue, and she bases her defense on the premise that the husband would have been exempt from prosecution if the roles were reversed. In front of her district attorney husband, she turns the courtroom and the trial into a hilarious forum for a public debate on the "double standard" and the narrowness of sexual stereotypes. In the meantime, the courtroom competition begins to threaten the Bonner's marriage.

Much of the film's humor arises from the many sex-role reversals. Through such reversals, the movie simultaneously comments on how traditional social roles are defined by stereotypes of masculinity and femininity. The film literally takes this notion to its extreme when it depicts what the unwitting husband, wife, and lover (Jean Hagen), who are the subjects of the trial, would be like if their sexes were reversed. Meanwhile, the Bonner's crumbling marriage, one based on mutual respect and liberation from sexual stereotypes, requires a series of further role reversals to be put back together again. Adam wins his wife's sympathies by crying; Amanda apologizes by sending her husband a new hat.

Amanda ultimately wins her case and husband without giving up her principles. Adam learns about humility without losing his masculinity. But when the reconciled Bonners finally fall into bed together behind a curtain, the on-screen veil and their final unresolved argument about sex roles, competition, and sex differences cinematically deny their absolute integration as a unified couple. Like many screwball comedies that preceded it, *Adam's Rib* ends with a marital reconciliation that establishes the couple's unity without resolving the individuals' ongoing differences.

The writing, acting, and directing team that made *Adam's Rib* a success reunited in 1952 for a screwball comedy about a manager and his professional female athlete in *Pat and Mike*. The successful story formula from *Adam's Rib* further inspired a 1973 television series with the same name.

—Lauren Rabinovitz

THE ADVENTURES OF PRINCE ACHMED. Originally black and white, 35mm, silent, animation; running time: 65 mins. Released 1926, Berlin. Re-released with color tinted backgrounds and a musical score by Freddy Phillips.

Produced by by Louis Hagen; scenario by Lotte Reiniger; from the stories of the *Arabian Nights*; directed by Lotte Reiniger; musical score which originally accompanied the film by Wolfgang Zeller; special effects assistance by Walter Ruttmann and Berthold Bartosch; animation team included Reiniger, Carl Koch, Berthold Bartosch, Walter Ruttmann, and Alexander Kardan.

Filmed 1923-26 above the garage of Louis Hagen in Potsdam, Germany.

Publications:

Review—"*Adventures of Prince Achmed*" by Mordaunt Hall in *The New York Times*, 27 February 1931; books—*Walking Shadows* by Eric Walter White, London 1931; *Shadow Theatres and Shadow Films* by Lotte Reiniger, New York 1970; *Die Abenteuer des Prinzen Achmed* by Lotte Reiniger, with an insert of text translated into English, Ontario 1975; *Experimental Animation: An Illustrated Anthology* by Robert Russett and Cecile Starr, New York 1976; articles—"*Prince Achmed and Other Animated Silhouettes*" by Randolph T. Weaver in *Theatre Arts Monthly* (New York), June 1931; "Lotte Reiniger and Her Art" by E.W. White in *Horn Book* (Boston), January 1939; "Flatland Fairy Tales" by Guy Coté in *Film* (London), October 1954; "She Made First Cartoon Feature" in *Films and Filming* (London), December 1955; "The Films of Lotte Reiniger" in *Film Culture* (New York), no.9, 1956; "Animated Women" by H. Beckerman in *Filmmakers Newsletter* (Ward Hill, Massachusetts), summer 1974; "Lotte Reiniger et les ombres chinoises" by L; Bonneville in *Sequences* (Montreal), July 1975; "Lotte Reiniger au pays des ombres" in *Image et son* (Paris), December 1981.

Lotte Reiniger's silhouette cut-out film, *The Adventures of Prince Achmed*, based on stories from the *Arabian Nights*, is the world's first full-length animated film, preceding by a decade Walt Disney's *Snow White*, (sometimes mistakenly credited as the first in that category).

The multi-plane animation stand, often called another first for Disney's animators, was used throughout the making of *Prince Achmed*, as is well documented in photographs of the time. It allowed for what Reiniger called one of the rarest collaborations in animation history, with Walter Ruttmann creating special effects on one level (the grotesque transformations in the battle of the monsters, for example), and Berthold Bartosch working on another level, animating the waves of a sea-storm or the stars twinkling in the sky, which Reiniger's Prince Achmed, on still another level, traverses on the magic wooden horse. In the monster scene Ruttmann created an abstract background using the wax slicing machine he recently had purchased from the young and future animation genius, Oskar Fishinger. It was indeed the rarest of collaborations.

Reiniger's episodic scenario for *The Adventures of Prince Achmed* tells the story of the handsome son of the Caliph of Bagdad; his attempts to rescue the beautiful maiden Peri Banu from assorted monsters and witches; and, his meeting with Aladdin, whose magic lamp facilitates a happy ending for all.

The film's first showing was held privately on a Sunday morning at the Volksbuehne, a theater in the north of Berlin. Reiniger later wrote that "our friend Bert Brecht helped us invite the right people"—press and artists—who would launch the film as an artistic, if not commercial, event. A six-month run followed in Paris, at Louis Jouvet's experimental Champs-Elysées Theatre. The first performance was a gala charity affair, for which leading French personalities sold programs, in elegant attire. Some film historians have cited René Clair and Jean Renoir among them, but Reiniger later said this was not so. The long, close friendship between Renoir and Reiniger and her husband Carl Koch seems to date from this time, however.

Randolph T. Weaver wrote in *Theatre Arts Monthly*, in June 1931, that the film had been called to his attention by Renoir and that he found it to have "extraordinary taste and imagination...a spirit and grace...a fine feeling for detail, which made the film as a whole almost faultless." Introducing the film to a New York audience in the mid-1970s during a U.S.-Canadian tour under the auspices of the Goethe Institute, Lotte Reiniger was somewhat more critical: "It starts rather clumsily, but gets better towards the end."

A new musical score by Freddy Phillips has recently been added to the film which was originally silent with an orchestral score by Wolfgang Zeller, who conducted at the first showing. Color has also been added to the backgrounds through the use of luminous color filters. An English sound track is now being prepared for American showings, based on Reiniger's version of the story as published in her book; the film's original lack of dialogue or narration, together with the austerity of the silhouette cut-out technique itself, made the film difficult for many movie audiences to follow. *The Adventures of Prince Achmed*, however, remains without peer, precedent or progeny historically, technically, and artistically—a major event in cinematic creativity, as timeless and everlasting as the stories on which the film is based.

—Cecile Starr

*   *   *

THE AFRICAN QUEEN 13

THE ADVENTURES OF ROBIN HOOD. Production: Warner Bros. Pictures Inc.; 1938; Technicolor, 35mm; running time: 102 mins. Released 1938.

Produced by Hal Wallis; screenplay by Norman Reilly Raine and Seton I. Miller from the Robin Hood legends; directed by Michael Curtiz and William Keighley; photography by Tony Gaudio, Sol Polito, and W. Howard Green; edited by Ralph Dawson; art direction by Carl Weyl; music by Eric Wolfgang Korngold with orchestrations by Hugo Friedhofer and Milan Roder; costumes designed by Milo Anderson.

Filmed at Warner Bros. studios. Academy Awards for Interior Decoration, Best Original Score, and Best Editing, 1938.

Cast: Errol Flynn (*Robin Hood, or Sir Robin of Locksley*); Olivia de Havilland (*Lady Marian Fitzwalter*); Basil Rathbone (*Sir Guy of Gisbourne*); Claude Rains (*Prince John*); Alan Hale (*Little John*); Eugene Pallette (*Friar Tuck*); Ian Hunter (*King Richard the Lion-Hearted*); Melville Cooper (*High Sheriff of Nottingham*); Patric Knowles (*Will Scarlett*); Herbert Mundin (*Much the miller's son*); Una O'Connor (*Bess*); Montagu Love (*Bishop of Black Canon*).

Publications:

Books—*Hollywood Without Makeup* by Pete Martin, New York 1948; *My Wicked, Wicked Ways* by Errol Flynn, New York 1959; *Errol Flynn* edited by J.R. Parish, Kew Gardens, New York 1969; *The Films of Errol Flynn* by Tony Thomas, Rudy Behlmer, and Clifford McCarty, New York 1969; *Cads and Cavaliers—The Film Adventurers* by Tony Thomas, New York 1973; articles—"Errol Flynn" by Anthony Thomas in *Films in Review* (New York), January 1960; "Comparative Anatomy of Folk-Myth Films: *Robin Hood* and *Antonio das Mortes*" by Ernest Callenbach in *Film Quarterly* (Berkeley), winter 1969-70; "The Way to Make a Future: A Conversation with Glauber Rocha" by Gordon Hitchens and Elliot Stein in *Film Quarterly* (Berkeley), fall 1970; "Michael Curtiz" by Jack Edmund Nolan in *Films in Review* (New York), November 1970; "Swashbuckling" by Gordon Gow in *Films and Filming* (London), January 1972; "Michael Curtiz" by Kingsley Canham in *The Hollywood Professionals, Vol. 1*, London 1973; "Les Aventures de Robin des Bois" by J. Carcédo in *Image et son* (Paris), 331 bis, 1978; "*Les Aventures de Robin des Bois*" by F. Chevassu in *Image et son* (Paris), February 1978; "Sherwood, USA (A propos des *Aventures de Robin des Bois*)" by O. Eyquem in *Positif* (Paris), April 1978; "*Les Aventures de Robin des Bois*" by T. Renaud in *Cinéma* (Paris), February 1978; "*The Adventures of Robin Hood*" by Robert Morsberger in *Magill's Survey of Cinema: Vol 1* edited by Frank N. Magill, Englewood Cliffs, New Jersey 1980.

*   *   *

The Adventures of Robin Hood, a Warner Brothers studio production, reveals many facets and details of the studio system. The film was originally planned as a vehicle for James Cagney following the success of *Midsummer Night's Dream*, but contract problems with Cagney and the success of *Captain Blood* prompted the studio to cast Errol Flynn as the rogue outlaw. Once production on the film began, a directorial change occurred after original director William Keighley led the production over budget and behind schedule. He was replaced by Michael Curtiz, though both men share the director's credit.

The film reflects the studio's plan to produce a more prestigious product than the musicals and gangster films of the early thirties. Even so, the film does show the studio's frequent thematic concern with common folk banding together to achieve a goal of correcting an injustice, economic or otherwise.

The film's cast members have generally been acclaimed for matching the literary image of their characters. Even the supporting characters such as Alan Hale's Little John and Eugene Pallette's Friar Tuck seem to be perfectly suited for their roles. Under the direction of Curtiz and Keighley, the principal actors play off each other and promptly reveal much of their characters in this straight-forward narrative. Claude Rains portrays Prince John as a schemer, a man with a thirst for power; while Basil Rathbone's Sir Guy, with his good looks and his sinister bearing, makes an equal adversary for Flynn's Robin. Olivia de Havilland as Marian seems to be a pure aristocrat whether in the court or in the forest, or when facing death or confessing her love for Robin.

Errol Flynn's Robin is a man of action but also of wit. Following Douglas Fairbanks's silent film portrayal of Robin, Flynn's Robin engages in daring deeds but not on such a large scale (in part due to Warner's tight budget). The film also follows Fairbanks's lead in giving Robin a sense of humor as Robin throws verbal arrows at any villains in sight. Even in the love scenes, Robin can joke with and tease Marian.

The Adventures of Robin Hood, a very successful film when first released, has become something more than an accomplished film from the thirties. For many, the influence of this film is immense. There is, for example, a great deal of similarity between the action of Robin's men in the forest capturing a gold shipment and the attack of the Ewoks against the Stormtroopers in *Return of the Jedi*. Not only does it remain one of the quintessential films of the swashbuckling genre but it is also the definitive Robin Hood legend for scores of film-goers and television viewers. Much like *The Wizard of Oz*, *Robin Hood*'s audience has grown through repeated and successful television screenings. *TV Guide* once listed it as one of the top five films on television as selected by station programmers.

—Ray Narducy

THE AFRICAN QUEEN. Production: Horizon Romulus Productions; 1951; Technicolor, 35mm; running time: 103 mins. Released 1951.

Produced by Sam Spiegel; screenplay by James Agee and John Huston with Peter Viertel; from the novel by C.S. Forester; directed by John Huston; photography by Jack Cardiff; edited by Ralph Kemplen; sound engineered by John Mitchell; art direction by John Hoesli; music by Allan Gray, executed by the Royal Philharmonic Orchestra under the direction of Norman del Mar; special effects by Cliff Richardson; costumes designed by Doris Langley Moore.

Filmed at various film studios in London; exteriors shot along the Ruiki River in the Belgian Congo; and what was then the British protectorate of Uganda. Academy Award, Best Actor (Bogart), 1951.

Cast: Katharine Hepburn (*Rose Sayer*); Humphrey Bogart (*Charlie Allnut*); Robert Morley (*Rev. Samuel Sayer*); Peter Bull (*Captain of the 'Luisa'*); Theodore Bikel (*1st Officer of the 'Luisa'*); Walter Cotell (*2nd Officer of the 'Luisa'*); Gerald Ohn (*Officer of the 'Luisa'*); Peter Swanwick (*1st Officer of the 'Shoona'*); Richard Marner (*2nd Officer of the 'Shoona'*).

Publications:

Reviews—by Clarissa Bowen in *Sight and Sound* (London), April/June 1952; review by Henry Hart in *Films in Review* (New York), February 1952; "*The African Queen*" by Georges Sadoul in *Les Lettres françaises* (Paris), 10 April 1952; books—*John Huston* by Paul Davay, Paris 1957; *John Huston* by Jean-Claude Allais, Paris 1960; *Let There Be Light* in *Film: Book 2* by Robert Hughes, New York 1962; *Agee on Film* by James Agee, Boston 1964; *John Huston, King Rebel* by William Nolan, Los Angeles 1965; *Agee on Film: 5 Film Scripts* by James Agee, foreword by John Huston, Boston 1965; *Bogart* by Richard Gehman, Greenwich, Connecticut, 1965; *Humphrey Bogart: The Man and his Films* by Paul Michael, Indianapolis, 1965; *Bogey: The Films of Humphrey Bogart* by Clifford McCarty, New York 1965; *John Huston* by Robert Benayoun, Paris 1966; *John Huston* by Riccardo Cecchini, 1969; *John Huston, A Picture Treasury of his Films* by Romano Tozzi, New York 1971; *The Films of Katharine Hepburn* by Homer Dickens, New York 1971; *Humphrey Bogart* by Alan Barbour, New York 1973; *Katharine Hepburn* by Alvin Marill, New York 1973; *Humphrey Bogart* by Nathaniel Benchley, Boston 1975; *John Huston: Maker of Magic* by Stuart Kaminsky, London 1978; *John Huston* by Axel Madsen, Garden City, New York 1978; *An Open Book* by John Huston, New York 1980; articles—"Life Goes on Location in Africa" in *Life* (New York), 7 September 1951; "The African Queen" in *Theatre Arts* (New York), February 1952; "Interview with Huston" by Karel Reisz in *Sight and Sound* (London), January/March 1952; special Huston issue of *Positif* (Paris), January 1952; "*The African Queen*, John Huston, and Humphrey Bogart" by Jacques Demeure and Michel Subiela in *Positif* (Paris), August 1952; special Huston issue of *Positif* (Paris), January 1957; special number of *Bianco e nero* (Rome), April 1957; "A Monograph on John Huston: Part I—A Touch of Hemingway" by Eugene Archer in *Films and Filming* (London), September 1959; "Part II—Small People in a Big World" by Eugene Archer in *Films and Filming* (London), October 1959; "Beating the Devil: 30 Years of John Huston" by DuPre Jones in *Films and Filming* (London), January 1973; "*African Queen*" by L. de Selva in *Image et son* (Paris), 331 bis, 1978; "*The African Queen*" by Ellen J. Snyder in *Magill's Survey of Cinema Vol. 1* edited by Frank N. Magill, Englewood Cliffs, New Jersey, 1980.

*   *   *

From the beginning, director John Huston insisted that *The African Queen* be shot on location. To find a river identical to the one in C.S. Forester's novel, he logged 25,000 flying miles criss-crossing Africa until he settled on the Ruiki in the then Belgian Congo. At a time (1951) when on-location shooting was nowhere near as common as today, traveling 1,100 miles up the Congo to make what is essentially a filmed dialogue must have seemed fanatical. And subsequent encounters with blood flukes, crocodiles, soldier ants, wild boars, stampeding elephants, malaria, and dysentery were hardly reassuring.

Yet *The African Queen* is more than a simple encounter between a man and a woman. It is a story of two very different people growing to love and respect one another after sharing and surviving severe hardships. Huston maintained that on-location shooting was the only way to make that suffering and subsequent romance believable and authentic. At Huston's insistence even the scenes shot off location were filmed under realistic conditions. For example, although Humphrey Bogart actually emerged from London rather than Ugandan waters (after pulling the

African Queen), the leeches that covered him were the genuine article. Bogart's revulsion and shivering during that particular scene are convincing arguments for Huston's point-of-view.

Indeed, *The African Queen*'s main strength is the acting of the two principal players—Humphrey Bogart as the seedy Canadian boat captain, Charlie Allnut, and Katharine Hepburn as the "Psalm-singing skinny old maid," British missionary Rose Sayer. According to Huston, although Bogart initially resisted and didn't like his character, after mimicking the director's gestures and expressions, "all at once he got under the skin of that wretched, sleazy, absurd, brave little man." Hepburn, too, had trouble at the beginning; her portrayal was brittle, cold, and humorless. However, once Huston suggested that she play her part as if she were that Grand Lady Eleanor Roosevelt, she became both funny and refined, and a humor inherent in neither the novel nor the screenplay emerged between the two characters.

The humor is essential to the success of the film not because it makes the film more entertaining, but because it arises out of the equality and individuality of two eccentric and strong-willed adversaries. They may end up falling in love, but not without an often hysterical struggle. Bogart's character begins as a self-indulgent drunk who mimics the missionary's prim ways; she, on the other hand, frowns upon his drinking and cowardice, disagreeing with his lax views on human nature: "Nature is what we were put on earth to rise above." But in courageously facing and solving problems together, the two head towards a middle ground. Allnut stops drinking (Rose has thrown his gin overboard) and shaves, while Rose changes her mind about human nature. After encountering her first rapids, for example, she ecstatically exclaims, "I never dreamed any mere physical experience could be so stimulating!...I don't wonder you love boating, Mr. Allnut." Finally, after escaping both the Germans and the allegedly uncrossable rapids, the two impulsively embrace and fall in love. The humor does not stop here, however. After their first tender night together, Rose shyly asks Allnut, "Dear, what is your first name?" Their mutual delight in his response is completely captivating.

Our captivation with the two characters allows us to accept many of the film's more improbable moments—the quick dispatch of Brother Samuel Sayer, the sun shining in the eyes of a German sharpshooter as naively predicted by Rose, heavy rains freeing the mired *African Queen* after Rose prays to God, and the *deus ex machina* ending. In fact, the ending had been changed several times. Writer James Agee hadn't written it yet when he suffered a heart attack, so Huston tried to write one with Peter Viertel; before the fourth and final ending was conceived, three others were apparently considered: (1) a British warship rescues Rose and Charlie after a heroic battle with the *Louisa*, (2) Rose proposes marriage before the first available British consul, (3) Charlie remembers the wife he had left behind in England and hadn't thought of for 20 years. The first and second endings combined were similar to what occurred in the original novel (that is, Forester's second ending—even he had problems resolving the plot).

Huston's fourth and happy ending—which miraculously saves Rosie and Charlie from their postnuptial death by hanging—is atypical, as are other elements in the script. Many of Huston's previous films had a bleaker view of humanity and ended unhappily (e.g., *The Maltese Falcon*, *The Treasure of the Sierra Madre*). Both Charlie and Rose exhibit an honesty and integrity at odds with such Hustonian liars and tricksters as Sam Spade, Brigid O'Shaughnessy, Rick Leland, and Dobbs. The two survive because of an internal nobility that Huston's seedier characters outwardly lack.

Huston's new optimism/idealism struck the right note with the public. *The African Queen* became one of 1952's top moneymakers, having been nominated for Best Actor (Bogart won), Best Actress, Best Direction, and Best Screenplay. British readers of *Picturegoer* voted Bogart the year's best actor, and Hepburn experienced the greatest box office hit of her career. A film that began as a vehicle for Charles Laughton and Elsa Lanchester, and later Bette Davis and David Niven, had found the perfect couple for its improbable romance.

—Catherine Henry

L'AGE D'OR. The Golden Age. Black and white, 35mm; running time: 60 mins. (some French sources list 80 mins.). Released 28 November 1930, Paris.

Produced by Charles Vicomte de Noailles; screenplay by Luis Buñuel and Salvador Dali; directed by Luis Buñuel; photography by Albert Duverger; edited by Luis Buñuel; production design by Pierre Schilzneck; original music by Van Parys, montage of extracts from Mozart, Beethoven, Mendelssohn, Debussy, and Wagner. Filmed in Studios Billancourt-Epinay, France.

Cast: Lya Lys (*The Woman*); Gaston Modot (*The Man*); Max Ernst (*Bandit Chief*); Pierre Prévert (*Péman, a Bandit*); Caridad de Labaerdesque; Madame Noizet; Liorens Artigas; Duchange; Ibanez; Lionel Salem; Pancho Cossio; Valentine Hugo; Marie Berthe Ernst; Jacques B. Brunius; Simone Cottance; Paul Eluard; Manuel Angeles Ortiz; Juan Esplandio; Pedro Flores; Juan Castañe; Joaquin Roa; Pruna; Xaume de Maravilles.

Scripts—"*L'Age d'or*" (scenerio) in *The Secret Life of Salvador Dali*, London 1948; "*L'Age d'or*" in *L'Avant-Scène du Cinéma* (Paris), July 1963; "*L'Age d'or* and *Un Chien andalou* by Luis Buñuel, translated by Mariane Alexander, New York 1968; books—*En marge du cinéma français* by Jacques B. Brunius, Paris 1947; *Luis Buñuel* by Luc Moullet, Brussels 1957; *Luis Buñuel* by Ado Kyrou, Paris 1962; *Luis Buñuel* by Frédéric Grange and Charles Rebolledo, Paris 1964; *Le Surréealisme au cinéma* by Ado Kyrou, Paris 1967; *Luis Buñuel: biografia critica* by Francisco Aranda, Madrid 1969; *Manifestoes of Surrealism* by André Breton, translated by R. Seaver and H.R. Lane, Ann Arbor, Michigan 1969; *Luis Buñuel* by Freddy Bauche, Lyon 1970; *Surrealism and the Film* by J. H. Matthews, Ann Arbor, Michigan 1971; "Luis Buñuel: Spaniard and Surrealist" in *6 European Directors* by Peter Harcourt, London 1974; *Luis Buñuel: A Critical Biography* by Francisco Aranda, London 1975; *Luis Buñuel* by Raymond Durgnat, Berkeley, California, revised 1977; *The Shadow and Its Shadow: Surrealist Writings on Cinema* edited by Paul Hammond, London 1978; *The World of Luis Buñuel: Essays in Criticism* edited by Joan Mellen, New York 1978; *Luis Buñuel* by Virginia Higginbotham, Boston 1979; articles—"Les Influences de *L'Age d'or*" by Louis Chavance in *Revue du cinéma* (Paris), 1 January 1931; article by Henry Miller in *The New Review* (Paris), 1931, reprinted in Spanish in *Contracampo* (Madrid), October/November 1980; "Surrealism and Spanish Giant" by Francesco Aranda in *Films and Filming* (London), October 1961; issue devoted to Buñuel, *La Methode* (Paris), January 1962; article by Raymond Durgnat

in *Films and Filming* (London), April 1962; "Manifeste des surréalistes à propos de *L'Age d'or*" in *L'Avant-Scène du cinéma* (Paris), 15 July 1963; "The Process of Dissociation in Three Films" by E.H. Lyon in *Cinema Journal* (Evanston, Illinois), fall 1973; "*L'Age d'or*" by Jean-Claude Bonnet in *Cinématographe* (Paris), July 1981; "*L'Age d'or* aujourd'hui" by P. Kral in *Positif* (Paris), October 1981; "Un Film irrécupérable: *L'Age d'or*" by L. Logette in *Jeune Cinéma* (Paris), October 1981; "Surréalisme et cinéma" by L. Logette in *Jeune Cinéma* (Paris), April/May 1981; "*L'Age d'or*: un manifeste de la subversion devenu pièce de musée" by J. Magny in *Cinéma* (Paris), July/August 1981.

AGUIRRE, DER ZORN GOTTES. Aguirre, the Wrath of God. Production: Werner Herzog Filmproduktion; Eastman color, 35mm; running time: 93 mins. Released 1973.

Produced by Werner Herzog; screenplay by Werner Herzog; from the journal of Gaspar De Carvajal; directed by Werner Herzog; photography by Thomas Mauch; edited by Beate Mainka-Jellinghaus; sound by Herbert Prasch; music by Popol Vuh; special effects by Juvenal Herrera and Miguel Vasquez.

Filmed in the jungles of Peru, along the Amazon.

Cast: Klaus Kinski (*Don Lope de Aguirre*); Helena Rojo (*Inez de Atienza*); Ruy Guerra (*Pedro de Ursua*); Del Negro (*Caspar de Carvajal*); Don Fernando de Guzman (*Peter Berling*); Cecilia Rivera (*Flores de Aguirre*); Dany Ades (*Perucho*); Armando Polanah (*Armando*); Edward Roland (*Okello*); Daniel Farafan, Alejandro Chavez, Antonio Marquez, Julio Martinez, and Alejandro Repulles (*The Indians*); and 270 Indians from the Cooperative of Lauramarca.

Publications:

Script—"*Aguirre, La Colère de Dieu*" by Werner Herzog in *L'Avant-Scène du cinéma* (Paris), 15 June 1978; reviews— "*Aguirre, der Zorn Gottes*" by R. Combs in *Monthly Film Bulletin* (London), January 1975; "*Aguirre, Wrath of God*" by D. Elley in *Films and Filming* (London), February 1975; "*Aguirre*" by G. Gauthier and D. Elley in *Films and Filming* (London), April 1975; "*Aguirre, Wrath of God*" by T. Rayns in *Sight and Sound* (London), winter 1974-75; "*Aguirre, The Wrath of God*" by M. McCreadie in *Films in Review* (New York), June/July 1977; "La Presse française..." in *L'Avant-Scène du cinéma* (Paris), 15 June 1978; books—*Herzog/Kluge/Straub* by Wolfram Schütte and others, Vienna 1976; *Heart of Glass* by Alan Greenberg, Munich 1976; *The New German Cinema* by John Sandford, Totowa, New Jersey 1980; articles—"Werner Herzog" by B. Baxter in *Film* (London), spring 1969; "Werner Herzog: 'Comme un rève puissant...'" by N. Ghali in *Jeune Cinéma* (Paris), September/October 1974; "Werner Herzog: Le Réel saisi par le rève" by N. Ghali in *Jeune Cinéma* (Paris), November 1974; "Un pouvoir qui ne pense, ne calcule, ni ne juge?" by J.P. Oudart in *Cahiers du cinéma* (Paris), July/August 1975; "*Aguirre, le Colère de Dieu*" by N. Simsolo in *Ecran* (Paris), April 1975; "Entretien avec Warner Herzog" by J. Zimmer in *Image et son* (Paris), March 1975; "*Aguirre*, den gale erobrer" by P. Schlepelern in *Kosmorama* (Copenhagen), no.132, 1976; "Une Juste Reparation: *Aguirre* remporte le Grand Prix de L.U.C.C." by D. Sotiaux in *Apec—Revue belge du cinéma* (Brussels), no.5, 1976; "*Aguirre, La Colère de Dieu*" by A. Garel in *Image et son* (Paris), 308bis, 1976; "The Cosmos and Its Discontents" by D. Benelli in *Movietone News* (Seattle), November 1977; "*Aguirre, La Colère de Dieu*" by M. Clarembeaux in *Revue Belge du cinéma* (Brussels), June 1977; "The Enigma of Werner Herzog" by J.H. Dorr in *Millimeter* (New York), October 1977; "Un Radeau nommé Délire" by Jean-Pierre Esquenazi in *L'Avant-Scène du cinéma* (Paris), 15 June 1978; "2 Films by Werner Herzog" by D. Coursen in *Cinemonkey* (Portland, Oregon), no.1, 1979.

*   *   *

Aguirre der Zorn Gottes is Werner Herzog's hypnotic epic of megalomania and delusional myths. The story concerns the search of Spanish conquistadors for El Dorado in the jungles of South America. The journey is made with the assistance of native slaves over mountains and down an uncharted river. Initiated under the aegis of the Spanish crown, the expedition experiences progressive disintegration. Aguirre, originally named second-in-command, usurps control in pursuit of a golden territory to rule on his own. At the same time, the very instruments and characters sustaining the journey are gradually eliminated. Food, rafts, supplies, and crew members are lost; the landscape changes until there is no land properly speaking to conquer, only river and swamps. In the face of desolation, Aguirre maintains obsessive faith in the reality of his dreams, weaving tales of his future glory.

This journey, with its imaginary goal, is presented in the guise of an historical account. An opening title explains that the events come from a journal kept by a monk during the course of the expedition. The diary provides the text of a voice-over narration which intermittently comments on events. But El Dorado—the goal of the journey, purpose of the expedition, and subject of the diary—is a known fiction, an eternal dream destined to failure. Moreover, the journal is described as the remaining record of an expedition which disappeared in the depths of the Amazonian jungle; it can not, in fact, exist. Thus from the outset the film defines its subject as a doomed journey and spurious history. Indeed, history is immediately construed in terms of myth.

As the film posits this mythical history and a goal-less journey, *Aguirre* transforms its world into a realm of hallucination. Crew members are attacked by arrows and darts from invisible sources. When the monk is struck by an arrow near the end of the film he denies its very being, "This is no arrow." The monk and Okello, one of the native slaves, also deny the existence of a boat hull ("There is no boat") which is shown suspended in a tree. In the face of an uncontrollable phenomenal world what counts above all else is the faith one sustains in fictions of one's own making. And it is this quality that defines Aguirre as a hero. The greatest and only believer in the myths of his own creation, he stands as the quintessential heroic figure of history.

With its striking images the film successfully constructs an impression of having entered an unworldly territory. The opening is particularly effective, as the expedition is seen in extreme long shots weaving its way down the mountains through the fog to the banks of the river. The audience is positioned with the expedition throughout the journey. What lies beyond the river on its overgrown banks—a source of beauty, monotony, and danger—remains a mystery throughout the film. The final shot of the film re-inforces the tenacity of the journey's confining vision, as the camera circles rapidly around the raft. Littered with dead bodies, overrun with monkeys, the raft is locked into an aimless drift as the hero and self-proclaimed "great traitor" asserts his power for the last time: "I am the wrath of God."

—M.B. White

AI NO CORRIDA. Ai no koriida. In the Realm of the Senses. L'Empire des Sens. Production: Argos Films (Paris), Oshima Productions (Tokyo), and Océanique Productions (some sources list Shibatu Organization as one of the production companies involved); Eastmancolor, 35mm, Vistavision; running time: 110 mins., some versions 115 mins. Released 1976.

Produced by Anatole Dauman; screenplay by Nagisa Oshima; directed by Nagisa Oshima; photography by Hideo Itoh; edited by Keiichi Uraoka; art direction by Shigemasa Toda; music by Minoru Miki; lighting by Ken'ichi Okamoto.

Filmed in Japan. Cannes Film Festival, Best Director, 1978.

Cast: Tatsuya Fuji (*Kichizo*); Eiko Matsuda (*Sada Abe*); Aoi Nakajima; Taiji Tonoyama (*Tramp*); Kanae Kobayashi; Akiko Koyama; Naomi Shiraishi; Machiko Aoki; Kyoko Okada; Yasuko Matsui; Katsue Tomiyama.

Publications:

Reviews—"*Empire of the Senses*" in *Cinema Papers* (Melbourne, Australia), September/October 1976; "*L'Empire des sens*" by J. Zimmer in *Image et son* (Paris), September 1976; "*L'Impero dei sensi*" by E. Bruno and others in *Filmcritica* (Rome), September 1976; "*In the Realm of the Senses*" by Richard Eder in *The New York Times*, 1 October 1976; "Nagisa Oshima's *In the Realm of the Senses*" by B. Berman in *Take One* (Montreal), March 1977; "*L'Empire des sens*" by M. Silverman in *Film Quarterly* (Berkeley), winter 1976-77; "*Empire des sens*" by J. Dawson in *Monthly Film Bulletin* (London), May 1978; books—*Japanese Film Directors* by Audie Bock, New York 1978; articles—"U.S. Bans Showing of Festival Movie" by A.E. Clark in the *New York Times*, 2 October 1976; interview with Oshima in the *New York Times*, 3 October 1976; "Customs Barred from Interfering with Japanese Film" by A. Lubasch in the *New York Times*, 10 November 1976; "L.A. Filmex Got *Senses*: Turned It Over to Dauman" in *Variety* (New York), 6 October 1976; "Segal Scores Customs Censors" in *Variety* (New York), 6 October 1976; "Customs in Encore as N.Y. Fest Goes for Porn" by A. Verrill in *Variety* (New York), 6 October 1976; "Okay *Senses* for Adults in Japan" in *Variety* (New York), 13 October 1976; "Belgian Police Hit *Senses*, Not *1900*" in *Variety* (New York), 20 October 1976; "Dauman Sues U.S. Customs: Also Wants Judge to Declare *In the Realm of the Senses* Not Obscene" in *Variety* (New York), 3 November 1976; "*Realm of the Senses* Free of Customs" in *Variety* (New York), 10 November 1976; "Entretien avec Nagisa Oshima" by N.L. Bernheim in *Cinématographe* (Paris), June 1976; "*L'Empire des sens*" by P. Bonitzer in *Cahiers du cinéma* (Paris), March/April 1976; "L'Essence du pire" by P. Bonitzer in *Cahiers du cinéma* (Paris), September/October 1976; "*L'Empire des sens*" by J.C. Bonnet in *Cinematographe* (Paris), October/November 1976; "Una Nota sul rito dell'eros" by E. Magrelli in *Filmcritica* (Rome), September 1976; "Sada e il rifiuto della scrittura porno" by M. Mancini in *Filmcritica* (Rome), September 1976; "I Sansernes vold" by Ib Monty in *Kosmorama* (Copenhagen), no.132, 1976; "*L'Empire des sens*" by J.L. Passek in *Cinéma 76* (Paris), November 1976; article by G. Perella in *Filmcritica* (Rome), September 1976; "*Empire of the Senses*" in *Cinema Papers* (Australia), September/October 1976, and in *Positif* (Paris), May 1976; "Film Festival Preview: *In the Realm of the Senses*" by T. Rayns in *Film Comment* (New York), September/October 1976;

"In the Realm of the Censors" by J. Bouras in *Film Comment* (New York), January/February 1977; "*In the Realm of the Senses*" by R. McCormick in *Cineaste* (New York), winter 1976-77; "Flamingo Hours: Enthusiasm" by Gene Youngblood in *Take One* (Montreal), July/August 1977; "The Question Oshima" by Stephen Heath in *Wide Angle* (Athens, Ohio), no.1, 1978; "Oshima: A Vita Sexualis on Film" by P.B. High in *Wide Angle* (Athens, Ohio), no.4, 1978; "L'Empire de la passion" by N. Oshima in *Cahiers du cinéma* (Paris), May 1978; "L'Erotismo segragato dell'impero dei sensi" by E. Garroni in *Cinema nuovo* (Turin), October 1979; "Ecco l'impero dei sensi" by G. Grossini in *Cinema nuovo* (Turin), June 1979; "El Fantasma del amor" by J.M. Company, "Ante del tribunal de la obscenidad" by N. Oshima, and "La Utopía de los cuerpos" by J.G. Requena in *Contracampo* (Madrid), July/August 1980.

* * *

The first film to break down the barriers between the commercial art film and hard-core pornography, the all-explicit *Ai no corrida* was for Japanese director Nagisa Oshima both a political and a psycho-cultural exploration. In keeping with his consistent treatment of sensitive issues in the guise of dramatic films, Oshima conceived this project at the suggestion of French producer Anatole Dauman to do a hard-core film. Immediately subsequent to the abolition of anti-obscenity laws in France, *Corrida* was the sensation of the 1976 Cannes International Film Festival, where an unprecedented thirteen screenings were mounted to meet the demand. Shot entirely in Japan, where police ordinarily seize films revealing so much as a pubic hair in the developing laboratory, the exposed footage was sent to France for processing. When re-imported to Japan as a French production, with every explicit scene air-brushed into white haze by the censors, it was nevertheless hailed as the first porno film for women. Oshima was therefore arrested and prosecuted for obscenity in the screenplay, which had been published in book form in Japan. After four years in court, he was found innocent by the supreme court, but he did not succeed in overturning the legal concept of obscenity.

Like all of Oshima's films, *Corrida* is based on a true story, the apprehension of Sada Abe, who strangled her lover with his consent and then cut off his genitals in 1936, months before Japan's full-scale aggression against China would open World War II. The appearance of Japanese flags and marching soldiers elucidate a background theme of sexuality as escape from political and social oppression, one of Oshima's persistent concerns.

Corrida is an exploration of the limits of sexuality. Sada (Eiko Matsuda) and Kichizo (Tatsuya Fuji) gradually reject the outside world in order to pursue the ultimate in sexual pleasure. Couched in a linear narrative with few but important stylistic deviations from a conventional exposition, the sexual exploits quickly lose any prurient quality. These lovers are too analytical; they comment too much; they allow and seek out too much intrusion upon their acts. Finally, they develop too much need for violence to stimulate themselves as over-indulgence dulls the pleasure. The desire to possess another person ends in Kichizo's death.

The major reversal of the conventions of the porno film lie in Kichizo's aim of giving pleasure to Sada. She gradually changes from addressing him as "master" (of the inn where she has worked as a maid) to adopting male speech and giving him orders. Some psychiatrists have seen this as a calculated role reversal, in which Kichizo takes on first a passive quality, then a maternal aspect for Sada. Indeed Sada becomes the aggressor, initiator and possessor in every sense. But Oshima characteristi-

cally ends the film without any comment but the historical facts: Sada was arrested with Kichizo's genitalia on her person, tried and jailed for murder. But she became celebrated as a folk heroine.

Aside from the universal interest of the possession urge in sexuality, Oshima layers his film with cultural references. He uses the formula of the Kabuki theater, the lovers' journey (michiyuki), (as they go to the inn that will be their refuge and site of the murder) to presage a doomed alliance. He taps the rich pornographic history of feudal Japan in the voyeurism, exploitation and sado-masochistic play of the geisha and maids at the inns, and he mocks the elaborate ritual of the Japanese wedding ceremony. Use of traditional Japanese musical instruments on the sound track, lush color photography even in the confinement of the small inn room, and superb acting from non-stars and amateurs add to the disturbing appeal of this psychological landmark of the cinema.

—Audie Bock

L'ALBERO DEGLI ZOCCOLI. The Tree of the Wooden Clogs. Production: RAI (Rete I)-Italnoleggio Cinematografico; Gevacolor, 35mm; running time: 175 mins.; length: 65,000 meters. Released 1978, Cannes Film Festival.

Production directed by Attilio Torricelli; screenplay, direction, photography, and editing by Ermanno Olmi; sound by Amedeo Casati; art direction by Enrico Tovaglieri, set dressing by Franco Gamborana; music by J.S. Bach, executed on the organ by Fernando Germani; costumes designed by Francesca Zucchelli. Filmed on location in Lombardy, Italy. Cost: lire 320,000,000. Palme d'Or, Cannes Film Festival, 1978; David of Donatello special plaque award to Olmi, Italy, 1978; New York Film Critics Award, Best Foreign Film, 1979.

Cast: Luigi Ornagli (*Batisti*); Francesca Moriggi (*Batisti's wife*); Omar Brignoli (*Minek, the son*); Antonio Ferrari (*Toni*); Teresa Brecianini (*Widow Runc*); Giuseppe Brignoli (*Grandpa Anselmo*); Carlo Rota (*Peppino*); Pasqualina Brolis (*Teresina*); Massimo Fratus (*Pierino*); Francesca Villa (*Annetta*); Maria Grazia Caroli (*Bettina*); Battista Trevaina (*Finard*); Giuseppina Sangaletti (*Mrs. Finard*); Lorenzo Pedroni (*Grandpa Finard*); Felice Cervi (*Usti*); Pierangelo Bertoli (*Secondo*); Brunella Migliaccio (*Olga*); Franco Pilenga (*Stefano, Maddalena's husband*); Guglielmo Badoni and Laura Locatelli (*Stefano's parents*); Carmelo Silva (*Don Carlo*); Mario Brignoli (*Landowner*); Emilio Pedroni (*Farm bailiff*); Vittorio Cappelli (*Frichi*); Francesca Bassurini (*Suor Maria*); Lina Ricci (*Woman of the "Segno"*).

Publications:

Script—"A facida faja: reszletch a forzatokonyvbol" (script extract) in *Filmkultura* (Budapest), January/February 1979; reviews—"Film: Olmi's *The Tree of the Wooden Clogs* Opens" by Vincent Canby in *The New York Times*, 1 June 1979; "Films: Miss Froy Rides Again" by J. Coleman in the *New Statesman* (London), 11 May 1979; "The Current Cinema: The Wheel of Time" by B. Gill in the *New Yorker*, 18 June 1979; "Curious Career" by Stanley Kauffmann in the *New Republic* (New York), 2 June 1979; "An Italian Classic" by Jack Kroll in *News-*

week (New York), 4 June 1979; "Films in Focus: Unclogging the Spirit" by Andrew Sarris in the *Village Voice* (New York), 4 June 1979; "*L'Abre aux sabots*" by C. Borseno in *Revue du cinéma* (Paris), series 23 1979; "Movies: A Vision of the Good Life" by D. Denby in *New York*, 11 June 1979; "*Tree of the Wooden Clogs*" by R. Martin in *Films in Review* (New York), August/September 1979; "The Soil and the Soiled" by John Simon in the *National Review* (New York), 3 August 1979; books—*L'albero degli zoccoli* by Ermanno Olmi, Bergamo 1979; *L'albero degli zoccoli nell'Italia 1978* by Gian Piero Dell' Acqua, Milan 1979; articles—"Träskor och diktatorer Rapport från Cannes 78" by L. Ahlander in *Chaplin* (Stockholm), XX/4, no.157, 1978; "Ermanno Olmi" by M. Devillers and others in *Cinématographe* (Paris), no.40, 1978; "*L'Arbre aux sabots*" by A. Masson and others in *Positif* (Paris), September 1978; "The Tree of the Wooden Clogs" by D. Castell in *Films Illustrated* (London), June 1979; "*Albero degli zoccoli, L'* (The Tree of the Wooden Clogs)" by J. Pym in *Monthly Film Bulletin* (London), June 1979; "Ermanno Olmi und sein neuer Film *Der Holzschuhbaum*" by G. Salje in *Film und Ton* (Munich), May 1979; "Das Land verliert, die Stadt gewinnt, der Bauer wird vertrieben" by G. Seesslen in *Film und Ton* (Munich), June 1979; "Kino Journal" by G. Seesslen and B. Seesslen-Hurler in *Medium* (Frankfort), May 1979; "*L'Arbre aux sabots*" by L. Bonneville in *Sequences* (Montreal), April 1979; "*Tree of the Wooden Clogs*" by J.K. Loutzenhiser in *Boxoffice* (Kansas City, Missouri), 10 September 1979; "*Tree of the Wooden Clogs*" by R. McCormick in *Cinéaste* (New York), no.4, 1979; article by Michael B. Gladych in *Film Quarterly* (Berkeley), winter 1980/81.

At the same time, Italy produced two films about peasant life at the turn of the century: Bertolucci's *1900* and Olmi's *Tree of the Wooden Clogs*, yet Olmi's work received more unqualified praise and caused more fierce debate than did the opus of his younger colleague. After *Tree* won the Golden Palm at Cannes, there were those who declared it a masterpiece, a supreme vision of beauty and poetry, a profoundly humanist testament. The film didn't deal directly with history; it was history. Other critics viewed it as an egocentric and myopic vision, dealing with personal nostalgia, negating historical and social issues, and taking refuge in a strict Catholicism. Everyone, no matter what their ideological bias, did agree that it was an exceedingly beautiful work of formal perfection. With this, his ninth feature, Olmi shared the limelight that had not been his since the time of *Il posto* and *I fidanzati*.

Tree of the Wooden Clogs belongs to the finest works of the tradition of cinematic realism. Olmi has stated that the masters who had greatly influenced him were Robert Flaherty (especially *Louisiana Story* and *Man of Aran*) and Roberto Rossellini. One could also draw Georges Rouquier's study of French Catholic farmers in *Farrebique* and Luchino Visconti's epic-length film on Sicilian fishermen, *La terra trema*. In regard to this tradition, Olmi's film has both similarities and differences. Like all the above, Olmi feels a deep dedication to his work and often spends years carefully choosing his subject matter and planning each film project. Olmi had conceived the idea 20 years before he realized this film; he had based his subject on stories told to him by his grandfather. For the film, like Visconti, Olmi spent months living in villages, and interviewing thousands of peasants, a score of which became the principal actors of the film. Olmi began without a definite script; the actions and dialogue came from the actors themselves. Rare to Italian cinema, Olmi insisted upon

shooting with direct sound and utilizing only the Bergamesque dialect, although, like Visconti in 1948, marketing difficulties demanded that Olmi produce a version in Italian as well. In this case, however, the Italian version was dubbed by the actors themselves. Olmi obtained a completely natural performance from his characters who are all framed in centrally-based compositions in the film. Although there are many close-ups, the eyes of the characters are rarely aimed directly at the camera and thus do not confront the spectator. The richly-saturated colors— russets, deep greens, browns and tans—are earth tones natural to the countryside and peasant life.

Except in a few isolated cases, the Italian cinema has rarely dealt directly with the peasantry, but Olmi has added nothing extra to what would normally occur in the pre-industrial countryside. As in the best of the realist tradition, all shooting was done on location and natural lighting prevails. Contrary to Rossellini and Visconti, and much closer to Rouquier, for example, is the fact that almost nothing happens in the film. Given its episodic nature that follows seasonal changes in the lives of five families in Lombardy, the highlights are the birth of a baby, the slaughtering of a pig, the discovery of a gold coin in the dirt, a couple's honeymoon trip on a barge to Milan, and a father who cuts down a tree in order to make a sandal for his son, from whence comes the film's title. One particular scene caused much of the divided critical opinion—the miracle of the cow. A woman's cow is ill; she prays for it and it miraculously regains its health. Olmi here stressed the primacy of religious faith; a Catholicism which offered a world of culture and learning to the peasantry as well as providing a source of magic and myth, symbols and stories.

—Elaine Mancini

ALEKSANDR NEVSKII. Alexander Nevsky. Production: Mosfilm; black and white, 35mm; length: 3044 meters. Released 23 November 1938.

Scenario by Sergei Eisenstein and Pyotr Pavlenko; directed by Sergei Eisenstein with collaboration by D.I. Vasiliev; photography by Edward Tisse; edited by Sergei Eisenstein; sound by B. Volsky and V. Popov; production design by Isaac Shpinel, Nikolai Soloviov, and K. Yeliseyev from Eisenstein's sketches; music by Sergei Prokofiev; costumes designed by Isaac Shpinel, Nikolai Soloviov, and K. Yeliseyev from Eisenstein's sketches; consultant on work with actors: Elena Telesheva.

Filmed June-November, 1938 in Moscow. Order of Lenin award, Soviet Union, 1939.

Cast: Nikolai Cherkasov (*Prince Alexander Yaroslavich Nevsky*); Nikolai Okhlopkov (*Vasili Busali*); Alexander Abrikosov (*Gavrilo Oleksich*); Dmitri Orlov (*Ignat, Master Armorer*); Vasili Novikov (*Pavsha, Governor of Pskov*); Nikolai Arsky (*Domash Tverdislavich*); Vera Ivasheva (*Olga, a Novogorod girl*); Varvarra Massalitinova (*Amelfa Timofeyevna*); Anna Danilova (*Vasilisa, a girl of Pskov*); Vladimir Yershov (*Von Blak, Grand Master of the Livonian Order*); Sergei Blinnikov (*Tverdilo, traitorous Mayor of Pskov*); Ivan Lagutin (*Ananias*); Lev Fenin (*Bishop*); Naum Rogozhin (*Black-robed Monk*).

Publications:

Script—*Eisenstein: 3 Films* edited by Jay Leyda, translated by

Diana Matias, New York 1974; reviews—by Herman Weinberg in *Sight and Sound* (London), spring 1939; "Alexander Nevsky" by Frank S. Nugent in *The New York Times*, 23 March 1939; books—*Eisenstein, 1898-1948* by Paul Rotha, Ivor Montagu and John Grierson, London 1948; *Film Form* by Sergei Eisenstein, New York 1949; *Notes of a Film Director* by Sergei Eisenstein, translated by X. Danko, London 1959; *Kino* by Jay Leyda, London 1960; *Sergei Eisenstein—Künstler der Revolution*, Berlin 1960; *S.M. Eisenstein* by Jean Mitry, Paris 1961; *Sergej Michailowitsch Eisenstein*, edited by Konlecher and Kubelka, Vienna 1964; *Sergei Eisenstein* by Léon Moussinac, translated by Sandy Petrey, New York 1970; *The Complete Works of Sêrgeî Eisênŝtein* by Marcel Martin, Guy Lecouvette, and Abraham Segal, New York 1971; *Eisenstein* by Yon Barna, Bloomington, Indiana 1974; *Eisenstein* by Dominique Fernandez, Paris 1975; *Sergei M. Eisenstein: Materialien zu Leben und Werk* by W. Sudendorf and others, Munich 1975; *Sergei M. Eisenstein in Selbstzeugrissen und Bilddokumenten*, edited by E. Weise, Reinbek bei Hamburg 1975; *Film Sense* by Sergei Eisenstein, New York 1975; *Eisenstein: A Documentary Portrait* by Norman Swallow, New York 1977; *Sergei M. Eisenstein* by Marie Seton, London 1978; *Eisenstein at Work* by Jay Leyda and Zina Voynow, New York 1982; articles—"Eisenstein's Resurgence" by J. Kunitz in the *New Republic* (New York), 29 March 1939; "Eisenstein Has Been Subordinated to the Orders of the Monolithic State" by F. Hoellering in *Nation* (New York), 8 April 1939; "Eisenstein and the Historical Films" by B. Maddow in *Hollywood Quarterly*, October 1945; "The End of Sergei Eisenstein: Case History of an Artist under Dictatorship" by Waclaw Solski in *Commentary* (New York), March 1949; article by Dennis Kawicki in *Cineaste* (New York), fall 1968; "Sergei Eisenstein's *Alexander Nevsky*" by D. Devensky in *Classic Film Collections* (Indiana, Pennsylvania), winter 1973; "Cuvstvo Rodiny" by R. Jurenev in *Iskusstvo Kino* (Moscow), November 1973; "The Eisenstein-Prokofiev Correspondence" by R. Levaco in *Cinema Journal* (Iowa City), fall 1973; "Eisenstein's *Alexander Nevskij*" by S. Kjorup in *Kosmorama* (Copenhagen), no. 136, 1977; "Prokofiev's Score and Cantata for Eisenstein's *Alexander Nevsky*" by P.D. Roberts in *Semiotica* (New York), no. 1-2, 1977; "The Prokofiev-Eisenstein Collaboration: 'Nevsky' and 'Ivan' Revisited" by D.W. Gallez in *Cinema Journal* (Evanston, Illinois), no. 2, 1978.

*   *   *

The cinematic works of Sergei Eisenstein demonstrate a continuous effort to explore and develop the elements of his theory of montage. Two marked phases of style and technique are evident in this development. The first phase consists of Eisenstein's silent films of the 1920s, and the second is comprised of his 1930s and 1940s sound films. In the first phase of his cinematic career Eisenstein introduces the formal concepts of intellectual montage, mise-en-scene, and a revolutionary new narrative concept: the portrayal of the mass as hero. With *Alexander Nevsky* Eisenstein enters a second phase in which the individual within the collective becomes the dominant narrative theme, and vertical montage and pictorial composition replace intellectual montage as the primary formal force in his films. These new techniques are not totally divorced from Eisenstein's early film methods, but have evolved from them.

The narrative theme of the individual within the collective in *Alexander Nevsky* can be seen as the maturing of the early concept of the portrayal of the mass as hero. Reflecting upon Soviet silent cinema, Eisenstein writes that the films are flawed in that they fail to fully represent the concept of collectivity: "collec-

tivism means the maximum development of the individual within the collective...Our first mass films missed this deeper meaning." In the depiction of "the general-revolutionary slogan" of the twenties the mass as hero functioned well, but to convey the more specific Communist message of the thirties, images of leading individuals were needed.

In *Alexander Nevsky* the theme of the patriotism of the Russian people is emphasized through such exemplary characters as Prince Alexander, Bouslay, and Govrilo. Even though this narrative device resembles more traditional cinema, Eisenstein's characters embody patriotic ideals to such an extreme that they become symbols rather than hero personalities. The subject matter of *Alexander Nevsky* contributes to this larger-than-life portrayal of its characters by presenting historical figures and events in such mythic proportions that, while the viewer may sympathize with the characters, he does not easily identify with them. An individual character never takes the viewer's attention away from the general theme of the film. It is intended that the ideas the characters represent will be remembered rather than their individual personalities. The characters, in the film must support, even succumb to, the dominant theme of the strength and patriotism of the Russian people.

Structuring a film such that a dominant theme controls all the individual elements of that film is a formal concern which made the transition from silent to sound film in Eisenstein's work. In the early silent films this formal method was referred to as overtonal montage. This method of montage dictates that all the visual images of film, which have been developed through the use of intellectual, metric, rhythmic, and tonal montage, serve to reveal and illustrate the dominant theme. The controlling formal method in *Alexander Nevsky*, vertical montage, is much the same as overtonal, but with the additional element of sound. Vertical montage, according to Eisenstein, "links different spheres of feeling—particularly the visual image with the sound image, in the process of creating a single, unifying sound-picture image. The audio and visual elements are not only governed by the dominant theme of the film, but work together to convey that theme in a strongly emotional manner.

The attack by the German wedge on the Russian army in "The Battle on the Ice" sequence in *Alexander Nevsky* demonstrates this appeal to the emotions. The musical score contributes greatly to the pacing and emotional tone of this sequence. Any speeding up or slowing down of the pictorial movement is complimented by the melodic movement. In addition, Eisenstein uses the combination of sound with its corresponding image to suggest an image to the viewer that is not actually visible on the screen. Although this concept resembles intellectual montage, it functions on a more metaphorical level For example, Eisenstein likens the leaping and pounding of horses' hooves to the motion and the sound of an agitated heart, a heart experiencing the increasing terror of the battle on the ice.

The most dramatic use of vertical montage in *Alexander Nevsky* is in the relationship throughout the film between the musical score and the pictorial composition. This relationship was developed through several different methods. For some sequences the music was written with a general theme or idea in mind. In other sequences the music was written for an already assembled visual episode. In yet other sequences, the visual images were edited to music already on the sound track. The final result of these editing methods is a connection between the visuals and the musical score that goes beyond the enhancement of the mood of a sequence. Throughout *Alexander Nevsky* Eisenstein strives for a "complete correspondence between the movement of the music and the movement of the eye over the lines of the plastic composition. The same motion found within the image composition of a shot sequence can be found in the complementary musical score for that sequence. That is, the ascending or descending shape the notes of the written musical score form correspond directly to the movement of the eye over the planes of the composition within each shot of a film sequence. Although the details of this complex sound-image relationship may not be apparent while viewing *Alexander Nevsky*, what is apparent is the control this relationship lends to the film. The sound and visual elements combine to create a very solid, unified whole.

Eisenstein states that, in comparison to the films of the twenties, the new Soviet sound-cinema appeared more traditional "and much closer to the foreign cinema than those films that once declared war to the death against its (the foreign cinema's) very principles and methods." Two elements that contribute to this traditional appearance are story and pictorial composition as Eisenstein borrowed conventional techniques from literature and painting for *Alexander Nevsky*, his first sound film. In the thirties Eisenstein became interested in the application of other art forms to film. Literature, he felt, offered "the dramatics of subject." Cinema should again be concerned with story and plot—concepts Eisenstein had condemned in the twenties. This was not a call to return to conventional content. Eisenstein felt that conventional forms could be utilized to present fresh content. The new story would not be centered around a traditional bourgeois hero, but instead, around the modern hero-characters who represent the individual within the collective. And, as in *Alexander Nevsky*, these individuals would embody the ideology of the proletariat.

The other art form referred to is painting. In contrast to the photographic quality of Eisenstein's earlier films, the individual frames of *Alexander Nevsky* are reminiscent of painted battle scenes and landscapes. This is why the battle scenes may appear unrealistic: they are highly stylized, like paintings. An example of this is the creation of "The Battle on the Ice." Not only was the frame composition of the sequence stylized, but the landscape was totally simulated. The winter battle scene was actually shot in the heat of July; the ice simulated using melted glass, alabaster, chalk, and salt. The appearance of the summer sky was altered with the use of a filter on the camera lens. The scene was almost literally painted on a blank canvas.

Although some critics were disappointed with Eisenstein's variations on, or departure from, his early film methods, *Alexander Nevsky* was a success upon its release in 1938. Probably Eisenstein's most commercially popular film in his own country, it also survived the scrutiny of Joseph Stalin, earning the symbol of official government approval, the Order of Lenin, in February of 1939. Soviet and foreign critics alike applauded the film as the work which, after more than six years of unproductivity, not all of it voluntary, returned Eisenstein to his former status as one of the foremost creative talents of the Soviet cinema.

Alexander Nevsky is viewed in much the same manner today as it was upon its original release. It is not touted as Eisenstein's best film but its epic qualities and cinematic achievement, the "Battle on the Ice" sequence in particular, are appreciated. The concept of vertical montage, however, has come under closer examination than in past years. Although critics may disagree on the extent to which the sound-image unity of vertical montage is at work in this particular film, they do seem to agree on the significance of Eisenstein's theory: he was one of the first theorists to give serious consideration to the relationship between sound and image in cinema.

—Marie Saeli

ALL ABOUT EVE. Production: 20th Century Fox; 1950; black and white, 35mm; running time: 138 mins. Released 1950.

Produced by Darryl F. Zanuck; screenplay by Joseph L. Mankiewicz; from the short story and radio play "The Wisdom of Eve" by Mary Orr; directed by Joseph L. Mankiewicz; photography by Milton Krasner; edited by Barbara McLean; art direction by Lyle Wheeler and George Davis, set decoration by Thomas Little and Walter M. Scott; music by Alfred Newman; costumes designed by Edith Head and Charles LeMaire.

Filmed at 20th Century-Fox studios and on location in a San Francisco theater. New York Film Critics' Awards, Best Picture, Best Direction (Mankiewicz), and Best Actress (Davis), 1950; Academy Awards, Best Picture, Best Direction (Mankiewicz), Best Supporting Actor (Sanders), Best Screenplay, Best Sound Recording, Best Costume Design—Black and White, 1950; Cannes Film Festival, Special Jury Prize and Best Actress (Davis), 1951.

Cast: Bette Davis (*Margo Channing*); Anne Baxter (*Eve Harrington*); George Sanders (*Addison De Witt / Narrator*); Celeste Holm (*Karen Richards*); Gary Merrill (*Bill Sampson*); Hugh Marlowe (*Lloyd Richards*); Marilyn Monroe (*Miss Caswell*).

Publications:

Reviews—by Ann Griffith in *Films in Review* (New York), December 1950; review by Penelope Houston in *Sight and Sound* (London), January 1951; Books—*Film in the Battle of Ideas* by John Howard Lawson, New York 1953; *Joseph L. Mankiewicz: An Index to His Work* by John Taylor, London 1960; *The Lonely Life: An Autobiography* by Bette Davis, New York 1962; *The Films of Bette Davis* by Gene Ringgold, New York 1965; *More About ALL ABOUT EVE*, by Joseph L. Mankiewicz with Gary Carey, New York 1972; *Bette Davis* by Jerry Vermilye, New York 1973; articles—"The Case of Joseph L. Mankiewicz" by Hollis Alpert in the *Saturday Review* (New York), 21 October 1950; "The Filming of All About Eve" by Arthur Gavin in *American Cinematography* (Hollywood), January 1951; "All About Joe" by F.S. Nugent in *Colliers* (New York), 24 March 1951; article by Richard Winnington in *Sight and Sound* (London), January 1951; "Mannerisms—in the Grand Manner" by Michell Raper in *Films and Filming* (London), September 1955; "Bette Davis" by Lawrence Quirk in *Films in Review* (New York), December 1955; "All About Bette" by Peter Baker in *Films and Filming* (London), May 1956; "Cleo's Joe, Part I" by John Howard Reid in *Films and Filming* (London), September 1963; "Whatever Happened to Bette Davis" by David Shipman in *Films and Filming* (London), April 1963; "Part II—*All About Eve* and Others" by John Howard Reid in *Films and Filming* (London), September 1963; "What is a Star?" by Bette Davis in *Films and Filming* (London), September 1965; "Bette Davis" by Lawrence J. Quirk in *Films in Review* (New York), December 1965; "Measure for Measure: Interview with Joseph L. Mankiewicz" by Jacques Bontemp and Richard Overstreet in *Cahiers du Cinema in English* (New York), May 1966; "Measure for Measure: Interview with Joseph L. Mankiewicz" by Jacques Bontemps and Richard Overstreet in *Cahiers du Cinema in English* (New York), February 1967; "Cocking a Snoot" by Gordon Gow in *Films and Filming* (London), November 1970; "The Films of Joseph Mankiewicz" by John Springer in *Films in Review* (New York), March 1971; "Mankiewicz: The Thinking Man's Director" by K. Geist in *American Film* (Washington, D.C.), April 1978; "Dossier-auteur (II): Joseph L. Mankiewicz—le temps et la parole" by A. Charbonnier in *Cinéma* (Paris), July/August 1981.

* * *

By 1950 television has made a heavy claim on America's entertainment dollar. The studio system, shaken at its base by the Supreme Court order to separate production and exhibition, will linger for a few years, but it has been dealt a mortal blow. In its annual self-canonization, the Academy Awards ceremonies, Hollywood reflects the industry's enforced self-awareness. Writer-directors Billy Wilder and Joseph Mankiewicz vie for the Best Film award with *Sunset Boulevard* and *All About Eve*, examinations of the entertainment profession and the phenomenon of stardom. Their respective stars, Gloria Swanson and Bette Davis, both making comebacks (Swanson after nearly two decades, Davis after being unceremoniously dethroned as Queen of Warners) are rivals for the Best Actress award. The fact that Judy Holliday wins for *Born Yesterday* takes nothing away from the impact made by Swanson and Davis. And if *All About Eve* is named Best Film, it only suggests that Hollywood is not ready to canonize a self-examination quite as acerbic as *Sunset Boulevard*.

The "literary," "East Coast" qualities of Mankiewicz's script (he was rewarded the previous year for his work as director and writer of *A Letter to Three Wives*) give *All About Eve* a patina of sophistication and Broadway savvy that do little to mask its Hollywood provenance. Even location shooting at a legitimate theater (in San Francisco, not New York) does not detract from the true reflexivity of *All About Eve*—its sense of itself as a movie. From the initial close-up of the stage actress, Margo Channing, to the final shot, a series of reflections of Phoebe, the ambitious fan who bows to an imaginary audience, we are brought to an apprehension of how cinema specifically captures modes of performance. The film may make blatant its condescension to Hollywood, often referred to as the place where talent demeans itself, but it does so while disavowing that assertion through its own cinematic status.

Many critics have found fault with Mankiewicz precisely for the script, the presumed reliance on words rather than images, the talkiness. And one of the reasons for which the film has achieved a certain cult following is its quotability. Margo Channing's "Fasten your seat belts. It's going to be a bumpy night" is a sing-along line, one of many that give viewers intimate access to the text. We are allowed to savor the verbality of *All About Eve* through the immediately apparent patterns of its wit. To achieve maximum effect in the movies, witty lines require contexts that favor our hearing, and in this film the unfussy stagings sustain the dynamics of individual discourse and conversation. When the director seats six actors on a staircase, (among whom are "talkers" as memorable as Celeste Holm, George Sanders, Anne Baxter and Marilyn Monroe) and has them exchange words with Bette Davis, he has created a filmic/aural event.

Beyond its general reflexivity about Hollywood, we also see and are moved by the specific mythology of *All About Eve*— Marilyn Monroe, on the verge of stardom, playing the dumb blonde, the persona that haunts her life; Bette Davis, in a role that echoes her own status as a mature star (one that she would not have played had Claudette Colbert not injured her back just prior to production), a role for which she is universally admired, a role just as universally perceived as the last great one of her career.

—Charles Affron

ALL QUIET ON THE WESTERN FRONT. Production: Universal Pictures Corp.; 1930; Movietone sound, black and white, 35mm (also silent version with synchronized music); running time: 140 mins.; length: 14 reels, 12,423 feet (with synchronized music 15 reels). Released April 1930, Los Angeles. Re-released 1939 but reduced to 10 reels, re-released 1950 in the U.S., re-released 1963 in France.

Produced by Carl Laemmle, Jr.; screenplay by Dell Andrews, Maxwell Anderson, and George Abbott; from the novel by Erich Maria Remarque; titles by Walter Anthony; directed by Lewis Milestone; photography by Arthur Edeson, Karl Freund, and Tony Gaudio; edited by Edgar Adams and Milton Carruth; sound technician: William W. Hedgecock; art direction by Charles D. Hall and William Schmidt; music and synchronization by David Broekman, recording engineered by C. Roy Hunter; special effects by Frank Booth; dialogue direction by George Cukor.

Filmed 1930 in Universal Studio backlots; battle scenes shot at Irvine Ranch, California. Academy Awards for Best Picture and Best Direction, 1929/30.

Cast: Louis Wolheim (*Katczincky*); Lew Ayres (*Paul Baumer*); John Wray (*Himmelstoss*); George (Slim) Summerville (*Tiaden*); Russell Gleason (*Muller*); Raymond Griffith (*Gerard Duval*); Ben Alexander (*Kemmerich*); Owen Davis, Jr. (*Peter*); Beryl Mercer (*Mrs. Baumer*), (in silent version Zasu Pitts is Mrs. Baumer); Joan Marsh (*Poster girl*); Yola d'Avril (*Suzanne*); Arnold Lucy (*Kantorek*); Scott Kolk (*Leer*); Walter Browne Rogers (*Behm*); Richard Alexander (*Westhus*); Renee Damonde and Poupee Andriot (*French girls*); Edwin Maxwell (*Mr. Baumer*); Harold Goodwin (*Detering*); Marion Clayton (*Miss Baumer*); G. Pat Collins (*Lieutenant Berlenck*); Bill Irving (*Ginger*); Edmund Breese (*Herr Mayer*); Heinie Conklin (*Hammacher*); Bertha Mann (*Sister Libertine*); William Bakewell (*Albert*); Bodil Rosing (*Watcher*); Tom London (*Orderly*); Vince Barnett (*Cook*); Fred Zinnemann (*Man*).

Publications:

Books—*An Index to the Films of Lewis Milestone* by Charles Shibuk, T. Huff Memorial Society 1959; *The Great Films: 50 Golden Years of Motion Pictures* by Bosley Crowther, New York 1967; *The Celluloid Muse: Hollywood Directors Speak* by Charles Higham and Joel Greenberg, Chicago 1969; "Lewis Milestone" in *Close Up: The Contract Director* edited by Jon Tuska, Metuchen, New Jersey 1976; *Lewis Milestone* by Joseph R. Millichap, Boston 1981; articles—"*All Quiet on the Western Front*" by Loretta K. Dean in *American Cinematographer* (Hollywood), March 1930; "Should Auld Acquaintance Be Forgot?" by Welford Beaton in *Hollywood Spectator*, 25 September 1937; "Milestone and War" by Karel Reisz in *Sequence* (London), 1950; "War Without Glory" by Dorothy Jones in *Quarterly of Film, Radio, and Television* (Berkeley), spring 1954; "*All Quiet on the Western Front*" by John Cutts in *Films and Filming* (London), April 1963; "*A l'ouest rien de nouveau*" in *Avant-Scène du cinéma* (Paris), 15 November 1963; "An Interview with Lewis Milestone" by Digby Diehl in *Action* (Los Angeles), July/August 1972; "Louis Wolheim" by Jack Spears in *Films in Review* (New York), March 1972; "*All Quiet on the Western Front*: A History Teacher's Reappraisal" by Eugene P.A. Schleh in *Film and History*, December 1978; "*All Quiet on the Western Front*" in *Films and Filming* (London), September 1979; "*All*

Quiet on the Western Front" by John Pym in Monthly Film Bulletin, May 1980; "All Quiet on the Western Front" by J. Fox in Films and Filming (London), April 1980; "All Quiet on the Western Front" by G. Weemaes in Filme en televisie (Brussels), May/June 1981.

*   *   *

All Quiet on the Western Front made Lew Ayres a star and was responsible for the start of George Cukor's screen career and the establishment of Lewis Milestone as a director of international repute. Milestone directed four further films concerned with war, notably A Walk in the Sun, but none measured up to All Quiet, and, indeed, the director never achieved the same success as this film brought. The film also boded well for the production career of Carl Laemmle, Jr., a much derided executive, who turned out a surprising number of major artistic features at his father's studio in the early through mid-thirties.

A passionate portrayal of the horror of war, which for the first time depicted the "hun" as simply a scared boy, All Quiet can be divided into four distinct parts. The first details the enlistment of the young recruits; the second their arrival at the front; the third the various incidents of war; and, finally, the hero Paul Baumer's return home and his hastened retreat back to the front and his death. The film remains faithful to the Erich Maria Remarque novel and was the most successful of a trio of features taking a pacifist approach to World War I at this time, the other two being the British Journey's End and the German Westfront, 1918.

All Quiet on the Western Front was the first sound film to use a giant mobile crane, particularly for filming the realistically-staged battle sequences, and one of the first talkies to boast a mobility of camerawork in general. Credit for this must, of course, go to Lewis Milestone, but George Cukor's contribution to the film should not be—as it is so often—overlooked. It was Cukor who rehearsed the actors and established a neutrality to their accents which is of inestimable value in putting across the production's emotional message.

There are no real stars in All Quiet, with each actor delivering a passionate cameo performance, be it Louis Wolheim as the brusque yet sympathetic Katczinsky, Raymond Griffith as the French soldier killed by Baumer, William Bakewell as Baumer's pal, Albert, or Beryl Mercer as Baumer's mother (a role played in the silent version by ZaSu Pitts).

Released initially in a 140-minute version, All Quiet on the Western Front has been successively cut through the years, until most prints today run as short as 90 or 110 minutes. These truncated versions fail to capture the film's momentum as the recruits become more and more involved in the war and its horrors. The most extraordinary cut-version of the feature, however, was a 1939 reissue which included an anti-Nazi narration.

—Anthony Slide

ALL THE KING'S MEN. Production: Columbia Pictures Corp., 1949; black and white, 35mm; running time: 109 mins. Released 1949.

Produced and directed by Robert Rossen; screenplay by Robert Rossen from the novel by Robert Penn Warren; photography by Burnett Guffey; edited by Al Clark and Robert Parrish; produc-

tion design by Sturges Carne and Louis Diage; music by Louis Gruenberg and Morris Stoloff; costumes designed by Jean Louis; consultant: Robert Parrish.

Filmed in Columbia studios. Academy Awards for Best Film, Best Actor (Crawford), and Best Supporting Actress (McCambridge), 1949; New York Film Critics' Awards for Best Film and Best Actor (Crawford), 1949.

Cast: Broderick Crawford (Willie Stark); Joanne Dru (Anne Stanton); John Ireland (Jack Burden); John Derek (Tom Stark); Mercedes McCambridge (Sadie Burke); Sheppard Strudwick (Adam Stanton); Anne Seymour (Lucy Stark); Raymond Greenleaf (Judge Stanton); Ralph Dumke (Tiny Duffy); Katherine Warren (Mrs. Burden); Walter Burke (Sugar Boy); Will Wright (Dolph Pillsbury); Grandon Rhodes (Floyd McEvoy); H.C. Miller (Pa Stark); Richard Hale (Hale); William Bruce (Commissioner).

Publications:

Script—"All the King's Men" by Robert Rossen in Three Screenplays, edited by Steven Rossen, New York 1972; reviews—by Peggy Hitchcock in Films in Review (New York), February 1950; review by Richard Winnington in Sight and Sound (London), June 1950; books—Our Modern Art: The Movies by Ernest Callenbach, Chicago 1955; The Films of Robert Rossen by Alan Casty, New York 1969; articles—"The Face of Independence" by Robert Rossen in Films and Filming (London), August 1962; articles by H. Hart, J. Springer, and H. Burton on Rossen's career and films in Films in Review (New York), June/July 1962; "The Films of Robert Rossen" by Alan Casty in Film Quarterly (Berkeley), winter 1967-68; "Lessons Learned in Combat: Interview with Robert Rossen" by Jean-Louis Noamès in Cahiers du Cinema in English (New York), Janury 1967; "Robert Rossen, A Retrospective Study of His Films" by Alan Casty in Cinema (Beverly Hills), fall 1968; "Reflections of Robert Rossen" by C. Dark in Cinema (London), August 1970; "Fascism in the Contemporary Film" by Joan Mellen in Film Quarterly (Berkeley), summer 1971; "Robert Rossen" by M. Wald in Films in Review (New York), August/September 1972.

*   *   *

All the King's Men is one of the best political films of all time and one of the few to seriously consider politics as a corrupting force. Based on Robert Penn Warren's Pullitzer Prize-winning novel of the same name which became a major best-seller, and has retained its reputation as one of the great works of American fiction, the film is a riveting account of the career of Willie Stark. Stark is a character loosely based on Louisiana's notorious governor Huey Long, the "kingfish" of Southern politics in the 1920s and 1930s. Although Penn Warren's novel considered the rise and fall of Stark from small-town lawyer to governor, Stark himself was a secondary character. The protagonist as well as narrator of the novel was newspaper reporter Jack Burden whose life, thoughts, and reactions to the politics of the time were related with frquent jumps back and forth in time.

In Robert Rossen's film version, Willie Stark becomes the main character and Burden, although still the narrator, is much less important. The film also follows the story in chronological order, making it a more traditional plot. Although in recent years many films have successfully used devices such as flashbacks and flashforwards without regard to traditional chronological story progression, in 1949 this would have been startling and probably unsuccessful. By shifting the emphasis in characters and re-ordering the development of the story, Rossen was able to adapt the spirit of the Penn Warren novel while still making a highly dramatic and entertaining film. Unlike many adaptations of the novels of Ernest Hemingway or F. Scott Fitzgerald, which invariably have been unsuccessful because they were either too close or too removed from the original, *All the King's Men* as a film is different, but equally as effective as the novel.

Another major reason for the success of the film is the quality of the acting. In the role of Stark, Broderick Crawford gives a dynamic performance in the only major starring role of his career. His Academy Award for Best Actor of the year was well deserved; as the meek naive country lawyer trying to help the members of his small community and as the spell-binding, power-hungry governor he is equally believable. The shift in his character's personality could have been a major flaw in the film yet Crawford's acting makes both sides of the man acceptable. Mercedes McCambridge also won an Academy Award for her performance as the hard-shelled Sadie Burke. Others, including John Ireland as Burke, were very good, but none had the opportunities for great performances as did Crawford and McCambridge.

While many films which make political or sociological statements tend to date badly in a few years, *All the King's Men* still seems fresh and powerful. The dichotomies of Stark's character—a man who wanted to do good but out of proximity to corruption, or out of his own ambition, became the embodiment of corrupt politics—are still as relevant today as they were in 1949. The character of the demagogue has been known in literature for centuries, but few works have attempted to show the how and why as successfully as *All the King's Men.*

—Patricia King Hanson

ALPHAVILLE. Production: Chaumiane (Paris) and Filmstudio (Rome); black and white, 35mm; running time: 98 mins., some sources list 100 mins. Released 1965.

Produced by André Michelin; screenplay by Jean-Luc Godard; based a character created by Peter Cheney; directed by Jean-Luc Godard; photography by Raoul Coutard; edited by Agnès Guillemot; sound by René Levert; music by Paul Misraki; assistant directors included Charles Bitsch, Jean-Paul Savignac, and Hélène Kalouguine.

Filmed January through February 1965 in Paris. Best Film, Berlin Film Festival, 1965.

Cast: Eddie Constantine (*Lemmy Caution*); Anna Karina (*Natasha von Braun*); Howard Vernon (*Professor von Braun*); Akim Tamiroff (*Henri Dickson*); Laszlo Szabo (*Chief Engineer*); Michel Delahaye (*Von Braun's Assistant*); Jean-André Fieschi (*Professor Heckell*); Jean-Louis Comolli (*Professor Jeckell*); Alpha 60 (*Itself*).

Publications:

Scripts—*Alphaville* by Jean-Luc Godard, translation and description of action by Peter Whitehead, New York 1966; reviews—"Current Cinema" by B. Gill in the *New Yorker*, 21 August 1965; review by Jonas Mekas in the *Village Voice* (New York), 16 September 1965; review by Andrew Sarris in the *Village Voice* (New York), 3 November 1965; review by Gordon Gow in *Films and Filming* (London), May 1966; books—*Jean-Luc Godard* by Richard Roud, New York 1967; *Jean-Luc Godard: A Critical Anthology* edited by Tony Mussman, New York 1968; *The Films of Jean-Luc Godard* edited by Ian Cameron, London 1969; *Jean-Luc Godard* edited by Jean Collet, translated by Ciba Vaughan, New York 1970; *Focus on Godard* edited by Royal Brown, Englewood Cliffs, New Jersey 1972; *Godard on Godard* edited and translated by Tom Milne, London 1972; *Jean-Luc Godard* by Alberto Farassino, Florence, Italy 1974; *The Great Spy Pictures* by James Robert Parrish, Metuchen, New Jersey 1974; *The New Wave* by James Monaco, New York 1976; articles—"Anguish: *Alphaville*" by Richard Roud in *Sight and Sound* (London), autumn 1965; article by Gilles Jacob and Claire Clouzot in *Sight and Sound* (London), autumn 1965; "Light of Day" by Raoul Coutard in *Sight and Sound* (London), winter 1965-66; article by Kirk Bond in *Film Society Review* (New York), March 1966; article by John Thomas in *Film Quarterly* (Berkeley), fall 1966; "Jean-Luc Godard and Americanism" by Raymond Federman in *Film Heritage* (Dayton, Ohio), spring 1968; "Eddie Constantine" by Jack Edmund Nolan in *Films in Review* (New York), August/September 1968; "The Films of Jean-Luc Godard" by Stephen Crofts in *Cinema* (London), June 1969; article by Max Kozloff in *Film Culture* (New York), winter/spring 1970; "Loss of Language" by M.C. Ropars-Wuillerumier in *Wide Angle* (Athens Ohio), no.3, 1976; "Wittenstein and Godard's *Alphaville*" by R. MacLean in *Sight and Sound* (London), winter 1977-78.

*   *   *

Since the early 1950s a tendency has begun to manifest itself in the genre of science fiction: there has been an increase in the number of important directors who are using the sci-fi form to express their views on society, mankind, the present and the future. One of these is the French director Jean-Luc Godard, who in 1965 contributed to science fiction the film *Alphaville*, a story which unfolds in a utopian world of the future. Godard's vision is not a world of joy and happiness; Alphaville is governed by a totalitarian system in which the individual counts for almost nothing, and an alienated society has no use for art, poetry, love, or even thought. People are reduced essentially to the level of robots, without their own will, ideas or feelings, and identified only by numbers.

Even though it belongs to the category of science fiction, Godard's film does not closely follow the conventional patterns of the genre. As a member of the French New Wave, Godard has held, since his debut, an individual and well-defined view of the cinema. One of the most important features of his work is his emphasis on the contemporary world. All of his films deal with modern man; we do not find a return to the past in his entire work. The stamp of the present can also be seen in his sole excursion into the future, *Alphaville*, which is less about what the world will be like tomorrow than what it it like today, and what it is gradually becoming before our very eyes without our realizing it. In the present and the past Godard sees the potential germs of a future world, and therefore the story has an admonitory subtext. From this thematic interpretation flows the film's realization, its formal execution and visual aspect. The viewer encounters on the screen nothing that appears to be unusual or extraordinary, and Godard even forgoes any futuristic mise-en-scène. His Alphaville of the future is the Paris of 1965, in which the dehumanized atmosphere is expressed through the camera work of Raoul Coutard, who uses light contrastively when shooting buildings of concrete and glass, alternates positive and negative in very short takes, and particularly zeroes in on images of Paris by night. The most unusual aspect of the film is the sound, particularly the monotonous voice of the central brain governing Alphaville, a voice in contrast to the somewhat ingratiating music of Paul Misrak.

A characteristic feature of the entire French New Wave was a certain admiration for the American cinema—its perfect craftsmanship and its ability to entertain, move, or thrill with suspense. In *Alphaville*, Godard's affinity for popular film can be seen, for example, in the choice of Eddie Constantine for the starring role—viewers know him chiefly from gangster films—and in the dramatic structure influenced by both film serials of the 1930s and by comic strips. Another striking feature of Godard's direction is his free use of ideas and resources borrowed from other films and other art forms; Godard summons these according to his own needs. In *Alphaville* we find links with the work of Jean Cocteau in the sequence in which Lemmy converses with Alpha 60; the labyrinths of passages recall the phantasmic world of the novels of Franz Kafka; and we find a reference to the ancient myth of Eurydice and the Biblical story of Lot's wife. There are also references to the unforgotten Fascist past, as in the tattooed numbers of the city's inhabitants, the name of the designer of the central brain—Professor von Braun, or the use of actual rooms of the Parisian Hotel Continental, where the Gestapo was quartered during the Occupation. These references in the film are not incidental; they are utilized intentionally to broaden and deepen the picture and shift the story to another, more relevant level. However, they do not destroy the integrity and unity of the film even when the viewer is aware of them.

Godard's films of the 1960s were often received by a portion of the public and by some critics with an enthusiasm that was almost excessive. In the course of time, some of these films have lost their appeal. This has not happened in the case of *Alphaville*, which remains part of a valuable current of science fiction while holding its place in the history of cinema.

—B. Urgosíková

LES AMANTS. The Lovers. Production: Nouvelles Editions des films; black and white, 35mm, Cinemascope; running time: 90 mins. Released 1958.

Produced by Louis Malle; screenplay by Louis Malle and Louise Vilmorin; from "Point de lendemain" by Dominique Vivant and Baron de Denon; directed by Louis Malle; photography by Henri Decaë; edited by Léonide Azar; production design by Bernard Evein and Jacques Saulnier; music from Johannes Brahms.

Filmed in Paris. Venice Film Festival, Silver Prize, 1958.

Cast: Jeanne Moreau (*Jeanne Tournier*); Alain Cuny (*Henri Tournier*); Jose-Luis de Villalonga (*Raoul Torres*); Jean-Marc Bory (*Bernard Langlois*); Judith Magre (*Maggy*); Gaston Modot (*Servant*).

Publications:

Script—"*Les Amants*" in *L'Avant-Scène du cinéma* (Paris),

March 1961; review—"*The Lovers*" by Bosley Crowther in the *New York Times*, 27 October 1959; books—*Louis Malle* by Henri Chapier, Paris 1964; *French Cinema Since 1946: The Personal Style Vol. Two*, by Roy Armes, New York 1976; *Cinema, The Magic Vehicle: A Guide to Its Achievement: Journey Two: The Cinema of the Fifties* edited by Adam Garbicz and Jacek Klinowski, Metuchen, New Jersey 1979; articles—"Louis Malle's France" by Gordon Gow in *Films and Filming* (London), August 1964; "Night and Solitude: The Cinema of Louis Malle" by James Price in *London Magazine*, September 1964; "Louis Malle" by Russell Lej in the *New Left Review* (New York), March/April 1965; "Louis Malle" by D. McVay in *Focus on Film* (London), summer 1974; article in the *Guardian*, 10 August 1974; article in *New York Post*, 19 October 1974; "Louis Malle" in *Current Biography*, New York 1976.

*   *   *

Truly one of the most controversial films ever distributed in France, *Les Amants* remains startlingly evocative even when viewed for its historical importance. As the last in a series of pre-New Wave efforts, *Les Amants* exhibits several traits that would come to define that movement.

First is its subject matter. *Les Amants*, as every critic was quick to point out, is concerned with the emancipatory power of eroticism. Jeanne Moreau's tedious provincial life and her equally tedious Parisian high life are blown to bits by a sudden inexplicable sexual passion. Both her husband and her lover are left looking aghast as she drives off at the end with the young student who rescued her when her car broke down and then stayed to dinner.

French cinema has always been noted for its eroticism. Both the cinema of quality (Autant-Lara's *Blé en herbe*, for instance) and its challengers (Vadim's *And God Created Women*) were frequently explicit in their treatment of the topic. But Malle brought something new, something mystical, to eros. Instead of trying to shock (Autant-Lara) or titillate (Vadim), Malle seems genuinely lost in the power of his subject. Attacks against the naiveté of the film and its adolescent obsessions are genuinely to the point. The tone of *Les Amants* is the opposite of the all-knowing cinema of quality or the fashionable amorality conveyed by Brigitte Bardot; it is instead a tone of discovery, the discovery of the miracle of eroticism and what that miracle might mean for the complete revolution of a life. While Jeanne Moreau is not young in the film, her encounter with Bernard gives her a youth she has never before had.

One can hardly imagine a more straightforward rhetorical organization. Tedium and suffocation are shown in Paris and on the provincial estate until Moreau is sudddenly swept into rapture. What is unexpected is the extent of the expression of that rapture. Malle definitely goes beyond all standards of taste and morality in pressing their love on a moonlit walk, then across a lake in a boat, then in the chateau in bed. Endlessly they love while Brahms soars in the background. Only such an excessive presentation of the pure facts of eros could hope to convince us of the dramatic propriety of the finale, when Jeanne Moreau, without a second thought, without subterfuge, puts a suitcase in the student's 2-CV and changes her life.

Obviously such sentiments are limited, (today they even embarrass Louis Malle), but the authenticity of their presentation is crucial to the moment at which they were expressed. This was the age of the "cult of youth" celebrated in French journals and talk shows; this was the age of the popularity of existentialism with its pleas for authentic rebellion against outdated institutions; and this was the time of transition to a new government, in hopes of getting out of the morass of the Algerian war. This was in short the beginning of the culture of the New Wave.

Malle's film reflects this through and through. It does so in its star Jeanne Moreau and its production personnel (Vilmorin as scriptwriter, Decaë as cameraman). The flowing Cinemascope and surging lyricism of the Brahms score seek to convey directly the tenderness that finally erupts from the stagnant world picture of the film's first half.

Many critics were not convinced by the logic of the film's events. Others were outraged that explicit eroticism could be a film's goal as well as its means. *Les Amants* was censored everywhere: England, Switzerland, Italy, and in many towns in France. Still it made a fortune in Paris and its specially re-cut version played to packed houses in New York.

While Louis Malle was never in the New Wave group (and *Cahiers du cinéma* only modestly supported him), his audacity founded on a trust in authenticity over inhibitions, spontaneity over caution, and youth over age, put him in the entryway of that movement. *Les Amants* is an excessive and youthful film. That is its charm and its value.

—Dudley Andrew

AMERICAN GRAFFITI. Production: A Universal-Lucasfilm Ltd.-Coppola Production, 1973; color, 35mm; running time: 110 mins. Released 1973.

Produced by Francis Ford Coppola and Gary Kurtz; screenplay by George Lucas, Gloria Katz, and Willard Huyck; from an idea by George Lucas; directed by George Lucas; photography by Ron Eveslage and Jan D'Alquen; edited by Verna Fields and Marcia Lucas; sound by Walter Murch; musical score comprised of original versions of several rock-and-roll "classics" from early 1960s.

Filmed 1972 in Petaluma and San Rafael, California. Cost: about $700,000. New York Film Critics Award, Best Screenwriting, 1973.

Cast: Richard Dreyfuss (*Curt Henderson*); Ron Howard (*Steve Bolander*); Paul Le Mat (*John Milner*); Charles Martin Smith (*Terry Fields*); Cindy Williams (*Laurie Henderson*); Candy Clark (*Debbie*); Mackenzie Phillips (*Carol*); Suzanne Sommers (*Girl in T-Bird*); Wolfman Jack (*Disc jockey*); Harrison Ford (*Drag racer*).

Publications:

Reviews—"*American Graffiti*" by M. Dempsey in *Film Quarterly* (Berkeley), fall 1973; "*American Graffiti*" by R. Combs in *Monthly Film Bulletin* (London), February 1974; "*American Graffiti*" by J. Dawson in *Sight and Sound* (London), spring 1974; "*American Graffiti*" by S. Rosenthal in *Focus on Film* (London), spring 1974; "*American Graffiti*" by A. Warner in *Films and Filming* (London), May 1974; articles—in *The New York Times*, 7 October 1973; "Films" by J. Ney in *Interview* (New York), September 1973; "The Filming of *American Graffiti*" by Larry Sturhahn in *Filmmakers Newsletter* (Ward Hill, Mass.), March 1974; "George Lucas: The Stinky Kid Hits the Big Time" by Steven Farber in *Film Quarterly* (Berkeley), spring 1974; "*American Graffiti*" by B. Houston and M. Kinder in *Film*

Heritage (Dayton, Ohio), winter 1973-74; "Lettre de Londres (*De L'Exorciste* à *Gatsby le magnifique*)" by J. Segond in *Positif* (Paris), September 1974; "The Epic World of *American Graffiti*" by A. Sodowsky, R. Sodowsky, and S. Witte in *Journal of Popular Film* (Bowling Green, Ohio), IV/1, 1975; "Theory of Film: Principles of Realism and Pleasure" by C. MacCabe in *Screen* (London), no.3, 1976; "George Lucas" in *Current Biography Yearbook*, New York 1978; "Songs of Innocence and Experience: The Blakean Vision of George Lucas" by B.H. Fairchild, Jr. in *Literature/Film Quarterly* (Salisbury, Maryland), no.2, 1979; "The Man Who Made *Star Wars*" by M. Pye and L. Miles in *Atlantic Monthly* (Greenwich, Conn.), March 1979; "*American Graffiti*" by Howard H. Prouty in *Magill's Survey of Cinema* edited by Frank N. Magill, Englewood Cliffs, New Jersey 1980; "George Lucas—Burden of Dreams" by Aljean Harmetz in *American Film* (Washington, D.C.), June 1983.

*   *   *

If *Star Wars* is George Lucas's idealized dream of the future, *American Graffiti* is his idealized dream of the past, a past in which optimism and naiveté were cherished sentiments before cynicism became a national past time. What joins these two films, however, is a devotion to entertainment, to the depiction of glorious worlds in which adventure is triumphant.

With the assistance of Francis Ford Coppola, Lucas's remembrance of teenage life in his home town of Modesto, California was brought to the screen, ushering in a wave of nostalgia for the music and lifestyle of an era ten years past, an era which subsequently became a staple of television situation comedies such as *Happy Days* and *Laverne and Shirley*, Ronnie Howard and Cindy Williams moving easily from this film to their television roles.

The central organizing device of this film is the musical score, permissions for which totalled $80,000 of the $700,000 budget. Music, which functions as the narrator of teen dreams and frustrations, as omnipresent companion, and as motivator of lifestyle, joins the various narrative threads and the three central locales: the hop where you danced to a band, the diner where you played the jukebox, and the strip where you listened to Spiritual Father Wolfman Jack on the car radio. To accentuate the over-riding function of the music, Lucas strove for a visual quality which resembled the aura of a 1962 "Hot-Rods-to-Hell" jukebox. For many growing up is a musical experience and, along with Barry Levinson's *Diner*, *American Graffiti* is the best evocation of that idea.

The narrative of *American Graffiti* is that of a day in the life of four central male characters coming of age after indulging in a series of misadventrues. Lucas located a mood of optimism and naiveté by setting the film in 1962, the period immediately prior to the Kennedy assassination and the resultant politicization of American youth and music. Naive optimism was so firmly entrenched that individuals refused to admit the necessity for personal development. Kurt, who's avowed dream was to shake the hand of JFK, almost succumbs to the complacent notion of "why leave home to find a new home?" At the end of the film after much indecisiveness, he does leave in pursuit of a future beyond the confines of family and security. As such he is representative of those students of the sixties who overcame their innocence and ventured forth.

In Lucas's sentimental view of growing up, he lovingly portrayed the innocence and freedom of life-before-twenty and perhaps unwittingly, the seductive mythology of the teen dream. Audiences bought the dream overwhelmingly. *American Graffiti* grossed over 50 million in its first year, making it, to that point, the most successful film made for under one million dollars. Recently its release in Japan has helped foster a booming business there in American musical and fashion nostalgia.

—Doug Tomlinson

AN AMERICAN IN PARIS. Production: Metro-Goldwyn-Mayer Picture Corp.; 1950; Technicolor, 35mm; running time: 113 mins. Released 1950.

Produced by Arthur Freed; screenplay by Alan Jay Lerner; directed by Vincente Minnelli; photography by Al Gilks, final ballet by John Alton; edited by Adrienne Fazan; art direction by Preston Ames and Cedric Gibbons, set decoration by Keogh Gleason and Edwin B. Willis; music by George and Ira Gershwin, music direction by Johnny Green and Saul Chaplin; costumes designed by Orry-Kelly, the Beaux-Arts Ball costumed by Walter Plunkett, and the final ballet costumed by Irene Sharaff; choreography by Gene Kelly.

Filmed 1 August 1950-fall 1950 at MGM studios, Culver City, California; also on location in Paris. Academy Awards for Best Picture, Story and Screenplay, Cinematography-Color, Art Direction-Color, Scoring, Costume Design-Color, 1951.

Cast: Gene Kelly (*Jerry Mulligan*); Leslie Caron (*Lise Borvier*); Oscar Levant (*Adam Cook*); Georges Guetary (*Henri Baurel*); Nina Foch (*Milo Roberts*); Eugene Borden (*Georges Mattieu*); Martha Bamattre (*Mathilde Mattieu*); Mary Young (*Old woman dancer*); Ann Codee (*Therese*); George Davis (*Francola*); Hayden Rourke (*Tommy Baldwin*); Paul Maxey (*John McDowd*); Dick Wessel (*Ben Macrow*).

Publications:

Review—by Edward Jablonski in *Films in Review* (New York), October 1951; books—*Vincente Minnelli* by Catherine de la Roche, New Zealand 1959, reprinted in *Film Culture* (New York), June 1959; *The Cinema of Gene Kelly* by Richard Griffith, New York 1962; *Vincente Minnelli* by François Truchaud, Paris 1966; *All Talking, All Singing, All Dancing* by John Springer, New York 1966; *Gotta Sing, Gotta Dance* by John Kobal, New York 1970; *Gene Kelly* by Michael Burrows, Cornwall, England 1971; *The MGM Years* by Lawrence B. Thomas, New Rochelle, New York 1972; *The Magic Factory* by Donald Knox, New York 1973; *The Movie Musical* by Lee Edward Stern, New York 1974; articles—"Vincente Minnelli" by Simon Harcourt-Smith in *Sight and Sound* (London), January/March 1952; "The Films of Vincent Minnelli" by A. Johnson in *Film Quarterly* (Berkeley), winter 1958 and spring 1959; "The Rise and Fall of the Film Musical" by Vincente Minnelli in *Films and Filming* (London), January 1962; "*Un Américain à Paris*" by François Truchaud in *Télérama* (Paris), 13 December 1964; "Gene Kelly" by Rudy Behlmer in *Films in Review* (New York), January 1964; "Dancer, Actor, Director" by John Cutts in *Films and Filming* (London), August 1964 and September 1964; "Ruekblende" by W. Steinhauer in *Film und Ton* (Munich), March 1973; "*An American in Paris*" in *Classic Film Collector* (Indiana, Pennsylvania), fall 1976; "*An American in Paris*" by Julia Johnson in *Magill's Survey of Cinema, Vol. 1* edited by Frank N. Magill, Englewood Cliffs, New Jersey 1980.

*　　*　　*

An American in Paris, one of the most successful and popular musicals in the history of film, is also one of the few Technicolor musicals to be taken seriously by critics during the Golden Age of Hollywood when many such films were made. Its grand finale, a 17-minute ballet, focused attention on the fact that films did not have to contain a serious message to be worthy examples of the art form. *An American in Paris* won the Academy Award for Best Picture of 1951, captured five other Academy Awards, and was placed on most lists of best films for that year. It stands as a prime example of a type of musical collaboration made during the studio system.

Difficult critical questions arise regarding the complicated assigning of credit involved in evaluating such movies. First of all, *An American in Paris* is an example of "producer cinema," being one of a list of musicals made by the famous Arthur Freed unit at Metro-Goldwyn-Mayer. The Freed unit was also responsible for *The Bandwagon, Singin' in the Rain, The Pirate, Meet Me in St. Louis,* and many others. Secondly, the creative input of star Gene Kelly, who did the choreography of the ballet, is undeniable, as are the myriad contributions made by MGM's outstanding roster of technicians—costume designer Irene Sharaff, cinematographer John Alton, art director Preston Ames, musicians Johnny Green and Saul Chaplin, and many more. Finally, it is most certainly a film by director Vincente Minnelli as it contains his recurring theme of characters in pursuit of their dreams, as well as his typical use of color, costume, and decor. Minnelli's musicals are among the most elegant and polished of the MGM musicals and his flair for camera movement, elaborately constructed long takes, and richly styled backgrounds contribute much to the film.

The opening scenes of *An American in Paris*, in which its characters wake up in "this star called Paris" and go about their daily routines, constitute an hommage to Rouben Mamoulian's 1932 film *Love Me Tonight*. In addition to the famous ballet, the innovative musical numbers contain a subjective characterization of Leslie Caron, presented through music, dance, and color. As she is described, images of her appear on screen each with a different Gershwin tune, different color, costume, setting and color-coordinated background. She is portrayed as sexy, studious, demure, athletic, etc., while the style of dance interprets her inner quality. Other musical numbers include the pas de deux "Our Love is Here to Stay", which is a beautiful blend of music, setting, costume and dance, photographed simply with a tight frame around the two dancers as the camera follows their movements. The old-fashioned "I'll Build a Staircase to Paradise" is a tribute to an earlier tradition, the Zeigfield Follies musical number. The musical highlight of the film is the ballet itself, which is based visually on a series of famous paintings by Dufy, Utrillo, Toulouse-Lautrec and others. Structually, the ballet carries out the story and theme of the film's narrative in an oblique manner. An ex-G.I., who has stayed on in Paris after the war, meets a young French girl, falls in love with her, and loses her. Following the ballet, a brief scene provides reconciliation to allow for the inevitable happy ending.

An American In Paris has undergone something of a critical devaluation in the past decade. Other Minnelli musicals (*Meet Me in St. Louis, The Pirate, The Bandwagon*) are considered superior works, and the Kelly/Stanley Donen *Singin' in the Rain* is more popular with general audiences. *An American in Paris* is frquently criticized as being too sentimental, too romantic and, because of the ballet, too pretentious. Nevertheless, the film undoubtedly contributed to the maturing process of the musical genre. By challenging the idea that audiences would not understand or accept a long ballet deeply linked to the narrative of the film it helped to free the dance visually and to expand the horizons of viewers as well as the creative possibilities for the artists making musical films.

—Jeanine Basinger

DER AMERIKANISCHE FREUND. The American Friend. Production: Road Movies Filmproduktion GmbH (Berlin), Les Films du Losange (Paris), Wim Wenders Produktion (Munich), and Westdeutschen Rundfunk (Cologne); Eastmancolor, 35mm; running time: 123 mins (some sources list 127 mins.). Released 1977.

Produced by Wim Wenders; screenplay by Wim Wenders; from the novel *Ripley's Game* by Patricia Highsmith; directed by Wim Wenders; photography by Robby Müller; edited by Peter Przygodda; art direction by Sickerts; music by Jürgen Knieper. Filmed in Paris.

Cast: Bruno Ganz (*Jonathan Zimmerman*); Dennis Hopper (*Tom Ripley*); Lisa Kreuzer (*Marianne Zimmerman*); Gérard Blain (*Raoul Minot*); Nicholas Ray (*Derwatt*); Samuel Fuller (*The American*); Peter Lilienthal (*Marcangelo*); Daniel Schmid (*Ingraham*); Jean Eustache (*Man in restaurant*); Sandy White-law (*Man in Paris*); Wim Wenders (*Mafia member);* Lou Castel (*Rodolphe*); Andreas Dedecke (*Daniel*).

Publications:

Reviews—"*Der amerikanische Freund*" by G. Moskowitz in *Variety* (New York), 8 June 1977; "*Der amerikanische Freund*" by H. Niogret in *Positif* (Paris), July/August 1977; "*L'Ami américan*" by D. Sauvaget in *Image et son* (Paris), November 1977; "*The American Friend*" by M. McCreadie in *Films in Review* (New York), December 1977; "Traquenards" by J. Narboni in *Cahiers du cinéma* (Paris), November 1977; "*The American Friend*" by Vincent Canby in *The New York Times*, 23 September 1977; "*The American Friend*" by Gordon Gow in *Films and Filming* (London), July 1978; "*Der Amerikanische Freund*" by T. Milne in *Monthly Film Bulletin* (London), January 1978; "*The American Friend*" by G. Morris in *Take One* (Montreal), January 1978; books—*Wim Wenders* (brochure) by Jan Dawson, Toronto 1976; *The New German Cinema* by John Sandford, Totowa, New Jersey 1980; articles—"German Helmer Wenders Rolls Co-Production for Theatrical and TV Release" in *Variety* (New York), 3 November 1976; "Awaiting *Big Red*, Sam Fuller Acts" in *Variety* (New York), 24 November 1976; "Germany's Wenders Using 3 Actors-Helmers in His $1,000,000 Frame" in *Variety* (New York), 1 December 1976; "King of the Road: Wim Wenders Interviewed" by C. Clarens in *Film Comment* (New York), September/October 1977; "Wim Wenders" by L. Dahan in *Cinématographe* (Paris), June 1977; "Le Romanesque et le spectaculaire" by A. Masson in *Positif* (Paris), October 1977; "Entretien avec Wim Wenders" by A. Masson and H. Niogret in *Positif* (Paris), October 1977; "*Der amerikanische Freund*" by O. Caldirone in *Bianco e nero* (Rome), May-/June 1978; "*The American Friend*" in *Films and Filming* (London), July 1978; "Filming Highsmith" by J. Dawson in *Sight and Sound* (London), winter 1977-78; "*The American Friend*" by K. Jaehne in *Sight and Sound* (London), spring 1978; "De emotionele reizen van Wim Wenders" by L. D. Winter in *Skrien* (Ams-

terdam), April 1978; "Im Laden ces Bilderrahmers" in *Film und Ton* (Munich), December 1979; "The Image of America in German Literature and in the New German Film: Wim Wenders *Der Amerikanische Freund* by J.D. Schlunk in *Literature/Film Quarterly* (Salisbury, Maryland), no.3 1979; "*The American Friend*" by M. Kinder in *Film Quarterly* (Berkeley), no.2 1979.

*   *   *

After his successful trilogy *Alice in the Cities*, *False Movement*, and *Kings of the Road*, Wim Wenders sought to give expression to his boundless admiration, extraordinary love and perfect formal command of American cinema with a thriller based on Patricia Highsmith's *Ripley's Game*.

The American Friend concerns two men: the picture framer Jonathan Zimmermann (Bruno Ganz) and Tom Ripley (Dennis Hopper), who wears a cowboy hat even in Hamburg and seems intentionally to caricature himself. Nicholas Ray and Samuel Fuller also appear, both in very short but unforgettable episodes, and there is a series of quotes, cliches, allusions, and analogies recalling typical Hollywood products—Hitchcock, *Johnny Guitar, Taxi Driver.*

This list of antecedents was proposed by the West German critic H.C. Blumenberg, who remarked further, "If mathematical formulae could be applied to cinema, there would be a new theorem: Hitchcock plus Ray plus Scorsese = Wenders." Witty and to the point: this is *The American Friend.*

A gloomy Hamburg, its old, destroyed houses, the filthy area of the fishmarket; Paris, in turn, consisting of escalators, narrow airless streets; then a deteriorating New York, skyscrapers and dirt, noise and dust—these are not single cities but a megalopolis, the modern city: hostile, deserted, ghostly. Man is alone, relationships don't work out. The tentative attempt at friendship between Zimmermann and Ripley remains essentially unspoken, half-hearted, unfulfilled. Jonathan is seriously ill, confused; he gets involved in a situation with a gangster. Of course Jonathan inflates him into a hero, becomes dependent, and is condemned. But by who, why, for what?

Wim Wenders gives no answer, because it doesn't concern him. He reproduces, reconstructs, falls in love again with the images, the colors, and sounds that have fascinated him: the Hollywood film myth. Hitchcock, Ray, Scorsese...

Blumenberg had continued: "The influence of the American cinema is not an isolated instance here, but combines with the outlook formulated in the three previous Wenders films to make a new unity. Its elements are thirties film, a laconic pessimism, pointless flight through run-down neighborhoods, agonizing identity crises, fear of women, and the myth of male comradeship, here brought to its culmination by Ripley and Jonathan, who get to know each other with a precarious tenderness, and who, out of the collision of two styles of performance—Hopper completely laid-back, spontaneous, Ganz very disciplined and restrained—achieve a further dimension of uncertainty: 'A little older, a little more confused...' "

That is the problem with this film: a faultlessly constructed work, suspenseful and fascinating, with good casting and well-known faces. For what purpose is such a film made? *The American Friend* has nothing to do with individuality, the personal, the auteur cinema. Its success is based on a myth: that Hollywood film is the best in the world. In West Germany this opinion is considered self-evident and indisputable. Students in film school are taught to make films following the American model, mainly because authentic German films do so much poorer financially than the big American films. So German directors try to match the receipts of American blockbusters.

A series of young, gifted artists such as Vadim Glowna, Christel Buschmann, and Peter Lilienthal shoot their films in America and attempt to attract an audience. *The American Friend* was the first and most succesful of this type of film, but it nevertheless is a secondary work—a carefully amateurish myth, spontaneously supported by critics because they immediately recognized in it everything they had already come to know as beautiful.

—Maria Racheva

AMOR DE PERDICÃO. Amour de perdition. Doomed Love. Production: Instituto Portuguese de Cinema; color, originally shot in 16mm; running time: 260 mins. Released 1978.

Produced by Anabela Goncaldes; screenplay by Manoel de Oliveira; from the novel by Camilo Castelo Branco; directed by Manoel de Oliveira; photography by Manuel Costa e Silva; edited by Soldeig Nordlund; art direction by Antonio Casmiro; music by João Paes and Handel.

Filmed in Portugal.

Cast: Antonio Sequeira Lopes (*Simão*); Cristina Hauser (*Tereza*); Elsa Wallencamp (*Mariana*); Antonio Costa (*Juao de Cruz*); Pedro Dinheiro and Manuela de Melo (*Narrators*).

Publications:

Reviews—"*Amour de perdition*" by B. Desclimont in *Revue du cinéma* (Paris), Series 23, 1979; "*Amor de perdicao*" by D. Holloway in *Variety* (New York), 15 October 1980; books—*Manoel de Oliveira*, Cinemateca Portuguesa, Lisbon 1981; *Introdução à de M. de Oliveira* by J.A. França , L. Pina, and A. Costa, Lisbon 1982; articles—"O voto de Simão e Teresa" by Jaõo Lopes in *Diário de Noticias* (Lisbon), November 1979; "*Amour de perdition*" by R. Bassan in *Ecran* (Paris), 15 June 1979; "Manoel de Oliveira et *Amour de perdition*" by S. Daney in *Cahiers du cinéma* (Paris), June 1979; "*Amour de perdition*" by E. Bachellier in *Cahiers du cinéma* (Paris), September 1979; "*Amour de perdition*" by J.C. Bonnet in *Cinematographe* (Paris), July 1979; "*Amour de perdition*" by J. Frenais in *Cinéma 79* (Paris), July/August 1979; "M. de Oliveira: Le Passé et le present" by F. Ramasse in *Positif* (Paris), March 1980; "Det stillstående kamera" by K. Alnaee in *Film & Kino* (Oslo), no.4, 1981; "Manoel de Oliveira and *Doomed Love*" by C. Clarens in *Film Comment* (New York), May/June 1981; interview with Oliveira by J.C. Bonnet and E. Decaux in *Cinématographe* (Paris), November 1981; interview with Oliveira by C. Tesson and J.C. Biette in *Cahiers du cinéma* (Paris), October 1981; "Artificio, enunciácion, emocion: la obra de M. de Oliveira" by S. Zunsunegui in *Contracampo* (Madrid), January 1981; "Manoel de Oliveira" by John Gillett in *Sight and Sound* (London), summer 1981; "M. de Oliveira, o cinema e a crueldade" by M.S. Fonseca in *Expresso* (Lisbon), October 1981.

*   *   *

At the age of 70 Manoel de Oliveira completed *Amor de perdicão*, a 260-minute version of Camilo Castelo Branco's 19th century, hyper-romantic novel of the same name. It was the twelfth film in the career of Portugal's most famous filmmaker, a

career which began in 1931.

As meticulously as the novel, the film renders events in a procession of extremely long sequence-shots, often between five and ten minutes each. *Amor de perdicão* consciously occupies a precarious historical position: in a style wholly characteristic of the advanced cinema of the 1970s, with a startling original use of the zoom lens, it depicts events of the late 18th and early 19th centuries, mediated by the deliberately anachronistic language of the 1861 novel. The film resonates with allusions to the Iberian pictorial tradition (Velázquez and Goya are the most obvious references), yet it calls attention to the modalities of camera position, shot duration, illusionary movement created by the zoom, and the artificiality of its museum-like sets and occasional painted backdrops. Oliveira is indebted to the major historical films of the previous decade, especially *La Prise du pouvoir de Louis XIV, Il Gattopardo*, and *Barry Lyndon* in his use of the zoom and his historical distanciation, but he is far more systematic and abstract than his major predecessors. More obviously, he follows Robert Bresson in his cool resistance to imitating the histrionics of the text he adapts; but he avoids the truly radical deflation of drama typical of the later films of Straub and Huillet. Yet, perhaps he has learned something from their early work; for the breathtaking pace with which the Botelho family history is recounted, in elliptical jumps, in the first half hour of the film, recalls the most disorienting moments of *Nicht versont*.

The novel and the film recount the miseries of the star-crossed lovers, Simão Botelho and his neighbor Tereza, whose father forbids their marriage because of a family feud. In an intricate plot, which would be long in summary, Simão goes to jail for killing the man Tereza's father wants her to marry. In jail he is attended by the peasant girl, Mariana da Cruz, whose devotion to him takes the form of obsessive love. Eventually Simão dies en route to the Indies, as a penal worker; Tereza, already withdrawn into a convent, dies as his boat passes; and Mariana jumps overboard to her death. Only Oliveira's genius transmutes this morbid excess into a cinema of sustained beauty and restraint.

Though he shot the film in 16mm because he couldn't afford 35mm for the first time in his career, he exploited the loss of definition and the grain brilliantly. His compositions are consistently artificial, evoking enlarged indoor spaces by posing the characters far from the camera or, following the examples of Velázquez's *Las Meninas*, using a mirror to reflect offscreen depths. The continual interlacing of the voice-overs of narrators Simão and Tereza bring a stylistic device already abstracted by Bresson and Hanoun to a new level of intensity and abstraction.

The very duration of the film, its plethora of information spread over so many nearly static compositions, the extended meditation on confinement, and the beauty of its deliberate rhythms and compositions make *Amor de perdicão* one of the most impressive films of the 1970s, and one of the very greatest historical fiction films.

—P. Adams Sitney

ANDREI RUBLIOV. Andre Rublev. Andrei Roublev. Production: Mosfilm Studio (Moscow); black and white with a color sequence, 35mm, Cinemascope; running time: 185 mins.; length: 5180 meters. Released 1969 in France, not released in USSR until 1972 though the film had been screened in Moscow in 1965.

Screenplay by Andrei Mikhalkov-Konchalovsky and Andrei Tarkovsky; directed by Andrei Tarkovsky; photography by Vadim Youssov; edited by N. Beliaeva and L. Lararev; sound by

E. Zelentsova; production design by Eugueni Tcheriaiev; music by Viatcheslac Ovtchinnikov. The film was censored and re-edited (not by Tarkovsky) several times between production and release in 1969. Filmed 1965. Cannes Film Festival, International Critics Award, 1969.

Cast: Anatoli Solonitzine (*Rubliov*); Ivan Lapikov (*Dirill*); Nikolai Grinko (*Daniel the Black*); Nikolai Sergueiev (*Theophane the Greek*); Irma Raouch Tarkovskaya (*Deaf-mute*); Nikolai Bourliaiev (*Boriska*); Youri Nasarov (*Grand Duke*); Rolan Bykov (*Buffoon*); Youri Nikulin (*Patrikey*); Mikhail Kononov (*Fomka*); S. Krylov; Sos Sarkissyan; Bolot Eichelanev; N. Grabbe; B. Beijenaliev; B. Matisik; A. Oboukhov; Volodia Titov.

Publications:

Reviews—"*Andrej Rublijov*" by M. Cetinjski in *Ekran* (Ljubljana, Yugoslavia), no.104-105, 1973; "*Andrei Rubliov*" by M. Tarratt in *Films and Filming* (London), November 1973; "*Andrei Rublev*" by J. O'Hara in *Cinema Papers* (Australia), March/April 1975; books—*Young Soviet Film Makers* by Jeanne Vronskaya, London 1972; *The Cultural-Political Traditions and Developments of the Soviet Cinema: 1917-1972* by Louis H. Cohen, New York 1974; *Cinema Beyond the Danube: The Camera and Politics* by Michael Jon Stoil, Metuchen, New Jersey 1974; *The Most Important Art: East European Film After 1945* by Mira and Antonin Liehm, Berkeley 1977; articles—"*Andrei Rublev*" by Jeanne Vronskaya in *Monogram* (London), summer 1971; "Artysta na gościńcu epoki: *Andriej Rublow*" by W. Wiersewski in *Kino* (Warsaw), November 1972; "Man and Experience: Tarkovsky's World" by Ivor Montagu in *Sight and Sound* (London), spring 1973; "*Andrej Rublov*—film projekcije po projekciji" by J. Povše in *Ekran* (Ljubljana, Yugoslavia), no.108-110, 1973; "Allégorie et Stalinisme dans quelques films de l'est" by B. Amengual in *Positif* (Paris), January 1973; issue on *Andre Rubliov* in *Filmrutan* (Sweden), no.2, 1973; articles by S. Gerasimov and S. Yutkevich and others on *Andre Rubliov* in *Filmkultura* (Budapest), March/April 1973; "*Andrej Rublev*" by M. Grande in *Filmcritica* (Rome), January-/February 1976; "*Andrej Rubljov*" by F. Prono in *Cinema Nuovo* (Turin), March/April 1976; "*Andrei Roublev*" by G. Rineldi in *Cineforum* (Bergamo), January/February 1976; "*Andrei Roublev*" by Henry Chapier in *Combat* (Paris), 20 November 1979, excerpt repeated in *L'Avant-Scène du cinéma* (Paris), 15 December 1979; "Richesse et diversité du nouveau cinéma soviétique" by Michel Ciment in *L'Avant-Scène du cinéma* (Paris), 15 December 1979.

ANEMIC CINEMA. Black and white, 35mm, silent; running time: 6 mins. Released 1926 or 1927.

Directed by Marcel Duchamp; photography by Man Ray and Marc Allegret; disks by Marcel Duchamp.

Filmed 1926 or 1927.

Publications:

Books—*Art in Cinema* edited by Frank Stauffacher, San Francisco: Museum of Modern Art, 1947; *The World of Marcel Duchamp* by Calvin Tomkins, New York 1966; *Marcel Duchamp: 66 Creative Years* by Astruc Schwartz, Milan, Italy 1972; *Marcel Duchamp in Perspective* by Joseph Masheck, Englewood Cliffs, New Jersey 1974; *Abstract Film and Beyond* by Malcolm Le Grice, Cambridge, Massachusetts 1977; *Duchamp et la photographie: essai d'analyse d'un primat technique sur le developpement d'une oeuvre* by Jean Clair, Paris 1977; *Visionary Film: The American Avant-Garde* by P. Adams Sitney, New York 1979; articles—"Dots and Dashes, Circles and Splashes" by Cecile Starr in *Saturday Review* (New York), 8 March 1952; "Early Surrealist Expression in the Film" by Toby Mussman in *Film Culture* (New York), summer 1966; "The Surrealist Film" by Toby Mussman in *Film Culture* (New York), September 1966.

* * *

Anemic Cinema, Marcel Duchamp's only film remains one of the great oddities of the history of the cinema. It has had a great influence, particularly on avant-garde filmmakers of the 1970s. Its dada spirit mocks, by example, the "anemia" of cinematic representation.

The title is an anagram in the mode of Rose Selavy (Eros, c'est la vie!) the Duchampian persona who signs the film. The rearrangement of the letters of the word "cinema" reveals a half-French, half-English epithet "anemic" which defines the illusionary nature of cinema. Furthermore the alteration of disks of optical ilusions with those words printed spirals parodies the dependency of the silent cinema on inter-titles.

In a way all of the film's nineteen images or shots are essentially the same: the unbudging camera stares at a rotating disk perched above a turntable. The montage consists of nothing more than changing the disk. However, Duchamp exploits the eye's automatic response to eccentric circles and spirals in motion; it perceives them as protruding or receding forms. The spiral texts, on the other hand, look flat.

The texts are elaborate puns which imply an auditory response to the purely optical phenomenon. This pale invocation of the voice is another measure of the "anemia" of cinema. Almost all of the puns are erotic. One flagrant example is "Avez-vous déja mis la poelle de l'epée dans la moëlle de l'aimée? (Have you already put the marrow of the sword in the oven of the girlfriend?)" The very tendency of erotic associations to spread from blatant jokes to more gnomic utterances is yet another dimension of the film.

In short, *Anemic Cinema* cultivates a tedious, unchanging and minimalized surface in order to force its viewers to recognize how much their film experience is a reflection of the spatial, linguistic, and erotic conditioning of the mind.

—P. Adams Sitney

ANGST ESSEN SEELE AUF. Ali: Feat Eats the Soul. Production: Tango-Film Productions; color, 35mm; running time: 90 mins. Released 1973.

Produced by Rainer Werner Fassbinder; screenplay by Rainer Werner Fassbinder; directed by Rainer Werner Fassbinder; photography by Jürgen Jüges; edited by Thea Eymes; sound by Fritz Müller-Scherz; art direction by Rainer Werner Fassbinder; costumes designed by Helga Kempke.

Filmed in Germany. Cannes Film Festival, International Critics' Award (shared with Bresson's *Lancelot du Lac*), 1974.

Cast: Brigitte Mira (*Emmi*); El Hedi ben Salem (*Ali/El Hedi ben Salem M'Barek Mohammed Mustapha*); Barbara Valantin (*Barbara*); Irm Hermann (*Krista*); Peter Gauhe (*Bruno*); Karl Scheydt (*Albert*); Rainer Werner Fassbinder (*Eugen*); Marquand Bohm (*Herr Gruber*); Walter Sedlmayer (*Herr Angermeyer*); Doris Mattes (*Frau Angermeyer*); Liselotte Eder (*Frau Munchmeyer*); Gusti Kreissl (*Paula*); Elma Karlowa; Anita Bucher; Margit Symo; Katharina Herberg; Lilo Pompeit; Hannes Gromball; Hark Bohm; Rudolf Waldemar; Peter Moland.

Publications:

Reviews—"Tous les autres s'appellent Ali" by B. Amengual in *Positif* (Paris), September 1974; "*Angst essen Seele auf*" by R. Combs in *Monthly Film Bulletin* (London), November 1974; "*Tous les autres s'appellent Ali*" by J. Grant in *Cinéma* (Paris), July/August 1974; "*Fear Eats the Soul*" by T. Rayns in *Sight and Sound* (London), autumn 1974; review by Vincent Canby in *The New York Times*, 7 October 1974; "Todos nos llamamos alí" by J.V.G. Santamaria in *Contracampo* (Madrid), September 1980; books—*Fassbinder* by Wolfgang Limmer, Munich 1973; *I Fassbinders Spejl* by Christian Thomsen, Copenhagen 1975; *Fassbinder* by Tony Rayns, London 1976; *Das bisschen Realität, das ich brauche. Wir Filme entstehen* by Hans Pflaum, Munich 1976; *Reihe Film 2: Rainer Werner Fassbinder*, edited by Peter Jansen and Wolfram Schütte, Munich 1979; *The New German Cinema* by John Sandford, Totowa, New Jersey 1980; articles—"Fassbinder's Holy Whores" by Christian Braad Thomas in *Take One* (Montreal), July/August 1973; article by E. Hepnerová in *Film a Doba* (Prague), September 1974; "Sur 3 films allemands" by D. Sauvaget in *Image et son* (Paris), September 1974; "Die Darstellung alter Frauen in Film" by Helke Sander in *Frauen & Film* (Berlin), no.3, 1974; "Rainer Werner Fassbinder" by Manny Farber and Patricia Patterson in *Film Comment* (New York), November/December 1975; "A New Realism: Fassbinder Interviewed" by John Hughes and Brooks Riley in *Film Comment* (New York), November/December 1975; "Fassbinder—The Poetry of the Inarticulate" by Paul Thomas in *Film Quarterly* (Berkeley), winter 1976-77; "*Angst Essen Seele Auf*" by Ed Lowry in *Cinema Texas Program Notes* (Austin), 3 November 1977; "Method and Message: Forms of Communication in Fassbinder's *Angst Essen Seele Auf*" by J.C. Franklin in *Literature/Film Quarterly* (Salisbury, Maryland), no. 3, 1979.

*   *   *

Rainer Werner Fassbinder's fifteenth film, *Angst essen Seele auf*, represents perhaps the peak of his renowned domestic melodrama period, bracketed approximately by *The Merchant of Four Seasons* and *Angst von Angst*. The story of an improbable romance between Ali, a young black *Gastarbeiter* in Munich, and Emmi, an elderly, widowed German cleaning woman, *Angst essen Seele auf* is patterned rather explicitly on the Hollywood "women's pictures" of Douglas Sirk; in this case, *All That Heaven Allows*, where bourgeois widow Jane Wyman falls in love with her younger gardener, Rock Hudson, and finds herself ostracized by her children as well as the country club set. Admiring Sirk for his ability to deal with interpersonal politics in the context of melodrama (a genre animated by personal crisis in a

social/familial context), Fassbinder was equally impressed by the visual stylization of Sirk's mise-en-scène.

Employing a Sirkian stylization in camera angle, framing, color and lighting, Fassbinder takes on the conventions of melodrama in *Angst essen Seele auf*, yet exaggerates them in the direction of Bertolt Brecht, emphasizing the social typage of the characters, arranging characters in frozen tableaux at key moments, and distancing the viewer by constantly framing through doorways and in long shot. The effect is to force the contradictions of the story to reveal themselves on an intellectual level, to remove the viewer from the level of pure empathy to that of understanding the ways in which the characters' lives are determined by age, social status and economic class. Like Sirk's characters, Ali and Emmi face social ostracism for their love—the harrassment of neighbors, co-workers and merchants, and the horror of family and friends. After returning from a trip to get away from it all, they finally find themselves accepted; but only to the extent that returning them to their "proper" social roles allows them to be exploited once again by those around them.

It is a very cold world which Fassbinder depicts, a world in which emotion and love are exploited. Writing on Sirk, Fassbinder (whose first film is appropriately titled *Love is Colder Than Death*) asserted his conviction that "love is the best, most insidious, most effective instrument of social repression"; and *Angst essen Seele auf* is an unblinking illustration of his point. Once relieved of the social pressure which brought the lonely Ali and Emmi together, they find their personal relationship determined by many of the same prejudices and assumptions, playing out their "types" and becoming more like those who despised them.

What emerges is a scathing critique of social repression seen from the lowest rungs of society's ladder. The ungrammatical title, translated literally "fear eat up soul," is a phrase used by Ali to describe the pain he is suffering in his relationship with Emmi, a pain which eventually manifests itself as an ulcerated stomach—a malady, a doctor tells Emmi, suffered by many foreign workers. The irony that this strange, almost grotesque couple must suffer a fate which is normal, typical and utterly anti-romantic adds a chilling sense of truth to the film's epigraph, "Happiness is not always fun."

It would be incorrect to assert that the analytic aspects of the film preclude an emotional response; for if Fassbinder makes it almost impossible to empathize with Ali and Emmi in the conventional sense, it is only to provoke more deeply disturbing feelings. Fassbinder has been quoted to the effect that "films that say the feelings you believe you have don't really exist, they are only the sentiments which you think you ought to have as a well-functioning member of society—such films have to be cold." Yet the coldness of *Angst essen Seele auf* is not emotionless; far from dulling the viewer, it produces a profound shiver, marking the success of Fassbinder in constructing a film which will make audiences both think *and* feel.

—Ed Lowry

L'ANNÉE DERNIÈRE À MARIENBAD. Last Year at Marienbad. Production: Terra Films, Société Nouvelle des Films Cormoran, Argos Films, Précitel, Como Films, Les Films Tamara, Cinetel, Silver Films (Paris), and Cineriz (Rome), 1961; black and white, 35mm, Dyaliscope; running time: 100 mins; English version: 93 mins. Released September 1961, Paris.

Produced by Pierre Courau and Raymond Froment; screenplay by Alain Robbe-Grillet; main titles by Jean Fouchet and English subtitles by Noele Gillmor; directed by Alain Resnais; photography by Sacha Vierny; edited by Henri Colpi and Jasmine Chasney; sound by Guy Villette; art direction by Jacques Saulnier, set decoration by Georges Glon, André Piltant, and Jean-Jacques Fabre; music by Francis Seyrig, musical direction by André Girard; costumes designed by Bernard Evein and Chanel; 2nd assistant director: Volker Schlöndorff.

Filmed September-November 1960 in Photosonar Studios, Paris and on location in Munich at various chateaux including Nymphenburg and Schleissheim. Lion of St. Mark, Venice Film Festival, 1961.

Cast: Delphine Seyrig (A); Giorgio Albertazzi (X); Sacha Pitoëff (M); Françoise Bertin; Luce Garcia-Ville; Hélèna Kornel; Françoise Spira; Karin Toech-Mittler; Pierre Barbaud; Wilhelm Von Deek; Jean Lanier; Gérard Lorin; Davide Montemuri; Gilles Quéant; Gabriel Werner.

Publications:

Scripts—*L'Année dernière à Marienbad* by Alain Robbe-Grillet, Paris 1961; *Last Year at Marienbad* by Alain Robbe-Grillet, translated by Richard Howard, London 1962; reviews—"*Last Year at Marienbad*" by Bosley Crowther in *The New York Times*, 8 March 1962; "*L'Année dernière à Marienbad*" by Penelope Houston in *Sight and Sound* (London), winter 1961-62; "On Last Year at Marienbad" by Henri Colpi in *New York Film Bulletin*, no.2, 1962; books—*Alain Resnais, ou la création au cinéma* by Stéphane Cordier, Paris 1961; *Alain Resnais* by Bernard Pingaud, Lyon 1961; *Alain Resnais* by Gaston Bounoure, Paris 1962; *Antonioni, Bergman, Resnais* by Peter Cowie, London 1963; *Robbe-Grillet* by Jean Miesch, Paris 1965; *Alain Robbe-Grillet* by Bruce Morrissette, New York 1965; *La Vision du monde d'Alain Robbe-Grillet* by J.V. Alter, Geneva, Switzerland 1966; *Nouvelle Vague: The First Decade* by Raymond Durgnat, Loughton, England 1966; *Film Makers on Filmmaking* edited by Harry M. Geduld, Bloomington, Indiana 1967; *The Cinema of Alain Resnais* by Roy Armes, London 1968; *Alain Resnais, or the Theme of Time* by John Ward, New York 1968; *The New Wave* by Peter Graham, Garden City, New York 1968; *Resnais, Alain Resnais* by Paolo Bertetto, Italy 1976; *Alain Resnais* by John Francis Kreidl, Boston 1977; *Alain Resnais: The Role of Imagination* by James Monaco, New York 1978; *In the Theory and Practice of the Ciné-Roman* by William F. Van Wert, New York 1978; *The Film Narratives of Alain Resnais* by Freddy Sweet, Ann Arbor, Michigan 1981; articles—interview with Resnais by Yvonne Baby in *Le Monde* (Paris), 29 August 1961; "Introduction à la methode d'Alain Resnais and d'Alain Robbe-Grillet in *Les Lettres françaises* (Paris), 10 August 1961; interview with Resnais in *Cahiers du cinéma* (Paris), September 1961, reprinted in *Films and Filming* (London), March 1962; "Marienbad Année Zéro" by André Labarthe in *Cahiers du cinéma* (Paris), September 1961; "*L'Année dernière à Marienbad*" by Alain Robbe-Grillet in *Sight and Sound* (London), autumn 1961; interview with Resnais by Eugene Archer in *The New York Times*, 18 March 1962; article by Jacques Brunius and interview with Resnais by Penelope Houston in *Sight and Sound* (London), winter 1961-62; "Last Word on Last Year" in *Films and Filming* (London), March 1962; "Trying to Understand My Own Film" by Alain Resnais in *Films and Filming* (London), February 1962; "A Conversation with Alain Resnais and Alain Robbe-Grilliet" by André S. Labarthe and Jacques Rivette in *New York Film Bulletin*, no.2, 1962; "Every Year at Marienbad or the Discipine of Uncertainty" by Jacques Brunius in *Sight and Sound* (London), summer 1962; "*Marienbad* Revisited" by Neal Oxenhandler in *Film Quarterly* (Berkeley), fall 1963; "Alain Robbe-Grillet" in *Vogue* (New York), 1 January 1963; "The Time and Space of Alan Resnais" by Alan Stanbrook in *Films and Filming* (London), January 1964; "Alain Resnais" in *Cinema Eye, Cinema Ear* by John Russell Taylor, New York 1964; "Film et roman: problèmes du récit" by Jean Ollier in *Cahiers du cinéma* (Paris), December 1966; "Nouveau roman and nouveau cinéma" by Bernard Pingaud in *Cahiers du cinéma* (Paris), December 1966; "Memories of Resnais" by Richard Roud in *Sight and Sound* (London), summer 1969; "Interview with Delphine Seyrig" by Rui Noguera in *Sight and Sound* (London), fall 1969; "10 Years After Marienbad" by Richard Blumengerg in *Cinema Journal* (Evanston, Illinois), spring 1971; "*Muriel*" and "*L'Année dernière à Marienbad*" in *Cinéma et Société* by Annie Goldmann, Paris 1971; "Aspects of Cinematic Consciousness" by D. Skoller in *Film Comment* (New York), September/October 1972; "Memory is Kept Alive with Dreams" by Peter Harcourt in *Film Comment* (New York), November/December 1973; "Le Symbolisme du noir et blanc dans *L'Année dernière à Marienbad*" by D. Rocher in *Etudes cinématographiques* (Paris), no.100-103, 1974; "*L'Année dernière a Marienbad*" by Lorrie Oshatz in *Cinema Texas Notes* (Austin), 30 March 1978; "Lieux du cinéma: de Versailled à Marienbad" by G. Dupont in *Cinématographe* (Paris), February 1979; "Ricardou and *Last Year at Marienbad*" by Roy Armes in *Quarterly Review of Film Studies* (New York), winter 1980.

*   *   *

Alain Resnais's *Last Year at Marienbad* shares, with a handful of other films (notably Truffaut's *The 400 Blows* and *Jules and Jim*, Godard's *Breathless*, and Resnais's own *Hiroshima Mon Amour*), the distinction of being a landmark of the French New Wave, and as such, a major influence upon later film styles. Unlike those other films, it remains controversial as it is often dismissed or despised as pretentious nonsense by some while admired as a masterpiece by others. In any case, it remains far more than the other films, distinctly avant-garde in its conception of narrative.

Co-authorship of the film must be assigned to screenwriter Alain Robbe-Grillet, whose earlier novels (notably *Jealousy*, 1959) share themes and narrative techniques with *Marienbad*. Robbe-Grillet's later works—films he directed as well as novels—have an even stronger resemblance to this first screenplay. This is not to deny major credit to Resnais, whose fascination with themes of time and memory runs through virtually all his films, and who had already displayed in an earlier feature and in a series of short subjects a mastery of montage and gliding camera movements characteristic of *Marienbad*.

Marienbad's initial fame was based on certain surface qualities: the baroque palace setting with its eerie formal gardens (Poe's Haunted Palace brought to life), the frozen postures of the guests, the "Marienbad" game the guests play (a brief fad after the film's release), and the puzzling plot of a man ("X") who attempts to convince a languid woman ("A") to leave her sinister husband or lover as—X claims—she had already agreed to do last year at Marienbad. A, however, claims not to know X. A radical feature of the film is the frequent number of flashbacks, and possible flashforwards, which may in fact be fantasy scenes: the subjective visions of X or A or both. The film is also radical in its use of narrative voice. At times descriptions by the voice do not correspond to the actions on the screen; or the narrator's sentence is finished by the dialogue of an actor in an amateur play; or minor characters repeat earlier speeches of the narrator verbatim.

Faced with the impossibility of working out a linear, coherent narrative from this material, some have rejected the entire work as deliberately incoherent, while others have reveled in its intoxicating images and rhythms: the splendid black-and-white cinemascope compositions; the sweeping, occasionally dizzying tracking shots; the abrupt yet controlled contrasts of light and shadow. The film need not, however, be taken as an abstract or "contentless" work. It simply demands to be considered in terms of its significant images and rhythms, and the matters discussed by the characters and the narrator, rather than in terms of a traditional narrative and psychological analysis of the characters.

The film is clearly epistomological in its interests. It is about how one constructs "reality" for oneself, as X evidently so convinces A that they did meet at Marienbad that his possible fantasy becomes her reality. In his valuable preface to his film script, Robbe-Grillet suggests that whatever a film shows is "present tense," unlike the novel's past and conditional tenses; hence what may be X's or A's fantasies become reality not only for them but for the viewer as well. The film can also be said to be about how people attach meanings to existence. Characters in the film discuss the possible symbolism of a mysterious, hauntingly expressive statue. This artwork surely corresponds to the film itself. The viewer must interpret the characters and their motives, must decide what among the scenes witnessed is fantasy or lies, and what, if anything, is fact. Indeed, in the first 15 minutes of the film, the viewer must figure out which of the large number of "guests" investigated by the roaming camera are to be the main characters: the camera teasingly eavesdrops and gives misleading hints.

The film is also about the relation of life to art and artifice. As we make an effort to remember the past, we "freeze" an image of it which is not reality, but a picture, an artwork, or perhaps a fantasy. This epistemological theme is developed by the film not only in its basic drama but in its constant attention to works of art and to the artificiality of the characters: statuary and people who pose like statues; a theatrical production even more stylized than the actual performances in the film; engravings and photographs; and the palace-hotel itself with its formal gardens. The baroque setting is perfect. Its curvilinear forms suggest frozen and symmetrical plant life, while the geometrical gardens are an exceedingly artificial arrangement of real plants. Ultimately the film suggests that perception itself is the creation of artifice.

Marienbad may be read on other, but not necessarily incompatible, levels as well. Freudians may see it as a fantasia on an Oedipal triangle, with both veiled and explicit images of sexual violence. Or it may be taken as a drama of entrapment or self-entrapment, like Jean-Paul Sartre's *No Exit*: a spectacle of people who cannot escape the prison of their own egos or the dominance of others.

It is difficult to trace the precise influence of Marienbad on later films, except for some specific cases such as the films of Robbe-Grillet, beginning with *L'Immortelle* (1963). Also included are the structures and rhythms in the films of Nicholas Roeg from *Performance* (1970) to *Bad Timing/A Sensual Obsession* (1981); and Edward Dmytryk's *Mirage* (1965), a spy/murdermystery in which an amnesia victim's memories, actual and false, are periodically flashed forth in *Marienbad* style. Thanks largely to *Marienbad* and other films by Resnais, the instant flashback (as opposed to the traditional slow ones signaled by dreamy music and blurred frames) and the interweaving of past and

present events in a continuous flow have become a basic part of the vocabulary of contemporary filmmaking.

—Joseph Milicia

ANNIE HALL. Production: Jack Rollins-Charles H. Joffe Productions; 1977; Deluxe color, 35mm, Panavision; running time: 93 mins. Released 1977 by United Artists.

Produced by Charles H. Joffe and Jack Rollins with Robert Greenhut and Fred T. Gallo; screenplay by Woody Allen and Marshall Brickman; directed by Woody Allen; photography by Gordon Willis; edited by Ralph Rosenblum; sound engineered by James Sabat; production design by Robert Drumheller and Justin Scoppa Jr.; art direction by Mel Bourne; costumes designed by Ruth Morley.

Filmed 1976 in New York City, and Los Angeles. Academy Awards for Best Picture, Best Director, Best Actress (Keaton), and Best Original Screenplay, 1977; New York Film Critics' Awards for Best Film, Best Director, Best Actress (Keaton), and Best Screenplay, 1977.

Cast: Woody Allen (*Alvy Singer*); Diane Keaton (*Annie Hall*); Tony Roberts (*Rob*); Paul Simon (*Tony Lacey*); Carol Kane (*Allison*); Janet Margolin (*Robin*); Shelley Duvall (*Pam*); Christopher Walken (*Duane Hall*); Colleen Dewhurst (*Annie's mother*); Donald Symington (*Annie's father*); Helen Ludlam (*Grammy Hall*); Joan Newman (*Alvy's mother*); Mordecai Lawner (*Alvy's father*); Jonathan Munk (Alvy as a child); Ruth Volner (*Alvy's aunt*); Martin Rosenblatt (*Alvy's uncle*); Hy Ansel (*Joey Nichols*); Rashel Novikoff (*Aunt Tessie*); Russel Horton (*Man in line at movies*); Marshall McLuhan (Himself); Dick Cavett (Himself); Christine Jones (*Dorrie*); Mary Boland (*Miss Reed*); Wendy Gerard (*Janet*); John Doumanian (*Man with drugs*); Bob Maroff (*1st Man in front of the movie theater*); Rick Petrucelli (*2nd Man in front of the movie theater*); Lee Callahan (*Cashier*); Chris Gampel (*Doctor*); Mark Lenard (*Marine officer*); Dan Ruskin (*Comic at the "Rallye"*) John Glover (*Actor friend of Annie's*); Bernie Styles (*Comic's business manager*); Johnny Haymer (*Comic*); Ved Bandhu (*Maharishi*); John Dennis Johnston (*L.A. policeman*); Lauri Bird (*Tony Lacy's girl*); Jim McKrell, Jeff Goldblum, William Callawy, Roger Newman, Alan Landers, and Dean Sarah Frost (*Party-goers*); Vince O'Brien (*Hotel doctor*); Humphrey Davis (*Alvy's psychiatrist*); Veronica Radburn (*Annie's pschiatrist*); Robin Mary Paris (*Girl in Alvy's play*); Charles Levin (*Man in Alvy's play*); Wayne Carson (*Stage manager of Alvy's play*); Michael Karm (*Director of Alvy's play*); Beverly D'Angelo (*Actress in Rob's TV show*); Tracy Walter (*Actor in Rob's TV show*); Sigourney Weaver (*Alvy's friend at the movies*); Walter Bernstein (*Annie's friend at the movies*).

Publications:

Scripts—"*Annie Hall*" by Woody Allen and Marshall Brickman in *L'Avant-Scène du cinéma* (Paris), 15 December 1977; *Woody Allen: Opus 9-10-11* (includes partial script of *Annie Hall*), Paris 1981; reviews—"*Annie Hall*" by G. Brown in *Sight and Sound* (London), autumn 1977; "Portrait de l'artiste en masochiste serein" by E. Carrère in *Positif* (Paris), November 1977; "*Annie*

Hall" by J. Dawson in *Monthly Film Bulletin* (London), October 1977; "*Annie Hall*" by A. Garel in *Image et son* (Paris), November 1977; "*Annie Hall*" by A. Stuart in *Films and Filming* (London), November 1977; "A Film About a Very Funny Man" by G.W.S. Trow in *Film Comment* (New York), May/June 1977; "*Annie Hall*" by J. MacBride in *Variety* (New York), 30 March 1977; articles—"Woody Allen is Feeling Better", interview by B. Drew, in *American Film* (Washington, D.C.), May 1977; "Comedy Directors: Interviews with Woody Allen" by M. Karman in *Millimeter* (New York), October 1977; "*Annie Hall*" by A. Remond in *Avant-Scène du cinéma* (Paris), 15 December 1977; "De la première personne du singulier à celle du pluriel..." by Alain Remond in *L'Avant-Scène du cinéma* (Paris), 15 December 1977; "Mig og Annie og moneterne" by P. Malmjaer in *Kosmorama* (Copenhagen), autumn 1977; "Le Rire et la culture: (le citoyen Allen et Spinoza) (*Annie Hall*)" by Robert Benayoun in *Positif* (Paris), November 1977; "Le Cinéphile à la voix forte" by S. Daney in *Cahiers du cinéma* (Paris), November 1977; "Scenes from a Mind", interview by I. Halberstadt in *Take One* (Montreal), November 1978; "In Search of *The Goodbye Girl*" by D. Baker in *Cinema Papers* (Melbourne, Australia), August/September 1978; "Forms of Coherence in the Woody Allen Comedies" by M. Yacowar in *Wide Angle* (Athens, Ohio), no.2, 1979; "L'Un dit gestion de ca, voire (sur *Annie Hall* de Woody Allen)" by J. Funck in *Positif* (Paris), February 1979; "I Share My Characters' Views on Men—And Stuff Like That", interview by Janet Maslin in *The New York Times*, 20 May 1979; "*Annie Hall*" by Timothy Johnson in *Magill's Survey of Cinema, Vol. 1* edited by Frank N. Magill, Englewood Cliffs, New Jersey 1980; "Producing Woody: an Interview with Charles H. Joffe" by D. Teitelbaum in *Cinema Papers* (Melbourne), April/May 1980; "El cine de Woody Allen" by R. Median de la Serna in *Cine* (Mexico), March 1980.

*   *   *

In *Annie Hall* Woody Allen finally delivered a unified work, one that relied on more than his episodic one-liner format. In the film he brought together many of his past obsessions, among them his love of New York, his lack of affection for L.A., the inability to handle success; but this time, he merged them with an in-depth examination of his feelings about family and relationships. It was as if, after 21 years of Freudian analysis, he finally decided to deal with his neuroses on the screen. Occasionally speaking with a confessional directness that destroys the film's illusion of reality and separates him momentarily from the episodic ramblings of his stream-of-consciousness narrative, he situates the spectator as analyst. Throughout the film the customary Allen episodes are cleverly linked together through memory, with dialogue precipitating flashbacks.

The film opens with a monologue which pays hommage to three key individuals: Groucho Marx, Sigmund Freud, and Annie Hall. He pays respects to Groucho, from whom he learned comedy; to Freud, from whom he learned how to deal with his childhood; and to Annie, from whom he learned of both love and despair. At the end of the monologue, he moves from comedy to melancholy as he states: "...Annie and I broke up...I keep sifting the pieces of the relationship through my mind...." Searching for the answer to the breakup, he begins by sifting through the wreckage of his childhood—a Freudian analysis laced with (Groucho) Marxian wit.

With *Annie Hall*, Allen the director is absorbed with his past, as is Alvy Singer, the character Allen portrays in this film. He uses many strategies to comment on the past, from interjecting himself as Alvy into a scene aurally, to interjecting himself visu-

ally. Early on both strategies are situated. Alvy's first childhood memories concern depression and his recurring difficulty of distinguishing between fantasy and reality. These scenes use a voice-over narration by Alvy as if to dispel any notion that he is unable to distinguish between the two as an adult. Immediately, however, he begins a strategy of interjecting himself physically into the past, proving that the inability does indeed exist. In a classroom scene he moves from observing himself as a child to participating in the scene as an adult attempting to clarify his childhood actions to his classmates.

Another key aspect of the film is Allen's ability to remove himself from the on-screen reality. This he achieves in a number of ways, from voice-over commentary and/or subtitles which contradict the on-screen dialogue, to physically stepping out of the scene either to comment on the narrative action or to correct the flow of events. After Annie and Alvy meet for the first time their dialogue is heard on the soundtrack but their real thoughts are shown in subtitles at the bottom of the screen: while Alvy says "The medium enters in as a condition of the art form itself," a subtitle reads "I don't know what I'm saying—she senses I'm shallow." At other points in the film Alvy simply uses voice-over to comment on the ridiculousness of an on-screen event: when the comic who wants Alvy to write his material minces around the office, Alvy, in voice-over, comments, "Look at him mincing around, like he thinks he's real cute...." In other scenes he is much more assertive. Unable to bear another moment of academic pretension from a man standing behind him in a theater lobby, he directly addresses the audience: "What do you do when you get stuck in a movie line with a guy like this behind you?" After embarrassing the academic by having Marshall McLuhan step out from behind a marquee to say: "How you got to teach a course in anything is totally amazing," Alvy turns to the camera once again and states: "Boy if life were only like this!"

At the film's end Alvy is writing a play about his breakup with Annie. Where in *Manhattan* the book he is writing becomes the film we are seeing, here the play he is writing becomes, in retrospect, the film we've just seen. In this film Allen stretched the limits of his narrative technique by developing strategies for showing how the past and present interact in life and art as well as analysis. The film succeeded beyond any of Allen's earlier work, brought new life to the romantic comedy genre, gave American audiences a new leading lady, Diane Keaton, and fashion designers a new look to market.

—Doug Tomlinson

ANTÔNIO DAS MORTES. O dragão da maldade contra o santo querreiro. Production: Produções Cinematográficas Mapa; Eastmancolor, 35mm; running time: 100 mins. Released June 1969, Rio de Janeiro.

Produced by Zelito Viana (executive producer), Claude-Antoine Mapa, and Glauber Rocha; screenplay by Glauber Rocha; from the legends about the bounty hunter who killed the famous bandit Corisco in 1939; directed by Glauber Rocha; photography by Alfonso Beato; edited by Eduardo Escorel; sound by Walter Goulart; art direction by Glauber Rocha; music by Marlos Nobre, Walter Queiroz, and Sérgio Ricardo. Filmed on location in Milagres in the Brazilian Northwest. Best Director (tied with Vojtech Jasny), Cannes Film Festival, 1969.

Cast: Maurício do Valle (*Antônio das Mortes*); Odete Lara

(*Laura*); Hugo Carvana (*Police Chief Mattos*); Othon Bastos (*The Professor*); Jofre Soares (*Colonel Horacio*); Lorival Pariz (*Coirana*); Rosa Maria Penna (*Sanata Bárbara*); Mário Gusmão (*Antão*); Vinivius Salvatori ("*Mata Vaca*"); Emanuel Cavalcanti (*Priest*); Sante Scaldaferri (*Batista*); the people of Milagres.

Publications:

Reviews—by Richard McGuinness in *The Village Voice* (New York), 21 May 1970; review by Mike Wallington in *Sight and Sound* (London), autumn 1970; books—*Second Wave*, New York 1970; *Nuevo cine latinoamericano* by Augusto Martinez and Manuel Perez Estremera, Barcelona 1973; *Glauber Rocha* edited by Raquel Gerber, Rio de Janiero 1977; *Brazilian Cinema* by Randal Johnson and Robert Stam, New Brunswick, New Jersey 1982; articles—"Comparative Anatomy of Folk-Myth Films: *Robin Hood* and *Antônio das Mortes*" by Ernest Callenbach in *Film Quarterly* (Berkeley), winter 1969-70; interview with Rocha by Gordon Hitchens in *Film Quarterly* (Berkeley), fall 1970; interview with Rocha in *Afterimage* (New York), April 1970; "The Aesthetics of Violence" by Glauber Rocha in *Afterimage* (New York), April 1970; interview with Rocha in *Cineaste* (New York), summer 1970; "Politics by Magic: *Antônio das Mortes*" by Jack Fisher in *Film Journal* (New York), spring 1971; "*Antônio Das Mortes*, de mooie revolutie" by A. Haakman in *Skoop* (The Hague), vol.8, no.5, 1972; "*Antônio das Mortes*" by N. Simsolo in *Image et son* (Paris), March 1972; "Cinema Novo: Pitfalls of Cultural Nationalism" by Hans Proppe and Susan Tarr in *Jump Cut* (Chicago), June 1976; "The History of Cinema Novo" by Glauber Rocha, translated by John Davis, in *Framework* (London), summer 1980; "Music in Glauber Rocha's Films: Brazilian Renaissance, Part 2" by Bruce Graham in *Jump Cut* (Chicago), May 1980; "The Role of Myth in *Antônio Mortes*" by Deborah Mistron in *Enclitic* (Minneapolis), fall 1981 and spring 1982.

*   *   *

In his lyric-mythic epic, *Antônio das Mortes*, Glauber Rocha creatively integrates elements of Brazilian popular religious culture, politics, folklore, social history, music, literature, and dance. Because of this thoroughly Brazilian context, the film is difficult for foreign viewers. Furthermore, the emblematic characters are not simple allegories but rather complex, synthetic creations representing real or fictional persons, social types, mystical or mythic motifs, social movements, or ideas.

The complexity of these unusual characterizations is exemplified by the protagonist, Antônio das Mortes. This figure had appeared in Rocha's earlier film *Deus e o Diabo na Terra do Sol*. According to Rocha, Antônio das Mortes is based on a historical figure, the bounty-hunter who in 1939 succeeded in killing Corisco, a famous *cangaceiro* (bandit) of the Northeastern backlands. In the film Antônio first appears as a *jagunço* (hired gunman) contracted to kill *cangaceiros* and protect a powerful landowner. After mortally wounding the *cangaceiro* Coirana, Antônio undergoes a political conversion and becomes a revolutionary who uses his rifle against the forces of oppression represented by the landowner and his hired gunslingers. The ending of the film is ambiguous in terms of the possible future role of the lone revolutionary. Antônio is last seen as a solitary figure walking—rifle in hand—down a backlands highway past a Shell Oil sign; the suggestion may be that a lone gunman can provoke a revolutionary situation in an underdeveloped regional setting, but he will be unable to halt massive exploitation in the new era of the multi-nationals.

In *Antônio das Mortes*, Rocha reworks the Christian myth of St. George versus the dragon in terms of Brazil's mythical consciousness. The St. George and the dragon myth is announced in the film's opening triptych and alluded to in a closing sequence: in three rapid montage shots, Antão lances the landowner from horseback. Antônio das Mortes is not the only warrior saint, or St. George figure, in the film Antão, whose name is similar to Antônio's, is a black associated with Afro-Brazilian religions. Antão's conversion from passive religious follower to armed warrior continues the tradition of black revolt in Brazil.

In order to ritually reenact the St. George and the dragon myth, Rocha theatricalizes the continuity of his film and its mise-en-scène. Many of the scenes take place in stage-like settings such as the cavern-amphitheater or the village square. The costuming, choreography, and the use of color, poetry, and music recall theater and opera. Rocha's method of shooting imitates theatrical time and space. He prefers either lengthy sequences with a few cuts or long sequence shots. Conventional shot-reverse shot or cross-cutting are generally rejected in favor of capturing the scene's significant elements within the shot and the frame.

Rocha has argued that Brazilian filmmakers should not use European and American cinematic strategies and techniques to depict Latin America's unique social problems. In *Antônio das Mortes*, Rocha seeks to contribute to the decolonization of Brazilian cinema by meshing new cinematic strategies with Brazilian reality. One such strategy is Rocha's use of a Brazilian color code: the bright colors of buildings and costumes are natural and authentic colors that convey cultural significance for Brazilian audiences. During the location filming, Rocha drew directly on the knowledge and experience of the backlanders. The music and the dancing of the Antônio-Coirana duel scene are largely a creation of the local people.

Antônio das Mortes was well received by the Brazilian filmgoing public. In Europe and the United States, the film was widely acclaimed by critics, and a debate erupted concerning the film's revolutionary qualities (or lack thereof). Today most critics regard the film as one of the greatest achievements—both aesthetically and culturally—of the Brazilian Cinema Novo.

—Dennis West

APOCALYPSE NOW. Production: United Artists; 1979; initial release in color, 70mm, Dolby sound; later releases in color, 35mm, Dolby sound with added footage of large-scale air attack which serves as backdrop for credit sequence; running time: 153 mins., also 139 mins. Released 1979.

Produced by Francis Ford Coppola; screenplay by John Milius and Francis Ford Coppola, narration by Richard Marks; suggested by the novella *Heart of Darkness* by Joseph Conrad; directed by Francis Ford Coppola; photography by Vittorio Storaro; edited by Richard Marks; sound by Walter Murch, Mark Berger, Richard Beggs, and Nat Boxer; production design by Dean Tavoularis, set decoration by Bob Nelson; art direction by Angelo Graham; original music by Carmine Coppola and Francis Ford Coppola, song "This is the End" by the Doors; special effects by A.D. Flowers.

Filmed 1976-77, though pre-production work began mid-1975 and post-production lasted until 1979; on location in the Philippines; cost: about $30,000,000. Academy Awards for Cinematography and Sound, 1979; Palme d'Or (shared with *The Tin Drum*), Cannes Film Festival, 1979.

Cast: Marlon Brando (*Colonel Walter E. Kurtz*); Robert Duvall (*Lieutenant Colonel Kilgore*); Martin Sheen (*Captain Benjamine L. Willard*); Frederic Forrest (*Chef*); Albert Hall (*Chief*); Sam Bottoms (*Lance*); Larry Fishburne (*Clean*); Dennis Hopper (*Freelance photographer*); G.D. Spradlin (*General*); Harrison Ford (*Colonel*).

Publications:

Script—*L'apocalisse e poi* (from the collection "Cinema e cinema, vol. 24), Venice 1980; reviews—"Film View: The Heart of *Apocalypse* is Extremely Misty" by Vincent Canby in the *New York Times*, 19 August 1979; "The Screen: *Apocalypse Now* by Vincent Canby in *The New York Times*, 15 August 1979; "*Apocalypse Now* by S. Daney and P. Bonitzer in *Cahiers du cinéma* (Paris), October 1979; "*8 1/2* Now: Coppola's *Apocalypse*" by D. Denby in *New York*, 28 May 1979 and "Hollow Movie" in *New York*, 27 August 1979; "The Current Cinema: Mistah Kurtz—He Dead" by V. Geng in the *New Yorker*, 3 September 1979; "*Apocalypse Now*" by Gordon Gow in *Films and Filming* (London), November 1979; "*Apocalypse Now*" by J. Heijs in *Skrien* (Amsterdam), November 1979; "Coppola's War" by Stanley Kauffmann in the *New Republic* (New York), 15 September 1979; "Coppola's War Epic" by J. Kroll in *Newsweek* (New York), 20 August 1979; "*Apocalypse Now*" by R. McCormick in *Cineaste* (New York), no.4, 1979; "$30 Million in Search of an Author" by John Simon in the *National Review* (New York), 28 September 1979; "Apocalypse Finally" by Bruce Williamson in *Playboy* (Chicago), October 1979; books—*Guts and Glory: Great American War Movies* by Lawrence H. Suid, Reading, Massachusetts 1978; *Notes* by Eleanor Coppola, New York 1979; *Overexposures: The Crisis in American Filmmaking* by David Thomson, New York 1981; *Vietnam on Film: From 'The Green Berets' to 'Apocalypse Now'* by Gilbert Adair, New York 1981; articles—"Christian Marguana, A. Clement Join *Apocalypse Now*" in *Boxoffice* (Kansas City, Missouri), 11 October 1976; "Entretien avec Francis Ford Coppola" in *Cahiers du cinéma* (Paris), July/August 1979; "Testimonianze: la storia di *Apocalypse Now*" in *Filmcritica* (Rome), May 1979; "Journey Up the River", interview by G. Marcus, in *Rolling Stone* (New York), 1 November 1979; "Zoetrope and *Apocalypse Now*" by A. Bock in *American Film* (Washington, D.C.), September 1979; "Dossier: Hollywood 79: Francis Ford Coppola" by P. Carcassone in *Cinématographe* (Paris), March 1979; "Francis Coppola Discusses *Apocalypse Now*" by G.R. Levin in *Millimeter* (New York), October 1979; "*Apocalypse Now*: 2 Views" by P. Anderson and J. Wells in *Films in Review* (New York), October 1979; "*Apocalypse* Booms Along with $1.2 mil posted in 20 days" in *Variety* (New York), October 1979; "Apocalypse is Now" in *Boxoffice* (Kansas City, Missouri), 20 August 1979; "*Apocalypse* reserved seats sell big" in *Boxoffice* (Kansas City, Missouri), 6 August 1979; "*Apocalypse* stumble, coin" in *Variety* (New York), 7 November 1979; "*Apocalypse* takes $2.5 million, but drops off in 4th week" in *Boxoffice* (Kansas City, Missouri), 15 October 1979; "Apocalypse Forever" by R. Baker in the *New York Times*, 26 August 1979; "Bell Tells" by A. Bell in the *Village Voice* (New York), 20 August 1979; "*Apocalypse Now*" by H. Bitomsky in *Filmkritik* (Munich), December 1979; "Briefs on the Arts: *Apocalypse* Praised by the Soviet Press" in the *New York Times*, 23 August 1979; "Getting Bigger Bang at the End of *Apocalypse*" by T. Buckley in the *New York Times*, 12 October 1979; article by L. Bennets and Albert Hall in *The New York Times*, 24 August 1979; "Francis Coppola's Cinematic *Apocalypse* is Finally at Hand" by T. Chiu in *The New York Times*, 12 August 1979; "CinemaScore's 781 Interviews on *Apocalypse Now*" in *Variety* (New York), 22 August 1979; "Apocalypse...at last" by J. Cleary and J. Sack in *Penthouse* (New York), August 1979; "Diary of a Director's Wife" by E. Coppola in *The New York Times*, 5 August and 7 August 1979; "Coppola's Words at Moscow" in *Variety* (New York), 29 August 1979; "Dolby Develops SA5 Stereo Surround Unit for Francis Ford Coppola's *Apocalypse*" in *Boxoffice* (Kansas City, Missouri), 17 September 1979; "Exhibs Asked to Buy Dolby Unit for 70mm *Apocalypse*" in *Variety* (New York), 5 September 1979; "Exhibs Bid for *Apocalypse*: UA Analyzing Offers for 2d Wave Bookings" in *Variety* 5 September 1979; "Separate 35mm *Apocalypse Now*: Coppola Explains O'Seas Urging: Big UA Promos: Lots of Angles" by G. Fabrikant in *Variety* (New York), 15 August 1979; "Francis Ford Coppola's *Apocalypse Now*" in *Films and Filming* (London), November 1979; "Cannes 79" by J. Grant in *Cinéma 79* (Paris), July/August 1979; "United Artists Now Sees *Apocalypse* Recoupment" by H. Hollinger in *Variety* (New York), 3 October 1979; "Die *Apokalypse* in unserer Zeit" by T. Honickel in *Film und Ton* (Munich), August 1979; "The Major Stunts of *Apocalypse Now*" by T. Leonard in *Filmmaker's Monthly* (Ward Hill, Massachusetts), August 1979; "At the Movies: Novelist Encounters Hollywood" by J. Maslin in *The New York Times*, 31 August 1979; "*Apocalypse Now*" by D. Munroe in *Film Bulletin* (Philadelphia), September 1979; "*Apocalypse* Never on Tube: 1986 Release May Not Be UA's: Maker on Past and Future" by D. Pollock in *Variety* (New York), 24 October 1979; "Reaction to Edited *Apocalypse*: Coppola Improves His Odds" by D. Pollock in *Variety* (New York), 15 August 1979; "The Making of a Quagmire" by F. Rich in *Time* (New York), 27 August 1979; "Heart Transplant" by B. Riley in *Film Comment* (New York), September/October 1979; "Wie is Willard?" *Apocalypse Now*" by M. Salzgeber in *Skrien* (Amsterdam), November 1979; "7 Months Later, Sagan Says *Apocalypse* Win was Pressured" in *Variety* (New York), 19 December 1979; "Soviets Dicker for *Apocalypse* Rights" and "Steal 35mm Print of *Apocalypse*" in *Variety* (New York), 10 October 1979; "The Literary Roots of *Apocalypse Now*" by J. Tessitore in *The New York Times*, 21 October 1979; "Francis Ford Coppola: Courte histoire d'un scenario: entretien avec John Milius" by R. Thompson, translated by L. Barbier, in *Ecran* (Paris), 15 September 1979; "*Apocalypse Now*: Au Coeur Des tenebres" by S. Toubiana in *Cahiers du cinéma* (Paris), July/August 1979; "The *Apocalypse* at Cannes and *Apocalypse Now*" by D. Toumarkine in *Film Bulletin* (Philadelphia), July 1979; "Martin Sheen: Heart of Darkness, Heart of Gold" by J. Vallely in *Rolling Stone* (New York), 1 November 1979; "Coppola Now" by C.L. Westerbeck in *Commonweal* (New York), 28 September 1979 and "Coppola Tomorrow" by C.L. Westerbeck in *Commonweal* (New York), 12 October 1979; "*Apocalypse Now*" by M. Wood in the *New York Review of Books*, 11 October 1979; "Les Apocalypses du Viet-Nam" by J. Zimmer in *Revue du cinéma* (Paris), October 1979; "Apocalypse Within" by R.A. Blake in *America* (New York), 8 September 1979; "*Apocalypse Now* Film Stuns Cannes" by S.H. Anderson in *The New York Times*, 21 May 1979; "Coppola Donates *Apocalypse* Print to Castro's Cuba" in *Variety* (New York), 20 June 1979; "Waiting for *Apocalypse*" by Molly Haskell in the *Village Voice* (New York), 21 May 1979; "Finally *Apocalypse Now*" by C. Michener in *Newsweek* (New York), 28 May 1979; "An Archival Detailing of UA's *Apocalypse Now* Since 1967 Start" by D. Pollack in *Variety* (New York), 23 May 1979; "Films in Focus: First Assault on

"The Sneaking of *Apocalypse*" in *Newsweek* (New York), 21 May 1979; "Zoetrope and *Apocalypse Now*" by A. Bock in *American Film* (Washington, D.C.), September 1979; "Coppolas dommedag" by N. Jensen in *Kosmorama* (Copenhagen), winter 1979; "The Major Stunts of *Apocalypse Now*" by T. Leonard in *Filmmakers Monthly* (Ward Hill, Massachusetts), August 1979; "*Apocalypse Now*" by Pat H. Broeske in *Magill's Survey of Cinema, Vol. 1* edited by Frank N. Magill, Englewood Cliffs, New Jersey 1980; "Francis Ford Coppola habla de *Apocalypse Now*", interview, in *Cine* (Mexico), March 1980; "Banality Now" by K. Boehringer in *Australian Journal of Screen Theory* (Kensington), no.8, 1980; "*Apocalipsis* e ideología" by N. Casullo in *Imagines* (Mexico), May 1980; "*Apocalypse Now*: The Absence of History" by M. Klein in *Jump Cut* (Chicago), October 1980; "*Apocalypse Now* and *The Deerhunter*: The Lies Aren't Over" by R.C. Franz in *Jump Cut* (Chicago), October 1980; "*Apocalypse Now*: Coppola's American Way" by B. Ruby Rich in *Jump Cut* (Chicago), October 1980; "Operation Mind Control: *Apocalypse Now* and the Search for Clarity" by C. Sharrett in *Journal of Popular Film and Television* (Bowling Green, Ohio), spring 1980; "*Apocalypse Now* / Capital Flow" by S. Yurick in *Cineaste* (New York), winter 1979-80; "*Apokalipsa przed prgiem wielkości*" by M. Przylipiak in *Kino* (Warsaw), March 1981; "*Apocalypse Now* Viewed by a Vietnamese" by N. K. Vien in *Framework* (Norwich, England), spring 1981.

* * *

Francis Coppola's *Apocalypse Now*, plagued by numerous delays and cost overruns during its four-year production, eventually emerged as the definitive Vietnam War film and demonstrated, as had his earlier two-part *Godfather* saga, Coppola's ability to combine serious art and popular entertainment.

When Coppola began shooting *Apocalypse Now* in the Phillipines in March, 1976, the film's budget was $12 million and the film was set for release in April, 1977. However, a series of setbacks slowed down production and drove up costs: a typhoon halted the shooting schedule for seven weeks; Marlon Brando, whose character was originally a lean, physically fit Green Beret showed up in the Phillipines weighing 285 pounds; Martin Sheen had a heart attack and could not work for seven weeks; and throughout the scriptwriting, shooting, and dieting phases of the production, Coppola had difficulty in choosing an ending for the film. By the time *Apocalypse Now* was released in August, 1979, its budget had climbed to over $30 million, $18 million of which came from Coppola's personal assets and loans for which he was accountable.

Apocalypse Now did well at the box office, earning at present over $37 million in domestic rentals and a similar amount in the foreign market. Critics also liked the film, although they generally considered it a flawed masterpiece because of the alleged pretentious and confusing ending.

Flawed or not, *Apocalypse Now* is both a technical and artistic achievement. The film won Academy Awards for its stunning cinematography and sound. The scene in which U.S. Army helicopters play Wagner over loudspeakers while attacking a Vietnamese village is perhaps the most spectacular battle sequence ever filmed. The napalm destruction of the Kurtz compound seen during the final credits of the 35mm version of the film involved the biggest explosion ever staged for a film. The opening dissolves and superimpositions of Martin Sheen's face with a rotating ceiling fan and a helicopter attack demonstrate one advantage of Coppola's video editing system (in which he transferred the *Apocalypse Now* footage to videotape, edited the tape, and then conformed the film to the edited tape). On the video editing machine, the filmmaker can quickly and easily build up the visual image in layers, avoiding the expensive, time-consuming optical printer and the film lab normally needed for superimpositions.

Finally, *Apocalypse Now* explores such themes as the horror and madness of war—of the Vietnam War in particular. Going beyond the traditional war genre themes of bravery versus cowardice and victory versus defeat, the film also examines man's recognition of, and struggle with, his dual sane/insane, civilized/savage nature.

—Clyde Kelly Dunagan

THE APU TRILOGY.

PATHER PANCHALI. Father Panchali. Father Panchali: Song of the Road. Production: Government of West Bengal; black and white, 35mm; running time: 112 mins. Released 1956.

Screenplay by Satyajit Ray; from the novel by Bibhuti Bannerji; directed by Satyajit Ray; photography by Subrata Mitra; edited by Dulal Dutta; art direction by Bansi Chandragupta; music by Ravi Shankar.

Begun in 1950, though principal filming done in 1952 in a small village in southern India. Best Human Document, Cannes Festival, 1956; Selznick Golden, Berlin Festival, 1957; Kinema Jumpo Award as Best Foreign Film, Tokyo Film Festival, 1966; Bodil Award as Best Non-European Film, Denmark, 1966.

Cast: Kanu Banerji (*The Father*); Karuna Banerji (*The Mother*); Subir Banerji (*Apu*); Uma Das Gupta (*The Daughter*); Chunibali Devi (*Old woman*).

Publications:

Scripts—"*Pather Panchali*" by Satyajit Ray in *L'Avant-Scène du cinéma* (Paris), 1 February 1980; "*Zalozpěv stecky*" (script extract) in *Film a doba* (Prague), December 1981; reviews—by Henry Hart in *Films in Review* (New York), February 1958; review by Jonas Mekas in *The Village Voice* (New York), 12 November 1958; "La Presse" in *L'Avant-Scène du cinéma* (Paris), 1 February 1980; books—*Indian Film* by Erik Barnouw and S. Krishnaswamy, New York 1963; *I Lost It at the Movies* by Pauline Kael, New York 1966; *The Great Films: 50 Golden Years of Motion Pictures* by Bosley Crowther, New York 1967; "A Long Time on the Little Road" by Satyajit Ray in *Film Makers on Film Making* edited by Harry Geduld, Bloomington, Indiana 1967; *Portrait of a Director—Satyajit Ray* by Marie Seton, Bloomington, Indiana 1971; *The Apu Trilogy* by Robin Wood, New York 1971; *Satyajit Ray*, Directorate of Advertising and Visual Publicity, Ministry of I and B, New Delhi, India 1976; *Satyajit Ray: Study Guide* by American Film Institute, Washington, D.C. 1979; *Satyajit Ray's Art* by Firoze Rangoonwalla, Shadara, Delhi 1980; articles—by Satyajit Ray in *Sight and Sound* (London), spring 1957; "Personality of the Month" in *Films and Filming* (London), December 1957; "Journey Through India" by Marie Seton in *Sight and Sound* (London), spring 1957; article by Peter Dyer in *Films and Filming* (London), February 1958; "*Pather Panchali* and *Aparajito*" by Arlene Croce in *Film Culture* (New York), no.19, 1959; "The Ray Trilogy" by Douglas McVay in *Film* (London), March/April 1960; "Talk with the Director" in *Newsweek* (New York), 26

September 1960; "Satyajit Ray: A Study" by Eric Rhode in *Sight and Sound* (London), summer 1961; "From Film to Film" by Satyajit Ray in *Cahiers du Cinema in English* (New York), February 1966; "Satyajit Ray" by James Blue in *Film Comment* (New York), summer 1968; "An Interview with Satyajit Ray's Cinematographers" by K. Dutta in *Filmmaker's Newsletter* (Ward Hill, Mass.), January 1975; "Satyajit Ray" by John Gillett in *Film* (London), October/November 1975; "A Voyage in India: Satyajit Ray Interviewed" by John Hughes in *Film Comment* (New York), September/October 1976; "*Pather Panchali*" by A. Williams in *Movietone News* (Seattle,), April 1976; "Dialogue on Film" by Satyajit Ray in *American Film* (Washington, D.C.), July/August 1978; "Un Film légendaire" by Henri Micciollo in *L'Avant-Scène du cinéma* (Paris), 1 February 1980.

APARAJITO. The Unvanquished. Production: Epic Films; black and white, 35mm; running time: 108 mins. Released 1957.

Screenplay by Satyajit Ray; from a novel by Bibhuti Bannerji; directed by Satyajit Ray; photography by Subrata Mitra; edited by Dulal Dutta; art direction by Bansi Chandragupta; music by Ravi Shankar.

Filmed 1956. Best Film: Lion of St. Mark, Venice Festival, 1957; Bodil Award, Denmark, Best Non-European Film, 1967.

Cast: Kanu Banerji (*The Father*); Karuna Banerji (*The Mother*); Pinaki Sen Gupta (*Apu, as a boy*); Smaran Ghosal (*Apu, as an adolescent*); Ramani Sen Gupta (*1st Uncle*); Subodh Ganguly (*Headmaster*); Ramani Sen Gupta (*2nd Uncle*).

Publications:

Reviews—by Peter Dyer in *Films and Filming* (London), February 1958; "*Aparajito*" by Henry Hart in *Films in Review* (New York), February 1959; review by Jonas Mekas in *The Village Voice* (New York), 13 May 1959; articles— "Journey Through India" by Marie Seton in *Sight and Sound* (London), spring 1957; "*Pather Panchali* and *Aparajito*" by Arlene Croce in *Film Culture* (New York), no.19, 1959; article by Albert Johnson in *Film Quarterly* (Berkeley), summer 1959; "The Ray Trilogy" by Douglas McVay in *Film* (London), March/April 1960; "Talk with the Director" in *Newsweek* (New York), 26 September 1960; "Indian Family" by Kobita Sarka in *Films and Filming* (London), April 1960; "Satyajit Ray: A Study" by Eric Rhode in *Sight and Sound* (London), summer 1961; "The Great 3-in-1" by Kobita Sarka in *Films and Filming* (London), December 1964; "From Film to Film" by Satyajit Ray in *Cahiers du Cinema in English* (New York), no.3, 1966. Also see books and articles following *Pather Panchali* credits.

APUR SANSAR. The World of Apu. Satyajit Ray Productions; black and white, 35mm; running time: 103 mins. Released 1959.

Screenplay by Satyajit Ray; from a story by Satyajit Ray, based on the novel by Bibhuti Bannerji; directed by Satyajit Ray; photography by Subrata Mitra; edited by Dulal Dutta; art direction by Bansi Chandragupta; music by Ravi Shankar.

Filmed 1959. Southerland Award Trophy, London Film Festival, 1960.

Cast: Soumitra Chatterjee (*Apu*); Sharmila Tagore (*Wife of Apu*); Alok Chakravarty (*Kajol*); Dhiresh Mazumaer (*Grandfather*).

Publications:

Reviews—"*Apur Sansar*" by Henry Hart in *Films in Review* (New York), March 1960; review by Jonas Mekas in *The Village Voice* (New York), 6 October 1960; articles—by Arlene Croce in *Film Culture* (New York), summer 1960; article by Jonathan Harker in *Film Quarterly* (Berkeley), spring 1960; "Talk with the Director" in *Newsweek* (New York), 26 September 1960; "The Ray Trilogy" by Douglas McVay in *Film* (London), March/April 1960; article by Raymond Durgnat in *Films and Filming* (London), May 1961; article by John Gillett in *Sight and Sound* (London), winter 1960-61; "Satyajit Ray: A Study" by Eric Rhode in *Sight and Sound* (London), summer 1961. Also see books and articles following *Pather Panchali* credits.

*   *   *

Satyajit Ray's *Apu Trilogy*, made over a period of eight years and not originally conceived of as a trilogy, had a profound effect on filmmaking within India and an important effect on the attention paid to Indian films outside India. Within India, the unobtrusive style of lighting, dialogue and action employed in the *Trilogy* challenged the prevailing operatic style and led to new conventions of realism. Abroad, the *Trilogy* stirred interest in other Indian cinema, and led to a wider market for Indian films as well as to significant contact between Indian and non-Indian filmmakers.

After returning to India from a business trip to London for Keymer's advertizing agency, Ray set about finding a crew and finances for a film based on the famous Bengali novel, *Pather Panchali*. In his work as a graphic artist, Ray had already illustrated a Bengali abridgement of the novel and he was able to obtain rights for a modest sum (about $1300) on the basis of his active interest. Finances proved more difficult to procure for the film itself: Ray pawned his wife's jewelry and was finally advanced money to complete the film by the government of West Bengal. For its first two weeks in Calcutta, the film played to small audiences. Then the theater filled and the film recovered its costs in Ray's native city within the first thirteen weeks. In Bombay, in 1956, the film was reviewed by Adib in the following terms: "It is banal to compare it with any other Indian picture— for even the best of the pictures produced so far have been cluttered with clichés. *Pather Panchali* is pure cinema. There is no trace of the theater in it. It does away with plot, with grease and paint, with the slinky charmer and the sultry beauty, with the slapdash hero breaking into song on the slightest provocation or no provocation at all." For many critics, Ray's completion of *Aparajito* in 1956, confirmed the novelty of his approach and the strength of his talent. Stanley Kauffmann reported that Ray was forging in the Apu films the uncreated conscience of his race.

All three films of the trilogy are organized by an open form: the progression of events is episodic and interest in the narrative derives from character and location rather than from the dynamics of plot. In *Pather Panchali*, the poor Brahmin priest and his wife have a son born to them, the father must leave home to make a living, their daughter dies, the son watches the world change around him, the family is forced to leave the village. The viewer's attention is engaged less by what is going to happen than by the way in which things do happen. The editing allows the viewer to soak in the atmosphere of a landscape or an evening. As son and daughter (Apu and Durga) run to the edge of the village to watch a steam train, the camera registers soft white tufts of flax waving in the air. When the train appears, it hurtles not only past the village, but across the viewer's inner rhythms which had been slowed by the waving flax. The episode of the train in *Pather Panchali* also indicates Ray's classicism, his practice of creating a strong response in the viewer and subsequently disciplining that response. During the course of the *Trilogy*, the viewer's empathetic experience of an event is frequently punctuated by a distancing perspective. In *Pather Panchali*, when the father breaks down in grief over his dead daughter, Ray cuts to the young Apu standing apart, watching his sorrowing father. In *Apur Sansar*, Ray cuts from the climactic reconciliation of Apu and his son Kajal to the dour father-in-law, who will add this episode to the many other curious episodes he has witnessed in his life.

The open form also allows Ray to annotate the feelings of his characters by referring to the natural world. At their simplest, these references function as analogies. When Apu's mother is happy, the water skates and dragonflies dance an insect version of happiness. But at their best, images of the natural world become surcharged with meaning: the monsoon clouds in *Pather Panchali* gather to themselves the pent-up emotions of the mother and the children; the fireflies in *Aparajito* signify the beauty and the remoteness of nature; and the river gleaming behind Apu, in *Apur Sansar*, while Apu debates whether to marry his friend's cousin, signifies both the burden of the moment and the flow of time into which individual moments run indistinguishably.

Although Ray and his cameraman, Subrata Mitra, made remarkable experiments towards recreating the effect of daylight on sets (by bouncing studio lights off of cotton sheeting stretched above the set), the *Apu Trilogy* did not constitute innovation in cinematic technique. The excellence of the *Trilogy* derived from its tact. Using long takes, reaction shots and unhurried action, Ray was able to place in suspension before the viewer multiple points of view: that of the aged aunt who must cadge food to survive and that of the young mother Sarbojaya, who will not extend herself indefinitely and who refuses to help the aged aunt pour water from a pitcher. The multiple points of view are validated by an evenness of regard: the camera attends as calmly to the ailing aunt as to the determined mother, to the griefstricken father as fully as to the observing Apu.

Ray's cinema has developed considerably in complexity and scope since the *Apu Trilogy*. Nonetheless, his first films retain their capacity to move the viewer. Their power derives from the internal consistency of Ray's style and from the cultural importance of Ray's story. The *Apu Trilogy* epitomizes the migration of many poor, Third World families from the village to the city. In the *Apu Trilogy*, Ray leaves the outcome of the migration open: Apu has not yet made his peace with the brisk anonymous ways of the city as, later, the protagonist of *Seemabaddha* is to embrace the city's modernity. When Ray turns, in his mid-career films, to examine the opportunities the city offers to idealistic young men, the optimism of the early films is lost.

In Bengal the effect of Ray's realism (his scaling of dialogue, action and lighting closer to everyday reality) was felt immediately in the work of Mrinal Sen and Tapan Sinha, but his example took 15 years to reach the principal film production center of Bombay. Only in the late sixties and early seventies did new directors begin making Hindi films without melodrama, trusting the subtlety of action, atmosphere and editing to transmit their intentions. The new movement, known as "parallel cinema," did not defeat the operatic style—most Hindi films are still extravaganzas—but they enabled Hindi cinema to begin inquiry into the conditions of ordinary life in India. The way

towards this inquiry was first explored by Ray in the *Apu Trilogy*.

—Satti Khanna

L'ARGENT. Production: Cinemondial and Cineromans; black and white, 35mm, silent; length: 5344 meters. Released 10 January 1929.

Produced by Simon Schiffrin; screenplay by Marcel L'Herbier; from the novel by Emile Zola; directed by Marcel L'Herbier; photography by Jules Kruger; production design by Lazare Meerson and André Barsacq; art direction by Jacques Manuel; costumes designed by Jacques Manuel.

Filmed in Francouer studios at Joinville; exteriors shot at La Bourse, Place de l'Opera, the Paris Stock Exchange, and Le Bourget; cost: over 3 million francs.

Cast: Mary Glory (*Line Hamelin*); Brigitte Helm (*Baron Sandorf*); Yvette Guilbert (*Le Méchain*); Marcelle Pradot (*Countess Alice de Beauvilliers*); Esther Kiss, Elaine Tayar, and Josette Racon (*Switchboard operators*); Mona Goya, Yvonne Dumas, Maries Costes (*Extras*); Pierre Alcover (*Nicolas Saccard*); Alfred Abel (*Alphonse Gunderman, the banker*); Henry Victor (*Jacques Hamelin*); Pierre Juvenet (*Baron Defrance*); Antonin Artaud (*Mazaud*); Jules Berry (*Huret, the reporter*); Alexandre Mihalesco (*Salomon Massias*); Raymond Rouleau (*Jantrou*); Jean Godard (*Dejoie*); Armand Bour (*Daigremont*); Roger Karl (*Banker*); Jimmy Gaillard (*The groom*); plus Les Rocky Twins, Raymond Dubreuil, Garaudet, and Tardif.

Publications:

Script—"*L'Argent*" (includes list of scenes, some dialogue) by Marcel L'Herbier in *L'Avant-Scène du cinéma* (Paris), 1 June 1978; review—"La Presse: lors de la sortie en 1929" in *L'Avant-Scène du cinéma* (Paris), 1 June 1978; books—*French Film* by Georges Sadoul, London 1953; *French Film* by Roy Armes, New York 1970; articles—"The Camera as Snowball: France 1918-1927" by R.H. Blumer in *Cinema Journal* (Evanston), spring 1970; "*L'Argent* de Marcel L'Herbier" by P. Jouvet in *Cinématographe* (Paris), May 1977; "Modernité de *L'Argent*" by Michel Marie in *L'Avant-Scène du cinéma* (Paris), 1 June 1978; "Marcel L'Herbier ou l'intelligence du cinématographe" by Claude Beylie in *L'Avant-Scène du cinéma* (Paris), 1 June 1978; "Entretien avec Marcel L'Herbier" by Claude Beylie and Marcel Martin in *L'Avant-Scène du cinéma* (Paris), 1 June 1978; "Archéologie du cinéma" by S. Trosa in *Cinématographe* (Paris), December 1978; "La Gratuite ce *L'Argent*" by J. Petat in *Cinéma 79* (Paris), March 1979; "Marcel L'Herbier" by J. Fieschi in *Cinématographe* (Paris), December 1979.

*   *   *

Marcel L'Herbier is a key figure of 1920s French cinema and his modernization of Emile Zola's novel, *L'Argent*, released in

1929 on the eve of the sound revolution, is his most ambitious work. The scope of the film is inspired by Abel Gance's *Napoléon*, but rather than talk of heroes, L'Herbier has chosen to attack what he hated most, the power of money. Though he took Zola's novel as his starting point, he retained little beyond the title and the outline of the plot. The film's action is transferred to the 1920s and unfolds within opulent, oversized sets built by Lazare Meerson and André Barsacq. The film's largest set, however, is an actual location, the Paris Stock Exchange borrowed for three days over Easter and filmed with a complex multi-camera style by a team led by Jules Kruger, who had earlier worked on *Napoléon*. The visual style's echoes of the major spectacles of 1920s German cinema are enhanced by the presence of Brigitte Helm and Alfred Abel, as the villains in L'Herbier's cast. Despite the enormous resources deployed—the film cost over three million francs—*L'Argent*'s plot line is remarkably straightforward: a young aviator and his wife become involved in a dubious financial scheme set up by the lecherous and unscupulous Saccard. The latter in turn is destroyed by an even more sinister figure, the banker Gunderman, abetted by the Baroness Sandorf. Though thwarted in his attempt to seduce the wife and destroy the aviator when he is ruined, Saccard is left in prison plotting his next financial coup, while Gunderman rules untroubled.

The 1920s were a period in which directors like Gance and L'Herbier seized the opportunities for individual expression offered by the disorganization of the French film industry. This was a cinema in which the key contributions of noted set designers were set against a continuing interest in location filming. As *L'Argent* shows, a preoccupation with visual effects—decor and movement, masking and superimpositions, slow motion photography, symbolic lighting and so on—did not imply any disregard for the real social world or for nature. *L'Argent* was not particularly highly esteemed by traditional film historians, but recent critical work, especially that of Noël Burch, has pointed to the great richness of the film even if the "modernity" claimed for it remains a problematic concept.

L'Herbier, like other 1920s filmmakers, refused to subordinate the visual style of his filmmaking to the demands of narrative continuity, which was already dominant in the United States and elsewhere. The type of cinema of which *L'Argent* is a key example can only be understood if the claims to primacy of narrative are disregarded and film is accepted as a mode of expression which may legitimately captivate its audience by other means. In this sense a work like *L'Argent* forces upon us a widening of the conception of cinema to take in forms fundamentally alien to the Hollywood tradition. The question of what value is to be attached to this alternative approach is, however, more complex. Noël Burch and others have prized *L'Argent* very highly as an example of a vitally important modernist cinema. But in a sense this distorts history, since the conventions L'Herbier was disregarding were not as fully established in France, and the Hollywood-style production practices which would have supported them were totally lacking. Moreover the weight of nineteenth century traditions of art and literature weighs heavily on L'Herbier, and a true evaluation of *L'Argent* would need to take into account also the conventional content, subject matter and ideological assumptions, as well as the visual and rhythmical audacities. But Burch's claims do make a refreshing alternative to the customary denigration of 1920s French cinema and open fascinating perspectives for future research.

—Roy Armes

ARSENAL. Arsenal: The January Uprising in Kiev in 1918. Production: VUFCO-Odessa; black and white, 35mm, silent; length: 7 reels, 1820 meters. Released 25 February 1929, Kiev.

Scenario, direction, and editing by Alexander Dovzhenko; photography by Danylo Demutsky; production design by Isaac Shpinel and Vladimir Mueller; music score for performance by Ihor Belza; assistant directors: Alexei Kapler, Lazar Bodyk. Filmed during the second half of 1928 in and around Kiev.

Cast: Semen Svashenko (*Tymish*); Amvroziy Buchma (*German soldier*); Mykola Nademsky (*Official*); M. Kuchynsky (*Petlyura*); D. Erdman (*German officer*); O. Merlatti (*Sadovsky*); A. Yevdakov (*Nicholas II*); S. Petrov (*German soldier*); Mykhaylovsky (*Ukrainian nationalist*); H. Kharkov (*Red Army soldier*).

Publications:

Reviews—"*Arsenal*" by Mordaunt Hall in *The New York Times*, 11 November 1929; review by James Shelley Hamilton in *National Board of Review Magazine* (New York), November 1929; books—*Alexander Dovz, henko* by R. Yourenev, Moscow 1958 (name transliterated as R. Jurenew in German translation, 1964); *Kino: A History of the Russian and Soviet Film* by Jay Leyda, London 1960; *Poetika Dovzhenko* by Igor Rachuk, Moscow 1964; *Dovjenko* by Luda and Jean Schnitzer, Paris 1966; *Alexandre Dovjenko* by Marcel Oms, Lyon 1968; *Dovjenko* by Alexandr Mariamov, Moscow 1968; *Alexandre Dovjenko* by Barthélemy Amengual, Paris 1970; *Alexander Dovzhenko: The Poet as Filmmaker*, edited by Marco Carynnyk, Cambridge, Mass. 1973; articles—"Film in Work" by O. Borisov in *Kino* (Moscow), no.10, 1928; "Pabst, Dovzhenko: A Comparison" by John C. Moore in *Close Up* (London), September 1932; "Index to the Creative Work of Alexander Dovzhenko" by Jay Leyda in *Sight and Sound* (London), supplement, index series, November 1947; issue on Dovzhenko of *Film* (Venice), August 1957; "Dovzhenko—Poet of Life Eternal" by Ivor Montagu in *Sight and Sound* (London), summer 1957; "The Films of Alexander Dovzhenko" by Charles Shibuk in *New York Film Bulletin*, no.11-14, 1961; "The Dovzhenko Papers" by Marco Carynnyk in *Film Comment* (New York), fall 1971; special issue devoted to Dovzhenko of *Iskusstvo Kino* (Moscow), September 1974; "Fin unserer Epoch" and "Ein Poet des Films" by S. Frejlih in *Film und Fernsehen* (Berlin), August and September 1974; "*Arsenal*" by I. Christie in *Monthly Film Bulletin* (London), September 1977; "Zu Problemen des stilistischen Einflusses der bildenden Kunst auf die Stummfilme Alexander Dowshenko" by A. Krautz in *Information* (Berlin), no.2, 1977.

*   *   *

In *Arsenal*, Alexander Dovzhenko, perhaps the most radical of the Soviet directors of the silent period, altered the already extended conventions of cinematic structure to a degree greater than had even the innovative Sergei Eisenstein in his bold *October*. The effect of this tinkering with the, more or less, accepted proprieties of motion picture construction produced a work that is actually less a film than it is a highly symbolic visual poem. For example, in a more linearly structured piece like *October*, the metaphors, allusions and analogies that arise through the construction of the various montages replace rather than comment on essential actions within the film. In *Arsenal*, however, the symbolism is so purposely esoteric, with seemingly deliberate barriers established to block the viewer's perception, that the relationship of individual symbols or sequences to the various actions of the film is not immediately clear.

The film's central theme obviously revolves around the idea of the sheer horror of war and is most fundamentally incarnate in the physical symbol of an arsenal in the midst of Russia's civil war. Yet, this theme is fragmented throughout the film within three distinct visual contexts. First, Dovzhenko exploits the inherent metaphorical potential of the individual shot as it is brilliantly exemplified in an opening image of a barbed wire trench barrier suddenly and unexpectedly exploding after a prolonged period of stasis. The contrast thus established between the transfixed image and the force of the off-camera shell explosion sets the stage for an interaction of fixed and moving images that runs the course of the film and establishes a semblance of poetic meter.

Second, the area between shots which is normally used in silent films for dialogue, location, or explanation is used here by Dovzhenko for thematic purposes. In an early scene, a series of three titles reading: "There was a mother who had three sons," "There was a war," "...and the mother had no sons," are interspersed between shots of a solitary woman and two camera angles of men on a moving train. This combination effected in sets of three (a recurrent image pattern throughout the film) not only establishes the concept of men going off to face the horrors of war but also ingrains in the audience a particular sentiment toward the idea.

A final thematic employment of symbolic images and one that runs through the entire course of the film in one form or another is the director's juxtaposition of stasis and movement within individual shots and between shots as well. Images of a train, of a platoon of soldiers moving almost relentlessly forward, a religious procession and a number of other dynamic elements are interjected around and between relatively static shots (usually grim), and effectively frame each immobile image as an individual symbolic and poetic unit with a meaningful parallel somewhere else in the film. In one sequence, a catatonic soldier is shot by an officer for not moving. The static shots of his execution are broken up by shots of a faceless platoon of soldiers moving forward. We never see the execution only still images of each stage. The isolated shots, however, pre-figure a parallel execution, again done in a sequence of three images, in turn foreshadows the fall of the arsenal itself. The middle shot in the execution sequence is nothing more than a highly symbolic pile of empty cartridges, but, as it turns out, the strikers who have taken over the arsenal are doomed by a lack of ammunition. Their plight is subsequently dramatized by three titles injected between shots of the men. The titles read: "The 24th hour," "The 48th hour," and "The 72nd hour," to show that time and ammunition is running out.

Arsenal is a difficult film that makes many demands upon the viewer and is stubbornly resistant to easy interpretation. Consequently it rewards a number of viewings and repeated analysis. Under intense scrutiny its thematic patterns emerge and the real genius of its creator becomes apparent. Although many of its images now appear dated as, in fact, do Eisenstein's, ample power remains to substantiate the relatively untutored Dovzhenko's reputation as one of the early giants of Soviet cinema on a plane with both Eisenstein and Pudovkin.

—Stephen L. Hanson

L'ATALANTE. Black and white, 35mm; running time: 89 mins.

(originally 82 mins.); length: 7343 feet. Released 1934 as *Le Chaland qui passe* with 7 mins. cut out. Re-released 1945 restored to its original form.

Produced by J.L. Nounez; screenplay by Jean Vigo and Blaise Cendrars (some sources list Albert Riéra as a collaborator); from a scenario by Jean Guinée; directed by Jean Vigo; photography by Boris Kaufman; edited by Louis Chavance; production design by Francis Jourdain; music by Maurice Jaubert. Filmed in Paris.

Cast: Jean Dasté (*Jean*); Dita Parlo (*Juliette*); Michel Simon (*Père Jules*); Gilles Margaritis (*Peddler*); Louis Lefèvre (*Boy*); Raya Diligent (*Bargeman*); Maurice Gilles (*Barge owner*).

Publications:

Books—*Le Surréalisme au cinéma* by Ado Kyrou, Paris 1953; *Amour, erotisme et cinéma* by Ado Kyrou, Paris 1957; *Jean Vigo* by P.E. Salès-Gomès, Paris 1957; *Hommage à Jean Vigo* edited by Freddy Bauche, Vinicio Beretta, and Franco Vercelotti, Lausanne 1962; *Anarchist Cinema* by Alan Lovell, London 1967; *Jean Vigo* by Pierre Lherminier, Paris 1967; *Jean Vigo* by P.E. Salès-Gomès, revised English ed., Los Angeles 1971; *Jean Vigo* by John M. Smith, London 1972; *Cinema, The Magic Vehicle: A Guide to Its Achievement. Journey One: The Cinema Through 1949* edited by Jacek Klinowski and Adam Garbicz, Metuchen, New Jersey 1975; *A History of Film* by Jack C. Ellis, Englewood Cliffs, New Jersey 1979; articles—in *Les Nouvelles Littéraires* (Paris), 29 September 1934; "Jean Vigo" by Alberto Cavalcanti in *Cinema Quarterly* (Edinburgh), winter 1935; "Life and Work of Jean Vigo" by James Agee in *The Nation* (New York), 12 July 1947; "The Films of Jean Vigo" by H.G. Weinberg in *Cinema* (Beverly Hills), July 1947; "Jean Vigo" by Siegfried Kracauer in *Hollywood Quarterly*, April 1947; special issue on Vigo of *Ciné-club* (Paris), February 1949; "Revaluations: L'Atalante, 1934" by Roger Manvell in *Sight and Sound* (London), February 1951; article in *Positif* (Paris), May 1953; "Jean Vigo et ses films" by Bernard Chardère in *Cinéma 55* (Paris), March 1955; "An Interview with Boris Kaufman" by Jonas Mekas in *Film Culture* (New York), no.4, 1955; *Premier Plan* (Lyon), no.19, 1961; "The Anarchism of Jean Vigo" by John Ellerby in *Anarchy 6* (London), August 1961; "The Playground of Jean Vigo" by B. Teush in *Film Heritage* (Dayton, Ohio), fall 1973.

*   *   *

The subject of *L'Atalante*—Vigo's only feature-length film completed just before his death—was not of his own choosing. The interest of the film lies in his engagement with material that was partly congenial in its unconventionality (life on a barge, with its freedom from the restrictions of established society, its alternative community of unsocialized eccentrics), and partly highly conventional (problems of the heterosexual couple, mutual adjustment to marriage, break-up and reunion). The subject enabled him to develop the love of anarchic behaviour already expressed in *Zéro de conduite*, but within the confines of an archetypal classical narrative of order (equated with marriage)/ disruption of order/restoration of order.

Crucial to Vigo's personal background was his allegiance to his anarchist father, who died in prison under mysterious circumstances, and about whom Vigo wanted to make a film:

crucial to his aesthetic background was the Surrealist movement. he wrote an adulatory review of *Un Chien andalou* and, while not Surrealist in the strict sense, his films are faithful to the spirit of Surrealism, with its commitment to Freudian theories of dream and the unconscious and to the overthrow of repressive bourgeois social and moral codes. *L'Atalante* opens with a wedding procession, which Vigo presents as if it were a funeral: everyone is in black, everyone looks glum, almost everyone is coupled. The only brief outburst of spontaneous energy comes from the one single man, who tries to pinch the behind of the woman in front of him and is sternly reprimanded. This is Vigo's succinct depiction of established society. Against it, in the same sequence, he sets the characters from the barge: *"le père Jules,"* whose relationship to mainstream culture and its rituals is summed up in his quick dash back into the church to splash himself with holy water and pronounce the couple man and wife; and the (nameless) boy who, having knocked the wedding bouquet into the canal, runs off to find a substitute and returns bearing great festoons of wild creeper, looking like a juvenile pagan nature god.

The barge departs, the social order is left behind, and the film swiftly establishes the bride, Juliette, as its central character and central problem. The film's great distinction lies partly in the honesty with which that problem is confronted, its ultimate failure lies in the way it withdraws from its implications. The Surrealist movement, while dedicated to sexual liberation, failed to develop any viable feminist theory and never successfully conceptualized the position of women: its commitment to *l'amour fou* was never disengaged from an emphasis on machismo. What is especially remarkable about *L'Atalante* is not only the intense erotic charge it conveys between its central couple (it could be described as an attempt to reconcile *l'amour fou* with domesticity), but also the way it foregrounds the position of the woman, raising the question of what this liberation means for *her*. For Juliette really has no place on the barge. Its little community appears to have functioned perfectly well before her appearance, the traditionally "feminine" reforms she effects (such as washing Jules's underwear) seem superfluous, and she never finds a role within the male work-world.

The culmination of the first half of the film is the marvellous scene in which Jules shows Juliette the treasures of his cabin (a veritable Surrealist world of unexpected juxtapositions). It ends with the brutal intervention of Jean, his smashing of Jules's collection of mementoes, and his striking of Juliette. He is re-establishing conjugal possession, and we register his behaviour as thoroughly negative. The nature of the threat Jean feels is extremely complex, not at all the simple one of erotic rivalry; and to understand it, we must consider the character of Jules and what he represents. Presented without ambiguity as an admirably robust and healthy figure, Jules transgresses, directly or by implication, every major bourgeois rule. (1) Money-value: his souvenirs are treasured solely for the associations they evoke, not for monetary worth. (2) Cleanliness: his physical robustness is unaffected by his living among cats which produce litters in the beds, and by his total lack of interest in bourgeois standards of hygiene. (3) Physical squeamishness: to demonstrate the efficiency of a native knife, he casually slices open his own hand. (4) Patriarchal dominance: he relates to Juliette as an equal, reducing the notion of male authority to a game (the tattered puppet of an orchestral conductor). (5) Death: he keeps the fore-arms of his best friend pickled in a jar, treating the souvenir without the least morbidity, but simply as a memento to live with. (6) Monogamy: he shows Juliette a photograph of himself with two women, telling her, "There's a story to that". We never get to hear it, but it is clear that Jules is unattached yet strongly sexual. (Neither does he *exploit* women: witness the later scene with the fortune-teller,

where the seduction is delightfully mutual). (7) Sexual identity: the dead friend was the person he was closest to, and although bisexuality is not necessarily implied, it is perfectly in keeping with the freedom from bourgeois conditioning Jules represents. (8) Property: Jules shows great affection for his souvenirs, but is not in the least bound to them. After Jean wrecks his cabin he casually picks up an unbroken piece of bric-à-brac, remarks, "there's one he missed", and smashes it. What Juliette is attracted to, and what her husband experiences as a threat, is precisely Jules's freedom—a freedom that can easily encompass loyalty, affection and loving relationship, but that quite precludes the exclusivity of marriage. Further, through Jean's behavior, the film clearly establishes marriage as characterized by the man's possession of, and assumption of absolute right over, the woman.

It is scarcely surprising that a film made within the capitalist production/distribution system for a bourgeois audience could not pursue further the implications of its own liberating perceptions. In fact, its second half is largely devoted to a retraction of those implications. Two related strategies are involved: the substitution of the peddler for "le père Jules," and the partial transformation of Jules's function. The bistro sequence with the peddler is clearly a repetition of/variation on the cabin scene. Juliette is attracted to the promise of freedom, the display of wonders, and Jean intervenes to reclaim her. But the peddler is not Jules: he is a slight figure, explicitly described as the "peddler of dreams," and the freedom and glamour with which he tempts Juliette are quite illusory. Jean is proved right in rejecting him. If Jules poses a substantial and formidable threat to the institution of marriage, the peddler only *seems* to, and the film can deal with him easily. Finally, Jules becomes indeed 'le père' Jules: the father-figure who retrieves the fugitive Juliette, slings her over his shoulder, restores her to her husband, and pulls shut the hatch over them. The film is quite explicit about Juliette's imprisonment, but the narrative resolution demands that she be shown to accept it gladly. The famous last shot—the phallic symbol of the barge pushing on through the sunlit canal—represents a celebration of sexuality about which we cannot help, today, feeling deeply uneasy.

—Robin Wood

L'AVVENTURA. The Adventure. Production: Produzioni Cinematografiche Europee, Cino del Duca, (Rome), and Société Cinématographique (Paris), 1959; black and white, 35mm; running time: 139 mins., also 130 mins. Released 25 September 1960, Bologna and Paris.

Produced by Amato Pennasilico; screenplay by Michelangelo Antonioni, Elio Bartolini, and Tonino Guerra; from an original story by Michelangelo Antonioni; directed by Michelangelo Antonioni; photography by Aldo Scavarda; edited by Eraldo da Roma; sound by Claudio Maielli; scene design by Piero Polletto; music by Giovanni Fusco; costumes designed by Adriana Berselli.

Filmed September 1959-January 1960 in Rome and Sicily (the isles of Lipari, Milazzo, Catania, and Taormina). Special Jury Prize, Cannes Festival, 1960.

Cast: Monica Vitti (*Claudia*); Gabriele Ferzetti (*Sandro*); Lea Massari (*Anna*); Dominique Blanchar (*Giulia*); Renzo Ricci

(*Anna's Father*); James Addams (*Corrado*); Dorothy De Poliolo (*Gloria Perkins*); Lelio Luttazzi (*Raimondo*); Giovanni Petrucci (*Young Painter*); Esmeralda Ruspoli (*Patrizia*); Enrico Bologna; Franco Cimino; Giovanni Danesi; Rita Molé; Renato Pincicoli; Angela Tommasi di Lampedusa; Vincenzo Tranchina; Joe, Fisherman from Panarea (*Old man on the island*); Prof. Cucco (*Ettore*).

Publications:

Scripts—*Screenplays of Michelangelo Antonioni* with an introduction by Antonioni, New York 1963; *Sei Film* by Michelangelo Antonioni, Turin 1964; reviews—"L'Avventura" by Ellen Fitzpatrick in *Films in Review* (New York), May 1961; review by Gordon Gow in *Films and Filming* (London), January 1961; "L'Avventura" by Penelope Houston in *Sight and Sound* (London), winter 1960-61; review by Andrew Sarris in *The Village Voice* (New York), 23 March 1961; books—*Michelangelo Antonioni: An Introduction* by Pierre Leprohon, New York 1963; *Antonioni, Bergman, Resnais* by Peter Cowie, New York 1963; *Cinema Eye, Cinema Ear* by John Russell Taylor, New York 1964; *Antonioni* by Philip Strick, London 1965; *Interviews with Film Directors* by Andrew Sarris, New York 1967; *Encountering Directors* by Charles Thomas Samuels, New York 1972; articles—by Michelangelo Antonioni in *Films and Filming* (London), January 1961; "L'avventura" by Robert Sandall in *Film Quarterly* (Berkeley), summer 1961; "Exploring the World Inside" by John Francis Lane in *Films and Filming* (London), January 1961; "An Interview with Antonioni" by Michele Manceaux in *Sight and Sound* (London), winter 1960-61; "Making a Film is My Way of Life" by Michelangelo Antonioni in *Film Culture* (New York), spring 1962; "*La Notte* and *L'Avventura*" by Guido Aristarco in *Film Culture* (New York), spring 1962; article by Raymond Durgnat in *Films and Filming* (London), March 1962; article by Marc Schleifer in *Film Culture* (New York), fall 1962; "Oh, Oh Antonioni" by John Francis Lane in *Films and Filming* (London), December 1962; issue on Antonioni in *Film Quarterly* (Berkeley), fall 1962; "The Face of '63—Italy" by John Francis Lane in *Films and Filming* (London), April 1963; "*L'Avventura*: A Closer Look" by Simon O. Lesser in *Yale Review* (New Haven), fall 1964; "The Event and the Image: Michelangelo Antonioni" by Geoffrey Nowell-Smith in *Sight and Sound* (London), winter 1964-65; "The R-H Factor and the New Cinema" by Jacques Doniol-Valcroze in *Cahiers du Cinema in English* (New York), January 1966; "Michelangelo Antonioni and the Imagery of Disintegration" by Thomas Hernacki in *Film Heritage* (Dayton, Ohio), spring 1970; "*L'Avventura*" by Stanley Kauffmann in *Horizon* (Los Angeles), autumn 1972; "Empêchement visuel et point de fuite dans *L'Avventura* and *Professione: Reporter*" by Kimball Lockhart in *Camera/Stylo* (Paris), November 1982.

* * *

When *L'avventura* was screened at the 1960 Cannes Film Festival its audience whistled, stamped, and shouted. They were not expressing enthusiasm. Antonioni's film had proved incomprehensible to them, as it was to prove to many an audience all over Europe. Significantly, however, this did not prevent the film from finding admirers and achieving remarkably large audience figures in several countries. This was the beginning of the age of the art-movie, and *L'avventura* was perfectly suited to the growing number of art-houses. After the debacle at Cannes,

35 critics and filmmakers issued a statement of support for *L'avventura* and its director, a view which was echoed in film criticism around the world. Within a year *L'avventura* had secured its place in film history.

What was it about the film that encouraged such extremes of disgust and admiration. The most common charge of the dissenters was that *L'avventura* was quite meaningless and, consequently, utterly boring. Foolishly, some defenders sought to turn that argument by making a virtue out of meaninglessness itself. To them *L'avventura* was the perfect aesthetic object: beautiful to observe but devoid of any cognitive or moral import. Apart from the fact that it is patently not devoid of such features, this view (not uncommon in art-house circles) makes the peculiar assumption that the look of a film is somehow independent of meaning, that beauty and meaning are separate elements in art. Others argued more cogently that *L'avventura* worked with and developed a new language of cinema, and that to understand it was to master an alien form. Hence the anger at Cannes among those not prepared to make that effort.

This claim does have some truth to it, though it overstates the film's innovatory qualities. *L'avventura* shares much with its two immediate predecessors, *Le amiche* and *Il grido*, both in theme and style. It hardly emerged from nowhere, though it is perhaps more unremittingly austere than anything its director had previously made. But it clearly does play down conventional narrative to the point of extinction. The "plot" of *L'avventura* (and the term is barely applicable) can be described in a couple of sentences. A young woman, Anna, disappears while cruising near Sicily in the company of a group of rich Italians. Her lover, Sandro, and her friend, Claudia, search unsuccessfully for her, developing a tenous relationship in the process. There is no resolution of the conventional type. Anna's disappearence is never explained, and ceases to be of any interest. At the end of the film Claudia and Sandro achieve a bleak sympathy, but hardly a consummation. Nor are we permitted any semblance of orthodox narrative involvement. The film is paced very slowly, much of its action seen in real time. Its characters communicate little in dialogue, and more often than not, are to be found looking away from each other out into the bleak and arid Sicilian landscape. We are invited to contemplate them, but not to identify. Point-of-view shots are rare, and shot-reverse shot sequences, where they exist, usually include both parties fully in shot. In these and other ways *L'avventura* excludes us from emotional involvement in any but the most cerebral sense.

Perhaps, then, the Cannes reception is unsurprising. In the two decades since *L'avventura*'s first appearance, narrative conventions have changed, but they have still nowhere near approached Antonioni's limit. In respect of its form *L'avventura* is as striking today as it was then, its invitation to contemplate its agonized characters as demanding as ever. Its meanings, however, are less elusive than they appeared to many in 1960. Hindsight and the cultural changes of the intervening years have rendered the film more transparent, its ideas more clearly part of their period. Antonioni himself, in a statement accompanying the film at Cannes, said that *L'avventura* charted a world in which "we make use of an aging morality, of outworn myths, of ancient conventions." The world had changed, yet human beings were trapped by the old standards. His characters, accordingly, can find no meaningful way to relate to each other, finally arriving, as he describes it, "at a sort of reciprocal pity."

Embedded in this diffuse account of modern social ills is a more specific lament at the degradation of creativity and sexuality. The love-making in *L'avventura* (except, briefly, for Claudia, the only fleetingly optimistic figure in a deeply depressing film) is without meaning or joy. Creative aspirations are stultified. As Sandro observes in a rare moment of self-perception, "I saw myself as a genius working in a garret. Now I've got two flats and I've neglected to become a genius." Materialism, alienation, and neurosis are the watchwords of this world. These were not new ideas, of course, and by 1960 there was a well established tradition of such despair in European art. What was new, and remains hugely impressive, was Antonioni's facility at expressing such ideas in a cinema shorn of conventional narrative aids. A sense of the alienation of people from their environment and from each other is conveyed in every stark composition, in every studied camera movement. The meaning of the film is there in its very fabric. *L'avventura* is never meaningless; if anything it is overloaded with meaning.

In an interview with Georges Sadoul, Antonioni made this observation, "when I finished *L'avventura* I was forced to reflect on what it meant." The lasting impact of the film has been to force the rest of us to take seriously the idea of a genuinely reflective cinema.

—Andrew Tudor

BALADA O SOLDATE. Ballad of a Soldier. Production: Mosfilm; black and white, 35mm; running time: 89 mins.; length: 8045 feet. Released 1959.

Screenplay by Grigori Chukhrai and Valentin Yoshov; directed by Grigori Chukhrai; photography by V. Nikolaev and Era Savelieva; edited by M. Timofeieva; art direction by B. Nemechek; music by Mikhail Siv.

Filmed 1958. Cannes Film Festival, Special Jury Prize, 1960; Honored at All-Union Film Festival of Russia and at the Czechoslovak Film Festival for Working People, 1960; Lenin Prize to Grigori Chukhrai, 1961.

Cast: Vladimir Ivashov (*Alyosha*); Shanna Prokhorenko (*Shura*); Antonina Maximova (*Mother*); Nikolai Kruchkov (*General*); Evgeni Urbanski (*Crippled soldier*).

Publications:

Script—extract in *Films and Filming* (London), July 1961; reviews—"*Ballad of a Soldier*" by Bosley Crowther in *The New York Times*, 26 December 1960; "*Balada o soldate*" in *Film a doba* (Prague), no.11, 1960; review in *Saturday Review* (New York), 24 December 1960; review by Arthur Clark in *Films in Review* (New York), January 1961; books—*An Example of Modern Revisionism in Art: A Critique of the Films and Statements of Grigori Chukhrai* by Chang Kuang-nien, Peking 1965; *The Most Important Art: East European Art After 1945* by Mira Liehm and Antonín J. Liehm, Berkeley, 1977; *Cinema, The Magic Vehicle: A Guide to Its Achievement: Journey Two: The Cinema of the Fifties* edited by Adam Garbicz and Jacek Kalinowski, Metuchen, New Jersey 1979; articles—by Albert Johnson in *Film Quarterly* (Berkeley), winter 1960; "Views of Life Compared: Chukhrai and Fellini" by Sergeî Gerasimov in *Films and Filming* (London), March 1961; article by Richard Whitehall in *Films and Filming* (London), July 1961; "A Talk with Grigori Chukhrai" by Hermann Herlinghaus in *Film Culture* (New York), no.26, 1962; "Keeping the Old on Their Toes" by G. Chukhrai in *Films and Filming* (London), October 1962; "Dis-

cussion in Villepre" in *Iskusstvo Kino* (Moscow), no.5, 1962; "Grigori Chukhrai" by D.J. Badder in *Film Dope* (London), April 1975.

LE BALLET MÉCANIQUE. Black and white, 35mm, silent; running time: about 14 mins.; length: 1260 meters. Released 1924. When shown in Berlin in 1925, part or all of *Ballet mécanique* was exhibited under the title *Images Mobile*.

Produced and directed by Fernand Léger; photography by Dudley Murphy (some sources credit Man Ray as well); sources indicate the editing was probably handled by Dudley Murphy; music by George Antheil; assistant director: Dudley Murphy.

Filming probably began with the "Charlot Cubiste" (Cubist Charlie Chaplin) sequence in 1923; filming completed in November 1924, most likely in Paris. Cost: about 5000 francs.

Cast: Kiki; Dudley Murphy.

Publications:

Books—*Bad Boy of Music* by Georges Antheil, New York 1945; *Underground Cinema* by Parker Tyler, New York 1969; *Experiment in the Film* edited by Roger Manvell, revised edition, New York 1970; *Experimental Cinema* by David Curtis, New York 1971; *Experimental Cinema: A 50 Year Evolution* by David Curtis, New York 1971; *The Cubist Cinema* by Standish Lawder, New York 1975; *Abstract Film and Beyond* by Malcolm Le Grice, Cambridge, Massachusetts 1977; *Visionary Film: The American Avant-Garde 1943-1978* by P. Adams Sitney, New York 1979; articles—"Léger, Dreyer, and Montage" by Kirk Bond in *Creative Art* (New York), October 1932; "The Avant-Garde Film Seen From Within" by Hans Richter in *Hollywood Quarterly*, fall 1949; "Epizod filmowy w dziele Fernanda Léger" by A. Jackiewicz in *Kino* (Warsaw), March 1974; book review of S.D. Lauder's *The Cubist Cinema* in *Quarterly Journal of Speech* (Falls Church, Virginia), no.4, 1976; "*Ballet mécanique*" by G. Brown in *Monthly Film Bulletin* (London), April 1977; "*Le Ballet mecanique*", translated by F. Lachenal from D. Cooper's *Fernand Léger*, in *Travelling* (Lausanne), summer 1979.

*   *   *

Contemporary film scholarship recognizes at least three major types of production. Most familiar and most popular is the fictive narrative, with roots back beyond Griffith's 1915 feature, *The Birth of a Nation*. Comparably familiar, though less popular, is the actuality film, with its documentary tradition at least as old as the 1920s work of artists like Flaherty and Grierson. Least familiar and least understood by popular audiences is the experimental film, which had its beginnings in the European avant-garde of the 1920s.

The European avant-garde was based largely upon the efforts of painters and other artists in Germany and France. Thus certain stylistics which mark the strategies of European painting during the 1920s often mark European avant-garde films: the stylistics of Futurism, Cubism, Dadaism, and Surrealism.

One of the best books on this period of experimental film is Standish Lawder's *The Cubist Cinema*. In part, Lawder's purpose was to relate classic European avant-garde films by Richter, Eggeling, Ruttman, and Léger to classic paintings of the period by Picasso, Kandinsky, Duchamp, and Léger. Indeed, it is especially interesting to find Léger's name common to both lists in light of the fact that his film *Ballet mécanique* constitutes one of the most famous and most successful examples surviving this brief-lived but highly innovative, highly influential period of experimental production.

Typically, experimental films are brief, independently-financed productions which tend toward innovative techniques and non-narrative structures. Often they are acollaborative, being the sole product of but one or two artists. *Ballet mecanique* is no exception to these characteristics. While the camerawork is attributed to the American Dudley Murphy, the 1924 French production is otherwise the work of one man, Fernand Léger.

Before he was 20, Léger had become a Cubist painter whose subject matter eventually centered on mechanical devices and urban imagery. *Ballet mécanique* is his sole film (although he did some work with Hans Richter on *Dreams that Money Can Buy* two decades later). He recalls that the film cost him some 5,000 francs, independent financing allowing him control comparable to that which he enjoyed with his paintings. *Ballet mécanique* is a difficult film to describe, though countless film scholars have embraced that very task. It is a brief, non-narrative exploration of cubist form, black and white tonalities, and various vectors through its constant, rapidly cut movements and compositions. As Lawder details in his study, many of the film's forms and compositions are reflected in—or themselves reflect—forms and compositions in Léger's famous cubist paintings from the period. Clearly the film allowed Léger cinematic extension of the formal problems he continued to explore in his single canvases.

The film flashes through over 300 shots in less than 15 silent minutes. The subjects of these fleeting images are diverse and difficult to quickly catalog: bottles, hats, triangles, a woman's smile, reflections of the camera in a swinging sphere, prismatically crafted abstractions of light and line, gears, numbers, chrome machine (or kitchen) hardware, carnival rides, shop mannequin parts, hats and shoes, etc. All interweave a complex cinematic metaphor which bonds man and machine. Further, *Ballet mécanique's* whimsical, witty, dadaist portrait seems to center on the looped repetition of a large woman repeatedly and mechanically ascending a stair (one of the first known examples of loop-printing, a technique later to become a mainstay of international experimental film after the 1960s).

Throughout its history, *Ballet mécanique* has always been a film more for other film artists or film scholars than for a general public. Still, it continues to enjoy critical attention and acclaim, and continues to influence the ongoing expression of experimental filmmakers throughout the industrialized free world.

—Edward S. Small

THE BAND WAGON. Production: Metro-Goldwyn-Mayer Picture Corp., 1953; Technicolor, 35mm; running time: 112 mins. Released 1953.

Produced by Arthur Freed; screenplay by Betty Comden and Adolph Green; from a radio show by Arthur Askey and Richard Murdoch; directed by Vincente Minnelli; photography by Harry Jackson; edited by Albert Akst; production design by Edwin Willis and Keogh Gleason, set designs for musical numbers by Oliver Smith; art direction by Cedric Gibbons and Preston Ames; music by Howard Dietz and Arthur Schwartz, music direction by Adolph Deutsch; costumes designed by Mary Ann Nyberg; dance direction by Michael Kidd. Filmed in the MGM studios.

Cast: Fred Astaire (*Tony Hunter*); Cyd Charisse (*Gabrielle Gerard*); Nanette Fabray (*Lily Marton*); Oscar Levant (*Lester Marton*); Jack Buchanan (*Jeffrey Cordova*); James Mitchell (*Paul Byrd*).

Publications:

Reviews—by Edward Jablonski in *Films in Review* (New York), August/September 1953; review by Gavin Lambert in *Sight and Sound* (London), January/March 1954; books —*Steps in Time* by Fred Astaire, New York 1959; *Vincente Minnelli* by Catherine de la Roche, New Zealand 1959, reprinted in *Film Culture* (New York), June 1959; *Vincente Minnelli* by François Truchaud, Paris 1966; *All Talking, All Singing, All Dancing* by John Springer, New York 1966; *Gotta Sing, Gotta Dance* by John Kobal, New York 1970; *Fred Astaire: A Pictorial Treasury of His Films* by Howard Thompson, New York 1970; *The MGM Years* by Lawrence B. Thomas, New Rochelle, New York 1972; *I Remember It Well*, with Hector Arce, New York 1974; articles—"L'Oeuvre de V.M." by Etienne Chaumeton in *Positif* (Paris), November/December 1954; "Fred Astaire's Film Career" by Gerald Pratley in *Films in Review* (New York), January 1957; "Entretien avec Vincente Minnelli" by Charles Bitsch and Jean Domarchi in *Cahiers du cinéma* (Paris), August/September 1957; "The Films of Vincente Minnelli" by Albert Johnson in *Film Quarterly* (Berkeley), winter 1958 and spring 1959; "Invitation à la danse" by François Tranchant in *Image et Son* (Paris), January 1958; "2 Feet in the Air" by Derek Conrad in *Films and Filming* (London), no.3, 1959; "Rencontre avec Vincente Minnelli" by Jean Domarchi and Jean Douchet in *Cahiers du cinéma* (Paris), February 1962; "The Rise and Fall of the Musical" by V. Minnelli in *Films and Filming* (London), January 1962; "There's No One Quite Like Astaire" by John O'Hara in *Show* (New York), October 1962; Minnelli issue of *Movie* (London), June 1963; "Vincente Minnelli ou le peintre de la vie rêvée" by Jean-Paul Torok and Jacques Quincey in *Positif* (Paris), March 1963; "Vincente Minnelli" by Catherine de la Roche in *Premier Plan* (Paris), March 1966; "Show-Making" by D. Giles in *Movie* (London), spring 1977; "Films: Fred Astaire's 'Dancing in the Dark'" by J. Mueller in *Dance Magazine* (New York), May 1979; "*The Band Wagon*" by Julia Johnson in *Magill's Survey of Cinema, Vol. 1* edited by Frank N. Magill, Englewood Cliffs, New Jersey 1980.

*   *   *

The Bandwagon is a marvelously engaging and delightful film, and has been recognized as such since its premiere in 1953. This film has been described as "a show that respectfully bids for recognition as one of the best musical films ever made" (New York *Times* movie reviewer Bosley Crowther, 1953), as "a series of urbane delights" (film critic Pauline Kael, 1968), as "the apotheosis of the backstage musical" (English arts critic Clive Hirschhorn, 1981), and as Fred Astaire's "best MGM musical" (film historian Ted Sennett, 1981).

The plot, fragile and almost inconsequential but laced with

some marvelous dialogue, deals with a faded movie star (Astaire) trying for a comeback in a musical written by his friends, played by Nanette Fabray and Oscar Levant who are almost the mirror image of scenarists Betty Comden and Adolph Green. Under the direction of a celebrated arty director-performer-impressario, portrayed by English musical comedy star Jack Buchanan, the skidding star is teamed with a well-known ballerina, played by Cyd Charisse. At first only sparks of dislike fly between them. Their show, moreover, is an unmitigated failure in its first performance on the road thanks to the artistic pretentions of the impressario. Due to the star's energy and intelligence, however, the show becomes a success and his relationship with the ballerina turns from antipathy to mutual love.

What distinguishes *The Bandwagon* from its many immediate predecessors produced by MGM, as well as from the many backstage musicals that have been made, is obviously not the plot, despite some delicious and some moving scenes. The strengths of the film lie in the zestful performances of the leads, especially Buchanan and Astaire, as well as the wonderfully tuneful score and the riveting choreography by Michael Kidd. Vincente Minnelli brought to the film a control, flair, and vitality that has seldom been surpassed by directors of musicals, resulting in a flawless harmony of the film's various parts. The superb score by the veteran composers Howard Dietz and Arthur Schwartz includes such standards as "Dancing in the dark," "I Love Louisa," "By Myself," "You and the Night and the Music," and "That's Entertainment" (the latter written especially for this film by Dietz and Schwartz in less than an hour). Among the many inventive and vital dance numbers was the "Girl Hunt" jazz ballet—an extremely enjoyable spoof on the then very popular blood and guts, over-sexed fiction of best selling novelist Mickey Spillane.

The Bandwagon represents the best efforts of the movie industry in producing musicals. Talent, energy, imagination all came together in the early 1950s to produce a number of fine musicals. Among the best of them is this classic film, which for sheer variety and vitality has rarely been equalled.

—Daniel J. Leab

BATAILLE DU RAIL, LA. Battle of the Rails. Production: Coopérative Générale du Cinéma Français; black and white, 35mm; running time: 87 mins.; length: 7800 feet. Released 1945 or 1946. Screenplay by René Clément and Colette Audry, with Jean Daurand; based on stories told to Colette Audry by members of the Resistance; directed by René Clément; photography by Henri Alekan; edited by Jacques Desagneaux; music by Yves Baudrier. The film contains documentary footage shot by an unknown amateur filmmaker.

Filmed, for the most part, in 1945 on location in France. Cannes Film Festival, voted among the Best Films, 1946.

Cast: Antoine Laurent (*Camargue*); Jacques Desagneux (*Maquis Chief*); Leroy (*Station master*); Redon (*Mechanic*); Pauléon (*Station master at St. André*); Rauzena (*Shunter*); Jean Clarieux (*Lampin*); Barnault and Kronegger (*Germans*); and the French Railwaymen. Some sources list a narration by Charles Boyer.

Publications:

Review—"*La Bataille du rail*" in *The New York Times*, 27

December 1949; books—*René Clément* by Jacques Siclier, Brussels 1956; *René Clément* by André Farwagi, Paris 1967; *Cinema, The Magic Vehicle: A Guide to Its Achievement: Journey One: The Cinema through 1949* edited by Adam Garbicz and Jack Klinowski, Metuchen, New Jersey 1975; *French Cinema Since 1946: Volume One: The Great Tradition* by Roy Armes, New York 1976; articles—by Jean Queval in *L'Écran français* (Paris), 16 October 1946; article by Roger Régent in *L'Écran français* (Paris), 14 October 1947; "Interview with Clément" by Francis Koval in *Sight and Sound* (London), June 1950; "Style of René Clément by Lotte Eisner in *Film Culture* (New York), no. 12 and 13, 1957; issue on Clément of *Avant-Scène du cinéma* (Paris), 1 February 1981.

*   *   *

Le Bataille du rail stands out as the only seriously realist film which the French made at the Liberation in 1945. At the first Cannes Festival in 1946 it took the grand prize. For a time its director René Clément was called a French neorealist, and it is true that he was much interested in and influenced by the Italian school. But Clément and his associates (Colette Audry as scriptwriter and Henri Alekan as cameraman) had thought about making this film when they had organized a discussion club in Nice well before 1945. This club later became IDHEC, the French film school.

Bataille du rail was shot out of doors with non-actors. Its script is episodic, involving separate sets of characters for each incident. The incidents include: 1) a meeting of the Resistance in the railyards and their narrow escape thanks to a timely air raid, 2) the planting of a bomb on a train despite discovery by German guards, and 3) the taking of hostages by Germans and their pitiful death by firing squad.

Midway through the film an overall dramatic direction is given when we learn that the Allies have landed and that the Germans must get their trains to Normandy. Despite heavy losses in skirmishes with armored trains and troops, the maquis, a military branch of the French underground, destroy four of the seven trains. The film concludes with the most elaborate incident, the derailing of a huge rail convoy, shot from three different angles. This spectacular destruction concludes with a closeup of an accordion slowly falling on itself, providing a musical sigh, as in Dovzhenko's *Arsenal*.

Other comparisons come to mind, especially Malraux' *Espoir* which, while shot in 1935, came out only in 1945. *Bataille du rail* remains fresh in comparison with dramatic resistance films like Henri Calef's *Jericho* because of its immediacy, speed, and detail. Despite its spectacular violence, the derailment is less memorable than the heroic closeups of the hostages lined up to be shot. At the instant before his death, we are given an extreme close-up from the vantage point of one of these anonymous patriots. He (and we) watch the indifferent but marvellous motions of a spider on the wall inches away. As the shots ring out, every engine in the railyard lets out a jolt of steam signalling, by its smoke and whistle, the spirit of resistance within the trains themselves.

This 85 minute film was fabled; nevertheless it didn't produce any imitations. Doubtless it had an effect on its director and cameraman who in turn were to rise to the top of the industry in France.

—Dudley Andrew

LA BATALLA DE CHILE: LA LUCHA DE UN PUEBLO SIN ARMAS, Part 1: La insurreccion de la burguesia. The Battle of Chile. Production: Equipo "Tercer Año," in collaboration with Chris Marker and the Instituto Cubano del Arte e Industria Cinematográficos (ICAIC); Kodak black and white, 16mm (subsequently blown up to 35mm). Released 1975, Cannes Film Festival.

Produced by Federico Elton; narration by Matías Rodríguez; directed by Patricio Guzmán; photography by Jorge Müller Silva; edited by Pedro Chaskel; sound engineered by Bernardo Menz; special effects by Jorge Pucheux, Delia Quesada, and Alberto Valdés; consultants: Julio García Espinosa and Marta Harnecker. Filmed 1973 in Santiago, Chile

Cast: Readers: Pedro Fernández Vila, Jacques Bonaldi and Bruno Colombo.

Publications:

Script—"*The Battle of Chile*: A Schematic Shooting Script" by Zuzana Pick in *Cine-Tracts* (Montreal), winter 1980; reviews— "*La Bataille du Chile*" by M. Cardenac in *Ecran* (Paris), December 1975; "*The Battle of Chile*" by P. Anderson in *Films in Review* (New York), June/July 1978; books—*La insurrección de la burgesia*, edited by Racinante, Caracas 1975; *La batalla de Chile: La lucha de un pueblo sin armas*, Madrid 1977; *Chile: El cine contra el fascismo*, by Patricio Guzmán with P. Sempere, edited by Fernando Torres, Valencia 1977; articles—"Más vale una sólida formación política que la destreza artesanal", interview by S. Salinas and H. Soto in *Primer plano* (Valparaiso), vol.2, no.5, 1973; "Chili: la première année" by Guy Gauthier in *Image et son* (Paris), March 1973; "Chili: le cinéma de l'unité populaire", interview by H. Ehrmann and others in *Ecran* (Paris), February 1974; "Le Cinéma dans la politique de l'Unité Populaire" in *Jeune Cinéma* (Paris), November 1974; "Stadion Chile" in *Film und Fernsehen* (Berlin), February 1974; "Il cinema cileno nel periodo del governo popolare" in *Quaderno informativo* (Pesaro), September 1974; "*La Bataille du Chili*" by Ginette Delmas in *Jeune Cinéma* (Paris), July/August 1975; "*La Bataille du Chili*, première partie: *L'Insurrection de la bourgeoisie*" by Guy Gauthier in *Image et son* (Paris), January 1976; "In Latin America They Shoot Filmmakers" by Peter Biskind in *Sight and Sound* (London), summer 1976; "Politics and the Documentary in People's Chile", interview by Julianne Burton in *Socialist Review*, October 1977; "Patricio Guzmán—ein Filmschöpfer der Unidad Popular" by J. Hönig in *Information* (Berlin), no.1, 1977; "*La batalla de Chile: La lucha de un pueblo sin armas*" by S. Meek in *Monthly Film Bulletin* (London), April 1977; "América Latina: Vigencia del documental politico Chile: Analista de una batalla" by P. Chaskel in *Cine al dia* (Caracas), November 1977; "*La batalla de Chile*", interview by Carlos Galiano in *Cine Cubano* (Havana), no.91-92, 1978; "La batalla de Chile", special section of *Cine Cubano* (Havana), March 1978; "Documenting the End of the Chilean Road to Socialism: *La batalla de Chile*" by Dennis West in *The American Hispanist*, February 1978; "An Interview with Patricio Guzmán, Director of *The Battle of Chile*" by Udayan Gupta and *FLQ* Staff in *Film Library Quarterly* (New York), no.4, 1978; "*Battle of Chile* in Context" by Angry Arts group in *Jump Cut* (Chicago), November 1979; "*Battle of Chile*: Struggle of People without Arms" by V. Wallis in *Jump Cut* (Chicago), November 1979; "Introduction to Latin America I: Chile" by Don Ranvaud in *Framework* (London), spring 1979; "Chilean Cinema in Exile" by Peter Schumann in *Framework* (London), spring 1979; "Wirklichkeit und Dokument", interview by C. Galiano in *Film und Fernsehen* (Berlin), November 1980; "*The Battle of Chile*: The Origins of the Project" by P. Guzmán in *Ciné-Tracts* (Montreal), winter 1980; "Chile: The Cinema of Resistance, 1973-1979" by Zuzana Pick in *Ciné-Tracts* (Montreal), winter 1980; "Letter from Guzman to Chris Marker" and "Reflections Previous to the Filming of *The Battle of Chile*" by Zuzana Pick in *Ciné-Tracts* (Montreal), winter 1980; "*The Battle of Chile*" by Dennis West in *Cineaste* (New York), no.2, 1981.

*　　*　　*

LA BATALLA DE CHILE: LA LUCHA DE UN PUEBLO SIN ARMAS, Part 2: El golpe de estado. The Battle of Chile, Part 2: A Blow Against the State. Production: Equipo "Tercer Año," in collaboration with Chris Marker and the Instituto Cubano del Arte e Industria Cinematográficos (ICAIC); Kodak black and white, 16mm (subsequently blown up to 35mm). Released 1976, Cannes Film Festival.

Produced by Federico Elton; screenplay by Patricio Guzmán; directed by Patricio Guzmán; photography by Jorge Müller Silva; edited by Pedro Chaskel; sound by Bernardo Menz, mixing by Carlos Fernández Vila, sound transfer by Jacinto Falcón and Ramón Torrado; special effects by Jorge Pucheux, Delia Quesada, and Alberto Valdés; advisors included Julio Garcia Espinosa and Marta Harnecker; foreign language versions by Matias Rodriguez. Filmed 1973 in Santiago, Chile.

Publications:

Script—"*The Battle of Chile*: A Schematic Shooting Script" by Zuzana Pick in *Ciné-Tracts* (Montreal), no.9, vol.3, no.1; reviews—"De l'histoire déjà (*La Bataille du Chile*)" by P.-L. Thirard in *Positif* (Paris), February 1977; "*La Bataille du Chile: 2e partie: Le coup d'etal*" in *Image et son* (Paris), April 1977; "*La Bataille du Chile: 2e partie: Le coup d'etat*" in *Jeune Cinéma* (Paris), February 1977; articles—"*La batalla du Chili: el golpe de estado*" by Hubert Niogret in *Positif* (Paris), July/August 1976; "La Bataille du Chili II", interview by Marcel Martin in *Ecran* (Paris), January 1977 "*Battle of Chile*: Struggle of People without Arms" by V. Wallis in *Jump Cut* (Chicago), November 1979; see Publications section for *La batalla de Chile* Part 1.

*　　*　　*

LA BATALLA DE CHILE: LA LUCHA DE UN PUEBLO SIN ARMAS, Part 3: El poder popular. The Battle of Chile, Part 3: The Power of the People. Production: Equipo "Tercer Año", in collaboration with Chris Marker and the Instituto Cubano del Arte e Industria Cinematográficos (ICAIC); Kodak black and white, 16mm (subsequently blown up to 35mm); running time: 90 mins. Released 1979.

Produced by Federico Elton; screenplay by Patricio Guzmán; directed by Patricio Guzmán; photography by Jorge Müller Silva; edited by Pedro Chaskel; sound by Bernardo Menz, mixing by Carlos Fernández, sound transfer by Jacinto Falcón and Ramón Torrado; advisors included Julio Garcia Espinosa, Pedro Chaskell, Marta Harnecker, and José Pino; other collaborators included Saul Yelin, Beatriz Allende, Harald Edelstam, Lilian Indseth, Juan José Mendy, Roberto Matta, Chris Marker, Rodrigo Rojas, Estudio Haynowsky, and Scheumann. Filmed 1973 in Santiago, Chile.

Cast: Reader: Pedro Luis Fernández Vila.

Publications:

Script—"*The Battle of Chile*: A Schematic Shooting Script" by Zuzana Pick in *Ciné-Tracts* (Montreal), winter 1980; review— "*La Batalla de Chile—III*" by T. MacCarthy in *Variety* (New York), 7 May 1980; article—"Chile 3. Guzmán" by P. Guzmán, translated by D. Ranvaud, in *Framework* (Norwich, England), spring 1979; see Publications section following *La batalla de Chile* Part 1.

* * *

The *Battle of Chile*, which consists of three feature-length parts, uses actuality footage to record the socio-economic and political turmoil preceding the fall of Chile's Marxist-socialist president, Salvador Allende, in 1973. While the film is an outstanding example of the documentary as a *record* of history-in-the-making, it is also a carefully conceived and clearly organized *analysis* of these events. Guzmán structured the first two parts of his film around selected "battlegrounds" (e.g., a strike of copper miners) where class interests clashed. The major issues and strategies in these clashes are generally presented in a dialectical fashion: for instance, the film may first show the tactics of the rightest forces and then the counter-measures with which the left responds. The filmmakers infiltrated the entire political spectrum and succeeded in showing events from multiple political perspectives as they unfolded. Part three of the film is structured differently in that it focuses on a single phenomenon—a people's power movement which first arose as a response to a bosses' strike.

This monumental documentary is Guzmán's most important film. It was made by a politically committed five-person team who faced overwhelming obstacles. Available to this film collective were one Nagra tape recorder, one 16mm Eclair camera, and film stock which had been sent from abroad by a colleague. In spite of the strict semi-clandestine measures they followed, the filmmakers at times risked their lives. After the right-wing military coup toppled Allende, all the sound tape and film footage were smuggled out of Chile. The film was edited at the Cuban Institute of Cinematographic Art and Industry in Havana.

The extensive use of the sequence-shot, *The Battle of Chile*'s predominant stylistic feature, is unusual in documentary films. Pedro Chaskel's low-key editing preserves the unity of these sequence-shots and maximizes their effect.

The Battle of Chile is one of the greatest Marxist documentaries. The influence of Marx's *The Civil War in France* and Lenin's *State and Revolution* is evident in the type of political analysis applied in the first two parts of the film. These two segments illustrate the Marxist-Leninist revolutionary lesson that there can be no peaceful transition to socialism before the repressive machinery of the bourgeois state (e.g., a standing army) is broken up and replaced. In accordance with this view, the filmmakers closely follow the military's drift to the right as well as the anti-Allende activities of the opposition-dominated legislature. Marx and Engels in the *Manifesto of the Communist Party*

viewed classes as the protagonists of history, and conflict as an inherent dimension of class societies. Guzmán follows this Marxist conception in that classes are the protagonists of his film and events are framed in terms of class conflict.

This film has reportedly never been seen in Chile. In countries where the documentary has been shown, both Marxist and non-Marxist critics have hailed it as a landmark in the history of the political documentary. Because of its vast scope, *The Battle of Chile* is surely the single most valuable historical document on the final months of the Vía Chilena, Chile's unique experiment in building socialism peacefully and democratically. Marxist critics have praised the film for its attack on the bourgeois ideology of cinema, an ideology which represents the capitalist mode of production and the bourgeois social order as "givens" and discourages viewers from challenging or questioning analytically the socio-economic status quo. In *The Battle of Chile*, the individual star of bourgeois cinema has been replaced by workers who are depicted as a class struggling to alter the capitalist mode of production and to change the world the bourgeoisie created.

—Dennis West

LA BATTAGLIA DI ALGERI. The Battle of Algiers. Production: Igor Films (Rome) and Casbah Film Company (Algiers), 1966; black and white, 35mm; running time: 123 mins. Released 1966.

Produced by Antonio Musu and Yacef Saadi; screenplay by Franco Solinas and Gillo Pontecorvo; directed by Gillo Pontecorvo; photography by Marcello Gatti; edited by Mario Serandrei and Mario Morra; art direction by Sergio Canevari; music by Gillo Pontecorvo and Ennio Morricone; special effects by Tarcisio Diamanti and Aldo Gasparri; Algerian assistants: Ali Yahia, Moussa Haddad, Azzedine Ferhi, Mohamet Zinet; Algerian "opérateurs": Youssef Bouchouchi, Ali Maroc, Belkacem Bazi, Ali Bouksani. Filmed 1965 in Algiers; cost: $800,000. Award: Venice Film Festival, Lion of St. Mark, 1966.

Cast: Yacef Saadi (*Djafar*); Brahim Haggiag (*Ali La Pointe*); Jean Martin (*Colonel Mathieu*); Tommaso Neri (*Captain Dubois*); Mohamed Ben Kassen (*Le Petit Omar*); Fawzia El Kader (*Hassiba*); Michele Kerbash (*Fathia*).

Publications:

Reviews—by Bosley Crowther in *The New York Times*, 23 September 1967; "Truthtelling" by Brendan Gill in the *New Yorker*, 23 September 1967; "So Long at the Festival" by Philip Hartung in *Commonweal* (New York), 20 October 1967; "Recent Wars" by Stanley Kauffmann in *The New Republic* (New York), 16 December 1967; "The Terror" by Joseph Morgenstern in *Newsweek* (New York), 23 October 1967; books— *Souvenirs de la bataille d'Alger: December 1956—September 1957* by Yacef Saadi, Paris 1962; *Filmguide to The Battle of Algiers* by Joan Mellen, Bloomington, Indiana 1973; articles— "Une si jeune paix", interview by Guy Hennebelle, in *Cinéma 65* (Paris), December 1965; "Le Cinéma algérien et *La Bataille d'Alger*" by Pierre Porin in *Positif* (Paris), October 1966; "*The Battle of Algiers*: An Adventure in Filmmaking" by Gillo Pontecorvo in *American Cinematographer* (Los Angeles), April 1967;

"*La battaglia di Algeri*" by Luisa Castelli in *Occhio critico* (Rome), May/June 1967; "Shooting at Wars: 3 Views" by Max Kozloff in *Film Quarterly* (Berkeley), winter 1967/68; "Gillo Pontecorvo" by Toby Mussman in *Medium* (New York), winter 1967-68; "Politics and Pontecorvo" by David Wilson in *Sight and Sound* (London), fall 1970; "Are the Revolutionary Techniques Employed in The Battle of Algiers Applicable to Harlem?" by Francee Covington in *The Black Woman*, New York 1970; "Politics and Pontecorvo" by David Wilson in *Sight and Sound* (London), fall 1970; "Battle of Algiers" by Peter Sainsbury in *Afterimage: Third World Cinema* (London), summer 1971; "An Interview with Gillo Pontecorvo" by Joan Mellen in *Film Quarterly* (Berkeley), fall 1972; "Valóság és modell. Pontecorvo: Az algiri csata és a Queimada" by E. Miklay in *Filmkultura* (Budapest), September/October 1972; "*La Bataille d'Alger*" by C. Bosséno in *Image et son* (Paris), February 1981.

*   *   *

In 1966, revolutionary filmmaker Gillo Pontecorvo released his stunning chronicle of one of the major clashes of the Algerian struggle for independence: *The Battle of Algiers*. The film's fictionalized account of this crucial three-year period in Algeria's history draws on actual people and events as the basis for its story, and adopts an impressively convincing documentary style in its presentation.

The film's opening credits contain a message stating that "not one foot" of actual newsreel footage was used in the making of the picture, yet Pontecorvo achieves a naturalistic, cinema-verité quality in his direction which conveys the immediacy of a television news broadcast. Marcello Gatti's grainy, black and white photography captures the look and texture of a newsreel, as does the jarring realism of the hand-held camerawork in many of the film's explosive crowd scenes. The use of non-professional actors (with the exception of Jean Martin as the French Colonel Mathieu) also contributes to the film's overall impression of events recorded as they occur.

This documentary-like effect has evoked both praise and condemnation for Pontecorvo, with some critics expressing admiration for the film's achievement and others questioning the ethics of filming a partly fictional scenario in such strikingly realistic terms. For Pontecorvo and his screenwriting partner, Franco Solinas, however, the question of the "truth" of *The Battle of Algiers* is answered by the film's political impact as an anti-imperialist statement. If isolated moments in the film, such as its central character's harassment by a group of arrogant young Frenchmen, are the products of the author's imaginations, they are nevertheless representative of events which occurred countless times during France's 130-year occupation of Algeria. Indeed, the film's most harrowing scenes-those of captured rebels undergoing torture at the hands of the military—demand to be shown, from a humanistic standpoint alone, at the full measure of the inhuman brutality they represent.

Yet Pontecorvo's political stance regarding the Algerian struggle does not lead him to resort to the caricatures of heroism and villainy which so often mar the impact of otherwise fine political films. Even as he reviles the policies of the French government, he forces us to confront the painful fact that these are human lives that are being lost and not mere pawns in a revolutionary uprising. His camera lingers on the faces of those who will die moments later from a planted rebel bomb, bringing home with wrenching clarity the bitter price of violent conflict. This rare approach, in a genre which frequently averts its eyes from these hard truths, places *The Battle of Algiers* at the forefront of political filmmaking by allowing each viewer to re-examine his or her own position on political violence in the harsh light of the images on the screen.

In the years since its release, *The Battle of Algiers* has become a staple of film classes and revival house theatres. Its political merits have been widely discussed and debated, with the individual outlook of each critic coming very much into play in any evaluation of the film. The film's cinematic achievements, however, remain as powerful as they first appeared in 1966, and subsequent armed revolts in other Third World countries have only served to reinforce the universality of Pontecorvo's remarkable work.

—Janet E. Lorenz

LA BELLE ET LA BÊTE. Beauty and the Beast. Black and white, 35mm; running time: 96 mins. (90 mins. according to some sources). Released 29 October 1946, Paris.

Produced by André Paulvé; screenplay by Jean Cocteau; from the fairy tale of Jean Marie Prince de Beaumont; directed by Jean Cocteau; photography by Henri Alekan; edited by Claude Iberia; sound engineered by Jean Lebreton, sound effects by Rouzenat; production design by René Moulaert and Lucien Carré; art direction by Christian Berard; music by Georges Auric, music directed by Roger Desormière; costumes designed by Christian Bérard, executed by Escoffier and Castillo from the House of Paquin; technical assistant to Cocteau: René Clément. Filmed in Saint-Maurice studios; exteriors shot at Rochecorbon in Touraine.

Cast: Jean Marais (*The Beast* and *The Prince*); Josette Day (*Beauty*); Marcel André (*The Father*); Mila Parély (*Félicie*); Nane Germon (*Adélaïde*); Michel Auclair (*Ludovic*); Raoul Marco (*The Usurer*); Gilles Watteaux and Noel Blin.

Publications:

Scripts—*Beauty and the Beast*, script edited by Robert Hammond, New York 1970; *Jean Cocteau: 3 Screenplays* [*The Eternal Return, Beauty and the Beast* and *Orpheus*], New York 1972; "*La Belle et la bête*" by Jean Cocteau in *L'Avant-Scène du cinéma* (Paris), July/September 1973; reviews—by André Bazin in *Le Parisien Libéré*, 11 January 1946; "*La Belle et la bête*: La critique" in *L'Avant-Scène du cinéma* (Paris), July-September 1973; books—*Diary of a Film* by Jean Cocteau, New York 1950; *Jean Cocteau* by Margaret Crosland, London 1955; *Jean Cocteau chez les sirènes* by Jean Dauven, Paris 1956; *Cocteau* by Jean-Jacques Kihm, Paris 1960; *Jean Cocteau tourne son dernier film* by Roger Pillaudin, Paris 1960; *Cocteau* by André Fraigneau, New York 1961; *Jean Cocteau: The History of a Poet's Age* by Wallace Fowlie, Bloomington, Indiana 1968; *Jean Cocteau: The Man and the Mirror* by Elizabeth Sprigge and Jean-Jacques Kihm, New York 1968; *Jean Cocteau* by Roger Lannes, Paris 1968; *Cocteau* by René Gilson, translated by Ciba Vaughn, New York 1969; *Cocteau* by Francis Steegmuller, Boston 1970; *Professional Secrets: An Autobiography of Jean Cocteau* edited by Robert Phelps and translated by Richard Howard, New York 1970; articles—"Jean Cocteau et le cinéma", special issue by C. Gauteur, of *Image et son* (Paris), June/July 1972; "Surréalisme et symbolisme" by Jean Decock in *L'Avant-Scène du cinéma*

(Paris), July/September 1973; "Cocteau face a *La Belle et la bête*" in *L'Avant-Scène du cinéma* (Paris), July/September 1973; "*La Belle et la bête* de Jean Cocteau" by J.C. Bonnet in *Cinématographe* (Paris), April/May 1976; "Jean Cocteau's *Beauty and the Beast*" in *American Imago* (Detroit), no.2, 1976; "*Beauty* and *The Thief*" by R.A. Wilson Jr. in *Audience* (Hollywood), November 1976.

*   *   *

La Belle et la bête, the film which marked Jean Cocteau's return to directing after an interval of 15 years, is a work which continues the vein of fantasy which had characterised his scriptwriting during the wartime years. To this extent the film is typical of its period, for the early postwar years in France saw a basic continuity with approaches established during the Vichy period (there was no resurgence of realism in France to compare with the emergence of neorealism in Italy). But in all other ways this appropriation of a fairy tale to the filmmaker's own personal mythology is a totally individual work.

The film is based on the tale as told by Madame Leprince de Beaumont, but there is little evidence in Cocteau's approach of the childlike innocence which the director demands of his audience in his brief introduction to the film. Visually, the film is one of Cocteau's most sophisticated works. The costumes designed by Christian Bérard and the lighting and framing devised by Henri Alekan are decorative rather than functional and take their inspiration from classic Dutch painting, particularly the work of Vermeer. Despite the presence of René Clément as technical supervisor, the film shows none of the reliance on complexity of scripting and use of heavy irony so characteristic of French cinema in the late forties. The legend is handled in a dazzlingly eclectic style. The home life of Belle's family is parodied and often broadly farcical in tone, as, for instance, in the use of cackling ducks to comment on the attitudes of her sisters. By contrast, the departure of Belle for the Beast's castle and her entry there are totally stylised, with Cocteau employing slow motion photography to obtain a dreamlike effect.

La Belle et la bête is an excellent example of Cocteau's continual concern in his film work to provide a "realism of the unreal." The fairytale world of Beast's castle is given great solidity, and indeed it is arguable that the setting has been given too much weight, with the result that there is a degree of ponderousness about the film which Georges Auric's music serves only to emphasise. In evoking the magical qualities of the castle, Cocteau has made surprisingly little use of the film's trick shot potentialities which form so crucial a part of so many of his other works. Here the living faces of the statuary and the disembodied human arms that act as Beast's servants are essentially theatrical devices.

One of the great difficulties facing Cocteau was that of sustaining interest for 90 minutes in the oversimplified and largely unpersonalised characters of his source material. The solution found for the minor characters is caricature and humour. For the Beast, Cocteau and Bérard use the make-up of Jean Marais to emphasise his bestial nature, a strategy which is particularly effective in such scenes as those in which he drinks or scents game. Belle is by comparison a fairly dull figure, despite Josette Day's beauty, but the ambiguities of her attitude toward the Beast do add interest and complexity to the character. The double use of Jean Marais as both the Beast and Belle's dissolute lover avoids the danger of too easy an explanation of the film's symbolism, and the transformation into a princely figure at the end shows a characteristically lyrical approach to death on the filmmaker's part. Particularly when seen in conjunction with the intimate diary of the shooting which Cocteau published in 1946 to coincide with the release of the film, *La Belle et la bête* provides an excellent introduction to the work of one of the screen's subtlest and most evocative poets.

—Roy Armes

BERLIN: DIE SINFONIE DER GROSSSTADT. Berlin: Symphony of a City. Berlin: Symphony of a Great City. Production: Fox-Europa-Film; black and white, 35mm; running time: 53 mins.; length: 1440 meters. Released September 1927.

Produced by Karl Freund; screenplay by Karl Freund and Walter Ruttmann; from an idea by Carl Meyer; directed by Walter Ruttmann; photography by Reimar Kuntze, Robert Baberske, and Laszlo Schaffer; edited by Walter Ruttmann; sets by Erich Kettelhut; music by Edmund Meisel. Filmed in Berlin.

Publications:

Reviews—by Leo Hirsch in *Berliner Tageblatt*, 24 September 1927; review by Harry Kahn in *Die Weltbühne* (Germany), 4 October 1927; review by Kurt Pinthus in *Tagebuch* (Germany), 8 October 1927; books—*The Film Till Now* by Paul Rotha, London 1930; *Der Geist des Films* by Béla Balázs, Halle, Germany 1930; *Documentary Film* by Paul Rotha, London 1936; *Film as Art* by Rudolph Arnheim, Berkeley 1957; *Nonfiction Film: A Critical History* by Richard Barsam, New York 1973; *Documentary: A History of the Nonfiction Film* by Erik Barnouw, New York 1974; *From Caligari to Hitler: A Psychological History of the German Film* by Siegfried Kracauer, Princeton 1974; *The Rise and Fall of the British Documentary* by Elizabeth Sussex, Berkeley 1975; *Abstract Film and Beyond* by Malcolm Le Grice, Cambridge, Massachusetts 1977; *Film as Film: Formal Experiment in Film, 1910-1975*, exhibition catalog, London 1979; articles—"Wie ich meinen *Berlin*—Film drehte" by Walter Ruttmann in *Lichtbild-Bühne* (Germany), no.241, 1927; article by Ruttmann in *Illustrierter Film-Kurier* (Germany), 9, no.658, 1927; "*Berlin—die Symphonie der Grosstadt*" by Paul Friedlander in *Die rote Fahne* (Germany), 25 September 1927; "Interview with Carl (Karl) Freund" by Oswell Blakeston in *Close Up* (Territet, Switzerland), January 1929; "The Rise and Fall of the German Film" by Harry Alan Potamkin in *Cinema* (New York), April 1930; "It's in the Script" by Paul Rotha in *World Film News* (London), September 1938; "Karl Freund, Candid Cinematographer" by Wick Evans in *Popular Photography* (Chicago), February 1939; "*Berlin*" by Peter Cowie in *Films and Filming* (London), August 1961; "Sound Montage: A Propos de Ruttmann" by Paul Falkenberg in *Film Culture* (New York), no.22-23, 1961; "*Berlin: The Symphony of a City* as a Theme of Visual Rhythm" by J. Kolaja and A.W. Foster in *Journal of Aesthetics and Art Criticism* (Cleveland), spring 1965; "Film 1928" in *Das Ornament der Masse* by Siegfried Kracauer, Frankfurt 1974; "Two Aspects of the City: Cavalcanti and Ruttmann" by Jay Chapman in *The Documentary Tradition* edited by Lewis Jacobs, 2nd ed., New York 1979; "Walter Ruttmann" in *Travelling* (Lausanne), summer 1979.

*   *   *

Underlying the totality of Walter Ruttmann's work in *Berlin, die Sinfonie der Grossstadt* was the aesthetic predicated on the wish to kineticize abstract forms as well as a concern for movement, rhythm, and alluring surface appearances. Orginally embodied in a series of innovative animated abstract films *Opus I-IV*, Ruttmann's eminently permutable aesthetic enabled him to emerge as one of the exemplars of the so-called New Objectivity in film during the middle years of the Weimar Republic. In *Berlin*, a rhapsodic, quasi-documentary record of a day in the life of Germany's capital, Ruttmann's fetishization of the rhythmic and visual as ends in themselves, fused with the cult of technology and urban modernity that characterized the New Objectivity, took on the aspects of an omniverous cinematic hubris seeking gratification by the manipulation of what Ruttmann termed the "living material" of a metropolis and the "absolute, purely filmic visual motifs" it yielded.

Berlin, then, is the film's true protagonist, a vibrant, pulsating, yet organic totality whose every component—animate or inanimate—is mediated and defined by the periodicity of the whole. The film portrays a day in the life of the city, beginning with panoramic shots of the sleeping metropolis as dawn breaks and concluding with a late-night fireworks display. Compressed between these diurnal poles is a brilliantly edited optical phantasmagoria of life in Berlin. The virtuosity with which cinematic tools are employed to stress certain leitmotifs—for example, the abstract beauty of modern technology—masterfully complements the film's structure, which replicates that of a symphony inasmuch as the alleged rhythms and oscillations of urban activity are organized into a series of movements. Yet, consonant with Ruttmann's aesthetic, within this rhythmic whole certain icons of modernity are isolated, abstracted, and transformed into purely ornamental images devoid of content and context. The recurring shots of machines, industrial facilities, and the facades of buildings, ripped out of any discernible context and deprived of any function save that of ornamentation, are typical leitmotifs in the film. Now luminous, now in shadow, now static, now in energetic but purposeless motion, they have been ruthlessly pressed into the service of Ruttmann's unrestrained formalism and thus stripped of all independent integrity and meaning.

This fetishism is accompanied by a contempt for human autonomy and subjectivity. Berlin's human inhabitants are placed on the same existential plane as its industrial and technological icons and the traffic that repeatedly criss-crosses the screen. Soulless ornaments, the people are but another source of optical titillation. Such a dehumanizing approach accounts for the gratuitous juxtaposition of shots of chattering monkeys and people conversing on the telephone, of department store mannequins or bobbing mechanical dolls with the anonymous inhabitants of the city, of the legs of workers with those of cattle being herded into a courtyard. Far from representing any rational critique of the contradictions that inhere in and have produced this particular manifestation of urban modernity, such juxtapositions are integrated into a visual rhapsody that, though brilliant in a narrow technical sense, emanates from an obsessive interest in the richness of forms and rhythm yielded by the city. Ruttmann's view of modern life is as a purely aesthetic phenomena, constituting abstract raw material for the filmmaker and entertaining optical cuisine for the public. This view represents not a denunciation of reification and dehumanization but their apotheosis.

Hailed upon its release as a revolutionary work of art, one that "flays our retinas, our nerves, our consciousness," *Berlin* is still venerated by film historians for its brilliant editing and imaginative structure. However, in the 1920's some perceptive critics, including Siegfried Kracauer and Paul Friedländer, lambasted its failure to establish any meaningful connections among the phenomena it portrayed. Such censure was well-founded, for *Berlin* reduced urban modernity to the spurious common denominators of dynamism, rhythm, and an aestheticized, reified technology, all of which were enveloped in a vacuous display of optical pyrotechnics. Indeed, these ideas and attitudes came to full fruition within the embrace of National Socialism. Ruttmann's world of abstract forms and stylized technology was fully integrated into the National Socialist public sphere and thereby into the latter's consummation: the mythologization and heroicization of imperialism and barbarism. Thus *Berlin*, far from being simply another "great film", must also be regarded as a precursor of a genre in which Ruttmann himself later specialized—the Nazi documentary film.

—Barry Fulks

THE BEST YEARS OF OUR LIVES. Production: Goldwyn Productions, 1946; black and white, 35mm; running time: 172 mins. Released 1946.

Produced by Samuel Goldwyn; screenplay by Robert Sherwood; from the novel *Glory for Me* by MacKinley Kantor; directed by William Wyler; photography by Gregg Toland; edited by Daniel Mandell; sound recorded by Gordon Sawyer; art direction by George Jenkins with Perry Ferguson; music by Hugo Friedhofer.

Filmed in RKO studios. Academy Awards for Best Picture, Best Direction, Best Actor (March), Best Supporting Actor (Russell), Best Screenplay, Best Editing, Best Music, and a Special Award to Harold Russell for "bringing hope and courage to his fellow veterans, 1946; New York Film Critics Awards for Best Motion Picture and Best Direction, 1946.

Cast: Myrna Loy (*Milly Stephenson*); Fredric March (*Al Stephenson*); Dana Andrews (*Fred Derry*); Teresa Wright (*Peggy Stephenson*); Virginia Mayo (*Marie Derry*); Cathy O'Donnell (*Wilma Cameron*); Harold Russell (*Homer Parrish*); Hoagy Carmichael (*Butch Engle*).

Publications:

Reviews—"*The Best Years of Our Lives*" by Abraham Polonsky in *Hollywood Quarterly*, April 1947; books—*William Wyler, An Index* edited by Karel Reisz, BFI, London 1958; *The Immediate Experience: Movies, Comics, Theater, and Other Aspects of Popular Culture* by Robert Warshow, New York 1962; *Directors at Work* edited by Bernard Kantor and Irwin Blacker, New York 1970; *William Wyler* by Axel Madsen, New York 1973; *Hollywood Directors: 1941-76* by Richard Koszarski, New York 1977; *Close-up: The Hollywood Director* edited by John Tuska, Metuchen, New Jersey 1978; *William Wyler* by Michael A. Anderegg, Boston 1979; articles—in *The New York Times*, 17 November 1946; "William Wyler: Director with a Passion and a Craft" by Hermine Rich Isaacs in *Theater Arts* (New York), February 1947; "Gregg Toland Film-Maker" by Lester Koenig in *Screen Writer* (London), December 1947; "Best Director of the Month" by L.O. Parsons in *Cosmopolitan* (New York), January 1947; "The Anatomy of a Falsehood" by Robert Warshow in the *Partisan Review* (New Brunswick), May/June 1947;

"The Hollywood Picture" by Peter Lyon in *Hollywood Quarterly*, summer 1948/summer 1949; "Wyler, Wellman, and Huston" by Richard Griffith in *Films in Review* (New York), February 1950; "The Later Films of William Wyler" by Karel Reisz in *Sequence* (London), no.13, 1951; "Fredric March" by Romano Tozzi in *Films in Review* (New York), December 1958; "A Little Larger Than Life" by John Howard Reid in *Films and Filming* (London), February 1960, and "A Comparison of Size", March 1960; "Myrna Loy" by Gene Ringgold in *Films in Review* (New York), February 1963; article by Andrew Sarris in *The Village Voice* (New York), 15 July 1965; "William Wyler" by Ken Doeckel in *Film in Review* (New York), October 1971; interview with Wyler by Charles Higham in *Action* (Los Angeles), September/October 1973; "Dialogue on Film" in *American Film* (Washington, D.C.), April 1976; "A Life in Film" by Larry Swindell in *American Film* (Washington, D.C.), April 1976; "The Sound Track" by P. Cook in *Films in Review* (New York), May 1979; "*The Best Years of Our Lives*" by Joan Cohen in *Magill's Survey of Cinema, Vol. 1* edited by Frank N. Magill, Englewood Cliffs, New Jersey 1980.

* * *

Acclaimed by critics and audiences at its release and awarded eight Academy Awards, *The Best Years of Our Lives* is imbued with the personal commitment that director William Wyler brought to his first project after his experience of shooting two documentaries for the U.S. Army Air Corps during World War II. Wyler was as much of a returning serviceman as are the heroes of this film. His problems in reintegrating himself into the community were perhaps not the same as those of Homer, the amputee, Fred, the captain who can only find work as a soda jerk and Al, the banker who confuses idealism and collateral, but the director's identification with their predicaments cannot be doubted. It is expressed in the film's unconventional structure and tone.

The film is, of course, about homecoming, and emphatically so when we realize that nearly one-third of its considerable length is exclusively devoted to that subject. The unfolding of the narrative, a slim narrative, is deferred until the film has thoroughly spatialized the notion of the return. In his pre-war films, Wyler's meticulous mise-en-scène served psychological porraiture in the context of melodrama. In *Best Years*, what we conventionally identify as theatrical tension is replaced by the nearly plotless placement of characters in locale and in relationship to each other. Wyler's stagings make dramatic events of the performers' positions in the frame. The three male protagonists, distinctive from each other in class, backgrounds, age and profession, are emblemized as an entity in the way their faces fit together in a bombadier's bay, during their journey back to Boone City. A taxi, with its windows and rear view mirror, provides a series of variations on their unity and singularity as it deposits them at their respective homes. Homer is caught in significant isolation, standing before his front porch, between the clear eyes of his buddies and the pitying ones of his family and sweetheart. When he waves goodbye with his prosthetic hook he *places* everyone in this less than triumphant homecoming. Al's reception, in one of the film's most famous shots (in a film full of famous shots), is a happier one. He embraces his wife Milly in a hallway whose length is a function of narrative time and camera placement rather than physical dimension.

One of the elements for which the film is distinguished is the use of quite limited spatial contexts—the bedrooms, living rooms and kitchens of the middle class. Wyler's blockings and the deep-focus photography of Gregg Toland, then, transcend the modest areas of middle-American domesticity, without betraying or distorting their shape, finding in them the coordinates that express this drama of placement. The emotional peak of the embrace of Al and Milly is followed by Al's nervousness at being a civilian and a husband. Milly sits comfortably in a wing chair, at place in the frame; Al shifts nervously from one side of the frame to the other. His homecoming, as well as that of Fred and Homer, is incomplete. It will require the duration of the whole film to achieve something like a narrative homecoming. And even that is ambiguous in this film that so disrupts the conventions of Hollywood storytelling.

The story that is told is charted in the distances our eyes traverse in the frame. Here, as in other examples of screen narrative that exploit staging in deep fields, we are required to make sense out of what is apparently a fully constituted frame, without the distraction of frequent inter-cutting. This access to the wholeness of the cinematic image is what prompted André Bazin to consider *Best Years* a model of his realist aesthetic. Bazin pays particular attention to the scene where the foreground is occupied by Homer, playing the piano with his hooks, while in the background Fred is phoning Al's daughter to break off their relationship. The mediating figure in the frame is Al, presumably looking at Homer, yet just as much aware of what is going on behind his back. We see and understand all the elements simultaneously, just as we do at the film's end, at the wedding of Homer and Wilma in one side of the frame, and the reconciliation of Fred and Peggy in the other.

The Best Years of Our Lives represents the kind of production for which Samuel Goldwyn was renowned. No expense or effort was spared; the lighting of the cramped playing spaces required enormously complicated procedures to create the deep-focus effects. Hugo Friedhofer's score is one of the most admired in the history of film music. A star actress, Myrna Loy, played Milly, essentially a supporting role. The embodiment of one kind of American wife in the "Thin Man" series, she is just as well remembered for the variation she brings to the type in *Best Years*. Fredric March won his second Academy Award (the first 15 years previously in *Dr. Jekyll and Mr. Hyde*) for his portrayal of Al. Harold Russell, the non-professional chosen to play Homer, gives a performance that is as much a function of the director's ability to place him in the frame and preserve his simplicity as it is a creation of the "actor."

While it is impossible to ignore the non-professional status of Harold Russell or to ignore the way the fiction addresses an important social problem in 1946 America, it is equally impossible to ignore the film's formal and perceptual challenges. With almost mannerist insistence, Wyler reminds us that the screen is an *image* of depth, not the real thing. He tests that quality of the image in the long and short of the fiction's expressive physical contexts—an ex-flier (Fred) wandering through a graveyard of planes slated for demolition, an amputee finally embracing his sweetheart with the stumps of his arms, a gigantic drug store that seems to sum up the crassness of post-war America, a neighborhood bar that collects the feelings of a film unsure about its "best years."

—Charles Affron

THE BIG HEAT. Production: Columbia Pictures Corp., 1953; black and white, 35mm; running time: 89 or 90 mins. Released 14 October 1953.

Produced by Robert Arthur; screenplay by Sidney Boehm; from

a novel by William P. MacGivern; directed by Fritz Lang; photography by Charles Lang, Jr.; edited by Charles Nelson; sound by George Cooper; art direction by Robert Peterson, set decoration by William Kiernan; music by Daniele Amfitheatrof, directed by Mischa Bakaleinikoff; costumes designed by Jean Louis. Filmed from about 21 March to 18 April 1953 in Columbia studios.

Cast: Glenn Ford (*David Bannion*); Gloria Grahame (*Debby Marsh*); Jocelyn Brando (*Katie Bannion*); Alexander Scourby (*Mike Lagana*); Lee Marvin (*Vince Stone*); Jeanette Nolan (*Bertha Duncan*); Peter Whitney (*Tierney*); Willis Buchey (*Lieutenant Wilkes*); Robert Burton (*Gus Burke*); Adam Williams (*Larry Gordon*); Howard Wendall (*Higgins*); Cris Alcaide (*George Rose*); Carolyn Jones (*Doris*); Michael Granger (*Hugo*); Dorothy Green (*Lucy Chapman*); Ric Roman (*Baldy*); Dan Seymour (*Atkins*); Edith Evanson (*Selma Parker*).

Publications:

Reviews—by Bosley Crowther in *The New York Times*, 15 October 1953; review in *Time* (New York), 2 November 1953; review by Lindsay Anderson in *Sight and Sound* (London), summer 1954; books—*Fritz Lang* by Francis Courtade, Paris 1963; *Fritz Lang* by Luc Moullet, Paris 1963; *Fritz Lang* edited by Alfred Eibel, Paris 1964; *The Cinema of Fritz Lang* by Paul M. Jensen, New York 1969; *Fritz Lang* by Claire Johnston, London 1969; *Fritz Lang in America* by Peter Bogdanovich, London 1969; *Violent America: The Movies Between 1946-1964* by Lawrence Alloway, New York 1971; *Underworld U.S.A.* by Colin McArthur, London 1972; *Fritz Lang* by Frieda Grafe, Enno Patalas, and Hans Helmut Prinzler, Munich 1976; *Fritz Lang* by Lotte Eisner, London 1977; *Fritz Lang* by Robert Armour, Boston 1978; *The Films of My Life* by François Truffaut, translated by Leonard Mayhew, New York 1978; *The Films of Fritz Lang* by Frederick W. Ott, Secaucus, New Jersey 1979; *Fritz Lang* edited by Stephen Jenkins, London 1979; *Film Noir* edited by Alain Silver and Elizabeth Ward, Woodstock, New York 1979; *Fritz Lang: A Guide to References and Resources* by E. Ann Kaplan, Boston 1981; articles—"Aimer Fritz Lang" by François Truffaut in *Cahiers du cinéma* (Paris), January 1954; "Fritz Lang's America" by Gavin Lambert in *Sight and Sound* (London), summer 1955; "Trajectoire de Fritz Lang" by Michel Mourlet in *Cahiers du cinéma* (Paris), September 1959; "Notes pour un éloge de Fritz Lang" by Gérard Legrand in *Positif* (Paris), March 1963; "Wirklichkeit statt Menschheitsfragen" by Rainer Hartmann in *Frankfurter Neue Presse*, 26 May 1964; "Fritz Lang, der Unbekannte: Jahrestreffen der deutschen Filmclubs" by Enno Patalas in *Frankfurter Allegemeine Zeitung*, 7 May 1964; "L'Oeuvre Américaine de Fritz Lang (1936-1956)" by Claude Beylie in *L'Avant-Scène du cinéma* (Paris), February 1968; "Aspects of Fritz Lang" by Paul Joannides in *Cinema* (London), August 1970; "*The Big Heat* and *The Big Combo*: Rogue Cops and Mink-Coated Girls" by Tom Flinn in the *Velvet Light Trap* (Madison, Wisconsin), no.11, 1974; "Règlement de comptes" by Claude Beylie in *Ecran* (Paris), January 1975; "American Nightmare: The Underworld in Film" by Mark Hennelly Jr. in *Journal of Popular Film* (Bowling Green, Ohio), no.3, 1978; "*The Big Heat*" by Valentin Almendarez in *Cinema Texas Notes* (Austin), 20 March 1978; "Fritz Lang: Only Melodrama" by Don Willis in *Film Quarterly* (Berkeley), winter 1979-80; article by William P. MacGivern in *American Film* (Washington, D.C.), October 1983.

*   *   *

The Big Heat is generally remembered as the Fritz Lang film in which a hoodlum (played by Lee Marvin) scalds and ultimately scars the face of a beautiful woman (Gloria Grahame). Like many of the films done in the film noir style, it is a complex morality play set in the city and populated with characters who represent good and bad, or often a mixture of both.

The hero-policeman Dave Bannion (Glen Ford) is clearly the forerunner of Don Siegel's *Dirty Harry* and numerous characters portrayed by Charles Bronson in the 1970s, particularly the urban vigilante of Michael Winner's *Death Wish*. Bannion is shown to be under pressure from his job. The investigation of the suicide of a fellow policeman, Duncan, leads Bannion to confront the mobster who controls the city. In direct battle with the crook, Bannion's normal restraints are released one by one. His understanding and supportive wife is killed by a car bomb that was meant for him. When he disobeys the order by his superiors to stop the investigation, he is taken off the force. His only weakness, his love and fear for his daughter, is eliminated when she is placed in complete safety, guarded by a group of tough ex-soldiers. Bannion, now free of ties and responsibilities and obsessed with the revenge motive, is ready to play the savage game by the rough and tough rules. But when faced with taking the law into his own hands and murdering, Bannion does not. For if he did, he knows he would not be any different than the mobsters he wants to destroy.

This difference is pointed out to him and clearly shown in the relationship between Bannion and the disfigured gangster's moll Debbie. The character of Debbie is the middle woman, the counterbalance between the two extremes of womanhood depicted in the film. She is not the schemer or shrew the widow Duncan is, nor is she pure and good like Bannion's wife. Departing from many film noir films, *The Big Heat* does not have the beautiful woman as the center of evil, though Debbie's role is just as important here as she is the key to the moral balance of the film. Her character straddles the line between good and bad. She is "good" in that she appreciates Bannion's kindness and humanity and sees that he is an honorable man; she is "bad" because she understands the criminal side of the struggle, and sees that by killing the blackmailing Mrs. Duncan, she will help Bannion. It will also be a fitting retaliation for her scarred face. Even in film noir though, murderers can not go free. Her death is her punishment for her crimes just as Bannion's acceptance of her at her death is fitting reward for her good deeds. This is unlike other film noir plots where the hero's acceptance of the beautiful woman leads to his downfall.

At the film's end, the moral balance is back to normal. Bannion has regained control of his life, has had his revenge, and he is back on the job. The criminals have met their end and fallen from power. At much human cost, the city is now safe.

—Ray Narducy

THE BIG PARADE. Production: Metro-Goldwyn Mayer Pictures Corp., 1925; originally black and white with tinted sequences, 35mm, silent with music score; running time: about 125 mins.; length: 13 reels at 12,550 feet originally, later 12 reels at 11,519 feet. Released selectively November 1925, released generally 1927. Re-released 1931 with synchronized music and sound effects.

Produced by Irving G. Thalberg; scenario by by Harry Behn, story by Laurence Stallings; from the play by Joseph W. Farnham, and also loosely based on the novel *Plumes* by Laurence Stallings; titles by Joseph W. Farnham; directed by King Vidor; photography by John Arnold; edited by Hugh Wynn; art direction by Cedric Gibbons and James Basevi; music score by William Axt and David Mendoza.

Cast: John Gilbert (*James Apperson*); Renée Adorée (*Mélisande*); Hobart Bosworth (*Mr. Apperson*); Claire McDowell (*Mrs. Apperson*); Claire Adams (*Justyn Reed*); Robert Ober (*Harry*); Tom O'Brien (*Bull*); Karl Dane (*Slim*); Rosita Marstini (*French Mother*).

Publications:

Books—*The Parade's Gone By...* by Kevin Brownlow, New York 1968; *King Vidor* by John Baxter, New York 1976; *A Tree is a Tree* by King Vidor, New York, reprinted 1977; *American Silent Film* by William K. Everson, New York 1978; articles— "Tells How *The Big Parade* Was Made" by F.J. Smith in *Motion Picture Classic* (Brooklyn), May 1926; "Interview" by Jim Tully in *Vanity Fair* (New York), June 1926; "John Gilbert" by Lawrence J. Quirk in *Films in Review* (New York), March 1956; "A John Gilbert Index" by Henry Davis in *Films in Review* (New York), October 1962; "King Vidor" by Kevin Brownlow in *Film* (London), winter 1962; "King Vidor" by Charles Higham in *Film Heritage* (Dayton, Ohio), summer 1966; "War, Wheat, and Steel" by Joel Greenberg in *Sight and Sound* (London), autumn 1968; "King Vidor at NYU" in *Cineaste* (New York), spring 1968; "Renee Adoree" by Roi A. Uselton in *Films in Review* (New York), June/July 1968; "King Vidor" by C. Barr in *Brighton* (London), March 1970; "King Vidor: A Career That Spans Half a Century" by Herbert G. Luft in *Film Journal* (Dayton, Ohio), summer 1971; "*The Big Parade*" by Raymond Durgnat in *Film Comment* (New York), July/August 1973; issue on Vidor in *Positif* (Paris), September 1974; "Entre l'horizon d'un seul et l'horizon de tous" by B. Amengual in *Positif* (Paris), September 1974.

*   *   *

Ironically, the film that established King Vidor as a major director is hardly typical of a man concerned almost entirely with obsession, sensuality and the subconscious. Having convinced Irving Thalberg he should abandon "ephemeral films" in favor of those on eternal subjects like "war, wheat and steel," Vidor in fact created in *The Big Parade* a box-office comedy romance similar in tone to Fox's hit *What Price Glory?*, and a vehicle for matinee idol John Gilbert.

MGM imported the co-author of *What Price Glory?*, Laurence Stallings, and accepted a script outline drawn mostly from his post-war novel *Plumes*, a protest at public indifference to returning veterans maimed in the war; like his hero Jim Apperson, Stallings had lost a leg.

The vision of trench warfare offered by *The Big Parade* is unabashedly romantic. Southern gentleman Apperson amiably condescends to egalitarian friendship with Tom O'Brien and a tobacco-chewing Karl Dane, and to love of the bouncy Mélisande (Renée Adorée), a parody of Gallic cuteness dressed, one French critic snapped, "like a burlesque miller's wife." The film's big scene, where she kneels in the road clutching his old boot as the Army streams by, was played, Vidor acknowledges, "to jerk a tear," and does so to some effect, as does their concluding reunion in a soft-focus rural France.

Vidor began shooting with the scene of a terrified Apperson trapped in a shell hole with a dying German. Impressed, Thalberg demanded a romantic framing story and additional battles—the price of splash release through the same chain that had made *Ben Hur* MGM's biggest hit. Vidor obligingly added the sub-plot of Apperson's fiancée and her affair with his brother. The film made a fortune for MGM, and might have done the same for Vidor had he not signed his percentage away at the behest of a smart studio lawyer.

The Big Parade belongs in the tradition of Hollywood's post-World War I romances, a companion piece to Griffith's *Hearts of The World* and Ford's *Pilgrimage*. Not anti-war so much as indifferent to it, the film, as Vidor wrote at the time, is about "the heartbeats of the doughboy, his girl and the parents of the two.... I do not wish to appear to be taking any stand about war...." The film's $18 million profit elevated him to the top echelon of Metro directors. For a reward, he was given, not films of "significance," but *Bardelys the Magnificent* and *La Boheme*, star vehicles for John Gilbert.

—John Baxter

———

THE BIG SLEEP. Production: Warner Bros. Pictures Inc., 1946; black and white, 35mm; running time: 114 mins. Released 31 August 1946.

Produced by Howard Hawks; screenplay by William Faulkner, Leigh Brackett, and Jules Furthman; from the novel by Raymond Chandler; directed by Howard Hawks; photography by Sidney Hickox; edited by Christian Nyby; sound by Robert B. Lee; production design by Fred M. MacLean; art direction by Carl Jules Weyl; music by Max Steiner; special effects by Roy Davidson and Warren E. Lynch. Filmed in Warner Bros. studios.

Cast: Humphrey Bogart (*Philip Marlowe*); Lauren Bacall (*Vivian*); John Ridgely (*Eddie Mars*); Martha Vickers (*Carmen*); Dorothy Malone (*Bookshop girl*); Peggy Knusden (*Mona Mars*); Regis Toomey (*Bernie Ohls*); Charles Waldren (*General Sternwood*); Charles D. Brown (*Norris*); Bob Steele (*Canino*); Elisha Cook, Jr. (*Jones*); Louis Jean Heydt (*Joe Brody*); Sonia Darrin (*Agnes*); Theodore von Eltz (*Geiger*); Tom Rafferty (*Carol Lundgren*); James Flavin (*Captain Cronjager*); Thomas Jackson (*Wilde*); Don Wallace (*Owen Taylor*); Joy Barlowe (*Chauffeur*); Tom Fadden (*Sidney*); Ben Weldon (*Pete*); Trevor Bardette (*Art Huck*); Marc Lawrence.

Publications:

Scripts—*The Big Sleep* by William Faulkner, Leigh Brackett, and Jules Furthman, New York 1971; *Howard Hawks: Tote schlafen fest*/"*The Big Sleep*", Tübingen, 1981; books—*The Cinema of Howard Hawks* by Peter Bogdanovich, New York 1962; *Bogart* by Richard Gehman, Greenwich, Connecticut 1965; *Humphrey Bogart: The Man and His Films* by Paul Michael, Indianapolis 1965; *The Films of Humphrey Bogart* by Clifford McCarty, New York 1965; *Howard Hawks* by Jean-Claude Missiaen, Paris 1966; *Howard Hawks* by Robin Wood, London 1968; *Howard Hawks* by Jean A. Gili, Paris 1971; *Focus on Howard Hawks* edited by Joseph McBride, Englewood Cliffs, New Jersey 1972; *The Films of Howard Hawks* by Donald Willis, Metuchen, New Jersey 1972; *Humphrey Bogart* by Alan G. Barbour, New York 1973; *Bogart and Bacall* by Joe Hyams, New York 1975; articles—"Today's Hero: A Review" by John Houseman in *Hollywood Quarterly*, January 1947; "The World of Howard Hawks" by Andrew Sarris in *Films and Filming* (London), July 1962 and August 1962; "Howard Hawks" by Henri Agel in the *New York Film Bulletin*, no.4, 1962; "Howard Hawks" by Peter Bogdanovich, Jacques Rivette, Mark Shivas, V.F. Perkins, and Robin Wood in *Movie* (London), December 1962; article by Claude-Jean Philippe in *Télérama* (Paris), June 1966; article by Bertrand Tavernier in *Humphrey Bogart* by Bernard Eisenschitz, Paris 1967; "*The Big Sleep*" by John Blades in *Film Heritage* (Dayton, Ohio), summer 1970; "Bogart, Hawks, and *The Big Sleep*" by Paxton David in *Film Journal* (New York), summer 1971; "Bogart, Hawks, and *The Big Sleep* Revisited-Frequently" by Paxton Davis in *Film Journal* (New York), summer 1971; "*Le Grand Sommeil*" in *Ecran* (Paris), July 1972; "Howard Hawks—Masculine Feminine" by Molly Haskell in *Film Comment* (New York), April 1973; "From *The Big Sleep* to *The Long Goodbye* and More or Less How We Got There" by Leigh Brackett in *Take One* (Montreal), January 1974; "Film Noir: The Writer: The World You Live In" by P. Jensen in *Film Comment* (New York), November/December 1974; "The Obvious and the Code" by Raymond Bellour in *Screen* (London), winter 1974-75; "Notes on *The Big Sleep*/30 Years After" by James Monaco in *Sight and Sound* (London), winter 1974/75; "En écoutant *Le Grand Sommeil*" by P. Carcassonne in *Cinématographe* (Paris), December 1978; "Chandler and *The Big Sleep*" by P. Hogue in *Movietone News* (Seattle), 22 February 1978; "*The Big Sleep*" by J. Pym in *Monthly Film Bulletin* (London), September 1978; "*The Big Sleep*" by Rita TheBerge in *Cinema Texas Notes* (Austin), 1 March 1978; "Teaching About Narrative" by G. Davies in *Screen Education* (London), winter 1978-79; "*Le Grand Sommeil*" by D. Sauvaget in *Revue du cinéma* (Paris), January 1979; "*The Big Sleep*" by Janey Place in *Magill's Survey of Cinema, Vol. 1* edited by Frank N. Magill, Englewood Cliffs, New Jersey 1980; "At the Acme Bookshop" by D. Thomson in *Sight and Sound* (London), spring 1981.

*   *   *

An unidentified finger presses the doorbell of the Sternwood mansion. A butler answers. The guest intones: "My name is Marlowe. General Sternwood sent for me."

This introduction thrusts us into immediate alliance with private detective Philip Marlowe, and throughout the film we traverse the world of crime as he does. As the central character, he is in every scene: we know what he knows, nothing more, nothing less. We share his experience as if on a detective training course: we see the way he works, the way he choreographs his moves and orchestrates his space to provoke a desired reaction from his opponent; we share his cognitive processes by identification with his visual point of view; we adopt his attitude by osmosis.

This is the world of film noir in which the existential hero (here played by noir favorite Humphrey Bogart) moves through oppressive atmospheres and dangerous locales, encounters wicked men and women and strives to earn his salary by solving a minor-league murder while wading through a complex and confusing series of clues. Despite a blackmail premise which exposes a whodunnit plot, this Howard Hawks film concerns itself less with why or who, than with how, more with process than result. The story line is extremely complicated (even the author of the novel, Raymond Chandler, was reputedly unable to answer a certain key question about the plot), and unfolds at breakneck speed forcing the spectator to assimilate facts and assess situations quickly or succumb to confusion. Does it really matter who is blackmailing General Sternwood, or what happened to Sean Regan, or who shot Arthur Gwynne Geiger?

In adapting the Chandler novel for the screen, many details were altered and the directly political material erased, but an essential pessimism and cynicism remained. An atmosphere of corruption was pervasive, and more than an investigation of a crime, this is an investigation into modern treachery: Marlowe is deceived, beat up, and threatened with extermination as he searches for the truth of a criminal situation. We are concerned not so much with what happened to others as what is happening to Marlowe.

What does happen to him is true in spirit to the novel except in the realm of romance, Marlowe's misogynistic streak replaced by a cynicism which erodes as the developing romance with Vivian consolidates. In a typical film noir, male/female relationships are doomed, severed by the conclusion of the film—typified by Fred MacMurray's condition at the end of *Double Indemnity* or Bogart's loss of Gloria Grahame at the end of *In a Lonely Place*. In *The Big Sleep* Hollywood romance prevailed in Hawksian style; Bogart and Bacall lived out their celebrated off-screen romance on screen.

The Big Sleep was a Warner Brother's big budgeted film, not an RKO low budget "B"; box office stars, a top notch crew and three major writers was not the usual treatment accorded to films of this genre. This studio treatment elevated the film to "A" status, but ultimately the box office was fuelled by a movie-going public anxious to witness romantic reality amidst Hollywood fiction.

—Doug Tomlinson

THE BIRDS. Production: Alfred J. Hitchcock Productions, 1963; Technicolor, 35mm; running time: 120 mins. Released 28 March 1963, New York, through Universal Pictures.

Produced by Alfred Hitchcock; screenplay by Evan Hunter; from "The Birds" by Daphne Du Maurier; main titles by James S. Pollak; directed by Alfred Hitchcock; photography by Robert Burks; edited by George Tomasini; sound by Remi Gassman and Oskar Sala, sound recorded by Waldon O. Watson and William Russell, sound supervised by Bernard Herrmann; production design by Robert Boyle, set decoration by George Milo; music by Bernard Herrmann; special effects by Lawrence A. Hampton; costumes designed by Edith Head; special photography advisor: Ub Iwerks; birds trained by Ray Berwick. Filmed mostly on location in Bodega Bay, California.

Cast: Rod Taylor (*Mitch Brenner*); Tippi Hedren (*Melanie Daniels*); Jessica Tandy (*Mrs. Brenner*); Suzanne Pleshette (*Annie Hayworth*); Veronica Cartwright (*Cathy Brenner*); Ethel Griffies (*Mrs. Bundy*); Charles McGraw (*Sebastian Sholes*); Ruth McDevitt (*Mrs. MacGruder*); Joe Mantell (*Traveling salesman*); Doreen Lang (*Hysterical woman*); Malcolm Atterbury (*Deputy Al Malone*); Karl Swenson (*Drunk*); Elizabeth Wilson (*Helen Carter*); Lonny Chapman (*Deke Carter*); Doodles Weaver (*Fisherman*); John McGovern (*Postal clerk*); Richard Deacon (*Man in elevator*); William Quinn.

Publications:

Reviews—by Sterling Foote in *Films in Review* (New York), May 1963; review by Andrew Sarris in the *Village Voice* (New York), 4 April 1963; books—*The Cinema of Alfred Hitchcock* by Peter Bogdanovich, New York 1962; *Hitchcock's Films* by Robin Wood, London 1965; *The Films of Alfred Hitchcock* by George Perry, London 1965; *Le Cinéma selon Hitchcock* by François Truffaut, Paris 1966; *Alfred Hitchcock* by Noel Simsolo, Paris 1969; *Movie Reader* edited by Ian Cameron, New York 1972; *Hitch* by John Russell Taylor, New York 1978; *L'Analyse du film* by Raymond Bellour, Paris 1979; *Hitchcock—The Murderous Gaze* by William Rothman, Cambridge, Mass. 1982; *The Dark Side of Genius: The Life of Alfred Hitchcock* by Donald Spoto, New York 1983; articles—"Echoes from *The Birds*" by Albert Johnson in *Sight and Sound* (London), spring 1963; "*The Birds*" by Peter Bogdanovich in *Film Culture* (New York), spring 1963; "Hitchcock on Style: Interview" in *Cinema* (Beverly Hills), August/September 1963; "The Face of 63—United States" by G. Fenin in *Films and Filming* (London), March 1963; article by Peter Baker in *Films and Filming* (London), September 1963; interview with Hitchcock by Ian Cameron and V.F. Perkins in *Movie* (London), January 1963; "*The Birds*" by Carl Belz in *Film Culture* (New York), winter 1963-64; article by John Thomas in *Film Society Review* (New York), September 1966; "*The Birds*" by Alfred Hitchcock in *Take One* (Montreal), no.10, 1968; "Caliban and Bodega Bay" by R.C. Cumbow in *Movietone News* (Seattle), May 1975; "Poe, Hitchcock and the Well-wrought Effect" by D. Simper in *Literature/Film Quarterly* (Salisbury, Maryland), summer 1975; "Hitchcock entre l'être et le néant" by J. Magny in *Téléciné* (Paris), April 1976; "Paranoia and the Film System" by J. Rose in *Screen* (London), winter 1976-77; "The Sound of One Wing Flapping" by E. Weis in *Film Comment* (New York), September/October 1978; "Enunciation and Sexual Difference" by J. Bergstrom in *Cinema Obscura* (Berkeley), summer 1979; "Alfred Hitchcock" by G. Bikácsy in *Filmkultura* (Budapest), September/October 1979; "*The Birds*: At the Window" by B. Nichols in *Film Reader* (Evanston, Illinois), no.4, 1979; "*The Birds*" in *Texas Cinema Notes* (Austin), 23 April 1979.

*   *   *

Of *The Birds*, Peter Bogdanovich has written, "If (Alfred Hitchcock) had never made another motion picture in his life, *The Birds* would place him securely among the giants of the cinema." Directed by Alfred Hitchcock in 1962, *The Birds* represents only one in a series of Hitchcock collaborations with composer Bernard Herrmann, cinematographer Robert Burks, and editor George Tomasini. As well, it is the director's first film with blonde actress Tippi Hedren, who would later star in *Marnie*, perhaps the most criticaly controversial film of Hitchcock's career.

The Birds seems to be a film which is almost beyond criticism, or, more precisely, to be a film which functions as a Rorschach test, in which everyone sees something different and of which virtually anything can be said. *The Birds* has been discussed as a generic work of horror which inaugurated a whole series of armageddon-oriented films, as a film of special effects and state-of-the-art mattework representing the ingenuity of Hollywood, as Hitchcock's most sophisticated example of his ability to manipulate his audiences and to play upon the spectators' fears, as a profound and personal work on the fragility of human experience and the importance of commitment in human relationships, as a philosophical treatise—influenced by Kafka and Poe—on the existential human condition, as a structural work examining the point-of-view shot and its relationship to the gaze of the spectator, as a psychoanalytic repository of ideology and meaning, and as the American film most influenced by and celebrative of the montage theories promulgated by the Russian cinema theorists. That this film has been interpreted in so many ways, that its memory remains so strong for so many filmmakers and critics, and that the film continues to excite and provoke new generations of filmgoers, offers the surest sign that *The Birds* may indeed be a great and lasting film.

Those who see the film for the first time are often surprised by the strength of their visceral response, but those who see the film an additional time are inevitably surprised by how much of the film has actually little to do with bird attacks, and takes, instead, the relationships between human beings as its subject. Certainly *The Birds* contains some of the most disturbing and almost surreally beautiful images Hitchcock has ever put on film: the children's party disrupted by a bird attack; the camera's treatment of Tippi Hedren as a fetish object; the surprising aerial view of Bodega Bay which shows the city from the birds' point of view; the three virtually still shots—each catching a discreet moment of time—of Tippi Hedren watching helplessly through the window of a cafe; and especially, the final exterior scene, aided by the poetic yet mysterious and ambiguous matte paintings of Al Whitlock, as the protagonists drive off into an unearthly bird-populated landscape and an uncertain future.

—Charles Derry

THE BIRTH OF A NATION. Original title: The Clansman. Production: Epoch Producing Corporation, 1915; black and white, 35mm, silent; length: 13,058 feet, later cut to 12,000 feet. Released 8 February 1915, Los Angeles. Re-released 1930 with musical soundtrack.

Produced by D.W. Griffith; scenario by D.W. Griffith, Thomas Dixon, and Frank Woods; from the play *The Clansman* by the Rev. Thomas Dixon; directed by D.W. Griffith; photography by G.W. (Billy) Bitzer and Karl Brown; edited by James Smith; music for the sound version compiled by Joseph Carl Breil, assisted by D.W. Griffith; costumes supplied by Robert Goldstein; assitants to the director include: Eric von Stroheim, Raoul Walsh, Jack Conway, and George Siegman. Filmed 4 July-24 September 1914 in Reliance-Majestic Studios, Los Angeles, and various outdoor locations around Los Angeles; cost: $110,000.

Cast: Henry B. Walthall (*Ben Cameron, the "Little Colonel"*); Mae Marsh (*Flora*); Miriam Cooper (*Margaret, the older sister*); Violet Wilkey (*Flora as a child*); Josephine Crowell (*Mrs. Cameron*); Spottiswoode Aitken (*Dr. Cameron*); Andre Beranger

(*Wade Cameron*); Maxfield Stanley (*Duke Cameron*); Jennie Lee (*Mammy*); William De Vaull (*Jake*); Lilliam Gish (*Elsie Stoneman*); Ralph Lewis (*The Hon. Austin Stoneman*); Elmer Clifton (*Phil Stoneman*); Robert Harron (*Ted Stoneman*); Mary Alden (*Lydia Brown, Stoneman's housekeeper*); Tom Wilson (*Stoneman's Negro servant*); Sam De Grasse (*Senator Sumner*); George Siegmann (*Silas Lynch*); Walter Long (*Gus*); Elmo Lincoln (*White Arm Joe*): Wallace Reid (*Jeff, the blacksmith*); Joseph Henaberry (*Abraham Lincoln*); Alberta Lee (*Mrs. Lincoln*); Donald Crisp (*Gen. Ulysses S. Grant*); Howard Gaye (*Gen. Robert E. Lee*); William Freeman (*Sentry*); Olga Grey (*Laura Keene*); Raoul Walsh (*John Wilkes Booth*); Eugene Palette (*Union Soldier*);); Bessie Love (*Piedmont Girl*); Charles Stevens (*Volunteer*); Erich von Stroheim (*Man who falls off Roof*).

Publications:

Scripts—*A Shot Analysis of D.W. Griffith's 'Birth of a Nation'* by Theodore Huff, New York 1961; "*La Naissance d'une Nation*" (outline of action plus some dialogue) by D.W. Griffith and Frank Woods in *L'Avant-Scène du cinéma* (Paris), 15 October 1977; *The Birth of a Nation* by John Cunibert (a shot by shot analysis), Woodbridge, Connecticut 1979; reviews—"Birth of a Nation" in *The New York Times*, 4 March 1915; "A Stirring Film Drama Shown" in the *New York Tribune*, 4 March 1915; "The Birth of a Nation: Summit of Picture Art" in *New York Dramatic Mirror*, 10 March 1915; review in *Variety* (New York), 12 March 1915; "After the Play" in *New Republic* (New York), 4 December 1915; "Brotherly Love" in *New Republic* (New York), 20 March 1915; books—*Life and Lillian Gish* by Albert Bigelow Paine, New York 1932; *The Rise of the American Film* by Lewis Jacobs, New York 1939; *Agee on Film. Vol. I* by James Agee, New York 1948; *The Negro in Films* by Peter Noble, London 1948; *The Movies in the Age of Innocence* by Edward Wagenknecht, Norman, Oklahoma 1962; *The Birth of a Nation Story* by Roy Aitken as told to Al P. Nelson, Middleburg, Virginia, 1965; *D.W. Griffith: American Film Master* by Iris Barry, New York 1965; *Spellbound in Darkness* by George C. Pratt, Connecticut 1966; *The Great Films: 50 Golden Years of Motion Pictures* by Bosley Crowther, New York 1967; *The Parade's Gone By* by Kevin Brownslow, New York 1968; *Fire from the Flint* by Raymond Allen Cook, Winston-Salem, North Carolina 1968; *Lillian Gish: The Movies, Mr. Griffith, and Me* by Lillian Gish with Ann Pinchot, Englewood Cliffs, New Jersey 1969; *The Art of the Moving Picture* by Vachel Lindsey, New York reprinted 1970; *Focus on Birth of a Nation* edited by Fred Silva, New York 1971; *Adventures with D.W. Griffith*, New York 1973; articles—"The Civil War in Film" in *Literary Digest* (New York), 20 March 1915; "The World's Master Picture Producer" by Selwyn Stanhope in *The Photoplay Magazine* (Hollywood), January 1915; "D.W. Griffith Recalls the Making of *The Birth of a Nation*" by Henry Stephen Gordon in *The Photoplay Magazine* (Hollywood), October 1916; "The Rise and Fall of Free Speech in America" by D.W. Griffith, (a pamphlet written in answer to the reaction against *The Birth of a Nation*), Los Angeles 1916; "*The Birth of a Nation* in Retrospect" by Seymour Stern in *International Photographer* (Hollywood), April 1935; "*The Birth of a Nation*" by Milton Mackaye in *Scribner's Magazine* (New York), November 1937; "The Negro in Hollywood" by David D. Platt in *Daily Worker* (New York), 19-28 February 1940; "Cultural History Written with Lightning: The Significance of *The Birth of a Nation*" by Everett Carter in *American Quarterly* (Unversity of Pennsylvania), fall 1960; "Editing in The

Birth of a Nation" in *Motion Pictures: The Development of an Art from Silent Pictures to the Age of Television* by A.R. Fulton, Norman, Oklahoma 1960; "The Reaction of the Negro to the Motion Picture, *Birth of a Nation*" by Thomas R. Cripps in *The Historian*, May 1963; "Griffith: I. *The Birth of a Nation*" by Seymour Stern in the Special Griffith Issue of *Film Culture* (New York), spring/summer 1965; "*Birth of a Nation* or White Power Back When" by Andrew Sarris in *The Village Voice* (New York), 17 and 24 July 1969; "*Naissance d'une Nation*: La Piste du Geant" by Claude Beylie in *Cinéma 71* (Paris), March 1971; "The Impact of Griffith's *Birth of a Nation* on the Modern Ku Klux Klan" by Maxim Simcovitch in *Journal of Popular Film* (Bowling Green, Ohio), winter 1972; "The Films of D.W. Griffith: A Style for the Times" by Alan Casty in *Journal of Popular Film* (Bowling Green, Ohio), spring 1972; "In Defense of Minority Group Stereotyping in the Popular Film" by Maurice Yacowar in *Literature/Film Quarterly* (Salisbury, Maryland), spring 1974; "G.P. and D.W.G...in dare e l'avere" by D. Turconi in *Bianco e nero* (Rome), summer 1975; issue on *Birth of a Nation* in *Kosmorama* (Copenhagen), summer 1975; "*Naissance d'une nation*: Opéra maçonnique" by M. Oms in *Cahiers du cinéma* (Paris), Christmas 1975; "Griffithiana: Material della e per la storia del cinema..." in *Filmcritica* (Rome), January/February 1976; "*The Birth of a Nation* Case" in *Classic Film Collector* (Indiana, Pennsylvania), fall 1976; "La naissance d'une Nation ou la reconstruction de la famille" by Pierre Sorlin in *L'Avant-Scène du cinéma* (Paris), 15 October 1977; "Histoire d'un film" by Pierre Sorlin in *L'Avant-Scène du cinéma* (Paris), 15 October 1977; "Le Témoignange de Raoul Walsh: 'Maturité d'Hollywood'" in *L'Avant-Scène du cinéma* (Paris), 15 October 1977; "La Guerre de Sécession dans le cinéma américain avant *La Naissance d'une Nation*" by Pierre Sorlin in *L'Avant-Scène du cinéma* (Paris), 15 October 1977; "The Battle" by D.W. Griffith in *L'Avant-Scène du cinéma* (Paris), 15 October 1977; "Two Lincoln Assassinations by D.W. Griffith" by Vlada Petric in *Quarterly Review of Film Studies* (Pleasantville, New York), summer 1978; "*Birth of a Nation*" by R. Combs in *Monthly Film Bulletin* (London), May 1979; "In Defence of the KKK" in *Monthly Film Bulletin* (London), May 1979; "Answering Film with Film..." by N. Fleener in *Journal of Popular Film and Television* (Bowling Green, Ohio), no.4, 1980; "Dixon, Griffith, and the Southern Legend: A Cultural Analysis of *The Birth of a Nation*" by Russell Merritt in *Cinema Examined*, New York 1982.

* * *

For people with only a casual interest in film, *The Birth of a Nation* remains Griffith's monument, but one that discredits its maker as much as it honors him. Griffith's movie still holds all silent box office records. By 1931, the film earned slightly under $18 million, and by 1946, when the last count was taken, more than 200 million people had seen it. No one knows how many more have seen it since.

Yet, even in its heyday it was never shown without apology or protest and today it is generally passed over in embarrassed silence, an antiquated dragon whose force has been spent. When *Sight and Sound* polled 89 critics in 1972 for a top ten list, the film once called America's greatest epic mustered a pitiful two votes. In *Sight and Sound*'s 1982 poll, no one included the film anywhere on their lists.

Those who do praise *Birth* usually hail it as an important landmark in film narrative technique. In praise of its spectacle and Griffith's contribution to film grammar, there is hardly anything new to say. These are the aspects, along with the film's racist portrait of Reconstruction, that are best known; the only aspects most people know. No one who writes on film history fails to pay hommage to Griffith's talents as a craftsman and inventor. In the early 1970s, however, scholars began paying serious attention to broader historical and social issues: the dynamics, sources, and effects of the narrative itself as well as the cultural and political context in which the film was made. Increasingly, the film has been seen as a popularizer of American history that perpetuated powerful and frequently dangerous American myths.

The initial and determining impulse behind *The Birth of a Nation* was the dramatization of a familiar American legend generally known as the romance of the Old South, America's historic Arcadia, defined by plantations and inhabited by wise old men, beautiful Southern belles, and handsome young soldiers. Griffith's immediate source was the notorious Reconstruction melodrama, *The Clansman*, a play in turn based on two turn-of-the-century novels, *The Clansman* and *The Leopard's Spots*. These works may be regarded as prime specimens of the depths to which the Southern romance had sunk by the turn of the century. The author was Thomas Dixon, Jr. of North Carolina, a professional Southerner, sometime preacher, novelist, and fervent Negrophobe. Dixon's story was familiar to Griffith as both a novel and a play. The Kinemacolor Company had earlier tried to turn *The Clansman* into a movie, starring Griffith's wife; and, as a play in 1906, it had attracted Griffith's attention because of the widely-publicized black agitation.

The first part of *The Birth of a Nation*, however, is largely Griffith's own work. Here, where Griffith portrayed life in the ante-bellum south, the influence of Dixon's play proved minimal, and what emerges is an extraordinary mixture of traditional Southern motifs cast in a fresh light. The feature of the Southern legend that Griffith found most appealing was the emphasis on the closely-knit home, an absolute faith in the values of family life, a view which he turns into the story's mainspring. When Griffith wants to show what the Old South is like, he need go no further than the porch of his hero's family estate. What he finds there sums up life's worthwhile pleasures: a family completely at ease, using its spare time to talk, play, and be together. Everyone knows and accepts his or her place, not only the slaves, but the children and parents too.

The woman-centered home was a perpetual preoccupation with Griffith, as anyone knows who has seen Griffith's Biograph short films. Over and again, the filmgoer comes across Biograph titles like *For a Wife's Honor*, *His Wife's Mother*, *The Girls and Daddy*, *The Honor of His Family*, *Her Father's Pride*, *The Two Brothers*, *The Three Sisters*, and *Her Mother's Oath*. Even before *The Birth of a Nation* was released, Griffith was filming a story about a mother and her baby called *The Mother and the Law*—later, part of *Intolerance*, where the central image would be a mother rocking her cradle.

The Civil War and its aftermath gave Griffith an opportunity to expand his vision of the family and its antagonists to heroic proportions. The South as a whole becomes a kind of family, an informal folk society made up of front porches, picket fences, and family balls held in the living room. Even the North. nominally the enemy, is defined in similar terms. Wherever he could—in the North-South love affairs between the protagonists, on the Civil War battlefields where brothers fight brothers, or at the climactic rescue scene where those from North and South fight side by side—Griffith illustrates that Northerners and Southerners are essentially the same, fundamentally part of the same family.

It is in this context that the inflammatory second half of the film, dominated by Dixon's play, may be best understood. Dixon had discovered an ingenious and extremely effective means to dramatize the fears of northern audiences concerned about their new black neighbors migrating from the South. Dixon simply expanded the old Southern legends, so familiar to American audiences, and used them to illustrate not only the black man's supposed social and political incompetence, but his continuing threat to the American family. Dixon's Reconstruction becomes a testing ground to see what black people were really like when left to govern themselves and others. The familiar picture of the Civil War's aftermath now took on new implications. The black's allegedly bestial behavior during Reconstruction could now be interpreted as a warning for the country as a whole and the North in particular—an argument for strict segregation laws and renewed talk about Negro colonization.

By 1915, when Griffith released *The Birth of a Nation*, the legend itself had already become old-fashioned. In the same years that *The Birth of a Nation* enjoyed its greatest popularity, 1915-1926, Southern writers like Ellen Glasgow and James Branch Cabell were taking hard and introspective looks at the South. The growing popularity of the new writers and their broad swipes at the old legends helped prepare for the later and even deadlier blows dealt in the 1930s.

—Russell Merritt

BIRUMA NO TATEGOTO. Harp of Burma. Production: Nikkatsu (Japan); black and white, 35mm; running time: 116 mins. Released 1956.

Screenplay by Natto Wada; from an original story by Michio Takeyama; directed by Kon Ichikawa; photography by Minoru Yokoyama; edited by Masonori Truju; production design by Takashi Matsuyama; music by Akira Ifukube. San Giorgio Prize, Venice Film Festival, 1956.

Cast: Shoji Yasui (*Private Mizushima*); Rentaro Mikuni (*Captain Inouye*); Taniye Kita Bayashi (*Old woman); Tatsuya Mihashi (*Defensive commander*); Yunosuke Ito (*Village head*).

Publications:

Books—*The Japanese Film: Art and Industry* by Joseph Anderson and Donald Richie, Rutland 1959; *Japan* by Arne Svensson, New York 1971; *Voices from the Japanese Cinema* by Joan Mellen, New York 1975; *Kon Ichikawa* by Angelo Soumi, La Nuova, Italy 1975; *Japanese Film Directors* by Audie Bock, New York 1978; articles—by Peter Baker in *Films and Filming* (London), April 1960; "The Several Sides of Kon Ichikawa" by Donald Richie in *Sight and Sound* (London), spring 1966; "The Skull Beneath the Skin" by Tom Milne in *Sight and Sound* (London), autumn 1966; "The Uniqueness of Kon Ichikawa" by Kon Ichikawa and others in *Cinema* (Beverly Hills), fall 1970; "Ichikawa and the Wanderers" by W. Johnson in *Film Comment* (New York), September/October 1975.

*   *   *

Biruma no Tategoto, directed by Kon Ichikawa, won the San Giorgio Prize at the 1956 Venice Film Festival. Although Ichikawa had been directing since 1945, this was the first film to bring him international recognition.

The film, starring Shoji Yasui as Private Mizushima and

Rentaro Mikuni as Captain Inouye, concerns the last days of World War II on Burma. When Mizushima's unit is taken as prisoners-of war, he is reported missing. Actually he has been commissioned to convince a group of Japanese soldiers to surrender rather than incur further bloodshed. Unsuccessful in his mission, the garrison is attacked and Mizushima becomes the sole survivor. He is nursed back to health by a Buddhist priest whose robes he steals in an effort to return to his unit. Crossing the island he comes upon several abandoned corpses and is compelled to bury them. For the Japanese, to die on foreign soil and to remain unburied, is the most ignoble of deaths. By the time he meets his former companions, he is committed to his new mission of burying the dead and refuses to be repatriated.

In concept the film reflects the post-World War II pacificism prevalent in Japan as well as a spirit of international humanism. Both Japanese and British are portrayed as caring individuals caught up in an inhuman war. War and death are the enemies. Mizushima's decision to remain in Burma is an act of contrition, which emerges in part from a sense of Japanese post-war shame and guilt. Throughout his wanderings, Mizushima carries a Burmese harp. This serves as a source of inspiration, a signal and a means of communication which unites both British and Japanese. The tune, "There's No Place like Home," an American melody, is sung alternatively by both groups, signifying the peaceful commitment to home and family which Mizushima will be sacrificing by remaining in Burma. Ultimately the harp becomes Mizushima's voice.

In addition to the interplay of light and shadow, suggestive close-ups and point-of-view shots, *Biruma no Tategoto* is noteworthy for its fragmented narrative structure. The story unfolds through a series of flashbacks and parallel action depicting Mizushima's plight in contrast to the experiences of the unit.

Like Ichikawa's next film, *Nobi*, the film documents the human suffering, brutality and carnage which are inevitable results of war. However, whereas *Nobi* ends on a pessimisstic note with the death of the hero, *Biruma no Tategoto* closed on an inspirational note, signaling the goodness of man and universal brotherhood. Ideologically the film speaks to the value of life and survival in opposition to the pre-World War II official position of allegiance to the Emperor and dishonor in surrender.

The film plays upon the traditional conflict between *giri* and *ninjo* (desire and duty). Here Mizushima longs to rejoin his friends and to return to Japan. But he is equally pulled by a higher duty which calls for the burial of the dead. As in all Japanese narratives, *ninjo* wins out after an emotional struggle. Mizushima's choice is especially difficult because his voluntary isolation deprives him of group support and comradery, a crucial aspect of Japanese society. Ichikawa's emphasis upon the warmth of group solidarity makes Mizushima's loss all the more heartrending. Further, Ichikawa, in an exception to the ironic attitude which pervades the majority of his other works, expresses an emotionalism, especially in the scenes where the men beg Mizushima to return with them and in Mizushima's silent determination to remain.

The film ends as the ship taking the soldiers home pulls away from shore. It is a subjective shot from Mizushima's point of view. On board the men talk of the Ginza and movies. They have already turned to the future. Only Mizushima remains to remember the past. His solitary sadness reflects a traditional view of the acceptance of life's tragedies. Yet equally, *Biruma no Tategoto* marks Japan's postwar conversion from one value system to another. Its implicit critique of feudal values reflects Japan's decision to become a full member of the international democratic community.

—Patricia Erens

BLACKMAIL. Production: British International Pictures, black and white, 35mm; running time: 96 mins. Released 1929.

Produced by John Maxwell; screenplay by Alfred Hitchcock, Charles Bennett, Benn W. Levy, and Garnett Weston; from the play by Charles Bennett; directed by Alfred Hitchcock; photography by Jack Cox; edited by Emile Ruello; production design by Wilfred C. Arnold and Norman Arnold; music by Campbell and Connely, finished and arranged by Hubert Bath and Henry Stafford, performed by the British Symphony Orchestra under the direction of John Reynders. Filmed in studios in London; and on location in the British Museum.

Cast: Anny Ondra (*Alice White*); Sara Allgood (*Mrs. White*); John Longden (*Frank Webber*); Charles Paton (*Mr. White*); Donald Calthrop (*Tracy*); Cyril Ritchard (*The artist*).

Publications:

Reviews—by Kenneth MacPherson in *Close Up* (London), October 1929; review by Ernest Marshall in the *New York Times*, 14 July 1929; books—*An Index to the Creative Work of Alfred Hitchcock* by Peter Noble, supplement to *Sight and Sound*, index series, London 1949; *Hitchcock* by Eric Rohmer and Claude Chabrol, Paris 1957; *Alfred Hitchcock* by Barthélémy Amengual and Raymond Borde, Paris 1957; *The Cinema of Alfred Hitchcock* by Peter Bogdanovich, New York 1962; *Hitchcock's Films* by Robin Wood, London 1965; *The Films of Alfred Hitchcock* by George Perry, London 1965; *Le Cinéma selon Hitchcock* by François Truffaut, Paris 1966; *Focus on Hitchcock* edited by Albert J. LaValley, Englewood Cliffs, New Jersey 1972; *The Strange Case of Alfred Hitchcock: Or, the Plain Man's Hitchcock* by Raymond Durgnat, Cambridge, Mass. 1974; *Hitchcock's British Films* by Maurice Yacowar, Hamden, Conn. 1977; *Hitch* by John Russell Taylor, New York 1978; *L'Analyse du film* by Raymond Bellour, Paris 1979; *Hitchcock—The Murderous Gaze* by William Rothman, Cambridge, Mass. 1982; *The Dark Side of Genius: The Life of Alfred Hitchcock* by Donald Spoto, New York 1983; articles—"My Own Methods" in *Sight and Sound* (London), summer 1937; "Alfred Joseph Hitchcock" by Russell Maloney in the *New Yorker*, 10 September 1938; "Alfred Hitchcock" by Lindsay Anderson in *Sequence* (London), autumn 1949; special issue on Hitchcock in *Cahiers du cinéma* (Paris), October 1953; special issue on Hitchcock in *Cahiers du cinéma* (Paris), August/September 1956; "Hitchcock's World" by Charles Higham in *Film Quarterly* (Berkeley), winter 1962-63; "An Alfred Hitchcock Index" by Jerry Vermilye in *Films in Review* (New York), April 1966; "The Other Alfred Hitchcock" by Kirk Bond in *Film Culture* (New York), summer 1966; "The Strange Case of Alfred Hitchcock" by Raymond Durgnat in *Films and Filming* (London), 10-part series beginning February 1970 and ending November 1970; "4 Inedits d'Alfred Hitchcock" by Claude Beylie in *Ecran* (Paris), November 1976; "Sur 4 Films d'Hitchcock" by G. Dagneau in *Revue du cinéma* (Paris), December 1976; "Les Premiers films parlants d'Alfred Hitchcock" by R. Lefevre in *Cinéma 76* (Paris), November 1976; "4 Films anglais d'Hitchcock" by L. Dahan in *Cinématographe* (Paris), January 1977; "*Blackmail*" by John Henley in *Cinema Texas Notes* (Austin), 29 January 1979; "*Blackmail*" by Anthony Slide in *Magill's Survey of Cinema*, Vol. 1 edited by Frank N. Magill, Englewood Cliffs, New Jersey 1980.

*   *   *

Hitchcock's last silent film, *Blackmail* was also Hitchcock's first sound effort—and one of the first British "talkies," as well. A resounding popular and critical success, *Blackmail* prefigures some of the director's most famous themes and demonstrates the technical style for which he would be noted.

As critic Eric Rohmer points out, the entire film "focuses on the relationships among characters." Victims and victimizers alternate from scene to scene (a technique Hitchcock would later perfect in his 1951 film, *Strangers on a Train*). Sometimes within a single shot, for example, the moral positions of the characters shift, while the placement of the characters illustrates visually the relationship that we also know from context. As many other critics have detailed, this type of shift is "pure Hitchcock": scenes such as those between the blackmailer and the detective parallel scenes from the director's future work, most notable the relationship between a tennis pro and his psychotic "fan" in *Strangers on a Train*.

This visual affirmation of moral ambiguity and transfer of guilt combines with other elements—such as the use of visual, cinematic means to direct point of view, often at the expense of a linear storyline—that would later be termed "typical Hitchcock." In addition, *Blackmail* serves as a prototype for some of Hithcock's Hollywood films, particularly in terms of such thematic concerns as the depiction of a woman's torments, as in *Suspicion*.

Blackmail demonstrates an intriguing use of sound, especially since it was originally conceived and produced as a silent film. One notable example occurs in the use of sound for scene-to-scene continuity: the protagonist's shriek becomes the basis for transition to the next scene in which a charwoman finds a dead body. (This technique, too, was incorporated into another film, *The Thirty-Nine Steps*.) Even in this very early sound venture, Hitchcock's imagination for the possibilities of sound represents a major experimental development in his ability to "make the inexpressible tangible."

Hitchcock said that he used a good many trick shots in the picture. During a sequence in the British Museum, he told Francois Truffaut, "we used the Shuftan process because there wasn't enough light in the museum to shoot there. You set a mirror at an angle for 45 degrees and you reflect a full picture of the British Museum in it." Hitchcock had nine of the pictures made, showing various rooms. But the producers knew nothing of the Shuftan process, and since they might have objected, Hitchcock performed his magic without their knowledge.

Blackmail has an important place in cinematic and Hitchcockian film history. Not only is it one of the first British talking pictures, but it is also a prototype for Hitchcock films to follow in terms of theme, the use of sound, and cinematic style. *Blackmail* initiated the suspense sub-genre many call the "Hitchcock film," while transforming innovative use of the then-new sound medium within an established visual style and unique, thematic purpose.

—Deborah H. Holdstein

BLADE RUNNER. Production: Ladd Company in association with Sir Run Run Shaw, 1982; Technicolor, 35mm, Panavision, Dolby Stereo; running time: about 2 hours. Released June, 1982.

Produced by Michael Deeley; screenplay by Hampton Fancher and David Peoples; from the novel *Do Androids Dream of Electric Sheep* by Philip K. Dick; directed by Ridley Scott; photography by Jordan Cronenweth; edited by Terry Rawlings; sound mixed by Bud Alper, sound edited by Peter Pennell, dialogue edited by Michael Hopkins; production design by Lawrence G. Paull; art direction by David Snyder; music composed, arranged, performed and produced by Vangelis; special effects supervised by Douglas Trumbull, Richard Yuricich, and David Dryer; costumes designed by Charles Knode and Michael Kaplan; visual futurist: Syd Mead. Filmed 1981 in Pinewood and Twickenham Studios, England and on location in Los Angeles.

Cast: Harrison Ford (*Deckard*); Rutger Hauer (*Batty*); Sean Young (*Rachael*); Edward James Olmos (*Gaff*); M. Emmet Walsh (*Bryant*); Daryl Hannah (*Pris*); William Sanderson (*Sebastian*); Brion James (*Leon*); Joe Turkel (*Tyrell*); Joanna Cassidy (*Zhora*); James Hong (*Chew*); Morgan Paull (*Holden*); Kevin Thompson (*Bear*); John Edward Allen (*Kaiser*); Hy Pyke (*Taffey Lewis*); Kimiro Hiroshige (*Cambodian Lady*); Robert Okazaki (*Sushi Master*); Carolyn DeMirjian (*Saleslady*); Charles Knapp (*Bartender No.1*); Leo Gorcey, Jr. (*Bartender No.2*); Thomas Hutchinson (*Bartender No.3*); Kelly Hine (*Show Girl*); Sharon Hesky (*Barfly No.1*); Rose Mascari (*Barfly No.2*); Susan Rhee (*Geisha No.1*); Hiroko Kimuri (*Geisha No.2*); Kai Wong (*Chinese Man No.1*); Kit Wong (*Chinese Man No.2*); Hiro Okazaki (*Policeman No.1*); Steve Pope (*Policeman No.2*); Robert Reiter (*Policeman No.3*).

Publications:

Reviews—"The Pleasures of Texture" by Richard Corliss in *Time* (New York), 12 July 1982; "Baby, the Rain Must Fall" by Pauline Kael in the *New Yorker*, 12 July 1982; "High Tech Horror" by Jack Kroll in *Newsweek* (New York), 28 June 1982; "When High Tech Meets Squalor" by Lawrence O'Tool in *Maclean's* (Toronto), 28 June 1982; "Cold Wars and Cold Futures" by Andrew Sarris in the *Village Voice* (New York), 8 July 1982; articles—"21st Century Nervous Breakdown" by Harlan Kennedy in *Film Comment* (New York), July/August 1982; "The Brave New World of Production Design" by Bart Mills in *American Film* (Washington, D.C.), January/February 1982; "*Blade Runner*" by Michael Dempsey in *Film Quarterly* (Berkeley), winter 1982-83; "Art for Film's Sake" by Raymond Durgnat in *American Film* (Washington, D.C.), May 1983.

*　　　*　　　*

Although set in the year 2019, *Blade Runner*, Ridley (*Alien*) Scott's film adaptation of Philip K. Dick's 1968 science fiction novel seems to take place in the recent past as much as the near future. The setting is Los Angeles, a dark, seedy, rain-drenched, gadget-filled metropolis. The anti-hero is Deckard (Harrison Ford), a down-and-out ex-cop who once hunted down and "retired" all robot/human-like "replicants" who refused to accept the fact that 21st-century Earth is off-limits. One of Deckard's tasks is to spot people's eye movements during a lie detector test as a means of determining whether they are human beings. Programed with artificial memories, some replicants do not know what they really are. When a female replicant, who has just realized what she is, asks Deckard if he's ever taken the humanity test himself, he cannot help being filled with self-doubt. In a genre of cardboard comic-strip heroes, Deckard is, refreshingly, very real.

Technically, *Blade Runner* is an extraordinary accomplishment. Rarely has a film reached such a high level of artistic excellence in so many different areas. The wide-screen photography, art direction, set design, costumes and visual effects are surpassed only by the Vangelis (Papathanassiou) music score, a once-in-a-lifetime achievement of such penetratingly haunting fatalism that, in order to *feel*, as well as see, *Blade Runner*, only Dolby stereo will do.

Although *Blade Runner* was nominated for eight British Academy Awards, the film was treated with cold indifference by the American Academy of Motion Picture Arts and Sciences. No doubt influenced by the film's failure to find much critical or audience support during its brief summer release (when *E.T.* was highly successful), *Blade Runner* was nominated only for Best Art Direction and visual effects Academy Awards—and won nothing.

Ironically, it was last-minute tampering that may have contributed to *Blade Runner's* critical failure once it opened at 1295 theaters. Following several disastrous sneak previews, a narration was added in order to clarify the anti-hero's plight. This attempt at achieving viewer-identification backfired because Ford's carefree voice-over clashes significantly with his bleak, dogged performance. An alternate, upbeat ending was also added, contradicting everything else in the film.

Despite its lack of camp elements of quotable dialogue, *Blade Runner* could very well become a cult classic. It has, for example, played for several consecutive weeks as a Thursday midnight movie at the St. Mark's Cinema in New York City. Perhaps distributor Warner Brothers will eventually be persuaded to reissue a 70mm print of what is easily the finest *adult* fantasy film since Stanley Kubrick's *2001: A Space Odyssey*.

—Marco Starr Boyajian

DER BLAUE ENGEL. The Blue Angel. Production: Universum-Film-Aktiengesellschaft Studios (UFA), Berlin; black and white, 35mm; running time: 90 mins.; length: 2920 meters. Released 31 March 1930, Germany; American version released 3 January 1931 by Paramount.

Produced by Erich Pommer; scenario by Josef von Sternberg, Robert Liebmann, and Karl Vollmoeller; dialogue by Carl Zuckmayer; from the novel *Professor Unrath* by Heinrich Mann; directed by Josef von Sternberg; photography by Günther Rittau and Hans Schneeberger; edited by Sam Winston; sound effects by Fritz Thiery; production design by Otto Hunte and Emil Hasler; music by Friedrich Holländer and lyrics by Robert Liebmann, music played by The Weintraub Syncopators.

Filmed (concurrently in English and German) in late winter of 1929, UFA studios, Berlin.

Cast: Emil Jannings (*Immanuel Rath*); Marlene Dietrich (*Lola Frolich*); Rosa Valetti (*Guste*); Hans Albers (*Mazeppa*); Kurt Gérron (*Kiepert*); Karl Huzar Puffy (*Proprietor*); Reinhold Bernt (*Clown*); Rolf Mueller (*Angst*); Roland Verno (*Lohmann*); Karl Bolhaus (*Ertzum*); Hans Roth (*Caretaker*); Gerhard Bienart (*Policeman*); Robert-Klein Loerk (*Goldstaub*); Wilheim Diegelmann (*Captain*); Ilsu Fuerstenbeg (*Rath's Maid*); Edward V. Winterstein (*Headmaster*).

Publications:

Scripts—"*L'Ange bleu*" in *L'Avant-Scène du cinéma* (Paris),

March 1966; *The Blue Angel* (continuity script), New York 1968; reviews—by Mordaunt Hall in *The New York Times*, 6 December 1930; "*L'Ange bleu*" in *Revue du cinéma* (Paris), October 1930; books—*Marlène Dietrich, femme énigme* by Jean Talky, Paris 1932; *From Caligari to Hitler* by Siegfried Kracauer, New York 1947; *An Index to the Films of Josef von Sternberg* by Curtis Harrington, London 1949; *Marlene Dietrich—Image and Legend* by Richard Griffith, New York 1959; "Sternberg et Marlène" in *Le Surrealism au cinéma* by Ado Kyrou , Paris 1963; *Fun in a Chinese Laundry* by Josef von Sternberg, New York 1965; *The Films of Josef von Sternberg* by Andrew Sarris, New York 1966; *Josef von Sternberg* by Herman G. Weinberg, Paris 1966; *Josef von Sternberg: A Critical Study* by Herman G. Weinberg, New York 1967; *The Great Films: Fifty Golden Years of Motion Pictures* by Bosley Crowther, New York 1967; *The Parade's Gone By* by Kevin Brownlow, New York 1968; *The Haunted Screen* by Lotte Eisner, Berkeley, California 1969; *The Cinema of Josef von Sternberg* by John Baxter, New York 1971; *Anthologie du cinéma, Vol. 6*, Paris 1971; articles—"10 Days à Berlin" by Jean Lenauer in *Revue du cinéma* (Paris), June 1930; article by Heinrich Mann in *La Revue du cinéma* (Paris), December 1930; "Les Grands Rôles de Marlène Dietrich" in *Cinémonde* (Paris), 4 February 1932; "Arrogant Gesture" by Curtis Harrington in *Theatre Arts* (New York), November 1950; article by Geoffrey Wagner in *Quarterly of Film, Radio, and Television* (Berkeley), fall 1951; "Josef von Sternberg" by Curtis Harrington in *Cahiers du cinéma* (Paris), October/November 1951; "Revaluation: *The Blue Angel*" by Geoffrey Wagner in *Sight and Sound* (London), August/September 1951; "Marlene Dietrich's Beginning" by Manfred George in *Films in Review* (New York), February 1952; "L'Amour dans le cinéma" by Jacques Audibert in *Cahiers du cinéma* (Paris), December 1954; "Der Schopfer des *Blauen Engels*" in *Der Kurier* (Berlin), 28 June 1960; "*The Blue Angel*" by Richard Whitehall in *Films and Filming* (London), October 1962; "A Taste for Celluloid" in *Films and Filming* (London), July 1963; "6 Films of Josef von Sternberg" by O.O. Green in *Movie* (London), no.13, 1965; "*Der Blaue Engel*" in *Filmkritik* (Frankfurt, Germany), April 1965; "L'Oeuvre de Josef von Sternberg" in *L'Avant-Scène du cinéma* (Paris), March 1966; article on von Sternberg and Dietrich in *Positif* (Paris), May 1966; "Josef von Sternberg" by Herman G. Weinberg in *Film Heritage* (Dayton, Ohio), winter 1965-66; "*L'Ange bleu*" by André Cornaud in *Image et son* (Paris), no.214, 1968; "Thoughts about the Objectification of Women" by Barbara Martineau in *Take One* (Montreal), November/December 1970; "Emil Jannings—A Personal View" by Harold Truscott in *Silent Picture* (London), autumn 1970; "Translations and Adaptations of Heinrich Mann's Novel in 2 Media" by Ulrich Weisstein in *Film Journal* (Evanston, Illinois), fall/winter 1972; "Josef von Sternberg: The Scientist and the Vamp" by Joyce Rheuban in *Sight and Sound* (London), autumn 1972-73; "On the Naked Thighs of Miss Dietrich" by P. Baxter in *Wide Angle* (Athens, Ohio), no.2, 1978; "Literary Origins: Sternberg's Film *The Blue Angel*" by R.A. Firda in *Literature/Film Quarterly* (Salisbury, Maryland), no.2, 1979; "L'Ombre du son" by L. Audibert in *Cinématographe* (Paris), June 1979; "Filmprotokoll: *Der blaue Engel*" in *Film und Fernsehen* (Berlin), December 1980; "L'Armature sonore de *L'Ange bleu* de Sternberg" by C. Laurens in *Image et son* (Paris), December 1981; "Elogio de la sombra" by J.L. Téllez in *Contracampo* (Madrid), June/July 1981.

*　　　*　　　*

When Josef von Sternberg arrived in Berlin in the autumn of 1929, his career was tottering. The two years since his 1927 success with *Underworld* had been spent making box-office failures in imitation of his pioneering gangster film now outdated by the coming of sound. A brief high-spot, the production of *The Last Command* with Emil Jannings, had led to this providential invitation for Erich Pommer of UFA to visit Germany and direct Jannings in his first sound picture.

A drama about Rasputin was suggested, partly to placate UFA's backer Alfred Hugenberg's right-wing sensibilities, but Sternberg finally chose a novel by Heinrich Mann written in 1905 as an attack on the period's reactionary politics. An upright professor is seduced by a night-club singer, becomes a pawn of her political friends, but finally fights off their influence and re-establishes himself in the community. *Professor Unrath* was essentially a protest against the false morality and corrupt values of the German middle class, but in it Sternberg saw the possibility of a film far closer to his personal obsessions, his sensuality, his love of decoration and photographic style.

Mann wrote a script, which Sternberg rejected. The popular comic playwright Carl Zuckmayer wrote another, whose dialogue Sternberg liked. UFA's resident dramaturg, Robert Liebmann, incorporated the dialogue into a story which cut the novel in half, showing only the professor's surrender to the beautiful cabaret singer and his destruction at her hands. Jannings, famous for his love of lavish emotionalism, raised no objection to the many scenes of hysteria and public humiliation—material for which he had become famous in films like *The Last Laugh*.

Sternberg proved difficult in his choice of a star to play Lola. Mann's friend Trude Hesterberg was considered. So was stage actress Greta Massine, singer Lucie Mannheim, even Brigitte Helm. Finally, with time running out, Pommer signed Kathe Haack. Then, though Karl Vollmoller, Sternberg met Marlene Dietrich, a minor actress in films and on stage but better known as the companion of the star Willy Forst. The meeting with the 25-year old married woman was the beginning of a life-long sexual obsession for Sternberg, as well as the end of his marriage and the foundation of his true career.

Der blaue Engel became, like most of Sternberg's films, an autobiographical excursion. In the material on Rath's autocratic teaching methods, Sternberg paid back his own early torment at the hands of his father, who had forced him to learn Hebrew with frequent physical punishment to drive home the lessons. By choosing a turn of the century setting, Sternberg placed the story in his own childhood, and decorated it with images of adolescent eroticism. Taking Otto Hunte's designs for the set of *The Blue Angel* cabaret, he plastered them with scores of posters, hung the cafe with nets, dangling cardboard angels, stuffed birds—a familiar Sternberg archetype—and, everywhere, low-hung lamps that give the whole film an air of scented, smoky claustrophobia.

Sternberg poured all his energy and imagination into the role of Lola, creating a star vehicle for the young Dietrich. Borrowing from the drawings of the erotic artist Felicien Rops, he created a figure out of a teenager's sexual fantasy, a vision in black stockings, heavy make-up and an arrogantly tilted top hat. Her poses and movements on stage were mapped out with choreographic care, her songs crafted for her uninspiring voice by Frederich Hollander, who found tunes needing only two or three notes. Her feline stroll on stage, her pointed, mocking stares, her casual use of her own sexual allure to beguile the giggling, simpering Jannings became elements in a screen persona Dietrich was to exploit for the rest of her career.

By contrast, Jannings is feeble and monochromatically comic. The shadings he might have hoped to receive from Sternberg's direction did not materialize. Instead, he found himself little more than a character player to this unknown young woman. Throughout the shooting, he threw tantrums, threatening to walk off the film and doing everything he could to break down

the rapport between director and star. After the film, he was to demand successfully of UFA that he have total control over the material in all his subsequent films, a decision which destroyed him as a screen star.

Shot concurrently in English and German, *Der blaue Engel* confronted Sternberg with a technical challenge of awesome complexity. nor could he fall back on conventional methods of inducing tension. Never a skilful editor or direction of action, he was committed to a style where lighting and atmosphere conveyed the story, and where each performer's "dramatic encounter with light" spelled out their thought. To achieve this, he added to the script a number of minor but important characters, notably the clown who morosely observes life in the cafe, and who is revealed later (when Rath is forced into the same costume) to be another of Lola's discarded lovers. When the film was remade in 1959 with Mai Britt and Kurt Jergens, Sternberg successfully sued 20th Century-Fox for plagiarism of his interpolated scenes, not found in the original screenplay.

Even before *Der blaue Engel* was finished, its success was obvious. Sternberg had shown tests of Dietrich to Paramount head B.P. Schulberg on a Berlin visit, and the studio immediately signed her to a two-picture contract. The premiere on April, 1930, was a sensation; that night, she and Sternberg sailed for America, to be met on the dock at New York by the former's wife, and a process server with writs—against Dietrich for libel and alienation of affections. Neither director nor star were unduly concerned. Dietrich had found a vehicle to achieve international stardom, Sternberg a subject on which he could focus his contradictory but prodigious talent. *Der blaue Engel* became the foundation of perhaps the most remarkable collaboration between actress and filmmaker that the cinema had ever seen.

—John Baxter

BLOW-UP. Production: Metro Goldwyn Mayer Pictures Corp.; Metrocolor, 35mm; running time: 111 mins.; length: 9974 feet. Released December 1966, New York.

Produced by Carlo Ponti; screenplay by Michelangelo Antonioni and Tonino Guerra; from a short story by Julio Cortazar; directed by Michelangelo Antonioni; photography by Carlo di Palma; edited by Frank Clarke; sound recorded by Robin Gregory; art direction by Assheton Gorton; music by Herbie Hancock; costumes designed by Jocelyn Rickards (dresses); photographic murals by John Cowan.

Filmed during 1966 on location in London, and at MGM Studios, Boreham Wood. Palme d'Or, Cannes Film Festival, 1967.

Cast: David Hemmings (*Thomas, the photographer*); Vanessa Redgrave (*Jane*); Sarah Miles (*Patricia*); John Castle (*Bill*); Peter Bowles (*Ron*); Jane Birkin (*Blonde*); Gillian Hills (*Brunette*); Harry Hutchinson (*Old Man*); Verushka, Jill Kennington, Peggy Moffitt, Rosaleen Murray, Ann Norman, and Melanie Hampshire (*Models*); Julian and Claude Chagrin (*The Tennis Players*).

Publications:

Scripts—*Blow-Up* by Antonioni and T. Guerra, Turin, Italy

1968; *Blow-Up* by Antonioni and T. Guerra, New York 1971; reviews—by Andrew Sarris in the *Village Voice* (New York), 29 December 1966; review by Henry Hart in *Films in Review* (New York), January 1967; review by Jay Cocks in *Take One* (Montreal), April 1967; "*Blow-Up*" by Carey Harrison in *Sight and Sound* (London), spring 1967; books—*Interviews with Film Directors* by Andrew Sarris, New York 1967; *Man and the Movies* edited by W.R. Robinson, Baton Rouge, Louisiana 1967; *The Great Films: Fifty Golden Years of Motion Pictures* by Bosley Crowther, New York 1967; *Michelangelo Antonioni de Gente del Po a Blow-Up* by Aldo Bernardini, Milan, Italy 1967; *Antonioni* by Ian Cameron and Robin Wood, New York 1969; *Focus on 'Blow-Up'* edited by Roy Huss, Englewood Cliffs, New Jersey 1971; *Film as Film: Critical Responses to Film Art* edited by Joy Boyum and Adrienne Scott, Boston 1971; *Encountering Directors* by Charles Thomas Samuels, New York 1972; *Cinéma et société moderne* by Annie Goldman, Paris 1974; articles—"On the Scene: Michelangelo Antonioni" in *Playboy* (Chicago), June 1967; article by Robin Bean in *Films and Filming* (London), May 1967; "Antonioni's Hypnotic Eye on a Frantic World" in *Life* (New York), 27 January 1967; "Antonioni in Transit" by Marsha Kinder in *Sight and Sound* (London), summer 1967; "*Blow-Up*" by Arthur Knight in *Film Heritage* (Dayton, Ohio), spring 1967; "*Blow-Up*" by Hubert Meeker in *Film Heritage* (Dayton, Ohio), spring 1967; "Interview" in *Playboy* (Chicago), November 1967; article by Thomas Hernacki in *Film Heritage* (Dayton, Ohio), spring 1970; article by Max Kozloff in *Film Quarterly* (Berkeley), spring 1967; article by Claire Clouzot in *Cinéma 67* (Paris), May 1967; article by Raymond Lefevre in *Image et son* (Paris), November 1967; article in *Cahiers du cinéma* (Paris), no.186, 1967; "*Blow-Up*: Sorting Things Out" by Charles Samuels in *American Scholar* (Washington, D.C.), winter 1967-68; "*Blow-Up*: Medium, Message, Mythos and Make-Believe" by George Slover in the *Massachusetts Review*, autumn 1968; "Still Legion, Still Decent?" by Richard Corliss in *Commonweal* (New York), 23 May 1969; "*Blow-Up*" by Henry Fernandez in *Film Heritage* (Dayton, Ohio), winter 1968-69; article by Charles Hampton in *Film Comment* (New York), fall 1970; "Antonioni Men" by Gordon Gow in *Films and Filming* (London), June 1970; "Michelangelo Antonioni and the Imagery of Disintegration" by T. Hernacki in *Film Heritage* (Dayton, Ohio), autumn 1970; "Re-Sorting Things Out" by Hubert Cohen in *Cinema Journal* (Evanston, Illinois), spring 1971; "Signs and Meanings in *Blow-up*: From Cortázar to Antonioni" by M. D'Lugo in *Literature/Film Quarterly* (Salisbury, Maryland), winter 1975; "*Blow-Up*: The Game with No Balls" by W.J. Palmer in *Literature/Film Quarterly* (Salisbury, Maryland), no.4, 1979; "Antonioni: Moving On" by Clarke Taylor in the *Los Angeles Times Calender*, 17 October 1982.

*   *   *

The plot level of Michelangelo Antonioni's *Blow-Up* is quickly and easily summarized. A photographer (David Hemmings) chances upon a romantic couple in a secluded park. From concealment, he photographs their playfulness. When the girl (Vanessa Redgrave) demands the negatives, he refuses. Her insistence provokes him to scrutinize the photographs. As he successively enlarges selected areas of the shots (the blow-ups of the title), he discovers evidence that she has been complicit in the murder of the man with whom she shared the interlude. Before he can decide what to do with the documentation, his studio is vandalized and the photographs are missing.

A superficial mystery story, the plot is not what interests

Antonioni in *Blow-Up*. His concern is directed toward the interplay between philosophical concepts of reality-illusion-appearance that manifest themselves through metaphors of photography, painting and pantomime. For Antonioni in *Blow-Up*, as in many of his other films (most notably *L'avventura* and *The Passenger*), the narrative is a vehicle upon which the director can investigate the gossamer thin and delicate nature of perception and interpretation.

London in the mid-sixties was the self-proclaimed capital of pop art; it boasted trends set by the Beatles, Twiggy and Carnaby Street. It was chic, hip, mod; it was filled with clashing colors and swinging youths. A technological surge in photographic equipment complemented this environment. Equipped with more compact cameras that used faster film stock, photographers could snap their subjects with greater rapidity and agility. This liberation offered the photographer the facility to capture life's raw candor in all its spontaneous shapes and form. Thus the radical new concepts of photography that prevailed in the sixties were characterized by the informal and unposed look of fact rather that the illusion of it.

Although the life-styles represented in *Blow-Up* may seem dated by contemporary comparison, that, of course, is not Antonioni's attraction to the situation. In fashionable London and with the candid photography of the mid-sixties, Antonioni found one of his most memorable metaphors. *Blow-Up* is a film about both a society decaying from within and a photograph that records an instant of truth. Both of these forces affect the young and successful photographer who is at the center of the film and his milieu.

The photographer, only rarely identified by a name (Thomas), is uncommitted, hostile, indifferent. He is professionally successful and an expert with his camera. He is in control of himself and situations only when he is armed with his camera; without it, he is at his weakest and most vulnerable. His uncertain sexuality is especially evident in the contemptuous pattern with which he treats women; dominating and humilitating them without any personal involvement. (The single exception to this is the nonsexual relationship with his neighbor's lover.) He is a model of duplicity: a voyeur, a deceiver, a performer. He is, for Antonioni, the Everyman of the unaffected generation: obsessed with surfaces, but blind to the interior value of the people and events he so skillfully and passionately records with his camera.

The character of the photographer is central to Antonioni's interest in *Blow-Up* because it is his transformation that provides the sustaining meaning of the film. The ambiguities of reality-illusion-appearance are ever-present but ignored by the photographer and his generation, and the photographer—beyond his will—is forced to confront this mystery, a mystery more perplexing and shattering than the murder he believes he has documented. The process by which the insulated, self-confident, self-seeking, self-indulging, self-absorbing photographer (so typical of his time) is changed by a set of circumstances he neither comprehends nor controls is examined by Antonioni with the skill and care of a surgeon. The photographer's casual assumptions are discredited and his values are toppled. He is a different person at the end of the film than he was at the beginning.

The photographer's transformation, as he wanders through the ambiguous zones of the reality-illusion-appearance syndrome, is embedded in the act of seeing. In *Blow-Up*, seeing is manifest on three parallel levels: camera sight, revealed in the photography; imaginary sight, revealed in the paintings and the mime troupe; and ocular sight, which moves freely but easily between them. The concept of seeing is emphasized through the corresponding use of silence. *Blow-Up* is arguably a completely visual expression; nothing more than implied significance is verbalized. For such an obviously searching film, it is indeed unusual that there are no metaphysical discussions, no intimate exchanges, no analytical speculations. The dialogue track, divorced from the image track, exposes the extraneous or frivolous words that are used between the interacting participants.

This attention to the visual dimensions of perception underscores the subtext represented by the mime troupe. If words are indeed superficial to the photographer, they are totally superfluous to (and consequently discarded by) the mimes. The mimes are presented to us as a framing device—they open and close the film. At the beginning, they are seen gadding about the bustling streets panhandling; at the end, the same troupe engages in a mock tennis match. At the beginning, the photographer simply finds them a momentary amusement; by the ending, however, he actually shares their experience. It is, in fact, the mime troupe that serves as the spiritual barometer by which we measure the photographer's transformation. The act of miming is crucial for Antonioni and *Blow-Up* because it is the mime who brings our attention to objects by their absence. For the mime, the imaginary tennis ball is every bit as "real" as the evidential photograph is "illusory".

It is, of course, significant that the tennis match takes place at the end. It is less a conclusion than a speculation. The photographer, an outer-directed man in the beginning, would never have retrieved the tennis ball and thrown it back at the outset of the film. He is only able to perform this act of assistance to the players because of what has happened to him in the interim. However, Antonioni does not have him abandon his camera as he fetches the ball; rather, he carries it with him. What the photographer has learned is that the camera and the tennis ball can (and do) exist in the same plane of perception—reality, illusion and appearance do not fall into neat and convenient categories.

The rejection of categories is given the final placement in *Blow-Up*. The blow-ups of the murder incident are visually related by Antonioni to the absract designs of his neighbor's paintings—the grain of the photographic enlargements bear an uncanny reseamblance to the color dots on the painter's canvas. Antonioni underscores this motif when, in the film's final shot, the photographer is left as isolated and indistinct as the microcosmic emulsion grains he has enlarged. Antonioni masterfully frames him in the composition of this shot to resemble a visual element in one of his own blow-ups.

As a consequence of his spiritual awakening, the photographer is a different person. His slumbering world of possessions and exploitations have been dislodged. By the film's final shot, he is awake to the dualities and complexities of life, and, ironically, that wakefulness isolates him. He can no longer return to the blind-sighted comfort of his complacent and gluttonous life; he can no longer use his camera or look at photographs in quite the same way as before.

—Stephen E. Bowles

BODY HEAT. Production: The Ladd Company in association with Warner Bros., 1981; Technicolor, 35mm; running time: 113 mins. Released August 1981.

Produced by Fred T. Gallo; screenplay and direction by Lawrence Kasdan; photography by Richard H. Kline; edited by Carol Littlejohn; sound mixed by Maury Harris; production design by Bill Kenney; music composed and directed by John Barry; special effects supervised by Howard Jensen; costumes designed by Renie Conley. Filmed on location in Florida.

Cast: William Hurt (*Ned Racine*); Kathleen Turner (*Matty Walker*); Richard Crenna (*Edmund Walker*); Ted Danson (*Peter Lowenstein*); J.A. Preston (*Oscar Grace*); Mickey Roarke (*Teddy Lewis*); Kim Zimmer (*Mary Ann*); Jane Hallaren (*Stella*); Lanna Saunders (*Roz Kraft*); Carola McGuinness (*Heather Kraft*); Michael Ryan (*Miles Hardin*); Deborah Lucchessi (*Beverly*); Lynn Hallowell (*Angela*); Thom J. Sharp (*Michael Glenn*).

Publications:

Reviews—"*Body Heat*" in *Variety* (New York), 19 August 1981; review by Pauline Kael in the *New Yorker*, 9 November 1981; review by Richard Corliss in *Time* (New York), 24 August 1981; review by Andrew Sarris in *The Village Voice* (New York), 2 September 1981; review by Janet Maslin in *The New York Times*, 28 August 1981; articles—"Film View: The Pleasures of *Body Heat*" by Vincent Canby in *The New York Times*, 15 and 25 October 1981; "Topic of Kasdan" by D. Chute in *Film Comment* (New York), September/October 1981; "*Body Heat*" by J. Dadroff in *Film Journal* (New York), 24 August 1981; "Films in Focus: New Twists to the Film Noir" by Andrew Sarris in *The Village Voice* (New York), 2-8 September 1981; "*Body Heat*" by D. Toumarkine in *Monthly Film Bulletin* (London), October 1981; "Dialogue on Film: Lawrence Kasdan" in *American Film* (Washington, D.C.), April 1982; "La Fieure au corps" by A. Philippon in *Cahiers du cinéma* (Paris), February 1982; "*Body Heat*" by Pat H. Broeske in *Magill's Cinema Annual* edited by Frank N. Magill, Englewood Cliffs, New Jersey 1982.

*   *   *

Fire trucks wail as a distant building blazes in the night. An air conditioning unit rattles feverishly, fans circle, french fries are lowered into sizzling fat, lights blare inside a popcorn machine. People sit dirpping with sweat, their faces illumined by a red EXIT sign. During its first ten minutes, *Body Heat* throws up image after image of intolerable heat. Some form of explosion, into eroticism or violence, is obviously imminent, and in due course we get both.

The steaming, sultry atmosphere, though, is not intended soley as an evocation of sub-tropical Florida. Director Kasdan is also aiming, quite explicitly, at a re-creation of the claustrophobic conventions of 1940s *film noir*—an intention made evident by the first appearance of the *femme fatale*, Matty Walker, shimmering into view in white from the darkness of a boardwalk jazz concert, as a Dorsey-style band plays "That Old Feeling". The plot is borrowed openly from a classic of the genre, Wilder's *Double Indemnity*; but Kasdan updates his narrative with enough style, and drive, to ensure that audience interest is held to the end. Not that we are left in much doubt (even without a knowledge of Wilder's film) what that end will be. "You're not too smart," Matty tells Ned Racine, third-rate lawyer and local stud, "I like that in a man." Matty, quite clearly, is more than smart enough for both of them, and Ned never stands a chance against her. "Some day," Ned's friend, the Assistant District Attorney, remarks worriedly, "your dick is going to lead you into a very big hassle"—but after murder, arson and faked wills, the warning has come a little late.

Kasdan's script is tight and stylised, packed with conscious ambiguities. As Ned, William Hurt gives a flawless portrayal of a man a lot less bright than he thinks he is, well matched by Kathleen Turner's smouldering, Bacall-like Matty. Their erotic scenes together play with a compulsive intensity which makes Ned's doomed obsession wholly credible. The sensual mood is heightened by John Barry's bluesy, saxophone-rich score, as Kasdan sends his camera roaming and prowling around the lovers, occasionally swooping ceilingwards for a detached, god's-eye stare at them as they plot the murder of Matty's husband. The night sequences especially are distinguished by virtuoso lighting effects, most notably in the final showdown, with Matty, Ned and the approaching police detective each picked out at different depths against a soft, black-velvet ground.

"I wanted this film to have the intricate structure of a dream," Kasdan explained, "the density of a good novel, and the texture of recognizable people in extraordinary circumstances." In these aims the film largely succeeds, marred only by a few nudging images—a spider's web, a prison door clanging premonitorily shut—and an over-explicit ending. It could be maintained that *Body Heat*'s very considerable pleasures are mainly on the surface, that it offers no more than an accomplished replaying of the film noir tradition—rather than a creative reworking, as in Roman Polanski's *Chinatown*, or the radical and disturbing re-evaluation of the genre achieved by Arthur Penn's *Night Moves*. But for its sheer richness of character, sustained narrative power, and sense of atmosphere, *Body Heat* must stand as one of the most assured and promising directorial debuts of recent years.

—Philip Kemp

BONNIE AND CLYDE. Production: Tatira-Hiller, 1967; Technicolor, 35mm; running time: 111 mins. Released August 1967.

Produced by Warren Beatty; screenplay by David Newman and Robert Benton; directed by Arthur Penn; photography by Burnett Guffey; edited by Dede Allen; sound by Francis E. Stahl; art direction by Dean Tavoularis, set decoration by Raymond Paul; music by Charles Strouse, theme "Foggy Mountain Breakdown" by Lester Flatt and Earl Scruggs; special effects by Danny Lee; costumes designed by Theodora Van Runkle; consultant: Robert Towne.

Filmed during 1967 on location in Texas. Academy Awards for Best Supporting Actress (Parsons) and Best Cinematography, 1967; New York Film Critics Award, Best Screenwriting, 1967.

Cast: Warren Beatty (*Clyde Barrow*); Faye Dunaway (*Bonnie Parker*); Gene Hackman (*Buck Barrow*); Estelle Parsons (*Blanche*); Michael J. Pollard (*C.W. Moss*); Dub Taylor (*Ivan Moss*); Denver Pyle (*Frank Hamer*); Evans Evans (*Velma Davis*); Gene Wilder (*Eugene Grizzard*).

Publications:

Reviews—by Bosley Crowther in *The New York Times*, 14 August 1967; "View through Splintered Glass" by Derek Prouse in the *London Sunday Times*, 10 September 1967; "*Bonnie and Clyde*" by Pauline Kael in the *New Yorker*, 21 October 1967; "Crime Wave" by Hollis Alpert in *Saturday Review* (New York), 5 August 1967; "Montreal 1967, le règne de l'image" by Michel Ciment in *Positif* (Paris), November 1967; "*Bonnie et Clyde*" by Jacques Chevallier in *Image et Son* (Paris), April 1968; "*Bonnie and Clyde*" by Stephen Farber in *Sight and Sound* (London), autumn 1968; books—*The Bonnie and Clyde Scrapbook* by B. Gelman and R. Lackman, New York 1967; *Arthur Penn* by Robin Wood, New York 1969; *The Director's Event* by Martin Rubin and Eric Sherman, New York 1970; *24 Times a Second* by William S. Pechter, New York 1971; *The Bonnie and Clyde Book* by Sandra Wake and Nicola Hayden, New York 1972; *Focus on 'Bonnie and Clyde'* edited by John G. Cawelti, Englewood Cliffs, New Jersey 1973; *Dreams and Dead Ends: The American Gangster/Crime Film* by Jack Shadoin, (London 1977); *10 Film Classics* by Edward Murray (New York 1978); *A Cinema of Loneliness: Penn, Kubrick, Coppola, Scorsese, Altman* by Robert Phillip Kolker, New York 1980; *Arthur Penn: A Guide to References and Resources* by Joel S. Zuker, Boston 1980; articles—"Study in Infantilism" by Marion Armstrong in *Christian Century* (Chicago), 18 October 1967; "*Bonnie and Clyde*: Society vs. the Clan" by Carolyn Geduld in *Film Heritage* (Dayton, Ohio), winter 1967-68; "A Trip with Bonnie and Clyde" by Robert Towne in *Cinema 3*, summer 1967; "*Bonnie and Clyde*" by Moira Walsh in *America* (New York), 2 September 1967; "*Mickey One* and *Bonnie and Clyde*" by Albert Johnson in *Film Quarterly* (Berkeley), winter 1967-68; "Director Arthur Penn Weighs Balance of *Bonnie and Clyde*" in *Variety* (New York), 30 August 1967; "Bonnie and Clyde" by Paul Glushanok in *Cineaste* (New York), fall 1967; "An Interview with Warren Beatty" by Curtis Lee Hanson in *Cinema* (Beverly Hills), summer 1967; "Raw Cinematic Realism in the Photography of *Bonnie and Clyde*" by Herb Lightman in *American Cinematographer* (Hollywood), April 1967; "*Bonnie and Clyde*: Beyond Violence to Tragedy" by Anthony Macklin in *Film Heritage* (Dayton, Ohio), winter 1967-68; "Sur *Bonnie and Clyde*" by Arthur Penn in *Positif* (Paris), November 1967; "A Middle Western" by Eric Rhode in *The Listener* (London), 14 September 1967; "Bonnie and Clyde" by Andrew Sarris in *The Village Voice* (New York), 24 August 1967, and additional comments in 31 August 1967 issue. "*Bonnie and Clyde*: An Interview with Arthur Penn" by Jean-Louis Comolli and André S. Labarthe in *Evergreen Review* (New York), June 1968; "Violent Movies" by Frank Conroy in *The New York Review of Books*, 11 July 1968; "Aesthetic and Moral Value in *Bonnie and Clyde*" by William J. Free in *Quarterly Journal of Speech* (Fall's Church, Virginia), October 1968; "Our Film and Theirs: *Grapes of Wrath* and *Bonnie and Clyde*" by John Howard Lawson in *American Dialog*, winter 1968-69; "The American Scene: *Bonnie and Clyde*" by Charles T. Samuels in *Hudson Review* (Nutley, New Jersey), spring 1968; "The Good-bad and the Bad-good in Movies: *Bonnie and Clyde* and *In Cold Blood*" by Robert Steele in *The Catholic World* (Paramus, New Jersey), May 1968; "Billy-Bonnie et Clyde-Hyde" by Robert Benayoun in *Positif* (Paris), March 1968; "Reflections on the Tradition of the Western" by Douglas Brode in *Cinéaste* (New York), fall 1968; "Gangster Story" by Ermanno Comuzio in *Cineforum* (Bergamo, Italy), September 1968; "Bonnie and Clyde" by Michel Delahaye in *Cahiers du cinéma* (Paris), March 1968; "Bonnie and Clyde" by Stanley Kauffmann in *New American Review*, (Cranford, New Jersey) January 1968; "Bonnie and Clyde" by Ernesto G. Laura in *Bianco e nero* (Rome), March-/April, 1968; "Non faccio l'avvocato della violenza" by Arthur Penn in *Cineforum* (Bergamo), September 1968; "Foggy Bottom" by Jerry Richard in *Antioch Review* (Yellow Springs, Ohio), fall 1968; "*Bonnie and Clyde*" by Jim Cook in *Screen* (London), July/August 1969; "Bonnie and Clyde" in *Film as Film: Critical Responses to Film Art* by Joy Gould Boyum and Adrienne Scott, Boston 1971; "Bonnie and Clyde" in *Movies into Film: Film Criticism 1967-70* by John Simon, New York

1971; "Bonnie and Clyde Revisited" by John Cawelti in *Focus!* (Chicago), spring 1972 and Part II, autumn 1972; "Bonnie and Clyde" in *Close-up: A Critical Perspective on Film* by Marsha Kinder and Beverle Houston, New York 1972; "Closet Outlaws" by James Childs in *Film Comment* (New York), March/April 1973; "Bonnie and Clyde" by J.D. Rintoul in *Films Illustrated* (London), August 1975; "Bonnie and Clyde" in *Talking Pictures: Screenwriters in the American Cinema* by Richard Corliss, New York 1975; "*Bonnie and Clyde* Set Trend: Penn Shuns 'Violence Pioneer' Role" by David Payette in *Montreal Star*, 24 March 1977; "Dick, Jane, Rocky and T.S. Eliot" by M. Yacowar in *Journal of Popular Film and Television* (Bowling Green, Ohio), winter 1977; "The Shock of Freedom in Films" in *Time* (New York), 8 December 1978; "The Hollywood Screenwriter, Take 2" by Richard Corliss in *Film Comment* (New York), July/August 1978; "Veszelyes egyensuly: Penn: *Bonnie and Clyde*" by I. Eorsi in *Filmkultura* (Budapest), March/April 1979.

*   *   *

To speak of Arthur Penn is to address the question of what might be termed, somewhat paradoxically, the "post-classical" American cinema. On the one hand Penn belongs with that group of post-World War II directors which came to cinema from the stage and from the early days of television—people like Nicholas Ray, Sam Peckinpah, Franklin Schaffner, Martin Ritt, and Joseph Losey. In that respect Penn is indeed an inheritor of the traditions and forms of the classical Hollywood cinema, the western (*The Left Handed Gun*), the biography picture (*The Miracle Worker*), the gangster/detective film (*Night Moves*), etc. Perhaps Penn's loyalty to Hollywood tradition is most clearly seen in his frequent reliance upon the star system to infuse his films with certain qualities of intensity and resonance—Dustin Hoffman's performance in *Little Big Man* and Marlon Brando's and Jack Nicholson's in *The Missouri Breaks* stand out in this regard. Yet on the other hand Penn is also frequently associated with the more overtly intellectual traditions of the European art film, especially those of the French New Wave films of the early sixties. Penn's *Mickey One*, for example, is frequently discussed in such "art film" terms. But arguably it was with *Bonnie and Clyde* that Penn's special status as a post-classical director was most forcefully asserted and confirmed.

In her classic essay on the film, Pauline Kael situates *Bonnie and Clyde*'s place in American film history by reference primarily to Fritz Lang's *You Only Live Once*, itself a version of the Bonnie and Clyde story, and to Frank Capra's *It Happened One Night*. Kael's essay was written in reply to those who saw *Bonnie and Clyde* as a glorification of violence as personified in the actions of Warren Beatty's Clyde Barrow and Faye Dunaway's Bonnie Parker, and Kael quite rightly points out that "Bonnie and Clyde are presented not as mean and sadistic, [but] as having killed only when cornered." Indeed, most of the film's explicitly graphic violence is directed *not* at society but rather at the members of the Barrow gang. This is especially clear in the film's last two ambush scenes, the first of which concludes with Buck Barrow's death throes and Blanche Barrow's agonized screams, the last of which sees Bonnie and Clyde riddled with machine gun fire. Kael's larger point, however, involves the particularly American theme of innocence at hazard and on the run, which makes Lang's melodrama and Capra's screwball comedy spiritual ancestors of Penn's alternately comic and tragic parable of the outlaw couple. The central characters in all three films long mightily, often awkwardly, to realize aspirations of spiritual and

social stature. But in Lang and Penn society provides no real outlet or model for the realization of such dreams. And even in Capra it takes an act of theft (like Bonnie and Clyde, Gable and Colbert literally steal a car at one point; Ellie's father has a "getaway" car standing by during the wedding ceremonoy) to ensure the dream's survival.

In terms of its *story*, then, *Bonnie and Clyde* is quite properly considered a classical Hollywood film. But this story of Bonnie and Clyde is mediated by or through a very self-conscious form of visual *discourse*; hence the critical commonplace of Penn's indebtedness to the generically-derived films of Truffaut and Godard. Partly this self-consciousness is seen *within* the film's depicted world: Bonnie writes her own legend in doggerel verse throughout the film, and she and Clyde both willingly pose for Buck Barrow's Kodak. Or consider the moment after the first killing, after the scene in the movie theatre, when Bonnie dances in front of her motel room mirror while singing "We're in the Money," as if she were herself a character in a film, La Cava's *Golddiggers of 1933* perhaps. The limited self-consciousness of Penn's characters is set in thematic context by the more inclusive self-consciousness of the film's discourse. For both the characters and the director, it's a matter of images—of living up to them, of taking responsibility for them.

Perhaps the greatest irony in *Bonnie and Clyde* is the degree to which the characters drift into big-time crime, without real premeditation. Clyde's first hold-up is undertaken in response to Bonnie's sexually loaded dare. And the first bank job—from which all else follows inexorably—evolves from a similarly innocent responsiveness on Clyde's part. He and Bonnie are taking target practice when a farmer and his family pull up in their truck to take a final look at their repossessed farm. Out of sympathy Clyde puts a slug into the Midlothian State Bank's "No Trespassing" sign. Clyde offers the gun to the farmer and to his black field hand. As the farmer turns to leave, Clyde says, almost hesitantly though somewhat boastfully, as if to cement the bond between them, "we rob banks." He hasn't robbed one yet—but now he is committed to trying; though the first bank he tries is empty both of money and customers. More significantly, in wanting to live up to his "bank robber" image Clyde unknowingly begins the progress of his own entrapment, an entrapment made chillingly clear in Penn's images. As Clyde steps through the door, gun drawn, Penn frames him through the teller's cage. Perhaps Clyde *thinks* of the holdup as an expression of his own freedom from restraint; but Penn's framing of him within the constriction of the teller's cage and through its bars, shows how wrong Clyde is. This motif of freedom delimited and constrained is elaborately developed through the course of the film via a whole range of internal frames—windows, mirrors, doors, car windows, etc.

Implicit in Penn's framing is the question of responsibility—of Clyde's for stepping into the frame, of Penn's (and ours) for standing on the other side and choosing to see him framed. The film's self-awareness is most clearly evident in the way it critiques the camera, as if our need to see Bonnie and Clyde as images of a freedom we both envy and fear were very directly responsible for their deaths. "Shooting" with a gun and "shooting" with a camera are explicitly equated in the sequence with Texas Ranger Hamer, where Bonnie proposes to humiliate Hamer by taking his picture ("He'll wish he were dead," as Buck puts it). In the credit sequence, moreover, Penn's name is immediately proceeded by a snapshot of three riflemen kneeling, as if he (the camera) were a gunman. And in the final ambush sequence we see Bonnie and Clyde's agonized death from a vantage point almost identical to that of Hamer and his deputies, from across the road, as if *we*, like Penn, were "shooting" the scene. No wonder the film was condemned; who wants to take that kind of responsibility? Arthur Penn, for one.

—Leland Poague

BOUDU SAUVE DES EAUX. Boudu Saved from Drowning. Production: Société Sirius; running time: 83 mins. Released November 1932, Paris.

Screenplay by Jean Renoir with Robert Valentin; from a work by René Fauchois; directed by Jean Renoir; photography by Marcel Lucien; edited by Marguerite Renoir and Suzanne de Troye; sound by Igor B. Kalinowski; production design by Jean Castanier and Hugues Laurent; music by Raphael and Johann Strauss; song "Sur les bords de la Riviera" by Leo Daniderff; assistants to the director: Jacques Becker and Georges Darnoux. Filmed summer 1932 in Epinay studios; exteriors filmed at Chennevières and in Paris.

Cast: Michel Simon (*Boudu*); Charles Granval (*Edouard Lestingois*); Marcelle Hainia (*Emma Lestingois*); Séverine Lerczinska (*Anne-Marie*); Jean Dasté (*The Student*); Max Dalban (*Godin*); Jean Gehret (*Vigour*); Jacques Becker (*Poet on the river bank*); Jane Pierson (*Rose*); Régine Lutèce (*Woman walking the dog*); Georges Darnoux (*Guest at the wedding*).

Publications:

Books—*Jean Renoir* by Paul Davay, Brussels 1957; *Jean Renoir* by Armand-Jean Cauliez, Paris 1962; *Jean Renoir* edited by Bernard Chardère in *Premier Plan* (Lyon), no.22-24, May 1962; *Analyses des films de Jean Renoir*, Institut des Hautes Etudes Cinématographiques, Paris 1966; *Study Unit 8: Jean Renoir* by Susan Bennett, London 1967; *Renoir 1938 ou Jean Renoir pour rein. Enquête sur un cinéaste* by François Poulle, Paris 1969; *Jean Renoir* by Pierre Leprohon, translated by Brigid Elson, New York 1971; *Jean Renoir* by Pierre Leprohon, New York 1971; *Jean Renoir: The World of His Films* by Leo Braudy, New York 1972; *Jean Renoir* by André Bazin, edited by François Truffaut, Paris, translated ed. 1973. *Jean Renoir* by Raymond Durgnat, Berkeley 1974; *Jean Renoir: le spectacle, la vie* by Claude Beylie, Paris 1975; *Jean Renoir: Essays, Conversations, Reviews* by Penelope Gilliatt, New York 1975; *French Cinema Since 1946: Volume One: The Great Tradition* by Roy Armes, New York 1976; *Jean Renoir: A Guide to References and Resources* by Christopher Faulkner, Boston 1979; articles—special Renoir issue, *Cahiers du cinéma* (Paris), January 1952; special Renoir issue, *Cahiers du cinéma* (Paris), Christmas 1957; "Painting Life with Movement" by Richard Whitehall in *Films and Filming* (London), June 1960 and "The Screen is his Canvas", July 1960; "Why Renoir Favors Multiple Camera, Long Sustained Take Technique" by Jean Belanger in *American Cinematographer* (Los Angeles), March 1960; "Jean Renoir" by Peter Harcourt in *London Magazine*, December 1962; "Jean Renoir" by Lee Russell in *New Left Review* (New York), May-/June 1964; "How I Came to Film *Boudu*" by Jean Renoir in *Film Society Review* (New York), February 1967; "*Boudu Saved From Drowning*" by Andrew Sarris in *Cahiers du Cinema in English* (New York), March 1967; "The Cinema of the Popular Front in France" by Goffredo Fofi in *Screen* (London), winter 1972/73: "Collapsing Columns: Mise-en-scene in *Boudu*" by R. Abel in *Jump Cut* (Chicago), January/February 1975

* * *

Boudu sauvé des eaux makes abundantly clear why Jean Renoir's work was so admired by André Bazin, and why the filmmakers of the New Wave regarded him as their sumpreme antecedent and father-figure. Bazin's theory of Realism—especially in so far as it is concerned with the preservation of the physical realities of time and space—is repeatedly exemplified by the use in *Boudu* of long takes, camera movement and depth-of-field, relating action to action, character to character, foreground to background, and continuously suggesting the existence of a world beyond the frame. The subversive implications of the material, the use of real locations instead of studio sets, the sense of a moral freedom combining inevitably with technical freedom, the evident love of actors and performance, and the resulting effect of spontaneity—all could add up to a model for the ambitions of the New Wave.

Leo Braudy has interpreted Renoir's work in terms of a dialectic of nature and "theatre" (the latter to be understood both literally and metaphorically), the two concepts achieving a complex interplay. *Boudu* works very well in this light. Indeed, the film opens with a *theatrical* representation of *nature* rites (Lestingois as satyr, Anne-Marie as nymph). If Renoir shows great affection for the world of nature surrounding, and epitomized by, Boudu—the freedom of the tramp without restrictions, the play of sunlight on water, the lush fertility of the imagery of the film's final scene—he is equally charmed by the bourgeois household of the Lestingois—by the artificial birds that Anne-Marie must dust, by Lestingois's reverence for Balzac (on whose works Boudu casually spits, not with the slightest animus but simply because it is natural to spit when you feel the need). One might add that he finds the Lestingois household charming because of the lingering traces of a subjugated, sublimated nature that continue to animate it. At the same time, he sees that it is the subjugation that makes culture possible. Windows—the barrier between nature and culture but also the means of access—are a recurrent motif throughout Renoir's work. In the films of Ophuls (with whom Renoir has so many points of contact while remaining so different) windows are always being closed; in those of Renoir they are always being opened. He is centrally concerned with the possibility of free access and interchange between the two worlds, the uncertainty being crucial.

The desire to negotiate between nature and culture encounters problems which the film can't resolve, and partially evades. On the one hand, the comic mode enables Renoir to avoid confronting the psychic misery produced by bourgeois repressiveness: Madame Lestingois, in particular, *can only* be a comic character for the film to continue to function. If her position were allowed to be explored seriously, the laughter would die immediately. The scene in which she is "liberated" by being raped by Boudu is saved from distastefulness solely by being played as farce. On the other hand, Renoir's equivocation in evaluating the bourgeois world results in some confusion over Boudu himself: does he or does he not represent a serious threat to it? The point gains force when one compares Michel Simon's characterization here with his père Jules in Vigo's *L'Atalante*. Jules is at once more formidable and more consistent, and Vigo's radicalism more sharply defined. Boudu, in contrast, seems little more than a pre-socialized (and pre-sexual) child, essentially harmless. The sudden ascription to him of great sexual potency jars, considering that we are told earlier that he has never kissed anyone except his dog.

The film is typical of Renoir's work in its warmth, humanity, generosity; it also suggests the close relation between that generosity and impotence. If every way of life can be defended, then nothing need be changed.

—Robin Wood

BRIEF ENCOUNTER. Production: Cineguild; black and white, 35mm; running time: 85 mins.; length: 7750 feet. Released 1945 by General Film Distributors, London,and in 1946 by Prestige Pictures. Re-released 1948 by ABFD, London.

Produced by Noel Coward; screenplay by Noel Coward, David Lean, and Anthony Havelock-Allan; from the one-act play *Still Life* by Noel Coward; directed by David Lean; photography by Robert Krasker; edited by Jack Harris; sound by Stanley Lambourne and Desmond Dew, sound edited by Harry Miller; production design by L.F. Williams; music from the 2nd Piano Concerto of Rachmaninoff. Filmed in England. New York Film Critics' Award, Best Actress (Johnson), 1946.

Cast: Celia Johnson (*Laura Jesson*); Trevor Howard (*Dr. Alec Harvey*); Cyril Raymond (*Fred Jesson*); Joyce Carey (*Myrtle Bagot*); Stanley Holloway (*Albert Godby*); Everly Gregg (*Dolly Messiter*).

Publications:

Scripts—"*Brief Encounter*" by Noel Coward, David Lean, and Anthony Havelock-Allan in *Masterworks of the British Cinema*, London 1974; books—*A Comparative Study of the Changes of 15 Film Plays Adapted from Stage Plays* by Charles John Gaupp, Jr., Doctoral study, University of Iowa, 1950; *Noel Coward* by Milton Levin, New York 1968; *A Talent to Amuse* by Morley Sheridan, New York 1969; *Motion Pictures: The Development of an Art from Silent Films to the Age of Television* by A.R. Fulton, Norman, Oklahoma 1970; *The Cinema of David Lean* by Gerald Pratley, New York 1974; *David Lean and His Films* by Alain Silver and James Ursini, London 1974; *Cinema, The Magic Vehicle: Journey One: The Cinema Through 1949* edited by Adam Garbicz and Jacek Klinowski, Metuchen, New Jersey 1975; *David Lean: A Guide to References and Resources* by Louis Castelli and Caryn Lynn Cleeland, Boston 1980; articles—"The Up and Coming Team of Lean and Neame" by C.A. Lejeune in *The New York Times*, 15 June 1947; "*Brief Encounter*" by David Lean in *The Penguin Film Review* (New York), no.4, 1947; "David Lean" in *Current Biography Yearbook*, New York 1953; "A Study of David Lean" by J. Holden in *Film Journal* (New York), April 1956; "Living Down a Classic" by Derek Conrad in *Films and Filming* (London), May 1958; "David Lean" by Stephen Watts in *Films in Review* (New York), April 1959; "Gallery of Great Artists: Trevor Howard" by Richard Whitehall in *Films and Filming* (London), February 1961; "*Brief Encounter*" by Kenneth T. Burles in *Magill's Survey of Cinema, Vol. 1* edited Frank N. Magill, Englewood Cliffs, New Jersey 1980.

*   *   *

In 1929 Leon Moussinac could, in his *Panoramique du cinéma*, declare "L'Angleterre n'a jamais produit un vrai film anglais." The remarkable renaissance of the British film which emerged after World War II requires a very different judgement. In 1944 David Lean made *Brief Encounter*, the most characteristic and perfect British film of all time. Its debt to Noel Coward must not be underestimated, but it is Lean's film. Lean, having worked as an editor on films by Michael Powell and Anthony Asquith, began his career as a director in association with Coward on *In Which We Serve*, *This Happy Breed* and *Blithe Spirit*. He then directed *Brief Encounter*, the infatuation between a housewife and a married man, with such uncanny human awareness and real creative skill that it stands out against his later more ambitious and elaborate films.

Brief Encounter is on a small scale, intimate and probing. Everything is obvious and yet nothing is. Laura Jesson, its suburban heroine, may not reach the dramatic solution of an Anna Karenina but what she does experience is no less poignant. We share her joys and sorrows of the moment until they carry her to the edge of tragedy. It cannot be seen entirely, however, as tragedy for there is an element of values and choice. Life is not simple and the greatness of the film lies in its awareness of this complexity. An insensitive critic once described the film as, "Two characters in search of a bed." French critics failed to see that there *was* a problem. But for characters like Laura and Alec, there were values that they honoured even at the expense of pain. It is, in a way, a triumph for their common humanity. Very simply the end did not justify the means.

The happy unification of this tale of star-crossed lovers, the intense reality of their attraction and the universal nature of the experience is played against a background that is deeply and truly British. If being British is the spirit of the "stiff upper lip," then it is belied by the passionate note that runs through the film. The small joys of love, the impetus towards realization and fulfillment, the sense of threatened pleasures haunts the viewer from beginning to end. The perfect performances of that most subtle of all actresses, Celia Johnson, and of Trevor Howard contribute greatly to the success of the film. It is, though, the happy fusion of all the elements that give it a perspective and unity rare in the cinema.

The setting of the suburban railway station and its vicinity sees a great human drama take place. Everything about it is authentic down to the familiars who haunt it, the funny little people with their airs and graces and their trivial jokes and quarrels. Other dramatic incidents which occur in the film include the visit to the restaurant and the cinema; the humiliation and shame when reality shatters the dream; and the unexpected friend who turns up to interrupt their one possible night together. The film thus opens with the climax which is not fully understood until the gentle pain-filled voice of Laura relives the happy but poignant days of a moment of life she will never forget.

There is one element that enhances the film in a most felicitous way. When Rachmaninoff wrote his 2nd Piano Concerto he could little have guessed that he was providing the theme music for a very beautiful and inspiring British film. Though it was not a commercial success in America, it was successful for the British cinema in terms of prestige.

—Liam O'Leary

BRINGING UP BABY. Production: RKO Radio Pictures Inc., 1938; black and white, 35mm; running time: 102 mins. (some sources state 100 mins.). Released 1938.

Produced by Cliff Reid; screenplay by Dudley Nichols and Hagar Wilde; from a story by Hagar Wilde; directed by Howard Hawks; photography by Russell Metty; edited by George Hively; music score by Roy Webb. Filmed in RKO studios and backlots.

Cast: Cary Grant (*David Huxley*); Katharine Hepburn (*Susan Vance*); May Robson (*Mrs. Carlton Random*); Charles Ruggles (*Major Applegate*); George Irving (*Alexander Peabody*); Virginia Walker (*Alice Swallow*); Barry Fitzgerald; Walter Catlett.

Publications:

Review—in *The New York Times*, 4 March 1938; books—*The Cinema of Howard Hawks* by Peter Bogdanovich, New York 1962; *Howard Hawks* by Jean-Claude Missiaen, Paris 1966; *Howard Hawks* by Robin Wood, London 1968, revised 1977; *Howard Hawks* by Jean A. Gili, Paris 1971; *Cary Grant Album* compiled by Allen Eyles, Shepperton, Surrey, England 1971; *The Films of Katharine Hepburn* by Homer Dickens, New York 1971; *Cary Grant* by Jerry Vermilye, New York 1973; *The Films of Cary Grant* by Donald Deschner, Secaucus, New Jersey 1978; *Katharine Hepburn* by Alvin H. Marill, New York 1973; *The RKO Gals* by James Robert Parish, New Rochelle, New York 1974; *Howard Hawks, Storyteller* by Gerald Mast, New York 1982; articles—"Katharine Hepburn" by Romano V. Tozzi in *Films in Review* (New York), December 1957; "Howard Hawks" by Henri Agel in the *New York Film Bulletin*, no.4, 1962; "The World of Howard Hawks" by Andrew Sarris in *Films and Filming* (London), July 1962 and August 1962; article by V.F. Perkins in *Movie* (London), December 1962; "Man's Favorite Director, Howard Hawks" (interview) in *Cinema* (Beverly Hills), November/December 1963; issue devoted to Hawks of *Cahiers du cinéma* (Paris), January 1963; "A Comment on the Hawksian Woman" by Leigh Brackett in *Take One* (Montreal), July/August 1971; "The Hawksian Woman" by Naomi Wise in *Take One* (Montreal), January/February 1971; "Of Babies, Bones, and Butterflies" by K. Murphy in *Movietone News* (Seattle), June 1977; "*Bringing Up Baby*" by Julia Johnson in *Magill's Survey of Cinema, Vol. 1* edited by Frank N. Magill, Englewood Cliffs, New Jersey 1980.

*   *   *

Bringing Up Baby is the zaniest screwball comedy of the 1930s. It employs the successful formula of such classic films as *It Happened One Night* and *My Man Godfrey* in which madcap heiresses pit their senses of fun, irreverence, and total irresponsibility against the seriousness, logic and dignity of working class heroes. In such screwball comedies of the 1930s, the leading couples' courtships of verbal battles provide a series of humorous sexual conflicts that are overcome but unresolved in their reconciliations during the "happy endings." *Bringing Up Baby* takes the antagonisms and extremes embodied in the screwball comedy a little further than any of the other films of the genre.

Starring Katharine Hepburn as the completely dotty heiress and Cary Grant as an overly stuffy, self-important paleontologist *Bringing Up Baby* exaggerates the lover-antagonist formula of the screwball comedy for a humorous battle between the sexes in which the stereotypes of sex roles are reversed. Hepburn's character is the aggressor, and her relentless pursuit of Grant engages him in a series of comic misadventures which become increasingly foolish as the movie progresses. Grant's character, who by nature is docile, submissive, and dutiful, has his dignity stripped away layer by layer in the course of Hepburn's bizarre schemes. But director Howard Hawks uses the division of his characters into masculine and feminine stereotypes in order to allow each to have a liberating effect on the other. When the two are united as a couple at the film's end, the effect is an uneasy integration of sex-role principles.

The Hawksian formula of sex-role reversals contained in comic opposites provided the underpinnings for Hawk's screwball comedies from the 1930s through the 1950s. In such movies as *Twentieth Century*, *Bringing Up Baby*, *His Girl Friday*, *Ball of Fire*, *I Was A Male War Bride*, and *Monkey Business*, Hawks relied on assertive heroines to peel away the dignity and mock seriousness of bumbling feminized heroes. As each hero's sense of identity and self-image crumbles, the ensuing confusion provides the comedy and the key to his liberation from a narrow restrictive code of behavior. In such films as *Bringing Up Baby* and *I Was A Male War Bride*, Hawks pushes his male characters' sexual confusion to such extremes that they are forced to parade around in women's clothing.

Bringing Up Baby enjoys frequently revived popularity today due to its breakneck pace, superb comic timing, humorous swipes at sex roles, and partnering of Hepburn and Grant. But when the film was initially released in 1938, it met harsh criticism and indifferent audiences. Hepburn, who headed the Independent Theatre Owners Association list of "box-office poison" movie stars, grated on the critics' nerves. In addition to Hepburn's seeming unpopularity, a critical disdain for what the *New York Times* reviewer called a "zany-ridden product of the goofy farce school" may have contributed to the film's lack of success. However, in 1962, *Sight and Sound* critic Peter Dyer attested to the reversal in status and popularity of *Bringing Up Baby*: "The durability of Hawks's films lies in the way that they have a mysterious life of their own going on under their familiar, facile surfaces. It is the constant cross-graining of cliche and inventive detail which produces the shock of pleasure his best work provides."

—Lauren Rabinovitz

BROKEN BLOSSOMS. Production: D.W. Griffith, Inc., 1919; black and white, 35mm, silent; running time: about 95 mins.; length: 6 reels. Released 1919 through United Artists.

Produced by D.W. Griffith; scenario by D.W. Griffith; from the story "The Chink and the Child" by Thomas Burke; directed by D.W. Griffith; photography by G.W. Bitzer; edited by James Smith; music arranged by Louis F. Gottschalk; special effects by Hendrick Sartov. Filmed December 1918-January 1919; cost: $88,000.

Cast: Lilliam Gish (*Lucy, the Girl*); Richard Barthelmess (*Cheng Huan*); Donald Crisp (*Battling Burrows*); Arthur Howard (*Burrows' Manager*); Edward Peil (*Evil Eye*); George Beranger (*The Spying One*); Norman Selby or "Kid McCoy" (*A Prize Fighter*); George Nicholls (*London policeman*); Moon Kwan (*Buddhist monk*).

Publications:

Books—*Life and Lillian Gish* by Albert Bigelow, New York 1932; *The Movies in the Age of Innocence* by Edward Wagenknecht, Oklahoma 1962; *D.W. Griffith: American Film Master* by Iris Barry and Eileen Bowser, New York 1965; *Griffith* by Jean Mitry in *Anthologie de Cinéma*, Paris 1966; *Lillian Gish: The Movies, Mr. Griffith, and Me* by Lillian Gish with Ann Pinchot, Englewood Cliffs, New Jersey 1969; *Griffith and the Rise of Hollywood* by Paul O'Dell, New York 1970; *The Man Who Invented Hollywood: The Autobiography of D.W. Griffith* edited by James Hart, Louisville, Kentucky 1972; *D.W. Griffith: His Life and Work* by Robert Henderson, New York 1972; *Billy Bitzer: His Story* by G.W. Bitzer, New York 1973; *Adventures with D.W. Griffith* by Karl Brown, New York 1973; *Dorothy and Lillian Gish* by Lillian Gish, New York 1973; *Spellbound in Darkness* by George C. Pratt, Connecticut 1973; *The Films of D.W. Griffith* by Edward Wagenknecht and Antony Slide, New

York 1975; *Star Acting: Gish, Garbo, Davis* by Charles Affron, New York 1977; *Griffith: 1st Artist of the Movies* by Martin Williams, New York 1980; articles—"The Origins of United Artists" by A.L. Mayer in *Films in Review* (New York), August-/September 1959; "Lillian Gish" by Romano Tozzi in *Films in Review* (New York), December 1962; special Griffith issue, *Film Culture* (New York), spring/summer 1965; "Billy Bitzer—Pioneer and Innovator" by George J. Mitchell in *American Cinematographer* (Hollywood), December 1964 and January 1965; "The Films of David Wark Griffith: The Development of Themes and Techniques in 42 of His Films" by Richard Meyer in *Film Comment* (New York), fall/winter 1967; "*Broken Blossoms*" by Eileen Bowser and Iris Barry in *Film Notes*, New York 1969; "D.W. Griffith and the Making of an Unconventional Masterpiece" by Arthur Lenning in *Film Journal* (New York), fall/winter 1972; "The Films of D.W. Griffith" by Alan Casty in *Journal of Popular Film* (Bowling Green, Ohio), spring 1972; "Quelques remarques sur Le Lys brisé" by B. Amengual in *Cahiers du cinéma* (Paris), spring 1972; "Le Lys brisé" by G. Braucourt in *Ecran* (Paris), February 1973; issue on Griffith in *Films in Review* (New York), October 1975; "*Broken Blossoms*, Or the Yellow Man and the Girl" by R. Combs in *Monthly Film Bulletin* (London), November 1975; "Griffith's *Broken Blossoms* and the Problem of Historical Specificity" by Vance Kepley, Jr. in *Quarterly Review of Film Studies* (Pleasantville, New York), winter 1978; "*Broken Blossoms*: Artful Racism, Artful Rape" by Julia Lesage in *Jump Cut* (Chicago), 1981; "*Broken Blossoms*: The Art and Eros of a Perverse Text" by Dudley Andrew in *Quarterly Review of Film Studies* (Pleasantville, New York), winter 1981; "Griffith's Family Discourse: Griffith and Freud" by Nick Browne in *Quarterly Review of Film Studies* (Pleasantville, New York), winter 1981.

*   *   *

Broken Blossoms is Griffith's most intricate film, a delicate mood piece that is set within a sharply confined space and delimited amount of time. The film opened to critical acclaim in this country with reviewers responding particularly to Lillian Gish's bravura performance and Hendrick Sartov's soft-focus photography. Its most profound effect, however, was felt by European filmmakers. In France, where the film premiered in 1921, it became something of a cult object. French impressionist directors like Louis Delluc, Marcel L'Herbier, and Germaine Dullac tried consciously to emulate its stylized lighting and atmospheric effects. As Vance Kepley stated, "*Broken Blossoms* may have been to the early French experimenters what *Intolerance* was to the Soviets." Louis Moussinac summed up the admiration French filmmakers felt for Griffith's film: "C'est le chef-d'oeuvre du cinema dramatique."

Broken Blossoms came as something of a surprise to critics who knew Griffith only through *The Birth of a Nation*, *Intolerance*, or his World War I extravaganza, *Hearts of the World*. In fact, this modest film shot in 18 days on a shoe-string budget, was at first considered box office poison. When Griffith approached Paramount to distribute the film as a special, Adolph Zukor unhesitatingly turned him down. "Everybody in it dies," he wrote. Mindful of the recent failure of Nazimova's *The Red Lantern* and Sessue Hayakawa's waning popularity, Zukor concluded that the brief vogue for film *chinoiserie* had passed and was eager to let Griffith distribute it himself. Griffith paid Zukor $250,000 for it, and eventually released it through the newly formed United Artists; dressed up with an elaborate live prologue, three separate orchestras and choirs, and a specially tinted screen, the film garnered a small fortune.

Today, the film's critical stock is soaring; *Broken Blossoms* is widely regarded as Griffith's masterpiece, eclipsing even his better known epics. Lillian Gish's masterful performance aside, critics have been especially impressed by the formal sophistication and narrative complexity of Griffith's film. It is, above all, a film marked by terrific compression. The concentration of time and space gives characters, objects, and decor sustained metaphorical power that is never dissipated. Just as skillful is the dramatic structure which gives the impression of simple straightforwardness while camouflaging an intricate intertwining of expository and narrative sequences.

Thematically, the film is perhaps Griffith's most adventurous work. Susan Sontag has called Griffith "an intellect of supreme vulgarity and even inanity," whose work ordinarily reeks of fervid moralizing about sexuality and violence. But in *Broken Blossoms* he lowers his guard, nearly breaching his cherished Victorian convictions. Activities obviously taboo in *The Birth of a Nation* and *Intolerance*—a racially mixed love-affair, auto-eroticism, opium eating, sado-masochism, revenge killing—are transformed here into sensually satisfying pastimes that resonate in dangerously non-conformist ways. For once in Griffith's work, racial bigotry is a target for reproach. The few citations to post-war 1919 American culture, far from catering to the rampant xenophobia and mood of self-congratulation, hint at the dark side of American provincialism. The glancing references to munition workers, American sailors, and First World War battles illustrate the west's penchant for self-destructiveness and violence.

—Russell Merritt

BRONENOSETS POTEMKIN. Battleship Potemkin. Production: First Goskino; black and white, 35mm, silent; running time: 86 mins. at silent speed; length: 1850 meters, or 6070 feet. Released 18 January 1926. Re-released 1956 with a second musical score by Nikolai Kryukov.

Produced by Jacob Bliokh; scenario and screenplay by Sergei Eisenstein; from an outline by Nina Agadzhanova-Shutko in collaboration with Sergei Eisenstein; titles by Nikolai Asseyev; directed by Sergei Eisenstein; photography by Edward Tisse; edited by Sergei Eisenstein; art direction by Vasili Rakhals; music (original background score) by Edmund Meisel.

Filmed from July through November, 1925, in Leningrad, Odessa, and aboard the *12 Apostles* (the sister ship of the *Prince Potemkin of Taurida*.)

Cast: Sailors of the Red Navy; Citizens of Odessa; Members of the Proletkut Theatre, Moscow; Alexander Antonov (*Vakulinchuk*); Grigori Alexandrov (*Chief Officer Gilerocsky*); Vladimir Barsky (*Captain Golikov*); Alexander Lyovshin (*Petty Officer*); Beatrice Vitoldi (*Mother with baby carriage*); I. Bobrov (*Humiliated soldrier*); Andrei Fait (*Officer on piano*); Konstantin Feldman (*Student Fel'dman*); Protopopov (*Old man*); Korobei (*Legless veteran*); Yulia Eisenstein (*Lady bringing food to mutineers*); Prokopenko (*Mother of wounded Aba*); A. Glauberman (*Aba*); N. Poltautseva (*School teacher*); Brodsky (*Intellectual*); Zerenin (*Student*); Mikhail Gomarov (*Militant sailor*).

Publications:

Scripts—*Potemkin* with an introduction by Sergei Eisenstein, translated by Gillon R. Aitken, New York 1968; *Eisenstein: 3 Films* edited by Jay Leyda, translated by Diana Matias, New York 1974; reviews—review by Herbert Jehring in *Berliner Börsencourier*, 30 April 1926, reprinted in *The Battleship Potemkin* edited by Herbert Marshall; "Russia All Around Us—Whoop, 3 Blows, and a Frown" in *The New Yorker*, 18 December 1926; "Panzerschiff Potemkin" by George Victor Mendel in *Kinemathek* (Berlin), 5 January 1926, reprinted in *The Battleship Potemkin* edited by Herbert Marshall; review by Mordaunt Hall in *The New York Times*, December 1926; books—*S.M. Eisenstein* by Marie Seton, New York 1960; "Artistic Imagery in the Film *The Battleship Potemkin*" in *The History of the Film* by S.S. Ginzburg, Moscow 1960; "On *Potemkin*" in *Kino, a History of The Russian and Soviet Film* by Jay Leyda, London 1960; *The Selected Works of S.M. Eisenstein* edited by S.I. Yutkevitch, Moscow 1964; *Bronenosets Potemkin—shedevry Sovetskogo kino* [The Battleship Potemkin, Masterpieces of Soviet Cinema] edited by N.I. Kleiman and K.B. Levina, Moscow, 1969; *Eisenstein's Potemkin* by David Mayer, New York 1972; *Autobigraphy* by S.M. Eisenstein, translated by H. Marshall and Toby Wright, London 1978; *The Battleship Potemkin* edited by Herbert Marshall, New York 1978; "*Potemkin*" by Edward Murray in *10 Film Classics*, New York 1978; articles—"First Thoughts on *Potemkin*" by Wilton A. Barrett in *National Board of Review Magazine* (New York), November 1926; "Studio News and Gossip East and West" by Cal York in *Photoplay* (Los Angeles), October 1926; "With *Potemkin* the Russians Have Gained Film Precedence" by John Grierson in *New York Herald Tribune*, 5 December 1926; "The End of Eisenstein" by Solski in *Commentary* (New York), March 1949; "Soviet Films in Pre-September Poland" by Vladislav Evsevitsky in *Kwartalnik Filmowy* (Warsaw), nos.3-4, 1951; "A Comparison of *Potemkin* and *Ivan the Terrible*: Eisenstein Today" by Semyon Freilich in *Soviet Literature Monthly*, 1965; "*Potemkin* in Print" by Ivor Montagu in *Sight and Sound* (London), summer 1970; "Kuleshov, Eisenstein, and the others. Part II: Kuleshov on Eisenstein" by L. Kuleshov in *Film Journal* (New York), fall/winter 1972; "Eisenstein's *Potemkin*" by Stanley Kauffmann in *Horizon* (London), spring 1973; "Dwunastu apostolów" by S. Eisenstein in *Kino* (Warsaw), November 1973; "*El Acorazado Potemkin*" in *Cine Cubano* (Havana), no.89-90, 1974; article by Eisenstein on *Bronenosets Potemkin* in *Ecran* (Paris), December 1975; "Epos Revolucii" in *Iskusstvo Kino* (Moscow), December 1975; "A for a es a tartalom egysegenek iskoklapeldaja" in *Filmkultura* (Budapest), May/June 1976; "Tol'ko piatnadstat 'kadrov" by N. Kieiman in *Iskusstvo Kino* (Moscow), no.3, 1976; "Wohin führt *Panzerkreuzer Potemkin*" by J. Chanjutin in *Film und Fernsehen* (Berlin), November 1977; "Massenkino" by S. Eisenstein in *Film und Fernsehen* (Berlin), January 1978; "Nur 15 Einstellungen" by N. Klejman in *Filmwissenschaftliche Beitrage* (Berlin), no.2, 1978; "Fotogrammi" by A. Imponente in *Filmcritica* (Rome), February 1979; article by W.F. Van Wert in *Sight and Sound* (London), summer 1980; "Křižník pluje desetiletími" by V. Sklovski in *Film a Doba* (Prague), November 1981.

*   *   *

Sergei M. Eisenstein's *Battleship Potemkin* is one of the most influential films ever made as well as one of the finest examples of film art. On its release, the film brought immediate worldwide fame to Eisenstein and the new Soviet cinema and made an important contribution to the language of the cinema—the concept of montage editing.

After the Bolshevik Revolution in 1917 the new Soviet government assumed control of the film industry, denounced the capitalist cinema of pre-Revolution Tsarist Russia, and decreed that the Soviet cinema was to be used for education and propaganda—to indoctrinate the Russian masses and to promote class consciousness throughout the world. *Battleship Potemkin* was made in order to celebrate the 20th anniversary of the unsuccessful 1905 Revolution against the Tsar. Although the film was originally supposed to chronicle the entire rebellion, Eisenstein decided to limit the story to just one representative episode—the mutiny on the Potemkin and the subsequent civilian massacre on the steps leading down to Odessa harbor.

Battleship Potemkin, like Eisenstein's earlier film, *Strike*, has several documentary-like qualities. For example, Eisenstein cast most of the characters in the film according to the notion of typage—the selection of a non-actor to play a role because he/she is the correct physical type for the part. Eisenstein preferred to use non-actors since, as he explained, "A 30 year-old actor may be called upon to play an old man of 60. He may have a few days' or a few hours' rehearsal. But an old man will have had 60 years' rehearsal." Eisenstein shot the film on location—on the Odessa steps and aboard the Potemkin's sister ship, The Twelve Apostles (the Potemkin had already been dismantled). The film has a collective hero: the Russian masses—the mutineers on the Potemkin, the people of Odessa, the sailors who mutiny on the other ships—who rebel against Tsarist oppression.

Despite the film's documentary look, it was very carefully constructed on every level, from the distribution of line, mass, and light in individual shots to the perfectly balanced five-act structure of the overall film. The most remarkable feature of the film's construction, however, is the montage editing.

Eisenstein's theory of montage—based on the Marxist dialectic, which involves the collision of thesis and anti-thesis to produce deals with the juxtaposition of shots, and attractions (e.g., lighting, camera angle, or subject movement) within shots, to create meaning. Rather than the smooth linkage of shots favored by many of his contemporaries (e.g., V.I. Pudovkin and D.W. Griffith), Eisenstein was interested in the collision and dialectical synthesis of contradictory shots as a way to shock and agitate the audience.

Eisenstein identified five methods of montage: metric, rhythmic, tonal, overtonal, and intellectual. Metric montage concern conflict caused by the lengths of shots. Rhythmic montage concerns conflict generated by the rhythmn of movement within shots. In tonal montage, shots are arranged according to the "tone" or "emotional sound" of the dominant attraction in the shots. In overtonal montage, the basis for joining shots is not merely the dominant attraction, but the totality of stimulation provided by that dominant attraction and all of its "overtones" and "undertones"; overtonal montage is, then, a synthesis of metric, rhythmic, and tonal montage that does not appear at the level of the individual frame, but only at the level of the projected film. Finally, intellectual montage involves the juxtaposition of images to serve as a visual metaphor.

All five types of montage may be found in *Potemkin*'s Odessa Steps sequence—in which Tsarist soldiers massacre Odessa citizens who are sympathetic to the Potemkin mutineers. An example of metric montage is the increase in editing tempo for intensifying audience excitement during the massacre. Rhythmic montage occurs in the conflict between the steady marching of the soldiers—the editing rhythm, which is out of synchronization with the marching rhythm plus the chaotic scrambling of the fleeing crowd, and the rolling movement of a runaway baby carriage. Tonal montage occurs in the many conflicts of planes, masses, light and shadow, and intersecting lines as in the shot depicting a row of soldiers pointing their rifles down at a mother and her son, their shadows cutting transversely across the steps and the helpless pair. Although Eisenstein claimed to have discovered overtonal montage while editing *Old and New* four years after *Battleship Potemkin*, overtonal montage can be detected in the Odessa Steps sequence in the development of the editing along simultaneous metric, rhythmic, and tonal lines—the increase in editing tempo, the conflict between editing and movement within the frame, and the juxtapositions of light and shadow, intersecting lines, etc. Finally, there is an example of intellectual montage at the end of the sequence, after the Potemkin has responded to the massacre by firing on the Tsarist headquarters in Odessa. Three shots of marble lions—the first is sleeping, the second waking, and the third rising—seen in rapid succession give the impression of a single lion rising to its feet, a metaphor for the rebellion of the Russian masses against Tsarist oppression.

When *Battleship Potemkin* was first released, it drew mixed reactions in the Soviet Union; many people praised the film, while others denounced it, charging Eisenstein with "formalism"—a preference for aesthetic form over ideological content. However, once they realized that foreign audiences loved the film, Soviet officials began to support the film, and it soon became a popular and critical success, both inside and outside the Soviet Union. Today *Battleship Potemkin* ranks among *The Birth of a Nation* and *Citizen Kane* as one of the most important films in cinema history.

—Clyde Kelly Dunagan

DIE BÜCHSE DER PANDORA. Pandora's Box. Loulou. Production: Nero Film A.G. (Berlin); black and white, 35mm, silent; running time: 140 mins. originally, other versions are 131 mins. and 120 mins.; length: 3254 meters originally. Released 30 January 1929.

Produced by George C. Horsetzky; scenario by Ladislaus Vajda and Joseph R. Fliesner; from 2 plays, *Erdgeist* and *Die Büchse der Pandora*, by Frank Wedekind; directed by Georg Wilhelm Pabst (G.W. Pabst); photography by Günther Krampf; edited by Joseph R. Fliesler; art direction by Andrei Andreiev and Gottlieb Hesch; music by Curtis Ivan Salke; costumes designed by Gottlieb Hesch. Filmed 1928 in Berlin.

Cast: Louise Brooks (*Lulu*); Fritz Kortner (*Dr. Peter Schön*); Franz Lederer (*Alwa Schön, the Son*); Carl Götz (*Schigolch, Papa Brommer*); Alice Roberts (*Countess Anna Geschwitz*); Daisy d'Ora (*Marie de Zarnika*); Krafft Raschig (*Rodrigo Quast*); Michael von Newlinsky (*Marquis Casti-Piani*); Siegfried Arno (*Stage manager*); Gustav Diessl (*Jack the Ripper*).

Publications:

Scripts—*Pandora's Box* (*Lulu*): A Film by G.W.Pabst translated by Christopher Holme, New York 1971; "*Loulou*" by L. Vajda and J. Fliesler in *L'Avant-Scène du cinéma* (Paris), 1 December 1980; review—"La Presse" in *L'Avant-Scène du cinéma* (Paris), 1 December 1980; books—*From Caligari to Hitler, A Psychological History of the German Film* by Siegfried Kracauer, Princeton, New Jersey 1947; *Index to the Creative Work of Pabst* by H. Weinberg and L. Boehm, New York 1955; *G.W. Pabst* by Freddy Buache, Lyon, France 1965; *Georg Wil-*

helm Pabst by Barthelemy Amengual, Paris 1966; "G.W. Pabst" by Yves Aubry and Jacques Pétat in *Anthologie du cinéma* vol.4, Paris 1968; *The German Cinema* by Roger Manvell and Heinrich Fraenkel, New York 1971; *50 Years of German Film* by H.H. Wollenberg, London 1972; *G.W. Pabst* by Lee Atwell, Boston 1977; *Lulu in Hollywood* by Louise Brooks, New York 1982; articles—"G.W. Pabst's *Lulu*" by Krazna-Kraus in *Close-up* (London), April 1929; "Loulou" by J. Bouissounousse in *La Revue du cinéma* (Paris), 1 May 1930; "Umanesimo di Pabst" by N. Chiaramonte in *Scenario* (Rome), no.8, 1932; "Pabst and the Social Film" by Harry Alan Potamkin in *Hound and Horn* (London), January/March 1933; "Lulù" by G. Viazzi in *Cinema* (Rome), no.170, 1943; "Lulù" by V. Pandolfi in *Cinema* (Rome), no.26, 1949; "G.W. Pabst" edited by Gideon Bachmann in *Cinemages* (New York), May 1955; "Out of Pandora's Box" by James Card in *Image* (Rochester, New York), September 1956; "G.W. Pabst" by Herbert Luft in *Films in Review* (New York), February 1964; article by Louise Brooks in *Sight and Sound* (London), summer 1965; "G.W. Pabst" by Herbert Luft in *Films and Filming* (London), April 1967; "*Die Büchse der Pandora*" by T. Rayns in *Monthly Film Bulletin* (London), May 1974; "De Wedekind à Pabst" by Barthélémy Amengual in *L'Avant-Scène du cinéma* (Paris), 1 December 1980; "Loulou à la scène et à l'écran" in *L'Avant-Scène du cinéma* (Paris), 1 December 1980; "*Loulou*" by J. Petat in *Cinéma* (Paris), April 1980; "*Loulou*" by D. Serceau in *Image et son* (Paris), March 1980; "Le Retour de Loulou" by O.-R. Veillon in *Cinématographe* (Paris), March 1980; "Le sexe de pandore" by F. Ramasse in *Positif* (Paris), July/August 1981.

*   *   *

Pandora's Box brings to mind familiar questions about film-as-art—whether the art arises from the director's work, from the performances, from the editor's decisions, or from a combination of all of these elements. *Pandora's Box* might well be an unremarkable film without the magnificent presence of Louise Brooks, but then again, this presence was never evoked by any director other than G.W. Pabst. The source of the magic is elusive.

Nothing about the film is obvious, least of all Pabst's technique. Pabst is known for having promoted the practice of cutting on movement as a means of minimizing the jarring effect of editing. Rather than carry the practice to a lyrical extreme, Pabst exercised restraint and made only subtle use of the technique. Yet, in his hands, cutting on even the slightest movement can communicate significantly and almost subliminally. For example, after Schigolch gives Alva cards to put up his sleeve during the gambling ship sequence, Schigolch begins to creep away screen-right. As the scene changes, his movement is continued by Rodrigo as he creeps in the same direction toward Lulu in another part of the ship. Above and behind Rodrigo is a sculpture of a crocodile mounted high on the wall. With great economy Pabst has identified Schigolch and Rodrigo as slimy beasts of prey. At no time do the camera work and the editing call attention to themselves. Even when watching with the express purpose of detecting technical patterns, one must constantly pull back from the hypnotic fluidity of the film. Pabst weaves the perfect story-teller's spell with his technique.

The film's style is as elusive as its technique. *Pandora's Box* seems to be composed of several segments, each with its own distinct style. There is psychological realism in Lulu's relationship with Dr. Schön. Expressionistic elements darken and distort the London coda with Jack the Ripper. A presentation to a Hollywood show-business tale makes the backstage sequence a delightful play of high spirits and frantic energies crossing and colliding. It is a self-consciously comical scene, especially in the antics of the beleaguered stage manager.

This same sequence illustrates another notable quality of the film—a closeness or an inwardness which confines without being oppressive. During the revue we see the action on stage from the wings, and once from the front of the stage itself, but never from the audience's perspective. Space is claustrophobic in this film. The rare outdoor scenes are hemmed in by night and/or fog, as in the London Salvation Army scenes and the escape in a rowboat from the smoke-filled, crowded gambling ship. This sense of closeness is heightened by Pabst's avoidance of any but the most sparing and economical use of camera movement.

The camera is restricted in terms of mobility, but its perspective of Lulu is privileged. Rarely is she observed from another character's point of view. The camera is a separate party in the action, a witness to all aspects of Lulu's behavior. She is watched both as a participant and as an observer, giving the viewer a rich sense of personal knowledge of the character, a familiarity which far surpasses the surface acquaintanceships secured with the other characters.

The film was not received with any enthusiasm in its debut. Perhaps its proximity to the two Frank Wedekind plays on which it was based, *Erdgeist* and *Die Büchse der Pandora*, prevented viewers from approaching the film on its own terms. The character of Lulu in the plays was characterized through her speech, while Pabst's and Brooks's Lulu was presented in a manner appropriate to the film medium, in a performance which today is recognized as one of the finest, most provocative in all of film.

—Barbara Salvage

CABARET. Production: Allied Artists, 1972; color, 35mm; running time: 123 mins. Released 1972.

Produced by Cy Feuer; screenplay by Jay Presson Allen; from the musical play of the same name by Joe Masterhoff, adapted from the play *I Am a Camera* by John Van Druten and the collection of short stories *Goodbye to Berlin* by Christopher Isherwood; directed by Bob Fosse; photography by Geoffrey Unsworth; edited by David Bretherton; sound by Robert Knudson and David Hildyard; art direction by Jurgen Kiebach and Rolf Zehetbauer, set decoration by Herbert Strabel; music by Fred Ebb and John Kander, music direction by Ralph Burns; costumes designed by Charlotte Flemming.

Filmed on location in West Germany. Academy Awards for Best Actress (Minnelli), Best Supporting Actor (Grey), Best Directing, Best Cinematography, Best Art Direction-Set Decoration, Best Sound, Best Editing, and Best Scoring-Adaptation and Original Song Score, 1972.

Cast: Liza Minnelli (*Sally Bowles*); Michael York (*Brian Roberts*); Helmut Griem (*Maximilian von Heune*); Fritz Wepper (*Fritz Wendel*); Joel Grey (*Master of Ceremonies*); Marisa Berenson (*Natalia Landauer*); Elisabeth Neumann-Viertel (*Fraulein Schneider*).

Publications:

Reviews—"Grinning" by Pauline Kael in the *New Yorker*, 19

February 1972; "*Cabaret*" by P. Buckley in *Films and Filming* (London), August 1972; "*Cabaret*" by L. Codelli in *Positif* (Paris), November/December 1972; "*Cabaret*" by A.H. Marill in *Films in Review* (New York), March 1972; "*Cabaret*" by Tom Milne in *Sight and Sound* (London), summer 1972; "*Cabaret*" by T. Vallance in *Focus on Film* (London), summer 1972; "*Cabaret*" by Stephen Farber in *The New York Times*, 20 February 1972; books—*The Films of Liza Minnelli* by Susan d'Arcy, London 1973; *The Great Movies* by William Bayer, New York 1973; *Liza* by James Robert Parish and Jack Ano, New York 1975; *The Hollywood Musical* by Ethan Mordden, New York 1972; *The Hollywood Musical* by Clive Hirschhorn, New York 1981; articles—by Foster Hirsch in *Take One* (Montreal), September/October 1971; "Interview with Bob Fosse" by L. Picard in *Interview* (New York), March 1972; "The Many Facets of Bob Fosse" by G. Loney in *After Dark* (Boston), June 1972; "Inter-/view with Bob Fosse" by L. Picard in *Inter/View* (New York), March 1972; "Bob Fosse" by J. Stegelmann in *Kosmorama* (Copenhagen), October 1972; "*Cabaret Isadora*" by P. Vecchiali in *Image et son* (Paris), November 1972; "Bob Fosse" in *Current Biography* (New York), 1972; "The Evolution of *Cabaret*" by J. Blades in *Literature/Film Quarterly* (Salisbury, Maryland), summer 1973; "Kortörténet-musicalban" by G. Thurzó in *Film-kultura* (Budapest), January/February 1974; "*Cabaret*" in *Living Images* by Stanley Kauffmann, New York 1975; "*Cabaret* Uncut in a German 'First', TV Version That Is" in *Variety* (New York), 17 November 1976; "*Cabaret* and *Nashville*: the Musical as Social Comment" by S.E. Bowles in *Journal of Popular Culture* (Bowling Green, Ohio), no.3, 1978-79; "*Cabaret*" by Leslie Taubman in *Magill's Survey of Cinema, Vol. 1* edited by Frank N. Magill, Englewood Cliffs, New Jersey 1980.

*   *   *

The release of the film version of *Cabaret* has been heralded as an important milestone in the history of the musical genre. Stanley Green called it a "dazzlingly stylized concept musical," and Stephen Farber championed its use of "...an intimate, experimental style rather than the conventional slick, splashy musical format...." This critical acclaim was based on the fact that for the preceding 30 years, musicals were elaborate affairs that followed the tenets of Arthur Freed; production numbers were integrated into the narrative. Characters would simply shift from conversation to song and dance as a natural form of everyday discourse. *Cabaret* changed all that. As Pauline Kael said, "...it is not merely that *Cabaret* violates the wholesome approach of big musicals but that it violates the pseudo-naturalistic tradition ...which requires that the songs appear to grow organically out of the story."

Bob Fosse's decision to totally separate the music from the story and choreograph all performance on a diegetic stage—the seedy Kit Kat Club (except for "Tomorrow Belongs to Me")—was not, however, a completely new or original idea. *Cabaret* borrowed its structure from the backstage musicals of the 1930's, where the song and dance routines were also separated from the narrative and occurred on a theatrical stage. *Cabaret* differed in that its production numbers never left the stage upon which they were set, and more significantly, served not as essentially irrelevant musical fantasies, but as grim metaphors and commentaries on the action of the story. This separation was the beginning of a contemporary drive towards a new "realism" or, to paraphrase Fosse, "plausible believability" in the movie musical.

Based on Christopher Isherwood's collection of short stories, *Goodbye to Berlin* (1939), John van Druten's drama *I Am A Camera* (1951), and musical play *Cabaret* (1966), the film dealt with the decadence of the last days of the Weimar Republic and the ensuing rise of Nazism. Gone is the sweetness and light of Rodgers and Hammerstein and the happiness and *joie-de-vivre* of MGM. In its place, a tough, satirical, bitter, and diamond-edged look at the sensual power of decadence and its mothering of fascism. *Cabaret* is akin to Brecht and Weill's *The Threepenny Opera* and as such, according to Stephen Farber, "...deserves to be called the first adult musical...."

Cabaret won 3 Golden Globe Awards, was listed as the best film of 1972 by the National Board of Review, and won 8 Academy Awards. Not only was it a critical success, but a financial one as well: it broke sales records in New York City and Boston and was the #8 money-making film of 1972.

—Greg S. Faller

DAS CABINET DES DR. CALIGARI. Das Kabinett Des Doktors Caligari. The Cabinet of Dr. Caligari. Production: Decla Filmgellschaft (Berlin); black and white, 35mm, silent, originally tinted in green, brown, and steely-blue; length: 4682 feet. Released February 1920, Berlin.

Produced by Erich Pommer; screenplay by Carl Mayer and Hans Janowitz; from an original story by Carl Mayer and Hans Janowitz; directed by Robert Wiene; photography by Willy Hameister; production design by Hermann Warm, Walter Reimann, and Walter Röhrig; costumes designed by Walter Reimann. Filmed winter 1919 in Decla studios; cost: $18,000.

Cast: Werner Krauss (*Dr. Caligari*); Conrad Veidt (*Cesare*); Friedrich Feher (*Francis*); Lil Dagover (*Jane*); Hans Heinz von Twardowski (*Alan*); Rudolf Lettinger (*Dr. Olsen*); Rudolph Klein-Rogge (*Criminal*).

Publications:

Scripts—*Films of Tyranny* (shot description) by Richard B. Byrne, Madison, Wisconsin 1966; *The Cabinet of Dr. Caligari* translated and description of action by R.V. Adkinson, New York 1972; *Masterworks of the German Cinema* (script), New York 1974; "*Le Cabinet du Docteur Caligari*" (plus photos) by Carl Mayer in *L'Avant-Scène du cinéma* (Paris), July/September 1975; books—*From Caligari to Hitler: A Psychological History of the German Film* by Siegfried Kracauer, Princeton, New Jersey 1947; *50 Years of German Cinema* by Hans H. Wollenberg, London 1948; *The Sociology of Film Art* by George A. Huaco, New York 1965; *The Great Films: 50 Golden Years of Motion Pictures* by Bosley Crowther, New York 1967; *The Haunted Screen* by Lotte Eisner, Berkeley 1969; *The German Cinema* by Roger Manvell and Heinrich Fraenkel, New York 1971; *Weimar: A Cultural History 1918-1933* by Walter Laqueur, New York 1974; *Classics of the Horror Film* by William K. Everson, Secaucus, New Jersey 1974; articles—"Caligari" by Siegfried Kracauer in *Partisan Review* (New Brunswick, New Jersey), March/April 1947; "Aspects of War and Revolution in the Theater and Film of the Weimar Republic" by William Melnitz in *Hollywood Quarterly*, no.3, 1948-49; "*The Cabinet of Dr. Caligari*" by Jerome Ashmore in *College Art Journal*, summer 1950; article by Herbert Luft in *Quarterly of Film, Radio, and Television* (Berkeley), summer 1954; "Caligari: Its Innovations in Editing" by C. Denis Pegge in *Quarterly of Film,* *Radio, and Television* (Berkeley), winter 1956; "From *Caligari* to *Caligari*" by Herb A. Lightman in *American Cinematographer* (Hollywood), July 1962; "Expressionism in the Cinema" by Frank Whitford in *Studio International* (Lugano), January 1970; "Robert Wiene czyli pozory niefilmowości" by A. Helman in *Kino* (Warsaw), April 1974; "Historique du film" in *L'Avant-Scène du cinéma* (Paris), July/September 1975; "Caligari et la critique" in *L'Avant-Scène du cinéma* (Paris), July/September 1975; "Les Charlatans et les hysteriques" by Catherine Clément in *Communications* (Paris), no.23, 1975; "Die Scharlatane und die Hysteriker" by C.B. Clément in *Filmkritik* (Munich), March 1977; "*Kabinett des Dr. Caligari, Das*" by R. Combs in *Monthly Film Bulletin* (London), June 1979; "Retrospective Narration in Film: Re-Reading *The Cabinet of Dr. Caligari*" by M. Budd in *Film Criticism* (Edinboro, Pennsylvania), no.1, 1979; "*The Cabinet of Dr. Caligari*" by M. Budd in *Ciné-tracts* (Montreal), winter 1981.

*   *   *

The Cabinet of Dr. Caligari is usually identified as the first significant German Expressionist film, exemplifying the narrative and visual traits of that movement. The primary story concerns a series of murders which occur in a German town, coinciding with the arrival of Dr. Caligari who runs a side-show at the local fair. Alan and Francis, friends and rivals for the affection of the same woman, Jane, witness his show; there the somnambulist Cesare predicts the future, and forecasts Alan's impending death. That night, Alan is murdered. Francis pursues the mysterious Caligari as Cesare kidnaps Jane. In the ensuing chase, Cesare collapses and dies. The investigation then leads to a local asylum from which Cesare has reportedly escaped. Dr. Caligari is discovered to be the director of the hospital, gone mad in his obsessive efforts to re-enact an 18th century showman's murders-by-proxy. This story is presented as the narrative account of Francis. The film opens in a park; Francis sits with another man as Jane, in a trance-like state, walks by. To explain her condition, Francis recounts the bizarre events of central story. At the end of the film, the scene returns to Francis, who is revealed to be an inmate at the asylum. His doctor is actually the Caligari figure from his tale. Upon hearing Francis's ravings in the courtyard, the doctor declares that he now understands the case.

The history of the framing device is well known, and is discussed by Siegfried Kracauer in his study of post-World War I German cinema, *From Caligari to Hitler*. It was not a part of the initial script, by Carl Mayer and Hans Janowitz, but was presumably added by the producer Erich Pommer. According to Kracauer this framing contrivance served to contain the inherent horror of the original story. A study of authoritative madness and abusive power was recast as the delusion of an insane narrator; the evil doctor was re-defined as a benign, ministering figure who can cure the lunatic. At the same time Kracauer sees the final film as a powerful expression of the inherent tensions of the collective German psyche of the period—the fear that individual freedom will lead to rampant chaos which can only be constrained by submission to tyrannical authority. If the original script depicted the potential abuses of absolute authority, the framing scenes concede to this authority and suggest it may be beneficial.

But the narrative significance of the film is not necessarily an either/or proposition as Kracauer suggests. The film does start by presenting Francis as a credible narrator. His reliability as a source is only called into question in the final scenes. In this sense the film is more equivocal and expresses a more disturbed sensibility than even Kracauer allows. Indeed, the film simultaneously presents at least two viewpoints on the depicted events: 1) Francis is in fact mad and his story totally or partially delusional; 2) Francis is a reliable source, a position assumed through most of the film. From this second perspective the director of the asylum might be considered a psychotic tyrant whose power extends to include Francis' confinement. One is not, however, led directly to this conclusion. Rather, this version of the narrative causes a disruption of any stable or conclusive perception of character status and narrational authority within the film. This in turn opens the film to a range of possible readings. The film has been seen, for example, in terms of a female fantasy, focusing on Jane as the enigmatic source of the narrative.

In other words, the film is structured in such a way that it represents contradictory ways of understanding the central sequence of events. This is supported by the consistency of the film's mise-en-scene. The artificiality and stylized exaggeration of acting, decor, and lighting are maintained throughout the film. There are no visual cues to indicate that the world of the framed tale of past events is different from the framing scenes in the asylum. The film's visual style is crucial to its exemplary status within the context of the German Expressionist film movement. In *The Haunted Screen* Lotte Eisner explains that the overall design scheme of the film creates a pervasive feeling of anxiety and terror. It is characterized by extreme contrasts in light and dark, distorted angles, exaggerated perspective and scalar relations within the decor, and painted backdrops and shadows. The basic tone of the decor extends to costume and make-up.

These qualities came to be known as the defining stylistic trait of German Expressionist film. Some critics have argued that German film producers consciously adopted this "arty" style to differentiate German film from other national cinemas (notably American) in order to compete in the international film market. Others have stressed the fact that this movement expresses the troubled state of the German national psyche after the war, or represents a retreat to Romantic despair. In addition, the film's artificiality and subversion of realistic codes of representation have led to discussion of the film as an early example of self-reflexivity and deconstructive processes in the cinema.

The film's equivocal narrative and visual stylization combine to create a disturbing fictional world. Moreover, its position in German cinema, and in German history, makes it a compelling case for examining relations between films and their social context. In these terms *The Cabinet of Dr. Caligari* provides a wealth of material to be mined by film critics and historians.

—M.B. White

CABIRIA. Production: Itala Film (Turin); black and white, 35mm, silent; running time: originally 210 mins.; length: originally 14,746 feet, later versions cut to 8345 feet. Released 18 April 1914, Turin.

Screenplay by Giovanni Pastrone and Gabriele D'Annunzio (though D'Annuzio's contributions to the script were reportedly minimal if not non-existent); titles by Gabriele d'Annunzio; directed by Giovanni Pastrone (under the name Piero Fosco); photography by Segundo de Chomon, Giovanni de Chomon, Giovanni Tomatis, Augusto Batagliotti, and Natale Chiusano; musical score which originally accompanied the film by Ildebrando Pizzetti; literary and dramatic advisor: Gabriele D'Annunzio.

Filmed 1913 in Turin on specially constructed sets; exteriors shot in Tunisia, Sicily, and the Alps. Cost: 1 million lire ($100,000).

Cast: Italia Almirante Manzini (*Sophonisba*); Vitale de Stefano (*Massinissa*); Bartolomeo Pagano (*Maciste*); Lidia Quaranta (*Cabiria*); Umberto Mozzato (*Fulvio Axilla*); Enrico Gemelli (*Archimedes*); Alex Bernard (*Siface*); Raffaele di Napoli (*Bodastoret*); Luigi Chellini (*Scipione*); Ignazio Lupi (*Arbace*).

Publications:

reviews—in *Bioscope*, 30 April 1914; review in *Kine Monthly Film Record*, June 1914; review in *Kine Monthly Film Record*, July 1915; books—*The Italian Cinema* by Vernon Jarratt, London 1951; *The Silent Cinema* by Liam O'Leary, London 1965; *Cinema, The Magic Vehicle: A Guide to Its Achievement: Journey One: The Cinema Through 1949* edited by Adam Garbicz and Jacek Klinowski, Metuchen, New Jersey 1975; *Cabiria*, the Museo Nazionale del Cinema Torino, Turin 1977; *A History of Narrative Film* by David Cook, New York 1981; articles—in *Bianco e nero* (Rome), July/August 1952; "*Cabiria e Intolerance* tra il serio e il faceto by A. Bellucio in *Bianco e nero* (Rome), summer 1975; "Pastrone e Griffith: mito di un rapporto" by F. Montesanti in *Bianco e nero* (Rome), summer 1975; "G.P. and D.W.G.: il dare e l'avere" by D. Turconi in *Biance e nero* (Rome), summer 1975; "Discours de l'ideologie, ideologie du discours" by A. Cugier in *Cahiers de la cinématheque* (Perpignan, France), no.26-27, 1979; article in *Classic Images* (Indiana, Pennsylvania), July 1982.

*   *   *

Standing out from all the stumbling efforts toward a new expression of cinema, Giovanni Pastrone's story of the 2nd Punic War, *Cabiria*, demands special attention. Compared to the other colossal Italian spectacles of its time, it had an integrity and sense of purpose. From the beginning it was regarded as something special, and its premiere at the Teatro Vittorio Emanuele, Turin, on the 18th April 1914 was a great occasion. The Film's accompanying score by Ildebrando Pizzetti, performed by an orchestra of 80 and a choir of 70, added to the excitement. Looking at the film today it has lost little of its epic poetry to the Zeitgeist, though the acting performances may seem dated.

This story of a young girl lost amidst the clashes of two great nations retains its human interest as well as its power to amaze and astonish. The association of Gabriele d'Annunzio's name with the film reminds us of his dictum, "The Cinema should give spectators fantastic visions, lyric catastrophies and marvels born of the most audacious imagination," though in fact, d'Annunzio's actual contribution to this film was very little. He was paid a large sum for the use of his name in promotion. What does bear his mark are the highly poeticized sub-titles which are a part of the film's continuity, as they harmonize style and feeling with the images. The film is consistently and stylishly in the grand manner. When the servant describes Massinissa to her mistress Sophonisba she says, "He is like a wind from the desert bringing the scent of dust and lions and the message of Astarte." Few film heros have had such a build-up.

Apart from the magnificence of the sets and the pulsating action of the story, the film is important for the patient research that produced such striking results and gave conviction to the historical setting. The great Temple of Moloch must have been one of the largest structures for a film up to that time. It and the

Carthaginian palaces certainly influenced Griffith's Babylon in *Intolerance*. Infinite pains were taken with details which fitted effectively into the vast canvas.

Technically the film is also remarkable for its photography by the Spaniard, Segundo de Chomon. The use of the moving camera has never been so effective in its almost imperceptible transitions. Every device of camera craft is used to produce a smoothly flowing narrative.

There is so much richness in this film: the great scenes of Hannibal crossing the Alps with his army and elephants; the eruption of Etna; and the destruction of the Roman fleet at Syracuse by means of the sun-reflectors of Archimedes. Most of these effects were achieved by multiple exposure. The acting is fairly theatrical, but the performances of Italia Almirante Manzini as Sophonisba and Vitale de Stafano as Massinissa are moving and impressive, while Bartolomeo Pagano, as Maciste the strong man, adds a new figure to the mythology of the movies. *Cabiria* therefore stands as a major filmic achievement at a time when the cinema was fighting for its place among the other arts.

—Liam O'Leary

LA CADUTA DEGLI DEI. The Damned. The Fall of the Gods. Götterdämmerung. Production: Pegaso Film-Italnolggio (Italy), Eichberg Film-Praesidens (West Germany); Eastmancolor, 35mm; running time: 164 mins., English version: 155 mins. Released December 1969.

Produced by Alfredo Levy and Ever Haggiag, executive producer: Pietro Notarianni; screenplay by Nicola Badalucco, Enrico Medioli, and Luchino Visconti; directed by Luchino Visconti; photography by Armando Nannuzzi and Pasquale De Santis; edited by Ruggero Mastroianni; sound mixed by Renato Cadueri, recording directed by Vittorio Trentino; art direction by Pasquale Romano, set designed by Enzo Del Prato; music composed and directed by Maurice Jarre; special effects by Aldo Gasparri; costumes designed by Piero Tosi and Vera Marzot.

Cast: Dirk Bogarde (*Friedrich Bruckmann*); Ingrid Thulin (*Baroness Sophie von Essenbeck*); Helmut Griem (*Aschenbach*); Helmut Berger (*Martin von Essenbeck*); Charlotte Rampling (*Elisabeth Thallman*); Florinda Bolkan (*Olga*); Reinhard Kolldehoff (*Baron Konstantin von Essenbeck*); Umberto Orsini (*Herbert Thallman*); Albrecht Schönhals (*Baron Joachim von Essenbeck*); Renaud Verley (*Guenther von Essenbeck*); Nora Rici (*Governess*); Irina Wanka (*Lisa Keller*); Valentina Ricci (*Thilde Thallman*); Karin Mittendorf (*Erika Thallman*); Peter Dane (*Steelworks employee*); Wolfgang Hillinger (*Yanek*); Bill Vanders (*Commissar*); Howard Nelson Rubien (*Rector*); Werner Hasselmann (*Gestapo official*); Mark Salvage (*Police inspector*); Karl Otto Alberty, John Frederick, Richard Beach (*Army officers*); Claus Höhne, Ernst Kühr (*SA officers*); Wolfgang Ehrlich (*SA soldier*); Esterina Carloni and Antonietta Fiorita (*Chambermaids*); Jessica Dublin (*Nurse*).

Publications:

Script—*Caduta degli dei* by Nicola Badalucco, Enrico Medioli, and Luchino Visconti, Capelli 1969; reviews—by Andrew Sarris in *The Village Voice* (New York), 18 December 1969; review by Norman Cecil in *Films in Review* (New York), February 1970; review in *Film Society Review* (New York), February 1970; books—*Visconti* by Giuseppe Ferrara, translated by Jean-Pierre Pinaud, Paris, 2nd ed. 1970; *A Discovery of Cinema* by Thorold Dickinson, Toronto, 1971; *Luchino Visconti* by Pio Baldelli, Milan, Italy 1973; *Visconti: il cinema*, edited by Adelio Ferrero, Modena, Italy 1977; *Maestri del cinema* by Pietro Bianchi, Milan, Italy 1977; *Album Visconti* edited by Lietta Tornabuoni, foreword by Michelangelo Antonioni, Milan, Italy 1978; *A Screen of Time: A Study of Luchino Visconti* by Monica Stirling, New York 1979; articles—by John Hofsess in *Take One* (Montreal), May/June 1969; "Visconti's *The Damned*: Words, Sights, Echoes" by J. Fischer in *Contempora*, October/November 1970; article by Gary Crowdus in *Film Society Review* (New York), February 1970; article by Brenda Davies in *Films and Filming* (London), May 1970; article by David Wilson in *Sight and Sound* (London), winter 1969-70; *The Damned*: Visconti, Wagner, and the Reinvention of Reality" by Margaret Tarratt in *Screen* (London), summer 1970; issue of *Cinema* (Rome) devoted to Visconti, April 1970; "Marxism and Formalism in the Films of Luchino Visconti" by Walter F. Korte in *Cinema Journal* (Evanston, Illinois), fall 1971; "Fascism in the Contemporary Film" by Joan Mellen in *Film Quarterly* (Berkeley), summer 1971; "Ingrid Thulin Comments on Visconti" in *Dialogue on Film* (Washington, D.C.), no.3, 1972; "A tragédia alkonya" by J. Marx in *Filmkultura* (Budapest), November/December 1973; "Visconti's Magnificent Obsessions" by D. Lyons in *Film Comment* (New York), March/April 1979.

* * *

The legacy of neorealism, deriving from a combination of the "realism" inherent in that movement and the lingering influence of early Italian spectacles, centers on a cinema at once passionately political and lyrical. While history has indelibly marked Roberto Rossellini and Vittorio DeSica as the fathers of neorealism, Luchino Visconti, while less prolific, must also be counted among its progenitors—his directorial debut with *Ossessione* being a landmark production of neorealism.

Though born into one of Italy's most aristocratic families, Visconti was influenced by Communism at an early age, and a recurring theme throughout his work has been "moral disintegration" of the family unit. This dichotomy of the aristocracy versus the proletariat, coupled with his love of the florid artifice of opera, made his films a unique combination of the baroque and the naturalistic.

With *The Damned*, Visconti adopted Acton's dictum that "all power corrupts, and absolute power corrupts absolutely." The result is his most controversial film mostly due to the repellent and fascinating subject matter: homosexuality, pedophilia, transvestism, incest and Nazism. Through the microcosm of the von Essenbecks, a Krupp-like munitions dynasty, Visconti endeavored to portray the decadence which gave rise to Nazi Germany during 1933-34. In his own words, "I want to ask in this picture where lay the responsibility for the Nazis in Germany. The most grave responsibility was with the bourgeoisie the industrialists, because if Hitler had not had their help, he would never have arrived to real power. Books say that the Krupps paid Hitler, so I don't invent. And I like in all my films to have a *cellula* of humanity, a family. I try to explain in the development of this family the parallel of what happens in all Germany and later in all the world. That is all I try to say. I don't know if I shall manage to say it." Drawing upon *Macbeth*, *Hamlet*, Thomas Mann's *Buddenbrooks*, The *Nibelungenlied*, Dostoyevsky's *The Possessed* and *Oedipus Rex*, Visconti fashioned a view of Nazi power in his inimitable grand operatic style.

The film's opening birthday party sequence coincides with the burning of the Reichstag, and the dramatic highlight of the film is Visconti's depiction of the "night of the long knives" on June 30, 1934, when Roehm and his S.A. Brown Shirts were massacred at the Hotel Hanselbauer in Wiesse, a lakeside resort near Munich. This homosexual orgy has become the most famous scene in the Visconti *oeuvre*. While the rest of the film is shot in English, this lengthy, 15-minute sequence is shot in German with English subtitles.

Despite the "X" rating, or possibly because of it, *The Damned* was the first of two Visconti films, the other being *Death in Venice*, to be successful in the U.S. outside the art house circuit. *The Damned* received very mixed reviews with many critical of its attempt to equate sexual perversion with the rise of Nazism, an interpretation obviously too simplistic. Visconti meant the corruption of the von Essenbeck family to be metaphor for Nazism and not an explanation in itself. The American distributor had no qualms in advertising the film with a poster showing Helmut Berger, in his Marlene Dietrich drag, with the capiton: "He was soon to become the second most powerful man in Nazi Germany."

The film received an Academy Award nomination for Best Original Screenplay and cited among the year's ten-best by *The New York Times*. While the cast is generally excellent throughout, some critics felt the great variety of international accents prevented the characters from seeming homogenously German. Helmut Griem, who is German, was praised by most critics and Helmut Berger caused *The New York Times'* Vincent Canby to opine, "(He) gives, I think, the performance of the year."

—Ronald Bowers

CAMILLE. Production: Metro-Goldwyn-Mayer Pictures Corp.; 1936; black and white, 35mm; running time: 115 mins., some sources state 108 mins. Released 1936.

Produced by Irving G. Thalberg, some sources list David Lewis as producer; screenplay by Zoe Akins, Frances Marion, and James Hilton; from the novel and play *La Dame aux camélias* by Alexandre Dumas (fils); directed by George Cukor; photography by William Daniels and Karl Freund; edited by Margaret Booth; music by Herbert Stothart; costumes designed by Adrian.

Filmed in the MGM studios. New York Film Critics' Award, Best Actress (Garbo), 1937.

Cast: Greta Garbo (*Marguerite Gautier/Camille*); Robert Taylor (*Armand Duval*); Lionel Barrymore (*Monsieur Duval*); Henry Daniell (*Baron de Varville*); Lenore Ulric (*Olympe*); Jessie Ralph (*Nanine*); Laura Hope Crews (*Prudence Duvernoy*); Elizabeth Allan (*Nichette*); Russell Hardie (*Gustave*).

Publications:

Books—*Garbo* by John Bainbridge, New York 1955; *Hommage à George Cukor* by Henri Langlois and others, Paris 1963; *The Films of Greta Garbo* by Michael Conway, Dion McGregor, and Mark Ricci, New York 1963; *George Cukor* by Jean Domarchi, Paris 1965; *Greta Garbo* by Raymond Durgnat and

John Kobal, New York 1965; *The Great Films: Fifty Golden Years of Motion Pictures* by Bosley Crowther, New York 1967; *Cukor and Company: The Films of George Cukor and His Collaborators* by Gary Carey, New York 1971; *Greta Garbo* by Richard Corliss, New York 1974; *George Cukor* by Carlos Clarens, London 1976; *George Cukor* by Gene Phillips, Boston 1982; articles—"How Cukor Directs Garbo" in *Lion's Roar* (Hollywood), November 1941; "The Career of Greta Garbo" by Theodore Huff in *Films in Review* (New York), December 1951; "Garbo" by Kenneth Tynan in *Sight and Sound* (London), spring 1954; "Camille" by Derek Prouse in *Sight and Sound* (London), summer 1955; "George Cukor: His Success Directing Women Has Obscured His Other Directorial Virtues" by Romano Tozzi in *Films in Review* (New York), February 1958; "George Cukor" by Romano Tozzi in *Films in Review* (New York), February 1958; "Gish and Garbo—the Executive War on Stars" by Louise Brooks in *Sight and Sound* (London), winter 1958-59; "So He Became a Lady's Man" by John Reid in *Films and Filming* (London), August 1960; "Women and Still More Women" by John Reid in *Films and Filming* (London), September 1960; "George Cukor: de Garbo à Marilyn il a instauré le Star-System", interview by Gilbert Guez, in *Cinémonde* (Paris), 1 January 1963; "Garbo—How Good Was She?" by Richard Whitehall in *Films and Filming* (London), September 1963; "Robert Taylor" by Ronald Bowers in *Films in Review* (New York), January 1963; "Retrospective Cukor" issue of *Cahiers du Cinéma* (Paris), February 1964; "George Cukor" by Charles Higham in *London Magazine*, May 1965; "Conversation with George Cukor" by John Gillett and David Robinson in *Sight and Sound* (London), autumn 1965; "Greta Garbo's Secret" by Carl Eric Nordberg in *Film Comment* (New York), summer 1970; "George Cukor: An Interview" by Gene Phillips in *Film Comment* (New York), spring 1972; "George Cukor ou comment le désir vient aux femmes" by M. Grisolia in *Cinéma* (Paris), February 1974; "Dialogue on Film: George Cukor" edited by James Powers in *American Film* (Washington, D.C.), February 1978; "Camille" by DeWitt Bodeen in *Magill's Survey of Cinema, Vol. 1* edited by Frank N. Magill, Englewood Cliffs, New Jersey 1980; "George Cukor" by DeWitt Bodeen in *Films in Review* (New York), November 1981; "Le Roman de Marguerite Gautier" by D. Païni in *Cinéma* (Paris), May 1981.

*   *   *

Garbo's *Camille* not only contains her best screen performance, but hers remains the definitive Camille. No actress in her right mind would dare do a re-make, because she would be inviting comparisons with the Garbo performance, which would not be to her advantage. In fact, some years ago, when Tallulah Bankhead was asked, along with other stars of the stage, to name what she considered the greatest of all theatrical performances, she led off instantly with "Garbo in *Camille*," and no one argued her choice.

The role of Camille has always been thought of as the supreme test for the dramatic actress, just as Hamlet has become "a consummation devoutly wished" for the actor. As a character, she not only runs the gamut of emotion, she explores every facet of all emotion. Cukor saw *Camille* again after a long period of time, and remarked of Garbo's performance: "I was staggered...her lightness of touch...the wantonness, the perversity of the way she played Camille, she played it as if she were the author of her own misery." Even Irving Thalberg, seeing her performance, remarked that she had never been so good. It was the scene where she sits in a box in the theatre, and Cukor demurred, "Irving, how can you tell? She's just sitting there," to which

Thalberg remarked, "I know, but she's *unguarded*." The key to her entire performance of Marguerite Gautier, the Parisian cocotte known among her coterie as "Camille," can be summed up in that one word—"unguarded," held safe against all time. It was in the finest tradition of thoughtful restraint in acting for the camera.

In the theatre, the story of Marguerite Gautier has been acted by all the greats, including Eleonora Duse and Sarah Bernhardt. On the screen, its various versions starred such actresses as Clara Kimball Young, Theda Bara, Nazimova, Norma Talmadge. American actresses resisted it as a talking role. Garbo alone, with Cukor's faith in her, wanted to do the part, knowing that it could be her greatest, and it was. Henry James wrote of the story that it had been written by Alexander Dumas *fils* when he was only 25, and added: "The play has been blown about the world at a fearful rate, but has never lost its happy juvenility, a charm that nothing can vulgarize...It is all champagne and tears, fresh perversity, fresh credulity, fresh passion, fresh pain...It carries with it an April air!"

In 1855, an American actress Matilda Heron, was in Paris, and saw *La Dame aux Camellias* played there. She made her own acting version, called it *Camille*, or *The Fate of a Coquette*, and played it all over the English-speaking world. She married and gave birth to a daughter known as Bijou Heron, who married Henry Miller. Their son, Gilbert Miller, was one of the best producers Broadway and London ever knew. The stories surrounding *Camille* onstage and in films are endless, and involve nearly every important player's name. Either as *Camille* or as *The Lady of the Camellias*, it has been played by all the best actresses from Tallulah Bankhead to Ethel Barrymore, from Eva Le Gallienne to Lillian Gish, so that what they created onstage was revealed in the performance Garbo brought to the screen.

With her the part became not just about a heroine who lives well but unwisely; she became a beautiful worldly creature fated to find real love with a young man, whom she deserts because she knows that in staying with him, she is ruining his life. The lovers are reunited on her deathbed, and the audience is always dissolved in to tears. Seeing Garbo's death scene, an admirer remarked, "What a pity that Garbo had to die! We shan't see her again." After that last fadeout, it was not easy to believe that at least two of Garbo's best roles were still ahead, with her performances as Marie Waleska, Napoleon's love, in *Conquest*, and as the title role in Lubitsch's *Ninotchka*.

Camille, however, remained her triumph for all time. It was her finest hour.

—DeWitt Bodeen

CARROSSE D'OR, LE. The Golden Coach. Il Carozzo d'ore. Production: Panaria Films and Roche Productions; Technicolor, 35mm; running time: 100 mins., some sources list 98 mins.; length: 2800 meters. Released 27 February 1953, Paris.

Produced by Francesco Alliata and Ray Ventura; screenplay by Jean Renoir, Renzo Avenzo, Giulio Macchi, Jack Kirkland, and Ginette Doynel; from the work *Le Carrosse du Saint-Sacrement* by Prosper Mérimée; directed by Jean Renoir; photography by Claude Renoir and Ronald Hill; edited by Mario Serandrei and David Hawkins; sound by Joseph de Bretagne and Ovidio del Grande, recorded by Mario Ronchetti; production design by Mario Chiari with De Gianni and Polidori; music by Vivaldi, Archangelo Corelli, and Olivier Metra, arranged by Gino Marinuzzi; costumes designed by Mario de Matteis.

Filming began 4 February 1952 in Cinecitta studios.

Cast: Anna Magnani (*Camilla/Colombine*); Duncan Lamont (*Ferdinand, the Viceroy*); Odoardo Spadaro (*Don Antonio, the head of the troupe*); Riccardo Rioli (*Ramon*); Paul Campbell (*Felipe Aquirre*); Nada Fiorelli (*Isabelle*); Georges Higgins (*Martinez*); Dante (*Arlequin*); Rino (*Doctor Balanzon*); Gisela Mathews (*Irène Altamirano*); Lina Marengo (*Comedienne*); Ralph Truman (*Duke of Castro*); Elena Altieri (*Duchess of Castro*); Renato Chiantoni (*Captain Fracasse*); Giulio Tedeschi (*Balthazar, the barber*); Alfredo Kolner (*Florindo*); Alfredo Medini (*Pulcinella*); John Pasetti (*Captain of the Guard*); William Tubbs (*Innkeeper*); Cecil Matthews (*Baron*); Fredo Keeling (*Viscount*); Jean Debucourt (*Bishop of Carmol*); Raf de la Torre (*Procurer*); Medini Brothers (*4 children*); Juan Perez.

Publications:

books—*Jean Renoir* by Paul Davay, Brussels 1957; *Jean Renoir* by Armand-Jean Cauliez, Paris 1962; *Analyses des films de Jean Renoir*, Institut des Hautes Etudes Cinématographiques, Paris 1966; *Jean Renoir* by Pierre Leprohon, Paris 1967; *Jean Renoir und seine Film: eine Dokumentation* compiled and edited by Ulrich Gregor, Bad Ems 1970; *Humanidad de Jean Renoir* by Carlos Cuenca, Valladolid, Mexico 1971; *Jean Renoir: The World of his Films* by Leo Braudy, New York 1972; *Jean Renoir* by André Bazin, edited by François Truffaut, Paris, translated ed. 1973; *Jean Renoir* by Raymond Durgnat, Berkeley 1974; *Jean Renoir: le spectacle, la vie* by Claude Beylie, Paris 1975; *Jean Renoir: Essays, Conversations, Reviews* by Penelope Gilliatt, New York 1975; *Jean Renoir: A Guide to References and Resources* by Christopher Faulkner, Boston 1979; articles—special Renoir issue, *Cahiers du Cinéma* (Paris), January 1952; "Commedia all'improviso" by Jean de Baroncelli in *Le Monde* (Paris), 4 March 1953; "Je n'ai pas tourné mon film au Pérou" by Jean Renoir in *Radio-Cinéma* (Paris), 15 March 1953; article by Georges Sadoul in *Les Lettres françaises* (Paris), 5 March 1953; special Renoir issue, *Cahiers du cinéma* (Paris), Christmas 1957; "The Renaissance of the French Cinema—Feydor, Renoir, Duvivier, Carné" by Georges Sadoul in *Film: An Anthology* edited by Daniel Talbot, New York 1959; "Renoir and Realism" by Peter John Dyer in *Sight and Sound* (London), summer 1960; "Why Renoir Favors Multiple Camera, Long Sustained Take Technique" by Jean Belanger in *American Cinematographer* (Los Angeles), March 1960; article by Richard Whitehall on Renoir's films in *Films and Filming* (London), June 1960 and July 1960; "Gallery of Great Artists: Anna Magnani" by Richard Whitehall in *Films and Filming* (London), July 1961; "Theater Life Film" by G. Petrie in *Film Comment* (New York), May/-June 1974; "Smukke Marie" by I. Lindberg in *Kosmorama* (Copenhagen), October 1980.

*   *   *

Jean Renoir regarded *Le Carrossse d'or* as a mere *feux d'esprit*, but in fact the film, while one of Renoir's lighter efforts, has been greatly underrated. Its *commedia dell'arte*-inspired picturesqueness encompasses one of Renoir's lifelong themes—the disaffinity between illusion and reality, life and theatre, what people really are versus the roles they play. Most important to the creative sensibility of Renoir the artist, the film concerns the artist's duty to give, not take, and by doing so he experiences his greatest power and true humanity.

The film based on Prosper Merimee's one-act play, *Le Carrosse du Saint-Sacrement* which derived from a real-life Peruvian incident. Merimee's play was also the inspiration for an episode in Thornton Wilder's *The Bridge of San Luis Rey*.

On the surface, *Le Carrosse d'or* is a simple story of love, but Renoir gives it a Pirandellian twist with its confusion of identities while restoring new meaning to Shakespeare's phrase, "All the world's a stage." The plot centers around Camilla (Anna Magnani), the Columbine of a troupe of traveling theatre players in 18th century Peru, and her three loves: the Peruvian viceroy, a matador, and a young Spanish nobleman/soldier. The viceroy has just incurred the wrath and envy of his court and the church council by importing a golden coach from Europe. As Renoir stated, "In Merimee's play, La Perichole is an actress, and in my movie, Camilla is an actress. In the play and in the film the coach stands for world vanity, and in both works the conclusion is precipitated by the bishop." As was his practice, Renoir used his scripts as a starting point, then wove the plot around his own special view of life and human nature.

Here Renoir's point was to present a serio-comic masque, referring to the game of appearances, as the true basis for all human activity. In a play within a play within a film, Camilla plays at love. She becomes the center of attention when the viceroy presents the coach to her as a gift, an act he hopes will dissipate the jealousies of his court. Camilla wears a variety of faces as she waivers between her three romantic choices: she can opt for the life of luxury with the viceroy; she can choose a simpler life among the Peruvian Indians with the faithful soldier; or she can elect a volatile relationship with the adored and fiery matador. But the *theatre* is her real life, her real love and she astonishes all three lovers by presenting the coach to the Bishop of Lima so it can be used to carry the last sacraments to the dying. Renouncing desire, she stands, alone, center stage as the curtain falls. When asked if she misses her three lovers, she replies wryly, "Just a little."

Le Carrosse d'or is the first of Renoir's three theatre films of the 1950s—the others being *French Cancan* and *Elena et les hommes*. In each he fills the stage/screen with a spectacle of action, sets and costumes, with a childlike glee at his powers of manipulation. In keeping with the *commedia dell'arte* flavor, he chose Vivaldi's music for its lightness of spirit making the music an integral part of the film.

Renoir drew forth the finest performance of Anna Magnani's career with this picture and called her "the greatest actress I have ever worked with." Her Camilla is a brilliant *tour de force. Le Carrosse d'or* is a charming film, and while minor Renoir, it is a testament to his warmth, good humor and sense of whimsy.

—Ronald Bowers

CASABLANCA. Production: Warner Bros. Pictures, Inc.; 1942; black and white, 35mm; running time: 102 mins. Released November 1942.

Produced by Hal B. Wallis; screenplay by Julius J. and Philip G. Epstein and Howard Koch, contributions by Aeneas Mackenzie and Hal Wallis among others; from an unpublished play *Everybody Comes to Rick's* by Murray Burnett and Joan Alison; directed by Michael Curtiz; photography by Arthur Edeson; edited by Owen Marks; sound by Francis J. Scheid; production design by Carl Jules Weyl, set decoration by George James Hopkins; music by Max Steiner, songs by Herman Hupfeld and M.K. Jerome; special effects by Laurence Butler and Willard Van Enger; costumes designed by Orry-Kelly (gowns); technical advisor: Robert Alsner; opening montage by Don Siegel.

Filmed at Warner Bros. studios. Academy Awards for Best Film, Best Director, and Best Screenplay, 1943.

Cast: Humphrey Bogart (*Rick*); Ingrid Bergman (*Ilsa Lund*); Paul Henreid (*Victor Laszlo*); Claude Rains (*Captain Louis Renault*); Conrad Veidt (*Major Strasser*); Sydney Greenstreet (*Senor Ferrari*); Peter Lorre (*Ugarte*); S.Z. Sakall (*Carl, a Waiter*); Madeleine LeBeau (*Yvonne*); Dooley Wilson (*Sam*); Joy Page (*Annina Brandel*); John Qualen (*Berger*); Leonid Kinsky (*Sascha, a Bartender*); Helmut Dantine (*Jan*); Curt Bois (*Pickpocket*); Marcel Dalio (*Croupier*); Corinna Mura (*Singer*); Ludwig Stössel (*Mr. Leuchtag*); Ilka Gruning (*Mrs. Leuchtag*); Charles La Torre (*Tonelli, the Italian officer*); Frank Puglia (*Arab vendor*); Dan Seymour (*Abdul*); Lou Marcelle (*Narrator*); Martin Garralaga (*Headwaiter*); Olaf Hytten (*Prosperous man*); Monte Blue (*American*); Paul Procasi (*Native*); Albert Morin (*French officer*); Creighton Hale (*Customer*); Henry Rowland (*German officer*); Richard Ryen (*Heinz*); Norma Varden (*Englishwoman*); Torben Meyer (*Banker*); Oliver Blake (*Blue Parrot waiter*); Gregory Gay (*German banker*); William Edmunds (*Contact*); George Meeker (*Friend*); George Dee (*Casselle*); Leo Mostovoy (*Fydor*); Leon Belasco (*Dealer*).

Publications:

Scripts—*Best Film Plays of 1943-44* edited by Dudley Nichols and John Gassner, New York 1945; *Casablanca: Script and Legend* (script plus other) by Howard Koch, Woodstock, New York 1973; *Michael Curtiz's 'Casablanca'* (partial script plus other) by Richard Anobile, New York 1975; books—*Hollywood Without Makeup* by Pete Martin, New York 1948; *My 1st 100 Years in Hollywood* by Jack Warner, New York 1965; *Bogey: The Films of Humphrey Bogart* by Clifford McCarty, New York 1965; *Humphrey Bogart: The Man and His Films* by Paul Michael, Indianapolis 1965; *Persistence of Vision: A Collection of Film Criticism* edited by Joseph McBride, Madison, Wisconsin 1968; *The Films of Ingrid Bergman* by Lawrence J. Quirk, New York 1970; *Favorite Movies: Critics' Choice* edited by Philip Nobile, New York 1972; *Humphrey Bogart* by Alan G. Barbour, New York 1973; *Ingrid Bergman* by Curtis F. Brown, New York 1973; *The Great Spy Pictures* edited by James Robert Parish and Michael R. Pitts, Metuchen, New Jersey 1974; articles—"Humphrey Bogart 1899-1957" by Clifford McCarty in *Films in Review* (New York), May 1957; "Epitaph for a Tough Guy" by Alistair Cooke in *Atlantic* (Greenwich, Connecticut), May 1957; "Peter Lorre" by Herbert Luft in *Films in Review* (New York), May 1960; "Likable but Elusive" by Andrew Sarris in *Film Culture* (New York), spring 1963; "Claude Rains" by Jeanne Stein in *Films in Review* (New York), November 1963; article by Harris Dienstfrey in *Film Culture* (New York), fall 1964; "Ingrid Bergman" by Ronald L. Bowers in *Films in Review* (New York), February 1968; article by Andrew Sarris in *The Village Voice* (New York), 8 January 1970; "Michael Curtiz" by Jack Edmund Nolan in *Films in Review* (New York), no.9, 1970; "It Lingers Deliciously in Memory as Time Goes By" by Leonid Kinsley in *Movie Digest*, September 1972; "Michael Curtiz" by Kingsley Canham in *The Hollywood Professionals, Vol. 1*, London 1973; short article in *Téléciné* (Paris), March 1973; "Casablanca" by M. Vernhes in *Cinéma* (Paris), March 1973; "The Cult Movies: Casablanca" by B. Day in *Films and Filming* (London), August 1974; interview with Ingrid Bergman in *Michael Curtiz's 'Casablanca'* by Richard Anobile, New York 1975; "*Casablanca* Revisted: 3 Comments" (letters to the editor) in *American Film* (Washington, D.C.), October 1976; "*Casablanca*" by L. Rubinstein in *Cineaste* (New York), summer 1977; "*The Maltese Falcon* and *Casablanca*" by D. McVay in *Focus on Film* (London), no.30, 1978; "*Casablanca*" by Dan Ackerman in *Cinema Texas Program Notes* (Austin), 5 September 1978; "Writing for the Movies: Casey Robinson" by J. Greenberg in *Focus on Film* (London), April 1979; "A Memory: *Casablanca* at the Rivoli" by W.J. Robson in *Classic Film Collector* (Indiana, Pennsylvania), September 1979; "*Casablanca*" by Stephen L. Hanson in *Magill's Survey of Cinema, Vol. 1* edited by Frank N. Magill, Englewood Cliffs, New Jersey 1980; "*Casablanca*" by A. Apon in *Skrien* (Amsterdam), March 1981.

* * *

"I have discovered the secret of successful filmmaking," says Claude Chabrol sarcastically, "Timing!" Casablanca belongs in the vanguard of films created by the era they so flawlessly reflect. Assured and expert, it is not in either substance or style superior to its director Michael Curtiz's *Mildred Pierce* or *Young Man With a Horn*. Bogart, Bergman. Rains and Henreid all gave better performances; of those by Greenstreet, Lorre, Kinsky and Sakall, one can only remark that they seldom gave any others. Producer Robert Lord categorized the story on the first reading as "a very obvious imitation of *Grand Hotel*"; Jerry Wald saw parallels with *Algiers*. Both were right.

Hal Wallis wanted George Raft to star and William Wyler to direct. Both declined. (There is some evidence he also planned it as a vehicle for the *Kings Row* team of Ronald Reagan and Ann Sheridan, with Dennis Morgan in the Henreid role. And both Lena Horne and Ella Fitzgerald had a chance at the singing part taken eventually by Dooley Wilson.) Vincent Sherman and William Keighley likewise refused the project before it went to Curtiz.

Casablanca might have joined *Sahara* and *Istanbul* on the shelf of back-lot travelogues had an Allied landing and summit conference in the north African city not coincided with the film's November 1942 release. Topicality fed its fame. Curtiz, accepting an unexpected Academy Award in March 1944, betrayed his surprise. "So many times I have a speech ready, but no dice. Always a bridesmaid, never a mother. Now I win, I have no speech." The broken English was entirely appropriate to a film where only Bogart and Dooley Wilson were of American origin.

Beyond its timing, *Casablanca* does show the Warners machine and Curtiz's talent at their tabloid best. The whirling glove of Don Siegel's opening montage and the portentous *March of Time* narration quickly define the city as a vision of the wartime world in microcosm. The collaborative screenplay, signed by Julius and Philip Epstein, and Howard Koch, but contributed to by, among others, Aeneas Mackenzie and Wallis himself (who came up with Bogart's final line) draws the characters in broad terms, each a compendium of national characteristics.

Bogart, chain-smoking, hard-drinking, arrogant, is the classic turned-off Hemingway American. Henreid, white-suited and courteous, is a dissident more akin to a society physician, untainted by either Communism or bad tailoring. The Scandinavian virgin, untouchable in pale linen and communicating mainly through a range of schoolgirl grins, Bergman's Ilsa succumbs to passion only when she pulls a gun on the unconcerned Rick, triggering not the weapon but a revival of their old affection.

The remaining regulars of Rick's Cafe Americain, mostly accented foreigners, dissipate their energies in Balkan bickering,

petty crime and, in the case of Claude Rains's self-satisfied Vichy policeman, some improbable lechery dictated by his role as the token naughty Frenchman, all moues and raised eyebrows. Cliche characterization leads to a range of dubious acts, notably the fawning Peter Lorre, an arch intriguer and murderer, entrusting his treasured "letters of transit" to Bogart's moralizing ex-gunrunner, a gesture exceeded in improbability only by Bogart's acceptance of them.

As with most formula films, technique redeems *Casablanca*. Arthur Edeson's camera cranes sinuously through Carl Jules Weyl's Omar Khayyam fantasy of a set. Typical of Curtiz's work is the razor-sharp "cutting on action" by Owen Marks, a legacy of the former's Hungarian and Austrian training. He forces the pace relentlessly, even to dissolving the back projection plate in mid-scene during the Parisian flash-back, an audacious piece of visual shorthand.

Narrative economy distinguishes the film. As its original material (an unproduced play by Murray Burnett and Joan Alison) suggests, *Casablanca* in structure is a one-set play; many events take place off-stage, from the murder of the couriers to the resistance meeting attended by Henreid and Sakall that is broken up by the police. *Everybody Comes to Rick's* is an apt title, since it's the ebb and flow of people through the cafe's doors that gives the story its sole semblance of vitality. As an entity, *Casablanca* lives on the artificial respiration of ceaseless greetings, introductions and farewells. Even the Parisian flashback does little to elucidate the characters of Rick and Ilsa. They remain at the end of the film little more than disagreeable maitre d' and troublesome patron.

In 1982, journalist Chuck Ross circulated *Casablanca*'s script as a new work to 217 American literary agents. Of those who acknowledged reading it (most returned it unread) 32 recognized the original, while 38 did not. Clearly this betrays the profound ignorance of the agenting community. But also implicit in their ignorance is *Casablanca*'s unsure standing as a work of art. Unremarkable in 1942, it rose to fame through an accident of timing. No better written or constructed today, it exists primarily as a cultural artifact, a monument of popular culture. Woody Allen was right in his *Play It Again Sam* to show the film as one whose morality, characters and dialogue can be adapted to social use; icons now, they transcend their original source. It is as folklore rather than as a cinematic masterwork that *Casablanca* is likely to survive.

—John Baxter

CASQUE D'OR. Production: Spéva Films and Paris-Film-Production; black and white, 35mm; running time: 96 mins. Released 16 April 1952, Paris.

Produced by Henri Baum; screenplay by Jacques Becker and Jacques Companéez; directed by Jacques Becker; photography by Robert Le Fèbvre; edited by Marguerite Renoir; sound engineered by Antoine Petitjean; art direction by Jean d'Eaubonne; music by Georges Van Parys; costumes designed by Mayo.

Filmed fall 1951 in Paris-Studio-Cinema studios at Billancourt; and at Annet-Sur-Marne, France.

Cast: Simone Signoret (*Marie*); Serge Reggiani (*Manda*); Claude Dauphin (*Félix Leca*); William Sabatier (*Roland*); Gaston Modot (*Danard*); Loleh Bellon (*Léonie Danard*); Paul Azais (*Ponsard*); Jean Clarieux (*Paul*); Roland Lesaffre (*Anatole*); Emile Genevois (*Billy*); Claude Castaing (*Fredo*); Daniel Mendaille (*Patron Guinguette*); Dominque Davray (*Julie*); Pierre Goutas (*Guillaume*); Fernand Trignol (*Patron of l'Ange Gabriel*); Paul Barge (*Inspector Juliani*); Leon Pauleon (*Conductor*); Tony Corteggiani (*Commissioner*); Roger Vincent (*Doctor*); Marcel Melrac (*Policeman*); Marcel Rouze (*Policeman*); Odette Barencey (*Adèle*); Yvonne Yma (*Patron of l'Ange Gabriel*); Paquerette (*Grandmother*); Pomme (*Concierge*).

Publications:

Scripts—"*Casque d'or*" (screenplay) by Jacques Becker and Jacques Companeez in *Avant-Scène du cinéma* (Paris), December 1964; books—*French Cinema Since 1946: Vol.I—The Great Tradition* by Roy Armes, New York 1970; *Cinema, the Magic Vehicle: A Guide To Its Achievement: Journey II* edited by Adam Garbicz and Jacek Klinowski, Metuchen, New Jersey 1979; articles—"The Stylist" by Catherine de la Roche in *Films and Filming* (London), March 1955; "Microscope Director" by Joseph Lisbona in *Films and Filming* (London), December 1956; "Becker" in *Sight and Sound* (London), spring 1960; "De Vraies Moustaches" by François Truffaut in *Avant-Scène du cinéma* (Paris), December 1964; "Jacques Becker: 2 Films" by Gilberto Perez Guillermo in *Sight and Sound* (London), summer 1969; "*Casque d'or*" by B. Amengual in *Cahiers de la Cinémathèque* (Perpignan, France), spring 1976.

*   *   *

The benign influence of Jean Renoir, with whom Jacques Becker worked for eight years as assistant director, can be clearly felt in the warm humanity that suffuses *Casque d'or*. Not that the film is in the least derivative; it is unmistakably a Becker film in its central concern with love and friendship (shown here as entirely complementary affections, not as opposed loyalties), and in its richly detailed evocation of period and milieu. The world of petty criminals and prostitutes in *fin-de-siècle* Paris is presented simply and directly—not romaticized, nor rendered gratuitously squalid, but seen as a complex, living community in its own right. And although the plot (based on a true story, which Becker found in court reports of the period) recounts a tragic sequence of treachery, murder, and death by guillotine, *Casque d'or* is far from depressing; on the contrary, its lasting impression is of optimism and affirmation.

This effect derives from the strength and veracity with which Becker delineates the film's central relationship. As Marie, from whose golden hair the film takes its title, Simone Signoret gives a performance of ripe sensuality, well matched by Serge Reggiani's Manda, convincingly revealing both tenderness and tenacity beneath an appearance of taciturn frailty. Their brief, sunlit idyll together in the countryside is shot through with an erotic intensity that eschews the least trace of prurience. That the power of such love can outlast even death is suggested by the film's final image, in which, after Marie has watched Manda die on the guillotine, we see the lovers dancing slowly, endlessly down the now empty terrace of the riverside cafe at which they first met, to the ghostly strains of their first waltz.

"My characters obsess me much more than the story itself. I want them to be true." *Casque d'or* is notably free of caricatures or stock types; around his two protagonists, Becker assembles a vivid gallery of subsidiary characters, each one individually depicted, no matter how briefly. There is no weakness in the story, either: the narrative moves with steady, unforced momentum from the opening sunlit scene on the river (irresistibly recalling *Une Partie de campagne*), through the gathering darkness of the fatal confrontation in a drab backyard when Manda stabs Marie's former lover, to end with Marie's bleak nocturnal vigil in a room overlooking the place of execution—before the brief coda returns us to the sunshine and the riverbank. "In my work," Becker wrote, "I do not want to prove anything except that life is stronger than everything else."

Surprisingly, *Casque d'or* was coldly received by the French critics on its initial release. In Britain, however, the film was enthusiastically acclaimed for its visual beauty, evocative period atmosphere, and fine performances. It is now generally agreed to be the outstanding masterpiece of Becker's regrettably short filmmaking career, offering the most completely realized statement of his abiding concern with, and insight into, the rich complexity of human relationships.

—Philip Kemp

CAT PEOPLE. Production: RKO Radio Pictures Inc.; 1942; black and white, 35mm; running time: 73 mins. Released December 1942.

Produced by Val Lewton; screenplay by DeWitt Bodeen; directed by Jacques Tourneur; photography by Nicholas Musuraca; edited by Mark Robson; music by Roy Webb.

Filmed 1942 in RKO/Radio studio in Hollywood; RKO-Pathe studio in Culver City; swimming pool scene shot at a hotel in the Alvarado district of Los Angeles; and zoo scenes shot at Central Park Zoo. Cost: $134,000.

Cast: Simone Simon (*Irena Dubrovna*); Kent Smith (*Oliver Reed*); Tom Conway (*Dr. Louis Judd*); Jane Randolph (*Alice Moore*); Jack Holt (*Commodore*); Elizabeth Russell (*Cat Woman*); Alan Napier; Elizabeth Dunne.

Publications:

Books—*An Illustrated History of the Horror Film* by Charles Clarens, New York 1967; *The Celluloid Muse: Hollywood Directors Speak* edited by Charles Higham and Joel Greenberg, London 1969; *Horror and Science Fiction Films: A Checklist* by Donald C. Willis, Metuchen, New Jersey 1972; *Reference Guide to Fantastic Films: Vol. 1, A-F* compiled by Walt Lee, Los Angeles 1972; *Val Lewton: The Reality of Terror* by Joel E. Siegel, New York 1973; *Movie Fantastic: Beyond the Dream Machine* by David Annan, New York 1975; articles—"Weird and Wonderful" by Henry Myers in *Screen Writer* (London), July 1945; "Taste Without Clichés" by Jacques Tourneur in *Films and Filming* (London), November 1956; "Esoterica" by Andrew Sarris in *Film Culture* (New York), spring 1963; "3 Faces of Fear" by Harlan Ellison in *Cinema* (Beverly Hills), March 1966; "The Shadow Worlds of Jacques Tourneur" by Robin Wood in *Film Comment* (New York), summer 1972; "3 Femmes" by C. Vianni in *Cahiers de la cinémathèque* (Perpignan), summer 1976; "Cat People" by DeWitt Bodeen in *Magill's Survey of Cinema, Vol. 1* edited by Frank N. Magill, Englewood Cliffs, New Jersey 1980; "Cat People" by R. Combs in *Monthly Film Bulletin* (London), July 1981.

*   *   *

While analysts of horror have long examined its psychological roots in a displacement of sexual drives and desires, few films make the link between horror and sexuality as explicit as *Cat People* (at least until the 1970s where the link becomes a central theme as in *Carrie*, for example). The film's central conceit— that the arousal of emotion could turn a woman into a panther— is a dramatic literalization of a metaphor of sexual energy as a living force.

Yet *Cat People* represents no simple endorsement of a sexist stereotype in which feminine sexuality is connected to a notion of unbridled devouring animality (as is the case in film noir's figuration of the independent woman as a kind of spider). Quite the contrary, through a reversal of horror's usual convention where an ostensibly normal world is threatened by a monstrosity, *Cat People* puts the cat woman, Irena, in the position of a victim whose "monstrous" reaction to the encroachments of the world upon her is viewed by the film with a degree of pathos-filled empathy and even perhaps a positive envy.

Irena becomes a mark of difference, an exotic other, that bourgeois society cannot understand and so ignores, represses, or controls through a force of domination. As in Hitchcock's films where the villain is often more attractive than the boring good guys, so too in *Cat People,* the middle class world appears as a dull, dulling banality whose own self-confidence only partially masks an inability to recognize either its own problems or those of outsiders to its circumscribed value system. This process is most explicit in a painful scene where Oliver Reed and Alice Moore literally exile Irena from their company during a supposedly pleasant visit to a museum.

Moreover, the very force that promotes itself as a cure in such a world—that is, the force of medicine (here the psychiatrist, Dr. Judd)—reveals itself to be more of a danger than the supposed illness that it sets out to cure. Not only does Judd fail to recognize Irena's problem, but he provokes its continuation, betraying his ostensibly professional objectivity by an aggressive sexual desire. If we traditionally associate the monster with the freak, it is significant that it is Judd, not Irena, who comes off as the monstrous figure, his crippled gait a mark of deformity, an abormality within the field of an imputed normality. Indeed, one can even suggest that the film portrays male sexuality as more dangerous than female sexuality, Irena at least tries to control rationally her own condition while the men around her advance heedlessly (for example, Oliver refuses her arguments against marriage; Judd refuses her protestations against a kiss). Thus, while *Cat People* has many of the conventional trappings of the horror film such as shadowy photography, a subtle creation of suspense (the panther's presence is often more felt than seen), and a concatenation of mysterious events, the film is finally most significant less as an efficient source of scary jolts than as a meditation on the very forces that menace us, that call into question the limits of the lives we construct for ourselves. It is also a dissection of the ways a supposedly normal world sustains itself by defining some other world as abnormal. *Cat People* is a tragedy about a world's inability to accept, or even to attempt to understand, whatever falls outside its defining frames.

—Dana B. Polan

LE CHAGRIN ET LA PITIÉ. Le Chagrin et la Pitié: Chronique d'une ville français sous l'occupation. The Sorrow and the Pity. Production: Television Rencontre (Lausanne), Nordeutscher Rundfunk (Hamburg), and Société Suisse de Radiodiffusion (Lausanne); black and white, 16mm; running time: original version: 270 mins., commercial release: 256 mins., other versions: 245 mins. Released 5 April 1971, Paris.

Produced by André Harris and Alain De Sedouy; screenplay by Marcel Ophuls and Andre Harris; directed by Marcel Ophuls; photography by Andre Gazut and Jurgen Thieme; edited by Claude Vajda; sound by Bernard Migy; songs sung by Maurice Chevalier; documentarists: Eliane Filippi (France), Christoph Derschau (Germany), and Suzy Benghiat (Great Britain), film also includes newsreel footage from the 1940s.

Interview material filmed in the late 1960s in Clermont-Ferrand. New York Film Critics' Special Citation as the year's best documentary.

Interviews: French witnesses: Emmanuel d'Astier de la Vigerie; Georges Bidault; Charles Braun; Pierre le Calvez; Comte Rene de Chambrun; Emile Coulaudon; MM. Danton and Dionnet; Jacques Duclos; Marcel Fouché-Degliame; Raphael Geminiani; Alexis and Louis Grave; R. du Jonchay; Marius Klein; Georges Lamirand; M. Leiris; Dr. Claude Lévy; Christian de la Mazière; Pierre Mendès-France; Commandant Menut; Monsieur Mioche; Maitre Henri Rochat; Madame Solange; Roger Tounze; Marcel Verdier; English witnesses: The Earl of Avon (Sir Anthony Eden); General Sir Edward Spears; Maurice Buckmaster; Flight Sergeant Evans; Denis Rake; German witnesses: Matheus Bleibinger; Dr. Elmar Michel; Dr. Paul Schmidt; Helmuth Tausend; General A.D. Walter Warlimont.

Publications:

Scripts—"*Le Chagrin et la pitié*" in *Avant-Scène du cinéma* (Paris), July/September 1972; *The Sorrow and the Pity*, translated by Mireille Johnston, New York 1972; reviews—"*Le Chagrin et la pitié*: La Critique" in *Avant-Scène du cinéma* (Paris), July/September 1972; "*The Sorrow and the Pity*" by C.P. Reilly in *Films in Review* (New York), April 1972; "*The Sorrow and the Pity*" by L. Rubenstein in *Cineaste* (New York), winter 1971-72; "*Le Chagrin et la pitié*" by M. Silverman in *Film Quarterly* (Berkeley), summer 1972; book—*Documentary: A History of the Non-Fiction Film* by Erik Barnouw, New York 1974; articles—"Jean-Pierre Melville Talks to Rui Nogueira about *Le Chagrin et la pitié*" in *Sight and Sound* (London), winter 1971-72; "Regardez donc dans vos greniers" by Marcel Ophuls in *Avant-Scène du cinéma* (Paris), July/September 1972; "*The Sorrow and the Pity*, A Sense of Loss, A Discussion with Marcel Ophuls" by B.J. Demby in *Filmmakers Newsletter* (Ward Hill, Massachusetts), December 1972; "Kosmorama Essay, Apropos virkeligheden" by E. Gres in *Kosmorama* (Copenhagen), October 1972; "*The Sorrow and the Pity*" by H.J. Gans in *Film Critic* (New York), November/December 1973; "Why Should I Give You Political Solutions. Marcel Ophuls: An Interview" in *Film Critic* (New York), November/-December 1973; "Marcel Ophuls and *The Sorrow and the Pity*" by Frederick Busi in *Massachusetts Review* (Amherst), winter 1973; "Razrušenie mifov" by S. Jutkevič in *Iskusstvo Kino* (Moscow), June 1974.

*　　*　　*

French postwar cinema is not remarkable for its social or political analysis, and the number of films offering a critical re-examination of the Occupation during the first 25 years after the Liberation is minimal. But as part of the aftermath of the confrontations setting the authorities against students and workers in May, 1968, a move towards a more realistic approach occurs on a variety of levels. *Le Chagrin et la pitié* is a key example of this new mood, and its particular value is that it offers perhaps the first comprehensive filmic analysis of 1940-44, probing the too easily accepted myths of heroic French resistance.

The film is the work of three men who had worked together in 1967 for the current affairs programming of the French television service (ORTF): the director Marcel Ophuls (the son of the great director Max Ophüls), and the producers André Harris and Alain de Sedouy. When their programme was discontinued, the trio continued to work independently, shooting on 16mm and designing their work for television. ORTF refused *Le Chagrin et la pitié*, however, acting in a quite ingenious manner to avoid charges of censorship. Since the film had been produced independently, it would have to be viewed before it could be bought for French showing, and ORTF simply refused to set up a viewing session, even after the film had received widespread praise. *Le Chagrin et la pitié*, a work designed for an audience of millions, received its first showing in a tiny art cinema on the Left Bank, but its power and originality made it one of the most controversial films of the year.

Le Chagrin et la pitié takes as its focal point the town of Clermont-Ferrand, chosen because it was both located close to Vichy and to the center of French resistance in the Auvergne. Ophuls's method was to base his investigation on a combination of interview material shot in the late 1960s with newsreel material from the 1940s. The particular situation of Clermont—Ferrand, initially part of the "free zone" and not occupied by the Wehrmacht until 1942, allows the twin themes of French response to Henri Pétain's policies and reaction to German occupation to be separated out. While the central focus is Clermont-Ferrand, Ophuls has also included statements by leading political figures of the period, such as Pierre Mendès-France and Anthony Eden, who put the local developments into a wider context.

The strength of the film however, lies in its human detail, in the interviews which relate directly to the situation in Clermont-Ferrand. Those interviewed cover the whole spectrum from aristocrats to peasants, from active collaborators and German occupying troops to resistance members and ordinary people who claim to be without politics. To set against the newsreels and the proven statistics are some startling testimonies, such as the champion cyclist who does not remember ever seeing any Germans in the town, the German ex-commanding officer, wearing his wartime service medals at his daughter's wedding, who denies any army involvement in the imprisonment and deportation of Jews, and a peasant who still has as his neighbor the man who denounced him for his resistance activities. All the easy half-truths are demolished: the crowds cheering De Gaulle's entry into the town in 1944 are indistinguishable from those who had earlier saluted Marshal Pétain.

Throughout the four hours of *Le Chagrin et la pitié* Ophuls's skillful selection from some 60 hours of interview material and apposite juxtapositions make a fascinating presentation of the facts beneath the legend, the still current evasions of self-evident truth, of the sorrow and the pity of the Occupation.

—Roy Armes

CHAPAYEV. Chapaev. Tchapaïev. Production: Lenfilm (USSR); black and white, 35mm; running time: 97 mins.; length: 2600 meters or 8760 feet. Released 1934.

Screenplay by Sergei and Georgi Vasiliev; from a published diary by Dmitri Furmanov detailing his experiences of the Russian Civil War of 1919; directed by Sergei and Georgi Vasiliev; photography by A. Sigayev and A. Xenofontov; sound by A. Bekker; production design by I. Makhlis; music by Gavrill Popov.

Filmed 1934.

Cast: B. Babochkin (*Chapayev*); Boris Blinov (*Fourmanov*); Varvara Myasnikova (*Anna*); Leomind Kmit (*Petka*); I. Pevtsov (*Colonel Borozdin*); Stepon Shkurat (*Potapov, a Cossack*); Nikolai Simonov (*Zhikhariev*); Boris Chirkov (*Peasant*); G. Vasiliev (*Lieutenant*); V. Volkov (*Yelan*).

Publications:

Scripts—*Tchapaïev* (includes notes on the direction) by the Vasiliev brothers, U.S.S.R. 1936; "*Tchapaïev*" by the Vasiliev brothers in *Scénarios choisis du cinéma soviétique*, France 1951; books—*Chapayev*, Moscow 1936; *Tchapaïev* (the story of the creation of the film) by I. Dolinski, U.S.S.R. 1945; *Kino: A History of the Russian and Soviet Film* by Jay Leyda, London 1960; *Soviet Cinema* by Thorold Dickinson and Catherine de la Roche, London, reissued 1972; *Cinema, the Magic Vehicle: A Guide to Its Achievement: Journey One: The Cinema Through 1949* edited by Adam Garbicz and Jacek Klinowski, Metuchen, New Jersey 1975; articles—"New Trends in Soviet Cinema" by Marie Seton in *Cinema Quarterly* (London), spring 1935 and summer 1935; "Soviet Cinema 1930-1940" by Dwight MacDonald in *Partisan Review* (New Brunswick, New Jersey), summer 1938 and winter 1939; "The Soviet Film Industry" by Ivor Montagu in *Sight and Sound* (London), autumn 1941; "Sunflowers and Commissars" by Robert Vas in *Sight and Sound* (London), summer 1962; "Bracia Wasiliew albo ideologiczna interpretacja rzeczywistości" by A. Helman in *Kino* (Warsaw), June 1973; special issue on *Chapayev* in *Iskusstvo Kino* (Moscow), July 1975; article by Z. Stábla in *Film a doba* (Prague), January 1975; "L'idéologie du régime stalinien au travers d'un film *Tchapaïev*" by Marc Ferro in *La Sociologie de l'art et sa vocation interdisciplinaire*, France 1976; "*Tschapajew*—Wir erlebten ihn wie unser eigenes Leben" by B. Uhse in *Film und Fernsehen* (Berlin), July 1977; "Les Frères Vassiliev" by E. Schmulevitch in *Avant-Scène du cinéma* (Paris), 1 and 15 January 1977; "Les Frères Vassiliev" by Eric Schmulèvitch in *Anthologie du cinéma, Vol. X*, Paris 1979.

*   *   *

Chapayev was directed by Georgi and Sergei Vasiliev who, although unrelated, worked together as "the Vasiliev Brothers." The film which won instant acclaim during the height of one of the Soviet film industry's *critical* periods, exploded like some bright miracle amidst the prevailing gloom. To achieve such an unalloyed and rapturous welcome simultaneously from the public, the intellectuals, the Party, the government and even fellow filmmakers was a miracle in itself. Stalin praised the film for its "successful portrayal of the great historical importance of the struggle for power of workers and peasants." V.I. Pudovkin wrote that it "depicted with meticulously developed economy the stormy inner achievement of maturity by a human being." Sergei Eisenstein—not just out of loyalty to two hard-working alumni of his directorial master-classes—was even stronger in his praise, claiming that the "Vasiliev Brothers," in combining the cinema of the masses (the first, silent period of the Soviet cinema) with the more intimate and naturalistic Soviet cinema (reflected in the sound era), had thus created an entirely new, third period.

How did the two directors win such spontaneous praise; more importantly, how did they create such an apparently spontaneous movie, which combined artistic, ideological and box-office requirements into a unified and highly-organized structure.

The literary basis of this story about a legendary Civil War hero comes from the writer Dmitri Furmanov, who was sent to join Chapayev's Red Army brigade as a political commissar in 1919. He kept a diary of his experiences and later published the diary in novel form which, despite its simple documentary style, "enhanced rather than diminished the hero's legendary glory"—according to a critic at the time. Later, the novel as a basis for the film would inspire a mass of comparisons between the two, including an entire volume by I. Dolinski devoted to the "Dramaturgy of *Chapayev*." In addition to a detailed history, this volume included the first scenario for the film, the second treatment, the shooting script and the final script set in four parallel columns for comparison.

Furmanov was absolutely conscious of the pitfalls he risked in writing about the exploits of an individualistic, swashbuckling guerilla leader, and of the problem of finding the correct mixture of heroism and humanity, of epic and documentary. The writer dealt with what he called the "decorative" (spectacular) side of heroism, by relying on the facts and including the details of ordinary everyday living. For the film, the Vasilievs would follow this approach as well.

In the mid-1920s, Furmanov had himself submitted a script, which was never developed and was later lost, to the Leningrad studios. After his death, his widow Anna put together another version and submitted it to Lenfilm where the Vasilievs eventually decided to make the film. They enlisted her help by persuading her to supply them with Furmanov's diaries and other source material. The directors, themselves Civil War veterans, faced an interesting problem: not only had Chapayev's status as a folk-hero increased and the mythology surrounding him emphasized, but recent Soviet historical-revolutionary films had, by this time, established a rather grandiose and melodramatic tradition.

The solution they put forward was to make the film intimate, a sort of "chamber work," which their contemporaries would have considered ludicrous in the context of a cast-of-thousands battling each other all over the steps. But, by continuously returning to the original source material, by including the author as a participant (a character rather than a narrator), and by spending much time on the actual location among the survivors and descendents of the people to be portrayed, the Vasilievs built up the "chamber" aspect of the drama. The spectacular deeds of derring-do were presented with a web of humor and humanity that wove together all the superficially disparate strands into a believable and satisfying whole. In one amusing sequence, for instance, Chapayev is literally cut down to size, making him a much more lovable hero.

Among the spectaculars made in the early days of sound, *Chapayev* was a rare break-through and an object lesson, not only to the Russians but also to all filmmakers, who so often find that their sensitivity and good intentions are submerged by the sheer weight, expense and misplaced reverence demanded by historical and biographical subjects—or by those who finance them.

—Robert Dunbar

LE CHARME DISCRET DE LA BOURGEOISIE. The Discreet Charm of the Bourgeoisie. Production: Greenwich Film (Paris), Jet Film (Barcelona), and Dean Film (Rome); Eastmancolor, 35mm, Panavision; running time: 105 mins. Released 15 September 1972, Paris.

Produced by Serge Silberman; screenplay by Luis Buñuel and Jean-Claude Carriere; directed by Luis Buñuel; photography by Edmond Richard; edited by Helen Plemiannikov; sound engineered by Guy Villette, sound effects by Luis Buñuel; production design by Pierre Guffroy; music edited by Galaxie Musique; costumes designed by Jacqueline Guyot.

Filming began 23 May 1972 in France. Academy Award for Best Foreign-Language Film, 1972.

Cast: Fernando Rey (*Ambassador*); Paul Frankeur (*M. Thévenot*); Delphine Seyrig (*Mme. Thévenot*); Bulle Ogier (*Florence*); Stephane Audran (*Mme. Sénéchal*); Jean-Pierre Cassel (*M. Sénéchal*); Julien Bertheau (*Bishop*); Claude Pieplu (*Colonel*); Michel Piccoli (*Minister*); Muni (*Peasant*); Georges Douking (*The moribund gardener*); Pierre Maguelon (*Police sergeant*); François Maistre (*Commissioner*); Milena Vukotic (*Inès*); Maria Gabriella Maione (*Guerilla*); Bernard Musson (*Waiter in the tea room*); Robert Le Beal (*Tailor*).

Publications:

Script—"*Le Charme discret de la bourgeoisie*" by Luis Buñuel and Jean-Claude Carriere in *L'Avant-Scène du cinéma* (Paris), April 1973; reviews—by Robert Benayoun in *Positif* (Paris), January 1973; "*Le Charme discret de la bourgeoisie*" by F. Chevassu in *Image et son* (Paris), November 1972; "*The Discreet Charm of the Bourgeoisie*" by S. Rice in *Take One* (Montreal), December 1972; "*Le Charme discret de la bourgeoisie*" by L. Bonneville in *Séquences* (Montreal), April 1973; "*The Discreet Charm of the Bourgeoisie*" by Gordon Gow in *Films and Filming* (London), March 1973; "*The Discreet Charm of the Bourgeoisie*" by C.P. Reilly in *Films in Review* (New York), January 1973; "*The Discreet Charm of the Bourgeoisie*" by S. Kovacs in *Film Quarterly* (Berkeley), winter 1972-73; "Interpretabilità (A proposito del *Fascino discreto della borghesia*" by N. Ciarletta in *Filmcritica* (Rome), August/September 1974; books—*The Cinema of Luis Buñuel* by Freddy Buache, revised London 1973; *Buñuel (Cine e ideología)* by Manuel Alcalá, Madrid 1973; *Luis Buñuel: A Critical Biography* by Francisco Aranda, New York 1975; *El ojo de Buñuel* by Fernando Cesarman, Barcelona 1976; *Luis Bunuel* by Raymond Durgnat, revised Berkeley 1977; *The World of Luis Buñuel: Essays in Criticism* edited by Joan Mellen, New York 1978; *Luis Buñuel, architecte du rêve* by M. Drouzy, Paris 1978; *Luis Buñuel* by Virginia Higginbotham, Boston 1979; *Luis Buñuel* by Ian Cameron, Berkeley 1979; articles—"Luis Buñuel anticapitalista romantico" by Fiesole in *Cinema nuovo* (Turin), September/October 1972; "La discreta sovversione di Bunuel" by M. Buffa in *Filmcritica* (Rome), October 1972; article by L. Oliva in *Film a Doba* (Prague), December 1972; "Le Charme discret de Luis Buñuel" by Michel Delain in *Avant-Scène du cinéma* (Paris), April 1973; "Spain, Catholicism, Surrealism and Anarchism: The Discreet Charm of Luis Buñuel" by Carlos Fuentes in *The New York Times Magazine*, 11 March 1973; special Buñuel issue of *Cine Cubano*, no.78-80, 1973; "*Fascino discreto della borghesia* "L'impenetrabilità di Bunuel" by E. Bruno in *Filmcritica* (Rome), April 1973; "*The Discreet Charm of the Bourgeoisie*" by G. Minish in *Take One* (Montreal), March 1973; "Interruption as Style: Buñuel's *Le Charme discret de la bourgeoisie*" by Jonathan Rosenbaum in

Sight and Sound (London), winter 1972-73; "*Il fascino (discreto) della borghesia*" by G. Turroni in *Filmcritica* (Rome), April 1973; articles discussing dream imagery in Buñuel films in *Filmcritica* (Rome), April 1973; "Bunuels Oscar" by José Francisco Aranda in *Kosmorama* (Copenhagen), August 1973; "The Discreet Charm of Luis Buñuel" by G.L. George in *Action* (Los Angeles), November/December 1974; "Erotic Moments in the Films of Luis Buñuel" by S. Murray in *Cinema Papers* (Melbourne), July 1974; "*The Discreet Charm of the Bourgeoisie*" by Raymond Durgnat in *Film Comment* (New York), May/June 1975; "*Charme discret de la bourgeoisie*" by R.C. Jameson in *Movietone News* (Seattle), February 1975; "A Magnificent and Dangerous Weapon: The Politics of Luis Buñuel's Later Films" by Randall Conrad in *Cineaste* (New York), no.8, 1976; "Pkt z diablem albo wdziek zwat pienia" by W. Wertenstein in *Kino* (Warsaw), November 1976; special Buñuel issue of *Contracampo* (Madrid), October/November 1980.

*   *   *

Recent critical attacks on Realism have tended, at their most extreme, to collapse it with narrative itself, as if to tell a story were an act of oppression. During the 1960s and 1970s there appeared a number of important and diversified European films (Bergman's *Persona*, Pasolini's *Teorema*, Herzog's *Even Dwarfs Started Small*, Godard's *Tout Va Bien*, Rivette's *Céline et Julie vont en bateau* are prominent examples) whose project involved retaining narrative while calling into question its realist/illusionist tyranny. Attention was drawn to process, and the pleasure, of narration, detaching it from the traditional support of a coherent diegetic world. *The Discreet Charm of the Bourgeoisie* belongs in this group, of which it is a particularly fascinating and delightful member.

Four levels of narrative can be distinguished within the film. (1.) "Reality"—for want of a better word. Like any traditional fiction *Discreet Charm* begins by establishing characters and plausible action (a car-load of guests driving to a dinner-party). This "reality-level" is never entirely undermined; the action, however, becomes increasingly implausible and absurd, a principle built mainly on the motif of meals frustrated or interrupted. (2.) Dream. At four points in the film male characters wake up, and the spectator is jolted into realizing that what has preceded that moment has been a dream. The boundary between this and the "reality" of (1) is ingeniously blurred: the dreams are scarcely more fantastic than reality; their beginnings are never signalled. Retrospectively, we can work out by the use of "common sense" where each dream started; but there remains the lingering doubt as to whether common sense can validly be applied to the film at all. One of the dreams is definitely established as being contained within the dream of another character. It is not impossible to read the entire film (until the last couple of minutes) as Fernando Rey's dream. (3.) Inserted narratives. During the film three stories are told (always by peripheral male characters) and rendered visually by Buñuel. Offered as truth, they are just as fantastic as the dreams or the reality; they are also the three most intense and disturbing episodes of the film. (4.) The country road. Barely a "narrative," (the "story" would amount to no more than "These people went for a walk in the country"), this remains the most enigmatic aspect of the film, unrelated to reality, dreams or narrations. It seems to express the ambivalence of Buñuel's attitude to his bourgeois characters, as to whether they are redeemable or not. On the one hand, they appear to be wandering aimlessly, lost, going nowhere; on the other, they are shown outside their artificial and constricted environment, amid images of natural fertility (perhaps, after all, they could be going somewhere?).

The dreams and the narratives work in a dialectical relationship. The three narratives all have strong Oedipal connotations. Two are literally about parent/child relationships, the third about a symbolic father, the "bloody sergeant" and a rebellious son, the young revolutionary. As fantasies, they represent the reality underlying the patriarchal order, the strain and horror upon which that order is constructed. The four dreams (all dreamt by middle-aged patriarchal authority figures) are single-mindedly concerned with anxieties about the collapse of authority. This explains why no dreams are dreamt, or stories told, by the women, who have no authority to lose.

Finally, the food motif. Buñuel uses the dinner-party to epitomize bourgeois rituals: its purpose is not to eat but to assert one's status. The frustration of every meal—until the last moments of the film—represents the bourgeoisie's collapse of confidence depicted in other ways in the dreams and narratives. Why can Fernando Rey eat at last, at the end of the film? He is alone; he eats because he is hungry not as part of a bourgeois ritual. He is not waited on—he serves himself out of the refrigerator—hence is acting outside the class oppression that is an essential factor in bourgeois ritual. Finally, he has just dreamed the annihilation of his entire circle, including himself. There has always been a close relationship between Buñuel and the characters Rey plays in his films: something less than identification but more than compassion.

—Robin Wood

CHARULATA. The Lonely Wife. Production: R.D. Bansal (company); black and white, 35mm; running time: 115 mins. Released 1964.

Produced by R.D. Bansal; screenplay by Satyajit Ray; from the novel by Rabindranath Tagore; directed by Satyajit Ray; photography by Subrata Mitra; edited by Dulal Dutta; art direction by Bansi Chandragupta; musical score by Satyajit Ray.

Filmed late 1963-early 1964 in India. Berlin Film Festival, Best Direction, 1965.

Cast: Soumitra Chatterjee (*Amal*); Madhabi Mukherjee (*Charulata*); Sailen Mukherjee (*Bhupati Dutt*); Shyamal Ghosal (*Umapeda*); Geetali Roy (*Mandakini*).

Publications:

Reviews—"*Charulata*" by G. Gauthier in *Image et son* (Paris), July/August 1981; "*Charulata*" by D. Goldschmidt in *Cinématographe* (Paris), July 1981; "*Charulata*" by A. Kieffer in *Jeune Cinéma* (Paris), October 1981; "Le Bruit du vent contre la jalousie" by I. Jordan in *Positif* (Paris), September 1981; "*Charulata*: De la géométrie des sentiments dans l'espace et dans le temps" by J. Magny in *Cinéma* (Paris), July/August, 1981; books—*Interviews with Film Directors* edited by Andrew Sarris, New York 1967; *Film Makers on Filmmaking* by Harry M. Geduld, Bloomington, Indiana 1967; *Portrait of a Director: Satyajit Ray* by Marie Seton, Bloomington, Indiana 1971; *Satyajit Ray*, Directorate of Advertising and Visual Publicity, New Delhi, India 1976; *Satyajit Ray: Study Guide*, American Film Institute, Washington, D.C. 1979; *Satyajit Ray's Art* by Firoze Rangoonwalla, Shahdara, Delhi, India 1980; articles—

article by John Gillett in *Monthly Film Bulletin* (London), December 1965; "The World of Ray" by Alan Stanbrook in *Films and Filming* (London), November 1965; "Satyajit Ray on Himself" in *Cinema* (Beverly Hills), July/August 1965; "Ray's *Charulata*" by Penelope Houston in *Sight and Sound* (London), winter 1965-66; "From Film to Film" in *Cahiers du Cinema in English* (New York), no.3, 1966; "Satyajit Ray: Genius Behind the Man" by B. Hrusa in *Film* (London), winter 1966; special issue of *Montage* on Ray, July 1966; "Satyajit Ray" by James Blue in *Film Comment* (New York), summer 1968; "India's Chekhov" by William S. Pechter in *Commonweal* (New York), 16 October 1970; "Cinéma Bengali de Ray, Cinéma Hindi de Bombay" by C. Haham in *Image et son* (Paris), July/August 1981.

*   *   *

Charulata is the most successful film of a group Satyajit Ray made in the mid-1960s with the actress Madhabi Mukherjee. Whereas the director's first films—especially the Apu trilogy—trace the education and growth to maturity of young male heroes, these mid-1960s films treat, in a variety of periods and social contexts, the problems of women in Indian society. As in the early films, Ray's method is to use a mass of brilliantly observed and often very funny details to build a single strand of plot. *Charulata*, one of Ray's undoubted masterpieces, is adapted from a story by Rabindranath Tagore and set in a period of particular significance to the director: the last quarter of the nineteenth century. Charulata, the sensitive but bored wife of a westernized newspaper publisher finds herself drawn sexually to her husband's young cousin who comes to stay and shares her taste for literature. The film moves with beautiful precision from flirtation and almost childish competitiveness to near tragedy amid a lovingly reconstructed period setting. While Tagore's story ends in disaster, Ray is less conclusive, choosing to freeze the film's last frame as husband and wife are about to come together again. This refusal of tragedy points to the characteristic form of Ray's films. One of the creative tensions in his work is that between the often rambling narratives he adapts and the tight shaping impulse of his imagination, which produces story patterns to match the most finely wrought classical Hollywood movies. But just as villains are absent from his work, so too is narrative closure and *Charulata* is typical in its rejection of finality where the characters are concerned.

In considering Ray as a filmmaker it is important to remember that his work has no roots in the traditions of Indian cinema. His early films are resolutely independent of the devices and conventions of the Hindi movie, of which he had little if any direct knowledge at this time. Ray's is a personal synthesis of an Indian sensibility and the formal lessons of western cinema. Though he is often seen as the heir to Italian neorealism and works like Vittorio De Sica's *Bicycle Thieves* have made a profound impression on him, there are fundamental differences. In particular Ray refuses actuality—the living presence of contemporary society—which was so crucial to filmmakers like De Sica and Rossellini. Ray habitually turns to the past, and the particular significance of *Charulata*, beyond its incredibly sensitive study of personal interaction, is the period to which Ray turns. Both Ray's ancestors and the Tagore family belonged to the educated elite of the Bengali middle classes who formed the "middle men" between the colonizers and the colonized. Their knowledge of English gave them key posts in education and administration under the British, and also made them a channel through which the new intellectual ideas from Europe (democracy, liberalism, nationalism, the liberation of women and social equality) flowed into Indian society. *Charulata* celebrates this moment of interaction: the husband Bhupati devotes his wealth and energy to his

English-language newspaper which will disseminate the new ideas. A key moment is the party that he throws to celebrate the Liberal election victory in London. But the nineteenth century Bengali Cultural Renaissance was not merely an assimilation of western ideas. Its participants combined this with a re-examination of traditional arts at his college—now a university—in Santineketan. Here too, Ray is faithful to his family traditions, for all his finest films are explorations of Indian society. Finally *Charulata*'s power comes from the sense of Ray's personal discovery of a key moment of fusion between India and the West.

—Roy Armes

CHELOVEK S KINO APPARATOM. The Man With the Movie Camera. L'Homme à la caméra. Production: Vufku (Ukraine); black and white, 35mm, silent; running time: 67 mins. Released 1929.

Screenplay and direction by Dziga Vertov; photography by Mikhail Kaufman; edited by Dziga Vertov, assisted by Yelizaveta Svilova; special effects by Dziga Vertov and Mikhail Kaufman.

Filmed 1929 mostly in Moscow.

Publications:

Scripts—"*The Man with the Movie Camera*" (treatment) by Dziga Vertov in *Film Comment* (New York), spring 1972; "Dziga Vertov: L'homme à la caméra" (photographic continuity), by M. Marie in *Avant-Scène du cinéma* (Paris), 1 December 1978; books—*Soviet Cinema* by Thorold Dickinson and Catherine De La Roche, London 1948; *Kino: A History of the Russian and Soviet Film* by Jay Leyda, London 1960; *Dziga Vertov* by Nikolai Abramov, edited and translated by B. Amengual, French ed., Lyon 1965; *Dziga Vertov* by Georges Sadoul, Paris 1971; *Nonfiction Film: A Critical History* by Richard Barsam, New York 1973; *Documentary: A History of the Non-Fiction Film* by Erik Barnouw, New York 1974; *Evolution of Style in the Early Work of Dziga Vertov* by Seth Feldman, New York 1977; articles—"*The Man with a Movie Camera*" by Dai Vaughn in *Films and Filming* (London), November 1960; "Bio-Filmographie de Vertov" by Georges Sadoul in *Cahiers du cinéma* (Paris), August 1963; "The Man With the Movie Camera" by Herman G. Weinberg in *Film Comment* (New York), fall 1966; "Dziga Vertov" by Christopher Giercke in *Afterimage* (New York), April 1970; article by David Bordwell in *Film Comment* (New York), spring 1972; "The Man With the Movie Camera: From Magician to Epistomologist" by Annette Michelson in *Art Forum* (New York), March 1972; "Dziga Wiertow albo wszechobecność kamery. Nasz kamery." by A. Helman in *Kino* (Warsaw), May 1973; "*L'Uomo con la macchina da presa*" by Dziga Vertov in *Bianco e Nero* (Rome), January/February 1973; "The Man Without a Movie Camera" by Jean Vronskaya in *Film* (London), May 1973; "Sur deux films de Dziga Vertov" by J. Cornand in *Image et son* (Paris), 297bis, June/July 1975; "Vertov and the Picaresque Spirit: *Man with the Movie Camera*" by R. Tuch in *Film Library Quarterly* (New York), no.1, 1975; "Kino-truth and Kino-praxis: Vertov's *Man with a movie Camera*" by Judith Mayne in *Ciné-tracts* (Montreal), summer 1977; "An Essay Towards *Man with a Movie Camera*" by S. Crofts and O. Rose in *Screen* (London), spring 1977; "*L'Homme à la caméra*: Continuité photographique présentée par Michel Marie" in *Avant-Scène du cinéma* (Paris), December 1978; "Slikovno polje in podoba v filmu" by T. Brejc in *Ekran* (Ljubljana, Yugoslavia), no.9-10, 1979; "An Interview with Mikhail Kaufman" in *October* (Cambridge, Mass.), winter 1979; "*L'Homme à la camera* de Dziga Vertov in *Image et son* (Paris), June 1980; "The Camera Eye and the Film: Notes on Vertov's 'Formalism'" by A. Williams in *Wide Angle* (Athens, Ohio), no.3, 1980.

*　　*　　*

The product of post-revolutionary Russia, *Man with a Movie Camera* reflects that era's excitement with film and anticipates modern techniques and concern for capturing actuality. Its creator Dziga Vertov, in the film's treatment, called *Man with a Movie Camera* an "experiment in conveying visual phenomena without the aid of titles..., scenario..., or theatre (a film without actors or sets)." The result of Vertov's experiment is a film about filmmaking and the illusions it can create.

Without the usual props of plot, titles, or sound, Vertov gives the film its structure by using the format of the city symphony films of the mid-twenties, but he brackets the scenes with references to the cinematic process. The film's protagonist is the cameraman, a picaro travelling through the city, involving himself in its daily dawn-to-dusk activities, and observing all walks of life through the eye of his camera. The camera eye takes on a persona of its own by turning frequently to the audience as though addressing it. The camera is the same apparatus Vertov personified in his early manifestos on film: "I am a mechanical eye. I, a machine, am showing you a world, the likes of which only I can see." In an almost virtuoso performance of camera and editing techniques, the audience is treated to superimpositions, animation, split screens, fast motion, varying camera angles, trolleying and dollying, quick cutting, montage, and prismatic lenses, all in a rapid succession which gives the film an inherent vitality.

The scenes themselves are actualities—people working, playing, resting—but always with the constant reminder that these are *filmed* actualities. The film opens on an empty theatre; the audience arrives; the projectionist readies his film; the orchestra begins to play; and we see a film come on the screen, the film we will in fact watch. Throughout the film, we are always aware of the camera's presence; we see the camera reflected in windows and in shadows. We see the cameraman with his machine climbing a smokestack, climbing out of a beer mug, being hoisted by a crane, walking into the sea, running across roof tops, and going down a mine shaft. The self-reflexive aspects of the film become more complex as we see shots of a motorcyclist, then of the cameraman filming the motorcyclist, then the same scene being projected in the theater. Later in the midst of an active sequence, the frame freezes; there follows a series of stills which lead us to a strip of film in an editor's hands. Now in the editing room, we see the editor hang the strip of film on a rack with other strips, some of which are shots we have already seen. At the end, we return to the theatre, the camera and tripod assemble on the screen, take a bow, and walk off. In the finale, we see a jumbling of shots from previous scenes intercut with shots of the audience watching these scenes, and finally the camera lens turned toward us with a human eye superimposed over the iris. Vertov's point is firmly established—he has shown us reality, he has expanded our vision of life, but it is a reality that only exists on film.

Greeted in 1929 as an exciting view into film's future, *Man with a Movie Camera* is still exciting to audiences because of its sophisticated approach to the art of filmmaking. The camera and editing pyrotechnics, in fact, seem quite contemporary. It is also strikingly modern in its basic concerns about the relationship between film and reality and the role the camera and cameraman play. These are also the concerns of the cinema verité filmmakers today.

—Sharon Lee

———————

CHELSEA GIRLS. Production: Andy Warhol Films; black and white and Eastmancolor, 16mm; running time: 195 mins., other versions are 210 and 205 mins. Released 15 September 1966, uncut reels were projected side by side. In the general release version, the 1st reel appeared screen right, and a few minutes later, the second appeared screen left.

Produced, directed, and photographed by Andy Warhol; screenplay by Andy Warhol and Ronald Tavel; music by The Velvet Underground; production assistant: Paul Morrissey.

Filmed 1966 in the Chelsea Hotel, New York City; other parts of New York City; and Cambridge, Massachusetts.

Cast: "The Pope Ondine Story": Ondine (*Pope*); Angelina Davis (*Pepper*); Ingrid Superstar; Albert René Ricard; Mary Might; International Velvet; Ronna. "The Duchess": Brigid Polk. "The John": Ed Hood (*Ed*); Patrick Flemming (*Patrick*); Mario Montez (*Transvestite*); Angelina "Pepper" Davis; International Velvet; Mary Might; Gerard Malanga; Albert René Ricard; Ingrid Superstar. "Hanoi Hanna (Queen of China)": Mary Might (*Hanoi Hanna*); International Velvet; Ingrid Superstar; Angelina ("Pepper") Davis. "The Gerard Malanga Story": Marie Menken (*Mother*); Gerard Malanga (*Son*); Mary Might (*Girlfriend*). "The Trip" and "Their Town (Toby Short)": Eric Emerson; "Afternoon": Edie Sedgwick (*Edie*); Ondine; Arthur Loeb; Donald Lyons; Dorothy Dean. "The Closet": Nico; Randy Borscheidt. "Reel 1": Eric Emerson; Ari.

Publications:

Books—*Andy Warhol* by John Coplans, New York 1970; *Andy Warhol* by Rainer Crone, New York 1970; *The Autobiography and Sex Life of Andy Warhol* by John Wilcock, New York 1971; *Andy Warhol's World and His Friends* by Stephen Koch, New York 1973; *Stargazer: Andy Warhol and his Films* by Stephen Koch, New York 1973; articles—"Beyond Cinema: Notes on Some Films by Andy Warhol" by J. Steller in *Film Quarterly* (Berkeley), fall 1966; "Room Service (*The Chelsea Girls*)" by David Ehrenstein in *Film Culture* (New York), fall 1966; articles by Jonas Mekas in the *Village Voice* (New York), 29 September and 24 November 1966; article by Andrew Sarris in the *Village Voice* (New York), 15 December 1966; issue devoted to *Chelsea Girls* and *Hedy-Hollywood's Goetterdaemmerung* in *Film Culture* (New York), summer 1967; "Dragtime or Drugtime: or Film à la Warhol" by Parker Tyler in the *Evergreen Review* (New York), April 1967; article by Ron Burnett in *Take One* (Montreal), April 1967; "My Favorite Superstar, Notes on My Epic, *Chelsea Girls*" by Andy Warhol in *Arts Magazine* (New York), February 1967; "On Andy Warhol" by Andrew Lugg in *Cineaste* (New York), winter 1967-68; article by Ernest Callenbach in *Film Quarterly* (Berkeley), winter 1967-68; article by Patricia Crawford in *Cineaste* (New York), winter 1967-68; article by James Price in *Sight and Sound* (London), spring 1968; "What's a Warhol" by Paul Carroll in *Playboy* (Chicago), September 1969; article by Raymond Durgnat in *Films and Filming* (London), August 1969; "It's Hard to be Your Own Scripts" edited by Leticia Kent in *Vogue* (New York), 1 March 1970; "My Life and Times with the Chelsea Girls" by Bob Cowan in *Take One* (Montreal), September/October 1971; "Part 1 of an Analysis of the Films of Andy Warhol" by Peter Gidal in *Films and Filming* (London), April 1971; "Warhol as Filmmaker" by David Bourdon in *Art in America* (New York), May/June 1971; "Andy Warhol: Iconographer" by D.J. Cipnic in *Sight and Sound* (London), summer 1972; "A Retrospective Look at the Films of D.W. Griffith and Andy Warhol" by R. Larson in *Film Journal* (New York), fall/winter 1972; essay on Morrissey in *Directors and Directions: Cinema for the 70s* by John Taylor, New York 1975.

* * *

A bonafide milestone of the American underground film, *Chelsea Girls* marks the apogee of the film career of pop artist Andy Warhol. Consisting of twelve 35-minute reels, each representing the activities of one room in New York's Chelsea Hotel, the film is projected two reels at a time, side by side, bringing its seven hours of footage to a running time of 3-1/2—as fans have noted, the same length as *Gone with the Wind*. The comparison is facetious, but apt, for *Chelsea Girls* not only represents one of the most significantly cultural/aesthetic touchstones for the 1960's underground, but also its first "blockbuster," drawing audiences large enough for *Variety* to begin listing its grosses.

Each of the film's 12 reels consists of a single, unedited shot in which various personalities from the Warhol factory (junkies, rock singers, camping homosexuals, professional poseurs) talk and/or act out sketchy vignettes. The cinema-verité aimlessness of the recorded performances is set in contrast to the strict, though seemingly arbitrary, structure of the film. While the length and continuity of each scene is identical (with actors instructed only to remain within the frame and to occupy the allotted time), the framing and camera movement vary between them, from the perfectly static to the eternally zooming. In a similar spirit of randomness, eight of the reels are in black-and-white, while four are in color. The dual projection, suggesting the simultaneity of action in two rooms at once, represents Warhol's final renunciation of the cinema of montage, by making cross-cutting superfluous.

Apparently, the decision to show *Chelsea Girls* two reels at a time was made only after the footage was shot; and Warhol provided no clue as to their order or as to which of the competing soundtracks should receive precedence. Thus, the projectionist took an active part in the creative process; as does the audience, which never fails to detect correspondence and contrasts between the randomly juxtaposed images. More recently, the film's projection has become conventionalized, based on the instructions of its sole distributor Ondine, star of one of the film's "climactic" scenes. The beginning of the first two reels is staggered by about five minutes, with the reel change on the first projector taking place while the second image continues, and vice versa. As currently presented, the order of the reels is structured along a line of increasingly dramatic (though basically non-narrative) scenes, and from black-and-white toward color. The first of the film's six coupled reels features Velvet Underground cohort Nico meticulously cutting her hair on the left screen, and superstar Ondine on the right. The last two reels mirror the first, with Nico on the right (in color) and Ondine on the left playing out the film's most emotional scene, wherein the fiction of Ondine as "Pope," taking confessions from various Factory types, flares into a genuine confrontation with one woman, followed first by a refusal to complete the scene and then by a sequence in which Ondine

makes use of the camera as confessor. The episodes in between include scenes of Factory regulars Ed Hood, Mario Montez, Ingrid Superstar and International Velvet lolling on a bed; of Brigid Polk shooting up speed through her jeans; of later exploitation queen Mary Woronov playing Hanoi Hannah, haranguing several women from a revolutionary tract; of avant-garde filmmaker Marie Mencken verbally abusing factory pretty-boy Gerard Malanga; and of young Eric Emerson doing a sort of slow striptease under psychedelic lights as he delivers an LSD-induced rap to the camera.

Seen outside the context of New York sixties' underground chic, *Chelsea Girls* still seems more than deserving of its reputation, not only as a document of a period, or even as the apotheosis of a certain influential part of the counterculture, but moreso as the epitome of Warhol's democratic notion of stardom for everyone placed in brashly contradictory juxtaposition to a passively mechanical aesthetic structured to the specifications of the culture of mass production and consumption.

—Ed Lowry

UN CHIEN ANDALOU. Andalusian Dog. Black and white, 35mm, silent; running time: 17 mins., some sources state 24 mins.; length: 430 meters. Released April 1929, Paris. Re-released 1960 with musical soundtrack.

Produced, directed, and edited by Luis Buñuel; screenplay by Luis Buñuel and Salvador Dali; photography by Albert Dubergen; production design by Pierre Schilzneck; music by Wagner with some Argentine tangos (for 1960 version).

Filmed March 1928 in Le Havre and Paris.

Cast: Pierre Batcheff (*Young Man*); Simone Mareuil (*Girl*); Jaime Miravilles; Salvador Dali (*Marist priest*); Luis Buñuel (*Man with razor*).

Publications:

Scripts—"Un chien andalou" (scenerio) in *The Secret Life of Salvador Dali*, London 1948; "Un chien andalou" in *L'Avant-Scène du Cinèma* (Paris), July 1963; *'L'age d'or'* and *'Un chien andalou'* by Luis Buñuel, translated by Marianne Alexander, New York 1968; review—"*Un Chien andalou*" by Jean Vigo reprinted in *L'Avant-Scène du cinéma* (Paris), July 1963; books—*Luis Buñuel* by Luc Moullet, Brussels 1957; *Luis Buñuel* by Ado Kyrou, Paris 1962; *Le Surréealisme au cinéma* by Ado Kyrou, Paris 1967; *Luis Buñuel* by Raymond Durgnat, Berkeley 1968; *Manifestoes of Surrealism* by André Breton, translated by R. Seaver and H.R. Lane, Ann Arbor, Michigan 1969; *Surrealism and the Film* by J. H. Matthews, Ann Arbor, Michigan 1971; *Buñuel (Cine e ideologia)* by Manuel Alcalá, Madrid 1973; *The Cinema of Luis Buñuel* by Freddy Bauche, translated by Peter Graham, New York 1973; *3 European Directors* by Peter Schillaci, Grand Rapids, Michigan 1973; *6 European Directors* by Peter Harcourt, Baltimore 1974; *Luis Buñuel: A Critical Biography* by Francisco Aranda, translated by David Robinson, London 1975; *Luis Buñuel* by Raymond Durgnat, Berkeley, revised 1977; *The Shadow and Its Shadow: Surrealist Writings on Cinema* edited by Paul Hammond, London 1978; *The World of Luis Buñuel: Essays in Criticism* edited by Joan Mellen, New York 1978; *Luis Buñuel* by Virginia Higginbotham, Boston 1979; articles—"The Films of Luis Buñuel" by

Tony Richardson in *Sight and Sound* (London), January/-March 1954; "The Eternal Rebellion of Luis Buñuel" by Emilio Riera in *Film Culture* (New York), summer 1960; "Interviewing Buñuel" by Derek Prouse in *Sight and Sound* (London), summer 1960; "Surrealist and Spanish Giant" by Francesco Aranda in *Films and Filming* (London), October 1961; article by Pierre Kast in *Cahiers du cinéma* (Paris), December 1961; issue devoted to Buñuel, *La Methode* (Paris), January 1962; article by Raymond Durgnat in *Films and Filming* (London), April 1962; "The Old Surrealist" by David Robinson in *London Magazine*, November 1962; article by Ken Kelman in *Film Culture* (New York), summer 1963; "Un itinèraire exemplaire" by Ado Kyrou in *L'Avant-Scène du cinéma* (Paris), July 1963; "Luis Alcoriza and the Films of Luis Buñuel" by Robert Hammond in *Film Heritage* (Dayton, Ohio), fall 1965; "Luis Buñuel: Spanish and Surrealist" by Peter Harcourt in *Film Quarterly* (Berkeley), spring 1967; article by Gordon Gow in *Films and Filming* (London), January 1969; "Pointed Horror: The Films of Luis Buñuel and Georges Franju" by Alf MacLochlainn in *Film Journal* (New York), summer 1971; "L'Exil de Bunuel à New-York" by R. Gubern in *Positif* (Paris), January 1973; "Luis Bunuel: The Process of Dissociation in 3 Films" by E. H. Lyon in *Cinema Journal* (Iowa City), fall 1973; "Textual Space in *Un Chien Andalou*" by P. Drummond in *Screen* (London), autumn 1977; "Surrealism's Enduring Bite: *Un Chien Andalou*" by A. Thiher in *Literature / Film Quarterly* (Salisbury, Maryland), winter 1977; "The Prologue to *Un Chien Andalou*: A Surrealist Film Metaphor" by L. Williams in *Screen* (London), winter 1976-77; "Bunuel's Half Century, Once Upon a Time..." by I. Walker in *Sight and Sound* (London), winter 1977-78; "*Un Chien Andalou*" in *Travelling* (Lausanne), summer 1979; "Surréalisme et cinéma" by L. Logette in *Jeune Cinéma* (Paris), April/May 1981; "The Discreet Charm of Luis Buñuel" by Michael Wood in *American Film* (Washington, D.C.), September 1982.

*   *   *

Un Chien andalou in probably the most renowned surrealist film. A collaborative work by Luis Buñuel and Salvador Dali, the film, intended as "a desperate and passionate appeal to murder," was immediately acclaimed for its poetry and beauty. Its enduring canonical status in film history is due not only to the reputation of its directors but also to its complex structure as a text. The film's disturbing imagery and transformation of narrative and continuity conventions help account for its appeal as a subject for critical scrutiny.

The film does present something on the order of narrative, if elusively; continuity is sustained primarily through the recurrence of the same actor-characters. However the connection between events is decidedly ambiguous. Title cards running through the film undermine any sense of coherent organization by randomly changing the temporal order and standard of reference throughout the course of the film—"Once upon a time," "Eight years later," "Towards 3 a.m.," etc. This level of narrative disorientation is supported by the film's visual construction, with its frequent use of point-of-view and continuity cutting to link ambiguously related spaces. Near the end of the film, the female character leaves an apartment which is presumably located on an upper floor of an urban building; a slight breeze blows through her hair, She smiles and waves at someone off-screen, as next shot places her on a beach.

This kind of illogical transition and unexpected conjunction is commonly associated with Surrealism. It is also in line with Buñuel's attitudes about the potential of cinema: "It is the best instrument to express the world of dreams, of emotions, of instinct." Indeed, most analyses of the film follow cues offered by dream interpretation to explain the film. In some cases this has led to reading the film as a symbolic conglomeration in which each bizarre image or event stands for something else. The deciphering process leads to an understanding of the film's "hidden" meanings—usually construed as an attack on bourgeois modes of behavior, an anti-religious diatribe, and/or a study of repressed sexual impulses. One of the key images here is that of the man, after he has been rebuffed by the woman, dragging the "baggage" of modern society with him, including two priests and two pianos surmounted by dead donkeys.

More recently, critical attention has shifted to the film's processes of development and transformation, emphasizing the ways in which the film opens up possibilities of meaning (rather than containing it through a series of symbolic equivalents). These approaches draw on unconscious thought processes, instead of symbolization, to organize critical understanding. In this context the driving forces of the text are described in terms of condensation and displacement. In this same vein, greater consideration is devoted to the relationship between the film and its audience. By disrupting familiar patterns of spatial and narrative development, *Un Chien andalou* focuses attention on filmic processes of constructing and dismantling meaning. In fact the film opens with a brutal assault on vision, with the image of a razor blade cutting an eye. This not only throws into question the whole notion of sight as the locus of meaning, but more crucially shocks and disturbs an audience which is looking at the screen.

—M.B. White

CHIKAMATSU MONOGATARI. A Story from Chikamatsu. The Tale of the Crucified Lovers. Production: Daiei (Tokyo); 35mm; running time: 102 mins.; length: 9144 feet. Released 1954.

Produced by Masaichi Nagata; screenplay by Matsutaro Kawaguchi and Yoshikata Yoda; from a puppet play by the 18th century playwright of puppet theater, Monsaemon Chikamatsu; directed by Kenji Mizoguchi; photography by Kazuo Miyagawa; edited by Kanji Sugawara; art direction by Hiroshi Mizutani; music by Fumio Hayasaka, Tamezo Mochizuki, and Eijiro Toyosawa.

Filmed in 29 days in Japan.

Cast: Kazuo Hasegawa (*Mohei*); Kyoko Kagawa (*Osan*); Yoko Minamida (*Otama, a servant girl*); Eitaro Shindo (*Ishun*); Sakae Ozawa (*Sukeyemon*); Ichiro Sugai (*Genbei*); Haruo Tanaka (*Doki*); Chiekok Naniwa (*Oko*); Ishiguro Tatsuya (*Isan*); Kimiko Tachibana (*Ocho*); Hisao Toake (*Chamberlain Morionkoji*); Shinobu Araki (*Nobleman's major-domo*); Ryunsuke Azuma (*Bairyu Akamatsu*); Koichi Katsuragi (*Priest*); Hirochi Mizumo (*Chief State Councillor Kuroki*).

Publications:

Books—*The Japanese Film: Art and Industry* by Joseph Anderson and Donald Richie, New York 1960; *Kenji Mizoguchi* by Ve-Ho, Paris 1963; *Anthologie du cinéma, Vol.3,* Paris 1968; *Mizoguchi Kenji no hito to geijutsu* [Kenji Mizoguchi: The Man and His Art] by Yoshikata Yoda, Tokyo 1970; *Kenji Mizoguchi* edited by Michel Mesnil, Paris 1971; *Voices from the Japanese Cinema* by Joan Mellen, New York 1975; *The Waves at Genji's*

Door: Japan Through Its Cinema by Joan Mellen, New York 1976; Japanese Film Directors by Audie Bock, New York 1978; Cinema, the Magic Vehicle: A Guide to Its Achievement: Journey II edited by Adam Garbicz and Jacek Klinowski, Metuchen, New Jersey 1979; articles—special issue of Cinéma 55 (Paris) on Mizoguchi, no.6, 1955; "Kenji Mizoguchi" by Donald Richie and Joseph Anderson in Sight and Sound (London), autumn 1955; special issue of Cahiers du cinéma (Paris) on Mizoguchi, March 1958; "L'Art de Kenji Mizoguchi" by Jean-Luc Godard in Art (Paris), no.656, 1958; "Souvenirs sur Mizoguchi" by Yoshikata Yoda in Cahiers du cinéma (Paris), no.174, 1966; "The Density of Mizoguchi's Scripts", interview with Yoshikata Yoda, in Cinema (Los Angeles), spring 1971; "Memories of Mizoguchi" in Cinema (Los Angeles), spring 1971; "Chikamatsu Monogatari" by I. Christie in Monthly Film Bulletin (London), May 1977; "Revers de la quiétude (sur 4 films de Mizoguchi)" by A. Masson in Positif (Paris), November 1978; "Mizoguchi and Modernism" by R. Cohen in Sight and Sound (London), spring 1978; "Notes sur Kenji Mizoguchi" by Noel Simsolo in Image et son (Paris), March 1979.

*   *   *

In 1954 Mizoguchi was at the peak of his career. In three of the past four years, he had won the Venice Film Festival's highest award and was touted in Europe as the world's greatest director. At home, he was revered as one of Japan's most venerable artists and his success in pushing open the door to export films gave him literally a free hand in choosing his subjects.

A Story from Chikamatsu, also known as The Tale of the Crucified Lovers, represents Mizoguchi's classic maturity. It was filmed without his usual anguish in only 29 days. Several sets of memoirs speak of the uncharacteristic atmosphere of relaxation on the set. It was a rare moment of happy labor for his cast and crew, all of whom knew they were working on a project very close to Mizoguchi's heart.

It was natural for Mizoguchi to adapt Chikamatsu. Considered the Japanese Shakespeare, this early eighteenth century puppet theater genius was both incalculably popular and deeply reflective, exactly in the way Mizoguchi wanted to be. Though separated by 250 years, both men took the middle class as their subject and both concentrated on the plight of women in a restrictive society. Most of Chikamatsu's 160 puppet plays pit giri (indebtedness) against authentic feeling, usually love. Many of these stories end in double suicide. Indeed, in 1722 his plays were banned in an attempt to curb the suicide fad they were though to have helped provoke.

In Chikamatsu Monogatari, Mizoguchi and his trusted writers, Matsutaro Kawagushi and Yoshikata Yoda, sought to maintain the simplicity of the original story, introducing very few changes into the plot. Of particular interest is the intersection of a public intrigue with an intimate love story. Hardly concerned about the immorality of Mohei and Osan, the court nobles are nevertheless only too glad to use their love affair as a way of destroying Osan's husband to whom all owe debts despite his middle class rank. While these nobles do not escape censure in the film, the social order upholding their rights and crushing the lovers is never directly questioned. Most disturbing is the pathetic incident in which Mohei's rustic, sympathetic father is brought to betray the couple because of his allegiance to the law and the rigidly conventional morality it sustains.

Mizoguchi's deep focus style is ideally suited to render the dynamics of this public/private plot, for he repeatedly films not only the developing drama, but the constant eavesdropping that actually deflects the direction of direction of that drama. Mohei approaches Osan for the first time only because he sees her with her profligate brother and thereby knows of her financial woes. The chestnut seller who comes upon them on the road gives them away. Spies are everywhere in this oppressive society; and houses are too small. The first half of the film plays with the architecture of Ishun's printing shop and home. Despite its luxury there is nowhere for the lovers to meet. It is a life of perpetual surveillance. Mizoguchi shows us silent spectators in many scenes. The women who work for Ishun form a kind of chorus to comment on the action, as do the women on the street who are moved by the spectacle of the lovers' crucifixion at the end.

In contrast the lovers' flight is visually liberating. The stifling indoors is replaced with misty lake settings and winding mountain trails. Here Mizoguchi's craning camera effortlessly glides to keep all action in view without disturbing the space in which it takes place. The ultimate transcendence of the lovers as they go to their death is prepared for by the loving camera, which has so many times raised them above their surroundings. Thus the purity of their love is shown to issue directly from the circumstances of life which seek to crush that love.

A Story from Chikamatsu brought Mizoguchi a coveted award from the Minister of Education. It won many other Japanese citations and it generally deemed by Japanese critics as his greatest film.

—Dudley Andrew

CHIMES AT MIDNIGHT. Falstaff. Campanadas a medianoche. Production: Internacional Films Española and Alpine Productions, presented by Harry Saltzman; black and white, 35mm; running time: 119 mins., English version 115 mins. Released May 1966.

Produced by Emiliano Piedra and Angel Escolano, executive producer: Alessandro Tasca; screenplay by Orson Welles; from Henry IV, Parts I and II, Henry V, Richard III, The Merry Wives of Windsor by William Shakespeare and the Chronicles of England by Raphael Holinshed; directed by Orson Welles; photography by Edmond Richard; edited by Fritz Muller; sound recorded by Peter Parasheles; art direction by José Antonio de la Guerra and Mariano Erdorza; music by Angelo Francesco Lavagnino, music conducted by Pierluigi Urbini, music directed by Carlo Franci; costumes designed by Orson Welles.

Filmed in Barcelona, Madrid, and other Spanish locations.

Cast: Orson Welles (Sir John (Jack) Falstaff); Jeanne Moreau (Doll Tearsheet); Margaret Rutherford (Hostess Quickly); John Gielgud (King Henry IV); Keith Baxter (Prince Hal, later King Henry V); Marina Vlady (Kate Percy); Norman Rodway (Henry Percy, called Hotspur); Alan Webb (Justice Shallow); Walter Chiari (Mr. Silence); Michael Aldridge (Pistol); Tony Beckley (Poins); Fernando Rey (Worcester); Beatrice Welles (Falstaff's Page); Andrew Faulds (Westmoreland); José Nieto (Northumberland); Jeremy Rowe (Prince John); Paddy Bedford (Bardolph); Ralph Richardson (Narrator); Julio Peña; Fernando Hilbeck; Andrés Meguto; Keith Pyott; Charles Farrell.

Publications:

Reviews—review by Gordon Gow in Films and Filming (London), May 1967; review by James Price in Sight and Sound (London), summer 1967; review by Andrew Sarris in the Village

Voice (New York), 30 March 1967; books—*Orson Welles* by Maurice Bessy, Paris 1970; *The Films of Orson Welles* by Charles Higham, Berkeley 1971; *Shakespeare and the Film* by Roger Manvell, New York 1971; *Orson Welles* by Joseph McBride, London 1972; *A Ribbon of Dreams: The Cinema of Orson Welles* by Peter Cowie, New York 1973; *Focus on Orson Welles* edited by Ronald Gottesman, Englewood Cliffs, New Jersey 1976; *Shakespeare on Film* by Jack Jorgens, Bloomington, Indiana 1977; *The Magic World of Orson Welles* by James Naremore, New York 1978; articles—"*Chimes at Midnight*" by Pierre Billard in *Sight and Sound* (London), spring 1965; "Welles and Falstaff" by Juan Cobos and Miguel Rubio in *Sight and Sound* (London), autumn 1966; "A Trip to Don Quixoteland" by Juan Cobos and Miguel Rubio in *Cahiers du Cinéma in English* (New York), no.5, 1966; "Welles on *Falstaff*" by Juan Cobos and Miguel Rubio in *Cahiers du Cinéma in English* (New York), September 1967; "Falstaff as Orson Welles" by J. Morgenstern and R. Sokolov in *Newsweek* (New York), 27 March 1967; interview with Welles in *Playboy* (Chicago), March 1967; "Welles' *Chimes at Midnight*" by Joseph McBride in *Film Quarterly* (Berkeley), fall 1969; "The Long Take" by Brian Henderson in *Film Comment* (New York), summer 1971; "Citizen Kane" by David Bordwell in *Film Comment* (New York), summer 1971; "Welles/Falstaff/Shakespeare/Welles: The Narrative Structure of *Chimes at Midnight*" by Stanley S. Rubin in *Film Criticism* (Edinboro, Pennsylvania), winter/spring 1978; "Reading the Prince: Shakespeare, Welles, and Some Aspects of *Chimes at Midnight*" by Leland Poague in *The Iowa State Journal of Research*, August 1981.

*　　*　　*

Among film scholars *Citizen Kane* is often regarded as the greatest film of all time; among Welles scholars, by contrast, *Chimes at Midnight* is often accorded pride of place as "the fullest, most completely realized expression of everything [Welles] had been working toward since *Citizen Kane*." Partly such praise can be understood as admiration for the fact that Welles managed to make the film at all, coming, as it did, late in a career long plagued by financial and commercial difficulties. And certainly auteurist film critics are prone to praise films generally discounted by journalistic reviewers and contemporary audiences, as *Chimes at Midnight* was discounted if not derided at the time of its initial (somewhat haphazard, if not half-hearted) release. The evaluative paradox cannot be readily settled, nor need it be; but the comparison to *Citizen Kane* can be helpful in highlighting those aspects of *Chimes at Midnight* which urge attention.

The central paradox of the Wellesian cinema involves a conflict between energy and dissipation or constraint; Charles Foster Kane, for instance, is shown as a youth of boundless imagination, but that imaginative energy is evidenced in a narrative which begins with Kane's own death and which portrays his overall inability to put that energy to real use. In *Chimes at Midnight* there is a similar contrast of youth and age—though the contrast involves two different characters drawn from Shakespeare's Lancaster plays, Falstaff, played by Welles himself, and Prince Hal, played by Keith Baxter. Furthermore, the terms of the constrast are reversed; all in all it is Falstaff who labors to be (or seem) young, while it is Hal who most clearly appreciates the fact that his aging father (John Gielgud) will soon die, and, thus, Hal himself will soon be England's king.

In both films the energy expended in the doomed effort to outwit the facts of time finds its presentational equivalent in the remarkable wit and energy of Welles's film style. It is generally accepted that film style is more muted in *Chimes at Midnight*

than in *Citizen Kane*; style does not carry the burden of mystery in the later film that it does in the earlier one. But the energy and intelligence remain evident in *Chimes at Midnight* nevertheless—not only in the justly famous Shrewsbury battle sequence (often likened, in Welles's favor, to that in Eisenstein's *Alexander Nevsky*), but also in the use Welles makes of moving camera (in the Gadshill robbery scene), of interior space (the Windsor castle sequences, as well as those at the Boar's Head tavern), and of camera angle (especially in the tavern scene where Hal plays King Henry to Falstaff's Prince. Especially moving and appropriate in this regard is the film's last shot, the intelligence of which (the camera craning slowly up to frame Falstaff's coffin against the castle in the deep background of the frame) serves to memorialize the energy lost at Falstaff's passing. Welles has long been noted for his use of such "deep focus" sequence shots—but the "depth" connoted by this shot, as by the whole of *Chimes at Midnight*, is equally as much emotional as technical.

—Leland Poague

* * *

CHINATOWN. Production: Paramount Pictures, Penthouse, and The Long Road Productions; 1974; Technicolor, 35mm, Panavision; running time: 131 mins. Released 21 June 1974.

Produced by Robert Evans; screenplay by Robert Towne; titles by Wayne Fitzgerald; directed by Roman Polanski; photography by John A. Alonzo; edited by Sam O'Steen; sound by Larry Jost and Bud Grenzbach, sound edited by Robert Cornett; production design by Richard Sylbert; set designed by Gabe and Robert Resh, set decorated by Ruby Levitt; art direction by W. Stewart Campbell; music score by Jerry Goldsmith; special effects by Logan Frazee; costumes designed by Anthea Sylbert; assistant director: Howard Koch, Jr.

Filmed on location in Los Angeles. Academy Award, Best Original Screenplay, 1974; New York Film Critics' Award, Best Actor (Nicholson, award also in conjunction with his role in *The Last Detail*), 1974.

Cast: Jack Nicholson (*J.J. Gittes*); Faye Dunaway (*Evelyn Mulwray*); John Huston (*Noah Cross*); John Hillerman (*Yelburton*); Perry Lopez (*Lieutenant Escobar*); Burt Young (*Curly*); Darrell Zwerling (*Hollis Mulwray*); Diane Ladd (*Ida Sessions*); Roy Jensen (*Mulvihill*); Roman Polanski (*Man with knife*); Dick Bakalyan (*Loach*); Joe Mantell (*Walsh*); Bruce Glover (*Duffy*); Nandu Hinds (*Sophie*); James Hong (*Evelyn's butler*); Belinda Palmer (*Katherine*); Fritzie Burr (*Mulwray's secretary*); Elizabeth Harding (*Curly's wife*).

Publications:

Reviews—"*Chinatown*" by M.S. Cohen in *Take One* (Montreal), July 1974; "*Chinatown*" by R. Combs in *Monthly Film Bulletin* (London), August 1974; "*Chinatown*" by Gordon Gow in *Films and Filming* (London), October 1974; "*Chinatown*" by Tom Milne in *Sight and Sound* (London), autumn 1974; "L'occhio e il ragno. Note su *Chinatown* e *Il fantasma della libertà*" by A. Cappabianca in *Filmcritica* (Rome), January/February 1975; "La Ville des feintes" by P. Kane in *Cahiers du cinéma* (Paris), February/March 1975; books—*Jack Nicholson—Face to Face* by Robert David Crane and Christopher Fryer, New York 1975; *Jack Nicholson: The Search for a Superstar* by

Norman Dickens, New York 1975; *Roman Polanski: A Guide to References and Resources* by Gretchen Bisplinghoff and Virginia Wexman, Boston 1979; *Film Noir* edited by Alain Silver and Elizabeth Ward, Woodstock, New York 1979; *The Roman Polanski Story* by Thomas Kiernan, New York 1980; *Polanski: A Biography* by Barbara Leaming, New York 1981; articles— *Dialogue on Film: Roman Polanski*, American Film Institute, August 1974; "Penthouse Interview: Roman Polanski" by Richard Ballad in *Penthouse* (New York), August 1974; "The Restoration of Roman Polanski", interview by Tom Burke in *Rolling Stone* (New York), 18 July 1974; "Hot Writer" by Martin Kasindorf in *Newsweek* (New York), 14 October 1974; "Roman Polanski, *Chinatown*" by C. Boost in *Skoop* (Wageningen, Netherlands), December 1974; "The Sound Track" by P. Cook in *Films in Review* (New York), November 1974; "Film Noir: Today, Son of Noir" by R.T. Jameson in *Film Comment* (New York), November/December 1974; "*Chinatown*: Other Places, Other Times" by J. Kavanagh in *Jump Cut* (Chicago), September/October 1974; "Paris-London Journal" by Jonathan Rosenbaum in *Film Comment* (New York), November/-December 1974; "*Chinatown*: Do As Little as Possible: Polanski's Message and Manipulation" by M. Sperber in *Jump Cut* (Chicago), September/October 1974; "Villains and Victims" by Mitchell Cohen in *Film Comment* (New York), November/December 1974; "*The Long Goodbye* from *Chinatown*" by Garrett Stewart in *Film Quarterly* (Berkeley), winter 1974; "Violence and the Bitch Goddess" by Stephen Farber in *Film Comment* (New York), vol.X, 1974; "Pieces of Mind" by Jonathan Baumbach in *Partisan Review* (New Brunswick, New Jersey), vol.XLI, 1974; "Behind the Scenes of *Chinatown*" by John Alonzo in *American Cinematographer* (Hollywood), May 1975; "Amerika" by W. Andersson and K. Josef in *Filmrutan* (Liding, Sweden), vol. XVIII, no.1, 1975; "Vuoto e fiction (Wyler, Polanski, Peckinpah)" by M. Mancini in *Filmcritica* (Rome), January/February 1975; "*Chinatown*" by W.D. McGinnis in *Literature/Film Quarterly* (Salisbury, Maryland), summer 1975; "*The Long Goodbye* and *Chinatown*: Debunking the Private Eye Tradition" by B. Oliver in *Literature/Film Quarterly* (Salisbury, Maryland), summer 1975; "The Long Goodbye from *Chinatown*" by G. Stewart in *Film Quarterly* (Berkeley), winter 1975; "*Chinatown* and the Detective Story" by R.B. Palmer in *Literature/Film Quarterly* (Salisbury, Maryland), spring 1977; "Contemporary Film Noir: Questing in *Chinatown's* Maze" by D. Benelli in *Cinemonkey* (Portland, Oregon), no.4, 1978; "*Chinatown*" by Olive Graham in *Cinema Texas Program Notes* (Austin), 3 May 1978; "*Chinatown*" by Charles Albright, Jr. in *Magill's Survey of Cinema, Vol. 1* edited by Frank N. Magill, Englewood Cliffs, New Jersey 1980.

*　　*　　*

Chinatown deals at plot level with the character of J.J. Gittes, a 1930's private eye in what seems to be the familiar wisecracking Raymond Chandler-cum-Bogart mould. The film's significance, however, lies over and above the excellence of this surface story and the vitality and readiness of Jack Nicholson's wit in this role, involving eventually a profoundly moving assessment of twentieth century American culture and corruption. Although set in Los Angeles in 1937, its urgent contemporary relevance is shaped by a use of nostalgia which avoids self-indulgence: the film effectively but sparingly recreates the feel of the city in the 1930's but is never a mere period piece.

The Chinatown of the title is a neighborhood district of Los Angeles, though this suburb hardly figured in the action and only the last scene is played out there. All we know is that Gittes once worked in Chinatown as a policeman, and those experiences led to his resignation from the police force. In Chinatown, it is suggested, the ordinary social and moral rules don't operate. Murders aren't investigated, graft and corruption are taken for granted. What Gittes learns as he tries to puzzle out answers is that all of Los Angeles has now—by 1937—become like Chinatown. What we learn, in the last frightening moments of the film, is even more disturbing: the amoral values of Chinatown are in complete control and apparently have power over the future. "Why are you doing it?...What can you buy that you can't already afford?" Gittes asks villain Noah Cross as the full horror dawns on him. "The future, Mr. Gittes, the future," is the chilling reply.

At first impression Gittes is a worldly cynical, coarse, smart-talking wise guy who earns his living investigating seedy adulteries. Yet as the film progresses he is revealed as a comparatively ingenious but naive quester seeking answers to questions he can barely comprehend. "You're an innocent," Evelyn Mulwray exclaims at one point, to our surprise and his; if the film has a fault it could lie in the ambivalence with which Gittes is presented. This is not to denigrate Jack Nicholson's excellent portrayal. Nicholson takes full advantage of Robert Towne's fine script and compellingly develops Towne's description of Gittes as a "brash, cynical and also very naive character." This naiveté is often presented to be an innocence of sorts but the actual quality and consistency of this "innocence" isn't readily apparent. For what is it which drives J.J. Gittes on to unravel the situation? At the surface level of the story it's hardly a moral drive to rid Los Angeles of corruption, and often he explains it to himself simply as a desire to protect his reputation after the initial trick has been pulled on him. Partly this is so, but his real motivation is never clear. Though he seems to be a figure in the Philip Marlowe mould, he is too naive: until the resolution of the film he remains unaware of the enormity of Noah Cross's power and momentarily believes he is free of the pervasive corruption after the police take him into custody. Marlowe would never have made that error.

On the wider symbolic level of the film the ambivalence of his presentation is still disturbing: presumably a quester in search of an answer to what is destroying the city, there are numerous parallels with the myth of the Fisher King and T.S. Eliot's *The Waste Land*—the land consumed with drought, corruption rife, the bringing of water as the key to the city's salvation. But Gittes is too ingenious to play Parsifal, and the beauty and delicacy of the camerawork and direction make the world he inhabits an attractive backdrop. The tone of the film is undoubtedly pessimistic, and aims toward the higher reaches of tragedy. It arrives much closer to the level of high art than some of Polanski's other films of this period, and has not yet received the full critical attention it deserves.

—Tony Slade

CHRISTOPHER STRONG. Production: RKO Radio Pictures Inc.; 1933; black and white, 35mm; running time: 77 mins. Released 1933.

Produced by David O. Selznick, with Pandro S. Berman; screenplay by Zoë Akins; from the novel by Gilbert Frankau; directed by Dorothy Arzner; photography by Bert Glennon, uncredited photography by Sid Hickox; edited by Arthur Roberts, uncredited editing by Jane Lorring; sound recorded by Hugh McDowell, Jr.; production design by Van Nest Polglase and Charles Kirk; music score by Max Steiner; special effects by Vernon Walker, transitions by Slavko Vorkapich; costumes designed by Howard Greer, uncredited costume design by Walter Plunkett; technical advisor: Sir Gerald Grove. Note: film's working title was *The Great Desire*.

Cast: Katharine Hepburn (*Lady Cynthia Darrington*); Colin Clive (*Sir Christopher Strong*); Billie Burke (*Lady Strong*); Helen Chandler (*Monica Strong*); Jack LaRue (*Carlo*); Desmond Roberts (*Bryce Mercer*); Gwendolyn Logan (*Bradford, the maid*); Agostino Borgato (*Fortune teller*); Margaret Lindsey (*Girl at party*); Donald Stewart (*Mechanic*); Zena Savina (*Second maid*).

Publications:

Books—*The Films of Katharine Hepburn* by Homer Dickens, New York 1971; *Katharine Hepburn* by Alvin H. Marill, New York 1973; *Notes on Women's Cinema* by Claire Johnston, London 1973; *Popcorn Venus: Women, Movies, and the American Dream* by Marjorie Rosen, New York 1973; *From Reverence to Rape* by Molly Haskell, New York 1974; *The Work of Dorothy Arzner: Towards a Feminist Cinema*, edited by Celia Johnston, London 1975; *Kate: The Life of Katharine Hepburn* by Charles Higham, New York 1975; *Early Women Directors* by Anthony Slide, South Brunswick, New Jersy 1977; articles— "Katharine Hepburn" by Romano V. Tozzi in *Films in Review* (New York), December 1957; "Approaching the Art of Arzner" by F. Parker in *Action* (Los Angeles), July/August 1973; interview with Arzner by G. Peary in *Cinema* (Beverly Hills), no.34, 1974; "Dorothy Arzner" by G. Peary in *Cinema* (Beverly Hills), no.34, 1974; "Re-reading the work of Claire Johnston" by J. Bergstrom in *Camera Obscura* (Berkeley), summer 1979; "Feminine Discourse in *Christopher Strong*" by J. Suter in *Camera Obscura* (Berkeley), summer 1979; "*Christopher Strong*" by M. Auty in *Monthly Film Bulletin* (London), August 1980.

*   *   *

There is little doubt that Dorothy Arzner's *Christopher Strong* is more highly regarded now than it was upon its release in 1933. What seemed to contemporary audiences and critics to be a competent, fairly effective but otherwise unexceptional melodrama, now seems an important and articulate step toward the formation of a feminist perspective in the male-oriented, mainstream of Hollywood. There is a freshness to *Christopher Strong* that stems directly from its unique point of view; while a great many movies of the 1930s and 1940s were known as "women's pictures", *Christopher Strong* really is one. Directed, written and edited by women, the film resonates a certain integrity and honesty towards the female character that few other films, then or now, can boast.

There is something slightly subversive about *Christopher Strong* in the way it so openly uses the soap-opera form as a base. Consequently, it works quite well as a standard "weepie" even as the filmmakers mold, transform and, ultimately, transcend the genre. Gilbert Frankau's novel, on which the film was based, was about a man torn between two women, his wife of many years and a young, daring aviatrix; the film is about the two women and how they face their love for the same man. It is, on the face of it, a minor shift in perspective, but Arzner and screenwriter Zoë Akins use it to examine the limited options open to women who

submit their own wills and abilities to those of their husbands and lovers.

Interestingly, Dorothy Arzner never admitted to having much interest in feminist philosophy, though she certainly owes the recent re-evaluation of her career to it. Of *Christopher Strong* she said, "I was more interested in Christopher Strong, played by Colin Clive, than in any of the women characters. He was a 'man on a cross'. he loved his wife and he fell in love with the aviatrix. He was a man on a rack. I was really more sympathetic with him, but no one seemed to pick that up."

Such a statement does not hold up as one views the film. The women of *Christopher Strong* are vital, adventurous, complex and emotional while the men are rarely more than stodgy and dull. This is due in part to the demands of the script, but is reinforced by the performances. Lady Cynthia Darrington, the aviatrix, was Katharine Hepburn's first starring role and her command of the part fluctuates wildly. There is, though, enough of Hepburn in the part to make it intelligent, perceptive and, electric. Billie Burke, as Strong's neglected wife, gives the performance of her career and Helen Chandler, as their daughter, gives a rather winsome role some unexpectedly dark shadings. Colin Clive, on the other hand, is stiff and ultimately uninteresting; naming the film after this character seems perversely ironic.

Despite Arzner's claim to the contrary, it is Cynthia Darrington who is "on the cross," torn between her great bravery and achievements and her desire for love and a normal life. She finds the resolution to her dilemma only in death, yet *Christopher Strong* is an important step toward a more reasonable presentation of men and women in film.

—Frank Thompson

CHRONIK DER ANNA MAGDALENA BACH. Chronicle of Anna Magdalena Bach. Chronique d'Anna Magdalena Bach. Production: Franz Seitz, Filmproduktion-Kuratorium Junger Deutscher Film, Hessiches Rundfunk, Radio-Televisionbessoise, Filmfonds, and Telepool (West Germany), IDI Cinematografica, PAI (Rome); black and white, 35mm; running time: 94 mins. Released 1968, West Germany.

Produced by Gian Vittorio Baldi, with Jean-Marie Straub; screenplay by Jean-Marie Straub and Danièle Huillet; directed by Jean-Marie Straub; photography by Ugo Piccone, Saverio Diamanti, and Giovanni Canfarelli; edited by Jean-Marie Straub and Danièle Huillet; sound by Louis Houchet and Lucien Moreau; music conducted by Nikolaus Harnoncourt, Schola Cantorum Basilienses concert group conducted by August Wenzinger, Hanover Boys Choir directed by Heinz Hennig; costumes designed by Casa d'Arte Fierenze, Vera Poggioni, and Renata Morroni.

Cast: Gustav Leonhardt (*Johann Sebastian Bach*); Christiane Lang (*Anna Magdalena Bach*); Paolo Carlini (*Hölzel*); Hans-Peter Boye (*Born*); Joachim Wolf (*Rector*); Rainer Kirchner (*Superintendent*); Eckart Brüntjen (*Prefect Kittler*); Walter Peters (*Prefect Krause*); Kathrien Leonhardt (*Catherina Dorothea Bach*); Anja Fährmann (*Regine Susanna Bach*); Katja Drewanz (*Christine Sophie Henrietta Bach*); Bob van Aspern (*Johann Elias Bach*); Andrea Pangritz (*Wilhelm Friedemann Bach*); Bernd Weikl (*Singer in Cantata No. 205*); Wolfgang Schöne (*Singer in Cantata No. 82*); Karl-Heinz Lampe (*Singer in Cantata No. 42*); Nikolaus Harnoncourt (*Prince of Anthalt-Cöthen*).

Publications:

Book—*Jean-Marie Straub* by Richard Roud, New York 1972; articles—"Frustration of Violence" in *Cahiers du Cinema in English* (New York), January 1967; article by Richard Roud in *Sight and Sound* (London), summer 1968; "Jean-Marie Straub" by B. Baxter in *Film* (London), spring 1969; article by Harriet Polt in *Film Quarterly* (Berkeley), winter 1968-69; "Jean-Marie Straub" by Roy Armes in *London Magazine*, September 1970; "Jean-Marie Straub" by Andi Engel in *Second Wave*, New York 1970; "Gespräch mit Danièle Huillet und Jean-Marie Straub" by W. Roth and G. Pflaum in *Filmkritik* (Munich), February 1973; "Die Filmographie—Jean-Marie Straub" in *Information* (Wiesbaden), January 1974; "Political Formations in the Cinema of Jean-Marie Straub" by M. Walsh in *Jump Cut* (Chicago), November/December 1974; "La Famille, l'histoire, le roman" by L. Seguin in *Cahiers du cinéma* (Paris), October/November 1975; "Report from Vienna: Cinema and Ideology" by N. Greene in *Praxis* (Berkeley), no.2, 1976; "Danièle Huillet Jean-Marie Straub's Fortini/Cani", special issue of *Filmkritik* (Munich), January 1977; "Straub/Huillet: The Politics of Film Practice" by S. Dermody in *Cinema Papers* (Melbourne), September/October 1976; "Jean-Marie Straub et Danièle Huillet" by Noel Simsolo in *Cinéma* (Paris), March 1977; "Le Combat conte l'impression" by J. Grant in *Cinéma* (Paris), January 1978; "Die Kunst des Filmesehens" by P. Nau in *Filmkritik* (Munich), June 1979.

*   *   *

The *Chronicle of Anna Magdalena Bach* is Jean-Marie Straub and Danielle Huillet's version of film biography. The film presents biography as the rewriting and juxtaposition of prior documents; in this instance music and a chronicle are most prominent. Defined in this way, through a range of documents, Bach does not emerge as a conventional dramatic character. The importance of music in the film, which was performed and recorded during the filming rather than dubbed, stresses its centrality to the contemporary knowledge and appreciation of the historical figure Bach. In fact, Straub has said that the music was considered the basic raw material of the film, and not simply background accompaniment.

Personal aspects of the composer's life are presented, along with the musical performance, through the agency of a diary. A voice-over narration, purportedly reciting the text of Anna Magdalena's journal, provides information about financial and familial affairs in a matter-of-fact monotone. No such chronicle really exists, and the narration was constructed from various sources including letters written by and to Bach. However the actual status of the spoken text is less important than its effect in the film as a document.

Through the use of these prior texts as its basic structuring principle, the film constructs a biographical portrait while asserting its distance from its subject. In line with this approach, the film refuses to engage the viewer emotionally in its characters as psychologized individuals. To undermine any sense of realistic depiction, the actors are dressed in period costumes but do not visibly age in the course of the film. The film as a whole is visually austere and verbally reticent, and the music stands as the major mechanism of viewer involvement. The actors rarely speak and the narration is void of emotional sentiment. This "silence" is expressed in several visual pauses punctuating the film; two shots of the sea, one of the sky, and one of a tree intervene in the course of the film. These images serve as moments of meditation. Removed from the musical, familial, and financial concerns developed in the narrative, they offer the possibility to speculate on,

among other things, the relation of these images to the filmic depiction of Bach's life; the relationship of nature to social and cultural life; and the nature of cinema. With regard to the latter, Straub is known for quoting D.W. Griffith: "What the modern movies lack is the wind in the trees."

The framing and lighting convey an almost academic sense of beauty, a calculatingly striking surface that denies the depth of space or character. While many of the images involve composition-in-depth, they are often so extreme and self-conscious that their status as artificial constructions—through the conjunction of set construction, lens choice, and character placement—is obvious. In addition, various camera and lens movements frequently manipulate and shift apparent depth within the course of such shots. The formal contrast and counterpoint guiding the editing are often seen as the visual counterpart of the structure of Bach's music. However, this approach to editing, insisting on the process of spatial construction, is characteristic of Straub and Huillet's films. It is a way of underscoring the artificiality of the film's visual world.

—M.B. White

CHRONIQUE DES ANNÉES DE BRAISE. Chronicle of the Years of Embers. Production: O.N.C.I.C. (Algeria); Eastmancolor, 70mm, Panavision; running time: 170 mins. Production manager: Mohammed (sometimes Mohamed) Lakhdar Hamina; screenplay by Mohammed Lakhdar Hamina and Tewfik Fares; directed by Mohammed Lakhdar Hamina; photography by Marcello Gatti; edited by Youcef Tobni; music by Philippe Arthuys. The film is divided into 6 parts: "The Years of Ashes," "The Year of the Tumbril," "The Years of the Embers," "The Year of Choice," "The Years of Fire," and "November 11, 1954."

Filmed in Algeria. Grand Prix, Cannes Film Festival, 1975.

Cast: Mohammed Lakhdar Hamina (*Miloud*); Jorgo Voyagis (*Ahmed*); Leila Shenna (*Wife*); Cheik Nourredine (*Friend*); Larbi Sekkai (*Larbi*); Hassan Hassani; M. Kouiret; Francois Maistre.

Publications:

Reviews—"*Chronique des années de braise*" by G. Moskowitz in *Variety* (New York), 21 May 1975; review in *Cinématographe* (Paris), August/September 1975; "Filmeposz hat tételben" by Z. Horváth in *Filmkultura* (Budapest), May/June 1977; 2 reviews by A. Mănoiu and V. Sava in *Cinema* (Bucharest), August 1977; articles—"*Chronique des années de braise*" by J. Magny in *Téléciné* (Paris), November/December 1975; "*Chronique des années des braise*" by G. Allombert in *Image et son* (Paris), November 1975; "Entretien avec Lakhdar Hamina" by C. Dupont in *Cahiers du cinéma* (Paris), spring 1975; interview with Lakhdar Hamina in *Ecran* (Paris), July/August 1975; special issue of *Cahiers de la cinémathèque* (Lyon), on the film and Lakhdar Hamina, summer 1975; article in *Cineforum* (Bergamo), June/July 1975; article in *Ecran* (Paris), October 1975; article in *Hollywood Reporter*, 29 October 1975; article in *Cahiers du cinéma* (Paris), May 1976; "De la prima incercare o lovitură de maestru" by A. Mănoiu in *Cinema* (Bucharest), June 1977; "Leiden und Empörung dann Alltag..." by C. Prochnow in *Film und Fernsehen* (Berlin), April 1978.

*   *   *

Mohamed Lakhdar Hamina is a key figure in the development of Algerian cinema, and one of the most talented and ambitious of Arab directors. Trained in Czechoslovakia, he began his career as a documentary filmmaker. His first feature, released in 1966, was one of the very first Algerian national productions. *Chronique des années de braise*, his fourth feature, made almost ten years later and designed to celebrate the outbreak of the Algerian Revolution on November 1, 1954, is without question one of the most striking of all third world films. Winning a Grand Prix at Cannes in 1975, it created a new international awareness for Algerian cinema, but for Arab critics and for some of Lakhdar Hamina's fellow directors it has remained a controversial work. Particular attention was focused in the 1970s on its enormous cost, with critics claiming that a dozen modest features could have been made with the funds squandered on this extravagant epic.

Certainly *Chronique des Années de braise* is an impressive work, with production values to match its cost. A monumental three-hour study of recent Algerian history, it gives a clear illustration of the high technical capability of the young Algerian film industry while confronting international cinema on its own terms. It is beautifully shot, with all the gloss of a Hollywood epic, but in achieving this result the director has had to sacrifice much of the specific national quality. In particular critics were hostile to the lushly orchestrated musical score by the French composer Philippe Arthuys, which owes nothing to Algerian musical traditions. It is fair to say that Lakhdar Hamina achieves something of the epic quality of the later David Lean. This is a remarkable feat in a country with a filmmaking history of barely a dozen years; but at the same time, this approach is questionable in terms of the priorities of a third world country like Algeria which in the 1970s began to take on an increasingly important international role.

In retrospect, the principal questions concerning this film derive less from its cost than from its narrative stance. Lakhdar Hamina defines his work as a personal vision and brushes aside questions of historical accuracy as mere quibbles. The film, he claims, is a poetic statement which grows directly out of his own childhood experiences (he was twenty in 1954). But the film's half-dozen or so intertitles drawing attention to the key dates in the historical development of Algeria between 1939 and 1954 deny the validity of a purely personal reading: *Chronique des années de braise* demands interpretation as an epic of the national consciousness. In this sense the film's inadequacies become clear. It offers less political insight that a purely lyrical protest; and the poverty and sufferings of the colonized are presented in lushly beautiful images which negate or, at least, defuse, the film's anger. The narrative intertwines two stories. One is that of a key Arab literary figure—the knowing madman (played with enormous gusto by Lakhdar Hamina himself)— who dies on the eve of revolution. The other concerns Ahmed, a totally mythologised figure, who is successively an uneducated peasant driven from his land, a skilled urban worker and—in a transformation all too reminiscent of western romantic melodrama—an unbelievably skilful horseman and swordsman defending his people against the savagery of the colonizers. Despite all Lakhdar Hamina's eloquence and directorial self-assurance, nothing could be more mystificatory than such a depiction of the 15 year origin of the national revolution.

—Roy Armes

CHRONIQUE D'UN ÉTÉ. Chronicle of a Summer. Production: Agros Films; black and white, 35mm; running time: 85 mins., English version is 90 mins. Released October 1961, Paris.

Produced by Anatole Dauman and Philippe Lifschitz; screenplay by Jean Rouch and Edgar Morin; directed by Jean Rouch and Edgar Morin; photography by Roger Morillère, Raoul Coutard, Jean-Jacques Tarbès, and Michel Brault; edited by Jean Ravel, Nèna Baratier, and Françoise Colin; sound by Guy Rophe, Michel Fano, and Barthèlèmy.

Filmed summer 1960 in Paris and Saint-Tropez. International Critics' Prize, Cannes Film Festival, 1961.

Cast: Jean Rouch; Edgar Morin; Marceline; Angelo; Marilou; Jean-Pierre; Jean (factory worker); Jacques (factory worker); Régis (student); Céline (student); Jean-Marc (student); Nadine (student); Landry (student); Raymond (student); Jacques (office worker); Simone (office worker); Henri (artist); Madi (artist); Catherine (artist); Sophie (model).

Publications:

Books—*French Cinema Since 1946: Vol. 2—The Personal Style* by Roy Armes, New York 1966; *Cinema Verite* by M. Ali Issari, East Lansing, Michigan 1971; *Documentary: A History of the Non-Fiction Film* by Erik Barnouw, New York 1974; articles— "Films by Jean Rouch" by Roger Sandell in *Film Quarterly* (Berkeley), winter 1961-62; article by David Gerard in *Films and Filming* (London), August 1962; "*Chronicle of a Summer*" by Tom Milne in *Sight and Sound* (London), summer 1962; "*Chronicle of a Summer*" by Mark Shivas in *Movie* (London), September 1962; interview with Rouch in *Movie* (London), April 1963; "Cinéma Véité in France" by Peter Graham in *Film Quarterly* (Berkeley), summer 1964; article by Peter Graham in *Film Quarterly* (Berkeley), summer 1964; "The Films of Jean Rouch" by James Blue in *Film Comment* (New York), fall-winter 1967; "Jean Rouch in Conversation with Jacqueline Veuve" in *Film Comment* (New York), fall 1967 and winter 1967; article by Ellen Freyer in *The Documentary Tradition* edited by Lewis Jacobs, New York 1971; interview with Rouch in *Documentary Explorations: 15 Interviews with Filmmakers* by G. Roy Levin, Garden City, New York 1971; "Je suis mon premier spectateur", interview by L. Marcorelles in *Avant-Scène du cinéma* (Paris), March 1972.

*   *   *

Substantially distinguished as an ethnographic filmmaker, a studious if somewhat unscientifc observer of rituals among the hunter-gatherers of post-Colonial Africa, Jean Rouch returned to his native Paris at 40 in 1959 to encounter a new and stimulating intellectual climate. His friend, critic and filmmaker Edgar Morin, challenged him to make a film about "his own tribe." Rouch responded with *Chronique d'un été*, one of the most evocative films from the makers of that ragbag of student excess and self-aggrandizement which Françoise Giroud christened the *nouvelle vague*.

Trained in the hard school of location shooting, Rouch knew the challenge of making an urban ethnographic film was largely technical. He persuaded André Coutant at Eclair to lend him the prototype of a lightweight camera under development for the military. After use by day, it was returned to the Eclair factory at night for modification and repairs. Raoul Coutard, who worked only one day on the film, disparages Rouch's search for "cinema verité." The effort to duplicate Alexandre Astruc's ideal of the "*caméra stylo*," a camera as flexible as a pen, required as much hardware as any feature film.

Chronique betrays the constraints of technique and the caution of its makers. Set-ups are studied, montage formal, photography often imitative of the cinema of performances, while a side trip to St. Tropez for an alleged holiday to observe the beautiful at play exposes the deficiencies of Rouch's philosophy of enquiry. The film is open to the same criticism of formalism as the now-historic Drew-Leacock-Pennebaker exercise in spontaneous cinema. A delight in the exercise of technique turns the aleatory by-products of low-light wild-sound filming into elements of a new style. Grain, rambling vox.pop. interviews, walking tracks are chosen, rather than merely being tolerated in the pursuit of truth.

But *Chronique* is a brilliant pre-vision of a style and approach to actuality filming that would sweep away the standard formal Grierson documentary. To begin by asking people at random "Are you happy?" was a stroke of genius. Their reactions, puzzled, truculent, thoughtful, sing with spontaneity. Nor is Rouch afraid to follow a plainly disturbed girl down into the wallow of self-pity and hysteria, leaving the watcher to make a personal determination of her sincerity. The refusal to take sides is *Chronique*'s strength, and the conclusion, as Rouch and Morin pace around a museum, wondering if the experiment proved anything, aptly conveys their genuine doubts. By then, however, their work had made the question largely irrelevant. The technique they created was to be the New Wave's most powerful and durable legacy.

—John Baxter

CITIZEN KANE. Production: RKO Radio Pictures Corp.; 1941; black and white, 35mm.; running time: 120 mins. Released 1 May 1941, New York.

Produced by Orson Welles; original screenplay by Herman J. Mankiewicz and Orson Welles; directed by Orson Welles; photography by Gregg Toland; edited by Robert Wise and Mark Robson; sound recorded by Bailey Fesler and James G. Stewart; art direction by Van Nest Polglase; music composed and conducted by Bernard Herrmann; special effects by Vernon L. Walker; costumes designed by Edward Stevenson.

Filmed 30 July-23 October 1940 in RKO studios. Cost: $686,033. Academy Award, Best Original Screenplay, 1941; New York Film Critics' Award, Best Picture, 1941.

Cast: Orson Welles (*Charles Foster Kane*); Buddy Swan (*Kane, Aged 8*); Sonny Bupp (*Kane 3rd*); Harry Shannon (*Kane's Father*); Joseph Cotten (*Jedediah Leland*); Dorothy Comingore (*Susan Alexander*); Everett Sloane (*Mr. Bernstein*); Ray Collins (*James W. Gettys*); George Coulouris (*Walter Parks Thatcher*); Agnes Moorehead (*Kane's Mother*); Paul Stewart (*Raymond*); Ruth Warrick (*Emily Norton*); Erskine Sanford (*Herbert Carter*); William Alland (*Thompson*); Georgia Backus (*Miss Anderson*); Philip Van Zandt (*Mr. Rawlston*); Gus Schilling (*Head Waiter*); Fortunio Bonanova (*Signor Matiste*).

Publications:

Scripts—"Citizen Kane" (shooting script) in *Avant-Scène du Cinéma* (Paris), January 1962; extract from *Citizen Kane* in *Cinéma d'Aujourd'hui* (Paris), no.6 1963; "The Shooting Script" in *The Citizen Kane Book* by Pauline Kael, Boston 1971; reviews—by Bosley Crowther in *The New York Times*, 2 May 1941; review by John O'Hara in *Newsweek* (New York), 17 March 1941; review in *Time* (New York), 17 March 1941; books—*Orson Welles* by André Bazin, Paris 1950; *The Fabulous Orson Welles* by Peter Noble, London 1956; *The Cinema of Orson Welles* by Peter Bogdanovich, New York 1961; *Orson Welles* by Maurice Bessy, *Cinéma d'Aujourd'hui* series, Paris 1963; *Orson Welles, l'éthique et l'esthétique* by various authors (for *Études cinématographiques*), Paris 1963; *The Cinema of Orson Welles* by Peter Cowie, London 1965; *The Citizen Kane Book* by Pauline Kael, Boston 1971; *The Films of Orson Welles* by Charles Higham, Berkeley 1971; *Focus on Citizen Kane* edited by Ronald Gottesman, Englewood Cliffs, New Jersey 1971; *This is Orson Welles* by Peter Bogdanovich and Orson Welles, New York 1972; *Orson Welles* by Joseph McBride, London 1972; *A Ribbon of Dreams* by Peter Cowie, New York 1973; *Focus on Orson Welles* edited by Ronald Gottesman, Englewood Cliffs, New Jersey 1976; *Orson Welles* by Joseph McBride, New York 1977; *The Magic World of Orson Welles* by James Naremore, New York 1978; *Mindscreen: Bergman, Godard, and First-Person Film* by Bruce Kawin, Princeton, New Jersey 1978; articles—in *Life* (New York), 17 March 1941; "How I Broke the Rules in *Citizen Kane*" by Gregg Toland in *Popular Photoplay Magazine* (New York), June 1941; article by Bernard Herrmann in *The New York Times*, 25 May 1941; "Orson Welles and *Citizen Kane*" by Emile Pritt in the *New Masses* (New York), 4 February 1941; "Hearst Over Hollywood: Matter of Orson Welles' Film *Citizen Kane*" by M. Sage in the *New Republic* (New York), 24 February 1941; "Realism for *Citizen Kane*" by Gregg Toland in *American Cinematographer* (Hollywood), February 1941, reprinted April 1975; article by Alva Johnston in *Saturday Evening Post* (New York), 1942; "Essai dur le style d'Orson Welles" by Jacques Manuel in *La Revue du cinéma* (Paris), December 1946; "Le triomph d'une bonne intention" by Jacques Doniol-Valcroze in *La Revue du Cinéma* (Paris), December 1964; "*Citizen Kane*" by Roger Leenhardt in *L'Ecran Français* (Paris), 3 July 1946; "Les films à la première personne' et l'illusion de la réalité au cinéma" by Jean-Pierre Chartier in *La Revue du Cinéma* (Paris), January 1947; "L'opérateur de prises de vues" by Gregg Toland in *La Revue du cinéma* (Paris), January 1947; interview with Welles by André Bazin and Jean-Charles Tacchella in *L'Ecran Français* (Paris), 21 September 1948; "*Citizen Kane*" by Glauco Viazzi in *Bianco e Nero* (Rome), July 1948; "Orson Welles from *Citizen Kane* to Othello" by Roberto Pariante in *Bianco e Nero* (Rome), March 1956; article by Manny Farber in *The Village Voice* (New York), 7 March 1956; "*Citizen Kane: American Baroque*" by Andrew Sarris in *Film Culture* (New York), no.2, 1956; "L'Oeuvre d'Orson Welles" in *Cahiers du Cinéma* (Paris), September 1958; "America" by Jean Domarchi in *Cahiers du cinéma* (Paris), July 1959; "*Citizen Kane*" by J.-P. Coursodon in *Cinéma 60* (Paris), no.43 1960; "The Heroes of Welles" by Alan Stanbrook" in *Film* (London), no.28, 1961; issue devoted to Welles in *Image et Son* (Paris), no.139 1961; "*Citizen Kane*" in *Avant-Scène du Cinéma* (Paris), January 1962; issue devoted to Welles in *Cine Forum* (Venice), no.19 1962; "Citizen K" by Michel Capdenac in *Les Lettres Françaises* (Paris), 27 December 1962; "*Citizen Kane*" by John Cutts in *Films and Filming* (London), December 1963; "*Citizen Kane*" by Joseph McBride in *Film Heritage* (Dayton, Ohio), fall 1968; "Orson Welles' Use of Sound" by Phyllis Goldfarb in *Take One* (Montreal), July/August 1971; "The Long Take" by Brian Henderson in *Film Comment* (New York), summer 1971; article by David Bordwell in

Film Comment (New York), summer 1971; article by Joseph McBride in *Film Heritage* (Dayton, Ohio), fall 1971; article by Andrew Sarris in *The Village Voice* (New York), 15 April 1971; article by Andrew Sarris in *The Village Voice* (New York), 27 May 1971; article by Andrew Sarris in *The Village Voice* (New York), 3 June 1971; "The Heart of Darkness in *Citizen Kane*" by H. Cohen in *Cinema Journal* (Evanston, Illinois), fall 1972; "Technique et Idéologie: Caméra, perspective, profondeur de champ" by J.-L. Comolli in *Cahiers du cinéma* (Paris), January/-February 1972; "issue on *Citizen Kane* in *Chaplin* (Stockholm), Vol. XV/2 (121), 1973; "Propositions" by Noel Burch in *Afterimage* (London), spring 1974; "A Linking of Legends: *The Great Gatsby* and *Citizen Kane*" by R. Mass in *Literature/Film Quarterly* (Salisbury, Maryland), summer 1974; "Orson Welles and the Great American Dummy..." by J. Smith in *Literature/-Film Quarterly* (Salisbury, Maryland), summer 1974; "More About *Citizen Kane*" by Charles Champlin in *American Cinematographer* (Hollywood), April 1975; "Ouragans autour de Kane" by Michel Ciment in *Positif* (Paris), March 1975; issue on "Semiotics and *Citizen Kane*" in *Film Reader* (Evanston, Illinois), no. 1, 1975; "*Citizen Kane, The Great Gatsby*, and Some Conventions of American Narrative" by Robert Carringer in *Critical Inquiry* (Chicago), winter 1975; "*Citizen Kane*" by Robert Carringer in *The Journal of Aesthetic Education* (Urbana, Illinois), April 1975; "*Citizen Kane*" by P. Pitiot and H. Béhar in *Image et Son* (Paris), 308bis, 1976; "A Rose is a Rose is a Columbine: *Citizen Kane* and William Styron's *Nat Turner*" by B.M. Firestone in *Literature/Film Quarterly* (Salisbury, Maryland), spring 1977; "Making Up Kane" by N. Gambill in *Film Comment* (New York), November/December 1978; "Film as Narration of Space: *Citizen Kane*" by I.S. Jaffe in *Literature/-Film Quarterly* (Salisbury, Maryland), no.2, 1979; "Von einem, der Karriere macht: Orson Welles in Hollywood der dreissiger Jahre" by J. Toeplitz in *Film und Fernsehen* (East Berlin), no.2, 1979; "Screen: Studio Studies: Part 2: Boohoo for Hollywood" by C.L. Westerbeck Jr. in *Commonweal* (New York), 22 June 1979; "Art and Nature in Welles' Xanadu" by L. J. Clipper in *Film Criticism* (Edinboro, Pennsylvania), spring 1981; "*Citizen Kane*" by G. Haustrate in *Cinéma* (Paris), July/August 1981; "Power and Dis-Integration in the Films of Orson Welles" by Beverle Houston in *Film Quarterly* (Berkeley), summer 1982.

*   *   *

"Everything that matters in cinema since 1940," François Truffaut has suggested, "has been influenced by *Citizen Kane*." It is not surprising, then, that *Citizen Kane* should be one of the most written about films in cinema history; nearly every major critic since André Bazin has felt compelled to discuss it, among them Andrew Sarris, Peter Cowie, David Bordwell, Joseph McBride and Bruce Kawin.

Of the various critical approaches taken to the film the most trivial, though in some respects the most common, is to understand *Citizen Kane* as an only slightly disguised biography of William Randolph Hearst. Hearst certainly took it that way, and was largely responsible, through the influence of his newspaper syndicate (which refused to review RKO films for a time), for the film's box office failure, despite the generally enthusiastic response of the critics. Pauline Kael did much to revive this line of thinking in her 1971 "Raising Kane" essay. Kael's point is essentially negative. Movies in general "are basically *kitsch*," though on one occasion *kitsch* "redeemed." *Citizen Kane* is a case in point, especially given its reputation, and that of Orson Welles. Indeed, much of Kael's essay is devoted to showing that aspects of *Kane* normally attributed to Welles really represented

or were indebted to the work of others—to Gregg Toland's cinematography, to the conventions of Hollywood newspaper comedy, and especially to Herman J. Mankiewicz, to whom Kael attributes the entire script. Her point even here, however, is that Mankiewicz largely retold the story of William Randolph Hearst ("What happened in Hearst's life was far more interesting" Kael argues at one point)—so that the process of making *Citizen Kane* is pictured largely as a process of disguise and oversimplification, begun by Mankiewicz and only finished by Welles. What Kael clearly fails to see is the irrelevance of her whole approach (not to mention its basic inaccuracy in regard to historical fact). As François Truffaut puts it: "It isn't San Simeon that interests me but Xanadu, not the reality but the work of art on film." To see the film as a denatured version of some past reality is simply not to see the film.

In sharp contrast to Kael's variety of historicism is the approach taken by André Bazin in his work on Welles. Rather than read the "story" of *Citizen Kane* against the background provided by the life of Hearst, Bazin focuses on film style in *Citizen Kane*, especially on the degree to which style "places the very nature of the story in question." And rather than describe film style in *Citizen Kane* as being consistent with that of Hollywood generally (as Kael does in part), Bazin suggests that Welles's reliance on the sequence shot (or long take) and deep focus represents an important *break* with classical cinematic practice and with the viewing habits derived from it. Classical editing, according to Bazin, "substituted mental and abstract time" for the "ambiguity of expression" implicit in reality; whereas "depth of focus reintroduced ambiguity into the structure of the image" by transferring "to the screen the continuum of reality," in regards both to time and space. "Obliged to exercise his liberty and his intelligence, the spectator perceives the ontological ambivalence of reality directly, in the very structure of its appearances."

There are problems with such an ontological approach to cinema (it focuses on sequences rather than on whole films, for instance); but Bazin's emphasis on the ambiguity of appearances in Welles is consistent with a third approach to *Citizen Kane* which sees the film as an early instance of the fragmented modernist narrative. In the words of Robert Carringer, the fact that Kane's story in the film is told from several perspectives, by several different characters, "reflects the Modernist period's general preoccupation with the relativism of points of view." Indeed, the film's "main symbolic event" is not the burning of Kane's "Rosebud" sled but rather the shattering of the little glass globe, which thus stands "for the loss of 'Kane-ness,' the unifying force behind the phenomenon of Kane." Accordingly, the effort undertaken by Thompson, the newsreel reporter, to uncover the secret of Kane's life by tracking down the meaning of "Rosebud" through interviewing Kane's friends and associates can be seen as a paradigm of the human desire to simplify the complex, though Thompson himself becomes increasingly cynical about the prospect of making sense of Charles Foster Kane.

It is arguable, however, that Thompson's cynicism—summed up when he says "I don't think any word can sum up a man's life"—is itself suspect for assuming that complexity is antithetical to intelligibility. Central to such a view of *Kane* is the premise that multiple narratives serve to cast doubt. And in a film such as Kurosawa's *Rashomon* (to which *Kane* is often compared) such is certainly the case. But the narrative of *Citizen Kane* may well work differently, at different "levels" of narration. The reporter himself comprises the first "level" of narration—in the newsreel he watches, and in the interviews he conducts. The interviews, then, constitute a second level of narration, in that they are embedded in the first. It is arguable, however, that a third level of narration exists. It can be seen in the "framing" sequences, which take us up to and then away from the gates of Xanadu; it can also be seen in the fact that the narratives of all those interviewed contain material that the person telling the tale could not have known, even at second hand (as if each such narrative were being "re-narrated"). But the third level of narration is most clearly evident in a series of visual metaphors (the recurrent visual figure of the window or door frame, for example, which repeatedly serves to cut one character off from others) which remain constant throughout the film, both in the flashbacks and in the reporter's narrative, regardless of who is ostensibly narrating the sequence. Accordingly, we can say that the entire film constitutes a single narrative with other narratives embedded; that the narratives work at different levels disallows easy assumptions that they cancel each other out, no matter how partial or biased any one narrative might be.

In terms of style and narative, then, *Citizen Kane* is a film of remarkable complexity and depth; yet, in thematic terms, *Citizen Kane* is also a hymn to failure, Kane's failure to put his remarkable energy to real use, Thompson's failure to find real meaning in Kane's life story. The shame, in Kane's case, is that his tremendous capacities and resources are wasted, used up; the closing shot of Xanadu, the smoke of Kane's burning possessions pouring from a chimney, recalls the factory smokestacks of the film's newsreel sequence, as the chainlink fence recalls the factory fences. The shame in Thompson's case is that he contributes to this waste by refusing to get to the point, refusing to see how thoroughly Kane was a product of his circumstances, as much victim as victimizer. But we need not follow Thompson's lead in this, however cinematically marvellous *Citizen Kane* might be. The sense is ours to make.

—Leland Poague

THE CITY. Production: American Documentary Films, Inc., for the American Institute of Planners, in conjunction with the Carnegie Corporation; Civic Films, a non-profit corporation within the American Institute of Planners, is often listed as the production company; black and white; running time: about 55 mins.; there are about 5 versions with times given ranging from 10 to 55 mins. Released 1939 at the World's Fair in New York.

Produced by Ralph Steiner, associate producer: Henwar Rodakiewicz; screenplay by Henwar Rodakiewicz, though Lewis Mumford is often credited as co-scriptwriter his participation was most likely centered on writing the narration; from an outline by Pare Lorentz; narration written by Lewis Mumford; directed by Willard Van Dyke and Ralph Steiner; photography by Willard Van Dyke and Ralph Steiner; edited by Henwar Rodakiewicz and Theodor Lawrence; music by Aaron Copland, conducted by Max Goberman; supervision by Oscar Serlin.

Filmed mostly in Greenbelt, Maryland; opening sequences shot in New England.

Cast: Morris Carnovsky (*Narrator*).

Publications:

Reviews—review by Franz Hoellering in the *Nation* (New York), 3 June 1939; review in *Sight and Sound* (London), 6 June 1939; books—*Films of the World's Fair: 1939* by Richard Grif-

fith. American Film Center, New York 1940; *Grierson on Documentary* edited by Forsyth Hardy, London 1947; *Documentary Film* by Paul Rotha, London 1952; *The Film Till Now* by Paul Rotha in collaboration with Richard Griffith, New York 1960; *Pare Lorentz and the Documentary Film* by Robert L. Snyder, Norman, Oklahoma 1968; *American City Planning Since 1890* by Mel Scott, Berkeley 1971; *The New Deal in the Suburbs: A History of the Greenbelt Town Program, 1935-1954* by Joseph L. Arnold, Columbus, Ohio 1971; *Documentary Explorations: 15 Interviews with Filmmakers* edited by G. Roy Levin, Garden City, New York 1971; *Nonfiction Film: A Critical History* by Richard Barsam, New York 1973; *Documentary: A History of the Non-Fiction Film* by Erik Barnouw, New York 1974; *Film on the Left: American Documentary Film from 1931-1942* by William Alexander, Princeton, New Jersey 1981; articles—"The Interpretive Camera in Documentary" by Willard Van Dyke in *Hollywood Quarterly*, July 1946; "The American Documentary—Limitations and Possibilities: An Interview with Willard Van Dyke" by Edouard De Laurot and Jonas Mekas in *Film Culture* (New York), no.3, 1956; "Focus on Willard Van Dyke" by Art Zuckerman in *Popular Photography* (Boulder, Colorado), April 1965; "30 Years of Social Inquiry: An Interview with Willard Van Dyke" by Harrison Engle in *Film Comment* (New York), spring 1965; "The Treatment of Sound in *The City*" by Henwar Rodakiewicz in *The Movies as Medium* edited by Lewis Jacobs, New York 1970; "Glancing Backward...Without Nostalgia" by Lora Hays in *Film Library Quarterly* (New York), summer 1971; "Willard Van Dyke" in *Documentary Explorations* edited by G. Roy Levin, Garden City, New York 1971; "Film as Architect: *The City*" by Howard Gillette, Jr. in *American Studies*, fall 1977.

*   *   *

Historically, *The City* was a culmination of private and public efforts to reflect in nonfiction films the agony of the depression years and the yearning for humane solutions. Pare Lorentz had surprised America with his intuitive grasp of visual communication in *The Plow That Broke the Plains* and *The River*, sponsored by the Farm Security Administration. These documentaries spoke forcefully and poetically of the need to protect the land from erosion by wind and water. Both were paid for by federal relief funds and were as much concerned with man-made poverty as with natural disasters.

Lorentz was occupied with other projects for his newly created U.S. Film Service when the American Institute of Planners, armed with $50,000 from the Carnegie Corporation, asked him to make a film on city planning for the 1939 World's Fair in New York City. He turned down the offer, but eventually made an important contribution in the form of a script outline. Clarence Stein then approached a private production group, Frontier Films, though Ralph Steiner, who had worked for Lorentz (along with Leo Hurwitz and Paul Strand) on *The Plow*. Steiner and Willard Van Dyke were just then on the point of withdrawing from Frontier, for personal and political reasons. This dedicated marxist cooperative (formerly called Nykino) made radical newsreels, sponsored the premiere of Strand's documentary about Mexican workers, *The Wave*, and later produced as a cooperative venture the civil rights film, *Native Land*. Frontier was too radical for the Carnegie Corporation or the A.I.P. but Van Dyke and Steiner, who agreed to fit the sponsor's needs, still made the film into a strong liberal statement about slums, smoke pollution and the exploitation of the poor by industrial capitalism. Part of the point of view came from Lewis Mumford's rather grim script for the narration. "Year by year," the printed foreword declared, "our cities grow more complex and less fit for living. The age of rebuilding is here."

This message was perfectly congruent with the vested interests of professional planners, architects, wrecking companies, and building engineers who have down through the years participated in the processes of urban renewal. The film made its point every day in the theater of the Science and Education Building at the fair and has been widely used through 16mm libraries ever since. An informative account of the making of the film is found in William Alexander's *Film on the Left*. A provocative review by John Grierson appeared in the first issue of the shortlived U.S. quarterly *Films*, reprinted in *Grierson on Documentary* (1947). Although Grierson always claimed to prefer education over aesthetics, he admitted the paradox of *The City* in his comment that the filmmakers' cameras "get an edge on and defeat their theories."

The City begins with nostalgic scenes: a water wheel, a hay wagon, a blacksmith, and a town meeting. It ends with equally idyllic pictures of a planned community, in which factory and suburb fit cheerfully together, children play and learn in scrubbed surroundings, and all is well under an indulgent sun. Between these two views of ideal living, a series of sequences show us how grim, dangerous and nerve-racking life in the city is supposed to be. Coal towns and steel mills reveal their smoke-laden air. Noisy traffic is bottle-necked downtown and crawls through the countryside for the weekend. Most effective of all, and one of the most famous achievements in the history of film, is the noon lunch-counter sequence. Beginning with a horse chewing its rations (a parody borrowed from the German silent documentary, *Berlin*), the editor has intercut close-ups of people chewing with shots of meat being sliced, coffee being poured, toast popping upward, and pancakes being turned by an automatic machine. Prunes and pie, plates and people—the images zip past with increasing speed, underscored by Aaron Copland's rollicking music. Some of the final shots are less than ten frames long.

These anti-city sequences of *The City* have kept the film alive. Yet they are remembered not because of their message but because of their jaunty cinematic style. The overt message of the film can never be out-dated, since it is unlikely that we shall ever succeed in remaking cities—or their suburbs—according to the heart's desire. But *The City* will continue to be shown and imitated—and stock footage from it included in other films—until long after other films in favor of city planning are forgotten. This is because *The City* is more than an editorial, more than a social document. Under the creative hand of its writer-editor, Henwar Rodakiewicz, the centerpiece of this half-hour film has become a classic example of the power of montage, a permanent poem about the behavior of humanity under stress. We remember it with appropriate distaste—and with delight.

—Richard Dyer MacCann

CITY LIGHTS. Production: Charles Chaplin Studio; 1931; black and white, 35mm, synchronized music and sound effects; running time: 86 mins.; length: 2380 meters. Released 6 January 1931 in New York City by United Artists Corp. Re-released 8 April 1950.

Produced, scripted, directed, and edited by Charles Chaplin; photography by Rollie Totheroh, Gordon Pollack and Mark Markatt; art direction by Charles D. Hall; music composed by Charles Chaplin, arranged by Arthur Johnston, and conducted by Alfred Newman; assistant directors: Harry Crocker, Henry Bergman, and Albert Austin.

Filmed 1930 in Hollywood.

Cast: Charles Chaplin (*Little Tramp*); Virginia Cherrill (*Flower Girl*); Florence Lee (*Grandmother*); Harry Myers (*Eccentric millionaire*); Allan Garcia (*Valet*); Hank Mann (*Boxer*); Eddie Baker (*Referee*); Henry Bergman (*Doorman*); Albert Austin (*Swindler*); Stanhope Wheatcroft (*Distinguished man at the café*); John Rand (*Another tramp*); James Donnelly (*Foreman*); Robert Parrish (*Newspaper boy*); Jean Harlow (*Nightclub girl*); Stanley Sanford (*Elevator boy*).

Publications:

Reviews—"Chaplin Hilarious in his *City Lights*" by Mordaunt Hall in *The New York Times*, 7 February 1931; "*City Lights*" by R.D. Skinner in *Commonweal* (New York), 18 March 1931; "Charlie Chaplin Falters" by Alexander Bakshy in the *Nation* (New York), 4 March 1931; "Charlie—As Ever Was" by Alexander Woolcott in *Collier's* (New York), 28 March 1931; books—*Charlie Chaplin: His Life and Art* by William Dodgson Bowman, New York 1931; *Charlie Chaplin: King of Tragedy* by Gerith von Ulm, Idaho, 1940; *Grierson on Documentary* edited by Forsyth Hardy, New York 1947; *Charlot* by Peter Cotes and Thelma Niklaus, Paris 1951; *Charlie Chaplin* by Theodore Huff, New York 1951; *Vie de Charlot* by Georges Sadoul, Paris 1953; *Chaplin et le rire dans la nuit* by M. Bessy and R. Florey, Paris 1953; *Chaplin, Last of the Clowns* by Parker Tyler, 2nd ed., London 1954; *The Great Charlie* by Robert Payne, 2nd ed., Paris 1954; *Charles Chaplin, le self-made Mythe* by José Augusto Franca, Lisbon 1954; *Pages pour Chaplin* by Henri Pichette, Paris 1950-54; *Charlot* by Pierre Leprohon, 2nd ed., Paris 1957; *Charlot et la fabulation chaplinesque* by Jean Mitry, Paris 1957; *Charles Chaplin* by Barthelemy Amengual, Paris 1963; *My Autobiography* by Charles Chaplin, New York 1964; *The Little Fellow: The Life and Work of Charles Spencer Chaplin* by Peter Cotes and Thelma Niklaus, New York 1965; *The Films of Charlie Chaplin* edited by Gerald D. McDonald, Michael Conway and Mark Ricci, New York 1965; *Charles Chaplin* by Marcel Martin, Paris 1966; *Interviews with Film Directors* by Andrew Sarris, New York 1967; *Magic, Myth, and the Movies* by Parker Tyler, New York 1970; *Focus on Chaplin* edited by Donald W. McCaffrey, Englewood Cliffs, New Jersey 1971; *Tout Chaplin* by Jean Mitry, Paris 1972; *Chaplin's Films* by Uno Asplund, London 1973; *Chaplin* by Roger Manvell, London 1974; *My Life in Pictures* by Charlie Chaplin, New York 1975; *Charlie Chaplin* by Robert F. Moss, New York 1975; articles—by Gladys Hall in *Motion Picture Magazine* (New York), May 1929; "No Talkies for Charlie" in *Photoplay* (New York), May 1930; "Charlie Chaplin and Talking Pictures" in *Theatre Arts* (New York), November 1930; "Charlie's Masterpieces: City Lights" by G. Seldes in the *New Republic* (New York), 25 February 1931; "Charlie Chaplin Defies the Talkies" in *Literary Digest* (New York), 28 February 1931; "If Charlie Plagiarized, What Then?" in *Literary Digest* (New York), 12 September 1931; article by Theodore Huff in *Films in Review* (New York), September 1950; article by Arthur Knight in *Films in Review* (New York), May/June 1950; article by Andrew Sarris in the *Village Voice* (New York), 5 December 1963; "*City Lights*" by Stanley Kauffmann in *Film Comment* (New York), September/October 1972; "*Les Lumières de la ville*" by R. Lefèvre in *Cinéma* (Paris), March 1972; "*Les Lumières de la ville*" by R. Lefévre in *Image et son* (Paris), March 1972; "Roland

Totheroh Interviewed: Chaplin Films" by T.M. Lyons in *Film Culture* (New York), spring 1972; "L'Assassin de Charlot" by Robert Benayoun in *Positif* (Paris), July/August 1973; "*Les Lumieres de la ville*" by F. Quenin in *Téléciné* (Paris), December 1976; "Chaplin as satyr..." by D.J. Gorsaro in *University Film Association Journal* (Houston, Texas), no.1, 1979; "Fighting Words" by I.S. Jaffe in *University Film Association Journal* (Houston, Texas), no.1, 1979; "*City Lights*" by Lynn Woods in *Magill's Survey of Cinema, Vol. 1* edited by Frank N. Magill, Englewood Cliffs, New Jersey 1980; "*City Lights*" by George Lellis and"*City Lights*" by Charles Berg in *Cinema Texas Program Notes* (Austin), 29 January 1981.

* * *

Early in 1931 an extraordinary event took place in New York City at the George M. Cohan Theatre. Though the talking picture had been firmly established, a new silent film premiered at the Cohan that became the talk of the town—Charles Chaplin's *City Lights*, in which he starred as the beloved Little Tramp. He was also the producer, the director, the author and scenarist, the editor, and had written the music which accompanied it. Chaplin was the solitary hold-out against the talking film, and *City Lights* was successful because it was a nine-reel comedy which revelled in its silence.

Though it had a sound track and musical accompaniment, it was, first and foremost, a tribute to the pantomimic art. Audiences loved it, and critics named it Chaplin's finest accomplishment, the perfect combination of hilarious comedy and pure pathos. One critic, Rose Pelwick, of the *New York Evening Journal*, remarked: "*City Lights* has no dialogue. And it's just as well, because if the picture had words, the laughs and applause of last evening's audience would have drowned them out."

In the first year of the Academy Awards, 1927-28, Chaplin had been nominated as Best Actor for *The Circus*; he was also nominated for Comedy Direction (a category which was discontinued after the first year of the Academy's existence); and a special statuette was awarded him "for versatility and genius in writing, acting, directing, and producing *The Circus*." Now two years later, the Academy ignored *City Lights*, although critics everywhere acknowledged that it might very well be the best of all Chaplin's films.

City Lights had an uncomfortable genesis. Chaplin had started shooting it in 1928 as a silent film; when it became obvious that talking pictures were neither a fad nor a fancy, he closed down production temporarily. When he decided to continue with it as a silent, everybody cautioned him that he was fighting a losing battle. He told Sam Goldwyn: "I've spent every penny I possess on *City Lights*. If it's a failure, I believe it will strike a deeper blow than anything else that has ever happened to me in this life."

During its production the stock market crashed, and Chaplin's situation became even more precarious, but he persisted in his distaste for talking pictures, confiding in an interview with Gladys Hall in *Motion Picture Magazine* (May, 1929): "They are spoiling the oldest art in the world—the art of pantomime. They are ruining the great beauty of silence. They are defeating the meaning of the screen, the appeal that has created the star system, the fan system, the vast popularity of the whole—the appeal of beauty. It's beauty that matters in pictures—nothing else."

In 1931, when *City Lights* was internationally premiered, Chaplin's world was younger, more innocent, ready to laugh, willing to weep, and they did both, totally succumbing to this romance of the devotion of the Little Tramp to a beautiful blind girl, charmingly played by a young divorcée, Virginia Cherrill.

The plot line is very simple. The picture opens with an introductory gag, showing a group of pompous dignitaries who have assembled for the dedication of an ugly civic statue. When it is unveiled, the Little Tramp is discovered sleeping blissfully in the lap of the central figure. He is chased away, but is attracted by the beauty of a young girl selling flowers from her sidewalk stand. He spends his last coin for a flower for his buttonhole, and only then realizes that the girl is blind.

That night he saves the life of a millionaire (Harry Myers), who is drunk and determined to throw himself in the river. The Tramp persuades him to live, and they spend the rest of the night celebrating in a night club. The millionaire invites the Tramp home, and their limousine passes the blind girl, who is setting up her flower stand on the sidewalk. The Tramp gets money from the millionaire, and buys all the flowers in the girl's basket. The millionaire also lends his limousine and driver to the Tramp, so he can take the girl home after he has dropped off the millionaire at his mansion. She thinks the Tramp must be a very rich man, and he is content to let her believe that. But when the Tramp returns to the millionaire's residence, the millionaire, now sober does not recognize him. This is a gag which is used several times effectively. Sober, the millionaire never knows who the Tramp is, but when he is drunk, he always greets the Tramp like an old buddy.

The Tramp now has a purpose in life: making enough money so the girl can have an operation and regain her sight. He gets a job as a street cleaner, and even enters the ring as a prizefighter, believing that the fight is fixed in his favor; but he is in error and ends up unconscious.

When he meets the millionaire again, the millionaire is happily drunk and willing to give the Tramp the money for the girl's eye surgery. They go to the mansion, and as the Tramp is given the money, two thugs enter the room and try to steal it, but are vanquished when the police arrive. The millionaire, knocked unconscious briefly, is revived, but, sobered, does not recognize the Tramp, who thereupon grabs the cash, and runs away at once to the blind girl's flower stand. He puts the money in her hands and runs away, but soon afterwards is arrested and jailed for robbery.

When he has served his term and is released, he discovers the girl working in a flower shop. She sees the Little Tramp outside, and overcome with pity, she gets some money from her cash register and goes outside to give it to the Tramp. As she puts the money in his hands, she recognizes the touch of his fingers, and realizes the truth at once. He has made everything possible for her. There follows an exchange of dialogue in subtitles that provides for one of the most moving finales in all Chaplin films. "You?" she asks. He nods, and smiles shyly, and asks, "You can see now?" She nods as her smile widens, "Yes, I can see now." The scene fades out with a radiant smile from the Little Tramp.

Thornton Delehanty, reviewing *City Lights* for the "New York Evening Post," remarked: "*City Lights* confirms the indestructibility of Chaplin's art, not only as an actor but as a director. And he has done it without making any concessions to dialogue; he remains the supreme pantomimist."

—DeWitt Bodeen

CIVILIZATION. Production: Triangle Film Corp.; black and white, 35mm, silent; running time: about 100 mins., originally about 130 mins.; length: about 10 reels. Released 1916. Re-released 1931 in re-edited version with sound track.

Produced by Thomas H. Ince; screenplay by C. Gardner Sullivan; directed by Raymond B. West and Reginald Barker (Ince is often erroneously given directorial credit); photography by Irvin Willat, Dal Clawson and others; edited by LeRoy Stone; music by Victor Schertzinger.

Filmed 1915-16 in Ince's studios in Culver City, Calfornia (the physical plant of MGM 10 years later); naval sequences shot on location in San Diego. Cost: $100,000, though this figure cannot be validated by any reliable sources.

Cast: Herschel Mayall (*King of Wredpryd*); Lola May (*Queen Eugenie*); Howard Hickman (*Count Ferdinand*); Enid Markey (*Katheryn Haldemann*); George Fisher (*The Christus*); J. Frank Burke (*Luther Rolf, the peace advocate*); Charles K. French (*Prime Minister*); J. Barney Sherry (*Blacksmith*); Jerome Storm (*Blacksmith's son*); Ethel Ullman (*Blacksmith's daughter*); Kate Bruce; Fannie Midgely; Gertrude Claire.

Publications:

Review—by Julian Johnson in *Photoplay* (New York), August 1916; books—*Thomas H. Ince, maître du cinéma* by Jean Mitry, Paris 1956; *The Movies in the Age of Innocence* by Edward Wagenknecht, Norman, Oklahoma 1962; *A Million and One Nights* by Terry Ramsaye, New York 1964; *The Parade's Gone By...* by Kevin Brownlow, New York 1968; *History of the American Film Industry From Its Beginnings to 1931* by Benjamin B. Hampton, New York 1970; *Dreams for Sale* by Kalton Lahue, New York 1971; *Spellbound in Darkness* by George C. Pratt, New York 1973; articles—"Ince Completes a World Drama" in *Photoplay* (New York), May 1916; sketch by R. Grau in the *American* (New York), August 1916; "Making an 8th Wonder" by Kenneth O'Hara in *Picture Play*, August 1916; "A Few More Inches About Ince" in *Photoplay* (New York), January 1919; "Thomas H. Ince" by W.K. Everson in *Cinemages* (New York), June 1955; "See Mr. Ince" by George Pratt in *Image* (Rochester, New York), May 1956; "Thomas H. Ince" by George Mitchell in *Films in Review* (New York), October 1960; "*Civilization*" by Richard Griffith in *Film Notes* edited by Eileen Bowser, New York 1969; "*Civilization*" by Henry Hart in *Films in Review* (New York), December 1969; "The Life of Thomas H. Ince: 1882-1924" in *Silent Picture* (London), spring 1972; "*Civilization*" by Tom Milne in *Monthly Film Bulletin* (London), April 1975; "Dividing Labor for Production Control: Thomas Ince and the Rise of the Studio System" by J. Staiger in *Cinema Journal* (Evanston), spring 1979.

*   *   *

Civilization, probably the best known film of Thomas H. Ince, is an epic drama which mixes allegory and realism in an attempt to justify pacifism and answer the cries for preparedness and participation in the World War I expounded by such features as *The Battle Cry of Peace* and *The Fall of a Nation*. Ince and his scenarist C. Gardner Sullivan prepared a script, followed blindly by directors Raymond B. West and Reginald Barker working under the close supervision of the producer, which tells of a Teutonic count and inventor of a newer, deadlier torpedo. After the submarine in which the count is travelling is destroyed, Christ enters the body of the inventor and shows to the ruler of the country the devastation and misery for which his warlike policies are responsible. The King sues for peace, and the final, pastoral scene is of a shepherd releasing a white dove from his hands beside a cannon overgrown with bushes.

Critical reaction to *Civilization* was somewhat mixed, with the general feeling, expressed, for example, by *Photoplay*'s Julian Johnson, that the film lacked intimacy and failed to involve the viewer. From today's viewpoint, the critics were overly kind, for *Civilization* is the type of epic which shows the silent cinema at its worst, with the acting ranging from dreary to wildly melodramatic and the direction lacking in emotion and an understanding of basic cinematic techniques. Only in some of the crowd sequences do the directors seem to have control of their material. To compare *Civilization* to *Intolerance* is akin to considering *Topsy and Eva* with *Gone with the Wind*. The basic premise may be the same, but the approach is totally different.

Civilization features many of the members of the Ince stock company, and was shot at the producer's studio, Inceville, in Pacific Palisades, California. The naval sequences were filmed on location in San Diego. The film was almost a year in planning and production. Its importance lies primarily in its contemporary value as a work of propaganda. Ince described *Civilization* as "a direct appeal to the mothers of men," an unabashed plea for peace, and certainly the film drew a large audience on those terms. What that audience saw was an allegorical story set in a mythical kingdom, whose soldiers bore a remarkable resemblance to Germans. But allegory does not stand the test of time too well as *Civilization* all too easily proves.

From an historical viewpoint, *Civilization* marks the close of Thomas H. Ince's career as a leading producer of both popular and critically acclaimed films. Though his career continued for another eight years, Ince concentrated more on minor program pictures and never again produced an epic such as *Civilization*, nor, a drama with the same artistic standards as displayed in his films from the early teens.

—Anthony Slide

CLÉO DE CINQ À SEPT. Cleo from 5 to 7. Production: Rome-Paris Films; black and white and Eastmancolor, 35mm; running time: 90 mins. Released April 1962, Paris.

Produced by Georges de Beauregard and Carlo Ponti, associate producer: Bruna Drigo; screenplay by Agnès Varda; English titles by Rose Sokol; directed by Agnès Varda; photography by Jean Rabier; edited by Janine Verneau; sound engineered by Jean Labussière and Julien Coutellier, sound edited by Jacques Maumont; art direction by Bernard Evein; music by Michel Legrand, lyrics by Agnès Varda; costumes designed by Bernard Evein.

Filmed in Paris.

Cast: Corinne Marchand (*Cleo*); Antoine Bourseiller (*Antoine*); Dorothée Blank (*Dorothée*); Michel Legrand (*Bob, the Pianist*); Dominique Davray (*Angèle*); José-Luis de Vilallonga (*Cleo's Lover*); Jean-Luc Godard; Anna Karina; Eddie Constantine; Sami Frey; Danièle Delorme; Jean-Claude Brialy; Yves Robert; Alan Scott; Robert Postec; Lucienne Marchand.

Publications:

Scripts—"*Cléo de 5 à 7*—Script Extract" in *Films and Filming* (London), December 1962; "*Cléo de Cinq à Sept*", Paris 1962;

reviews—in *Time* (New York), 14 September 1962; review by Joseph Morgenstern in the *New York Herald Tribune*, 5 September 1962; books—*French Cinema Since 1946: Vol. 2—The Personal Style* by Roy Armes, New York 1966; *Women in Focus* by Jeanne Betancourt, Dayton, Ohio 1974; *Caligari's Cabinet and Other Grand Illusions: A History of Film Design* by Léon Barsacq, New York 1976; articles—"*Cléo de 5 à 7* and Agnès Varda" by M. Shivas in *Movie* (London), October 1962; article by Richard Roud in *Sight and Sound* (London), summer 1962; article by Roger Manvell in *Films and Filming* (London), December 1962; "*Cléo de 5 à 7*" in *Avant-Scène du cinéma* (Paris), 15 May 1962; "The Face of '63—France" by P. Graham in *Films and Filming* (London), May 1963; "The Left Bank" by Richard Roud in *Sight and Sound* (London), winter 1962-63; "Pasolini-Varda-Allio-Sarris-Michelson" in *Film Culture* (New York), fall 1966; "The Underground River" by Gordon Gow in *Films and Filming* (London), March 1970; "Agnes Varda" in *Current Biography* (New York), 1970; interview with Varda by Barbara Confino in *Saturday Review* (New York), 12 August 1972; "Mother of the New Wave", interview by J. Levitin in *Women and Film* (Santa Monica), v.1, no.5-6, 1974; "Visual Pleasure and Narrative Cinema"" by Laura Mulvey in *Women and Film: A Critical Anthology* edited by Karyn Kay and Gerald Peary, New York 1977; "*Cléo de 5 à 7*" by Marjorie Baumgarten in *Cinema Texas Program Notes* (Austin), 13 April 1978.

*　　*　　*

With *Cléo de cinq à sept*, Agnès Varda reached international recognition for a film once called "the most beautiful film ever made about Paris."

Cléo is a young pop singer who suspects she has cancer. The film chronicles the time, minute by minute, that Cléo waits for her doctor's diagnostic report. Varda's intentions for *Cléo* were to integrate Cléo's concept of death with her fear of it, while at the same time freeing herself of that fear. While she waits for the medical verdict, Cléo restlessly moves about Paris, walking and riding in buses and cabs, transported not only from the Rue de Rivoli to Salpetriere Hospital but from self-conceited ignorance to an incipient understanding of her private self and public image.

The co-ordinates of time and space dominate Cléo's and her audiences' consciousnesses with expanding tension and enlightenment. Like a novel, *Cléo* is comprised of chapters, titled for the chapter's dominant character, i.e. Chapter Five: Cléo from 5:26 to 5:33. Events in the film occur at the pace of actual life. Varda's rendering of *physical* time in *Cléo* is unique. To physical, subjective time, she adds objective space, the peopled places of Paris. Varda begins with fate indicators: Cléo has her fortune told from Tarot cards. She then buys a hat, meets her lover, confers with her songwriting team, visits a girlfriend. Cléo discovers a wall separating her from her friends: she cannot communicate the terror she feels. Finally, she encounters a soldier on furlough in the park. To him, Cléo can voice her anxieties.

Jeanne Betancourt commends *Cléo*'s use of music, especially Cléo's rendition of a sad, new song in a Judy Garland-like style, "Dead, alone and ugly without you." The soldier goes to the hospital with Cléo, where her doctor orders two months of radiation therapy.

Critical comments varied widely. "Varda has made a sensational debut..." (Richard Roud) "This pic marks...Varda as a fine addition to French film ranks." (*Variety*) Hollis Alpert in *Saturday Review* asserts "her attempt to convey a more luminous reality, has led her to neglect her story...she hasn't brought off what she has tried in this first large film attempt." Joseph Morin in the *New York Herald Tribune* observes, "The camera sees a lot and tells a lot from an unusual variety of viewpoints." Stanley Kauffmann (*New Republic*) faults *Cléo* for its overly sentimental soap-opera ambience. Bosley Crowther (*The New York Times*) considers that the film "fairly glitters with photographic and cinematic 'style,' yet fails to do more than skim the surface of a cryptic dramatic theme..." Crowther asserts that Varda is so preoccupied with camera techniques that her focus upon Cléo is fragmented, and the viewers' interest in her is weakened.

Cléo evidences typical New Wave traits: the tendency to depart from a conventional storyline; the use of idiosyncratic filming techniques, the attempt to use the camera to establish fresh cinematic conventions, and a concern for socio-economic conditions.

Cléo's binary (subjective/objective) structure; its literary and documentary affinities, its use of physical time, its loving use of Paris as locale, and its depiction of a young woman's confrontation with death, make it, as Roger Manvell has noted, "a considerable achievement for Agnes Varda."

—Louise Heck-Rabi

A CLOCKWORK ORANGE. Production: Hawk Films; 1971; Warnercolor, 35mm; running time: 135 mins., some sources list 137 mins. Released 20 December 1971 in New York by Warner Bros.

Produced by Stanley Kubrick with Max L. Raab and Si Litvinoff serving as executive producers; screenplay by Stanley Kubrick; from the novel by Anthony Burgess; directed by Stanley Kubrick; photography by John Alcott; edited by Bill Butler; sound by John Jordan; production design by John Barry; art direction by Russell Hagg and Peter Shields; music by Ludwig van Beethoven, Edward Elgar, Gioacchino Rossini, Terry Tucker, and Erika Eigen, original electronic music by Walter Carlos; costumes designed by Milena Canonero; make-up by Fred Williamson, George Partleton, and Barbara Daly; paintings and sculptures by Herman Makking, Cornelius Makking, Liz Moore and Christiane Kubrick; stunt arranger: Roy Scammer.

Filmed September 1970-March 1971 in MGM British Studios, Boreham Wood, England. New York Film Critics' Awards for Best Film and Best Direction, 1971.

Cast: Malcolm McDowell (*Alex*); Partick Magee (*Mr. Alexander*); Michael Bates (*Chief Guard*); Warren Clark (*Dim*); John Clive (*Stage actor*); Adrienne Corri (*Mrs. Alexander*); Carl Duering (*Dr. Brodsky*); Paul Farrell (*Tramp*); Clive Francis (*Lodger*); Michael Gover (*Prison governor*); Miriam Karlin (*Cat lady*); James Marcus (*George*); Aubrey Morris (*Deltroid*); Godfrey Quigley (*Prison chaplain*); Sheila Raynor (*Mum*); Madge Ryan (*Dr. Barnom*); John Savident (*Conspirator*); Anthony Sharp (*Minister of the Interior*); Philip Stone (*Dad*); Pauline Taylor (*Psychiatrist*); Margaret Tyzack (*Conspirator*); Steven Berkoff, Lindsay Campbell, Michael Tarn, David Prowse, Barrie Cookson, Jan Adair, Gaye Brown, Peter Burton, John J. Carney, Vivienne Chandler, Richard Connaught; Prudence Drage, Carol Drinkwater, Lee Fox, Cheryl Grunwald, Gilliam Hills, Craig Hunter, Shirley Jaffe, Virginia Wetherell, Neil Wilson, and Katya Wyeth.

Publications:

Script—*Stanley Kubrick's A Clockwork Orange, Based on the Novel by Anthony Burgess* (shot by shot script), New York 1972; reviews—"*A Clockwork Orange* Dazzles the Senses and Mind" by Vincent Canby in *The New York Times*, 20 December 1971; "Kubrick: Degrees of Madness" by Jay Cocks in *Time* (New York), 20 December 1971; "Films in Focus" by Andrew Sarris in the *Village Voice* (New York), 30 December 1971; "Stanley Kubrick le libertin" by Robert Benayoun in *Positif* (Paris), June 1972; review by Jackson Burgess in *Film Quarterly* (Berkeley), spring 1972; "A Clockwork Orange" by Don Daniels in *Sight and Sound* (London), winter 1972; review by Gordon Gow in *Films and Filming* (London), February 1972; "Stanley Strangelove" by Pauline Kael in *New Yorker*, 1 January 1972; books— *Stanley Kubrick Directs* by Alexander Walker, 2nd edition, New York, 1972; *The Cinema of Stanley Kubrick* by Norman Kagan, New York 1972; *The Films of Stanley Kubrick* by Daniel Devries, Grand Rapids, Michigan 1973; *The Movie Makers: Artists in Industry* by Gene D. Phillips, Chicago 1973; *Elements of Film* by Lee R. Bobker, New York 1974; *From Reverence to Rape* by Molly Haskell, New York 1974; *Stanley Kubrick: A Film Odyssey* by Gene D. Phillips, New York 1975; *Directors and Directions: Cinema for the '70's* by John Russell Taylor, New York 1975; *The Novel and the Cinema* by Geoffrey Wagner, Madison, New Jersey 1975; *The Science Fiction Pictures* edited by James Robert Parish, Metuchen, New Jersey 1977; articles—"Milk-Plus and Ultra-Violence" by Hollis Alpert in *Saturday Review* (New York), 25 December 1971; "Mind's Eye" by John Hofsess in *Take One* (Montreal), May/June 1971; "Kubrick Country" by Penelope Houston in *Saturday Review* (New York), 25 December 1971; "The Decor of Tomorrow's Hell" by Robert Hughes in *Time* (New York), 27 December 1971; "London Junkets for Kubrick Fans" by Addison Verrill in *Variety* (New York), 22 December 1971; "*Clockwork Orange* Wins Critics Prize" by A.H. Weiler in *The New York Times*, 29 December 1971; "*Detroit News* Submits a Jog to Conscience" in *Journal of the Producers Guild of America* (Los Angeles), September 1972; "A Clockwork Orange" in *Playboy* (Chicago), January 1972; "*Straw Dogs, A Clockwork Orange*, and the Critics" by C. Barr in *Screen* (London), summer 1972; "Les avatars du cercle" by Jean-Loup Bourget in *Positif* (Paris), March 1972; "Kubrick's *A Clockwork Orange*: Some Observations" by Robert Boyers in *Film Heritage* (Dayton, Ohio), summer 1972; "Clockwork Marmalade" by Anthony Burgess in *Listener* (London), 17 February 1972; "Sur *A Clockwork Orange*" by Anthony Burgess, translated by Jeannine Cement,in *Positif* (Paris), June 1972; "Juice from *A Clockwork Orange*" by Anthony Burgess in *Rolling Stone* (San Francisco), 8 June 1972; "Malcolm McDowell: The Liberals, They Hate *Clockwork*" by Tom Burke in *The New York Times*, 30 January 1972; "Orange, Disorienting, but Human Comedy" by Vincent Canby in *The New York Times*, 9 January 1972; "Entretien avec Stanley Kubrick" by Michel Ciment in *Positif* (Paris), June 1972; "From Counter-Culture to Anti-Culture" by Donald Costello in *Commonweal* (New York), 14 July 1972; "Pop Nihilism at the Movies" by David Denby in *Atlantic* (Greenwich, Connecticutt), March 1972; "*A Clockwork Orange*:Novel into Film" by Arthur Gumenik in *Film Heritage* (Dayton, Ohio), summer 1972; "Oranges, Dogs, and Ultraviolence" by Robert Philip Kolker in *Journal of Popular Culture* (Bowling Green, Ohio), summer 1972; "*A Clockwork Orange*" by P. Krassner, J. Burks, and S. Feldman in *Take One* (Montreal), April 1972; "Nice Boy from the Bronx" by Craig McGregor in *The New York Times*,- January 1972; "Treatment and Ill Treatment" by Gavin Millar in *Listener* (London), 20 January 1972; "Kubrick" by Gene Philips

in *Film Comment* (New York), winter 1972; "Or, a Dangerous, Criminally Irresponsible Horror Show" by Clayton Riley in the *New York Times*, 9 January 1972; "The Context of *A Clockwork Orange*" by Charles Thomas Samuel in *American Scholar* (Washington, D.C.), summer 1972; "Kubrick's Horrorshow" by Phillip Strick in *Sight and Sound* (London), winter 1972; "Interview with Stanley Kubrick" by Penelope Houston and Phillip Strick in *Sight and Sound* (London), spring 1972; "Kubrick Tells What Makes *Clockwork Orange* Tick" by Bernard Weinraub in *The New York Times*, 4 January 1972; "Kubrick's Brilliant Vision" by Paul Zimmerman in *Newsweek* (New York), 3 January 1972; "Burgess, Originator of 'Clockwork' says, 'Let Kubrick Defend Himself'" in *Variety* (New York), 22 August 1973; "Unstuck in Time: *Clockwork Orange* and *Slaughterhouse 5*" by Neil D. Isaac in *Literature/Film Quarterly* (Salisbury, Maryland), spring 1973; "Novel Into Film: Novelist Into Critic: *A Clockwork Orange*...Again" by Samuel McCracken in *Antioch Review* (Yellow Springs, Ohio), no.3, 1973; "A Clockwork Orange" by Stephen Mamber in *Cinema* (Los Angeles), winter 1973; "Has Film Violence Gone Too Far" by David Denby in *Film 72/73: An Anthology by the National Society of Film Critics* edited by David Denby, Indianapolis 1973; "Kubrick and the Structures of Popular Cinema" by Harriet and Irving Deer in *Journal of Popular Films*, summer 1974; "Violence and Film: The Thesis of Kubrick's *A Clockwork Orange*" by W. Evans in *Velvet Light Trap* (Madison, Wisconsin), fall 1974; "Interview: Anthony Burgess" by Robert Jennings in *Playboy* (Chicago), September 1974; "Something More" by Gordon Gow in *Films and Filming* (London), October 1975; "All Time Film Rental Champs" in *Variety* (New York), 7 January 1976; "Clockwork Orange Gross May Exceed $1 mil in Spain Run" in *Variety* (New York), 21 April 1976; "Kubrick and His Discontents" by H. Feldmann in *Film Quarterly* (Berkeley), no.1, 1976; "*A Clockwork Orange*" by K. Moskowitz in *Velvet Light Trap* (Madison, Wisconsin), fall 1976; "Clockwork Violence" by Ken Moskowitz in *Sight and Sound* (London), winter 1977; "*Orange mécanique*" by D. Sotiaux in *Revue Belge du Cinema* (Brussels), January 1977; "Decor as Theme: *A Clockwork Orange*" by V.C. Sobcharck in *Literature/Film Quarterly* (Salisbury, Maryland), no.2, 1981.

*   *   *

Stanley Kubrick has achieved a reputation among both film critics and the general public for creating films of a highly controversial nature. Kubrick's ninth feature, *A Clockwork Orange*, is no exception. Descriptions of this film range from "brilliant" to "sick." There can be no denying that the film is extremely manipulative in the presentation of its themes and images. It is part of Kubrick's style to manipulate, through editing and camera technique, in order to direct the audience to a specific point of view. However, when that point of view is too shocking (and perhaps too real), Kubrick may alienate some of his audience, which seems to be the case with *A Clockwork Orange*.

The theme of *A Clockwork Orange* deals with freedom of choice; specifically the question is, "should freedom of choice be for everyone." Kubrick's answer is an unequivocal yes, even for a character as repugnant and loathsome as the film's protagonist, Alex. Alex represents absolute anti-social behavior, yet Kubrick shows through the course of the film that one man's choice to be anti-social is more important than society itself.

Although Alex is a socially unacceptable person, the audience is manipulated into sympathizing with his character. The first person narrative structure of the film is the first step in winning the audience over to Alex's side. Through this narration members of the audience become Alex's confidants and "only friends." The photographic style of the film also helps to align the audience with Alex. Kubrick makes frequent use of hand-held camera and point-of-view shots in the film to place the audience within Alex's space.

The portrayal of sex and violence in *A Clockwork Orange* has been criticized for its brutality and explicitness. Although the content in these scenes may be horrifying, their presentation on the screen is extremely stylized. Kubrick's editing, along with the use of music, creates a kind of choreographed "dance" out of the violence. On one level the violence may be very alarming to the normal viewer, but Kubrick disguises it within a more elegant presentation of style.

Alex's subjection to the Ludovico Treatment continues to manipulate the audience to Alex's side. The scenes of Alex strapped helpless to a chair with electrodes protruding from his head are reminiscent of the Frankenstein films. The "evil" scientists in this scene sit in the darkness of the back of the auditorium while Alex is "cured" of his bad tendencies in a bright spotlight. Kubrick's use of lighting in these scenes plays upon the meanings of good and evil conventionally attributed to light and dark to turn Alex into the innocent and sympathetic victim.

Once Alex has been completely brainwashed, he is no longer capable of any violent thoughts. He has become the "true Christian" citizen and is ready to take his place in society. However, the question of choice becomes the issue at hand. "When a man cannot choose, he ceases to be a man." Kubrick has cleverly backed his audience into a corner: whether to protect the rights of the individual at the risk of destroying society, or to protect society at the risk of destroying the individual. Although Alex is a dispicable character, the odds have been stacked in his favor. Kubrick's use of lighting, camera work, music, and editing have created a "hero" out of an anti-hero. *A Clockwork Orange* is a keen example of Kubrick's style of filmmaking in which he leads the audience to accept his personal point of view on a controversial issue.

—Linda J. Obalil

CLOSE ENCOUNTERS OF THE THIRD KIND. Production: Steven Spielberg Film Productions for Columbia Pictures; 1977; Metrocolor, 70mm, Dolby; running time: 134 mins. Released 9 November 1977. Re-released 1980 with additional footage under the title *Close Encounters of the Third Kind, Special Edition.*

Produced by Julia Phillips and Michael Phillips; screenplay by Steven Spielberg; directed by Steven Spielberg; photography by Vilmos Zsigmond, and Douglas Trumball, William A. Fraker, Douglas Slocombe, John Alonzo, Laszlo Kovacs, Richard Yuricich, Dave Stewart, Robert Hall, Don Jarel, and Dennis Muren; edited by Michael Kahn; sound by Buzz Knudson, Don MacDougall, Robert Glass, Gene Cantamessa, and Steve Katz, sound edited by Frank Warner; production design by Joe Alves, sets decorated by Phil Abramson; art direction by Dan Lomino; music by John Williams; special effects by Douglas Trumball; costumes designed by Jim Linn; consultant: Dr. J. Allen Hynek; stunts coordinated by Buddy Joe Hooker; "Extraterrestrials" realized by Carlo Rambaldi.

Filmed in U.S. and foreign locations. Cost: about $19 million. Academy Award, Cinematography (Zsigmond), 1977; Special Achievement Award from the Academy of Motion Picture Arts and Sciences to Frank Warner for Sound Effects Editing, 1977.

Cast: Richard Dreyfuss (*Roy Neary*); Melinda Dillon (*Jilian Guiler*); François Truffaut (*Claude Lacombe*); Cary Guffey (*Barry Guiler*); Teri Garr (*Ronnie Neary*); Bob Balaban (*David Laughlin*).

Publications:

Reviews—"The Greening of the Solar System" by Pauline Kael in the *New Yorker*, 28 November 1977; "Epiphany" by Stanley Kauffmann in the *New Republic* (New York), 10 December 1977; "The UFO's Are Coming" by Jack Kroll in *Newsweek* (New York), November 1977; "*Rencontres du troisième type*" by J.C. Biette in *Cahiers du cinéma* (Paris), April 1978; "*Close Encounters of the Third Kind*" by R. Combs in *Monthly Film Bulletin* (London), April 1978; "*Close Encounters of the Third Kind*" by Gordon Gow in *Films and Filming* (London), May 1978; "*Close Encounters of the Third Kind* by C.P. Reilly in *Films in Review* (New York), December 1977; "*Close Encounters of the Third Kind*" by John Simon in *Take One* (Montreal), January 1978; "The Third Coming" by Martin Gardner in the *New York Review of Books*, 26 January 1978; books—*Story telling and Mythmaking: Images from Film and Literature* by Frank McConnell, New York 1979; articles—"*Close Encounters of the Third Kind*" in *Films Illustrated* (London), December 1976; "Columbia Asks Bids on *Deep, Close Encounters* Carrying Hopes" by F. Segers in *Variety* (New York), 8 December 1976; "Steven Spielberg Wants You" by D. Shay and R.M. Stewart in *Cinemafantastique* (Oak Park, Illinois), no.3, 1976; "Weissman Named to Direct Projects for *Encounters*" in *Boxoffice* (Kansas City, Kansas), 8 November 1976; article in *Newsweek* (New York), 21 November 1977; article in *The New York Times*, 15 May 1977; "*Po Celistech UFO*" by J. Cieslar in *Film a Doba* (Prague), October 1977; "Close Encounters with Steven Spielberg" by B. Cook in *American Film* (Washington, D.C.), November 1977; "First Sightings of *Close Encounters of the Third Kind*" by D. Murray in *Millimeter* (New York), September 1977; special section on *Close Encounters* in *Filmmakers Newsletter* (Ward Hill, Massachusetts), December 1977; interview with Spielberg in *Penthouse* (New York), February 1978; "Rencontre express avec Steven Spielberg" by H. Béhar in *Image et son* (Paris), April 1978; "Hoe *Close Encounters of the Third Kind* gemaakt werd" by S. Brilleslijper in *Skoop* (Amsterdam), March 1978; special issue on *Close Encounters* in *American Cinematographer* (Hollywood), January 1978; "*Close Encounters of the Third Kind*" in *Films and Filming* (London), March 1978; "*Close Encounters of the Third Kind*: Close Encounters of the Third Reich" by F. Seymour and R. Entman in *Jump Cut* (Chicago), August 1978; "Trumball the Magician" by S. Eyman in *Take One* (Montreal), May 1978; "An Event Sociologique: *Close Encounters*"" by B. H. Fairchild in *Journal of Popular Culture* (Bowling Green, Ohio), no.4, 1978; "Steven Spielberg" by G. Heathwood in *Cinema Papers* (Melbourne, Australia), April/June 1978; "Close Encounters of a Quibbling Kind" by Ernest Lehman in *American Film* (Washington, D.C.), April 1978; "The Middle American Sky" by J. Pym in *Sight and Sound* (London), spring 1978; "Close Encounters of the 4th Kind" by G. Stewart in *Sight and Sound* (London), summer 1978; "The Forerunners of *CE3K*" by Alex Eisenstein in *Fantastic Films*, April 1978; interview with Spielberg by Mitch Tuchman in *Film Comment* (New York), January/February 1978; "Encounter Espionage" in *Film Comment* (New York), January/February 1978; "*Close Encounters* and *Star Wars*" by David Gerrold in *Science Fantasy Film Classics*, spring 1978; "Basn dwudziestego wieku" by J. Skwara in *Kino* (Warsaw), February

1979; "Montare, smontare, ircollare..." by S. Carlo in *Filmcritica* (Rome), April 1979; "*Close Encounters of the Third Kind*" by James Ursini in *Magill's Survey of Cinema, Vol. 1* edited by Frank N. Magill, Englewood Cliffs, New Jersey 1980; "Style vs. 'Style'" by R.T. Jameson in *Film Comment* (New York), March/April 1980; "*Close Encounters*: The Gospel According to Steven Spielberg" by A. Gordon in *Literature/Film Quarterly* (Salisbury, Maryland), no.3, 1980.

*   *   *

Following the financial success of *Jaws*, director Steven Spielberg was able to obtain funding for *Close Encounters of the Third Kind*, a large personal project about the UFO experience. Spielberg had explored this topic in a 2½ hour 8mm film he had made as a youth, called *Firelight*.

Close Encounters tells the story of Roy Neary, a middle class American who becomes alienated from his family and his suburban lifestyle when he sees actual flying saucers, apparently controlled by intelligent beings from outer space. The aliens have implanted a mysterious vision in Neary's mind, the meaning of which puzzles and frustrates him. Accompanied by Jillian Guiler, a woman whose son has been kidnapped by the aliens, Neary pursues his vision to Devil's Tower, an incredible mountain formation in Wyoming. There, they witness the first physical contact between a team of UFO investigators, led by French scientist Claude Lacombe, and the alien visitors. With a dazzling display of special effects, the film presents a host of small spaceships led by a gigantic mother ship. According to Spielberg, the inspiration for the mother ship's design was an oil refinery in India and the city lights of the San Fernando Valley in California. At the end of the film, Jillian is reunited with her son and Neary attains his dream by flying away with the mother ship.

The "Special Edition" of the film added scenes of Neary inside the mother ship, but cut the sequence where Neary throws dirt into his family's home in order to re-create his vision of Devil's Tower. Both versions of the film were combined in a special presentation for network television.

Critical reaction to the film was largely favorable, although there were some strong complaints about gaps in the narrative. Critics especially noted the religious overtones in the film.

But *Close Encounters* is more than just a quasi-religious celebration of childlike innocence—it is also a celebration of communication, expressed in the film through the interplay of light and music. The film opens with a splash of light and music and closes with an intensified version of these images and sounds, as the aliens and their human counterparts use flashing lights and a specific combination of musical tones to communicate with one another. Reportedly, composer John Williams actually started work for the film two years before it was finalized, and in many instances, he wrote his music first while Spielberg constructed the scenes to it later.

Close Encounters combines light and music to show how communication can transcend the boundaries between the known and the unknown, the human and the alien, the real and the imagined. As Frank McConnell suggests in his *Storytelling and Mythmaking*, the film "is not so much about aliens as about our imagination of aliens, or, rather, about the myths of film culture itself and their power to energize and ennoble our lives beyond the point of irony and dissatisfaction."

—Tom Snyder

COMO ETA GOSTOSO O MEU FRANCES. How Tasty Was My Little Frenchman. Production: Eduardo Embassahy, Manfred Colassanti, José Cléber (Brazil); 35mm; running time: 100 mins.; length: 2390 meters. Released 1971.

Produced by Luis Carlo Barreto and Nélson Pereira Dos Santos; scripted, directed, and edited by Nélson Pereira Dos Santos; photography by Dib Lufti; art direction by Regis Tontairo; music by Guilherme Mangalhaes Vaz; costumes designed by Nara Chaves.

Filmed in Brazil.

Cast: Arduino Colassanti (*Frenchman*); Ana Maria Magalhaes (*Girl*); Ital Natur (*Chief*).

Publications:

Reviews—in *Variety* (New York), 14 July 1971; "*Comme il était bon mon petit Francais*" by C.M. Cluny in *Cinéma* (Paris), May 1974; "*Qu'il était bon, mon petit Francais*" by M. Martin in *Ecran* (France), May 1974; "*Qu'il était bon mon petit Francais*" by D. Sauvaget in *Image et son* (Paris), May 1974; articles—in *Cinéma 71* (Paris), July/August 1971; article in *Positif* (Paris), September 1971; article in *Hablemos de Cine* (Lima, Peru), no.66, 1974; "The New Brazilian Film" by John Mosier in *The New Orleans Review*, no.1, 1978; article in *Take One* (Montreal), March 1979; "Brazilian Cinema Re-awakens: An Interview with Nelson Pereira Dos Santos" by Sebastian Dominguez in *Film Library Quarterly* (New York), no.1, 1979.

*   *   *

The scene is Brazil, 1557. The French and the Portuguese are battling for control of the area around Guanabara Bay, where the city of Rio de Janeiro is now located. A Frenchman is captured, along with some Portuguese, by the Tupinamba, a tribe supposedly allied to the French. Although he does his best to convince them otherwise, the Tupinamba declare the Frenchman their enemy and prisoner. As is their custom, he is taken into the tribe, given a wife, allowed to live and even fight beside them; meanwhile, he makes furtive plans to escape from Brazil with the help of a French merchant. In the end, his escape attempt is foiled, and the Tupinamba kill and cannibalize him during a victory celebration.

How Tasty Was My Little Frenchman marks a kind of watershed moment in the history of Brazilian cinema. Made during the darkest, most repressive period of a military dictatorship which had taken over Brazil in 1964, the film sought to combine the critical social analysis which had characterized the Brazilian cinema novo with an upbeat, more accessible style of filmmaking.

How Tasty... is essentially a complex metaphor for the whole of Brazilian history, with each of the major characters representing a large-scale social and political force. At the center of this maelstrom stands the Frenchman, a figure who, in his nakedness and with his shaved head, *looks* like the Tupinamba, yet who emotionally and (more importantly) economically is identified with the Europeans (in the film symbolized by the old French merchant). Pereira dos Santos plays on the audience's expectations; knowing full well that the Brazilian audience would identify with the Frenchman as a "hero," he continually undercuts the ease of this identification. Rather than accepting the Frenchman as a hero—the white-skinned European colonizer who is imagined as the "hero" of Brazilian history—the audience is asked instead to stand back and critically evaluate the Frenchman's position within the whole colonial experience.

How Tasty... begins with a declaration that it is the "latest news from Terra Firme" which was one of Brazil's colonial names, and indeed Pereira dos Santos attempts to expand the relevance of his political analysis of colonial forces into the seventies. The film is meant to be a portrait of contemporary Brazil as well, and this motif of "presentness" or actuality is re-emphasized throughout by the exceptional camera work of Dib Lutfi. The long, uninterrupted hand-held shots, quick zooms, and use of natural light are clearly evocative of the techniques of cinéma verité; *How Tasty...* is a historical film that's shot as if it were the evening news. Another of the film's interesting conceits is its use of language; the film is mainly in French and Tupi-Guarani, significantly not in Portuguese—as if Brazilians must read subtitles to understand their own history. Throughout the film the dialogue switches back and forth between French and Tupi-Guarani; for example, when the myth of Mair, the Indian's "great ancestor," is recounted, we hear the Frenchman's version, including images of him as a kind of white god readily accepted by the Indians, in French. At a key moment, the narration is taken over by Sebiopepe, the Frenchman's Indian wife, who speaks in Tupi-Guarani and gives a very different vision of the relations between her tribe and this "white god."

It is in this context that the film's notorious cannibalism must be understood. The cannibalism is a gesture of defiance, a special kind of revolt against the European invasion of Brazil. It represents the ultimate act of assimilation; the Frenchman, finally, does become part of the tribe, but in such a way that he is no longer able to be perceived as the Frenchman.

—Richard Peña

UN CONDAMNÉ À MORTE S'EST ECHAPPE. Le Vent souffle où il vent. A Man Escaped. The Spirit Breathes Where It Will. Production: SNE Gaumont/NEF (Paris); black and white, 35mm; running time: 102 mins. Released 1956, France.

Produced by Jean Thuillier and Alain Poiré; screenplay by Robert Bresson; from the account by André Devigny as published in *Le Figaro Littéraire*, 20 November 1954; directed by Robert Bresson; photography by Léonce-Henry Burel; edited by Raymond Lamy; sound by Pierre-André Bertrand; art direction by Pierre Charbonnier; music by Mozart, conducted by I. Disenhaus.

Filmed in France. Cannes Film Festival, Best Director, 1957.

Cast: François Leterrier (*Fontaine*); Roland Monod (*Le Pasteur*); Charles Le Clainche (*Jost*); Maurice Beerblock (*Blanchet*); Jacques Ertaud (*Orsini*).

Publications:

Books—*The Films of Robert Bresson* edited by Ian Cameron, London 1969; *The Films of Robert Bresson* by 5 reviewers, New York 1969; *French Cinema Since 1946, Vol. I* by Roy Armes, New York 1970; *Transcendental Style on Film: Ozu, Bresson, Dreyer* by Paul Schrader, Los Angeles 1972; *Notes sur le cinématographe* by Robert Bresson, Paris 1975, English edition

Notes on the Cinema, New York 1977; *Robert Bresson o cinematografo e o sinal* by C. de Pontes Leca, Lisbon 1978; articles— "Working with Bresson" by Roland Monod in *Sight and Sound* (London), summer 1957; "The Quest for Realism" by Gordon Gow in *Films and Filming* (London), December 1957; "Robert Bresson" by Brian Baxter in *Film* (London), September/October 1958; "Robert Bresson" by Charles Ford, translated by Anne and Thornton Brown in *Films in Review* (New York), February 1959; "Robert Bresson" by Marjorie Green in *Film Quarterly* (Berkeley), spring 1960; "An Interview with Robert Bresson" by Ian Cameron in *Movie* (London), February 1963; "Spiritual Style in the Films of Robert Bresson" by Susan Sontag in *Seventh Art* (New York), summer 1964; "Robert Bresson" in *Interviews with Film Directors* by Andrew Sarris, New York 1967; "Praxis as a Cinematic Principle in the Films of Robert Bresson" by Donald S. Skoller in *Cinema Journal* (Evanston, Illinois), fall 1969; "Spiritual Style in the Films of Robert Bresson" by Susan Sontag in *Against Interpretation*, New York 1969; "The Art of Robert Bresson" by Roy Armes in *London Magazine*, October 1970; "Robert Bresson" in *Current Biography Yearbook*, New York 1971; "Bresson's Stylistics Revisited" by M. Prokosch in *Film Quarterly* (Berkeley), v.15, no.1, 1972; "Matter and Spirit in the Films of Robert Bresson" by H.M. Polhemusin *Film Heritage* (Dayton, Ohio), spring 1974; "The Rhetoric of Robert Bresson" by P. Adams Sitney in *The Essential Cinema*, New York 1975; "For a Close Cinematic Analysis" by V. Petric in *Quarterly Review of Cinema Studies* (Pleasantville, New York), no.4, 1976.

*   *   *

In the words of Jesus to Nicodemus in the third chapter of St. John, "the spirit breathes where it will." This alternate title for the film speaks the director's intentions with greater clarity, for here Bresson illustrates the dictum that heaven helps the man who helps himself.

Basing his screenplay on a true incident involving the successful 1943 escape of André Devigny from Fort Monluc prison in Lyons just hours before he was to have been executed, Bresson fashioned an escape film which has none of the embellishments of other films with that subject. Disavowing grand scale action sequences and focusing on the intimate details of the process of escape, Bresson elucidates the *how* rather than the *why*, the details of the physical process rather than the psychological motivations. Beginning with fact and striving for authenticity, Bresson employed Devigny as an advisor, secured permission to film in the actual prison, and gained access to the ropes and hooks used by Devigny in his escape.

Having made two films in which performance and dialogue were central, Bresson began to develop an alternate narrative strategy with *Diary of a Country Priest*. In this and later films he disavowed all notions of theatricality, refusing to employ professional performers and insisting upon writing his screenplays in a stripped down, elliptical form. In *Un Condamné à Mort s'est échappé*, a voice-over monologue almost entirely replaced diegetic dialogue.

The protagonist, here named Fontaine, is the focus of the film, and yet the performance of the man who portrays him is only partially responsible for the central impact of the main character. Using first person voice-over narration and shifting the dramatic emphasis to a close examination of manual dexterity, Bresson was able to eliminate any dependence on the standard conventions of vocal and facial expression to impart dramatic emphasis. In so doing, and by avoiding a persistent use of point-of-view shots, Bresson was able to impart a spiritual dimension, making the spectator aware of the workings of fate as well as those of the individual. Fontaine's actions during the process of escape are thus transformed from a manual enterprise to a collaboration betweeen the physical and the spiritual.

Bresson creates an "escape" from traditional narrative form as well by the transformation of subjects and objects, creating meaning for those performers or objects which did not previously exist; certain items are transformed into the tools of escape, prisoners are transformed into free men, non-actors are turned into credible screen characters.

Visually alternating between scenes of solitary incarceration and minimal communication, Bresson used sound to allude to the possibility of freedom. In line with his belief that the ear is more creative than the eye, sound is used sparingly, generally to conjure up, for both Fontaine and the spectator, images that refer to ideas associated with escape: the guns of execution, the rattling of the prison guards keys, and the sound of a distant train. In the final moments of the film, as indicated by the title, Fontaine does realize his quest.

Less a film about the French Resistance, Un Condamné... is an evocation of Bresson's belief in man's existence as being governed by a combination of predestination and human will. Elucidated without embellishment, this unusually suspenseful film celebrates the mystery of fate and the power of individual will.

—Doug Tomlinson

IL CONFORMISTA. The Conformist. Production: Mars Film SPA (Rome), Marianne Productions (Paris), and Maran Film GMBH (Munich); Technicolor, 35mm; running time: 112 mins. Released 1970.

Produced by Maurizio Lodi-fe with Giovanni Bertolucci as executive producer; screenplay by Bernardo Bertolucci; from the novel by Alberto Moravia; directed by Bernardo Bertolucci; photography by Vittorio Storaro; edited by Franco Arcalli; production design by Ferdinando Scarfiotti, set decoration by Nedo Azzini; music by Georges Delerue; costumes designed by Gitt Margrini.

Filmed in Italy and Paris.

Cast: Jean-Louis Trintignant (*Marcello*); Stefania Sandrelli (*Giulia*); Dominique Sanda (*Anna Quadri*); Pierrel Clementi (*Nino Seminara*); Gastone Moschin (*Manganiello*); Enzo Tarascio (*Professor Quadri*); Jose Quaglio (*Halo*); Milly (*Marcello's mother*); Giuseppe Addobbati (*Marcello's father*); Yvonne Sanson (*Giulia's mother*); Fosco Giachetti (*The Colonel*); Benedetto Benedetti (*Minister*); Gio Vagni Luca (*Secretary*); Christian Alegny (*Raoul*); Antonio Maestri (*Priest*); Christian Belegue (*Gypsy*); Pasquale Fortunato (*Marcello as child*); Marta Lado (*Marcello's daughter*); Pierangelo Givera (*Male nurse*); Carlo Gaddi, Franco Pellerani, Claudio Cappeli, and Umberto Silvestri (*Hired killers*).

Publications:

Reviews—"*The Conformist*" by Gordon Gow in *Films and Filming* (London), January 1972; "*Medløberen*" by O. Hjort in *Kosmorama* (Copenhagen), February 1972; books—*Women and Sexuality in the New Film* by Joan Mellen, New York 1973; *The Great Spy Pictures* edited by James Robert Parish and

Michael R. Pitts, Metuchen, New Jersey 1974; *Bertolucci* by F. Casetti, Florence 1975; articles—"Jean-Louis Trintignant" by Molly Haskell in *Show* (Hollywood), 20 August 1970; "Bernardo Bertolucci, an Italian young master" by R. Kreitzman in *Film* (London), spring 1971; "Bernardo Bertolucci" by N. Purdon in *Cinema* (London), no.8, 1971; "Bertolucci on *The Conformist*" by Marilyn Goldin in *Sight and Sound* (London), spring 1971; "Bernardo Bertolucci: An Interview" by Amos Vogel in *Film Comment* (New York), fall 1971; "Fathers and Sons" by Richard Roud in *Sight and Sound* (London), spring 1971; "Bertolucci: Sobre *El Conformista*" by M. Goldin in *Hablemos de Cinema* (Lima), April/June 1972; "Skyggerne på vaeggen" by J.B. Jensen in *Kosmorama* (Copenhagen), December 1972; "Methoden & technieken van Brechts epies theater" by A. Apon in *Skrien* (Amsterdam), November/December 1973; "Bernardo Bertolucci Seminar" in *Dialogue on Film* (Washington, D.C.), April 1974; "*Le Conformiste* de Bernardo Bertolucci" by F. Paenhuijsen in *APEC-Revue Belge du cinema* (Brussels), no.3, 1974-75; "Novel into Film: Bertolucci's *The Conformist*" by D. Lopez in *Literature/Film Quarterly* (Salisbury, Maryland), fall 1976; "The Father Figure in *The Conformist* and in *Last Tango in Paris*" by D. Lopez in *Film Heritage* (Dayton, Ohio), summer 1976; special issue on Bertolucci in *Cinema* (Zurich), December 1972; "The Father Figure in The Conformist and in Last Tango in Paris" by D. Lopez in *Film Heritage* (New York), summer 1976; "Bertolucci's Gay Images" by W. Aitken in *Jump Cut* (Berkeley), November 1977; "Ideology and Narrative Strategy in Bertolucci's *The Conformist*" by C. Orr in *Film Criticism* (Edinboro, Pennsylvania), spring 1980.

*   *   *

Bernardo Bertolucci's films are often centered on the "split" protagonist. Sometimes (*Before the Revolution, The Conformist* and—if we take Maria Schneider as the central figure—*Last Tango in Paris*) the split is dramatized within a single individual torn between two lovers/ways of life/political allegiances; sometimes (*Partner, 1900*) it is dramatized by simultaneously paralleling and opposing two protagonists, inverted "doubles."

The Conformist repeats the essential structure of *Before the Revolution.* The protagonist is torn between alternatives on two levels: political—Marxism vs. conservative Fascism; and sexual—bourgeois marriage vs. a form of sexual deviancy (incest in the earlier film and homosexuality in the later, though this is touched on in the first section of the earlier film also). There are also important differences. In *The Conformist* the choice has already been made, and Marcello is presented with the quandary of whether to re-confirm or reverse it; also, because the protagonist is a (precariously) committed Fascist, Bertolucci is able to distance himself from him more successfully, achieving a degree of irony that eluded him in *Before the Revolution.*

What gives the films both richness and confusion is the failure of the political and sexual levels to become coherently aligned. One expects the straightforward opposition of Marxism/sexual liberation vs. conservatism/sexual conformity, but this never quite materializes. In *Before the Revolution* the protagonist's aunt/lover (and before her, his young male friend/potential lover) is presented as apolitical and neurotic. In *The Conformist* the "liberated" woman with left-wing commitments and explicit lesbian tendencies is associated (via the lesbianism) with decadence and irresponsibility. The homosexual chauffeur who seduced an already sexually ambiguous Marcello in childhood is also presented as decadent and exploitive. Yet the film is quite clear in connecting Marcello's *repression* of his homosexuality with his espousal of Fascism. The tension is never resolved in the film, or elsewhere, in Bertolucci's work so far.

Fundamental to the "Bertoluccian split" is a tension within his cinematic allegiances. Avowedly a disciple of Godard, his stylistic affinities are with a tradition of luxuriance and excess that might be represented by Welles, Ophuls and von Sternberg—a tradition totally alien to Godard's filmic practice. When Bertolucci obtained financing from Paramount for *The Conformist*, Godard (then at his most intransigent, in the period immediately following the upheavals of May, 1968) denounced him. Bertolucci took his revenge by giving Marcello's left-wing mentor, Professor Quadri, Godard's telephone number, then having the character violently assassinated. It is not surprising that the same film sees the full flowering of Bertolucci's stylistic flamboyance—elaborate camera movements, strange baroque angles, luxuriant color effects, a profusion of ornate décor, the intricate play of light and shadow. This abandonment, however, never ceases to be troubled and uneasy: baroque excess collides with Godardian distanciation. The film at once intellectually disavows "decadence" yet acknowledges an irresistible fascination for it. The split is not merely thematic (hence under the artist's control): it manifests itself at every level of his filmmaking.

—Robin Wood

LA COQUILLE ET LE CLERGYMAN. The Seashell and the Clergyman. Production: Delia Film (Dulac's company) may have produced it, but there is no concrete evidence to that fact; black and white, 35mm, silent; running time: 42 mins., some sources list 38 mins. Released 9 February 1928.

Scenario by Antonin Artaud, revised by Germaine Dulac; directed by Germaine Dulac; photography by Paul Guichard; edited by Paul Parguel; assisted by Louis Ronjat.

Filmed at Studio de Ursulines in Paris.

Cast: Alex Allin (*Priest*); Bataille (*Officer*); Gerica Athanasiou (*Woman*);

Publications:

Scripts—*La Coquille et le clergyman* (Artaud's version) in *Nouvelle Revue française* (Paris), November 1927; books—*The Cubist Cinema* by Standish D. Lawder, New York 1975; *Abstract Film and Beyond* by Malcolm Le Grice, Cambridge, Massachusetts 1977; articles—"Sur le cinéma visuel" by Germaine Dulac in *Le Rouge et le noir* (Paris), July 1928; "Jouer avec les bruits" by Germaine Dulac in *Cinéa-Ciné por tous* (Paris), 15 August 1929; biography by Charles Ford in *Anthologie du cinéma* (Paris), no.31, January 1968; "Maya Deren and Germaine Dulac: Activists of the Avant-Garde" by Regina Cornwell in *Film Library Quarterly* (New York), winter 1971/72; "Germaine Dulac: 1st Feminist Filmmaker" by W. Van Wert in *Women and Film* (Santa Monica, Calif.), v.1, no.5-6, 1974; "Dulac vs. Artaud" by W. Dozoretz in *Wide Angle* (Athens, Ohio), no.1, 1979; "*La Coquille et le clergyman*" in *Travelling* (Lausanne, Switzerland), summer 1979; "Rediscovering French Film: Part II" by Eileen Bowser and Marjorie Baumgarten in *Museum of Modern Art Department of Film* (notes on the films), January and February 1980.

*   *   *

La Coquille et le clergyman, made by Germaine Dulac, may now be regarded as the first surrealist film. Dulac filmed it two years prior to the Buñuel-Dali film *Le Chien andalou*, which contains the image of an eye sliced by a razor. In *Coquille*, Dulac used trick photography to split an officer's head in half. Both films are surrealist specimens, sharing several basic qualities.

Antonin Artaud wrote the scenario for the film Dulac planned to direct. Artaud wanted to act the role of the priest, but did not want to direct the film. Vacillating, he changed his mind. He wrote to Dulac that he was annoyed that the shooting and editing of *La Coquille* were done without him. Dulac had revised his scenario, casting Alex Allin in the priest's role, Bataille as the officer, and Gerica Athanasiou as the woman. The film represents the subconscious sexual cravings of the priest in dream-like enviornments. In one shocking scene the clothed priest is shown masturbating. Elsewhere, the priest meets a frightening woman's ghost in a ballroom. He runs away, pulling up the skirts of his cassock; his cassock lengthens and stretches like a tail behind him. The clergyman and the woman then run through darkness, their progress marked by visions of the woman in varying forms, once with her tongue sticking out, another time with her cheek ballooning outward.

In another scene, the priest wears a frockcoat in a wine cellar. He empties an array of glasses of red wine, then shatters all of them. With no transition, he then crawls on his hands and feet on the streets of Paris. It is believed Artaud was infuriated by Dulac's direction of this scene. He criticized Dulac for softening the lean strength of his script. When Dulac premiered *La Coquille* on February 9, 1928, as "a dream of Antonin Artaud," Artaud denounced the film. According to Wendy Dozoretz in her article in *Wide Angle*, it was André Breton who yelled out, as the film's credits appeared on the screen, "Mme. Dulac is a cow." Led by Artaud, critic Georges Sadoul, novelist Louis Aragon and others stopped the film projector, threw objects at the screen and walked out in protest, leaving a bewildered audience behind. In Dozoretz's words, *La Coquille* was "the unique product of two incongruous minds."

Certain contemporary critics contend that Artaud's scenario was superior to Dulac's interpretation. David Curtis in *Experimental Cinema* faults Dulac's pictorial conceptions as oversimplified, and her editing as too well measured, subtracting from Artaud's visions. J.H. Matthews in *Surrealism and Film* affirms that Dulac did not comprehend Artaud's artistic intentions, and did distort his script. "...She did not succeed altogether in emptying Artaud's scenario of surrealist content. For this reason alone, her *Coquille*... deserves mention among the first surrealist films..."

Wendy Dozoretz admits that the feminist Dulac's direction of the film could have revised the misogynist, Artaud scenario. However, the optical tricks that Dulac used were inherent in the scenario. As for Artaud's charge that Dulac "feminized" his script, Dozoretz agrees that Dulac probably did weaken the harsh brutality of Artaud's work.

Presently, *La Coquille* is more widely known and more often shown because Henri Langlois, head of the Cinemathéque Française, rediscovered it, after decades of oblivion. *La Coquille* has aged gracefully, its potency intact, in its deserved niche as a classic of surrealist cinema.

—Louise Heck-Rabi

THE COVERED WAGON. Production: Famous Players-Lasky (later Paramount); 1923; black and white, 35mm, silent;

length: 10 reels, 9407 feet. Released 8 September 1924 (premiered 16 March 1923, New York).

Presented by Jesse L. Lasky and Adolph Zukor, produced by James Cruze (note: Zukor's name was added later); scenario by Jack Cunningham; from the novel by Emerson Hough; directed by James Cruze; photography by Karl Brown; edited by Dorothy Arzner; music arranged by Hugo Riesenfeld; advisor: Co. T. J. McCoy. The film is dedicated to the memory of Theodore Roosevelt.

Filmed in, among other locales, Nevada's Sun Valley and Antelope Island in the Great Salt Lake.

Cast: Lois Wilson (*Molly Wingate*); J. Warren Kerrigan (*Will Banion*); Ernest Torrence (*Jackson*); Charles Ogle (*Mr. Wingate*); Ethel Wales (*Mrs. Wingate*); Alan Hale (*Sam Woodhull*); Tully Marshall (*Bridger*); Guy Oliver (*Kit Carson*); John Fox (*Jed Wingate*); 1000 Indians as extras.

Publications:

Books—*The Western: From Silents to Cinerama* by William Everson and George N. Fenin, New York 1962; *The Great Films: 50 Golden Years of Motion Pictures* by Bosley Crowther, New York 1967; *A Pictorial History of the Western Film* by William K. Everson, New York 1969; *Westerns—Aspects of a Movie Genre* by Philip French, New York 1973; *The Great Western Pictures* edited by James Robert Parish and Michael Pitts, Metuchen, New Jersey 1976; *American Silent Film* by William Everson, New York 1978; articles—"Cruze, Trail-breaker" by D. Donnel in *Motion Picture Classic* (Brooklyn), September 1925; "Cruze, Director" by Frank Condon in *Collier's* (New York), 28 March 1936; "James Cruze" by George Geltzer in *Films in Review* (New York), July 1954; "The Covered Wagon" by Alan Stanbrook in *Films and Filming* (London), May 1960; "*The Covered Wagon*" by John Perry in *Film Heritage* (Dayton, Ohio), spring 1969; "Fantasy and Form in the Western by T.J. Ross in *December*, nos.1-2, 1970.

*   *   *

When viewed today, *The Covered Wagon* seems to be just another static, clichéd western, hampered by a familiar storyline, one-dimensional characterizations and an annoyingly slow pace. But the film is something more, much more. It is the original of its type, the first real epic western, the model on which hundreds of future westerns were based.

The scenario of *The Covered Wagon* may be hackneyed: it details pioneer hardships on a trek across America to settle the west. The film is decidedly lacking in drama, with the titles relying more on dates and references to familiar period names than on character development and interaction. It is never actually clear why these brave settlers have undertaken their journey: their sense of purpose in pioneering Oregon and California is nonexistent.

Overall, *The Covered Wagon* is not as vividly authentic as the earlier William S. Hart westerns, with director James Cruze more concerned with spectacle than realism. As Hart himself pointed out when *The Covered Wagon* was released, no sane wagon train leader, aware of a threat of indian attack, would camp his charges in a boxed-in canyon. Cruze's direction is also crude, and *The Covered Wagon* does not differ from most of the director's films in this respect. He ignores the technical innova-

tions of the day, securing his camera to the ground. Most annoyingly, he shoots an errant horse not from various angles or in closeup, but in one boring longshot.

The visual grandeur of *The Covered Wagon*, however, easily overrides any objection to Cruze's failings. The film was shot outdoors, in such impressive locales as Nevada's Sun Valley and Antelope Island in the Great Salt Lake. The spectacular camerawork of Karl Brown, a former assistant cinematographer for D.W. Griffith who shot all of Cruze's films between 1921 and 1926, effectively captures the settlers' trials in an almost documentary-like manner. Brown's panoramic shots of the wagons rolling one after the other across the plain or Indians attacking the settlers under an ominous gray sky are no less than majestic. Buffalo hunts, river crossings, campfire singing, burials and births all add to the film's splendor.

Early on, *The Covered Wagon* was rightfully regarded as a classic. The film, begun as a programmer with the script rewritten and expanded during production, received critical praises. Audiences were convinced that they had never really experienced the Old West on celluloid—despite the earlier efforts of Hart, Griffith and others. As a result, the film was a box office success. It helped renew the career of its star, J. Warren Kerrigan, a leading screen hero of the early silent years, who had retired after starring in *Captain Blood* in 1924. It also revived the western genre at a time when such films had suffered a major decline in audience interest. In 1922, 50 western features were completed; and, with the exception of those starring Hart and Tom Mix, most were plodding "B" efforts. By 1924, the production of westerns tripled. The largest success was John Ford's *The Iron Horse*, far richer than *The Covered Wagon* in most every detail. Without the success of *The Covered Wagon*, however, *The Iron Horse* might simply never have been made.

The Covered Wagon is a western spectacle, the likes of which audiences in 1923 were unaccustomed. It may have lost its critical luster over the years, yet it remains a milestone in the evolution of its genre.

—Rob Edelman

———————

CRIA CUERVOS... Production: Elías Querejeta Production Company (Madrid); Eastmancolor, 35mm; running time: 112 mins.; length: 2740 meters. Released Cannes Film Festival, 1976.

Produced by Elías Querejeta; screenplay by Carlos Saura; directed by Carlos Saura; photography by Teodoro Escamilla; edited by Pablo del Amo; sound engineered by Bernardo Menz; production design by Rafael Palmero; music by Federico Mompou and Valverde Leon Y Quiroga, songs sung by J.L. Perales and Jeanette; costumes designed by Maiki Marin.

Filmed in Madrid. Cannes Film Festival, Special Jury Prize, 1976.

Cast: Ana Torrent (*Ana*); Conchita Pérez (*Irene*); Mayte Sánchez (*Juana*); Geraldine Chaplin (*Ana, Madre-Mujer*); Mónica Randall (*Paulina*); Florinda Chico (*Rosa*); Héctor Alterio (*Anselmo*); Germán Cobos (*Nicolás*); Mirta Miller (*Amelia*); Josefina Díaz (*Abuela*).

Publications:

Scripts—*Cria cuervos...* by Carlos Saura, 2nd edition, Madrid

1976; "*Cria Cuervos*" by Carlos Saura in *Avant-Scène du cinéma* (Paris), 15 October 1978; reviews—"*Cria Cuervos* by C. Braucourt and others" in *Ecran* (Paris), July 1976; "*Cria Cuervos*" by C.M. Cluny in *Cinéma 76* (Paris), July 1976; "*Cria Cuervos*" by L. Jajeunesse in *Revue du cinéma* (Paris), october 1976; "*Cria Cuervos*" by P. Maraval in *Cinématographe* (Paris), summer 1976; "Carlos Saura's *Cria Cuervos*" by W. Aitken in *Take One* (Montreal), July/August 1977; "*Cria Cuervos*" by R.C. Bérubé in *Séquences* (Montreal), April 1977; "*Cria*" by DeWitt Bodeen in *Films in Review* (New York), October 1977; "La Presse" in *Avant-Scène du cinéma* (Paris), 15 October 1978; "*Cria cuervos*" by I. Pauks in *Cinema Papers* (Melbourne, Australia), October 1977; "*Cria cuervos*" by T. Pulleine in *Sight and Sound* (London), autumn 1978; "*Cria cuervos*" by J. Pym in *Monthly Film Bulletin* (London), September 1978; books—*Carlos Saura* by Enrique Brasó, Madrid 1974; *Venturas y desventuras de la prima Angélica* by Diego Galan, Valencia 1974; *Homenaje a Carlos Saura* by Roman Gubern, Huelva 1979; articles—"Pleurons, pleurons, c'est le plaisir des dieux..." by R. Duval in *Ecran* (Paris), September 1976; "Entretien avec Carlos Saura" by E. Braso in *Positif* (Paris), June 1977; "Carlos Saura" by D. Maillet in *Cinématographe* (Paris), July/August 1977; "L'Anti-vie..." by Daniel Jolly-Mange in *Avant-Scène du cinéma* (Paris), 15 October 1978; "L'Album de famille" by Carlos Saura in *Avant-Scène du cinéma* (Paris), 15 October 1978; "Prostor a čas v posledních dílech Carlose Saury" by J. Foll in *Film a Doba* (Prague), July 1978; "*Cria Cuervos* de Carlos Saura in *Revue Belge du Cinéma* (Brussels), December/March 1977-78; interview with Saura in *Film und Fernsehen* (East Berlin), no.3, 1979; "Carlos Saura: The Political Development of Individual Consciousness" by M. Kinder in *Film Quarterly* (Berkeley), no.3, 1979; article by J. Schnelle in *Medien und Erziehung* (Munich), no.2, 1979; "*Cria Cuervos*" by I.L. Frias in *Hablemos de cine* (Lima, Peru), no.70, 1979; "Carlos Saura: Constructive Imagination in the Post-Franco Cinema" by Marvin D'Lugo in *Quarterly Review of Film Studies* (Pleasantville, New York), spring 1983.

LE CRIME DE MONSIEUR LANGE. L'Ascension de M. Lange. Sur la coeur. Dans la coeur. The Crime of Monsieur Lange. Production: Obéron; black and white, 35mm; running time: about 2 hours. Released 24 January 1936, Paris.

Screenplay by Jacques Prévert and Jean Renoir; from an idea by Jean Castanier; directed by Jean Renoir; photography by Jean Bachelet; edited by Marguerite Renoir; sound by Guy Moreau, Louis Bogé, Roger Loisel, and Robert Tesseire; production design by Jean Castanier and Robert Gys assisted by Roger Blin; art direction by Marcel Blondeau; music by Jean Wiener, orchestra directed by Roger Desormières; still photography by Dora Maar.

Filmed October-November 1935 in Billancourt studios, exteriors shot in and around Paris.

Cast: Jules Berry (*Paul Batala*); René Lefèvre (*Amédée Lange*); Florelle (*Valentine Cardès*); Nadia Sibirskaia (*Estelle*); Sylvia Bataille (*Edith*); Henri Guisol (*Meunier's son*); Marcel Leveseque (*Landlord*); Odette Talazac (*Landlady*); Maurice Baquet (*Landlord's son*); Jacques Brunius (*Baigneur*); Marcel Duhamel (*Foreman*); Jean Dasté (*Dick*); Paul Grimault (*Louis*); Guy Decomble, Henri Saint-Isles, and Fabien Loris (*Workers at the publishing house*); Claire Gérard (*Prostitute*); Edmond Beau-

champ (*Priest on the train*); Sylvain Itkine (*Inspector Julian*); René Génin (*Client*); Janine Loris (*Worker*); plus Jean Brémand, Pierre Huchet, Charbonnier and Marcel Lupovici, Michel Duran, and Dora Maar.

Publications:

Books—*Jean Renoir* by Paul Davay, Brussels 1957; *Jean Renoir* by Armand-Jean Cauliez, Paris 1962; *Jean Renoir* edited by Bernard Chardère in *Premier Plan* (Lyon), no.22-24, May 1962; *Analyses des films de Jean Renoir* by Institut des Hautes Etudes Cinématographiques, Paris 1966; *Study Unit 8: Jean Renoir* by Susan Bennett, London 1967; *Renoir 1938 ou Jean Renoir pour rein. Enquête sur un cinéaste* by François Poulle, Paris 1969; *Jean Renoir* by Pierre Leprohon, New York 1971; *Humanidad de Jean Renoir* by Carlos Cuenca, Valladolid, Mexico 1971; *Jean Renoir: The World of his Films* by Leo Braudy, New York 1972; *Jean Renoir* by André Bazin, edited by François Truffaut, Paris, translated ed. 1973. *Jean Renoir* by Raymond Durgnat, Berkeley 1974; *Jean Renoir: le spectacle, la vie* by Claude Beylie, Paris 1975; *Jean Renoir: Essays, Conversations, Reviews* by Penelope Gilliatt, New York 1975; *French Cinema Since 1946: Vol. I, The Great Tradition* by Roy Armes, New York 1976; *Jean Renoir: A Guide to References and Resources* by Christopher Faulkner, Boston 1979; articles—special Renoir issue, *Cahiers du Cinéma* (Paris), January 1952; special Renoir issue, *Cahiers du cinéma* (Paris), Christmas 1957; "The Renaissance of the French Cinema—Feyder, Renoir, Duvivier, Carné" by Georges Sadoul in *Film: An Anthology* edited by Daniel Talbot, New York 1959; "Why Renoir Favors Multiple Camera, Long Sustained Take Technique" by Jean Belanger in *American Cinematographer* (Los Angeles), March 1960; "Renoir and Realism" by Peter Dyer in *Sight and Sound* (London), summer 1960; article by Richard Whitehall on Renoir's films in *Films and Filming* (London), June 1960 and concluded in July 1960; "The Cinema of the Popular Front in France" by Goffredo Fofi in *Screen* (London), winter 1972/73; "Renoir's *Crime de Monsieur Lange*: Visual Environments" by B. Klinger in *Wide Angle* (Athens, Ohio), no.2, 1979; "Alain Tanner's *Jonah...*: Echoes of Renoir's *M. Lange*" by A. Horton in *Film Criticism* (Edinboro, Pennsylvania), spring 1980; "Jean Renoir's *Crime of Monsieur Lange*" by P. Pappas in *Cineaste* (New York), summer 1980; "A Reconsideration of Renoir's Film" by E.G. Streubel in *Sight and Sound* (London), winter 1979-80.

* * *

For nearly three decades Jean Renoir's *Le Crime de Monsieur Lange* was a film which failed to garner the recognition it so richly deserved. At the time of its release, it was received indifferently and suffered the vicissitudes of political censorship. It was not until 1964 that the film enjoyed a U.S. release, and belatedly earned its reputation as a pivotal work in Renoir's career.

Le Crime de Monsieur Lange is the film which solidified Renoir's political reputation as the film director of the left. In sympathy with France's Popular Front, this film was Renoir's statement that the ordinary working man, through united action, can overcome the tyranny of fascism. Renoir's films were always imbued with a humanism and love for all mankind. With this film he uses a small group of Parisian workers, their families and neighbors, as a microcosm for the French common man.

Lange, played by René Lefevre, is the author of a western pulp fiction series entitled *Arizona Jim*. When Batala (played magnificently by the great Jules Berry), the head of the nearly-bankrupt publishing company, absconds with the company funds, Lange organizes a "cooperative" with the help of the other employees. Their venture is so successful it prompts the scoundrel publisher to return in the guise of a priest and reap the monetary rewards of the cooperative. In a brave and mandatory move, the naive and humble Lange kills the publisher to prevent the destruction of their venture. Lange and his girlfriend flee the country, are caught by border guards, but allowed to go free when the girl explains the details of Lange's crime.

The script of *Monsieur Lange* was written by Jacques Prévert from an idea by Renoir and Jean Castanier. As with all Renoir films, the script was simply a starting point around which Renoir composed his films. To emphasize the sense of community, Renoir centers all the action on the courtyard which surrounds the publishing firm as well as the homes of the workers. Thus the courtyard becomes an integral part of Renoir's mise-en-scene, as much a character in the film as any of the actors, representing a united world which in turn evokes Renoir's philosophical aspirations for all mankind. Renoir is thus able to demonstrate the importance of the interaction of his characters for the benefit of all. The beginning of the film is devoted mostly to scenes of characters one-on-one, emphasizing the lack of any central goal. When Lange begins his efforts to form the cooperative, Renoir shifts his scenes to those of group relationships. Throughout, he uses his extraordinarily fluid and cyclical camera movements to create a unity of both time and purpose.

While *Monsieur Lange* is both an intriguing story of crime and an exercise in black humor, the film encompasses much more. It is an attack on class superiority and prejudice, an attack on the church, and although Lange does commit murder, it is a crime of poetic justice exonerated by the victim's avarice and the altruism of Lange's goal. Despite its indifferent reception at its release, *Le Crime de Monsieur Lange* is today regarded as one of Renoir's best films and one which significantly captures the social consciousness of the day.

—Ronald Bowers

CROSSFIRE. Production: RKO Radio Pictures Corp.; 1947; black and white, 35mm; running time: 86 mins. Released 22 July 1947.

Produced by Adrian Scott, executive producer: Dore Schary; screenplay by John Paxton; from the novel *The Brick Foxhole* by Richard Brooks; directed by Edward Dmytryk; photography by Roy Hunt; edited by Harry Gerstad; sound by John E. Tribby and Clem Portman; art direction by Albert D'Agostino and Alfred Herbert, set decoration by Darrell Silvera and John Sturteurant; music by Roy Webb, music direction by Constantin Bakaleinikoff; special effects by Russell A. Cully.

Filming completed 28 March 1947 in RKO studios. Best Social Film, Cannes Film Festival, 1947.

Cast: Robert Young (*Finlay*); Robert Mitchum (*Keeley*); Robert Ryan (*Montgomery*); Gloria Grahame (*Ginny*); Paul Kelly (*The Man*); Sam Levene (*Samuels*); Jacqueline White (*Mary Mitchell*); Steve Brodie (*Floyd*); George Cooper (*Mitchell*); Richard Benedict (*Bill*); Richard Powers (*Detective*); William Phipps (*Leroy*); Lex Barker (*Harry*); Marlo Dwyer (*Miss Lewis*).

Publications:

Reviews—by Elliot E. Cohen in *Commentary* (New York), August 1947; review by Bosley Crowther in *The New York Times*, 23 July 1947; review by James Agee in the *Nation* (New York), 2 August 1947; books—*Agee on Film*, Vol. 1, by James Agee, New York 1958; *Kings of the B's: Working Within the Hollywood System* by Todd McCarthy and Charles Flynn, New York 1975; *The Films of the Forties* by Tony Thomas, Secaucus, New Jersey 1975; *It's a Hell of a Life But Not a Bad Living* by Edward Dmytryk, New York 1978; *Film Noir* edited by Alain Silver and Elizabeth Ward, Woodstock, New York 1979; articles—"Some of My Worst Friends" by Adrian Scott in *Screen Writer* (London), October 1947; "You Can't Do That" by Adrian Scott in *Screen Writer* (London), August 1947; reply by Dore Schary to Elliot Cohen review in *Commentary* (New York), no.4 1947; article by John Houseman in *Hollywood Quarterly*, fall 1947; article by Richard Brooks in *Films in Review* (New York), February 1952; "Edward Dmytryk" by Romano Tozzi in *Films in Review* (New York), February 1962; "Robert Mitchum" by Gene Ringgold in *Films in Review* (New York), May 1964; "Robert Ryan" by Jeanne Stein in *Films in Review* (New York), January 1968; *Crossfire*" by Eileen Bowser in *Film Notes* edited by Eileen Bowser, New York 1969; "The Cinema of Edward Dmytryk" in *Films Illustrated* (London), October 1971; "Odio implacabile" by E. Magrelli in *Filmcritica* (Rome), May/June 1976; *Crossfire* and the Anglo-American Tradition" by C. McArthur in *Film Form* (Newcastle-upon-Tyne, England), autumn 1977; *Crossfire*: A Dialectical Attack" by K. Kelly and C. Steinman in *Film Reader* (Evanston, Illinois), no.3, 1978; *Crossfire*" by Louis Black in *Cinema Texas Notes* (Austin), 20 February 1978.

*   *   *

A fascinating and biting film noir, *Crossfire* is a good example of the message film disguised as entertainment. It is one of a series of films produced in the later 1940s when the American motion picture industry discovered that adult themes and social problems could produce good box office. The first of two films released in 1947 dealing with anti-Semitism, *Crossfire* was both a commercial smash and a critical success. It was RKO's most lucrative production, earning over $1,000,000 in profits. It also garnered outstanding reviews: film critic James Agee called it "the best Hollywood movie in a long time" and *Newsweek* magazine judged it "one of the year's best films."

The film opens on a soldier, shrouded in shadows, viciously beating a man to death. The victim was Jewish, and his killer is a pathological sadist and rabid Jew-hater (stunningly portrayed by Robert Ryan). *Crossfire* is actually concerned with why the man is beaten to death, rather than who did the killing, as less than halfway through the film the killer's identity becomes known. The setting has been described by two film historians as "that peculiar midnight-to-dawn atmosphere that ordinary surroundings acquire in those mute subdued hours," and includes still, almost deserted city streets, all-night movie theatres, seedy bars, and cheap apartments—as well as the disparate and somewhat shady types who inhabit this world. Before the killer is brought to justice by an avuncular but hardnosed police captain (played by Robert Young in a role against type), he also brutally strangles a fellow soldier who might have given him away. Assisting the police captain is an army sergeant (Robert Mitchum) who serves in part as a sounding board for the captain in his comments on racial prejudice.

The movie is based on *The Brick Foxhole* by Richard Brooks, who later gained a certain well-deserved fame as a screenwriter and director. The novel focused on the brutal murder of a homosexual, but as that subject was just too controversial for a Hollywood still under the domination of the Motion Picture Production Code, the filmmakers changed the victim to a Jew. The "message" of the film is presented by the police captain. In perhaps a too didactic sermon, he preaches the need for tolerance and an end to prejudice, and summarizes the role of bigotry in American history. The film's message and its good intentions deserve respect but, over time, have lost their forcefulness. What remains striking and powerful is the framework in which the message of the film was set. *Crossfire* is a well-crafted, carefully organized, beautifully presented melodrama which still retains its audience's interest in the story's unfolding.

—Daniel Leab

THE CROWD. Production: Metro-Goldwyn-Mayer Pictures Corp.; 1928; black and white, 35mm, silent with music score; running time: about 93 mins.; length: 9 reels, 8538-8548 feet. Released 3 March 1928.

Produced by King Vidor; scenario by King Vidor, John V.A. Weaver and Harry Behn; titles by Joseph Farnham; directed by King Vidor; photography by Henry Sharp; edited by Hugh Wynn; production design by Cedric Gibbons and Arnold Gillespie; music score by Carl Davis.

Cast: Eleanor Boardman (*Mary*); James Murray (*John*); Bert Roach (*Bert*); Estelle Clark (*Jane*); Daniel G. Tomlinson (*Jim*); Dell Henderson (*Dick*); Lucy Beaumont (*Mother*); Freddie Burke Frederick (*Junior*); Alice Mildred Puter (Daughter).

Publications:

Books—*The Great Films: Fifty Golden Years of Motion Pictures* by Bosley Crowther, New York 1967; *The Parade's Gone By...* by Kevin Brownlow, New York 1968; *King Vidor* by John Baxter, New York 1976; *A Tree is a Tree* by King Vidor, New York, reprinted 1977; articles—interview with Vidor by B. Beach in *Motion Picture Classic* (New York), June 1928; interview with Vidor by M. Cheatham in *Motion Picture Classic* (New York), June 1928; "Work of King Vidor" by W.E. Mulligan in the *National Review* (New York), July 1928; "Collectivism More or Less" by W. Troy in *Nation* (New York), 24 October 1934; "King Vidor" by Kevin Brownlow in *Film* (London), winter 1962; article by John Thomas in *AFFS Newsletter* (New York), November 1964; "King Vidor" by Charles Higham in *Film Heritage* (Dayton, Ohio), summer 1966; "King Vidor at NYU: Discussion" in *Cineaste* (New York), spring 1968; "James Murray" by Vernon Schonert in *Films in Review* (New York), December 1968; "A Career that Spans Half a Century" by H.G. Luft in *Film Journal* (New York), summer 1971; "*The Crowd*" by Raymond Durgnat in *Film Comment* (New York), July/August 1973; issue on Vidor in *Positif* (Paris), September 1974; "Entre l'horizon d'un seul et l'horizon de tous" by B. Amengual in *Positif* (Paris), September 1974; "L'Acteur" by King Vidor in *Positif* (Paris), December/January 1978; "Crowd Music" by M. Ellis in *Sight and Sound* (London), autumn 1981.

*   *   *

King Vidor's career wavered between the lure of romantic, erotic melodrama and the stricter morality of the Christian Science background. After three John Gilbert vehicles, including the popular *The Big Parade*, Vidor was able to sell MGM on a bleak, expressionist urban tragedy of the sort made fashionable by the novels of Sinclair Lewis, Theodore Dreiser and John Dos Passos. Other studios, notably Fox, already enjoyed considerable success in this area due to their importation of German and Austrian directors like Murnau and Dupont. MGM, committed to a policy of mainly Scandinavian recruitment, lacked such experts in the relentless art of the "city film." Vidor persuaded Irving Thalberg to permit this single excursion into the field by offering to produce "*The Big Parade* of peace"—clearly a stratagem, since *The Crowd* is as cynical and relentless as his World War I romantic drama was soft-centered and sentimental.

The Crowd is a remarkable aberration to come from optimistic, cheerful MGM machine, mocking as it does all American fictions of self-advancement and ambition. John Sims's birth on July 4th, 1900, is greeted with elation by his father. "He's a little man the world's going to hear from," he crows. But social circumstances, Vidor points out, guide our life from childhood. John's schoolboy friends already have their careers mapped out for them, especially the black boy who boasts in comic minstrel patter of the time "I detend to be a preacher man. Hallelujah!"

No less a social stereotype, John is forced by his father's early death to join the crowd who fill the streets of New York. "You've got to be good in that town if you want to beat the crowd," remarks a gaunt stranger as John watches the skyline from a ferry. As a huge office building swallows up the young Sims, we realize he has become another victim of the city, subject to its whims, threatened by its pressures.

John's early enthusiasm for city life, fuelled by visits to Coney Island, an early marriage and the unexpected windfall of a $500 slogan-writing contest prize, is crushed by the random death of his child, then unemployment and a slide to the humiliation of selling vacuum cleaners door to door, until he becomes a juggling sandwich-board man—a character seen before and mocked by Sims, but who returns like the clown in *The Blue Angel* as a *memento mori*. Interfering relatives nearly destroy Sims's marriage, but the love of his son saves him from a suicide attempt and he's finally reunited with his wife. "The crowd laughs with you always," warns a title, "but it will cry with you for only a day."

Vidor tried seven endings before shooting one incorporating this bleak moral. Sims and his family visit a vaudeville show, and are last seen howling at the antics of two clowns, swallowed in a mindless laughing crowd.

Always attracted by expressionism and stylisation, Vidor exercised his penchant for both in *The Crowd*. Characters seem swallowed by their environment; the office building where John works (actually a model) is one of thousands in the city, and the camera zooms in through a window, apparently at random, to choose him, just another wage slave in an office of identical desks reaching in forced perspective to infinity. Earlier in the film, when John hears of his father's death, Vidor creates a vision of his threatened status by placing the boy on a staircase constructed against a distorted impression of a corridor actually painted on the back wall of the set. John, sustained by a relative, seems to hover between the inquisitive crowd huddled around the doorway and a threatening, unknown future.

James Murray, a minor featured performer (and not, as Vidor claimed, an extra) superbly conveys the feckless, ukelele-plucking John Sims mindlessly letting the world carry him along. (He was never to be offered work of this standard again, and drowned in the Hudson River in 1936; used to his gagging, watchers thought he was joking and failed to attempt a rescue.) Eleanor Boardman, later Vidor's wife, is an effective support.

But, as in all "city films," the individuals are dwarfed by an unfeeling capitalist society. Vidor emphasises this isolation in the film's most striking images; trying to quiet the crowd to soothe his dying child, Sims plunges blindly against the hurrying mob, hands thrust out, eyes blind; clocks dictate the coming and going of the city people with a relentless Langian power; even the couple's honeymoon is dwarfed by the torrent of Niagara plunging past the ledge on which they sit. A mis-step and it will carry them away.

Thalberg was alarmed at the bleak vision Vidor presented to him. The film was delayed for a year, and released to respectful reviews but little profit. Vidor went straight on to two Marion Davies comedies for William Randolph Hearst's Cosmopolitan Pictures, then based on the MGM lot. It was not until *An American Romance* that he had a chance to deal with the larger quasi-political issues he addressed in *The Crowd*, and by then the moment had passed.

—John Baxter

CSILLAGOSOK, KATONÁK. The Red and the White. Zvyozdy i soldaty. Production: Mafilm Studios (Hungary) and Mosfilm (USSR); black and white, 35mm, Agascope; running time: 92 mins.;, Russian version about 70 mins.; length: 2545 meters. Released November 1967, Hungary.

Production managers: Jeno Götz, Yuri Rogozovskiy, Andras Nemeth, M. Shadur, Kirill Siruauev, and Istvan Daubner; screenplay by Georgiy Mdivani, Gyula Hernádi, and Miklós Jancsó; directed by Miklós Jancsó; photography by Tamás Somló; edited by Zoltán Farkas; sound by Zoltán Toldy; art direction by Boris Chebotaryov; costumes designed by Mayya Abar-Baranovskaya and Gyula Várdai. assistant directors: Zsolt Kezdi Kovacs, Ferenc Grunwalski, Vladimir Glazkov, and Liliya Kelshteyn.

Filmed 1967 in the Kostroma Region of central Soviet Russia.

Cast: József Madaras (*Hungarian Commander*); Tibor Molnár (*András*); András Kozák (*László*); Jácint Juhász (*István*); Anatoliy Yabbarov (*Captain Chelpanov*); Sergey Nikonenko (*Cossack officer*); Mikhail Kozakov (*Nestor*); Bolot Beyshenaliyev (*Chingiz*); Tatyana Konyukhova (*Yelizaveta, the matron*); Krystyna Mikolajewska (*Olga*); Viktor Avydyushko (*Sailor*); Gleb Strizhenov (*Colonel*); Nikita Mikhalkov (*White officer*); Vladimir Prokofyev; Valentin Bryleyev; Vera Bykova; Yermolayeva; Vitaliy Konyayev; Valeriy Glebov; K. Karyolskikh; Pyotr Savin; Nikolay Sergeyev; Sándor Szili; Roman Khomyatov; Károly Eizler; Mika Ardova.

Publications:

Reviews—in *Variety* (New York), 22 November 1977; review by Calvin Green in *Film Society Review* (New York), 2 October 1968; "Current Cinema" by Penelope Gilliatt in the *New Yorker*, 29 March 1969; review by R. Hatch in the *Nation* (New York), 9 June 1969; review in *Filmfacts* (New York), no.12, 1969; review by Penelope Gilliatt in the *New Yorker*, 29 March 1969; books—*Id. Jancsó Miklós és Ifj, a Két Orvostudós* by Béla Issekutz, Budapest 1968; *Le Nouveau Cinema Hongrois* edited by Michel Estève, Paris 1969; *New Cinema in Eastern Europe* by Alistair

Whyte, London 1971; *Fényes Szelek Fujjátok!* by Szekfu András, Budapest 1974; *Jancso: Miklos Jancso* by Giovanni Buttava, Firenze, Italy 1974; *Directors and Directing: Cinema for the Seventies* by John Russell Taylor, New York 1975; *The Ambiguous Image: Narrative Style in Modern European Cinema* by Roy Armes, London 1976; *Il Vertice Della Parabola: Cinema Bianconevo de Miklos Jancso* by Ennio Castaldini, Bologna 1976; *The Most Important Art: Eastern European Film After 1945* by Mira Liehm and Antonín Liehm, Berkeley 1977; *Miklos Jancso* by Yvette Bird, Paris 1977; *History Must Answer to Man: The Contemporary Hungarian Cinema* by Graham Petrie, London 1978; *Adalékok az Ideológia és a Jelentés Elméletéhez* edited by Péter Józsa, Budapest 1979; articles—plot synopsis and credits in *Avant-Scène du cinéma* (Paris), December 1968; "The Horizontal Man" by Penelope Houston in *Sight and Sound* (London), summer 1969; "Polarities: The Films of Miklós Jancsó" by James Price in *London Mag*, August/September 1969; article by Peter Cowie in *International Film Guide: 1969*, London 1969; "Quite Apart from Miklos Jancso" by D. Robinson in *Sight and Sound* (London), spring 1970; "Jancso Country: Miklos Jancso and the Hungarian New Cinema" by Lorant Czigany in *Film Quarterly* (Berkeley), fall 1972; "Un 'Rouge' noir sur blanc" by Marcel Martin in *Ecran* (Paris), December 1972; "*Rouges et blanc*" by M.C. Mercier in *Image et son* (Paris), no.269, 1973; "Jancso naguère er aujourd'hui. Retour sur *Mon Chemin* et *Rouges et Blancs*" by B. Amengual in *Etudes Cinématographiques* (Paris), no.104-108, 1975; "L'Espace le Mouvement et la Figure du Cercle (de *Les Sans-Espoir* et *Rouges et Blancs*" by Michel Esteve in *Etudes Cinematographe* (Paris), no.104-108, 1975; "Ripensando Alla Violenza dei *Rossi e dei Bianchi*" by R. Alemmano in *Cinema Nuovo* (Torino, Italy), January/February 1975; "Miklos Jancso" by C. Losada in *Cinema 2002* (Madrid), December 1979.

*　　*　　*

The films of Miklós Jancsó have come to represent the New Hungarian Cinema for moviegoers in the West. Since the mid-sixties with the release of his first feature film *My Way Home*, Jancsó has attracted a wide, and appreciative, audience of cinéastes and critics alike. Through his distinctive style, primarily his use of a constantly moving camera, one which probes and circles and twists its way through his cinematic landscape, and through his almost obsessive return to the Hungarian past for his plots, and his repeated use of the broad, Hungarian plain as a setting, Jancsó has fashioned a highly individual *oeuvre*. He has been accused of creating an obscure, private world accessible only to those who are steeped in history, conversant with Marxist dialectic, and fascinated by the experiments of avant-garde filmmakers. At his worst, Jancsó's highly-mannered style, his limited range of recurrent images and themes, and his idiosyncratic camera make it seem as though he were making the same film over and over. Yet at his best, Jancsó can evoke an hallucinatory power within his own private world, one which produces an effect so daring and extraordinary, that his films are unlike anything else in cinema. It is for this sublime quality that Jancsó has become a director of international stature.

The Red and the White is Jancsó's third feature film. He shot it in the Soviet Union when he was invited to make a film celebrating the 50th anniversary of the October Revolution. Although, as one critic has put it, the movie is hardly a celebration of much of anything, it nevertheless exhibits Jancsó's distinctive thematic and stylistic preoccupations. Although the script at times seems a bit thin and the narrative disjunctive, the film is technically remarkable. Jancsó extends his use of long takes and increases the fluidity of his camera movements over his previous films. The perpetual motion, which would become even more hypnotic in *The Confrontation*, helps to provide a visual equivalent to the forces which criss-cross and interweave throughout the movie when time and history are collapsed as we see a "cinematic ballet of violence and oppression" acted out between the Hungarians and the Russians.

In all of Jancsó's films there is a tension between the "beauty" of artistic stylization and the "ugliness" of the testimony of history. This rival claim between realism and formalism has proven to be a rich source of the filmmaker's power. Through the tension he has been able to generate a unique fusion of ritual and dialectic which elevates his projects beyond the predictable social realism of so many Eastern-bloc films. Jancsó's films are political in every sense of that term, but they are also stylish and exhibit a technical virtuosity unique among his contemporaries.

Of the directors who have influenced Jancsó (including Ingmar Bergman, Jean-Luc Godard, and Andrzej Wajda), the most important is Michelangelo Antonioni from whom he discovered the long take. Jancsó uses it to reveal the class struggle and to link visually often seemingly disparate ideas. Although he is an authentic national filmmaker, Jancsó is nevertheless thoroughly a modernist; first, in his rejection of cross-cutting and of montage in general, and second, in his insistence on audience involvement in his films. The ambiguity of his movies fostered by their minimal plots, elliptical style, and artistic self-consciousness demand attention. This is never more evident than in *The Red and the White* where the story is presented episodically without a specific moral reference; both reds and whites are depicted in shades of gray. In this film Jancsó studiously avoids an emotional involvement.

Although the critics were generally excited by his films on their initial release, and *The Red and the White* was no exception, in retrospect they seem less enthusiastic. In part this is a result of Jancsó's obsessive use of locale and imagery; it is an obsession which has prompted one critic to note that, although the hallmark of an *auteur* is the making of the same film in different guises, Jancsó seems to be making the same film in the same guise. The films which he has made outside Hungary since *Red Psalm* have not fared well with the critics. However, *The Red and the White* remains an interesting, even technically brilliant, film which has proved frustratingly elusive to critical analysis, much like the rest of the films of Miklós Jancsó.

—Charles L.P. Silet

CZŁOWIEK Z MARMURU. Man of Marble. Production: Enterprise de Realization de Films: Ensembles Cinematographiques and Ensemble X; 1976; Eastmancolor, 35mm; running time: 160 mins. Released February 1977, Warsaw.

Produced by Andrzej Wajda; screenplay by Aleksander Scibor-Rylski; directed by Andrzej Wajda; photography by Edward Kłosinski; edited by Halina Pugarowa and Maria Kalinciska; sound operated by Piotr Zawadski; production design by Allan Starski, Wojciech Majda, and Maria Osiecka-Kuminek; music by Andrzej Korzyński, songs performed by the group Ali Babki and the Groupe Instrumental; costumes designed by Lidia Rzeszewska and Wiesława Konopelska. The documentary sequences were provided by the Archives des Actualites, Cinematographiques Polonaises.

Filmed in Poland. Prix de la Critique International, Cannes Film Festival, 1978.

Cast: Jerzy Radziwilowicz (*Mateusz Birkut and his son Maciek Tomcyzyk*); Michal Tarkowski (*Wincenty Witek*): Krystyna Zachwatowicz (*Hanka Tomczyk*); Piotr Cieślak (*Michalak*); Wieslaw Wojcik (*Jodia*); Krystyna Janda (*Agnieszka*); Tadeusz Lomnicki (*Jerzy Burski*); Jacek Lomnicki (*Young Burski*); Leonard Zajaczkowski (*Leonard Frybos*); Jacek Domanski (*Sound Man*); Grzegorz Skurski (*Chauffeur/Lighting man*); Magda Teresa Wojcik (*Editor*); Boguslaw Sobczyk (*TV Writer*); Zdzislaw Kozien (*Agnieszka's father*); Irena Laskowska (*Museum employee*); Jerzy Moniak (*Moniak*); Wieslaw Drzewicz (*Manager of the restaurant*); Kazmierz Kaczor (*Security man*); Eva Zietek (*Secretary*); B. Fronczkowiak (*Official from the Minstry of the Interior*).

Publications:

Scripts—"*L'Homme de marbre*" in *Avant-Scène du cinéma* (Paris), 15 January 1980; reviews—"*Człowiek z marmuru*" by D. Holloway in *Variety* (New York), 1 June 1977; review by Paul Louis Thirard in *Positif* (Paris), November 1978; review by Jean-Paul Fargier in *Cahiers du cinéma* (Paris), December 1978; "*Mensch aus Marmor*" by R. Keller in *Filmfaust* (Frankfurt), no.7, 1978; "*Człowiek z marmuru*" by M. Holthof in *Film en Televisie* (Brussels), February 1979; "*L'Homme de marbre et de celluloid*" by R. Linehart in *Cahiers du cinéma* (Paris), March 1979; "*Man of Marble*" by J. Dawson in *Sight and Sound* (London), no.4, 1979; "*La Presse*" in *Avant-Scène du cinéma* (Paris), 15 January 1983; "*El Hombre de mármol*" by A. Torres Fernandez in *Contracampo* (Madrid), February 1980; review in *The New York Times*, 23 January 1981; review in *Newsweek* (New York), 9 February 1981; articles—"O tê ludzká dzielność nam szlo...Mówiâ Aleksander Scibor-Rylski i Andrzej Wajda" by L. Bajer in *Kino* (Warsaw), May 1977; "Entretien avec Andrzej Wajda" by J. Demeure and H. Niogret in *Positif* (Paris), October 1978; "Short Notes: Wajda's *Man of Marble*" by P. Waterman in *Cineaste* (New York), no.2, 1978-79; "Andrzej Wajda: Alltfer kvalefererad for Sverige?" by K.A. Abrahamson in *Chaplin* (Stockholm), no.1964, 1979; "L'Homme (de marbre) est le capital le plus precieux, pensait planov" by B. Amengual in *Positif* (Paris), June 1979; interview with Wajda in *Ecran* (Paris), no. 1, 1979; article by D. Castell in *Films Illustrated* (London), November 1979; article by P.Pap in *Filmkultura* (Budapest), November/December 1979; "*Man of Marble*" by L. Quart in *Cineaste* (New York), no.4, 1979; article by W. Ruf in *Medium* (Frankfurt), October 1979; "Wajda's *Man of Marble* Delineates Heroic Laborer" by Vincent Canby in *The New York Times*, 17 March 1979; "*Człowiek Z Marmaru*" by Ryszard Konicek in *International Film Guide 1979* edited by Peter Cowie, New York 1979; "L'Épopée inachevée d'un stakhanoviste: le romantisme en question" by Jerzy Borkowski in *Avant-Scène du cinéma* (Paris), 15 January 1980; "Andrzej Wajda—ikke socialrealist men stilist" by D. Nissen in *Kosmorama* (Copenhagen), October 1980; "*Marmornati človek*" by Z. Vrdlovec in *Ekran* (Ljubljana, Yugoslavia), no.4, 1980; "Språkrör för vardagsmänniskan" by K.A. Abrahamson in *Chaplin* (Stockholm), no.5 (176), 1981; "Between the Permissible and the Impermissible: An Interview with Andrzej Wajda" by D. Bickley and L. Rubinstein in *Cineaste* (New York), winter 1980-81; "Men of Wajda" by G. Fox in *Film Criticism* (Edinboro, Pennsylvania), fall 1981; "*Man of Marble*" by Joan Cohen in *Magill's Cinema Annual* edited by Frank N. Magill, Englewood Cliffs, New Jersey 1982.

After many successful and mature historical films, describing different crucial moments of the fate of the Polish, and many screen versions of famous literary pieces, Andrzej Wajda with *Man of Marble* succeeds in creating nearly as great and important a work as *Ashes and Diamonds*. Analogically, *Man of Marble* is a success in the spirit of the actual moment; the film is important in understanding all the Polish troubles and disasters of the 1980s.

The film is the story of a student, Agnieszka, who wants to make her graduation film about a former "exemplary worker" of the late Stalin years. Being a modern, bright and courageous girl, she is astonished at the many tresholds and difficulties she has to overcome in order to learn the whole truth about the forgotten idol. Many who had previously worked with him are currently successful, but not eager to recall the past. The television managers even intervene in order to stop her. At the end, Agnieszka does manage to present the complete biography of the man.

The forgotten hero, Mateusz Birkut, was a peasant boy who went to the city, like millions of youngsters during the 1950s, in order to earn their bread. Birkut was lucky enough to catch the eye of an ambitious filmmaker, who decided to make Birkut a legend and a star. During the Stalinistic epoch, a star could only be a perfect worker; and Birkut became such through the invisible help of his fellow workers who remained anonymous. His problems occurred when he himself began to believe in his own importance. He interfered in various political activities in a way that his bosses never anticipated. He disappeared from view, and his image and memory were brutally degraded. He eventually died though no one knew when and how.

Wajda manages in this story, masterfully written by Aleksander Scibor-Rylski, to paint a very detailed, ambivalent and strongly emotional picture of the development of his country during the last 30 years, and to portray two generations—fathers and sons—who formed the socialist system in Poland.

The structure of the film is rather sophisticated. Wajda here renounces the use of visual symbols, so typical of his usual style. He replaces the symbols with documentation—chronicles and news items—from the period; his narrative structure consists of three parallel stories, each of them taking place in a different historical time.

In spite of this complicated form, the film enjoyed an enormous audience success. One of the aims of the socialist culture is to educate people to understand an art which participates in the life and the problems of society. The artist themselves, in this case Wajda, feel themselves obliged to function as the consciousness of their compatriots, while at the same time presenting to them refined, aesthetic works.

For all the negative events shown in the film Wajda declares himself to be among the responsible. The character of Burski, the filmmaker in *Man of Marble* who gained prominence with his film on Birkut and later became a world renowned Polish artist, is a conscious allusion to Wajda himself. Wajda continues today to ask the question: Is the cinema something more than just a creator of myths?

—Maria Racheva

LES DAMES DU BOIS DE BOULOGNE. L'Opinion Publique. Les Dames de Port-Royal. Production: Films Raoul Ploquin; black and white, 35mm; running time: originally 96 mins., but edited down to 84 mins. for initial release, current versions are usually 90 mins. Released 21 September 1945.

Produced by Robert Lavallée; screenplay by Robert Bresson,

dialogue by Jean Cocteau; from a passage in "Jacques le fataliste et son maitre" by Denis Diderot; directed by Robert Bresson; photography by Philippe Agostini; edited by Jean Feyte; sound by Rene Louge, Robert Ivonnet, and Lucien Legrand; production design by Max Douy; music by Jean-Jacques Grunenwald.

Filmed summer 1944 in France. Louis Delluc Award, France, 1945.

Cast: Paul Bernard (*Jean*); Maria Casares (*Hélène*); Elina Labourdette (*Agnès J*); Lucienne Bogaert (*Madame D*); Jean Marchat (*Jacques*); Yvette Etievant (*Chamber maid*); Bernard Lajarrige, Nicole Regnault, Marcel Rouzé, Emma Lyonnel, Lucy Lancy, Marguerite de Morlaye, and the dog Katsou.

Publications:

Scripts—dialogue from the film presented in *Cahiers du cinéma* (Paris), October 1957, November 1957, and December 1957; *Les Dames du bois de Boulogne*" by Robert Bresson in *Avant-Scène du cinéma* (Paris), 15 November 1977; reviews—by Georges Sadoul in *Les Lettres françaises* (Paris), 29 September 1945; "Points de vue..." in *Avant-Scène du cinéma* (Paris), 15 November 1977; books—*The Films of Robert Bresson* by 5 reviewers, New York 1969; *French Cinema Since 1946, Vol. I* by Roy Armes, New York 1970; *The Films of Robert Bresson* by Ian Cameron, London 1970; *Transcendental Style on Film: Ozu, Bresson, Dreyer* by Paul Schrader, Los Angeles 1972; *Notes sur le cinématographe* by Robert Bresson, Paris 1975, English edition *Notes on the Cinema*, New York 1977; *Cinema, the Magic Vehicle: A Guide to Its Achievement: Journey One: The Cinema Through 1949* edited by Adam Garbicz and Jacek Klinowski, Metuchen, New Jersey 1975; *Robert Bresson o cinematografo e o sinal* by C. de Pontes Leca, Lisbon 1978; articles—"Hommage à Robert Bresson" by Jacques Becker in *L'Ecran français*, 17 October 1946; "Notes on Robert Bresson" by Gavin Lambert in *Sight and Sound* (London), summer 1953; article by François Truffaut in *Arts* (Paris), 22 September 1954; "The Quest for Realism" by Gordon Gow in *Films and Filming* (London), December 1957; "Robert Bresson" by Brian Baxter in *Film* (London), September/October 1958; "The Early Work of Robert Bresson" by Richard Roud in *Film Culture* (New York), no.20, 1959; "French Outsider with an Insider Look" by Richard Roud in *Films and Filming* (London), April 1960; "Spiritual Style in the Films of Robert Bresson" by Susan Sontag in *Seventh Art* (New York), summer 1964; "Robert Bresson" in *Interviews with Film Directors* by Andrew Sarris, New York 1967; "Praxis as a Cinematic Principle in the Films of Robert Bresson" by Donald S. Skoller in *Cinema Journal* (Evanston, Illinois), fall 1969; "Robert Bresson" in *Current Biography Yearbook*, New York 1971; "Robert Bresson" in *Encountering Directors* by Charles Thomas Samuels, New York 1972; "Matter and Spirit in the Films of Robert Bresson" by H.M. Polhemusin *Film Heritage* (Dayton, Ohio), spring 1974; "Le Film Bressonnien, 'bel objet'" by Jean Sémolué in *Avant-Scène du cinéma* (Paris), 15 November 1977; *Les Dames du Bois de Boulogne*: Eléments d'un dossier critique" by Jean Sémolué in *Avant-Scène du cinéma* (Paris), 15 November 1977.

* * *

Les Dames du Bois du Boulogne, Robert Bresson's second film, premiered just at the moment of the Liberation of France. Considered a difficult and extraordinary work, it was the first recipient of the Louis Delluc Award for the year's most important French film. What was it that made this film so difficult, and how could Bresson's severe style have attracted the attention it did?

First of all, the stifling studio look, by which Bresson was able to control every shadow, was perfectly suited to the hermetic era of the Occupation in which the film was made and to the strict moral drama of the film's literary source. The story was pulled from Diderot's eighteenth century classic *Jacques Le fataliste*. Seemingly updated to include automobiles, electric lights, etc., Bazin once claimed that Bresson's adaptation is in fact backdated, that it is the aesthetic equivalent of Racine. Bresson has indeed essentialized a picaresque, ironic drama into a tragic struggle of absolutes. More accurately, he has pitted the absolute and tragic world view of Hélène, the injured, icy heroine played elegantly by Maria Casares, against the more modern and temperate worldviews held by the lover who has left her, and by the two women she vengefully introduces him to in the Bois du Boulogne.

Here is the crux of the film's difficulty for twentieth century spectators are required to identify with the hardened Hélène as she spins the web of her trap, using modern, attractive characters as bait. Yet the film succeeds because Bresson has supported her with his style, if not his moral sympathy. We experience her anguish and determination within the decisive clarity of each shot and within the fatal mechanism made up by the precise concatenation of shots. No accident or spontaneous gesture is permitted to enter either Hélène's world or Bresson's mise-en-scene.

Jean Cocteau's dialogue, compressed like some dense radioactive element, continually points up the absolute stakes at play; furthermore, the lines he has written play antiphonally with the images to produce a reflective space in which every perception has already been oralized. A good example of this process is found when Jean enters Agnes's room. He takes in this closed space and then transforms it in words: "This is her lamp, her flowers, her frame, her cushion.... This is where she sits to read, this, her piano...." And yet throughout this recitation we see only his face. The dialogue sums up and closes off sentiments, cooling passions, abstracting emotions. We observe Hélène lying wrathful on her bed for some time before she leans forward to speak her incredibly cold, "Je me vengerai."

Although this style insists on the overpowering strength of Hélène's response to life (in which a single errant word warrants death and damnation), the plot supports the more ordinary characters whom she has manipulated to the end. For after her plans have run their course, after she has announced to Jean at the church that he has married a loose woman, her power is spent. The grace of love, of the love born between these two humble and minor mortals, points to a life or a purpose beyond Hélène. Bresson's Jansenism mixes severity (style) and the disclosure of grace (plot).

Only the dead-time of the Occupation could have permitted such a refined and distant love story. Its timeless values, though, reflect on that period, particularly its concern with weakness, forgiveness, and the future in a world controlled by absolute political powers. More important is the full expression of a style that demands to be taken morally. Even if Bresson has since rejected this effort as too theatrical (with its music, acting, and studio lighting), the fact is that *Les Dames du Bois du Boulogne* showed the world the value of his search, a search that is at once stylistic and metaphysical, and one his later work has justified. It is a tribute to the French film community that they recognized the presence and importance of something truly different.

—Dudley Andrew

DAYS OF HEAVEN. Production: O.P. Productions; Metrocolor, 35mm, Dolby sound; running time: 95 mins. Released 13 September 1978.

Produced by Bert and Harold Schneider, executive producer: Jacob Brickman; screenplay by Terrence Malick; directed by Terrence Malick; photography by Nestor Almendros, additional photography by Haskell Wexler; edited by Billy Weber; sound mixed by George Ronconi, Barry Thomas, special sound effects by James Cox; set decoration by Robert Gould; art direction by Jack Fisk; music by Ennio Morricone, additional music by Leo Kottke; special effects by John Thomas and Mel Merrells; costumes designed by Patricia Norris; Dolby consultants: Steve Katz, Philip Boole, Clyde McKinney.

Filmed on location in the Midwest. Cost: $2.5 million. Academy Award, Cinematography, 1978; New York Film Critics' Award, Best Director, 1978; Cannes Film Festival, Best Director, 1979.

Cast: Richard Gere (*The Brother*); Brooke Adams (*The Girl*); Sam Shepard (The Farm owner); Linda Manz (The Sister); Robert Wilke (The Foreman); Jackie Shultis; Stuart Margolin; Tim Scott; Gene Bell; Doug Kershaw (*Fiddle player*).

Publications:

Reviews—in *Films in Review* (New York), November 1978; "The Last Ray of Light" by T.C. Fox in *Film Comment* (New York), September/October 1978; *Days of Heaven*" by C. Schreger in *Variety* (New York), 13 September 1978; *Days of Heaven*" by A. Insdorf in *Take One* (Montreal), November 1978; *Days of Heaven*" by M. Morris in *Cinema Papers* (Melbourne, Australia), September/October 1979; *Days of Heaven*" by John Coleman in the *New Statesman* (London), 1 June 1979; *Days of Heaven*" by Richard Corliss in the *New Times* (New York), 8 January 1979; articles—*Days of Heaven*" by R. Combs in *Sight and Sound* (London), spring 1978; *Days of Heaven*" in *Films and Filming* (London), December 1978; "Nestor Almendros Interviewed" by B. Riley in *Film Comment* (New York), September/October 1978; "Terrence Malick: *Days of Heaven's* Image Maker" by Chris Hodenfield in *Rolling Stone* (New York), 16 November 1978; "The Eyes of Texas: Terrence Malick's *Days of Heaven*" by R. Combs in *Sight and Sound* (London), no.2, 1979; *Les Moissons du ciel*" by P. Carcassonne in *Cinématographe* (Paris), June 1979; "Le Jardin de Terrence Malick" by M. Ciment and B. Riley in *Positif* (Paris), December 1979; "Dossier: Hollywood 79: Terence Malick" by P. Maraval in *Cinématographe* (Paris), March 1979; "*Days of Heaven*" in *Christian Century* (Chicago), 3 January 1979; "Days of High Seriousness" by Arthur M. Schlesinger in the *Saturday Review* (New York), 6 January 1979; "Sweeping Cannes" in *Time* (New York), 4 June 1979; "Días de Gloria y Badlands. Terrence Malick, nueva personalidad del cine norteamericano" by T. Pérez Turrent in *Cine* (Mexico), March 1980.

*   *   *

Of Terrence Malick's two feature films to date, *Badlands* is perhaps the more satisfying, *Days of Heaven* the more remarkable. Malick's achievement must be seen first and foremost in terms of its opposition to the dominant Hollywood shooting and editing codes of the period. Those codes are centered on the television-derived misuse and overuse of the telephoto (plus zoom) lens, in the interests of speed and economy rather than from any *aesthetic* interest in its intrinsic properties; this is seconded by the lyrical use of shallow focus and focus-shifts as an instant signifier of "beauty" (flowers in focus in the foreground, out-of-focus lovers in the background, shift focus to the lovers behind a foreground of out-of-focus flowers). Bo Widerberg's use of this in *Elvira Madigan* (the decisive influence) had a certain authenticity and originality, but it quickly lapsed into automatic cliché. Within such a context the sharp-etched, crystal-clear, depth-of-field images of Malick and his magnificent cameraman, Nestor Almendros, in *Days of Heaven* assume the status of protest and manifesto. They restore the concept of "beauty" from its contemporary debasement.

There is a further consequence of this—what one might call the resurrection of mise-en-scène, theorized in the 1950's and 1960's as the essential art of film, and seemingly a lost art since. In place of the "one shot—one point" of the flat, perfunctory images derived from television, Malick suddenly has a frame within which to compose in depth, where every segment of the image potentially signifies. The desire for precision and definition within the image here combines naturally with a most delicate feeling for nuances of emotion and interchange between the characters. Joseph Conrad's description of Henry James as "the historian of fine consciences" comes to mind. Aptly enough; for what is *Days of Heaven* but a re-working of the subject of James's *The Wings of the Dove*, with the sexes reversed and the protagonists transposed to the working-class?

Given the film's concern with the realities of democratic capitalism—manifest inequality, poverty, class oppression—the "beauty" is a potential problem. Indeed it comes perilously close (especially in its opening sequences) to aestheticizing misery in the manner of, for example, Lean's *Doctor Zhivago*, where the response "Isn't that terrible?" is completely superseded by "Isn't that beautifully photographed?." The distinction of *Days of Heaven* lies partly in its careful separation of its sense of beauty from the human misery and tension depicted. The pervasive suggestion is that human existence could correspond to the natural and aesthetic beauty the film celebrates, were it not for the oppressive systems of organization that men [sic] have developed: the film's sense of tragedy is firmly grounded in an awareness of class and gender oppression. As in *Heaven's Gate*, the woman expresses her ability and freedom to love both men. It is the men who precipitate catastrophe by demanding exclusivity and ownership as their right, and as a means of bolstering their threatened egos.

Badlands explicitly acknowledged, in its final credits, the influence of Arthur Penn; in fact, its relation to *Bonnie and Clyde* is at once obvious and tenuous, restricted to its subject. Far more important seemed the influence of Godard, especially in *Les Carabiniers* and *Pierrot le fou*. The film's counterpointing of verbal narration and image is extremely sophisticated and, in relation to classical Hollywood narrative, audaciously unconventional. *Days of Heaven* simultaneously modifies and develops this strategy: the verbal narration of Linda Manz represents a less jarring dislocation than the use of Sissy Spacek's diary in the earlier film, but provides a continuous and subtle distanciation which contributes significantly to the film's unique flavor, in which irony co-exists with intense involvement.

—Robin Wood

DE CIERTA MANERA. One Way or Another. Production: Instituto Cubano del Arte e Industria Cinematográficos (ICAIC);

black and white, 35mm, originally shot in 16mm; running time: 79 mins.; length: 2147 meters. Released 1977.

Produced by Camilo Vives; scenario by Sara Gómez and Tomas González Pérez; screenplay by Tomas Gutíerrez Alea and Julio García Espinosa; directed by Sara Gómez; photography by Luis García; edited by Iván Arocha; sound by Germinal Hernádez; production design by Roberto Larraburre; music by Sergio Vitier, songs by Sara González; assistant directors: Rigoberto López and Daniel Díaz Torres.

Cast: Mario Balmaseda (*Mario*); Yolanda Cuellar (*Yolanda*); Mario Limonta (*Humberto*).

Publications:

Reviews—"*De cierta manera*" by A. Marrosu in *Cine al Día* (Caracas, Venezuela), June 1980; "*De cierta manera*" by J. Pym in *Monthly Film Bulletin* (London), July 1980; articles—"Special Section on 20 Years of Revolutionary Cuban Cinema, Part 1" in *Jump Cut* (Chicago), December 1978; "*One Way or Another*: The Revolution in Action" by Carlos Galiano in *Jump Cut* (Chicago), December 1978; "*One Way or Another*: Dialectical, Revolutionary, Feminist" by Julia Lesage in *Jump Cut* (Chicago), May 1979; "Special Section on 20 Years of Revolutionary Cuban Cinema, Part 3" in *Jump Cut* (Chicago), May 1980; "*De Cierta Manera*" by Geraldo Chijona in *Cine Cubano* (Havana), no. 93; "*Hablar de Sara, De Cierta Manera*" by Rigoberto López in *Cine Cubano* (Havana), no.93.

*   *   *

Here is a revolutionary film: dialectical in form and content, humble in the face of real human experience, proposing no final answers except the unending struggle of a people to make something out of what history has made of them. *De Cierta Manera* is that powerful hybrid—the fictional documentary set to a tropical beat—for which the cinema of revolutionary Cuba is justifiably famous. In this instance, the documentary deals with the destruction of slum housing and the struggle against the culture of marginality generated in such slums through the creation of a new housing project (Miraflores) and an accompanying educational program. The fictional embodiment of this historical process is seen in the clash of attitudes between Mario (a product of the slums), his lover Yolanda (a teacher who has come to Miraflores to help integrate such marginal elements into the revolution), and his friend Humberto (a fun-loving slacker). In the course of telling these stories, and others, *De Cierta Manera* demolishes the categories of fiction and documentary, insisting that both forms are equally mediated by the intention of the filmmaker, and that both thus require a critical stance.

This insistence on a critical attitude is conveyed, first of all, in the dialectical resonance of the film, a structure characteristic of the best of the Cuban cinema. Visually this resonance is achieved through a rich blending of fictional present and historical re-creation with documentary and semi-documentary. In fact, it becomes impossible to distinguish the different forms; fictional characters are set in documentary sequences where they interact with real people and real people re-enact historical re-constructions which are not visually in accordance with their *own* telling of the stories. Further, the film repeats various sequences several times, twisting the film back on itself and requiring the audience to participate actively in analyzing the different perspectives offered on the problems posed by the film.

The sound track is as creatively textured as are the images, and is every bit as demanding of the audience. The film sets up a tension between the classical documentary and its omniscient narrator, cinema-verité interviews, and fictional cinema. The omniscient documentary provides sociological data on different facets of marginality. Although this data establishes one framework for the "fictional" core of the film, its deliberately pompous tone warns us that we must critically question even such "official" pronouncements.

This omniscient narrator is juxtaposed to the conversations which take place around different aspects of marginalism. The manifestations of the culture of marginality are seen to be manifold—work absenteeism, machismo, delinquency—and the problem is hotly debated by everyone. Humberto is criticized for taking off from work on an unauthorized four-day jaunt with a girl friend, while lying about his "sick mother." Mario is criticized for denouncing Humberto, not because his attitude was counter-productive, but because Humberto accused him of being an informer—a violation of male-bonding rules. Yolanda criticizes the mothers of children who misbehave in school, and is in turn criticized by her co-workers for her inability to empathize with women whose background is so different from hers. Although trenchant and acute, these critiques are also loving and constructive. Just as individuals in the film leave these confrontations with a clearer understanding of the revolutionary process to which they are committed, so too does the audience leave tne film with a more precise notion of dialectical film.

At the end of the film, the workers in the factory meeting where the fictional confrontation of Mario and Humberto took place enter into a discussion of the case. They seem to rise up and incorporate themselves into the actual production of the film itself. This is as it should be, for this film demands the participation of all: real people and actors, workers and marginal elements, teachers and housewives, audience and filmmaker. The wrecking ball (in a sequence repeated several times during the film) is not only destroying the slums and (metaphorically) the slum mentality, it may also be demolishing some of the more cherished assumptions of moviegoers in bourgeois cultures.

—John Mraz

LA DENTELLIÈRE. The Lacemaker. Production: Citel Films (Geneva), Actions Films (Paris), and Filmproduktion (Frankfort); Eastmancolor, 35mm; running time: 108 mins. Released May 1977, France.

Produced by Yves Peyrot with Yves Gosser; screenplay by Claude Goretta and Pascal Laine; from the novel by Pascal Laine; directed by Claude Goretta; photography by Jean Boffety; edited by Joelle Van Effenterre; sound by Pierre Gemet and Bernard Chaumeil; production design by Serge Etter and Claude Chevant; music by Pierre Jansen, edited by Georges Bacri.

Filmed in France. Cannes Film Festival, Ecumenical Prize, 1977.

Cast: Isabelle Huppert (*Béatrice*); Yves Beneyton (*François*); Florence Giorgietti (*Marylène*); Anne-Marie Duringer (*Béatrice's mother*); Jean Obe (*François'father*); Monique Chaumette (*François'mother*); Michel de Re (*The painter*); Renata Schroeter (*François'friend*); Sabine Azema (*Student*); and with: Christian Baltauss, Christian Pytieu, Heribert Sasse, Jeanne Allard, Odile Poisson, Gilberte Geniat, Valentine Albin, Agnes Chateau, Bretrand de Hauteport; Suzanne Berthois, Yvon Brian, Barbara Cenche, Luc Chessex, Nicole Chomo, Maud Darsy, Martine Mauclair, Rebecca Potok, Joelle Robin, Simone Roche, Simone Saniel; Jacques Dichamp, Gilbert Gaffiot, Daniel Guillaume, Michele Hamelin, Lucienne Legrand, Sophie Thiery, France Valery, Catherine Vidon, Jean-Pierre Viviane; and the voices of Anne Deleuze and Rosine Rochette.

Publications:

Scripts—"*La Dentelliere*" by Claude Goretta and Pascal Laine in *Avant-Scène du cinéma* (Paris), 15 April 1981; *Goretta, Claude: La Dentellière*, Paris 1981; reviews—*La Dentellière*" by F. Chevassu in *Image et son* (Paris), September 1977; *La Dentellière*" by Tom Milne in *Monthly Film Bulletin* (London), November 1977; *La Dentellière*" by G. Moskowitz in *Variety* (New York), 25 May 1977; *La Dentellière*" by C. Roulet in *Cinématographe* (Paris), June 1977; "Verlorenes Schweigen" by J. Günter in *Films & Fernsehen* (Berlin), October 1978; *La Dentellière*" by A. Leroux in *Séquences* (Montreal), January 1978; *The Lacemaker*" by G. Parker in *Film Quarterly* (Berkeley), fall 1978; *The Lacemaker*" by I. Pruks in *Cinema Papers* (Melbourne, Australia), April/June 1978;'; "La Presse" in *Avant-Scène du cinéma* (Paris), 15 April 1981; articles—"Claude Goretta en *La Dentellière*" by A. Jong in *Skoop* (Amsterdam), June/July 1977; "Claude Goretta" by D. Maillet in *Cinématographe* (Paris), June 1977; "Jeg elsker dig" by B. Peterson-Schultz in *Kosmorama* (Copenhagen), summer 1978; article in *International Film Guide 1978;* (London), 1978; "Claude Goretta and Isabelle Huppert", interview by Judith Kass in *Movietone News* (Seattle), 14 August 1978; "Trotz allem hoffe ich", interview by J.-P. Brossard in *Film und Fernsehen* (Berlin), October 1978; "Une Martyre de l'amour" by Gilles Cèbe in *Avant-Scène du cinéma* (Paris), 15 April 1981.

*   *   *

Claude Goretta's third feature film, his first made in France, tells a deceptively simple story of lost innocence against the picturesque background of the Normandy coast and the contemporary ambience of Paris. *The Lacemaker* is marked by the economy, close observation, and compassion of its director and the virtuoso performance of its star, Isabelle Huppert, who plays Beatrice, nicknamed "Pomme," a shy young assistant in a Paris beauty parlor. The film depicts her first romance with a well-bred Sorbonne student named François (Yves Beneyton), who meets her while on vacation in the resort town of Cabourg and rejects her some months later, bringing on an emotional and physical collapse. Goretta has synthesized several potentially sentimental genres—*Bildungsroman*, pastoral, seduction story, poor-meets-rich romance—and managed to evoke fresh responses to his film's own particular time and place.

The Lacemaker begins by exploring the friendship between Pomme and Marylene (Florence Giorgetti), a slightly older and far more experienced beautician. Like her illustrious namesake, Marilyn Monroe, whose poster adorns a wall in her high-rise apartment, Marylene is blonde, restless, and seductive, a compulsive poseur. Pomme seems her complete opposite: small, quiet, utterly guileless. While Marylene's extroverted personality, sensuousness, and superior position in the shop clearly present her as a foil in the opening sequences, she is soon shown to be no less vulnerable to men than Pomme will become. The opening movement of *The Lacemaker* thus concludes with Marylene being jilted by her married boyfriend and deciding to forget her troubles by taking Pomme along on a vacation at the seacoast.

Marylene soon meets a new man and moves out of the hotel room she briefly shared with Pomme, who acquiesces silently. François sees her eating an ice cream at an outdoor cafe and introduces himself to the shy girl as a brilliant student of literature from Paris. Goretta departs from his customary unobtrusive cinematic style at this point with a beautiful sequence of long tracking shots and cross-cutting to depict François and Pomme looking for each other the next day. The distance between them in the panoramic vistas and the high camera placements suggest both the separate worlds they inhabit and the fate that draws them together. When they finally meet on the boardwalk, Pomme wears a white dress and François a dark t-shirt and jeans, visually underscoring their differences at the very moment their romance begins.

Goretta depicts the development of their relationship through a series of delicately woven vignettes, the most clearly symbolic of which involves a game of blindman's bluff on a steep cliff overlooking the Channel. François leads her to the very edge, but Pomme continues to follow his commands without ever opening her eyes. When she finally does, standing at the very edge of the precipice, François has to grab her to keep her from falling with fright. Soon after this strangely disturbing interlude, Pomme agrees to sleep with him, her first time with a man.

Back in Paris and now living in François' flat near the university, Pomme happily cleans and cooks after her own work at the beauty parlor is done so that he might pursue his studies. Their life together seems epitomized in a scene where she tries to eat an apple silently (her nickname, "pomme," means "apple") without disturbing his concentration, and he becomes annoyed not so much by the sound as by her effort at self-effacement. The film's pivotal scene occurs during the couple's visit with François' parents in the country. When the dinner conversation turns to news about François' successful young friends and questions about what she does for a living, Pomme is overcome by a violent fit of choking. In moments such as these, Goretta reveals the subtle unraveling of their romance, without a single argument between them. In a high-angle long shot foreshadowing their parting, and mirroring the panoramic views of Cabourg, François rushes across a city boulevard, leaving Beatrice stranded on a traffic island. Some time after François explains how breaking up will be best for both of them and returns her to her mother's apartment, Beatrice collapses in the middle of a busy intersection.

The Lacemaker's final sequence takes place in a sanatorium where François comes to visit Beatrice, whose altered appearance is profoundly disquieting. She wears a shapeless black dress like a shroud; she moves and speaks mechanically, drained of all her former charm. As they pass the time together in a park filled with fallen yellow leaves, François asks what she has been doing since they parted. When Beatrice tonelessly describes a trip to Greece with someone she met, François seems relieved to learn she has taken other lovers. In the closing shot, however, the camera tracks in on the therapy room where Beatrice sits alone in a corner knitting in front of a bright poster of Mykonos. Her foreign travel was an illusion, both a deception and farewell gift for the guilt-ridden François. As the truth dawns, she turns to the camera with a chilling expression which Goretta then freezes. The closing title appears, with its reference to the anonymous working women—seamstresses, water-girls, lacemakers—of the paintings of the Old Masters.

Goretta's film, like his heroine's face, is deceptively simple. While seemingly inviting interpretation as a modern parable of innocence betrayed, a Marxist allegory on the plight of the working class, feminist tract against patriarchal society, or even a

clinical study of mental breakdown, *The Lacemaker* remains ultimately less moralistic than Eric Rohmer's films, less political than Godard's or Tanner's, less intellectual than Resnais's. Goretta's deepest concern—and the film's ultimate "meaning"—lies with Beatrice herself, with what she has lost and, just possibly, what she has gained.

—Lloyd Michaels

DER VAR ENGANG EN KRIG. Once There Was a War. Production: Nordisk Films Kompagni; black and white, 35mm, widescreen; running time: 94 mins.; length: 2565 meters, or 8460 feet. Released 16 November 1966, Copenhagen.

Produced by Bo Christensen; screenplay by Klaus Rifbjerg; directed by Palle Kjaerulff-Schmidt; photography by Claus Loof; edited by Ole Steen; sound by Niels Ishsy and Hans W. Søensen; art direction by Henning Bahs; music by Chopin, Beethoven, and Leo Mathisen; costumes designed by Lotte Dandanell; assistant director: Tom Hedegaard.

Filmed in Denmark.

Cast: Ole Busck (*Tim*); Kjeld Jacobsen (*Father*); Astrid Villaume (*Mother*); Katja Miehe Renard (*Kate, the sister*); Birgit Bendix Madsen (*Jane*); Christian Gottschalck (*Grandfather*); Yvonne Ingdal (*Lis*); Karen Marie Løwert (*Lis' mother*); Gregers Ussing (*Frank*); Jan Heinig Hansen (*Markus*); Birgit Brüel (*Markus' mother*); Jørgen Beck (*Friend*); Elsa Kourani (*Friend's wife*); Henry Skjar (*Headmaster*); Holger Perfort (*Teacher in gymnastics*).

Publications:

Script—*Der var engang en krig—en film af Klaus Rifbjerg og Palle Kjaerulff*, Copenhagen 1966; reviews—in *Variety* (New York), 30 November 1966; review in *Kosmorama* (Copenhagen), December 1966; review in *Hollywood Reporter*, 2 November 1967; books—*Danish Films* edited by Uffe Stormgaard and Soren Dyssegaard, Danish Film Institute and the Press and Cultural Relations Department of the Royal Danish Ministry of Foreign Affairs, 1973; *Le Cinéma danois* edited by Jean-Loup Passek, France 1979; articles—in *Film Quarterly* (Berkeley), winter 1967-68; article in *Films and Filming* (London), September 1969; article in *Monthly Film Bulletin* (London), no.427, 1969; article in *Today's Cinema*, 13 June 1969. "Danish Film" by Ib Monty in *Factsheet Denmark* (pamphlet published by Royal Danish Ministry of Foreign Affairs), Copenhagen 1983.

*   *   *

Apart from Carl Th. Dreyer's *Gertrud*, *Der var engang en krig* is the most important Danish film of the sixties. It is a portrait of a 15-year old boy from middle class Copenhagen during the German occupation. The German occupation of 1940-45 has been described in several documentaries, most notably in the unique *Your Freedom Is at Stake*, based on illegally shot material and reflecting the views of the resistance movement—a view quite critical towards the official Danish collaboration policy. Sixteen feature films were inspired by this important period in recent Danish history, most of them stressing the heroic aspects of the resistance. Contrary to this approach, *Der var engang en krig* uses the war as a background, but reflects that daily life of the Danes in a more authentic and honest manner.

The film is structured as a chain of incidents, showing the boy in relation to family, friends, teachers and girls. The main story centers on the boy's love for one of his older sister's girlfriends. To her he is a boy, to him she is the object of his adolescent dreams. He fantasizes about her, seeing himself as a resolute hero in a number of daydream sequences, which are among the most problematic scenes in an otherwise beautifully controlled film. It is based on a meticulous care for authentic detail, and its intensity of feeling grows out of these carefully recollected views of the past. Though visually it can be considered within a realistic tradition, it is the situations, the excellently written dialogue, the characters, and the way it brings a period to life which make the film engaging and emotionally rich. The film is not without humor; but as the narrative is from the boy's point of view, he is never presented in an ironic way. The stronger feelings are condensed in the long travelling shots and pans, when the boy is cycling, expressing his feelings in physical activity.

The film was written by Klaus Rifbjerg who, like Palle Kjarulff-Schmidt, the director, takes advantage of personal experiences to enhance his work. Rifbjerg is the finest poet and author of his generation, and he and Kjarulff-Schmidt started collaborating on films in 1959. In 1962 they made *Weekend*, a study of young adults and their emotional problems. *Weekend* was considered one of the films heralding a new, more modern era in the Danish cinema. Reality had finally returned to Danish film after a long barren period. The collaboration between Rifbjerg and Kjarulff-Schmidt culminated with *Der ver engang en krig*, their finest achievement and one of the highlights of contemporary Danish cinema. Influenced by Truffaut (especially *Les 400 Coups*) and similar to films by Ermanno Olmi and Milos Forman, *Der var engang en krig* represents the best in intimate realism. The film was received very well by Danish critics and also got very fine reviews abroad, especially in England.

—Ib Monty

IL DESERTO ROSSO. The Red Desert. Production: Film Duemila, Cinematografica Federiz (Rome) and Francoriz (Paris); Eastmancolor (print by Technicolor), 35mm; running time: 120 mins, some versions are 116 mins. Released 1964, Venice Film Festival.

Produced by Antonio Cervi; screenplay by Michelangelo Antonioni and Tonino Guerra; directed by Michelangelo Antonioni; photography by Carlo Di Palma; edited by Eraldo Da Roma; sound by Claudio Maielli and Renato Cadueri; production design by Piero Poletto; music by Giovanni Fusco, sung by Cecilia Fusco, electronic music by Vittorio Gelmetti; special effects by Franco Freda; costumes designed by Gitt Magrini.

Filmed October-December 1963 in Ravenna and Sardinia, Italy. Venice Film Festival, Best Film: Lion of St. Mark and International Film Critics Award, 1964.

Cast: Monica Vitta (*Giuliana*); Richard Harris (*Corrado Zeller*); Carlo Chionetti (*Ugo*); Xenia Valderi (*Linda*); Rita Renoir (*Emilia*): ALdo Grotti (*Max*); Giuliano Missirini (*Radiotelescope operator*); Lili Rheims (*His wife*); Valerio Bartoleschi (*Son of Giuliana*); Emanuela Paola Carboni (*Girl in the fable*); Bruno Borghi; Beppe Conti; Giulio Cotignoli; Giovanni Lolli; Hiram Mino Madonia; Arturo Parmiani; Carla Ravasi; Ivo Cherpiani; Bruno Scipioni.

Publications:

Reviews—by Jules Cohen in *Film Comment* (New York), winter 1965; review by Henry Hart in *Films in Review* (New York), March 1965; "The Red Desert" by Penelope Houston in *Sight and Sound* (London), spring 1965; review by Andrew Sarris in the *Village Voice* (New York), 11 February 1965; books—*Antonioni* by Philip Strick, London 1965; *Interviews with Film Directors* by Andrew Sarris, New York 1967; *Antonioni* by Ian Cameron and Robin Wood, London 1968; *Encountering Directors* by Charles Thomas Samuels, New York 1972; articles—"In the Red Desert" by Michèle Manceaux in *Sight and Sound* (London), summer 1964; "Most Controversial Director" by Melton Davis in the *New York Times Magazine*, 15 November 1964; interview with Antonioni by Jean-Luc Godard in *Movie* (London), spring 1965; article by Gordon Gow in *Films and Filming* (London), June 1965; article in *Films and Filming* (London), April 1965; "The Red Desert" by Richard Roud and Penelope Houston in *Sight and Sound* (London), spring 1965; "Il Deserto rosso" by Robin Wood in *Movie* (London), summer 1965; "The Red Desert" by Colin Young in *Film Quarterly* (Berkeley), fall 1965; article by John Bragin in *Film Culture* (New York), summer 1966; article by Stanley Solomon in *Film Heritage* (Dayton, Ohio), winter 1965-66; "Night, Eclipse, Dawn" by Jean-Luc Godard in *Cahiers du Cinema in English* (New York), January 1966; article by John Thomas in *Film Society Review* (New York), April 1967; "Antonioni Talks About His Work" in *Life* (New York), 27 January 1967; "The Stature of Objects in Antonioni's Films" by J. Dudley Andrew in *TriQuarterly*, winter 1968; "Michaelangelo Antonioni and the Imagery of Disintegration" by Thomas Hernacki in *Film Heritage* (Dayton, Ohio), spring 1970; "Le desert rouge" by G. Colpart in *Téléciné* (Paris), October 1976; special Antonioni issue of *Caméra/Stylo* (Paris), November 1982.

*   *   *

Antonioni's first color film also marks his turn from subjective and social dramas to the representation of the world through the eyes of a psychologically disturbed protagonist. Monica Vitti, in her last role for Antonioni, plays Guilia, the wife of the director of a Ravenna factory and the mother of a young boy. She has attempted suicide after a near fatal automobile accident. The film describes the damaging effect of her brief affair with the owner of the factory her husband directs.

Il Deserto rosso is a remarkable experiment in color cinematography. Admittedly inspired by Hegel's color theories, Antonioni spray painted dump heaps and the fruit of a street peddlar to a neutral gray to transmit the neurosis of his protagonist directly to the viewer. Corrado, the factory owner play by Richard Harris, finds Guilia nervously stymied in her empty shop in which she has slapped patches of different colors on the wall without deciding which to use for the décor. She doesn't even know what sort of "things" she wants to sell. The painful sequence in which she rushes to his hotel room to make love to him is a tour de force of color deformations: a starkly blanched corridor leads to the room in which the vivid red of the bedframe stands out against the subdued interior. During their nervous lovemaking, we see a murky spectrum on the ceiling, and afterward the entire interior is bathed in pink.

In contrast to the lushly disturbing colors of the film as a whole, Guilia frames a story or dream of her childhood, which she narrates to her son when she thinks (or he pretends—we cannot be sure) he has become crippled. This episode, filmed in the conventionally slick colors of an advertisement for beach resorts, evokes a period of girlish purity, innocence, and isolation, so that we can interpret the color disfunctions of the rest of the film as a sign of a trauma induced by puberty. The fantasy she narrates to her son is a version of the flying Dutchman legend. Her encounter with an unmanned ship marks a psychical change in her and terminated her idyll. The sexual nature of this fantasy becomes explicit when she makes a feeble effort to run away on a Norwegian freighter immediately after sleeping with Corrado.

The entire film is permeated with allusions to Dante's *Divine Comedy*. It is shot at Chiassi, the port of Ravenna, which was Dante's model for the earthly paradise at the summit of Purgatory. But Antonioni emphasizes the pollution and filth of the spot, as if to declare that Dante's Eden has become our Hell. Furthermore, the figure of Corrado is modeled on Dante's Ulysses, as the wanderer who seeks to conquer realms only accessible by grace. Corrado is in Ravenna to recruit workers for a factory in the far south Atlantic, where Dante's Ulysses sunk his ship trying to assail the mount of Purgatory. The film repeats Antonioni's fascination with erotic disasters.

—P. Adams Sitney

THE DEVIL IS A WOMAN. Production: Paramount Pictures; black and white, 35mm; running time: 80 mins., some sources list 82 mins. Released 1935.

Screenplay by Josef von Sternberg, adapted by John Dos Passos and S. K. Winston; from the novel *The Woman and the Puppet* by Pierre Louys; directed by Josef von Sternberg; photography by Josef von Sternberg and Lucien Ballard; production design by Hans Dreier; music and lyrics by Ralph Rainger and Leo Robin.

Filmed in Paramount studios.

Cast: Marlene Dietrich (*Concha Perez*); Cesar Romero (*Antonio Galvan*); Lionel Atwell (*Don Pasqual*); Edward Everett Horton (*Don Paquito*); Alison Skipworth (*Señora Perez*); Don Alvarado (*Morenito*); Morgan Wallace (*Dr. Mendez*); Tempe Pigott (*Tuerta*); Jil Dennett (*Maria*); Lawrence Grant (*Conductor*).

Publications:

Books—*Marlène Dietrich, femme-énigme* by Jean Talky, Paris 1932; *An Index to the Films of Josef von Sternberg* by Curtis Harrington, London 1949; *Marlene Dietrich—Image and Legend* by Richard Griffith, New York 1959; *Fun in a Chinese Laundry*, New York 1965, published in France as *Souvenirs d'un montreur d'ombres*, Paris 1966; *The Films of Josef von Sternberg* by Andrew Sarris, New York 1966; *Josef von Sternberg, Dokumentation, Eine Darstellung*, Mannheim, Germany 1966; *Josef von Sternberg* by Herman G. Weinberg, Paris 1966; *Marlene*

Dietrich by John Kobal, New York 1968; *The Films of Marlene Dietrich* by Homer Dickens, New York 1968; *The Cinema of Josef von Sternberg* by John Baxter, New York 1971; *Anthologie du cinéma, Vol 6*, Paris 1971; *Marlene Dietrich* by Charles Silver, New York 1974; articles—"Creative Film Director" in *Cue* (New York), 14 December 1935; "Comment Marlène Dietrich est devenue star" by Maurice Dekobra in *Cinémonde* (Paris), 16 April 1939; "Marlene Dietrich" by Arthur Knight in *Films in Review* (New York), December 1954; "The Lost Films, Part 1" by Herman G. Weinberg in *Sight and Sound* (London), August 1962; filmography on von Sternberg in *Cahiers du cinéma* (Paris), July 1965; "Josef von Sternberg" by Herman G. Weinberg in *Film Heritage* (Dayton, Ohio), winter 1965; "6 Films of Josef von Sternberg" by O.O. Green in *Movie* (London), summer 1965; article on von Sternberg and Dietrich in *Positif* (Paris), May 1966; "L'Oeuvre de Josef von Sternberg" by Bernard Eisenschitz in *Avant-Scène du cinéma* (Paris), March 1966; "Dietrich in Sydney" by Charles Higham in *Sight and Sound* (London), winter 1965-66; *The Devil is a Woman*" by Eileen Bowser and Richard Griffith in *Film Notes* edited by Eileen Bowser, New York 1969; "Thoughts on the Objectification of Women" by Barbara Martineau in *Take One* (Montreal), November/December 1970; "Joe, Where Are You?" by Tom Flinn in *Velvet Light Trap* (Madison, Wisconsin), fall 1972; "Josef von Sternberg: The Scientist and the Vamp" by Joyce Rheuban in *Sight and Sound* (London), autumn 1973; "La femme et le pantin" by J. Magny in *Téléciné* (Paris), November 1976; *The Devil is a Woman*" by R. Combs in *Monthly Film Bulletin* (London), May 1978.

*   *   *

The Devil Is a Woman is the final film starring Marlene Dietrich made by director Joseph von Sternberg. The identifying characteristics of the von Sternberg/Dietrich collaboration, including the ambiguity, often difficult for viewers to accept, are evident here. *The Devil Is a Woman* is a perfect culmination to an enigmatic relationship and a breathtaking series of visually stunning films.

Based on Pierre Louys's novel, *The Woman and the Puppet*, the film is a quintessential example of the von Sternberg filmed universe. To follow the story is to travel through a narrative labyrinth, following the many changes of mood, mind, character and costume of the central character, Concha (Dietrich), the devilish woman of the title. The contradictory Concha is all surface and no depth, a beautiful, fickle, unpredictable woman, or at least that is how she is presented as Don Pasqual (Lionel Atwill) tells Antonio (Cesar Romero) about her. Concha exists at the center of the film, and von Sternberg favors the audience with as few fulfilled expectations and explanations as she has favored her lovers. At the end, Concha (through von Sternberg) has demonstrated the same cruel control over viewers as she has over her lovers, leaving an audience with nothing to grasp, much less to embrace or understand.

The Devil Is a Woman defines the von Sternberg approach to cinema, which is unique. As a film artist, he defies the conceptions most have about what film is or what it can or should do. He seldom develops a logical narrative pattern, with ordinary character motivations. On the contrary, a von Sternberg character frequently makes an abrupt shift that, in literary terms, is unexpected and unjustified. "I changed my mind," Concha offers as an explanation when she turns back across the border to rejoin her rejected former lover. This arbitrary change of mind is the essence of the von Sternberg film, which forces viewers to realize that the act of seeing is itself the truest meaning of the film. By removing conventional forms of dramatic tension, character development and plot motivation, he asks viewers to accept the things that usually supplement a film story as if they were the story themselves. In never fully explaining Concha, he seduces viewers into observing her more and more closely.

The Devil Is a Woman presents an illusionary world, filled with irony, mockery, androgyny, and a certain amount of implied decadence. As is true of all his films with Dietrich, it is somewhat of a von Sternberg autobiography, with Atwill, a von Sternberg look-alike, playing the character who is toyed with by Concha. The relationship of these two characters is a complicated interplay of master and victim, puppet and manipulator, with no clear indication of which is truly the master and which the puppet.

With *The Devil Is a Woman*, von Sternberg worked against the tradition of Hollywood in the 1930s, in that he reduced narrative tension to a state in which very little seemed to be happening. "The best source for a story," he said, "is an anecdote." Although *The Devil Is a Woman* is based on a famous novel, von Sternberg liked trivial plots, and never took up great social or political themes. This led to an inevitable rejection of von Sternberg by both critics and audiences, and *The Devil Is a Woman* was a failure. Seen today, it is a stunning example of pictorial beauty. The use of light and shadow in intricate interplay, the long takes connected by luxuriously slow dissolves, the ironic music, the elegant compositions, and the complicated, layered images make it the work of a major visual artist.

—Jeanine Basinger

DIABLE AU CORPS. Devil in the Flesh. Production: Transcontinental Films; black and white, 35mm; running time: 110 mins. Released 1947.

Screenplay by Jean Aurenche and Pierre Bost; from a novel by Raymond Radiguet; directed by Claude Autant-Lara; photography by Michel Kelber; edited by Madeleine Gug; production design by Max Douy; music by René Cloërec. Filmed in France.

Cast: Gérard Philipe (*François*); Micheline Presle (*Marthe*); Denise Grey; Jean Debucourt.

Publications:

Book—*French Cinema Since 1946: Volume One: The Great Tradition* by Roy Armes, New York 1976; articles—"Styles du cinéma français" in *La Livre d'or du cinéma français 1947-48* edited by René Jeanne and Charles Ford, Paris 1948; "In the Margin" by Gérard Philipe in *Sequence*, spring 1949; "Gérard Philipe" by Ginette Billard in *Films and Filming* (London), October 1955; "The Rebel with Kid Gloves" in 2 parts by Raymond Durgnat in *Films and Filming* (London), October and November 1960; "Comment j'ai pu réaliser *Le Diable au corps*" by Claude Autant-Lara in *Ikon* (Milan), January/March 1972; "La Chasse aux escargots" by Claude Autant-Lara in *Cahiers de la cinémathèque* (Paris), spring 1973; "La Parole est à Claude Autant-Lara", interview by M. Oms, in *Cahiers de la cinémathèque* (Paris), summer 1973.

*   *   *

Le Diable au Corps was certainly *the* French film of 1947. Winner of several European awards, the film was also banned in communities across the Continent. While a proud tribute to the French Literary tradition, it posed as the most avant-garde example of postwar cinema in that country.

There is no paradox here, for the aesthetic ideology of the "cinema of quality," of which this film serves as an outstanding example, openly mixes an interest in iconoclastic subject matter, high art tradition, and a refined studio treatment. Aurenche and Bost's careful reworking of a youthful and rebellious novel points up its key social and psychological oppositions. Claude Autant-Lara was then able to put these oppositions into play through the psychological realism of his handling of actors, and through the narrational commentary wrung out of décor, music, and cinematic figures.

Their grim intelligence and determined passion made Gérard Philipe and Micheline Presle an instantly legendary couple; he as a precocious teenage malcontent, son of an upright bourgeois, she, the older woman whose husband is off at the front in World War I. Autant-Lara evinces sympathy for their questionable moral position by rendering the action through a series of flashbacks for the boy's point of view. The war is over and the town celebrates the return of its veterans, but he must hide in the room of their forbidden love and go through the anguish of recalling that love. This flashback structure, together with the doomed love of the couple, reminded critics of *Le Jour se Lève* and made the public see Gérard Philipe as the heir of Jean Gabin. But the Limpid expressiveness of the prewar poetic realism had been complicated after the war. Philipe's gestures were calculated to display his passion and anguish, whereas Gabin had moved and spoken instinctively, without the hesitation of either good taste or intelligence, hallmarks of the postwar style. The same holds true for the direction. While Carné and Prévert had devised a number of highly charged objects, Autant-Lara multiplies effects wherever he can. The incessant play of reflections in mirrors and by the ferry insists on the significance of the dramas but does so from the outside. Similarly the famous 360-degree camera movement that circles the bed of the couple's lovemaking demands to be noticed as a figure supplied by an external narrator, especially since it begins on a crackling fire and ends on dying embers. This is more than a metaphor for passion, it is a poetic display that lifts an ordinary drama into telling significance.

Altogether *Le Diable au Corps* stuns its audience with the cockiness of its presentation as well as with the audacity of its subject matter. This is its conquest as well as its loss; for in only a few years the New Wave critics, led by Truffaut, would clamor for the downfall of psychological realism and of the paternalistic, elitist narration that preaches a liberal morality. If Radiguet, the novelist, likewise condemned a suffocating society, he did so from within, from the perceptions and language of his hero. Autant-Lara has used Radiguet's rebelliousness, has packaged it approvingly, but has made of it a mature, stylish film. Radiguet, legend has it, put everything of himself into this novel and then died. The movie pays tribute to his effort and his views, but is just another very good movie.

—Dudley Andrew

LES DIABOLIQUES. Production: Filmsonor (Paris); black and white, 35mm; running time: 110 mins. Released 1954.

Produced by Louis de Masure; screenplay by Henri-Georges Clouzot, Jérôme Géronimi, René Masson, and Frédéric Grendel; from the novel *Celle qui n'était plus* by Boileau and Narcejac; directed by Henri-Georges Clouzot; photography by Armand Thirard; edited by Madeleine Gug; sound by William-Robert Sivel; production design by Léon Barsacq; music by Georges van Parys.

Filmed in France. Prix Louis Delluc (France), 1955; New York Film Critics' Award, Best Foreign Film (tied with *Umberto D*), 1955.

Cast: Simone Signoret (*Nicole*); Véra Clouzot (*Christina*); Paul Meurisse (*Michell*); Charles Vanel (*Fichet*); Jean Brochard (*Plantiveau*); Noël Roquevert (*M. Herboux*); Georges Chamarat (*Dr. Loisy*); Jacques Varennes (*Professor Bridoux*); Michel Serrault (*M. Raymond*).

Publications:

Review—"A propos de Clouzot et de ses *Diaboliques*" by André G. Brunelin in *Cinéma 55* (Paris), November 1954; books—*Le Procès Clouzot* by Francis Lacassin and Raymond Bellour, Paris 1964; *H.G. Clouzot* by Philippe Pilard, Paris 1969; *French Cinema Since 1946: The Great Tradition, Vol. 1* by Roy Armes, New York 1976; articles—"Frenchman's Horror" in *Newsweek* (New York), 28 November 1955; "The Necrophilist" by Stanley Goulder in *Films and Filming* (London), December 1955; "Clouzot est-il vraiment diable?" by Claude Brulé in *Ciné-revue* (Paris), 1955; "Henri-Georges Clouzot" by Sylvia Tennant in *Film* (London), March/April 1956; "H.G. Clouzot, l'homme diabolique du cinéma français" by J. Forestier and G.P. Richer in *Les Lettres françaises* (Paris), July 1960; "An Interview with Henri-Georges Clouzot" by Paul Schrader in *Cinema* (Beverly Hills), no.4, 1969; "Henri-Georges Clouzot, 1907-1977" by Roland Lacourbe in *Anthologie du cinéma, Vol. X*, Paris 1979.

*   *   *

Henri-Georges Clouzot is a key member of the generation of filmmakers who emerged during the Occupation and dominated French cinema for a dozen years or so after the war. *Les Diaboliques* is not a masterpiece to rank with such earlier Clouzot films as *Le Corbeau* or *Le Salaire de la Peur*, but its particular contradictions allow the principal aspects of what was later to be dubbed the "tradition of quality" to be clearly observed.

The political events of these years—the war in Indo-China leading to the fall of Dien Bien Phu, and the beginning of the Algerian revolution which was to lead to eight years of savage fighting and eventually bring down the Fourth Republic—are ignored and Clouzot, like so many of his contemporaries, offers a studio reconstruction of the world which is meticulously realist in detail, but essentially timeless. *Les Diaboliques* is set in one of Clouzot's favorite locations—a shabby, rundown provincial school—and the tensions here between a bullying headmaster, his ailing wife and forceful mistress are methodically set up. The craftsmanship involved in the creation of this world is enormous, and nothing is allowed to stand between the director and his conception of his film. Before 1939 actors had been the *monstres sacrés* of French cinema and every aspect of a film was subordinate to their will. But Clouzot was from the first renowned for the harsh treatment he meted out to his actors. If the story that he served bad fish to the actors in *Les Diaboliques* and made them eat it so as to capture an authentic sense of disgust is probably apocryphal, it certainly conveys perfectly his essential attitude.

The 1940s and early 1950s was also a time of the totally scripted film in which the diversity and contradictions of life were reduced to a single narrative line relentlessly followed. Though there might be a rich counterpoint of incident as well as the creation of multiple ironies, there was no space for gaps within the plot which would unfold with all the precision of a watch mechanism. In works like *Le Corbeau* and *Quai des Orfèvres*, Clouzot had shown himself to be a master of the thriller structure, with all the subtle manipulation of audience responses which that implies. But as so often in other aspects of his work, Clouzot seems to have been driven by a desire to take the creation of suspense to extreme limits. For him, as for his contemporary, Alfred Hitchcock, whom he much admired, there could be no half measures. In *Les Diaboliques* Clouzot is tempted into a display of his own narrative skills, and the logic of the film, which has plotted its first murder with brutal precision, is slowly taken apart. Inexplicable things start to happen, and the spectator's confidence in his own perceptions, in the truth of what he has seen and heard, is undermined. The contradictions are resolved in a virtuoso passage of plot twisting in the final reel, but this very ingenuity destroys the psychological realism on which the film's opening is constructed. *Les Diaboliques* is exhilarating at first viewing, and proved to be both commercially successful and controversial on its first release. For most critics, however, the contrivance of the ending renders a second viewing meaningless, since it underlines the film's remoteness from a lived reality and even makes Clouzot's deeply felt black vision seem trite and superficial.

—Roy Armes

————

DO BIGHA ZAMIN. Two Acres of Land. Black and white, 35mm; running time: 138 mins. Released 1953.

Produced by Bimal Roy; screenplay by Hrishikesh Mukerjee; from a story by Salil Chaudhury; directed by Bimal Roy; photography by Kamal Bose; edited by Hrishikesh Mukerjee; music by Salil Chaudhury.

Filmed in India. Prize for Social Progress, Karlovy Vary Film Festival, 1954. Cannes Film Festival, received one of the 10 international awards, 1954.

Cast: Balraj Sahni (*Sambhu*); Nirum Roy; Rattan Kumar.

Publications:

Books—*Indian Film* by Erik Barnouw and S. Krishnaswamy, New York 1980; *The New Generation: 1960-1980* edited by Uma da Cuncha , New Delhi 1981; articles—"The Indian Film" by Marie Seton in *Film* (London), March 1955; "New Indian Directors" by S.K. Ray in *Film Quarterly* (Berkeley), fall 1960; "Discovering India" by Kolita Sarha in *Films and Filming* (London), December 1960; "The Bimal Roy Only I Knew" by Manobina Roy in *The Illustrated Weekly of India*, 3 August 1980; "Film India: Indian Film Festival, Part Two—Historical Perspective" in *Museum of Modern Art Department of Film* (film notes), summer 1981.

*   *   *

Into a cinema devoted chiefly to gaiety and adventure, Bimal Roy's *Do Bigha Zamin* introduced an element of seriousness and naturalism. Roy did not break with tradition in his film: *Do Bigha Zamin* includes songs and dances and the usual patterned dialogue. But Roy enlarged the operatic scope of popular films to include: location shots of an ordinary, undramatic character (e.g. the look of trees and fields as the peasant leaves the country for Calcutta); well-observed natural actions (e.g. the habitual manner in which the peasant's wife puts out a pan to catch fresh rainwater); and grave subject matter (e.g. the stacking of legal justice against those unskilled in legalities). Roy's use of the familiar musical and melodramatic style enabled audiences to comprehend his films; at the same time the new naturalistic elements prepared the ground for the more uncompromising and formally innovative political cinema of the seventies.

Do Bigha Zamin tells the story of a peasant whose meager two acres come in the way of the landlord's scheme to sell a large parcel of the village land to speculators. The landlord fabricates evidence of an unpaid debt and the peasant must leave for the city to earn the cash the landlord requires. The acting in the film veers between the rapid responsiveness of performers in a melodrama and the slow surfacing of responses characteristic of naturalism. At the landlord's, the peasant (played by the deeply intelligent actor Belraj Sahni) acts by formula, but his leave-taking from his wife is simple; his fears for her emerge into natural, unemphatic expression on his face and in his bearing. The lighting, too, varies between the full lighting characteristic of Bombay sets and the chiaroscuro of available light cinematography. The landlord's house is amply lit, but the rickshaw-puller's quarters in Calcutta retain a natural look of charcoal dilapidation.

In sum, an important, earnest, transitional film, which bespeaks the influence of Italian neorealism on Hindi cinema. It won the Prix Internationale at the 1954 Cannes film festival and the Prize for Social Progress at the Karlovy Vary film festival.

—Satti Khanna

DR. JEKYLL AND MR. HYDE. Production: Paramount Pictures; black and white, 35mm; running time: 82 mins., some sources list 90 mins. Released 1931.

Produced by Rouben Mamoulian; screenplay by Samuel Hoffenstein and Percy Heath; from the novel by Robert Louis Stevenson; directed by Rouben Mamoulian; photography by Karl Struss; edited by William Shea; sound by the Paramount sound department; production design by Hans Dreier.

Filmed in Paramount studios. Venice Film Festival citations for Most Original Film and Favorite Actor (March), 1932, note: there were not official awards that year, but acknowledgements were by public referendum; Academy Award, Best Actor (March), 1932.

Cast: Fredric March (*Dr. Henry Jekyll/Mr. Hyde*); Miriam Hopkins (*Ivy Pearson*); Rose Hobart (*Muriel Carew*); Halliwell Hobbes (*Brigadier General Carew*); Holmes Herbert (*Dr. Lanyan*); Edgar Norton (*Poole*).

Publications:

Script—*Dr. Jekyll and Mr. Hyde* (screenplay and blow-ups

from film) edited by Richard Anobile, New York 1976; books— *An Illustrated History of the Horror Film* by Carlos Clarens, New York 1967; *Interviews with Film Directors* by Andrew Sarris, Indianapolis 1967; *Hollywood in the Thirties* by John Baxter, New York 1968; *Rouben Mamoulian* by Tom Milne, London 1969; *Charles Laughton and Fredric March* by Michael Burrows, New York 1970; *Rouben Mamoulian: Style is the Man* edited by James Silke, Washington, D.C. 1971; *The Films of Fredric March* by Lawrence J. Quirk, New York 1971; *Horror and Science Fiction Films: A Checklist* by Donald C. Willis, Metuchen, New Jersey 1972; *Reference Guide to Fantastic Films: Volume 1, A-F* compiled by Walt Lee, Los Angeles 1972; *Classics of the Horror Film* by William K. Everson, Secaucus, New Jersey 1974; *Movie Monsters* by Thomas G. Aylesworth, Philadelphia 1975; articles—"Personalities Prominent in the Press" by M. Merrick in *Cinema Digest*, 25 July 1932; "Fredric March" by Romano Tozzi in *Films in Review* (New York), December 1958; "Painting the Leaves Black" by David Robison in *Sight and Sound* (London), summer 1961; "Fallen Idols" by Andrew Sarris in *Film Culture* (New York), spring 1963; "Mamoulian on His Dr. Jekyll and Mr. Hyde" in *Cinefantastique* (Oak Park, Illinois), summer 1971; "*Dr. Jekyll and Mr. Hyde*" by T. Atkins in *Film Journal* (Hollins College, Virginia), January/March 1973; "Book into Films: *Dr. Jekyll and Mr. Hyde*" by S.S. Prawer in the *Times Literary Supplement* (London), 21 December 1979; "*Dr. Jekyll and Mr. Hyde*" by D. Gail Huskins in *Magill's Survey of Cinema, Vol. 1* edited by Frank N. Magill, Englewood Cliffs, New Jersey 1980.

*   *   *

Rouben Mamoulian's *Dr. Jekyll and Mr. Hyde* is perhaps the most stylish and technically innovative of any of the several versions of Robert Louis Stevenson's classic novel, for Mamoulian integrated both the new and established film technologies into his individual filmmaking style. Dissolves, superimpositions, camera movements, and expressionistic lighting are synthesized into his vision of the struggle within man, which is the heart of Stevenson's tale.

While other directors seemed shackled by the then infant sound technology, Mamoulian freely moved the camera within the frame. *Dr. Jekyll and Mr. Hyde* in fact opens with an extensive tracking shot that the viewer quickly realizes represents the subjective point of view of Dr. Jekyll. The effect of characters directly addressing the camera (as Dr. Jekyll) is disarming. Not only is such a shot a masterful technical innovation, in light of the obstacle posed by sound recording, but it is a striking narrative device as well. Mamoulian's subjective camera foreshadows the use, some 50 years later, of the same device to similar ends by John Carpenter in *Halloween*. Since *Halloween*, it has become a characteristic element of those kinds of films which indeed bear resemblance to *Dr. Jekyll and Mr. Hyde*.

No less striking is the 360-degree pan which accompanies Dr. Jekyll's initial transformation to Hyde. The shot underscores the duration of the transformation, solidly placing it in time and space. Mamoulian claims that the pan was the first of its kind in Hollywood film. The shot not only presented the obvious challenge of lighting, but also posed unique problems for recording sound. Mamoulian overcame this by mixing a sound effects track. The track is dominated rhythmically by a heartbeat (Mamoulian's own) and serves as an early example of a complex sound mix in a Hollywood film. In addition, as he had done earlier in *City Streets* and particularly in *Applause*, Mamoulian utilized multiple microphones for recording live sound. He even pioneered a mobile microphone used in situations such as the opening shot of *Dr. Jekyll and Mr. Hyde.*

This version of *Dr. Jekyll and Mr. Hyde* is ahead of its time in Mamoulian's exploitation of the potential eroticism of Stevenson's novel. Miriam Hopkins streetwalker, Ivy, is at once sympathetic and highly sensual. Unlike Stevenson's gnarled, diminuitive Hyde, Mamoulian's representation of Hyde is that of an enlarged, powerful, bestial man. Both characterizations heighten the intensity of their moments together on screen. Jekyll first meets Ivy in her room where he has gone to return a discarded garter. He finds her nearly undressed as she slips beneath the bedcovers and taunts him coquettishly. The scene closes with Ivy's leg, dangling from beneath the covers deliciously—superimposed—over the image of Jekyll and his friend Lanyon departing below.

Superimpositions and dissolves were not new to the cinema in 1932. However, Mamoulian's use of them to heighten aesthetically the impact of various scenes was not characteristic of Hollywood in the thirties. For example, the superimpositions used in the scene where Jekyll meets Ivy suggest that the image of Ivy's leg lingers in Jekyll's mind. Mamoulian's use of dissolves may be somewhat more traditional in that they are the primary means for showing Jekyll's transformations into Hyde.

Dr. Jekyll and Mr. Hyde represents the strengths of Mamoulian's style. Perhaps as an extension of his experience directing theater and opera, where the proscenium limits space, Mamoulian's style emphasizes lighting and framing. In the film, when Hyde's passion for Ivy becomes rage, he begins to strangle her. The two figures fall, struggling below the frame. Only when Hyde returns to frame does the viewer understand Ivy's fate. Similarly, when Jekyll undergoes his first transformation, he falls, writhing out of frame. Mamoulian combines this technique with lighting in a later scene to create an enormous shadow—Hyde. The shadow is formed as Hyde runs from the frame, his departure signalled by his ever increasing shadow on the wall. This shot echoes a similar shot in F.W. Murnau's *Nosferatu* where Count Dracula's shadow gradually engulfs the cowering figure of Jonathan Harker.

Several nuances of Mamoulian's style are also reinforced with this film. Split-screen is used, for example, to suggest a symbolic proximity between otherwise distant spaces and events. Another characteristic is the use of counterpoint to heighten dramatic effect. When Jekyll arrives to tell his fiancée, Muriel, that they must separate it is accompanied not by a dirge, but by the waltz to which they had danced earlier. Counterpoints such as this create a dynamism between the visuals and the sound. The waltz serves as a powerful reminder of Jekyll's price for tampering with nature. Perhaps the strongest example of Mamoulian's individuality as a filmmaker is the final shot, where Lanyon and the authorities stand over the body of the fallen Jekyll. Shot from inside and behind the flames of the fireplace, it is a complete synthesis of the medium's potential for narrative discourse.

Critical reaction to *Dr. Jekyll and Mr. Hyde* was enthusiastic. *The New York Times* called it "splendidly produced" and "masterfully photographed." Fredric March, for his performance as Jekyll and Hyde, received the Academy Award as Best Actor.

—Robert Winning

DR. NO. Production: Eon Productions Ltd. Technicolor, 35mm; running time: 111 mins. Released 1962 in England through United Artists.

Produced by Harry Saltzman and Albert R. Broccoli; screen-play by Richard Maibaum, Johanna Harwood, and Berkeley Mather; from the novel by Ian Fleming; main titles designed by Maurice Binder; directed by Terrence Young; photography by Ted Moore; edited by Peter Hunt; production design by Ken Adam; art direction by Syd Cain; music composed by Monty Norman, orchestrated by Burt Rhodes, and conducted by Eric Rodgers; special effects Frank George; animation by Trevor Bond and Robert Ellis.

Filmed on location around the world. Cost: just under $1 million.

Cast: Sean Connery (*James Bond*); Ursula Andress (*Honey*); Joseph Wiseman (*Dr. No*); Jack Lord (*Felix Leiter*); Bernard Lee (*M*); Anthony Dawson (*Professor Dent*); John Kitsmiller (*Quarrel*); Zena Marshall (*Miss Taro*); Eunice Gayson (*Sylvia*); Lois Maxwell (*Miss Moneypenny*); Lester Prendergast (*Pussfeller*); Tim Moxon (*Strangeways*); Margaret LeWars (*Girl photographer*); Reggie Carter (*Jones*); Peter Burton (*Major Boothroyd*); William Foster-Davis (*Duff*); Louis Blaazer (*Playdell-Smith*); Michele Mok (*Sister Rose*); Dolores Keator (*Mary*).

Publications:

Books—*The Great Spy Pictures* edited by James Robert Parish and Michael Pitts, Metuchen, New Jersey 1974; *James Bond in the Cinema* by John Brosnan, San Diego 1981; *The James Bond Films* by Steven Jay Rubin, Westport, Connecticutt, 1981; articles—"Ursula Andress: She Said Yes to Dr. No." in *Cinema* (Beverly Hills), June/July 1963; "The Bond Wagon" in *Newsweek* (New York), 11 May 1964; "James Bond's Girls" in *Vogue* (New York), July 1964; "Interview: Sean Connery" in *Playboy* (Chicago), November 1965; "007" by Penelope Houston in *Sight and Sound* (London), winter 1964-65; "Bondomania" in *Time* (New York), 11 June 1965; "007 Girls" in *Time* (New York), 10 September 1965; "007 plus 4" by Ian Johnson in *Films and Filming* (London), October 1965; "007-The Spy with the Golden Touch" by James Stewart Gordon in *Reader's Digest* (Pleasantville, New York), October 1965; "Young Romantic" by John Francis Lane in *Films and Filming* (London), February 1967; "007 and the Myth of the Hero" by Richard Carpenter in *Journal of Popular Culture* (Bowling Green, Ohio), no.2, 1967.

*   *   *

When *Dr. No* was first released in 1963, an entirely different kind of film hero was introduced. James Bond was a new breed of super spy who could, against incredible odds, outwit and defeat seemingly invincible enemies. Although the basic theme of *Dr. No* (and all the James Bond films) was simply good vs. evil, Bond was not the typical moral and upright "good guy." He had a license to kill and used it without hesitation. Although perhaps a bit tame when compared to later films, the violence in *Dr. No* was considered shocking in 1963. Two graphic murders occur in the first five minutes of the film (one of the victims is a woman who is shot in the breast, leaving a pool of blood on the floor). This style of cold-blooded murder brought forth a number of editorials against the film. The Vatican City newspaper called the film "a dangerous mixture of violence, vulgarity, sadism, and sex." Apparently this was just the combination the public was looking for in a motion picture because *Dr. No* was a huge success.

All of the James Bond films are based on formula filmmaking and *Dr. No* helped establish many of the ingredients in this formula. Part of the success of the James Bond films is their tongue-in-cheek approach which can be attributed to director Terence Young. Young realized that since the Bond stories were fantasies they should not take themselves too seriously. Thus Bond exhibited a rather dry wit, often understating the facts to contrast his fantastic surroundings. The performance of Sean Connery also helped to establish the popularity of the Bond character. Connery's Bond never lost his touch in any situation. He could be suave and debonaire yet cold and calculating in the same scene. Another reason for the appeal of the Bond films is the presentation of sex. Not only is Bond a super spy, but is is a super lover as well. He often uses sex as a weapon, as can be seen in *Dr. No.* Bond keeps one of Dr. No's accomplices, a beautiful oriental woman, occupied in bed until the police come to arrest her; he then turns her over to the authorities with a cool "so long" as though sending her off to summer camp.

Dr. No also introduced the science fiction elements to the James Bond films. Dr. No, who is working for SPECTRE (Special Executive for Counter-Intelligence, Terrorism, Revenge, and Extortion) has built his own atomic reactor with plans to destroy the United States's missile program. Each successive James Bond film has introduced more elaborate science-fantasy elements, such as specially equipped cars and flying jet packs. These fanciful gadgets which Bond encounters in each film have become a trademark of the series.

The producers of *Dr. No* originally planned to do a series of James Bond pictures if the first one was successful. Produced with a budget of under $1 million, the film grossed six times that amount in its initial release. Subsequent re-issues continue to add to its box office total. All of the James Bond films have subsequently been huge box office successes, making James Bond the most successful and longest running film series. The success of *Dr. No* and the James Bond films have inspired a string of film and television imitations, such as "The Man from U.N.C.L.E.", Tony Rome, Matt Helm, Derick Flint, and Maxwell Smart, However, none of these characters have been as successful as James Bond.

—Linda J. Obalil

DR. STRANGELOVE OR: HOW I LEARNED TO STOP WORRYING AND LOVE THE BOMB. Production: Hawk Films, a Stanley Kubrick Production; black and white, 35mm; running time: originally 102 mins., edited down to 93 mins. Released 30 January 1964.

Produced by Stanley Kubrick, associate producer: Victor Lyndon; screenplay by Stanley Kubrick, Terry Southern, and Peter George; originally conceived as a serious adaptation of *Red Alert* by Peter George; main titles by Pablo Ferro; directed by Stanley Kubrick; photography by Gilbert Taylor; edited by Anthony Harvey; sound supervised by John Cox, sound recorded by Richard Bird, dub mixed by John Aldred, sound edited by Leslie Hodgson; production design by Ken Adam; art direction by Peter Murton; music by Laurie Johnson, song "Try a Little Tenderness" is the original recording by Vera Lynn; special effects Wally Veevers, travelling matte by Vic Margutti; costumes designed by Pamela Carlton; aviation adivisor: Capt. John Crewdson.

Cost: $1,500,000. New York Film Critics' Award, Best Direction, 1964.

Cast: Peter Sellers (*Group Capt. Lionel Mandrake/President Muffley/Dr. Strangelove*); George C. Scott (*Gen. Buck Turgidson*); Sterling Hayden (*Gen. Jack D. Ripper*); Keenan Wynn (*Col. Bat Guano*); Slim Pickens (*Maj. T.J. "King" Kong*); Peter Bull (*Ambassador de Sadesky*); Tracy Reed (*Miss Scott*); James Earl Jones (*Lieut. Lothar Zagg*); Jack Creley (*Mr. Staines*); Frank Berry (*Lieut. H.R. Dietrich*); Glenn Beck (*Lieut. W.D. Kivel*); Shane Rimmer (*Capt. G.A. "Ace" Owens*); Paul Tamarin (*Lieut. B. Goldberg*); Gordon Tanner (*General Faceman*); Robert O'Neil (*Admiral Randolph*); Roy Stephens (*Frank*); Laurence Herder, John McCarthy, Hal Galili (*Burpelson defense team members*).

Publications:

Reviews—by Bryan Forbes in *Films and Filming* (London), February 1964; review by Jackson Burgess in *Film Quarterly* (Berkeley), spring 1964; review by Bosley Crowther in *The New York Times*, 31 January 1964; review by Tom Milne in *Sight and Sound* (London), winter 1963-64; books—*The Cinema of Stanley Kubrick* by David Austen, London 1969; *The Film Director as Superstar* by Joseph Gelmis, New York 1970; *Stanley Kubrick Directs* by Alexander Walker, New York 1972; *The Cinema of Stanley Kubrick* by Norman Kagan, New York 1972; *The Films of Stanley Kubrick* by Daniel Devries, Grand Rapids, Michigan 1973; *Elements of Film* by Lee Bobker, New York 1974; *Stanley Kubrick: A Film Odyssey* by Gene Phillips, New York 1977; *Voices of Film Experience* edited by Jay Leyda, New York 1977; *How to Read a Film* by James Monaco, New York 1977; articles—by Henry Hart in *Films in Review* (New York), February 1962; "How I Learned to Stop Worrying and Love the Cinema" by Stanley Kubrick in *Films and Filming* (London), June 1963; "Contradicting the Hollywood Image" by Lyn Tornabene in the *Saturday Review* (New York), 28 December 1963; "Take Aim: Fire at the Agonies of War" by T. Prideaux in *Life* (New York), 20 December 1963; "Stanley Kubrick's Divided World" by James Price in *London Magazine*, May 1964; "How I Learned to Stop Worrying and Love Stanley Kubrick" by Tom Milne in *Sight and Sound* (London), spring 1964; "Dr. Kubrick" by Joe Goldberg in *Seventh Art* (New York), spring 1964; articles by Andrew Sarris in *The Village Voice* (New York), 13 February and 11 June 1964; article by Stephen Taylor in *Film Comment* (New York), winter 1964; "Stanley Kubrick" by Lee Russell in *New Left Review* (New York), summer 1964; "Sex and Dr. Strangelove" by F.A. Macklin in *Film Comment* (New York), summer 1965; article by Patrick MacFadden in *Film Society Review* (New York), January 1967; "Dr. Strangelove" by Frank Manchel in *Media and Methods* (Philadelphia), December 1967; "Dr. Strangelove: Or, How I Learned to Stop Worrying and Love the Bomb" by Linda Obalil in *Cinema Texas Program Notes* (Austin), 1 May 1978; "Dr. Strangelove, or How I Learned to Stop Worrying and Love the Bomb" by Rob Edelman in *Magill's Survey of Cinema, Vol. 1* edited by Frank N. Magill, Englewood Cliffs, New Jersey 1980; "Dr. Strangelove: Analyse op de montagetafel" by W. Verstappen in *Skoop* (Amsterdam), October 1980.

* * *

Stanley Kubrick's *Dr. Strangelove*, which has won wide and continued public acceptance from the time of its release, has come to be considered one of the screen's great masterpieces of black comedy. Yet Kubrick had originally planned the film as a serious adaptatin of Peter George's *Red Alert*, a novel concerned with the demented General Jack D. Ripper (Sterling Hayden) and his decision to order a troupe of B-52 bombers to launch an attack inside Russia. Gradually Kubrick's attitude toward his material changed: "My ideal of doing it as a nightmare comedy came in the early weeks of working on the screenplay. I found that in trying to put meat on the bones and to imagine the scenes fully, one had to keep leaving out of it things which were either absurd or paradoxical, in order to keep it from being funny; and these things seemed to be close to the heart of the scenes in question."

Kubrick remembers that he kept revising the script right through the production period. "During shooting many substantial changes were made in the script, sometimes together with the cast during improvisations. Some of the best dialogue was created by Peter Sellers himself." Sellers played not only the title role of the eccentric scientist, but also the president of the United States and Captain Mandrake, a British officer who fails to dissuade General Ripper from his set purpose.

General Ripper's mad motivation for initiating a nuclear attack is his paranoid conviction that the explanation of his diminishing sexual potency can be traced to an international Communist conspiracy to poison the drinking water. Kubrick subtly reminds us of the general's obsession by a series of suggestive metaphors that occur in the course of the film. The very opening image of the film shows a nuclear bomber being refueled in mid-flight by another aircraft, with "Try a Little Tenderness" appropriately playing on the sound track to accompany their symbolic coupling. As Ripper describes to Mandrake his concern about preserving his potency, which he refers to as his "precious bodily essence," Kubrick photographs him in close-up from below, with a hugh phallic cigar jutting from between his lips while he is talking. Later, when the skipper of a B-52 bomber (Slim Pickens) manages to dislodge a bomb that has been stuck in its chamber and unleash it on its Russian target, he sits astride this mighty symbol of potency clamped between his flanks, as it hurtles toward the earth.

Black ironies abound throughout the picture. During an emergency conference called by President Muffley, a disagreement between General Buck Turgidson (George C. Scott) and the Russian ambassador (Peter Bull) threatens to turn into a brawl, and the president intervenes by reminding them, "Please, gentlemen, you can't fight here; this is the War Room!" Later, when Mandrake tries to reach the president in order to warn him about the imminent attack on Russia, he finds that he lacks the correct change for the pay telephone he is using, and that the White House will not accept a collect call! He then demands that Colonel Bat Guano (Keenan Wynn) fire into a Coca-Cola machine in order to obtain the necessary coins. Guano reluctantly agrees, ruefully reminding Mandrake that it is he who will have to answer to the Coca-Cola Company. Guano blasts the machine, bends down to scoop up the silver—and is squirted full in the face with Coca-Cola by the vindictive machine.

Kubrick had originally included a scene in which the Russians and the Americans in the War Room engage in a free-for-all with custard pies, but deleted it from the final print of the film when he decided that "it was too farcical, and not consistent with the satiric tone of the rest of the film." Very much in keeping with the satiric, dark humor of the picture is the figure of Dr. Strangelove himself, Kubrick's grim vision of man's final capitulation to the machine: he is more a robot than a human being, with his mechanical arm spontaneously saluting Hitler, his former employer, and his mechanical hand, gloved in black, at one point trying to strangle the flesh and blood still left in him.

In the end a single U.S. plane reaches its Russian target, setting off the Russian's retaliatory Doomsday machine. There follows a series of blinding explosions, while on the sound track we hear a popular song which Kubrick resurrected from World War II: "We'll meet again, don't know where, don't know when...." (Kubrick used the original World War II recording by Vera Lynn, which brought popularity back not only to the song but to Ms. Lynn as well.)

One critic summed up the film by saying that the black comedy which Kubrick had originally thought to exclude from *Dr. Strangelove* provides some of its most meaningful moments. "They are made up of the incongruities, the banalities, and misunderstandings that we are constantly aware of in our lives. On the brink of annihilation, they become irresistibly absurd."

The theme that emerges from *Dr. Strangelove* is the plight of fallible man putting himself at the mercy of his "infallible" machines and thus bringing about his own destruction. Kubrick, who is always on the side of humanity in his films, indicates here, as in *2001: A Space Odyssey* that human fallibility is less likely to destroy man than the relinquishing of his moral responsibilities to his supposedly faultless machinery. Summing up his personal vision as it is reflected in *Dr. Strangelove*, the director has said: "The destruction of this planet would have no significance on a cosmic scale. Our extinction would be little more than a match flaring for a second in the heavens. And if that match does blaze in the darkness, there will be none to mourn a race that used a power that could have lit a beacon in the stars to light its funeral pyre."

—Gene D. Phillips

DOG STAR MAN. Black and white and Eastmancolor, 16mm, silent; running time: 83 mins. for entire film, some sources list 78 mins.; including the final section of the film, entitled *The Art of Vision*, the film runs 270 mins. Released 22 February 1965.

Produced, scripted, directed, and edited by Stan Brakhage; photography by Stan Brakhage, with additional photography by Jane Brakhage.

Filmed in 5 sections, beginning in 1960 and concluding in 1964, for the most part in Colorado.

Cast: Stan Brakhage (*Dog Star Man*); Jane Brakhage (*Woman*); Sirius (*Dog*).

Publications:

Books—*Metaphors on Vision* by Stan Brakhage, New York 1963; *Brakhage* by Dan Clark, New York 1966; *Stan Brakhage* by Donald Richie, New York 1970; *The Brakhage Lectures*, Chicago 1972; *Movie Journal, The Rise of a New American Cinema, 1959-1971* by Jonas Mekas, New York 1972; *A History of the American Avant-Garde Cinema* edited by The American Federation of Arts, New York 1976; *Abstract Film and Beyond* by Malcolm Le Grice, Cambridge, Massachusetts 1977; *Stan Brakhage* by Marie Nesthus, Minneapolis/St. Paul 1979; *Visionary Film* by P. Adams Sitney, New York 1979; *Brakhage Scrapbook: Collected Writings 1964-1980*, New Paltz, New York 1982; articles—"A Note on Stan Brakhage" by Donald Sutherland in *Film Culture* (New York), no.24, 1962; "*Anticipation of the Night* and *Prelude*" by P. Adams Sitney in *Film Culture* (New York), no.26, 1962; "Interview with Stan Brakhage" by P. Adams Sitney in *Film Culture* (New York), fall 1963; "*Dog Star Man*" by Michael McClure in *Film Culture* (New York), summer 1963; article by P. Adams Sitney in *Film Culture* (New York), winter 1963-64; article by Robert Kelly in *Film Culture* (New York), summer 1965; "Robert Kelly on *The Art of Vision*" in *Film Culture* (New York), summer 1965; "Notes and Writings" by Carl Linder in *Film Culture* (New York), spring 1967; "*The Art of Vision*, a Film by Stan Brakhage" by Fred Camper in *Film Culture* (New York), autumn 1967; "Stan and Jane Brakhage Talking" by Hollis Frampton in *Artforum* (New York), January 1973.

*   *   *

The most important of Stan Brakhage's films of the early 1960s, and the most widely discussed of all of his films, *Dog Star Man* was the first of his works to have a serial form; it has a *Prelude* and four separate parts, which roughly correspond to the seasons. It is a tour de force of minute editing and elaborate superimposition, with two layers in the *Prelude* and *Part Two*, three in *Part Three*, and four in the final part. *The Art of Vision* expands the 83-minute *Dog Star Man* into two hundred and seventy minutes by showing all the layers separately and by projecting all the possible combinations of layers within each of the parts.

Brakhage and his family are the only human figures in this cosmological myth of cyclic quests and defeats. They are gradually introduced in the *Prelude* after a leisurely exposition of the "elements" of the natural world. As in some of Brakhage's later films, the myth of the creation of mankind is collapsed upon a fantasy of origins of an individual consciousness. *Part One* dissects Brakhage's climb up a snow-covered mountain, accompanied by a dog. Images of internal organs, often enlarged by microscopy, control the rhythm of the section, where the montage reflects the back and forth movement of the capillaries and the movements of heart and lungs. It is the andante section of the film, the only one without superimpositions.

In the second part, the face of a baby boy, filmed in black and white, with colored fragments of film actually collaged into holes Brakhage made in the original 16mm film, dominates the imagery. The collage elements draw attention to his developing sense organs, while the superimposition seems to represent the world from the child's perspective, with the mother's breast playing a large role. The counterpart to this metaphor for innocent vision is the sexual imagery of *Part Three* in which a layer of images of a male body and another of a female are superimposed over a beating heart. The filmmaker handpainted over the heart layer to emphasize a rhythmic figure corresponding to an orgasm.

The fourth section rapidly picks up where the first and the frame of the second left off, with the collapsed man. Now, he rises in autumn, wrestles with a dead tree, and, as he is chopping it up, falls down the mountain only to rise as a figure in the sky.

Throughout the film Brakhage intercuts and superimposes images which allude to the imagined evolution of artistic and architectural forms. All through the work he stresses the ad hoc status of his images, eschewing illusionary narrative, and exploring the dynamics of film construction.

Dog Star Man is a film of enormous ambition and intricacy, the American avant-garde's equivalent of Vertov's *The Man with a Movie Camera*.

—P. Adams Sitney

DR. MABUSE, DER SPIELER. Part I: Der Grosse Spieler—Ein Bild der Zeit, Part II: Inferne—Ein SpielVon Menschen Unserer Zeit. Production: Uco-Film Studios; black and white, 35mm, silent; length: originally 3496 meters (Part I) and 2560 meters (Part II). Released 27 April 1922 (Part I) and 26 May 1922 (Part II).

Screenplay by Fritz Lang and Thea von Harbou; from a novel by Norbert Jacques published in *Berliner Illustrirte Zeitung*; directed by Fritz Lang; photography by Carl Hoffman; art direction by Carl Stahl Urach (died during production), Otto Hunte, Erich Kettelhut, and Karl Vollbrecht; costumes designed by Vally Reinecke.

Filmed 1921-1922, Part I in 8 weeks and Part II in 9 weeks; in Uco-Film studios in Berlin.

Cast: Rudolf Klein-Rogge (*Dr. Mabuse*); Aud Egede Nissen (*Cara Carozza, the dancer*); Gertrude Welcker (*Countess Told*); Alfred Abel (*Count Told*); Bernhard Goetzke (*Detective von Wenk*); Paul Richter (*Edgar Hull*); Robert Forster-Larringa (*Dr. Mabuse's servant*); Hans Adalbert Schlettow (*Georg, the chauffeur*); Georg John (*Pesche*); Karl Huszar (*Hawasch, manager of the counterfeiting factory*); Grete Berger (*Fine, Mabuse's servant*); Julius Falkenstein (*Karsten, Wenk's friend*); Lydia Potechina (*Russian woman*); Jululius E. Herrman (*Schramm, the proprietor*); Karl Platen (*Told's servant*); Anita Berber (*Dancer*); Paul Biensfeldt (*Man with the pistol*); Edgar Pauly (*Fat man*); Lil Dagover.

Publications:

Reviews—in the *Berliner Tageblatt*, 30 April 1922; "Filmfragen (*Dr. Mabuse*)" by Herbert Ihering in *Berliner Börsen-Courier*, 11 June 1922, reprinted in his *Von Reinhardt bis Brecht, Vol. 1*, East Berlin 1958; review by Fritz Goetz in *The New York Times*, 9 August 1928; books—*The Film Till Now* by Paul Rotha, London 1930; *Celluloid* by Paul Rotha, London 1931; *An Index to the Creative Work of Fritz Lang* by Herman Weinberg, supplement to *Sight and Sound* (London), index series, 1946; *From Caligari to Hitler: A Psychological History of the German Film* by Siegfried Kracauer, Princeton, New Jersey 1947; *Film Form* by Sergei Eisenstein, New York 1949; *Film as Art* by Rudolf Arnheim, Berkeley 1957, originally published in 1933; *Fritz Lang* by Francis Courtade, Paris 1963; *Fritz Lang* by Luc Moullet, Paris 1963; *Fritz Lang* edited by Alfred Eibel, Paris 1964; *The Cinema of Fritz Lang* by Paul M. Jensen, New York 1969; *The Haunted Screen* by Lotte Eisner, Berkeley 1969; *Fritz Lang* by Claire Johnston, London 1969; *Fritz Lang in America* by Peter Bogdanovich, New York 1969; *The German Cinema* by Roger Manvell and Heinrich Fraenkel, New York 1971; *Le Cinéma Expressioniste Allemand* by Michael Henry, Paris 1971; *Fritz Lang* by Frieda Grafe, Enno Patalas, and Hans Helmut Prinzler, Munich 1976; *Fritz Lang* by Lotte Eisner, London 1977; *Fritz Lang* by Robert Armour, Boston 1978; *The Films of Fritz Lang* by Frederick W. Ott, Secaucus, New Jersey 1979; *Fritz Lang* edited by Stephen Jenkins, London 1979; *Fritz Lang: A Guide to References and Resources* by E. Ann Kaplan, Boston 1981; articles—"Kitsch—Sensation-Kultur und Film" by Fritz Lang in *Das Kulturfilmbuch* edited by E. Beyfuss and P. Kossowsky, Berlin 1924, reprinted in *UFA und der frühe deutsche Film*, Zurich 1963; "Some New German Films" by Trask C. Hooper in *The New York Times*, 20 May 1928; "Notes sur le Style de Fritz Lang" by Lotte Eisner in *Revue du cinéma* (Paris),

1 February 1947; "The Genius of Fritz Lang" by Harry Wilson in *Film Quarterly* (London), summer 1947; "Fritz Lang: Suggestion und Stimmung" in *Gestalter der Filmkunst, von Asta Nielsen bis Walt Disney* by Ludwig Gesek, Vienna 1948; article by Fritz Lang in *Penguin Film Review* (Harmondsworth, Middlesex), vol.V, 1948; "Dämonie des Untergangs: Das Abgründige in Herrn Fritz Lang" by Ulrich Seelman-Eggebrecht in *Der Mittag* (Dusseldorf), 22 March 1951; "Fritz Lang—Endstation 'Indisches Grabmal'?" by Enno Patalas in *Kirche und Film* (Germany), 11 October 1958; "Le Style de Fritz Lang" by Georges Franju in *Cahiers du cinéma* (Paris), November 1959; "Über *Dr. Mabuse, der Spieler*" by Franz Everschor in *Film-Dienst* (Düsseldorf), 5 April 1961; "The Nine Lives of Dr. Mabuse" by John Russell Taylor in *Sight and Sound* (London), winter 1961; "Deutschland: Expressionismus und Neue Sachlichkeit" by Ulrich Gregor and Enno Patalas in *Geschichte des Films*, Gütersloh, Germany 1962; "Fritz Lang Talks About Dr. Mabuse" by Mark Shivas in *Movie* (London), November 1962; "Zwischen Kunst und Kolportage" by Rudolf Freund in *Filmspiegel* (East Berlin), 1 December 1965; "La Nuit Viennoise: Une Confession de Fritz Lang, Part 2" edited by Gretchen Berg in *Cahiers du cinéma* (Paris), August 1965; "Nouvelles Notes pour un éloge de Fritz Lang" by Gérard Legrand in *Positif* (Paris), April 1968; "Selbstdarstellung: Fritz Lang" in *Frankfurter Rundschau*, 15 May 1971; "*Dr. Mabuse* by J. Toeplitz in *Kino* (Warsaw), March 1972; "De Mabuse à M: Le Travail de Fritz Lang" by Noel Burch in *Revue d'Esthétiwue* (Paris), special issue 1973; "*Dr. Mabuse*" by Nora Sayre in *The New York Times*, 15 October 1973; article by Tom Milne in *Monthly Film Bulletin* (London), May 1974; "Von Siegfried bis Mabuse. Filmklassiker Fritz Lang zum 80" by Henning Harmssen in *Lübecker Nachrichten* (Germany), 6 December 1975; "Fritz Lang" by C. Boost in *Skoop* (Amsterdam), February 1975; "Kino der Angst" by Hans Blumenberg in *Die Zeit* (Hamburg), 13 September 1976; "Lang and Parole: Character and Narrative in *Doktor Mabuse, der Spieler*" by J. Jubak in *Film Criticism* (Edinboro, Pennsylvania), no.1, 1979; "Dr. Mabuse and Mr. Lang" by Lucy Fischer in *Wide Angle* (Athens, Ohio), winter 1980; "Notes on Fritz Lang's first Mabuse" by Noel Burch i n *Ciné-tracts* (Montreal), spring 1981.

DAS TESTAMENT DES DR. MABUSE. The Last Will of Dr. Mabuse. Production: Nero-Film A.G. Studios; black and white, 35mm; running time: about 122 mins.; length: 3334 meters. Released 5 December 1933 in Vienna, a French version (95 mins.) was shot simultaneously with the same technical crew and released April 1933 in Paris. Re-released 1943 in U.S., Eisner states that unassembled footage from the French version was smuggled out of Germany and edited by Lothar Wolff in France in a less complete version, and this was the version released in the U.S. 24 August 1951, Germany.

Produced by Seymour Nebenzal; screenplay by Thea von Harbou and Fritz Lang; from the characters in a novel by Norbert Jacques; directed by Fritz Lang; photography by Fritz Arno Wagner and Karl Vass; art direction by Karl Vollbrecht and Emil Hasler; music by Hans Erdmann.

Filmed in 10 weeks in 1932 in Nero-Film A.G. studios in Berlin.

Cast: Rudolf Klein-Rogge (*Dr. Mabuse*); Oskar Beregi (*Dr. Baum*); Karl Meixner (*Landlord*); Theodor Loos (*Dr. Kramm*,

assistant to Baum); Otto Wernicke (*Detective Lohmann*); Klaus Pohl (*Müller, Lohmann's assistant*); Wera Liessem (*Lilli*); Gustav Diessl (*Thomas Kent*); Camilla Spira (*Jewel-Anna*); Rudolf Schündler (*Hardy*); Theo Lingen (*Hardy's friend*); Paul Oskar Höcker (*Bredow*); Paul Henckels (*Lithographer*); Georg John (*Baum's servant*); Ludwig Stössel (*Worker*); Hardrian M. Netto (*Nicolai Grigoriew*); Paul Bernd (*Blackmailer*); Henry Pless (*Dunce*); A.E. Licho (*Dr. Hauser*); Karl Platen, Anna Goltz, and Heinrich Gretler (*Sanitarium Assistants*); Gerhard Bienart, Paul Bernd, Enrst Ludwig, Klaus Pohl, and Paul Rehkopf (*Detectives*); Franz Stein, Ludwig Stössel, Eduard Wesener, Bruno Ziener, Michael Von Newlinski, Heinrich Gotho, and Josef Dahmen (*Detectives*).

Publications:

Reviews—in *Variety* (New York), 9 May 1933; review by Bosley Crowther in *The New York Times*, 20 March 1943; review by Martin Ruppert in *Frankfurter Allgemeine Zeitung*, 13 September 1951; books—*An Index to the Creative Work of Fritz Lang* by Herman Weinberg, supplement to *Sight and Sound* (London), index series, 1946; *From Caligari to Hitler: A Psychological History of the German Film* by Siegfried Kracauer, Princeton, New Jersey 1947; *Film Form* by Sergei Eisenstein, New York 1949; *Film as Art* by Rudolf Arnheim, Berkeley 1957, originally published in 1933; *Fritz Lang* by Francis Courtade, Paris 1963; *Fritz Lang* by Luc Moullet, Paris 1963; *Fritz Lang* edited by Alfred Eibel, Paris 1964; *The Sociology of Film Art* by George Huaco, New York 1965; *The Haunted Screen* by Lotte Eisner, Berkeley 1969; *Film in the Third Reich* by David Stewart Hull, Berkeley 1969; *The Cinema of Fritz Lang* by Paul M. Jensen, New York 1969; *Fritz Lang in America* by Peter Bogdanovich, New York 1969; *The German Cinema* by Roger Manvell and Heinrich Fraenkel, New York 1971; *Le Cinéma Expressioniste Allemand* by Michael Henry, Paris 1971; *Fritz Lang* by Frieda Grafe, Enno Patalas, and Hans Helmut Prinzler, Munich 1976; *Fritz Lang* by Lotte Eisner, London 1977; *Das gab's nur einmal: Die grosse Zeit des deutschen Films, Vol. II* by Curt Reiss, Vienna-Munich 1977; *Fritz Lang* by Robert Armour, Boston 1978; *The Films of Fritz Lang* by Frederick W. Ott, Secaucus, New Jersey 1979; *Fritz Lang: A Guide to References and Resources* by E. Ann Kaplan, Boston 1981; articles—"Last Will of Dr. Mabuse" by Paul Rotha in *Cinema Quarterly* (London), autumn 1934; "Fritz Lang Discusses Two of His Films: *Hangmen Also Die* and a Very Old One" by Eileen Creelman in the *Sun* (New York), 20 March 1943; "Notes sur le Style de Fritz Lang" by Lotte Eisner in *Revue du cinéma* (Paris), 1 February 1947; "The Genius of Fritz Lang" by Harry Wilson in *Film Quarterly* (London), summer 1947; "*The Testament of Dr. Mabuse*" by Sergio Romano in *Cinema* (Rome), 10 November 1948; article by Fritz Lang in *Penguin Film Review* (Harmondsworth, Middlesex), v.V, 1948; "One Facet of Lang's Art Prophetic of Hitlerism" in the *Herald Tribune* (New York), 21 March 1949; article by J.G. in *Monthly Film Bulletin* (London), January 1954; "Gespräch Mit Fritz Lang" by Erwin Kipfmuller in *Film* (Munich), December 1956; "Fritz Lang—Endstation 'Indisches Grabmal'?" by Enno Patalas in *Kirche und Film* (Germany), 11 October 1958; "Le Style de Fritz Lang" by Georges Franju in *Cahiers du cinéma* (Paris), November 1959; "Über *Dr. Mabuse, der Spieler*" by Franz Everschor in *Film-Dienst* (Düsseldorf), 5 April 1961; "Le Diabolique Docteur Mabuse" by Michel Mardore in *Cinéma 61* (Paris), August/September 1961; "The Nine Lives of Dr. Mabuse" by John Russell Taylor in *Sight and Sound* (London), winter 1961; "Recontre avec Fritz Lang: Ce que vous ne saississez pas, jamais vous ne le comprenez" by Yvonne Baby in *Le Monde* (Paris), 3 July 1961; "Rapporti fra Uomo e Societa: Fritz Lang" by Maurizio Ponzi in *Filmcritica* (Rome), September 1964; "Fritz Lang (The German Period, 1919-1933)" in *Tower of Babel* by Eric Rhode, London 1966; "La Nuit Viennoise: Une Confession de Fritz Lang, Part 2" by Gr Berg in *Cahiers du cinéma* (Paris), June 1966; "Review of *Das Testament des Dr. Mabuse*" by Nora Sayre in *The New York Times*, 6 December 1973; "Film Favorites: Roger Greenspun on *The 1000 Eyes of Dr. Mabuse*" by Roger Greenspun in *Film Comment* (New York), March/April 1973; article by Paul Wiliam in *The Village Voice* (New York), 12 September 1974; "Review of *Dr. Mabuse, der Spieler*" by Tom Milne in *Monthly Film Bulletin* (London), May 1974; "Fritz Lang" by C. Boost in *Skoop* (Amsterdam), February 1975; "Fritz Lang Gives His Last Interview" by Gene D. Phillips in *The Village Voice* (New York), 16 August 1976; "Fritz Lang on Dr. Mabuse" by Fritz Lang in *Monthly Film Bulletin* (London), April 1978; "L'ecriture du mal: *Le testament du Docteur Mabuse*" by L. Audibert in *Cinematographe* (Paris), no.53, 1979; "Dr. Mabuse and Mr. Lang" by Lucy Fischer in *Wide Angle* (Athens, Ohio), winter 1980; "L'Ecriture du mal" by L. Audibert in *Cinématographe* (Paris), December 1979; "*Le Testament du Dr. Mabuse*" by C.M. Cluny in *Cinéma* (Paris), January 1980; "Le Nom de l'innommable" by G. Legrand in *Positif* (Paris), March 1980.

*   *   *

The popular novelist, Thea von Harbou began her unbroken 12-year scripting association with Fritz Lang in 1920. Divorcing the actor Rudolf Klein-Rogge, she married Lang in 1924, working with him until 1932 when they separated and subsequently divorced after Lang's hasty departure from Germany. Lang had already gained considerable success as the writer-director of *Die Spinnen*. In Thea von Harbou, he found an ideal writing partner to develop the psychological potentiality of a psychotic genius and master-criminal, Dr. Mabuse. Mabuse became the protagonist in Lang's two celebrated films of 1922 and 1932.

Dr. Mabuse the Gambler, Part I began by showing Mabuse making a fortune on the stock market and using hypnotism to win $50,000 from Edgar Hull, whom Mabuse finally murders after inducing his own exotic mistress, the dancer Cara Carezza, to seduce him. He induces Cara to commit suicide when she is faced with arrest. Opposed to Mabuse is von Wenck, the public prosecutor; in Part II Wenck manages to resist Mabuse's attempts to hypnotise him and traces the criminal to his headquarters, a building placed under siege by the police. When arrested, Mabuse goes insane. Reviving the character of Mabuse ten years later in *The Last Will of Dr. Mabuse* Lang and Harbou show how the insane Mabuse uses his hypnotic powers to induce Dr. Baum, director of the asylum where he is being held, to maintain his criminal activities outside and indeed, on Mabuse's death, to accept that he is the reincarnation of the mad doctor. Commissioner Lehmann (the dedicated police superintendent Lang had introduced in *M*), exposes Baum, who finally goes mad after the model of Mabuse and inhabits the criminal's original cell. Mabuse was revived, according to Lang, as a projection of Hitler: "I put all the Nazi slogans into the mouth of the ghost of the criminal." he has stated. In 1933 Goebbels banned both Mabuse films. "Out of the Mabuses," Lang wrote later when *The Last Will of Dr. Mabuse* was salvaged and released in America in 1943, "came the Heydrichs, the Himmlers and the Hitlers." He added, "This film was made as an allegory to show Hitler's processes of terrorism."

Lang always insisted that the original character of Mabuse had contemporary significance even in 1922. He seems to represent an arch criminal of that period of galloping inflation that destroyed the German currency, and with it German social morale. According to Lotte Eisner, Lang's friend and biographer, the Berlin critics accepted this reference to the times without demur. Writing of the period, Lang himself said, "The First World War brought changes.... In Europe, an entire generation of intellectuals embraced despair...young people, myself among them, made a fetish of tragedy." This helps to account for the fact that insanity in various forms became a recurrent theme in German cinema of the 1920s. Lang regarded his film not merely as a box-office thriller but as a document of the time, and Siegfried Kracauer terms Mabuse, "a contemporary tyrant," a symbol of mad, anti-social domination, combining a lust for absolute tyranny with the desire to effect social chaos. Like Caligari before him, he is insane and makes continual use of hypnosis to overcome his victims: an attempt is even made to hypnotise the audience. Lang indeed was concerned to give his film a contemporary psychological touch; Mabuse's thirst for power and his Protean manifestations in a ceaseless flow of disguises make him seem ever-present and ever-active in society. Eric Rhodo, writing in *Tower of Babel* (1966), sees the original film and the character of Mabuse as a myth of its time reflecting "not only the confusion and anxieties of the Weimar Republic," but also Oswald Spengler's romantic, fatalistic thesis in his bestseller, *The Decline of the West* (1918), in which he claimed that city-bound man is doomed through his power-lust for money. This was relevant not only to Lang's *Mabuse* but to his most spectacular work of the 1920s, *Metropolis*. In *Mabuse* his primary settings are gambling dens, depraved nightclubs, and the Stock Exchange. Mabuse is a vampire gambler and cheat extraordinary, operating against society on a universal scale, typified here by such characters as the wealthy, degenerate Count and Countess Told. As played by Rudolf Klein-Rogge, Mabuse has all the appearance of an actor-like, romantic genius—the penetrating eyes and the flowing mane of hair swept back from a towering brow.

Lang, whose father was a Viennese architect and whose training had been in art, had a strongly developed visual and structural "was far ahead of its time in Décor." He writes of "the perfection of camerawork and lighting effects" in Lang's films. Lang employed the irising device to dramatic effect, double, triple and quadruple exposures, and chiaroscuro lighting; for visual effect, Eric Rhodo instances the scene when the "mad count wanders with a candelabra through his twilight mansion." Lang, he points out, "favours middle or long distance shots, and a rim lighting that gives his characters both dimension and solidity.... In *Dr. Mabuse* rooms tend to be ample, while streets are so narrow that cars jam and bump into each other." Sergei Eisenstein, who had assisted Esther Schub in re-editing *Dr. Mabuse* for Russian audiences, commented on "the mystic criminal...reaching out towards us from our screens...showing us a future as an unrelieved night crowded with sinister shadows."

Lang was to make one further film featuring Mabuse in 1960, working again in Germany. Though adroitly made, *The Thousand Eyes of Dr. Mabuse*, a somewhat pale revival of Mabuse in the form of a madman who believes himself the reincarnation of the dead criminal but turns out to be Mabuse's son, seemed out of place by the 1960s.

—Roger Manvell

LA DOLCE VITA. La Douceur de vivre. Production: Riama Film (Rome) and Pathé Consortium Cinéma (Paris); black and white, 35mm, Totalscope; running time: 180 mins. Released February 1960, Rome.

Produced by Giuseppe Amato with Angelo Rizzoli, and Franco Maglis as executive producer; screenplay by Federico Fellini, Tullio Pinelli, Brunello Rondi, and Ennio Flaiano; from an original story by Federico Fellini, Tullio Pinelli and Ennio Flaiano; directed by Federico Fellini; photography by Otello Martelli; edited by Leo Cattozzo; sound by Agostino Moretti; art direction by Piero Gherardi; music by Nino Rota, conducted by Franco Ferrara with the assistance of I. Campanino and Adriano Celentano; costumes designed by Piero Gherardi; artisic collaborator: Brunello Rondi.

Filmed 16 March-27 August 1959 in Rome, the Odescalchi Palace, Fregene, and in the studios of Cinecittà, Rome. Cannes Film Festival, Gold Palm, 1960; Academy Award, Best Foreign Picture, 1961; New York Film Critics Award, Best Foreign Film, 1961.

Cast: Marcello Mastroianni (*Marcello Rubini*); Walter Santesso (*Paparazzo, the photographer*); Anouk Aimée (*Maddalena*); Adriana Moneta (*Prostitute*); Yvonne Furneaux (*Emma, Marcello's mistress*); Anita Ekberg (*Sylvia, a Hollywood star*); Lex Barker (*Robert, Sylvia's fiancée*); Alan Dijon (*Frankie Stout*); Alain Cuny (*Steiner*); Valeria Ciangottini (*Paola*); Annibale Ninchi (*Marcello's father*); Magali Noel (*Fanny, a chorus girl*); Nadia Gray (*Nadia*); Jacques Sernas (*Matinee idol*); Polidor (*Clown*).

Publications:

Scripts—*La dolce vita di Federico Fellini* edited by Tullio Kezich, Bologna, Italy 1960; *La Dolce Vita* translated by Oscar DeLiso and Bernard Shir-Cliff, New York 1961; *La douceur de vivre* edited by Giuseppe Lo Duca, translated by Maria Charlotte Guillaume, Paris 1961; *Quattro film: I vittelloni, La dolce vita, 8 ½, Giulietta degli spiriti* by Federico Fellini, Turin 1974; reviews—"*La Douceur Vivre*" by Raymond Lefèvre in *Image et son* (Paris), October 1960; "*La Dolce Vita*" by Eric Rhode in *Sight and Sound* (London), winter 1960; "Adventures of a Journalist" by Hollis Alpert in *Saturday Review* (New York), 15 April 1961; "*La Dolce Vita*" by Bosley Crowther in *The New York Times*, 20 April 1961; "*La Dolce Vita*" by Raymond Durgnat in *Films and Filming* (London), January 1961; "*La Dolce Vita*" by R.L. Franchi in *Film Quarterly* (Berkeley), summer 1961; "*La Dolce Vita*" by Henry Hart in *Films in Review* (New York), June/July 1961; "A Catalogue of Deadly Sins" by Stanley Kauffmann in *New Republic* (New York), 1 May 1961; "Movie Journal" by Jonas Mekas in *The Village Voice* (New York), April 1961; "Fellini: Moviemaker as Moralist" by Ronald Steel in *Christian Century* (Chicago), 19 April 1961; books—*La dolce vita di Federico Fellini* by Tullio Kezich, Bologna 1960; *Federico Fellini* by Renzo Renzi, translatd by P.L. Thirard, Lyons, France, reprinted 1960; *Le cinèma et le sacré* by Henri Agel, Paris 1961; *La Dolce Vita* edited by Giuseppe Lo Duca, Paris 1961; *Classics of the Foreign Film* by Parker Tyler, New York 1962; *Nouveau Cinéma italien* by Raymond Borde and André Bouissy, Lyons, France, 1963; *Italian Cinema Today* by Gian Luigi Rondi, Rome 1966; *Fellini* by Suzanne Budgen, London 1966; *The Great Films: 50 Golden Years of Motion Pictures* by Bosley Crowther, New York 1967;

The Film Experience by Roy Huss and Norman Silverstein, New York 1968; *Literature and Film* by Robert Richardson, Bloomington, Indiana, 1969; *Federico Fellini: The Search for a New Mythology* by Charles Ketcham, New York 1976; *The Cinema of Federico Fellini* by Stuart Rosenthal, London 1976; *Fellini on Fellini* edited by Christian Strich, translated by Isabel Quigley, New York 1976; *Federico Fellini: A Guide to References and Resources* by John Stubbs, Boston 1978; articles—"La Douceur de vivre" by Henri Agel in *Etudes cinèmatographiques* (Paris), summer 1960; "Su *La dolce vita* la parola a Fellini" in *Bianco e Nero* (Rome), January/February 1960; "*La dolce vita*" by Guido Aristarco in *Cinema nuovo* (Torino, Italy), January/February 1960; "*La Douceur de vivre*" by Georges-Albert Astre in *Etudes cinèmatographiques* (Paris), summer 1960; "*La dolce vita*" by Edoardo Bruno in *Filmcritica* (Rome), February 1960; "Cannes" by Dominque Delouche in *Cinema nuovo* (Turin), May/June 1960; "Un Fellini Baroque" by Dominque Delouche in *Etudes cinèmatographiques*, spring 1960; "Filming *La Dolce Vita* in Black-and-White and Wide-Screen" by Libero Grandi in *American Cinematographer* (Los Angeles), April 1960; "3 Adventurous Italiens" by Cynthia Grenier in *Saturday Review* (New York), December 1960; "Fellini Tells Why" by John Francis Lane in *Films and Filming* (London), June 1960; "Il dolce Fellini" by Jean-Louis Laugier in *Cahiers du Cinéma* (Paris), July 1960; "La stagione delle mele d'oro" by Ernesto Laura in *Bianco e Nero* (Rome), March/April 1960; "Essai sur *La dolce vita*" by Mardore in *Positif* (Paris), July/August 1960; "L'irrazionalismo cattolico di Fellini" by Pier Paolo Pasolini in *Filmcritica* (Rome), February 1960; "Dialettica de *La dolce vita*" by Brunello Rondi in *Filmcritica* Rome, February 1960; "*La Douceur de vivre*" by Gilbert Salachas in *Téléciné* (Paris), September/October 1960; "Letter from Italy" by William Weaver in *Nation* (New York), 19 March 1960; "Quattro domande sul cinema italiano" in *Cinema nuovo* (Turin), January/February 1961; "The Lonely Crowd in *La Dolce Vita*" by Eric Bergtal in *America* (New York), 7 October 1961; "Bergman and Fellini, Explorers of the Modern Spirit" by Richard Duprey in *Catholic World* (Paramus, New Jersey), October 1961; "The Follies Fellini" by Norman Holland in *Hudson Review* (Nutley, New Jersey), autumn 1961; "*La* (The) *Dolce* (Sweet) *Vita* (Life)" by John Francis Lane in *Films and Filming* (London), June 1961; "Poet-Director of the Sweet Life" by Robert Neville in *The New York Times Magazine*, 14 May 1961; "Federico Fellini: An Interview" by Enzo Peri in *Film Quarterly* (Berkeley), fall 1961; "*La Dolce Vita*" by John Flaus in *Film Journal* (Evanston, Illinois), April 1962; "2 Movies and Their Critics" by William Pechter in *Kenyon Review* (Gambier, Ohio), spring 1962; "Fellini's La Dolce Italia" by John Navone in *Commonweal* (New York) 15 March 1963; "Fellini's 8 ½, Holland's 11" by Norman Holland in *Hudson Review* (Nutley, New Jersey), autumn 1963; "The Come-Dressed-As-the-Sick-Soul-of-Europe Parties" by Pauline Kael in the *Massachusetts Review* (Amherst), winter 1963; "The Secret Life of Federico Fellini" by Peter Harcourt in *Film Quarterly* (Berkeley), spring 1966; "I Was Born for the Cinema" by Irving R. Levine in *Film Comment* (New York), fall 1966; "The Question of Fellini Continues" by Robin Wood in *December* (London), nos. 2-3, 1967; "Psychanalyse de Fellini" by Jacques Julia in *Cinéma 71* (Paris), May 1971; "Un Artiste sous le chapiteau" by Marcel Martin in *Cinéma 71* (Paris), May 1971; "Dilatazione visionaria del documento e nostalgia della madre chiesa in Fellini" in *Cinema dell'ambiguità: Rossellini, De Sica e Zavattini, Fellini* by P. Baldelli, Rome 1971; "Fellini" by Raymond Lefèvre in *Image et son* (Paris), January 1971; "*La Dolce vita*" by A. Torres Fernández in *Contracampo* (Madrid), June/July 1981; "*La Dolce vita*" by B. Villien in *Cinématographe* (Paris), September 1981.

Fellini's epic study of the loss of values at the climax of the Italian "economic miracle," delineates the daily activities of a writer, turned reporter for a sensationalist journal, who is too deeply compromised by the degeneracy around him to see it, never mind report on it. The opening and closing scenes of the film are cleverly matched allusions to Dante which underscore the moral loss and its consequences for Italy, at the very moment when the revival of Fascism was beginning to make a difference in the balance of political powers.

Marcello follows a helicopter delivering a monumental statue of Christ, on a tow line, to the Vatican. From his own helicopter, he flirts with women sunbathing on a roof. The noise of the machine drowns out his voice as he tries to shout for their telephone numbers. In a parallel scene of shot-countershot the film ends with Marcello accosted by a charming and innocent girl who had once waited on his table. A stretch of water separates them and the noise of the sea makes her words inaudible to him. An Italian audience might recognize the allusion to the Medusa of the *Inferno* in the grotesquely reified image of Christ soaring through the Roman sky; even more evident would be the figure of Matilda at the top of *Purgatorio* who represents the summit of earthly beauty, irradiated by divine grace, Marcello has lost the ability to react to the grossness of the former and the saving promise of the latter. The world he inhabits is as lost as he is: Marcello moves from prostitutes to aristocratic women while, at the same time, deceiving his girlfriend; his intellectual friend, Steiner, who had urged him to find more fulfilling work, kills himself and his children; he covers for his newspaper the scene of a false miracle where someone is trampled by the enthusiastic crowd; he follows an American movie star as she utters banalites and poses for the press. In the center of the film Marcello accompanies his father on his first night in Rome since he was one of Mussolini's blackshirts (this is subtly suggested by the old man's references, never bluntly stated). The father's physical collapse and profound embarrassment when he fails to perform with a prostitute predicts the hero's eventual confrontation with the limitation of his values, just as it suggests that the playboy figure of 1959, brilliantly represented by Marcello Mastroianni, is a modern version of the Fascist ideal.

The moral atmosphere of *La Dolce Vita* reflects that of all of Fellini's films, but the grandeur of its scale, the refusal to resort to a pitiful or lovable protagonist, and the accuracy of its caricatures make it one of his most enduring achievements. Its initial success was, however, due in great part to the supposed daring and sensational manner with which it dealt with sexual themes. Actually, it was one of three films to emerge from Italy at the end of the 1950s which heralded a powerful renewal of that national cinema. The others were Michelangelo Antonioni's *L'Avventura* and Luchino Visconti's *Rocco e i suoi fratelli*, both released in 1960.

—P. Adams Sitney

DOUBLE INDEMNITY. Production: Paramount Pictures; 1944; black and white, 35mm; running time: 107 mins. Released 7 September 1944.

Produced by Joseph Sistrom; screenplay by Billy Wilder and Raymond Chandler; from the novel *3 of a Kind* by James M. Cain; directed by Billy Wilder; photography by John F. Seitz; edited by Doane Harrison; sound by Stanley Cooley; art direction by Hal Pereira, supervised by Hans Dreier, set decoration by Bertram Granger; music by Miklos Rozsa; costumes designed by Edith Head.

Filmed 27 September—24 November 1943 in Paramount studios, and on location in Jerry's Market in Los Angeles.

Cast: Fred MacMurray (*Walter Neff*); Barbara Stanwyck (*Phyllis Dietrichson*); Edward G. Robinson (*Barton Keyes*); Porter Hall (*Mr. Jackson*); Jean Heather (*Lola Dietrichson*); Tom Powers (*Mr. Dietrichson*); Byron Barr (*Nino Zachette*); Richard Gaines (*Mr. Norton*); Fortunio Bonanova (*Sam Gorlopis*); John Philliber (*Joe Pete*); Clarence Muse (*Black man*).

Publications:

Books—*Billy Wilder* by Oreste del Buono, Parma, Italy 1958; *Billy Wilder* by Axel Madsen, Bloomington, Indiana 1969; *The Bright Side of Billy Wilder, Primarily* by Tom Wood, New York 1970; *Starring Miss Barbara Stanwyck* by Ella Smith, New York 1973; *Barbara Stanwyck* by Jerry Vermilye, New York 1975; *Billy Wilder in Hollywood* by Maurice Zolotow, New York 1977; *The Film Career of Billy Wilder* by Steve Seidman, Boston 1977; *Film Noir* edited by Alain Silver and Elizabeth Ward, Woodstock, New York 1979; articles—"End of a Journey" by Thomas Pryor in *The New York Times*, 23 September 1945; "2 Views of a Director—Billy Wilder" by Herbert Luft and Charles Brackett in *Quarterly of Radio, Television, and Film* (Berkeley), fall 1952; "The Eye of a Cynic" by Douglad McVay in *Films and Filming* (London), January 1960; "I've Been Lucky" by Fred MacMurray and Pete Martin in the *Saturday Evening Post* (Philadelphia), February 1962; "Entretien avec Billy Wilder" by Jean Domarchi and Jean Douchet in *Cahiers du cinéma* (Paris), August 1962; "Cast a Cold Eye: The Films of Billy Wilder" by Charles Higham in *Sight and Sound* (London), spring 1963; "Barbara Stanwyck" by Gene Ringgold in *Films in Review* (New York), December 1963; "The Films of Billy Wilder" in *Film Comment* (New York), summer 1965; "The Films of Billy Wilder" by Stephen Farber in *Film Comment* (New York), winter 1971; "7 Réflexions sur Billy Wilder" by Michel Ciment in *Positif* (Paris), May 1971; "*Assurance sur la mort*" in *Ecran* (Paris), July 1972; "Le Dernier carré?" by Jean-Loup Bourget in *Positif* (Paris), April 1973; "Raymond Chandler and the World You Live In" by Paul Jensen in *Film Comment* (New York), November/December 1974; "The Author-Auteurs" in *Talking Pictures: Screenwriters in the American Cinema* by Richard Corliss, New York 1975; "Assurance sur la mort" by R. Borde and E. Chaumeton in *Avant-Scène du cinéma* (Paris), 1 October 1979; "*Double Indemnity*" by Elizabeth Leese in *Magill's Survey of Cinema, Vol. 1* edited by Frank N. Magill, Englewood Cliffs, New Jersey 1980.

*   *   *

Billy Wilder's *Double Indemnity* marks the apotheosis of film noir thematic concerns and narrative construction. It emphasizes a man's obsession with shaping a woman's desire, and his slow realization that he had never been able to do it. It also effects a remarkable shift in the status of the hero, Walter Neff, an insurance salesman. He goes from a self-assured aggressor at the start of the film to a confused victim at the end. Neff himself, as a voice-over narrator, tells the story of his own transformation. In films noirs, the protagonist frequently acts as the narrator. This double duty emphasizes the difference between what the hero knows while the story unfolds, and what he knows once it has ended and begins relating it to us. This imbalance, which Wilder presents so skillfully in *Double Indemnity*, makes the film noir perhaps the most ironic of all movie genres.

Walter wants Phyllis Dietrichson, and works to make her love him. He apparently succeeds, and not only seems to chart the course of her desire, but also expresses it for her. When they discuss, early on, the insurance policies that could cover Phyllis's husband, Walter says, "You want him dead, don't you?" This is precisely what Phyllis wants, but it is also, for her, unspeakable.

Following Walter's plans, Neff and Phyllis murder Mr. Dietrichson. Afterward, Phyllis stops relying on Walter to speak her desire. With her husband freshly dead, she asks him, "Won't you give me a kiss?" Later, she explicitly states her feelings, and lets Walter know precisely who is responsible for the murder. She tells him, "I loved you and I hated him. But I didn't do anything about it until you came along." Like the women in *The Maltese Falcon, Out of the Past*, and other films noir, Phyllis is setting up the hero to be the classic film noir fall guy, done in by the woman he loved.

Wilder marks the shift in Walter's status during a scene just after the murder. As part of the plan, Neff takes Mr. Dietrichson's place on a train ride. He dresses just like Dietrichson, a sign that Neff, despite his apparent control over events so far, will finish no differently from the man whose clothes he wears. In his own household, Dietrichson had represented despotic, repressive masculine power. Walter, too, as the orchestrator of events and by controlling Phyllis, becomes a model of male strength. But when, on the train, he plays the part of the husband, Walter can no longer expect treatment any better than that which Phyllis gave to the original Mr. Dietrichson.

At the end of the voice-over story, Phyllis matter-of-factly tells Neff that, "No, I never loved you," her final expression of a complete lack of desire. Then she shoots him, completing the identification between Walter and Phyllis's late husband. First, Neff had dressed like him and taken his place on the train; then, at the end, just like Dietrichson, he becomes Phyllis's victim.

Considered a film noir masterpiece today, critics recognized *Double Indemnity* as one of the better examples of the genre even upon its original release. It received outstanding reviews, and was nominated for several major Academy Awards, including Best Picture, Actress, Directing, Screenplay, and Cinematography.

—Eric Smoodin

DRACULA. Production: Universal Pictures; black and white, 35mm; running time: 84 mins., some sources list 76 mins.; length: 6978 feet. Released Valentine's Day, 1931. Re-released 1938.

Produced by Carl Laemmle Jr.; screenplay by Garrett Fort, dialogue by Dudley Murphy; from Hamilton Deane's and John L. Balderston's stage adaptation of the novel by Bram Stoker; directed by Tod Browning; photography by Karl Freund; edited by Milton Carruth, editing supervised by Maurice Pivar; sound by C. Roy Hunter; production design by Charles Hall; music by Peter Tachikovsky, music directed by David Broekman; make-up by Jack P. Pierce.

Filmed in Universal studios.

Cast: Bela Lugosi (*Count Dracula*); Helen Chandler (*Mina*); David Manners (*Jonathan Harker*); Dwight Frye (*Renfield*);

Edward Van Sloan (*Professor Van Helsing*); Herbert Bunston (*Dr. Seward*); Frances Dade (*Lucy Weston*); Joan Standing (*Briggs*); Charles Gerrard (*Martin*); Moon Carroll (*Maid*); Josephine Velez (*Nurse*); Donald Murphy (*Man in coach*); Michael Visaroff (*Innkeeper*).

Publications:

Books—*Horror* by Drake Douglas, New York 1966; *An Illustrated History of the Horror Film* by Carlos Clarens, New York 1967; *The Horror Film* by Ivan Butler, New York 1967; *Persistence of Vision: A Collection of Film Criticism* edited by Joseph McBride, Madison, Wisconsin 1968; *Movie Monsters* by Denis Gifford, London 1969; *Focus on the Horror Film* by Roy Huss and T.J. Ross, Englewood Cliffs, New Jersey 1972; *Great Monsters of the Movies* by Edward Edelson, Garden City, New York 1973; *Pictorial History of the Horror Film* by Denis Gifford, London 1973; *Transylvanian Catalogue* by Mark Lamberti, Mount Vernon, New York 1974; *Horror Movies* by Alan G. Frank, Secaucus, New Jersey 1974; *Classics of the Horror Film* by William K. Everson, Secaucus, New Jersey 1974; *The Count—The Life and Films of Bela "Dracula" Lugosi* by Arthur Lenning, New York 1974; *The Seal of Dracula* by Barrie Pattison, New York 1975; *Movie Fantastic—Beyond the Dream Machine* by David Annan, New York 1975; *Monsters of the Movies* by Denis Gifford, London 1977; articles—"Tod Browning" by George Geltzer in *Films in Review* (New York), October 1953; "Movie Monster Rally" by Charles Addams in the *New York Times Magazine*, 9 August 1953; "A Family Tree of Monsters" by William K. Everson in *Film Culture* (New York), no.1, 1955; "The Browning Version" by Rory Guy in *Cinema* (Beverly Hills), June/July 1963; "The Baron, The Count, and Their Ghoul Friends" by Leslie Halliwell in *Films and Filming* (London), June 1969; "Schept vreugde met mij, horror freaks" by H. Verstappen in *Skoop* (Amsterdam), no.2, 1972; "Monster Movies: A Sexual Theory" by W. Evans in *Journal of Popular Film* (Bowling Green, Ohio), fall 1973; "Tod Browning" by Stuart Rosenthal in *The Hollywood Professionals, Vol. 4*, London 1975; "Tod Browning: à la recherche de la réalité" by A. Garsault in *Positif* (Paris), July/August 1978; "*Dracula*" by V.I. Huxner in *Magill's Survey of Cinema, Vol. 1* edited by Frank N. Magill, Englewood Cliffs, New Jersey 1980.

*   *   *

Released on Valentine's Day of 1931, *Dracula* was directed by Tod Browning and photographed by Karl Freund. Bela Lugosi's performance has been called "the definitive interpretation of the Count," and the film began Universal's trio of famous horror films, completed by *Frankenstein* and *The Mummy*.

Broodingly and darkly photographed, *Dracula* is the story of the Transylvanian count vampire who has lived forever, and continues to live by sucking the blood of human beings (turning them, too, into vampires). Laced with simple and then-frightening effects, *Dracula* has become a cult film in the last 15 years. It is important also as a historical document and as an illustration of the early horror film, the genre which would eventually spawn more sophisticated films such as *Jaws*.

After this film the Transylvanian count of Bram Stoker's 1897 novel would appear in countless other versions, ranging from *Dracula's Daughter* to *Abbott and Costello Meet Frankenstein* to *Dracula A.D.* Max Schreck played the Count in F.W. Murnau's silent film, *Nosferatu* , but after these early 1920s and 1930s versions, the quality and essence of the films deteriorate.

Dracula is also a valuable film in terms of its visual style. It merges stylized versions of British gothic horror with German Expressionism—dark shadows; extensive cross-cutting for suspense; mysterious, unpredictable. almost sympathetic villains; brooding, atmospheric, and forbidding surroundings—while creating a horror film that became a hallmark of the genre.

—Deborah H. Holdstein

DIE DREIGROSCHENOPER. The Threepenny Opera. Production: Warner Bros. First National (USA), Tobis Klang-Film, and Nero-Film (Germany); black and white, 35mm; running time: 111 mins. (German version) and 104 mins. (French version); length: 3097 meters (German version). Released 19 February 1931, Berlin.

Produced by Seymour Nebenzahl; screenplay by Leo Lania, Bela Balàsz and Ladislaus Vajda; from the play by Berthold Brecht; adaptation for the French version by Solange Bussi, André Mauprey, and Ninon Steinhoff; directed by Georg Wilhelm Pabst (G.W. Pabst); photography by Fritz Arno Wagner; edited by Hans Oser (German version), Henri Rust (French version); sound by Adolf Jansen; production design by Andrei Andreiev; music by Kurt Weill, orchestration by Theo Mackeben.

Filmed in Berlin.

Cast: *German:* Rudolf Forster (*Mackie Messer*); Carola Neher (*Polly*); Reinhold Schünzel (*Tiger Brown*); Fritz Rasp (*Peachum*); Valeska Gert (*Mrs. Peachum*); Lotte Lenya (*Jenny*); Hermann Thimig (*Vicar*); Ernst Busch (*Street-singer*); Vladimir Sokolov (*Smith*); Paul Kemp. Gustav Puttjer, Oskar Höcker, and Kraft Raschig (*Mackie's Gang*); Herbert Grünbaum (*Filch*); *French:* Albert Préjean (*Mackier Messer*); Florelle (*Polly*); Jack Henley (*Tiger Brown*); Gaston Modot (*Peachum*); Jane Markem (*Mrs. Peachum*); Margo Lion (*Jenny*); Antonin Artaud, Vladimir Sokolov, and Merminod (*Mackie's Gang*).

Publications:

Scripts—*Masterworks of the German Cinema* with an introduction by Roger Manvell, London 1973; "*L'Opéra de quat'sous*" by L. Lania, B. Balàsz, and Laszlo Vajda in *Avant-Scène du cinéma* (Paris), 1 December 1976; reviews—"Un Mystérieux musée de figures de cire" by Louis Chavance in *La Revue du Cinéma* (Paris), 1 May 1931; "*L'Opéra de quat'sous et la presse*" in *Avant-Scène du cinéma* (Paris), 1 December 1976; books—*Celluloid, the Film Today* by Paul Rotha, London 1933; *From Caligari to Hitler* by Siegfried Kracauer, Princeton, New Jersey 1947; *Der Regisseur: G.W. Pabst* edited by Rudolph Joseph, Munich 1963; *G.W. Pabst*, Premier Plan no.39, by Freddy Buache, Lyons 1965; *Georg Wilhelm Pabst* by Barthelemy Amengual, Paris 1966; "G.W. Pabst" by Yves Aubry and Jacques Pétat in *Anthologie du cinéma, Vol. 4*, Paris 1968; *The Haunted Screen* by Lotte Eisner, Berkeley 1969; *Caligari's Cabinet and Other Grand Illusions: A History of Film Design* by Léon Barsacq, New York 1976; *G.W. Pabst* by Lee Atwell, Boston 1977; articles—"Pabst and the Social Film" by Harry

Potamkin in *Hound & Horn* (New York), January/March 1933; "6 Talks on G.W. Pabst" edited by Gideon Bachmann in *Cinemages* (New York), no.3, 1955; special issue of *Filmkunst* (Vienna), no.18, 1955; article by Arlene Croce in *Film Quarterly* (Berkeley), fall 1960; article by Mark Seitling in *Films in Review* (New York), August/September 1960; "Die Dreigroschenoper" by Alan Stanbrook in *Films and Filming* (London), April 1961; essays on *Don Quichotte* and *The Threepenny Opera* in *Classics of the Foreign Film* by Parker Tyler, New York 1962; "G.W. Pabst" by Herbert Luft in *Films and Filming* (London), April 1967; "Het Driestuiversproces—een sociologies experiment" by B. Brecht and G. Verhage in *Skrien* (Amsterdam), November/December 1973; "*Die Dreigroschenoper*" by T. Rayns in *Monthly Film Bulletin* (London), July 1974; "Quelques Notes sur l'Opera de quat'sous" in *Avant-Scène du cinéma* (Paris), 1 December 1976; "La Fête noire" by Claude Beylie in *Avant-Scène du cinéma* (Paris), 1 December 1976; "Les remake" in *Avant-Scène du cinéma* (Paris), 1 December 1976; "Proces za trzy grosze" by Z. Pitera in *Kino* (Warsaw), August 1976; "Three Penny Opera: Brecht vs. Pabst" by J.C. Horak in *Jump Cut* (Chicago), no.15, 1977; "Proces za trzy grosze" by Z. Pitera in *Kino* (Warsaw), August 1976.

*   *   *

G.W. Pabst's film version of Bertolt Brecht and Kurt Weill's *The Threepenny Opera* is a fascinating though flawed curio. The property, initially presented on the stage in 1928, is an adaptation of John Gay's *The Beggar's Opera*, a parody of Italian musical dramas first performed 200 years earlier.

While Brecht retained the basic plot of *The Beggar's Opera*, he updated it and related the satirical elements to his own era. At the same time, he was concerned more with ideas than coherent storyline or character development. In cinematizing the play, Pabst treated the plot and characters far more realistically, with greater emphasis on the feelings and motivations of the principal roles; in this regard, the film bears more the mark of Pabst than Brecht or Weill.

The sets, lighting and props are very stylized (except for the sequence detailing a beggar's demonstration) resulting in an odd conglomeration of surrealism and reality. Brecht originally collaborated on the film, but the script was rewritten when his ideas clashed with those of Pabst. Brecht and Weill were displeased with the filmmaker's interpretation, and took out a lawsuit over the material's copyright.

Brecht's social satire is still preserved though, along with this unaffected lyricism. The theme is as relevant to 1983 as to 1928 or 1728: the government and the underworld are as equally amoral in terms of self-interest. A once orderly world—which may only exist in the fantasies of those nostalgic for the "good old days" that in reality were never really so good—has been polluted by economic and political chaos. The setting is a dreary Victorian London of pimps and prostitutes, thieves and killers, and crooked politicians. (*The Threepenny Opera* was banned in London after a single showing.) Polly Peachum, with the members of Mackie Messer's gang, opens a bank, in the belief that "honest" thievery is more profitable than larceny outside the law. In the end Polly's father (who is king of the beggars), Tiger Brown (the corrupt police commissioner) and Mackie become partners in the bank—and mainstays of society.

Weill's songs, so important in the stage production, seem less so here: some—"Ballad of Sexual Dependency," "The Tango Ballad," and "The Ballad for the Hangman"—were omitted by Pabst. On one level the film is difficult to evaluate because current prints are faded; and the soundtrack seems archaic because of the technology then available for recording dialogue and music. But the disunity of style (a fault) and the keenly realized satire (an asset) are both lucidly apparent.

The Threepenny Opera is one of a trio of films Pabst directed in the 1930s that were anti-capitalist, stressing the importance of friendship and the moral obligation to oppose the forces of evil. The others were *Westfront 1918* and *Kameradschaft*, Though *The Threepenny Opera* is far more romantic and stylized than the first two, all are united thematically.

The film was released on the eve of Hitler's seizure of power in Germany. Pabst captured the essence of the atmosphere which allowed the existence of the Nazi state, and all original German prints were destroyed by the Third Reich. The film was shot simultaneously in both German and French, with different casts; the French *Threepenny Opera* became a success in Paris, and was hailed as a masterpiece, but the German version is more well-known in America. A complete negative of the latter was reconstructed by film distributor Thomas J. Brandon in 1960, after a decade-long search through Europe for sections and scenes.

—Rob Edelman

DRIFTERS. Production: New Era Studios for the Empire Marketing Board; black and white, 35mm; running time: about 40 mins. Released 10 November 1929, premiered at the London Film Society.

Produced, scripted, directed, and edited by John Grierson; Photographed by John Grierson and Basil Emmott.

Filmed 1929 in a small fishing village in Northern England, and on board a herring boat at sea. Cost: Grierson declares cost to have been about 2500 pounds, while Rotha remembers it as being less than 2000 pounds.

Publications:

Books—*Documentary Film* by Paul Rotha, London 1952; *Films Beget Films: Compilation Films From Propaganda to Drama* by Jay Leyda, New York 1964; *Grierson on Documentary* by John Grierson, edited by Forsyth Hardy, 2nd. edition, London 1966; *The Documentary Tradition: From Nanook to Woodstock* edited by Lewis Jacobs, New York 1971; *Nonfiction Film: A Critical History* by Richard Barsam, New York 1973; *Documentary: A History of the Non-Fiction Film* by Erik Barnouw, New York 1974; *The Rise and Fall of the British Documentary: The Story of the Film Movement Founded by John Grierson* by Elizabeth Sussex, Berkeley 1975; *Nonfiction Film: Theory and Criticism* by Richard Barsam, New York 1976; *John Grierson: Film Master* by James Beveridge, New York 1978; *John Grierson: A Documentary Biography* by Forsyth Hardy, London 1979; *A History of Film* by Jack C. Ellis, Englewood Cliffs, New Jersey 1979; articles—"E.M.B. Film Unit" by John Grierson in *Cinema Quarterly* (London), summer 1933; "I Derive My Authority from Moses" by Ronald Blumer in *Take One* (Montreal), no.9, 1970; article by Grierson's associates on the EMP and GPO films units in *Sight and Sound* (London), summer 1972; "Grierson's Hammer" in *Films and Filming* (London), July 1972; "John Grierson" by Elizabeth Sussex in *Sight and Sound* (London), spring 1972; "Grierson on Documentary: Last Interview" by Elizabeth Sussex in *Film Quarterly* (Berkeley), fall 1972; "*Drifters*" in *Travelling* (Lausannne, Switzerland), summer 1979.

*   *   *

Drifters was John Grierson's first film, and the only one of thousands of films for which he was responsible that he completely controlled creatively. Not only did he write the script, produce, direct and edit, but, according to Forsyth Hardy in his biography of Grierson he shot much of the film himself. In its editing he was assisted by Margaret Taylor, who would become his wife.

About the work of herring fishermen in the North Sea, *Drifters* has a simple narrative structure. The men board their ships in harbor, sail to the banks, lay the nets, haul in the catch in the midst of a storm, race homeward to the auction of the catch at quayside. It includes images of Scotland and the sea, both important in Grierson's life and recurring in the films he produced. Herring fishing was a canny choice since the Financial Secretary to the Treasury was an authority on the subject.

Drifters marked the beginning of the British documentary film and served as a prototype for many of the films that followed. But, rather than evidence of an innovative genius, it represents the work of a brilliant analyst who had absorbed what was at hand for the making of the kind of films he wanted to see made. In it are reflections of Flaherty's *Nanook of the North*, with brave men eking out their existence in the face of the elements. Eisenstein's *Potemkin* is even more heavily called upon. In *Drifters* the loving long takes of a Flaherty are cut up and banged together in Eisensteinian montage to provide a modern energy and rhythm, and the individual accomplishments of Nanook are replaced by the collective efforts of a crew as in *Potemkin*. It is unlike both models, however, in eschewing the exotics of Flaherty and the heroics of the Soviets. In *Drifters* the drama is in the everyday workaday. By ending on the fish being sold at market, Grierson sets the fishermen's work within the context of the economic actualities of contemporary Britain.

Its premiere at the Film Society in London was as the first half of a double bill on which the British premiere of *Potemkin* was the main attraction, with Eisenstein in attendance. Though risking the comparison must have taken considerable nerve on Grierson's part, he knew that the audience for that event would comprise the intellectual elite and correspondents for the national press. *Drifters* was very well received and went on to modest commercial distribution. It was the first instance in English cinema in which work had been given this sort of importance and that members of the working class were presented with dignity rather than as comic relief. As a silent film it was severly handicapped, however; at the time of its release the transition from silence to sound was becoming complete.

Rather than continuing as a personal filmmaker, as he might have done, Grierson used the success of *Drifters* as the basis for establishing the Empire Marketing Board Film Unit, for hiring others who would make more films and develop the British documentary film movement.

—Jack C. Ellis

DU RIFIFI CHEZ LES HOMMES. Rififi. Production: Miracle Productions for Indus, Pathé, and Prima (France); black and white, 35mm; running time: 113 mins, some sources list 116 mins. Released 1955 in France.

Screenplay by René Wheeler, Jules Dassin, and Auguste le Breton; from the novel by Auguste le Breton; directed by Jules Dassin; photography by Philippe Agostini; edited by Roger Dwyre; sound by J. Lebreton; art direction by Auguste Capelier; music by Georges Auric.

Cannes Film Festival, Best Director (shared with Serge Vasilierv), 1955.

Cast: Jean Servais (*Tony le Stephanois*); Carl Mohner (*Jo le Suedois*); Robert Manuel (*Mario*); Perlo Vita (*Cesar*); Magali Noe (*Viviane*); Marie Subouret (*Mado*); Janine Darcy (*Louise*); Pierre Grasset (*Louise*); Robert Hossein (*Remi*); Marcel Lupovici (*Pierre*); Dominique Maurin (*Tonio*); Claude Sylvain (*Ida*).

Publications:

Reviews—by Michael Raper in *Films and Filming* (London), September 1955; review by John Wilcox in *Sight and Sound* (London), autumn 1955; review by Vance Bourjaily in *The Village Voice* (New York), 4 July 1956; review by Henry Hart in *Films in Review* (New York), June/July 1956; review by Andrew Mayer in *Quarterly of Film, Radio, and Television* (Berkeley), winter 1956; "Rififi" by Bosley Crowther in *The New York Times*, 6 June 1956; books—*Jules Dassin* by Adelio Ferrero, Parma 1961; *Underworld USA* by Colin McArthur, London 1972; *The Great Gangster Pictures* by James R. Parish and Michael R. Pitts, Metuchen, New Jersey 1976; *The Contemporary Greek Cinema* by Mel Schuster, Metuchen, New Jersey 1979; articles—interview with Dassin by Claude Chabrol and François Truffaut in *Cahiers du cinéma* (Paris), April and May 1955; "Jules Dassin" by Cynthia Grenier in *Sight and Sound* (London), winter 1957-58; "An Interview with Jules Dassin" by George Bluestone in *Film Culture* (New York), no.17, 1958; article by Ian Johnson in *Films and Filming* (London), April 1963; "Style and Instinct" by Jules Dassin in *Films and Filming* (London), February 1970; "Trois Hommes du milieu" by P. Carcassonne in *Cinématographe* (Paris), December 1980; "Los vaivenes de Jules Dassin" by M. Martínez Carril in *Cinemateca revista* (Andes), July 1981.

*   *   *

Despite his Gallic-like name, *Du Rififi chez les hommes* was Jules Dassin's first French film. In the late 1940s he had pioneered a vivid new style of urban thriller, bringing an incisive, documentary-influenced realism to the mean streets of New York (*The Naked City*)and San Francisco (*Thieves' Highway*). Forced into exile by McCarthyism, he discovered an equally stark vision of London (*Night and the City*) before crossing the Channel to make (in the opinion of most critics) the finest film of his career. The richly textured evocation of Paris which Dassin created for *Rififi* perhaps betrays, in the sheer profusion of its detail, the eye of a fascinated visitor rather than the intimate glance of a native. But the film is convincingly authentic in its exact sense of milieu, its close attention to the tawdry glitter and stoic conventions of the small-time underworld it describes.

Along with Jean-Pierre Melville's *Bob le flambeur* and Jacques Becker's *Touchez Pas au Grisbi*, *Rififi* stands as one of the most accomplished French thrillers of the 1950s all three films acknowledging, while never slavishly imitating, their American sources.

Like *Grisbi*, *Rififi* derives from a novel by Auguste le Breton, and shares the same downbeat, doom-laden atmosphere. The characters of *Rififi* inhabit a small, hermetic world, bounded by rigid precepts, in which even the police scarcely seem to figure. Danger threatens, not from the forces of law and order, but from rival gangs: the final shoot-out takes place in a half-built villa on the outskirts of Paris, a setting as ramshackle, bleak and devoid of bystanders as any Main Street in a western. From the first reel, the final outcome of events is never in doubt. With his racking cough and his air of aging, existential gloom, Tony le Stephanois is marked down for destruction. The best he can hope for is a good death, according to his own strict code of honor.

The plot follows the accepted caper format, as laid down by John Huston's *The Asphalt Jungle*. A robbery is meticulously planned, flawlessly executed—but the gang is subsequently betrayed by its own weaknesses or internal dissensions, and all is lost. *Rififi*'s most notable innovation, for which the film is still best remembered, is the classic half-hour sequence covering the robbery, executed in unprecedented detail and total silence, mesmerizing in its coolly sustained suspense. The gang members are depicted as conscientious craftsmen, carrying out their task steadily and skillfully, to a predetermined system. This sequence has since been much imitated (not least by Dassin himself, in *Topkapi*), but never yet surpassed.

Dassin portrays his doomed criminals with warmth and sympathy, aided by fine performances from a cast which includes (under the stage-name of Perlo Vita) the director himself, as the dapper Italian cracksman whose susceptibility to women brings about the gang's downfall. *Rififi* marks the high point—and, regretably, the conclusion—of Dassin's urban thriller cycle. Soon afterwards came the meeting with Melina Mercouri, and his descent into the pretensions of *Phaedra* and the cheerful rubbish of *Never on Sunday*. Nothing in his subsequent career has recaptured a fraction of the atmosphere and control of *Rififi*.

—Philip Kemp

———————

DUCK SOUP. Production: Paramount Pictures; 17 November 1933; black and white, 35mm; running time: 72 mins., some sources list 68 mins. Released 22 November 1933.

Screenplay by Bert Kalmar and Harry Ruby, dialogue by Nat Perrin and Arthur Sheekman; directed by Leo McCarey; photography by Henry Sharp; edited by Leroy Stone; sound by H.N. Lindgren; art direction by Hans Dreier and W.B. Ihnen; music by Bert Kalmar, Harry Ruby, and Arthur Johnston, music directed by Arthur Johnston.

Cast: Groucho Marx (*Rufus T. Firefly*); Harpo Marx (*Brownie*); Chico Marx (*Chicolini*); Zeppo Marx (*Bob Rolland*); Raquel Torres (*Vera Marcal*); Louis Calhern (*Ambassador Trentino*); Margaret Dumont (*Mrs. Teasdale*); Edgar Kennedy (*Leomande Seller*); Edmund Breese (*Zander*); Edwin Maxwell (*Minister of War*); William Worthington (*Minister of Finance*); Leonid Kinsky (*Agitator*); Vera Hillie (*Secretary*); George MacQuarrie (*Judge*); Fred Sullivan (*Judge*); Davison Clark

(*Minister*); Charles B. Middleton (*Prosecutor*); Eric Mayne (*Judge*).

Publications:

Script—*Monkey Business and Duck Soup*, London 1972; reviews—"The Four Marx Brothers" by M.H. in *The New York Times*, 23 November 1933; books—*The Marx Brothers* by Kyle Crichton, New York 1951; *50 Years of American Comedy* by Bill Treadwell, New York 1951; *Comedy Films* by John Montgomery, London 1954; *The Laugh Makers* by William Cahn, New York 1957; *Harpo Speaks* by Harpo Marx, New York 1961; *The Marx Brothers, Their World of Comedy* by Allen Eyles, London 1966; *The Marx Brothers and the Movies* by Paul Zimmerman and Burt Goldblatt, New York 1968; *Why a Duck: Visual and Verbal Gems from the Marx Brothers Movies* by Richard Anobile, New York 1971; *Anthologie du cinéma* vol.7, Paris 1973; *Leo McCarey and the Comic Anti-Hero in American Film* by Wes Gehring, New York 1980; articles—"American Classic" by Richard Rowland in *Hollywood Quarterly*, April 1947; "Return of the Marx Brothers" by Harry Kurnitz in *Holiday*, January 1957; "Taking Chances: Interview with Leo McCarey" by S. Davey and J.L. Noames in *Cahiers du Cinema in English* (New York), February 1965; "*Duck Soup*" by Gary Carey in *Film Notes* edited by Eileen Bowser, New York 1969; "Duck Soup for the Rest of Your Life" by Joseph Adamson in *Take One* (Montreal), September/October 1970; "Leo McCarey: From Marx to McCarthy" by C. Silver in *Film Comment* (New York), September/October 1973;; "Taking Stock of *Duck Soup*" by R. Rosenblatt in the *New Republic* (New York), 20 November 1976.

*   *   *

Probably the most successful of all of the Marx Brothers's films in terms of its gaggery and timing, *Duck Soup* features Groucho, Chico, Harpo, and Zeppo in their most famous film. Directed by Leo McCarey, the film's gags were written by Nat Perrin and Arthur Sheekman, with music by Harry Ruby and Bert Kalmar.

Groucho plays Rufus T. Firefly, the soon-to-be leader of the small country called Freedonia ("Hail, hail Freedonia, Land of the Brave and Free"). The thin plot includes Margaret Dumont in her recurring role as the rich matron Groucho unabashedly tries to bilk out of her fortune, and Louis Calhern as the obligatory villian out to trounce Groucho and company.

Most notably *Duck Soup* contains one of the most famous examples of Marx Brothers comedy: the mirror sequence. During one particularly frenetic scene which results in a full wall mirror being broken to bits, Groucho and Chico, dressed alike in stocking cap, nightgown, painted mustache, and white socks, act out a "mirror image" of each another in perfect unison. Years later, Harpo would duplicate this famous sequence with Lucille Ball in one of the "gone Hollywood" episodes of "I Love Lucy."

While the brothers' first and second films, *Coconuts* and *Animal Crackers*, suffer from staginess and inconsequential plotting, *Duck Soup* transcends its meager plot to give the brothers the characterizations that would stay with them in other films: Groucho, the master of zany one-liners and double-entendres, whose shadiness is exceeded only by his humor; Harpo, the silent, loony girl-chaser; Chico, the "Italian" foil for Groucho's complicated conversations; and Zeppo, the rather

wooden "go-fer," whose talents were often overshadowed by his more outrageous brothers. The film's weakness lies primarily in its sudden, abrupt ending, a disappointment after the insane, relentless comedy of the earlier scenes.

Duck Soup is historically important in the legacy it has left for more recent comics and their films. Woody Allen, for example, borrows from the Marx Brothers, merging one-liners and zany humor with the physical comedy characteristic of Chaplin. Further *Duck Soup*'s satire on government and its inconsistencies continues the Marx tradition of attacking society's institutions, continued in 1936, with *A Night at the Opera* assault on high culture.

—Deborah H. Holdstein

EAST OF EDEN. Production: Warner Bros. Pictures, Inc. and First National; 1955; Technicolor (Warnercolor), 35mm, Cinemascope; running time: 115 mins.; length: 3415 meters. Released 9 April 1955, New York.

Produced by Elia Kazan; screenplay by Paul Osborn, dialogue by Guy Tomajean; from the novel by John Steinbeck; directed by Elia Kazan; photography by Ted McCord; edited by Owen Marks; sound engineered by Stanley Jones; art direction by James Basevi and Malcolm Bert, set decoration by George James Hopkins; music by Leonard Rosenman; costumes designed by Anna Hill Johnstone; Technicolor consultant: John Hambleton.

Cannes Film Festival, Prix du Film Dramatique, 1955; Academy Award, Best Supporting Actress (Van Fleet), 1955.

Cast: James Dean (*Cal Trask*); Julie Harris (*Abra*); Raymond Massey (*Adam Trask*); Richard Davalos (*Aron Trask*); Jo Van Fleet (*Kate*); Burl Ives (*Sam Cooper, the sheriff*); Albert Dekker (*Will Hamilton*); Lois Smith (*Ann*); Harlod Gordon (*Mr. Albrecht*); Timothy Carey (*Joe*); Mario Siletti (*Piscora*); Roy Turner (*Lonny Chapman*); Nick Dennis (*Rantany*).

Publications:

Script—"*L'Est d'Eden*" by Paul Osborn in *Avant-Scène du cinéma* (Paris), November 1975; reviews—by Ralph Gerstle in *Films in Review* (New York), March 1955; review by Derek Prouse in *Sight and Sound* (London), summer 1955; review by Andrew Sarris in *Film Culture* (New York), May/June 1955; "L'Indéniable Puissance lyrique de Kazan" by André Bazin in *France-Observateur* (Paris), 3 November 1955, reprinted *Avant-Scène du cinéma* (Paris), November 1975; books—*James Dean Album*, New York 1956; *The Official James Dean Anniversary Book* edited by Peter Myerson, New York 1956; *Jimmy Dean Returns*, New York 1956; *The Real James Dean Story*, New York 1956; *James Dean: A Biography* by William Bast, New York 1956; *I, James Dean* by T.T. Thomas, New York 1957; *Elia Kazan* by Roger Tailleur, revised edition, Paris 1971; *Working with Kazan* edited by Jeanine Basinger, John Frazer, and Joseph W. Reed, Jr., Middletown, Connecticut 1973; *Kazan on Kazan* by Michel Ciment, New York 1974; *The Films of James Dean* by Mark Whittman, London 1974; *James Dean—The Mutant King* by David Dalton, San Francisco 1974; *James Dean—A*

Short Life by Venable Herndon, New York 1974; articles—"The Photography of *East of Eden*" by Arthur Gavin in *American Cinematographer* (Los Angeles), March 1955; article by Clayton Cole in *Films and Filming* (London), April 1955; "The Genesis of a Style" by Eugene Archer in *Film Culture* (New York), no.8, 1956; "*Les Haricots du Mal*" by François Truffaut in *Cahiers du cinéma* (Paris), February 1956; "Genesis of a Genius" by Eugene Archer in *Films and Filming* (London), January 1957; "The Young Agony" by Robin Bean in *Films and Filming* (London), March 1962; "Eden Revisited" by Ray Connolly in *Motion*, winter 1961-62; "Raymond Massey" by Jeanne Stein in *Films in Review* (New York), August/September 1963; "The Life and Times of Elia Kazan" by Robin Bean in *Films and Filming* (London), May 1964; "*East of Eden*" by Robin Bean in *Films and Filming* (London), May 1964; "Dean—10 Years After" by Robin Bean in *Films and Filming* (London), October 1965; "Preface to an Interview" by Michel Delahare in *Cahiers du Cinema in English* (New York), October 1966; "A Natural Phenomenon: Interview with Elia Kazan" in *Cahiers du Cinema in English* (New York), November 1966; "Cain, Abel et le dollar" by Robert Benayoun in *Positif* (Paris), May 1967; "Elia Kazan Interview" by Stuart Byron and Martin L. Rubin in *Movie* (London), winter 1971-72; "*East of Eden*" by Jim Hillier in *Movie* (London), winter 1971-72; "Elia Kazan: A Structuralist Analysis" by Jim Kitses in *Cinema* (Los Angeles), winter 1972-73; "James Dean est mort" by François Truffaut in *Avant-Scène du cinéma* (Paris), November 1975; "*East of Eden*" by J.M. Lardinois in *Apec-Revue belge du cinéma* (Brussels), no. 1-2, 1975; "*East of Eden*" by Edward S. Small in *Magill's Survey of Cinema, Vol. 1* edited by Frank N. Magill, Englewood Cliffs, New Jersey 1980.

*   *   *

If *East of Eden* is remembered only for its introduction to the screen of the extraordinary talents of its legendary star, James Dean, its place in film history would be assured. As it is, however, the techniques developed by the director to capture and translate the actor's performance most effectively within the 70 millimeter frame also allowed it to achieve the artistic distinction of being one of the first serious attempts at a creative use of CinemaScope. Elia Kazan's bag of stylistic tricks, regarded by many critics as technical abnormalities, consisted of such devices as canting the camera to distort angles, swinging pans to sustain a sense of movement in stagey scenes, unusually moody lighting effects, horizontal pans and experiments with soft focus lenses. Through these techniques, the director juxtaposed his camera with his actors' styles of performance, effectively and imaginatively enhancing their work. At the same time, he effected a visual impression of continuous movement while constantly redirecting the viewer's attention to the appropriate area of the screen, maximizing the dramatic advantages of its vast expanses. The resulting effect is an amplification of the film's symbolic motifs though their placement in shifting but highly visual contexts.

In a sense, the effective translation of *East of Eden* to the large screen required a visual equivalent to the theatrical acting style known as the Stanislavsky or Actors Studio method in which the performer actually becomes a character. A number of Kazan's actors, particularly Dean and Marlon Brando (In *Streetcar Named Desire*,) were practitioners of "the method" which placed greater demands on the camera than it placed on the stage. Through Kazan's visual style in *East of Eden*, the camera, too, in a process similar to that used in the German expressionist films of the 1920s, reflects the psychological aspects of the characters under its scrutiny. For example, the story, a modern reinterpreta-

tion of the Biblical Cain and Able tale, centers on the relationship between a father and his two sons. Its point of view is that of the youngest son Cal who, like his Biblical counterpart Cain, performs certain acts that are subject to at least two different interpretations. Viewed simplistically, they can, in the case of both characters, be seen as the vile deeds of a genetically flawed son. Yet, through Dean's eccentric interpretation, the modern boy can be recognized as a psychologically complex, insecure child who is starved for parental love. In scenes in which Cal appears with his father Adam (Raymond Massey), Kazan tilts the camera to dramatically characterize both figures as being in an essentially aberrant, distorted relationship. Both actor and camera combine to place the character's actions within an abnormal family context and reveal Cal's actions to be those of a boy consumed by an overwhelming need to win his father's approval. It is highly significant that the angle of vision is most distorted in the scene in which Adam refuses his son's heartfelt but slightly tainted gift of money. He can not look beneath the surface of the act to assess its meaning in terms of their relationship.

Interspersed throughout the film are long, almost theatrical, scenes derived from the director's stage experience, which provide the film with its thematic unity as ideas are raised which will later result in violent confrontations. Even in these scenes, there is a constant sense of movement expressed through the camera often by setting it in a ferris wheel or swing. Additional coherence is provided by the film's glimpse of the plight of California's immigrant population, a subject close to Kazan's heart. Some scholarship makes a case for *East of Eden* as the first series of the director's studies of various psychological and sociological aspects of the immigrant experience which he continues in *Wild River*, *America, America* and *The Arrangement*.

—Stephen L. Hanson

EASY RIDER. Production: Raybert Productions and Pando Company; 1969; Technicolor, 35mm (LSD sequence shot in 16mm); running time: 94 mins.; length: 2561 meters. Released 14 July 1969, New York.

Produced by Peter Fonda with Bert Schneider and William L. Hayward; screenplay by Peter Fonda, Dennis Hopper, and Terry Southern; main titles by Cinefx; directed by Dennis Hopper; photography by Laszlo Kovacs; edited by Donn Cambern; sound by Ryder Sound Service, sound mixed by Leroy Robbins, sound boom by James Contrares, sound effects by Edit-Rate Inc; art direction by Jerry Kay; music by Hoyt Axton ("The Pusher"), Mars Bonfire ("Born to be Wild"), Gerry Goffin and Carole King ("Wasn't Born to Follow"), Robbie Robertson ("The Weight"), Antonia Duren ("If You Want to Be a Bird"), Elliot Ingber and Larry Jay Wagner ("Don't Bogart That Joint"), Jimi Hendrix ("If 6 Was 9"), Gerry Goffin and Jack Keller ("Let's Turkey Trot"), David Axelrod ("Kyrie Eleison"), Mike Bloomfield ("Flash, Bam, Pow"), Bob Dylan ("It's All Right Ma, I'm Only Bleeding"), and Roger McQuinn ("The Ballad of Easy Rider"); songs sung by Steppenwolf, The Byrds, The Band, The Holy Modal Rounders, Fraternity of Man, The Jimi Hendrix Experience, Little Eva, The Electric Prunes, The Electric Flag, and Roger McGuinn; special effects by Steve Karkus; stunt gaffer: Tex Hall.

Filmed 1968-69 on location between California and New Orleans. Cost: about $375,000. New York Film Critics' Award,

Best Supporting Actor (Nicholson), 1969; Cannes Film Festival, Best First Film, 1969.

Cast: Peter Fonda (*Wyatt*); Dennis Hopper (*Billy*); Antonio Mendoza (*Jesus*); Phil Spector (*Connection*); Mac Mashourian (*Bodyguard*); Warren Finnerty (*Rancher*); Tita Colorado (*Rancher's wife*); Luke Askew (*Stranger on highway*); Luana Anders (*Lisa*); Sabrina Scharf (*Sarah*); Sandy Wyeth (*Joanne*); Robert Walker, Jr. (*Jack*); Robert Ball, Carmen Phillips, Ellie Walker, and Michael Pataki (*Mimes*); Jack Nicholson (*George Hanson*); George Fowler Jr. (*Guard*); Keith Green (*Sheriff*); Hayward Robillard (*Cat man*); Arnold Hess Jr. (*Deputy*): Buddy Causey Jr., Duffy Lamont, Blase M. Dawson, and Paul Guedry (*Customers in the cafe*); Toni Basil (*Mary*); Karen Black (*Karen*); Lea Marmer (*Madame*); Cathi Cozzi (*Dancing girl*); Thea Salerno, Anne McClain, Beatriz Monteil, and Marcia Bowman (*Hookers*); David C. Billodeau and Johnny David (*Men in pickup truck*).

Publications:

Scripts—*Easy Rider: Original Screenplay by Peter Fonda, Dennis Hopper, Terry Southern, Plus Stills, Interviews and Articles* edited by Nancy Hardin and Marilyn Schlossberg, New York 1969; *Easy Rider* by Dennis Hopper, Peter Fonda, and Terry Southern, New York 1970; "*Easy Rider*" by Peter Fonda, Dennis Hopper, and Terry Southern in *Avant-Scène du cinéma* (Paris), September 1971; reviews—by Tom Milne in *Sight and Sound* (London), autumn 1969; review and article by Andrew Sarris in *The Village Voice* (New York), 3 July 1969 and 14 August 1969; "*Easy Rider*: La Critique" in *Avant-Scène du cinéma* (Paris), September 1971; books—*The Americans* by David Frost, New York 1970; *The Fondas: The Films and Careers of Henry, Jane, and Peter Fonda* by John Springer, New York 1970; *A Short History of the Movies* by Gerald Mast, New York 1971; articles—"Thoughts and Attitudes About *Easy Rider*" by Peter Fonda and Leslie Reyner in *Film* (London), autumn 1969; "Fonda" by Tony Reif and Iain Ewing in *Take One* (Montreal), no.3, 1969; "*Easy Rider*: The Initiation of Dennis Hopper" by F.A. Macklin in *Film Heritage* (Dayton, Ohio), fall 1969; "Not so Easy Riders: Dennis Hopper and Peter Fonda" in *Vogue* (New York), 1 August 1969; "What Directors Are Saying" in *Action* (Los Angeles), September/October 1969; "Dennis Hopper, Riding High" in *Playboy* (Chicago), December 1969; article by Harriet Polt in *Film Quarterly* (Berkeley), fall 1969; article by Frederic Tuten in *Film Society Review* (New York), May 1969; "Interview: Peter Fonda" in *Playboy* (Chicago), no.9, 1970; "*Easy Rider*: Comic Epic Poem in Film" by Tom R. Sullivan in *Journal of Popular Culture* (Bowling Green, Ohio), spring 1970; "*Easy Rider*" by Paul Warshow in *Sight and Sound* (London), winter 1969-70; article by Stephen Farber in *Film Quarterly* (Berkeley), winter 1969-70; article by Charles Hampton in *Film Comment* (New York), fall 1970; "The Current Cinema" by Pauline Kael in the *New Yorker*, 3 October 1970; "*Easy Rider*: Critique of the New Hedonism" by Mary Rose Sullivan in *Western Humanities Review*, no.24, 1970; "Un Film de portée universelle" by Marie-Angèle Williams in *Avant-Scène du cinéma* (Paris), September 1971; "The Corporate Style of BBS" by M.S. Cohen in *Take One* (Montreal), November 1973.

*   *   *

Easy Rider remains a cinematic hallmark primarily for negative reasons: the preeminent film dealing with the subject and style typifying the late 1960s, it remains an interesting cultural and historical document of the industry's response to "youth culture." Unfortunately, the film seemed trite even two years after its initial critical and public triumph. Produced for $375,000, it made over $50,000,000 and spawned a number of less-effective imitators; the film's profits convinced even the most reticent backers in Hollywood that the youth market was ready to be tapped. In fact, it may have been its imitators that made the original date so quickly: many of the films produced after *Easy Rider* were of such inferior quality that they couldn't be sold to television after their initial release in regular theaters.

The film is not completely without value. Film historian Gerald Mast sees *Easy Rider* as a landmark of the "New Hollywood" as well as the culmination of films representing our American West/journey motif experience—a sort of New Wave cowboy epic. The film reflects the sexual and social values of American film audiences of its period: the protagonists are social misfits, even outlaws. The heros become the villians and vice-versa. However, unlike the outlaws of the past—Little Caesar, Scarface—these protagonists are also charming, good-humored, warm, and often compassionate. Their pursuers, predictably, represent the "older generation" and seem inhuman, humorless. In Mast's words, "Given the outlaw protagonists, the new obligatory ending was the unhappy rather than happy one. The protagonists die; law triumphs over lawlessness. However, good did not triumph over evil, for law and good were antithetical."

Easy Rider dealt openly with violence and paranoia, appropriate themes given the ideological divisions of the United States in the late 1960s. As David Cooks notes, the film "was praised for its radical social perspective far beyond its value as a film." And it is the western/quest film revisited: two "hippies," their journey facilitated through motorcycles rather than horses, go "in search of America." The film concerns freedom, or the illusion of freedom—for ultimately the bikers "can't find it anywhere," as the ad copy itself reads.

At its best, *Easy Rider* merges the American past and present, city and country, gangster and cowboy through the two main characters played by Dennis Hopper and Peter Fonda. Interestingly, the horse has become the chopper motorcycle; and civilization is personified by the small-town bigots, the country sheriff, institutionalized love (a whorehouse), and even institutionalized death (a very large cemetery). The romantic, free journey seems less than it should be; a commune of hip kids from the city acts with as much hostility towards the easy riders as the "straights" from the towns. Freedom is represented by the road, but as the ending of the film illustrates, even that will not last.

Andrew Sarris stressed the "assortment of excellences...that lift (*Easy Rider*) above the run and ruck of its genre. The first and foremost is the sterling performance of Jack Nicholson as George Hanson, a refreshingly civilized creature from Southern comfort and interplanetary fantasies." Among the film's other strengths is its roadside traveling shots interspersed with rock music: Jimi Hendrix, The Byrds, Steppenwolf, The Band, Bob Dylan, Roger McGuinn and others. But Sarris' main point is as follows: "With all the rousingly rhythmic revelry and slendiferously scenic motorcycling, *Easy Rider* comes to resemble a perceptual precredit sequence, but reasonably pleasant withal... there is something depressingly *deja vu* about the moralistic view of America from a motorcycle." And all this from a critic who essentially *likes* the film.

Critical approbrium of its time notwithstanding, *Easy Rider's* jury still hasn't returned a less than contradictory verdict. For all its apparent triteness, for all of its "Man-cool mumbles," even mainstream critics like Sarris warn, "beware of all generalizations, including this one...the *nouvelle vague* tricks and Bergman-Fellini-Antonioni mannerisms are no more voguish today than the UFA German Expressionist and Soviet montage tricks were in the late twenties..." The film has dated badly, yet its value lies in capturing one of the United States' most divisive times, illustrating where the frontier legacy begun with *Stagecoach* seems to have led. It's often impossible to tell the heros from the villains in *Easy Rider*, as now.

—Deborah H. Holdstein

L'ECLISSE. The Eclipse. Production: Interopa Film and Cineriz (Rome) and Paris Film Production (Paris); black and white, 35mm; running time: 125 mins. Released 1962.

Produced by Robert and Raymond Hakim; screenplay by Michelangelo Antonioni and Tonino Guerra with Elio Bartolini and Ottiero Ottieri; directed by Michelangelo Antonioni; photography by Gianni Di Venanzo; edited by Eraldo Da Roma; sound by Claudio Maielli and Mario Bramonti; production design by Piero Poletto; music by Giovanni Fusco.

Filmed in Italy. Cannes Film Festival, Special Jury Prize and Catholic Film Office Award, 1962.

Cast: Alain Delon (*Riccardo*); Monica Vitti (*Vittoria*); Francisco Rabal; Lilla Brignone; Rossana Rory; Mirella Ricciardi; Louis Seignier.

Publications:

Scripts—*L'Eclisse* by Michelangelo Antonioni and Tonino Guerra, Italy 1962; *Screenplays of Michelangelo Antonioni*, introduction by Antonioni, New York 1963; review—"L'lapse" by Donald Barthelme in the *New Yorker*, 2 March 1963; books—*Michelangelo Antonioni: An Introduction* by Pierre Leprohon, New York 1963; *Antonioni, Bergman, Resnais* by Peter Cowie, New York 1963; *Antonioni* by Philip Strick, London 1965; *Antonioni* by Ian Cameron and Robin Wood, New York 1969; *Encountering Directors* by Charles Thomas Samuels, New York 1972; articles—issue on Antonioni of *Film Quarterly* (Berkeley), fall 1962; "Antonioni Diary" by John Francis Lane in *Films and Filming* (London), March 1962; "Antonioni" by L. N. Gerard in *Films in Review* (New York), April 1963; "The Antonioni Trilogy" by Terrance McNally, "The Music of Sound" by Gary Carey, and "To Be, Not to Understand" by Sibyl March in *7th Art* (New York), spring 1963; issue devoted to Antonioni of *Motion*, no.5, 1963; "The Event and the Image" by Geoffrey Nowell-Smith in *Sight and Sound* (London), winter 1964-65; "Keeping Up with the Antonionis" by Penelope Houston in *Sight and Sound* (London), autumn 1964; "Shape Around the Black Point" by Geoffre Nowell-Smith in *Sight and Sound* (London), winter 1963-64; "Night, Eclipse, and Dawn: An Interview with Michelangelo Antonioni" by Jean-Luc Godard in *Cahiers du Cinema in English* (New York), January 1966; "The Stature of Objects in Antonioni's Films" by J. Dudley Andrew in *Triquarterly*, winter 1968; "Michelangelo Antonioni and the Imagery of Disintegration" by T. Hernacki in *Film Heritage* (Dayton, Ohio), autumn 1970; "Antonioni Men" by Gordon Gow in *Films and Filming* (London), June 1970; "A Contextual Analysis of M. Antonioni's *L'Eclisse*" by Ted Perry in *Speech Monographs*, June 1970; "Antonioni: The Road to Death" by Andrew Tudor in *Cinema* (London), August 1970; "Une Musique: *L'eclipse*" by E. Decaux in *Cinématographe* (Paris), November 1980;

* * *

Michelangelo Antonioni's *L'eclisse* is the most succinct expression of moral ambiguities of the Italian "economic miracle" of the late fifties and early sixties to come from the national cinema. It is the complement of Federico Fellini's *La dolce vita*. Whereas Fellini dwells upon the hellish and grotesque dimensions of Roman life during that period, Antonioni focuses upon its inauthenticity and its impermanence. The "eclipse" of the title refers primarily to the brief affair of the protagonists Vittoria, a translator, and Piero, a stock jobber; and secondarily to a brief tailspin in the stockmarket which forms the backdrop of their liaison. In an even wider sense, it alludes to the brief span of human life on earth, literalized in a scene in a natural history mueum which the filmmaker had to cut perhaps under pressure from the producers. The sole vestige of this dimension is a fossil Vittoria hangs as a decoration on her wall.

From the opening scene of Vittoria arranging objects in a frame to the final, magnificent montage of the nearly empty, vespertinal streets of Rome's fashionable and modernistic E.U.R. district, Antonioni's typical love of composition and attention to significant detail is in evidence. In this film, things overwhelm people. Even the accidental meeting of Piero and Vittoria for the first time occurs during an ominous pause—a literal "minute of silence" in the stock exchange honoring a dead broker—and they whisper to each other around a monumental pillar (the Roman stock market is built in the ruins of an ancient temple).

The rootlessness of this couple is emphasized in the scenes of their mutual seduction which take place, not in their modern apartments, but in their parents' stuffier dwellings in the center of the city. By locating their amours in the vacant parental apartments, Antonioni underlines the dimensions of compulsion and regression in their relationship. Without pain, almost cheerfully, they exploit each other, playing at seriousness and constancy.

The ironic counterpoint to their homelessness is Vittoria's neighbor, Marta, who longs for her family plantation in Kenya. Her home is decorated with African trophies and giant enlargements of photographs of East Africa. A nostalgist and a racist, who refers to the natives as "apes", she has reified her environment. Antonioni underscores the illusory status of her feeling for Africa by depicting her hysterical attitude to her effeminately mannered poodle amid the vestiges of safaries.

The final minutes of the film sustain a remarkable suspense as the viewer is lead to expect either Vittoria or Piero to appear at the corner of their assignations. Instead, the camera focuses upon the objects and people that had been backdrops and tangents of their actions. As we come to realize that neither will appear, we get a glimpse of a man reading a newspaper (one of the many false identifications of the protagonists) with the headline about the threat of atomic war. The final, sustained closeup of a street light suggests the nuclear explosion which can eclipse human time.

—P. Adams Sitney

DIE EHE DER MARIA BRAUN. The Marriage of Maria Braun. Production: Albatros Film (M. Fengler), Trio Film, WDR, and Filmerlog Der Autoren (all of West Germany); Fujicolor, 35mm; running time: 120 mins.; length: 10,764 feet. Released 1978, Germany, and 28 February 1979, United States.

Produced by Michael Fengler; screenplay by Peter Märthesheimer and Pea Fröhlich, dialogue by Rainer Werner Fassbinder; from an idea by Rainer Werner Fassbinder; directed by Rainer Werner Fassbinder; photography by Michael Ballhaus; edited by Juliane Lorenz and Franz Walsch (Fassbinder); sound recorded by Jim Willis and Milan Bor; art direction by Norbert Scherer, Helga Ballhaus, Claus Kottmann, and Georg Borgel, set decoration by Andreas Willim, Arno Mathes, and Hans Sandmeier; music by Peer Raben; costumes designed by Barbara Baum, Susi Reichel, George Kuhn, and Ingeborg Pröller.

Filmed in Germany. Berlin Film Festival, Best Actress (Schygulla) and Best Technical Team, 1979.

Cast: Hanna Schygulla (*Maria Braun*); Klaus Löwitsch (*Hermann Braun*); Ivan Desny (*Karl Oswald*); Gottfried John (*Willi Klenze*); Gisela Uhlen (*Mother*); George Byrd (*Bill*); Elisabeth Trissenaar (*Betti Klenze*); Rainer Werner Fassbinder (*Dealer*); Isolde Barth (*Vevi*); Peter Berling (*Bronski*); Sonja Neudorfer (*Red Cross nurse*); Lieselotte Eder (*Frau Ehmke*); Volker Spengler (*Train conductor*); Michael Ballhaus (*Counsel, Anwalf*); Günther Kaufmann (*American on train*); Karl-Heinz von Hassel (*Prosecuting counsel*).

Publications:

Reviews—"The Current Cinema" by Renata Adler in the *New Yorker*, 29 October 1979; "On Screen: Love Crazed" by R. Asahina in *New Leader* (New York), 19 November 1979; "Films/TV: Limited Visibility" by R.A. Blake in *America* (New York), 24 November 1979; "Film: Maria Braun from Fassbinder" by Vincent Canby in *The New York Times*, 14 October 1979; "*The Marriage of Maria Braun*" by T. Curran in *Films in Review* (New York), November 1979; "Films" by R. Hatch in *Nation* (New York), 27 October 1979; "*Die Ehe der Maria Braun*" by M. Holthot in *Film en televisie* (Brussels), October 1979; "Stanley Kauffmann on Films: Through the War Years" in the *New Republic* (New York), 29 September 1979; "The Boom Goes Bust" by Jack Kroll in *Newsweek* (New York), 29 October 1979; "High Camp: *The Marriage of Maria Braun*" by F. Rich in *Time* (New York), 22 October 1979; "Film Festival II: Nostalgic Gamble" by Andrew Sarris in *The Village Voice* (New York), 15 October 1979; "*Le Mariage de Maria Braun*" by J.C. Bonnet in *Cinématographe* (Paris), March 1980; "*Ehe der Maria Braun*" by R. Combs in *Monthly Film Bulletin* (London), August 1980; "*The Marriage of Maria Braun*" by D. Elley in *Films* (London), December 1980; "*The Marriage of Maria Braun*" by R. McCormick in *Cineaste* (New York), spring 1980; "*Le Mariage de Maria Braun*" by D. Sauvaget in *Image et son* (Paris), February 1980; "Comment désire la femme au temps du miracle allemand" by J.P. Domecq in *Positif* (Paris), March 1980; "*Le Mariage de Maria Braun*" by Y. Lardeau in *Cahiers du cinéma* (Paris), February 1980; books—*The New German Cinema* by John Sandford, Totowa, New Jersey 1980; articles—"At the Movies: Last Match of Director and Actress" by T. Buckley in *The New York Times*, 26 October 1979; "Den kvinnohatande feministen: om Fassbindfer's kvinnosyn och *Die Ehe der Maria Braun* by J. Dawson in *Chaplin* (Stockholm), no. 2, 1979; "Fassbinder

Makes with Boxoffice Hit" in *Variety* (New York), 14 November 1979; interview with Fassbinder by H. Hosman in *Skoop* (Amsterdam), August 1979; "*The Marriage of Maria Braun*" by A.M. Widem in *Boxoffice* (Kansas City, Kansas), 19 November 1979; "*Die Ehe der Maria Braun*" by G. Moskowitz in *Variety* (New York), 28 February 1979; article in *Cineforum* (Bergamo, Italy), May 1980; article in *Film Quarterly* (Berkeley), spring 1980; "*The Marriage of Maria Braun*" in the *Monthly Film Bulletin* (London), August 1980; article in *Journal of Popular Film and Television* (Bowling Green, Ohio), fall 1981.

*　　*　　*

The importance of *The Marriage of Maria Braun*, released in Germany in 1978, can be seen on a number of levels. It is the first of Rainer Werner Fassbinder's works to win him popularity not only in his own country but also in foreign lands. Prior to this film, Fassbinder's success was limited to the audience of foreign art house. *The Marriage of Maria Braun* belongs to the trilogy of films in which Fassbinder portrays post World War II Germany. These films unfold through the stories of three women whose names are also the titles—*The Marriage of Maria Braun*, *Veronica Voss*, *Lola*. These films present a glimpse into the post war Germany and a history of the building of the Federal Repulic.

Maria Braun also belongs to a special group of Fassbinder films which are indebted in a structure to the melodramas of Douglas Sirk. Fassbinder gave the conventional melodrama style, of which Sirk's films are a prime example, new life by infusing it with the social and political concerns of modern Germany. At the same time he foregrounded and laid bare the melodramatic structures of the film. The structure of this film is so closely embedded in the content that a study of one leads inevitably to a study of the other. It is the successful fusing of these two elements which lead to the popularity of the film; audiences could easily relate to the highly charged, emotional story of a woman struggling to survive, and simultaneously, through the same actress in the same film, understand Germany's options for survival.

Fassbinder, born in 1945, grew up in Germany which was quickly rebuilding itself with American aid into the "economic miracle" of the 1950s. Germany was surfeited with American films during this time, including the melodramas of Douglas Sirk. Fassbinder, familiar with these films, attempted to discover what made them so successful, and to duplicate that success with his own work in Germany.

The structure of *Maria Braun* allows for the intensely emotional scenes of Maria's story (for example, her marriage, her search for her husband, her realization of his death) to be emphasized by the lighting, music and camera angles. All of these elements stretch the limits of the conventional style of melodrama. Yet, they are all undercut by the dead-pan acting of Hanna Schygulla in the role of Maria Braun, and the sheer multiplicity of the heart-rending situations in which Maria finds herself. The audience is drawn into the emotionally charged moment, then distanced from it and forced to look elsewhere for content. It looks instead to the social and political situation which built the Germany economic miracle for its history and Maria's story are so closely intertwined, that the audience may hardly notice it is shifting its gaze. The scene, for example, in which Maria announces to her American G.I. lover that her husband is dead, implying that she is now free to go with him, is one that seems feverish with emotion, but it is completely cooled by Schygulla's dead-pan deliverance of the line "Mein Mann ist tot." The scene is also heavy with the symbolism of a despondent

Germany which, after the war, turned to America. Maria comes to her G.I. lover not out of love but out of need to be cared for and because he is there and willing to give. All the trappings of great emotion are present, but there is no emotion on her face or in her voice. Likewise, Germany follows America out of the same need down the capitalistic road but with no thought or emotion that would imply that it is a true alliance.

Schygulla, with a great deal of class, moves through scene after scene of a devastated Germany. Surrounded by bombed-out buildings and broken walls, she moves through the debris with courage and skill, but no integrity. The camera follows her in long sweeping movements which reflect the aplomb of her transactions; the same way, the rigid, frequently off-centered cinematography reflects the starkness of the world around her. Vincent Canby sums up the essence of Schygulla'a character when he refers to Maria as a Mother Courage type who wouldn't be caught dead pulling a cart.

The most important characteristic of *The Marriage of Maria Braun* is its ability to successfully blend the elements of classical melodrama with aspects of modernist theory and contemporary social-political themes. Fassbinder has not only prolonged the life of the melodramatic mode, but has also embedded the sometimes confusing characteristics of an alienating modernism into the romance of the melodrama.

—Gretchen Elsner-Sommer

LES ENFANTS DU PARADIS. The Children of Paradise. Production: S.N. Pathé Cinema; black and white, 35mm; running time: originally 195 mins. for both parts, current versions—Part I is 100 mins., Part II is 86-88 mins.; length: current versions—Part I is 9066 feet, Part II is 7762 feet. Released 9 March 1945, Paris. Re-released later in 188 min. version.

Screenplay by Jacques Prévert, scenario structure by Marcel Carné; from an original idea by Marcel Carné and Jacques Prévert; directed by Marcel Carné; photography by Marc Fossard and Roger Hubert; edited by Henri Rust and Madeleine Bonin; sound engineered by Robert Teisseire; production design by Léon Barsacq, Raymond Gabutti, and Alexandre Trauner; music by Joseph Kosma, Maurice Thierte and Georges Mouque, music directed by Charles Munch; costumes designed by Antoine Mayo.

Filming began August 1943, but was interrupted by WWII, resuming 9 November 1943; filmed in Joinville studios, Paris, La Victorine studios in Nice, and on an outdoor set constructed by Carné's crew in Nice. Venice Film Festival, Special Mention, 1946.

Cast: Jean Louis Barrault (*Baptiste Deburau*); Arletty (*Garance*); Pierre Brasseur (*Frederick Lamaître*); Marcel Herrand (*Lacenaire*); Pierre Renoir (*Jericho*); Fabien Loris (*Avril*); Louis Salou (*Count de Montray*); Maria Cassares (*Nathalie*); Etienne Decroux (*Anselm Deburau*); Jeanne Marken (*Madame Hermine*); Gaston Modot (*Blind man*); Pierre Palau (*Director*); Albert Remy (*Scarpia Barigni*); Paul Frankeur (*Inspector of Police*).

Publications:

Scripts— *Children of Paradise* by Jacques Prévert, with interview of Carné, New York 1968; "*Les Enfants du paradis*" by Jacques Prévert and Marcel Carné in *Avant-Scène du cinéma* (Paris), July/September 1967; reviews—by Georges Sadoul in *Les Lettres Françaises* (Paris), 17 March 1945; review by Roger Manvell in *Sight and Sound* (London), spring 1946; books— *Marcel Carne* by Jean-Louis Béranger, Paris 1945; *French Film* by Georges Sadoul, Paris 1947; *Marcel Carne* by Robert Chazal, Paris n.d. *Marcel Carné* by Jean Quéval, Paris 1952; *Marcel Carné, sa vie, ses films* by Bernard Landry, Paris n.d. *The Great Films: 50 Golden Years of Motion Pictures* by Bosley Crowther, New York 1967; *Cinema, the Magic Vehicle: A Guide to its Achievement: Journey One, The Cinema Through 1949* edited by Jacek Klinowski and Adam Garbicz, Metuchen, New Jersey 1975; *French Cinema Since 1946: The Great Tradition*, Vol. I, by Roy Armes, New York 1976; *Caligari's Cabinet and Other Grand Illusions: A History of Film Design* by Léon Barsacq, New York 1976; articles—by James Phillips in *Hollywood Quarterly*, July 1946; "Marcel Carné" by Roger Manvell in *Sight and Sound* (London), spring 1946; "Marcel Carné" by Gavin Lambert in *Sequence* (London), spring 1948; article by Alan Bodian in *The Village Voice* (New York), 23 November 1955; "Classics Revisited: Reaching for the Moon" by William Hedges in *Film Quarterly* (Berkeley), summer 1959; "The Carné Bubble" by Alan Stanbrook in *Film* (London), November/December 1959; article by Raymond Durgnat in *Films and Filming* (London), October 1965; interview with Marcel Carné and interview with Jacques Prévert in *Avant-Scène du cinéma* (Paris), July/September 1967; "En Guise de préface" by Jacques-G. Perret in *Avant/Scène du cinéma* (Paris), July/September 1967; "Petite histoire d'un grand film" in *Avant/Scène du cinéma* (Paris), July/September 1967; "*Les Enfants du paradis*" by E. Chaumeton in *Cahiers du cinéma* (Paris), winter 1973; "*Les Enfants du paradis*" by R. Lefévre in *Cinéma* (Paris), February 1974; "The Birth of *Children of Paradise*" by E.B. Turk in *American Film* (Washington, D.C.), July/August 1979; "*Les Enfants du paradis*: la mutation cinematographique du melodrame" by M. Oms in *Cahiers de la cinématheque* (Perpignan, France), no.28, 1979.

*   *   *

It is reported that director Marcel Carné had described his greatest work, *Les Enfants du Paradis*, as being "a tribute to the theatre," meaning the French theater, for the entire story breathes with the very life and soul of the French drama. Three of its characters are based on historical figures famous during the reign of Louis-Philippe (two actors, the pantomimist Deburau and the ambitious romantic actor, Frederic Lemaitre; and a debonair but ruthless criminal known as Lacenaire). Their meeting ground is Paris in the vicinity of the theatre Funambules, in the Boulevard du Temple, sometimes called the Boulevard du Crime because it was the scene for many unsolved thefts and murders. A quarter of a mile of street fronts, as well as the full theatre of the Funambules along the Boulevard du Temple, was reconstructed at great cost for the picture's production.

The most remarkable thing about the making of the film was that it took over two years to be made, during a time when Paris was occupied by the Nazis. Production was often deliberately sabotaged, halted because actors had disappeared and had either to be found again or their roles re-cast. The Nazis, anxious to keep film production active in France, were more than willing to co-operate. Some actors working in the French Underground arranged to have their scenes shot secretly when they were daring enough to temporarily come out from hiding. German-speaking films were not patronized by the French people, and the Nazis determined that making films in the French language was an important part of the "Occupation" of the nation. Over 350 feature films, some like *Les Enfants du Paradis*, were shot in occupied France. During the War the Nazis could not get films from the USA or England, and the French people boycotted all movies not made in Hollywood or London; they would only see films made in their native tongue. The most ambitious of all these was *Les Enfants du Paradis*, just as it was the most Parisian of them all; yet director Marcel Carné and scenarist Jacques Prévert contrived to slow up production, sometimes deliberately hiding key reels already shot from their Nazi supervisors, waiting hopefully for the Germans to be forced to evacuate Paris before they premiered what they knew was going to be a masterpiece of the French film world.

On March 9, 1945, *Les Enfants du Paradis* was finally premiered in Paris, the first important movie premiere since the end of the Occupation. It was received with adoration by its public. The film's running time was originally 195 minutes. This was shortened by 45 minutes when the picture was first premiered in New York; but most of the edited film was later restored, and prints of *Les Enfants du Paradis* now run 188 minutes.

The genesis for the story occurred in Cannes during the second year of the Occupation when actor Jean-Louis Barrault met over lunch with director Carné and screenwriter Prévert. When Barrault learned that they were seeking a subject for filming, he suggested a story to be written about Debureau, who had been France's greatest pantomimist. (In 1950, Sacha Guitry, forced to be inactive during the Occupation, would create such a plot in verse.) The scope of the movie envisioned by Carné, Prévert, and Barrault was very wide, indicating that the drama could only flourish where men are free, a subtlety of interpretation that eluded the Nazi mind; otherwise, they would never have authorized production of the film.

In French, "paradis" is the colloquial name for the gallery or second balcony. Roughly, it symbolized the common man. This was where the French people sat and viewed a play, responding openly and vociferously to its message and interpretation. They were like gallery gods, and the actors played to them, hoping to win their favor, thus elevating the actor himself to an Olympian status.

The French theatre at the time was very much as Dumas knew it, and Balzac subsequently wrote about it. It was a free theatre for the people, catering to their own romantic and extravagant tastes. Mountebanks, clowns, courtesans quickened its rich blood. Debureau, whose father was an actor, became the idol of his time for, with a few well-timed gestures, he touched the emotions of his public. He rose to fame just as Lemaitre caught the fashionable fancy of the nation. Their fates mingled with the daring criminal, Lacenaire. All three loved and were loved, however briefly, by Garance, the beautiful adventuresss idolized as an actress. In the film she is presented as a woman who rejected those men who tried to possess her, moving on to other countries and other men who did not attempt to dictate her lifestyle. Only when she learns that Debureau is also the father of a young son does she abandon her hold on him, relinquishing him to his wife and child while she pursues a new chapter in her life, praying that it will lead her to ultimate freedom. Garance becomes a popular example of this century's emancipated woman, a true sophisticate knowing everything about living, resisting all bonds of dictation.

Had the then-victorious German Army even faintly realized that in authorizing production of *Les Enfants du Paradis*, they

were condoning the exploits of a free woman like Garance, they would have withdrawn their approval of the film immediately. She symbolized tha activating spirit of the Free French, a spirit of revolt and independence, a spirit that can never be broken or subjugated, as Hilter's generals soon learned.

Beautifully cast with the triumphant Arletty as Garance, the picture also boasted the presence of Jean-Louis Barrault as Debureau. In his own right he was the finest pantomimist in the French theatre, and he simply transferred his special gifts to the role he was playing. Handsome Pierre Brasseur was an immaculate Lemaitre, and Marcel Herrand offered a stunning portrayal of the criminal. Lovely Maria Casarès was very appealing as the wife of Debureau.

All in all, *Les Enfants du Paradis*, in spite of its large canvas, remains a very special study of the French theatre, inviting its audience not only to know and appreciate its people, but to acquaint them with the free French spirit.

—DeWitt Bodeen

ENTOTSU NO MIERU BASHO. The Four Chimneys. Where Chimneys Are Seen. Production: Studio 8 Productions and Shin Toho Co.; black and white, 35mm; running time: 108 mins.; length: 9678 feet. Released 5 March 1953, Japan.

Produced by Yoshishige Uchiyama; screenplay by Hideo Oguni; from the novel *Mujaki na Hitobito* by Rinzo Shiina; directed by Heinosuke Gosho; photography by Mitsuo Miura; edited by Nobu Nagata; sound by Yuji Dogen; art direction by by Tomoo Shimogahara; music by Yasushi Akutagawa; assistant director: Akira Miwa.

Filmed in Japan. Kinema Jumpo, Tokyo Citizen Film Concours Prize "Best One Award," 1953; Berlin Film Festival, International PeacePrize, 1954.

Cast: Ken Uehara (*Ryukichi Ogata*); Kinuyo Tanaka (*Hiroko Ogata*); Hiroshi Akutagawa (*Kengo Kubo*); Hideko Takamine (*Senko Azuma*); Cheiko Seki (*Yukiko Ikeda*); Haruo Tanaka (*Chujiro Tsukahara*); Ranko Hanai (*Katsuko Ishibashi*).

Publications:

Books—*The Waves at Genji's Door* by Joan Mellen, New York 1976; *Japanese Film Directors* by Audie Bock, New York 1978; *Cinema, The Magic Vehicle: A Guide to its Achievement: Journey Two* edited by Jacek Klinowski and Adam Garbicz, Metuchen, New Jersey 1979; *The Japanese Film: Art and Industry* (expanded version) by Joseph Anderson and Donald Richie, Princeton, New Jersey 1982; articles—"The Films of Heinosuke Gosho" by J.L. Anderson and Donald Richie in *Sight and Sound* (London), autumn 1956; "Coca-Cola and the Golden Pavilion" by John Gillett in *Sight and Sound* (London), summer 1970; "Heinosuke Gosho", with biofilmography, by John Gillett in *Film Dope* (London), April 1980; "Heinosuke Gosho" by Max Tessier in *Image et son* (Paris), June 1981.

*   *   *

The film's title *Where Chimneys Are Seen*, refers to an industrial-residential area in Tokyo's downtown, where a set of huge chimneys is a familiar sight to its lower middle class inhabitants. The protagonist discovers that, according to where you are, the number of these chimneys varies from one to four. This observation typifies the philosophy of Rinzo Shiina (who wrote the original story) that nothing is absolutely true or false; everybody has to believe something or pretend to. Director Heinosuke Gosho takes splendid advantage of his most familiar subject, the life of ordinary people, and elegantly their humor and pathos.

The story develops around the four main characters: Ryukichi, an honest salesman at a wholesale socks store; his diligent wife Hiroko whose previous marriage was unoffically terminated by her husband's disappearance during the war; their young upstairs lodgers, Kengo, a serious and good natured tax officer and Senko, a pretty and vivacious bargain announcer on a commercial street. As Gosho seems to be more interested in depicting each character's personality and emotional situation, and their interrelationships than in detailing a completed plot, he successfully makes the viewer feel intimate with these likable and good willed people.

The film's light and humorous tone is first manifested in the opening narration by Ryukichi. In an aerial shot, the camera shows us downtown Tokyo, focusing on Ryukichi's busy neighborhood with its small houses packed together; his usual neighbors are presented as a constant yet unwitting source of humor (e.g., the weird, loud morning chanting of a religious leader and the radio repairman with seven children). Finally his modest household, is shown, and the habitual peace is broken by the sudden appearance of the baby left by Hiroko's previous husband to Hiroko and Ryukichi. Though it obviously creates tension between the couple, ultimately the baby becomes a symbol of unification: the childless couple confirms their love through their care for the sick baby; Kengo's (the young man upstairs) voluntary efforts to locate the baby's parents make Senko aware of his character, thus drawing the couple closer together; and the baby's mother finally realizes her responsibility to reclaim the baby.

The film's narrative structure involves numerous episodes which look simplistic, but cumulatively show the charms of everyday life. A memorable example is the scene in which Senko plays with pencils on Kengo's desk during their conversation on his daily, frustrating search for the baby's parents. This scene is noteworthy not only for its intimate humor, but also for its meditative effect, for the pencils, like the chimneys, make Senko realize the relativity of life. Another good example is the scene in which Senko's modern girlfriend follows an older woman on the river bank—after the older one's sandal gets broken, the other also takes off one of her shoes. This lame pair create a wryly humorous image through their leisurely walking in the airy, bright morning light.

Gosho here, as in his other films, makes use of many closeups to indicate the subtle expressions of its characters. He also uses occasional long shots and long takes. Particularly effective is a long-shot sequence from a bus window where Kengo, after an exhausting search, notices the mystery of the chimneys. The fluidly vibrating image of the chimneys as the scenery swiftly passes is visually refreshing.

This film, produced by Gosho himself, distinctively reflects the Japanese film's *shomin-geki* genre (films about the lives of ordinary people), with its superb characterizations, successful portrayal of everyday life and emotions, a rich depiction of details, and the particular bittersweet atmosphere created by skillful timing, confortable pace and excellent acting. Overall, the film displays Gosho's belief that the sincere efforts of good people are understood and rewarded. This film not only has won the highest critical acclaim, but has also remained one of the most beloved of Gosho's films in Japan.

—Kyoko Hirano

ENTR'ACTE. Black and white, 35mm, silent; running time: 22 mins. Released 1924, at the Theatre des Champs Elysées between acts of the ballet "Relâche" by Francis Picabia as performed by the Ballets Suédois, Paris. Re-released 1968 with musical soundtrack directed by Henri Sauguet.

Produced by Rolf de Maré; scenario from an outline by Francis Picabia, adapted by René Clair; directed by René Clair; photography by Jimmy Berliet; edited by René Clair; music composed specially for the film by Erik Satie.

Filmed 1924 in and around Paris.

Cast: Jean Borlin; Francis Picabia; Man Ray; Marcel Duchamp; Erik Satie; Marcel Achard; Pierre Scize; Louis Touchagues; Rolf de Maré; Roger Lebon; Mamy; Georges Charensol; Mlle. Friis.

Publications:

Scripts—*A Nous la liberté and Entr'acte: Films by René Clair* translated and description of action by Richard Jacques and Nicola Hayden, New York 1970; *Clair: Four Screenplays* translated by Piergiuseppe Bozzetti, New York 1970; books—*René Clair* by G. Viazzi, Milan 1946; *René Clair* by J. Bourgeois, Geneva 1949; *Un Maître du cinéma* by Georges Charensol and Roger Régent, Paris 1952; *René Clair: An Index* by Catherine de la Roche, London 1958; *René Clair* by Jean Mitry, Paris 1960; *René Clair* by Barthelemy Amengual, revised edition, Paris 1969; *Encountering Directors* by Charles Thomas Samuels, New York 1972; *French Cinema Since 1946: The Great Tradition*, Vol. 1, by Roy Armes, New York 1976; *René Clair* by Celia McGerr, Boston 1980; articles—"René Clair and Film Humor" by Harry Potamkin in *Hound and Horn* (New York), October/December 1932; "Conversations with René Clair" by Bernard Causton in *Sight and Sound* (London), winter 1932-33; "The Films of René Clair" by Louis Jacobs in *New Theatre* (New York), February 1936; "René Clair" by Gavin Lambert in *Sequence* (London), winter 1948-49; issue devoted to Clair, *Bianco e nero* (Rome), August/September 1951; "Cinema's First Immortal" by Charles Ford in *Films in Review* (New York), November 1960; "Picabia, Satie et la première d'*Entr'acte*" in *Avant-Scène* (Paris), November 1968; "Entr'acte, le film sans maître" by Claude Beylie in *Cinema 69* (Paris), February 1969; "Satie's *Entr'acte*: A Model of Film Music" by D.W. Gallez in *Cinema Journal* (Evanston, Illinois), no.1, 1976; "*Entr'acte*, Paris, and Dada" by N. Carroll in *Millenium* (New York), winter 1977-78; "Rene Clair's *Entr'acte*, or Motion Victorious" by R.C. Dale in *Wide Angle* (Athens, Ohio), no.2, 1978; "*Entr'acte*" by J. Brunius in *Travelling* (Lausanne, Switzerland), summer 1979; "Parodic Narration in *Entr'acte*" by P. Sandro in *Film Criticism* (Edinboro, Pennsylvania), no.1, 1979.

*　　*　　*

In November of 1924, Paris anticipated another performance by The Swedish Ballet, a company which had outraged its audience since its residency began in 1920. The centerpiece of one particular evening was to be a new work created by Francis Picabia, the Dadaist artist. When Picabia learned that the opening night might be obstructed by censors, he ruefully entitled the work *Relâche*, or *Theatre Closed* or *Performance Suspended*. When the event did not take place on the announced night (due to an illness rather than censorship), patrons surmised this to be simply another Dadaist prank. Opening night finally did occur, and the events became firmly inscribed in French cultural history.

That infamous evening included a screening of the film *Entr'acte*. Shown between the two acts of *Relâche*, it was greeted with as much hissing and booing as it was with applause; the Dadaist philosophy, based in part on offending its audience, was once again triumphantly realized.

While *Relâche* remained mostly unknown until the Joffrey Ballet revived it in New York City during its 1980 season, *Entr'acte* has long since become a staple of film classes as an example of the French avant-garde cinema of the 1920s and as the prime exemplification of the Dada spirit in the film.

In his search for "pure" cinema, René Clair followed the Dadaist approaches of photomontage (as advocated by John Heartfield—a technique which involved "the meeting place of a thousand spaces"), and the random (as advocated by Tristan Tzara). True to those premises, Clair juxtaposed images and events as disparate as a chess game played by Marcel Duchamp and Man Ray, a cannon ignited by Erik Satie and Francis Picabia, a funeral where the coat of arms bearing the initials of Satie and Picabia was displayed, a ballerina, a sniper, inflatable balloon heads, the Luna Park rollercoaster, etc. These events were shot from a number of angles (including the ballerina from below through a plate of glass), and at varying speeds (from Satie and Picabia jumping toward the cannon in slow motion to the funeral procession racing off at the speed of the Keystone cops). While the images stressed the content as play, the director stressed the style as playfulness.

Through his film Clair invoked the entire catalogue of available cinematic technique, abandoned the notion of narrative causality, and in true Dadaist style, espoused the overthrow of the bourgoise norm. The audience was assulted with a series of non-related and often provocative images—from a "legless" man rising from his wagon and running away at full tilt to a ballerina transformed into a bearded man—within a work which stressed the pleasure of inventing new spatial and temporal relations while provoking random laughter. While Clair often referred to this film as "visual babblings," audiences of today can see the film as a serious attempt to subvert traditional values, both cinematic and social.

—Doug Tomlinson

EROICA. Production: Film Polski, ZAF "Kadr", and WFD (Warsaw); black and white, 35mm; running time: 87 mins.; length: 7787 feet. Released January 1958.

Produced by Stanisław Adler; screenplay by Jerzy Stefan Stawiński; from the collection of Stawiński's short stories, *Węgrzy* and *Ucieczka*; directed by Andrzej Munk; photography by Jerzy Wójcik; edited by Jadwiga Zajiczek and Mirosława Garlicka; sound by Bohdan Jankowski; art direction by Jan Grandys; music by Jan Krenz.

Filmed in Poland. Prize of the International Film Press, the "Fipresci," 1959.

Cast: *Scherzo alla polacca:* Edward Dziewoński (*Dzidziuś Górkiewicz*); Barbara Polomska (*Zosia Górkiewicz*); Ignacy Machowski (*Major Grzmet*); Leon Niemszyk (*Hungarian officer*); Kazimierz Opaliński (*Commander of Mokotów*); *Ostinato lugubre:* Kazimierz Rudzki (*Turek*); Henryk Bak (*Krygier*); Mariusz Dmochowski (*Korwin Makowski*); Roman Kłosowski (*Szpakowski*); Bogumił Kobiela (*Lieutenant Dabecki*); Józef Kostecki (*Zak*); Tadeusz Łomnicki (*Lieutenant Zawistowski*); Józef Nowak (*Kurzawa*); Wojciech Siemion (*Marianek*).

Publications:

Review—"Az úrakezdés öröme" by K. Gyula in *Filmkultura* (Budapest), July/August 1975; books—*Nouveaux cinéastes polonais* by Philippe Haudiquet, Premier Plan no.27, Lyon 1963; *Andrzej Munk*, collective work, Warsaw 1964; *The Most Important Art: East European Film After 1945* by Mira Liehm and Antonín Liehm, Berkeley 1977; *Cinema, The Magic Vehicle: A Guide to its Achievement: Journey Two* edited by Adam Garbicz and Jacek Klinowski, Metuchen, New Jersey 1979; *Historia filmu polskiego IV*, Warsaw 1981; articles—"Expérience du cinéma polonais", interview by P.-L. Thirard in *Les Lettres françaises* (Paris), no.790, 1959; "Andrzej Munk" by Georges Sadoul in *Les Lettres françaises* (Paris), no.894, 1961; "Andrzej Munk" issue of *Études cinématographiques* (Paris), no.45, 1965; "Andrzej Munk" by Luc Moullet in *Cahiers du cinéma* (Paris), February 1965; "Andrzej Munk (1921-1961)" by J. Cieslar in *Film a Doba* (Prague), October 1981.

*   *   *

Eroica, Andrzej Munk's third film, is based on the contemporary drama *Człowiek na torze*. As in his debut *Blekitny krzyz*, he returns again to World War II for subject matter. The film consists of two parts, both of which deal with the theme of heroism which in a certain historical situation becomes myth.

The initial episode, centered on the tragic Warsaw uprising of 1944, sounds a new note in Munk's artistic method as well as for Polish cinema. It is the presentation of an ironic, sarcastic anti-hero and his deeds, a view that is quite exceptional within the body of Polish film that treated either the uprising or the war in general. The protagonist is a Warsaw good-for-nothing who is calculating, and forever oscillating between cowardice and a utilitarian world view. Suddenly and against his will he becomes a hero. In drawing his character Munk does not obscure a single negative feature; in certain sections of the story Munk consistently emphasizes aspects of character and plot that lead the protagonist to greedy calculations of profit and loss. However, the hero is not a schematic one-dimensional character. At the moments when he sets aside his own principles to defend the uprising, Munk lends him a certain grandeur, which flows from the tragedy of the solitary deed that is ultimately useless and unnecessary. The director's ability to find elements of the comic and the grotesque even in tragic events has enabled him to catch some of the paradoxes of the Warsaw uprising. However, the film is not a satire, as has been charged by some Polish critics. Munk does not mock his hero but shows how the atmosphere of the time can influence a totally unheroic individual and impel him to act.

The second episode unfolds on a tragic plane. It takes place in a POW camp, where a significant moment in the joyless lives of the Polish officers occurs when the rumor that one of their comrades has managed to escape is heard. The story is false—the fugitive hides until his death inside the camp. Here Munk contemplates the meaning of an artificially sustained myth and, in this connection, examines and traces its influence on the entire camp. In this case, too, he is not demeaning the importance of the rumor; from the outset he even ascribes to it a certain power that should help the captives in their struggle for survival. Analysis of the mechanics of the story, however, gradually reveals its destructive nature, for it paralyzes activity and displaces courage and the will to act.

The structure of *Eroica* is loosely built according to the rules of musical composition using contrastive means. The tragi-comic hero of the first novella, who belongs nowhere and to nobody, is placed in the boundless space of a large city in ruins, among streets that no longer have names; the viewer does not learn where these streets lead, where they end or where they begin. The officers of the second novella, on the other hand, move within a strictly limited geometric space tightly compressed into a tense order accented by non-dynamic compositions. These images not only convey hopelessness but also show the sophistication of the enemy, who suppress their opponents through psychological stress. They understand quite well that the worst punishment for prisoners is having to live with each other.

One further note of interest: *Eroica* was supposed to have had three parts. The third section had a rather intricate and elusive story that unfolded in a mountain setting and involved a spurious nun. This novella, however, did not come up to the level of the first two, and Munk himself eliminated it from the film.

—Mrs. B. Urgosíkova

EROTIKON. Bonds That Chafe. Vers le bonheur. Production: Svensk Filmindustri; black and white, 35mm, silent; length: 5998 feet. Released 8 November 1920, Sweden.

Screenplay by Mauritz Stiller and Arthur Norden; from the play *A Kék Róka* by Ferenc Herczeg; directed by Mauritz Stiller; photography by Henrik Jaenzon; production design by Mauritz Stiller and Axel Esbensen; musical score which accompanies film by Kurt Atterburg.

Filmed in Sweden, theater scenes shot in Royal Opera House, Stockholm.

Cast: Tora Teje (*Irene Charpentier*); Lars Hanson (*Preben*); Karin Molander (*Marthe, the niece*); Anders de Wahl (*Prof. Leo Charpentier*); Wilhelm Bryde (*Baron Felix*); Elin Lagergren (*Irene's mother*); Torsten Hammaren (*Prof. Sedonius*); Stina Berg (*Servant*); Gucken Cederborg (*Cook*); Vilhelm Berntsson (*Butler*); Bell Hedqvist (*Friend of Baron Felix*); John Lindlof (*Friend of Preban's*); Greta Lindgren (*Model*); Carl Wallin (*Furrier*); Carina Ari and Martin Oscar (*Ballet dancers*).

Publications:

Books—*Den Svenska Filmens Drama: Sjöström och Stiller* by Bengt Idestam-Almquist, Stockholm 1938; *Scandinavian Film* by Forsyth Hardy, London 1951; *Swedish Cinema* by Rune Waldekranz, Stockholm 1959; *La Grande Aventure du Cinema Suédois* by Jean Béranger, Paris 1960; *Swedish Film* by Einar Lauritzen, New York 1962; *Swedish Cinema* by Peter Cowie, London 1966; *Anthologie du cinéma* Vol. III, Paris 1968; *Seastrom and Stiller in Hollywood* by Hans Pensel, New York 1969; *Mauritz Stiller och hans filmer* by Gösta Werner, Stockholm 1969; *Cinema, The Magic Vehicle: A Guide to its Achievement: Journey One, The Cinema Through 1949* edited by Jacek Klinowski and Adam Garbicz, Metuchen, New Jersey 1975; articles—"The Golden Age of Scandinavian Film" by M.C. Potamkin in *Cinema* (London), September 1930; "The Man Who Found Garbo" by Bengt Idestam-Almquist in *Films and Filming* (London), August 1956; "*Erotikon*" by R. Combs in *Monthly Film Bulletin* (London), November 1977.

*   *   *

By 1920 the artistic achievements of the Swedish cinema, under the inspired leadership of Victor Sjöström and Mauritz Stiller, were universally recognized. Most of these films reflected the life of rural Sweden. Stiller, a cultured man, decided to make a film set in a sophisticated urban milieu. His scriptwriter Arthur Norden brought to his attention Ferenc Herczeg's play *Der Blaufuchs*, which he and Norden adapted to their purpose, dropping any acknowledgement to the author. From its premiere at the Roda Kvarn Cinema in Stockholm on the 8th November 1920, its success was assured.

Stiller lavished attention on this film, building elaborate sets and commissioning a special exotic ballet for the theatre scenes which were shot in the Royal Opera House of Stockholm, with a host of society extras for an audience. The film reflected the fashionable life of the city and a modernity indicated by the inclusion of scenes with airplanes.

The story about a professor of entomology who is sustained in his work by his devoted niece while his neglected wife seeks consolation elsewhere, seemed more like the work of Noel Coward than Selma Lagerlöf, who contributed so much to the Swedish cinema. It was handled with the lightest of touches; the irony of the scene where the man who tries to reconcile the married pair becomes the wife's lover is reminiscent of Ernst Lubitsch. Stiller's stylish direction worked well with his talented players. Tore Teje's delightful portrayal of the wife was witty, wise and worldly. It was in striking contrast with the peasant role she had played the previous year in Sjöström's *Karin Ingmarsdotter*. Karin Molander's charming performance as the young niece was equally effective; Torsten Hammaren's caricature of a dry old stick was inspiring; and Lars Hanson and Anders de Wahl maintained the elegant style of the film.

Erotikon helped create a new genre of social comedy, and attracted considerable attention in the movie world. Jean Renoir admired it very much; Lubitsch mentioned it as one of the best films he had ever seen and it may well have influenced his work from *The Marriage Circle* onwards; Chaplin would have seen it during his European tour and the style of *A Woman of Paris* may have been influenced by it. On the other hand, while admiring its freshness of approach, the socially conscious critic Georges Sadoul regretted that the social satire had not gone further, "There is no satiric intention in *Erotikon*: the humor is gentle and pleasant, defensive rather than attacking....we are far from Beaumarchais or even Marivaux."

Stiller never made another film like *Erotikon*, which is curious for it represented his own outlook on life. His next great success was the monumental *Gösta Berling Saga* which introduced Greta

Garbo to the world. The delicacy and subtlety of the acting and the gentle observation of human foibles make *Erotikon* a film that transcends its time and fashion.

—Liam O'Leary

EL ESPIRITU DE LA COLMENA. Spirit of the Beehive. Eastmancolor, 35mm; running time: 98 mins.; length: 8785 feet. Released 1973.

Produced by Elias Querejeta; screenplay by Francisco J. Querejeta; from an idea by Victor Erice and Angel Fernandéz Santos; directed by Victor Erice; photography by Luis Cuadrado; edited by Pablo G. del Amo;; sound by Luis Rodriguez, sound effects by Luis Castro and Sire Castro; art direction by Adolfo Cofiño, set decoration by Ramon de Diego; music by Luis de Pablo; assistant director: José Ruiz Marcos.

Filmed in Spain.

Cast: Fernando Fernan Gomez (*Fernando*); Terésa Gimpera (*Teresa*); Ana Torrent (*Ana*); Isabel Telleria (*Isabel*); Lady Soldevilla (*Don Lucia*); Miguel Picazo (*Doctor*); José Villasante (*Frankenstein*); Juan Margallo (*Outlaw*).

Publications:

Reviews—"*The Spirit of the Beehive*" by J. Gillett in *Sight and Sound* (London), winter 1973-74; "*El Espiritu de la colmena*" in *Monthly Film Bulletin* (London), November 1974; "*The Spirit of the Beehive*" by Gordon Gow in *Films and Filming* (London), autumn 1974; "Grown Up Movies About Children" by Vincent Canby in *The New York Times*, 10 October 1976; "Der Geist des Bienenkorb" by W. Guenther in *Medium* (Frankfurt), December 1976; "Beeswax" by R. McGuinness in *The Thousand Eyes Magazine* (New York), October 1976; "A Spanish Haunt" by C. Michener in *Newsweek* (New York), 11 October 1976; "From Ineptitude to Incompetence" by John Simon in *New York*, 4 October 1976; "*L'esprit de la ruche*" by J. Chevalier in *Image et son* (Paris), March 1977; "*La Lumière et l'ombre*" by D. Dubroux in *Cahiers du cinéma* (Paris), March 1977; "La Couleur du rêve" by I. Jordan in *Positif* (Paris), February 1977; "*L'Esprit de la ruche*" by R. Prédal in *Jeune Cinéma* (Paris), March 1977; books—*A History of Film* by Jack C. Ellis, Englewood Cliffs, New Jersey 1979; articles—"Spain: Out of the Past" by R. Mortimore in *Sight and Sound* (London), autumn 1974; "Film in Spanje" by J. Rábago in *Skoop* (Wageningen' Netherlands), February 1974; "L'espirit de la ruche..." by A. Abet in *Cinéma 76* (Paris), December 1976; "*The Spirit of the Beehive*" by Dewitt Bodeen in *Films in Review* (New York), November 1976; "Mysteries of the Organism. Character consciousness and film form in *Kasper Hauser* and *Spirit of the Beehive*" by D. Benelli in *Movietone News* (Seattle), June 1977; "*El espiritu de la colmena*" by S. Rotker in *Cine al día* (Caracas, Venezuela), November 1977; "Ånden i bistaden" by A. Troelsen in *Kosmorama* (Copenhagen), winter 1977; "Duh panja" by Z. Vrdlovec in *Ekran* (Ljubljana, Yugoslavia), no.9-10, 1979; "*O espírito da colmeia*" by F. Duarte and J. Matos-Cruz in *Celulóide* (Rio Major, Portugal), May 1980.

*   *   *

In Spain at the time of its release, *El espíritu de la colmena* was a major popular and critical success because it was one of the new films since the end of the Spanish Civil War (1939) to accurately portray the oppressive atmosphere of the postwar Spain under the Caudillo, Francisco Franco. Today Spanish and other critics continue to hold the film in high regard not only because of this convincing portrait of one period of Spanish history, but also because of the director's unusual ability to mesh his cinematic style with the themes of the film and because of the outstanding performance by the lead child actress Ana Torrent.

El espíritu de la colmena is culturally significant in that it is one of the finest Spanish works of art to explore the psychological effects of the Spanish Civil War. In *El espíritu de la colmena*, the war has created an unbridgeable gulf between parents and children. After the war, the parents have retreated into private worlds—the father's obsession with understanding the ways of the bees, and the mother's persistent correspondence with a loved one, who may in fact be dead. The parents seldom communicate with their children; and, as a result, the young protagonist must seek to understand the mysteries of life and death as best she can. After seeing James Whale's *Frankenstein*, the impressionable and imaginative child dreams of meeting with Frankenstein's monster, an expression of her desire to understand and to communicate.

The film advocates no specific political position, and important political questions are deliberately left with no explicit answers: what exactly were the politics of the protagonist's father during the war, and what is the postwar political position; who is the fugitive, and why does he hide in the abandoned house? Such political ambiguity allowed Erice to avoid problems with Franco's censors.

Erice and his cinematographer successfully employ two notable stylistic devises to enhance the thematic thrust of the film. The many carefully composed, stationary-camera long shots reflect the slow-paced monotony of life in the village and contribute to the contemplative tone of the film. The skillfully lit faces seen in underlit interiors reflect the play of light and shadow in an unelectrified manor and suggest a child's metaphorical groping in darkness.

—Dennis West

ET... DIEU CRÉA LA FEMME. And... God Created Woman. And Woman...Was Created. Production: Iena-Films-U.C.I.L.-Cocinor; Eastmancolor, 35mm, Cinemascope; running time: 95 mins. Released 28 November 1956, Paris.

Produced by Raoul-J. Levy; screenplay by Roger Vadim and Raoul-J. Levy; directed by Roger Vadim; photography by Armand Thirard; edited by Victoria Mercanton; sound engineered by Pierre-Louis Calvet; production design by Jean Andre with Jean Forestier and Georges Petitot; music by Paul Misraki, directed by Marc Lanjean.

Filmed in St. Tropez.

Cast: Brigitte Bardot (*Juliette Hardy*); Curt Jergens (*Eric Carradine*); Jean-Louis Trintignant (*Michel Tardieu*); Christian Marquand (*Antoine Tardieu*); Georges Poujouly (*Christian Tardieu*); Jeanne Marken (*Mme. Morin*); Isabelle Corey (*Lucienne*); Jean Lefebvre (*René*); Philippe Grenier (*Perri*); Jacqueline Ventura (*Mme. Vigier-Lefranc*); Jean Tissier (*M. Vigier-Lefranc*); Jany Mourey (*Young Girl*); Mary Glory (*Mme. Tar-*

dieu); Jacques Giron (*Roger*); Paul Faivre (*M. Morin*); Leopoldo Frances (*Dancer*); Toscano (*René*).

Publications:

Script—"*Et...Dieu Créa la Femme*" (excerpts from screenplay) by Roger Vadim and Raoul-J. Levy in *Avant-Scène du cinéma* (Paris), 15 November 1962; reviews—by François Truffaut in *Arts* (Paris), November 1956; review by Jacques Rivette in *Cahiers du cinéma* (Paris), May 1957; review by Jean-Luc Godard in *Cahiers du cinéma* (Paris), July 1957; books—*Roger Vadim* by Michel Mardore in *Premier Plan* (Paris), October 1959; *The Brigitte Bardot Story* by George Carpozi, New York 1961; *Brigitte Bardot and the Lolita Syndrome* by Simone de Beauvoir, London 1961; *The Dreams and the Dreamers* by Hollis Alpert, New York 1962; *Nouvelle Vague* edited by Raymond Borde, Freddy Bauche, and Jean Curtelin in *Premier Plan* (Paris), 1962; *Roger Vadim* by Maurice Frydland, Editions Pierre Segher, Paris 1963; *French Cinema Since 1946: The Personal Style*, Vol. 2, by Roy Armes, New York 1966; *Films and Feelings* by Raymond Durgnat, Cambridge, Massachusetts 1973; *Bardot: Eternal Sex Goddess* by Peter Evans, New York 1973; *Memoirs of the Devil* by Roger Vadim, New York 1977; articles—"Qu'est-ce que la Nouvelle Vague?" by Noël Burch in *Film Quarterly* (Berkeley), winter 1959; "Ban on Vadim" by G. Billard in *Films and Filming* (London), November 1959; "Two Actors" in *Films and Filming* (London), October 1960; special edition on the *nouvelle vague* in *Cahiers du cinéma* (Paris), December 1962; "B.B." by Rayond Durgnat in *Films and Filming* (London), January 1963; "Jean-Louis Trintignant" by Molly Haskell in *Show* (Hollywood), 20 August 1970; "Conversation with Roger Vadim" in *Oui* (Chicago), October 1975; "*Et Dieu créa la femme*" in *Copie Zero* (Montreal), no.3, 1979.

*   *   *

Conventional accounts of the *nouvelle vague* commence with the *annus mirabilis* of 1959, when the new directors Truffaut, Camus and Resnais swept the Cannes Film Festival. But the true beginning took place three years earlier, when ex-*Paris Match* journalist Roger Vadim, then 28, released his debut feature *Et...Dieu créa la femme*. Its initial *succès de scandale* was reflected at the box office, and for the first time independent producers opened their purses to the frustrated generation of the new French filmmakers.

In 1952, Vadim had married 19-year-old Brigitte Bardot. After working as assistant to Marc Allegret, he felt confident enough to direct a vehicle for her sullen, bitchy beauty. Producer Raoul Levy helped raise funds via ex-band leader Ray Ventura. German actor Kurt Jurgens agreed to take a role and guarantee the obligatory international appeal. Jean-Louis Trintignant, then unknown, played opposite the provocative Bardot, and would soon have a well-publicized affair with her.

Vadim wrote the story, based on fact, of two fisherman brothers feuding over a girl in the remote town of St. Tropez. Bardot, nude, pouting, deceitful, embodied the popular public stereotype of dissident youth. Christian Marquand and Trintignant were the brothers, Jurgens the rich man fascinated by a woman he can't buy. Pursuing his theories about the dramatic and erotic impact of color, Vadim set the tanned Bardot against white—sand, linen—to spectacular effect. Her appearance sun-bathing behind sun-dried bed sheets, and later at her own wedding break-

fast, wrapped in a sheet, were spectacular proof of Vadim's skill.

Shrewdly shot in Eastmancolor and CinemaScope, *Et...Dieu créa la femme* sold speedily to international markets, its notoriety feeding Bardot's fame and announcing to audiences everywhere that a new spirit was stirring in French cinema. Vadim's career did not flourish, but Bardot's did: in creating a character who followed her instincts in her contempt for money and for the sensibility of others, Vadim produced an emblem for the "me decade."

Jeanne Moreau is unequivocal about the significance of *Et...Dieu créa la femme* and Bardot's potency as a symbol. "Brigitte was the real modern revolutionary character for women. And Vadim, as a man and a lover and a director, felt that. What was true in the New Wave is that suddenly what was important was vitality, eroticism, energy, love and passion. One has to remember it was Vadim who started everything, with Bardot."

—John Baxter

E.T.—THE EXTRATERRESTRIAL. Production: Universal Pictures; 1982; De Luxe color, 70mm, Dolby sound; running time: 115 mins. Released June 1982.

Produced by Steven Spielberg and Kathleen Kennedy, associate producer: Melissa Mathison, production supervisor: Frank Marshall; screenplay by Melissa Mathison; directed by Steven Spielberg; photography by Allen Daviau; edited by Carol Littlestone; production design by James D. Bissell; music by John Williams; special effects produced at Industrial Light and Magic, supervised by Dennis Muren; E.T. created by Carlo Rambaldi.

Cast: Dee Wallace (*Mary*); Henry Thomas (*Elliott*); Peter Coyote (*Keys*); Robert MacNaughton (*Michael*); Drew Barrymore (*Gertie*); K.C. Martel.

Publications:

Books — *Halliwell's Film Guide* edited by Leslie Halliwell, 4th edition, New York 1983; articles—"The Making of E.T." in *Cinefantastique* (Chicago), November/December 1982; "Sand Castles: An Interview with Steven Spielberg" by Todd McCarthy in *Film Comment* (New York), May/June 1982.

*   *   *

In itself, *E.T.* would hardly concern us: if not entirely negligible (it manifests certain skills, and contains a few memorable turns of dialogue, such as the question of how one explains "school" to a "higher intelligence"), it has no greater claim on the attention than countless other minor Hollywood movies. It does demand consideration as a cultural phenomenon: not merely the film itself and what it signifies, but the commercial hype, the American critics' reviews, the public response, the T-shirts, the children's games, the candy advertisements. It represents a moment in American cultural history. The film is distinguishable from the Disney live action movies it otherwise so closely resembles only by virtue of Steven Spielberg's evident commitment to his own infantile fantasy. Where the Disney films seemed more or less shrewd commercial exploitations of the child-audience, we have the sense here of a filmmaker infatuated with what he is doing. Just what difference that makes is open to argument: bourgeois society sets a high value on "sincerity," regardless of what the possessor of that virtue is being "sincere" about. Suffice it to comment that the precise *quality* of Spielberg's sincerity remains open to question. I am not convinced that it is entirely innocent and uncompromised.

E.T. belongs to the Reagan era as surely as the genuinely distinguished works of the period (the films of Martin Scorsese and Michael Cimino, or even of a minor figure like Brian De Palma) do not. It is an era profoundly inimical to serious art, especially within the field of popular culture. "Serious art" is, by definition, challenging and progressive; what is wanted now—after the upheavals of the 1970s, the era of Vietnam and Watergate, the era when every American institution was called into question and radical movements suddenly flourished—is reassurance, the restoration of the symbolic Father, preferably in a form that allows one simultaneously to believe and disbelieve.

The premise of *E.T.* is essentially the appearance of the "Other" within the bourgeois home. Roland Barthes suggests in *Mythologies* that bourgeois ideology has two ways of coping with Otherness: it either denies it, and if possible exterminates it, or converts it into a replica of itself. American civilisation was founded upon the denial/extermination of the Other (in form of the Indians); during the 1970s, the Other erupted in numerous forms—women, blacks, gays—demanding recognition. Now, in the Reagan era, Spielberg presents the Other in the shape of a lovable, totally innocuous little extra-terrestrial, who just wants to go home (to his own nuclear family?). The treatment of E.T. himself is shamelessly opportunistic for he becomes whatever is convenient to the development of the narrative from scene to scene: mental defective, higher intelligence, child figure, father figure.

The film is extremely sexist. Spielberg seems unable to conceive of women as anything but wives and, in particular, mothers. Apart from almost dying, the worst thing that happens to E.T. is being dressed in female clothes, an event which is shown to deprive him of his dignity. At the end of the film, as all purpose friend, Christ figure and patriarch, he lays his finger on Elliott's head to transmit to him his power and knowledge, but tells the boy's younger sister to "be good." (I have not yet found a woman who likes the film: the fantasy about childhood that it enacts is heavily male-orientated.)

Crucially, the cultural phenomenon presented in *E.T.* signifies a choice made by the critical establishment, the public and Motion Picture Academy, who nominated it for many Academy Awards even though they ultimately found in *Ghandhi* an even more respectable and archetypal liberal/bourgeois recipient of honors. One must compare *E.T.* with the commercial/critical failure of the infinitely more interesting *Blade Runner* (released the same week) and its troubling and complex presentation of the Other. The most pertinent comparison remains, however, with the two *It's Alive* films of Larry Cohen, which provide numerous suggestive parallels. Critically depised, they lack *E.T.'s* aura of expensiveness, an essential component of reassurance within the context of capitalism's decline.

—Robin Wood

ETOILE DE MER, L'. Star of the Sea. Black and white, 35mm, silent. Released 1928.

A poem by Robert Desnos, as seen by Man Ray; directed, photographed, and edited by May Ray; assisted by J.A. Boiffard. Filmed in France.

Cast: Alice (*Kiki*); André de la Rivière (*A man*); Prin (*A woman*); Robert Desnos (*Another man*).

Publications:

Books—*Works of Man Ray* by London Institute of Contemporary Arts with text by Man Ray, London 1959; *Painting, Photography, Film* by Laszlo Maholy-Nagy, translated by J. Seligman and Lund Humphries, Cambridge, Massachusetts 1969; *Man Ray* by Robert Penrose, Boston 1975; *Abstract Film and Beyond* by Malcolm Le Grice, Cambridge, Massachusetts 1977; *Visionary Film: The American Avant-Garde* by P. Adams Sitney, New York 1979; articles—"Film Poetry of Man Ray" by C.I. Belz in *Criticism* 7, spring 1965; "The Surrealist Film" by Tony Mussman in *Artforum* (New York), September 1966; "Man Ray" in *Etudes cinématographiques* (Paris), no.38-39, 1979; article in *Travelling* (Lausanne, Switzerland), summer 1979.

*   *   *

L'Etoile de mer, Man Ray's cinematic interpretation of a poem by Robert Desnos is the finest example of a canonical Surrealist film, just as the films of Dali and Buñuel represent the later, international phase of Surrealism at its pinnacle. Characteristically for surrealist art of the mid-twenties, the film depends heavily upon the language of its intertitles (which are probably all the lines of Desnos' otherwise lost poem), but its meaning depends upon the disjunctive combination of those words with images.

The organizing "image" of the whole film, that of the *vagina dentata*, has to be invoked by the initial juxtaposition of the poetic texts, "Women's teeth are such chaming objects/that they should be seen only in a dream or at the instant of love," with the filmic image of a woman lifting her dress. Like André Breton's surrealistic novella, *Nadja*, and like the poems of Desnos, *A la mysterieuse* (*To the Mysterious Woman*), the film describes a casual sexual encounter as a model for poetic experience. The main character of the film picks up a woman selling newspapers, but when she undresses for him in her room, he merely bids her "Adieu." He is a quester after imaginative rather than physical satisfaction, who fetishistically takes and examines in private the weight she used to kept her stack of newspapers from blowing away. It is a starfish, enclosed in a cylinder of glass.

Just as the interaction of texts and images make it apparent that the starfish brings to his mind associations of the *vagina dentata* (which simultaneously renders him impotent from fear and aroused with voyeuristic passion), Man Ray develops a montage that suggests that the entire experience of cinema is that a world viewed through the distorting glass lens. The most obvious way he achieves this is by alternating so-called normal shots with others shot through stippled lens. More subtly, there is a pun on "verre" (glass) and "vers" (poetry) which aligns the world of poetic images induced by the surrealistic distortion of langauge and the symbolical and often distorted images of the cinema.

L'Etoile de mer shares aesthetic and ideological affinities with *Anemic Cinema*. Man Ray had helped Duchamp and Allégret film the disks; Desnsos had written a book of puns and anagrams entitled *Rrose Selavy* in hommage to Duchamp. But the stress of *L'Etoile de mar* comes from the superiority of an imaginative, masturbational eros, over any "real" sexual encounter, while Duchamp's film had been ironical criticism of the limits of filmic represention.

—P. Adams Sitney

DER EWIGE JUDE. Production: Deutsche Film Gesellschaft; black and white, 35mm, documentary; running time: 78 mins., other versions include a 67-min. print; length: 1753 feet, other versions include a 1830-foot print. Released 4 November 1940 in Uraufführung, Germany.

Scenario by Eberhard Taubert; from an idea by Eberhard Taubert; directed by Fritz Hippler; photography by A. Endrejat, A. Hafner, A. Hartman, F.C. Heere, H. Kluth, E. Stoll, and H. Winterfield; edited by Hans Dieter Schiller and Albert Baumeister; music by Franz R. Friedl.

Filmed in Poland and Germany, with library footage from many sources, including the United States.

Publications:

Books—*Nationalsozialistische Filmpolitik: Eine Soziologische Untersuchung über die Spielfilme des Dritten Reichs* by G. Albrecht, Stuttgart, Germany 1969; *Film in the Third Reich* by David Stewart Hull, Berkeley 1969; *The Mythical World of Nazi War Propaganda* by J.W. Baird, Minneapolis 1974; *Nazi Cinema* by Erwin Leiser, New York 1974; *Propaganda and the German Cinema, 1933-1945* by David Welch, New York and London 1983; articles—"Goebbels' Principles of Propaganda" by L.W. Doob in *Public Opinion and Propaganda* edited by D. Katz, New York 1954; "Manipulation of the Masses Through the Nazi Film" by Hilmar Hoffmann in *Film Comment* (New York), fall 1965; article in *Filmstudio*, January 1966; "An Analysis of *Der Ewige Jude*: Its Relationship to Nazi Anti-Semitic Ideas and Policies" by G. Walker in *Wide Angle* (Athens, Ohio), no.4, 1980; "Nazi Wartime News-Reel Propaganda" by David Welch in *Film and Radio Propaganda* edited by K.R.M. Short, London 1983.

*   *   *

Fritz Hippler's *Der ewige Jude* was an exemplary moment in the history of Nazi cinema. A dutiful Nazi Party functionary, Hippler was unrestrained by considerations of objectivity, balance, or even the sensibilities of the less fanatical members of his audience. Indeed, his virulent anti-Semitic excesses so repelled some German audiences that in a few cities the film attracted "only the politically active" segments of the populace.

Artistically, the film is a "black masterpiece" of the cinematic conventions of 1940; a German version of *The March of Time* style that included animated maps, falsely labeled stock footage, segments of feature films borrowed to make some ideological point, stills, decoupages of evocative bookjackets and headlines, and an omniscient voice-over narration.

The importance of *Der ewige Jude* lies not in its technique but in its brutal service to the cause of Nazi racism. Hippler, after reading law and sociology at Heidelberg, entered the German Propaganda Ministry, specializing in military films such as *Westwall*, *Feldzug in Polen*, and *Sieg im Westen*. On orders from Joseph Goebbels himself, Hippler in 1940 began an anti-Semitic film that, according to its official synopsis, would "fill the spectator with a feeling of deep-seated gratification for belonging to a people whose leader has absolutely solved the Jewish problem." In fact, it has been asserted that *Der ewige Jude* helped prepare the German people to accept the eventual policy of genocide inflicted upon Jews.

The controlling metaphor—the Jew as parasite in an otherwise healthy host—is found throughout the film in several forms, all of them designed to reveal to Germans the "true" Jew underneath the veneer of European culture that concealed Jewish parasitism. Jews are introduced as a foreign, swarthy, hook-nosed, untidily bearded, sullen presence that clogs the teeming streets of middle Europe. They haggle, squabble over food at the table, hoard wealth, conceal it from tax collectors, and grow sleek and fat at the expense of good Germans. Their religion and culture are seen as cabalistic sources of secret powers.

Animated maps alive with pulsing, arterial tentacles extending outward from Palestine invoke a history of Jewish expansion into Europe. Even distant America offers no immunity from the spread of Jewish power. Stockshots of Wall Street and outtakes from the American movie, *The House of Rothschild*, throb with new meaning given them by the voice-over. The world seems in the thrall of a network of great Jewish banking houses whose interlocking pedigrees are traced in animated diagrams. Reinforcing the image of the Jew as international parasite, Hippler punctuates the film with cutaways to rats crawling out of sewers, plundering granaries, and scurrying pellmell through the streets of Europe. So compelling was the imagery, the government reported the collective relief expressed by audiences at the appearance of Hitler at the end, comforting the nation with the news that Nazi race laws had saved the day.

The Nazi period of Hippler's life ended with his capture by the British in 1944. He escaped prosecution as a criminal when Allied tribunals failed to convict other filmmakers, notably Veit Harlan. After a process of "de-Nazification" Hippler served the American Army as a translator. In later life, he lived apart from cinema circles, earning a living as a travel agent.

—Thomas Cripps

FANTASIA. Production: Walt Disney Productions; Technicolor, 35mm, animation, Fantasound; running time: 126 mins., British version cut to 105 mins., later versions cut to 81 mins.; length: originally 11,361 feet, cut to 9405 feet for British version. Released 13 November 1940 by RKO/Radio. Re-released every 5-7 years, beginning in 1946. Re-released in 1982 with soundtrack in digital audio.

Produced by Walt Disney. Stories developed by Lee Blair, Elmer Plummer, and Phil Dike ("Toccata and Fugue in D Minor" episode); Sylvia Moberly-Holland, Norman Wright, Albert Heath, Bianca Majolie, and Grahm Heid ("The Nutcracker Suite" segment); Perce Pearce and Carl Fallberg ("The

Sorcerer's Apprentice" segment); William Martin, Leo Thiele, Robert Sterner, and John Fraser McLeish ("The Rite of Spring" segment); Otto Englander, Webb Smith, Erdman Penner, Joseph Sabo, Bill Peet, and George Stallings ("Pastoral Symphony"); Martin Provensen, James Bodrero, Duke Russell, and Earl Hurd ("Dance of the Hours"); Campbell Grant, Arthur Heinemann, and Phil Dike ("Night on Bald Mountain/Ave Maria" segment). Story direction by Joe Grant and Ben Sharpsteen. Directed by Samuel Armstrong ("Toccata and Fugue in D Minor" and "The Nutcracker Suite" segments); James Algar ("The Sorcerer's Apprentice" segment); Bill Roberts and Paul Satterfield ("The Rite of Spring" segment); Hamilton Luske, Jim Hangley, and Ford Beebe ("Pastoral Symphony"); T. Hee and Norman Ferguson ("Dance of the Hours" segment); Wilfred Jackson ("Night on Bald Mountain/Ave Maria" segment). Animation directed by Samuel Armstrong ("Toccata and Fugue in D Minor" and "The Nutcracker Suite"); Bill Roberts ("The Rite of Spring"); James Algar ("The Sorcerer's Apprentice"); Hamilton Luske, Jim Handley, and Ford Beebe ("Pastoral Symphony"); T. Hee and Norman Ferguson ("Dance of the Hours"); and Wilfred Jackson ("Night on Bald Mountain/Ave Maria"). Musical film editor: Stephen Csillag; sound and music recorded by William E. Garity, C.O. Slyfield, and J.N.A. Hawkins, sound system, called Fantasound, designed especially for the film. Art direction by Robert Cormack ("Toccata and Fugue in D Minor" segment); Robert Cormack, Al Zinnen, Curtiss D. Perkins, Arthur Byram, and Bruce Bushman ("The Nutcracker Suite" segment); Tom Codrick, Charles Phillippi, and Zack Schwartz ("The Sorcerer's Apprentice" segment); McLaren Stewart, Dick Kelsey, and John Hubley ("The Rite of Spring" segment); Hugh Hennesy, Kenneth Anderson, J. Gordon Legg, Herbert Ryman, Yale Gracey, and Lance Nolley ("Pastoral Symphony" segment); Kendall O'Connor, Harold Doughty, and Ernest Nordli ("Dance of the Hours" segment); Kay Nielson, Terrell Stapp, Charles Payzant, and Thor Putnam ("Night on Bald Mountain/Ave Maria" segment). Music directed by Edward H. Plumb, music conducted by Leopold Stokowski, music conducted by Irwin Kostal for 1982 release; music selections include Bach's "Toccata and Fugue in D Minor"; Tchaikovsky's "The Nutcracker Suite"; Dukas' "The Sorcerer's Apprentice"; Stravinsky's "The Rite of Spring"; Beethoven's "Pastoral Symphony"; Ponchielli's "Dance of the Hours"; Mussorgsky's "Night on Bald Mountain"; and Schubert's "Ave Maria." Special animation effects by Joshua Meador, Miles E. Pike, John F. Reed, and Daniel Leonard Pickely; animation supervisers: Fred Moore and Vladamir Tytla ("The Sorcerer's Apprentice" segment); Wolfgang Reitherman and Joshua Meador ("The Rite of Spring"); Fred Moore, Ward Kimball, Eric Larsen, Arthur Babbitt, Oliver Johnson Jr., and Don Townsley ("Pastoral Symphony" segment); Norman Ferguson ("Dance of the Hours" segment); Vladamir Tytla ("Night on Bald Mountain/Ave Maria" segment); animators: Cy Young, Art Palmer, Daniel MacManus, George Rowley, Edwin Aardal, Joshua Meador, and Cornett Wood ("Toccata and Fugue in D Minor" segment); Arthur Babbitt, Les Clark, Don Lusk, Cy Young, and Robert Stokes ("The Nutcracker Suite" segment); Les Clark, Riley Thompson, Marvin Woodward, Preston Blair, Edward Love, Ugo D'Orsi, George Rowley, and Cornett Wood ("The Sorcerer's Apprentice" segment); B. Wolf, J. Campbell, J. Bradbury, J. Moore, M. Neil, B. Justice, J. Elliotte, W. Kelly, D. Lusk, L. Karp, M. McLennan, R. Youngquist, and H. Mamsel ("Pastoral Symphony" segment); J. Lounsbery, H. Swift, P. Blair, H. Fraser, H. Toombs, N. Tate, H. Lokey, A. Elliott, G. Simmons, R. Patterson, and F. Grundeen ("Dance of the Hours" segment); John McManus, W.N. Shull, Robert Carlson Jr., Lester Novros, and Don Patterson ("Night on Bald Moun-

tain/Ave Maria" segment).

Filmed in Walt Disney Studios. Cost: $2,280,000. New York Film Critics' Special Award, 1940; Academy Awards, Special Awards (certificates), to Walt Disney, William Garity, John N.A. Hawkins, and RCA for Contributions to the Advancement of Sound in Motion Pictures, 1941; Academy Award, Special Award (certificate), to Leopold Stokowski for his Achievement in the Creation of a New Form of Visualized Music, 1941; Irving G. Thalberg Award to Walt Disney by the Academy of Motion Picture Arts and Sciences, 1941.

Cast: Deems Taylor (*Narrative Introductions*).

Publications:

Reviews—"Once in a Lifetime: *Fantasia* is a Rare Treat" by P.T. Hartung in *Commonweal* (New York), 29 November 1940; review in the *New Republic* (New York), 25 November 1940; review in *Time* (New York), 18 November 1940; review in the *Nation* (New York), 23 November 1940; books—*Walt Disney's 'Fantasia'* by Deems Taylor, New York 1940; *The Art of Walt Disney* by Robert D. Field, New York 1942; *The Technique of Film Music* by Roger Manvell and J. Huntley, New York 1957; *Dictionnaire des cinéastes* by Georges Sadoul, Paris 1965; *Animation in the Cinema* by Ralph Stephenson, New York 1967; *The Great Films: 50 Golden Years of Motion Pictures* by Bosley Crowther, New York 1967; *The Disney Version: The Life, Times, Art and Commerce of Walt Disney* by Richard Schickel, New York 1968; *Walt Disney* by Maurice Bessy, Paris 1970; *The Art of Walt Disney, from Mickey Mouse to the Magic Kingdoms* by Christopher Finch, New York 1973; *The Disney Films* by Leonard Maltin, New York 1973; "Disney and Animation" in *Film and Reality* by Roy Armes, Baltimore 1974; *Walt Disney: An American Original* by Bob Thomas, New York 1976; *Full Length Animated Features* by Bruno Edera, edited by John Halas, New York 1977; *Walt Disney: A Guide to References and Resources* by Elizabeth Leebron and Lynn Gartley, Boston 1979; *Disney Animation: The Illusion of Life* by Frank Thomas and Ollie Johnston, New York 1982; articles—"Disney Again Tries Trailblazing" by S. Robins in the *New York Times Magazine*, 3 November 1940; "Disney's Cinesymphony: *Fantasia*" in *Time* (New York), 18 November 1940; "*Fantasia*: Walt Disney plus Bach or Beethoven" by F. Hoolering in the *Nation* (New York), 23 November 1940; "Both Fantasy and Fancy: Disney's *Fantasia*" by O. Ferguson in the *New Republic* (New York), 25 November 1940; "Class in Fantasia" by Robert Gessner in the *Nation* (New York), 30 November 1940; "Walt Disney, Genius at Work" by P. Hollister in *Atlantic* (Greenwich, Connecticut), December 1940; article in *Variety* (New York), 21 August 1940; "Mickey Mouse Goes Classical" by Andrew R. Boone in *Popular Science Monthly* (New York), January 1941; "*Fantasia*" by B.H. Haggin in the *Nation* (New York), 11 January 1941; "What Makes *Fantasia* Click?" by A.P. Peck in *Scientific American* (New York), January 1941; "New Horizons: *Fantasia* and Fantasound" by H.R. Isaacs in *Theatre Arts* (New York), January 1941; "Movie Cartoons Come to Life" by Ub Iwerks in *Popular Mechanics* (New York), January 1942; "Walt Disney" by Peter Ericsson in *Sequence* (London), no.10, 1950; "Animated Film Technique" (series of 9 articles) by Carl Fallberg in *American Cinematographer* (Hollywood), July 1958 issue through March 1959 issue; "*Fantasia*" by Jimmie Hicks in *Films in Review* (New York), November 1965; "Walt Disney's Psychedelic *Fantasia*" by W. Zinsser in *Life* (New York), 3 April 1970; special Disney issue of *Kosmorama* (Copenhagen), November 1973; "Art, Music, Nature and Walt Disney" by W. Paul in *Movie* (London), spring 1977; "Fischinger at Disney: Or, Oscar in the Mousetrap" by W. Moritz in *Millimeter* (New York), February 1977; "Disney Animation: History and Technique" by J. Canemaker in *Film News* (New York), January/February 1979; "Disney Design: 1928-1979;" by J. Canemaker in *Millimeter* (New York), February 1979; "Films: Nutcrackers" by J. Coleman in *New Statesman* (London), 30 march 1979; "*Fantasia*" by A. Stuart in *Films and Filming* (London), April 1979; "*Fantasia*" by J.M. Andrault in *Revue du cinéma* (Paris), November 1979; "*Fantasia*" by Howard H. Prouty in *Magill's Survey of Cinema, Vol. II* edited by Frank N. Magill, Englewood Cliffs, New Jersey 1980; "Lens Caps: Finding *Fantasia*" by S. Mallow in *Filmmakers Newsletter* (Ward Hill, Massachusetts), March 1980.

*   *   *

According to Deems Taylor, writing in 1940 (though the story was later denied by Disney sources), *Fantasia* first began as a comeback vehicle for Mickey Mouse after the Disney Studio had turned from modest cartoon production to large-scale animation features. Certainly Disney had used the Silly Symphony format to introduce additional cartoon figures—Pluto in 1930, the Three Pigs in 1933, and then Donald Duck in 1934, who went on to challenge Mickey's top billing. Also in 1934 Disney began work on *Snow White and the Seven Dwarfs*, a considerable gamble that came to be regarded as "Disney's Folly," but went on to turn a profit of $8 million in its first release in 1937-38 and earned a special Oscar from the Motion Picture Academy. *Pinocchio* followed the success of *Snow White*, introducing Jiminy Cricket as an ingenuous narrator. At this point, then, in 1938, Disney began thinking about a new role for Mickey.

Disney's solution, the story goes, was to make Mickey the lead figure of a special cartoon rendering of "The Sorcerer's Apprentice," a fairy tale that had been set to music by the French composer Paul Dukas. Needing musical advice, Disney broached the project to the conductor of the Philadelphia Orchestra, Leopold Stokowski, who was interested not only in the Dukas/Mickey idea but also in extending the project to an animated concert feature. Disney then began thinking in terms of "The Concert Feature" that was to become *Fantasia*. Whether the idea to expand was Disney's or Stokowski's has also been disputed.

At any rate, Deems Taylor, the radio voice of the Metropolitan Opera, was brought in to provide further advice and to handle the narrative transitions among the concert film's various "movements," involving eight different musical compositions. Disney presumably saw the project as a challenging experiment in animated technique rather than an opportunity to use animation merely as a means of popularizing classical music for the masses. In the Bach *Toccata and Fugue* portion, for example, Disney artists were encouraged to experiment visually and boldly, in ways never before imagined. This sequence, early in the film, signals its experimentalism, departing from the usual Disney style and moving in abstract directions, imitating the techniques of Oscar Fischinger, who was originally to direct that sequence but left the project before completing it, after discovering the studio had altered his original designs. Other experiments are elsewhere in evidence, as when the sound track is visualized through animation midway through the film, recalling the abstract experiments of Len Lye and anticipating those of Norman McLaren. More conventional Disney whimsy is elsewhere in evidence, however, and there is perhaps the danger of vulgarizing the music through the imposed visual patterns. In fact, the sequences are diverse and uneven.

The film has been criticized for its "ponderous didacticism" (the visualization of the "paleontological cataclysm" in the Stravinsky *Rite of Spring* sequence, for example, and the simplistic contrasts of the final sequences—Moussorgsky's *Night on Bald Mountain* against Shubert's *Ave Maria*, with Good triumphing over Evil in a finale of Christian tranquility) and praised for those sequences in which Disney contented himself with being Disney and avoided self-conscious attempts at being "artistic."

Fantasia came to Disney at a time when risks were being taken. After the demonstrated success of "Disney's Folly," animation began on *Fantasia* early in 1938. The production cost $2,280,000, including $400,000 for the music alone. Disney began thinking in terms of wide-screen production, multiplane Technicolor, and "Fantasound," representing a major technical innovation involving the use of stereophonic sound and employing a new four-track optical stereophonic system. The achievement of "Fantasound" was something of a compromise: according to Peter Finch, Disney "developed a sound system utilizing seven tracks and thirty speakers," but the system was "prohibitively expensive" and only installed in a few theatres. The score was recorded at the acoustically splendid Academy of Music in Philadelphia.

For the first time, moreover, Disney became his own distributor with *Fantasia*, since, as *Variety* reported, the film was so different as to require a different sales approach. It premiered on November 13, 1940, at the Broadway Theatre in New York, and was not an immediate success. Its original running time, with an intermission, was about 130 minutes, later cut to 81 minutes. It was reissued in 1946, but it would only build its audience strength over time. By 1968, for example, it had earned $4.8 million in North American markets, more than doubling its original investment, and finally taking its place among the top 200 grossing films.

In musical terminology, a *Fantasia* is "a free development of a given theme." The achievement, though often impressive and no doubt ahead of its time, has nonetheless had its detractors. Stravinsky was not pleased that his music had been restructured and that the instrumentation had been changed. "I will say nothing about the visual complement," Stravinsky remarked, "as I do not wish to criticize an unresisting imbecility...." The film succeeds the best when it is at its most playful—the hippopotamus ballerinas in the "Dance of the Hours" sequence, for example, which Richard Schickel has described as "a broad satirical comment on the absurdities of high culture." The visuals for Beethoven's *Pastorale* Symphony strain for contrived mythic charm in an Arcadian setting populated by fabulous creatures. Far more interesting are the animated dances from Tchaikovsky's *Nutcracker* and the whimsical treatment of Ponchielli's "Dance of the Hours," or Mickey's struggle with the dancing brooms in *The Sorcerer's Apprentice*, the conceptual core of the picture. John Tibbetts has written that the results of Mickey's "union with high art were questionable for some, just as Walt's collision with the likes of Stravinsky, Beethoven, and Moussorgsky raised (or lowered) many a brow."

Disney's undertaking *Fantasia* brings to mind an artisan who has only a superficial knowledge of religion undertaking to sculpt a monumental pieta out of sand as the tide moves in, threatening to erode it. Some passers-by will no doubt pause to watch out of curiosity, but the spectacle will not for most of them constitute a conversion. If anything, *Fantasia* does not teach a musical lesson, but it often fascinates and delights the eye.

Reviewing *Fantasia* in 1940, Otis Ferguson called it "a film for everybody to see and enjoy," despite its "main weakness—an absence of story, of motion, of interest." Bosley Crowther was less harsh, remarking that the images often tended to overwhelm the music, but praising the film for its "imaginative excursion" and concluding that it was a milestone in motion picture history. Despite its sometimes elaborate pretensions, its many innovations, the boldness of its concept quite overrides the "disturbing jumble" of its achievement. It is, indeed, a "milestone" in the history of animated film.

—James M. Welsh

FANTÔMAS; (first film in Fantômas series). Production: Gaumont; black and white, 35mm, silent; running time: 37 mins. at 16 frames per second, the speed at which it was filmed; length: 1007 meters. Released May 1913.

Scenario by Louis Feuillade; from the novel by Pierre Souvestre and Marcel Allain; directed by Louis Feuillade; photography by Guerin; edited by Guerin. Filmed in Paris.

Cast: Rene Navarre (*Dr. Chaleck, Fantômas*); Breon (*Inspector Juve*); Renee Carl (*Lady Beltham*); Jane Faber (*Princess Sonia Danidoff*); Georges Melchior (*Jérôme Fandor*); Naudier (*Nibet*).

* * *

JUVE CONTRE FANTÔMAS (second film in Fantômas series). Production: Gaumont; black and white, 35mm, silent; running time: 45 mins. at 24 frames per second at which speed it was filmed; length: 1227 meters. Released 1913.

Scenario by Louis Feuillade; from the novel by Pierre Souvestre and Marcel Allain; directed by Louis Feuillade; photography by Guerin; edited by Guerin. Filmed in Paris.

Cast: Rene Navarre (*Dr. Chaleck, Fantômas*); Breon (*Juve*); Melchior (*Fandor*); Renee Carl (*Lady Beltham*); Yvette Andreyor (*Joséphine*).

* * *

LE MORT QUI TUE (third in the Fantômas series). Production: Gaumont; black and white, 35mm, silent. Released 1913.

Scenario by Louis Feuillade; from the novel by Pierre Souvestre and Marcel Allain; directed by Louis Feuillade; photography by Guerin; edited by Guerin. Filmed 1913 in Paris.

Cast: Rene Navarre (*Banker Nanteuil, Fantômas*); Breon (*Juve*); Melchior (*Jérôme Fandor*); Andre Luguet (*Jacques Dollon*); Luitz Morat (*Thomery*); Naudier (*Nibet, the gardener*); Renee Carl (*Lady Beltham*); Jane Faber (*Princess Sonia*); F. Fabreges (*Elisabeth Dollon*).

* * *

FANTÔMAS CONTRE FANTÔMAS (fourth in the Fantômas series). Production: Gaumont; black and white, 35mm, silent. Released February 1914.

Scenario by Louis Feuillade; from the novel by Pierre Souvestre and Marcel Allain; directed by Louis Feuillade; photography by Guerin; edited by Guerin; music adaptation which accompanies screenings by Paul Fosse. Filmed in Paris.

Cast: Rene Navarre (*Father Moche, Tom, Bob, Black Man, Fantômas*); Breon (*Juve*); Melchior (*Fandor*); Naudier (*Nibet, the gardener*); Maury (*Chief of security*); Renee Carl (*Grand Duchess*).

* * *

LE FAUX MAGISTRAT (last in the Fantômas series). Production: Gaumont; black and white, 35mm, silent. Released April 1914 (some sources list July).

Scenario by Louis Feuillade; directed by Louis Feuillade; photography by Guerin (?); edited by Guerin (?). Filmed 1914 in Paris.

Cast: Rene Navarre (*False Magistrate, Fantômas*); Breon (*Juve*); Melchior (*Fandor*); Morlas (*Nestor, the young hooligan*); Martial (*Ribonard*); Mesnery (*Marquis of Tergall*); Melle Pelisse (*Marguise of Tergall*); Le Bret (*Rosa*).

Publications:

Scripts—for all 5 films in the Fantômas series in *Avant-Scène du cinéma* (Paris), 1 July 1981; books—*Cinéma et Compagnie* by Louis Delluc, Paris 1919; *Images du Cinéma français* by Nicole Védrès, Paris 1945; *Louis Feuillade* by Francis Lacassin, Paris 1964; *French Film* by Georges Sadoul, London 1953, reprinted 1972; *French Film* by Roy Armes, New York 1970; *Caligari's Cabinet and Other Grand Illusions: A History of Film Design* by Léon Barsacq, New York 1976; articles—"Louis Feuillade" by Claude Beylie in *Ecrans de France* (Paris), 15 May 1959; "Louis Feuillade" by Francis Lacassin in *Sight and Sound* (London), winter 1964/65; "Feuillade" in *Anthologie du Cinéma* vol.2, Paris 1967; "*Fantômas* de Paul Fejos by P. Guibbert in *Cahiers du cinéma* (Paris), winter 1974; "*Fantomas*" by F. Lacassin in *Ecran* (Paris), January 1975; "Guirlande pour *Fantômas*" by Michel Boujut in *Avant-Scène du cinéma* (Paris), 1 July 1981; "Louis Feuillade poète de la réalité" by Jacques Champreux in *Avant-Scène du cinéma* (Paris), 1 July 1981; "Le Comédiens de *Fantômas*" in *Avant-Scène du cinéma* (Paris), 1 July 1981; "De Feuillade à Chabrol: les avatars de Fantômas" by Claude Beylie in *Avant-Scène du cinéma* (Paris), 1 July 1981.

* * *

Although the credit for introducing the episodic tale of the master criminal into French cinema belongs to Victorian Jasset, whose *Zigomar* appeared in 1911, it is with Louis Feuillade's *Fantômas* that the form finds its initial culmination. *Fantômas* was produced at a period of deep crisis in French filmmaking, when the world dominance of Pathé and Gaumont was already crumbling. Feuillade, who had been head of the production at Gaumont since 1906, turned for the source of his work to the popular steam of feuilletonesque novels which Pierre Souvestre and Marcel Allain had begaun publishing in Paris a few years earlier. The organisation of the production of *Fantômas* gives fascinating insight to the difficulties of the French cinema at a period when it was about to receive the full impact of American competition.

Though *Fantômas* is often described as a serial and given showings as if it were a single, huge, continuous work, in fact it comprises five separate films of about an hour's length each. Indeed, Feuillade was unable to work in any concentrated way on the series, and the five films were individually released at irregular intervals over a period of some twelve months, between May 1913 and April 1914. Even though France had been the major film producing and distributing nation in the world since 1908, French production had not undergone an intense restructuring of the kind that Thomas Ince had pioneered in the United States, and the industry was unable to organise production sufficiently to handle a weekly or even monthly serial. Nor was the integration with the popular press achieved at this time: *Fantômas* did not benefit from the simultaneous publication of the story in the daily newspapers which was such a key feature of the success of the later serials in both France and the United States. The separation of management from production was not common in France at this period, and like most of his principal contemporaries, Feuillade combined the artistic role of leading director with that of administrator of the whole of the studio's output.

The first of the five part series, called simply *Fantômas*, introduces the master criminal, recounts some of his misdeeds and leads to his seduction of Lady Beltham and the murder of her husband. The climax comes when Fantômas, faced with imprisonment and execution, manages to exchange places with the hapless actor Valgrand, who is currently enjoying a popular success by impersonating Fantômas on stage. The subsequent episodes follows much the same pattern, and almost all of them contain one totally memorable situation: the gun battle among barrels on the quai de Bercy and the struggle with the boa constrictor in *Juve contre Fantômas*: the glove made from the dead mans hand in *Le Mort qui tue*: the tormenting of the now discredited Inspector Juve by Fantômas, master of many disguises, in *Fantômas contre Fantômas*: the rain of blood and pearls from a church tower in *Le Faux Magistrat*.

Fantômas was made within the mainstream of French commercial production by a director unconcerned with questions of art, working within the customary constraints of Gaumont's budgets with a well-tried team of actors. Nothing could be less subversively intended, but with its intertwined worlds of police and criminals, its susceptible aristocratic ladies, corrupt bankers and phony magistrates, *Fantômas* can easily be read as an ararchistic celebration of revolt. Certainly it was the film's derisory picture of the bourgeois world and its reversal of normal logic and order that endeared the film series to the group of young poets and artists grouped around the surrealists. Their praise—echoed later by such film makers as Franju and Resnais—has given the solidly bourgeois Feuillade his paradoxical fame.

—Roy Armes

FARREBIQUE. Production: L'Ecran Française and Les Films Etienne Lallier; black and white, 35mm; running time: 100 mins., some versions are 85 mins. Released 11 February 1947.

Produced by Jacques Girard; screenplay by Georges Rouquier; from an idea by C. Blanchard; directed by Georges Rouquier; photography by André Danton; edited by Madeleine Gug; sound by Lecuyer; music by Henri Sauguet, conducted by Roger Desormieres; special effects by Jean Painleve, Daniel Senade, and Jean-Jacques Rebuffet.

Filmed from about 1944 to 1946 on location at the farm Farrebique.

Cast: The Owners of the farm of Farrebique and some of their neighbors as themselves.

Publications:

Script—*Rouquier: Album de Farrebique*, Paris, Editions Fortuny 1947; reviews—in *Cinéma Français* (Paris), 15 February 1947; review in *Sight and Sound* (London), winter 1946-47; review in *Review du cinéma* (Paris), January 1947; review in *Monthly Film Bulletin* (London), 30 April 1948; books—*Documentary: A History of Non-Fiction Film* by Erik Barnouw, New York 1974; *French Film Since 1946: The Great Tradition*, Vol. 1, by Roy Armes, New York 1976; articles—"New Picture" in *Time* (New York), 15 March 1948; "New Acquisitions: *Le Tempestaire* and *Farrebique* by Eileen Bowser in *Museum of Modern Art* film notes, (New York), 2 and 4 April 1978; "An Innocent Eye? The Career and Documentary Vision of Georges Rouquier" by J.H. Weiss in *Cinema Journal* (Evanston), spring 1981.

*   *   *

The roots of the style which George Rouquier brought to full maturity with his first feature-length film, *Farrebique*, released in 1946, lie in a number of short documentary studies of rural crafts, such as *Le Tonnelier* and *Le Charron*, which the director had made during the Occupation years. In the immediate postwar years *Farrebique's* picture of French farming life was hailed as a break with the past, its deeply felt concern to present realist detail being constrasted with the escapist fantasy that was felt to characterise the cinema of the Pétain years. Certainly this aspect of the film remains impressive. The everyday activity of the farming family is precisely observed—the breadmaking, ploughing and harvesting, evening prayers and trips to church or bistro—and forms the context for the film's fictionalised sequence of events. They include the grandfather's account of the family history, his death and the birth of a baby, the younger son's injury and engagement, and they are staged in a slightly clumsy fashion which is in perfect keeping with the film's strategy of presenting its story as a "real" document. The understatement of joys and sorrows and the unemphatic playing reinforce this tone. But the film as a whole does not have any of the coldness or objectivity that such a stance might lead one to expect, for these family events are not presented neutrally but are fitted into what can be aptly characterised as a pageant of the seasons. The director views nature with true poetic intensity, stressing always its dynamic aspect, particularly in the long lyrical passage celebrating the coming of the spring. This vision allows the film to remain optimistic and affirmative despite the inclusion of such events as the grandfather's death, which can be seen as part of a rhythm of change and development. Though moving in itself, this death is merely part of the process of seasonal renewal and can be supplanted by the son's engagement and the promise of spring.

In the mid and late 1940's *Farrebique* was generally seen as belonging alongside René Clément's documentary drama of the railway workers' efforts at the resistance to their German occupiers as an example of the postwar French realism which failed to develop on the lines of that emerging during these years in Italy. Comparisons with Italian neo-realism are fruitful, for it is immediately apparent that Rouquier has not attempted to integrate rural life into a wider social framework. In *Farrebique* virtually the only contact with the outside world is the installation of electricity and even this is treated as a comparatively minor incident and icorporated in the film's conception of change as part of a natural rhythm. Certainly Rouquier offers none of the social analysis which characterises Luchino Visconti's *La terra trema*, a study of an equally isolated fishing community made some two years later. But while such an approach to *Farrebique* has great relevance and considerable value, relating closely to André Bazin's 1940's advocacy of realist styles, it can be seen in retrospect as somewhat limited. Bazin's formulation of the problematics of realism leaves out of the account any consideration of political issues. Yet from today's perspective one of the most fascinating aspects of *Farrebique* is the way it questions the neat separation of Occupation years from the postwar renewal that underpins so many accounts of France in the 1940's. Planned during the Occupation years, *Farrebique* reflects the all-persuasive influence of the Pétainist ideology of "work, family and fatherland" at least as strongly as it affirms a new postwar realist approach. Far from lessening the value and significance of *Farrebique*, this essential ambiguity makes it a key document for a re-examination of French culture that looks beneath the comfortable myths of Occupation and Resistance.

—Roy Armes

LA FEMME DU BOULANGER. The Baker's Wife. Production: Les Films Marcel Pagnol; black and white, 35mm; running time: 120 mins., some sources list 110 mins. Released 1938.

Screenplay by Marcel Pagnol; from *Jean le Bleu* by Jean Giono; directed by Marcel Pagnol; photography by G. Benoît, R. Lendruz, and N. Daries; edited by Suzanne de Troye, Marguerite Houllé, and Suzanne Cabon; music by Vincent Scotto.

Cast: Raimu (*Aimable Castenet*); Ginette Leclerc (*Aurélie Castenet*); Charpin (*M. de Monelles*); Robert Vattier (*Priest*); Bassac (*Teacher*); Charles Moulin (*Dominique*); Delmont (*Mailleterre*); Alida Rouffe (*Marie*); Maximilliene (*Angèle*); Maupi, Dullac, Blavette, Odette Roger, Castan, Maffre, and Charblay.

Publications:

Books—*French Film* by Roy Armes, New York 1970; *Marcel Pagnol* by P. Domeyne, Paris 1971; *Marcel Pagnol* by Claude Beylie, Paris 1972; *French Film* by Georges Sadoul, London 1953, revised 1972; *Marcel Pagnol m'a raconté...* by Raymond Castans, Paris 1975; *Marcel Pagnol* by Pierre Leprohon, Paris 1976; *Il etait une fois Marcel Pagnol* by R. Castans, Paris 1978; articles—"Adieu à Raimu" in *L'Ecran française* (Paris), 3 October 1951; "Marcel Pagnol" in *Current Biography Yearbook 1956*, New York 1957; "Souvenirs sur Raimu" in *Le Figaro Littéraire* (Paris), 7 September 1963; "Spécial Guitry-Pagnol" issue of *Cahiers du cinéma* (Paris), 1 December 1965; "L'adieu de Marcel Pagnol à Raimu" in *Avant-Scène du cinéma* (Paris), July/September 1970; "Marcel Pagnol" by Charles Ford in *Films in Review* (New York), April 1970; "Marcel Pagnol: Un Cinéaste mineur?" by F. Gévaudan in *Cinéma* (Paris), June 1974.

* * *

La Femme du boulanger is a work which can stand as a summation of Marcel Pagnol's work in the cinema and of a certain style of 1930s cinema. It was a period in which the star and his or her attendant dialogue writer reigned supreme in French cinema. Despite the film's title, the sultry Ginette Leclerc has only a small role as the errant wife, but in compensation we are given Raimu at the height of his powers in a part shaped by Pagnol so as to give the maximun relief and humanity to the figure of a village baker deceived by his faithless wife, who runs off with a stranger. The plot could hardly be simpler: the husband now refuses to bake bread, the villagers have to join forces to "engineer" the wayward wife's return and acceptance by the baker.

In terms of Marcel Pagnol's own work, *La Femme du boulanger*, though it holds together remarkably well, is in many ways a hybrid work, combining two divergent tendencies. The source of the film lies in a novel by Jean Giono, who had earlier provided the stimulas for the rural epics of *Angèle* and *Regain*. Once more the film breathes an authentic country atmosphere, with its open air meetings and sense of real village community. But here the epic qualities of Giono's vision are scaled down, and the village, though remote, is a microcosm of the city, with its social stratifictions and religious differences. The performance of Raimu forcibly calls to mind the atmosphere of Pagnol's marvellous Marseilles trilogy—*Marius*, *Fanny* and *César*—which the director and the star had completed just two years previously. This trilogy had its roots in Pagnol's writing for the stage, and it was essentially a studio work, in which the atmosphere of the Mediterranean port was summoned up through vivid dialogue and accent. Raimu's role in *La Femme du boulanger* has the same verbal richness. These are speeches written to be performed—as in the theatre—and since Raimu was unhappy acting in the open air, many of them were restaged in the studio, giving the film its sometimes awkward combination of location and studio work. As always, the themes of Pagnol's work are simple, bordering on the melodramatic, but they are captured in dialogue of such verbal felicity and shaped so cunningly as drama that they hold the attention effortlessly, especially when—as here—they are set against a vividly drawn background.

The controversy which surrounded Marcel Pagnol's work in the late 1930s, the result of his enthusiastic welcoming of sound cinema as no more than a perfected means of recording and distributing theatrical works, has now subsided. His own work proved richer than the polemical positions which he adopted at the time. Despite his advocacy of the studio, he was in fact one of the first to record sound on location and take his players into the countryside around Marseilles. Formerly regarded as a marginal provincial figure, cut off from the mainstream of Parisian cinema, Pagnol was in fact consistently able to produce two or three films a year: That made him a major figure at a time when the major production companies had long since vanished and most films were made by ephemeral companies set to organise just a single production. Owning his own production and distribution companies, his own laboratories and cinemas, Pagnol created his films *en famille* in a uniquely personal atmosphere. *La Femme du boulanger*, his last film of the 1930s, conveys perfectly the strengths of this spontaneous, uninhibited approach to production.

—Roy Armes

LA FEMME INFIDÈLE. The Unfaithful Wife. Production: Les Films La Boétie and Cinégay; Eastmancolor (print by DeLuxe), 35mm; running time: 105 mins., English version: 98 mins.; length: 2900 meters. Released January 1969, Paris.

Produced by André Génovès and Georges Casati; screenplay by Claude Chabrol; directed by Claude Chabrol; photography by Jean Rabier; edited by Jacques Gaillard; sound by Guy Chichignoud; art direction by Guy Littaye, set decoration by Raoul Guiraud; music by Pierre Jansen, music conducted by André Girard and Dominique Zardi; costumes designed by Maurice Albray.

Filmed 1968 in and around Paris.

Cast: Stéphane Audran (*Hélène Desvallées*); Michel Bouquet (*Charles Desvallées*); Maurice Ronet (*Victor Pegala*); Serge Bento (*Bignon*); Michel Duchaussoy (*Police officer*); Guy Marly (*Police Officer Gobert*); Stéphane Di Napoli (*Michel Desvallées*); Louise Chevalier (*Maid*); Louise Rioton (*Mother-in-Law*); Henri Mateau (*Paul*); François Moro-Giafferi (*Frédérdic*); Dominique Zardi (*Truck driver*); Michel Charrel (*Policeman*); Henri Attal (*Man in cafe*); Jean-Marie Arnoux (*False witness*); Donatella Turri (*Brigitte*).

Publications:

Script—"*La Femme Infidele*" by Claude Chabrol in *Avant-Scène du cinéma* (Paris), May 1969; reviews—by Gavin Millar in *Sight and Sound* (London), autumn 1969; review by Andrew Sarris in *The Village Voice* (New York), 13 November 1969; review by Gordon Gow in *Films and Filming* (London), October 1969; review by Jean-Louis Comolli in *Cahiers du cinéma* (Paris), February 1969; books—*Claude Chabrol* by Robin Wood and Michael Walker, New York 1970; *Claude Chabrol* by Guy Braucourt, Paris 1971; *Directors and Directions* by John Taylor, New York 1975; *Reihe Film 5: Claude Chabrol*, [Carl Hanser] 1975; *French Cinema Since 1946: The Personal Style*, Vol. 2, by Roy Armes, New York 1976; *The New Wave* by James Monaco, New York 1976; articles—"Chabrol Rides the Waves" by Langdon Dewey in *Film* (London), summer 1969; special Chabrol issue of *Avant-scène du cinéma* (Paris), May 1969; "Claude Chabrol" by Brian Baxter in *Film* (London), spring 1969; "An Interview with Claude Chabrol" in *Take One* (Montreal), September/October 1970; "Chabrol's Schizophrenic Spider" by Tom Milne in *Sight and Sound* (London), spring 1970; "Claude Chabrol" by D. Allen in *Screen* (London), February 1970; "This Man Must Commit Murder" by Roger Ebert in

The New York Times Biography Edition, 29 November 1970; article by Margot Kernan in *Film Quarterly* (Berkeley), summer 1970; article by Robin Wood in *Movie* (London), winter 1969-70; "The Films of Chabrol—A Priest among Clowns" by Molly Haskell in *The Village Voice* (New York), 12 November 1970; interview with Chabrol by G. Legrand, M. Ciment, and J. Torok in *Movie* (London), winter 1970-71; "Conversation with Claude Chabrol" by R. Nogueira and N. Zalaffi in *Sight and Sound* (London), winter 1970-71; "*Une Femme infidele*" by P. Harcourt in *Film Comment* (New York), November/December 1976; "Middle Chabrol" by P. Harcourt in *Film Comment* (New York), November/December 1976.

*   *   *

Claude Chabrol's *La Femme infidèle* is perhaps the director's most characteristic film: an extraordinarily spare thriller emphasizing the subtle psychologies of its few major characters. Although the film presents Chabrol's typical triangle—Charles and his wife, Hélène, who has taken a lover—the members of the triangle never all come together; and the film is organized very formally: one scene between Hélène and her lover, one scene between Charles and her lover, and many scenes between Hélène and Charles. The film is almost completely subtext: although the film's primary subject is the relationship between Charles and Hélène (and the sociopolitical implications of its failings), not one word ever passes between Charles and Hélène about her love affair or the problems in their marriage.

The indirectness of the film seems apposite, since Chabrol indicates that the violence which erupts so suddenly in the film is repressed beneath the apparently civilized surface of bourgeois society. Chabrol emphasizes those surfaces: the beautiful greens of the couple's landscaped garden, the shine on the silverware, the bouquets of flowers, the outside and informal family grouping which is masked by cheery blue canopy. True to his manner, Chabrol entirely eschews sentiment, and yet—although apparently cold and distant—condemns no one. Neither Hélène nor Charles are completely responsible for her affair and the act of violence it precipitates serves to rekindle the couple's passions for each other, as each suddenly sees the other in a new light. By the end of the film, Hélène is all too willing to cover up her husband's crime and lovingly accept the kind of tranference of guilt typical of the Hitchcock films Chabrol so obviously admires.

There are very few emotional outbursts or expressions of feeling in the film: the murder of Hélène's lover, which comes unexpectedly; three choked sobs that Hélène gives when she discovers her lover has been killed; and one truly heartfelt repressed as the natural instincts of the characters, is displaced instead onto the decor: indeed, there are flashes of red throughout—Hélène's earrings, a bedroom wall, a beauty shop awning, a bright dress, a lampshade, a cabinet, and so forth. As usual for Chabrol, objects are consistently used as symbols: a white, aloof statue that Charles tries to cleanse of red blood and which stands, perhaps, for Hélène; a huge cigarette lighter, which represents the passion Hélène has transferred from her husband to her lover; and the jigsaw puzzle, put together by the couple's son, which seems clearly to represent their marriage and/or the narrative.

The cinematography by Jean Rabier and the score by Pierre Jansen are impeccable and provoctive. So too are the performances, especially by Chabrol's wife, Stéphane Audran, as Hélène (note the cool expressiveness of her beauty as she descends the stairs at the end of the film), and Michel Bouquet as

Charles. A small but perfect film, *La Femme infidèle* represents only one variation on the theme in a series of films directed by Chabrol in the late 1960s and 1970s in collaboration with Audran, Rabier, and Jansen.

—Charles Derry

FEU MATHIAS PASCAL. The Late Matthew Pascal. Production: Cinégraphic Albatross/ Films L'Herbier; black and white, 35mm, silent; running time: English version is 192 mins.; length: 4617 feet.

Produced by Alexandre Kamenka; screenplay by Marcel L'Herbier; from the novel *Il fu Mattia Pascal* by Luigi Pirandello; directed by Marcel L'Herbier; photography by René Guichard, Jean Letort, Bourgassof, and Berliet; art direction by Alberto Cavalcanti and Lazare Meerson.

Filmed in Paris.

Cast: Ivan Mosjoukine (*Mathias Pascal*); Marthe Belot (*Maria Pascal, Mathias's mother*); Pauline Carton (*Scolastique Pascal, Mathias's aunt*); Michel Simon (*Jérôme Pomino*); Marcelle Pradot (*Romilde Pescatore*); M. Barsac (*Mariana Dondi Pescatore*); Isaure Douvane (*Batta Maldagna*); Georges Terof (*Gambler*); Lois Moran (*Adrienne Paleari*); Philippe Hériat (*Anselmo Paleari*); Irma Perrot (*Saldia Caporale*); Jean Hervé (*Térence Papiano*); Pierre Batcheff (*Scipion Papiano*).

Publications:

Review—in *Theatre Arts* (New York), April 1927; books—*Cavalcanti* by Wolfgang Klaue and others, Berlin 1952; *French Film* by Roy Armes, New York 1970; *French Film* by Georges Sadoul, London 1953, revised 1972; *Caligari's Cabinet and Other Grand Illusions: A History of Film Design* by Léon Barsacq, New York 1976; articles—"Ivan Mosjoukine" by Liam O'Leary in *Silent Picture* (London), summer 1969; "The Camera as Snowball: France 1918-1927" by R.H. Blumer in *Cinema Journal* (Evanston), spring 1970; "Marcel L'Herbier" (Edition Seghers) by Noël Burch in *Cinéma d'aujourd'hui* (Paris), 1973; article in *Ecran* (Paris), January 1976; article in *Monthly Film Bulletin* (London), February 1976; issue on L'Herbier of *Avant-Scène du cinéma* (Paris), 1 June 1978; "Marcel L'Herbier" by J. Fieschi in *Cinématographe* (Paris), December 1979.

*   *   *

Marcel L'Herbier's *Feu Mathias Pascal* is a key work of French cinema of the 1920's, valuable both for its intrinsic merits and its representative qualities. It was a period of some uncertainty in the French film industry, but the very lack of any organised studio structure on the lines similar to those which had emerged in Hollywood offered film makers a rare degree of freedom. This freedom was exploited to the full by film makers such as L'Herbier, Abel Gance and Jean Epstein, all of whom produced highly personal works the experimental and innovative visual style of which continues to astonish even today.

Feu Mathias Pascal was made in conditions that the director has described as completely ideal, produced by his own Cinégraphic company in collaboration with the Société Albatros, founded three years before by the Russian émigré producer, Alexandre Kamenka. The highly talented group around Kamenka had considerable influence on the work of French-born filmmakers, and for this film L'Herbier had the advantage of the collaboration of two of the most gifted of the exiles: his star, the great silent actor Ivan Mosjoukine, and his designer, Lazare Meerson, who had arrived in Paris just one year before and was to have a crucial shaping impact on the development of French cinema over the next dozen years through his work with Clair and Feyder. The choice of subject matter points to the literary origins of film makers of this generation. Like Gance and Clair, L'Herbier had envisaged a career as a writer before turning to the cinema under the influence of the American films which began to be widely shown in France after World War I. *Feu Mathias Pascal* was the first work by Luigi Pirandello to be adapted for the screen, and it is clear from later accounts that the author's literary prestige was one of the motivating impulses behind L'Herbier's decision to undertake a production which was never likely to be more than a *succès d'estime*.

In terms of L'Herbier's own artistic development, *Feu Mathias Pascal* is remakable for its unity and balance. The director was attracted by the challenge of creating a complex narrative structure, and for once the story is not simply a pretext for that play with the whole panoply of visual effects—superimpositions, masking, dream sequences and so on—so beloved of French film makers of the period. L'Herbier has not pushed his film towards psychological realism, however; he was evidently fascinated, rather, by the fantastic aspects of his picaresque hero's adventures. Mosjoukine's masterly performance and magnetic personality hold the film together, and the shifts and changes of Mathias's life offer full scope for his virtuoso talents. In other ways—in the mixture of studio work and location shooting and the resultant combination of play with shadows and at times almost documentary style realism—the film shows characteristic eclecticism of the kind which had reached its extreme point in L'Herbier's previous film, *L'Inhumaine*.

The qualities of the story and performance made *Feu Mathias Pascal* one of L'Herbier's most accessible works and gave it its high reputation among traditional historians. Ironically it is precisely these factors that have to some extent worked against the film in current critical evaluations. The pioneering studies by Noël Burch, which have done so much to re-establish the director's status as a major silent film maker, prize L'Herbier's work for the alternative he offers, in a film like *L'Argent*, to the dominant codes of Hollywood cinema, while *Feu Mathias Pascal* is in this sense one of the director's more conventional pieces of film narrative.

—Roy Armes

FILM D'AMORE E D'ANARCHIA. Film d'amore e d'anarchia, ovvero Stamattina alle 10 in via dei fiori nella nota casa di tolleranza.... Film of Love and Anarchy, or This Morning at 10 in the Via dei Fiori at the Well-Known House of Tolerance. Love and Anarchy. Production: Europ International (Italy); Technicolor, 35mm; running time: 108 mins., some versions are 125 mins. Released 1973.

Produced by Romano Cardarelli; screenplay and direction by

Lina Wertmüller; photography by Giuseppe Rotunno; edited by Franco Fraticelli; sound by Mario Bramonti; production design by Enrico Job; music by Carlo Savina, songs by Nino Rota; costumes designed by Enrico Job.

Filmed in Italy. Cannes Film Festival, Best Actor (Giannini), 1973.

Cast: Giancarlo Giannini (*Tunin*); Mariangela Melato (*Salomé*); Lina Polito (*Tripolina*); Eros Pagni (*Spatoletti*); Pina Cei (*Madame Aida*); Elena Fiore (*Donna Carmela*); Isa Bellini; Giuliana Calandra; Isa Danieli; Anna Bonaiuto; Mario Scaccia.

Publications:

Script—*The Screenplays of Lina Wertmüller*, translated by Steven Wagner, introduction by John Simon, New York 1977; reviews—"*Film d'amour et d'anarchie*" by J. Delmas in *Jeune Cinéma* (Paris), July/August 1973; "*Film o milości i anarchii*" by J. Fuksiewicz in *Kino* (Warsaw), February 1974; "*Love and Anarchy*" by L. Rubinstein in *Cineaste* (New York), no.3, 1974; articles—"*Love and Anarchy*: Passion and Pity" by Patricia Erens in *Jump Cut* (Chicago), July/August 1974; "Love, Anarchy, and the Whole Damned Thing" by W. Van Wert in *Jump Cut* (Chicago), November/December 1974; "*Love and Anarchy*" by C. Gorbman in *Movietone News* (Seattle), April 1975; article by Diane Jacobs in *Film Comment* (New York), March/April 1976; "5 Directors: Lina Wertmüller" by Diane Jacobs in *International Film Guide* (London), 1977.

*   *   *

Film d'amore e d'anarchia is Lina Wertmüller's fourth feature and the first work to bring her critical attention in the United States. The film reveals the influence of Federico Fellini for whom Wertmüller worked as an assistant director on *8 1/2*, and it incorporates most of the elements that were to become trademarks of the Wertmüller canon. From Fellini she inherited a tendency towards comic exaggeration, both in creating type and in producing broad performances. Typical to her own concerns are the thematic interest in sexual politics, frequently set against a political backdrop; commanding heroines; and flawed, vulnerable heroes.

D'amore e d'anarchia is framed by two scenes: the first depicts the childhood trauma of the peasant Tunin (Giancarlo Giannini). When Tunin's father, a rural anarchist, is shot by the police, the young boy assumes his father's mission to assassinate Mussolini. The second framing scene is his death in a Roman prison some decades later. The remainder of the film takes place in a Roman bordello where the adult Tunin meets Salome (Mariangela Melato), an anarchist sympathizer, and Tripolino (Lina Polito), a young prostitute.

As protector and lover, Salome provides Tunin with information that she extracts from a self-important client, Spatoletti, the head of Mussolini's secret police. Yet, gradually, Tunin falls in love with Tripolino. The climax of the film takes place on the day appointed for Mussolini's assassination. Tripolino hides the key to Tunin's bedroom: she hopes that by allowing him to oversleep, she will prevent both the deed and its punishment. She and Salome fight over the "key" to Tunin's fate: a struggle between love and anarchy. Finally Tripolino succeeds in convincing Salome that she should opt for personal happiness. But that is

not to be: once Tunin discovers their collusion, he goes beserk, shooting widely at some policemen who have come to check the prostitutes for V.D. The film ends with Tunin's execution, as the police repeatedly strike Tunin's head against the stone walls of his cell.

D'amore e d'anarchia is part of that outpouring of Italian films, released between 1969 and 1972, that examines the relations of individuals and authoritative institutions, particularly during the Fascist period. Included in this group are Bertolucci's *Il conformista* and *Strategia del ragno*, Bellochio's *Nel nome del padre* and Visconti's *La caduta degli dei*. In contrast to her compatriots or the Greek Constantin Costa-Gavras (*Z* and *The Confession*, also released at this time), Wertmüller provides only minimal insight into the words of political tyranny. Further, it is difficult to decipher her position from the evidence of the film. An end quotation from the 19th century anarchist Malatesta cautions against assassination as a political expendient; it refers to assassins as saints as well as heroes. Yet the one clear message of the film remains the certain failure of political naiveté and the ineffectuality of individual action.

The film's most original moments are three lyrical interludes which crystalize mood rather than further plot; they demonstrate Wertmüller's ability to expose humor in the midst of dark circumstances. The interludes include a break-neck motorcycle ride through the Italian countryside; a series of seduction scenes as the prostitutes begin their day's business; and a filmic and poetic chronicle of a holiday that Tunin and Tripolino take before the final tragedy.

D'amore e d'anarchia is most memorable for its spirited performances: the lusty Salome, the freckled and wide-eyed Tunin (Giannini won the Best Actor Award at Cannes in 1973), the angelic Tripolino, and the bombastic Spatoletti. And Giuseppe Rotunno's fluid camerawork, Nino Rota's music, and Wertmüller's exuberant scenario combine to create an overall impression of a fine Italian opera.

—Patricia Erens

FIRES WERE STARTED. I Was a Fireman. Production: Crown Film Unit, with the co-operation of the Home Office, Ministry of Home Security, and National Fire Service; black and white, 35mm; running time: 63 mins., some sources state 60 mins. Released 1943.

Produced by Ian Dalrymple; screenplay and direction by Humphrey Jennings; photography by C. Pennington-Richards; edited by Stewart McAllister; sound recorded by Ken Cameron and Jock May; production design by Edward Carrick; music by William Alwyn, musical direction by Muir Mathieson.

Filmed in London.

Cast: Officer George Gravett (*Sub-Officer Dykes*); Lt. Fireman Philip Dickson (*Fireman Walters*); Lt. Fireman Fred Griffiths (*Johnny Daniels*); Lt. Fireman Loris Rey (*J. Rumbold*); Fireman Johnny Houghton (*S.H. Jackson*); Fireman T.P. Smith (*B.A. Brown*); Fireman John Barker (*J. Vallance*); Fireman W. Sansom (*Barrett*); Asst. Group Officer Green (*Mrs. Townsend*); Firewoman Betty Martin (*Betty*); Firewoman Eileen White (*Eileen*).

Publications:

Books—*Humphrey Jennings: A Tribute* by John Grierson, London 1951; *Grierson on Documentary* by Forsyth Hardy, revised edition London 1966; *Studies in Documentary* by Alan Lovell and Jim Hillier, New York 1972; *Nonfiction Film: A Critical History* by Richard Barsam, New York 1973; *Documentary: A History of Non-Fiction Film* by Erik Barnouw, New York 1974; *The Rise and Fall of British Documentary: The Story of the Film Movement Founded by John Grierson* by Elizabeth Sussex, Berkeley 1975; *Humphrey Jennings: More than a Maker of Films* by Anthony Hodgkinson and Rodney Sheratsky, Hanover, New Hampshire 1982; *Humphrey Jennings: Film-Maker/Painter/Poet* edited by Mary-Lou Jennings, London 1982; articles—"Humphrey Jennings" by Basil Wright in *Sight and Sound* (London), December 1950; "Humphrey Jennings—A Memoir" by Nicole Védréas and "Jennings' Britain" by Gavin Lambert in *Sight and Sound* (London), May 1951; "Index to the Creative Work of Humphrey Jennings" by Jonas Mekas in *Film Forum* (Mesdetten, Germany), 8 July 1954; "Britain's Screen Poet" by Charles Dand in *Films in Review* (New York), February 1955; "*Fires Were Started*" by Philip Strick in *Films and Filming* (London), May 1961; special issue on Jennings in *Film Quarterly* (London), winter 1961-62; "*Fires Were Started*" by Daniel Millar in *Sight and Sound* (London), spring 1969; "Humphrey Jennings, 1907-1950" by Jacques Belmans in *Anthologie du cinéma, Vol. VI*, Paris 1971; "Über Humphrey Jennings und einige seiner Filme" by H. Bitomsky in *Filmkritik* (Munich), November 1975; "Humphrey Jennings: Artist of the British Documentary", special issue, by R.E. Sharatsky in *Film Library Quarterly* (New York), v.8, no.3-4, 1975; "Only Connect: Some Aspects of the Work of Humphrey Jennings" by Lindsay Anderson in *Non Fiction Film Theory and Criticism* edited by Richard Barsam, New York 1976; article by O. Barrot in *Cinéma d'Aujourd'hui* (Paris), February/March 1977.

*   *   *

Fires Were Started was one of the semi-documentary features produced in Britain during World War II by both the government Crown Film Unit and the commercial studios following the success of such prototypes a *Target for Tonight* (1941) and *In Which We Serve* (1942). This film combined the actuality of documentary (a recreated or composite and representative event; the actual people involved in such an event) with the narrative line and dramatic heightening of fiction.

Fires Were Started is about the work of the Auxiliary Fire Service during the dreadful German fire raids on London. It follows a new recruit through a 24-hour shift with one unit. During the day the men train and perform menial chores. Following dinner they briefly relax and their camaraderie and understated humor become fully evident. As the raid begins, they proceed to their perilous and exhausting work, on this occasion putting out a fire raging near a munitions ship docked along the Thames. Though one of their number falls from a burning building to his death, the fire is finally extinguished. The films ends with the burial of the dead fireman intercut with the munitions ship moving out to sea.

As was usual with the British wartime films, the emphasis is given to the togetherness of the British people (with the cast a cross-section of classes). The propaganda function of this particular film seems to have been to show the quaility and courage of the brave men and women who were working to insure that

Britain would withstand the enemy assault. The enemy remains offscreen, and none of the hatred is portrayed which might have seemed an appropriate response to the bombing; instead, the destruction is treated almost as if it were a natural disaster.

By using the device of the new recruit, the director Humphrey Jennings can let us see and learn not only about the functioning of this fire fighting service but also about the diverse and likable personalities it brings together. When the raid begins, we are able to follow without aid of commentary, the tactics of the firefighters, their actions and conversations, the phone calls from headquarters, the maps with pins stuck in them, the chalked lists of equipment. Among other things, *Fires Were Started* is a model of teaching without didacticism.

But where its true greatness lies is in the way it simultaneously informs, persuades, and moves us. In this film Jennings goes beyond other of the semi-documentaries in differentiating and developing the characters of his non-actor firemen. Besides being very skillful at narrative, Jennings was a visual-aural poet who captured the precise image for a feeling, which also contained symbolic reverberations of English tradition and wartime exigencies—a poet who offered the exact words men might have spoken and even the songs they might have sung in the circumstances. The mood of this film may have well matched the mood of its wartime audience. It has lasted as a supplement to the national memory of what wartime England felt like.

—Jack Ellis

42ND STREET. Production: Warner Bros. Pictures, Inc.; 1933; black and white, 35mm; running time: 85 mins., some sources list 89 mins. Released 4 March 1933 (premiere).

Produced by Hal B. Wallis; screenplay by James Seymour and Rian James; from the novel by Bradford Ropes; directed by Lloyd Bacon; photography by Sol Polito; edited by Thomas Pratt; art direction by Jack Okey; music numbers by Al Dubin and Harry Warren; costumes designed by Orry-Kelly; choreography by Busby Berkeley.

Filmed in Warner Bros. studios in Hollywood. cost: budgeted at $400,000.

Cast: Warner Baxter (*Julian Marsh*); Bebe Daniels (*Dorothy Brock*); George Brent (*Pat Denning*); Una Merkel (*Lorraine Fleming*); Ruby Keeler (*Peggy Sawyer*); Guy Kibbee (*Abner Dillon*); Ned Sparks (*Barry*); Dick Powell (*Billy Lawler*); Ginger Rogers (*Anytime Annie*); George E. Stone (*Andy Lee*); Eddie Nugent (*Terry*); Allen Jenkins (*MacElroy*); Robert McWade (*Jones*); Harry Axt (*Jerry*); Clarence Nordstrum (*Leading man*); Henry B. Whitehall (*The actor*).

Publications:

Script—*42nd Street* by Rocco Fuments, Madison, Wisconsin 1980; review—"Putting on a Show" by Mordaunt Hall in *The New York Times*, 10 March 1933; books—*The Blue Book of Hollywood Musicals* by Jack Burton, Watkins Glen, New York 1953; *All Talking, All Singing, All Dancing* by John Springer, New York 1966; *Gotta Sing, Gotta Dance: A Pictorial History of the Film Musical* by John Kobal, New York 1970; *We're in the*

Money: Depression America and Its Films by Andrew Bergman, New York 1971; *The Busby Berkeley Book* by Tony Thomas, Jim Terry, and with Busby Berkeley, New York 1973; *The Genius of Busby Berkeley* by Bob Pike and Dave Martin, Resada, California 1973; *The Movie Musical* by Lee Edward Stern, New York 1974; *The Movie Musical from Vitaphone to 42nd Street* edited by Miles Kreuger, New York 1975; *Warner Brothers Directors* by William Meyer, New York 1978; *The Warner Bros. Story* by Clive Hirschhorn, New York 1979; articles— "Lloyd Bacon...Warner Brothers' Ace" in *Cue* (New York), 6 April 1935; obituary for Lloyd Bacon in *The New York Times*, 16 November 1955; "Dick Powell" by Anthony Thomas in *Films in Review* (New York), May 1961; article by Raymond Durgnat in *Films and Filming* (London), January 1962; "The Great Busby" by P. Jenkinson in *Film* (London), spring 1966; "Dancing Images" by J.-L. Comolli and "A Style of Spectacle" by P. Brion and R. Gilson in *Cahiers du Cinema in English* (New York), no.2, 1966; "The 3 Ages of the Musical" by George Sidney in *Films and Filming* (London), June 1968; interview with Berkeley in *Close-up* by John Gruen, New York 1968; "Busby and Ruby" by D. Gorton in *Newsweek* (New York), 3 August 1970; "*42: a gatan*" by Y. Bengtsson in *Filmrutan* (Sweden), no.1, 1973; "Busby Berkeley" by Arthur Knight in *Action* (Los Angeles), May/June 1974; "*Forty-second Street* New Deal: Some Thoughts About Early Film Musicals" by A.W. Hodgkinson in *Journal of Popular Film* (Bowling Green, Ohio), no.1, 1975; "*42nd Street*" by G. Turroni in *Filmcritica* (Rome), March 1975; "The Image of Women: The Optical Politics of Dames" by Lucy Fischer in *Film Quarterly* (Berkeley), fall 1976; "Some Warners Musicals and the Spirit of the New Deal" by M. Roth in *Velvet Light Trap* (Madison, Wisconsin), winter 1977; "The Backstage Musical" by J. Belton in *Movie* (London), spring 1977; "Entertainment and Utopia" by Richard Dyer in *Movie* (London), no.24, 1977; "Busby Berkeley: an American Surrealist" by J. Delameter in *Wide Angle* (Athens, Ohio), v.1, no.1, 1979; "*42nd Street*" by Julia Johnson in *Magill's Survey of Cinema, Vol. II* edited by Frank N. Magill, Englewood Cliffs, New Jersey 1980.

* * *

42nd Street was the first of three films released in quick succession by Warner Brothers in 1933 (the other two were *Gold Diggers of 1933* and *Footlight Parade*) that are generally regarded as having revitalized the musical as a genre. *42nd Street* gave Busby Berkeley (known for his unique overhead camera shots in Eddie Cantor films) full reign to develop his ideas of choreography. The Depression-weary public was obviously fascinated: *Variety* listed *42nd Street* as one of the top six money-making films of 1933, and it was nominated for an Oscar as best picture. Based to some extent on *The Broadway Melody* (MGM, 1929), *42nd Street* continued the sub-genre of the "backstage musical" but added new dimensions with its hard-hitting references to the Depression and with Berkeley's opulent staging of the musical numbers.

The film refuses to be completely escapist: the main thrust of the narrative is the need to get a job, create a viable product (the show *Pretty Lady*), and to make money. The structural tension results from the separation of the production numbers (glimpses of *Pretty Lady*) from the narrative; those numbers are indeed escapist in nature. Richard Dyer, in "Entertainment and Utopia" (*Movie* 24, 1977), regards this separation as an ideological method of suggesting that the musical numbers are the Utopia we all seek from the hard work of the narrative reality—that the "ills" of capitalism (the Depression) can be resolved through the "means" of capitalism (putting on a successful show). Mark Roth, in "Some Warners Musicals and the Spirit of the New Deal" (*Velvet Light Trap* 17, 1977), puts forward a similar theory; he notes a social connection betwen *42nd Street* and newly-elected President Roosevelt's New Deal: by working together under a strong leader (the director), the United States (the cast and crew) can lift itself out of the Depression and towards prosperity. (*42nd Street* opened in Washington, D.C. on March 4, 1933, the day on which Roosevelt was inaugurated.)

Regardless of these factors, *42nd Street* is usually labelled a "Busby Berkeley musical." Backstage musicals had existed since the beginning of sound, but they were always shot straight-on, as if on stage. Berkeley freed the camera and took advantage of its mobility. He was not a trained dancer, and consequently his "dancers" did not dance so much as move about; the camera did the dancing. By disrupting spatial integrity (the production numbers would begin and end on a theatrical stage but would inevitably move into a realm of limitless dimensions), Berkeley created a surrealistic world that thrilled movie audiences. His predilection for beautiful women resulted in some of the most voyeuristic fantasies ever put on film. Recent feminist film criticism (particularly Lucy Fischer's "The Image of Woman as Image: The Optical Politics of *Dames*" in *Film Quarterly*, fall 1976) has justifiably attacked Berkeley's objectification of the female body.

42nd Street also introduced Ruby Keeler and Dick Powell to movie audiences and contains that immortal line, "...You're going out a youngster, but you've got to come back a star!"

—Greg S. Faller

———

THE FOUR HORSEMEN OF THE APOCALYPSE. Production: Metro Pictures Corp.; black and white, 35mm, silent; running time: about 150 mins.; length: 11 reels. Released 6 March 1921 at the Lyric Theatre, New York.

Produced by Rex Ingram; scenario by June Mathis; from the novel *Los cuatros jinetes del Apocalipsis* by Vicente Blasco-Ibáñez; art titles by Jack W. Robson; directed by Rex Ingram; photography by John F. Seitz; edited by Grant Whytock and June Mathis; art direction by Walter Mayo and Curt Rehfeld; music for accompanying film by Louis F. Gottschalk; technical assistants: Amos Myers and Joseph Calder; make-up by Jean Hersholt.

Cast: Rudolph Valentino (*Julio Desnoyers*); Alice Terry (*Marguerite Laurier*); Pomeroy Cannon (*Madariaga, the Centaur*); Josef Swickard (*Marcelo Desnoyers*); Brinsley Shaw (*Celendonio*); Alan Hale (*Karl von Hartrott*); Bridgetta Clark (*Doña Luisa*); Mabel Van Buren (*Elena*); Nigel De Brulier (*Tchernoff*); Bowditch Turner (*Argensola*); John Sainpolis (*Laurier*); Mark Fenton (*Senator Lacour*); Virginia Warwick (*Chichi*); Derek Ghent (*René Lacour*); Stuart Holmes (*Captain von Hartrott*); Jean Hersholt (*Professor von Hartrott*); Henry Klaus (*Heinrich von Hartrott*); Edward Connelly (*Lodgekeeper*); Georgia Woodthorpe (*Lodgekeeper's wife*); Kathleen Key (*Georgette*); Wallace Beery (*Lieutenant-Colonel von Richthoffen*); Jacques D'Auray (*Captain d'Aubrey*); Curt Rehfeld (*Major Blumhardt*); Harry Northrup (*The Count*); Claire De Lorez (*Mademoiselle Lucette, the model*); Bull Montana (*French butler*); Isabelle Keith (*German woman*); Jacques Lanoe (*Her husband*); Noble

Johnson (*Conquest*); Minnehaha (*Old nurse*); Arthur Hoyt (*Lieutenant Schnitz*); Beatrice Dominquez (*Dancer*); also featuring Ramon Samaniegos (later Novarro) in small role.

Publications:

Books—*Motion Picture Directing: The Facts and Theories of the Newest Art* by Peter Milne, New York 1922; *Valentino* by Irving Shulman, New York 1967; *The Rise of the American Film: A Critical History* by Lewis Jacobs, revised edition, New York 1968; *Rex Ingram* by Rene Predal, Paris 1970; *Gentlemen to the Rescue: The Heroes of the Silent Screen* by Kalton C. Lahue, New York 1972; *American Silent Film* by William K. Everson, New York 1978; *Rex Ingram, Master of the Silent Cinema* by Liam O'Leary, Dublin 1980; articles—interview with Ingram by J. Robinson in *Photoplay* (New York), August 1921; "Fairbanks and Valentino: The Last Heroes" by Gavin Lambert in *Sequence* (London), summer 1949; "Hollywood's Handsomest Director" by George Geltzer in *Films in Review* (New York), May 1952; "The Career of Rudolph Valentino" by Theodore Huff in *Films in Review* (New York), April 1952; article by Mervyn McPherson in *Films and Filming* (London), May 1956; "Rex Ingram and the Nice Studios" by Liam O'Laoghaire in *Cinema Studies* (England), December 1961; "Rex Ingram and Alice Terry" in 2 parts by Dewitt Bodeen in *Films in Review* (New York), February and March 1975.

* * *

When screenwriter June Mathis campaigned among the executives of the then none-too-sound Metro Film Company to have Blasco Ibáñez's best-selling novel *The Four Horsemen of the Apocalypse* transferred to the screen, she was on shaky ground. The war had been over for two years, there had been a surfeit of war films, and people wanted to forget. She succeeded, however, and she also had the intelligence to recognize the talents of two young men—the director, Rex Ingram, and the actor, Rudolph Valentino. In production the film gathered momentum; there was an air of expectation. Ingram, who had hitherto produced distinguished work without achieving full recognition, had a talent for moulding actors, and the young and largely inexperienced Valentino, lithe and graceful as a dancer, with style and charm and a touch of the devil, proved ideal material for the screen. Ingram, who had come from an Irish rectory and an artistic training at the Yale School of Fine Arts, had inherited his father's capacity for study and research. He had never been to France, knew nothing of European culture, and yet he succeeded in creating in Hollywood the atmosphere of Paris in wartime and the tragedy of the destruction that had ravaged Europe.

The Four Horsemen was an immediate sensation, comparable in its success only to the major films of D.W. Griffith some years earlier. In all the large cities it was sumptuously presented with large orchestras and backstage sound effects for the battle scenes. Its story had all the ingredients for success. A dazzling gigolo hero. A tragic story of frustrated illicit love. It ranged from the pampas of South America and the glittering world of Paris, to the horrors of war and the invasion of a French village by the Germans. Pervading everything was the anti-war theme and the mystical element of the four terrible horsemen. It was also anti-German to the point of caricature: it was banned in Germany and indeed withdrawn from circulation many years later when a campaign was launched to suppress films promoting hatred between nations.

But for years it was the major box-office attraction, and was revived on the death of Valentino. Indeed, it is now remembered more for its star than for the genuine achievement of Ingram himself. Yet today's viewers even those whose main interest is in nostalgia for Valentino, will be struck by the excellence of the film itself. With the help of his constant collaborator, the cameraman John Seitz, Ingram infused the film with great visual beauty, a sensitivity to light and shade, and an unusual feeling for composition.

The effect of the film was to shore up the finances of the shaky Metro company, recently taken over by Marcus Loew. It established Valentino as a star, and it established Ingram as a major director who henceforth had carte blanche and full control of his films. A "Rex Ingram Production" thereafter carried as much weight as the star's billing, and indeed Ingram can be said to have set an aesthetic standard for the screen image.

—Liam O'Leary

FRANKENSTEIN. Production: Universal Pictures; 1931; black and white, 35mm; running time: 71 mins. Released 1931.

Produced by Carl Laemmle, Jr.; screenplay by Garrett Fort, Francis Faragoh, and John L. Balderston, uncredited first draft by Robert Florey; from John Balderston's adaptation of Mary Shelley's novel, adapted from the play by Peggy Webling; directed by James Whale; photography by Arthur Edeson; edited by Clarence Kolster; sound recording supervised by C. Roy Hunter; art direction by Charles Hall; music by David Broekman; makeup by Jack Pierce; laboratory equipment by Ken Strickfadden.

Filmed in Universal studios. Cost: $250,000.

Cast: Colin Clive (*Dr. Henry Frankenstein*); Boris Karloff (*The Monster*); Mae Clarke (*Elizabeth*); John Boles (*Victor*); Edward Van Sloan (*Dr. Waldman*); Dwight Frye (*Fritz*); Frederick Kerr.

Publications:

Script—*James Whale's 'Frankenstein'* by Richard Anobile, New York 1974; books—*Le Fantastique au Cinéma* by Michel Laclos, Paris 1958; *Horror* by Drake Douglas, New York 1966; *An Illustrated History of the Horror Film* by Carlos Clarens, New York 1968; *Movie Monsters* by Denis Gifford, New York 1969; *Science Fiction in the Cinema* by John Baxter, New York 1970; *Horror in the Cinema* by Ivan Butler, 2nd revised ed., New York 1970; "Monster Films" by Lawrence Alloway in *Focus on the Horror Film* edited by Roy Huss and T.J. Ross, Englewood Cliffs, New Jersey 1972; *Monsters from the Movies* by Thomas Aylesworth, Philadelphia 1972; *Karloff: The Life of Boris Karloff* by Peter Underwood, New York 1972; *Great Monsters of the Movies* by Edward Edelson, Garden City, New York 1973; *Karloff: The Man, the Monster, the Movies* by Denis Gifford, New York 1973; *The Frankenstein Legend: A Tribute to Mary Shelley and Boris Karloff* by Donald Glut, Metuchen, New Jersey 1973; *The Films of Boris Karloff* by Richard Bojarski and Kenneth Beale, Secaucus, New Jersey 1974; *Classics of the Horror Film* by William Everson, Secaucus, New Jersey 1974; *Hor-*

ror Movies by Alan Frank, London 1974; Boris Karloff and His Films by Paul Jensen, New York 1974; Caligari's Cabinet and Other Grand Illusions: A History of Film Design by Léon Barsacq, translated by Michael Bullock, revised and edited by Elliott Stein, Boston 1976; Mary Shelley's Monster: The Story of Frankenstein by Martin Tropp, Boston 1976; Dark Dreams: A Psychological History of the Modern Horror Film by Charles Derry, New York 1977; Classic Movie Monsters by Donald Glut, Metuchen, New Jersey 1978; Journey into Darkness: The Art of James Whale's Horror Films by Reed Ellis, New York 1980; articles—"James Whale and Frankenstein" in The New York Times, 20 December 1931; "Movie Gothick: A Tribute to James Whale" by Roy Edwards in Sight and Sound (London), autumn 1957; "My Life as a Monster" by Boris Karloff in Films and Filming (London), November 1957; "James Whale" by Robert Fink and William Thomaier in Films in Review (New York), May 1962; "Memories of a Monster" by Boris Karloff in Saturday Evening Post (New York), 3 November 1962; "Frankenstein, Or the Modern Prometheus: A Review" by Harold Bloom in Partisan Review (New Brunswick, New Jersey), fall 1965; "Boris Karloff" by Robert C. Roman in Films in Review (New York), August/September 1969; "Frankenstein" by Paul Jenson in Film Comment (New York), fall 1970; "Boris Karloff: The Man Behind the Myth" by Lillian Gerard in Film Comment (New York), spring 1970; "Some Historical Notes on Dr. Frankenstein and his Monster" by Gordon Hitchens in Film Comment (New York), spring 1970; "James Whale" by Paul Jensen in Film Comment (New York), spring 1971; "Schept vreugde met mij, horror freaks" by H. Verstappen in Skoop (Amsterdam), no.2, 1972; "Monster Movies: A Sexual Theory" by Walter Evans in Journal of Popular Film (Bowling Green, Ohio), fall 1973; "Drawing the Circle: A Devolution of Values in 3 Horror Flims" by R.H.W. Dillard in Film Journal (Hollins College, Virginia), January/March 1973; "Frankenstein" by P. Schpelern in Kosmorama (Copenhagen), March 1973; "Monster Movies and Rites of Initiation" by Walter Evans in Journal of Popular Film (Bowling Green, Ohio), spring 1975; "Frankenstein" by D. Gail Huskins in Magill's Survey of Cinema, Vol. I edited by Frank N. Magill, Englewood Cliffs, New Jersey 1980.

*   *   *

The 1931 version of Frankenstein has on many occasions been referred to as the greatest horror film ever produced. Whether that judgement is correct, it can not be denied that Frankenstein has had a tremendous influence on the horror genre ever since its release. The film has spawned literally dozens of sequels and remakes, some by Universal (Bride of Frankenstein, Ghost of Frankenstein, Frankenstein Meets the Wolf Man), others by Hammer Films (Curse of Frankenstein, Horror of Frankenstein, Frankenstein and the Monster from Hell), some cheap exploitation films (I Was a Teenage Frankenstein, Jesse James Meets Frankenstein's Daughter) and even some comedies (Abbott and Costello Meet Frankenstein, Young Frankenstein, The Munsters). Frankenstein also established some important concepts that have been carried into other horror films: as the scientist who emulates God and delves into matters that "man was not meant to know"; the "monster" who is not truly evil, but rather a victim of circumstances that are beyond his control.

Frankenstein was originally to have been directed by Robert Florey with Bela Lugosi as the star. Florey even wrote the first draft of the script. Although the final draft of the script retains many important elements from Florey's version, his work on the film was uncredited. Disagreements with the studio led to a change of personnel, and the film was reassigned to James Whale. To play the role of the monster, Whale chose a relative unknown, Boris Karloff. (The studio executives felt that the monster was only a supporting role and that the star of the film was Colin Clive. Only later were they to realize that the real "star" was Frankenstein's creation.) The success of the film provided a tremendous boost to both Karloff's and Whale's careers.

Visually, the Frankenstein monster was the creation of make-up artist Jack Pierce. Mary Shelley's novel did not give a detailed description of the monster, so Pierce consulted with surgeons to design a realistic version of a man who was sewn together out of dead bodies. He originated the square-top head which has been copied in so many of the sequels. The entire make-up took hours to apply, and included padded shoulders, metal leg braces, and built-up boots to make Karloff appear taller. In spite of this heavy and grotesque make-up, Karloff's talent as an actor brought a very human quality to the "monster."

Many of the themes and images in Frankenstein may seem clichés to viewers today, but in its initial release Frankenstein introduced some shocking ideas to contemporary audiences. Stories were circulated of women screaming and fainting in the theatres. No doubt some of these stories were planted by the publicity department at Universal, but the shocks were real enough. Indeed, the film opens with a "friendly warning" delivered by Edward Van Sloan who tells us that Frankenstein "is one of the strangest tales ever told...it may shock you...it might even horrify you." Certainly by today's standards the film is extremely tame. But as the pioneer of the "mad scientist" stories, Frankenstein introduced a number of concepts and themes which are still the basis of horror films today.

—Linda J. Obalil

––––––––––

FREAKS. Barnum ou la Monstrueuse Parade. Production: Metro-Goldwyn-Mayer Pictures Corp.; black and white, 35mm; running time: 90 mins. originally, later 64 mins., some sources state that existing copies are 53 mins. Released February 1932, New York and San Francisco. Re-released 1940's.

Produced by Irving Thalberg with Harry Sharock (some filmographies state Dwain Esper as producer but he was responsible for the 1940's re-issue, other sources list Browning as producer); screenplay by Willis Goldbeck, Leon Gordon, Al Boasberg, and Edgar Allen Woolf; from the book Spurs by Clarence Tod Robbins; directed by Tod Browning; photography by Merritt B. Gerstad; edited by Basil Wrangell; sound engineered by Gavin Barns; art direction by Cedric Gibbons with Merrill Pye; music by Gavin Barns.

Filmed in Hollywood. Honored at the Venice Film Festival, 1962.

Cast: Olga Baclanova (Cleopatra); Henry Victor (Hercules); Wallace Ford (Phroso); Harry Earles (Hans); Leila Hyams (Venus); Roscoe Ates (Roscoe); Rose Dione (Mme. Tetralini); Daisy and Violet Hilton (Siamese Twins); Schlitze (Herself); Peter Robinson (Human Skeleton); Elisabeth Green (Bird Woman); Randion (Larva Man, or Living Torso); Joseph-Josephine (Androgyne); Johnny Eck (Trunk Man); Frances O'Connor and Martha Morris (Women without arms); Olga

Roderich (*Bearded Woman*); Koo-Koo (*Herself*); Edward Brophy and Mat-Mac Huch (*The Rollo Brothers*); Angelo Rossitto (*Angeleno*). Daisy Earles (*Frieda*); Zip and Flip (*Pinheads*).

Publications:

Scripts—"*Freaks*" by W. Goldbeck, L. Gordon, E.A. Woolf, and A. Boasberg (2 scenes only) in *Avant-Scène du cinéma* (Paris), July/September 1975; "*Freaks*" by W. Goldbeck, L. Gordon, E.A. Woolf, and A. Boasberg in *Avant-Scène du cinéma* (Paris), 15 March 1981; reviews—"La Presse" in *Avant-Scène du cinéma* (Paris), 15 March 1981; books—*Kiss Kiss Bang Bang* by Pauline Kael, Boston 1968; *Focus on the Horror Film* by John Thomas, New Jersey 1972; *Classics of the Horror Film* by William K. Everson, Secaucus, New Jersey 1974; articles—"Tod Browning" by George Geltzer in *Films in Review* (New York), October 1953; "Tod Browning" by Jean-Claude Romer in *Bizarre* (Paris), no.3, 1962; "Horror: The Browning Version" by Rory Guy in *Cinema* (Beverly Hills), June/July 1963; "*Freaks*" by K. Schmidt in *Kosmorama* (Copenhagen), September 1972; "Tod Browning" by Eli Savada in *Photon* (New York), no.23, 1973; "*Freaks* ou la monstrueuse parade" by Claude Beylie in *Ecran* (Paris), July/August 1973; "Ni Fantastique ni 'normal'" by Jean-Marie Léger in *Avant-Scène du cinéma* (Paris), July/September 1975; "*Freaks* et la critique" in *Avant-Scène du cinéma* (Paris), July/September 1975; "Tod Browning" by Stuart Rosenthal in *The Hollywood Professionals, Vol. 4*, London 1975; "*Freaks* Was Weird" by N. James in *Classic Film Collector* (Indiana, Pennsylvania), fall 1976; "Tod Browning and *Freaks*" by J.-C. Biette and F. Ziolkowski in *Cahiers du cinéma* (Paris), May 1978; "*Freaks*: La monstrueuse parade" by P. Carcassonne in *Cinématographe* (Paris), April 1978; "*Freaks* dans l'oeuvre de Tod Browning" by C.M. Cluny in *Cinéma* (Paris), May 1978; "*Freaks*" by D. Sauvaget in *Image et Son* (Paris), May 1978; "Tod Browning's Side Show" by James Hoberman in *The Village Voice* (New York), 17 September 1979; "Le Jour où les maudits prirent la parole" by jacques Goimard in *Avant-Scène du cinéma* (Paris), 15 March 1981.

* * *

Although it has been seldom shown in the fifty years since its introduction in 1932 as a "masterpiece of horror," Tod Browning's *Freaks* has achieved near legendary cult status and continues to exert a major influence on modern attempts at the baroque film. Certainly the power of its wedding feast sequence was not lost on Luis Buñuel when he staged the tramps "last supper" in his 1961 *Viridiana*. And such diverse film makers as Max Ophuls, Federico Fellini and Ingmar Bergman have all shown vestiges of *Freaks* in various of their works.

Today it is difficult to believe that the film was produced at MGM. It more closely resembles the kind of horror films that were being released during the 1930's by Universal Studios, which had in fact made a fortune with Browning's earlier *Dracula* as well as James Whale's *Frankenstein*. However, Irving Thalberg, MGM's president, noting the success of these two efforts, purchased Clarence Robbin's grisly tale *Spurs*, hired Browning and, over considerable objections within the studio, adapted it for the screen as *Freaks*. Yet in the transition to film, the story deviated from traditional horror format and evolved into gothic social comment that closely resembled the kind of

sociological treatments being attempted by Warner Bros. in their great gangster films of the period.

If *Freaks* is not totally satisfactory to audiences of today, that is perhaps due, for the most part, to the fundamental conflicts inherent in merging horror and social criticism. Although Browning was successful in portraying his deformed subjects sympathetically and causing his viewer to re-evalute their concepts of what is normal, he succumbs to the obvious temptation to "scare the pants" off his viewers in the film's final scene. For most of the film, he portrays the freaks as human beings going about their daily rituals. (Significantly, we never see them on stage as sideshow performers.) At the wedding feast, however, when one of their number marries a "normal" person, we sense their solidarity as they go through an elaborate ritual to admit Cleo to their circle. This triggers a course of events in which the innate humanity of the freaks is juxtaposed with the inherent ugliness, evil and abnormality of the so-called normal people.

But in the film's final sequences, Browning emphasizes the physical grotesqueness of the freaks as they slither and crawl through the mud to exact their revenge on Cleo and the strong man Hercules after she has betrayed them. At the end of the film, we find that Cleo has turned into a freak herself at the hands of the little people. The scene, contrived as it is, clouds the image of the humanity of the deformed creatures by emphasizing the enormity of their vengeance, and because the costuming of Cleo as a freak is technically crude, it erodes the worthwhile themes of the film and makes its subjects objects of scorn.

Still, individual scenes, in their power and construction, provide unforgettable images and truly extend the boundaries of baroque filmmaking. The film is still today a virtual textbook on the horror film, and enough of its nobler aspirations come through to allow it to remain as undoubtedly the ultimate challenge to the old fiction that beauty is necessarilly synonymous with truth. Although it was banned in many countries throughout the world for its graphic display of this theme, it was honored in 1962 at the Venice Film Festival and has been shown periodically thereafter.

—Stephen L. Hanson

THE FRESHMAN. Production: Harold Lloyd Corp.; 1925; black and white, 35mm, silent; running time: about 75 mins.; length: 7 reels, 6883 feet. Released 20 September 1925.

Scenario by Sam Taylor, John Grey, Ted Wilde, and Tim Wheelan; directed by Sam Taylor and Fred Newmeyer; photography by Walter Lundin and Henry Kohler.

Cast: Harold Lloyd (*Harold Lamb*); Jobyna Ralston (*Peggy*); Brooks Benedict (*College Cad*); James Anderson (*College Hero*); Hazel Keener (*College Belle*); Joseph Harrington (*College Tailor*); Pat Harmon (*Football coach*).

Publications:

Books—*Harold Lloyd's World of Comedy* by William Cahn, New York 1964; *The Great Films: 50 Golden Years of Motion Pictures* by Bosley Crowther, New York 1967; *Four Great Comedians: Chaplin, Lloyd, Keaton, Langdon* by Donald W. McCaffrey, New York 1968; *An American Comedy* by Harold

Lloyd, New York re-issued 1971; *Yesterday's Clowns* by Frank Manchel, New York 1973; *Harold Lloyd: The Shape of Laughter* by Richard Schickel, Greenwich, Connecticut 1974; *American Silent Film* by William K. Everson, New York 1978; *The Silent Clowns* by Walter Kerr, New York 1979; *The Comic Mind: Comedy and the Movies* by Gerald Mast, Chicago, revised edition, 1979; articles—"Obit for Samuel Taylor" in *Screen World* (New York), no.10, 1959; "Harold Lloyd" by Nelson E. Garringer in *Films in Review* (New York), August/-September 1962; "Interview with Harold Lloyd" by Arthur Friedman in *Film Quarterly* (Berkeley), summer 1962; "The Funny Side of Life" by Harold Lloyd in *Films and Filming* (London), January 1964; article by Allen Eyles in *Films and Filming* (London), May 1964; "The Serious Business of Being Funny" by Harold Lloyd in *Film Comment* (New York), fall 1969; "Harold Lloyd Talks to Anthony Slide about His Early Career" in *Silent Picture* (London), summer/autumn 1971.

*   *   *

The Freshman was one of Harold Lloyd's situation comedies, rather than one of his thrill comedies—a type best exemplified by *Safety Last* (1923) with Lloyd's climactic climb up the side of a skyscraper. In a situation comedy, like *The Freshman*, probably Lloyd's best of that type (others might prefer *Grandma's Boy*, 1922), Lloyd generates laughs from plunging the character he fashioned into a familiar social situation, building lengthy comic sequences from the contrast of Harold's energetic, pushy, and unselfconscious behavior and the particular demands of the social group around him. At the base of Lloyd's comic persona with his embodiment of American pep, the zippy go-getter who succeeded by the unflagging application of incurable optimism and determined zeal. Harold looked at the world not only through glasses physically, but through metaphorically rose-colored ones as well. Harold's optimistic energy faced formidable foes—physical, mental, or social tasks for which he was unsuited and at which he was unskilled; a large group of comrades or colleagues thought him ridiculous. But Harold's energy, determination, and unflappable cheerfulness inevitably vanquished all adversaries and inadequacies.

In *The Freshman*, Harold dreams of becoming the embodiment of a 1920s American hero: the most popular man on the college campus. He intends to accomplish this by performing a little jig step and handshake he saw in a movie, followed by the line, "Step right up and call me Speedy." The film's major comic sequences show his comic failure at every attempt to jig-step his way to this pinnacle. He is tricked into delivering the welcoming address to all the other freshmen on the first day of school, replacing the authoritative dean whom Harold has already offended. His opening address turns into comic chaos when a pair of kittens interrupt his speech and the entire student body howls with laughter at his ridiculous jig-step. He shows up at football practice, wearing his familiar spectacles beneath his football helmet, only to be used as a tackling dummy. Though woozy, the game and chipper Harold cheerfully submits to the abuse. At the big dance, the "Fall Frolic," Harold has invited the entire campus as his guests. His tuxedo, however, has not been properly sewn because of his tailor's fainting spells. The tailor accompanies Harold to the Frolic to repair any seams that rip, and the ensuing dance scene becomes one of the classic comic sequences of the American silent cinema as Harold must simultaneously deal with the sneers of his college "chums," the social demands of dancing, the inevitable ripping of one seam after another, and the perpetual spells of his sinking tailor.

The film's final sequence, the big football game between Harold's school, Tate College, and the rival school, Union State, is probably the most famous comic football sequence ever filmed. Harold, the team's waterboy, is pressed into service when all the other substitutes are disabled. Harold succeeds in scoring several touchdowns that are negated—one when he drops the ball just before crossing the goal line because he believes a factory whistle to be the official's that stops the action; another when he races for a touchdown with a balloon rather than the ball. But in the end Harold's sheer drive allows him to dodge his way through the enemy to cross the goal line with the winning touchdown at the last second. And the entire campus celebrates the victory by adopting Harold's ridiculous jig-step and handshake.

As is typical of Lloyd comedies, Harold's unrelating pep, though silly, is inevitably successful—perhaps an affirmation of its audience's belief that eventually not brains, nor skill, nor luck count very much, but that push and pep and positive thinking will win the day.

—Gerald Mast

FRÖKEN JULIE. Miss Julie. Production: Sandrew Bauman Produktion; black and white, 35mm; running time: 87 mins., some sources list 90 mins. Released 1950.

Produced by Rune Waldekranz; screenplay by Alf Sjöberg; from the play by August Strindberg; directed by Alf Sjöberg; photography by Göran Strindberg; edited by Lennart Wallén; art direction by Bibi Lindström; music by Dag Wirén.

Filmed in Sweden. Cannes Film Festival, Best Film (shared with *Miracolo a Milano*), 1951; Honored at Venice Film Festival, as part of a retrospective program, 1964.

Cast: Anita Björk (*Miss Julie*); Ulf Palme (*Jean*); Anders Henrikson (*The Count*); Marta Dorff (*Christine*); Lissi Alandh (*Berta, the Countess*); Inga Gill (*Viola*); Kurt-Olof Sundstrom (*The fiance*); Ake Claessens (*Doctor*); Jan Hagerman (*Jean as a child*); Inger Norberg (*Julie as a child*); Ake Fridell (*Robert*); Max von Sydow (*Groom*).

Publications:

Books—*Swedish Cinema* by Peter Cowie, New York 1966; *Sweden I/II* by Peter Cowie with Arne Svensson, New York, 1970; *Caligari's Cabinet and Other Grand Illusions: A History of Film Design* by Léon Barsacq, New York 1976; *Cinema, The Magic Vehicle: A Guide to its Achievement: Journey Two* edited by Jacek Klinowski and Adam Garbicz, Metuchen, New Jersey 1979; *Filmregi Alf Sjöberg* by G. Lundin, Lund, Sweden 1979; articles—in *Variety* (New York), 16 May 1951; article in *Cinématographe français* (Paris), 28 July 1951; article in *Cahiers du cinéma* (Paris), July/August 1951; article in *Sight and Sound* (London), fall 1951; article in *Sight and Sound* (London), January/March 1952; article in *Monthly Film Bulletin* (London), no.216, 1952; article in *Variety* (New York), 4 September 1952; article in *Films in Review* (New York), May 1952; "Swedish Films" by Catherine De La Roche in *Films in Review* (New

York), November 1953; "The Swedish Paradox" by Ann Morrisett in *Sight and Sound* (London), autumn 1961; article in *Cinema Nuovo* (Turin), August 1965.

* * *

In *Miss Julie*, there is a prolific use of "flashbacks," one flash forward and two dream sequences, all of which serve to articulate the opposing but also disintegrating class values of Miss Julie, who represents the feudal aristocracy, and of her father's valet, Jean, who is of lower class, servant background. The difference in director Alf Sjöberg's use of the flashback device in *Miss Julie* from its standard employment in strictly conventional, i.e., "Hollywood" films, is that there is not the usual cinematic punctuation demarcating exactly when the narrative is speaking about the present and when it is referring to the past.

In the play, the past is evoked through the use of dialogue, which characteristically involves an exchange among two or more people seeking mutual understanding. However, the key to the success of dialogue, insofar as its communicative status is predicated upon the arrival of this understanding, is one of intentionality. The speakers must be able to make one another recognize the meaning intended in what they are trying to express. In *Miss Julie* the dialogue—as a means of describing for example, the conflicts Miss Julie harbors about morality, class distinction, and sexual roles—has been translated cinematically into the flashback. That the flashbacks in the film are not marked off in the traditional manner indicates that they are not to be understood in the usual sense, i.e., not as simply retrogressive delineations of time. Instead, they are intended by the filmmaker to illustrate in formal terms the indecisive and confused nature of Miss Julie's conception of herself, of her conception of how others see her, and of what she should do or be in the world.

The rules of verbal communication must be followed by the speakers involved. If they are not, of course, an incorrect meaning or set of meanings will be derived from the exchange. Specifically, flashbacks in *Miss Julie* are constructed so that there is no spatial and thus temporal differentiation made between the people, objects and places of the present and those of the past. Miss Julie's mother, who is dead in the present time of her daughter's affair with Jean, walks into the "frame" of this time from the midst of one from the past. The camera moves with her across these two temporal dimensions passing on its way people of the present who are speaking about her in the past. This overlapping occurs as a rule of the flashback structure in the film. Its meaningful effect is one of instability, of alternating balances and contrasts of moods. The viewer understands ultimately that *Miss Julie* will remain an illusionary and impenetrable fiction.

To further create a sense of the basic unreality and illusion of imagination in the diegesis, landscapes, objects, and the natural elements (wind, etc.) are not represented or portrayed as things existing merely in themselves. Rather, Sjöberg manipulates them in such a way that they take on a symbolic life of their own. They become anthropomorphized conveyors of the character's emotions as well as expressive means of the larger and more pervasive moods of the film. This anthropomorphization process, which affords significance to objects usually represented statically, as devoid of meaning, does not in the overall perception of the film simply consign the narrative and its means of presentation to the realm of the melodramatic.

—Sandra L. Beck

FROM HERE TO ETERNITY. Production: Columbia Pictures Corp.; 1953; black and white, 35mm; running time: 118 mins. Released 1953.

Produced by Buddy Adler, executive producer: Harry Cohn; screenplay by Daniel Taradash; from the novel by James Jones; directed by Fred Zinnemann; photography by Burnett Guffey; edited by William A. Lyon; sound by John P. Livadary and Columbia Studio Sound Department; art direction by Cary Odell; music by George Duning.

Filmed in Hawaii at the Schofield Barracks. Academy Awards for Best Picture, Best Supporting Actor (Sinatra), Best Supporting Actress (Reed), Best Director, Best Screenplay, Best Cinematography-Black and White, Best Sound Recording, and Best Editing, 1953; New York Film Critics' Awards for Best Motion Picture, Best Actor (Lancaster), and Best Direction, 1953; Cannes Film Festival, Out of Competition Prize, 1954.

Cast: Burt Lancaster (*Sergeant Milton Warden*); Montgomery Clift (*Robert E. Lee "Prew" Prewitt*); Deborah Kerr (*Karen Holmes*); Frank Sinatra (*Angelo Maggio*); Donna Reed (*Alma "Lorene"*); Philip Ober (*Captain Dana Holmes*); Ernest Borgnine (*Sergeant "Fatso" Judson*).

Publications:

Reviews—by Robert Kass in *Films in Review* (New York), October 1953; review by Karel Reisz in *Sight and Sound* (London), January/March 1954; books—*Fred Zinnemann* by Richard Griffith, New York 1958; *King Cohn* by Bob Thomas, New York 1967; *Burt Lancaster: A Pictorial Treasury of His Films* by J. Vermilye, New York 1970; *The Films of Frank Sinatra* by Gene Ringgold and Clifford McCarty, New York 1971; *The Movie Makers: Artists in an Industry* by the Rev. Gene D. Phillips, Chicago 1973; *Burt Lancaster* by Tony Thomas, New York 1975; articles—"Censored: *From Here to Eternity*" in *Look* (New York), 25 August 1953; "Fred Zinnemann, Oscar Winner" in *Vogue* (New York), 1 May 1954; "Screen Adaptation" by Jerry Wald in *Films in Review* (New York), February 1954; "Into Another World" by Daniel Taradash in *Films and Filming* (London), May 1959; "A Conflict of Conscience" by Fred Zinnemann in *Films and Filming* (London), December 1959; "*From Here to Eternity*: Letter" by Fred Zinnemann in *Films and Filming* (London), November 1961; "Montgomery Clift" by Fred Zinnemann in *Sight and Sound* (London), autumn 1966; "Montgomery Clift" by Robert C. Roman in *Films in Review* (New York), November 1966; "A Man for All Movies: The Films of Fred Zinnemann" by John Howard Reid in *Films and Filming* (London), May and June 1967; "Burt Lancaster" by Mel Schuster in *Films in Review* (New York), August/September 1969; "From Here to Esteem" by Eric Braun in *Films and Filming* (London), May 1970 (see also April and June issues); "Tant qu'il y aura des hommes" by G. Colpart in *Cinéma* (Paris), November 1978; "*From Here to Eternity*" by Jeffry Michael Jensen in *Magill's Survey of Cinema, Vol. II* edited by Frank N. Magill, Englewood Cliffs, New Jersey 1980.

* * *

James Jones's novel *From Here to Eternity* was a best seller. Portraying Army life immediately before Pearl Harbor, its racy sex scenes, lively and rough language, and vivid characterizations of man under stress made it one of the most widely-read books to come out of World War Two. Hollywood was interested but felt that the book would be a difficult project. Obviously the realistic and explicit sex scenes were the basis for much of the book's appeal. The book was also very lengthy and somewhat rambling. If one could conquer the problems of translating the language and sex to the screen, could a film be made that captured the spirit of the book? Hollywood wanted to try because the loss of audience to television and the lack of ready-made theatrical circuit was forcing Hollywood to provide forms of entertainment that could not be found elsewhere.

Columbia's chief executive Harry Cohn bought the rights and directly worked on the project with producer Buddy Adler, director Fred Zinnemann, and writer Dan Taradash. Cohn felt that he really contributed to the project; he appeared on the set to make suggestions. For the first time and only time in his career, his name was included in the ads for the film. But Cohn and his director did not have a smooth relationship. Zinnemann had his own ideas about how to handle the film.

Zinnemann was an excellent choice as a director. He was known for his respect of actors, and the film was one that for success would depend on the performance of the cast. Zinnemann had also worked on short subjects earlier in his career and had developed a technique of cutting away everything but the necessities—important in bringing *From Here to Eternity* down to a workable but effective size. Already evident in his work (*High Noon*, 1952), the thematic concern of *From Here to Eternity*, how an individual fights for what he believes to be right, was important to Zinnemann and a theme he would return to in later films (*A Nun's Story*, 1959; *A Man for All Seasons*, 1966).

Surprisingly, considering the Cold War temperament of the times, the film is not a glorification of military life. Although the problems of bad leadership and abuse of authority are solved by the army in the film (unlike the book), officers are shown to be pompous, arrogant and ignorant. Only some of the enlisted men are shown heroically. No glorious battles are depicted, and the climax is the Japanese sneak attack on Pearl Harbor. With love affairs involving an officer's wife and an enlisted man, a military outcast and a prostitute, the melodrama of military life is the focus of the film. The beach love scene of Burt Lancaster and Deborah Kerr has become a cliché, although at the time it was considered very risqué and erotic.

The film was a very big moneymaker for Columbia, and the production won 8 academy awards. One of those awards, for Best Supporting Actor, marked the comeback of Frank Sinatra. Probably most important of all, Hollywood learned that the American audience would support films that attempted to deal with adult situations and problems. The next year Columbia verified this theory with another successful adult drama, *On the Waterfront*.

—Ray Narducy

FUKUSHU SURU WA WARE NI ARI. Vengeance Is Mine. Production: Shochiku Co. Ltd.; color, 35mm; running time: 128 mins. Released 1979.

Produced by Kazuo Inoue; screenplay by Masaru Baba; from a book by Ryuzo Saki; directed by Shohei Imamura; photography by Shinsaku Himeda; edited by Keiichi Uraoka; music by Shinichiro Ikebe.

Filmed in Japan. Kinema Jumpo Award, Best Film, 1979-80.

Cast: Ken Ogata (*Iwao Enokizu*); Rentaro Mikuni (*Shizuo Enokizu*); Chocho Mikayo (*Kayo Enokizu*); Mitsuko Baisho (*Kazuko Enokizu*); Mayumi Ogawa (*Haru Asano*); Nijiko Kiyokawa (*Hisano Asano*).

Publications:

Reviews—"*Vengeance is Mine*" by F. Sartor in *Film en Televisie* (Brussels), May/June 1980; "*Vengeance is Mine*" by "Cart." in *Variety* (New York), 26 March 1980; articles—"New Directors/-New Films" in *The Museum of Modern Art* film notes, 11-23 April 1980; interview with Imamura by S. Hoaas in *Cinema Papers* (Melbourne), September/October 1981; "Shohei Imamura" by John Gillett in *Film Dope* (London), January 1983.

*   *   *

After a long search, in *Vengeance is Mine*, the Japanese police finally capture Iwao Enokizu, an almost legendary criminal who's left a trail of corpses to mark the last year of his murderous rampage across Japan. As the police drive him to prison, a flashback recounts the key moments in Enokizu's life: The humiliation of his father, a Japanese Catholic, by the military during the war; his brutal murders; and his relationship with the proprietress of a small inn at Hamamatsu, where he has avoided the police dragnet by passing himself off as a professor from Kyoto University. After finally being brought to justice, Enokizu confronts his wife and father—who have entered into an incestuous relationship—and declares that he finally understands the reason behind his rage.

Considered by many critics to be his masterpiece, *Vengeance is Mine* marked a return to feature filmmaking for director Shohei Imamura after an eight year "retirement" during which time he worked exclusively on documentaries for Japanese television. The film was extremely successful with both Japanese audiences and critics, who voted it "Best Japanese Film of the Year" in the prestigious film journal *Kinema Jumpo*. Its box-office success allowed Imamura to enter in an advantageous financial relationship with Shochiku Studios, which gave him the possibility of a better level of production while creating new national and international outlets for his work.

Imamura's work up until 1970 can be characterized as highly textured, almost baroque narratives which freely intertwined the sociological, the sexual, and the political; this was followed by a period in which he explored the outer limits of the documentary and the possibility of attaining a kind of "truth" on film. *Vengeance is Mine* introduced a new stage in Imamura'a development, one which returns to the narratological complexity of the pre-1970 work, but which unlike those films lacks the strong central character (in those early films, usually female) whose odyssey structures the film. Instead, *Vengeance is Mine* introduced a new series of films built on patterns of continuous disorientation, which causes each spectator to question the relation of each image to the next. Often, the beginnings and ends of actions only are shown; it is only later that we discover what actually happened. The focus of the action glides between Enokizu, his father, the proprietress at Hamamatsu, and the police investigation; deliberately undercutting any concentration on a single main character, Imamura instead creates a portrait of a world, of which Enokizu is perhaps the ugliest, yet most revealing, manifestation. Brilliantly photographed by Shinsaku Himeda, one of the greatest of all Japanese cinematographers and a frequent collaborator of Imamura's, *Vengeance is Mine* also features a superb performance by Ken Ogata as Enokizu.

—Richard Peña

OS FUZIS. Les Fusils. The Guns. Production: Copacabana Films, Embracine, and Daga Filmes (Brazil); black and white, 35mm; running time: 110 mins.; length: 3300 meters. Released 1964.

Produced by Jarbas Barbosa; screenplay by Miguel Torres and Ruy Guerra; from an adaptation by Pierre Pelegri, Demosthenes Theokary, and Philippe Dumarçay from an original story by Ruy Guerra; directed by Ruy Guerra; photography by Ricardo Aronovich; edited by Ruy Guerra; music by Moacyr Santos.

Filmed in Milagres.

Cast: Atila Lorio (*Gaura, the truck driver*); Nelson Xavier (*Mario*); Maria Gladys (*Luisa*); Leonides Bayer (*Sergeant*); Paulo Cesar (*Soldier*); Mauricio Loyola (*Bearded prophet*); Rui Polanah (*Civilian*); Hugo Carvana (*Soldier*); Joel Barcelos (*Father of the dead baby*); Ivan Candido.

Publications:

Book—*Brazilian Cinema* edited by Randal Johnson and Robert Stam, East New Brunswick, New Jersey 1982; articles—interview with Guerra by F. Leduc on *Os Fusis* in *Jeune cinéma* (Paris), April 1967; interview with Guerra by J.A. Fieschi and J. Narboni in *Cahiers du cinéma* (Paris), April 1967; interview with Guerra by G. Langlois in *Cinéma* (Paris), June 1967; interview with Guerra by P. Pelegri in *Positif* (Paris), July 1967; "Os Fuzis" by Van Zele in *Image et son* (Paris), November 1969; "Ruy Guerra" by Michel Ciment in *Second Wave*, New York 1970; "The Guns" by M. Tarratt in *Films and Filming* (London), December 1972; "Interview with Ruy Guerra" by Thomas Elsaesser in *Monograph* (London), April 1974; "History in the Brazilian Cinema" by Bradford E. Burns, Fred Estevez, Peter L. Reich, and Anne Fleck in *Luso-Brazilian Review* (Madison, Wisconsin), summer 1977; "The Fall: Formal Innovation and Radical Critique" in *Jump Cut* (Chicago), May 1979.

*   *   *

Os Fuzis (*The Guns*) is, arguably, Ray Guerra's greatest political film. This landmark work is unusual in that it relies primarily on a tradition of mainstream commercial cinema—the linear narrative—to convey profoundly political themes. Guerra imaginatively and effectively blends this tradition with features typical of documentary filmmaking.

The action is set in Brazil's semi-arid, underdeveloped Northeastern backlands (the *sertão*), and Guerra uses numerous devices, in addition to location shooting, to give his film the look of documentary. Early in the film, a subtitle appears that specifies the time and place of the action. The sub-plot of the holy man and his bull is, according to Guerra, based on a historical incident. Local customs (a procession of people praying for rain) and types (the leather-clad *vaqueiros*) are observed. In interview-like sequences, elderly inhabitants recall past events and personages in the region's history, such as religious zealot Antônio Conselheiro and the government he established and defended at Canudos.

The film's plot and sub-plot weave together the political problems of the oppression of the villagers by the military and the forces of fanatic religious mysticism. Gaúcho's solution, to battle the soldiers, fails because it springs from emotional impulse rather than from any revolutionary consciousness. Gaúcho—himself an outsider—is not a revolutionary leader; his response is personal, and it is not supported by the masses. The butchering of the sacred bull, however, is a collective revolutionary action reflecting a change of consciousness on the part of the villagers. The followers of the holy man had been seeking a fantastic solution (worshipping an animal) instead of a political and/or economic solution to their problem of hunger. The crowd's cry, "It's meat!," heralds the downfall of the holy man: his bull has been discarded as a religious symbol; it is now perceived as a source of food.

Unlike many Latin American political films *Os Fuzis* not only avoids facile political solutions, but it also features complex characters and interpersonal relations. Gaúcho initially acts like a typically exploitative truck driver, but his moral behavior evolves when he sinks as low as the starving villagers. The tortuous mise-en-scène of the love scene between Mario and his girlfriend brilliantly reflects the complex approach-avoidance conflict the girl faces: she loves Mario, but she is restrained in expressing this love by her identification with the villagers and by her revulsion over Mario's complicity in the cover-up. At the end of the film, the villagers have derived no political profit from Gaúcho's suicidal act, and they will continue to be subject to military oppression. The soldiers themselves remain the corrupt victims of the system.

Many Brazilians see *Os Fuzis* as a forceful condemnation of the needless killing, the corruption, and the ties to powerful landowning and entrepreneurial interests that have characterized their country's military. The references in the film to Antônio Conselheiro's rebellion (1896-97) remind viewers that the Brazilian military in the 1960's still operated much as it did during the infamous Canudos compaign—a totalitarian crime perpetrated against a backlands community.

When first shown in Brazil in 1963, *Os Fuzis* did poorly because many viewers considered the film's narrative needlessly obscure and complex. Today, however, critics recognize the film as a great, typical work of the first phase of Brazil's highly regarded Cinema Novo. Guerra, like other filmmakers of this period, opposed the ideology and aesthetics of Hollywood and Brazilian commercial cinema by favoring low-budget, independently produced films shot on location. For Guerra and his colleagues, filmmaking was a key political-cultural activity in the battle against Brazil's neo-colonialism.

—Dennis West

THE GENERAL. Production: Buster Keaton Productions and United Artists; 1926; black and white, 35mm, silent; running time: about 74 minutes; length: 8 reels, 7500 feet. Released 18 December 1926, New York. Re-released after 1928 with musical soundtrack and sound effects.

Produced by Joseph Schenck and Buster Keaton; scenario by Al Boasberg and Charles Smith after a storyline by Buster Keaton and Clyde Bruckman, adapted by Al Boasberg and Charles Smith; from *The Great Locomotive Chase* by William Pittinger; directed by Buster Keaton and Clyde Bruckman; photography by Dev Jennings and Bert Haines; edited by Sherman Kell with Harry Barnes; production design by Fred Gabourie; technical direction by Fred Gabourie.

Filmed during 1926 in Oregon. Cost: $250,000 (estimated).

Cast: Buster Keaton (*Johnnie Gray*); Marion Mack (*Annabelle Lee*); Glen Cavender (*Capt. Anderson*); Jim Farley (*General Thatcher*); Frederick Vroom (*Southern general*); Charles Smith (*Annabelle's father*); Frank Barnes (*Annabelle's brother*); Joe Keaton, Mike Denlin, Tom Nawm (*Union generals*).

Publications:

Scripts—"*Le Mécano de la 'General'*" by Buster Keaton in *Avant-Scène du cinéma* (Paris), February 1975; books—*Buster Keaton* by Davide Turconi and Francesco Savio, Venice 1963; *Buster Keaton* by Jean-Patrick Lebel, Paris 1964; *Buster Keaton* by Marcel Oms, Premier Plan No.31, Lyon 1964; *Keaton* by Rudi Blesh, New York 1966; *My Wonderful World* by Buster Keaton with Charles Samuels, London 1967; *The Great Films: 50 Golden Years of Motion Pictures* by Bosley Crowther, New York 1967; *The Parade's Gone By* by Kevin Brownlow, New York 1968; *Hollywood in the Twenties* by David Robinson, New York 1968; *4 Great Comedians* by Donald McCaffrey, New York 1968; *Buster Keaton* by David Robinson, London 1968; *A Short History of the Movies* by Gerald Mast, New York 1971; *Filmguide to The General* by E. Rubinstein, Bloomington, Indiana 1973; *The Silent Clowns* by Walter Kerr, New York 1975; *The Best of Buster* edited by Richard Anobile, New York 1976; *Buster Keaton and the Dynamics of Visual Wit* by George Wead, New York 1976; *Keaton: The Silent Features Close Up* by Daniel Moews, Berkeley, California 1977; *The Film Career of Buster Keaton* by George Wead and George Ellis, Boston 1977; *Keaton: The Man Who Wouldn't Lie Down* by Tom Dardis, New York 1979; *The Comic Mind: Comedy and the Movies* by Gerald Mast, Chicago, revised edition, 1979; articles—"Sketch" by Joseph Keaton in *Photoplay* (New York), May 1927; article by Penelope Houston in *Sight and Sound* (London), April/June 1953; "The Great Stone Face" by Christopher Bishop in *Film Quarterly* (Berkeley), fall 1958; "Buster Keaton" by Brian Baxter in *Film* (London), November/December 1958; "Comedy's Greatest Era" in *Agee on Film* by James Agee, New York 1958; special Keaton issue of *Cahiers du cinéma* (Paris), August 1958; "*The General*" by Philip Strick in *Films and Filming* (London), September 1961; "Rétrospective Buster Keaton" by Claude Beylie and others in *Cahiers du cinéma* (Paris), April 1962; "Le Mécano de la générale" by Georges Sadoul in *Les Lettres Françaises* (Paris), 28 June 1962; article by Allen Eyles in *Films and Filming* (London), October 1963; "Keaton at Venice" by John Gillett and James Blue in *Sight and Sound* (London), winter 1965-66; "Le Génie de Buster Keaton" by Georges Sadoul in *Les Lettres Françaises* (Paris), 10 February 1966; article by Gerald

Mast in *Cinema Journal* (Evanston, Illinois), spring 1970; "Buster Keaton" by Anne Villelaur in *Dossiers du cinéma: Cinéastes* I, Paris 1971; "Buster Keaton" in *The Primal Screen* by Andrew Sarris, New York 1973; "Le Général Buster" in *Avant-Scène du cinéma* (Paris), February 1975; "The Limits of Silent Comedy" by Jeremy Cott in *Literature/Film Quarterly* (Salisbury, Maryland), spring 1975; "More is Less: Comedy and Sound" by P. Warshow in *Film Quarterly* (Berkeley), fall 1977; "The Great Locomotive Chase" by G. Wead in *American Film* (Washington, D.C.), July/August 1977.

*   *   *

The General is by far the most famous of the comedy features in which Buster Keaton starred, and in several cases directed or co-directed, between 1923 and 1928. It is also one of the finest; and has appeared on many 10-best-films list. All of his silent features followed a basic story formula (a popular one in silent comedy): a young "failure" finally displays prowess and wins the girl. In addition, his films demonstrated, in part or in whole, a striking cinematic imagination as well as superb comic acting. While *The General may* not be a greater artistic achievement than *The Navigator* or *Sherlock, Jr.*, it has a number of features that have made it a special favorite of silent film fans.

The film is distinctive for its Civil War setting and location shooting. It was shot mostly in Oregon, where necessary narrow-gauge railroad tracks were still to be found. (Compare, for contrast, the studio look of Chaplin's *The Gold Rush*, made at about the same time.) The usually fine photography (Matthew Brady comparisons are inevitable), the extensive action involving the trains, the ambitious subject based on history—the theft and recovery of the locomotive, "The General"—and, the serious element of the drama combined to give this film an epic sweep that is surely unique in silent comedy.

In the typical Buster Keaton comedy the hero is at first anything but heroic: he is callow, bumbling, and even in some films effete. Through perseverance, self-teaching and luck he becomes a success and—sometimes as a bonus but usually as the original goal—he is united with the woman of his dreams. *The General* is distinctive in that Johnnie Gray is an expert in at least one field, railroad engineering. In fact his competence at his job is what prevents him from being accepted into the Confderate army, setting the rest of the plot in motion. Of course, he must still demonstrate bravery to win the heart of Annabelle Lee; and, to satisfy himself, must succeed as a soldier as well. And to be sure, even in railroading he makes some spectacularly comic miatakes in pursuing the Yankee train-nappers. He does, however, demonstrate early on the kind of hilariously smooth efficiency that other Keaton characters learn only with time (as in *The Navigator*) or achieve in fantasy (*Sherlock, Jr.*): e.g., his clambering aboard the General and pressing the starting lever in one swift movement; or his deft way of knocking out a Yankee guard face to face. The unselfconscious heroism and expertise of Johnnie Gray are simultaneously touching and amusing—though much of his success is also due to good fortune (as with the flyaway blade of his sword in the battle scene).

The heroine of the film, delightfully played by Marion Mack, has a larger and more unusual role than in the other Keaton features (excepting *The Navigator*). Usually a Keaton heroine is either haughty or sweet, but in each case little more than the goal to be attained. Annabelle is forced by circumstances to become skilled in railroading while fleeing southward with the "General." There is arguably some stereotype of the foolish female in some of Annabelle's earlier efforts to block the pursuers and feed the engine, but the evolving of her role from the "unattainable goal" to a partner in action is still refreshing. The moment in which the exasperated Johnnie feigns strangling his dream girl and then swiftly kisses her is one of the most memorable romantic gestures in silent film.

The General is filled with surprising moments: brilliant comic gags or fine touches of sentiment that never go on long enough to become maudlin. Perhaps the comedy is especially striking because it grows out of a serious melodramtic pursuit—but it is particularly satisfying because it stems from the characters of the hero and heroine or from the ironic perspective of the camera. The point has been made that the camera in Chaplin's films was used mainly to record the body or facial movements of its pantomine hero while in Keaton's film the comedy often depends on special placement of the camera, or on special visual effects. A classic example in *The General* occurs when Johnnie has accidentally caused the cannon attachment to be aimed directly at his own train. However, he and his train are spared, and better yet, the Yankees are convinced of the powers of their pursuer(s), when the forepart of Johnnie's train curves left and the cannon fires directly ahead—nearly blasting the back car of the train on the track ahead. The elegance of the gag centers on the placement of the camera behind and above the cannon car, grandly recording the beautifully timed action in one shot. Another famous moment in the film—this one visually simple and emotionally complex—occurs when Johnnie, rejected by Annabelle, sits disconsolately on the crossbar of the engine's wheels as the train starts up and carries him up and down twice before he realizes what is going on. His forlorn, unmoving body posture is at once astonishingly sad and funny; any drift into sentimentality is destroyed by Johnnie's sudden stare of awareness as he passes into the train shed. The overall wit and irony of the shot are dependent on the camera placement at a sufficient distance to show the small size of Johnnie's body against the sublimely unaware and ongoing machine.

Much more could be said about this shot, and has been said by analysts of the film: e.g., the way it stresses a "togetherness" between Johnnie and his beloved engine which is a major subject of the film; and the way that the final shot of the film is a counterpart to it, with both Johnnie and Annabelle sitting on the crossbar. This correspondence of shots is a reminder that the construction of the film is unusually tight and balanced in its overall arc of chase and return. The more one attempts to analyze the comedy, or merely describe certain brilliant shots—such as the one of Johnnie on the cowcatcher removing logs from the tracks—the more one admires the classic assurance and economy of the film.

—Joseph Milicia

GERTIE THE DINOSAUR. black and white, 35mm, animation, silent; running time: about 7 mins. (length varies). Released as one-reel film in 1914, though the character was created and seen in a short cartoon in McCay's vaudeville act circa 1909.

Scripted, animated, photographed, and edited by Winsor McCay; assisted by John Fitzsimmons.

Publications:

Review—"People of the Stage: Winsor McCay" by Montgomery Phester (?) in the *Cincinnati Commercial Tribune*, 28 November 1909; books—*Animated Film: Concepts, Methods, Uses* by Roy Madsen, New York 1969; *American Silent Film* by William K. Everson, New York 1978; articles—"The History of the Animated Cartoon" in *The Journal of Motion Pictures Inventors*, 24 September 1933; "Movie Cartoons" by Winsor McCay in the *New York Evening Journal*, 27 July 1934; "McCay Before Disney" by H. Wilson in *Time* (New York), 10 January 1938; "Drawings That Are Alive" by Jules Schwerin in *Films in Review* (New York), September 1950; "In Search of Winsor McCay" by Judith O'Sullivan in *American Film Institute Report* (Washington, D.C.), summer 1974; "The Animated Art of Winsor McCay" by Michael Patrick Hearn in *American Artist* (New York), May 1975; "The Birth of Animation" by J. Canemaker in *Millimeter* (New York), April 1975; "Winsor McCay" by J. Canemaker in *Film Comment* (New York), January/February 1975; "Le Festival d'Annecy et les Rencontres internationales du cinéma d'animation" by A. Cornand in *Image et son* (Paris), January 1977.

*   *   *

Gertie the Dinosaur is the masterpiece of early animation. It employed 10,000 animated drawings inked on rice paper and mounted on cardboard. Artist Winsor McCay used *full animation*—a new drawing for each individual frame of film—and while he himself did all the drawings of Gertie, he hired his young neighbor John Fitzsimmons to assist him in tracing the stationary background of trees rocks, and water. *Gertie* is the improvement and development of McCay's animation experiments in his first two films, *Little Nemo* and *The Story of a Mosquito*.

McCay originally made *Gertie* for his vaudeville act as a lightning-sketch artist. In the routine, McCay announced that he could make a drawing come to life; then a projected film depicting an animated dinosaur walking from the background into the foreground appeared. McCay talked to the cartoon Gertie and gave her commands to which she would respond. Gertie raised her left leg, devoured a tree stump, became distracted by a sea serpent, lay down and rolled over, tossed a passing elephant into the lake, cried like a child when scolded, and caught a pumpkin supposedly tossed to her by McCay. As the first cartoon star, she displayed the charm, personality, and mischievousness of a playful puppy. For the finale, Gertie bent down and as she got up and walked away, carried an animated man on her back, thus appearing to take McCay into the screen with her.

For wider distribution, McCay turned his *Gertie the Dinosaur* into a one-reel film which frames the animated sequence with a live-action story. In the live-action portion, McCay accepts a bet from fellow cartoonist George McManus that he can make the dinosaur come to life. McCay is then shown with his stacks of cards demostrating the laborious process by which he made *Gertie*. At a dinner of cartoonists, he unveils his masterpiece, and the animated sequence incorporates a series of title cards for McCay's dialogue with Gertie. After the animation ends, the dinner party toasts McCay's achievement, and McManus winds up losing the bet as well as footing the bill for dinner.

In its own time, *Gertie the Dinosaur* overshadowed all prior animated films, and it inspired a generation of animators who would begin their careers over the next decade. Audiences today still marvel at the fluidity of the movement and the amount of animated detail—Gertie's sides expanding and contracting as she breathes, particles of dirt falling from the tree trunk she devours, Gertie swaying back and forth. The shimmering or vibrating lines in the background (due to a primitive retracing process) hardly matter and do not detract from the captivating dinosaur in the foreground.

McCay also used for the first time an animation method known as the *split system*. Instead of drawing an "action" in sequential order, he split it up into poses, drawing the first pose, the last pose, the halfway pose, and then continuing to draw the poses in between the last two drawn. In this manner, he was able to simplify timing and placement with a method that underwent further refinement only after the advent of sound cartoons in 1928, when Walt Disney insisted upon its use. McCay also discovered another labor saving device in *Gertie* by re-using drawings for repeated cycles of action. He drew Gertie making a gesture—breathing or swaying—and rephotographed the same series of drawings several times.

While it was neither the first animated cartoon nor McCay's first animated cartoon, *Gertie the Dinosaur* is generally regarded as the first *important* cartoon in film history.

—Lauren Rabinovitz

GERTRUD. Production: Palladium (Denmark); black and white, 35mm; running time: 115 mins.; length: 3440 meters. Released 8 December 1964, Paris.

Produced by Jørgen Nielsen with John Hilbard as executive producer; screenplay by Carl Theodor Dreyer; from the play by Hjalmar Söderberg; directed by Carl Theodor Dreyer; photography by Henning Bendtsen with Arne Abrahamsen; edited by Edith Schlüssel; sound by Knud Kristensen; art direction by Kai Rasch; music and solo numbers by Jørgen Jersild, songs by Grethe Risbjerg Thomsen, "Ich grolle nicht" by Robert Schumann, lyrics by Heinrich Heine; costumes designed by Berit Nykjaer; assistants: Solveig Ersgaard and Jens Ravn.

Cast: Nina Pens Rode (*Gertrud Kanning*); Bendt Rothe (*Gustav Kanning*); Ebbe Rode (*Gabriel Lidman*); Baard Owe (*Erland Jansson*); Axel Strøbye (*Axel Nygren*); Anna Malberg (*Kanning's Mother*); Edouard Mielche (*The Rector Magnificus*); Vera Gebuhr (*Kanning's Maid*); Karl Gustav Ahlefeldt; Lars Knutzon; William Knoblauch; Valsø Holm; Ole Sarvig.

Publications:

Script—"*Gertrud*" in *Cinque Film* edited by Giulio Einaudi, Torino, Italy 1967; reviews—"A Contre-courant" by Georges Sadoul in *Les Lettres françaises* (Paris), no. 1061, 1964; "Circulaire" by Michel Delahaye in *Cahiers du cinéma* (Paris), no. 164, 1965; "*Gertrud*" by Henry Hart in *Films in Review* (New York), no. 8, 1965; "*Gertrud*" by Ib Monty in *Kosmorama* (Copenhagen), no. 69, 1965; "*Gertrud*" by Elliot Stein in *Sight and Sound* (London), no. 2, 1965; review by Andrew Sarris in *The Village Voice* (New York), 2 June 1966; books—*Om Filmen* by Carl Theodor Dreyer, Copenhagen 1964; *The Films of Carl Dreyer* by Eileen Bowser, New York 1964; *Portrait of Carl Th. Dreyer* by Ib Monty, Copenhagen 1965; *Carl Th. Dreyer, Danish Film Director*, edited by Soren Dyssegaard, Copenhagen 1968; *Carl Th. Dreyer* by Claude Perrin, Paris 1969; *Carl Theodor Dreyer*, Amsterdam 1970; *Carl Th. Dreyer* by Jean Sémolué, Paris 1970; *The Cinema of Carl Dreyer* by Tom Milne, New York 1970;

Dreyer in Double Reflection, edited by Donald Skoller, New York 1973; *Dreyer*, edited by Mark Nash, London 1977; *Carl Theodor Dreyer* by Pier Giorgio Tone, Florence 1978; *The Films of Carl-Theodor Dreyer* by David Bordwell, Berkeley, California 1981; articles—"Dreyer" by Ken Kelman in *Film Culture* (New York), no.35, 1964-65; "La Parole de la fin" by André Téchiné in *Cahiers du cinéma* (Paris), no.164, 1965; "*Gertrud*" by Andrée Tournés in *Jeune Cinéma* (Paris), no.5, 1965; "Ett spel om en dröm. En analys av Carl Th. Dreyers film *Gertrud*" by Børge Trolle in *Filmrutan* (Liding, Sweden), no.1, 1965; "Between Heaven and Hell: Interview with Carl Dreyer" by Michel Delahaye in *Cahiers du Cinema in English* (New York), no.4 1966; "An Interview with Carl Dreyer" by Borge Trolle in *Film Culture* (New York), summer 1966; "The Basic Demand of Life for Love" by Kirk Bond in *Film Comment* (New York), fall 1966; "To Rescue *Gertrud*" by Donald Skoller in *Film Comment* (fall 1966); "*Gertrud*" by Elsa Gress Wright in *Film Quarterly* (Berkeley), spring 1966; "My Working is in Relation to the Future: A Conversation with Carl Dreyer" by Carl Lerner in *Film Comment* (New York), fall 1966; article by Alexander Sesonske in *Film Society Review* (New York), March 1967; "Corenza e modernità di Gertrud" by Giuseppe Perruzzi in *Cinema nuovo* (Turin), no.190, 1967; article by Chris Jones in *Films and Filming* (London), January 1969; "Propositions" by Noel Burch in *Afterimage* (Rochester, New York), no.5, 1974.

* * *

For the last 20 years of his career, Dreyer worked on a film about Jesus Christ. It was never realized, though his script was published posthumously in 1968. Near the end of his life, Dreyer was also planning a film of *Medea*. He was aiming at tragedy, reflected again in *Gertrud*, which was to be his last film.

Dreyer's last four films were based on plays. *Gertrud* is a 1906 play by Hjalmar Söderberg. It is a problem-drama in the manner of Ibsen, but while the play is naturalistic, the film is not. Dreyer considered the film an experiment; he wanted to co-ordinate the word and the image, to create harmony between what is seen and what is heard. The function of the images is to open up a perspective on the characters, who manifest themselves in the way they speak and move. *Gertrud* contains almost no close-ups; it is a film of travelling shots and long, uncut scenes. The film has only 89 shots, with very few sets and only one exterior scene. The film's depiction of life/reality is antinaturalistic and stylized, and Dreyer treats the story as a tragedy. He called the film "a portrait of time from the beginning of the century," and he has stressed typical features of that period and milieu. As in *La Passion de Jeanne d'Arc* he has tried to transform the whole of "the past reality into camera-reality," to quote Siegfried Kracauer.

Gertrud is the last of Dreyer's many portraits of women. Gertrud, however, is not a suffering woman, submissive to men; she is superior to them. A free intellectual woman with strong will-power, she rejects the men in her life. While these men prefer their careers and pleasures, for Gertrud love is all. Gertrud knows she will always come second, and prefers to abandon men and withdraw into solitude. She knows that her demands on life cannot be fulfilled, so she chooses to live in accordance with her inner demands. In Gertrud, Dreyer finds a greatness which had also fascinated him about Jeanne d'Arc. This is not a naturalistic portrayal, but a tragic one—Gertrud is bound for defeat. Both she and the men are presented in a disquieting double light.

In many ways the 75-year-old Dreyer was in harmony with the modern, younger directors. In films by Antonioni, Godard and

Truffaut the women characters often demand a love which should be placed above everything else, a love which was more than most men could or would grant. *Gertrud* is also amazingly in harmony with the stylistic trends of the films of the sixties. Because Dreyer never consciously tried to keep up with his time, but kept his integrity, he was more modern in his last film than many of the directors were who tried to adjust to their time.

Gertrud, premiering in Paris, was badly received by most of the Danish and French reviewers. However, in the film magazines *Gertrud* did find more understanding critics. With his last film, Dreyer once again caused great controversy, even if he did not ask for it. *Gertrud* is still a film which divides its audience.

—Ib Monty

IL GIARDINO DEI FINZI-CONTINI. The Garden of the Finzi-Contini. Le Jardin des Finzi-Contini. Production: Documento Film (Italy) and CCC Filmkunst (West Germany); Eastmancolor, 35mm; running time: 95 mins., some sources list 103 mins. Released 1970.

Produced by G.H. Lucari and Arthur Cohn; screenplay by Tullio Pinelli, Valerio Zurlini, Franco Brusati, Ugo Pirro, Vittorio Bonicelli, and Alain Katz; from the novel by Giorgio Bassani; directed by Vittorio De Sica; photography by Ennio Guarnieri; edited by A. Novelli; production design by Giancarlo Bartolini Salembini; music by Manuel De Sica.

Filmed in Italy. Berlin Film Festival, Best Film, 1971.

Cast: Dominique Sanda (*Micol*); Lino Capollichio (*Giorgio*); Helmut Berger (*Alberto*); Fabio Testi (*Bruno Malnate*); Romollo Valli (*Giorgio's father*); Katina Morisani (*Barbara*); Camillo Angelini-Rota (*Professor Finzi-Contini*); Katina Viglietti (*Olga Finzi-Contini*).

Publications:

Reviews—by Gerard Langlois in *Les Lettres françaises* (Paris), 15 December 1971; "*Le Jardin des Finzi-Contini*" by G. Allombert in *Image et son* (Paris), February 1972; "*Le Jardin des Finzi-Contini*" by G. Braucourt in *Ecran* (Paris), February 1972; "*The Garden of the Finzi-Continis*" by L. Corbin in *Films in Review* (New York), February 1972; "*Le Jardin des Finzi-Contini*" by G. Legrand in *Positif* (Paris), March 1972; "*The Garden of the Finzi-Continis*" by A. Stuart in *Films and Filming* (London), August 1972; books—*Encountering Directors* by Charles Thomas Samuels, New York 1972; *La Mia Vita con Vittorio De Sica* by Maria Mercader, Milan, Italy 1978; *Anthologie du cinéma* vol.10, Paris 1979; articles—"Inter/View with Vittorio de Sica" by D. Lyons in *Inter/View* (New York), February 1972; "What Directors are Saying" in *Action* (Los Angeles), May-June 1972; "*The Garden of the Finzi-Continis*" by S.G. Eskin in *Literature/Film Quarterly* (Salisbury, Maryland), spring 1973; issue devoted to De Sica edited by O. Caldiron, *Bianco e nero* (Rome), September/December 1975; "Le Fantasme dans le cinéma 'Retro'" by L. Frenkel in *Cahiers de la Cinématheque* (Perpignan, France), spring 1976; "Vittorio de Sica 1902-1974" by Henri Agel, special issue of *Avant-Scène du*

cinéma (Paris), 15 October 1978; "Vittorio de Sica" by J. Passalacqua in *Films in Review* (New York), April 1978.

*   *   *

During the postwar years, Vittorio De Sica directed a trio of classic neorealistic dramas: *Shoeshine*, *The Bicycle Thief* and *Umberto D*, all shot on actual locations, using non-professionals as actors and dealing with real problems. His style, however, failed to evolve, and his films became exercises in commercialism. For two decades, De Sica did not produce a film to compare with his earlier masterpiece. (*Two Women*, released in 1960, is perhaps the only exception.)

In the last years of his career, the filmmaker returned to the limelight with a superior drama, *The Garden of the Finzi-Contini*. The film is set in the late 1930s, and depicts the members of the wealthy Finzi-Contini family of Ferrara who are beautiful, cultured—and Sephardic Jews. While a middle-class Jewish family tries to accommodate itself—but not escape from—the pervading anti-Semitism of Mussolini's fascist state, the Finzi-Continis ignore the political realities of their time. They feel safe, secure in their money and status. The high walls of their estate, with its private park, stable and tennis courts, will keep them immune from fascism; their garden becomes a metaphor for all that is good and beautiful in the world. Meanwhile Jews are banned from clubs, libraries, and business activities. Finally, the aristocratic Finzi-Continis and their bourgeois neighbors are herded together with thousands of other Jews, and dispatched to the concentration camps. Their formality, their outdated 19th century liberalism, will not save them.

The film's scenario is slowly and gracefully unravelled, and novelistic in structure. *The Garden of the Finzi-Contini*, from Georgio Bassani's semi-autobiographical novel, is told from the point of view of Georgio, a middle-class boy in love with Micol, the Finzi-Contini daughter. Thus, the film is different from *Shoeshine*, *The Bicycle Thief* and *Umberto D*, in which events simply are brought to a climax. The leading players are professional actors and, unlike the earlier films, the story is told from a distance of over 30 years. De Sica evokes a nostalgic ambience: there is soft-focus cinematography, with pastel hues and sunlight filtering through trees; Micol constantly plays a 78 rpm record of "I'm Getting Sentimental Over You." As Richard Schickel wrote, "The film looks as if it had been photographed through the mists of time."

The Garden of the Finzi-Contini may not for these reasons be a pure neorealistic film, but it is unmistakably rooted in the movement. De Sica shot it on authentic locations, and some of the cast are non-professionals: for example, the elder Finzi-Continis are played by Turin aristocrats. Most importantly, the scenario relates thematically to the social vision and truth of human interaction that typifies neorealism. In all, the characters in a neo-realist world are victimized by an impersonal, inhumane world: the boys in *Shoeshine*; the poor man who loses his bicycle in *The Bicycle Thief*; the old man in *Umberto D*; and finally the Finzi-Continis.

—Rob Edelman

GIANT. Production: Warner Bros. Pictures Inc.; 1956; Warner-color, 35mm; running time: 198 mins. Released 1956.

Produced by George Stevens and Henry Ginsberg; screenplay by Fred Guiol and Ivan Moffat; from the novel by Edna Ferber; directed by George Stevens; photography by William C. Mellor and Edwin DuPar; edited by William Hornbeck, Philip W. Anderson, and Fred Bohanen; art direction by Ralph S. Hurst; music by Dmitri Tiomkin; costumes designed by Moss Mabry and Marjorie Best.

Filmed in Texas. Academy Award, Best Direction, 1956.

Cast: Elizabeth Taylor (*Leslie Lynnton Benedict*); Rock Hudson (*Bick Benedict*); James Dean (*Jett Rink*); Mercedes McCambridge (*Luz Benedict, the older*); Jane Withers (*Vashti Snythe*); Chill Wills (*Uncle Bawley Benedict*); Carroll Baker (*Luz Benedict, the younger*); Dennis Hopper (*Jordan Benedict III*); Elsa Cardenas (*Juana Benedict*); Fran Bennett (*Judy Benedict*).

Publications:

Reviews—"*Giant*" by Andrew Sarris in *Film Culture* (New York), no.10, 1956; review by Courtland Phipps in *Films in Review* (New York), November 1956; review by Penelope Houston in *Sight and Sound* (London), winter 1956-57; books—*The Official James Dean Anniversary Book* edited by Peter Myerson, New York 1956; *The Real James Dean Story*, New York 1956; *James Dean: A Biography* by William Bast, New York 1956; *George Stevens: An American Romantic* by Donald Richie, New York 1970; *The Movie Makers: Artists in the Industry* by Rev. Gene D. Phillips, Chicago 1973; *Elizabeth Taylor* by Foster Hirsch, New York 1973; *The Films of James Dean* by Mark Whittman, London 1974; *James Dean—The Mutant King* by David Dalton, San Francisco 1974; *James Dean—A Short Life* by Venable Herndon, New York 1974; *The Films of Elizabeth Taylor* by Susan d'Arcy, London 1974; articles—"New Pictures" in *Time* (New York), 22 October 1956; "*Giant* Enhanced by Bold, Offbeat Photography" by Arthur Rowan in *American Cinematographer* (Hollywood), March 1956; "Liz Taylor as Edna Ferber's Heroine" by Jon Whitcomb in *Cosmopolitan* (New York), August 1956; "A Tale of Rich Land and Its Lords" in *Life* (New York), 15 October 1956; "George Stevens and the American Dream" by E. Archer in *Film Culture* (New York), no.1, 1957; article by Paul Rotha in *Films and Filming* (London), February 1957; "George Stevens" by Herbert H. Luft in *Films in Review* (New York), November 1958; "Hollywood Romantic" by J. Stang in *Films and Filming* (London), July 1959; article by Paul Mayersburg in *Movie* (London), November 1962; article by V.F. Perkins in *Movie* (London), November 1962; article by Richard Whitehall in *Films and Filming* (London), August 1962; "Sentiment and Humanism" by N. Bartlett in *Film* (London), spring 1964; interview with Stevens in *Cinema* (Beverly Hills), December/January 1965; "The Picture" by James R. Silke in *Cinema* (Beverly Hills), December/January 1965; "Greatest—Stevens" by Douglas McVay in *Films and Filming* (London), April 1965 and May 1965; "George Stevens" by B. Beresford in *Film* (London), summer 1970; *George Stevens: An American Romantic* by Donald Richie, New York 1970; "Elizabeth Taylor" by Gabe Essoe in *Films in Review* (New York), August/September 1970; issue devoted to Stevens in *Dialogue on Film* (AFI, Washington, D.C.), no.1, 1972; "*Giant*" by J.M. Lardinois in *Apec-Revue belge du cinéma* (Brussels), no.1-2, 1975; "George Stevens",

special issue of *Dialogue on Film* (Washington, D.C.), May/-June 1975; "*Giant*" by Maria Soule in *Magill's Survey of Cinema, Vol. II* edited by Frank N. Magill, Englewood Cliffs, New Jersey 1980.

*   *   *

In 1956 George Stevens released his monumental film of Edna Ferber's novel *Giant*, which was not only a great box office success, but won him his second Academy Award as best director and the Screen Directors' Guild Award as well. *Giant* is made with the same skilled craftsmanship which marks every Stevens film; and his painstaking care seems to inspire his actors to give performances that often surpass their work for other directors. As Bick and Leslie Benedict, a couple maturing into middle age on a ranch in modern Texas, Rock Hudson and Elizabeth Taylor have never been better.

Moreover, James Dean, who died in an auto accident just after finishing *Giant*, received a posthumous Academy Award nomination for his role as Jett Rink, the cowhand on the Benedict ranch who becomes a Texas oil magnate. Jett is an outsider from the start, and is as remote from the other cowhands on the ranch as he is from the Benedict clan, though he secretly loves Leslie. Even after he strikes it rich, Jett is not accepted by the Texas "artistocracy." who patronize him for his inability to adopt the pretensions of the *nouveaux riches*.

Though Jett has grown calloused and selfish in his rise to power, he continues to win our sympathy; for we are able to perceive in him the same lonely and vulnerable cowboy that he has always been, despite all of his bravado. This is emphisized in his last scene, when he appears blind drunk at a banquet in his honor, and passes out at the speakers' table. By the time he awakens, the embarrassed guests have all departed. In a stupor he delivers his speech to an empty dining hall, and Stevens photographs him in looming long shots which encompass the huge banquet hall and dwarf Jett in his isolation. The melancholy harmonica theme, associated earlier with Jett's days as a cowhand, accompanies his speech, reminding us that, underneath, he remains the man he always has been. Jett finally collapses, overturning the whole speakers' table, as his bid for status comes crashing down on him.

By reflecting on the tragedy of Jett's life, Bick seems to have finally realized the truth of a remark made by his son-in-law earlier in the film which serves as an ironic comment on the film's title: the acquisitive Texas millionaires have confused bigness with greatness, and have become less human in the bargain.

That Bick is becoming more concerned for others is reflected in one of the film's last sequences. Bick fights wih the proprietor of a highway luncheonette who refuses to serve Mexican-Americans; to his credit, Bick goes down swinging, but for the first time in his life he loses a fight. In Bick's case, Stevens suggests, bigness may at last come to mean greatness.

—Gene D. Phillips

———————

GIMME SHELTER. 1970; color, 35mm; running time: 90 mins. Released 1970.

Produced by Albert Maysles, David Maysles, and Charlotte Zwerin, with Porter Bibb; directed by Albert Maysles, David

Maysles, and Charlotte Zwerin; photography by Albert and David Maysles, Peter Adair, Baird Bryant, Joan Churchill, Ron Dorfman, Robert Elfstrom, Elliot Erwitt, Bob Fiori, Adam Giffard, William Kaplan, Kevin Keating, Stephen Lighthill, George Lucas, Jim Moody, Jack Newman, Pekke Niemela, Robert Primes, Eric Saarinen, Peter Smokler, Paul Ryan, Coulter Watt, Gary Weiss and Bill Yarrus; edited by Ellen Giffard, Robert Farren, Joanne Burke and Kent McKinney; sound by Michael Becker, John Brumbaugh, Howard Cheslet, Pepper Crawford, Stanley Cronquist, Paul Deason, Tom Goodwin, Peter Pilafin, Orly Lindgren, Walter Murch, Art Rochester, Nelson Stoll, David Thompson and Alvin Tokunow; sound mixed by Bill Blachy; music by the Rolling Stones.

Filmed 1969 in Altamont Speedway in northern California; Madison Square Garden, New York City; and Muscle Shoals, Alabama.

Publications:

Script—"*Gimme Shelter*: Production Notes" by Albert and David Maysles in *Filmmakers Newsletter* (Ward Hill, Massachusetts), December 1971; reviews—in *Hollywood Reporter*, 25 November 1970; "The Current Cinema/Beyond Pirandello" by Pauline Kael in the *New Yorker*, 19 December 1970; "*Gimme Shelter*" by Patrick McFaddin in *Film Society Review* (New York), November 1970; books—*Nonfiction Film: A Critical History* by Richard Barsam, New York 1973; *Up and Down with the Rolling Stones* by Tony Sanchez, New York 1979; articles— "Rock's 'We Are One' Myth" by Craig McGregor in *The New York Times*, 9 May 1971; "*Gimme Shelter*: A Corkscrew or a Cathedral?" by David Sadkin in *Filmmakers Newsletter* (Ward Hill, Massachusetts), December 1971; "Delicately Handled Dynamite" by Peter Schjeldahl in *The New York Times*, 3 January 1971; "A Whitewash of Jagger" by Albert Goldman in *The New York Times*, 3 January 1971; "Why Are We Fighting? A Closer Look at *Gimme Shelter*" by Peter Buckley in *Films and Filming* (London), August 1971; "Circumstantial Evidence: An Interview with David and Albert Maysles" in *Sight and Sound* (London), autumn 1971; "*Gimme Shelter*" by P.J. Bagh in *Filmihullu* (Helsinki), no.2, 1972; "*Dame refugio*" by I.L. Frias in *Hablemos de Cine* (Lima), January/March 1972; "Cinéma vérité and Social Concerns" by S. Mamber in *Film Comment* (New York), November/December 1973.

*   *   *

If Woodstock epitomized the optimism of the sixties youth movement with its peace and love rhetoric, the concert at Altamont a few months later displayed the underside of that era of rebellion and revolution. Where the film of Woodstock concentrated on detailing the harmony between performers and the assembled masses, *Gimme Shelter*, the film which includes the events at Altamont, presents evidence that violence is as possible as love and peace in such a setting, and that the on-stage gods are powerless in the face of shifting emotions.

The fiasco at Altamont has been documented by a number of writers including Sol Stern and Lester Bangs who attempted to uncover the before and after facts and assess responsibility. While the film also attempts to document the events preceding the violence at Altamont, it never assigns responsibility. Nor does it begin to accurately assess the ego which propelled this entire

project. Rather than consider that it may have been Mick Jagger's rivalry with The Who that caused the careless and cavalier preparation for the Altamont event, the film attempts to relieve him of any responsibility. Jagger was determined to have his film released before *Woodstock*, and it was. *Gimme Shelter* showed the Rolling Stones as powerful performers, but also showed them as victims of fate.

While the film is an excellent demonstration of the potential for disaster if large rock concerts are not adequately organized or policed, the dishonesty of the approach to depicting the events of 6 December 1969, is harrowing. The directors do not contort the facts so much as present them in a biased way. The blame is shoved squarely onto the broad shoulders of the Hell's Angels, the hired peacekeepers for the concert. Jagger is depicted as a sympathetic bystander; the filmmakers never deal with their own complicity as recorders of the event.

Often acknowledged as a classic of cinéma verité, the filmmakers have adequately captured the frenzy of performance and ruthlessly exposed aspects of the back stage drama. Where the film begins to fail is in the presentation of the preparation of the film, self-consciousness belying the supposed intentions of setting the record straight. Intercut throughout we see Mick Jagger viewing the footage of their tour: a Madison Square Gardens Concert, listening to Muscle Shoals demos, conferring with lawyer Melvin Belli. Throughout these reflexive sections Jagger looks uncomfortable while trying to act sincere. Where his persona breaks is when he repeatedly views the murder at Altamont, where 18-year-old black Meredith Hunter was stabbed by Hell's Angel Alan Passaro. His sincerity is opaque, his attempt to remove himself from the arena of the responsibility a heinous act; his sincerity is no more convincing than his act of naiveté.

In court, the Maysles footage was used as evidence, the jury viewing it repeatedly before acquitting Passaro on the grounds of self-defense. Mick Jagger had planned greater celebrity with this film and begged shelter on its release. He received both.

—Doug Tomlinson

GION NO SHIMAI. Sisters of the Gion. Production: Daiichi Eiga (Tokyo); black and white, 35mm; running time: 70 mins. Released October 1936.

Produced by Masaichi Nagata; screenplay by Yoshikata Yoda; from an idea by Kenji Mizoguchi; directed by Kenji Mizoguchi; photography by Minoru Miki.

Filmed in Japan.

Cast: Isuzu Yamada (*Umekichi, the elder sister*); Yoko Umemura (*O-Mocha, the younger sister*); Eitaro Shindo; Benkei Shiganoya; Namiko Kawahima; Fumio Okura; Taizo Fukami; Reido Aoi.

Publications:

Books—"Mizoguchi" by Akira Iwazaki in *Anthologie du cinéma* vol.3, Paris 1968; *Mizoguchi Kenji no hito to geijutsu* [Kenji Mizoguchi: The Man and His Art] by Yoshikata Yoda, Tokyo 1970; *Kenji Mizoguchi* edited by Michel Mesnil, Paris 1971; *Cinema, The Magic Vehicle: A Guide to Its Achievement: Jour-*

ney One: The Cinema Through 1949 edited by Jacek Klinowski and Adam Garbicz, Metuchen, New Jersey 1975; *Voices from the Japanese Cinema* by Joan Mellen, New York 1975; *The Waves at Genji's Door: Japan Through Its Cinema* by Joan Mellen, New York 1976; *Japanese Film Directors* by Audie Bock, New York 1978; *Il cinema di Kenji Mizoguchi*, Venice 1980; *The Japanese Film: Art and Industry* by Joseph Anderson and Donald Richie, (expanded edition), Princeton, New Jersey 1982; *Kenji Mizoguchi* by Dudley Andrew, Boston, in press; *Kenji Mizoguchi* by Keiko McDonald, Boston, in press; articles—"Kenji Mizoguchi" by Donald Richie and Joseph Anderson in *Sight and Sound* (London), autumn 1955; special issue of *Cinéma 55* on Mizoguchi (Paris), no.6, 1955; special issue of *Cahiers du cinéma* on Mizoguchi (Paris), March 1958; special issue of *L'Ecran* on Mizoguchi(Paris), February/March 1958; "Dossier Mizoguchi" in *Cahiers du cinéma* (Paris), August/September 1964; "Souvenirs sur Mizoguchi" by Yoshikata Yoda in *Cahiers du cinéma* (Paris), no.174, 1966; "The Density of Mizoguchi's Scripts", interview with Yoshikata Yoda, in *Cinema* (Los Angeles), spring 1971; "On Kenji Mizoguchi" by Tadao Sato and Dudley Andrew in *Film Criticism* (Edinboro, Pennsylvania), spring 1980.

*　　*　　*

Sisters of the Gion is the second of two great films made by Kenji Mizoguchi in 1936, the year which marks the beginning of his serious career as an artist. The year before, Mizoguchi and several other directors had set up an independent production company, Daiichi, for whom Mizoguchi had made three films. When censorship problems and major studio jealousy led to limited distribution of *Osaka Elegy*, Daiichi spent its remaining finances lavishly on its last film, this story of two Kyoto geishas. For the second time, Mizoguchi was working with Yoshikata Yoda, who would collaborate on nearly all his subsequent films. Together they researched the setting in the Gion quarter of Kyoto, carefully rendering its dialect in the three or four revisions of the script. This film, too, displeased the censors, who cut 90 meters from its realistic story. When it was released in October, the film attracted only mediocre attendance, but critics applauded it, even naming it best film of the year. Serious filmgoers, and Mizoguchi himself, realized that a new style had been born.

The sisters of the title are Umekichi, geisha and longtime lover of the just bankrupt merchant Furushawa, and Omocha, a younger geisha who sees the modern business more coldly and refuses to get involved with her customers. When Umekichi needs a beautiful kimono for an important function, Omocha obtains one from Kimura, a kimono shop clerk who is infatuated with her. His "borrowing" is discovered, but Omocha placates the Kimono shop owner by accepting him as a patron. Kimura, angered by this, confronts the pair and is scorned and fired. He vows revenge.

Omocha in the meantime has also been working to discourage the relationship between Umerkichi and Furusawa, but the two finally decide to live together, away from Omocha, who advises against it. Alone, at night, a taxi calls for Omocha, claiming to be from the shop owner. She gets in; Kimura comes out of hiding behind the seat, ready to take his revenge.

Umekichi is summoned to the hospital, where she is told that her sister was lucky to have survived Kimura's terrible beating. Umekichi is horrified, but not surprised, saying this is what comes from treating men badly. She returns home to collect her things so that she may stay with her sister in the hospital, only to find that Furusawa has left her to rejoin his wife in the north.

At the hospital it is the battered Omocha's turn to say "I told you so." She declares her hatred for all men and her misery as a woman of pleasure in the geisha quarters of Gion. Neither sister has the key to escape.

—Dudley Andrew

THE GO-BETWEEN. Production: EMI Films and World Film Services; Technicolor, 35mm; running time: 116 mins. Released 1970 by Metro-Goldwyn-Mayer.

Produced by Johy Heyman and Norman Priggen, executive producer: Robert Velaise; screenplay by Harold Pinter; from the novel by L.P. Hartley; directed by Joseph Losey; photography by Gerry Fisher; edited by Reginald Beck; sound by Peter Handford; art direction by Carmen Dillon; music by Michel Legrand and Richard Rodney Bennett; costumes designed by John Furniss and Camilla Farmer.

Filmed in England. Cost: budgeted at $1,000,000. Cannes Film Festival, Palme d'or, 1971.

Cast: Julie Christie (*Marian Maudsley*); Dominic Guard (*Leo Colston, the younger*); Michael Redgrave (*Leo Colston, the older*); Alan Bates (*Ted Burgess*); Margaret Leighton (*Mrs. Maudsley*); Edward Fox (*Hugh Trimingham*); Richard Gibson (*Marcus Maudsley*); Michael Gough (*Mr; Maudsely*); Simon Hume-Kendall (*Denys*); Amaryllis Garnett (*Kate*); Roger Lloyd Park (*Charles*).

Publications:

Script—*The Go-Between* by Harold Pinter, London 1971; reviews— by Norman Cecil in *Films in Review* (New York), October 1971; review by Andrew Sarris in *The Village Voice* (New York), 12 August 1971; review by Gordon Gow in *Films and Filming* (London), October 1971; review by Alexandre Astruc in *Paris-Match*, 26 June 1971; "Messaggero d'amore" by I. Cantacuzino in *Filmcritica* (Rome), January 1972; "*The Go-Between*" by T. Elsaesser in *Monogram* (London), no.3, 1972; "*The Go-Between*" by R. Jordan in *Film Quarterly* (Berkeley), spring 1972; books—*Le Livre de Losey: entretiens avec le cinéaste*, Paris 1979; *Joseph Losey* by Foster Hirsch, Boston 1980; articles—"*The Go-Between*" by John Russell Taylor in *Sight and Sound* (London), autumn 1970; "Entretiens" in *Positif* (Paris), no.128, 1971; "Weapons" by Gordon Gow in *Films and Filming* (London), October 1971; "From the Go-Between to Trotsky" by A. Guerin in *Show* (Hollywood), October 1971; "Going Between" by Richard Roud in *Sight and Sound* (London), summer 1971; article by Gérard Langlois in *Les Lettres français* (Paris), 2 June 1971; "*Poslaniec*" by Z. Klaczyński and "Loseya czas przesly opóźniony" by J. Plażewski in *Kino* (Warsaw), September 1972; "Losey a względność czasu" by J. Skwara in *Kino* (Warsaw), December 1972; "Angoscia d'un amore represso e sfruttato" by C. Tiso in *Filmcritica* (Rome), February 1972; "Summer of 1900: A la Recherche of *The Go-Between*" by Edward T. Jones in *Literature-Film Quarterly* (Salisbury, Maryland), April 1973; "Losey, Galileo, and the Romantic English-woman" by Richard Combs in *Sight and Sound* (London), summer 1975; "*Le Messenger*: Un Film de Joseph Losey" in *APEC-Revue belge du cinéma* (Brussels), November 1975-76; "The Losey-Pinter Collaboration" by B. Houston and Marcia Kinder in *Film Quarterly* (Berkeley), fall 1978; "*The Go-Between*" by Ruth Hirayama in *Magill's Survey of Cinema, Vol.II* edited by Frank Magill, Englewood Cliffs, New Jersey 1980; "Dialogue on Film: Joseph Losey" in *American Film* (Washington, D.C,), November 1980.

*   *   *

Adapted from the novel by L.P. Hartley, *The Go-Between* is an unusually provocative and sensuous film, representing a primary collaboration between director Joseph Losey and screenwriter Harold Pinter. Losey has always been interested in the organization of social classes and the harmful effects of society's dictums on the natural and healthy development of the individual. In *The Go-Between*, that theme is represented in the way the film chronicles the extraordinary repressiveness of a Victorian-influenced society, especially in relationship to sex and to class, and the traumatic effect of this repressiveness on a young boy who is exploited by his elders to such an extent that he is never able to overcome the trauma of his initiation into the secret rites of sexuality.

Losey's interests certainly complement Pinter's, but here they are especially augmented by Pinter's own unique contribution to the film: an exploration of time. Pinter has manipulated this concept in his unproduced screenplay for Proust's *Remembrance of Things Past*; his screenplay for *The French Lieutenant's Woman*, which cross-cuts between a real present and a fictional past; his play and subsequent screenplay, *The Betrayal*, which presents its scenes in reverse chronological order; and here in *The Go-Between*, where the narrative alternates between scenes in the past and scenes in the present, separated by over a half-century of time.

"The past is a foreign country, They may do things differently there..." intones the film's narrator, an old man, who is actually the young boy presented in the flashbacks. What makes the time component of *The Go-Between* so intriguing, however, is that the whole fits together like a gigantic puzzle, with perhaps, several pieces missing. The audience must work not only to make the connections between the two narratives, but also to understand exactly what is taking place when. That certain pieces seem almost repeated and unusually scrambled gives the film mystery and forces the spectator to consider time philosophically; that *The Go-Between* ends in the middle of a sentence and with an unacted-upon command relates this mainstream film to an almost avant-garde sensibility.

Ultimately, the emotional effect of *The Go-Between* is profoundly depressing, for its chronicles how a single event within a particular social fabric can ruin several lives, including some which are technically innocent to blame. Beauty fades, love dies, and although times past can be reclaimed in memory, events cannot be changed nor consequences undone. Affecting too is the jumping in time from the beautiful, if cold image of Julie Christie (as Marian) to the incredibly winkled image of that same face, now aged; from the optimistic and expectant face of the young Dominic Guard (as Leo) to the dull and fearful face of the aged Michael Redgrave, playing the same character many years later. Notable too is the performance of Margaret Leighton as

Mrs. Maudsley, the music by Michel Legrand, and the cinematography by Gerry Fisher.

—Charles Derry

THE GODFATHER. Production: Paramount Pictures; 1972; Technicolor, 35mm; running time: 176 mins. Released 11 March 1972.

Produced by Albert S. Ruddy; screenplay by Francis Ford Coppola and Mario Puzo; from the novel by Mario Puzo; directed by Francis Ford Coppola; photography by Gordon Willis; edited by William Reynolds, Peter Zinner, Marc Lamb, and Murray Solomon; sound by Bud Granzbach, Richard Portman, Christopher Newman, and Les Lazarowitz; production design by Philip Smith; art direction by Warren Clymer; music by Nino Rota; costumes designed by Anna Hill Johnstone.

Filmed in New York City and in Sicily. Cost: over $5 million. Academy Awards for Best Picture, Best Actor (Brando), Best Screenplay, 1972; New York Film Critics' Award, Best Supporting Actor (Duvall), 1972; Directors Guild of America, Director Award (Coppola), 1972.

Cast: Marlon Brando (*Don Vito Corleone*); Al Pacino (*Michael Corleone*); James Caan (*Sonny Corleone*); Richard Castellano (*Clemenza*); Robert Duvall (*Tom Hagen*); Diane Keaton (*Kay Adams*); Sterling Hayden (*McCluskey*); Talia Shire (*Connie Rizzi*); John Cazale (*Fredo Corleone*).

Publications:

Reviews—by Gary Arnold in *Filmfacts* edited by Ernest Parmentier (New York), no.15, 1972; "Un Coup de barre, Mars, et ça repart" by M. Amiel in *Cinéma* (Paris), November 1972; "Gudfadern" by P. Berglund in *Chaplin* (Stockholm), VXIV/5 (116), 1972; "*The Godfather*" by R. Chappetta in *Film Quarterly* (Berkeley), summer 1972; "*The Godfather*" by Peter Cowie in *Focus on Film* (London), autumn 1972; "*The Godfather*" by C.P. Reilly in *Films in Review* (New York), April 1972; review by Stanley Kauffmann reprinted in *Living Images*, New York 1975; books—*The Godfather* by Mario Puzo, New York 1969; *The Godfather* (about the making of the film), New York 1972; *The Godfather Journal* by Ira Zuckerman, New York 1972; "How Brando Brought Don Corleone to Life" in *Films 72-73* edited by David Denby, Indianapolis 1973; "Alchemy" in *Deeper Into Movies* by Pauline Kael, Boston 1973; "Keeping Up With the Corleones" in *Films 72-73* edited by David Denby, Indianapolis 1973: *The Making of the Godfather* by Mario Puzo, Greenwich, Connecticut 1973; *Marlon Brando* by René Jordan, New York 1973; *The Films of Marlon Brando* by Tony Thomas, Secaucus, New Jersey 1973; *Brando* by Gary Carey, New York 1973; *Brando* by David Shipman, London 1974; "The Godfather" in *Beyond Formula* by Stanley Solomon, New York 1976; *Francis Ford Coppola* by Robert K. Johnson, Boston 1977; articles—by John Kane and Bruce Rubenstein in *Take One* (Montreal, Canada), March/April 1971; "Coppola and *The Godfather*" by Stephen Farber in *Sight and Sound* (London), autumn 1972; "4/HF" by H. Faltysová in *Film & Doba* (Prague), May 1972; "*The Godfather*" by J. Kane and B. Rubenstein in *Take One* (Montreal), June 1972; "Produktion in Hollywood" by S. Schober in *Filmkritik* (Munich), October 1972; "Två filmer om Maffian" by G. Rosengren in *Filmrutan* (Stockholm), XV/3, 1972; "Directors Guild Winner: Francis Ford Coppola" by Charles Higham in *Action* (Hollywood), May/June 1973; "*The Godfather*: Metaphor and Microcosm" by J.P. Latimer in *Journal of Popular Film* (Bowling Green, Ohio), spring 1973; "Une Gigantesque métaphore" by F. Vitoux in *Positif* (Paris), January 1973; "Motifs of Image and Sound in *The Godfather*" by J. Vogelsang in *Journal of Popular Film* (Bowling Green), spring 1973; "Godfather of the Movies" by Maureen Orth in *Newsweek* (New York), 24 November 1974; "Francis Ford Coppola" in *Film Comment* (New York), July/August 1974; "Playboy Interview:Francis Ford Coppola" by William Murray in *Playboy* (Chicago), July 1975; "Godfather Saga: The Death of the Family" by John Yates in *Journal of Popular Film* (Bowling Green, Ohio), no.4 1975; "Toyota Refuses Offer NBC Hasn't Made" in *Broadcasting* (Washington, D.C.), 30 August 1976; "The Godfather Saga" by C. Clarens in *Film Comment* (New York), January/February 1978; "Films on TV" by A.H. Marill in *Films in Review* (New York), January 1978; "The Discreet Charm of *The Godfather*" by D. Thomson in *Sight and Sound* (London), spring 1978; "Dialogue on Film: Mario Puzo" in *American Film* (Washington, D.C.), May 1979; "Francis Ford Coppola: La Mafia, l'orare et l'Amerique" by G. Cebe in *Ecran* (Paris), 15 September 1979; "*The Godfather*" by Leslie Taubman in *Magill's Survey of Cinema, Vol. II* edited by Frank N. Magill, Englewood Cliffs, New Jersey 1980.

*   *   *

THE GODFATHER, PART 2. Production: Paramount Pictures; 1974; Technicolor, 35mm; running time: 200 mins. Released 12 December 1974, New York.

Produced by Francis Ford Coppola, Gary Frederickson, and Fred Roos; screenplay by Francis Ford Coppola and Mario Puzo; from the novel by Mario Puzo; directed by Francis Ford Coppola; photography by Gordon Willis; edited by Peter Zinner, Barry Malkin, and Richard Marks; production design by Dean Tavoularis, set decoration by George R. Nelson; art direction by Angelo Graham; music by Nino Rota, additional music by Carmine Coppola; costumes designed by Theodora Van Runkle.

Filmed in 9 months, 1973-74, on location in New York City, Lake Tahoe and Las Vegas Nevada, Washington, Sicily, and the Dominican Republic. Academy Awards for Best Picture, Best Director, Best Supporting Actor (De Niro), Best Screenplay, Best Art Decoration, Best Original Dramatic Score, 1974; Directors Guild of America, Director Award (Coppola), 1974.

Cast: Al Pacino (*Michael Corleone*); Robert Duvall (*Tom Hagen*); Diane Keaton (*Kay Adams*); Robert DeNiro (*Vito Corleone*); John Cazale (*Fredo Corleone*); Talia Shire (*Connie Corleone*); Lee Strasberg (*Hyman Roth*); Michael V. Gazzo (*Frankie Pentangeli*); Troy Donahue (*Connie's boyfriend*).

Publications:

Reviews—"*Parrain no.2*" by H. Béhar in *Image et Son* (Paris), September 1975; "*The Godfather, Part II*" by Stephen Farber in *Take One* (Montreal), December 1975; "*The Godfather, Part II*" by Gordon Gow in *Films and Filming* (London), July 1975; "*Godfather, Part II*" by Tom Milne in *Monthly Film Bulletin* (London), June 1975; "*The Godfather, Part II*" by L. Quart and A. Auster in *Cineaste* (New York), VI/4, 1975; "*The Godfather, Part II*" by C.P. Reilly in *Films in Review* (New York), February 1975; "*The Godfather, Part II*" by Jonathan Rosenbaum in *Sight and Sound* (London), summer 1975; books—*Francis Ford Coppola* by Robert K. Johnson, Boston 1977; articles—"The Final Act of a Family Epic" in *Time* (New York), 16 December 1974; "Fathers and Sons" by Pauline Kael in *New Yorker*, 23 December 1974; "Godfather of the Movies" by Maureen Orth in *Newsweek* (New York), 14 November 1974; "Francis Ford Coppola" in *Film Comment* (New York), July/August 1974; "Outs" by J. Cocks in *Take One* (Montreal), December 1974; "*Godfather II*: Zelfkritiek van Coppola" by Gideon Bachmann in *Skoop* (Wageningen, Netherlands), December 1974; "Playboy Interview: Francis Ford Coppola" by William Murray in *Playboy* (Chicago), July 1975; "Godfather Saga: The Death of the Family" by John Yates in *Journal of Popular Film* (Bowling Green, Ohio), no.4 1975; "Strømere og stoddere" by P. Calum in *Kosmorama* (Copenhagen), autumn 1975; "L.A. Journal" by Stephen Farber in *Film Comment* (New York), March/April 1975; "*Godfather II*: A Deal Coppola Couldn't Refuse" by John Hess in *Jump Cut* (Chicago), May/July 1975; "*Le Parrain, 2ème partie*" by D. Rabourdin in *Cinéma* (Paris), September/October 1975; "Toyota Refuses Offer NBC Hasn't Made" in *Broadcasting* (Washington, D.C.), 30 August 1976; "*Le Parrain II*" by G. Allombert in *Revue du cinéma* (Paris), October 1976; "*Boter II*" by V. Konjar in *Ekran* (Ljubljana, Yugoslavia), no. 1 1976; "*El Padrino II*: Lucky Luciano" by A. Marrosu in *Cine al Dia* (Caracas, Venezuela), February 1976; "De Invloed van televisie op het filmen: *The Godfather II*" by P. Bueren in *Skoop* (Wageningen, Netherlands), January 1977; "Het missen van de essentie als principe" by W. Verstappen in *Skoop* (Wageningen, Netherlands), January 1977; "The Godfather Saga" by C. Clarens in *Film Comment* (New York), January/February 1978; "Films on TV" by A.H. Marill in *Films in Review* (New York), January 1978; "The Discreet Charm of *The Godfather*" by D. Thomson in *Sight and Sound* (London), spring 1978; "Dialogue on Film: Mario Puzo" in *American Film* (Washington, D.C.), May 1979; "Francis Ford Coppola: La Mafia, l'orare et l'Amerique" by G. Cebe in *Ecran* (Paris), 15 September 1979; "The Italian Connection in American Film: Coppola, Cimino, Scorsese" by P. Rule in *America* (New York), 17 November 1979; "*Godfather, Part II*" by Leslie Taubman in *Magill's Survey of Cinema, Vol. II* edited by Frank N. Magill, Englewood Cliffs, New Jersey 1980.

*   *   *

The Godfather and *The Godfather II* are epics that chronicle the union and discord between family ties and our social system. With the latter film Coppola made the term "sequel" respectable by exploiting the resources which made possible its beautiful images in order to show "the corruption and perversion of the system which supplied those means" (John Hess). For Coppola the films seem to have been personal and professional labor of love; critical and audience response was overwhelming.

Taken from Mario Puzo's novel, *The Godfather* has been called a "realistic depiction of the Mafia," "more than just a gangster film," and "a depiction of the Mafia as metaphor for the decay of the United States." These claims obscure the film's more favorable features; however, both *Godfather* films do enhance the romantic, often murderous glamour of the men in the "family" by making the non-Mafia men weak or repulsive, and the women more acquiescent than their counterparts in reality. Women in the film are little more than one-dimensional stereotypes. As for the glamourized violence, one critic writes, *The Godfather* "is saturated with a combination of the threat of violence, the plans to commit violence, the fear of violence, and the actual committing of violence..," though Coppola *is commended* for the ways in which the violence appears—the story centers, literally, on life-and-death struggles.

Most interestingly, however, *The Godfather* details the themes of individual and community "moral" codes and the loyalty and transformation of power these codes demand. Early in the film, through Coppola's exceptional mastery of parallel action, we witness the power and favor-giving of Don Corleone during his daughter's wedding. All during the festivities the reception serves merely as another framework for the Don in his home office, receiving and giving favors, or "justice" for family, friends, and business associates. His son Michael, unlike the older sibling, "hot-headed" Sonny, seems to reject the family business. As he tells his non-Italian girlfriend, Kay, "It's not me."

By the end of the film, however, various events—inextricably tied with loyalty and immediate family needs for an heir apparent to Don Vito—transform Michael in his father's image. The final sequence brilliantly points towards the sequel. Wife Kay asks Michael if what she's heard is true—that he has arranged the murder of his sister's husband. He lies to her, condescending and patronizing as if to a child. During an especially tightly-framed, pregnant pause in the narrative, he lies to her, "No." She leaves the room, and as critic Stephan Farber notes, "...she sees the other mafiosi come in to pay tribute to their new godfather...we feel she is excluded forever from everything important in her husband's life."

The Godfather remains a powerfully conceived and created film. Coppola proves himself to be a master of irony through such simple yet telling devices as cross-cutting. Just as the wedding sequence bears a double message (family ties, personal happiness versus family ties, "business"), so do other telling sequences. As his child is being christened at mass, Michael's orders of execution are simultaneously carried out elsewhere in the city.

Coppola was disappointed that many in the audience missed the moral implications of the film's ending: "I felt I was making a harsh statement about the Mafia and power at the end of *Godfather I* when Michael murders all those people, then lies to his wife and closes the door. But...many people didn't get the point.... I felt *Godfather II* was a chance to rectify that."

Many filmgoers and critics feel that *Godfather II* overshadows its predecessor in its epic scope, alternating scenes and events from the past and present, the old country and the new. *Godfather II* also elaborates and extends the themes and concerns of *I*: family, business, loyalty, and the search for security. *Godfather II* is also a painful look at the increasing isolation and determination of Michael Corleone, whose adherence to the "code" costs him his family and his soul. The sequel, then, focuses on Michael's simultaneous rise and moral deterioration.

Elaborate flashbacks and parallel action chronicle in epic proportions the history and characters revolving within and around the Corleone family. *Godfather II* presents the eras before and after the time of *Godfather I*, and through the use of lighting and framing the sequel offers unforgettable "spots of time": young Vito Corleone, his family recently murdered in Sicily, sits in an oversized chair in a quarantine cell at New York's Ellis Island on a brightly lit afternoon with his back to the camera. He swings his thin small legs while singing a folk song in a frail, young boy's voice—the first time he is heard in the flashback. *Godfather II* becomes a film of poignant *moods* as

well as characterization and events.

The film's virtues outweigh any of its serious flaws. (Critics sometimes accuse Coppola of improbable characterization in some of the peripheral characters.) The film's complex narrative details how the murder of Michael's grandparents in Sicily decades earlier has subsequently led to Michael's destruction of his family and his "family business." While the family is the impetus for the most, if not all the Corleone' actions, it is by Michael's hands that several of them have died or left him. The desire for revenge is part of the code, a code that explains Michael's entrapment by the family business, a code that ultimately leads to his own moral destruction.

Acts of vengeance dominate most of *The Godfather II*, and yet the most singularly effective scene remains the confrontation between Michael and Kay. She has had an abortion—she had previously lied, telling him it was a miscarriage—and gives Michael his most stunning blow. Kay's actions threaten the religious, moral, and social sanctity of Michael's patriarchal domination, and she is banished from his life.

John Hess writes that "The film works, makes its statement, through juxtaposition." He notes that the major effort in both *Godfather* films is the "construction of families, which are ultimately destroyed by business." The business destroys ethnic communities—Michael's move to Las Vegas symbolizes this. But ultimately, "Michael's own nuclear family is destroyed by the very requirements of doing the business that is supposed to secure it." This is the ultimate point of Coppola's masterful chronicles of familial affiliations and tragedy.

—Deborah Holdstein

THE GOLD RUSH. Production: Charles Chaplin Studio; 1925; black and white, 35mm, silent with musical score; running time: 74 mins.; length: 2720 meters. Released 16 August 1925, New York, by United Artists. Re-released 18 April 1942 in edited version of 2150 meters with music by Chaplin, and re-released again April 1956.

Produced, scripted, and directed by Charles Chaplin; photography by R.H. Totheroh and Jack Wilson; art direction by Charles D. Hall; artistic consultant: Harry d'Abbadie d'Arrast, Chaplin also assisted by Charles Reisner.

Filmed January 1924-May 1925 in various studios, and on location in the Sierra Nevadas.

Cast: Charles Chaplin (*The Lone Prospector*); Mack Swain (*Big Jim McKay*); Tom Murray (*Black Larsen*); Georgia Hale (*The Girl*); Betty Morissey (*Chum of the Girl*); Malcolm White (*Jack Cameron*); Henry Bergman (*Hank Curtis*). John Rand, Albert Austin, Heine Conklin, Allan Garcia and Tom Wood (*Prospectors*).

Publications:

Script—shot record put together by Timothy Lyons in *Cinema* (Beverly Hills), summer 1968; review—"New Chaplin Comedy" by E. Wilson in the *New Republic* (New York), 2 September 1925; books—*Charles Chaplin: A Portrait* by Waldo David Frank, New York 1929; *Charlie Chaplin: His Life and Art* by

William Dodgson Bowman, New York 1931; *Charlie Chaplin: King of Tragedy* by Gerith von Ulm, Idaho, 1940; *Charles Chaplin, el Genio del Ciné* by Manuel Villegas Lopez, Buenos Aires 1943; *Charlot* by Peter Cotes and Thelma Niklaus, Paris 1951; *Charlie Chaplin* by Theodore Huff, New York 1951; *Vie de Charlot* by Georges Sadoul, Paris 1953; *Chaplin et le rire dans la nuit* by M. Bessy and R. Florey, Paris 1953; *Chaplin, Last of the Clowns* by Parker Tyler, 2nd ed., London 1954; *The Great Charlie* by Robert Payne, 2nd ed., Paris 1954; *Charles Chaplin, le self-made Mythe* by José Augusto Franca, Lisbon 1954; *Pages pour Chaplin* by Henri Pichette, Paris 1950-54; *Charlot* by Pierre Leprohon, 2nd ed., Paris 1957; *Charlot et la fabulation chaplinesque* by Jean Mitry, Paris 1957; *Charles Chaplin* by Barthelemy Amengual, Paris 1963; *My Autobiography* by Charles Chaplin, New York 1964; *The Little Fellow: The Life and Work of Charles Spencer Chaplin* by Peter Cotes and Thelma Niklaus, New York 1965; *The Films of Charlie Chaplin* edited by Gerald D. McDonald, Michael Conway and Mark Ricci, New York 1965; *Charles Chaplin* by Marcel Martin, Paris 1966; *The Great Films: 50 Golden Years of Motion Pictures* by Bosley Crowther, New York 1967; *Interviews with Film Directors* by Andrew Sarris, New York 1967; *Focus on Chaplin* edited by Donald W. McCaffrey, Englewood Cliffs, New Jersey 1971; *Tout Chaplin* by Jean Mitry, Paris 1972; *Chaplin's Films* by Uno Asplund, London 1973; *Chaplin* by Roger Manvell, London 1974; *My Life in Pictures* by Charlie Chaplin, New York 1975; *Charlie Chaplin* by Robert F. Moss, New York 1975; articles— "Chaplin as Composer" by Theodore Huff in *Films in Review* (New York), September 1950; "The True Face of the Man" by Peter John Dyer in *Films and Filming* (London), September 1958; "Classics Revisited" by Ernest Callenbach in *Film Quarterly* (Berkeley), fall 1959; "Il circo, il clown et la tristezza del mondo" by José Carlos Mariategui in *Cinema Nuovo* (Rome), September/October 1969; "*The Gold Rush* and *The General*" by Gerald Mast in *Cinema Journal* (Evanston, Illinois), spring 1970; "*The Gold Rush*" by W. Paul in *Film Comment* (New York), September/October 1972; "La Ruée vers l'or: Little big man" by T. Renuad in *Cinéma* (Paris), June 1972; "The Preparation and Use of Study Guides for the Mass Media, with a Study Guide to *The Gold Rush*" by J. Mersand in *Literature/Film Quarterly* (Salisbury, Maryland), spring 1975; "*The Gold Rush*" by N. Carroll in *Wide Angle* (Athens, Ohio), no. 2, 1979; "*La Ruee vers l'or*" (shot analysis) in *Avant-Scène du cinéma* (Paris), 1 January 1979; "Chaplin and Brecht: *The Gold Rush* and the *Rise and Fall of the City of Mahagonny*" by J.E. Michaels in *Literature/Film Quarterly* (Salisbury, Maryland), no. 3, 1980.

*   *   *

The Gold Rush was Chaplin's favorite among his own films, so much a favorite that he deliberately did not copyright it, allowing it to pass into the public domain as a gift to his future public. As a result, the film has been seen more frequently than any other Chaplin feature, especially between 1952 and 1972, the two decades of Chaplin's disenchantment with America when he withdrew all his other feature films from public circulation. Inspired by stories of the Donner Party, trapped in a desert of ice, and perhaps by the icy landscapes of Robert Flaherty's popular documentary feature, *Nanook of the North*, Chaplin took his Tramp character to the frozen gold fields where human beings endure great hardships so that they might strike it rich. As usual in a Chaplin film, the Tramp is very much an outsider in the world of *The Gold Rush*, even in this society of outsiders and outcasts. The Tramp is too kind, too sensitive to human needs, and too spiritual for that isolated, materialistic world. The Tramp's kindness in befriending Georgia, an abused dance-hall girl, contrasts with other human actions in the film—with those of Jack, Georgia's handsome boyfriend who treats her as his sex object: or with those of Black Larsen, a man so hungry for gold that he robs and kills others.

Despite the serious moral issues which the film raises in it contrast of material and spiritual human pursuits, its popularity derives from the power of its comedy sequences. In one of the most famous of Chaplin's transpositions of objects—his conversion of one kind of physical object into another—the Tramp cooks a dinner for himself and his starving friend, Big Jim McKay. Lacking anything else to eat, the Tramp sacrifices one of his own symbols, his floppy shoe, which he boils carefully in a pot, testing it with a fork for tenderness. He then carves it like a roast beef, twirls the shoestrings around his fork like spaghetti and sucks on the nails like chicken bones. In a later sequence, lacking even a shoe to eat, Charlie converts himself into a mammoth chicken—or so Big Jim imagines. The contrast of Charlie's chickenish actions with the cannibalistic dreams of his sometimes friend reveals the typical Chaplin method of making comedy out of the most basic and elemental human needs—love, shelter, hunger.

Balancing the comedic scenes is one of the most effective and powerful sequences of pathos and poignancy in the entire Chaplin canon. Charlie has invited Georgia, whose picture he preserves under his pillow next to a rose, and several of her friends at the dance hall to supper on New Year's Eve. They, making fun of the pathetic little Tramp, have teasingly promised to attend supper. As he waits for them, Charlie falls asleep and dreams of the delightful dinner that will never be. He entertains the girls by sticking two rolls on the ends of two forks and using them to dance the "Oceana Roll." The sight of Charlie's playful face, coyly peering over the tops of these two tiny, dancing legs is one of the most memorable single images in Chaplin's work. But Charlie awakens to find that a social success has only been a dream—like his many dreams of love and success in earlier films. The pathos of his loneliness is emphasized by the communal society of revelers singing "Auld Lang Syne," while Charlie, shown isolated within the frame stands outside the circle of their friendship and observes.

However, almost miraculously, the Tramp eventually finds both love and wealth in this film. Charlie, now rich from his gold strike, discovers Georgia on board the same ship on which he is travelling home. She has had enough of the frozen wasteland (Chaplin typically uses the hired dance-hall girl as a metaphor for prostitution, the conversion of female sexuality into a commodity to be bought and sold.) Georgia reveals her kindness when she protects Charlie from the ship's captain, believing him to be a stowaway. And Charlie, in turn, returns the girl's kindness by embracing her, now that he can offer her money as well as love. In what seems Chaplin's own conscious comment on the film's happy ending, a group of shipboard photographers, taking pictures of the former Tramp now a millionaire, criticize a photograph of the Tramp's kissing Georgia: "You've spoiled the picture." Chaplin seemed to have been anticipating the film's critics whom he expected to attack this last scene.

The issue that the ending raises is whether the Tramp can ever find happiness with a romantic-sexual mate. Must the Tramp, as outcast and outsider, also be disqualified from the consummation of love, which in our society, is formulized by marriage? The previous Chaplin films to end with a happy, affirmative answer to this question (*The Vagabond, A Dog's Life, The Kid*) also suggest something dreamlike and impossible about such a solution. This dreamlike suggestion about the Tramp's attainment of marital happiness becomes explicit in films like *The Bank* or

Shoulder Arms, in which his attainment of the lady of his dreams literally turns out to be a dream. His next three films, *The Circus*, *City Lights*, and *Modern Times*, will return to the marriage theme with far more ambiguity and uncertainty. *The Gold Rush*, which lies at the crossroads of Chaplin's lighter early work and his more mature and darker features, is probably his most successful film at producing a completely happy ending without "spoiling the picture."

—Gerald Mast

GOLD DIGGERS OF 1933. Production: Warner Bros. Pictures, Inc.; 1933; black and white, 35mm; running time: 96 mins. Released June 1933.

Produced by Robert Lord; screenplay by Erwin Gelsey and James Seymour, dialogue by David Boehm and Ben Markson; from a play by Avery Hopwood; directed by Mervyn LeRoy; photography by Sol Polito; edited by George Amy; art direction by Anton Grot; music and lyrics by Harry Warren and Al Dubin, Vitaphone Orchestra conducted by Leo F. Forbstein; costumes designed by by Orry-Kelly; choreography by Busby Berkeley.

Filmed in Warner Bros. studios.

Cast: Warren William (*J. Lawrence Bradford*); Joan Blondell (*Carol King*); Aline MacMahon (*Trixie Lorraine*); Ruby Keeler (*Polly Parker*); Dick Powell (*Robert Treat Bradford, or Brad Roberts*); Guy Kibbee (*Faneuil H. Peabody*); Ned Sparks (*Barney Hopkin*); Ginger Rogers (*Fay Fortune*); Clarence Nordstrom (*Don Gordon*); Robert Agnew (*Dance director*); Tammany Young (*Gigolo Eddie*); Sterling Holloway (*Delivery boy*); Ferdinand Gottschalk (*Elderly gentleman*); Lynn Browning (*Gold Digger girl*); Charles C. Wilson (*Sheriff*); Billy Barty ("*Pettin' in the Park*" *baby*); Fred Tones and Theresa Harris (*Black couple*); Joan Barclay (*Chorus girl*); Wallace MacDonald (*Stage manager*); Wilbur Mack, Grace Hayle, and Charles Lane (*Society reporters*); Hobart Cavanaugh (*Dog salesman*); Bill Elliot (*Dance extra*); Dennis O'Keefe (*Critic during intermission*); Busby Berkeley (*Callboy*); Fred Kelsey (*Detective Jones*); Frank Man (*1st forgotten man*).

Publications:

Scripts—*Gold Diggers of 1933* by Erwin Gelsey and James Seymour, edited with an introduction by Arthur Hove, Madison, Wisconsin 1980; reviews—in *Newsweek* (New York), 18 March 1933; books—*The Blue Book of Hollywood Musicals* by Jack Burton, Watkins Glen, New York 1953; *It Takes More Than Talent* by Mervyn LeRoy as told to Alyce Canfield, New York 1953; *All Talking, All Singing, All Dancing* by John Springer, New York 1966; *The Musical Film* by Douglas McVay, New York 1967; *Hollywood in the 30s* by John Baxter, New York 1968; *Gotta Sing, Gotta Dance: A Pictorial History of Film Musicals* by John Kobal, New York 1970; *We're in the Money: Depression America and Its Films* by Andrew Bergman, New York 1971; *The Hollywood Musical* by John Russell Taylor and Arthur Jackson, New York 1971; *The Genius of Busby Berkeley* by Bob Pike and Dave Martin, Resada, California

1973; *The Busby Berkeley Book* by Tony Thomas, Jim Terry, and with Busby Berkeley, New York 1973; *The Complete Encyclopedia of Popular Music and Jazz: 1900-1950* by Roger D. Kinkle, New Rochelle, New York 1974; *The Movie Musical* by Lee Edward Stern, New York 1974; *Mervyn LeRoy: Take One* by Mervyn LeRoy, New York 1974; *The Warner Bros. Story* by Clive Hirschhorn, New York 1979; articles—"The Making of Mervyn LeRoy" in *Films in Review* (New York), May 1953; "Filmusicals" by Edward Jablonski in *Films in Review* (New York), February 1955; "Dick Powell" by Anthony Thomas in *Films in Review* (New York), May 1961; "Dancing Images" by Jean-Louis Comolli in *Cahiers du cinéma in English* (New York), no.2, 1966; "Interview with Busby Berkeley" by Patrick Brion and René Gilson in *Cahiers du cinéma in English* (New York), no.2, 1966; "The Return of Busby Berkeley" by William Murray in the *New York Times Magazine*, 2 March 1969; "Warner Brothers in the '30's" by Russell Campbell and Michael Roth in the *Velvet Light Trap* (Madison, Wisconsin), June 1971; "*Gold Diggers of 1933*" by Jules Feiffer in *Film Comment* (New York), May/June 1974; "Movie Musicals in the Thirties" by Miles Kreuger in *High Fidelity and Musical America* (Marion, Ohio), no.24, 1974; "Mervyn LeRoy: Star-making, Studio Systems and Style" by Kingsley Canham in *The Hollywood Professionals Vol. 5*, London 1976; "Review Essay" by T.E. Scheurer in *Journal of Popular Film* (Bowling Green, Ohio), summer 1981; "Commodity Fetishism: Women in *Gold Diggers of 1933*" by Lauren Rabinowitz in *Film Reader 5* (Evanston, Illinois), 1982.

*   *   *

Gold Diggers of 1933 was the second of three films released in quick succession by Warner Brothers in 1933 (the other two were *42nd Street* and *Footlight Parade*) that are regarded as having revitalized the musical genre. Its roots reach back to a silent movie (and play) called *The Gold Diggers* (1919) and a musical film version, *Gold Diggers of Broadway* (1929). Originally titled *High Life*, it was put into production before *42nd Street* without any special musical numbers. After the runaway success of *42nd Street*, Busby Berkeley was called in to reproduce his brand of elaborate choreography.

Berkeley's style of dance depended very little on actual dancing but more on the camera's mobility and its power to create a surrealistic world of limitless dimensions; the main part of the production numbers could never have taken place on any stage. Berkeley's predilection for beautiful women resulted in the most voyeuristic fantasies ever committed to celluloid, and recent feminist criticism has justifiably attacked Berkeley's objectification of the female body.

Miles Kreuger notes in "Movie Musicals in the Thirties" that musicals of this period were an indicator of "...the individual style of the studio, as determined by its stars, staff, choice of subject matter, and to a certain degree, its image of itself." Keeping Kreuger's thesis in mind, these three Warners musicals (and *Dames*) all dealt with the contemporary economic crisis, were created by essentially the same staff and crew. Warner Brothers musicals were even linked narratively: in the films' stories, the leading performer was always replaced by another just before the big finale. Though what can be said theoretically and critically of one film can be said of the others, "the *Gold Diggers of 1933* was the one to deal most directly with the Depression." (Stanley Green) Even opening and closing production numbers dealt specifically with the economy. The first, "We're in the Money", presented a prematurely optimistic (that is governmental) and cynical attitude that the Depression was almost over. It clearly wasn't since the number is halted when the sheriff and a crew of workmen begin to disassemble the elaborate stage because the bills have not been paid. The latter, "Remember My Forgotten Man," was a stirring piece of social commentary which expressed the problems of World War I veterans who were unemployed due to the Depression.

—Greg S. Faller

GONE WITH THE WIND. Production: Selznick International Pictures; 1939; Technicolor, 35mm; running time: 220 mins.; length: 20,300 feet. Released 15 December 1939 in Atlanta by MGM, some sources list the premiere date as 18 November 1939. Re-released 1947, 1954, 1967, 1969.

Produced by David O. Selznick; screenplay by Sidney Howard, with structural innovations by Jo Swerling and some dialogue by Ben Hecht and John van Druten; from the novel by Margaret Mitchell; directed by Victor Fleming (with uncredited direction by George Cukor and Sam Wood); photography by Ernest Haller, cameramen included Lee Garmes, Joseph Ruttenberg, Ray Rennahan, and Wilfred Cline; edited by Hal C. Kern and James E. Newcom; sound recorded by Frank Maher; production design by William Cameron Menzies; art direction by Lyle Wheeler; musical score by Max Steiner; special effects by Jack Cosgrove and Lee Zavitz; costumes designed by Walter Plunkett, Scarlett's hats by John Frederics; consulting historian was Wilbur G. Kurtz; dance direction by Frank Floyd and Eddie Prinz.

Filmed 10 December 1938-August 1939 in RKO backlots and studios (rented to Selznick International for the film), and on location at Old Laskey Mesa, California. Cost: $4,250,000. Academy Awards for Best Picture, Best Director, Best Actress (Leigh), Best Supporting Actress (McDaniel), Best Screenplay, Best Cinematography-Color, Best Editing, Interior Decoration, 1939; Academy of Motion Pictures Arts and Sciences Special Awards to William Cameron Menzies for Color Achievement and to Don Musgrave and Selznick International Pictures for pioneering use of coordinated equipment, 1939; New York Film Critics' Award, Best Actress (Leigh), 1939.

Cast: Vivien Leigh (*Scarlett O'Hara*); Clark Gable (*Rhett Butler*); Lesley Howard (*Ashley Wilkes*); Olivia deHavilland (*Melanie Hamilton*); Hattie McDaniel (*Mammy*); Thomas Mitchell (*Gerald O'Hara*); Barbara O'Neil (*Ellen O'Hara*); Caroll Nye (*Frank Kennedy*); Laura Hope Crews (*Aunt Pittypat*); Harry Davenport (*Dr. Meade*); Rand Brooks (*Charles Hamilton*); Ona Munson (*Belle Watling*); Ann Rutherford (*Careen O'Hara*); George Reeves (*Stuart Tarleton*), wrongly credited on screen as Brent Tarleton; Fred Crane (*Brent Tarleton*); Oscar Polk (*Pork*); Butterfly McQueen (*Prissy*); Evelyn Keyes (*Suellen O'Hara*); Jane Darwell (*Mrs. Merriweather*); Leona Roberts (*Mrs. Meade*); Everett Brown (*Big Sam*); Eddie Anderson (*Uncle Peter*); Ward Bond (*Tom, a Yankee Captain*); Cammie King (*Bonnie Blue Butler*); J.M. Kerrigan (*Johnny Gallagher*); Isabel Jewell (*Emmy Slattery*); Alicia Rhett (*India Wilkes*); Victor Jory (*Jonas Wilkerson*); Howard Hickman (*John Wilkes*); Mary Anderson (*Maybelle Merriweather*); Paul Hurst (*Yankee Looter*); Marcella Martin (*Cathleen Calvert*); Mickey Kuhn (*Beau Wilkes*); Zack Williams (*Elijah*).

Publications:

Script—*Gone With The Wind*, Munich 1981-82; reviews—by Frank S. Nugent in *The New York Times*, 20 December 1939; books—*Selznick* by Bob Thomas, New York 1950; *The Oliviers* by Felix Barber, Philadelphia 1953; *A Quite Remarkable Father* by Leslie Ruth Howard, New York 1959; *Every Frenchman Has One* by Olivia De Havilland, New York 1962; *The King: A Biography of Clark Gable* by Charles Samuels, New York 1963; *Margaret Mitchell of Atlanta: The Author of 'Gone with the Wind'* by Finis Farr, New York 1965; *Gable: A Complete Gallery of His Screen Portraits* compiled by Gabe Essoe and Ray Lee, Los Angeles 1967; *Vivien Leigh: A Bouquet* by Alan Dent, London 1969; *The Films of Clark Gable* by Gabe Essoe, New York 1970; *Light of a Star* by Gwen Robyns, New York 1970; *Classic Motion Pictures: The Stuff That Dreams Are Made Of* by David Zinman, New York 1970; *Vivien Leigh* by Gwen Robyns, New York 1971; *Memo from David O. Selznick* edited by Rudy Behlmer, New York 1972; *GWTW* by Gavin Lambert, Boston 1973; *Scarlett, Rhett, and a Cast of Thousands: The Filming of 'Gone with the Wind'* by Roland Flamini, New York 1975; *Margaret Mitchell's 'Gone with the Wind' Letters* edited by Richard Harwell, New York 1976; *Hollywood Costume Design* by David Chierichetti, New York 1976; *Long Live the King: A Biography of Clark Gable* by Lyn Tornabene, New York 1976; *Scarlett Fever* by William Pratt, New York 1977; *Vivien Leigh: A Biography* by Anne Edwards, New York 1977; articles—"Director's Dilemma" by Richard Watts in *Cinema Arts* (New York), June 1937; "Finished at Last" by H.F. Pringle in *Ladies' Home Journal* (New York), January 1940; "Directed by Victor Fleming" in *Lion's Roar* (Los Angeles), September 1941; article by David Curtis and Richard Goldhurst in *Film Culture* (New York), May/June 1955; "Gone With the Wind" by Tom Dyer in *Films in Review* (New York), May 1957; "Leslie Howard" by Homer Dickens in *Films in Review* (New York), April 1959; "Clark Gable" by Carlos Clarens in *Films in Review* (New York), December 1960; "Gone With the Wind" by Henry Hart in *Films in Review* (New York), May 1961; "Olivia De Havilland" by Neil Doyle in *Films in Review* (New York), February 1962; "Vivien Leigh" by Ronald Bowers in *Films in Review* (New York), August/September 1965; article by Andrew Sarris in *The Village Voice* (New York), 26 October 1967; "Box Office Belle Makes Its 3rd Debut" in *Business Week* (New York), 14 October 1967; "Creating the New 70mm Stereophonic Sound Version of *Gone With the Wind*" by Herb A. Lightman in *American Cinematographer* (Hollywood), November 1967; "Dream That Never Died" by Olivia de Havilland in *Look* (New York), 12 December 1967; "The Man who Made *Gone With the Wind*" by John Howard Reid in *Films and Filming* (London), December 1967; article by Gordon Gow in *Sight and Sound* (London), November 1968; "The Black Reaction to *Gone With the Wind*" by J.D. Stevens in *Journal of Popular Film* (Bowling Green, Ohio), fall 1973; "*Gone With the Wind* and *The Grapes of Wrath* as Hollywood Histories of the Depression" by T.H. Pauly in *Journal of Popular Film* (Bowling Green, Ohio), summer 1974; "Now Hollywood Stars Achieve Success in Spite of Themselves" by E. Finney in *Classic Film Collector* (Indiana, Pennsylvania), fall 1976; "*GWTW* Knocks ABC Out of First for Week, Sets Modern Nielsen Record" in *Broadcasting* (Washington, D.C.), 15 November 1976; "*GWTW* Surprise Aussie Click in its 9th Revival There" in *Variety* (New York), 3 November 1976; "Pay Cable Gets TV Premiere of Film Classic" in *Broadcasting* (Washington, D.C.), 3 May 1976; "Frankly My Dear, We Do Give a Damn" by Andrew Sarris in *The Village Voice* (New York), 29 November 1976; "Films on TV" by A.H. Marill in *Films in Review* (New York), January 1977; "A propos d'un film célèbre..." by C. Gelé in *Ecran* (Paris), March 1978; "Scarlett e altro: le stagioni di un nostro amore" by M. De Benedictis in *Bianco e Nero* (Rome), January/February 1979; "Reunion Recalls Those 'Gone with the Wind'" by R. Lindsey in *The New York Times*, 31 December 1979; "GWTW Quiz" in *Films in Review* (New York), December 1979; "*Gone with the Wind*" by Rudy Behlmer in *Magill's Survey of Cinema, Vol. II* edited by Frank N. Magill, Englewood Cliffs, New Jersey 1980.

* * *

Gone With the Wind, based on Margaret Mitchell's best-selling novel about the South during the Civil War and Reconstruction, made producer David O. Selznick's name a box-office draw, made the relatively unknown Vivien Leigh an international star, and became the most popular motion picture of all time.

Soon after Selznick brought the movie rights to Mitchell's novel in July, 1936, thousands of fan letters began to arrive at Selznick International Pictures, most of them demanding that Clark Gable play the role of Rhett Butler. In order to get Gable, Selznick had to make a deal with MGM and Louis B. Mayer who held Gable's contract—in exchange for Gable's services and $1,125,000 of the film's budget, MGM would receive the distribution rights and half the profits of *GWTW*.

Since Selznick had a contract with United Artists to distribute all his films until the end of 1938, principal shooting on *GWTW* could not start before 1939. In order to maintain public interest in the film before shooting could begin, Selznick launched a nationwide talent search to find an unknown actress to play Scarlett O'Hara. In the course of the two-year search, 1400 candidates were interviewed and 90 were tested, at a total cost of $92,000. Among those considered for the part were Katharine Hepburn and Paulette Goddard. The role eventually went to Vivien Leigh, a British actress who was largely unknown to American audiences.

The production phase of *GWTW* began auspiciously in December, 1938, with the Atlanta fire scene—the largest fire ever staged in a film up to that time. Principal shooting which started six weeks later, was plagued by numerous problems and required seven months to complete. The main problem was the script, which despite the efforts of more than a dozen writers, remained a confusing mass of revisions, and revisions of revisions, until after shooting was completed. The disorganized condition of the script made shooting difficult and created tension among the production personnel. After only three weeks of principal shooting, Selznick replaced director George Cukor with Victor Fleming. Two months later, Fleming, upset by Selznick's handling of the script, went home and refused to work. Selznick quickly hired Sam Wood to direct and when Fleming decided to return to the film two weeks later, Selznick let the two men split the directorial chores.

When *GWTW* was finally completed, it turned out to be a monumental film in almost every respect. Its technical achievements included the Atlanta fire sequence, the use of matte paintings to provide distant backgrounds and to complete partially constructed sets (*GWTW* marked the second use in Technicolor film of the matte process in which painted backgrounds are blended with filmed scenes of live actors), and the railroad depot crane shot, in which the camera pulls back and up to reveal Scarlett O'Hara walking among thousands of wounded Confederate soldiers—about 2000 live extras and dummies. Its total cost was $4.25 million—equivalent to $50 million today. It had the longest running time (3:40) of its day and the largest titles in cinema history—each word of the film's title fills the screen itself.

It was also the first major film to successfully challenge the Production Code's prohibition of profanity—with Rhett Butler's final line, "Frankly, my dear, I don't give a damn."

When *GWTW* premiered in Atlanta on December 15, 1939, over one million people poured into the city of 300,000, hoping to see Clark Gable, Vivien Leigh, and the other stars who attended the premiere. After three days of parades, celebrations, and Confederate flag-waving, a select audience of 2500 people saw the film, and they loved it. *GWTW* quickly became worldwide critical and box-office success and won ten Academy Awards, a record that stood until 1959, when *Ben Hur* won eleven.

As of 1983, *GWTW* has earned $76.7 million in domestic rentals. In 1976 NBC paid $5 million for the film's television premiere. The program, aired over two nights in November, 1976, received a 47.6 Neilsen rating—the highest rating ever received by a movie on television. CBS subsequently paid $35 million for 20 airings of *GWTW* over a 20-year period. When appropriate adjustments for inflation are made, *GWTW* is the biggest box-office success in cinema history. The current critical consensus is that *GWTW* is the quintessential Hollywood studio system product.

—Clyde Kelly Dunagan

THE GOOD, THE BAD, AND THE UGLY. Il buono, il brutto, il cattivo. Production: P.E.A.; Technicolor, 35mm, Techniscope; running time: 180 mins., English version is 162 mins. Released 1966 in Italy, released 1968 in US.

Produced by Alberto Grimaldi; screenplay by Luciano Vincenzoni and Sergio Leone; from a story by Age Scarpelli, Sergio Leone, and Luciano Vincenzoni; titles designed by Ardani; directed by Sergio Leone; photography by Tonino Delli Colli; edited by Nino Baragli and Eugenio Alabiso; art direction by Carlo Simi; music by Enneio Morricone, music conducted by Bruno Nicolai; special effects Eros Bacciucchi; costumes designed by Carlo Simi.

Filmed 1965-66 in Spain.

Cast: Clint Eastwood (*Joe*); Eli Wallach (*Tuco*); Lee Van Cleef (*Setenza*); Aldo Giuffrè; Chelo Alonso; Mario Brega; Luigi Pistilli; Rada Rassimov; Enzo Petito; Claudio Scarchilli; Al Mulock; Livio Lorenzon; Antonio Casas; Sandro Scarchilli; Angelo Novi; Benito Stefanelli; Silvana Bach; Antonio Casas; Aldo Sambrell.

Publications:

Reviews—"*The Good, the Bad, and the Ugly*" by Raymond Durgnat in *Films and Filming* (London), November 1968; "*Le Bon, la Brute et le Truand*" by Sylvie Pierre in *Cahiers du cinéma* (Paris), April/May 1968; books—*Italian Westerns* by Laurence Staig and Tony Williams , London 1975; *The Great Western Pictures* edited by James Robert Parish and Michael R. Pitts, Metuchen, New Jersey 1976; *Sergio Leone* by Oreste de Fornari, Milan 1977; *Spaghetti Westerns: Cowboys and Europeans: From Karl May to Sergio Leone* by Christopher Frayling, London 1981; articles—"Hi-Ho, Denaro!" in *Time* (New York), 4 August 1967; "Western à l'Italienne" by Pio Baldelli in *Image et* son (Paris), May 1967; "Western und Italowestern" by Klaus Badekerl in *Filmkritik* (Munich), October 1969; "Sergio Leone" by Jean Gili in *Cinéma 69* (Paris), November 1969; "Sergio Leone" by C. Frayling in *Cinema* (London), August 1970; "Western Italiono-Western Americano" by Sandro Graziani in *Bianco e nero* (Rome), September/October 1970; "Italian Westerns—a concordance" by Mike Wallington in *Cinema* (London), August 1970; "Idéologie du western italien" by Pierre Baudry in *Cahiers du cinéma* (Paris), November 1971; "L'anti-Western e il caso Leone" by Franco Ferrini in *Bianco e nero* (Rome), September/October 1971; article by Stuart Kaminsky in *Take One* (Montreal), January/February 1972; "Clint Eastwood" by DeWitt Bodeen in *Focus on Film* (London), spring 1972; "Something To Do With Death" by Richard Jameson in *Film Comment* (New York), March/April 1973; "Notes sur les Westerns de Sergio Leone" by Noel Simsolo in *Image et son* (Paris), September 1973; "Ennio Morricone" by François Chevassu in *Image et son* (Paris), spring/summer 1974; "The Italian Western Beyond Leone" by Stuart Kaminsky in the *Velvet Light Trap* (Madison, Wisconsin), no.12, 1974; "From Spaghetti Cowboys to the Jewish Gangsters of New York" by Lewis Beale in the *Los Angeles Times Calendar*, 7 November 1982.

*   *   *

The western for Italian Sergio Leone is a genre in which he can explore his own sad, comic, grotesque and surreal vision of life. Leone is no more interested in what could or did happen in the West than he is in any conception of surface reality in his films. *The Good, the Bad, and the Ugly* is a comic nightmare more in tradition of Kafka than that of John Ford or Howard Hawks.

Although Clint Eastwood had, with Leone, established the anti-hero in *A Fistful of Dollars* and *For a Few Dollars More*, it was here, in their third and final film together, that they set out to destroy the more simplistic image so successfully that they contributed to the decline of the western in cinema. In the film, the Eastwood character ("the Good" of the title), called "Blondie" quite ironically by Tuco ("the Ugly"), is both amused by and aloof from the grotesque world. The massive destruction of the film as exemplified by the Civil War (against which the quest for buried gold is played) demonstrates an evil beyond "the Good" man's capacity to control it. With this totally corrupt world around him, he is more interested in living according to a certain style, showing others that he knows how to face danger with amusement and without fear. In this sense, the Eastwood/Leone hero becomes an almost mystic survivor, a new ironic Christ offering a way to face life.

"The Bad" in the film (Lee Van Cleef's "Angel Eyes," itself an ironic appellation) is in many ways similar to "the Good." Neither is defined in his goodness or badness by the traditional morality. Between the two non-extremes stands, or rather scurries, Tuco, "the Ugly"—physically coarse, bearded, a bit dirty, but vibrant and alive in contrast to the other two cold characters. Tuco is hyper-human, and can show great affection as well as great hatred and violence. He has no cunning, is open and direct with an earthy simplicity and sense of humor. Good and Bad are false moral extremes. The ugly represents the human who acts out of animal immediacy without recourse to postures or guilt. Whenever Tuco resorts to poses (as a soldier, a friend) he suffers.

In the film, Leone's use of the extreme close-up is a major device for getting to character; plot is of minimal interest. What is important is the examination of these characters. The close-up is used as ironic balance and the pan for thematic emphasis. For example, the dizzying pan which follows Tuco around the graves near the end of the film indicates the frenzy of Tuco in the midst of death as he seeks the hidden gold.

In an interview Leone said that in "*The Good, the Bad, and the Ugly*, I demystified the adjectives. What do Good, Bad or Ugly mean? What does it mean when these characters are three killers thrown into the midst of a civil war? In that film, I was pursuing the theme that Chaplin so masterfully exposed in *Monsieur Verdoux*."

The film is filled with a number of vivid and powerful visual moments: the opening sequence ending with Tuco in freeze-frame, chicken leg in hand, flying through a window; Angel Eyes' calm murder of the man (and his family) who hired him for the job; Tuco's confrontation with his priest brother; Tuco and Blondie's trek through the desert; the battle at the river; the graveyard search for gold; and Tuco's theft of a gun from a frightened gunsmith.

The feeling of unreality is central to the film and Leone's work in general. The film is a world of bizarre coincidence and horror. The apparent joy and even comedy in the destruction and battle scenes are often followed by some personal touch that underlies the real meaning of the horror which only moments before had been amusing. The dynamiting of the bridge between the Union and Confederate troops is presented as a touch of low comedy with Blondie pushing down Tuco's rear end before the moment of explosion. Yet this scene is preceded by the death of the sympathetic Union officer and followed immediately by an encounter with the dying young man to whom Blondie gives his poncho and his cigar, the two central marks of his minimal identity. The comedy and horror of meaninglessness are thus important in the film.

The Good, the Bad, and the Ugly is a series of contradictions. It is serious and comic, moral and amoral, concerned with the meaning of history while indifferent to the facts of history, unconcerned with reality while filled with moments of tangible character and objects. Like the triumvirate it establishes in the title, the film is not about right or wrong, good or bad, just or unjust. It is a comic vision not far removed from the literature of Kafka or Celine in which we walk on the visual boundary line of comic ugliness.

That the popular press found the film amusing but meaningless upon its release is but an expected footnote in the history of works of popular culture which were unrecognized by critics who thought that a violent, comic, and highly popular work could not possibly by worthy of serious attention.

—Stuart M. Kaminsky

GÖSTA BERLINGS SAGA. The Story of Gösta Berling. Production: Svensk Filmindustri; black and white, 35mm, silent, shown in two parts; running time: 137 mins.; length: first part-2346 meters, second part-2189 meters, eventually edited by Stiller down to about current length. Released 10 and 17 March, 1924. Re-released 1933-1934 in a re-edited version by Ragner Hylten-Cavallius, with sound.

Scenario by Mauritz Stiller and Ragner Hyltén-Cavillius; from the novel by Selma Lagerlöf; directed by Mauritz Stiller; photography by Julius Jaenzon; art direction by Wilhelm Bryde.

Filmed fall 1923 in Sweden.

Cast: Lars Hanson (*Gösta Berling*); Gerda Lundequist-Dahlstrom (*Majorskan Samzelius*); Otto Elg-Lundgren (*Major Sem-*

zelius); Sixten Melmerfelt (*Melchior Sinclaire*); Karin Swanstrom (*Gustafva Sinclaire*); Jenny Hasselqvist (*Marianne Sinclaire*); Ellen Cedarstrom (*Countess Martha Dohna*); Mona Martenson (*Countess Ebba Dohna*); Torsten Hammeren (*Count Hendrick Dohna*); Greta Garbo (*Countess Elizabeth Dohna*).

Publications:

Books—*Den Svenska Filmens Drama: Sjöström och Stiller* by Bengt Idestam-Almquist, Stockholm 1938; *Scandinavian Film* by Forsyth Hardy, London 1951; *Classics of the Swedish Cinema* by Bengt Idestam-Almquist, Stockholm 1952; *Garbo* by John Bainbridge, New York 1955; *Swedish Cinema* by Rune Waldekranz, Stockholm 1959; *La Grande Aventure du Cinema Suédois* by Jean Béranger, Paris 1960; *The Films of Greta Garbo* by Michael Conway, New York 1963; *Swedish Cinema* by Peter Cowie, London 1966; *The Great Films: 50 Golden Years of Motion Pictures* by Bosley Crowther, New York 1967; *Seastrom and Stiller in Hollywood* by Hans Pensel, New York 1969; *Mauritz Stiller och hans filmer: 1912-1916* by Gösta Werner, Stockholm 1969; articles—"The Golden Age of Scandinavian Film" by M.C. Potamkin in *Cinema* (London), September 1930; "Stiller" by Mario Verdone in *Cinema* (Milan), no.126, 1954; "The Man Who Found Garbo" by Bengt Idestam-Almquist in *Films and Filming* (London), August 1956; "Greta Garbo and My Book" by A. Gronowicz in *Contemporary Review* (London), December 1960; "Checklist 110—Mauritz Stiller" and "Mauritz Stiller" by J. Robertson in *Monthly Film Bulletin* (London), December 1977; "Svenska giganter" by G. Werner in *Filmrutan* (Stockholm), no.3, 1981.

*   *   *

Gösta Berlings Saga is regarded by many as Sweden's *Gone With the Wind*. With an epic sweep, episodic structure, and numerous characters, it evokes 19th century Swedish life and is imbued with a lyricism and vibrancy which places its director Mauritz Stiller among the masters of silent film. The film represents both the pinnacle and the swan song of the "golden age" of Swedish cinema—1913-24. With its plot centering on the search for redemption by Gösta Berling, the defrocked priest, and the several women who disastrously fall in love with him, it numbers, along with Griffith's *Intolerance*, among the earliest important films of social protest and one of the masterpieces of silent cinema.

Stiller was a flamboyant dandy whose early reputation was built on sophisticated comedies exhibiting visual dexterity and artful editing. In 1919, he directed what is generally regarded as his foremost masterpiece—*Sir Arne's Treasure (The Three Who Were Doomed)*, based on a novel by the popular Nobel Prizewinning Selma Lagerlof. He directed the De Mille-like sex comedy *Erotikon* and then returned to adapting Lagerlof's novels with *Gunnar Hede's Saga* and finally *Gösta Berlings Saga*.

Gösta Berlings Saga was a formidable undertaking which encompassed many characters and themes, required elaborate sets and costumes and resulted in a four-hour production shown in two parts on consecutive evenings. Stiller eventually conceded this impracticality and edited the film to 137 minutes. His editing, while judiciously shortening many scenes rather than eliminating them, nonetheless imposed a disjunction which ultimately mars the continuity. Despite this shortcoming, *Gösta Berlings Saga* remains a remarkable evocation of life among the

Swedish aristocracy and mirrors its repression and hypocrisy. The first half of the film is devoted to exposition and the introduction of the many characters while the second half is highlighted by the dramatic fire in Ekeby Hall, a flight from wolves by sleigh across a frozen lake, and the brilliant acting of the venerable Gerda Lundequist-Dahlstrom as the shamed mistress of the manor.

Stiller's directorial technique was displayed through an expressive visual lyricism, an artistic use of light contrasted with shadowy darker hues and a picturesque depiction of the beauty and variety of the Swedish landscape. These elements are particularly evident in his photographing (with the masterful cinematographer Julius Jaenzon) of the then unknown Greta Garbo, who played Elizabeth. Stiller's scenes of Garbo picking flowers in the garden, carrying a lamp through the mansion hallways at night, and her first close-up in the sleigh scene capture the luminescence and radiance that made her the most unique female screen image of all time.

The success of *Gösta Berlings Saga* resulted in both Stiller and Garbo being hired by MGM in 1925. His three years in Hollywood destroyed Stiller and he returned to Sweden to die at the age of 45 in 1928. That same year *Gösta Berlings Saga* was released in the United States where a number of religious groups denounced it as "a glorified Elmer Gantry."

Lagerlof disdained Stiller's interpretation of her novel, claiming he had seen "too many poor serials." For the most part *Gösta Berlings Saga* is remembered today as the film which introduced Garbo to the screen. However, it is a major work of the silent screen and as French critic Jean Beranger wrote: "If all but one Swedish silent film were to perish, this, probably, would be the one to save as the best witness of its period. All the charm, intelligence, profound human resonance and technical dexterity, here blend into an indissoluble bloc."

—Ronald Bowers

LA GRANDE ILLUSION. Grand Illusion. Production: Réalisations d'Art Cinématographique (R.A.C.); black and white, 35mm; running time: 117 mins.; length: 10,530 feet. Released 4 June 1937, Paris. Re-released 1946 with much footage deleted, re-released in 1959 with most original footage restored, and again in 1972.

Produced by Frank Rollmer and Albert Pinkovitch; screenplay by Charles Spaak and Jean Renoir; directed by Jean Renoir; photography by Christian Matras (1st operator) and Claude Renoir (2nd operator); edited by Marguerite Marthe-Huguet; sound engineering by Joseph de Bretagne; production design by Eugène Lourié; music by Joseph Kosma, lyrics by Vincent Tully and A. Valsien; costumes designed by Decrais; technical advisor: Carl Koch; assistant director: Jacques Becker.

Filmed from about 30 January-2 April 1937 in Billancourt Studios, Tobis Studios, and Eclair Studios, Epinay; and on location near Neuf-Brisach, the Colmar barracks, and Haut-Koenigsbourg, Alsace. Venice Film Festival, Best Artistic Ensemble, 1937; New York Film Critics Award, Best Foreign Film, 1938.

Cast: Erich von Stroheim (*von Rauffenstein*); Jean Gabin (*Maréchal*); Pierre Fresnay (*de Bœildieu*); Marcel Dalio (*Rosenthal*); Julien Carette (*Actor*); Gaston Modot (*Engineer*); Jean Daste (*Teacher*); Georges Peclet (*French soldier*); Jacques Becker

(*English officer*); Sylvain Itkine (*Demolder*); Dita Parlo (*Elsa*); Werner Florian; Michel Salina; Carl Koch.

Publications:

Scripts—*La Grande Illusion* (screenplay) by Jean Renoir, translated by Marianne Alexandre and Andrew Sinclair, London 1968; *La Grande Illusion* by Jean Renoir, Paris 1971; *La Société français (1914-45)* (partial screenplay) edited by René Prédal, Paris 1972; *La Grande Illusion* by Jean Renoir and Charles Spaak, Paris 1974; *La Grande Illusion*, Zurich 1981; reviews—"*La Grande Illusion*" in *Bianco e Nero* (Rome), September 1937; books—"The Renaissance of the French Cinema—Feydor, Renoir, Duvivier, Carné" by Georges Sadoul in *Film: An Anthology* edited by Daniel Talbot, New York 1959; *Jean Renoir* by Armand-Jean Cauliez, Paris 1962; *Jean Renoir* by Bernard Chardère, Lyon, France 1962; *I Lost It at the Movies* by Pauline Kael, Boston 1965; *Analyses des films de Jean Renoir* by Institut des Hautes Etudes Cinématographiques, Paris 1966; *Study Unit 8: Jean Renoir* by Susan Bennett, London 1967; *The American Cinema* by Andrew Sarris, New York 1968; *70 Years of Cinema* by Peter Cowie, New York 1969; *Jean Renoir* by Pierre Leprohon, New York 1971; *Jean Renoir: The World of his Films* by Leo Braudy, New York 1972; *Guerre et cinéma: grandes illusions et petits soldats, 1895-1971* by Joseph Daniel, Paris 1972; "Grand Illusion" by Archer Winsten in *American Film Criticism* edited by Stanley Kauffmann, New York 1972; *La Société français (1914-45)* edited by René Prédal, Paris 1972; *Jean Renoir* by André Bazin, edited by François Truffaut, Paris, translated ed. 1973. *My Life and My Films* by Jean Renoir, translated by Norman Denny, New York 1974; *Jean Renoir* by Raymond Durgnat, Berkeley 1974; *Film and the Critical Eye* by Dennis DeNitto and William Herman, New York 1975; *Godard and Others: Essays on Film Form* by Louis D. Giannetti, Rutherford, New Jersey 1975; *Les Films de ma vie* by François Truffaut, Paris 1975; articles—"Jean Renoir fait son examen de conscience" by Benjamin Fainsilber in *Cinémonde* (Paris), 20 May 1937; "A Guide to the Discussion and Appreciation of the French photoplay *Grand Illusion*" edited by Rita Hochheimer in *Photoplay Studies* (New York), no.1, 1939; issue devoted to Renoir in *Cahiers du cinéma* (Paris), January 1952; "American Commentary: Says M. Renoir" by Fred Hift in *Today's Cinema* (United Kingdom), 9 August 1956; issue devoted to Renoir in *Cahiers du cinéma* (Paris), Christmas 1957; "Où est la liberté?" by Claude Beylie in *Cahiers du cinéma* (Paris), November 1958; "Reprise: *La Grande Illusion*" by Claude Beylie in *Cinéma 58* (Paris), November 1958; "Un film—*La Grande Illusion*—restauré comme un tableau" in *Les Lettres français* (Paris), 6 March 1958; "Renoir and Realism" by Peter John Dyer in *Sight and Sound* (London), summer 1960; "Jacques Becker, ou la trace de l'homme" by André-G. Brunelin in *Cinéma 60* (Paris), July 1960; "The Screen in His Canvas" by Richard Whitehall in *Films and Filming* (London), July 1960; "*The Elusive Corporal* and *Grand Illusion*" in *A World on Film* by Stanley Kauffmann, New York 1966; article by Claude Beylie in *Cinéma 69* (Paris), November 1969; "Directors Go to their Movies: Jean Renoir" by Digby Diehl in *Action* (Los Angeles), May/June 1972; "Q & A: Jean Renoir" by Digby Diehl in *Los Angeles Times West Magazine*, 16 April 1972; "*La Grande Illusion*" by Jean-Jacques Dupuich in *Image et son* (Paris), November 1972; "Jean Renoir's *La Grande Illusion*" by Stanley Kauffmann in *Horizon* (Los Angeles), summer 1972; "The Cinema of the Popular Front in France, (1934-38)" by Goffredo Fofi in *Screen* (London), winter 1972-73; "Jean Renoir de *Nana* à *La Grande Illusion*" by

Claude Gauteur in *Image et son* (Paris), May 1975; "Jean Renoir's *La Grande Illusion*" by Alexander Sesonske in *The Georgia Review* (USA), spring 1975; "*La Grande Illusion* de Jean Renoir" by R. Viry-Babel in *Cahiers de la cinématheque* (Perpignan, France), spring 1976; "Theatricals in Jean Renoir's *Rules of the Game* and *Grand Illusion*" by P.R. Perebinossoff in *Literature/Film Quarterly* (Salisbury, Maryland), winter 1977.

*   *   *

The critical estimate of *La Grande Illusion* has fluctuated with the vicissitudes of critical theory. In the days when film's importance was attributed to the importance of its subject, it was widely regarded as Renoir's masterpiece, a noble humanist anti-war statement. With the development of the *auteur* theory in the late 1950s, its reputation dwindled. It came to be perceived as a less personal, less intimate and less complex work than *La Règle du jeu*, which superceded it as marking the summit of Renoir's achievement. Though opposed, these views are based on the same misconception. *La Grande Illusion* is much too complex to be reduced to a thesis film, and although an anti-war statement can certainly be read from it (Renoir's detestation of war is not in doubt), that is incidental rather than essential to the film's meaning. In fact, it has a great deal in common with *La Règle du jeu*: Renoir's own account of the thematic premise of the later film applies equally to earlier ("My preoccupation is with the meeting; how to belong, how to meet"); both have similiar four-part structures, moving to a big climactic scene at the end of part two, placing the major climax at the end of part three, with a quieter, more intimate fourth part in which the action moves out of doors or into the countryside.

"How to belong, how to meet"—another way of putting it is to say that Renoir's perennial concern is with the boundaries that keep people apart and the possibility of transcending them. The four-part structure enables him to develop this theme through a network of shifting, interlocking relationships presented consistently in terms of difference and the overcoming of difference.

The first part consists of a prologue that introduces three of the four main characters and two of the main boundaries, class and nationality. Bœildieu and Maréchal are connected because both are French and involved in a war against Germany; Bœildieu and von Rauffenstein are connected because both are aristocrats and share a particular code that excludes the proletariat Maréchal. The film's basic assumption—that "difference is socially constructed but so thoroughly internalized and so strongly institutionalized as to be very difficult to overcome—is dramatized in the parallels between the two headquarters (French/German) which are identical in structure but different in every detail, the details insisting upon "Frenchness" and "German-ness" respectively.

The second part occurs in the Prison Camp. Another main character, Rosenthal, is introduced, along with a host of minor ones who illustrate diverse aspects of the theme in the particularities of social position, profession, outlook, etc. With Rosenthal a third main boundary is established, that of race and religion. The pattern of alignments/separation becomes more complex: Maréchal/Bœildieu are linked by race and religion (Aryan, Christian) but separated by class position; Bœildieu/Rosenthal are linked by privilege but separated by class tradition (aristocrat/*nouveau riche*); Rosenthal/Maréchal are linked as non-aristocratic but separated by race/religion and social status. This section of the film makes frequent and expressive use of a favorite Renoir motif, the window, which stresses separation (outside/inside), but is also a boundary that can be crossed or communicated across. The second part culminates in the first big climax, the celebrated scene of the prisoners' camp show and defiant singing of the "Marseillaise." Most important here, however, is the film's raising of the last main issue of boundary, that of gender/sexuality, especially in the extraordinary moment when the young prisoner is seen in women's clothes (for the show) and all activity and conversation abruptly cease. Its intensity exceeds anything explainable in terms of nostalgia for absent women: the androgynous figure becomes the center of the men's fascination and attraction.

The third section re-introduces von Rauffenstein (now with broken vertebrae, in a sense as much a prisoner as the men he is in charge of) and the development and culmination of the Bœildieu/von Rauffenstein alignment/separation. A leading concern here again connects the film to *Règle du jeu*: the notion that the aristocratic order the two men represent will not survive the war. The aristocracy of *Règle du jeu* is significantly different; they no longer are informed and guided by a clearly defined code of nobility. *Règle du jeu*'s Marquis is connected, not to Bœildieu, but to Rosenthal (not only are the two characters played by the same actor, we are told that "Rosenthal" was the name of the Marquis' grandfather). Renoir views this inevitable destruction of a way life with marked ambivalence. The aristocratic code is seen at once as based upon an untenable privilege and as embodying a fineness without which civilization will be poorer. This part of the film moves to the second major climax, in which Renoir magnificently ties all the major thematic and dramatic threads together: the escape of Maréchal and Rosenthal, secured by Bœildieu who sacrifices his life by compelling von Rauffenstein to shoot him. The scene echoes the climax of the second section by centering on a "theatrical" performance (Bœildieu playing his penny whistle on the battlements, the searchlights trained on him as "star"). Together with the ensuing scene of Bœildieu's death and his class friend/national enemy's grief, the scene enacts the theme of the end of the aristocratic order (the proletarian Maréchal and the *nouveau riche* Rosenthal are the embryonic future). It achieves the film's supreme irony in its play on the intimate understanding and affection between two men, one of whom must kill the other.

The last section involves the escape/the farm/the border. The relation of *La Grande Illusion* to classical narrative (with its traditional pattern of order-disturbance of order-restoration of order) is complex and idiosyncratic. The narrative actually takes place in the hiatus between two orders: the order the war has destroyed and the new order that will be built when it is over. Between the two, Renoir manages at once to suggest the social order that was left behind and the possibility of a different order no longer based on artificial divisions. In the camps, the boundaries of class, race, nationality are repeatedly crossed and eroded as new alignments (based on human need and sympathy) are formed. The last section restores what was crucially absent earlier: the presence of a woman. A series of three immediately consecutive scenes can be read as "answering" and containing the eruption of a possible bisexuality in part two: Maréchal and Rosenthal sleep in each other's arms (the motive is warmth, not sexuality, but nonetheless they are in close bodily proximity); awakening, they quarrel violently, Maréchal calls Rosenthal a "dirty Jew," they separate, then tentatively come together again; hiding in a barn, they hear someone coming and spring to either side of the door; the door opens and, exactly between them, the woman appears. The ensuing scenes restore the heterosexuality that, at the outset, was present only as a song ("Frou-Frou") and a memory (Maréchal's Joséphine, the woman recalled by both Bœildieu and von Rauffenstein). This leads to the ultimate expression of togetherness/division: the Christmas celebration in which Rosenthal assists, only to be excluded as the lovers leave to go to bed. If the film celebrates the possibility of demolishing boundaries, it also acknowledges, within the existing social system, their inevitability.

—Robin Wood

THE GRAPES OF WRATH. Production: Twentieth Century-Fox; 1940; black and white, 35mm; running time: 128 mins., some prints are 115 mins. Released 24 January 1940, New York.

Produced by Darryl F. Zanuck; screenplay by Nunnally Johnson; from the novel by John Steinbeck; directed by John Ford; photography by Gregg Toland; edited by Robert Simpson; art direction by Richard Day and Mark Lee Kirk; music arranged by Alfred Newman; special sound effects by Robert Parrish.

Filmed late summer-early fall 1939 in Twentieth Century-Fox studios and lots; with some footage shot on location on Highway 66 between Oklahoma and California. Cost: $750,000 (estimated). Academy Awards for Best Director and Best Supporting Actress (Darwell), 1940; New York Film Critics' Awards for Best Picture and Best Direction, 1940.

Cast: *The Joad Party*—Henry Fonda (*Tom*); Jane Darwell (*Ma*); Russell Simpson (*Pa*); Charley Grapewin (*Grampa*); Zeffie Tilbury (*Granma*); Frank Darien (*Uncle John*); Frank Sully (*Noah*); O.Z. Whitehead (*Al*); Dorris Bowdon (*Rosasharn*); Eddie Quillan (*Connie Rivers*); Shirley Mills (*Ruthie*); Darryl Hickman (*Winfield*); *Others*—John Carradine (*Casey*); John Qualen (*Muley Graves*); Ward Bond (*Policeman*); Paul Guilfoyle (*Floyd*); Charles D. Brown (*Wilkie*).

Publications:

Script—*20 Best Film Plays* edited by John Gassner and Dudley Nichols, New York 1943; reviews—in *Collier's* (New York), 23 January 1940; review by Thomas Benton in *Life* (New York), 22 January 1940; "Slumming with Zanuck" by M. Mok in *Nation* (New York), 3 February 1940; review by Otis Ferguson in the *New Republic* (New York), 12 February 1940; review in *The New York Times*, 25 January 1940; books—*John Ford* by Jean Mitry, Paris 1954; *Novels into Films* by George Bluestone, Baltimore 1957; *Theory of Film: The Redemption of Physical Reality* by Siegfried Kracauer, New York 1960; *A Companion to "The Grapes of Wrath"* by Warren French, New York 1963; *John Ford* by Philippe Haudiquet, Paris 1966; *John Ford* by Peter Bogdanovich, Los Angeles 1968; *John Steinbeck and His Films* by Michael Burrows, (Primestyle "Formative Films" series) 1970; *The Fondas: The Films and Careers of Henry, Jane, and Peter Fonda* by John Springer, New York 1970; *The Cinema of John Ford* by John Baxter, New York 1971; *Filmguide to "The Grapes of Wrath"* by Warren French, Bloomington, Indiana 1973; *John Ford* by Joseph McBride and Michael Wilmington, London 1975; *The John Ford Movie Mystery* by Andrew Sarris, London 1976; *John Ford* by Peter Bogdanovich, Berkeley 1978; *John Ford* by Andrew Sinclair, New York 1979; *Pappy: The Life of John Ford* by Dan Ford, Englewood Cliffs, New Jersey 1979; articles—"John Ford Wants It Real" by Frank Daugherty in *Christian Science Monitor Magazine* (Boston), 21 June 1941; "The Film Since Then" by Richard Griffith in *The*

Film Till Now by Paul Rotha, revised edition, New York 1949; "Press Conference" by Derek Hill in *Sight and Sound* (London), summer 1957; "Henry Fonda" by John Springer in *Films in Review* (New York), November 1960; "The Five Worlds of John Ford" by Douglas McVay in *Films and Filming* (London), June 1962; "Fonda" by Peter Cowie in *Films and Filming* (London), April 1962; "Fonda on Fonda" by Henry Fonda in *Films and Filming* (London), February 1963; issue devoted to Ford, *Focus on Film* (London), spring 1971; issue on "Ford's Stock Company" in *Filmkritik* (Munich), January 1972; "*Gone With the Wind* and *The Grapes of Wrath* as Hollywood Histories of the Depression" by T.H. Pauly in *Journal of Popular Film* (Bowling Green, Ohio), summer 1974; "A Family in a Ford: *The Grapes of Wrath*" by J. Place in *Film Comment* (New York), September/-October 1976; "The Ideology of the Social Consciousness Movie: Three Films of Darryl F. Zanuck" by R. Campbell in *Quarterly Review of Film Studies* (Pleasantville, New York), winter 1978.

*   *   *

A pet project of Darryl Zanuck's, *The Grapes of Wrath* exercised the packaging talents of Fox's studio head for a large part of 1939 as he put together a team appropiate to a book with the stature of Steinbeck's novel. John Ford was an obvious choice to direct, Dudley Nichols to write the script, and Henry Fonda to star as Tom Joad, the uneducated ex-convict "Oakie" who becomes the personification of flinty Midwestern integrity and moral worth. Knowing Fonda's wish to play Joad, Zanuck lured him into signing an eight-picture contract by advertising his intention to cast in the role either Don Ameche or Tyrone Power.

Ford, Nichols, Fonda and the supporting cast transformed Steinbeck's novel to the screen with proper fidelity, the distortions far outweighed by the spectacular rightness of Fonda's casting and the remarkable cinematography of Gregg Toland, clearly influenced by the dust bowl photographs of Walker Evans and Margaret Bourke-White. The film's opening image is of Tom Joad walking with tireless application out of the flat Midwestern landscape against a counterpoint of leaning telephone poles, of society confronted by an ecological and historical disaster against which it is helpless to act. Accustomed to such material from his frontier films, Ford took instinctive and instant command.

Clearly he felt an affinity with the plight of the dispossessed Kansas farmers of Steinbeck's story, which mirrored that of his Irish forebears turned off the land in the potato famine of the 19th century. And he had already established in films like *Four Men and a Prayer* the image of the family as not only unbreakable but an instrument for change, an institution that could act to improve social conditions. Throughout the film, it is the independents like John Carradine's itinerant preacher Casey and the half-mad fugitive Muley (John Qualen) who seem lost, desperate for companionship, while Jane Darwell and Russell Simpson as Ma and Pa Joad exhale a sense of calm and confidence. As Ma affirms at the end of the film, in a scene added by Zanuck to underline the moral and blunt the harsh dying fall of the novel, no force can destroy the will of people who are determined to live.

The picture Ford and Nichols draw of Depression America pulls few punches. Disinterested banks employ local strong-arm men to dispossess the share croppers and evict farmers unable to keep up mortgage payments on their own over-used, poorly maintained properties. Muley's futile stand against the bulldozers wilts when he recognizes one of his neighbors in the driving seat. One has to eat even if it means betraying one's own kind. Deprived of his sacred kinship with the earth, sanctified by "living on it and being born on it and dying on it," Muley becomes "just an ol' graveyard ghost" flitting about his crumbling house in the light of Tom Joad's lamp.

The Joads set out for California, their lurching truck loaded up with possessions, relatives and, in a touching gesture, the preacher Casey, invited along after a brief and hurried calculation of the vehicle's strength. Casey is a classic Fordian figure, a religious madman who acts as custodian of principles, the celebrant of rituals like Mose Harper (Hank Worden) in *The Searchers*. He says the brief funeral oration over Grandpa Joad when he succumbs to the trials of the journey. He also turns into a primitive union organiser when greedy employers exploit the itinerants desperate for work as fruit-pickers. He's no natural radical—just a man with a proper sense of right and wrong. Amused, he says of the bosses' thugs who hunt him, "They think I'm the leader on account of I talk so much." When he dies, murdered by the employers, it is Tom who carries on his duty, instinctively sensing his destiny. "Maybe it's like Casey says. A feller ain't got a soul of his own, but only a piece of a big soul..." And he walks off again, as he entered the story, undramatically spreading the gospel of social reform.

The Grapes of Wrath abounds with examples of Ford's skill in visual language. Poor talkers, the Joads express much in a way of standing, looking, responding to the land through which they pass. Ma Joad's cleaning up of the old house is shown largely without dialogue, but her careful turning out of a box of mementoes, the discovery of a pair of earrings and her action of putting them on her ears and looking up into the dark at some half-forgotten moment of youthful pleasure could hardly be bettered with words. Jane Darwell is perhaps too plump, matriarchal, too *Irish* for her role, and Ford's first choice, Beulah Bondi, had a greater physical claim to the part with her gaunt, stringy resilience, but so effective is Ford's use of the actress that one can no longer imagine anyone else playing it.

Fonda remains the focus of the film, his clear-eyed sceptical gaze reaching out to the camera no matter where he stands in the frame. The strength of his moral convictions is all the more striking for the imperfection of the character which supports them. Just released from jail for a murder, Tom is unrepentant: "Knocked his head plumb to squash," he recalls to an alarmed truck driver who gives him a lift. He has little understanding of politics ("What's these 'Reds' anyway?"), enjoys a drink and a dance, but has no time for abstract discussions. That such a man can be roused to moral wrath by injustice dramatizes the self-evident corruption of the system, and the belief in his conviction carries an audience to a conclusion startling radical by the standards of time. Ford's reactionary politics, his populism and republicanism, must have stood in direct contradiction of the book's harsh message, which may explain his acceptance of the final sugar-coated scene. Yet in Ford's world, to keep faith meant more than any political creed; better to believe in an error than not to believe at all. When Ma Joad at the end of *The Grapes of Wrath* professes the absolute faith of a peasant people in simple survival, one hears Ford's voice as clearly as that of writer, producer or star.

—John Baxter

THE GREAT DICTATOR. Production: United Artists; 1940; black and white, 35mm; running time: 127 mins. Released 1940.

Produced, scripted, and directed by Charles Chaplin; photography by Karl Struss and Rollié Totheroh; edited by Willard Nico; art direction by J. Russell Spencer; music by Meredith Wilson.

Cast: Charles Chaplin (*Adenoid Hynkel, Dictator of Ptomania/A Jewish Barber*); Paulette Goddard (*Hannah*); Jack Oakie (*Benzini Napaloni, Dictator of Bacteria*); Reginald Gardiner (*Schultz*); Henry Daniell (*Garbitsch*); Billy Gilbert (*Herring*).

Publications:

Reviews—by Herman Weinberg in *Sight and Sound* (London), autumn 1940; review in *Sight and Sound* (London), winter 1940-41; books—*Charlie Chaplin* by Theodore Huff, New York 1951; *Monsieur Chaplin ou le rire dans la nuit* by Maurice Bessy and Robert Florey, Paris 1952; *Vie de Charlot* by Georges Sadoul, Paris 1952; *Charlot et la "fabulation" chaplinesque* by Jean Mitry, Paris 1957; *Charles Chaplin* by Barthelemy Amengual, Paris 1963; *My Autobiography* by Charles Chaplin, London 1964; *The Films of Charlie Chaplin* by Gerald McDonald and others, Secaucus, New Jersey 1965; *Charlie Chaplin* by Marcel Martin, Paris 1966; *Chaplin, Last of the Clowns* by Parker Tyler, New York 1947; *Charles Chaplin* by Pierre Leprohon, Paris 1970; *Focus on Chaplin* edited by Donald McCaffrey, Englewood Cliffs, New Jersey 1971; *Chaplin's Films* by Uno Asplund, Newton Abbot, Devon 1971; *Tout Chaplin: Tous les films, par le texte, par le gag et par l'image* by Jean Mitry, Paris 1972; *My Life in Pictures* by Charles Chaplin, London 1974; *Chaplin* by Roger Manvell, Boston 1974; *Charlie Chaplin* by Robert Moss, New York 1975; *Chaplin, Genesis of a Clown* by Raoul Sobel and David Francis, London 1977; *Charlie Chaplin* by P. Baldelli, Florence 1977; *Charles Chaplin—a Guide to References and Resources* compiled by T.J. Lyons, Boston 1977; *Charlot: ou, Sir Charles Chaplin* by J. Lorcey, Paris 1978; articles—"Charlie Chaplin" by Alistair Cooke in *Atlantic* (Greenwich, Connecticut), August 1939; "About Chaplin's Film" by Daniel Todd in the *New Masses* (New York), 17 December 1940; "Story of 2 Mustaches" by H.F. Pringle in *Ladies Home Journal* (New York), July 1940; "Charlie Chaplin's Dictator" in *Life* (New York), 2 September 1940; "Chaplin Draws a Keen Weapon" by R. Van Gelder in the *New York Times Magazine*, 8 September 1940; "Hitler and Chaplin at 54" in the *New York Times Magazine*, 18 April 1943; "A Feeling of Sad Dignity" by Robert Warshow in the *Partisan Review* (New Brunswick, New Jersey), November/December 1954; "Clown with a Frown" by Peter Baker in *Films and Filming* (London), August 1957; "The True Face of Man" by Peter John Dyer in *Films and Filming* (London), September 1958; "Film Chronicle (1940): Chaplin Again, Again, and Again" by Paul Goodman in *Movie* (London), winter 1964; articles by Andrew Sarris in *The Village Voice* (New York), 5 March and 12 March 1964; "Roland H. Totheroh Interviewed" by Timothy J. Lyons in *Film Culture* (New York), spring 1972; "Le Dictateur" by F. Chevassu in *Image et son* (Paris), November 1972; "The Great Dictator" by S. Harvey in *Film Comment* (New York), September/October 1972; "Le Dictateur: Un culot inouï" by R. Lefévre in *Cinéma* (Paris), November 1972; "Chaplin's The Great Dictator" by C. Boost in *Skoop* (The Hague), August 1973; "L'Art des transitions dans Le Dictateur" by J.L. Bourget in *Positif* (Paris), July/August 1973; "Die letzte Tortenschlacht. Chaplins Grosser

Diktator und das Ende des Slapstacks" by J. Friedrich in *Filmkritik* (Munich), November 1973; "*The Great Dictator*" by M. Tarratt in *Films and Filming* (London), March 1973; "La negazione del dittatore come fenomeno di massa" by G. Giuricin in *Cinema nuovo* (Turin), January/February 1974; "Charlot et *La Dictature*" by G. Blanco in *Ecran* (Paris), December 1977; "Charles Chaplin (en) français" by C. Chaplin in *Image et son* (Paris), January 1977; special issue of *Film und Fernsehen* (Berlin), March 1978; "*De dictator*" by Sergei Eisenstein in *Skrien* (Amsterdam), February 1978; special Chaplin issue of *University Film Association Journal* (Houston), no.1, 1979; "Chaplin's *Dictator* Finally Plays Chile Screens After Censor Lag" in *Variety* (New York), 31 October 1979; "Adolf Hitler as Portrayed in Drama and Film" by A. Goldfarb in *Journal of Popular Culture* (Bowling Green, Ohio), no.1, 1979; "*The Great Dictator*" by R.M. Goldstein in *Film News* (New York), March/April 1979; "The Comedy of Ozu and Chaplin—a Study in Contrast" by T. Sato, translated by G. Barrett, in *Wide Angle* (Athens, Ohio), no.2, 1979; "*The Great Dictator*" by DeWitt Bodeen in *Magill's Survey of Cinema*" edited by Frank N. Magill, Englewood Cliffs, New Jersey 1980.

*   *   *

The Great Dictator was Chaplin's first dialogue film, the first film for which he wrote a script in advance, and the first film in two decades in which he does not star as the Tramp. Instead Chaplin plays a double role—a little Jewish barber, who closely resembles the Tramp, and the great dictator of Ptomania, Adenoid Hynkel, an obvious parody of Adolf Hitler, whom Chaplin ironically resembled. The funniest sequences of the film are Chaplin's burlesques of Hitler's rhetoric, mannerisms, and delusions of grandeur. In one of those comic sequences, Hynkel delivers a political speech that is so scorching that the microphones melt and bend. Hynkel is so inflamed by his rhetorical passion that he not only has to cool his throat with water but also splashes water down the front of his pants—a brilliantly subtle Freudian suggestion that much of the fire of Hitler's political persuasion derives from the urgings of his genitals. In perhaps the most memorable sequence of the film, Hynkel converts the globe of the earth into his balloon-like plaything, performing a languid, romantic, dreamlike ballet with the floating globe, revealing his aspirations to possess the earth in almost sexual terms. This comic sexuality is reinforced by both the suggestions of masturbation in Hynkel's solo dance with the globe, and in the fact that the sort of actions he performs precisely mirror the twirls and gyrations of a bubble dancer, teasingly playing with the circular globe that hides her most mysterious parts from her leering audience.

In contrast to the delusions of the dictator is the earthy, pragmatic activity of the barber, a German soldier injured in World War I, suffering from amnesia, who awakens and returns to "Ptomanian" society only to find himself in an unfamiliar world where Jews are outcasts. In immediate response to the dictator's dance with the globe is the Jewish barber's snappy shaving of a customer to the precise rhythms of a Brahms Hungarian dance. The barber's snappy, vital, human-oriented actions contrast deliberately with the dictator's masturbatory solo. The barber also contrasts with the dictator in his relationship to language. As opposed to flaming rhetoric, the barber talks very little—another clear parallel to the Tramp. But at the end of the film, the barber, because of his physical resemblance, is mistaken for the dictator and asked to deliver the victorious speech to celebrate the invasion of "Austerlich." The barber becomes very talkative, summoning his courage and feelings to deliver a direct appeal to all his viewers for hope, peace, and humanity. Although the lengthy, explicit political speech is deliberately woven into the film's action—which has contrasted the barber and the dictator in their relationship to human speech—the monologue struck many critics as overly explicit and impassioned, inadequately translated into Chaplin's tools of comedy, irony, and physical action.

Chaplin claims that he was unaware of the horrors of the Nazi death camps when he made the film. The outrageous sense of burlesque in the film implies the general American belief that Hitler was more a clown to be laughed at than a menace to be feared. The reduction of Hitler's associates and allies to buffoons reveals the same pattern—Goering becomes Herring, Goebbels becomes Barbitsch, Mussolini becomes Benzino Napaloni, impersonated by a pasta-slinging Jack Oakie. Chaplin later stated that if he had known about the seriousness and murderousness of the Nazi threat he would have never made the film.

—Gerald Mast

GREAT EXPECTATIONS. Production: Rank/Cineguild (London); black and white, 35mm; running time: 118 mins. Released May 1947 by Universal-International Pictures.

Produced and directed by David Lean; screenplay by David Lean and Ronald Neame with Anthony Havelock-Allan, Kay Walsh and Cecil McGivern; from the novel by Charles Dickens; photography by Guy Green; edited by Jack Harris; art direction by John Bryan; music score by Walter Goehr.

Academy Awards for Best Cinematography-Black and White and Best Art Direction, 1947.

Cast: John Mills (*Mr. Pip*); Anthony Wager (*Pip as a boy*); Valerie Hobson (*Estella*); Jean Simmons (*Estella as a girl*); Bernard Miles (*Joe Gargery*); Francis L. Sullivan (*Jaggers*); Finlay Currie (*Magwitch*); Alec Guinness (*Herbert Pocket*); John Forrest (*Herbert as a boy*); Martita Hunt (*Miss Havisham*); Ivor Bernard (*Wemmick*); Freda Jackson (*Mrs. Joe*); Torin Thatcher (*Bentley Drummil*); Eileen Erskine (*Biddy*); Hay Petrie (*Uncle Pumblechock*); George Hayes (*Compeyson*); Richard George (*Sergeant*); Everley Gregg (*Sarah Pocket*); John Burch (*Mr. Wopsie*); O.B. Clarence (*Aged parent*).

Publications:

Books—*Alec Guinness* by Kenneth Tynan, New York 1954; *Motion Pictures: The Development of an Art from the Silent Films to the Age of Television* by Albert Fulton, Norman, Oklahoma 1960; *A Mirror for England: British Movies from Austerity to Affluence* by Raymond Durgnat, New York 1971; *The Cinema of David Lean* by Gerald Pratley, New York 1974; *David Lean and His Films* by Alain Silver and James Ursini, London 1974; *David Lean: A Guide to References and Resources* by Louis Castelli and Caryn Lynn Cleeland, Boston 1980; articles—by Stanley Ellin in *Hollywood Quarterly*, fall 1947; article by Irving Pichel in *Hollywood Quarterly*, July 1947; "The Up and Coming Team of Lean and Neame" by C.A. Lejeune in *The New York Times*, 15 June 1947; "Career Inventory From the Lean Viewpoint" by Howard Thompson in the *New York Times*, 9 November 1952; "A Study of David Lean" by J. Holden in *Film Journal* (New York), April 1956; "David Lean—Lover of Life" by Douglas McVay in *Films and Filming* (London), August 1959; "David Lean" by Stephen Watts in *Films in Review* (New York), April 1959; "Alec Guinness" by Douglas McVay in *Films and Filming* (London), May 1961; "Mills" by Ian Johnson in *Films and Filming* (London), June 1962; "John Mills" by Alvin Marill in *Films in Review* (New York), August/-September 1971; "The Untranquil Light: David Lean's *Great Expectations*" by A. Silver in *Literature/Film Quarterly* (Salisbury, Maryland), spring 1974; "*Great Expectations*" by A.L. Zambrano in *Literature/Film Quarterly* (Salisbury, Maryland), spring 1974; "Gag Bag" by D. Wilson in the *New Statesman* (London), 9 January 1976.

* * *

The picturesque novels of Charles Dickens have a marked affinity for cinematic translation. There are literally dozens of filmed versions of Dickens's work dating back to silent films, but two interpretations stand out above all the others: first and foremost is David Lean's *Great Expectations* and the second is Noel Langley's *The Pickwick Papers*.

Lean was one of the predominant figures in post-World War II England, first gaining recognition as co-director, with Noel Coward, of *In Which We Serve*. There followed three Coward adaptations—*This Happy Breed*, *Blithe Spirit* and the memorable *Brief Encounter*, and then his two adaptations of Dickens—*Great Expectations* and *Oliver Twist*. Lean worked with meticulously crafted scripts and had a keen sense of the importance of cinematic editing, which he defines as "a kind of magic...the most important job" in filmmaking.

Those two elements of filmic style are paramount to the success of *Great Expectations*. He co-authored the script with Ronald Neame, Anthony Havelock-Allan, Kay Walsh and Cecil McGivern, and their truncation of Dickens's expansive novel captures the essence of both the fairy-tale aspect of the author's familiar story and his succinct social commentary. While many of Dickens's minor characters had to be eliminated in this 118-minute film, none of Dickens's literary finesse was eschewed. Lean's interpretation has a light and charming touch, though critic James Agee, while an admirer of the film, felt an even more faithful rendering would have elicited more of Dickens's darker psychology. He wrote: "I thought it very provocative a a symbolized intuitive image of nineteenth-century England, with the century (represented by Pip and Estella) moving as if hypnotized by the vengefulness, gratitude, and deviousness of great ancestral forces: Magwitch as the archetype of the nameless swarm; Miss Havisham as the embittered Virgin Queen; the sinister-benign Jaggers as Law and Government."

However, if not as psychologically penetrating as Agee wished, the intelligent script and the expert editing serve Dickens exceedingly well. The film contains numerous scenes of atmosphere and vitality, such as the opening sequence in the graveyard where Pip first meets the fugitive Magwitch.

The film was nominated for five Academy Awards including Best Picture, Best Direction and Best Screenplay and won two awards: Best Cinematography (Guy Green) and Best Art Direction (John Bryan) with Set Decoration by Wilfred Shingleton.

Great Expectations remains the high point of Lean's enigmatic career. Following these intimate and personalized films in England during the 1940s, Lean turned to internationally cast epic films such as *The Bridge on the River Kwai*, *Lawrence of Arabia* and *Dr. Zhivago* which, while extraordinarily popular, diminished his critical acclaim.

—Ronald Bowers

THE GREAT TRAIN ROBBERY. Production: The Edison Company; black and white, 35mm, silent; running time: about 10-12 mins. Released about 1903.

Scenario, direction, and editing by Edwin S. Porter. Filmed about 1903 in and around Dover, New Jersey.

Cast: George Barnes; A.C. Abadie; Marie Murray; G.M. Anderson.

Publications:

Script—"English Influences on the Work of Edwin S. Porter" (includes condensed script) by Georges Sadoul in *Hollywood Quarterly*, fall 1947; books—*The Western: From Silents to Cinerama* by William Everson and George N. Fenin, New York 1962; *A Million and One Nights* by Terry Ramsaye, New York 1964 edition; *Film Makers on Filmmaking* edited by Harry M. Geduld, Bloomington, Indiana 1967; *The First 20 Years: A Segment of Film History* by Kemp R. Niver, Los Angeles 1968; *The Silent Voice—A Text, Golden Age of the Cinema* by Arthur Lennig, Troy 1969; *History of the American Film History From Its Beginnings to 1931* by Benjamin B. Hampton, New York 1970; *Spellbound in Darkness* by George C. Pratt, Greenwich, Connecticut 1973; *The Early Develpment of the Motion Picture: 1887-1909* by Joseph H. North, New York 1973; *American Silent Film* by William Everson, New York 1978; *A History of Film* by Jack C. Ellis, Englewood Cliffs, New Jersey 1979; articles—Porter obituary in *Current Biography Yearbook*, New York 1941; "Porter and Griffith" by D. Drum in *Films in Review* (New York), March 1956; "Edwin S. Porter: 5 Films" by Eileen Bowser and "*The Great Train Robbery*" by Iris Barry in *Film Notes*, New York 1969; "Edwin S. Porter" by Jack Spears in *Films in Review* (New York), June/July 1970; "Detours in Film Narrative: The Development of Cross-Cutting" in *Cinema Journal* (Evanston, Illinois), no. 1, 1979; "A 1903 Pic on the Right Track: 100th Anni of Edison's Bulb Recalls His Epochal *Great Train Robbery*" by H. Hollinger in *Variety* (New York), 14 March 1979.

*   *   *

The Great Train Robbery, directed by Edwin S. Porter, holds a position of importance in the history of film for many reasons: it was the first American film to gain a wide popularity among audiences in nickelodeons across the country; it was one of the first American films to contain a narrative, and it helped to establish the chase scene as a staple of adventure films. *The Great Train Robbery* had a running time of almost 12 minutes, a length of epic proportions compared to the single-shot, 50-foot films so common at the turn of the century.

Of utmost importance in the film is the technique of editing that it introduced. Instead of presenting the story in linear time, the film cross-cuts between different scenes to represent simultaneous actions. (Porter used this technique of cross-cutting in an earlier film, *The Life of an American Fireman*, but it was the wide-spread popularity of *The Great Train Robbery* that brought it to the forefront.)

The story presented in the film is relatively simple: bandits break into the telegraph office, tie up the operator, and force a train to make an unscheduled stop; they board the train, rob the express car and passengers, and make their escape. *Meanwhile*, the telegraph operator, freed by his daughter, alerts the townspeople. A posse is formed, and the bandits are killed after an exciting chase scene, climaxed by an exchange of gunfire. The final image of the film is a striking point-of-view shot from one of the bandits firing his gun at the camera and into the audience.

Porter's exact editing sequence is unknown because the film exists in more than one version. However, the original intent is quite clear: through the use of editing, Porter tells the story from two points of view. The action cuts back and forth between the robbers and the posse. Porter discovered that each scene need not be self-contained, but that scenes can lead into each other to create a new meaning.

Individually, each scene remains a single shot. The film is comprised of 14 scenes which contain no editing within. For the most part, they retain the eye level, twelfth-row point of view so prevelant in the early silent films. The exterior scenes do show some inventive camerawork, probably due to circumstances of outdoor location shooting. For example, as the robbers made their escape on horseback, the camera pans to follow them along. The exterior scenes seemed to require more inventiveness to maintain the composition and action, while the interior scenes remained more stagey and flat.

Technically speaking, Porter had a strong interest in camerawork and "special effects," especially the trick films of George Méliès. Porter did use some trick photography in *The Great Train Robbery*. For example, in the telegraph office (which is an interior set) Porter uses a travelling matte (done in the camera) in the window to indicate the train pulling into the station outside. In the later scene, two men are struggling on top of a moving train. Porter makes a cut in the middle of the scene so that a dummy can be substituted for one of the actors, and then thrown off the train to his "death." Whereas Méliès uses trick photography as "magic," Porter tried to use special effects in a more realistic manner.

Surprisingly, after *The Great Train Robbery*, Porter did little else directorially to advance the art of filmmaking. *The Great Train Robbery*, however, was so innovative that it became a dramatic step in the evolution of film.

—Linda J. Obalil

GREED. Production: begun under Goldwyn-von Stroheim Productions for Goldwyn Pictures; released by Metro-Goldwyn Corporation as a Louis B. Mayer Presentation; black and white, 35mm, silent; running time: about 150 mins., a 109 min. version also exists; originally 7 hours, but Stroheim was forced to edit further, first into a 4 hour version, then into a 3 hour version supervised by Rex Ingram, and finally cut to 2 ½ hours by the studio; length: 10,212 feet (some sources list length as 10,067 feet or 10,500 feet); originally 47,000 feet, then 45,000 feet, then 42,000 feet, then 24,000 feet, then 18,000 feet, then 16,000 feet, and finally present length. Released December 1924, New York;

all scenes with gold or gold-related objects were hand-tinted in original release prints.

Produced by Erich von Stroheim and Samuel Goldwyn, some sources list Irving Thalberg as producer; screenplay by Erich von Stroheim and June Mathis; from the novel *McTeague* by Frank Norris; original titles written by Erich von Stroheim and June Mathis, released titles written by Joseph Farnham; directed by Erich von Stroheim; photography by William H. Daniels, Ben F. Reynolds, and Ernest B. Schoedsack; edited by Frank Hull, final version edited by Joseph Farnham and reputedly June Mathis; production design by Capt. Richard Day and Erich von Stroheim (no actual sets used); art direction by Louis Germonprez and Edward Sowders; music by James and Jack Brennan.

Filmed in 9 months, 1922-23 and edited in 1 year, 1923-24. Filmed in Oakland, California, and in Death Valley and the Panamint Mountains, California. Cost: over $450,000.

Cast: *In the Prologue:* Jack Curtis (*McTeague, Sr., Shift Boss at the Big Dipper Mine*) (role cut from film); Tempé Piggot (*Mother McTeague*); Gibson Gowland (*McTeague, the Son*); Günther von Ritzau (*Dr. "Painless" Potter*); Florence Gibson (*Hag*); *In the Play:* Gibson Gowland (*Doc McTeague*); Jean Hersholt (*Marcus Schouler*); Chester Conklin (*Popper Sieppe*); Sylvia Ashton (*Mommer Sieppe*); Zasu Pitts (*Trina*); Austin Jewell (*"Owgoost" Sieppe*); Oscar and Otto Gotell (*"Der Tervins", the twin brothers*); Joan Standing (*Selina*); Frank Hayes (*Old Grannis*); Fanny Midgley (*Miss Baker*); Max Tyron (*Mr. Oelbermann*); Hughie Mack (*Heise, the Harness Maker*); Tiny Jones (*Mrs. Heise*); J. Aldrich Libbey (*Mr. Ryer*); Rita Revela (*Mrs. Ryer*); Dale Fuller (*Maria Miranda Macapa, a Scrubwoman*); Cesare Gravina (*Zerkow, a Junkman*); Lon Poff (*Lottery Agent*); S.S. Simon (*Joe Frenna, the Saloon Keeper*); William Mollenheimer (*The Palmist*); Hugh J. McCauley (*The Photographer*); Jack McDonald (*Cribbens, a Prospector*); James Gibson (*Deputy Sheriff*).

Publications:

Scripts—*Greed* by Erich von Stroheim (entire scenario), Brussels 1958; "*Greed*" by Erich von Stroheim in *Avant-Scène du cinéma* (Paris), September 1968; *Greed* edited by Joel W. Finler, New York 1972; books—*McTeague* by Frank Norris, New York 1899; *Erich von Stroheim, sa vie, ses films* by Georges Fronval, Paris 1939; *An Index to the Creative Work of Erich von Stroheim* by Herman G. Weinberg, supplement to *Sight and Sound*, index series, London 1943; *Hollywood Scapegoat* by Peter Noble, London 1951; *Erich von Stroheim* by Bob Bergut, Paris 1960; *Film: The Creative Process* by John Howard Lawson, New York 1964; *Hommage à Erich von Stroheim* edited by Charlotte Gobeil, Ottawa, Canada 1966; *Stroheim* by Jon Barna, Vienna 1966; *The Great Films: 50 Golden Years of Motion Pictures* by Bosley Crowther, New York 1967; *Erich von Stroheim* by Michel Ciment, Paris 1967; *What is Cinema*, Vol. I, by André Bazin, translated by Hugh Grey, Berkeley 1967; *The Parade's Gone By...* by Kevin Brownlow, New York 1968; *Stroheim* by Joel Finler, Berkeley 1968; *The Complete 'Greed' by Erich von Stroheim* by Herman G. Weinberg, New York 1972; *Erich von Stroheim* by Freddy Bauche, Paris 1972; *Stroheim: A Pictorial Record of his 9 Films* by Herman G. Weinberg, New York 1975; *American Silent Film* by William K. Everson, New York 1978; articles—"Estimate" in *Photoplay* (New York), January 1925; article in *Variety* (New York), 10 December 1924;

"Notes sur les principaux films de Stroheim" by Paul Davay in *L'Ecran des arts* (Paris), 1947; "Erich von Stroheim, His Work and Influence" in *Sight and Sound* (London), winter 1947-48; "The Resurgence of von Stroheim" by Jules Schwerin in *Films in Review* (New York), April 1950; "Stroheim Revisited" by G. Lambert in *Sight and Sound* (London), April/June 1953; "Stroheim's *Greed*" by A.R. Fulton in *Films in Review* (New York), June/July 1955; "*Greed*" by Herman G. Weinberg in *Cinemages* (New York), Vol. 1955; "Notes sur le style de Stroheim" by Lotte Eisner in *Cahiers du cinéma* (Paris), January 1957; "The Career of Erich von Stroheim" by W.K. Everson in *Films in Review* (New York), August/September 1957; issue on von Stroheim in *Film Culture* (New York), April 1958; issue on von Stroheim in *Bianco e Nero* (Rome), February/March 1959; issue of *Premier Plan* (Lyon), August 1963; issue of *Etudes cinétographiques* (Paris), no. 48-50, 1966; "*Les Rapaces (Greed)*" by G. Recassens in *Téléciné* (Paris), January 1957; "Count von Realism" by R. Lee in *Classic Film Collector* (Indiana, Pennsylvania), spring 1969; "*Les Rapaces (Greed)*" by Luis Buñuel in *Positif* (Paris), summer 1970; "Stroheim's *Greed*" by P. Schepelern in *Kosmorama* (Copenhagen), March 1973; "An Introduction to *Greed*" by H.G. Weinberg in *Focus on Film* (London), spring 1973; "Resurrecting *Greed*" by C. Wolfe in *Sight and Sound* (London), summer 1975; "*Greed*" by Nick Barbaro in *Cinema Texas Program Notes* (Austin), 29 September 1975; "Les rapaces d'Eric von Stroheim" by L. Dahan in *Cinématographe* (Paris), April 1977. "*Greed*" by John Henley in *Cinema Texas Program Notes* (Austin), 25 September 1978;

*   *   *

Frank Norris' novel, *McTeague*, was the basis for Erich von Stroheim's film *Greed*. Though he had purchased the rights to it, he never got the production off the ground until Irving Thalberg, disgusted with von Stroheim's method of extravagant production on *Merry-Go-Round*, quarreled with him, and von Stroheim was dismissed as Universal's most prestigious director/producer. It did not take long for von Stroheim to sign with Goldwyn studios, where it was soon announced that his first production would be a film depiction of *McTeague*.

The Norris novel is a dramatic and sordid but realistic preachment of the evils of greed. Heretofore von Stroheim had epitomized the grand scene. At Universal he had directed three big features that showed life on an extravagant scale: his characters were all venal and recklessly amoral; they were decadent, and offered to the public under such lurid titles as *Blind Husbands*, *The Devil's Passkey*, and *Foolish Wives*. His characters were the rich in an Alpine playground, on the boulevards and in the boudoirs of Paris, and in the gambling casino at Monte Carlo, which was reconstructed on the Universal lot. *McTeague* took place wholly in California, specifically in San Francisco, Oakland and the Bay area, and Death Valley, in a very lower middle class, even depressed, society. The title character was a dentist from the lower classes who practiced his dentistry illegally. Both he and the girl he marries, Trina, are crass, uneducated vulgarians possessed and destroyed by a love for gold. It seemed unlike anything von Stroheim had attempted in his previous films.

Early in pre-production, the project was referred to as *Greed*, and the name soon became the accepted title. Deliberately doing a turnabout, von Stroheim saw it as a venture completely shot in its natural setting, the Bay area, as far as he could get from the studios of Hollywood. The company would even go to Death Valley to film the bitterly ironic finale of the story. He saw the project as a faithful adaptation of the Norris novel, an almost page by page re-creation of a well-known American novel of the naturalist type. The film grew in monstrous proportions eventually reaching an estimated nine and a half hours! The studio forced von Straheim to severely edit it. Secretly, his good friend, Rex Ingram, saw the film and helped him cut one version, but June Mathis was later called in to edit it down to under three hours. It remained, however, a hopeless gargantuan project. Characters had to be eliminated so that the main story of McTeague, Trina, and Schouler became entirely the story of *Greed*.

Ironically, it was Irving Thalberg who ordered the drastic cuts in *Greed*. Thalberg had moved from his berth with Carl Laemmle at Universal to join the new Metro-Goldwyn. He was soon to become head of production at the amalgamated Metro-Goldwyn-Mayer Studios, where after Louis B. Mayer officially became head of production, he had his own unit. His first concern was to shape *Greed* out of the mountainous reels of footage which von Stroheim had so recklessly shot. It was at his order that *Greed* was released in 1924, but only a quarter of it contained footage shot by von Stroheim. That savaged edition is the only one unreeled at von Stroheim retrospectives nowadays. The unused film was ordered melted down so that the silver in the negative could be salvaged. There would be no ultimate rediscovery of footage unused and fitted into subsequent re-issues of the picture. It would be another chapter in the obliteration of von Stroheim's name as a great director. Not one film he made exists as he originally envisioned it. All have been cut either maliciously or out of necessity. Only one may have escaped obliteration— Universal's *The Devil's Passkey*, but it is a lost picture. To date, no print whatsoever has survived.

The legend surrounding von Stroheim's name as a great creative director survives, however, nurtured by those who have read the original *McTeague* written by Frank Norris. There are moviegoers who can relate whole sequences of the film that just are not in the final print. Memorable, however, in the released film are such treasured moments as the wooing of Trina under sedation in a dental chair; the miserably unromantic, even comic, wedding of Trina and McTeague; the brutalization of Trina by McTeague, leading to her murder and his escape with the gold she had even slept with; McTeague's meeting with onetime friend, Marcus Schouler, and their journey across Death Valley. Schouler is slain by McTeague, but before Schouler dies, he handcuffs himself to McTeague, and the picture fades out on McTeague sitting in the murderous heat of Death Valley handcuffed to a corpse he slew.

Greed made no profit either domestic or foreign. Costing $585,000 to film (a fortune in the mid-twenties), *Greed* showed a gross of only $277,000 domestically, and the foreign receipts were even more disappointing. The world's moviegoing public simply resisted *Greed*. Von Stroheim and his few faithful cohorts could quite honestly say that the picture as he filmed it was never released. The studio also alibied that *Greed* never stood a chance of success as a product from a studio noted for creating stars. There were no box-office names in *Greed*. The cast was handchosen by von Stroheim himself—ZaSu Pitts, Gibson Gowland, and Jean Hersholt, who had never brought in a dime on their own. They were more often featured in comedies, as were fellow cast members Dale Fuller, Chester Conklin, and Hughie Mack, and *Greed* was certainly no comedy.

A few years later, when von Stroheim had chalked up a few more disasters, he abandoned his directorial career for a successful one as an actor. He had often played in some of his own

pictures, but as an actor he is a recognizable star in Renoir's *La Grande Illusion* and in Hollywood's *Sunset Boulevard*.

—DeWitt Bodeen

GYCKLARNAS AFTON. The Naked Night. Sawdust and Tinsel. La Nuit des forains. Production: Sandrews for Svensk Filmindustri; black and white, 35mm; running time: 92 mins.; length: 2520 meters. Released 14 September 1953, Sweden.

Produced by Rune Waldekranz; screenplay by Ingmar Bergman; directed by Ingmar Bergman; photography by Hilding Bladh, Göran Strindberg, and Sven Nykvist; edited by Carl-Olav Skeppstedt; art direction by Bibi Lindström; music by Karl-Birger Blomdahl; costumes designed by Mago.

Filmed early summer 1953 in Sandrews studios in Stockholm; and exteriors shot in Arild, Sweden.

Cast: Harriet Andersson (*Anne*); Ake Grönberg (*Albert Johansson*); Hasse Ekman (*Frans*); Anders Ek (*Frost*); Gudrun Brost (*Alma*); Annika Tretow (*Agda, Albert's wife*); Gunnar Björnstrand (*Mr. Sjuberg*); Erik Strandmark (*Jens*); Kiki (*Dwarf*); Ake Fridell (*Officer*); Majken Torkeli (*Mrs. Ekberg*); Vanjek Hedberg (*Ekberg's son*); Curt Löwgren (*Blom*).

Publications:

Books—*Ingmar Bergman et ses films* by Jean Béranger, Paris 1959; *Ingmar Bergman: teatermannen och filmskaparen* by Fritiof Billquist, Stockholm 1960; *Thèmes d'inspiration d'Ingmar Bergman* by Jos. Burvenich, Brussels 1960; *Ingmar Bergman* by Jacques Siclier, Paris 1960; *Ingmar Bergman* by Marianne Höök, Stockholm 1962; *Ingmar Bergman* by Jean Béranger and François Guyon, Lyon 1964; *The Personal Vision of Ingmar Bergman* by Jörn Donner, Bloomington, Indiana 1964; *Ingmar Bergman: The Search for God* by David Nelson, Boston 1964; *La Solitudine di Ingmar Bergman* by Guido Oldrini, Parma 1965; *Ingmar Bergman* by Birgitta Steene, New York 1968; *The Silence of God: Creative Response to the Films of Ingmar Bergman* by Arthur Gibson, New York 1969; *Ingmar Bergman* by Robin Wood, New York 1969; *Regi: Ingmar Bergman* by Henrik Sjögren, Stockholm 1970; *Cinema Borealis: Ingmar Bergman and the Swedish Ethos* by Vernon Young, New York 1971; *Ingmar Bergman Directs* by John Simon, New York 1972; *The Films of Ingmar Bergman* by Jörn Donner, New York 1972; *Bergman on Bergman* edited by Stig Björkman and others, translated by Paul Austin, New York 1973; *Ingmar Bergman* by Tino Ranieri, Florence 1974; *Ingmar Bergman: Essays in Criticism* edited by Stuart Kaminsky, New York 1975; *Ingmar Bergman* by Denis Marion, Paris 1979; *Ingmar Bergman: An Appreciation* by Roger Manvell, New York 1980; *My Story* by Ingrid Bergman with Alan Burgess, New York 1980; *Ingmar Bergman: The Cinema as Mistress* by Philip Mosley, Boston 1981; *Film and Dreams: An Approach to Bergman* edited by Vlada Petrić, South Salem, New York 1981; *Ingmar Bergman: A Critical Biography* by Peter Cowie, New York 1982; *A Reference Guide to Ingmar Bergman* by Birgitta Steene, Boston 1982; articles— "Ingmar Bergman, Magician of Swedish Cinema" by Paul Austin in *Anglo-Swedish Review* (London), April 1959; "The Rack of Life" by Eugene Archer in *Film Quarterly* (Berkeley), summer 1959; "Style is the Director" by Hollis Alpert in *Saturday Review* (New York), 23 December 1961; "Photographing the Films of Ingmar Bergman" by Sven Nykvist in *American Cinematographer* (Los Angeles), October 1962; *Ingmar Bergman* by Raymond Lefèvre in *Image et son* (Paris), March 1969; "Biography, Ingmar Bergman" in *Film Comment* (New York), summer 1970; "Valorile de ieri s#0i de alaltáieri" by P. Rado in *Cinema* (Bucharest), March 1975; "¶Gøglernes aften & *Ansigtet*" by A. Koustrup in *Kosmorama* (Copenhagen), spring 1978.

*　　*　　*

The films of Ingram Bergman have largely been considered "intellectual" films rather than "pure entertainment." The themes which Bergman has chosen to present in his work—death, fate, love, loneliness—are often thought-provoking and hence their intellectual appeal. *The Naked Night* exhibits many typical Bergman themes and has been selected by some critics as his best film. However, this favorable acceptance of the film was not the initial reaction.

The Naked Night was the first of Bergman's films to be given a wide release in the United States (although it was his eighteenth film as a director). A few of his early films had a limited distribution here, but they were mainly exploited for their nudity as soft-core pornography. *The Naked Night* was also publicized in this manner, as evidenced by the American title. A more literal translation of *Gycklarnas Afton* is "twilight of the jugglers." France released the film as *Night of the Clowns* and England released the film as *Sawdust and Tinsel*. Only the American version was labeled with a suggestive title.

As in many of Bergman's films, the main theme of *The Naked Night* is the idea of fate. Fate dictates the kind of lives the characters must lead and they cannot escape their destinies. Their attempts to do so only make their lives more miserable. For example, Albert, the owner of a travelling circus, seeks a more secure life in the traditional family unit. When he tries to make amends with his estranged wife, she rejects him and even thanks him for having left her in the first place. Albert's visit to his wife prompts his mistress, Anne, to have an affair with a local actor. The actor later humiliates Albert in public by bragging about his new conquest. Albert's humiliation leads him to attempt suicide, but he cannot escape his fate and the attempt fails. This string of events eventually comes full circle, until Albert once again sets out on the road with Anne, following the only choice fate allows him.

The Naked Night, not surprisingly, considering the subject matter, does not have a happy ending. Obviously 1953 audiences were not ready for this kind of film as it was quite unsuccessful, not just financially but critically. The film was also unsuccessful in Sweden, as well as in most foreign markets. Critics termed the film too "complex" and "depressing." The failure of *The Naked Night* affected Bergman deeply. He knew he would have to make changes if his was going to continue to find financial backing for his films. As a result, Bergman's next three pictures were comedies (*A Lesson in Love*, *Dreams*, and *Smiles of a Summer Night*). These films continued to address the issues of his earlier work (fate, love, etc.), but in a lighter vain. This new approach made his films more popular and critically recognized. The change in the reaction to his films encouraged Bergman to turn toward "serious" films again, such as *Persona* and *Cries and Whispers*.

In the mid-sixties critics rediscovered *Gycklarnas Afton* in a new, more positive light as one of the more significant films of his career.

—Linda J. Obalil

HADAKA NO SHIMA. The Island. Production: Kindai Eiga Kyokai (Japan); black and white, 35mm; running time: 92 mins., English version is 96 mins. Released 1961, Japan.

Produced by Kaneto Shindo and Eisaku Matsura; screenplay by Kaneto Shindo; directed by Kaneto Shindo; photography by Kiyoshi Kuroda; edited by Toshio Enoki; sound by Kunie Maruyama; music by Hikaru Hayashi.

Cast: Nobuko Otowa (*Toyo*); Taiji Tonoyama (*Senta*); Shinji Tanaka (*Taro*); Masanori Horimoto (*Jiro*).

Publications:

Review—by Helen Kuhn in *Films in Review* (New York), October 1962; book—*Japanese Cinema: Art and Industry* by Joseph Anderson and Donald Richie, expanded edition, Princeton, New Jersey 1982; articles—by Gordon Gow in *Films and Filming* (London), December 1962; "About the Moviemaker" in *Newsweek* (New York), 10 September 1962; article by Gerald Noxon in *Cinema Journal* (Iowa City, Iowa), no.3, 1963; "Dialogue on the Film *The Island*" by George Fradier in *UNESCO Courier*, April 1963; "Note" in *International Film Guide* (London), no.2, 1965; "L'ile nue" by M.L. Potrel-Dorget in *Image et son* (Paris), July/August 1978.

*　　*　　*

Hadaka no shima (The Island) is the thirteenth feature written and directed by Kaneto Shindo, best known for his depictions of women's lives. The film stars Nobuko Otowa who has appeared in most of his films. Released in 1961, it is Shindo's best known work outside of Japan.

Constructed like a documentary drama, the film tells the story of a husband (Senta) and wife (Toyo), who live on a small island with their two sons. Their lives are consumed by the necessity of obtaining water from a nearby island twice a day. Like Robert Flaherty's *Nanook* and *Man of Aran*, the film focuses on the family's struggle against nature for survival. *Hadaka no shima* is innovative on two levels. First, the narrative is presented without dialogue. Like F.W. Murnau's silent classic, *Der letzte Mann*, which is rendered without inter-titles (save one), *Hadaka no shima* is almost purely visual. Shindo utilizes action, gesture, camera movement, rhythmic editing, close-ups, music and sound effects to make his points.

Second, Shindo experiments with elliptical editing. One scene in particular is noteworthy. On the road Senta and Toyo move towards the audience, carrying their buckets. As soon as they come close to the camera, Shindo cuts and they are once again seen in the distance in the exact position of the opening shot. This device gives the impression of a film loop, serving to emphasize the Sisyphean effort of repeating arduous chores in a never-ending cycle.

The film contains only minimal action. The main events are the accidental spilling of water, which prompts Senta to knock Toyo to the ground; the death of the oldest son after a brief illness; Toyo's reaction to this loss (she deliberately dumps water on the ground and tramples the plants); and, finally, the family's visit to the mainland where they unsuccessfully attempt to sell a fish. The remainder of the film details the twice daily trips to the main island, the slow climb up the hill, the watering of plants, and the family's eating and bathing.

Shindo is fond of close-ups inter-cut between long sequence shots. He uses parallel editing, connecting the dining of the family with the eating of the animals, to provide a commentary on the simplicity and poverty of their lives. Shindo likewise includes "pillow shots" similar to the insertions found in Yasujiro Ozu films. Primarily these consist of the image of a small boat which the family uses to row to the main island. The shot functions as a meditative moment which possesses associational meaning like images in a *haiku* poem.

Shindo offers a portrayal of a primitive way of life, which is contrasted to the frantic mechanized life of the main island. Despite the hardships on the island, the family possess dignity, perseverance and stamina. Their lives have purpose and meaning. There is joy at the day's end when their labors cease and they can relax with a bath and the communal meal. The couple exhibit a stoicism bred of necessity and the knowledge that life must go on. After Toyo angrily spills the water, she picks herself up and resumes work. Throughout the family personifies a Buddhist attitude toward life: a sense of harmony with nature, resignation to man's insignificance in the universe, the flux of life and the acceptance of death. *Hadaka no shima* is thus pervaded with a sense of *mono no aware*, a sad awareness of the transience of all things worldly. This attitude is logically expressed in the film's dominant metaphor—the island, a small sanctuary surrounded by a vast body of water. Like the famous Zen sand gardens composed of rocks surrounded by racked sand, the island represents everything from the isolated family, to the Japanese people of the island nation, to mankind itself.

Hadaka no shima was critically acclaimed in the United States. Most of the popular critics were taken with its quiet power and simplicity. Only Pauline Kael questioned whether less was really more and wondered at the adulation of such a primitive way of life. Such sentiments were also shared by several Japanese commentators who wondered at the the film's foreign popularity and worried about the effect of portraying Japan as an esoteric, primitive people rather than a modern industrial nation. After *Hadaka no shima*, Shindo turned to new subject matter.

—Patricia Erens

———————

HALLELUJAH. Production: Metro-Goldwyn-Mayer Pictures Corp.; 1929; black and white, 35mm, sound and silent versions; running time: about 100 mins., some sources list 107 mins.; length: 6579 ft. (silent), 9711 ft. (sound). Released 20 August 1929.

Produced by King Vidor; scenario by Wanda Tuchock, treatment by Richard Schayer, dialogue by Ranson Rideout; from an original story by King Vidor; titles for silent version by Marian Ainslee; directed by King Vidor; photography by Gordon Avil; edited by Anson Stephenson (silent), Hugh Wynn (sound); sound recorded by Douglas Shearer; art direction by Cedric Gibbons; music traditional with 2 songs by Irving Berlin; costumes designed by Henrietta Frazer.

Filmed 1929 in MGM Studios in Culver City, California and on location in and around Memphis, Tennessee.

Cast: Daniel Haynes (*Zeke*); Nina Mae McKinney (*Chick*); William Fountaine (*Hot Shot*); Harry Gray (*Parson*); Fannie B. DeKnight (*Mammy*); Everett McGarrity (*Spunk*); Victoria Spivey (*Missy Rose*); Milton Dickerson (*One of the Johnson kids*); Robert Couch (*One of the Johnson kids*); Walter Tait (*One of the Johnson kids*); Dixie Jubilee Singers.

Publications:

Review—by Mordaunt Hall in *The New York Times*, 21 August 1929; books—*Around Cinemas* by James Agate, Amsterdam 1948; *The Negro In Films* by Peter Noble, London 1950; *The Film Till Now* by Paul Rotha and Richard Griffith, New York 1960; *The Rise of the American Film: A Critical History* by Lewis Jacobs, New York 1968; *Blacks in the Cinema—The Changing Image* by Jim Pines, London 1971; *To Find an Image* by James Murray, Indianapolis 1973; *Toms, Coons, Mulattoes, Mammies, and Bucks: An Interpreteive History of Blacks in American Films* by Donald Bogle, New York 1973; *The Black Man on Film: Racial Stereotyping* edited by Richard A. Maynard, Rochelle Park, New Jersey 1974; *From Sambo to Superspade: The Black Experience in Motion Pictures* by Daniel J. Leab, Boston 1975; *Black Films and Film-Making: A Comprehensive Anthology from Stereotype to Superhero* by Lindsay Patterson, New York 1975; *Blacks in Film: A Survey of Racial Themes And Images in the American Film* by Jim Pines, London 1975; *The Men Who Made the Movies* by Richard Schickel, New York 1975; *King Vidor* by John Baxter, New York 1976; *A Tree is a Tree*, New York, reprinted 1977; *Blacks in Black and White: A Source Book on Black Films* by Henry T. Sampson, Metuchen, New Jersey 1977; *Slow Fade to Black: The Negro In American Film, 1900-1942* by Thomas Cripps, New York 1977; articles—"Vidor and Evasion" by B.G. Braver-Mann in *Experimental Cinema*, v.1, no.3, 1931; "The Later Years: King Vidor's Hollywood Progress" by Curtis Harrington in *Sight and Sound* (London), April/June 1953; "Hollywood Hallelujah" by King Vidor in *Films and Filming* (London), May 1955; "King Vidor" by Charles Higham in *Film Heritage* (Dayton, Ohio), summer 1966; "King Vidor at NYU: Discussion" in *Cineaste* (New York), spring 1968; "A Career that Spans Half a Century" by H.G. Luft in *Film Journal* (New York), summer 1971; "*Hallelujah*" by Raymond Durgnat in *Film Comment* (New York), July/August 1973; issue on Vidor in *Positif* (Paris), September 1974; "*Hallelujah*" by R. Combs in *Monthly Film Bulletin* (London), September 1974; "Saints noirs" by M. Leiris in *Positif* (Paris), November 1974; "*Hallelujah*" by Marjorie Baumgarten in *Cinema Texas Program Notes* (Austin), 11 October 1977; "*Hallelujah!*" by John Cocchi in *Magill's Survey of Cinema, Vol. II* edited by Frank N. Magill, Englewood Cliffs, New Jersey 1980.

*   *   *

Hallelujah has fair claim to being the first masterpiece of the sound era. Certainly King Vidor could have realized his frequently-proposed all-black film only at a moment when the Broadway success of Rouben Mamoulian's *Porgy*, rumors of a similar project at Fox (*Hearts of Dixie*), and Vidor's own willingness to gamble his salary all combined with corporate confusion at MGM—the last major studio to equip for sound. Unitmately, however, *Hallelujah*'s accompanying music couldn't quite make it a musical, nor defuse its savagery; and it had as much trouble with bookings in the North as in the South.

The film tends to be remembered now under a *Birth of a Nation* stigma common to "Southerns"—admired technically while damned for its racism. It is true that the contented matriarchial family of cotton-pickin' blacks, singing while they work their patch of land, can seem an image of slave-based Southern prosperity, and the violence of the melodramatic plot can seem straight out of Mrs. Stowe. But the characters are Uncle Tom-ish only outside the context of Vidor's other work: the same documentary of an agrarian lifestyle is at the root of his idealized white co-operative in *Our Daily Bread*; emotional intensity is everywhere a Vidorian trademark; and an identical ferocity characterizes *Northwest Passage* and *Duel in the Sun*. *Ruby Gentry*, with another murder-in-the-swampwater finale, comes closest to being his whitefolks version of *Hallelujah* One needs to repress how Vidor was working at a time when respectable British critic James Agate could dismiss the film with: "Personally, I don't care if it took Mr. Vidor ten years to train these niggers; all I know is that ten minutes is all I can stand of nigger ecstasy." If the film *is* flawed morally, it's for the *complete* exclusion of whites, which renders imprecise the family's relationship to the land they apparently sharecrop. Additionally, the four brief shots which make an elipsis of Zeke's prison term for murdering his rival "Hot Shot" deny the experience of punishment—he's soon strummin' on the ol' banjo riding home to Mammy.

Whatever Vidor may have said in interviews about the film's "good vs. evil" structure, its tension comes from pitting against each other two mutually-exclusive "goods": family-as-religion vs. passionate sexuality. And the temptress Chick, whose dance-hall sensuality elevates easily into religious fervor, isn't inauthentic in either incarnation. She tempts Zeke from his revivalist preaching, but considering Vidor's very consistent repudiation of narrow religion from *The Sky Pilot* (1921) right through *Solomon and Sheba* (1959), that too might be for the best. The surrealist Ado Kyrou is close to the mark in reading *Hallelujah* as a celebration of desire.

Early sound equipment limits the musical numbers to relatively static takes, but by any criterion *Hallelujah* is technically remarkable—the ironic result of Vidor's having had to shoot location sequences silent and post-synch the often expressionistic sound effects of ecstatic wails or broken bodies (a procedure which, so Vidor claims, drove his sound editor to a nervous breakdown). The aural expressionism might be written off as unavoidable accident if it hadn't its visual equivalent in such shots as the featureless black half-screen into which Zeke futilely shouts for aid for his dying brother. But to stress expressionism is to ignore the ways *Hallelujah* anticipates the early-Visconti variety of neorealism, with its authentic dialects, its quirky, slack dialogue, its inexperienced actors, its documentary tracing of rural life, and its relentless analysis of the *crime passionel*.

—Scott Simmon

A HARD DAY'S NIGHT. Production: Proscenium Films; 1964; black and white, 35mm; running time: 85 mins. Released July 1964, London.

Produced by Walter Shenson and Denis O'Dell; screenplay by Alun Owen; title design by Robert Freeman; directed by Richard Lester; photography by Gilbert Taylor; edited by John Jympson and Pamela Tomlin; sound recorded by H.L. Bird and Stephen Dalby, sound edited by Gordon Daniel; art direction by Ray Simm; music direction by George Martin, songs by John Lennon and Paul McCartney and George Harrison, songs sung by The Beatles; costumes designed by Julie Harris.

Filmed 1964 in London.

Cast: John Lennon (*John*); Paul McCartney (*Paul*); George Harrison (*George*); Ringo Starr (*Ringo*); Wilfrid Brambell (*Grandfather*); Norman Rossington (*Norm*); Victor Spinetti (*Television director*); John Junkin (*Shake*); Deryck Guyler (*Police inspector*); Anna Quayle (*Millie*); Kenneth Haigh (*Simon*); Richard Vernon (*Man on train*); Michael Trubshawe (*Club manager*); Eddie Malin (*Hotel waiter*); Robin Ray (*Television floor manager*); Lionel Blair (*Television choreographer*); Alison Seebohm (*Secretary*); David Jaxon (*Young boy*); Marianne Stone (*Society reporter*); David Langton (*Actor*); Clare Kelly (*Barmaid*).

Publications:

Reviews—by Peter Baker in *Films and Filming* (London), August 1964; review by Andrew Sarris in *The Village Voice* (New York), 27 August 1964; books—*New Cinema in Britain* by Roger Manvell, New York 1969; *Directors at Work: Interviews with American Film-Makers* edited by Bernard Kantor, New York 1970; *The Film Business: A History of the British Cinema* by Ernest Betts, New York 1973; *Hollywood U.K.* by Alexander Walker, New York 1974; *Richard Lester: A Guide to References and Resources* by Diane Rosenfeldt, Boston 1978; articles—"What are the Beatles Really Like?" by Edwin Miller in *Seventeen* (New York), August 1964; article by Ray Hagen in *Films in Review* (New York), October 1964; article by Geoffrey Nowell-Smith in *Sight and Sound* (London), autumn 1964; article by John Seelye in *Film Quarterly* (Berkeley), fall 1964; "Keeping Up with the Beatles" by Robin Bean in *Films and Filming* (London), February 1964; "Richard Lester" by Philip French in *Movie* (London), autumn 1965; "Lunch with Lester" by George Bluestone in *Film Quarterly* (Berkeley), summer 1966; "The Beatles and Film Art" by Alfred Sugg in *Film Heritage* (Dayton, Ohio), summer 1966; "The Art of Comedy" by Richard Lester in *Film* (London), spring 1967; "Richard Lester" in the *New Yorker*, 28 October 1967; "An Interview with Richard Lester" by Mark Shivas and Ian Cameron in *Movie* (London), winter 1968-69; "What's Richard Lester Trying to Do" by B. Prelutsky in *Holiday* (New York), April 1969; "*A Hard Day's Night*: 10 Years After" by Richard Corliss in *Film Comment* (New York), May/June 1974; "*A Hard Day's Night*" by Timothy Johnson in *Magill's Survey of Cinema, Vol. II* edited by Frank N. Magill, Englewood Cliffs, New Jersey 1980.

*   *   *

Before *A Hard Day's Night* rock and roll films were of two main kinds, the revue film and the star vehicle. The revue films had plots that usually involved a national fad like the twist; they allowed a showcasing of a variety of performers and their songs. Frank Tashlin's *The Girl Can't Help It* (1956) and Sam Katzman's *Twist around the Clock* (1961) are examples of this form. The star vehicle was designed to showcase the recording image and talents of the star. Elvis Presley's early films, *Jailhouse Rock* (1957) and *King Creole* (1958), followed this form.

A Hard Day's Night has traits of both forms. The plot, a day in the life of the Beatles, allows 12 Beatle songs to be heard, and since the group plays itself, to say the film was tailored to them is an understatement. Unlike many of the earlier rock and roll films where the music and the performers had to be justified and shown to be "good and clean and fun," the Beatles never have to prove anything. They simply are. There is no need to validate their rock and roll; their music and performances are not something that upsets parents. At times, it appears the Beatles don't even need an audience when they perform. The Beatles playing music is part of the Beatles playing with the world.

This is not to say the Beatles are conventional figures and do not rebel, a major theme of much of the rock and roll culture. Their rebellion is against dishonesty and against pompous adults. With their weapons of music, fashion, wit and humor, they defeat authority figures who attempt to thwart the group's drive for pleasure. The Beatles simply make fun of any distasteful situation. A session with an overly-anxious television director leads to a romp in a field.

Romance was frequently an aspect of the earlier rock and roll films. The "romantic interest" was in part taken from the traditional musical genre plot of boy meets girl, boy loses girl, and boy and girl are reunited. In the early rock films, the reunion usually took place against a background of rock music; there was a happy ending for all concerned. In *A Hard Day's Night* romance is barely mentioned. Certainly the boyishness of the Beatles is part of their image at this point in their career, but they are not innocent of sexual matters. Notice the showgirls John Lennon and Paul McCartney are shown leading around and the many homosexual jokes and references. But the group is not involved in romance. Romance might weaken its unity.

For in *A Hard Day's Night* the focus of the film is the group. There are four individuals in the film and each of the individuals is distinctive. John has his wit. Paul has his good looks and his mischievous grandfather. Ringo Starr has his drums and his waif image. George Harrison deflates the television producer's arrogant attitude. Yet the Beatles as a group are the center of the film. Their songs and performances reinforce this dominance, but what the film really shows is a world into which four common lads unified in a social and musical group can escape. This differs from the goals suggested by other film rock heroes. Previously rock and roll heroes have looked for traditional success—in show business by acceptance from the audience and on a personal level with romantic love. The Beatles do not need these rewards though it is implied they could have them if they wanted them. The Beatles simply live for fun. It is a fantasy of rock and roll that reached audiences in 1964 and continues to be successful in revivals and on television.

—Ray Narducy

HÄXAN. Witchcraft Through the Ages. Production: Svensk Filmindustri; black and white, 35mm, silent; running time: 76 mins., some sources list 83 mins.; length: 6840 feet (sound version). Released 1921. Re-released 1967 with sound and an English commentary read by William Burroughs, version re-released with French commentary read by Philippe Noiret and adapted by Claude Seignolle.

Scenario by Benjamin Christensen; directed by Benjamin Christensen; photography by Johan Ankerstjerne; art direction by Richard Louw; music for French re-release by Daniel Humair, featuring Jean-Luc Ponty, Bernard Lubat, Michel Poratl, Guy Pedersen, and Daniel Humair.

Filmed in Copenhagen-studios.

Cast: Maren Pedersen (*The Witch*); Clara Pontoppidan (*Nun*); Tora Teje (*Modern hysteric*); Elith Pio (*Young monk*); Benjamine Christensen (*Devil, and Fashionable doctor*); Oscar Stribolt (*Fat doctor*); Johs Andersen (*Chief Inquisitor*); Karen Winther (*Dame Anna*); Emmy Schønfield (*Marie, a seamstress*); Alice O'Fredericks (*Woman possessed by the Devil*).

Publications:

Books—*Histoire du cinéma mondial* by Georges Sadoul, Paris 1959; *Benjamin Christensen* by John Ernst, Copenhagen 1967; *Histoire du cinéma mondial* by Jean Mitry, Paris 1967; *Scandinavian Film* by Forsyth Hardy, revised edition, New York 1972; *The History of World Cinema* by David Robinson, New York 1974; *Cinema, The Magic Vehicle: A Guide to Its Achievement: Journey One: The Cinema Through 1949* edited by Jacek Klinowski and Adam Garbicz, Metuchen, New Jersey 1975; articles—*La Sorcellerie à traversles âges* by Max Tessier in *Cinéma 68* (Paris), no.130, 1968; "La Sorcellerie à travers les âges" by G. Gourdon in *Cinématographe* (Paris), December 1978; "La Sorcellerie a travers les ages" by P. Canniere in *Cinéma 79* (Paris), January 1979.

* * *

From the beginning, Benjamin Christensen's *Häxan* was an extraordinary conception. It was Christensen's idea to present a well-documented critical account of superstition and fanaticism, and he spent more than two years researching his subject before he began. Shot in studios in Copenhagen but financed with Swedish money, *Häxan* was the most expensive film ever to be produced in Scandinavia. Although the completed film is markedly uneven, it is still a unique work, the peak of Christensen's career, and the only one of his films that is famous.

Christensen considered his film an historical document, "a lecture on cultural history in moving pictures," and *Häxan* has a place in the history of both the documentary and the feature film. It is an ambitious attempt to break down the barriers between art and science. It is also a complete realization of the writer-director himself (he even acts in the film; he plays Satan): Christensen's highly-original personality, his views, passions and idiosyncrasies all have their most perfect expression in *Häxan*.

The film attempts to present an historical and psychological account of the belief in witches down through the ages, partly in narrative and partly in dramatic form. It offers a poetically imaginative description of historical witches, black sabbaths, etc., leading up to our own time and modern superstition. Obviously, Christensen found the section on the modern age the most important, but, from a critical point of view, that part is the least successful. Here Christensen's materialistic view of the world and his utterly unscientific approach to modern phenomena lead to a naive, didactic style that verges on self-parody.

It is in the sequences about the Middle Ages, in which wild fantasy is mingled with harsh realism, that Christensen's vision unfolds most spectacularly. Assisted by the eminent cameraman Johan Ankerstjerne, Christensen creates passionate and magical scenes of hysteria, perversion and madness. For these sequences alone *Häxan* must be considered the most inspired and original work in the entire history of the Danish cinema, many years ahead of its time.

As an attempt to create a synthesis of the documentry and the imaginative, the film can not be called a success. As a documentary, it is not very reliable. But the film's shortcomings are richly compensated for in its marvellous fantasy and in the sweeping way in which it compels us. It was Christensen's intention that *Häxan* should be the first part of a trilogy, but the two other parts were never realized. Even so, *Häxan* on its own is a major experimental film in the history of the cinema.

—Ib Monty

———

HEAVEN AND EARTH MAGIC. No. 12. The Magic Feature. Distributed through the New York Filmmakers Cooperative; black and white, animated collage; running time: 62 mins., sometimes shown in shorter segments and sometimes with additional ones. Released late 1950's or early 1960's.

Directed, photographed, edited, and animated by Harry Smith. Filmed between 1950 and 1961.

Publications:

Books—*Abstract Film and Beyond* by Malcolm Le Grice, Cambridge, Massachusetts 1977; *Visionary Film: The American Avant-Garde* by P. Adams Sitney, New York 1979; articles— "Harry Smith Interview" by P. Adams Sitney in *Films in Review* (New York), no.37, 1965; "Smith's *Heaven and Earth* at Whitney" by Vincent Canby in *The New York Times*, 24 April 1975; "Mind, Medium and Metaphor in Harry Smith's *Heaven and Earth Magic*" by N. Carroll in *Film Quarterly* (Berkeley), winter 1977-78; "The Spatial Strategies of Harry Smith's *Heaven and Earth Magic*" by J.A. Switzer in *Film Reader* (Evanston, Illinois), no.3, 1978.

*   *   *

Harry Smith's eccentric and brilliant hour-long animation was originally entitled *No. 12*; as with all his works, Smith prefers the simple opus number. Jonas Mekas seems to have given it the title *Heaven and Earth Magic* or *The Magic Feature*, although the expression may have been derived from the way in which Smith referred to his film.

In its most available form, it is an animation of cutout figures, in white, against a flat black background. There is almost no movement into the illusionary vanishing point; instead gradations of depth are registered by figures moving in front of or behind fixed architectural forms. The overall optical impression of the film resembles the collage books of Max Ernst, *La Femme 100 têtes* and *Une Semaine de Bonte*. The central figure, a stage director of sorts, or a magician, who ushers other figures onto the scene and performs endless acts of transformation on them, is derived from images of a model of physical fitness in Daniel

Gottlob Moritz Schreber's *Medical Indoor Exercises*. The author of that best-selling health guide was also the father of the jurist Daniel Paul Schreber, whose *Memoirs of My Nervous Illness* was the subject of Freud's classical study of paranoia. Smith's film may have nothing to do with Freud's analysis, but it certainly has the psychotic son in mind in its fantastic elaboration of a paranoid system. In fact, the massive accumulation of detail, and the bewildering repetition of acts of transformation, deliberately draws our attention away from the overall schema of the film and induces us to enter its surreal labyrinth.

The schema is actually rather simple, once it is isolated from the plethora of its variations. The magician subjects a woman to a violent operation until an hydraulic dentist's chair elevates her into heaven. There she is dismembered and gradually reconstituted through an expansive process of permutations. Everything and everyone except the magician is capable of transformation. Eventually the parts of the women are swallowed up by an enormous head (a cutout of the historian of religion and philologist, Max Muller) and brought down through his body in an elevator, ultimately to be defecated into a sewer along with innumerable fragments of apparatus seen previously in the film. The entire process is clearly circular, and Smith goes to great lengths to emphasize the illusionary and *ad hoc* status of images. They are figures for the invisible and unrepresentable.

In his original plan the entire film was to have been much longer, slower in its animated movements, projected through masks that would alter the shape of the screen, and even presented in a specially designed theatre in which the very seats were sculpted versions of the images of the film and the fidgeting of the viewers would trigger electrical responses which changed the masks! Of course, it was never exhibited in this manner.

No. 12 can be seen as one moment—certainly the most elaborately crafted moment—of the single alchemical film which is Harry Smith's life work. In its seriousness, its austerity, it is one of the strangest and most fascinating landmarks in the history of cinema.

Its elaborately constructed soundtrack in which the sounds of various figures are systematically displaced onto other images reflects Smith's abiding concern with auditory effects.

—P. Adams Sitney

———

HENRY V. Production: Two Cities Film, presented by Eagle-Lion; Technicolor, 35mm; running time: 153 mins., some versions are 137 mins. Released 22 November 1944, Carlton Theatre, London.

Produced by Laurence Olivier with Dallas Bower; screenplay by Laurence Olivier and Alan Dent; from the play by William Shakespeare; directed by Laurence Olivier; photography by Robert Krasker; edited by Reginald Beck; sound recorded by John Dennis and Desmond Drew; art direction by Paul Sheriff assisted by Carmen Dillon, scenic art by E. Lindgaard; music by William Walton, conducted by Muir Mathieson, played by the London Symphony Orchestra; special effects by Percy Day; costumes designed by Roger Furse assisted by Margaret Furse; the film is dedicated to the Commandos and Airborne Troops of Great Britain—"the spirits of whose ancestors it has humbly attempted to recapture..."

Filmed 9 June 1943-12 July 1944 in Enniskerry, Eire; and at Denham and Pinewood Studios, England. Cost: about 400,000 pounds. Special Academy Award to Laurence Olivier for his Outstanding Achievement as Actor, Producer, and Director in bringing *Henry V* to the screen, 1946; New York Film Critics Award, Best Actor, 1946; Venice Film Festival, Special Mention, 1946.

Cast: Leslie Banks (*Chorus*); Felix Aylmer (*Archbishop of Canterbury*); Robert Helpmann (*Bishop of Ely*); Vernon Greeves (*English Herald*); Gerald Case (*Earl of Westmorland*); Griffith Jones (*Earl of Salisbury*); Morland Graham (*Sir Thomas Erpingham*); Nicholas Hannen (*Duke of Exeter*); Michael Warre (*Duke of Gloucester*); Laurence Olivier (*King Henry V*); Ralph Truman (*Montjoy, the French Herald*); Ernest Thesiger (*Duke of Berri, French Ambassador*); Frederick Cooper (*Corporal Nym*); Roy Emerton (*Lieutenant Bardolph*); Robert Newton (*Pistol*); Freda Jackson (*Mistress Quickly, the Hostess*); George Cole (*Boy*); George Robey (*Sir John Falstaff*); Harcourt Williams (*King Charles VI of France*); Leo Genn (*Constable of France*); Francis Lister (*Duke of Orleans*); Max Adrian (*Dauphin*); Jonathan Field (*French Messenger*); Esmond Knight (*Fluellen*); Michael Shepley (*Gower*); John Laurie (*Jamy*); Nial MacGinnis (*Macmorris*); Frank Tickle (*Governor of Harfleur*); Renee Asherson (*Princess Katherine*); Ivy St. Helier (*Lady Alice*); Janet Burnell (*Queen Isabel of France*); Brian Nissen (*Court, camp-boy*); Arthur Hambling (*John Bates*); Jimmy Hanley (*Michael Williams*); Ernest Hare (*Priest*); Valentine Dyall (*Duke of Burgundy*); and Infantry and Cavalry by members of the Eire Home Guard.

Publications:

Script—*Film Scripts One* edited by George P. Garrett, New York 1971; books—*Where We Came In: 70 Years of the British Film Industry* by C.A. Oakley, London 1964; *Olivier-Shakespeare* by Peter Whitehead and Robin Bean, London 1966; *Laurence Olivier* by W.A. Darlington, London 1968; *Focus on Shakespearian Films* by Charles W. Eckert, Englewood Cliffs, New Jersey 1972; *A Filmguide to Henry V* edited by Harry M. Geduld, Bloomington, Indiana 1973; *Laurence Olivier* by Logan Gourlayi, London 1973; *The Great British Picture Show, from the 90s to the 70s* by George Perry, New York 1974; *Caligari's Cabinet and Other Grand Illusions: A History of Film Design* by Léon Barsacq, New York 1976; *Olivier: The Films and Faces of Laurence Olivier* edited by Margaret Morley, Godalming 1978; *Laurence Olivier* by Forster Hirsch, Boston 1979; *Laurence Olivier Directs Shakespeare: A Study in Film Authorship* by Sandra Subawman Singer, Northwestern University Dissertation, 1979; *Laurence Olivier: Theater and Cinema* by Robert Daniels, London 1980; *Sir Larry: The Life of Laurence Olivier* by Thomas Kiernan, New York 1981; *Confessions of an Actor: An Autobiography* by Laurence Olivier, New York 1982; articles—"Hamlet to Clown" by Douglas McVay in *Films and Filming* (London), September 1962; "Laurence Olivier" by Henry Hart in *Films in Review* (New York), December 1967; "Olivier's *Richard III*: A Reevaluation" by Constance Brown in *Film Quarterly* (Berkeley), summer 1967; "Onstage and On Film" by M. McCreadie in *Literature/Film Quarterly* (Salisbury, Maryland), fall 1977.

*   *   *

At the beginning of his career Laurence Olivier did not specialize in interpreting Shakespearean roles on the screen. He had played many of Shakespeare's greatest characters on stage, and was especially praised for having alternated with John Gielgud in the roles of Romeo and Mercutio in the 1935 production of *Romeo and Juliet* at London's New Theatre. He was charming in the 1936 film production of *As You Like It* as Orlando, but he really didn't take his film career seriously until 1939, when he played Heathcliff in Goldwyn's production of *Wuthering Heights*.

With the coming of war, his filmmaking was curtailed, but more than halfway through the conflict, when the Allied victory seemed certain, Olivier was released from his military duties to produce, direct, and star in a film to be made from Shakespeare's *Henry V*. Because the play is so patriotic, it was thought by the British government that the project would create a wonderful piece of nationalistic propaganda. Olivier had already played *Henry V* at the Old Vic, and knew what he wanted to achieve—a movie version that would restore glory to the common man's thinking about his own country.

There were some preliminary setbacks. David O. Selznick refused to allow Vivien Leigh to play the role of the French Princess Katharine; he thought too small a role for the star of *Gone with the Wind*. Olivier chose Renée Asherson, Robert Donat's wife, for the part. He wanted William Wyler as director, because Wyler had directed him in *Wuthering Heights*. But Wyler was busy on another project, and suggested that Olivier himself direct the film. Olivier thought about it, then said, "Why not?" and began preproduction work. The film might never have been made, however, were it not for the efforts of an Italian lawyer, Filippo del Guidice, who had been the driving force behind Nöel Coward in *In Which We Serve*. Del Giudice wanted another patriotic classic to coincide with the D-Day landings in Normandy, and he eased Olivier's working budget of 300,000 pounds upward more than another 100,000 pounds for *Henry V*.

Olivier, preparing his own screenplay from the Shakespearean text, cut the play nearly a quarter so that he could give ample time to the staging of the Battle of Agincourt. Olivier lifted the death of Falstaff from the last scenes of *Henry IV, Part II*, wisely casting a music hall comedian, George Robey, as Falstaff. He decided to begin his picture and end it as if it were a performance at the Globe Theatre in Shakespeare's time. Shakespeare had created the device himself when in the lines of the Chorus in the Prologue, he instructs the audience, "On your imaginary forces work," leaving the way open for a very inventive cinematic trick: the camera pulls back, widens, and we are out of the Globe and immediately into the real conflict itself.

The critic for *Time* wrote: "At last there has been brought to the screen, with such sweetness, vigor, insight and beauty that it seemed to have been written yesterday, a play by the greatest dramatic poet who ever lived." *Henry V* ran for five months in London, and it played on Broadway for 46 weeks. It opened the door for Olivier to other Shakespearean films. His *Hamlet* (1948) came next; then *Richard III* (1955). Ten years later in 1965 it was *Othello*, with Olivier as the Moor of Venice. For television he played Shylock in *The Merchant of Venice* in 1972, and the title role in *King Lear* in 1983.

—DeWitt Bodeen

HIGH NOON. Production: Stanley Kramer Productions; 1952; black and white, 35mm; running time: 84 mins. Released 1952 by United Artists.

Produced by Stanley Kramer; screenplay by Carl Forman; from the story "The Tin Star" by John W. Cunningham; directed by

Fred Zinnemann; photography by Floyd Crosby; edited by Elmo Williams and Harry Gerstad; sound by James Speak; art direction by Rudolph Sternad, set decoration by Emmett Emerson; music by Dmitri Tiomkin, song "High Noon" by Dmitri Tiomkin and Ned Washington, sung by Tex Ritter.

Academy Awards for Best Actor (Cooper), Best Film Editing, Best Scoring of a Dramatic or Comedy Picture, and Best Song, 1952; New York Film Critics Awards for Best Motion Picture and Best Direction, 1952.

Cast: Gary Cooper (*Will Kane*); Thomas Mitchell (*Jonas Henderson*); Lloyd Bridges (*Harvey Pell*); Katy Jurado (*Helen Ramirez*); Grace Kelly (*Amy Kane*); Otto Kruger (*Percy Mettrick*); Ian MacDonald (*Frank Miller*). Lon Chaney (*Martin Howe*); Harry Morgan (*Sam Fuller*); Eve McVeagh (*Mildred Fuller*); Harry Shannon (*Cooper*); Lee Van CLeef (*Jack Colby*); Bob Wilke (*James Pierce*); Sheb Wooley (*Ben Miller*); Tom London (*Sam*); Ted Stanhope (*Station master*); Larry Blake (*Gillis*); William Phillips (*Barber*); Jeanne Blackford (*Mrs. Henderson*); James Millican (*Baker*); Jack Elam (*Charlie*).

Publications:

Scripts—*High Noon* by Carl Foreman, New York 1971; "*High Noon*" by Carl Foreman in *3 Major Screenplays* edited by Malvin Ward and Michael Werner, New York 1973; *High Noon* by Carl Foreman, New York 1974; "*High Noon*" by Carl Forman in *Values in Conflict* edited by Richard A. Maynard, New York 1974; reviews—in *Films in Review* (New York), May 1952; books—*Princess of Monaco: The Story of Grace Kelly* by Gant Gaither, New York 1957; *Fred Zinnemann* by Richard Griffith, New York 1958; *The Western: From Silents to Cinerama* by George N. Fenin, New York 1962; *The Tall American, The Story of Gary Cooper* by Richard Gehman, New York 1963; *A Pictorial History of the Western Film* by William K. Everson, New York 1969; *The Films of Gary Cooper* by Homer Dickens, New York 1970; *Westerns—Aspects of a Movie Genre* by Philip French, New York 1973; *Gary Cooper* by René Jordan, New York 1974; *Focus on the Western* edited by Jack Nachbar, Englewood Cliffs, New Jersey 1974; *Sixguns and Society: A Structural Study of the Western* by Will Wright, Los Angeles 1975; *The Great Western Pictures* edited by James Robert Parish and Michael Pitts, Metuchen, New Jersey 1976; *Westerns* by Philip French, New York 1977; *Gary Cooper, An Intimate Biography* by Hecton Arle, New York 1979; *Coop: The Life and Legend of Gary Cooper* by Stuart Kaminsky, New York 1980; *The Last Hero: A Biography of Gary Cooper* by Larry Swindell, New York 1980; articles—"Choreography of a Gunfight" by Fred Zinnemann in *Sight and Sound* (London), summer 1952; "*High Noon*: Everyman Rides Again" by Howard Burton in *Quarterly of Film, Radio, and Television* (Berkeley), fall 1953; "Fred Zinnemann" in *Current Biography Yearbook* (New York), 1953; "Movie Chronicle: The Westerner" by Robert Warshow in *Partisan Review* (New Brunswick, New Jersey), March 1954; "The Olympian Cowboy" by Harry Schein in *American Scholar* (Washington, D.C.), summer 1955; "Interview with Carl Foreman" by Penelope Houston and Kenneth Cavender in *Sight and Sound* (London), summer 1958; "A Conflict of Conscience" by Fred Zinnemann in *Films and Filming* (London), December 1959; "Gary Cooper" by Carlos Clarens in *Films in Review* (New York), December 1959; "*High Noon*" by A.W. Hodgkinson in *The Film Teachers Handbook*, London 1960; "Son of Uncle Sam" by George Fenin in *Films and Filming* (London), October 1962; "A Question of Standard" by John A. Barsness in *Film Quarterly* (Berkeley), fall 1967; "A Man for All Movies" by John Howard Reid in *Films and Filming* (London), May 1967 and June 1967; "Westerns as Social and Political Alternatives" by James Folsom in *Western American Literature*, fall 1967; "Le Train sifflera trois fois" by P. Allombert in *Image et son* (Paris), no.269, 1973; interview with Carl Foreman in *American Film* (Washington, D.C.), April 1974; "*High Noon*" by Mike Selig in *Cinema Texas Program Notes* (Austin), 28 February 1979; "*High Noon*" by DeWitt Bodeen in *Magill's Survey of Cinema, Vol. II* edited by Frank N. Magill, Englewood Cliffs, New Jersey 1980.

*   *   *

High Noon was responsible for moving the career of Gary Cooper upward again and is considered by many the single most important film in his career. However, no one knew or thought the film was destined for big things when it was first conceived.

Cooper was not producer Stanley Kramer's first choice to play Marshal Will Kane. In fact, he was fairly far down the line below Marlon Brando and Montgomery Clift. Charlton Heston was also offered the role. The chief financial backer of the film, however, a Salinas lettuce tycoon, wanted Cooper. The backer threatened to pull his money out and Kramer couldn't change his mind about using Cooper, so the script had been sent to Coop. Later Cooper said he took the film, even though he was ill and emotionally troubled, because it represented what his father had taught him, that law enforcement was everyone's job.

In an interview, Fred Zinnemann gave his recollections of Cooper and *High Noon*: "His recurring hip problem bothered him on one or two occasions. It made it difficult for him to do the fight with Lloyd Bridges, but it didn't stop him from working very hard and very long hours under some trying conditions. If I remember correctly, we made the entire film in 31 shooting days. Not once were we delayed or held up by him for whatever reason. For most of the time he had seemed in good health, and it was only two or three months after shooting had been completed that he became ill.

"He did in fact look quite haggard and drawn, which was exactly what I wanted for the character, even though this was in contrast to the unwritten law, then still in force, that the leading man must always look dashing and romantic. If I remember correctly, we used a minimum of makeup for Coop, which was perhaps a bit of a novelty in those days.

"Cooper seemed absolutley right for the part. It seemed completely natural for him to be superimposed on Will Kane."

According to Zinnemann, *High Noon* "is the one picture I directed which more than any other was a team effort. There was a marvelous script by Carl Foreman, a brilliant job of cutting by Elmo Williams, an inspired musical score by Dimitri Tiomkin, a solid contribution by Stanley Kramer. And Gary Cooper was the personification of the honor-bound man. He was in himself a very noble figure, very humble at the same time, and very inarticulate. And very unaware of himself." (Interestingly, in a 1979 interview in *American Film*, Carl Foreman claimed that he and Zinnemann had made the film apart from the Kramer company. According to Foreman, "neither Kramer nor anyone around him had any use for the film from the beginning."

In the film, Coop's first line is the same as the first line he had ever uttered in a film back in 1928 in *Shopworn Angel*—"I do." Kane is marrying Amy on a Sunday morning. It is just past 10:30 when the tale begins, and it ends a few minutes after noon. The length of the story and the length of the film almost coincide. The film is filled with reminders of the passing time, time that brings Marshal Kane closer to having to face Frank Miller when he gets off the noon train in Hadleyville and seeks revenge against Kane, who sent him to prison. Clocks in the background show the time and tick ominously. People refer to meetings in five minutes. One by one the people whom Kane assumes he can count on in the battle against Miller and his gang find reasons or excuses to stay out of the coming fight. Only the town drunk comes forth, but Kane turns him dowm, realizing he is more of a liability than an asset.

At one point Kane, alone in his office, puts his head down on his desk, possibly to weep, and then wearily pulls himself up again. In the final confrontation with Miller and his gang, Kane does stand alone until the last moment, when Amy saves his life by shooting Frank Miller. Kane then throws down his badge in a sign of contempt for the town and rides out with his bride.

For his performance in *High Noon*, Cooper would win his second Academy Award. Yet it is a performance in which he does less with the character than he had done with almost any of his major roles before. His walk is stiff and pained. His arms remain at his sides through most of the film. He hasn't a single extended speech. What audiences apparently responded to was the look that Zinnemann had captured and that Cooper, with years of experience, had played on. They also responded to the simple story of a man who is not supported by his community in a time of mortal crisis and who triumphs alone through courage and determination.

Will Kane and Gary Cooper were tired, sick men of 51. Cooper's performance is basically put together in relatively short takes and scenes. This was exactly what Zinnemann wanted and what he got, and it was interpreted by a public that loved Cooper as a supreme performance.

Cooper later said that when *High Noon* was finished, he was "acted out," and that pained weariness is exactly what is seen on the screen. Perhaps for the first time, he had truly become the character he portrayed, for Gary Cooper and Will Kane were the same persona. Kane's pain came from fear and his betrayal by others. Cooper's was a result of illness and domestic and career worries.

As he got older, Cooper tended more and more to be concerned about the West and its portrayal and tended to be disturbed by the lack of historical authenticity in western films. Since his own career as a western star had helped to reinforce the myth of the American fictional West rather than a re-creation of historical data, it is ironic that Cooper should turn to that position.

High Noon is indeed not a tale about the true West, but like so many westerns a presentation of contemporary ideas in the most durable popular genre, the western. In a sense, the myths of the West—and Cooper as an actor is one of them—are as culturally important as what actually transpired on the frontier a century ago. Will Kane tells us more about how we view our history and myths than any real data we might find out about Wild Bill Hickok, Billy the Kid or Buffalo Bill. Cooper's career as a western figure lasted 35 years, as long in fact as the time between the end of the Civil War and the start of the twentieth century, as long as the historical time of the real West.

—Stuart Kaminsky

HIROSHIMA, MON AMOUR. Production: Argos Films-Como Films (Paris), Pathé Overseas, and Daiei (Tokyo); 1959; black and white, 35mm; running time: 91 mins., some sources list 88 mins. Released June 1959.

Produced by Sacha Kamenka, Shirakawa Takeo, and Samy Halfon; screenplay by Marguerite Duras; directed by Alain Resnais; photography by Sacha Vierny and Michio Takahashi; edited by Henri Colpi, Jasmine Chasney, and Anne Sarraute; sound Pierre Calvet and Yamamoto, and Rene Renault; art direction by Esaka, Mayo, and Petri; music by Giovanni Fusco and Georges Delerue; costumes designed by Gérard Collery; literary adviser: Gerard Jarlot.

Filmed September-December 1958 in film studios in Tokyo and Paris, and on location in Hiroshima and Nevers. Cannes Film Festival, International Critics Award and Film Writers' Award, 1959; New York Film Critics Award, Best Foreign Film, 1960.

Cast: Emmanuelle Riva (*She*); Eiji Okada (*He*); Bernard Fresson (*The German*); Stella Dassas (*The Mother*); Pierre Barbaud (*The Father*).

Publications:

Scripts—*Hiroshima, Mon Amour* by Marguerite Duras, Paris 1960; "*Hiroshima, Mon Amour*" by Marguerite Duras, translated into German in *Spektakulum: Texte Moderner Filme*, Frankfurt 1961; *Hiroshima, Mon Amour* by Marguerite Duras, translated by Richard Seaver, New York 1961; *Hiroshima, Mon Amour* by Marguerite Duras, London 1966; "*Hiroshima, Mon Amour*" by Marguerite Duras in *Avant-Scène du cinéma* (Paris), summer 1966; reviews—"Hiroshima" by A.H. Weiler in *The New York Times*, 17 May 1960; review by Henry Hart in *Films and Review* (New York), June/July 1960; review by Jonas Mekas in *The Village Voice* (New York), 25 May 1960; books—*Alain Resnais, or la Création au Cinéma* by Stéphane Cordier, Paris 1961; *Alain Resnais* by Bernard Pingaud, Lyon 1961; *Alain Resnais* by Gaston Bounoure, Paris 1962; *Tu n'as rien vu à Hiroshima* edited by Raymond Ravar, Brussels 1962; *Antonioni, Bergman, Resnais* by Peter Cowie, London 1963; *Cinema Eye, Cinema Ear* by John Russell Taylor, New York 1964; *The Cinema of Alain Resnais* by Roy Armes, London 1968; *Alain Resnais, or the Theme of Time* by John Ward, New York 1968; *On Movies* by Dwight MacDonald, Englewood Cliffs, New Jersey 1969; *Resnais, Alain Resnais* by Paolo Bertetto, Italy 1976; *Alain Resnais* by John Francis Kreidl, Boston 1977; *Alain Resnais: The Role of Imagination* by James Monaco, New York 1978; *The Film Narratives of Alain Resnais* by Freddy Sweet, Ann Arbor, Michigan 1981; articles—interview with Resnais by Michel Delahaye in *Cinéma 59* (Paris), July 1959; "*Hiroshima, Mon Amour*, film scandaleux?" in *Les Lettres françaises* (Paris), 14 May 1959; "Hiroshima, notre amours" in *Cahiers du cinéma* (Paris), July 1959; "Un Grand film, un grand homme" by Georges Sadoul in *Les Lettres françaises* (Paris), 14 May 1959; "Alain Resnais and *Hiroshima, Mon Amour*" by Louis Marcorelles, Henri Colpi and Richard Roud in *Sight and Sound* (London), winter 1959-60; interview with Resnais by Max Egly in *Image et son* (Paris), February 1960; "Conversation with Marguerite Duras" by Richard Roud in *Sight and Sound* (London), winter 1959-60; "Editing *Hiroshima, Mon Amour*" by Henri Colpi in *Sight and Sound* (London), winter 1960; "Musique d'Hiroshima" by Henri Colpi in *Cahiers du cinéma* (Paris), January 1960; "A Conversation with Alain Resnais" by Noël Burch in *Film Quarterly* (Berkeley), spring 1960; interview with Resnais by André Labarther and Jacques Rivette in *Cahiers du cinéma* (Paris), September 1961; "Fantasies of the Art House Audience" by Pauline Kael in *Sight and Sound* (London), winter 1961-62; article by A.J. Alexander in *Film Culture* (New York), summer 1961; article by Howard Hart in *The Village Voice* (New York), 4 October 1961; article by Raymond Durgnat in *Films and Filming* (London), May 1962; "The Time and Space of Alain Resnais" by Alan Stanbrook in *Films and Filming* (London), January 1964; "Does the Camera Lie? Notes on *Hiroshima Mon Amour*" by K. Hanet in *Screen* (London), autumn 1973; "*Hiroshima, Mon Amour*" by J. Le Troquer in *Téléciné* (Paris), February 1973; "Klasszikus vagy 'szép' film a Hirosima?" by P. Pór in *Filmkultura* (Budapest), March/April 1973; "Alain Resnais albo obrazowanie rzeczywistości" by A. Helman in *Kino* (Warsaw), September 1974; "*Hiroshima Mon Amour*" by David Hansard in *Cinema Texas Program Notes* (Austin), 13 October 1977; "Point Counterpoint in *Hiroshima, Mon Amour*" by W.F. Van Wert in *Wide Angle* (Athens, Ohio), no.2, 1978; "Destruction and Reconstruction in *Hiroshima, Mon Amour*" by C. Mercken-Spaas in *Literature/Film Quarterly* (Salisbury, Maryland), no.4, 1980; "*Hiroshima, Mon Amour*" by L. Boer in *Skoop* (Amsterdam), December/January 1980-81.

*   *   *

Hiroshima mon amour was the first feature directed by Alain Resnais. Besides establishing the director's international reputation, the film was one of several released in 1959 signalling the emergence of a new generation of French filmmakers working in a modernist narrative vein. Indeed, the film is considered something of a landmark in the history of modernist cinema. The film is also seen as an exemplary instance of artistic collaboration. The scenario by Marguerite Duras, photography of Sacha Vierny, editing of Henri Colpi, and musical score by Giovanni Fusco and George Delerue contribute to its dense patterns of repetition and counterpoint.

In the film, an initially casual romantic encounter between a Japanese architect ("He"), and a French actress ("She") working in Hiroshima on a film about peace provides the basis for exploring the nature of memory, experience, and representation. The love affair is important primarily for the chain of memory it triggers, as the woman gradually discloses the story of her first love, a story she has never told before. During World War II, in Nevers, she fell in love with a German soldier. On the day the city was liberated, he was shot and killed. She was subsequently submitted to public disgrace, followed by a period of imprisonment and near-madness in her parents' home. She finally recovered enough to leave home permanently, arriving in Paris on the day the war ended after the bombing of Hiroshima and Nagasaki.

This story is only revealed in stages, and establishes a complex of metaphoric relations between the past and present. The woman's first memoryimage is prompted by a direct visual comparison: the twitching hand of her sleeping Japanese lover resembles, and motivates a cut to, the twitching hand of the dying German soldier. This transition is a specific instance of a more complex network of comparisons constructed throughout the course of the film, a concise figure for the film's general pattern of development. A structure of metaphoric logic takes the place of the linear causality, clearly defined goals, and conscious motivation associated with dominant narrative.

For example, the German lover from the past and Japanese lover in the present are comparable as former mutual enemies of France. At the same time, we see the woman victimized in the past for her relations with the German. Her victimization is likened to the victims of the atom bomb seen in the film's opening sequence in a series of images—documentary and reconstructed—depicting the effects of the bomb. These images of destruction and deformity include loss of hair and burnt, distorted skin. Later, we see the woman's head shaved in the public square in Nevers to mark her illicit "collaboration" and her skin broken and bloody as she scrapes it on the walls of her parents' cellar. While the woman is thus "like" the Japanese, a victim of the war's end, she is nevertheless liberated from her private torture, allowed to go free, at the same time the bomb is dropped on Hiroshima.

Through the accumulation of images and narrative information, *Hiroshima mon amour* provides material for recognizing a complex network of comparison and contrast linking disparate events. As the film progresses, the terms of association become more abstract, a function of formal repetition, as tracking shots through the streets of Hiroshima are intercut with tracking shots through the streets of Nevers. Two places and times converge through the continuity afforded by the camera's point of view. At the same time the relationship between the man and woman in the present is infused with the potency of memory. The Japanese man asks the woman to stay in Hiroshima (not a viable option in any conventional sense, since she has a family in France and his wife is due home from a trip shortly), as she comes to emblemize the inconsolable memory of the past.

Yet her story, once told, transforms the experience and its memory into the order of history. The woman acknowledges this shift in value. She confronts herself in the mirror and addresses her dead lover, announcing her betrayal. At one point, she refers to the event as a "two-penny romance," a common, even trivial affair. This change is a function of narration; having been recounted, the experience has undergone a change in nature. This is one way in which the film explores the nature of representation in relation to experience and memory.

In the course of exploring this issue *Hiroshima mon amour* clearly suggests that the mediated account, whether verbal or visual, is qualitatively different from, and supplants, personal experience. The very opening of the film promotes this view, challenging any easy equation of representation and experience. Images of the Hiroshima museum and its repository of documents are accompanied by a woman's voice saying she saw and felt everything in Hiroshima—the heat, the suffering, and so on. Voice and image seem to confirm and validate one another. But a male voice denies her assertions, insisting, "No, you saw nothing." The viewer not only wonders who is speaking, but also is forced to question the woman's certainty, and his own, about the nature of what he is watching. Seeing, in this way, may become misbelieving.

If the woman's narrative of her past displaces the event as pure experience, the initial recounting is not an easy task. Bringing the experience to the level of verbal presence involves the painful eruption of the past ("inconsolable memory") into the present. Temporal distinctions get provisionally confused, and past and present seem to merge, as she first tells the story to her Japanese lover. Her language involves shifts in tense and pronoun use, as past events are spoken of in the present tense and the woman replaces the "he" of her story (referring to the past German lover) with "you" (an apparent address to her present Japanese lover). In this way the nature and act of narrating emerge as a further concern of the film. If the process of narrative is a personal and difficult activity, merging the speaking subject with event, the product eludes the control of the teller. The woman's deeply personal experience, once told, counts as a public story to be judged in the context of narrative history.

For all of these reasons the film is seen to exemplify practices associated with modernist aesthetics. It rejects linear, causal narrative progression, constructs its characters as figures involved in the process of representation, and problematizes the nature of this process. The implications of this investigation extend beyond the characters in the fiction to include the film and its audience, as *Hiroshima mon amour* challenges the viewer to recognize the metaphoric relations that confer its coherence, and also to question the value and meaning of its own representations.

—M.B. White

HIROSHIMA-NAGASAKI: AUGUST, 1945. Production: Columbia University Press; black and white, 16mm; running time: 16 mins. Released March 1970, Japan.

Produced by Erik Barnouw, associate producer: Barbara Van Dyke; screenplay by Paul Ronder; edited by Paul Ronder, associate editor: Geof Bartz; musical effects by Linea Johnson and Terrill Schukfraft; acknowledgements: Harold M. Agnew, Prof. Henry F. Graff, Albert W. Hilberg, Lucy B. Lemann, and Shigeko Niimoto.

Filmed 1945 in Hiroshima and Nagasaki by Japanese cameramen, and produced by Akira Iwasaki. (note: at that time, the film was confiscated by the U.S. Army).

Cast: Paul Ronder and Kazuko Oshima (*Narrators*).

Publications:

Books—*Nonfiction Film: A Critical History* by Richard Barsam, New York 1973; *Documentary: A History of the Nonfiction Film* by Erik Barnouw, New Yrok 1974; *The Occupied Screen* (in Japanese) by Akira Iwasaki, Tokyo 1975; footnote in *Film on the Left: American Documentary Film from 1931 to 1942* by William Alexander, pp. 188-189, Princeton, New Jersey 1981; articles—"Films" by John Dowling in *The Bulletin of the Atomic Scientists*, October 1980; "The Case of the A-Bomb Footage" by Erik Barnouw in *Studies in Visual Communication*, winter 1982; "Columbia and the A-Bomb Film" by Erik Barnouw in *Columbia* (New York), November 1982; "On Television and Nuclear War" by Robert Gottlieb in *Emmy Magazine*, January/February 1982.

*   *   *

Hiroshima-Nagasaki, August 1945 is a 1970 film based on long-suppressed footage shot by Japanese cameramen in 1945. The cameramen belonged to the Nippon Eiga Sha documentary unit, commissioned by the Japanese government to document the effects of the two mysterious bombs dropped on Hiroshima and Nagasaki. The cameramen were at work in both cities before the occupation forces arrived. The work was halted by the occupation, then ordered resumed under its supervision, then all footage was impounded, classified SECRET, and moved to the United States. Its existence was known to few.

In 1968 Columbia University, having received information about the material, applied to the U.S. Department of Defense for access to it, and was allowed to duplicate the surviving 2

hours and 40 minutes along with detailed shot lists. The SECRET stamps on these lists had been crossed out and another stamp substituted: "NOT TO BE RELEASED WITHOUT APPROVAL OF DOD." It was undated. The Columbia University compilation used 15 minutes of the footage. Japanese television (TBS) premiered the Columbia film in March 1970; American public television followed in August. ABC, CBS, and NBC declined to show it.

The film did not concern itself with the theme, "Should we have dropped the bomb?", which had dominated several previous television programs about Hiroshima; instead, it aimed, through selected footage and a narrative sound track—using, in one portion, the words of a Hiroshima girl—to give audiences the sense of experiencing atomic war. Thus it addressed future—rather than past—policy, and came into wide use during the 1981-83 anti-nuclear agitation, with telecasts sponsored by Physicians for Social Responsibility, the Union of Concerned Scientists, and religious and environmental groups, who challenged the U.S. government's projections of a "winnable" nuclear war. For two months, May 12-July 12, 1982, New York's Cathedral of St. John the Divine held continuous daily showings.

Distributed by the Museum of Modern Art, New York, the film was for more than two years the most active film in its collection, both in sales and rentals. Among American independent filmmakers, the film stirred wide discussion concerning network policies toward independent documentary work and government misuse of the SECRET classification. The Japanese historian and film critic Akira Iwasaki, who supervised the Nippon Eiga Sha unit, was not mentioned in earliest release prints of *Hiroshima-Nagasaki, August 1945*, but received an acknowledgement in later prints.

—Erik Barnouw

HIS GIRL FRIDAY. Production: Columbia Pictures Corp.; 1940; black and white, 35mm; running time: 92 mins. Released 18 January 1940.

Produced by Howard Hawks; screenplay by Charles Lederer, with uncredited assistance by Ben Hecht; from the play *Front Page* by Ben Hecht and Charles MacArthur; directed by Howard Hawks; photography by Joseph Walker; edited by Gene Havlick; art direction by Lionel Banks; music by Morris W. Stoloff; costumes designed by (gowns) by Kalloch.

Cast: Cary Grant (*Walter Burns*); Rosalind Russell (*Hildy Johnson*); Ralph Bellamy (*Bruce Baldwin*); Gene Lockhart (*Sheriff Hartwell*); Helen Mack (*Mollie Malloy*); Porter Hall (*Murphy*); Ernest Truex (*Benslinger*); Cliff Edwards (*Endicott*); Clarence Kolb (*Mayor*); Roscoe Karns (*McCue*); Frank Jenks (*Wilson*); Regis Toomey (*Sanders*); Abner Biberman (*Louis*); Frnk Orth (*Duffy*); John Qualen (*Earl Williams*); Alma Kruger (*Mrs. Baldwin*); Billy Gilbert (*Joe Pettibone*); Pat West (*Warden Cooley*); Edwin Maxwell (*Dr. Egelhoffer*).

Publications:

Review—in *The New York Times* by Frank S. Nugent, 12 January 1940; books—*The Cinema of Howard Hawks* by Peter Bogdanovich, New York 1962; *Howard Hawks* by Jean-Claude

Milliaen, Paris 1966; *Howard Hawks* by Robin Wood, London 1968; *Howard Hawks* by Jean Gili, Paris 1971; *Cary Grant Album* compiled by Allen Eyles, Shepperton, Surrey, England 1971; *Focus on Howard Hawks* edited by Joseph McBride, Englewood Cliffs, New Jersey 1972; *Cary Grant* by Jerry Vermilye, New York 1973; *The Films of Cary Grant* by Donald Deschner, Secaucus, New Jersey 1978; *The Comic Mind* by Gerald Mast, New York 1973; *Notes on Women's Cinema* by Claire Johnston, London 1973; *From Reverence to Rape* by Molly Haskell, New York 1974; *Rosalind Russell* by Nicholas Yanni, New York 1975; *The Films of Howard Hawks* by Donald Willis, Metuchen, New Jersey 1975; *The Men Who Made the Movies* by Richard Schickel, New York 1975; articles—"Howard Hawks de *Scarface* à *La Terre des Pharaons*" by Daniel Kostoveski in *Radio, Cinéma, Télévision* (Paris), 4 December 1955; "Cary Grant" by Robert Roman in *Films in Review* (New York), December 1961; "Analysis of Hawks' Work for the Cinéma" in *Films and Filming* (London), July 1962 and August 1962; "Howard Hawks" by Henri Agel in the *New York Film Bulletin*, no.4, 1962; "The World of Howard Hawks" by Andrew Sarris in *Films and Filming* (London), July 1962 and August 1962; issue devoted to Hawks in *Cahiers du cinéma* (Paris), January 1963; "Howard Hawks by Jacques Rivette and François Truffaut in *Interviews with Film Directors* by Andrew Sarris, New York 1967; "Rosalind Russell" by Gene Ringgold in *Films in Review* (New York), December 1970; "A Comment on the Hawksian Women" by Leigh Brackett in *Take One* (Montreal), July/August 1971; "The Hawksian Women" by Naomi Wise in *Take One* (Montreal), January/February 1971; "Demonology" by K. Cooney in *Movietone News* (Seattle), April 1975; "*His Girl Friday*" by Lauren Rabinovitz in *Cinema Texas Program Notes* (Austin), 21 November 1977; "Screwball Liberation" by T. Powers in *Jump Cut* (Chicago), April 1978; "*His Girl Friday*" by Joanne L. Yeck in *Magill's Survey of Cinema, Vol. II* edited by Frank N. Magill, Englewood Cliffs, New Jersey 1980.

*   *   *

Hollywood director Howard Hawks said he got the idea for *His Girl Friday* at a dinner party at which the guests were doing a reading of the Ben Hecht and Charles MacArthur play, *The Front Page*. Hawks had handed the male reporter's part (Hildy Johnson) to one of the women while he took the managing editor's lines (Walter Burns). After a few pages of dialogue, Hawks grew excited and decided that the play was better with a girl playing Hildy Johnson. He called Hecht and suggested changing the reporter's sex for a future film project. Hecht liked the idea, but he had other project commitments; so Hawks hired Charles Lederer to write additional dialogue for a new script. Lederer had written the script of the 1931 movie version of *The Front Page*, directed by Lewis Milestone, and had co-written other Hollywood screenplays with Hecht. On *His Girl Friday*, he worked with Hecht (who receives no screen credit) to revamp characters and dialogue while preserving the wit and style of the original.

His Girl Friday's pivotal plot issue is Hildy's (Rosalind Russell) decision whether to marry the tepid, dull Bruce Baldwin (Ralph Bellamy) or team up with her ex-boss and ex-husband, newspaper editor Walter Burns (Cary Grant). Although film critic Molly Haskell praised the way that the movie allows a woman to find her identity in a non-domestic sphere, Hildy still faces rather restrictive options—marriage to home, children and pallid Bruce or marriage to career and ego with a maniacal Walter. Hildy's choice to remain with the press is less a decision

to relinquish her "feminine" longings for home and family than a commitment to the continued excitement and kinetic activity of the world of journalism. Her decision to remarry Walter grows out of their mutual understanding, respect and love for professionalism. Hildy's ultimate decision for an active, motion-filled life is her only possible choice in a "Hawksian" world. As Hawks himself suggested, her solution is the only way that she can work up enough sense of speed so that she won't have to think about how limited her options really are and how bad life really is.

When *His Girl Friday* premiered in 1940, it baffled and excited critics and public alike for just one reason—its speed. Hawks' actors overlapped their dialogue; they spoke in lower tones of voice; conversations ran almost simultaneously. Hawks reinforced the sensation of speed by keeping his characters in constant activity. For example, when he finds out that Hildy is getting married, Walter nervously reacts by rubbing his hand, touching the phone, picking up a carnation from a vase and slipping it into his buttonhole. All the while, he struggles to keep an impassive face. When he tries to convince Hildy to postpone her wedding plans so that she can write an important story, his impassioned, aggressive speech drives her around the room, first clockwise and then counter-clockwise. When Hawks cannot rely on his characters' motions, he uses such techniques as rapid cuts between the reporters talking into their telephones or a searchlight sweeping across the room to keep the pace frenetic. Hawks' comedy clocks in at 240 words-per-minute, about 100-140 words per minute faster than the average speaking rate; but his timing, camerawork and editing make it seem still faster.

The film is so mannered, especially in its pacing, that the degree of stylization calls attention to itself. When Walter Burns describes Bruce Baldwin, he says that he looks like "That actor—Ralph Bellamy." He later quips to one of the film's characters, "The last man that said that to me was Archie Leach just a week before he cut his throat." (Archie Leach is Cary Grant's real name.) Such references do not really disrupt the film but merely add to the movie's hilarious message on the absurdity of believing in the characters as real people. Coupled with the timing and acting, the parodic elements contribute to the development of an essay on the absurdity of any kind of ethical or moral commitments—any commitments to "normal values"—in the modern world.

His Girl Friday was the first screwball comedy to depart form the money-marriage-ego conflicts of *Holiday*, *My Man Godfrey*, and *The Philadelphia Story*, inserting into the same comic structure and pattern of action a conflict between career and marriage. Throughout the 1940's, career-marriage decisions for women provided the crises in several screwball comedies. *His Girl Friday* marked the transition from the subversion of women working for ends other than marriage to more explicit statements regarding money-marriage-sex roles in the genre in the 1940's.

—Lauren Rabinovitz

LA HORA DE LOS HORNOS. subtitled: (Notas y testimonios sobre el neocolonialismo, la violencia y la liberación). The Hour of the Furnaces. L'Heure des Brasiers. Production: Grupo Cine Liberación; black and white, 16 and 35mm; running time: 260 mins., French version: 200 mins.; the film is composed of 3 parts: "Neocolonialismo y violencia"-90 mins., "Acto para la liberación"-120 mins., and "Violencia y liberación"-45 mins. Released 1968.

Produced, directed, and edited by Fernando E. Solanas; screenplay by Fernando E. Solanas and Octavio Getino; photography by Juan Carlos de Sanzo with Fernando E. Solanas; sound by Octavio Getino; music by Fernando E. Solanas.

Filmed in Argentina.

Publications:

Books—*Cine, cultura y descolonización* by Fernando E. Solanas and Octavio Getino, Mexico City 1973; "Latin American Films: Fourth Frontier" by Leonardo Luxemburg in *Films of a Changing Worlds* edited by Jean Marie Ackerman, Washington, D.C. 1977; *Latin American Filmmakers and the Third Cinema* edited by Zuzana Pick, Ottawa, Canada 1978; articles—"*L'Heure des brasiers*" in *Avant-Scène du cinéma* (Paris), October 1969; "Cinema as a Gun: An Interview with Fernando Solanas" in *Cineaste* (New York), fall 1969; "Solanas: Film as a Political Essay" by Louis Marcorelles in *Evergreen* (New York), July 1969; "*La Hora de los Hornos*' by James Roy MacBean in *Film Quarterly* (Berkeley), fall 1970; "Fernando Solanas: An Interview" in *Film Quarterly* (Berkeley), fall 1970; "Fernando Solanas: An Interview" by James Roy MacBean in *Film Quarterly* (Berkeley), winter 1971; "Notes on Solanas and Godard" by Joel Haycock in *Film Society Review* (New York), November 1971 and December 1971; "Towards a Third Cinema" by Octavio Getino and Fernando Solanas in *Cineaste* (New York), winter 1971; "...And After?: A Response to Solanas and Getino" by John Matthews in *Afterimage* (London), summer 1971; "Algunas preguntas a Octavio Getino" in *Cine Cubano* (Havana), no.73-75, 1972; "Voor een derde cinema" by F. Solanas and O. Getino in *Skrien* (Amsterdam), spring 1972; "*The Hour of the Furnaces*" in *Films and Filming* (London), November 1972; "Aspects of Latin American Political Cinema" by David Wilson in *Sight and Sound* (London), summer 1972; "*L'Heure des brasiers*" by A. Sibon-Blanc in *Image et son* (Paris), no.269, 1973; "The New South American Cinema: From Neo-Realism to Expressive Realism" by Concetta Carestia Greenwood in *Latin American Library Review*, spring 1973; "Screening the Movies in Argentina" by Steve Kovacs in *New Boston Review*, December 1977; "Le Realisme magique et les elans du coeur" by G. Hennebelle in *Ecran* (Paris), 15 March 1979; "Fernando Solanas: An Interview" by Dan Ranvaud in *Framework* (London), spring 1979; "The Cinema: Art Form or Political Weapon" by Fernando Solanas, Bertrand Tavernier, Rene Vautier, and Guy Hennebelle in *Framework* (London), autumn 1979.

* * *

The liberation struggles of the 1960's were a fertile seedbed for *La hora de los hornos*. Independence movements in the colonies and neo-colonies of the Third World, student revolts in the United States and Western Europe, and the brief protest by Czechoslovakians against the dull grey bureaucracy of the Soviet Union were the world context in which Fernando E. Solanas and Octavio Getino's film exploded. Argentina moved closer to a social revolution that it ever had before (or since), and *Hora* was an important expression of that movement, as well as a pivotal example for cineastes involved in national liberation movements throughout the world.

The film is a documentary of such length (4½ hours) that most viewers outside of Argentina have probably seen only the first part. Perhaps influenced by the work of the Cuban documentarist, Santiago Alvarez, the directors have created a film that takes the form of a didactic collage, committed to the denunciation of imperialism and its cultural influences. As is stated in the film: "Mass communications are more effective for neo-colonialism than napalm. What is real, true, and rational is to be found on the margin of the Law, just as are the people."

That which is most interesting about the film's form is its relation to the audience. Rather than the conventional finished cinematic product, ready for viewer consumption, the work is conceived as an open-ended militant act, in which the film itself is only important as a "detonator" or "pretext for dialogue." Parts 2 and 3 were structured with pauses in which the projector was to be turned off and discussion was to take place; groups using the film were encouraged to employ their own visual or sound accompaniment and to cut or add to the film as they saw fit. Of course, the very context in which the film was shown contributed to the sense of audience participation. Because the film was illegal, no one in the audience was a mere spectator: "On the contrary, from the moment he decided to attend the showing, *from the moment he lined himself up on this side* by taking risks and contributing his living experience to the meeting, he became an actor, a more important protagonist than those who appeared in the films....The situation turned everyone into accomplices of the act."

Argentina's climate of political repression also required a novel approach to production. Conceiving of their work as a guerrilla act, Solanas and Getino "provided a model for clandestine activity under an aggressively hostile regime which no filmmakers in Latin America or elsewhere have surpassed," noted the American critic Julianne Burton. Strict discipline and tight security were the rule, and all who participated in the film's production were required to develop interchangeable skills. One example of the measures required by the situation was that the film's footage had to be constantly disassembled and reassembled so that technicians in the processing laboratories would have no hint as to its subversive content.

The film's strident manichaeism ("*our* culture and *their* culture, *our* films and *their* films, *our* sense of beauty and *their* sense of beauty") and its puerile historical analysis seem dated today. But, the current situation in Latin America leaves little room for doubt that more such films are both needed and forthcoming. As Solanas and Getino stated in *Hora*, "At this time in Latin America there is room for neither passivity nor innocence. The intellectual's commitment is measured in terms of risks as well as words and ideas; what he does to further the cause of liberation is what counts." What Solanas and Getino did for the cause of liberation was make *La hora de los hornos*, which, as they reminded us in their first public statement about the film "is an *act* before it is a film—an act of liberation."

—John Mraz

LAS HURDES. Terre sans pain. Land Without Bread. Black and white, 35mm; running time: 27 mins.; length: about 865 meters. Released 1937, France.

Produced by Ramon Acin; screenplay by Luis Buñuel, commentary by Pierre Unik and Julio Acin; directed by Luis Buñuel; photography by Eli Lotar; edited by Luis Buñuel; soundtrack by Charles Goldblatt and Pierre Braunberger, 1937; music by Brahms; assistants: Pierre Unik and Sanchez Ventura.

Filmed 20 April-24 May 1932 in the Las Hurdes region of Spain. Cost: rumored to be 20,000 pesetas that a friend won in a lottery.

Cast: Abel Jacquin (*Commentator*).

Publications:

Script—"*Las Hurdes* (Terre sans Pain)" by Luis Buñuel in *Avant-Scène du cinéma* (Paris), 15 April 1964; books—*Luis Buñuel*, edited by Michel Esteve, Paris 1962-63; *Luis Buñuel* by Ado Kyrou, Paris 1962; *Luis Buñuel: odisea del demoledor* by Eduardo Lizalde, Mexico 1962; *Luis Buñuel* by Frédéric Grange and Charles Rebolledo, Paris 1964; *Luis Buñuel: eine Dokumentation* by Alice Goetz and Helmut Banz, Verband der Deutschen Filmclubs 1965; *Luis Buñuel* by Raymond Durgnat, Berkeley 1968; *Luis Buñuel: Biografia Critica*, Madrid 1969; *The Cinema of Luis Buñuel* by Freddy Buache, translated by Peter Graham, London 1973; *Buñuel (Cine e ideología)* by Manuel Alcalá, Madrid 1973; *Luis Buñuel: A Critical Biography* by José Aranda, translated by David Robinson, New York 1975; *El ojo de Buñuel* by Fernando Cesarman, Barcelona 1976; *The World of Luis Buñuel: Essays in Criticism* edited by Joan Mellen, New York 1978; *Luis Buñuel* by Virginia Higginbotham, Boston 1979; *Luis Buñuel* by Ian Cameron, Berkeley 1979; articles— "The Films of Luis Buñuel" by Tony Richardson in *Sight and Sound* (London), January/March 1954; special Buñuel issue, *Cinemages* (Paris), no.1, 1955; "Buñuel espagnol" by J.-F. Aranda in *Cinema 57* (Paris), Christmas 1957; special Buñuel issue, *Positif* (Paris), November 1961; special Buñuel issue, *Image et son* (Paris), December 1962; special Buñuel issue, *La Methode* (Paris), January 1962; "Luis Buñuel" by Alan Lovell in *Anarchist Cinema*, London 1964; "Une Seule Certitude, la mort" by Marcel Oms in *Avant-Scène du cinéma* (Paris), 15 April 1964; special Buñuel issue, with interviews, *Image et son* (Paris), May 1971; special Buñuel issue, *Cine Cubano*, no.78-80, 1973; "L'Exil de Buñuel à New York" by R. Gubern in *Positif* (Paris), January 1973; "Luis Buñuel: The Process of Dissociation in 3 Films" by E.H. Lyon in *Cinema Journal* (Iowa City), fall 1973; "Erzählende Dokumentarfilme" by P. Nau in *Filmkritik* (Munich), October 1974; "Un Chien andalou, L'Age d'or, Las Hurdas, Los Olvidados" by R.C. Dale in *Movietone News* (Seattle), February 1975; "The Minister of the Interior is on the Telephone: The Early Films of Luis Buñuel" by Randall Conrad in *Cineaste* (New York), no.7, 1976; special Buñuel issue of *Contracampo* (Madrid), October/November 1980.

*   *   *

Las Hurdes or *Land without Bread* is a pseudo-documentary by Luis Buñuel. It was his first film after his committed surrealist collaborations with Salvador Dali, *Un chien andalou* and *L'Age d'or*. Most of the film's critics have treated this investigation of the squalor of people living in the isolated Hurdanos region of Spain as a simple, but powerful, documentary of the injustice of neglect. Although the film does present a devastating image of the wretchedness of Hurdane life, it even more powerfully indicts the documentary genre itself and the urbane audiences who respond to it.

Buñuel deliberately adopts the tone of a travelogue moving into the interior of an unknown region, with a dispassionate voice-over narration, and the incongruous music of Brahms. Lest sophisticated viewers miss the parody, the film ends with a spoof on the most famous of such documentaries, Flaherty's *Nanook of the North*, as *Las Hurdes*'s most perceptive critic, Ken Kelman, first pointed out. Along the way, there are hilarious clues for the observant viewer, which are generally overlooked; Buñuel realized that audiences respond to the preconceptions of a genre more thoroughly than they do to the details before them. The most notorious deception offered to the half-aware viewer is an image of a goat falling off a mountain. Anyone aware of cinematic technique would realize that the alternation of two shots, one from the side of the mountain, another from above, negates the idea of an accidental fall (unless the viewer is gullible enough to believe that two different cameras, hidden from each other, happened to catch the same rare accident); but even more nonchalantly, Buñuel allows a puff of gunsmoke to remain in the frame, giving away how the "accident" reached the screen.

There is a lesson in malaria control, for the film viewer rather than for the Hurdano victims of the disease; dying children, a dead infant, and brain-damaged shepherds are carefully posed before the camera and even manipulated in shot-countershot interactions. At one point the moving camera glides past a file of hiking Hurdanos although we are told they have no roads.

The surrealist poet and communist, Pierre Unik, accompanied Buñuel on the shooting expedition and is often credited with the composition of the voice-over (for which there are several versions with significant variations in different languages). The text as a whole is an example of the surrealist doctrine of the transfiguring power of language. Here it blinds us to the evident manipulations of the montage, which Buñuel implies are identical with those of fiction films, and it consoles us with variations on how the helpless film crew could do nothing for the suffering subjects of the film. There is no doubt that the filmmaker felt compassion for the plight of the Hurdanos, but he was fiercely and hilariously vicious toward the comfortable liberal audience for its interest in "real life" horror stories.

—P. Adams Sitney

_____

HUSBANDS. Production: Faces Music Inc.; De Luxe color, 35mm; running time: originally 154 mins., edited to 138 mins. for general release. Released 8 December 1970, New York.

Produced by Al Ruban with Sam Shaw; screenplay by John Cassavetes; directed by John Cassavetes; photography by Victor Kemper; edited by Peter Tanner; sound by Dennis Maitland (New York) and Barrie Copland (London); art direction by René D'Auriac, scenic artist: Robert Hamlin; music direction by Stanley Wilson, additional music by Ray Brown; costumes designed by Louis Brown (New York).

Filmed 1969-70 in London and New York City.

Cast: Ben Gazzara (*Harry*); Peter Falk (*Archie*); John Cassavetes (*Gus*); Jenny Runacre (*Mary Tynan*); Jenny Lee Wright (*Pearl Billingham*); Noelle Kao (*Julie*); John Kullers (*Red*); Meta Shaw (*Annie*); Leola Harlow (*Leola*); Delores Delmar (*Countess*); Eleanor Zee (*Mrs. Hines*); Claire Malis (*Stuart's wife*); Peggy Lashbrook (*Diana Mallabee*); Eleanor Gould ("*Normandy*"); Sarah Felcher (*Sarah*); Gwen Van Dam ("*Jeannie*"); John Armstrong ("*Happy Birthday*"); Antoinette Kray ("*Jesus Loves Me*"); Lorraine McMartin (*Annie's mother*); Carinthia West (*Susanna*); Edgar Franken (*Ed Weintraub*); Joseph Boley (*Minister*); Judith Lowry (*Stuart's grandmother*);

Joe Hardy (*"Shanghai Lil"*); David Rowlands (*Stuart Jackson*); Rhonda Parker (*Margaret*); K.C. Townsend (*Barmaid*); Anne O'Donnell and Gena Wheeler (*Nurses*); Nick Cassavetes (*Nick*); Alexandra Cassavetes (*Xan*); Bill Britton; Arthur Clark; Charles Gaines; Fred Draper.

Publications:

Reviews—*"Husbands"* by Robert Benayoun in *Positif* (Paris), May 1972; *"Husbands"* by G. Braucourt in *Ecran* (Paris), May 1972; *"Husbands"* by J. Magny in *Cinéma* (Paris), June 1972; *"Husbands"* by D. Sauvaget in *Image et son* (Paris), May 1972; book—*John Cassavetes, Peter Falk* edited by Bruce Henstell, Washington, D.C. 1972; articles—*"After Faces"* by Ann Guerin in *Life* (New York), 9 May 1969; "The Faces of the Husbands" in the *New Yorker*, 15 March 1969; "New Hollywood Is the Old Hollywood" in *Time* (New York), 7 December 1970; "Interview: John Cassavetes" in *Playboy* (Chicago), July 1971; *"Maridos y Así habla el amor"* by Léon Frías in *Hablemos de cine* (Lima, Peru), no.65, 1973; "Femmes et maris dans l'oeurvre de Cassavetes" by C. Benoit and A. Tournes in *Jeune Cinéma* (Paris), September/October 1976; "John Cassavetes" in *Hollywood Renaissance* by Diane Jacob, New York 1977; "Notes sur le cinéma de John Cassavetes" by Noel Simsolo in *Cahiers du cinéma* (Paris), May 1978; "The Cinema of John Cassavetes" by M. Landy and S. Shostack in *Ciné-Tracts* (Montreal), winter 1980.

*   *   *

The films of John Cassavetes are, at their worst, occasionally irritating and confusing. But, most always, they are original and thought-provoking, with moments of undeniable brilliance. In a quick shot, or camera angle or movement, the filmmaker eloquently captures the anguish, fear, paranoia, intimacy and hope of his characters.

Husbands is a representative Cassavetes work. Plotless, and shot in cinema verité style, it is an observation of the lives of a trio of average, middle-aged American men (superbly played by Ben Gazzara, Peter Falk and the filmmaker himself; in all Cassavetes films, the performances are extraordinary) who find themselves strangely upset by the death of a close friend. This tragedy—and the fact and finality of death—becomes for them profoundly real. As a result, they begin a search for freedom, for the essence of being and feeling alive. Specifically, they attempt to recapture the joy of boyhood camaraderie; they escape their everyday realities, their jobs and wives and children and cars, by striking off for London. They drink, flirt, party and gamble, in an attempt to belatedly reject the conventions thrust upon them by their adulthood and quest for the American Dream. Reality intrudes, though, in the form of their own awareness of time lost, their ages and situations and failings. Two of the characters eventually return home, while the third decides to forsake all responsibilities and remain abroad.

Most significantly, *Husbands* is a celebration of male bonding, male friendship and love. Its characters are more comfortable with men than with women, because men are undemanding of each other. They do not really exist as separate entities, but are linked by their camaraderie. *Husbands* is, ultimately, an examination of the manner in which men love each other. Gazzara, Falk and Cassavetes are not Butch Cassidy and the Sundance Kid, or Batman and Robin. They are neither superheroes, nor superlovers, nor supermen. They are only men.

While Cassavetes understands his characters, he also understands the actors playing them. In all of his films he allows his performers to improvise (supposedly from the dialogue he writes), to literally work out the problems of their characters on screen. As a result, the actors inhabit the lives and souls of the roles they play; often, it seems as if they are playing themselves. This is never more so than in *Husbands*.

Husbands is Cassavetes's third film (after *Shadows* and *Faces*) produced independently of the Hollywood establishment. He shot the film, which he also conceived, scripted and edited, with privately raised funding, and at his own pace. Columbia Pictures acquired distribution rights, and Cassavetes had to fight with the studio to retain his final cut.

With its almost two-and-a-half hour running time, *Husbands* is sometimes meandering; the viewer must often consciously concentrate on Cassavetes's words and images. But the reward is an honesty rarely found in movies.

—Rob Edelman

I AM A FUGITIVE FROM A CHAIN GANG. Production: Warner Bros. Pictures, Inc.; 1932; black and white, 35mm; running time: 93 mins. Released 10 November 1932.

Produced by Hal Wallis; screenplay by Howard J. Green and Brown Holmes; from the autobiography *I Am a Fugitive from a Georgia Chain Gang* by Robert E. Burns; directed by Mervyn LeRoy; photography by Sol Polito; edited by William Holmes; art direction by Jack Okey; music conducted by Leo F. Forbstein; costumes designed by Orry-Kelly; technical advisors: S.H. Sullivan and Jack Miller, uncredited assistance by Robert E. Burns.

Filmed 28 July-7 September 1932 in Warner Bros. studios. Cost: $195,845.

Cast: Paul Muni (*James Allen*); Glenda Farrell (*Marie*); Helen Vinson (*Helen*); Noel Francis (*Linda*); Preston Foster (*Pete*); Allen Jenkins (*Barney Sykes*); Edward Ellis (*Bomber Wells*); John Wray (*Nordine*); Everett Brown (*Sebastian*); Hale Hamilton (*The Reverend Robert Allen*); Louise Carter (*Mother*); Sally Blane (*Alice*); Berton Churchill (*Judge*); David Landau (*Warden*); Willard Robertson (*Prison Board Chairman*); Robert McWade (*Attorney*); Robert Warwick (*Fuller*).

Publications:

Scripts—*I Am a Fugitive from a Chain Gang* by Howard J. Green and Brown Holmes, edited with an introduction by John E. O'Connor, Madison, Wisconsin 1981; reviews—in *The New York Times*, 11 November 1932; review in *Variety*, 15 November 1932; books—*I Am a Fugitive from a Georgia Chain Gang* by Robert E. Burns, New York 1932; *It Takes More Than Talent* by Mervyn LeRoy, New York 1953; *My First Hundred Years In Hollywood* by Jack L. Warner with Dean Jennings, New York 1964; *Don't Say Yes Until I Finish Talking: A Biography of Darryl F. Zanuck* by Mel Gussow, New York 1971; *The Warner Bros. Golden Anniversary Book*, New York 1973; *Actor: The Life and Times of Paul Muni* by Jerome Lawrence, New York

1974; *Mervyn LeRoy: Take One* by Mervyn LeRoy with Dick Kleiner, New York 1974; *Lorentz on Film: Movies 1927-1941* by Pare Lorentz, New York 1975; *Film Noir* edited by Alain Silver and Elizabeth Ward, Woodstock, New York 1979; articles—about Robert Burns upon whom film is based in *New York Herald Tribune*, 27 November 1932; "Champion of the Underdog" in *Silver Screen* (New York), December 1932; "The Making of Mervyn LeRoy" by Mervyn LeRoy in *Films in Review* (New York), May 1953; "*I Am a Fugitive From a Chain Gang*" by Russell Campbell in *Velvet Light Trap* (Madison, Wisconsin), June 1971; "Kracauers Abbildtheorie" by J. Ebert in *Filmkritik* (Munich), April 1977; "*I Am a Fugitive from a Chain Gang*" by T. Pulleine in *Monthly Film Bulletin* (London), March 1979; "*Je suis un evade*" by J. Siclier in *Avant-Scène du cinéma* (Paris), 1 October 1979; "*I Am a Fugitive from a Chain Gang*" by Joan Cohen in *Magill's Survey of Cinema, Vol. II* edited by Frank N. Magill, Englewood Cliffs, New Jersey 1980.

*   *   *

During the 1930s Warner Brothers earned a well-deserved reputation of being a studio with a strong social conscience. Hal Wallis, who was production chief at the studio for much of that decade, recalled that "the general impression was that we were very liberal in our selection of material." Among the Warners' productions which helped to create that image was *I Am A Fugitive From A Chain Gang*, a well-made film which earned the studio's sound department and Paul Muni Oscar nominations. This production ranks, to use the words of film historian Clive Hirschhorn, as "one of the most vehement, eloquent, and far-reaching of social protest films."

I Am A Fugitive From A Chain Gang is based on a book by Robert E. Burns, who recounts his adventures with the prison system in Georgia and his two escapes from the chain gangs. The movie is generally faithful to its sources (although for various reasons Georgia is never mentioned), with some melodramatic flourishes added. The story is deceptively simple: a World War I veteran from a good family returns home after the war and becomes dissatisfied with his circumstances. He takes to the road and becomes innocently involved in a stickup; found guilty he is sentenced for some years to a chain gang. The film in stark fashion depicts the sadistic brutality and dehumanizing violence with which chain gang inmates are treated. He escapes, goes North, makes something of himself, but is forced into marriage with a woman who has discovered his past; when ultimately he tries to leave her for another woman she denounces him to the authorities. Attempting to clear his record by going South voluntarily to serve a nominal term, he is doublecrossed and returned to the chain gang. He escapes once more, and comes out of hiding one night to see his sweetheart. Restless, fear-ridden, terrified of being returned to the chain gang, he is but a haunted shadow of his former self. In what film critic Pauline Kael has called "one of the great closing scenes in the history of films," he retreats into the shadows at hearing a sound, and responds to his sweetheart's question of how he lives by saying "I steal" as the movie ends.

The film is a harsh indictment of the chain gang, and American movie audiences were made aware of the terrible conditions prevalent in the penal system of the South. Moreover, these audiences were presented with a bleak view of contemporary American life in keeping with the harsh realities of the Great Depression which was just then peaking in terms of its impact on life in the United States. Although the bulk of the film's action is set in the 1920s the indictment and conditions depicted easily translated to the hard times of the early 1930s. *I Am A Fugitive*

From A Chain Gang, thanks to a thoughtful script, taut direction, and vibrant central performance remains a powerful indictment and pungent commentary on social ills.

—Daniel J. Leab

———

IF... Production: Memorial Enterprises; color with tinted black and white sequences (EastmanColor), 35mm; running time: 112 mins., American version 111 mins. Released December 1968, London.

Produced by Roy Baird with Michael Medwin and Lindsay Anderson; screenplay by David Sherwin; from the original script "Crusaders" by David Sherwin and John Howlett; directed by Lindsay Anderson; photography by Miroslav Ondricek; edited by David Gladwell; sound recorded by Christian Wangler; production design by Jocelyn Herbert; art direction by Brian Eatwell; music composed and conducted by Marc Wilkinson; costumes designed by Shura Cohen.

Filmed beginning 8 March 1968 at Cheltenham College, England. Cost: budgeted at £250,000. Cannes Film Festival, Grand Prix, 1969.

Cast: Malcolm McDowell (*Mick*); David Wood (*Johnny*); Richard Warwick (*Wallace*); Christine Noonan (*Girl*); Rupert Webster (*Bobby Philips*); Robert Swann (*Rowntree*); Hugh Thomas (*Denson*); Michael Cadman (*Fortinbras*); Peter Sproule (*Barnes*); Peter Jeffrey (*Headmaster*); Arthur Lowe (*Mr. Kemp*); Mona Washbourne (*Matron*); Mary MacLeod (*Mrs. Kemp*); Geoffrey Chater (*Chaplain*); Ben Aris (*John Thomas*); Graham Crowden (*History Master*); Charles Lloyd Pack (*Classics Master*); Anthony Nicholls (*General Denson*); Tommy Godfrey (*Finchley*); Guy Ross (*Stephans*); Robin Askwith (*Keating*); Richard Everett (*Pussy Graves*); Philip Bagenal (*Peanuts*); Nicholas Page (*Cox*); Robert Yetzes (*Fisher*); David Griffen (*Willens*); Graham Sharman (*Van Eyssen*); Richard Tombleson (*Baird*); Richard Davis (*Machin*); Brian Pettifer (*Biles*); Michael Newport (*Brunning*); Charles Sturridge (*Markland*); Sean Bury (*Jute*); Martin Beaumont (*Hunter*);

Publications:

Script—*If...: A Film by Lindsay Anderson* by Lindsay Anderson and David Sherwin, New York 1969; reviews—by Gavin Miller in *Sight and Sound* (London), winter 1968; "Much Virtue in *If*" by Dilys Powell in *Sunday Times* (London), 22 December 1968; review by Paul Schrader in *Cinema* (London), no.3, 1968; review by Mark Shivas in *Movie* (London), winter 1968; review by Elizabeth Sussex in the *London Times*, 29 November 1968; "*If...*: Pop Rebellion Fantasy, and Snob Appeal" by Gary Arnold in *Washington Post*, 13 June 1969; "Give Me Back My Yo-Yo" by Vincent Canby in *The New York Times*, March 1969; "School Days, School Days" by Pauline Kael in the *New Yorker*, March 1969; review by David Spiers in *Screen* (London), March/April 1969; "Students vs. the System in Bloody Vision" by Roger Ebert in the *Chicago Sun Times*, 1 June 1969; books—*Lindsay Anderson* by Elizabeth Sussex, New York 1969; *New Cinema in Britain* by Roger Manvell, New York 1969; *The Film Director as Superstar* by Joseph Gelmis, New

York 1970; *Dictionary of Film* by Georges Sadoul, translated, edited, and updated by Peter Morris, Berkeley 1972; *The British Film Industry in the Sixties* by Alexander Walker, New York 1974; *Lindsay Anderson: A Guide to References and Resources* by Charles L. P. Silet, Boston 1979; articles—"Anderson Shooting *If...*" by David Robinson in *Sight and Sound* (London), summer 1968; "Observer: Youth Without Rose-Colored Glasses" by Russell Baker in *The New York Times*, 13 May 1969; "British Film Breaks Hold On Cannes Fete" by Vincent Canby in *The New York Times*, 26 May 1969; "The Importance of Being Oscar" by Vincent Canby in *The New York Times*, 20 April 1969; "*If* Does Not Equal Zero" by Jay Cocks in *Time* (New York), 21 March 1969; "Hollywood and the Student Revolt" by Richard Corliss in *National Review* (New York), 17 June 1969; "*If...*High School Unless" by John Craddock in *Film Society Review* (New York), September 1969; "Before the Revolution" by Stephen Farber in *Hudson Review* (Nutley, New Jersey), autumn 1969; "If Youth But Knew" by Philip Hartung in *Commonweal* (New York), 21 March 1969; "Aspects of Love" by Robert Kotlowitz in *Harper's* (New York), April 1969; "Film Chronicle: Notes on the Compulsive Revolution" by Vernon Young in *Hudson Review* (Nutley, New Jersey), winter 1969; "Editing Anderson's *If...*" by David Gladwell in *Screen* (London), January/February 1969; "Bergman and Anderson for Sophomores" by James Welsh in *Cinema Journal* (Evanston, Illinois), fall 1971; "Lindsay Anderson—romantisk ironiker" by N. Jensen in *Kosmorama* (Copenhagen), November 1973; "Lindsay Anderson" by Rafal Marszalek in *Kino* (Warsaw, Poland), October 1974; "Un Filme que Evoca Jean Vigo" by Jose Jorge Rumalho in *Celuloide* (Rio Maior, Portugal), November 1974; "Brecht in Britain—Lindsay Anderson" by Alan Lovell in *Screen* (London), winter 1975; "Britannia Waives the Rules" by Raymond Durgnat in *Film Comment* (New York), July/August 1976.

*   *   *

Lindsay Anderson's film *If...*, related to Rudyard Kipling's poem of the same name, has frequently raised much debate politically, stylistically, structurally, and particularly concerning his use or misuse of Brechtian theory. Based on a script by David Sherwin and John Howlett entitled *Crusaders*, the film uses the British public school system as a microcosm of society to demonstrate the repression of the individual by authority. In the published screenplay of *If...*, Anderson also credits another source of inspiration for the film, Jean Vigo: "We especially saw *Zero de conduite* again, before writing started, to give us courage."

The mid-1950s marked significant changes in Britain. The New Left emerged, the Free Cinema began, John Osborne was energizing the theater, and Brecht was re-discovered. It was also the period Anderson was writing for *Sight and Sound*. Not unexpectedly, the influences of that period can be traced to *If...*. The film has a sense of "documentary realism" (Osborne), surprising surrealistic passages (Free Cinema), a drive to overthrow authority (New left), and a use of self-reflexive devices (Brecht).

If... functions predominantly within a kind of realism typical of classic narrative films, but one that is undercut by Brechtian concerns and surrealistic images. Anderson himself declared that "...I think that *If...* is a rather Brechtian film." There are inherent difficulties with this statement (and regarding "Brechtian cinema" in general), but *If...* does exhibit two ostensible examples of the well-known *verfremdungseffekt*: the oft-cited black and white sections and the title cards. The film is constructed in a series of eight vignettes, each one introduced by a title card. The overall design conveys some idea of a chronology, but the ordering of the scenes could be altered without changing the thematic drive. This type of structural flexibility was central to Brecht's early writings. The use of black and white sections within a color film was entirely random, based on economic and practical considerations. Notwithstanding, both devices are meant to distance the spectator from the film, calling into question the production of the film as text and, theoretically, permitting cool observations of societal machinations. The fact that the fantasy sequences scattered throughout *If...* (the chaplin in a drawer, the naked woman at the cafe, the headmaster's wife wandering the empty corridors, and possibly the ending) are not delineated from the accepted diegetic reality reflects Anderson's belief that there are no rigid distinctions between what is real and what is fantasy. This use of surrealism blends nicely with the Brechtian aspects of the film in that it raises similar questions about constructed images and the supposed truth of realism.

To a lesser degree, *If...* also deals with sexuality, especially the repression of desires with its deleterious effects, and the covert homosexuality of an all male school brought to the fore in certain relationships.

Anderson has said that no authority is necessary and that his sympathies are always with the revolutionaries. *If...* presents contradictions inherent in any authoritarian system and states that without resolution, radical action will be the only means of change—the quite literal "if" of the film.

—Greg S. Faller

IKIRU. Living. To Live. Doomed. Vivre. Vivre enfin. Un seul jour. Production: Toho (Tokyo); black and white, 35mm; running time: 143 mins.; length: 3918 meters. Released 9 October 1952.

Produced by Shojiro Motoki; screenplay by Shinobu Hashimoto, Hideo Oguni, and Akira Kurosawa; directed by Akira Kurosawa; photography by Asakazu Nakai; edited by Koichi Iwashita; sound by Fumio Yanoguchi; art direction by So Matsuyama; music by Fumio Hayasaka; lighting by Shigeru Mori.

Filmed 1952 in Tokyo. The David O. Selznick "Golden Laurel" Award, 1961.

Cast: Takashi Shimura (*Kanji Watanabe*); Nobuo Kaneko (*Mitsuo Watanabe*); Kyoko Seki (*Kazue Watanabe*); Makoto Kobori (*Kiichi Watanabe*); Kumeko Urabe (*Taysu Watanabe*); Yoshie Minami (*Maid*); Miki Odagiri (*Toyo Odagiri*); Kamatari Fugiwara (*Ono*); Minosuke Yamada (*Saito*); Haruo Tanaka (*Sakai*); Bokuzen Hidari (*Ohara*); Shinichi Himori (*Kimura*); Nobuo Nakamura (*Deputy Mayor*); Kazuo Abe (*City assemblyman*); Masao Shimizu (*Doctor*); Ko Kimura (*Intern*); Atsushi Watanabe (*Patient*); Yunosuke Ito (*Novelist*); Yatsuko Tanami (*Hostess); Fuyuki Murakami (*Newspaperman*); Seiji Miyaguchi (*Gang-Boss*); Daisuke Kato (*Gangmember*); Kin Sugai, Eiko Miyoshi, Fumiko Homma (*Housewives*); Ichiro Chiba (*Policeman*); Minoru Chiaki (*Noguchi*); Toranosuke Ogawa (*Park Section Chief*); Tomoo Nagai and Hirayoshi Aono (*Reporters*); Akira Tani (*Old man at bar*); Toshiyuki Ichimura (*Pianist at cabaret*).

Publications:

Scripts—*Ikiru: A Film by Akira Kurosawa*, English translation by Donald Richie, New York 1969; "*To Live (Ikiru)*" (scenario) in *The Complete Works of Akira Kurosawa* by Takamaro Shimaji, translated by Don Kenny, Tokyo 1971; "*Ikiru*" in *Contemporary Japanese Cinema* edited by Howard Hibbet, New York 1977; reviews—"Vivre" by André Bazin in *Cahiers du cinéma* (Paris), March 1957; "Ikiru" by Peter John Dyer in *Films and Filming* (London), August 1959; "*Ikiru*" in *Time* (New York), no.3, 1960; "*Ikiru*" by William Bernhardt in *Film Quarterly* (Berkeley), summer 1960; review by Jonas Mekas in *The Village Voice* (New York), 10 February 1960; "*Ikiru*" by Bosley Crowther in *The New York Times*, 30 January 1960; "*Ikiru*" by Robert Roman in *Films in Review* (New York), March 1960; books—*Japanese Movies* by Donald Richie, Tokyo 1961, reprinted as *Japanese Cinema: Film Style and National Character*, New York 1971; *Kurosawa* by Sacha Ezratti, Paris 1964; *The Films of Akira Kurosawa* by Donald Richie, 2nd edition, Berkeley 1970; *The Complete Works of Akira Kurosawa*, translated and edited by Don Kenny, Tokyo 1971; *Kurosawa* by Michel Mesnil, Paris 1973; *Akira Kurosawa: A Guide to References and Resources* by Patricia Erens, Boston 1979; *The Japanese Film: Art and Industry* by Joseph Anderson and Donald Richie, expanded edition, Princeton, New Jersey 1982; articles—"The History of Japanese Movies" by Joseph Anderson in *Films in Review* (New York), June/July 1953; "The Films of Kurosawa" by Jay Leyda in *Sight and Sound* (London), fall 1954; "Japanese Film in Modern Dress" by Earl Roy Miner in *Quarterly of Film, Radio, and Television* (Berkeley), summer 1956; "2 Inches Off the Ground" by Lindsay Anderson in *Sight and Sound* (London), winter 1957; "Ikiru" in *Filmfacts* (New York), no.3, 1960; "The Fact of Mortality" by Stanley Kauffmann in the *New Republic* (New York), no.10, 1960; "The Rebel in a Kimono" Douglas McVay in *Films and Filming* (London), July 1961 and August 1961; "Akira Kurosawa" by Donald Richie in *Orient-West* (Tokyo), summer 1962; special issue on Kurosawa in *Études cinématographiques* (Paris), spring 1964; "Kurosawa on Kurosawa" by Donald Richie in *Sight and Sound* (London), summer 1964 and autumn 1964; "*Ikiru*" in *A World of Film: Criticism and Comment* by Stanley Kauffmann, New York 1966; "Dodes'caden" by Jean-Loup Passek in *Cinéma 74* (Paris), December 1974; "The Mythos of 'The Sickness Unto Death'..." by R. Thomas Simone in *Literature/Film Quarterly* (Salisbury, Maryland), winter 1975; "Éloge de la folie" by Michel Sineaux in *Positif* (Paris), January 1975; "*Ikiru*" by S. van Beek in *Skoop* (Amsterdam), August 1980; "Humilié et initié" by C. Labre in *Positif* (Paris), October 1980; "*Vivre*" by J. Magny in *Cinéma* (Paris), March 1980; "*Vivre*" by M. Martin in *Image et son*" (Paris), February 1980.

*   *   *

Akira Kurosawa's popularity in the West has been based primarily on his *jidai-geki* (period films). The *gendai-geki* (contemporary dramas), despite the championship of many critics, have been relatively neglected. *Ikiru* is the major exception to this rule. Its reputation rested initially on the seriousness of its subject (how does a man with only a few months left to live find meaning in life?), its humanism (Kurosawa's commitment to individual heroism, discovered in an apparently insignificant and undistinguished person), its social criticism (the satire on bureaucracy), and the power and directness of its emotional appeal. The film also became central to the anti-Kurosawa back-lash led by certain *auteur* critics bent on attacking the notion that the importance of a film had any connection with the importance of its subject; to them, the humanism seemed naive, the social satire obvious, the emotional effects contrived, laborious and rhetorical. Neither view accounts for the particularity—in some ways the *oddity*—of Kurosawa's work.

The emphasis on a formal analysis of *Ikiru* in Nöel Burch's brilliant book on Japanese cinema, *To the Distant Observer*, goes some way towards rectifying the inadequacy of previous approaches. Burch discusses the film in terms of its elaborate and rigorous formal system of symmetries and asymmetries contained within the overall "rough-hewn geometry" that he sees as Kurosawa's most distinctive general characteristic. The film falls into two strongly demarcated sections, the break coming about two-thirds of the way through. The first part begins and ends with the voice of an off-screen narrator, who tells us that Watanabe has only six months to live, and, later, that he has died. The intervening narrative takes us through Watanabe's discovery of his situation and his search to find a meaning for his life, culminating in his moment of decision. The second part (marked formally by the narrator's last intrusion and, in terms of narrative, by the death of the film's hero and central consciousness) shows Watanabe's funeral wake. The two parts are linked by a formal device: each contains five flashbacks the precise pattern of which is inverted in part two. At the same time, each part has its own highly organized formal structure. Part one consists of a prologue which includes the time preceding Watanabe's discovery of his fatal disease, and three sections. The prologue is clearly marked off from the rest by the only use in the film of a striking technical device: the shutting off of the soundtrack in the shot where Watanabe leaves the clinic in a state of shock, totally absorbed by his plight, and is nearly run down by a truck (the sound crashing in again at that moment). The ensuing three sections show the three phases of his search for meaning, each ending in disillusionment: his revaluation of his relationship with the son to whom his life has been devoted; his plunge into the hedonism of Tokyo's nightlife; his relationship with the young girl who used to work in his office. The first part, then, covers a considerable extent of time and space; the second part (flashbacks and a brief epilogue apart) is contained within a single night and a single room. The three-section structure of part one is "answered" in part two by the three intrusions of outsiders into the wake: the reporters, the women from the district that has benefited from Watanabe's achievement, and the policeman who recounts the manner of his death. Where each of the three sections of part one marked a phase in the search for meaning, each of the intrusions marks a stage in the revelation of the truth about his achievements.

The "rough-hewn geometry," the use of the narrator, the abrupt narrative break, and the frequently disruptive editing all combine to produce a strong sense of distanciation. What is remarkable about *Ikiru*, and crucial to the Kurosawa "flavor," is the way in which this collides with the film's equally strong emotional rhetoric, setting up a continuous tension between involvement and distance.

—Robin Wood

IM LAUF DER ZEIT. Kings of the Road. Production: Wim Wenders Produktion; black and white, 35mm; running time: 165 mins., some sources list 176 mins.; length: 15,740 feet. Released 17 March 1976.

Produced by Wim Wenders, executive producer: Michael Wiedemann; screenplay by Wim Wenders; directed by Wim Wenders; photography by Robbie Müller and Martin Schäfer; edited by Peter Przygodda; sound recorded by Martin Müller and Bruno Bollhalder, sound re-recorded by Paul Schöler; art direction by Heidi Lüdi and Bernd Hirskorn; music by Axel Linstädt and performed by Improved Sound Limited.

Filmed along the border regions between West and East Germany. Cannes Film Festival, International Critics Award, 1976.

Cast: Rüdier Vogeler (*Bruno Winter*); Hanns Zischler (*Robert Lander*); Lisa Kreuzer (*Cashier*); Rudolf Schündler (*Robert's father*); Marquard Böhm (*Man who has lost his wife*); Dieter Traier (*Garage owner*); Franziska Stömmer (*Cinema owner*); Patrick Kreuzer (*Little boy*).

Publications:

Script—"Casem..." (script extract) by Wim Wenders in *Film & Doba* (Prague), August 1977; reviews—"Folies bourgeoises" by G. Braucourt in *Ecran* (Paris), July 1976; "*Au fil du temps*" by J. Grant in *Cinéma 76* (Paris), June 1976; "*Au fil du temps*" by P. Maraval in *Cinematographe* (Paris), June 1976; "Movies: Of Men and Justice: A Platonic Friendship" by John Simon in *New York*, 25 October 1976; "Das Freiheitsversprechen und die Frustration: *Im Lauf der Zeit* von Wim Wenders" by H. Wiedemann in *Film und Ton Magazine* (Munich), May 1976; review in *Variety* (New York), 17 March 1976; "*Im Lauf der Zeit* (Kings of the Road)" by R. Combs in *Monthly Film Bulletin* (London), July 1977; "*Kings of the Road*" by M. Tarratt in *Films and Filming* (London), May 1977; books—*The New German Cinema* by John Sandford, Totowa, New Jersey 1980; articles— "Allemagne, annees errantes (*Au fil au temps*)" by P. Bonitzer in *Cahiers du cinéma* (Paris), July/August 1976; "*Kings of the Road* Has Opening at NY Theatre" in *Boxoffice* (Kansas City, Kansas), 11 October 1976; "Cannes 1976...l'ancien & le nouveau" by M. Martin in *Cinema Pratique* (Paris), August/September 1976; "*Au fil du temps*" (interview with Wenders) by H. Wiedemann and F. Mueller-Scherz, translated by B. Hervo, in *Cinéma 76* (Paris), December 1976; "Wim Wenders ueber *Im Lauf der Zeit*" by H. Wiedemann and F. Mueller-Scherz in *Film und Ton Magazine* (Munich), May 1976; article in *Skoop* (Amsterdam), May 1976; article in *Filmkritik* (Munich), July 1976; article in *Hollywood Reporter*, 13 October 1976; "Wim Wenders on *Kings of the Road*" by Wim Wenders in *Monthly Film Bulletin* (London), July 1977; "Den vita duken" by S. Hällen in *Chaplin* (Stockholm), Vol. XX/4, no.(157), 1978; "At Home on the Road: Wim Wenders" by J.M. Kass in *Movietone News* (Seattle), 22 February 1978; "De Emotionele reizen van Wim Wenders" in *Skrien* (Amsterdam), April 1978; "*Nel corso del tempo*" by R. Alvarez in *Filmcritica* (Rome), February 1979; "*Nel corso del tempo*" by G. Fanara in *Cinema Nuovo* (Rome), June 1979.

*   *   *

The first image of *Im Lauf der Zeit* is a title specifying where and when the film was shot. The importance of location becomes obvious from the length of screen time devoted to images of the land, the road, and the small towns along the itinerary which, rather than a script, was the organizing structure of the film.

The choice of subject was made early in the production. The preeminence of the itinerary insured that the spatial dimension would structure the narrative. The choice of route allowed the filmmakers to photograph the east/west borderline guard towers, providing a visual metaphor that functions on several levels. Wenders claims to have chosen the area because it was seldom photographed, an underpopulated, forgotten area he wanted to record on film. He was also able to preserve images of the disappearing small town cinema houses, which served as subject matter in terms of both the condition of the German film industry in 1975 and the history of German cinema. These two facets of the same subject are introduced in a pseudo-interview conducted with an actual movie house owner by a fictional character. Just as important as location is an exactness of time. Wenders and cameraman Robbie Müller were able to make use of the natural light to evoke a precise sense of time of day.

Another significant production decision was to shoot chronologically, allowing the crew to react to what was found along the route—to react to their subject in the sense of documentary filmmaking. It allowed for the workings of chance.

The film does not attempt to reveal the characters psychologically through the editing style. While the film does to a certain extent represent the consciousnesses of its two protagonists, a distance is maintained. The acting is relatively unrevealing, there is little dialogue, and the camera pulls out to extreme long shot at intervals. Most important is an editing style that de-emphasizes point-of-view techniques. This includes the frequent absence of either the glance or reaction shot, a lack of signification registered in the reaction when it is present, and a tendency to cut just after the glance has turned away, rather than on the look.

A primary characteristic of the film is its length, or more exactly the length of time between "events", resulting in its slowness, or sense of duration. The film covers six and a half days in three hours. It is the time between events that shifts the emphasis from story to setting. These are the summary sequences, transition scenes punctuated by wipes and dissolves. The sense of duration also comes from the types of events portrayed on the screen. It is as if Wenders wanted to record actions which usually are excluded from films—the time it takes to enter a room, climb a stairway or the process of an everyday task—in the same way that he wanted to film in an area that is usually ignored as a film location. Elipses in this film tend to be between scenes, not within them.

The third part of a loosely connected trilogy (with *Alice in den Städten* and *Falsche Bewegung*), *Im Lauf der Zeit* possesses a documentary quality dependent primarily on its descriptive nature, a preoccupation with recording and preserving events and a concern for surfaces. Its ending suggests the possibility of change for its protagonists, but it is not so optimistic for the future of film in Germany. The last movie house owner has closed her theater, waiting for a change in the industry, but at least no longer complacent and willing to exhibit whatever given.

—Ann Harris

IN WHICH WE SERVE. Production: Two Cities Productions; black and white, 35mm; running time: 113 mins. Released 1942, released in the U.S. by United Artists.

Produced by Noel Coward; screenplay by Noel Coward; from the experiences of Lord Louis Mountbatten and his ship the H.M.S. Kelly, sunk during the Battle of Crete; directed by Noel

Coward and David Lean; photography by Ronald Neame; edited by Thelma Myers and David Lean; music by Noel Coward.

Filmed in Denham studios, England. Special Academy Award (certificate) to Noel Coward for his Outstanding Production Achievement in *In Which We Serve*, 1942; New York Film Critics Award, Best Film, 1942.

Cast: Noel Coward (*Captain Kinross*); Bernard Miles (*Chief Petty Officer Walter Hardy*); John Mills (*Ordinary Seaman Shorty Blake*); Celia Johnson (*Alix Kinross*); Kay Walsh (*Freda Lewis*); Joyce Carey (*Mrs. Hardy*); Michael Wilding (*Flags*); Richard Attenborough (*Young sailor*); Juliet Mills (*Shorty's daughter*); Daniel Massey (*Kinross's son*).

Publications:

Books—*Noel Coward* by Milton Levin, New York 1968; *A Talent to Amuse* by Morley Sheridan, New York 1969; *A Mirror for England: British Movies from Austerity to Affluence* by Raymond Durgnat, New York 1971; *20 Years of British Film: 1925-1945* by Michael Balcon, New York 1972; *The Cinema of David Lean* by Gerald Pratley, New York 1974; *David Lean and His Films* by Alain Silver and James Ursini, London 1974; *The Rise and Fall of the British Documentary: The Story of the Film Movement Founded by John Grierson* by Elizabeth Sussex, Berkeley 1975; *David Lean: A Guide to References and Resources* by Louis Castelli and Caryn Lynn Cleeland, Boston 1980; articles—"H.M.S. Torrin" in *Newsweek* (New York), 21 December 1942; "Noel Coward Writes, Directs and Gets Very Wet for British Navy" in *Life* (New York), 25 May 1942; "Noel Coward Presents" by C.A. Lejeune in *The New York Times*, 25 October 1942; "Sliding Down the Ways" by C.A. Lejeune in *The New York Times*, 5 April 1942; "Academy Will Not Consider Coward Film" by Thornton Delehanty in the *Herald Tribune* (New York), 10 January 1943; "The Up and Coming Team of Lean and Neame" by C.A. Lejeune in *The New York Times*, 15 June 1947; "Career Inventory From the Lean Viewpoint" by Howard Thompson in *The New York Times*, 9 November 1952; biography of David Lean in *Current Biography Yearbook*, New York 1953; "A Study of David Lean" by J. Holden in *Film Journal* (New York), April 1956; "David Lean" by Stephen Watts in *Films in Review* (New York), April 1959; "Lean—Lover of Life" by Douglas McVay in *Films and Filming* (New York), August 1959; "John Mills" by Alvin Marill in *Films in Review* (New York), August/September 1971; "*In Which We Serve*" by Anthony Slide in *Magill's Survey of Cinema, Vol. II* edited by Frank N. Magill, Englewood Cliffs, New Jersey 1980.

*   *   *

In Which We Serve is one of the better examples of World War II patriotic propaganda. Despite its "stiff upper lip" attitude, it is still moving and memorable unlike *Mrs. Miniver*, for example, which involves a similar upper middle class English group but fails to make them believable.

For his story, Noel Coward turned to the experiences of his friend Lord Mountbatten on board the destroyer H.M.S. Kelly, which was sunk during the Battle of Crete. Coward's film is basically a study of the men of what might have been a sister ship to the Kelly, the H.M.S. Torrin. The family backgrounds of the

men of the Torrin are recalled as the ship sinks. Although the men range from the aristocratic captain down to the ordinary able seaman, the ideology and the lifestyle which the group represents are distinctly middle-class and very much in the tradition that Coward had established with *Cavalcade* and would continue in *This Happy Breed* and *Brief Encounter*.

In Which We Serve is exclusively Noel Coward's film not only because of his involvement as producer, co-director, screenwriter, composer, and star, but also because Coward uses the film to illustrate what he believes Englishmen were fighting for: a love of home, family and country. He claimed there were no heroes in his story and only one heroine—the ship. In reality, the hero of *In Which We Serve* is England and all that England once stood for, and which Coward was to see destroyed by this war and the Socialist government which followed.

Aside from an opening, semi-documentary sequence in which the viewer sees the birth and launching of the destroyer, Coward offers nothing spectacular in the way of camerawork or cinematic technique. The story is told through a series of flashbacks which rely on the dialogue and acting to grip the audience. As the captain who holds the narrative together, Coward is singularly asexual in his relationship with his wife, his ship and his men. He is an Englishman, bringing national pride to his countrymen and understanding of the Coward vision of the English spirit to the world.

In Which We Serve helped to alleviate much of the negative publicity which Coward had been receiving up to this time in Britain. In addition, it aroused considerable praise in the United States, where United Artists purchased the film for release for the unprecedented amount of $750,000. So impressed was Hollywood by *In Which We Serve* that, because it was ineligible for Academy Award consideration, Noel Coward was voted a Special Oscar for "his outstanding production achievement."

—Anthony Slide

———————

INDIA SONG. Production: Sunchild, Les Films Armorial, S. Damiani and A. Cavaglione; color, 35mm; Released 1975.

Produced by Stephane Tchalgaldjeff; screenplay by Marguerite Duras; directed by Marguerite Duras; photography by Bruno Nuytten; edited by Solange Leprince; sound by Michel Vionnet; original music by Carlos D'Alessio, recording at the ORTF by Gaston Sylvestre, Beethoven selection by Gerard Fremy, and "India Song Blues" interpreted by Raoul Verez.

Cast: Delphine Seyrig (*Anne-Marie Stretter*); Michel Lonsdale (*Vice-Counsel of France*); Matthieu Carriere (*Young attaché to the Ambassador*); Didier Flamand (*Young escort to Stretter*); Claude Mann (*Michael Richardson*); Vernon Dobtcheff (*Georges Crawn*); Claude Juan (*A guest*); Satasinh Manila (*Voice of the beggar*); Nicole Hiss, Monique Simonet, Viviane Forrester, Dionys Mascolo, and Marguerite Duras (*Voices of Time*); François Lebrun, Benoit Jacquot, Nicole-Lise Bernheim, Kevork Kutudjan, Daniel Dobbels, Jean-Claude Biette, Marie-Odile Briot, and Pascal Kane (*Voices from the reception*).

Publications:

Scripts—*India Song—texte—theatre—film*, Paris 1973; *India

Song, New York 1976; "*India Song*" (list of shots) by in *Avant-Scène du cinéma* (Paris), 1 April 1979; reviews—"*India Song*" by M. Amiel in *Cinéma* (Paris), June 1975; "D'une Inde à l'autre" by P. Bonitzer in *Cahiers du cinéma* (Paris), July/August 1975; "*India Song*" by A. Lanol in *Jeune Cinéma* (Paris), July/August 1975; "*India Song*" by G. Moskowitz in *Variety* (New York), 18 June 1975; "La Press: *India Song*" in *Avant-Scène du cinéma* (Paris), 1 April 1979; books—*Marguerite Duras tourne un film* by N.-L. Bernheim, Paris 1976; *La Texte divisé* by Marie-Claire Ropars-Wuilleumier, Paris 1981; articles—"Les Yeux fertiles" by B. Amengual in *Positif* (Paris), July/August 1975; "*India Song* and Marguerite Duras* by C. Clarens in *Sight and Sound* (London), winter 1975-76; "Planète Vénus" by C. Clouzot in *Ecran* (Paris), April 1975; "*India Song, A Chant of Love and Death: Marguerite Duras Interviewed*" by J. Dawson in *Film Comment* (New York), November/December 1975; "Marguerite Duras tourne un film" by N.L. Bernheim in *Cinéma 76* (Paris), April 1976; "Marguerite Duras" in *Film en Televisie* (Brussels), November 1976; "Review and Interview: *India Song*" by M. Tarantino in *Take One* (Montreal), no.4, 1976; "*India Song*" by D. McWilliams in *Wide Angle* (Athens, Ohio), no.4, 1977; "*India Song*" by J. Pym in *Monthly Film Bulletin* (London), November 1977; "Tanner and Duras" by P. Straram in *Cinéma Québec* (Montreal), no.10, 1977; "*India Song*" by P. Schepelern in *Kosmorama* (Copenhagen), summer 1978; "La Mort des miroirs: *India Song* and *Son Nom de Venise dans Calcutta désert*" by Marie-Claire Ropars-Wuilleumier in *Avant-Scène du cinéma* (Paris), 1 April 1979; "*India Song*" by I. Escudero in *Cinema 2002* (Madrid), October 1979; "Marguerite Duras" by A. Förster in *Skrien* (Amsterdam), September 1980; "*India Song*" by E. de Kuyper in *Skrien* (Amsterdam), May 1981.

India Song is radical in both form and content. Like Alain Resnais's *L'Année dernière à Marienbad*, Duras's film offers an ambiguity of narrative—a type of enigma which paradoxically calls for a reading and yet makes any reading tentative. The film asks, who is Anne-Marie Stretter, the protagonist? What is her relation to men? To India? Or to a beggar woman whose destiny somehow parallels her own? In answering these questions or, more precisely, in eluding any definitive answer, the film expresses some important feminist perspectives while making innovations in film narrative.

Duras, in this film, finally puts into full practice what Sergei Eisenstein posed in theory 45 years earlier—non-synchronous sound. She separates the verbal track of the film from the visual track in such a way that either the narrator or the dialogue is over-voiced with images that do not correspond on a simple story level. Both the verbal and visual tracks offer us fragmented and disparate pieces of the puzzle of Anne-Marie Stretter that the viewer must re-assemble.

Duras has structured the plot in layers. Madame Stretter, wife of the French Ambassador to colonial India, has a *doppelgänger* in an insane beggar woman who haunts the embassy gardens. While we never see the woman, we hear her distant off-camera cries. Often these cries are juxtaposed with the restrained stance and expression of Madame Stretter. It is as if these cries spring from Madame Stretter's inner self, which has no outlet in the oppressive society she inhabits. The beggar woman, whom we learn has followed Madame Stretter from French Indo-China, perhaps is emblematic of India or other lands burdened by European imperialism; her cries may also be theirs.

A sense of the oppressive lends unity to the film. While we never see colonial India beyond the embassy walls. Duras conveys, through actors' movements and details in the mise-en-scene, the oppressively humid atmosphere. Colonialism is shown oppressing not only the Indians but the Europeans who seem in power. There is a double meaning in Madame Stretter's sexual enslavement of the men around her—all members of the apparent ruling-class. She and India are ineluctable forces that elude and, even to some degree, control the male hierarchy which only seems to oppress them.

Duras explores stasis in all of its forms and ramifications. The characters often remain immobile under the influence of both the sultry atmosphere and class-imposed decorum. *India Song* treats death and life at once, or more precisely, death in life; for, Madame Stretter lives a death amid a mise-en-scene filled with funeral objects and flowers. Further, since sound and visuals do not match in a realistic sense, narration and dialogue seem something vaguely heard from beyond the tomb.

Interlacing the destiny of one woman with another and then comparing their situation to nations occupied by foreigners suggests that *India Song* be read as a film about political oppression on all levels—from personal to national. While some might find Duras's view—that women and, by extension, nations are able to transcend oppression—somewhat naive, the innovative techniques she uses gives this work a haunting quality beyond mere polemics.

—Rodney Farnsworth

THE INFORMER. Production: RKO/Radio Pictures Inc.; 1935; black and white, 35mm; running time: 91 mins.; length: 10 reels. Released 1935.

Produced by Cliff Reid; screenplay by Dudley Nichols; from the novel by Liam O'Flaherty; directed by John Ford; photography by Joseph H. August; edited by George Hively; sound by Hugh McDowell Jr.; art direction by Van Nest Polglase and Charles Kirk; music by Max Steiner; costumes designed by Walter Plunkett.

Academy Awards for Best Director, Best Actor (McLaglen), Best Screenplay, Best Score, 1935; Best Screenplay, Venice Film Festival, 1935; New York Film Critics Awards for Best Picture and Best Director, 1935.

Cast: Victor McLaglen (*Gypo Nolan*); Heather Angel (*Mary McPhillip*); Preston Foster (*Dan Gallagher*); Margot Grahame (*Katie Madden*); Wallace Ford (*Frankie McPhillip*); Una O'Connor (*Mrs. McPhillip*); J.M. Kerrigan (*Terry*); Joseph Sauers (*Bartly Mulholland*); Neil Fitzgerald (*Tommy Connor*); Donald Meek (*Peter Mulligan*); D'Arcy Corrigan (*Blind man*); Gaylord Pendleton (*Dennis Daly*); May Boley (*Madame Betty*); Leo McCabe (*Donahue*); Francis Ford (*Flynn*); Grizelda Harvey (*The Lady*); Dennis O'Dea.

Publications:

Scripts—*The Informer* (condensed screenplay) by Dudley Nichols in *Theatre Arts* (New York), August 1951; "*Le Mouchard*" (screenplay) by Dudley Nichols in *Avant-Scène du cinéma* (Paris), February 1965; books—*Express to Hollywood* by Victor McLaglen, London 1934; *John Ford* by Jean Mitry, Paris 1954; *Our Modern Art* by Ernest Callenbach, Chicago 1955; *Novels into Films* by George Bluestone, Berkeley 1961; *John Ford* by Philippe Haudiquet, Paris 1966; *The Cinema of John Ford* by John Baxter, New York 1971; *John Ford* by Joseph McBride and Michael Wilmington, London 1975; *John Ford* by Claude Beylie in *Anthologie du Cinéma*, Paris 1976; *John Ford* by Peter Bogdanovich, Berkeley 1978; *John Ford* by Andrew Sinclair, New York 1979; *Pappy: The Life of John Ford* by Dan Ford, Englewood Cliffs, New Jersey 1979; articles— "John Ford" by Jean Mitry, translated by Anne and Thornton K. Brown, in *Films in Review* (New York), August/September 1955; "The Informer" by Alan Stanbrook in *Films and Filming* (New York), July 1960; "The 5 Worlds of John Ford" by Douglas McVay in *Films and Filming* (London), June 1962; "Notes on the Art of John Ford" by Michael Barkun in *Film Culture* (New York), no.25, 1962; John Ford issue, *Présence du Cinéma* (Paris), March 1965; "L'Univers familier de John Ford" by Philippe Haudiquet in *Avant-Scène du cinéma* (Paris), February 1965; "Special John Ford" in *Cahiers du cinéma* (Paris), October 1966; John Ford issue, *Velvet Light Trap* (Madison, Wisconsin), August 1971; issue devoted to Ford, *Focus on Film* (London), spring 1971; "John Ford" by Lindsay Anderson in *Cinema* (Beverly Hills), spring 1971; issue on "Ford's Stock Company" in *Filmkritik* (Munich), January 1972; "The Informer" by Dan Scapperotti in *Magill's Survey of Cinema, Vol. II* edited by Frank N. Magill, Englewood Cliffs, New Jersey 1980.

*   *   *

John Ford was the perfect choice to direct the film version of Liam O'Flaherty's novel about the Sinn Fein Rebellion in Dublin in 1922 as Ford's Irish heritage proved invaluable in setting the background for the film. *The Informer* was Ford's 74th film as a director and he would do 48 more before his retirement in 1966.

Flaherty's novel was first filmed as an early talkie in Great Britain in 1929 with Lars Hansen in the leading role. Six years later, Ford's version was released through RKO Radio Pictures. The mood piece surprised everyone, including the studio, by winning four Academy Awards and moving John Ford into the top echelon of Hollywood directors and Victor McLaglen into the role of one of the film industry's most trusted character actors.

Strictly observing the unities of time and space, the film traces Gypo Nolan from betrayal to death in just one 12-hour period. Whether Ford was aware he was making a *film noir* or not, he preceded the forties spate of "dark" films by having *The Informer* take place entirely at night.

The film opens with Gypo encountering a poster stating that there is a reward out for information leading to the capture of Frankie McPhillip, his rebel friend. Tearing the sign down and tossing it away, Gypo goes on his way only to discover, in one of Ford's most brilliant visual moments, that the poster takes on a life of its own and follows him down the street, eventually blowing onto his leg and clinging to it. The visual imagery continues as the viewer is introduced to Gypo's girlfriend Katie as a lovely madonna who suddenly changes into a bleach-blonde streetwalker by merely removing her scarf.

Reasoning that he and Katie would be able to get a boat to the United States with the money offered to turn Frankie in, Gypo informs on the fugitive to the police. As Frankie visits clandestinely with his mother and sister, he is ambushed and killed. Gypo gets his reward, but is soon under suspicion by rebel leader Dan Gallagher. Celebrating by getting drunk, Gypo is caught and, having spent all the blood money, confesses. He hides in Katie's apartment and when she innocently reveals his whereabouts, he is shot. The wounded Gypo staggers to a church where Frankie's mother is praying. She forgives him and he dies under the altar.

Much has been said about composer Max Steiner's contribution to *The Informer*. The music suitably underscores all the action from the atmospheric beginning to the religious ending. The flawless cast, composed mainly of Irish-born actors, make the film and the plot believable, and the lighting, costuming, art direction and cinematography all contribute to the stifling and tense atmosphere. Although over 50 years old, this melodrama still holds up well in a period when another Irish rebellion has been raging in the 1980s.

—James Limbacher

———————

INTOLERANCE. Production: Wark Producing Company, some sources list studio as Epoch Releasing Corp.; black and white (with some scenes tinted in original release prints), 35mm, silent; running time: about 220 mins., some versions are 129 mins., original version 8 hrs. Released 5 September 1916, New York.

Produced and directed by D.W. Griffith; scenario by D.W. Griffith; photography by G.W. (Billy) Bitzer and Karl Brown; edited by James and Rose Smith; production design by (set decorator and architect) Frank Wortman; art direction by Walter L. Hall and others; music score which accompanied the film on its initial release arranged by Joseph Carl Breil and D.W. Griffith; assistants included Eric von Stroheim, W.S. Van Dyke, Tod Browning, Joseph Henabery, Edward Dillon, George Siegman, Lloyd Ingraham, and others.

Filmed fall 1914-July 1916 in Hollywood, basically on outdoor sets constructed by Griffith and his crew. Cost: about $386,000, though figures differ in various sources.

Cast: The Modern Story: Mae Marsh (*The Dear One*); Robert Harron (*The Boy*); Fred Turner (*The Girl's Father*); Sam de Grasse (*Jenkins*); Vera Lewis (*Miss Jenkins*); Walter Long (*Musketeer of the Slums*); Ralph Lewis (*The Governor*); Monte Blue (*Strike Leader*); Tod Browning (*Race car owner*); Miriam Cooper (*The Friendless One*). The Babylonian Story: Alfred Page (*Belshazzar*); Constance Talmadge (*The Mountain Girl*); Elmer Clifton (*The Rhapsode*); Seena Owen (*The Princess Beloved*); George Siegman (*Cyrus the Persian*); Tully Marshall (*High Priest of Bel*); Carl Stockdale (*King Nabonidus*); Elmo Lincoln (*Mighty Man of Valor*); Jewel Carmen, Carol Dempster, Mildred Harris, Alma Rubens, Pauline Starke, Eve Southern, Natalie Talmadge, and Anna Mae Walthall (*Slave girls and dancers*); Frank Campeau, Donald Crisp, Douglas Fairbanks, DeWolfe Hopper, Wilfred Lucas, Owen Moore, Sir Herbert Beerbohm Tree, Tammany Young, others (*Soldiers, courtiers, etc.*). The French Story: Margery Wilson (*Brown Eyes*); Eugene Pallette (*Prosper Latour*); Spottiswoode Aitken (*Father*); Ruth Handford (*Mother*); Josephine Crowell (*Catherine de Medici*); Frank Bennett (*Charles IX*); Maxfield Stanley (*Duc d'Anjou*); Constance Talmadge (*Marguerite de Valois*). The Judean Story:

Howard Gaye (*The Nazarene*); Lillian Langdon (*Mary*); Olga Grey (*Mary Magdalene*); Bessie Love (*Bride of Cana*); George Walsh (*Bridegroom*); W.S. Van Dyke (*Wedding guest*). Lillian Gish (*The Woman Who Rocks the Cradle*).

Publications:

Scripts—*Intolerance: The Film by David Wark Griffith, Shot-by-Shot Analysis* by Theodore Huff, New York 1966; "*Intolerance*: Schéma narratif d'un drame de comparaisons" in *Cahiers du cinéma* (Paris), spring 1972; books—*An Index to the Creative Work of D.W. Griffith* by Seymour Stern, supplement to *Sight and Sound*, index series, London 1946-47; *Film Form* by Sergei Eisenstein, New York 1949; *The Movies in the Age of Innocence* by Edward Wagenknecht, Norman, Oklahoma 1962; *The Art of the Film* by Ernest Lindgren, New York 1963; *The Great Films: 50 Golden Years of Motion Pictures* by Bosley Crowther, New York 1967; *The Parade's Gone By...* by Kevin Brownlow, New York 1968; *The Movies, Mr. Griffith and Me* by Lillian Gish, New York 1969; *Griffith and the Rise of Hollywood* by Paul O'Dell, New York 1970; *The Man Who Invented Hollywood: The Autobiography of D.W. Griffith* edited by James Hart, Louisville, Kentucky 1972; *D.W. Griffith: His Life and Work* by Robert Henderson, New York 1972; *Spellbound in Darkness* by George C. Pratt, Connecticut, 1972; *Billy Bitzer: His Story* by G.W. Bitzer, New York 1973; *Adventures with D.W. Griffith* by Karl Brown, New York 1973; *The Films of D.W. Griffith* by Edward Wagenknecht and Antony Slide, New York 1975; articles—in *The New York Times*, 6 September 1916; "*Intolerance*" by Floyd Dell in *The Masses* (New York), November 1916; "After the Play" by George Soule in the *New Republic* (New York), 30 September 1916; "*Intolerance*: The Sun Play of the Ages" by G.W. Bitzer in *International Photographer* (Hollywood), October 1934; "Rush Hour in Babylon" by J.C. Trewin in *Sight and Sound* (London), spring 1949; "*Intolerance*" by C.E.M. Joad in *New Statesman and Nation* (London), February 1949; "The D.W. Griffith Influence" by Joseph and Harry Feldman in *Films in Review* (New York), July/August 1950; "Lillian Gish" by Romano Tozzi in *Films in Review* (New York), December 1962; "Bessie Love" by Harold Dunham in *Films in Review* (New York), February 1959; "*Intolerance*" by Philippe Esnault in *Cinéma* (Paris), 1960; "Blanche Sweet" by DeWitt Bodeen in *Films in Review* (New York), November 1965; "The Films of David Wark Griffith" by Richard J. Meyer in *Film Comment* (New York), fall/winter 1967; "Les Aventures de l'idée" by P. Baudry in *Cahiers du cinéma* (Paris), July/August 1972; "Les Aventures de l'idée, Part II" by P. Baudry in *Cahiers du cinéma* (Paris), September/October 1972; "*Intolerance*" by D.W. Griffith, reprinted in *Cahiers du cinéma* (Paris), January/February 1972; "Note su alcuni fotogrammi di *Intolerance*" by E. Bruno in *Filmcritica* (Rome), November/December 1972; "The Films of D.W. Griffith: A Style for the Times" by Alan Casty in *Journal of Popular Film* (Bowling Green, Ohio), spring 1972; "Essai de lecture thématique de *Intolerance*" by M. Oms in *Cahiers du cinéma* (Paris), spring 1972; "Tolérance de la critique" in *Cahiers du cinéma* (Paris), spring 1972; "D.W. Griffith: Some Sources" by Bernard Hanson in *The Art Bulletin* (New York), December 1972; "Dossier Intolerance" in *Les Cahiers de la Cinémathèque* (Lyons), spring 1972; "*Intolerance*" by Claude Beylie in *Ecran* (Paris), February 1973; issue on Griffith in *Films in Review* (New York), October 1975; "*Cabiria e Intolerance* tra il serio ed il faceto" by A. Belluccio in *Bianco e Nero* (Rome), May/August 1975; "*Cabiria e Intolerance*" by A. Belluccio in *Bianco e Nero* (Rome), May/August 1975; "D.W. Griffith's *Intolerance*: A Sun-Play of the Ages" by Seymour Stern in *The Essential Cinema*, New York 1975; "*Intolerance* and the Soviets: A Historical Investigation" by V. Kepley Jr. in *Wide Angle* (Athens, Ohio), no.1, 1979; "On First Looking into Griffith's Babylon: A Historical Investigation" by Russell Merritt in *Wide Angle* (Athens, Ohio), no.1, 1979; "*Intolerance*" by J. Pym in *Monthly Film Bulletin* (London), May 1979.

*   *   *

Critical judgment remains sharply divided on *Intolerance*, Griffith's most expensive and flamboyant spectacle. Those critics who pronounce the film a failure generally point to the four stories which, they claim, are thematically too diverse to be effectively collated. Taking their cue from Eisenstein's famous indictment, they argue that the film suffers from purposeless fragmentation and thematic incoherence. Others, notably Vachel Lindsay, George Sadoul, Edward Wagenknecht, and more recently Pauline Kael, list *Intolerance* among the masterworks, stressing its formal complexity, experimental daring, and thematic richness. René Clair, taking a middle position, writes, "it combines extraordinary lyric passages, realism, and psychological detail, with nonsense, vulgarity, and painful sentimentality."

Historians agree, however, that *Intolerance* remains Griffith's most influential film, and that among its most precocious students were the Soviet directors of the 1920s. As Vance Kepley states, "When *Intolerance* was shown in the Soviet Union in 1919, it popularized a montage style already evolving in the hands of Soviet artists. It was reputedly studied in the Moscow Film Institute for the possibilities of montage and "agitational" cinema (agit-film) and leading Soviet directors, including Eisenstein, Pudovkin, and Kuleshov, acknowledged a debt to Griffith in their writings."

True to his customary practice of starting one film while finishing another, Griffith began work on *Intolerance* while editing *The Birth of a Nation* in the fall of 1914. *Intolerance* began with the modern story, originally entitled "The Mother and the Law." It was intended as a companion piece to *The Escape* (released by Mutual earlier that year), a study of white slavery and the corruption of city slums.

"The Mother and the Law" was virtually completed before *The Birth of a Nation* was released. not until May, 1915, after *Birth*'s controversies were at their peak, did he resume work on it. Determined to surpass the Civil War movie, he decided to expand his modern story to epic proportions. He built lavish sets (notably, the Mary Jenkins ballroom and the Chicago courtroom) and—most important—expanded the story to include the famous strike sequence.

This was, in part, an effort to capitalize on the headlines surrounding John D. Rockefeller, Jr., who had been called up before the Commission on Industrial Relations to explain his role in the 1914 Ludlow massacre. *Intolerance*'s strike is loosely based on this incident, in which 23 striking employees of Rockefeller's Colorado Fuel and Iron Company were shot down by the national guard. In these new sequences, Griffith also attacked the Rockefeller Foundation, which, like its founder, came under severe public criticism as the creation of a hypocritical plutocrat, a philanthropy paid for by the exploitation of workers to enhance the reputation of their taskmaster.

Griffith continued shooting his modern story through the summer of 1915. Meanwhile, he began work on a French story, directly patterned after Meyerbeer's *Les Huguenots* which had enjoyed great popularity at the Metropolitan Opera with Caruso and Toscanini. Originally, this was to be the lustrous counterpoint to the drab modern story. In original prints, the interiors of the Louvre palace were hand-tinted, while considerable attention was paid to royal costumes and lavish Paris sets.

Not until the end of the year did he begin his most elaborate and expensive story. The Hall for Belshazzar's Feast has become perhaps the best-known set created for a silent film. Griffith had his set festooned with Egyptian bas-reliefs, Hindu elephant gods, and Assyrian bearded bulls. Practically every Near Eastern style was represented somewhere on the walls or in the costumes— except the styles of Babylon. Until Douglas Fairbanks's castle set for Robin Hood, it remained the largest backdrop ever created for a movie scene.

The result, when combined with the Passion sequence, was a conglomerate of stories and styles in search of a unifying principle. Part morality play and part three-ring circus, the movie was part of the new eclectic aesthetic that had all but buried the older ideal of organic synthesis. Along with Scott Joplin's "Treemonisha" and Charles Ives's Third Symphony, it remains one of the period's great hybrids.

As such, it won uniformly enthusiastic critical notices, but proved disappointing at the box office. Produced at a cost of $386, 000 (almost four times the expense of *The Birth of a Nation*) and endowed with an extraordinary cast, it left audiences cold. Although the film cost considerably less and earned more than historians have generally reported, Griffith himself was convinced he had failed. Two years after its release, he released the modern and Babylonian episodes as two separate films. Traditionally, these productions have been dismissed as footnotes to *Intolerance*, simple attempts to relieve the producer of *Intolerance*'s burden of debt. Several recent critics, however, have argued that the modern story—released as *The Mother and the Law*—is improved when separated from the other stories and should be evaluated as a self-contained feature.

Griffith was the most eclectic of American directors, an artist whose work consistently absorbed and reflected American popular culture. Of all his films, *Intolerance* remains the one most firmly rooted in its own time, a work representing the cultural phenomena of its day. Probably no film before *Citizen Kane* touched on as many aspects of American popular taste.

Griffith's instincts cannot be called infallible. In his sweeping dragnet of the fine arts, he intuitively missed every important art movement of his time; the raw materials he gathered were an unsorted miscellany of official art treasures (like the Cluny unicorn tapestries and the Assyrian winged bulls) and parochial 19th century *kitsch*. As a muckraker, he had trouble distinguishing important social evils (like America's bloody labor wars and horrible prison conditions) from ephemeral parochial problems. The demons he fought most bitterly, like the Anti-Saloon League, the Rockefeller Foundation, and settlement workers, represented issues far more complex than he ever perceived. He had infinite charity for prodigals, but none for Pharisees, and he depicts "uplifters" as onesidedly in *Intolerance* as he depicted blacks in *The Birth of a Nation*.

Today, *Intolerance* is usually discussed according to memorable isolated sequences, notably Belshazzar's feast, beginning with its famous crane shot; the strike sequence; the courtship of Mae Marsh and Bobby Harron; the courtroom scene with the famous close-ups of Mae Marsh's hands; and the Babylonian battles. Although considerable attention has recently been paid to Griffith's treatment of mise-en-scene, the most durable aesthetic debate continues to center on his intercutting techniques, especially the rhythmic climax built on four intertwined catastrophes, one averted, the others not.

—Russell Merritt

INVASION OF THE BODY SNATCHERS. Production: Allied Artists Pictures Corp.; 1956; black and white, 35mm, Superscope; running time: 80 mins. Released 5 February 1956.

Produced by Walter Wanger; screenplay by Daniel Mainwaring, and according to some sources uncredited scriptwriting by Sam Peckinpah; from the novel *The Body Snatchers* by Jack Finney; directed by Don Siegel; photography by Ellsworth Fredericks; edited by Robert S. Eisen; sound engineered by Ralph Butler, sound edited by Del Harris; production design by Joseph Kish; art direction by Edward Haworth; music by Carmen Dragon, music edited by Jerry Irvin; special effects by Milt Rice.

Filmed 1955.

Cast: Kevin McCarthy (*Dr. Miles Bennel*); Dana Wynter (*Becky Driscoll*); Larry Gates (*Dr. Dan Kauffmann*); King Donovan (*Jack*); Carolyn Jones (*Theodora*); Jean Willes (*Sally*); Ralph Dumke (*Nick Grivett*); Virginia Christine (*Wilma Lentz*); Tom Fadden (*Uncle Ira Lentz*); Kenneth Patterson (*M. Driscoll*); Whit Bissell (*Dr. Hill*); Sam Peckinpah (*Charlie, Buckholtz, gas company employee*); Guy Way (*Sam Janzek*); Eileen Stevens (*Mrs. Grimaldi*); Beatrice Maude (*Grandmother Grimaldi*); Bobby Clark (*Jimmy Grimaldi*); Jean Andren (*Aunt Eleda Lentz*); Everett Glass (*Dr. Ed Percy*); Richard Deacon (*Dr. Harvey Bassett*); Dabbs Greer (*Mac*); Marie Selland (*Martha*); Pat O'Malley (*Man carrying baggage*); Guy Rennie and Harry J. Vejar (*with man carrying baggage*).

Publications:

Script—"*L'Invasion des profanateurs de sepultures*" by Daniel Mainwaring in *Avant-Scène du cinéma* (Paris), 15 July 1979; reviews—by Marcel Martin in *Les Lettres Françaises* (Paris), 15 November 1967; "La Presse" in *Avant-Scène du cinéma* (Paris), 15 July 1979; books—*Filmgoer's Companion: An International Encyclopedia* by Leslie Halliwell, New York 1970; *Cinema of the Fantastic* by Chris Steinbrunner and Burt Goldblatt, New York 1972; *Focus on the Science Fiction Film* edited by William Johson, Englewood Cliffs, New Jersey 1972; *Don Siegel: Director* by Stuart M. Kaminsky, New York 1974; *American Film Genres* by Stuart Kaminsky, Dayton, Ohio 1974; *The Science-Fiction Pictures* edited by James Robert Parish, Metuchen, New Jersey 1977; articles—"Esoterica: Filmography" by Andrew Sarris in *Film Culture* (New York), spring 1963; "Out for the Kill—Part 1" by David Austen in *Films and Filming* (London), May 1968; article by Raymond Durgnat in *Films and Filming* (London), February 1969; "Don Siegel: Time and Motion, Attitudes and Genre" by Robert Mundy in *Cinema* (London), February 1970; "The Films of Don Siegel and Sam Fuller" by Manny Farber in *December* (Los Angeles), nos.1-2, 1970; "Monsters from the Id" by Margaret Tarratt in *Films and Filming* (London), December 1970; article by Guy Braucourt in *La Revue de Cinéma-Image et son* (Paris), April 1970; "The Pod Society Vs. the Rugged Individualist" by Charles T. Gregory in *Journal of Popular Film* (Bowling Green, Ohio), winter 1972; "Don Siegel" by Stuart Kaminsky and "The B-Movie as Art" by Peter Bogdanovich in *Take One* (Montreal), June 1972; "Don Siegel" by Judith M. Kass in *The Hollywood Professionals, Vol. 4*, London 1975; "De stjålne kroppe" by P. Nørgaard in *Kosmorama* (Copenhagen), summer 1975; article by Jean-François Tarnowski in *L'Ecran Fantastique* (Paris), no.3, 1977; "Les Profanateurs de titres" by Jean-Claude Romer in *Avant-Scène du cinéma* (Paris), 15 July 1979; "We'd Fight...We Had To: The

Body Snatchers" by G.M. Johnson in *Journal of Popular Film and Television* (Bowling Green, Ohio), no.1, 1979; "*Midnight Marquee* Review: *Invasion of the Body Snatchers*" by G.J. Svehla in *Midnight Marquee* (Baltimore), September 1979; "*Body Snatchers* op de montagetafel: pseudo-lijken in peulen", (shot analysis), by W. Verstappen in *Skoop* (Netherlands), December/January 1979; "Hoe Siegel tijd weet te rekken" by W. Verstappen in *Skoop* (Netherlands), December/January 1979; "Pods Over San Francisco" by C. Freund in *Film Comment* (New York), January/February 1979; "*Invasion of the Body Snatchers*" by Elizabeth McDermott in *Magill's Survey of Cinema, Vol. II* edited by Frank N. Magill, Englewood Cliffs, New Jersey 1980; "El otro, el mismo" by A. Beltrán in *Contracampo* (Madrid), February 1981; "*Invasion of the Body Snatchers*: Pods Then and Now" by S. Higashi in *Jump Cut* (Chicago), March 1981.

*   *   *

There are no moments of great violence in *Invasion of the Body Snatchers*. We see no one die on screen and, technically, no one dies in the film. There are no monsters and only a few special effects, which are confined totally to the construction of a few pods shown but briefly. The essence of *Invasion of the Body Snatchers* is its aura of normalcy. It is normalcy, the acceptance of the status quo, the desire to escape from the pain of the abnormal that creates the sense of horror in the film.

The thematic goals of *Invasion of the Body Snatchers* are beautifully expressed in content (the dialogue primarily) and style (the visual body). The fact that one cannot escape from the body-snatching pods is indicated by the director, Don Siegel, in the way the pods are hidden before they take over the minds of the humans. We see them in basements, automobile trunks, a greenhouse, and on a pool table. That the pods are virtually indestructible is shown by Dr. Miles Bennel's repeated attempts to destroy them. When Miles discovers the pods growing in the greenhouse, we are shown a ritual vampire killing. The camera is low in the point of view of the pod. We see Miles's anguished face as he drives the pitchfork down and leaves it like a stake through the heart. But it is not enough. Other pods appear in his trunk. He burns them in much the same way we have seen so many monsters burning in films, only to rise again in a sequel. The pods are not traditional terrors; they are indestructible modern terrors. There is no catharsis in the presentation of a monster being destroyed by love or religious ritual. Here it is the monsters who will prevail.

Siegel expects that his warning of a "pod invasion" will not be heeded. This is indicated in the film in a variety of ways. Perhaps the most striking is that of the small boy, Jimmy Grimaldi, whom we meet along with Miles at the beginning of the picture. As Jimmy runs down the road, he is stopped by Miles. Jimmy informs him that Mrs. Grimaldi (who has become a pod) is not his mother any more. Miles doesn't believe him. The world will not believe him and eventually the boy becomes a pod. Near the end of the film we also see Miles running down the road, searching for someone to tell that the people of Santa Mira (the very name of the town—"mira" in Spanish means "look"—calls attention to itself, and cries to be understood or heeded as a warning) have been consumed by pods. Like Jimmy, we know Miles will not be believed.

A sense of impending doom, or a sense of helplessness in combatting the pods, is indicated by depicting Miles as constantly being driven into dark corners and forced to hide. His world is threatened by the pods, and he is reduced to constricted areas of existence. For example, he and Becky Driscoll have to hide in a closet in his office; the camera moves with them into the closet. Through a small hole in the door we see a human-turned-pod turn on a light outside. Later Miles and Becky are forced to hide in a hole in the floor of a cave which they cover with boards. We see the pod people rush over them from Miles's and Becky's point of view. In effect, the places to run have been repeatedly reduced and we suffer the confinement of choices with the protagonists.

One of the most striking and famous sequences in the film is where Miles, having finally escaped from Santa Mira, suddenly finds himself on a highway with hundreds of cars passing him, full of people who are unwilling to listen to him, and thus unwilling to save themselves. The setting is dark with Miles in a sea of machines; the people are hiding within these machines, perhaps the first step toward becoming pods. As he stands on the highway, a truck passes with the names of various cities on it. In the truck, Miles finds the pods, and he realizes they are being taken to the big cities listed on the side of the truck. We feel as hopeless in the face of the image as Miles.

Finally, an important contribution to the total power of the film lies in the performances. Kevin McCarthy (as Miles) conveys a growing frenzy combined with an unfaltering sense of determination. A less restrained actor might well have proved a disaster. The other actors have the burden of appearing normal while at the same time suggesting that they are not. It is in the performances that this ambiguity is carried. Siegel seldom relies on low key lighting, ominous shadows, radical camera angles or shock cutting to carry the terror of the situation. It is in the matter-of-fact quality of the presentation that the film holds its power; and it is Siegel's handling of actors which contributes considerably to the film which Leslie Halliwell calls "the most subtle film in the science-fiction cycle, with no visual horror whatever."

—Stuart M. Kaminsky

THE IRON HORSE. Production: Fox Film Corp.; 1924; black and white, 35mm, silent; running time: about 119 mins.; length: 12 reels, 11,335 feet, later cut for release to ll reels, 10,424 feet. Released 4 October 1925 (premiered 28 August 1924, New York).

Produced by William Fox; scenario by Charles Kenyon; from an original story by Charles Kenyon and John Russell; titles by Charles Darnton; directed by John Ford; photography by George Schneiderman, additional photography by Burnett Guffey; production design; music score by Erno Rapee.

Filmed on location in the Nevada desert.

Cast: George O'Brien (*Davy Brandon*); Madge Bellamy (*Miriam Marsh*); Cyril Chadwick (*Jesson*); Fred Kohler (*Deroux*); Gladys Hulette (*Ruby*); J. Farrell MacDonald (*Corporal Casey*); James Marcus (*Judge Haller*); James Welch (*Private Schultz*); Walter Rogers (*General Dodge*); George Waggner (*Col. Buffalo Bill Cody*); Jack Padjan (*Wild Bill Hickok*); Charles O'Malley (*Major North*); Charles Newton (*Collis P. Huntington*); Charles Edward Bull (*Abraham Lincoln*); Colin Chase (*Tony*); Delbert Mann (*Charles Crocker*); Chief Big Tree (*Cheyenne Chief*); Chief White Spear (*Sioux Chief*); Edward Piel (*Old Chinaman*); James Gordon (*David Brandon, Sr.*); Winston Miller (*Davy, as* child); Peggy Cartwright (*Miriam, as a child*); Thomas Durant (*Jack Ganzhorn*); Stanhope Wheatcroft (*John Hay*); Frances Teague (*Polka Dot*); Will Walling (*Thomas Marsh*); and, according to publicity releases, about 4800 extras.

Publications:

Review—in *The New York Times*, 29 August 1924; books—*An Index to the Films of John Ford* by W.P. Wooten, supplement to *Sight and Sound Index* series, London 1948; *John Ford* by Jean Mitry, Paris 1954; *The Westerns: From Silents to Cinerama* by George N. Fenin and William K. Everson, New York 1962; *John Ford* by Philippe Haudiquet, Paris 1966; *Hollywood in the 20s* by David Robinson, New York 1968; *The Cinema of John Ford* by John Baxter, New York 1971; *John Ford* by Joseph McBride and Michael Wilmington, London 1975; *The Great Western Pictures* by James Robert Parish and Michael Pitts, Metuchen, New Jersey 1976; *John Ford* by Peter Bogdanovich, Berkeley 1978; *John Ford* by Andrew Sinclair, New York 1979; *Pappy: The Life of John Ford* by Dan Ford, Englewood Cliffs, New Jersey 1979; articles—"The 5 Worlds of John Ford" by Douglas McVay in *Films and Filming* (London), June 1962; "George O'Brien" by David Martin in *Films in Review* (New York), November 1962; "The Films of John Ford" by George Mitchell in *Films in Review* (New York), March 1963; special Ford issue of *Présence du cinéma* (Paris), March 1965; "Special John Ford" in *Cahiers du cinéma* (Paris), October 1966; "Our Way West", interview by Burt Kennedy in *Films and Filming* (London), October 1969; special Ford issue of *Focus on Film* (London), spring 1971; special Ford issue of *Velvet Light Trap* (Madison, Wisconsin), August 1971; "Film Favorites" by Stuart Byron in *Film Comment* (New York), November/December 1972; "Straight Shooting" by J. McBride in *Silent Picture* (London), winter/spring 1972; "The Birth of a Style" by J. Mitry in *Wide Angle* (Athens, Ohio), no.4, 1978; "*The Iron Horse*" by J. Pym in *Monthly Film Bulletin* (London), June 1980.

*   *   *

John Ford in *The Iron Horse* deals with an actual event, the building of the transcontinental railroad. Rather than as an historical document, however, the film is more interesting as the beginning of Ford's efforts at mythologizing Abraham Lincoln, and as an example of D.W. Griffith's influence on Ford's early work.

In such films as *The Prisoner of Shark Island* and *Young Mr. Lincoln*, Ford's interest in Lincoln can be seen as a unifier of opposing forces, whether they be North and South during the Civil War, or two participants in a pie-cooking contest. In *The Iron Horse*, Lincoln plays the same role on both a grand and trivial scale. Long before becoming president, he encourages a young boy, who is about to move away, and his girlfriend to pledge that they will find one another once again as adults. Even in adolescent affairs of the heart, Ford posits Lincoln as a reconciler. Later, as president, he begins the building of the railroad, with tracks starting from both the east and the west but designed to met in the middle. Not only does Lincoln unify the nation politically after the Civil War, but he unifies it literally, as a champion of the Industrial Revolution.

In the beginning of the film, after the pledge by the young couple, Lincoln tells a skeptic that there will indeed, one day, be a

cross-country railroad. A title card says of Lincoln, "He sees the inevitable—a great nation pushing Westward." Lincoln is like a soothsayer, able to predict his country's future. At the end of the film, after Lincoln has died and the rails have been joined, another title card says of the late president, "His truth is marching on." Here, Ford eternalizes Lincoln. Even after his death, he will nonetheless effect the future of his country.

The narrative of *The Iron Horse* takes its shape from *Birth of a Nation*. Like Griffith's film, this one is a personal story told against an historical backdrop. While Griffith dealt with the Little Colonel's family during the Civil War and Reconstruction, here the prime concern is whether Davy, the boy who left at the beginning and who now, as an adult, works on the railroad, will be able to avenge the death of his father. Certainly, the epic scale of *The Iron Horse* is also reminiscent of Griffith's film. And so, too, is the handling of the villains. In *Birth of a Nation*, the newly-freed blacks, whose leader was half white, were the vengeful enemies of Southern whites. In Ford's film, the railroad workers must constantly fight the Indians, whose leader is a white man pretending to be a tribal member.

The film was well received at its release, both as history and as drama. *The New York Times* said that Ford shows things "truthfully," and "with thoroughness and pleasing imagination...This is an instructive and inspiring film." Today, the film is one of Ford's less appreciated works, overshadowed by the masterpieces from the sound era.

—Eric Smoodin

———

IT HAPPENED ONE NIGHT. Production: Columbia Pictures Corp.; 1934; black and white, 35mm; running time: 105 mins. Released 23 February 1934.

Produced by Harry Cohn; screenplay by Robert Riskin; from the story "Night Bus" by Samuel Hopkins Adams; directed by Frank Capra; photography by Joseph Walker; edited by Gene Havlick; sound recorded by E.E. Bernds; art direction by Stephen Gooson; music direction by Louis Silvers; costumes designed by Robert Kalloch.

Filmed between Thanksgiving and Christmas 1933. Academy Awards, Best Picture, Best Actor (Gable), Best Actress (Colbert), Best Directing, and Best Writing-Adaptation, 1934.

Cast: Clark Gable (*Peter Warne*); Claudette Colbert (*Ellie Andrews*); Walter Connolly (*Alexander Andrews*); Roscoe Karns (*Mr. Shapely*); Jameson Thomas (*King Westley*); Alan Hale (*Danker*); Wallis Clark (*Lovington*); Harry Bradley (*Henderson*); Arthur Hoyt (*Zeke*); Blanche Frederic (*Zeke's wife*); Ward Bond (*Bus driver*).

Publications:

Review-by Mordaunt Hall in *The New York Times*, 23 February 1934; books—*Frank Capra* by Richard Griffith, London 1951; *Hollywood in the Thirties* by John Baxter, New York 1968; *The Films of Clark Gable* by Gabe Essoe, New York 1970; *Name Above the Title* by Frank Capra, New York 1971; *The Films of Frank Capra* by Donald Willis, Metuchen, New Jersey 1974; *Frank Capra: The Man and his Films* by John Raeburn and

Richard Glatzer, Ann Arbor, Michigan 1975; *Talking Pictures* by Richard Corliss, New York 1975; *The Cinema of Frank Capra* by Leland Poague, New York 1975; *The Films of Frank Capra* by Victor Scherle and William Turner Levy, Secaucus, New Jersey 1977; articles—"Hollywood's New Miracle Man" by Kirtley Baskette in *Photoplay* (Los Angeles), December 1934; interview with Frank Capra in *Motion Picture* (New York), July 1935; "Comedy's Greatest Era" by James Agee in *Life* (New York), 4 September 1949; "*It Happened One Night*" in *Films and Filming* (London), May/June 1958; "Clark Gable" by Carlos Clarens in *Films in Review* (New York), December 1960; article by Marcel Martin in *Les Lettres françaises* (Paris), 27 December 1962; "Capra and the American Dream" by James Price in *London Magazine*, January 1964; "Frank Capra and the Cinema of Populism" by Jeffrey Richards in *Cinema* (London), February 1970; "Claudette Colbert" by Joseph B. Pacheco Jr. in *Films in Review* (New York), May 1970; special Capra issue of *Positif* (Paris), December 1971; "Capra, 74, Looks Back at Film Career" by Howard Thompson in *The New York Times*, 24 June 1971; "Capra and Riskin" by Richard Corliss in *Film Comment* (New York), November/December 1972; "A Decade of Good Deeds and Wonderful Lives: Under Capracorn" by Stephen Handzo in *Film Comment* (New York), vol.8, no.4, 1972; "Capra Counts His Oscars" by Elliott Stein in *Sight and Sound* (London), vol.41, no.3, 1972; "The Making of Cultural Myths: Walt Disney and Frank Capra" in *Movie-Made America* by Robert Sklar, New York 1975; "Now Hollywood Stars Achieve Success In Spite of Themselves" by E. Finney in *Classic Film Collector* (Indiana, Pennsylvania), fall 1976; "Det stulna paradiset" by T. Manns in *Chaplin* (Stockholm), no.4, 1976; interview with Capra in *American Film* (Washington, D.C.), October 1978; "*It Happened One Night*" by G. Brown in *Monthly Film Bulletin* (London), February 1978; "*As You Like It* and *It Happened One Night*: The Generic Pattern of Comedy" by Leland Poague in *Literature/Film Quarterly* (Salisbury, Maryland), fall 1977; "McCarey vs. Capra: A Guide to American Film Comedy of the '30s" by Wes Gehring in *The Journal of Popular Film and Television* (Bowling Green, Ohio), vol.7, no.1, 1978; "The 'Populist' Films of Frank Capra" by G.A. Phelps in *Journal of American Studies* (London), no.3, 1979; "Adaptation as Rhetorical Process: *It Happened One Night* and *Mr. Deeds Goes to Town*" by L. Self and R. Self in *Film Criticism* (Edinboro), winter 1981.

*　　　*　　　*

It Happened One Night is the film generally credited with launching the "screwball comedy" genre popular in the 1930s and 1940s. A difficult genre to define, the screwball comedy revolves around the characters' contradictory desires for individual identity and complete union in heterosexual romance. The films pit the couple's erotic moments of courtship against their verbal combats, battles of wit spiced with rapid-fire, brilliant repartee. Because of the resurgence of censorship in 1934 coupled with an American reluctance to be frank about sex, screwball comedies capitalized on the necessity to mask and to express *verbally* sexual tensions and conflicts. Screwball comedies usually relied upon a final reconciliation or marriage to establish the couple's unity but undercut it as a resolution to the couple's ongoing differences. *It Happened One Night* established these generic rules and provided a model for incorporating into a comic structure attitudes, fears, and tensions about social, sexual, and economic roles.

It Happened One Night, the story of a runaway madcap heiress who is befriended by an individualistic journalist so he can "scoop" her story, simply adapted for a Depression-era context a popular movie formula of the 1920s. Movies such as *Dancing Mothers* or *A Woman of the World* presented man-woman, husband-wife relationships in which both parties were witty, intelligent, charming, and thoroughly at odds with each other. Unlike the screwball comedies that arose later, these films extolled aristocratic life styles and proper behavior while resolving the sexual issues on superficial terms. German-emigré director Ernst Lubitsch strengthened the structural integrity of the formula and created the prototype for the screwball comedy in *Trouble in Paradise* and *Design for Living*. Impressed and influenced by Lubitsch's films, Frank Capra borrowed the comic romantic structure that Lubitsch had evolved in order to deal with middle-class sexual and social proprieties. But Capra used the formula as a vehicle for the resolution of all economic and social differences in one vast American middle class united by the virtues of caring and sharing.

Capra's simple Depression-era philosophy, often labelled "Capra-corn," is conveyed in *It Happened One Night* as a modern folk tale reversal of Cinderella. Rich girl Ellie Andrews flees her father so she can marry the worthless playboy of her dreams. Penniless and thrown on her own, she runs into the out-of-work ace reporter Peter Warne. In exchange for her "story," Warne helps her return to the playboy. Traveling by bus, foot, and auto across the backroads of thirties America, they discover a mutual independence of spirit, feistiness, and resilience. Warne gets the story, Andrews get her playboy, but both discover that what they had really been seeking they had found in each other. The rich girl ultimately gets the poor boy proving that even the wealthy, if given a chance, will subscribe to the working class values that were deemed a prescription for fighting the Depression.

One of the most successful films of its time, *It Happened One Night* is in its making and reception a "rags-to-riches" story. When Capra first proposed the film based on a story serialized in *Cosmopolitan*, Columbia Pictures executives disliked the idea and thought that the fad had passed for bus movies. At least five Hollywood stars turned down the leading roles. Colbert initially hated the picture, and Gable only made the movie because angry MGM executive Louis B. Mayer had loaned him to Columbia as a punishment. When the finished film finally opened, poor reviews and indifferent moviegoers led to the movie's closing after only one week. The film resurfaced, however, and went on to win the top five Academy Awards. The film made stars of Colbert, Gable, and Capra, and Gable's bare-chested appearance in one scene has been said to be responsible for a 50 percent drop in undershirt sales within the year. Critics have since tried to explain the secret of the film's enduring popularity. They have generally credited Capra with inventing a message that audiences wanted to hear. The nutty romance, a down-to-earth courtship that maintains a spirit of crazy adventure in spite of adversities, showed audiences then as well as today, as critic Andrew Sarris said, "the private fun a man and a woman could have in a private world of their own making."

—Lauren Rabinovitz

IT'S A WONDERFUL LIFE. Production: Liberty Films; 1946; black and white, 35mm; running time: 129 mins. Released 1946 by RKO/Radio.

Produced by Frank Capra; screenplay by Frances Goodrich, Albert Hackett, and Frank Capra with additional scenes by Jo Swerling; from the story "The Greatest Gift" by Philip Doren Stern; directed by Frank Capra; photography by Joseph Walker and Joseph Biroc; edited by William Hornbeck; sound by Richard Van Hessen, Clem Portman, and John Aalberg; art direction by Jack Okey, set decoration by Emile Kuri; music by Dmitri Tiomkin; special effects by Russell A. Cully; costumes designed by Edward Stevenson.

Cast: James Stewart (*George Bailey*); Donna Reed (*Mary Hatch*); Lionel Barrymore (*Mr. Potter*); Thomas Mitchell (*Uncle Billy*); Henry Travers (*Clarence*); Beulah Bondi (*Mrs. Bailey*); Gloria Grahame (*Violet Bick*); H.B. Warner (*Mr. Gower*); Ward Bond (*Bert*); Frank Faylan (*Ernie*); Samuel S. Hinds (*Pa Bailey*); Mary Treen (*Cousin Tilly*); Frank Hagney (*Bodyguard*); Sheldon Leonard (*Nick*); Alfalfa Switzer (*Freddie*).

Publications:

Books—*Frank Capra* by Richard Griffith, London 1951; *The Films of James Stewart* by Ken D. Jones, New York 1970; *The Name Above the Title*, New York 1971; *Frank Capra: One Man—One Film* by James Silke, Washington, D.C. 1971; *The Films of Frank Capra* by Donald Willis, Metuchen, New Jersey 1974; *James Stewart* by Howard Thompson, New York 1974; *Frank Capra: The Man and His Films*, edited by Richard Glatzer and John Raeburn, Ann Arbor 1975; *The Cinema of Frank Capra* by New York 1975; *The Men Who Made the Movies* by Richard Schickel, New York 1975; *The Films of Frank Capra* by Victor Scherle and William Levy, Secaucus, New Jersey 1977; *American Visions: The Films of Chaplin, Ford, Capra, and Welles* by Charles J. Malard, New York 1977; *Frank Capra Study Guide*, edited by Dennis Bohnenkamp and Sam Grogg, Washington, D.C. 1979; *Frank Capra* by Charles Maland, Boston 1980; articles—"Cosmopolitan's Citation as One of the Best Directors of the Month" by L.Q. Parsons in *Cosmopolitan* (New York), January 1947; "Frank Capra Sticks by the Little Man" by A. Rivkin in *U.N. World* (New York), March 1947; article by P.L. Mannock in *Films and Filming* (London), September 1956; "Capra and the American Dream" by James Price in *The London Magazine*, vol.3, no.10, 1964; "James Stewart" by William R. Sweigart in *Films in Review* (New York), December 1964; special Capra issue of *Positif* (Paris), December 1971; "A Decade of Good Deeds and Wonderful Lives: Under Capracorn" by Stephen Handzo in *Film Comment* (New York), vol.8, no.4, 1972; "Frank Capra and the Cinema of Populism" by Jeffrey Richards in *Film Society Review* (New York), vol.7, no.6 and no.7-9, 1972; "Under Capracorn" by Stephen Handzo in *Film Comment* (New York), November/December 1972; "The Telephone Company, the Nation, and Perhaps the World" by Mark Bergman in *Velvet Light Trap* (Madison, Wisconsin), winter 1971-72; "The Making of Cultural Myths: Walt Disney and Frank Capra" in *Movie-Made America* by Robert Sklar, New York 1975; "Frank Capra and the Popular Front" by Leonard Quart in *Cineaste* (New York), summer 1977; "It's a Wonderful Life: The Stand of the Capra Hero" by B. Rose in *Journal of Popular Film* (Bowling Green, Ohio), v.6, no.2, 1977; "Ideology, Genre, Auteur" by Robin Wood in *Film Comment* (New York), January/February 1977; "*It's a Wonderful Life*" by Lauren Rabinovitz in *Cinema Texas Program Notes* (Austin), 31 October 1977; "Dialogue on Film" in *American Film* (Wshington, D.C.), October 1978; "The

'Populist' Films of Frank Capra" by G.A. Phelps in *Journal of American Studies* (London), no.3, 1979; "*It's a Wonderful Life*" by DeWitt Bodeen in *Magill's Survey of Cinema, Vol. II* edited by Frank N. Magill, Englewood Cliffs, New Jersey 1980; "It's a Wonderful Life, But..." by M. Dickstein in *American Film* (Washington, D.C.), May 1980; special Capra issue of *Film Criticism* (Edinboro, Pennsylvania), winter 1981; "*Its a Wonderful Life*" by K. Silverman in *Framework* (Norwich, England), spring 1981.

* * *

When Frank Capra returned to Hollywood after coordinating the *Why We Fight* propaganda series during the war, he resumed the total artistic control over his films for which he had fought during the 1930s. *It's a Wonderful Life* was made for Liberty Films, the production company organized by Capra, George Stevens, William Wyler and Sam Briskin. The film exemplifies the concept of the independent producer-director, and Capra has called it his favorite film. In the year of its release its importance was overshadowed by Wyler's *The Best Years of Our Lives* (not made for Liberty Films), but it has since gone on to be one of the most frequently revived of Capra's works.

The impetus and structure of *It's a Wonderful Life* recall the familiar model of Capra's pre-war successes. *Mr. Deeds Goes to Town*, *Mr. Smith Goes to Washington* and *Meet John Doe*. In each of these films, the hero represents a civic ideal and is opposed by the forces of corruption. His identity, at some point misperceived, is finally acclaimed by the community at large. The pattern receives perhaps its darkest treatment in *It's a Wonderful Life*. The film's conventions and dramatic conceits are misleading. An idyllic representation of small-town America, a guardian angel named Clarence and a Christmas Eve apotheosis seem to justify the film's perennial screenings during the holiday season. These are the signs of the ingenuous optimism for which Capra is so often reproached. Yet they function in the same way "happy endings" do in Moliere, where the artifice of perfect resolution is in ironic disproportion to the realities of human nature at the core of the plays.

George Bailey is presumably living the "wonderful life" of the title. Having abandoned his ambition to become an architect in order to run a benevolent building and loan association, and facing arrest for a discrepancy in the books, George is on the verge of suicide. His guardian angel offers him the chance to find out what would have happened had he not been born. George then sees the town as a nightmarish vision of corruption. No one knows him. Even his mother, a benevolent image through the rest of the film, appears hard-bitten and cruel, and refuses to recognize him in a scene that dramatizes a primal identity crisis. George does regain his identity and is euphorically acknowledged by everyone. But this joyous finale caps a film that so often represents pain and despair—from a slap that draws blood from young George's ear, to a marriage proposal expressed in utter frustration, to the images (both inside and outside the fantasy section of the film) of George in a rage, furious with himself and with those he loves. Here, as in *Mr. Smith Goes to Washington*, James Stewart embodies the hysterical energy of Capra's quintessential American hero, thereby conveying, along with the director, the ambiguities of the American dream along with its promises.

—Charles Affron

IVAN GROZNYI. Ivan the Terrible. Production: Part I—Alma-Ata Studio, Part II—Mosfilm Studio; Part I—black and white, 35mm, Part II—black and white and Agfacolor, 35mm; length: Part I—2745 meters, Part II—2373 meters. Released Part I—1944, Part II—1958.

Scenario by Sergei Eisenstein; directed by Sergei Eisenstein; photography by A. Moskvine and E. Tisse; edited by E. Tobak; sound by V. Bogdankevitch and B. Volsky; production design by I. Chpinel; music by S. Prokofiev, songs by V. Louzowsky, and orchestra led by A. Stassevitch; costumes designed by L. Naoumova and N. Bouzina for Part I, and L. Naoumova and M. Safonova for Part II; ballet choreographed by R. Zakharov.

Shooting for Part I was begun 1 February 1943; Part II was shot September-December 1945, though not released until 1958.

Cast: N. Tcherkassov (*Ivan*); M. Jarov (*Maluta Skouratov*); A. Boutchma (*Alexei Basmanov*); M. Kouznetzov (*Fedor Basmanov*); Kolychev (*Monk Philippe*); A. Mguebrov (*Pimen, Architect of Novgorod*); V. Balachov (*Piotr Volynetz*); S. Birman (*Efrossinia Staritzkaïa*); P. Kadotchnikov (*Vladimir Andrevitch*); M. Nazvanov (*Prince Andrei Kourbsky*) (Part II only); P. Massalsky (*Sigismond, King of Pologne*) (Part II only); Erik Pyriev (*Ivan as a child*) (Part II only); L. Tzelikovskaïa (*Czarina Anastassia Romanovna*) (Part I only); Vladimir Staritsky (*Son of Staritzkaïa*) (Part I only); M. Mikhaïlov (*Archdeacon*) (Part I only); V. Pudovkin (*Nikolai*) (Part I only); S. Timochenko (*Ambassador of the Livonien Order*) (Part I only); A. Roumnev (*The Stranger*) (Part I only).

Publications:

Scripts—*Ivan the Terrible: A Screenplay* translated by Herbert Marshall and Ivor Montagu, New York 1962; *Ivan the Terrible: Oratorio* edited by A. Stasevich, translated by Herbert Marshall, Moscow 1962; *Ivan the Terrible* by Sergei Eisenstein, New York 1970; books—*Sergei Eisenstein* by Marie Seton, London 1952; *Notes of a Film Director* by Sergei Eisenstein, translated by X. Danko, London 1959; *Kino: A History of the Russian and Soviet Film* by Jay Leyda, London 1960; *Film Form* by Sergei Eisenstein, reissue, New York 1969; *Film Sense* by Sergei Eisenstein, reissue, New York 1969; *Sergei Eisenstein: An Investigation into His Films and Philosophy* by Leon Moussinac, translated from the French by D. Sandy Petrey, New York 1970; *Eisenstein* by Yon Barna, Bloomington, Indiana 1973; *Eisenstein* by Dominique Fernandez, Paris 1975; *Sergei M. Eisenstein: Materialien zu Leben und Werk* by W. Sudendorf and others, Munich 1975; *Eisenstein: a Documentary Portrait* by N. Swallow, London 1976; *S.M. Eisenstein* by Jean Mitry, Paris 1978; *Montage Eisenstein* by Jacques Aumont, Paris 1979; *Eisenstein's Ivan the Terrible: A Neoformalist Analysis* by Kristin Thompson, Princeton, New Jersey 1981; *Eisenstein at Work* by Jay Leyda and Zina Voynow, New York 1982; articles—by Ben Maddow in *Hollywood Quarterly*, October 1945; "Ivan le Terrible" by Jean-Pierre Chartier in *La Revue du cinèma* (Paris), 1 October 1946; article by B.D.Garga in *Sight and Sound* (London), spring 1958; article in *Film and Filming* (London), November 1959; article by Jay Leyda in *Film Quarterly* (Berkeley), spring 1959; article by Jonas Mekas in *The Village Voice* (New York), 9 December 1959; article by Liam O'Laoghaire in *Films and Filming* (London), January 1959; article by Herman Weinberg in *Film Culture* (New York), no.20, 1959; "Ivan the Terrible" by David Robinson in *Sight and Sound*

(London), spring 1960; "Ivan the Terrible" by Gregory Valentin in *Films in Review* (New York), January 1960; "Eisenstein" by Rostislav Yourenev, translated by Luda Schnitzer in *Anthologie du cinéma* (Paris), no.44 1964; article by Evelyn Gerstein in *Film Comment* (New York), fall 1968; "Sur *Ivan le Terrible*" by Jean-Pierre Oudart in *Cahiers du cinèma* (Paris), March 1970; "Style in *Ivan the Terrible*" by David Morse in *Monogram*, April 1971; "*Ivan*, una tragedia atea dello storico S.M. Eisenstein" by G. Aristarco in *Cinema Nuovo* (Turin), July/August 1973; "The Eisenstein-Prokofiev Correspondence" by R. Levaco in *Cinema Journal* (Iowa City), fall 1973; "Eisenstein's Epistemological Shift" by David Bordwell in *Screen* (London), winter 1974-75; "*Ivan the Terrible* and Stalinist Russia: A Reexamination" by K. Thompson in *Cinema Journal* (Iowa City), fall 1977; "Historyczne dramaty Sergiusza Eisensteina" by Z. Machwitz in *Kino* (Warsaw), November 1979; "Stanislavskij prodolžaetsja" by P. Massal'skij and V. Tereškovič in *Iskusstvo Kino* (Moscow), May 1980.

*   *   *

Ivan the Terrible is in structure an unfinished trilogy of three films: *Part I, Ivan the Terrible; Part II, the Boyars; Part III, Ivan's Struggles.* Recent criticism has made the mistake of viewing the two extant parts as one film. Each part presented to Eisenstein different formal and ideological problems which he solved with varying degrees of success; thus, *Part I* and *II* will be considered separately in this essay before any generalizations will be made on the trilogy as a whole.

Part I takes up the history of Ivan when he is about to take on the trappings of the Byzantine Emperors and the title of Czar (Caesar) instead of the title of his predecessors—Grand Prince of Moscow. The first scene shows his second coronation—that as Czar. This scene also sets the style of the trilogy, in that it prepares the audience for the extremely stylized expression and gestures modeled on Wagnerian music-drama, Marinsky ballet, and Japanese Kabuki theatre. Further, the first scene acts as a sort of overture introducing the three main themes of the trilogy: the personal life of Ivan; domestic problems within Russia and foreign problems of war and trade. The interweaving of these themes into a complex tapestry makes *Part I* one of the supreme masterpieces of cinematic art.

Ivan, in the solitude of absolute power, is often shown seeking companionship: with two friends, Kolychev and Kourbsky, who eventually betray him and side with his enemies, the boyars; in Anastasia, who is poisoned by Efrossinia, the leader of the boyars; finally, near the end of the film, in the Oprichniki, problems with the boyars is crucial to the structure and ideology of the work because Ivan seeks to create a monarchy with a centralized power at the expense of the fragmented powers of the aristocracy. The film is an attempt at embodying in art a part of Marxist theory—the step from the feudal order to the stage in which the urban merchants (that is, budding capitalists) form an alliance with the monarch to break the power of the aristocrats. Of equal importance is Ivan's desire to change Russia's foreign policy from that of a princedom to that of an empire. He seeks to break the backs of the Poles and Germans to the west, as well as the Tartars to the south and east. Important too is the idea of foreign trade; for in an essay written in 1928, Eisenstein said that if he ever made a film on *Ivan*, it would show a "merchant-czar" rather than a character from a horror story by Poe. In *Part I*, Eisenstein seeks to establish trade with the other great developing European nation-state—England; but his way is blocked by the Poles and Germans.

All three themes come together in the finale of the film: Ivan, after forming the *Oprichniki*, retreats to a monastery outside Moscow; word is brought that English trading ships have bypassed the Germans and Poles by means of a northern route through the White Sea; and, the townspeople arrive from Moscow to join with their monarch in the great alliance against the boyars. This final scene, which Ivan refers to as his true coronation by the people, formally recapitulates the coronation in the opening scene of the film. The shots of the large figure of the Czar and the tiny figures of the people beyond and below—capture the quintessential relationship between the people and their leader.

Part II remains flawed by its problematic genesis: both it and the aborted *Part III* were to form one film and were to carry forth the three main themes. Unfortunately, the decision was made to divide this original second part into two and expand the material of the boyars' plot. *Part II* unfortunately resulted in a hypertrophy of the "cloak and dagger" material. Since Ivan's final victory against the Poles and the Germans was now saved for the third part, only two out of the three themes were allowed to be developed in the second part.

The personal aspects of the Czar, as Eisenstein admitted himself, are developed at the expense of the public figure. At one point, this symbol of ineluctable power all but grovels before his childhood friend Kolychev. The *Oprichniki*, important figures in his war against the boyars, are shown as mere companions for an orgy. There is nothing inherently wrong with any of these aspects of Ivan's character, except that each, when developed out of proportion to the whole, sacrifices any formal and psychological integrity found in *Part I*. The *Oprichniki*-orgy scene proved to be a perfect chance for Eisenstein to experiment for the first time with color film stock. At several points in this scene, the filmmaker transcends the usual naturalistic use of color in order to suggest psychological states. In keeping with its excessive emphasis on the private man, the second part makes Ivan's power struggle seem more like a palace soap-opera, and less like a political struggle of national significance. Family jealousies and murder/revenge become the motive of what in the first part had been a fully rounded historical figure, Ivan IV. Worst of all, the theme of foreign policies is awkwardly tacked onto the conclusion of the film in the form of a speech by Ivan.

Taking both parts as a unity, *Ivan the Terrible* stands as one of the most courageous experiments in film art. The two completed parts of the trilogy (particularly the first) stand as a testimony against film theorists who claim that filmmaking demands by its very nature a realistic approach. *Ivan* also demonstrates that film can draw upon the other arts and yet not lose its aesthetic integrity. In this work, the great talents of Eisenstein were supplemented by those of the important Soviet composer Sergei Prokofiev to create a work that can be termed operatic—a film in which words, image, and music achieve a perfect dramatic union. Moreover, *Part I* taken by itself stands as perhaps the only masterpiece of any art which fully embodies the aesthetics preached by Stalin—namely, Soviet Socialist Realism. The first part of *Ivan the Terrible* offers a figure who is both positive and fully-rounded in human complexities, yet who does not wallow excessively in the darker side of the human psyche.

—Rodney Farnsworth

J'ACCUSE. Production: Charles Pathé (major investor); black and white, 35mm, silent; length: 1500 meters. Released 1919.

Scenario at least in part by Abel Gance; directed by Abel Gance; photography by L.H. Burel, Bujord, and Forster; edited by André Danis; assistant director: Blaise Cendrars. Cost: about 456,000 francs.

Cast: Séberin Mars (*François Lauron*); Romuald Joubé (*Jean Diaz*); Maryse Dauvray (*Edith*); Desjardins; Blaise Cendrars.

Publications:

Scripts—*J'Accuse* in *La Cinématographie Française* (Paris), April 1919; *J'Accuse*, Paris 1922; books—*Abel Gance, hier et demain* by Sophie Daria, Paris 1959; *Abel Gance* by Roger Icart, Toulouse 1960; *The Parade's Gone By* by Kevin Brownlow, New York 1968; *French Film* by Georges Sadoul, revised edition, New York 1972; *Cinema and Society: France and Germany during the 20s* by Paul Monaco, New York 1976; *Abel Gance* by Steven Kramer and James Welsh, Boston 1978; articles—in *Kine Weekly*, 29 April 1920; article in *Bioscope*, 29 April 1920; "Filmographie d'Abel Gance" by Philippe Esnault in *Cahiers du cinéma* (Paris), January 1955; special Gance issue, *L'Ecran* (Paris), April/May 1958; *Abel Gance: Spark of Genius"* by Kevin Brownlow in *Films and Filming* (London), November 1969; "The French Film—Abel Gance" in *The Silent Voice: A Text* by Arthur Lenning, New York 1969; "Film as Incantation: An Interview with Abel Gance" in *Film Comment* (New York), March/April 1974; "Abel Gance's Accusation Against War" by J.M. Welsh and Herbert Curiël in *Cinema Journal* (Iowa City), spring 1975; "Dossier: La Censure, Monsieur J. Brunin, *J'Accuse*" by J. Debacker in *Apec-Revue Belge du Cinema* (Brussels), no.4, 1976; "Abel Gance" by Kevin Brownlow, with biofilmography, in *Film Dope* (London), September 1979; "Abel Gance: trop grand pour le cinéma?" by C.M. Cluny in *Cinéma* (Paris), December 1981.

*   *   *

Abel Gance was one of the most innovative filmmakers of the silent era. Most famously, in his masterpiece *Napoleon*, he projected three images on screen at once in a process he called Polyvision. But this film is not Gance's only epic. Eight years before *Napoleon*, there was *J'Accuse!*

While *Napoleon* celebrates the exploits of its title character, *J'Accuse!* is unabashedly anti-military. The setting is a small French town. A gentle poet, who opposes war and all hostility, loves the wife of a hunter. War is declared, and the husband goes off to fight; jealous of his rival, he dispatches his wife to the Ardennes. When she is captured by the Germans, the poet himself enlists. By the finale, the hunter has been killed in battle, the wife is raped, and the poet, driven mad by the destruction that has destroyed his life, drops dead. While he does not die in combat, his demise—and the tainting of his spirit, his zest for life, his inner peace and love of beauty—becomes the symbol of the pointlessness of war.

J'accuse is one of the earliest cinematic indictments of war. This fact alone earns the film its status in cinema history. But, additionally, it is the first French film to utilize montage and superimposed shots. In a stunning series of images, closeups of hands grasp each other, pray and raise glasses of wine as soldiers leave to fight. Gance communicates with his audience visually, in abstractions: at the film's outset, the head of a dog is placed over the head of the hunter and, at the declaration of war, the Grim

Reaper is placed over the poet's work; the filmmaker's rapid montage cutting highlights the horror of the battle sequences, shot by Gance after joining a French army unit. (He perfected this last technique in *La Roue*, a melodrama released in 1923, and in *Napoleon*.) The most famous sequence in *J'accuse* occurs near the finale, when the crazed poet imagines the ghosts of his dead comrades returning from the battlefield and through the countryside to observe the results of their sacrifices. Tragically, many of the real soldiers Gance utilized as extras did not themselves survive the conflict. (The film was shot during the final stages of the conflict. They were hired while on leave, just prior to their slaughter at Verdun.)

J'accuse was, upon its release, condemned for its anti-war sentiment by those basking in the German defeat. Gance wanted to make two sequels, to be called *The Scars* (*Les Cicatrices*) and *The League of Nations* (*La Société des Nations*). Although these films were never completed, he did revise *J'accuse* four years after its release, most notably comparing the return of the dead soldiers sequence with a victory celebration.

Gance remade *J'accuse* with sound in 1937. He wrote that this new version was "intended as a challenge to the countries of Europe for permitting the gradual development of a situation that made war inevitable. Before the present menace became a reality, I wrote an introduction to the film which expresses the prophetic message it conveys from the screen: 'This film is dedicated to those who will die in the new war of tomorrow, although I am sure that they will view it skeptically and will fail to recognize themselves in it....' "

Unfortunately, like Renoir's *Grand Illusion*, *J'accuse* had no effect on altering the events which resulted in the next Great War.

—Rob Edelman

JAWS. Production: Universal Pictures; 1975; Technicolor, 35mm; running time: 124 mins. Released 20 June 1975.

Produced by Richard D. Zanuck and David Brown with William S. Gilmore Jr.; screenplay by Peter Benchley and Carl Gottlieb; from the novel by Peter Benchley; directed by Steven Spielberg; photography by Bill Butler; edited by Verna Fields; sound by Robert L. Hoyt, Roger Herman, Earl Madery, and John Carter; music by John Williams.

Filmed summer 1974 on location on Martha's Vineyard. Academy Awards, Best Sound, Best Editing, and Best Original Score, 1975.

Cast: Roy Scheider (*Brody*); Robert Shaw (*Quint*); Richard Dreyfuss (*Hooper*); Lorraine Gary (*Ellen Brody*); Murray Hamilton (*Vaughan*); Carl Gottlieb.

Publications:

Reviews—"*Jaws*" by M. Magill in *Films in Review* (New York), August/September 1975; "*Jaws*" by Tom Milne in *Monthly Film Bulletin* (London), December 1975; "*Jaws*" by James Monaco in *Sight and Sound* (London), no.1, 1975-76; "*Jaws*" by A.D. Murphy in *Variety* (New York), 18 June 1975; "*Jaws*" by D. Shear in *Film Heritage* (Dayton, Ohio), autumn 1975; "*Les*

Dents de la mer" by G. Dagneau in *Revue du cinéma* (Paris), October 1976; "La Religion du monstre" by J. Fieschi in *Cinematographe* (Paris), April/May 1976; "Jeszcze o szczekach" by B. Michalek in *Kino* (Warsaw), December 1976; books—*Jaws* by Peter Benchley, New York 1975; *The JAWS Log* by Carl Gottlieb, New York 1975; *On Location On Martha's Vineyard: The Making of the Movie Jaws* by Edith Blake, New York 1975; articles—"On Location with *Jaws*—Tell the Shark We'll Do It One More Time" by R. Riger in *Action* (Hollywood), July/August 1974; "What Directors Are Saying" in *Action* (Hollywood), September/October 1974; "On Location with *Jaws*" by M. Cribben in *American Cinematographer* (Hollywood), March 1975; "Le Point de vue d'jun psychiatre su *Les Dents de la mer*" by R. Blacher in *Cinéma 76* (Paris), April 1976; "L'Ecran fantasme (*Jaws*)" by P. Bonitzer and S. Daney in *Cahiers du cinéma* (Paris), March/April 1976; "The Great American Eating Machine" by R.C. Cumbow in *Movietone News* (Seattle), 11 October 1976; "*Jaws* Breaks B.O. Mark in Singapore" in *Variety* (New York), 8 December 1976; "*Jaws* Grosses $6.6-Mil in UK on 90-10 Deals" in *Variety* (New York), 22 December 1976; "Verites et mensonges du cinéma americain" by M. Martin and others in *Ecran* (Paris), September 1976; "Toujours a propos des *Dents de la mer*" by D. Paini in *Cinéma 76* (Paris), May 1976; "*Jaws* as Submarine Movie" by R. Willson in *Jump Cut* (Chicago), no.15, 1977; "In the Teeth of *Jaws*" by M.S. Dworkin in *Ikon* (Milan), January/March 1977; "Celjusti: mif, biznes, politika" by G. Kapralov in *Iskusstvo Kino* (Moscow), October 1977; interview with Spielberg in *Penthouse* (New York), February 1978; "*Jaws* as Patriarchal Myth" by J.E. Caputi in *Journal of Popular Film and Television* (Bowling Green, Ohio), no.4, 1978; "Spielberg schept 100 percent spanning met 6 ½ procent haai: *Jaws I* op de montagetafel" by W. Verstappen in *Skoop* (Amsterdam), February 1978; "*Jaws* Played to 80 Million on ABC" by L. Brown in *The New York Times*, 7 November 1979; "Readers' Forum" in *Journal of Popular Film and Television* (Bowling Green, Ohio), no.2, 1979; "*Jaws*" by Glenn Erickson in *Magill's Survey of Cinema, Vol. II* edited by Frank N. Magill, Englewood Cliffs, New Jersey 1980.

*　　　*　　　*

Jaws formally initiated the era of the Hollywood blockbuster. This tale of shark terror, which earned more than 100 million dollars in six months, easily surpassed *The Godfather* as the all-time Hollywood box-office champ. Although *Star Wars*, *E.T.* and *Raiders of the Lost Ark* set new records, *Jaws* created marketing precedents that became Hollywood standards: it proved that one film under careful guidance from its distributor, could precipitate a national pop cultural "event."

Universal opened *Jaws* in 409 American houses in June 1975, establishing late May/early June as the beginning of the movie season. To milk the most from its "national" premiere, Universal fully utilized "saturation advertising" on television. The company purchased at least one 30-second ad on every "prime time" network television program during the evening of the three days preceding the premiere; the cost was a million dollars. So successful was this advertising campaign that it became standard operating procedure in the American film industry (thereafter New York premieres and limited newspaper advertising were the exceptions, not the rule). *Jaws* convinced movie executives that television should be fully exploited for advertising, not avoided as in the past.

In 17 days *Jaws* earned an extraordinary $36,000,000. House records were established in cities around the country, and record grosses continued through the summer. Indeed, Universal turned 1975 into the year of the shark. The film inspired pop songs and other films. And there were, of course, the ubiquitous spin-offs: posters, T-shirts, beach towels, shark tooth pendants. The stock of Universal's parent company, MCA, moved up 22½ points in less than a month. *Jaws* proved that a single film, marketed in the right way, could make millions of dollars for everyone connected with it.

One direct beneficiary was director Steven Spielberg, who completed the film before his 30th birthday. This film school graduate learned the Hollywood system with his television work for Universal; he directed episodes of *Owen Marshall, Marcus Welby, Columbo*, and television movies such as the now cult film *Duel*. The dollars generated by *Jaws* and by his other films, *Close Encounters of the Third Kind, Raiders of the Lost Ark*, and *E.T.*, have made Spielberg the most successful box-office director of all time.

But *Jaws* won few awards, for critics did not consider it a complex artefact. Rather, *Jaws* was singled out as an example of the success of Hollywood as an entertainment machine. Social and cultural critics have "read" the film in two different ways. *Jaws* can be seen as a "Watergate" film. In it a public official (the mayor) seeks to hush up a threat to the public good (a shark attack); it takes an heroic outsider (the chief of police) to kill the shark and return things to normal. The overt message seems clear enough: the world does indeed work, if "true heroes" stand up to be counted. But *Jaws* also skillfully exploits the machine of modern cinema. From the opening sequences Spielberg associates the camera's point-of-view (under the water) and the major musical motif with the danger of the shark attack. *Jaws* manipulates our gaze, simultaneously providing the viewee with both enjoyment and fear. It remains a remarkable example of how well Hollywood can control a viewer's vision to produce pain and pleasure. *Jaws* is about Watergate America, but it is also about the experience of filmgoing in the 1970's.

—Douglas Gomery

JAZZ SINGER, THE. Production: Warner Bros. Pictures, Inc.; black and white, 35mm, silent with synchronized musical numbers; running time: 89 mins. Released October 1927, New York.

Scenario by Alfred A. Cohn; from the story and play *The Day of Atonement* by Samson Raphaelson; titles written by Jack Jarmuth; directed by Alan Crosland; photography by Hal Mohr; edited by Harold McCord; sound by George R. Groves; music score and direction by Louis Silvers.

Filmed during June through August 1927 in Warner Bros. studios, and on location in Hollywood, and the Lower East Side and in front of Shuberts' Winter Garden theater in New York City. Cost: $500,000. Special Academy Award to Warner Bros. for Producing *The Jazz Singer* "which revolutionized the industry," 1927-28.

Cast: Al Jolson (*Jakie Rabinowitz, later Jack Robin*); Warner Oland (*Cantor Rabinowitz*); Eugenie Besserer (*Sara Rabinowitz*); Otto Lederer (*Moisha Yudelson*); Bobby Gordon (*Jakie, age 13*); Richard Tucker (*Harry Lee*); May McAvoy (*Mary Dale*); Nat Carr (*Levi*); William Demarest (*Buster Billings*); Anders Randolf (*Dillings*); Will Walling (*Doctor*); Roscoe Karns (*Agent*); Myrna Loy, Audrey Ferris (*Chorus girls*); Cantor Josef Rosenblatt (*Himself, in concert number*); Jane Arden, Violet Bird, Ernest Clauson, Marie Stapleton, Edna Gregory, and Margaret Oliver (*Extras in Coffee Dan's sequence*).

Publications:

Scripts—*The Jazz Singer* edited with an introduction by Robert Carringer, Madison, Wisconsin 1979; books—*Okay for Sound: How the Screen Found Its Voice* by Frederick Thrasher, New York 1946; *Jolson, As Told to Alban Emley*, Hollywood 1951; *The Blue Book of Hollywood Musicals* by Jack Burton, Watkin's Glen, New York 1953; *The Immortal Al Jolson* by Pearl Sieben, New York 1962; *All Singing, All Talking, All Dancing* by John Springer, New York 1966; *Jolson* by Michael Freedland, New York 1972; *The Talkies: Articles and Illustrations from Photoplay Magazine* edited by Richard Griffith, New York 1972; *Al Jolson* by Michael Freedland, London 1972; *The Movie Musical* by Lee Edward Stern, New York 1974; *Birth of the Talkies: From Edison to Jolson* by Harry M. Geduld, Bloomington, Indiana 1975; *The Movie Musical from Vitaphone to 42nd Street* edited by Miles Kreuger, New York 1975; *Sonny Boy!: The World of Al Jolson* by Barrie Anderton, London 1975; *American Silent Film* by William K. Everson, New York 1978; *A History of Film* by Jack C. Ellis, Englewood Cliffs, New Jersey 1979; articles—"Warner Brothers Studios" in *Moving Picture World*, 26 March 1927; "Vitaphone Activity in Hollywood" by Edwin Schallert in *Moving Picture World*, 8 July 1927; "How the Vitaphone Enters In" in *The New York Times*, 28 August 1927; "Sketch on Alan Crosland" by D. Calhoun in *Motion Picture Classic* (Brooklyn), June 1928; "Flicker Veteran" in *Cue* (New York), 20 July 1935; "Confrontation 8: le cinéma et les juifs" by B. Amengual in *Positif* (Paris), September 1972; "The Cultural Guilt of Musical Movies: *The Jazz Singer*, 50 years After" by Andrew Sarris in *Film Comment* (New York), September/October 1977; "The Day the Silents Stopped" by L. Swindell in *American Film* (Washington, D.C.), October 1977; "Sonore, parlant et chantant" by C. Beylie in *Ecran* (Paris), January 1978; "Psst: Tišina v dvorani govori vam film" by A. Farassino in *Ekran* (Ljubljana, Yugoslavia), no.2, 1978; "*The Jazz Singer*" by A. Kupferberg in *Take One* (Montreal), January 1978; "*Le Chanteur de jazz*" by C. Bosseno in *Revue du cinéma* (Paris), series 23, 1979; "*The Jazz Singer*" by Anthony Slide in *Magill's Survey of Cinema, Vol. II* edited by Frank N. Magill, Englewood Cliffs, New Jersey 1980.

* * *

As it is generally stated, *The Jazz Singer*'s place in film history as the first talkie is an erroneous one. It was not the first sound picture—sound films are as old as the cinema itself—and it was not the first Vitaphone feature—that was *Don Juan*—nor was it the first all-talking Vitaphone feature—that was *The Lights of New York*. *The Jazz Singer is* important because it was the first film with sound to catch the imagination of an audience. As one contemporary critic, Welford Beaton, wrote, "*The Jazz Singer* definitely establishes the fact that talking pictures are imminent."

Unlike the sound films which had preceded it, *The Jazz Singer* boasted all the right components in the right mixture. It had a sentimental—silly, even by the standards of the day—story involving mother love, honor and a young man's striving for success. The film featured such songs as "Toot, Toot, Tootsie,"

"Mother o' Mine," "Mammy," and "Blue Skies," which were to become lasting successes. (Irving Berlin had written "Blues Skies" a year earlier, but it became a standard after it was featured in *The Jazz Singer*.) Above all, *The Jazz Singer* starred Al Jolson, a legendary performer, on stage from the early years of the century, whose presence somehow lent validity to the production and gave it something special. Robert Benchley, writing in the old humor magazine *Life*, jokingly summed up the power of Jolson's performance: "When Jolson enters, it is as if an electric current had been run along the wires under the seats where the hats are stuck. The house came to tumultuous attention. He speaks, rolls his eyes, compresses his lips, and it is all over.... He trembles his lip, and your hearts break with a loud snap. He sings, and you totter out to send a night letter to your mother." And as if Jolson's presence was not enough, Warner Bros. wisely cast a major silent screen actress, Mae McAvoy, to play opposite him.

Supposedly based on Al Jolson's own life, *The Jazz Singer* first saw life as a magazine story, "The Day of Atonement," by Samson Raphaelson. Raphaelson—who was to become a prominent screen writer in the 30's—adapted his story into a stageplay, which became a major success for its star George Jessel (who was initially cast in the film version, but backed out at the last minute apparently in a dispute over money). The story of *The Jazz Singer* concerns Jakie Rabinowitz who yearns to sing popular songs, but whose father, a cantor, wishes him to follow in his footsteps. Jakie leaves home changes his name to Jack Robin (selecting a Gentile name in rejection not only of his father but also of his Jewish faith), and goes on the stage. As he is about to get his big break, opening as the star of a Broadway musical, Jakie learns that his father has been taken seriously ill. Realizing his true feelings and his place in his Jewish family, serious Jakie sings the "Kol Nidre" that night, delaying the opening of his show. The musical eventually opens, starring Jakie and his Gentile girlfriend, Mary Dale, and that night Jakie's mother realizes, "He is not my boy any more. He belongs to the world."

The plot is ludicrous, and was treated as such even by contemporary critics, many of whom complained that the story was "too Jewish." (Of course, it is worth noting that despite the awfulness of the story, *The Jazz Singer* has been twice remade.) What *is* exciting about the film is its use of sound—not only the interpolated dialogue and songs, but also the musical score and sound effects arranged by Louis Silvers (who skillfully blends elements of popular music with elements of serious music by Tchaikovsky, Debussy and others).

Jolson's first spoken words—"Wait a minute, wait a minute, you ain't heard nothing yet. Wait a minute, I tell you. You ain't heard nothing yet. Do you want to hear 'Toot, Toot, Tootsie?' "—electrifying in their intensity, even today, some 50 or more years since they were first uttered. It is as if the viewer were participating, in a very personal way, in a moment of historic significance. Similarly, there is something embarrassingly private about Jolson's remarks to his mother as he sits at the piano and sings "Blue Skies" to her. Jolson's apparently improvised ramblings are perhaps a little too real and, therefore, almost a little too artificial and stilted. The impact of this last dialogue sequence is further emphasized by its abrupt ending as Warner Oland (in the role of Cantor Rabinowitz) enters the scene. He looks at his wife and son, and through a title, shouts "Stop." The dialogue, the human voice, is stilled, and *The Jazz Singer* once again becomes a silent film with musical accompaniment.

Alan Crosland brings almost a documentary quality to many of the scenes, particularly the opening sequences in which Jakie, as a child, sings at a local saloon. (It is the voice of Jakie as a child, played by Bobby Gordon, that is the voice first heard in the film.) The director is obviously a highly competent technician,

and gets the best from his players, even such notorious purveyors of melodrama as Warner Oland and Eugenie Besserer.

The critics admired the film, but *loved* Al Jolson. One commented that "He is as solitary upon the heights of an art he has made peculiarly his own as Chaplin is upon his." Indeed, with *The Jazz Singer* Jolson heralded a new era which was to bring about the ultimate decline of Chaplin and his contemporaries, destroying one art form and creating another. Perhaps the one irony is that despite its place in the history of the sound film, the sound system utilized for *The Jazz Singer*—Vitaphone—was not the system that ultimately became standard in the industry. Vitaphone utilized sound on disc, and the future of the industry lay with sound on film.

—Anthony Slide

JEDER FUR SICH UND GOTT GEGEN ALLE. L'Enigme de Kaspar Hauser. The Enigma of Kaspar Hauser. Every Man for Himself and God Against All. Production: Werner Herzog Film-Product and ZDF (German television); Eastmancolor, 35mm; running time: 110 mins. Released 1974.

Produced, scripted, and directed by Werner Herzog; photography by Jorg Schmidt-Reitwein; edited by Beate Mainka-Jellinghaus; sound by Haymo Henry Heyder; production design by Henning V. Gierke; music by Pachelbel, Orlandi di Lasso, Albinoni, and Mozart; costumes designed by Gisela Storch and Ann Poppel.

Cannes Film Festival, Special Jury Prize, the International Critics' Award, and the Ecumenical Prize, 1975.

Cast: Bruno S. (*Kaspar Hauser*); Walter Ladengast (*Daumer*); Brigitte Mira (*Kate, the governess*); Hans Musaus (*The stranger*); Willy Semmelrogge (*Circus Master*); Michael Kroecher (*Lord Stanhope*); Henry Van Lyck (*Captain of the cavalry*); Enno Patalas (*Pastor Führmann*); Elis Pilgrim (*Pastor*); Volker Prechtel (*Hiltel, prison guard*); Kidlat Tahmik (*Hombrecito, the Indian*); Gloria Doer (*Madame Hiltel*); Helmut Doring (*Little King*); Andi Gottwald (*Young Mozart*); Herbert Achternbusch (*Farmboy*); Wolfgang Bauer (*Farmboy*); Walter Steiner (*Farmboy*); Florian Fricke (*Monsieur Florian*); Clemens Scheitz (*Registrar*); Johannes Buzalski (*Police officer*); Dr. Willy Meyer-Furst (*Doctor*); Wilhelm Bayer (*Captain of the cavalry, domestic*); Franz Brumbach (*Bear trainer*); Alfred Edel (*Professor of Logic*); Heribert Fritsch (*Mayor*); Peter Gebhart (*Shoemaker who discovers Kaspar*); Reinhard Hauff (*Farmer*); Dorothea Kraft (*Little girl*); Markus Weller (*Julius, son of Hiltel*); Dr. Heinz H. Niemoller (*Pathologist*); Dr. Walter Pflaum (*Pathologist*); Otto Heinzle (*Old priest*); Peter-Udo Schonborn (*Swordsman*).

Publications:

Script—*L'énigme de Kaspar Hauser*, cutting continuity and dialogue, in *Avant-Scène du cinéma* (Paris), June 1976; reviews—by Gérard Legrand in *Positif* (Paris), May 1975; review by Noureddine Ghali in *Cinéma 75* (Paris), September 1975; reviews by H. Farocki and N. Ghali in *Filmkritik* (Munich), November 1975; "*Jeder für sich und Gott gegen alle*" by Tom Milne in *Monthly Film Bulletin* (London), December 1975; "*Jeder für sich und Gott gegen alle*" by G. Moskowitz in *Variety* (New York), 14 May 1975; "*L'Enigme de Kaspar Hauser*" by A. Garel in *Revue du cinéma* (Paris), October 1976; "La Presse..." in *Avant-Scène du cinéma* (Paris), 15 November 1976; "*L'Enigme de Kaspar Hauser*" by C. Bronchain in *Apec-Revue Belge de Cinema* (Brussels), October 1976; books—*Herzog/Kluge/Straub* by Wolfram Schütte and others, Vienna 1976; *The New German Cinema* by John Sandford, Totowa, New Jersey 1980; articles—"Herzog in Dinkelsbühl" by Lotte Eisner in *Sight and Sound* (London), autumn 1974; "Entretien avec Werner Herzog" by Michel Ciment in *Positif* (Paris), May 1975; "*L'Enigme de Kaspar Hauser*-Entretien avec Werner Herzog" by C. Clouzot in *Ecran* (Paris), November 1975; "Werner Herzog: *Jeder fü sich und Gott gegen alle*" by A. Haakman in *Skoop* (Amsterdam), February 1975; "Every Man for Himself", interview by D.L. Overbey in *Sight and Sound* (London), spring 1975; "Une Enigme qui ne se résout pas" by Jacques Lourcelles in *Avant-Scène du cinéma* (Paris), 15 November 1976; "Le 'comédien' Bruno S." in *Avant-Scène du cinéma* (Paris), 15 November 1976; "Ce Jour la à Nuremberg" by J. Leirens in *Amis du Film & de la Television* (Brussels), March 1976; "Bilderarbeit" by M. Schaub in *Cinema* (Zurich), no.3, 1976; "Mysteries of the Organism: Character Consciousness and Film Form in *Kaspar Hauser* and *Spirit of the Beehive*" by D. Benelli in *Movietone News* (Seattle), June 1977; "The Enigma of Werner Herzog" by John Dorr in *Millimeter* (New York), October 1977; "Werner Herzog" by George Morris in *International Film Guide 1979*, London 1978; "Kaspar Hauser Doubly Portrayed..." by E. Finger in *Literature/Film Quarterly* (Salisbury, Maryland), no.3, 1979; "Werner Herzog's ecran absurde" by J.C. Horak in *Literature/Film Quarterly* (Salisbury, Maryland), no. 3, 1979; "The Cinema of the Grotesque" by R. Perlmutter in *Georgia Review* (Athens, Georgia), no.1, 1979; "Woyzeck and Kaspar: The Congruities in Drama and Film" by M. Bloom in *Literature/Film Quarterly* (Salisbury, Maryland), no.4, 1980; "Kritiken av förnuftet" by I. Koršič in *Chaplin* (Stockholm), no.3 (174), 1981.

*   *   *

In many countries *Jeder für sich und Gott gegen alle* (*Every Man for Himself and God Against All*) is distributed under the title *Kaspar Hauser*—the name of the hero of this film based on the history of a man who in 1828 was found by chance living in a dark cave where he had apparently grown up without any contact with other human beings. Brought to civilization, he experiences many of the events of ordinary life, all of which make him feel equally uneasy.

Werner Herzog, the director, unlike François Truffaut in *The Wild Child*, is not interested in showing the painful process of adaptation to civilized surroundings; Kaspar has a special consciousness in which the laws of nature have a central place and in which the conventions and norms of civilized behavior are as artificial and inconvenient to him as the black dinner jacket he is forced to wear. His difficulties in communication are not the result of any linguistic inadequacies; simply, he is "different" from other men. That is why Herzog seems to wish to persuade us that, despite being gratuitous, both the early isolation and the surprising death of his hero are somehow logical.

An examination of Herzog's earlier films suggests that he always moves within the same closed circle of his imagination. All of his heroes are in some way related. The deafmutes in *Land of Silence and Darkness*, the dwarfs in *Even Dwarfs Started Small* or the half-crazy conquistador in *Aguirre, the Wrath of God*—like Kaspar Hauser—are outsiders, unable to adapt, creatures who have no place in human society.

His later films, if anything, stress this similarity of characters and continuity of motifs. In *Stroszek* the main characters from Kaspar Hauser reappear but in another historical context—that of our own time. Stroszek—played by Bruno S., the same Berlin hobo who played Kaspar—and his two companions, the old man (Clemens Scheitz) and the girl (Eva Mattes), can no longer find a "place" in their native Germany, so they emigrate to America, where they also fail. This would be the fate of Kaspar Hauser today. Aguirre, the greedy colonist, appears again in *Fitzcarraldo*—a corrective to the pessimistic conclusion of *Aguirre*. The wisdom and integrity of the Indians have profound effect on the conqueror, and he comes to see his confrontation with the jungle and the natives as a blessing that saves him from the abyss.

This summary of plot sounds like a fairy tale—and it is. Most of Herzog's films recall fables, and that is surely one of the reasons for their success. There is a kind of magical charm in the way that Herzog composes his shots: these films contain much natural beauty and slow rhythm that evokes splendor and transience. When one speaks of Herzog, one speaks of "mystical cinema, transcendent, an idealistic vision of reality." The film *Kaspar Hauser* is an example of a kind of narration in which realistically-realized shots are perceived as a perfect, even though unrealistic, fiction.

—Maria Racheva

JEUX INTERDITS, LES. Forbidden Games. The Secret Game. Production: Silver-Film; black and white, 35mm; running time: 102 mins., some sources list 90 mins., others 84 mins. Released 9 May 1952.

Produced by Robert Dorfmann; screenplay by François Boyer, adaptation and dialogue by Jean Aurenche, Pierre Bost, and René Clement; from the novel by François Boyer; directed by René Clement; photography by Robert Juillard; edited by Roger Dwyre; sound engineered by Jacques Lebreton; art direction by Paul Bertrand; music adaptation and intepretation by Narciso Yepes; costumes designed by Majo Brandley.

Filmed fall 1951. Cannes Film Festival, Grand Prix Indépendant, 1952; Venice Film Festival, Best Film—Gold Lion of St. Mark, 1952; New York Film Critics' Award, Best Foreign Film, 1952; Honorary Academy Award, Best Foreign-Language Film, 1952.

Cast: Brigitte Fossey (*Paulette, age 5*); Georges Poujouly (*Michel Dolle, age 11*); Lucien Herbert (*Père Dolle*); Suzanne Courtal (*Mère Dolle*); Jacques Marin (*Georges Dolle*); Laurence Badie (*Berthe Dolle*); Andre Wasley (*Père Gouard*); Amedee (*Francis Gouard*); Denise Peronne (*Jeanne Gouard*); Louis Sainteve (*Le curé*); Madeleine Barbulee; Pierre Merovee; Violette Monnier; and Fernande Roy.

Publications:

Script—"*Jeux Interdits*" (excerpts from script) by François Boyer, Jean Aurenche, Pierre Bost, and René Clement in *Avant-*

Scène du cinéma (Paris), 15 May 1962; books—*René Clément* by Jacques Siclier, Brussels 1956; *René Clément* by André Farwagi, Paris 1967; *French Film* by Roy Armes, New York 1970; *French Cinema Since 1946: The Great Tradition*, Vol. I, by Roy Armes, New York 1976; *Caligari's Cabinet and Other Grand Illusions: A History of Film Design* by Léon Barsacq, New York 1976; articles—"Style of René Clément" by Lotte Eisner in *Film Culture* (New York), no.12 and no.13, 1957; "Pourquoi j'ai tourné *Jeux Interdits*" by René Clement in *Avant-Scène du cinéma* (Paris), 15 May 1962; "Monsieur Ripois" in *Avant-Scène du cinéma* (Paris), January 1966; "The Darker Side of Life" by Douglas McVay in *Films and Filming* (London), December 1966.

*   *   *

For English-speaking audiences, *Les Jeux interdits* remains one of the two or three most important French films. Of the pre-New Wave era. Under Clement's direction, the two children are inestimably fresher and more engaging than almost any other child actors of the time. But beyond its immediate appeal, *Fobidden Games* remains important as an early conjunction of the realist style of director René Clement on the one side and the cinema of quality of the Aurenche/Bost script on the other. A tension is created by the film's hesitation between social allegory and anthropology and between a natural and a prettified style.

The film's allegory is transparent from the outset when German Stuckas strafe a line of fleeing Parisians. In the gorgeous French countryside at the waning of spring, man's urge to destroy strews bodies around the landscape. Having set a brutal tone, Clement turns to his tender drama and to Brigitte Fossey, already irresistible at five years old. Wandering away from the bodies of her parents and into a pasture of lowing cows, she narrows the film's focus from public to private morals and mores, for her subsequent adoption by a peasant family displaces the social context from international war to domestic strife.

Now Little Brigitte and her soulmate, played by Georges Poujouly, observe the stupid bickerings, rituals, and greed both within their household and between the households of the village. Particularly memorable is the death of the older brother who had been kicked by a horse. The children are amused by his ugly demise and the religious trappings of his funeral. Soon they develop rituals of their own, "les jeux interdits." In an abandoned barn they construct an elaborate burial ground for every sort of creature. So fascinated are they by death that they eagerly await (even bring about) the final end of insects, dogs, etc. The religious compensation of their candles and crosses is at once a grotesque and authentic displacement of the petty comforts of adult religion.

This ridicule of peasant life, particularly of religion, distinguishes the film as serious production, as does the obvious irony at work in comparing a Parisian girl and her rural foster parents. Much of Clement's compositional strategy reinforces supercilious sentiments as when he cuts among rural families at the cemetery from a number of low angles. Such pretty shots progressively make a mockery of the mourners; finally, one shot is taken literally from the bottom of the grave. Clement also ridicules romance: the children discover the older sister in the hay with the boy next door, who has been recently demilitarized. Altogether the dialogue is terribly pointed, even pithy, despite coming from the mouths of peasants. This whole "quality" flavor is summed up in the credits which are rendered over the pages of a book, as if insisting on the literary stature of the film.

But Clement's roots in realism and his command of location shooting also pull the film in other directions, some of which might be thought to presage the New Wave. Close-ups of the children are excessively lengthy and attain a documentary interest beyond their narrative motivation. They give the viewer a rather direct emotional access to these children apart from the story we find them in. The full power of this technique is reserved for the film's final sequence in which we observe, without any artifice of editing, the little girl dissolve in tears amidst hundreds like her at the Paris orphanage to which she has been taken. In short, we trust the tears of this child.

A New Wave attitude is associated with the music as well. Not only in the employment of a simple, lyrical guitar, but also in its haunting melody, which often triggers meditation on a recent dramatic action. Frequent promenades to the accompaniment of guitar are dramatic resting places wherein the film addresses the spectator in a new and more direct way.

Altogether then the film highlights in its style(s) and subject the conflicts of purity and the grotesque, of children and adults, of nature and man, of realism and parody.

—Dudley Andrew

JIGOKUMON. Gate of Hell. Production: Daiei (Tokyo); Eastmancolor, 35mm; running time: 89 mins. Released 1953, Japan.

Produced by Masaichi Nagata; screenplay by Teinosuke Kinugasa; from a 20th century play by Kan Kikuchi; directed by Teinosuke Kinugasa; photography by Kohei Sugiyama; art direction by Kisaku Itoh; music direction by Yasuchi Akutagawa; costumes designed by Sanzo Wada; color consultant: Sanzo Wada.

Filmed in Japan. Academy Award for Best Costume Design-Color and Special Academy Award for Best Foreign Film, 1954; New York Film Critics' Award, Best Foreign Film, 1954; Cannes Film Festival, Best Film, 1954.

Cast: Machiko Kyo (*Wife*); Kazuo Hasegawa (*Husband*); Koreya Senda; Isao Yamagata; Yataro Kurokawa; Kataro Bando.

Publications:

Books—*Le Cinéma japonais* by Marcel de Shinobu Giuglaris, Paris 1956; *Invitation au cinéma japanois* by Cinémathèque français, Paris 1963; *The Japanese Film: Art and Industry* by Joseph Anderson and Donald Richie, Princeton, New Jersey 1982; articles—"Japan's Film Revolution" by Arthur Knight in *Saturday Review* (New York), 11 December 1954; "Exquisite New Films from Japan" in *Life* (New York), 15 November 1954; "Reflections on the Japanese Film" by Vernon Young in *Art Digest*, August 1955; "Popular Entertainments of Japan" by Koji Ozaki in *Atlantic* (Boston), January 1955; "1954 in Japan" by Masayoshi Iwabutchi in *Sight and Sound* (London), spring 1955; "Seven from the Past" by J.L. Anderson in *Sight and Sound* (London), autumn 1957.

*   *   *

Although today Teinosuke Kinugasa's *Jigokumon* is seldom treated as an important film, its historical position is secure. It was one of the first post-World War II Japanese films to be accepted and honored by the international film community. Not only did it win the Grand Prize at the 1954 Cannes International Film Festival but also it received two Academy Awards in the United States. The great commercial and critical success of Akira Kurosawa's *Rashomon* (1950), Kenji Mizoguchi's *Ugetsu* (1953), and *Jigokumon* made the Western world begin to take notice of Japanese films.

Jigokumon was especially noteworthy to Western audiences because it was the first Japanese color film released in the West. Although the Eastmancolor film stock came from the United States, Kinugasa and his cinematographer, art director, and color consultant used it with an artistry and subtlety that was seldom seen in the American films of that time. Many critics praised the filmmakers for giving the color a distinctly Japanese look that was a welcome contrast to the flamboyance of Hollywood.

Although *Jigokumon* is set in the 12th century, it is based on 20th century Japanese play by Kan Kikuchi. The film begins with a war between rival clans, and then, when the war is over, concentrates on only three characters in a story of love, sacrifice, and grief.

The direction of Kinugasa gives intimacy to both parts of the film, even the battle scenes. Kinugasa often highlights the large-scale sequences with small details in the foreground or at the end of a scene. In one scene, for example, the march of warriors in the background is accentuated by a number of chickens fighting in the foreground, and many scenes that involve large numbers of fighting men end with a quiet close-up of an inanimate object.

The second part of the film contrasts the emotion and brutality of the warrior Moritah with the restraint of a man and his wife who value self-sacrifice above violence and revenge. When Moritah tries to take the wife away from her husband, she sacrifices her life rather than accept the warrior; after her death, the husband refuses to take vengeance. The warrior finally realizes that he must atone for his sin by continuing to live with the knowledge of what he has done. This is not a familiar theme for Western audiences, but under Kinugasa's direction the performers who play the couple convey the depth of their feeling without much overt show of emotion. (The wife, incidentally, is played by Machiko Kyo, who also was featured in *Rashomon*.)

Jigokumon is only one of the many fine films directed by Teinosuke Kinugasa in a career that spanned five decades, but to Western audiences it was a revelation in the artistry of its color and the strength of its story. The audiences that had appreciated the black-and-white masterpieces of Kurosawa and Mizoguchi were astonished by Kinugasa's use of color film. The American Motion Picture Academy gave Sanzo Wada its award for costume design, and because at that time the Academy had no foreign film category, it gave *Jigokumon* a special award as Best Foreign Film.

—Timothy Johnson

JOHNNY GUITAR. Production: Republic Pictures; 1954; Trucolor, 35mm, Cinemascope; running time: 110 mins; Released November 1954;

Produced by Herbert J. Yates; screenplay by Philip Yordan; from the novel by Roy Chanslor; directed by Nicholas Ray; photography by Harry Stradling, Jr.; edited by Richard L. Van Enger; sound by T.A. Carmen and Howard Wilson; production design by John McCarthy, Jr. and Edward G. Boyle; art direction by James Sullivan; music by Victor Young, title song by Victor Young and Peggy Lee, song sung by Peggy Lee; special effects by Howard and Theodore Lydecker; costumes designed by by Sheila O'Brien.

Filmed 1953.

Cast: Joan Crawford (*Vienna*); Sterling Hayden (*Johnny Guitar*); Mercedes McCambridge (*Emma Small*); Scott Brady (*Dancin' Kid*); Ben Cooper (*Turkey*); Ward Bond (*John McIvers*); Ernest Borgnine (*Bart Lonergan*); John Carradine (*Tom*); Royal Dano (*Corey*); Frank Ferguson (*Sheriff*); Paul Fix (*Eddie*); Rhys Williams (*Mr. Andrews*); Ian McDonald (*Zeke*); Will Wright (*Ned*); John Maxwell (*Jake*); Robert Osterloh (*Sam*); Frank Marlowe (*Frank*); Trevor Bardette (*Jenks*); Sumner Williams, Sheb Wooley, Denver Pyle, and Clem Harvey (*Possemen*).

Publications:

Scripts—"*Johnny Guitar*" by Philip Yordan in *Avant-Scène du cinéma* (Paris), March 1974; reviews—in the *Hollywood Reporter*, 5 May 1954; review by Bosley Crowther in *The New York Times*, 28 May 1954; "L'Adolescent et l'homme" by Jean-Luc Godard in *Image et son* (Paris), July 1956; "La Belle et la bête du western" by François Truffaut in *Arts* (Paris), February 1955; books—*A Portrait of Joan: The Autobiography of Joan Crawford* by Joan Crawford with Jane Kesner, Garden City, New York 1962; *The Western: From Silents to Cinerama* by George N. Fenin and William K. Everson, New York 1962; *The Immediate Experience* by Robert Warshow, Garden City, New York 1962; *Wanderer* by Sterling Hayden, New York 1965; *The Films of Joan Crawford* by Lawrence J. Quirk, New York 1968; *What is Cinema* by André Bazin, translated by Hugy Gray, Berkeley 1971; *The Western: From Silents to the 70's* by George N. Fenin and William K. Everson, New York 1973; *Joan Crawford* by Stephen Harvey, New York 1974; *Westerns* by Philip French, New York 1974; *Focus on the Western* edited by Jack Nachbar, Englewood Cliffs, New Jersey 1974; *Sixguns and Society* by Will Wright, Berkeley 1975; *The Great Western Pictures* edited by James Robert Parish, Metuchen, New Jersey 1976; *Nicholas Ray* by John Kreidl, Boston 1977; *Cinema, The Magic Vehicle: A Guide to Its Achievement: Journey One: The Cinema Through 1949* edited by Jacek Klinowski and Adam Garbicz, Metuchen, New Jersey 1979; articles—"Joan Crawford" by Lawrence J. Quirk in *Films in Review* (New York), December 1956; "Entretien avec Nick Ray" by Charles Bitsch in *Cahiers du cinéma* (Paris), November 1958; "Nicholas Ray" by Henri Agel in *New York Film Bulletin*, no.11, 1961; "Mercedes McCambridge" by Ray Hagen in *Films in Review* (New York), May 1965; "The Cinema of Nicholas Ray" by Victor Perkins in *Movie Reader* edited by Ian Cameron, New York 1972; "Circle of Pain: The Cinema of Nicholas Ray" by Jonathan Rosenbaum in *Sight and Sound* (London), autumn 1973; "Cinemascope Before and After" by Charles Barr in *Film Theory and Criticism* edited by Gerald Mast and Mark Cohen, New York 1974; "Rebel Without a Cause: Nicholas Ray in the Fifties" by Peter Biskind in *Film Quarterly* (Berkeley), fall 1974; "Johnny Guitar", special issue of *Avant-Scène du cinéma* (Paris), March 1974; "*Johnny Guitar*" by Ann Laemmle in *Cinema Texas Program Notes* (Austin), 7 March 1979; "*Johnny Guitar*" by Janey Place in *Magill's Survey of Cinema, Vol. II* edited by Frank N. Magill, Englewood Cliffs, New Jersey 1980. "Dos Miradas sobre *Johnny Guitar*" by A. Fernandez Santos and J.G. Requena in *Contracampo* (Madrid), December 1980.

*   *   *

Johnny Guitar is a film that can be studied and appreciated from several different points of view. As a political text, it clearly is a metaphor of the McCarthy era from the point of view of the persecuted. As an example of how the presence of a powerful star can be used to provide meaning, its use of Joan Crawford and her previous accumulated film roles is classic. Psychologically, it is a startling portrait of how a mob is manipulated; generically, it is an unusual example of a western film that does not fit a mold. It is probably best interpreted, however, as a powerful and beautiful film by a director whose name signifies a unique kind of kinetic cinema—Nicholas Ray.

Ray's work, like that of many other great film artists, is more personal than social or political. His strength as a director was in presenting characters isolated from the main stream of the social world around them. The extremes of their behavior, from lyrical happiness to total despair illustrate Ray's world of alienation and insecurity, and *Johnny Guitar* is a typical example. It is one of the most emotional films ever made.

Upon release, Johnny Guitar was treated with contempt, as a joke that starred an over-the-hill leading lady whose increasing tendency to look like a tough cowboy was being utilized without her understanding. However, François Truffaut prophesied, "In five years, those same people who snickered" would revere *Johnny Guitar*. It took considerably more years than that for the film to find a respectful audience, and even today, it is a film that separates those who appreciate visual power on screen from those who appreciate a film more as a scripted, literary work.

The opening sequence of the film presents a visual statement of character and situation. The hero rides along a narrow path on a mountain side. Above him, men are blasting the side out of the mountain with dynamite. Below him, other men are robbing a stagecoach. Although he observes both actions, he neither runs for cover from the blasts nor attempts to help the beleaguered coach below. He merely observes, treads his narrow path, passes by and survives.

The film's heroine, Joan Crawford, is costumed both in men's clothes and in long, flowing gowns. Crawford contributes a meaning to the film that reaches beyond any such limited view as "performance." In addition to her acting, which suitably provides the sense of a tough, desperate, yet vulnerable woman, she provides a film persona of enormous sexual complexity. The anger and rage that seem to be barely controlled beneath her Mount Rushmore facade is finally expiated in the final shootout between herself and Mercedes McCambridge, a fitting end to a film that contains subtle questions about male and female roles.

Johnny Guitar was filmed in Trucolor, a two-color process using Dupont color stock which was a trademark of Republic Studios for a period of years. Ray's symbolic and expressive use of color in the film adds to its complexity of meanings, and *Johnny Guitar* is considered by color experts to be the finest example of Republic's many Trucolor films.

Johnny Guitar is clearly ahead of its time in combining a lyrical, poetic attitude toward its images with a mocking, almost parodistic attitude toward its plot. It contains calmly staged scenes, acted out in cadenced style by actors posed like statues, talking directly into the camera. It also contains passionate action sequences that seem to swirl and dance before the eye.

Such scenes are not alternated with one another. Rather, as opposite as they are in style, they have been effectively integrated into a meaningful whole. The sophisticated viewer perceives power and madness in *Johnny Guitar*, a delirious film.

—Jeanine Basinger

JOHNNY GOT HIS GUN. Production: Robert Rich Productions for World Entertainment Ltd.; black and white with color sequences, 35mm; running time: 111 mins. Released 1971.

Produced by Bruce Campbell; screenplay by Dalton Trumbo; from the 1939 novel by Dalton Trumbo; directed by Dalton Trumbo; photography by Jules Brenner; music by Jerry Fielding.

Cannes Film Festival, Prix Spécial du Jury (shared with Milos Forman's *Taking Off*), 1971.

Cast: Timothy Bottoms (*Joe Bonham*); Jason Robards (*Mr. Bonham*); Marsha Hunt; Donald Sutherland; Kathy Fields; Diane Varsi.

Publications:

Reviews—"*Johnny Got His Gun*: Ou le miracle de l'impossible" by A. Cervoni in *Cinéma* (Paris), May 1972; "*Johnny Got His Gun*" by P. Gaulier in *Image et son* (Paris), May 1972; "*Johnny Got His Gun*" by C. Lundberg in *Chaplin* (Stockholm), no.5 (116), 1972; "*Johnny Got His Gun*" by A. Stuart in *Films and Filming* (London), December 1972; "*Johnny Got His Gun*" by T. Ryan in *Lumiere* (Melbourne, Australia), April 1973; "*E Johnny prese il fucile*" by G. Giuricin in *Cinema Nuovo* (Turin), September/December 1975; books—*Johnny Got His Gun* by Dalton Trumbo, New York 1939; articles—"Diary of a Dead Bavarian" by J. Zinnamon in *Esquire* (New York), December 1970; "Dalton Trumbo: An Interview" by William Starr in *Film Society Review* (New York), October 1971; "*Johnny s'en va-t-en guerre*" by G. Braucourt in *Ecran* (Paris), April 1972; "*Johnny Got His Gun*" by N. Jensen in *Kosmorama* (Copenhagen), winter 1975; "*E Johnny prese il fucile*" by E. Comuzio in *Cineforum* (Bergamo, Italy), November 1975; "Oscar-statyetten kom sent, 19 ar for att vara esakt och nu ar Robert Rich dod." by B. Wredlund in *Filmrutan* (Tyreso, Sweden), no.4, 1976; "Una Experiencia quizás irreptible" by M. Carril Martínez in *Cinemeteca Revista* (Andes, Uraguay), July 1981.

*   *   *

In 1939, the distinguished screenwriter Delton Trumbo published *Johnny Got His Gun*, easily the best of his four novels and one of the great works of fiction of that decade. It is a poignant outcry against war; although set during World War I, and written in reaction to the horrors rapidly unfolding in Europe, the story is equally as relevant to any conflict at any other time in history.

Johnny Got His Gun's youthful hero, Joe Bonham, has been maimed in battle. He has lost all use of his limbs and senses, except touch. All the action takes place within Joe's head.

Because he cannot in any way communicate with anyone or anything, he can exist only in his own memories and fantasies. And, because he has no arms, legs or face, and is dumb, blind and deaf, he realizes that he must remain aware of time's passage, must think and constantly use his mind; otherwise, he will go mad. Finally, Joe learns to communicate by tapping out signals in Morse Code. He asks to be put on public display, as a remnant of war, but of course he is not allowed this wish. His presence outside his hospital room will, after all, certainly not increase army enlistments. New wars must continue replacing old ones; the old will continue sending the young to die.

Joe Bonham is, in his relationship to others, a dead man. Yet he can still think and feel. Trumbo unravels his world by moving in and out of the character's awareness in a manner that can be best described as stream of consciousness. Additionally, he employs his screenwriting skills to handle the book's flashback sequences, in which he cuts away to create clear, crisply-described incidents. He verbally incorporates montage, mixing dialogue between characters with sounds from the world moving on around them. Via words, Trumbo makes the reader smell smells, hear sounds. Appropriately, *Johnny Got His Gun*, besides being both an eloquent anti-war statement and a work of art, is almost a cinematic novel.

Curiously, the story could not be easily visualized, and the resulting film is not without flaws. Thirty years elapsed between the book's publication and the film's release. Trumbo had always hoped to adapt *Johnny Got His Gun* into a motion picture, a goal that might have been realized immediately following World War II, if it were not for the writer's having been blacklisted for alleged Communist Sympathies. Years later he was inspired to mount the project when the light at the end of the Vietnam tunnel proved to be ever more tragically elusive. No major studio would finance the film; Trumbo was supposedly turned down by 17 companies. So he established an independent organization and solicited relatively small contributions from a variety of sources. (*Johnny Got His Gun* was made under the banner of Robert Rich Productions; Rich was the pseudonym used by the then-blacklisted Trumbo on his Academy Award-winning script for *The Brave Bulls*.) Finally, the film was completed with Trumbo as director. It is truly an auteur effort in that a writer not only adapted his novel for the screen but directed as well.

Despite a Prix Spécial du Jury at the 1971 Cannes Film Festival, *Johnny Got His Gun* received mixed reviews in America and promptly died. The film is uneven: Trumbo realized the necessity to visualize both the subjective reality of Joe's consciousness and activity around him, while somehow cohesively uniting the two. To accomplish this, he shot the film's hospital scenes in black and white and all the rest—flashbacks of Joe, in adolescence, with his father, mother girlfriend—in color. There is no real movement, and the film is often plodding.

But *Johnny Got His Gun* is still touching, particularly when Joe breaks through to the outside world. The subject matter by itself is so powerful that the viewer cannot help but be moved. It is an honest, gutsy piece of filmmaking, in its own way an even stronger anti-war statement than *All Quiet on the Western Front* or *Paths of Glory*. As Pete Hamill—not a movie critic—was moved to write in a column in the *New York Post*, the film is a "work of art that tears, lifts, rips, and cuts; it is savage in its single-mindedness, but it is also most terribly human." For *Johnny Got His Gun* is, after all, about the "filthy little secret of war."

—Rob Edelman

LE JOLI MAI. Production: Sofracima; black and white, 35mm; running time: 110 and 140 mins., American version 124 mins. Released May 1963, Paris.

Produced by Catherine Winter; screenplay by Catherine Varlin and Chris Marker; directed by Chris Marker; photography by Pierre Lhomme; edited by Eva Zora; music by Michel Legrand, title song by B. Mokkoussov and Michel Legrand, sung by Yves Montand.

Filmed spring 1962 in Paris. Venice Film Festival, Best First Film, 1963; Cannes Film Festival, International Critics' Prize, 1963.

Cast: Commentators: Yves Montand (the French commentary); Simone Signoret (the English commentary).

Publications:

Review—by Gordon Gow in *Films and Filming* (London), May 1964; books—*Cinema Verité* by Ali Issari, East Lansing, Michigan 1971; *Documentary: A History of Non-Fiction Film* by Erik Barnouw, New York 1974; *French Cinema Since 1946: The Personal Style*, Vol. II, by Roy Armes, New York 1976; articles—"The Face of '63—France" by P. Graham in *Films and Filming* (London), May 1963; article by Michael Kustow in *Sight and Sound* (London), spring 1964; "Cinéma Vérité in France" by Peter Graham in *Film Quarterly* (Berkeley), summer 1964; "Chris Marker and the Mutants" by Gilles Jacob in *Sight and Sound* (London), autumn 1966; article by John Thomas in *Film Society Review* (New York), January 1967; "*Le Joli mai*" by G. Gauthier in *Image et son* (Paris), no.274 (fiche), 1973; "The Left Bank Revisited" by Richard Roud in *Sight and Sound* (London), summer 1977; "Marker and Resnais: Myth and Reality" by S. Gaggi in *Literature/Film Quarterly* (Salisbury, Maryland), no.1, 1979.

*   *   *

Released in 1963, Chris Marker's *Le Joli Mai* was one of the first and finest examples of cinema verite to come out of France. Poetic, witty, complex, the film uses as its initial focus the spring of 1962, the first spring of peace for France since 1939. With roof top shots of Paris on the screen, the narrator in the opening commentary tells us: "For two centuries happiness has been a new idea in Europe, and people are not used to it." In the very political film which follows, Marker examines that idea of happiness on the small, private scale and on a larger, societal scale.

Divided into two parts, *Le Joli Mai* first concerns itself with individual happiness in a series of interviews with people from a range of social backgrounds. We meet a nervous clothing salesman concerned about money in the till, a pompous inventer intoning his philosophy of hard work and success, a young couple speaking of eternal happiness. Marker's interviewers are adept, able to elicit revealing statements about individual hopes and beliefs without overpowering the subjects. Some segments need no such devices to make a statement: the glum bride at the jolly wedding party, the joyous mother of eight showing her family their government flat, well-dressed literary types releasing a flock of doves to celebrate a poetry prize.

Part II places the small slices of life from the first half of the film onto a larger canvas for clearer definition. We see the shared political and social turmoil of France in 1962 in newsreel-like segments of police charges, demonstrations, and strikes. Cut against the newsreel footage are scenes from a Parisian nightclub where the dancing takes on an almost tribal quality. One of the dancers tell us: "While scientists concentrate on microbes, I concentrate on the twist." The interviews in this section also contribute to the larger canvas. A black student from Dahomey reveals his first thought on seeing white people, "So these are the people who conquered us," and his second, "Some day we will conquer them." A communist worker-priest says he no longer has time to consider whether God exists.

Le Jole Mai is distinguished by the witty artistry of its director. A poet and essayist as well as filmmaker, Marker has a wonderful flair for visual asides. When a grumbler disrupts the interview going on with two stock exchange apprentices, Marker turns the camera on the man and, complete with clapper, starts shooting as the interviewer asks the man the same question—what does money mean? When two consulting engineers in their discussion of work refer to nonworkers, Marker shows us shots of marvelously luxuriant, sleek cats. When the inventor propounds his philosophy of life, the camera watches the progress of a daddy longlegs across the man's lapel. A salesman's description of new luxury apartments is counterpointed by older people in the background washing in the street.

Throughout, the film is permeated by a bittersweet quality as it evokes the troubles of the past and present and hopes for a better future. That bittersweet tone underscores the inability of the individuals in the first part to cope with the larger reality around them. How can statements on the value of hard work, the meaning of money, the eternal quality of happiness deal with a police charge that kills eight people on the Metro? As one of the consulting engineers at the end of the film comments, "Our dreams are too small for what already exists." One of the distinctions of *Le Joli Mai* is that it is able to present disparate episodes from real life involving many different people and yet pull them together into a cohesive statement about the milieu in which those individuals exist.

—Sharon Lee

JONAH QUI AURA 25 ANS EN L'AN 2000. Jonah Who Will Be 25 in the Year 2000. Production: Citel Films and SSR Télévision Suisse (Geneva), Action Films and Société Français de Production (Paris); Eastmancolor, 35mm; running time: 110 mins., some sources list 116 mins.; length: 10,401 feet. Released 25 August 1976.

Produced by Yves Gasser and Yves Peyrot, executive producer: Roland Jouby; screenplay by John Berger and Alain Tanner; directed by Alain Tanner; photography by Renato Berta; edited by Brigitte Sousselier and Marc Blavet; sound recorded by Pierre Gamet, sound re-recorded by Christian Londe; music by Jean-Marie Senia.

Cast: Jean-Luc Bideau (*Max Sitigny*); Myriam Boyer (*Mathilde Vernier*); Myriam Mzière (*Madeleine*); Rufus (*Mathieu Vernier*); Roger Jendly (*Marcel Certoux*); Jacques Denis (*Marco Perly*); Miou-Miou (*Marie*); Raymond Bussieres (*Charles*); Dominique Labourier (*Marguerite*); Jonas (*Himself*); Pierre Holdener; Maurice Aufair; Jean Schlegel; Gilbert Costa; Christine Wipf; Guillaume Chenevière; Robert Schmid; Daniel Stuffel; Francis Reusser; Michel Fidanza; Nicole Dié; Domingo

Semedo; Mady Deluz; Jiairo Daghini; Albino Palumbo; Cécile; Coralie; Nathalie; David; Lionel; Nicholas; Sten; and the theater group from Calvin College.

Publications:

Scripts—"*Jonah Who Will Be 25 in the Year 2000*" (script extract) in *Ciné-tracts* (Montreal), fall/winter 1977-78; *Jonas qui aura 25 ans en l'an 2000*, Lausanne 1978; reviews—"*Jonas qui aura 25 ans en l'an 2000*" by C. Colpart in *Revue du cinéma* (Paris), November 1976; "Kids Are Hot Again" by Molly Haskell in *The Village Voice* (New York), 1 November 1976; "En Route vers la terre promise: zu Alain Tanners *Jonas-qui aura 25 ans en l'an 2000*" by B. Jaeggi in *Cinema* (Zurich), no.3, 1976; "The Current Cinema: A Cuckoo Clock That Laughs" by Pauline Kael in the *New Yorker*, 18 October 1976; "*Jonas*" by J.P. Le Pavec in *Cinéma 76* (Paris), December 1976; "Movies: A Kiss for Cinderella" by John Simon in *New York*, 15 November 1976; review in *Variety* (New York), 25 August 1976; "*Jonas qui aura 25 ans en l'an 2000*" by J. Dawson in *Monthly Film Bulletin* (London), January 1978; "*Jonas Who Will Be 25 in the Year 2000*" by T. Pulleine in *Sight and Sound* (London), spring 1978; articles—in *Image et son* (Paris), November 1976; "Les huit 'Ma'" by S. Daney in *Cahiers du cinéma* (Paris), January/February 1977; "*Jonah Who Will Be 25 in the Year 2000*" by T. Gitlin in *Film Quarterly* (Berkeley), spring 1977; "Alain Tanner's *Jonah Who Will Be 25 in the Year 2000*" by M. Tarantino in *Take One* (Montreal), March 1977; "Dialektisches Spiel mit den Ausdrucksformen" by J.P. Brossard in *Film und Fernsehen* (Berlin), December 1977; "*Jonas...qui aura 25 ans en l'an 2000*" by N. Heinic in *Cahiers du cinéma* (Paris), January/February 1977; "Keeping Hope for Radical Change Alive" by L. Rubenstein in *Cineaste* (New York), winter 1976-77; "*Jonah Who Will Be 25 in the Year 2000*: The Subversive Charm of Alain Tanner" by Robert Stam in *Jump Cut* (Chicago), no.15, 1977; "*Jonah...*: Subversive Charm Indeed!" by L. Greene in *Jump Cut* (Chicago), no.15, 1977; article in *Sequences* (Montreal), July 1977; article in *Positif* (Paris), January 1977; article in the *Listener* (London), 23 February 1978; "*Jonas qui aura 25 ans en l'an 2000*" by A. Tanner in *Ecran* (Paris), 15 January 1979; article in *Monthly Film Bulletin* (London), July 1979; "Tanner-Jonah-Ideology" by A.E. Harrild in *Film Directions* (Belfast, Northern Ireland), no.11, 1980; "Alain Tanner's *Jonah...*: Echoes of Renoir's *M. Lange*" by A. Horton in *Film Criticism* (Edinboro), spring 1980; article in *Cineforum* (Bergamo, Italy), January/February 1980; "Going Inside with Tanner" by M. Tarantino in *Movietone News* (Seattle), March 1981.

*   *   *

Jonah Who Will Be 25 in the Year 2000 is both a succinct commentary on the disillusionment experienced by the "generation of 1968" and a utopian series of vignettes that looks forward to a more egalitarian future. *Jonah* is Tanner's most successful collaboration with his frequent scenarist, the Marxist art critic John Berger, and this film follows the great promise shown by the two earlier Berger-Tanner collaborations, *La Salamandre* and *The Middle of the World*.

All of Tanner's films can be viewed as critiques of the intellectual aridity of Swiss society, and *Jonah* is his buoyant rejoinder to the complacency of the Swiss bourgeoisie. *Jonah* celebrates the communitarian idealism of eight disparate individuals at a moment of alleged historical "stasis". Yet the vitality of Tanner's protagonists helps to vitiate standard *Time* magazine clichés concerning the essentially "ephemeral" radical politics of the 1960's. For example, Max (all of the protagonists' names begin with prefix "Ma"), the disillusioned ex-Trotskyist, and his mystically inclined girlfriend, Madeleine, would seem to represent antithetical extremes of the counter-cultural spectrum. Yet Tanner's qualified optimism enables the politicized (if temporarily sidetracked) Max and the occultish Madeleine to share the same universe of discourse.

As Robert Stam has pointed out, *Jonah*'s emphasis on the need for a radical pedagogy to replace the outmoded strictures of bourgeois discourse has deep affinities with the anarchic spirit of negation embedded in Jean Vigo's classic *Zéro de conduite*. The spirit of Rousseau's *Emile* (despite its inherent contradictions, perhaps the first primer of libertarian approaches to education) permeates *Jonah*, and critical potential that is always latent (but rarely appropriated) in the educational process is highlighted in one of the film's most brilliant sequences. Marco, a charmingly gauche high school teacher, demonstrates how the hallowed "truths" of history tend to dissolve when compared to the indisputably tangible, *material* folds of a sausage link. Subsequently, Marco teaches his class the harsh realities of economic hardship by having his girlfriend lecture on the daily annoyances of her job as a supermarket cashier. This synthesis of the personal and political is (surprisingly) never cloying, and always reiterates with pointed humor Tanner's desire for social transformation.

Jonah is ultimately one of the most astonishing examples of "Brechtian cinema" to have been engendered by the ongoing re-examination of the late playwright's theoretical corpus. Unlike many other contemporary directors, Tanner realizes that "Brechtian" does not necessarily connote humorless diatribes in the manner of "the master's" most sterile, didactic works. (The dreadful *The Measures Taken* comes to mind in this context.) Miou-Miou's spontaneous cabaret song, on the other hand, suggests the exuberance of Brecht and Weill, and Tanner's playful, and always unobtrusive, use of quotations from such contemporary savants a Pablo Neruda, Jean Piaget, and Walter Benjamin helps to make *Jonah* a particularly exhilarating example of 70's *Lehrstücke*.

—Richard Wharton

LE JOUR SE LÈVE. Daybreak. Production: VOG Sigma (Paris); 1939; black and white, 35mm; running time: 85 mins.; length: 7995 feet. Released 1939.

Produced by Brachet; screenplay by Jacques Viot, adaptation and dialogue by Jacques Prévert; directed by Marcel Carné; photography by Curt Courant, Philippe Agostini, and André Bac; edited by René le Henaff; sound recorded by Arman Petitjean; production design by Alexandre Trauner; music composed by Maurice Jaubert; costumes designed by Boris Bilinsky.

Filmed in Paris Studios Cinema, Billancourt.

Cast: Jean Gabin (*François*); Jacqueline Laurent (*Françoise*); Arletty (*Clara*); René Génin (*Concierge*); Mady Berry (*Concierge's wife*); Jules Berry (*M. Valentin*); Marcel Pérè (*Paulo*); Jacques Baumer (*Inspector*); René Bergeron (*Cafe proprietor*); Gabrielle Fonton (*Woman on the stairs*); Arthur Devère (*M. Gerbois*); Georges Douking (*Blind Man*); Bernard Blier (*Gaston*).

Publications:

Scripts—"*Le Jour se lève*" in *Avant-Scène du cinéma* (Paris), October 1965; *Le Jour Se Lève: A Film by Marcel Carné and Jacques Prévert* translated by Dinah Brooke and Nicola Hayden, New York 1970; books—*Marcel Carne* by Jean-Louis Béranger, Paris 1945; *Marcel Carné* by Jean Quéval, Paris 1952; *Arletty* by Michel Perrin, Paris 1952; *Marcel Carne* by Robert Chazal, Paris 1965; *Marcel Carné, sa vie, ses films* by Bernard Landry, Paris n.d. *Marcel Carné* by Jacques Meillant, Paris n.d. *Jacques Prévert* by Guy Jacob, *Premier Plan* no.14, Lyon, November 1960; *French Film* by Roy Armes, New York 1970; *French Film* by Georges Sadoul, revised edition, New York 1972; *Cinema, The Magic Vehicle: A Guide to Its Achievement: Journey One: The Cinema Through 1949; A History of Film* by Jack C. Ellis, Englewood Cliffs, New Jersey 1979; articles—"The Cinema of Marcel Carné" by J.F. Lodge in *Sequence* (London), 1946; article by Georges Sadoul and J. Boul in *Ecrans français* (Paris), 12 June 1946; "Le Jour se lève" by Roger Manvell in *Sight and Sound* (London), autumn 1947; "Marcel Carné" by Gavin Lambert in *Sequence* (London), spring 1948; "Jean Gabin's Instinctual Man" by Pierre Duvillars in *Films in Review* (London), March 1951; "Les Films de Marcel Carné, expression de notre époque" by Georges Sadoul in *Les Lettres françaises* (Paris), 1 March 1956; "The Carné Bubble" by Alan Stanbrook in *Film* (London), November/December 1959; "Les Visiteurs du Soir" by Gérard Guillot in *Avant-Scène du cinéma* (Paris), February 1962; "Jean Gabin" by Jack E. Nolan in *Films in Review* (New York), April 1963; "Jean Gabin" by Peter Cowie in *Films and Filming* (London), February 1964; "Marcel Carné czyli rzeczywistość upozorowana: Nasz iluzjon" by A. Helman in *Kino* (Warsaw), August 1973; "*Le Jour se lève*" by F. Quenin in *Téléciné* (Paris), December 1976; "Gabin dans *Le Jour se lève*" by J. Fieschi in *Cinématographe* (Paris), January 1977.

*　　*　　*

Coming at the very end of a decade in which the French cinema reigned intellectually supreme, *Le Jour Se Lève* was the culminating achievement of the school known as "poetic realism." Forty years on, the realism looks uncommonly like romanticism, but there can be little doubt about the poetry. The film is suffused with a bitter-sweet fatalism, a soft, drifting melancholy that invests the drab settings of factory and tenement with its own sad romance. The characters, hero and villain alike, seem to move in a dream, progressing with stoic resignation towards their inescapable destiny. The parallel with pre-war France, awaiting defeat with mesmerised passivity, has often been drawn, and is indeed hard to avoid.

The circularity of the film's structure mirrors its fatalistic mood—what will happen, must happen, for we have already seen it happen. In the opening seconds, a man is shot, reeling mortally wounded down the tenement stairs. As police arrive and a crowd gathers, the killer barricades himself in his attic room; and through the long night, smoking his last cigarettes, he recalls events that led him to kill. By way of a carefully structured series of flashbacks, we return full circle to the shooting, seeing it this time from inside the room. As dawn breaks, the police prepare an assault. A final shot is heard; a cloud of rear-gas creeps over a lifeless body in the early rays of the sun; and abruptly, the noise of the dead man's alarm-clock breaks the silence.

Gabin's performance, as the besieged killer, stands as the epitome of his pre-war persona as doomed proletarian anti-hero, developed through Duvivier's *Pépé le Moko*, Renoir's *La Bête*

Humaine, and his previous Carné film, *Quai des Brumes*. Equally outstanding is Jules Berry's portrayal of his victim, the sadistic animal trainer so compulsively dedicated to destruction that he even brings about his own death in order to destroy others. *Le Jour Se Lève*—like *Quai des Brumes* and all Carné's other early films—was made in close collaboration with his scriptwriter, the poet Jacques Prévert, whose wit, love of language, and fatalistic poetry permeate the film to such a degree that his name should stand with the director's as co-creator.

Le Jour Se Lève was banned under the Vichy regime, accused of having contributed to the debacle of 1940. (Carné responded that the barometer should hardly be blamed for the storm it foretells.) Widely shown and acclaimed after the war, it was then suppressed again in 1947, this time by RKO, to make way for Anatole Litvak's crass re-make, *The Long Night* (with Henry Fonda in the Gabin role). Rumours that all prints had been destroyed proved mercifully unfounded. Carné's film resurfaced during the 1950's, and is now generally acknowledged, together with *Les Enfants du Paradis*, as the finest product of his partnership with Prévert. The film's pre-war despair has transmuted into nostalgic melancholy, closer now to Ophuls than Renoir; its romantic appeal seems likely to survive undimmed.

—Philip Kemp

JOURNAL D'UN CURÉ DE CAMPAGNE. Diary of a Country Priest. Production: Union Générale Cinématographique; black and white, 35mm; running time: 120 mins. Released 1950.

Produced by Léon Carré; screenplay by Robert Bresson; from the novel by Georges Bernanos; directed by Robert Bresson; photography by Léonce-Henry Burel; edited by Paulette Robert; production design by Pierre Charbonnier; music by Jean-Jacques Grüenwald.

Prix Louis-Delluc, France, 1950; Venice Film Festival, Best Photography and International Prize, 1951.

Cast: Claude Laydu (*Priest of Ambricourt*); Nicole Ladmiral (*Chantal*); Nicole Maurey (*Mademoiselle Louise*); Marie-Monique Arkell (*Countess*); Armand Guibert (*Priest of Torcy*); Jean Riveyre (*Count*); Jean Danet (*Olivier*); Antoine Balpêtré (*Doctor Delbende*); Martine Lemaire (*Séraphita*); Yvette Etiévant (*Young girl*).

Publications:

Books—*The Film* edited by Andrew Sarris, Indianapolis, Indiana 1968; *The Films of Robert Bresson* by 5 reviewers, New York 1969; *French Cinema Since 1946, Vol. I* by Roy Armes, New York 1970; *The Films of Robert Bresson* by Ian Cameron, London 1970; *Transcendental Style on Film: Ozu, Bresson, Dreyer* by Paul Schrader, Los Angeles 1972; *Robert Bresson o cinematografo e o sinal* by C. de Pontes Leca, Lisbon 1978; articles—"Bresson on Location: Interview" by Jean Douchet in *Sequence* (London), no.13, 1951; "Notes on Robert Bresson" by Gavin Lambert in *Sight and Sound* (London), summer 1953; "The Quest for Realism" by Gordon Gow in *Films and Filming* (London), December 1957; "Robert Bresson" by Brian Baxter in *Film* (London), September/October 1958; "Robert Bresson" by

Charles Ford, translated by Anne and Thornton Brown in *Films in Review* (New York), February 1959; "Robert Bresson" by Marjorie Green in *Film Quarterly* (Berkeley), spring 1960; "Conventional/Unconventional" by Colin Young in *Film Quarterly* (Berkeley), spring 1960; "French Outsider with the Inside Look" by Richard Roud in *Films and Filming* (London), April 1960; "Puritans Anonymous" by Ian Johnson and Raymond Durgnat in *Motion* (London), autumn 1963; "Spiritual Style in the Films of Robert Bresson" by Susan Sontag in *Seventh Art* (New York), summer 1964; "The Two Chambermaids" by Tom Milne in *Sight and Sound* (London), autumn 1964; "The Question: Interview with Robert Bresson" by Jean-Luc Godard and Michel Delahaye in *Cahiers du Cinéma in English* (New York), May 1966; "*Diary of a Country Priest*" by Raymond Durgnat in *Films and Filming* (London), December 1966; "Robert Bresson" in *Interviews with Film Directors* by Andrew Sarris, New York 1967; "Praxis as a Cinematic Principle in the Films of Robert Bresson" by Donald S. Skoller in *Cinema Journal* (Evanston, Illinois), fall 1969; "The Art of Robert Bresson" by Roy Armes in *London Magazine*, October 1970; "The Suicide of Robert Bresson" by Marvin Zemon in *Cinema* (London), spring 1971; "Robert Bresson" in *Encountering Directors* by Charles Thomas Samuels, New York 1972; "Bresson's Stylistics Revisited" by M. Prokosch in *Film Quarterly* (Berkeley), winter 1971-72; "Matter and Spirit in the Films of Robert Bresson" by H.M. Polhemusin *Film Heritage* (Dayton, Ohio), spring 1974; "Burel and Bresson" by R. Nogueira in *Sight and Sound* (London), winter 1976-77; "Léonce H. Burel", interview by R. Prédal, in *Cinéma* (Paris), July/August 1974; "Das *Tagebuch eines Landfarrers* und die Stilistik von Robert Bresson" by A. Bazin, translated by A. Spingler, in *Filmkritik* (Munich), May 1979.

*   *   *

In the politics of adaptation, Robert Bresson's *Diary of a Country Priest* must stand out as a revolutionary event. Taking over the project of this novel after its author, Georges Bernanos, had repudiated the version offered by Aurenche and Bost, Bresson promised to get beyond the cinema in order to embody, or act out, the spiritual drama that was at its core. Initially supported by producer Pierre Gerin, Bresson found himself abandoned after Bernanos's death in 1948. Nevertheless, he obtained the rights, finished his austere and unconventional script, and appealed to Bernanos's literary executor, Albert Beguin. Not only did Beguin accept Bresson's project, but this influential editor of the journal *Esprit* also helped him secure financing through the recently established national production agency, Union Générale Cinématographique.

Bresson chose for his hero a young Swiss actor from among a great many candidates, all of them practicing Catholics. For over a year Bresson and Laydu met each Sunday to discuss the role. Laydu went so far as to live for a time in a monastery to accustom himself to priestly garb and gestures. Bresson insisted that he cease acting and become a "model," an instinctive presence to be sculpted by light and camera.

The French press covered the production and premiere of the film with pride. They helped guide it to a new audience, of intellectuals and of the pious, two groups that had never frequented the cinema. Cinephiles were encouraged to see the film twice. In this way *Diary of a Country Priest* opened up new options in the conception, realization, and exploitation of a film.

Using fidelity of adaptation as an issue, Bresson actually challenged the entire aesthetics of French cinema of quality. His film overturns received notions of "the primacy of the image" and of the "cinematic story," abandoning the theatirical, public and architectural ostentation of quality for a fluid, musical, interior, and ascetic expression. Bresson spoke of his work as an "ecriture" (Sartre) demanding new notions of the actor, the shot, and the soundtrack. Most critics could barely digest the film, for as Bazin said, it is a film not so much to read as to directly feel. While one can analyse the subject "christologically" according to the Stations of the Cross (the curé's falls, the wiping of his face by Seraphita, his glorious motorcycle ride to the big city where he will die, that death occurring between two outcasts in a high attic room), Bresson's is the opposite of an allegorical film. He cut 45 minutes without hesitation because the true drama was internal and was present in the quality of each of its moments. The spirituality every critic feels emanating from the film is really an effect produced by the accumulation of details rather than by dramatic plotting. A spiritual rhythm invades the images through the repetition of scenes, gestures, sounds, lighting and decor. Dialogue, monologue, landscape shots, scenes of writing, intensely composed music and natural sounds orchestrate a meditation rather than a story.

The diary form itself becomes the true site of meditation. It is variously represented as written pages on the screen, as a voice which situates the actions we see, and as those actions themselves, when through fades, ellipses and the like we realize that what is represented is reflection upon an event, not the event itself. In the penultimate sequence at the cafe, all three diary forms are present simultaneously: we see him writing, hear him say "I must have dozed off for a while," and sense that doze through a slight reframing after a dissolve. In this key moment we realize that he is recording the very episode we are watching, Layering reflection on reflection as he sums up his life just before it ends.

But the diary is also treated as one physical object among others. Bresson capitalizes on the cinema's indifferent attachment to the objects of the world by filming lamps, winebottles, furniture, and prayerbooks in closeup. Bazin always claimed that style is a pattern of selection. If this is so, then Bresson gets to the interior via these objects as they interact with the hands, feet, and eyes of characters in a landscape of barren trees, narrow roads and the interiors of cold houses the doors and windows of which are at once invitations and warnings.

The gray and spongy atmosphere that lights this world is transcended by the priest in his diary. Certain scenes let us sense this transcendence in their lighting. The dialogue with Chantal in the confessional is the greatest such scene, for Bresson allows us to witness the luminosity of two faces and two hands in a dark space where only voice and intention matter. Light is the metaphor of the curé's discourse as he passes dark nights and is drawn to the warmth of lamps in windows and to the promise of dawn. At times light is not even a clarifying medium but a substance surrounded by darkness.

The curé's homelessness is seldom pictured in a single image, but exists as a rhythm of entrances and exits in which the world seems distant from him. The diary shapes a life in transit, at home only with itself and its meditation. *Diary of a Country Priest* is a landmark in subjective cinema. No establishing shots put the priest in context. Characters accelerate away from him. Bresson refuses to situate him dramatically, sociologically, or theologically. We are locked within his point of reflection. The soundtrack alone reminds him and us of the wider world. The natural sounds of feet on cobblestones, of a motorcycle, of people whispering, or of a breeze blowing constitute the true atmosphere of a search for grace. Together with the voice of the diary and the finality of the musical score (the last time Bresson would lean on a score), these natural sounds present the whole of the curé's world in each moment of the film: its pastness, its responsiveness,

its fidelity, its limitation of vision, its productive loneliness and suffering.

The stakes of this film are high. Like the curé, Bresson is banking on the power of humility and discipline. Instead of achieving a life, Bresson would achieve a film. He would do so by thwarting the cinema. Many believers, especially the young *cahiers* critics Truffaut and Godard, have had to defend their faith against those outraged by a film emanating in fragments from an obscure and obsessive mind. *Diary of a Country Priest* remains a watershed film in the history of adaptations and in the politics of style.

—Dudley Andrew

JUJIRO. Crossroads. Shadows of the Yoshiwara. Crossways. Production: Kinugasa Motion Pictures Association and Shochiku; black and white, 35mm, silent; running time: about 80 mins.; length: 7 reels. Released 11 May 1928. Re-released 1976.

Produced, scripted, and directed by Teinosuke Kinugasa; photography by Kohei Sugiyama; art direction by Yozo Tomonari, some sources list Bonji Taira; lighting: Masao Uchida and Kinshi Tsuruta.

Cast: Junosuke Bando (*Rikiya, the brother*); Akiko Chihaya (*Older sister*); Yukiko Ogawa (*O-une, woman of Yoshiwara*); Ippei Soma (*Man with the Constable's stick*); Yoshie Nakagawa (*Woman who sells women*); Misao Seki (*Old landlord*); Myoichiro Ozawa (*Man who quarrels*); Teruko Sanjo (*Mistaken woman*).

Publications:

Books—*Le Cinéma japonais* by Marcel de Shinobu Giuglaris, Paris 1956; *Invitation au cinéma japanois* by Cinémathèque français, Paris 1963; *Cinema, The Magic Vehicle: A Guide to Its Achievement: Journey One: The Cinema Through 1949* edited by Jacek Klinowski and Adam Garbicz, Metuchen, New Jersey 1975; *The Japanese Film: Art and Industry* by Joseph Anderson and Donald Richie, Princeton, New Jersey 1982; articles— "Seven from the Past" by J.L. Anderson in *Sight and Sound* (London), autumn 1957. "*Crossways*" by Douglas McVay in *Films and Filming* (London), June 1960.

*   *   *

After the commerical disaster of the experimental *Page of Madness* (1926), Kinugasa's independent production company made its last film, *Jujiro*, in 1928. Thus freed somewhat from the pressure of maintaining the company's image (and solvency), everybody in the staff decided to explore whatever he wanted in the company's swan song. The result was this unique avant-garde *jidaigeke* (period film): Kinugasa completely eliminated from this film sword play, which was then the norm, and concentrated on the depiction of the characters' psychology, thus creating a new style in this genre.

Visually, the film is one of astonishing effects and powerful images. Because of financial limitations, old boxes and wood used in the previous films were collected, painted and deliberately reused to create a bizarre atmosphere of poverty. The whole set design is based on unbalanced and distorted images, which happen to be similar to those of German Expressionism. Parallel lines are carefully avoided in the shapes of roofs, at the window lines and in the interior architecture.

The strong contrast of light and shadow is also expressionistic. Particularly skillful is the highlighting of characters' dramatic emotion by exploiting a heightened effect of counterlight. Raindrops are captured dripping from the hair of the doomed sister and brother, shining in the strong counterlight. The grotesque and nasty face of the man with the constable who is trying to make advances to the helpless sister is illuminated from behind in the dark as he ascends the stairs to the attic. The chiaroscuro photography, by the then young and ambitious Kohei Sugiyama, is exquisite.

The upstairs room is symbolically presented as the only sanctuary from the lower world of evil and malice. The tragedies of the sister and the brother both originate in credulous mistakes (she believes the false identity of the man with the constable; he believes that he committed a murder which in fact never took place). This theme is conveyed by the numerous scenes of fantasy and dream, as well as by the use of the flash-back and flash-forward techniques. The boundary between reality and imagination is left ambiguous in mesmerising effects created by camera movements, such a quick tracking shots, quick panning shots and numerous superimpositions.

An especially sophisticated sequence is the scene in which ashes are thrown in the brother's face dazzling him. Interrupting the fight sequence is a sequence of black and white designs, used to create a flickering effect: there then follows a close-up shot of the brother's agonized face within the image of a storm of falling ashes. This is followed by a shot of him staggering, frames with black and white lightning-like shapes, and then the shot of an object accelerating toward the camera. Finally, the camera tilts almost 90 degrees and captures the tottering brother crashing into objects. This complicated process of mixing the establishing shots and close-up shots of him staggering with images from his subjective point-of-view succeeds in conveying his despair and disorientation.

The recurrent spinning image is prevalent throughout the film. It is suggested by the image of targets at an archery shop where the woman the hero loves works. This shop is surrounded by other round and spinning images such as umbrellas and lanterns. The pattern of the woman's kimono suggests playfully those targets and arrows (relevant to the theme of stalking of a love partner). At the house of the brother and his sister, there is a big spinning wheel in the upstairs room; the downstairs is filled with round objects such as mats and straw hats.

The image of the crossroads is strikingly simple: only a few naked trees along the white roads in the dark. This set conveys artificiality, yet it also successfully suggests the helplessness and desperation of the sister finally waiting alone in vain for her brother.

Kinugasa's ambitious film was received far more appreciatively in Europe than in his home country. The re-release of *Jujiro* in Japan in 1976, however, created an excitement appropriate to the re-discovery of an avant-garde clasic.

—Kyoko Hirano

JULES ET JIM. Jules and Jim. Production: Films du Carosse and SEDIF; 1962; black and white, 35mm, Franscope; running time: 105 mins. Released 23 January 1962, Paris.

Produced by Marcel Berbert; screenplay by François Truffaut and Jean Gruault; from the novel by Henri-Pierre Roché; directed by François Truffaut; photography by Raoul Coutard; edited by Claudine Bouche; sound by Témoin; music by Georges Delerue, song "Le Tourbillon" by Bassiak; costumes designed by Fred Capel.

Filmed 1963 Alsace, Paris, and Venice.

Cast: Jeanne Moreau (*Katherine*); Oscar Werner (*Jules*); Henri Serre (*Jim*); Vanna Urbino (*Gilberte*); Boris Bassiak (*Albert*); Sabine Haudepin (*Sabine*); Marie Dubois (*Thérèse*); Jean-Louis Richard (*1st Customer in café*); Michel Varesano (*2nd Customer in café*); Pierre Fabre (*Drunkard in the café*); Danielle Bassiak (*Albert's friend*); Bernard Largemains (*Merlin*); Elen Bober (*Mathilde*); Michel Subor (*Narrator*).

Publications:

Scripts—"Jules et Jim" in *Avant-Scène du Cinéma* (Paris), 1962; *Jules and Jim: A Film by François Truffaut* translated by Nicholas Fry, New York 1968; *Jules et Jim*, translated into German by E. Elling, L. Kaczmarek and K.-D. Möller and H.J. Wulff, Munich 1981; reviews—by Peter Baker in *Films and Filming* (London), June 1962; review by Richard Roud in *Sight and Sound* (London), summer 1962; review by Andrew Sarris in *The Village Voice* (New York) 3 May 1962; books—*The New Wave* by Peter Graham, New York 1968; *The Cinema of François Truffaut* by Graham Petrie, New York 1970; *François Truffaut* by C.G. Crisp and Michael Walker, New York 1971; *Film as Film: Critical Responses to Film Art* by Joy Boyum and Adrienne Scott, Boston 1971; *François Truffaut* by C.G. Crisp, London 1972; *L'Univers de François Truffaut* by Dominique Fanne, Paris 1972; *Truffaut* by Don Allen, New York 1974; *The New Wave* by James Monaco, New York 1976; *Le Cinéma de François Truffaut* by Jean Collet, Paris 1977; *François Truffaut* by Annette Insdorf, Boston 1978; articles—by Parker Tyler in *Film Culture* (New York), summer 1962; "Les Tourbillons élémentaires" by Michel Delahaye in *Cahiers du cinéma* (Paris), March 1962; "Interview with Truffaut" by L. Marcorelles in *Sight and Sound* (London), winter 1961-62; "Conversation with François Truffaut in the *New York Film Bulletin*, no.3, 1962; "*Jules and Jim*: Sex and Life" by F. Truffaut in *Films and Filming* (London), no.10, 1962; article by Roger Greenspun in *Sight and Sound* (London), spring 1963; "François Truffaut—The Anarchist Imagination" by Judith Shatnoff in *Film Quarterly* (Berkeley), spring 1963; "The Face of 63—France" by P. Graham in *Films and Filming* (London), May 1963; "The Stars They Couldn't Photograph" by Alan Stanbrook in *Films and Filming* (New York), February 1963; "La Peau douce..." by André Téchiné in *Cahiers du cinéma* (Paris), July 1964; "The Literary Sophistication of François Truffaut" by Michael Klein in *Film Comment* (New York), summer 1965; article by Stanley Solomon in *Film Heritage* (Dayton, Ohio), winter 1965-66; article by Daniel Rosenblatt in *Film Society Review* (New York), November 1968; "Art and Film in François Truffaut's *Jules and Jim* and *2 English Girls*" by Barbara Coffee in *Film Heritage* (Dayton, Ohio), spring 1974; "Truffaut's Gorgeous Killers" by Beverle Houston and Marsha Kinder in *Film Quarterly* (Berkeley), winter 1973-74; "*Jules et Jim*" by G. Colpart in *Téléciné* (Paris), November 1976; "From *400 Blows* to *Small*

Change" by Gerald Mast in the *New Republic* (New York), 2 April 1977; "The Existential Play in Truffaut's Early Films" by A. Thiher in *Literature/Film Quarterly* (Salisbury, Maryland), summer 1977; "From Virgin to Dynamo: The 'Amoral Woman' in European Cinema" by D. Davidson in *Cinema Journal* (Iowa City), fall 1981.

*   *   *

Jules and Jim is among the masterpieces of the French New Wave and may be considered the high achievement of that movement. The first films of Truffaut, Godard, Chabrol & Co. had astonished the world with a vitality that seemed evanescent, while too many of the films after 1962 are generally thought to be decadent and cloying in their search for novel effects. But with *Jules and Jim* we have a film that is at once vital, astonishing, and mature. Its solidity as well as its richness have kept it from fading even under the intense light of scholarship and criticism to which it has been continually subject.

In some respects it is not characteristic New Wave film, for it chronicles 30 years in the lives of its characters, opening brightly in La Belle Epoque and closing in the grim era of the Depression and the rise of Hitler. Whereas most New Wave films sought to express the rhythms of their own epoch with complete freshness, Truffaut in this film retreated to the past. But in its own way *Jules and Jim* is faithful to the existentialist ethic and aesthetic of the New Wave period, for no film strives more obviously for authenticity in its quest to tap the feelings of a liberated generation whose morality must be achieved on the run.

Oddly, it was through the intermediary of a 75-year-old sensibility, that of novelist Henri-Pierre Roché, that Truffaut was able to shape this past into a pure picture of his own generation. When he read the novel upon its publication in 1955, he immediately contacted Roché, initiating a correspondence that continued until the latter's death which occurred just before the film went into production. Of course in 1955 Truffaut was but a minor critic who could only dream of the film this novel might become. Nevertheless, even at that time he mentioned it as an example of the kind of living, breathing story he claimed was missing from the moribund "Cinema of Quality" which dominated the 1950's in France.

What was it that gave this novel its vigor, and how did Truffaut succeed in letting its spirit animate his film when at length he was able to make it? One must begin with the plethora of incidents spilling out of the novel's first pages. While Truffaut has drastically reduced their number and, more certainly, the number of characters he introduces, both works dizzy their audience. La Belle Epoque is carefree and exciting as lived through Jules and Jim. It becomes more dangerous and even more exciting once they attach themselves to Katherine.

The bubbling first third of the film is a textbook in photographic and editing effects (stop frame, swish pans, stock footage, jump cuts). Only the narrator who ties together these fragments hints wistfully at the trouble to come. The film makes its inevitable descent just as Katherine accepts Jules' marriage proposal. For his dream has been attained on the eve of the outbreak of the Great War, a war so graphically documented that it brutalizes the earlier sentiments of the film, tossing its characters off their merry-go-round where they land, still and stunned. This second movement shows the reality of living with Katherine, the dream they had so hectically pursued. Her fickleness makes them prisoners of their own desires, and their imaginations, still rich with inventiveness, are tethered to one who is neither beautiful nor intelligent but for whom they would surrender their lives because

she is pure woman (spontaneous, tender, cruel). The conclusion is more somber still, as each character achieves a compensating wisdom, a sense of self. Katherine is both fire and water, the vitriol she pours down the sink. She chooses water for death, cremation for burial. Jim is romantic, a dashing Parisian novelist who travels after the war in search of the 20th century. Comfortable with his shifting feelings, he runs from Gilberte to Katherine whenever she calls him. Finally there is Jules who treasures their lives to the full. A Buddhist in sensibility, he possesses Katherine through patience. An entomologist, he would write of the loves that insects aspire to. Nothing is too small for his attention. His resignation and nostalgia place him nearest the narrator, as he looks back at a time when life was full of freedom and promise.

If the film's plot is a progressive decline, its images set off these oppositions at every turn. The film's first enthusiasts pointed to the interplay of circles and triangles. The lovers directly illustrate the triangle they are living as they welcome the morning from three separate windows at the seashore. The sharp angular pans of the camera keep us wondering in which direction love must flow. But it is the spinning circularity of the cinemascope most viewers recall, a circularity repeated in the cafe tables, the tadpoles swimming round their bowl, in Katherine's cosmology which holds the world to be an inverted bowl. Bicycles are in circles; Sabine rolls over and over to the music which culminates in Katherine's prophetic song, her "Rondo of love."

These two master graphic forms come together. Roger Greenspun observed, in the hourglass measuring out the final days of La Belle Epoque and the preciousness of the briefest instants of life. Art is another such measure, and *Jules and Jim* is a catalogue of the arts. Scattered through its texture are references to old films, to photography and slideshows, to statues, paintings, novels, the theater, and music. This is a story about the drive to raise life to art and art to eternity. In the abundance of its episodes, symbols, citations, and tales, and in its mixture of excitement and resignation, *Jules and Jim* never lets up in its own drive to give meaning to and express the vitality of life. This was the ambition of the New Wave, and this film is its apotheosis.

—Dudley Andrew

<hr>

KAGEMUSHA. The Double. The Shadow Warrior. Production: Toho Films-Kurosawa Productions (Tokyo) and Twentieth Century-Fox; Eastmancolor, 35mm; running time: 179 mins. Released 21 May 1980.

Produced by Akira Kurosawa; screenplay by Akira Kurosawa and Masato Ide; directed by Akira Kurosawa; photography by Takao Saito and Masaharu Ueda, supervised by Kazuo Miyagawa and Asaichi Nakai; art direction by Yoshiro Muraki; music by Shinichiro Ikebe.

Cost: $6 million.

Cast: Tatsuya Nakadai; Tsutomu Yamazaki; Kenichi Hagiwara; Kota Yui; Hideji Otaki; Hideo Murata; Daisuke Ryu.

Publications:

Reviews—"*Kagemusha*" by Rob Edelman in *Films in Review* (New York), December 1980; "A Shaggy Ghost Story" by R. Combs in *Sight and Sound* (London), winter 1980; "4 from the New York Film Festival": *Kagemusha: The Shadow Warrior*" by Gary Growdus in *Cineaste* (New York), fall 1980; "*Kagemusha*" by G. Moskowitz in *Variety* (New York), 21 May 1980; "*Kagemusha*" by J. Pym in *Monthly Film Bulletin* (London), December 1980; "Der Schatten eines Kriegers" by E. Schumacher in *Fern und Fernsehen* (Berlin), June 1981; articles— "Toho Shoots $7,000,000 Bankroll on Kurosawa, Fox Buys Stake, Coppola-Lucas Will Re-edit" in *Variety* (New York), 9 May 1979; "*Kagemusha*" by P. Bueren in *Skoop* (Amsterdam), August 1980; "De keizer en de samurai: Kurosawa filmt tussen de glazen whiskey door: een reportage" by I. Buruma in *Skoop* (Amsterdam), March/April 1980; "Kurosawa's Army" by J. Gillett in *Sight and Sound* (London), spring 1980; "Akira Kurosawa—Humanist uden illusioner" by E. Iversen in *Kosmorama* (Copenhagen), December 1980; "*Kagemusha*" in *Films* (London), December 1980; "Kurosawa tourne *Le Double*" by M. Martin in *Image et son* (Paris), January 1980; "Apocalypse nô ou la fin d'un humanise" by F. Ramasse and A. Tassone in *Positif* (Paris), October 1980; "La Fascination des grandes ambitions des grands héros, des grands brigands" by A. Tassone in *Cinéma* (Paris), October 1980; "Kurosawa. *Kagemusha*" by M. Tessier in *Image et son* (Paris), October 1980; "The Warrior Returns" by D. Yakir in *Film Comment* (New York), November/December 1980; "Vom gewöhnlichen Dieb zum echten Takeda" by M. Martin in *Film und Fernsehen* (Berlin), June 1981; "*Kagemusha*" in *International Film Guide* (London), 1981.

*   *   *

Although most Japanese filmmakers have regarded the period film as an unrewarding, languishing genre, Akira Kurosawa has repeatedly produced and directed such films, set against a background of 16th—century feudal Japanese society, during his career of almost 40 years. In *Kagemusha*, at six million dollars the most expensive film yet made in Japan, Kurosawa again demonstrates that the period film can manifest a vitality that it has apparently lost for his contemporaries.

Running more than two and a half hours, *Kagemusha* can be characterized as genuinely epic. Not only does it deal with warfare on a massive scale as do epics in western literary tradition, but, also, like those long narrative poems, it narrows its focus to a consideration of how warfare affects and is affected by the individual. While the film's title character may not be as valorous as Achilles or Aeneas, he still emerges as an "epic hero" who changes throughout the course of the narrative.

Based on an incident from Japanese history, *Kagemusha*—the title means "shadow warrior"—relates how Shingen, warlord of one of the three clans that are struggling for control of Japan, ensures that the effect of his presence will persist even after his death. Recognizing that his presence is essential for the clan's military success, Shingen has been using his younger brother to double for him. Thus he can be at two different parts of the battlefield at the same time. When a nameless thief, facing execution by crucifixion, is found to bear an exact resemblance to Shingen, though, the criminal is chosen as the double. The warlord is killed by a sniper, and the thief must assume the dead leader's identity. Gradually mastering the etiquette of the feudal nobility as well as convincing some of Shingen's intimates—

especially his grandson and mistresses—that he is the actual warlord, the thief manages to hold the clan together until Shingen's envious son exposes the imposture. But by this time the thief, unwilling at first to be Shingen's double, has become closely identified with the warlord. Even though he is exiled from court, the thief tries to rally the clan's army in a climactic last battle. Wounded fatally, he sinks dying into the lake where Shingen had been buried.

Like *The Iliad* and *The Aeneid*, Kurosawa's film has its scenes of sweeping grandeur: an early sequence in which a messenger rushes through what seems to be acres of bivouacking soldiers, the disposal of Shingen's body in the mist-enshrouded waters of the lake, the pomp of the feudal warlord's court, and the vistas of the final battle, for example. But these scenes are balanced by those that depict the thief's growth into his role as substitute warlord. He gradually progresses from reluctant participant in the charade, to a shadow of the warlord, and, finally, to a figure of real stature. His growth, though, occurs mainly because of his personal relationships with members of the feudal aristocracy. For instance, the thief's deepening fondness for Shingen's grandson, a feeling which is reciprocated, parallels his commitment to the role assigned to him. The grandson initially recognizes that the thief is a fake, but before long the two have formed a warm friendship. The child seems to represent the clan for which the thief ultimately sacrifices his life.

With *Kagemusha*, Kurosawa reasserts the idea that period films may be more than soap operas or mindless adventures in antique dress. He uses the period background as an apt milieu for the development of a figure who finally becomes heroic and self-sacrificing. The film assumes epic quality as its central figure attains stature.

—Frances M. Malpezzi

KAMERADSCHAFT. Comradeship. Production: Nero-Film (Berlin) and Gaumont-Franco (Paris), the collaboration of these two companies frequently referred to as Nero-Film AG; black and white, 35mm; running time: 85 mins., French version is 93 mins.; length: 3060 feet (German version). Released 1931.

Produced by Seymour Nebenzel; screenplay by Ladislaus (Laszlo) Vajda, Karl Otten, Peter Martin Lampel and Fritz Eckardt; from a story by Karl Otten; directed by G.W. Pabst; photography by Fritz Arno Wagner and Robert Baberski; edited by Hans Oser; sound recorded by A. Jansen; production design by Ernö Metzner and Karl Vollbrecht; French advisor: Robert Beaudoin.

Cast: Alexander Granach (*Kaspar*); Fritz Kampers (*Wilderer*); Daniel Mendaille (*Pierre*); Ernst Busch (*Kaplan*); Elisabeth Wendt (*Françoise*); Gustav Püttjer (*Jean*); Oskar Höcker (*Emile*); Hélèna Manson (*Albert's wife*); Andrée Ducret (*François*); Alex Bernard (*Grandfather*); Pierre Louis (*George*).

Publications:

Books—*Der Regisseur: G.W. Pabst* edited by Rudolph Joseph, Munich 1963; *Le Cinéma réaliste allemande* by Raymond Borde and others, Lyons 1965; *G.W. Pabst*, Premier Plan No.39, by Freddy Buache, Lyons 1965; *The Haunted Screen* by Lotte

Eisner, Berkeley 1969; *From Caligari to Hitler: A Psychological History of the German Film* by Siegfried Kracauer, Princeton 1969; *The German Cinema* by Roger Manvell and Heinrich Fraenkel, New York 1971; *50 Years of German Film* by H.H. Wollenberg, reissued, New York 1972; *G.W. Pabst* by Lee Atwell, Boston 1977; articles—"A Mining Film" by Ernö Metzner in *Close Up* (London), March 1932; "Pabst and the Social Film" by Harry Alan Potamkin in *Hound and Horn* (New York), January/March 1933; "Revaluations: *Kameradschaft*" by Roger Manvell in *Sight and Sound* (London), November 1950; special Pabst issue of *Cinemages* (New York), May 1955; special Pabst issue of *Filmkunst* (Vienna), no.18, 1955; fiche in *Image et son* (Paris), November 1960; article in *Cineforum* (Bergamo, Italy), no.14, 1962; "G.W. Pabst" by Herbert Luft in *Films in Review* (New York), February 1964; "G.W. Pabst" by Herbert Luft in *Films and Filming* (London), April 1967; "Lang, Pabst, and Sound" by N. Carroll in *Ciné-tracts* (Montreal), fall 1978; "*Kameradschaft*" by T. Pulleine in *Monthly Film Bulletin* (London), March 1978; article in *Filmkunst* (Vienna), no.86, 1980; "La Tragedie de la mine" by D. Sauvaget in *Image et son* (Paris), March 1981; article in *Cinématographe* (Paris), February 1981.

*   *   *

Kameradschaft is a noble film—in theme and execution. It reflects the proletarian idealism of its time. It smacks of Toller and Rolland, and like them it has at the back of its mind a shadow of doubt. In 1931 in Germany events were moving slowly to the rise of Hitler, which all the good will in the world could not stop, and the film does in fact end on an ironic note.

The action turns on a single event. On the borders of France and Germany a vein of coal cuts through the frontier. Above ground a frontier post separates two communities; in the mine a brick wall separates the German and French workers. From very first shots of boys quarreling over a game of marbles to those of three German workers who decide to spend a Saturday night in a French dance hall, the director G.W. Pabst sets the mood of the film. Action is sparked off when an explosion in the French mine is reported to the German miners as they stand naked in the great shower room with their clothes raised above the sprinklers by chains. Ernst Busch, their spokesman, decides to lead a rescue party which ultimately breaks through the frontier barrier and arrives at the gates of the French mine to the astonishment of the waiting and despairing relatives. "Les Allemands. Ce n'est pas possible". The rest of the film is concerned with the rescue.

Pabst has stamped the exterior and interior of the mine with uncompromising realism. The people are the protagonists, and individual characters never leave the ambience which shapes them and to which they belong. With the brilliant cooperation of his designer, Ernő Metzner, Pabst has achieved a triumph of studio construction. Life in the mine and the terror of the disaster are translated into film terms that remain unforgettable. No music is used. The noises of the mine, the clanking of chains, metal rubbing against metal, the whirring sounds of lifts—all this brings the strange world of the miner vividly before the spectator. It is a shared and illuminated experience. Pabst's great humanity shines through the film. Its technical virtuosity is no less. Wagner's camera catches the light shining in darkness, follows the ravaged, terrified faces. It gives significance to darkness.

There is no plot as such. Human relations are hinted at. But the mine disaster leaves us in no doubt as to those relationships. Fançoise and her lover. The old man and his grandson. The three German friends. All are people we know, and from the event

Pabst creates a richly textured canvas of life and reality.

Faces haunt us. The hysterical miner, tap tapping a signal on metal pipe, who hears the guttural sounds of his German rescuer wearing a gasmask; he thinks he is back in the war and hurls himself on his rescuer. Anna dragging her child beside the lorry that carries her husband to the dangers of rescue work. The actors do not play in this film; they are embedded in it.

The technical problems of creating movement in a narrow space were superbly overcome, as were the problems of proportioning light in dark areas. But above all it is the great spirit of Pabst that is the real triumph of the film.

Sadly, as the miners celebrate their new found friendship— "Why must we cooperate only at times of disaster. Why not every day"—below ground the brick wall which was smashed to allow the German rescuers through is rebuilt with much official rubber-stamping and exchanging of documents. A new shadow was falling on the German people.

—Liam O'Leary

KANAL. Canal. They Loved Life. Production: Film Polski and ZAF; black and white, 35mm; running time: 95 mins., some sources list 97 mins.; length: 8569 feet. Released April 1957.

Produced by Stanisław Adler; screenplay by Jerzy Stefan Stawiński; from a short story by Jerzy Stawiński; directed by Andrzej Wajda; photography by Jerzy Lipman; art direction by Roman Mann and Roman Wołzniec; music by Jan Krenz, Ocarina theme by Adam Pawlikowski.

Filmed 1957 in Poland. Cannes Film Festival, Special Prize, 1957; Moscow International Film Festival of Youth and Students, Golden Medal, 1957.

Cast: Wieńczysław Gliński (*Lt. Zadra*); Tadeusz Janczar (*Korab*); Teresa Iżewski (*Stokrotka*); Emil Karewicz (*Madry*); Władysła Sheybal (*Composer*); Tadeusz Gwiazdowski (*Kula*); Stanisław Mikulski (*Slim*); Teresa Berezowska (*Halinka*); Adam Pawlikowski (*German officer*).

Publications:

Reviews—"*Kanal*" by R. Holloway in *Variety* (New York), 5 September 1979; books—*Tower of Babel: Speculations on the Cinema* by Eric Rhode, New York 1967; *Film Makers on Filmmaking* edited by Harry M. Geduld, Bloomington, Indiana 1967; *Andrzej Wajda: Polish Cinema* edited by Colin McArthur, London 1970; *The Cinema of Andrzej Wajda* by Bolestaw Michatek, translated by Edward Rothert, London 1973; *Cinema Beyond the Danube: The Camera and Politics* by Michael Jon Stoil, Metuchen, New Jersey 1974; *The Most Important Art: East European Film After 1945* by Mira Liehm and Antonín Liehm, Berkeley 1977; *Cinema, The Magic Vehicle: A Guide to Its Achievement: Journey One: The Cinema Through 1949* edited by Jacek Klinowski and Adam Garbicz, Metuchen, New Jersey 1979; articles—"Destroying the Commonplace" by Andrzej Wajda in *Films and Filming* (London), November 1961; "Grasping the Nettle: The Films of Andrzej Wajda" by C. Higham in *Hudson Review* (Nutley, New Jersey), autumn 1965; special Wajda issue of *Etudes Cinématographique* (Paris), no.69-72, 1968; "*Kanal*—kirottujen tie" by A. Hauru in *Filmihullu* (Helsinki, Finland), no.2, 1979; special Wajda issue of *Avant-Scène du cinéma* (Paris), 1 January 1980; portrait of Wajda in *The New York Times*, 11 October 1981; portrait of Wajda in *The Village Voice* (New York), 20 December 1981; "Andrzej Wajda" in *Current Biography* (New York), 1982.

*   *   *

Kanal, Andrzej Wajda's second film, is based on a story by Jerzy Stefan Stawiński which appeared in the magazine *Twórczość*. The events of the story are drawn from the writer's personal experience. Stawiński had taken part in two battles for Warsaw, as an 18-year-old in 1939 and then in the Warsaw Uprising of 1944.

Wajda quite purposely renounced any possibility of producing an exhaustive chronicle of the Uprising or commemorative poem on the heroic insurgents. His approach to examining this event was different. From the outset he limited himself to the time in which the story itself is set. The Uprising lasted 63 days, and he followed his heroes from the fifty-seventh day, just a few days and nights before the Uprising was suppressed. Defeat is present in the film from the introductory commentary which presents the individual characters: "These are the main heroic tragedies. Watch them closely; these are the last hours of their lives." It is from this point of view that we see the unfolding story of one group of fighters who are no longer able to hold off the enemy and must retreat through underground sewers.

The film is structured in two parts which differ from one another in their use of cinematic techniques. The first part is documentary in nature. It acquaints the viewer with the heroes and briefly conveys something of their lot before the Uprising. The camera follows them through everyday situations: they prepare their food, shave, make love, and talk about their loved ones and about their past. The effects of the war are everpresent as these apparently everyday moments occur amid the ruins of the city where not a single house has been left standing. The war itself intrudes only with occasional explosions and small-scale attacks. This relative quiet is expressed through long takes, tracking shots and the use of only a minimum of detail. The actual tragedy commences only after the group has withdrawn underground. There is also a change in the style of representation, which takes on an expressive eloquence; the lighting changes, there are more contrasts of light and dark, the camera focuses on the heroes in detail, the sequences of reality alternate with scenes that have symbolic meaning. A comparison of the two parts brings out the specific use of sound, light, and darkness.

Above ground in the film's beginning, the basic component of the soundtrack is the staccato of firearms, while underground the sound component is far richer—the distorted voices of the heroes, dissonant sounds which the viewer is often unable to identify, even a solitary harmonic note of an ocarina. Here, sound has the extra function of heightening the drama, for the underground odyssey must take place in absolute stillness so that the insurgents do not betray their positions to the Germans who are lurking above. Light and shadow play a similar role. The first part is depicted in light, non-contrasting shades of grey, while darkness and sharp flashes of light are assigned to the underground sequences. Traditionally, the light/sun is a symbol of hope. For Wajda, the symbol has the opposite meaning, for the fulfillment of longing for light would mean death for the heroes. Therefore, at the conclusion both symbolic meanings—light as good, darkness as threat—flow together and empty into tragedy; both extremes of the light spectrum bring the ineluctable ending.

Kanal had it Polish premiere in the spring of 1957, the same year it was introduced at the International Festival at Cannes, where it won a prize. Its reception abroad was decidedly positive, while its appearance in Poland stirred discussions that included both positive and negative views. The country still had a tragic reminder of the Uprising; people who had been direct participants in this tragedy of modern history were still living. Their attitude towards the film was sometimes too uncompromising; they wanted it to be a literal depiction of what they had experienced. However, Wajda could not make such a film. He emphasized his personal approach as a director by presenting the experiences of a specific group of people whom he divests of heroism but does not condemn, for they chose their fate freely and fought not for glory but against bondage and enslavement, and paid the highest price.

Kanal occupies a crucial position in the Polish cinema. It ushered in a series of films noted for their sober view of the myths engendered by the war and the Uprising. From this standpoint the film is similar in function to a declaration of policy.

—B. Urgošíkova

LA KERMESSE HÉROÏQUE. Die klugen Frauen. Carnival in Flanders. Production: Film Sonores Tobis, distributed through Films Sonor; black and white, 35mm; running time: 115 mins. French version released 3 December 1935, Paris; German version released 16 January 1936, Berlin.

Screenplay by Charles Spaak, adapted by Charles Spaak and Jacques Feyder, dialogue by Bernard Zimmer (French) and A. Rabenalt (German); from a story by Charles Spaak; directed by Jacques Feyder; photography by Harry Stradling, Louis Page and André Thomas; edited by Jacques Brillouin; sound by Hermann Storr; art direction by Lazare Meerson, Alexandre Trauner, and Georges Wakhévitch; music by Louis Beydte; costumes designed by Georges K. Benda and J. Muelle; artistic consultant: Charles Barrois; history consultant: M. Sterling of the Louvre; technical assistant: Marcel Carné.

Filmed June-July and September 1935 in Tobis d'Epinay-sur-Seine studios (France). Venice Film Festival, Best Direction, 1936; Le Grand Prix du Cinéma Français, 1936.

Cast: French version: Louis Jouvet (*Chaplain*); Françoise Rosay (*Madame, the Burgomaster*); Jean Murat (*Duke of Olivares*); André Alerae (*Burgomaster*); Lyne Clévers (*Fishmonger's wife*); Micheline Cheirel (*Siska*); Maryse Wendling (*Baker's wife*); Ginette Gaubert (*Innkeeper's wife*); Marguerite Ducouret (*Brewer's wife*); Bernard Lancret (*Jean Breuchel*); Alfred Adam (*Butcher*); Pierre Labry (*Innkeeper*); Arthur Devère (*Fishmonger*); Marcel Carpentier (*Baker*); Alexandre Darcy (*Captain*); Claude Sainval (*Lieutenant*); Delphin (*Midget*); German version: Wilhelm Holsboer (*Chaplain*); Françoise Rosay (*Burgomaster's wife*); Paul Hartmann (*Duke*); Will Dohm (*Burgomaster*); Charlott Daubert (*Siska*); Albert Lieven (*Bernard Lancret*); Paul Westermeier (*Butcher*); Carsta Loegk (*Fishmonger's wife*); Trude Marlen (*Innkeeper*); Erika Helmke (*Baker's wife*); Hans Henninger (*Fishmonger*); Wilhelm Gombert (*Innkeeper*); Heintz Forster Ludwig (*Baker*); Werner Scharf (*1st Spanish Lieutenant*); Paul Wolka Walker (*Midget*).

Publications:

Scripts—"*La Kermesse héroïque*" in *Téléciné* (Paris), nos. 27-28, 1951; "*Kermesse Heroique*" in *Avant-Scène du cinéma* (Paris), May 1963; "*La Kermesse héroïque*" in *Antologia di Bianco e nero*, Vol. 4, Rome 1964; reviews—in *Monthly Film Bulletin* (London), October 1936; review in *Sight and Sound* (London), autumn 1936; review in *Motion Picture Herald*, 3 October 1936; review in *Today's Cinema*, 15 October 1936; books—*La Kermesse eroica* (photographs) by Aldo Buzzi, Milan 1945; *Jacques Feyder ou le cinéma concret*, Cinémathèque royale de Belgique, Brussels 1949; "Jacques Feyder" by Victor Bachy, *Anthologie du cinéma*, no.18, 1966; *Jacques Feyder, artisan du cinéma* by Victor Bachy, Louvain 1968; *French Film* by Georges Sadoul, revised edition, New York 1972; *Jacques Feyder* by Charles Ford, Paris 1973; *Caligari's Cabinet and Other Grand Illusions: A History of Film Design* by Léon Barsacq, New York 1976; *A History of Film* by Jack C. Ellis, Englewood Cliffs, New Jersey 1979; articles—"Hommage à Jacques Feyder" in *L'Ecran français* (Paris), 8 June 1948; special issue of *Ciné-Club* (Paris), 2 November 1948; "L'Art du costume dans le film" by J.-G. Auriol and Mario Verdone in *Revue du cinéma* (Paris), autumn 1949; article in *Today's Cinema*, 31 December 1952; article in *Avant-Scène du cinéma* (Paris), May 1963; article in *Skrien* (Amsterdam), December 1977.

* * *

Jacques Feyder had already made two sound films in France; his creative skills were by no means diminished by the new dimension. His successful collaboration with Charles Spaak was to further produce one of the wittiest, most colourful and amusing comedies to reach the screen, *La Kermesse héroïque*. Taking as his subject the period of the great Renaissance of Flemish painting and the less happy era of Spanish domination, Feyder made a major contribution to "women's lib." The film satirizes political, religious, and moral pretentiousness, and the men come off second best when a strong-minded and realistic woman encounters a tricky diplomatic situation.

The little town of Boom's fussy Burgomaster and his officials cannot cope with the threat to their town when the news comes of the approach of the Spanish army under the command of a Duke. Cornelia has a plan. The Burgomaster will pretend to be dead, and she will receive the Duke and hope that in the sad circumstances he will be gentleman enough not to overstay his leave. The possibilities for comedy are wide open.

From this situation Feyder fashioned a film full of sly and subtle comment on human foibles, designed with lavish elegance, at all times a feast for the eye. Feyder, himself a Belgian, created a monument to the great visual artist of his country. The film was a crowning jewel in the great flowering of the French cinema of the 1930's. The designs of Lazare Meerson and the costumes of Benda come alive with the superb acting Feyder extracts from his players. The subtle and delicate humour, the gentle implications of the dialogue, are epitomised in the sly performance of Louis Jouvet as the Duke's chaplain. Needless to say, the Flemish ladies thoroughly enjoy the elegant manners of the Spaniards while their menfolk look helplessly on. There is a little sadness in the air as the Duke and his army leave. One feels life in the little town of Boom will never be the same again.

In making this film, of course Feyder trod on the toes of his fellow countrymen. The reaction was much like that of the Irish to *The Playboy of the Western World*, and chauvinistic sensibilities were not easily smoothed. But the success of the film was universal, and Feyder was established as a great director.

Through an irony of history the significance of the film was soon to change. Belgium was, in fact, invaded by a less charming enemy than the Spanish Duke. Collaboration soon became a very ugly word indeed. But time was on Feyder's side, and today his masterpiece is secure in the annals of film history.

—Liam O'Leary

THE KID. Production: Charles Chaplin Productions for First National; 1921; black and white, 35mm, silent; running time: about 52 mins.; length: 6 reels, 5300 feet. Released 6 February 1921.

Produced, scripted, and directed by Charles Chaplin; photography by Rollie Totheroh.

Cast: Jackie Coogan (*The Kid*); Edna Purviance (*The Woman*); Carl Miller (*The Man*); Charles Chaplin (*The Tramp*); Tom Wilson (*The Policeman*); Chuck Reisner (*The Bully*); Thelbert Theustin (*The Crook*); Nellie Bly Baker (*Slum Woman*); Henry Bergman (*Proprietor of lodging house*); Lita Grey (*Flirting angel*).

Publications:

Books—*Chaplin, Last of the Clowns* by Parker Tyler, New York 1947; *The Great God Pan: A Biography of the Tramp Played by Charlie Chaplin* by Robert Payne, New York 1952; *My Autobiography* by Charles Chaplin, London 1964; *The Films of Charlie Chaplin* by Gerald McDonald and others, Secaucus, New Jersey 1965; *My Life With Chaplin* by Lita Grey Chaplin, New York 1966; *The Parade's Gone By* by Kevin Brownlow, London 1968; *Charlie Chaplin: Early Comedies* by Isabel Quigly, London 1968; *Chaplin's Films* by Uno Asplund, Newton Abbot, Devon 1971; *Tout Chaplin: Tous les films, par le texte, par le gag et par l'image* by Jean Mitry, Paris 1972; *My Life in Pictures* by Charles Chaplin, London 1974; *Etude de sémiologie stylistique portant sur l'oeuvre cinématographique de Charles Chaplin* by Adolphe Nysenholc, Brussels 1975; *Cinema, The Magic Vehicle: A Guide to Its Achievement: Journey One: The Cinema Through 1949* edited by Jacek Klinowski and Adam Garbicz, Metuchen, New Jersey 1975; *Chaplin, Genesis of a Clown* by Raoul Sobel and David Francis, London 1977; *Charles Chaplin—a Guide to References and Resources* compiled by T.J. Lyons, Boston 1977; *Charlie Chaplin* by J. McCabe, Garden City, New York 1978; *Vie de Charlot: Charles Spencer Chaplin, ses films et son temps* by Georges Sadoul, Paris 1978; *Charlot: ou, Sir Charles Chaplin* by J. Lorcey, Paris 1978; articles—"Charlie Chaplin's Art Dissected" in the *Literary Digest* (New York), 8 October 1921; "Chaplin as Film Producer" by J.T. Grein in the *Illustrated London News*, 15 March 1924; "Charlie Chaplin's Films and American Culture Patterns" by Harry A. Grace in *Journal of Aesthetics and Art Criticism* (Cleveland), June 1952; "The Early Days of Charlie Chaplin" by Kevin Brownlow in *Film* (London), summer 1964; "Roland H. Totheroh Interviewed: Chaplin Films" edited by T.J. Lyons, in *Film Culture* (New York), spring 1972; "Hail Chaplin—The Early Chaplin" by Richard Schickel in the *New York Times*

Biography Edition*, 2 April 1972; "*The Kid*" by G. Carey in *Film Comment* (New York), September/October 1972; "*The Kid*" by A. Ferrari in *Télécine* (Paris), March 1974; "*Le Kid*" by R. Lefèvre in *Cinéma* (Paris), February 1974; "Chaplinin poika" by S. Salko in *Filmihullu* (Helsinki, Finland), no.2, 1979.

*   *   *

The Kid was the first feature film that Charles Chaplin devised and directed, the longest film in which he had appeared since Keystone's *Tillie's Punctured Romance* seven years earlier, three times longer than the typical two-reeler at which he had specialized for six years, and almost twice as long as his other major films produced for First National since 1918. The film's greater length reveals Chaplin's expansion of his comic focus to include more powerful and more personal social, moral, and emotional material. At the center of the film is the Tramp's relationship to little Jackie (Jackie Coogan), a five-year-old child who has been abandoned by his unwed mother, found and raised by the Tramp as his own surrogate son. Like the mongrel, Scraps, of *A Dog's Life* (1918), Jackie is a smaller, alternate version of the Tramp himself—a social outcast, defined as illegitimate by the laws and conventions of organized society, able to survive because he is tough though small, mentally agile though uneducated, alternately hard-headed and soft-hearted when it becomes necessary to be either.

Chaplin transferred many of the Tramp's traits, as well as many of his own comedic skills, to little Jackie. Coogan's brilliant performance, responsible for much of the success and popularity of the film, was the first by another performer that Chaplin totally dominated and controlled, in effect creating an alternative Chaplin in a different physical guise (Edna Purviance's performance in *A Woman of Paris*, Virginia Cherrill's in *City Lights*, and Paulette Goddard's in *Modern Times* would be three later such transmutations). Beneath the fictional material in the film one can strongly sense the influence of Chaplin's own personal experiences—his own life as an abandoned child of the London slums, the death of his own first child, born prematurely, and the collapse of his own first marriage, at least partially resulting from the child's death.

Framing the serio-comic study of Charlie and Jackie's domestic bliss, their poor but tranquil existence vivified by love, is material of an entirely different sort. The film begins with a sequence on the unwed mother's (Edna Purviance) difficult decision to abandon her child, depicting her relationship to the callous father (a painter who no longer thinks of the woman) and to the conventional societal definitions of morality and legitimacy (fraught with explicit Christian symbolism). Whereas the woman observes a socially "legitimate" marriage that pairs a young woman with an old, rich man, her own sort of affair is considered illegitimate, even if the action resulted from love and not money. The Christian symbolism returns at the end of the film when Charlie, searching for the child who has been stolen from him, falls asleep to dream of a more pleasant place where, as in so many other Chaplin dream sequences, the painful realities of earthly existence no longer exist. In this dream, considered irrelevant by some critics, Chaplin recreates a comic version of "the Fall" as a group of heavenly angel-people, including the Tramp and all his other neighbors in the slum, fly through the now white-washed and flower-garlanded streets of a utopian city. The dream collapses and the perfect peace turns to bitter chaos when the Satanic spirits of lechery and jealousy sneak through the gates of the heavenly city. Although the sleeping Tramp is roused from this dream to be reunited with Jackie and Edna, the dream sequence suggests Chaplin's sense of the fragility and transience of the true moments of human love and happiness, only temporary escapes from the sordid realities and painful necessities of earthly life.

—Gerald Mast

THE KILLERS. Production: Mark Hellinger Productions; 1946; black and white, 35mm; running time: 105 mins., some sources list 102 mins. Released 28 August 1946 by Universal.

Produced by Mark Hellinger; screenplay by by Anthony Veiller; from the short story by Ernest Hemingway; directed by Robert Siodmak; photography by Woody Bredell; special photography by David S. Horsely; edited by Arthur Hilton; sound by Bernard Brown and William Hedgecock; art direction by Jack Otterson and Martin Obzina, set decoration by Russell A. Gausman and E.R. Robinson; music by Miklos Rozsa; costumes designed by Vera West.

Filming completed 28 June 1946 in Universal studios.

Cast: Edmond O'Brien (*Riordan*); Ava Gardner (*Kitty Collins*); Albert Dekker (*Colfax*); Sam Levene (*Lubinsky*); John Miljan (*Jake*); Virginia Christine (*Lilly*); Vince Barnett (*Charleston*); Burt Lancaster (*Swede*); Charles D. Brown (*Packy*); Donald MacBride (*Kenyon*); Phil Brown (*Nick*); Charles McGraw (*Al*); William Conrad (*Max*); Queenie Smith (*Queenie*); Garry Owen (*Joe*); Harry Hayden (*George*); Bill Walker (*Sam*); Jack Lambert (*Dum Dum*); Jeff Corey (*Blinky*); Wally Scott (*Charlie*); Gabrielle Windsor (*Ginny*); Rex Dale (*Man*).

Publications:

Review—"Mister Siodmak" by D. Marshman in *Life* (New York), 25 August 1947; books—*Underworld U.S.A.* by Colin McArthur, London 1972; *American Film Genres* by Stuart Kaminsky, Dayton, Ohio 1974; *Film Noir* edited by Alain Silver and Elizabeth Ward, Woodstock, New York 1979; articles—"Hemingway on the Screen" by Richard Lillich in *Films in Review* (New York), April 1959; "Hoodlums: The Myth and Their Reality" by Robert Siodmak and Richard Wilson in *Films and Filming* (London); "Encounter with Siodmak" by John Russell Taylor in *Sight and Sound* (London), summer/autumn 1959; "Esoterica" by Andrew Sarris in *Film Culture* (New York), spring 1963; "Robert Siodmak" by Jack Nolan in *Films in Review* (New York), April 1969; "Burt Lancaster" by Mel Schuster in *Films in Review* (New York), August/September 1969; "3 Faces of Film Noir" by Tom Flinn in *Velvet Light Trap* (Madison), summer 1972; "*Les Tueurs*" in *Ecran* (Paris), July 1972; "Hemingway's *The Killers*" by Stuart Kaminsky in *Take One* (Montreal), November 1974; "*The Killers*" by Greg Beal in *Cinema Texas Program Notes* (Austin), 7 October 1976; "*The Killers*" by S. Jenkins in *Monthly Film Bulletin* (London), October 1981.

*   *   *

Based on the 1927 Ernest Hemingway short story, *The Killers* is frequently cited as an example of the film noir style. Greatly influenced by German expressionism and often directed by transplanted Germans (such as Fritz Lang, Edward Dmytryk, and Billy Wilder), film noir involved a pessimistic vision of life in gereral and often centered on urban crime and criminals. Urban life is not glorified: back streets, alleys and small apartments, are shown to be dirty, full of grime, and dimly lit. Lighting is a key element in film noir. The films are filled with shadows. The city is dark and cramped; brightly lit scenes are infrequent, and smoke and fog are always present.

Much of the pessimism of the films comes from their depiction of corruption. Crime is no longer found only in the underworld; it has spread throughout society, and mob bosses are often respectable businessmen. Women are no longer to be trusted. They are shown to be treacherous, selfish, and frequently the center of evil in elaborate criminal schemes.

Because film noir is a phenomenon of the post-war period, some film critics have suggested that it represents the doubts and concerns that America felt after the horror of the first use of the atom bomb. The appearance of evil and vicious women, it has been suggested, may be a backlash reaction to the growing independence and breaking of traditional roles that women had experienced during the war years.

Producer Mark Hellinger bought *the Killers* from Hemingway and initially put John Huston along with Anthony Veiller to work on a screenplay. Huston's plans to direct the picture did not materialize, and Robert Siodmark, another of the Germans now working in America, was given the job.

The Killers is the story of an insurance agent (Edmund O"Brien) investigating the death of "The Swede" (Burt Lancaster in his first role), a man who has allowed himself to be killed by two gunmen. The investigation reveals how Swede gets involved in a robbery, is made to look like a traitor within the caper, and is killed to cover up for the real villains.

The film certainly has many of the film noir elements. Set in the city, it is photographed in a shadowy style (oddly enough, one of the few brightly lit scenes is the robbery). The general tone of the film is not optimistic; the Swede is shown to be a man who knows that he did something wrong once and must be punished. Fate is not very comforting in film noir, and by the end of *The Killers* many of the criminals involved in the robbery have been destroyed. A woman (Ava Gardner) is the main motivator for the crime. It is for her that the Swede gets involved in crime, is set up as a traitor and is finally killed.

An interesting footnote is that one of Hellinger's choices for director was Don Siegel. At the time Siegel was an editor just beginning to direct, but his Warner Bros. contract prevented him from working on the film. In 1964 Siegel remade the film with Lee Marvin and Ronald Reagan. The two films make for an interesting study in comparisons. While the story remains basically the same, the differences between the two films provides for an examination of the ways in which a work is modified by an artist and by his time. A worthwhile discussion along these lines can be found in *American Film Genres* by Stuart Kaminsky.

—Ray Narducy

KIND HEARTS AND CORONETS. Production: Ealing Studios; black and white, 35mm; running time: 106 mins.; length: 9529 feet. Released 1949.

Produced by Michael Balcon; screenplay by Robert Hamer and John Dighton; from the novel *Israel Rank* by Roy Horniman; directed by Robert Hamer; photography by Douglas Slocombe; edited by Peter Tanner; music by Wolfgang Mozart.

Filmed in England. Venice Film Festival, Best Scenography, 1949.

Cast: Dennis Price (*Louis Mazzini/Mazzini's father*); Joan Greenwood (*Sibella*); Valerie Hobson (*Edith*); Alec Guinness (*Ascoyne d'Ascoyne/Henry d'Ascoyne/Canon d'Ascoyne/ Admiral d'Ascoyne/General d'Ascoyne/Lady Agatha d'Asc oyne/Lord d'Ascoyne/Ethelbert/the Old Duke*); Audrey Fildes (*Mrs. Manzini*); John Penrose (*Lionel*); Miles Malleson (*Hangman*); Clive Morton (*Prison governor*).

Publications:

Scripts—"*Kind Hearts and Coronets*" (script extract) in *Sight and Sound* (London), November/December 1951; *Kind Hearts and Coronets* by Robert Hamer and John Dighton, New York 1974; "*Kind Hearts and Coronets*" by Robert Hamer and John Dighton in *Masterworks of the British Cinema*, New York 1974; reviews—by Jules Schwerin in *Films in Review* (New York), March 1950; books—*Michael Balcon's 25 Years in Films* edited by M. Danieschewsky, London 1947; *Alec Guinness* by Kenneth Tynan, New York 1955; *(Michael Balcon Presents) A Lifetime of Films* by Michael Balcon, London 1969; *Cinema in Britain* by Ivan Butler, New York 1973; *The Film Business—A History of British Cinema* by Ernest Betts, New York 1973; *Cinema, The Magic Vehicle: A Guide to Its Achievement: Journey One: The Cinema Through 1949* edited by Adam Garbicz and Jacek Klinowski, Metuchen, New Jersey 1975; articles—"Interview with Hamer" by Freda Bruce Lockart in *Sight and Sound* (London), October/December 1941; "Man of Many Faces" by Derek Hill in *Films and Filming* (London), February 1955; "Ealing: The Studio in Surburbia" by Kenneth Tynan in *Films and Filming* (London), November 1955; "Ealing's Way of Life" by Kenneth Tynan in *Films and Filming* (London), December 1955; "Filmography" (Hamer) in *Film* (London), November/December 1957; "British Feature Directors: an Index to Their Work" in *Sight and Sound*, supplement, index series, autumn 1958; "Alec Guiness" by Douglas McVay in *Films and Filming* (London), May 1961; "Survivor" by Penelope Houston in *Sight and Sound* (London), winter 1962-63; "*Kind Hearts and Coronets*" by Alan Stanbrook in *Films and Filming* (London), April 1964; "Noblesse oblige" by J. Mazoyer in *Image et son* (Paris), no.274, 1973; "Projecting Britain and the British Character: Ealing Studios" by Charles Barr in *Screen* (London), summer 1974; "*Kind Hearts and Coronets*" by Charles Hopkins in *Magill's Survey of Cinema, Vol. II* edited by Frank N. Magill, Englewood Cliffs, New Jersey 1980; "*Kind Hearts and Coronets*" in *Ealing Studios* by Charles Barr, London, n.d.

*   *   *

Kind Hearts and Coronets is an Ealing Comedy in name only. True, it is a comedy, and it was produced by Michael Balcon's Ealing Studios. Even so, the film has little in common with its stablemates. Ealing comedies (with the partial exception of Mackendrick's) were cosy; *Kind Hearts* is callous, even cruel. The humour of Ealing comedies was generally warm, cheerful, and folksy; *Kind Hearts* is cool, ironic and witty. Sex, in Ealing comedies, was kept at a safe distance, and handled (if at all) with embarrassed jocularity; *Kind Hearts* includes scenes that carry a powerful erotic charge.

Hamer stated his intentions as: "Firstly, that of making a film not noticeably similar to any previously made in the English language. Secondly, that of using this English language, which I love, in a more varied and...more interesting way... Thirdly that of making a picture which paid no regard whatever to established, although not practised, moral convention." Much of the humour is indeed verbal, elegantly Wildean, carried by the hero's voice-over narration—yet always aptly counterpointed by the visual effects. The shape of the film is satisfyingly classic, a long flash-back. It opens with Louis Mazzini (Dennis Price) in prison, condemned to death for a murder of which he is innocent, composing his memoirs, in which he recounts all the murders of which he is guilty. His mother, a member of the proud d'Ascoyne clan, had married an Italian singer; for this they disowned her, condemning her to poverty and eventual death. At her grave, Louis vows vengeance, and gradually eliminates every d'Ascoyne (all played by Alec Guinness) between himself and the dukedom.

Louis's narration serves as a unifying factor, effectively sustaining the tone of cool irony throughout the film. Cool—but not cold; there is a pervasive undercurrent of passion beneath the urbane wit, motivating Louis in his systematic slaughter, and surfacing both in the erotic passages with his mistress Sibella (Joan Greenwood), and in his embittered outburst before shooting the Duke, his final victim. The Duke, most repellent of the d'Ascoynes, has been decoyed by Louis into one of his own mantraps; but Louis, too, is caught in his own trap. In revenging himself on the d'Ascoynes for their heartlessness, he has become as heartless, cold and calculating as they.

But the film can readily be enjoyed without any such consideration of its serious undertones. *Kind Hearts* is very funny, wickedly subversive, and probably the finest black comedy the British cinema has ever produced. It is certainly Hamer's masterpiece, a highly successful fusion of his dominant influences: Wildean comedy, and classic French cinema (notably, in this case, Sacha Guitry and the Renoir of *La Règle du Jeu*). The film made Alec Guiness's international reputation, and rapidly attained the status of a classic—which it has consistently maintained. Such polished excellence makes it even more regrettable that Hamer's masterpiece was also the last good film of his sadly blighted career.

—Philip Kemp

KING KONG. Production: RKO Radio Pictures Inc.; 1933; black and white, 35mm; running time: 100 mins. Released 2 March 1933, Radio City Music Hall and RKO Roxy Theatre, New York. Re-released 1938 with a few scenes censored.

Produced by Merian C. Cooper and Ernest B. Schoedsack with David O. Selznick as executive producer; screenplay by James Creelman and Ruth Rose; from a story by Merian C. Cooper and Edgar Wallace based on an idea conceived by Cooper; directed by Merian C. Cooper and Ernest B. Schoedsack; photography by Edward Linden, Vernon L. Walker, and J.O. Taylor, optical photography by Linwood C. Dunn and William Ulm; edited by Ted Cheesman; sound recorded by E.A. Wolcott, sound effects by Murray Spivack; production technicians: Mario Larrinaga and Byron L. Crabbe; art direction by Archie

S. Marshek and Walter Daniels, art direction supervised by Van Nest Polglase; music by Max Steiner; chief technician: Willis H. O'Brien, special effects by Harry Redmond Jr.; Dunning Process supervision by Carroll H. and C. Dodge Dunning; Williams Matte supervision by Frank Williams; technical artwork by Juan Larrinaga, Zachary Hoag, and Victor Delgado; projection process by Sydney Saunders; costumes designed by Walter Plunkett; technical staff included E.B. Gibson, Orville Goldner, Marcel Delgado, Fred Reefe, and Carroll Shepphird.

Filmed 1932-33 in RKO Studios and backlots, also in San Pedro Harbor and Shrine Auditorium, Los Angeles. Cost: $670,000.

Cast: Fay Wray (*Ann Darrow*); Bruce Cabot (*Jack Driscoll*); Sam Hardy (*Weston*); James Flavin (*2nd mate*); Victor Wong (*Charley*); Paul Porcasi (*Fruit vendor*); Dick Curtis (*Crewman*); Robert Armstrong (*Carl Denham*); Frank Reicher (*Captain Englehorn*); Noble Johnson (*Native chief*); Steve Clemento (*Witch king*); Roscoe Ates (*Press photographer*); Leroy Mason (*Theater patron*).

Publications:

Reviews—by Mordaunt Hall in *The New York Times*, 5 March 1933; "Beauty and the Beast" by William Troy in the *Nation* (New York), no.136, 1933; books—*The Bad Guys: A Pictorial History of the Movie Villain* by William K. Everson, New York 1964; *The Great Films: Fifty Golden Years of Motion Pictures* by Bosley Crowther, New York 1967; *Persistence of Vision* by Joseph McBride, Madison, Wisconsin 1968; *Movie Monsters* by Denis Gifford, New York 1969; *50 Classic Motion Pictures: The Stuff That Dreams are Made of* by David Zinman, New York 1970; *Cinema of the Fantastic* by Chris Steinbrunner and Burt Goldblatt, New York 1972; *Homenaje a King Kong* by Roman Gubern, Barcelona, Spain 1974; *The Making of King Kong* by Orville Goldner and George E. Turner, New York 1975; *The Girl in the Hairy Paw* edited by Ronald Gottesman and Harry Geduld, New York 1976; articles—"Prehistoric Monsters Roar and Hiss for the Sound Film" by Andrew R. Boone in *Popular Science Monthly* (New York), 1933; "Who Killed King Kong" by X.J. Kennedy in *Dissent* (New York), spring 1960; "Willis O'Brien, or the Birth of a Film from Design to Still" by Jean Boullet in *Midi-Minuit Fantastique* (Paris), October/November 1962; "A King in New York" by Claude Ollier in *Cahiers du cinèma* May/June 1965; "Merian C. Cooper" by Rudy Behlmer in *Films in Review* (New York), January 1966; "King Kong Was a Dirty Old Man" in *Esquire* (New York), September 1971; obituary for Cooper by W.-E. Bühler in *Filmkritik* (Munich), November 1973; "Father of Kong" by A. Osborne in *Cinema Papers* (Richmond, Australia), July 1974; "A Speculation: The Historicity of *King Kong*" by G. Peary in *Jump Cut* (Chicago), November/December 1974; "Orphan in the Storm: Son of Kong" by G. Peary in *Film Heritage* (Dayton, Ohio), winter 1973-74; "Films on 8 & 16" by S.A. Peoples in *Films in Review* (New York), January 1974; "The Cult Movies: *King Kong*" by Gordon Gow in *Films and Filming* (London), January 1975; "Race, Sex, and Rebellion" by D.N. Rosen in *Jump Cut* (Chicago), March/April 1975; "The Beast" (poem) by Ray Bradbury in *Producers Guild of America Journal* (Los Angeles), no. 3, 1976; "La Religion du monstre" by J. Fieschi in *Cinematographe* (Paris), April/May 1976; "Horror im Kino" by A. Gerely in *Film und Ton Magazine* (Munich), November 1976; "Trucages profilmiques et filmiques dans *King Kong*" by P. Maraval in *Cinematographe* (Paris), April/May 1976; "The Kong and I" by W.

Markfield in *The New York Times*, 12 December 1976; "*King Kong* and the Ideology of the Spectacle" by Judith Mayne in *Quarterly Review of Film Studies* (Pleasantville, New York), no.4, 1976; "The Science Fiction Image: *A Trip to the Moon* to *2001: A Space Odyssey*" by Fred Chappell in *Science Fiction Films* edited by Thomas Atkins, New York 1976; "*King Kong*" by J.-M. Sabatier in *Image et son* (Paris), 308bis, 1976; "Creating Film Magic for the Original *King Kong*" by L.G. Dunn in *American Cinematographer* (Los Angeles), January 1977; "Sound Track: And the Beast Goes On" by R. Fiedel in *American Film* (Washington, D.C.), March 1977; "Le Singe est nu (sur *King Kong* 1 et 2)" by A. Garsault in *Positif* (Paris), February 1977; "Doctor, I Have These Strange Dreams..." by F. Jackson in *Take One* (Montreal), January 1977; "The Making of the Original *King Kong*" in *American Cinematographer* (Los Angeles), January 1977; "*King Kong*" by A. Marty in *Image et Son* (Paris), February 1977; "*King Kong*-Then and Now" by H. Wellman in *American Cinematographer* (Los Angeles), January 1977; "*King Kong*" by Pat H. Broeske in *Magill's Survey of Cinema, Vol. II* edited by Frank N. Magill, Englewood Cliffs, New Jersey 1980.

*   *   *

Few films can compete with the longevity of *King Kong*. The film is as popular today, on television and in revival theaters, as it first was in its initial release in 1933. Ironically, the film's contemporary setting of 1933 has now made it a period piece, though the ideas and themes have never aged.

The story was conceived by producer/director Merian C. Cooper and inspired by his trips to Africa and Southeast Asia to shoot documentary films. Cooper imagined setting a primitive giant ape against the civilization of a modern New York City. This vision was eventually realized on the screen with the aid and collaboration of special visual effects artist and innovator, Willis H. O'Brien.

The special visual techniques developed for *King Kong* were numerous. One of the more important technical advances was the development of a safe (cellulose-acetate) rear-projection screen by Sidney Saunders. Although earlier films had used a more primitive glass rear-projection screen (which, if accidently broken, could cause serious injuries to actors and crew), the cellulose-acetate screen allowed *King Kong* to be the first film to use large-scale rear projection. Another innovation was the invention and use of the optical printer by Vernon Walker and Linwood Dunn. The optical printer presented a new way of combining optical mattes that was superior to the old, and more complex, Dunning process. The enormous amount of matte work in the film (used to combine the special effects with the live action) would not have been feasible without the help of the printer.

Although stop-motion animation had been used previously in other films (such as O'Brien's *The Lost World* in 1925), *King Kong* was the first feature film to use stop-motion to create a continuous character. The model of King Kong was constructed by artist Marcel Delgado out of metal, rubber, cotton and rabbit fur, yet it was truly an "actor." He could express emotions and react logically to the situation around him.

The making of *King Kong* also presented a problem in the area of sound effects. Kong had to sound believable, yet unlike any other creature on earth. The sound department at RKO headed by Murray Spivak, ran dozens of new and innovative experiments to create the right soundtract. Kong's roar was a combination of a lion and tiger sounds slowed down and played backwards. The music is still another example of the film originality. Many films in the early 1930s used classical music as background accompaniment. *King Kong* was one of the first films for which an entire score was created. Composer Max Steiner carefully plotted out each scene in the film so that he could synchronize his music with the action.

The technical innovations found in *King Kong* are not the only reasons for its success; every good film must start with a good story. *King Kong* has a universal appeal, making it one of the most popular and well-known films in American culture,

—Linda J. Obalil

KINO-PRAVDA. Film-Truth. Black and white, 35mm, series of 23 newsreels-documentaries released over a period of 3 years; First issue released 21 May 1922, the 23rd and last issue released 1925.

Directed by Dziga Vertov; photography by Mikhail Kaufman, I. Belyakov and A. Lemberg; edited by Dziga Vertov, assisted by Yelizaveta Svilova; assitant director: Ilya Kopalin.

Filmed in the Soviet Union.

Publications:

Books—*Kino: A History of Russian and Soviet Film* by Jay Leyda, London 1960; *Dziga Vertov* by Nikolai Abramov, edited and translated by B. Amengual, French ed., Lyon 1965; *Dsiga Wertow: aufsätze, tagebücher, skizzen* edited by Sergej Drobaschenko, Berlin 1967; *Dziga Vertov* by V. Borokov, Moscow 1967; *Documentary Film* by Paul Rotha and Sinclair Road, and Richard Griffith, New York 1968; *Film Culture Reader* edited by P. Adams Sitney, New York 1970; *Dziga Vertov* by Georges Sadoul, Paris 1971; *Cinema Verite* by M. Ali Issari, East Lansing, Michigan 1971; *Soviet Cinema* by Catherine De La Roche and Thorold Dickinson, revised edition, New York 1972; *Cinema in Revolution: The Heroic Era of the Soviet Film* by Luda Schnitzer, Jean Schnitzer, and Marcel Martin, New York 1973; *The Motion Picture in the Soviet Union, 1918-1952* by John Rimberg, New York 1973; *The Cultural-Political Traditions and Developments of the Soviet Cinema, 1917-1972* by Louis Harris Cohen, New York 1974; *Evolution of Style in the Early Work of Dziga Vertov* by Seth Feldman, New York 1977; *A History of Film* by Jack C. Ellis, Englewood Cliffs, New Jersey 1979; articles—"Dziga Vertov es a dokumentufilm muveszete" by Nikolai Abramov in *Filmkultura* (Budapest, Hungary), January 1961; "The Writings of Dziga Vertov" in *Film Culture* (New York), no.25, 1962; "Dziga Vertov: An Introduction" by David Bordwell in *Film Comment* (New York), spring 1972; "Cinema Weekly and Cinema Truth" by Seth Feldman in *Sight and Sound* (London), winter 1973-74; "Kinoletopis' epohi" by A. Lebedev in *Iskusstvo Kino* (Moscow), October 1977; "Kino-truth and Kino-praxis: Vertov's *Man with a Movie Camera*" by J. Mayne in *Ciné-Tracts* (Montreal), summer 1977.

*   *   *

Communicating its ideals and achievements was a major problem for the new government of the Russian Revolution. In that vast country with a disparate and, in the 1920's, largely illiterate population, film was almost the only means of reaching the broad mass of Russians with information about the changes being brought about by the Revolution. Following his declaration in 1918 that cinema was the art of the Revolution, Lenin in 1922 underlined the importance of the nonfiction film by calling for a fixed production allotment favoring the production of documentary films over fiction or entertainment films. Four months after Lenin's decree, Dziga Vertov, a brilliant young filmmaker, released the first issue *Kinopravda*, which was to become the most imaginative newsreel of the silent era.

Although the early issues of *Kinopravda* followed a fairly conventional front page approach to the news, the series from its very beginning was distinguished by filmic innovation. *Kinopravda* included the first examples of Soviet animation, was among the pioneers in its use of montage to develop a narrative line, experimented with camera speeds and different vehicles for trolleying and dollying effects, used superimpositions for symbolic effect, and intergrated title cards into the pictorial flow of the film. The editing at times was dazzling. In one 30-second sequence in the 18th issue, Vertov used 65 shots of machines and workers singing the "Internationale" to create not only an emotional climax but also the illusion of sound and a sense that man and machine can be harmoniously linked.

By its 13th issue, *Kinopravda* was no longer a news-oriented series but a documentary series dealing with questions of current concern. In a departure from the standard newsreel, *Kinopravda 13* uses shots from different time periods and different locations to cover the fifth anniversary of the October Revolution. To give a sense of the breadth of the Revolution, Vertov includes aerial footage of cities, factories, and villages from all over Russia. To give further depth to the coverage, Vertov in the second segment focuses on the years of struggle leading to the establishment of the new regime. An even more interesting example of the series' experimentation with the newsreel form is seen in *Kinopravda 17*, which covers the *Agricultural and Home Exhibition* in Moscow. Departing from a straight coverage of the exhibition, the introduction presents a rationale for the exhibit with a sequence showing a famine followed by a harvest with the then Soviet President standing amidst a group of peasant children. The next sequence focuses on two telegrams: the first sent by a group of school children to wish Lenin a speedy recovery and the second from Lenin to wish the exhibition success. Since all the footage of the exhibition was shot before its opening, Vertov in the last section shows the construction of the exhibition site, the preparation of projects at factories and in villages, the final inspection of the site, the raising of the flag, and an animated map of the exhibition.

Kinopravda devoted a great deal of attention to capturing the details of everyday life, and in that, too, it separated itself from the typical newsreel's concentration on important people and events. Vertov sought out what he called "life caught unawares." Sometimes he used a hidden camera, sometimes he let people become so accustomed to the camera that they forgot its presence, but more often he relied on people's absorption in their own lives to give him the shots of reality he wanted. In his rejection of artificiality and staging in films, and in his efforts to record uncontrolled life, Vertov anticipated the cinema verite movement of the present (which, in fact, takes its name from Vertov's newsreel).

Realeased between 1922 and 1925, the 23 issues of *Kinoprava* not only excited film critics, they also played a major role in educating the Russian people about the changes in their society. In its focus on everyday life, the series reinforced as nothing else

could the meaning of that Revolution. Rather than seeing film stars and officials on the screen, the audience saw people like themselves engaged in activities like their own.

—Sharon Lee

KONYETS SANKT-PETERBURGA. The End of St. Petersburg. Production: Mezhrabpom-Russ; black and white, 35mm, silent; running time: about 110 mins.; length: 8202 feet. Released 1927.

Screenplay by Nathan Zarkhi; from the poem "The Bronze Horseman" by Pushkin and the novel *St. Petersburg* by Andrey Biely; directed by Vsevolod Pudovkin; photography by Anatoli Golovnya and K. Vents; art direction by S. Kozlovsky.

Cast: A.P. Chistyakov (*Worker*); Vera Baranovskaya (*His wife*); Ivan Chuvelov (*Ivan, a peasant*); V. Chuvelov (*Friend from the village*); V. Obolensky (*Lebedev, steel magnate*); A. Gromov (*Revolutionary*); Vladimir Tzoppi (*Patriot*); Nikolai Khmelyov and M. Tzibulsky (*Stockbrokers*).

Publications:

Books—*Poudovkine, "Pouti Tvortchestva," les voies de la création* by N. Yezuitov, Moscow 1937; *Vsevolod Pudovkin* by A. Mariamov, Moscow 1952; *Kino: A History of Russian and Soviet Film* by Jay Leyda, New York 1960; *Vsevolod Poudovkine* by Luda and Jean Schnitzer, Paris 1966; *V.I. Poudovkine* by Barthélémy Amengual, Premier Plan, Lyon 1968; *Soviet Cinema* by Catherine De La Roche and Thorold Dickinson, revised edition, New York 1972; *Cinema in Revolution: The Heroic Era of the Soviet Film* by Luda Schnitzer, Jean Schnitzer, and Marcel Martin, New York 1973; *The Motion Picture in the Soviet Union, 1918-1952* by John Rimberg, New York 1973; *Pudovkin's Films and Film Theory* by Peter Dart, New York 1974; *The Cultural-Political Traditions and Developments of the Soviet Cinema, 1917-1972* by Louis Harris Cohen, New York 1974; *Cinema, The Magic Vehicle: A Guide to Its Achievement: Journey One: The Cinema Through 1949* edited by Jacek Klinowski and Adam Garbicz, Metuchen, New Jersey 1975; articles—"Pudovkin and the Revolutionary Film" by Harry Potamkin in *Hound and Horn* (New York), April/-June 1933; "Index to the Creative Work of Vsevolod Pudovkin" by Jay Leyda in *Sight and Sound* (London), November 1948; special Pudovkin issue of *Cahiers du cinéma* (Paris), August/-September 1953; "Vsevolod Pudovkin" by Herman Weinberg in *Films in Review* (New York), August/September 1953; special Pudovkin issue of *Iskusstvo Kino* (Moscow), February 1973; "Film Language: Pudovkin and eisenstein and Russian Formalism" by E. Hudlin in *Journal of Aesthetic Education* (Urbana, Illinois), no.2, 1979; "Linkage: Pudovkin's Classics Revisited" by P.E. Burns in *Journal of Popular Film and Television* (Washington, D.C.), summer 1981.

*   *   *

Pudovkin made *The End of St. Petersburg* in 1927 for the tenth anniversary of the Soviet Revolution. From an earlier conception of the film as a 200-year history of St. Petersburg and its changing political climate, Pudovkin focused instead on the struggle for that city at the time of the revolution. As in *Mother*, Pudovkin charted the emergence of the (mass) protagonist from political naiveté to Marxist consciousness. The film's distinction is in the conjunction of this personal mode of Marxist analysis with two othe major points of reference: the St. Petersburg cityscape itself and its representation in the Russian literary tradition; and Pudovkin's theoretical writings *(Film Technique and Film Acting)*, particularly on the role of editing.

The portrayal of a protagonist who interacts with the animated architecture of St Petersburg is within the tradition of Pushkin's poem "The Bronze Horseman" and Andrey Biely's symbolist novel *St. Petersburg*, written in 1910-11 but set during the unsuccessful rebellion in 1905. Pudovkin superimposes a Marxist interpretation on to Puskin's Bronze Horseman, the "Soul of Russia." Through editing, he causes the statue to cry during the bombardment of the Czar's Winter Palace. Biely's vivid city geometry becomes in the film a maze of revolutionary activity. Pudovkin shifts the major site of conflict from the homes of the workers (in Biely) to the foundries in which they work. The realism of the photographic image would serve him well, allowing him to rely on the spectator's familiarity with the architecture of the city. He vivifies the city's monumental buildings and squares (as well as its famous statues), lending credibility to his political narrative. The tradition of romanticized urbanism, from Dickens through Griffith, takes on a Marxist ideological thrust in *The End of St. Petersburg*.

Pudovkin conveys the revolutionary and urban themes through precise techniques of editing, which he had codified in *Film Technique*. His re-assemblage of filmed reality recalls Constructivism in its tight integration of form and content. The camera records real space and time; the director creates filmic space and time through editing. Pudovkin called this the "linkage" of the film strips, "brick by brick." Kuleshov had taught him the importance of the legibility of individual shots when trying to emphasize the relationships among shots. Pudovkin would elaborate important details and eliminate others, often stressing the metaphorical nature of a particular detail. It is the editing that gives film its strong metaphorical potential.

The various ways in which Pudovkin alternates these details in the editing gives the film its distinctive rhythm. He establishes oppositions, cutting for contrast between day and night, as well as between large open spaces and clastrophobic interiors. He inserts ironic intertitles to contrast with visual images. Most significantly, he employs parallel editing to contrast static shots with dynamic activity. Pudovkin maintains this rhythm throughout the film, often cutting on human movement to provide fluid continuity.

Pudovkin's conception of the mass hero would unfortunately set the pattern for what would become the official aesthetic of Socialist Realism. His cinematic dynamization of St. Petersburg would remain a more enduring contribution.

—Howard Feinstein

KÖRKARLEN. The Phantom Chariot. Thy Soul Shall Bear Witness. Clay. The Stroke of Midnight. La Charette fantome. Il Caretto fantasma. Il Carrehiere della Morte. Production: Svensk Bio; black and white, 35mm, silent; length: 5 reels, 6122 feet. Released 1 January 1921. Re-released in a re-edited version in America in 1922.

Screenplay by Victor Sjöström (Seastrom); from the novel by Selma Lagerlöf; directed by Victor Sjöström (Seastrom); photography by Julius Jaenzon; art direction by Aleksander Bako and Axel Esbensen.

Filmed 1920 in Sweden.

Cast: Victor Sjöström (*David Holm*); Hilda Borgstrom (*His wife*); Astrid Holm (*Sister Edith*); Tor Weijden (*Gustafsson*); Tore Svenberg (*Georg*); Concordia Selander (*Edith's mother*); Lisa Lundholm (*Sister Maria*); Olaf Aas (*Coachman*): Nils Aréhn (*Prison chaplain*).

Publications:

Books—*40 Ans de cinéma, 1895-1935* by Georges Charensol, Paris 1935; *Den Svenska Filmens Drama: Sjöström och Stiller* by Bengt Idestam-Almquist, Stockholm 1952; *Scandinavian Film* by Forsyth Hardy, London 1951; *Classics of the Swedish Cinema* by Bengt Idestam-Almquist, Stockholm 1952; *Swedish Cinema* by Rune Waldekranz, Stockholm 1959; *Swedish Films* by Einar Lauritzen, New York 1962; *Sjöström* by René Jeanne and Charles Ford, Paris 1963; *Swedish Cinema* by Peter Cowie, London 1966; *Anthologie du cinéma* Vol. I, Paris 1966; *Seastrom and Stiller in Hollywood* by Hans Pensel, New York 1969; *Cinema, The Magic Vehicle: A Guide to Its Achievement: Journey One: The Cinema Through 1949* edited by Jacek Klinowski and Adam Garbicz, Metuchen, New Jersey 1975; *Caligari's Cabinet and Other Grand Illusions: A History of Film Design* by Léon Barsacq, New York 1976; *A History of Film* by Jack C. Ellis, Englewood Cliffs, New Jersey 1979; articles—"The Golden Age of Scandinavian Film" by M.C. Potamkin in *Cinema* (London), September 1930; "Victor Sjöström" by Bengt Idestam-Almquist in *Biografbladet* (Stockholm), summer 1950; "Victor Sjöström" by Charles L. Turner in *Films in Review* (New York), May 1960 and June 1960.

*   *   *

Although it was made more than 60 years ago, *The Phantom Chariot* still considered to be a film remarkable for its sophisticated narrative structure. Though flashbacks were not unheard-of narrative devices in the cinema of that time, *The Phantom Chariot* was not understood by many audiences, and had to be re-edited to facilitate comprehension. The narrative is developed according to a mise-en-abŷme construction, wherein flashback issues from flashback, and stories are contained by or within other stories. Audiences of the time were sufficiently educated viewers, cinematically speaking, to grasp one temporal level of flashback description, but beyond that had some difficulty in deciphering further narrative complexities.

The articulation of the different temporal layers in the film serves to fill out its penultimate meaning (the ultimate one being concerned with repentance and redemption of the soul), which has to do with the notion that time is multi-dimensional and multi-perspectival. In *La Jetée*, Chris Marker pursues this concept, and in doing so suggests that the Western world's current perception of time is not only too restrictive but needlessly fatal as well. In *The Phantom Chariot* David Holm, the main character, is "given another chance" at life via a "non-linear" portal, the point at which the time cycle begins and also can be arrested; in this case it is New Year's Eve.

Most of the filmic narrative actually takes place or at least is generated in a cemetery where David Holm and two drinking buddies are getting ready to toast the incoming year. A shot of a nearby clock tower lets us know that it is 20 minutes to midnight. Then David Holm tells a story about how one gets to be driver of "the phantom chariot." The tale has it that any man who breathes his last at the stroke of midnight before the beginning of a new year must then take over the ghastly chore of gathering up departed souls during the coming year. Another shot of the clock tower reveals that ten minutes have elapsed during the telling of this story within the diegesis of the film. A policeman comes along to ask David if he would please come and visit Edith, a salvation army nurse who had once been kind to him and is now dying of consumption. He refuses, then fights with his two companions. They knock him out and leave quickly, presuming him dead. A magnificient superimposition of David Holm's spirit leaving his body follows. At that moment the phantom chariot arrives, driven by an old drinking buddy, Georg, who has died the previous New Year's Eve at precisely midnight.

The narrative then proceeds through a series of flashbacks: we see how David Holm met Georg, and that Georg was a bad influence on him, encouraging him to drink heavily and consequently mistreat his wife and two young children; we are introduced to Edith and the Salvation Army Mission where David Holm stayed after being released from prison and finding that his wife had left him.

Returning to the cemetery once again, the film is now three fourths complete or (roughly an hour and a half into the total viewing time), and Georg has one last soul to collect—David Holm's. But, according to the time registered by the clock tower in the film it is midnight, ten minutes after David Holm had finished telling the story about the phantom chariot. Georg ties up his body with invisible yet binding rope and loads him into the carriage. David Holm's spirit rides up front with Georg as they ride to the house where Edith is about to die. Georg also "shows" David Holm that his wife is about to take her own life as well as the lives of their children. At the moment of Edith's death, David Holm breaks down into tears, praying desperately to God for another chance in life so that he can prevent the death of his innocent family. An abrupt cut back to the cemetery shows him waking up, his body and spirit intact. He rubs his head and eyes for an instant, then gets up—a bit shakily at first, for he is still drunk from all the liquor he has consumed this New Year's Eve. He arrives home just in time to stop his wife from going through with the fatal poisonings.

In 1920, "zero-degree" writing or a "zero-degree" narrative structure was still 40 odd years away from being invented, yet *The Phantom Chariot* is clearly an example of just such a representational construct.

—Sandra Beck

KOROL LIR. King Lear. Production: Lenfilm; black and white, 35mm, scope; running time: 140 mins.; length: 12,500 feet. Released 1971, USSR.

Produced, scripted, and directed by Grigori Kozintsev; from Boris Pasternak's translation of the play by William Shakespeare; photography by Jonas Gritsius; sound by Eduard Vanunts; production design by Yevgeny Yenei (Jenöcek Jenei), sets by Vsevolod Ulitko; music by Dmitri Shostakovich; costumes designed by Suliko Virsaladze.

Filmed 1970 the USSR. Teheran Film Festival, Grand Prix, 1972.

Cast: Yuri Yarvet (*King Lear*); Elsa Radzinya (*Goneril*); Galina Volchek (*Regan*); Valentina Shendrikova (*Cordelia*); Oleg Dal (*The Fool*); Karl Sebris (*Earl of Gloucester*); Leonard Merzin (*Edgar*); Regimantas Adomaitis (*Edmund*); Vladimir Emelyanov (*Earl of Kent*); Alexander Volkach (*Duke of Cornwall*); Alexei Petrenko (*Oswald*); Yumas Budraitis (*King of France*); Donatas Banionis (*Duke of Albany*).

Publications:

Reviews—in *Variety* (New York), 29 September 1971; "*King Lear*" by N. Andrews in *Sight and Sound* (London), summer 1972; "*King Lear*" by Gordon Gow in *Films and Filming* (London), August 1972; "*King Lear*" by M. Yacowar in *Take One* (Montreal), April 1972; review in *Monthly Film Bulletin* (London), August 1972; "Lear" by G. Braucourt in *Ecran* (Paris), March 1974; "*Le Roi Lear*" by J.C. Guiguet in *Image et son* (Paris), March 1974; books—*Shakespeare: Time and Conscience* by Grigori Kozintsev, translated by Joyce Vining, New York 1966; *Focus on Shakespearean Film* edited by Charles Eckert, Englewood Cliffs, New Jersey 1972; *King Lear: The Space of Tragedy: The Diary of a Film Director* by Grigori Kozintsev, translated by Mary Mackintosh, Berkeley 1977; *The Most Important Art: East European Film After 1945* by Mira Liehm and Antonín Liehm, Berkeley 1977; *Grigori Kozintsev* by Barbara Leaming, Boston 1980; *La Feks: Kozintsev e Trauberg* edited by Giusi Rapisarda, Rome n.d. articles—"One Day with *King Lear*" by Yevgeniya Barteneva in *Soviet Film* (Moscow), no.9, 1969; "The Conscience of the King: Konsintsev's *King Lear*" by Sergei Yutkevitch in *Sight and Sound* (London), autumn 1971; article in *Filmfacts* (New York), no.24, 1971; "Az interpretálás: a rendezo életrajza" by T. Koltain in *Filmkultura* (Budapest), May/June 1972; "Prostranstvo tragedii" by G. Kozincev, series of articles in *Iskusstvo Kino* (Moscow), January, April, June, August, November issues, 1972; "Kozincew: lekcja kina i Szekspira" by Z. Pitera in *Kino* (Warsaw), March 1972; "Spór o Króla Lira" by A. Tatarkiewicz in *Kino* (Warsaw), March 1972; Director of the year entry in *International Film Guide*, London 1972; "Er widmete sein Talent der Revolution" in *Film und Fernsehen* (Berlin), September 1973; "Prostaranstvo tragedii" by G. Kozincev in *Iskusstvo Kino* (Moscow), last article in series, January 1973; "*Le Roi Lear*" by J.C. Guiguet in *Image et son* (Paris), March 1974; "Deux Versions du roi Lear" by R. Marienstras in *Positif* (Paris), April 1974; article in *Literature Film Quarterly* (Salisbury, Maryland), spring 1976; "Kozintsev's *King Lear*" by B. Hodgdon in *Literature/Film Quarterly* (Salisbury, Maryland), fall 1977.

*　　*　　*

Karol Lir was the last film of Kozintsev's long career, which began with the delirious experimentalism of the early 1920's, and ended with two towering adaptations of Shakespeare. His version of *Hamlet* is probably the better-known of the two, but some critics have considered his *Lear* even finer. In its austere grandeur the film conveys, more effectively perhaps than any stage production could ever do, the majestic stature of the play, extending it to its utmost range without in the least distorting it. Kozintsev's *Lear* remains, with all its gritty strength, still very much Shakespeare's *Lear*.

"This is not the story of one man," Kozintsev commented; "everything occurs among many other people." His aim is to place *Lear* in context, showing that the schemes and caprices of royalty bring disaster not only to themselves, but also to the whole nation. In the opening sequence a meandering procession of ragged vagabonds (immediately recalling the line of suppliants winding through the snow in *Ivan the Terrible*) make their painful way to Lear's castle. Later, as war and destruction rage across the stark landscape, the entire populace of Britain has apparently been reduced to such scurrying wretchedness, with the king himself now one among their number. The closing scenes take place amid the scorched and shattered ruins of Dover, whose inhabitants continue while Lear dies to forage gloomily among the rubble, indifferent to one more death after so many.

Pictorially the film is consistently superb. Kozintsev deploys his widescreen monochrome photography to impressive effect, creating panoramic compositions which echo the elemental forces unleashed by the play. In one vivid overhead shot, the camera seems even to become one with the elements as it glares down on the cowering figures of Lear and the Fool stumbling blindly across the storm-swept heath. At other times it identifies with the king in his changing moods, sweeping vertiginously upwards with him to the mad heights of the battlements, or panning slowly across a darkening horizon as if in apprehension of the coming storm.

In the title role, the Estonian actor Yure Jarvet is imaginatively cast: a diminutive, bird-like man with quick eyes, he seems at first almost childishly unfitted for kingship, yet by the end of the film has acquired a touchingly frail nobility, transcending his own inadequacies as he gains in understanding. The other roles are equally individually characterised, drawing on a wealth of personal detail, from the gossipy fussiness of Goucester to the Fool's crop-haired innocence. Pasternak's sinewy translation audibly recaptures, even for those with no Russian, the rhythms and inflections of Shakespeare's verse; while in its power and energy, Shostakovich's music (the last of his many outstanding film scores) perfectly complements Kozintsev's epic conception of the play.

There are no compromises in *Karol Lir*. In its visual style it is thoroughly Russian, very much Kozintsev. (The hand of the director, 40 years earlier, of *New Babylon*, is clearly evident.) It conforms to a Marxist reading of the text, but without being in any way doctrinaire, nor perverting Shakespeare's intentions. Along with Kurosawa's *Throne of Blood*, and Kozintsev's own *Hamlet*, it provides a rare example of a Shakespeare film that succeeds in being at once superb cinema and superb Shakespeare.

—Philip Kemp

KOSHIKEI. Death by Hanging. Production: Sozo-sha and A.T.G.; black and white, 35mm, Vistavision size; running time: 117 mins. Released 1968, Japan.

Produced by Masayuki Nakajima, Takuji Yamaguchi and Nagisa Oshima; screenplay by Tsutomu Tamura, Mamoru Sasaki, Michinori Fukao and Nagisa Oshima; from a newspaper story; directed by Nagisa Oshima; photography by Yasuhiro Yoshioka; edited by Sueko Shiraishi; sound by Hideo Nishizaki, sound effects by Akira Suzuki; production design by Jusho Toda; music by Hikaru Hayashi; assistant director: Kiyoshi Ogasawara.

Cost: 10 million yen. Kinema Jumpo's Best Screenplay Prize and one of Kinema Jumpo's Best Films of 1968.

Cast: Kai Sato (*Officer in charge of the execution*); Fumlio Watanabe (*Official educator*); Yun do-Yun (*R*); Mutsuhiro Toura (*Doctor*); Hosei Komatsu (*Prosecutor*);); Akiko Koyama (*Woman*); Toshiro Ishido (*Priest*); Masao Adachi (*Security officer*); Masao Matsuda (*Official witness*).

Publications:

Script—"*Koshikei*" (Japanese) in *Sekai no Eigasakka No.6: Nagisa Oshima*, Tokyo 1972; reviews—by Jean de Baroncelli in *Le Monde* (Paris), 4 October 1969; review by Hubert Niogret in *Positif* (Paris), October 1969; review by René Gardies in *Image et son* (Paris), February 1970; "L'impicciagion—Diario di un ladro di Shinjuku—Storia..." by G. Corbucci in *Cinema Nuovo* (Turin) January/February 1972; "Døden ved haengning" by P. Schepelern in *Kosmorama* (Copenhagen), December 1972; books—*Voices from the Japanese Cinema* by Joan Mellen, New York 1975; *Second Wave* by Ian Cameron et al., New York 1975; *The Waves at Genji's Door* by Joan Mellen, New York 1976; *Japanese Film Directors* by Audie Bock, New York 1978; *To the Distant Observor: Form and Meaning in the Japanese Cinema* by Noel Burch, Berkeley 1979; articles—by Jean-Louis Bory in *Le Nouvel Observateur* (Paris), 29 September 1969; "Entretien avec Oshima" by Max Tessier in *Cinéma 69* (Paris), no.140, 1969; article and interview by Andrée Tournes in *Jeune Cinéma* (Paris), November/December 1969; "Nagisa Oshima" by Ian Cameron in *Movie* (London), winter 1969-70; "Entretien avec Oshima" in *Cahiers du cinéma* (Paris), March 1970: "Narrative Space" by S. Heath in *Screen* (London), no.3, 1976; "Anato mo" by Stephen Heath in *Screen* (London), winter 1976-77; "*La Pendaison*" in *Image et son* (Paris), 331bis, 1978.

* * *

Death by Hanging is an excellent example of the marriage of Oshima's stylistic experiments to his thematic concerns. Inspired by the true story of a Korean youth condemned and hanged for raping and murdering two Japanese girls, Oshima confronts us with the problems of discrimination against Koreans in Japan, the protagonist's discovery of his own identity, nationalism and the function of the state, and the relationship of imagination and reality.

Oshima cleverly arranges a situation in which the execution of R (identified by his initial to symbolize all Koreans in Japan) fails, or as a written title explains, body of R refuses to die." The dismayed officers try to stimulate his memory by re-enacting the roles of R and the people around him. While R, in a state of amnesia, keeps asking them naive questions, thus confronting the officers and the audience with fundamental problems—for example, the meaning of the state, the definition of a "Korean." Through their discussions and actions, the executioners' prejudice, their dishonorable past lives as war-criminals, their sexual frustrations and blind faith in the authorities are revealed. As well, the poverty and internal struggles of R's family are illustrated, as is the historical context of Japanese importation of Koreans as forced laborers.

The intensity of the mise-en-scene is related to the closed and fixed space of the set of the execution ground. This set's artificiality and claustrophobic atmosphere (partly necessitated by the film's low budget) is marvelously contrasted with the open space, natural light and sound of the outdoor sequences. When the film returns to the original prison setting, it becomes more abstract and surrealistic.

The victim's body, which is visible to the audience from the beginning, is recognized by the officers one by one, and finally, it comes to life as a symbolic "sister" of R. Her role is to agitate R politically, and awaken in him his identity as a Korean in Japan. R, then, refuses to be executed, condemning the nation as the murderer if the execution is carried out. Although he believes he is innocent, R returns to be executed, accepting "all the R's in the world." Obviously, the scene with the empty noose after the execution conveys the idea that the authorities are not capable of executing R.

The Japanese authorities, and Oshima's ideological position in relation to them are symbolized by the director's favorite symbol, e.g., the national flag in which the rising sun appears black (because the film is black-and white). The flag appears on the wall, frequently behind the faces of the public prosecutor and R.

Oshima also employs various experimental methods. Single actions are portrayed twice from different angles. Hand-written titles accompanied by discordant music are used to divide the film into sequences or to express the protagonist's emotions. The continuity of action between shots is intentionally broken during the first half of the film. Often, the characters, particularly R, talk to the camera directly. Oshima's ideological concerns require this Brechtian style.

The film's primary purpose is to provoke the audience through the visual and auditory images—yet, though it won the highest critical acclaim, *Death by Hanging* was not commerically successful in Japan.

—Kyoko Hirano

KOZIYAT ROG. Kozijat Rog. The Goat Horn. Production: Studiya za igralni filmi (Sofia, Bulgaria); 1971; black and white, 35mm, wide-screen; running time: 105 mins., some versions 95 mins.; length: 2824 meters. Released February 1972.

Screenplay by Nikolai Haitov; from the short story by Nikolai Haitov; directed by Métodi Andonov; photography by Dimo Kolarov; edited by Evgeniya Radeva; sound by Mithen Andreev; production design by Konstantin Dzhidrov; music by Siméon Pironkov, song composed and performed by Maria Neikova; special effects pyrotechnics by Ivan Angelov; costumes designed by Vladislav Schmidt; stunts headed by Petar Klyavkov.

Filmed 1971 in Bulgaria. Bulgarian Film Festival at Varna, Prize of the Audience, 1972; First Prize of the Central Committee of the Youth Communist League, 1972; Chicago Film Festival, Silver Hugo (2nd prize), 1973.

Cast: Katya Paskaléva (*Maria*); Anton Gorchev (*Kara-Ivan*); Kliment Denchev, Stefan Manrodiev, Todor Kolev, Marin Yanev (*Turk rapists*); Milèn Pénev (*The Shepherd*); Nevena Andonova (*Maria as a girl*); Krasimira Petrova (*Turk's wife*); Ivan Obretenov (*Poor man*); Ivan Yanchev (*Man with scar*).

Publications:

Reviews—"*Koziyat Rog*" by V. Ignatovski in *Kinoizkustvo* (Sofia, Bulgaria), March 1972; "Cornul de capră" by A. Ivasiuc in *Cinema* (Bucharest), September 1972; "*Kozijat Rog*" in *Variety* (New York), 16 August 1972; "*La Corne de chèvre*" in *Cinéma* (Paris), May 1973; "Zrozumieć siebie umierjąc" by B. Mruklik in *Kino* (Warsaw), May 1973; "Bulgarian Film Proves Excellent" by Lawrence Van Gelder in *The New York Times*, 23 August 1973; review by Martin Malina in the *Montreal Star*, 27 January 1973; "*Das Ziegenhorn*" by B. Jaeggi in *Cinema* (Zurich), no.4, 1976; books—*The Most Important Art: East European Film After 1945* by Mira Liehm and Antonín Liehm, Berkeley 1977; articles—"Karlovarské rozhovory: Metodi Andonov" by G. Kopanêvová in *Film a Doba* (Prague), October 1972; article in *Variety* (New York), 30 May 1973; article by Roger Greenspun in *The New York Times*, 3 April 1973; article by Peter Cowie in the *International Film Guide* (London), 1973; "*Kozji rog*" by T. Gomiscek in *Ekran* (Ljubljana, Yugoslavia), no.9-10, 1979.

*   *   *

One of the most successful Bulgarian films ever made and probably the best known abroad, *Koziyat Rog* was based on a legend that was first retold and later worked into a short story by Nikolai Haitov. He emerged in the 1960's as one of the most popular of Bulgarian writers, especially famous for his descriptions of the people and traditions in the somewhat isolated and "wild" region of the Rhodope mountains in the southern part of the country. The screenplay drifted yet further from historical and psychological accuracy in search of a larger truth, that of a shattering human tragedy. An introductory title ("This bloody story happened in the XVII century. It starts with an act of violence...") makes apparently intentional the shift from the original story of blood revenge to a more ambitious study of the devastating chain-reaction effect of violence on man's soul— which gradually becomes the film's main theme.

In parallel with the thematic evolution is a formal development: the film discards what was perhaps considered a "more cinematic" dramatization with flashbacks and intriguing tension for a straightforward narration with very sparse dialogue and a more predictable yet moving plot. In the role of both shepherd Karaivan's wife, raped and eventually killed by a band of Turks, and their daughter Maria, who is brought up by her father to be a man and a revenger but falls in love and commits suicide after Karaivan kills her lover, Katya Paskaleva gives a memorable performance. The bold treatment of sex and violence made the film a box-office record-breaker, while the critics praised its rhythm, stark black-and-white photography and its inherent Bulgarian-ness. It touched, no doubt, a very intimate chord in the collective consciousness of a country in which the last hundred years of its independence had been painfully dominated by the consequences of a fierce Ottoman oppression, threatening at times its very existence.

The song from the film, with lyrics added, became a hit, and ten years after the film's release the short story was successfully made into a ballet at the National Opera and Ballet Theatre in Sofia. *Koziyat Rog* is now widely recognized by Bulgarian critics and public alike as not only the best screen adaptation of Haitov's work and the best film of director Metodi Andonov (whose untimely death in 1974 put an end to a promising career) but also as a landmark in Bulgarian cinema, one that raised its prestige for a generation of film-goers and helped it move to the forefront of the country's contemporary culture.

—Dimitar Bardarsky

KWAIDAN. Kaidan. Production: Bungei Production/Ninjin Club for Toho Co. (Tokyo); Eastmancolor, 35mm, Tohoscope; running time: versions which include all 4 short stories are 164 mins., English version which includes only 3 stories is 125 mins. Released 1964, Japan.

Produced by Shigeru Wakatsuki; screenplay by Yoko Mizuki; from Lafacadio Hearn's (Yagumo Koizumi) collection of traditional Japanese ghost stories; including "Kurokami" (Black Hair), "Chawan no naka," "Miminashi Hoichi," and "Yuki-onna"; directed by Masaki Kobayashi; photography by Yoshio Miyajima; edited by Hisashi Sagara; sound by Hideo Nishizaki; art direction by Shigemasa Toda; music by Toru Takemitsu.

Cannes Film Festival, Special Jury Prize, 1965.

Cast: "Black Hair" ("Kurokami") episode: Rentaro Mikuni (*Samarai*); Michiyo Aratama (*1st wife*); Misako Watanabe (*2nd wife*); "The Woman of the Snow" ("Yuki-onna") episode: Keiko Kishi (*The Woman*); Tatsuya Nakadai (*Minokichi*); Mariko Okada; "Hoichi, the Earless" ("Mimi-nashi-Hoichi") episode: Katsuo Nakamura (*Hoichi*); Rentaro Mikuni (*Samurai*); Ganjiro Nakumara (*Head priest*); Takashi Shimura (*Priest*); Joichi Hayashi (*Yoshitsune*); Tetsuro Tamba; "In a Cup of Tea" ("Chawan no naka") episode: Ganemon Nakamura (*Kannai*); Noburo Nakaya (*Heinai*).

Publications:

Reviews—"*Kwaidan*" by Jean-André Fieschi in *Cahiers du cinéma* (Paris), July 1965; review by Diana W. Cope in *Films in Review* (New York), January 1966; review by Rory Guy in *Cinema* (Beverly Hills), March 1966; review by Richard Davis in *Films and Filming* (London), October 1967; books—*Les Classiques du cinéma fantastique* by Jean-Marie Sabatier, Paris 1973; *Voices from the Japanese Cinema* by Joan Mellen, New York 1975; *Japanese Film Directors* by Audie Bock, New York 1978; articles—"Note" in *International Film Guide*, London 1965; "Un Grand Film de marionnettes" by Pierre Philippe in *Cinéma 65* (Paris), December 1965; "Fantómes à revendre" by Pierre Billard in *Cinéma 65* (Paris), June 1965; article by John Thomas in *Film Society Review* (New York), December 1966; "Les Artifices de la légende" by Jean Sirodeau in *Positif* (Paris), June 1966; article by James Price in *Sight and Sound* (London), autumn 1967; "Kobayashi, l'homme et l'oeuvre" by C.R. Blouin and "Kobayashi, à l'uquam: anarchiste ou utopiste?" by G. Thérien in *Cinéma Québec* (Montreal), February/March 1974; "*Kwaidan*" by L. Merckx in *Film en Televisie* (Brussels), October 1981; "*Kwaidan*" by P. Delpeut in *Skrien* (Amsterdam), winter 1981-82.

Uniquely among Kobayashi's mature works, *Kaidan* is free from any social or political dimension. In its place, the director aimed "to explore the juxtaposition between man's material nature and his spiritual nature, the realm of dream and aspiration," and "to express... the ultimate in stylised film method." How far the first of these ambitions was fulfilled is debatable; but the film has a good claim to have achieved the second.

The film is based on four tales from Lafcadio Hearn's collection of traditional Japanese ghost stories, *Kwaidan* (although some release prints omit the second episode). Ghost stories form a long and respectable tradition in Japanese cinima, with Mizoguchi's *Ugestsu Monogatare* the classic example; Kobayashi brought to the genre his own exceptionally acute eye for superb visual composition. Remarkably, *Kaidan* was his first film in colour; bent on attaining maximum tonal control, the director had all the sets constructed inside a disused aircraft hangar, and painted everything himself. Not since Hermann Warm's sets for *Caligari* had stylised backdrops been so strikingly deployed, and *Kaidan's* influence is clearly evident in the sets for Kurosawa's *Dodes'ka-den*. Realism is deliberately eschewed in favour of atmospheric expressionism: in the second episode, *Yuke-onna* (*Woman of the Snow*), a huge eye peers impassively down from the sky on the events of the story, to disconcerting effect.

Kobayashi took equal pains over the soundtrack, working closely with the composer Toru Takemitsu for six months to achieve the desired mix of sound and image. For each story Takemitsu chose a different sound as the basis of his electronically synthesised music—wood being split, pebbles being struck together, the non-verbal vocal accompaniments to *Noh* drama, and the playing of a *shamisen* (a banjo-like instrument)—to produce eerie and unsettling tones that combine evocatively with the haunting visuals.

Each of the stories sustains its own distinct mood: the elegiac sorrow of *Kurokami* (*Black Hair*), the icy remoteness of *Yuki-onna*, the sardonic humour of *Chawan no naka* (*In a Cup of Tea*). Perhaps the most memorable is the third tale, *Miminashi Hoichi* (*Hoichi the Earless*), in which a blind young monk is compelled by ghostly warriors of the Heike clan to recount each night the saga of the battle of Daira-no-ora. To break the spell, the priests paint his body with sacred writings, which will render him invisible to the ghosts. But they forget to paint his ears, which the thwarted ghosts tear from his head in their fury.

Although it lacks the wider—and perhaps ultimately more satisfying—social implications of Kobayashi's finest films, such as *Seppuku (Harakiri)* and *Joiuchi (Rebellion)*, *Kaidan* certainly stands as his most sheerly beautiful and visually enchanting work. It also proved his most commercially successful picture to date, and won him a Special Jury Prize at Cannes. Characteristically, Kobayashi rejected the obvious temptation to produce further films in this vein, preferring to return to his social and philosophic preoccupations. *Kaidan* remains an isolated tour-de-force, dazzling exception in his output.

—Philip Kemp

LADRI DI BICICLETTE. The Bicycle Thief. Le Voleur de Bicyclette. Production: Produzioni De Sica; 1948; black and white, 35mm; running time: 90 mins. Released 1948.

Produced by Umberto Scarpelli; screenplay by Cesare Zavattini with Oreste Biancoli, Suso Cecchi d'Amico, Vittorio De Sica, Adolfo Franci, Gherardo Gherardi, and Gerardo Guerrieri;

*   *   *

from a novel by Luigi Bartolini; directed by Vittorio de Sica; photography by Carlo Montuori; edited by Eraldo da Roma; production design by Antonino Traverso; music by Alessandro Cicognini, orchestra directed by Willy Ferraro.

Filmed in Rome. New York Film Critics Award, Best Foreign Film, 1949; Belgium World Festival of Film and Arts, Grand Prix, 1949; Festival of Film at Locarno, Social Prize, 1949; Special Academy Award as Most Outstanding Foreign Film, 1949.

Cast: Lamberto Maggiorani (*Antonio Ricci*); Enzo Staiola (*Bruno Ricci*); Lianella Carell (*Maria Ricci*); Elena Altieri; Gino Saltamerenda; Vittorio Antonucci; Guilio Chiari; Michele Sakara; Carlo Jachino; Nando Bruno; Fausto Guerzoni; Umberto Spadaro; Massimo Randisi.

Publications:

Scripts—"*Le Voleur de Bicyclette*" in *Avant-Scène du Cinèma* (Paris), December, 1967; "*Le voleur de bicyclette*" (extracts), with C. Zavattini and others in *Cinémathèque belge* (Brussels), 1958; *The Bicycle Thief: A Film by Vittorio de Sica* translated by Simon Hartog, New York 1968; "Zlodĕji kol" (script extract) in *Film a Doba* (Prague), July 1981; books—*Il Cinema Italiano* by Carlo Lizzani, Firenze, Italy 1954; *Il Cinema Neorealistico Italiano* by G.C. Castello, Turin, 1956; *Il Neorealismo Italiano* by Brunello Rondi, Parma, Italy 1956; *Il Nuovo Cinema Italiano* by Giuseppe Ferrara, Firenze, Italy 1957; *Le Néo-Réalism italien et ses créateurs* by Patrice G. Hovald, Paris 1959; *Le Néo-Réalism italien* by Borde-Bouissy, Lausanne, France 1960; *Qu'est-ce que le cinèma* by Andre Bazin, Les Editions du Cerf, Paris 1962; *Vittorio De Sica* by Henri Agel, 2nd ed., Paris 1964; *Vittorio De Sica* by Pierre Leprohon, Paris 1966; *The Great Films: 50 Golden Years of Motion Pictures* by Bosley Crowther, New York 1967; *Patterns of Realism: A Study of Neo-Realist Cinema* by Roy Armes, New York 1971; *Encountering Directors* by Charles Thomas Samuels, New York 1972; *Neorealismo e Vita Nazionale: Antologia di Cinema Nuovo* edited by Mario Guaraldi-Rimini, Firenze, 1975; *La Mia Vita con Vittorio De Sica* by Maria Mercader, Milan 1978; *Anthologie du cinéma*, vol.10, Paris 1979; articles—"De Sica's *Bicycle Thief* and Italian Humanism" by Herbert L. Jacobson in *Hollywood Quarterly*, fall 1949; article by Richard Winnington in *Sight and Sound*, March 1950; "Interview with De Sica" by Francis Koval in *Sight and Sound* (London), April 1950; "*Le voleur de bicyclette*", with C. Zavattini and others in *Ciné-Club* (Paris), January 1950; article by André Bazin in *Cahiers du cinéma* (Paris), March 1954; article by Vittorio de Sica in *Films and Filming* (London), January 1956; article by J. Chevallier in *Image et son* (Paris), December 1956; "Why Neo-Realism Failed" by Eric Rhode in *Sight and Sound* (London), winter 1960-61; "Poet of Poverty" by Douglas McVay in *Films and Filming* (London), October 1964, concludes in November 1964; "Film Critique no.6: *Bicycle Thief*" by Peter Harcourt in *Screen Education* (London), July/August 1965; "La pérennité du *Voleur de bicyclette*" by Pierre Leprohon in *Avant-Scène du cinéma* (Paris), December 1967; issue on De Sica edited by O. Caldiron, *Bianco e nero* (Rome), September/December 1975; "Le Cinéma du néo-realisme italien est en berne: Vittorio de Sica" by J.-L. Passek in *Cinéma* (Paris), January 1975; "*Le Voleur de bicyclette*" by L. La Fuente in *Cinéma* (Paris), November 1978; "Vittorio de Sica 1902-1974" by Henri Agel, special issue of *Avant-Scène du cinéma* (Paris), 15 October 1978; "Fahrrad-

diebe" by A. Bazin, translated by A. Spingler in *Filmkritik* (Munich), May 1979; "Italian Neo-Realism: A Mirror Construction of Reality" by B. Lawton in *Film Criticism* (Edinboro, Pennsylvania), no.2, 1979; "Dossier: le neo-realisme: De Sica 'le menteur'" by P. Carcassonne in *Cinématographe* (Paris), January 1979.

*   *   *

Before examining the film, it is important to point out that the oft-used English language title "The Bicycle *Thief*" is misleading and injurious to the meaning to the film. *Ladri di biciclette* translates as "Bicycle Thieves", the plural marking an allegorical intention. Vittorio De Sica's film suggests a universe interrelated inextricably by perverse economic ties—the bicycle one man needs to work and support his family, another man steals to support his, and still another sells. Singulars will not do in this film. De Sica presents the story in terms of a man's relation to a crowd, but this crowd is more than just a picturesque background. It is the modern equivalent of a Greek chorus and represents both the higher and lower aspects of human character. It is an extension of the protagonist.

Ricci, the victimized worker emerges from this crowd at the beginning of the film, called to work after months of unemployment, but his accession to the status of modern tragic hero is a matter of random choice and necessity, not of birth, self-determination, or desire. For a while, endowed with the promise of a steady salary and the ability to once again be the bread-winner in his family, Ricci is permitted to dream of material success. When he retrieves his bicycle from the municipal pawn-shop, exhanging for it the family linen, the camera pans up, following the clerk as he climbs to deposit the sheets at the top of what seems like thousands of similar bundles. Ricci is not the exception—and thus, the traditional tragic hero—he is the rule, one of thousands or more. Searching desperately all over the city, he will again encounter this societal chorus: as workers readying a strike; as the denizens of a black market; as a mass of poor people praying in a church; as a crowd lamenting a drowned child; as a gang of toughs in a crowded street protecting a local boy from Ricci's accusations; as a pack of football fans who thwart Ricci's feeble attempt to steal a bicycle himself in a rash, despairing decision to reject moral restraint; and finally, as an anonymous, everyday crowd, walking, going about their business peacefully, hopefully—the crowd to which Ricci is returned.

Ricci's relation to society, in general, and the political and economic proportions of postwar Italian society, in partiuclar, is reflected as a series of encounters with crowds to which the protagonist's membership is cyclically articulated at the beginning and end of the film. In *Crowds and Power*, Elias Canetti offers a taxonomy of such groups: "baiting crowds" intent on blood; "prohibition crowds;" "feast crowds," the "lamenting pack;" and the "hunting pack." Most importantly, the activities of these crowds are to be considered as historically construed.

One significance of *Ladri di biciclette*, and to a larger extent that of neorealism, then, lies in the predominance of the role of representation, not only of those inexhaustible details of every-day existence, but also of popular life in all its diversity. Still, *Ladri di biciclette* does not explore the area of popular, political action. Any solidarity among people in the film is a matter of personal friendship (between Ricci and the sanitation workers who help him search Rome in their truck) or that between father and son. The effectiveness of political struggle to improve the inequitable economic conditions at fault here is not considered beyond the brief glimpse of the strike preparations.

The story was brought to De Sica's attention by Cesare Zavattini, screenwriter for the film and one of the seven who adapted the novel by Luigi Bartolini; yet, no film adaptation was ever so disrespectful of its original as this one. Bartolini's protagonist is *not* a man brought forward from the crowd, a man like any other, he is a disgruntled and supercilious artist who opines the most reactionary prejudices about the poor. Moreover, in order to find his stolen bicycle, the protagonist gets about on a second one which apparently he kept around for just such emergencies.

De Sica and Zavattini use the bicycle as a "vehicle" to organize the narrative. The theft of a bicycle authorizes a wide search through Rome; hence, the narrative discloses itself as an odyssey structure (there are interesting parallels between Ricci and Ulysses, too). The filmmakers' immense capacity to introduce metaphor into the most everyday context and the puissance of that metaphor (we recall the white stallion in *Sciusciá*) becomes clear when we attempt to bracket the idea of the bicycle. For example, if we substitute a worker's tool box for the bicycle, the narrative loses much of its momentum, its mythical implications, and even part of its effectiveness as a tragedy.

Veteran actor De Sica's talent for molding the raw material of the non-professional actor is prominently displayed. He knew it would be difficult for the trained actor to forget his/her highly coded technique to become the man in the street. He felt that better results were to be obtained by teaching the non-actor just enough to serve the purposes of the scene being shot. Compare, for example, the lattitude of his actors with those of Visconti's in *La terra trema*. In that film, the non-professionals are stiff and gesturally inarticulate; their inexperience tends to stand in the way of a heightened dramatic communication. On the other hand, De Sica's actors signal physically a greater alertness and sensitivity to their immediate problems and awareness of the social and psychological conformations of their characters. Ricci was played by Lamberto Maggiorani, a factory worker who had brought his small son to audition for the role of Bruno; his wife, Maria (Lianella Carell) was a journalist who had approached the director for an interview. Bruno (Enzo Staiola), the last cast member to be found, was watching the shooting when De Sica noticed him. The scene in which Ricci takes his son to a trattoria in order to make up for having scolded him involves some of the most subtly nuanced and believable expression of a father-son relationship in the history of cinema.

—Joel E. Kanoff

THE LADY FROM SHANGHAI. Production: Columbia Pictures Corp.; 1948; black and white, 35mm; running time: 86 mins. Released 10 June 1948.

Produced by Orson Welles with Richard Wilson and William Castle; screenplay by Orson Welles; from the novel *Before I Die* by Sherwood King; directed by Orson Welles; photography by Charles Lawton, Jr. edited by Viola Lawrence; sound by Lodge Cunningham; art direction by Stephen Goosson and Sturges Carne, set decoration by Wilbur Menefee and Herman Schoenbrun; music by Heinz Roemheld, music directed by Morris Stoloff; special mirror effects by Lawrence Butler; costumes designed by Jean Louis.

Filmed for the most part in fall 1946, in Central Park and the Maritime Union Headquarters, New York; the Aquarium and the Chinese Mandarin Theatre, San Francisco; the Walhalla Bar and Cafe, Sausalito; various locations in Acapulco; and aboard the yacht "Zaca" owned by Errol Flynn.

Cast: Rita Hayworth (*Elsa Bannister*); Orson Welles (*Michael O'Hara*); Everett Sloane (*Arthur Bannister*); Glenn Anders (*George Grisby*); Ted de Corsia (*Sidney Broome*); Erskine Sanford (*Judge*); Gus Schilling (*Goldie*); Carl Frank (*District attorney*); Louis Merrill (*Jake*); Evelyn Ellis (*Bessie*); Harry Shannon (*Cab driver*); Wong Show Chong (*Li*); Sam Nelson (*Yacht captain*).

Publications:

Books—*Orson Welles* by André Bazin, Paris 1950; *The Fabulous Orson Welles* by Peter Noble, London 1956; *The Cinema of Orson Welles* by Peter Bogdanovich, New York 1961; *Orson Welles, l'éthique et l'esthétique* by various authors in *Études cinématographiques*, Paris 1963; *The Cinema of Orson Welles* by Peter Cowie, London 1965; *The Films of Orson Welles* by Charles Higham, Berkeley 1971; *Orson Welles* by Maurice Bessy, New York 1971; *Orson Welles* by Joseph McBride, London 1972; *Orson Welles* by Joseph McBride, New York 1977; *The Magic World of Orson Welles* by J. Naremore, New York 1978; *Film Noir* edited by Alain Silver and Elizabeth Ward, Woodstock, New York 1979; *Orson Welles* by André Bazin, revised edition, translated and annotated by Jonathan Rosenbaum, Berkeley 1979; articles—"Orson Welles from *Citizen Kane* to *Othello*" by Roberto Pariante in *Bianco e nero* (Rome), March 1956; "L'Oeuvre d'Orson Welles" in *Cahiers du cinéma* (Paris), September 1958; "Orson Welles" by Peter Cowie in *Films and Filming* (London), April 1961; "The Heroes of Welles" by Alan Stanbrook" in *Film* (London), no.28, 1961; issue devoted to Welles in *Image et son* (Paris), no.139, 1961; issue devoted to Welles in *Cineforum* (Venice), no.19, 1962; interview with Everett Sloane in *Film* (London), no.37, 1965; "A Trip to Don Quixoteland: Conversations with Orson Welles" by Juan Cobos, Miguel Rubio, and J.A. Pruneda in *Cahiers du Cinema in English* (New York), June 1966; "Orson Welles' Use of Sound" by Phyllis Goldfarb in *Take One* (Montreal), July/August 1971; "The Long Take" by Brian Henderson in *Film Comment* (New York), summer 1971; "The Inaccessibility of *The Lady from Shanghai*" by M. Graham in *Film Criticism* (Edinboro, Pennsylvania), spring 1981; "Power and Disintegration in the Films of Orson Welles" by Beverle Houston in *Film Quarterly* (Berkeley), summer 1982.

* * *

The difficulty a viewer faces in interpreting Orson Welles's *The Lady from Shanghai* may be the first sign of its complexity. As in *Touch of Evil* ten years later, the film spins such intricate webs in terms of plot that several viewings are needed for anyone to find its crucial junctures and crossovers. The viewer's task is impeded by the self-conscious and intricate use of the frame, the lush compositions in foreground and background, and the abrupt ruptures of continuity between the image and sound tracks. In sum, Michael O'Hara is victimized in a skein of machinations wrought by Elsa Bannister with and against a brilliant criminal lawyer, a cane-swaggering cripple who happens to be her aged husband. Framed in a plot of fake self-murders reminiscent of *Double*

Indemnity, Welles portrays a tough, soft-hearted anti-Franco refugee, an Irish innocent who wants to walk through life with independence and adventure.

Simplicity and complication are of the same essence in this film. As we listen to the tales of cross-purpose concocted by Hayworth in the sequence taking place in the San Francisco aquarium, the closeups of her icy beauty are offset by lurid projections of monstrous fish of colossal stature. A segment less famous but no less important than that of the "Hall of Mirrors" that crowns the plot, the uncanny illuminations and chiaroscuro reveals Welles's style at its best: the female is both a menacing figure of deceit but also an agent of sardonic hilarity, of metaphysical farce that even Renoir or Hitchcock could not attain in their frontal closeups of spellbinding women. The glass that separates the bizarre creatures from the two lovers is what will splatter and crash at the final meeting of the three protagonists in the "crazy-house," where prismatic multiplication of the images of the characters foregrounds the two spouses shooting their phantom images to bits. "If I kill you, I kill myself," murmurs Bannister in closeup where the frame places his reflection adjacent to Elsa's. A carnival of destruction ensues, mirrors blasted until the bullets finally reach the two figures. A cinematic potlatch, The *Lady from Shanghai* celebrates and consumes its madness, only to allow O'Hara to slip out of the amusement park of horrors and to ambulate towards the airy cityscape of San Francisco in the last shot. "The only way to grow wise is to get old," he predicts, as we see him pacing off into a world whose immensity dwarfs him.

The film uses a high contrast of black and white, essaying compositional angles that are more zany and unpredictable than those of *Citizen Kane*. It establishes important relations between figures and objects in extreme closeup and great depth with keen attention to editing in a fashion that makes Welles's masterpiece of 1941 look already standard: shots of Hayworth on the rocks off Acapulco are in such extreme depth of field that we can barely recognize her adjacent to Welles's nose in closeup. An obsessively self-conscious use of optical instruments in the film—monocular devices, water tumblers, anamorphic mirrors, windshields, projections of shadows on screen illuminated from behind—make the film theorize its own process as it narrates its baroque plot. And, as usual in Welles's major works, the play within the play multiplies the diegesis as it conflates its entirety. The lady who will "shanghai" O'Hara catches the hero observing a hieratic spectacle in a Chinese playhouse near Union Square just as he had been evading the police after a scandalous frame-up in a courtroom. As Elsa and the police seek O'Hara, a field of theatrical and scriptural enigmas dazzle in frame. The sound of gongs and cymbals, the stylized dances of players fixed upon by wizened Asiatic bums, the blonde beauty of Elsa accompanied by her incomprehensible whispers of Chinese exchanged with her underworld cronies: the display of the sequence supersedes any central or calming influence either of narrative or formal approaches to perspective and composition. The theater doubles, then infinitizes, the frame; it allows us to speculate on cinema as no studio film had ever done up to 1947, with *Citizen Kane* excepted.

Classifying *The Lady from Shanghai* as a pervasive *film noir*, a variant of the same principal of film at the core of Welles's *oeuvre*, as a modern Shakespeare of Hugolian experiment would seem useless. Its genre is its own, and the film must be viewed independently of the models of editing one remembers from *the Magnificent Ambersons* or *Citizen Kane*.

—Tom Conley

THE LAND. Production: Agricultural Adjustment Agency, U.S. Department of Agriculture; 1942; black and white, 35mm; running time: 42 mins. Though it has been shown non-theatrically, the film has never had a general release; its premiere showing was in April 1942, at the Museum of Modern Art, New York.

Screenplay by Robert J. Flaherty, commentary by Russell Lord; directed by Robert Flaherty; photography by Irving Lerner, Douglas Baker, Floyd Crosby, and Charles Herbert; edited by Helen Van Dongen; sound engineered by A. Dillinger and Reuben Ford; music by Richard Arnell, played by The National Youth Administration Symphony under the direction of Fritz Mahler; consultant: Wayne Darrow; collaborator: Frances Flaherty; research and field assistance: W.H. Lamphere and Lamp Hart.

Filmed summer 1939-March 1940 in the American South and Midwest.

Cast: Robert Flaherty (*Narrator*).

Publications:

Books—*The Film Till Now* by Paul Rotha, New York 1949; *Forever the Land: A Country Chronicle and Anthology* by Russell and Kate Lord, New York 1950; *Robert Flaherty: Nota biografica, filmografica e bibliografica...* by Mario Gromo, Parma, Italy 1952; *Documentary Film* by Paul Rotha, Sinclair Reed, and Richard Griffith, 3rd ed., London 1952; *The World of Robert Flaherty* by Richard Griffith, New York 1953; *Robert Flaherty e le Documentaire Poetique: Etudes Cinematographiques no.5* by Fuad Quintar, Paris 1960; *The Film Till Now: A Survey of World Cinema* by Paul Rotha with Richard Griffith, New York 1960; *Robert Flaherty* by Jose L. Clemente, Madrid 1963; *Robert Flaherty* by Carlos Fernandez Cuenca, Madrid 1963; *Robert Flaherty* compiled by Wolfgang Klaue, East Berlin 1964; *Robert J. Flaherty* by Henri Agel, Paris 1965; *Pare Lorentz and the Documentary Film* by Robert Snyder, Norman, Oklahoma 1968; *The Innocent Eye: The Life of Robert Flaherty* by Arthur Caldwell-Marshall, revised ed., London 1970; *Nonfiction Film: A Critical History* by Richard Barsam, New York 1973; *Documentary: A History of Non-Fiction Film* by Erik Barnouw, New York 1974; *The Long View* by Basil Wright, New York 1974; *Robert J. Flaherty* by Antonio Napolitano, Florence 1975; *Robert Flaherty: A Guide to References and Resources* by William T. Murphy, Boston 1979; *Grierson on the Movies* edited by Forsyth Hardy, London and Boston, 1981; articles—"Flaherty and the Future" by Richard Griffith in *New Movies* (formerly *National Board of Review Magazine*) (New York), January 1943; "Documentare a lotta per la vita" by Vito Pandolfi in *Cinema* (Rome), 15 December 1950; "Gli uomini hanno fame mella terra de Flaherty" by M.T.L. in *Cinema* (Rome), November 1951; "Il film proibito di Flaherty" by Davide Turconi in *Bianco e Nero* (Rome), no.2, 1962; "Robert J. Flaherty, 1884-1951" by Helen Van Dongen in *Film Quarterly* (Berkeley), summer 1965; "Robert J. Flaherty: 1884-1951" by Helen Van Dongen in *Nonfiction Film: Theory and Criticism* edited by Richard Barsam, New York 1976; "Helen Van Dongen: An Interview" by Ben Achtenberg in *Film Quarterly* (Berkeley), winter 1976; "The Giant Shinnies Down the Beanstalk: Flaherty's *The Land*" by Theodore Strauss in *The Documentary Tradition* edited by Lewis Jacobs, New York 1979.

*   *   *

The Land, the least typical, least known and most controversial of Robert Flaherty's films, depicts a vast and vague territory across the southern and midwestern United States. Here, in the period between the Depression's end and the beginning of World War II, abandoned farmhouses lined dusty roadways, and forgotten farm people had almost ceased to hope for a better life. On the face of it, *The Land* might have become the earthly counterpart to Pare Lorentz's *The River* easily the best known and most widely praised American documentary film. But as it turned out, *The Land* pleased few people, least of all Flaherty himself.

As head of the new U.S. Film Service, Lorentz had invited Robert Flaherty (perhaps at John Grierson's suggestion) to make a film on the New Deal's efforts to restore American farmers and farmlands to their productive fullness. Flaherty and his wife collaborator, Frances, welcomed the chance to explore their homeland as they had previously explored many distant corners of the world. Flaherty's brief experience with government sponsorship while making *Industrial Britain*, or most of it, for Grierson's E.M.B. Film Unit in 1931 had not prepared him for the frustrations and troubles that lay ahead.

To make *The Land* Robert and Frances Flaherty travelled some 100,000 miles, shooting 25,000 feet of 35mm film—all silent (narration and music were added later). "A long and gruelling job," Flaherty later described it. While he was still filming, Lorentz started a new film of his own (*The Fight for Life*) and in his absence Congress abruptly dismantled the U.S. Film Service. *The Land* was shunted to Henry Wallace's Department of Agriculture. All through the summer and fall of 1941, the Department's experts tinkered with Flaherty's footage, trying to make it conform to the government's rapidly changing needs and policies. As the U.S. came closer to entering the war, unemployment gave way to a farm labor shortage, mechanization became part of the solution to the farm problems rather than a threat. It fell to Helen van Dongen (who had edited Joris Ivens' later European films, and his just finished *Power and the Land*) to find structure for Flaherty's random footage and make sense of the changing government directives.

The film's most memorable scenes are those in which Flaherty (narrating the film himself) briefly dramatizes poignant human incidents: a young couple with two small children packing their pitiful belongings on a mule cart; an old Negro man living alone on a once-abundant plantation, wondering where everyone has gone; a boy sleeping, while his mother explains that his hands move because he thinks he's shelling peas. Flaherty conceded that the film had no specific solutions for what the camera saw; he found it amazing that so critical a film could be made at all. "It shows that democracy can face itself in the mirror without flinching," he told an interviewer a short while before the film's intended release.

Within a few short weeks, however, democracy flinched. With the U.S. now at war, government officials feared that so dismal a picture would serve mainly to aid the enemies' propaganda campaigns. A prestige premiere was held at The Museum of Modern Art in early 1942, but the film's release was permanently denied. (The Museum still distributes 16mm prints for study purposes. Calder-Marshall's *The Innocent Eye*, Appendix 4, contains the final narration, written by Russell Lord based on Flaherty's comments, interspersed with critical descriptions of each sequence by Paul Rotha and Basil Wright.)

Critical opinion about *The Land* has been divided, then as now, into two more or less exclusive areas: style and content. Basil Wright has called it "the most important film in Flaherty's development as an artist...a cry of protest...impressive because of its passionate incoherence." Siegfried Kracauer found its "plot" lacking precision and failing to get hold of the very problems it attacked; its true merits (deep honesty, the beauty of its pictures,

and its avoidance of hasty conclusions) added up to "fragments of a lost epic song." Frances Flaherty did not mention *The Land* in her book, *The Odyssey of a Film-maker* considering only their four "free" films as bearing the true Flaherty mark.

Although the first credit after the main title on *The Land* reads "Directed by Robert J. Flaherty in collaboration with Frances H. Flaherty," her name often does not appear in books listing those credits. Richard Griffith, in *The World of Robert Flaherty*, details the nature of the Flahertys' "filmmaking partnership" in creating a film method which Frances later called "non-pre-conception," which she championed after Flahert's death through her writings and her talks and through the Flaherty Seminars which she founded in 1955.

The Land was Flaherty's major effort to align himself with the social-minded documentarists. If he failed, it was no more or less a failure than his efforts to become part of the commercial movie world. Like the great Sergei Eisenstein, Flaherty was a man of mythic vision; his films were mythic too, despite earnest efforts to conform to pre-determined rules and counter-regulations. At Flaherty's death in 1951, Grierson re-assessed Flaherty's "handful of lovely films" with the thousands of educational and propaganda productions, made by the "documentary people who went the other way," financed by the million in government services all over the world. "I look at it all today and think with the gentler half of my head that Flaherty's path was right and the other wrong." Certainly Flaherty's path was right for Flaherty, if for no others.

—Cecile Starr

LÁSKY JEDNÉ PLAVOVLÁSKY. Loves of a Blonde. Production: Barrandov Film Studio for Ceskoslovenský Film; black and white, 35mm; length: 2195 meters. Released November 1965, Prague.

Produced by Rudolf Hajek; screenplay by Jaroslav Papoušek, Ivan Passer, Miloš Forman, and Václav Sašek; directed by Miloš Forman; photography by Miroslav Ondříček; edited by Miroslav Hájek; sound by Adolf Böhm; art direction by Karel Cerný; music by Evžen Illín; assistant director: Ivan Passer.

Filmed 1965 in Zruč and Sázavou, Czechoslovakia. Venice Film Festival, Prize of CIDALAC, 1965.

Cast: Hana Brejchová (*Andula*); Vladimir Pucholt (*Milda*); Vladimir Menšík (*Vacovský*); Ivan Kheil (*Maňas*); Jiří Hrubý (*Burda*); Milada Ježková (*Milda's Mother*); Josef Sebáek (*Milda's Father*); Marie Salačová (*Marie*); Jana Nováková (*Jana*); Jana Crkalová (*Jaruška*); Zdeňka Lorencová (*Zdena*): Táňa Zelinkaová (*Girl*); Jan Vostřeil (*Colonel*); Josef Kolb (*Prkorný*); Antonín Blažejovský (*Tonda*); M. Zedníčková (*Educator*).

Publications:

Reviews—by Saul Kahan in *Cinema* (Beverly Hills), December 1966; review by Andrew Sarris in *The Village Voice* (New York), 10 November 1966; "*Loves of a Blonde*" by Claire Clouzot in *Film Quarterly* (Berkeley), fall 1967; review by Graham Frazer in *Take One* (Montreal), February 1967; books—*Modern Czechoslovak Film 1945-1965* by Jaroslav Boček, Prague 1965; *New*

Cinema in Eastern Europe by Alistar Whyte, New York 1971; *Outline of Czechoslovakian Cinema* by Langdon Dewey, London 1971; *Miloš Forman, Ingrid Thulin* edited by Bruce Henstall, Washington, D.C. 1972; *Closely Watched Films* by Antonín Liehm, White Plains, New York 1974; *Cinema Beyond the Danube* by Michael Jon Stoil, Metuchen, New Jersey 1974; *The Milos Forman Stories* by Antonin Liehm, White Plains, New York 1975; *The Most Important Art: East European Film After 1945* by Mira Liehm and Antonín Liehm, Berkeley 1977; articles—"Putování za holčči vujní" by J. Janousěek in *Film a doba* (Prague), no.5, 1965; "Pár docela obyčejných věcí" by A.J. Liehm in *Flim a doba* (Prague), no.11, 1965; "Star-Crossed in Prague" by Peter John Dyer in *Sight and Sound* (London), winter 1965-66; "Red Youth" by Gordon Gow in *Films and Filming* (London), February 1966; "Adula's Dream" in *Newsweek* (New York), 19 September 1966; article by Gordon Gow in *Films and Filming* (London), July 1966; "Interview with Miloš Forman" by James Blue and Gianfranco de Bosio in *Cahiers du Cinéma in English* (New York), February 1967; "Getting the Great 10%" by Harriet Polt in *Film Comment* (New York), fall 1970; "Milos Forman's America is Like Kafka's—Basically Comic" by James Conaway in the *New York Times Magazine*, 11 July 1971; "A Czech in New York: An Interview with Milos Forman" by Gordon Gow in *Films and Filming* (London), September 1971; "Idotallo kerdesek: Forman: *Feketer Peter*, egy szoszi szerelme" by A. Foldes in *Filmkultura* (Budapest), September/October 1979.

*   *   *

The heroes of Milos Forman's first films are quite ordinary young people, like most of the young people in the world. They do not stand out; they are not too good and not too bad, not particularly clever, but not particularly stupid either. In *Konkurs* (*The Competition*) they are girls who long to sing in the popular theater of Prague but are incapable of assessing their own abilities. In *Cerny Petr* (*Black Peter*) the hero is a young man who is learning to be a salesman because he has no precise goals in life. In *Loves of a Blonde* the central figures are young women who work in a shoe factory. All they want is a little happiness and a nice romantic love. Forman systematically chooses these non-heroic heroes for his films; he is interested precisely in the kind of people who will never be astronauts, outstanding scientists, actors or professional singers. In his opinion, they, too, are worthy of filmmakers' attention. This is the underlying premise of his early films, which derive their form from it, a form obviously different from traditional cinema not only in its conception of the hero but also in its distinct type of narrative. In these films Forman builds his style on the conviction that the most ordinary banalities of life contain more drama and more truth than the carefully elaborated form of a classically developed drama.

It is such everyday banalities that constitute the simple action of *Loves of a Blonde*. Its heroine, the young girl Andula, longs for love. She tries to find it with several men she happens to meet in her neighborhood. But she finds true love—or so she thinks—only after meeting a pianist from Prague. After a few beautiful moments, however, disappointment sets in, and Andula must once again content herself with her dreams. Her story, this slice of her life, is based on a linear succession of episodic situations with no gradations whatsoever. The director then develops these situations before the camera, and it is the viewer who combines them into a mosaic that has narrative value. Forman first took up filmmaking with a documentary bent; his quest for drama and truth in his films' characters in banal situations therefore has, to a certain extent, the nature of a documentary record. He follows his heroine and her comrades during their conversations at boarding school, at work in the factory, at a dance party, in talks with parents, and at meetings. The camera jumps from one face to another, fixing on them in an attempt to catch those imperceptible signs of inner feelings—boredom, longing, sadness, bitterness. The indifferent gaze of the camera could have a cruel effect, but it is softened by Forman's spontaneous sense of humor, which flows from the recognition that the most tragic occurrence, experienced and examined from without—and Forman looks at it with the same distance as the viewer—has comic and grotesque aspects. He finds and reveals the comedy in every situation involving the worker Andula, and even makes it the foundation of a love scene in which malfunctioning blinds undercut the significance Andula attaches to her feelings in her relationship with the pianist. However, Forman's humor is not malicious. He observes his heroes without ridiculing them, with kind sympathy and with the conviction that through laughter there is always a greater hope of penetrating beneath the surface of things. But he does not stop at the level of humorous portrayal. Through intimately familiar detail he brings the viewer to an understanding of the more general essence of the situations he depicts. And this essence is neither banal nor sentimental. Against the background of everyday activity, with all its comic situations, there is the weighty social problem of the isolated life of young women working in a remote Bohemian town where there are no opportunities to find acquaintances or love, resulting in the playing out of their emotional lives in cheap, demeaning short-term affairs. Ultimately, despite all the film's lighter moments, the viewer is left with a slight sense of sadness and bitterness.

Forman embarks on his subjects and themes with a thorough knowledge of the matter at hand; the life of the young women factory workers is depicted without the slightest artificiality. A contributing factor is the measured guidance of the actors, which makes one forget that, except for a few professionals, most of the actors had never been in front of a camera before. Another virtue of Forman's films of this period is the lively dialog, which becomes a vital element for enhancing the verisimilitude of the film situations.

In the history of Czechoslovak cinematography Forman's films represent a new achievement, from the standpoint of the choice of theme and content as well as techniques of expression. They have signaled a deviation from previous filmmaking and the start of a new course.

—B. Urgosiíková

THE LAST PICTURE SHOW. Production: BBS Production and Last Picture Show Productions; 1971; black and white, 35mm; running time: 118 mins. Released 1971 by Columbia-Warner.

Produced by Stephen F. Friedman, executive producer: Burt Schneider; screenplay by Larry McMurtry and Peter Bogdanovich; from the novel by Larry McMurtry; directed by Peter Bogdanovich; photography by Robert Surtees; edited by Don Cambern; sound by Tom Overton; production design by Polly Platt; art direction by Walter Scott Herndon; music by Hank Williams, Bob Wills and the Texas Playboys, Eddy Arnold, Eddie Fisher, Phil Harris, Pee Wee King, Hank Snow, Tony

Bennett, Lefty Frizzell, Frankie Laine, Johnnie Ray, Johnny Strindley, Kay Starr, Hank Thompson, Webb Pierce, and Jo Stafford.

Filmed in Texas. Academy Awards for Best Supporting Actor (Johnson) and Best Supporting Actress (Leachman), 1971; New York Film Critics Awards for Best Supporting Actor (Johnson), Best Supporting Actress (Burstyn), and Best Screenwriting (tied with *Sunday Bloody Sunday*), 1971.

Cast: Timothy Bottoms (*Sonny Crawford*); Jeff Bridges (*Duane Jackson*); Cybill Shepherd (*Jacy Farrow*); Ben Johnson (*Sam the Lion*); Cloris Leachman (*Ruth Popper*); Ellen Burstyn (*Lois Farrow*); Eileen Brennan (*Genevieve*); Clu Gulager (*Abilene*); Sam Bottoms (*Billy*); Sharon Taggart (*Charlene Dugs*); Randy Quaid (*Lester Marlow*); Joe Heathcock (*Sheriff*); Bill Thurman (*Coach Popper*); Barc Doyle (*Joe Bob Blanton*); Jessie Lee Fulton (*Miss Mosey*); Gary Brockette (*Bobby Sheen*); John Hillerman (*Teacher*); Helena Humann (*Jimmie Sue*); Loyd Catlett (*Leroy*); Robert Glenn (*Gene Farrow*); Janice O'Malley (*Mrs. Craig*); Floyd Mahaney (*Policeman*); Kimberly Hyde (*Annie Martin*); Noble Willingham (*Chester*); Pamela Kelier (*Jackie Lee French*); Gordon Hurst (*Monroe*); Mike Hosford (*Johnny*); Charlie Seybert (*Andy Fanner*); Grover Lewis (*Mr. Crawford*); Rebecca Ulrick (*Marlene*); Merrill Shephard (*Agnes*); Buddy Wood (*Bud*); Leon Brown (*Cowboy in the cafe*).

Publications:

Reviews—"*The Last Picture Show*" by J. Dawson in *Sight and Sound* (London), spring 1972; "*The Last Picture Show*" by M. Goodwin in *Take One* (Montreal), April 1972; "*The Last Picture Show*" by G. Haustrate in *Cinéma* (Paris), June 1972; "*La Dernière Séance*" by I. Jordan in *Positif* (Paris), June 1972; "*The Last Picture Show*" by T. Pulleine in *Film Quarterly* (Berkeley), spring 1972; "*L'Ultimo spettacolo*" by S. Piro in *Cinema Nuovo* (Turin), May/June 1973; books—*The Last Picture Show* by Larry McMurtry, New York 166; *Pieces of Time* by Peter Bogdanovich, New York 1974; *Bogdanovich* by V. Giacci, Florence 1975; articles—"*The Last Picture Show*" by G. Allombert in *Image et son* (Paris), May 1972; "*The Last Picture Show*: A Study in Black and White" in *American Cinematographer* (Los Angeles), January 1972; "Inter/View with Peter Bogdanovich" by G. O'Brien and R. Feiden in *Inter/View* (New York), March 1972; "The Corporate Style of BBS" by M.S. Cohen in *Take One* (Montreal), November 1973; "Den sista föreställningen" by L. Duprez in *Filmrutan* (Tyreso, Sweden), no.2, 1973; "Il Fiume rosso" by G. Turroni in *Filmcritica* (Rome), November/December 1972; "*The Last Picture Show* and One More Adaptation" by John Cerlich in *Literature/Film Quarterly* (Salisbury, Maryland), April 1973; "Peter Bogdanovich Remembered and Assessed" by C. Starr in *Filmmakers Newsletter* (Ward Hill, Mass.), September 1973; "Cybill and Peter", interview by Andy Warhol and others in *Interview* (New York), June 1974; "*Die letzte Vorstellung*" by I. Pietzsch in *Fern und Fernsehen* (Berlin), January 1977; "Dialogue on Film: Peter Bogdanovich" in *American Film* (Washington, D.C.), December/January 1978/79; "*The Last Picture Show*" by Tom O'Guinn in *Cinema Texas Program Notes* (Austin), 16 January 1979.

The Last Picture Show is director Peter Bogdanovich's painful and moving look at life in a small Texas town. Adapted by Bogdanovich and Larry McMurtry from McMurtry's novel, the film chronicles the coming of age of two young men in an era that saw the final fadeout of the American frontier.

Underlying the film's story is its haunting theme of lost hopes and half-forgotten dreams. Bogdanovich captures the mood of desolation and boredom that grips the town of Anarene, contrasting it with the frustrated energy of the local teenagers as they struggle toward a future which holds only the emptiness they see in the lives of the adults around them. The end of their youth will bring death of their belief in a brighter life ahead, just as the passage of time has brought about the disappearance of the Old West and left a bleak, dying town in its place. Sam the Lion, the theatre and poolhall owner who had been a cowboy in his youth, is the story's link to an earlier time. His wisdom and innate dignity provide a role model for the boys, and his death marks the close of a chapter in their lives as well as the severing of the town's past and present.

The Last Picture Show is also a film about the decline of the "Golden Age" of Hollywood moviemaking. Set in 1951, it presents a view of a culture on the verge of change when the arrival of television signalled the end of the studio system. The "last picture show" to play the local movie house before lack of business closes it down is Howard Hawks's *Red River*, one of the final epics of frontier life. Bogdanovich, a former film critic and the author of books on John Ford and Orson Welles, pays tribute in the film to the work of the legendary directors he admires. The style he adopts is reminiscent of the classic "invisible" approach to filmmaking favored by such directors as Ford and Hawks, his camera remains an unobstrusive observer of the story. Like Ford, he makes use of occasional sweeping long shots, although here the shots record only the deserted, dusty streets of the town, providing a sad coda to Ford's majestic Western landscapes.

In 1970, Bogdanovich's decision to shoot his film in black and white was a somewhat radical choice. By the end of the 1960s, black and white photography had all but vanished from the American cinema and a trend toward colorful, showy films was much in evidence. Yet the powerful dramatic possibilities of the format, as well as the contrasts and shadings it offers, are ideally suited to the film's subject matter, and Robert Surtee's cinematography suggests documentary-like realism.

This illusion is enhanced by the film's soundtrack of 1950s pop and country-western tunes and by the remarkable naturalism of its performers. From Cloris Leachman as the lonely, affection-starved coach's wife to Cybill Shepherd as the beautiful, self-centered Jacy, the film is an example of ensemble playing at its finest. Particularly memorable among a host of strong performances is veteran character actor Ben Johnson's portrayal of Sam the Lion. Johnson, who received an Academy Award for his work, embodies the independence and strength of character which are the hallmarks of the heritage the town has lost.

The Last Picture Show is a film rich in both style and substance. Bogdanovich recaptures the atmosphere of his 1950s setting with careful attention to detail, and creates a stunning portrait of a town slowly dying as America moves into a new age.

—Janet E. Lorenz

* * *

LAST TANGO IN PARIS. Le Dernier Tango a Paris. Ultimo Tango a Parigi. Production: P.E.A. (Rome) and Artistes Associés (Paris); 1972; Technicolor, 35mm; running time: 126 mins. Released 15 December 1972, Paris.

Produced by Alberto Grimaldi; screenplay by Bernardo Bertolucci and Franco Arcalli; directed by Bernardo Bertolucci; photography by Vittorio Storaro; edited by Franco Arcalli; sound by Antoine Bonfanti; production design by Ferdinando Scarfiotti; music by Gato Barbieri; costumes designed by Gitt Magrini.

Filmed 1971-72 in Paris. New York Film Critics Award, Best Actor (Brando), 1973.

Cast: Marlon Brando (*Paul*); Maria Schneider (*Jeanne*); Jean-Pierre Léaud (*Tom*); Massimo Girotti (*Marcel*); Maria Michi (*Rosa's mother*); Giovanna Galetti (*Prostitute*); Catherine Allegret (*Catherine*); Darling Legitimus (*Landlady*); Marie-Hélène Breillet (*Monique*); Catherine Breillet (*Mouchette*); Veronica Lazare (*Rosa*); Luce Marquand (*Olympia*); Gitt Magrini (*Jeanne's mother*); Rachel Kesterber (*Christine*); Armand Ablanalp (*Prostitute's client*); Mimi Pinson (*Jury president*); Ramon Mendizabal (*Orchestra leader*); Stephane Kosiak (*Small dancer*); Gérard Lepennec (*Large dancer*); Catherine Sola (*TV script girl*); Mauro Manchetti (*TV cameraman*); Dan Diament (*TV sound engineer*); Peter Schommer (*TV assistant cameraman*).

Publications:

Reviews—"*Le Dernier Tango a Paris*" by Jean de Baroncelli in *Le Monde* (Paris), 16 December 1972; "*Le Dernier Tango a Paris*" by Robert Benayoun in *Le Point* (Paris), 11 December 1972; "Tango" by Pauline Kael in the *New Yorker*, 28 October 1972; excerpts from French reviews in *Avant-Scène du cinéma* (Paris), February 1973; "The Unvistable Past" by Julian Jebb in *Sight and Sound* (London), spring 1973; "*Ultimo Tango a Parigi*" by M. Buffa in *Filmcritica* (Rome), April 1973; "*Dernier Tango à Paris*" by A. Cornand in *Image et son* (Paris), February 1973; "*Ultimo Tango a Parigi*" by G. Cremonini in *Cinema Nuovo* (Turin), January/February 1973; "*Letzter Tango in Paris*" by J. Ebert in *Filmkritik* (Munich), July 1973; "*Last Tango in Paris*" by Gordon Gow in *Films and Filming* (London), May 1973; "*Last Tango in Paris*" by S. Kovacs in *Take One* (Montreal), March 1973; "*The Last Tango in Paris*" by H. Robinson in *Films in Review* (New York), April 1973; books—v*Close Up—Last Tango in Paris* edited by Kent E. Carroll, New York 1973; *Women and Sexuality in the New Film* by Joan Mellen, New York 1973; *Bertolucci* by F. Casetti, Florence 1975; articles—by Steven Kovacs in *Take One* (Montreal), November/December 1971; "*Last Tango in Paris*" by Richard Roud in *Sight and Sound* (London), summer 1972; "Conversazione con Bertolucci" by G. Bachmann in *Filmcritica* (Rome), September 1972; "Mon film n'est pas pornographique" by Bernardo Bertolucci in *Avant-Scène du cinéma* (Paris), February 1973; "*Le Dernier Tango a Paris*: Credits" in *Avant-Scène du cinéma* (Paris), February 1973; "Every Sexual Relationship is Condemned: Interview" by Gideon Bachmann in *Film Quarterly* (Berkeley), spring 1973; "Sexual Politics and *Last Tango in Paris*" by Joan Mellen in *Film Quarterly* (Berkeley), spring 1973; cover story in *Time* (New York), 22 January 1973; "Bernardo Bertolucci: 'Au cinéma le temps se glisse entre les choses et les gens...'" by M. Amiel in *Cinéma* (Paris), January 1973; "En Passion" by S. Björkman in *Chaplin* (Stockholm), no.1 (120), 1973; "L'Expérience en intérieur" by P. Bonitzer in *Cahiers du cinéma* (Paris), July/August 1973; "Entretien avec Bernardo Bertolucci" by M. Ciment and G. Legrand in *Positif* (Paris),

March 1973; "Bertolucci and the Dance of Danger" by M. Kinder and B. Houston in *Sight and Sound* (London), autumn 1973; "The Last Time I Saw Hollywood" by G. Legrand in *Positif* (Paris), March 1973; "Entretien avec Bernardo Bertolucci" by M. Martin in *Ecran* (Paris), February 1973; "Censorship and the Press" by G. Phelps in *Sight and Sound* (London), summer 1973; "*Dernier Tango à Paris*" by S. Schober in *Filmkritik* (Munich), April 1973; "Tango tra un'incognita e un passato irrecuperabile" by R. Speziale-Bagliacca in *Cinema Nuovo* (Turin), May/June 1973; "*Ultimo Tango a Parigi*" by G. Turroni in *Filmcritica* (Rome), January/February 1973; "A Woman of Paris in 1973" by H.G. Weinberg in *Take One* (Montreal), May 1973; "Bernardo Bertolucci Seminar" in *Dialogue on Film* (Beverly Hills), April 1974; "The Importance and Ultimate Failure of *Last Tango in Paris*" by E. A. Kaplan in *Jump Cut* (Chicago), November/December 1974; "Bertolucci's *Last Tango in Paris*" by J.C. Rice in *Journal of Popular Film* (Bowling Green, Ohio), spring 1974; "Theme and Structure: *Last Tango Untangled*" by D. Sadkin in *Literature/Film Quarterly* (Salisbury, Maryland), spring 1974; "Ik houd niet echt van acteren" by G. Bachmann in *Skoop* (Netherlands), March 1976; "*Last Tango* Short Term Mex Scandal" in *Variety* (New York), 6 October 1976; "The Father Figure in *The Conformist* and in *Last Tango in Paris*" by D. Lopez in *Film Heritage* (Dayton, Ohio), summer 1976.

*   *   *

Last Tango in Paris is a landmark motion picture, an essay on primitive sexuality that surprised and fascinated audiences in 1973. It may not be the initial film of its era to include frequent nudity or a sexual theme, and it is never blatantly pornographic; but, in many ways, it is the original sex movie. Director Bernardo Bertolucci, who co-authored the screenplay, made a film about sex without romance—or, sex as it often is in the actual world.

Marlon Brando stars as Paul, a 45-year-old American living in Paris, whose wife has just committed suicide. He meets Jeanne (Maria Schneider), a young Frenchwoman 25 years his junior, while hunting for an apartment. Paul and Jeanne do not exchange names or engage in small talk, but make love in the large, empty flat. They approach each other like animals, as if their sexual desires have been long repressed and only now are allowed to surface. Throughout the film, their sexual encounters are presented as raw, unadulterated lust, with a complete lack of romance. Paul and Jeanne do not communicate in a traditional cinematic manner. There is no repartee between them, with their personalities revealed via the dialogue. Jeanne exists in Paul's life for one reason: orgasm, total sexual subservience. She may be engaged to a man (Jean-Pierre Leaud) closer to her in age, but she becomes a willing prisoner of Paul's lust. However, to her, the older man is only a sexual interlude. After burying his wife, Paul wants to continue on with his life—and with Jeanne, but on a more emotional and loving level. Outside the apartment, Paul is to Jeanne just another middle-aged has-been.

The vulnerability of Paul, the hurt and pain of an aging, anguished, isolated man, becomes known to the viewer not through his dialogue with Jeanne, but in his lengthy monologues, revealing as much about the actor as the character. The film's most shattering sequence is the scene where Paul raves at his dead wife as she rests in a bed of flowers. He is a far more interesting character than Jeanne, perhaps because Maria Schneider is not a very good actress. Jeanne is ultimately little more than a presence an object whose availability is the impetus that sets Paul in motion. As a result, *Last Tango in Paris* is far more revealing with regard to male sexuality. (Ironically, despite the film's unabashed eroticism, Brando never appears nude while Schneider's breasts and buttocks are everpresent.) In his monologues, Brando plays Paul as a tragic hero, yet in his sexual confrontations he is a brute—selfish and unloving in his demands of Jeanne. It is unfortunate that she is not allowed to make any intellectual demands on him.

Marlon Brando's performance in *Last Tango in Paris* ranks with his work in *On the Waterfront* as the greatest of his career and one of the most impressive performances on celluoid. His career had been in commercial and critical decline prior to his Academy Award-winning performance in *The Godfather*. His follow-up was *Last Tango in Paris*, earning him another Oscar nomination. It is to Bertolucci's credit that he allows his actors to improvise, so that their characters might grow out of their own feelings and experiences; it is to Brando's credit that he does not allow his reputation to prevent him from creating a character so gritty and real. As Pauline Kael wrote, in her legendary essay on *Last Tango in Paris*, Brando "brings the character a unity of soul. Paul feels so "real" and the character is brought so close that a new dimension in screen acting has been achieved."

Since *Last Tango in Paris*, graphic—but not pornographic—sex has been depicted in other features. In Bob Rafelson's remake of James M. Cain's *The Postman Always Rings Twice*, Jack Nicholson and Jessica Lange appear in particularly revealing sexual scenes. While there is the barest minimum of nudity, the actors exploit the sexual tension and the resulting lovemaking is about as explicit as can be found in a film with Oscar-winning stars. This version of *Postman* could never have been made prior to *Last Tango in Paris*. Kael writes, "This *Last Tango* must be the most powerfully erotic movie ever made, and it may turn out to be the most liberating movie ever made...Bertolucci and Brando have altered the face of an art form."

—Rob Edelman

THE LAST WAVE. Production: Ayer Productions Pty. Ltd., McElroy production, South Australian Film Corp., and the Australian Film Commission. Atlab color, 35mm; running time: 106 mins.; length: 9513 feet. Released 16 November 1977.

Produced by Hal and James McElroy; screenplay by Tony Morphett, Petru Popescu, and Peter Weir; from an idea by Peter Weir; directed by Peter Weir; photography by Russell Boyd, additional photography by Ron Taylor, George Greenough and Klaus Jaritz; edited by Max Lemon; sound edited by Greg Bell, sound recorded by Don Connolly, sound re-recorded by Phil Judd; production design by Goran Warff; art direction by Neil Angwin; set decoration by Bill Malcolm; music by Charles Wain; special effects by Monty Fieguth and Bob Hilditch; costumes designed by Annie Bleakley; color consultant: James Parsons; adviser on tribal Aboriginal matters: Lance Bennett.

Filmed in Australia.

Cast: Richard Chamberlain (*David Burton*); Olivia Hammett (*Annie Burton*); Gulpilil (*Chris Lee*); Frederick Parslow (*Rev. Burton*); Nandjiwarra Amagula (*Charlie*); Vivean Gray (*Dr. Whitburn*); Walter Amagula (*Gerry Lee*); Roy Bara (*Larry*); Cedric Lalara (*Lindsey*); Morris Lalara (*Jacko*); Peter Carroll (*Michael Zeadler*); Athol Compton (*Billy Corman*); Hedley Cullen (*Judge*); Michael Duffield (*Andrew Potter*); Wallas Eaton (*Morgue doctor*); Jo England (*Babysitter*); John Frawley (*Policeman*); Jennifer de Greenlaw (*Zeadler's secretary*); Richard Henderson (*Prosecutor*); Penny Leach (*Schoolteacher*); Merv Lilley (*Publican*); John Meagher (*Morgue clerk*); Guido Rametta (*Guido*); Malcolm Robertson (*Don Fishburn*); Greg Rowe (*Carl*); Katrina Sedgwick (*Sophie Burton*); Ingrid Weir (*Grace Burton*).

Publications:

Reviews—"*The Last Wave*" by G. Moskowitz in *Variety* (New York), 16 November 1977; "*The Last Wave*" by H. Béhar in *Image et son* (Paris), February 1978; "*The Last Wave*" by J. Clancy in *Cinema Papers* (Melbourne, Australia), January 1978; "*The Last Wave*" by R. Combs in *Sight and Sound* (London), spring 1978; "*The Last Wave*" by A. Garsault in *Positif* (Paris), March 1978; "*The Last Wave*" by Gordon Gow in *Films and Filming* (London), April 1978; "*The Last Wave*" by T. Pulleine in *Monthly Film Bulletin* (London), April 1978; "*The Last Wave*" by D. Bartholomew in *Film Bulletin* (Philadelphia), March 1979; "Film View: Chilling Truths About Scaring" by Vincent Canby in *The New York Times*, 21 January 1979; "*The Last Wave*" by J.R. Fox in *Cinefantastique* (Oak Park, Illinois), no.2/3, 1979; "*The Last Wave*" by M. Holthof in *Film en televisie* (Brussels), March 1979; "The Current Cinema: Doused" by Pauline Kael in the *New Yorker*, 22 January 1979; "*The Last Wave*" by S. de Romreee in *Amis du Film et de la Television* (Brussels), March 1979; articles—about the producers and the special effects by S. Murray in *Cinema Papers* (Melbourne), October 1977; article in *Cinema Papers* (Melbourne), April 1977; "Rencontre avec Peter Weir autour de *La Dernière Vague*" by H. Béhar in *Image et son* (Paris), February 1978; "Photographing *The Last Wave*" by R. Boyd in *American Cinematographer* (Los Angeles), April 1978; "*The Last Wave*" in *Films and Filming* (London), February 1978; "Naissance d'un cinéma australien" by A. Tournès in *Jeune Cinéma* (Paris), March 1978; "At the Movies: Giannini Talks of Guru, Visconti, and Italian Madness" by T. Buckley in *The New York Times*, 12 January 1979; "New Wave Director Peter Weir Rides *The Last Wave* into U.S. Market" by P. Childs in *Millimeter* (New York), March 1979; "Director Peter Weir's *Last Wave* Makes Impressive Showings W'Wide" by J. Cocchi in *Boxoffice* (Kansas City, Missouri), 29 January 1979; "His Subject—Mysteries of Different Cultures" by D. Jacobs in *The New York Times*, 14 January 1979; "Films, TV: Horror" by R.A. Blake in *America* (New York), 27 January 1979; "It Doesn't Take Any Imagination at All to Feel Awed: Peter Weir" by J.M. Kass in *Movietone News* (Seattle), December 1979.

*   *   *

"Hasn't the weather been strange?" muses the advertizing slogan for Peter Weir's *The Last Wave*. "Could it be a warning?" This tone of covert menace, of nasty things unseen by naive protagonists, characterizes Weir's films, but none more than this atmospheric thriller. Troubled by dreams of his home city, Sydney, inundated by a vast flood, lawyer Richard Chamberlain is drawn into the underground world of Sydney's aboriginals who still live a tribal life in the slums. To them, the city is merely a transient facade obscuring ancient mysteries, the ritual objects of which remain buried in forgotten catacombs. Chamberlain's discovery of these tunnels and the resulting revelation give the film its final enigmatic scenes.

Weir conceived the film after discovering (by precognition, he feels) a piece of statuary on a Tunisian beach. Early drafts of the script represented, in a Von Daniken-like manner, ancient races dragging rafts across the Australian desert. In collaboration with various writers, Weir shaped a story of city aboriginals protecting ritual stones brought to Australia by a long dead race. As Australia is gripped by fierce storms and an unrelenting downpour, Chamberlain finds his way to the caves where ancient wall paintings foretell the world's destruction by water. He emerges on a beach to face the ultimate reality of the prophecy.

Australian backers derided the film, and a shortage of money forced many compromises—notably in the last sequence, where Weir used a clip from the surfing film *Crystal Voyager* to stand in for the tidal wave. The Aztec ruins lost something in their rough and ready construction. The use of aboriginal myths led to picketing by militant black groups who charged Weir with debasing their mythology. However, Weir acknowledged that his contact with aboriginal performers led to a widening and deepening of the script. Gulpilil's appearance in a dream, the rain streaming down, with a scored sacred stone in his out-thrust hand, is particularly striking.

Weir calls *The Last Wave* his "roughest, most awkward" film. But despite a certain tentativeness in the use of large resources, it is significant as the first new Australian film to reveal an interest in wider issues and a less chauvinistic sensibility.

—John Baxter

LAURA. Production: Twentieth Century-Fox; 1944; black and white, 35mm; running time: 88 mins. Released 1944.

Produced by Otto Preminger; screenplay by Jay Datler, Samuel Hoffenstein, and Betty Reinhardt; uncredited collaboration on screenplay by Ring Lardner, Jr. and Jerome Cady; from the play and novel by Vera Caspary; directed by Otto Preminger; photography by Joseph LaShelle; edited by Louis R. Loeffler; sound by E. Clayton Ward and Harry M. Leonard; production design by Thomas Little and Paul S. Fox; art direction by Lyle Wheeler and Leland Fuller; music by David Raksin, music directed by Emil Newman; special effects photography by Fred Sersen; costumes designed by Bonnie Cashin.

Filmed 24 April-29 June 1944, (retakes 15-20 July 1944), in Fox studios. Academy Award, Best Cinematography, 1944.

Cast: Gene Tierney (*Laura Hunt*); Dana Andrews (*Mark McPherson*); Clifton Webb (*Waldo Lydecker*); Vincent Price (*Shelby Carpenter*); Judith Anderson (*Anne Treadwell*); Dorothy Adams (*Bessie Clary*); James Flavin (*McAvity*); Clyde Fillmore (*Bullitt*); Tom Dillon replaced Ralph Dunn as (*Fred Callahan*); Kathleen Howard (*Louise*); Lee Tung Foo (*Waldo's Servant*); Harold Schlickenmayer, Harry Strang, and Lane Chandler (*Policemen*); Non-Credited Roles: Frank La Rue (*Hairdresser*); Dorothy Christy, Aileen Pringle, Terry Adams, Jean Fenwick, Kay Linaker, and Yolanda Lacca (*Women*); Cara Williams, Gloria Marlin, Beatrice Gray, Kay Connors, and Frances Gladwin (*Young girls*); Buster Miles (*Johnny*); Jane Nigh (*Secretary*); William Forrest, Alexander Sacha, Forbes Murray, Cyril Ring, and Nestor Eristoff (*Men*); John Dexter (*Jacoby*); Bess Flowers (*Girl in the hall of the theater*); Major Sam Harris (*Anne Treadwell's escort*).

Publications:

Scripts—"*Laura*" by Jay Dratler, Samuel Hoffenstein, and Betty Reinhardt in *Avant-Scène du cinéma* (Paris), July/September 1978; reviews—"La Presse" in *Avant-Scène du cinéma* (Paris), July/September 1978; books—*Otto Preminger* by Jacques Lourcelles, Paris 1965; *The Cinema of Otto Preminger* by Gerald Pratley, New York 1971; *The Fox Girls* by James Robert Parish, New Rochelle, New York 1971; *Behind the Scenes of Otto Preminger* by Willi Frischauer, London 1973; *Preminger: An Autobiography*, Garden City, New York 1977; articles—*Panorama du Film Noir* by Raymond Borde and Etienne Chaumeton, Paris 1955; article in 2 parts on Preminger's career by John Howard Reid in *Films and Filming* (London), February 1961 and March 1961; special issue on Preminger in *Présence du cinéma* (Paris), February 1962; special issue on Preminger in *Movie* (London), September 1962; special issue on Preminger in *Movie* (London), no.4, 1963; special issue on Preminger in *Visages du cinéma* (Paris), March 1963; "*Laura* ou l'épanchement de la mort dans la vie" by Henri Agel in *Romance Amérique*, Paris 1963; "Preminger's 2 Periods—Studio and Solo" by Andrew Sarris in *Film Comment* (New York), summer 1965; "Clifton Webb" in *Films in Review* (New York), January 1970; "Gene Tierney" by Jonathan Shields in *Films in Review* (New York), November 1971; "My *Laura* and Otto's" by Vera Caspary in *Saturday Review* (New York), 26 June 1971; "*Laura*: The Story Behind the Picture" by B. Borok in *Thousand Eyes* (New York), November 1976; "*Laura*: scénario d'un scénario" by Jacques Lourcelles in *Avant-Scène du cinéma* (Paris), July/September 1978; "Closure Within a Dream: Point of View in *Laura*" by K. Thompson in *Film Reader* (Evanston, Illinois), no.3, 1978; "Faithful in his Fashion: Otto Preminger's *Laura*" by D. McVay in *Bright Lights* (Los Angeles), no. 4, 1979; "*Laura*" by Elizabeth Leese in *Magill's Survey of Cinema, Vol. II* edited by Frank N. Magill, Englewood Cliffs, New Jersey 1980.

*   *   *

Given its inauspicious beginnings, there was little reason to predict that *Laura* would become a critical and commercial success and capture the Academy Award for Best Cinematography. In the beginning, there were problems with the script. Vera Caspary was displeased with the adaptation because all it retained from her novel was the gimmick of the supposed victim later becoming the chief suspect. Studio officials at Twentieth-Century Fox shared her low opinion, and *Laura's* B-movie status seemed assured. Darryl Zanuck, however, liked the script, and despite a feud between him and producer Otto Preminger, promoted the film to an A-production. Nevertheless, he disagreed with Preminger over casting, direction, and the ending.

Preminger wanted Clifton Webb for the role of the murderer, but Zanuck wanted Laird Cregar. Zanuck finally agreed to see a screen test of Webb, but Webb refused to make one, declaring that Zanuck could come watch him in the play *Blithe Spirit*, which, of course, Zanuck refused to do. Preminger, unbekownst to Zanuck, filmed Webb's monologue in the play, which convinced Zanuck to cast him.

Zanuck still refused to let Preminger direct, and hired Rouben Mamoulian, the only legitimate director apparently willing to take the project. After viewing two abysmal examples of Mamoulian's progress on the film, Zanuck fired him and hired Preminger, who proceeded to scrap Mamoulian's sets and costumes. Mamoulian retaliated by telling the cast that Preminger thought they were all poor actors.

Once the resultant ill will from the actors was settled, the sets and costumes redesigned, and the film reshot, Zanuck decided to have *Laura's* ending reshot from Laura's point of view. No one—actors or director—agreed, but they complied with Zanuck. Luckily, Walter Winchell saw the unreleased film with Zanuck and told him it was great except for the ending, at which point Zanuck allowed the original ending to stand.

What could have been a film ruined by studio manipulation emerges as an innovation in the genre of the American detective thriller. For example, there is Caspary's victim-to-suspect transition, improved upon in the film by having the murderer narrate the first part through flashbacks. Having the heroine absent for a significant portion of the film poses a problem that Preminger solves both visually and aurally. A large portrait of Laura over her fireplace dominates several scenes, and a piece of music she had liked—the "Laura theme"—is played repeatedly: in the film's beginning, on Laura's record player, at a restaurant, etc. The haunting and classical quality of both the portrait and the theme not only explains the detective's increasing obsession with Laura, whose death he is investigating but also keeps her foregrounded for the audience as well.

The other major innovation is the setting of the murder in the cool, sophisticated world of New York *haute société*, with its chic Park Avenue apartments and elegant restaurants. A world in which the *bon mot*, wit and charm under pressure, and self control are the most important means for survival.

Indeed, more than anything else, *Laura* is about control and repressing dangerous feelings. Laura, a cool and self-possessed career woman has been brutally murdered in her apartment, her face blown away by a shotgun; the self-controlled young woman has apparently been eliminated by someone who has irrevocably and inexplicably lost control. As the film unfolds we learn that the real victim was a model in love with Laura's fiance; a woman more victimized by her emotions than Laura and thus Laura's social inferior and less worthy of survival.

This emphasis on control appears in several ways. Whenever he fears he is no longer in command of himself, particularly in his encounters with the waspish columnist Waldo Lydecker, homicide detective Mark McPherson pulls out a pocket baseball game whose object is to place, simultaneously, metal balls in half a dozen small holes. When Lydecker asks him if he obtained the game "in a raid on a kindergarten," McPherson stalwartly replies, "It takes a lot of control."

Lydecker himself is a master controller, making or destroying people and careers in his columns and broadcasts. A verbal swordsman, he appoints himself as Laura's guide and counselor. When she begins seeing other men, Lydecker ridicules and excoriates her first suitor in his column, Thereafter, according to Lydecker, "Laura's own discrimination ruled out other men." However, with the arrival of Shelby Carpenter, Laura's fiancé, Lydecker fears he has lost his hold and influence on Laura. He therefore shoots her, or so he believes, and settles down to write her story, the ultimate way to direct her destiny. The detective, Mark McPherson, is the final threat to Lydecker's authority.

Other characters exhibit the same sort of restraint. Anne Treadwell, Laura's aunt, is in love with Laura's fiancé, yet nothing other than a smooth politeness ever passes between the two women. She calmly admits to Laura (at a sophisticated soirée given by the murderer to celebrate his victim's resurrection) that she and Shelby understand one another because of their shared deficiencies: "Shelby's no good for you. He's better for me. I can afford him. We're both weak." As for the murder of the other rival, Treadwell answers Laura's unspoken query: "No, my dear, I didn't, but I thought of it."

Shelby himself is an enigma—all things to all women. He dallies with Laura, Anne Treadwell, and Diane Redfern, and we are never the wiser as to where his true affections, if any, lie. Since actually falling in love with a woman might endanger his economic survival, we are left to conclude that his form of control is to avoid such emotions.

The cool detachment and moral ambiguity of *Laura's* surface glitter, we care little for the characters themselves. The one exception is Bessie, Laura's maid, who supplies the film's only two genuinely affecting moments—she cries when she sees Laura returned from the dead, and again when Laura is arrested. Unlike the others, Bessie has no desire to dissimulate, ("I'm a domestic and I'm not ashamed of it"), or to control her emotions; it is she, not the central characters, who engages our sympathy.

—Catherine Henry

LETYAT ZHURAVLI. The Cranes Are Flying. Production: Mosfilm; black and white, 35mm; running time: 94 mins., some sources list 97 mins.; length: about 8697 feet. Released October 1957.

Screenplay by Victor Rozov; from the work *Eternally Alive* by Victor Rozov; directed by Mikhail Kalatozov; photography by Sergei Urusevsky; edited by M. Timofeyeva; production design by E. Svidetelev; music by Moisei Vaynberg.

Cannes Film Festival, Palme d'Or, 1958.

Cast: Tatyana Samoĭlova (*Veronika*); Alexeĭ Batalov (*Boris Borozdine*); Vassili Merkuriev (*Dr. Fedore Ivanovitch Borodzine*); A. Shvorin (*Mark*); S. Kharitonova (*Irina*); K. Nikitine (*Volodia*); Valentin Zubkov (*Stépan*); Anna Bogdanova (*Grand mother*); K. Nikitin (*Volodya*); B. Kokobkin (*Tyernov*); E. Kupriyanova (*Anna Mikhailovna*).

Publications:

Reviews—"Un Authentique Chef-d'Oeuvre" by Martine Monod in *Les Lettres françaises* (Paris), 19 June 1958; "*The Cranes Are Flying*" by Peter John Dyer in *Films and Filming* (London), November 1958—books—*Vingt ans de cinéma soviétique* by Luda and Jean Schnitzer, Paris 1964; *The Film Till Now* by Paul Rotha and Richard Griffith, New York 1967; *The Most Important Art: East European Film After 1945* by Mira Liehm and Antonín Liehm, Berkeley 1977; *Cinema, The Magic Vehicle: A Guide to Its Achievement: Journey Two* edited by Jacek Klinowski and Adam Garbicz, Metuchen, New Jersey 1979; articles—by Pierre Billard in *Cinéma 58* (Paris), June 1958; "Un An de cinéma" by J. Louis Cros in *Image et son* (Paris), November 1958; "Par la grâce du formalisme" by Jacques Doniol-Valcroze in *Cahiers du cinéma* (Paris), July 1958; article by André Martin in *Cahiers du cinéma* (Paris), June 1958; "Qui est Kalatozov" by Jay Leyda in *Cinéma 58* (Paris), July/August 1958; article in *Image et son* (Paris), December 1959; "*The Cranes Are Flying*" by Michael Lifton in *Film Quarterly* (Berkeley), spring 1960; "*Ivan the Magnificent*" by Nina Hibbin in *Films and Filming* (London), February 1963; article by L. Anninsky in *Film a Doba* (Prague), 1971; "Kann, 1958 god..." by S. Yutkevich in *Iskusstvo Kino* (Moscow), March 1980.

*   *   *

The Cranes are Flying is one of the major post-Stalinist soviet features. A work of grace and intelligence, the story is refreshingly free of propaganda. It is romantic, lyrical, a tale of war and lost love, of individuals who suffer because of the follies of their leaders.

The heroine is a young Russian girl, Veronica, whose sweetheart, Boris, volunteers to fight for his country at the outbreak of World War II. She marries her fiance's cousin, a draft dodger she does not love but who seduced her during a bombing raid. Veronica is evacuated to Siberia, and eventually learns of Boris's death. As her beloved's life has so tragically ended, Veronica cannot comprehend that she has essentially been abandoned, to live out her days in isolation. She waits for Boris to return to her; though, at the end, she realizes that she must continue with her life—if not for herself, than for others. She must accept the reality of Boris's death in order to find peace.

The Cranes are Flying, an international hit, is universal in its anti-war sentiment. Veronica's tragedy is the symbolic outgrowth of the collective tragedy any nation must endure during wartime. Sons and brothers, husbands and lovers, all die. Their existence remains alive in the minds of the women who bury them and plant flowers on their graves.

This scenario is not original, but similar to a number of Hollywood weepers produced 15 years earlier. The film is flawed, in that Veronica's marriage to the cousin is not credible: she is, after all, still yearning for Boris. The characterizations of various hoodlums and profiteers are caricatured, too broad to be believable. Yet *The Cranes are Flying* is still unique for its time in its concern for individual rights and feelings rather than public pronouncements. Whether communist or capitalist, liberal or conservative, Veronica's plight is meaningful and touching. Her role in life is not just to toil in the fields and produce children. She is allowed to love, to feel passion, to seek joy. There is also an acknowledgment that not all Russians are brave and heroic, that draft dodgers do exist in the Soviet Union. No system is without defects; no nation is ever without its share of shirkers and criminals.

Sergei Urusevski's cinematography is superior. His camera is forever restless, moving along with and examining the actions of the characters while establishing an intimacy with the viewer. At the film's center is Samoilova's exciting performance; she makes Veronica a truly tragic heroine.

The Cranes are Flying was the first film released in the United States as part of a cultural exchange program with Russia; *Marty* and other Hollywood productions were exhibited in Moscow. In its own modest way, it was a breakthrough for the Soviet cinema.

—Rob Edelman

DER LETZTE MANN. The Last Laugh. Production: Universum-Film-Aktiengesellschaft (Ufa); black and white, 35mm, silent; running time: about 73 mins.; length: 2036 meters, 8 reels. Released 23 December 1924, Berlin.

Screenplay by Carl Mayer, under the supervision of Erich Pommer; directed by Friedrich Wilhelm Murnau (F.W. Murnau); photography by Karl Freund; production design by Robert Herlth and Walter Röhrig; accompanying musical score by Giuseppe Becce.

Filmed 1924 in UFA studios.

Cast: Emil Jannings (*Doorman*); Maly Delschaft (*His daughter*); Max Hiller (*Her fiancé*); Emilie Kurtz (*His aunt*); Hans Unterkircher (*Manager*); Olaf Storm (*Young hotel resident*); Hermann Valentin (*Hotel resident*); Emmy Wyda (*Thin neighbor*); Georg John (*Night watchman*).

Publications:

Books—*From Caligari to Hitler, A Psychological History of the German Film* by Siegfried Kracauer, New York 1947; *An Index to the Films of F.W. Murnau* by Theodore Huff, supplement to *Sight and Sound*, index series, London 1948; *Le Cinéma réaliste allemand* by Raymond Borde, Freddy Bauche, François Courtade, and Marcel Tariol, Paris 1959; *Murnau* by Charles Jameux, Paris 1965; *Anthologie du cinéma*, Vol. VII, 1965; *The Haunted Screen* by Lotte Eisner, Berkeley 1969; *Carl Mayer e l'espressionismo*, edition by *Bianco e Nero*, Rome 1969; *The German Cinema* by Roger Manvell and Heinrich Fraenkel, New York 1971; *50 Years of German Film* by H.H. Wollenberg, revised edition, New York 1972; *Murnau* by Lotte Eisner, translated ed., Berkeley 1973; *Cinema and Society: France and Germany during the Twenties* by Paul Monaco, New York 1976; articles—"F.W. Murnau—The German Genius of the Films" by Matthew Josephson in *Motion Picture Classic* (New York), October 1926; "The Last Laugh is on Hollywood" by Tamar Lane in *Motion Picture Magazine* (New York), November 1926; "Murnau—ses films" by Roger Blin in *La Revue du cinéma* (Paris), July 1931; "F.W. Murnau" by Kenneth White in *Hound and Horn* (New York), July/September 1931; "Carl Mayer" by Wolfgang Wilhelm in *Sight and Sound* (London), July 1944; "Un Hommage au scénariste de Caligari, Carl Mayer" by Jacques-B. Brunius in *La Revue du cinéma* (Paris), spring 1947; "Notes on the World and Work of Carl Mayer" by Herbert Luft in *Quarterly of Film, Radio, and Television* (Berkeley), summer 1954; "Quarante ans après" by Pierre Billard in *Cinéma 65* (Paris), November 1965; "Fire and Ice" by F.W. Murnau in *Cahiers du Cinema in English* (New York), January 1966; "*Le Dernier des hommes*" in *Image et son* (Paris), no.214, 1968; "Emil Jannings—A Personal View" by Harold Truscott in *Silent Picture* (London), autumn 1970; "F.W. Murnau: An Introduction" by Gilberto Perez Guillermo in *Film Comment* (New York), summer 1971; "Friedrich Murnau albo semantyka filmowych środków wyrazu" by A. Helman in *Kino* (Warsaw), April 1973; issue on *Der letzte Mann* in *Filmcritica* (Rome), July 1974; "*Der letzte Mann*" by T. Rayns in *Monthly Film Bulletin* (London), March 1974; "F.M. Murnau: Zadnji mož" by V. Koch in *Ekran* (Ljubljana, Yugoslavia), no.3-4, 1977; issue on Murnau in *Avant-Scène du cinéma* (Paris), July/September 1977; "*The Last Laugh*" by Cicely Wynne in *Cinema Texas Program Notes* (Austin), 3 October 1978.

*   *   *

Had scenarist Carl Mayer not quarrelled with director Lulu Pick, his collaborator on two previous films, *Scherben* and *Sylvester*, *Der letzte Mann* would undoubtedly have been more like its *kammerspiel* (literally "chamber play") predecessors. In these two films Mayer and Pick had abandoned the Expressionist concern for subjective vision and instead dealt with the intimate details of petit bourgeois existence. Mayer and Pick together create a *Stimmung* or "mood" of inevitable domestic tragedy brought on by the workings of instinct, a force so natural and all-conquering that it cannot even he expressed in language (hence, in part, the films' lack of intertitles). This treatment of the workings of obsession, of course, suggests a *rapprochement* between the psychologism of *Caligari* and the Zolaesque determinism suitable for presenting a social critique. In fact, it is often noted that the *Kammerspielfilme* as a group can be viewed as continuing the Expressionist examination of disturbed minds and emotions within settings and with characters that are essentially realistic. In the case of Pick's two efforts with Mayer, this realism even takes on socio-political overtones, developed by the contrast between the miseries of lower-middle class existence and the easy, but unattainable life of the rich.

Even with F.W. Murnau as director, *Der letzte Mann* has much in common with Mayer's two previous films, which together form a triptych. Once again, the narrative deals with the hardships suffered by the petit bourgeois. The central character is a hotel doorman, who, as such, must serve the rich, but is still admired by his fellow tenement dwellers because of the status implied by his ornate uniform. Removed from his post because of old age, the doorman cannot adjust to his new position as lavatory attendant. His desperate struggle to retain his former standing in the neighborhood eventually fails, and he becomes an object of ridicule and shame. The doorman's decline takes on a larger socio-political significance as he seems the only mediator between life in the slums and in the luxury hotel. The film's ending, however, undercuts this sharp critique of lower middle-class disenchantment, symbolized, in a specifically German fashion, by the loss of the uniform. When the doorman is reduced to utter abjectness, the film's only intertitle declares that although in the real world he would have no chance, the filmmakers will have mercy on him. What follows defies the film's carefully developed *vraisemblance*. The doorman becomes the beneficiary of an eccentric American millionaire who, having willed his fortune to the "last man" to serve him, had died in the hotel lavatory. The film ends with the doorman and his partner, the nightwatchman, enjoying a suitably vulgar and ostentatious dinner in the hotel dining room and leaving for parts unknown in a huge limousine. The carnival celebration of *Der letzte Mann*'s conclusion finds no equivalent in the unrelieved grimness of the earlier *Kammerspielfilme*.

The differences between *Der letzte Mann* and its predecessors, however, are not simply those of narrative construction. *Scherben* and *Sylvester* attained only limited critical and commercial success. *Der letzte Mann* was hailed as a masterpiece both in Germany and abroad. It became one of the most important films to emerge from Weimar Germany and was influential upon the Hollywood establishment, where it aroused an enthusiasm for German filmmaking that was to last for many years. Much of the acclaim centered around the cinematic techniques devised by Mayer, Murnau, and cameraman Karl Freund to present the narrative.

Murnau often receives full credit for inventing the "unchained camera" that explores both the inner and outer worlds of *Der letzte Mann*, but the innovations resulted from collaborative effort. Murnau, more than Pick, was able to realize Mayer's ideas about dynamic and flexible point of view; his previous work particularly in *Nosferatu*, reveals an expert handling of camera placement and angles. Griffith may have invented both tracking movements and point-of-view editing, but these elements of film grammar are refined and extended in *Der letzte Mann*. In the famous drunk scene, the camera records the doorman's distorted perceptions, an effect Freund achieved by strapping the camera to his chest and staggering about the set. In the dream sequence that follows, Murnau suggests an even more subjective experience, the distortions imposed by the unconscious upon conscious concerns; here the Expressionist influence is strongest and is achieved largely through special effects, not, as in *Caligari*, through set design.

This linkage between the camera and the doorman's perceptions or feelings in not sustained. Several sequences suggest the camera's independence from both narrative and character. In the opening sequence, a long travelling shot, entirely unmotivated, takes the spectator down the hotel elevator, through the lobby, and out the revolving door that serves as a symbol of fate. Freund achieved this effect by mounting the camera on a bicycle. Later, at a crucial moment in the story, the camera positions itself outside a glass wall and, by means of a discreet dissolve, gradually moves into the room to record the interview between the doorman and manager. When the doorman is later accused of slackness by an irate customer, the camera refuses to follow the manager down to the lavatory. In these sequences and others, the camera calls attention to itself rather than presenting the narrative through the doorman's experience. This reflexivity finds its culmination in the artificiality of the film's conclusion.

Der letzte Mann is noteworthy not simply because it inaugurated the use of subjective camera, but because it revealed the potentially complex relationship between camera and narrative. If it's elaborate and virtuoso production exceeds the intimate atmosphere of *Kammerspielfilme*, lending the doorman's simple story a grandiosity it can hardly sustain, it is because Murnau, Mayer, and Freund discovered storytelling techniques that could barely be contained by the limitations of that genre.

—R. Barton Palmer

LIMELIGHT. Production: United Artists; 1952; black and white, 35mm; running time: 138 mins. Released fall 1952, London.

Produced, scripted, directed, and music written by Charles Chaplin; photography by Karl Struss; edited by Joe Inge; art direction by Eugene Lourié; photographic consultant: Roland Totheroh; choreography of ballet sequences by Charles Chaplin.

Academy Award, Best Original Motion Picture Score, 1972.

Cast: Charles Chaplin (*Calvero*); Claire Bloom (*Terry*); Sydney Chaplin (*Neville*); Buster Keaton (*Piano accompanist*); Andre Eglevsky (*Harlequin*); Melissa Hayden (*Columbine*); Charles Chaplin, Jr. (*Clown in ballet*); Wheeler Dryden (*Doctor*); Geraldine Chaplin, Michael Chaplin, and Josephine Chaplin (*Street urchins*).

Publications:

Reviews—by Theodore Huff in *Films in Review* (New York), November 1952; books—*Chaplin, the Immortal Tramp* by Rubeigh Minney, London 1954; *Charlot et la "fabulation" chaplinesque* by Jean Mitry, Paris 1957; *Charles Chaplin* by Barthelemy Amengual, Paris 1963; *My Autobiography*, London 1964; *The Films of Charlie Chaplin* by Gerald McDonald and others, Secaucus, New Jersey 1965; *Charlie Chaplin* by Marcel Martin, Paris 1966; *Charles Chaplin* by Pierre Leprohon, Paris 1970; *Chaplin's Films* by Uno Asplund, Newton Abbot, Devon 1971; *Tout Chaplin: Tous les films, par le texte, par le gag et par l'image* by Jean Mitry, Paris 1972; *Chaplin* by Roger Manvell,

Boston 1974; *My Life in Pictures*, London 1974; *Charlie Chaplin* by Robert Moss, New York 1975; *The Silent Clowns* by Walter Kerr, New York 1975; *The Film Career of Buster Keaton* by George Wead and George Ellis, Boston 1977; *Chaplin, todo sobre un mito* by H.A. Thevenet, Barcelona 1977; *Charles Chaplin—a Guide to References and Resources* compiled by T.J. Lyons, Boston 1977; *Charlie Chaplin Story ou Charlot l'immortel* by P. Lemoine and F. Pedron, Bologna 1978; *Charlie Chaplin* by J. McCabe, Garden City, New York 1978; *Charlot: ou, Sir Charles Chaplin* by J. Lorcey, Paris 1978; articles— "Buster Keaton: 'On ne peut pas faire ça à Charlie Chaplin'", interview by José Zendel in *Les Lettres Françaises* (Paris), 2 October 1952; "How Mr. Chaplin Makes a Movie" by Thomas M. Pryor in *The New York Times Magazine*, 17 February 1952; "Chaplin at Work" in *Life* (New York), 17 March 1952; "Letter from London" by Mollie Panter-Downes in the *New Yorker*, 1 November 1952; "Lineage to *Limelight*" by Walter Kerr in *Theatre Arts* (New York), November 1952; "*Limelight*: A Great Comedian Sums Up His Life" by E. Miller in *Theatre Arts* (New York), November 1952; "The Process of Dissolution" in *Commonweal* (New York), 6 February 1953; "Limelight out" in *Time* (New York), 9 February 1953; "The Elegant Melancholy of Twilight" by Gavin Lambert in *Sight and Sound* (London), January/March 1953; "*Limelight*: Chaplin and His Censors" by William Murray in the *Nation* (New York), 21 March 1953; "Then and Now", interview by Milton Shulman in the *New York Times Magazine*, 9 May 1954; "Film Chronicle: A Feeling of Sad Dignity" by Robert Warshow in *Partisan Review* (New Brunswick, New Jersey), November/December 1954; "Buster Keaton" by Brian Baxter in *Film* (London), November/December 1958; article by Andrew Sarris in *The Village Voice* (New York), 1 October 1964; "*Limelight*" by E. Sieger in *Film Comment* (New York), September/October 1972; "*Limelight*" by M. Tarratt in *Films and Filming* (London), October 1973; "*Limelight*" by S. Le Puyat in *Téléciné* (Paris), July/August 1976; special Chaplin issue of *University Film Association Journal* (Houston), no.1, 1979; "*Limelight*" by Janet E. Lorenz in *Magill's Survey of Cinema, Vol. II* edited by Frank N. Magill, Englewood Cliffs, New Jersey 1980.

* * *

Limelight was the last of Charlie Chaplin's films made in America and, for most critics, the last major Chaplin film of artistic significance. Like Shakespeare's *The Tempest*, *Limelight* seems very much a deliberate summing up, the artist's conscious look backward at his aims and his art. That look backwards is especially striking in *Limelight*, set in London, the city of Chaplin's birth, depicting a drunken music-hall entertainer, like his own father, in the year 1914, the year Chaplin left for Hollywood. Chaplin plays the former music-hall comedian, Calvero, his name almost a synthesis of Chaplin's own and that of the great nineteenth century clown, Grimaldi. Calvero, a great comic star in his youth, is now apparently a drunken has-been, out of touch with his audience, his times and his own failure. Chaplin seemingly put many of his fears and reactions to his public into this film: the critical comments that his films were old-fashioned (a typical reaction to his dialogue films); that his new films were failures (a dominant critical response to *Monsieur Verdoux*), and that his life was a mess (public reactions both to his political and marital affairs). Rather than surrender to self-pity, Chaplin made a film re-affirming his belief in his craft, his art, and himself.

The old drunk, Calvero, saves the life of a young dancer,

Terry, who has tried to commit suicide. Calvero nurses her back to mental and physical health, at the same time discovering that his own hopes for a comeback are groundless and that the audience no longer seems interested in his kind of comedy. Calvero fears that his kindness has obligated Terry into loving a man whom she really does not or cannot love (an echo of the final question in *City Lights*, as well as Chaplin's own marriage to Oona O'Neill, over 30 years his junior). Calvero believes that Terry really loves the young composer, played in one of those nice Chaplin twists in which life and art become inextricable, by Chaplin's own son, Sydney. (Three of Chaplin's other children also play roles in the film as street urchins.)

In the film's final sequence, Calvero's friends organize a special performance for the entertainer—to reintroduce him to his public, to honor him for his past accomplishments, and to express their thanks for what he has given them. Chaplin, in the guise of Calvero, re-enacts several classic music-hall sketches for his audience, including a magnificent comic sketch with another "has-been" of the silent era, Buster Keaton. These sketches are comic marvels, for both the theater and movie audiences, proving the vitality and power of this style of comedy for those audiences who are prepared for it, who are able and willing to see it in a historical context rather than demand its adherence to the comic fashions of the day. Calvero collapses and dies at the end of the film, while his protégée Terry continues to dance on stage, in the limelight, making perpetual pirouettes that describe Chaplin's favorite figure—the circle. Chaplin suggests that a specific kind of comic entertainment is indeed dead—the 200 year tradition of physical comedy that evolved from circuses and music halls into silent films even, with his own work, into sound films. Although that tradition may be dead, it remains alive in other forms: in modern dance, and in movies themselves—in which one can see not only newer forms of comedy but the preservation of the traditions of the past, whether in Chaplin's and Keaton's silent comedies or in this very film. *Limelight* is a film that, in several different senses, literally encloses, preserves, honors and revitalizes the past.

—Gerald Mast

LISTEN TO BRITAIN. Production: Crown Film Unit, for the Ministry of Information; black and white, 35mm; running time: 20 mins. Released 1942.

Produced by Ian Dalrymple; screenplay, direction, and editing by Humphrey Jennings and Stewart McAllister; photography by Henry Fowle; sound recorded by Ken Cameron; foreword spoken by Leonard Brockington added in Canada for North American versions, it was not part of the original film.

Filmed summer 1941 in and around London.

Publications:

Books—*Humphrey Jennings: A Tribute* by John Grierson, London 1951; *Studies in Documentary* by Alan Lovell and Jim Hillier, New York 1972; *Documentary: A History of the Nonfiction Film* by Erik Barnouw, New York 1974; *The Rise and Fall of British Documentary: The Story of the Film Movement Founded by John Grierson* by Elizabeth Sussex, Berkeley 1975;

Humphrey Jennings: More than a Maker of Films by Anthony Hodgkinson and Rodney Sheratsky, Hanover, New Hampshire 1982; Humphrey Jennings: Film-Maker/ Painter/ Poet edited by Mary-Lou Jennings, London 1982; articles—"British Documentaries and the War Effort" by H.D. Waley in Public Opinion Quarterly (London), December 1942; "Humphrey Jennings" by Basil Wright in Sight and Sound (London), December 1950; "Jennings' Britain" by Gavin Lambert in Sight and Sound (London), May 1951; "Some Aspects of the Work of Humphrey Jennings" by Lindsay Anderson in Sight and Sound (London), April/June 1954; "Index to the Creative Work of Humphrey Jennings" by Jonas Mekas in Film Forum (Mesdetten, Germany), 8 July 1954; "Britain's Screen Poet" by Charles Dand in Films in Review (New York), February 1955; issue devoted to Jennings in Film Quarterly (Berkeley), winter 1961-62; "Humphrey Jennings, 1907-1950" by Jacques Belmans in Anthologie du cinéma, Vol. VI, Paris 1971; "Humphrey Jennings: Artist of the British Documentary", special issue, by R.E. Sharatsky in Film Library Quarterly (New York), v.8, no.3-4, 1975; "Listen to Britain" by O. Barrot in Cinéma d'aujourd'hui (Paris), February/March 1977.

*　　*　　*

If Listen to Britain had to be categorized according to its film mode, it would qualify as both propaganda and as avant-garde; the sponsor's message and experimentation are quiet, subtle, and interesting. Audiences could have been easily accepting of both.

What the film is demonstrating is that in wartime Britain everyone is doing his or her job with good cheer. It was no doubt designed to reassure a public who remembered that the losses and deprivations of World War I had not affected the retention of privilege by the upper classes. This time the war was being fought for everyone and everyone was playing an equal part in it, the film is saying. The people in this one nation indivisible are not only working together, they are enjoying recreation (mostly music) together. The music hall team of Flanagan and Allen perform at lunchtime in a factory while Dame Myra Hess plays Mozart in the National Gallery (with the Queen quite casually in the audience, incidentally). A huge ballroom in Blackpool is full of dancers circling to "The Beer Barrel Polka"; a military parade marches through the streets of a town watched by the populace. The film is also letting its audience know that Britain has survived and will endure, that its present war effort is set within honored tradition and rich cultural heritage. "England never, never shall be slave" are the final words of "Rule, Britannia" sung by a chorus over the final image looking down on the English countryside from on high.

As for its experimentation, as the title suggests, the sounds of Britain serve to link the various human groupings and activities shown. The impressionist form and 24-hour survey of the avant-garde city symphonies of the 1920s are recalled here, it is a national symphony (though in fact shot mostly in and around London) with sound added. There is no commentary nor composed musical score; the ubiquitous BBC radio of wartime Britain frequently serves a connective function. The sounds are all source sounds though they often precede and lead into the scene from which they emanate (we hear the pop tune "Yes, My Darling Daughter" and shortly see that it is coming from a public address loud speaker in a factory), or carry over into the next scene (Mozart chords cross-fading into the banging and crunching of heavy machinery).

Another of its remarkable artistic characteristics is the way virtually every image contains symbols of both war and peace. A narrow, cobbled street lined with Tudor houses has an armored column moving along it; on the walls of an art gallery are frames which no longer hold paintings; inside a train sit Canadian soldiers chatting and singing "Home on the Range"; massive industrial smokestacks near the end make one think not only of the wartime productivity of Britain but of its solidity and lasting power. Each image, rich and complex with meaning, carries a symbolic weight that is much greater than the reality of the everyday thing itself. At the same time there are moments of concise emotional intensity associated with certain kinds of poetry. Though this poetry is firmly rooted in a time and place, it has a universality and a timelessness that made it last, as did the country it celebrates.

—Jack C. Ellis

———————

LITTLE CAESAR. Production: Warner Bros. Pictures, Inc.; 1930; black and white, 35mm; running time: 77 mins. Released January 1931.

Screenplay by Frances Faragoh and Robert E. Lee; from a novel by William B. Burnett; directed by Mervyn LeRoy; photography by Tony Gaudio; edited by Ray Curtiss; art direction by Anton Grot; music direction by Erno Rapee. Filmed summer-fall 1930 in Warner Bros. studios. cost: Budgeted at $700,000.

Cast: Edward G. Robinson (Cesare Bandello, alias Rico); Douglas Fairbanks, Jr. (Joe Massara); Glenda Farrell (Olga Stassoff); Sidney Blackmer (Big Boy); Thomas Jackson (Sergeant Flaherty); Ralph Ince (Pete Montana); William Collier, Jr. (Tony Passa); Maurice Black (Little Arnie Lorch); Stanley Fields(Sam Vettori); George E. Stone (Otero); Armand Kaliz (DeVoss); Nick Bela (Ritz Colonna); Noel Madison (Pepi); Ben Hendricks, Jr. (Kid Bean); Lucille LaVerne (Ma Magdalena); Landers Stevens (Commissioner McClure); George Daly (Machine gunner); Ernie Adams (Cashier); Larry Steers (Cafe guest); Louis Natheaux (Hood); Kerman Cripps (Detective).

Publications:

Script—Little Caesar edited by Gerald Peary, Madison, Wisconsin 1981; reviews—"Little Caesar" by Bige in Variety (New York), 14 January 1931; review by Mordaunt Hall in The New York Times, 10 January 1931; books—Little Caesar by W.R. Burnett, New York 1929; The Hollywood Hallucination by Parker Tyler, New York 1944; It Takes More Than Talent by Mervyn LeRoy as told to Alyce Canfield, New York 1953; The Bad Guys by William K. Everson, New York 1964; The Gangster Film by John Baxter, New York 1970; Underworld U.S.A. by Colin McArthur, London 1971; Gangsters and Hoodlums: The Underworld in Cinema by Raymond Lee and B.C. Van Hecke, foreword by Edward G. Robinson, New York 1971; We're in the Money: Depression America and Its Films by Andrew Bergman, New York 1971; The Cinema of Edward G. Robinson by James Robert Parish and Alvin H. Marill, South Brunswick, New Jersey 1972; All My Yesterdays by Edward G. Robinson and Leonard Spigelgass, New York 1973; American Film Genres by Stuart Kaminsky, Dayton, Ohio 1974; Mervyn LeRoy: Take

One by Mervyn LeRoy and Dick Kleiner, New York 1974; *The Great Gangster Pictures* by James R. Parish and Michael Pitts, Metuchen, New Jersey 1976; *Born to Lose* by Eugene Rosow, New York 1978; *Crime Movies* by Carlos Clarens, New York 1980; articles—"The Making of Mervyn LeRoy" in *Films in Review* (New York), May 1953; "Edward G. Robinson" by Allen Eyles in *Films and Filming* (London), January 1964; "Edward G. Robinson" by Robert Roman in *Films in Review* (New York), August/September 1966; "*Little Caesar* and Its Role in the Gangster Film Genre" by Stuart Kaminsky in *Journal of Popular Culture* (Bowling Green, Ohio), summer 1972; "Klassiske gangsterfilm og deres baggrund" by S. Kjørup in *Kosmorama* (Copenhagen), August 1973; "Vers une definition du 'film de gangster'" by Gerald Peary, translated by Olivier Eyquem in *Positif* (Paris), July/August 1975; "Mervyn LeRoy: Star-making, Studio Systems and Style" by Kingsley Canham in *The Hollywood Professionals Vol. 5*, London 1976; "*Little Caesar*" by M. Perez in *Avant-Scène du cinéma* (Paris), 1 October 1979.

*   *   *

Mervyn LeRoy's *Little Caesar* is a vanguard film in motion picture history as it is the prototype for the gangster genre. D.W. Griffith's one-reel *The Musketeers of Pig Alley* is generally acknowledged as the "first" gangster film and Josef von Sternberg's silent *Underworld* is conceded to be an early cinematic depiction of the modern gangster, that uniquely American racketeer which came to power as a result of Prohibition and the Depression; but it is *Little Caesar*, with its hard-hitting irony and grim humor, which spawned the format for the gangster film of the sound era.

Darryl F. Zanuck, Warner Brother's production supervisor at the time, favored scenarios of social drama "straight from the headlines." The myth, romanticism and autonomy of organized crime and its leaders, e.g., Al Capone, were a popular part of American pulp culture. W.R. Burnett's novel on which the film is based crystallized a gangster's milieu through its Capone-like anti-hero. Director LeRoy took the book to Zanuck who immediately recognized its box office potantial, "Every other underworld picture has had a thug with a little bit of good in him. He reforms before the fade-out. This guy is no good at all. It'll go over big." It is this total lack of redeeming qualities in the character of Enrico Bandello and the multifaceted portrayal by Edward G. Robinson that created the extraordinary impact which *Little Caesar* still holds today.

Sternberg's *Underworld*, and many of the subsequent gangster films which followed *Little Caesar*, frequently examined the social forces which drove men to a life of crime. Such is not the case with *Little Caesar*. From the very beginning, when we first see him robbing a gas station, Rico is a full-fledged criminal whose credo is power at all cost. Rico is just what he seems—a ruthless, pugnacious punk. His only friend, Joe, is his partner who wants to give up the life of crime. It is Rico's emotional attachment to Joe which ultimately does him in.

In recent years some film historians have inferred a latent homosexual bond between Rico and Joe, but it is highly improbable that any such implication was intended by the filmmakers.

In its depiction of the meteoric rise and fall of Rico, *Little Caesar's* opening title quotes St. Matthew: "For all them that take the sword shall perish by the sword." The retribution implied in this quote is evident throughout the film; nevertheless, this and subsequent gangster films, had a tendency to glamorize the lives of these men who flaunted authority and lived outside the social structure in a world bound by their own rules. Death, too, had a sense of nobility to it as evidenced by Rico's dying words: "Mother of mercy, is this the end of Rico?"

LeRoy's direction is completely fast-paced and straight to the point, but by no means exceptional. As a director LeRoy was a proficient studio craftsman with a shrewd sense of what the public wanted, but he was not highly innovative. While *Little Caesar* was indeed a hallmark film, it was later surpassed in quality by such memorable films as *The Public Enemy* and *Scarface: The Shame of the Nation*.

—Ronald Bowers

THE LITTLE FOXES. Production: RKO/Radio Pictures; 1941; black and white, 35mm; running time: 115 mins. Released 1941.

Produced by Samuel Goldwyn; screenplay by Lillian Hellman, additional scenes and dialogue by Dorothy Parker, Alan Campbell, and Arthur Kober; from the play by Lillian Hellman; directed by William Wyler; photography by Gregg Toland; edited by Daniel Mandell; production design by Stephen Goosson; music by Meredith Wilson.

Cast: Bette Davis (*Regina Giddens*); Herbert Marshall (*Horace Giddens*); Teresa Wright (*Alexandra Giddens*); Richard Carlson (*David Hewitt*); Charles Dingle (*Ben Hubbard*); Carl Benton Reid (*Oscar Hubbard*); Dan Duryea (*Leo Hubbard*); Patricia Collinge (*Birdie Hubbard*).

Publications:

Books—*Bette Davis: A Biography* by Peter Noble, London 1948; *Samuel Goldwyn: The Producer and His Films* by Richard Griffith, New York 1956; *William Wyler, An Index* edited by Karel Reisz, BFI, London 1958; *The Lonely Life* by Bette Davis, New York 1962; *The Films of Bette Davis* by Gene Ringgold, New York 1965; *What is Cinema, Vol. II* by André Bazin, translated by Hugh Gray, Berkeley 1971; *William Wyler* by Axel Madsen, New York 1973; *Bette Davis* by Jerry Vermilye, New York 1973; *Uil'iam Uailer* by V. Kolodiazhnaia, Moscow 1975; *Samuel Goldwyn Presents* by Alvin R. Marill, South Brunswick, New Jersey and New York 1976; *Close-up: The Hollywood Director* edited by John Tuska, Metuchen, New Jersey 1978; *William Wyler* by Michael A. Anderegg, Boston 1979; articles—"Gregg Toland Film-Maker" by Lester Koenig in *Screen Writer* (London), December 1947; "William Wyler: Director with a Passion and a Craft" by Hermine Rich Isaacs in *Theater Arts* (New York), February 1947; "The Work of Gregg Toland" by Douglas Slocombe in *Sequence* (London), summer 1949; "Wyler, Wellman, and Huston" by Richard Griffith in *Films in Review* (New York), February 1950; "The Later Films of William Wyler" by Karel Reisz in *Sequence* (London), no.13, 1951; "Bette Davis" by Lawrence J. Quirk in *Films in Review* (New York), December 1955; "A Great Cameraman" by George Mitchell in *Films in Review* (New York), December 1956; "A Little Larger Than Life" by John Howard Reid in *Films and Filming* (London), February 1960 and March 1960; "William Wyler" by Curtis Lee Hanson in *Cinema* (Beverly Hills), summer 1967; "The Lady and the Director: Bette Davis and

William Wyler" by Gary Carey in *Film Comment* (New York), fall 1970; "William Wyler" by Ken Doeckel in *Films in Review* (New York), October 1971; "William Wyler" by Charles Higham in *Action* (Los Angeles), September/October 1973; "Dialogue on Film" in *American Film* (Washington, D.C.), April 1976; "Les Immortels du cinéma: William Wyler" by J. von Cottom in *Ciné revue* (Brussels), 30 August 1979; "*The Little Foxes*" by Cheryl Karnes in *Magill's Survey of Cinema, Vol. II* edited by Frank N. Magill, Englewood Cliffs, New Jersey 1980.

* * *

Lillian Hellman's play, a prime example of the "well-made" variety, is precisely the kind of successful middle-brow property that appealed to Samuel Goldwyn. He had already produced Hellman's controversial *The Children's Hour* (also directed by William Wyler, with cinematographer Gregg Toland), a play that handsomely survived a title change to *These Three* and the transformation of the issue of lesbianism into an illicit hetero-sexual affair. No major alterations were required for *The Little Foxes*. The film even resists the conventional "opening up" so often applied to theatrical texts, in the mistaken notion that fundamental cinematic values are expansively pictorial ones.

Wyler's directional energies are deployed in the concentrated focus that suits the closed-in nature of this fiction. He exploits the closure of a house, its rooms and furniture to convey the power struggles of ambitious siblings, a rotten marriage, and the coming-of-age of the daughter, in the turn-of-the-century South. The family is the scene of an action whose violence (and theatri-cally) is augmented by the tightness of the area in which it is enacted. The various postures of Regina Giddens provide the fulcrum for the shots of which she is the center, and of the family configuration that she dominates. She exercises her intelligence and her desire in the manipulation of the figures around her, plotting and placing them with an expertise and a tyranny that is matched by the director himself.

The expertise was recognized by André Bazin in his essay on Wyler included in the French edition of *What is Cinema?*. Bazin analyzes the properties of hard and soft focus in the scene where Regina refuses to give her husband his medicine, while he is in the throes of a heart attack. She remains rooted in her divan during his struggle from the foreground to the background of the frame. Here, the famous Wyler-Toland deep-field staging eschews hard focus on the background. Horace's death on the staircase is a function of the hard focus on Regina's face and torso. This sort of strategy is what constitutes the cinematic in *The Little Foxes*, a film that requires great attention in order to be read in its fullness. The explicit dramaturgy is contained, of course, in the dialogue and plot. But this bourgeois drama truly challenges us in the nuances of its staging, in what must be seen rather than said about family relationships—the slight camera pan on a group of four characters as Aunt Birdie confesses her drinking, the duplic-itous play of the faces of the father and son in a shaving mirror, the low camera placement that captures Regina's swaying pro-gess up her lonely staircase.

The care of the staging and the long shot durations are what make Wyler an actor's director, and no more so than in this ensemble film, where the strength of the company enhances and is enhanced by the star performance of Bette Davis. To the actress's regret, this was her last collaboration with Wyler, the director of her great successes, *Jezebel* and *The Letter*.

—Charles Affron

LOLA. Production: Rialto Film-Preben-Philipsen and Trio FilmWestdeutschen Rundfunk; color, 35mm; running time: 115 mins.; length: 10,313 feet. Released 1981, West Germany.

Produced by Rainer Werner Fassbinder with Horst Wendlundt; screenplay by Peter Märthesheimer, Pea Fröhlich, and Rainer Werner Fassbinder; directed by Rainer Werner Fassbinder; pho-tography by Xaver Schwarzenberger; edited by Juliane Lorenz and Franz Walsch (Rainer Werner Fassbinder); sound recorded by Vladimir Vizner and Milan Bor; art direction by Helmut Gassner; music by Peer Raben; costumes designed by Barbara Baum and Egon Strasser; artistic consultant: Harry Baer; cho-reography by Dieter Gackstetter; staging by Peter Marklewitz and Uwe Ringler.

Cast: Lola (*Barbara Sukowa*); Von Bohm (*Armin Mueller-Stahl*); Schukert (*Mario Adorf*); Matthias Fuchs (*Esslin*); Helga Feddersen (*Frau Hettich*); Karin Baal (*Lola's mother*); Ivan Desny (*Wittich*); Elisabeth Volkmann (*Gigi*); Hark Böhm (*Völker*); Karl-Heinz von Hassel (*Timmerding*); Rosel Zech (*Frau Schukert*); Sonja Neudorfer (*Frau Fink*); Christine Kaufmann (*Susi*); Y Sa Lo (*Rosa*); Günther Kaufmann (*GI*); Isolde Barth (*Frau Völker*); Harry Baer (*1st demonstrator*); Rainer Will (*2nd demonstrator*); Karsten Peters (*Editor*); Her-bert Steinmetz (*Concierge*); Nino Korda (*TV delivery man*); Raul Gimenez (*1st waiter*); Udo Kier (*2nd waiter*); Andrea Heuer (*Librarian*); Ulrike Vigo (*Mariechen*); Helmut Petigk (*Bouncer*); Juliane Lorenz (*Saleswoman*); Marita Pleyer (*Rahel*); Maxim Oswald (*Grandfather Berger*).

Publications:

Reviews—"*Lola*" by "Klad" in *Variety* (New York), 2 September 1981; "*Lola, une femme allemande*" by D. Serceau in *Image et son* (Paris), November 1981; "*Lola*" by L. Audibert in *Cinéma-tographe* (Paris), November 1981; articles—"*Lola, une femme allemande*: Des fantasmes de la petite-bourgeoisie liberale et des leurs consequences politiques" by J. Magny in *Cinéma* (Paris), November 1981; "Den das ist meine Welt, und sonst gar nichts..." by Y. Tobin in *Positif* (Paris), December 1981; "Explorations" by J. Hoberman in *American Film* (Washington, D.C.), Sep-tember 1982.

* * *

Rainer Werner Fassbinder was by far the most prolific of Germany's *Neue Welle* directors, a group which includes Volker Schlöndorff, Werner Herzog, Hans-Jürgen Syberberg, and Wim Wenders. During his short life, the controversial and ico-noclastic Fassbinder directed 41 feature films of which *Lola* is arguably his best, perhaps his masterpiece.

Fassbinder's prodigious cinematic *oeuvre* abounded in politi-cal statements protesting psychological and material corruption. He held a lifelong contempt for those who lived for profit. The subject matter of the majority of his films is the post-World War II Adenauer years of Fassbinder's youth when Germany under-went its economic miracle. Fassbinder's political stance was not that of a great thinker. His socio-political philosophies eman-ated from his personal feelings, and his dissection of Germany's materialism was saved from total misanthropy by his abrasive wit and sense of the ironic. He disavowed those who called him a cynic by explaining, "My work is not cynical; it is realistic.

Pessimistic. Life is pessimistic in the end because we die, and pessimistic in between because of corruption in our daily lives.... It is still the fact that you win by playing by the rules, and the pure person doesn't have much of a chance."

His depiction of the corruption which permeated his homeland was never more satisfying than in his allegorical quartet: *The Marriage of Maria Braun, Lili Marleen, Lola* and *Veronika Voss.* These films span the social history of Germany from 1938 to the late 1950s and each is told from the point of view of a strong-willed woman (the mother country).

In *Lola,* a small town in Bavaria is controlled by the power elite, birds of prey who extort the poor and underprivileged. Led by Schukert, the building contractor, these officials conspire to gain political control over von Bohm, the new building comissioner. Their *deus ex machina* is Lola, Schukert's mistress, the mother of his illegitimate daughter and the singer in his whorehouse/cabaret. Von Bohm's moral and physical seduction by Lola is Fassbinder's cinematic metaphor for German corruption.

Lola obviously is a derivation of von Sternberg's *Der blaue Engel,* but it is only a derivation and not a re-make. The film expertly employs all of Fassbinder's filmic devices—his vivid use of color, his circular moving camera and long pans, his penchant for melodrama, his expert handling of actors, and most of all the distancing of himself and his camera from the subjects on the screen. All come together to better advantage here than in his previous works, making this easily his most accessible film.

Lola is a combination of themes from *Der blaue Engel,* Lillian Hellman's *The Little Foxes,* Ibsen's *An Enemy of the People,* and the many influences of directors Fassbinder admired, such as Godard and Douglas Sirk, and stands as the best expression of his extraordinary personal cinema.

—Ronald Bowers

LOLA MONTÈS. Lola Montez. Production: Gamma-Films, Florida-Films (Paris), and Oska Films (Munich); Eastmancolor, 35mm, Cinemascope; running time: original version 110 mins;, later cut to 90 mins.; length: originally 9900 feet, later cut to 8100 feet. Released 23 December 1955. Re-released 1968 with 30 mins. missing.

Produced by Albert Caraco, some sources list Ralph Baum; screenplay by Jacques Natanson, Annette Wademant, Max Ophuls, and (for the German version) Franz Geiger; from the novel *La Vie extraordinaire de Lola Montès* by Cecil St.-Laurent; directed by Max Ophuls; photography by Christian Matras; edited by Madeleine Gug; sound by Antoine Petitjean with J. Neny and H. Endrulat; production design by Jean d'Eaubonne, Jacques Guth, and (for the German version) William Schatz; music by Geoges Auric; costumes designed by Georges Annenkov, Monique Plotin, and Marcel Escoffier; choreography by Helge Pawlinin.

Filmed 28 February-29 July 1955 in Studio Joinville, Paris, Studio Geiselgasteig, Munich, Studio Victorine, Nice, and on location in Bavaria, Côte d'Azur, and around Paris. Cost: 650 million francs.

Cast: Martine Carol (*Maria Dolorès Porriz y Montèz, alias Lola Montèz*); Peter Ustinov (*Anton Walbrook, King Louis 1st of Bavaria*); Ivan Densy (*Lt. James, 1st husband of Lola Montèz*); Lise Delamare (*Mrs. Craigie*); Henri Guisol (*Maurice, Lola's* driver); Paulette Dubost (*Josephine, servant to Lola*); Will Quadflieg (*Franz Liszt*); Oscar Werner (*The student*); Jacques Fayet (*Steward*); Daniel Mendaille (*Captain*); Jean Gallard (*Secretary to the Baron*); Claude Pinoteau (*Orchestra leader*); Béatrice Arnac (*Circus rider*); Willy Eichberger (*Carl Esmond*); Werner Finck (*Painter*); Germaine Delbat (*Stewardess*): Helena Manson (*James's sister*); Walter Kiaulehn (*Attendant in the theater*); Willy Rösner (*1st Minister*); Friedrich Domin (*Director of the circus*); Hélène Iawkoff; Gustav Waldou (*Rhino trainer*); Betty Philipsen.

Publications:

Scripts—"*Lola Montès*: Scenerio and Adaptation" edited by Claude Beylie in *Avant-Scène du Cinéma* (Paris), January 1969; reviews—by François Truffaut in *Arts* (Paris), December 1955; reviews in *Cahiers du cinéma* (Paris), January 1956; review by Jacques Audiberti in *Cahiers du cinéma* (Paris), February 1956; books—*Présences Contemporaines-Cinema* by Pierre Leprohon, Paris 1957; *Index to the Work of Max Ophuls* by Richard Roud, London 1958; *Max Ophuls* by Claude Beylie, Brussels, 1958; *Max Ophuls* by G. Annenkov, Paris 1962; *Max Ophuls par Max Ophuls* edited by Robert Laffont, Paris 1963; *Interviews with Film Directors* by Andrew Sarris, New York 1967; *From Reverence to Rape* by Molly Haskell, Baltimore 1974; *Caligari's Cabinet and Other Grand Illusions: A History of Film Design* by Léon Barsacq, New York 1976; *Ophuls* edited by Paul Willemen, London 1978; *Max Ophuls and the Cinema of Desire* by Alan Larson Williams, New York 1980; articles—"Fiche Lola Montès" by Dominque Delouche in *Téléciné* (Paris), no.55-56; "Le Dossier de presse de *Lola Montès* in *Cahiers du cinéma* (Paris), January 1956; "Lola au bûcher" by Andrew Sarris in *Cahiers du cinéma* (Paris), January 1956; "Ophuls and the Romantic Tradition" by Eugene Archer in *Yale French Studies*, summer 1956; interview with Ophuls in *Cahiers du cinéma* (Paris), June 1957; article by John Cutts in *Films and Filming* (London), January 1958; article by David Robinson in *Sight and Sound* (London), winter 1957-58; articles on Ophuls in *Cahiers du cinéma* (Paris), March 1958; "*Lola Montes*" by G. Weinberg in *Films in Review* (New York), summer 1963; article by Roger Greenspun in *Film Society Revue* (New York), October 1968; "Lola du bûcher au pavois" by Claude Beylie in *Avant-Scène du cinéma* (Paris), January 1969; "The Current Cinema" by Penelope Gilliatt in the *New Yorker*, 3 May 1969; "The Mastery of Movement: An Appreciation of Max Ophuls" by Forrest Williams in *Film Comment* (New York), winter 1969; "The Long Take" by Brain Henderson in *Film Comment* (New York), summer 1971; "Max Ophuls: An Introduction" by Andrew Sarris in *Film Comment* (New York), summer 1971; "*Lola Montès*" by N. Simsolo in *Image et son* (Paris), March 1972; "*Lola Montès*" by K. Schmidt in *Kosmorama* (Copenhagen), August 1973; "*Lola Montès*" by H. Bitomsky in *Filmkritik* (Munich), June 1974; special issue devoted to Ophuls in *Filmkritik* (Munich), November 1977; "*Lola Montes*" by Marjorie Baumgarten in *Cinema Texas Program Notes* (Austin), 6 October 1977; "*Lola Montès*" by Gordon Gow in *Films and Filming* (London), October 1978; "*Lola Montès*" by Tom Milne in *Monthly Film Bulletin* (Lonodon), October 1978; "*Lola Montès*" by D. Robinson in *Sight and Sound* (London), autumn 1978; "La Dernière femme de Max Ophuls" by L. Audibert and J. Tonnorred in *Cinématographe* (Paris), May 1980; "*Lola Montès*" by J.P. Le Pavec in *Cinéma* (Paris), May 1980; "*Lola Montès*" by R. Lefèvre in *Image et son*" (Paris), May 1980; "Ich bin die Fesche lola..." by Y. Tobin in *Positif* (Paris), July/August 1980;

"Schein und Sein—Glanz und Grausamkeit der Repräsentation" in *Frauen und Film* (Berlin), February 1981.

* * *

From the time of its premiere in Paris in December of 1955, *Lola Montès* has created controversy with the critics and the public alike. During its initial release audiences booed the film. Some grew so rowdy that the exhibitors were forced to call in the police. An open letter appeared in *Le Figaro* pleading for restraint on the part of those patrons who remained perplexed by the film. It argued that a film as technically new and audacious as *Lola* was just the breath of fresh air the cinema needed, and that to condemn the film was to do a disservice not merely to this film but to the cinema in general. The letter was signed by, among others, Jean Cocteau, Robert Rossellini, Jacques Tati, and Jacques Becker. The critical response while less impassioned was no less polarized. On one side the film was dismissed as boring and incoherent because of its sumptuous excess of decor, mise-en-scene, and narrative convolution. On the other, by reason of this same excess, it was hailed as a masterpiece of the baroque.

Much of this controversy can be attributed to the way in which the film was touted. Hoping to capitalize on the popularity of such lush costume spectacles as *Lucrece Borgia* and *Madame Du Barry*, Gamma Films advertised a super-production based on the life and loves of the most scandalous woman of all time, Lola Montès—the Spanish-Irish cabaret dancer who became the mistress of Franz Liszt and Ludwig I, King of Bavaria. The film would feature Martine Carol, France's foremost sex goddess at the pinnacle of her career, and would be adapted from a novel by Cecil St. Laurent, author of a series of tastefully erotic novels, including *Caroline and Cherie*. It would boast an all-star supporting cast headed by Peter Ustinov, Anton Walbrook, and the latest heart-throb from Germany, Oskar Werner. Finally, the film was to be directed by Europe's most urbane master of the "woman's film," Max Ophuls, in lavish Eastmancolor and Cinemascope. All of these ingredients promised a blockbuster, a film which would provide a titillating view of tragic love among the aristocratic classes while never overstepping the boundries of good taste and middle-class morality.

However, this was not the film that Ophuls delivered. Instead, he chose to take aim at the very mechanism that Gamma Films was using to market the film: lurid publicity. In an interview with François Truffaut, Ophuls cites the fate of Judy Garland and Diana Barrymore, which he blamed on the public's appetite for scandal and on the entrepreneurs who shamelessly exploit scandals. "We must kill publicity...I find it dreadful, this vice of wanting to know every thing, this irreverence in the face of mystery. It is on this theme that I have built my film: the annihilation of the personality through the cruelty and indecency of spectacles based on scandal." Cinema made a voyeur of everyone—producer, performer, and spectator alike. For Ophuls the true subject of *Lola Montès* became the demystification of publicity and exhibitionism that characterizes our era. To achieve this, he turns his customary style on its head. He sets the glittering display of his previous films against itself, and transforms his formerly refined depiction of a decadent world into a virulent condemnation of itself.

All aspects of the film's technique attempt to subvert the spectators' voyeuristic gaze and turn it back on itself. The framing device of the mammoth circus serves to distance the spectator from the events of Lola'a life presented in flashback. Lola, confined in a cage, is introduced by the suitably oily ringmaster as a beast more dangerous than any other found in circus's menag-

erie. Lola's entrance had been preceded by a parade of clowns representing a caricature of a parade of Lola's lovers. She is displayed on a pedestal revolving in one direction, while the camera orbits about her in a 360-degree track moving in the opposite direction. A short mimeshow prefaces each flashback undermining the suspense of the episodes. Even the woodenness of Martine Carol's performance, which many critics felt marred the film, is turned to advantage. Lola is treated as an object, a beautiful but hollow doll, an empty manikin, to be invested with the fantasies of the men who possess her. Like the earrings in Ophuls's earlier *Madame De...* the character of Lola functions as a focal point around which the desires of the other characters (especially those of the circus spectators) are gathered and then reflected back with striking clarity.

Ophuls mustered all of his expertise in mounting this, his final film. Though it marked his first use of color and CinemaScope, what he is able to accomplish is often stunning. Each flashback is set off by a dominant hue to suggest Lola's psychological state. These range from the blue of the episode of Lola as a young girl to the autumnal yellow and ocher of her sojourn at the court of Ludwig. In his encounter with wide-screen format, Ophuls discovered solutions to compositional problems which had perplexed users of the unwieldy aspect ratio since its inception which look forward to effects that Anthony Mann, Nicholas Ray and Douglas Sirk would realize in the late 1950s. Of course in his use of moving camera Ophuls remains without peer. The circular track which opens the film, the camera's plunge which duplicates Lola's at the climax of her performance, and the final track back which reveals the line of men queuing up to pay for a brush with immortality at Lola'a hand, still prove capable of taking the breath away.

When *Lola Montès* failed so miserably with Parisian audiences, the producers decided to recall all prints and, despite Ophuls's protests, recut the film. Their version reduced the film from 140 to 90 minutes by abandoning the flashback structure in favor of a strict chronological rendering of the story. Also a happy epilogue spoken by Martine Carol was added. This mutilated version open in Monte Carlo in February, 1957, and succeeded only in calling forth the unanimous disapprobation of both critics and the public. It was withdrawn from further distribution. By a bitter coincidence, Ophuls died in March, 1957, without completing another film. *Lola Montès* remained unseen in any version for nearly a decade. In 1966 a group of scholars purchased the prints that remained available and patched together a version which, as far as possible, corresponds to the cut Ophuls had authorized, though it still lacks 30 minutes of the original. This version premiered in 1968, and has since become a staple of film societies and re-run houses around the world. It has been justly hailed as Ophuls's masterpiece and, as Claude Beylie has writen, after *Rules of the Game* and *Citizen Kane*, it is "the third and decisive stage in the development of modern cinema."

—Dennis Nastav

LOOK BACK IN ANGER. Production: Woodfall Films; black and white, 35mm; running time: 99 mins. Released 1959.

Produced by Harry Saltzman; screenplay by Nigel Kneale, additional dialogue by John Osborne; from the play by John Osborne; directed by Tony Richardson; photography by Oswald Morris; edited by Richard Best; art direction by Peter Glazier; music performed by Chris Barber.

Filmed in London.

Cast: Richard Burton (*Jimmy Porter*); Claire Bloom (*Helena Charles*); Mary Ure (*Alison Porter*); Edith Evans (*Mrs. Tanner*); Gary Raymond (*Cliff Lewis*); Glen Byam Shaw (*Colonel Redfern*); Phyllis Neilson-Terry (*Mrs. Redfern*); Donald Pleasence (*Hurst*); Jane Eccles (*Mrs. Drury*); S.P. Kapoor (*Kapoor*).

Publications:

Scripts—"*Look Back in Anger*" (extract) in *Sight and Sound* (London), summer/autumn 1959; reviews—by Henry Hart in *Films in Review* (New York), October 1959; review by Gavin Lambert in *Film Quarterly* (Berkeley), summer 1959; review by Roger Manvell in *Films and Filming* (London), June 1959; "*Look Back in Anger*" by Bosley Crowther in *The New York Times*, 16 September 1959; books—*Where We Came In: 70 Years of the British Film Industry* by C.A. Oakley, London 1964; *Filmmakers on Filmmaking* edited by Harry M. Geduld, Bloomington, Indiana 1967; *A Mirror for England: British Movies from Austerity to Affluence* by Raymond Durgnat, New York 1971; *Behind the Scene: Theatre and Film Interviews From Transatlantic Review* by Joseph F. McCrindle, New York 1971; *The Film Business: A History of the British Cinema* by Ernest Betts, London 1973; *A History of Film* by Jack C. Ellis, Englewood Cliffs, New Jersey 1979; articles—"Two New Directors" by Penelope Houston and Louis Maracorelles in *Sight and Sound* (London), winter 1958-59; "*Look Back in Anger*" by David Robinson in *Sight and Sound* (London), summer/autumn 1959; "The Man Behind an Angry-Young-Man" by Tony Richardson in *Films and Filming* (London), February 1959; "Tony Richardson: An Interview" by Colin Young in *Film Quarterly* (Berkeley), summer 1960; "Britain's Angry Young Directors: Interview" by Hollis Alpert in the *Saturday Review* (New York), 24 December 1960; "Talking About Acting: Albert Finney and Mary Ure" by Louis Marcorelles in *Sight and Sound* (London), spring 1961; "A Modern Hero: The Nongenue" by A.J. Alexander in *Film Culture* (New York), summer 1961; article by Pauline Kael in *Film Quarterly* (Berkeley), fall 1961; "Britain's Busiest Angry Young Man" by David Moller in *Film Comment* (New York), winter 1964.

*   *   *

Tony Richardson came to motion pictures after directing for the stage and television, writing for the British film magazine *Sight and Sound*, and helping found Britain's Free Cinema Movement. Through his work in television, he met playwright John Osborne and directed the stage version of Osborne's *Look Back in Anger*, a shocking and vitriolic diatribe about the hopeless plight of the working class in England. The play opened on May 8, 1956, and marked what has come to be know as the "dramatic renaissance" of English theatre and the age of "the Angry Young Men," with Osborne their leading exponent.

In translating Osborne's play for the screen, Richardson hired Mary Ure from the original stage cast to play the pregnant wife, Alison, and enlisted Richard Burton to play the loquacious part of Jimmy Porter, the angry, pessimistic sweet-stall vendor, and the lovely Claire Bloom to play Helena, the actress who vacillates between lust and hate for Jimmy.

On the surface, *Look Back in Anger* ia a patent melodrama about a working-class bloke who has married above his social station and cries out in anger and self-pity against a society which blithely ignores the plight of the commoner as long as it can remain enveloped in its cocoon of tradition and servility—similar to *A Streetcar Named Desire*. However, Osborne's play lacks the sensuality and poetic fantasy of William's play. Instead he opts for an abrasive, provocative and brutal realism which he sets his work apart from the mannered subterfuge of British restraint.

Osborne's Jimmy Porter is spokesman for a generation of post-World War II Englishmen constrained by the restrictions of a caste-ridden welfare state. Their lives are dismal, seemingly without hope for the future. The boorish, uneducated Jimmy feels trapped in his menial job; he tests his wife's affection for him until his anger and his infidelity with Helena drives her away. Only after he learns that their child was stillborn does he realize that he "needs" Alison, and even then, makes her beg to return to him.

This was trenchant fare for English theatre and filmgoers of the late 1950s, but today the film seems incomplete. Though Richardson has imbued the film with a startling authentic realism, its success owes less to Richardson than to the excellent cast. Richard Burton plays one of his finest roles as Jimmy Porter, a part which tapped his brooding intensity and marvelous vocal instrument. Mary Ure and Claire Bloom each give splendid performances. Also memorable is Dame Edith Evans as Mrs. Tanner, the Cockney mother of one of Jimmy's friends, a character only mentioned in the play. What dates the film is Osborne's sophomoric philosophical stance. As critic Stanley Kauffmann wrote: "It is a recognition of the lonely condition of contemporary Western man—minus the additional recognition that this condition is a grave opportunity, not a final defeat."

Look Back in Anger was only moderately well-received in England, and was dismissed in the U.S., for the most part, as a depressing and irritating story about people for whom the audience shared little sympathy. While Osborne's frustrated idealism seemed to have misfired over the long term, *Look Back in Anger*, as a play and a film, was important in its time. It led to Richardson's adaptation one year later of Osborne's *The Entertainer*, which features one of Laurence Olivier's most vivid and accomplished performances.

—Ronald Bowers.

LOST HORIZON. Production: Columbia Pictures; 1937; black and white, 35mm; running time: 118 mins. Released 1937. Re-released 1943 in an edited version of 109 mins.

Produced by Frank Capra; screenplay by Robert Riskin; from the novel by James Hilton; directed by Frank Capra; photography by Joseph Walker; edited by Gene Havlick and Gene Milford; sound recorded by John Livadary; art direction by Stephen Goosson; music by Dmitri Tiomkin.

Cost: about $2,000,000. Academy Awards for Interior Decoration and Editing, 1937.

Cast: Ronald Colman (*Robert Conway*); Jane Wyatt (*Sondra*); Edward Everett Horton (*Alexander P. Lovett*); John Howard (*George Conway*); Thomas Mitchell (*Henry Barnard*); Margo (*Maria*); Isabel Jewell (*Gloria Stone*); H.B. Warner (*Chang*); Sam Jaffe (*High Lama*).

Publications:

Books—*Frank Capra* by Richard Griffith, London 1951; *Hollywood in the Thirties* by John Baxter, New York 1968; *Frank Capra: One Man—One Film* by James Silke, Washington, D.C. 1971; *The Name Above the Title* by Frank Capra, New York 1971; *We're in the Money: Depression America and Its Films* by Andrew Bergman, New York 1972; *The Films of Frank Capra* by Donald Willis, Metuchen, New Jersey 1974; *Frank Capra: The Man and His Films*, edited by Richard Glatzer and John Raeburn, Ann Arbor 1975; *Ronald Colman: A Very Private Person* by Juliet Benita Colman, New York 1975; *The Films of Frank Capra* by Victor Scherle and William Levy, Secaucus, New Jersey 1977; *Frank Capra Study Guide*, edited by Dennis Bohnenkamp and Sam Grogg, Washington, D.C. 1979; *Frank Capra* by Charles Maland, Boston 1980; articles—"Columbia's Gem" in *Time* (New York), 8 August 1938; "Mr. Capra's Short Cuts to Utopia" by Harold Salemson in *Penguin Film Review* (London), no.7, 1948; "Ronald Colman" by Jack Jacobs in *Films in Review* (New York), April 1958; "Ronald Colman and the Cinema of Empire" by Jeffrey Richards in *Focus on Film* (London), September/October 1970; issue on Capra of *Positif* (Paris), December 1971; "Capra and Riskin" by Richard Corliss in *Film Comment* (New York), vol.8, no.4, 1972; "Colman..." by Julian Fox in *Films and Filming* (London), March 1972 and April 1972; "Jane Wyatt" by Roger Dooley in *Films in Review* (New York), January 1972; "Frank Capra" by D.J. Dadder in *Film Dope* (London), November 1974; "Lost and Found: The Films of Frank Capra" in *Film* (London), June 1975; "Dialogue on Film" in *American Film* (Washington, D.C.), October 1978; "*Lost Horizon*" by Harold Meyerson in *Magill's Survey of Cinema, Vol.III* edited by Frank N. Magill, Englewood Cliffs, New Jersey 1980; issue on Capra of *Film Criticism* (Edinboro, Pennsylvania), winter 1981.

*   *   *

From the middle to the late 1930s, Frank Capra was Hollywood's Golden director. During a five year period, he won three Academy Awards for Best Direction, had a steady succession of box office hits, and, as his autobiography notes, was the first director to have his "name above the title" of his films. His movies exuded a populist philosophy which preached the goodness of the common man, the evil of big business and fascism, and the power of true love. Yet, one film, *Lost Horizon*, made in 1937 stands apart from Capra's Depression-era output (cynically labeled by some critics "Capra-corn"). Based on James Hilton's popular novel, the motion picture was an allegorical fantasy which delivered essentially the same messages as Capra's other films but employed a different style. Although set in contemporary times and beginning during the early stages of the Sino-Japanese war, its principal action takes place in Shangri-La, a mythical country in the Himilayas, which gives the film the appearance of a costume drama. Along with Capra'a other film using a non-American setting, *The Bitter Tea of General Yen*, it shows the violent struggles of the Chinese people and then shifts the action to an idyllic, peaceful haven to establish a meaningful contrast.

The use of violence contrasted with a peaceful retreat, however, is not the only deviation from Capra's usual formula. The protagonist, Robert Conway, is also not a typical Capra hero. Analyzing the director's films as a body, his protagonist seems to represent an idealized model of the American male: tall, handsome, uneducated and somewhat naive, but decent and down to earth, as in those characters played by Clark Gable, James Stewart, or Gary Cooper. Although tall and handsome, Coleman's Conway was an aristocratic Englishman, highly educated and worldly.

Another point of difference is its lack of extensive comic relief. Edward Everett Horton as Alexander P. Lovett does provide a certain amount of humor but these moments stand apart, almost negatively, from the rest of the film. There are many examples of Capra's famous "reaction shots," but they do not provide the marvelous blend of types and characters usually seen in his films.

Critics have noticed that Shangri-La is actually the final solution to the problems of the world, an escape to a Utopian community where war, disease, and even aging, have virtually disappeared. Yet it is not a true Utopia. Some members of the group marooned in Shangri-La are not content and yearn for the more troubled world they had left behind. Maria wants to return to "civilization," unaware that her return also means that she will quickly grow old, and ultimately die. She tricks Conway and his brother George into taking her away from Shangri-La. After their departure, and after Maria's death, George leaps (or possibly falls as he is overcome by grief) off the mountain to his death. Conway then resolves to return to Shangri-La forever. Conway's resolution through suicide, is similar in theme to John Doe's in *Meet John Doe* and George Bailey's in *It's a Wonderful Life*; only after facing death, or oblivion, can the hero survive.

It is not a particularly happy ending when Conway eventually finds his way back to Shangri-La. Rather than accepting life and reality, Conway prefers to escape to a fantasy world. *Lost Horizon* remains, after almost 50 years, Capra's most critically controversial film. While many view it on the level of romantic fantasy, its less obvious meanings are more complex and more cynical.

—Patricia King Hanson

LOUISIANA STORY. Production: Robert Flaherty Productions, Inc (Standard Oil of New Jersey); 1948; black and white, 35mm; running time: 77 mins. Released September 1948, New York by Lopert Pictures, premiered at Edinburgh Film Festival, August 1948.

Produced by Robert Flaherty with Richard Leacock and Helen Van Dongen; screenplay by Robert Flaherty and Frances Flaherty; from their original story; directed by Robert Flaherty; photography by Richard Leacock; edited by Helen van Dongen, assisted by Ralph Rosenblum; sound by Benjamin Donniger; music by Virgil Thompson, music performed by Philadelphia Orchestra under Eugene Ormandy.

Filmed in Louisiana bayou country. Cost: $258,000. Venice International Film Festival, International Award for its lyrical beauty, 1948.

Cast: Joseph Boudreaux (*Boy*); Lionel Le Blanc (*Father*); Mrs. E. Bienvenu (*Mother*); Frank Hardy (*The driller*); C.T. Guedry (*His boilerman*).

Publications:

Reviews—"*Louisiana Story*" by Robert Hatch in the *New Republic* (New York), 11 October 1948; "More Seeing, Less

Selling" by Mary Losey in *Saturday Review* (New York), 9 October 1948; "*Louisiana Story*: nouveau film de Flaherty" by Serge Roullet in *La Revue du cinéma* (Paris), April 1948; "*Louisiana Story*" by Gaetano Carancini in *Bianco e nero* (Rome), April 1949; books—*Robert Flaherty: Nota biografica, filmografica e bibliografica...* by Mario Gromo, Parma, Italy 1952; *The Technique of Film Editing* by Karel Reisz and Gavin Miller, New York 1953; *The Odyssey of a Film-Maker: Robert Flaherty's Story* by Frances Flaherty, Urbana, Illinois 1960; *Robert Flaherty* by Jose Clemente, Madrid 1963; *Robert Flaherty* by Carlos Fernandez Cuenca, Madrid 1963; *Robert Flaherty* compiled by Wolfgang Klaue, Berlin (East) 1964; *Robert J. Flaherty* by Henri Agel, Paris 1965; *Virgil Thomson* by Virgil Thomson, London 1967; *The World of Robert Flaherty* by Richard Griffith, reprinted New York 1970; *The Innocent Eye: The Life of Robert Flaherty* by Arthur Calder-Marshall, London 1970; *Nonfiction Film: A Critical History* by Richard Barsam, New York 1973; *Film and Reality: An Historical Survey* by Roy Armes, Baltimore 1974; *Documentary: A History of the Non-Fiction Film* by Erik Barnouw, New York 1974; *Robert J. Flaherty* by Antonio Napolitano, Florence 1975; *Robert Flaherty: A Guide to References and Resources* by William T. Murphy, Boston 1978; articles—"Old Master" in *Time* (New York), 20 September 1948; "Movie of the Week: *Louisiana Story*" in *Life* (New York), 4 October 1948; "*Louisiana Story* and Melody Time by Hermann Weinberg in *Sight and Sound* (New York), autumn 1948; "Interview with Flaherty" by Penelope Houston in *Sight and Sound* (London), December 1949; "How He Made the *Louisiana Story* in the Bayous of Louisiana" in *Travel* (New York), May 1949; "Robert Flaherty and the Naturalist Documentary" by Hugh Gray in *Hollywood Quarterly*, fall 1950; "Flaherty—Education for Wanderlust" in *The Running Pianist* by Robert Lewis Taylor, New York 1950; "Film: Language of the Eye" by Robert Flaherty in *Theatre Arts* (New York), May 1951; "Flaherty at Abbeville" by Edward Sammis in *Sight and Sound* (London), November/December 1951; "350 Cans of Film" by Helen Van Dongen in *Cinema 51*, London 1951; "The World of Robert Flaherty" by George L. George in *Film News* (New York), no.4, 1953; "*Louisiana Story*" in *The Film and the Public* by Roger Manvell, Harmondsworth 1955; "Explorations" by Frances Flaherty and "Robert Flaherty—The Man and the Filmmaker" by Charles Siepmann in *Film Book I: The Audience and the Filmmaker* edited by Robert Hughes, New York 1959; "*Louisiana Story*" by Alan Stanbrook in *Films and Filming* (London), December 1961; "*Louisiana Story*" by Ralph Stephenson in *Films and Filming* (London), December 1961; "Robert J. Flaherty 1884-1951" by Helen van Dongen in *Film Quarterly* (Berkeley), summer 1965; article by Gretchen Weinberg in *Film Culture* (New York), summer 1966; "A Flaherty Mystery" by Georges Sadoul in *Cahiers du Cinema in English* (New York), September 1967; "Bob Flaherty Remembered" by Harvey Fondiller in *Popular Photography* (Boulder, Colorado), March 1970; "Remembering Frances Flaherty" by Ricky Leacock in *Film Comment* (New York), November/December 1972; "Helen Van Dongen: An Interview" by Ben Achtenberg in *Film Quarterly* (Berkeley), winter 1976; "*Louisiana Story*" by Sally V. Holm in *Magill's Survey of Cinema, Vol. III* edited by Frank N. Magill, Englewood Cliffs, New Jersey 1980.

*   *   *

Robert Flaherty's last film is a fitting culmination to a long career. It is less a documentary about the Cajun people of Louisiana's bayou country than an autobiographical film about Flaherty himself. From the viewpoint of a Cajun boy the film reveals the mysteries of the bayou wilderness, portrayed as an enchanting work of fantasy, filled with beauty and danger. The film is a poetic reflection of Flaherty's youth, in which he explores his own life-long relationship to the wilderness and natural environment, and to the people who lived there.

The opening sequence is one of the most celebrated in film history. Shots of alligators, magnificent birds, floating lily ponds, slithering snakes, and other wildlife and flora are given unity, continuity, and a sense of graceful movement. The brilliance of these sequences was the result of the troubled but highly successful collaboration between Flaherty and his talented editor, Helen Van Dongen. The nightime oil drilling sequence, another outstanding sequence, succeeds because of the interplay of images of the derricks accompanied by an atonal sound track. Flaherty's strength was in direction and shooting; Van Dongen's in her outstanding skill as an editor.

The film's visual beauty is so effective that it overshadows the sponsor's message. Oil drilling technology, first seen as an unknown threat to the tranquility of the bayou, in the end appears benign, leaving the impression that the unspoiled wilderness is safe.

The simple visual beauty of this film pleased most of the contemporary critics, though the film's theme or message bewildered some. Many recognized that the scenes with speaking parts were not terribly convincing. As in other Flaherty films, the cast was chosen from the locals, more for their appearance than acting ability. Making them speak their roles showed the limitation of using real people in dialogue situations that are necessary to rehearse. They become stilted and artificial before the camera.

Louisiana Story remains an enduring work of art for its shear visual beauty, though some have argued its qualifications as a documentary, due to the manipulation of events depicted. For any film essentially based in reality, however, it remains one of the most successful collaborations of all time with an impressive amalgamation of talent in direction, photography, editing, writing, and music.

—Willian T. Murphy

THE LOVE PARADE. Parade d'amour. Production: Paramount Famous Lasky Corp.; 1930; black and white, 35mm, Movietone sound (also released in silent version); running time: about 112 mins.; length: 12 reels, 10,022 feet (silent version: 7094 feet). Released 18 January 1930, but premiered 19 November 1929 in New York.

Produced by Ernst Lubitsch; scenario by Ernest Vajda and Guy Bolton; from the play *The Prince Consort* by Leon Xanrof and Jules Chancel; directed by Ernst Lubitsch; photography by Victor Milner; edited by Merrill White; sound engineered by Franklin Hansen; art direction by Hans Dreier; music (songs) by Victor Schertzinger and Clifford Grey; dialog directed by Perry Ivens.

Cast: Maurice Chevalier (*Count Alfred*); Jeanette MacDonald (*Queen Louise*); Lupino Lane (*Jacques*); Lilian Roth (*Lulu*); Edgar Norton (*Master of Ceremonies*); Lionel Barrymore (*Prime Minister*); Albert Roccardi (*Foreign Minister*); Carlton Stockdale (*Admiral*); Eugene Pallette (*Minister of War*); Russell Powell (*Afghan ambassador*); E.H. Calvert (*Ambassador*);

André Sheron (*Le Mari*); Yola D'Avril (*Paulette*); Winter Hall (*Priest*); Ben Turpin (*Cross-Eyed lackey*); Anton Vaverka, Albert De Winton, and William von Hardenburg (*Cabinet ministers*); Margaret Fealy, Virginia Bruce, Josephine Hall, Rosalind Charles, and Helene Friend (*Ladies in waiting*).

Publications:

Reviews—in *Variety* (New York), 27 November 1929; review in *Time* (New York), 2 December 1929; books—*An Index to the Films of Ernst Lubitsch* by Theodore Huff, supplement to the *Sight and Sound* index series, London 1947; *Ernst Lubitsch* by Mario Verdone, Lyon 1964; *The Lubitsch Touch: A Critical Study* by Herman Weinberg, revised edition, New York 1971; *The Movie Musical from Vitaphone to 42nd Street*, edited by Miles Kreuger, New York 1975; *The Hollywood Exiles* by John Baxter, New York 1976; *The Cinema of Ernst Lubitsch: The Hollywood Films* by Leland Poague, London 1977; *Ernst Lubitsch: A Guide to References and Resources* by R. Carringer and B. Sabath, Boston 1978; *The Cinema of Ernst Lubitsch* by Leland Poague, South Brunswick, New Jersey 1978; articles— "Concerning Cinematography...as Told to William Stull" in *American Cinematographer* (Los Angeles), November 1929; "Contributo alla storia della 'Sophisticated Comedy'" by Giulio Castello in *Bianco e Nero* (Rome), September 1949; "A Tribute to Lubitsch" by Herman G. Weinberg in *Films in Review* (New York), August/September 1951; "The Films of Ernst Lubitsch", special issue of *Film Journal* (Australia), June 1959; "Origins of the Lubitsch Style" by Lotte Eisner in *Film Journal* (Australia), March 1960; "Jeanette MacDonald" by DeWitt Bodeen in *Films in Review* (New York), March 1965; "Chez Ernst" by Jean-Georges Auriol in *Cahiers du cinéma in English* (New York), March 1967; "Lubitsch (1892-1947)" by Bernard Eisenschitz in *Anthologie du Cinéma* vol.3, Paris 1968; "The 'Lubitsch Touch' and the Lubitsch Brain" in *The Comic Mind: Comedy and the Movies* by Gerald Mast, Indianapolis, Indiana 1973; "Ernst Lubitsch" in *Passport to Hollywood: Film Immigrants: Anthology* by Don Whittemore and Philip Cecchettini, New York 1976; "Lubitsch: The American Silent Films" by D. McVay in *Focus on Film* (London), April 1979; issue on *The Love Parade* of *Avant-Scène du cinéma* (Paris), 15 March 1980.

*   *   *

Musicals produced following the introduction of sound were essentially of one type: the recording of song and dance routines performed on stage. There was no variety to these "100% all-singing, all-dancing, all-talking" musicals and the American public grew weary of them. Theater owners frequently advertised that the films they were showing were not musicals. General film histories suggest that it was Warner Brothers and Busby Berkeley's backstage musicals of 1933 that ended a 3-year drought and revived the genre. During the period from 1929 to 1932, however, Ernst Lubitsch created a vital film format that is still a major influence on musicals today.

The Love Parade was Lubitsch's first musical, and according to *Variety*, "the first true screen musical." With it, he eliminated the proscenium-bound style characteristic of most musicals by employing a moving camera, sophisticated editing, and non-synchronous sound.

This final consideration freed the camera even more; Lubitsch could shoot whatever and wherever he chose and add a musical or sound score later. The camera movement was not as fluid as Lubitsch was to achieve in his next film, *Monte Carlo*, but it was an important initial step. *The Love Parade* also signalled Lubitsch's method of integrating performance into the narrative line. He used music that advanced the plot and developed the characters so that the shift from narrative to song and dance would seem a "natural" emotional expression. Fred Astaire and Arthur Freed would use the same formula with only minor changes.

The Love Parade was a further extension of the themes Lubitsch had investigated in his silent marriage comedies: the roles of men and women in society, sex as part of everyday life, the psychology of relationships, and the undercutting of conventional morality. The famous "Lubitsch touch" was again manifest in the suave characters, witty dialogue, and urbane situations. *Time* called the film a "...boldly amorous, decorative, and at times amusing combination of drawing room farce and Balkan operetta."

The film starred Jeanette MacDonald and Maurice Chevalier in the first of their four musicals for Lubitsch. Chevalier was a screen personality in demand in Hollywood after his first musical, *Innocents of Paris*. *The Love Parade* was his second musical and in it he sang "Nobody's Using It Now," the first musical soliloquy in a talking picture. MacDonald was an ingenue prima donna from Broadway known for such stage musicals as *Boom Boom* and *Yes, Yes Yvette*. *The Love Parade* was her screen debut.

The Love Parade was one of the first "$2.00 talkies" and set new records at the box office. After nine weeks it was still playing to standing-room-only crowds at the Criterion in New York City. The film continues to be popular; *The Love Parade* and *Monte Carlo* are among the most frequently revived films.

—Greg S. Faller

———

LUCIA. Production: Instituto Cubano del Arte e Industria Cinematograficos (ICAIC); black and white, 35mm; running time: 160 minutes. Released 1968.

Produced by Raúl Canosa; screenplay by Humberto Solás, Julio García Espinosa, and Nelson Rodríguez; directed by Humberto Solás; photography by Jorge Herrera; edited by Nelson Rodríguez; sound engineered by Ricardo Istueta and Carlos Fernáandez; music by Leo Brower; costumes designed by María Elena Molinet.

Filmed 1967 in Cuba. Moscow Film Festival, Gold Medal, 1969.

Cast: Raquel Revuelta (*Lucia, Part 1*); Eslinda Núñez (*Lucia, Part 2*); Adela Legrá (*Lucia, Part 3*); Adolfo Llauradó (*Tomás*).

Publications:

Scripts—"*Lucia 196(Part III)*" in *Memories of Underdevelopment: The Revolutionary Films of Cuba* edited by Michael Myerson, New York 1973; books—*Memories of Underdevelopment: The Revolutionary Films of Cuba* edited by Michael Myerson, New York 1973; articles—by Geoffrey Minish in *Take One* (Montreal), July/August 1969; "Solidarity and Violence" by Andi Engel in *Sight and Sound* (London), autumn 1969; "The Cuban Cinema" by M.E. Douglas in *Take One* (Montreal), July/August 1969; interview with Solás in *Atlas* (New York), April 1970; "3 Cuban Cultural Reports with Films Somewhere in Them" by Renata Adler in *A Year in the Dark*, Berkeley 1971; "*Lucia*: Struggles with History" by P. Biskind in *Jump Cut* (Chicago), July/August 1974; "*Lucia*" by M. Matthews in *Films in Review* (New York), May 1974; "Cine Cubano: Revaluaciones, Devaluaciones y Presentaciones" by Jorge Ayala Blanco in *Movietone News* (Seattle), November 1974; "*Lucia*: Style and Meaning in Revolutionary Film" by Steven Kovacs in *Monthly Review* (New York), June 1975; "*Lucia*" by A.M. Taylor in *Film Quarterly* (Berkeley), winter 1974-75; "Latin American Films: 4th Frontier" by Leonardo Luxemburg in *Films of a Changing World: A Critical International Guide*, Vol. II, edited by Jean Marie Ackerman, Washington, D.C. 1977; "The Role of Film in Cuban Development" by Andres Hernandez in *Films of a Changing World: A Critical International Guide* edited by Jean Marie Ackerman, Washington, D.C. 1977; "*Lucia*: Visual Style and Historical Portrayal" by John Mraz in *Jump Cut* (Chicago), December 1978; "Introduction to Revolutionary Cuban Cinema" by Julianne Burton in *Jump Cut* (Chicago), December 1978; "Every Point of Arrival is a Point of Departure: An Interview with Humberto Solás" by Marta Alvear in *Jump Cut* (Chicago), December 1978; "Cuba. 3. Humberto Solás—An Interview" by J. King, translated by C. Weller, in *Framework* (Norwich, England), spring 1979.

* * *

Robert Phillip Kolker has called Humberto Solás's *Lucia* "something of an encyclopedia of progressive film in the sixties," and this invigoratingly feminist trilogy is indeed one of the greatest examples of stylistic virtuosity to emerge from any national cinema in recent years. Solás's film depicts three women, all named Lucia, in their gradual acquisition of revolutionary consciousness, as they confront the specific historical dilemmas of their respective epochs-1895, 1932, and the postrevolutionary era of the 1960s. The film is remarkable in its ability to integrate diverse cinematic styles with an almost seamless fluidity. *Lucia* is a unique amalgam of Soviet style montage, hand-held shots in the manner of the early New Wave, and baroque stylization that recalls Antonnioni and Bertolucci.

The first episode (1895) is the most ambitious in its epic grandeur, although Solás's directoral restraint prevents his mise-en-scène from becoming hopelessly florid. This segment is superficially a revenge tragedy, although the emphasis on the suffering engendered by Spanish imperialism serves as tragic counterpoint to the central, doomed love affair. The frenetic shots of impoverished black soldiers on horseback remind the viewer of the travails of war at the very point that a Hollywood film would revert to a political escapism.

After the inspired grandiosity of the 1895 segment, the second episode is conceived within the more modest requirements of Hollywood melodrama. Yet, paradoxically, this segment is perhaps the most subtly subversive of Solás's film. He has absorbed all of the mannerisms of melodramatic kitsch, but subverts them in order to make a political statement that transcends the common, soap-operaish woes of the isolated individual. The 1932 Lucia's romantic disillusion coincides with her disillusion with the regime that replaces that of the dictatorial Machado. Personal happiness and societal goals have become dialectically interwined.

Lucia's last episode is understandably the most upbeat,

although it is curiously the most dated of the trilogy. This exuberant study in "consciousness raising" takes place during the ambitious literacy campaign of the 1960s. This was the time when many Cuban women first grasped the ways in which sexism continued to contaminate their lives during the postrevolutionary period. Although the third episode of *Lucia* seems relatively minor when contrasted with the other two, its comic brio and good-natured didacticism make it enjoyable.

Julianne Burton has remarked that "post-revolutionary Cuban cinema strives to unite cultural expression and political consciousness." *Lucia* is one of the most admirable results of this aspiration since Solás's narrative genius succeeds in explaining the much remarked-upon fusion of personal and political motivations during periods of revolutionary upheaval.

—Howard Feinstein

M. M, Mörder unter uns. M, Murderer Among Us. Production: Nero-Film A.G. Verlag Star Film-G.m.b.H.; black and white, 35mm; running time: originally 117 mins., according to Eisner an 89 min. version is most commonly shown now, though some sources list current version as 99 mins. Released 11 May 1931, Berlin. Re-released 1933 in the U.S. in a dubbed version.

Produced by Seymour Nebenzal; scenario by Thea von Harbou and Fritz Lang; from an article by Egon Jacobson, based on the Düsseldorf child murder case; directed by Fritz Lang; photography by Fritz Arno Wagner and Gustav Rathje; edited by Paul Falkenberg; sound by Adolf Jansen; production design by Emil Hasler and Karl Vollbrecht; music (*Murderer's Theme*) by Edward Grieg, based on an extract from *Peer Gynt*; backdrop photographs by Horst von Harbou.

Filmed during 6 weeks of 1931 in Nero-Film A.G. Verlag Star Film-G.m.b.H. studios in Berlin.

Cast: Peter Lorre (*Hans Beckert, the murderer*); Gustaf Gründgens (*Schränker*); Ellen Widmann (*Mrs. Beckman*); Inge Landgut (*Elsie Beckman*); Otto Wernicke (*Inspector Lohmann*); Franz Stein (*Minister*); Theodor Loos (*Inspector Groebor*); Fritz Gnass (*Burglar*); Fritz Odemar (*Safecracker*); Paul Kemp (*Pickpocket*); Theo Lingen (*Con-Man*); Georg John (*Blind beggar*); Karl Platen (*Night watchman*); Gerhard Bienart (*Inspector's secretary*); Rosa Valetti (*Landlady of the Crocodile Club*); Hertha von Walther (*Prostitute*); Ernst Stahl-Nachbaur (*Chief of Police*); Rudolf Blümner (*Lawyer*).

Publications:

Scripts—*M* by Thea von Harbou and Fritz Lang, edited by Gero Gandert and Ulrich Gregor, Hamburg 1963; *M: El Vampiro de Dusseldorf* by Thea von Harbou and Fritz Lang, Barcelona 1964; *M / Fritz Lang* by Theo von Harbou, English translation and description of action by Nicholas Garnham, London 1968; *Masterworks of the German Cinema* with an introduction by Roger Manvell, London 1973; reviews—by Leo Hirsch in *Berliner Tageblatt*, 12 May 1931; review by Rudolf Arnheim in *Die Weltbühne* (Germany), 19 May 1931; review by Magnus in *Variety* (New York), June 1931; review by Mordaunt Hall in *The New York Times*, 3 April 1933; review by Willian Troy in the

Nation (New York), 19 April 1933; books—*An Index to the Creative Work of Fritz Lang* by Herman Weinberg, supplement to *Sight and Sound* (London), index series, 1946; *From Caligari to Hitler: A Psychological History of the German Film* by Siegfried Kracauer, Princeton, New Jersey 1947; *Fritz Lang* by Francis Courtade, Paris 1963; *Fritz Lang* by Luc Moullet, Paris 1963; *Fritz Lang* edited by Alfred Eibel, Paris 1964; *The Sociology of Film Art* by George Huaco, New York 1966; *The Cinema of Fritz Lang* by Paul M. Jensen, New York 1969; *The Haunted Screen* by Lotte Eisner, Berkeley 1969; *Fritz Lang* by Claire Johnston, London 1969; *The German Cinema* by Roger Manvell and Heinrich Fraenkel, New York 1971; *Fritz Lang* by Frieda Grafe, Enno Patalas, and Hans Helmut Prinzler, Munich 1976; *Fritz Lang* by Lotte Eisner, London 1977; *Fritz Lang* by Robert Armour, Boston 1978; *The Films of Fritz Lang* by Frederick W. Ott, Secaucus, New Jersey 1979; *Fritz Lang* edited by Stephen Jenkins, London 1979; *Fritz Lang: A Guide to References and Resources* by E. Ann Kaplan, Boston 1981; articles—"Mein Film *M*: Ein Tatsachenbericht" by Fritz Lang in *Die Filmwoche* (Berlin), May 1931; article by Iris Barry in the *Museum of Modern Art Bulletin* (New York), June 1933; "Notes sur le style de Fritz Lang" by Lotte Eisner in *Revue du cinéma* (Paris), 1 February 1947; "The Genius of Fritz Lang" by Harry Wilson in *Film Quarterly* (London), summer 1947; "Fritz Lang: Suggestion und Stimmung" in *Gestalter der Filmkunst, von Asta Nielsen bis Walt Disney* by Ludwig Gesek, Vienna 1948; "One Facet of Lang's Art Prophetic of Hitlerism" in the *Herald Tribune* (New York), 21 March 1949; "Il Parabola di Fritz Lang" by Leonardo Autera in *Cinema* (Rome), 15 January 1954; "Lang, Director of *M*, Seeks Escape Net" by Don Ross in the *Herald Tribune* (New York), 20 May 1956; "Le Style de Fritz Lang" by Georges Franju in *Cahiers du cinéma* (Paris), November 1959; "Trajectoire de Fritz Lang" by Michel Mourlet in *Cahiers du cinéma* (Paris), September 1959; article by Andrew Sarris in *The Village Voice* (New York), 1 September 1960; "30 Jahre alt und alterlos: In der Urania ist Fritz Langs *M* jetzt wieder greifbar" by Georg Ramseger in *Die Welt* (Hamburg), 16 January 1960; "*M*, Le Maudit" by Raymond Bellour in *Cinéma 61* (Paris), no.58, 1961; "*M*: Wieder in Deutschland" by Dietrich Kuhlbrodt in *Filmkritik* (Munich), no.3, 1961; "Avec *M*, Le Maudit*, Fritz Lang en 1932 Annonçait la Destinée de L'Allemagne" by Jean Domarchi in *Arts* (Paris), 26 April 1961; "*M*, Le Maudit" by Rene Gilson in *Cinéma 61* (Paris), August/September 1961; "Kein Mörderspiel: Fritz Lang's *M* von 1931" in *Frankfurter Allgemeine Zeitung*, 11 December 1961; "*M*, Le Maudit" by Raymond Lefèvre in *Image et son* (Paris), June 1962; "Fritz Lang über *M*" by Gero Gandert in *M* (script) edited by Gandert and Ulrich Gregor, Hamburg 1963; "Le Style de *M*, Le Maudit" by Lotte Eisner in *Avant-Scène du cinéma* (Paris), 15 July 1964; "La Estructura Profètica en *M*" by Miguel Porter in *M: El Vampiro de Dusseldorf* (Spanish edition of the script), Barcelona 1964; "M, Le Maudit et L'Expressionisme" by Michel Sandras in *Image et son* (Paris), January 1964; "*M*" by Peter Jensen in *Classics of the Film* edited by Arthur Lennig, Madison, Wisconsin 1965; "Fritz Lang's *M*" by Eckart Jahnke in *Film* (East Berlin), no.6, 1965; "Fritz Lang (The German Period: 1919-1933)" in *Tower of Babel: Speculations on the Cinema* by Eric Rhode, New York 1966; "Aspects of Fritz Lang" by Paul Joannides in *Cinema* (London), August 1970; "Der Regisseur von *M*" by Wilfried Wiegand in *Frankfurter Allgemeine Zeitung*, 5 December 1970; "*M*" in *Close-Up: A Critical Perspective on Film* by Marsha Kinder and Beverly Houston, New York 1972; "De Mabuse à M: Le Travail de Fritz Lang" by Noel Burch in *Revue d'Esthétique* (Paris), special issue 1973; "Reply to Thierry Kuntzel's 'The Treatment of Ideology in the Textual Analysis of Film'" by Nicolas Garnham in *Screen* (London),

autumn 1973; "The Treatment of Ideology in the Textual Analysis of Film" by Thierry Kuntzel in *Screen* (London), autumn 1973; "Le Pouvoir et 'sa' folie" by R. Dadon in *Positif* (Paris), December 1976; "Deux textes pour servir une problématique: L'ouvrier dans le cinéma allemand des années 20" by V. Basset and D. Sotiaux in *Revue Belge du cinéma* (Brussels), June 1977; "Lang, Pabst, and Sound" by Noel Carroll in *Ciné-tracts* (Montreal), fall 1978; "Dossier: cu muet au parlant: l'ombre du son" by L. Audibert in *Cinematographe* (Paris), June 1979; "Uma obra-prima de Fritz Lang" by L. de Barros in *Celuloide* (Rio Major, Portugal), August 1979; "*M*: A Reconsideration" by J.S.M.J. Chang in *Literature/Film Quarterly* (Salisbury, Maryland), no.4, 1979.

* * *

Fritz Lang's films are marked by an uneasy tension between moral opposites: light and dark, innocence and evil, order and chaos. No subject is too mean or sordid to be outside or beneath human experience or to be illuminated, ultimately, by the vision of the artist. According to Lang, his films are like "the loveliest German fairy tales," which, despite their beauty, accumulate "an enormous amount of brutality, of cruelty and crime." Lang explains why this tension works, both in children's stories and in his films:

> ...In fairy tales the most simple and most moral law of mankind is upheld. The good are rewarded, the evil punished. The good becomes more touching through sorrow, the evil more hateful by the initial success of their wickedness.... Film yields the satisfaction of the fulfilled law just as naively as does the fairy tale, only in a form which conforms with its time.

Certainly *M*, Lang's first sound film, functions in this manner. Considered by most critics to be Lang's masterwork, *M* concerns the fulfillment of moral law while amply reflecting the horrors of its time: the years following World War I in Germany, a period, according to Lang, "of the deepest despair, hysteria, cynicism, unbridled vice." Rampant inflation and other chaotic elements gradually eroded the public order. By 1930, the year before Lang made *M*, Nazi paramilitary groups, with their own police and tribunals, murdered, bombed, and sabotaged while the Weimar bureaucracy slowly strangled in its own red tape.

Through a highly ordered juxtaposition of visual and aural images, and through an effective blending of expressionistic and realistic styles, Lang explores the effects of this growing chaos by depicting it on personal and social planes. On the personal plane, *M's* central character, child murderer Hans Beckert, embodies the struggle between a weakening order and an increasingly malevolent and powerful chaos. Possessed by a *doppelgänger*, Beckert is a childish, soft-bellied, petit bourgeois seized by uncontrollable homicidal passions:

> I can't help myself! I haven't any control over this evil thing that's inside me.... It's there all the time, driving me out to wander through the streets...It's me, pursuing myself...I want to escape...to escape from myself!...but it's impossible...I have to obey.

When persued by this *doppelgänger*, he whistles a theme from *Peer Gynt*, an appropiate leitmotif for his personal demon. A capricious and irreponsible character with no sense of self, Gynt saved his own life by allowing another man to drown. Similarly,

Beckert keeps his own divided psyche intact by killing young girls, by submitting irresponsibly to his most primal urges.

Lang portrays Beckert as both *doppelgänger*, victim and victimizer, and Gynt, a self-absorbed child, in a series of images, the chief ones being mirrors and other reflective surfaces. While the police attempt to develop a psychological profile of Beckert the camera cuts to Beckert peering and making faces at himself in the mirror. In another scene the camera catches Beckert eating an apple and looking into a store window where we see him surrounded by a diamond-shaped display of knives; when the camera shifts back to Beckert's point of view, we see a mirror at the back of the window display—again surrounded by knives— where a little girl, a potential victim, suddenly appears. Beckert then begins to whistle the theme from *Peer Gynt*, indicating that his *doppelgänger* has assumed control. Finally, Beckert doesn't know that his *doppelgänger* has become visible to others as well until he sees reflected in the window the mark of Cain, the "M," chalked on his shoulder.

Beckert's shadow is also a projection of the *doppelgänger*. As Elsie's ball bounces against a billboard posting a reward for the murderer, his shadow falls across the pillar—a visual echo of the "evil man in black" (with a chopper) portrayed in the opening children's ditty.

Such images suggest two ideas: 1) Beckert is self-absorbed and involuted, and 2) Beckert can be known only through his projections. The first point is conveyed through various visual and aural images: the target in a toy window spiralling endlessly into its own center (recalling the circles on the policemen's map); Beckert's oral fixations (eating apples and candy, drinking brandy, smoking cigarettes, biting his hand after a foiled abduction attempt); Beckert's relative silence until the last scene when he is forced to come to his own defense (that is, he can only speak to himself or to children). His projections and oral obsessions ultimately reveal and trap him: a pack of cigarettes puts the police on his trail, and his compulsive whistling alerts the beggars to his presence. He is trapped by his own "garbage" as it were (another example being the red pencil shavings). Lang repeats this theme by locating Beckert's final hiding place in a small locker full of junk—a vivid metaphor both for the meaningless disorder of his mind and for his self-confinement. Other scenes reinforce this notion: Beckert is stalked by beggers who live off the refuse of others, and he is ultimately brought to trial in an abandoned brewery by society's outcasts.

Beckert's personal chaos aggravates the chaos existing on the social plane: the apparent struggle between the police (who symbolize the Weimar Republic) and the underworld (who symbolize the Nazi organization). The real struggle, however, is between the two groups, who represent control, and Beckert, who represents lack of control. The erosion of control in postwar Germany is thus reflected in the growing *similarity*, not struggle between the two orginizations. Lang conveys this resemblance through skillful editing and scripting and by the use of similar settings, camera angles, and images for the two groups.

Lang's portrayal of their parallel investigations emphasizes the complementary nature of the police and the underworld. The camera cuts back and forth between police conferences and underworld meetings to show the following: a gesture and remark begun by the head of the underworld are completed by the chief of police. After a safecracker declares that the police must stop looking for Beckert in the underworld, an elderly detective concludes that the murderer must be a "peaceful little family man who wouldn't hurt a fly." A burglar stands up and leans against the back of his armchair, while the scene shifts to an inspector leaning over the back of his chair. Both rooms are slowly engulfed by cigarette smoke as the meetings progress, and the people get up and wander about as the parallel discussions unfold. Identical camera angles reinforce the similarities in dialogue and settings. The ultimate exchange of identities comes near the end of the manhunt and involves the leaders of the two groups: Schränker, the head of the underworld, disguises himself as a policeman to penetrate Beckert's hiding place, and Lohmann, the chief of police, uses "illegal" methods (lies and blackmail) to determine where the underworld has taken Beckert to be "tried."

Not content to make a "talking picture" as such, Lang again uses the technical innovation of sound to complement the message of the camera. Film scholar Thierry Kuntzel has argued that, to connect the police and the underworld, Lang employs two separate chains of visual and aural clues. At first, the underworld's surveillance (visual) and the police interrogations (aural) yield no results. Then two important clues emerge: the letter to the press (visual) and the whistling in front of the blind man (aural). The letter ultimately yields two visual clues for the police—the cigarette pack and the pencil shavings—whereas the underworld narrows in on Beckert through two aural clues— Beckert's second whistling in front of the blind man of the *Peer Gynt* theme and the sounds he makes while trying to escape from his hiding place.

In equating the police with the underworld Lang muddies the distinction between good and evil, order and chaos, on the social plane. In *M*'s final judgment scene, the distinctions are obscured on the personal plane as well. In his eloquent plea before the kangaroo court, Beckert changes from villain to helpless victim, both of his *doppelgänger* and of the criminal element of society. How can Lang deliver his fairy tale ending of a fulfilled moral law when innocence and guilt have become so hopelessly confounded? Lang's solution is to move "above" the action aurally, just as in earlier scenes he moved above the action visually— employing overhead or crane shots to imply omniscience or a divine perspective. We hear off-camera, "In the name of the law," and the action freezes. Because we do not see the speaker, higher law is implied—one that will stop the criminal elements of society and protect both innocent children and the murderous child within Beckert.

—Catherine Henry

MADAME DE... The Earrings of Madame de... Production: Franco-London Films, Indus, and Rizzoli; black and white, 35mm; running time: 105 mins. Released 1953.

Produced by Ralph Baum; screenplay by Max Ophüls, Marcel Achard, and Annette Wademant; from a novella by Louise de Vilmorin; directed by Max Ophüls; photography by Christian Matras; edited by Boris Lewin; production design by Jean d'Aubonne; music by Oscar Strauss and George Van Parys.

Cast: Danielle Darrieux (*Madame De*); Charles Boyer (*Monsieur De*); Vittorio De Sica (*Baron Donati*); Lia de Léa (*Monsieur De's mistress*); Jean Debucourt.

Publications:

Books—*Max Ophüls: An Index* by Richard Roud, London 1958; *Max Ophüls* by Georges Annenkov, Paris 1962; *Max Ophüls par Max Ophüls*, Paris 1963; *Max Ophüls* by Claude

Beylie, Paris 1963; *French Film* by Roy Armes, New York 1970; *French Cinema Since 1946: The Great Tradition*, Vol. I, by Roy Armes, New York 1976; *Ophüls* edited by Paul Willemen, London 1978; *Max Ophüls and the Cinema of Desire* by Alan Williams, New York 1980; articles—"*Madame de...*" by Lindsay Anderson in *Sight and Sound* (London), April/June 1954; "Ophüls and the Romantic Tradition" by Eugene Archer in *Yale French Studies* (Hartford, Connecticut), summer 1956; issue on Ophüls of *Cahiers du cinéma* (Paris), March 1958; "Danielle Darrieux" by Richard Whitehall in *Films and Filming* (London), December 1961; "*The Earrings of Madame de...*" by Robert Giard in *Seventh Art* (New York), summer 1964; "Max Ophüls" by Claude Beylie in *Anthologie du cinéma* (Paris), June 1965; "Memory and Max Ophüls" by Andrew Sarris in *Moviegoer*, summer 1966; "The Long Take" by Brian Henderson in *Film Comment* (New York), summer 1971; "Max Ophüls" by Andrew Sarris in *Film Comment* (New York), summer 1971; "*Madame de...*" by Foster Hirsch in *Film Comment* (New York), summer 1971; "Max Ophüls" by Andrew Sarris in *Film Comment* (New York), summer 1971; "Rythmes et masques" by P. Jouvet in *Cinématographe* (Paris), December 1977; 2 issues devoted to Ophüls of *Filmkritik* (Munich), November and December 1977.

* * *

The Earrings of Madame de... is one of the four films—all made in the 1950s shortly before his death—that constitute the highest expression of Max Ophüls's personal style. Along with *La Ronde*, *Le Plaisir*, and *Lola Montès*, the film combines all the technical ingredients and thematic concerns that had preoccupied Ophüls throughout his rather "up and down" career. Foremost among these interests, of course, was the intricate blending of complex, dazzling camera work with the themes of mankind's obsession with material objects—and a kind of poignant romanticism usually miscontrued by critics attempting to pigeonhole him as a director of women's films much like Douglas Sirk.

In *Madame de* there is a notion of mutability: the earrings, being material, remain constant, but the changing emotional circumstances of their possessors increase their symbolic value until they become the emblems of a domestic catastrophe. To some extent, however, the characters also remain static: they are unchanging in surface demeanor, yet the rush of time alters each one's status and effects a transition in their personalities. Madame de, for example, matures from a supercilious young girl into a truly passionate woman betrayed by the depth of her emotion, while, at the same time, her husband and lover evolve correspondingly but somewhat less noticeably because they are more reluctant than Madame de to deviate from their sense of propriety.

One element in the clash between relentless time and the seeming intransigence of objects and events is Ophul's tenacious tracking camera and its unrelenting interchange of shots and episodes. Another is the brisk unfolding of the narrative, which delicately balances a lush, rich atmosphere with lean camera technique. This interplay is particularly evident in the film's opening scene: the camera follows a woman's hand as it glides along a rack of expensive clothes in a lavishly appointed wardrobe, and then, without a pause, the camera clings to the woman as she admires her earrings in the mirror of her dressing table. In one continuous shot, Ophüls establishes a world of extravagant material possessions and then hones in on the frivolous, silly woman who seems virtually a part of them as she sits reflected in the mirror.

Later, however, in the ball sequence, the camera dazzlingly plays against the sumptuous surroundings to create a rush of time that encapsulates Madame de's progress from frivolity to tragedy without her having changed the tempo of her dance (a parallel to the changing value of the symbolic earrings as they float from hand to hand while remaining materially constant.) With her lover she dances round and round from one elegant ballroom to another under the constant gaze of the encircling camera, which reveals the deepening feelings of the couple. Finally, as they slowly glide through the last dance in the sequence, the air of gaiety disappears. The camera then, moves to follow a servant in one long continous shot as he goes from light to light, extinguishing them; the sequence ends in darkness as he throws a cover over a harp.

The party is over. Frivolity has became romance, and love becomes tragedy. As in all of Ophüls's best films, every element is interconnected—technique, pacing, theme and character—to intertwine both the light and tragic strains and to resolve the seemingly divergent tensions into a final mood of desolation.

—Stephen L. Hanson

MÄDCHEN IN UNIFORM. Girls in Uniform. Production: Deutsches Film Gemeinschaft; black and white, 35mm; running time: 98 mins.; length: 8799 feet. Released 1931. A new, reconstructed print was released in the 1970s.

Screenplay by Christa Winsloe and F.D. Andam; from the play *Yesterday and Today* by Christine Winsloe; directed by Leontine Sagan under the supervision of Carl Froelich; photography by Reimar Kuntze and Franz Weihmayr; music by Hansom Milde-Meissner.

Cast: Dorothea Wieck (*Fraülein von Bernburg*); Hertha Thiefe (*Manuela von Meinhardis*); Emilie Unda (*Headmistress*); Ellen Schwanneke (*Ilse von Westhagen*); Hedwig Schlichter (*Fraülein von Kosten*); Gertrud de Lalsky (*Manuela's aunt*).

Publications:

Reviews—"*Mädchen in Uniform*" in the *National Board of Review Magazine* (New York), September/October 1932; "*Madchen in Uniform*" by Watts in *Herald Tribune* (New York), 21 September 1932; books—*From Caligari to Hitler: A Psychological History of the German Film* by Siegfried Kracauer, Princeton, New Jersey 1974; *Cinema, The Magic Vehicle: A Guide to Its Achievement: Journey One: The Cinema Through 1949* edited by Jacek Klinowski and Adam Garbicz, Metuchen, New Jersey 1975; articles—"Leontine Sagan", interview by Forsyth Hardy in *Cinema Quarterly* (London), winter 1932; "4 Films from Germany" by Kraszna-Krausz in *Close Up* (London), March 1932; "Pabst and the Social Film" by Harry Potamkin in *Hound and Horn* (New York), January/March 1933; "42 Ans de cinéma" by Valerio Jahier in *Le Rôle intellectuel du cinéma*, Paris 1937; "Piger i uniform" by S. Kjørup in *Kosmorama* (Copenhagen), December 1972; "Maedchen in Uniform" by N. Scholar in *Women in Film* (Berkeley), summer 1975; "From Repressive Tolerance to Erotic Liberation" by B. Ruby Rich in *Jump Cut* (Chicago), March 1981; "Vorbemerkung" by H. Schlüpmann and K. Gramann in *Frauen und Film* (Berlin), June

1981; "Gestern und Heute", interview with Hertha Thiele in *Frauen und Film* (Berlin), June 1981.

* * *

Mädchen in Uniform was directed by Leontine Sagan under the supervision of Carl Froelich in 1931; it was based on the play *Yesterday and Today* by Christine Winsloe. Its subversive anti-Fascist, anti-patriarchal themes seem astonishing when one realizes that the film was shot in Germany just two years before Hitler's rise to power.

Mädchen in Uniform achieved great popularity in Paris, London and Berlin, but it was later banned in Germany by Goebbels, Hitler's cultural minister, for its unhealthy moral conclusions. For the next few decades, the film was almost forgotten and received little critical attention. It seems to have been lost somewhere in film history between German expressionism and the Nazi cinema. In the early 1970s interest in the film was revived by women's film festivals; it has come to be seen as the first truly radical lesbian film; and in the last decade *Mädchen in Uniform* has finally received the recognition it deserves.

The structure of the film is a mixture of montage and narrative sequences which inform each other and create an atmosphere which perhaps could not have been achieved by the use of one of these methods alone. The montage sequence at the beginning of the film—stone towers, statues, and marching soldiers—sets up a compliance and strength, a tone that introduces the audience to the life of the girls at school. From the constricting montage shots, the camera turns immediately to the girls' school. Periodically, still shots of the militaristic, patriarchal world outside the school are interspersed with the narrative. The audience is reminded that although the school is a feminine space (indeed, there are no male characters in the film), it is surrounded and even permeated by ubiquitous male authority. Yet, that authority is itself called into question by the narrative, the defiance that continues despite the prevalence of authoritarianism. By its structure, the film succeeds in creating a feminine space enclosed in the literal walls (as exemplified by the montage) of the outside world.

In her utilization of the new sound medium, Sagan was the most advanced director in pre-war Germany. Lotte Eisner said: "With this work, the German sound film reached its highest level." Not only Sagan's precise use of dialogue but also her use of sound as metaphor (the sounding trumpet at the beginning and end of the film) and her creation of atmosphere, the whispers of the girls exchanging secrets, their final desperate chanting of Manuela's name—all attest to the accuracy of Eisner's statement.

Siegfried Kracauer also praised Sagan for her cinematography. He noted her ability to impart the "symbolic power of light" to her images. Sagan's use of shadows adds not only depth to the flat screen but also meaning and atmosphere. Sagan's cinematography is an excellent example of what Eisner calls "*stimmung*" (emotion), which suggests the vibrations of the soul through the use of light. The lighting and shooting of the stairway is a notable example. Its ascending shadows and its center depth creates a tension in which the girls must operate, for the front, well-lighted stairs are off limits to them. The staircase is then a symbol of the girls' confinement, and its darkness literally shadows all of their activities.

Sagan also pioneered the cinematic convention of superimposition of one character's face over that of another to symbolize a deep psychological connection between them. She uses this technique in the film to convey moments of deep attraction between the teacher Fraulein von Bernburg and her student Manuela.

The fusion of their images suggests the strength of their bond. It was a technique used 30 years later by Bergman in *Persona* to achieve the same effect.

Mädchen in Uniform was the first film in Germany to be cooperatively produced. The Deutsches Film Gemeinschaft was created especially for this project—a cooperative film company formed by the cast and crew in which shares rather than salaries were distributed.

—Gretchen Elsner-Sommer

THE MAGNIFICENT AMBERSONS. Production: Mercury Productions; 1942; black and white, 35mm; running time: 88 mins. Released 1942 by RKO Radio Pictures Inc.

Produced by Orson Welles; screenplay by Orson Welles; from the novel by Booth Tarkington; directed by Orson Welles; photography by Stanley Cortez; edited by Robert Wise; sound by Bailey Fesler and James G. Stewart; art direction by Mark-Lee Kirk; music by Bernard Herrmann; special effects by Vernon L. Walker; costumes designed by Edward Stevenson. New York Film Critics' Award, Best Actress (Moorehead), 1942.

Cast: Joseph Cotten (*Eugene Morgan*); Dolores Costello (*Isabel Amberson Minafer*); Anne Baxter (*Lucy Morgan*); Tim Holt (*George Minafer*); Agnes Moorehead (*Fanny Amberson*); Ray Collins (*Jack Amberson*); Richard Bennett (*Major Amberson*); Don Dillaway (*Wilbur Minafer*).

Publications:

Books—*Orson Welles* by André Bazin, Paris 1950; *The Fabulous Orson Welles* by Peter Noble, London 1956; *The Cinema of Orson Welles* by Peter Bogdanovich, New York 1961; *Orson Welles* by Maurice Bessy, *Cinéma d'aujourd'hui* series, Paris 1963; *Orson Welles, l'éthique et l'esthétique* by various authors for *Études cinematographiques*, Paris 1963; *The Cinema of Orson Welles* by Peter Cowie, London 1965; *The Films of Orson Welles* by Charles Higham, Berkeley 1971; *Orson Welles* by Maurice Bessy, New York 1971; *This is Orson Welles* by Peter Bogdanovich and Orson Welles, New York 1972; *Orson Welles* by Joseph McBride, London 1972; *The Magic World of Orson Welles* by James Naremore, New York 1978; articles—"Controversy with RKO" in *Time* (New York), 20 July 1942; "Welles Labors Over *The Magnificent Ambersons* and Emerges with Good Film but Minus RKO Job" in *Newsweek* (New York), 20 July 1941; "La Splendeur des Amberson" in *La Revue du Cinéma* (Paris), December 1946; "The Magnificent Orson W." by G.C. Castello in *Bianco e nero* (Rome), January 1949; "Agnes Moorehead" in *Sight and Sound* (London), autumn 1955; "Notes on Film Acting" by Derek Prouse in *Sight and Sound* (London), spring 1955; "Orson Welles from *Citizen Kane* to *Othello*" by Roberto Pariante in *Bianco e nero* (Rome), March 1956; "L'Oeuvre d'Orson Welles" in *Cahiers du cinéma* (Paris), September 1958; "The Heroes of Welles" by Alan Stanbrook in *Film* (London), no.28, 1961; issue devoted to Welles in *Image et son* (Paris), no.139, 1961; issue devoted to Welles in *Cine Forum* (Venice), no.19, 1962; "Agnes Moorehead" by Ronald Bowers in *Films in Review* (New York), May 1966; "Orson Welles: Of Time and Loss" by William Johnson in *Film Quarterly* (Berkeley), fall 1967; "The Long Take" by Brian Henderson in *Film Comment* (New York), summer 1971; "Orson Welles' Use of Sound" by Phyllis Goldfarb in *Take One* (Montreal), July/August 1971; "Orson Welles: An Introduction" by Mike Prokosch in *Film Comment* (New York), summer 1971; "*The Magnificent Ambersons*" by Stephen Farber in *Film Comment* (New York), summer 1971; "Orson Welles and the Great American Dummy—Or, the Rise and Fall and Regeneration of Benjamin Franklin's Model American" by J. Smith in *Literature/Film Quarterly* (Salisbury, Maryland), summer 1974; "An American Film Institute Seminar with Stanley Cortez, ASC" by H. Schwartz in *American Cinematographer* (Los Angeles), November 1976; "*La Splendour des Ambersons*" by G. Vialle in *Image et son* (Paris), 308bis, 1976; "*The Magnificent Ambersons*" by Susan Karnes Passler in *Magill's Survey of Cinema, Vol. III* edited by Frank N. Magill, Englewood Cliffs, New Jersey 1980.

*   *   *

The Magnifient Ambersons has been called Orson Welles's near-masterpiece, second to *Citizen Kane*. That qualified description derives more from the fact that the film was "butchered" by RKO, rather than from any intrinsic shortcoming on the part of its director.

Following the financial disaster of *Kane*, RKO executives compelled Welles to choose as his next film a subject with commercial appeal. Welles wanted to film *The Pickwick Papers* with W.C. Fields but Fields's schedule would not permit it. As Booth Tarkington was a favorite novelist of Welles, he selected instead the author's 1919 Pulitzer Prize-winning novel about the decline and fall of an aristocratic family brought on by the encroaching industrial revolution at the turn of the century. Welles had already presented a radio version of the novel in 1939 starring himself and Walter Huston.

Welles wrote the script in nine days, deleting much of Tarkington's sentimentality, and with a Proustian remembrance of a life of gentility now past, concentrated on the psychological darkness which destroyed the Amberson clan. His was a literary rendering of what was essentially a second-rate novel, a lament, he says, "not so much for an epoch as for the sense of moral values which are destroyed." The film centers on the ill-fated love between the gentlemanly horseless carriage manufacturer Eugene Morgan and the exquisitely beautiful Amberson matriarch, Isabel; the reaction of her spoiled son George Minafer, whose "come-uppance" eventually transpires; and the fate of neurotic spinster aunt Fanny Minafer.

Welles's completed version ran 148 minutes which he reduced to 131. RKO then sent him to Brazil to direct the aborted *It's All True* and proceeded to edit the film to 88 minutes, including the insertion of the hospital scene at the end. This scene had not been written by Welles and was directed by Freddie Flick and scored by Roy Webb, instead of Bernard Herrmann whose haunting score is so essential a part of the film. This truncated version, says Welles, destroyed "the whole heart of the picture really."

Nevertheless what remains is a luxuriant motion picture combining Welles's unique directorial flair with what Jean Cocteau called "calm beauty." The beginning of the film provides a picture of a bygone era with its good humor and homey virtues, after which Welles slowly and deliberately unmasks the Ambersons' imperfections. The dramatic use of light and shadow in Stanley Cortez's deep-focus photography accentuates and enhances the characters' conflicts. Welles employed a nostalgic irising in and out to begin and end scenes, and he edited the film in the camera—scene by scene, vignette by vignette—rather than relying on the cutting room after the fact. He spoke the voice-over narration himself, a skill honed through his vast experience with radio, a narration he likened to the titles in silent films. He also incorporated overlapping dialogue and street noises as part of the sound track and used groupings of the townspeople in the film as a Greek chorus, whose chattering, gossipy observations of the vicissitudes of the Amberson-Morgans provided succinct commentary and embellished the storyline.

Paramount to the success of *Ambersons* is the excellent acting. Welles worked meticulously with his cast. Using his script as a guide, he discussed their characters with the actors, rehearsed them at length and then shot the scenes, often allowing them to improve the actual dialogue based on their understanding of their parts. The cast constituted a first-rate ensemble with Joseph Cotten a standout as the gentle, suave Eugene, though the acting honors unequivocally belong to Agnes Moorehead. Her virtuoso performance is one of the finest on the American screen and earned her the New York Film Critics Award.

Reviews of *Ambersons* were less than enthusiastic. Many seemed to expect a depiction of the typical family wrapped in sugar-spun Americana, rather than the in-depth analysis which revealed warts and all. *The New York Times* opined that Welles had wasted his abundant talents on "a relentlessly somber drama on a barren theme." The picture was not the commercial success that RKO had hoped for and it was well over a decade before the film was received and appreciated for the master stroke it is.

—Ronald Bowers

***

THE MALTESE FALCON. Production: Warner Bros. Pictures, Inc.; 1941; black and white, 35mm; running time: 100 mins. Released 3 October 1941.

Produced by Hal B. Wallis with Henry Blanke; screenplay by John Huston; from the novel by Dashiell Hammett; directed by John Huston; photography by Arthur Edeson; edited by Thomas Richards; sound by Oliver S. Garretson; art direction by Robert Haas; music by Adolph Deutsch, musical direction by Leo. F. Forbstein; costumes designed by Orry-Kelly.

Filmed June-July, 1941 in Warner Bros. studios. Cost: budgeted at $300,000.

Cast: Humphrey Bogart (*Sam Spade*); Mary Astor (*Brigid O'Shaughnessy*); Sidney Greenstreet (*Kasper Gutman, the Fat Man*); Peter Lorre (*Joel Cairo*); Elisha Cook, Jr. (*Wilmer Cook*); Lee Patrick (*Effie Perine*); Barton MacLane (*Detective Lieutenant*); Jerome Cowan (*Miles Archer*); Gladys George (*Iva Archer*); Ward Bond (*Detective Polhaus*); James Burke (*Luke*); Murray Alper (*Frank Richman*); John Hamilton (*Bryan*); Walter Huston (*Ship's officer*).

Publications:

Books—*The Maltese Falcon* by Dashiell Hammett, New York 1929; *John Huston* by Paul Davay, Paris 1957; *John Huston* by Jean-Claude Allais, Paris 1960; *John Huston, King Rebel* by William Nolan, New York 1955; *Bogey, The Man, The Actor, the Legend* by Jonathan Hill and Jonah Ruddy, London 1965;

Bogie by Joe Hyams, New York 1966; *John Huston* by Robert Benayoun, Paris 1966; *The Great Films: 50 Golden Years of Motion Pictures* by Bosley Crowther, New York 1967; *John Huston* by Riccardo Cecchini, Viridiana 1969; *John Huston, A Picture Treasury of His Films* by Romano Tozzi, New York 1971; *Movie-Made America* by Robert Sklar, New York 1975; *John Huston* by Axel Madsen, New York 1978; *John Huston: Maker of Magic* by Stuart Kaminsky, London 1978; *Film Noir* edited by Alain Silver and Elizabeth Ward, Woodstock, New York 1979; articles—"John Huston" in *Films and Filming* (London), October 1954; "Gunman no.1" by Peter Barnes in *Films and Filming* (London), September 1955; "The Private Eye" by Penelope Houston in *Sight and Sound* (London), summer 1956; article by Eugene Archer in *Film Culture* (New York), no.19, 1959; article by Eugene Archer in *Films and Filming* (London), September 1959 and October 1959; "Le Faucon maltais" by Marcel Martin in *Cinéma 62* (Paris), no.64, 1962; "The Maltese Falcon" by Allen Eyles in *Films and Filming* (London), November 1964; article by David Mallory in *Film Society Review* (New York), February 1966; "John Huston and the Figure in the Carpet" by John Russell Taylor in *Sight and Sound* (London), spring 1969; "Notes on Film Noir" by Paul Schrader in *Film Comment* (New York), spring 1972; "John Huston and *The Maltese Falcon*" by James Naremore in *Literature/Film Quarterly* (Salisbury, Maryland), July 1973; "Pursuit of the Falcon" by Gordon Gow in *Films and Filming* (London), March 1974; "John Huston and *The Maltese Falcon*" by J. Naremore in *Literature/Film Quarterly* (Salisbury, Maryland), summer 1973; "The Maltese Falcon" by Greg Beal and Peg Masterson in *Cinema Texas Program Notes* (Austin), 16 September 1976; "Le Falcon maltais" by F. Guérif in *Lumière du Cinéma* (Paris), March 1977; "The Maltese Falcon and Casablanca" by D. McVay in *Focus on Film* (London), no.30, 1978; "Le Faucon Maltais" by R. Benayoun in *Avant-Scène du cinéma* (Paris), 1 October 1979; "Rediscovery: Blues in the Night" by William K. Everson in *Films in Review* (New York), March 1980.

*   *   *

The Maltese Falcon opens with credits appearing over the falcon statue, which casts a shadow into the depth of the frame. There follows a printed commentary, over the image, about the falcon's history. A shot of San Francisco, the Golden Gate Bridge, establishes location, and we move to the Spade and Archer sign on the window of their office. The shadow letters "Spade and Archer" appear on the office floor throughout the opening scene. Spade and Archer share the same office, are inextricably linked, and, we discover, even share Archer's wife, Iva (Gladys George). John Huston, in his first directing effort, quickly establishes the link between the two men so that later, when Spade (Humphrey Bogart) denounces Brigid (Mary Astor) for Archer's murder, we understand that it has nothing to do with Spade's like or dislike of his partner. The situation and atmosphere have been economically achieved.

To emphasize the constriction of investigation, Huston frequently limits the space in which Spade must move. Spade's office is small; so is his apartment. In fact, in a departure from convention, Huston chose to build some of his sets with ceilings. (The more usual procedure during that period of filmmaking was not to show the ceiling so that lights could be placed above the action and the camera could be free to move upward.) Huston also explored a unique style of framing with *The Maltese Falcon*. Following his own sketches, he set up shots as if they were paintings. For instance, Huston placed characters in the foreground of a shot, their faces often covering half the screen. Frequently, too, the character is not talking, but listening. His reactions thus become more important than those of the person who is speaking or moving.

The Maltese Falcon presented situations that Huston would return to again and again. Spade is the obsessed professional, a proud man who will adhere to a principle unto death. Women are a threat, temptations that can only sway the hero from his professional commitment. They may be wilfully trying to deceive, as Brigid and Iva, or (as in later Huston films), they may be the unwitting cause of the protagonist's defeat or near-defeat. Protagonists in Huston films frequently take risks, gamble with their lives. Spade constantly taunts the mad Wilmer, even using Huston's favorite personal referent—"kid"—to goad him. The taunting is potentially dangerous, but Spade enjoys it.

As Huston was to develop as a director, the image of the ill-fated group that begins with *Falcon* was to emerge more strongly. Gutman, Cairo, Wilmer, and Brigid are parts of an alliance of greed. They distrust each other but also respect each other. Spade refuses to join the group and survives. The others don't. Huston was to increasingly develop the idea that groups are doomed families, the survivors of which most learn to accept defeat with grace and dignity.

The idea of appreciating expert deception also emerges in *Falcon*. Bogart's admiration for Brigid's ability to lie is part of his love for her "You're good, you're real good," he says with a smile after a particular lie. In contrast, Spade is scornful of Iva because her lies are so transparent. A Huston hero, like Huston, appreciates wit, intelligence, and a good performance even if they come from a consummate villain.

Although Huston and others have suggested that *The Maltese Falcon* is almost a line-by-line filming of the novel, there are important technical and sequential, as well as plot and character, differences between the two versions of the story. Hammett's original novel was written and set in 1928-1929; the Huston version is clearly updated to 1940. Also, the conclusions of Hammett's novel is quite different from that of Huston's film. The film ends with Sam Spade watching Brigid disappear through the prisonlike bars of the elevator of his apartment building. Hammett's novel ends with Spade back in his office, where he puts his arm around the waist of his secretary, Effie, and she pulls away from him in confusion because he has turned Brigid in. The novel's last few lines indicate that Spade will have to deal with Iva Archer, who has come to see him again.

Such alterations are, however, less important than the film's dark humor, the deceit and paranoia of it characters, and the brooding darkness and matter-of-fact presentation that made *The Maltese Falcon* the first clear step into film noir.

—Stuart M. Kaminsky

THE MAN IN THE WHITE SUIT. Production: Ealing Studios; black and white, 35mm; running time: 85 mins., some sources list 81 mins. Released 1952 by Universal-International.

Produced by Michael Balcon with Sidney Cole; screenplay by Roger MacDougall, John Dighton, and Alexander Mackendrick; directed by Alexander Mackendrick; photography by Douglas Slocombe; edited by Bernard Gribble; sound edited by Mary Habberfield; music by Benjamin Frankel; white suit designed by Anthony Mendleson.

Cast: Alec Guiness (*Sidney Stratton*); Joan Greenwood (*Daphne Birnley*); Cecil Parker (*Alan Birnley*); Michael Gough (*Michael Corland*); Ernest Thesiger (*Sir John Kierlaw*); Vida Hope (*Bertha*); Howard Marion Crawford; Miles Malleson; George Benson; Edie Martin.

Publications:

Scripts—"*The Man in the White Suit*" (script extract) by Roger MacDougall, John Dighton, and Alexander Mackendrick in *Sight and Sound* (London), November/December 1951; reviews—by Gavin Lambert in *Sight and Sound* (London), November/December 1951; review by B.G. Marple in *Films in Review* (New York), March 1952; books—*Michael Balcon's 25 Years in Films* edited by M. Danieschewsky, London 1947; *Alec Guiness* by Kenneth Tynan, New York 1955; *(Michael Balcon Presents) A Lifetime of Films* by Michael Balcon, London 1969; *Cinema in Britain* by Ivan Butler, New York 1973; *The Film Business—A History of British Cinema* by Ernest Betts, New York 1973; *Ealing Studios* by Charles Barr, London 1977; articles—"A Day in the Life of a Film: *The Man in the White Suit*" in *Sight and Sound* (London), April 1951; illustrations in *Sight and Sound* (London), April 1951; "Ealing: The Studio in Surburbia" by Kenneth Tynan in *Films and Filming* (London), November 1955; "Man of Many Faces" by Derek Hill in *Films and Filming* (London), February 1955; "Ealing's Way of Life" by Kenneth Tynan in *Films and Filming* (London), December 1955; "Mackendrick Finds the Sweet Smell of Success" by John Cutts in *Films and Filming* (London), June 1957; "British Feature Directors: an Index to Their Work" in *Sight and Sound*, supplement, index series, autumn 1958; "Alec Guiness" by Douglas McVay in *Films and Filming* (London), May 1961; "*The Man in the White Suit*" by J.B. Hoare in *Screen Education Yearbook*, 1960-61; "Survivor" by Penelope Houston in *Sight and Sound* (London), winter 1962-63; "Alexander Mackendrick" in *Films and Filming* (London), January 1963; AFI University Advisory Committee Seminar in *Dialogue on Film* (Washington, D.C.), entire issue 1972; "Projecting Britain and the British Character: Ealing Studios" by Charles Barr in *Screen* (London), summer 1974; "*The Man in the White Suit*" by David Bartholomew in *Magill's Survey of Cinema, Vol. III* edited by Frank N. Magill, Englewood Cliffs, New Jersey 1980.

*   *   *

The Man in the White Suit was one of a number of post-World War II comedies produced by London's Ealing Studios under the supervision of production chief Michael Balcon, who upgraded the company's image from that of a prewar producer of music hall comedy vehicles to one that produced films of a more substantial if somewhat insular nature. Loosely termed "The Ealing Comedies," these light films employed original scripts from the studio's cadre of talented writers, which included T.E.B. Clarke, William Rose, Roger MacDougall and John Dighton. Utilizing techniques and styles evolved from the highly realistic films produced by the company during the war, the writers created films like *Passport to Pimlico* (1949), *Whisky Galore* (1949) and *The Lavender Hill Mob* (1951) which redefined the boundaries of filmed comedy.

These small films were masterful blends of English domesticity, irreverent understated wit and unassuming production values which drew their subject matter from actual events.

According to the formula, the typical screenplay establishes a realistic, completely believable setting and introduces into it one or more bizarre events. The humor thus arises from the reactions of relatively normal human beings to occurrences that they don't fully understand. In *The Man in the White Suit*, the realistic milieu is a textile mill. Into this smooth functioning operation comes a chemist who invents a super fabic that will not wear out, tear or get dirty. The reaction to this unbelievable development is initially one of optimism until the eventual panic sets in.

In every Ealing comedy, resistance is normally applied by the established order, usually a business or governmental bureaucracy, but in *The Man in the White Suit* Sidney Stratton (Alec Guinness), the miracle fabric's inventor, is threatened from all sides, and the film is developed more as a vehicle for social satire than are the others in the series. As might be expected, the fabric industry is pictured as wanting to destroy a fabric that will cause it to lose profits, but the workers and potential consumers are also against it because it will mean unemployment and depressed economic conditions for an industry that depends on clothing's wearing out. The film, therefore, unites labor, management and government as objects of satire; they are banded together to prevent technological progress.

The director, Alexander Mackendrick, shifts the barb of his satire subtly from observations of the workers and their union representatives led by the burly shop steward Bertha (Vida Hope) to the almost aristocratic captains of industry as they exercise the political machinations of their respective power bases. Lost in the shuffle, however, is the obvious truth that the vagaries of fashion and sheer physical growth will always create a need for new clothes and keep the industry afloat. Such is the greed and duplicity of all of the factions depicted that they are easy targets for the film's droll observations.

The Man in the White Suits was, with *Kind Hearts and Coronets* (1949), also featuring Alec Guinness, one of two films that went beyond the norm of Ealing comedies and developed humor into acerbic social criticism. Although both employed the successful formula of the genre, through subtle modifications they produced in the first instance a deft social satire and in the second the definitive "black comedy." Employing relatively spartan scripts and directed with an eye for a steady, unhurried pacing of the action, both films have become minor classics of the comedy genre, and *The Man in the White Suit* in particular has achieved the distinction of being perhaps the sharpest production from a studio that was synonymous with postwar comedy.

—Stephen L. Hanson

MAN OF ARAN. Production: Gainsborough Pictures, Ltd. for Gaumont-British Corp.; black and white, 35mm; running time: 76 mins. Released 25 April 1934, London.

Produced by Michael Balcon; screenplay by Robert Flaherty with Frances Flaherty, with scenarist credit for John Goldman; directed by Robert Flaherty; photography by Robert Flaherty, David Flaherty, and John Taylor; edited by John Goldman; sound by H. Hand; music by John Greenwood.

Filmed approximately 1931-33 in the Aran Islands, off the coast of Ireland. Venice International Film Festival, Best Foreign Film, 1934.

Cast: Colman "Tiger" King (*A man of Aran*); Maggie Dirrane (*His wife*); Michael Dillane (*Their son*); Pat Mullin (*Himself*);

Patch Ruadh (*Red Beard*); Patcheen Flaherty and Tommy O'Roarke (*The shark hunters*); Patcheen Conneely, Stephen Dirrane, Mac McDonough (*The curragh men*).

Publications:

Scripts—*Man of Aran* by Pat Mullen, Cambridge, Massachusetts 1970; reviews—"Rock and Water" by Otis Ferguson in *The New Republic* (New York), 7 November 1934; "The Play and the Screen" by Vernon Grenville in *Commonweal* (New York), 9 November 1934; "*Man of Aran*" by Brian O'Neil in the *New Masses* (New York), 30 October 1934; "*Man of Aran*" by Paul Rotha in *Sight and Sound* (London), summer 1934; "*Man of Aran*" by Andre Sennwald in *The New York Times*, 19 October 1934; books—*Man of Aran* by Pat Mullen, New York 1935; *The World of Robert Flaherty* by Richard Griffith, New York 1953; *The Odyssey of a Film-Maker: Robert Flaherty's Story* by Frances Flaherty, Urbana, Illinois 1960; *Robert Flaherty* by Jose Clemente, Madrid 1963; *Robert Flaherty* by Carlos Fernandez Cuenca, Madrid 1963; *Robert Flaherty* compiled by Wolfgang Klaue, Berlin (East), 1964; *Robert J. Flaherty* by Henri Agel, Paris 1965; *The Innocent Eye: The Life of Robert Flaherty* by Arthur Calder-Marshall, London 1970; *Nonfiction Film: A Critical History* by Richard Barsam, New York 1973; *Robert J. Flaherty* by Antonio Napolitano, Florence 1975; *Robert Flaherty: A Guide to References and Resources* by William T. Murphy, Boston 1978; articles—"Primitive Life on Aran Islands" in the *Herald Tribune* (New York), 24 June 1934; "Subjects and Stories" by Graham Greene in *Footnotes to the Film* edited by Charles Davy, New York 1938; "Hommage a Robert Flaherty" by Georges Sadoul in *Les Lettres françaises* (Paris), 13 September 1951; "Robert Flaherty und seine Film" by Fritz Kempe in *Film Bild Ton* (Munich), December 1952; "How *Man of Aran* Came Into Being" by Frances Flaherty in *Film News* (New York), no.3, 1953; "Flaherty's Finest Film" by Rohama Lee in *Film News* (New York), no.3, 1953; "Robert Flaherty" by Marcel Martin in *Anthologie du cinéma*, Vol. I, Paris 1965; "Flaherty and the Idea of Documentary" in *Film and Reality: An Historical Survey* by Roy Armes, Baltimore 1974; "How the Myth Was Made" by G. Hitchens in *Film Library Quarterly* (New York), no.3, 1978; "Independents" by A. Vogel in *Film Comment* (New York), March/April 1979.

*   *   *

Robert Flaherty's third major film portrayed the lives of a family of fisher folk on the Aran Islands, located off the coast of Galway, Ireland. Flaherty selected this location and subject, because of its isolation, as the western outpost of European civilization. In addition, the daily struggle between the islanders and the sea perfectly suited his interests and concerns. The struggle and conflict that he naively sought in Samoa while making *Moana* were evident everywhere on the Aran Islands. A way of life was threatened and already changing. Consequently, Flaherty recreates the patterns of life as they might have existed in an earlier age.

The re-creation is carried out with a fair amount of poetic license. The family is not a real one. They were selected from the locals because of their photogenic appearance. The boating sequences were shot during rough seas that the fishermen would normally avoid. And fishing for basking sharks was a skill that the islanders had not used in many years.

Nevertheless, the merits of this documentary are many. There is Flaherty's usual concern for photographic detail and tonal values; and his continued experimentations with long-lens photography created some of the best marine footage ever made, capturing the sea's menacing power.

This film precipitated an interesting critical debate. There was sharp disagreement between the popular press and the documentary specialists who wrote for magazines, journals, and other publications. The former praised the film for its simple beauty, nobility of purpose, and its powerful portrayal of a family striving to eke out a living from unrelenting nature. Other critics, influenced by Grierson, film developments in the Soviet Union, and the dismal economic depression of 1930s, chastized Flaherty at great length for not portraying the real struggle of the islanders, at its core an economic one against absentee landlords. Such critics viewed the film as an anachronism that ignored the real life of the islanders, their customs, traditions, and ceremonies, in favor of some romantic notion about man againt sea. For such writers, the documentary was obligated to be a means to a social end. Grierson came to the film's defense, partially to pay homage, but also to underscore Flaherty's powerful sense of observation and his ability to stretch the conventions of commercial cinema. *Man of Aran*, he concluded, reflected Flaherty's own personality.

Man of Aran remains a wonderful visual experience that easily captures one's curiosity but ultimately fails to interest us in the personal lives of his heros. More humanity and less myth are needed.

—William T. Murphy

THE MAN WHO SHOT LIBERTY VALANCE. Production: Ford Productions-Paramount; 1962; black and white, 35mm; running time: 122 mins. Released April 1962.

Produced by Willis Goldbeck; screenplay by Willis Goldbeck and James Warner Bellah; from the story by Dorothy M. Johnson; directed by John Ford; photography by William H. Clothier; edited by Otho Lovering; sound by Philip Mitchell; set decoration by Sam Comer and Darrell Silvera; art direction by Hal Pereira and Eddie Imazu; music by Cyril Mockridge, music directed by Irvin Talbot, theme from *Young Mr. Lincoln* by Alfred Newman; costumes designed by Edith Head.

Filmed September 1961 in Paramount studios. Cost: budgeted at $3.2 million, (according to Ford's grandson).

Cast: James Stewart (*Ransom Stoddard*); John Wayne (*Tom Doniphon*); Vera Miles (*Hallie Stoddard*); Lee Marvin (*Liberty Valance*); Edmond O'Brien (*Dutton Peabody*); Andy Devine (*Link Appleyard*); Ken Murray (*Doc Willoughby*); John Carradine (*Starbuckle*); Jeanette Nolan (*Nora Ericson*); John Qualen (*Peter Ericson*); Willis Bouchey (*Jason Tully*); Carleton Young (*Maxwell Scott*); Woody Strode (*Pompey*); Denver Pyle (*Amos Carruthers*); Strother Martin (*Floyd*); Lee Van Cleef (*Reese*); Robert F. Simon (*Handy Strong*); O.Z. Whitehead (*Ben Carruthers*); Paul Birch (*Mayor Winder*); Joseph Hoover (*Hasbrouck*); Jack Pennick (*Barman*): Anna Lee (*Passenger*); Charles Seel (*President, Election Council*); Shug Fisher (*Drunk*); Earle Hodgins; Stuart Holmes; Dorothy Phillips; Buddy Roosevelt; Gertrude Astor; Eva Novak; Slim Talbot; Monty Montana; Bill Henry; John B. Whiteford; Helen Gibson; Major Sam Harris.

Publications:

Reviews—by DuPre Jones in *Sight and Sound* (London), summer 1962; review by Wilfred Mifflin in *Films in Review*, May 1962; books—*Indian Country* by Dorothy Johnson, New York 1949; *The Films of John Ford* by Geoge J. Mitchell, 1963; *John Ford* by Philippe Haudiquet, Paris 1964; *John Ford* by Peter Bogdanovich, Berkeley 1968; *Horizons West* by Jim Kitses, Bloomington, Indiana 1970; *The Cinema of John Ford* by John Baxter, New York 1971; *The Six-Gun Mystique* by John Cawelti, Bowling Green, Ohio 1971; *24 Times a Second* by William Pechter, New York 1972; *The Western Films of John Ford* by Janey Place, Secaucus, New Jersey 1973; *American Film Genres* by Stuart Kaminsky, Dayton, Ohio 1974; *John Ford* by Joseph McBride and Michael Wilmington, New York 1975; *The John Ford Movie Mystery* by Andrew Sarris, London 1976; *John Ford* by Andrew Sinclair, New York 1979; *Pappy: The Life of John Ford* by Dan Ford, Englewood Cliffs, New Jersey 1979; articles—"Cactus Rosebud or the Man Who Shot Liberty Valance" by Andrew Sarris in *Film Culture* (New York), summer 1962; "The 5 Worlds of John Ford" by Douglas McVay in *Films and Filming* (London), June 1962; article by Ernest Callenbach in *Film Quarterly* (Berkeley), winter 1963-64; "James Stewart" by William Sweigart in *Films in Review* (New York), December 1964; "*Der Mann, der Liberty Valance erschloss*" by F.W. Vöbel in *Filmanalysen 2* edited by Franz Everschor, Düsseldorf, 1964; issue devoted to John Ford of *Cahiers du cinéma* (Paris), October 1966; "Our Way West" by Burt Kennedy in *Films and Filming* (London), October 1969; "Tall in the Saddle" by Dennis John Hall in *Films and Filming* (London), October 1969; "Shall We Gather at the River: The Late Films of John Ford" by Robin Wood in *Film Comment*, fall 1971; "*The Man Who Shot Liberty Valance*" by David Bordwell in *Film Comment* (New York), fall 1971; "Persistence of Vision" by William Pechter in *24 Frames a Second*, New York 1971; "The Auteur Theory" in *Signs and Meaning in the Cinema* by Peter Wollen, London 1972; "John Ford's Wilderness—*The Man Who Shot Liberty Valance*" by D.F. Coursen in *Sight and Sound* (London), autumn 1978; "Genre and History—*Fort Apache* and *Liberty Valance*" by D. Pye in *Movie* (London), winter 1977-78; "*The Man Who Shot Liberty Valance*" by Ed Lowry in *Cinema Texas Program Notes* (Austin), 9 November 1978; "La Structure de l'églantine" by B. Amengual in *Positif* (Paris), June 1981.

*   *   *

John Ford's *The Man Who Shot Liberty Valance* opened to mixed reviews in 1962, and played on the second half of many double bills. But two decades later critics see this film quite differently. *The Man Who Shot Liberty Valance* is now regarded as one of the greatest works of one of America's greatest filmmakers. It reaffirms John Ford's reputation as the master of the most American of the film genres, the western.

Coming late in the career of a director with a long-standing reputation as a creator of popular films, *The Man Who Shot Liberty Valance* was completely an auteur project. Ford located the property, developed a script with long-time associates Willis Goldbeck and James Warner Bellah, and raised half the proposed $3.2 million budget needed for an all-star cast which included John Wayne and James Stewart in their first film together. Because Wayne had just signed a ten picture contract with Paramount (for which he was paid $6 million in advance), Ford took his package deal to that particular studio. Shooting commenced in September 1961. The completed film was released

in April 1962, and quickly played out, to be resurrected a decade later in revivals and retrospectives.

The Man Who Shot Liberty Valance presents a very dark view of the western legend. Although the opening sequence is of an "iron horse," confidently moving through the desert, the rest of the film is by and large confined to sequences indoors, usually taking place at night—recorded on a Hollywood sound stage. The Old West has lost the epic proportions of Monument Valley, and moved to a ramshackle town, populated by a handful of people. (An unseen range war occurs off-screen.) The West has been settled; the myth of the western hero is remembered only in flashbacks. Indeed, the western era has already past when the film begins. Senator Ransom Stoddard (James Stewart) and his wife Hallie (Vera Miles) journey to hometown Shinbone to attend the funeral of an old friend, the true western hero Tom Doniphon (John Wayne). Through a long flashback (one that comprises most of the film) we learn how progress came to the West. On his first journey to Shinbone, Stoddard, an earnest young lawyer from the East, is robbed and beaten by archetypal outlaw Liberty Valance (Lee Marvin). Stoddard seeks revenge by trying to civilize the community. But in the end Stoddard can bring the civilized values of the East only through deception and violence. He earns his fame not through the law but as a man who stood up to and killed evil incarnate, Liberty Valance.

Tom Doniphon is more tragically caught up in the conflict between civilization and chaos, order and violence: Doniphon is doomed to live in a world to which he can not adapt. Structurally, the film counterpoints the rise of Stoddard with the fall of Doniphon. Gradually Stoddard educates and draws Doniphon's "girl" to him through his teachings. (Stoddard literally becomes the school teacher.) Ultimately, when Stoddard does face off with Liberty Valance, the film tells the viewer that it is Doniphon, in a last heroic act, who shoots Liberty Valance. If a viewer looks closely, however, nowhere does the film actually show us who killed Liberty Valance. It is impossible to tell visually whether the bullet was from the gun of Tom Doniphon or that of Ransom Stoddard. But the myth continues. The out-of-date western hero loses his girl, and settles into a life of obscurity, while the lawyer from the East rises to heights of political power, becoming a senator in Washington, D.C.

At the nominating convention for statehood, Stoddard assumes authority. In this sequence Ford mocks the heart of the American political process. This becomes clear when the cattle-baron candidate, one Buck Langhorn, is nominated. Dressed in western dude fashion, this grotesque cowboy "image" is all that remains of the values and honor associated with a western hero like Tom Doniphon. Aptly, when the doors swing shut on the convention, that is the last time we see Doniphon alive. As the newspaper editor notes later about Stoddard's rise to power, "When the legend becomes fact, print the legend." The desert is now a garden, full of the symbolic cactus rose. The myth is complete with "progress" coming to the old West. The honor and values of *Stagecoach*, the *Iron Horse*, and earlier Ford westerns will never return again.

To deconstruct the western as story, Ford finally acknowledged its role as a myth and legend in the history and development of the United States. To create a timeless world of formal artifice, Ford filmed *The Man Who Shot Liberty Valance* in black and white on a studio soundstage. Furthermore, Ford's distinction between fact and legend also involved the restructuring of the film's time by placing the act of telling between past and present, thus reinforcing the process of deconstructing mythmaking. This narrative framework, the stark stylization of mise-en-scène, and the use of lighting render the flashback (and the flashback in the flashback) into nightmare. This is a stripped down western; the colorful legend and look of Monument Valley have become a barren world of broken dreams.

In the end *The Man Who Shot Liberty Valance* is a great filmmaker's own critique of the form in which he did his best work. It probably now ranks second to *The Searchers* (1956) in Ford's oeuvre, and is part of what critics and historians now consider Ford's greatest period, the film—especially the westerns—made after World War II. Ford's career is now seen as a slow, steady parabola of change, beginning with certainties about the values of civilization and ending with abject filmmaking, always seeming to follow the rules, yet always breaking with them. *The Man Who Shot Liberty Valance* must be seen as a great achievement of a filmmaker at the height of his power and understanding.

—Douglas Gomery

MANHATTAN. Production: A Jack Rollins-Charles H. Joffe Production for United Artists; 1979; black and white, 35mm, Panavision; running time: 96 mins. Released 1979.

Produced by Charles H. Joffe; screenplay by Woody Allen and Marshall Brickman; directed by Woody Allen; photography by Gordon Willis; edited by Susan E. Morse; production design by Mel Bourne; music by George Gershwin; costumes designed by Albert Wolsky.

Filmed 1978 in New York City. New York Film Critics Awards for Best Direction (shared with Robert Benton for *Kramer Vs. Kramer*) and Best Supporting Actress (Streep, award also includes her performances in *Kramer Vs. Kramer and Seduction of Joe Tynan*), 1979.

Cast: Woody Allen (*Isaac Davis*); Diane Keaton (*Mary Wilke*); Mariel Hemingway (*Tracy*); Michael Murphy (*Yale*); Meryl Streep (*Jill*); Anne Byrne (*Emily*).

Publications:

Script—*Four Films of Woody Allen*, New York 1982; reviews—"*Manhattan*" by D. Bartholomew in *Film Bulletin* (Philadelphia), June 1979; "*Manhattan*" by S. Ginsberg in *Variety* (New York), 25 April 1979; "The Screen: Woody Allen's *Manhattan*" by Vincent Canby in *The New York Times*, 25 April 1979; "A Little Faith in People" by R. Corliss in *Film Comment* (New York), May/June 1979; "The Current Cinema: The Black-and-White Apple" by Penelope Gilliatt in the *New Yorker*, 30 April 1979; "Stanley Kauffmann on Films: Exteriors" in the *New Republic* (New York), 19 May 1979; "Woody's Big Apple" by J. Kroll in *Newsweek* (New York), 30 April 1979; "*Manhattan: A Cerebral Approach to Filmmaking"* by G. Morris in *Take One* (Montreal), no.6, 1979; "Film: Nattaham" by John Simon in the *Nation* (New York), 22 June 1979; "Films in Focus: 'S Wonderful" by Andrew Sarris in *The Village Voice* (New York), 30 April 1979; "Rhapsody in Blue" by D. Denby in *New York*, 7 May 1979; "*Manhattan*" by Gordon Gow in *Films and Filming* (London), August 1979; "*Manhattan*" by M. Letremble in *Sequences* (Montreal), August 1979; "*Manhattan*" by J. Pym in *Sight and Sound* (London), no.4, 1979; "*Manhattan*" by L. Quart in *Cineaste* (New York), no.4, 1979; articles—"Woody Allen: Seit 50 Jahren hält der amerikanische Film den Mythos am Leben,

dass gleich um die Ecke das Glück auf dich wartet", interview by J. Kritz, in *Filmfaust* (Frankfurt), October 1979; "The Autobiography of Woody Allen" by M. Dempsey in *Film Comment* (New York), May/June 1979; "Woody Allen's Jewish American Gothic" by D.M. Friend in *Midstream* (New York), June/July 1979; "The Maturing of Woody Allen" by N. Gitelson in *The New York Times*, 22 April 1979; "United Artists' *Manhattan* Wins NSC Blue Ribbon Award" by S. Goldstein in *Boxoffice* (Kansas City, Missouri), 25 June 1979; "Woody Allen's Friends Were All There" by J. Klemesrud in *The New York Times*, 20 April 1979; "I Share My Character's Views on Men—And Stuff Like That" by J. Maslin *The New York Times*, 20 May 1979; "Woody Allen: God's Answer to Job" by H. Weidner in *Christian Century* (Chicago), 6 June 1979; "The Editing Room" by H. Alpert in *American Film* (Washington, D.C.), September 1979; "Cannes 79: *Manhattan*" by M. Amiel in *Cinéma 79* (Paris), July/August 1979; "Liebeserklaerung an eine Stadt" by W. Baer in *Film und Ton Magazine* (Munich), October 1979; "Films/TV: Islands" by R.A. Blake in *America* (New York), 12 May 1979; "*Manhattan*" by D. Castell in *Films Illustrated* (London), September 1979; "Woody Allen: Portrait de l'acteur en cineaste: *Manhattan* ou le temps retrouve" by G. Cebe in *Ecran* (Paris), 15 September 1979; "Foreign Fans Dig *Manhattan*: 14 Markets Yield UA $10.8-Mil" in *Variety* (New York), 26 December 1979; "Woody Allen—pamflecista wspolszesnej Ameryki" by J. Fuksiewicz in *Kino* (Warsaw), November 1979; "The Current Cinema: As Long as It Works" by V. Geng in the *New Yorker*, 6 August 1979; "Woody Allen in the Limelight" by R. Grenier in *Commentary* (New York), July 1979; "Images de la ville: Allen and Duras" by P. Maraval and J.C. Bonnet in *Cinématographe* (Paris), no.53, 1979; "*Manhattan* Wins Best Picture Award" by J. Maslin in *The New York Times*, 29 December 1979; "Comment: Woody Allen, Neighborhood Filmmaker" by L. McMurty in *American Film* (Washington, D.C.), September 1979; "The New Phase of Intelligence" by Andrew Sarris in *The Village Voice* (New York), 3 December 1979; "On Screen: The Canonization of Woody Allen" by L. Quart in *USA Today* (New York), September 1979; "Our Aliens and Theirs" by John Simon in the *National Review* (New York), 6 July 1979; "Films: *Manhattan*: Chic Obsessions" by J. Thurman in *MS* (New York), July 1979; "Woody Allen in *Manhattan*" by W.R. Wolf in *Film en Televisie* (Brussels), December 1979; "Woody Allen's *Manhattan*" in *Films and Filming* (London), July 1979; "Lens Cap: Making Sense in Metuchen" by S. Mallow in *Filmmakers Monthly* (Ward Hill, Massachusetts), July 1979; "*Manhattan*" by Douglas Blau in *Magill's Survey of Cinema, Vol. III* edited by Frank N. Magill, Englewood Cliffs, New Jersey 1980; "El cine de Woody Allen" by R. Median de la Serna in *Cine* (Mexico), March 1980; "Producing Woody: an Interview with Charles H. Joffe" by D. Teitelbaum in *Cinema Papers* (Melbourne), April/May 1980; "Dos encuentros con Woody Allen" by J. Ruiz in *Casablanca* (Madrid), February 1981; "Avatar del buhonero" by M. Fuster in *Contracampo* (Madrid), February 1981.

*   *   *

Manhattan opens with images of New York City over which the voice of Woody Allen, as writer Isaac Davis, begins chapter one of his new book: "He adored New York City. He idolized it out of proportion." The film is an homage to "Allen-town," to the city that spawned him, but unlike Allen's homage to the woman of his dreams (*Annie Hall*), here he idolizes the good while systematically removing the obviously negative. In the prologue he presents us with New York City's most glorious vistas: fireworks over Central Park, the skyline at dawn, the Empire State Building, the Brooklyn Bridge, all to the lush romantic sound of George Gershwin's *Rhapsody in Blue*. Gone are the messy vistas, the untidy streets, the horrors of the subway system, people of non-white lineage.... His book, an expanded version of an article he had written about his mother entitled "The Castrating Zionist," is, one can assume, this movie, and Isaac Davis is its author.

With typical deprecation, Isaac decides that the best way to achieve success is to write an autobiographical novel that is neither preachy nor angry, which focuses on an explication of his desired self-image. That image, like his image of the city, is a castrated one. While dwelling on the city's physical beauty, Isaac proceeds to effect an autopsy on his social set, his ultimate desire being an exposé of the decay of contemporary culture.

That social set consists of writers. Four of the main characters belong to that occupation: Isaac Davis is a television writer who quits his job to write his book; Yale is a teacher who is working on a biography of O'Neill; Mary Wilke is a journalist who writes on art and a variety of other topics; Jill is Isaac's ex-wife who publishes a feminist tract on their marriage entitled *Marriage, Divorce and Selfhood*. Throughout the film the names of great writers are bandied about, each one cited as if he were a reference point in the psychological development of the character. Thus Isaac refers to Strindberg, Bergman, Fellini, Kafka and Groucho Marx, his strategy being both reverential and referential. As he says to Yale: "I gotta model myself after someone!" The blend of writers cited certifies Isaac's neurotic condition. His problems, like those of the city, are intellectual.

As with other Allen films, this one also dwells on the impossibilty of lasting relationships. If Bergman and Fellini were the influences of *Interiors* and *Stardust Memories*, Orson Welles seems to be the working model here, most specifically the Welles of *The Lady from Shanghai*. A reflection of the real-life decay of Welles's marriage to Rita Hayworth, *Lady* abounds with bitter commentary on relationships. References to Hayworth, the buggy ride in Central Park, the use of the planetarium for a love scene, the romantic voice-over which begins *Manhattan*, and themes of decay all point to this film as an influence. In fact, the last line of dialogue from *Shanghai* could have been used to end *Manhattan*.

Filmed in Panavision on Technicolor stock, then printed in black and white, this film is Allen's most complex reflection on the artist as romantic—his draining of its color the most bittersweet stroke.

—Doug Tomlinson

THE MARCH OF TIME. Production: Time Inc.; black and white, 35mm; running time: about 20 mins. per episode. First episode released 1 February 1935, New York, by First Division Exchanges, Inc. After 1935 *The March of Time* was distributed through RKO/Radio, and later 20th Century Fox. The last episode was released in August, 1951.

Produced by Louis de Rochemont and Roy Larsen, but during WWII Louis resigned and was replaced by his brother Richard de Rochemont; edited by Louis de Rochemont and Roy Larsen, Louis replaced by brother Richard during WWII; technical management by Jack Bradford and Lothar Wolff.

Cost: the first 3 reels cost approximately $40,000, while $150,000 was used to launch the series. Special Academy Award for the series' significance to motion pictures for having revolutionized one of the most important branches of the industry—the newsreel, 1936.

Cast: Westbrook Van Voorhis (*Narrator*).

Publications:

Reviews—"Pictorial Journalism" (review of first episode) in *The New York Times*, 2 February 1935; "Pictorial Journalism" (review of first episode) by William Troy in the *Nation* (New York), 20 February 1935; "What Pictures Mean" (review of episode entitled "Inside Nazi Germany") by Mark Van Doren in the *Nation* (New York), 29 January 1938; books—*Documentary in American Television* by A. William Bluem, New York 1965; *Time Inc.: The Intimate History of a Publishing Enterprise, 1923-41* by Robert T. Elson, New York 1968; *The American Newsreel, 1911-1967* by Raymond Fielding, Norman, Oklahoma 1972; *The World of Time Inc.: The Initimate History of a Publishing Enterprise, Volume Two, 1941-60* by Robert T. Elson, New York 1968; *Nonfiction Film: A Critical History* by Richard Barsam, New York 1973; *Documentary: A History of the Nonfiction Film* by Erik Barnouw, New York 1974; *The March of Time, 1935-1951* by Raymond Fielding, New York 1978; articles—by Alistair Cooke in *Sight and Sound* (London), autumn 1935; "Re-enacted Events Make Bow" in *Newsweek* (New York), 9 February 1935; "Pictorial Journalism by Janet Mabie in *Christian Science Monitor Monthly* (Boston), 30 October 1935; "Celluloid Censorship" in *Time* (New York), 1 June 1936; "Time Muddles On" by George Dangerfield in *New Republic* (New York), 19 August 1936; "Freedom of Film and Press" in *Christian Century* (Chicago), 2 February 1938; "Inside Nazi Germany, 1938: The March of Time" by Peter Galway in *New Statesman and Nation* (London), 30 April 1938; "Time Marches Back: Propaganda for Defense" by Margaret Frakes in *Christian Century* (Chicago), 16 October 1940; "New March of Time Program Features Books" in *Publishers Weekly* (New York), 28 October 1944; "The Magazine Film" by Edgar Anstey in *Penguin Film Review*, May 1949; article by Raymond Fielding in *Quarterly of Film, Radio, and Television* (Berkeley), summer 1957; "Mirror of Discontent: The *March of Time* and Its Politically Controversial Film Issues" by Raymond Fielding in *Wisconsin Political Quarterly*, March 1959; "*The March of Time*: News as Drama" by L.W. Lichty and T.W. Bohn in *Journal of Popular Film* (Bowling Green, Ohio), fall 1973; "This is America" by Richard Barsam in *Cinema Journal* (Evanston, Illinois), spring 1973; "Time Marches on the Screen" by Robert T. Elson in *Nonfiction Film: Theory and Criticism* edited by Richard Barsam, New York 1976; "Whatever Happened to Westbrook Van Voorhis?" by B. Cook in *American Film* (Washington, D.C.), March 1977; "Ideology and Film Rhetoric: 3 Documentaries of the New Deal Era" by P.C. Rollins in *Journal of Popular Film* (Bowling Green, Ohio), no.2, 1977; "*The March of Time*, 1935-51" by R. Fielding in *Filmmakers Monthly* (Ward Hill, Massachusetts), February 1979; "Florence Fest Nod to *March of Time*" in *Variety* (New York), 28 November 1979; "Histoire: *March of Time*" by M. Martin in *Ecran* (Paris), 20 October 1979;

* * *

The March of Times had the most substantial and sustained success of any documentary-like film series prior to television; it lasted from 1935 to 1951. It offered a new and distinctive kind of screen journalism, a cross between the newsreel and the documentary. At its peak, in the late 1930's and during the years of World War II, it was seen in the United States alone by more than 20 million people a month in 9,000 theaters. It was distributed internationaly as well.

The *MOT* was sponsored by the *Time-Life-Fortune* organization of Henry Luce. The monthly film series was preceded by a weekly radio series of the same title. Roy Larsen of *Time* was responsible for the initiation of both series; Louis de Rochemont became the principal creator of the film series.

Though originating from a conservative organization, the *MOT* was identified with a liberal stance, more so than *Time* magazine. This was particularly true in foreign affairs; the films tended to be more conservative or erratic on domestic issues. Still, while features in the 1930's ignored or dealt only convertly with the Depression, *MOT* acknowledged the bread lines, unemployment, and political demagoguery that it gave rise to. Internationally, while the newsreel avoided controversial political and military developments, *MOT* tackled the machinations of Hitler, Stalin, Mussolini, and Tojo. One of the most politically controversial films in the history of American cinema was *Mot*'s "Inside Nazi Germany" (1938). It examined in some detail (16 minutes) the regimentation of the German people, the control and consolidation of nationalistic allegiances, and the preparations being made for future military and economic expansion. This was at a time when the majority of the American public was still strongly isolationiist and the government maintained a careful impartiality.

The success of *The March of Time*—fueled by the controversy it aroused by its press agentry as well as by its energetic innovations—encouraged imitations, especially after world War II began. Created along the same lines were the National Film Board of Canada's monthly *Canada Carries On* (1939-50) and *The World in Action* (1940-45). When the distribution of *The March of Time* moved from RKO to Twetieth Century-Fox in 1942, RKO replaced it with its own series. *This Is America* (1942-51). Immediately after the war, in England, the J. Arthur Rank organization produced and distributed *This Modern Age* (1946-50). The influence of *March of Time* extended into American documentaries of World War II as well, the most important being the *Why We Fight* series. *MOT* is the principal American model for what is now called the "compilation documentary."

A standard format for *The March of Time* was worked out early and varied little, regardless of subject. The fixed form may have been necessitated by the pressures of monthly production with modest resources; it must also have come to seem desirable given the considerable popularity of the series in the form in which it was offered. One of the most important ingredients was the voice and delivery style of its commentator, Westbrook van Voorhis. His "Voice of Time" (sometimes irreverently referred to as the "Voice of God") was deep and commanding, ominous and reassuring at the same time. Spoken words carried the weight of the communication; the footage (largely stock), music (obvious and clichéd), and sound effects (sparse and highly selective) were cut to them. Often the pictures were given their meaning by the words, as part of "the dramatization of the news" that *MOT* practiced. An extreme close-up of a face and mouth at a telephone becomes "An angry refusal"; a long shot of a city street at night with a few electric signs becomes "That evening Shanghai is tense" ("War in China," 1937). Editing was the key. The pace is fast, with a hard rhythmic impact; a great deal of information is presented dramatically to capture the attention of the popcorn-chewing Friday night audience.

Structurally, each issue had four parts, with its titles announcing each part. The first established the magnitude and urgency of the problem being dealt with. The second offered a historical survey of its origins and causes. Part three presented the immediate complications, confirming its newsworthiness. The concluding part looked to the future, stressing that the problem was a matter for continuing and serious concern.

By 1951 the losses of *The March of Time* had become to heavy for even the Luce organization to sustain. It was suffering from the competition of television news and public affairs programs, which could do the same thing as *MOT* films in theaters with much greater immediacy. It was suffering even more from rising costs and inadequate rentals paid for shorts by the theaters, geared largely to the selling of feature films. And finally it was no doubt suffering from its own fixed style and approach which, through repetiton of 160 issues over 16 years, had lost much of the freshness and excitment of its earlier days.

The March of Time must be acknowledged, however, as an event in the history of popular American culture. Its influence has extended down to much of the documentary and public affairs programming on television today.

—Jack C. Ellis

MARÌA CANDELARIA. Xochilmilco. Production: Films Mundiales; 1943; black and white, 35mm; running time: 101 mins. Released 20 January 1944.

Scenario and direction by Emilio Fernández; screenplay by Emilio Fernández and Mauricio Magdaleno; photography by Gabriel Figueroa; edited by Gloria Schoemann; sound by Howard Randall, Jesús González Gancy and Manuel Esperón; production design by Jorge Fernández; music by Francisco Domínguez; costumes designed by Armando Valdés Peza.

Filmed in the CLASA studios in Mexico City and in Xochimilco. Cannes Film Festival, Best Film (shared with several other films), 1946.

Cast: Dolores Del Rio (*María Candelaria*); Pedro Armendáriz (*Lorenzo Rafael*); Alberto Galán (*Painter*); Margarita Cortés (*Lupe*); Miguel Inclán (*Damián*); Beatriz Ramos (*Reporter*); Rafael Icardo (*Priest*); Arturo Soto Rangel (*Doctor*); Julio Ahuet (*Jose Alfonso*): Lupe del Castillo (*Huesera*).

Publications:

Books—*El cine mexicano* by Emilio Garcia Riera, Mexico 1963; *Historia documental del cine mexicano*, Vol. II, by Emilio Garcia Riera, Mexico City 1970; *The Mexican Cinema: Interviews with 13 Directors* by Beatriz Reyes Nevares, Albuquerque 1976; *La aventura del cina mexicano* by Jorge Ayala Blanco, Mexico City 1979; *Mexican Cinema: Reflections of a Society, 1896-1980* by Carl J. Mora, Berkeley 1982; articles—"El Indio" in *Time* (New York), 11 November 1946; "The 2 Kinds of Mexican Movies" by Natalia Askenazy in *Films in Review* (New York), May 1951; "Mexican Cinema: A Panoramic View" by Michel Manuel in *Film Quarterly* (Berkeley), summer 1965; "Dolores Del Rio" by DeWitt Bodeen in *Films in Review* (New York), May 1967; "Courte History du cinéma mexicain ens sept films étapes" by G. Talon in *Cinéma* (Paris), November 1973.

*   *   *

The first Mexican film to receive international (European and U.S.) attention, *María Candelaria* could have been a caricature of what the world expected from Mexico. Directed by Emilio "El Indio" Fernández and focusing on the travails of an Indian maiden in the floating flower gardens of Xochimilco, the work was praised by French film critic, Georges Sadoul, for "its authentic portrayal of Mexican rural life." Sadoul considered it the "most fascinating" of the films at the 1946 Cannes Film Festival, but more recent writers on the work criticize it for having both contributed and corresponded to a folkloric and picturesque image of Mexico and its "noble savages."

The best thing about the film is its impressive visual aesthetic. Fernández and Gabriel Figueroa, the cinematographer, are the creators of the classical Mexican film form. Influenced by Sergei Eisenstein (*Que viva México*) and Paul Strand (*Redes*), this visual style is characterized by monumental cloud formations, statuesque cactuses, and stoic Indian faces set off by white dresses and dark rebozos. Although *María Candelaria* may not quite measure up to the outstanding optical qualities of *Flor Silvestre* or *La perla*, it does offer some lovely moments in its images of boats loaded with flowers slowly moving past thatched huts, long lines of tall poplar trees reflected in the waters of Xochimilco, and the faces of Dolores del Rio and Pedro Armendáriz set off against luminous banks of rolling clouds.

The story is a lacrimous melodrama, typical of Fernández's works, and saved only by his lyricism and the presense of del Rio and Armendáriz. But, as an "Indianist" film, it offers an interesting example of the portrayal given to these "purest Mexicans"— the nation's ethnic base; and, because of its simplistic Manicheanism, the film affords an uncomplicated structural analysis. The "good guys" are Maria and Lorenzo (saintly, if simple-minded, incarnations of the Indian's traditional humiliation and resignation), and three white men: the artist who helps María, the doctor who cures her, and the priest who protects her from Damián, the evil mestizo (mixed-blood) shopkeeper who exploits the Indians. The government is also generally good (even though the film is conspicuously placed in 1909, the eve of the revolution), it makes quinine available to the people. However, its good intentions are thwarted by Damián—presumably something that will not happen after 1909.

The "bad guys" are Damián, who curses the Indians as "despicable aborigines," and the Indian *pueblo* (people) as a whole. The *pueblo* obstructs María and prevents her from selling her flowers because her mother was "a woman of the streets." Later, believing that María has posed in the nude for the painter, they stone her to death. The message is clear: culturally (if not mentally) retarded, the Indians require a strong state to protect them from their own savagery as well as from the (inexplicably) wicked mestizos who prey on them. That firm fatherly hand (surely the state erected after the revolution) will be provided by rational, white, Christian men—the familiar paternalist response of nationalist cinema.

There is, of course, a tragic element to the story. The modern, city-dwelling artist inadvertently causes María's death by having her pose for him, a violation of traditional morality. Thus, modernity results in the death of primitive beauty—although it will presumably also serve to restrain barbaric savagery. Although Mexican racism is such that Fernández was ousted from Films Mundiales for having made "such shit about Indians," he considers this paean to primitivism "a completely Mexican film." And, while it appeared as such to many in the late 1940's, its nationalist and folkloric populism have worn a little thin today.

—John Mraz

THE MARK OF ZORRO. Production: Douglas Fairbanks Pictures Corp. for United Artists; 1920; black and white, 35mm, silent; running time: about 85-90 mins. Released 1920.

Produced by Douglas Fairbanks; from the story "The Curse of Capistrano" by Johnson McCulley; directed by Fred Niblo; photography by William McGann and Harry Thorpe; art direction by Edward Langley; musical score which accompanies film by William Perry.

Cast: Douglas Fairbanks (*Don Diego Vega/ Señor Zorro*); Noah Beery (*Sergeant Pedro*); Charles Hill Mailes (*Don Carlos Pulido*); Claire McDowell (*Dona Catalina*); Marguerite de la Motte (*Lolita*); Robert McKim (*Captain Juan Ramon*); George Periolat (*Governor Alvarado*); Walt Whitman (*Fray Felipe*); Sydney de Grey (*Don Alejandro*); Snitz Edwards; Tote Du Crow.

Publications:

Books—*Douglas Fairbanks: The Making of a Screen Character* by Alistair Cooke, New York 1940; *The Parade's Gone By* by Kevin Brownlow, New York 1968; *The Matinee Idols* by David Carroll, New York 1972; *Gentlemen to the Rescue: The Heroes of the Silent Screen* by Kalton C. Lahue, New York 1972; *His Picture in the Papers* by Richard Schickel, New York 1973; *Cads and Cavaliers—The Film Adventurers* by Tony Thomas, New York 1973; articles—interview with Fred Niblo by M. Cheatham in *Motion Picture Classic* (Brooklyn), July 1920; "Sketch" by K. McGaffey in *Motion Picture Classic* (Brooklyn), October 1921; obituary for Fred Niblo in *The New York Times*, 12 November 1948; "Fairbanks and Valentino: The Last Heroes" by Gavin Lambert in *Sequence* (London), summer 1949; "Homespun Superman" by John Minchinton in *Films and Filming* (London), December 1954; "*The Mark of Zorro*" by Eileen Bowser in *Film Notes* edited by Eileen Bowser, New York 1969; "Douglas Fairbanks" by DeWitt Bodeen in *Focus on Film* (London), winter 1970; "Buried Directors" by W.D. Route in *Focus* (Chicago), spring 1972; "The Hero" by David Robinson in *Sight and Sound* (London), spring 1973; "*Le Signe de Zorro*" by C. Beylie in *Ecran* (Paris), March 1973; "*The Mark of Zorro*" by C.M. Cluny in *Cinéma* (Paris), February 1973; "Zorro" by J.J. Dupuich in *Image et son* (Paris), March 1973; "Zorro Rides Again...And Again...And Again" by B. Rainey and others in *Classic Film Collector* (Indiana, Pennsylvania), November 1979.

*   *   *

The Mark of Zorro is the most significant credit in the filmography of its star, the legendary Douglas Fairbanks. Prior to its release, the boyish, energetic, ever-smiling and optimistic Doug had played boyish, energetic, ever-smiling and optimistic all-American heroes in friendly comedies, westerns and satires, most of them written by Anita Loos. But *The Mark of Zorro* was a complete departure for Fairbanks. The film is a period costume fantasy with the actor, liberated from suit, tie and western getup, dazzling audiences with athletic exploits. It established the screen persona for which he is best remembered today, and altered his career permanently, irrevocably.

The sheer spectacle of Fairbanks's subsequent adventure epics sometimes overwhelms the star's robust personality and physical prowess. However, while Errol Flynn's *Adventures of Robin Hood* and the Ludwig Berger-Tim Whelan-Michael Powell *Thief of Bagdad* are more definitive than the Fairbanks versions, his Zorro portrayal has never been topped. Others have played the role: Tyrone Power, Reed Hadley, Frank Latimore, George Turner, Robert Livingston, John Carroll, Clayton Moore (who was soon to become television's Lone Ranger), Guy Williams, Alain Delon, Frank Langella and, most recently George Hamilton. But none has played it better.

Zorro is an American folk hero, the ancestor of Superman and soul-brother of Robin Hood. He is a dashing knight without armor in mid-19th century Spanish California; disguised by a costume all his own, a purple cloak and black mask, he is a master swordsman who foils the nefarious activities of corrupt politicians. Like Superman, he has an alter ego, Don Diego Vega, who is more concerned with music and poetry than with oppression: Heroine Marguerite de la Motte, like Lois Lane, thinks little of this fop, whom her parents wish her to wed; instead, she adores the mysterious Zorro, unaware that he and Vega are the same person. And, like Robin Hood, Zorro is an outlaw who rights injustices inflicted on the common folk. He has his own special calling card: with his sword, he carves a "Z" on the bodies of his adversaries.

Fairbanks's characterization is lighthearted, and the storyline in *The Mark of Zorro* is, despite its confrontational aspects, delightfully silly. When he made the film, Fairbanks was unsure of how it would be received; in fact, upon its completion he starred in what was then a more typical Fairbanks project, *The Nut*. When *The Mark of Zorro* became both a critical and financial smash, the actor decided to make thereafter only elaborately produced costume adventures.

Five years after *The Mark of Zorro*, Douglas Fairbanks appeared in a sequel, *Don Q, the Son of Zorro*, which featured both the character and his offspring. But the original is the traditional film in the Fairbanks career, the seed that sprouted into his heroics as D'Artagnan in *The Three Musketeers* and the title characters in *Robin Hood*, *The Thief of Bagdad* and *The Black Pirate*. It is also the forerunner of all swashbucklers, and the cinematic swordsmanship of Flynn, Power, Douglas Fairbanks, Jr., and Burt Lancaster (most famously in *The Crimson Pirate*, which could have starred no one but Fairbanks, Sr, had it been produced 30 years earlier).

—Rob Edelman

M*A*S*H. Production: 20th Century-Fox; 1970; color, 35mm, Panavision; running time: 116 mins. Released 1970.

Produced by Ingo Preminger; screenplay by Ring Lardner, Jr.; from the novel by Richard Hooker; directed by Robert Altman; photography by Harold E. Stine; edited by Danford Greene; art direction by Jack Martin Smith and Arthur Lonergan; music by Johnny Mandel, song "Suicide is Painless" by Mike Altman and Johnny Mandel.

Academy Award, Best Screenplay-Material from another medium, 1970; Best Film, Cannes Film Festival, 1970.

Cast: Donald Sutherland (*Hawkeye*); Elliott Gould (*Trapper John*); Tom Skerritt (*Duke*); Gary Burghoff (*Radar O'Reilly*); Sally Kellerman (*Major Margaret "Hot Lips" Houlihan*); Robert Duvall (*Major Frank Burns*); John Shuck (*Painless Pole*); Roger Bowen (*Colonel Henry Blake*); René Auberjonois (*Dago Red*); Jo Ann Pflug (*Lieutenant Dish*).

Publications:

Reviews—by Jan Dawson in *Sight and Sound* (London), summer 1970; review by Gordon Gow in *Films and Filming* (London), August 1970; books—*Persistence of Vision: The Films of Robert Altman* by Neil Feineman, New York 1976; *Robert Altman: American Innovator* by Judith M. Kass, New York 1978; *Guts and Glory: Great American War Movies* by Lawrence H. Sind, Reading, Massachusetts 1978; *A Cinema of Loneliness: Penn, Kubrick, Coppola, Scorsese, Altman* by Robert Phillip Kolker, New York 1980; *Robert Altman* by Jean-Loup Bourget, Paris 1980; *The Films of Robert Altman* by Alan Karp, Metuchen, New Jersey 1981; articles—"D.W. Griffith se porte bien, moi aussi, merci!" by Bertrand Tavernier in *Positif* (Paris), October 1970; "*M*A*S*H*" by G. Trutta in *Harper's Bazaar* (New York), March 1970; "*M*A*S*H* Notes" by Ingo Preminger in *Esquire* (New York), August 1970; "Creation in Chaos" in *Time* (New York), 13 July 1970; "What Directors are Saying" in *Action* (Los Angeles), July/August 1970; "What Directors are Saying" in *Action* (Los Angeles), November/December 1970; article by Louise Bartlett in *Films and Filming* (London), March 1970; article by William Johnson in *Film Quarterly* (Berkeley), spring 1970; interview by Aljean Harmetz in *The New York Times*, 20 June 1971; "*MASH, McCloud, and McCabe*" by John Cutts in *Films and Filming* (London), November 1971; "Entretien avec Robert Altman" by M. Grisolia in *Cinéma* (Paris), July/August 1972; "The Theme of Structure in the Films of Robert Altman" by C.A. Baker in *Journal of Popular Film* (Bowling Green), summer 1973; "Outlaws, Auteurs, and Actors" by Richard Corliss in *Film Comment* (New York), May/June 1974; "Smart-ass and Cutie-pie: Notes Toward an Evaluation of Altman" by Robin Wood in *Movie*, autumn 1975; issue on Altman in *Film Heritage* (Dayton, Ohio), fall 1975; Robert Altman seminar in *Dialogue on Film* (Beverly Hills), February 1975; "Improvisations and Interactions in Altmanville" by Jonathan Rosenbaum in *Sight and Sound* (London), spring 1975; "Tracking Altman's Movies (on his sound techniques) by Bruce Pittman in *Take One* (Montreal), August 1976; "Robert Altman de *Mash* a *Nashville*" by P. Pitiot and H. Talvat in *Jeune cinéma* (Paris), September/October 1976; "Robert Altman" in *Hollywood Renaissance* by Diane Jacobs, New York 1977; interview with Altman by Charles Michener in *Film Comment* (New York), September/October 1978; "*M*A*S*H*" by James J. Desmarais in *Magill's Survey of Cinema, Vol. III* edited by Frank N. Magill, Englewood Cliffs, New Jersey 1980; "Actors as Conventions in the Films of Robert Altman" by M. Yacowar in *Cinema Journal* (Evanston, Illinois), fall 1980.

*   *   *

MASH, one of the most popular films of the early seventies, achieved stardom for Donald Sutherland and Elliott Gould, spawned a successful television series, and gave its innovative director, Robert Altman, his first financial and critical success.

In *MASH*—and to a greater extent in his later films—Altman abandons conventional Hollywood narrative techniques in favor of a very personal style characterized by overlapping dialogue, improvisational acting, elliptical editing, wide-screen Panavision compositions, telephoto shots (specifically shots through windows and past obstructing foreground objects), and the development of a large community and of major characters within a limited time and space. These techniques alter conventions of narrative structure in two ways. First, the improvisational acting, the multiple babble of overlapping dialogue, and the frequently voyeuristic telephoto shots (particularly the shots of explicit gore in the operating scenes) generate a sense of spontaneity and authenticity usually found in documentary, rather than narrative, films. Second, the large number of characters arranged within the wide Panavision frame, the compression of space caused by the telephoto lens, and the continuous barrage of overlapping dialogue, music, and P.A. announcements on the soundtrack combine to create an aural and visual denseness that demands much more of a viewer's attention and active participation than does the shallow-focus cinematography, the separation of major characters from peripheral characters, and the one-speaker-at-a-time dialogue of conventional narrative.

When *MASH* appeared in 1970, audiences—caught up in the spirit of rebellion generated by the civil rights movement, the women's movement, the drug culture, the demonstratrions against the Vietnam War, etc.—revelled in the film's iconoclastic humor, its joyous deflation of patriotism, religion, heroism, and other values cherished by the establishment. The film became an immediate box office success, earning over $36 million in domestic rentals by 1983. The critics also favored *MASH*, but while they praised its innovative techniques, some critics thought that the film's humor was too smug and the scenes involving the trip to Tokyo and the football game were flaws in the film's structure. Today critics feel that *MASH* is inferior to most of Altman's later films (none of which proved as successful at the box office), though the film is still highly regarded for its innovative narrative techniques and its effective humor.

—Clyde Kelly Dunagan

MAT. Mother. Production: Mezhrabpom-Russ.; black and white, 35mm, silent; running time: about 90 mins.; length: 1800 meters, or 5906 feet. Released 11 October 1926. Re-released 1935, with musical soundtrack.

Scenario by Nathan Zarkhi; from the novel by Maxim Gorky; directed by V.I. Pudovkin; photography by Anatoli Golovnya; art direction by Sergei Kozlovsky; music (1935) by S. Blok; assistant directors: Mikhail Doller and V. Strauss.

Cast: Vera Baranovskaya (*Pelageya Vlasova, the mother*); A. Tchistyakova (*Vlasov, her husband*); Nikolai Batalov (*Pavel, her son*); Alexander Savitsky (*Isaika Gorbov, the foreman*); Ivan Koval-Samborsky (*Vesovshchikiv, Pavel's friend*); Anna Zemstova (*Anna, a girl student*); Vsevolod Pudovkin (*Police officer*); N. Vidonov (*Misha*).

Publications:

Script—*Mother: A Film by V.I. Pudovkin and Earth: A Film by Alexander Dovzhenko*, New York 1973; books—*Poudovkine, "Pouti Tvortchestva, Les Voies de la création"* by N. Yezuitov, Moscow 1937; *Vsevolod Pudovkin* by A. Mariamov, Moscow

1952; *Kino: A History of the Russian and Soviet Film* by Jay Leyda, London 1960; *Vsevolod Poudovkine* by Luda and Jean Schnitzer, Paris 1966; *V.I. Poudovkine* by Barthélémy Amengual, Premier Plan, Lyon 1968; *Soviet Cinema* by Thorold Dickinson and Catherine de la Roche, New York 1972; *Cinema in Revolution: The Heroic Era of the Soviet Film* edited by Luda and Jean Schnitzer and Marcel Martin, New York 1973; *Pudovkin's Films and Film Theory* by Peter Dart, New York 1974; *The Cultural-Political Traditions and Developments of the Soviet Cinema* by Louis Harris Cohen, New York 1974; *Cinema, The Magic Vehicle: A Guide to Its Achievement: Journey One: The Cinema Through 1949* edited by Jacek Klinowski and Adam Garbicz, Metuchen, New Jersey 1975; articles—"Soviet Film *Mother* Acclaimed in Vienna" in *The New York Times*, 8 January 1928; "Index to the Creative Work of Vsevolod Pudovkin" by Jay Leyda in *Sight and Sound* (London), November 1948; "Mother" by Roger Manvell in *Sight and Sound* (London), August 1950; issue on Pudovkin of *Cahiers du cinéma* (Paris), August/September 1953; "Vsevolod Pudovkin" by Herman Weinberg in *Films in Review* (New York), August/September 1953; issue on Pudovkin of *Iskusstvo Kino* (Moscow), February 1973; "Pravato na tvorchesko druznobenie" by G. Stoianov-Bigor in *Kinoizkustvo* (Sofia, Bulgaria), July 1979; "Film Language: Pudovkin and Eisenstein and Russian Formalism" by E. Hudlin in *Journal of Aesthetic Education* (Urbana, Illinois), no.2, 1979; "Linkage: Pudovkin's Classics Revisited" by P.E. Burns in *Journal of Popular Film and Television* (Washington, D.C.), summer 1981.

* * *

Mother might rightfully be labelled Soviet propaganda. It is the story of a poor working-class woman at the time of the 1905 Revolution who, through her relationship with her worker son, becomes politicized. At first, she is oppressed. just another anonymous pawn of the power structure; at the finale she is exultant, a heroine and a martyr. However, the film is no boring treatise on the wonders of revolutionary spirit. *Mother* is a drama of love and conflict that can be universally understood and appreciated. In the scenario, based on a Maxim Gorky novel, a traditional theme—a mother's concern for her beloved son—may be stretched to fit into a propagandistic framework. But this fact does not obscure the heart-wrenching storyline and superior cinematic techniques of its maker, Vsevolod Illareonovitch Pudovkin.

Mother is Pudovkin's first feature produced on his own, independent of his colleagues at the State Film School. Here, under the tutelage of Lev Kuleshov, the filmmaker had defined and sharpened his cinematic grammer, and this film became his initial major achievement; he followed it a year later with *The End of St. Petersburg* and, thereafter with *The Heir to Genghis-Khan*. *Mother*, made when Pudovkin's relative inexperience prevented him from initially receiving adequate funding, is a superior example of the filmmaker's concern with camera angles, montage and editing. He and his cinematographer, Anatoli Golovnya, photographed the actors from every which angle: a military officer's self-importance would be conveyed by shooting him from below; the mother's early fruatration would be emphasized by shooting her from above, and at the end, her triumph and liberation is highlighted by shooting from below. When Pudovkin places his camera in this position, the character's upper body and head seem further away, more inaccessible, reaching to the sky and towering over the viewer; when the actor is beneath the camera he becomes inferior, in that the viewer is literally looking down on him. Pudovkin does not shoot his performance straight on, as if he is recording a stage play. Mood and characterization are communicated in *Mother* not by the actor emoting before the camera; the performer is almost a passive participant in the filmmaking process.

Pudovkin believed that the manner and order in which pieces of film are spliced together can have the most powerful effect on the viewer. *Mother* is structured like a musical composition: a balance of action and reaction, seemingly disconnected shots— opposites, if you will—coming together to form a coherent whole. For example, the son receives some happy news while in prison. Instead of just editing in a simple reaction shot of his actor, Nikolai Batalov, Pudovkin combines shots of hands energetically in motion and a close-up of the bottom part of Batalov's face with scenes of a sun-lit stream, birds cavorting in a pond, and a happy child. *Mother* is a creative leap in the advancement of the editing process as an important filmmaking tool.

Pudovkin's individual images are, when contrasted to his cutting, relatively insignificant. But they are not uninteresting. One example: the mother visits the bier of her just-deceased husband. The filmmaker conveys a stark, sad mood by shooting only the dark shape of Vera Baranovskaya (who plays the role) casting an ominous shadow on the nearby grey wall, and a white sheet covering the body.

Pudovkin was also allegedly inspired by artists, painters and printmakers. The mother's characterization is modelled after the creations of Kathe Kollwitz, Picasso (especially the works of his Blue Period) and Degas. A sequence in a prison has its roots in Van Gogh's "Prison Courtyard." The film's influences are also literary: the trail scenes are based more on Tolstoy's *Resurrection* than in anything from the original source material.

Mother is expertly cast, from the actors playing mother and son (Baranovskaya and Batalov were recruited from the Moscow Art Theather) to the extras on screen for a split second. Pudovkin favored using non-actors in smaller roles, people whose real-life experience would provide a heightened sense of reality. In a sequence depicting the son's arrest after a search of his home, a former tsarist officer plays the colonel supervising the interrogation. After all, who else but an authentic career military man would know how to look the part of a professional soldier?

Interestingly, *Mother* might easily have been made by another director. Yuri Zhelyabuzhsky was initially assigned to direct the film, but was unable to cast the title role and even requested that scenarist Nathan Zarkhi transform her into a father. Finally, the project came to Pudovkin, who could never have worked independently within, or outside, the Soviet cinema establishment. His films are not pure works of art: *Mother* is similar to *The End of St. Petersburg* and *The Heir to Genghis-Khan* in that its motives are unabashedly political. Every great Russian film of the era, including Eisenstein's *Battleship Potemkin*, *Strike* and *October*, are in some way linked to the Revolution. But *Mother* is the most personalized, and most poetic, of them all.

—Rob Edelman

MATKA JOANNA OD ANIOŁÓW. Joan of the Angels. Mothe Joan of the Angels. Production: Kadr Film Unit for Film Polski; black and white, 35mm; running time: 125 mins. and 105 mins., English version is 101 mins. Released 1961, Poland.

Screenplay by Tadeusz Konwicki and Jerzy Kawalerowicz; from a novel by Jarosław Iwaszkiewicz which in turn was based on 17th century documents about the events at the convent in Loudon, France; directed by Jerzy Kawalerowicz; photography by Jerzy Wójcik; edited by Wiesława Otocka and Felicja Ragowska; sound recorded by Józef Bartczak, Zygmunt Nowak, and Jozef Kensikowski; art direction by Roman Mann and Tadeusz Borowczyk (some sources list Tadeusz Wybult); music by Adam Walaciński.

Cast: Lucyna Winnicka (*Mother Joan*); Mieczysław Voit (*Father Jozef Suryn/the Rabbi*); Anna Ciepielewska (*Sister Margaret*, or *Małgorzata*); Maria Chwalibóg (*Awdosia*); Kazimierz Fabisiak (*Father Brym*); Stanisław Jasiukiewicz (*Chrzaszczewski*); Zygmunt Zintel (*Wołodkowicz*); Franciszek Pieczka (*Odryl*); Jerzy Kaczmarek (*Kaziuk*); Jarosław Kuszewski (*Juraj*); Lech Wojciechowski; Marian Nosek.

Publications:

Reviews—"*Mère Jeanne des anges*" by Jean Douchet in *Arts* (Paris), 7 June 1961; "*Mère Jeanne des anges*" by Michel Flacon in *Cinéma 61* (Paris), no.57, 1961; "*Mère Jeanne des anges*" by Georges Sadoul in *Les Lettres françaises* (Paris), May 1961; review by Henry Hart in *Films in Review* (New York), May 1962; books—*Jerzy Kawalerowicz: Filmtexte*, Munchen 1963; *20 Years of Polish Cinema* by Stanislaw Grzelecki, Warsaw 1969; *The Oxford Companion to Film*, London 1976; *The Most Important Art: East European Film After 1945* by Mira Liehm and Antonín Liehm, Berkeley 1977; *Contemporary Polish Film* by Stanislaw Kuszewski, Warsaw 1978; articles—"Angles on the Angels" by Jerzy Kawalerowicz in *Films and Filming* (London), November 1961; "Paphnuce et les Chacals" by Jacques Siclier in *Cahiers du cinéma* (Paris), July 1961; "Le Père Joseph et la Mère Jeanne" by Paul-Louis Thirard in *Positif* (Paris), September 1961; "*Mother Joanna of the Angels*" by Gordon Hitchens in *Vision* (New York), spring 1962; article by Jonas Mekas in *The Village Voice* (New York), 17 May 1962; article by Raymond Durgnat in *Films and Filming* (London), May 1962; "*Mère Jeanne des anges*" by R. Lefèvre in *Image et son* (Paris), October 1962; article by Ernest Callenbach in *Film Quarterly* (Berkeley), winter 1963-64; "Czy istnieje swiat Kawalerowicza" by Boleslaw Michalek in *Kino* (Warsaw), no.6, 1967; "Persrektywa moralna 'Szkoly polskiej'" by Maryla Hopfinger in *Kino* (Warsaw), no.11, 1971.

*   *   *

"The revolt of oppressed humanity" is how one Polish critic described *Mother Joan of the Angels* and with this definition various levels of meaning may be glimpsed. The novel of the same name by the well-known author Jarosław Iwaszkiewicz, deals with an occurence in the eastern region of Poland in the 17th century. The young ascetic priest Suryn ventures into a cloister where, it is said, all of the nuns are in the terrible grip of Satan. Four exorcists have made every effort, but in vain, to drive out the evil.

In his first encounter with the Mother Superior Joan, the priest is somewhat disappointed—instead of a miserable creature in the Devil's grasp, he is greeted by a beautiful, dignified, and proud woman who engages him in a serious philosophical discussion. Between the two a shy, tender affection develops, a kind of halting love which they cannot resolve. The closed world of religious dogma and ritual shut out such a love. (Another nun, Małgorzata, has let herself be led astray by a nobleman who later abandons her, and she despairs of returning to the convent.)

Suryn, in a tragic conflict with himself, with his feelings and his principles, decides on radical measures; to begin with he builds a screen in the attic where he meets with Joan, so that she can not come too near. Then he brings in two innocent boys with the aim of concentrating the satanic might onto them, thereby freeing Joan. In his holy foolishness, he suspects no tragic consequences; for him everything is only a game, a challenge to moral norms and customs, to the mendacity of his surroundings. For the clever woman, religion is not a calling but an opportunity to live free of the burden of a woman's fate at that time.

Even in the cloister, in the perfect, uniformed and regulated system, Joan has rebelled against a one-dimensional, determinedly average existence. She unleashes this theater of darkness, with its possession by the devil and exorcisms, in order to express her need for love and spiritual contact. That is her vengeance on the cruel world; and as is the rule in the great tragedies, she causes the sacrifice of her beloved.

Kawalerowicz has succeeded in creating a poetically stylized work full of contrasts, elevated in its sincerity. The impressive, emotionally-laden, subtle interpretations by Lucyna Winnicka (Joan) and Mieczysław Voit (Suryn), grab the viewer and awake similar feelings. Without any physical contact, only through close-ups, eyes, glimpses, hands, the film refracts a delicate, but elusive eroticism. The film is full of erotic allusions, indirect, unprovoked, transmitted through atmosphere and images. As a pure art work, *Mother Joan* embodies an almost mystic ambivalence which releases intense feelings and many-layered thoughts. It is completely wrong to view the film as a critique of the church or religion. Rather, this Polish film should be seen as a lyrical tragedy of human existence, as a striving toward spiritual freedom, toward emotion and dreams. The director's visual symbolism and his means of expression all point to this. Plagued by the contradictions of his situation, Suryn goes looking for a rabbi. Astonishingly, he discovers that the rabbi is himself (played by the same actor). He sees the situation with more wisdom and composure, realizing that there are no solutions to the existential questions of life. *Mother Joan of the Angels* is a film about the eternal quest for those answers.

—Maria Racheva

THE MAXIM TRILOGY

YUNOST MAXIMA. The Youth of Maxim. Also referred to as Part 1 of the Maxim Trilogy. Production: Lenfilm (Leningrad); black and white, 35mm; running time: 98 mins., some versions are 86 mins.; length: 2678 meters. Released 27 January 1935.

Scenario, screenplay and direction by Grigori Kozintsev and Leonid Trauberg; photography by Andrei Moskvin; sound by I. Volk; art direction by Evgeny Enei; music by Dmitri Shostakovich; assistant directors: N. Kosheverova, Kh. Lokshina, and M. Nesterov. Order of Lenin to Lenfilm studios for producing *Yunost Maxima*, 1935.

Cast: Boris Chirkov (*Maxim*); Valentina Kibardina (*Natasha*); A. Kulakov (*Andrei*); Mikhail Tarkhanov (*Polivanov*); M.

Shchelkovsky (*Foreman*); S. Leontyev (*Engineer*); P. Volkov (*Worker*); Stepan Kayukov (*Dyoma*); V. Sladkopevtsev.

*   *   *

VOZVRASHCHENIYE MAXIMA. The Return of Maxim. Also referred to as Part 2 of the Maxim Trilogy. Production: Lenfilm; black and white, 35mm; running time: about 112 mins.; length: 3082 meters. Released 23 May 1937.

Scenario by Grigori Kozintsev and Leonid Trauberg; screenplay by Grigori Kozintsev, Leonid Trauberg and Lev Slavin; directed by Grigori Kozintsev and Leonid Trauberg; photography by Andrei Moskvin; art direction by Evgeny Enei; music by Dmitri Shostakovich; assistant directors: N. Kosheverova, Kh. Lokshina, an M. Nesterov.

Cast: Boris Chirkov (*Maxim*); Valentina Kibardina (*Natasha*); Alexandr Zrazhevsky (*Yerofeyev*); A. Kuznetsov (*Turaev*); Mikhail Zharov (*Dymba, the anarchist*); Vasily Vanin (*Nikolai*); A. Chistyakov (*Mishchenko*); Yuri Tolubeyev (*Bugai*); A. Bondi (*Menshevik*): Vasily Merkuriev (*Student*); N. Kriuchkov (*Soldier*).

*   *   *

VYBORGSKAYA STORONA. The Vyborg Side. New Horizons. Also referred to as Part 3 of the Maxim Trilogy. Production: Lenfilm; black and white, 35mm; running time: about 120 mins.; length: 3276 meters. Released 2 February 1939.

Scenario, screenplay and direction by Grigori Kozintsev and Leonid Trauberg; photography by Andrei Moskvin with G. Filatov; sound by I. Volk; art direction by V. Vlasov; music by Dmitri Shostakovich; assistant directors: N. Kosheverova and Kh. Lokshine.

Stalin Prize awarded to the entire trilogy in 1941.

Cast: Boris Chirkov (*Maxim*); Valentina Kibardina (*Natasha*); Maxim Strauch (*Lenin*); Mikhail Gelovani (*Stalin*); Natalia Uzhvi (*Yevdokia*); L. Lyubashevski (*Sverdlov*); A. Kuznetsov (*Turaev*); Mikhail Zharov (*Dymba, the anarchist*); A. Chistyakov (*Mishchenko*); Yuri Tolubeyev (*Bugai*); B. Zhukovski (*Attorney*); D. Dudnikov (*Ropshin*); M. Nazarov (*Lapshin*).

Publications:

Reviews-of *The Vyborg Side* by William Boehnel in *New York World Telegram*, 13 May 1939; review of *The Vyborg Side* (or *New Horizons*) in *Daily Worker* (New York), spring 1939; review of *The Vyborg Side* (*New Horizons*) in *Variety* (New York), 17 May 1939; review of *The Vyborg Side* (*New Horizons*) in *The New York Times*, 12 May 1939; books—*Kino: A History of the Russian and Soviet Film* by Jay Leyda, London 1960; *Cinema, The Magic Vehicle: A Guide to Its Achievement: Journey One: The Cinema Through 1949* edited by Jacek Klinowski and Adam Garbicz, Metuchen, New Jersey 1975; *Grigori Kozintsev* by Barbara Leaming, Boston 1980; articles—by V.I. Pudovkin in *New Theatre*, February 1935; "Over the Parisiana" by Grigori Kozintsev in *Sight and Sound* (London), winter 1962-63; "The Soviet Film" in *Museum of Modern Art Department of Film Program Notes* (New York), 25 September-11 November 1969; "Grigori Kozintsev, 1905-1973;" by David Robinson in *Sight and Sound* (London), summer 1973; "A Child of the Revolution" in *Cinema in Revolution* edited by Luda and Jean Schnitzer, New York 1973; "Films from the Archive" by Sonia Volochova in *Museum of Modern Art Department of Film Program Notes* (New York), 26-27 February 1976.

*　　*　　*

The first episode of *The Maxim Trilogy* was released a few months after *Chapaev* and provided an alternative, equally successful, answer to that perennial but seldom soluble obsession of the Soviet arts establishment: the search for an ideal Communist hero. Whereas the Vasiliev brothers had patiently re-created Chapaev, a real-life champion, the directorial team of Grigori Kozintsev and Leonid Trauberg came up with an entirely synthetic hero, their own invention, Maxim. First envisaged as a conventional proto-Bolshevik—in an early treatment described as "a lean lad, of intelligent appearance, with a sharp nose and a shock of straight hair, withdrawn...a bookworm...self-taught..."—he grew in the hands of the young but highly experienced and original filmmakers into a very different, more interesting and much more believable individual, with a touch of Til Eulenspiegel perhaps, or, as Kozintsev himself observed, with his roots in the favourite characters of Russian folklore, of fairground farces, Petrushka and Ivan Durak (Ivan the Fool), the holy innocent and the dumb youngest brother who always gets the Princess in the end.

This, of course, was only Maxim's ancestry: his personality grew, as might be expected, from the workings of two creative and complementary minds. But Maxim was no test-tube baby: together with the scripts as a whole he was developed against a background of thorough research into the history and actual documents of the period and locale—pre-revolutionary St. Petersburg. Once cast in the role, Boris Chirkov joined the process and was made, for instance, to try out any number of pre-1914 songs before one was found to fit the character: it was to become a leit-motif for the whole trilogy—but the composer, Shostakovich, and the directors were well aware of the oft-neglected truth that "music from nowhere," however inspired, whatever its contribution to mood, is the enemy of reality. In the first film, *The Youth of Maxim*, therefore, except for the opening prologue, there is little symphonic "background," only the actual sounds of song, accordion and guitar that belonged to the environment and the era.

Sense of period is also enhanced by Andrei Moskvin's photography and Evgeny Enei's art direction; both men were regular members of K and T's team. A memorable example is the scene in which police break up a demo in front of a huge bill-board announcing "ARA PILLS—THE BEST IN THE WORLD," giving us in one bold brush-stroke, as it were, an uncluttered background to the action, a sharp stab of visual irony and, in the simplistic advertising message, so remote in time and space from Madison Avenue, a glimpse of a complacent and unsuspecting "bourgeois" society. By such juxtapositions, by a succession of apparently disparate, even "unimportant" images, by a series of incidents rather than a relentless plot, the whole trilogy is allowed to grow. There is, however, a stylistic unity, and the strong central character helps to hold the kaleidoscope together.

On the other hand, Maxim is not continuously shoved into the centre of things. Dovzhenko (even Donzhenko!) reproached K

and T for this: "Maxim is frequently out of focus!" he complained, comparing the film, in a sense, unfavourably with *Chapaev*: that film's "secret of success" was said to be that "the Commander is always to be found at the centre of things." But within a much freer framework, and throughout the whole trilogy, Maxim is never too far away. The *real* "secret of success" shared by both teams of directors (but absent from most attempts to idealize revolutionary heros) was a warm and liberating sense of humour.

Most of the belly laughs are in the first film: open and innocent, the youthful Maxim, chasing a clucking chicken or a pretty girl, singing his "Blue Globe" song, provides plenty of fun himself, and there are many humorous confrontations as the future revolutionary learns who his enemies are—masters, bosses, police, informers.

In Part II, *The Return of Maxim*, although he still appears to be the same naive youth, his naiveté has become a sort of disguise: for Maxim is now a revolutionary, working in the "underground." In the course of this dangerous activity he has to learn who are his "new enemies—Mensheviks and dissidents," says a Soviet film historian, who adds: "Maxim shows himself unable to reconcile himself with any kind of ideological vacillation." But the heavy political message is made much lighter (in both senses) by a masterly evocation of the glorious summer of 1914, the last before "the lights went out all over Europe," particularly poignant perhaps in Saint Petersberg.

In Part III, *The Vyborg Side* (the slummier side of St. Petersberg), although never allowed to forget, or regret, his working-class origins, and not entirely denied his sense of humour, Maxim is already a commissar somewhat sober, dignified and strict. In the final significant sequence, which is played for laughs, he confronts some definitely "vacillating" bank employees, who plead "We are peaceful Russian people." "What's Russian about you?" he replies—"Messrs Schumacher, Andersen, etc. Your surnames are German: you have consorted with English spies and have thought about setting up Japanese accounting systems...." An odd piece of dialogue, one might think, when one of the directors was called Trauberg: but, with the Nazi menace already building up, it is an early example of the shift from the "class struggle" towards the more chauvinistic "patriotic" propaganda of the following decade.

And even the immensely popular "synthetic" hero was not allowed to die. By popular demand the somewhat reluctant Boris Chirkov was made to re-enact Maxim (by now a member of the Central Committee) in Ermler's two-part *Great Citizen*, just before World War II and, in 1941, still singing his "Blue Globe" song (with appropiate new lyrics), he opened the first "Fighting Film Album," under Gerasimov's direction, in *Meeting with Maxim*.

Indeed, the outstanding excellence of the *Maxim Trilogy* (and the first part, at least, is a true classic) has been almost overshadowed by the authors' successful creation of their "Communist hero"—one of the few fictitious characters who, like Sherlock Holmes, is obstinately believed, against all the evidence, to have actually existed.

—Robert Dunbar

MEAN STREETS. Production: Taplin-Perry-Scorsese; Technicolor, 35mm; running time: 110 mins. Released 1973.

Produced by Jonathan T. Taplin; screenplay by Martin Scorsese and Mardik Martin; directed by Martin Scorsese; photography by Norman Gerard; edited by Sid Levin.

Filmed in New York City.

Cast: Harvey Keitel (*Charlie*); Robert De Niro (*Johnny Boy*); David Proval; Amy Robinson; Richard Romanus; Cesare Danova.

Publications:

Reviews—"*Mean Streets*" in *Films in Review* (New York), November 1973; "*Mean Streets*" by J. Ney in *Interview* (New York), November 1973; "*Mean Streets*: The Sweetness of Hell" by David Denby in *Sight and Sound* (London), winter 1973-74; "*Mean Streets*" by Gordon Gow in *Films and Filming* (New York), May 1974; "*Mean Streets*" by L. Rubenstein in *Cineaste* (New York), no.2, 1974; "*Mean Streets*" by J. Stein in *Film Heritage* (Dayton, Ohio), spring 1974; "*Les Rues chaudes*" by J.L. Cros in *Revue du cinéma* (Paris), October 1976; "Eastside Story: *Hexenkessel* von Martin Scorsese" by P.W. Jansen in *Film und Ton Magazine* (Munich), December 1976; "*Mean Streets*" by T. Renaud in *Cinéma 76* (Paris), July 1976; "*Mean Streets*" by G. Turroni in *Filmcritica* (Rome), January/February 1976; book—*Hollywood Renaissance* by Diane Jacobs, New York 1977; articles—"*Mean Streets*" by J. Delson in *Take One* (Montreal), November 1973; "The Filming of *Mean Streets*" by A.C. Bobrow in *Filmmakers Newsletter* (Ward Hill, Massachusetts), January 1974; "*Alice n'est plus ici* et *Mean Streets*" by Claude Beylie in *Ecran* (Paris), July/August 1975; "La Passion de Saint Martin Scorsese" by M. Henry in *Positif* (Paris), June 1975; "It's a Personal Thing for Me" by F.A. Macklin in *Film Heritage* (Dayton, Ohio), spring 1975; "Martin Scorsese Seminar" in *Dialogue on Film* (Beverly Hills), April 1975; "Rebel Heroes der 70er Jahre: Kontaktlos und gewalttaertig: zu zwei Filmen von Martin Scorsese" by K. Eder in *Medium* (Frankfurt), July 1976; "Gaden uden nade" by I. Lindberg in *Kosmorama* (Copenhagen), no.131, 1976; "Een eindeloos verhaal zonder punten en komma's: de films van Martin Scorsese" by H. Hosman in *Skoop* (Amsterdam), February/March 1976; "*Mean Streets*: Martin Scorsese" by G. Rinaldi in *Cineforum* (Bergamo, Italy), March 1976; "Rules of the Game: Martin Scorsese's *Mean Streets*" by R. Hermann in *Cinemonkey* (Portland, Oregon), no.4, 1979.

*   *   *

Mean Streets is the film that established director Martin Scorsese's reputation, and it is often considered his most personal and emblematic work. In comparison with his later films, however, *Mean Streets* seems more like a rough sketch (both thematically and stylistically) than a fully-realized achievment, despite the film's distinction when viewed as an isolated work.

At the center of *Mean Streets* is Charlie (Harvey Keitel). Of all of Scorsese's male protagonists he is arguably the least mentally unstable and the least prone to movement and action. Like Travis Bickle in *Taxi Driver*, Charlie's responses to his surroundings are so internalized that the film must utilize devices like voice-over monologues and subjective slow-motion shots in order to clarify those responses. But unlike Travis (or even unlike Ellen Burstyn's Alice), there is no point in the film at which Charlie is jolted out of his inactive state. While the protagonists

of Scorsese's later films almost continually create the action and upheaval that set in motion and propel foward the narrative, Charlie remains in an almost constant state of indecision and stasis, as does the movement of the narrative in *Mean Streets*.

It is the presense of Johnny Boy (Robert De Niro) that suggests Scorsese's later protagonists with their propensity towards emotional and physical violence that they are unable to fully comprehend. In Scorsese's collaborations with De Niro after *Mean Streets* the two men were able to fuse the masochistic Charlie with the violent, inarticulate Johnny Boy. But in *Mean Streets* Johnny Boy's almost total inarticulateness results in his being slightly displaced from the center of the narrative by his more "normal" friend Charlie, even though Johnny Boy's accumulated actions lead to the shoot-out on Charlie, Theresa and himself.

The shoot-out itself leaves the unanswered question whether Charlie will ever become active rather than (essentially) passive. In all of Scorsese's subsequent narrative films, the extremely violent and/or emotional upheavals that serve as a climax have a kind of cleansing effect, unleashing all of the psychological problems, the private demons, of the main characters. Nevertheless, the epilogues in each of these post-*Mean Streets* films tend to re-state the essential problems of the characters, giving an impression of apparent unity and order precariously on the brink of collapsing once again and thus denying any "true" catharsis. *Mean Streets* simply ends with the shoot-out, an act of violence perpetrated not *by* the central characters but *on* them, with Scorsese playing their would-be assassin, ending the film on a note of total disorder. Charlie, with a confused and uncertain future before him, is essentially the "hero" of an extraordinary work-in-progress.

—Joseph McElhaney

———

MEDIUM COOL. Production: H & J Pictures; Technicolor, 35mm; running time: 110 mins. Released 27 August 1969 by Paramount.

Produced by Jerrold Wexler, Haskell Wexler, Steven Nort, and Michael Philip Butler (executive producer: Tully Friedman); screenplay by Haskell Wexler; from the novel *The Concrete Wilderness* by Jack Couffer; titles by James Talbot; directed by Haskell Wexler; photography by Haskell Wexler; edited by Verna Fields; sound mix by Chris Newman, sound edited by Kay Rose; art direction by Leon Erickson; music by Mike Bloomfield, incidental music by The Mothers of Invention; Chicago consultant: Studs Turkel.

Filmed 1967-68 in Kentucky; Minnesota; Chicago; and Washington, D.C.

Cast: Robert Forster (*John Cassellis*); Verna Bloom (*Eileen Horton*); Peter Bonerz (*Gus*); Marianna Hill (*Ruth*); Harold Blankenship (*Harold Horton*); Sid McCoy (*Frank Baker*); Christine Bergstrom (*Dede*); Robert McAndrew (*Pennybaker*); William Sickingen (*News Director Karlin*); Beverly Younger (*Rich lady*); Marrian Walters (*Social worker*); Edward Croke (*Plainclothesman*); Sandra Ann Roberts (*Blonde in car*); Doug Kimball (*Newscaster*); Janet Langhart (*Maid*); Peter Boyle (*Gun clinic manager*); Georgia Tadda (*Secretary*); Charles Geary (*Buddy, Harold's father*); Jeff Donaldson, Richard Abrams, Felton Perry, Val Grey, Bill Sharp, Robert Paige, Walter Bradford, Russell Davis, Livingston Lewis, Barbara Jones, and John S. Jackson (*Black militants*); Simone Zorn, Madeleine Marcou, Mickey Pallas, Lynn Erlich, Lester Brownlee, Morris Bleckman, Wally Wright, Sam Ventura, and George Boulet (*Reporters and photographers*); James Jacobs, Spence Jackson, Dorien Suhr, Kenneth Whitener, Connie Fleischauer, Mary Smith, and Nancy Lee Noble (*Kennedy students*); Linda Handelman, Moira Friedman, Kathryn Schubert, Barbara Brydenthal, Elizabeth Moisant, and Rose Bormacher (*Gun clinic ladies*); Roger Phillips; Robert Blankenship; China Lee; Sirri Murad.

Publications:

Reviews—by Andrew Sarris in *The Village Voice* (New York), 28 August 1969; "Salute of the Week" in *Cue* (New York), 27 September 1969; "Dynamite" in *Time* (New York), 22 August 1969; articles—"Haskell and the Cool Medium" by R.B. Jones in *Take One* (Montreal), May/June 1969; "Film of Social Reality" by H. Alpert in the *Saturday Review* (New York), 6 September 1969; "Before the Revolution" by Stephen Farber in the *Hudson Review* (Nutley, New Jersey), autumn 1969; article by Stephen North in *Take One* (Montreal), July/August 1969; "Stay with Us, NBC" by Richard Corliss in *Film Quarterly* (Berkeley), winter 1969-70; "A View of the Future" by R.B. Jones in *Making Films* (New York), June 1970; "The Filming of *Medium Cool*" by Herb Lightman in *American Cinematographer* (Hollywood), January 1970; article by Philip French in *Sight and Sound* (London), spring 1970; article by Gordon Gow in *Films and Filming* (London), April 1970; article by Judith Shatnoff in *Film Quarterly* (Berkeley), winter 1969-70; "Haskell Wexler" by Michael Shedlin in *Take One* (Montreal), July/August 1971; "*Medium Cool*" by N. Gabler in *Film Society Review* (New York), March/May 1972.

*   *   *

Medium Cool is as timely as tomorrow's headlines. As the film opens, a cameraman for a Chicago television news department happens to pass by an automobile that has just crashed. A woman, injured, perhaps dying, lies just outside the car's open door. The cameraman, John Cassellis, does not attempt to assist her, or immediately summon an ambulance. Instead, he films the accident, then calls for aid. Cassellis, who "loves to shoot film," is a voyeur, insensitive to violence and unable to become involved in the life of a woman whose fate he controls. The cameraman is ruled by his camera, his technology, and the point is distressingly clear: the man operating the machine has lost his humanity.

As the film progresses, Cassellis becomes radicalized, a participant rather than just a passive recorder of events. He covers a tactical exercise in a National Guard riot training camp, where he films a mock clash between soldiers and war protesters. He learns about black militancy while shooting a story in the ghetto. He becomes aware of the hopeless poverty in Appalachia when he begins a relationship with Eileen, a welfare mother who has moved to the city from West Virginia. Once Cassellis sees, he is able to feel.

The cameraman becomes outraged after learning that the FBI and CIA have automatic access to his footage. Eventually, he finds himself at the 1968 Democratic National Convention, where the National Guardsmen and war protesters clash. Distracted by these events, he loses control of his car and crashes into a tree. Eileen is dead; he is seriously injured. A passing motorist pauses to photograph the scene, and then drives away.

The change in Cassellis parallels that of *Medium Cool*'s maker, Haskell Wexler, from distinguished cinematographer to screenwriter and director. His screenplay evolved partially in anticipation that "it was going to be very bad" at the Democratic Convention. Wexler brought his cameras to the International Amphitheatre, where the convention was held, and, most tellingly, to Grant Park, where the major rioting occurred. Ironically, the Justice Department requisitioned the 20 hours of footage shot at the site.

Medium Cool—the title evolved from a reversal of Marshall McLuhan's then fashionable term for television—is an undeniably truthful film, one of the forgotten gems of its era. It is refreshingly unconventional, almost revolutionary for a film released by a major studio: a non-documentary feature set within, and shot during, an actual news event. All the dialogue and dubbing were recorded on the spot, with not a word or sound edited in or eliminated.

Additionally, Wexler paints a frightening, vividly realistic portrait of a nation in conflict with itself, in one of the most critical years in its history. *Medium Cool* is among the first films to examine the power of television, its ability to trivialize actual events and numb the masses to actual feelings. At the same time, it is an eloquent statement on the moral responsibilities of those who record those events.

In a chilling example of life imitating art—or, in this case, life imitating life—Wexler himself became a participant in his film when he was teargassed. As a National Guardsman fires a canister at him, one of Wexler's crew members is heard to shout off camera, "Watch out, Haskell, it's real." Like John Cassellis, Haskell Wexler is a recorder of events. And, like Cassellis as *Medium Cool* reaches its climax, Wexler is passionately concerned about, and actively involved with, the reality he photographs.

—Rob Edelman

MEET ME IN ST. LOUIS. Production: Metro-Goldwyn-Mayer Picture Corp.; 1944; color, 35mm; running time: 113 mins. Released 1944.

Produced by Arthur Freed; screenplay by Irving Brecher and Fred F. Finklehoffe; from the novel by Sally Benson; directed by Vincente Minnelli; photography by George J. Folsey; edited by Albert Akst; art direction by Cedric Gibbons, Lemuel Ayers, and Jack Martin Smith; music direction by George Stoll, music numbers by Ralph Blane and Hugh Martin, song "Meet Me in St. Louis" by Sterling and Mills, song "Under the Bamboo Tree" by Bob Cole, and "You and I" by Arthur Freed and Nacio Herb Brown; costumes designed by Irene Sharaff; choreography by Charles Walters.

Filmed in MGM studios. Cost: $1,700,000. Academy Award to Margaret O'Brien for Outstanding Child Actress, 1944.

Cast: Judy Garland (*Esther Smith*); Margaret O'Brien (*Tootie Smith*); Lucille Bremer (*Rose Smith*); Mary Astor (*Mrs. Anna Smith*); Leon Ames (*Mr. Alonzo Smith*); Tom Drake (*John Truett*); Harry Davenport (*Grandpa Potter*); Marjorie Main (*Katie*); Henry H. Daniels, Jr. (*Lon Smith, Jr.*); Joan Carroll (*Agnes Smith*); Robert Sully (*Warren Sheffield*); Chill Wills (*Mr. Neely*); Hugh Marlowe (*Colonel Darly*).

Publications:

Books—*The Blue Book of Hollywood Musicals* by Jack Burton, Watkins Glen, New York 1953; *Vincente Minnelli* by François Truchaud, Paris 1966; *All Talking, All Singing, All Dancing* by John Springer, New York 1966; *Judy: The Films and Career of Judy Garland* by Joe Morella and Edward Epstein, New York 1969; *Gotta Sing, Gotta Dance: A Pictorial History of Film Musicals* by John Kobal, New York 1970; *The MGM Years* by Lawrence B. Thomas, New Rochelle, New York 1972; *Little Girl Lost—The Life and Hard Times of Judy Garland* by Al Di Orio, Jr., New Rochelle, New York 1973; *I Remember It Well* by Vincente Minnelli with Hector Arce, New York 1974; *The Movie Musical* by Lee Edward Stern, New York 1974; *The Films of Judy Garland* by Brian Baxter, London 1974; *Judy Garland* by James Juneau, New York 1974; articles—"His Engagement to Judy Garland" by A.R. St. Johns in *Photoplay* (New York), April 1945; "Minnelli's Talents" in *Time* (New York), 14 May 1945; "Vincente Minnelli" by Simon Harcourt-Smith in *Sight and Sound* (London), January/March 1952; "Judy Garland" by Robert Rosterman in *Films in Review* (New York), April 1952; "L'Oeuvre de V.M." by Etienne Chaumeton in *Positif* (Paris), November/December 1954; "The Films of Vincente Minnelli" by Albert Johnson in *Film Quarterly* (Berkeley), winter 1958 and spring 1959; "The Rise and Fall of the Musical" in *Films and Filming* (London), January 1962; Minnelli issue of *Movie* (London), June 1963; "Vincente Minnelli" by Dennis Lee Galling in *Films in Review* (New York), March 1964; "Minnelli e l'architettura del tempo (a proposito di Meet Me in St. Louis*" by G. Torroni in *Filmcritica* (Rome), April 1976; "*Meet Me in St. Louis*: Smith, or, the Ambiguities" by A. Britton in *Australian Journal of Screen Theory* (Kensington), no.3, 1977; "Nuove retrospettive: due film di Judy Garland" by O. De Fornari in *Filmcritica* (Rome), February 1979; "The American Family Comedy: From *Meet Me in St. Louis* to *Texas Chain Saw Massacre*" by R. Wood in *Wide Angle* (Athens, Ohio), no. 2, 1979; "*Meet Me in St. Louis*" by Kathleen Karr in *Magill's Survey of Cinema, Vol. III* edited by Frank N. Magill, Englewood Cliffs, New Jersey 1980.

*   *   *

As with many of the finest Hollywood films, the richness of *Meet Me in St. Louis* derives from the interaction of a number of sources and determinants, some of them complex in themselves, producing a filmic text to which no single, "coherent" reading can do justice. A few of these determinants include:

The dominant ideological project. Bordwell and Thompson give a clear account of this aspect in *Film Art* (unfortunately, they give the impression that there is nothing more to the film). They stress the film's release date (1944), a time when "families were often forced apart.... In context *Meet Me in St. Louis* appeared as a nostalgic look back at America in 1903.... It suggested an ideal of family unity for the future." The superficial level of familial celebration is the most easily perceived, and Bordwell and Thompson are doubtless correct in assuming that it was responsible for the film's contemporary popularity. Today, it is obvious that it is disrupted by numerous other factors.

Ideological contradiction. Throughout American art and culture the concepts "home" and "family," are central to ideological tension and conflict, perceived at once as the repositories of security and happiness where "good" values are preserved and as prisons in which energy is repressed, human beings trapped and frustrated. Beneath its level of affirmation, this tension is dramatized in *Meet Me in St. Louis* more thoroughly than in almost any other American film. To give one example only: the "happy ending" can be achieved only through the symbolic castration of the father (the "snow-people" scene), his capitulation expressing itself in the line, "We'll stay here till we rot."

Genre. The film basically crosses two genres, the musical (often regarded in terms of "celebration of vitality") and the small town domestic comedy (traditionally concerned with the *containment* of energy). Instead of concealing the potential tension here, the film consistently exploits it, making it its central principle. Even more remarkable is the eruption of a third (totally incompatible) genre: the famous Halloween sequence is built unambiguously on the iconography of the horror film and can now be seen to be the antecedent of the "demon child" movies of the 70's (*The Exorcist, The Omen, Halloween*).

Stars. The film draws particularly on the personalities/star images of two performers: Judy Garland, with her combination of energy, neuroticism and precariously-suppressed hysteria, and Margaret O'Brien, who became famous overnight in her first film, *Journey for Margaret*, especially for her scene of prolonged hysterical breakdown.

Director. There was a time when Minnelli's musicals were critically downgraded in favour of those by Donen and Kelly: the latter certainly, correspond more unproblematically to the simple "celebration of vitality" formula. Minnelli's musicals—full, like melodramas, of tension, excess, dislocation—produce continuous uneasiness. Virtually every number in *Meet Me in St. Louis* (including the famous "Trolley Song") ends not in the ultimate release of exuberance but in frustration. "Release" in Minnelli, in fact, usually takes the form of the explosion of hysteria (see, for example, the frenetic car-rides of *The Bad and the Beautiful* and *Two Weeks in Another Town*, the fairground climax of *Some Came Running*, the "goldfish" scene of *Courtship of Eddie's Father*, the "Mack the Black" fantasy of *The Pirate*). Both the major sequences of *Meet Me in St. Louis* centred on Margaret O'Brien (Halloween and the smashing of the snow people) have this function; both are also concerned with the symbolic destruction of parent-figures. Even the apparent affirmation of the end of the film is severely undercut—by its anti-climactic nature, by Tootie's dream of apocalyptic destruction, by John's casual remark that he "liked it better when it was just a swamp."

Meet Me in St. Louis, then, must be read not as a simple celebration of family life but as the point of intersection of some of the major ideological tensions in American culture. For a detailed account, the reader is referred to Andrew Britton's "Smith, or the Ambiguities" in *The Australian Journal of Screen Theory*, one of the most comprehensive and intelligent readings of a Hollywood film so far attempted.

—Robin Wood

MEG KER A NEP. Red Psalm. Production: Mafilm Studio; Eastmancolor, 35mm; running time: 88 mins.; length: 7920 feet. Released 1971, Hungary.

Screenplay by Gyula Hernádi; directed by Miklós Jancsó; photography by János Kende; edited by Zoltán Farkas; art direction by Tamás Banovich; musical arrangements by Ferenc Sebo; choreography by Ferenc Pesovár.

Filmed 1971. Cannes Film Festival, Best Director, 1972.

Cast: Lajos Balázsovits (*Officer Cadet*); András Bálint (*Count*); Gyöngyi Büros (*Young peasant woman*); Andrea Drahota (*Militant girl*); József Madoras; Tibor Molnár; Tibor Orbán; Bertalan Solti.

Publications:

Reviews—"Álom a szabadságról": Jancsó Miklós: *Még kér a nép*" by V. Varga in *Filmkultura* (Budapest), November/December 1972; "*Psaume rouge*: la tactique et le rite" by J.L. Passek in *Cinéma* (Paris), December 1972; "*Red Psalm*" by Gordon Gow in *Films and Filming* (London), May 1973; "*Psaume rouge*" by P. Desmet and J.C. Guiguet in *Image et son* (Paris), January 1973; "Vers Le Corpus sacré de la révolution" by J.P. Jeancolas in *Positif* (Paris), February 1973; "*Psaume rouge*" by J. Magny in *Téléciné* (Paris), January 1973; book— *The Most Important Art: East European Film After 1945* by Mira Liehm and Antonín Liehm, Berkeley 1977; articles— "L'Idéologie, la technique et le rite" by Claude Beylie in *Ecran* (Paris), December 1972; "*Les Maelstroms de la liberté*" by *Claude Beylie in Ecran* (Paris), July/August 1972; "Miklos Jancso: 'Le plan séquence: le rythme le plus près de la réalité...'" by G. Langlois in *Cinéma* (Paris), December 1972; "A fanatizmus ritusai" by M. Szabó in *Filmkultura* (Budapest), March/April 1972; article in *Variety* (New York), 24 May 1972; article in *Hollywood Reporter*, 3 October 1972; "Entretien avec Miklos Jancso" by A. Cornaud in *Image et son* (Paris), January 1973; article in *Cinématographe* (Paris), February 1973; article in *Monthly Film Bulletin* (London), April 1973; "Röd hymn" by W. Andersson in *Filmrutan* (Lidingö, Sweden), no.3, 1974; "Circolarità della rivoluzione" by R. Tomasino in *Filmcritica* (Rome), August/September 1974; "*Psaume rouge*" by B. Gay in *Image et son* (Paris), June/July 1975; "Miklos Jancso: i riti della rivoluzione la morte, la resurrezione, il futuro" by R. Escobar and V. Giacci in *Cineforum* (Bergamo), November 1976; article in *Cinema Papers* (Melbourne, Australia), June/July 1976; article in *Film Form* (New Castle, England), spring 1976.

*   *   *

Of all of his films, *Meg ker a nep* perhaps best exemplifies the stylistic hallmarks with which Miklós Jancsó is most often associated: long takes (frequently 5 to 8 minutes in length), a constantly moving camera which weaves in and out of groups of moving figures, and an array of visual metaphors and exotic images rooted in Hungarian folklore and his own personal mythology.

On its most simple level, *Meg ker a nep* is set in Hungary in the 1890s and presents the emergence of agrarian socialist movements—but Jancsó isn't interested in a realistic depiction of isolated historical events. Through his unconventional cinematic style, Jancsó creates a "ritualistic portrayal of revolution" which takes on universal significance, and the success of the film derives from the manner in which its form *becomes* its content.

For Jancsó, "one can imagine a film other than in the form of a story. We must try to widen the limits of expression." With his reduction of the primacy of narrative, Jancsó also diminishes depth of characterization, the importance of individual action, and complex psychological explanations of behavior. In spite of these simplifications, Jancsó claims that his films are still "a

means of expression with several dimensions." His undercutting of an audience's emotional identification with characters and situations creates, in his mind, "active" viewers and "makes.- ..[them] think"—and presumably take action at a later time.

If, in *Meg ker a nep*, Jancsó reduces traditional cinematic elements to a minimum, his style creates a heightened sense of the importance of movement, both in aesthetic and ideological terms. "It seems to me that life is a continual movement. In a procession, a demonstration, there's movement all the time, isn't there? It's physical and it's also philosophical: the contradiction is founded on movement, the movement of ideas, the movement of the masses.... A man also is always surrounded, threatened by oppression: the camera movements I create suggest that too." In *Meg ker a nep*, the complex interweaving of the moving camera with the carefully choreographed groups of soldiers, horsemen, and villagers reflects the ideological conflicts central to the film. The long takes and the examples of nearly invisible editing allow the spectator to concentrate on non-verbal devices to understand the unfolding action. For example, foreground activity becomes background activity only to return minutes later to the foreground of the screen as a manifestation of the continual shifting nature of power. Geometric shapes (most notably vertical lines and circles) are also in constant conflict and in constant movement, and the shifting fortunes of ideological struggles are also indicated in the clash of various types of music in the film.

Music is especially important in *Meg ker a nep*; the narrative action is delineated as much by music and song as by the film's rather abstract, depersonalized dialogue. Beyond that, music universalizes the film's theme. Aside from Hungarian folk songs that tell of the events depicted in the film and the repetition of a key song in multiple contexts, Jancsó's music, which includes the Scottish ballad "Charlie Is My Darling" and the French "Marseillaise," suggests that all revolutions are part of one continuing revolution.

Miklós Jancsó, like Sergei Eisenstein and Sergei Paradzhanov, is a master of synesthesia, a director who fuses multiple art forms to create in film the perfect medium for Wagner's *Gesamtkunstwerk. Meg ker a nep*, which won the "Best Director" award at the 1972 Cannes Film Festival, is perhaps Jancsó's best example of "fusion of the arts" and has been justly praised as Jancsó's best film by critics John Russell Taylor and Roy Armes.

—Joseph A. Gomez

MEMORIAS DEL SUBDESAROLLO. Memories of Underdevelopment. Production: Instituto Cubano del Arte e Industria Cinematograficos (ICAIC); black and white, 35mm; running time: 104 minutes. Released 1968.

Produced by Miguel Mendoza; screenplay by Tomás Gutiérrez Alea and Edmundo Desnoes; from the novel by Edmundo Desnoes; directed by Tomás Gutiérrez Alea; photography by Ramón Suárez; edited by Nelson Rodríguez; sound engineering by Eugenio Vesa, Germinal Hernández, and Carlos Fernández; production design by Julio Matilla; music by Leo Brower, conducted by Manuel Duchezne Cuzán, recorded by Medardo Montero; optical effects by Jorge Pucheux; costumes designed by Elba Perez; animation by Roberto Riquenes.

Filmed in Havana. Warsaw Festival, Mermaid Prize, 1970.

Cast: Sergio Corrieri (*Sergio*); Daisy Granados (*Elena*); Eslinda Núñez (*Noemi*); Omar Valdés; René de la Cruz; Yolanda Farr;

Ofelia Gonzáles; José Gil Abad; Daniel Jordan; Luis López; Rafael Sosa.

Publications:

Script—*Memories of Underdevelopment: The Revolutionary Films of Cuba* (screenplay) edited by Michael Myerson, New York 1973; reviews—"*Mémoires du sous-développement*" by R. Bassan in *Téléciné* (Paris), December 1974; "*Mémoires du sous-développement*" by G. Colpart in *Image et son* (Paris), November 1974; "*Memories of Underdevelopment*" by A.F. Nussbaum in *Movietone News* (Seattle), February 1975; "*Mémoires du sous-développement*" by P.L. Thirard in *Positif* (Paris), January 1975; articles—"The Cuban Cinema: Filmography" by M.E. Douglas in *Take One* (Montreal), July/August 1968; article by Don Allen in *Sight and Sound* (London), autumn 1969; article by Brian Murphy in *Films and Filming* (London), September 1969; "Solidarity and Violence" by Andi Engel in *Sight and Sound* (London), autumn 1969; "*Memorias del subdesarrollo*" by Juan M. Bullita in *Hablemos de Cine* (Lima, Peru), no.54, 1970; "3 Cuban Cultural Reports with Films Somewhere in Them" in *A Year in the Dark* by Renata Adler, Berkeley 1971; "Egy polgár vallomásai" by O. Hámori in *Filmkultura* (Budapest), January/February 1972; "Two Third World Films" by W. Murphy in *Take One* (Montreal), April 1972; "Images of Underdevelopment" by Julia Lesage in *Jump Cut* (Chicago), May/June 1974; *Cine Cubano en EEUU"* by D. Torres Diaz in *Cine Cubano* (Havana), no.89-90, 1974; "*Mémoires du sous-dévelopment*" by M. Martin in *Ecran* (Paris), December 1974; "The Alea Affair in *Film 73/74* edited by David Denby and Jay Cocks, Indianapolis 1974; "3 on 2: Henry Fernandez, David I. Grossvogel and Emir Rodriguez Monegal on Desnoes and Alea" in *Diacritics: A Review of Contemporary Cinema*, v.4, no.4, winter 1974; "Women: *The Memories of Underdevelopment*" by S. Lieberman in *Women and Film* (Berkeley), summer 1975; "*Memories of Underdevelopment*: Alienation and Critical Response, or Can a Bourgeois Intellectual Find Happiness in a Revolutionary Society?" by Julianne Burton in *Review* (Center for Inter-American Relations), fall 1976; "Cuban Cinema: Tomas Guiterrez Alea" by Margot Kernan in *Film Quarterly* (Berkeley), winter 1976; "About *Memories of Underdevelopment*" in *Memories of Underdevelopment: The Revolutionary Films of Cuba* edited by Michael Myerson, New York 1977; "Individual Fulfillment and Collective Achievement: An Interview with Tomás Gutiérrez Alea" by Julianne Burton in *Cinéaste* (New York), January 1977; "*Memories of Underdevelopment*: In the Land of Overdevelopment" by Julianne Burton in *Cineaste* (New York), summer 1977; "Dialectics and the Textuality of Class Conflict" by Tho. M. Kavanagh in *Journal of Latin American Lore*, v.4, no.1, 1978; "Revolutionary Cinema and the Self-Reflections on a Disappearing Class" by Albert Michaels in *Journal of Latin American Lore*, v.4, no.1, 1978; "Witnesses Everywhere: The Rhetorical Strategies of *Memories of Underdevelopment*" by Enrique Fernandez in *Wide Angle* (Athens, Ohio), winter 1980; "*Memorias del subdesarrollo*, Notas de trabajo" by Tomás Gutiérrez Alea in *Cine Cubano* (Havana), no.45/6, n.d. "Se llamaba Sergio" by Edmundo Desnoes in *Cine Cubano* (Havana), no.45/6, n.d.

*   *   *

The self and society, private life and history, individual psychology and historical situation—this is the core of *Memories*, and the film has rarely (if ever) been used so effectively to portray this relationship. The dialectic of consciousness and context is presented through the character of Sergio, a wealthy but alienated member of the bourgeoisie who stays in Cuba after the triumph of the revolution and whose experiences, feelings, and thoughts in being confronted by the new reality form the basis of the film.

The formal inventiveness of the film has its origin in the dialectical resonance created through the juxtaposition of various cinematic forms, a characteristic of revolutionary Cuban cinema at its best. Here, the film begins by re-working the book which inspired it, taking the form of the novel—Sergio's subjective revolutionary Cuba, presented in documentary footage. Through this formal juxtaposition, the film "objectifies" the internal monologue of Sergio—criticizing and contextualizing his psychological subjectivism and confronting his attempts to retreat into his pre-revolutionary psychology and ways of seeing with the "fact of history" presented by the revolutionary situation.

Visually, the film's dialectic is presented through the use of three forms of cinematic structure. Documentary and semi-documentary footage is used to depict the "collective consciousness" of the revolutionary process, a consciousness that is pre-eminently historical. This footage presents us with the background of the revolution and establishes the historical context of the film's fictional present by placing it between the 1961 exodus in the aftermath of the failed Bay of Pigs invasion and the defensive preparations for the Missile Crisis of 1962. Fictional footage is used in two ways. The majority of the fictional sequences are presented in the traditional form of narrative cinema, in which the camera functions as omniscient narrator. However, at times the camera presents us with Sergio's point-of-view, the way in which his consciousness realizes itself in his forms of perception—what he looks at and how he sees it. Thus, the film shows and creates an identification with what it is simultaneously criticizing. Through this juxtaposition of visual forms, and through the visual contradiction of Sergio's reflections, the film insists that what we see is a function of how we believe, and that how we believe is what our history has made of us.

Sergio's way of seeing was formed in pre-revolutionary Cuba. As a member of the educated elite, he developed a disdain for Cuban reality and a scorn for those who believe that it could be changed. Critical of his bourgeois family and friends (who are, however, capable of making the commitment to leave Cuba), he is nonetheless unable to overcome his alienation and link himself to the revolution. The "ultimate outsider," he attempts to content himself by colonizing and exploiting women—a metaphor for the colonization of Cuba. His personal fate is finally and paradoxically irrelevent, for as the film ends the camera moves out from his individual vision to the larger revolution beyond.

The film "shocked" U.S. critics when released there in 1973, and they described it variously as "extremely rich," "hugely effective," "beautifully understated," and "a miracle." No "miracle" at all, but simply one of the finest examples of revolutionary Cuban cinema, *Memories* has also received a warm reception from Cuban audiences, some film-goers returning to see it again and again. *Memories'* complex structure and dialectical texture merit such repeated viewings, for it transforms the now familiar themes of alienation and the "outsider" by placing them within a revolutionary setting. We identify with and understand Sergio, who is capable of moments of lucidity. However, we also understand that his perspective is neither universal nor timeless but a specific response to a particular situation. *Memories of Understanding* insists that such situations are not permanent and that things can be changed through commitment and struggle. History is a concrete, material process which, ironically, is the salvation of the Sergios.

—John Mraz

MENILMONTANT. Production: Dimitri Kirsanoff's production company; black and white, 35mm, silent; running time: about 50 mins.; length: 1800 feet. Released 1924, France.

Produced, written, and directed by Dimitri Kirsanoff; photography by Léonce Crouan (uncredited) and Dimitri Kirsanoff; edited by Dimitri Kirsanoff (uncredited).

Filmed in Paris.

Cast: Nadia Sibirskaia (*Younger sister*); Yolande Beaulieu (*Elder sister*); Guy Belmont (*Young man*); Jean Pasquier; Maurice Ronsard.

Publications:

Book—*Leslie Halliwell's Film Guide*, (credits only), 4th edition, New York 1983; articles—"*Menilmontant*" in *Travelling* (Lausanne, Switzerland), summer 1979; "*Ménilmontant*" by G. Brown in *Monthly Film Bulletin* (London), October 1981.

*   *   *

Menilmontant, the best known and the most impressive film of the Russian émigré cellist, Dimitri Kirsanoff, takes its title from the working-class district of Paris where its drama occurs. This short film is remarkable for the honesty with which it represents seduction, jealousy, and prostitution, and, even more so, for its economical and powerful use of montage to narrate a complex story completely without intertitles.

The film opens with an unexplained axe murder, brilliantly conceived in a montage of violent details. The remainder of the film describes the life of the two daughters of the murdered couple, who both fall in love with a Parisian thug; one ends up with a baby and the other becomes a prostitute. In the final moments of the film they are reconciled and return to their first job in a sweatshop, while the thug, unbeknownst to them, is murdered in an obscure brawl, the mystery and violence of which reflect the opening murders.

A series of hand-held views of Paris, together with superimpositions, simultaneously propels the story elliptically and gives us insights into the psychology of the two girls. The first such sequence marks the abrupt transition from the country to the city, and conveys in its rhythm the excitement Paris possesses for the two new arrivals. When the sister who eventually will have a baby spends her first night with her lover, another moving camera sequence, superimposed over the other sister, vividly portrays her jealousy, and her fantasy, of her sister's initiation into the excitements of the city. A gloomier version of the same dynamic camera movement is superimposed over the face of the young mother when she leaves the maternity ward, thinking (as the montage makes perfectly clear) of killing herself and her baby. The final round of this stylistic trope introduces the idea of prostitution and culminates in the meeting of the two sisters.

They had become estranged when the first one to be seduced saw, from a distance, her sister also seduced by the thug. Kirsanoff brilliantly emphasizes her shock by cutting to a series of progressively closer shots of her face, in precisely the manner that he had earlier edited the scene in which she comes upon her slaughtered parents. By reserving this figure for those two scenes alone, he urges the viewer to connect the two traumas psychologically. The entire film is constructed around an elaborate network of such cinematic figures, making it one of the most interesting psychological narratives of its period.

—P. Adams Sitney

MEPHISTO. Production: Mafilm-Objektiv Studio (Budapest) in cooperation with Manfred Durniok Productions (West Berlin); Eastmancolor, 35mm; running time: 146 mins., some sources list 144 mins. Released 1981.

Produced by Manfred Durniok; screenplay by István Szabó and Péter Dobai; from the novel by Klaus Mann; directed by István Szabó; photography by Lajos Koltai; edited by Zsuzsa Zsa Kany; music by Zdenkó Tamássy.

Filmed in Germany. Academy Award, Best Foreign Film.

Cast: Klaus Maria Brandauer (*Hendrik Höfgen*); Krystyna Janda (*Barbara Bruckner*); Ildikó Bánsági (*Nicoletta von Niebuhr*); Karin Boyd (*Juliette Martens*); Rolf Hoppe (*The General*); Christine Harbort (*Lotte Lindenthal*); Gyögy Cserhalmi (*Hans Miklas*); Martin Hellberg (*Professor*).

Publications:

Reviews—in *The New York Times*, 29 September 1981; "*Mephisto*" by M. Auty in *Monthly Film Bulletin* (London), October 1981; "*Mephisto*" by J. Forbes in *Films and Filming* (London), December 1981; "A jó magaviselet megszállottja" by M. Györffy in *Filmkultura* (Budapest), September/October 1981; "*Mephisto*" in the *Hungarofilm Bulletin* (Budapest), no.2, 1981; "*Mephisto*" by G. Moskowitz in *Variety* (New York), 18 March 1981; "My Homeland" by D. Robinson in *Sight and Sound* (London), autumn 1981; review in the *New Yorker*, 17 May 1982; review in the *New Republic* (New York), 7 April 1982; review in *Variety* (New York), 17 March 1982; review in *Newsweek* (New York), 12 April 1982; review in *Time* (New York), 3 May 1982; articles—"Mephistopheles" by István Szabó in *Hungarofilm Bulletin* (Budapest), no.5, 1980; "Leider kann man einen Film nur einmal drehen..." by G. Fenyves in *Film und Fernsehen* (Berlin), March 1981; "*Mephisto*" by R. Frey in *Filmfaust* (Frankfurt), November 1981; "Méphisto de István Szabó" by Louis Marcorelles in *Le Monde* (Paris), July 1981; "*Mephisto*" by Derek Elley in *International Film Guide 1982* edited by Peter Cowie, New York 1982; "*Mephisto*" by Rob Edelman in *Magill's Cinema Annual* edited by Frank N. Magill, Englewood Cliffs, New Jersey 1982; "Analízis jelképek nélkül" by György Szabó in *Filmkultura* (Budapest), no.3, 1982.

*   *   *

István Szabó, probably the most engagingly intelligent of the younger Hungarian filmmakers who began working after 1956, earned a reputation among serious observers of the international cinema during the 1960s—most of all for the wonderfully bright and inventive *The Father* (1966). More than a decade later, his *Confidence* (1979) was nominated for an Academy Award; an exceptional film, its subtle complexities and quiet beauty did not win either the Oscar or the wider public his work deserves. Both trophies did, however, come soon thereafter with *Mephisto*, the director's first major international production.

The idea behind *Mephisto* is a promising one—to explore the psyche of a chameleon-like actor living through the rise of Nazism in Germany (the filmmakers actually choose not to specify the precise time or place) and accommodating himself to the new regime in any way necessary to maintain his position and acclaim. Most promising of all is the fact that this central character is based on the life of Gustav Gründgens (1899-1963), Germany's most commanding actor, theatrical director, and impresario of his generation. (Among his film roles, Gründgens played the wily chief of the underworld in Fritz Lang's *M* in 1931.) The screenplay, which Szabó wrote with Péter Dobai, is based on the 1936 *roman à clef*, also titled *Mephisto*, by Klaus Mann, the son of Thomas Mann and brother of Erika, to whom Gründgens was married before she fled from Hitler's Germany. (The title is an ironic reference to the actor's celebrated role, Mephistopheles in *Faust*.)

In Szabó's film, the Gründgens character is named Hendrik Höfgen. There are intimations that the fictional Höfgen shares some of Gründgens's early leftist learnings as he embarks on a propitious acting career. To keep that career afloat in the mounting tide of fascism, Höfgen ingratiates himself with a powerful leader in the new regime—a proxy for Göring, whose pretégé Gründgens became. And, like Gründgens, Höfgen chooses to remain in his position rather than avail himself of an opportunity to emigrate. *Mephisto* ends before the war, as its version of the Gründgens character begins to see himself becoming a puppet of his protectors.

The film is brilliant and enthralling, a whirlwind of color and motion that suggests its protagonist's rapid success and self-absorption. A virtuosic achievement as a succession to Szabó's finely modulated previous work, *Mephisto* is near-perfect within the scope of its ambition—to delineate the course of an opportunist whose life is nothing more or less than the sum of all the roles he plays. But its tone of moral indignation is all too easy, its moral crux so very familier and predictable, and its rendering of the central figure a pat oversimplification of the unacknowledged character who inspired it. Klaus Maria Brandauer's manic performance in the part of Höfgen, as is apt for this film, represents a self-illuminating style of acting that one esteems or rejects according to one's critical disposition toward work of its kind. Neither the role nor Brandauer's portrayal suggests whether Höfgen is a genuinely great actor (as Gründgens was) or simply an effectively truculent and narcissistic one. (The other performers are quite fine, although the many Hungarians in the cast have been dubbed into German for the film's distribution outside Hungary.)

Klaus Mann's aim was to condemn Gründgens. Szabó sought to universalize the character, "a man who considers it his only possiblity in life to make people accept him." But beyond the simple figure who appears in *Mephisto* lies the complex and ambivalent case of Gründgens himself. Despite his tacit support for Hitler, he was cleared after the war and continued his prominence in the theaters of both West and East Germany. He was even credited with upholding artistic standards during the Third Reich (Höfgen participates in plays reinterpreted to fit fascist ideology) and with helping many who were threatened by the Nazis (Höfgen does obtain an exit visa for his lover, a black actress).

In the shadow of Stalinism, many Eastern European directors have made films set around the time of World War II, with safe, anti-Nazi topics, when current issues could not be broached. Szabó understands very well the real difficulties and ambiguities of individuals who chose to continue living and working under compromising political circumstances, and in fact his own contemporary films have frequently focused on their dilemmas with sympathy and resonance. With *Mephisto* and the aspiration for wide popularity, it seems he has limited his scrutiny to an extreme case and held it at a safe distance.

—Herbert Reynolds

THE MERRY WIDOW. Production: Metro-Goldwyn-Mayer Pictures Corp.; 1925; black and white, 35mm, silent; running time: 111 mins.; length: 10 reels, 10,027 feet. Released 26 August 1925.

Produced by Irving Thalberg; scenario by Erich von Stroheim and Benjamine Glazer; from the opera *Die lustige Witwe: Operette in drei Akten* by Leo Stein and Victor Léon, music by Franz Lehar; titles by Marian Ainslee; directed by Erich von Stroheim; photography by Oliver T. Marsh, Ben Reynolds, and William Daniels; edited by Frank E. Hull; production design by Cedric Gibbons and Richard Day; musical score which accompanies film by William Axt and David Mendoza; costumes designed by Richard Day and Erich von Stroheim.

Filmed during 12 weeks of 1925 in Hollywood.

Cast: Mae Murray (*Sally*); John Gilbert (*Prince Danilo*); Roy D'Arcy (*Crown Prince Mirko*); Josephine Crowell (*Queen Milena*); George Fawcett (*King Nikita*); Tully Marshall (*Baron Sadoja*); Albert Conti (*Danilo's adjutant*); Sidney Bracy (*Danilo's footman*); Don Ryan (*Mirko's adjutant*); Hughie Mack (*Innkeeper*); Ida Moore (*Innkeeper's wife*); Lucille von Lent (*Innkeeper's daughter*); Dale Fuller (*Sadoja's chambermaid*); Charles Magelis (*Flo Epstein*); Harvey Karels (*Jimmy Watson*); Edna Tichenor (*Frenchie Christine*); Jacqueline Gadsdon (*Madonna*); Estelle Clarke (*French barber*); D'Arcy Corrigan (*Horatio*); Clara Wallacks and Frances Prim (*Hansen Sisters*); Zack Williams (*George Washington White*); Edward Connelly (*Ambassador*); Merewyn Thayer (*Ambassador's wife*); Lon Poff (*Sadoja's lackey*).

Publications:

Books—*Erich von Stroheim, sa vie, ses films* by Georges Fronval, Paris 1939; *An Index to the Creative Work of Erich von Stroheim* by Herman G. Weinberg, supplement to *Sight and Sound*, index series, London 1943; *Hollywood Scapegoat: The Biography of Erich von Stroheim* by Peter Noble, London 1951; *Erich von Stroheim* by Bob Bergut, Paris 1960; *Erich von Stroheim* by Jon Barna, Vienna 1966; *Hommage à Erich von Stroheim* edited by Charlotte Gobeil, Ottawa, Canada 1966; *Erich von Stroheim* by Michel Ciment, Paris 1967; *Stroheim* by Joel Finler, Berkeley 1968; *Erich von Stroheim* by Thomas Quinn Curtiss, Paris 1969; *Irving Thalberg: Life and Legend* by Bob Thomas, New York 1969; *Erich von Stroheim* by Freddy

Buache, Paris 1972; *Stroheim: A Pictorial Record of his 9 Films* by Herman G. Weinberg, New York 1975; articles—"Erich von Stroheim" by Jim Tully in *Vanity Fair* (New York), March 1926; "Stroheim Revisited: The Missing Third in American Cinema" by Gavin Lambert in *Sight and Sound* (London), April/June 1953; "John Gilbert" by Lawrence Quirk in *Films in Review* (New York), March 1956; "Erich von Stroheim: 1885-1957" by William K. Everson in *Films in Review* (New York), August/-September 1957; "Erich von Stroheim introduces *The Merry Widow*" by von Stroheim in *Film Culture* (New York), April 1958; "Notes on the Style of Stroheim" by Lotte Eisner in *Film Culture* (New York), April 1958.

*   *   *

It was almost more trouble than it was worth, but Irving Thalberg and Louis B. Mayer were convinced that there was tremendous box-office potential in a film version of Franz Lehar's operetta, *The Merry Widow*, to star MGM's most expensive star, Mae Murray. The increasingly popular John Gilbert was to be her Prince Danilo, and Erich von Stroheim was to be given one last chance to prove his worth as director, for on the surface a film version of *The Merry Widow* seemed perfect for him. Actually, it meant 12 weeks of very stormy shooting time.

All was sweetness and light when the production started. As the year was 1925, it was a silent picture—but MGM would prove that there was lyricism in a silent with such productions as this film, *The Student Prince* (1927), and *Rose Marie* (1928). The big moment in *The Merry Widow* was to come when Murray and Gilbert danced the famous waltz, which would be pounded out in theatres by a live orchestra, or a Wurlitzer, or at least by a piano accompaniment. Miss Murray's main interest was in that sequence, and her idea of *The Merry Widow* was certainly not that of von Stroheim. He saw the picture as entirely realistic, an openly vulgar exposé of all the depravity and decadence in high court life, and wanted to cut the famous waltz sequence in its entirety.

Miss Murray had some power in those days. She hadn't been too happy with the scenario von Stroheim and Benjamin Glazer had constructed, which bore little resemblance to the operetta's book. She wasn't to be a heroine named Sonia; she was just the lead dancer named Sally in an American touring company appearing in the mythical kingdom of Marsovia with her show "Manhattan Follies." She catches the eye of the richest man in the country, and becomes both bride and widow on her wedding night, when her senile, fetish-ridden husband (Tully Marshall) has a stroke and conveniently expires, leaving her all his wealth. Prince Danilo is sent to follow her to Paris, because Marsovia does not want her vast wealth to leave the country. This becomes the set-up, climaxing when the waltz is danced by the widow and her Danilo.

Von Stroheim threatened not to shoot the waltz, but was compelled to set up the scene. Turning his back on his actors, he said, "Tell me when the damned thing is done." Unfortunately, Gilbert, who was not a trained dancer, stumbled once, and the waltz had to be halted momentarily for another take. Von Stroheim said, loud enough for everyone to hear, "What can you expect from a showgirl and a rank amateur?" Miss Murray flew into a temper, and stormed off to her dressing-room.

Everyone went slightly crazy then, but eventually an unsteady peace was achieved. The picture was finished under stress, and von Stroheim left the lot with his picture in 90 reels that had to be cut down to 10 before it could be released. Gone was the mockery and decadence von Stroheim had filmed, and the released picture was just what Miss Murray wanted—an innocent confection of gossamer romance.

Shortly thereafter, when talking pictures came in, no studio would hire von Stroheim, and he went back to acting, and was superb in both French and Hollywood films. *The Merry Widow* made money, a great deal. It has twice been re-made, once in 1934, with Jeanette MacDonald and Maurice Chevalier, directed by Ernst Lubitsch; and then disastrously in Technicolor with Lana Turner and Ricardo Montalban, with Curtis Bernhardt directing as if he only wanted to get it out of the way.

—DeWitt Bodeen

MESHES OF THE AFTERNOON. Black and white, 16mm; running time: 18 mins., some sources list 14 mins. Released 1943.

Screenplay by Maya Deren and Alexander Hammid; directed and editing by Maya Deren; photography by Alexander Hammid.

Cast: Maya Deren (*Woman*); Alexander Hammid (*Man*).

Publications:

Books—*An Anagram of Ideas on Art, Form and the Film* by Maya Deren, New York 1946; *Introduction to the Art of the Movies: An Anthology of Ideas on the Nature of Movie Art* edited by Lewis Jacobs, New York 1960; *Underground Film* by Parker Tyler, New York 1969; *A History of the American Avant-Garde Cinema* edited by The American Federation of Arts, New York 1976; *The Legend of Maya Deren* by VeVe Amasasa Clark and others, New York 1978; *Visionary Film* by P. Adams Sitney, 2nd edition, New York 1979; articles—"Maya Deren's Films" by Manny Farber in the *New Republic* (New York), 28 October 1946; "Experimental Film: A New Growth" by Parker Tyler in *Kenyon Review* (Gambier, Ohio), no.1, 1949; "Writings of Maya Deren and Ron Rice" in *Film Culture* (New York), winter 1965; "Maya Deren and Germaine Dulac: Activists of the Avant-Garde" by Regina Cornwell in *Film Library Quarterly* (New York), v.5, no.1, 1971; "The Idea of Morphology" by P. Adams Sitney in *Film Culture* (New York), nos.53, 54 and 55, 1972; "The Legend of Maya Deren: Champion of the American Independent Film by T. Mayer in *Film News* (New York), September/October 1979.

*   *   *

Meshes of the Afternoon launched the American avant-garde film movement after World War II. Made in collaboration by Maya Deren and her husband Alexander Hammid, the film depicts a woman's imaginative dream and the way it eventually destroys the woman herself. The film established dream imagery and visual poetic devices as the chief type of cinematic language for a new generation of postwar filmmakers and their audiences.

The story of *Meshes* is this: a woman (played by Deren) enters her home and falls asleep in a chair. As she sleeps and dreams, she repeatedly encounters a mysterious hooded figure whom she chases but cannot catch. With each failure, she re-enters her house, where the household objects she employs in her waking state—a key, a knife, a flower, a phonograph, and a telephone— assume intensifying potency in an environment that becomes increasingly disoriented. Through such filmic means as creative editing, extreme camera angles, and slow motion, the movie creates a world in which it is more and more difficult for the woman to master the space and rooms around her. Finally, multiplied into three versions of herself, the woman attempts to kill her sleeping body. But she is awakened by a man (played by Hammid) only to find that physical reality, too, gives away to the dream logic of her imagination, ultimately causing her death.

Made privately in Deren's and Hammid's home over a few weeks and for a few hundred dollars, *Meshes of the Afternoon* revived a European cinematic tradition established in the 1920's, a tradition in which Hammid participated in his native Czechoslavakia. *Meshes of the Afternoon* sustained and developed the cinematic style of such leading European avant-garde filmmakers of the 1920's as Germaine Dulac, Luis Buñuel, and Jean Cocteau.

Meshes is a landmark film that has provided an important model, setting the tone and style for other individual efforts over the next decade. It launched Deren's career as one of the leading avant-garde filmmakers of the 1940's and 1950's. She showed the film at colleges, museums, and film societies across Canada and the United States. Her numerous bookings encouraged many younger artists interested in a personal cinema controlled by the individual artists. The film consequently inspired poetic self-exploratory films by such other filmmakers as Kenneth Anger, Stan Brakhage, and Willard Maas.

Meshes of the Afternoon is still one of the most popular of all American experimental films. It is revered as a classic mood poem which investigates a person's psychological reality.

—Lauren Rabinovitz

METROPOLIS. Production: Universum-Film-Aktiengesellschaft (Ufa) studios; black and white, 35mm, silent; running time: about 2 hours originally, no complete master copy now exists but the Staatliches Archiv in East Berlin has compiled a new copy from all remaining footage; length: 4189 meters originally, current copies are now 3170 meters. Released 10 January 1927, Berlin.

Screenplay by Fritz Lang and Thea von Harbou; from the novel by Thea von Harbou, (Eisner disputes this in *The Haunted Screen*, 1969, claiming the film preceded the novel); directed by Fritz Lang; photography by Karl Freund and Günther Rittau; art direction by Otto Hunte, Erich Kettelhut, and Karl Vollbrecht; music by Gottfried Huppertz; special effects by Eugene Schüfftan; costumes designed by Anne Willkomm; sculptures by Walter Schultze-Mittendorff.

Filmed 1925-26, in 310 days and 60 nights, in UFA Studios, Berlin. Cost: $2,000,000.

Cast: Brigitte Helm (*Maria/the Mechanical Maria*); Alfred Abel (*John Fredersen*); Gustav Fröhlich (*Freder*); Rudolf Klein-Rogge (*Rotwang*); Fritz Rasp (*Slim*); Theodor Loos (*Josaphat/*

Joseph); Heinrich George (*Grot, the foreman*); Olaf Storm (*Jan*); Hanns Leo Reich (*Marinus*); Heinrich Gotho (*Master of Ceremonies*); Margarete Lanner (*Woman in the car*); Max Dietze, Georg John, Walter Kühle, Arthur Reinhard, and Erwin Vater (*Workers*); Grete Berger, Olly Böheim, Ellen Frey, Lisa Gray, Rose Lichtenstein, and Helene Weigel (*Female workers*); Beatrice Garga, Anny Hintze, Margarete Lanner, Helen von Münchhofen, and Hilde Woitscheff (*Women in the Eternal Garden*); Fritz Alberti (*Robot*); 750 secondary actors; and over 30,000 extras.

Publications:

Script—*Metropolis* in *Avant-Scène du cinéma* (Paris), 1 December 1977; reviews—in *The New York Times*, 7 March 1927; "*Metropolis*" by Iris Barry in *Spectator* (London), 26 March 1927; "*Metropolis*" by Axel Eggebrecht in *Die Weltbühne* (Berlin), 18 January 1927; "*Metropolis*" by Evelyn Gerstein in the *Nation* (New York), 23 March 1927; "*Metropolis*" by Robert Herring in *London Mercury*, May 1927; "Mr. Wells reviews a Current Film" by H.G. Wells in *The New York Times*, 17 April 1927; books—*The Film Till Now* by Paul Rotha, London 1930; *Vom Werden deutscher Filmkunst, Part I: Der Stummfilm* by Oskar Kalbus, Altona-Bahrenfeld, Germany 1935; *An Index to the Creative Work of Fritz Lang* by Herman Weinberg, supplement to *Sight and Sound*, index series, London 1946; *From Caligari to Hitler: A Psychological History of the German Film* by Siegfried Kracauer, Princeton 1947; *Fritz Lang* by Francis Courtade, Paris 1963; *Fritz Lang* by Luc Moullet, Paris 1963; *Tower of Babel* by Eric Rhode, London 1966; *Les Grands Cinéastes que je Propose* by Henri Agel, Paris 1967; *Films and Feelings* by Raymond Durgnat, London 1967; *The Cinema of Fritz Lang* by Paul Jensen, New York 1969; *The Haunted Screen* by Lotte Eisner, Berkeley 1969; *American Film Criticism* by Stanley Kauffmann and Bruce Henstall, New York 1972; *Histoire du Cinéma: Art et Industrie, Vol. 3, 1923-30* by Jean Mitry, Paris 1973; *Fritz Lang* by Frieda Grafe, Enno Patalas, Hans Helmut Prinzler, Munich, Germany 1976; *Fritz Lang* by Lotte Eisner, translated by Gertrud Mander, edited by David Robinson, London 1977; *Fritz Lang* by Robert Armour, Boston 1978; *The Films of Fritz Lang* by Frederick W. Ott, Secaucus, New Jersey 1979; *Fritz Lang* edited by Stephen Jenkins, London 1979; *Fritz Lang: A Guide to References and Resources* by E. Ann Kaplan, Boston 1981; articles—"*Metropolis* Film Seen. Berlin Witnesses a Grim Portrayal of Industrial Future" in *The New York Times*, 10 January 1927; "*Metropolis*" by Rudolf Arnheim in *Das Stachelschwein* (Germany), 1 February 1927; "German Film Revision Upheld as Needed Here" by Randolph Bartlett in *The New York Times*, 13 March 1927; "*Metropolis*" by Fred Hildebrandt in *Berliner Tageblatt*, 11 January 1927; "Was ich noch zu sagen habe" by Fritz Lang in *Mein Film* edited by Frederick Proges, Vienna 1927; "Claims *Metropolis* Play. Plagiarism Charge" in *The New York Times*, 23 December 1928; issues devoted to *Metropolis* of *La Petite Illustration* (Paris), no.372, 1928 and *Cinéma* (Paris), 3 March 1928; "*Metropolis*" in *Scrutiny of Cinema* by William Hunter, London 1932; "Notes sur le Style de Fritz Lang" by Lotte Eisner in *La Revue du cinéma* (Paris), 1 February 1947; "Fritz Lang: Suggestion and Stimmung" in *Gestalter der Filmkunst, von Asta Nielsen bis Walt Disney* by Ludwig Gesek, Vienna 1948; "Fritz Lang Today" by H. Hart in *Films in Review* (New York), June/July 1956; "L'Oeuvre de Fritz Lang à la Cinémathèque. Le Piège Considéré Comme l'un des Beaux-Arts" by Jean Douchet in *Arts* (Paris), 1 July 1959; "Le Style de Fritz Lang" by Georges

Franju in *Cahiers du cinéma* (Paris), November 1959; "Eric Pommer: Part 2" by Herbert Luft in *Films in Review* (New York), November 1959; "Entretien avec Fritz Lang" by Jean Domarchi and Jacques Rivette in *Cahiers du cinéma* (Paris), September 1959; "Notes on Lang's *Metropolis*" by David De Laura in *Film Notes of the Wisconsin Film Society* edited by A. Lennig, Madison, Wisconsin 1960; "Avec *M, Le Maudit*, Fritz Lang en 1932 Annonçait la Destinée de L'Allemagne" by Jean Domarchi in *Arts* (Paris), April/May 1961; "Karl Freund" by Herbert Luft in *Films in Review* (New York), February 1963; "Fritz Lang" by Andrew Sarris in *Film Culture* (New York), spring 1963; "Kolportage, Stilisierung, Realismus. Anmerkungen zum werk Frtiz Langs..." by Wolfram Schütte in *Filmstudio* (Frankfurt), September 1964; "La Nuit Viennoise: Une Confession de Fritz Lang, Part 1 " by Gretchen Berg in *Cahiers du cinéma*, August 1965; "Introduction" and "German Expressionism" in *Sociology of the Film* by George Huaco, New York 1965; "L'Écran Démoniaque" by André-Peyre De Mandiarques in *Cinéma 66* (Paris), no.100, 1966; "La Nuit Viennoise: Une Confession de Fritz Lang, Part 2 " by Gretchen Berg in Cahiers du cinéma (Paris), June 1966; "*Metropolis*" by Paul Jensen in *Film Heritage* (Dayton, Ohio), winter 1968; "*Metropolis*" by Luis Buñuel reprinted in *Cahiers du cinéma* (Paris), August/September 1971 and in *Luis Buñuel: A Critical Biography* by Francis Arnanda, New York 1976; "Structures of Narrativity in Fritz Lang's *Metropolis*" by Alan Williams in *Film Quarterly* (Berkeley), summer 1974; "Fritz Lang: An Interview" in *Focus on Film* by Gene Phillips, London 1975; "Genetic Structuralism and the Cinema: A Look At Fritz Lang's *Metropolis*" by John Tulloch in *Australian Journal of Screen Theory*, no.1, 1976; "Wat doet een ingenieur met een infantiel scenario van zijn vrouw?" by C. Boost in *Skoop* (Wageningen, Netherlands), March 1976; "Deux textes pour servir une problématique: L'ouvrier dans le cinéma allemand des années 20" by V. Basset and D. Sotiaux in *Revue Belge du cinéma* (Brussels), June 1977; "*Metropolis*: The Lights Fantastic: Semiotic Analysis of Lighting Codes in Relation to Character and Theme" by Lane Roth in *Literature/Film Quarterly* (Salisbury, Maryland), fall 1978; "Fritz Lang: Only Melodrama" by Don Willis in *Film Quarterly* (Berkely), winter 1979-80.

*   *   *

The year 1927 witnessed the appearance in Germany of the most significant utopian film of the silent era —*Metropolis*. In the film, director Fritz Lang achieves the realization of his ideas about the possible future organization of society. The introductory sequences present this social organization in a very attractive light. In a magnificent, gigantic city with gleaming skyscrapers, suspension bridges, and bustling streets, people live in comfort and plenty, with every possibility for intellectual and physical development. However, Metropolis is not a city of freedom and equality. Below ground, working for the chosen elite, are masses of nameless workers who have no more value within the social order than a cog in a machine or a tool of production. It is for this reason that the workers revolt and almost destroy the city; only then is there a reconciliation and an equalization of rights for the two strata, the elite and the workers. Lang honestly believed in this idea of reconciliation, and his attitude to a certain extent reflected the German reality, in which there were growing indications of stabilization and attempts to resolve social problems. But Lang's views on these questions, conveyed finally in the reconciliation of the two classes under the slogan "the heart must serve as intermediary between the brain and the hands," did not sound convincingly progressive, either when the film was made or in the years that followed. Lang himself acknowledged this when, after the Nazi *Putsch*, Propaganda Minister Goebbels had him summoned: "(Goebbels)... told me that years before, he and Hitler had seen my film *Metropolis* in some small town and that at that time Hitler declared that he would like me to make Nazi films." (Siegfried Kracauer: *From Caligari to Hitler: A Psychological History of the German Film*.)

In the 1920s Lang was strongly influenced by Expressionist film, particularly its artistic forms. Originally an architect, Lang was a man of unusually sensitive visual perceptions. His films of those years show an expressionistic sense for the plastic and for lighting, which emphasized architectonic lines and conveyed a sense of geometric construction that not only extends to the sets and the depicted milieu but even influenced the positioning of the actors in individual shots. In *Metropolis* the artistic techniques of expressionism were more in evidence than in Lang's previous films, which were temporally closer to the greatest blossoming of that movement in the cinema. In keeping with the conventions of expressionism, the inhabitants of the subterranean city have no individuality, and the crowd represents a compact mass from which personality projects only as a stark exception and only in a definite rhythm. Extreme stylization is used in scenes depicting the alternation of work shifts. Lang also shapes space with the help of human bodies and uses light in accordance with the principles of expressionism. Sometimes he uses light so intensively that it takes the place of sound; for example, reflectors replace a siren with light functioning as an outcry. The pictorial formulation also reflects the antagonism between the ideas in the film. A salient example is the contrast between the supermodern metropolis of the future and the house of the scientist Rotwan, the spiritual creator of Metropolis. His dwelling in the shadows of the skyscrapers belongs more to the age when alchemists attempted to discover the philosophers' stone and the elixir of life, and the clay figure of the Golem roamed the streets. Also in his appearance and behavior, Rotwang does not fit the stereotype of a modern scientist, and there are indications that he may be in league with the devil.

Metropolis inaugurated a series utopias on film that attempted to resolve the difficulties of the contemporary state of society by projecting them into a story with a futuristic setting. The film was preceded by a large public relations campaign which stressed the grandiose nature of what was at the time a super-production by detailing and enumerating all the costs of production and the individual components (how many costumes were used in the film, how many wigs, how many extras, etc.). The premiere took place in an atmosphere of great expectation. However, the reactions of contemporary critics and reviews show that the film was, to some extent, a disappointment. There were great reservations about the plot and content, and the script by Lang's wife, Thea von Harbou, came under sharp attack. H.G. Wells, the well-known English writer of science fiction novels, criticized the film in unusually harsh terms.

Despite the reservations about the film voiced by its contemporaries and by other generations, it cannot be denied that the story of *Metropolis* is told in refined cinematic language. On this point even some critics of the 1920s agree. With the passage of time it has become possible to ascertain the film's contribution and its influence on the development of filmmaking. The film contained a number of technical innovations and influenced, for example, the narrative Hollywood films of the 1930s and 1940s. From the standpoint of film as visual art, one could cite sequences which remain to the present day examples of the potential of the film image to generate meaning. *Metropolis* particularly influenced the development of the science fiction genre. German expressionism brought new codes of artistic expression to the whole current of fantasy —uneven lines, contrasts of light and dark, half-shadows and silhouettes— which serve to suggest mysterious and menacing actions, events, and emotions. Lang applied these techniques effectively and successfully to one of the varieties of the fantasy genre —the utopian work (in modern terminology, science fiction). Some of these elements were still used in the science fiction genre when the rest of the cinema was no longer influenced by expressionism. The amorphous mass or the nameless crowd, as depicted by Lang, found its continuation in anti-utopian films of the postwar years. The wondrous atmosphere of the scene in which Rotwang brings a robot to life is encountered in a number of subsequent science fiction films, especially those that border on horror, as in *The Bride of Frankenstein*. Of course, Lang's robot, with its glittering female body, stylized breasts and inhuman mask instead of a face, is unsurpassed in its artistic beauty. The personality of the scientist Rotwang belongs to one of the most interesting antagonists of the screen. The possibility of an ambivalent interpretation of his character —he is a scientist, but also something of a sorcerer allied with satanic forces —gives him greater complexity. This character type recurs in films of the 1930s and 1940s (*Son of Frankenstein*) and continues without major changes into the most recent science fiction films, as well as into numerous horror and fantasy films.

Diverse audience response to the film's premiere influenced its fate in later years. For its time, *Metropolis* was a lengthy work. Its partial failure resulted in its release often with modifications, cuts, and abridgements. In the 1970s the film archive of the German Democratic Republic in Berlin undertook a reconstruction of the film; the work was completed in 1981 with the collaboration of several member archives of the International Federation of Film Archives (F.I.A.F.) and other film collectors. The result was an approximation of Lang's original version.

—B. Urgošíková

LE MILLION. Production: Films Sonores Tobis (France); black and white, 35mm; running time: 89 mins. Released 1931.

Produced by Frank Clifford; screenplay by René Clair; from the musical comedy by Georges Berr and M. Guillemaud; directed by René Clair; photography by Georges Périnal and Georges Raulet; production design by Lazare Meerson; music by Georges Van Parys, Armand Bernard and Philippe Parès.

Cast: René Lefèvre (*Michel*); Annabella (*Beatrice*); Louis Allibert (*Prosper*); Vanda Gréville (*Vanda*); Paul Olivier (*Father Tulipe, a gangster*); Odette Talazac (*Prima donna*); Constantin Stroësco (*Sopranelli, the tenor*); Raymond Cordy (*Taxi driver*).

Publications:

Books—*René Clair* by G. Viazzi, Milan 1946; *René Clair* by J. Bourgeois, Geneva 1949; *Un Maître du cinéma: René Clair* by Georges Charensol and Roger Régent, Paris 1952; *Tre maestri del cinema* by A. Solmi, Milan 1956; *René Clair, an Index* by Catherine De La Roche, London 1958; *René Clair* by Jean Mitry, Paris 1960; *René Clair* by Barhélemy Amengual, Paris 1969; *Cinema, The Magic Vehicle: A Guide to Its Achievement: Journey One: The Cinema Through 1949* edited by Jacek Klinowski and Adam Garbicz, Metuchen, New Jersey 1975; *René Clair's Grand Maneuver* by Nancy Warfield, New York 1982; articles—"René Clair and Film Humor" by Harry Potamkin in *Hound and Horn* (New York), October/December 1932; "A Conversation with René Clair" by Bernard Causton in *Sight and Sound* (London), winter 1933; "The Films of René Clair" by

Louis Jacobs in *New Theatre* (New York), February 1936; "The Films of René Clair" by G. Lambert in *Sequence* (London), no.6, 1949; issue on Clair of *Bianco e nero* (Rome), August/September 1951; "L'arte del comico in René Clair" by V. Berti in *Bianco e nero* (Rome), March/April 1968; "René Clair albo uroki geometrii" by A. Helman in *Kino* (Warsaw), June 1974; "René Clair, *Le Million* and the Coming of Sound" by L. Fischer in *Cinema Journal* (Iowa City), spring 1977; "*Le Million*" by Tom Milne in *Monthly Film Bulletin* (London), November 1977; "Utopia Ltd., the Cinema of René Clair" by G. Adair in *Sight and Sound* (London), summer 1981.

*   *   *

Of the series of comedies that René Clair made for Tobis Films at the beginning of the sound era, *Le Million* remains the most satisfying. It was preceded by the half-silent/half-musical *Under the Roofs of Paris* and followed by *À nous la liberté*, making Clair the first internationally acclaimed sound film director.

Clair had become one of the most vociferous opponents of the sound film, claiming that it could only mire down the silent film's flights of images. He had begun his career with the anarchic *Paris qui Dort* (1923) and *Entr'acte* (1924), and he feared the added equipment and personnel, the excessively wordy scripts, and the close-ups of the actors speaking those scripts. It took someone as skeptical as Clair to overcome these problems in the early sound film. In *Under the Roofs of Paris* he freed the camera from street singers and let it scale an apartment house, peering in at every floor to watch the effects of their song. He joked with the medium by cutting the sound when a door was closed. In this way he made the first international talkie a success by keeping talk to a minimum.

With *Le Million* his ambitions grew. Every element (sets, lighting, acting, noise, speech, and camerawork) was broken into parts capable of fitting an overriding rhythm that didn't properly belong to any of them. Characters don't walk or gesture so much as half-dance their way from scene to scene. Double chases, near misses, and parallel plots give Clair the chance to syncopate the action with his razor-edge cutting. Scenes are stopped just as one character leaves the frame, and another enters the next. Every shot offers a single dramatic or rhythmic jolt. Ultimately these tidy bits collect on stage for the delightful denouement.

The plot is as symmetrical as the decor. The lyric opera is set off against the bohemian life of two poor artists both in love with a ballerina. Their happiness depends on finding a lottery ticket which through a clever series of reversals finds its way into the jacket of the lead singer in "The Bohemians." The struggle to grab the ticket involves the police and a Robin Hood band led by the master of the underworld, the master of Paris, the master of ceremonies, Père Tulipe. At its height Clair abandons even the abstract tone of natural sound and lays the noise of a rugby crowd over the madcap actions as the jacket is passed from person to person until it appears in the hands of Père Tulipe who produces the winning ticket for our hero.

Afraid of the talkie, Clair gave cinema its purest example of what a lyrical film might be.

—Dudley Andrew

THE MIRACLE OF MORGAN'S CREEK. Production: Paramount Pictures; 1944; black and white, 35mm; running time: 99 mins. Released 1944.

Produced by Preston Sturges, executive producer: Buddy De Sylva; screenplay by Preston Sturges; directed by Preston Sturges; photography by John F. Seitz; edited by Stuart Gilmore; music by Leo Shuken and Charles Bradshaw.

Cast: Eddie Bracken (*Norval Jones*); Betty Hutton (*Trudy Kockenlocker*); Diana Lynn (*Emmy Kockenlocker*); William Demarest (*Officer Kockenlocker*); Brian Donlevy (*Governor McGinty*); Akim Tamiroff (*The Boss*); Georgia Caine (*Mrs. Johnson*); Emory Parnell (*Mr. Tuerck*).

Publications:

Books—*Interviews with Film Directors* by Andrew Sarris, New York 1967; *Preston Sturges: An American Dreamer* by James Ursini, New York 1973; articles—biography of Preston Sturges in *Current Biography Yearbook*, New York 1941; "Where Satire and Slapstick Meet" by Bosley Crowther in the *New York Times Magazine*, 27 August 1944; "Preston Sturges" by Peter Ericsson in *Sequence* (London), summer 1948; "Preston Sturges or Laughter Betrayed" by Siegfried Kracauer in *Films in Review* (New York), February 1950; "Preston Sturges" by Penelope Houston in *Sight and Sound* (London), summer 1965; "Notes on Preston Sturges and America" by Michael Budd in *Film Society Review* (New York), January 1968; "List of Screenplays" by P. Zucker in *Films in Review* (New York), March 1971; "Preston Sturges" by Richard Corliss in *Cinema* (Beverly Hills), spring 1972; "*The Miracle of Morgan's Creek*" by James Ursini in *Magill's Survey of Cinema, Vol. III* edited by James N. Magill, Englewood Cliffs, New Jersey 1980.

*   *   *

For those who think of Hollywood films as simple-minded celebrations of all things American, *Miracle of Morgan's Creek* is a useful challenge. Made and released during the depths of World War II, it offers a satirical portrait of American small-town life. It is a comic masterpiece, beloved in its day, which has currently been restored to critical favor after a period of time in which both it and its writer-director, Preston Sturges, were considered too shrill, too frenzied, and too violent to be respected.

At the core of *Miracle of Morgan's Creek* is its heroine, Trudy Kockenlocker, whose name warns viewers of the basic attitude toward censorship the film embodies. Brilliantly played by Betty Hutton, Trudy is the dreadful truth about the All-American Sweetheart, that girl next door who was usually presented with over-written sentiment during the war years. She's a little brainless, a little man crazy (especially if the man wears a uniform), and more than a little careless during a big night out on the town about which she remembers nothing except that she thinks she married a "Sergeant Ratszky-Watszky." Hutton, the blonde bombshell of the 1940's, was a wild performer who seemed willing to hang herself from the chandelier if only the audience would applaud the act. She was the perfect embodiment of the Sturges spirit.

Miracle of Morgan's Creek is a typical Preston Sturges comedy. His ability to observe the foibles of ordinary people and record them with a comic acuity that would be cruel in a lesser talent is ably demonstrated. On parade is the usual series of superbly written portraits of "normal" Americans, ably played by his stable of character actors, Porter Hall, Jimmy Conlin, Esther Howard, and Akim Tamiroff. The line-up of the leading characters includes, besides the jitterbugging Trudy, the hero (Eddie Bracken) who sees spots in times of stress ("The spots! The spots!", he cries when Hutton tells him of her dilemma), Trudy's beleaguered father (William Demarest), and her venal little sister (Diana Lynn) who ruthlessly gives advise on how to manipulate Bracken into marriage.

The blend of sophistication and slapstick that marks the work of Sturges can be seen in *Morgan's Creek*. It is a highly sophisticated sex comedy, pulling off a real trick in cheating the rigid censors of the day. Its keen eye for the contradictions and delusions of American small-town life show it to be the work of a knowing sophisticate, and its sharp dialogue exchanges frequently surpass the best of 1930's screwball comedy. At the same time, well-directed pratfalls and physical shenanigans are skillfully woven into the plot, so that an audience also experiences the free-rolling, knockabout physical comedy of the great tradition of silent films.

As a director, Sturges was not only a great writer and interpreter of his own scripts. He was also a master of the overall tempo of a comic film, and his technical skill in cutting and framing contributes to the success of *Morgan's Creek*. When Trudy deceives her father to go out with a rowdy group of soldiers, her evening is presented through a series of dissolves and rapid cuts. As her world disintergrates into a hot evening on the town, the audience sees an equivalent loss of narrative coherence. Although *Morgan's Creek* sets a frenetic pace, when two characters are exchanging a particularly well-written set of lines, Sturges is careful to protect both the script and the players. In such moments, he keeps the actors in medium range, in two-shots, letting the funny dialogue provide the energy. However, Sturges also knew how to use the camera, the sound track, and the cutting table as tools of comedy. A series of long tracking shots appear in *Morgan's Creek*, with the main characters walking from one end of town to the other, allowing viewers to watch the characters in their natural habitat at the same time as they are absorbing the meaning and humor of the dialogue.

To use the jargon of the 40's, *Miracle of Morgan's Creek* got away with murder. By presenting itself as an exaggerated satire of American mores, it managed to make jokes about not only an unwed pregnancy but also the Nativity. It makes a shambles of the world "our boys" were supposed to be fighting to preserve. It is a purely American film—self-critical, loaded with energy, packed with dialogue and event, perfectly timed, and literally reeling with comedy.

—Jeanine Basinger

MIRACOLO A MILANO. Miracle in Milan. Production: Soc. Produzioni De Sica, in cooperation with Ente Nazionale Industrie Cinematografiche (Rome); black and white, 35mm; running time: 101 mins., some versions are 95 mins. Released 1951.

Screenplay by Cesare Zavattini and Vittorio De Sica with Suso Cecchi d'Amico, Mario Chiari, and Adolfo Franci; from the novel *Totò, il buono* by Cesare Zavattini; directed by Vittorio De Sica; photography by G.R. Aldo; edited by Eraldo da Roma; sound by Bruno Brunacci; art direction by Guido Fiorini; music direction by Alessandro Cicognini; special effects by Ned Mann.

Filmed in Milan. Cannes Film Festival, Grand Priz, 1951; New York Film Critics' Award, Best Foreign Film, 1951.

Cast: Emma Grammatica; Francesco Golisano; Paolo Stoppa; Gugliemo Barnabò; Brunella Bovo; Anna Carena; Alba Arnova; Flora Cambi; Virgilio Riento; Arturo Bragaglia; Ermino Spalla; Riccardo Bertazzolo; Francesco Rizzone; Angelo Priolil.

Publications:

Scripts—"*Miracle a Milan*" (extract), with C. Zavattini and others in *Cinémonde* (Paris), 1953; *Miracle in Milan* (plus filmography and 2 articles by De Sica), with C. Zavattini and others, New York 1968; reviews—"De Sica's New Film" by Antonia Petrucci in *Sight and Sound* (London), April 1951; "De Sica Dissected" by Robert Hawkins in *Films in Review* (New York), May 1951; books—*The Italian Cinema 1945-1951* edited by Luigi Malerba, Rome 1951; *Vittorio De Sica* by Henri Agel, 2nd ed., Paris 1964; *Vittorio De Sica* by Pierre Leprohon, Paris 1966; *Patterns of Realism: A Study of Italian Neo-Realist Cinema* by Roy Armes, Cranbury, New Jersey 1971; *Italian Cinema Since the War* by Ken Wlaschin, Cranbury, New Jersey 1971; *Encountering Directors* by Charles Thomas Samuels, New York 1972; *La mia vita con Vittorio De Sica* by Maria Mercader, Milan, Italy 1978; *Anthologie du cinéma* vol.10, Paris 1979; articles—"The Case of De Sica" by John Maddison in *Sight and Sound* (London), June 1951; "Miracle Man" in the *New Yorker*, 5 April 1952; "Miracle of Milan: Some Psychoanalytic Notes on a Movie" by Alexander Grinstein in *American Imago* (Detroit), fall 1953; "Profiles: Bread, Love, and Neo-Realismo" by Winthrop Sargeant in the *New Yorker*, 29 June and 6 July 1957; "Poet of Poverty" by Douglas McVay in *Films and Filming* (London), October 1964, concludes in November 1964; issue on De Sica edited by O. Caldiron of *Bianco e nero* (Rome), September/December 1975; "La città e lo spazio" by F. La Polla in *Bianco e nero* (Rome), fall 1976; "Vittorio De Sica" by J. Passalacqua in *Films in Review* (New York), April 1978; "Neorealist Aesthetics and the Fantastic..." by P. Bondanella in *Film Criticism* (Edinboro, Pennsylvania), no. 2, 1979.

*   *   *

Miracolo a Milano, which won the Grand Prize at the Cannes Film Festival and was named Best Foreign Film by the New York Film Critics, is one of Vittorio De Sica's lesser masterpieces, not so renowned as *Sciuscia* (1946), *The Bicycle Thief* (1948) and *Two Women* (1960). Today De Sica's reputation as a filmmaker has been diminished by a climate of film criticism which maintains that much of Italian neorealism was little more than an idealistic masquerade. Nonetheless, De Sica contributed much that was powerful and authentic in neorealism, especially with the shattering, stark drama of both *Sciuscia* and *The Bicycle Thief*.

The whimsy and fairy tale atmosphere that pervade *Miracolo a Milano* were De Sica's respite from the severity of his earlier films, an exercise in satire and irony which he linked to the world of Hans Christian Anderson wherein "virtue triumphs and evil is punished." He also said that he drew his inspiration from Chaplin and René Clair, an observation confirmed by the first paragraph of the *New York Times* review of the film; but he did not abandon neorealism in *Miracolo a Milano*, as so many critics have suggested. The first half of the film, (based on the

novel, *Toto, il buono*, by Cesare Zavattini, De Sica's frequent collaborator) adheres to the documentary re-creation of Milan's impoverished outcasts.

Miracolo a Milano is a modern-day fable which implies that the "pure in heart" must seek their heaven apart from earth. Toto the Good (Francesco Golisano) is an orphan who is discovered as a baby in the cabbage patch of the kindly old Lolotta (wonderfully played by the great Emma Granatica), who teaches him to be good and pure of heart. When she dies, he spends several years in an orphanage after which he becomes an apostle for the beggars of Milan, aided by a white dove which possesses the power of miracles—the dove being a gift from Lolotta, now his guardian angel and benefactress. As he endeavors to improve the life of the beggars he discovers seeds of caste dissent, then their sense of unity is further disrupted by the discovery of oil on their adopted encampment. When they are forced to fight the landowner's police who are armed with billy clubs and tear gas, Toto's only resource is to have his band of hobos snatch up the brooms of street cleaners and fly to a land "where there is only peace, love, and good."

De Sica's combination of realism and fantasy is seductive, and his use of the fanciful sometimes overshadows the social commentary about the exploitation and dispossession of the innocent when confronted by the vagaries of poverty and the industrial society. And although De Sica steadfastly refused to admit it, the film has an element of despair, of spiritual quandary, as a dominant theme.

Miracolo a Milano was greeted with sharp denunciation from critics on the Italian right, all of whom accused De Sica of Communist leanings. It was much more wholeheartedly received in the United States, although its many levels of meaning were no less discussed here than in Italy. It is a transitional film in De Sica's career, for with it he moved out of the mainstream of neorealism. It remains a charming salute to the hope and perseverance of the common man, enhanced by the consummate cinematography of G.R. Aldo, a melodious score by Alessandro Cicognini and the wholly believable and unprepossessing acting of a cast made up of professional and non-professional actors.

—Ronald Bowers

MR. SMITH GOES TO WASHINGTON. Production: Columbia Pictures Corp.; black and white, 35mm; running time: 130 mins. Released 1939.

Produced by Frank Capra; screenplay by Sidney Buchman; from a story by Lewis R. Foster; directed by Frank Capra; photography by Joseph Walker; edited by Gene Havlick and Al Clark; sound engineered by Ed Bernds; art direction by Lionel Banks; music score by Dimitri Tiomkin, musical direction by M.W. Stoloff; costumes designed by (gowns) Kalloch; montage effects by Slavko Vorkapich.

Filmed in Columbia Pictures studios. Academy Award, Best Original Story, 1939; New York Film Critics Award, Best Actor (Stewart), 1939.

Cast: Jean Arthur (*Saunders*); James Stewart (*Jefferson Smith*); Claude Rains (*Senator Joseph Paine*); Edward Arnold (*Jim Taylor*); Guy Kibbee (*Governor Hopper*); Thomas Mitchell (*Diz Moore*); Eugene Pallette (*Chick McGann*); Beulah Bondi (*Ma Smith*); H.B. Warner (*Senate Majority Leader*); Harry Carey

(*President of the Senate*); Astrid Allwyn (*Susan Paine*); Ruth Donnelly (*Mrs. Hopper*); Grant Mitchell (*Senator MacPherson*); Porter Hall (*Senator Monroe*); Pierre Watkin (*Senate Minority Leader*); Charles Lane (*Nosey*); William Demarest (*Bill Griffith*); Dick Elliot (*Carl Cook*); Billy Watson, Delmar Watson, John Russell, Harry Watson, Gary Watson, and Baby Dumpling (*the Hopper Boys*).

Publications:

Books—*Frank Capra* by Richard Griffith, London 1951; *The Films of James Stewart* by Ken D. Jones, New York 1970; *The Name Above the Title* by Frank Capra, New York 1971; *Frank Capra: One Man—One Film* by James Silke, Washington, D.C. 1971; *The Films of Frank Capra* by Donald Willis, Metuchen, New Jersey 1974; *James Stewart* by Howard Thompson, New York 1974; *Frank Capra: The Man and His Films*, edited by Richard Glatzer and John Raeburn, Ann Arbor 1975; *American Visions: The Films of Chaplin, Ford, Capra and Welles, 1936-1941* by Charles Maland, New York 1977; *The Films of Frank Capra* by Victor Scherle and William Levy, Secaucus, New Jersey 1977; *Frank Capra Study Guide*, edited by Dennis Bohnenkamp and Sam Grogg, Washington, D.C. 1979; *Frank Capra* by Charles Maland, Boston 1980; articles—"Mr. Capra Goes Someplace" by Otis Ferguson in *The New Republic* (New York), 1 November 1939; "A Guide to the Appreciation of *Mr. Smith Goes to Washington*" edited by Max J. Herzberg in *Photoplay Studies* (New York), no.21, 1939; "Democracy at the Box Office" by Otis Ferguson in *The New Republic* (New York), 24 March 1941; "Frank Capra's Characters" by Herbert Biberman in *New Masses* (New York), 8 July 1941; "Do I Make You Laugh?" by Frank Capra in *Films and Filming* (London), September 1962; "Capra and the American Dream" by James Price in *The London Magazine*, v.3, no.10, 1964; issue devoted to Capra, *Positif* (Paris), December 1971; "A Decade of Good Deeds and Wonderful Lives: Under Capracorn" by Stephen Handzo in *Film Comment* (New York), v.8, no.4, 1972; "Frank Capra and the Cinema of Populism" by Jeffrey Richards in *Film Society Review* (New York), v.7, no.6 and no.7-9, 1972; "Mr. Smith Goes to Washington: Capra, Populism and Comic-Strip Art" by J. Nelson in *Journal of Popular Film* (Bowling Green, Ohio), summer 1974; "The Making of Cultural Myths: Walt Disney and Frank Capra" in *Movie-Made America* by Robert Sklar, New York 1975; "Frank Capra and the Popular Front" by Leonard Quart in *Cineaste* (New York), summer 1977; "It's a Wonderful Life: The Stand of the Capra Hero" by B. Rose in *Journal of Popular Film* (Bowling Green, Ohio), v.6, no.2, 1977; "The 'Populist' Films of Frank Capra" by G.A. Phelps in *Journal of American Studies* (London), no.3, 1979; "It's a Wonderful Life, But..." by M. Dickstein in *American Film* (Washington, D.C.), May 1980; "The Politics of Narrative Form: Capra's *Mr. Smith Goes to Washington*" by N. Browne in *Wide Angle* (Athens, Ohio), no.3, 1980; special Capra issue of *Film Criticism* (Edinboro, Pennsylvania), winter 1981.

*   *   *

The title of *Mr. Smith Goes to Washington* gives a sense of one of the basic elements of a Frank Capra film in the late 1930's—a hero whose individual identity is defined by the community and who ultimately redefines that community. Ingenuous Jefferson Smith (James Stewart) is chosen by the political machine to fill out a senator's term. When he becomes aware of the bosses' corruption and threatens to expose it, they try to silence him. Inspired by Saunders, Capra's prototypical wise woman figure (here and elsewhere played by Jean Arthur), Smith learns how to pitch the honest voice of one man loudly enough for it to be heard by the nation at large. The democratic man exemplifies the democratic society and makes that society understand truly what it ought to be.

The film is structured in terms of Smith's voice and its effect on its audiences. Tall James Stewart, with his stammerings, hesitations and regional accent, makes speech problematic; his adversary in the Senate is short, eloquent Claude Rains. Merely seeing/hearing these actors in the same scene makes us sensitive to the sound/image dynamics of *Mr. Smith Goes to Washington*. When Smith is first named senator, at a political banquet, the novice is hesitant to speak, and then moved to emotional speech by the tribute of his Boy Rangers. Upon his introduction to the Senate, and later, reading his first bill to that august body, he is comical, tongue-tied, too loud or too soft. He has no control over his voice and no power over the forum. Filled with ardor about his plan for a boy's camp, he converts the cynical Saunders to his cause. And when he sets out to explore his adversaries his speech becomes a matter of life and death in a filibuster during which he must hold the floor or forever be silenced.

Filmed in a meticulous reconstruction of the Senate chamber, making full use of the various levels of speech and audition (floor, podium, gallery, senators and visitors at first harshly critical of Smith, then attentive and visibly moved by him), even marking the connections between the individual speaker and the outside world, this sequence exemplifies Capra's affinity for the dynamics of sound film, of drama in which speech is spatialized. The variations of that space are expressed in the ways communication is effected—vocal utterance, signs perceived with the eyes, telephones, printed words. When Smith falters he looks to the gallery for reassurance from Saunders, who also sends him parliamentary advice along with a declaration of love. Smith is a man whose first day in Washington is climaxed at the Lincoln Memorial, where he hears a child reading Lincoln's words inscribed in stone; he nearly destroys himself by "writing" and "reading" a bill; he is buried by harshly critical telegrams just before his final triumph.

At the film's gala première in Washington it was seen as a bad reflection on the "dignity" of government, but it went on to great success. Like many of Capra's others films, *Mr. Smith* has invited accusations of facile sentimentality and facile populism, judgements that must be outweighed against the power of its emotional trajectory and its disquietingly bleak vision of the realities of political life. The first-night audience of dignitaries had cause to feel threatened.

—Charles Affron

———————

MOANA. Production: Famous Players-Lasky; 1926; black and white, 35mm, silent; running time: about 85 mins.; length: 7 reels, 6133 feet. Released 7 January 1926.

Scenario and direction by Robert Flaherty; titles by Robert Flaherty and Julian Johnson; photography by Robert Flaherty and Bob Roberts; edited by Julian Johnson; assistant director: Frances Flaherty.

Filmed in the village of Safune on the island of Savai'i in Polynesia.

Cast: Ta'avale; Fa'amgase; Tu'ugaita; Moana; Pe'a.

Publications:

Books—*The Odyssey of a Film-Maker: Robert Flaherty's Story* by Frances Flaherty, Urbana, Illinois 1960; *Robert Flaherty* by Jose Clemente, Madrid 1963; *Robert Flaherty* by Carlos Fernandez Cuenca, Madrid 1963; *Robert J. Flaherty* by Henri Agel, Paris 1965; *The World of Robert Flaherty* by Richard Griffith, reprinted New York 1970; *The Innocent Eye: The Life of Robert Flaherty* by Arthur Calder-Marshall, London 1970; *Nonfiction Film: A Critical History* by Richard Barsam, New York 1973; *Documentary: A History of the Non-Fiction Film* by Erik Barnouw, New York 1974; articles—"Interview with Flaherty" by S.M. Weller in *Motion Picture Classic* (Brooklyn), October 1927; "Moviemaker" by Robert Lewis Taylor in the *New Yorker*, 11 June, 18 June, and 25 June 1949; "Flaherty as Innovator" by John Grierson in *Sight and Sound* (London), October/December 1951; "The Flaherty Way" by Frances Flaherty in the *Saturday Review* (New York), 13 September 1952; "Un poete de l'exotisme: Robert J. Flaherty" in *L' exotisme et le cinéma* by Pierre Leprohon, Paris 1945; "Robert Flaherty (Barnouw's File)" by Erik Barnouw in *Film Culture* (New York), spring 1975; "Moana" by J. Rosenbaum in *Monthly Film Bulletin* (London), December 1975; "Films" by L.D. Holmes in *American Anthropologist* (Washington, D.C.), no.3, 1979; "Moana" in *Travelling* (Lausanne, Switzerland), summer 1979; "Moana: Version 1980" in *Image et son* (Paris), October 1981.

* * *

Shot in the Samoan Islands, *Moana* is the story of a young Polynesian, his family, friends, and relations; how they live their everyday lives; and how Moana gains manhood and the respect of his community. Robert Flaherty's second major film, *Moana* established a consistant pattern in his work. To writers like Grierson it showed that film could be a "document" of daily life. Its photographic realism rendered creditably this portrayal of an entire people, enhanced by the use of panchromatic film which was sensitive to color, long lenses for close-up work, and exceptional tonal values. Its strength was its pictorial loveliness, perfect composition, and a rhythm or movement perfectly suited to the beautiful surroundings.

Its structure relies on a few detailed sequences built around Moana's daily life. These culminate in the tattooing of Moana, a long and painful ceremony, a rite of passage to manhood. Harking back to an earlier age, again a typical Flaherty theme, the tattooing demonstrates the ways in which the Samoans cling to their traditional values and culture in the face of threats from western civilization; never shown on the screen, the presence of those threats is felt. Flaherty captured an age of innocence before its demise.

The preconceptions of Flaherty's experiences in the Arctic were dispelled. The drama of life was more subtle in Samoa. Life was not an everyday struggle and conflict in this would-be land of abundance and benevolence. The drama had to be discovered from within, by living with the people and achieving a profound understanding of their psyche and rituals. The drama could not be imposed by the filmmaker.

Contemporary critics praised Moana's photographic qualities, its poetry and visual beauty. Even so, it was never a commercial success. More importantly, it served as a focal point for the emerging documentary film movement. Grierson and Paul Rotha could agree that the documentary must emerge from the location and that documentary photographed from real life was not mere recorded reality but a special dramatization of reality based on an intimate understanding of a culture and a profound sensitivity to its nuances.

Today, *Moana* is the least regarded of Flaherty's major films. One reason may be that the prints in circulation rarely convey the photographic perfection that Flaherty achieved. Consequently, modern critics have placed less emphasis on its photographic realism and have pointed to its static, undramatic theme and lack of conflict. *Moana* may not be as enduring as *Nanook of the North* or *Louisiana Story*, but its place in the historical development of the documentary film is well established.

—William T. Murphy

MODERN TIMES. Production: United Artists-Charles Chaplin; 1935; black and white, 35mm, mostly synchronized musical soundtrack; running time: 85 mins.; length: 7634 feet. Released 1936.

Produced, scripted, directed and edited by Charles Chaplin; photography by Rollie Totheroh and Ira Morgan; art direction by Charles D. Hall and J. Russell Spencer; music direction by Alfred Newman, music by Charles Chaplin, music arranged by David Raksin and Edward Powell, "Je Cherche Apres Titine" by Leo Daniderff.

Cast: Charles Chaplin (*A Worker*); Paulette Goddard (*A Gamine*); Henry Bergman (*Café propreitor*); Chester Conklin (*Mechanic*); Stanley Sandford, Louis Natheux, and Hank Mann (*Burglars*); Allan Garcia (*President of a steel corporation*).

Publications:

Books—*Garbo and the Night Watchman: A Selection from the Writings of British and American Film Critics* edited by Alistair Cooke, London 1937; *Chaplin, Last of the Clowns* by Parker Tyler, New York 1947; *The Little Fellow* by Peter Cotes and Thelma Niklaus, London 1951; *Charlie Chaplin* by Theodore Huff, New York 1951; *The Great God Pan: A Biography of the Tramp Played by Charlie Chaplin* by Robert Payne, New York 1952; *Chaplin, the Immortal Tramp* by Rubeigh Minney, London 1954; *Charlot et la "fabulation" chaplinesque* by Jean Mitry, Paris 1957; *Charles Chaplin* by Barthelemy Amengual, Paris 1963; *My Autobiography*, London 1964; *The Films of Charlie Chaplin* by Gerald McDonald and others, Secaucus, New Jersey 1965; *Charlie Chaplin* by Marcel Martin, Paris 1966; *Chaplin's Films* by Uno Asplund, Newton Abbot, Devon 1971; *Tout Chaplin: Tous les films, par le texte, par le gag et par l'image* by Jean Mitry, Paris 1972; *My Life in Pictures*, London 1974; *Etude de sémiologie stylistique portant sur l'oeuvre cinématographique de Charles Chaplin* by Adolphe Nysenholc, Brussels 1975; *Cinema, The Magic Vehicle: A Guide to Its Achievement: Journey One: The Cinema Through 1949* edited by Jacek Klinowski and Adam Garbicz, Metuchen, New Jersey 1975; *Chaplin, Genesis of a Clown* by Raoul Sobel and David Francis, London 1977; *Charlie Chaplin Story ou Charlot l'immortel* by P. Lemoine and F. Pedron, Bologna 1978; *Vie de*

Charlot: Charles Spencer Chaplin, ses films et son temps by Georges Sadoul, Paris 1978; *Charlot: ou, Sir Charles Chaplin* by J. Lorcey, Paris 1978; *Charles Chaplin—a Guide to References and Resources* compiled by T.J. Lyons, Boston 1979; articles— "Charlie Chaplin's New Picture" by B. Shumiatski, translation from *Pravda*, in *New Masses* (New York), 24 September 1935; "Chaplin's Critics" by Edward Newhouse in *Partisan Review* (New Brunswick, New Jersey), April 1936; "Bewildered Little Fellow Bucking Modern Times" in *Newsweek* (New York), 8 February 1936; "Charlie Chaplin" by M. Van Doren in *Nation* (New York), 19 Feburary 1936; "Charlie Chaplin" by Alistair Cooke in *Atlantic Monthly* (Greenwich, Connecticut), August 1939; "Charlie the Grown Up" by S.M. Eisenstein in *Sight and Sound* (London), summer 1946; "Charlie Chaplin's Films and American Culture Patterns" by Harry A. Grace in *Journal of Aesthetics and Art Criticism* (Cleveland), June 1952; article by Louis Marks in *Films and Filming* (London), October 1954; article by William Whitebait in *Sight and Sound* (London), January/March 1955; "Interview with Chaplin" by Margaret Hinxman in *Sight and Sound* (London), autumn 1957; article by Andrew Sarris in *The Village Voice* (New York), 21 May 1964; "L'Uomo in pericolo nei tempi moderni di Chaplin" by G. Aristarco in *Cinema Nuovo* (Turin), May/June 1972; "*Modern Times*" by David Denby in *Film Comment* (New York), September/October 1972; *Modern Times* by Gordon Gow in *Films and Filming* (London), April 1972; "Voir et revoir *Les Temps modernes*" by R. Lefèvre in *Cinéma* (Paris), January 1972; "*Modern Times*" by David Robinson in *Sight and Sound* (London), spring 1972; "*Les Temps modernes*" in *Téléciné* (Paris), January 1972; "Roland H. Totheroh Interviewed: Chaplin Films" edited by T.J. Lyons, in *Film Culture* (New York), spring 1972; "Style et conscience de classe" by B. Amengual in *Positif* (Paris), July/August 1973; issue on Chaplin of *Film und Fernsehen* (Berlin), March 1978; issue on Chaplin of *University Film Association Journal* (Houston), no.1, 1979; "*Modern Times*" by Charles Berg in *Magill's Survey of Cinema, Vol. III* edited by Frank N. Magill, Englewood Cliffs, New Jersey 1980.

*　　*　　*

Charles Chaplin was the last holdout in an industry that had uncritically turned its mode of production away from the visual developments of the end of the silent period to the spoken word and the theatrical trappings which that change entailed. In 1931, two years after the end of the silent period, Chaplin directed *City Lights*; five years later came *Modern Times*, his last film to extensively and specifically employ silent film strategies. A stylistic anachronism, the film was both a tribute to the glories of the silent period and a sociological perspective on industrialized society. If Chaplin considered sound likely to become an enslavingly mechanized aspect of movie making, he rendered that vision nonsensically by portraying himself as the factory worker forced to undergo a new approach to factory life—eating while working, using both mouth and body simultaneously. Not surprisingly, this experiment in modernization has disastrous consequences for our hero, the machine designed to feed the worker running disastrously amuck, serving food but rendering it inedible. Having been served by a machine, Charlie is later literally served *to* a machine. The film becomes a satire on the mechanization of thought and industry, a plea for the reinstitution of human individual values over those of industrialization and mass production.

The year of Chaplin's *City Lights*—1931—was also the year of *À nous la liberté*, René Clair's film attacking mechanized society. Both films share an assembly line scene of humorous yet socially critical implications; both directors posit a rather utopian ending in which man abandons the mechanized world for a life of individual freedom outside the urban landscape; both resist the use of dialogue as a naturalistic element of filmmaking. Although *À nous la Liberté* contains some dialogue, the strength of the soundtrack is an operetta of sounds and music, occasional pieces of dialogue being part of that source. In *Modern Times*, machines, not people, are allowed voice, Chaplin using the musical soundtrack to evoke the sentimental nostalgia inherent in all of his films and ultimately to introduce us to the tramp's heretofore unheard voice, when, near the end of the film, he finds employment as a singing waiter. In this scene Chaplin defies the law of naturalism by singing a lyric totally in gibberish, preferring to detail the song's narrative through the brilliance of his pantomine. Here he recapitulates his belief that actions speak louder than words by rendering the words superfluous.

When *Modern Times* was released, Tobis, the company that controlled the rights to *À nous la liberté*, brought suit against Chaplin for his "borrowing" from Clair. The suit, however, was never brought to court because of Clair's refusal to sanction the action: Clair claimed that he had been greatly inspired by Chaplin, and that if that director had been inspired by him in return, he was greatly honored. Critics of the day generally noted the similarities between the two films but rarely to the detriment of either.

The staple Chaplin narrative involved a struggle, and in *Modern Times* the tramp is shown encountering the modern urban landscape with its overabundance of menacing institutions. He assumes a variety of occupations from nightwatchman to singing waiter, from worker on the assembly line to worker at a shipyard. Each time his employment is short-lived, not because Charlie is incapable but because his human qualities interfere with the system. In the factory, the monotony of his job as a bolt tightener reduces him to a machine off the job—he is unable to stop fulfilling his mechanized duties, continuing to tighten everything in sight: noses, waterplugs, buttons, etc. This problem takes him to a hospital where, after recovering, he returns to the streets. There, picking up a red warning flag which has fallen off a truck, he unwittingly becomes the front man in a parade of radicals, his carrying of the flag landing him in jail. He unwittingly thwarts a jailbreak for which he is rewarded first with more luxurious quarters, then to his dismay, with an honorable discharge. Back in the work force, he gets a job at a shipyard, only to be fired when he accidently and prematurely launches a new ship. Continuing along the path where good intentions misfire, he meets the gamin. He witnesses her act of thievery, realizes that it is provoked by hunger, and attempts to take the rap. Unfortunately, an eye witness thwarts Charlie's intentions, and the girl is taken away. Incensed, he goes about purposely commiting a crime: he enters a restaurant and, after eating a large meal and smoking the best cigars, admits to having no money to pay. Gamin and tramp meet through their mutual arrests and escape together to the (dis)comfort of her waterfront shack, the location of which allows Chaplin some of his most elegant balletics, notably his dive into two feet of water in an attempt to cleanse himself.

Once again Charlie attempts to integrate himself into the modern system, this time by taking a job as a nightwatchman in a department store. Misplaced confidence in some friendly burglars ends in his being sent back to prison. When he is released, the gamin is waiting and takes him to his next job, that of a singing waiter. No sooner does he enjoy some success at this job than a juvenile court officer comes looking for the gamin. Deciding to forsake this entertainment industry job, he and the girl go arm in arm into the sunset, unemployed but happy. Optimism infuses this final image, but as always, pessimism has been firmly situated throughout: his aesthetic rejection of cinematic advances, his moral rejection of industrialization.

This last scene, the indestructible tramp walking into the sunset empty of hand but full of heart, is but one of many references in this film to Chaplin's silent comedies. In the factory he converts the moment of despair into one of humor, notably when the feeding machine goes beserk, and by so doing refers to the slapstick comedy of the teens when food was used as an arsenal rather than as goods for consumption. In the parade scene he reinterprets the meaning of an object—the flag's being transformed from a warning of danger to a symbol of freedom from incarceration; in the toy store he reinvents his roller skating scene from *The Rink* (1916); in the restaurant he recreates his *Gold Rush* dinner scene, changing the food from sustenance for the stomach to sustenance for the spirit by using the duck first as a football then a chandelier ornament rife with delight rather than calories. Throughout the film Chaplin continues to assert his belief that actions speak louder than words, that the dictum "don't bite the hand that feeds you" is fallacious, that optimism must prevail despite omnipresent pessimism and adversity, and that one must continue to uphold the values that have served him well in the past. The reappearance of Chester Conklin and other silent film players in this film further strengthens Chaplin's ode to the past and past values.

Initially a financial failure, *Modern Times* has since been hailed as one of Chaplin's most eloquent social statements. Accused of embodying Red propaganda, the film was banned in Germany and Italy, and in Austria it was trimmed of the flag waving scene by incensed censors. At best a flirtation with radical politics, its real message lies in the rejection of modern urban life and the need for the reinstitution of human rather than mechanical values. With *Modern Times* Chaplin retained his position as spokesman for the underprivledged.

—Doug Tomlinson

DIE MÖRDER SIND UNTER UNS. The Murderers Are Among Us. Production: DEFA (East Germany); black and white, 35mm; running time: 86 mins.; length: 2400 meters. Released 1946.

Produced by Herbert Uhlich; screenplay by Wolfgang Staudte; directed by Wolfgang Staudte; photography by Friedl Behn-Grund and Eugen Klagemann; edited by Lilian Seng; sound recorded by Dr. Klaus Jungk; production design by Otto Hunte and Bruno Monden; music by by Ernst Roters.

Filmed spring 1946 in Berlin.

Cast: Hildegard Knef (sometimes Neff) (*Susanna Wallner*); Ernst Fischer (*Dr. Mertens*); Arno Paulsen (*Captain Bruckner*); Erna Sellmer (*Frau Bruckner*); Robert Forsch (*Herr Mondschein*); Albert Johann (*Herr Timm*).

Publications:

Reviews—in *Bianco e nero* (Rome), September 1948; review in *Today's Cinema*, 9 April 1948; review in *Kine Weekly*, 15 April 1948; review in *Monthly Film Bulletin* (London), no.172, 1948; review by N.B. in *Cue* (New York), 21 August 1948; books—*Deutscher Spielfilm Almanach, 1929-1950* edited by Dr. Alfred Bauer, Germany; *The German Cinema* by Roger Manvell and Heinrich Fraenkel, New York 1971; *50 Years of German Film* by H.H. Wollenberg, London 1972; articles—by Vorwärts in *Tiefernste Mahnung zur Wachsamkeit* (West Germany), 17 October 1946; "Hildegarde Neff" by Manfred George in *Films in Review* (New York), November 1955; article in *Filmkritik* (Munich), no.1, 1960; "Wolfgang Staudte" by J. Bachmann in *Film* (London), summer 1963; "Films From the German Democratic Republic" by Adrienne Mancia in *The Museum of Modern Art Department of Film* (New York), 20 November-29 December 1975; article in *Information* (Wiesbaden), no.3-6, 1976; "Wolfgang Staudte" by K. Karkosch in *Film und Ton* (Munich), March 1976; article in *Die Information* (Wiesbaden), January/-February 1978.

*　　*　　*

By March 1946, nine months after the armistice, a film crew dominated by veterans of the Nazi industry was out in the streets of devastated Berlin, in front of Stettiner railway station and on flattened Alexanderplatz, shooting the first postwar German film, *Die Mörder sind unter uns*. The director, Wolfgang Staudte, worked under the auspices of DEFA, the only production company licensed in the Soviet Zone. Founded on the remains of the old Ufa empire, DEFA had a distinct material advantage over its western counterparts: what remained of giant studios and even raw stock plants was concentrated in the eastern, Soviet Zone, of Germany. *Mörder* is both an exposé denouncing the ability of Nazi war criminals to bury their pasts and to enjoy respected positions in the new German society and a romance between a returning concentration camp survivor and a doctor whose participation in the war has left him an alcoholic with no will to rebuild his life.

The prominence of the love story and the casting of Hildegard Knef (a very unlikely looking camp victim) effectively mutes the political criticism implied by the film. Nevertheless, *Mörder* was well received by contemporary critics as a serious and realistic drama. The arrival of this film in Western Europe and America occasioned speculation that a new German film industry would soon spring to life. This prediction was, of course, premature.

Today, in spite of the location shooting, it is the leftovers of an older expressionist style that seem to permeate Staudte's work. The ruins of Berlin were a ready-made horror film set, and expressionist stylization sets the tone in this film much as it did in postwar American film noir—the heavy shadows, the weird angles, the use of frames within frames. Ravaged Berlin is used as a metaphor for the broken people who live there. In one emphatic cut, the film switches from the hero's confession of his own war guilt to a long held shot of a crumbling building, dust rising from the rubble beneath it. Staudte indulges in heavy irony. The camera zooms in on a poster advertizing "beautiful Germany" in the midst of desolation through the rubble; he quips, "The city is coming back to life." With oblique camera angles, the film also creates a subjective view of the doctor's drunken interludes.

Mörder was the first in a cycle of *"Trümmerfilme"* or "rubble films," produced mainly by DEFA,, using the streets of Berlin as backdrops for melancholy dramas concerning contemporary issues—the returning soldier, the black market, war criminals. Meanwhile, as the many competing companies licensed in the west went into action, more escapist, apolitical films began to dominate German production. Staudte, who had worked in the

Nazi film industry, may have retreated from a clear coming to terms with the issue of war guilt in *Die Mörder sind unter uns*, but he did produce a serious drama securely moored in a contemporary milieu, something German filmmakers had refused to do for years. What seems lacking is a break with the past in style as well as subject matter.

—Ann Harris

MORTE A VENEZIA. Death in Venice. Production: Alfa Cinematografica (Rome) and P.E.C.F. (Paris); Technicolor, 35mm, Panavision; running time: 131 mins., some versions are 128 mins. Released 1971.

Produced by Mario Gallo with Luchino Visconti, Nicolas Badalucco, and Robert Gordon Edwards; screenplay by Luchino Visconti and Nicolas Badalucco; from the novel by Thomas Mann; directed by Luchino Visconti; photography by Pasquale De Santis; edited by Ruggero Mastroianni; sound by Vittorio Trentino with Giuseppe Muratori; art direction by Ferdinando Scarfiotti; music by Gustav Mahler, directed by Franco Mannino; costumes designed by Piero Tosi.

Cannes Film Festival, Special Prize, 1971.

Cast: Dirk Bogarde (*Gustav von Aschenbach*); Romolo Valli (*Director of the 'Hotel Des Bains'*); Nora Ricci (*Governess of Tadzio*); Mark Burns (*Alfried*); Marisa Berenson (*Mogol of G.V.A.*); Carole André (*Esmeralda*). Leslie French (*Cook's agent*); Sergio Garfagnoli (*Jasciu*); Franco Fabrizi (*Barber*); Dominque Darel (*English tourist*); Masha Predit (*Russian tourist*); Silvano Mangano (*Tadzio's mother*); Ciro Cristogoletti; Antonio Apicella; Bruno Boschetti; Luigi Battaglia; Mirella Pompili; Björn Andersen.

Publications:

Script—*Morte a Venezia* by Luchino Visconti, edited by Lino Miccichè, Bologna, Italy 1971; books—*Luchino Visconti* by Pio Baldelli, Milan 1973; *Visconti: il cinema*, edited by Adelio Ferrero, Modena, Italy 1977; *Maestri del cinema* by Pietro Bianchi, Milan 1977; *Album Visconti* edited by Lietta Tornabuoni, foreward by Michelangelo Antonioni, Milan 1978; *A Screen of Time: A Study of Luchino Visconti* by Monica Stirling, New York 1979; *Luchino Visconti* by Gaia Servadio, New York 1983; articles—"Visconti in Venice" by Hollis Alpert in *Saturday Review* (New York), 8 August 1970; "*Death in Venice*" by Margaret Hinxman in *Sight and Sound* (London), autumn 1970; "*Death in Venice*: At the End of the Path of Beauty Lies Eros" by Kathleen Tynan in *Vogue* (New York), December 1970; issue on Visconti of *Cinema* (Rome), April 1970; "Visconti" by K. Radkai in *Vogue* (New York), 1 November 1970; "Luchino Visconti" by T. Elsaesser in *Brighton* (London), February 1970; "*Mort a Venise*" (synopsis, background, the music, bio-filmography of Visconti) in *Avant-Scène du cinéma* (Paris), July 1971; "Marxism and Formalism in the Films of Luchino Visconti" by Walter Korte in *Cinema Journal* (Evanston, Illinois), fall 1971; "Le Nom-de-l'auteur" by J.P. Oudart and S. Daney in *Cahiers du cinéma* (Paris), January/February 1972; "A propos de *Mort à Venise* de Luchino Visconti" by J.C. Guiguet in *Image et son*

(Paris), February 1972; "Luchino Visconti's *Death in Venice*" by A. Hutchinson in *Literature/Film Quarterly* (Salisbury, Maryland), winter 1974; "Nachkomme eines alten Herrschergeschlechts", 5-part series by G. Bogemski in *Film und Fernsehen* (Berlin), October and December, 1979, and January, April and June 1980.

*   *   *

Director Luchino Visconti's screen adaption of Thomas Mann's *Death in Venice* is both a triumph of visual style and a problematic study of literature-into-film translations. In collaboration with cinematographer Pasquale De Santis, Visconti captures Mann's haunting story in images of hypnotic beauty, yet they are images which the film's verbal exposition cannot always equal.

One of the themes of Mann's brilliant novella has to do with the artist's recognition of the power and validity of physical beauty, and Visconti's cinematic approach conveys his understanding of this theme in every frame. The splendor of Venice, the elegance of Aschenbach's seaside hotel, the androgynous perfection of the boy Tadzio—all are photographed in a lush, unhurried manner that allows the viewer to linger on a detail or to simply absorb the richness of the scene as a whole. This is a story—and a film—of contemplation, and Visconti permits his audience to share in the overwhelming sensuality that will penetrate Aschenbach's emotional reserve and shatter his lifelong convictions about philosophy and art.

Yet as this is also a story of death—Aschenbach's own, as well as the destruction of his rigidly-held ideas—Visconti has permeated his film with an atmosphere of decay. Images of death are everywhere. Indeed, when Aschenbach at last allows himself to be powdered and rouged into a pathetic parody of youthfulness, his face resembles nothing so much as a death mask, streaked with black as the sun melts the paint around his eyes. This pairing of beauty and death, which lies at the heart of the story itself, lends the film an unsettling, almost oppressive air, reminiscent of flowers on the verge of wilting. Visconti himself was close to 70 when *Death in Venice* was made and would complete only three more pictures after its release. It is clear from the film's painful illumination of the gulf between youth and old age that it was a concern much on the filmmaker's own mind.

The shortcomings of *Death in Venice* are those which every film adaption must face, i.e. the nearly insurmountable difficulties inherent in transposing interior thoughts into visible images. To understand the effect that his obsession with Tadzio has on Aschenbach, one must first grasp the rejection of emotion and the physical senses that has informed Aschenbach's work as an artist. Mann conveys this information through straight-forward description of his character's meditations on art, a method not available to Visconti. Instead, the director resorts to a series of flashbacks in which Aschenbach and a friend argue bitterly over their opposing views on art and life. The resulting scenes seem static and talky when juxtaposed with Visconti's fluid—and virtually wordless—presentation of the delicate interplay between Aschenbach and the enigmatic Tadzio.

The flashbacks, however, merely lay the groundwork for most of the film's action, and in depicting Aschenbach's growing love for Tadzio and the older man's subsequent decline, Visconti's strong cinematic sense serves him well. He is aided by a finely textured performance from Dirk Bogarde, who has been made up to resemble composer Gustav Mahler, upon whom Mann is said to have based his character, and by Mahler's stirring Fifth Symphony which is the basis of the film's soundtrack. Despite its flaws, *Death in Venice* remains an absorbing and visually stunning adaption of Mann's challenging work.

—Janet E. Lorenz

MUERTE DE UN CICLISTA. Death of a Cyclist. Production: Cesareo Gonzalez (Madrid), Trionfalcine (Rome), and Guion PC (Paris); black and white, 35mm; running time: originally 91 mins. but cut by Spanish censors to 88 mins. Released 9 September 1955, Madrid.

Screenplay by Juan Antonio Bardem and Luis F. De Igoa; from the novel by Luis F. De Igoa; directed by Juan Antonio Bardem; photography by Alfredo Fraile; edited by Margarita Ochoa; sound by Alfonson Carvajal, sound for French version by Jacques Bonpaint; art direction by Enrique Alarcon, art direction for French version by Jacques Willemetz; music by Isidro B. Maztegui.

Filmed 29 November 1954-29 March 1955. Cannes Film Festival, Critics Prize, 1955.

Cast: Lucia Bose (*Maria Jose de Castro*); Alberto Closas (*Juan*); Carlos Casaravilla (*Rafael Sandoval, called Rafa*); Otello Toso (*Miguel de Castro*); Bruna Corra (*Matilde*); Alicia Romay (*Cristina*); Julia Delgado Caro (*Dona Maria*); Matilde Muñoz Sampedro (*Neighbor*); Mercedes Albert (*Cristina*); Emilio Alonso (*Jorge*).

Publications:

Script—"*Mort d'un cycliste*" (screenplay) by Juan Antonio Bardem in *Avant-Scène du cinéma* (Paris), 15 February 1964; book—*Cinema, The Magic Vehicle: A Guide to Its Achievements: Journey Two* edited by Jacek Klinowski and Adam Garbicz, Metuchen, New Jerey 1979; articles—"New Names: Spain" in *Sight and Sound* (London), spring 1956; "Spanish Highway" by Juan Bardem in *Films and Filming* (London), June 1957; "Bardem: Une Méthode de travail" by J.F. Aranda in *Cinéma 59* (Paris), no.33, 1959; "Juan Antonio Bardem, homme d'Espagne" by Philippe Durand in *Image et son* (Paris), October 1959; "Un Evénement important" by Georges Sadoul in *Avant-Scène du cinéma* (Paris), 15 February 1964.

*   *   *

At a meeting in Salamanca in 1955 Spain's young filmmakers declared: "We want to struggle for a national cinema.... Through our cinema we want to enter into contact with the people and the regions of Spain, with the people and the regions of the entire world." The spirit of Salamanca was manifested in a film released that same year, *Muerte de un ciclista*. Directed by Juan Antonio Bardem, *Muerte de un ciclista* won the critics grand prize at the Cannes Film Festival. It established contact not only with the people of Spain but also with international audiences and marked the rebirth of Spain cinema in the post-Civil War period.

The style of *Muerte de un ciclista* attests to the influence of a number of diverse filmmakers. In its dramatic use of cross-cutting it follows Eisenstein's principle of montage by collision; in its themes and subject matter it resembles such Italian neorealist works as Antonioni's *Cronaca di un Amore* (1950). Indeed, some critics have criticized Bardem's style for being too eclectic and derivative. Nevertheless, *Muerte de un ciclista* is of exceptional interest as a document of the early 1950's in Spain. It reveals how privileged members of the Franco regime lived and provides a critical view of those who profited socially and financially from the dictatorship. It also offers brief glimpses of Madrid's lower classes and of university students impatient for change. Both of these groups would reject the assertion made by one of the upper class characters that they are living in a "golden age."

Muerte de un ciclista begins as a domestic drama. A car speeding down a windswept, deserted highway hits a man on a bicycle. After stopping and confirming that the victim is still alive, the couple in the car speed away, leaving the stricken man on the road. We subsequently learn that Juan, the man in the car, is a university professor; the woman who was driving is the wife of a wealthy businessman. Afraid that the accident will reveal their adulterous affair, they choose to let the cyclist die, thereby touching off a chain of events that leads the protagonist, a former soldier on the Falange side, to re-examine his life and to see the compromises that he has made and the ideals that he has sacrificed.

Juan is both an individual and a representative of a social class and a particular generation. He stands in sharp contrast to the university students whom he teaches. These students, like the real students in Madrid in the 1950's, hold demonstrations and denounce what they perceive to be injustices in the system. By alternating scenes between the university students and the upper class world of the lovers, Bardem expands the focus of his story and explores the social and political dimensions of the protagonists' actions.

Although the ending of the film remains ambiguous (because of conditions imposed by the censor, some would argue), Bardem's point of view is clear. *Muerte de un ciclista* is a parable on the selfishness of the ruling classes, a meditation on the impact of Spain's past upon the present, and an expression of Bardem's fervent hope that the future will be different.

—Katherine Singer Kovács

MY DARLING CLEMENTINE. Production: Twentieth Century-Fox; 1946; black and white, 35mm; running time: 97 mins. Released November 1946.

Produced by Samuel G. Engel; screenplay by Samuel G. Engel and Winston Miller based on a story by Sam Hellman; from the novel *Wyatt Earp, Frontier Marshal* by Stuart N. Lake; directed by John Ford; photography by Joseph P. MacDonald; edited by Dorothy Spencer; set decoration by Thomas Little and Fred J. Rode; art direction by James Basevi and Lyle R. Wheeler; music by Cyril Mockridge and David Buttolph, orchestrated by Edward B. Powell; special effects by Fred Sersen; costumes designed by Rene Hubert.

Filmed on location in Monument Valley, Utah and in New Mexico.

Cast: Henry Fonda (*Wyatt Earp*); Linda Darnell (*Chihuahua*); Doc John Holliday (*Victor Mature*); Old Man Clanton (*Walter*

Brennan); Tim Holt (*Virgil Earp*); Ward Bond (*Morgan Earp*); Cathy Downs (*Clementine Carter*); Alan Mowbry (*Granville Thorndyke*); John Ireland (*Billy Clanton*); Grant Withers (*Ike Clanton*); Roy Roberts (*Mayor*); Jane Darwell (*Kate Nelson*); Russell Simpson (*John Simpson*); Francis Ford (*Dad, old soldier*); J.Farrell McDonald (*Mac the barman*); Don Garner (*James Earp*); Ben Hall (*Barber*); Arthur Walsh (*Hotel clerk*); Jack Pennick (*Coach driver*); Louis Mercier (*Francois*); Micky Simpson (*Sam Clanton*); Fred Libby (*Phin Clanton*); Harry Woods (*Luke*); Charles Stevens (*Indian Joe*); Danny Borzage (*Accordian player*); Mae Marsh.

Publications:

Books—*John Ford* by Jean Mitry, Paris 1954; *The Film Till Now: A Survey of World Cinema* by Paul Rotha with Richard Griffith, New York 1960; *The Westerns: From Silents to Cinerama* by William K. Everson and George N. Fenin, New York 1962; *La Grande Aventure du western* by Jean-Louis Rieupeyrout, Paris 1964; *John Ford* by Philippe Haudiquet, Paris 1966; *John Ford* by Peter Bogdanovich, Berkeley 1968; *John Steinbeck and His Films* by Michael Burrows, (Primestyle "Formative Films" series) 1970; *The Fondas: The Films and Careers of Henry, Jane, and Peter Fonda* by John Springer, New York 1970; *The Cinema of John Ford* by John Baxter, New York 1971; *John Ford* by Michael Wilmington and Joseph McBride, London 1975; *The John Ford Movie Mystery* by Andrew Sarris, London 1976; *John Ford* by Andrew Sinclair, New York 1979; articles—"Lettre à John Ford sur *My Darling Clementine*" by Jean-Georges Auriol in *La Revue du Cinéma* (Paris), spring 1947; article by Jean-Louis Rieuperout in *Quarterly of Film, Radio, and Television* (Berkeley), winter 1952; "Henry Fonda" by John Springer in *Films in Review* (New York), November 1960; "The Five Worlds of John Ford" by Douglas McVay in *Films and Filming* (London), June 1962; "Fonda" by Peter Cowie in *Films and Filming* (London), April 1962; "Fonda on Fonda" by Henry Fonda in *Films and Filming* (London), February 1963; article by Douglas Brode in *Cinéaste* (New York), fall 1968; article by Robin Wood in *Film Comment* (New York), fall 1971; issue devoted to "John Ford's Stock Company" in *Filmkritik* (Munich), January 1972; "Per una rilettura del cinema classico americano" by M. Buffa and C. Scarrone in *Filmcritica* (Rome), October/December 1973; "Mise-en-scène in John Ford's *My Darling Clementine*" by Douglas Gomery in *Wide Angle* (Athens, Ohio), vol.2, no.4, 1978.

*　　　*　　　*

My Darling Clementine is considered the archetype of the classic western. In retelling the familiar story of the Earp brothers standing up to the evil Clanton family, director John Ford proved Hollywood genre films would become great cultural artifacts. However, Ford, one of the industry's most honored directors, is usually better remembered for other masterworks. While *My Darling Clementine* is considered one of his better films, it is only one of many in a truly remarkable career.

Ford, however, did not want to direct this classic work originally. After World War II Ford, like many of Hollywood's highly rated directors, formed an independent company, in this case Argosy Pictures. But he still owed Twentieth Century-Fox one more film. (Fox's production chief Darryl F. Zanuck tried to tempt Ford to re-negotiate his Fox contract for a guaranteed

$600,000 per year plus limited freedom but Ford refused.) Zanuck assigned Ford to *My Darling Clementine* starring Fox stars Henry Fonda and Victor Mature. Shooting began in Monument Valley in May, 1946, and was completed within 45 days. Zanuck found Ford's version too long, and the story unclear, so he cut 30 minutes, and re-structured some of the remaining material. Released in November, 1946 the film received favorable reviews, and earned respectable, but not record-breaking revenues.

The structure of *My Darling Clementine* is straight-foward, and symmetrical, opening with the ominous meeting of the Earps with the Clantons, and closing with the gun-fight at the OK Corral (and Wyatt's half-hearted promise to return). All this seems to take place in three or four days. Although the events are grounded in history (Ford claimed to have gotten this version directly from friend Wyatt Earp), the details were transformed to make a popular film. The Doc Holliday figure was transfigured the most. Like central characters in *The Searchers* and *The Man Who Shot Liberty Valance*, Holliday tragically stands between primitivism and civilization. Unlike the Earps this character fails to find a way to reconcile his place in the changing world, and turns to alcohol and a desire for death.

Disintegration of the family was a dominant theme in Ford's work prior to World War II. In *My Darling Clementine* the contrast between the Earps and Clantons is clearly drawn, with death at the ultimate shootout predestined. The Earps are diametrically opposed to the Clantons, yet strong similarities exist. In both cases, the father holds powerful authority. "Old Man" Clanton beats his sons with a whip, bullying them like animals. The Earps, however, are more civilized, and continually appeal to their unseen father ("How will we tell Pa?"). In the end Wyatt and Morgan, the surviving brothers choose to return to tell Pa of recent events rather than remain to help civilize Tombstone.

My Darling Clementine seems to present a well known story, set in the familiar context of the western. Upon closer examination of the film, however, one can still see the confusion Zanuck must have sensed, such as the sequence in which the Earps come to town. Wyatt settles down for a shave when gunshots arouse him. He goes through the hotel (next to the barber shop) and emerges, in a medium long shot, alone on the sidewalk. A barber pole serves as a reference to locate him in the darkness. Wyatt goes across the street to the source of the trouble. We see him with the Oriental Saloon in the background, its doors clearly seen in deep space. Wyatt enters the Oriental saloon to capture Indian Joe, the perpetrator of the trouble. Wyatt then gathers the barber from the crowd of spectators and seeks a continuation of his shave. Later in the film we learn, through several long establishing shots, that there is *no* Oriental saloon on the other side of the street. This absence of the continual "referential focus" disrupts the film's visual rhythm, setting this sequence apart from the rest of the film. There are numerous other examples of visual discontinuity in this film, all violating rules of classical Hollywood style. Indeed in this seemingly simple work Ford develops a complex visual pattern of stability and disruption in the world of Tombstone. Ford seems to be foreshadowing his autocritiques of the western genre made throughout the 1950s and 1960s.

In its use of generic elements *My Darling Clementine* suggests the western myth might not be as stable as it was prior to World War II. Although in the end the film seems to promise the formation of a utopian community, the western hero does not seem to be able to reconcile his individual and social roles. He rides off in the closing sequence with only a vague suggestion he will return to Clementine and the community. To further play on the hero's ambiguous character Ford continually reminds us that he does not fit in. *My Darling Clementine*'s most cited sequence is not its elaborate gunfight, but rather a dance in which Wyatt

Earp displays his lack of grace on the dance floor. This Eastern ritual is here to stay, whether the western hero fits in or not. Ford seems to have been influenced in *My Darling Clementine* by his recent military experience during World War II. Despite the fact Ford made seven films about the United States Cavalry, *My Darling Clementine* seems to be his most militarist western, both in theme and action. The Earps represent a new type of law—cold and calculating. They operate within the law, yet always clearly able to kill in a most efficient manner. Family ties and a sense of justice seem all that is necessary to justify action. Civilization defends itself only by obliterating the other side, and then leaving when the job is done, much as the popular image of the role of the American military during World War II.

In the end, in structure, theme and style Ford seems to be undercutting the anarchic spirit of the western, so celebrated in 1939 with his *Stagecoach*. The style seems classical but upon closer inspection is not. The themes seem classical, but contradictions and loose ends abound. Even closure, the Hollywood system's point of "wrapping the package," is confused and ambiguous. *My Darling Clementine* represents the work of a filmmaker ready to break out of the studio system and go onto more complex projects, as Ford would. In an uneven path he would make his way to his masterworks, westerns of complexity and ambiguity: *The Searchers* (1956) and *The Man Who Shot Liberty Valance* (1962). *My Darling Clementine*, a masterwork in its own right, foreshadows Ford's greatest films.

—Douglas Gomery

THE NAKED CITY. Production: Hellinger Productions for United-International Pictures; black and white, 35mm; running time: 96 mins. Released 4 March 1948.

Produced by Mark Hellinger with Jules Buck; screenplay by Malvin Wald and Albert Maltz; from an unpublished story by Malvin Wald; directed by Jules Dassin; photography by William Daniels; edited by Paul Weatherwax; sound by Leslie I. Carey and Vernon W. Kramer; art direction by John F. DeCuir, set decoration by Russell Gausman and Oliver Emert; music by Miklos Rozsa and Frank Skinner, music supervised by Milton Schwarzwald; costumes designed by Grace Houston.

Filmed in Stillman's Gym, the Roxy Theater, the Whitehall Building, the City Morgue, Roosevelt Hospital, the Universal Building, and Williamsburg Bridge in New York City.

Cast: Barry Fitzgerald (*Lt. Dan Muldoon*); Howard Duff (*Frank Niles*); Dorothy Hart (*Ruth Morrison*); Don Taylor (*Jimmy Halloran*); Ted De Corsia (*Garzah*); House Jameson (*Dr. Stoneman*); Anne Sargent (*Mrs. Halloran*); Adelaide Klein (*Mrs. Batory*); Grover Burgess (*Mr. Batory*); Tom Pedi (*Detective Perelli*); Enid Markey (*Mrs. Hylton*); Frank Conroy (*Captain Donahue*).

Publications:

Script—*The Naked City* by Malvin Wald and Albert Maltz, edited by Matthew J. Bruccoli, afterword by Malvin Wald, Carbondale, Illinois 1979; books—*Jules Dassin* by Adelio Ferrero, Parma 1961; *Underworld USA* by Colin McArthur, London 1972; *Film Noir* edited by Alain Silver and Elizabeth Ward, Woodstock, New York 1979; articles—by Richard Brooks on Mark Hellinger in *Screen Writer* (Hollywood), March 1948; "Jules Dassin" by Cynthia Grenier in *Sight and Sound* (London), winter 1957-58; "I See Dassin Make the Law" by John Francis Lane in *Films and Filming* (London), September 1958; "Style and Instinct" by Jules Dassin in *Films and Filming* (London), February 1970 and March 1970; "Los vaivenes de Jules Dassin" by M. Martínez Carril in *Cinemateca revista* (Andes), July 1981.

*　　*　　*

The Naked City is New York, a metropolis of playgrounds and police precincts, fire escapes and brownstones and neon lights, rush-hour subways packed like sardine cans and fire hydrants sprinkling the streets on a sweltering summer day. It is most definitely not a city constructed on a Hollywood back lot, not a set designer's stylized or otherwise exaggerated vision of Manhattan canyons. To paraphrase Mark Hellinger, the film's producer and narrator, the actors play their roles in the actual apartments, skyscrapers and city streets—107 total locations in all.

At the close of and after World War II, several Hollywood thrillers were shot in a documentary-like manner, away from the studio in actual urban locales: *The House on 92nd Street* (the trendsetter, filmed in New York and released three years before *The Naked City*), *Panic in the Streets* and *Walk East on Beacon* (which were shot in, respectively, New Orleans and Boston). Jules Dassin's *The Naked City* may not be the first of its type, but its almost revolutionary union of actors and real people, on real streets, has inspired scores of films ever since. The camera crew worked inside a van equipped with a one-way mirror, enabling them to film the city while remaining invisible to passersby. New York, and New Yorkers, become the leading performers, the film's major attraction.

The Naked City is a series of powerful scenes, first depicting the murder of a pretty, man-hungry, larcenous young model, and then detailing the efforts of the cops to sniff out her killers. Of course, they unravel the case, which culminates in a thrilling chase sequence across the Williamsburg Bridge from Manhattan's Lower East Side to Brooklyn. The homicide detectives are meticulous, but their labors are decidedly tedious and unglamorous. They are not heroically superhuman Clint Eastwoods, and they do not exchange sexy banter with voluptuous heroines whom they bed before the final reel. The major role is played by Barry Fitzgerald; he could be only May Robson's idea of a sex symbol, but his character is a sharp, 30-odd year veteran at the New York Police Department. His associate, young eager-to-please Don Taylor, might be more attractive, but he lives in an undistinguished working class neighborhood and kisses his wife goodbye each morning. Fitzgerald tells a co-worker that he hasn't had a busy day since yesterday; he and his fellow flatfoots forever "ask a question, get an answer, ask another." *The Naked City* does not contain street language or bloody corpses; it is no *Sharky's Machine* or *True Confessions* or *Prince of the City*. But it is as realistic as a major studio film could be in 1948.

The leading actors are familiar faces, but not stars. Except for, perhaps, Barry Fitzgerald, their names were unfamiliar to audiences. *The Naked City* is peopled not so much by performers as faces, everyday faces. The murder victim's parents appear in several key scenes, and the actors portraying them give heart-wrenching performances. But, most importantly, they *look* like an anonymous couple from the New Jersey boondocks who have lost their only child to the glitter of the big city.

From *Brute Force* to *Rififi* to *Never on Sunday*, director Jules Dassin's career has been disconnected: *The Naked City* is more the cousin of *The House on 92nd Street* than anything else in Dassin's filmography (with the possible exception of *Night and the City*, shot in London). All have their roots more in Italian neorealism—or even the ashcan paintings of Robert Henri, George Bellows, John Sloan, George Luks and William Glackens—than in anything from Hollywood.

—Rob Edelman

NANIWA EREJI. Osaka Elegy. Production: Daiichi Eiga; black and white, 35mm. Released 1936.

Screenplay by Yoshikata Yoda; from the story "Mieko" by Saburo Okada; directed by Kenji Mizoguchi; photography by Minoru Miki; sound by Hisashi Kase and Yasumi Mizoguchi.

Cast: Isuzu Yamada (*Ayako Murai*); Benkei Shinganoya (*Sonosuke*); Eitaro Shindo (*Yoshizo Fujino*); Kensaku Hara (*Susumu Nishimura*); Seiichi Takegawa (*Ayako's father*); Shinpachiro Asaka (*Ayako's brother*); Chiyoko Okura (*Ayako's sister*); Yoko Umemura (*Sonosuke's wife*); Shizuko Takezawa (*Mine Fukuda*); Kuneo Tamura (*Doctor Yoko*); Kiyoko Okubo (*Doctor's wife*).

Publications:

Books—*Kenji Mizoguchi* by Ve-ho, Paris 1963; *Kenji Mizoguchi* by Michel Mesnil, Paris 1965; *Mizoguchi Kenji no hito to geijutsu* [Kenji Mizoguchi: The Man and His Art] by Yoshikata Yoda, Tokyo 1970; *Kenji Mizoguchi* by Max Tessier, Paris 1971; *Voices from the Japanese Cinema* by Joan Mellen, New York 1975; *The Waves at Genji's Door: Japan Through Its Cinema* by Joan Mellen, New York 1976; *Japanese Film Directors* by Audie Bock, New York 1978; *The Japanese Film: Art and Industry* by Joseph Anderson and Donald Richie, revised edition, Princeton 1982; articles—"Kenji Mizoguchi" by Donald Richie and Joseph Anderson in *Sight and Sound* (London), autumn 1955; issue on Mizoguchi of *Cinéma 55* (Paris), no.6, 1955; issue on Mizoguchi of *Cahiers du cinéma* (Paris), March 1958; issue on Mizoguchi of *L'Ecran* (Paris), February/March 1958; "Mizoguchi" by Akira Iwasaki in *Anthologie du cinéma*, Vol. 29, Paris 1967; "The Density of Mizoguchi's Scripts", interview with Yoshikata Yoda, in *Cinema* (Los Angeles), spring 1971; "3 cinéastes de la femme" by G. Braucourt and others in *Ecran* (Paris), August/September 1974; "Pour ne pas oublier Mizoguchi Kenji: 6 films inédits de Mizoguchi au Centre Georges Pompidou" by J.L. Cros in *Image et son* (Paris), April 1978; "Kenji Mizoguchi" by Donald Richie in *Cinema: A Critical Dictionary* edited by Richard Roud, London 1980; "On Kenji Mizoguchi" by Tadao Sato and Dudley Andrew in *Film Criticism* (Edinboro, Pennsylvania), spring 1980; article in *Film Criticism* (Edinboro, Pennsylvania), winter 1982.

The term "feminist" has been applied to the films of Kenji Mizoguchi frequently and somewhat indiscriminately. The term can involve three rather different approaches: 1) films that explicitly confront and endorse the theories and values of the women's liberation movement; 2) films that analyze the ways in which women are oppressed within society; and 3) films in which the director appears to identify with, show special sympathy for, female characters. The interest in Mizoguchi's work is that it covers this entire spectrum of approaches. Only two of his films that have become accessible in the West (*Victory of Women* and *My Love Has Been Burning*) employ the first approach (both belong to the immediate aftermath of World War II and to the enforced "democratization" of Japan under the American occupation). The late films, especially, are examples of the third approach, and involve the constant risk of succumbing to traditional male-created myths of women, especially woman-as-redeemer, with the emphasis on female sacrifice. *Osaka Elegy* (as it is generally known in the West), like *Sisters of Gion* made later in the same year, is that of the second approach. Here the risk is that the films will become "melodramas of defeat," reinforcing myths of woman-as-victim, with an emphasis on female masochism.

The importance of *Osaka Elegy* lies in its position within the series of increasingly radical feminist films that culminates in the magnificent *My Love Has Been Burning* (1949), one of Mizoguchi's greatest achievements, for which no equivalent exists within the commercial cinema of the West. *Osaka Elegy* marks, in many respects, a point of hesitation prior to the director's total (if temporary) commitment to feminist principles. Noel Burch is clearly correct (in *To the Distant Observer*) in arguing for the superiority of *Sisters of Gion*, though it is a pity the argument is conducted on purely formal grounds: the formal and stylistic rigour of the later film is paralleled in its altogether tougher and more uncompromising treatment of women's oppression, central to which is its female protagonist, whom the film credits with a rebelliousness and ideological awareness far beyond that of Ayako in *Osaka Elegy* (the two characters are played, splendidly, by the same actress, Isuzu Yamada, which underlines the continuity between the two films).

As Noel Burch suggests, *Osaka Elegy* is stylistically torn between a capitulation to the codes of dominant cinema—Hollywood—and the repudiation of them marked so emphatically by *Sisters of Gion*. It is also torn, thematically and dramatically, between the female masochism of earlier Mizoguchi films (such as *Taki No Shiraito*, 1933) and the feminist protest to come—marvellously anticipated in the final shot, in which Ayako walks and stares straight into camera, with a look combining defiance with denunciation of the society (i.e., the film's contemporary audience) that has condemned her to prostitution. The film also has a dimension lacking in its successors: an analysis of the oppression of women within the family, in the name of familial "loyalty" and "duty"—the duty of the daughter to serve, unquestioningly, father and brother.

Where *Sisters of Gion* breaks with the codes of western cinema, *Osaka Elegy* evokes direct comparison with certain Hollywood films of the same period, especially the films of von Sternberg with Marlene Dietrich, where the resemblance is stylistic as well as thematic. It lacks the extraordinary excess and obsessiveness that give the von Sternberg films their unique distinction; on the other hand, the political rigour that was to characterize the Mizoguchi films centred on women up to 1950 is here more than embryonic.

—Robin Wood

*   *   *

NANOOK OF THE NORTH. Production: Révillon Frères; 1922; black and white, 35mm, silent; running time: 75 mins.; length: 1525 meters. Released 11 June 1922, New York. Re-released July 1947 with narration and music. Re-released 1976 with music track only.

Produced, conceived (scenario), directed and photographed by Robert Flaherty; titles by Robert Flaherty and Carl Stearns Clancy; edited by Robert and Frances Flaherty.

Filmed August 1920-August 1921 in the area around the Hudson Strait, Canada; and along the shores of the Hopewell Sound, Quebec, Canada. Cost: $55,000.

Publications:

Reviews—"*Nanook of the North*" by Frances Taylor Patterson in the *New Republic* (New York), 9 August 1922; "*Nanook of the North*" by Fritz Tidden in *Moving Picture World* (New York), 24 June 1922; books—*Moving Pictures* by Frederick A. Talbot, Philadelphia 1923; *My Eskimo Friends* by Robert Flaherty, New York 1924; *Representative Photoplays Analyzed* by Scott O'Dell, Hollywood 1924; *Let's Go to the Movies* by Iris Barry, London 1926; *L'Usine aux images* by Ricciotto Canudo, translated by Harold J. Salemson, Paris 1927; *The Standardization of Error* by Vilhjalmur Stefansson, London 1928; *2 Pioneers: Robert Flaherty, Hans Richter* by Herman Weinberg, supplement to *Sight and Sound*, index series, London 1946; *Grierson on Documentary* by John Grierson, edited by Forsyth Hardy, New York 1947; *Robert Flaherty* by Mario Gromo, Parma, Italy 1952; *Documentary Film* by Paul Rotha, London 1952; *The World of Robert Flaherty* by Richard Griffith, New York 1953; *The Odyssey of a Filmmaker* by Frances Flaherty, Urbana, Illinois, 1960; *Robert Flaherty* by Paolo Gobetti, Turin 1960; *Robert Flaherty et le documentaire poétique* by Fuad Quintar, Paris 1960; *The Cinema and Social Science: A Survey of Ethnographic and Sociological Films* by Luc De Heusch, Paris 1962; *Robert Flaherty* by Jose Clemente, Madrid 1963; *Robert Flaherty* by Carlos Fernandez Cuenca, Madrid 1963; *Robert Flaherty* by Jay Leyda and Wolfgang Klaue, Berlin 1964; *Spellbound in Darkness: A History of the Silent Film* by George C. Pratt, New York 1966; *The Great Films: 50 Golden Years of Motion Pictures* by Bosley Crowther, New York 1967; *The Innocent Eye: The Life of Robert J. Flaherty* by Arthur Calder-Marshall, London 1970; *Nonfiction Film: A Critical History* by Richard Barsam, New York 1973; *Documentary: A History of the Non-Fiction Film* by Erik Barnouw, New York 1974; *Robert J. Flaherty* by Antonio Napolitano, Florence, Italy 1975; articles—"*Nanook of the North*" in *Moving Picture Herald* (New York), 24 June 1922; "Robert Flaherty's *Nanook of the North*" in *The Best Moving Pictures of 1922-23* by Robert Sherwood, Boston 1923; "The Future of American Cinema" by Wilbur Needham in *Close-Up* (London), June 1928; "Flaherty, Great Adventurer" by Terry Ramsaye in *Photoplay* (New York), May 1928; interview with Flaherty in *Sight and Sound* (London), no.71, 1949; "*Nanook of the North*" by Osvaldo Campassi in *Cinema* (Rome), 15 July 1949; "Profile of Flaherty" by Robert Lewis Taylor in the *New Yorker*, 11, 18 and 25 June 1949; "Flaherty—Education for Wanderlust" in *The Running Pianist* by Robert Lewis Taylor, New York 1950; "Hommage à Robert Flaherty" by Georges Sadoul in *Les Lettres françaises* (Paris), 13 September 1951; "Flaherty in Review" in *Sight and Sound* (London), November/December 1951; "The Flaherty Way" by Frances Flaherty in *Saturday Review* (New York), 13 Sep-

tember 1951; "A Flaherty Festival" by Arthur Knight in *Saturday Review* (New York), 6 January 1951; "Vanité que la Peinture" by Maurice Scherer (Eric Rohmer) in *Cahiers du cinéma* (Paris), June 1951; "The Film Forum: Documentary Masterpiece" by Cecile Starr in *Saturday Review* (New York), 6 January 1951; "Robert Flaherty, Geographer" by Roger Manvell in *The Geographical Magazine* (New York), February 1957; "Flaherty's Quest for Life" by Frances Flaherty in *Films and Filming* (London), January 1959; "Explorations" by Frances Flaherty and "Robert Flaherty—The Man and the Film-maker" by Charles Siepmann in *Film Book no.1: The Audience and the Filmmaker* edited by Robert Hughes, New York 1959; article by Robert Flaherty on *Nanook* in *The Emergence of Film Art* edited by Lewis Jacobs, New York 1969; "Robert Flaherty (Barnouw's File)" by Erik Barnouw in *Film Culture* (New York), spring 1972; "Robert Flaherty: The Man in the Iron Myth" by Richard Corliss in *Film Comment* (New York), November/December 1973; "Robert Flaherty albo rytual odkrywania formy" by A. Helman in *Kino* (Warsaw), March 1973; "A Re-examination of the Early Career of Robert J. Flaherty" by J. Ruby in *Quarterly Review of Film Studies* (Pleasantville, New York), fall 1980.

* * *

Through the everyday life of one family, *Nanook of the North* typifies Eskimo life in the Arctic; it uses a number of sequences that demonstrate Eskimo ingenuity and adaptability in one of the world's harshest climates. Flaherty filmed his documentary during the years 1920-1921 on the eastern shore of Hudson Bay's Ungava Peninsula. He brought with him a Carl Akeley gyroscope camera which required minimum lubrication in cold climates to facilitate pans and tilts; Flaherty was something of a pioneer in the camera's use. He also brought along printing equipment to process and develop the film on location and a portable theater to involve the Eskimos more intimately in the film's production, to enable them to understand its purpose.

Despite the license that Flaherty took in portraying some events and conditions, the film's most important feature was its very basis in reality. Nanook and his family were real persons who re-enacted their lives before Flaherty's camera. Not to be confused with cinema verité, Flaherty carefully selected his "cast" and directed them to "play" their own roles and to carry out tasks that would demonstrate to the outside world how they conducted their lives. Through a careful selection of details, Flaherty succeeded in conveying the drama, the struggle, underlying their daily existence.

Nanook was a significant departure both from the fiction and nonfiction films that preceded it. It departs from fiction because it lacks a plot or story. The background comes to the fore. Man's struggle to survive in this bleak environment becomes an inseparable part of the film's dramatic development. Its photographic detail was also far superior to other films of actuality. The film departs from nonfiction, newsreels and other actualities, in its narrative editing (for 1922), its ability to tell a story through images, and its use of the shot as the basis of a sequence. The film provides detailed pictorial information of the environment, narrative structure, and the filmmaker's art with its implicit emotive statement.

Nanook is a reflection of Flaherty's life-long interest in the interaction of diverse cultures. To be sure, Flaherty wanted to give the outside world a glimpse of Eskimo life as he had experienced it during his years as an explorer, surveyor, and prospector in the lower Arctic region. However, he also wanted to capture on film a way of life threatened by encroaching civilization. *Nanook*, like other Flaherty films, is not depicted in a particular historical setting or context; the timeless appearance was deliberate. He also wanted to capture the Eskimos' essential nobility, to portray them as they saw themselves.

The building of the igloo sequences serves to illustrate Flaherty's technique. Detail upon detail demonstrates Nanook's amazing ingenuity. He builds a shelter out of ice and snow. The sequence is not overexplained. The audience is left to discover each new step and its significance—such as the way in which the translucent block of ice is used as a window. What perhaps has sparked the most discussion is Flaherty's shooting of the interior shots inside the igloo. Restricted to camera negative stock with relatively slow speed or slow sensitivity to light, he had an igloo constructed to twice the average size with half of it cut away to permit sunlight to brighten the scene. The Nanook family goes to sleep during the day for the benefit of Flaherty's camera. This sequence illustrates Flaherty's dictum that sometimes it is necessary to exaggerate reality in order to capture its real essence.

Professor Frances Taylor Patterson of Columbia University was one of the first to recognize the documentary value of *Nanook*. It differed from travel exotica, she wrote, because it did not wander but used one location and one hunter to present an entire culture. Later in the decade some writers criticized *Nanook* for lack of authenticity. However, most modern writers have been delighted with the film's emotive powers which have made audiences identify with the fundamental struggle to survive with all its sociological and philosophical implications.

Nanook, opening to rave reviews, almost immediately was considered one of the greatest films of all times; it quickly received worldwide distribution. Robert Sherwood, for example, called it "literally in class by itself." No one called it a documentary, though, until as a result of the release of *Moana* (1926) and the writings of John Grierson, parallels could be seen in Flaherty's work. They became the foundation for the development of documentary film as an art form and as a new filmic sensibility. It is perhaps Edmund Carpenter, the cultural anthropologist, who best elucidated *Nanook of the North* and Flaherty's work in general by noting a relationship between this film and Eskimo art. To the Eskimo, he wrote, the creation of art is "an act of seeing and expressing life's values; it's a ritual of discovery by which patterns of nature and of human nature are revealed by man." The drama of daily existence in the North is not imposed from the outside but discovered by exploration, a process that takes into account the natural environment and a philosophy of life.

Nanook remains the most enduring of all Flaherty's films for its simplicity of purpose, structure, and design. It ennobles its subjects rather than exploits them. It relies on a few well-developed sequences. The images, sharp and uncluttered, are still memorable.

—William T. Murphy

NAPOLÉON. Napoléon vu par Abel Gance. Production: Westi/Société générale de films, Paris; black and white, 35mm, Polyvision (some versions without Polyvision); running time: originally about 270 mins., but the film has always existed in several versions, some up to 5 hours in length; length: originally about 32 reels. Released 7 April 1927, Paris. Released without Polyvision 1929, New York. Re-released 1934 with sound. In 1971 *Napoléon—Bonaparte et la Revolution* was re-released

with sound and with some footage added and some eliminated. In 1981 *Napoléon*, the original version, was restored by Kevin Brownlow and re-released in its entirety with music by Carl Davis, also re-released in the US by Francis Ford Coppola with some footage cut and music by Carmine Coppola.

Produced by Wengoroff and Hugo Stinnes; screenplay by Abel Gance; directed by Abel Gance; photography by Jules Kruger, Léonce-Henry Burel, Jean-Paul Mundwiller, and assisted by Lucas, Briquet, Emile Pierre, and Roger Hubert; edited by Marguerite Beaugé and Henritte Pinson; production design by (set decorators) Alexandre Benois, Schildnecht, Jacouty, Meinhardt, and Laourie; music by Arthur Honegger; consultants: Jean Arroy, Jean Mitry, and Sacher Purnal; assistant directors: Henry Krauss, Alexandre Volkov, and Viatcheslaw Tourjansky.

Filmed 1925-26 in France.

Cast: Albert Dieudonné (*Bonaparte*); Vladimir Roudenko (*Young Bonaparte*); Edmond van Daele (*Robespierre*); Alexandre Koubitsky (*Danton*); Antonin Artaud (*Marat*); Abel Gance (*Saint-Just*); Pierre Batcheff (*Hoche*); Maxudian (*Barras*); Chakatouny (*Pozzo di Borgo*); Philippe Hériat (*Salicetti*); Nicolas Koline (*Tristan Fleuri*); Daniel Mendaille (*Fréron*); Alexandre Bernard (*Dugommier*); Philippe Rolla (*Masséna*); Robert Vidalin (*Camille Desmoulins*); Roger Blum (*Talma*); Paul Amiot (*Fouquier-Tinvillle*); Boudreau (*La Fayette*); Georges Lampin (*Joseph Bonaparte*); Alberty (*J.-J. Rousseau*); R. de Ansorena (*Desaix*); Jack Rye (*Louis XVI*); Armand Bernard (*Jean-Jean*); Albert Bras (*Monge*); Georges Cahuzac (*Beauharnais*); Favière (*Fouché*); Harry Krimer (*Rouget de Lisle*); Genica Missirio (*Murat*); Rauzena (*Lucien Bonaparte*); Viguier (*Couthon*); Vonelly (*André Chenier*); Jean d'Yd (*La Bussière*); Gina Manès (*Joséphine de Beauharnais*); Annabella (*Violine Fleuri*); Suzanne Blanchetti (*Marie-Antoinette*); Eugénie Buffet (Letizia Bonaparte); Damia (*la Marseillaise*); Yvette Dieudonné (*Elisa Bonaparte*); Marguerite Gance (*Charlotte Corday*); Simone Genevois (*Pauline Bonaparte*); Andrée Standard; Pierrette Lugan; Francine Mussey; Suzy Vernon; Mlle. Carvalho; Sylvie Gance; Boris Fastovitch; M. Guibert; Maupin; Blin; Bonvallet; Daniel Burret; Silvio Gavicchia; Caillard; M. de Canolle; Chabez; Roger Chantal; M. Pérès; Pierre Ferval.

Publications:

Scripts—*Napoléon vu par Abel Gance* (sequence description and scenerio) by Abel Gance, Paris 1927; selections from the shooting script in "Special Gance Issue" of *L'Écran* (Paris), April/May 1958; reviews—"Shadow Version of Napoleon's Life" by James Graham in *The New York Times*, 5 June 1927; review of Ameican version of *Napoléon* by Mordaunt Hall in *The New York Times* 12 February 1929; review of *Bonaparte and the Revolution* by Roger Greenspun in *The New York Times*, 16 October 1971; review of *Bonaparte et la révolution* by Michael McKegney in *The Village Voice* (New York), 11 November 1971; books—*En tourant 'Napoléon' avec Abel Gance. Souvenirs et impressions d'un sans-culotte* by Jean Arroy, Paris 1927; *French Film* by Georges Sadoul, London 1953; *Abel Gance* by Roger Icart, Toulouse, France 1960; *The Parade's Gone By....* by Kevin Brownlow, New York 1969; "Abel Gance's *Bonaparte and the Revolution*" in *Film 71/72* by Vincent Canby, New York 1972; *Film/Cinema/Movie* by Gerald Mast, New York 1977; *Abel Gance* by Steven Kramer and James Welsh, Boston 1978; articles—"France Films Her

Napoleon" in *The New York Times*, 4 March 1928; "Les Nouveaux Chapitres de notre syntaxe" by Abel Gance in *Cahiers du cinéma* (Paris), October 1953; "Départ vers la polyvision" by Abel Gance in *Cahiers du cinéma* (Paris), December 1954; "*Napoléon*" in *Classics of the Foreign Film* by Parker Tyler, New York 1962; "Film Festival: 1927 Vintage" by Howard Thompson in *The New York Times*, 25 September 1967; article by Kevin Brownlow in *Films and Filming* (London), November 1969; "The French Film—Abel Gance" in *The Silent Voice: A Text* by Arthur Lenning, New York 1969; "The Camera as Snowball" by R.H. Blumer in *Cinema Journal* (Evanston, Illinois), spring 1970; "Bonaparte et la révolution" by Kevin Brownlow in *Sight and Sound* (London), winter 1971-72; "Abel Gance's *Bonaparte and the Revolution*" in *Film 71/72* by Vincent Canby, New York 1972; "The Current Cinema: Work of a Master" by Penelope Gilliatt in *New Yorker*, 6 September 1976; "Napoléon—A Personal Involvement" by Kevin Brownlow in *Classic Film Collector* (Indiana, Pennsylvania), 23 August 1977; "Abel Gance, At Age 90, Hit of Telluride: *Napoleon* on 3 Screens, Runs Until 3 A.M." by W.K. Everson in *Variety* (New York), 12 September 1979; "History Made Again" by F. Grant in *Broadcast* (London), 8 December 1980; "Abel Gance's epic *Napoléon* Returns from Exile" by Kevin Brownlow in *American Film* (Washington, D.C.), January/February 1981; "The Music of Time: From *Napoléon* to New Babylon" by B. Eisenschitz in *Afterimage* (London), no.10, 1981; "Gance's *Napoléon* Returns in Style" by D. Elley in *Films* (London), February 1981; "The Many Lives of *Napoléon*" by W.K. Everson in *Film Comment* (New York), January/February 1981; "The Superimposition of Vision: *Napoléon* and the Meaning of Fascist Art" by P. Pappas in *Cineaste* (New York), no.2, 1981; "*Napoléon*" by James Welsh in *Films in Review* (New York), March 1981.

*   *   *

The showing of *Napoléon vu par Abel Gance* on 7 April 1927 at the Opéra in Paris was in every sense a triumphant occasion. For the invited audience it meant the culminating point of the restoration of French cinema after its virtual annihilation in 1914. For writer-director Able Gance himself it was the climax to 18 years work in the cinema and 10 years of rigorous and innovative exploration of the visual potential of the medium. *Napoléon* alone had taken three years of unremitting research, writing and shooting, cost several million francs, involved thousands of extras and a team of a dozen assistants and at least eight cameramen and directors of photography.

The project had been initially conceived as a massive six-part work which was to include the whole of Napoleon's life. The eventual six hours of edited footage in fact covers only a portion of the first part of this grandiose scheme, so the scale of Gance's imagination is immediately apparent. The truncation of the project means that though *Napoléon* has a greater sweep than any other Gance epic, it lacks the tragic resolution which usually completed Gance's tales of heroic endeavour, whether that of Jean Diaz in *J'accuse*, Savaronola in *Lucrèce Borgia*, or Beethoven in *Un Grand amour de Beethoven*. Despite its length, the film offers only the education and shaping of its hero, leaving him at an early point of triumph—the entry of his armies into Italy.

It is the technical aspects of *Napoléon* that have always received the most attention. The context in which Gance was working was one highly receptive of visual experimentation. After the constriction of the pre-1914 system organised by Charles Pathé and Léon Gaumont, in which Gance had made his debut, the new postwar generation to which he belonged strove to give a new dignity to the cinema. Despising the underfinanced, totally commerically oriented cinema of the early 1910's, with its philistine disregard for artistic aspiration and its conception of films as products to be made as if they were tinned peas, Gance and his contemporaries strove to develop the visual potential of the new medium, experimenting with mobile cameras and the new editing techniques pioneered by the emergent Hollywood narrative cinema and indulging in a profusion of optical effects—masks and superimpositions, distorting lenses and pulled focus. All of these tendencies reach their climax in *Napoléon*. To help with the massive project and the manipulation of the crowd scenes, Gance sought the assistance of fellow directors Henry Krauss, Alexandre Volkov and Viatcheslaw Tourjansky. With the aid of a team of cinematographers led by Jules Kruger, Léonce-Henry Burel and Jean-Paul Mundwiller, Gance moved his camera in every conceivable fashion—to imitate a ship tossed by a storm, the view from a galloping horse or even a snowball in flight. As if this welter of visual effects were not in itself sufficiently dazzling, Gance arranged for the screen width to be tripled at the end, so that Napoleon's entry into Italy, recorded in widescreen and with triptych effects, becomes a stunningly unique visual experience.

The climate of French 1920's cinema was very conducive to Gance's project, and there was nothing to restrain his exuberant imagination. The most successful films of the decade were superproductiqns with an exotic, literary or historical flavour, and *Napoléon* was designed to outmatch them all. It combined breathtaking virtuosity with a totally personal conception of the subject, and not until the 1970's masterpieces of Coppola and Spielberg do we find a similar harnessing of the entire resources of an industry to an unfettered personal vision. Central to Gance's conception was a very 19th-century romantic view of the artist. It has been well observed that just as *Un Grand Amour de Beethoven* depicts the artist as hero, *Napoléon* offers a view of the hero as artist. Though Gance himself played the role of Saint Just, he identified himself as creator of the film with Napoleon (played by Albert Dieudonné) as creator of a new France and master of the forces of history. Napoleon, the man of action, the politician and military genius, becomes a largely passive figure, a pensive visionary. Much stress is placed on Napoleon's childhood, and the hero's ability to crush dissent with a steely gaze is anticipated in early scenes of the schoolboy leading his side in a snowball fight. The boy is endowed with an all-too-symbolic pet eagle. But if these early scenes are often lively and well-realised, the most remarkable feature of this inevitably uneven work is the handling of action, nowhere better shown than in the celebrated scenes which intercut shots of Napoleon at sea in a tiny boat rocked by a storm with the human storm in the Convention in revolution-torn Paris.

In the 1980's *Napoléon* has become probably the most celebrated of all silent masterpieces. Kevin Brownlow's 20-year self-imposed task of bringing together all extant footage of the film is a remarkable endeavour, but for film historians it raises a whole host of questions about authenticity and authorship. There are now two quite different *Napoléon* restorations, Brownlow's own English version with its music by Carl Davis and preservation of silent running speed, and the version distributed in the United States by Francis Ford Coppola's company which is cut, run at the inappropriate speed of 24 frames a second and endowed with a questionable score by Coppola's father. Moreover, far from simply constituting a restoration of a mutilated film and a recreation of the viewing conditions of silent cinema with full orchestral accompaniement, Brownlow's five-hour version is as much a modern interpretation and distortion as Henri Langlois's seven or eight hour compilations of episodes from *Judex* or *Les Vam-*

pires. These versions led to the rediscovery of Louis Feuillade's work and the restoration of his reputation, but by compressing up to a dozen episodes, designed to be seen separately at fortnightly intervals, into a single massive viewing session, Langlois created a work that owed nothing to 1920's conceptions of film narrative and time-span. This new relationship of film and spectator can have an immediate "modern" impact, as the films of Jacques Rivette, one of the Cinémathèque Francaise's most faithful habitués, show, but it is not a recreation of the 1920's experience.

Similarly, Brownlow's "original" version corresponds to none that was ever shown in Paris in the 1920's, and there is nothing to indicate that audiences then would have accepted this five-hour endurance test. The actual Napoléon, like so many silent films, existed in several versions, and the 1927 showings were either of a shortened version with triptych effects (as at the premiere in the Opéra) or a four or six episode version without triple screen and shown over a period of weeks. Despite such paradoxes, the Brownlow version has many virtues, not least of which has been its revival of interest in silent cinema. Moreover, whereas Gance's own reworkings of his material—the 1934 sound version, the re-edited 1971 compilation Bonaparte et la revolution—like his 1960's feature Austerlitz, are simplifications and at times trivialisations, this 1980's version restores the work to full complexity and to its status of one of the 1920's most remarkable achievements.

—Roy Armes

NASHVILLE. Production: Paramount Pictures; 1975; Metrocolor, 35mm, Panavision; running time: 159 mins. Released 1975.

Produced by Robert Altman; screenplay by Joan Tewkesbury; title design by Dan Perri; directed by Robert Altman; photography by Paul Lohmann; edited by Sidney Levin and Dennis Hill; sound by Jim Webb and Chris McLaughlin; music direction by Richard Baskin; songs "200 Years" and "Keep a Goin'" by Henry Gibson; song "Yes I Do" by Lily Tomlin; songs "Down to the River," "Bluebird," "Tapedeck in His Tractor," "Dues," and "My Idaho Home" by Ronee Blakley; songs "Honey," "I'm Easy," and "It Don't Worry Me," by Keith Carradine; song "Rose's Cafe" by Allan Nichols; songs "Memphis," "Rolling Stone," and "I Don't Know If I Found It in You" by Karen Black; song "The Day I Looked Jesus in the Eye" by Robert Altman.

Filmed on location in Nashville. Academy Award, Best Song ("I'm Easy"), 1975; New York Film Critics Awards for Best Motion Picture, Best Direction, and Best Supporting Actress (Tomlin), 1975.

Cast: David Arkin (Norman); Barbara Baxley (Lady Pearl); Ned Beatty (Delbert Reese); Karen Black (Connie White); Ronee Blakley (Barbara Jean); Timothy Brown (Tommy Brown); Keith Carradine (Tom Frank); Geraldine Chaplin (Opal); Robert Doqui (Wade); Shelley Duvall (L.A. Joan); Allen Garfield (Barnett); Henry Gibson (Haven Hamilton); Scott Glenn (Pfc. Glen Kelly); Jeff Goldblum (Tricycle man); Barbara Harris (Albuquerque); David Hayward (Kenny Fraiser); Michael Murphy (John Triplette); Allan Nichols (Bill); Dave Peel (Bud Hamilton); Christina Raines (Mary); Bert Remsen (Star); Lily Tomlin (Linnea Reese); Gwen Welles (Sueleen); Keenan Wynn (Mr. Green).

Publications:

Reviews—"Nashville" by V. Glaessner in Focus on Film (London), autumn 1975; "Nashville" by Gordon Gow in Films and Filming (London), October 1975; "Nashville" by A.D. Murphy in Variety (New York), 11 June 1975; "Nashville" by C.P. Reilly in Films in Review (New York, August/September 1975; "Nashville" by Jonathan Rosenbaum in Sight and Sound (London), autumn 1975; "Nashville" by P. Strick in Monthly Film Bulletin (London), October 1975; "Nashville" by M. Blaedel in Kosmorama (Copenhagen), no.131, 1976; "Nashville" by G. Colpart in Téléciné (Paris), July/August 1976; "Robert Altman's Nashville" by A. Frezzato in Cineforum (Bergamo), October 1976; "Nashville" by D. Sauvaget in Revue du cinéma (Paris), October 1976; reviews by E. Magrelli and G. Turroni in Filmcritica (Rome), April 1976; books—Persistence of Vision: The Films of Robert Altman by Neil Feineman, New York 1976; Robert Altman: American Innovator by Judith M. Kass, New York 1978; The Films of Robert Altman by Alan Karp, Metuchen, New Jersey 1981; articles—"Entretien avec Robert Altman" by Michel Ciment and M. Henry in Positif (Paris), February 1975; Robert Altman seminar in Dialogue on Film (Beverly Hills), February 1975; "Altman, U.S.A." by Robert Benayoun in Positif (Paris), December 1975; "Jouer avec Altman (rencontres avec Ronee Blakley et Keith Carradine)" in Positif (Paris), December 1975; "Entretien avec Joan Tewkesbury" by Michael Henry in Positif (Paris), December 1975; "Nashville: America's Voices" in Film Heritage (Dayton, Ohio), fall 1975; "Improvisations and Interactions in Altmanville" by Jonathan Rosenbaum in Sight and Sound (London), spring 1975; "Smart-ass and Cutie-pie: Notes Toward an Evaluation of Altman" by Robin Wood in Movie, autumn 1975; issue on Altman of Film Heritage (Dayton, Ohio), fall 1975; "London Journal" by Jonathan Rosenbaum in Film Comment (New York), September/October 1975; "The Artist and the Multitude Are Natural Enemies", interview by F.A. Macklin, in Film Heritage (Dayton, Ohio), winter 1976/77; "Playboy Interview: Robert Altman" by Bruce Williamson in Playboy (Chicago), August 1976; "Invention and Death: The Commodities of Media in Robert Altman's Nashville" by Robert Self in Journal of Popular Film (Bowling Green, Ohio), no.5, 1976; "Nashville (An Interview Documentary) by Connie Byrne and William O. Lopez in Film Quarterly (Berkeley), winter 1975-76; "Robert Altman de Mash à Nashville" by P. Pitiot and H. Talvat in Jeune Cinéma (Paris), September/October 1976; "Pour bientot de Robert Altman" by J. Belmans in Amis du Film et de la Television (Brussels), January 1976; "The Space in the Distance: A Study of Altman's Nashville" by R.J. Cardullo in Literature/Film Quarterly (Salisbury, Maryland), no.4, 1976; "Buffalo Bill und die Indianer: Nashville" by W. Knorr in Medien und Padagogik (Munich), no.4, 1976; "Nashville: Il sonoro e il genere" by E. Magrelli in Filmcritica (Rome), April 1976; "Un film 'non-altro'" by G. Turroni in Filmcritica (Rome), April 1976; "Waarom is het rood-wit-blauw in Amerika intenser dan hier?" by W. Verstappen in Skoop (Wageningen, Netherlands), March 1976; "R. Altman & Co." by R. Levine in Film Comment (New York), January/February 1977; "Ou Finit le spectacle?..." by T. Elsaesser in Positif (Paris), September 1977; "Knocert trwa nadal" by J. Płażewski in Kino (Warsaw), March 1977; "Bob and Pauline: A Fickle Affair" by B. Cook in American Film (Washington, D.C.), December/January 1978-79; "Joan Tewkesbury on Screenwriting: An

Interview" by C. Sack in *Literature/Film Quarterly* (Salisbury, Maryland), winter 1978; "Dialogue on Film" by Joan Tewkesbury in *American Film* (Washington, D.C.), March 1979; "*Cabaret* and *Nashville*..." by S.E. Bowles in *Journal of Popular Film and Television* (Bowling Green, Ohio), no.3, 1978-79; "*Saturday Night Fever* and *Nashville*: Exploring the Comic Mythos" by R. Masbany in *Journal of Popular Film and Television* (Bowling Green, Ohio), no.3, 1978-79; "The Discursive and the Ideological in Film: Notes on the Conditions of Political Intervention" by C. MacCabe in *Screen* (London), no.4, 1978-79; "*Nashville*" by Leslie Taubman in *Magill's Survey of Cinema, Vol. III* edited by Frank N. Magill, Englewood Cliffs, New Jersey 1980; "Actors as Conventions in the Films of Robert Altman" by M. Yacowar in *Cinema Journal* (Evanston), fall 1980.

*　　*　　*

Robert Altman's Bicentennial epic about one week-end in the lives of 24 people in Nashville, Tennessee conveys his personal reflection on the state of the nation and his political call to fellow Americans on the nature of the state. Altman's artistic success results from the way he shapes uniquely American materials and sensibilities into a complex ideological network.

After three prologue scenes, Altman introduces a staggering total of 24 characters in one long location sequence at the Nashville airport (only Connie White—Karen Black—is not there, but her poster image represents her.) The interweaving of characters, music, sights, and sounds in the airport and freeway sequences establishes them and their lives within a modernist context, a barrage of sensory impressions which Altman choreographs into a bombardment of movement and timing. The continuously moving camera, rhythmic cuts between characters, background band music, TV announcer both on screen and as off-screen voice-over commentator, airport noises, characters talking and overlapping each other, continue to build in momentum until all characters are on the freeway on the way to town. The freeway sequence incorporates wider perspectives in aerial and high angle shots, highway noises, conversations and arguments until, as screenwriter Joan Tewksbury said, "Everything has whirled and spun and played through your senses."

Following this barrage-like exposition, Altman departs from stylistic sensational overload and moves to a "floating narrative," much like the style of TV soap operas in which the lives and events of many characters are presented by cutting back and forth between them. Altman periodically brings together and connects his 24 characters through devices of communication: telephones and telephone conversations, radio programs, tape recorded songs, the p.a. announcements of a presidential campaign van. He presents events happening simultaneously while slowly allowing for the evolution of time. Altman then cuts between four simultaneous church scenes, offering perspectives on as many characters as possible, then moves forward by cutting events into a progressive 24-hour period. Fewer things occur simultaneously as the camera begins more and more to catch each character impressionistically rather than following them all at the same time.

Cutting back and forth between gestures, reactions, and responses, their dynamic personalities of the characters emerge. But nothing is hinted at of their internal workings. They remain the sum of their exposed surfaces as no psychological or narrative meaning is assigned to their existences. Country singing star Barbara Jean (Ronee Blakely) comes the closest to exposing an internal emotional depth, but that is because her emotions have become her raw surface, both as a star and as a person, turning her into a fragile human being. Because she is the key narrative character, her fate and its meaning is more unresolved than anyone else's at the film's end.

In the last sequence of the film, the rally at the Nashville Parthenon, Altman reunites and refocuses on all his characters in one place. Unlike the airport scene, here the characters are united by a single event of which their reactions and responses depend. The Parthenon rally and the subsequent assassination act as the narrative's culminating hub, while all the characters move like spokes of a wheel in relation to it. Altman moves from the barrage of simultaneous moments in many characters' lives to a progressively more linear pattern until he is once again able to present many perspectives simultaneously responding to one single unifying element.

By creating a mosaic of contemporary American life, *Nashville* suggests a cultural view of reality that is made up of fragmented images and their incomprehensibility. But Altman overturns a bleak finale with the optimism that learning to live with uncertainty yields an affirmation and assignment of meaning to life in and of itself.

When influential *New Yorker* critic Pauline Kael first saw the film, she applauded Altman's vision, "I've never before seen a movie I loved in quite this way." Her laudatory review, based on a screening of a pre-release version of the film, caused a minor flurry of controversy about critical responsibility and was not able to help the film out of its box office doldrums. But despite its lack of popular success, *Nashville* has since been heralded as one of director Altman's finest films and one of the quintessential American movies of the 1970's.

—Lauren Rabinovitz

NEOBYCHANYE PRIKLYUCHENIYA MISTERA VESTA V STRANE BOLSHEVIKO.

The Extraordinary Adventures of Mr. West in the Land of the Bolsheviks. How Will This End? Mr. West. Production: Goskino; black and white, 35mm, silent; running time: 80 mins. Released 1924.

Scenario by Nikolai Aseyev and V.I. Pudovkin; directed by Lev Kuleshov; photography by Alexander Levitsky; production design by V.I. Pudovkin; assistants: Alexandra Khokhlova, Leonid Obolensky, Sergei Komarov, Porfiri Podobed, and Leo Mur.

Cast: Porfiri Podobed (*Mr. J.S. West*); Boris Barnet (*Jeddy, the cowboy*); Alexandra Khokhlova (or Chochlowa) (*Countess*); V.I. Pudovkin (*Zhban, the con-man*); S. Komarov (*One-eyed man*); Leonid Obolensky (*The dandy*); V. Lopatina (*Ellie, the American girl*); G. Kharlampiev (*S'enka Svisch*); P. Galadzhev, S. Sletov, and V. Latyshevskii (*Con-men*); A. Gorjchilin (*Millionaire*); Vladimir Fogel.

Publications:

Books—*Kino: A History of the Russian and Soviet Film* by Jay Leyda, London 1960; *The Motion Picture in the Soviet Union, 1918-1952: A Sociological Anaylsis* by John Rimberg, New York 1973; *Cinema in Revolution: The Heroic Era of the Soviet Film* edited by Luda and Jean Schnitzer and Marcel Martin,

New York 1973; *Kuleshov on Film* translated and edited by Ronald Levaco, Berkeley 1974; *The Cultural-Political Traditions and Developments of the Soviet Cinema* by Louis Harris Cohen, New York 1974; articles—"From 'West' to 'Canary'", in Russian, in *Sovietski Ekran* (Moscow), 12 March 1929; "Lev Koulechov" by Neïa Zorkaia in *Cahiers du cinéma* (Paris), May/June 1970; "Kuleshov" by Ronald Levaco in *Sight and Sound* (London), spring 1971; "The Classic Period of Soviet Cinema" in *Film Journal* (New York), fall/winter 1972; "Soviet Silent Cinema: Part I: 1918-1925" in *Museum of Modern Art Department of Film Notes* (New York), 7 March-15 April 1974.

*   *   *

It is doubtful whether many historians would regard a Soviet filmmaker of the twenties as having delivered an opening salvo in what is now termed the "cold war." Yet Lev Kuleshov's *The Extraordinary Adventures of Mr. West in the Land of the Bolsheviks* so completely foreshadows the attitudes inherent in the current East-West tensions that it has lost little of its satiric bite today almost 60 years after its original release. At the same time, it has grown in stature to become one of the pivotal films in the early development of cinema.

Conceived initially as a demonstration of the theory of montage developed by Kuleshov's experimental film group, the "Kuleshov Workshop," which operated outside the formal curriculum of the Soviet State Film School, it advanced the art of the film on a number of fronts. Not the least of these, was its employment of a number of brilliant young directors including Vsevolod Pudovkin who with Sergei Eisenstein would develop variations on the theory of montage that would produce most of the outstanding Soviet films of the 1920s. For three years preceding the production of *The Extraordinary Adventures*, the group, because of a scarcity of film stock, conducted filmless exercises in editing and reconstructing imported films such as D.W. Griffith's *Intolerance* in an effort to analyze the precise manner in which a film produces meaning.

The Extraordinary Adventures, however, provided the first lengthy, practical opportunity to put the workshop's theories into practice. Interestingly, one of the group's overriding concerns was to demonstrate that a different type of actor was needed for the screen than for the stage—still a major issue in the Soviet Union which had been relatively cut off from the films of Griffith and other innovators. Since, in Kuleshov's view, film creates meaning through a number of interacting images of which the actor constitutes only one, the acting technique must support the visual images that are intercut with it—an idea unheard of on the stage. His characters themselves, however, shared one characteristic obviously borrowed from the theater, that of personification. Mr. West, the most obvious example of this trait, is a typical American holding views representative of most of his countrymen. But his views or, more precisely, fears become personified in the symbolic characters that his entourage encounters in the Soviet Union and, though the actors deftly underplay their roles, the satiric undertones come through. For the most part the staging of West's misadventures is inspired by American Westerns and action comedies of the late teens— although probably not by the films of Charlie Chaplin or Buster Keaton, as some have suggested; few such films were exported to the Soviets during and immediately after the revolution.

The Extraordinary Adventures of Mr. West in the Land of the Bolsheviks proved that Kuleshov's theories were viable. Although he had somewhat miscalculated the degree of sophistication needed by his actors to fully carry out his goals, it was a good

start. Further, it gave an emerging generation of directors the impetus that would eventually result in the great classics of theoretical montage, *Storm Over Asia* (1928) and *October* (1927).

—Stephen L. Hanson

DIE NIBELUNGEN. PART I: SIEGFRIED. Siegfried. Production: Decla-Bioscop-Ufa Studios (Decla-Bioscop and Ufa merged during production); black and white, 35mm, silent; length: 3216 meters originally. Released 14 February 1924. Re-released 1925 in shortened version of 2743 meters with music from Wagner's *Der Ring des Nibelungen* as arranged by Hugo Reisenfeld. Re-released 1933 in even shorter version of 688 meters under title *Siegfrieds Tod*.

Screenplay by Thea von Harbou and Fritz Lang; from the opera *Das Nibelungenlied* by Richard Wagner and Norse sagas; directed by Fritz Lang; photography by Carl Hoffman and Günther Rittau, and Walter Ruttmann for the "Dream of the Falcon" sequence; art direction by Otto Hunte, Erich Kettelhut, and Karl Vollbrecht; music by Gottfried Huppertz; costumes designed by Paul Gerd Guderian (who died during production) and Anne Willkomm, armor and weapons by Heinrich Umlauff.

Filmed 1922-24 simultaneously with *Die Nibelungen, Part II: Kriemhilds Rache* in Decla-Bioscop-Ufa studios in Berlin.

Cast: Paul Richter (*Siegfried*); Margarethe Schön (*Kriemhild*); Theodor Loos (*King Gunther*); Hanna Ralph (*Brunhild*); Georg John (*Mime, the Smith* and *Alberich*); Gertrud Arnold (*Queen Ute*); Hans Carl Müller (*Gerenot*); Erwin Biswanger (*Giselher*); Bernhard Goetske (*Volker von Alzey*); Hans Adalbert Schlettow (*Hagen Tronje*); Rudolf Rittner (*Markgraf Rüdiger von Bechlarn*); Hardy von Francois (*Dankwart*); Fritz Alberti (*Dietrich von Bern*).

Publications:

Reviews—in *Berliner Tageblatt*, 15 February 1924; review by Mordaunt Hall in *The New York Times*, 24 August 1925; review by J.W. Krutch in the *Nation* (New York), 16 September 1925; review in the *New Republic* (New York), 13 August 1930; books—*Das Nibelungenbuch* by Thea von Harbou, Berlin and Munich 1923; *The Film Till Now* by Paul Rotha, London 1930; *An Index to the Creative Work of Fritz Lang* by Herman Weinberg, supplement to *Sight and Sound* (London), index series, 1946; *From Caligari to Hitler: A Psychological History of the German Film* by Siegfried Kracauer, Princeton, New Jersey 1947; *Fritz Lang* by Francis Courtade, Paris 1963; *Fritz Lang* by Luc Moullet, Paris 1963; *Fritz Lang* edited by Alfred Eibel, Paris 1964; *The Cinema of Fritz Lang* by Paul Jensen, New York 1969; *Fritz Lang* by Claire Johnston, London 1969; *The Haunted Screen* by Lotte Eisner, Berkeley 1969; *Le Décor de Film* by Léon Barsaq, Paris 1970; *Film in the Third Reich* by David Steward Hull, Berkeley 1973; *Fritz Lang* by Frieda Grafe, Enno Patalas, and Hans Helmut Prinzler, Munich 1976; *Fritz Lang* by Lotte H. Eisner, London 1977; *Fritz Lang* by Robert A. Armour, Boston 1978; *The Films of Fritz Lang* by Frederick Ott, Secaucus, New Jersey 1979; *Fritz Lang* edited by Stephen

Jenkins, London 1980; *Fritz Lang: A Guide to References and Resources* by E. Ann Kaplan, Boston 1981; articles—"The Nibelungs" by Iris Barry in *Spectator* (London), 14 June 1924; "*Die Nibelungen* Meets Disaster in Berlin" by T.R. Ybarra in *The New York Times*, 29 April 1924; "How *Siegfried* was Produced" in *The New York Times*, 6 September 1925; "The Story of Fritz Lang, Maker of *Siegfried*" by Heinrich Fraenkel in *Motion Picture Classic* (Brooklyn), March 1926; "The Genius of Fritz Lang" by Harry Wilson in *Film Quarterly* (London), summer 1947; "Notes sur le Style de Fritz Lang" by Lotte Eisner in *Revue du cinéma* (Paris), 1 February 1947; "Fritz Lang: Suggestion und Stimmung" in *Gestalter der Filmkunst, von Asta Nielsen bis Walt Disney* by Ludwig Gesek, Vienna 1948; "Fritz Lang" by Tom Granich in *Ferrania* (Milan), August 1950; "*Siegfried 1922-1924*" by Roger Manvell in *Sight and Sound* (London), April 1950; "Il Parabola di Fritz Lang" by Leonardo Autera in *Cinema* (Rome), 15 January 1954; "La Cinquième Victime" by François Truffaut in *Arts* (Paris), 22-24 August 1956; "Eric Pommer: Part Two" by Herbert G. Luft in *Films in Review* (New York), November 1959; "Notes on Lang's *Nibelungen Saga*" in *Film Notes of the Wisconsin Film Society* edited by A. Lennig, Madison, Wisconsin 1960; "Fritz Lang (The German Period, 1919-1933)" in *Tower of Babel* by Eric Rhode, London 1966; "La Nuit Viennoise: Une Confession de Fritz Lang, Part II" edited by Gretchen Berg in *Cahiers du cinéma* (Paris), June 1966; "Fritz Lang" in *Les Grands Cinéastes que je Propose* by Henri Agel, Paris 1967; "*Die Nibelungen* on Screen Tonight" by Kevin Thomas in the *Los Angeles Times*, 10 October 1969; "Toward a Film Aesthetic: Sweden and Germany 1917-1922" by Léon Barsacq in *Le Décor de Film*, Paris 1970; "Selbstdarstellung: Fritz Lang" in *Frankfurter Rundschau* (Frankfurt), 15 May 1971; "Fritz Lang: An Interview" by Gene D. Phillips in *Focus on Film* (London), spring 1975; "Fritz Lang Gives His Last Interview" by Gene D. Phillips in *The Village Voice* (New York), 16 August 1976; "The Siegfried Legend and the Silent Screens...Fritz Lang's Interpretation of a Hero Saga" by V.M. Stiles in *Literature/Film Quarterly* (Salisbury, Maryland), no.4, 1980.

* * *

DIE NIBELUNGEN. PART II: KRIEMHILDS RACHE.

Kriemhild's Revenge. Production: Decla-Bioscop-Ufa Studios (Decla-Bioscop and Ufa merged during production of the *Die Nibelungen* films; black and white, 35mm, silent; length: 3576 meters. Released 26 April 1924, Berlin. Re-released 1928 in shortened version of 2743 meters.

Screenplay by Thea von Harbou and Fritz Lang; from the opera *Das Nibelungenlied* by Richard Wagner and from Norse sagas; directed by Fritz Lang; photography by Carl Hoffman and Günther Rittau; art direction by Otto Hunte, Erich Kettelhut, and Karl Vollbrecht; music by Gottfried Huppertz; costumes designed by Paul Gerd (who died during production) and Anne Willkomm, armor and weapons manufactured by Heinrich Umlauff.

Filmed 1922-1924 simultaneously with *Die Nibelungen, Part I: Siegfried* in Decla-Bioscop-Ufa studios in Berlin.

Cast: Paul Richter (*Siegfried*); Margarethe Schön (*Kriemhild*); Theodor Loos (*King Gunther*); Hanna Ralph (*Brunhild*); Georg John (*Blaodel*); Gertrud Arnold (*Queen Ute*); Hans Carl Müller

(*Gerenot*); Erwin Biswanger (*Giselher*); Bernard Goetzke (*Volker von Alzey*); Hans Adalbert Schlettow (*Hagen Tronje*); Rudolf Rittner (*Markgraf Rüdiger von Bechlarn*); Hardy von Francois (*Dankwart*); Fritz Alberti (*Dietrich von Bern*); Georg August Koch (*Hildebrand*); Rudolph Klein-Rogge (*King Etzel*); Hubert Heinrich (*Werbel*); Grete Berger (*Hun*); Frida Richard (*Lecturer*); Georg Jurowski (*Priest*); Iris Roberts (*Page*); Rose Lichtenstein.

Publications:

Reviews—by E.H. in the *Berliner Tageblatt*, 2 May 1924; "Ufa Palast: *Kriemhilds Rache*" by Remy Hardt in *Der Kritiker* (Berlin), May/June 1924; review in *The New York Times*, 16 October 1928; books—*Das Nibelungenbuch* by Thea von Harbou, Berlin and Munich 1923; *An Index to the Creative Work of Fritz Lang* by Herman Weinberg, supplement to *Sight and Sound* (London), index series, 1946; *From Caligari to Hitler: A Psychological History of the German Film* by Siegfried Kracauer, Princeton 1947; *Fritz Lang* by Francis Courtade, Paris 1963; *Fritz Lang* by Luc Moullet, Paris 1963; *Fritz Lang* edited by Alfred Eibel, Paris 1964; *The Haunted Screen* by Lotte Eisner, Berkeley 1969; *Film in the Third Reich* by David Stewart Hull, Berkeley 1969; *The Cinema of Fritz Lang* by Paul M. Jensen, New York 1969; *Fritz Lang* by Claire Johnston, London 1969; *The German Cinema* by Roger Manvell and Heinrich Fraenkel, New York 1971; *Fritz Lang* by Frieda Grafe, Enno Patalas, and Hans Helmut Prinzler, Munich 1976; *Fritz Lang* by Lotte Eisner, London 1977; *Fritz Lang* by Robert Armour, Boston 1978; *The Films of Fritz Lang* by Frederick W. Ott, Secaucus, New Jersey 1979; *Fritz Lang* edited by Stephen Jenkins, London 1979; *Fritz Lang: A Guide to References and Resources* by E. Ann Kaplan, Boston 1981; articles—"The Nibelungs" by Iris Barry in *Spectator* (London), 14 June 1924; "*Die Nibelungen* Meets Disaster in Berlin" by T.R. Ybarra in *The New York Times*, 29 April 1924; "An Artistic Production" by Mordaunt Hall in *The New York Times*, 21 October 1928; "Notes sur le Style de Fritz Lang" by Lotte Eisner in *Revue du cinéma* (Paris), 1 February 1947; "The Genius of Fritz Lang" by Harry Wilson in *Film Quarterly* (London), summer 1947; "Fritz Lang: Suggestion und Stimmung" in *Gestalter der Filmkunst, von Asta Nielsen bis Walt Disney* by Ludwig Gesek, Vienna 1948; "Fritz Lang" by Tom Granich in *Ferrania* (Milan), August 1950; "*Siegfried 1922-1924*" by Roger Manvell in *Sight and Sound* (London), April 1950; "La Cinquième Victime" by François Truffaut in *Arts* (Paris), 22 August 1956; "Eric Pommer: Part Two" by Herbert Luft in *Films in Review* (New York), November 1959; "Notes on Lang's *Nibelungen Saga*" in *Film Notes of the Wisconsin Film Society* edited by A. Lennig, Madison, Wisconsin 1960; "Fritz Lang (The German Period, 1919-1933)" in *Tower of Babel* by Eric Rhode, London 1966; "La Nuit Viennoise: Une Confession de Fritz Lang, Part II" edited by Gretchen Berg in *Cahiers du cinéma* (Paris), June 1966; "Fritz Lang" in *Les Grands Cinéastes que je Propose* by Henri Agel, Paris 1967; "La Sature" by Jean Pierre Oudart in *Cahiers du cinéma* (Paris), April 1969 and May 1969; "*Die Nibelungen* on Screen Tonight" by Kevin Thomas in the *Los Angeles Times*, 10 October 1969; "Toward a Film Aesthetic: Sweden and Germany 1917-1922" by Leon Barsacq in *Le Décor de Film*, Paris 1970; "Selbstdarstellung: Fritz Lang" in *Frankfurter Rundschau* (Frankfurt), 15 May 1971; "Fritz Lang: An Interview" by Gene D. Phillips in *Focus on Film* (London), spring 1975; "Fritz Lang Gives His Last Interview" by Gene D. Phillips in *The Village Voice* (New York), 16 August 1976; "Les Images de Kriemhild" by P. Jouvert in *Cinématographe* (Paris), January 1977; "The Siegfried Legend and the Silent Screens...Fritz Lang's Interpretation of a Hero Saga" by V.M. Stiles in *Literature/Film Quarterly* (Salisbury, Maryland), no.4, 1980.

* * *

The filming of a national epic was a large undertaking even for Fritz Lang. *Die Nibelungen* emerged as a masterpiece of design based on a script by the talented Thea von Harbou, Lang's wife. It was an architectural concept from beginning to end (Lang himself had been an architect), and it was a triumph of studio craftsmanship at which the Germans excelled. The castles, the forests, the brooks and caverns were all studio-made.

The story fell naturally into two parts: the love of Siegfried and Kriemhild ending in his death; the vengeance of Kriemhild wreaking destruction on her husband's murderers: to this end she gives herself to the barbarian Attila and uses her power to destroy her brothers and the sinister Hagen Tronje. The essential drama of the film lies in the contrast between the stately formal beauty of the first part and the desolate and arid lovelessness of part two. The formal patterns, magnificent though they are, exclude dynamic development, and the progress of the film is slow and static. The Soviet critic Vladimir Nilsson faults the film on these grounds. In Part 2, however, the revenge of Kriemhild hastens the pace until the final holocaust.

The version of the saga used by Lang is very different from that used by Wagner. It is less concerned with Gods and more with human beings. In their symmetrical patterned costumes Lang's people are still human; the world of magic which he evokes does not diminish them. Without any tricks of editing or visual fireworks, Lang approaches his subject with sober observation. It is nevertheless a magic world. The tall stately trees of the forest, the flower laden banks of streams, the great steps of the cathedral, the drawbridges high in the air, the armour of the knights are all part of a world designed by Lang and his architect, Kettelhut. Scene after scene is memorably beautiful: the fight with the dragon; the flaming fortress of Brunhilde; the great cathedral of Worms.

The acting is strong and firm with a finely contrasted performance by Margarethe Schön as Kriemhild, the gentle lover who becomes the half-demented fury. In the final castastrophe, as the crazed widow of Siegfried sways in front of the blazing hostel, one thinks of the fanatical woman outside the burning jail in Lang's first American film, *Fury*. The theme of the dual nature of woman is a recurring one with Lang to which he returns in *Metropolis* in which Maria and the Robot represent the forces of love and destructiveness.

It is interesting to compare this early film with John Boorman's *Excalibur* (1981), because they have so many elements in common. But the tautness of Lang's structure gains over the looser and more diffused film by Boorman. *Die Nibelungen* is a film without offspring, a beautiful pageant by a master, to be admired and enjoyed for its own sake.

—Liam O'Leary

A NIGHT AT THE OPERA. Production: Metro-Goldwyn-Mayer Picture Corp.; 1935; black and white, 35mm; running time: 96 mins. Released 1935.

Produced by Irving Thalberg; screenplay by George S. Kaufman and Morrie Ryskind, uncredited assistance by Bert Kalmar and Harry Ruby, with gagwriter Al Boasberg; from a screen story by James Kevin McGuiness; directed by Sam Wood; photography by Merritt B. Gerstad; edited by William Levanway; sound recording directed by Douglas Shearer; art direction by Cedric Gibbons; music score by Herbert Stothart; song "Alone" by Nacio Herb Brown and Arthur Freed; song "Cosi-Cosa" by Bronislau Kaper, Walter Jurmann, and Ned Washington; costumes designed by Dolly Tree; dances by Chester Hale.

Filmed in MGM studios.

Cast: Groucho Marx (*Otis B. Driftwood*); Chico Marx (*Fiorello*); Harpo Marx (*Tomasso*); Kitty Carlisle (*Rosa Castaldi*); Allan Jones (*Ricardo Baroni*); Walter Woolf King (*Rudolfo Lassparri*); Sig Rumann (*Herman Gottlieb*); Margaret Dumont (*Mrs. Claypool*); Edward Keane (*Captain*); Robert Emmett O'Connor (*Detective Henderson*); Gino Corrado (*Steward*); Purnell Pratt (*Mayor*); Frank Yaconelli (*Engineer*); Billy Gilbert (*Engineer's assistant/peasant*); Sam Marx (*Extra on ship and at dock*); Claude Peyton (*Police captain*); Rita and Rubin (*Dancers*); Luther Hoobyar (*Ruiz); Rodolfo Hoyos (Count di Luna*); Olga Dane (*Azucena, Gypsy woman*); James J. Wolf (*Ferrando*); Ines Palange (*Maid*); Jonathan Hale (*Stage manager*); Otto Fries (*Elevator man*); William Gould (*Captain of police*); Leo White, Jay Eaton, and Rolfe Sedan (*Aviators*); Wilbur Mack and George Irving (*Committee*); George Guhl (*Policeman*); Harry Tyler (*Sign painter*); Phillip Smalley and Selmer Jackson (*Committee*); Alan Bridge (*Immigration inspector*); Harry Allen (*Doorman*); Lorraine Bridges (*Louisa*).

Publications:

Script—*A Night at the Opera* (original script, plus dialogue and description of action) by George S. Kaufman and Morrie Ryskind, New York 1972; review—"*A Night at the Opera*" by Andre Sennwald in *The New York Times*, 7 December 1935; books—*50 Years of American Comedy* by Bill Treadwell, New York 1951; *The Marx Brothers* by Kyle Crichton, New York 1952; *The Laugh Makers* by William Cahn, New York 1957; *The Marx Brothers: Their World of Comedy* by Allen Eyles, New York 1966; *The Marx Brothers and the Movies* by Paul D. Zimmerman and Burt Goldblatt, New York 1968; *Thalberg: Life and Legend* by Bob Thomas, New York 1969; *Why a Duck? Visual and Verbal Gems from the Marx Brothers Movies* edited by Richard Anobile, New York 1971; *Groucho, Harpo, Chico and Sometimes Zeppo: A History of the Marx Brothers and a Satire on the Rest of the World* by Joseph Adamson, New York 1973; *The Comic Mind: Comedy and the Movies* by Gerald Mast, Chicago, revised edition, 1979; articles—"Sam Wood" in *Current Biography Yearbook*, New York 1944; "American Classic" by Richard Rowland in *Hollywood Quarterly*, April 1947; "*A Night at the Opera*" by Allen Eyles in *Films and Filming* (London), February 1965; "Die Marx Brothers in der Oper: Skandal in der Oper" in *Filmkritik* (Munich), August 1973; "Sam Wood" in *The Hollywood Professionals-Vol. 2* by Clive Denton and others, New York 1974; "*A Night at the Opera*" by Howard H. Prouty in *Magill's Survey of Cinema, Vol. III* edited by Frank N. Magill, Englewood Cliffs, New Jersey 1980; "*Una Noche en la ópera*" by J. Vega in *Contracampo* (Madrid), October 1981.

* * *

A Night at the Opera is the sixth Marx Brothers movie and their first with MGM Studios. *Duck Soup* (1933) had been a critical and commercial failure, and marked the end of the Marx Brothers' contract with Paramount. Zeppo Marx had left the team, and for a time it appeared that the brothers' movie career was at an end. However, producer Irving Thalberg became interested in them, and an MGM contract was negotiated. It was Thalberg's contention that the audience for Marx Brothers movies could be broadened by bringing the story line, characterizations, musical numbers, and production values up to the high standard already set by their comedy sequences; that is, by putting the Marx Brothers into a musical comedy, rather than surrounding a collection of their vaudeville-style routines with a sketch intended only to glue them together. The Marx Brothers, who had attempted something similar on Broadway without finding an appropriate property, agreed with him, and an excellent working relationship was established.

The script of *A Night at the Opera* provides sympathetic, integrated characters for all of the Marx Brothers, and the operatic and shipboard settings make an appropriate contrast to the team's anarchic comedy style and offer opportunities for good roles for regular Marx Brothers supporting players Margaret Dumont and Sig Rumann. Final credit for the screenplay went to George S. Kaufman and Morrie Ryskind, but the concept was apparently also treated earlier by Bert Kalmar and Harry Ruby, and received significant additions from gagwriter Al Boasberg. Zeppo was replaced as romantic lead by Allan Jones, a convincing actor and excellent singer who, with ingenue Kitty Carlisle, managed to supply both a believable love story and strong musical numbers.

Thalberg also suggested trying out the comedy numbers on the road for audiences, a system that the team continued to use in later productions. The Marx Brothers, with part of the rest of the cast, took a tabloid version of the show on a short tour of four western cities, accompanied by writers Ryskind and Boasberg (Kaufman, who disliked Hollywood, had returned to New York). Audience reactions were monitored and scenes rewritten for maximum effect. Filming included not only the perfected routines, but also reaction times for laughs, which had been timed by stop-watch during live performances. It appears that the completed film owes little to director Sam Wood; the concept was Thalberg's, and the execution was chiefly by the writers and the Marx Brothers themselves.

The resulting film was the Marx Brothers' most successful with both critics and the public. It contains some of the team's best comedy routines, including the famous stateroom scene; the contract scene, in which Groucho and Chico edit a legal document by simply tearing off the offending clauses; and a spectacular finale in which the three Marx Brothers demolish a full-scale production of *Il Trovatore*. However, it also has straight musical numbers which became hit songs outside the film; logical places in the plot for Harpo's and Chico's musical specialties; and an overall polish and integrity which had not been present in their earlier movies. Its success prompted the team to apply the same formula to most of their subsequent films, but only *A Day at the Races* comes close to matching its quality. Thalberg died during the making of *A Day at the Races*, and no other producer was willing to invest the same resources in a Marx Brothers comedy.

Recent critical opinion allows *A Night at the Opera* to retain status as one of the best, if not absolutely the best, of the Marx Brothers films. *Duck Soup*, despite its early failure, has become a favorite of those Marx Brothers audiences who feel that any interruption of comedy sequences is a waste of time, and of those who profess to see it as a powerful statement against war. However, *A Night at the Opera* is generally considered to equal *Duck Soup* in the perfection of its comedy routines and dialogue, and

certainly to surpass it in the quality of the film as a whole.

—Annette Fern

NIGHT MAIL. Production: GPO Film Unit; black and white, 35mm; running time: 25 mins. Released 1936.

Produced by John Grierson; screenplay by John Grierson, Harry Watt, and Basil Wright, verse by W.H. Auden; directed by Harry Watt and Basil Wright; photography by Henry Fowle and Jonah Jones; edited by Basil Wright and R.Q. McNaughton; sound supervised by Alberto Cavalcanti, sound recorded by A.E. Pawley; music by Benjamin Britten.

Filmed on the mail train journeying from London to Glasgow, Scotland.

Cast: John Grierson and Stuart Legg (*Narrators*).

Publications:

Books—*Documentary Film* by Paul Rotha and Richard Griffith, revised edition, New York, 1952; *Studies in Documentary* by Alan Lovell and Jim Hillier, New York 1972; *20 Years of British Film: 1925-1947* by Michael Balcon, et al., New York 1972, originally published 1947; *Nonfiction Film: A Critical Study* by Richard Barsam, New York 1973; *Don't Look at the Camera* by Harry Watt, London 1974; *The Rise and Fall of British Documentary: The Story of the Film Movement Founded by John Grierson* by Elizabeth Sussex, Berkeley 1975; *John Grierson: A Documentary Biography* by Forsyth Hardy, London 1979; articles—"Sound in Films" by Alberto Cavalcanti in *Film* (London), November 1939; "Alberto Cavalcanti" by Emir Rodriguez Monegal in *Nonfiction Film: Theory and Criticism* by Richard Barsam, New York 1976; article by O. Barrot in *Cinéma d'Aujourd'hui* (Paris), February/March 1977.

*   *   *

Night Mail records the journey of the postal train from London to Glasgow; it is an example of the "drama of the doorstep" that John Grierson wrote about—everyday and close to home, yet lovely and lasting. It may be the ultimate fusion of the ethic and aesthetic of British documentary, a paradigm of propaganda so entertwined with art that the viewer absorbs the message (painlessly, effortlessly, and probably even unconsciously) while experiencing pleasure. What this film is saying, simply, is 1) that mail delivery is a large and complicated undertaking requiring the attention of the national government on behalf of all of us; 2) that this government service is a splendid thing involving speed, efficiency and intricate processes faultlessly learned and carefully regulated; and 3) that the government employees who perform these multifarious and interesting tasks for us are a pretty good bunch, patient and caring but not without an occasional irritability or little joke. That's the story, one might say, and *Night Mail* is more narrative than preceding British documentary had tended to be.

Within this slight odyssey of a working journey, expository

and poetic sequences are embedded. The poetic interpolations include the rhythmic montage of the mail bags discharged and picked up by the speeding train, the climb up into Scotland, "past cotton grass and moorland boulder, shovelling white steam over her shoulder." These latter words are from one of the passages of verse written for the film by Auden (Grierson himself speaks the final passage, incidentally; Stuart Legg speaks the rest) which are fused with the music of Britten; sound supervision is by Cavalcanti. Interlaced with Auden's poetry is a factual statistical commentary, as if from the General Post Office itself, and the dialogue of the postal workers' conversations with each other while doing their jobs. This whole mélange of sound, diverse in its components and complex in its assemblage, accompanies the visuals in a manner that makes this seem a lively and natural way to describe the working of this mail train on its nightly journey.

Night Mail started a narrative trend, and Cavalcanti and Watt became leaders of this new tendency in British documentary. Watt's creative personality seems, on the basis of his subsequent films, to have been dominant in *Night Mail*, though he shares directorial credit with Basil Wright. Watt would go on in a direct line of increasing narrative elements culminating in *Target for Tonight* (1941), the first of the Crown Film Unit wartime semi-documentaries. In 1942 he and Cavalcanti left government documentary for Ealing Studios and feature film making.

Night Mail well represents the advances of British documentary in the 1930s and the uses to which it could be put. Grierson was tickled, much later, when a Yugoslavian film maker told him that the beginning of Yugoslavian documentary occurred when some partisans came across a print of *Night Mail* during World War II and had, lacking any means of projection, run it through their fingers, studying it frame by frame. *Night Mail* and the other British documentaries of the 1930s—in their subjects, purposes, and forms, as well as in their government sponsorship and nontheatrical distribution—were enormously influential in the growth and development of documentary throughout the world.

—Jack C. Ellis

THE NIGHT OF THE HUNTER. Production: United Artists; 1955; black and white, 35mm; running time: 93 mins. Released 1955.

Produced by Paul Gregory; screenplay by James Agee, re-written by Charles Laughton; from the novel by Davis Grubb; directed by Charles Laughton; photography by Stanley Cortez; edited by Robert Golden; art direction by Hilyard Brown, set decoration by Al Spencer; music by Walter Schumann; special effects by Jack Rabin and Louis De Witt.

Cast: Robert Mitchum (*"Preacher" Harry Powell*); Shelley Winters (*Willa Harper*); Lillian Gish (*Rachel*); Billy Chapin (*John*); Pearl (*Sally Jane Bruce*); Peter Graves (*Ben Harper*); Evelyn Varden (*Icey Spoon*); Don Beddoe (*Walt Spoon*); James Gleason (*Uncle Birdie*); Gloria Castillo (*Ruby*).

Publications:

Scripts—"*Night of the Hunter*" by James Agee in *Agee on Film: Vol. II*, New York 1960; "*La Nuit du chasseur*" by James Agee in

Avant-Scène du cinéma (Paris), 15 February 1978; reviews—by Eugene Archer in *Film Culture* (New York), winter 1955; "*The Night of the Hunter*" by Henry Hart in *Films in Review* (New York), August/September 1955; review by Gavin Lambert in *Sight and Sound* (London), winter 1955-56; review by François Truffaut in *Arts* (Paris), 23 May 1956; review by André S. Labarthe in *Cahiers du cinéma* (Paris), June 1956; "La Presse" in *Avant-Scène du cinéma* (Paris), 15 February 1978; books—*Kiss Kiss Bang Bang* by Pauline Kael, Boston 1968; *Charles Laughton: A Pictorial Treasury of His Films* by William Brown, New York 1970; *Charles Laughton and Frederic March* by Michael Burrows, Cornwall, England 1970; *The Robert Mitchum Story* by Mike Tomkies, Chicago 1972; *The Oxford Companion to Film* edited by Liz-Ann Bawden, New York 1976; *Charles Laughton: An Intimate Biography* by Charles Higham, Garden City, New York 1976; *Elsa Lanchester Herself* by Elsa Lanchester, New York 1983; articles—"Freud au pays de l'ogre" by Robert Benayoun in *Demain* (Paris), 1956, reprinted in "18 Propos Américains" in *La Méthode* (Paris), March 1962; "Lillian Gish" by Romano Tozzi in *Films in Review* (New York), December 1962; "Charles Laughton" by Jerry Vermilye in *Films in Review* (New York), May 1963; "Puritans Anonymous" edited by Ian Johnson and Raymond Durgnat in *Motion* (London), autumn 1963; "Robert Mitchum" by Gene Ringgold in *Films in Review* (New York), May 1964; "*Night of the Hunter: Novel into Film*" by Robin Wood in *On Film*, 1970; "The Cult Movies: *The Night of the Hunter*" by Gordon Gow in *Films and Filming* (London), February 1975; "Plus Noir que vous nne pensez" by Jacques Goimard in *Avant-Scène du cinéma* (Paris), 15 February 1978; "Melmoth in Norman Rockwell Land...*The Night of the Hunter*" by P. Hammon in *Sight and Sound* (London), no.2, 1979; "*Night of the Hunter*" by Blake Lucas in *Magill's Survey of Cinema, Vol. III* edited by Frank N. Magill, Englewood Cliffs, New Jersey 1980.

*   *   *

The only complete film Charles Laughton ever directed, *The Night of the Hunter* is a cinematic fairy tale (Laughton called it a "nightmarish sort of Mother Goose tale"): the protagonists are children pursued by a dark and evil stranger who has murdered their mother and now seeks to steal from and eliminate them. Pauline Kael has called him a Pied Piper in reverse because adults trust and accept him as the God-fearing preacher he claims to be, whereas the children try to escape him. Their storybook flight is broken by the appearance of a Christian fairy godmother who ensures that good triumphs over evil in the end. Her declaration to the camera at the film's conclusion sums up a major theme of the movie: the innocence and durability of children, who survive no matter what adults do to them.

A related theme is also implied: the superior wisdom of innocent children over adult society. Only John (Billy Chapin) recognizes "Preacher" Harry Powell (Robert Mitchum) for what he is—the "hate" written on the fingers of his left hand rather than the "love" inscribed on his right. Because she is female, Pearl (Sally Jane Bruce) is as trusting as her mother (Shelley Winters) and is therefore weakened, rather than strengthened, by her innocence. Indeed, the only woman in the film to penetrate the false prophet's disguise is Rachel (Lillian Gish), the reverent protector of children and animals—society's strays—an older woman whose maturity and true Christian spirit place her above the sexuality that would otherwise cloud her vision. (Thus, Eve escapes the serpent.)

Laughton's artistic choices beautifully enhance the magical, timeless, and dreamlike qualities of the fairy tale. Borrowing both from German expressionism and such silent film greats as D.W. Griffith (using Gish emphasizes this connection), the atmospheric photography and unusual use of music are stunning vehicles for this complex allegory of good and evil. Examples include the peaceful clips (shot from the bottom of the river looking up—one of many unusual, "arty" camera angles) of the dead mother floating in her watery grave, her hair and some plants tendrilling about her; the creatures of nature—a vulnerable, twitching rabbit and a croaking frog—in the foreground of the children's escape down the river; the fragile, glittering spider web through which we watch their flight; the long shadow of the dark pursuer on horseback; his inhuman moaning as he plunges blindly into the black waters; and the haunting refrain of the preacher's distortion of the hymn "Leaning" (resung correctly by Rachel later in the film—only the true Christian, and not the false prophet, can sing God's words).

Despite, or in part because of, these artistic touches, the film does not succeed completely. (When it was released, most critics thought it an "interesting failure.") The problem lies in Laughton's failure to pull the three parts of the film together. The first part is a straightforward murder and suspense narrative; the second (the children's flight down the river), a timeless dream sequence; and the third (the children's rescue by the spinster) is an uneasy combination of straight narrative and symbol, culminating in a disembodied epilogue by Rachel to the audience.

That the film succeeds as well as it does is due in large part to the acting. Combining his usual restraint with the dramatic delivery of a preacher, Mitchum gives the best performance of his career. Gish gives a controlled and technically proficient performance, and Winters is affecting as the confused, soon-to-be-murdered young mother. Evelyn Varden as a hypocritical gossip, and James Gleason, as a drunken boatman, also perform well. Only the children seem somewhat wooden, but in a curious way this helps the film: the difference in their mood and acting style separates them rather effectively from the adults. (Actually it has been reported, both by Mitchum and by Elsa Lanchester, Laughton's widow, that Laughton loathed the children and had Mitchum direct them. This would explain why they almost appear to be in a different film.)

The Night of the Hunter is usually described as James Agee's last screenplay. Elsa Lanchester recently challenged this assumption in her autobiography. According to her, Laughton first worked on a screenplay with Davis Crubb, the author of the original novel, but later pulled in an acknowledged scenarist, Agee, to ensure studio backing. Agee turned in "a script as big as a telephone book," and he and Laughton had terrible disagreements about it. In the end, Laughton rewrote it and Agee was paid $30,000 for a script that was never used. If, indeed, there was this sort of dissension and confusion over the screenplay, that fact may help to explain the uneven treatment of the three sections.

When it was released in 1955, *The Night of the Hunter* was a commercial and critical failure, effectively ending Laughton's chances of directing subsequent films. Since then, it has garnered a considerable following and is now generally admired for its suspense, beauty, and idiosyncratic vision.

—Catherine Henry

NINGEN NO JOKEN, PART I. No Greater Love. The Human Condition. Production: Shochiku Co.; black and white, 35mm,

Shochiku Grandscope; running time: 208 mins. (doesn't include Parts II and III.); length: 5501 meters. Released 1959, Japan. Re-released 1969, with Parts II and III.

Produced by Shigeru Wakatsuki; screenplay by Zenzo Matsuyama and Masaki Kobayashi; from *Ningen no joken, Vols. 1 and 2* by Jumpei Gomikawa; directed by Masaki Kobayashi; photography by Yoshio Miyajima; edited by Keiishi Uraoka; sound recorded by Hideo Nishizaki; art direction by Kazue Hirataka; music by Chuji Kinoshita.

Cast: Tatsuya Nakadai (*Kaji*); Michiyo Aratama (*Michiko*); So Yamamura (*Okishima*); Eitaro Ozawa (*Okasaki*); Akira Ishihama (*Chen*); Shinji Nambara (*Kao*); Ineko Arima (*Yang Chun Lan*); Chikage Awashima (*Jin Tung Fu*); Keiji Sada (*Kageyama*); Toru Abe (*Watai*); Masao Mishima (*Kuroki*); Koji Mitsui (*Furya*); Kyu Sazanka (*Cho Meisan*); Seiji Miyaguchi (*Wang Heng Li*); Nobuo Nakamura (*Chief of Head Office*).

* * *

NINGEN NO JOKEN II: ZOKO NINGEN NO JOKEN. Road to Eternity. Production: Ningen Productions for Shochiku Co.; black and white, 35mm, Shochiku Grandscope; running time: 181 mins.; length: 4938 meters. Released 1959, Japan. Re-released 1969, as Part II with Parts I and III.

Produced by Tatsuo Hasoya; screenplay by Masaki Kobayashi and Zenzo Matsuyama; from *Ningen no joken, Vols. 3 and 4* by Jumpei Gomikawa; directed by Masaki Kobayashi; photography by Yoshio Miyajima; edited by Keiishi Uraoka; sound recorded by Hideo Nishizaki; art direction by Kazue Hirataka; music by Chuji Kinoshita.

Cast: Tatsuya Nakadai (*Kaji*); Michiyo Aratamo (*Michiko*); Keija Sada (*Kageyama*); Michio Minami (*Yoshida*); Hideo Kisho (*Kudo*); Kei Sato (*Shinjo*); Taketoshi Naito (*Tange*); Kunie Tanaka (*Obara*); Kokinjo Katsura (*Sasa*); Kaneko Iwasaki (*Nurse*); Yusuke Kawazu; Hideo Kidokoro; Jun Tatara.

* * *

NINGEN NO JOKEN III. A Soldier's Prayer. Production: Bungei Production/Ningen Club for Shochiku Co.; black and white, 35mm, Shochiku Grandscope; running time: 190 mins.; length: 5197 meters. Released 1961. Re-released 1969 with Parts I and II.

Produced by Shigeru Wakatsuki and Masaki Kobayashi; screenplay by Masaki Kobayashi, Zenzo Matsuyama, and Koichi Inagaki; from *Ningen no joken, Vols. 5 and 6* by Jumpei Gomikawa; directed by Masaki Kobayashi; photography by Yoshio Miyajima; edited by Keiishi Uraoka; art direction by Kazue Hirataka; music by Chuji Kinoshita.

Cast: Tatsuya Nakadai (*Kaji*); Michiyo Aratama (*Michiko*); Taketoshi Naito (*Private Tange*); Keijiro Morozumi (*Corporal Hironaka*); Yusuke Kawazu (*Private Terada*); Kyoko Kishida (*Ryuko*); Reiko Hitomi (*Umeko*); Fijio Suga (*Captain Nagata*); Nobuo Kaneko (*Corporal Kirahara*); Tamao Nakamura (*Female *refugee*); Hideko Takamine (*Woman in settlers'village*); Chishu Ryu (*Village elder*).

Publications:

Review—review of *Ningen No Joken* (Part I) in *Films and Filming* (London), December 1960; book—*Voices from the Japanese Cinema* by Joan Mellen, New York 1975; articles— "The Youngest Talents" by Donald Richie in *Sight and Sound* (London), spring 1960; article by Peter John Dyer in *Sight and Sound* (London), spring 1961; "Japanese Cinema 1961" by M. Iwabutchi in *Film Culture* (New York), spring 1962; "Kobayashi's Trilogy" by M. Iwabuchi in *Film Culture* (New York), spring 1962; "Kobayashi, l'homme et l'oeuvre" by C.R. Blouin and "Kobayashi, à l'uquam: anarchiste ou utopiste?" by G. Thérien in *Cinéma Québec* (Montreal), February/March 1974; "Masaki Kobayashi" by Richard Tucker in *International Film Guide*, London 1975.

NINOTCHKA. Production: Metro-Goldwyn-Mayer Pictures Corp.; 1939; black and white, 35mm; running time: 110 mins. Released 3 November 1939. Re-released 1947.

Produced by Ernst Lubitsch; screenplay by Charles Brackett, Billy Wilder, and Walter Reisch; from the story by Melchior Lengyel; directed by Ernst Lubitsch; photography by William Daniels; edited by Gene Ruggiero; sound recording directed by Douglas Shearer; production design by (set decorations) Edwin Willis; art direction by Cedric Gibbons; music score by Werner R. Heymann; costumes designed by Adrian.

Filmed 19 May 1939-16 July 1939 in MGM studios.

Cast: Greta Garbo (*Ninotchka*); Melvyn Douglas (*Count Léon d'Algout*); Ina Claire (*Grand Duchess Swana*); Sig Rumann (*Iranoff*); Felix Bressart (*Buljanoff*); Alexander Granach (*Kopalski*); Bela Lugosi (*Commissar Razinin*); Gregory Gayle (*Count Rakonin*); Rolfe Sedan (*Hotel Manager*); Edwin Maxwell (*Mercier*); Richard Carle (*Gaston*).

Publications:

Scripts—*Ninotchka* by Charles Brackett, Billy Wilder, and Walter Reisch, New York 1972; *Ninotchka* (script, stills, and screen dialog) edited by Richard Anobile, New York 1975; reviews—in the *New York Times*, 10 November and 19 November 1939; review in *Variety* (New York), ll October 1939; review in *Newsweek* (New York), 30 October 1939; review in *Sight and Sound* (London), winter 1939-40; review in *Monthly Film Bulletin* (London), 31 January 1940; books—*Best Pictures 1939-40* edited by Jerry Wald and Richard Macaulay, New York 1940; *Garbo* by John Bainbridge, New York 1955; *Here Lies the Heart* by Mercedes de Acosta, New York 1960; *The Films of Greta Garbo* by Michael Conway, New York 1963; *Ernst Lubitsch* by Mario Verdone, Lyon 1964; *The Great Films: 50 Golden Years of Motion Pictures* by Bosley Crowther, New York 1967; *The Lubitsch Touch: A Critical Study* by Herman Weinberg, New York 1968; *The Kindness of Strangers* by Salka Viertel, New

York 1969; *Garbo* by Norman Zierold, New York 1969; *Memoirs of the 40's* by Cecil Beaton, New York 1972; *Hollywood* by Garson Kanin, New York 1974; *People in a Diary: A Memoir* by S.N. Behrman, Boston 1972; "The 'Lubitsch Touch' and the Lubitsch Brain" in *The Comic Mind: Comedy and the Movies* by Gerald Mast, Indianapolis 1973; *Talking Pictures: Screenwriters in the American Cinema, 1927-73* by Richard Corliss, Woodstock, New York 1974; *Passport to Hollywood: Film Immigrants Anthology* edited by Don Whittemore and Philip Alan Cecchettini, New York 1976; *The Cinema of Ernst Lubitsch: The Hollywood Films* by Leland Poague, London 1977; *Billy Wilder in Hollywood* by Maurice Zolotow, New York 1977; articles—in *The New York Times*, 16 April 1939; article by Greta Garbo and Ernst Lubitsch in *The New York Times*, 22 October 1939; article in *The New York Times*, 12 November 1939; article in *Variety* (New York), 15 November 1939; article in *The New York Times*, 8 April, 1940; article in the *New Yorker*, 29 June 1940; article in the *New Yorker*, 10 August 1940; article in *Variety*(New York), 25 September 1940; article in *The New York Times*, 25 May, 1941; article in *Variety* (New York), 21 May 1941; article in *Variety* (New York), 12 March 1947; article in *Variety* (New York), 26 November 1947; article in *Variety* (New York), 29 October 1947; article in *Variety* (New York), 5 November 1947; article in *The New York Times*, 2 April 1948; article in *Variety* (New York), 14 April, 1948; interview with Melchior Lengyel in *The New York Times*, 4 January 1948; "Parere su Lubitsch" by Gianni Pozzi in *La critica cinematografica* (Parma, Italy), May 1948; "Ernst Lubitsch, regista del tempo perduto" by Roberto Paolella in *Bianco e nero* (Rome), January 1958; article in *The New York Times*, 3 February 1951; "A Tribute to Lubitsch" by Herman Weinberg in *Films in Review* (New York), August/September 1951; issue on Ernst Lubitsch in *Film Journal* (Australia), June 1959; "*Ninotchka*" by John Cutts in *Films and Filming* (London), March 1962; "Garbo— How Good Was She?" by Richard Whitehall in *Films and Filming* (London), September 1963; issue on Lubitsch of *Cahiers du cinéma* (Paris), February 1968; "Lubitsch in the 30's: Part One" by Andrew Sarris in *Film Comment* (New York), winter 1971-72.

*   *   *

The advertising campaign for *Ninotchka* is proof of a publicist's faith in the collective amnesia of the American public. "Garbo Laughs" was treated as momentously as was "Garbo Talks," the slogan that announced her first sound film, *Anna Christie*. The marketing of *Ninotchka* takes no account of Greta Garbo's frequent laughter, her smile and the lightness of her touch throughout her 1930s films. Just three years before, in *Camille*, playfulness and humor inflect her doomed "lady of the camellias." *Ninotchka* is, however, her first comedy. Its principal comic ploy is a paradoxial reflection on Garbo as actress. Here she is made to play, through the first part of the film, a woman who apparently has no emotions. Audiences must read this as they would a scene that suggests that Fred Astaire is clumsy or that John Wayne is a coward. *Ninotchka* extracts much of its humor from the deadpan expression of an actress whose presence is a sign of deep emotional resonance.

The story of the rigid, businesslike commissar who awakens to luxury and love in Paris is coherent with director Ernst Lubitsch's stylistics. His major films demonstrate the connections between an elegance of decor, elegance of manner, and elegance of the heart. The film's narrative pretext is the sale of jewels; Ninotchka falls in love with an absurd hat just as she falls in love with Léon. Much humor is drawn from the contrast between a lush Parisian hotel and the austere Moscow room Ninotchka shares with a cello player and a streetcar conductor.

As is usually the case in the films of Luitsh, the comedy reflects back upon the characters. The director uses the comedy of manners to authenticate and dramatize the feelings of the protagonists, and in this, he is at odds with the hard-edged, satirical bent that is characteristic of the writers of *Ninotchka*, Charles Brackett, Billy Wilder and Walter Reisch, a mode that becomes particularly apparent when Wilder turns to directing their scripts. The appeal of *Ninotchka* is in the mix of talents, from Garbo's emotional complexity, to Lubitsch's wry sentiment, to the writer's acerbic wit. The range of the performances includes the broadness of the three bumbling commissars and the drawing-room bitchery of the Grand Duchess Swana (to which Ina Claire brings her distinctively brittle sophistication). Melvyn Douglas provides the pratfall that inspires Garbo's celebrated laugh, and the warm charm that inspires her love.

Very successful at its release, it seemed to promise a new direction in Garbo's faltering career. Her next and final film, *Two Faced Woman*, also co-starring Melvyn Douglas, proved that considerable comic talents also require a comic script. But *Ninotchka* was reborn, first as a Cole Porter's Broadway musical, *Silk Stockings*, with film stars Hildegarde Knef and Don Ameche, and then as a musical film with Cyd Charisse and Fred Astaire.

—Charles Affron

NOBI. Fires on the Plain. Production: Daiei (Tokyo); black and white, 35mm, CinemaScope; running time: 105 mins. Released 3 November 1959.

Produced by Masaichi Nagata, "planned" by Komei Fujii; screenplay by Natto Wada; from the original story by Shohei Ooka; directed by Kon Ichikawa; photography by Setsuo Shibata; edited by Tatsuji Nakashizu; art direction by Tokuji Shibata; music by Yasushi Akutagawa; special effects by Toru Matoba.

Kinema Jumpo Awards, #2 on Best Films List and Best Actor's Award (Funakashi), 1959.

Cast: Eiji Funakashi (*Tamura*); Osamu Takizawa (*Yasuda*); Micky Curtis (*Nagashima*); Hikaru Hoshi (*First soldier*); Mantaro Ushio (*Master sergeant*); Jun Hamamura (*Crazy officer*).

Publications:

Review—"Fires on the Plain and Odd Obsessions" by John Gillett in *Sight and Sound* (London), spring 1962; books—*Voices from the Japanese Cinema* by Joan Mellen, New York 1975; *The Waves at Genji's Door* by Joan Mellen, New York 1976; *Japanese Film Directors* by Audie Bock, New York 1978; articles—"Japan: The Younger Talents" by Donald Richie in *Sight and Sound* (London), spring 1960; "Portrait de Kon Ichikawa" by Donald Richie in *Cinéma 60* (Paris), June 1960; "The Several Sides of Kon Ichikawa" by Donald Richie in *Sight and Sound* (London), spring 1966; "The Skull Beneath the Skin" by Tom Milne in *Sight and Sound* (London), autumn 1966; "The

Uniqueness of Kon Ichikawa" by Kon Ichikawa, et al. in *Cinema* (Los Angeles), no.2, 1970; "Ichikawa and *The Wanderers*" by William Johnson in *Film Comment* (New York), September/-October 1975.

*   *   *

Fires on the Plain is about the last campaign of the defeated Japanese army in the Philippines during World War II, as seen through the eyes of the tubercular Private Tamura. This film, along with the same year's *The Human Condition* (by Kobayashi), initiated the war film genre in Japan with its exhaustive depiction of the physical devastation of the environment and the physical and mental devastation of human beings at the front.

Employing CinemaScope photography (which he frequently used during his career), and using many bleak images of fighting and death, through heat, rain, mud and jungle, director Ken Ichikawa succeeds in conveying Tamura's dismay, exhaustion, fear and desperation. To the same end, he frequently uses close-up shots of the private's face, and juxtaposes his monologues with the horrible war images. Yet the overall tone of the film is one of detachment.

Ichikawa's film adaptation dismisses the original novel's theme of Christian salvation and focuses on the brutality of the war front. However, the images of the cross at the village church roof are skillfully juxtaposed with the scene of the murder of the village girl, ominously preceded by the image of Tamura killing a dog. In the murder scenes, the viewers are shown only the spreading of blood on the body, after the sound of the gunshot. Ichikawa's concentration is rather on expressing the traumatic reaction of Tamura to the scenes of bloodshed.

All of Tamura's murders are rather impulsive. After killing the girl, his deep remorse is revealed by his subtle act of arranging her disturbed dress and by his dropping his gun into the river afterward. Tamura's personality is in fact, depicted as rather peaceful and humanistic. Even though he faces hunger and a constant threat of death, he chooses to be on the side of victims, rather than the victimizers (he gives away his scarce food, salt, and his hand grenade). His obedient attitude towards other aggressive soldiers is somehow wryly funny. When he cannot find a decent pair of boots, he decides to walk barefoot. Later, he ransacks the boots from a soldier who dies in front of his eyes. By portraying the many sides of Tamura's character, Ichikawa makes his personality credible.

Tamura tries to maintain his human feelings against all the odds. One of the most impressive scenes is that of his taking a rest at a brook; there are close-up shots of his feet soaking in the gentle flow of water, and his soft smile as he observes an ant crawling on his body. The viewer can feel almost tangibly Tamura's joy in life as a respite from the hell around him, even when his reverie is interrupted playfully by the ant's bite. Such occasional humorous scenes serve to release the otherwise continuous tension of the desolation surrounding Tamura. The crazy officer under the tree is presented as a frightening image, especially when he offers his arm to be eaten, but his manner is simultaneously humorous and horrible.

Fires on the plain, seemingly guerrillas' signals, occasionally appear accompanied by ominous music, creating uneasiness and fear. The last scene, despite its physical bleakness on the battlefield, is one of liberation, terminating Tamura's plight. His moral victory is in his refusal to join in cannibalism.

The sensational subject of *Fires on the Plain* attracted widespread attention. Some critics said that the theme of cannibalism was not treated philosophically, though Ichikawa does handle these scenes skillfully. Through such detailed depictions of human feelings in circumstances of wartime horror and ubiquitous death, this film (along with his *Harp of Burma*) successfully conveys Ichikawa's humanistic anti-war message.

—Kyoko Hirno

* * *

LA NOIRE DE.... Production: Les films Domirev (Dakar) and Les Actualités Françaises (Paris); black and white, 35mm; running time: 70 mins. Released March 1966, France; English version released 1969, New York.

Produced by André Zwobada; scripted and directed by Ousmane Sembene; from a short story by Ousmane Sembene first published in *Voltaïque* (1961); photography by Christian Lacoste; edited by André Gaudier; assistant director: Ibrahima Barro; 2nd assistant: Pathé Diop.

Prix Jean Vigo, Paris, 1966; Festival mondial des Arts nègres, Antilope d'argent, 1966; Journées cinématographiques de Carthage, Tanit d'Or, 1966.

Cast: Thérèse N'Bissine Diop (*Diouana*); Robert Fontaine (*The patron*); Momar Nar Sene (*Friend*); Anne-Marie Jelinek (*The patroness*); Ibrahima Boy (*Boy with mask*); Philippe, Sophie, and Damien (*Infants*); plus the voices of Toto Bissainthe, Robert Marcy, and Sohie Leclerc; Bernard Delbaro; Nicole Donati; Raymond Lemery; Suzanne Lemery.

Publications:

Articles—"On Films and Filmmakers" by H. Morgenthau in *Africa Report*, May/June 1969; "Engaged Film-Making for a New Society" by Robert Mortimer in *Africa Report*, November 1970; "Ousmane Sembene. Les 'francs-tireurs' sénégalais"by A. Pâquet and G. Borremans in *Cinéma Québec* (Montreal), March/April 1973; interview with Sembene by G.M. Perry in *Film Quarterly* (Berkeley), spring 1973; "'Film-makers have a great responsibility to our people'", interview with Sembene by H.D. Weaver, Jr., in *Cineaste* (New York), v.6, no.1, 1973; "Ousmane Sembene, Carthage et le cinéma africain" and "Problématique du cinéaste africain: l'artiste et la révolution", interviews by T. Cheriaa in *Cinéma Québec* (Montreal), August 1974; "Ousmane Sembene" by N. Ghali in *Cinématographe* (Paris), April 1976; interview with Sembene by J.-C. Bonnet in *Cinématographe* (Paris), June 1977; interview with Sembene by R. Grelier in *Image et son* (Paris), November 1977; interview with Sembene by C. Bosseno in *Image et son* (Paris), September 1979; "Ousmane Sembène" in *Avant-Scène du cinéma* (Paris), 1 June 1979.

* * *

La Noire de..., by the Senegalese filmmaker Ousmane Sembene, is the first feature-length film to come out of sub-Saharan Africa. Technically flawed, it is nevertheless a cultural and cinematographic achievement, and it marks an important date in the history of African cinema. Based on a short story of the same title, written by Sembene and published in *Voltaïque* (1961), *La*

Noire de... tells the story of a young African woman who goes to France to work for the French couple who have employed her in Dakar. Filled with joy at the prospect of the trip, she soon becomes disillusioned, and finally, feeling imprisoned and isolated from the support of her own community, kills herself.

The film is remarkable in several ways. The force of this tragic tale, itself based on a real life incident, is developed with considerable skill, especially for a filmmaker with only two short subjects to his credit at the time. The visual impact is great—an accomplishment that is especially noteworthy when one considers that Sembene first told the story in another form, then adapted it into a film that stands completely on its own merits. Sembene's ability at adaptation distinguishes this work from unsuccessful film adaptations in general and marks his progress from the making of his second film *Niaye*, in which the original literary text is still respected to the detriment of the visual presentation. One major difference between *La Noire de...* and the original short story is in the powerful emphasis placed on an African mask, raising it to the level of a symbol. We see the mask first in its African context, then see it given joyfully by Diouana, the African maid and central character, to the European couple after she begins to work for them. It appears again in Antibes, hung on a very white wall in the couple's apartment. When Diouana breaks into open revolt at her dismal situation, she reclaims it, and we see the two women—one white, one black—fighting over the mask. The mask is returned by the Frenchman to Diouana's family, along with her other belongings, after her death. The film closes with a wonderfully dramatic sequence in which the dead woman's younger brother, wearing the mask, pursues the Frenchman out of the African residential area, as the music in the background rises in pace and intensity.

The conditions of the making of this film are unusual, if not unique, and speak directly to Sembene's vision of cinema as both art and politics: the African actors, including the woman who plays Diouana, were all non-professionals. The film sequences—despite the extensive use of flashbacks—had to be shot in strictly chronological order because of the lack of experience and sophistication with regard to the medium, and this circumstance engendered further problems with lighting in the film. In addition, the sound was dubbed in France. Despite all of these difficulties, the film succeeds admirably in conveying, through the life of one otherwise unremarkable African woman, the brutal realities of neo-colonialism on the African continent.

Sembene's conception of his role as African artist is central to an understanding of his work. Known first as a writer of novels and short stories, he was moved to study cinema at the age of 38 by the realization that, for several reasons, his French-language writings were reaching only a minute segment of his African compatriots. Film allows him to reach many more people, and he sees it as the best way to educate the masses: he claims that he can reach more people with cinema than are likely to attend all the political rallies, all the Christian and Muslim religious gatherings. The fact that *La Noire de...* is in French shows that the metamorphosis was incomplete at this point in his career. *Le Mandat* (*Mandabi*), his next film, would be in Wolof, a language spoken by some 90% of his fellow Senegalese.

—Curtis Schade

* * *

NORTH BY NORTHWEST. Production: Metro-Goldwyn-Mayer Pictures Corp.; 1959; Technicolor, 35mm; running time: 136 mins.; length: 12,256 feet. Released 1959.

Produced by Alfred Hitchcock; screenplay by Ernest Lehman; titles designed by Saul Bass; directed by Alfred Hitchcock; photography by Robert Burks; edited by George Tomasini; sound recording supervised by Franklin Milton; production design by Robert Boyle, set decorations by Henry Grace and Frank McKelvey; art direction by William A. Horning and Merrill Pye; music by Bernard Herrmann; special effects by A. Arnold Gillespie and Lee LeBlanc; color consultant: Charles K. Hagedon.

Filmed in New York City, Long Island, Chicago, and at the Mount Rushmore National Memorial, South Dakota.

Cast: Cary Grant (*Roger Thornhill*); Eva Marie Saint (*Eve Kendall*); James Mason (*Phillip Vandamm*); Jessie Royce Landis (*Clara Thornhill*); Leo G. Carroll (*Professor*); Philip Ober (*Lester Townsend*); Josephine Hutchinson (*Handsome woman*); Martin Landau (*Leonard*); Adam Williams (*Valerian*); Edward Platt (*Victor Larrabee*); Robert Ellenstein (*Licht*); Les Tremayne (*Auctioneer*); Philip Coolidge (*Dr. Cross*); Edward Binns (*Captain Junkett*); Pat McVey, Ken Lynch (*Chicago policemen*); John Beradino (*Sgt. Emile Klinger*); Nora Marlowe (*Housekeeper, Anna*); Doreen Lang (*Maggie*); Alexander Lockwood (*Judge Anson B. Flynn*); Stanley Adams (*Lt. Harding*); Larry Dobkin (*Cartoonist*); Madge Kennedy (*Housewife*); Tommy Farrell (*Elevator starter*); Maudie Prickett (*Maid, Elsie*); Ned Glass (*Ticket agent*); Alfred Hitchcock (*Man who misses bus*); Harvey Stephens (*Stockbroker*): Walter Coy (*Reporter*); Harry Seymour (*Captain of waiters*): Frank Wilcox (*Weltner*); Robert Shayne (*Larry Wade*); Carleton Young (*Fanning Nelson*); Paul Genge (*Lt. Hagerman*); Robert B. Williams (*Patrolman Waggoner*); James McCallion (*Valet*); Baynes Barron (*Taxi driver*); Doris Singh (Indian girl); Sally Fraser (*Girl attendant*); Susan Whitney (Girl attendant); Maura McGiveney (*Girl attendant*).

Publications:

Script—*North by Northwest* by Ernest Lehman, New York 1972; reviews—by Ellen Fitzpatrick in *Films in Review* (New York), August/September 1959; "*North by Northwest*" by Penelope Houston in *Sight and Sound* (London), summer/autumn 1959; review by Peter Baker in *Films and Filming* (London), September 1959; books—*The Cinema of Alfred Hitchcock* by Peter Bogdanovich, New York 1962; *Alfred Hitchcock* by Hans-Peter Manz, Zurich 1962; *Hitchcock's Films* by Robin Wood, London 1965; *The Films of Alfred Hitchcock* by George Parry, London 1965; *Le Cinéma selon Hitchcock* by François Truffaut, Paris 1966; *Alfred Hitchcock* by Jean Douchet, Paris 1967; *Interviews with Film Directors* edited by Andrew Sarris, New York 1967; *Alfred Hitchcock* by Noel Simsolo, Paris 1969; *Focus on Hitchcock* edited by Albert J. LaValley, Englewood Cliffs, New Jersey 1972; *The Strange Case of Alfred Hitchcock* by Raymond Durgnat, Cambridge, Massachusetts 1974; *Hitch* by John Russell Taylor, New York 1978; articles—interview with Hitchcock in *Films and Filming* (London), July 1959; "Alfred Hitchcock: Je suis prisonnier des compromis commerciaux: je veux revenir à la comédie" by Charles Bitsch in *Arts* (Paris), January 1959; "La nouvelle vague, c'est moi" by Luc Moullet in *Arts* (Paris), October 1959; "La troisième clé d'Hitchcock" by Jean Douchet in *Cahiers du cinéma* (Paris), December 1959; "*North by Northwest*" by A.W. Richardson in *Screen Education Yearbook*, 1963; "The Cult Movies: *North by Northwest*" by Gordon Gow in *Films and Filming* (London), October 1974; "Bookkeeping on an Analyst's Couch: A French

Critic's Approach to Hitchcock" by David Bombyk in *Take One* (Montreal), 21 May 1976; "The Cinema and Its Double: Alfred Hitchcock" by James Monaco in *Take One* (Montreal), 21 May 1976; "How He Does It" by Michael Tarantino in *Take One* (Montreal), 21 May 1976; "La Mort aux trousses" by J. Magny in *Cinéma* (Paris), October 1978; "La Mort aux trousses" by M. Sator in *Cahiers du cinéma* (Paris), December 1978; "*North by Northwest*" by Ed Lowry in *Cinema Texas Program Notes* (Austin), 11 November 1978; "Enunciation and Sexual Difference (Part I)" by J. Bergstrom in *Camera Obscura* (Berkeley), summer 1979; "Hitchcock blijft voortbestaan" by C. Boost and W. Verstappen in *Skoop* (Amsterdam), May/June 1980; "En el unbral de lo in verosimil" by J.G. Roquena in *Contracampo* (Madrid), September 1981; "*North by Northwest* de Bernard Herrmann" in *Séquences* (Montreal), April 1981.

* * *

North by Northwest features one of the cinema's most celebrated and recognizable sequences: the reverse tracking shot of Roger Thornhill (Cary Grant), New York advertising man, running for his life from a "killer" cropdusting plane. Thornhill, away from his usual sophisticated milieu in the city, is lured to his possible doom not in a dark alley or dimly-lit street, but in an open Indiana cornfield in broad daylight. Thus the sequence encapsulates a treatment of two of director Alfred Hitchcock's most famous themes: the innocent person caught in circumstances he or she doesn't understand, and the unpredictability—actually, the "reversal"—of those things and places we assume to be safe, reliable, and comforting.

The cornfield sequence epitomizes a characteristic Hitchcockian motif—"doubles"—through mise-en-scène, characterization, cinematic structure, and even the nature of the sequences themselves. Merging contradictory emotions in what Louis Giannetti calls "a rather bizarre paradox," the episode is simultaneously terrifying and ridiculously funny.

North by Northwest represents the foremost example of Hitchcock's emphasis on character, suspense, and style over plot: how did beautiful, treacherous Eve Kendall (Eva Marie Saint) know to which train Roger Thornhill would happen to run? The film ofter parallels *The 39 Steps* in its attractive, charming, clever protagonists, and in its situations in which the heros or heroines must rely on wits and sheer nerve to extricate themselves from danger. Robert Donat in *Steps* temporarily escapes the police and others by losing them in a passing parade; Thornhill is trapped by his pursuers after he follows them to an auction in Chicago. Aware that if he tries to leave he will be killed, Thornhill deliberately creates a nuisance so that the police will come and arrest him for disorderly conduct. As he passes the most sinister of the henchmen, he says, "Oh, sorry, old boy, keep trying."

Roger Thornhill is a modern-day man who becomes a Hitchcock hero only after he's been put through his paces, which serve as a learning process. As Robin Wood writes, "He is a man who lives purely on the surface, refusing all commitment or responsibility (appropriately he's in advertising), immature for all his cocksureness, his life all the more a chaos for the fact that he doesn't recognise it as such...." Within ten minutes of the start of the film, his world is literally cut from under him. The remainder of the film serves to strip away all of Thornhill's protective veneer as a modern "city" man.

Apart from its value as fabulous entertainment and as a summation of Hitchcock's most characteristic themes and visual techniques, the films climax comes as a result of two extended suspense sequences: Thornhill's attempted rescue of Eve from

Vandamm's (the spy's) house, and the chase on top of Mount Rushmore. (The latter sequence done entirely in a studio with the help of the Shüfftan process.) The stone faces of the presidents suggest "stability and order forming a background to Thornhill's desperate struggle to save himself and Eve for life." And even within this anxiety-ridden scene, the humor, the absurdity, is characteristic Hitchcock. Thornhill tells Eve: "My wives divorced me...they said I led too dull a life."

North by Northwest is a successful summing-up for Alfred Hitchcock in terms of theme, style, and characterization. Its constant invention, humor, and quick pace help it to keep its position as a Hitchcockian favorite with audiences and critics alike.

—Deborah H. Holdstein

NOSFERATU. Nosferatu, a Symphony of Horror. Production: Prana-Film (Berlin); black and white, 35mm, silent; running time: about 74 mins. Released 5 March 1922, Germany. Re-released as *Die zwölfte Stunde* or *Eine Nacht des Grauens* in 1930 in a sound version, but it was re-released under mysterious circumstances as the original negative had been taken by a Dr. Waldemar Roger some time earlier.

Scenario by Henrik Galeen; from the novel by Bram Stoker (out of copyright); directed by Fredrich Wilhelm Murnau (F.W. Murnau); photography by Fritz Arno Wagner and Gunther Krampf; production design by Albin Grau; original music by Hans Erdmann; costumes designed by Albin Grau.

Filmed in Jofa studios, Berlin-Johannistal; exteriors shot in the Upper Tatras, Czechoslovakia, near Zakopane, Propad, and Smokovec; also at Wismar, Rostock, and Lübeck.

Cast: Max Schreck (*Nosferatu, or Graf Orlok*); Alexander Granach (*Jonathan Knock, an estate agent*); Gustav von Wangenheim (*Hutter*); Greta Schröder (*Nina*); G.H. Schnell (*Harding, a shipbuilder*); Ruth Landshoff (*Annie Harding*); John Gottowt (*Professor*); Gustav Botz (*Town doctor*); Max Nemetz (*Captain of the "Demeter"*); Wolfgang Heinz (*1st mate*); Albert Venohr (*2nd mate*); Hersfeld (*Innkeeper*); Hardy von François (*Hospital doctor*); Heinrich Witte.

Publications:

Scripts—*Masterworks of the German Cinema* with an introduction by Roger Manvell, London 1973; *Murnau* (includes script from *Nosferatu*) by Lotte Eisner, Berkeley 1973; "*Nosferatu*" (list of shots) in *Avant-Scène du cinéma* (Paris), 15 May 1979; review—"La Presse" in *Avant-Scène du cinéma* (Paris), 15 May 1979; books—*From Caligari to Hitler, A Psychological History of the German Film* by Siegfried Kracauer, New York 1947; *An Index to the Films of F.W. Murnau* by Theodore Huff, supplement to *Sight and Sound*, index series, London 1948; *Murnau* by Charles Jameux, Paris 1965; *Films of Tyranny* by Richard B. Byrne, Madison, Wisconsin 1966; *Anthologie du cinéma*, Vol. 1, Paris 1966; *The Haunted Screen* by Lotte Eisner, London 1969; *Murnau* by Lotte Eisner, Berkeley 1973; articles—"Murnau—Ses Films" by Roger Blin in *La Revue du Cinéma* (Paris), July 1931; article by Phil Mori in *Bianco e Nero* (Rome), April 1951; "L'enigme des deux Nosferatus" by Lotte Eisner in *Cahiers du cinéma* (Paris), January 1958; article by Gilberto Perez Guillermo in *Sight and Sound* (London), summer 1967; article by Gilberto Perez Guillermo in *Film Comment* (New York), summer 1971; article by Robin Wood in *Film Comment* (New York), summer 1971; "*Nosferatu*" by J. Toeplitz in *Kino* (Warsaw), February 1972; "*Nosferatu le vampire*" by Claude Beylie in *Ecran* (Paris), July/August 1973; "*Nosferatu—Eine Symphonie des Grauens*" by Tom Milne in *Monthly Film Bulletin* (London), February 1974; "Le grand Nocturne" by Tony Faivre in *Avant-Scène du cinéma* (Paris), 15 May 1979; "Narrative/Structure/Ideology in Murnau's *Nosferatu*—Another Start from Propp" by J. Tulloch in *Australian Journal of Screen Theory* (Kensington), no. 5/6, 1979; "A Symphony of Terror: F.W. Murnau" by J. McCarty in *Classic Film Collector* (Indiana, Pennsylvania), November 1979; "De Murnau a Herzog: l'eternel retour de Nosferatu le vampire" by J. Petat and others in *Cinéma 79* (Paris), March 1979; "Dracula Meets the 'Zeitgeist': *Nosferatu* as Film Adaptation" by L. Roth in *Literature/Film Quarterly* (Salisbury, Maryland), no. 4, 1979; "Una scrittura su palinsesto: il *Nosferatu* di Herzog" by L. Termine in *Cinema Nuovo* (Rome), October 1979; "La Lettre oubliee de *Nosferatu*" by S. Exertier in *Positif* (Paris), March 1980; "Vápírok ujjáaszületése" by G. Bíró in *Filmkultura* (Budapest), January/February 1981.

*   *   *

Nosferatu was the first film version of *Dracula*; more than 60 years later, it remains easily the most intelligent adaptation of Bram Stoker's novel (its nearest, not very close, rival being John Badham's 1978 version with Frank Langella).

Given the way in which Stoker's vampire aristocrat has haunted popular culture since the appearance of the novel in 1890, the figure's social/ideological significance can scarcely be exaggerated. Conceived at the height of Victorian sexual repression, the Count Dracula of the novel embodies, to varying degrees of explicitness, all the sexual dreads that our culture has still not exorcised or come to terms with: non-procreative sexuality, promiscuity, bisexuality, the so-called "perversions," incest, even (indirectly, through the preferences of the vampirized Lucy) the sexuality of children. Much of our sexual social history can be traced through the transformations the Count has undergone from Stoker's novel to Badham's movie. With his origins in sexual repression, he transplants very logically and easily into the climate and ethos of German expressionism.

Between Stoker's novel and Murnau's film came Freud, to whose theories of repression and the unconscious the Expressionist movement, like the Surrealist movement later, was heavily indebted. The essential difference between the two movements lies in their contrasting inflections of Freudian theory: the Surrealists were committed to liberation and the overthrow of repressive bourgeois norms whatever the costs, whereas the Expressionists consistently conceived the repressed forces as evil, their release cataclysmic. The extraordinary power, and continuing fascination, of Murnau's film are rooted in this vision.

The distinction of *Nosferatu* can be partly suggested by examining the changes Murnau and his scriptwriter Galeen made from novel to film. What novel and film have in common (and no other film version to the same degree except the Badham) is the perception that it is the woman who is the centre of the conflict, that the work is really about *her*. The uses made of this insight are, however, quite different. In Stoker's novel the battle is fought *for* the woman; in Murnau's film she becomes the vampire's active antagonist and destroyer. In Stoker the battle is fought between van Helsing and Dracula (conceived, in the terms of Victorian sexual morality, as "good" and "evil"—in Freudian terms they represent superego and Id); Murnau reduces van Helsing to an ineffectual old fuddy-duddy who lectures on Venus fly-traps but contributes nothing whatever to the vampire's overthrow. In the novel, the woman (Mina) must be saved from contagion and corruption: the Victorian dread of a released female sexuality is basic to the conception; in the film, the woman (now called Nina) realizes that only she can save civilization from the vampire's contagion, by offering herself to him. Murnau's Nina is a character of quite extraordinary ambivalence: emaciated, as if drained of blood, she suggests both vampire and Christian martyr; the strange abandon with which she gives herself to Dracula (first throwing open a window, then prostrating herself on the bed) suggests the close relationship between religious ecstasy and sensual fulfilment. The ambiguity is set up much earlier in the film, in the protracted and elaborate cross-cutting between Nina (ostensibly awaiting Jonathan's return) and the journeys of Jonathan and Dracula (a sequence that makes nonsense of Bazin's claim that ". . . in neither *Nosferatu* nor *Sunrise* does editing play a decisive part"). Jonathan, who travelled by land, is returning by land; the vampire (having taken over a ship) is coming by sea. Nina sits by the shore, gazing out to sea, awaiting her "husband." Her exclamation, as she awakens from sleepwalking ("He is coming! I must go to meet him!") follows a shot, not of Jonathan, but of Dracula's ship.

Jonathan and Dracula also undergo significant alteration from their originals. Stoker's Jonathan is a conventional "noble hero" (although he doesn't actually achieve much of note). Murnau transforms him into the vampire's double, through an intricate series of "mirror" images involving arch-structures: at their first meeting, for example, Jonathan enters the castle under one arch, and this is immediately "answered" by Dracula emerging out of darkness under another. Murnau, following Freud, dramatizes the vampire quite explicitly in terms of repression: he is the repressed under-side of Jonathan, of civilization. As he falls under Dracula's influence, Jonathan is reduced to total impotence: even when he discovers the vampire asleep in his coffin, during the day, he can do nothing but cower back; when Dracula visits his bedchamber at night, to suck his blood, he can do nothing but prostrate himself. At the film's climax, when Nina reveals to him the vampire's presence at the window of the house directly opposite, across the water (another mirror-image), he once again collapses, helpless.

In the novel, Dracula himself is at first quite old, becoming progressively rejuvenated in England by fresh blood; but he is never as grotesque as Max Schreck in Murnau's version and never as romantically attractive as Frank Langella in Badham's—the two films inflect him, significantly, in precisely opposite directions. Murnau's most striking development of the original material is his elaboration of the vampire. In the novel, Dracula disappears quite early from the surface of the narrative (which is told entirely through letters, diaries, etc.), appearing only in brief glimpses; in the film he becomes the dominant figure, a development especially clear in the long central section of the voyage (for which the novel has no equivalent). Murnau greatly extends Dracula's association with animals, and with a dark, nocturnal underside of nature: he has pointed ears, is visually connected with a jackal, emerges from his castle as out of the blackness of an animal's lair. Above all, the film associates him with rats and plague: wherever he goes, rats swarm, and the precise nature of the spreading pestilence is kept carefully ambiguous.

The re-thinking of Dracula in Badham's film offers a fascinating comparison, an attempt at a "progressive" re-interpretation with a far more positive view of the repressed forces the vampire represents: the heroine becomes a "liberated" woman who freely chooses Dracula as her lover, and it is the father-figure, van Helsing, who is finally impaled on a stake. In fact, what Badham's film proves is the intractability of the material for such a purpose: Dracula becomes a kind of sexual superman, the film develops disturbing Fascist overtones, and many of the complex connotations of the vampire are eliminated. While Murnau's film—heavily determined by its Expressionist background—can depict repressed sexuality and its release only in the most negative terms, it manages to endow it with far greater force and potency, dramatizing the basic Freudian quandary—the necessity for repression, yet the appalling cost of repression—with a much more suggestive complexity.

—Robin Wood

LA NOTTE. The Night. Production: Nepi Film (Rome), Sofitedip (Paris), and Silver Films (Paris); black and white, 35mm; running time: 120 mins. Released February 1961, Italy.

Produced by Emanuele Cassuto; screenplay by Michelangelo Antonioni, Ennio Flaiano, and Tonino Guerra; English subtitles by Rose Sokol; directed by Michelangelo Antonioni; photography by Gianni Di Venanzo; edited by Eraldo Da Roma; sound by Claudio Maielli; art direction by Piero Zuffi; music by Giorgio Gaslini and his Quartette.

Filmed 1960 in Milan. Berlin Film Festival, Best Film, 1961.

Cast: Jeanne Moreau (*Lidia*); Marcello Mastroianni (*Giovanni*); Monica Vitti (*Valentina Gerardini*); Bernhard Wicki (*Tommaso*); Rosi Mazzacurati (*Resy*); Maria Pia Luzi (*Nymphomaniac*); Vincenzo Corbella (*Gerardini*); Gitt Magrini (*Signora Gerardini*); Giorno Negro (*Roberto*); Guido Aimone Marsan (*Fanti*); Roberta Speroni (*Beatrice*); Vittorio Bertolini; Ugo Fortunati; Pompiani.

Publications:

Scripts—*La Nuit: La Notte* by Antonioni, T. Guerra, and E. Flaiano, translated by Michèle Causse, Paris 1961; *Screenplays by Michelangelo Antonioni*, New York 1963; reviews—by Ellen Fitzpatrick in *Films in Review* (New York), December 1961; review by Guido Aristarco in *Film Culture* (New York), spring 1962; review by Jonas Mekas in *The Village Voice* (New York), 15 February 1962; review in *Cinema* (Beverly Hills), no.2, 1963; books—*Antonioni, Bergman, Resnais* by Peter Cowie, New York 1963; *Michelangelo Antonioni: An Introduction* by Pierre Leprohon, New York 1963; *Antonioni, Bergman, Resnais* by Peter Cowie, New York 1963; *Cinema Eye, Cinema Ear* by John Russell Taylor, New York 1964; *Antonioni* by Philip Strick, London 1965; *Antonioni* by Ian Cameron and Robin Wood, New York 1969; articles—"Making a Film is My Way of Life" in *Film Culture* (New York), spring 1962; "A Talk with Antonioni on His Work" in *Film Culture* (New York), spring 1962; "Talk with Antonioni" by H. Alpert in the *Saturday Review* (New York), 27 October 1962; issue on Antonioni of *Film Quarterly* (Berkeley), fall 1962; "*La Notte*" by Geoffrey Nowell-Smith in

Sight and Sound (London), winter 1961-62; "*La Notte* and *L'Avventura*" by Guido Aristarco in *Film Culture* (New York), spring 1962; "Of Night, Fire, and Water" by Vernon Young in *The Hudson Review* (Nutley, New Jersey), summer 1962; "Most Controversial Director" by Melton S. Davis in the *New York Times Magazine*, 15 November 1964; "Night, Eclipse, Dawn..." by Jean-Luc Godard in *Cahiers du Cinema in English* (New York), January 1966; "Antonioni Men" by Gordon Gow in *Films and Filming* (London), June 1970; "Antonioni: The Road to Death Valley" by Andrew Tudor in *Cinema* (London), August 1970; "Michelangelo Antonioni and the Imagery of Disintegration" by T. Hernacki in *Film Heritage* (Dayton, Ohio), autumn 1970; "The Natural Enmity of Words and Moving Images: Language, *La Notte*, and the Death of the Light" by F. Burke in *Literature/Film Quarterly* (Salisbury, Maryland), no. 1, 1979.

*   *   *

Michelangelo Antonioni's *La notte* is about an artist's life at the height of Italy's economic miracle; it depicts several hours, including a whole night, in the life of Giovanni Pontano, a novelist, on the day of the publication of his latest book.

The film opens with a visit by Pontano and his wife, Lidia, to the most sympathetic figure of the film, the Marxist editor Tommaso, who is in a hospital dying of cancer. Later, during a long and tedious all-night party at the home of a Milanese industrialist, who wants to buy Pontano's services to promote his business, Lidia learns that Tommaso has died.

The fascination of the film lies in its representation of boredom: a routine book party unenlivened by the actual appearance of Salvatore Quasimodo, then a recent Nobel laureate; Lidia's aimless walk at the outskirts of Milan, while Giovanni tries to nap in his study; an unsatisfying visit to a nightclub; and the endless meanderings and regroupings of the affluent guests at the party.

Within that matrix Pontano's sexual adventures becomes an index of his moral, and even artistic, collapse. He allows himself to be grabbed and caressed by a nymphomniac in the hospital until two brutal nurses separate them and beat the woman; he trails the dilettante daughter of the industrialist around her mansion and ultimately fails to seduce her: and, in the film's last moments, on what appears to be the host's private golf course, he starts to make love to his wife, after she reads him an old love letter which he does not recognize as his own.

Antonioni manipulates entrances and exits and ambiguous shifts of scale, in order to shift regularly between his principal characters while maintaining the impression that their independent actions are linked together, almost as if they could see each other in their privacy. This impression is furthered by the well-ordered system of countershots which stress distance between characters even when they are behaving intimately. This is the most emphatic in the increasing lengths at which the camera is placed from the couple at the film's conclusion.

—P. Adams Sitney

1900. Novecento. Production: TCF, PEA, Artistes Associés, and Artemis Productions; Technicolor, 35mm; running time: originally 320 mins., US version is 245 mins., usually shown in two parts. Released Cannes Film Festival, 1976.

Produced by Alberto Grimaldi; screenplay by Bernardo Bertolucci, Franco Arcalli, and Giuseppe Bertolucci; directed by Bernardo Bertolucci; photography by Vittorio Stovaro; edited by Franco Arcalli; art direction by Enzo Frigiero; music by Ennio Morricone.

Cast: Robert De Niro (*Alfredo, the grandson*); Burt Lancaster (*Alfredo, the grandfather*); Romolo Valli (*Giovanni*); Anna-Marie Gherardi (*Eleonora*); Laura Betti (*Regina*); Paolo Pavesi (*Alfredo, as a child*); Dominique Sanda (*Ada*); Sterling Hayden (*Leo Dalco*); Gérard Depardieu (*Olmo Dalco*); Roberto Maccanti (*Olmo, as a child*); Stefania Sandrelli (*Anita Foschi*); Donald Sutherland (*Attila*); Werner Bruhns (*Octavio*); Alida Valli (*Signora Pioppi*); Francesca Bertini (*Sister Desolata*).

Publications:

Script—"*Dvadesetijat vek (1900)*" (script extract) in *Kinoizkustvo* (Sofia, Bulgaria), November 1977 and December 1977; reviews—"*1900*" by A. Cornand in *Image et son* (Paris), November 1977; "Dokumentation" in *Filmfaust* (Frankfurt), April/May 1977; "*1900*" by Vincent Canby in *The New York Times*, 8 October 1977; "*1900*" by W. Aitken in *Take One* (Montreal), March 1978; "*1900*" by D. Dean in *Films in Review* (New York), January 1978; "*1900*" by J. Forbes in *Monthly Film Bulletin* (London), January 1978; "*1900*" by Gordon Gow in *Films and Filming* (London), April 1978; "*1900*" by Geoffrey Nowell-Smith in *Sight and Sound* (London), spring 1978; book—*Bertolucci* by F. Casetti, Florence 1975; articles—special section of *Filmcritica* (Rome) on *1900*, July 1976; "History as Myth and Myth as History in Bertolucci's *1900*" by A. Horton in *Film and History* (Newark, New Jersey), February 1980; "Bertolucci interview 1." by G. di Bernardo in *Skrien* (Amsterdam), July/August 1977; "*1900*" by D. Bickley and others in *Cineaste* (Paris), winter 1976-77; "Bertolucci: Interview 2" by F. De Vico and R. Degni in *Skrien* (Amsterdam), September 1977; "Bertolucci's *1900*: Stormy Beginnings" by B. Gilbert in *Cinema Papers* (Melbourne), January 1977; "*1900*" by S. Le Puyat and M. Olmi in *Téléciné* (Paris), October 1976; "Bernardo Bertoluccis zweiteiliges Epos und das Unbehagen der Bourgeoisie" by G. Netzeband in *Film und Fernsehen* (Berlin), June 1977; "Bernardo Bertolucci og den falske folkelighed" by P. Schepelern in *Kosmorama* (Copenhagen), spring 1977; "*1900* rosarote Dollars—gefälschte Bauern?" by B. Steinborn in *Filmfaust* (Frankfurt), April/May 1977; "Bernardo Bertolucci's s'explique" in *Cinéma Québec* (Montreal), no.4, 1978; "Bernardo Bertolucci's *1900*" in *Films and Filming* (London), April 1978; "Cannes—vinneren Treskotreet" by W. Blomberg in *Filmavisa* (Oslo), nos.1-2, 1978; "Bernardo Bertolucci's *1900*: klasse mot klasse" by S. Erikson in *Filmavisa* (Oslo), nos.1-2, 1978; "Vom Monolog zum Epos" by A. Karaganov in *Film und Fernsehen* (Berlin), April 1978; article by R. Paret in *Cinéma Québec* (Montreal), no.4 and no.5, 1978; "*1900*—Bertolucci's Marxist Opera" by L. Quart in *Cineaste* (New York), winter 1977-78; "Bertolucci's *1900* ett dialektiskt experiment" by A. Sevensson in *Filmrutan* (Lidingö, Sweden), no.1, 1978; "History Lessons" by D. Young in *Film Comment* (New York), November/December 1977; "Como si la cáara fuese un lápiz que escribiese al viento" by A. Arbasino in *Cine* (Mexico), May 1979.

*   *   *

The films of Bernardo Bertolucci are audacious, lyrical and passionately political. One of the most talented progeny of Italian neorealism, Bertolucci invests his films with technical virtuosity, a rich, visual patina and a poetic use of people and landscapes. With *Novecento* (20th Century), Bertolucci has created an immense, operatic socio-political document of Italian history from 1901 to 1945. It is 'a family saga of truly epic proportions, shown at the Cannes Film Festival in its 5-hour, 20-minute entirety and released in the United States as *1900* in a 245-minute version. *1900* is a vivid, sumptuous, complex study of the rise of Fascism, and arguably it is Bertolucci's masterpiece.

"The basis of *1900*," explains Bertolucci, "is the dialectic of class, the dialetic between the landowner's class and the peasant class and the collision of these two classes." To illustrate this subject, Bertolucci tells his story through the lives of two boys both born on January 27, 1901, the day Verdi died. He opens his film on Liberation Day, April 25, 1945, then goes back to the day of their birth. Alfredo is the pampered bourgeois son of the landowning Berlinghieri family headed by Alfredo, the boy's grandfather (Burt Lancaster). Olmo, the bastard son of the daughter of the peasants who farm the land and whose patriarch is Leo Dalco (Sterling Hayden). The boys grow up together, and their love/hate relationship is Bertolucci's representation of the death of feudalism and the birth of socialism. Alfredo (Robert De Niro) grows into a dilettante who shrinks from confronting Attila, his fascistic foreman (Donald Sutherland), and Olmo (Gérard Depardieu) becomes a union organizing Marxist. Their paths intertwine throughout their lives, as do the lives of other members of the two families.

The film is set in Parma in north central Italy, and the entire action takes place within a 20-mile radius of that city with dramatic scenes depicting the peasant uprising of 1908, the end of World War I and the rise of Fascism. In the first half of the film Bertolucci emphasizes the human relationships and struggles of the two families. In the second half of the movie Bertolucci becomes bogged down in political philosophizing—he sincerely (although to some, misguidedly) believes in a socialist Utopia—but his didactic approach diminishes the human element. He ends *1900* with the death of the elder Alfredo and jubilant celebration by the peasants welcoming in a new era—picturesque, but politically naive.

Bertolucci endows *1900* with the epic sweep of grand opera and Hollywood spectacles. The numerous characters and the dubbing of an international cast lend a certain confusion, yet there are scenes of magnificence unexcelled by any of today's directors. And the cast is for the most part more than competent. De Niro and Depardieu are first-rate, even though some critics have said that De Niro is too "bland;" he was, after all, playing a wimp. Also memorable are Lancaster, Hayden, Dominique Sanda (as Alfredo's alcoholic wife), and Alida Valli as an anguished aristocrat.

All of Bertolucci's films are autobiographical, and each one exhibits what Robin Wood calls the "divided hero." And *1900*, Bertolucci's most complex and complete political statement to date, is likewise a strongly personal statement with the two young men representing conflicting aspects of Bertolucci's psyche—the bourgeois Alfredo and the proletarian Olmo.

—Ronald Bowers

NOW VOYAGER. Production: Warner Bros. Pictures, Inc. black and white, 35mm; running time: 117 mins. Released 1942.

Produced by Hal B. Wallis; screenplay by Casey Robinson; from the novel by Olive Higgens Prouty; directed by Irving Rapper; photography by Sol Polito; edited by Warren Low; art direction by Robert Haas; music by Max Steiner.

Academy Award, Music—Scoring of a Dramatic or Comedy Picture, 1942.

Cast: Bette Davis (*Charlotte Vale*); Paul Henreid (*Jerry Durrance*); Claude Rains (*Dr. Jaquith*); Gladys Cooper (*Mrs. Henry Windle Vale*); Bonita Granville (*June Vale*); Ilka Chase (*Lisa Vale*); John Loder (*Elliot Livingston*); Lee Patrick (*Deb McIntyre*); Franklin Pangborn (*Mr. Thompson*); Katherine Alexander (*Miss Trask*); James Rennie (*Frank McIntyre*); Mary Wickes (*Dora Pickford*); Janis Wilson (*Tina Durrance*); Michael Ames (*Dr. Dan Regan*); Charles Drake (*Leslie Trotter*): Frank Puglia (*Manoel*); David Clyde (*William*).

Publications:

Review—"*Now Voyager* with Bette Davis, Paul Henreid, Claude Rains at the Hollywood—*Flying Tigers* Featured at Capitol" by T.S. in *The New York Times*, 23 October 1942; books—*The Lonely Life: An Autobiography* by Bette Davis, New York 1962; *The Films of Bette Davis* by Gene Ringgold, New York 1966; articles—"Bette Davis" by Janet Flanner in the *New Yorker*, February 1943; "Mannerisms—in the Grand Manner" by Michell Raper in *Films and Filming* (London), September 1955; "Bette Davis" by L. Quirk in *Films in Review* (New York), December 1955; "Claude Rains" by Jeanne Stein in *Films in Review* (New York), November 1963; article by Allen Eyles in *Films and Filming* (London), February 1965; "Bette Davis: Part One" by Ann Guerin in *Show*, April 1971; "Bette Davis: Part Two" by Ann Guerin in *Show*, May 1972; "Semiotic Constraints in *Now Voyager*" by Sam Rhodie in *Australian Journal of Screen Theory* (Kensington), no.4, 1978; "Writing for the Movies: Casey Robinson" by J. Greenberg in *Focus on Film* (London), April 1979; "*Now Voyager*" by P. Merigeau in *Revue du cinéma* (Paris), September 1979; "*Now Voyager*" by J. Narache in *Cinéma 79* (Paris), July/August 1979; "*Now Voyager*" by B. Villien in *Cinematographe* (Paris), July 1979;

* * *

Now Voyager is today one of the best remembered and best loved woman's films," or "weepies,"of the 1930's and 1940's. Bette Davis remembers it as one of her most satisfying movies. But during its initial release in 1942, the film received a mixed critical response; the *New York Times* called the film a "prudish fantasy." The low esteem in which critics held the film seems in retrospect to be due to the low regard in which critics held the "woman's picture." *Now Voyager* succeeds, not because it explores any new thematic or formal areas within the genre of "woman's pictures," but because it utilizes generic conventions in a highly polished manner.

The "woman's film" is characterized by a central female protagonist whose concerns revolve around a romantic or materal relationship. In the case of *Now Voyager*, the film weaves both into the narrative. The first half of the film documents Charlotte Vale's (Bette Davis) growth into a sexually mature and attractive woman who must overcome the repressive influence of her mother. In the first segment, Charlotte's mother, psychiatrist, and sister-in-law discuss Charlotte before she appears, making her the center of the story without necessitating her on-screen presence. The camera introduces Charlotte with a closeup of her hands working on an ivory box, then discloses her feet walking down the stairs, finally offering a long shot of her entering the parlor. In the second segment, Dr. Jaquith (Claude Rains) and the sister-in-law discuss Charlotte before she is actually seen. The camera here introduces her with a closeup of her hands operating a loom. In the third segment, which takes place on an ocean liner, the passengers discuss Charlotte prior to the camera's introductory closeup panning from her feet up to her head. Upon Charlotte's return to New York City in the film's fourth segment, a discussion of Charlotte precedes the medium shot introducing her. Each discussion creates a sense of expectancy and interest about the character, while the introductions themselves follow a course that visually parallels Charlotte's character development from disjointed close-ups of fragmented body parts to the completely integrated portrait in one shot. It is only after an innocent shipboard romance with a married man has sexually awakened her that Charlotte achieves her sense of identity as a woman and a person. In the second half of the movie, Charlotte supplants her earlier womanly hobbies—carving ivory boxes, weaving and knitting—with socializing, mothering and philanthropy, completing her journey toward the assumption of her socially acceptable roles.

Several motifs provide a symbolic continuity to the film. The most notable, Paul Henreid lighting Davis's cigarette, operates as a poetic visual sign that may be likened to the intricate musical dances of Fred Astaire and Ginger Rogers. Only during the shared intimacies of the couple's "cigarette breaks" does the camera break from the almost continuous objective viewpoint to a series of subjective shot-reverse shots of Davis and Henreid. In this way, the camera forces the audience to shift from its fixation on Davis as an object-to-be-consumed to an alternating identification with her and Henreid. The audience vicariously participates as both parties in their fleeting and harmless romantic moments. Thus, the viewer retains a distance from Charlotte Vale that makes her problems seem as though they are happening to someone else, while fully identifying with her few moments of idealized romantic pleasure.

Max Steiner's Academy Award-winning score and the references to the relationship between Charlotte's life and the art of fiction reinforce an idealized discovery of sexuality. Steiner's melodramatic lover's theme song appears not only when Henreid and Davis get together, but also as the piece the orchestra plays when the two must sit next to each other without acknowledging their love; and after Jerry (Henreid) returns to his wife and family, it comes over the radio reminding Davis and the audience of her emotional ties to him while she chats with another man. The music helps set up a world that seems to exist only to underscore the poignancy of their situation. The ludicrousness of such an idea is overcome by equating how one acts and lives with the way that novels work. Charlotte repeatedly refers to her understanding of life, and especially her life, as having come from novels, and the dissolves into and out of the flashbacks are accomplished via the turning pages of a book. Charlotte's life and world fulfill one's expectations of the romance formula, and they are believable because she believes and acts as if life is a romance formula.

The credit for making Charlotte Vale's identity and life appear so attractive should go largely to Bette Davis for suggestively giving, through gestures, movements, rhythms, timing and articulation, an assertive and independent awareness to the role of Charlotte Vale. Secondly, the film preserves much of the dialogue from Olive Higgins Prouty's 1941 novel on which it is based; its rhythms, tempo and the words themselves underscore a

developing assertiveness, control and mastery in Charlotte Vale's speech.

In the end, Charlotte Vale may not be able to achieve complete fulfillment of her destined womanly role through marriage to the man she loves, but she hangs on to her independence, her own identity, while she captures the semblance of a nuclear family. The resolution allows Charlotte to become adoptive mother to Jerry's unhappy daughter while he remains faithful to his legal wife. In one of the great screen romance endings of all time, Charlotte Vale's compromised balance between self-sufficient independence and romantic longing provides an impossible illusory alternative to the unmasking of romance and the loss of independence that would result in daily married life with Jerry and his daughter.

—Lauren Rabinovitz

NÓŻ W WODZIE. Knife in the Water. Production: Kamera Film Unit for Film Polski; black and white, 35mm; running time: 94 mins. Released Poland, 1962.

Produced by Stanisław Zyewicz; screenplay by Jerzy Skolimowski, Jakub Goldberg, and Roman Polanski; directed by Roman Polanski; photography by Jerzy Lipman; sound by Halina Paszkowska; music by Krzysztof Komeda.

Filmed 1962 in Poland. International Film Critics Award (Fipresci), Venice Film Festival, 1962.

Cast: Leon Niemczyk (*Andrzej*); Jolanta Umecka (*Christine/Krystanal*); Zygmunt Malanowicz (*Young man*).

Publications:

Reviews—by Andrew Sarris in *The Village Voice* (New York), 31 October 1963; review by Peter Baker in *Films and Filming* (London), February 1963; review in *Cinema* (Beverly Hills), February/March 1964; books—*The Cinema of Roman Polanski* by Ivan Butler, New York 1970; *Roman Polanski* by Pascal Kané, Paris 1970; *Roman Polanski* by Jacques Belmans, Paris 1971; *The Most Important Art: East European Cinema After 1945* by Mira Liehm and Antonín Liehm, Berkeley 1977; *Roman Polanski: a Guide to References and Resources* by Gretchen Bisplinghoff and Virginia Wexman, Boston 1979; *The Roman Polanski Story* by Thomas Kiernan, New York 1980; *Polanski: A Biography* by Barbara Leaming, New York 1981; articles—"Nouveaux Cinéastes Polonais: Roman Polanski" by Philippe Haudiquet in *Premier Plan* (Lyon), no.27, 1962; "Prélude à Polanski" by Jean-Paul Torok in *Positif* (Paris), March 1962; "Interview with Roman Polanski" by Gretchen Weinberg in *Sight and Sound* (London), winter 1963/64; "*Knife in the Water*" by Sibyl March in the *Seventh Art* (New York), winter 1963; "Landscape of the Mind: Interview with Roman Polanski" by Michel Delahaye and Jean-André Fieschi in *Cahiers du Cinema in English* (New York), no.3 1966; "On the Scene: Roman Polanski, Pole Vaulting" in *Playboy* (Chicago), October 1966; "Jerzy Skolimowski: Portrait of a Debutant Director" by K.-T. Toeplitz in *Film Quarterly* (Berkeley), fall 1967; "Polanski in New York" by Harrison Engle in *Film Comment* (New York), fall 1968; "Roman Polanski" by Tom Nairn in *Cinema* (London), June 1969; "Satisfaction—A Most Unpopular Feeling" by Gordon Gow in *Films and Filming* (London), April 1969; "The Polanski Puzzle" by John Alan McCarty in *Take One* (Montreal), no.5, 1969; "*Le Couteau dans l'eau*" by L. Cugny in *Cinématographe* (Paris), no.40, 1978; "*Le Couteau dans l'eau*" by H. Guibert in *Cinématographe* (Paris), no.40, 1978; "The Double...a Doestoevskian Theme in Polanski" by A.M. Lawton in *Literature/Film Quarterly* (Salisbury, Maryland), no.2, 1981.

* * *

Roman Polanski emerged as a highly individual artist when he made his directorial debut with a few short films —*Dwaj ludzie z szafa*; his graduation project *Gdy spadaja aniloy*; *Gros et le maigre*, produced in France; and the grotesque *Ssaki*. These films startled audiences and critics alike and won praise at various film festivals. They amazed viewers with their unusually innovative approach of pure experiment combined with elaborated philosophical import and elements of absurd humor. The critics anxiously awaited his first feature-length film which came in 1962 and was entitled *Nóż w wodzie (Knife in the Water)*.

What was so startling about *Nóż w wodzie*? At first glance, it seems to be a simple story with neither an attractive setting nor much external dramatic action. However, within the ordinary plot a bitter internal drama is played out in the form of a minor allegory. It is an intimate drama of three people in the enclosed space of a sailboat in the middle of a lake, and it takes place over the 24 hours of a single Sunday. A young hitchhiker steps out in front of the car of an elegant married couple, Andrzej and Christine. The hitchhiker's clumsiness appeals to the older man, who finds in it an opportunity to show off his own strength, make fun of the hitchhiker and provoke him. Andrzej invites him to go out sailing with him and his wife. Their relationship gradually comes to a critical point; more and more, Andrzej asserts his role as captain and forces the youth into an audacious reprisal. Somewhere in the relationship between the two men stands Christine. The conflict reaches a climax when, in one of their quarrels, Andrzej throws the boy's knife into the water. The boy jumps in after it but doesn't come up. Andrzej attempts to rescue the boy, but the latter had only pretended to drown and has returned to the boat, where he again confronts Christine. With morning the drama ends. The boy goes off, and the husband and wife, having cleared up the situation, fall back into the routine of their peculiar conjugal life.

Nóż w wodzie is a cold work that exposes the general norms of human relations defined by generational conflicts and social factors. The drama is characterized by short, clipped pieces of dialogue, each of which serves to determine the character and conduct of the protagonists. Both the beginning and end of the film are wrapped in silence and the quiet, disturbing isolation of the "heroes." Some critics noted, at the time of the film's release, the similarity between Polanski's development and the directorial style of Michelangelo Antonioni. Nevertheless, this work bears a uniquely individual directorial stamp. The film opens with an automobile ride; across the windshield and the faces of the husband and wife flit the shadows of branches and tree trunks. The image is cold and grey. So, too, are the world and the relationship of the central couple into which the hitchhiker intrudes. The enclosed space of the boat surrounded by water intensifies the drama of the situation and the coldness and hopelessness of the human relationships. There is an intrinsic drama hidden somewhere beneath the exterior of these people who have nothing to say to each other. The boy serves as a kind of catalyst for the development of the action, for the exposure of relationships and character. But the authors present everything as a mere game which, in the end, can start all over again despite the malicious accusations and the disclosure of egoism and cowardice; in spite of the pain and

cruelty of an empty conjugal existence, everything remains as it had been. The drama is heightened by the brilliant camera work of Jerzy Lipman, which captures both the surroundings and the people in cold, grey tones; looks at them as a tangle of ropes, objects and bodies; and uses discrete images to portray the contrasts between expressions and utterances. The attention concentrated on the strangeness of human communication is emphasized further by the jazz elements in Krzysztof Komeda's music.

Nóż w wodzie was the confession of a generation, the warning of dangerous trends of philistinism, thoughtlessness, and authoritarianism. It is at this general level that the film is important today as well, and it has lost nothing of its suggestiveness in the years since its first appearance. It is a masterpiece which has risen above generational conflict to confront the viewer with the universal problem of human intolerance.

—G. Merhaut

NUIT ET BROUILLARD. Night and Fog. Production: Argos-Como-Cocinor (Paris); Eastmancolor, some sequences in black and white, 35mm; running time: 32 mins. Released 1955.

Text written by Jean Cayrol; directed by Alain Resnais; photography by Ghislain Choquet S. Vierny (Sacha Vierny); edited by Alain Resnais; music by Hans Eisler; historical consultants: André Michel and Olga Wormser.

Filmed near Auschwitz. Prix Jean Vigo, France, 1956.

Cast: Michel Bouquet (*Narrator*).

Publications:

Script—"*Nuit et Brouillard*" (text) by Jean Cayrol in *Avant-scène du cinéma* (Paris), February 1961; books—"Alain Resnais" in *Qu'est-ce que le cinéma* by André Bazin, Paris 1959; *Alain Resnais, ou la Création au Cinéma* edited by Stéphane Cordier, Paris 1961; *Alain Resnais* by Bernard Pinguad, Lyon 1961; *Alain Resnais* by Gaston Bournoure, Paris 1962; *Film: Book 2: Films of Peace and War* edited by Robert Hughes, New York 1962; *Antonioni, Bergman, Resnais* by Peter Cowie, London 1963; "Alain Resnais" in *Cineme Eye, Cinema Ear* by John Russell Taylor, New York 1964; *French Cinema Since 1946: Vol. 2—The Personal Style* by Roy Armes, New York 1966; *The Cinema of Alain Resnais* by Roy Armes, London 1968; *Alain Resnais, or the Theme of Time* by John Ward, New York 1968; *Documentary: A History of the Non-Fiction Film* by Erik Barnouw, New York 1974; *Resnais: Alain Resnais* by Paolo Bertetto, Italy 1976; *Alain Resnais: The Role of Imagination* by James Monaco, New York 1978; *Alain Resnais, arpenteur de l'imaginaire* by Robert Benayoun, Paris 1980; *The Film Narratives of Alain Resnais* by Freddy Sweet, Ann Arbor, Michigan 1981; articles—interview with Resnais in *Arts* (Paris), 20 February 1956; "*Nuit et brouillard*" by Louis Marcorelles in *Sight and Sound* (London), spring 1956; "*Night and Fog*" by Roger Sandall in *Film Quarterly* (Berkeley), spring 1961; issue on Resnais of *Avant-Scène du cinéma* (Paris), summer 1966; "Memories of Resnais" by Richard Roud in *Sight* and Sound (London), summer 1969; issue on Resnais of Cinéma (Paris), July/August 1980.

*   *   *

Two closely related problems; How does one make a film about the concentration camps? and how does one write a reference book entry about a film about the concentration camps? The facts are too appalling to be aesthetically encompassed; any *attempt* to encompass them seems almost beyond criticism. The word that rises automatically to one's lips to describe what was done in the camps is "inhuman"; yet it was human beings who performed those acts. For both the film-maker and the critic, it is one's own "humanity" that is in question.

In making *Night and Fog* director Alain Resnais and his writer Cayrol confronted a problem that is simultaneously aesthetic and moral: how does one adequately represent the enormity of the camps without so overwhelming the spectator that the only possible response is a despairing impotence?—how to achieve and sustain a contemplative distance without softening or/trivializing the material? Their solution, curiously *seductive* (and the strangeness of that word in such a context is deliberate), is ultimately unsatisfying. The failure lies in the fact that the kind of distance achieved is aesthetic rather than analytical: we find ourselves invited to contemplate, not the historical/material realities, but an art-object.

The film is built on a systematic pattern of related oppositions: present/past, colour/black-and-white, tranquillity/horror, natural environment/buildings, footage shot for the film/archive material. Particularly stressed is the recurrent Resnais theme: importance of memory/difficulty of remembering. Nothing can mitigate the appalling impact of the newsreel material incorporated in the film, with the horrors carefully built up to, yet introduced almost casually, so that we at once expect them and are taken unawares. The problem arises from the attitude to the horror that the film, overall, constructs.

One omission—startling today, though no one seems to have commented on it at the time—is symptomatic in more than one way of the film's failure. One sequence carefully specifies the various coloured triangles that identified different groups of victims, distinguishing the Jews from other ethnic groups, political prisoners, etc.. Presumably Resnais and Cayrol had very thorough documentation at their disposal, yet no reference is made to the *pink* triangle: the filmmakers surround the deaths of the (approximately) 300,000 homosexuals who died in the camps with their own "night and fog" of silence. A sinister enough comment on the "liberal" conscience in itself, this omission has implications that lead much further. The fact that the Nazis attempted to exterminate gays as well as Jews points to certain fundamental traits of Fascism that our culture generally prefers to gloss over for its own comfort. Alongside the demand for racial purity went the insistence on extreme sexual division: "masculinity" and "femininity" must strictly differentiated, women relegated to the subordinate position of the mothers who would produce future generations of "pure" aryans. The reason why patriarchal capitalist society is so reluctant to confront this aspect of Nazism is clearly that it has its own stake in the same assumptions.

The problem, however, is not simply that Resnais and Cayrol cannot make that analysis (though it is a fundamental one); they really offer no analysis at all (with the result that they tend to repress the possibility of really understanding the camps). The final moments of the film are extremely moving: at the post-war trials, we are led through the whole hierarchy of camp authority;

everyone denies responsibility; we are left with the question, "Then who is responsible?" Yet the implication is something like: "These things have always happened; they have happened again; they will always happen." Denied concrete material/historical analysis, we are thrown back on "the human condition." The answer the film (without much hope) proposes is eternal vigilance. Yet no "liberal" vigilance is going to prevent the recurrence of the camps (or related phenomena) until the fundamental premises and structures of our culture are radically transformed.

This account of *Night and Fog* is perhaps ungenerous, the problems inherent in the undertaking being so daunting. The film is intensely moving. Yet to confront the human monstrousness of the camps demands the utmost rigour from both the film-maker and the critic. Ultimately, the kind of "distance" constructed by Resnais and Cayrol seems less honourable, as a response, than the direct emotional assault of work like Schönberg's "A Survivor From Warsaw."

—Robin Wood

———

UNE NUIT SUR LE MONT CHAUVE. Night on Bald Mountain. Black and white, 35mm, animation; running time: 8 mins., some sources list 9 mins. Released 1933, Paris.

Narrative developed by Alexander Alexeieff; inspired in part by Moussorgsky's music and notes, and a short story based on a Slavic fairy tale by Gogol; directed by Alexander Alexeieff, some sources list Alexeieff and Claire Parker both as directors; music by Moussorgsky, arrangement by Rimski-Korsakov, "His Master's Voice" interpreted by the London Symphony Orchestra under the direction of Albert Coates; animation by Alexandre Alexeieff and Claire Parker.

Publications:

Books—*Alexandre Alexeieff*, exhibition catalogue, National Library of Scotland, Edinburgh 1967; *Alexandre Alexeieff*, exhibition catalogue, by G. Rondolino, Cinema incontri abano terme, Este 1971; *Discovering the Movies* by Cecile Starr, New York 1972; *Alexandre Alexeieff*, exhibition catalogue, edited by G. Bendazzi, Ente provinciale per il turismo di Milano, Milan 1973; *A. Alexeieff, C. Parker: Films et eaux-fortes, 1925-75*, exhibition catalogue, Chateau d'Annecy, 1975; *Experimental Animation* by R. Russett and C. Starr, New York 1976; *Pages d'Alexeieff* edited by G. Bendazzi, Milan 1983; *A. Alexeieff ou la gravure animée*, exhibition catalogue, Chateau d'Annecy, 1983; articles—by John Grierson in *Cinema Quarterly* (London), autumn 1934; "*Une Nuit sur le Mont Chauve*, film en gravure animée par A. Alexeieff et C. Parker" by L. Cheronnet in *Art et décoration* (Paris), no.63, 1934; "Gravure animée" by S. Priacel in *L'Art vivant* (Paris), no.188, 1934; "Alexandre Alexeieff et les cinémas possibles" by A. Martin in *Cinéma 63* (Paris), no.81, 1963; "Reflections on Motion Picture Animation" by Alexandre Alexeieff in *Film Culture* (New York), no.32, 1964; "The Synthesis of Artificial Movements in Motion Picture Projection" by Alexandre Alexeieff in *Film Culture* (New York), no.48-49, 1970; "Le Chant d'ombres et de lumières de 1 250 000 épingles", edited by H. Arnault, in *Cinéma pratique* (Paris), no.123, 1973;

"A. Alexeieff" by J.P. Jouvanceau and C. Gaudillière in *Banc-Titre*, no.25, 1982.

*   *   *

The power of *Night on Bald Mountain* derives from the extraordinary versatility that Alexander Alexeieff and Claire Parker brought to their unusual medium. Their "pinboard" (l'*ecran d'epingles*) is an upright perforated screen, three by four feet, with 500,000 (one million in later films) headless steel pins as its physical matrix. Images created on the pinboard take their character from the depth of the pins and their oblique lighting. Pushed forward, the pins create an entirely dark surface; when fully recessed, they produce a white ground. By varying the depth of the pins, one creates between the extremes of white and black a wide variety of subtle shades the brilliance and delicacy of which exceed that of engravings. The pinboard screen yields a single picture at a time which must be photographed as part of a sequence of thousands of such shots to shape the cumulative effect.

This frame-by-frame creation during the process of filming, rather than before it, is the earliest form of direct animation. Alexeieff acknowledges the pontillism of Seurat as analogous to the character of his images. The delicacy of this process of image-building becomes apparent when one realizes that four minutes of production requires a year of work. Since the artist can see only the current frame, the procedure is akin to writing a short story sentence-by-sentence and locking away each one until completion of the narrative. During the interactive process of creating and filming, the only original of a pinboard picture that remains is its photographic negative; there are almost 12,000 for this eight-minute film.

It is important to note that *Night on Bald Mountain* has about as much affinity to Walt Disney's evocation of the same Moussorgsky work in *Fantasia* (1940) as Lotte Reininger's *Cinderella* has to Disney's version, i.e., the relationship is one of contrast more than of comparison. While Disney's *Fantasia* used cel animation in a direct and explicit way, which includes a sketching from life of Bela Lugosi as a Moussourgsky demon, Alexeieff and Parker employ indirection and impression, eminently conscious of art's power to universalize experience, of animation's power to create movement that is not "live" in the conventional ways of narrative, feature-length films. Their technique is most closely akin to the music that they visualize in their manipulation of time and space through shadowy referents. More physicists than engineers, their mobile structures reflect the changing character of thought and feeling, depict imaginary rather than static worlds. To photography and painting's laws of perspective they add the suggestive movement of implicit images. To the dance they add weightless figures whose unlimited metamorphoses invokes the license of Ovid's epic poem or the transitory, spatial and temporal fluidity of musical patterns. More than do other approaches to cinema, that of Alexeieff and Parker embody Suzanne Langer's description of cinema as a dream mode.

Night on Bald Mountain is a nightmare, a *Walpurgisnacht*, inspired by Moussorgsky's music and written notes, by childhood recollections, by the Russian short-story writer Gogol's record of an ages-old Slavic fairytale, and by a dancing windmill in Pushkin's *Eugene Onegin*. The film's witches, demons and skeletal horses, in contrasting day and night reflection of each other, create a feverish tone poem that Moussorgsky's music "describes" as powerfully as would a verbal soundtrack. The description, however, of both sight and sound is poetic and lyric rather than narrative and prosaic. The correlative and opposing patterns of visual and musical images create unexpected harmonies whose tonalities are both elastic and balanced. The clash of old and new realities, of expected and unexpected sights and sounds that regularly, rather than continually, complement each other provides the conceptual unity that is finally as satisfying as it is initially troubling. The audience comes to realize that the animation and the music are metaphorical equivalents to one another and that in combination they tell a tragicomic story of life and death, which calls upon the vertical complexity of poetic allusion and brevity for its thrilling and very temporary resolution of basic human contradictions.

The first pinboard was built in 1932, for *Night on Bald Mountain*, and was used by Alexeieff and Parker for all their noncommercial films. Jacques Drouin's *Le Paysagiste* (*Mindscape*: National Film Board of Canada, 1976) continues their tradition. Because of the difficulty of the technique, however, Alexeieff and Parker have had many more admirers than cinematic descendants.

Following the traditional path of successful experimenters, they earned well deserved critical acclaim, but the applause only gradually expanded beyond the ranks of film experts and film-society aficionados. Initial success in Paris did not yield widespread distribution in spite of John Grierson's generous praise in the Autumn 1934 issue of *Cinema Quarterly*. In 1970 Norman McLaren proclaimed *Night on Bald Mountain* "first and foremost" on his list of the world's best animated films, and in 1980 it earned inclusion on a list of the eight best short animation films of all time.

—Arthur G. Robson

THE NUTTY PROFESSOR. Production: Jerry Lewis Enterprises for Paramount; 1963; Technicolor, 35mm; running time: 107 mins.; length: 3200 meters. Released 4 June 1963, Houston.

A Jerry Lewis Production, produced by Ernest D. Glucksman and Arthur P. Schmidt; screenplay by Jerry Lewis and Bill Richmond, dialogue by Jerry Lewis and Marvin Weldon; directed by Jerry Lewis; photography by W. Wallace Kelley; edited by John Woodcock; sound by Hugo Grenzbach and Charles Grenzbach; art direction by Hal Pereira and Walter Tyler, set decorated by Sam Comer and Robert Benton; music by Walter Scharf, "We've Got a World That Swings" by Louis Brown and Lil Mattis; special effects by Paul K. Lerpal; costumes designed by Edith Head, men's wardrobe by Sy Devore and Nat Wise; college consultant: Richard Mueller.

Filmed in Tempe, Arizona on location at Arizona State University.

Cast: Jerry Lewis (*Prof. Julius F. Kelp/Buddy Love*); Stella Stevens (*Stella Purdy*); Del Moore (*Dr. Hamius Warfield*); Kathleen Freeman (*Millie Lemmon*); Med Flory, Norman Alden, and Skip Ward (*Football Players*); Howard Morris (*Father Kelp*); Elvia Allman (*Mother Kelp*); Milton Frome (*Dr. Lee-Vee*); Buddy Lester (*Bartender*); Marvin Kaplan (*English boy*); David Landfield, Julie Parish, and Henry Gibson (*College students*); Dave Willock (*Bartender*); Doodles Weaver (*Rube*); Mushy Callahan (*Cab driver*); Gavin Gordon (*Salesman/clothier*); Celeste Yarnell and Francine York (*Students*); Joe Forte (*Faculty Member*); Terry Higgens (*Cigarette girl*); Murray Alper (*Judo instructor*); Gary Lewis; Les Brown and His Band.

Publications:

Script—"Docteur Jerry et Mister Love" (screenplay) by Jerry Lewis and Bill Richmond in *Avant-Scène du cinéma* (Paris), 15 March 1964; reviews—by Raymond Durgnat in *Films and Filming* (London), October 1963; review by John Gillett in *Sight and Sound* (London), summer 1964; books—*That Kid—The Story of Jerry Lewis* by Richard Gehman, New York 1964; *Directors at Work* edited by Bernard R. Kantor, Irwin R. Blacker, and Anne Kramer, New York 1970; *The Total Film-Maker* by Jerry Lewis, New York 1971; articles—"Search for Jerry Lewis" by E. Linn in the *Saturday Evening Post* (Philadelphia), 12 October 1963; "Une Revanche de 'l'homo americanus'" by Robert Benayoun in *France-Observateur* (Paris), October 1963; "Jerry pense rose" by Robert Benayoun in *Positif* (Paris), December 1963; "Un Comique d'epouvante" by Pierre Marcabru in *Arts* (Paris), November 1963; "Nutty Professor Contest Winners" by L. Hill in *Photoplay* (New York), January 1964; "Don Juan et son double" by Robert Benayoun in *Avant-Scène du cinéma* (Paris), 15 March 1964; "Un Beau Ténébreux" by Paul-Louis Thirard in *Positif* (Paris), February 1964; "Jerry Lewis" by John Russell Taylor in *Sight and Sound* (London), spring 1965; "Le Roi du Crazy" by Hollis Alpert in the *New York Times Magazine*, February 1966; "Jerry Lewis as Auteur" by S. Manes in *Focus* (Chicago), no.3-4, 1968; "La Morale de Jerry" by Jacques Siclier in *Télérama* (Paris), no.720, 1970; "*The Nutty Professor*" by Blake Lucas in *Magill's Survey of Cinema, Vol. III* edited by Frank N. Magill, Englewood Cliffs, New Jersey 1980.

*   *   *

The generic significance of *The Nutty Professor* lies not in any superficial blending of comedy and horror, but rather in the ways the film discovers a deep psychological affinity between the two genres. *The Nutty Professor* maps the comic convention of buffoon and straight man—the convention that Martin and Lewis had perfected as a comic team—onto the horror convention of the double, or the monster that is released from the protagonist's darker, other side. At the same time, the film renders the notion of doubling more complex by blurring the boundries between the two sides: Buddy Love may be another part of Professor Kelp but Kelp's craziness already sets the scientific community apart from any world of everyday reason. Love and Kelp are equally outsiders to a life of "respectable normality." Just as Love is a performer—someone who makes a presentation to others—so too is Kelp in his role as professor. In both cases, performing to an audience is counterposed against a world geared to utility, control, balance; Kelp and Love are equally sources of non-utility, of the uncontrollable, and the unbalanced.

Buddy Love, a Dean Martin-type figure, simultaneously encapsulates the hidden desires and dreams of the klutzy, chaos-causing Professor Kelp *and* reveals a horrific dimension to those dreams—in the desperate machismo that drives Love on, making him a nightclub hit but simultaneously alienating him from his fans on a personal level. Love's nightclub banter only inadequately conceals a self-doubt and anxiety that, for the film, is self-reflexively not only a comment on the Martin-Lewis team but also on the whole psychology and fate of the American popular performer.

Stylistically, *The Nutty Professor* works out its concern with doubling through a rigorous color scheme—white for Kelp, garish blue and red for Love, and shades or blends in between for Stella. Kelp's white lab coat, in particular, suggests a force that battles external, assailing forces; significantly, Kelp's coat is continually sullied by bright colors. For example, a gag where Kelp, having switched his white lab coat for a white evening jacket, accidently immerses his jacketed arm in a bowl of bright red punch, can suggest the ways in which an individual personality is torn between the conflicting needs and desires; soon after this scene, Kelp will lose all control over his own power to determine when he is Kelp and when he is Love.

Just as Lewis's television work has given him a reputation that some critics find in conflict with his comic identity, so too a number of viewers have criticized Love/Kelp's final speech, in which he exhorts his listener's to search for happiness in their own lives rather than in fantasy, as a betrayal to the film's overall comic, non-moralistic tone. Yet the film continues after the speech to show some of the characters have not abandoned the dream of a miracle release from the lives they lead; for example, a last scene shows Kelp's father discovering new potentials from the wonder-potion and, just before the fade-out, we see Stella with bottles of the potion in her pocket. The ending clearly suggests the inadequacy of Kelp's speech. Such an ending calls into question any notion of the film as the transmission of a single, simple message, and pinpoints rather the complex manner in which *The Nutty Professor* deals with issues of desire, morality, scientific and human commitment.

—Dana B. Polan

O SLAVNOSTI A HOSTECH. A Report on the Party and the Guests. Production: Barrandov Film Studio for Československý Film; black and white, 35mm; running time: 70 mins. Released Czechoslovakia, 1968.

Presented by Carlo Ponti; screenplay by Ester Krumbachová and Jan Němec; directed by Jan Němec; photography by Jaromír Sofr; edited by Miroslav Hájek; sound by Jiří Pavlik; art direction by Oldřich Bosák; music by Karel Mareś.

Filmed 1966 in Czechoslovakia.

Cast: Ivan Vyskočil (*Host*); Jan Klusák (*Rudolf*); Jiří Němec (*Josef*); Zdena Skvorecká (*Eva*); Pavel Bosek (*František*); Helena Pejškova (*Marta*); Karel Mareš (*Karel*); Jana Pracharová (*Wife*); Evald Schorm (*Husband*).

Publications:

Books—*Closely Watched Films* by Antonín Liehm, White Plains, New York 1974; *The Most Important Art: East European Art After 1945* by Mira Liehm and Antonín Liehm, Berkeley 1977; articles—by Calvin Green in *Film Society Review* (New York), October 1968; "Director of the Year" and "Jan Němec: Filmography" in *International Film Guide*, London 1968; article by Gordon Gow in *Films and Filming* (London), March 1969; "Allégorie et Stalinisme dans quelques films de l'est" by B. Amengual in *Positif* (Paris), January 1973.

*   *   *

O Slavnosti a hostech is the best-known and most respected of the feature films directed by Jan Němec in Czechoslovakia. The film is his second feature and was co-scripted by Ester Krumbachová, his wife at that time.

The work is a thinly veiled critique of the Communist regime and a parable on authoritative oppression and the nature of conformity. Although the movie was completed in 1966, it was not exhibited in Czechoslovakia until 1968, following a two-year struggle supported by many of the country's leading intellectuals to have it shown. Its subsequent appearance in the 1968 New York Film Festival brought Němec to world attention.

The plot begins as a group of ordinary men and women frolic in the countryside, enjoying an afternoon picnic. Suddenly several men appear from behind the trees. Despite their smiles, the men forcefully direct the group to a clearing. A leader appears and takes up a position of authority behind a small table. He sets forth the rules by which the group will be governed and their movements confined. The women comply readily; the men make attempts to protest, but in the end acquiesce as well. Tension and incipient violence hang in the air when suddenly an older man appears, apologetic for the stridency of his hirelings, particularly the leader whom he refers to as his adopted son, Rudolph. He invites the group to a birthday celebration in the forest.

Among the trees which line the lake, banquet tables have been set with elaborate dishes and candelabras. The host speaks about the small differences in shape and design which distinguish the tables, but proudly points out how all fit together into one distinguishable whole. The host is openly paternalistic and all present toast his benelovence. The harmony is interrupted when one woman discovers she is sitting at the wrong place. Her desire to move sets a chain reaction which disturbs the entire group, much to the dismay of the host. More urgent is the discovery that one of the guests has disappeared. Finding his departure intolerable, the host instructs Rudolph to bring him back. Delighted with this opportunity, Rudolph leaves with a sharp-toothed dog and is joined in the chase by the entire party. The tables are abandoned and the film closes with the sound of the barking dog.

O Slavnosti a hostech deals with the themes common to all of Němec's films, although they are the best developed here. Most prominent are the restriction on human freedom, the reactions of human beings under stress, and the ease with which man utilizes violence. In *O Slavnosti a hostech*, however, Němec goes a step further and treats the degree to which men are complicit in their own fate. Like his other works, the film possesses a surreal quality, especially in its presentation of extraordinary occurrences in a realistic manner, such as the fairy tale-like outdoor court scene and the elaborate banquet.

The film was critically praised and Němec was considered among the front ranks of the new Czech directors. His sensibility was compared to that of Franz Kafka, his compatriot, and Feodor Dostoevski.

However, following the fall of the short-lived Dubcek government which allowed for artistic freedom in Czechoslovakia, Němec was blacklisted and unable to make films after 1968. More than his other two features, *O Slavnosti a hostech* was seen as a direct attack on Eastern European Communism and was responsible for his being barred from directing.

—Patricia Erens

OBCHOD NA KORZE. The Shop on Main Street. The Shop on the High Street. Production: Barrandov Film Studio for Československý Film; black and white, 35mm; running time: 128 mins.; length: 3428 meters. Released Czechoslovakia, 1965.

Presented by Marie Desmarais and Eurofilm Ltd.; head of production: Ladislav Hanuš; associate producer: Jaromír Lukáš and Jordan Balurov; screenplay by Ladislav Grosman, Ján Kadár, and Elmar Klos; from the book *Obchod na korze* by Ladislav Grosman; English sub-titles by Lindsay Anderson; directed by Ján Kadár and Elmar Klos; photography by Vladimír Novotný; edited by Jaromir Janáček and Diana Heringová; sound by Dobroslac Srámek; art direction by Karel Skvor; music by Zdeněk Liška; costumes designed by Marie Rosenfelderová.

Filmed 1964 Barrandov Film Studio; location scenes filmed in Sabinov, Czechoslovakia. Academy Award, Best Foreign Film, 1965; New York Film Critics Award, Best Foreign Film, 1966.

Cast: Jozef Króner (*Tono Brtko*); Ida Kamińska (*Rozálie Lautmannová*); Hana Slivková (*Evelyna Brtková*); František Zvarík (*Markus Kolkocká*); Elena Zvaríkova (*Ružena Kolkocká*); Martin Hollý (*Imro Kuchar*); Martin Gregor (*Katz, the barber*); Adam Matejka (*Piti Báči*); Mikuláš Ladižinský (*Marian Peter*); Eugen Senaj (*Blau, the printer*); František Papp (*Andorić*); Gita Mišurová (*Andoričová*).

Publications:

Reviews—by Andrew Sarris in *The Village Voice* (New York), 10 March 1966; review by Flavia Wharton in *Films in Review* (New York), March 1966; books—*Modern Czechoslovak Film 1945-1965* by Jaroslav Boček, Prague 1965; *Eastern Europe: An Illustrated Guide* by Nina Hibbin, New York 1970; *Closely Watched Films* by Antonín Liehm, White Plains, New York 1974; *The Most Important Art: East European Film After 1945* by Mira Liehm and Antonín Liehm, Berkeley 1977; articles—by Peter Cowie in *Films and Filming* (London), August 1965; article in *Films and Filming* (London), June 1965; "Director" in the *New Yorker*, 12 February 1966; article by John Seelye in *Film Quarterly* (Berkeley), summer 1966; "Elmar Klos and Ján Kadár" by Jules Cohen in *Film Comment* (New York), fall and winter 1967; article by Howard Livingston in *Film Society Review* (New York), December 1967; "The New Czech Film" by Kirk Bond in *Film Comment* (New York), fall 1968; "Czechs in Exile" in *Newsweek* (New York), 27 July 1970; "The Czech Who Bounced Back" in *Films Illustrated* (London), April 1972; "En för alla..." by A.J. Liehm in *Chaplin* (Stockholm), XIV/1 (112), 1972; "Interview with Jan Kadar" by R.A. Haller in *Film Heritage* (Dayton, Ohio), spring 1973; obituaries for Kadár by G. Gervais in *Jeune Cinéma* (Paris), July/August 1979, by H. Moret in *Ecran* (Paris), 15 July 1979; obituary for Kadár in *The New York Times*, 4 June 1979.

* * *

In the mid-sixties, young, creative artists appeared on the Czech film scene with fresh film and projected a new conception of the present and the past in a new way. *The Shop on Main Street*, however, was made by Jan Kadar and Elmar Klos in the tradition of classical film, without any particular formal innovations such as complicated dramatic structure, impressive camera work, and even without any visible influence of the international trends of those days, e.g. cinema verité, the French New Wave, etc. The modernity of *The Shop on Main Street* was not based on any technical characteristics but on its content on another way of viewing the reality of the Second World War. After a series of movies about the occupation years of 1939-1945, narrating or describing this period in a linear and uniform way, opposing heroism and cowardice, *The Shop on Main Street* concentrates instead on profoundly penetrating the thoughts and feelings of people who lived at that time and experienced a fear which broke their will to resist and led them to criminal acts. It asks the question of whether a human being has the right to build his happiness and personal security on the misfortune of others, and answers that question with a story of someone who committed a crime because he did not have the strength to resist evil.

The locale of the story is a typical small town in the so-called Slovak State (established by secession of Slovakia from the Czechoslovak Republic at the beginning of the Second World War), where the citizens gradually come under the disintegrative influence of the new order organized by the government under the protection of the expanding German empire. Seemingly—at least in the beginning—this influence manifests itself in comical and provincial ways. However, behind all this funny business is a tragic reality—the Jewish residents of the town will be deported to concentration camps and face death. In this situation the moral conflict unfolds, the conflict of the main protagonist whom the viewer meets at the moment when the new society distributes power, rank and wealth. This fellow acquires a portion of the loot and although it is very negligible and almost worthless, still it signifies the first step toward a compromise which, in the end, logically leads him to crime. At the beginning of the story, he is scarcely distinguishable from his victim. Both of them—he a common little businessman, she an aging owner of a small store and a Jewess—used to accept the same moral code and honor the same rules of living together. Their collision does not take place at the intellectual level but rather in the deeper layers of life. Its roots are really misunderstanding and misinterpretation of one's own actions and also of the actions of others. The old lady does not comprehend anything taking place before her eyes, anything of what looms ahead. The carpenter Brtko does not understand the senselessness and criminality of his compromise. They both pay for it by their death.

The film is made with an unusual sensitivity toward the need to alternate bearable doses of the tragicomic, with fully tragic elements and situations. It has outstanding editing and music, and shows a fine sense for detail. The acting performances of the Slovak actor Jozef Kroner and the Polish actress Ida Kaminska mesh beautifully. The picture was honored by a number of prizes including the 1965 Academy Award for Best Foreign Language Film.

—Mrs. B. Urgošíkova

OKTIABR. October. 10 Days That Shook the World. Production: Sovkino; black and white, 35mm, silent; running time: 103 mins.; length: 2000-2200 meters, originally 3800 meters and then 2800 meters in the U.S.S.R. Released 20 January 1928. Rereleased with musical soundtrack by Chostakovitch, 1966, Paris.

Scenario by Sergei Eisenstein with Grigori Alexwithrov; from *10 Days That Shook the World* by John Reed; directed by Sergei Eisenstein with Grigori Alexwithrov; photography by Edward Tisse; production design by Vladimir Kovrighine; camera assistants: Vladimir Nilsin and Vladimir Popov.

Filmed in spring, 1927 in Leningrad.

Cast: V. Nikandrov (*Lenin*); N. Popov (*Kerensky*); Boris Lianov (*Minister Tereshchenko*); Chibisov (*Minister Kishkin*); Smelsky (*Minister Verderevsky*); N; Podvoisky (*Bolshevik Podvoisky*); Eduard Tisse (*A German*).

Publications:

Scripts—"*Octobre*" by Sergei Eisenstein in *Avant-Scène du cinéma* (Paris), October 1967; *Octobre* (original script, screenplay, Eisenstein's comments on directing the film, filmography) by Sergei Eisenstein, edited by Jacques Charrièere, Paris 1971; *Eisenstein: 3 Films* edited by Jay Leyda, translated by Diana Matias, New York 1974; review—by Mordaunt Hall in *The New York Times*, 3 November 1928; books—*Kino, A History of the Russian and Soviet Film* by Jay Leyda, New York 1942; *Eisenstein* by Paul Rotha, John Grierson, and Ivor Montagu, London 1948; *Eisenstein* by Marie Seton, London 1957; *Panorama du cinéma soviétique* by Marcel Martin, Brussels 1960; *Sergei Eisenstein—Künstler der Revolution*, Berlin 1960; *Lessons with Eisenstein* by Vladimir Nizhny, London 1962; *Sergej Michailowitsch Eisenstein*, edited by Konlecher and Kubelka, Vienna 1964; *Film Form and Film Sense* by Sergei Eisenstein, New York and Cleveland 1965; *Eisenstein* by Yon Barna, Bloomington, Indiana 1973; *Eisenstein* by Dominique Fernandez, Paris 1975; *Cinema, The Magic Vehicle: A Guide to Its Achievement: Journey One: The Cinema Through 1949* edited by Jacek Klinowski and Adam Garbicz, Metuchen, New Jersey 1975; *Octobre. Ecriture et idéologie* by Marie-Claire Ropars-Wuilleumier and others, Paris 1976; *Eisenstein: A Documentary Portrait* by Norman Swallow, New York 1977; *Montage Eisenstein* by Jacques Aumont, Paris 1979; *Eisenstein at Work* by Jay Leyda and Zina Voynow, New York 1982; articles—"Sergei Michailovitch Eisenstein" by Alfred Barr, Jr. in *The Arts* (New York), December 1928; article by Derick Grigs and Guy Cote in *Sight and Sound* (London), November/December 1951; "Quand le souffle de l'histoire passe par le baroque cinématographique" by Samuel Lachize in *Avant-Scène du cinéma* (Paris), October 1967; "Eisenstein and Pudovkin in the 20s" and "Soviet Cinema, 1930-1940" by Dwight Macdonald in *On Movies*, New York 1969; article by Raymond Durgnat in *Films and Filming* (London), March 1970; "October" by O.M. Beck and V.B. Sklovskij in *Screen* (London), winter 1971-72; "*Octobre*" by N. Simsolo in *Image et Son* (Paris), March 1972. "Storia non come memoria ma presente a realtà in atto" by G.C. Argan in *Cinema nuovo* (Turin), January/February 1972; "October" by O.M. Brik and V.B. Sklovskig in *Screen* (London), winter 1971-72; "*Octobre:* quelle histoire?!" by M. Lagny, M.C. Ropars and P. Sorlin in *Image et son* (Paris), December 1976; "La Lettre et le cinématographe" by M. Marie in *Image et son* (Paris), April 1977; "Eisenstein's *October*" by M. Sperber in *Jump Cut* (Chicago), March 1977; "Yhteistyoni Eisensteinin kanssa" by E. Meisel in *Filmihullu* (Helsinki, Finland), no. 5, 1977; "Das russische Volk filmt" by S.M. Eisenstein in *Film und Fernsehen* (Berlin), January 1978; "Eisenstein: Ideology and Intellectual Cinema" by J. Goodwin in *Quarterly Review of Film Studies* (Pleasantville, New York), spring 1978; "*Ten Days That Shook the World*" by Charles Berg in *Cinema Texas Program Notes* (Austin), 14 February 1978.

*   *   *

In 1927 Sergei Eisenstein, along with V.I. Pudovkin and Esther Shub, was commissioned to make a film to contribute to the celebration commemorating the tenth anniversary of the 1917 Revolution. Eisenstein and Eduard Tisse were called away from the production of *The General Line* to begin work on the anniversary project. The film that resulted, *Oktiabr*, was not the anticipated popular successor to *Potemkin* but instead a bold experiment in intellectual montage.

Preparation for *Oktiabr* included research into newspaper reports, news photographs, newsreels, Esther Shub's footage taken in Petrograd during the revolution, and historical memoirs. An additional source was John Reed's *Ten Days That Shook The World* (the title used for the version of *Oktiabr* prepared for release abroad). The initial scenario covered the events leading up to the 1917 Revolution through post-Civil War reconstruction. Although the scope of the film was eventually narrowed, an abundance of information remains, which according to critics both in the Soviet Union and abroad was still too extensive. Much of the power of the film is lost because the viewer is faced with not only too much detail, but also with too large a vista—too large a vision to comprehend.

Portions of the film brought criticism even before *Oktiabr* was screened. As Eisenstein explains, "the timing was accidentally unfortunate. A crisis in the Communist Party and among Government leaders coincided with the completion of a film in which both the now-divided factions were unmistakably represented on the screen." The two factions Eisenstein referred to were the government group headed by Joseph Stalin and the Opposition led by Leon Trotsky. As the date for the anniversary celebration approached, Stalin's offensive against Trotsky and the Opposition reached its peak. Eisenstein, as Yon Barna states, was "expected (by Stalin) to take account of the 'new historical facts.'" As a result, only certain select reels of *Oktiabr* were ready to be screened at the jubilee on November 7, 1927. The film was re-edited and publicly released in March of 1928. Although scenes of Opposition leaders were cut from the film, Trotsky does appear in two scenes of the final version of *Oktiabr*, but not as a significant figure.

Government leaders, critics, and the general public were anticipating another *Potemkin* from Eisenstein. *Oktiabr*, however, never approached the popular appeal of that previous work. Reaction inside Russia to the completed version of the film was mixed. *Oktiabr* was praised as being the beginning of the Soviet cinema art of the future and also criticized as being too abstract for the masses—the working class population—to comprehend, often within the same review. The elements of typage and intellectual montage, the main reasons for both the praise and the condemnation of *Oktiabr*, were first developed in *Potemkin* and are basic to Eisenstein's theory of the "montage of attractions."

Typage, a concept originating with Vsevolod Meyerhold, involves the use of persons whose physical appearance conveys the personality or spirit of a character as opposed to using trained actors. Through the use of typage, Eisenstein wanted to create visual impressions of models or representative figures so perfect that an audience could know the character at the first glimpse of him on the screen. The use of typage to represent Lenin on the screen in *Oktiabr* brought much criticism. The worker chosen to play Lenin, V. Nikandrov, resembled him physically but was criticized for an empty portrayal that did not convey the inner character of the man. Rather than a poor representation, however, this use of typage seems to be an attempt by Eisenstein to create a model character that embodies the mass rather than a single individual acting apart from the collective. (Eisenstein is more successful with this particular use of typage in *Alexander Nevsky*.) Eisenstein's contemporaries and critics since have argued that the symbolism was not comprehensible by the masses. Nevertheless, they did recognize Eisenstein's technique and purpose in the sequence in *Oktiabr*

that are developed through intellectual montage.

Intellectual montage, the use of visual images to express abstract ideas, is the core of Eisenstein's film theory. The specific idea behind intellectual montage is that the juxtaposition of two separate images can convey an idea which is not represented by either of those images when viewed separately. Such sequences in *Oktiabr*, of which there are many, brought a wider range of responses from the film's reviewers. In one sequence, Eisenstein ridicules the concept of God through a series of symbolic deities in which a Baroque Christ figure is ultimately equated with a primitive idol. The idea of the gradual debasement of the Christ figure is conveyed through the relationships between the images of the deities and not by the individual images themselves. While acknowledging the artistic and cinematic value of this sequence and others like it (Kerensky's climb up the stairs leading to the Tsar's apartment, the association of Kerensky and Napoleon), reviewers criticized the fact that these sequences could not be interpreted by the masses. *Oktiabr* was commissioned to be part of the celebration of the proletarian revolution but the proletariat could not understand the film.

—Marie Saeli

THE OLD DARK HOUSE. Production: Universal Pictures; 12 October 1932; black and white, 35mm; running time: 71 mins.; length: 6451 feet. Released October 1932.

Produced by Carl Laemmle Jr.; screenplay by Benn W. Levy, dialogue by R.C. Sherriff; from the novel *Benighted* by J.B. Priestley; directed by James Whale; photography by Arthur Edeson; edited by Clarence Kolster; art direction by Charles D. Hall; special effects by John P. Fulton; make-up by Jack P. Pierce.

Filmed in Universal studios.

Cast: Boris Karloff (*Morgan*); Charles Laughton (*Sir William Porterhouse*); Melvyn Douglas (*Roger Penderel*); Gloria Stuart (*Margaret Waverton*); Raymond Massey (*Philip Waverton*); Lillian Bond (*Gladys DuCane*); Ernest Thesiger (*Horace Femm*); Eva Moore (*Rebecca Femm*); Brember Wills (*Saul Femm*); John (Elspeth) Dudgeon (*Sir Roderick Femm*).

*   *   *

Review—"Boris Karloff, Charles Laughton and Raymond Massey in a Film of Priestley's *The Old Dark House*" by Mordaunt Hall in *The New York Times*, 28 October 1932; books—*Hollywood in the Thirties* by John Baxter, New York 1968; *Charles Laughton: A Pictorial Treasury of his Films* by William Brown, New York 1970; *Karloff: The Life of Boris Karloff* by Peter Underwood, New York 1972; *Karloff: The Man, The Monster, The Movies* by Denis Gifford, New York 1973; *The Films of Boris Karloff* by Richard Bojarski and Kenneth Beale, Secaucus, New Jersey 1974; *Journey into Darkness: The Art of James Whale's Horror Films* by Reed Ellis, New York 1980; articles—"Movie Gothick: A Tribute to James Whale" by Roy Edwards in *Sight and Sound* (London), autumn 1957; "James Whale" by Robert Fink and William Thomaier in *Films in Review* (New York), May 1962; "Charles Laughton" by Jerry Vermilye in *Films in Review* (New York), May 1963; "Boris

Karloff" by Robert Roman in *Films in Review* (New York), August/September 1969; "James Whale" by Paul Jensen in *Film Comment* (New York), spring 1971; "One Man Crazy: James Whale" by Tom Milne in *Sight and Sound* (London), summer 1973; "*Old Dark House*" by J. Pym in *Monthly Film Bulletin* (London), July 1979.

*   *   *

The Old Dark House was possibly James Whale's most personal horror feature, in that it contains elements of fear combined with a cynical humor hinted at in Whale's earlier *Frankenstein* and given full reign in *The Bride of Frankenstein*. Indeed, *The Old Dark House* is better considered as a classic black comedy than as a straight horror feature. The film also demonstrates Whale's attention to detail in creating his native Britain (in this case a very English-dominated Welsh location) on a Hollywood soundstage. The majority of the players are British; Charles Laughton even speaks with his native Yorkshire accent. Ernest Thesiger, at that time virtually unknown to American audiences, is delightfully camp as Horace Femm, with his querulous demands of "Have a potato!" and his obvious distaste for the uninvited houseguests. "We make our own electricity, but we're not very good at it," he explains pathetically as the lights go out.

Based on and faithful to a novel by J.B. Priestley, *The Old Dark House* is a highly implausible story of a group of travellers (Melvyn Douglas, Charles Laughton, Raymond Massey, Gloria Stuart, and Lillian Bond) forced by a storm to spend the night in an isolated home inhabited by Horace Femm, his sister Rebecca (who wanders around spitefully declaiming, "No beds, no beds") an insane butler (Boris Karloff), the Femm's 102-year-old father (played by stage actress Elspeth Dudgeon, and billed in the credits as John Dudgeon), and his pyromaniac son, Saul. The butler gets drunk, Saul sets fire to the house, and the travellers change romantic partners in a hectic finale.

The Old Dark House was obviously produced to take advantage of Karloff's fame as the Frankenstein monster, and here, as in *Frankenstein*, the actor remains mute, relying on eloquent and subtle pantomine. As a Karloff vehicle, *The Old Dark House* did well at the box-office, although the critics were mixed in their comments, chiefly complaining that the film was not horrific enough and that the English accents were incomprehensible to American audiences. With the passing of years, *The Old Dark House* has become less of a Karloff feature and more a perfect example of James Whale's tasteful, unobtrusive direction, at its best, here and in the upper class English drama, *One More River*, filmed two years later.

The Old Dark House disappeared from distribution when the story rights reverted back to J.B. Priestley and the film was remade as a William Castle horror thriller, starring Tom Poston and released by Columbia in 1963. Whale's friend and fellow cult director Curtis Harrington was responsible for rediscovery of the negative in 1968. As a result the film was preserved by George Eastman House and is once again delighting film buffs.

—Anthony Slide

LOS OLVIDADOS. The Young and the Damned. Production: Ultramar Films, SA for Tepeyac Studios; black and white,

35mm; running time: 88 mins.; length: 8020 feet. Released 9 November 1950, Mexico.

Produced by Oscar Dancigers; screenplay by Luis Buñuel, Luis Alcoriza, and Oscar Dancigers; directed by Luis Buñuel; photography by Gabriel Figueroa; edited by Carlos Savage; sound engineered by Jesus Gonzalez and Jose B. Carles; art direction by Edward Fitzgerald; music composed by Gustavo Pitaluga, music arranged by Rodolfo Halfter.

Filmed 6 February-9 March 1950 in Mexico. Cost: budgeted at 450,000 pesos. Cannes Film Festival, Best Director, 1951.

Cast: Estela Inda (*Marta, Pedro's mother*); Miguel Inclán (*Don Carmelo, the blind man*); Alfonso Mejia (*Pedro*); Roberto Cobo (*Jaibo*); Alma Delia Fuentes (*Meche*); Francisco Jambrina (*Farm school director*); Mario Ramírez (*Big-Eyes*); Efrain Arauz (*Pockface*); Javier Amezcua (*Julian*); Jesus Garcia Navarro (*Julian's father*); Jorge Perez ("*Pelón*"); Sergio Villareal.

Publications:

Scripts— "*Los Olvidados*" by Luis Buñuel, Luis Alcoriza, and Oscar Dancigers in *Exterminating Angel, Nazarin, and Los Olvidados: Three Films by Luis Buñuel* translated by Nicholas Fry, London 1972; "*Los Olvidados*" by Luis Buñuel and Luis Alcoriza in *Avant-Scène du cinéma* (Paris), June 1973; review— by Jacques Doniol-Valcroze in *Cahiers du cinéma* (Paris), December 1951; books—*Luis Buñuel*, edited by Michel Esteve, Paris 1962-63; *Luis Buñuel* by Ado Kyrou, Paris 1962; *Luis Buñuel: odisea del demoledor* by Eduardo Lizalde, Mexico 1962; *Luis Buñuel* by Frédéric Grange and Charles Rebolledo, Paris 1964; *Luis Buñuel: eine Dokumentation* by Alice Goetz and Helmut Banz, Verband der Deutschen Filmclubs 1965; *Luis Buñuel* by Freddy Buache, Lausanne 1970; *The Cinema of Luis Buñuel* by Freddy Buache, translated by Peter Graham, London 1973; *Buñuel (Cine e ideología)* by Manuel Alcalá, Madrid 1973; *El ojo de Buñuel* by Fernando Cesarman, Barcelona 1976; *Luis Buñuel, architecte du rêve* by M. Drouzy, Paris 1978; *Luis Buñuel* by Raymond Durgnat, Berkeley 1978; *The World of Luis Buñuel: Essays in Criticism* edited by Joan Mellen, New York 1978; *Luis Buñuel* by Virginia Higginbotham, Boston 1979; *Luis Buñuel* by Ian Cameron, Berkeley 1979; *Cinema, The Magic Vehicle: A Guide to Its Achievement: Journey Two* edited by Jacek Klinowski and Adam Garbicz, Metuchen, New Jersey 1979; articles—"Une fonction de constat: notes sur l'oeuvre de Buñuel" by Pierre Kast in *Cahiers du cinéma* (Paris), December 1951; "Luis Buñuel's *Los Olvidados*" by J. Rubia Barcia in *Quarterly of Film, Radio, and Television* (Berkeley), summer 1953; "The Films of Luis Buñuel" by Tony Richardson in *Sight and Sound* (London), January/March 1954; special Buñuel issue, *Cinemages* (New York), no.1, 1955; "The Eternal Rebellion of Luis Buñuel" by Emilio Garcia Riera in *Film Culture* (New York), no.21, 1960; "*Los Olvidados*" by R.C. Dale and "*Viridiana*" by Frederick Hoffman in *Classics of the Film*, Madison, Wisconsin 1965; "The Mexican Buñuel" by Tom Milne in *Sight and Sound* (London), winter 1965/66; "Louis Alcoriza and the Films of Luis Buñuel" by Robert Hammond in *Film Heritage* (Dayton, Ohio), fall 1965; "Luis Buñuel: Spaniard and Surrealist" by Peter Harcourt in *Film Quarterly* (Berkeley), spring 1967; "Donner a voir" by André Cornand in *Avant-Scène du cinéma* (Paris), June 1973; "*Los Olvidados*" by D. Diaz Torres in *Cine Cubano* (Havana), nos.78-80, 1973; "*Los Olvi-*

dados" by J. Lord in *Lumiere* (Melbourne, Australia), April/-May 1974; "Un Chien andalou, L'Age d'or, Las Hurdes, Los Olvidados" by R.C. Dale in *Movietone News* (Seattle), February 1975; special Buñuel issue of *Contracampo* (Madrid), October/November 1980; "Take Two: *Los Olvidados*" by J. Hoberman in *American Film* (Washington, D.C.), June 1983.

*   *   *

Los Olvidados was Luis Buñuel's favorite film, and the one with which he returned to mainstream motion picture directing after a 17-year hiatus. The film shocked many audiences for its pessimistic, unrelentingly realistic depiction of the futility in the lives of the abandoned children of Mexico City's slums. It is the first film of any reputation to present a realistic picture of what life was like in the Third World; its unequivocal soberness and its topicality not only make it the prototype of Hector Babenco's *Pixote* and Yilmaz Guney's *Yol*, but allows it to stand on its own as a viable and seering indictment of society's ills.

Buñuel ended his exiled inactivity by signing a contract with Mexican producer Oscar Dancigers in 1947. The first film for Dancigers was *Gran Casino*, "a film with songs" which proved unsuccessful; the second was the comedy, *El Gran Calavera*. The success of the latter encouraged Danciger to back Buñuel's production of *Los Olvidados*, a film which Buñuel said he had to make. The budget was a meagre 450,000 pesos.

The idea for the film came from Buñuel's exploration of Mexico City where he witnessed the "wretchedness in which many of its inhabitants lived." He researched the project in the files of a local reformatory and explained, "My film is entirely based on real cases. I tried to expose the wretched condition of the poor in real terms, because I loathe films that make the poor romantic and sweet."

Using a combination of professional and non-professional actors, Buñuel focuses his story on the bond of power and duplicity between two young Mexican boys—Jaibo (Roberto Cobo), a hardened murderer, and Pedro (Alfonso Mejia), an innocent drawn into a life of crime by the cruelty of his environment. When Pedro's father abandons him, the boy is befriended by a ruthless, miserly blind beggar. Jaibo, recently escaped from reform school robs and stones the beggar; soon after, Pedro sees Jaibo kill another youth who had informed on him. This shared experience leads to Jaibo becoming Pedro's mentor/master as the innocent boy falls into petty thievery. Imprisoned for stealing a knife, Pedro is tested by his liberal school director and sent on the outside on an errand. He encounters Jaibo who robs and kills him; Pedro in turn is shot down by the police. Buñuel ends his film with the devastating scene of Pedro's body thrown into the sewer by Jaibo's grandfather.

Buñuel's semi-documentary approach is mediated somewhat by the picturesque, studio-influenced cinematography of Gabriel Figueroa, but the penetrating, unsentimental surrealism of Buñuel is omnipresent. In the forward to the film, Buñuel states: "The task of finding a solution lies with the force of progress," and *Los Olvidados* offers no romantic answers for the social ills he records. The film is not without Buñuel's sense of symbolism, however, as evidenced by Pedro's Oedipal dream sequence and Jaibo's dying hallucinations.

Los Olvidados earned Buñuel the Best Director prize at the Cannes Film Festival and was greeted with astonishment by critics internationally. André Bazin called it "a film that lashes the mind like a red-hot iron and leaves one's conscience no opportunity for rest." Its pessimism and violence was too much for *The New York Times*'s conservative Bosley Crowther.

Released in the U.S. under the title, *The Young and the Damned*, Crowther called the film "brutal and unrelenting" and added, "Although made with meticulous realism and unquestioned fidelity to facts, its qualifications as dramatic entertainment—or even social reportage—are dim." Obviously Crowther missed the point of the film entirely, for while Buñuel wisely chose not to, soften his interpretation by providing pat answers, the abiding message here, as in much of his work, is, as his biographer, Francisco Aranda states, "By creating a society which is not criminal, we shall ourselves cease to be criminal."

—Ronald Bowers

OLYMPIA. Production: Tobis Cinema (Germany); black and white, 35mm; running time: Part I, 100 mins. and Part II, 105 mins.; length: Riefenstahl's final cut was 18,000 feet. Released 20 April 1938.

Produced by Walter Traut and Walter Grosskopf; scripted, photographed, and edited by Leni Riefenstahl; photography by Hans Ertl, Walter Frentz, Guzzi Lantschner, Kurt Neubert, Hans Scheib, Willy Zielk; music by Herbert Windt.

Filmed 20 July-4 August 1936 in Berlin at the Olympic Games. Cost: 2.2 million Reichsmarks (approximately $523,810 in 1938). Biennale Film Festival, Venice, 1st Prize, 1938; State Prize (Staatspreis) of Germany, 1938; Polar Prize, Sweden, n.d.

Publications:

Books—*Schönheit im Olypischen Kampf* by Leni Riefenstahl, Berlin 1937; *Notes on the Making of Olympia* by Leni Riefenstahl, London (?), 1958; *Interviews with Film Directors* edited by Andrew Sarris, Indianapolis, Indiana 1967; *Film in the Third Reich* by David Stewart Hull, Berkeley 1971; *Nazi Olympics* by Richard D. Mandell, 1971; *Vernon Young on Film: Unpopular Essays on a Popular Art* by Vernon Young, Chicago 1972; *Dictionary of Films* by Georges Sadoul, Berkeley 1972; *Nonfiction Film: A Critical History* by Richard Barsam, New York 1973; *Documentary: A History of Non-Fiction Film* by Erik Barnouw, New York 1974; *Film: Space, Time, Light, and Sound* by Lincoln F. Johnson, New York, 1974; *Leni Riefenstahl, the Fallen Film Goddess* by Glenn Infield, New York 1976; *Leni Riefenstahl* by Charles Ford, Paris 1978; *Leni Riefenstahl et le 3e Reich* by G.B. Infield, Paris 1978; *Leni Riefenstahl* by Renata Berg-Pan, Boston 1980; articles—"Leni Riefenstahl" by D. Gunston in *Film Quarterly* (Berkeley), fall 1960; article by Robert Gardner in *Film Comment* (New York), winter 1965; "Statement on Sarris-Gessner Quarrel about *Olympia*" in *Film Comment* (New York), fall 1967; interview with Riefenstahl on *Olympia* by Norman Swallow (for the BBC) but discussed in *Listener* (London), 19 September 1968; "Leni Riefenstahl: A Bibliography" by Richard Corliss in *Film Heritage* (Dayton, Ohio), fall 1969; "Leni Riefenstahl: Style and Structure" by J. Richards in *Silent Pictures* (London), autumn 1970; "Leni Riefenstahl: Artifice and Truth in a World Apart" by R.M. Barsam in *Film Comment* (New York), November/December 1973; "*Olympiad 1936*—Andrew Sarris and Dick Schaap Discuss Riefenstahl Film" by G. Hitchens in *Film Culture* (New York), spring 1973; "Henry Jaworsky, Cameraman for Leni Riefenstahl Interviewed" by G.

Hitchens, K. Bond and J. Hanhardt in *Film Culture* (New York), spring 1973; "The Production of the Olympia Films" by Leni Riefenstahl in *Film Culture* (New York), spring 1973; "Footnote to the History of Riefenstahl's *Olympia*" by H. Barkhausen in *Film Quarterly* (Berkeley), fall 1974; "Notes on the Making of *Olympia*" by Leni Reifenstahl in *Nonfiction Film: Theory and Criticism* edited by Richard Barsam, New York 1976; interview with Riefenstahl in the *Montreal Star*, 20 July 1976; "Berlin versus Tokyo" by D. Vaughn in *Sight and Sound* (London), autumn 1977; "Leni Riefenstahl's *Olympia*" by Parker Tyler in *The Documentary Tradition* edited by Lewis Jacobs, 2nd ed., New York 1979.

*   *   *

Few films have been praised as highly as Leni Riefenstahl's *Olympia*, the official film of the 1936 Olympics in Berlin. Riefenstahl gained permission to film the events from the International Olympic Committee, obtaining consents from all national committees and from each contestant. In her *Notes on the Making of Olympia*, which outlined the schedule she and her crew completed during the 16 days of the competition, she noted that determining the positions from which to shoot was as arduous as the actual filming. Cameras were attached to towers, balloons, placed in ditches, on air, land, and water vehicles, below and above water.

Riefenstahl decided to divide the filming into two parts, allocating specific amounts of footage to each sport. *Olympia I* entitled *Festival of the Nations*, has 13 segments; *Olympia II, Festival of Beauty*, has 11 segments. She did not follow the actual sequence of the sports events, and the numerous versions of *Olympia* vary in the number of events included. She planned the editing first, "I had the whole thing in my head...I was like an architect building a house...You must alternate tension with relaxation for both sound and picture; when one is up, then the other must be down." The secret of *Olympia*'s success, Riefenstahl asserts, is its sound, all sythetic and studio-produced, as in the simulated horses' breathing and panting of the runners. Seventy percent of the footage was not used.

The opening of *Olympia I*, filmed from the Zeppelin Hindenberg, was 15 minutes of visuals with a musical background. Carrying an ignited torch, a runner traverses landscapes of stone and shore, recalling ancient Greece. The torch is handed from runner to runner, the last arriving in the stadium to light the Olympic flame in a large cauldron. The contestants then march before Hitler, a scene which prefaces the athletic events—throwing the discus, high and long jumps, javelin throwing, pole vaulting, and relays—that peak with Jesse Owen's record-breaking performance.

Olympia II begins with scenes from the Olympic Village. Men and women exercise in an exhibition of calisthenics. Then the competitions commence: yacht racing, cross-country bicycle racing, decathlon, and pentathlon. However, just as Jesse Owen's prestigious track feat climaxed viewer excitement in *Olympia I*, the diving scenes do so in *Olympia II*. These diving scenes represent the pinnacle of Riefenstahl's cinema career. They are unsurpassed miracles of documentation requiring quick changes of camera captured, as Richard Mandell describes, "the athlete from his take-off, down the 33 feet to the water to trace his bubbling change of trajectory beneath the surface, and finally emerged with him from the pool."

Lincoln F. Johnson in *Film: Space, Time, Light and Sound*, analyzes the diving sequences. Reifenstahl begins by viewing the customary movements of the divers: the walk to the end of the board, the spring into air, the plunge into the water, climbing out of the pool. Three changes are then introduced: the cutting rate is altered, time condensed, and camera angles varied to form a rhythmical pattern. The divers are seen as suspended silhouettes soaring in space. Riefenstahl strove for liberated movement, a free-from-earth illusion, the release of beauty through motion. By omitting the splashes of divers' bodies into water, Riefenstahl presents bodies defying gravity, flying as if dancing in air. As Johnson points out, diving is the least competitive of the Olympic sports, based on beauty of form, not scores or points.

After the games and filming were done, the 1,300,000 feet (400,000 meters) of film went to the laboratory to be developed and edited. Riefenstahl alone edited *Olympia* for 18 months. Her final cut was 6,151 meters (about 18,000 feet) long.

Olympia was premiered on Hitler's birthday, April 20, 1938, and unanimously declared a masterpiece, winning a number of prizes. (Riefenstahl also compiled photographs and wrote a book commemorating the event, *Schoenheit im Olympischen*.) The question as to whether *Olympia* is Nazi propaganda elicits a varity of replies. Most likely the viewer must decide the political significance of the film as a personal matter. Robert Gardner in *Film Comment* states: "Neither *Triumph* nor *Olympia* could have been made by a propagandist pure and simple...." Richard Meran Barsam in *Nonfiction Film*, admits that "the Nazi comes through...Like all great art, it (*Olympia*) defies simple explanation." Georges Sadoul observes that *Olympia* "provides strange glimpses of the Nazi mystique and about idealization of the young male body whose implications may seem disturbing today...." Ulrich Gregor claims *Olympia* is "outspokenly fascistic in spirit. The films celebrate sport as an heroic, superhuman feat, a kind of ritual...apparent in the narration, which constantly resounds with words like 'fight' and 'conquest'...."

Norman Swallow, BBC Producer, interviewed Riefenstahl while preparing a TV program about *Olympia*. Swallow affirms that the film can "only be described as Nazi propaganda by those who are determined to find what they seek." Swallow agrees with critic Andrew Sarris's assessment of *Olympia*: "The film as a whole is distinguished from most other documentaries by the power of its unifying idea...whether you agree with its sentiments, or its ultimate implications or not it does flourish coherently as a work of art."

Riefenstahl has attended all Olympic events since 1936. At the 26th Oylmpiade in Montreal, the Canadian Jewish Congress telegrammed its protests at her presence. Interviewed in the *Montreal Star*, Riefenstahl stated that she had gone to court more than 50 times to secure a retraction from a newspaper that declared her a Nazi, and also to stop the distribution and exhibition of her films without her permission, without payment of royalties to her.

—Louise Heck-Rabi

ON THE TOWN. Production: Metro-Goldwyn-Mayer Picture Corp.; 1949; Technicolor, 35mm; running time: 98 mins. Released 1949.

Produced by Arthur Freed; screenplay by Adolph Green and Betty Comden; from the musical play by Comden and Green based on an idea by Jerome Robbins; directed by Gene Kelly and Stanley Donen; photography by Harold Rossen; edited by Ralph E. Winters; art direction by Cedric Gibbons and Jack Martin Smith; music directed by Lennie Hayton, songs by

Roger Edens, Adolph Green, and Betty Comden, additional original music by Leonard Bernstein; orchestrations by Conrad Salinger; vocal arrangements by Saul Chaplin; costumes designed by Helen Rose; choreography by Gene Kelly and Stanley Donen.

Filmed in MGM studios and some location shots in New York City. Academy Award, Music-Scoring of a Musical Picture, 1949.

Cast: Gene Kelly (*Gabey*); Frank Sinatra (*Chip*); Betty Garrett (*Brunhilde Esterhazy*); Ann Miller (*Claire Huddesen*); Jules Munshin (*Ozzie*); Vera-Ellen (*Ivy Smith*).

Publications:

Books—*The Blue Book of Hollywood Musicals* by Jack Burton, Watkins Glen, New York 1953; *The Cinema of Gene Kelly* by Richard Griffith, New York 1962; *All Talking, All Singing, All Dancing* by John Springer, New York 1966; *Gotta Sing, Gotta Dance: A Pictorial History of Film Musicals* by John Kobal, New York 1970; *The Compleat Sinatra* by Albert I. Lonstein and Vito R. Marino, Monroe, New York 1970; *Gene Kelly* by Michael Burrows, Cornwall, England 1971; *The Films of Frank Sinatra* by Gene Ringgold and Clifford McCarty, New York 1971; *Singin' in the Rain*, script, by Betty Comden and Adolph Green, New York 1972; *The MGM Years* by Lawrence B. Thomas, New Rochelle, New York 1972; *The Movie Musical* by Lee Edward Stern, New York 1974; *Gene Kelly* by Clive Hirschhorn, Chicago 1975; articles—"From Dance to Film Director" by Arthur Knight in *Dance* (New York), August 1954; "The 10th Muse in San Francisco" by Albert Johnson in *Sight and Sound* (London), summer 1956; "Making Musicals" by Arthur Freed in *Films and Filming* (London), January 1956; "Dance in the Movies" by Arthur Knight in *Dance* (New York), October 1958; "Donen at Work" by Herbert Luft in *Films in Review* (New York), February 1961; "Gene Kelly" by Rudy Behlmer in *Films in Review* (New York), January 1964; "Dancer, Actor, Director" by John Cutts in *Films and Filming* (London), August 1964 and September 1964; "Stanley Donen" by P. Lloyd in *Brighton Film Review* (London), March 1970; "*On the Town*" by Blake Lucas in *Magill's Survey of Cinema, Vol. III* edited by Frank N. Magill, Englewood Cliffs, New Jersey 1980.

*   *   *

On the Town may not be the greatest Hollywood musical ever produced; *Singin' in the Rain, The Wizard of Oz, The Band Wagon* and several others would all garner consideration with *Singin' in the Rain* probably receiving the most attention. But *On the Town*, so unconventional for its time, is separate from the rest for several very special reasons. Most significantly, the film was partically shot outdoors; it instigated the use of increased on-location shooting for films of that genre. *On the Town* is one of the few features in which the talents of two filmmakers are so happily blended; Gene Kelly and Stanley Donen, the co-directors, later went on to make *Singin' in the Rain* and *It's Always Fair Weather*. The songs and dances—modern, as well as ballet and tap—were not necessarily by and of themselves, but were related to character development and assisted in moving along the story.

On the Town was a ground-breaking property in the theater. It

was initially presented as *Fancy Free*, a modernistic ballet with music by Leonard Bernstein and choreography by James Robbins, in which a trio of sailors dance their experiences while on shore leave. From this, Betty Comden and Adolph Green fashioned a musical comedy storyline, adding a book and lyrics. The resulting Broadway musical, which opened three days after Christmas, 1944, successfully united story, song, music, comedy and dance. In this respect, it is a theatrical first.

Both Kelly and Donen made their directorial debuts with the film version, released five years later with several songs eliminated and six new ones added. Kelly pressured MGM into allowing him to film in New York, though some of the musical and dance numbers were shot on sets. Donen allegedly worked mainly with the non-dance material. Kelly, Frank Sinatra and Jules Munshin, cast as the carefree sailors who partake in various romantic escapades while on 24-hour passes, cavort outdoors on Wall Street, near Grant's Tomb and the Statue of Liberty, in Rockefeller Center, the RCA Building, Central Park and, most, memorably, while singing the praises of the city—"New York, New York, it's a wonderful town"—in the Brooklyn Navy Yard. The action never halts for an elaborate production number. Characterizations are established not only by dialogue and performance but in terms of song and dance: "Prehistoric Man," set in the Museum of Natural History and tap-danced by anthropology student Ann Miller, displays her character's aggressiveness in pursuing Manshin; in "Come Up to My Place," shy Sinatra finally succumbs to the charms of taxi driver Betty Garrett. These two women are certainly no standard, passive heroines, and are unusually liberated for their day by the manner in which they relate to, and compete with, men.

Most of those involved in the production had worked together previously in *Take Me Out to the Ball Game*. *Ball Game*'s credits include, in similar and different capacities from *On the Town*, Kelly, Sinatra, Munshin, Donen, Comden, Green, Cedric Gibbons, Roger Edens and Arthur Freed (who produced most of Kelly's musicals from *For Me and My Gal*, 1942, through *It's Always Fair Weather*, 1955, and allowed him creative freedom here.) From *Anchors Away* (also featuring Kelly and Sinatra in the navy) to *Words and Music* (in which Kelly and Vera-Ellen are superb in the "Slaughter on Tenth Avenue" dance sequence), various combinations of *On the Town*'s talent collaborated on other films. Yet, excluding *Singin' in the Rain*, none is as delightful or memorable. Without question, these two are the key musicals of their period rather than the then more highly regarded *An American in Paris*, which won the Best Picture Academy Award.

On the Town is an energetic, effervescent combination of reality and fantasy. *West Side Story, Funny Girl*, and so many other subsequent musicals owe their very existence to the creativity and vision of Gene Kelly and company.

—Rob Edelman

ON THE WATERFRONT. Production: Horizon Productions; black and white, 35mm, Cinemascope; running time: 108 mins. Released 1954, by Columbia Pictures Corp.

Produced by Sam Spiegel; screenplay by Budd Schulberg; from an original story by Budd Schulberg, suggested by a series of newspaper articles by Malcolm Johnson; directed by Elia Kazan; photography by Boris Kaufman; edited by Gene Milford; art direction by Richard Day; music score by Leonard Bernstein.

Filmed in New York and Hoboken, New Jersey. Academy Awards for Best Picture, Best Director, Best Actor (Brando), Best Supporting Actress (Saint), Best Writing-Story and Screenplay, Best Cinematography-Black and White, Best Art Direction-Black and White, and Best Editing, 1954; New York Film Critics Awards for Best Picture, Best Direction, and Best Actor (Brando); Venice Film Festival, Silver Prize, 1954.

Cast: Marlon Brando (*Terry Malloy*); Eva Maria Saint (*Edie Doyle*); Karl Malden (*Father Barry*); Lee J. Cobb (*Johnny Friendly*); Rod Steiger (*Charley Malloy*); John Hamilton (*"Pop" Doyle*); Pat Henning (*"Kayo" Dugan*); James Westerfield (*Big Mac*); Leif Erickson (*Glover*); Martin Balsam (*Gilette*); Tony Galento (*Truck*); Tami Maurriello (*Tillio*); Abe Simon (*Barney*); John Heldabrand (*Mott*); Rudy Bond (*Moose*); Thomas Handley (*Tommy*); Anne Hegira (*Mrs. Collins*); Don Blackman (*Luke*); Arthur Keegan (*Jimmy*); Barry Macollum (*J.P.*); Mike O'Dowd (*Specs*); Fred Gwynn (*Slim*); Pat Hingle (*Bartender*).

Publications:

Script—*On the Waterfront*, New York 1955; reviews—by Penelope Houston in *Sight and Sound* (London), October/December 1954; "*On the Waterfront*" by Steve Sondheim in *Films in Review* (New York), September 1954; review by A.H. Weiler in *The New York Times*, 29 July 1954; review by Lindsay Anderson in *Sight and Sound* (London), 1955; books—*Elia Kazan* by Roger Tailleur, Paris 1966, revised 1971; *The Great Films: 50 Golden Years of Motion Pictures* by Bosley Crowther, New York 1967; *Kazan on Kazan* by Michel Ciment, New York 1974; *The Great Gangster Pictures* by James R. Parish and Michael Pitts, Metuchen, New Jersey 1976; articles—series of articles entitled "Crime on the Waterfront" by Malcolm Johnson in the *New York Sun*, 8 November-10 December 1948; article by Peter Brinson in *Films and Filming* (London), October 1954; article by Edouard De Laurot in *Film Culture* (New York), summer 1955; article by Gordon Hendricks in *Film Culture* (New York), January 1955; "*On the Waterfront*: A Defense" by Robert Hughes in *Sight and Sound* (London), spring 1955; "Brooder" by Peter Brinson in *Films and Filming* (London), October 1954; "The Last Sequence of *On the Waterfront*" by Lindsay Anderson in *Sight and Sound* (London), January/March 1955; "The Brando Mutiny" by Douglas McVay in *Films and Filming* (London), December 1962; "Elia Kazan and the House Un-American Activities Committee" by Roger Tailleur in *Film Comment* (New York), fall 1966; "Method Master: Rod Steiger's Career-Part I" by John Dennis Hall in *Films and Filming* (London), December 1970, "Part II," January 1971; special Kazan issue of *Movie* (London), spring 1972; *3 Liberal Films* by J.M. Smith in *Movie* (London), winter 1971-72; series of articles on Brando by Molly Haskell in *The Village Voice* (New York), 14 June 1973 through 30 August 1973; "The Politics of Power in *On the Waterfront*" by Peter Biskind in *Film Quarterly* (Berkeley), autumn 1975; "Ammattiyhdistyslike ja elokuva" by R. Borde in *Filmihullu* (Helsinki, Finland), no. 5, 1976; "*On the Waterfront*" by Rita TheBerge in *Cinema Texas Program Notes* (Austin), 1 December 1976; special section on Kazan of *Positif* (Paris), April 1981.

*   *   *

The genesis of *On the Waterfront* is nearly as fascinating as the film itself. In April 1948, a New York dock hiring boss was murdered; it was the second killing in a short time. Reporter Malcolm Johnson was assigned by the now-defunct *New York Sun* to cover the story. Johnson's initial inquiries developed into a full investigation of waterfront crime. His findings were revealed in a series of 24 pieces, called "Crime on the Waterfront," published in the *Sun* between November 8-December 10, 1948. The exposé revealed rampant thievery, bribery, shakedowns, kickbacks, payoffs, shylocking and murder that was costing the port of New York millions of dollars in lost shipping trade. The articles earned Johnson a Pulitzer Prize.

Elia Kazan was among the most successful and influential directors on Broadway and in Hollywood at this time. Despite his considerable reputation, Kazan had fallen into disfavor with many for his cooperation with the House Un-American Activities Committee during their investigations of communist activity in the film industry. Budd Schulberg was an established author who had won esteem for his novel about motion picture business *What Makes Sammy Run?*, and his hard-hitting exposé of prizefighting, *The Harder They Fall*, as well as the best-seller *The Disenchanted*. Like Kazan, Schulberg had also flirted with communism in the thirties and voluntarily testified before HUAC in 1951.

Schulberg had already drafted a script based on Johnson's articles when Kazan approached him about doing a film on the east coast. Their collaboration resulted in a script based on the waterfront scandals but imbued with a message about the virtues of "right-thinking men in a vital democracy." Although the project was supported by the combined expertise of Kazan/Schulberg, no Hollywood studio would finance the venture; some argued that the issues were too depressing, others that filming on actual locations would be too dangerous, but ultimately the reason for rejection seemed to be the meager commercial prospects. Just as the project seemed unrealizable, independent producer Sam Spiegel, looking for a property, accepted the challenge and financed the film.

In keeping with the documentary nature of its source material, *On the Waterfront* was to be filmed on the streets and docks of Hoboken, New Jersey, where it takes place. With a singularity of purpose, the film was to expose not only the corruption of the waterfront unions but also reflect the day-to-day struggle for work and dignity among the longshoremen. Frank Sinatra was approached for the leading role of a slow-witted dockworker who, through a strange brew of conscience and vengeance, emerges from the group to break the stranglehold maintained by the corrupt union. When terms with Sinatra could not be reached, Marlon Brando, who had won Oscar nominations in two previous Kazan films, was signed. A substantial array of acting talent was recruited for supporting roles, including Lee J. Cobb, Rod Steiger, Karl Malden and Eva Marie Saint. The production cost $820,000 and made an immediate and astonishing impression on both audiences and critics when released in 1954.

The narrative centers around Terry Malloy, a former boxer turned dockworker, who becomes the unwitting pawn in the murder of a fellow longshoreman preparing to testify against gangsters who tyrannize the docks. Through the insistent priest, Father Barry, Terry is drawn into a moral dilemma. His loyalties to the racketeers, led by Johnny Friendly and Terry's brother Charlie, have been weakened by the murder. His growing affection for Edie and the persuasive tactics of Father Barry gradually draw his allegiance away from the gangsters. Terry is served with a subpoena to testify before the Waterfront Crime Commission about the Joey Doyle murder. In love with Edie, manipulated by the priest and in disfavor with the mob, Terry's conversion is completed when his own brother is brutally murdered as a warning to him. Terry testifies against Friendly and is ostracized as a "stoolie." When he confronts Friendly and his cohorts, he is brutally beaten. In a final effort of will, Terry rallies and leads the loitering longshoremen to work as an act of defiance against the racketeers.

The technique of the film is as basic and effective as the story. There are no attempts at a self-conscious aesthetics or pyrotechnics. There are no compromises in rendering the locale as anything but the urban jungle that it is. We follow the story as it takes us into the cargo holds of the ships, the slum dwelling of the workers, the shack that serves as headquarters for the union leaders, the seedy bars, the littered streets, the rooftops, the alleyways. Everything about the film is grimy and oppressive. The waterfront is presented as a harsh place where violence and betrayal have become an accepted way of life; it is a place where the strong prey upon the weak and a self-defeating code of silence prevails. We not only see and hear the sub-human malaise of the neighborhood, but we feel the suffering of the dockworkers as they mull about in a fraternal hopelessness.

At the center of *On the Waterfront* is Terry Malloy. Terry is a man in his thirties, always exploited by others; Johnny Friendly callously uses him to set up Joey Doyle just as Father Barry manipulates him against his loyalties. Terry initiates nothing of his own, yet he is redeemed through love from the limitations of his background. Left to himself, it is probable that he would remain just another likable but expendable dockworker and errand boy.

At the beginning of the film, Terry is barely articulate and painfully confused about himself and his situation. Not only is he mired in the urban jungle of greed, deceit and betrayal, but he is at loss to understand it or change himself. As he tells Edie in the tavern: "Wanta know my philosophy of life?" Yet beneath his layered exterior of toughness, Terry possesses traits that seem contradictory to his own philosophy: his fondness for pigeons, the tender way he wears Edie's glove, the rejection he feels at being excluded from the protection and confidence of his brother.

As Brando inteprets him, Terry Malloy also possesses a touch of sadness. He is a man who, at one time, had the opportunity to rise above his condition through his skill as a prizefighter. Although he could have had a personal sense of self-respect and self-worth as a contender for the title, he was prevented from it by others (including his brother). Embittered but not self-piteous, he reveals his self-awareness in a touching scene with his brother in the back seat of a cab. Although well suppressed, the seed of something better resides in him. It is Edie's love that nurtures that seed.

Reduced to its basics, *On the Waterfront* is a morality tale about how corruption *can* (indeed *must*) be fought and defeated when a man of courage and conscience emerges from the crowd to oppose the corruption. Although the narrative progresses in a linear manner without flashbacks and subplots, the power of the film is announced from the opening scene, with its assertive orchestral percussion, in which Terry is dispatched to lure Joey Doyle into a setup. In addition to dominating the Academy Awards of 1954, it garnered some additional laurels. It brought credibility to the method technique of acting taught at the Actors Studio. It certified the acting credentials of a number of talents trained for the theater. It brought acclaim and stardom to Marlon Brando, and even briefly made mumbling fashionable. It also created at least one enduring vignette ("I coulda been a contender") which has frequently been parodied.

Even though *On the Waterfront* is universally hailed as a milestone, the film's denouement still taints its reputation as a classic. Terry informs before a congressional committee on those who have exploited him and the other longshoremen. In the context of the narrative, he is elevated to heroic proportions (even though his heroism is misunderstood by others) through a

behavior that is typically classified by both the film and society as reprehensible. As a result of his informing through public testimony, Terry is considered an outcast by everyone from the police assigned to protect him to his friends who now refuse to speak to him. But after he confronts Friendly, he is the lone man of strength who wins the support of the longshoremen. In a turn-about, the act of informing is not only justified but sanitized and made admirable.

The fact that Terry moves, perhaps too conveniently, from a complex individual through the act of informing to an emblem of Christian integrity and suffering has aggravated certain viewers. Some have argued that the optimistic ending is a reversal of the film's narrative premise. In another attack, critic-filmmaker Lindsay Anderson, writing in *Sight and Sound*, considered the film's violent conclusion to be "implicitly (if unconsciouly) fascist." Others have cited the parallels to Kazan-Schulberg's own situation and objected to the ending as an unconvincing effort to vindicate their own informing to HUAC. Whatever interpretation one prefers, it is interesting to observe that in writing the novelization of his screenplay, Schulberg chose to end it not with Terry's heroic leadership but with his ignoble death (stabbed 27 times with an ice pick and then deposited in a barrel of lime left in a Jersey swamp).

None of these criticisms, however, has diminished the dramatic power of the film. Regardless of political considerations or implications, the film has found its way into the ranks of cinema classics.

—Stephen E. Bowles

ONCE UPON A TIME IN THE WEST. C'era una volta il West. Production: Rafran Cinematografica and Euro International Films; Technicolor, 35mm, Techniscope; running time: 165 mins., other versions 132 and 144 mins. Released 1968, Italy.

Produced by Bino Cicogna with Fulvio Morsella; story by Dario Argento, Bernardo Bertolucci, and Sergio Leone; screenplay by Sergio Leone and Sergio Donati; directed by Sergio Leone; photography by Tonino Delli Colli; edited by Nino Baragli; sound recorded by Claudio Maielli; art direction by Carlo Simi, set decoration by Carlo Leva; music composed and directed by Ennio Morricone; costumes designed by Carlo Simi; make-up by Alberto De Rossi.

Filmed in Arizona, Utah, and Spain.

Cast: Henry Fonda (*Frank*); Claudia Cardinale (*Jill McBain*); Jason Robards (*Cheyenne*); Charles Bronson (*The Man/Harmonica*); Frank Wolff (*Brett McBain*); Gabriele Ferzetti (*Morton*); Keenan Wynn (*Sheriff*); Paolo Stoppa (*Sam*); Marco Zuanelli (*Wobbles*); Lionel Stander (*Barman*); Jack Elam (*Knuckles*); John Frederick (*Member of Frank's gang*); Woody Strode (*Stony*); Enzio Santianello (*Timmy*); Dino Mele (*Harmonica as a boy*); Robert Hossein; Benito Stefanelli; Livio Andronico; Salvo Basile; Aldo Berti; Marilú Carteny; Luigi Ciavarro; Spartaco Conversi.

Publications:

Reviews—by David Austen in *Films and Filming* (London),

October 1969; "*C'era una volta il West*" in *Bianco e nero* (Rome), January/February 1969; review by Andrew Sarris in *The Village Voice* (New York), 6 August 1970; books—*The Fondas: The Films and the Careers of Henry, Jane, and Peter Fonda* by John Springer, New York 1970; *The Western: From Silents to the 70's* by George N. Fenin and William K. Everson, New York 1973; *The Great Western Pictures* by James Robert Parish and Michael Pitts, Metuchen, New Jersey 1976; *Sergio Leone* by Oreste de Fornari, Milan 1977; *Spaghetti Westerns: Cowboys and Europeans: From Karl May to Sergio Leone* by Christopher Frayling, London 1981; articles—"Western and Italowestern" by Klaus Badekerl in *Filmkritik* (Munich), October 1969; interview with Leone in *Cinéma 69* (Paris), November 1969; interview with Leone in *Image et son* (Paris), December 1969; "Sergio Leone" by C. Frayling in *Cinema* (London), August 1970; "Western Italiano-Western Americano" by Sandro Graziani in *Bianco e nero* (Rome), September/October 1970; "Idéologie du western italien" by Pierre Baudry in *Cahiers du cinéma* (Paris), November 1971; interview with Charles Bronson in *Cinéma 71* (Paris), January 1971; "L'anti-Western e il caso Leone" by Franco Ferrini in *Bianco e nero* (Rome), September/October 1971; "Faut-il brûler les Westerns Italiens?" by Gaston Haustrate in *Cinéma 71* (Paris), March 1971; article by Stuart Kaminsky in *Take One* (Montreal), January/February 1972; interview with Leone in *Take One* (Montreal), January/February 1972; "Something to do with Death" by Richard Jameson in *Film Comment* (New York), March/April 1973; "Pastalong Cassidy Always Wears Black" by Cynthia Grenier in *Oui* (Chicago), April 1973; "Tenkrát na západě" by Sergio Leone in *Film & Doba* (Prague), July 1973; interview with Henry Fonda in *Dialogue on Film* (Washington, D.C.), November 1973; "Notes sur les Westerns de Sergio Leone" by Nick Simsolo in *Image et son* (Paris), September 1973; "Update: Sergio Leone" by D. Jameson in *Film Comment* (New York), March/April 1974; "Ennio Morricone" by François Chevassu in *Image et son* (Paris), spring/summer 1974; "*Once Upon a Time in the West*" by B.T. Pedersen, translated by L. Ahlander in *Chaplin* (Stockholm), vol. 21, issue 3, no. 162, 1979; article in *Sight and Sound* (London), winter 1980-81.

*   *   *

Sergio Leone's *Once Upon a Time in the West*, made during the peak of Italian Western production, is regarded as the best of the "spaghetti" Westerns.

Here Leone pays tribute to classic Hollywood Westerns by means of numerous cinematic quotes from the films of John Ford, Nicholas Ray, and others: for example, the opening credit sequence parodies the three-men-waiting-for-a-train situation of *High Noon*; Brett McBain's wooden model of a railroad station and surrounding town is similar to a wooden model in *Johnny Guitar*; and the appearance of Monument Valley ("Ford country") and veteran Western actors Jack Elam, Woody Strode, and Henry Fonda recalls John Ford.

OUTW, however, is much more than an homage to Hollywood: as in his earlier Westerns, *Fistful of Dollars*, *For a Few Dollars More*, and *The Good, the Bad, and the Ugly*, Leone toys with Western conventions and creates a version of the American West that is quite different from that of Hollywood. Leone avoids the traditional Good/Bad (Hero/Villain) polarization, and replaces it with a triangular Good/Bad/Ugly conflict in which the Good (Harmonica in *OUTW*) is so labeled only because he is less evil than the Bad (Frank in *OUTW*) or the Ugly (Cheyenne in *OUTW*)—all three characters seem a bit unsavory

when compared with most Hollywood Western heroes.

The visual style that Leone developed in his earlier Westerns, a style frequently copied by other Italian Western directors, is much in evidence in *OUTW*. Leone explores spatial relationships with sweeping pans (McBain scanning the horizon), tracking shots (Frank's walk from one end of Morton's train to the other), and crane shots that suddenly reveal huge open spaces (Jill's walk from the railroad depot into the busy main street of Flagstone.) In the opening, the camera lingers interminably on a fly on one man's face, water dripping onto another man's head, and the loud knuckle-cracking of a third man to suggest the idea of three bored men waiting for a train. In the final gunfight, Leone cuts together alternating shots of Harmonica and Frank to the rhythmn of the Ennio Morricone musical score; as the confrontation progresses, the music builds and the camera moves closer and closer to the characters, until an extreme closeup of Harmonica's eyes fills the screen at the climax of the gunfight.

At the time of its release, *OUTW* was popular with European and Japanese audiences and critics, but failed in the United States. American audiences thought the film too long and too slow; other Italian Westerns had been much more action-packed. American critics generally felt that an Italian lacked the "cultural roots" necessary for dealing with American history and mythology. Recently, however, *OUTW* has generated a cult following in America, and many critics—in America and abroad—consider it to be one of the best Westerns ever made.

—Clyde Kelly Dunagen

ORDET. The Word. Production: Palladium (Copenhagen); black and white, 35mm; running time: 124 mins.; length: 3440 meters. Released 10 January 1955, Denmark.

Screenplay by Carl Theodor Dreyer; from the play by Kaj Munk; directed by Carl Theodor Dreyer; photography by Henning Bendtsen; edited by Edith Schlüssel; sound by Knud Kristensen; art direction by Erik Aaes; music by Poul Schierbeck; costumes designed by N. Sanat Jensen; dialogue expert: Svend Pousen.

Filmed in and near Veders, Denmark. Venice Film Festival, Leone d'Oro, 1955.

Cast: Henrik Malberg (*Morten Borgen*); Emil Hass Christensen (*Mikkel, his son*); Preben Lerdorff Rye (*Johannes, his son*); Cay Kristiansen (*Andre, his son*); Birgitte Federspiel (*Inger, Mikkel's wife*); Ann Elisabeth (*Maren*); Susanne (*Little Inger*); Ove Rud (*The priest*); Ejnar Federspiel (*Peter the tailor*); Sylvia Eckhausen (*Kirstine, the tailor's wife*); Gerda Nielsen (*Anne, the tailor's daughter*); Henry Skjaer (*The doctor*); Hanne Ågesen (*Karen*); Edith Thrane (*Mette Maren*); Kirsten Andreasen and the peasants and fisherman of the district of Veders.

Publications:

Scripts— *Cinque Film* by Carl Theodor Dreyer, Turin 1967; "*Ordet*" by Carl Theodor Dreyer in *Carl Theodor Dreyer: Four Screenplays* translated by Oliver Stallybrass, London 1970; reviews—"Carl Dreyer's New Film" by Mogens Fønns in *Films in Review* (New York), no.1, 1955; "*Ordet* di Carl Dreyer in

Bianco e nero (Rome), no.9-10, 1955; "*The Word*" by Ebbe Neergaard in *Sight and Sound* (London), no.4, 1955; "Une Alceste chrétienne" by Erik Rohmer in *Cahiers du cinéma* (Paris), no. 55, 1956; "*Ordet*" by Louis Seguin in *Positif* (Paris), no. 16, 1956; books—*Carl Theodor Dreyer: A Film Director's Work* by Ebbe Neergaard, London 1950; *The Art of Carl Dreyer: An Analysis* by Børge Trolle, Copenhagen 1955; *Om Filmen* by Carl Theodor Dreyer, Copenhagen 1964; *The Films of Carl Dreyer* by Eileen Bowser, New York 1964; *Portrait of Carl Th. Dreyer* by Ib Monty, Copenhagen 1965; *Carl Th. Dreyer, Danish Film Director*, edited by Soren Dyssegaard, Copenhagen 1968; *Carl Th. Dreyer* by Claude Perrin, Paris 1969; *Carl Theodor Dreyer*, Amsterdam 1970; *Carl Th. Dreyer* by Jean Sémolué, Paris 1970; *The Cinema of Carl Dreyer* by Tom Milne, New York 1971; *Dreyer in Double Reflection*, edited by Donald Skoller, New York 1973; *Dreyer*, edited by Mark Nash, London 1977; *Carl Theodor Dreyer* by Pier Giorgio Tone, Florence 1978; *The Films of Carl-Theodor Dreyer* by David Bordwell, Berkeley 1981; articles—special issue of *Écran français* (Paris), 11 November 1947; "*Ordet* og billederne" by Jan Wahl in *Kosmorama* (Copenhagen), no.3, 1954; "The World of Carl Dreyer" by Børge Trolle in *Sight and Sound* (London), winter 1955/56; "Mankind on the Border" by Harry Schein in *Quarterly of Film, Radio, and Television* (Berkeley), spring 1956; "Carl Dreyer—A Master of His Craft" by Herbert Luft in *Quarterly of Film, Radio, and Television* (Berkeley), winter 1956; "*Ordet*" by Jonas Mekas in *Film Culture* (New York), no.1, 1958; "*Ordet*, la critica e Kierkegaard" by Armando Montanari in *Cinema nuovo* (Turin), no.134, 1958; "*Ordet*" by Edoardo Bruno in *Filmcritica* (Rome), no.88, 1959; "Dreyer" by Herbert Luft in *Films and Filming* (London), June 1961; "The World of Carl Dreyer" by Kirk Bond in *Film Quarterly* (Berkeley), fall 1965; issue on Dreyer, *Cahiers du cinéma* (Paris), December 1968; special issue of *Kosmorama* (Copenhagen), June 1968; "Metaphysic of *Ordet*" in *The Film Culture Reader*, edited by P. Adams Sitney, New York 1970; "Carl Dreyer and the Theme of Choice" by Dai Vaughan in *Sight and Sound* (London), summer 1974; "Dreyer's Concept of Abstraction" by Vlada Petric in *Sight and Sound* (London), spring 1975.

*   *   *

Carl Dreyer wanted to make a film based on the play *Ordet*, written in 1925 by the pastor-poet Kaj Munk, immediately after he saw it in a Copenhagen theatre in 1932. However, it wasn't until 23 years later, and after he saw the 1943 Swedish *Ordet* by Gustaf Molander, that Dreyer attempted his film.

The drama is about a young woman who dies in childbirth, but is brought back to life by an act of faith. The story is set among peasants in the rough Western Jutland. Dreyer cut the dialogue to half of the original, and otherwise cleansed Munk's drama, which had been written in a more realistic tradition. In the film, as well as in the play, the dramatic nucleus is in the contrasts: there is a strong division between the men's and the women's world; and between the bright optimistic Christianity of the family Borgen and the dark pessimistic fanaticism of the village tailor. Contrasts are also reflected in the stern authority of the old peasant as opposed to the rebellion of his sons: the youngest wants to marry the tailor's daughter; the second son is not able to share the faith of his father and his wife, and the third son has crossed the border into madness after having read Soren Kierkegaard as a student of theology.

The crucial scene of the film is the miracle, the awakening of the dead, and ever since the film's initial release, this has been the major point of contention. Dreyer is deliberately vague. From a rationalistic point of view the miracle could be explained as a psychic phenomenon. It is obvious that Dreyer does not want the miracle to be a proof of God's existence, rather it should be interpreted as a sign. In earlier films, such as *Vampyr*, Dreyer has shown a fascination for the unreal or the fantastic, and a main theme of many of his films is the ambiguous border between the real and the unreal, the physical world and the spiritual world. But it is possible to call *Ordet* a Christian film, even a religious one, and it has often been interpreted as such. The miracle is worked out by the lunatic and the child. It is through the smile of the innocent child that the miracle is revealed to us, and this short scene is one of the most beautiful Dreyer has ever created. The young woman who literally conquers death and returns to life represents another of Dreyer's triumphant women.

Dreyer aimed for simplification in *Ordet*. The quiet acting, the simple sets, the floating close-ups, the long uncut sequences (up to 8 minutes), the calm pans and travelling shots, and the deliberate slow rhythm of the film are means of establishing the milieu and its people in the most convincing way. At the same time it represents Dreyer's protest against the hectic speed of modern life and modern films.

Ordet was an immediate success, and Dreyer's greatest. Although the film was met with accusations of formality and questioned by theologians, the audience was fascinated by it, particularly in France and Italy.

—Ib Monty

_____

ORFEU NEGRO. Black Orpheus. Production: Dispatfilm (Paris), Gemma Cinematografica (Rome), and Tupan; Eastmancolor, 35mm, Cinemascope; running time: 103 mins., some sources list 106 mins. Released 1958.

Produced by Sacha Gordine; screenplay by Vinicius de Moraes, adapted by Jacques Viot and Marcel Camus; from the play *Orfeu da Conceição* by Vinicius de Moraes; directed by Marcel Camus; photography by Jean Bourgoin; sound by Lenhart; music by Luis Bonfa and Antonio Carlos Jobim.

Filmed in Rio de Janeiro during Carnival in both 1957 and 1958, footage with actors shot September-December 1958. Cannes Film Festival, Palme d'or, 1959; Academy Award, Best Foreign Film, 1959.

Cast: Brenno Melio (*Orphée*); Marapessa Dawn (*Eurydice*); Ademar da Silva (*Death*); Lourdes de Oliveria (*Mira*); Lee Garcia (*Serafina*).

Publications:

Books—*Orfeu da Conceição* by Vinicius da Moraes, Rio de Janeiro, 1960; *French Film* by Roy Armes, New York 1970; *Dictionary of Films* by Georges Sadoul, Berkeley 1972; *The Oxford Companion to Film* edited by Liz-Ann Bawden, New York 1976; *Halliwell's Film Guide* by Leslie Halliwell, New York 1983; articles—"New Wave at Cannes" by C. Grenier in *Reporter*, 23 July 1959; "Notes on a New Generation" by Georges Sadoul in *Sight and Sound* (London), summer/autumn 1959; "An Escapist Realism" by Eugen Weber in *Film Quarterly*

(Berkeley), winter 1959; "New Wave: Orpheus in Rio" by Hollis Alpert in the *Saturday Review* (New York), 19 December 1959; "Orpheus Distending" in *Time* (New York), 19 September 1960; "Comment Camus a tourne: *Orfeu Negro*" by Claude-Marie Tremois in *Les Nouveaux Films français* (Paris), no.474, 1960.

*   *   *

By transplanting the myth of Orpheus and Eurydice to the boisterous, colorful atmosphere of Brazil's Carnaval, Marcel Camus rejuvenates it and infuses its universal themes with a vibrant particularity born of its interweavings with Vodoun and other Brazilian traditions.

Film anthologies routinely report that *Orfeu Negro* is based on *Orfeu da Conceiçnao*, a play written two years earlier by the Brazilian Vinicius de Moraes. Actually there is only a slight correspondence between the two; the play follows the original myth far more closely. Although Camus borrows two principal elements from the play—Mira as the other love interest and an avenging Maenad, and a black woman as the voice of Eurídice after death—he translates these elements as freely as those borrowed from the original myth, other Greek legends, and Brazilian customs.

The principal motif in the film is that of Orfeu as a sun god, and the film itself as a modern solar myth. In an opening scene, a boy flies a kite that looks like a sun, shouting to Serafina to "look at the sun!" Umbrellas (necessary only when there is no sun) are hung rapidly, one by one, by Orfeu's guitar in a pawnshop. Orfeu tells the boy, Benedetto, that he makes the sun rise, which is the principal task of a solar god; the morning after Orfeu first sleeps with Eurídice, Benedetto and a friend leave Orfeu's guitar by the door so that he'll remember to make the sun rise; the boys themselves make it rise the next day when Orfeu dies before daybreak. Orfeu's songs reflect solar themes: "Morning when the run rises...come and place tenderly your pearls of dew on nature in bloom," as well as "Happiness lasts a day," a day being the birth-death-rebirth cycle of a sun god. At the rehearsal for the upcoming dance, Benedetto tells Eurídice that Orfeu is the sun god and his fiancée Mira is the Queen of the Day: "Look, the sun will kiss the day." Orfeu's costume for Carnaval is that of a golden warrior with a gold foil sun as his shield. Finally, at Carnaval a number of dancers carry sun-like wands. Other motifs—Eurídice's scarf of the constellations ("houses of Heaven") and the float of the stars, moon, and the planets that passes Orfeu after Eurídice's death—reinforce the astral themes.

The film also relates more specifically to the Orphic myth. Though he plays a more modern stringed instrument, Orfeu, like Orpheus before him, is a musician. When he discovers the name of his new-found goddess—Eurídice—he tells her, "I have loved you a thousand years." Eurídice flees from Death just as Eurydice fled from Aristaeus, a shepherd intent on seducing her. While fleeing, she is electrocuted by a live wire she has seized in panic, just as Eurydice was poisoned by a viper she trod upon in her haste. After Eurídice's death, Orfeu descends to the underworld as did Orpheus. Indeed, the overhead shot of him descending a long, dark spiralling staircase, flowing red at its base, is one of the eeriest moments in the film (the final encounter with Death being the other). A dog named Cereberus guards the gate of a house where a *Vodoun* ceremony is being held, Orfeu's destination. Just as Orpheus had to sing to animate the shades of the underworld, so does Orfeu's guide urge him, once they are inside: "Call her. She'll come. Call her, Orfeu...Sing to her." (It is here, incidentally, that Greek myth and Brazilian religion neatly coincide; in *Vodoun* the appropriate gods are expected to appear when devotees summon them by songs in their honor.) As in the original myth, Orfeu is warned not to look behind him when he is retrieving Eurídice. But when he hears her voice—"Do not turn around, Orfeu. You'll lose me forever"—he is desperate to see her and, in turning, loses her as did Orpheus before him. Finally, he is killed by a vengeful and jealous woman, just as Orpheus was killed by the Maenads.

Other elements from Greek mythology are liberally employed. The principal characters live on an Olympian mountain. A blind balloon man/guide appears at the beginning of the film to give Eurídice directions: "I know the way without sight." Hermes, who functions, appropriately, as a messenger tells Eurídice the way to Serafina's and offers her sanctuary when she is threatened. He then goes to find Orfeu, tells Orfeu of Eurídice's death, and finally discovers Orfeu collapsed on the street, giving him the necessary papers to claim Eurídice's body.

It is to Camus's credit that the incorporation of all these mythic elements is rarely heavy-handed. (Only the intermittent appearance of Death seems strained, perhaps because it has no Brazilian context.) This is largely due to his lively, detailed depiction of local custom—the opening scenes of women carrying cans on their heads and shopping, the commotion of the pawnshop, the rustic huts of Orfeu and Serafina, the wild and colorful dancing and music of Carnaval, and the scenes of Brazilian bureaucracy. The spontaneity is enhanced by Camus's use of native Brazilian actors, many not professionals.

The vivid cinematography of Jean Bourgoin also helps to enliven the mythic themes. The day/night dichotomy is handled brilliantly—spectacular technicolor sunrises and glorious panoramas of Rio in the daylight contrast with the dimly-lit scenes of night, particularly in the encounters with Death which heighten the sense of impending doom. The scene at the tram depot is particularly frightening: we see Death, large and ominous in the foregound. Eurídice runs through the dark, and we hear more clearly than we see what is happening—Eurídice's screams of "No!" and "Orfeu!," the creepy hum of electricity, the stacatto sound of Eurídice's high heels in flight. Such darkness is appropriate to night and it is only when Orfeu tries to turn night into day, by throwing the electric switch, that Eurídice dies.

Orfeu Negro is an effective translation of an ancient Greek myth to a modern Brazilian love story. The film was an instant commercial success worldwide and won the Palme d'or at Cannes.

—Catherine Henry

ORPHEE. Orpheus. Production: Palais-Royal Films; black and white, 35mm; running time: 112 mins. Released 1950.

Produced by André Paulvé; screenplay by Jean Cocteau; from Cocteau's play; directed by Jean Cocteau; photography by Nicolas Hayer; sound by Calvet; production design by Jean d'Eaubonne, models by Christian Bérard; music by Georges Auric; costumes designed by Marcel Escoffier.

Filmed in the ruins of the Ecole de Saint-Cyr.

Cast: Jean Marais (*Orphée*); Maria Casarès (*The Princess*); Marie Déa (*Eurydice*); François Périer (*Heurtebise*); Juliette Gréco (*Aglaonice*); Edouard Dermit (*Cégeste*); Henri Crémieux (*Editor*); Pierre Bertin (*Police commissioner*); Roger Blin (*Poet*); Jacques Varennes, André Carnège, René Worms (*Judges*);

Renée Cosima (*A bacchant*); René Lacour (*The factor*); Maffre (*An agent*); Jean-Pierre Melville (*Hotel director*); Claude Mauriac, Jean-Pierre Mocky, Jacques Doniol-Valcroze, Claude Borelli, Philippe Bordier, Victor Tabournol, and the voice of Jean Cocteau.

Publications:

Scripts—*Orphée* by Jean Cocteau, Paris 1961; *Jean Cocteau: 3 Screenplays*, New York 1972; books—*Jean Cocteau* by Margaret Crosland, London 1955; *Cocteau* by Jean-Jacques Kihm, Paris 1960; *Cocteau* by André Fraigneau, New York 1961; *The Journals of Jean Cocteau* edited and translated by Wallace Fowlie, Bloomington, Indiana 1964; *Jean Cocteau: The History of a Poet's Age* by Wallace Fowlie, Bloomington, Indiana 1968; *Jean Cocteau: The Man and the Mirror* by Elizabeth Sprigge and Jean-Jacques Kihm, New York 1968; *Jean Cocteau* by Roger Lannes, Paris 1968; *Cocteau* by René Gilson, translated by Ciba Vaughn, New York 1969; *French Cinema Since 1946: Vol.1—The Great Tradition* by Roy Armes, New York 1970; *Professional Secrets: An Autobiography of Jean Cocteau* edited by Robert Phelps and translated by Richard Howard, New York 1970; *Cocteau* by Francis Steegmuller, Boston 1970; *Jean Cocteau and His Films of Orphic Identity* by Arthur Evans, Philadelphia 1977; articles—"Interview with Cocteau" by Francis Koval in *Sight and Sound* (London), August 1950; "Cocteau and Orpheus" by Gavin Lambert in *Sequence* (London), autumn 1950; "Cocteau's *Orpheus* Analyzed" by Jean R. Debrix, translated by Edith Morgan in *Films in Review* (New York), June/July 1951; "Cocteau" by Jean Cocteau in *Film* (London), March 1951; "People of Talent (1): Maria Casarès" in *Sight and Sound* (London), spring 1955; "*Orphée*" by Raymond Durgnat in *Films and Filming* (London), October 1963; "Cocteau's *Orphée*: From Myth to Drama to Film" by Chester Clayton Long in *Quarterly Journal of Speech*, October 1965; "The Mysteries of Cocteau's *Orpheus*" by R. M. Hammond in *Cinema Journal* (Iowa City), spring 1972; "Jean Cocteau et le cinéma", special issue by C. Gauteur, of *Image et son* (Paris), June/July 1972; "Rétrospective. Jean Cocteau. Un cinéaste? Peut-être. Un autear? Certainement." by T. Renaud in *Cinéma* (Paris), December 1973; issue on Cocteau of *Avant-Scène du cinéma* (Paris), July/September 1973.

*   *   *

No discussion of modern European cinema can be complete without the inclusion of Jean Cocteau's *Orphée*. It is not only the capstone of Cocteau's artistic career but also a foremost example of poetry on film which influenced an entire generation of young filmmakers. The film represents the artistic zenith of Cocteau's lifelong pre-occupation with the myth of Orpheus. In the words of Pauline Kael, "It was with *Orpheus* that Cocteau orchestrated the themes of the dreams and ecstasies of the poet and his obsession with the unknown."

Orphée is Cocteau's most philosophically complete film and the second in his trilogy of *films à clef* dealing with the "orphic identity." The first was the milestone *Le Sang d'un poete*, an enigmatic and surreal work of art which André Bazin described as a "documentary of the imagination." Cocteau completed his trilogy in 1960 with *Le Testamanet d'Orphée*, a personalized coda to his poetic quest in which Cocteau himself played the poet.

To Cocteau "poet" meant the creative artist, and the Opheus of Greek mythology—the god of the lyre, song, and poetry—was Cocteau's personal muse. For Cocteau the plight of the poet was an unending search for truth and immortality, a life of suffering and martyrdom during which the poet must experience many deaths. In his introduction to *Orphée*, Cocteau wrote: "The poet must die several times in order to be reborn. Twenty years ago I developed this theme in *The Blood of a Poet*. But there I played it with one finger, in *Orpheus* I have orchestrated it."

The film, derived from Cocteau's 1925 play *Orphée*, revolves around the Poet Orpheus, the conflict with his wife Eurydice, and his struggle with the unknown world of "inspiration" personified by the Princesses. Like the mythical Opheus's journey to Hades, Cocteau's Orphée must journey to the unknown—herein called the "zone"; which Cocteau, rather than building an artificial set, filmed in the bombed-out military academy of Saint-Cyr.

Cocteau's modernization of this fable is delineated much like a whodunit; Cocteau himself described it as "a detective story, bathed on one side in myth, and on the other is the supernatural." To evoke the supernatural Cocteau employed a number of cinematic tricks reminiscent of Méliès, most notably the vat of mercury to depict his mirror. He was, however, no mere filmic prestidigitator. These devices were simply the technical means by which he transcended the ordinary boundaries of the narrative film to create a "cinematograph" (a term he invented) detailing the "frontier incidents between one world and another."

Orphée was greeted with indifference and ambivalence by many critics who thought Cocteau a dilettante and a visual trickster, though perhaps their animosity derived from their own homophobia. The film, however, did receive the International Critics Award at the Venice Film Festival, and through the years has achieved the deserved status of masterpiece.

—Ronald Bowers

————

OSSESSIONE. Les Amants diaboliques. Production: Industrie Cinematografiche Italiane S.A.; black and white, 35mm; running time: 135 mins. originally, other versions are 110 mins. Released 1942.

Screenplay by Antonio Pietrangeli, Luchino Visconti, Mario Alicata, Giuseppe De Santis, and Gianni Puccini; from the novel *The Postman Always Rings Twice* by James M. Cain; directed by Luchino Visconti; photography by Aldo Tonti and Domenico Scala; edited by M. Serandrei; art direction by Gino Franzi,- and Ferrare and Ancône; music by Giuseppe Rosati, directed by Maestro Fernando Previtali; costumes designed by Maria De Matteis.

Cast: Dhia Cristiani (*Anita, the dancer*); Elio Marcuzzo (*The Spaniard*); Vittorio Duse (*Truck driver*); Clara Calamai (*Giovanna*); Massimo Girotti (*Gino*); J. de Landa (*Giovanna's husband*); M. Sakara; Michele Riccardini.

Publications:

Script—*Ossessione* by Luchino Visconti, Mario Alicata, Giuseppe De Santis, and Gianni Puccini, Bologna 1977; books—*Cinema Italiano* by Mario Gromo, Milan 1954; *Luchino Visconti* by Lorenzo Pellizzari, Milan 1960; *I film di Luchino*

Visconti by Pio Baldelli, Manduria, Italy 1965; *Visconti* by Yves Guillaume, Paris 1966; *Luchino Visconti* by Geoffrey Nowell-Smith, New York 1968; *Visconti* by Giuseppe Ferrara, translated by Jean-Pierre Pinaud, Paris, 2nd ed. 1970; *Luchino Visconti* by Pio Baldelli, Milan 1973; *Cinema, the Magic Vehicle: A Guide to Its Achievement: Journey One: The Cinema Through 1949* edited by Jacek Klinowski and Adam Garbicz, Metuchen, New Jersey 1975; *Visconti: il cinema*, edited by Adelio Ferrero, Modena, Italy 1977; *A Screen of Time: A Study of Luchino Visconti* by Monica Stirling, New York 1979; *Luchino Visconti* by Gaia Servadio, New York 1983; articles—"Luchino Visconti" by Giulio Cesare Castello in *Sight and Sound* (London), spring 1956; "Luchino Visconti and the Italian Cinema" by Gianfranco Poggi in *Film Quarterly* (Berkeley), spring 1960; issue on Visconti of *Premier Plan* (Paris), May 1961; issue on Visconti of *Etudes cinématographique* (Paris), no.26-27, 1963; issue on Visconti of *Cinema* (Rome), April 1970; "Authorized Cain: *Postman* Done by French, Pirated by Visconti's *Ossessione*" by T.T. Foose in *Variety* (New York), 10 November 1976; "Luchino Visconti, 1906-1976" by J. Cabourg in *Avant-Scène du cinéma* (Paris), 1 and 15 March 1977; "Visconti années quarante" by J. Fieschi in *Cinématographe* (Paris), December 1978; "Luchino Visconti, 1906-1976" by Jean Cabourg in *Anthologie du cinéma, Vol. X*, Paris 1979; "Visconti's Magnificent Obsessions" by D. Lyons in *Film Comment* (New York), March/April 1979; "Huit coups de sonnette" by J. Fieschi and others in *Cinématographe* (Paris), September 1981; "Den fatala âgterkomsten" by C.J. Malmberg in *Chaplin* (Stockholm), no.4 (175), 1981.

*   *   *

A majority of critics and theoreticians locate the first, significant instance of the neorealist aesthetic in *Ossessione*, Luchino Visconti's first directorial effort. (The term "neorealism" appeared initially in 1942, the same year as the film, in Umberto Barbaro's article on French pre-war cinema.) Whether or not we choose to view *Ossessione* as elementally neorealist, it does succeed in demonstrating many of the appropriate traits of that mode.

That the film is a version of James M. Cain's thriller *The Postman Always Rings Twice* is less surprising when we realize the impact that the gritty toughness and brutal edge of Cain's prose and narrative, as well as that of the hardboiled school in general, had in Italy at that time. The idea to adapt the work probably came from Jean Renoir (whose *La Bete humaine* is fraught with similarities), during the period that Visconti acted as his assistant. A legend, disputed by Geoffrey Nowell-Smith in *Visconti*, has grown up around the film to the effect that the director chose to subvert Fascist censorship and criticize the regime; however, it is believed that when Mussolini's son walked out on a preview screening, exclaiming that this was not Italy, the film was abruptly withdrawn from distribution and went unseen until the peak of neorealist interest after the war.

As would become his general practice in adapting the work of others, Visconti changes dramatic motivations and much of the story itself. He "Italianized" the novel's setting and characters so that the film is unique to its historical moment. *Ossessione* amalgamates operatic melodrama and realism as in later films (*Senso*, *Il gattopardo*, *La Caduta degli dei*) except here it is the naturalistic, verist potential that is stressed in the mise-en-scène, not the theatrical. Instead of indulging in the palpable, material sensuality of the later works, the director does not shirk the squalid prosaicism associated with neorealism at its most ingenuous and idealized. A monocrome countryside, devoid of pictorial charge, emphasizes the dismal life of provincials. Even the

sexual attraction of Gino and Giovanna, relatively unmediated by the kind of clever banter found in Wilder's *Double Indemnity* (another Cain piece with a comparable story made that year), reveals itself as a human fact, another aspect setting the film apart from the coldly sophisticated sensuality of the Fascist era films. This irrational but human passion, alluded to in the title, plays an active role in transforming these unhappy economically marginal people into murderers, and will eventually destroy them.

Characters are drawn with a deft exactitude falling just this side of sterotype or exaggeration. Giovanna has traded the uncertain and demeaning life of a casual prostitute ("I used to get men to invite me to supper") for the vapid existence of a defeated slave. She sits in her depressing kitchen, hopelessly embattled by the boredom and servitude of a loveless marriage. On his part, Bragana adds to the claustrophobia of the relationship with his repulsive corpulence and spiteful personality. Behind him—and due in part to his association with the local priest, somewhat sinister-looking, almost Buñuelian, with his hunting rifle—we sense a whole class of greasy Braganas only too willing to impose sexual hegemony and the will of the bourgeoisie. Social signification surfaced through exacting psychological determinations and the resultant interpersonal conflict is at the root of Visconti's "anthropomorphic cinema," an idea laid out around the time of this film.

Metonymic signifiers of the desires of the pair pepper the narrative in an almost Antonionian fashion: while they are making love, a wardrobe door swings open to reveal Bragana's good clothing; Bragana rushes out to shoot a troublesome cat, and as the shot rings out, we read on the lovers' faces the fear of discovering within themselves the power to do away with him in the same brutal manner.

—Joel Kanoff

OSTRE SLEDOVANÉ VLAKY. Closely Watched Trains. A Difficult Love. Production: Smída-Fikar group for the Barrandov Film Studio; black and white, 35mm; running time: 92 mins., English version is 89 mins.; length: 2509 meters. Released 1966, Czechoslovakia.

Presented by Carlo Ponti, produced by Zdeněk Oves; screenplay by Jiří Menzel and Bohumil Hrabal; from the novel *Ostre sledované vlaky* by Bohumil Hrabal; English sub-titles by M. A. Gebert; directed by Jiří Menzel; photography by Jaromír Sofr; edited by Jiřina Lukešová; sound by Jiří Pavlík; art direction by Oldřich Bosák, sets by Jiří Cvrček; music by Jiří Sust, music conducted by Stěpán Koníček, music of the Czech army conducted by Eduard Kudelašek; costume production by Ružena Bulicková; advisers: J. Simák and Colonel Golyšev.

Filmed 1965 in the Loděnice train station. Grand Priz, International Film Week at Mannheim, 1966; Academy Award, Best Foreign-Language Film, 1967; Grand Prix, International Film Festival at Addis Ababa, 1967.

Cast: Václav Neckář (*Trainee Miloš Hrma*); Jitka Bendová (*Conductor Maša*); Vladimír Valenta (*Stationmaster*); Libuše Havelková (*Stationmaster's wife*); Josef Somr (*Train Dispatcher Hubĺcka*); Alois Vachek (*Station assistant*); Jitka Zelenohorská (*Telegraphist*); Vlastimil Brodský (*Councilor Zedníček*); Ferdinand Kruta (*Uncle Noneman*); Květa Fialová (*The Countess*); Naďa Urbánková (*Victoria Freie*); Jiří Menzel (*Dr. Brabec*).

Publications:

Script—*Closely Watched Trains: A Film by Jiri Menzel and Bohumil Hrabal* translated by Josef Holzbecher, New York 1971; reviews—in *Films and Filming* (London), July 1968; reviews by Joseph Morgenstern and John Simon in *Film 67-68* edited by Richard Schickel and John Simon, New York 1968; books—*Closely Watched Films* by Antonín Liehm, White Plains, New York 1974; *The Most Important Art: East European Film After 1945* by Mira Liehm and Antonín Liehm, Berkeley 1977; articles—"Movers" by Andrew Sarris in the *Saturday Review* (New York), 23 December 1967; "The Man Who Made *Closely Watched Trains*" by I. Kolodny in *Action* (Los Angeles), May/June 1968; "A Promised Land..." by Alan Levy in the *New York Times Magazine*, 9 February 1969; "Jiri Menzel" by John Zalman in *Closely Watched Trains: A Film by Jiri Menzel and Bohumil Hrabal* translated by Josef Holzbecher, New York 1971; "A Track All Its Own" by John Simon in *Closely Watched Trains: A Film By Jiri Menzel and Bohumil Hrabal* translated by Josef Holzbecher, New York 1971.

*   *   *

In 1963, Bohumil Hrabal, almost fifty years old, made his first contribution to Czech literature with a collection of short stories entitled *Perličky na dně* (Pearls of the Deep). These diminutive prose pieces, remarkable for concentrating on the destinies of little people on the edges of society, the original manner of narration, and a masterly use of most varied niceties and refinements of the Czech language, immediately gained popularity with both readers and critics. The stories also captivated film people. In 1965, a group of emerging directors shot a film based on *Perličky*. One of these was Jiří Menzel who was charmed by the world of Hrabal's characters to such an extent that he has returned to it throughout his creative career. In 1966 he completed *Closely Watched Trains* from Hrabal's book of the same year. In 1980, he made *Postřižiny* and soon worked on another picture inspired by Hrabal's work, *Slavnosti sněženek* ("The Feast of the Snowdrops").

The adaptation of Hrabal's prose, based on an uninterrupted flow of speech, monologues in which the word has an enormous significance, is not a simple matter. *Closely Watched Trains* flows in several layers: ridiculous aspects of life are permeated by cruelty, tragedy, and pathos as well as tenderness; time is treated freely, the reader being led, without obvious transitions, into various depths of the past. Menzel succeeded in transposing this multi-layered story into an art with a visual foundation. He retained almost all the conflicts of the narrative but he translated the story into a linear time sequence, arranging the succession of events according to his own needs, and gave up a multitude of *hrabalesque* details which had literally begged to be expressed. He did not allow himself to be seduced by Hrabal's magical vocabulary and he consistently pursued a visual mode of expression.

Together with Hrabal, he leads the reader to a small railroad station at a time near the end of the Second World War. Life seems to flow without great excitement. The entire story is derived from the idea that human grief, fear, and joy has its place in times of profound peace as well as in the years of a cruel war. The story of a young clerk Miloš who has problems with his love life, as well as the petty destinies of the other characters who live and work at the railroad station, are therefore linked very factually and soberly with the overwhelming events of the Second War. Menzel reminds us of the war, at the beginning, by a view of military trains, but soon it seems as if it did not exist. However, he progressively develops this theme, first in the ridiculous form in a sequence where a supervisor explains to his employees how cunningly the German army victoriously retreats, then more and more intensively through Miloš's experience of a bombardment and the dead people in the train. Together with the increasingly frequent and terrifying reminders of war, there unfolds Miloš's erotic suffering which culminates in his liberation in love but also in his death. The film unfolds at a slow pace which accelerates only at the conclusion by the paralleling and alternating the investigation of dispatcher Hubiček's "immoral" act and Miloš dispassionate acts of sabotage. The comical, obscene, and tragical alternate to create a peculiar mixture of pathos and tragicomedy which represents a new concept in Czech film. Jaromír Sofr's camera work is understated; it stresses the lyric in contrast to *hrabalesque* naturalism. The film director himself expressed accurately the poetry of his film: "Film is too imperfect to be capable of recording everything that takes place in our fantasy when we read Hrabal's texts... It is necessary to compensate for the poetry of these imaginings. In my opinion, poetry of this movie is not the absurd situations themselves but in their juxtaposition, the confrontation of obscenity and tragedy."

In the sixties, this picture was one of the most successful Czech films, both at home and abroad. This is demonstrated by many honors at both domestic and international festivals. It still remains in the repertory of Czech movie theaters and still has not lost its audience.

—Mrs. B. Urgošíkova

EL OTRO FRANCISCO. The Other Francisco. Production: Instituto Cubano del Arte e Industria Cinematográficos (ICAIC); black and white, 35mm; running time: 100 mins. Released 1975.

Screenplay by Sergio Giral; from the novel *Francisco* by Anselmo Suárez y Romero written in 1838-9; directed by Sergio Giral, *Variety* lists the director as Santiago Liapur; photography by Livio Delgado; edited by Nelson Rodriguez; music by Leo Brouwer.

Filmed in Cuba.

Cast: Miguel Benavides (*Francisco*); Ramon Veloz (*Ricardo*); Alina Sanchez (*Dorotea*); Margarita Balboa; Adolfo Llaurado.

Publications:

Review—"*El otro Francisco*" by H. Werb in *Variety* (New York), 6 August 1975; articles—"Les Films" by R. Grelier in *Image et son* (Paris), March 1977; "The Other Francisco" by Dennis West in *Cineaste* (New York), fall 1977; article in *Hollywood Reporter*, 7 July 1977; "Cuban Cinema and the Afro-Cuban Heritage: An Interview with Sergio Giral" by Gary Crowdus and Julianne Burton in *The Black Scholar*, summer 1977; "*The Other Francisco*: Film Lessons on Novel Reading" by Francine Masiello in *Ideologies and Literature*, Vol. I, January/February 1978.

*   *   *

Cuba's first anti-slavery novel, *Francisco*, was written in 1838-39 by Anselmo Suárez y Romero, who came from a family of slaveowners. The novel portrays an interplay of personal emotions and passions—those of masters and slaves—and contains scenes stressing the harsh lot of plantation slaves. This depiction of plantation life was submitted to Richard Madden, a British agent investigating slavery in Cuba at that time.

The film *El otro Francisco* is not a mere adaptation of the novel *Francisco*. *El otro Francisco* is a Marxist analysis of the book and its ideological framework. The film rejects the novel's liberal bourgeois idealism and uses a historical materialist perspective in an attempt to reveal the true conditions of slavery. The first half of the film may be seen as a critical "re-reading" of the book. The novel's melodramatic plot is followed, but two key ingredients are added: scenes illustrative of the economic situation and the class conflict, and voice-over critical commentary which underscores the novel's Romantic frame work and important social and economic facts ignored by Suárez y Romero. The second half of the film is a de-romanticized, historical materialist re-creation of the 19th century plantation where life was governed by the economics of sugar production, by class antagonism, and by Britain's overseas mercantile expansion. This section of the film also dramatizes methods of slave resistance, a subject which remained unexamined in Suárez y Romero's work. To critique history and art, Giral imaginatively drew on typical resources of the fiction film (interesting characters, plot, powerful music) and of documentary (statistics, interviews, voice-over explanation).

Giral, who is a Black, believes that his fellow Cubans know little about the history of slavery in their country. To fill this gap, Giral made *El otro Francisco* as well as two other features on Cuban slavery. Giral and his colleagues at the Instituto Cubano del Arte e Industria Cinematográficos have supported these projects because the film institute is committed to reexamining and reassessing the nation's history. The subject of Afro-Cuban slavery merits cinematic treatment because the Black tradition of resistance (both to slavery and to the Spanish colonial powers) represents a significant but little-known contribution to the formation of today's socialist Cuba, whose proclaimed goals include an end to all forms of domination and escape from the oppressive legacy of colonialism.

In *El otro Francisco*, Giral strived for authenticity in his depiction of the Black slave experience. Black speech patterns, chants, ceremonies, and dances were researched with the aid of the University of Havana Folklore Group. Certain information, such as the slaves' scheduled hours of work and sleep, was drawn from Richard Madden's published documents on Cuba.

The convoluted structure and critical digressions of *El otro Francisco* appealed to critics and intellectuals but not to Cuba's general movie-going public. Because Giral proposes to reach a wide audience with his films, in his subsequent features on slavery he abandoned the structural and narrative experimentation which characterized *El otro Francisco*. Giral's cinematic experiment stands as a unique example of cinema as an instrument through which to critique literature.

—Dennis West

———————

8 ½. Otto e Mezzo. Production: Cineriz (Rome) and Francinex (Paris); black and white, 35mm; running time: 135 minutes. Released February 1963, released in the United States on 25 June 1963 by Joseph E. Levine, Embassy Pictures.

Produced by Angelo Rizzoli; screenplay by Federico Fellini, Ennio Flaiano, Tullio Pinelli, and Brunello Rondi; from a story by Federico Fellino and Ennio Flaiano; directed by Federico Fellini; photography by Gianni di Venanzo; edited by Leo Cattozzo; sound by Mario Faraoni and Alberto Bartolomei; production design (scenery) by Piero Gherardi; music by Nino Rota; costumes designed by Piero Gherardi; artistic collaboration by Brunello Rondi, assistant directors were Lina Wertmuller and Guidarino Guidi.

Filmed 9 May 1962-14 October 1962, in Titanus-Appia Studios and the Cecchignola military reservation in Rome, and on location in Tivoli, Filacciano, Viterbo, and the beaches between Ostia and Fiumicino. Academy Award, Best Foreign-Language Film, 1963; New York Film Critics Award, Best Foreign Film, 1963; Moscow Film Festival, Grand Prize, 1963.

Cast: Marcello Mastroianni (*Guido Anselmi*); Anouk Aimée (*Luisa Anselmi*); Sandro Milo (*Carla*); Claudia Cardinale (*Claudia*); Rosella Falk (*Rosella*); Madeleine Lebeau (*The actress*); Caterina Boratto (*The fashionable, unknown woman*); Barbara Steele (*Gloria Moran*); Mario Pisu (*Mario Mezzabotta*); Guido Alberti (*Pace, the producer*); Mario Conocchia (*Conocchia*); Jean Rougeul (*Fabrizio Carini, Daumier*); Edra Gale (*La Saraghina*); Ian Dallas (*Maurice, the magician*); Annibale Ninchi (*Guido's father*); Giuditta Rissone (*Guido's mother*); Tito Masini (*The Cardinal*); Frazier Rippy (*The Cardinal's secretary*); Georgia Simmons (*Guido's grandmother*); Palma Mangini (*Old peasant relative*); Roberta Valli (*Little girl at the farmhouse*); Riccardo Guglielmi (*Guido at the farmhouse*); Marco Gemini (*Guido as a schoolboy*); Yvonne Casadei (*Jacqueline Bonbon*); Cesarino Miceli Picardi (*Cesarino, the production supervisor*); Bruno Agostino (*Bruno Agostino, the production director*); Olimpia Cavalli (*Miss Olympia, as Carla in the screen tests*); Maria Antonietta Beluzzi (*La Saraghina in some screen tests*); Comtesse Elisabetta Cini (*The Cardinal in the screen tests*); Polidor (*One of the clowns in the parade*); Mino Doro (*Claudia's agent*). The entire technical staff participated in the final circus scene.

Publications:

Scripts—*8 ½ de Fellini* (contains screenplay plus a recounting of the filming) by Camilla Cederna, translated by H. de Mariassy and C. de Lignac, Paris 1963; *8 ½* by Federico Fellini, edited by Camilla Cederna, Bologna 1965; "Special Fellini" (screenplay in French) in *Avant Scène du Cinéma* (Paris), no.63, 1966; reviews—by Bosley Crowther in *The New York Times*, 26 June 1963; review by Peter John Dyer in *Monthly Film Bulletin* (London), October 1963; review by Brendan Gill in the *New Yorker*, 29 June 1963; "Fantastic Fellini" by Penelope Gilliatt in *London Observer*, 25 August 1963; review by Stanley Kauffmann in *The New Republic* (New York), 13 July 1963; books—*Nouveau Cinéma italien* by Raymond Borde and André Bouissy, Lyons, 1963; *The 200 Days of 8 1/2* by Deena Boyer, New York 1964; *Fellini* by Suzanne Budgen, London 1966; *Fellini* by Angelo Solmi, New York 1968; *Film as Film: Critical Responses to Film Art* by Joy Gould Boyum and Adrienne Scott, Boston, 1971; *Dibattiti di film* by Antonio Covi, Padua 1971; *Close-up: A Critical Perspective on Film* by Marsha Kinder and Beverle Houston, New York 1972; *Critical Approaches to Federico Fellini's 8 1/2* by Albert Edward Benderson, New York 1974; *Filmguide to 8 1/2* by Ted Perry, Bloomington, Indiana 1975; *Federico Fellini: The Search for a New Mythology*, New York

1976; *Federico Fellini: A Guide to References and Resources* by John C. Stubbs, Boston 1978; articles—"*8 1/2*" by Peter Baker in *Films and Filming* (London), October 1963; "Fellini 8 1/2" by Gideon Bachmann in *Film Journal* (Melbourne), April 1963; "*8 1/2*: Director in Mid-Journey" by Gary Carey in *The 7th Art*, fall 1963; "A Fresh Interpretation of Fellini's *8 1/2*" by Roberta Cohen in *Film*, winter 1963; "Dizzy Doings on a Set: Making a Movie—*8 1/2*" in *Life* (New York), 19 July 1963; "Federico Fellini: *8 1/2* by M. Estève in *Etudes cinématographiques* (Paris), winter 1963; "*8 1/2*" by Jack Hirschman in *Film Quarterly* (Berkeley), fall 1963; "Fellini's *8 1/2*: Holland's 11" by Norman Holland in *Hudson Review* (Nutley, New Jersey), autumn 1963; "A Case of Artistic Inflation" by John Francis Lane in *Sight and Sound* (London), summer 1963; "*8 1/2*: A Quest for Ecstasy" by James Price in *London Magazine*, November 1963; "From 1/2 to 8 1/2" by Hollis Alpert in the *New York Times Magazine*, 21 July 1963; "Confessione in publico: colloquio con Federico Fellini" in *Bianco e nero* (Rome), April 1963; "Fellini: *8 1/2*" in *Cinema* (Beverly Hills), August/-September, 1963; "Il gattopardo e il telepata" by Guido Aristarco in *Cinema nuovo* (Turin), March/April 1963; "La colonna sonora di *Fellini otto e mezzo*" by Ermanno Comuzio in *Cineforum* (Bergamo), March 1963; "Un caso clinico" by Fernaldo Di Giammatteo in *Bianco e nero* (Rome), April 1963; "Si butto in ginocchio ad abbracchiarmi" by Federico Fellini in *Cinemo nuovo* (Turin), September/October, 1963; "L'anti-Marienbad" by Ernesto G. Laura in *Bianco e nero* (Rome), April 1963; article on *8 1/2* by Alberto Moravia in *Cinéma 63* (Paris), April 1963; "La mezza eta del socialismo?" by Renzo Renzi in *Cinema nuovo* (Turin), March/April 1963; "L'ora della veri è di un artista" by Mario Verdone in *Bianco e nero* (Rome), April 1963; "La musica di 8 e mezzo" by Mario Zucconi in *Filmcritica* (Rome), October 1963; "Fellini's Masterpiece" by Dwight MacDonald in *Esquire* (New York), January 1964; "Interview: Federico Fellini" in *Playboy* (Chicago), February 1966; "Masina contre Fellini" by Claude Gauteur in *Image et son* (Paris), April 1966; "Fellini: Analyst Without Portfolio" in *Man and the Movies* edited by W.R. Robinson, Baton Rouge, Louisiana, 1967; "Notes on Double Structure and the Films of Fellini" by Patrick Eason in *Cinema* (Cambridge), March 1969; "Wastelands: The Breakdown of Order" in *Literature and Film* by Robert Richardson, Bloomington, Indiana 1969; "Film Form: Situation, Articulation, Revelation" in *Reflections on the Screen* by George Linden, Belmont, California 1970; "Fellini" by Raymond Lefèvre in *Image et Son* (Paris), January 1971; "Le Clair et l'obscur" by René Micha in *L'Arc* (Aix-en-Provence), no.45, 1971; "*8 1/2* Times 2" in *24 Times a Second* by William S. Pechter, New York 1971; "Dilatazione visionaria del documenta e nostalgia della madre chiesa in Fellini" in *Cinema dell'ambiguità: Rossellini, De Sica de Zavattini, Fellini*, Rome 1971; "Signifiers in Fellini's *8 1/2*" by Ted Perry in *Forum Italicum* (Rome), March 1972; "Fellini *8 1/2* (A Jungian Analysis)" by Isabelli Conti in *Ikon* (Milan), January/March and July/December 1972; "Italian Film: Failure and Emergence" by Joseph Bennett in *Kenyon Review* (New York), autumn 1974; "*8 1/2* as an Anatomy of Melancholy" by T. Hyman in *Sight and Sound* (London), summer 1974; "The Secret Life of Federico Fellini" in *6 American Directors* by Peter Harcourt, Baltimore 1974; "Mirror Construction in Fellini's *8 1/2*" in *Film Language: A Semiotics of the Cinema* by Christian Metz, New York 1974; "Study Guide to *8 1/2*" by John Stubbs in *Journal of Aesthetic Education* (Urbana, Illinois), April 1975; "*8 1/2*—The Declensions of Silence" in *The Movies on Your Mind* by Harvey Greenberg, New York 1975; "The Pinocchio Motif in Federico Fellini's *8 1/2*" by Albert Benderson in *Film Studies Annual*, 1976; "Le Noir et blanc du rêve" by L. Audibert in *Cinématographe* (Paris), February 1978; "Subjectivity under Seige—from Fellini's *8 1/2* to Oshima's *The Story of a Man Who Left his Will on Film*" by E. Branigan in *Screen* (London), spring 1978; "Notes on Subjectivity: On Reading Edward Branigan's 'Subjectivity under Seige'" by P. Willemen in *Screen* (London), spring 1978; "Le Miroir et les ombres" by L. Audibert in *Cinematographe* (Paris), October 1979; "Magia w *8 1/2* Felliniego" by L.J. Majewski in *Kino* (Warsaw), April 1979 and June 1979; "*8 1/2* and the Evolution of the Neorealist Narrative" by J.P. Telotte in *Film Criticism* (Edinboro, Pennsylvania), no.2, 1979.

*   *   *

Otto e mezzo achieved its rather distinctive appellation as a result of its location within a Fellini canon which up to that point included seven films and two short pieces that the director had contributed to a pair of Italian anthology films. Given this personal linkage with its director and the film's apparent theme—one not unrelated to a case history of male menopause—as well as its numerous biographical parallels to Fellini's own life, it is tempting to regard *8 1/2* simply as a self-indulgent though highly creative attempt to fill a void in the director's progression of films. Instead this study of a filmmaker's creative and personal crises is now recognized as a masterpiece, and one of a very small number of cinematic efforts to utter a clear statement on the intricate nature of artistic inspiration.

8 1/2 is a film of cycles in which past, present and future are subtly intertwined in an endless continuum of meaning that exists within the mind of the artist as well as in the aesthetic itself. Utilizing a complex structure of multi-tiered symbolism common to works as diverse as Edmund Spenser's *Fairie Queene* and Herman Melville's *Moby Dick* but only rarely accomplished on the screen, the film revolves in a seemingly counter-clockwise direction pivoting on the character of Guido. It is he who imbues it with a different meaning on each level of interpretation. The various symbolic planes merge fully in the film's final scenes when all of the characters (and all that each represents) join hands to form a circle that revolves dizzily backwards until all that remains is Guido as a child, ready to begin the cycle again.

8 1/2 is a trip backward in preparation to go forward. The end of the film is also its beginning. On every level, it is a return of the artist and the aesthetic to the formative wellsprings of the art for the inspiration that will take each into the future. On its most accessible level, the biographical one, it is the story of Guido, a motion picture director not unlike Fellini himself (although most critics are too reverential of the similarities between the two) who has lost his source of inspiration both in his art and in his life. He inevitably turns inward to examine the generative events of his development—his boyhood, the Church, his relationship with his parents, and the women in his life—as well as the nightmares accompanying each. It is only when he symbolically returns to the womb at the end of the film, by crawling under the table at the press conference where he squeezes a revolver to his temple, that he can be reborn. Stating "Clean...disinfect," he pulls the trigger. Like an artistic phoenix, he is reborn in his own creative ashes and rises to receive the inspiration that will enable him to create an entirely new kind of film from the experiences of the old.

At this point, a second and more abstract level of meaning begins to become apparent. The film that Guido is ultimately inspired to make is, in fact, the film that we have been watching. Thus, at the end of the biographical cycle, the beginnings of the first aesthetic level emerge. The meaning of the film, on this tier, centers on our witnessing of the creative process—the thoughts, the memories, the incidents by which a new kind of film is born. As a number of scholars, most notably Christian Metz, have suggested, "8 1/2 is the film of 8 1/2 being made." This is most obvious in those scenes in which a sound stage buzzer intrudes on the action, or those in which bright set lights are all too obviously turned on, and in the film's critical final scene where lights, cameras and crews are visible.

The final scene initiates an even more abstract cycle of meaning that becomes a commentary on the aesthetic of Italian film itself. The entire scene unfolds before an enormous monolithic structure of a rocket gantry. In front of this structure, a large crowd mills about and the entire image becomes reflective of similar scenes in the great silent epics *Quo Vadis* (1912) and *Cabiria* (1913) which represented Italy's first "golden period" of cinema. During this era, reality manifested itself in the monumental, densely populated and often frenzied forms of the epics, as well as in the grim, suffering people and dirty streets of such forerunners of neorealism as *Sperduti nel Buio* (1914). This dichotomy is reflected in *8 1/2* in the artistic struggles Guido has with his producer who wants him to make an epic, and with himself in his expressed desire to make a film that tells the truth. Fellini merges and internalizes both concepts in *8 1/2* to create an epic of the psyche which adequately encompasses the gritty realism of the scenes of Guido's childhood.

On this broad aesthetic level, *8 1/2* is the journey of Italian film backward to re-establish its roots in the silent period and regain the inspiration to create a new direction for the films to come. What, on the biographical level, had been a re-examination of Guido's childhood, becomes, at this extreme, a history of Italian film returning through neorealism, the white telephone comedies, and even the side show demonstrations to its beginnings. At the end of the film, as workers are dismantling the huge gantry after the press conference, Guido sits in his car with his scriptwriter Carni who discourses on the creative artist. "Any man", says the writer, "who is really worthy to be called an artist should swear to one thing in his creative life—dedication to silence." With the pronunciation of the word "silence," Guido's creative powers surge back and he is ready to begin the film that is *8 1/2*.

While this scene is significant on all levels of interpretation, in the broadest sense, it is indicative that Fellini has taken film back to its golden period when experimental approaches to film forms were daring and innovative. He is clearing the stage for a new kind of film represented by *8 1/2*, and its successor *Juliet of the Spirits*, an intertwining of reality and spectacle, but an internal one projecting the mind, imagination and emotions of its director. Although there are various other concerns in *Otto e mezzo* reflected in the musings and dialogues of its protagonist, they are generally supportive of the broader aesthetic levels of the film: the artist, the original work, and the tradition of the art itself. On all of these levels, Fellini has succeeded admirably in the creation of a new aesthetic from the materials of the old.

—Stephen L. Hanson

THE OX-BOW INCIDENT. Strange Incident (British). Production: Twentieth Century-Fox; 1942; black and white, 35mm; running time: 76 mins.; length: 6776 feet. Released 1942.

Produced by Lamar Trotti; screenplay by Lamar Trotti; from the novel by Walter van Tilburg Clark; directed by William Wellman; photography by Arthur Miller; edited by Allen McNeil; sound by Alfred Bruzzlin and Roger Heman; art direction by Richard Day and James Basevi; sets by Thomas Little and Frank E. Hughes; music by Cyril Mockridge; costumes designed by Earl Luick; make-up by Guy Pearce.

Cast: Henry Fonda (*Gil Carter*); Henry Morgan (*Art Croft*); Dana Andrews (*Martin*); Anthony Quinn (*Mexican*); Harry Davenport (*Davies*); Frank Conroy (*Major Tetley*); William Eythe (*Gerald Tetley*); Mary Beth Hughes (*Rose Mapen*); George Meeker (*Rose's Husband*); Jane Darwell (*Ma Grier*); Francis Ford (*Old Man*); Matt Briggs (*Judge*); Marc Lawrence (*Farnley*); Paul Hurst (*Monty Smith*); Victor Killian (*Darby*); Chris-Pin Martin (*Pancho*); Frank Orth (*Kinkaid*); Ted North (*Joyce*); Rondo Hatton (*Gabe Hart*); Leigh Whipper (*Sparks*); Dick Rich (*Mapes*). Almira Sessions (*Mrs. Swanson*); Margarit Hamilton (*Mrs. Larch*); Stanley Andrews (*Bartlett*); Billy Benedict (*Greene*); Paul Burns (*Winder*); George Lloyd (*Moore*); George Chandler (*Jimmy Cairnes*); Hank Bell (*Red*); Forrest Dillon *Mark*); George Plues (*Alec Small*); Willard Robertson *Sheriff*); Tom London (*Deputy*).

Publications:

Scripts—"*The Ox-Bow Incident*" in *Best Film Plays 1943-44* edited by John Gassner and Dudley Nichols, New York 1944; *The Ox-Bow Incident* by Lamar Trotti, New York 1972; reviews—by Manny Farber in the *New Republic* (New York), 17 May 1943; review by Bosley Crowther in *The New York Times*, 10 May 1943; books—*The Ox-Bow Incident* by Walter Van Tilburg Clark, New York 1940; *Our Modern Art: The Movies* by Ernest Callenbach, Chicago 1955; *Novels into Films* by George Bluestone, Berkeley 1961; *The Western: From Silents to Cinerama* by George N. Fenin and William K. Everson, New York 1962; *One Reel a Week* by Fred J. Balshofer and Arthur C. Miller, Berkeley 1967; *Hollywood in the Forties* by Charles Higham and Joel Greenburg, New York 1968; *The Fondas: The Films and the Careers of Henry, Jane, and Peter Fonda* by John Springer, New York 1970; *The Western: From Silents to the 70's* by George N. Fenin and William K. Everson, New York 1973; *A Short Time for Insanity: An Autobiography* by William Wellman, New York 1974; *The Men Who Made the Movies* by Richard Schickel, New York 1975; articles—"Wyler, Wellman, and Huston" by Richard Griffith in *Films in Review* (New York), February 1950; "Henry Fonda" by John Springer in *Films in Review* (New York), November 1960; "Fallen Idols" by Andrew Sarris in *Film Culture* (New York), spring 1963; "William Wellman" by Kevin Brownlow in *Film* (London), winter 1965-66; "A Memorable Visit with An Elder Statesman" by Curtis Lee Hanson in *Cinema* (Beverly Hills), July 1966; "Reflections on 40 Years of Make-Believe" by Curtis Lee Hanson in *Cinema* (Beverly Hills), December 1966; "The Essential Wellman" by J.M. Smith in *Brighton* (London), January 1970; "William Wellman: Director Rebel" by William Wellman, Jr. in *Action* (Los Angeles), March/April 1970; "Mary Beth Hughes" by T.P. Turton in *Films in Review* (New York), October 1971; "Movie Chronicle: The Westerner" by Robert Worshow in *The Immediate Experience*, New York 1975; "*The Ox-Bow Incident*" by Michael Selig in *Cinema Texas Program Notes* (Austin), 7 February 1979; "*The Ox-Bow Incident*" by David Bahnemann in *Magill's Survey of Cinema, Vol.III* edited by Frank N. Magill, Englewood Cliffs, New Jersey 1980.

*　　*　　*

Although William Wellman directed more popular box-office successes, *The Ox-Bow Incident* remains one of the high points of his 35-year Hollywood career, and has gained in stature since its initial release.

The film, based on the novel by Walter van Tilburg Clark, depicts an incident said to have actually happened in Nevada in 1885. Written and produced by Lamar Trotti, *The Ox-Bow Incident* features Henry Fonda and Henry (Harry) Morgan as drifters who ride into a small western town, where they overhear in a saloon that a rancher named Kinkaid has been killed by cattle rustlers. As the sheriff is out of town, a deputy organizes a posse whose members take the law into their own hands despite one or two ineffectual objections. The 28-member posse soon runs into three men encamped by the Ox-Bow and discover that one is in possession of some of Kinkaid's cattle and another has Kinkaid's gun.

Despite the circumstantial evidence and the trio's protestations of innocence, only seven people in the posse side with the three men and ask for a trial. The three are hanged at dawn and a few minutes later, the posse is informed that Kinkaid is not dead and the men who wounded him have been captured. Back at the saloon, Fonda reads the hanged man's letter written to his wife and vows to deliver it to her.

The film is not a western in the usual sense, but it is usually classified with that *genre*. The Ox-Bow itself is an obvious set, yet because it is symbolic, viewers can accept its artificiality.

It is the casting which helps the film attain classic status. Henry Fonda's deft underplaying of the sensible man who challenges the mob makes the contrast with the prejudiced out-for-action posse all the more dramatic. His friend Henry Morgan (who would soon change his screen name to Harry to distinguish him from the radio comedian of the same name) plays the kind but slow-witted friend to perfection—a portent of parts to come, including his role as the patient Colonel Potter in television's *M*A*S*H* series.

The complex personalities of the three men to be hanged are well developed and moving. Dana Andrews (young, sensitive, married), Anthony Quinn (Mexican, shifty, carrying a weapon, confident), and Francis Ford (elderly, senile, with no comprehension of what is going on) arouse audience sympathy. The elderly Ford was the brother of director John Ford. The casting of black actor Leigh Whipper as a preacher who does not cowtow to the pressures brought by the lynch mob was astute and unusual in that most black actors of the early 1940s were playing fawning servants or shuffling, dim-witted stooges.

Harry Davenport, always a distinguished character actor, becomes almost the only voice of reason in a town gone mad. Frank Conroy as the major who badgers his son into "being a man" is at his best, as are a cast of excellent supporting players. Only two women appear in the film—Jane Darwell as the racous Ma Grier who is "one of the boys" and delicate Mary Beth Hughes as Rose Mapen, who left Fonda for marriage to a rich man.

Arthur Miller's cinematography sustains the claustrophobic atmosphere through light and shadow and the excellent use of closeups. The clothing and atmosphere are properly gritty.

The Ox-Bow Incident dates very little because of the period in which it is sent and, despite its allusions to the Nazi death camps of World War II, could have happened anywhere in the world during any period of history—and probably did.

The film was among 10 motion pictures nominated for an Academy Award as Best Picture of the Year, but lost to *Casablanca*. Because of its cynical and downbeat qualities, the uncompromising ending, and a 76-minute running time, 20th Century-Fox released the film on the lower half of a double bill.

—James L. Limbacher

PAISÁ. Paisan. Production: Organization Films International in collaboration with Foreign Films Productions, some sources also credit Capitani Films; black and white, 35mm; running time: 117 mins., originally 124 mins.; length: 4195 feet. Released 1946.

Produced by Roberto Rossellini, Rod E. Geiger, and Mario Conti, production supervised by Ugo Lombardi; story by Victor Haines, Marcello Pagiero, Sergio Amidei, Federico Fellini, Roberto Rossellini, Klaus Mann (Florence episode), and Vasco Pratolini; screenplay by Sergio Amidei, Federico Fellini, and Roberto Rossellini; English dialogue by Annalena Limentani; English subtitles by Herman G. Weinberg; directed by Roberto Rossellini; photography by Otello Martelli; edited by Eraldo da Roma; sound by Ovidio del Grande; music by Renzo Rossellini; assistant directors: Federico Fellini, Massimo Mida, E. Handimar, and L. Limentani; English narrators: Stuart Legg and Raymond Spottiswoode.

Venice Film Festival, Special Mention, 1946; New York Film Critics Award, Best Foreign Film, 1948.

Cast: Carmela Sazio (*Carmela*); Robert Van Loon (*Joe from Jersey*); Alfonsino Pasca (*Boy*); Maria Michi (*Francesca*); Renzo Avanzo (*Massimo*); Harriet White (*Harriet*); Dots M. Johnson (*MP*); Bill Tubbs (*Captain Bill Martin*); Benjamin Emmanuel; Raymond Campbell; Albert Heinz; Harold Wagner; Merlin Berth; Leonard Parrish; Dale Edmonds (*Dale*); Carlo Piscane (*Peasant in Sicily story*); Mats Carlson (*Soldier in Sicily story*); Gar Moore (*Fred*); Gigi Gori (*Partisan*); Cigolani (*Cigolani*); Lorena Berg (*Maddalena*); Allen Dan; M. Hugo; Anthony La Penna.

Publications:

Scripts—"*Paisá*, Sixth Episode—Scenario and Dialogue by Roberto Rossellini and Federico Fellini" in *Film Culture* (New York), winter 1963-64; *The War Trilogy: Open City, Paisan, Germany—Year Zero* edited by Stefano Roncoroni, translated by Judith Green, New York 1973; reviews—by Lindsay Anderson in *Sequence*, winter 1947; review by Bosley Crowthers in *The New York Times*, 30 March 1948; "*Paisan*" by Robert Worshow in *Partisan Review* (New Brunswick, New Jersey), July 1948; review in *Variety* (New York), 2 November 1948; "*Paisa*" by Ian Johnson in *Films and Filming* (London), February 1966; books—*Roberto Rossellini* by Patrice Hovald, Paris 1958; *Roberto Rossellini* by Massimo Mida, Guanda, Parma, Italy 1961; *Roberto Rossellini* by Mario Verdone, Paris 1963; *Roberto Rossellini* by Jose Luis Guarner, translated by Elisabeth Cameron, New York 1970; *Patterns of Realism* by Roy Armes, South Brunswick, New Jersey 1971; *What is Cinema?* Vol. II, by André Bazin, selected and translated by Hugh Gray, Berkeley 1971; *The Italian Cinema* by Pierre Leprohon, translated by Roger Greaves and Oliver Stallybrass, New York 1972; *Roberto Rossellini* by Pio Baldelli, Rome 1972; *Roberto Rossellini* by Gianni Rondolino, Florence 1974; *Film and Revolution* by James Roy MacBean, Bloomington, Indiana 1975; *Cinema, The Magic Vehicle: A Guide to Its Achievement: Journey One: The Cinema Through 1949* edited by Jacek Klinowski and Adam Garbicz, Metuchen, New Jersey 1975; *Springtime in Italy: A Reader on Neo-Realism* edited by David Overby, Hamden, Connecticut 1978; *Italian Cinema: From Neorealism to the Present* by Peter Bondanella, New York 1983; articles—"Seven Americans" by Hugh Barty King in *Sight and Sound* (London), autumn 1946;

"Prophet with Honor: Roberto Rossellini" by Peter Ordway in *Theatre Arts* (New York), January 1949; "*Paisan*: How It Struck Our Contemporaries" by Roger Manvell in *Penguin Film Review*, May 1949; "Interview with Roberto Rossellini" by Francis Koval in *Sight and Sound* (London), February 1951; "Notes on a Definition of Neorealism" by Sergio J. Pacifici in *Yale French Studies*, summer 1956; "Why Neorealism Failed" by Eric Rhode in *Sight and Sound* (London), winter 1960-61; "The Achievement of Roberto Rossellini" in *Film Comment* (New York), fall 1964; "Roberto Rosselini albo synteza anty-nomjii: Nasz Iluzjon" by A. Helman in *Kino* (Warsaw), October 1973; "Roberto Rossellini, 1906-1977" by René Prédal in *Avant-Scène du cinéma* (Paris), 15 February 1979; "Italian Neorealism: A Mirror Construction of Reality" by B. Lawton in *Film Criticism* (Edinboro, Pennsylvania), no.2, 1979; "*Paisa*" by J. Pym in *Monthly Film Bulletin* (London), November 1980.

*   *   *

Roberto Rossellini's *Paisa*, along with his *Roma, Cittá Aperta* (1945), introduced post-war American audiences to Italian neo-realism, which proved to be the first wave in a series of European influences that altered the shape of American cinema. Neo-realism, a movement that emerged from the shattered Italian film industry immediately after the Second World War, concerned itself with an almost documentary-like depiction of the hardship and suffering of the Italian people during and after the Second World War. Directors like Rossellini, Victorio De Sica, and Luchino Visconti took to the streets in order to make their films. In the process they articulated an aesthetic of cinematic realsim that called for the use of non-professional actors, on-location shooting, the abandonment of slick "Hollywood" production values, and a self-conscious rejection of commercial considera-tions. What emerged was a fresh and energetic film style which largely rejuvenated the pre-war stagnation of the Italian cinema.

Years later Rossellini wrote that he used this new approach to attempt to understand the events of the fascist years, which had overwhelmed him personally and the Italian people generally. He chose the particular film style he did for its morally neutral approach; he simply wanted to observe reality objectively and to explore the facts that implicated his country in the fascist horror of the war. He also wanted to create a balance sheet on the experience so that Italians could begin to live life on new terms, could begin with a fresh page.

Paisa contains six episodes that trace the American invasion of Italy from the Allied landing in Sicily in 1934 until the Italian surrender in the spring of 1944. Rossellini does not present the war in terms of armies, strategies and grand plans but rather as a tragedy involving the death and the suffering of human beings caught in the crush of forces beyond their control. Although some of the critics, amoung them Robert Warshow, found the film too sentimental in places, the film received good reviews outside of Italy, and it has retained its place as one of the classics of neo-realism, especially in the United States.

Neo-realism and Rossellini's remarks concerning *Paisa* raise some interesting questions about the mimetic nature of film and about the significance of a point of view or doctrine in shaping the final cinematic product. *Paisa* is neither a doctrine film nor, as Rossellini would have it, a neutral one. The film is not a long documentary, as some critics have rather simple-mindedly sug-gested, nor is it a film guided by a manifesto. It is film which provides a new beginning, to borrow Rossellini's balance sheet metaphor, and does so by stripping film of the appurtenances of the pre-war studio world. Rossellini was striving for a basic

sincerity in his films, and it was primarily toward that end that he made *Paisá* with a truthful simplicity which is so effective.

—Charles L.P. Silet

———————

LES PARAPLUIES DE CHERBOURG. The Umbrellas of Cherbourg. Die Regenschirme von Cherbourg. Production: Madeleine Films, Parc Films, and Beta-Film; Eastmancolor, 35mm, Ultrascope; running time: 95 mins., English version about 90 mins. Released February 1964, Paris.

Produced by Mag Bodard; screenplay by Jacques Demy; directed by Jacques Demy; photography by Jean Rabier; edited by Anne-Marie Cotret; art direction by Bernard Evein; music composed and conducted by Michel Legrand, lyrics by Jacques Demy; costumes designed by Jaqueline Moreau.

Filmed in Cherbourg.

Cast: Catherine Deneuve (*Geneviève*); Nino Castelnuovo (*Guy*); Anne Vernon (*Madame Emery*); Ellen Farner (*Madeleine*); Marc Michel (*Roland Cassard*); Mireille Perrey (*Aunt Elise*); Jean Champion (*Aubin*); Harald Wolff (*Dubourg*); Dorothée Blank (*Girl in cafe*).

Publications:

Reviews—in *Film Comment* (New York), spring 1965; review by Adelaide Comerford in *Films in Review* (New York), January 1965; review by J.H. Fenwick in *Sight and Sound* (London), winter 1964-65; review by Gordon Gow in *Films and Filming* (London), January 1965; review by Andrew Sarris in *The Village Voice* (New York), 25 February 1965; books—*French Cinema Since 1946: Vol. 2—The Personal Touch* by Roy Armes, New York 1966; articles—"Jacques Demy and His Other World" by Ginette Billard in *Film Quarterly* (Berkeley), fall 1964; "Rondo Galant" by Richard Roud in *Sight and Sound* (London), summer 1964; "Phenomenon of *Les Parapluies de Cherbourg*" by Ginette Billard in *Vogue* (New York), 1 November 1964; "The Music in *Parapluies*" by Douglas McVay in *Film* (London), winter 1964; "The Colours in *Cherbourg*" by Lang Dewey in *Film* (London), winter 1964; "I Prefer the Sun to the Rain" by Jacques Demy in *Film Comment* (New York), spring 1965; article by Stephen Chodes in *Film Comment* (New York), spring 1965; article by Harriet Polt in *Film Quarterly* (Berkeley), spring 1966; article by Stanley Solomon in *Film Heritage* (Dayton, Ohio), winter 1965-66; interview with Demy in *Film Heritage* (Dayton, Ohio), spring 1967; "Lola in Los Angeles" by Jacques Demy in *Films and Filming* (London), April 1970; issue on Demy of *Cinéma* (Paris), July/August 1981.

*   *   *

The Umbrellas of Cherbourg is the centerpiece of Jacques Demy's triptych (*Lola* and *The Young Girls of Rochefort* are the other two films) which pays homage to Hollywood musicals of the 1950's such as *The Bandwagon* and *Singin' in the Rain*. Like *Lola*, a musical without songs, and *Les Demoiselles...*, a film in dance, *Umbrellas...*, "a film in color and song," turns the Hollywood formula inside out. Instead of being set among glamourous affluence of the show business world, *Umbrella...*'s milieu is that provincial, middle-class shopkeeper. And in place of the series of gaudy production numbers that express moments of heightened emotion while fracturing the film's narrative flow, *Umbrellas...* presents a seamless narrative, classic in structure, in which every line of dialogue is sung.

As Demy has said, the film is neither opera, musical comedy, nor operetta but a film of dialogue in song in which music underlays the text. All the words are audible without ever forcing the lyricism of the voice. In consequence, the music exposes simple themes that are at once popular and general. It is a jazz film. Or, more exactly, a film "en-chanted."

Like the fairy-tale, a genre which holds special appeal for Demy, *Umbrellas...*'s story is banal and almost embarrassingly sentimental. Its plot is fuelled by a string of wildly improbable coincidences. Roland Cassard's arrival in Cherbourg occurs just in time for him to rescue first Mme. Emery from the financial embarrassment of foreclosure, then Genevieve from the social embarrassment of bearing Guy's child out of wedlock. Though she admits her predicament, Cassard still agrees to marry Genevieve because he once abandoned a girl in a similar condition several years earlier in Nantes, a girl, oddly enough, named Lola. Aunt Elise's revelation on her deathbed of a secret cache of money she has been putting by for years opens Guy's eyes to the love Madeleine bears for him, a love that will redeem him. Aunt Elise's money allows Guy and Madeleine to be married and Guy to buy the gas station he has always coveted. Most improbable of all is the climactic meeting of the former lovers when Genevieve, on an infrequent drive through Cherbourg, happens to stop at Guy's station. The encounter sounds a cynical strain which has played throughout the film in counterpoint to its bright surface glitter. Guy and Genevieve in effect admit that their youthful passion was folly, that each is perfectly happy with the spouse that he or she has married and that happiness depends not on some love in the ideal but on the financial security each has now attained. Meanwhile snow settles lightly on the picture-postcard setting as violins swell in the background and the camera cranes up to the concluding high angle long shot.

Michel Legrand's music and the way it is used reinforces this counterpoint. Working with only five basic phrases, Legrand constructs a score that perfectly apes the pop idiom of the day— one of the tunes even became an international hit—while maintaining a melodic austerity reminiscent of Milhaud or Ravel. What is set to the music are not lyrics but rather unrhymed, unrhythmic, mundane dialogue of the most banal sort.

Bernard Evein's transformation of actual Chergourg locations into "sets" that look artificial enough to be found on any Hollywood sound stage completes Demy's satiric trope of the film musical.

Demy's musicals not only satirize the manners of provincial life, they also seek to dismantle the propelling mechanism of the genre itself.

—Dennis Nastav

UNE PARTIE DE CAMPAGNE. A Day in the Country. Production: Pantheon-Production; black and white, 35mm; running time: 45 mins.; length: 1100 meters, originally 1232 meters. Released 8 May 1946, Paris.

Produced by Pierre Braunberger, executive producer: Jacques B. Brunius, with Roger Woog; screenplay by Jean Renoir; from the story by Guy de Maupassant; directed by Jean Renoir; photography by Claude Renoir; edited by Marguerite Houle-Renoir, final version by Marienette Cadix under Marguerite Houle-Renoir's supervision, assisted by Marcel Cravenne; sound by Courme and Joseph de Bretagne; production design by Robert Gys; music by Joseph Kosma and Germaine Montero; assistants to the director: Jacques Becker and Henri Cartier-Bresson, other contributors to this film include: Claude Heymann, Luchino Visconti, and Yves Allegret.

Filmed July-August 1936 near Montigny and Marlotte.

Cast: Sylvia Bataille (*Henriette*); Georges Darnoux (*Henri*); Jeanne Marken (*Madame Dufour*); Jacques Borel (*Rodolphe*); Paul Temps (*Anatole*); Gabrielle Fontan (*Grandmother*); Jean Renoir (*Father Poulain*); Marguerite Renoir (*The servant*); Gabriello (*M. Cyprien Dufour*); Pierre Lestringuez (*Old priest*).

Publications:

Scripts—"*Une Partie de Campagne*" (excerpts from screenplay) in *Avant-Scène du cinéma* (Paris), 15 December 1962; "*Une Partie de Campagne*" in *Image et son* (Paris), April/May 1962; "*Partie de Campagne*" by Jacques Prevert in *Art et Essai* (Paris), April 1965, May 1965, and June 1965; "Excerpts from Screenplays: *Partie de campagne*" in *Jean Renoir: An Investigation into His Films and Philosophy* by Pierre Leprohon, New York 1971; reviews—by Bosley Crowther in *The New York Times*, 13 December 1950; review in *Variety* (New York), 20 December 1950; books—*Jean Renoir* by Paul Davay, Brussels 1957; *Jean Renoir* by Armand-Jean Cauliez, Paris 1962; *Jean Renoir* edited by Bernard Chardère in *Premier Plan* (Lyon), no.22-24, May 1962; *Renoir, My Father* by Jean Renoir, Boston 1962; *Analyses des films de Jean Renoir* by Institut des Hautes Etudes Cinématographiques, Paris 1966; *Study Unit 8: Jean Renoir* by Susan Bennett, London 1967; *Renoir, 1938* by Francois Poulle, Paris 1969; *Jean Renoir und seine Film: eine Dokumentation* compiled and edited by Ulrich Gregor, Bad Ems 1970; *Jean Renoir: An Investigation into His Films and Philosophy* by Pierre Leprohon, New York 1971; *Humanidad de Jean Renoir* by Carlos Cuenca, Valladolid, Mexico 1971; *Jean Renoir: The World of His Films* by Leo Braudy, New York 1972; *Jean Renoir* by André Bazin, edited by François Truffaut, Paris, translated ed. 1973. *Jean Renoir* by Raymond Durgnat, Berkeley 1974; *Six European Directors: Essays on the Meaning of Film Style* by Peter Harcourt, Baltimore 1974; *Jean Renoir: le spectacle, la vie* by Claude Beylie, Paris 1975; *Jean Renoir: Essays, Conversations, Reviews* by Penelope Gilliatt, New York 1975; *Jean Renoir: A Guide to References and Resources* by Christopher Faulkner, Boston 1979; *Jean Renoir: The French Films, 1924-1939* by Alexander Sesonske, Cambridge, Massachusetts 1980; *Cinema, A Critical Dictionary* edited by Richard Roud, two volumes, London 1980; articles—special Renoir issue, *Cahiers du cinéma* (Paris), January 1952; "The Illustrious Career of Jean Renoir" by Jean Berangert in *Yale French Studies*, summer 1956; special Renoir issue, *Cahiers du cinéma* (Paris), Christmas 1957; "The Renaissance of the French Cinema—Feydor, Renoir, Duvivier, Carné" by Georges Sadoul in *Film: An Anthology* edited by Daniel Talbot, New York 1959; "Renoir and Realism" by Peter John Dyer in *Sight and Sound* (London), summer 1960; "Painting Life with Movement" by Richard Whitehall in *Films and Filming* (London), June 1960;

"The Screen Is His Canvas" by Richard Whitehall in *Films and Filming* (London), July 1960; "Cette Male Gaîté" by Claude Beylie in *Avant-Scène du cinéma* (Paris), 15 December 1962; "Eroticism in Cinema—Part 7: Symbolism—Another Word for It" by Raymond Durgnat in *Films and Filming* (London), April 1962; article by R.G. Howard in *Film Journal* (New York), July 1964; "Interview with Jean Renoir" by Rui Nogueira and François Truchaud in *Sight and Sound* (London), spring 1968; "*En landtur*" by A. Bodelsen in *Kosmorama* (Copenhagen), October 1972; "Visconti and Renoir: Shadowplay" by Epi Wiese in *Yale Review*, December 1974; "Kaksi kertaa *Une Partie de campagne*" by P. von Bagh in *Filmihullu* (Helsinki, Finland), no.7, 1976; "*Partie de Campagne: Les Bas-Fonds*" by J. Magny in *Téléciné* (Paris), April 1977; "Jean Renoir: Enrevoyant *Une Partie de campagne...*" by J.L. Comolli in *Cahiers du cinéma* (Paris), April 1979.

* * *

André Bazin, in his unfinished study of the director Jean Renoir, described *Une Partie de Campagne* as a "perfectly finished work," one that is not only faithful in letter and spirit to the Maupassant story from which it was adapted but also actually improved by Renoir's additions and refinements to the original tale. This is high praise, indeed, when one realizes that the film's completion was highly problematic. Many of Renoir's films have had checkered careers, but none was quite so confusing as *Une Partie de Campagne*. Renoir originally intended to shoot a 35-or 40-minute story which he would make, he wrote later, just as if it were a full-length film. Renoir chose a gentle, 19th-century tale and planned to spend a relaxed summer shooting along the banks of the Loin near Marlotte, an area he knew extremely well. The entire experience should have provided him, as Alexander Sesonske has described it, with a "brief and pleasant respite in mid-career." Despite the rainiest summer in memory, an extremely volatile political climate, tensions on the set, and the fact that the film sat for nearly 10 years waiting for its final editing, *Une Partie de Campagne* is a remarkably fine film, some say a masterpiece; Sesonske thinks that no Renoir film seems "more unstudied, more a pure flow of life caught unaware."

There are sound reasons for the film's critical success: it is a film of uncommon gentleness and beauty, and it forms less of a "respite" in Renoir's career than a concentration of his most important themes and images: the river, the countryside, the loving scrutiny of bourgeois life. *Une Partie de Campagne* forms a poetic center for Renoir's French films. Rather than a sense of diversion, the film reflects a completeness. Renoir's rendering of his subject matter is incisive, his style mature, his vision complete; it is a seamless work of art. Many critics have called attention to the film's impressionistic quality, suggesting that it is a homage to the director's father, the painter Pierre Auguste Renoir. Indeed, impressionistic moments do grace the film—but for one to try to understand it as an attempt by the son to do what the father had already done with paint and canvas is to sadly underestimate the qualities of the movie. The "painterly" look of the films of Renoir *fils* have done much to strengthen his popular image as a director of surfaces, much to the detriment of his standing as a filmmaker of depth and perception.

The shortness of the film also has strengthened the perception of Renoir as an impressionistic filmmaker, and many critics today still respond to the film as incomplete, an interesting but unfinished experiment. The fact that Renoir left two scenes from the Maupassant story unshot has been used as evidence for regarding the film as a fragment, and considering Renoir's rela-tive fidelity to the events of Maupassant's story, it is an understandable, if mistaken, conclusion. Published versions of the screenplay for those "missing" scenes have further confused the issue. However, closer examination of the relationship between the story and the film will dispel such misconceptions. Renoir wrote in his autobiography, *My Life and My Films*, that when he was asked to increase the original footage to feature length, he refused because he felt that it would have been contrary to the intent of Maupassant's story and to his screenplay to lengthen it. Moreover, what many critics have failed to notice is that Renoir adapted the events of Maupassant's story faithfully, but he greatly altered the story's tone, which allowed him to drop the final scenes from the completed film without leaving the project incomplete.

Maupassant's tantalizingly brief tale is largely satiric in tone. He makes fun of the pretensions and foibles of his bourgeoisie often rather harshly; the natural setting is kept in the background; and the atmosphere of the country is diminished. Renoir not only places greater emphasis on the rural atmosphere and setting but also makes a film that by bringing such natural elements into the foreground turns Maupassant's rather strident attack on the Dufort family into a compassionate and understanding film about unrecoverable moments and the inevitable sadness of the loss of innocence and love. As André Bazin has noted, such changes do improve the original. The story is given a resonance, the characters motivation, and the ending a poignance lacking in the fictional source. As Pierre Laprohon has described it: "there is an overflowing tenderness, and extraordinary responsiveness to the existence of things, and a transformation of the commonplace into the sublime." In *Une Partie de Campagne*, Renoir has created a poetic compression of those things that he holds dear, which is one of the reasons the film evokes such fond memories and responses from its viewers. Although unhappy and somewhat ironic, the ending is nevertheless not unhopeful. Life and the river will both flow on and be renewed.

—Charles L.P. Silet

LA PASSION DE JEANNE D'ARC. The Passion of Joan of Arc. Production: Société Générale des Films (Paris); black and white, 35mm, silent; running time: originally 110 mins., later 86-88 mins.; length: 2400 meters. Released 21 April 1928, Paladsteatret, Copenhagen. Re-released 1952 in sound version produced by Gaumont Actualité and supervised by Lo Duca, musical accompaniment from works by Scarlatti, Albinoni, Gemianani, Vivaldi, and Bach.

Screenplay by Carl Theodor Dreyer and Joseph Delteil; from a book by Joseph Delteil; titles by Carl Theodor Dreyer; directed and edited by Carl Theodor Dreyer; photography by Rudolph Maté; art direction by Hermann Warm and Jean Hugo; costumes designed by Valentine Hugo; historical consultant: Pierre Champion; assistants: Paul la Cour and Ralph Holm.

Filmed May-October 1927 in Paris.

Cast: Maria Falconetti (*Joan*); Eugéne Silvain (*Pierre Cauchon*); André Berley (*Jean d'Estivet*); Maurice Schutz (*Nicolas Loyseleur*); Antonin Artaud (*Jean Massieu*); Michel Simon (*Jean Lemaître*); Jean d'Yd (*Guillaume Evrard*); Ravet (*Jean Beaupére*); André Lurville; Jacques Arma; Alexandre Mihalesco; R. Narlay; Henri Maillard; Leon Larive; Henri Gaultier; Paul Jorge.

Publications:

Scripts—*Cinque Film* by Carl Theodor Dreyer, Turin 1967; "*La Passion de Jeanne d'Arc*" by Carl Theodor Dreyer in *Carl Theodor Dreyer: Four Screenplays* translated by Oliver Stallybrass, London 1970; books—*Carl Theodor Dreyer: A Film Director's Work* by Ebbe Neergaard, London 1950; *The Art of Carl Dreyer: An Analysis* by Børge Trolle, Copenhagen 1955; *Om Filmen* by Carl Theodor Dreyer, Copenhagen 1964; *The Films of Carl Dreyer* by Eileen Bowser, New York 1964; *Portrait of Carl Th. Dreyer* by Ib Monty, Copenhagen 1965; *Carl Th. Dreyer, Danish Film Director*, edited by Soren Dyssegaard, Copenhagen 1968; *Le Cinéma et sa vérité* by Amédée Ayfre, Paris 1969; *Carl Th. Dreyer* by Claude Perrin, Paris 1969; *Carl Theodor Dreyer*, Amsterdam 1970; *The Cinema of Carl Dreyer* by Tom Milne, New York 1971; *Dreyer: Carl Th. Dreyer—en dansk filmskaber* by Helge Ernst, Copenhagen 1972; *Transcendental Style in Film: Ozu, Bresson, Dreyer* by Paul Schrader, Los Angeles 1972; *Filmguide to La Passion de Jeanne d'Arc* edited by David Bordwell, Bloomington, Indiana 1973; *Dreyer in Double Reflection*, edited by Donald Skoller, New York 1973; *Dreyer*, edited by Mark Nash, London 1977; *Carl Theodor Dreyer* by Pier Giorgio Tone, Florence 1978; *Carl Dreyer's La Passion de Jeanne D'Arc: A Comparison of Prints and Formal Analysis* by Anthony T. Pipolo, Ann Arbor, Michigan 1981; *The Films of Carl-Theodor Dreyer* by David Bordwell, Berkeley 1981; articles—special issue of *Écran Français* (Paris), 11 November 1947; "Interview with Dreyer" by John Winge in *Sight and Sound* (London), January 1950; "*La Passion de Jeanne d'Arc*" by Roger Manvell in *Sight and Sound* (London), no.8, 1950; "Les Voix du silence" by Amédée Ayfre in *Cahiers du cinéma* (Paris), no.17, 1952; "*Giovanna d'Arco restaurata*" by Corrado Terzi in *Cinema nuovo* (Turin), no.17, 1953; "*La Passion de Jeanne d'Arc*" by Chris Marker in *Regards Neufs sur le cinéma* edited by Jacques Chevallier, Paris 1953; "The World of Carl Dreyer" by Børge Trolle in *Sight and Sound* (London), winter 1955-56; "Rudy Maté—His Work with Carl Dreyer" by William Everson in *Films and Filming* (London), no.2, 1955; "Thoughts on My Craft" by Carl Dreyer in *Sight and Sound* (London), winter 1955-56; "Dreyer" by Herbert Luft in *Films and Filming* (London), June 1961; "'Douleur, Noblesse Unique' ou la passion chez Carl Dreyer" by Jean Sémolué in *Etudes cinématographiques* (Paris), fall 1961; "Great Films of the Century: The Passion of Joan of Arc" by Alan Stanbrook in *Films and Filming* (London), June 1961; "Passion et procès (de Dreyer à Bresson)" by Jean Sémolué in *Etudes cinématographiques* (Paris), no.18-19, 1962; "*The Trial of Joan of Arc*" by Robert Vas in *Sight and Sound* (London), no.4, 1963; "Rudolph Maté. Photographed Dreyer's *Passion of Joan of Arc* and Became Director on His Own" by Herbert Luft in *Films in Review* (New York), no.8, 1964; "Dreyer at 65" by Peter Cowie in *Films and Filming* (London), March 1964; "The World of Carl Dreyer" by Kirk Bond in *Film Quarterly* (Berkeley), fall 1965; "*La Passion de Jeanne d'Arc*" by Jean Delmas in *Jeune Cinéma* (Paris), no.5, 1965; "Interview med Herman Warm" by Werner Zurbuch in *Kosmorama* (Copenhagen), no.71, 1965; "Darkness and Light: Carl Dreyer" by Tom Milne in *Sight and Sound* (London), autumn 1965; "Thoughts on My Craft" By Carl Dreyer in *Sight and Sound* (London), winter 1955/56; "My Way of Working is in Relation to the Future: A Conversation with Carl Dreyer" by Carl Lerner in *Film Comment* (New York), fall 1966; "Fonctions

du gros plan et du cadrage dans *La Passion de Jeanne d'Arc*" by Barhélémy Amengual in *Etudes cinématographiques* (Paris), no.53-56, 1967; "Carl Dreyer: Utter Bore or Total Genius?" by Denis Duperly in *Films and Filming* (London), February 1968; special issue on Dreyer, *Cahiers du cinéma* (Paris), December 1968; special issue of *Kosmorama* (Copenhagen), June 1968; "Carl Dreyer", interview by Michel Delahaye in *Interviews with Film Directors*, edited by Andrew Sarris, New York 1969; "*The Passion of Joan of Arc*" by Harry Alan Potamkin in *The Emergence of Film Art* by Lewis Jacobs, New York 1969; "Historique du film" in *Avant-Scène du cinéma* (Paris), February 1970; "Jeanne d'Arc a l'écran" in *Avant-Scène du cinéma* (Paris), February 1970; "Historiens et critiques" in *Avant-Scène du cinéma* (Paris), February 1970; "Carl Th. Dreyer" by Jacques-Pierre Amette in *Dossiers du cinéma: Cinéasts I*, Paris 1971; article by Luis Buñuel in *Postitif* (Paris), February 1973; "Carl Dreyer and the Theme of Choice" by Dai Vaughan in *Sight and Sound* (London), summer 1974; "Carl Dreyer" by Robin Wood in *Film Comment* (New York), March/April 1974; "Dreyer's Concept of Abstraction" by Vlada Petric in *Sight and Sound* (London), spring 1975; "Joseph Delteil: The Passion of Joan of Arc" by Wilhelmina Van Ness in *Literature/Film Quarterly* (Salisbury, Maryland), no.4, 1975; "Dreyer's Joan" by David Bordwell in *Sight and Sound* (London), autumn 1975; "*La Passion de Jeanne d'Arc*" by V. Hugo, J. de Lacretelle, and P. Morand in *Avant Scène du cinéma* (Paris), 1 December 1977; "Une Peur active" by Jean-Pierre Oudart in *Cahiers du cinéma* (Paris), no.292, 1978; "*La Passion de Jeanne d'Arc*" by J.L. Cros in *Image et son* (Paris), September 1978; "Uncoded Images in the Heterogeneous Text" by Deborah Linderman in *Wide Angle* (Athens, Ohio), no.3, 1980.

* * *

Carl Dreyer's last silent film is one of the most famous films in the history of cinema. It is seldom missing on "World's Ten Best" Films" lists. Few films have been studied and analyzed as thoroughly in articles and books, and one sometimes feels that the real film is buried in theory and aesthetics. But, a true classical work of art, *La Passion de Jeanne d'Arc* appeals to and moves the spectator with its beautiful simplicity. It is a pure tragedy of a young suffering woman fighting a hostile world. The finest homage to the film is perhaps that of Jean-Luc Godard: in his film *Vivre sa vie* the prostitute (played by Anna Karina) is deeply moved by Dreyer's portrait of the legendary heroine when she sees the film in a Paris cinema in the 60's. She can identify with the tormented young woman in this timeless film.

From the time he started his script in October 1926 until the film was finished, Dreyer worked on it for a year and a half. The historical trial of Jeanne lasted for more than a year. Dreyer concentrated the actual 29 interrogations into one long interrogation, and in the film it takes place on May 30 1431, the last day of Jeanne's short life; Dreyer thus keeps to the unities of time, place and story.

The style of the film, which has been called a film in closeups, is derived directly from his sources and evokes the protocol of the trial. When the film was released, the closeup technique was regarded as shocking. Dreyer defended his method by stating: "The records give a shattering impression of the ways in which the trial was a conspiracy of the judges against the solitary Jeanne, bravely defending herself against men who displayed a devilish cunning to trap her in their net. This conspiracy could be conveyed on the screen only through hugh closeups that exposed, with merciless realism, the callous cynicism of the judges hidden behind hypocritical compassion—and on the other hand there had to be equally huge closeups of Jeanne, whose pure features would reveal that she alone found strength in her faith in God." As in all of Dreyer's major films the style grew out of the theme of the film. In *La Passion de Jeanne d'Arc* Dreyer wanted "to move the audience so that they would themselves feel the suffering that Jeanne endured." It was by using closeups that Dreyer could "lead the audience all the way into the hearts and guts of Jeanne and the judges."

The closeup technique is the core of the film, because it lifts the drama above a given place and a given time. It is a satisfactory way of abstracting from an historically defined reality without abandoning a respect for authenticity and realism. But this striving for timelessness is reflected in all the components of the film. And there is more to the film than closeups. Dreyer uses medium closeups, tilts, pans, travelling shots and intricate editing. Crosscutting is used to great effect, especially in the last part of the film, and the hectic rhythm and swiftly changing shots towards the end of the film are as masterfully controlled as the closeups. The visual language is very complex and not in the least monotonous. The sets and the costumes were consciously created in a way that furthered the balance between the historical and the modern. The lighting, the over-all whiteness of the images, contributes to the film's emphasis on the simple and the lucid.

Dramatically, *La Passion de Jeanne d'Arc* is composed as one long scene. This is Jeanne's last struggle, and the battle is for her life and her soul. The film is dramatically and psychologically intensified in two scenes. The first is when Jeanne breaks down mentally and, to save her life, signs a confession as a heretic. The second is the scene in which she regrets what she has done and withdraws the confession. She knows then that her death is certain, but she saves her soul, and she triumphs in her faith.

La Passion de Jeanne d'Arc is an intense description of the suffering of an individual, the drama of a soul transformed into images. It is a "cool" look, and Dryer called his method "realized mysticism." With his sober objectivity Dreyer succeeded in making the difficult understandable and the irrationl clear. The film is about the necessity of suffering for the liberation of the individual human being. As do all of Dreyer's heroines, Jeanne suffers defeat, but for Dreyer defeat or victory in this world is of no importance. The essential thing is the soul's victory over life. Dreyer's view of the historical facts is, of course, not a balanced one. Jeanne is the heroine, and Dreyer is on her side in her struggle against a cruel, official world.

In Dreyer's oeuvre *La Passion de Jeanne d'Arc* brings together all the resources of the cinema at that time, and is the most pure and perfect expression of his art. Of none of his films is his own statement more fitting: "The soul is revealed in the style, which is the artist's expression of the way he regards his material."

The film was well received when it was released, but it was not a commercial success. Since then the film's reputation has grown, and for many years it has been continuously shown in film archives and film clubs all over the world. The original negative of *La Passion de Jeanne d'Arc* was destroyed in a fire in 1928 at UFA in Berlin. Film archeologists are still working on a restoration of the film, which has survived in many slightly differing versions—but even a definitive version should not drastically change our impression of this masterpiece.

—Ib Monty

PATTON. Production: 20th Century-Fox; 1970; Deluxe Color, 35mm and 70mm, Cinemascope, (dimension 150 process used only in 70mm roadshow prints); running time: 170 mins. Released 4 February 1970.

Produced by Frank McCarthy with Frank Caffey; screenplay by Francis Ford Coppola and Edmund H. North; main titles designed by Pacific Title; directed by Franklin J. Schaffner; photography by Fred Koenekamp; edited by Hugh Fowler; sound supervised by James Corcoran, sound re-recorded by Douglas O. Williams, Ted Soderburg, and Murray Spivack, sound production by Don Bassman; art direction by Urie McCleary and Gil Parrondo, set decoration by Antonio Mateos and Pierre-Louis Thévenet; music by Jerry Goldsmith, orchestrated by Arthur Morton; special photographic effects by L.B. Abbott and Art Cruickshank, mechanical effects by Alex Weldon; technical advisers: Gen. Paul D. Harkins, Col. Glover S. Johns Jr., and Sr. Military Adviser General Omar S. Bradley; Spanish military adviser: Lieut. Col. Luis Martin Pozuelo; action coordinated by Joe Canutt.

Filmed on location in Spain, England, Morocco, and Greece. Academy Awards for Best Picture, Best Director, Best Actor (Scott), Best Screenplay-based on material not previously published, Best Art Direction-Set Decoration, Best Sound, and Best Editing, 1970; New York Film Critics Award, Best Actor (Scott), 1970.

Cast: George C. Scott (*Gen. George S. Patton Jr.*); Karl Malden (*Gen. Omar N. Bradley*); Michael Bates (*Field Marshal Sir Bernard Law Montgomery*); Edward Binns (*Major General Walter Bedel Smith*); Lawrence Dobkin (*Col. Gaston Bell*); John Doucette (*Maj. General Lucian K. Truscott*); James Edwards (*Sgt. William George Meeks*); Frank Latimore (*Lieut. Col. Henry Davenport*); Richard Münch (*Col. Gen. Alfred Joll*); Morgan Paull (*Capt. Richard N. Jenson*); Siegfried Rauch (*Capt. Oskar Steiger*); Paul Stevens (*Lieut. Col. Charles R. Codman*); Michael Strong (*Brig. Gen. Hobart Carver*); Karl Michael Vogler (*Field Marshal Erwin Rommel*); Stephen Young (*Capt. Chester B. Hansen*); Peter Barkworth (*Col. John Welkin*); John Barrie (*Air Vice-Marshal Sir Arthur Conningham*); David Bauer (*Lieut. Gen. Harry Buford*); Tim Considine (*Soldier who gets slapped*); Albert Dumortier (*Moroccan minister*); Gerald Flood (*Air Chief Marshal Sir Arthur Teddler*); Jack Gwillim (*Gen. Sir Harold Alexander*); David Healy (*Clergyman*); Bill Hickman (*Gen. Patton's driver*); Douglas Wilmer (*Maj. Gen. Francis de Guingand*); Patrick J. Zurica (*1st Lieut. Alexander Stiller*); Lowell Thomas (*Narrator of Fox Movietone Newsreels*).

Publications:

Reviews—in *Film Society Review* (New York), March 1970; review by Gordon Gow in *Films and Filming* (London), July 1970; review by Henry Hart in *Films in Review* (New York), February 1970; review by Andrew Sarris in *The Village Voice* (New York), 26 February 1970; review by Bernard Weinberg in *Film Quarterly* (Berkeley), summer 1970; books—*Big Screen, Little Screen* by Rex Reed, New York 1971; *Figures of Light: Film Criticism and Comment* by Stanley Kauffmann, New York 1971; *Francis Ford Coppola* by Robert Johnson, Boston 1977; *Guts and Glory: Great American War Movies* by Lawrence H. Sind, Reading, Massachusetts 1978; *Storytelling and Mythmaking: Images from Film and Literature* by Frank McConnell, New York 1979; *A Cinema of Loneliness: Penn, Kubrick, Coppola, Scorsese, Altman* by Robert Phillip Kolker, New York

1980; articles—"An Interview with Franklin Schaffner" by Gerald Pratley in *Cineaste* (New York), summer 1969; article by Stanley Bielecki in *Films and Filming* (London), August 1969; "The Photography of *Patton*" by George J. Mitchell in *American Cinematographer* (Los Angeles), August 1970; "*Patton*" by Robert Steele in *Film Heritage* (Dayton, Ohio), August 1970; "Director of the Month" by Andrew Sarris in *Show* (Hollywood), April 1970; "Director Franklin Schaffner: From *Planet of the Apes* to *Patton*" by D. Munroe in *Show* (Hollywood), 6 August 1970; "What Directors are Saying" in *Action* (Los Angeles), November/December 1970; "*Patton*" by Michael Sragow in *Film Society Review* (New York), March 1970; article by David Wilson in *Sight and Sound* (London), summer 1970; "De der matte ofres—og de der kom tilbage" by N. Jensen in *Kosmorama* (Copenhagen), summer 1979.

*   *   *

Patton struck the American consciousness in 1970 with all the impact of a slap in the face. Arriving on the screen at the height of public disillusionment with the United States military involvement in Vietnam, it seemed to many a reaffirmation of the attitudes that had led the country into its entanglement in Southeast Asia. Others, however, including the producer and director, viewed it as an implicit statement against war in which battles served as a framework within which a complex human being could be deciphered. The emphasis was placed upon creating not only a dramatic but an accurate portrayal of the man so that audiences could fully comprehend the complexities and enigmatic character or perhaps the most colorful and misunderstood personality of World War II.

The effectiveness of the film in achieving its goals rests almost on the tour d'force performances of George C. Scott as Patton. What the actor did, in his Academy Award winning performance, was simply to make his character come across as a human being without resorting to clichés or manipulating the role into a vehicle for his own judgments. Scott, in fact, studied more than 3000 feet of film and every available book on the general to enhance his portrayal. By shaving his head daily, wearing false teeth to lengthen his jawline, and straightening his nose with plastic, he achieved a certain physical resemblance but made no attempt to raise the pitch of his own gravelly voice to the rather high, squeaky level of Patton's.

Scott's portrayal of Patton as a dominating personality was enhanced by the epic quality of much of the color photography, done in 70-millimeter, Dimension 150, a procedure that produced a profound aura of grandeur and a perception of immense depth. The resulting images of large scale battles became impersonal, even beautiful panoramas, that removed the viewer from an intimate perception of the war's brutality. The audience's attention is focused on one man, Patton, and his interpretation of the battles. In some instances, he ponders upon the toll that combat exacts in human lives and the squandering of the talents of the men who must fight. In others, he revels in the crusades of battle as a glorious adventure, a global chess game to be contested and mastered by an elite few. He admits "God help me, I do love it so." Audiences are accordingly left with an enigmatic picture of a man who wants to win so badly that he will slap one of his own soldiers for not sharing that resolve but who is also a tender and loving father to those who are close to him.

If Scott's interpretation of Patton (assisted by screenwriter Francis Ford Coppola and director Franklin Schaffer) was multi-leveled, so was critical and popular reaction to the film. There was a certain polarization between those who saw its main character as a reflection of the worst aspects of the military establishment and those who regretted that there was no one like him among the soldiers who fought in Vietnam. Finally, the film, which resembled a cinematic Rorschach test of the American temperament, did extremely well at the box office and won eight academy awards including Best Picture and a Best Actor award, refused by Scott, for his performance in the title role.

—Stephen L. Hanson

PEEPING TOM. Production: Anglo Amalgamated; Eastmancolor, 35mm; running time: 109 mins., other versions include 90 mins. and 86 mins. Released April 1960, London.

Produced by Michael Powell with Albert Fennell; screenplay by Leo Marks; directed by Michael Powell; photography by Otto Heller; edited by Noreen Ackland; sound by C.C. Stevens and Gordon McCallum; art direction by Arthur Lawson; set decoration by Ivor Beddoes; music composed and conducted by Brian Easdale.

Cast: Karl Boehm (*Mark Lewis*); Moira Shearer (*Vivian*); Anna Massey (*Helen Stephens*); Maxine Audley (*Mrs. Stephens*); Esmond Knight (*Arthur Baden*); Bartlett Mullins (*Mr. Peters*); Shirley Ann Field (*Diane Ashley*); Michael Goodliffe (*Don Jarvis*); Brenda Bruce (*Dora*); Martin Miller (*Dr. Rosan*); Pamela Green (*Milly*); Jack Watson (*Inspector Gregg*); Nigel Davenport (*Sergeant Miller*); Brian Wallace (*Tony*); Susan Travers (*Lorraine*); Maurice Durant (*Publicity chief*); Brian Worth (*Assistant director*); Veronica Hurst (*Miss Simpson*); Miles Malleson (*Elderly gentleman*); Alan Rolfe (*Store detective*); Michael Powell (*Mr. Lewis*); John Dunbar.

Publications:

Review—by Peter Baker in *Films and Filming* (London), May 1960; books—*Michael Powell* by Kevin Gough-Yates, London 1971; *Films and Feelings* by Raymond Durgnat, Cambridge, Massachusetts 1971; *A Mirror for England* by Raymond Durgnat, London 1971; *A Critical History of British Cinema* by Roy Armes, New York 1978; *Powell, Pressburger, and Others*, edited by I. Christie, London 1978; articles—"Michael Powell: Filmography" by O.O. Green in *Movie* (London), autumn 1965; article by Philip Chamberlin in *Film Society Review* (London), January 1966; "Private Madness and Public Lunacy" by Kevin Gough-Yates in *Films and Filming* (London), February 1972; "Interview with Michael Powell: The Expense of Naturalism" by R. Collins and I. Christie in *Monogram* (London), no.3 1972; "*Le Voyeur*" by J.C. Romer in *Ecran* (Paris), July/August 1973; "*Le Voyeur*" by T. Renaud in *Cinéma 76* (Paris), October 1976; "Film: Michael Powell's *Peeping Tom*" by Vincent Canby in *The New York Times*, 14 October 1979; "Film Festival II: Nostalgic Gamble" by Andrew Sarris in *The Village Voice* (New York), 15 October 1979; "Films" by N. Sayre in the *Nation* (New York), 10 November 1979; "A Very Tender Film, A Very Nice One: Michael Powell's *Peeping Tom*" by E. Stein in *Film Comment* (New York), September/October 1979; "*Peeping Tom*: Voyeurism, the Camera, and the Spectator" by R. Humphries in *Film*

Reader (Evanston, Illinois), no.4, 1979; "Mark of the Red Death" by D. Thomson in *Sight and Sound* (London), autumn 1980.

* * *

Almost the most remarkable thing about *Peeping Tom* is the critical reception it provoked. This film, disingenuously described by its director Michael Powell as "a very tender film, a very nice one," was uniformly abused in its own country. Derek Hill's infamous claim that "the only really satisfactory way to dispose of *Peeping Tom* would be to shovel it up and flush it swiftly down the nearest sewer" may have been the most violent of critical assessments, but it was all too typical. Powell's career as a feature-film director never recovered from the assault, and the road to critical re-assessment of *Peeping Tom* has been long and hard. Anyone concerned with the whys and wherefores of this process need look no further than Ian Christie (ed.) *Powell Pressburger and Others*, where the nature of the affront Powell offered to orthodox criticism is clearly analyzed. *Peeping Tom* was only the climactic case in a long series.

None of this is to suggest, however, that *Peeping Tom* is not a disturbing movie. In narrative terms alone it is immediately problematic: any story about a man who murders women with the sharpened leg of a tripod, filming them as they die, is likely to attract adverse attention. When the young man in question is played straight, as someone with whom we are invited to empathise, and not as some rolling eyed gothic horror, then the difficulties are redoubled. How can we empathise with such perverse pleasures? And when the film-maker involved is such a well-established talent, how can we reconcile his presumed "seriousness" with what is conventionally the subject for a shocker?

Today such difficulties would not be quite as pressing as they were in 1960. Ranges of acceptability have widened, and the line between Art and Exploitation is no longer so easily drawn. Yet even today *Peeping Tom* is genuinely disturbing. For all our familiarity with violent movie murder, with sexuality, with the psychology of perversion, Powell's movie can still leave a spectator profoundly uneasy. For *Peeping Tom* refuses to let us off the hook after the fashion of so many apparently horrific movies. Its elaborate structure of films within films implicates us as spectators in the voyeurism that fuels Mark's violence. We see the murders through his viewfinder; later we see them on screen as he projects them for his pleasure. We see his father's filmed record of experiments on the young Mark, experiments which have turned him into a voyeuristic killer. We see the movie studio where he works, the setting where he will murder (of all people) Moira Shearer, star of Powell's *The Red Shoes*. As the internal cross-references multiply (and they are endless) the implication insinuates itself into our awareness. In watching film, all film, the pleasures that we take are finally no different to Mark's; the gap between his and our voyeurism is too small for comfort.

It was Powell's misfortune to make *Peeping Tom* at a time when commitment to a one-dimensional notion of realist cinema was at its height. *Peeping Tom* , like all of Powell's cinema, is founded on a highly self-conscious manipulation of film itself, and it is impossible here to do justice to the resonating visual complexity of films like *A Matter of Life and Death*, *Black Narcissus*, and, of course, *Peeping Tom*. In this cinema it is the medium that is the source of pleasure and the focus of attention, not some instantly apparent moral ingredient. *Peeping Tom* turns that cinematic awareness back on itself, offering aesthetic satisfactions along with their disturbing implications. It is a film that is paramountly about cinema, about the experience of cinema, a film which makes voyeurs of us all. That *is* genuinely disturbing.

—Andrew Tudor

PEPE LE MOKO. Nuits blanches. Il bandito della Casbah. Production: Paris Film Production; black and white, 35mm; running time: 93 mins. Released 28 January 1937, Paris.

Produced by Robert and Raymond Hakim; screenplay by Julien Duvivier and d'Henri La Barthe (under pseudonym Detective Ashelbe) with Jacques Constant and Henri Jeanson; from the novel by Detective Ashelbe; directed by Julien Duvivier; photography by Jules Kruger and Marc Fossard; edited by Marguerite Beauge; sound by Antoine Archaimbaud; production design by Jacques Krauss; music by Vincent Scotto and Mohamed Yguerbouchen.

Filmed in Pathe studios in Joinville, exteriors shot in Algiers, Marseille, and Sete.

Cast: Jean Gabin (*Pépé le Moko*); Mireille Balin (*Gaby Gould*); Line Noro (*Inès*); Lucas Gridoux (*Inspector Slimane*); Gabriel Gabrio (*Carlos*); Fernand Charpin (*Régis*); Saturnin Fabre (*Grandfather*); Gilbert Gil (*Pierrot*); Roger Legris (*Max*); Gaston Modot (*Jimmy*); Marcel Dalio (*L'Arbi*); Frehel (*Tania*); Olga Lord (*Aïcha*); Renee Carl (*Mother Tarte*); Rene Bergeron (*Inspector Meunier*); Charles Granval (*Maxime Kleep*); Philippe Richard (*Inspector Janvier*); Paul Escoffier (*Commissioner Louvain*); Robert Ozanne (*Gendron*); Georges Peclet (*Barsac*); Frank Maurice (*An inspector*).

Publications:

Script—"*Pépé le Moko*" by Julien Duvivier and d'Henri La Barthe in *Avant-Scène du cinéma* (Paris), 1 June 1981; review—"La Presse" in *Avant-Scène du cinéma* (Paris), 1 June 1981; books—*Julien Duvivier* by Raymond Chirat, Lyon 1968; *Anthologie du cinéma* vol.4, Paris 1969; *French Film* by Georges Sadoul, London 1972; articles—"Jean Gabin's Instinctual Man" by Pierre Duvillars in *Films in Review* (New York), March 1951; "Julien Duvivier" by Michel Aubriant in *Cinémonde* (Paris), 28 November 1952; "Jean Gabin" by Jack Nolan in *Films in Review* (New York), April 1963; "Jean Gabin" by Peter Cowie in *Films and Filming* (London), February 1964; "Duvivier, le professionel" by Jean Renoir in *Le Figaro littéraire* (Paris), 6 November 1967; "*Pépé le Moko*" by N. Simsolo in *Image et son* (Paris), March 1972; "L'Auberge fameuse" by Claude Beylie in *Avant-Scène du cinéma* (Paris), 1 June 1981; "*Pépé le Moko*: la valse des caméras" by Michel Marie in *Avant-Scène du cinéma* (Paris), 1 June 1981.

* * *

Pepe le Moko had an immediate success scarcely rivalled in French film history. Its director, Julien Duvivier, was instantly hired by Hollywood, where the film itself was remade the next year, with Anatole Litvak directing Charles Boyer, as *Casbah*. *Pepe* ranked as the year's top film in many countries, including Japan, and it remains today a cult film of a stature similar to that which *Casablanca* enjoys in the United States.

A chronicle of the adventures of a dandy criminal hiding out in the casbah section of Algiers, *Pepe le Moko* is really a film about the bitterness of lost dreams. Pepe, as created by Jean Gabin, is in no way captive of the outlaw life he leads. Controlling his minions by dint of his authoritative personality and the notoriety of his name, he is above them all. Only Sliman, the Algiers police inspector, has an inkling of the real man and his motives. Pepe's gang is set off against the police force, while Pepe and Sliman struggle on a higher plane, respecting one another, respecting even more the fate that both believe rules them all.

The film opens with documentary footage and informational commentary about the Casbah. We learn of the mixture of races, the numbers and kinds of vices represented in the maze of alleys even the police fear to enter. Pepe's entrance is spectacular: a closeup of his hand holding a jewel, then his face tilted as he examines the jewel in the light. Soon after, while being pursued, he ducks into a secret hideaway and there encounters Gaby (Mireille Balin). Once again it is her jewels that attract both him and the camera in successive closeups of their faces. When Sliman enters to escort Gaby back to the safety of the grand hotels, the knot is tied. Sliman even remarks, "It is written, Pepe."

Duvivier treats the entire intrigue as if with Sliman's magistral comprehension. Never indulging in suspense, he nevertheless inflates key moments with an abundance of stylistic flourishes. Most famous is the death of the informer Regis at the hands of Pepe and his gang. Shoved back against a wall, hysterical and pathetic, Regis bumps into a jukebox, setting off a raucous song just as his own victim, aided by pals, pumps a revolver full of bullets into his thick body. Just before this scene Pepe and Gaby express their love by reciting antiphonally the Metro stops they know, moving through a remembered Paris from opposite ends until they say together "*La Place Blanche*." Sliman looks on, knowing that he has caught Pepe in the net of desire and nostalgia. The Casbah will no longer serve as a refuge now that Gaby and thoughts of Paris have corrupted Pepe. Later, in a moment of quiet just before the denouement, a homesick old singer, caught like Pepe in the Casbah, puts a record on the gramophone and, tears in her eyes, sings along with the record, a song about the glories of Paris. Duvivier pans along a wall from a picture of this woman when she was young and beautiful, to the record player, and then to the woman's tear-choked face. It is a magnificent summation of the film's ability to summon up unfulfilled desire and nostalgia.

The film's dynamic conclusion unrolls directly from these sentiments: Pepe's obligatory outburst against another informer (Marcel Dalio), his breaking away from his common-law wife, his descent from the Casbah—accompanied by the theme music of the film and a totally artificial rear-projection that places us inside his obsessed mind. Duvivier wrings all the pathos of the lost dream from the finale, as Pepe finds his way aboard Gaby's ship and then is arrested inches away from her, though neither of them realizes how close they are. As the ship pulls out, he sees Gaby on the deck but the whistle of the ship drowns out his call. She is looking far above him, at the Casbah he has left. He tears his stomach open with a pocketknife. Virtually a private masturbation, his suicide is the climax of his longings, represented by the mysterious and elegant Gaby and by the memory of home. Both these sentiments and their outcome are of the style and spirit of poetic realism. One can see why the film was banned as demoralizing and debilitating first by the French government at the start of the war and then by the Vichy government once the

new order had come to power. After the war it returned as a classic.

—Dudley Andrew

PERSONA. Production: AB Svensk Filmindustri; black and white, 35mm; running time: 84 mins; length: 2320 meters. Released 18 October 1966, Stockholm.

Produced, scripted, and directed by Ingmar Bergman; photography by Sven Nykvist; edited by Ulla Ryghe; sound engineered by P.O. Pettersson; production design by Bibi Lindström; music by Lars-Johan Werle; special effects by Evald Andersson; costumes designed by Mago.

Filmed 19 July 1965-17 September 1965, with some scenes shot in February and March 1966, in Svensk Filmindustri studios, Stockholm, and on location.

Cast: Bibi Andersson (*Alma*); Liv Ullmann (*Elisabeth Vogler*); Margaretha Krook (*Läkaren*); Gunnar Björnstrand (*Herr Vogler*); Jörgen Lindström (*The boy*).

Publications:

Scripts—*Persona* by Ingmar Bergman, Stockholm 1966; "*Persona*" in *Avant-Scène du cinéma* (Paris), October 1968; *Persona and Shame* translated by Keith Bradfield, New York 1972; reviews—by Raymond Durgnat in *Films and Filming* (London), December 1967; review in *Films in Review* (New York), April 1967; review by Andrew Sarris in *The Village Voice* (New York), 23 March 1967; review by Georges Sadoul in *Les Lettres françaises* (Paris), 12 July 1967; review by Michael Harris in *Take One* (Montreal), no.8 1967-68; books—*Ingmar Bergman på teatern* by Henrik Sjögren, Stockholm 1968; *Ingmar Bergman* by Birgitta Steene, New York 1968; *The Silence of God: Creative Response to the Films of Ingmar Bergman* by Arthur Gibson, New York 1969; *Ingmar Bergman* by Robin Wood, New York 1969; *Bergman on Bergman* by Stig Björkman, Torsten Manns, and Jonas Sima, translated by Paul Britten Austin, London 1970; *Regi: Ingmar Bergman* by Henrik Sjögren, Stockholm 1970; *Cinema Borealis: Ingmar Bergman and the Swedish Ethos* by Vernon Young, New York 1971; *Ingmar Bergman Directs* by John Simon, New York 1972; *Ingmar Bergman* by Tino Ranieri, Florence 1974; *Ingmar Bergman: Essays in Criticism* edited by Stuart Kaminsky, New York 1975; *Changing* by Liv Ullmann, New York 1976; *Ingmar Bergman and Society* by Maria Bergom-Larsson, San Diego 1978; *Mindscreen: Bergman, Godard and the First-Person Film* by Bruce Kawin, Princeton 1978; *Der frühe Ingmar Bergman* by Hauke Lange-Fuchs, Lübeck 1978; *Ingmar Bergman* by Denis Marion, Paris 1979; *Ingmar Bergman: An Appreciation* by Roger Manvell, New York 1980; *Ingmar Bergman: The Cinema as Mistress* by Philip Mosley, Boston 1981; *Film and Dreams: An Approach to Bergman* edited by Vlada Petrić, South Salem, New York 1981; *Ingmar Bergman: A Critical Biography* by Peter Cowie, New York 1982; *A Reference Guide to Ingmar Bergman* by Birgitta Steene, Boston 1982; articles—by Richard Corliss in *Film Quarterley* (Berkeley), summer 1967; article by Erwin Leiser in *Film Comment* (New York), fall/winter 1967; article by F.A. Macklin in *Film Heritage* (Dayton, Ohio), spring 1967; "The Phantom of Personality" by Jean-Louis Comolli in *Cahiers du cinéma* (Paris), September 1967; "*Persona*" by Susan Sontag in *Sight and Sound* (London), autumn 1967; article by John Hofsess in *Take One* (Montreal), August 1968; article by Robin Wood in *Movie* (London), spring 1968; "Ingmar Bergman: jugé par deux critiques suédois" in *Avant-Scène du cinéma* (Paris), October 1968; article by Kirk Bond in *Film Culture* (New York), winter/spring 1970; "Cinema Borealis" by Vernon Young in *Hudson Review* (Nutley, New Jersey), summer 1970; "Bergman's *Persona* and the Artistic Dilemma of the Modern Narrative" by C.J. Jones in *Literature/Film Quarterly* (Salisbury, Maryland), winter 1977; "*Persona*" by E. Iverson in *Kosmorama* (Copenhagen), spring 1978; "Anais Nin's *House of Incest* and Ingmar Bergman's *Persona*: Two Variations on a Theme" by N. Scholar in *Literature/Film Quarterly* (Salisbury, Maryland), no.1, 1979; "The Reflexive Function of Bergman's *Persona*" by P.N. Campbell in *Cinema Journal* (Evanston, Illinois), no.1, 1979; "Szemelykozi kudarcok—alarcban: Ingmar Bergman pszichologiai modellje" by S. Fejja in *Filmkultura* (Budapest), November/December 1979.

* * *

Persona may be Ingmar Bergman's most consciously crafted film; it may also be one of his most enigmatic. The plot is a tour-de-force distillation of an agon between two women, Alma (Bibi Anderson), a young nurse, and Elisabeth Vogler (Liv Ullman) her patient, a successful actress who has withdrawn into silence. The psychic tension between the two women, and the power of the silent one, reflect Stringberg's short play *The Stronger*, a source many critics of the film have noted. Yet Bergman is even more daring than Stringberg, for more is at stake in his film, and he sustains the one-sided conversation for the length of a feature film.

In many ways *Persona* is "about" the nature and conventions of the feature film—most obviously because Bergman begins the film by showing the ignition of an arc projector and the threading of a film, and ends it with the same projector's being turned off. The greatest visual shock in all of Bergman's often startling oeuvre must be the moment near the middle of *Persona* when the film rips (or seems to rip), burns, and introduces strange material, apparently foreign to the story of the two women.

Actually, the material comes largely from a pre-title sequence. By the time *Persona* was made, the pre-title sequence had ceased to be a novelty and was on the way to becoming a tired convention. Generally, a pre-title sequence presents some bit of action preliminary to the main action of the film, but not essential to its comprehension. The pre-title sequence of *Persona*, however, is utterly unique. It is composed of material completely foreign to the imagery of the film itself (except for the eruption after the burned film), so that one truly misses "nothing" of the plot by starting with the titles, yet it is crucial to an understanding of what is happening in that plot.

Early in the film we see a psychiatrist who talks to Alma about her future patient, and who talks to Elisabeth, alone, about her withdrawal. Bergman uses the psychiatrist to fill us in on the background of the silent woman. Late in the film we meet Elisabeth's husband, who may be blind, when he shows up on the island where his wife is recuperating—but apparently he cannot tell Alma from Elisabeth. By this time Bergman has laid so many clues about the imaginative or psychotic perspective of the plot that we must wonder whether the husband is himself imagined or indeed whether Alma and Elisabeth are two aspects of a divided

personality. This suspicion is encouraged by a repeated shot of a composite face, made up of half of each woman's face. It appears after a climactic scene in which Alma recites Elisabeth's faults to her face and ends up screaming that she is not Elisabeth Vogler herself. Interpretation of the film must depend on how one regards that scene.

Without judging the reality of any of the depicted events, however, once one sees the silent Elisabeth as a figure for the analyst and Alma as the patient, one can see that the sequence of the relationship between Alma and Elisabeth neatly corresponds to the stages of transference and counter-transference in classical psychoanalysis. Even more remarkable than the correspondence is the fact that Bergman has virtually suppressed shot-countershot in this film. This in itself is a considerable stylistic innovation for a film essentially about a single speaker and a single listener. But the few times that shot-countershot does occur, it underlines the stages of transference: first, when Alma initially makes contact with Elisabeth by reading her a letter from her husband; next, and with obsessive frequency, as Alma feels comfortable enough to describe her life and confess her excitement over an orgy and her subsequent abortion. Here shot-countershot underlines the positive transference: Alma is falling in love with Elisabeth. But when reading a private letter to Elisabeth's husband, Alma realizes that she is being coolly analyzed and her love turns to hatred (negative transference). It is when she deliberately causes harm to Elisabeth that a single instance of shot-countershot occurs and, with it, comes the ripping and burning of the film, along with all the "repressed" material from the pre-title scene. The climactic accusation is the final shot-countershot scene in the film. It is repeated twice as if to stress its importance and to show how a film-maker constructs shot-countershot.

As a psychoanalytic drama, *Persona* depends upon the relationship of the seemingly chaotic images of the beginning of the film to the accusations of Alma at the height of her transference anxiety. There the abortion, the rejection of Elisabeth's son, and the confusion over who sleeps with the husband are significant issues as are the frequent representations and discussions of love-making while someone looks on. The entire film actually turns on the perspective of a pre-adolescent male, seen waking up in a morgue in the pre-title scene, and reaching out, in the first initial shot-countershot structure, to touch the projected image of the faces of the two women flowing together. In the center of this labyrinthine film, there is a primal scene disturbance: a fantasy of intercourse as a violent act, yet exciting to watch, in which the child born out of it believes himself unwanted, even the victim of willed destruction.

No film so systematically reflects the psychoanalytical encounter, although many films of lesser intensity (such as Hitchcock's *Spellbound* or Bergman's own *Face to Face*) attempt it more directly; perhaps no other film offers as many decoys to hide its psychoanalytical core. The very clues that would engage the viewer in trying to sort out what is real and what is imagined by the two (or is it one?) women are distractions from its profound concern.

—P. Adams Sitney

THE PHANTOM OF THE OPERA. Production: Universal Pictures; black and white, (some sequences filmed in 2-strip Technicolor), 35mm, silent; running time: about 94 mins.; length: 10 reels, 8464 feet. Released 15 November 1925, premiered 6 September 1925 in New York. Re-released 1930 with some dialogue sequences and songs added.

Presented by Carl Laemmle; screenplay (adaptation) by Raymond Schrock and Elliott J. Clawson; from the novel by Gaston Leroux; titles written by Tom Reed; directed by Rupert Julian, additional direction by Edward Sedgwick (some sources list Sedgwick as the "associate director"); photography by Virgil Miller, Milton Bridenbecker, and Charles Van Enger; edited by Maurice Pivar; production design by Charles Hall and Ben Carre.

Filmed in Hollywood. Cost: budgeted at $1 million.

Cast: Lon Chaney (*Erik*); Mary Philbin (*Christine Dace*); Norman Kerry (*Raoul de Chagny*); Snitz Edwards (*Florine Papillon*); Gibson Gowland (*Simon*); John Sainpolis (*Philippe de Chagny*); Virginia Pearson (*Carlotta*); Arthur Edmund Carew (also Carewe) (*Ledoux*); Edith Yorke (*Madame Valerius*); Anton Vaverka (*Prompter*); Bernard Siegel (*Joseph Buguet*); Olive Ann Alcorn (*La Sorelli*); Edward Cecil (*Faust*); Alexander Bevani (*Mephistopheles*); John Miljan (*Valentin*); Grace Marvin (*Martha*); George Williams (*Ricard*); Bruce Covington (*Moncharmin*); Cesare Gravina (*Manager*); Ward Crane (*Count Ruboff*); Chester Conklin (*Orderly*); William Tryoler (*Conductor*).

Publications:

Review—"*The Phantom of the Opera*" by Mordaunt Hall in *The New York Times*, 7 September 1925; books—*An Illustrated History of the Horror Film* by Carlos Clemens, New York 1967, also see Clemens's *Horror Movies*, n.d. ; *Faces, Forms, Films: The Artistry of Lon Chaney* by Robert G. Anderson, South Brunswick 1971; *Classics of the Horror Film* by William K. Everson, Secaucus, New Jersey 1974; *American Silent Film* by William K. Everson, New York 1978; *American Film Institute Catalog of Feature Films*, Vol. F2, 1921-1930, Los Angeles, n.d.; articles—"Lon Chaney" by George Mitchell in *Films in Review* (New York), December 1953; article by Rudy Belmer in *Films in Review* (New York), October 1962; "Lon Chaney: Man of a Thousand Faces" by DeWitt Bodeen in *Focus on Film* (London), May/August 1970; "Lon Chaney ou la politique de l'acteur" by C. Viviani in *Positif* (Paris), July/August 1978; "Reflections in a Cinema Eye: Lon Chaney" by S. Meth in *Classic Film Collector* (Indiana, Pennsylvania), July 1979.

*   *   *

There have been several versions of *The Phantom of the Opera*, but none has remained as close to the original novel by Gaston Leroux as does the Lon Chaney film. Admittedly the film stays faithful to the original work sometimes more as a result of what is not shown that what is; for example, whereas later screen versions offer fanciful explanations for the phantom's grotesque appearance, the Chaney feature makes no effort to explain why the phantom is the way he is—by default, presumably going along with Leroux's story that he was "born that way."

Encouraged by the praise and box-office rewards heaped on Chaney's previous Universal feature, *The Hunchback of Notre Dame*. Carl Laemmle budgeted one million dollars for *The Phantom of the Opera*. Rupert Julian, a long-time Universal contract director who had made a career as an actor portraying Kaiser Wilhelm in various films, was assigned to direct, but he was replaced some time during the shooting by Edward Sedg-

wick, a minor comedy director. (Apparently Julian and Chaney did not get along, the result of a disagreement about the phantom's characterization.) Universal promoted the film by using the rather obvious device of permitting no advance photographs of Chaney to be shown, thus assuring an excited and enthusiastic audience for the New York premiere on September 6, 1925. Critical reaction was somewhat mixed, but the feature proved a tremendous success at the box office.

It is perhaps unfortunate that *The Hunchback of Notre Dame* and *The Phantom of the Opera* are the most frequently revived and easily accessible of Chaney's silent features, for neither film allows the actor much excuse for dramatics. His make-up, of course, is superb, but here there is no evidence of the kind of emotional range that Chaney displays, for example, in *Tell It to the Marines* (1927). Also, his supporting players, Mary Philbin and Norman Kerry, are singularly lacking in talent; Philbin, as the opera singer who unmasks the Phantom, is particularly weak.

The star of *The Phantom of the Opera* is not Chaney, but rather the magnificent sets of Charles D. Hall and Ben Carre, ranging from the awe-inspiring lobby and auditorium of the Paris Opera House to the eerie, subterranean home of the phantom. Equally impressive are the costumes, particularly the "Death" garment worn by Chaney in the Bal Masque sequence. This scene, together with the operatic numbers from Gounod's *Faust*, were filmed in two-strip Technicolor. The direction is weak, and the film is badly paced for a melodrama, although suspense is allowed to build, the result of Chaney's remaining masked until more than half-way through the film.

For a 1930 reissue of *The Phantom*, Universal filmed a number of dialogue sequences with Mary Philbin and Norman Kerry, and added a singing voice—not that of Philbin—to the operatic numbers. At that time some ten minutes were also cut from the film.

—Anthony Slide

THE PHILADELPHIA STORY. Production: Metro-Goldwyn-Mayer Pictures Corp.; 1940; black and white, 35mm; running time: 112 mins. Released December 1940.

Produced by Joseph Mankiewicz; screenplay by Donald Ogden Stewart and Waldo Salt (uncredited); from the play by Philip Barry; directed by George Cukor; photography by Joseph Ruttenberg; edited by Frank Sullivan; sound by Douglas Shearer; set decoration by Edwin Willis; art direction by Cedric Gibbons and Wade B. Rubottom; music by Frank Waxman; costumes designed by Adrian.

Filmed 1940 in MGM studios. Academy Awards for Best Actor (Stewart) and Best Screenplay, 1940; New York Film Critics Award, Best Actress (Hepburn), 1940.

Cast: Katharine Hepburn (*Tracy Lord*); Cary Grant (*C.K. Dexter Haven*); James Stewart (*Macauley Connor*); Ruth Hussey (*Liz Imbrie*); John Howard (*George Kittredge*); Roland Young (*Uncle Willie*); John Halliday (*Seth Lord*); Virginia Weidler (*Dinah Lord*); Mary Nash (*Margaret Lord*); Henry Daniell (*Sidney Kidd*); Lionel Pape (*Edward*); Rex Evans (*Thomas*); Russ Clark (*John*); Hilda Plowright (*Librarian*); Lita Chevret (*Manicurist*); Lee Phelps (*Bartender*); Dorothy Fay, Florine McKinney, Helene Whitney, and Hillary Brooks (*Mainliners*);

Claude King (*Uncle Willie's butler*); Robert de Bruce (*Dr. Parsons*); Veda Buckland (*Elsie*).

Publications:

Books—*Hommage à George Cukor* by Henri Langlois and others, Paris 1963; *George Cukor* by Jean Domarchi, Paris 1965; *Cukor and Company: The Films of George Cukor and His Collaborators* by Gary Carey, New York 1971; *The Films of Katharine Hepburn* by Homer Dickens, New York 1971; *On Cukor* by Gavin Lambert, New York 1972; *The Films of Cary Grant* by Donald Deschner, Secaucus, New Jersey 1978; *Katharine Hepburn* by Alvin H. Marill, New York 1973; *George Cukor* by Carlos Clarens, London 1976; *The Hollywood Professionals*, Cukor entry by Allen Estrin, New York 1980; *George Cukor* by Gene Phillips, Boston 1982; articles—"Katharine Hepburn" by Romano V. Tozzi in *Films in Review* (New York), December 1957; "George Cukor: His Success Directing Women Has Obscured His Other Directorial Virtues" by Romano Tozzi in *Films in Review* (New York), February 1958; "So He Became a Lady's Man" by John Reid in *Films and Filming* (London), August 1960; "*The Philadelphia Story*" by John Cutts in *Films and Filming* (London), July 1962; "Un Etincelant Cukor" by Patrick Bureau in *Les Lettres françaises* (Paris), 1 November 1962; "Où finit le théâtre" by Jean-André Fieschi in *Cahiers du cinéma* (Paris), February 1963; "Analyse d'un grand film: *Philadelphia Story*" by Claude Jean Philippe in *Télérama* (Paris), 8 December 1963; "Retrospective Cukor" issue of *Cahiers du cinéma* (Paris), February 1964; "James Stewart" by William Sweigart in *Films in Review* (New York), December 1964; "After Making 9 Films Together, Hepburn Can Practically Direct Cukor" by B. Nightingale in *The New York Times*, 28 January 1979; "Cukor and Hepburn" by Gene Phillips in *American Classic Screen* (Shawnee Mission, Kansas), fall 1979; "George Cukor" by DeWitt Bodeen in *Films in Review* (New York), November 1981.

*   *   *

The Philadelphia Story is the one of the most successful and best loved screwball comedies of the classical Hollywood era. It is based on the 1939 Broadway production of Philip Barry's play which starred Katharine Hepburn. The film employs the 1930s screwball plot device of the idle rich whose wealth has blinded them to the simple joys of life and the worthiness of middle-class values. Tracy Lord is the arrogant Philadelphia socialite who is planning her wedding to a stuffy social climber when her ex-husband, C.K. Dexter Haven, arrives at the mansion. Haven is a charming millionaire who openly displays his love of life and his disdain for pretentiousness while he secretly longs for the reunion with his ex-wife. Jimmy Stewart and Ruth Hussey are the reporters from the scandal sheet *Spy Magazine* who have been assigned to cover the wedding. Anti-romance, verbal and witty relationships, and the tendency to poke fun at the rich are all in abundance providing humorous distractions and obstacles to Tracy's and Dexter's final reconciliation.

Director Georges Cukor here shows his preference for understatement in romantic comedies through his emphasis on plot and performance. Following Frank Capra's example in *It Happened One Night* and his earlier success in *Holiday*, Cukor employs a screwball comic style which avoids explicit romance between two leading characters. He instead pits them against each other, creating romantic courtship through character tensions.

Because the audience knows that the characters are Hepburn and Grant, two movie stars who have been paired before in Cukor's *Sylvia Scarlett* and *Holiday* and the Howard Hawks's *Bringing Up Baby*, the audience is predisposed to want them to get together. Cukor plays with this expectation throughout the film but especially in the famous opening scene:

Grant is tossed out the front door; Hepburn appears at the door where she breaks one of Grant's golf clubs; she tosses the clubs after him and slams the door; Grant returns to the door and rings the bell; when Hepburn answers, he pushes her in the face.

Not a single word is spoken in this scene. Its comic success depends as much on Hepburn's star image as on the superb timing. During the latter 1930s, Hepburn headed the list by the Independent Theatre Owners Association of "box-office poison" movie stars. Critics found her grating, "mannish," or too intense. Cukor, who had directed Hepburn in five previous films, said that she was unattractive to audiences in the late 1930s because she "never was a 'love me. I'm a lovable little girl' kind of actress. She always challenged the audience, and....they felt something arrogant in her playing." In *The Philadelphia Story*, Hepburn and Cukor capitalized on these aspects of her image turning them to Hepburn's advantage by establishing Tracy as a haughty, inflexible snob who becomes lovable when she exposes her underlying vulnerability and fragility.

The Philadelphia Story broke attendance records at the Radio City Music Hall in New York City. The critical and popular success of the film was especially sweet to Hepburn, who had selected the film as a vehicle for her return to movies after a two year hiatus. After *Holiday* and *Bringing·Up Baby* had brought her additional negative reviews, she angrily left Hollywood. Hepburn vowed to return only if the role and circumstances were right. The Tracy Lord character in *The Philadelphia Story* not only provided the right role, but it afforded Hepburn the opportunity to create the right circumstances. During her Broadway stint in the play, she acquired the movie rights which she then sold to MGM in a deal that guaranteed her the movie role of Tracy Lord and choice of director and co-stars.

The Philadelphia Story's success led to its remake as a film musical in 1956. Though *High Society* features music and lyrics by Cole Porter and stars Bing Crosby, Frank Sinatra, and Grace Kelly, this 1956 film lacks the sparkle and comic tautness of the original.

—Lauren Rabinovitz

PICKPOCKET. Production: Lux Films; black and white, 35mm; running time: 75 mins. Released 1959.

Produced by Agnès Delahaie; screenplay by Robert Bresson; directed by Robert Bresson; photography by L.H. Burel; edited by Raymond Lamy; sound engineered by Antoine Archimbault; production design by Pierre Charbonnier; music by Lulli.

Cast: Martin Lassalle (*Michel*); Marika Green (*Jeanne*); Pierre Leymarie (*Jacques*); Jean Pelegri (*Instructor*); Kassagi (*Initiator*); Pierre Etaix (*2nd accomplice*); Mme. Scal (*Mother*).

Publications:

Books—*The Films of Robert Bresson* by 5 reviewers, New York 1969; *French Cinema Since 1946, Vol. I* by Roy Armes, New York 1970; *The Films of Robert Bresson* by Ian Cameron, London 1970; *Transcendental Style on Film: Ozu, Bresson, Dreyer* by Paul Schrader, Los Angeles 1972; *Robert Bresson o cinematografo e o sinal* by C. de Pontes Leca, Lisbon 1978; articles—"Robert Bresson" by Marjorie Green in *Film Quarterly* (Berkeley), spring 1960; "Spiritual Style in the Films of Robert Bresson" by Susan Sontag in *Seventh Art* (New York), summer 1964; "Praxis as a Cinematic Principle in the Films of Robert Bresson" by Donald S. Skoller in *Cinema Journal* (Evanston, Illinois), fall 1969; "The Art of Robert Bresson" by Roy Armes in *London Magazine*, October 1970; "Bresson's Stylistics Revisited" by M. Prokosch in *Film Quarterly* (Berkeley), v.15, no.1, 1972; "Matter and Spirit in the Films of Robert Bresson" by H.M. Polhemus in *Film Heritage* (Dayton, Ohio), spring 1974; "Léonce H. Burel", interview by R. Prédal, in *Cinéma* (Paris), July/August 1974; "Robert Bresson's Austere Vision" by Colin Westerbeck, Jr., in *Artforum* (New York), November 1976.

*   *   *

Pickpocket, made in 1959 by Robert Bresson, was not considered a "New Wave" film because it did not deal with the problems of what Jean-Luc Godard termed "psychological realism". *Pickpocket* did not address the then burgeoning question of cinematic reality, whether this status must be assigned according to the perception of reality or in terms of its impression. In fact, contrary to the expanding discipline of semiotics during the late 1950's and early 60's *Pickpocket* was so sufficiently depersonalized and unrealistic as to avoid being regarded as an example of a film that articulated the way in which film was a "language system." The filmmakers of this genre (as it is now recognized) were concerned with the deconstruction of the "Hollywood" fiction film and its idiosyncratic stylization of cinematic reality. Bresson was not attempting to contribute cinematically to the ideological canons of the period. Instead, he was interested in exploring themes of redemption, a bourgeois preoccupation that did not coincide with New Wave theories of "distancing" and "unrealization."

In elucidating the "road to redemption" in *Pickpocket*, Bresson employs the devices of ellipsis and temporal distention. Closeups of objects and actions are incriminating and clinical. He fragments the body frequently, compartmentalizing the parts shown into tight, claustrophobic realms of desire. One senses Michel's compulsion to "fill up" some kind of void; there is a relentless but carefully repressed feeling of urgency in the film to experience a wholeness. With each theft he both approaches and moves further away from this unrecognized (until the last moment of the film) spiritual yearning. It is the action of the crime itself that interests both the character Michel and director Bresson, rather than the material gains and narrative consequences it may bring.

In order that we clearly see the acts of "adding and subtracting" themselves, Bresson deftly shadows the movements of hands and eyes with his camera. At the moment of transference, i.e., when the money or the object ceases being owned by the "victim," the shot of this precarious exchange is held for a few "long" seconds. The distention of this moment denies verisimilitude to the representation of the theft and serves to call it to our attention on a symbolic level. It is at this level that the viewer comes closest,

through the metaphoric use of temporal distortion and fragmentation, to grasping the apostatic lengths to which Michel is blindly going, that his emptied soul might find redemption.

Pickpocket proves to be an excellent filmic discourse on the boundaries and rules of bourgeois perception. Space is repeatedly compartmentalized in the film, being marked out more and more constrictively as the main character becomes further dependent upon the illusionary efficacy of his displaced desire. Bresson reverses the denotational treatment of "public" and "private" space. The door to Michel's room has no lock or any kind of securing device, so throughout the film it remains ajar. Since western audiences are culturally attuned to the proprieties of bourgeois space and are accustomed to seeing them observed, it is disconcerting to accept the existence of this unguarded, undefined space.

Conversely, Bresson focuses without scruple on the scenes and bare moments of the crimes, thereby reconsolidating public space as private. The human eye can not objectively see a crime being committed. Instead, it perceives the act as it has been sedimented informationally through the media. Thus, television cameras have taken over the task. On film, the action of the crime is meta-communicated by its image. This image of the forbidden act is already motivated in terms of its signifying historicity. In *Pickpocket*, the functional status of this meta-communicated image is that of a palimpsest, allowing the viewer to see it as a diegetic trace. It shows but does not interpret or explain the main character's movements in the story. Further, this trace, insofar as it does not presuppose a narrative closure, re-posits the primordial status of pre-bourgeois, unassigned space. In terms of discovering the reason why Michel steals, Bresson intends that it be attributable anagogically, rather than accessible through scientific analysis.

—Sandra L. Beck

PIROSMANI. Production: Gruzia Films; Sovcolor, 35mm; running time: 100 mins. Released 1971.

Screenplay by Erlom Akhvlediani and Georgy Shengelaya; directed by Georgy Shengelaya; photography by Constantin Opryatine; music by V. Koukhianidzé.

Filming completed 1971.

Cast: Avtandil Varazi (*Niko Pirosmanichvili*); David Abachidzé; Zourad Capianidzé; Teimouraz Beridzé; Boris Tsipouria; Chota Daouchvili; Maria Guaramadzé; Nino Setouridzé; Rosalia Mintshine.

Publications:

Reviews—"*Pirosmani*" by I. Marazov in *Kinoizkustvo* (Sofia, Bulgaria), June 1972; "*Pirosmani*" by G. Matei in *Cinema* (Bucharest), April 1972; "*Pirosmani*" in *Variety* (New York), 12 June 1974; "*Pirosmani*" by D. Elley in *Films and Filming* (London), September 1974; "*Pirosmani*" by V. Glaessner in *Monthly Film Bulletin* (London), September 1974; "*Pirosmani*" by G. Gauthier in *Image et son* (Paris), December 1975; "*Pirosmani: Une osmose quasi pariaite*" by G. Haustrate in *Cinéma* (Paris), September/October 1975; "*Pirosmani*" by M. Portal in *Jeune Cinéma* (Paris), September/October 1975; book—*The Most Important Art: East European Film After 1945* by Mira Liehm and Antonín Liehm, Berkeley 1977; articles—by S. Bensch in *Film a Doba* (Prague), October 1972; "*Pirosmani*" by M. Trujillo in *Cine Cubano* (Havana), nos.86-88, 1973; "Unfamiliar Talents" by Gordon Gow in *Films and Filming* (London), February 1974; article by Michel Capdenac in *Ecran* (Paris), 15 November 1975, excerpt appears in *Avant-Scène du cinéma* (Paris), 15 December 1979; "*Pirosmani*" in *Ecran* (Paris), 15 November 1975; "*Pirosmani*" in *Avant-Scène du cinéma* (Paris), 15 December 1979; "Richesse et diversité du nouveau cinéma soviétique" by Michel Ciment in *Avant-Scène du cinéma* (Paris), 15 December 1979; "*Pirosmani*" by A. Horton in *Film Quarterly* (Berkeley), no.2, 1979.

*   *   *

Pirosmani is one of the works that has contributed to the reputation of recent Georgian Soviet film. The director, Georgi Shengelaya, is a member of a prominent film family. (His father was one of the pioneers of the Georgian industry; his mother was an early star; and his brother is also a director.) The film portrays the life of Georgian primitive artist Niko Pirosmanishvili, who died in 1918. Yet if the film is considered in terms of the familiar category of the art bio-pic, it is obvious that it minimizes the dramatic and psychologizing tendencies frequently associated with this genre. The film presents events from the artist's life in episodic form: through the accretion of individual scenes, the status of the artist is gradually defined. But the film's point of view toward, and explanation of, its main character is developed almost elliptically. A distinct reticence characterizes the film as a whole and the people within it. In part this is due to the measured pauses in dialogue and silences within specific scenes. In addition, the narrative is not developed in terms of strong casual links but can only be fully understood in terms of retrospective reconstruction; each sequence does not proceed clearly and unambiguously to the next. Instead, mid-way through a particular scene, some event or line of dialogue may indicate that it is now one week, or three years, later than the previous scene.

For example, at one point Pirosmani opens a diary store. Some time later his sister and her husband unexpectedly come for a visit; their conversation indicates it has been some time since they have seen one another. His sister suggests that he should get married. This scene is immediately followed by one of a wedding. In mostly long shots one sees guests arriving, receiving flour, dancing, toasting the couple, and generally enagaging in those activities associated with wedding receptions. The scene ends when Pirosmani gets up from a table and walks out. Back at his store he explains to his partner that the wedding was a trick, that the bride's relatives have stolen his flour. However, their treachery is not at all clear during the marriage scene; in context, the distribution of flour appears as something on the order of a social custom. Moreover, whatever reticence and uneasiness Pirosmani exhibits during the wedding scene is not any different from his appearance and behavior through most of the film. Thus, one can make sense of his departure and understand that something is wrong only after the fact; even then the extent of our comprehension is limited. Pirosmani subsequently causes his business to fall by raising prices exorbitantly on his steady paying customers and by giving his stock away to poor children. One gathers that these actions are a response to his wedding experience, an expression of general disgust and of feeling exploited. But his attitude is not fully clarified by the film.

Through such episodes the status of the artist is seen to be that of an outsider. Pirosmani never fits into any defined social group; he rejects his business and marriage. At one point some

artists are interested in his work and invite him to the city. But his glory is short-lived. He is uncomfortable and out of place in the world of salon intellectuals, and his work is ridiculed by a mainstream art critic in a newspaper.

The film uses painting to structure its narrative of the artist's life. The major segments of the film are indicated by images of Pirosmani paintings, "Giraffe," "White Cow," "Easter Lamb," and others. The paintings function as titles and transitional devices. For example, the picture of the white cow precedes a shot of the main character walking through the streets among a herd of cows. Later the painting is hung outside his store, "so people will know what we sell." In fact the filmic mise-en-scène is modeled on the paintings. Frontal medium and long shots predominate, with simple decor and stark lighting, imitating the primitivism of the paintings we seen in the film. In this way the art itself becomes the most significant structuring principle of the film and its central subject.

—M.B. White

A PLACE IN THE SUN. Production: Paramount Pictures; 1951; black and white, 35mm; running time: 122 mins. Released 1951.

Produced by George Stevens; screenplay by Harry Brown and Michael Wilson; from the novel *An American Tragedy* by Theodore Dreiser; directed by George Stevens; photography by William C. Mellor; edited by William Hornbeck; music by Franz Waxman; costumes designed by Edith Head.

Academy Awards for Best Director, Best Screenplay, Best Cinematography-Black and White, Best Editing, Best Music-Dramatic or Comedy Picture, and Best Costume-Black and White, 1951.

Cast: Montgomery Clift (*George Eastman*); Elizabeth Taylor (*Angela Vickers*); Shelley Winters (*Alice Tripp*); Anne Revere (*Hannah Eastman*); Sheppard Strudwick (*Anthony Vickers*); Frieda Inescort (*Mrs. Vickers*); Keefe Brasselle (*Earl Eastman*); Fred Clark (*Bellows*); Raymond Burr (*Frank Marlowe*).

Publications:

Reviews—by Stephen Lewis in *Films in Review* (New York), October 1951; review by Karel Reisz in *Sight and Sound* (London), January/March 1952; books—*George Stevens: An American Romantic* by Donald Richie, New York 1970; *The Movie Makers: Artists in the Industry* by Rev. Gene D. Phillips, Chicago 1973; *Elizabeth Taylor* by Foster Hirsch, New York 1973; *The Films of Elizabeth Taylor* by Susan d'Arcy, London 1974; *Monty: A Biography of Montgomery Clift* by Robert Laguaria, New York 1977; *Montgomery Clift: A Biography* by Patricia Bosworth, New York 1978; articles—"Revivals, Reissues, Remakes, and *A Place in the Sun*" by Irving Pichel in *Quarterly of Radio, Television, and Film* (Berkeley), summer 1952; "The Man Who Made the Hit Called *Shane*" by Pete Martin in the *Saturday Evening Post* (Philadelphia), 8 August 1953; "George Stevens and the American Dream" by E. Archer in *Film Culture* (New York), no.1, 1957; "George Stevens" by Herbert G. Luft in *Films in Review* (New York), November 1958; "Hollywood

Romantic" by J. Stang in *Films and Filming* (London), July 1959; "Monograph of George Stevens's Films" in *Cinema* (Beverly Hills), December/January 1965; "George Stevens, His Work" by Douglas McVay in *Films and Filming* (London), April 1965 and May 1965; "*A Place in the Sun*" by Penelope Houston in *Sight and Sound* (London), winter 1955-56; "Montgomery Clift" by Robert C. Roman in *Films in Review* (New York), November 1966; "George Stevens" by B. Beresford in *Film* (London), summer 1970; "Elizabeth Taylor" by Gabe Essoe in *Films in Review* (New York), August/September 1970; "Shelley Winters" by Michael Buckley in *Films in Review* (New York), March 1970; issue on Stevens in *Dialogue on Film* (AFI, Washington, D.C.), no.1, 1972; "An American Tragedy: Novel, Scenario, and Films" by B. Kliman in *Literature/Film Quarterly* (Salisbury, Maryland), summer 1977; "*A Place in the Sun*" by Judith M. Kass in *Magill's Survey of Cinema, Vol. III* edited by Frank N. Magill, Englewood Cliffs, New Jersey 1980.

* * *

Before George Steven's version as *A Place in the Sun*, Theodore Dreiser's *An American Tragedy* had inspired the work of two important directors in the history of film. During his brief sojourn in Hollywood, Sergei Eisenstein prepared a treatment of the novel. The project, in a completely modified form, was realized by Josef von Sternberg (in 1931). Steven's style could not be further from the critical montage of Eisenstein and the spirit of Sternberg's ironies (though, it must be admitted, Sternberg's characteristic tone is muted in his *An American Tragedy*). For Stevens, the story of the young man crushed by capitalism became one of the most lush romantic films of the 1950s. It won six Oscars (directing, screenplay, cinematography, editing, music, costumes); it increased the already great popularity of Montgomery Clift and Elizabeth Taylor; it was a major turning point in the career of Shelly Winters, who was cast against her showgirl type.

If Stevens violates the soul-killing drabness of Dreiser's novel by transforming George and Angela into star-crossd lovers, the glamor of the film is consistent with the director's new reading of the text. The hero's dilemma is conveyed in a nearly expressionistic play of cinematic light and dimension. The film's title refers to wealth and recognition, to the place where one is identified in bright light. George's relationship to a young woman of his own class, Alice, is a function of darkness and subterfuge. In order to succeed in the work place, George and Alice must keep their affair a secret. During their first sexual encounter the camera shows only a radio in Alice's window, the rain beating down in the dark night outside. Such obliquity was, of course, mandated by censorship and the cinema practice of the period, but the particular solution found by Stevens also reinforces the film's dialectic of concealment/display and the identification of characters in terms of darkness and light. Alice's death occurs on a lake, in the deep shadows of evening.

For George, Angela is the light of love and the acknowledgement of success. In fact, the privacy of love is, in their relationship, rendered as a grandiose erotic demonstration. George and Angela confess their feelings to each other at a dance. In panic, Angela imagines everyone has *seen* them and draws George out to the terrace. There, the manifestation of love is hyperbolic as the camera rolls back and forth between the faces of Taylor and Clift, faces that go beyond the measure of the closeup in the degree of magnification chosen by the director. The overwhelming emotion is conveyed in images that overwhelm the frame.

The kiss of George and Angela is recalled at the film's end. It is superimposed on George as he walks the "last mile" to his execution. Here, and elsewhere, Stevens saturates the text with emotional visual signs, augmented by Franz Waxman's score. What he achieves is a film designed to swamp the viewer with its excessive feelings and to envelop the viewer as fully in a romantic ethos as he does the characters. By the end of *A Place in the Sun* both the audience and George have been made to submit to the voluptuous raptures of Alice's murder and Angela's kiss.

—Charles Affron

PLAYTIME. Production: Specta Films; Eastmancolor, 70mm, stereophonic sound; running time: originally 155 mins., versions for United States release run about 108 mins. or 93 mins. Released 1967, France. Re-released 1972 in the United States in 35mm version.

Produced by René Silvera; screenplay by Jacques Tati and Jacques Lagrange; directed by Jacques Tati; photography by Jean Badal and Andreas Winding; edited by Gérard Pollicand; production design by Eugene Roman; music by Francis Lemarque, African themes by James Campbell, "Take My Band" by David Stein; artistic collaboration by Jacques Lagrange; English dialogue by Art Buchwald.

Filmed on specifically constructed sets just outside Paris.

Cast: Jacques Tati (*M. Hulot*); Barbara Dennek (*Young tourist*); Jacqueline Lecomte (*Her friend*): Valérie Camille (*M. Luce's secretary*); France Romilly (*Woman selling eyeglasses*); France Delahalle (*Shopper in department store*); Laure Paillette and Colette Proust (*Two women at the lamp*); Erika Dentzler (*Mme. Giffard*); Yvette Ducreux (*Hat check girl*); Rita Maiden (*Mr. Schultz's compainion*); Nicole Ray (*Singer*); Jack Gauthier (*The guide*); Henri Piccoli (An important gentleman): Léon Doyen (*Doorman*); Billy Kearns (*M. Schultz*).

Publications:

Reviews—"*Playtime*" by R.C. Dale in *Film Quarterly* (Berkeley), winter 1972-73; "*Playtime*" by D. Leach in *Films in Review* (New York), Septmember 1973; "Oldies but Goodies" by James Monaco in *Take One* (Montreal), September 1973; "Profiles: Playing" by Penelope Gilliatt in the *New Yorker*, 27 January 1973; books—*French Film* by Roy Armes, New York 1970; *French Cinema Since 1946*, Vol. I, by Roy Armes, New York 1970; *Jacques Tati* by Penelope Gilliatt, London 1976; *The Films of Jacques Tati* by Brent Maddock, Metuchen, New Jesey 1977; articles—"The Comic Art of Jacques Tati" by Roy Armes in *Screen* (London), February 1970; "Paris Journal" by J. Rosenbaum in *Film Comment* (Paris), winter 1971-72; "Tati's Democracy" by Jonathan Rosenbaum in *Film Comment* (New York), May/June 1973; "*Playtime*" by J.E. Siegel in *Film Heritage* (Dayton, Ohioi), spring 1974; "Beyond Freedom and Dignity: An Analysis of Jacques Tati's *Playtime*" by L. Fischer in *Sight and Sound* (London), no.4, 1976; "Afterword" by Jonathan Rosenbaum in *Sight and Sound* (London), no.4, 1976; "*Playtime*: Comedy on the Edge of Perception" by K. Thompson in *Wide Angle* (Athens, Ohio), no.2, 1979; "Jacques Tati: L'autre monde de Hulot" by B. Boland in *Cahiers du cinéma*

(Paris), September 1979; "Entretiers avec Jacques Tati: propos rompus" by S. Daney and others in *Cahiers du cinéma* (Paris), September 1979; "Jacques Tati: La vitrine" by J.L. Schefer in *Cahiers du cinéma* (Paris), September 1979; "*Playtime*" by Michael Selig in *Cinema Texas Program Notes* (Austin), 17 April 1979; "De Hulot a Mick Jagger: *Playtime*" by R. Bezombes in *Cinematographe* (Paris), July 1979; "Eloge de Tati" by S. Daney in *Cahiers du cinéma* (Paris), September 1979.

*   *   *

Jacques Tati's *Playtime* is perhaps the only epic achievement of the modernist cinema, a film that not only accomplishes the standard modernist goals of breaking away from closed classical narration and discovering a new, open form of story-telling, but also uses that form to produce an image of an entire society. After building a solid international audience through the 1950's with his comedies *Jour de fête*, *Mr. Hulot's Holiday*, and *Mon Oncle*, Tati spent ten years on the planning and execution of what was to be his masterpiece, selling the rights to all his old films to raise the money he needed to construct the immense glass and steel set—nicknamed "Tativille"—that was his vision of modern Paris. The film—two hours and 35 minutes long, in 70mm and stereophonic sound—opened in France in 1967, and was an instant failure. It was quickly reduced, under Tati's supervision, to a 108-minute version, and further reduced, to 93 minutes and 35 monaural, when it was released in the United States in 1972. Even in its truncated form, it remains a film of tremendous scope, density, and inventiveness.

Playtime is what its title suggests—an idyll for the audience, in which Tati asks us to relax and enjoy ourselves in the open space his film creates, a space cleared of the plot-line tyranny of "what happens next?", of enforced audience identification with star performers, and of the rhetorical tricks of mise-en-scene and montage meant to keep the audience in the grip of pre-ordained emotions. Tati leaves us free to invent our own movie from the multitude of materials he offers.

One of the ways in which Tati creates the free space of *Playtime* is by completely discarding conventional notions of comic timing and cutting. There is no emphasis in the montage to tell us when to laugh, no separation in the mise-en-scène of the gag from the world around it. Instead of using his camera to break down a comic situation—to analyze it into individual shots and isolated movement—he uses deep-focus images to preserve the physical wholeness of the event and long takes to preserve its temporal integrity. Other gags and bits of business are placed in the foreground and background; small patterns, of gestures echoed and shapes reduplicated, ripple across the surface of the image. We can't look at *Playtime* as we look at an ordinary films, which is to say, passively, through the eyes of the director. We have to roam the image—search it, work it, play with it.

With its universe of Mies van der Rohe boxes, *Playtime* is often described as a satire on the horrors of modern architecture. But the glass and steel of *Playtime* is also a metaphor for all rigid structures, from the sterile environments that divide city dwellers to the inflexible patterns of thought that divide and compartmentalize experience, separating comedy from drama, work from play. The architecture of *Playtime* is also an image for the rhetorical structures of classical filmmaking: the hard, straight lines are the lines of plot, and the plate glass windows are the shots that divide the world into digested, inert fragments. At one point in *Playtime*, M. Hulot stands on a balcony looking down on a network of office cubicles, seeing and hearing a beehive of human activity. As an escalator slowly carries him to the ground

floor, the camera maintains his point of view, and the change in perspective gradually eclipses the human figures and turns the sound to silence. It is one of the most profound images of death ever seen in a film, yet it is a death caused by nothing more than a change in camera placement. Tati's implication is that life can be restored to the empty urban desert simply by putting the camera in the right position, by finding the philosophical overview that integrates all of life's contradictory emotions, events, and movements into a seamless whole. His film is proof that such a point of view is possible.

—Dave Kehr

———————

POPIOL I DIAMENT. Ashes and Diamonds. Cendres et diamant. Production: Film Polski; black and white, 35mm; running time: 105 mins.; length: 2938 meters. Released October 1958.

Produced by Stanislaw Adler; screenplay by Jerzy Andrzejewski and Andrzej Wajda; from the novel by Jerzy Andrzejewski; directed by Andrzej Wajda; photography by Jerzy Wójcik; edited by Halina Nawrocka; sound engineered by Bogdan Bienkowski; production design by Roman Mann; music by the Rhythm Quintette of the Polish Radio of Warsaw, directed by Filip Nowak; costumes designed by Katarzyna Chodorowicz.

Filmed 1958. Cost: 5,000,000 zlotys. Award from the International Cinema Press, Venice Film Festival, 1959.

Cast: Zbigniew Cybulski (*Maciek Chelmicki*); Ewa Kryzjewska (*Krystyna*); Waclaw Zastrżezyński (*Szczuka*); Adam Pawlikowski (*Andrzej*); Jan Ciecierski (*The porter*); Bogumil Kobiela (*Drewnowski*); Stanislaw Milski (*Pieniazjek*); Arthur Mlodnicki (*Kotowicz*); Halina Kwiatkowska (*Mme. Staniewicz*); Ignacy Machowski (*Waga*); 'bigniew Skowroński (*Slomka*); Barbara Krafft (*Stefka*); Aleksander Sewruk (*Swiecki*).

Publications:

Scripts—"*Cendres et diament*" by Jerzy Andrzejewski and Andrzej Wajda in *Avant-Scène du cinéma* (Paris), April 1965; books—*Andrzej Wajda: Polish Cinema* edited by Colin McArthur, London 1970; *The Cinema of Andrzej Wajda* by Bolesław Michatek, translated by Edward Rothert, London 1973; *The Most Important Art: East European Film After 1945* by Mira Liehm and Antonín Liehm, Berkeley 1977; *A History of Film* by Jack C. Ellis, Englewood Cliffs, New Jersey 1979; *Historia Filmu Polskiego IV*, Warsaw 1981; articles—"Polish Notes" by Bolestaw Michatek in *Sight and Sound* (London), winter 1958-59; "Ashes Falsified" by Jan Zygmunt Jakubowski and "Ashes Simplified" by Zbigniew Zaluski in *Ekran* (Ljubljana, Yugoslavia), no.42, 1965; "Grasping the Nettle: The Films of Andrzej Wajda" by C. Higham in *Hudson Review* (Nutley, New Jersey), autumn 1965; "Zbigniew Cybulski" by John Minchinton in *Film* (London), spring 1967; issue on Andrzej Wajda in *Etudes cinématographiques* (Paris), no.69-72, 1968; "Realizm i symbolizm *Popiołu i diamentu* Andrzeja Wajdy" by M. Hendrykowski in *Kino* (Warsaw), January 1972; "Cenușă si diamant" by E. Sirbu in *Cinema* (Bucharest), May 1975; "Ashes and Diamonds" by Gordon Gow in *Films and Filming* (London), March 1977; "Andrzej Wajda" by M. Dipont in *Polish Film Polonaise* (Warsaw), no.4, 1979; "The Best Are Dead or Numb: A Second Look at Andrzej Wajda's *Ashes and Diamonds*" by E. Brill and L. Rubenstein in *Cinéaste* (New York), no.3, 1981; "Taamte filmy, tamte lata..." by E. Czesejko-Sochacka in *Kino* (Warsaw), September 1981.

*   *   *

The best work of Wajda begins in 1958, and his epic *Popioł i diament* represents the climax of the entire Polish school. The literary source for this film is the novel of the same name by Jerzy Andrzejewski published in 1948. The book, which openly speaks of the complicated Polish society at the end of the war and in the first days of peace, was initially criticized, but was eventually accepted as the best work of prose published in the postwar years. Filmmakers soon became interested, but several attempts at adapting it in the early 1950s fell through. In 1957, when a promising scenario appeared, its author was the young director Andrzej Wajda, and the novel was somewhat changed. The novel differs from the film in that it takes place in one day and one night. The setting of the story, with the exception of a few short scenes, is the hotel in town. The principal character in the novel is young Mack Chelmicki, a member of the guerilla group "Armii krajowej," which fought against the Germans during the war, jointly with the communists. The deep political differences between the two groups led to the communists engaging in acts of terrorism, aimed toward the forming of a new society for the people of Poland. Maciek is a bold young man, prepared to give up his life for higher ideals. After the end of the war, he is given orders to kill a man, and so is faced with the tragic choice between a growing awareness of the absurdity of the command and his loyalty to duty. The decision to kill or not creates a conflict of conscience. To kill is to violate the law of peace; if he does not go through with it, he creates discord in a situation of war.

Mack's counterpart is the communist, Szczuka, an ex-soldier of the Spanish revolution. Only a short time before they fought on the same side against their mutual foe. At the time when the film begins, they are confronting one another, foes in life and death, cruelly tied together by the past. Their conflict is obviously not a personal matter, but a conflict of two different conceptions of the future. It reflects a disorganized society at the boundary between war and peace. Wajda presents it with dramatic conciseness at a banquet held on the occasion of the signing of the German capitulation. At one table are gathered the former allies, and also the bourgeois politicians and an assortment of careerists and opportunists who are prepared for defeat while (at the same time) seeking the largest share of the spoils. Against the background of this gathering the fate of both heros is being decided. These two have a divided ideological orientation, differing experiences in life and in politics, and belong to different generations. Nevertheless, they have much more in common than is seen at first glance. First of all they share an allegiance to the ideal for which they fight and work, allegiance to those with whom they together fought, and a determination to strive for the best in the positions they have been entrusted with. Their relationship becomes an image of self-contradiction or paradox; for instance, Maciek has the order to kill; that he has mistakenly killed someone else instead of Szczuka means he has done his job badly. Szczuka and his friend realize that they are incapable of the art of governing, that they do not have the necessary experience; that depresses them, exhausts them, but they know they must work for their ideal until the end of their lives. The most obvious similarities between the two are seen in consecutive sequences. Maciek, at the bar, is lighting glasses filled with alcohol as a memorial to his fallen comrades and is remembering

with enthusiasm the years of fighting, which were so difficult and at the same time so simple, where everything was clearly understood because all activities were directed to one purpose—to annihilate the foe in war. So too, Szczuka reminisces with his friend about times past, and comrades that fell in Spain. Their reminiscing is marked with sadness and nostalgia, and they also realize how, after the victorious war, everything about their nationalistic ideals was uncomplicated. Maciek and Szczuka are kept distinct from the other guests that are gathered in the hotel, and from the closing sequence, when both rebels are dying and the drunken group at the banquet is mostly asleep, emerges the main idea of the work. By validating the character and deeds of both protagonists, Wajda avoided the infertile narrative conventions which place the hero in one system. The result of understanding the complications of the story is comprehension of how difficult it was for an honest person to find his way in that mixed up situation. Maciek and Szczuka are honest people, and beyond everything that pitted them against each other, they belonged to the best that existed in the land. That is why their death, unthinkable and absurd, is a tragedy of Poland.

A new look at reality characterized Wajda's unprecedented style which sprang out of two previous films, but here reaches the epitome of art. Immersing the film in actuality and concreteness, in contrast with *Kanał*, he returns to classic dramatic construction, the unity of place and time, and gradually uncovers the heros' character and motives. The picture is saturated with symbols and metaphors, which are capable of expressing the tension between objective actuality and the subjective aspect of expression. The use of narration and picturesque symbolic metaphors sharpens Wajda's drama and broadens the gamut of associations evoked by the conflicts depicted. This may be illustrated by two important sequences. The first takes place in a cemetery and in a half-demolished church. Maciek falls in love with the girl Krystyn, he spends a night with her, and before he departs, they walk to a church. Krystyn reads an inscription on a grave stone, verse of the Polish poet Cyprian Norwida, which explains Mack's situation and also provides the title of the film: "Here nothing but ashes will remain, the storm in an instant to oblivion will sweep them; from the ashes perhaps a diamond will emerge, shining victoriously for centuries, it will have blossomed for you." Dominating the church's interior is a picture of a statue of Jesus Christ, hung head down as a symbol of the overthrown values. It is a scene of extraordinary visual impact, but at the same time is very meaningful, because here end Mack's doubts, his loyalty to a lost cause and his yearning for a normal life, his thoughts conform to reality. With the same intensity, symbols also inform the ending of the film, depicting the death of both protagonists. Dying Szczuka, felled by Mack's shots, falls into Mack's arms, and his death is accompanied by the clanging fire engines celebrating victory. Mack is killed by a drunk from the banquet. In agony Mack stumbles to the huge rubbish heap, like the rubbish heap of history.

In the accomplished cast, it is impossible not to mention the significance of the main character. Wajda chose the unknown actor Zbigniew Cybulski who made his debut in the film *Pokolenie* in a cameo role. This choice proved to be a happy one. Cybulski, with his capability of making an effortless transition from a state of maximum concentration to being relaxed, managed to embody in his character the zeal of exultation, emotion, strength, and gentleness. Maciek, in his characterization is a boy who becomes involved with insignificant people and causes, but he is also a warrior, who is constantly in the line of fire, one who loves weapons because they give him a feeling of freedom. In that he is a man of the generation of 1945. But Cybulski, in realizing the director's intentions, communicates more. His hesitation in searching for meaning shields him from reality. The soft, thoughful charm, underlined by black glasses and a costume which does not represent that time, makes him representative of the young people of the late 1950s. With that he become a hero of two generations. This, let us say, double character as Cybulski grasps it, added markedly to the clamorous acceptance of the film by young people. Even Andrzejewski was satisfied. "The measure of my satisfaction is that during the writing of the book, I pictured Mack Chelmicki entirely differently. Now when I see the film, I see him only this way, as Cybulski played him."

In the postwar history of Polish film the premiere of *Popioł i diament* was the most extraordinary event in terms of opening up consideration of problems which up to that time were schematically or falsely pictured, leading to open criticism by the newer generation. Added to Wajda's success was the fact that he spoke with a new artistic tongue, without arrogance and declamation, and that he found a voice in harmony with the warmer political climate of the second half of the 1950s.

—Mrs. B. Urgošíkova

Harry Potamkin in *Hound and Horn* (New York), April/June 1933; "Index to the Creative Work of Vsevolod Pudovkin" by Jay Leyda in *Sight and Sound* (London), November 1948; issue on Pudovkin of *Cahiers du cinéma* (Paris), August/September 1953; "Vsevolod Pudovkin" by Herman Weinberg in *Films in Review* (New York), August/September 1953; "V.I. Pudovkin: 1893-1953" by Basil Wright in *Sight and Sound* (London), October/December 1953; "*Tempéte sur l'Asie*" in *Image et son* (Paris), no.143 bis, summer 1961; "*Tempéte sur l'Asie*" by Robert Desnos in *Cinéma* (Paris), 1966; "*Tempête sur l'Asie*" by Marcel Martin in *Cinéma 66* (Paris), April 1966; "Des Steppes aux rizières" by Georges Sadoul in *Les Lettres françaises* (Paris), 10 March 1966; "*Tempête sur l'Asie*" by J.J. Dupuich in *Image et son* (Paris), June/July 1972; issue on Pudovkin of *Iskusstvo Kino* (Moscow), February 1973; "*Temptête sur l'Asie*" by J.C. Mairal in *Image et son* (Paris), June/July 1975; "Storm Over Asia and *Bezhin Meadow* by Geoffrey Marks in *Cinema Texas Program Notes* (Austin), 27 September 1977; "Linkage: Pudovkin's Classics Revisited" by P.E. Burns in *Journal of Popular Film and Television* (Washington, D.C.), summer 1981.

POTOMOK CHINGIS-KHANA. The Heir of Genghis Khan. Storm Over Asia.

Production: Mezhrabpomfilm (USSR); black and white, 35mm, silent; running time: 93 mins., some sources list 102 mins.; length: 10,144 feet. Released 1928. Re-released 1949 with sound, music by Nicolas Krioukov and text and dialogue by Slavine and V. Koutchoukov.

Screenplay by Osip Brik; from a story by I. Novokshenov; directed by V.I. Pudovkin; photography by A. N. Golovnya; art direction by Sergei Koslovsky and N. Aaronson.

Cast: Valeri Inkishinov (*Bair, A Mongol huntsman*); I. Inkishinov (*Bair's father*); A. Chistyakov (*Commander of a partisan detachment*); A. Dedintsev (*Commander of the occupation forces*); Anna Sudakevich (*His daughter*); K. Gurnyak (*British soldier with leggings*); Boris Barnet (*British soldier with cat*); V. Tzoppi (*Mr. Smith, agent of the British fur company*); V. Ivanov (*Lama*); Vladimir Pro (*Missionary*); Paulina Belinskaya (*Wife of the commander of the occupation forces*).

Publications:

Books—*Poudovkine, "Pouti Tvortchestva," Les Voies de la création* by N. Yezuitov, Moscow 1937; *Vsevolod Pudovkin* by A. Mariamov, Moscow 1952; *Film Techniques and Film Acting* by V.I. Pudovkin, translated by Ivor Montagu, London 1958; *Vsevolod Poudovkine* by Luda and Jean Schnitzer, Paris 1966; *The Film Till Now* by Paul Rotha and Richard Griffith, London 1967; *V.I. Poudovkine* by Barthélémy Amengual, Premier Plan, Lyon 1968; *Kino: A History of the Russian and Soviet Film* by Jay Leyda, New York 1973; *Cinema in Revolution* edited by Luda Schmitzer, translated by David Robinson, New York 1973; *Pudovkin's Films and Film Theory* by Peter Dart, New York 1974; *Cinema, The Magic Vehicle: A Guide to Its Achievement: Journey One, Cinema Through 1949* edited by Jacek Klinowski and Adam Garbicz, Metuchen, New Jersey 1975; articles—"Pudovkin and the Revolutionary Film" by

---

PRIMARY.

Production: Drew Associates for Time-Life Broadcast (Time-Life Inc.); 1960. black and white, 16mm; running time: 60 mins. Released 1960.

Produced by Robert Drew; directed by Richard Leacock, D.A. Pennebaker, Al Maysles, Robert Drew, and Terrence McCartney Filgate; photography by Al Maysles and Ricky Leacock; edited by Drew, Maysles, Pennebaker, and Leacock; sound recorded by Robert Drew and D.A. Pennebaker.

Filmed 1960 in Wisconsin during the election primary.

Publications:

Books—*Cinema Verite* by M. Ali Issari, Ann Arbor, Michigan 1971; *Nonfiction Film: A Critical History* by Richard Barsam, New York 1973; *Living Cinema: New Directions in Contemporary Film Making* by Louis Marcorelles, New York 1973; *The World of Time Inc.: The Intimate History of a Publishing Enterprise, Volume Two, 1941-1960* by Robert T. Elson, New York 1973; *Documentary: A History of the Nonfiction Film* by Erik Barnouw, New York 1974; *Cinema Verite in America: Studies in Uncontrolled Documentary* by Stephen Mamber, Cambridge, Massachusetts 1974; *What is Cinema Verite?* by Issari and Paul, n.d. articles—"The Frontiers of Realist Cinema: The Work of Ricky Leacock", interview of Pennebaker by Gideon Bachmann in *Film Culture* (New York), summer 1961; "Going Out to the Subject: II" by Gideon Bachmann in *Film Quarterly* (Berkeley), spring 1961; article in *Movie* (London), April 1963; "One Man's Truth: Interview with Richard Leacock" by James Blue in *Film Comment* (New York), spring 1965; "Leacock-Pennebaker: The MGM of the Underground?" in *Show* (Hollywood), January 1970; "Richard Leacock" in *Documentary Explorations* edited by G. Roy Levin, Garden City, New York 1971; "Reportage a la historia Cubana" by J. Wainer in *Cine Cubano* (Havanna), nos.71-72, 1972; "Focus on Al Maysles" by Charles Reynolds in *The Documentary Tradition* edited by Lewis Jacobs, 2nd ed., New York 1979.

*   *   *

Primary was the first film using the cinéma vérité or direct cinema method to be widely seen. The method depended on new technology: a lightweight portable camera and synchronous sound recording equipment. *Primary* was produced for Time-Life Broadcast by Drew Associates—executive producer was Robert Drew, a former assistant picture editor and reporter for *Life* magazine. Most of the shooting was done by Al Maysles and Ricky Leacock; Drew and Pennebaker recorded the sound. Of *Primary*, Leacock said: "For the first time we were able to walk in and out of buildings, up and down stairs, film in taxi cabs, all over the place, and yet achieve synchronous sound" (*Movie*, April 1963). All of the crew worked on the editing; 18,000 feet of film were cut down to 2,000.

The film deals with the 1960 Wisconsin Democratic primary election contest between senators Hubert Humphrey and John F. Kennedy. It follows each candidate through his public appearances and activities, intercutting between them, but it also enters into the more private times when they are in their hotel rooms or in cars riding to the next engagement. Although the film contains many remarkable moments, perhaps the one that is most often mentioned is an uninterrupted shot that follows Kennedy from outside a building into it, down a long corridor, up some stairs, out onto a stage, ending with a view of the wildly applauding audience. The novelty at the time was breathtaking, this freely perambulating camera with synchronous sound opening up totally new possibilities to film makers.

Primary and *On the Pole*, the second of the Drew Associates films, were first shown on four Time Inc. television stations. Their success led to a contract with ABC for four more hour-long films (1960-61) which were telecast on the "Close-up" series: *Yanki, No!*, *X-Pilot*, *The Children Were Watching*, *Adventures on the New Frontier*.

Cinéma vérité developed early in two other countries. *Les Raquetteurs* (1959), produced by the National Film Board of Canada and made by Michel Brault and Gilles Groulx, preceded *Primary*. In France *Chronique d'un été* (1962), made by Jean Rouch and Edgar Morin, followed a little later. *Primary* was shot with modified 16mm Auricon with a zoom lens, using Nagra 1/4" magnetic tape recorder synchronized by means of a Bulova Accutron electronic watch. The Canadians used a modified and improved 16mm Arriflex. It was one of these Canadians, Michel Brault, who used the prototype version of the 16mm Eclair NPR in shooting *Chronique d'un été* for Rouch and Morin.

Ricky Leacock became the most articulate spokesman in this country for the use of this technique as an objective observational tool, preferring the term direct cinema to cinéma vérité. Jean Rouch, who first used the term cinéma vérité, thought of its possibilities more as objective, engaged film making with the film maker in active participation with the subject in the making of the film. Whatever the use or the term used, it has been the predominant documentary technique since the early 1960s.

—Jack C. Ellis

LA PRIMERA CARGA AL MACHETE. The First Charge of the Machete. Production: Instituto Cubano del Arte e Industria Cinematográficos (ICAIC); black and white, 35mm, Panoramic; running time: 84 mins. Released 1969.

Screenplay by Manuel Octavio Gómez, Alfredo L. Del Cueto, Jorge Herrera, and Julio García Espinosa; directed by Manuel Ocatavio Gómez; photography by Jorge Herrera; edited by Nelson Rodríguez; sound by Raúl Garcia; music by Leo Brouwer and songs by Pablo Milanés; costumes designed by Maria Elena Molinet.

Filmed in Cuba.

Cast: Adolfo Llauradó; Idalia Anreus; Eslinda Nuñez; Ana Viñas.

Publications:

Books—*Cuba: The Measure of a Revolution* by L. Nelson, Minneapolis 1972; articles—"*La Primera Carga al machete*" in *Hablemos de Cine* (Lima, Peru), no.54, 1970; "Cuba" by Pyhala Mikko in *International Film Guide* (London), 1971; "*La Primera Carga al machete*" by Daniel Díaz Torres in *Cine y revolución en Cuba* by Santiago Alvarez, et. al., Barcelona 1975; "Popular Culture and Perpetual Quest: An Interview with Manuel Octavio Gomez" by Julianne Burton in *Jump Cut* (Chicago), May 1979; "Entrevista a Manuel Octavio Gómez" by Enrique I. Colina in *Cine Cubano* (Havana), no.56/57.

*   *   *

Even within the context of revolutionary Cuban cinema—distinguished for its innovations in bringing history to the screen—*First Charge* is a whole new kind of historical film. Produced as a part of a cycle dedicated to the celebration of "One Hundred Years of Struggle," the film fuses the political and the poetic into a reconstruction of the 1868 uprising against Spanish colonials and in so doing redefines historical cinema.

The experimental nature of *First Charge* is immediately apparent in the richness of its formal structure. The film is designed to appear as if the technological capabilties (and resultant aesthetic) of cinema verité had been available in 1868. Light hand-held cameras and portable sound equipment produce "on-the-spot" interviews and follow the Cuban rebels into the very center of the battle. This eminently modern "TV documentary" style is complemented, however, by a high-contrast film that resembles ancient newsreel footage and by a manner of posing individuals at the beginning of sequences as if they were in old historical photos. The clash of aesthetics at once so up-to-the-minute and so archaic results in the formal "dialectical resonance" for which Cuban cinema has attained such renown.

This formal juxtaposition, and the various techniques contained within it, has a meaning beyond mere experimentation for its own sake. Manuel Octavio Gómez uses this confrontation of past and present to insistently remind viewers that they are seeing an interpretation of the historical event, not the event itself. The high-contrast film also functions metaphorically, for it connotes the extremes of the struggle and the reality of sharply opposed interests, in which compromise was impossible. This use of contrast is set up against the grey tones employed in the official pronouncements of the Spanish, which are intended to convey a false impression of tranquility. The hand-held camera and the provocative interviewing style also have connotative functions, for they take on the form of participating in and helping to precipitate the struggle. Gómez's rejection of the narrative structure traditional in historical cinema is important as well, for, in place of characters with whom one identifies, the film's central protagonist is the machete—the work tool become weapon in 1868 and the weapon of 1868 which is today the tool of Cuba's economic struggle.

Gómez combined extensive historical research with his use of such deliberately anachronistic devices. Cuban and Spanish archives were mined for materials dealing with the struggle, and historical photographs, etchings, and documentary footage were studied in depth. The film's dialogues are constructed entirely from documents, books, speeches, reports, letters, and anecdotes from the period, and, although it was not possible to reconstruct the language patterns of 1868, the actors were required to immerse themselves in this historical material.

Audiences inside and outside of Cuba responded favorably to the film, although some people were put off by the exaggerated expressionism of the visual style. At times—most notably in the final battle—the combination of extreme high-contrast film and the widely careening hand-held camera of Jorge Herrera reduce the screen image to a swirling mass of abstract patterns. One critic saw the technique as "obsessive and vampire-like" in detracting from the story-line; Gómez himself acknowledged that the "brusque and violent" camera movements "molest" viewers. However, Gómez defends his film's style as part of the struggle against the "routinization" of audience and filmmaker. If *First Charge* does not quite attain the goals set for it by Gómez, that is because he has aimed so high.

—John Mraz

THE PRIVATE LIFE OF HENRY VIII. Production: London Film Productions; black and white, 35mm; running time: 97 mins.; length: 8664 feet. Released 12 October 1933, Radio City Music Hall, released 24 October 1933 in London by United Artists.

Produced by Alexander Korda; screenplay by Lajos Biro and Arthur Wimperis; directed by Alexander Korda; photography by George Perinal; edited by Stephen Harrison and Harold Young; art direction by Vincent Korda; music by Kurt Schroeder; costumes designed by John Armstrong; historical adviser: Peter Lindsey; dance direction by Espinosa; falconry expert: Captain Knight.

Filmed in about 5 weeks in London. Cost: about 60,000 pounds. Academy Award, Best Actor (Laughton), 1932/33.

Cast: Charles Laughton (*Henry VIII*); Robert Donat (*Thomas Culpepper*); Franklin Dyall (*Thomas Cromwell*); Miles Mander (*Worthesly*); Lawrence Hanray (*Archbishop Cranmer*); William Austin (*Duke of Cleves*); John Loder (*Peynell*); Claude Allister (*Cornell*); Gibb McLaughlin (*French executioner*); Sam Livesy (*English executioner*); William Heughan (*Kingston*); Merle

Oberon (*Anne Boleyn*); Wendy Barrie (*Jane Seymour*); Elsa Lanchester (*Anne of Cleves*); Binnie Barnes (*Katherine Howard*); Everley Gregg (*Katherine Parr*); Lady Tree (*Nurse*).

Publications:

Script—*The Private Life of Henry VIII*, London 1934; review—by Charles Beard in *Sight and Sound* (London), winter 1934; books—*20 Years of British Films, 1925-45* by Michael Balcon and others, London 1947; *Nice Work: The Story of 30 Years in British Film Production* by Adrian Brunel, London 1949; *Alexander Korda* by Paul Tabori, London 1966; *Charles Laughton and Fredric March* by Michael Burrows, London 1970; *Alexander Korda: The Man who Could Work Miracles* by Karol Kulik, London 1975; *Charmed Lives: A Family Romance* by Michael Korda, New York 1979; *Charles Laughton and I* by Elsa Lanchester, New York 1983; articles—"Alexander Korda and the International Film" by Stephen Watts in *Cinema Quarterly* (London), autumn 1933; article by James Laver in *Sight and Sound* (London), summer 1939; "The Producer: Sir Alexander Korda" by Colin Campbell in *Sight and Sound* (London), summer 1951; "Sir Alexander Korda" by Sidney Gilliat and others in *Sight and Sound* (London), spring 1956; "Alexander Korda" by Ian Dalrymple and others in *Quarterly Review of Film, Radio, and Television* (Berkeley), spring 1957; "Charles Laughton" by Jerry Vermilye in *Films in Review* (New York), May 1963; "The Intolerant Giant" by Douglas McVay in *Films and Filming* (London), March 1963; "Alexander Korda" by Peter Cowie in *Anthologie du cinéma, Vol. VI*, Paris 1965; "*The Private Life of Henry VIII*" by Lewis Archibald in *Magill's Survey of Cinema, Vol. III* edited by Frank N. Magill, Englewood Cliffs, New Jersey 1980.

*   *   *

"An ace and certainly the finest picture which has come out of England to date," is the way that *Variety* hailed *The Private Life of Henry VIII*, a feature generally considered to be the first British film to have had an international impact (although certainly not the first British film to be screened in the United States, where English features had been seen from the early 'teens). *The Private Life of Henry VIII* was very much an international production: it starred Charles Laughton, a major stage and screen actor from England, and was produced by Hungarian-born Alexander Korda and photographed by the French Georges Perinal. Wisely, to emphasize that his film was no mere British feature, Alexander Korda gave *The Private Life of Henry VIII* its world premiere at New York's Radio Music Hall on October 12, 1933, two weeks prior to the London premiere.

A jovial film which equates the joy of sex with the pleasure of food, *The Private Life of Henry VIII* depicts the British Monarch's personal relationship with five of his six wives. The film does not bother with Henry's first wife, Catherine of Aragon: an opening title explains that she was too respectable. The actresses portraying three of the remaining wives—Merle Oberon, Binnie Barnes and Elsa Lanchester—were later to become familiar players in Hollywood films, as was Robert Donat (as Thomas Culpeper). Charles Laughton received an Academy Award for Best Actor for his performance, making *The Private Life of Henry VIII* the first British feature to be so honored.

Alexander Korda always maintained that the idea for the film came to him when he heard a London cab driver singing the popular Music Hall song, "I'm 'Enery the Eighth I Am." Another, more sensible, explanation for Korda's decision to make the film is that he was seeking a suitable vehicle for Charles Laughton and his wife, Elsa Lanchester, and a statue of Henry VIII made the producer aware of the resemblance between the Monarch and the actor. The film was shot in a mere five weeks at a reported cost of 60,000 pounds.

What contemporary audiences particularly enjoyed and what makes *The Private Life of Henry VIII* still entertaining is the film's comedy, particularly the dialogue between Henry and Anne of Cleves, with the former's oft-quoted line as he enters the bedchamber, "The things I've done for England!" The film has an elegance and a charm created in part by Vincent Korda's set and Perinal's photography. Alexander Korda's direction is little more than adequate and relies heavily on the quality performances delivered by his players.

—Anthony Slide

LE PROCÈS. The Trial. Der Prozess. Il processo. Production: Paris Europa Productions, Hisa-Film (West Germany), and FI.C.IT. (Italy); black and white, 35mm; running time: 120 mins., English and German versions: 118 mins., Italian version: 100 mins. Released December 1962, Paris.

Produced by Yves Laplanche, Miguel Salkind and Alexander Salkind with Robert Florat; screenplay by Orson Welles; from the novel by Franz Kafka; directed by Orson Welles; photography by Edmond Richard; edited by Yvonne Martin; sound engineered by Guy Vilette, sound mixed by Jacques Lebreton; art direction by Jean Mandaroux, set dressed by Jean Charpentier and Francine Coureau, scenic artist: André Labussière; music composed and arranged by Jean Ledrut; special effects edited by Denise Baby; costumes designed by Helene Thibault with Mme. Brunet and Claudie Thary.

Filmed 26 March 1962-June 1962 in the Studio de Boulogne; and on location in Paris and Zagreb.

Cast: Anthony Perkins (*Joseph K*); Jeanne Moreau (*Miss Burstner*); Romy Schneider (*Leni*); Elsa Martinelli (*Hilda*); Suzanne Flon (*Pittle*); Orson Welles (*Hastler*); Akim Tamiroff (*Bloch*); Madeleine Robinson (*Mrs. Grubach*); Arnoldo Foà (*Inspector A*); Fernand Ledoux (*Chief clerk*); Michel Lonsdale (*Priest*); Max Buchsbaum (*Examining magistrate*); Max Haufler (*Uncle Max*); Maurice Teynac (*Deputy manager*); Wolfgang Reichmann (*Courtroom guard*); Thomas Holtzmann (*Bert*); Billy Kearns and Jess Hahn (*Assistant inspectors*); Maydra Shore (*Irmie*); Carl Studer (*Man in leather*); Jean-Claude Remoleux and Raoul Delfosse (*Policemen*); Titorelli (*X*).

Publications:

Scripts—*Sed de Mal e Il Processo* (scripts for *Touch of Evil* and

The Trial), Madrid 1962; "*Le Procès* (The Trial)" (extracts from sreenplay) by Orson Welles in *Avant-Scèen du cinéma* (Paris), 15 February 1963; *The Trial*, script, New York 1970; reviews— by Ernest Callenbach in *Film Quarterly* (Berkeley), summer 1963; review by John Cutts in *Films and Filming* (London), December 1963; review by Henry Hart in *Films in Review* (New York), March 1963; review by Jonas Mekas in *The Village Voice* (New York), 21 February 1963; review by Mark Shivas in *Movie* (London), February/March 1963; review by Bosley Crowther in *The New York Times*, February 1963; review by Brian Nevitt in *Take One* (Montreal), September/October 1966; review by John Thomas in *Film Society Review* (New York), January 1967; books—*The Cinema of Orson Welles* by Peter Cowie, London 1965; *Orson Welles* by Peter Wollen, London 1969; *The Films of Orson Welles* by Charles Higham, Berkeley 1971; *Orson Welles: An Investigation into His Films and Philosophy* by Maurice Bessy, New York 1971; *Orson Welles* by Joseph McBride, London 1972; *This is Orson Welles* by Peter Bogdanovich and Orson Welles, New York 1972; *A Ribbon of Dreams* by Peter Cowie, New York 1973; *The Novel and the Cinema* by Geoffrey Wagner, Cranbury, New Jersey 1975; *Focus on Orson Welles* edited by Ronald Gottesman, Englewood Cliffs, New Jersey 1976; *Orson Welles: Actor and Director* by J. McBride, New York 1977; *Orson Welles: A Critical View* by André Bazin, translated by Jonathan Rosenbaum, New York 1978; *The Magic World of Orson Welles* by J. Naremore, New York 1978; articles—"The Heroes of Welles" by Alan Stanbrook in *Film* (London), March/April 1961; "The Trial of Orson Welles" by Enrique Martinez in *Films and Filming* (London), October 1962; "Case for the Defense" by Richard Fleischer in *Films and Filming* (London), October 1962; "Prodigal Revived" in *Time* (New York), 29 June 1962; "Orson Welles" in *Film* (London), autumn 1962; "Citizen Welles Rides Again" by J. Kobler in *Saturday Evening Post* (New York), 8 December 1962; "*The Trial* of Orson Welles by John Francis Lane in *Films and Filming* (London), March 1963; article by F. Gretchen and Herman Weinberg in *Film Culture* (New York), spring 1963; "Pour introduire au procès d'Orson Welles" by André S. Labarthe in *Avant-Scène du cinéma* (Paris), 15 February 1963; "Trials" by William Pechter in *Sight and Sound* (London), winter 1963-64; "A Trip to Quixoteland: Conversations with Orson Welles" by Juan Cobos, Miguel Rubio, and J.A. Pruneda in *Cahiers du Cinema* in English (New York), June 1966; "Welles in Power" by Serge Daney in *Cahiers du Cinema in English* (New York), September 1967; "*Le Procès*" by C. Bosseno in *Image et son* (Paris), May 1973; "Welles and Kafka" by N. Carroll in *Film Reader* (Evanston, Illinois), no.3, 1978.

*   *   *

Orson Welles would seem the perfect director to bring the tortured fiction of Franz Kafka to the screen. The deep chiaroscuro, mordant humor, and labyrinthian qualities of his films are sufficiently Kafkaesque to suggest a sympathetic match between novelist and filmmaker. Yet the filmed version of *The Trial* brought forth a chorus of negative reviews, especially from the Anglo-American press. Plagued by its own set of problems (as what recent Welles film has not been), *The Trial* elicited as violent and negative notices on its initial release as any garnered by a major director within recent memory. It was a critical lashing that has been salved only recently by those film commentators who have had the luxury of a broader perspective with which to consider *The Trial* within the context of the development of Welles' cinema.

The initial problems Welles encountered were due to his having adapted a modern literary classic, provoking a spate of reviews comparing Welles's adaptation to the original story, and since Welles had had the audacity to tamper with the novel's plot line, such as it is, he fell afoul the critics. The largest discrepancy between the film and the fiction, however, was in Welles's making of Joseph K into a more active character. Welles later admitted in an interview that the passivity of Kafka's anti-hero just did not fit with his own world view. And the war had happened between novel and film. After the death camps and advent of the atomic age, Welles felt that Kafka's morality tale needed updating, and in typical Wellsian style he did so.

The major problems the critics pounced on had less to do with the film's faithfulness, however, than with the film's opacity. A number of critics claimed that the movie was even less understandable than the book; furthermore, they found the movie boring. The attacks against *The Trial* remained fairly uniform in British and American papers and weekly magazines. In more recent assessments of Welles's career—James Naremore's *The Magic World of Orson Welles*, for example—the film has received much more careful and appreciative treatment. Naremore finds the movie a fascinating study of repressed sexuality, and he is at pains to place the film within the Welles canon, especially by making comparisons with *The Lady from Shanghai* and *Touch of Evil*. If the film remains little shown today, at least it has assumed a respected place for students of Welles's cinema.

The Trial may not be much liked, but at least it is now dealt with. Even one of the movie's most severe critics, William Pechter, admitted that in spite of its overall failure, Welles had pushed mise-en-scène beyond any concern for narrative or dramatic necessity into a realm of purely visual effects, into the realm of pure cinema. At least Pechter found the experiment an interesting one. The use of the railway as the central office set, which caused one critic to remark that the film seemed dominated by its decor, produced a brilliantly evocative visual representation of the post-war world. Moreover for Peter Cowie, *The Trial* is Welles's finest film since *Citizen Kane*, partly because it conveys so perfectly "the terrifying vision of the modern world" that is characteristic of Kafka's novel and partly because the film so clearly bears the stamp of Welles's personality, to rival only *Citizen Kane* and *Touch of Evil* in this respect. Cowie wrote that Welles had succeded in not only translating the book into film but also in creating a cinematic environment that revealed the complexity of Kafka's world and reflected the inability of the human mind to grasp complexity which is "the tragic moral of the novel and of this extraordinary, hallucinatory film."

Charles L.P. Silet

PROFESSIONE: REPORTER. The Passenger. Production: Compagnia Cinematografica Champion (Rome), Les Films Concordia (Paris), and C.I.P.I. Cinematografica (Madrid); Metrocolor, 35mm; running time: 126 mins. Released March 1975, Italy.

Produced by Carlo Ponti; screenplay by Mark Peploe, Peter Wollen, and Michelangelo Antonioni; from an original idea by Mark Peploe; directed by Michelangelo Antonioni; photography by Luciano Tovoli; edited by Franco Arcalli and Michelangelo Antonioni; sound by Cyril Collik, sound edited by Sandro Peticca and Franca Silvi, and sound mixed by Franco Ancillai; production design by Osvaldo Desideri; art direction by Piero Poletto; costumes designed by Louise St. Jensward.

Filmed on location in England, Spain, and Germany.

Cast: Jack Nicholson (*Locke*); Maria Schneider (*The Girl*); Jenny Runacre (*Rachel*); Ian Hendry (*Knight*); Stephen Berkoff (*Stephen*); Ambroise Bea (*Achebe*); Jose Maria Cafarel (*Hotel manager*); James Campbell (*Stregone*); Manfred Spies (*Tedesco*); Jean Baptiste Tiemele (*The African*); Chuck McVehill or Mulvehill (*Robertson*); Angel del Pozo (Police inspector); Narcisse Pula (*African's accomplice*).

Publications:

Scripts—*Professione: Reporter* by Michelangelo Antonioni, Mark Peploe, and Peter Wollen, edited by Carlo Di Carlo, introduction by Stefano Reggiani, Bologna 1975; "*Professione: Reporter*" (script extract) in *Cinema nuovo* (Turin), September/-December 1975; reviews— "*Professione: Reporter*" by D. Offroy in *Cinématographe* (Paris), August/September 1975; "*The Passenger*" by L. Atwell in *Film Quarterly* (Berkeley), summer 1975; "*The Passenger*" by Peter Cowie in *Focus on Film* (London), summer 1975; "*The Passenger*" by H.A. Giroux in *Cinéaste* (New York), fall 1975; "*The Passenger*" by Gordon Gow in *Films and Filming* (London), August 1975; "*The Passenger*" by C.P. Reilly in *Films in Review* (New York), May 1975; "*Profession: Reporter*" by Jonathan Rosenbaum in *The Monthly Film Bulletin* (London), June 1975; articles—" *Profession: Reporter: Un Film de Michelangelo Antonioni*" in *Avant-Scène du cinéma* (Paris), October 1975; "*Profession: Reporter*" by C. Benoit in *Jeune Cinéma* (Paris), September/-October 1975; issue on *Profession: Reporter* in *Filmcritica* (Rome), March 1975; "Michelangelo Antonioni Discusses *The Passenger*" by B.J. Demby in *Filmmakers Newsletter* (Ward Hill, Massachusetts), July 1975; "Antonioni Speaks...and Listens" by R. Epstein in *Film Comment* (New York), July/August 1975; "*The Passenger*: An Individual in History" by M. Gliserman in *Jump Cut* (Chicago), August/September 1975; "Men and Landscapes: Antonioni's *The Passenger*" by T. Perry in *Film Comment* (New York), July/August 1975; "*The Passenger*" by C. Plumb in *Take One* (Montreal), May 1975; "*The Passenger*" by Richard Roud in *Sight and Sound* (London), summer 1975; "*The Passenger*: Antonioni's Narrative Design" by M. Walsh in *Jump Cut* (Chicago), August/September 1975; "Maria Schneider: 'Ik houd niet echt van acteren'" by G. Bachmann in *Skoop* (Wagenengen, Netherlands), March 1976; "A riportut vege: Antonioni: *Figlalkozasa: Riporter*" by E. Bojtar in *Filmkultura* (Budapest), July/August 1976; "Desir desert (*Profession reporter*)" by P. Bonitzer in *Cahiers du cinéma* (Paris), January 1976; "Fuuga Antonionin tapaan, Michaelangelo Antonioni: *Ammatti: Reportteri*" by T. Tuominen in *Filmihullu* (Helsinki, Finland), no.1, 1976; "Exhumed Identity: Antonioni's Passenger to Nowhere" by G. Stewart in *Sight and Sound* (London), winter 1975-76; "*The Passenger* and Literary Existentialism" by B. Dick in *Literature/Film Quarterly* (Salisbury, Maryland), winter 1977; "*The Passenger* and Reporting: Photographic Memory" by R. MacLean in *Film Reader* (Evanston, Illinois), no.3, 1978; "Film Maudit: The Political and Religious Meaning of Antonioni's *The Passenger*" by T. Price in *Cinemonkey* (Portland, Oregon), volume 5, no.2, 1979; "Empêchement visuel et point de fuite dans *L'avventura* et *Profession: Reporter*" by Kimball Lockhart in *Caméra/Stylo* (Paris), November 1982.

*   *   *

After the general confusion prompted by *Zabriskie Point*, Michelangelo Antonioni's previous feature, *Professione: Reporter* (distributed in the United States as *The Passenger*) met with critical and popular acclaim. This success may have been due as much to the cast as to either a new "transparency" in Antonioni's direction or a suddenly acquired sophistication of the filmgoer. Though *Professione: Reporter*, like *Zabriskie Point* and for that matter any one of Antonioni's previous films, de-emphasizes classic cinematic narrative in favor of the presentation of an essentially static/dramatic situation through experimentation with expressive elements specific to film—thereby remaining what the general public would see as a "difficult" film: "nothing happens" with which one can "identify"—*Professione: Reporter*'s stars, Jack Nicholson and Maria Schneider, were two of 1975's biggest box-office draws. Their appearance guaranteed the film a degree of financial success (necessary after *Zabriskie Point*), but also introduced a marked artificiality into the fabric of the film's fiction—Jack Nicholson virtually plays himself, all the more emphasized by the implausible turning point of the film's plot: the Nicholson character gives up his own identity to assume the identity of a man who happens to die and happens to resemble him. The presumption that such an arbitrary exchange of identities might be either workable or desirabe seems to comment on the nature of acting; and later in the film when Maria Schneider finds a gun in Nicholson's luggage, he takes it away from her with an ironic monotone "no" which cannot fail to recall, intertextually, yet another gun, the one Schneider used to kill an even bigger box-office draw, Marlon Brando, in the film that made her famous and which is no doubt responsible for her appearance in this film, namely, Bertolucci's *Last Tango in Paris* (1972).

But the real interest in *Professione: Reporter* lies in its groundbreaking technique, one that explicitly works in opposition to the film's narrative continuity and impression of reality, effects that both mainstream critics and the general public expect of any feature film. The most discussed technical innovation concerns the film's next-to-the-last seven minute-long continuous traveling shot which moves foward into the frame at an almost imperceptible rate and which impossibly passes through the narrow iron bars of a window and into a courtyard only to come back to the same window to look through the same bars to view the same Nicholson the shot first framed but which upon return finds him dead. This shot is emblematic of a radical strategy Antonioni has since pursued in an even more global fashion in *Il mistero di Oberwald* (1979) and *Identificazione di una donna* (1982), whereby elements taken to belong exclusively to filmic technique, elements such as camera movement, framing, point of view, sound, and image tone, which are normally considered to be neutral vehicles for the transparent expression of a narrative—find themselves emphatically motivated, bearing the principal burden of signification in the face of an increasingly banal "story." Such is the case in *Professione: Reporter*. Preparing the ground for these later films, and perpetuating a research Antonioni has engaged since the films of the early 1950's, the innovative technique of *Professione: Reporter* proposes nothing short of the fictionalization of technique itself.

—Kimball Lockhart

PSYCHO. Production: Universal Pictures; 1960; black and white, 35mm; running time: 109 minutes. Released June 1960, originally by Paramount.

Produced by Alfred Hitchcock; screenplay by Joseph Stefano; from a novel by Robert Bloch; titles designed by Saul Bass; directed by Alfred Hitchcock; photography by John L. Russell; edited by George Tomasini; sound engineered by Walden O. Watson and William Russell; production design by Joseph Hurley, Robert Claworthy, and George Milo; music by Bernard Herrmann; special effects by Clarence Champagne; costumes designed by Helen Colvig; pictorial consultant: Saul Bass.

Filmed on Universal backlots, interiors filmed at Revue Studios, locations shot on Route 99 of the Fresno-Bakersfield Highway and in the San Fernando Valley. Cost: $800,000.

Cast: Anthony Perkins (*Norman Bates*); Janet Leigh (*Marion Crane*); Vera Miles (*Lila Crane*); John Gavin (*Sam Loomis*); Martin Balsam (*Milton Arbogast*); John McIntyre (*Sheriff Chambers*); Lurene Tuttle (*Mrs. Chambers*); Simon Oakland (*Dr. Richmond*); Frank Albertson (*Tom Cassidy*); Pat Hitchcock (*Caroline*); Vaughn Taylor (*George Lowery*); John Anderson (*Car salesman*); Mort Mills (*Policeman*); Sam Flint, Francis De Sales, George Eldredge (*Officials*); Alfred Hitchcock (*Man outside real estate office*).

Publications:

Script—*Alfred Hitchcock's Psycho* edited by Richard Anobile, New York 1974; reviews—by Peter Baker in *Films and Filming* (London), September 1960; review by Peter Dyer in *Sight and Sound* (London), autumn 1960; review by Andrew Sarris in *The Village Voice* (New York), 11 August 1960; review by Bosley Crowther in *The New York Times*, 17 June 1960; books—*The Cinema of Alfred Hitchcock* by Peter Bogdanovich, New York 1962; *Alfred Hitchcock* by Hans-Peter Manz, Zurich 1962; *The Films of Alfred Hitchcock* by George Perry, London 1965; *Alfred Hitchcock* by Jean Douchet, Paris 1967; *Hitchcock* by François Truffaut in collaboration with Helen Scott, New York 1967; *Alfred Hitchcock* by Noel Simsolo, Paris 1969; *Focus on Hitchcock* edited by Albert J. LaValley, Englewood Cliffs, New Jersey 1972; *A Filmguide to Psycho* by James Naremore, Bloomington, Indiana 1973; *The Strange Case of Alfred Hitchcock* by Raymond Durgnat, Cambridge, Massachusetts 1974; *The Art of Alfred Hitchcock* by Donald Spoto, New York 1976; *Dark Dreams: A Psychological History of the Modern Horror Film* by Charles Derry, New York 1977; *Hitchcock's Films* by Robin Wood, London 1977; *Hitchcock—The Murderous Gaze* by William Rothman, London 1982; *The Silent Scream: Alfred Hitchcock's Sound Track* by Elisabeth Weis, Rutherford, New Jersey 1982; articles—interview with Hitchcock by Jean Domarchi and Jean Douchet in *Cahiers du cinéma* (Paris), December 1959; article by Ernest Callenbach in *Film Quarterly* (Berkeley), fall 1960; "Je suis une légende" by Nally Kaplan in *Les Lettres françaises* (Paris), October 1960; "Pourquoi j'ai peur la nuit" by Alfred Hitchcock in *Arts* (Paris), June 1960; "Hitchcock et son public" by Jean Douchet in *Cahiers du cinéma* (Paris), November 1960; "Alfred Hitchcock" by Guillaume Allombert in *Image et son* (Paris), November 1960; "Lettre de New York" by Philippe Demonsablon in *Cahiers du cinéma* (Paris), September 1960; "Psychanalyse de Psycho" by Robin Wood in *Cahiers du cinéma* (Paris), November 1960; "Un certain Alfred Hitchcock" by Pierre Marcabru in *Arts* (Paris), February 1961; interview by Yves Boisset in *Cinéma 61* (Paris), January 1961; article by Raymond Durgnat in *Films and Filming* (London), January 1962; Interview with Hitchcock by Ian Cameron and V.F. Perkins in *Movie* (London), 6 January 1963;

"Pinning Down the Quicksilver" by Robin Bean in *Films and Filming* (London), July 1965; "The Rhetoric of Hitchcock's Thrillers" by O.B. Hardison in *Man at the Movies*, Baton Rouge, Louisiana 1967; article by Leo Braudy in *Film Quarterly* (Berkeley), summer 1968; "*Psycho*, Rosie and a Touch of Orson: Janet Leigh Talks" by Rui Nogueira in *Sight and Sound* (London), spring 1970; "Private Madness and Public Lunacy" by Kevin Gough-Yates in *Films and Filming* (London), February 1972; "*Psycho* Therapy" by Richard Corliss in *Favorite Movies: Critics' Choice*, New York 1973; "De Quelques Points de theorie du cinéma" by J.F. Tarnowski in *Positif* (Paris), September 1975; "Psycho" in *Hammer's House of Horrors* by Tony Crawley, London 1978; "*Psycho*" by Valentin Almendarez in *Cinema Texas Program Notes* (Austin), 21 September 1978; "Psychosis, Neurosis, Perversion" by Raymond Bellour, translated by N. Huston in *Camera Obscura* (Berkeley), summer 1979; "Psychosis, Neurosis, Perversion" by Raymond Bellour in *Camera Obscura* (Berkeley), nos.3-4, 1979; "The Big Hitch" by David Thomson in *Film Comment* (New York), March/April 1979; "Alfred Hitchcock" by G. Bikácsy in *Filmkultura* (Budapest), September/October 1979; "*Psycho*" by Louis Black in *Cinema Texas Program Notes* (Austin), 16 April 1979; "Faith and Idolatry in the Horror Film" by J.P. Telotte in *Literature/Film Quarterly* (Salisbury, Maryland), no.3, 1980; "De eenvoud van Hitchcock" by W. Verstappen in *Skoop* (Amsterdam), April 1981; "*Psycho*: The Institutionalization of Female Sexuality" by Barbara Klinger in *Wide Angle* (Athens, Ohio), no.1, 1982.

*   *   *

There are those for whom Alfred Hitchcock is a "master of suspense," the premier technician of the classical narrative cinema; there are those for whom Hitchcock's mastery of film technique, of "pure cinema" as he liked to call it, amounts to a species of pandering, or even of an audience-directed cruelty; there are others for whom Hitchcock's fables of emotions trapped and betrayed are seen as self-reflexive, enticing the viewer to participate in the drama of suspense only to call that participation into moral question; and, finally, there are those who find in Hitchcock's films submerged allegories of grace, of mistakes acknowledged, redeemed, and transcended. Despite such general differences of opinion, however, it *is* commonly agreed among Hitchcock scholars that *Psycho* raised the issue of Hitchcock's artistic status and intentions (or lack thereof) in its purest form, as if it were his most essential, most essentially Hitchcockian, film.

Indeed, the shower murder sequence in *Psycho*—wherein Janet Leigh's almost confessional cleansing is cut short by the knife wielding "Mrs. Bates"—is frequently cited as a textbook instance of cinematic suspense and formal (montage) perfection. Moreover, it is this murder of the film's ostensible heroine, roughly a third of the way through the narrative, that most critics focus on when discussing the significance of the entire film, as if it *were* the film writ small, as if the film were itself an act of murder that we are commanded, via Hitchcock's expert use of subjective camera, to take part and pleasure in.

Two kinds of evidence are typically invoked to support such a reading of *Psycho* and of Hitchcock generally. One of these is Hitchcock's lifelong commitment to popular cinematic genres, mainly the thriller. The underlying premise here is that Hitchcock had ample opportunity to break out of the thriller format, to became an "artist" in the way that Fellini and Antonioni are (it is often pointed out that *Psycho* and *L'avventura* were released within a year of each other), so that his apparent decision *not* to do so can be read as a matter either of obsession (as if he feared to) or satisfaction (as if he aspired no higher). And underlying *this* premise is the conviction that popular genres, of their very nature, are inimical to serious art, are too much the product of popular tastes and box-office calculation to allow for humane insights or serious artistic self-expression—hence O.B. Hardison's argument that Hitchcock is less an artist than a "rhetorician."

A second sort of evidence is also cited to support the claim that neither Hitchcock nor *Psycho* need be taken seriously—his comments to interviewers, especially regarding his working methods and intentions. Hitchcock's description of *Psycho* as "a *fun* picture," one that takes its audience through an emotional process "like taking them through the haunted house at the fairground" (in *Movie* 6), is a notorious instance of this apparent dissociation between the seriousness of his ostensible subjects (crime, murder, sexuality) and the triviality of Hitchcock's approach. As David Thomson puts it, "*Psycho* is just the cocky leer of evil genius flaunting tragic material but never brave enough to explore it."

The case against *Psycho* is grounded in a reading of intention and effect, the charge being that Hitchcock's intentions are mercenary and that the effect of the film is a kind of brutality, directed equally at the film's characters *and* its audience. The accepted case *for* the film follows a similar line of reasoning, though to different conclusions. Thus critics like Robin Wood and Leo Braudy would agree that in *Psycho* Hitchcock "forces the audience...to face the most sinister connotations of our audience role" by playing with, yet disturbing, our normal expectation "that our moral sympathies and our aesthetic sympathies [will] remain fixed throughout the movie." Our desire to "identify" with sympathetic characters is thus called increasingly into question as our "identification" shifts from the reasonably normal Marion Crane to the seemingly normal Norman Bates— who finally becomes "Mrs. Bates" in an epiphany of confused identity. Indeed, it is this voyeuristic tendency to identify with others, or to identify them *as* the views we take of them, often without their knowledge, that the film calls into ethical doubt, forcing viewers "to see the dark potentialities within all of us."

Such arguments both for and against *Psycho* are problematic, however, on several counts—not the least of which is the common assumption that film, of its very essence, is "naturally voyeuristic." Is it more or less voyeuristic than still photography, or painting, or sight generally? Also a problem is the clear implication in both arguments that audience response is so thoroughly under Hitchcock's control that "the spectator becomes the chief protagonist." Upon what grounds can we claim to know all members of a given audience, much less all members of all possible audiences, will respond to a particular film? Furthermore, what warrants our generalizing from predicted audience response to authorial intention? And of what relevance is intention to our evaluation of *Psycho* in any event? Much discussion of *Psycho* assumes that our decision to take *Psycho* seriously as a work of art *depends* upon our reading of Hitchcock's intentions regarding it; but one can more reasonably argue that the very decision to treat the film as an aesthetic object renders intention *ir*relevant. As Stanley Cavell puts it, all that matters for our *experience* of any film is "in front of your eyes."

A final reason for doubting the wisdom of the accepted approaches to *Psycho* is the focus they place on individual psychology, of the characters, of the viewer, at the expense of other facts of the text. One such fact, often read as an Hitchcockian irrelevancy (a "MacGuffin"), is money—as personified by the oil-rich Mr. Cassidy and as an implicit factor in the attitudes and actions of nearly every major character. It is Sam's lack of money that prompts Marion in the first place to steal Cassidy's $40,000. Sam and Lila assume that money is behind Norman's silence regarding Marion (Norman himself hints that money played a part in the relationship of his widowed mother to her lover); the Sheriff assumes that money is behind Arbogast's disappearance. Indeed, *Psycho* can be read as a meditation on money and its effects—negative effects as far as the film's characters are concerned, but also positive effects in regard to the audience, or at least in regard to those members of the audience who take *Psycho* seriously as a warning of the deadly effects that money can have. It is in such terms that the audience *can* become an implicit "character" in the film—the character who *does* benifit from past mistakes and who is therefore capable of transcending them.

—Leland Poague

THE PUBLIC ENEMY. Production: Warner Bros. Pictures Inc.; 1931; black and white, 35mm; running time: 96 mins. Released May 1931.

Produced by Darryl Zanuck; screenplay by Kubec Glasmon and John Bright, adaptation and dialogue by Harvey Thew; from a story "Beer and Blood" by Kubec Glasmon and John Bright; directed by William Wellman; photography by Dev Jennings; edited by Ed McCormick; art direction by Max Parker; music conducted by David Mendoza; costumes designed by Earl Luick.

Filmed February-March 1931 in Warner Bros. studios. Cost: $151,000.

Cast: James Cagney (*Tom Powers*); Jean Harlow (*Gwen Allen*); Edward Woods (*Matt Doyle*); Joan Blondell (*Mamie*); Beryl Mercer (*Ma Powers*); Donald Cook (*Mike Powers*); Mae Clark (*Kitty*); Leslie Fenton (*Nails Nathan*); Robert Emmett O'Connor (*Paddy Ryan*); Murray Kinnell (*Putty Nose*); Ben Hendricks, Jr. (*Bugs Moran*); Rita Flynn (*Molly Doyle*); Clark Burroughs (*Dutch*); Snitz Edwards (*Hack Miller*); Adele Watson (*Mrs. Doyle*); Frank Coghlan, Jr. (*Tom as a boy*); Frankie Darro (*Matt as a boy*); Purnell Pratt (*Officer Powers*); Mia Marvin (*Jane*); Robert E. Homans (*Pat Burke*); Dorothy Gee (*Nails's girl*); Lee Phelps (*Steve the bartender*); Ben Hendricks III (*Bugs as a boy*); Landers Stevens (*Doctor*); Eddie Kane (*Joe, the headwaiter*); Douglas Gerrard (*Assistant tailor*); Sam McDaniel (*Black headwaiter*); William H. Strauss (*Pawnbroker*); Snitz Edwards (*Hack*); Russ Powell (*Bartender*).

Publications:

Script—*The Public Enemy* edited with an introduction by Henry Cohen, Madison, Wisconsin 1981; books—*Harlow: An Intimate Biography* by Irving Shulman, New York 1964; *The Great Films: 50 Golden Years of Motion Pictures* by Bosley Crowther, New York 1967; *Don't Say Yes Until I'm Finished Talking: A Biography of Darryl F. Zanuck* by Mel Gussow, New York 1971; *Cagney* by Ron Ohen, Chicago 1972; *Cagney* by Andrew Bergman, New York 1973; *A Short Time for Insanity: An Autobiography* by William Wellman, New York 1974; *James Cagney* by Michael Freedland, London 1974; *Warner Brothers* by Charles Higham, New York 1975; *Cagney by Cag-*

ney by James Cagney, New York 1976; *Deliver Us From Evil: An Interpretation of American Prohibition* by Norman H. Clark, New York 1976; *The Great Gangster Pictures* by James R. Parish and Michael Pitts ,Metuchen, New Jersey 1976; *Warner Brothers Directors* by William R. Meyer, New Rochelle, New York 1978; *Cagney: The Actor as Acteur* by Patrick McGilligan, San Diego 1982; articles—"Ridding Local Movies of Gangster Films" by A. Edmund Williamson in *American City*, September 1931; "Cagney and the American Hero" by Lincoln Kirstein in *Hound and Horn* (New York), April 1932; "Cagney and the Mob" by Kenneth Tynan in *Sight and Sound* (London), May 1951; "James Cagney" by Don Miller in *Films in Review* (New York), August/September 1958; "A Memorable Visit with and Elder Statesman" by Curtis Lee Hanson in *Cinema* (Beverly Hills), July 1966; "William Wellman: Director Rebel" by William Wellman, Jr. in *Action* (Los Angeles), March/April 1970; "Warner Brothers in the Thirties" by Russell Campbell in *Velvet Light Trap* (Madison, Wisconsin), June 1971; "3 klassiske Gangsterfilm og deres Baggrund" by S. Kjørup in *Kosmorama* (Copenhagen), August 1973; "A Man's World: An Analysis of the Films of William Wellman" by Julian Fox in *Films and Filming* (London), March/April 1973; "More Than Meets the Eye" by Gerald Peary in *American Film* (Washington, D.C.), March 1976; "*Public Enemy*—Samhäallets fiende nr. 1" by S. Linnéll in *Chaplin* (Stockholm), no.4 (151), 1977; "Bullets, Beer and the Hays Office: *Public Enemy*" by Garth Jowett in *American History/American Film* edited by John E. O'Connor and Martin Jackson, New York 1979; "*L'Ennemi public*" by F. Guerif in *Revue du cinéma* (Paris), April 1979; "*The Public Enemy*" by Howard H. Prouty in *Magill's Survey of Cinema, Vol. III* edited by Frank N. Magill, Englewood Cliffs, New Jersey 1980.

*   *   *

Although *The Public Enemy* is now most remembered for the famous scene in which James Cagney smashes half a grapefruit into the face of actress Mae Clarke—an act that more than one critic has termed the most vicious in all of motion picture history—the film is, in fact, one of the first of the gangster genre to examine the sociological roots of crime in a serious way. Because of some unforgettable images and a charismatic performance by Cagney in the role that made him famous, the film achieved the rare distinction of being both a major box office success and a public-spirited statement.

The film's overall treatment of violence is implied rather than graphic. Most of the violence occurs off camera, but through an innovative use of sound—for example, in the chilling scene in which Cagney murders the horse that killed his friend—the effects of the savagery are actually heightened. Similarly, the scenes in which Cagney's gift-wrapped corpse is delivered to his brother or the bizarre scene in the rain after he is wounded (which prefigures the famous Gene Kelly "Singin' in the Rain" number from that 1952 film) stunned audiences and justified the film's social statement. When Cagney, riddled with bullets, falls face down in a rain gutter, his blood entering the torrent, and mutters "I ain't so tough," that is a restatement of the film's prologue that it is within the public's power to stamp out criminals.

Between the picture's framing prologue and epilogue, director William Wellman created powerful sequences that still retain much of their impact. Through the introduction of his characters as children and an elaborate opening pan that delineates their environment, Wellman establishes a relationship between sordid surroundings and the natural inclinations of children, that they sometimes interact to begin the evolution of the criminal. Yet much of the commentary surrounding these scenes seems simplistic to modern viewers. That the film retains much of its impact today is due largely to the performances, particularly those of Jean Harlow as Cagney's seductive mistress and Cagney himself as the gangster Tom Powers. Although the fortuitous pairing of the star with a role ideally suited to his talents was the result of one of Wellman's "gut" instincts, Cagney's magnetic performance made the film a smash hit and achieved some political repercussions as well: the picture unintentionally glamorized the criminal and indirectly hastened Hollywood's implementation of a self-imposed Production Code to prevent such undesirable social figures from being depicted in future in a sympathetic way. Although *The Public Enemy* may seem tame in comparison with some of the post-Code films of the last two decades, enough of its power survives to sustain it both as a film and as a creditable social document.

—Steve Hanson

I PUGNI IN TASCA. Fists in the Pocket. Production: Doria Cinematografica; 1965; black and white, 35mm; running time: 105 mins. Released 1965.

Production director: Ugo Novello; screenplay by Marco Bellocchio; directed by Marco Bellocchio; photography by Alberto Marrama; edited by Aurelio Mangiarotti (pseudonym of Silvano Agosti); production design by Gisella Longo; music by Ennio Morricone; assistant director: Giuseppe Lanci; artistic collaboration for dubbing and montage: Elda Tattoli.

Filmed in 9 weeks. Cost: 50,000,000 lira. Locarno Film Festival, Vela d'argento; Venice Film Festicval, Prize Outside of Competition, 1965.

Cast: Lou Castel (*Alessandro*); Paola Pitagora (*Giulia*); Marino Masé (*Augusto*); Liliana Gerace (*Mother*); Pier Luigi Troglio (*Leone*); Jennie MacNeil (*Lucia*); Maura Martini (*Child*); Giani Schicchi (*Tonino*); Alfredo Filippazzi (*Doctor*); Gianfranco Cella and Celestina Bellocchio (*2 Youths at the party*); Stefania Troglio (*Waitress*); Irene Agnelli (*Bruna*).

Publications:

Script—"*I pugni in tasca*" (scenario), Milan 1967; review—"*I Pugni in tasca*" by Jacques Bontemps in *Cahiers du cinéma* (Paris), September 1965; books—*Italian Cinema Since the War* by Ken Wlaschin, Cranbury, New Jersey 1971; *The Italian Cinema* by Pierre Leprohon, New York 1972; articles—" interview with Marco Bellocchio in *Cahiers du cinéma* (Paris), September 1965; "Le Cercle de famille" by Gilles Jacob in *Cinéma 66* (Paris), June 1966; "The Sterility of Provocation" by Marco Bellocchio in *Cahiers du Cinema in English* (New York), January 1967; "Les Poings dans les poches à travers les controverses" by Jean Delmas in *Jeune Cinéma* (Paris), nos.27-28, 1968; "Les Poings dans les poches" by A. Lisor in *Image et son* (Paris), (fiche), March 1972; "Entretien avec Marco Bellochio" by N. Zalaffi in *Image et son* (Paris), April 1973.

*   *   *

After attending the Centro Sperimentale film school in Rome and then studying (on a grant) at the Slade School of Fine Arts in London, Marco Bellocchio returned to his native town of Piacenza and sent out to make a feature film. Because he couldn't find a producer willing to underwrite the project, he borrowed money from one of his brothers and created a set in his family's country house near Bóbbio. He filmed for nine weeks on a shoestring budget of 50,000,000 lire (28,000 pounds sterling). The result, *Fists in the Pocket*, hit Italy like a bomb. The film was unanimously acclaimed for the skill of its direction and expressive camera work, and it received numerous awards at film festivals, thus ensuring international distribution. French critics compared the film favorably to *Zero for Conduct* by Jean Vigo and *L'Age d'or* by Luis Buñuel, and Italian critics announced that they had not seen such a powerful debut since Visconti's *Ossessione*. For the next ten years Bellocchio was regarded as one of Italy's leading political filmmakers whose films also performed respectably at the box office.

Fists in the Pocket is about a family living in the provinces, and is a bitter denunciation of bourgeois values from an angry young member of the bourgeoisie. Situations are shown at their most extreme: two of the five family members are epileptics, the youngest son is an idiot, and the mother is blind—all abnormal states working as commentaries upon what Bellocchio sees as normal conditions in family life. The sister's epilepsy, for example, is a metaphor for the agonizing emotions of jealousy, incestual desire, and the fear that she always feels. The mother is blind because, as Bellocchio explained, "When a son becomes 18, his mother no longer sees him, no longer understands him, and is no longer of use to him." The only family member who has normal contacts with the outside world is Augusto, but he is also clearly representative of the hypocrisy and emptiness of so-called "normalcy."

Alessandro, the main character, acts as catalyst in the film. He respects Augusto so much that, in order to relieve Augusto of the burden of being the patriarchal protector of the sick family, he decides to kill everyone else in the house. The tiny push he gives the mother in the cemetery (which sends her literally to her grave) is an allegorical act testifying that within the bourgeois system a minor action is sufficient enough to make the whole structure fall. Alessandro kills his younger brother in the bathtub, which, with its warm water and Freudian connotations, represents the womb from which Alessandro never wanted Leone to emerge. Alessandro also attempts to kill his sister, with whom he has had an incestuous relationship. Meanwhile Augusto, acting out his role as true patriarch, allows his underling brother to commit crimes the results of which will be advantageous to himself.

The characters are depraved, fanatical, and morbid. As well, the film's rough style makes no concession to the traditional rapport among artist/character/spectator; here the spectator must remain active and question the director's objectivity in presenting gruesome events and bizarre psychological states. Bellocchio said in an interview (in *Positif*) that, although his work had exorcised demons from his own past, he wished to present that past in the most objective and critical way so that it might then be of use to others.

—Elaine Mancini

PUTYOVKA V ZHIZN. Putevka v zhizn. The Road to Life. Production: Mezhrabpomfilm (USSR); black and white, 35mm; running time: about 100 mins.; length: 3330 meters. Released

June 1931. Re-released May 1957, re-edited and re-dubbed by Nikolai Ekk and Yakov Stollyar (2617 meters).

Screenplay by Nikolai Ekk, Alexander Stolper, and R. Yanushkevich; directed by Nikolai Ekk; photography by Vasili Pronin; sound by E. Nesterov; art direction by I. Stepanov and A. Evmenko; music by Yakov Stollyar.

Cast: Mikhail Zharjov (*Zhigan*); Nikolai Batalov (*Sergeev*); Ivan Kyrlya (*Mustafa*); A. Antropova (*Inspector*); M. Dzhagofavov (*Kolka*); V. Vesnovski (*His father*); R. Yanushkevich (*Mother*); Maria Gonka (*Lolka*); Alexander Nowikow (*Saschka*).

Publications:

Books—*Kino: A History of the Russian and Soviet Film* by Jay Leyda, London 1960; *Soviet Cinema* by Thorold Dickenson and Catherine De La Roche, revised edition, New York 1972; *The Motion Picture in the Soviet Union, 1918-1952: A Sociological Analysis* by John Rimberg, New York 1973; articles—"Film in Moscow" in *Spectator*, 31 October 1931; "The First Russian Sound Films" by A. Kraszna-Krausz in *Close-Up* (London), December 1931; "Der Weg ins Leben: Hin und zurueck ueber Gubenkos Film *Mit gebrochenen Schwingen*" by H. Holba in *Film und Fernsehen* (East Berlin), no.9, 1979; "*Putniiat list za zhivota*" by G. Stoianov-Bigor in *Kinoizkustvo* (Sofia, Bulgaria), August 1979.

*   *   *

One of the first Soviet sound films—with an imaginative sound track far ahead of its time—Nikolai Ekk's *Road to Life* was a smash hit both in Russia and in the West, where its impact generated some dozen spinoffs on its theme of "difficult" children. A Soviet critic, legitimising its official function, wrote that "the film's success depended on the social problems involved, problems of responsibility towards a new generation." But he added, more acutely, that the film broke new ground because "it did not merely manipulate the life stories of the people involved in order to illustrate social problems but let the problems grow out of these life stories and their dramatic development."

The film's theme is the reformation—or rescue—of one of the bands of *besprizorni* (homeless children) who roamed, and terrorised, city streets in the difficult post-civil war years. The gang loyalties are torn between Zhigan, a sort of Fagin character played by Mikhail Zharov, who urges them to carry on thieving, and Sergeev, the head of a "work-commune," played by Nikolai Batalov, who tries to lead them into the paths of righteousness. The children themselves were not from a stage school but were inmates, or pupils, of work-communes (reform schools or rehabilitation centres in which students were expected to work on real projects—in the film, the building of a railroad). Despite their superb performances, not one of these kids later became a professional actor, not even Ivan Kyrlya, who plays the gang leader Mustafa, whose Asian features, far from inscrutable, vividly expressed every emotion. Kyrlya grew up to become a famous poet, writing in Mari, his native language.

Highly professional, the actors who played hero and villain gave performances that seem equally natural and true to life. Zharov was no Dickensian villain, but used his powerful physical presence to portray a man governed by instinct, a man

able to attract as well as intimidate his teenage thieves. His moments of melancholy rapture, whenever he picks up his guitar, made the songs he sings top of the contemporary pops. Although accused therefore of romanticising thieves and their slang, Ekk had no Brechtian intention of updating the *Beggars' Opera* by introducing underworld folksongs as "production numbers": as he intended, they come across as spontaneous expressions of the character and are an integral part of the film.

If Zharov portrayed instinct, Batalov, the hero, portrayed thought. As, with imaginative accuracy, his dialogue is limited to the repetition of a few dozen pithy phrases, he has to convey much of his thinking with his eyes and facial expression. But Batalov arrived at this impressive performance only after spending much time at a work-commune, getting to know its Head and (in Batalov's words) "learning his method of handling the students, which had an enormous influence on my interpretation of the role."

Ekk steers his simple down-to-earth story of good and evil daringly close to, but (despite the tear-jerking presence of his band of boys) always clear of sentimentality, always remembering that the boys are wicked as well as innocent. He is never afraid of shock sequences—mutiny in the commune, smashing up the thieves' den, Mustafa's death on the railroad—for they seem to arise logically from the realistic documentary course of the story and fit smoothly into the somewhat spiky but deeply expressive rhythm of his editing technique. A talented but sensitive and retiring man, Ekk was never again to equal the success of *Road to Life*, which had so great an influence on filmmakers both at home and abroad.

—Robert Dunbar

LE QUAI DES BRUMES. Production: Ciné-Alliance (some sources state Sigma-Frogerais); black and white, 35mm; running time: 91 mins. Released 18 May 1938, Paris.

Produced by Grégor Rabinovitch (some sources list Simon Schiffrin); screenplay by Jacques Prévert; from the novel by Pierre MacOrlan; directed by Marcel Carné; photography by Eugene Schufftan; edited by René Le Hénaff; sound by Antoine Archaimbaud; production design by Alexandre Trauner with Paul Bertrand; music by Maurice Jaubert.

Filmed January-February 1938 in the Pathé-Nathan studios, exteriors shot in Le Havre. Prix Louis Delluc, 1938; Académie du Film, Prix Méliès, 1938; Grand Prix National du Cinéma Français, 1939.

Cast: Jean Gabin (*Jean*); Michèle Morgan (*Nelly*); Michel Simon (*Zabel*); Aimos (*Quart-Vittel*); René Génin (*Doctor*); Pierre Brasseur (*Lucien*); Edouard Delmont (*Panama*); Robert Le Vigan (*Michel Krauss*); Marcel Perès (*Chauffeur*); Kiki (the dog).

Publications:

Script—"*Le Quai des brumes*" by Jacques Prévert in *Avant-Scène du cinéma* (Paris), 15 October 1979; reviews—in *Cinématographie français* (Paris), 12 August 1938; review in *Sight and Sound* (London), spring 1939; review in *Monthly Film Bulletin*

(London), no.62, 1939; "La Presse" in *Avant-Scène du cinéma* (Paris), 15 October 1979; books—*Marcel Carne* by Jean-Louis Béranger, Paris 1945; *Marcel Carne* by Robert Chazal, Paris n.d. *Marcel Carné* by Jean Quéval, Paris 1952; *Marcel Carné, sa vie, ses films* by Bernard Landry, Paris 1952; *Marcel Carné* by Jacques Meillant, Paris n.d. *French Film* by Roy Armes, New York 1970; *French Cinema Since 1946: Volume One: The Great Tradition* by Roy Armes, 2nd edition, New York 1976; *A History of Film* by Jack C. Ellis, Englewood Cliffs, New Jersey 1979; articles—"Marcel Carné" by Roger Manvell in *Sight and Sound* (London), spring 1946; "The Cinema of Marcel Carné" by J.F. Lodge in *Sequence* (London), December 1946; "Marcel Carné" by Gavin Lambert in *Sequence* (London), spring 1948; *Jean Gabin's Instinctual Man" by Pierre Duvillars in Films in Review* (New York), March 1951; "Les 20 Ans de cinéma de Marcel Carné" by Louis Daquin in *Les Lettres françaises* (Paris), 1 March 1956; "Les Films de Marcel Carné, expression de notre époque" by Georges Sadoul in *Les Lettres françaises* (Paris), 1 March 1956; "The Carné Bubble" by Alan Stanbrook in *Film* (London), November/December 1959; "Jean Gabin" by Jack E. Nolan in *Films in Review* (New York), April 1963; "Jean Gabin" by Peter Cowie in *Films and Filming* (London), February 1964; issue on Carné of *Cahiers du cinematheque* (Paris), winter 1972; "Comment est né *Le Quai de brumes*" by Marcel Carné in *Avant-Scène du cinéma* (Paris), 15 October 1979.

*   *   *

Marcel Carné's *Le Quai des brumes* and *Le Jour se lève* are examples of "poetic realism," a filmic style and narration often located in the French cinema of the 1930's. The term is, however, an unreliable critical rubric since the generalities and imprecisions associated with "poetry" and "realism" mask the specific elements of the texts it presumes to characterize.

In the case of Carné, many of those specific elements can be traced to his collaborators. Assistant to Jacques Feyder, Carné was clearly influenced by the world-weariness of the older director's *Le Grand Jeu*, by the fascination of marginal lives in *Pension Mimosas*. Carné's first film, *Jenny*, stars Feyder's wife, Françoise Rosay. Other consistencies in Carné's films are provided by Jacques Prévert, who was responsible for all of Carné's scripts until the 1950's, as well as by the sets of Alexandre Trauner and the music of Maurice Jaubert. Jean Gabin, the hero of *Le Quai des brumes* and *Le Jour se lève*, is the actor whose persona most insistently dominates Carné's pre-war films.

One of Gabin's mid-'30's successes was in Duvivier's *La Bandéra*, based upon a novel of Pierre Mac Orlan, who was also the author of *Le Quai des brumes*. The most apparent changes wrought by Carné and Prévert in Mac Orlan's novel were the transpositions of time (from the turn-of-the-century to sometime vaguely contemporary) and place (from Paris to Le Havre). Carné, who would prove himself so expert in the rendition of period detail in *Les Enfants du paradis*, opts here for a nonspecific temporality, for an epoch that is both removed from and familiar to viewers. The port city is exploited for the degree to which it suggests the edge of the world, a jumping-off place (enacted in the suicide of one of the film's characters), the place for final decisions, the place for taking the last chance. Whatever might have been specific to the real city of Le Havre (location shooting was begun there on January 2, 1938) is sacrificed to the evocation of *port* per se, the port of all ports, and to the allegorization of place appropriate to the film's schematics of plot and character. The "realism" of Carné's "poetry" is shrouded in the dark shadows and fog that enhance the elusiveness of the fiction.

Plot is the skeleton required to sustain the trajectory of Jean, the hero, the deserter, from arrival (he materializes out of nearly pitch darkness on a deserted road) to departure (his death) through his encounter with the other desperate men and his love for a mysterious woman. The script provides little in terms of background or motivation beyond the basic tensions of its good/evil, outsider/bourgeois society oppositions. If lines such as "C'est difficile de vivre" (living is difficult) and "Oui...on est seul" (Yes, you're alone) suggest a proto-existentialism, the incorporeal nature of the film's texture is distant from the tangibilities of existential art.

But *Le Quai des brumes* does generate a specific density through its enactments and stagings. Gabin may appear from nowhere, but he bears with him the weight of a highly identifiable presence, that of the most bankable star in French cinema. (In fact, it was Gabin's faith in the project that kept it from foundering when, just a few days before shooting was about to begin, the head of the production company financing the film, Gregor Rabinovitch, read the script and tried to dissuade the star from doing such a downbeat subject. Gabin persisted. He undoubtedly saw in the role of Jean a rich variation of the type of doomed hero that had brought him such success in Duvivier's *Pépé-le-Moko*, Grémillon's *Gueule d'amour* and Renoir's *Les Bas-fonds*.) The very young Michèle Morgan matched enigma to Gabin's mixture of strength and tenderness. Their first meeting takes place in a café that seems to be in the middle of nowhere. Shots ring out. A deserter and a woman wearing a beret and a transparent raincoat exchange names and fall in love. This configuration defines French film noir, its style and milieu, its challenge to bourgeois aesthetics and ethics. Here, far from the light of the natural world (in this darkness a patch of light is a privilege), far from families and social contexts, even far from conventional plots with their careful, "logical" identifications of situation and character, there flourish these emblems of gallantry and beauty.

Gabin and Morgan retain something of their emblematic status for the duration of a fiction that so sharply designates good and evil. The lovers are tormented by the petty criminal (Pierre Brasseur, who figures so importantly in *Les Enfants du paradis*) and by the girl's guardian, the prototypical dirty old man. Played by Michel Simon (if Gabin is the most popular leading man in French cinema, Simon is its most popular character actor), Zebel, the character no one can bear to be with or see, locates the film's moral conflict in a contrast of surfaces, of beauty and ugliness.

It is the very notion of surface, however, that distinguishes the film, that makes *Le Quai des brumes* an examination of the concept of image. Near the beginning, Jean meets a painter who soon after commits suicide. He jumps off this "edge of the world" and provides Jean, the deserter, with the clothes and identity that take him through the rest of the film. The painter is tormented by the acuity of his own vision. He sees behind things, through things. He sees to the core of images, to their decay. He would paint Jean with his hands in his pockets, at night, in fog. This is a project for a portrait filled with signs of concealment. And in the space between the hidden and the·revealed lies the truth. The painter is a surrogate for Carné and Prévert. What he says clearly defines the relationship between image (both visual and verbal) and meaning in the film. It is from this expression of style that character, narrative and film are generated.

—Charles Affron

LES QUATRE CENTS COUPS. The 400 Blows. Production: Les Films du Carrosse and SEDIF; black and white, 35mm, Dyaliscope; running time: 94 mins. Released 3 June 1959, dedicated to André Bazin.

Produced by Georges Charlot; screenplay by Marcel Moussy; from an original story by François Truffaut; directed by François Truffaut; photography by Henri Decaë; edited by Marie-Joseph Yoyotte; sound by Jean-Claude Marchetti; art direction by Bernard Evein; music by Jean Constantin.

New York Film Critics Award, Best Foreign Film, 1959; Best Director and Catholic Film Office Awards, Cannes Film Festival, 1959.

Cast: Jean-Pierre Léaud (*Antoine Doinel*); Claire Maurier (*Gilberte Doinel*); Albert Rémy (*Julien Doinel*); Guy Decomble (*"Little Quiz"*); Georges Flamant (*Monsieur Bicey, René's Father*); Patrick Auffray (*René*); Daniel Couturier, François Nocher, Richard Kanayan, Michel Girard, Henri Moati, Bernard Abbou, Michael Lesignor, Jean-François Bergouignan (*the children*); special guest appearances by Jeanne Moreau and Jean-Claude Brialy.

Publications:

Scripts—*Les Quatre Cents Coups* by François Truffaut and Marcel Moussy, Paris 1959; *The 400 Blows* edited and translated by David Denby, New York 1969; *The Adventures of Antoine Doinel: 4 Screenplays by François Truffaut* translated by Helen Scott, New York 1971; reviews—"400 Blows" by Louise Corbin in *Films in Review* (New York), November 1959; review by Jonas Mekas in *The Village Voice* (New York), 25 November 1959; "400 Blows" by Eric Rhode in *Sight and Sound* (London), spring 1960; review by Arlene Croce in *Film Quarterly* (Berkeley), no.3, 1960; books—*Cinema Eye, Cinema Ear* by John Russell Taylor, New York 1964; "Interview with François Truffaut" in *The New Wave* by Peter Graham, New York 1968; *The Cinema of François Truffaut* by Graham Petrie, New York 1970; *François Truffaut* by C.G. Crisp, New York 1972; *L'Univers de François Truffaut* by Dominique Fanne, Paris 1972; *Truffaut* by Don Allen, New York 1974; *The New Wave* by James Monaco, New York 1976; *Le Cinéma de François Truffaut* by Jean Collet, Paris 1977; *10 Film Classics* by Edward Murray, New York 1978; "François Truffaut" by Annette Insdorf, Boston 1978; *The Cinematic Muse: Critical Studies in the History of French Cinema* by Allen Thiher, Columbia, Missouri 1979; *François Truffaut: A Guide to Reference and Resources* by Eugene P. Walz, Boston 1982; articles—interview in *L'Express* (Paris), 23 April 1959; "Du côte de chez Antoine" by Jacques Rivette in *Cahiers du cinéma* (Paris), May 1959; "Screen" by P.T. Hartung in *Commonweal* (New York), 27 November 1959; article by Paul Rotha in *Films and Filming* (London), April 1960; "On Film" in the *New Yorker*, 20 February 1960; "A Conversation with François Truffaut" by R.M. Franci and Marshall Lewis in the *New York Film Bulletin*, nos.12, 13 and 14 1961; interview with L. Marcorelles in *Sight and Sound* (London), winter 1961-62; "Conversation with François Truffaut" by R.M. Franci and Marshall Lewis in *The New York Film Bulletin*, no.3, 1962; "François Truffaut—An Interview" by Paul Ronder in *Film Quarterly* (Berkeley), fall 1963; "François Truffaut—The Anarchist Imagination" by Judith Shatnoff in *Film Quarterly* (Berkeley), spring 1963; "The Literary Sophistication of François Truffaut" by Michael Klein in *Film Comment* (New York), summer 1965; article by Paul Saw-

yer in *Cinéaste* (New York), winter 1967-68; "The 400 Blows of François Truffaut" by Gilles Jacob in *Sight and Sound* (London), autumn 1968; "Czterysta batów" by A. Helman in *Kino* (Warsaw), November 1973; "Dialogue on Film: Interview with Truffaut" in *American Film* (Washington, D.C.), May 1976; "On Time and Truffaut" by Leland Poague in *Film Criticism* (Edinboro, Pennsylvania), summer 1976; "From *400 Blows* to *Small Change*" by Gerald Mast in the *New Republic* (New York), 2 April 1977; "The Existential Play in Truffaut's Early Films" by A. Thiher in *Literature/Film Quarterly* (Salisbury, Maryland), summer 1977.

*   *   *

The film career of François Truffaut is marked by paradox. As the "enfant terrible" of French film criticism he was barred from attending the Cannes Film Festival of 1958. But in 1959 his first feature-length film, *Les Quatre Cents Coups*, earned him honors as Best Director. Similarly, Truffaut's role as champion of the "politique des auteurs" also involved a species of paradox, in his attacking the French "tradition of quality" while praising American film noir in traditional aesthetic terms, in his praising of individual self-expression while creating a "counter-tradition" of filmic reference points from sources as diverse as neorealism and Hollywood. Especially important in Truffaut—given the tensions implicit in his critical stance—is a fact of language, at once a social institution *and* a means of personal expression. Repeatedly it is through language that Truffaut's central characters—most of them loners of one sort or another—attempt to reconcile themselves to society, as Truffaut himself, perhaps, has used language, especially the language of cinema, to establish his position as the most consistently successful of the *Cahiers du cinéma* group of New Wave directors which included not only Truffaut but also Jean-Luc Godard, Claude Chabrol, and Jacques Rivette.

To see *Les Quatre Cents Coups* against the background of the European cinema is to become especially conscious of Truffaut's indebtedness to Vigo, Rossellini, and Renoir. Vigo's short documentary *A propos de Nice* is a study of a city, with particular emphasis on the contrast between rich and poor; *Les Quatre Cents Coups* is similarly concerned with Paris as a city, and again there is a contrast between affluence (the many shop windows against which Truffaut frames his action) and poverty (the cramped Doinel apartment; various acts of theft). Equally resonant are the oft-noted parallels between *Les Quatre Cents Coups* and Jean Vigo's *Zéro de conduite*. Though the action in *Les Quatre Cents Coups* is not limited to interiors—the exterior shots of Paris connote a sense of almost lyrical freedom (partly the result of Jean Constantin's greatly energetic score)—the film's action is effectively "framed" by two "institution" sequences, the first in the school where Antoine Doinel (Jean-Pierre Léaud) is constantly at odds with his teacher, the second in the "Observation Center for Delinquent Minors" to which Antoine is sent after stealing a typewriter. Both settings recall the boys' boarding school in Vigo's *Zéro de conduite*, as Antoine's revolt against his social and familial circumstances recalls that of Vigo's quartet of young rebels.

Truffaut's debts to Rossellini and Renoir are as much stylistic as thematic—in both cases it is a matter of camera mobility and take duration, as well as the use of real-world rather than studio sets. But the theme of rebellion against rigid social authority is common both to Rossellini's and Renoir's modes of "film realism." In this regard *Les Quatre Cents Coups* recalls Renoir's *Boudu sauvé des eaux* especially, in setting (Paris) and in its tone of affection for the innocent self-assertiveness of its central character; Boudu polishes his shoes with a fancy bedspread, while Antoine wipes his dirty hands on the dining room drapery. It is also worth remarking that water is an important image in both films—for Boudu, who is "saved" from drowning, only to escape his bourgeois rescuers by eventually returning to the river, and also for Antoine Doinel, who speaks longingly of the sea throughout *Les Quatre Cents Coups*, and who finds himself (ambiguously) at the seashore at the film's end.

Equally important to the texture and tone of *Les Quatre Cents Coup* are Truffaut's references to the American cinema, especially to Hitchcock and Welles. The entire sequence of Antoine's arrest and detention, for instance, recalls in spirit and detail (right down to Antoine's hat) a similar sequence in Hitchcock's *The Wrong Man*; questions are asked, fingerprints or mug shots are taken, and the prisoner is eventually led to his cell. And the sense of shock in both cases follows from the disproportion or dissonance of the accused (Manny is innocent; Antoine was *returning* the typewriter) and the accusation.

Far more central to *Les Quatre Cents Coups* are its submerged (almost retroactive) relations to the Wellesian cinema. In *La Nuit Américaine* the childhood figure of the director played by Truffaut dreams of stealing stills of *Citizen Kane* through the grill work protecting the front of a local cinema (in *Les Quatre Cents Coups* Antoine and René filch a still from Bergman's *Sommaren med Monika*); in several respects the basic situation in *Les Quatre Cents Coups* recalls that in Welles's *Citizen Kane* and *The Magnificent Ambersons*. In all three films a young boy endeavors to reconcile himself to his mother, and in each instance the father figure is weak to the point of desertion: Kane's father quickly gives in to the scheme which sends Charlie east with Thatcher, Georgie Amberson's father dies midway through the narrative, and Antoine Doinel's stepfather has neither the courage nor the insight to understand the basic honesty and earnestness of Antoine's attempts to please or to be independent.

All of which is especially important given the stylistic and thematic affinity of Truffaut to Welles. That stylistic energy of both Truffaut and Welles is evidenced by the range of their filmic devices; both are masters equally of montage and of long take. And yet in each case the energy evident in film style is set thematically against a lack of energy in the depicted world of the film. The danger is one of denial (as Antoine is eventually denied by his mother) or exhaustion (as Antoine reaches the verge of exhaustion in his long run to the seashore).

The alternative—at least for Truffaut—is to find a way of life which allows for repetition, as children "repeat" and hence "replace" their parents, without falling prey to mechanical regimentation or cynical bitterness. It is Madame Doinel's bitterness toward her own past, toward her son, which is most directly responsible for Antoine's delinquency and exile. By contrast, Truffaut always works in his films to incorporate the past creatively into the present, to sustain the past by revising and reviewing it. Hence, in *Les Quatre Cents Coups* he pays homage to the history of cinema (and also literature) in the very process of renewing it, of using it again. And *Les Quatre Cents Coups* is itself subsequently revised and thereby sustained in a series of films about further adventures of Antoine Doinel, a series that culminates in *L'Amour en fuite* in which footage from all of the earlier films in the Doinel saga (*Les Quatre Cents Coups*, *Antoine et Collete*, *Baisers volés*, and *Domicile conjugal*), as well as from *Les Deux Anglais et le continent* and *La Nuit Américaine*, is recombined with new footage to demonstrate with remarkable clarity and feeling the possibilities for human renewal.

—Leland Poague

RAIDERS OF THE LOST ARK. Production: Lucasfilm Productions; 1981; color, 35mm, Panavision; running time: 115 mins. Released summer 1981 by Paramount Pictures.

Produced by Frank Marshall, executive producers: George Lucas and Howard Kazanjian; screenplay by Lawrence Kasdan, story by George Lucas and Philip Kaufman; directed by Steven Spielberg; photography by Douglas Slocombe; edited by Michael Kahn; sound effects supervised by Richard L. Anderson, sound effects edited by Steve H. Flick and Mark Mangini; production design by Norman Reynolds; art direction by Leslie Dilley; music by John Williams; special effects supervised by Richard Edlund; costumes designed by Deborah Nadoolman; stunts coordinated by Glenn Randall.

Filmed 1980 in France, Tunisia, and Hawaii, and in Elstree Studios, England. Cost: about $20 million. Academy Awards for Sound, Visual Effects, Art Direction, and Editing, 1981.

Cast: Harrison Ford (*Indiana Jones*); Karen Allen (*Marion Ravenswood*); Paul Freeman (*Belloq*): John Rhys-Davies (*Sallah*); Wolf Kahler (*Dietrich*); Ronald Lacey (*Toht*); Denholm Elliot (*Marcus Brody*).

Publications:

Reviews—in *Newsweek* (New York), 15 June 1981; "Le Retour au plaisir" by R. Benayoun in *Positif* (Paris), September 1981; review in the *New Yorker*, 15 June 1981; review in *Variety* (New York), 5 June 1981; "Les Aventuriers de l'arche perdue" by D. Païni in *Cinéma* (Paris), September 1981; review in *Time* (New York), 15 June 1981; review in *The New York Times*, 12 June 1981; articles—"*Raiders of the Lost Ark*" by R. Combs in *Monthly Film Bulletin* (London), August 1981; "*Raiders of the Lost Ark*" by G. Furtak in *Films in Review* (New York), September/August 1981; "*Raiders of the Lost Ark*, an Interview with Steven Spielberg" by D. Reiss in *Filmmakers Monthly* (Ward Hill, Massachusetts), July/August 1981; "*Raiders of the Lost Ark*" in *Films* (London), August 1981; "*Les Aventuriers de l'arche perdue*" by P. Mérigeau in *Image et son* (Paris), September 1981; "*Raiders of the Lost Ark*" by "Step" in *Skrien* (Amsterdam), October 1981; "*Les Aventuriers de l'arche perdue*" by J. Tonnerre in *Cinématographe* (Paris), September 1981; article in the *Hollywood Reporter*, 5 June 1981; article in the *New Republic* (New York), 4-11 July 1981; article in the *Saturday Review* (New York), June 1981; "The Complete Spielberg?" by Chris Auty in *Sight and Sound* (London), autumn, 1982; "*Raiders of the Lost Ark*" by John Wilson in *Magill's Cinema Annual* edited by Frank N. Magill, Englewood Cliffs, New Jersey 1982.

*   *   *

Raiders of the Lost Ark is historically important because it marks the first collaboration between George Lucas and Steven Spielberg, the two most financially successful of American filmmakers. Released in the summer of 1981, the film garnered some of the best critical accolades in either man's career; it also continued their phenomenal success: it is now one of the top ten money-makers of all time.

A homage to old movie serials in much the same way as are George Lucas's *Star Wars* films, *Raiders* is also derivative of westerns, horror films, war films and James Bond films. In fact, Lucas reportedly mentioned his *Raiders* story to Spielberg in 1977 after Spielberg said that he had always wanted to make a James Bond film. *Raiders* even opens with an initial adventure scene unrelated to the main story of the film, a device used in the James Bond films.

Relying on Spielberg's TV experience and extensive "storyboarding," the elaborate action film was shot in 73 days in France, Tunisia, Hawaii, and the famed Elstree Studios in England, which Lucas also used for his *Star Wars* films. Special effects for the film were made at Industrial Light and Magic, Lucasfilms' own facility in Northern California. Spielberg used cinematographer Douglas Slocombe, who worked on his *Close Encounters*, and editor Michael Kahn, who edited *Close Encounters* and *1941*. Spielberg also brought screenwriter Lawrence Kasdan to Lucas's attention.

The primary distinction of *Raiders*, in addition to its constant high level of thrills and chills, is the vivid portrayal of its hero, Indiana Jones, played by Harrison Ford. As Spielberg himself has said, Ford in this film is a combination of Errol Flynn in *The Adventures of Don Juan* and Humphrey Bogart in *The Treasure of the Sierra Madre*. A vulnerable but heroic figure, Ford's Indiana Jones also has a shadowy side. Indiana's search for the Ark which contains the original Ten Commandments becomes a dark obsession, a passion that causes him to twice abandon the film's heroine, Marion Ravenswood, played by Karen Allen.

Around this larger than life hero, Lucas and Spielberg weave a tale of intrigue and adventure, full of Nazi villains, a nasty but engaging Frenchman who is Indy's rival and shadowy double, and numerous references to Biblical and Egyptian mythology. There is an atmosphere of evil and mysterious power, and a demonic transformation of many of the film's settings and props. Thus, the ancient city of Tanis in *Raiders* has become deserted wasteland, an Egyptian temple becomes the prison full of snakes for Indy and Marion, and the mysterious Ark of the Covenant brings fiery destruction to the Nazis.

In the end, the Ark eludes grasp and is tucked away in an immense warehouse, a scene reminiscent of the last shot in *Citizen Kane*. Through the course of the film, Indy discovers that he is both free and bound—although he loses the Ark, he does get Marion. In this respect the film seems to be saying, True love or friendship is its own reward.

—Thomas Snyder

RASHOMON. Production: Daiei Productions; 1950; black and white, 35mm; running time: 88 mins.; length: 2406 meters. Released 25 August 1950, Tokyo.

Produced by Jingo Minuro, later titles list Masaichi Nagata as producer; screenplay by Shinobu Hashimoto and Akira Kurosawa; from two short stories by Ryunosuke Akutagawa; directed by Akira Kurosawa; photography by Kazuo Miyagawa; art direction by So Matsuyama (some sources list Takashi Matsuyama); music by Fumio Hayasaka.

Filmed at Daiei Studios on outdoor sets. Venice Film Festival, Best Film: Lion of St. Mark, 1951; Academy Award, Honorary Award as most outstanding foreign film, 1951.

Cast: Toshiro Mifune (*Tajomaru, the bandit*); Masayuki Mori (*Takehiro, the samurai*); Machiko Kyo (*Masago, his wife*); Takashi Shimura (*Woodcutter*); Minoru Chiaki (*Priest*); Kichijiro Ueda (*The commoner*); Daisuke Kato (*Police agent*); Fumiko Homma (*The medium*).

Publications:

Script—*Rashomon: A Film by Akira Kurosawa* (includes original Rashomon stories, 3 essays, and part of screenplay for *The Outrage*), edited by Donald Richie and Robert Hughes, New York 1969; reviews—"Intriguing Japanese Picture, *Rashomon*" by Bosley Crowther in *The New York Times*, 27 December 1951; "What Happened in Those Woods" by John McCarten in the *New Yorker*, 29 December 1951; "*Rashomon* and the 5th Witness" by George Barbarow in *Hudson Review* (Nutley, New Jersey), autumn 1952; "*Rashomon*" by Manny Farber in the *Nation* (New York), 19 January 1952; "An Almost Forgotten Art" by Richard Griffith in *The Saturday Review* (New York), 19 January 1952; books—*Le Cinéma japonais (1896-1955)* by Shinobu and Marcel Giuglaris, Paris 1956; *The 3 Faces of Film* by Parker Tyler, New York 1960; "*Rashomon no Toji*" (*Rashomon*'s Own Time) by Shinobu Hashimoto in *Nihon Eiga Kaikoroku (A Retrospective of Japanese Cinema)*, Tokyo 1963; *The Films of Akira Kurosawa* by Donald Richie, Los Angeles 1965; *The Great Films: 50 Golden Years of Motion Pictures* by Bosley Crowther, New York 1967; *Rashomon: A Film by Akira Kurosawa* edited by Donald Richie, New York 1969; *Focus on Rashomon* by Donald Richie, New York 1972; *Japan: Film Image* by Richard Tucker, London 1973; *Akira Kurosawa: A Guide to References and Resources* by Patricia Erens, Boston 1979; articles—"Drama and Lesson of the Defeated" by Paolo Jacchia in *Bianco e nero* (Rome), October 1951; "*Rashomon*" by Bosley Crowther in *The New York Times*, 6 January 1962; "*Rashomon*" by Simon Harourt-Smith in *Sight and Sound* (London), July/September 1952; "*Rashomon* et le cinéma japonais" by Curtis Harrington in *Cahiers du cinéma* (Paris), May 1952; "The Movies" by William Whitebait in *The New Statesman* (London), 15 March 1952; "*Rashomon*" by Nino Ghelli in *Bianco e nero* (Rome), March 1952; "Japan's Great Movie" in *Life* (New York), 21 January 1952; "*Rashomon* et le pédantisme" by Pierre Mercier in *Cahiers du cinéma* (Paris), June 1953; "Existe-t-il un néorealism japonais?" by Georges Sadoul in *Cahiers du cinéma* (Paris), November 1953; "Memory of Defeat in Japan: A Reappraisal of *Rashomon*" by James F. Davidson in *The Antioch Review* (Yellow Springs, Ohio), December 1954; "Le cinema japonais" in *Cinéma 55* (Paris), June/July 1955; "*Rashomon*" by Jean-Louis Rieupeyrout in *Cinéma 55* (Paris), June/July 1955; "My Affair with Japanese Movies " by Harold Strauss in *Harper's Magazine* (New York), July 1955; "Modesty and Pretension in 2 New Films" by Jay Leyda in *Film Culture* (New York), no.10, 1956; "*Rashomon*" in *Classics of the Foreign Film: A Pictorial Treasury* by Parker Tyler, New York 1962; "Kurosawa" by Shinbi Iida, translated by Hideo Sekiguchi, in *Cinema* (Los Angeles), August/September 1963; "Akira Kurosawa" in *Etudes cinématographiques* (Paris), spring 1964; "Kurosawa on Kurosawa" by Donald Richie in *Sight and Sound* (London), summer and autumn 1964; "Films" by Andrew Sarris in *The Village Voice* (New York), 15 October 1964; "Kurosawa and his Work" by Akira Iwasaki in *Japan Quarterly*, January/March 1965; "Akira Kurosawa" by Alfonso Pinto in *Films in Review* (New York), April 1967; "*Rashomon* as Modern Art" by Parker Tyler in *Renaissance of the Film* edited by Julius Bellone, London 1970; "The Epic Cinema of Kurosawa" by Joan Mellen in *Take One* (Montreal), June 1971; "Rashomon" by Valentin Almendarez in *Cinema Texas Program Notes* (Austin), 19

March 1974; "*Rashomon*" by Stanley Kauffmann in *Horizon* (Los Angeles), spring 1974; "*Rashomon*" by G. Poppelaars in *Skoop* (Amsterdam), August 1980.

*   *   *

When *Rashomon* won the Grand Prix at the Venice International Film Festival in 1951, the event represented the opening of the Japanese cinema to the West, and the film itself was regarded as a revelation. Ironically, it has never been very highly thought of in Japan. This does not necessarily mean that the West was wrong (consider the number of major Hollywood films that had to wait to be discovered by the French). It should, however, make us pause to question the grounds for its acclamation.

The film's exotic appeal is very obvious, and in some respects inseparable from its genuine qualities—the originality of its structure, the bravura virtuosity of its camerawork, the strength and force of the performances—its success at Venice (and subsequently thoughout the western world) was doubtless due to its fortuitous knack of combining the exotic with the appearance of precisely the kind of spurious profundity that western intellectuals have tended to see as necessary for the validation of cinema as an art form. The film was (mis-)taken for a vast metaphysical statement (or, at least, question) along the lines of "What is truth?" Little wonder that there has been a considerable backlash. The initial mis-recognition of *Rashomon* no doubt played its part in the subsequent rejection of Kurosawa by numerous critics in the process of discovering Ozu and Mizoguchi. Reseeing the film now, one is apt to challenge both extremes.

The "What is truth?" school of *Rashomon* admirers always (quite understandably) felt some embarrassment at the film's ending: the film's "great subject" seemed suddenly displaced and evaded, the film collapsing in "sentimentality": certainly a poor woodcutter deciding to adopt an abandoned baby seems to have little relevance to a philosophical inquiry into the nature of truth and reality. It is, however, open to question whether a demonstration that different people will tell the same story in different ways to suit their own convenience really amounts to such philosophical inquiry in the first place. There is no evidence anywhere in Kurosawa'a work to suggest that he is a profound "thinker." That is not at all to belittle him as an artist, philosophy and art (though capable of intimate inter-relationships) being quite distinct human activities with quite distinct functions. To demand that a work of art be philosophically profound is merely a crass form of intellectual snobbery. (This is not of course to deny that all art has philosophical *implications*, which is another matter altogether.)

One must, as always, "Never trust the artist—trust the tale"; yet Kurosawa's own far more modest and earthly account of *Rashomon*'s subject (from his splendid and delightful *Something Like an Autobiography*) seems to me to tally more satisfactorily with the actual film:

Human beings are unable to be honest with themselves about themselves. They cannot talk about themselves without embellishing. This script portrays such human beings—the kind who cannot survive without lies to make them feel they are better people than they really are..... Egoism is a sin the human being carries with him from birth; it is the most difficult to redeem....

This account has a number of advantages. For one thing, it ties the film in closely with Kurosawa'a other work, as the "relativity of truth" account does not: for example, the last third of *Ikiru* is singlemindedly concerned with the gradual revelation of an unquestioned and authentic "truth" that the self-serving bureaucrats are bent on concealing. For another, it accords much more readily with the general tone and attitude of Kurosawa's films—what one might describe as a bitter humanism, a tenacious belief in the human spirit and in human goodness juxtaposed with a caustic and often savage view of human egoism, duplicity and pettiness. Thirdly, it is much more compatible than philosophical abstractions with one of *Rashomon*'s most immediately striking qualities, its intense physicality, the direct visual communication of sensory experience. It also makes perfect sense of the ending, which becomes, indeed, the logical and very moving culmination of the whole film.

Rashomon is adapted from two very short stories by Akutagawa. The first, "In a Grove," provides the basis for the main body of the film; the second, "Rashomon" (the name of the ruined stone gate), is the framing story; the two are brilliantly tied together by the woodcutter's narration of the final version of the story. What many westerners fail to recognize is how *funny* the film is—at least in part. The use of its premise by the Hollywood cinema is well-known: there are Martin Ritt's painstakingly literal (and somewhat laboured) translation of it to the American southwest (*The Outrage*), and George Cukor's marvellous transformation of its premise into the basis for a musical comedy (*Les Girls*). But the Hollywood movie that seems closest to *Rashomon* in structure actually antedates it: *Unfaithfully Yours*. Sturges's comedy gives us three quasi-serious episodes (Rex Harrison's fantasies) which prove to be but the necessary build-up to the final, comic, episode, in which the protagonist attempts to put his fantasies into action. *Rashomon* follows the same pattern: the first three "full" versions of the story (the bandit's, the wife's, the nobleman's)—which certainly contain their longeurs—are best read as the equally necessary preliminary to the explosion of savage farce in the woodcutter's version. The function of the farce in both films is strikingly similiar: the deflation of presumption and pretension. We are not invited to read the woodcutter's story as "the truth," yet its status is clearly different from that of the other three: its purpose is not that of bolstering his own ego. It is especially important that his version uses the woman as its central figure to make the two men look ridiculous: the proletarian and the woman fuse for the purpose of puncturing class pretension and male egoism.

The woodcutter is the real hero of the film and a fully characteristic Kurosawa hero, a point underlined by the casting, since Takashi Shimura also plays the heros of *Ikiru* and *The Seven Samurai*. His adopting the baby (although he and his family are near starvation-level) follows logically from the scathing denunciation of self-serving egoim that is the central impulse of his version of the story: rising above the moral squalor of his time and the physical squalor of his environment, he performs the action that at once establishes his heroic status and redeems the film's almost desperate, almost nihilist view of humanity.

—Robin Wood

REAR WINDOW. Production: Paramount Pictures; 1954; Technicolor, 35mm; running time: 112 mins. Released 1954.

Produced by Alfred Hitchcock; screenplay by John Michael Hayes; from the novel by Cornell Woolrich; directed by Alfred Hitchcock; photography by Robert Burks; edited by George Tomasini; sound by Harry Lindgren and John Cope; production design by Hal Pereira, Ray Mayer, Sam Comer, and MacMillan Johnson; music by Franz Waxman; special effects by John P. Fulton; costumes designed by Edith Head.

Filmed 1954 in Paramount studios and backlots. New York Film Critics Award, Best Actress to Grace Kelly for *The Country Girl*, *Rear Window*, and *Dial M for Murder*, 1954.

Cast: James Stewart (*L.B. Jeffries, or Jeff*); Grace Kelly (*Lisa Fremont*); Wendell Corey (*Detective Thomas J. Doyle*); Thelma Ritter (*Stella*); Raymond Burr (*Lars Thorwald*); Judith Evelyn (*Miss Lonely Hearts*); Ross Bagdasarian (*The Composer*); Georgine Darcy (*Miss Torso, the dancer*); Jesslyn Fax (*Sculptress*); Rand Harper (*Honeymooner*); Irene Winston (*Mrs. Thorwald*); Denny Bartlett; Len Hendry; Mike Mahoney; Alan Lee; Anthony Warde; Harry Landers; Dick Simmons; Fred Graham; Edwin Parker; M. English; Kathryn Grandstaff; Havis Davenport; Mike Mahoney; Iphigenie Castiglioni; Sara Berner; Frank Cady.

Publications:

Reviews—by Ernest Borneman in *Films and Filming* (London), November 1954; review by Derwent May in *Sight and Sound* (London), October/December 1954; review by Steve Sondheim in *Films in Review* (New York), October 1954; review in *Positif* (Paris), November 1955; books—*Hitchcock* by Eric Rohmer and Claude Chabrol, Paris 1957; *Hitchcock* by Barthélemy Amengual, Paris 1960; *The Cinema of Alfred Hitchcock* by Peter Bogdanovich, New York 1962; *Alfred Hitchcock* by Hans Peter Manz, Zurich 1962; *Hitchcock's Films* by Robin Wood, London 1965; *The Films of Alfred Hitchcock* by George Perry, London 1965; *Le Cinéma selon Hitchcock* by François Truffaut, Paris 1966; *Alfred Hitchcock* by Jean Douchet, Paris 1967; *Alfred Hitchcock* by Noel Simsolo, Paris 1969; *Hitch* by John Russell Taylor, New York 1978; *L'Analyse du film* by Raymond Bellour, Paris 1979; *Hitchcock—The Murderous Gaze* by William Rothman, Cambridge, Massachusetts, 1982; *The Dark Side of Genius: The Life of Alfred Hitchcock* by Donald Spoto, New York 1983; articles—by R.M. Arland in *Arts* (Paris), 6 April 1955; article by G. Garson in *Cahiers du cinéma* (Paris), April 1955; article by Claude Chabrol in *Téléciné* (Paris), May/June 1955; issue devoted to Hitchcock in *Cahiers du cinéma* (Paris), August/September 1956; "A Master of Suspense" by John Pett in *Films and Filming* (London), November 1959, and "Improving the Formula" in *Films and Filming*, December 1959; "Hitch and His Public" by Jean Douchet in *New York Film Bulltetin*, no.7, 1961; "Alfred Hitchcock" by Alfred Agel in *New York Film Bulletin*, no.15, 1961; "Hitchcock's World" by Charles Higham in *Film Quarterly* (Berkeley), December 1962/January 1963; "James Stewart" by William R. Sweigert in *Films in Review* (New York), December 1964; "Alfred Hitchcock: Master of Morality" by Warren Sonbert in *Film Culture* (New York), summer 1966; "*Rear Window*" by Alfred Hitchcock in *Take One* (Montreal), December 1968; "The Strange Case of Alfred Hitchcock" by Raymond Durgnat in 10 issue of *Films and Filming* (London), February through November 1970; special issue of *Camera/Stylo* on Hitchcock (Paris), November 1981; articles by P. Delpeut and E. Kuyper in *Skrien* (Amsterdam, Netherlands), September 1981; "Reissued Hitchcock Classics Reflect Obsessions of Genius" by Roger Ebert in *Sun-Times* (Chicago), 2 October 1983; "Fear of Spying" by Robin Wood in *American Film* (Washington, D.C.), November 1983.

*   *   *

In *Rear Window* Alfred Hitchcock placed a film in a confined setting, as he had already done in *Lifeboat* (1944) and *Rope* (1948). Temporarily incapacitated by a broken leg, Jeff Jeffries (James Stewart) indulges his press photographer's inclination to spy on other people's private lives by peeking into the windows of the apartment dwellings across the courtyard from his own Greenwich Village flat. Since the camera remains in Jeff's room throughout the picture, we see the inhabitants of the other apartments largely from Jeff's point of view. In fact, the wall of apartment windows that face Jeff's own rear window become for him a bank of television monitors, by means of which he is able to keep his neighbors under his voyeuristic surveillence without their being aware of it. Hitchcock thus extends the borders of the single set in a most ingenious way.

Among the assortment of people whom Jeff observes are a lonely spinster whom he calls Miss Lonelyhearts, and, by contrast, a gregarious composer with lots of friends — as well as Lars Thorwald (Raymond Burr), an adulterous husband whom Jeff comes to suspect of having killed his invalid wife.

Thorwald's ugly deed is eventually brought to light by the efforts of Jeff and his sometime fiancée Lisa (Grace Kelly), who finds Jeff's morbid curiosity catching. Ultimately they are not entirely proud of their meddling in other people's lives: for, as Lisa shamefacedly confesses late in the film, she and Jeff were deeply disappointed when it seemed for a time that Thorwald was not actually guilty of homicide after all. "I'm not much on rear window ethics," she says, "but we're two of the most frightening ghouls I have ever known."

Jeff's increasingly unwholesome interest in the affairs of his neighbors is mirrored in his switching, as his curiosity increases, from a simple pair of binoculars to the use of a telescopic lens as his means of prying more and more deeply into the private lives at as close a range as possible. One of his friends suggests that Jeff's fascination with the lives of others is his way of side-stepping his own pressing need to sort out his unsatisfactory relationship with Lisa — something he has yet to do by the end of the movie.

Besides the overall plot of the picture, dealing with the detection and apprehension of Thorwald, Hitchcock has created some interesting little subplots. In the course of the picture, for example, we hear snatches of a romantic ballad being composed by the song writer who lives in one of the flats across the way; at the end of the film we hear the number in its finished form. In the final scene we see Jeff, who has taken a new lease on life and given up spying on others, sitting with his back to the window.

An immediate critical and popular success, *Rear Window* has been out of circulation for several years because of litigation over the film's literary source. This unfortunate situation has at last been remedied.

— Gene D. Phillips

REBEL WITHOUT A CAUSE. Production: Warner Bros. Pictures, Inc.; 1955; Warnercolor, 35mm, Cinemascope; running time: 111 mins. Released 1955.

Produced by David Weisbart; screenplay by Stewart Stern; from an adaptation by Irving Shulman of a storyline by Nicholas Ray inspired from the story "The Blind Run"; title from a book by

Dr. Robert M. Lindner (1944); directed by Nicholas Ray; photography by Ernest Haller; edited by William Ziegler; production design by by William Wallace; music by Leonard Rosenman.

Filmed in 9 weeks in 1955.

Cast: James Dean (*Jim Stark*); Natalie Wood (*Judy*); Jim Backus (*Jim's father*); Ann Doran (*Jim's mother*); Rochelle Hudson (*Judy's mother*); William Hopper (*Judy's father*); Sal Mineo (*Plato*); Corey Allen (*Buzz*); Dennis Hopper (*Goon*); Ed Platt (*Ray*); Steffi Sydney (*Mil*); Marietta Canty (*Plato's nursemaid*); Virginia Brissac (*Jim's grandmother*); Beverly Long (*Helen*); Frank Mazzola (*Crunch*); Robert Foulk (*Gene*); Jack Simmons (*Cookie*); Nick Adams (*Moose*).

Publications:

Books—*The Official James Dean Anniversary Book* edited by Peter Myerson, New York 1956; *Jimmy Dean Returns*, New York 1956; *The Real James Dean Story*, New York 1956; *James Dean: A Biography* by William Bast, New York 1956; *I, James Dean* by T.T. Thomas, New York 1957; *The Films of James Dean* by Mark Whittman, London 1974; *James Dean—The Mutant King* by David Dalton, San Francisco 1974; *James Dean—A Short Life* by Venable Herndon, New York 1974; *Nicholas Ray* by John Kreidl, Boston 1977; *The JD Films: Juvenile Delinquency in the Movies* by Mark Thomas McGee and R.J. Robertson, Jefferson, North Carolina and London 1982; articles—"Portrait de l'acteur en jeune homme" in *Cahiers du cinéma* (Paris), no.66, 1956; "Rebels without Causes" by Penelope Houston in *Sight and Sound* (London), spring 1956; "Story into Script" by Nicholas Ray in *Sight and Sound* (London), autumn 1956; "Generation without a Cause" by Eugene Archer in *Film Culture* (New York), no.7, 1956; "The Dean Myth" by Clayton Cole in *Films and Filming* (London), January 1957; "Conversations with Nicholas Ray and Joseph Losey" by Penelope Houston and John Gillett in *Sight and Sound* (London), autumn 1961; "Enhancement of Punitive Behavior by Audio-Visual Displays" by R. Walters in *Science*, 8 June 1962; "Mother, Men and the Muse" by Murray Kempton in *Show* (Hollywood), March 1962; "Dean—10 Years After" by Robin Bean in *Films and Filming* (London), October 1965; "*La Fureur de vivre*" in *Arts et spectacles* (Paris), 15 May 1967; "Because They're Young—Parts I and II" by Lionel Godfrey in *Films and Filming* (London), October and November 1967; "The Current Cinema" by Pauline Kael in the *New Yorker*, 3 October 1970; "The Cinema of Nicholas Ray" by Victor Perkins in *Movie Reader* edited by Ian Cameron, New York 1972; "Circle of Pain: The Cinema of Nicholas Ray" by Jonathan Rosenbaum in *Sight and Sound* (London), autumn 1973; "Rebel Without a Cause: Nicholas Ray in the Fifties" by Peter Biskind in *Film Quarterly* (Berkeley), fall 1974; "*Rebel Without a Cause*" by J.M. Lardinois in *Apec-Revue Belge du cinéma* (Brussels), no.Î, 1975; "*Rebel Without a Cause*" by D. McVay in *Films and Filming* (London), August 1977; "Nicholas Ray, nattens diktare" by B.T. Pedersen, translated by L. Ahlander in *Chaplin* (Stockholm), vol.21, no.6, 1979; "Encore: *Rebel Without a Cause*" by D. Thomson in *Take One* (Montreal), no.4, 1979; article in *Cinema* (Bucharest), March 1979; "Nicholas Ray, Without a Cause" by Terry Fox in *The Village Voice* (New York), 9 July 1979.

*   *   *

In an overheated moment part-way through Laslo Benedek's 1953 film *The Wild One*, Johnny (Marlon Brando) responds to the question "What are you rebelling against?" with "Watcha got?" That film detailed the restless rebellion of two motorcycle gangs, one bent on havoc, the other on less violent forms of social rebellion, and in Johnny lay the seed of many a Hollywood rebel, the pose of many an aspiring Hollywood actor, and the essence of a new breed of teenager. The following year, two films were released that immediately secured a position for their star as spokesperson for and icon of America's frustrated youth. In both *East of Eden* and *Rebel Without a Cause* James Dean embodied a restless youngster unable to cope with his future because of the insecurity of the present and the failings of his parents. Unlike Johnny, his anger was still internalized, waiting for the moment of explosion. As director Nicolas Ray said: "When you first see Jimmy in his red jacket against his black Merc, it's not just a pose. It's a warning. It's a sign."
pose. It's a warning. It's a sign."

Ever in sympathy with the outsider, Ray fashioned a modern Romeo and Juliet story, a romance set among teenagers seeking satisfaction outside the traditional systems, misunderstood by their parents, misunderstanding and mistrusting of their parents values. Soon America would explode with the sound of rock 'n roll, and teens would find a form of social rebellion that was non-violent but nontheless highly charged. Ray caught both the immediate and timeless qualities of frustrated adolescence.

A plea for understanding of the day's younger generation, *Rebel Without a Cause* focused on three youngsters: Plato, whose divorced parents had abandoned him; Judy, who felt her father had withdrawn his love; and Jim, the offspring of a domineering mother and henpecked father. Disenchanted with their own families, these three alienated individuals sought a new sense of family, Plato and Judy looking to Jim as the head of the new unit. Unlike many of the teen rebel films which followed, *Rebel* placed a blame on the parents rather than the teens; teens were unbalanced by parents rather than the reverse.

The main action of the film is compressed into one day, a day in which Jim moves from confusion to a possible sense of clarity, from wanting to be a man to the beginning stages of becoming one. After going through the various initiation rights into manhood—knife fight, chicken run, girlfriend, homosexual advance, drinking, etc.—Jim begins to realize that perhaps responsibility for his life rests within himself. The end of the film, in which he asserts independence and self-determination rings slightly optimistic and therefore false, making the spectator wonder whether Jim has been liberated or tamed. If Jim-as-a-rebel refers to his status at the beginning of the film, what is his status after Plato's death?

In this, his first film in Cinemascope, Nicolas Ray signalled his reputation as the American master in the format. Having studied on Frank Lloyd Wright scholarship, Ray had a clearly defined sense of spatial relations, an ability which made much of his film noir work especially charged. In his Cinemascope features he developed an aesthetic of the horizontal which, particularly in *Rebel Without a Cause*, lent a sensuality to the images of alienation. If this feeling pervaded exteriors, a sense of claustrophobia permeated the spatial tensions of the cluttered interiors.

Ray is also just beginning his metaphorical use of color in this film. Originally begun in black and white, *Rebel* was changed to color while in production, and Ray began to code his characters through changes in costume. Among the obvious examples are Plato's wearing of one black and one red sock, signalling his confusion, Jim's move from neutral browns to his bright red jacket, Judy's move from red to soft pink.

Ray's ability to elicit strong performances is a key to the successes of his best films. Having trained as an actor and having come to film through a friendship and apprenticeship with Elia

Kazan, he was particularly attuned to the problems and the practices of performance. Previously he had worked in close collaboration with Humphrey Bogart for the actor's production company (Santana Films) on both *Knock on Any Door* and *In a Lonely Place*, and on *Rebel Without a Cause* he included Dean in the decisions of production. As actor Jim Backus wrote in his autobiography, Dean was practically the co-director of *Rebel*. Ray and Dean were so compatible that they had planned to collaborate on a second project on which Dean would serve as both actor and producer while Ray continued to direct (a project that was never realized because of Dean's death). Ray was later to establish that relationship with James Mason on *Bigger Than Life*.

Like Nick Romano in *Knock on Any Door* and Bowie in *They Live By Night*, Jim Stark is a misunderstood teenager seeking a better deal before it is too late. His gestures are those of alienation and pressurized anxiety, his overheated condition and need to cool down or explode best visualized by the scene in which he sensually presses a cold bottle of milk to his cheek. As much as any, that image became both a warning and a prediction.

—Doug Tomlinson

RED RIVER. Production: Monterey Productions; 1948; black and white, 35mm; running time: 125 mins., some sources list 133 mins. Released 1948.

Produced by Charles K. Feldman with Howard Hawks; screenplay by Borden Chase and Charles Schnee; from the story "The Chisholm Trail" by Borden Chase; directed by Howard Hawks; photography by Russell Harlan; edited by Christian Nyby; sound by Richard DeWeese and Vinton Vernon; art direction by John Datu Arensma; musical direction by Dimitri Tiomkin; special effects by Donald Stewart and Allan Thompson; an extract of the film is featured in *The Last Picture Show* directed by Peter Bogdanovich.

Filmed in 85 days.

Cast: John Wayne (*Thomas Dunson*); Montgomery Clift (*Matthew Garth*); Joanne Dru (*Tess Millay*); Walter Brennan (*Groot Nadine*); Coleen Gray (*Fen*); John Ireland (*Cherry Valence*); Noah Beery, Jr. (*Buster*); Harry Carey, Jr. (*Dan Latimer*); Mickey Kuhn (*Matt as an infant*); Paul Fix (*Teeler*); Hank Worden (*Slim*); Ivan Parry (*Bunk Kenneally*); Hal Taliaferro (*Old Leather*); Paul Fierro (*Fernandez*); Billie Self (*Cowboy*); Ray Hyke (*Walt Jergens*); Dan White (*Laredo*); Tom Tyler (*Cowboy*); Glenn Strange (*Naylor*); Lane Chandler (*Colonel*); Joe Dominguez (*Mexican guard*); Shelley Winters (*Girl in wagon train*).

Publications:

Books—*The Cinema of Howard Hawks* by Peter Bogdanovich, New York 1962; *Howard Hawks* by Jean-Claude Missiaen, Paris 1966; *Howard Hawks* by Robin Wood, Garden City, New York 1968; *What is Cinema?, Vol. II* by André Bazin, Berkeley 1971; *Howard Hawks* by Jean A. Gili, Paris 1971; *Movie Reader* edited by Ian Cameron, New York 1972; *Focus on Howard Hawks* edited by Joseph McBride, Englewood Cliffs, New Jersey 1972; *The Films of Howard Hawks* by D.C. Willis, Metuchen, New Jersey 1975; *The Great Western Pictures* by James Robert Parish and Michael Pitts, Metuchen, New Jersey 1976; *Howard Hawks, Storyteller* by Gerald Mast, New York 1982; articles—"Howard Hawks et le western" by Michel Perez in *Présence du cinéma* (Paris), July/September 1959; "The World of Howard Hawks" by Andrew Sarris in *Films and Filming* (London), July 1962 and August 1962; issue on Hawks of *Cahiers du cinéma* (Paris), January 1963; "Montgomery Clift" by Robert Roman in *Films in Review* (New York), November 1966; "Gunplay and Horses" by David Austen in *Films and Filming* (London), October 1968; "Reflections on the Tradition of the Movie Western" by Douglas Brode in *Cineaste* (New York), fall 1968; "Tall in the Saddle" by Dennis John Hall in *Films and Filming* (London), October 1969; "An Interview with Howard Hawks" by Michael Goodwin and Noami Wise in *Take One* (Montreal), November/December 1971; issue on Hawks of *Filmkritik* (Munich), May/June 1973; "Hawks Talks: New Anecdotes from the Old Master" by Jim McBride in *Film Comment* (New York), May/June 1974; "*Rîul rosu*" by A. Tiroiu in *Cinema* (Bucharest), September 1974; "Letter" by J. Belton in *Movietone News* (Seattle), 11 October 1976; "Hawks et le mythe de l'ouest améericain" by J.L. Bourget in *Positif* (Paris), July/August 1977; "All Along the River" by D. Thomson in *Sight and Sound* (London), winter 1976-77; "*Red River*: Empire to the West" by Robert Sklar in *Cineaste* (New York), fall 1978; "*Red River*" by Charles Ramirez Berg in *Cinema Texas Program Notes* (Austin), 14 February 1979; "Conflict of Interpretations: A Special Section on *Red River* by Howard Hawks" by R. Reeder and others in *Ciné-Tracts* (Montreal), spring 1980.

* * *

Red River is a film about a cattle drive. To depict this story of Texas cattlemen driving thousands of cattle across thousands of miles northward to Kansas, Howard Hawks, the film's director, in effect recreated that original task to make the film. In both 1865, when the narrative was set, and 1946, when the film was shot, the epic task confronting a group of men was that of moving all those animals across all that space. The epic task is mirrowed by the film's vast, epic shots of men, cattle, sky, and space.

The epic story is both a view of American history and a view of the American civilization as a successor of those of the past. Set just after the Civil War, the film's journey reaffirms and re-establishes the oneness of the American nation and the oneness of the American continent. The journey to bring Texas beef to the north reveals the conquest of space and the distance to produce one whole nation. But this journey has a relation to Homeric epic as well as to American history, for, like the *Odyssey*, the film chronicles a vast and epic task in which the threatened dangers are external (in *Red River*, the threat is from Indian attack and cattle rustlers) but the real dangers are internal (in the will, the judgment, and the dedication of the travelers themselves, and in the tension between the leader and his followers).

In converting a sprawling serialized story by Borden Chase into his own taut film, Hawks chose a metaphoric title, *Red River*, which has little specific meaning in the story (crossing the Red River signifies the departure from the familiar homeland and the journey into the unknown) but which has obvious Biblical parallels to the epic journey of the Israelites in "Exodus." Hawks anchors these epic and metaphoric suggestions with a sensitive psychological study of the joureny's two leaders, Thomas Dunson, the older man who founded the cattle spread in 1851, and Matthew Garth, his adopted son. In the role of Dunson, Hawks cast John Wayne, giving Wayne the kind of role that became indistinguishable from his own persona for three decades—tough, hard, absolutely committed to accomplishing the task before him no matter what the cost, old but not too old to get a tough job done, bull-headed but bound by personal codes of duty, honor, and morality, Opposite Wayne, Hawks cast the young Montgomery Clift in his first film role. The contrast between the sensitive, "soft," almost beautifully handsome Clift and the hard, determined, indomitable Wayne not only provides the essential psychological contrast required for the film's narrative but also provides two brilliant and brilliantly contrasted acting styles for the film's dramatic tension.

In the film's narrative, the more supple leader, Garth, replaces the unbending Dunson when the inflexible older man's decisions threaten the success of the enterprise. Dunson vows to take revenge on Garth for this ouster, and the climax of the film, after Garth has successfully delivered the cattle to market, promises a gun battle between the vengeful Dunson and his own spiritual son. In what has become the most controversial issue about the film, that gun battle never takes place. While some see Hawk's avoidance of the climatic duel as some kind of pandering to Hollywood tasted, Hawks has carefully built into his narrative pattern the terms that guarantee that a man with Dunson's sense of humor and morality could never kill a man who does not intend to kill him first. Matthew Garth demonstrates he could never kill his "father," and Dunson, despite his previous verbal threats and his unswerving commitment to his word, could never kill the "son" who loves him. As is typical of a Hawks film, beneath the superficial talk the two men love one another, and they demonstrate that love by what they do rather than what they say.

—Gerald Mast

LOS REDES. The Wave. Production: Secretaría de Educación Púlica, Mexico; black and white, 35mm; running time: 65 mins. Released 1936.

Produced by Carlos Chávez and Narciso Bassols (?); scenario by Agustín Velázquez Chávez and Paul Strand; adapted by Emilio Gómez Muriael, Fred Zinnemann, and Henwar Rodakiewicz; directed by Fred Zinneman and Emilio Gómez Muriel; photography by Paul Strand; edited by Emilio Gómez Muriel with Gunther von Fritsch; sound by Roberto and Joselito Rodríguez; music by Silvestre Revueltas.

Filmed beginning 9 April 1934, in natural settings at Alvarado, Tlacotalpan, and the mouth of the Papaloapan River. Cost: 55,000 pesos.

Cast: Silvio Hernández (*Miro*); David Valle González (*The packer*); Rafael Hinojosa (*The politician*); Antonio Lara (*El Zurdo*); Miguel Figueroa; and native fishermen.

Publications:

Books—*Fred Zinnemann* by Richard Griffith, New York 1958; *Historia documental del cine mexicano*, vol. 1, by Emilio García

Riera, Mexico City 1969; *Paul Strand: A Retrospective Monograph*, in 2 vols., *The Years 1915-1946* and *The Years 1950-1968*, New York 1971; *Nonfiction Film: A Critical History* by Richard Barsam, New York 1973; *Mexican Cinema: Reflections of a Society, 1896-1980* by Carl J. Mora, Berkeley 1982; articles— "Camera Reconnoiters" by B. Belitt in *Nation* (New York), 20 November 1937; "Films by American Government: Mexico" by Carlos Chavez in *Films*, summer 1940.

*   *   *

A progenitor of the classical Mexican visual style, *Redes* is also one of the very few instances of genuine social criticism in the history of Mexican cinema. The fact that *Redes* was directed and photographed by foreigners is ironic as well as illustrative of a neo-colonial tendency in Mexican films. *Redes* was born out the collaboration of Paul Strand, a photographer from New York who had come to mexico to do a book of photos on the country, and 2 Mexicans: Carlos Chávez, the noted composer who occupied a government post at the time, and narciso Bassols, a Marxist who was then the Secretary of Public Education. 1930-40 was the decade in which the social ideals of the Mexican Revolution (1910-17) achieved their greatest artistic and political expression. Many of the important murals were painted during this period, which was also the time of the expropriation of foreign oil companies and extensive land distribution by President Lazaro Cardenas. Bassols and Chávez desired to participate in this revolutionary process by financing films, which were to be "with the people and for the people," with government funds. In addition to Paul Strand, they hired a young Austrian, Fred Zinnemann (who later went on to a long distinguished career in Hollywood), to direct the film which was to portray life and struggle in a fishing village.

Redes combines many of the elements which were afterward to make up the classical Mexican film style. The excellent photography focuses on the beauty of natural and famous forms: rolling masses of luminous clouds, swirling eddies of water, fishermen's nets draped out on lines to dry, palm fronds against thatched huts, stoic native faces set off by white shirts or dark *rebozos*, their sinuous arms entwined with ropes. Both the images and the dialectical montage of the editing appear to be influenced by the work of Sergei Eisenstein, who had filmed the never-released *Que Viva Mexico* a couple of years earlier. Equally important, however, must have been Paul Strand's background in the National Film and Photo League, many of whose photographers went on to produce the extraordinary documentation of the depression in the United States under the auspices of the Farm Security Administration.

These radical influences from abroad fused with the evolutionary experience of Mexico to produce a work of penetrating social criticism. Incredibly exploited by the packer's monopoly, the fishermen attempt to form a union under the leadership of Miro, whose young son has died for lack of medicine. Miro is killed by the politician who has been paid by the packer, but the other fishermen continue the struggle. The film not only lays bare a situation of exploitation, it also criticizes religion, reformist politics, and anarchism by indicating that none of these provide as effective an answer as does organized resistance. The use of non-professional actors adds to the film's realism, and the intelligent employment of montage and music keeps the actors from being overwhelmed by the demands made upon them.

Although the film was an economic failure, critics both inside and outside Mexico have since percieved it to be an important work. Within Mexico, *Redes* and *Que Viva Mexico* are seen as the precursors of the style later mad internationally known in the films of Emilio Fernández and the cinematographer Gabriel Figueroa. Outside Mexico, several writers have stated that it may well have been a major influence on Italian neo-realism. Whatever its effects, *Redes* is an interesting example of socially committed art and a key film in the history of Mexican cinema.

— John Marz

REGLE DU JEU. Rules of the Game. Production: La Nouvelle Édition Française; black and white, 35mm; running time: 85 mins., restored version is 110 mins.; length: restored version is 10,080 feet. Released 7 July 1939, Paris. Re-released 1949 in Great Britain, and 1950 in New York. Restored to original form and released at 1959 Venice Film Festival.

Produced by Claude Renoir; screenplay by Jean Renoir with Camille François and Carl Koch; directed by Jean Renoir; photography by Jean Bachelet; edited by Marguerite Houlet-Renoir; sound engineered by Joseph de Bretagne; production design by Eugène Lourié, assistant designer: Max Douy; music arranged and directed by Roger Desormières; costumes designed by Coco Chanel; assistant directors: André Zwobada and Henri Cartier-Bresson.

Filmed February through the spring of 1939, in the Chateau de le Ferté-Saint-Aubin and at La Motte-Beuvron, Aubigny; interiors shot at the Billancourt Studios, Joinville. Cost: 5,000,000 F.

Cast: Marcel Dalio (*Robert de la Chesnaye*); Nora Grégor (*Christine de la Chesnaye*); Roland Toutain (*André Jurieu*); Jean Renoir (*Octave*); Mila Parély (*Geneviève de Marrast*); Paulette Dubost (*Lisette*); Gaston Modot (*Schumacher*); Julien Carette (*Marceau*); Anne Mayen (*Jackie*); Pierre Nay (*Saint-Auben*); Pierre Magnier (*The General*); Odette Talazac (*Charlotte*); Roger Forster (*The homosexual*); Richard Francouer (*La Bruyère*); Claire Gérard (*Madame de la Bruyère*); Tony Corteggiani (*Berthelin*); Nicolas Amato (*The South American*); Eddy Debray (*Corneille*); Lisa Elina (*Radio announcer*); André Zwobada (*Engineer*); Léon Larive (*Chef*); Célestin (*Kitchen servant*); Jenny Helia (*Serving girl*); Henri Cartier-Bresson (*English servant*); Lise Elina (*Female radio announcer*); André Zwobada (*Engineer at the Caudron*); Camille François (*Radio announcer*); friends of Jean Renoir as guests in the shooting party; local villagers as the beaters.

Publications:

Scripts— "Après la chasse (extrait de *La Regle du jeu)*" in *Cahiers du cinéma* (Paris), August/September 1954; "*La Regle du jeu*" in *Avant-Scène du Cinéma* (Paris), Ocotber 1965; *The Rules of the Game* by Jean Renoir, New York 1969; *Rules of the Game* by Jean Renoir, translated by John McGrath and Maureen Teitelbaum, New York 1970; *Jean Renoir* (contains early scenario) by André Bazin, Paris, translated ed. 1973; "*Pravidla hry*" (script extract) in *Film a doba* (Prague), June 1974; reviews—in *Variety* (New York), 30 August 1939; review in the *Financial Times* (London), 29 September 1961; review in *The New York Times*, 19 January 1961; books—*French Film* by

Georges Sadoul, London 1953; *Jean Renoir* by Armand-Jean Cauliez, Paris 1962; *Jean Renoir* by Bernard Chardère, Lyon, France 1962; *Classics of the Foreign Film: A Pictorial Treasury* by Parker Tyler, New York 1968; *Analyses des films de Jean Renoir* by Institut des Hautes Etudes Cinématographiques, Paris 1966; *Private Screenings* by John Simon, New York 1967; *The American Cinema* by Andrew Sarris, New York 1968; *70 Years of Cinema* by Peter Cowie, New York 1969; *Renoir 1938 ou Jean Renoir pour rein*. Enquête sur un cinéaste by François Poulle, Paris 1969; *Jean Renoir* by Pierre Leprohon, New York 1971; *Jean Renoir: The World of his Films* by Leo Braudy, New York 1972; *Jean Renoir* by André Bazin, edited by François Truffaut, Paris, translated ed. 1973; *The Classic Cinema* by Stanley Solomon, New York 1973; *Filmguide to The Rules of the Game* by Gerald Mast, Bloomington, Indiana 1973; *My Life and My Films* by Jean Renoir, translated by Norman Denny, New York 1974; *Jean Renoir* by Raymond Durgnat, Berkeley 1974; *Jean Renoir: Essays, Conversations, Reviews* by Penelope Gilliatt, New York 1975; *Theory of Film Practice* by Nöel Burch, n.d.; articles—"Il cinema e lo Stato: inter-vista con Françoise Rosay e Jean Renoir" by Giuseppe Lo Duca in *Cinema* (Rome), 25 March 1939; "Jean Renoir" by Richard Plant in *Theatre Arts* (New York), June 1939; "French Cinema: The New Pessimism" by Gavin Lambert in *Sequence* (London), summer 1948; "*La Règle du jeu*, film de Jean Renoir" by Louis Menard in *Les Temps Modernes* (Paris), no.43, 1949; issue on Renior of *Cahiers du cinéma* (Paris), January 1952; "A Last Look Round" by Gavin Lambert in *Sequence* (London), no.14, 1952; "Personal Notes" by Jean Renoir in *Sight and Sound* (London), April/-June 1952; issue on Renoir of *Cahiers du cinéma* (Paris), Christmas 1957; "The Renaissance of the French Cinema—Feydor, Renoir, Duvivier, Carné" by Georges Sadoul in *Film: An Anthology* edited by Daniel Talbot, New York 1959; "Renoir and Realism" by Peter John Dyer in *Sight and Sound* (London), summer 1960; "Histoire d'une malédiction" by André G. Brunelin in *Cinéma 60* (Paris), February 1960; article by Louise Corbin in *Films in Review* (New York), January 1961; article by Jonas Mekas in *The Village Voice* (New York), 26 January 1961; article by Richard Whitehall in *Films and Filming* (London), November 1961; article by Richard Whitehall in *Films and Filming* (London), November 1962; "Conversation with Jean Renoir" by Louis Marcorelles in *Sight and Sound* (London), spring 1962; "Jean Renoir" by Lee Russell (Peter Wollen) in *New Left Review* (United Kingdom), May/June 1964; "Bergman et Renoir: à propos des *Sourires d'une nuit d'eté" in Le Cinéma* edited by P. Adams Sitney, New York 1975; "Le jeu de la vérité" by Philippe Esnault in *Avant-Scène du cinéma* (Paris), October 1965; "Renoir, cinéaste de notre temps, à coeur ouvert" in *Cinéma 67* (Paris), May 1967 and June 1967; "Between Theatre and Life: Jean Renoir and *The Rules of the Game*" by J. Joly in *Film Quarterly* (Berkeley), winter 1967-68; "Some Notes on the Sources of *La Règle du jeu*" by Suzanne Budgen in *Take One* (Montreal), July/August 1968; "Dialogue avec une salle" by Robert Grélier in *Cinéma 68* (Paris), March 1968; "Game Without Umpire" by Penelope Gilliatt in the *New Yorker*, 20 September 1969; "Le Meneur de jeu" by Penelope Gilliatt in the *New Yorker*, 23 August 1969; "L'Analyse du film" by A. Mary in *Image et son* (Paris), December 1972; "The Cinema of the Popular Front in France, (1934-38)" by Goffredo Fofi in *Screen* (London), winter 1972-73; "Sound Track: *Rules of the Game*" by Michael Litle in *Cinema Journal* (Evanston, Illinois), fall 1973; "Game Theory and *The Rules of the Game*" by George A. Wood, Jr. in *Cinema Journal* (Evanston, Illinois), fall 1973; "*La Règle du jeu* et la critique en 1939" edited by Claude Gauteur in *Image et son* (Paris), March 1974; "Renoir: Impressions at Twilight" by Andrew Sarris in *The Village Voice*

(New York), 6 and 12 September 1974; "*La Règle du jeu*" by W. Jehle in *Cinema* (Zurich), no.4, 1975; "A Masterpiece on 8th Street" by Marshall Lewis in *The Essential Cinema* edited by P. Adams Sitney, New York 1975; "*La Règle du jeu*" by R. Allezaud in *Téléciné* (Paris), December 1976; "*La Règle du jeu*: Renoir's spelregel: de leugen" by C. Boost in *Skoop* (Wageningen, Netherlands), March 1976; "Hoe moet een acteur geregisseerd worden? ..." by A. Haakman in *Skoop* (Wageningen, Netherlands), March 1976; "*S/Z* and *Rules of the Game*" by Julia Lesage in *Jump Cut* (Chicago), 30 December 1976; "Theatricals in Jean Renoir's *Rules of the Game* and *Grand Illusion*" by P.R. Perebinossoff in *Literature/Film Quarterly* (Slalisbury, Maryland), winter 1977; "*La Règle du jeu*" by J. Roy in *Cinéma* (Paris), June 1978.

*   *   *

Detested when it first appeared (for satirizing the French ruling class on the brink of the Second World War), almost destroyed by brutal cutting, restored in 1959 to virtually its original form, *La Règle du jeu* is now universally acknowledged as a masterpiece and perhaps Renoir's supreme achievement. In the four international critics polls organized every ten years (since 1952) by *Sight and Sound*, only two films have been constant: one is *Battleship Potemkin*, and the other is *La Règle du jeu*. And in the 1982 poll *La Règle du jeu* had climbed to second place. Its extreme complexity (it seems, after more than 20 viewings, one of the cinema's few truly inexhaustible films) makes it peculiarly difficult to write about briefly; the following attempt will indicate major lines of interest:

Sources. The richness of the film is partly attributable to the multiplicity of its sources and influences (all, be it said, totally assimilated: there is no question here of an undigested eclecticism). It seems very consciously (though never pretentiously) the product of the vast and complex cultural tradition, with close affinities with the other arts, especially painting, theatre and music. If it evokes impressionist painting less directly than certain other Renoir films (for example *Partie de campagne* or *French Can-Can*), it is strikingly faithful to the *spirit* of impressionism, the desire to portray life-as-flux rather than as a collection of discrete objects or figures. The influence of theatre is much more obvious, since it directly affects the acting style, which relates to a tradition of French boulevard comedy. Renoir specifically refers to Musset's *Les Caprices de Marianne* as a source (indeed, it was to be the title of the film at an early stage of its evolution) and to Beaumarchais (the film is prefaced by a quotation from *The Marriage of Figaro*). This last points us directly to music, and especially to Mozart, whose music opens and closes the film, the "overture" (in fact the first of the "3 German Dances" K. 605) accompanying the Beaumarchais quotation. This is perhaps the most Mozartian of all films: it constantly evokes Bruno Walter's remark (in a celebrated rehearsal record of a Mozart symphony), "The expression changes in every bar."

Method. Every frame of *La Règle du jeu* seems dominated by Renoir's personality; yet the most appealing facets of that personality are generosity, openness, responsiveness. As a result, *La Règle* is at once the *auteur* film *par excellence* and a work of co-operation and active participation. In Renoir's words, "of all the films I have made, this one is probably the most improvised. We worked out the script and decided on the places we were going to shoot as we went along...." It is clear that much of the film's complexity derives from its improvisatory, co-operative

nature. Renoir cast himself as Octave (a role originally intended for his older brother Pierre), and developed Octave's relationship with Christine, because of his own pleasure in the company of Nora Grégor; the role of Geneviève was greatly extended (originally, she was to have left the château after the hunt) because of Renoir's appreciation of the talent of Mila Parély; the entire sub-plot involving the servants was similarly elaborated during shooting, partly because of Renoir's delight in Carette's characterization.

Stylistics. The film marks the furthest elaboration of certain stylistic traits developed by Renoir since his silent films: the use of off-screen space (see Nöel Burch's seminal account of *Nana* in *Theory of Film Practice*); the mobile camera, always at the service of the action and the actors yet unusually free in its movements, continuously tracking, panning, re-framing; the fondness for the group shot, in which several characters (sometimes several diverse but simultaneous actions) are linked; depth of field, enabling the staging of simultaneous foreground and background actions, which often operate like counterpoint in music; the re-thinking of "composition" in terms of time and movement (of the camera, of the actors) rather than static images; the constant transgressing of the boundaries of the frame, which actors enter and exit from during shots. There are various consequences of this practice: 1) Renoir's "realism" (a word we should use very carefully in reference to so stylized a film)—the sense of life continuing beyond the borders of the frame, as if the camera were selecting, more or less arbitrarily, a mere portion of a continuous "real" world. 2) A drastic modification of the habits of identification generally encouraged by mainstream cinema. Close-ups and point-of-view shots are rare (though Renoir does not hesitate to use them when he feels them to be dramatically appropriate—interestingly, such usages are almost always linked to Christine). The continual reframings and entrances/exits ensure that the spectator's gaze is constantly being transferred from character to character, action to action. If Christine is gradually defined as the film's central figure, this is never at the expense of other characters, and she never becomes our sole object of identification. 3) The style of the film also assumes a metaphysical dimension, the apprehension of life-as-flux. The quotation from Lavoisier that Renoir applied to his father is apt for him too: "In nature nothing is created, nothing is lost, everything is transformed...."

Thematics. *La Règle du jeu* defies reduction to any single statement of "meaning." As with any great work of art, its thematic dimension is inextricably involved with its stylistics. Renoir's own statements about the film indicate the complexity of attitude it embodies: on the one hand, "the story attacks the very structure of our society"; on the other, "I wish I could live in such a society—that would be wonderful." People repeatedly quote Octave's line. "Everyone has his reasons," as if it summed up the film (and Renoir), reducing its attitude to a simple, all-embracing generosity; they ignore the words that introduce it: "...*there's one thing that is terrible,* and that is that everyone has his reasons." As to the "rules" of the title, the attitude is again highly complex. On the one hand, the film clearly recognizes the need for order, for some form of "regulation"; on the other, the culminating catastrophe is precipitated by the application of opposed sets of rules by two characters (who happen to be husband and wife): Schumacher, who believes in punishing promiscuity with death, and Lisette, who believes in sexual game-playing but has rigid notions of propriety in questions of age and income. Not surprisingly, the film plays on unresolved (perhaps, within our culture, unresolvable) tensions and paradoxes: the Marquis "doesn't want fences" (restrictions), but also "doesn't want rabbits" (total freedom). Few films have treated the issue of sexual morality (fidelity, monogamy, freedom) with such openness: a film about people who go too far, or a film about people who don't go far enough?

—Robin Wood

———————

LE RÉTOUR À LA RAISON. black and white, 35mm, silent; running time: about 5 mins. Premiered at a 1923 Paris Dada program entitled *Le Coeur à Barbé*.

Directed and edited by Man Ray. The film is nothing more than an assemblage of unrelated images using the technique of cameraless photography on film.

Publications:

Books—*Works of Man Ray* by London Institute of Contemporary Arts with text by Man Ray, London 1959; *Painting, Photography, Film* by Laszlo Maholy-Nagy, translated by J. Seligman and Lund Humphries, Cambridge, Massachusetts 1969; *Man Ray* by Robert Penrose, Boston 1975; *Abstract Film and Beyond* by Malcolm Le Grice, Cambridge, Massachusetts 1977; *Visionary Film: The American Avant-Garde* by P. Adams Sitney, New York 1979; articles—"Film Poetry of Man Ray" by C.I. Belz in *Criticism 7*, spring 1965; special film issue of *Artforum* (New York), September 1971; "Man Ray" in *Etudes cinématographiques* (Paris), no.38-39, 1979.

*   *   *

Le Retour à la raison employs Man Ray's Rayograph process, a photographic procedure accidently discovered in 1922 when the photographer left some objects on developing unexposed negatives. The result was a series of photographic images of the objects' shape without the intervention of a camera. While the process to which Man Ray gave his name had been used earlier, Man Ray became the first to use it as aesthetic photographic means. *Le Retour à la raison* (The Return to Reason) uses the Rayograph process for the first time on moving film. Having "no idea what this would give on the screen," Man Ray placed salt and pepper, pins, and thumbtacks on undeveloped negative film stock and then combined the results with a few random shots.

Although hurriedly made and only a few minutes long, *Le Retour à la raison* establishes an aesthetic goal that Man Ray pursued in all four of his films. The initial footage of salt thrown across the film creates scattered shapes that negate the film's tie to representationalism. But the juxtaposition of the initial images with a field of daisies shot from a high angle indicates a visual similarity between the abstract and representational images.

Similar effects are achieved in the rest of the film by a series of geometric forms, abstract spirals and circles succeeded by a revolving paper spiral, a rotating egg crate, and a nude human torso moving from side to side. The emphasis on abstract and geometric shapes in these series tie together the sequences. The dynamic process of rotation unifies the second series of images and makes possible the emphasis on their abstract and geometric elements over their identification as objects. Man Ray heightened the process by superimposing one strip of film upon another

and by doing a sequence upside down to interrupt still further any possible identification of the subject as a utilitarian object.

Man Ray initially screened *Le Retour à la raison* at a 1923 Paris Dada program, entitled "Le Coeur à Barbé." The film kept breaking during the screening because Man Ray had naively used glue to hold together the strips of film. After the second break and interruption during the film's showing a fight broke out in the audience. The soirée turned into a riot that led to police intervention. Because the film caused the evening to end in chaos, the Dadaists hailed it as a great success.

—Lauren Rabinovitz

———————

RETRATO DE TERESA. Portrait of Teresa. Production: Instituto Cubano del Arte e Industria Cinematográficos (ICAIC); color, 35mm. Released 1979.

Screenplay by Ambrosio Fornet; directed by Pastor Vega.

Filmed in Cuba.

Cast: Ramón (*Adolfo Llauradó*); Daisy Grandados (*Teresa*).

Publications:

Reviews—"*Retrato de Teresa*" by G. Moskowitz in *Variety* (New York), 5 September 1979; "*Retrato de Teresa*" by F. Segers in *Variety* (New York), 7 November 1979; "*Portrait of Teresa*" by Julianne Burton in *Film Quarterly* (Berkeley), spring 1981; "*Retrato de Teresa*" by J. Imeson in *Monthly Film Bulletin* (London), August 1981; articles—"Pastor Vega: An Interview" by Don Ranvaud in *Framework* (London), spring 1979; "*Portrait of Teresa*: An Interview with Pastor Vega and Daisy Granados" by P. Peyton and C. Broullon in *Cineaste* (New York), no.1, 1979-80; "*Portrait of Teresa*: A Letter from Havana" by M. Randall in *Cineaste* (New York), no.1, 1979-80; "Con Teresa, punto y seguido..." by A. González Acosta in *Cine Cubano* (Havana), no.97, 1980; "*Portrait of Teresa*: Double Day, Double Standard" by B. Rich in *Jump Cut* (Chicago), May 1980; "*Retrato de Teresa*: de la realidad a la ficción" by L. Prieto in *Cine Cubano* (Havana), no.98, 1981.

*   *   *

The most polemical film in the history of Cuban cinema, *Portrait of Teresa* was seen by 500,000 spectators in less than two months and has been the focus of more than two dozen articles and the subject of innumerable marital discussions on the island. The reason for such controversy lies not in the form utilized by the film (it resembles as undistinguished "made-for-TV" movie), but in its content: a critique of *machismo* and its double standard for men and women. Ramón objects to Teresa's growing involvement in her work and politico-cultural activities, accusing her of neglecting her household duties. Despite the fact that they both work full-time, Teresa has to labor the familiar "doubleday" of women, doing the domestic chores before and after her shift in a textile factory. Her attempts to incorporate herself into some of the cultural activities offered by the revolution are met by Ramón's increasingly intransigent defense of his male privileges, and they separate.

The film is a criticism to the "Law of the Funnel" ("Ley del embudo"), under which a different set of rules apply for men than for women. Impelled by its female integrants, the Cuban revolution has made great efforts to overcome the traditional subservience of women, insisting on a coherence of theory and practice and the integration of political principles into daily life. In the film's pivotal scene, Teresa confronts Ramón's assertion that he has changed (and thus wants her to return to him) by asking him how he would feel if she had had a relationship with someone else, as he did. His answer, "It's not the same," confirms her suspicion that he continues to maintain a double standard, and determines her decision to remain separated from him.

The leading actors spent much time and effort familiarizing themselves with the lives of the workers they were to represent, and were caught up in the controversy that swept Cuba after the release of the film. Daisy Granados (Teresa) saw it as an issue of the Cuban revolution: "I think that we women still make too many concessions to men. However, Teresa is no feminist symbol, but the conclusive proof that a new type of human being is arising among us. The revolution needs Teresa, because she is a symbol to all of us who believe that the revolution is a constant and permanent advance toward a superior and more complex person." Adolfo Llauradó (Ramón) saw it somewhat differently: "I've grown, and I think that intellectually I'm totally in agreement with women's equality. I understand Teresa's necessities and aspirations, but when they clash with patterns and customs established throughout millenniums, I can't deny that, like Ramón, it disturbs me."

The Cuban revolution has consistently struggled against *machismo* and its repressive patterns, among other things by explicitly legislating against a double sexual morality and by requiring men to share in the housework. However, the profundity of male-dominance is perhaps nowhere expressed more ironically than in the fact that, although both the director and scriptwriter see themselves as battling against "paternalism," no women were included at decision-making levels in the film. *Portrait of Teresa* is a useful film, though hardly a radical one. The fact that it provoked such controversy in Cuba is indicative of how far we all have to go.

—John Mraz

RIEN QUE LES HEURES. Only the Hours. Production: Néofilm (Paris); black and white, 35mm, silent; running time: 45 mins. Released 1926.

Directed by Alberto Cavalcanti; photography by Jimmy Rogers; edited by Alberto Cavalcanti (?); art direction by M. Mirovitch.

Filmed in Paris.

Publications:

Books—*Cavalcanti* by Wolfgang Klaue and others, Berlin 1962; *Nonfiction Film: A Critical History* by Richard Barsam, New York 1973; *Documentary: A History of the Nonfiction Film* by Erik Barnouw, New York 1974; articles—"Documentary" by John Grierson in *Cinema Quarterly* (London), winter 1932; "Alberto Cavalcanti" by Emir Rodriguez Monegal in *Quarterly of Film, Radio, and Television* (Berkeley), summer 1955; "Cavalcanti: His Film Works" in *Quarterly of Film, Radio, and Television* (Berkeley), summer 1955; "Cavalcanti in Paris by Geoffrey Minish in *Sight and Sound* (London), summer 1970; "Alberto Cavalcanti" by Claude Beylie and others in *Ecran* (Paris), November 1974; "Alberto Cavalcanti" by Emir Rodriguez Monegal in *Nonfiction Film: Theory and Criticism* edited by Richard Barsam, New York 1976; "Two Aspects of the City: Cavalcanti and Ruttmann" by Jay Chapman in *The Documentary Tradition* edited by Lewis Jacobs, New York 1979.

*   *   *

Rien que les heures was the first of the "city symphony" films. It was followed by *Berlin: Die Sinfonie der Grossstadt (Berlin: Symphony of a Great City)* (1929, Walter Ruttmann), *Chelovek s kinoapparatom (The Man with a Movie Camera)* (Moscow, 1928, Dziga Vertov), and *Regen (Rain)* (Amsterdam, 1929, Joris Ivens). This genre grew out of the interest of 1920s avant-garde filmmakers in the interrelationship between space and time. The genre is related to the method of the earlier French impressionist painters in their attempt to capture quick views and concentration on surfaces and light. It is also related to novels of the time which offer a cross-section of city life during a limited period, e.g. Joyce's *Ulysses* (1922) and Dos Passos's *Manhattan Transfer* (1925). The "city symphony" films were one of the strands that led into the documentary; Cavalcanti, Ruttmann, Vertov, and Ivens all subsequently became identified with documentaries. Paul Rotha, of British documentary, called these filmmakers "continental realists." Cavalcanti moved from the avant-garde of France in the 1920s to the documentary of Britain in the 1930s.

Rien que les heures is a curious and fascinating mixture of the aesthetic and the social. It deals with Paris from pre-dawn to well into the following night—roughly 24 hours. The opening titles promise that we will not be looking at the elegant life but rather at that of the lower classes. Thus the social viewpoint is established. A philosophical thesis about time and space is also introduced and returned to. At the end we are asked, after we have seen what the filmmaker can show us of Paris, to consider Paris in relation to Peking. The titles assert that we can fix a point in space, immobilize a point in time, but that space and time both escape our possession. Life is ongoing and interrelated. Without their monuments you can't tell cities apart.

Mainly the film is devoted to contrasting scenes and changing activities of Paris during the passing hours: early morning revelers, deserted streets, the first workers appear; then there are workers at work; then lunchtime; some are swimming in the afternoon; work ceases, rest and recreation occupy the evening. But among these views of unstaged actuality are inserted three brief, staged, fragmented narratives. The subjects of all three are female—an old derelict (drunken or ill), a prostitute, a newspaper vendor—all of them sad, even tragic figures. The overall mood of the film is a bit downbeat; there is a sweet sadness, a sentimental toughness about it that looks ahead to the poetic realism of the 1930s and the films of Jacques Prévert and Marcel Carné.

Still, Cavalcanti's viewpoint about all of this seems to be one of detachment: "c'est la vie," he seems to be saying. Though some concern with social matters is evident, the considerable number and variety of highly stylized special effects—wipes, multiple exposures, fast motion, spinning images, split screen, freeze frame—seem to confirm that Cavalcanti's greatest interest was in the artistic experimentation.

—Jack C. Ellis

RIO BRAVO. Production: Armada Productions; Technicolor, 35mm; running time: 141 mins. Released 1959.

Produced by Howard Hawks; screenplay by Jules Furthman and Leigh Brackett; from a novelette by B.H. McCampbell; directed by Howard Hawks; photography by Russell Harlan; edited by Folmar Blangsted; sound by Robert B. Lee; art direction by Leo K. Kuter, sets decorated by Ralph S. Hurst; music direction by Dimitri Tiomkin, songs by Dimitri Tiomkin and Francis Webster; costumes designed by Marjorie Best; make-up by Gordan Bau.

Filmed in Old Tucson, Arizona.

Cast: John Wayne (*John T. Chance*); Dean Martin (*Dude*); Ricky Nelson (*Colorado Ryan*); Angie Dickinson (*Feathers*); Walter Brennan (*Stumpy*); Ward Bond (*Pat Wheeler*); John Russell (*Nathan Burdette*); Pedro Gonzalez-Gonzalez (*Carlos*); Estelita Rodriguez (*Consuelo*); Claude Akins (*Joe Burdette*); Malcolm Atterbury (*Jake*); Harry Carey, Jr. (*Harold*); Bob Steele (*Matt Harris*); Myron Healey (*Barfly*); Fred Graham and Tom Monroe (*Hired hands*); Riley Hill (*Messenger*); Bob Terhue, Nesdon Booth, Ted White, George Bruggeman, and Andy Brennon.

Publications:

Review—in *Films and Filming* (London), 1959; books—*The Cinema of Howard Hawks* by Peter Bogdanovich, New York 1962; *The Western: From Silents to Cinerama* by George N. Fenin, New York 1962; *Romance américaine* by Henri Agel, Paris 1963; *La Grande Aventure du western, 1894-1964* by Jean-Louis Rieupeyrout, Paris 1964; *Howard Hawks* by Jean-Claude Missiaen, Paris 1966; *Howard Hawks* by Robin Wood, Garden City, New York 1968; *Howard Hawks* by Jean A. Gili, Paris 1971; *Focus on Howard Hawks* edited by Joseph McBride, Englewood Cliffs, New Jersey 1972; *Westerns—Aspects of a Movie Genre* by Philip French, New York 1973; *The Films of Howard Hawks* by D.C. Willis, Metuchen, New Jersey 1975; *The Great Western Pictures* by James R. Parish and Michael Pitts, Metuchen, New Jersey 1976; *Westerns* by Philip French, New York 1977; *Howard Hawks, Storyteller* by Gerald Mast, New York 1982; articles—"H.H. and the western" by Michel Perez in *Présence du cinéma* (Paris), September 1959; "The World of Howard Hawks" by Andrew Sarris in *Films and Filming* (London), July 1962 and August 1962; "*Rio Bravo*" by Robin Wood in *Movie* (London), December 1962; "Howard Hawks" in *Movie* (London), December 1962; issue on Hawks of *Cahiers du cinéma* (Paris), January 1963; "Gunplay and Horses" by David Austen in *Films and Filming* (London), October 1968; "Tall in the Saddle" by Dennis John Hall in *Films and Filming* (London), October 1969; "*Rio Bravo*" by T. Renaud in *Cinéma* (Paris), January 1973; issue on Hawks of *Filmkritik* (Munich), May/June 1973; "Organiser le sensible" by A. Masson in *Positif* (Paris), July/August 1977; "Hawks et le mythe de l'ouest amée-icain" by J.L. Bourget in *Positif* (Paris), July/August 1977.

*   *   *

Rio Bravo is one of the supreme achievements (hence justifications) of "classical Hollywood," that complex network of determinants that includes the star system, the studio system, the system of genres and conventions, a highly developed grammer and syntax of shooting and editing, the interaction of which made possible an art at once personal and collaborative, one nourished by a rich and vital tradition: it is an art that belongs now to the past; the period of *Rio Bravo* was its last flowering.

The film at once is one of the greatest westerns and the most complete statements of the themes of director Howard Hawks. One can distinguish two main currents within the western genre, the "historical" and the "conventional": the western that is concerned with the American past (albeit with its mythology as much as its reality), and the western that plays with and develops a set of conventions, archetypes, "stock" figures. Ford's westerns are the finest examples of the former impulse, and in the westerns of Anthony Mann (for example, *Man of the West*) the two achieve perfect fusion. *Rio Bravo* is among the purest of all "conventional" westerns. Here, history and the American past are of no concern, a point amply demonstrated by the fact that the film is a virtual remake (in its thematic pattern, its characters and character relationships, even down to sketches of dialogue) of Hawks's earlier *Only Angels Have Wings* (set in the Andes mountains) and *To Have and Have Not* (set on Martinique). Hawks's stylized and anonymous western town is not a microcosm of American civilization at a certain point in its development but an abstract setting within which his recurrent concerns and relationships can be played out. All the characters are on one level "western" archetypes: the infallible sheriff, the fallible friend, the "travelling lady," the garrulous sidekick, the comic Mexican, the evil land-baron. On another level, however, they are Hawksian archetypes: the overlay makes possible the richness of characterization, the detail of the acting, so that here the archetypes (western and Hawksian) achieve their ultimate elaboration. With this goes the remarkable and varied use Hawks makes of actors' personas: Martin, Dickinson and Brennan have never surpassed (perhaps never equalled) their performances here, and the use of Wayne is extremely subtle and idiosyncratic, at once drawing on his "heroic" status and satirizing its limitations.

The film represents Hawks's most successful transcendence of the chief "binary opposition" of his work, its division into adventure films and comedies. Here the thematic concerns of the action pictures—self-respect, personal integrity, loyalty, stoicism, the interplay of mutual respect and affection—combines with the sexual tensions of the comedies (Wayne's vulnerability to women permitting a fuller development of this than is possible with, for example, Bogart in *To Have and Have Not*). The ambiguous relationship of Hawks's work to dominant American ideological assumptions (on the one hand the endorsement of individualism and personal initiative, on the other the rejection of established society in favour of the "primitive" male group, the total lack of interest in such central American ideals as marriage, home and family) permeates the whole film. The "gay subtext" that many critics have sensed in Hawks's films—their tendency to become (in his own words) "love stories between men"—surfaces quite clearly in the Dean Martin-Ricky Nelson relationship, though it is never allowed expression beyond the exchange of looks and is swiftly "contained" within the group (a progression beautifully enacted in the famous song-sequence). Within a system necessarily committed, at least on surface level, to reinforcing the status quo, Hawks's cinema continuously suggests the possibility of alternative forms of social and sexual organization.

—Robin Wood

THE RIVER. Production: Farm Security Administration, United States Government; 1937; black and white, 35mm; running time: 32 mins. Released 20 October 1937, premiering in New Orleans.

Screenplay by Pare Lorentz; directed by Pare Lorentz; photography by Floyd Crosby, Stacy Woodward, and Willard Van Dyke; edited by Pare Lorentz with Lloyd Nosler; music by Virgil Thomson, conducted by Alexander Smallens; contains footage from newsreels, and from the features *Come and Get It* and *Showboat*.

Filmed October 1936-1 March 1937 along the Mississippi River Valley, beginning in West Virginia and concluding in New Orleans. Cost: budgeted at $50,000, plus additional funds for shooting flood sequences. Venice International Film Festival, Best Documentary, 1938.

Cast: Thomas Chalmers (*Narrator*).

Publications:

Script—*The River: A Scenario* by Pare Lorentz, New York 1938; reviews—in *Time* (New York), 8 November 1937; "Old Man River" by Otis Ferguson in the *New Republic* (New York), 10 November 1937; review in the *Saturday Review of Literature* (New York), 9 April 1938; review by Harold Barnes in the *Herald-Tribune* (New York), 5 February 1938; "Pare Lorentz's *The River*" by Gilbert Seldes in *Scribner's* (New York), January 1938; review by Frank Nugent in *The New York Times*, 5 and 6 February 1938; books—*Pare Lorentz and the Documentary Film* by Robert L. Snyder, Norman, Oklahoma 1968; *Nonfiction Film: A Critical History* by Richard Barsam, New York 1973; *The People's Films: A Political History of U.S. Government Motion Pictures* by Richard Dyer MacCann, New York 1973; *Documentary: A History of the Nonfiction Film* by Erik Barnouw, New York 1974; *Film on the Left: American Documentary Film from 1931-1942* by William Alexander, Princeton, New Jersey 1981; articles—"The American Documentary" by Ezra Goodman in *Sight and Sound* (London), autumn 1938; "Award to Pare Lorentz" in the *Magazine of Art* (New York), July 1938; "Pare Lorentz" by W.L. White in *Scribner's* (New York), January 1939; "Pare Lorentz" in *Current Biography Yearbook*, New York 1940; "Letters from *The River*" by Willard Van Dyke in *Film Comment* (New York), March/April 1965; "The Narration of *The River*" by Pare Lorentz in *Film Comment* (New York), spring 1965; "Conscience of the 30's" in *Newsweek* (New York), 5 August 1968; "30 Years of Social Inquiry: An Interview with Willard Van Dyke" by Harrison Engle in *Nonfiction Film: Theory and Criticism* edited by Richard Barsam, New York 1976; "Ideology and Film Rhetoric: 3 Documentaries of

the New Deal Era" by P.C. Rollins in *Journal of Popular Film* (Bowling Green, Ohio), no.2, 1976.

THE ROARING TWENTIES. Production: Warner Bros. Pictures Inc.; 1939; black and white, 35mm; running time: 104 mins. Released 1939.

Produced by Hal B. Wallis with Sam Bischoff; screenplay by Jerry Wald, Richard Macaulay, and Robert Rossen, story foreword by Mark Hellinger; from a screen story by Mark Hellinger based on his experiences as a reporter in New York City; directed by Raoul Walsh and Anatole Litvak; photography by Ernie Haller; edited by Jack Killifer; sound by Everett A. Brown; art direction by Max Parker; music by Heinz Roemheld and Ray Heindorf, songs by Ernie Burnett and George A. Norton, Eubie Blake and Noble Sissle, Isham Jones and Gus Kahn, Jack Little, Joseph Young, and John Siras; special effects by Byron Haskin and Edwin B. DuPar.

Filmed in Warner Bros. studios.

Cast: James Cagney (*Eddie Bartlett*); Priscilla Lane (*Jean Sherman*); Humphrey Bogart (*George Hally*); Jeffrey Lynn (*Lloyd Hart*); Gladys George (*Panama Smith*); Frank McHugh (*Danny Green*); Paul Kelly (*Nick Brown*); Joe Sawyer (*Pete Jones*); Elisabeth Risdon (*Mrs. Sherman*); Ed Keane (*Pete Henderson*); Abner Biberman (*Lefty*); John Deering (*Commentator*); Ray Cooke (*Orderly*); Robert Dobson (*Lieutenant*); John Harron (*Soldier*); Vera Lewis (*Mrs. Gray*); Murray Alper and Dick Wessel (*Mechanics*); Joseph Crehan (*Fletcher the foreman*); Norman Willis (*Bootlegger*); Robert Elliott and Eddy Chandler (*Officers*); John Hamilton (*Judge*); Pat O'Malley (*Jailer*); Wade Boteler (*Policeman*); Arthur Loft (*Producer and proprietor of still*); Al Hill, Raymond Bailey, and Lew Harvey (*Ex-cons*); Creighton Hale (*Customer*); Major Sam Harris (*Man in club*); Cyril Ring (*Charlie the clerk*); Stuart Holmes (*Man for turkish bath*).

Publications:

Books—*Bogart* by Richard Gehman, Greenwich, Connecticut 1965; *The Films of Humphrey Bogart* by Clifford McCarty, New York 1965; *The Films of Robert Rossen* by Alan Casty, New York 1969; *Raoul Walsh* by Michel Marmin, Paris 1970; *The Films of James Cagney* by Homer Dickens, Secaucus, New Jersey 1972; *The Hollywood Professionals* by Kingsley Canham, New York 1973; *James Cagney* by Andrew Bergman, New York 1973; *Each Man in His Time* by Raoul Walsh, New York 1974; *The Great Gangster Pictures* by James R. Parish and Michael Pitts, Metuchen, New Jersey 1976; articles—"The Gangster as Tragic Hero" by Robert Worshow in *Partisan Review* (Nutley, New Jersey), February 1948; "Cagney and the Mob" by Kenneth Tynan in *Sight and Sound* (London), May 1951; "Gunman No.1" by Peter Barnes in *Films and Filming* (London), September 1955; "Humphrey Bogart" by Clifford McCarty in *Films in Review* (New York), May 1957; "James Cagney" by Don Miller in *Films in Review* (New York), August/-September 1958; issue on Walsh of *Présence du cinéma* (Paris), May 1962; issue on Walsh of *Cahiers du cinéma* (Paris), April 1964; "Raoul Walsh" by R. Lloyd in *Brighton* (London),

November 1969, December 1969, and January 1970; "*The Roaring Twenties*" by Dan Scapperotti in *Magill's Survey of Cinema, Vol. III* edited by Frank N. Magill, Englewood Cliffs, New Jersey 1980; article in *Casablanca* (Madrid), February 1981.

*   *   *

The Roaring Twenties is often grouped with other well-known gangster movies of the 1930's, among them *Little Caesar* (1930), *Scarface: The Shame of the Nation* (1932), and *Public Enemy* (1931), but it is different from them in a way that is more than chronological. All four are about gangsters, bootlegging, murder, betrayal, and all end with the protagonist's death, but *The Roaring Twenties* is a romantic reworking of themes prevalent in the early 1930's. Unlike the harsh, incorrigible existence of gangsters portrayed in films such as *Little Caesar*, there are shades of good and bad in *The Roaring Twenties*. Film historian Carlos Clarens has labeled the film a "revisionist" gangster movie, and this theory is certainly borne out by the historical fact that the era of the colorfully corrupt kingpins of the early 1930's had ended, its key figures, such as Al Capone and John Dillinger, having died or been permanently incarcerated.

The revisionist theme comes in large measure from the guiding hand of veteran director Raoul Walsh. One of the best of the so-called "studio directors," Walsh had an ability to make action films that combined sentimentality and humor with the harsher realities of crime or war. His romanticism was also characterized by a number of prominent roles for women in the otherwise male dominated genre.

In *The Roaring Twenties* the downfall of gangster Eddie Bartlett is not simply retribution for a misspent life. Eddie, unlike Rico, or Tony Camonte, is a "nice guy." Only after returning to civilian life after service in World War I and finding no jobs and little opportunity does he become a criminal. Even his entry into bootlegging is the result of his "character"—he refuses to turn in Panama Smith (Gladys George) and instead innocently takes the "rap" for her. The film seems to say that bootlegging, not the government or the Ameriacn public, can offer Eddie opportunities for success. Panama is the only one who rewards him for a job well done, and ironically she is the only one who stays by him until the end.

Eddie never does become completely corrupt, though. He remains sentimental about his cab company, his early honest venture, and also shows great devotion to his friends. Ironically, it is his loyalty to his World War I buddy Lloyd Hart (Jeffrey Lynn) and his idealized love Jean Sherman (Priscilla Lane) that causes his downfall. He cannot let them be killed by George Hally (Humphrey Bogart), another war buddy who wants them silenced; he offers one last gesture to save them by killing George. In the end, he dies in Panama's arms, symbolically on the steps of a church where Panama gives the film's most memorable line, "He used to be a big shot."

Eddie is a symbol not only of corruption of innocence, but also of the forgotten man of the 1930's. Like millions of former Dough Boys, Eddie was given little in return for his service. Yet, despite his venture into bootlegging, he remained part of society. This is shown in several ways in the film by his loyalty, his continuous operation of the cab company, and even his investments in the stock market. Walsh shows the audience a good man betrayed by the system rather than a bad man who scorns it.

This theme is reinforced by James Cagney's performance. Even when he pretends to be completely callous and corrupt, his soft center shows through. It is great tribute to Cagney's merits as an actor that he could move from film to film within the same genre and be believable in a variety of characterizations. His next performance as a gangster was in Walsh's *White Heat* (1949). There he was the total opposite of Eddie Bartlett, a psychotic and completely corrupt individual. It is also a tribute to Walsh's talents as a director that he could make two such opposite films within the same genre.

—Patricia King Hanson

ROCCO E I SUOI FRATELLI. Rocco and His Brothers. Production: Titanus and Les Films Marceau; 1960; black and white, 35mm; running time: 182 mins.; length: 4973 meters originally, usually distributed in versions of 3600 meters. Released 15 October 1960, premiered at Venice Film Festival on 6 September 1960.

Produced by Goffredo Lombardo; subject by Luchino Visconti, Vasco Pratolini, and Suco Cecchi D'Amico; screenplay by Luchino Visconti, Suso Cocchi d'Amico, Pasquale Festa Campanile, Massimo Franciosa, and Enrico Medioli; from the book *Il Ponte della ghisolfa* by Giovanni Testori; directed by Luchino Visconti; photography by Giuseppe Rotunno; edited by Mario Serandrei; sound by Giovanni Rossi; art direction by Mario Garbuglia; music by Nino Rota; costumes designed by Piero Tosi; production organized by Giuseppe Bordogni; assistant directors: Jerry Macc and Lucio Orlandini.

David di Donatello prize for best production, 1960; Venice Film Festival, Special Jury Prize and International Film Critics Award, 1960; Festival of Workers (Czechoslovakia), First Prize, 1961.

Cast: Alain Delon (*Rocco*); Renato Salvatori (*Simone*); Annie Girardot (*Nadia*); Katina Paxinou (*Rosaria*); Roger Hanin (*Morini*); Paolo Stoppa *Impresario*); Suzy Delair (*Luisa*); Claudia Cardinale (*Ginetta*); Spiros Focas (*Vincenzo*); Rocco Vidolazzi (*Luca*); Corrado Pani (*Ivo*); Max Cartier (*Ciro*); Alessandra Panaro (*Ciro's fiancée*); Claudia Mori (*Laundry worker*); Becker Masocro (*Nadia's mother*).

Publications:

Scripts—*Rocco e i suoi fratelli di Luchino Visconti* (includes introduction by Aristarco and chronicle of the filming), edited by G. Aristarco and G. Carancini, Milan 1960; script extract in *Tiempo de cine* (Buenos Aires), no.4, 1960 and no.6, 1961; script extract in *Films and Filming* (London), September 1961; *Rocco et ses freres*, Paris 1961; script in German in *Filmkritik* (Munich), no.7, 1961; *Luchino Visconti: 3 Screenplays* translated by Judith Green, New York 1970; *Rocco e i suoi fratelli*, Bologna 1978; reviews—by Albert Moravia in *L'espresso*, 6 March 1960; review by Henry Hart in *Films in Review* (New York), August/September 1961; review by Jonas Mekas in *The Village Voice* (New York), 22 June 1961; review by Derek Prouse in *Sight and Sound* (London), winter 1960-61; review by Peter Armitage in *Film* (London), winter 1961; review by Robert Benayoun in *Positif* (Paris), July 1961; review by Bosley Crowther in *The New York Times*, 28 June 1961; review by Vernon Young in *Film Quarterly* (Berkeley), fall 1961; review by Georges Sadoul in *Les Lettres françaises* (Paris), 9 March 1961;

books—*Luchino Visconti* by Salvador Elizondon, Mexico 1963; *I film di Luchino Visconti* by Pio Baldelli, Manduria, Italy 1965; *Luchino Visconti* by V. Sitova, Moscow 1965; *Visconti* by Yves Guillaume, Paris 1966; *Le cinéma italien, d'Antonioni à Rosi* by Freddy Bauche, Yverdon, Switzerland 1969; *L'Opera di Luchino Visconti* edited by M. Speranzi, Florence 1969; *Visconti* by Giuseppe Ferrara, translated by Jean-Pierre Pinaud, Paris, 2nd ed., 1970; *La crisi dell'uomo e della societé nei film di Visconti e di Antonioni*, Alba 1972; *Luchino Visconti* by Pio Baldelli, Milan 1973; *Visconti* by Geoffrey Nowell-Smith, 2nd ed., New York 1973; *Luchino Visconti*, Carl Hanser Verlag, Munich 1975; *Leggere Visconti* edited by G. Callegari and N. Lodato, Pavia, Italy 1976; *Visconti: il cinema* edited by Adelio Ferrera, Milan 1977; *Album Visconti* edited by Lietta Tornabuoni, foreword by Michelangelo Antonioni, Milan 1978; *A Screen of Time* by Monica Stirling, New York 1979; *Il mio teatro* by Luchino Visconti, Bologna 1979; *Luchino Visconti* by Gaia Servadio, Milan 1980; *Luchino Visconti* by Gianni Rondolino, Turin 1981; *Luchino Visconti* by Alessandro Bencivenni, Florence 1982; articles—by Grazia Livi in *L'Europeo*, 6 March 1960; article by Rino Dal Sasso in *Filmcritica* (Rome), October 1960; interview with Visconti in *Cinema nuovo* (Turin), September/October 1960; "Oltre il fato dei Malavoglia" by Luchino Visconti in *Vie nuove*, October 1960; article by Roger Manvell in *Films and Filming* (London), October 1961; issue on Visconti of *Premier Plan* (Paris), May 1961; "The Earth Still Trembles" by Guido Aristarco in *Films and Filming* (London), January 1961; "The Miracle That Gave Man Crumbs" by Luchino Visconti in *Films and Filming* (London), January 1961; "Visconti and Rocco" by P. Armitage in *Film* (London), winter 1961; article by Vito Pandolfi in *Film 61*, Milan 1961; "New Old Master" by L. Minoff in *Saturday Review* (New York), 29 December 1962; issue on Visconti of *Etudes cinématographiques* (Paris), no.26-27, 1963; articles in *Cinéma 63* (Paris), September/October 1963; article by Madina Buschkowsky in *Jahrbuch des Film 1962*, Berlin 1964; issue on Visconti of *Cinema* (Rome), April 1970; "Luchino Visconti" by T. Elsaesser in *Brighton* (London), February 1970; article by Helga Koppel in *Film in Italien, Italien in Film*, West Berlin 1970; "Marxism and Formalism in the Films of Luchino Visconti" by Walter Korte in *Cinema Journal* (Evanston, Illinois), fall 1971; "Treska i sintez" by I. Zolotuski in *Kinoizkustvo* (Sofia, Bulgaria), January 1972; "Visconti laat zich niet bij pilsje navertellen: *Rocco* op de montagetafel" by W. Verstappen in *Skoop* (Amsterdam), August/September 1978; article in *The New York Times*, 7 January 1979; "25 Years of Film: *Rocco*" by M. Shivas in *Film* (London), November 1979; "*Rocco en zijn broers*" by G. Verhage in *Skrien* (Amsterdam), May 1979.

emigrants and the social community to which they belong, as in his staging of Arthur Miller's *A View from a Bridge* (1958). Most Italian critics saw this film as the finest example of the critical realism called for in the writings of Lukacs. Visconti himself saw it as a further examination of Verga's characterizations and Gramsci's analysis of the Southern social and political condition. In fact, Visconti considered *Rocco* a sequel to *La terra trema*.

Visconti's critical realism takes the form of a study of each member of a Sicilian family of five sons and a mother (some characters receiving more emphasis than others) who have emigrated to the industrial Northern city of Milan. Each character responds to his or her situation in utterly different ways. Visconti thus achieved a complex structure that was to be attempted again by Bertolucci, one of his greatest admirers, in *1900*. Originally Visconti conceived of the film as built around the mother, but the final film analyzed more closely the two middle sons, Rocco and Simone, both of whom become boxers but have entirely opposite personalities. Simone is fierce and instinctual; Rocco is passive and thoughtful. Rocco sacrifices himself, his love (Annie Girardot's portrayal of Nadia was universally praised), and his dreams, for his brother and his family. The last scene is devoted to Ciro, the son who reaches political awareness, the only member of the family to become truly a part of the urban community. Ciro's final speech to his younger brother reveals Visconti's intention to "arrive at social and political conclusions, having taken during the film the road of psychological investigation and faithful reconstruction of a drama."

Visconti often had problems with the censors, and *Rocco* was no exception. During production he was forced to change a location because it was felt that to film Nadia's death scene there would harm the tourist trade. At its world premiere in Venice, the film was projected with scenes cut and run with the soundtrack only. Many cuts were required before general release, and later the city of Milan refused to have it distributed there. The prints circulated in Italy run 45 minutes shorter than the original version. Nevertheless, *Rocco* was the first Visconti film to achieve enormous commercial success in its national market, and it convinced the film community that Visconti was indeed a major film director. For the most part, the film earned praise throughout the world, though a few critics abhorred the portrayal of violence and considered the film morally questionable.

—Elaine Mancini

---

*   *   *

Rocco e i suoi fratelli appeared in the same year as Fellini's *La dolce vita*, and together they indicated, in opposite ways, the major possibilities for the Italian cinema of that decade. As artistically successful as director Visconti's earlier *La terra trema* (1948) and *Senso* (1954), *Rocco* is, however, even more rigorous and has its roots in a larger and richer cultural base. Although not an adaption of any particular literary piece, it draws from works as diverse as Dostoevsky's *The Idiot* (Myshkin inspiring the character of Rocco, Rogosin inspiring that of Simone), Giovanni Testori's stories of Milan (especially *Il Ponte della Ghisolfa*), and Thomas Mann's *Joseph and His Brothers*. The film also displays the interests and the realistic style of most of Visconti's theatre work from 1945, which included studies of

ROCKY. Production: United Artists; 1976; Technicolor, 35mm; running time: 119 mins. Released 1976.

Produced by Robert Chartoff and Irwin Winkler; screenplay by Sylvester Stallone; directed by John G. Avildsen; photography by James Crabe; edited by Richard Halsey; music by Bill Conti.

Cost: $960,000. Academy Awards for Best Picture, Best Director, and Best Editing, 1976; New York Film Critics Award, Best Supporting Actress (Shire), 1976.

Cast: Sylvester Stallone (*Rocky Balboa*); Talia Shire (*Adrian*); Burt Young (*Paulie*); Carl Weathers (*Apollo Creed*); Burgess Meredith (*Mickey*); Joe Spinell (*Gazzo*).

Publications:

Reviews—"The Current Cinema: Stallone and Stahr" by Pauline Kael in the *New Yorker*, 29 November 1976; "Poor Folk" by Stanley Kauffmann in the *New Republic* (New York), 27 November 1976; "Knockout" by Janet Maslin in *Newsweek* (New York), 29 November 1976; "*Rocky*" by D. Munroe in *Film Bulletin* (Philadelphia), November/December 1976; "*Rocky*" by A.D. Murphy in *Variety* (New York), 10 November 1976; "*Rocky*" by Andrew Sarris in *The Village Voice* (New York), 22 November 1976; "Movies: Stallone's Ring of Truth" by John Simon in *New York*, 29 November 1976; articles—"Blacklisting, Battling, and Bernhardt" by Judith Crist in the *Saturday Review* (New York), 27 November 1976; "*Rocky*: It Could Be a Contender" by L. Farr in *New York*, 18 October 1976; "*Rocky* KOs Tinseltown" by P. Hamill in *The Village Voice* (New York), 8 November 1976; "John G. Avildsen Describes *Rocky* as a Classic 'Capra-type' Picture" by R. Kaminsky in *Boxoffice* (Kansas City, Missouri), 20 December 1976; "Rocky isn't Based on Me, Says Stallone, But We Both Went the Distance" by J. Klemesrud in *The New York Times*, 28 November 1976; "Sylvester Stallone Profiled in 2 Weekly Magazines" in *Boxoffice* (Kansas City, Missouri), 15 November 1976; "*Rocky*" by Pat Aufderheide in *Cineaste* (New York), summer 1977; "*Rocky*" by O. Eyquem in *Positif* (Paris), June 1977; "*Rocky*" by Gordon Gow in *Films and Filming* (London), May 1977; "*Wytrwać*" by D. Karcz in *Kino* (Warsaw), June 1977; "The New Hoke" by James Monaco in *Take One* (Montreal), January 1977; "*Rocky*" by J. Pym in *Sight and Sound* (London), summer 1977; "The Industry: *Rocky* and His Friends" by S. Byron in *Film Comment* (New York), January/February 1977; "The Photography of *Rocky*" by J. Crabe in *American Cinematographer* (Los Angeles), February 1977; "*Rocky*" by V. Oravsky in *Filmrutan* (Lidingö, Sweden), no.2, 1977; "The Invisible Man of *Rocky*" by D. Schaefer in *Millimeter* (New York), September 1977; "*Rocky*: 2 Faces" by I. Shor in *Jump Cut* (Chicago), no.3 (150), 1977; "*Rocky* on CBS Draws 3rd Best Movie Audience" by L. Brown in *The New York Times*, 7 February 1979; "Stallone wraca do zywych" by K. Metrak in *Kino* (Warsaw), April 1979; "*Rocky*" by Pat H. Broeske in *Magill's Survey of Cinema, Vol. III* edited by Frank N. Magill, Englewood Cliffs, New Jersey 1980.

*   *   *

The phenomemal popular and critical success of *Rocky* seemed to mirror the Cinderella-like plot of the film. Similar to the title character, the film began in a small, insignificant way and became a champion—Academy Award for Best Picture, second highest grossing film of the year, and critical success.

The film was the brainchild of Sylvester Stallone, an actor of minor reputation who had appeared in *The Lords of Flatbush* both on Broadway and in the 1974 film. Stallone sold his screenplay to producers Robert Chartoff and Irwin Winkler, and was reportedly so eager to star in the production himself that he accepted a relatively small salary for both aspects of his work. The gamble paid off, for *Rocky*, which was filmed in the restrictive schedule of under one month, and for a budget of slightly under one million dollars, became a national sensation. The story of a minor down-and-out fighter who, through a fluke, receives an opportunity to fight the Mohammed Ali-like Apollo Creed (Carl Weathers) on the day of the American Bicentennial, *Rocky* is a quintessetial "rags-to-riches" story. Even the now trite words "go for it" and the stirring theme music by composer Bill Conti became instantly recognizable throughout the world as symbols of the will to win. The film is more than an uplifting diversion about tenacity, however, and can be appreciated even

more for its portrait of a boxer and modern boxing.

The boxing scenes in *Rocky* compare favorably with those in some of the earlier classic fight films such as *Golden Boy* (1939), *Body and Soul* (1947), and *Champion* (1949), even if the sociological themes examined within those other films are far more significant than those in *Rocky*. The long, final sequence of the championship match is realistic and emotionally involving for the audience, even though perhaps some people were revolted by the graphic punching and injuries of the two actors. The best portions of the film, however, are the training sequences. In the beginning they are gruelling and, like Rocky himself, almost pathetic. As his competence and confidence increase, though, his training becomes smooth and professional. In the climactic sequence in which Rocky runs through the streets of Philadelphia and easily races up the long steps to the city's Museum of Art, the audience begins to believe with him that he can win. By the end of the film, Rocky has become a "winner," by attaining a split-decision with Creed, and by gaining the love of the shy Adrian (Talia Shire).

Although the film is almost totally Stallone's, he failed to win an Oscar, even though he was nominated in the categories of Best Actor and Best Screenplay. The film, and director John G. Avildsen did win Oscars, however, and in the two sequels, Stallone's success in the original enabled him to direct as well as star and write the screenplays. *Rocky II* was completely forgettable, although it did do well at the box office. *Rocky III*, the last sequel to date, was well received as a mature progression of the Rocky saga and surpassed the original in box office receipts.

—Patricia King Hanson

THE ROCKY HORROR PICTURE SHOW. Production: Twentieth Century-Fox; Eastmancolor, 35mm; running time: 100 mins. Released 1975.

Produced by Michael White with John Goldstone, executive producer: Lou Adler; screenplay by Jim Sharman and Richard O'Brien; from the play by Richard O'Brien; directed by Jim Sharman; photography by Peter Suschitzky; edited by Graeme Clifford; art direction by Terry Ackland Snow, design consultant: Brian Thomson; songs by Richard O'Brien, music direction by Richard Hartley; special effects by Wally Veevers; costumes designed by by Richard Pointing and Gillian Dods, costume consultant: Sue Blane.

Cast: Tim Curry (*Dr. Frank N. Furter*); Barry Bostwick (*Brad Majors*); Susan Sarandon (*Janet Weiss*); Richard O'Brien (*Riff Raff*); Jonathan Adams (*Dr. Everett Majors*); Nell Campbell (*Columbia*); Peter Hinwood (*Rocky*); Meatloaf (*Eddie*); Patricia Quinn (*Magenta*); Charles Gray (*Narrator*); Hilary Labow (*Betty Munroe*); Jeremy Newson (*Ralph Hapschatt*): Frank Lester (*Wedding Dad*); Mark Johnson (*Wedding guest*); Koo Stark, Petra Leah, and Gina Barrie (*Bridesmaids*); John Marquand (*Father*).

Publications:

Reviews—in *Hollywood Reporter*, 26 October 1974; "*The Rocky Horror Picture Show*" by J. Pitman in *Variety* (New York), 24 September 1975; "*The Rocky Horror Picture Show*" by T. Rayns in *Monthly Film Bulletin* (London), August 1975; "*The Rocky Horror Picture Show*" by A. Stuart in *Films and Filming* (London), September 1975; review in the *Listener* (London), 28 August 1975; "*The Rocky Horror Picture Show*" by M. Porro in *Cineforum* (Bergamo), February 1977; articles— "*The Rocky Horror Picture Show*" by H. Behar in *Revue du cinéma* (Paris), October 1976; "*The Rocky Horror Picture Show*" by R. Care in *Cinefantastique* (Oak Park, Illinois), no.2, 1976; "Selective Audience Marketing Approach Credited for *Rocky Horror* Successes" in *Boxoffice* (Kansas City, Missouri), 22 November 1976; "South Africa Bans *Rocky Horror* Pic" in *Variety* (New York), 13 October 1976; article in *Monthly Film Bulletin* (London), March 1976; "*The Rocky Horror Picture Show*" by W. Baer in *Film und Ton Magazine* (Munich), July 1979; "Criticism: Film: *Rocky Horror*: The Newest Cult" by R. Bold in *Christian Century* (Chicago), 12 September 1979; "*Rocky Horror*: The Case of the Rampant Audience" by M. Segell in *Rolling Stone* (New York), 5 April 1979; "The RH Factor" by K. Von Gunden in *Film Comment* (New York), September/October 1979; "Film is too Horrible for North York" in *Boxoffice* (Kansas City, Missouri), 5 February 1979; "Midnights at *Rocky Horror*" by A. Quindlen in *The New York Times*, 9 March 1979; "*Rocky Horror* Taken Off Screen in W. Mass" in *Boxoffice* (Kansas City, Missouri), 5 February 1979; article in *Time Out*, April 1979; "*Le Rocky Horror Picture Show*: Cult-film" by Jonathan Rosenbaum in *Cahiers du cinéma* (Paris), January 1980; "The Rocky Horror Picture Cult" by Jonathan Rosenbaum in *Sight and Sound* (London), spring 1980; "Portrait of a Cult Film Audience: *The Rocky Horror Picture Show*" by B.A. Austin in *Journal of Communication* (Philadelphia), spring 1981; article in *Starburst*, no.36, 1981; article in *Screen International*, July 1982.

* * *

When *The Rocky Horror Picture Show* was first distributed in 1975, it proved to be a severe commercial disappointment for its producer, Lou Adler. Already firmly established as one of the most successful commercial exploiters of rock music and the youth market, Adler was quite naturally attracted (as a shrewd businessman) to Richard O'Brien's popular stage musical, which had opened in London in 1973. *The Rocky Horror Picture Show* combined glitter rock (popularized in the early 1970's by such performers as David Bowie, Gary Glitter, Alice Cooper, and The New York Dolls) with a camp sensibility founded on an acute awareness of gesture, costume, role-playing, extreme theatricality, and a kind of bisexual fantasy world of ambiguous sexual identity, humor, and sexual freedom—thus appealing to both a young and a gay audience.

When the film was released in 1975, however, the glitter subculture was waning, and the potential audience for a glitter rock musical was gradually shrinking. Adhering to the philosophy that, through proper advertising and distribution, a demand could be created for whatever film product one happened to have on hand, Adler rethought his strategy and decided to concentrate on a target audience of glitter devotees, limiting the film's release to midnight screenings in a few urban centers. The spectacular group of *Rocky Horror* fans who came to see the film over and over again eventually created their own media attention which attracted others to the film; conventional advertising was minimal. Money came pouring in from small venues catering to a repeat clientele; week-end *Rocky Horror* outings became the "thing to do." In fact, the film became an ideal for every small producer who dreams of a profitable, low-budget, "cult" hit. An

avid group of repeat viewers is, after all, the perfect means to maximize profits.

Rooted in camp humor and theatricality, *Rocky Horror*'s narrative involves an elaborate mechanism of irony—a shared understanding between the spectator and the film fantasy which allows free play with all sorts of taken-for-granted conventions— of gender and film genre, of social and sexual identity. It is an elaborate parody of Hollywood horror films and musicals, and a mild, but deliberate, satire on conventional notions of sexuality.

After their engagement, Brad Majors and Janet Weiss, two straight "innocents," decide to seek the blessing of their former science professor, Dr. Everett Scott. En route to his house, however, they are forced by a flat tire and a severe rainstorm to seek help at an ominous Gothic castle, the home of Dr. Frank N. Furter, a transvestite from another galaxy. Frank seduces both Brad and Janet, as well as his own creation, Rocky Horror, and a host of other guests and hangers-on. Eventually, after Dr. Scott appears, searching for his nephew Eddie, and also falls under the spell, Frank N. Furter is finally foiled by his own servants, Riff Raff and Magenta, who kill their former master and transport the entire castle back to its home planet. Janet and Brad are left behind, corrupted, and thus their hypocritical denial of sexuality is symbolically exposed.

The "cult"—the subcultural activity surrounding the film—is, however, perhaps more familiar to most people than the film itself. Outlandish costumes, shouted dialogues of insults and additions, and projectiles of toilet paper, toast, playing cards and streams of water accompany each screening of the film. The sexual fantasy presented by the film is both imitated and enjoyed and tacitly criticized and condemned by the audience, whose relation to the screen fantasy remains contradictory and ultimately ambivalent. The energy and carnival-like atmosphere which accompanies the film, however, did succeed in reviving the glitter subculture in the very specialized, high ritualized, and slightly sterile way. The film has been able to attract many who may not have been very interested in glitter when it was in vogue, and with the continued—though gradually declining—popularity of the film, it has even attracted people who were too young to really be aware of glitter when it was at its zenith in the early 1970s.

—Gina Marchetti

ROMA, CITTÀ APERTA. Rome, Open City. Rome, Ville ouverte. Production: Excelsa Film; black and white, 35mm; running time: 100 mins.; length: 9586 feet. Released September 1945, Rome.

Screenplay by Sergio Amidei with Federico Fellini and Roberto Rossellini; from an original story by Sergio Amidei in collaboration with Alberto Consiglio and Roberto Rossellini; directed by Roberto Rossellini; photography by Ubaldo Arata; edited by Eraldo da Roma; production design by R. Megna; music by Renzo Rossellini, directed by L. Ricci.

Filmed in part during the liberation of Rome by the Allies, the remainder shot during early 1944. Filmed in and around Rome, and in improvised studios at the "via degli Avignonesi" (Liborio Capitani) and at the home of Sergio Amidei. Cannes Film Festival, Best Film, 1946.

Cast: Anna Magnani (*Pina*); Aldo Fabrizi (*Don Pietro Pelle-*

grini); Marcello Pagliero (*Giorgio Manfredi, alias Luigi Ferraris*); Harry Feist (*Major Bergmann*); Maria Michi (*Marina Mari*); Francesco Grandjaquet (*Francesco, the typist*); Giovanna Galletti (*Ingrid*); Vito Annichiarico (*Marcello, son of Pina*); Carla Revere (*Lauretta*); Nando Bruno (*Agostino*); Carlo Sindici (*Treasurer from Rome*); Joop van Hulzen (*Hartmann*); Akos Tolnay (*Austrian deserter*); Eduardo Passarelli (*Police sergeant*); Amalia Pelegrini (*Landlady*).

Publications:

Scripts—"Cosi nacquero *Paisa* e *Roma città aperta*" in *Cinema nuovo* (Turin), 25 April 1955; "*Rome, Ville ouverte*" in *Avant-Scène du cinéma* (Paris), June 1965; "*Róm, otevřené město*" (script extract) in *Film a doba* (Prague), April 1975; books—*Roberto Rossellini* by Patrice Hovald, Paris 1958; *Roberto Rossellini* by Massimo Mida, Guanda, Parma, Italy 1961; *Roberto Rossellini* by Mario Verdone, Paris 1963; *Interviews with Film Directors* by Andrew Sarris, New York 1967; *Roberto Rossellini* by José Luis Guarner, translated by Elizabeth Cameron, New York 1970; *La Resistenza nel cinema italiano del dopoguerra* by Nedo Ivaldi, Rome 1970; *Patterns of Realism: A Study of Italian Neo-Realist Cinema* by Roy Armes, Cranbury, New Jersey 1971; *Italian Cinema Since the War* by Ken Wlaschin, Cranbury, New Jersey 1971; *Roberto Rossellini* by Pio Baldelli, Rome 1972; *The Italian Cinema* by Pierre Leprohon, New York 1972; *Roberto Rossellini* by Gianni Rondolino, Florence 1974; *Cinema, The Magic Vehicle: A Guide to Its Achievement: Journey One: The Cinema Through 1949* edited by Jacek Klinowski and Adam Garbicz, Metuchen, New Jersey 1975; articles—"Poésie et réalité" by Jean Desternes in *La Revue du cinéma* (Paris), December 1946; "*Rome, ville ouverte*" by Roland Martin in *Bulletin de l'Idhec* (Paris), March/May 1947; "Prophet with Honor: Roberto Rossellini" by Peter Ordway in *Theatre Arts* (New York), January 1949; "Roberto Rossellini" by Lauro Venturi in *Hollywood Quarterly*, fall 1949; "Rossellini' in the *New Yorker*, 19 February 1949; "Lo stil nuovo" by Ferruccio Parri in *Cinema nuovo* (Turin), April 1955; "The Quest for Realism" by Gordon Gow in *Films and Filming* (London), December 1957; "Une esthétique de la réalité: le Néo-Réalisme" in *Qu'est-ce que le cinéma* by André Bazin, 2nd edition, Paris 1962; "Rossellini Rediscovered" by Andrew Sarris in *Film Culture* (New York), no.32, 1964; "The Achievement of Roberto Rossellini" by Alan Casty in *Film Comment* (New York), fall 1964; "Le Neo-Réalisme italien, bilan de la critique" by François Debreczeni in *Etudes cinématographique* (Paris), nos.32-35, 1964; "*Rome, villa ouverte*: un film-clé" by Maurizio Ponzi in *Avant-Scène du cinéma* (Paris), June 1965; "Roberto Rossellini" in *Cinema* (Beverly Hills), fall 1971; "Rossellini's Materialist Mise-en-Scène" by J.R. MacBean in *Film Quarterly* (Berkeley), winter 1971-72; "*Roma, città aperta*" by J. Heijs in *Skrien* (Amsterdam), October 1977; "*Rome, Open City*: The Rise to Power of Louis XIV" by M. Walshi in *Jump Cut* (Chicago), no.15, 1977; "Italian Neorealism: A Mirror Construction of Reality" by B. Lawton in *Film Criticism* (Edinboro, Pennsylvania), no.2, 1979; "*Rome ville ouverte*" by O.R. Veillon in *Cinématographe* (Paris), June 1980.

*   *   *

Roberto Rossellini's *Roma, città aperta* emerged from the ashes of World War II to become Europe's first post-war master-

piece, and in doing so demonstrated once again an increasingly accepted axiom of filmmaking: cinema is perhaps the only one of the major art forms in which scarcity and deprivation periodically unite with genius to produce technical innovations that drastically influence the course of the art form for generations to follow. For example, the filmless experiments (caused by scarcities of film stock) of the Soviet Union's Kuleshow workshop, betweem 1922 and 1924, produced the concept of montage and led to the great works of Vsevolod Poduvkin and Sergei Eisenstein. Somewhat earlier, in Germany, director Robert Wiene utilized painted backdrops and shadowy lighting induced by a power failure to create *The Cabinet of Dr. Caligari* and popularize the film style known as Expressionism. Similarly, Rossellini, trying to produce a film in 1945 with fragments left from an industry decimated by war, pioneered a style that became known as neo-realism, the influence of which can still be seen in films as diverse as Ermanno Olmis' *Tree of Wooden Clogs* (1979) and Michael Cimino's *Heaven's Gate* (1981).

Roma, città aperta, which was begun within two months of the Allied liberation of Rome, was actually conceived and planned several months earlier when Rossellini and some colleagues were dodging Nazi patrols to avoid being conscripted for military service on the side of the Fascists. In a purely professional sense, the attempt to make the film itself should have been doomed: Rossellini could obtain a permit from the allied administrators to make a documentary film only, and the prohibitive cost of the sound film on the black market virtually mandated the use of cheaper stock normally reserved for silent films. In addition, all of the performers with the exception of Anna Magnani, a sometime music hall performer, were non-professionals.

The resulting film, unlike anything produced before, turned these seeming drawbacks into tenets of a major new mode of expression—neo-realism—which shook the Italian film industry from its doldrums and returned it to the forefront of cinematic innovation. But, *Roma, città aperta*'s employment of this mode of representation was not the end product of the application of conscious artistic principle in the manner of the less influential *Ossessione* (1943), which many feel was the real harbinger of neo-realism. Rossellini's version of the form placed heavy emphasis on the re-creation of incidents in, whenever possible, the exact locales in which such events had taken place and accordingly spotlighted the everyday occurrences of Italian life. It also featured real people in the actors' roles which served to convey a sense of the immediacy of the post-war Italian experience.

Yet, several features of *Roma, città aperta* make it difficult to classify its director as simply or purely a neo-realist, particularly given the way that the form was subsequently defined by such filmmakers as Luchino Visconti, Vittorio De Sica and others who took up the style in the late 1940's. Its plot is highly melodramatic in the worst sense of the word. Characters are clearly defined as either good or evil according to the strength of their commitment to a better tomorrow for Italy or, conversely, by their lack of faith in themselves and their cynicism in adhering to an obviously corrupt ideology.

Rossellini makes little pretense at objectivity in rendering even the surface appearance of things which characterized later neo-realistic works. His employment of his brother Renzo's music is emotionally manipulative in a number of scenes, while, in other instances, certain images represent a definite intrusion of the director's personal feelings. His use of babies and children, for example, as an embodiment of Italy's hopes for the future not only shapes our anguish in a scene such as the one in which pregnant Anna Magnani is murdered but it also reaffirms the validity of the sacrifice and the Italian cause in the final scene when the children are neatly juxtaposed with a shot of the dome of St. Peter's as they leave the execution of the priest Don Pietro.

Although these overly dramatic inconsistencies make it difficult to classify *Roma, città aperta* as a textbook example of the mode of expression it popularized, such contradictions actually heighten its powerful depiction of the conflicting realities inherent in the struggle against fascism. Rossellini's shifting perpectives alternating between comedy and pathos when focused upon a select number of crucial episodes in the lives of some real people effectively isolates a specific historical reality that exerted a profound effect upon filmgoers of the late 1940's.

Though the grainy, black-and-white images of *Roma, città aperta* are at least one step removed from actuality, conforming instead to a verity appropriate to documentary films, they promulgate a very real social humanism that prevades the entire body of Rossellini's work and transcends the narrow boundaries of specific modes of expression. The film is ultimately a hopeful vision of the future of Italy and indeed of mankind in general, and while it establishes techniques that would subsequently evolve into filmmaking codes, it reflects more the personality of its director and his belief in innate goodness than it does a rigid ideology of realistic representation.

—Stephen L. Hanson

to Its Achievement: Journey Two edited by Jacek Klinowski and Adam Garbicz, Metuchen, New Jersey 1979; *Max Ophüls and the Cinema of Desire* by Alan Williams, New York 1980; articles—"Interview with Ophüls" by Francis Koval in *Sight and Sound* (London), July 1950; "Ophüls and the Romantic Tradition" by Eugene Archer in *Yale French Studies* (New Haven), no.17, 1956; "Esquisse d'une théatrographie de Max Ophüls" by Claude Beylie in *Cahiers du cinéma* (Paris), March 1958; "Retrospective Ophüls" by Charles Bitsche and Jacques Rivette in *Cahiers du cinéma* (Paris), March 1958; issue on Ophüls of *Cahiers du cinéma* (Paris), March 1958; "De l'amour de l'art a l'art de l'amour" by Claude Beylie in *Avant-Scène du cinéma* (Paris), 15 April 1963; "Max Ophüls" by Claude Beylie in *Anthologie du cinéma* (Paris), June 1965; issue on Ophüls of *Film Comment* (New York), summer 1971; "Max Ophüls" by Andrew Sarris in *Film Comment* (New York), summer 1971; "The Circles of Desire: Narration and Representation in *La Ronde*" by A. Williams in *Film Quarterly* (Berkeley), fall 1973; "Interview with Ophüls (1950)" by Francis Koval in *Masterworks of the French Cinema* edited by John Weightman, New York 1974; "Distance and Style: The Visual Rhetoric of Max Ophüls" by Fred Camper in *Monogram* (London), no.5, 1974; 2 issues devoted to Ophüls of *Filmkritik* (Munich), November and December 1977.

*   *   *

LA RONDE. Production: Saint-Maurice; black and white, 35mm; running time: 97 mins.; length: 2600 meters. Released 17 June 1950, Paris.

Produced by Sacha Gordine; screenplay by Jacques Natanson and Max Ophüls; from the story "Der Reigen" by Arthur Schnitzler; directed by Max Ophüls; photography by Christian Matras; edited by Leonide Azar; sound operated by Pierre Calvet; production design by Jean d'Eaubonne; music by Oscar Straus, orchestrated by Joe Hajos; costumes designed by Georges Annenkov.

Filmed 23 January 1950-18 March 1950 in Saint-Maurice studios.

Cast: Anton Walbrook (*Master of Ceremonies*); Simone Signoret (*Léocardie, the prostitute*); Serge Reggiani (*Franz, the soldier*); Simone Simon (*Marie, the chambermaid*); Jean Clarieux (*Sergeant*); Daniel Gelin (*Alfred, the young man*); Robert Vattier (*Professor Schuller*); Dannielle Darrieux (*Emma Breitkopf*); Fernand Gravey (*Charles*); Odette Joyeux (*Working girl*); Marcel Merovee (*Toni*); Jean-Louis Barrault (*Robert Kühlenkampf*); Isa Miranda (*Charlotte, the comedienne*); Charles Vissiere (*Theater manager*); Gerard Philipe (*Count*); Jean Ozenne, Jean Landier, Rene Marjac, and Jacques Vertan (*Silhouettes*).

Publications:

Script—"*La Ronde*" (screenplay) by Max Ophüls and Jacques Natanson in *Avant-Scène du cinéma* (Paris), 15 April 1963; books—*Max Ophüls: An Index* by Richard Roud, London 1958; *Max Ophüls* by Georges Annenkov, Paris 1962; *Max Ophüls par Max Ophüls*, Paris 1963; *Max Ophüls* by Claude Beylie, Paris 1963; *French Cinema Since 1946: Vol. I, The Great Tradition* by Roy Armes, New York 1976; *Ophüls* edited by Paul Willemen, London 1978; *Cinema, The Magic Vehicle: A Guide*

With *La Ronde*, Max Ophüls returned home—to France, his adopted country, and in subject matter to Vienna, his spiritual home. After nine years of uneasy exile in America, the film marks the opening of the last, finest phase of his peripatetic career. Its mood of consummate artifice is established in the very first shot. In one long, unbroken take Anton Walbrook, dressed as an elegant man-about-town, strolls on to a sound stage, past lighting equipment, backdrops, and other paraphernalia, chatting urbanely to camera the while; hangs up hat, scarf and cape, wanders into the set of a small lamplit square, in which stands a carousel; steps on to it and—as Simone Signoret's prostitute emerges from the shadows—starts the mechanism. The merry-go-round of love is under way.

"Passion without love, pleasure without love, love without reciprocation"—these, according to Truffaut and Rivette, are the themes that engaged Ophüls, and certainly they sum up *La Ronde*. Each of his chain of characters pursues or is pursued, exploits or is exploited, loves or...is not loved, as the carousel turns; and each encounter centres around the act, or the acting, of love. Schnitzler's play *Reigen* furnished the basis of the film, but his bleak cynicism is transmuted by Ophüls into a bittersweet irony, viewed through a haze of poetic nostalgia. Schnitzler intended his play as a metaphor for the transmission of venereal disease; the film scarcely lends itself to any such reading.

The film, like the play, is set in the Vienna of 1900: present actuality for Schnitzler (though the play's first public performance was not until 1921), but for Ophüls a romantic, fairy-tale city, stylised and charmingly unreal. To the tune of Oscar Strauss's insidious waltz, the infinitely fluid camera which Ophüls made his own leads through an opulent world of boudoirs, cafés, misty streets and *chambres privées*, as each puppet-character repeats the same words, the same gestures, with different partners, at once deceiving and self-deceived. Only the master of ceremonies, the director's alter ego, is granted freedom, able to range through time and identity, proteanly appearing as waiter or coachman to nudge the action on its way, or share an epigram with the audience. Walbrook's subtle, delicate performance, gracefully avoiding the least hint of pretentiousness, holds the centre of the film, while around him circles a dazzling array of the finest acting talent of the period: Signoret, Serge Reggiani, Simone Simon, Danielle Darrieux, Jean-Louis Barrault, Gérard Philipe (the latter two, admittedly, not quite at their best).

La Ronda was Ophüls's most successful, and most widely distributed, film. To audiences everywhere, especially in Britain and North America, it represented the epitome of everything witty, sophisticated and elegant: quintessentially French and Viennese at once. The Oscar Straus waltz became a popular hit. For some years the film was unavailable, due to legal complications, and Vadim's meretricious remake of 1964 offered a distinctly poor substitute. The Ophüls version resurfaced early in the 1980s, its reputation enhanced by its long absence, and proved as stylish and compelling as ever in its exposition of the director's perennial theme: the gulf between the ideal of love and its imperfect, transient reality.

—Philip Kemp

ROOM AT THE TOP. Production: Romulus Films, Ltd.; black and white, 35mm; running time: 115 mins. Released 1958, Britain.

Produced by John and James Woolf; screenplay by Neil Paterson; from the novel by John Braine; directed by Jack Clayton; photography by Freddie Francis; edited by Ralph Kemplen; art direction by Ralph Brinton; music by Mario Nascimbene.

British Academy Awards for Best Film, Best British Film, and Best Foreign Actress (Signoret), 1958; Cannes Film Festival, Best Actress (Signoret), 1959; Academy Awards for Best Actress (Signoret) and Best Screenplay Based on Material from Another Medium, 1959.

Cast: Laurence Harvey (*Joe Lampton*); Simone Signoret (*Alice Aisgill*); Heather Sears (*Susan Brown*); Donald Houston (*Charles Soames*); Donald Wolfit (*Mr. Brown*); Hermione Baddeley (*Elspeth*); John Westbrook (*Jack Wales*).

Publications:

Reviews—by Peter John Dyer in *Films and Filming* (London), February 1959; review by Ellen Fitzpatrick in *Films in Review* (New York), May 1959; review by Jonas Mekas in *The Village Voice* (New York), 29 April 1959; books—*New Cinema in Britain* by Roger Manvell, New York 1969; *A Mirror for England: British Movies from Austerity to Affluence* by Raymond Durgnat, New York 1971; *The Film Business—A History of British Cinema: 1896-1972* by Ernest Betts, New York 1973; *The Great British Picture Show* by George Perry, New York 1974; *Hollywood U.K.* by Alexander Walker, New York 1974; articles—"*Room at the Top?*" by Penelope Houston in *Sight and Sound* (London), spring 1959; "A Free Hand" in *Sight and Sound* (London), spring 1959; article by A.J. Alexander in *Film Culture* (New York), summer 1961; "Commitment and Strait Jacket" by Pauline Kael in *Film Quarterly* (Berkeley), fall 1961; "Laurence Harvey: Following My Actor's Instinct" in *Films and Filming* (London), October 1961; "Clayton's Progress" by Peter Cowie in *Motion* (London), spring 1962; "On Being Under a Director's

Spell" by Simone Signoret in *Films and Filming* (London), June 1962; "The Face of 63: Britain" by Peter Cowie in *Films and Filming* (London), February 1963; "Laurence Harvey" by Alan Stanbrook in *Films and Filming* (London), May 1964; "There'll Always Be Room at the Top for Nothing But the Best" by C.T. Gregory in *Journal of Popular Film* (Bowling Green, Ohio), winter 1973; "*Room at the Top*" by Leslie Donaldson in *Magill's Survey of Cinema, Vol. III* edited by Frank N. Magill, Englewood Cliffs, New Jersey 1980.

* * *

From post-war Britain emerged the syndrome of the angry young man, one intent on overthrowing established social conventions and codes of behavior. In the theatre, John Osborne's *Look Back in Anger* set the pace; in fiction, John Braine's *Room at the Top*. With Jack Clayton's film of the Braine novel, the syndrome became known internationally to film audiences, its central character, Joe Lampton, becoming the epitome of the restless young Englishman fed up with social traditions that made life forever one situated in the lower or middle class.

In this his feature film debut, Clayton displayed a feeling for atmosphere and character delineation that made this study of social, political and sexual behavior one of the most significant and successful British films of the 1950s. Its failure to receive Code approval in the United States only increased its popularity, confirming the notion that the film-going public was ready for more mature films, films that involved a more realistic portrait of current social and sexual realities.

Having spent three years as a prisoner of war, Joe Lampton decides that he is owed more than slavery for his wartime duties and thus he seeks to break through the rigid provincial social structure of the industrial town of Warnley. Convinced that ability is not the key to advancement, he sets his sights on marriage to Susan Brown, the daughter of a local industrialist and community leader. The more his status-seeking is discouraged, the more actively he pursues his goals, bribery, public embarassment and removal of the object of affection all failing to curtail Joe's activities. Almost from the beginning it is clear that Joe's love is not for Susan but for the status she will provide.

Ever the opportunist, Joe takes advantage of the disastrous marital situation of Alice Aisgill, the leading lady of the village theatre group, and before long they are lovers. Alice falls in love; Joe continues to place his priorities on money and status. When Susan returns from her father-induced exile, Joe seduces her, subsequently realizing that while he desires what Susan can provide, his love is for Alice. Joe, however, must pay for his crime. When Susan becomes pregnant, her father attempts to bribe Joe, offering to set him up in business if he agrees never to see Susan again, and, when that fails, forcing him to marry Susan and agree never to see Alice again. Joe now finds himself caught in the web he has constructed, realizing too late that his freedom from social structures is not a function of money and status but of self, that before he can be outwardly free he must be inwardly free. His room at the top may be lined with gold, but the achievement of that position ensures not happiness but misery. The ending of this film is a bitter parody of the conventional happy ending: a two-shot situates the wedding couple, she in her joy, he in his misery, the tightness of the frame depicting the restrictiveness of Joe's new social position.

The success of *Room at the Top* set in motion a new genre of British cinema, the "kitchen sink drama" with its emphasis on social realism. Over the next five years such strong examples as

Saturday Night and Sunday Morning and *This Sporting Life* won international acclaim.

—Doug Tomlimson

ROSEMARY'S BABY. Production: William Castle Enterprises for Paramount Pictures; 1968; Technicolor, 35mm; running time: 137 mins. Released 12 June 1968, New York.

Produced by William Castle with Dona Holloway; screenplay by Roman Polanski; from the novel by Ira Levin; directed by Roman Polanski; photography by William Fraker; edited by Sam O'Steen and Robert Wyman; sound recorded by Harold Lewis and John Wilkinson; production design by Richard Sylbert; art direction by Joel Schiller, set decorated by Robert Nelson; music by Krzysztof Komeda; costumes designed by Anthea Sylbert; make-up by Allan Snyder.

Filmed on location in New York City and Playa del Rey, California. Academy Award, Best Supporting Actress (Gordon), 1968.

Cast: Mia Farrow (*Rosemary Woodhouse*); John Cassavetes (*Guy Woodhouse*); Ruth Gordon (*Minnie Castevet*); Sidney Blackmer (*Roman Castevet*); Maurice Evans (*Hutch*); Ralph Bellamy (*Dr. Sapirstein*); Angela Dorian (*Terry*); Patsy Kelly (*Laura-Louise*); Elisha Cook (*Mr. Nicklas*); Emmaline Henry (*Elsie Dunstan*); Marianne Gordon (*Joan Jellico*); Philip Leeds (*Doctor Shand*); Charles Grodin (*Dr. Hill*); Hanna Landy (*Grace Cardiff*); Hope Summers (*Mrs. Gordon*); Wende Wagner (*Tiger*); Gordon Connell (*Guy's agent*); Janet Garland (*Nurse*); Joan Reilly (*Pregnant woman*); Tony Curtis (*Voice of Donald Baumgart*); William Castle (*Man at telephone booth*).

Publications:

Reviews—by Penelope Gilliatt in the *New Yorker*, 15 June 1968; review by Henry Hart in *Films in Review* (New York), August/-September 1968; review by Rick Lynn in *Cineaste* (New York), fall 1968; review by Andrew Sarris in *The Village Voice* (New York), 25 July 1968; review by Gordon Gow in *Films and Filming* (London), March 1969; books—*The Cinema of Roman Polanski* by Ivan Butler, New York 1970; *Roman Polanski* by Pascal Kané, Paris 1970; *Roman Polanski* by Jacques Belmans, Paris 1971; *American Film Genres* by Stuart Kaminsky, Dayton, Ohio 1974; *Roman Polanski: A Guide to References and Resources* by Gretchen Bisplinghoff and Virginia Wexman, Boston 1979; *The Roman Polanski Story* by Thomas Kiernan, New York 1980; *Polanski: A Biography* by Barbara Leaming, New York 1981; articles—"Polanski in New York", interview by Harrison Engle in *Film Comment* (New York), fall 1968; "*Rosemary's Baby*" by Jack Hamilton in *Look* (Des Moines), 25 June 1968; article by Harlan Ellison in *Cinema* (Beverly Hills), fall 1968; article by Harrison Engle in *Film Comment* (New York), fall 1968; "Entretien avec Roman Polanski" by Michel Ciment and others in *Positif* (Paris), February 1969; "Satisfaction: A Most Unpleasant Feeling", interview by Gordon Gow in *Films and Filming* (London), April 1969; "An Interview with Roman Polanski" by Joel Reisner and Bruce Kane in *Cinema* (Los Angeles), no.2, 1969; "A New Ending to *Rosemary's Baby*"

by Ray Bradbury in *Films and Filming* (London), August 1969; "Still Legion, Still Decent" by Richard Corliss in *Commonweal* (New York), 23 May 1969; "*Rosemary's Baby*" by Marsha Kinder and Beverle Houston in *Sight and Sound* (London), winter 1968-69; "Roman Polanski, *Repulsion*, and the New Mythology" by T. J. Ross in *Film Heritage* (Dayton, Ohio), winter 1968-69; "The Polanski Puzzle" by John Alan McCarty in *Take One* (Montreal), May/June 1969; "Polanski" by Colin McArthur in *Sight and Sound* (London), winter 1968-69; "Roman Polanski" by Tom Nairn in *Cinema* (London), June 1969; "*Rosemary's Baby*" by Robert Chappetta in *Film Quarterly* (Berkeley), spring 1969; "'If You Don't Show Violence the Way It Is,' says Roman Polanski, 'I Think That's Harmful. If You Don't Upset People Then That's Obscenity.' by Bernard Weintraub in the *New York Times Magazine*, 12 December 1971; "Notes on Polanski's Cinema of Cruelty" by J. Leach in *Wide Angle* (Athens, Ohio), v.2, no.1, 1978; "L'Univers de Roman Polanski", special section by M. Amiel and others in *Cinéma* (Paris), February 1980.

*   *   *

That *Rosemary's Baby* was a success at the box office was somewhat surprising. Although based on a best selling book, it was just a "horror film" and the first Hollywood film for Roman Polanski. And though Mia Farrow was widely known because of the publicity surrounding her marriage to and divorce from Frank Sinatra, the film did not feature any major box office stars (an attempt to sign then rising star Robert Redford had not been successful). Perhaps a reason for the favorable response to the film was its emphasis on witches and demons at work in everyday life.

Unlike the traditonal horror setting of dark gloomy castles or strange old houses, *Rosemary's Baby* has a "normal" setting, an apartment building in the middle of New York City. The witches, the evil force behind the plot to "steal" (or at least worship) the baby, are not imposing mysterious figures. They are older men and women who upon first impression seem to be slightly out of step with contemporary fashion and society but otherwise quite harmless. Ruth Gordon's portrayal of Minnie (for which she won an Academy Award) is not that far removed from her role as the lovable Maude of *Harold and Maude* (1971).

The everyday quality is probably most evident in the character of Rosemary and in her pregnancy. The arrival of a baby to the young couple is anything but evil, especially from Rosemary's perspective. A loving wife and a fairly meek person, Rosemary seems to be a hardly likely candidate for a major role in a struggle of good and evil forces. But because the film is shown from her viewpoint, the audience is able to sense her anxiety about her marriage, her pregnancy and the baby conspiracy. By centering on Rosemary, the film creates an ambiguity that the novel lacks. The book clearly shows the devil's forces at work; the film only hints at supernatural powers, and they are mainly conveyed through the fears of an anxious woman. The ambiguity is carried right up to the end when Rosemary the victim behaves as Rosemary the mother.

Rosemary's Baby was very influential in causing the horror genre to focus on the child as evil or as an important element in the cosmic battle between good and evil, God and Devil. *The Other* (1972), *Don't Look Now* (1973), *The Exorcist* (1973) and *The Omen* trilogy certainly follow *Rosemary's Baby* lead. This trend, it has been suggested, may be a cultural reaction to the radical, protesting "children" of the 1960s. America could now see her children as evil and destructive.

—Ray Narducy

SAFETY LAST. Production: Hal Roach Studios; 25 January 1923; black and white, 35mm, silent; running time: about 70 mins.; length: 7 reels, 6300 feet. Released 1 April 1923.

Produced by Hal Roach; screenplay by Sam Taylor, Jean Havez, and Tim Whelan, some sources give script credit to Hal Roach; from an idea by Hal Roach and Sam Taylor; directed by Fred Newmayer and Sam Taylor; photography by Walter Lundin; edited by Fred L. Guiol; art direction by Fred L. Guiol.

Cast: Harold Lloyd (*The Boy*); Mildred Davis (*The Girl*); Bill Strothers (*The Pal*); Noah Young (*The Law*); Westcott B. Clarke (*The Floorwalker*); Anna Townsend (*The Grandma*); Mickey Daniels (*The Kid*).

Publications:

Review—"*Safety Last*" in *The New York Times*, 2 April 1923; books—*An American Comedy: An Autobiography* by Harold C. Lloyd and Wesley W. Stout, New York 1928; *Harold Lloyd's World of Comedy* by William Cahn, New York 1964; *Four Great Comedians: Chaplin, Lloyd, Keaton, Langdon* by Donald W. McCaffrey, New York 1968; *An American Comedy* by Harold Lloyd, New York re-issued 1971; *Yesterday's Clowns* by Frank Manchel, New York 1973; *Harold Lloyd: The Shape of Laughter* by Richard Schickel, Greenwich, Connecticut 1974; *Harold Lloyd: The King of Daredevil Comedy* by Adam Reilly, New York 1977; *The Silent Clowns* by Walter Kerr, New York 1979; *The Comic Mind: Comedy and the Movies* by Gerald Mast, Chicago, revised edition, 1979; articles—"Obit for Samuel Taylor" in *Screen World* (New York), no.10, 1959; "Harold Lloyd" by Nelson E. Garringer in *Films in Review* (New York), August/September 1962; "Interview with Harold Lloyd" by Arthur Friedman in *Film Quarterly* (Berkeley), summer 1962; "The Funny Side of Life" by Harold Lloyd in *Films and Filming* (London), January 1964; "The Serious Business of Being Funny" by Harold Lloyd in *Film Comment* (New York), fall 1969; "Harold Lloyd Talks to Anthony Slide about His Early Career" in *Silent Picture* (London), summer/autumn 1971; "Harold Lloyd, 1893-1971" by Roland Lacourbe in *Avant-Scène du cinéma* (Paris), 1 May 1979; "Harold Lloyd a travers *Hot Water* et *Safety Last*" by L. de la Fuente in *Cinéma 79* (Paris), February 1979.

*   *   *

Approximately one-fourth of *Safety Last* is devoted to a well-known scene involving Harold Lloyd's attempt to scale a skyscraper. Before that sequence, Lloyd is established as a brash young country boy working as a clerk in a big city department store. Audiences, as familiar with the spectacled character as they were with the Little Tramp, knew as soon as they saw Lloyd in the film that he was ambitious, resourceful and willing to do almost anything to make a name for himself.

Early in the film, Lloyd realizes that he is probably going to be late for work. Being ambitious but still afraid of facing the boss, he proceeds to make his way to work as rapidly as possible. The viewer begins to identify with him as the situation is a familiar one. Then the exaggeration comes, but it is the kind of nightmarish exaggeration which confronts the urban dweller—the streetcar is too crowded; he can't find an inch to hang on to. Finally, he lies down in the steet pretending to be sick or hit by a car, and an ambulance arrives to pick him up. As he passes the department store, Lloyd jumps out of the seat of the ambulance and rushes to punch in on the time clock.

A short time later Lloyd plucks up enough courage to see the boss. He pauses outside the door torn between fear and ambition, hesitates, reaches out, changes his mind, and turns in defeat as the door accidently begins to open. He grabs it in desperation and gently closes it, his heart pounding. These are typical Lloyd inventions—they are not simply comic bits, but part of a building of character as well as a striking home of the psychological traumas of modern American living.

The skyscraper sequence begins not with Lloyd choosing to climb the outside of the building, but agreeing to replace his friend, the human fly, who performs this stunt for money. The friend, suddenly pursued by a policeman, cannot begin to climb himself. Lloyd, frightened but loyal and expecting the friend to replace him on the first floor, begins the upward climb. It is psychologically important that Lloyd does not climb the building out of choice; in none of his thrill pictures does he climb out of choice. It is always to help someone else. He is not a fool, but a good friend. As Lloyd reaches each floor, he is met by a new obstacle while his friend passes by on the inside, still pursued by the policeman, and urges Lloyd ever upward. Lloyd's ascent of the skyscraper in *Safety Last* and other films is perhaps semiconsciously metaphorical. Ambition, friendship, and pride drive Lloyd upward as they drive Lloyd and others upward in business or social intercourse in other films. The crowds watch from below encouraging him, not thinking of the danger which increases with each step upward. The potential for falling makes the situation increasingly frightening. The reaction of fear and laughter as Lloyd dangles high above the crowd, clutching the hand of a huge clock, may be in the equivalent of that which is felt in reaction to the handless clock in Ingmar Bergman's *Wild Strawberries*. The reaction to the sequence stems in part from Lloyd's clinging to that mechanical manifestation of the passage of time. It is Lloyd's own time on earth to which he is metaphorically clinging and to which we react.

Safety Last is a comic nightmare that touches the core of human fear.

—Stuart M. Kaminsky

SAIKAKU ICHIDAI ONNA. The Life of Oharu. Production: Shintoho; black and white, 35mm; running time: 148 mins. originally, cut to 133 mins.; length: 13,339 feet originally, cut to 11,970 feet. Released 1952.

Produced by Hideo Koi, Yoshikata Yoda, and Kenji Mizoguchi; screenplay by Yoshikata Yoda and Kenji Mizoguchi; from the novel *Koshuku Ichidai Onna* by Saikaku Ihara; directed by Kenji Mizoguchi; photography by Yoshimi Hirano; edited by Toshio Goto; art direction by Hiroshi Mizutani; music by Ichiro Saito; historical consultant: Isamu Yoshi.

Venice Film Festival, International Prize, 1952.

Cast: Kinuyo Tanaka (*Oharu*); Toshiro Mifune (*Katsunosuke*); Hisako Yamane (*Lady Matsudaira*); Yuriko Hamada (*Yoshioka*); Tsukie Matsura (*Tomo, Oharu's mother*); Ichiro Sugai (*Shinzaemon, Oharu's father*); Toshiaki Konoe (*Lord Tokitaka Matsudaira*); Jukichi Uno (*Yakichi Senya*); Eitaro Shindo (*Kohei Sasaya*); Akira Oizumi (*Fumikichi, Sasaya's friend*); Masao Shimizu (*Kikuno Koji*); Daisuke Kato (*Tasaburo Hishiya*); Toranosuke Ogawa (*Yataemon Isobei*); Eijiro Yanagi (*Daimo Enaka*); Hiroshi Oizumi (*Manager Bunkichi*); Haruo Ichikawa (*Iwabashi*); Kikue Mori (*Myokai, the old nun*); Chieko Hagashiyama; Sadako Sawamura.

Publications:

Review—"*La Vie de O'Haru, femme galante*" by Georges Sadoul in *Les Lettres françaises* (Paris), 11 February 1954; books—*Kenji Mizoguchi* by Ve-Ho, Paris 1963; *Connaissance de Mizoguchi*, Documentation FFCC, no.2, Paris 1965; *Kenji Mizoguchi* by Michel Mesnil, Paris 1965; *Kenji Mizoguchi* by Max Tessier, Paris 1971; *Voices from the Japanese Cinema* by Joan Mellen, New York 1975; *The Waves at Genji's Door: Japan Through Its Cinema* by Joan Mellen, New York 1976; *Japanese Film Directors* by Audie Bock, New York 1978; *Cinema, The Magic Vehicle: A Guide to Its Achievement: Journey Two* edited by Adam Garbicz and Jacek Klinowski, Metuchen, New Jersey 1979; *Il cinema di Kenji Mizoguchi*, Venice 1980; *The Japanese Film: Art and Industry* by Joseph Anderson and Donald Richie, expanded edition, 1982; articles—"*La Vie de O'Haru, femme galante*" by André Bazin in *France Observateur* (Paris), February 1954; "Qui naquit à Newgate..." by Philippe Demonsablon in *Cahiers du cinéma* (Paris), March 1954; "Kenji Mizoguchi" by Donald Richie and Joseph Anderson in *Sight and Sound* (London), autumn 1955; "Retrospective Mizoguchi" by Louis Marcorelles in *Cahiers du cinéma* (Paris), March 1958; "Mes Films" by Kenji Mizoguchi in *Cahiers du cinéma* (Paris), May 1959; "Mizoguchi Kenji" in *Cinéma d'aujourd'hui* (Paris), no.31, 1965; "Souvenirs sur Mizoguchi" by Yoshikata Yoda in *Cahiers du cinéma* (Paris), January 1967; "The Density of Mizoguchi's Scripts", interview with Yoshikata Yoda, in *Cinema* (Los Angeles), spring 1971; "*Saikaku ichidai onna*" by Jonathan Rosenbaum in *Monthly Film Bulletin* (London), March 1975; "Revers de la quiétude" by A. Masson in *Positif* (Paris), November 1978; "Mizoguchi and Modernism" by R. Cohen in *Sight and Sound* (London), spring 1978; "Kenji Mizoguchi" by Donald Richie in *Cinema: A Critical Dictionary* edited by Richard Roud, London 1980; "On Kenji Mizoguchi" by Tadao Sato and Dudley Andrew in *Film Criticism* (Edinboro, Pennsylvania), spring 1980.

*   *   *

The Life of Oharu is surely Kenji Mizoguchi's most important film. Artistically it ended a series of critical failures and indicates the half-dozen masterpieces that close his career. Financially it ultimately made enough money to land Mizoguchi a carte blanche contract with Daiei films, resulting in the artistic freedom he enjoyed at the end. Critically, *Oharu* marks the recognition of Mizoguchi by the West for the film captured top prize at the Venice Film Festival and made him cult hero of *Cahiers du cinéma*. Mizoguchi may have made more perfect films (Wes-

terners prefer *Ugetsu monogatari*; the Japanese choose *Crucified Lovers*), but seldom has a film meant so much to a director and his future.

Beyond these practical considerations, *Oharu* was, of all his films, the one he struggled the longest to get on the screen. The idea of adapting Saikaku's seventeeth-century picaresque classic came to him at the beginning of the war, and he actively sought to produce it once the war had ended. But American restrictions against historical subjects and the evident expense this film would entail frightened all the studios he approached.

When the Americans pulled out of Japan in 1950, Mizoguchi could count eight films made during the occupation, not one of which satisfied him or pleased the critics. He needed a big success more than ever. While shooting the last of these films, he was galled to learn that Akira Kurosawa had received the top prize at Venice for *Rashomon*. How could a young director with only a handful of films and little personal experience win such a prize? In a rare interview Mizoguchi claimed that he had cut down his drinking to extend his life so that he could make at least one great film. No artist, he felt, achieved anything truly great until after he was 50. Mizoguchi was 52 when he said this, and it was clear that from then on he would waste no more time. He wanted greatness. His ambition was matched by that of his longtime leading actress, Kinuyo Tanaka, whose trip to the United States had halted a skid in her artistic reputation. Mizoguchi had been appalled at the gaudy welcome she received at the airport on her return. He shamed her into working with him, and together they agreed to risk their careers on this film.

Mizoguchi was able to subcontract the film from a newly established company through Shin Toho, assuring it some distribution though he would have no studio at his disposal for its production. Filming took place in a bombed-out park midway between Kyoto and Osaka. Every 15 minutes a train between these cities passed nearby, the noise allowing for no more than one of Mizoguchi's invariably long takes at a time; to Mizoguchi the idea of dubbing was unacceptable. Planning went on for days, since he refused to begin until his crane arrived from Kyoto, and until his assistants returned from museums, where they were trying to secure authentic props to replace the copies which had already been prepared. The concentration on the set was legendary. When his chief assistant argued with him over a problem in which Mizoguchi was clearly being unreasonable, he fired the assistant. After an unexpected snowfall he had 30 men spend an exhausting three hours clearing it away, only to scrap the proposed site when he noticed a snow-capped peak in the background.

The film took months to complete and cost 46 million yen. Japan had never seen a film to match its scope and rigor; it was perhaps too taxing a film for Japanese audiences. The intellectuals complained that Mizoguchi had lost Saikaku's irony and humor in his realistic and sympathetic treatment of Oharu. The populace was no doubt frustrated by its length, tempo, and inevitability. The film virtually sank Shin Toho, but the critics continued to discuss it. While it placed only ninth on the annual list of Japan's ten best films, it was selected to represent the country at Venice, where it stunned the jury who awarded it the grand prize.

What made the film so exceptional was the camera perspective which was omniscient yet sympathetic. As Oharu descends from a privileged life at court down the ladder to the untouchable, nameless mendicant nun at the end, she achieves nobility and wisdom. Where Saikaku had parodied her erotic exploits and used her to satirize all levels of Tokugawa culture, Mizoguchi finds her odyssey painful and sacred. She is the purest of all his sacrificing women who suffer at the hands of a male world not worthy of them.

This hagiographic tone is felt in the incredible camera flourishes that terminate so many sequences. The falling of the camera away from the beheading of Toshiro is the most hysterical fall; indeed, its point of rest is a perfect composition, including the sword still glistening from its bloody work. When the family flees in exile from the court, the camera cooly watches them cross the bridge, only to dip under the bridge at the last moment and catch a final glimpse of them passing a single tree far away. The graceful movement here serves to keep the subject in view, but more importantly, it is the melancholy reaction of an observer to a woeful tale. In the final shot Oharu, bowing to the temple, passes out of the frame, allowing the camera to hold on that temple in a sacramental finale that comprehends a life gone so low it is now forever out of view. Long and solemn, *The Life of Oharu* is an immensely mature work of art.

—Dudley Andrew

LA SALAMANDRE. The Salamander. Production: Svociné presented by NEF (Switzerland); black and white, 35mm; running time: 123 mins.; length: 3521 meters. Released 27 October 1971, Paris.

Produced by Alain Tanner; screenplay by Alain Tanner with John Berger; directed by Alain Tanner; photography by Renato Berta and Sandro Bernardoni; edited by Brigitte Sousselier and Marc Blavet; sound (direct) by Marcel Sommerer and Gérard Rhône; music by Patrick Moraz and the Main Horse Airline.

Cast: Bulle Ogier (*Rosemonde*); Jean-Luc Bideau (*Pierre*); Jacques Denis (*Paul*); Veronique Alain (*Suzanne*); Marblum Jéquier (*Paul's girlfriend*); Nathalie (*Paul's daughter*); Marcel Vidal (*Rosemonde's uncle*); Dominique Catton (*Roger*); Daniel Stuffel (*Patron of shoestore*); Violette Fleury (*Patron's mother*); Mista Prechac (*Rosemonde's mother*); Pierre Walker (*Inspector*); Antoine Bordier (*Inspector of civil defense*); Janine Christoffe (*Catherine, Pierre's friend*); Marcel Robert (*Max*); Claudine Berthet (*Zoé*); Guillaume Chenevière (*Poilice inspector*); Jaroslav Vizner (*Policeman*); Michel Viala (*Patron of the housepainter*); Pedro Penas (*Painter*); Jean-Christophe Malan (*Factory foreman*).

Publications:

Scripts—"*La Salamandre*" by Alain Tanner in *Avant-Scène du cinéma* (Paris), May 1972; reviews—"*La Salamandre*: La Critique*" in *Avant-Scène du cinéma* (Paris), May 1972; "*The Salamander*" by E. Callenbach in *Film Quarterly* (Berkeley), winter 1972-73; "*La Salamandre*" by D. Elley in *Films and Filming* (London), June 1973; "*The Salamander*" by V. Radin in *Sight and Sound* (London), spring 1973; "*La Salamandre*" by L. Rubenstein in *Cineaste* (New York), no.1, 1973; articles—"Entretien avec Alain Tanner" by Michel Delahaye, Bernard Eisenschitz, and Jean Narboni in *Cahiers du cinéma* (Paris), June 1969; "Petite Planète du cinéma suisse" by Freddy Bauche in *Cinéma 70* (Paris), September/October 1970; article by Mireille Amiel in *Cinéma 71* (Paris), December 1971; "Les Rideaux arrachés" by Jean-Louis Bory in *Le Nouvel Observateur* (Paris), 25 October 1971; interview with Tanner in *Les Lettres françaises* (Paris), 27 October 1971; "La Suisse en question" in *Avant-Scène du cinéma* (Paris), May 1972; "Entretien avec Alain Tanner" by L. Bonnard in *Positif* (Paris), February 1972; "Alain Tanner—L'Objectivité empêche le pari sur l'avenir" by M. Boujut in *Jeune Cinéma* (Paris), January 1972; "Autres distances longées" by G. Legrand in *Positif* (Paris), February 1972; "Tanner, Goretta, la Suisse et nous" by J. Delmas in *Jeune Cinéma* (Paris), September/October 1973; "The New Swiss Cinema" by F. Bucher in *Jeune/Young Cinema & Theatre* (Prague), winter 1974; "*La Salamandre*" by B. Lafon, D. Guffroy and others in *Image et son* (Paris), 331bis, 1978.

* * *

La Salamandre was Alain Tanner's first collaboration with the noted art critic John Berger, and despite its limitations it remains something of a minor *tour de force*. Tanner's eclectic integration of ersatz cinéma vérité for fictional purposes, elliptical voiceover, and comic vignettes that verge on slapstick make this film the most successfully experimental (and enjoyable) of Tanner's early features.

La Salamandre recounts the attempt of two charmingly inept journalists, Pierre and Paul, to discover the causes of a young working class woman's anti-social behavior. Rosemonde, the woman in question who is accused of attempting to murder her reactionary uncle, provides the film's narrative cynosure. Tanner himself has described Rosemonde as a woman who is unable to adjust to the "conditions of daily work." Her disgust toward the arid conformity that permeates Swiss life serves as the film's thematic focus.

Yet if Rosemonde's unwillingness to respect the strictures of Swiss society provides the film's thematic ballast, her admirable intransigence is always mediated by the bemused detachment of Pierre and Paul who comically struggle to unravel the strands of this enigmatic personality. These two men, essentially archetypal ineffectual intellectuals, are embodiments of Tanner's indictment of the myth of "objective truth" cherished by journalists and film directors alike. Pierre and Paul's pretensions eventually dissolve as Rosemonde, the "salamander," becomes an object of desire rather than an object of dispassionate inquiry.

Like an earlier Tanner feature, *Charles, Dead or Alive*, *La Salamandre* is concerned with a marginal figure's struggle with bureaucratic insensitivity. While the central character in *Charles* finds that his gentle non-conformism is construed as "madness," Rosemonde's half-hearted attempts to hold down a job ultimately politicize her. While she initially has contempt solely for her boss, the film concludes with Rosemonde's astonishingly astute critique of "the army, the state, and the President of the Republic."

La Salamandre is one of the many films of the late 1960s and early 1970s influenced by Jean-Luc Godard. Nonetheless, unlike many other Godard-like films of this period, *La Salamandre* is the product of a truly original sensibility. The film serves as a precursor to Tanner's subsequent, equally distinctive achievements, *Jonah Who Will Be 25 in the Year 2000* and *Messidor*.

—Richard Porton

SALT OF THE EARTH. Production: Independent Productions Corporation and the International Union of Mine, Mill, and Smelter Workers; black and white, 35mm; running time: 92 mins. Released 1954, New York City.

Produced by Paul Jarrico with Sonja Dahl Biberman and Adolfo Barela; screenplay by Michael Wilson with Herbert J. Biberman; directed by Herbert J. Biberman; photography by Leonard Stark and Stanley Meredith, some sources list director of photography as Simon Lazarus; edited by Ed Spiegel and Joan Laird; sound by Dick Stanton and Harry Smith; production design by Sonja Dahl and Adolfo Bardela; music by Sol Kaplan.

Filmed 1953 in the Bayard Region of New Mexico.

Cast: Professional actors: Rosaura Revueltas (*Esperanza Quintero*); Will Geer (*Sheriff*); David Wolfe (*Barton*); Melvin Williams (*Hartwell*); David Sarvis (*Alexander*); Non-professional actors: Juan Chacón (*Ramón Quintero*); Henrietta Williams (*Teresa Vidal*); Ernest Velásquez (*Charley Vidal*); Angela Sánchez (*Consuelo Rúiz*); Joe T. Morales (*Sal Rúiz*); Clorinda Alderette (*Luz Morales*); Charles Coleman (*Antonio Morales*); Virginia Jencks (*Ruth Barnes*); Clinton Jencks (*Frank Barnes*); E.A. Rockwell (*Vance*); William Rockwell (*Kimbrough*); Frank Talavera (*Lúis Quintero*); Mary Lou Castillo (*Estella Quintero*); Floyd Bostick (*Jenkins*); Victor Torres (*Sebastian Prieto*); E.S. Conerly (*Kalinsky*); Elvira Molano (*Mrs. Salazar*); Adolfo Barela and Albert Muñoz (*Miners*); and the men and women of Local 890, International Union of Mine, Mill, and Smelter Workers, Bayard, New Mexico.

Publications:

Scripts—*Il film nella battaglia delle idee* by John Howard Lawson, Milan 1955; "*Le Sel de la Terre*" by Michael Wilson in *Avant-Scène du cinéma* (Paris), June 1971; "*Salt of the Earth*" by Michael Wilson in *Salt of the Earth* compiled by Deborah Silverton Rosenfelt, New York 1978; review—"*Le Sel de la Terre*: La Critique" in *Avant-Scène du cinéma* (Paris), June 1971; books—*Report on Blacklisting I: Movies* by John Cogley, New York 1956; *Salt of the Earth, The Story of a Film* by Herbert Biberman, Boston 1965; *Salt of the Earth* compiled by Deborah Silverton Rosenfelt, New York 1978; articles— "Hollywood Film Writers" in the *Nation* (New York), 15 January 1949; "I.U.M.M.S.W. with Love" in *Time* (New York), 23 February 1953; "Silver City Troubles" in *Newsweek* (New York), 16 March 1953; "Vigilantism Plays the Villain, Silver City, N. Mex." by H. Bloom in the *Nation* (New York), 9 May 1953; "Comment fut tourné *Le Sel de la terre*" by Herbert Biberman and Paul Jarrico in *Cinéma 55* (Paris), March 1955; "Blacklisted" by Patrick McFadden in *Take One* (Montreal), no.5, 1967; interview with Herbert Biberman in *Positif* (Paris), summer 1969; interview with Herbert Biberman in *Jeune Cinéma* (Paris), November 1950; "Un Film qui a une ame" by Gaston Haustrate in *Avant-Scène du cinéma* (Paris), June 1971; "Le Sel de Biberman" (interview with Biberman) by Luce Sand in *Avant-Scène du cinéma* (Paris), June 1971; "*Salt of the Earth*" by R. McCormick in *Cineaste* (New York), no.4, 1973; "Dossier: *Le sel de la terre*" by J. Debacker in *Apec—Revue Belge du cinema* (Brussels), no.4, 1974-75; "Filmmodoffentlighed" by B. Fausing in *Kosmorama* (Copenhagen), autumn 1975; "Ammattiyhdistysliike ja elokuva" by R. Borde in *Filmihullu* (Helsinki, Finland), no. 5, 1976; "Ideology and Structure in *Salt of the Earth*" by D. Rosenfelt in *Jump Cut* (Chicago), 30 December 1979; "*Salt of the Earth*" by P. Jarrico and others in special issue of *Film und Fernsehen* (Berlin), July 1977; "*Du Sel de la terre* à la liste noire" by P. Haudiquet in *Image et son* (Paris), June 1978; "Jordens salt—en klassiker fram i lyset" by

P.R. Hoen in *Filmavisa* (Oslo), no.4, 1978; "*Il Sale della terra*" by G. Turroni in *Filmcritica* (Rome), May 1979; "*La Sal de la tierra*" by C.F. Heredero in *Cinema 2002* (Madrid), November 1979.

* * *

Salt of the Earth was produced as a self-consciously radical film during one of the most repressive periods in American political history. Started by a number of Hollywood's blacklisted, it soon attained the status of a truly collective film enterprise, employing the talent and experience of many of those involved in the real events the film portrays as well as the original group of ousted Hollywood professionals. Because it was conceived as a politically radical statement on working conditions, union organizing, and relations between the races and sexes, *Salt of the Earth* faced official and unofficial harassment from political and industrial leaders whose thinking characterized the McCarthy era.

Salt of the Earth began as a film project when blacklisted producer Paul Jarrico and his family visited a miners' strike in Grant County, New Mexico. Previously, a number of blacklisted Hollywood professionals, including some of the recently released Hollywood Ten, had formed Independent Productions Corporation in 1951 with $10,000 from theater operator Simon Lazarus, and another $25,000 from an array of sympathetic businessmen. The group was unable to decide on a project until Jarrico returned with his suggestion to film a story based on the miners' real experiences in the strike he had just witnessed. Screenwriter Michael Wilson then ventured to Grant County three months prior to the end of the almost one and a half year strike. Wilson made several trips between Los Angeles and Grant County, each time preparing a new script incorporating the input of the miners and their families. In its final form, the film tells a fictionalized story of New Mexico's Union of Mine, Mill, and Smelter Workers strike against Empire Zinc, lasting from October 1950 to January 1952. The strike was characterized by an especially tense and violent atmosphere between Anglos and Chicanos. Ultimately, the miners' wives took over the picket line to avoid a court injunction against the all male union of workers, an event which profoundly affected the Chicano community's attitudes about women's rights. The emotional tensions generated by the strike—between Chicano and Anglo, and when the women walked the picket line, between husbands and wives—are portrayed in their impact on a fictional married couple, Ramon and Esperanza Quintero.

Collective decision-making distinguished not only the script's preparation but all aspects of the film's production, marking an abrupt change in the hierarchical collaboration that characterized Hollywood filmmaking. Most of the roles were filled by the miners themselves and local Anglos, including the male lead Ramon, played by unionist Juan Chacon. The heroine was originally to be played by Gale Sondergaard, already involved in the project, but was finally cast with Rosaura Revueltas, a highly successful Mexican film star. Her participation in the film led to her deportation from the United States, and ultimately to the end of her film career.

The production and post-production of *Salt* was hampered by constant harassment from industrial and political leaders. Hiring a union crew proved impossible as Roy Brewer, red-baiter and head of the I.A.T.S.F., refused to allow union personnel to participate. During the film's shooting, the project and all those involved were denounced by union representatives in Hollywood, the trade press, and Congressman Donald Jackson in the

House of Representatives, all leading to increasing tension in Grant County which hindered the film's completion.

Post-production was impeded not only by Hollywood union recalcitrance but also by Howard Hughes's attempts to organize an industry-wide boycott of the film by post-production facilities throughout the country. The film's exhibition encountered such strong resistance from I.A.T.S.E. projectionists, who under Brewer's orders refused to project the finished film, that it was and still is seen most widely at union activities and outside the United States.

The film is marred aesthetically by these outside pressures, since the tension and violence that marked the final shooting days and Revueltas's deportation necessitated the inclusion of some poor sound footage and mismatched edits. Nevertheless, even today the film presents in its fictionalized account of the strike a powerful statement on workers' conditions, union organizing, and changing relations between women and men and Chicanos and Anglos.

—Michael Selig

SALVATORE GIULIANO. Production: Lux Film and Vides-Galatea (Italy); black and white, 35mm; running time: 125 mins., some sources list 135 mins. Released 1961.

Produced by Franco Cristaldi; screenplay by Francesco Rosi, Suso Cecchi D'Amico, Enzo Provenzale, and Franco Solinas; based on official court records and journalistic reports on the career of Salvatore Giuliano; directed by Francesco Rosi; photography by Gianni Di Venanzo; edited by Mario Serandrei; sound by Claudio Maielli; art direction by Sergio Canevari and Carlo Egidi; music by Piero Piccioni; costumes designed by Marilù Carteny.

Filmed in Sicily. Berlin Film Festival, Best Direction, 1962.

Cast: Frank Wolff (*Gaspare Pisciotta*): Salvo Randone (*President of Viterbo Assize Court*); Federico Zardi (*Pisciotta's defense counsel*); Pietro Camarata (*Salvatore Giuliano*); Fernando Cicero (*Bandit*); Sennuccio Benelli (*Reporter*); Bruno Ekmar (*Spy*); Max Cartier (*Francesco*); Giuseppe Calandra (*Minor official*); Cosimo Torino (*Frank Mannino*); Giuseppe Teti (*Priest of Montelepre*); Ugo Torrente.

Publications:

Reviews—in *Films and Filming* (London), December 1962; review by Robin Bean in *Films and Filming* (London), June 1963; books—*The Italian Cinema Today, 1952-1965* by Gian Luigi Rondi, New York 1966; *Italian Cinema Since the War* by Ken Wlaschin, Cranbury, New Jersey 1971; articles—"A Neapolitan Eisenstein" by John Lane in *Films and Filming* (London), August 1963; "The Face of '63" by J.F. Lane in *Films and Filming* (London), April 1963; article by Robin Bean in *Films and Filming* (London), June 1963; "Francesco Rosi: Interview" in *Film* (London), spring 1964; article by John Thomas in *Film Society Review* (New York), September 1966; article by Maria-Teresa Ravage in *Film Society Review* (New York), October 1971; "The Audience Should Not Be Just Passive Spectators" by Gary Crowdus and D. Georgakas in *Cineaste* (New York), no.1,

1975; "Sono lo psicologo del film e non del personaggio: colloquio con Francesco Rosi" by F.D. Baker in *Cinema nuovo* (Turin) October 1979; "Eisenstein, Rosi, Kieslowski und andere" by G. Netzeband in *Film und Fernsehen* (Berlin), no.12, 1979.

*   *   *

Salvatore Giuliano, a Sicilian bandit who became a force in that island's violent political affairs from the end of World War II until his violent death in 1950, is the subject of the third feature film by Francesco Rosi, former assistant director to Luchino Visconti. But in a real sense it is Sicily—the texture of its land and the interwoven social and political forces which shaped the career of this bandit—that is the true subject of the film.

In many ways *Salvatore Giuliano* produces the effect of documentary. The scenario is based on extensive research into official court records as well as historical and journalistic reports surrounding the career of Giuliano. The confusion of these reports and records is preserved by the fractured structure of the film's narrative.

The non-fictional subject is the basis of a complex structure which relies more on selection of events and reconstruction than on invention. The major structuring device is a voice-over narration, spoken by Rosi himself in the Italian version. This device, along with a few printed titles, accounts for much of the film's documentary impact and serves to specify space and time in the major narrative sections.

The structure alternates events following the bandit's death in 1950 with flashbacks chronicling his career from the end of World War II. Within both the present and the flashback segments, the development is chronological but sharply elliptical. Within the flashbacks, events are selected around certain themes in Sicilian politics and Giuliano's career—the Separatist movement, kidnapping, the attack on a leftist peasant gathering.

The voice-over with its verbal overload of information may contribute as much as the temporal structure to the film's ambiguity. The various sources of power in Sicily—government, Separatists, police, army—are all eventually linked with the mafia, a connection more often implied by juxtaposition of image and voice-over than by direct statement.

Salvatore Giuliano is concerned with Sicily not only in terms of its politics. The film was shot on location, using Sicilian non-professionals as actors. Sweeping camera movements describe the uneven terrain that concealed and protected the bandits from their opponents.

Rosi systematically withholds critical information. The bandit himself is on view as a corpse in the first sequence and then appears briefly several times in the flashbacks, his identity often obscured. And yet Rosi took pains to select an actor who resembled the real bandit. Giuliano's murderer is the closest approximation to a developed character, although he emerges from the background very late in the film.

The lack of emphasis on characters is one clear distinction between this 1961 film and Italian neorealism. There is also, despite the location shooting and the careful research that contributed to the film, a new scepticism regarding the status of photographic reality. In the opening scene, a city official reads a fastidiously detailed description of the death scene, its precision revealing absolutely nothing. In the course of the film the viewer is shown that these apparent circumstances mask a complicated system of deception.

—Ann Harris

SAMMA NO AJI. An Autumn Afternoon. The Widower. Production: Shochiku Co.; Agfacolor, 35mm; running time: 113 mins. Released November 1962, Japan.

Produced by Shizuo Yamanouchi; screenplay by Yasujiro Ozu and Kogo Noda; directed by Yasujiro Ozu; photography by Yushun (or, Yuharu) Atsuta; edited by Yoshiyasu Manamura; sound by Yoshisaburo Senoo; art direction by Tatsuo Hamada; music by Takanobu Saito.

Cast: Chisu Ryu (*Shuhei Hirayama*); Shima Iwashita (*Michiko Hirayama*); Shin-ichiro Mikami (*Kazuo Hirayama*); Keiji Sada (*Koichi Hirayama*); Mariko Okada (*Akiko Hirayama*); Nobuo Nakamura (*Shuzo Kawai*); Kuniko Miyake (*Nobuko Kawai*); Ryuji Kita (*Susumu Horie*); Eijiro Tono (*Sakuma*); Teruo Yoshida (*Miura*).

Publications:

Reviews—"*Le Gout du saké: Fin d'automne*" by R. Bezombes in *Cinématographe* (Paris), November 1978; "*Le Gout du saké*" by J. Magny in *Cinéma* (Paris), December 1978; "*Le Gout du saké et Fin d'automne*" by M. Tessier in *Ecran* (Paris), December 1978; books—*Ozu Yasujiro no Geijutsu* [The Art of Yasujiro Ozu] by Tadao Sato, Tokyo 1971; *Japanese Cinema: Film Style & National Character* by Donald Richie, New York 1971; *Ozu Yasujiro—Hito to Shigoto* [Yasujiro Ozu: The Man and His Work] edited by Jun Satomi and others, Tokyo 1972; *Transcendental Style in Film: Ozu, Bresson, Dreyer* by Paul Schrader, Berkeley 1972; *Anthologie du cinéma* vol.7, Paris 1973; *Ozu* by Donald Richie, Berkeley 1974; *Masters of Japanese Film* edited by Leonard Schrader and Haruji Nakamura, Tokyo 1975; *Japanese Film Directors* by Audie Bock, New York 1978; *To the Distant Observer* by Noel Burch, Berkeley 1979; articles—"Flavour of Green Tea over Rice" by Tom Milne in *Sight and Sound* (London), autumn 1963; "The Face of '63—Japan" by Donald Richie in *Films and Filming* (Lonon), July 1963; "Yasujiro Ozu: Syntax of His Films" by Donald Richie in *Film Quarterly* (Berkeley), winter 1963-64; special Ozu issue of *Kinema Jumpo* (Tokyo), February 1964; "Yasujiro Ozu" by Chisu Ryu in *Sight and Sound* (London), spring 1964; "Ozu" by Akira Iwasaki in *Film* (London), summer 1965; article by Tung in *Film Quarterly* (Berkeley), winter 1965-66; "Ozu" by Manny Farber in *Artforum* (New York), June 1970; "Ozu Spectrum" by Haruji and Leonard Schrader in *Cinema* (Beverly Hills), no.1, 1970; "Yasujiro Ozu" by Jean-Claude Philippe in *Dossiers du Cinéma: Cinéastes* no.1, Paris 1971; "The Zen Artistry of Yasujiro Ozu" by Marvin Zeman in *Film Journal* (New York), fall/winter 1972; "Ozu" by Jonathan Rosenbaum in *Film Comment* (New York), summer 1972; "The Zen Artistry of Yasujiro Ozu: The Serene Poet of Japanese Cinema" by Marvin Zeaman in *Film Journal* (New York), fall/winter 1972; "Space and Narrative in the Films of Ozu" by Kristin Thompson and David Bordwell in *Screen* (London), summer 1976; "*Le Gout du saké*" by J.C. Biette in *Cahiers du cinéma* (Paris), January 1979; "*Le Gout du saké*" by J. Delmas in *Jeune Cinéma* (Paris), December/January 1979; "Bien definir et bien peindre (sur *Le Gout du saké* et *Fin d'automne*)" by A. Masson in *Positif* (Paris), January 1979; "*Le Gout du saké*" by G. Colpart in *Revue du cinéma* (Paris), series 23, 1979; "Ozu" by Donald Richie in *Cinema, A Critical Dictionary* edited by Richard Roud, London 1980.

*　　*　　*

The title of Yasujiro Ozu's last film, *Samma no aji (An Autumn Afternoon)*, literally "taste of autumn swordfish," symbolizes the ordinary in life, and represents another contemplative study of the serenity of Japanese middle-class family life.

Ozu's characteristic stylistic techniques are evident here. The film begins with a series of shots of chimneys from different angles, and proceeds to the corridor of an office building preparing our introduction to a company executive, Mr. Hirayama—an editing pattern common in Ozu's work. Another characteristic Ozu device is the use of a number of shots of restaurant and bar signs appearing for several seconds before the story inside the restaurant develops. We soon lose track of how often we witness the character enjoying a conversation over food and drink. All of these scenes are very deliberately composed, including the placement of food, dishes, and beer bottles. The movements of the characters seem carefully choreographed throughout these scenes. We are shown in detail a high-school reunion, casual gossip between intimate friends, and discussions of household topics among couples and family members.

The film's central plot is the arrangement of the marriage of Hirayama's daughter, Michiko, further developed by other marriage-related subplots. For example, Hirayama's old high school teacher and his old maid daughter make Hirayama realize his duty to arrange Michiko's marriage despite his own loneliness which will surely continue. We also see Michiko's older brother's trifling marriage problems; Michiko's unsuccessful love for her brother's friend; Hirayama's friend's happy remarriage to a younger wife; Hirayama's secretary's marriage; and Hirayama's encounter with a bar maid who reminds him of his deceased wife.

Subplots such as these are developed in a lengthy, carefully edited conversation scenes. Ozu frequently uses frontal, close-up shot-reverse shots of characters' faces (occasionally including unmatching eyelines). Indeed, the film's narrative is developed more in these conversations and less by direct actions. Each dialogue is extremely concise, often omitting subjects and objects in the sentences, making it impossible to translate directly in the English subtitles.

Ozu is obsessed with showing the empty space after any action takes place. After Michiko leaves her house on the wedding day, a series of shots showing her empty room during the day and at night are used to accentuate the emptiness after her departure. Particularly, the close-up shots of the big mirror and the vacated stool force us to realize that she, sitting there in her wedding gown just moments before, is now gone. The pathos is suggested by the systematic arrangement of shots of inanimate objects.

Through the depiction of the non-dramatic atmosphere of peaceful human relationships between good-willed people, the film conveys the feeling of the quiet realization of the loneliness in life. It is deftly symbolized by the sequences at the bar where Hirayama drinks, listening nostalgically to the Japanese Navy march, and then, at home, drinks water silently in the kitchen at the end of the corridor.

The audience and critics appreciated the distinctive loneliness of Ozu's world all the more for the light and even humorous nature of many of *An Autumn Afternoon*'s individual scenes.

—Kyoko Hirano

———

LE SANG DES BÊTES. Blood of the Beasts. Production: Forces et Voix de France; black and white, 35mm; running time: about 20 mins.; length: 600 meters. Released 1949.

Produced by Paul Legros; screenplay by Georges Franju, commentary by Jean Painlevè; directed by Georges Franju; photography by Marcel Fradetal assisted by Henri Champion; edited by Andre Joseph; sound engineered by Raymond Vachere; music by Joseph Kosma; assistant directors: André Joseph and Julien Bonardier.

Filmed 1949 in a slaughterhouse outside Paris.

Cast: Nicole Ladmiral and Georges Hubert (*spoken parts*).

Publications:

Script—"*Le Sang des bêtes* by Georges Franju and Jean Painlevè in *Avant-Scène du cinéma* (Paris), October 1964; books—*Anarchist Cinema* by Alan Lovell, London 1962; *French Cinema Since 1946: The Personal Style*, Vol. II, by Roy Armes, New York, 1966; *Franju* by Raymond Durgnat, Berkeley 1968; *Georges Franju* by Gabriel Vialle, Paris 1968; articles—"Aspects of French Documentaries" by Claude Goretta in *Sight and Sound* (London), winter 1956-57; "Franju" by Cynthia Grenier in *Sight and Sound* (London), spring 1957; "Georges Franju" by Jean-Luc Godard in *Cahiers du cinéma* (Paris), December 1958; issue on Franju in *Image et son* (Paris), March 1966; "Franju" by G. Gow in *Films and Filming* (London), August 1971; "The Films of Luis Buñuel and Georges Franju" by A. MacLochlainn in *Film Journal* (New York), summer 1971; "Terrible Buildings: The World of Georges Franju" by Robin Wood in *Film Comment* (New York), November/December 1973; "*Le Sang des bêtes* de Franju" in *Avant-Scène du cinéma* (Paris), 15 October 1976; "*Thérèse Desqueroux* and *Le Sang des bêtes*" by Nick Barbaro in *Cinema Texas Program Notes* (Austin), 27 April 1978; "1952—*Bloedbad op de kring*" by C. Boost in *Skoop* (Amsterdam), August 1981.

*   *   *

The unique tone of Georges Franju's best work—which includes *Le Sang des Bêtes*—arises from its combination of hypersensitivity to pain (inseparable from an obsession with it) with an extraordinary poise. The peculiar distinction of his work goes inextricably with its very limited range: he is one of the cinema's authentic minor poets.

Although *Hôtel des Invalides* (Franju's masterpiece) is more complex, and although one would not wish to be without the other documentaries and many characteristic, privileged moments in the features, *Le Sang des Bêtes* already contains, in a form at once concentrated and comprehensive, all the major components of the Franju *oeuvre*. It is a film totally at odds with the Grierson school of documentary filmmaking (i.e. the task of documentary is to explain the world to us so that we can all understand each other): "understanding, " to Franju, is the realization that civilization is constructed upon pain and horror and cannot be extricated from them.

The opening of the film—typically casual and disarming—establishes the location of the slaughterhouse. It is carefully set apart from the city that depends upon its activities, so that those who devour its products may be spared awareness of its existence, and of the physical realities of its interior. Separating it from Paris is a no-man's land where a young worker kisses his girlfriend goodbye, and where the debris of civilization—a heterogeneous, quasi-Surrealist assortment of junk objects

divorced from their domestic contexts and deposited on the wasteland grass—is offered for sale, second-hand. The sequence (before we are introduced to any of the film's horrors) establishes with gentle irony and tenderness, a sense of the absurd and the arbitrary, of a world that never confronts the oddity of what it terms "reality."

The slaughterhouse itself is the first in the long succession of "terrible buildings" that provide Franju's work with one of its dominant recurrent motifs. It is a building at once thoroughly familiar as everyone knows that slaughterhouses exist, but also hidden away because no one wants to confront or know about them. We are briefly shown the tools of slaughter. Then a white horse is led in through the gate. No one who has seen the film ever forgets the moment when a so-called humane killer is casually applied to its head and fired. From that moment on, the film spares us nothing of the details of slaughter, disembowellment, dismemberment. What is remarkable about the film is the way in which it scrupulously avoids, on the one hand, sadistic relish, and, on the other, the note of protest. Everything is shown calmly, dispassionately, generally at a distance. If a close-up is used, it is to clarify a detail of method or procedure. If the film converts some spectators to vegetarianism, this is purely incidental, a by-product of the audience's exposure to material they would prefer not to know about. The film is at once far more ambitious and far less presumptuous: it wishes to make us confront, with neither hysteria nor coercion, an aspect of the material reality on which our civilization is based.

—Robin Wood

LE SANG D'UN POÈTE. The Blood of the Poet. Black and white, 35mm; running time: 58 mins. Released 1930.

Produced by Vicomte de Noailles; screenplay by Jean Cocteau; directed by Jean Cocteau; photography by Georges Périnal; sound by Henri Labrély; production design by Jean Gabriel d'Aubonne; music by Georges Auric.

Cast: Lee Miller (*The Statue*); Enrico Rivero (*The Poet*); Jean Desbordes (*The Louis XV Friend*); Féral Benga (*The Black Angel*); Pauline Carton; Odette Thalazac; Fernand Dichamps; Lucien Jager; Barbette; Jacques Cocteau (*Narrator*).

Publications:

Scripts—*The Blood of a Poet*, translated by Lily Pons, New York 1949; *Le Sang d'un poète* by Jean Cocteau, Monaco 1957; *Two Screenplays* by Jean Cocteau, translated by Carol Martin-Sperry, New York 1968; books—*Jean Cocteau* by Margaret Crosland, London 1955; *Jean Cocteau chez les sirènes* by Jean Dauven, Paris 1956; *Cocteau* by Jean-Jacques Kihm, Paris 1960; *Jean Cocteau tourne son dernier film* by Roger Pillaudin, Paris 1960; *Cocteau* by André Fraigneau, New York 1961; *Jean Cocteau: The History of a Poet's Age* by Wallace Fowlie, Bloomington, Indiana 1968; *Jean Cocteau: The Man and the Mirror* by Elizabeth Sprigge and Jean-Jacques Kihm, New York 1968; *Jean Cocteau* by Roger Lannes, Paris 1968; *Cocteau* by René Gilson, translated by Ciba Vaughn, New York 1969; *Professional Secrets: an Autobiography of Jean Cocteau Drawn from his Lifetime Writings* edited by R. Phelps, New York 1970; *French*

Cinema Since 1946: Vol. I, The Great Tradition by Roy Armes, 1970; *Cocteau* by Francis Steegmuller, Boston 1970; *Cocteau on the Film*, New York 1972; articles—"The Blood of a Poet" by C.G. Wallis in *Kenyon Review* (Gambier, Ohio), winter 1944; "On Cocteau" by Neal Oxenhandler in *Film Quarterly* (Berkeley), fall 1964; "*Le Sang d'un poète*" in *Image et son* (Paris), March 1972; "Jean Cocteau et le cinéma", special issue by C. Gauteur of *Image et son* (Paris), June/July 1972; "La vita del poeta" by M. Campigli in *Bianco e nero* (Rome), March/April 1973; "Rétrospective. Jean Cocteau. Un cinéaste? Peut-être. Un auteur? Certainement." by T. Renaud in *Cinéma* (Paris), December 1973; "*Sang d'un poète*" by T. Rayns in *Monthly Film Bulletin* (London), May 1977; "The Mirrors of Life" by Gordon Gow in *Films and Filming* (London), February 1978.

*   *   *

Though the 1920s are generally considered the most significant years of experiment with filmic forms in French cinema, two of the acknowledged masterpieces of the avant-garde, Jean Cocteau's *Le Sang d'un poète* and Luis Buñuel's *L'Age d'or*, both date from the beginning of the sound era in the early 1930s. The bitter opposition, feuds and mutual denunciations existing at this time between Cocteau and the Surrealists seem in retrospect of less importance than the common avant-garde impulse which unites them. Significantly both *Le Sang d'un poète* and Buñuel's film were funded in exactly the same way, through private commissions by the wealthly art lover and socialite, the Vicomte de Noailles. Despite their differences and incompatibilities both films have proved to be lasting works of cinematic imagination. They provide a common inspiration for later independent filmmakers throughout the world.

Jean Cocteau came to the cinema as an amateur who had already acquired a literary reputation, though he was never concerned with the application of literary ideas or practices to film. Instead he saw filmmaking as a manual craft and gave far greater weight to the qualities of the film image than to the demands of a conventional narrative development. As *Le Sang d'un poète* shows so clearly, he was a filmmaker able to disregard the conventionalities of cinematic construction simply because he never learned them in the first place. His essentially amateur approach is reflected in his choice of non-professional players for most of the key roles of the film. This did not preclude him from calling upon highly talented collaborators with real professional skills—such as George Périnal or Georges Auric—to assist him with the photography and music for *Le Sang d'un poète*.

Cocteau has often denied that *Le Sang d'un poète* contains either symbols or allegorical meaning. It uses some of the mechanics of the dream, not to explore social or psychological realities, but as ends in themselves. His concern is less to analyze than simply to recreate a state of inner consciousness, a world preceding rational thought. To this end he applies a whole range of trick devices—animation, mirrors, reverse action, false perspectives—and deliberately blurs the boundaries between the live action and graphic work or sculpture. Though haunted, like so much of Cocteau's work, by the omnipresence of death, *Le Sang d'un poète* is a lyrical, idyllic work without tension or conflict. In Cocteau's mythology, death is reversible, just one aspect of a constant play of transformation. It is the director's ability to present this in a totally personal manner—aided by the first-person narration spoken by Cocteau himself—which makes the film such a fascinating work.

Le Sang d'un poète introduces a distinctive new voice to world cinema. It contains an initial statement of virtually all the guiding themes of Cocteau's film work, and since it was followed by a dozen or more years of silence, it has a hauntingly premonitory quality. The wealth of themes and obsessions it contains is brought out clearly by the rich series of films from *La Belle et la bête* to *Le Testament d'Orphée* which Cocteau made when he returned to film directing after World War II. Both as a work in its own right and as a forerunner of the director's later feature work, *Le Sang d'un poète* has lost nothing of its power to fascinate and intrigue.

—Roy Armes

SANSHO DAYU. Sansho the Bailiff. Production: Daiei (Kyoto); black and white, 35mm; running time: 119 mins., some sources list 123 mins.; length: 11,070 feet. Released 1954.

Produced by Masaichi Nakata; screenplay by Yahiro Fuji and Yoshikata Yoda; from the novel by Ogai Mori; directed by Kenji Mizoguchi; photography by Kazuo Miyagawa; edited by Mitsuji Miyata; sound engineered by Iwao Otani; production design by Kisaku Ito with Uichiro Yamanoto and Nakajima Kozaburo; music by Tamekichi Mochizuki, Fumio Hayasaka, and Kanahichi Odera, traditional music by Shinichi; costumes designed by Yoshio Ueno; consultant on ancient architecture: Giichi Fujiwara.

Venice Film Festival, Silver Prize, 1954.

Cast: Kinuyo Tanaka (*Tamaki/Nakagimi*); Yoshiaki Hanayagi (*Zushio, his son*); Kyoko Kagawa (*Anju, his daughter*); Eitaro Shindo (*Sansho*); Ichiro Sugai (*Nio, Minister of Justice*); Bontaro Miyake (*Kichiji*); Yoko Kosono (*Kohagi*); Chieko Naniwa (*Ubatake*); Kikue Mori (*Miko*); Ken Mitsuda (*Morosane Fujiwara*); Masao Shimizu (*Masaji Taira, the father*); Ryosuke Kagawa (*Ritsushi Ummo*); Akitake Kono (*Tara, Sansho's son*); Kanji Koshiba (*Kudo*); Shinobu Araki (*Sadayu*); Masahiko Kato (*Zushio, a boy*); Keiko Enami (*Anju, young girl*); Naoki Fujima (*Zushio, as small boy*); Teruko Taigi (*The other Nakagimi*); Reiko Kongo (*Shiono*).

Publications:

Script—"*L'Intendant Sansho*" by Yoshikata Yoda and Yahiro Fuji in *Avant-Scène du cinéma* (Paris), 1 May 1979; reviews—"La Presse" in *Avant-Scène du cinéma* (Paris), 1 May 1979; "*L'Intendant Sansho*" by G. Gauthier in *Image et son* (Paris), April 1980; "*L'Intendant Sansho*" by G. Gourdon in *Cinematographe* (Paris), April 1980; "La Bruit des vagues" by Y. Tobin in *Positif* (Paris), November 1980; books—*Kenji Mizoguchi* by Ve-Ho, Paris 1963; *Mizoguchi Kenji* by Michel Mesnil, Paris 1965; *Mizoguchi Kenji no hito to geijutsu* [Kenji Mizoguchi: The Man and His Art] by Yoshikata Yoda, Tokyo 1970; *Kenji Mizoguchi* edited by Michel Mesnil, Paris 1971; *Kenji Mizoguchi* by Max Tessier, Paris 1971; *Voices from the Japanese Cinema* by Joan Mellen, New York 1975; *The Waves at Genji's Door: Japan Through Its Cinema* by Joan Mellen, New York 1976; *Cinema, The Magic Vehicle: A Guide to Its Achievement: Journey Two* edited by Jacek Klinowski and Adam Garbicz, Metuchen, New Jersey 1979; *Il cinema di Kenji Mizoguchi*, Venice 1980; *The Japanese Film: Art and Industry* by Joseph Anderson and

Donald Richie, revised edition, Princeton 1982; articles—issue on Mizoguchi of *Cinéma 55* (Paris), no.6, 1955; "Kenji Mizoguchi" by Joseph Anderson and Donald Richie in *Sight and Sound* (London), autumn 1955; "L'Art de Kenji Mizoguchi" by Jean-Luc Godard in *Art* (Paris), no.656, 1958; issue on Mizoguchi of *Cahiers du cinéma* (Paris), March 1958; issue on Mizoguchi of *Ecran* (Paris), February/March 1958; "Dossier Mizoguchi" in *Cahiers du cinéma* (Paris), August/September 1964; "Souvenirs sur Mizoguchi" by Yoshikata Yoda in *Cahiers du cinéma* (Paris), no.174, 1966; "Kenji Mizoguchi" by Akira Iwasaki in *Anthologie du cinéma* (Paris), November 1967; "The Density of Mizoguchi's Scripts", interview with Yoshikata Yoda, in *Cinema* (Los Angeles), spring 1971; "The Ghost Princess and the Seaweed Gatherer" by Robin Wood in *Film Comment* (New York), March/April 1973; "Keeping Our Distance" by J. Coleman in *New Statesman* (London), 20 February 1976; "L'Espace de Mizoguchi" by H. Bokanowski in *Cinématographe* (Paris), November 1978; "Mizoguchi and Modernism" by R. Cohen in *Sight and Sound* (London), spring 1978; "L'Intendant Sansho, ou des vertus de la piété filiale" by Max Tessier in *Avant-Scène du cinéma* (Paris), 1 May 1979; "On Kenji Mizoguchi" by Tadao Sato and Dudley Andrew in *Film Criticism* (Edinboro, Pennsylvania), spring 1980; "Kenji Mizoguchi" by Donald Richie in *Cinema: A Critical Dictionary* edited by Richard Roud, London 1980.

* * *

Sansho Dayu can be taken as representing the ultimate extension and one of the supreme achievements of a certain tendency in the world cinema, the tendency celebrated in the critical writings of André Bazin and associated with the term "realism." The only way in which the term is useful, and not actively misleading, is if it is applied to specific stylistic options. (Clearly, Mizoguchi's late films are not "realistic" in the sense in which a newsreel is "realistic.") The following features are relevant.

1. *The Long Take*, tending to the sequence-shot. Mizoguchi developed a long-take technique quite early in his career; in Japan, he was frequently criticized as old-fashioned ior not adopting the editing techinques of western cinema. One must distinguish, however, between the sequence-shots of *Sisters of Gion* (1936), for example, and those of *Sansho Dayu*. As Nöel Burch has convincingly argued in *To the Distant Observer*, the earlier type of long take, where the camera is held at a great distance from the characters, remaining static for long stretches of the action, with its occasional movements maintaining emotional and physical distance, is peculiarly Japanese, rooted in elements of a national aesthetic tradition. The sequence-shots of late Mizoguchi, on the contrary, are compatible with certain practices of western cinema, for example, the works of Wyler, Welles and Ophuls. Whether one is content to say, with Burch, that Mizoguchi *succumbed* to the Western codes of illusionism, or whether one places the stress on his plastic realization of their full aesthetic and expressive potential, doubtless depends on one's attitiude to the codes themselves.

2. *Camera Movement*. The clinical detachment with which the camera views the characters of *Sisters of Gion* is replaced in the late films by an extremely complex tension between comtemplation and involvement. The camera moves in the great majority of shots in *Sansho Dayu*, sometimes identifying us with the movements of the characters, sometimes (perhaps within a single shot) withdrawing us from them to a contemplative distance. The film's famous closing scene contains particularly beautiful examples in the two shots that frame it: in the first, the camera

begins to move *with* Zushio at the moment he hears his mother's voice and is drawn towards it, then cranes up to watch the movements towards reunion, until the mother is also visible within the frame; in the last shot of film, the camera moves upward away from the reunited couple, to reveal the vast seascape and the solitary figure of the old seaweed-gatherer, his task now completed.

3. *Depth of field*. Again and again Mizoguchi makes marvellously expressive use of simultaneous foreground and background action. That something is amiss with the priestess's plan for the family travel by sea is subtly hinted by the presense, in distant long-shots, of a small hunched figure sinisterly scuttling away as the family walks to the water. The impact of the following sequence of the kidnapping and separation of mother and children is largely created by their being kept consistently within the frame as Mizoguchi cuts back and forth between the mother's struggles and the children's struggles, so that we are continuously aware of the widening distance between them.

It is true that this bringing to perfection of a certain kind of cinematic art in Mizoguchi's last period coincides with a shift to a more conservative ideological position. The rage against oppression and cruelty is still there, but it is now heavily qualified by resignation, by a commitment to notions of spiritual transcendence. However, the tradition that feeds the film is rich and complex, and one must honor—whatever one's own political position—an art that brings such a tradition to its fullest realization.

—Robin Wood

SATURDAY NIGHT AND SUNDAY MORNING. Production: Woodfall Film Productions; black and white, 35mm; running time: 89 mins. Released October 1960, London.

Produced by Tony Richardson, executive producer: Harry Saltzman; screenplay by Alan Sillitoe; from the novel by Alan Sillitoe; directed by Karel Reisz; photography by Freddie Francis; edited by Seth Holt; sound by Peter Handford and Bob Jones, sound edited by Chris Greenham; art direction by Ted Marshall; music composed and conducted by John Dankworth.

British Academy Awards for Best British Film, Best British Actress (Roberts) and Most Promising Newcomer (Finney), 1960.

Cast: Albert Finney (*Arthur Seaton*); Shirley Ann Field (*Doreen Gretton*); Rachel Roberts (*Brenda*); Hylda Baker (*Aunt Ada*); Norman Rossington (*Bert*); Bryan Pringle (*Jack*); Robert Cawdron (*Robboe*); Edna Morris (*Mrs. Bull*); Elsie Wagstaff (*Mrs. Seaton*); Frank Pettitt (*Mr. Seaton*); Avis Bunnage (*Blowzy woman*); Colin Blakely (*Loudmouth*); Irene Richmond (*Doreen's mother*); Louise Dunn (*Betty*); Peter Madden (*Drunken man*); Cameron Hall (*Mr. Bull*); Alister Williamson (*Policeman*); Anne Blake (*Civil defense officer*).

Publications:

Reviews—by Gordon Gow in *Films and Filming* (London), December 1960; review by Harold Dunham in *Films in Review* (New York), April 1961; review by Peter John Dyer in *Sight and*

Sound (London), winter 1960-61; review by Elizabeth Sutherland in *Film Quarterly* (Berkeley), summer 1961; books—*New Cinema in Britain* by Roger Manvell, London 1969; *A Mirror for England* by Raymond Durgnat, London 197o; *Hollywood U.K.: The British Film Industry in the 60's* by Alexander Walker, New York 1974; *A Critical History of the British Cinema* by Roy Armes, New York 1978; *Karel Reisz* by Georg Gaston, Boston 1980; articles—in *Films and Filming* (London), August 1960; "From 'Free Cinema' to Feature Film: Interview" in the *London Times*, 19 May 1960; "Karel Reisz: Free Czech" in *Films and Filming* (London), February 1961; article by Pauline Kael in *Film Quarterly* (Berkeley), fall 1961; "Talking About Acting: Albert Finney and Mary Ure" by Louis Marcorelles in *Sight and Sound* (London), spring 1961; "Movie and Myth" by Geoffrey Nowell-Smith in *Sight and Sound* (London), spring 1963; "An Interview with Karel Reisz" by Gene Phillips in *Cinema* (Beverly Hills), summer 1968; "*Saturday Night and Sunday Morning*" by Alan Sillitoe in *Masterworks of the British Cinema*, New York 1974; "Minute Reisz: 6 Earlier Films" by H. Kennedy in *Film Comment* (New York), September/October 1981.

*   *   *

Saturday Night and Sunday Morning came roughly at the midpoint of the cycle of British social realist or "kitchen sink" films (so-called for their penchant for depicting working class domestic situations) which appeared in the late 1950s and early 1960s.The use of location shooting in the film—the streets of a Northern industrial town, a factory, blocks of row houses and their cramped interiors—suggest the documentary backgrounds of director Karel Reisz and producer Tony Richardson in the short-lived "Free Cinema" movement, and their debt to Italian neo-realism. Like other films of the cycle, the screenplay was adapted from a story by Alan Sillitoe, one of a new generation of British writers and playwrights who took working class characters as their subject matter; the narrative centers on a rebellious and fiercely individualistic character, Arthur Seaton (played by Albert Finney speaking in Northern dialect); and the film was characterized by a degree of sexual frankness new to the British cinema.

Critics in Britain and the United States praised *Saturday Night* enthusiastically at the time of its release and the low budget film was a significant financial success. Twenty years later, *Saturday Night* holds up better than many other films of this cycle. This is due in part to Albert Finney's charismatic performance in the leading role, as well as to Reisz's controlled style—he avoids attempts at pyschological realism through expressionist shots which badly date similar films directed by Richardson. The film offers an unusually sympathetic presentation of the female characters with whom Arthur is involved: the married woman, Brenda, who becomes pregnant and tries in vain to obtain an abortion, and the fiancee, Doreen, who tries to be cynical, smart and tough to avoid "getting caught" and ending up, as her mother did, with a husband who deserts her. *Saturday Night* avoids the usual "battle of the sexes" approach to the hero's relationship to the two women and explores the social implications of the dilemma facing working class women about sexuality and its consequences.

Most important, the film remains an exceptionally vivid portrait of British working-class life: how the tedium of Arthur's job as a lathe operator haunts him even during his precious leisure time, and the vital importance in his life of making love with women, drinking at the pub or fishing with a friend. Like the hero of *The Loneliness of the Long Distance Runner* (also written by

Sillitoe), Arthur's class consciousness and analysis of his own social position are astute, and he has none of the middle class aspirations and personal ambition of the angry young heros of *Room at the Top* and *A Kind of Loving*. "What I'm out for is a good time," Arthur says, "all the rest is propaganda." Like all the British social realist films of this period, *Saturday Night and Sunday Morning* envisions no means of resistance other than Arthur's not "letting the bastards grind you down," and the tone of the film is ultimately one of despair.

—Ellen Seiter

———————

SCARFACE. The Shame of the Nation. Production: Atlantic Pictures; 1932; black and white, 35mm; running time: 99 mins. Released April 1932, New York, as *Scarface: The Shame of the Nation*.

Produced by Howard Hughes and Howard Hawks; screenplay by Ben Hecht, Seton I. Miller, John Lee Mahin, and W.R. Burnett, with Fred Palsey; from the novel by Armitage Trail; directed by Howard Hawks; photography by Lee Garmes and L.W. O'Connell; edited by Edward Curtis; sound by William Snyder; production design by Harry Olivier; music by Adolph Tandler and Gus Arnheim; assistant director: Richard Rosson.

Filmed during spring and summer 1931.

Cast: Paul Muni (*Tony Camonte*); Ann Dvorak (*Cesca Camonte*); Karen Morley (*Poppy*); Osgood Perkins (*Johnny Lovo*); Boris Karloff (*Gaffney*); George Raft (*Guido Rinaldo*); Vince Barnett (*Angelo*); C. Henry Gordon (*Inspector Guarino*); Ines Palance (*Tony's mother*); Edwin Maxwell (*Commissioner*); Tully Marshall (*Editor*); Harry J. Vejar (*Big Louis Costello*); Bert Starkey (*Epstein*); Henry Armetta (*Pietro*); Maurice Black (*Sullivan*); Purnell Pratt (*Publisher*); Charles Sullivan and Harry Tembrook (*Bootleggers*); Hank Mann (*Worker*); Paul Fix (*Gaffney hood*); Howard Hawks (*Man on bed*); Dennis O'Keefe (*Dance extra*).

Publications:

Script—"*Scarface*" by Ben Hecht in *Avant-Scène du cinéma* (Paris), January 1973; reviews—excerpts of French reviews in *Avant-Scène du cinéma* (Paris), January 1973; books—*The Cinema of Howard Hawks* by Peter Bogdanovich, New York 1962; *Howard Hawks* by Jean-Claude Missiaen, Paris 1966; *Howard Hughes* by John Keats, London 1967; *Howard Hawks* by Robin Wood, London 1968, revised 1977; *Bashful Billionaire* by Albert B. Gerber, New York 1968; *Howard Hawks* by Jean A. Gili, Paris 1971; *We're in the Money: Depression America and Its Films* by Andrew Bergman, New York 1971; *Actor—The Life and Times of Paul Muni* by Jerome Lawrence, New York 1974; *Paul Muni—His Life and Films* by Michael B. Druxman, New York 1974; *George Raft* by Lewis Yablonsky, New York 1974; *The George Raft File: The Unauthorized Biography* by James Robert Parish and Steven Whitney, New York 1974; *The Films of Howard Hawks* by D.C. Willis, Metuchen, New Jersey 1975; *The Great Gangster Pictures* by James R. Parish and Michael Pitts, Metuchen, New Jersey 1976; *Howard Hawks, Storyteller* by Gerald Mast, New York 1982; articles—

"Community Stands on Its Rights" by C.M. Wright in *Christian Century* (Chicago), 3 August 1932; "The Gangster as Tragic Hero" by Robert Worshow in *Partisan Review* (Nutley, New Jersey), February 1948; "Howard Hawks" by Jacques Rivette and François Truffaut in *Films in Review* (New York), November 1956; "Paul Muni" by Jack Jacobs in *Films in Review* (New York), November 1961; "The World of Howard Hawks" by Andrew Sarris in *Films and Filming* (London), July 1962 and August 1962; "Howard Hawks" by Henri Agel in the *New York Film Bulletin*, no.4, 1962; issue on Hawks of *Cahiers du cinéma* (Paris), January 1963; issue on Hawks edited by W.-E. Bühler of *Filmkritik* (Munich), May/June 1973; "3 klassiske gangsterfilm og deres baggrund" by S. Kjørup i n *Kosmorama* (Copenhagen), August 1973; "Howard Hawks e le possibilità del cinema" by G. Frezza in *Filmcritica* (Rome), May 1974; "Scarface" by Claude Beylie in *Ecran* (Paris), January 1975; "Demonology" by K. Cooney in *Movietone News* (Seattle), April 1975; "Film Festival II: Nostalgic Gamble" by Andrew Sarris in *The Village Voice* (New York), 15 October 1979; "Scarface: Shame of a Nation" by Gregory William Mank in *Magill's Survey of Cinema, Vol. III* edited by Frank N. Magill, Englewood Cliffs, New Jersey 1980; "Un Maelstrom de violence" by A. Jourdat in *Cinématographe* (Paris), December 1980; "Scarface" by T. Pulleine in *Monthly Film Bulletin* (London), August 1980.

*   *   *

Scarface was one of the three major films (along with *Little Caesar* and *Public Enemy*) that defined the American gangster genre in the early 1930s. Of the three, *Scarface* was simultaneously the most violent and the most humorous; it was also the most controversial. Its gleeful depiction of the gangster's life as brutal fun lacked the mean, growling swagger of *Little Caesar* and the sociological analysis of *Public Enemy*. For two years, Howard Hughes, the film's producer, battled with the industry's censors, who only allowed the film's release with the deletion of some scripted material (for example, a scene showing an elected public official as a paid collaborator of the gangsters) and the addition of other material (a morally sententious scene in which the newspaper publisher implores a group of public-spirited citizens to stop the gangster menace by taking some sort of public action on election day). Even with the censorship and the changes, the film was cited as an example of what the industry would try to avoid when it implemented its Hollywood Production Code two years later. As a result of the controversy the film has been seen far less often in America (especially on television) than the other two major gangster films, and for decades the film could only be shown legally in Europe. (Hughes's death allowed his estate to find an American distributor for it.)

Much of the power of *Scarface* derives from its director, Howard Hawks, and the choices he made. Rather than make a film of snarling gangsters, he decided to treat the gangsters as children playing games, having fun—since Hawks felt that the gangsters who talked to him about their adventures always sounded like children. Another Hawks decision was to turn the leading gangster's affection for his sister into a repressed, unexplored, and unarticulated form of incest so that the gangster himself does not understand the power and shape of feelings for her. As Hawks told his chief writer for the film, Ben Hecht, the intention was to get the Borgia family into Chicago, and the script for the film made explicit references to incest and the Borgias (scenes either deleted by the censors or removed by Hawks himself, who preferred to give less away). The incest motif underlies the plot of the film, which turns when the leading gangster, Tony Camonte, kills his best friend, Guido Rinaldo, because he believes Guildo is sleeping with his sister.

In casting his film, Hawks found several minor or unknown players to fit the roles. Paul Muni, a noted actor from New York with roots in the Yiddish theater, played his first major film role as Tony Camonte. Hawks claimed that he found George Raft, who played Tony's best friend, at a prizefight. Raft's nervous, perpetual flipping of a coin occurs for the first time in this film; the action has since become a cultural icon of movie gangsterism duplicated decades later in the "Broadway Melody" ballet of *Singin' in the Rain*, when two dancing thugs flip coins in unison, and by a minor thug in *Some Like It Hot*, an act which occasions George Raft himself to ask, "Where'd you learn that cheap trick?" For the role of Cesca Camonte, Tony's sister, Hawks found Ann Dvorak, a lithe, sharp-talking mixture of toughness and softness who would become the prototype for all Hawksian women in future films. And for the role of "Dope," Tony's comic "seckatary," Hawks found the quirky character actor Vince Barnett, who provides most of the film's comedy by being a secretary who cannot write and can never even remember who the caller is or what the message might be.

The overall shape of *Scarface* reveals the classic narrative of the gangster's rise and fall, roughly patterned on the same tragic model as Shakespeare's *Macbeth*: the gangster climbs to the top by taking action against his betters, then falls from that summit when he is deserted by his own allies and underlings. The first scene of the film is one of its most memorable, a very lengthy traveling shot, extended in both time and space in which we watch a shadowy, whistling figure (only later identified as Tony) murder the gangster who then sits at the "top of the world." At the end of the film Tony himself will be gunned down (by the police, not by one of his own), and as he dies in the gutter an electric sign above him ironically flashes, "The World Is Yours—Cook's Tours." The shadowy irony of the film's opening shot and the cynical irony of its final image enclose a narrative full of other ironic, comic, or subtle touches that are clearly lacking from the other major films of this type. Tony's fall is precipitated not by the forces of law in the film (who are shown to be totally inept or unable to contain the gangster menace) but by Tony himself. The murder of his best friend (like Macbeth's murder of Banquo) and the death of his sister, whom he loved not wisely but well, lead to his emotional breakdown and collapse. His resolution to die "with harness on his back," like Macbeth, shooting gleefully at the police from his heavily armored lair, collapses when his sister dies from a stray police bullet—turning Tony into a puling, weeping coward.

Among the other memorable scenes in the film is a violently comic sequence which juxtaposes the brutal clashing of machine-gun bullets, spraying a restuarant with deadly destruction, with Dope's comic attempts to take a telephone message for Tony. Dope keeps complaining that he is unable to hear the message because of all the noise from the crashing glass around him. This method of deflection dominates the film to produce its wry, ironic, understated tone; deflecting a scene from a brutal gun battle to a comic telephone conversation, deflecting emotion from brutal words to a flipping coin, deflecting Tony's motivation to a smothered and incomprehensible love for his own sister, deflecting the gangster menace to a series of childhood games.

The irony and deflection not only makes *Scarface* unique among gangster films but makes it consistent with the other films of its director, Howard Hawks. Hawks enjoys depicting the lives of professionals who do their work well and love what they do. In this film, those professionals are gangsters. Hawks also comments on a related group of professionals in the film—newspaper reporters and editors—who do not condemn the gangster menace but excitedly exploit the gangsters' activities—to sell more newspapers. Hawks would return to this theme—the conflict between morality and professionalism in the newspaper world—in *His Girl Friday*. Still another of the film's delights (equally true of *Public Enemy* and *Little Caesar*) was the pleasure of simply listening to the private lingo and argot of tough gangsters. The gangster film was born with the talkies, at least partially because listening to the slang was a major delight of the genre.

—Gerald Mast

THE SCARLET EMPRESS. Production: Paramount Pictures, Inc.; black and white, 35mm; running time: 109 mins. Released 7 September 1934.

Screenplay credited to Josef von Sternberg; adapted from a diary of Catherine the Great by Manuel Komroff; directed by Josef von Sternberg; photography by Bert Glennon; production design by Hans Dreier, Peter Balbusch, and Richard Kollorsz; music by Tchaikovsky and Mendelssohn, music arranged by John Leipold and W. Frank Harling, additional music by Josef von Sternberg; special effects by Gordon Jennings; costumes designed by Travis Banton.

Cast: Marlene Dietrich (*Sophia Fredericka, or Catherine II*); John Lodge (*Count Alexei*); Sam Jaffe (*Grand-Duke Pierre*); Louise Dresser (*Elizabeth*); Maria Sieber (*Catherine as a child*); C. Aubrey Smith (*Prince August*); Ruthelma Stevens (*Countess Elizabeth*); Olive Tell (*Princess Johanna*); Gavin Gordon (*Gregory Orloff*); Jameson Thomas (*Lieutenant Ovtsyn*); Hans Von Twardowski (*Ivan Shuvolov*); Erville Anderson (*Chancelor Bestuchef*); Marie Wells (*Marie*); Edward Van Sloan (*Herr Wagner*).

Publications:

Review—"*The Scarlet Empress*" by Andre Sennwald in *The New York Times*, 15 September 1934; books—*An Index to the Films of Josef von Sternberg* by Curtis Harrington, London 1949; *Marlene Dietrich—Image and Legend* by Richard Griffith, New York 1959; *Fun in a Chinese Laundry* by Josef von Sternberg, New York 1965; *The Films of Josef von Sternberg* by Andrew Sarris, New York 1966; *Josef von Sternberg, Dokumentation, Eine Darstellung*, Mannheim, Germany 1966; *Josef von Sternberg* by Herman G. Weinberg, Paris 1966; *Josef von Sternberg: A Critical Study* by Herman G. Weinberg, New York 1967; *Anthologie du cinéma, Vol 6*, Paris 1971; *The Cinema of Josef von Sternberg* by John Baxter, New York 1971; articles—"Comment Marlène Dietrich est devenue star" by Maurice Dekobra in *Cinémonde* (Paris), 16 April 1939; "Josef von Sternberg" by Curtis Harrington in *Cahiers du cinéma* (Paris), October/November 1951; "Marlene Dietrich" by Arthur Knight in *Films in Review* (New York), December 1954; "Josef von Sternberg" by Herman G. Weinberg in *Film Heritage* (Dayton, Ohio), winter 1965; "6 Films of Josef von Sternberg" by O.O. Green in *Movie* (London), summer 1965; article on von Sternberg and Dietrich in *Positif* (Paris), May 1966; "On Sternberg" by Herman G. Weinberg in *Sight and Sound* (London), summer 1967; "Thoughts on the Objectification of Women" by Barbara Martineau in *Take One* (Montreal), November/December 1970;

"Alchemy: Dietrich + Sternberg" by Gordon Gow in *Films and Filming* (London), June 1974; "Sternberg's Empress: The Play of Light and Shade" by Robin Wood in *Film Comment* (New York), March/April 1975; "Riflessi in un occhio velato (*La Bestia—Scarlet Empress*)" by A. Cappabianca in *Filmcritica* (Rome), April 1976; "*The Scarlet Empress*" by T. Flinn in *Velvet Light Trap* (Madison, Wisconsin), fall 1976; "*The Scarlet Empress*" by T. Pulleine in *Monthly Film Bulletin* (London), June 1978; "Some Observations on Sternberg and Dietrich" by C. Zucker in *Cinema Journal* (Evanston), spring 1980; "Josef von Sternberg" by Herbert Luft in *Films in Review* (New York), January 1981.

*   *   *

The Scarlett Empress was the penultimate work in the series of six films Josef von Sternberg made with Marlene Dietrich for Paramount—a series made possible by the international success of *The Blue Angel*. The series must stand, taken *in toto*, as one of the most remarkable achievements within the Hollywood cinema, and *The Scarlett Empress* as one of its peaks, yet its relationship to that cinema is highly ambiguous. Scarcely conceivable outside the studio/star/genre system, the films were progessively unsuccessful at the box office, and increasingly frowned upon by the studio bosses. The reasons for this are complex. First, von Sternberg (like Orsen Welles after him) broke the fundamental rule of classical Hollywood cinema by attempting consistently to assert himself as an "artist" through elaboration of a highly idiosyncratic personal style; whereas Ford, Hawks and Lang, for example, were able to develop, quite unobtrusively, personal styles that did not conflict with the law of authorical invisibility. Secondly the tone of the films proved increasingly disconcerting. One superficial level, they seemed frivolous and cavalier (and audiences perhaps suspected that, if there *was* a joke, they themselves were its ultimate butt); on a deeper level the films were disturbingly intense and obsessional.

Critics, committed to characteristically unsophisticated bourgeois notions of what is serious (*The Blue Angel*) and what isn't (*The Scarlett Empress*), missed the deeper level altogether, repudiating the films as decadent exercises in "style" with no "content," as though the two were logically separable. Von Sternberg's own pronouncements have unfortunately endorsed this view, describing the film's subjects as "fatuous" and declaring his own exclusive interest in "the play of light and shade." Sergei Eisenstein acknowledged the influence of *The Scarlett Empress* on his own *Ivan the Terrible*, (leaving aside obvious similarities of imagery, they do have the same essential subject, the perversion of sexuality into the power drive). Generally, however, the two works have been assigned to quite distinct categories: *Ivan the Terrible* is a work of art, *The Scarlett Empress* an example of "camp." But in fact, a scrupulous analysis of the films will reveal that von Sternberg's is no less serious than Eisenstein's.

The matter of levels is important. *The Scarlett Empress* defines meticulously the level on which it is serious and the level on which it isn't. It is *not* serious about Russian history: the intermittent facetiousness (John Lodge ridiculing Catherine's old-fashioned notions of conjugal fidelity on the grounds that "this is the eighteenth century") is there to repudiate the meretricious solemnity of the Hollywood historical epic. It *is* serious about sexuality and gender roles. Dietrich's complex star persona involves the difficulties surrounding a woman's assertion of autonomy in a world created and dominated by men. *The Scarlett Empress* develops her persona to one of its extremes. The film's imagery is amazingly dense, suggestive and systematic: for example, the dissolve from the young Catherine innocently clutching her doll to the "adult" doll of the Iron Maiden; or the progression from the child's innocent question "Can I be a hangman some day?" through the intricate bell imagery that recurs throughout, to the moment when the adult Catherine rings the bell that is the sign for the assassination of her husband and her seizure of absolute power. The action of the film is dominated by women throughout, but by women who have accepted patriarchal roles and thereby become monstrous. Catherine herself, her natural desires frustrated and perverted, becomes the ultimate monster, cynically using her sexuality as a weapon. Her growing assumption of the male role is answered by the increasingly feminization of her husband (at the climax, she is in soldier's uniform, he in a flowing white nightgown). The culmination is one of Hollywood's most ambiguous and devastating happy endings: the heroine triumphs over all adversity—at the expense of her humanity, and perhaps her sanity.

—Robin Wood

SCHATTEN. Production: Pan-Film for Dafu Film Verlieh; black and white, 35mm, silent; running time: 62 mins. currently, but original version was longer. Released 1923.

Screenplay by Arthur Robison and Rudolf Schneider; from an idea by Albin Grau; directed by Arthur Robison; photography by Fritz Arno Wagner; edited by Arthur Robison; production design by Albin Grau; originally accompanied by a score by Ernst Riege; costumes designed by Albin Grau.

Cast: Fritz Kortner (*Husband*); Alexander Granach (*Mesmerist*); Ruth Weyher (*Wife*); Gustav von Wangenheim (*Lover*); Max Gülstorff, Eugen Rex and Ferdinand von Alten (*Cavaliers*); Fritz Rasp (*Manservant*); Lilli Herder (*Maid*); Karl Platen.

Publications:

Books—*The Film Till Now* by Paul Rotha, London 1930; *The Haunted Screen* by Lotte Eisner, Berkeley 1969; *From Caligari to Hitler: A Psychological History of the German Film* by Siegfried Kracauer, fifth printing, Princeton, New Jersey 1974; articles—in *Bioscope*, 20 November 1924; "The Rise and Fall of the German Cinema" by Harry Potamkin in *Cinema* (New York), April 1930; "I Believe in Sound Film" by Fritz Arno Wagner in *Film Art*, no.8, 1936; "*Schatten*" by T. Rayns in *Monthly Film Bulletin* (Paris), June 1975; article in *Close-Up* (London), October 1975.

* * *

Schatten combines with great power and unity of purpose the talents of painter Albin Grau, the film's originator who also designed the sets and costumes, the cameraman Fritz Arno Wagner, and the director-scriptwriter Arthur Robison. The action of the film is compressed to one evening and, apart from an introductory title and an explanation in the middle, the story is told in entirely visual terms. The plot concerns a flirtatious wife, a jealous husband, an indiscreet lover, three philanderers and a sinister servant. Tragedy is impending; a travelling shadow

theater showman hypnotizes the characters and lets them see the directions in which their follies will take them. The lesson is learned. The wife and husband are reconciled and the lover departs at dawn. The intensity of the action and the simplification of the characters is representative of Expressionism as is the chiaroscuro lighting which heightens the mood. An air of unreality is deliberately sought and mirror reflections take us further from the concrete action. This makes it quite easy to accept the marvellous scene of the dinner table viewed slightly from above and from the side, when the shadows of the characters stretch away from them and the magic of the unreal begins.

The beautiful period settings and costumes carry a romantic air, consistent with the film's style and action. The performances of the actors are controlled, and the powerful and dynamic Fritz Kortner dominates the film, creating a tension which never falters. Alexander Granach gives an impish performance as the Mesmerist. Though his contribution to the German Cinema was considerable, he will best be remembered as the disgruntled Commissar Kowalsky in the Garbo-Lubitsch *Ninotchka*.

A unity of space is preserved allowing the transactions from the dining room to hall and the corridors outside the bedroom to be effectively managed. Details impinge on our consciousness— the ropes that will bind the wife, the candelabra held by the husband, the swords that will be forced into the cavaliers' hands, all take on a new meaning and significance.

Expressionism was the simultaneous simplification and heightening of mood, atmosphere, and "feeling" to suggest the essence of an action or thought-process. As such it was highly subjective style—both exaggerated and neurotic. Expressionism came at the time of national tension in Germany and found its exponents in the theater as well as in literature and painting. Many of the actors from the stage were trained in Expressionist theater, and that influence is very evident in *Schatten*.

The fact that this film was made for ordinary cinema distribution indicates how rich popular film culture was at the time. Films such as *Schatten*, today viewed as rare classics in cineclubs and specialized cinemas, were in their day part and parcel of ordinary film-going entertainment.

Perfect films like this were not without their influence. Much of the innovative camera work and visual style has been absorbed into the accepted techniques of the cinema. But there is a special patina which the pioneer film has that can never be transmitted and that is the excitement generated by an original and creative spirit; *Schatten* is unique in the history of film, and unlike anything its creator, Arthur Robison, ever attempted again.

—Liam O'Leary

SCIUSCIA. Shoeshine. Production: Alfa Cinematografica (Italy); black and white, 35mm; running time: 93 mins.; length: 8340 feet. Released 1946.

Produced by P.W. Tamburella; screenplay by Cesare Zavattini, Sergio Amidei, A. Franci, Cesare Giulio Viola, and Vittorio De Sica; from a story by Zavattini; directed by Vittorio De Sica; photography by Anchise Brizzi; edited by Nicolo Lazzari; production design by Ivo Batteli; music by A. Cicognini.

Cost: less than 1 million lire.

Cast: Franco Interlenghi (*Pasquale*); Rinaldo Smordoni (*Giuseppe*); Amiello Mele (*Raffaele*); Bruno Otensi (*Archangeli*);

Anna Pedoni (*Nannarella*); Enrico de Silva (*Giorgio*); Antonio Lo Nigro (*Righetto*); Emilio Cigoli (*Staffera*); Angelo D'Amico (*The Sicilian*); Antonio Carlino (*Inhabitant of the Abruzzes*); Francesco De Nicola (*Ciriola*); Pacifico Astrologo (*Vittorio*); Maria Campi (*Palmreader*); Leo Garavaglia (*Commissioner*); Giuseppe Spadare (*The advocate*); Irene Smordoni (*Giuseppe's mother*).

Publications:

Review—by J. Doniol-Valcroze in *Revue du cinéma* (Paris), February 1947; books—*Italian Cinema 1945-1951* edited by Luigi Malerba, Rome 1951; *Il cinema neorealistico italiano* by G.C. Castello, Turin, 1956; *Il neorealismo italiano* by Brunello Rondi, Parma, 1956; *Il nuovo cinema italiano* by Giuseppe Ferrara, Florence 1957; *Vittorio De Sica* by Henri Agel, 2nd ed, Paris 1964; *Vittorio De Sica* by Pierre Leprohon, Paris 1966; *What is Cinema?, Vols. I and II* by André Bazin, translated by Hugh Gray, Berkeley 1971; *Patterns of Realism* by Roy Armes, Cranbury, New Jersey 1971; *Literary and Socio-Political Trends in Italian Cinema* by Benjamin Ray Lawton, Los Angeles 1971; *Italian Cinema Since the War* by Ken Wlaschin, Cranbury, New Jersey 1971; *Cinema, The Magic Vehicle: A Guide to Its Achievement: Journey One: The Cinema Through 1949* edited by Jacek Klinowski and Adam Garbicz, Metuchen, New Jersey 1975; articles—"De Sica Dissected" by R.F. Hawkins in *Films in Review* (New York), May 1951; "The Most Wonderful Years of My Life" by Vittorio De Sica in *Films and Filming* (London), December 1955; "Bread, Love, and Neo-Realism" by W. Sargeant in the *New Yorker*, 29 June 1957 and 6 July 1957; "Why Neo-Realism Failed" by Eric Rhode in *Sight and Sound* (London), winter 1960-61; "Poet of Poverty" by Douglas McVay in *Films and Filming* (London), October and November 1964; "Le Cinéma du néo-realisme italien est en berne: Vittorio de Sica" by J.-L. Passek in *Cinéma* (Paris), January 1975; issue on De Sica of *Bianco e nero* (Rome) edited by O. Caldiron, September/December 1975; "Shoeshine" by Nick Barbaro in *Cinema Texas Program Notes* (Austin), 22 November 1977; "Vittorio De Sica 1902-1974" by Henri Agel, special issue of *Avant-Scène du cinéma* (Paris), 15 October 1978; "Vittorio De Sica, 1902-1974" by Henri Agel in *Anthologie du cinéma, Vol. X*, Paris 1979; "Dossier: le neo-realisme: De Sica 'le menteur'" by P. Carcassonne in *Cinématographe* (Paris), January 1979.

*   *   *

Vittorio De Sica's first major film, *I bambini ci guardano*, the account of a broken marriage as seen through the eyes of a child, was also his first significant attempt at the social realism which would characterize his pre-1960s films. From the beginning he explained that his films were a protest "against the absence of human solidarity, against the indifference of society towards suffering. They are a word in favor of the poor and the unhappy." *I bambini ci guardano* was De Sica's first collaboration with screenwriter Cesare Zavattini. Their fruitful partnership produced the most admired films of neorealism—*Sciuscia* and *Ladri di biciclette*. Each is an extraordinary indictment of the social circumstances which existed during post-Fascist Italy; *Sciuscia* is uncompromisingly tragic, while *Ladri di biciclette*, tempered by less cruelty, conveys a sense of tenderness.

Sciuscia is a neologism coined by the shoe-shine boys of Rome. These youngsters plied their trade to American soldiers who were among those few able to afford this minor luxury in a country filled with unemployment and poverty following the war. The embryo for the film was the result of De Sica's close observation of two shoe-shine boys in the streets of Rome. He studied their habits, their hand-to-mouth existence, and their dealing in black market contraband. Inevitably, he recalled, the two boys were arrested for stealing a gas mask and sent off to a reformatory. They were victims, he said, of "the legacy from war...the drama was not invented by me but staged by life instead, drawing to its fatal conclusion." He related his story to Zavattini who fashioned it into a screenplay, resulting in a major neorealist film. *Sciuscia* emphasized the creators' commitment to showing, through actual incidents, "the indifference of humanity to the needs of others."

De Sica uses two non-professional actors and the streets of Rome to tell of the two boys, Pasquale and Giuseppe, who shine shoes and become involved in crime in order to raise money to buy a white horse. Their black market activities get them arrested and sent to reform school where, supposedly, they will be rehabilitated. Reformatory life turns out to be far more harsh and corrupt than life on the streets and in their struggle for survival they betray each other resulting in the death of Giuseppe. The anguish of all suffering humanity is displayed in Pasquale's unforgettable cry of despair at the end of the film.

Though *Sciuscia* was universally hailed by critics as a work of art, it was by no means a financial success. The Academy of Motion Picture Arts and Sciences presented De Sica with a special Academy Award describing the film as "an Italian production of superlative quality made under adverse circumstances." *Sciuscia* was successful only in art houses and De Sica would later say, "*Shoeshine* was a disaster for the producer. It cost less than a million lire but in Italy few people saw it as it was released at a time when the first American films were reappearing...."

At the time of its American release, James Agee's first response was, "*Shoeshine* is about as beautiful, moving, and heartening a film as you are ever likely to see." Soon after he recanted these remarks, describing it as "the raw, or at its best, the roughed-out materials of art" rather than the perfected work of art he had first thought. Such critical reassessment has diminished the reputation of most of De Sica's work and today he is often written off as a minor director. Yet for many, including Orsen Welles, his films retain a poeticism and sincerity. In 1960, Welles said, "I ran his *Shoeshine* recently and the camera disappeared, the screen disappeared; it was just life...."

—Ronald Bowers

SCORPIO RISING. Color, 16mm; running time: 29 mins. Released 1963.

Scripted, directed, photographed, and edited by Kenneth Anger; music by Little Peggy March, The Angels, Bobby Vinton, Elvis Presley, Ray Charles, The Crystals, The Ron-dells, Kris Jensen, Claudine Clark, Gene McDaniels, and The Surfaris.

Filmed in Brooklyn and Manhattan.

Cast: Bruce Bryon (*Scorpio*); Johnny Sapienza (*Taurus*); Frank Carifi (*Leo*); John Palone (*Pinstripe*); Ernie Allo (*Joker*); Barry Rubin (*Fall Guy*); Steve Crandall (*Blondie*); Bill Dorfman (*Back*); Johnny Dodds (*Kid*).

Publications:

Review—"The Current Cinema: Easeful Death" by Brendan Gill in the *New Yorker*, 23 April 1966; books—*Magick Lantern Cycle: A Special Presentation in Celebration of the Equinox Spring 1966* by Kenneth Anger, New York 1966; *Expanded Cinema* by Gene Youngblood, New York 1970; *History of the American Avant-Garde Cinema* edited by The American Federation of Arts, New York 1976; *Visionary Film: The American Avant-Garde* by P. Adams Sitney, New York 1979; articles— "*Scorpio Rising* (1st Impressions After a 1st Viewing)" by Gregory Markopoulos in *Film Culture* (New York), winter 1963-64; "Thanatos in Chrome" by Ken Kelman in *Film Culture* (New York), no.31, 1963-64; "Imagism in 4 Avant-Garde Films" by P. Adams Sitney in *Film Culture* (New York), winter 1963-64; "*Scorpio Rising*" by Gregory Markopoulos in *Film Culture* (New York), no.31, 1964; "Art in Court: City of Angels vs. *Scorpio Rising*" by Fred Haines in *Nation* (New York), 14 September 1964; "Kenneth Anger's *Scorpio Rising*" by Carolee Schneeman in *Film Culture* (New York), spring 1964; "2 Films and An Interlude by Kenneth Anger" by Harris Dietsfrey in *Artforum* (New York), 1965; "*Spider* Interviews Kenneth Anger" in *Spider*, 15 April 1965; interview with Anger in *Film Culture* (New York), spring 1966; "San Francisco's Hipster Cinema" by Thomas Kent Alexander in *Film Culture* (New York), no.44, 1967; "Kenneth Anger" by Bruce Martin and Joe Medjuck in *Take One* (Montreal), no.6, 1967; "On Kenneth Anger" by Regina Cornwall in *December*, no.1, 1968; "Lucifer: A Kenneth Anger Kompendium" by Tony Rayns in *Cinema* (Cambridge), October 1969; "The Avant-Garde: Kenneth Anger and George Landow" by P. Adams Sitney in *Afterimage* (Rochester, New York), no.2, 1970; "Kenneth Anger: Master in Hell" by Robin Hardy and "Kenneth Anger: Personal Traditions and Satanic Pride" by Michael Wade in *Body Politic*, April 1982.

*   *   *

Scorpio Rising, a landmark in the American underground film, confirmed Kenneth Anger's reputation as a major talent and, at the time of its release, created a stir which reached from the pages of New York's *Film Culture* to the courts of California, where it was judged obscene. It is testimony to the film's aesthetic power that 20 years later it continues to shock and dismay as many viewers as it amuses and exhilarates through its artfully subversive reinterpretation of the American mythos.

A product of the period which produced Andy Warhol's Brillo boxes and Roy Lichtenstein's comic-strip canvases, *Scorpio Rising* is a pop-art collage of found artifacts which submerges itself in the crome-and-leather, skull-and-swastika iconography of the motorcycle cult that provides its subject. (Anger shot many scenes using an actual Brooklyn biker's club.) Yet, almost instantly, the film extends these symbols of machismo to include the entirety of American culture via the re-reading of its popular imagery. Structured around 13 "top forty" songs from the period in which it was made (1962-63), *Scorpio Rising* mounts a dialectical collision between images and music to reveal the strains of romanticized violence, morbidity and homoeroticism just beneath the surface of "Dondi" and "Li'l Abner," of Brando's and Dean's rebels, of hit tunes by Rick Nelson, Elvis Presley and Martha and the Vandellas. The juxtaposition of the Angel's "My Boyfriend's Back" with shots of a biker working on his machine, for example, not only suggests the violent eroticism and fetishization inherent to the cycle cult, but reveals the open brutality of the song's lyrics as well, implicating the whole civilization in its imagery of obsession. And when Anger plays Bobby Vinton's "Blue Velvet" over a loving tilt up a biker's jeans as he zips his fly, the effect is both erotic and a savage parody of eroticism as it is packaged by the culture industry.

Scorpio Rising's short-circuitry of traditional readings of familiar objects ultimately represents the joyous celebration of the dawning of the Age of Scorpio, the erratic astrological sign associated with chaos, and the concomitant downfall of the ascetic and repressed reign of Christianity. In the film's most notorious juxtaposition, Anger poses this cosmological convulsion by a clever intercutting of a black-and-white Sunday School movie of the last days of Christ (set, in part, to the Crystals' "He's a Rebel") with profanely contrasting scenes from a biker's "Walpurgisnacht." The multiple layering of subversive associations generated by Anger's various techniques of collision provides the basically non-narrative means by which *Scorpio Rising* drives toward its disturbing, yet cathartic conclusion. It is a method equally explicit in his punning description of the film as "A conjuration of the presiding Princes, Angels and Spirits of the Sphere of MARS, formed as a 'high' view of the American Motorcyclist. The Power Machine seen as tribal totem, from toy to terror. Thanatos in chrome and black leather and bursting jeans."

Clearly, *Scorpio Rising* has had its influence, from the found-footage collages of Bruce Conner to the pop-flash sound and color imagery of *American Graffiti*. Yet the film remains one of a kind in terms of the immediacy and savagery of its critique. Anger's manipulations of the culturally overloaded imagery of Nazism, sado-masochism and the occult finally result in a film which refuses to comform to any dominant, edifying reading whatsoever—an almost unparalleled achievement which should earn *Scorpio Rising* an enduring place in the artistic annals of the 1960s, a decade remembered for the challenges it posed to the ruling ideology.

—Ed Lowry

* * *

THE SEARCHERS. Production: C.V. Whitney Pictures; 1956; Technicolor, 35mm, Vistavision; running time: 119 mins. Released 1956.

Produced by Merian C. Cooper and C.V. Whitney; associate producer: Patrick Ford; screenplay by Frank S. Nugent; from the novel by Alan LeMay; directed by John Ford; photography by Winton C. Hoch and Alfred Gilks; edited by Jack Murray; sound by Hugh McDowell and Howard Wilson; set decoration by Victor Gangelin; art direction by Frank Hotaling and James Basevi; music by Max Steiner, orchestrated by Murray Cutter, song "The Searchers" by Stan Jones, sung by the Sons of the Pioneers; special effects by George Brown; costumes designed by Frank Beetson and Ann Peck; Technicolor consultant: James Gooch.

Filmed from February through the summer of 1955 in Monument Valley, Utah and Colorado.

Cast: John Wayne (*Ethan Edwards*); Jeffrey Hunter (*Martin Pawley*); Vera Miles (*Laurie Jorgensen*); Ward Bond (*Capt. Rev. Samuel Clayton*); Natalie Wood (*Debbie Edwards*); John Qualen (*Lars Jorgensen*); Olive Carey (*Mrs. Jorgensen*); Henry Brandon (*Chief Scar*); Ken Curtis (*Charlie McCorry*); Harry Carey, Jr. (*Brad Jorgensen*); Antonio Moreno (*Emilio Figu-*

eroa); Hank Worden (*Mose Harper*); Lana Wood (*Debbie as a child*); Walter Coy (*Aaron Edwards*); Dorothy Jordan (*Martha Edwards*); Pippa Scott (*Lucy Edwards*); Pat Wayne (*Lt. Greenhill*); Beulah Archuletta (*Look*); Jack Pennick (*Private*); Peter Mamakos (*Futterman*); Cliff Lyons, Billy Cartledge, Chuck Hayward, Slim Hightower, Fred Kennedy, Frank McGrath, Chuck Roberson, Dale van Sickle, Henry Wills, and Terry Wilson (Stunt men); Away Luna, Billy Yellow, Bob Many Mules, Exactly Sonnie Betsuie, Feather Hat, Jr., Harry Black Horse, Jack Tin Horn, Many Mules Son, Percy Shooting Star, Pete Grey Eyes, Pipe Line Begishe, Smile White Sheep (*Comanches*); Mae Marsh; Dan Borzage.

Publications:

Reviews—by Peter Baker in *Films and Filming* (London), September 1956; review by Courtland Phipps in *Films in Review* (New York), June/July 1956; books—*The Western from Silents to Cinerama* by George Fenin and William Everson, New York 1962; *John Ford* by Philippe Haudiquet, Paris 1966; *John Ford* by Peter Bogdanovich, Berkeley 1968; *The Films of John Wayne* by Mark Ricci, Boris Zmijewsky, and Steve Zmijewsky, New York 1970; *The Cinema of John Ford* by John Baxter, New York 1971; *The Six-Gun Mystique* by John Cawelti, Bowling Green, Ohio 1971; *The Western Films of John Ford* by J.A. Place, Secaucus, New Jersey 1973; *The Western* edited by Jack Nachbar, Englewood Cliffs, New Jersey 1974; *The American West on Film: Myth and Reality* by Richard A. Maynard, Rochelle Park, New Jersey 1974; *John Wayne* by Alan Barbour, New York 1974; *American Film Genres* by Stuart Kaminsky, Dayton, Ohio 1974; *John Ford* by Joseph McBride and Michael Wilmington, London 1975; *The John Ford Movie Mystery* by Andrew Sarris, London 1976; *John Ford* by Claude Beylie in *Anthologie du cinéma*, Paris 1976; *Pappy: the Life of John Ford* by Dan Ford, Englewood Cliffs, New Jersey 1979; *John Ford* by Andrew Sinclair, New York 1979; articles—by Lindsay Anderson on *The Searchers* in *Sight and Sound* (London), autumn 1956; article in *Films and Filming* (London), June 1956; "Thrill Shot" in *American Cinematographer* (Hollywood), November 1956; "John Ford Makes Another Movie Classic in Monument Valley" by Allen C. Reed in *Arizona Highways*, April 1956; "Press Conference" by John Cutts in *Sight and Sound* (London), spring 1956; "Poet in an Iron Mask", interview by Michael Barkun in *Films and Filming* (London), February 1958; "Notes on the Art of John Ford" by Michael Barkun in *Film Culture* (New York), summer 1962; "The 5 Worlds of John Ford" by Douglas McVay in *Films and Filming* (London), June 1962; "The Films of John Ford" by George Mitchell in *Films in Review* (New York), March 1963; "Ford on Ford" in *Cinema* (Beverly Hills), July 1964; "Autumn of John Ford" by Peter Bogdanovich in *Esquire* (New York), April 1964; John Ford issue, *Présence du cinéma* (Paris), March 1965; issue on John Ford of *Cahiers du cinéma* (Paris), October 1966; interview by Jean Mitry in *Interviews with Film Directors*, edited by Andrew Sarris, New York 1967; "Our Way West", interview by Burt Kennedy in *Films and Filming* (London), October 1969; "Prisoner of the Desert" by Joseph McBride and Michael Wilmington in *Sight and Sound* (London), autumn 1971; "*The Searchers*" by Andrew Sarris in *Film Comment* (New York), spring 1971; "John Ford" by Lindsay Anderson in *Cinema* (Beverly Hills), spring 1971; issue on John Ford of *Velvet Light Trap* (Madison, Wisconsin), August 1971; "A Persistence of Vision" by William Pechter in *24 Times a Second: Films and Film-makers*, New York 1971; issue on Ford of *Focus on Film* (London), spring

1971; issue on Ford of *Velvet Light Trap* (Madison, Wisconsin), August 1971; "The West of John Ford and How it Was Made" by D. Ford in *Action* (Los Angeles), September/October 1971; "The American West of John Ford" by M. Zolotow in *TV Guide*, 4 December 1971; issue devoted to John Ford's "stock company" in *Filmkritik* (Munich), January 1972; "John Wayne Talks Tough" by Joe McInery in *Film Comment* (New York), September 1972; "The Auteur Theory" in *Signs and Meaning in the Cinema* by Peter Wollen, London 1972; "Forfolgeren" by U. Jorgensen in *Kosmorama* (Copenhagen), June 1974; "John Ford: A Reassessment" by Michael Dempsey in *Film Quarterly* (Berkeley), summer 1975; issue on *The Searchers* of *Screen Education* (London), winter 1975-76; "The Method of *The Searchers*" by Clay Steinman in *Journal of the University Film Association* (U.S.), summer 1976; "Prisoner of the Night" by D. Boyd in *Film Heritage* (Dayton, Ohio), winter 1976-77; "*The Searchers*" by Ed Lowry in *Cinema Texas Program Notes* (Austin), 2 November 1978; "*The Searchers*: Cult Movie of the New Hollywood" by S. Byron in *New York*, 5 March 1979; "*The Searchers*" by Michael Selig in *Cinema Texas Program Notes* (Austin), 21 March 1979.

*   *   *

A popular though critically ignored western at the time of its release, John Ford's *The Searchers* was canonized a decade later by auteur critics as the American masterpiece *par excellence*, exerting its influence as a cinematic touchstone and "cult film" among such directors of the New Hollywood as Martin Scorsese, Paul Schrader, Steven Spielberg and George Lucas. Representing Ford's most emotionally complex and generically sophisticated work, *The Searchers* manages to be both a rousing adventure movie and a melancholy film poem exploring the American values at the heart of the western genre.

At the center of the film is Ethan Edwards, a bitter, ruthless and frustrated crusader engaged in a five-year quest to retrieve a niece kidnapped by the Comanches. Edwards is perhaps John Wayne's most accomplished characterization, bringing to bear the iconography which has made Wayne synonymous with the western. Isolated by the violent individualism which defines his heroic status, Edwards is torn by the neurotic split inherent in the archetype: he belongs neither to the civilized community of settlers nor with the savages he fights on their behalf. A crusty, intolerant misanthrope, he occasionally betrays a wellspring of emotion which again and again is sublimated in violent action and an insane hatred of the red man.

Returning to his brother's Texas home after many years' absence, Edwards arrives just in time to be lured away by a Comanche trick while the homestead is burned, his brother, sister-in-law and nephew are slaughtered, and his two nieces are taken captive by the brutal chief Scar. Embarking with a posse to recover the kidnapped girls, Edwards is eventually left to pursue his search with a single companion, young Martin Pawley, an eighth-blood Cherokee who was the adopted son of the Ethan's brother. Though Edwards begins by despising Pawley as a "half-breed," their companionship eventually draws them together as father and son. Yet when they finally discover Debbie, the sole survivor of the raid, now grown and living as a Comanche squaw, Edwards is determined to kill her, and Pawley is forced to defy his wrath and his gun in order to save her.

For all his hatred of the Comanches, Edwards is clearly aligned with them psychologically. Not only can he speak their language, but on one occasion, he shoots the eyes of a dead warrior in tacit acknowledgement of an Indian belief that this will force the man's soul to "wander forever between the winds." Further, there is a strongly sexual undercurrent to Edwards's search, manifested on one hand by his obsession with revenge for the violation of his sister-in-law Martha, and on the other by his insistence on killing Debbie for "living with a Comanche buck." His ultimate decision to spare the girl and to temper his anger thus assumes the proportions of a kind of transcendental grace.

In one of the most poignant subtexts provided by any western, *The Searchers* suggests a source for Edwards's anger by hinting at his unspoken and unfulfilled love for his brother's wife Martha. Ford subtly conveys this attachment through gesture and staging alone in the early scenes, yet extends its ramifications to inform Pawley's treatment of Laurie, the fiancee he leaves behind. After years of waiting, Laurie finally opts for a less attractive suitor, an action which threatens to cut Pawley off from the civilized community much like Edwards. Without stating it in so many words, the film suggests that the situation echoes a frustrated romance, prior to the beginning of the story, between Edwards and Martha, who finally chose to marry his brother instead of waiting indefinitely for the man she loved.

Within the auteurist context, *The Searchers* assumes an even greater significance. Never before in a Ford western has the wilderness seemed so brutal or settlements so tenuous and threatened. There are no towns—only outposts and isolated homesteads, remote and exposed between the awesome buttes of Ford's mythic Monument Valley. And while the Comanches are depicted as utterly ruthless, Ford ascribes motivations for their actions, and lends them a dignity befitting a proud civilization. Never do we see the Indians commit atrocities more appalling than those perpetrated by the white man. Not only does Edwards perform the only scalping shown in the film, but Ford presents the bloody aftermath of a massacre of Indian women and children carried out by the same clean-cut cavalrymen he depicted so lovingly in films like *Fort Apache*.

The Searchers's status as a masterpiece of the genre may finally lie in its abundant poetic imagery: a massacre presaged by a startled covey of quail, a cloud of dust and an artificially reddened sunset; the echoing voices reverberating from the towering stones surrounding men who, 40 miles from home, realize they have been drawn away so that the Comanches can attack their families; the image of Debbie running down a distant dune, unseen by the searchers whom she approaches; the repetitive tossing of objects between Edwards and the garrulous preacher/Texas Ranger Captain Clayton, conveying the delicate balance between their mutual respect and enmity; the way in which Martha strokes Edwards's coat before their unplanned final farewell.

But the most significant visual motif in *The Searchers* is surely the doorway open onto the wilderness. It is the image which begins and ends the film. Ford introduces Edwards through the frame of an opening doorway in the first shot of the film, and repeats the image on several occasions: once to frame (and parallel) the introduction of Pawley, and twice again with the mouth of a cave as the framing doorway. It is an image which expresses both the subject and the conflict of the film: inside the door are the values cherished by civilization; outside, in the glaring sun, is the savage land which threatens them. *The Searchers* final shot watches the reunited family walk in through the door, while Edwards remains behind, looking after them. He starts to enter, then hesitates. Realizing that he has served his purpose, that there is really no place for the western hero by the hearthside within, he turns and walks away, as the door closes behind him.

—Ed Lowry

SEPPUKU. Harakiri. Production: Shochiku Co. (Kyoto); black and white, 35mm, Shochiku GrandScope; running time: 135 mins.; length: 3686 meters. Released 1962, Japan.

Produced by Tatsuo Hosoya with Gin-ichi Kishimoto; screenplay by Shinobu Hashimoto; from the novel by Yasuhiko Tokigushi; directed by Masaki Kobayashi; photography by Yoshio Miyajima; edited by Hisashi Sagara; sound by Hideo Nishizaki; art direction by Jun-ichi Ozumi and Shigemasa Toda; music by Toru Takemitsu.

Cannes Film Festival, Special Jury Prize, 1963.

Cast: Tatsuya Nakadai (*Hanshiro Tsugumo*); Shima Iwashita (*Mihio Tsugumo*); Akira Ishihama (*Motome Chijiiwa*); Yoshio Inaba (*Jinai Chijiiwa*); Rentaro Mikuni (*Kageyu Saito*); Masao Mishima (*Tango Inaba*); Tetsuro Tamba (*Hikokuro Omodaka*); Ichiro Nakaya (*Hayato Yazaki*); Yoshio Aoki (*Umenosuke Kawabe*); Jo Azumi (*Ichiro Shimmen*); Hisashi Igawa, Shoji Kobayashi, Ryo Takeuchi (*Young samurai*); Shichisaburo Amatsu (*Page*); Kei Sato (*Masakazu Fukushima*).

Publications:

Reviews—"Cela s'appelle l'horreur" by Pierre Billard in *Cinéma 63* (Paris), June 1963; "L'Armure vide" by Michel Ciment in *Positif* (Paris), November 1963; "Le Piège" by André S. Labarthe in *Cahiers du cinéma* (Paris), September 1963; "*Harakiri*" by Mark Shivas in *Movie* (London), July/August 1963; "*Harakiri*" by Hubert Arnault in *Image et son* (Paris), January 1964; books—*The Japanese Movie: An Illustrated History* by Donald Richie, Tokyo 1966; *Japanese Cinema: Film Style & National Character* by Donald Richie, New York 1971; *Voices from the Japanese Cinema* by Joan Mellen, New York 1975; *Japanese Film Directors* by Audie Bock, New York 1978; articles—"Kobayashi's Trilogy" by M. Iwabuchi in *Film Culture* (New York), spring 1962; "*Harakiri*, Kobayashi, Humanism" by James R. Silke in *Cinema* (Beverly Hills), June/July 1963; article in *Cinema* (Beverly Hills), August/September 1963; article by Geoffrey Donaldson in *Films and Filming* (London), March 1963; article by Georges Sadoul in *Les Lettres françaises* (Paris), 23 May 1963; article by Marcel Martin in *Les Lettres françaises* (Paris), 30 May 1963; "*Harakiri*" by Pierre Philippe in *Cinéma 63* (Paris), September/October 1963; article by Cid Corman in *Film Quarterly* (Berkeley), spring 1964; article by Allen Eyles in *Films and Filming* (London), May 1965; article in *Films and Filming* (London), March 1965; "L'Astre japonais" by Philippe Esnault in *Image et son* (Paris), February 1969; "Kobayashi, l'homme et l'oeuvre" by C.R. Blouin and "Kobayashi, à l'uquam: anarchiste ou utopiste?" by G. Thérien in *Cinéma Québec* (Montreal), February/March 1974; "*Harakiri*" by Max Tessier in *Image et son* (Paris), November 1981.

*   *   *

Seppuku marks Masaki Kobayashi's first venture into the genre of *jidai-geki* (costume drama). But his choice of an historical subject entails no lessening of the distinctive social and moral preoccupations which informed the contemporary subjects of his earlier films. Rather, those preoccupations are intensified by their placement in a historical perspective, their universal relevance underlined; while in the stylized conventions of the samurai ritual, Kobayashi found the ideal context for the slow, measured cadences of his cinematic language. The result was his finest film to date, a work of masterly narrative construction and outstanding visual beauty.

Through an intricate pattern of flashbacks, the story is revealed to us in reverse. The *ronin* (masterless, hence destitute, samurai) Tsugumo, who comes seeking to be allowed to commit ritual suicide in the house of Lord Iyi, is told a cautionary tale of the fate of another *ronin*, Chijiwa, who had made the same request. In his turn, Tsugumo relates his own story: he already knew of Chijiwa's brutal death, for the man was his son-in-law, and he has now come to take vengeance on the Iyi clan. The film culminates in a superbly choreographed explosion of violence.

As so often in his films, Kobayashi's concern is with the solitary, courageous individual who stands against a corrupt, inhuman and oppressive system. The vaunted samurai traditions of honor and nobility, as professed by the members of the Iyi clan, are shown to be a hollow sham, adhered to only in public view. In the film's opening shot, a huge suit of armor, surmounted by a horned battle helmet, looms out of the mist, to an eerie and impressive effect. This armor, it transpires, embodies the ancestral spirits of the Iyi household, who pay it exaggerated deference. But in the final headlong combat, Tsugumo contemptuously knocks it out of his way, then uses it as a shield. The armor, like the samurai system, is an empty show.

The recurrent image in *Seppuku* is of Tsugumo in his black robes (having refused the white ones appropriate to the ritual suicide), seated cross-legged on the white harakiri mat in the center of the courtyard, surrounded by the massed spears of the Iyi warriors, and speaking in calm, unhurried tones. Around this image of charged stillness, the action of the film proceeds through visual compositions of intense lyrical beauty: most notably in the duel between Tsugumo and Omadaka, finest of the Iyi swordsmen, breathtakingly staged as a formal ballet of stylized, sweeping gestures amid long wind-tossed grass. Kobayashi's coolly reticent camera perfectly matches the rhythms of his studied narrative, supported by Toru Takemitsu's evocative score and, in the central role, a performance of epic stature from Tatsuya Nakadai.

Seppuku was awarded the Special Jury Prize at the 1963 Cannes Festival, the first of Kobayashi's films to become widely known in the west. It was to be equalled in visual beauty by *Kaidan* (*Kwaidan*). In his most famous film, *Joiuchi*, he once again made telling use of the samurai system as the epitome of an ossified, authoritarian tradition. *Seppuku*, though, combines both elements in unsurpassable fashion, and remains the most achieved expression of Kobayashi's central belief that all systems, even the most malignant and entrenched, can be resisted by the power of "sheer human resilience."

—Philip Kemp

7TH HEAVEN. Production: Fox Film Corporation; 1927; black and white, 35mm; running time: 125 mins.; length: 9 reels, 8500 feet. Released 1927.

Screenplay by Benjamin Glazer; from the play by John Golden (other sources indicate the play was written by Austin Strong); titles by Katherine Hilliker and H.H. Caldwell; directed by Frank Borzage; photography by by Ernest Palmer and J.A. Valentine; edited by Barney Wolf; production design by Harry Oliver; music by Erno Rapee and Lew Pollock; costumes designed by Kathleen Kay; assistant directors: Lew Borzage and Park Frame.

Filmed in Fox Studios, Movietone City (now Century City). Academy Awards for Best Director, Best Actress (Gaynor, in conjunction with her roles in *Street Angel* and *Sunrise*), and Best Writing-Adaptation, 1927-28.

Cast: Janet Gaynor (*Diane*); Charles Farrell (*Chico*); Ben Bard (*Colonel Brissac*); David Butler (*Gobin*); Marie Mosquini (*Madame Gobin*); Albert Gran (*Boul*); Gladys Brockwell (*Nana*); Emile Chautard (*Père Chevillon*); George Stone (*Sewer rat*); Jessie Haslett (*Aunt Valentine Vulmir*); Brandon Hurst (*Uncle Georges Vulmir*); Lillian West (*Arlette*).

Publications:

Books—*The Fox Girls* by James Robert Parish, New Rochelle, New York 1971; *The Hollywood Professionals* vol.3 by John Belton, New York 1974; *Cinema, The Magic Vehicle: A Guide to Its Achievement: Journey One: Cinema Through 1949* edited by Jacek Klinowski and Adam Garbicz, Metuchen, New Jersey 1975; *American Silent Film* by William K. Everson, New York 1978; articles—interview by V. Tully in *Vanity Fair* (New York), February 1927; "Frank Borzage" in *Current Biography Yearbook*, New York 1963; "*Seventh Heaven* Revisited" in *Look* (New York), 10 April 1951; "Janet Gaynor" by Chauncey L. Carr in *Films in Review* (New York), October 1959; "Frank Borzage" by Henri Agel in *New York Film Bulletin*, no.12-14, 1961; "Frank Borzage" by A. Bease in *Film Journal* (Australia), April 1963; "*Seventh Heaven*" by Richard Griffith in *Film Notes* edited by Eileen Bowser, New York 1969; "*Seventh Heaven*" by J.L. Bourget in *Monogram* (London), no.4, 1972; "Souls Made Great By Love and Adversity: Frank Borzage" by J. Belton in *Monogram* (London), no.4, 1972; "L'Heure suprême de Frank Borzage" in *Cahiers de la Cinématheque* (Paris), winter 1974; "Difference and Displacement in *Seventh Heaven*" by P. Rosen in *Screen* (London), summer 1977; "7th Heaven" by Richard Combs in *Monthly Film Bulletin* (London), July 1980.

*   *   *

7th Heaven is an uplifting drama of the power of love over adversity, even death. As a title early in the film states, "For those who will climb it, there is a ladder leading from the depths to heights—from the sewer to the stars—the ladder of courage." Frank Borzage was one of the screen's great romantic directors, and nowhere is that romanticism more visible than in *7th Heaven*, perhaps his greatest achievemnet—certainly his finest silent feature. It made stars of its two leading players, Charles Farrell and Janet Gaynor, and led to a series of similar, if lesser, romantic dramas featuring the pair.

The film, based on a popular stage hit starring Helen Mencken, tells the story of a Paris waif, Diane, who is cruelly treated by her sister and taken in by a sewer worker named Chico. Chico is promoted to a street cleaner, and his love for Diane grows until World War I interrupts, separating the two. Each day, at 11:00 a.m., the two commune mentally through two religious medallions, while uttering the words, "Diane, Chico, Heaven." At the war's close, Diane learns of Chico's death (a death which the viewer appears to have witnessed). Just as she renounces God, Chico reappears, blinded, but very much alive.

Love has conquered even death!

Contemporary critics were much taken with the film's lyrical qualities, as well as with its ambitious sets which recreated a Paris street and the seventh floor garret of a French tenement where Chico and Diane live. Aside from the emotion which Frank Borzage wrings from both the story and the audience, the director deserves credit for his use of camera movement. The camera follows the action wherever appropriate, but never obtrusively, notably when Diane is about to be arrested as a prostitute and later when, using the courage Chico has given her, she is able to turn the tables on her sister and takes a whip to her, driving her from the pair's "seventh heaven."

7th Heaven is an intense drama which holds and grips its viewer, an impressive piece of romantic lyricism which overcomes both its maudlin and melodramatic aspects. Equally impressive is the music which is often ignored today. As with most late silent features, *7th Heaven* was released with an orchestral score as accompaniment. This music featuring the popular song "Diane," is an integral part of the drama, specifically the sequence where Diane and Chico declare their love for each other while the sacred music of Gounod is interrupted by the sounds of the march, just as Diane and Chico's sacred love for each other will be interrupted by a war which will scar both of them, one mentally and one physically.

—Anthony Slide

SHANE. Production: Paramount Pictures; 1953; Technicolor, 35mm; running time: 118 mins. Released 1953.

Produced by George Stevens, associate producer: Ivan Moffat; screenplay by A.B. Guthrie, Jr. with additional dialogue by Jack Sher; from the novel by Jack Schaefer; directed by George Stevens; photography by Loyal Griggs; edited by William Hornbeck and Tom McAdoo; sound recorded by Harry Lindgran and Gene Garwin; art direction by Hal Pereira and Walter Tyler, set decoration by Emile Kuri; music score by Victor Young; special effects by Gordon Jennings; costumes designed by Edith Head; Technicolor consultant: Richard Mueller; techical adviser: Joe DeYong.

Academy Award, Best Cinematography-Color, 1953; Irving G. Thalberg Award to George Stevens, 1953.

Cast: Alan Ladd (*Shane*); Jean Arthur (*Marion Starrett*); Van Heflin (*Joe Starrett*); Brian de Wilde (*Joey*); Jack Palance (*Wilson*); Ben Johnson (*Chris*); Edgar Buchanan (*Lewis*); Emile Meyer (*Ryker*); Elisha Cook Jr. (*Torrey*); Douglas Spencer (*Shipstead*); John Dierkes (*Morgan*); Ellen Corby (*Mrs. Torrey*); Paul McVey (*Grafton*); John Miller (*Atkey*); Edith Evanson (*Mrs. Shipstead*); Leonard Strong (*Wright*); Ray Spiker (*Johnson*); Janice Carroll (*Susan Lewis*); Martin Mason (*Howell*); Helen Brown (*Mrs. Lewis*); Nancy Kulp (*Mrs. Howell*); Howard J. Negley (*Pete*); Beverly Washburn (*Ruth Lewis*); George Lewis (*Ryker man*); Charles Quirk (*Clerk*); Jack Sterling, Henry Wills, Rex Moore, and Ewing Brown (*Ryker men*).

Publications:

Reviews—by Nina Stern in *Films in Review* (New York), April

1953; "*Shane*" in *Time* (New York), 13 April 1953; books—*The Western: From Silents to Cinerama* by George N. Fenin and William K. Everson, New York 1962; *The Hero* by David Babcock, Waltham, Massachusetts, 1968; *A Pictorial History of the Western Film* by William K. Everson, New York 1969; *George Stevens: An American Romantic* by Donald Richie, New York 1970; *The Six-Gun Mystique* by John Cawelti, Bowling Green, Ohio 1971; *What is Cinema?, Vol. II* by André Bazin, edited and translated by Hugh Gray, Berkeley 1971; *The Movie Makers: Artists in the Industry* by Rev. Gene D. Phillips, Chicago 1973; *The Western: From Silents to the 70's* by George N. Fenin and William K. Everson, New York 1973; *Westerns—Aspects of a Movie Genre* by Philip French, New York 1973; *Focus on the Western* edited by Jack Nachbar, Englewood Cliffs, New Jersey 1974; *The Great Western Pictures* by James Parish and Michael Pitts, Metuchen, New Jersey 1976; articles—"The Man Who Made the Hit Called *Shane*" by B. Martin in *Saturday Evening Post* (New York), 8 August 1953; "*Shane* and George Stevens" by Penelope Houston in *Sight and Sound* (London), fall 1953; "George Stevens" by H.G. Luft in *Films in Review* (New York), April 1953; "George Stevens and the American Dream" by Eugene Archer in *Film Culture* (New York), no.11, 1957; "Hollywood Romantic—A Monograph of George Stevens" by Joanne Stang in *Films and Filming* (New York), July 1959; "Movie Chronicle: The Westerner" by Robert Worshow in *The Immediate Experience*, New York 1962; "Alan Ladd" by Robert C. Roman in *Films in Review* (New York), April 1964; "Viewing Report of *Shane*" in *Screen Education* (London), September/-October 1964; "George Stevens—His Work" by Douglas McVay in *Films and Filming* (London), April 1965 and May 1965; "The Picture" by James R. Silke in *Cinema* (Beverly Hills), December/January 1965; "The Return of Shane" by Alan Stanbrook in *Films and Filming* (London), May 1966; "Jean Arthur" by Jerry Vermilye in *Films in Review* (New York), June/July 1966; issue on Stevens of *Dialogue on Film* (AFI, Washington, D.C.), no.1, 1972; "*Shane*" by Charles Albright, Jr. in *Magill's Survey of Cinema, Vol. IV* edited by Frank N. Magill, Englewood Cliffs, New Jersey 1980.

*   *   *

Narrative films can be generally categorized into those that are motivated by plot and those that are motivated by character. Many American films are often cited as belonging to the former category, particularly in comparison to some of the European films. *Shane* is pure plot and pure American. The characters, rather than autonomous individuals, are functions of the plot and move through their respective roles with the assurance of legend. They possess no depth or dimension beyond the surface; they are always and exactly what they seem to be. And, ironically, this is their strength and the strength of the film.

The plot of *Shane* is a masterpiece of simplicity. The Indian Wars have been fought and won. The homesteaders have settled in to farm the land, threatening the open range of the ranchers. The law is a three day ride from the community, and the tenuous co-existence waits for eruption into "gunsmoke." The ranchers, led by the Ryker brothers, try to intimidate the homesteaders in an effort to force them out of the valley, but the homesteaders are held together by the determination of a single man, Joe Starrett, who wants to build a life on the land for his wife Marion and young son Joey. Into this tension rides Shane, a stranger who is befriended by the Starretts. A gunfighter by profession, Shane tries to renounce his former trade and join the community of homesteaders. As the tension increases, another gunfighter is recruited to bait and kill the helpless homesteaders. When Starrett is left with no alternative but to meet the hired gunfighter, it is obvious that only Shane is a match for the final shootout. He overpowers Starrett and rides into town where he kills the gunman and the Rykers. Now that the valley is safe, Shane bids farewell to Joey and rides off into the distant mountains.

Of all American genres, the western is arguably the most durable. The western has tended to document not the history of the West but those cultural values that have become cherished foundations of our national identity. The western certifies our ideals of individualism, initiative, independence, persistence and dignity. It also displays some of our less admirable traits of lawlessness, violence and racism. Possibly more than any previous American film, *Shane* tries to encapsulate the cultural ethos of the western.

Rather than avoiding the cliches, platitudes and stereotypes of the genre, *Shane* pursues and embraces them. With the exception of a saloon girl and an Indian attack, all of the ingredients of the typical western are present: the wide open spaces, the ranchers feuding with the farmers, the homesteading family trying to build a life, the rival gunman, the absence of law, the survival of the fastest gun, even the mandatory shoulder wound. Embodying as it does the look and feel of the western, *Shane* becomes an essential rarity; it not only preserves but honors our belief in our heritage.

As myth, it is appropriate that *Shane* is seen through the eyes of a small boy. Joey is the first to see Shane ride into the community, more than the others he perceives the inner strength of the man, and he's the only one to bid Shane farewell as he leaves the valley. As both the child's idolization of an adult and the creative treatment of a myth, *Shane* is not a story of the West; it is, rather, *the* West as we believe it to have been.

Everything in the film favors its treatment of the myth. Alan Ladd—with his golden hair, his soft voice, his modest manner—is more the Olympian god than the rugged frontiersman or the outcast gunfighter. He rides down from the distant mountains and into lives of a settlement in need of his special talents. A stranger who doesn't belong and can never be accepted, he is a man without a past and without a future. He exists only for the moment of confrontation; and once that moment has passed, he has no place in the community. Even the way in which his movements are choreographed and photographed seem mythic—when riding into town for the final shootout, for example, the low angle tracking of the camera, the gait of his horse, the pulsing of the music with its heroic, lonely tones and the vast, panoramic landscapes all contribute to the classical dimensions of the film.

Shane is the generic loner who belongs to no one and no place. He possesses capability, integrity, restraint; yet there is a sense of despair and tragedy about him. Shane is that most characteristic of American anachronisms, the man who exists on the fringe of an advancing civilization. His background and profession place him on the periphery of law and society. The same skills as a warrior that make him essential to the survival of the community also make him suspect and even dangerous to that same community. In the tradition of William S. Hart, Tom Mix, John Wayne and Clint Eastwood, Shane is the embodiment of the western hero.

Shane is a reluctant mediator. There is a moral guilt about his profession that he carries with him as clearly as his buckskins. He wants to lay aside the violence of his past, but like the Greek heroes, of which he is kin, fate will not allow him to alter what is destined for him. Although he conspicuously tries to avoid the kind of confrontations he is best prepared to face, he suffers humiliation in doing so which is mistaken for cowardice. Once again he must prove himself, as if serving as the defender of those

weaker will atone for his past and his profession. Consequently, a paradox emerges; he is both necessary and a threat to the survival of the community. In the Starrett family, for example, he begins to be more important to Joey than his father and more attractive to Marion than her husband. If the community is to grow and prosper, it must do so without him. Once he has served his function, he has no place and must again move on.

Shane is a tapestry laced with contrasts. The gun and the ax, the horse and the land, the buckskins and the denims, the loner and the family. In the end, the ax (peace) replaces the gun (violence), the land (stability) replaces the horse (transience), the denims (work) replace the buckskins (wilderness), the family (future) replaces the loner (past).

The unheralded mythic god leaves and the community is safe. Good has triumphed over evil, the family has been preserved, all the guns have been silenced. And yet there is a sense of loss. We have admired and appreciated Shane, but he exists for a single purpose and a single moment. When he has departed, we know we're safer and better for his presence; but we also know that we're again vulnerable.

—Stephen E. Bowles

SHANGHAI EXPRESS. Production: Paramount Publix, Inc.; black and white, 35mm; running time: 84 mins. Released 12 February 1932.

Screenplay by Jules Furthman; from an idea by Harry Hervey; directed by Josef von Sternberg; photography by Lee Garmes; production design by Hans Dreier; music by W. Franke Harling; costumes designed by Travis Banton.

Academy Award, Best Cinematography, 1931-32.

Cast: Marlene Dietrich (*Shanghai Lily*); Clive Brook (*Donald Harvey*); Anna May Wong (*Hui Fei*); Warner Oland (*Henry Chang*); Eugene Pallette (*Sam Salt*); Lawrence Grant (*Mr. Carmichael*); Louise Closser Hale (*Mrs. Haggerty*); Gustav von Seyffertitz (*Eric Baum*); Emile Chautard (*Commandant Lenard*); Claude King (*Albright*); Nesheda Minoru (*Chinese spy*).

Publications:

Script—*Morocco and Shanghai Express: Two Films by Josef von Sternberg*, introduction by Andrew Sarris, New York 1973; review—"Marlene Dietrich in a Brilliantly Directed Melodrama Set Aboard a Train Running from Peiping to Shanghai" by Mordaunt Hall in *The New York Times*, 18 February 1932; books—*Marlène Dietrich, femme-énigme* by Jean Talky, Paris 1932; *An Index to the Films of Josef von Sternberg* by Curtis Harrington, London 1949; *Marlene Dietrich—Image and Legend* by Richard Griffith, New York 1959; *Fun in a Chinese Laundry* by Josef von Sternberg, New York 1965, published in France as *Souvenirs d'un montreur d'ombres*, Paris 1966; *The Films of Josef von Sternberg* by Andrew Sarris, New York 1966; *Josef von Sternberg, Dokumentation, Eine Darstellung*, Mannheim, Germany 1966; *Josef von Sternberg* by Herman G. Weinberg, Paris 1966; *Josef von Sternberg: A Critical Study* by Herman G. Weinberg, New York 1967; *The Cinema of Josef von Sternberg* by John Baxter, New York 1971; *Marlene Dietrich* by Charles

Silver, New York 1974; articles—"Les grands rôles de Marlène Dietrich" in *Cinémonde* (Paris), 4 February 1932; "Marlene Dietrich" by Arthur Knight in *Films in Review* (New York), December 1954; "Josef von Sternberg" by Herman G. Weinberg in *Film Heritage* (Dayton, Ohio), winter 1965; "Sternberg, avant, pendant, après Marlene" by Ado Kyrou in *Positif* (Paris), May 1966; "Thoughts on the Objectification of Women" by Barbara Martineau in *Take One* (Montreal), November/December 1970; "article by Jules Furthman and Richard Koszarski in *Film Comment* (New York), winter 1970-71; "Joe, Where Are You?" by Tom Flinn in *Velvet Light Trap* (Madison, Wisconsin), fall 1972; "Shanghaj expressen, några visuella karakteristika" by L.G. Thelestam in *Filmrutan* (Stockholm), no.2, 1972; "Shanghai Express" by M. Humbert in *Image et son* (Paris), June/July 1975; "Shanghai Express" by Tom Milne in *Monthly Film Bulletin* (London), May 1978; "Retrospettive: Shanghai Express" by T. Ratti and S. Carlo in *Filmcritica* (Rome), April 1979; "Josef von Sternberg" by Claude Oliver in *Cinema, a Critical Dictionary, Vol. II* edited by Richard Roud, New York 1980.

*   *   *

Shanghai Express is the fourth of the seven films that Josef von Sternberg made with Marlene Dietrich. Released to enormous commercial success in 1932, it stands at the chronological center of the series. More significantly, it stands at the center of the larger personal and artistic drama which, incorporating and transcending the seven fictional narratives on which Sternberg and Dietrich worked together, marked this legendary collaboration of director and star.

That larger drama was born in the relatively straightforward mise-en-scéne and direct emotional thrust of *The Blue Angel*; it died amid the neo-byzantine delirium of *The Scarlet Empress* and the acrid convoluted ironies of *The Devil Is a Woman*. It might be characterized as the conflict between Sternberg's increasingly ingenious efforts to reduce his *protégée* to little more than a figure in a field of unexampled iconographical complexity, and Dietrich's increasingly effortless assertion of her power to command the attention of the camera no matter what Sternberg may have had in mind. Of all their films, *Shanghai Express* represents perhaps the most nearly perfect balance of the claims of the filmmaker and the claims of the hypnotic screen presence. Sternberg's vision of Dietrich and Dietrich's vision of Dietrich are for once precisely adjusted.

Everything seems to work. The characteristic devices of Sternberg's assault upon dead cinematic space—the veils and the feathers and the smoke—succeed in dramatizing, not qualifying, the concealed anguish of Dietrich's Shanghai Lily. The sumptuous cinematography of Lee Garmes is not only breathtaking, but also creates a surface sensuality that validates any narrative excesses. Like the libretto of an opera, the script establishes a simple, familiar, indeed banal dramatic situation which Sternberg's visual imagination and Dietrich's face and voice invest with startling new resonances. Sternberg also draws upon Dietrich's sardonic public manner and upon the intensity of feeling she can convey in those rare moments when, isolated from the other figures in the film, the audience can witness her grief and her terror.

In its structure, the film embodies the ancient motif of the *Narrenschiff*, the Ship of Fools, which makers of motion pictures—pictures of motion—have for obvious reasons found congenial, whatever the particular mode of transportation in question. (It may at first seem peculiar to think that *Stagecoach*

and *Shanghai Express* belong to a single narrative mode, but, in this sense they do.) Creeping across the clotted landscape of Sternberg's China, the Shanghai Express is peopled with those to whom various deceptions, whether self-delusions or public mendacities, have become the very essence of existence. Sternberg's characters (his fools) include: the doctor who has allowed his broken faith in a woman, the woman who has become Shanghai Lily, to shrivel his emotional being; the Chinese prostitute who thinks she can cancel her past by means of a respectable marriage; and a Mao figure whose revolutionary fervor is apparently fueled by sexual conquest. However, The greatest fool of all, precisely because she is the victim of self-*awareness*, is the woman who seems alert to every nuance of her own words and her own voice when she states, in response to a question from Doc as to whether she has married since their separation, "It took more than one man to change my name to Shanghai Lily."

The progress of this woman from the pudgy incarnation of animal sexuality in *The Blue Angel* to the sleek embodiment of the knowledge of a too cruel world in *Shanghai Express* constitutes an important chapter in the history of public taste in the early 1930s. With uncharacteristic bluntness, Sternberg invokes the earlier Dietrich within the film itself. At one point, Doc reveals a photograph of the woman he loved and abandoned a few years before. The photograph is of Dietrich in her German, pre-Hollywood days. The sight of it temporarily distances us from the world of Sternberg's Oriental fantasia and reminds us of the geographical, stylistic and emotional distance that the director and his star have covered together since *The Blue Angel*.

—Elliot Rubenstein

SHCHORS. Shors. Chtchors. Production: Kiev Film Studio; black and white, 35mm; length: 3849.5 meters, 14 reels. Released 1 May 1939.

Screenplay by Alexander Dovzhenko; directed by Alexander Dovzhenko with Julia Solntseva; photography by Yuriy Yekelchik and Yuriy Goldabenko; sound recorded by Nikolai Timartsev; production design by Maurits Umansky and Y. Breskin; music by Dmitri Kabalevsky, lyrics by Andriy Malyshko, conducted by S. Gindin; assistants to the director: Lazar Bodyk, H. Zatvornytsky, and I. Ihnatovych.

Filmed February 1937 through 1938 in Kiev, Chernihiv, and Poltava.

Cast: Yevgeni Samolov (*Shchors*); Ivan Skuratov (*Bozhenko*); Amvroziy Buchma (*General Tereshkevich*); L. Lyashenko (*Chernyak and Chyzh*); D. Kadnikov (*Wurm*); O. Khvylya (*Savka Troyan*); Nikolai Komissarov (*Hofman*); Hans Klering (*Otto*); O. Glazunov (*German Delegate*); S. Komarov (*German Colonel*); G. Polezhayev (*Petlyura*); D. Milyutenko (*Volodymyr Vynnychenko*); Y. Vurmansky and R. Chalysh (*Members of the Directory*); R. Chalysh (*Nalyvayko and Roman*); N. Kryuchkov (*Provocateur*); Hnat Yura (*Otaman Konovalets*); Semen Shkurat (*Prokopenko*); O. Hrechany (*Mykhaylyuk*); H. Borysohlibska (*Woman weaver*); F. Ishchenko (*Petro Chyzh*); P. Krasylych (*Havrychenko*); M. Makarenko (*Antonyuk*); Y. Titov (*Burdenko*); Y. Bantysh, Petro Masokha, P. Tatarenko, and D. Kostenko (*Commanders*); V. Dukler (*Tyshler*); P. Radetsky, D. Barvinsky, and Y. Velichko (*Soldiers*); P. Kiyansky and N. Nikitina (*Nastya*); A. Yegorova (*Olena*); S. Levchenko (*Bor-*

kovsky); A. Gorunyov (*Officer in Hetman's army*); V. Khalatov, Y. Lavrov, and Mysloslavsky (*Inspectors*); F. Dubrovksy (*Bohdankevych*); O. Zahorsky (*Colonel Fedorov*); O. Nelidov (*Colonel Kucherenko*); T. Yavorsky (*Rohovenko*); A. Hubatenko (*Ocheredko*).

Publications:

Script—"*Chtchors*" by Alexander Dovzhenko in *Izbrannoié*, Moscow 1957; books—*An Index to the Creative Work of Alexander Dovjenko* by Jay Leyda, supplement to *Sight and Sound* (London), index series, 1947; *Alexander Dovzhenko* by R. Yourenev, Moscow 1958 (name transliterated as R. Jurenew in German translation, 1964); *Kino: A History of the Russian and Soviet Film* by Jay Leyda, London 1960; *Poetika Dovzhenko* by Igor Rachuk, Moscow 1964; *Dovjenko* by Luda and Jean Schnitzer, Paris 1966; *Alexandre Dovjenko* by Marcel Oms, Lyon 1968; *Dovjenko* by Alexandr Mariamov, Moscow 1968; *Alexandre Dovjenko* by Barthélemy Amengual, Paris 1970; *Alexander Dovzhenko: The Poet as Filmmaker*, edited by Marco Carynnyk, Cambridge, Massachusetts 1973; articles—"L'Esperienza del mio laovro nel film biografico" by Grigory Rochal in *Il mestiere di regista*, Milan 1954; "Dovjenko, Poet of Life Eternal" by Ivor Montagu in *Sight and Sound* (London), summer 1957; issue on Dovzhenko of *Film* (Venice), August 1957; "Julia Solntśva et la terre ukrainieene" by Michel Capdenac in *Les Lettres françaises* (Paris), 25 May 1961; "The Films of Alexander Dovzhenko" by Charles Shibuk in *New York Film Bulletin*, no.11-14, 1961; "La non indifférente nature" by S. M. Eisenstein in *Cahiers du cinéma* (Paris), July/August 1969; "The Dovzhenko Papers" by Marco Carynnyk in *Film Comment* (New York), fall 1971; issue on Dovzhenko of *Iskusstvo kino* (Moscow), September 1974.

*   *   *

Shchors, directed by Alexander Petrovich Dovzhenko, is one of the crop of Societ films designed, like *Chapaev* and *The Maxim Trilogy*, to create an ideal Communist hero as an example for a new generation. Dovzhenko had many advantages over his predecessors in the field. One of the greatest visual artists in world cinema, he was also a long-standing active member of the Communist Party, serving in his youth as a diplomat as well as a revolutionary, combining an international outlook with his Ukrainian patriotism.

Joseph Stalin had asked him to make the film. Despite endowing the director with resources not even Cecil B. DeMille dared dream, Stalin's involvement brought with it a host of difficulties. "Why not make a film about Shchors...," a Ukrainian *Chapaev*. Dovzhenko had praised *Chapaev* at some length at the 1935 Central Committee awards ceremony, stating, "...the authors have achieved an exposition, an example, of popular genius, the genius of the creative masses, the originators of the Revolution, today fulfilling the second Five-year Plan." Though these may be fine and appropriate sentiments, his decision to go ahead with *Shchors* involved him in a long and arduous struggle. He emerged surprisingly victorious, despite the continuous intervention of Stalin throughout the three years of scripting, shooting, and editing. Worse perhaps was the meddling of bureaucrats who claimed "to have Stalin's ear."

Matters were made more difficult by one of those frequent re-writes of Bolshevik history, this time due to the growing Nazi

menace and a consequent fear of defections to the enemy. Ukrainian nationalism was not a part of this interpretation and a number of its Civil War heros found themselves in serious trouble: had Shchors not been a *dead* hero the film might never have been completed. As nearly all the other actual participants in the drama were no longer to be mentioned, far less portrayed on the screen, the director disguised most of the roles. It is a tribute to Dovzhenko's obstinate genius that, despite frequent laundering and official whitewashing, he was able to make his central character human and believable. The first actor in the role, after months of hard work and a formidable waste of footage, was fired. When Yevgeni Samoilov took over the part, he found himself burdened with more monologues than Hamlet, although the monologues seemed a genuine facet of his character, an intellectual deeply committed to the cause. Samoilov gave a fine performance, but other members of the cast, especially Skuratov as his fellow freedom-fighter Old Bozhenko, had plenty of opportunities to steal his scenes.

The relationship between Shchors and Bozhenko, similar to that between Furmanov and Chapaev, formed an important central theme—the resolution of conflict between the worker/peasant and the educated college communist, leading to a complete understanding and co-operation. There was, however, something unique about this pair; if Shchors contained something of Dovzhenko, Bozhenko was partly based on the director's father. Skuratov took full advantage of this role, one filled with peasant humor and wisdom, which concluded with a full-scale death scene. Dovzhenko's script, in setting the death scene, gives some indication of the film style: "Towards (Batka Bozhenko's) stretcher ride the black horses, their riders enveloped in black cloaks. From right and left shells fall amongst the wheat. The horsemen rein in their lathered horses, take a look at him and move on: all around nothing but wheatfields and emptiness: on the horizon a village burns; artillery thunders. Raising himself on his stretcher Bozhenko looks around—'Goodbye Russia and Ukraine....Farewell...From the bottom of my heart forgive me for not dying on the battlefield...but on the shoulders of footsloggers...' Bozhenko dies." However, he doesn't die until he has given his stretcher-bearers a humorous comparison between Pushkin and Shevchenko (the Ukrainian poet) asking for one of the latters poems to be engraved on his tombstone.

Shchors transcends its political message with its poetry, its humor, its striking visual evocations of landscape, and the human figures in the Ukrainian landscape. As in all Dovzhenko's work we see how a committed artist can transcend any sectarian limitations in a way that is impossible for those who dutifully accept establishment pressures.

—Robert Dunbar

SHE DONE HIM WRONG. Production: Paramount Pictures; 1933; black and white, 35mm; running time: 65 mins. Released 1933.

Produced by William Le Baron; screenplay by Mae West with Harvey Thew and John Bright, some sources do not list West with script credit; from the play *Diamond Lil* by Mae West; directed by Lowell Sherman; photography by by Charles Lang; music and lyrics by Ralph Rainger.

Filmed in Paramount studios.

Cast: Mae West (*Lady Lou*); Cary Grant (*Captain Cummings*); Gilbert Roland (*Serge Stanieff*); Gus Jordan (*Noah Beery, Sr.*); Rafaela Ottiano (*Russian Rita*); David Landau (*Dan Flynn*); Rochelle Hudson (*Sally*); Owen Moore (*Chick Clark*); Fuzzy Knight (*Rag-Time Kelly*); Tammany Young (*Chuck Connors*); Dewey Robinson (*Spider Kane*); Grace La Rue (*Frances*).

Publications:

Books—*Goodness Had Nothing to Do with It* by Mae West, New York 1970; *The Wit and Wisdom of Mae West* edited by Joseph Weintraub, New York 1967; *Hollywood in the Thirties* by John Baxter, Cranbury, New Jersey 1968; *The Films of Cary Grant* by Donald Deschner, New York 1971; *Cary Grant Film Album* compiled by Allen Eyles, Shepperton, Surrey, England 1971; *The Hays Office* by Raymond Moley, New York 1971; *The Paramount Pretties* by James Robert Parish, New Rochelle, New York 1972; *Women and Sexuality in the New Film* by Joan Mellen, New York 1973; *The Films of Mae West* by Jon Tuska, Secaucus, New Jersey 1973; *Cary Grant* by Jerry Vermilye, New York 1973; articles—"Mae West" in *Vanity Fair* (New York), March 1933; "Mae West and the Classic Tradition" by William Troy in *Nation* (New York), 8 November 1933; "Cary Grant" by Robert Roman in *Films in Review* (New York), December 1961; "*She Done Him Wrong*" by Eileen Bowser and Richard Griffith in *Film Notes* edited by Eileen Bowser, New York 1969; "Doing What Comes Naturally" by Eric Braun in *Films and Filming* (London), October 1970 and November 1970; "*She Done Him Wrong*" by Elaine Raines in *Magill's Survey of Cinema, Vol. IV* edited by Frank N. Magill, Englewood Cliffs, New Jersey 1980.

* * *

Given the variety and richness of Hollywood in the 1930s and 1940s—the decades now called the classical period of American film—it is difficult to claim that any stretch of time belonged to any star, director, or studio. Still, it is tempting to proclaim the years from 1932 to 1934 as the age of Mae West.

From her movie debut in *Night after Night* (in a small part: the studios were not sure how the movie public would take to the woman whose contempt for all proprieties and censors was so manifest), Mae West asserted her force as a screen presence. However, It was not until her second film, *She Done Him Wrong*, that the audience could appreciate the range of West's appeal. Based on one of West's most celebrated stage vehicles, *Diamond Lil*, the film showed us a woman of uncanny sensitivity to verbal sex-play (she was responsible for transcribing the lines she wrote for herself in *Diamond Lil* to the screen); a woman whose self-assurance was matched only by her capacity for self-caricature; a woman who would give ground to no mere male; a woman who calmly overturned all the principles of what we now call sexism; and a woman with a voice like none other heard in the movies.

There is no overestimating the last of these characteristics. With the death of silent film, individuality of vocal inflection assumed paramount importance; with the demise specifically of silent comedy, the human voice substituted for some of the comic uniqueness implicit in the bodies of Chaplin, Keaton and the others. (Significantly, when Chaplin at last gave in to speaking on the screen, a new visual presence had to be devised.) The stage, radio and vaudeville comedians, for a while at least, could provide what was needed, but no one with more dazzling public

success than Mae West. There could be no separation of her dialogue from her voice. Her popularity was for a time so enormous that the movie censors waited to put her in her place, or rather the place the censors thought she ought to occupy. Eventually the censors had their way: with the advent of the Breen Office in 1934, Mae West was fated to become a rather bowdlerized memory of the star of *She Done him Wrong* and *I'm No Angel*.

The woman was indomitable; she continued making films through the 1930s and early 1940s. In the final years of her life, she made atrocities such as *Myra Breckenridge* and *Sextette*. Even in the later 1930s however, few of the pleasures of *She Done Him Wrong* and *I'm No Angel* were to be duplicated.

Aside from West herself, *She Done Him Wrong* is notable for West's "discovery" of Cary Grant (he had actually appeared in several earlier movies). Grant manages to make himself noticed despite his relative inexperience, despite his function as a foil for Mae West, and despite the fact that he has to impersonate a policeman impersonating a Salvation Army officer. And in the course of its preposterous little plot, involving such unlikely comic topics as white slavery, the film somehow manages to come up with a villainess called "Russian Rita." The real lure is, of course, Mae West, the woman who could make America howl by introducing herself as one of the finest women who ever walked the streets.

—Elliot Rubenstein

SHE WORE A YELLOW RIBBON. Production: Argosy Pictures-RKO Radio Pictures, Inc.; Technicolor, 35mm; running time: 103 mins. Released October 1949.

Produced by John Ford and Merian C. Cooper with Lowell Farrell; screenplay by Frank S. Nugent and Laurence Stallings; from the story "War Party" by James Warner Bellah; directed by John Ford; photography by Winton C. Hoch and Charles P. Boyle; edited by Jack Murray; production design by Joe Kish; art direction by James Basevi; music by Richard Hageman, directed by Constantin Bakaleinkoff, and orchestrated by Lucien Cailliet; special effects by Jack Cosgrove and Jack Caffee; costumes designed by Michael Meyers and Ann Peck; history consultant: D.R.O. Hastwell; military technique consultants: Cliff Lyons and Maj. Philip Kieffer.

Filmed 1949 in Monument Valley, Utah. Cost: budgeted at $1,851,290. Academy Award, Best Cinematography-Color, 1949.

Cast: John Wayne (*Captain Nathan Brittles*); Joanne Dru (*Olivia*); John Agar (*Lt. Flint Cohill*); Ben Johnson (*Sgt. Tyree*); Harry Carey, Jr. (*Lt. Pennell*); Victor McLaglen (*Sgt. Quincannon*); Mildred Natwick (*Mrs. Allshard*); George O'Brien (*Maj. MacAllshard*); Arthur Shields (*Dr. O'Laughlin*); Francis Ford (*Barman*); Harry Woods (*Karl Rynders*); Chief Big Tree (*Pony-That-Walks*); Noble Johnson (*Red Shirt*); Cliff Lyons (*Trooper Cliff*); Tom Tyler (*Quayne*); Michael Dugan (*Hochbauer*); Mickey Simpson (*Wagner*); Fred Graham (*Hench*); Frank McGarth (*Trumpeter*); Don Summers (*Jenkins*); Fred Libby (*Col. Krumrein*); Jack Pennick (*Sergeant major*); Billy Jones (*Courier*); Bill Gettinger (*Officer*); Fred Kennedy (*Badger*); Rudy Bowman (*Pvt. Smith*); Post Park (*Officer*); Ray Hyke (*McCarthy*); Lee Bradley (*Interpreter*); Chief Sky Eagle; Dan White.

Publications:

Books—*John Ford* by Jean Mitry, Paris 1954; *The Western from Silents to Cinerama* by George Fenin and William Everson, New York 1962; *John Ford* by Philippe Haudiquet, Paris 1966; *John Ford* by Peter Bogdanovich, Berkeley 1968; *The Films of John Wayne* by Mark Ricci, Boris Zmijewsky, and Steve Zmijewsky, New York 1970; *The Cinema of John Ford* by John Baxter, New York 1971; *The Six-Gun Mystique* by John Cawelti, Bowling Green, Ohio 1971; *The Western Films of John Ford* by J.A. Place, Secaucus, New Jersey 1973; *The Great Western Pictures* by James R. Parish and Michael Pitts, Metuchen, New Jersey 1976; *John Ford* by Andrew Sinclair, New York 1979; *Pappy: The Life of John Ford* by Dan Ford, Englewood Cliffs, New Jersey 1979; articles—"John Ford" by Lindsay Anderson in *Films in Review* (London), February 1951; "Recontre avec John Ford" by Jean Mitry in *Cahiers du cinéma* (Paris), March 1955; "Press Conference" by John Cutts in *Sight and Sound* (London), spring 1956; "No-Contract Star" by Martin Gray in *Films and Filming* (London), March 1957; "The Five Worlds of John Ford" by Douglas McVay in *Films and Filming* (London), June 1962; issue on John Ford of *Cahiers du cinéma* (Paris), October 1966; "Our Way West" by Burt Kennedy in *Films and Filming* (London), October 1969; "Tall in the Saddle" by Dennis John Hall in *Films and Filming* (London), October 1969; "*La Charge héroïque*" by B. Boudin in *Image et son* (Paris), no.274, 1973; "The Narrative Structure of *She Wore a Yellow Ribbon*" by M. Deutelbaum in *Cinema Journal* (Evanston, Illinois), no.1, 1979.

*   *   *

She Wore a Yellow Ribbon is the middle (and arguably finest) of three films that have come to be known as John Ford's "cavalry trilogy," the two outer panels being *Fort Apache* and *Rio Grande*. The relationship of the three films to each other is somewhat confusing. *Ford Apache* culminates in Ford's fictionalized version of the Custer massacre; *She Wore a Yellow Ribbon* opens with news of the massacre, establishing an apparently direct chronological continuity; *Rio Grande*, however, takes up characters (played by the same actors) from both the earlier films in a way that makes nonsense of that chronology. For example, the *captain* Kirby Yorke of *Ford Apache* becomes the *Colonel* Kirby Yorke of *Rio Grande*, but the *Sergeant* Tyree of *Yellow Ribbon* becomes the *Trooper* Tyree of the third film. The real connections between the three films should be seen as thematic rather than fictionally continuous. *Yellow Ribbon* is stylistically distinguished from its companions because it was filmed in color—a rich, mellow, and generally sombre color which diminishes austerity and intensifies the sense of nostalgia and elegy. If *Ford Apache* is the most complex of the three, *Yellow Ribbon* is the most satisfying; though its coherence is bought at the price of evading some of the issues (the problematic nature of heroism, the gulf between myth and reality) that give the earlier work its rich ironies and contradictions.

The conventional account of Ford's career—that it moves from idealism and optimism in the 1930s and 1940s through stoical resignation in the 1950s, to final disillusionment in the last period—is too simple. It fails to account for the already disillusioned attitude toward civilization in *Stagecoach*, or the already embittered stoicism of *The Long Voyage Home*. This is not to deny that some such chronological development is there, but it is continuously counterpointed and modified by a second chronology: the historical chronology of the periods in which the films

are set. Hence *Drums Along the Mohawk* is Ford's most optimistic and idealistic film about America not only because of its relatively early date (1939), but also because it has the earliest historical setting of all his films about American history: the Revolutionary War. Similarly, *The Man Who Shot Liberty Valance* is the most disillusioned of all the westerns, not only because of its late date (1962), but because it is about the moment (mythical as much as historical) when the Old West gave way to modern America.

These two films serve as markers between which to set *Yellow Ribbon*, made at almost exactly the midpoint. Four factors are relevant to defining its position within Ford's development: 1. The date it was made (1949), when the immediate post-war optimism registered in *My Darling Clementine* had subsided with the onset of the Cold War. 2. The date of its setting, in the immediate aftermath of the Custer massacre but also in the aftermath of the Civil War, which (as Douglas Pye has rightly stressed in his three articles in *Movie*, perhaps the finest work on Ford that has been done) is for Ford the great American trauma, leaving its indelible psychic scar. 3. The shift from westerns about the growth of settled communities, microcosms of America, to westerns about the cavalry, where the problem of America itself—the widening schism between the Fordian ideal and the contemporary reality—can be partly evaded. 4. The shift from Henry Fonda to John Wayne as the definitive Ford star (Wayne had of course appeared in earlier Ford films, but it is in the 1950s that he becomes central, with *Yellow Ribbon* as the decisive step).

All these factors inter-relate—Wayne's persona is as crucial to the stoicism of the cavalry movies as Fonda's was to the idealism of *Drums Along the Mohawk, Young Mr. Lincoln, My Darling Clementine*. The spectre of the Civil War haunts *She Wore a Yellow Ribbon* more than any previous Ford movie (for example, the magnificent sequence showing the death and burial of General Clay, the southern veteran re-enlisted in the cavalry as "Trooper Smith"—a sequence wholly extraneous to the film's narrative but central to its mood and its thematic). Post-Civil War melancholy fuses with post-World War II disturbance and disillusion.

The shift in tone can be very precisely defined by a comparison of specific scenes. A recurrent motif of Ford's work is a scene in which the hero visits the grave of someone beloved and lost and addresses the dead person intimately, as if in a two-way dialogue. There is one such scene in *Young Mr. Lincoln*, another in *She Wore a Yellow Ribbon*: respectively, Lincoln (Fonda) visiting the grave of Ann Rutledge, and Captain Brittles (Wayne) visiting the grave of his dead wife. In the background of the former scene is a rushing river (the ice has just broken up); in the background of the latter, the barren desert of Monument Valley. The spring of the earlier film contrasts with the setting sun of the later. Lincoln brings with him the first spring flowers, snowdrops, a local wild-flower; Brittles is interrupted by Olivia bringing the gift of a cyclamen in a pot—a flower imported from Europe. Lincoln talks to Ann about the future: she should decide his destiny, which we know to be that of one of America's national heroes. Brittles talks to his wife about the past, specifically about the men they knew who have just died in the Custer massacre. When Brittles refers to the future, it is to his own sense of having nowhere to go, nothing to do, no function in life, on his imminent retirement. Another, simpler comparison is offered by another favorite Fordian motif, the dance (a celebration of community): in *Drums Along the Mohawk* Fonda leaves the dance to visit the cradle of his infant son; in *She Wore a Yellow Ribbon* Wayne leaves the dance to visit, once again, his wife's grave (on which scene the film virtually ends).

Although its final battle is won (and bloodlessly, by the strategem of stampeding the Indians' horses), *She Wore a Yellow Ribbon* is overwhelmingly a film of defeat. Its "happy ending" (Brittles recalled from retirement to be given an honorary position as Chief of Scouts) is abrupt, illogical and uinsatisfying. The visual image which characterizes it is that of sunset and nightfall. There is no longer any conviction about the civilization for which the cavalry is fighting: all that remains is service (generally unrewarded) in a cause that no longer has much meaning, a stoical acceptance of duty to an ideal that no longer bears much looking into.

—Robin Wood

SHERLOCK JUNIOR. Production: Metro Pictures and Buster Keaton Productions; black and white, 35mm, silent; running time: about 45 mins. Released 1924.

Produced by Joseph M. Schenck; scenario by Clyde Bruckman, Jean Haves, and Joseph Mitchell; directed by Buster Keaton; photography by Elgin Lessley and Bryon Houck; edited by Buster Keaton.

Cast: Buster Keaton (*The projectionist*); Kathryn McGuire (*The girl*); Ward Crane; Joseph Keaton.

Publications:

Books—*My Wonderful World of Slapstick* by Buster Keaton with Charles Samuels, New York 1960; *L'Originalissimo Buster Keaton* by José Pantieri, Milan 1963; *Buster Keaton* by Davide Turconi and Francesco Savio. Venice 1963; *Keaton et Compagnie: Les Burlesques américaines du "muet"* by Jean-Pierre Coursodon, Paris 1964; *Buster Keaton* by Marcel Oms, Premier Plan No.31, Lyon 1964; *Keaton* by Rudi Blesh, New York 1966; *Buster Keaton* by Jean-Pierre Lebel, New York 1967; *4 Great Comedians* by Donald McCaffrey, New York 1968; *Buster Keaton* by David Robinson, London 1968; *Anthologie du cinéma*, vol.7, Paris 1971; *The Comic Mind* by Gerald Mast, New York 1973; *Buster Keaton* by Jean-Pierre Coursodon, Paris 1973; *The Silent Clowns* by Walter Kerr, New York 1975; *The Best of Buster* edited by Richard Anobile, New York 1976; *Buster Keaton and the Dynamics of Visual Wit* by George Wead, New York 1976; *Keaton: The Silent Features Close Up* by Daniel Moews, Berkeley, 1977; *The Film Career of Buster Keaton* by George Wead and George Ellis, Boston 1977; *Keaton: The Man Who Wouldn't Lie Down* by Tom Dardis, New York 1979; articles— "Why I Never Smile" in the *Ladies Home Journal* (New York), June 1926; "Comedy's Greatest Era" in *Agee on Film* by James Agee, New York 1958; "Buster Keaton" by Brian Baxter in *Film* (London), November/December 1958; issue on Keaton of *Cahiers du cinéma* (Paris), August 1958; "The Great Stone Face" by Christopher Bishop in *Film Quarterly* (Berkeley), fall 1958; "Buster Keaton" by Jean-Marc Leuwen in *Cinéma 60* (Paris), August/September 1960; "Keaton at Venice" by James Blue and John Gillett in *Sight and Sound* (London), winter 1965-66; "Le Colosse de silence" and "Le Regard de Buster Keaton" by Robert Benayoun in *Positif* (Paris), summer 1966; "Le Génie de Buster Keaton" by Georges Sadoul in *Les Lettres Françaises* (Paris), 10 February 1966; "Buster Keaton" by Anne Villelaur in *Dossiers du cinéma: Cinéastes* I, Paris 1971; "Sherlock Holmes,

junior og Buster som bokser" by I. Lindberg in *Kosmorama* (Copenhagen), March 1973; "Buster Keaton's Gags" by Sylvain de Pasquier in *Journal of Modern Literature* (Philadelphia), April 1973; "'Anything Can Happen—And Generally Did': Buster Keaton on His Silent Film Career", interview by George Pratt in *Image* (Rochester), December 1974; "*Sherlock Junior*: Le forcené de l'intelligence" by R. Lefevre in *Cinéma* (Paris), September/October 1975; article by Claude Beylie in *Ecran* (Paris), October 1975; "*Sherlock Junior*" by D. Sauvaget in *Revue du cinéma* (Paris), October 1976; "*Sherlock Junior*" by R. Lefèvre in *Image et son* (Paris), 308bis, 1976; "Keaton Through the Looking Glass" by G. Stewart in *Georgia Review* (Athens), no.2, 1979; "The Filmic Dream and Point of View" by R.T. Eberwein in *Literature/Film Quarterly* (Salisbury, Maryland), no.3, 1980; "Discours sur le cinéma dans quelques films de Buster Keaton: by J. Valot in *Image et son* (Paris), February 1980.

*   *   *

Although he had been popular with critics and the public for several years, Buster Keaton became a major star with *The Navigator*, released after *Sherlock Jr.*. Nevertheless, *Sherlock Jr.* is a masterpiece. It contains a story within a story, through which Keaton deals with oppositions central to Western culture: dream versus reality, and reality versus art.

The film starts routinely. Beginning the dream/reality opposition, we learn that Keaton yearns to be a detective, but works merely as a projectionist. The action of the story is instigated by the announcement of a missing object. The watch belonging to the father of Keaton's girlfriend has been stolen, and as Keaton is the prime suspect, the father expels him from the house. Developing a narrative around the absence (the watch) and an expulsion of the hero is much like nineteenth-century melodrama. Even in comedies, though, this structure is not extraordinary.

After Keaton's expulsion, the film takes on a less traditional structure. Keaton falls asleep on the job. In a dream, he looks out the projectionist's window, and sees his girlfriend, her father, and his rival as performers in a film. Though the dream mirrors "real life," there are some significant changes. The setting is aristocratic, and instead of a watch, a necklace is missing. The biggest change is with Keaton himself. Awake he is only an aspiring investigator with little Holmsian ability, but once he enters the story of the film within the film, he becomes a master detective.

After the dream begins, *Sherlock Jr.* takes on characteristics of an avant-garde film. The projectionist walks to the screen, and tries to become part of the film. Like a film spectator suspending disbelief, Keaton is fooled by the realistic effect of the cinema, so much so that he cannot separate life from the movies. However, unlike the ordinary spectator, Keaton is able to participate in the film he watches. This, however, has its hazards. As he is about to enter a house, the scene cuts to an African veldt where Keaton confronts a lion. Another cut places Keaton in a snowbank; with another he is transported to the ocean. Upon entering the film within the film, the projectionist believed he would be taking part in a narrative as neat and linear as his real life one. Instead, he is at the mercy of the most artificial of cinematic devices, the cut, which allows for instant changes of locale, or the ellision of large chunks of time.

A normal story eventually returns, and Keaton (the detective) solves the mystery. A normal visual style returns, too. During the quick-cutting sequence, the movie screen, the curtain around it, and the theater audience were visible in the frame. Once the detective story begins, however, the camera moves in, no longer showing any of the theater or the edges around the screen. The film within the film (Keaton's dream) comes to look just like the character's "real life" (the beginning, when Keaton works as a projectionist). Thus, art seems to imitate life.

When Keaton awakes, his girlfriend visits him in the projectionist's booth, and tells him he has been absolved of all guilt in the watch theft. Keaton looks at the film he has been showing, and sees a man and woman reconciling. He watches for instructions, doing everything the man does, kissing his girlfriend only after the man and woman have kissed on the screen. Here, in a final blurring of the two, life imitates art.

—Eric Smoodin

SHICHININ NO SAMURAI. The Seven Samurai. Les Sept Samouraïs. The Magnificent Seven (released in New York under this title in 1956). Production: Toho Productions (Tokyo); black and white, 35mm; running time: original version: 203 mins., international version: 160 mins. (no copies of 203 mins. print extant); length: original version: 5480 meters, international version: 4401 meters. Released 26 April 1954, Tokyo. Re-released 1982.

Produced by Shojiro Motoki; screenplay by Shinobu Hashimoto, Hideo Oguni, and Akira Kurosawa; directed by Akira Kurosawa; photography by Asakasu Nakai; sound engineered by Fumio Yanoguchi; art direction by So Matsuyama; music by Fumio Hayasaka; coordinator of wrestling and sword stunts: Yoshio Sugino; archery masters: Ienori Kaneko and Shigeru Endo.

Venice Film Festival, Silver Prize, 1954.

Cast: The Samurai: Takashi Shimura (Kambei, the leader); Toshiro Mifune (Kikuchiyo); Yoshio Inaba (Gorobei); Seiji Miyaguchi (Kyuzo); Minoru Chiaki (Heihachi); Daisuke Kato (Shichiroji); Isao (Ko) Kimura (Katsuchiro); The Peasants:; Kuninori Kodo (Gisaku, the old man); Kamatari Fujiwara (Manzo); Yoshio Tsuchiya (Rikichi); Bokusen Hidari (Yohei); Yoshio Kosugi (Mosuke); Keiji Sakakida (Gosaku); Jiro Kumagai, Haruko Toyama, Tsuneo Katagiri, and Yasuhisa Tsutsumi (Peasants and farmers); Keiko Tsushima (Shino, son of Manzo); Tcranosuke Ogawa (Grandfather); Noriko Sengoku (Wife from burned house); Yu Akitsu (Husband from burned house); Gen Shimizu (Small master); Jun Tasaki and Isao Yamagata (Other samurais); Jun Tatari (Laborer); Atsushi Watanabe (Guardian of the stable); Yukikok Shimazaki (Rikichi's woman); Sojin Kamiyama (Singer); The Bandits: Eijiro Higashino (Bandit chief); Kichijiro Ueda, Shimpei Takagi, Akira Tani, Haruo Nakajima, Takashi Narita, Senkichi Omura, Shuno Takahara, and Masanobu Okubo (Bandits).

Publications:

Scripts—The Seven Samurai by Akira Kurosawa, translated by Donald Richie, New York 1970; "Les Sept Samouraïs" in Avant-Scène du cinéma (Paris), April 1971; reviews—"Seven Samurai" by Peter Barnes in Films and Filming (London), April 1955; "Seven Samurai" by Tony Richard in Sight and Sound (London), spring 1955; "Japan-Style Western" in Newsweek (New York), 10 December 1956; "The New Picture" in Time (New York), 10 December 1956; "The Magnificent Seven" by Bosley Crowther in The New York Times, 20 November 1956; "Ode to the Warrior" by Philip T. Hartung in Commonweal (New York), 14 December 1956; "The Seven Samurai" by T.S. Hines in Films in Review (New York), December 1956; "The Japanese Do It Again" by Arthur Knight in Saturday Review (New York), 1 December 1956; "East is West" by John McCarten in the New Yorker, 1 December 1956; review by F. Gaffary in Positif (Paris), March 1957; "Wild West Out East: Fight and Fury Fill Japanese Film: The Magnificent Seven" in Life (New York), 14 January 1957; books—The Japanese Film: Art and Industry by Joseph Anderson and Donald Richie, Tokyo and Rutland, Vermont 1959; Kurosawa Retrospektive by Donald Richie and Werner Schwier, Munich 1961; Kurosawa by Sacha Ezratti, Classiques du cinéma no.15, Paris 1964; Kurosawa Akira no Sekai [The World of Akira Kurosawa] by Tadao Sato, Tokyo 1968; The Films of Akira Kurosawa by Donald Richie, Berkeley 1970; Japanese Cinema: Film Style and National Character by Donald Richie, New York 1971; Kurosawa by Michel Mesnil, Paris 1973; The Waves at Genji's Door: Japan Through Its Cinema by Joan Mellen, New York 1976; Akira Kurosawa: A Guide to References and Resources by Patricia Erens, Boston 1979; articles—"The Films of Kurosawa" by Jay Leyda in Sight and Sound (London), fall 1954; "The Seven Samurai" in the New York Times Magazine, 28 October 1956; "Modesty and Pretension in 2 Films" by Jay Leyda in Film Culture (New York), no.4, 1956; "Samurai and Small Beer" by Douglas McVay in Films and Filming (London), August 1961; "When the Twain Meet: Hollywood's Remake of Seven Samurai" by Joseph Anderson in Film Quarterly (Berkeley), spring 1962; "Kurosawa", translated by Yoshio Kamii, in Cinema (New York), August/September 1963; "Kurosawa and His Work" by Akira Iwasaki in Japan Quarterly (Tokyo), 1965; "Duel dans la boue" by Max Tessier in Avant-Scène du cinéma (Paris), April 1971; "The Samurai Film and the Western" by Stuart Kaminsky in The Journal of Popular Film (Bowling Green, Ohio), fall 1972; "Kurosawa and Ichikawa: Feudalist and Individualist" in Japan, Film Image by Richard Tucker, London 1973; "Samurai" by Alain Silver in Film Comment (New York), September/-October 1975; "The Western as Jidai-geki" by K. Nolley in Western American Literature (Logan, Utah),no.3, 1976; "Akira Kurosawa's Seven Samurai" by F. Kaplan in Cineaste (New York), no.1, 1979-80; "The Seven Samurai" by H. Hosman in Skoop (Amsterdam), August 1980; "Les Sept Samourais" by A. Carbonnier in Cinéma (Paris), February 1981; "Une Epopée de l'absurdité" by F. Ramasse in Positif (Paris), February 1981.

* * *

From its opening shot of silhouetted horsemen galloping across a horizon line, The Seven Samurai announces its sources. The setting may be a 16th-century Japan convulsed by civil war, but those wide-open, lawless spaces are immediately recognizable as those of the Hollywood west.

Kurosawa has made no secret of his debt to the western in general and John Ford in particular: the small farming village of The Seven Samurai, nestled between mountain and plain, might be the Tombstone of My Darling Clementine. The marauding brigands who wait in the woods could be the vicious Clantons of Ford's film, and the seven samurai hired by the villagers for their defense could be the band of deputies, saloon girls, and alcoholic hangers-on assembled by Henry Fonda's Wyatt Earp. There is, no doubt, a broad and general resemblance between the

American western and the Japanese samurai film—in terms of the themes both genres treat, and in the historical setting they choose for their work—but in *The Seven Samurai* the correspondences are strict and specific. We recognize the rules of the game that Kurosawa is playing in *The Seven Samurai*, where in a more arcanely Japanese samurai film such as Hideo Gosha's *Bandits vs. Samurai Squadron*, we do not.

Like Ford in his westerns, Kurosawa organizes the action of *The Seven Samurai* around three different elements: the civilized (the villagers), the savage (the brigands), and those who live in between (Ford's soldiers and lawmen, Kurosawa's samurai), defending civilization by savage, violent means. (This three-point, triangular structure is something personal to Kurosawa; it pops up in different contexts throughout his work, most decisively in *Kagemusha*.) By placing his samurai in the same mediating position as Ford's lawmen, Kurosawa is self-consciously breaking with the traditions of the genre, in which the samurai represent civilization at its most refined, entrenched, and aristocratic. The heroes of Kurosawa's films are masterless samurai, no longer attached to a royal house (and hence, I believe, no longer entitled to be called samurai—masterless samurai are called *ronin*). Both Ford's lawmen and Kuorsawa's samurai are profoundly marginal figures, prevented from fully entering society by the possession of the same skills they must employ upholding it. But where Ford in his middle-period films searches constantly for the ways to reintegrate the lawmen in to society (before resolving, in his late work, that such a reconciliation is impossible), Kurosawa in *The Seven Samurai* emphasizes the unbridgeable differences between the villagers and their hired defenders. Though the townpeople and the samurai can fight in temporary alliance, they can never fight for the same goals: the villagers fight for home and family, the samurai for professional honor. The only society allowed to the samurai is their own; if civilization has no place for them, they must make a place of their own. The formation of the samurai's separate, self-enclosed society—the professional group—is the subject of some of the finest passages in Kurosawa's film: once a suitable father has been found, in the form of the veteran warrior Kambei, the other members of the family fall into place, down to a wifely companion for Kambei (Shichiroji, an old comrade-in-arms), a dutiful son (the apprentice Katsushiro), and a black sheep (Kikuchiyo). The remaining samurai are distributed like the Three Graces—Wisdom (Gorobei), Skill (Kyuzo), and Hope (Heihachi). As schematic as this arrangement may sound, Kurosawa never lets it solidify; there is no flat sense of allegory here, bur rather an open vision of different talents and attributes brought into harmony. To distinguish bewteen the members of the group, Kurosawa gives each a defining gesture, much as Walt Disney differentiated his seven dwarfs: Kambei's reflective rubbing of his scalp, Kikuchiyo's leaps and whoops, Katsushiro's imploring eyes, etc. This, too, is classic Hollywood shorthand technique, in which a ritual gesture completely subsumes a character's psychology. And there is a pleasure in its repetition: each time Kambei scratches his head, he is reassuring the strength and constancy of his character. The gesture never changes, and neither does he. He is permanent, and in this one movement we know him and trust him.

At least one-quarter of *The Seven Samurai* is devoted to the relations between the townspeople and the professional group. Kurosawa seems to be looking for a stable, workable relationship, but he rejects each possibility in turn; there is always a dissonance, a contradiction, between the two groups. The samurai take charge of fortifying the village and training the farmers to fight, yet because they are, in the end, mere employees of the villagers, they are never in a position of genuine authority. The samurai tell themselves that they are fighting on behalf of the poor and helpless, but the cozy paternalism of this relationship is undermined by the suggestion that the farmers have been holding out—that they have secret reserves of rice and sake they refuse to share with their protectors. Two of the samurai have ties to the villagers—Kaksushiro, who falls in love with a village girl, and Kikuchiyo, who is revealed to be a farmer's son—yet neither of these bonds is allowed to endure. By insisting so strongly on the absolute separation of the groups, Kurosawa departs radically from the western archetype: the lawmen can no longer derive their values from the community, as they did in Ford and Hawks, but must now define those values for themselves. This sense of moral isolation—fresh and startling in the genre context of 1954—eventually became Kurosawa's gift to the American western, his way of giving back as much as he took. Even before *The Seven Samurai* was officially remade as a western (John Sturges's 1960 *The Magnificent Seven*), Kurosawa's variation had been incorporated in the genre, giving rise to the series of "professional" westerns that runs from Hawks's optimistic *Rio Bravo* to the final cynicism of Sergio Leone.

Separation is also the subject of Kurosawa'a mise-en-scene. Using both foreground-background separation of deep-focus shots and the flattening, abstracting effect of telephoto lenses, Kurosawa puts a sense of unbridgeable space in nearly all of his shots. Even in what should be the most intimate and open scenes among the samurai themselves, Kurosawa arranges his compositions in distinct rigid planes, placing one or two figures in the extreme foreground, two or three more in a row in the middle, the balances lined up in the background (this will also be the design applied to the burial mound at the film's conclusion). The primary visual motif is one of boundaries: the natural ones formed around the village by the mountains, woods, and flooded rice fields, the man-made boundaries of fences, stockades, and doorways. The extreme formality of Kurosawa's compositions also emphasizes the boundaries of the frame; there is only occasionally a sense of off-screen space, as if nothing existed beyond the limits of the camera's eye. The world of *The Seven Samurai* is carefully delineated, compartmentalized; not only are the characters isolated in their separate groups, but in separate spaces.

The compartmentalization reflects Kurosawa's theme, but it also works (more originally, I think) in organizing the film emotionally—in building its suspense and narrative power. Three hours pass between the announcement of the brigands' attack and its arrival—an impossibly long time to keep the audience waiting for a single event. But where most filmmakers would try to fill the interval with minor flurries of action, Kurosawa gives us only two: Kambei's rescue of a child and the guerilla foray into the brigands' camp. These incidents are so widely spaced (misplaced, even, in terms of conventional rhythm) that they don't serve at all to support the structure of crest and valley, crest and valley that the long form usually depends on. Instead, Kurosawa sticks to a strict linearity: the narrative has been divided (compartmentalized?) into discrete acts (the posing of the threat, the recruitment of the samurai, the fortification of the village, the battle), separated not by strongly marked climaxes but by the slow and subtle transitions. The rigorous chopping, dividing, and underlining of space is the only constant factor through these transitions: no matter what the characters may be doing, the visual style is bearing down on them, forcing them further into immobility, isolation, entrapment. The suspense builds visually, subliminally, until we long for the final battle with its promise of release.

The battle in the rain is the most celebrated passage in Kurosawa's work, justly famous for its overwhelming physicality—the sense of force and texture, of sensual immersion, produced by staging the sequence in the mud and confusion of a fierce storm. But the rain also accomplishes something else—it fills in the spaces that Kurosawa has so carefully carved off, creating a continuity, an even density, from foreground to background. The rain begins the night before the battle, during the greatest moment of divisiveness between the townspeople and the samurai—the confrontation over Kikuchiyo's right to love a village girl. By forcing the two groups to fight more closely together, the rain closes this gap during the battle. And suddenly, all other boundaries are broken open: as part of their strategy, the samurai allow some of the brigands to cross the fortifications (cut off from support, they can be killed more easily in the village square) and the camera loses its fixity and formality, panning wildly to follow details of action within the struggle. It is an ineffable moment of freedom, and of course it cannot last.

For his epilogue, Kurosawa returns to divided space. The surviving samurai are seen in one shot, standing still before the graves of those who fell; the villagers are seen in another, singing and moving in unison as they plant the new rice crop. There probably isn't a more plangent moment in all Kurosawa's work than this juxtaposition of two different tempos, two different worlds. They are separated only by a cut, but they are separated forever.

—Dave Kehr
©essay copyright Chicago Reader, Inc. 1983

SHOCK CORRIDOR. Production: F & F Productions (A Leon Fromkess-Sam Firks Production); 1963; black and white with Technicolor sequences, 35mm, Cinemascope without anamorphic lens; running time: 101 mins. Released 11 September 1963, New York.

Produced, scripted, and directed by Sam Fuller; titles designed by Ray Mercer; photography by Stanley Cortez, color sequences by Sam Fuller; edited by Jerome Thomas; sound recording supervised by Phil Mitchell, music and sound effects supervised by Gordon Zahler, sound effects by Joseph von Stroheim; art direction by Eugene Lourie, set decorated by Charles Thompson; music by Paul Dunlap; special effects by Charles Duncan, special optical effects by Lynn Dunn; costumes designed by Einar Bourman; choreography by Jon Gregory.

Filmed during 14 days in 1963 in Hollywood.

Cast: Peter Breck (*Johnny Barett*); Constance Towers (*Cathy*); Gene Evans (*Boden*); James Best (*Stuart*); Hari Rhodes (*Trent*); Larry Tucker (*Pagliacci*); William Zuckert (*Swanee*); Philip Ahn (*Dr. Fong*); Neyle Morrow (*Lloyd*); Frank Gerstle (*Police lieutenant*); Paul Dubov (*Dr. Menkin*); Rachel Romen (*Singing nympho*); Linda Randolph (*Dance teacher*); John Matthews (*Dr. Cristo*); Chuck Roberson (*Wilkes*); John Craig (*Lloyd*).

Publications:

Script—"*Shock Corridor*" by Samuel Fuller in *Avant-Scène du cinéma* (Paris), December 1965; reviews—in *Cinema* (Beverly Hills), August/September 1963; review by Andrew Sarris in *The Village Voice* (New York), 12 September 1963; books—*Samuel Fuller* edited by David Will and Peter Wollen, Edinburgh, Scotland 1969; *Samuel Fuller* by Phil Hardy, New York 1970; *The Director's Event: Interviews with Five American Film-makers*

by Eric Sherman and Martin Rubin, New York 1970; *Samuel Fuller* by Nicholas Garnham, New York 1972; articles—"Samuel Fuller" by Lee Russell in *New Left Review* (New York), January/February 1964; "Quelques notes sur un visionnaire" by Bertrand Tavernier in *Avant-Scène du cinéma* (Paris), December 1965; "Notes Toward a Structural Analysis of the Films of Samuel Fuller" by Peter Wollen in *Cinema* (London), December 1968; "The World of Samuel Fuller" by Kingsley Canham in *Film* (London), November/December 1969; article by Margaret Tarratt in *Films and Filming* (London), July 1970; "The Films of Sam Fuller and Don Siegel" by Manny Farber in *December* (New York), nos.1-2, 1970; "Love, Action, Death, Violence: Cinema Is Emotion (sur quelques films de Samuel Fuller)" by J. Valot in *Image et son* (Paris), July/August 1980; "La Violence de Fuller" by O.-R. Veillon in *Cinématographe* (Paris), September 1980; section on Fuller of *Image et son* (Paris), April 1981.

*   *   *

"My name is Johnny Barrett, and this is my story...as far as it went," says the opening narration of *Shock Corridor*. No more chilling words ever began a movie, and in retrospect, a viewer realizes that, just as each of the three insane characters has had a moment of lucidity in which to tell his story to the audience, this film has been nothing but the hero's similar moment. He is totally, frighteningly insane.

Shock Corridor has been described as a film involving only interiors, both literally and psychologically. Director Samuel Fuller has wielded a series of dynamic images and sounds into a striking presentation of the inner state of a group of insane inmates. As usual, Fuller follows no accepted "rules of cinema" in his presentation, but explores experimentally all the possibilities such a setting affords him creatively. To demonstrate madness, he uses many techniques in a bold manner. When an inmate conducts a symphony that is taking place only inside his head, Fuller chooses to show that only the crazy man hears the music through an unconventional method. Instead of employing cuts from character to character, he shows the different interior worlds of the mind by camera angle, panning, and manipulation of the sound track. When another inmate tells about his days as a prisoner of the Communists, his internal world is seen in color (the film is black and white) and as a distorted image. (Fuller used footage from his own anamorphic color film, *House of Bamboo.*)

The hero's slow descent into madness is expertly woven into a narrative story of how he has himself committed to an insane asylum in order to discover who committed a murder there. It is his hope to reveal the story and win the Pulitzer Prize. This obsession, which causes him to undertake such a dangerous and bizarre action, lays the foundation for the emotional state which will ultimately consume him. As he has to repress his intelligent, rational self in order to pretend sanity, his interior monologues become the audience's guide to reality. Eventually, it becomes clear that his interior world has truly become insane, and an audience watches in horror as his view of the "shock corridor," the hallway of his ward, turns from an ordinary space into a raging torrent of pouring water and distorted sound. The hero of the film has been turned inside out, as the film has moved deeper and deeper inside of him. Finally, it ends there. He has no external, sane self left at all; he has become a catatonic schizophrenic.

Since *Shock Corridor* is about the characters' internal selves, Fuller establishes a sophisticated level of subjective/objective presentation. He presents a character inside a setting, and then gives the viewer an objective look at what the character sees. By panning back to the character, and then re-returning to the same point of view, but presenting this time as the character sees it, he establishes an interior distorted state through one shot. By using such unorthodox film techniques, Fuller's films provide an onslaught of emotional impact. This iconoclastic style is effectively used in *Shock Corridor*, where the subject matter calls for Fuller's use of an inconsistent narrative structure, intense close-ups, extensive camera movement, long takes sustaining continuous action, and shock cutting.

Shock Corridor, like most of Fuller's work, has been dismissed by critics if treated at all. Over the years, Fuller has been appreciated by scholars who understand film as a visual art and by the general public, but never by critics. His influence on modern cinema, however, has been significant, and *Shock Corridor* is one of his major films.

—Jeanine Basinger

SHONEN. Boy. Production: Sozo-sha and A.T.G.; Eastmancolor with black and white sequences, 35mm, Cinemascope; running time: 97 mins.; length: 2676 meters. Released 1969, Japan.

Produced by Masayuki Nakajima and Takuji Yamaguchi; screenplay by Tsutomu Tamura; directed by Nagisa Oshima; photography by Yasuhiro Yoshioka and Seizo Sengen; edited by Sueko Shiraishi. sound by Hideo Nishizaki, sound effects by Akira Suzuki; art direction by Jusho Toda; music by Hikaru Hayashi.

Cast: Tetsuo Abe (*Toshio*); Fumio Watanabe (*Father*); Akiko Koyama (*Stepmother*); Tsuyoshi Kinoshita (*Little brother*).

Publications:

Books—*Second Wave* by Ian Cameron, New York 1970; *Cinema giapponese degli anni 60* (3 vols.), Pesaro, Italy 1972; *Oshima Nagisa no sekai* [The World of Nagisa Oshima] by Tadao Sato, Tokyo 1973; *Japanese Film Directors* by Audie Bock, New York 1978; articles—"Nagisa Oshima" by Ian Cameron in *Movie* (London), winter 1969/70; "Oshima" in *Film* (London), spring 1970; article by Margaret Tarratt in *Films and Filming* (London), August 1970; article by Philip Strick in *Sight and Sound* (London), summer 1970; "Cinéma japonais d'après-guerre" by J. Delmas in *Jeune Cinéma* (Paris), November 1972; "Nagisa Oshima and Japanese Cinema in the 60s" by Noël Burch in *Cinema: A Critical Dictionary* edited by Richard Roud, London 1980; "Nagisa Oshima", special section by J.G. Requena and others in *Contracampo* (Madrid), July/August 1980.

*　　*　　*

Based on a real event which shocked Japan in the mid-1960s, *Shonen* depicts a family that travels the country, collecting out-of-court settlement money in automobile accident scams. The film is clearly Nagisa Oshima's: thematically, it deals with crimes; it is based on a real event; and it develops many of his stylistic devices.

The character of the lazy and self-indulgent father, for example, represents the victim complex that Oshima sees as typical of the postwar Japanese mentality. The character serves as a microcosm of the problems of the patriarchal Japanese emperor state. Oshima's criticism is ultimately of a society where uneducated and unskilled parents can use and exploit their own children in illegal schemes. The cruelty of the authorities is shown by the arrest of the family after they have given up their life of crime and settled in the city. The omnipresence of state authority is conveyed by the Japanese national flags: in the street, in the hand of the baby, on the boat, and in the background.

Basically, the film follows a linear narrative though it includes many experimental stylistic devices, such as the occasional insertion of black and white footage. The first insert, showing the family's flight to a new town works like a fantasy scene. The second insert, a car accident, masks the colors of the blood and the victim's red boot. Later, when the film returns to color, the viewers are shocked by the red of the blood and the boot in the white snow (corresponding to the colors of the Japanese flag).

There are occasional suspensions of sound as well as the use of still photographs accompanied by the boy's narration reminiscent of a school composition, and newspaper clips accompanied by a newsreel-like narration. Other such techniques used to emphasize important points include: the slow-motion scene of the boy (never called by name throughout the film) destroying the snowman, one of the few scenes in which he displays strong emotion, and the theatrical setting where the father fights with the mother and the son beside what appears to be a funeral altar in front of a large national flag. In additon, Oshima often deliberately confuses the sense of time between shots.

Abstract music, often resembling actual sounds, is used disjointedly with the image, and the intentional decentralization of the Cinemascope composition is visually jarring as many actions take place on the far left or right side of the screen. Such stylistic techniques are intended to destroy our suspension of disbelief and therefore destroy our subconcious identification with (and sympathy for) the main characters. Oshima is careful not to trivialize his subject by sentimentalizing it. He avoids this all-too-easy trap by, for example, never using music to enhance the character's emotion.

Shonen does not make simplistic judgments on the characters or the situations. We simply see the boy's solitude, playing by himself and pretending to visit his grandmother. Only twice in the film do we see his tears, despite all the mental and physical exploitation he suffers. We are never told why the boy keeps silent after his family is arrested. Instead, on many levels and in many subtle ways, this film urges us to think. Perhaps for this reason, this film was more successful critically than commercially.

—Kyoko Hirano

SINGIN' IN THE RAIN. Production: Metro-Goldwyn-Mayer Pictures Corp.; 1952; Technicolor, 35mm; running time: 103 mins.; length: 9228 feet. Released 1952.

Produced by Arthur Freed; screenplay by Betty Comden and Adolph Green; from the play by Betty Comden and Adolph Green; directed by Gene Kelly and Stanley Donen; photography by Harold Rosson; edited by Adrienne Fazan; sound recording supervised by Douglas Shearer; set decoration by Edwin B. Willis and Jacques Mapes; art direction by Cedric Gibbons and

Randall Duell; music direction by Lennie Hayton, orchestrations by Conrad Salinger, Wally Heglin, and Skip Martin, songs by Arthur Freed, Nacio Herb Brown, Betty Comden, and Roger Edens, vocal arrangements by Jeff Alexander; special effects by Warren Newcombe and Irving G. Ries.

Filmed in MGM Studios and backlots.

Cast: Gene Kelly (*Don Lockwood*); Donald O'Connor (*Cosmo Brown*); Debbie Reynolds (*Kathy Selden*); Jean Hagen (*Lina Lamont*); Millard Mitchell (*R.F. Simpson*); Rita Moreno (*Zelda Zanders*); Douglas Fowley (*Roscoe Dexter*); Cyd Charisse (*Dancer*); Madge Blake (*Dora Bailey*); King Donovan (*Rod*); Kathleen Freeman (*Phoebe Dinsmore, diction coach*); Bobby Watson (*Diction coach*); Tommy Farrell (*Sid Phillips, ass't. director*); Jimmie Thompson (*Male lead in "Beautiful Girls" number*); Dan Foster (*Ass't. director*); Margaret Bert (*Wardrobe woman*); Mae Clark (*Hairdresser*); Judy Landon (*Olga Mara*); John Dodsworth (*Baron De La Bouvet De La Toulon*); Stuart Holmes (*J.C. Spendrill III*); Dennis Ross (*Don as a boy*); Bill Lewin (*Villian in western, Bert*); Richard Emory (*Phil, cowboy hero*); Julius Tannen (*Man on screen*); Dawn Addams and Elaine Stewart (*Ladies in waiting*); Carl Milletaire (*Villain, "Dueling Cavalier" and "Broadway Rhythm"*); Jac George (*Orchestra leader*); Wilson Wood (*Vallee impersonator*).

Publications:

Script—*Singin' in the Rain* (includes an introduction discussing the development of the storyline and script) by Betty Comden and Adolph Green, New York 1972; reviews—"Singin' in the Rain" by Edward Jablonski in *Films in Review* (New York), April 1952; "Singin' in the Rain" by James Morgan in *Sight and Sound* (London), July/September 1952; review by Jean de Baroncelli in *Le Monde* (Paris), 20 September 1953; books—*The Cinema of Gene Kelly* by Richard Griffith, New York 1962; *All Talking, All Singing, All Dancing* by John Springer, New York 1966; *Gotta Sing, Gotta Dance* by John Kobal, New York 1970; *Gene Kelly* by Michael Burrows, Cornwall, England 1971; *The MGM Years* by Lawrence B. Thomas, New Rochelle, New York 1972; *The Movie Musical* by Lee Edward Stern, New York 1974; *Gene Kelly* by Clive Hirschhorn, Chicago 1975; *The Best of MGM* by Parish and Mank, 1981; articles—"From Dance to Film Director" by Arthur Knight in *Dance* (New York), August 1954; "The 10th Muse in San Francisco" by Albert Johnson in *Sight and Sound* (London), summer 1956; special issue on musical comedy, *Cinéma 59* (Paris), August/September 1959; "Le Plus Beau Film du monde" by J.P. Coursodon in *Cinéma 59* (Paris), August/September 1959; article by René Gilson in *Cinéma 62* (Paris), May 1963; "Entretien avec Stanley Donen" by Bertrand Tavernier and Daniel Pallas in *Cahiers du cinéma* (Paris), May 1963; "Gene Kelly" by Rudy Behlmer in *Films in Review* (New York), January 1964; "Dancer, Actor, Director" by John Cutts in *Films and Filming* (London), August 1964 and September 1964; "Le Premier Film 'camp': *Singin' in the Rain*" by Gene Kelly in *Cinéma 71* (Paris), July/August 1971; "Chantons sous la pluie" by R. Lefevre in *Cinéma* (Paris), February 1973; "Chantons sous la pluie" by F. Pasche in *Travelling* (Lausanne, Switzerland), January/February 1974; article by Stephen Winer in *Velvet Light Trap* (Madison, Wisconsin), no.11, 1974; "Quelques Réflexions sur cinq 'Musicals' en réédition" by G. and A. Dagneau in *Image et son* (Paris), February 1977; "Cult Movies: *Singin' in the Rain*" by B. Day in *Films and Filming* (London), April 1977; "Entertainment and Utopia" by Richard

Dyer in *Movie* (London), no.24, 1977; "Show-Making" by Dennis Giles in *Movie* (London), no.24, 1977; "Come on with the Rain" by J. Mariani in *Film Comment* (New York), May/June 1978; "Making *Singin' in the Rain*" by W.R. Wolf in *Film en Televisie* (Brussels), March 1979; "*Singin' in the Rain*" by Julia Johnson in *Magill's Survey of Cinema, Vol. IV* edited by Frank N. Magill, Englewood Cliffs, New Jersey 1980; "Cenizas del sentido. Acerca de *Cantando bajo la iluvia*" by J.M. Company and J. Talens in *Contracampo* (Madrid), September 1981.

*   *   *

Traditionally, the film musical is said to have reached its pinnacle in the 1950s at MGM studios. The creative personnel at MGM responsible for this perfection were Arthur Freed, Vincent Minnelli, Stanley Donen and Gene Kelly. The "golden era" began with *On the Town* (1949) and ended with *Gigi* (1958); between were *An American in Paris, Singin' in the Rain, The Bandwagon, Seven Brides for Seven Brothers, It's Always Fair Weather*, and *Funny Face*. With the exception of *On the Town*, all were originally conceived for the screen. They were, in a sense, the last of their kind, because the early 1950s began the great mass adaptions of Broadway musicals. As television began to effect box office returns, the studios were hesitant to produce big budget musicals unless they were proven hits.

All were developments on Arthur Freed's concept of organic integration. The production numbers would, ideally, grow directly out of the emotional needs of the characters or would serve as plot motivation. Song and dance would replace dialogue as a means of discourse. Whether or not this is the perfect structure for the musical is debatable. Richard Dyer feels that critical stances which champion this form recapitulate the dominant ideology. In "Entertainment and Utopia," he states that entertainment is escapist/wish-fulfilling, a longing for something better—a literal Utopia. Musicals manage contradictions in the system (music/narrative, success/failure, love/hate, wealth/poverty, male/female) on all levels in such a way as to make them disappear. A film that offers no distinction between narrative (reality) and musical numbers (escapist fantasy) suggests that the narrative is also (already) Utopian. The films of the 1950s can be seen as the most ideologically repressive, because of the ease in which that ideology can be hidden.

Of the musicals of the 1950s, *Singin' in the Rain* is the best remembered. In 1977, the American Film Institute conducted a poll that listed *Singin' in the Rain* as one of the top ten American films. "*Singin' in the Rain* is generally accepted as the apogee of screen musical art, a virtually faultless film by any standards...," says Arthur Jackson, in *The Best Musicals*. Clive Hirschorn notes that *Singin' in the Rain*, released "...on the heels of *An American in Paris*, did not receive the glowing reviews of the Gershwin film.... Over the years, however, it has surpassed *An American in Paris* in popularity and is now recognized as one of the all time greats'...." Following so closely behind *An American in Paris, Singin' in the Rain* was not as generally well received. *Time* felt it was "... without much warmth or wit," and *Newsweek* called it "sluggish." It was nominated for only two Oscars; Jean Hagen for supporting actress and musical score. Notwithstanding, it was listed as one of the best films of 1952 by the National Board of Review and *Films in Review*, was the number one money-making film in April 1952, and number ten money-making film of the same year. Written by Betty Comden and Adolph Green (who also wrote *On the Town*), the screenplay won the award for best writing in an American musical from the Writers Guild of America.

The work of Comden and Green usually ridiculed an industry (filmmaking in *Singin' in the Rain*, theater in *The Bandwagon*, and television in *It's Always Fair Weather*) but without bitterness; "...there was always wit, and so they were able to create musical movies full of joy that were still effective satire," says Stephen Winer in *Velvet Light Trap*. Based on a catalogue of songs writen by Arthur Freed and Nacio Herb Brown during the late 1920s and early 1930s, the film spoofed the turmoils of the transition from silent to sound film. Originally planned for Howard Keel, who was extremely popular at that time, it eventually shifted to accommodate the persona of Gene Kelly, who also co-directed with Stanley Donen. Kelly's career is firmly rooted in film history not only for his solo routine to the title song, but also because of the "Broadway Rhythm" ballet. As expensive (in rehearsal/shooting time and overall cost) as the climactic ballet from *An American in Paris*, it was also as out of place. Gene Kelly commented on the "Broadway Rhythm" ballet at an American Film Institute symposium in 1979. Not being able to use Donald O'Connor or Debbie Reynolds, "...we got Cyd Charisse and just wrote a whole ballet and stuck it in. That's how it came about. We had to have a number there. We never meant it to be that long, but since we were introducing a new character into the show, we had to keep adding to it and adding to it. It went on for hours, it seems." Donald O'Connor is possibly best remembered for his song and dance solo "Make Em Laugh", an athletic *tour-de-force* that helped him win the Golden Globe for Best Actor in 1952. *Singin' in the Rain* was Debbie Reynolds's third film for MGM and her first major role. Reportedly her age (she was only 19) and lack of professional experience was problematic. Playing the role of an understudy who dubs the voice of a silent star, she was dubbed by Betty Noyes for the singing and by Jean Hagen for the lines Debbie was supposedly dubbing for Jean Hagen's character, Lina Lamont.

Dennis Giles, offers a psycho-analytical reading of *The Bandwagon* and *Singin' in the Rain* that is particularly interesting. He sees the successful production of the show (in *Singin' in the Rain*, the ravamping of *The Dueling Cavalier* into *The Singing Cavalier*) as a visually uncensored form of love-making. "The private show of love is displayed through the vehicle of the public spectacle: the lovers sing and dance to each other as if they were alone, at the same time that they openly display this love to the on-screen (diegetic) audience and to ourselves, the off-screen spectators." A successful show guarentees a consummated relationship between the male and female leads. Needless to say, *The Singing Cavalier* is a hit and Gene Kelly and Debbie Reynolds embrace as *Singin' in the Rain* fades out.

—Greg S. Faller

DET SJUNDE INSEGLET. The Seventh Seal. Production: Svensk Filmindustri; 1956; black and white, 35mm; running time: 96 mins. Released 16 February 1957, Stockholm.

Produced by Allan Ekelund; screenplay by Ingmar Bergman; from the dramatic sketch *Wood Painting* by Ingmar Bergman; directed by Ingmar Bergman; photography by Gunnar Fischer; edited by Lennart Wallén; sound by Aaby Wedin and Lennart Wallin, special sound effects by Evald Andersson; sets by P.A. Lundgren; music by Erik Nordgren, music directed by Sixten Ehrling; costumes designed by Manne Lindholm; make-up by Nils Nittel and Carl M. Lundh, Inc.

Filmed in the summer of 1956 in Svensk Filmindustri's studios, Råsunda, Sweden, and on location at Hovs Hallar, Sweden. Cannes Film Festival, Special Prize, 1957.

Cast: Bengt Ekerot (*Death*); Nils Poppe (*Jof*); Max von Sydow (*The Knight, Antonius Blok*); Bibi Andersson (*Mia*); Inga Gill (*Lisa*); Maud Hansson (*Tyan, the witch*); Inga Landgré (*Knight's wife*); Gunnal Lindblom (*The girl*); Berto Anderberg (*Raval*); Anders Ek (*Monk*); Ake Fridell (*Plog, the smith*); Gunnar Olsson (*Church painter*); Erik Strandmark (*Skat*); Benkt-Åke Benktsson (*The merchant*); Gudrum Brost (*Woman at the inn*); Ulf Johansson (*Leader of the soldiers*); Lars Lind (*The young monk*); Gunnar Börnstrand (*Jöns, the squire*).

Publications:

Scripts—*The 7th Seal: A Film By Ingmar Bergman* by Ingmar Bergman, translated by Lars Malstrom and David Kushner, New York 1960; *4 Screenplays of Ingmar Bergman* translated by Lars Malmstrom and David Kushner, New York 1960; *Ingmar Bergman: Oeuvres* translated by C.G. Bjurström and Maurice Pons, Paris 1962; reviews—"*The 7th Seal*" by John Peter Dyer in *Sight and Sound* (London), spring 1958; "Traduit du silence" by Jean Mambrino in *Cahiers du cinéma* (Paris), May 1958; "Wormwood for You and Me" by Dilys Powell in *The Sunday Times* (New York), 9 March 1958; "The 7th Seal" by Colin Young in *Film Quarterly* (Berkeley), spring 1959; "Apocalypse und Totentantz" by Theo Fürstenau in *Die Zeit*, 16 February 1962; books—*Ingmar Bergman et ses films* by Jean Béranger, Paris 1959; *Ingmar Bergman: teatermannen och filmskaparen* by Fritiof Billquist, Stockholm 1960; *Thèmes d'inspiration d'Ingmar Bergman* by Jos. Burvenich, Brussels 1960; *Ingmar Bergman* by Marianne Höök, Stockholm 1962; *Ingmar Bergman* by Tommaso Chiaretti, Rome 1964; *The Personal Vision of Ingmar Bergman* by Jörn Donner, Bloomington, Indiana 1964; *Ingmar Bergman* by Jean Béranger and François Guyon, Lyon 1964; *Ingmar Bergman: The Search for God* by David Nelson, Boston 1964; *La Crisi spirituali dell'uomo moderno nei film di Ingmar Bergman* by Massimo Maisetti, Varese 1964; *Ingmar Bergman* by Birgitta Steene, New York 1968; *The Silence of God: Creative Response to the Films of Ingmar Bergman* by Arthur Gibson, New York 1969; *Ingmar Bergman* by Robin Wood, New York 1969; *Regi: Ingmar Bergman* by Henrik Sjögren, Stockholm 1970; *Cinema Borealis: Ingmar Bergman and the Swedish Ethos* by Vernon Young, New York 1971; *Focus on 'The 7th Seal'* edited by Brigitta Steen, Englewood Cliffs, New Jersey, 1972; *Ingmar Bergman* by Tino Ranieri, Florence 1974; *Ingmar Bergman: Essays in Criticism* edited by Stuart Kaminsky, New York 1975; *Ingmar Bergman and Society* by Maria Bergom-Larsson, San Diego 1978; *Mindscreen: Bergman, Godard and the First-Person Film* by Bruce Kawin, Princeton 1978; *Ingmar Bergman* by Denis Marion, Paris 1979; *Bergman on Bergman: Interviews with Ingmar Bergman* by Stig Bjorkman, Torsten Lanns, and Jonas Sima, translated by Paul Britten Austin, New York 1970; *Ingmar Bergman: An Appreciation* by Roger Manvell, New York 1980; *Ingmar Bergman: The Cinema as Mistress* by Philip Mosley, Boston 1981; *Film and Dreams: An Approach to Bergman* edited by Vlada Petrić, South Salem, New York 1981; *Ingmar Bergman: A Critical Biography* by Peter Cowie, New York 1982; *A Reference Guide to Ingmar Bergman* by Birgitta Steene, Boston 1982; articles—"*The 7th Seal*" by Henry Hart in *Films in Review* (New York), November 1958; "Avec *Le Septième Sceau* Bergman nous offre son Faust" by Eric Rohmer in *Arts* (Paris), 23 April 1958;

"Death and the Knight" by William Whitebait in *The New Statesman* (London), 8 March 1958; *Le Septième Sceau*" by Guy Allombert in *Image et Son* (Paris), February 1959; "The Rack of Life" by Eugene Archer in *Film Quarterly* (Berkeley), summer 1959; "*The 7th Seal*: The Film as Iconography" by Norman Holland in *The Hudson Review* (Nutley, New Jersey), summer 1959; "Notes on the Films of Ingmar Bergman" by Ian Jarvie in *Film Journal* (Melbourne), November 1959; "*The 7th Seal*" by Andrew Sarris in *Film Culture* (New York), no.19, 1959; "Ingmar, the Image-Maker" by John Simon in *The Mid-Century* (New York), December 1960; cover story on Ingmar Bergman in *Time* (New York), 14 March 1960; "*Dal settimo sigillo* alle soglie della vita" by Antonio Napolitano in *Cinema nuovo* (Turin), May/June 1961; "Great Films of the Century: *The 7th Seal*" by Peter Cowie in *Films and Filming* (London), January 1963; "The Achievement of Ingmar Bergman" by James F. Scott in *The Journal of Aesthetics and Arts* (Cleveland, Ohio), winter 1965; "The Isolated Hero of Ingmar Bergman" by Birgitta Steene in *Film Comment* (New York), September 1965; "Bergman's *Shame* and Sartre's *Stare*" by Robert E. Louder in *Catholic World*, September 1969; "The Snakeskin" by Ingmar Bergman in *Film Comment* (New York), summer 1970; "The Milk and the Strawberry Sequence in *The Seventh Seal*" by B. Steene in *Film Heritage* (Dayton, Ohio), summer 1973; "As Normal as Smorgasbord" by Charles Marowitz in the *New York Times Magazine*, 1 July 1973; "Ingmar Bergman albo parabola pytań odwiecznych" by A. Helman in *Kino* (Warsaw), August 1974; "*The Seventh Seal*" by Darryl Wimberly in *Cinema Texas Program Notes* (Austin), 15 September 1977; "*Det syvende segl*" by P. Malmkjaer in *Kosmorama* (Copenhagen), spring 1978.

*   *   *

The Seventh Seal is one of the films in Ingmar Bergman's mature, highly individualized style, coming after an initial period he considers merely an imitative apprenticeship, in which he made films in the style of other directors. It was derived from a dramatic sketch, *Wood Painting*, which Bergman had written in 1954 for his drama students in Malmö. *The Seventh Seal* was made on a very low budget in 35 days.

In his late thirties, Bergman was still struggling with religious doubts and problems after having been reared very strictly in the Protestant Luthern tradition, his father having been a prominent Swedish pastor. *The Seventh Seal*, which Bergman has termed an oratorio, is the first of three films (the others being *The Face* and *The Virgin Spring*) made at this time in which he tried to purge the uglier aspects of religious practice and persecution, as well as confront the absence of any sign of response from God to human craving for help and reassurance. As the film makes clear at the beginning, the title refers to God's book of secrets sealed by seven seals; only after the breaking of the seventh seal will the secret of life, God's great secret, be revealed. In *Bergman on Bergman* he is quoted as saying, "For me, in those days, the great question was: Does God exist? or doesn't God exist?.... If God doesn't exist, what do we do then?.... What I believed in those days—and believed in for a long time—was the existence of a virulent evil, in no way dependent upon environmental or hereditary factors...an active evil, of which human beings, as opposed to animals, have a monopoly." He regards the 1950s as a period of personal convulsion, the remnants of his faith altering with a strengthening scepticism.

In *The Seventh Seal*, Antonius Blok, a 14th century knight, returns home with his earthy, sensual squire, Jöns, after a decade of crusading in the Holy Land. He finds his native country plague-striken and the people, haunted by a sense of guilt, given over to self-persecution, flagellation, and witch-hunting, a movement induced by a fantastic and sadistic monk, Raval. The Knight, God's servant-at-arms, finds that he has lost his faith and can no longer pray. In the midst of his spiritual turmoil he is suddenly confronted by the personification of Death, a figure cloaked and implacable, who coldly informs him that his time has come. The Knight, unable to accept demise when in a state of doubt, wins a brief reprieve by challenging Death to a game of chess, the traditional ploy adopted by those seeking more time on earth, for Death is supposedly unable to resist such a challenge.

The film, Bergman has said, is "about the fear of death." Bergman had been steeped since childhood in the kind of imagery portrayed in this film, with its legendary concepts and simple pictorial forms; he had looked endlessly at the mural paintings that decorate the medieval Swedish churches. A painter of such images appears in the film, contriving studies of death to frighten the faithful. The stark but theatrical Christian imagery comes to life in *The Seventh Seal*. The Knight wins a brief reprieve, but Death still stalks his native land as the plague takes hold, and continues to haunt him with constant reappearances. The Knight demands:

> Is it so cruelly inconceivable to grasp God with the senses? Why should he hide himself in a midst of half-spoken promises and unseen miracles?.... What is going to happen to those of us who want to believe but aren't able to?.... Why can't I kill God within me? Why does he live on in this painful and humiliating way even though I curse him and want to tear him out of my heart?.... I want knowledge, not faith....I want God to stretch out his hand toward me, reveal himself to me.... In our fear, we make an image and that image we call God.

But death has no anwers, and God is silent. As for Jöns, he is faithful to his master, but cynical about the horrors of the Crusades: "Our crusade," he says, "was such madness that only a genuine idealist could have thought it up.... This damned ranting about doom. Is that good for the minds of modern people?" He prefers the simplicity of drink and fornication. To him Christianity is just "ghost stories."

In total contrast to the Knight's fearful dilemmas concerning faith and self-persecution is the position of Joff, a poor traveling entertainer and his beautiful young wife Mia. Joff, in his simplicity of heart, has continual visions of the Virgin and Child. Although Mia laughs lovingly at his excitement following the vision, she is happy to share his unquestioning faith. Only with these unpretentious people does the Knight find solace, "Everything I have said seems meaningless and unreal while I sit here with you and your husband," he says. Mia gives him milk and wild strawberries to eat, the latter symbols of spring or rebirth. It is, as Brigitta Steene suggests in her book on Bergman, a kind of private Eucharist which momentarily redeems the Knight from his doubts. It is only to be expected that Joff is hunted and persecuted by the puritanical and guilt-ridden religious community he seeks innocently to amuse.

At the close, when the chain-dance of Death tops the horizon, it is Joff and Mia who are spared by the Knight's intervention when he distracts Death while they escape. The Knight and his Lady have to accept death, and the squire can do nothing but go along with them. In a program note released with the film, Bergman wrote: "In my film the crusader returns from the Crusades as the soldier returns from war today. In the Middle Ages men lived in terror of the plague. Today they live in fear of the atomic bomb. *The Seventh Seal* is an allegory with a theme that is quite simple: man, his eternal search for God, with death as his only certainty."

Bergman has turned against this group of films, especially *The Virgin Spring* whose motivations he now finds "bogus." "With its sparse stylized, thematic dialogue, its austere sound effects, and its dignified, melancholy music, *The Seventh Seal* survives as a compelling, if obsessive film, visually beautiful but permeated by the lighter as well as the darkest aspects of religious experience. It remains a powerful study in the cruelty of the religious impulse once it has soured in the human consciousness and merged with the darker aspects of the psyche. Bergman, at this spiritually troubled time in his live, was concerned with, "the idea of the Christian God as something destructive and fantastically dangerous, something filled with risk for the human being and bringing out in him the dark destructive forces instead of the opposite." Later, by 1960, he had adopted a more humanist position, and "life became much easier to live."

—Roger Manvell

SMULTRONSTÄLLET. Wild Strawberries. Production: Svensk Filmindustri; black and white, 35mm; running time: 90 mins.; length: 2490 meters. Released 26 December 1957.

Produced by (production supervisor) Allan Ekelund; screenplay by Ingmar Bergman; directed by Ingmar Bergman; photography by Gunnar Fischer; edited by Oscar Rosander; sound by Aaby Wedin and Lennart Wallin; art direction by Gittan Gustafsson; music by Erik Nordgren, music directed by E. Eckert-Lundin; costumes designed by Millie Ström.

Filmed summer 1957 in Svensk studios and backlots in Rosunda, some exteriors shot in and around Stockholm.

Cast: Victor Sjöström (*Professor Isak Borg*); Bibi Andersson (*Sara*); Ingrid Thulin (*Marianne*); Gunnar Björnstrand (*Evald*); Jullan Kindahl (*Agda*); Folke Sundquist (*Anders*); Björn Bjelvenstam (*Viktor*); Naima Wifstrand (*Isak's mother*); Gunnel Broström (*Mrs. Alman*); Gertrud Fridh (*Isak's wife*); Ake Fridell (*Her lover*); Sif Rund (*Aunt*); Max von Sydow (*Åkerman*); Yngve Nordwall (*Uncle Aron*); Per Sjöstrand (*Sigfrid*); Gio Petré (*Sigbritt*); Gunnel Lindblom (*Charlotta*); Maud Hansson (*Angelica*); Anne-Mari Wiman (*Mrs. Åkerman*); Eva Norée (*Anna*); Monica Ehrling (*The twins*).

Publications:

Scripts—*4 Screenplays of Ingmar Bergman* translated by Lars Malmstrom and David Kushner, New York 1960; *Wild Strawberries: A Film by Ingmar Bergman* (contains some alterations and additions from shooting script and cutting continuity script), translated by Lars Malmström and David Kushner, n.d.; reviews—by Peter John Dyer in *Films and Filming* (London), December 1958; "*Wild Strawberries*" by Kenneth Cavender in *Sight and Sound* (London), winter 1958-59; "*Wild Strawberries*" by Henry Hart in *Films in Review* (New York), April 1959; review by Jonas Mekas in *The Village Voice* (New York), 1 July 1959; books—*Ingmar Bergman et ses films* by Jean Béranger, Paris 1959; *Ingmar Bergman: teatermannen och filmskaparen* by Fritiof Billquist, Stockholm 1960; *Thèmes d'inspiration d'Ingmar Bergman* by Jos. Burvenich, Brussels 1960; *Ingmar*

Bergman by Jacques Siclier, Paris 1960; *Ingmar Bergman* by Marianne Höök, Stockholm 1962; *Ingmar Bergman* by Tommaso Chiaretti, Rome 1964; *The Personal Vision of Ingmar Bergman* by Jörn Donner, Bloomington, Indiana 1964; *Ingmar Bergman* by Jean Béranger and François Guyon, Lyon 1964; *Ingmar Bergman: The Search for God* by David Nelson, Boston 1964; *La crisi spirituali dell'uomo moderno nei film di Ingmar Bergman* by Massimo Maisetti, Varese 1964; *La solitudine di Ingmar Bergman* by Guido Oldrini, Parma 1965; *Ingmar Bergman* by Birgitta Steene, New York 1968; *The Silence of God: Creative Response to the Films of Ingmar Bergman* by Arthur Gibson, New York 1969; *Ingmar Bergman* by Robin Wood, New York 1969; *Cinema Borealis: Ingmar Bergman and the Swedish Ethos* by Vernon Young, New York 1971; *Ingmar Bergman Directs* by John Simon, New York 1972; *Ingmar Bergman* by Tino Ranieri, Florence 1974; *Ingmar Bergman: Essays in Criticism* edited by Stuart Kaminsky, New York 1975; *10 Film Classics* by Edward Murray, New York 1978; *Ingmar Bergman and Society* by Maria Bergom-Larsson, San Diego 1978; *Mindscreen: Bergman, Godard and the First-Person Film* by Bruce Kawin, Princeton 1978; *Ingmar Bergman* by Denis Marion, Paris 1979; *Ingmar Bergman: An Appreciation* by Roger Manvell, New York 1980; *Ingmar Bergman: The Cinema as Mistress* by Philip Mosley, Boston 1981; *Film and Dreams: An Approach to Bergman* edited by Vlada Petrić, South Salem, New York 1981; *Ingmar Bergman: A Critical Biography* by Peter Cowie, New York 1982; *A Reference Guide to Ingmar Bergman* by Birgitta Steene, Boston 1982; articles—in *Films and Filming* (London), October 1958; article by Eugene Archer in *Film Quarterly* (Berkeley), fall 1959; "An Aspect of Bergman" by Alan Stanbrook in *Film* (London), March/April 1959; "The Rhetoric of *Wild Strawberries*" by Eleanor McCann in *Sight and Sound* (London), winter 1960-61; "The Mystique of Ingmar Bergman" by Caroline Blackwood in *Encounter* (London), April 1961; "Puritans Anonymous" by Raymond Durgnat and Ian Johnson in *Motion*, autumn 1963; article by Birgitta Steene in *Film Comment* (New York), spring 1965; "The Achievement of Ingmar Bergman" by James Scott in *Journal of Aesthetics and Art Criticism* (Cleveland), winter 1965; "Ingmar Bergman: An Assessment at Mid-point" by W. Richard Comstock in *Film Society Review* (New York), April 1966; "Rags of Time: Ingmar Bergman's *Wild Strawberries*" by H.R. Greenberg in *American Imago*, spring 1970; "Cinema Borealis" by Vernon Young in *Hudson Review* (Nutley, New Jersey), summer 1970; "Images and Words in Ingmar Bergman's Films" by Birgitta Steene in *Cinema Journal* (Evanston, Illinois), fall 1970; article by James Welsh in *Cinema Journal* (Evanston, Illinois), fall 1971; "Images of Dying and the Artistic Role: Ingmar Bergman's *Wild Strawberries*" by J. Tulloch in *Australian Journal of Screen Theory* (Kensington), March 1977; "*Ved vejs ende*" by P. Schepelern in *Kosmorama* (Copenhagen), spring 1978; "*Les Faises Sauvages*" by J. Magny in *Cinéma* (Paris), October 1978; "The Filmic Dream and Point of View" by R.T. Eberwein in *Literature/Film Quarterly* (Salisbury, Maryland), no.3, 1980.

*   *   *

Wild Strawberries is to Ingmar Bergman what *King Lear* was to Shakespeare—a study in old age and the need for an old man to discover the errors and inhumane deeds of his life and, as he cannot mend them, come to terms with his own fallibility. Lear ("four score and upward") learns the truth about himself by passing through a violent period of deprivation and madness, occasioned by the cruelty of his two married daughters. Professor Isak Borg (played by Victor Sjöström in his late 70s) is an honored physician, and he learns his home-truths through a successions of dreams experienced during a drive by car to Lund, where he is to receive yet another academic honor. He is accompanied by his daughter-in-law, Marianne, who is estranged from her husband, Isak's son. She is quite unafraid of Isak, prompting in him the self-examination that the dreams, forming the principal action of the film, represent. Like Lear, Isak Borg emerges purged, if not wholly changed, from the subconscious confrontations with self-truth. Much of the film he narrates himself as part of the self-examination, as if under some form of analysis. The concept of the film was influenced by Strindberg's *Dream Play*, which Bergman had directed for the theater.

The title, *Wild Strawberries*, refers to the fruit that symbolizes for the Swedish the emergence of spring, the rebirth of life. The motif of wild strawberries frequently recurs in Bergman's films. Isak Borg is revealed as a cold-natured, egotistical, irascible and authoritarian old man, even though the journey should be a time of happiness for him in terms of academic recognition. The most macabre of the dreams comes before the journey has even begun; it is a dream Bergman claims frequently to have had himself, that of seeing a coffin fall free into the street from a driverless hearse and then breaking open. In the film a hand emerges from the coffin and grasps Isak; he finds the face of the corpse to be his own.

During the journey by car Marianne is very blunt with her father-in-law, whose cold nature and lack of humanity matches that of his son. The professor dozes as the car rides along the country highway. A succession of dreams reveals to him the shortcomings and losses of his youth. On the journey they pass the now empty house among the birchwoods where, in distant years, Isak had spent his youth. He dreams of the loss of the girl he had loved but was afraid to kiss, his cousin Sara, who picked wild strawberries for him to share with her during their failing courtship. He eventually loses her to his more ardent brother, Sigfrid. Another stop is made for the professor to see his 96-year-old mother. "We imagined her," says Bergman, "to be somewhere between 90 and 100—almost mythical." Marianne considered her to "ice-cold, in some ways more frightening than death itself"; Isak, then, is the product of a cold womb.

Sara is re-incarnated as a student who, hitch-hiking with a couple of young men, is offered a lift by the professor and his daughter-in-law. The presence of this double excites Isak to dream of the youthful Sara who shows him his now-aged face in a mirror, for in his dreams he remains his present age while those from his past are seen as they were when they were young. When he begs her not to leave him this time, he finds himself voiceless. She can no longer hear him. Though she leaves him for his brother, her seducer, in a later dream she takes him by the hand and shows him the joy of happy parenthood.

The professor's final dream is at once the most revealing and the most tormenting. Like a young student, he faces a humiliating oral examination which is somewhat like a trial. Those who have been most intimate with him are witnesses. He can make no sense of what is asked of him; even the female cadaver he is called upon to examine, rises and laughs in his face. He is forced to be the witness concerning his dead wife's unfaithfulness with her sensual, middle-aged lover, and to hear her bitter description of him as "completely cold and hypocritical." (There is a melancholy burlesque of this ill-fated marriage in the behavior of a bickering couple from an earlier scene.) At the conclusion of this trial-examination, Isak is condemned by the judge-examiner and sentenced to a punishment of loneliness. When he wakes, Marianne reveals she is pregnant and determined to go back to her husband, insisting on her right to have the child he, as the father, does not want her to have.

Wild Strawberries, for all the horror of certain moments, is a film full of compassionate understanding and the need for warmth and humanity. There is a compassion for this old man who cannot respond to people and who lacks the important quality of love and concern for others, particularly for women. Yet there is humor, even touches of light-heartedness, in the film, particularly in the scenes with the students and those between Isak and his aged housekeeper who proves his match when it comes to mutual criticism. It is indeed this overall compassion that makes *Wild Strawberries* so memorable, crowned by the magisterial performance of Victor Sjöström, the pioneer Swedish film director.

—Roger Manvell

SNOW WHITE AND THE SEVEN DWARFS. Production: Walt Disney Studios; 1937; Technicolor, 35mm, animation; running time: 83 mins. Released 4 February 1938, but premiered in December 1937, released through RKO Radio Pictures Inc. Re-released 1943, 1952, 1958, 1967, 1975, 1983.

Produced by Walt Disney; screenplay by Ted Sears, Otto Englander, Earl Hurd, Dorothy Ann Blank, Richard Creedon, Dick Richard, Merrill de Maris, and Webb Smith; from the fairy tale "Snow White" from *Grimm's Fairy Tales*; supervising director: David Hand, sequence directors: Perce Pearce, Larry Morey, William Cottrell, Wilfred Jackson, and Ben Sharpsteen; art direction by Charles Phillippi, Hugh Gennesy, Terrell Stapp, McLaren Stewart, Harold Miles, Tom Codrick, Gustaf Tenggren, Kenneth Anderson, Kendall O'Connor, and Hazel Sewell; music by Frank Churchill, Leigh Harline, Paul Smith, and Larry Morey; character designers: Albert Hunter and Joe Grant; supervising animators: Hamilton Luske, Vladamir Tytla, Fred Moore, and Norman Ferguson; animators: Frank Thomas, Dick Lundy, Arthur Babbitt, Eric Larson, Milton Kahl, Robert Stokes, James Algar, Al Eugster, Cy Young, Joshua Meador, Ugo D'Orsi, George Rowley, Les Clark, Fred Spencer, Bill Roberts, Bernard Garbutt, Grim Natwick, Jack Campbell, Marvin Woodward, James Culhane, Stan Quackenbush, Ward Kimball, Wolfgang Reitherman, and Robert Martsch; backgrounds: Samuel Armstrong, Mique Nelson, Merle Cox, Claude Coats, Phil Dike, Ray Lockrem, and Maurice Noble.

Filmed in Walt Disney Studios. Cost: $1,500,000. Academy Award, Special Award to Walt Disney, 1938; Venice Film Festival, Great Art Trophy, 1938; New York Film Critics Award, Special Award, 1938.

Cast (voices): Adriana Caselotti (*Snow White*); Harry Stockwell (*Prince Charming*); Lucille LaVerne (*The Queen*); Moroni Olsen (*Magic Mirror*); Billy Gilbert (*Sneezy*); Pinto Colvig (*Sleepy* and *Grumpy*); Otis Harlan (*Happy*); Scotty Mattraw (*Bashful*); Roy Atwell (*Doc*); Stuart Buchanan (*Humbert, the Queen's huntsman*); Marion Darlington (*Bird sounds and warbling*); The Fraunfelder Family (*Yodeling*).

Publications:

Reviews—"Current History in the World of the Arts: The Snow

White Fiasco" by V.F. Calverton in *Current History* (Philadelphia), June 1938; review by Otis Ferguson in the *New Republic* (New York), 26 January 1938; books—*The Art of Walt Disney* by Robert Field, New York 1942; *Dictionnaire de cinéastes* by Georges Sadoul, Paris 1965; *Animation in the Cinema* by Ralph Stephenson, New York and London 1967; *The Rise of the American Film* by Lewis Jacobs, New York 1968; *The Disney Version: The Life, Times, Art and Commerce of Walt Disney* by Richard Schickel, New York 1968; *Movies and Society* by J.C. Jarvie, New York 1970; *Films in America 1929-1969* by Martin Quigley Jr. and Richard Gertner, New York 1970; *Walt Disney: The Master of Animation* by Gerald Kurland, Charlottesville, New York 1971; *The Art of Walt Disney, from Mickey Mouse to the Magic Kingdoms* by Christopher Finch, New York 1973; *The Disney Films* by Leonard Maltin, New York 1973; *The Art of Walt Disney* by Christopher Finch, New York 1975; *Walt Disney: An American Original* by Bob Thomas, New York 1976; *Full Length Animated Features* by Bruno Edera, edited by John Halas, New York 1977; *Walt Disney: A Guide to References and Resources* by Elizabeth Leebron and Lynn Gartley, Boston 1979; *Of Mice and Magic* by Leonard Maltin, New York 1980; *The American Animated Cartoon* edited by Gerald Peary and Danny Peary, New York 1980; *Walt Disney's Snow White and the Seven Dwarfs*, New York 1980; *Disney Animation: The Illusion of Life* by Frank Thomas and Ollie Johnston, New York 1982; articles—"A Famous Fairytale is Brought to the Screen as the Pioneer Feature-length" by Andrew Boone in *Popular Science Monthly* (New York), January 1938; "The Snow White Debate Continues" by G.W. Grauer in *Christian Century* (Chicago), August 1938; "Walt Disney's $10,000,000 Surprise" by Miriam Stillwell in *The Reader's Digest* (Pleasantville, New York), June 1938; "*Snow White and the Seven Dwarfs*: First Full-Length Cartoon Movie" by A.R. Boone in *Popular Science* (New York), January 1938; "Walt Disney and the Art Form" by Christopher La Farge in *Theatre Arts* (New York), September 1941; "Make Mine Disney: A Review" by Kenneth MacGowan in *Hollywood Quarterly*, no.1, 1945; "A Wonderful World: Growing Impact of the Disney Art" in *Newsweek* (New York), 18 April 1955; "My Dad, Walt Disney" by Diane Disney, edited by Pete Martin, in *The Saturday Evening Post* (Philadelphia), 17 November 1956 through 5 January 1957; "Style and Medium in the Motion Picture" by Erwin Panofsky in *Film: An Anthology* edited by Daniel Talbot, New York 1959; "Sur le 'huitème art'" by Georges Sadoul in *Cahiers du cinéma* (Paris), June 1962; "Walt Disney, R.I.P." by Roy Brewer in the *National Review* (New York), 10 January 1967; "Walt Disney's Films" by Leonard Maltin in *Films in Review* (New York), October 1967; "Walt Disney de Mickey à Disneyland" by Marie-Therese Poncet in *Anthologie du cinéma, Vol. II*, Paris 1968; "*Albă ca zăpada*" by N. Cassian in *Cinema* (Bucharest), September 1973; "*De Blance Neige à la Planète Sauvage*" by S. Sorel in *Téléciné* (Paris), December/January 1973-74; "The Last of the Old 9 Men" by John Culhane in *American Film* (Washington, D.C.), June 1977; "Heigh Ho! Heigh Ho! Here Comes a Staged *Snow White*" by M. Cohen in *The New York Times*, 14 October 1979; "*Sneguljcica in sedam paltkov*" by T. Gomiscek in *Ekran* (Ljubljana, Yugoslavia), no.5/6, 1979; "*Snow White and the Seven Dwarfs*" by Nancy S. Kinney in *Magill's Suevey of Cinema, Vol. IV* edited by Frank N. Magill, Englewood Cliffs, New Jersey 1980.

*   *   *

In his years as an animator, director, producer, and magnate, Walt Disney did more than any other individual to influence and shape the look of animated films. As a pioneer he was willing to take risks by experimenting with various technical inventions. In almost every case these experiments were successful. By searching for new and different ways to expand and advance the cartoon format, Walt Disney kept several steps ahead of his competitors. His animated films became the technological standard of the industry and no one came close to matching them.

Among Disney's most innovative films is *Snow White and the Seven Dwarfs*, one of the first feature-length animated cartoons. Part of his reason for venturing into the feature film market was economic. Although Disney's eight-minute cartoons were among the most popular of their day, these shorts had a limited earning potential. Cartoons were only a secondary attraction at the movie theaters and did not receive top billing or top dollar. With accelerating production costs, Disney realized that it would soon become more and more difficult to turn a profit. Looking ahead to the future, he saw feature film production as a way to keep his studio in the black.

The production of his first feature-length cartoon proved to be an enormous undertaking. Many of Disney's competitors felt that the task was impossible and news spread throughout the trade papers about "Disney's Folly." By his own admission Disney was not totally aware of all the complexities that would accompany his new project. He viewed the film as a learning experience and tackled each obstacle with undaunted perseverance.

Disney soon discovered that the scope of a feature-length cartoon dictated some technical changes from the shorter length format. For example, the field size (the size of the painted cels) would have to be enlarged to make room for more detail. This not only required the manufacture of larger cels, but also new drawing boards. In addition, the animation cameras had to be adjusted to photograph the larger field size.

Another innovation used was the multi-plane camera. Actually, Disney's multi-plane camera was first used to a small extent in a short cartoon called *The Old Mill*. The ability of this tool to enhance a feeling of depth proved more useful in Disney's features. With conventional flat animation cels it is difficult to simulate a dolly or a pan. For example, when a camera dollys in on a flat animation cel, all the objects in the scene appear to grow larger at the same rate, whereas in reality the foreground would grow much quicker while the background objects would stay relatively the same size. Since the multi-plane camera holds the foreground and background cels on different planes, it is possible to manipulate the images on each cel at different speeds. Disney's first multi-plane camera was fourteen feet tall with seven different levels, all of which could be controlled independently of each other.

With the expansion of the screen time for *Snow White and the Seven Dwarfs*, Disney also had to expand the number of employees in his company. Approximately 750 artists worked on the two million drawings that made up the film. These artists worked in an assembly-line fashion, each group responsible for a specific task. Some artists worked on the layout, others on background, some worked as in-betweeners for the chief animators, and other artists were inkers and painters. One group worked in special effects animation. In the past, cartoon animators had paid little attention to special effects. However, *Snow White and the Seven Dwarfs* contains many examples of effects animation in the representation of lighting, smoke, rain, and other details.

Snow White was also different from other cartoons in that some of the characters were human. Most cartoons features animals, and although they had anthropomorphic traits, they were all removed from the actual world. The characters of the Queen, Prince, Snow White, and the Huntsman presented a special problem in their "realism." To help keep the animation natural, live-action reference footage was shot of actors as a rotoscope (where the animation is traced directly off the live-action film), but mainly as a guide for the animators to follow.

After three years in the making, *Snow White* was finally ready for a Christmas release in 1937. The film was an instant success and received nothing less than growing reviews. During its initial release the film grossed over $8 million and it continues to be a financial success with each subsequent re-issue. "Disney's Folly" proved to be the way of the future and feature-length animated films continue to be made today, long after the eight-minute theatrical cartoon format has died out. Once again, Walt Disney was proven to be a most important innovator and promoter of the art of animation.

—Linda J. Obalil

SOME LIKE IT HOT. Production: Ashton Productions and the Mirisch Company; 1959; black and white, 35mm; running time: 120 mins. Released 1959 by United Artists.

Produced by Billy Wilder with Doane Harrison and I.A.L. Diamond; screenplay by Billy Wilder and I.A.L. Diamond; from an unpublished story by R. Thoeren and M. Logan; directed by Billy Wilder; photography by Charles Lang; edited by Arthur Schmidt; sound by Fred Lau; art direction by Ted Haworth, set decoration by Edward G. Boyle; music by Adolph Deutsch, songs by A.H. Gibbs and Leo Wood, Herbert Stothart and Bert Kalmar, and Matty Malneck and Gus Kahn; special effects by Milt Rice; costumes designed by Orry-Kelly.

Academy Award, Costume Design-Black and White, 1959.

Cast: Marilyn Monroe (*Sugar Kane*); Tony Curtis (*Joe/Josephine*); Jack Lemmon (*Jerry/Daphne*); George Raft (*Spats Colombo*); Pat O'Brien (*Mulligan*); Joe E. Brown (*Osgood Fielding III*); Nehemiah Persoff (*Little Bonaparte*); John Shawlee (*Sweet Sue*); Billy Gray (*Sig Poliakoff*); George Stone (*Toothpick*); Dave Barry (*Beinstock*); Mike Mazurki and Harry Wilson (*Spats's henchmen*); Beverly Wills (*Dolores*); Barbara Drew (*Nellie*); Edward G. Robinson Jr. (*Paradise*); Tom Kennedy (*Bouncer*); John Indrisano (*Walter*).

Publications:

Books—*The Films of Marilyn Monroe* edited by Michael Conway and Mark Ricci, New York 1964; *Billy Wilder* by Axel Madsen, Bloomington, Indiana 1969; *The Bright Side of Billy Wilder, Primarily* by Tom Wood, New York 1970; *Marilyn Monroe: A Life on Film* by John Kobac, New York 1974; *Lemmon: A Biography* by Don Widenen, New York 1975; *The Great Gangster Pictures* by James R. Parish and Michael Pitts, Metuchen, New Jersey 1976; *Billy Wilder in Hollywood* by Maurice Zolotow, New York 1977; *The Film Career of Billy Wilder* by Steve Seidman, Boston 1977; articles—"The New Monroe" by Jon Whitcomb in *Cosmopolitan* (New York), March 1959; "We Like This Marilyn" in *Life* (New York), 20 April 1959; "The Wilder—and Funnier—Touch" by Murray Schumach in the *New York Times Magazine*, 24 January 1960; "The Eye of a Cynic" by Douglas McVay in *Films and Filming*

(London), January 1960; "Such Fun to Be Funny" by Jack Lemmon in *Films and Filming* (London), November 1960; "Marilyn Monroe" by Robert Roman in *Films in Review* (New York), October 1962; "Cast a Cold Eye: The Films of Billy Wilder" by Charles Higham in *Sight and Sound* (London), spring 1963; "The Films of Billy Wilder" in *Film Comment* (New York), summer 1965; "Interview with I.A.L. Diamond" by Robert Mundy and Michael Wallington in *Cinema* (London), October 1969; "The Private Life of Billy Wilder" by Joseph McBride and Michael Wilmington in *Film Quarterly* (Berkeley), summer 1970; "Jack Lemmon" by Joe Baltake in *Films in Review* (New York), January 1970; "The Films of Billy Wilder" by Stephen Farber in *Film Comment* (New York), winter 1971; "Interview with I.A.L. Diamond" in *The Screenwriter Looks at the Screenwriter* by William Froug, New York 1972; "Landmarks of Film History: *Some Like It Hot*" by Stanley Kauffmann in *Horizon* (Los Angeles), winter 1973; "Dialogue on Film: Billy Wilder and I.A.L. Diamond" in *American Film* (Washington, D.C.), July/August 1976; "*Some Like It Hot*" by Pat H. Broeske in *Magill's Survey of Cinema, Vol. IV* edited by Frank N. Magill, Englewood Cliffs, New Jersey 1980.

* * *

If there is a candidate for the funniest closing line in cinema history, it must surely be Osgood's declaration "Nobody's perfect!" at the end of Billy Wilder's spoof on sexual role playing, *Some Like It Hot*. Utterly unshakeable in his love for Daphne and trusting of his passionate instincts, Osgood overlooks all, including gender.

Men masquerading as women have been the source of great comic scenes and characters throughout the history of entertainment whether the sexual identity beneath the garments and makeup was straight or gay. Until recently, men in women's clothes have found acceptance on the screen only when their sexual identity was either ambiguous or categorically heterosexual: dressing up was only an extension of the act of performance. While sexual politics were not the focus of Wilder and Diamond's script, audiences were left with a closing line which was a non-resolution of the issue at hand. Of the two men whose lives were saved by dressing as women, one found love by maintaining that persona: Jerry's acceptance of Osgood's proposal was the best single example of *l'amour fou* since Buñuel. Many years later Hollywood is still putting straight men in dresses and then confirming their heterosexuality (albeit with a greater understanding of what it means to be a woman, as in *Tootsie*.)

While many of the comic scenes from *Some Like It Hot* revolve around a spoof of the gangster era (the film begins in Chicago, 1929 with Joe and Jerry witnessing a Valentine's Day-like massacre) and its screen incarnations (George Raft parodies his coin flip from *Scarface*), much of the best comedy results from an examination of sexual identity. In the beginning of the film, the all-girl band which Jerry and Joe have joined, is bedding down for the night in their train berths. Having erased their masculinity to avoid being erased by gangsters, Joe and Jerry (now Josephine and Daphne) participate in an evening of "berth rights." When Joe tries to assert his masculinity with Sugar, Jerry insists he maintain his female identity. Aware of their dilemma, our pleasure becomes dependent on the ramifications of gender identification and sexual exposure. In the course of the film Joe re-asserts his masculinity and finds love with Sugar while Jerry pursues his femininity and finds love with Osgood.

Legendary in Hollywood for the trouble Marilyn Monroe caused Wilder on the set, the film was a great commercial success and escalated Wilder's position in Hollywood. His esteem hit its peak with his next release, *The Apartment*. These two films signalled the beginning of one of the most successful director/actor teams in the history of American cinema. Until 1959 Jack Lemmon had been a talent in search of expansion; with Wilder he unleashed his neurotic mannerisms and became the director's favorite performer, appearing in seven Wilder films.

With *Some Like It Hot* Billy Wilder and his writing partner, I.A.L. Diamond, combined the physicality of the Mack Sennett era with the wit and complications of thirties screwball comedy to make the funniest American film of the fifties and one of the greatest of the genre.

—Doug Tomlinson

SOMMARNATTENS LEENDE. Smiles of a Summer Night. Production: Svensk Filmindustri; black and white, 35mm; running time: 108 mins.; length: 2975 meters. Released 26 December 1955.

Produced by Allan Ekelund; screenplay by Ingmar Bergman; directed by Ingmar Bergman; photography by Gunnar Fischer; edited by Oscar Rosander; sound by P.O. Petterson; art direction by P.A. Lundgren; music by Erik Nordgren; costumes designed by Mago.

Filmed summer 1955 in Svensk studios in Råsunda, exteriors shot in small towns such as Malmö and Ystad. Cost: Bergman states $75,000, other sources claim up to $150,000. Cannes Film Festival, Special Prize for Most Poetic Humor, 1956.

Cast: Ulla Jacobsson (*Anne Egerman*); Eva Dahlbeck (*Desirée Armfeldt*); Margit Carlquist (*Charlotte Malcolm*); Harriet Andersson (*Petra, the maid*); Gunnar Björnstrand (*Fredrik Egerman*); Jarl Kulle (*Count Malcolm*); Ake Fridell (*Frid, the groom*); Björn Bjelvenstam (*Henrik Egerman*); Naima Wifstrand (*Mrs. Armfeldt*); Gull Natorp (*Malla, Desirée's maid*); Birgitta Valberg and Bibi Andersson (*Actresses*); Anders Wulff (*Desirée's son*); Gunnar Nielsen (*Niklas*); Gösta Prüzelius (*Footman*); Svea Holst (*Dresser*); Hans Straat (*Almgen, the photographer*); Lisa Lundholm (*Mrs. Almgren*); Sigge Fürst (*Policeman*).

Publications:

Script—"*Sommarnattens Leende*" by Ingmar Bergman in *Four Screenplays of Ingmar Bergman*, translated by Lars Malmstrom and David Kushner, New York 1960; books—*Ingmar Bergman et ses films* by Jean Béranger, Paris 1959; *Ingmar Bergman: teatermannen och filmskaparen* by Fritiof Billquist, Stockholm 1960; *Ingmar Bergman* by Jacques Siclier, Paris 1960; *Ingmar Bergman* by Marianne Höök, Stockholm 1962; *The Personal Vision of Ingmar Bergman* by Jörn Donner, Bloomington, Indiana 1964; *Ingmar Bergman* by Jean Béranger and François Guyon, Lyon 1964; *La solitudine di Ingmar Bergman* by Guido Oldrini, Parma 1965; *Ingmar Bergman på teatern* by Henrik Sjögren, Stockholm 1968; *Ingmar Bergman* by Birgitta Steene, New York 1968; *The Silence of God: Creative Response to the Films of Ingmar Bergman* by Arthur Gibson, New York 1969; *Ingmar Bergman* by Robin Wood, New York 1969; *Cinema*

Borealis: Ingmar Bergman and the Swedish Ethos by Vernon Young, New York 1971; *Ingmar Bergman Directs* by John Simon, New York 1972; *Ingmar Bergman* by Tino Ranieri, Florence 1974; *Ingmar Bergman: Essays in Criticism* edited by Stuart Kaminsky, New York 1975; *Ingmar Bergman and Society* by Maria Bergom-Larsson, San Diego 1978; *Mindscreen: Bergman, Godard and the First-Person Film* by Bruce Kawin, Princeton 1978; *Der frühe Ingmar Bergman* by Hauke Lange-Fuchs, Lübeck 1978; *Ingmar Bergman* by Denis Marion, Paris 1979; *Ingmar Bergman: An Appreciation* by Roger Manvell, New York 1980; *Ingmar Bergman: The Cinema as Mistress* by Philip Mosley, Boston 1981; *Film and Dreams: An Approach to Bergman* edited by Vlada Petrić, South Salem, New York 1981; *Ingmar Bergman: A Critical Biography* by Peter Cowie, New York 1982; *Ingmar Bergman: 4 Decades in the Theatre* by Lise-Lone and Frederick Marker, Cambridge, England 1982; *A Reference Guide to Ingmar Bergman* by Birgitta Steene, Boston 1982; articles—"Dreams and Shadows" in *Films and Filming* (London), October 1956; "Ingmar Bergman" by Claude Gauteur in *Cinéma 58* (Paris), July/August 1958; "Bergman, an Uncertain Talent" by J.G. Weightman in *20th Century*, December 1958; "Ingmar Bergman, Magician of Swedish Cinema" by Paul Austin in *Anglo-Swedish Review* (London), April 1959; "An Aspect of Bergman" by Alan Stanbrook in *Film* (London), March/April 1959; "The Rack of Life" by Eugene Archer in *Film Quarterly* (Berkeley), summer 1959; "The Mystique of Ingmar Bergman" by Caroline Blackwood in *Encounter* (London), April 1961; "The Achievement of Ingmar Bergman" by James F. Scott in *Journal of Aesthetics and Art Criticism* (Cleveland), winter 1965; *Ingmar Bergman* by Raymond Lefevre in *Image et son* (Paris), March 1969; "Picture and Meaning in Bergman's *Smiles of a Summer Night*" by Simon Grabowski in *Journal of Aesthetics and Art Criticism* (Cleveland), winter 1970; "Cinema Borealis" by Vernon Young in *Hudson Review* (Nutley, New Jersey), summer 1970; "Surîsurile unei nopti de vară" by L. Pintilie in *Cinema* (Bucharest), February 1972; "Reprises: *Sourires d'une nuit d'été*" by G. Haustrate in *Cinéma* (Paris), November 1973; "*Sommernattens smil*" by Ib Monty in *Kosmorama* (Copenhagen), spring 1978.

*   *   *

Comedies have featured more frequently in Ingmar Bergman's output than in his popular image as a purveyor of Nordic gloom might suggest, but few of them have achieved wide success. The sole exception—and the first film to bring him international recognition when it was acclaimed at the 1956 Cannes Festival—is *Sommarnattens Leende*. Not without reason; for though the relative neglect of, for example, *En Lektion i Kärlek* or *Djävulens Öga* seems undeserved, *Sommarnattens Leende* is without doubt Bergman's most perfectly achieved comedy to date.

The tone of the comedy is formalized, openly theatrical in its pattern: four men and four women circle around each other, constantly changing partners in an elaborate dance of love played out amid the baroque splendor of a country mansion at the turn of the century. Presiding over the spectacle is the aged chatelaine, the former courtesan Madame Armfeldt, a burnt-out relic of bygone loves. Parallels are irresistibly suggested with Mozartian opera, especially *The Marriage of Figaro* and *The Magic Flute* (which Bergman was later to film), as well as with *A Midsummer Night's Dream*; the Swedish cinema also offers a precedent in Stiller's sexual comedy *Erotikon*. Yet the film is very much Bergman's in the skillful juxtaposition of its contrasting moods and event, most notably in the scene of Henrik Egerman's attempted suicide. The script, witty and epigrammatic, plays teasingly with such archetypically Bergmanesque themes as the nature of love, the problem of identity, and the impossibility of lasting emotional satisfaction.

Within the intricate plot, Bergman explores diverse attitudes towards love using each character, each pairing, to comment on and illuminate the others. In their direct, earthy pleasure the servants, Petra and Frid, expose the hollowness and pretensions of their supposed betters, yet they sense their own limitations beside the enchanted idealism of Henrik and Anne, the young lovers. Fredrik Egerman's futile infatuation with Anne, his virgin bride, weakened by the feline seductions of Countess Charlotte, finally crumbles before the sardonic maturity embodied in his ex-mistress, Desirée Armfeldt. Yet even Fredrik, an absurd and repeatedly humiliated figure, evinces in his perplexed strivings a humanity lacking in the poised and coldly brutal Count Malcolm. As so often in Bergman's films, the women come out of the whole affair distinctly better than the men.

Sommarnattens leende is a unified work; the studied elegance of the subject matter is complemented by the sinuously smooth camera technique, and by the seamless ensemble playing of a cast drawn largely from Bergman's regular "rep company." The film marks the culmination of his early work, and also paved the way, in its rich complexity, for the tortured Gothicism of *Det sjunde inseglet* and the symbolic dream-landscape of *Smulstronstället*. In his subseqeunt output comedies have become increasingly rare, and those that he has produced—such as *Ansiktet* and *För att inte tala om alla dessa kvinnor*—have tended to suffer distortion through the intensity of the director's personal preoccupations. But in *Sommarnattens leende* Bergman achieved the ideal balance between emotional invo!vement and ironic detachment to create a wholly satisfying comedy, and one which so far remains unsurpassed among his films.

—Philip Kemp

SONG OF CEYLON. Production: GPO Film Unit for Ceylon Tea Marketing Board, begun as an Empire Marketing Board film; black and white, 35mm; running time: 40 mins. Released 1934.

Produced by John Grierson; screenplay by John Grierson, Basil Wright, and others; based, in part, on a book about Ceylon written by traveller Robert Knox in 1680; directed, photographed, and edited by Basil Wright; sound supervised by Alberto Cavalcanti, sound recorded by E.A. Pawley; music composed and recorded under the direction of Walter Leigh; the "voices of commerce" heard in the sound track montage included the voices of John Grierson, Alberto Cavalcanti, Stuart Legg, and Basil Wright.

Filmed in Ceylon.

Cast: Lionel Wendt (*Narrator*).

Publications:

Reviews—in *Variety* (New York), 18 August 1937; review by John T. McManus in *The New York Times*, August 1937; books—*The Use of Film* by Basil Wright, London 1948; Grierson on Documentary* by John Grierson, edited by Forsyth Hardy, 2nd ed., London 1966; *Studies in Documentary* by Alan Lovell and Jim Hillier, New York 1972; *Nonfiction Film: A Critical History* by Richard Barsam, New York 1973; *Documentary: A History of the Nonfiction Film* by Erik Barnouw, New York 1974; *The Long View* by Basil Wright, London 1974; *The Rise and Fall of British Documentary: The Story of the Film Movement Founded by John Grierson* by Elizabeth Sussex, Berkeley 1975; articles—"Filming in Ceylon" by Basil Wright in *Cinema Quarterly* (London), summer 1934; "The Birth of British Documentary" by Stephen Tallents in *Journal of University Film*, nos.1,2, and 3, 1968; "Calvalcanti in England" by Elizabeth Sussex in *Sight and Sound* (London), autumn 1975; "Basil Wright and *Song of Ceylon*" by Cecile Starr in *Filmmakers Newsletter* (Ward Hill, Massachusetts), November 1975; article in *Cinéma d'aujourd'hui* (Paris), February/March 1977; "English Documentary Films" by Evelyn Gerstein in *The Documentary Tradition* edited by Lewis Jacobs, 2nd ed., New York 1979; "Jung/Sign/Symbol/Film" by D. Fredrickson in *Quarterly Review of Film Studies* (Pleasantville, New York), fall 1980.

*   *   *

One of the finest achievements of the British documentary movement, was Basil Wright's *Song of Ceylon*, which has been called the world's finest example of lyrical documentary. The film's theme, as its producer John Grierson described it, is "Buddhism and the art of life it has to offer, set upon by a Western metropolitan civilization which, in spite of all our skills, has no art of life to offer."

Graham Greene, reviewing the film when it played as the second feature in a London art theatre, described it as having an "air of absolute certainty in its object and assurance in its method." He singled out shots of birds in flight as "one of the loveliest visual metaphors I have ever seen on any screen." Wright later said that he had seen the birds at the end of a day's shooting, when the light was practically gone; he made his assistant unpack the cameras and get out the telephoto lens, though at the time he had no idea how the shots would be used.

Wright had been sent to Ceylon to film four one-reel travelogues as publicity for the Ceylon Tea Propaganda Board, but that purpose soon gave way to an "inner impulse" that made him film other sites and themes. In practical terms, he did not realize he was filming *Song of Ceylon* until he was back in London and had the material on a cutting bench. There was no shooting script for the film, and Wright could not screen his rushes in Ceylon. Without air transportation, it took a month just to get reports on the footage he had shot.

Wright worked with one assistant, three cameras and two tripods, one of which had a finely balanced free-head which he found tricky to use but once mastered was capable of very delicate movement. This permitted some of the most remarkable panning shots ever made in film, an art he had learned from Robert Flaherty a few years earlier.

The editing and sound in *Song of Ceylon* were done in England. Composer Walter Leigh created and recorded every effect in the film, as well as all the music. Combining as many as eight tracks was both difficult and costly on the primitive equipment available to documentary filmakers in the mid-1930s; at that time, sound was developed and edited on film, not on tape.

The film's narration was taken from a book written by Robert Knox in 1680, which Wright had discovered by chance in a store window. At the last minute, Wright inserted four titles which prescribes the film's symphonic structure: "The Buddha," "The

Virgin Island," "Voices of Commerce," and "The Apparel of the Gods." The first section, extremely slow, follows pilgrims up a mountainside to pray. The second shows the daily life of the people. "Voices of Commerce" juxtaposes two systems of labor, with the sound track ironically quoting British stock market prices and the arrival and departure times for ships while Ceylonese natives gather coconuts and tea leaves by hand. The last section returns to the religious and cultural life as it had been lived by the Ceylonese people centuries before the arrival of the British.

Not everyone responded favorably to the film's poetry and beauty. *Variety*'s reviewer called *Song of Ceylon* "a shade too arty," despite its "splendid camera work." Archer Winsten in *The New York Post* rated it midway between "fair" and "good" on the movie meter, and called it "interesting." John T. McManus, in *The New York Times*, attributed the film entirely to John Grierson (without mentioning Basil Wright's name) and seemed bothered by what he called the film's "basic aloofness." He objected not so much to the film ("beautiful job...striking in photographic values...painstaking in composition and montage") as to its approach. "It certainly deserves the prizes it has won, but there are prizes it could not win," McManus concluded. The same could be said, however, for any film which, like *Song of Ceylon*, is one of a kind.

Basil Wright summed up his feelings about the film in this way: "I think *Song of Ceylon* is the work of a young man exposed for the first time to an oriental as opposed to occidental way of life, and to a very impressive and convincing oriental religion.... Without any question it's the only film I've ever made that I can bear to look at." Wright directed or co-directed some 25 other documentaries (including the celebrated *Night Mail*, with Harry Watt, and *World Without End*, with Paul Rotha). He is author of many film articles and reviews, as well as two books—*The Use of Film* and *The Long View*.

—Cecile Starr

SOUFFLE AU COEUR. Murmur of the Heart. Production: NEF/Marianne Productions (Paris), Vides Cinematografica SAS (Rome), and Franz Seitz Productions (Munich); color, 35mm; running time: 118 mins. Released 1971.

Produced by Vincent Malle and Claude Nedjar; screenplay by Louis Malle; directed by Louis Malle; photography by Ricardo Aronovich; music by Charlie Parker and Sidney Bechet.

Cast: Lea Massari (*Mother*); Benoit Ferreux (*Laurent*); Daniel Gelin (*Father*); Marc Winocourt (*Marc*); Michel Lonsdale (*Father Henry*); Fabien Ferreux (*Thomas*).

Publications:

Reviews—in *Newsweek* (New York), 8 November 1971; review by Pauline Kael in the *New Yorker*, 23 October 1971; "*Le Souffle*: Lea Massari Portrays Non-French Mother" by Roger Greenspun in *The New York Times*, 17 October 1971; "Herzflimmern" by A. Brustellin in *Filmkritik* (Munich), March 1972; "*El soplo al corazón*" by J. Nuño in *Cine al dia* (Caracas, Venezuela), June 1972; "*Le Souffle au coeur*" by M. Silverman in *Take One* (Montreal), October 1972; books—*Louis Malle* by

Henri Chapier, Paris 1964; *Louis Malle par Louis Malle*, with S. Kant, Paris 1978; articles—"Louis Malle: Murmuring From the Heart", by N. Pasquariello in *Inter/View* (New York), July 1972; "There's More to Malle than Sex, Sex, Sex" by C. Grenier in the *New York Times*, 6 February 1972; "Louis Malle om den naturlige incest" by S. Kalmar in *Fant* (Oslo), no.21, 1972; article in *The New York Times*, 6 February 1972; "Sum na scru" by N. Muzić in *Ekran* (Ljubijana, Yugoslavia), no.100-103, 1973; "Louis Malle" by D. McVay in *Focus on Film* (London), summer 1974; article in the *Guardian*, 10 August 1974; "Louis Malle" in *Current Biography Yearbook*, New York 1976; "From The Lovers to Pretty Baby", interview by D. Yakir in *Film Quarterly* (Berkeley), summer 1978.

*   *   *

For all the deliberate diversity and stylistic versatility of Louis Malle's films—qualities for which he has often been criticized—certain clear thematic preoccupations can readily be seen to recur in his work. One such favorite theme is adolescence, which he handles with consistent sympathy and sensitivity—albeit from widely different standpoints—in *Zazie dans le Métro*, *Lacombe Lucien*, *Black Moon*, *Pretty Baby* and, most successfully of all, in *Le Souffle au coeur*.

Malle has described *Souffle au coeur* as "my first film." In fact it was his eighth feature; but it was the first which he had scripted entirely himself, and was also, he felt, "my first happy. optimistic film." Loosely based on reminiscences of Malle's own childhood, the film represents a world seen entirely from the viewpoint of its 15-year-old hero, Laurent, who is present in every scene. Little in the episodic plot is unpredictable: the boy hates his father, loves his mother, veers uncontrollably between infancy and adulthood, and is fascinated, perplexed and disconcerted by his own rampant, unfocused sexuality. The film's freshness lies in the complexity and ironic affection with which Malle depicts Laurent's fumbling attempts at self-definition, and in the physical immediacy of the family which surrounds him—a rich, convincing mixture of jokes, rows, awkwardness, horseplay, feuds and alliances.

Le Souffle au coeur also evocatively re-creates *haut-bourgeois* provincial society of the early 1950s—the adults obsessed with the imminent fall of Dien-Bien-Phu, their children far more interested in Camus or the latest Charlie Parker album. Beneath the light-hearted charm and the period detail, Malle's concern, as so often in his films, is with the struggle of the individual to assert an independent existence in the face of society's demands (and especially those of the family). Laurent's illness (the "heart murmur" of the title) is shown as a response to the insistent pressures of the world about him—a tactical withdrawal which corresponds, in the more tragic context of *Le Feu follet* or *La Vie privée*, with the protagonist's suicide. His liberation from this impasse comes through the act of incest with his mother, a crucial moment treated by Malle with exceptional subtlety and discretion, and played with total conviction by Benoît Ferreux and Lea Massari.

At the time, this scene caused considerable scandal. The French government refused the film its sanction as the official French entry at Cannes, and also banned it from being shown on ORTF (thus automatically entailing the loss of a sizable subsidy). Malle's fault, apparently, was not in having depicted mother-son incest, but in having presented it as an event to be looked back on, in the mother's words, "not with remorse, but with tenderness...as something beautiful." Had he shown the participants tormented by guilt, or driven to suicide, it would presumably have been found more acceptable.

Despite official disapproval, or possibly because of it—*Le Souffle au Coeur* was well received at Cannes, widely distributed in France and abroad, and nominated for an Acadeny Award for Best Script. With the controversy now long forgotten, the film can be taken on its own terms, and seen as one of Malle's most personal, engaging, and thoroughly accomplished works.

—Philip Kemp

THE SOUTHERNER. Production: United Artists; 1945; black and white, 35mm; running time: 91 mins. Released 1945.

Produced by David Loew and Robert Hakim; screenplay by Jean Renoir and Hugo Butler, uncredited assistance by William Faulkner; from the novel *Hold Autumn in Your Hand* by George Sessions Perry; directed by Jean Renoir; photography by Lucien Andriot; edited by Gregg Tallas; music by Werner Janssen.

Filmed in Hollywood. Venice Film Festival, Best Film, 1946.

Cast: Zachary Scott (*Sam Tucker*); Betty Field (*Nona Tucker*); Beulah Bondi (*Granny Tucker*); Bunny Sunshine (*Daisy Tucker*); Jay Gilpin (*Jot Tucker*); Percy Kilbride (*Harmie*); Blanche Yurka (*Ma Tucker*); Charles Kemper (*Tim*); J. Carrol Naish (*Devers*); Norman Lloyd (*Finlay*); Nestor Paiva (*Bartender*); Paul Harvey (*Ruston*).

Publications:

Script—*The Southerner* in *Best Film Plays—1945*, edited by Gassner and Nichols, New York 1946; books—*Jean Renoir* by Paul Davay, Brussels 1957; *Jean Renoir* by Armand-Jean Cauliez, Paris 1962; *Jean Renoir* edited by Bernard Chardère in *Premier Plan* (Lyon), no.22-24, May 1962; *Analyses des films de Jean Renoir* by Institut des Hautes Etudes Cinématographiques, Paris 1966; *Study Unit 8: Jean Renoir* by Susan Bennett, London 1967; *Jean Renoir und seine Film: eine Dokumentation* compiled and edited by Ulrich Gregor, Bad Ems 1970; *Jean Renoir* by Pierre Leprohon, New York 1971; *Humanidad de Jean Renoir* by Carlos Cuenca, Valladolid, Mexico 1971; *Jean Renoir: The World of his Films* by Leo Braudy, New York 1972; *Jean Renoir* by André Bazin, edited by François Truffaut, Paris, translated ed. 1973. *My Life and My Films* by Jean Renoir, translated by Norman Denny, New York 1974; *Jean Renoir* by Raymond Durgnat, Berkeley 1974; *Jean Renoir: le spectacle, la vie* by Claude Beylie, Paris 1975; *Jean Renoir: Essays, Conversations, Reviews* by Penelope Gilliatt, New York 1975; *Jean Renoir: A Guide to References and Resources* by Christopher Faulkner, Boston 1979; articles—"Jean Renoir à Hollywood", interview by Paul Gilson in *L'Ecran française* (Paris), 15 August 1945; "The Mistakes of David Loew" by Bernard Schoenfeld in *Screen Writer* (London), October 1945; issue on Renoir of *Cahiers du cinéma* (Paris), January 1952; "Renoir in America" by François Truffaut and Jacques Rivette in *Films in Review* (New York), November 1954, reprinted from *Sight and Sound* (London), July/September 1954; issue on Renoir of *Cahiers du cinéma* (Paris), Christmas 1957; "Why Renoir Favors Multiple Camera, Long Sustained Take Technique" by Jean Belanger in *American Cinematographer* (Los Angeles), March 1960; "Beulah Bondi" by John Springer in *Films in Review* (New York),

May 1963; "Jean Renoir" by Lee Russell in the *New Left Review*, May/June 1964; "*The Southerner*" by Judith M. Kass in *Magill's Survey of Cinema, Vol. IV* edited by Frank N. Magill, Englewood Cliffs, New Jersey 1980.

*   *   *

The Southerner was the third of Jean Renoir's American films (after *Swamp Water* and *This Land is Mine*), the first of his independent Hollywood productions, and the object of controversy from the start. The debates that surrounded the film upon its release and continued long thereafter, disparate as they are in origin and intent, bear one upon the other in defining the film's central critical issue.

The Southerner recounts the struggles of a family to live in independence on the land, if not their own, at least not belonging to another visible presence. The enemies are, as one expects, the extremities of weather, an unyielding soil, illness and—less conventionally—mean-spirited, even hostile neighbors. If "the southerner" is the couragous Sam Tucker, he is also the dour, stone-hearted Devers as well as the tight-fisted Harmie. The film's very title, in its generality (suggesting "the southerner" as a type) proved, perhaps as much as the story, a provocation.

The first of the controversies was local. Considered a sordid depiction of life in the southern states, the film was banned in Tennessee and attacked throughout the South. The Ku Klux Klan announced a boycott. To these inhabitants, *The Southerner* presented in realistic terms a derogatory image of the people of that region. The second of the controversies was critical. James Agee, who knew the South well, objected that, on the contrary there was nothing realistic in Renoir's depiction of the region; Renoir had failed to convey not only the character of the southerner, but the speech, the gait, the facial expressions. To Agee, in spite of William Faulkner's well-publicized consultation on dialogue, the film rang false. Agee's was, as Raymond Durgnat points out, an objection based on the definition of authenticity borrowed from naturalism: from appearance to essence, from the outside in. Renoir had understood none of the codes of the region or its people.

Renoir's South was clearly not one of surface verisimilitude, but neither did his definition of realism depend on what André Bazin called "the crust of realism which blinds us." The direction of realism is from the inside out. The camera work, particularly in the exterior locations often shot in deep focus, captures the desolate landscape of a southern winter. A foggy river bank; Beulah Bondi, alone, stubborn and miserable, atop a cart in the pouring rain; and a hut hardly fit for human shelter are a few of the quasi-surreal images that translate Renoir's vision of rural America as a land of loneliness and isolation, without the comfort of neighbor or faith, depressed materially and especially morally. It was on the spirit of the place and times, not on the accent or gesture, that Renoir based and defined his portrait of "the southerner."

—Mirella Jona Affron

THE SPANISH EARTH. Production: Contemporary Historians, Inc. (New York); black and white, 35mm; running time: 53 mins. Released 1937.

Screenplay by (commentary) Ernest Hemingway; narration for English version spoken by Ernest Hemingway, narration translated for French version by E. Guibert and spoken by Joris Ivens; directed by Joris Ivens; photography by John Ferno; edited by Helen Van Dongen; sound supervised by Irving Reis at Columbia workshop at CBS; music by Marc Blitzstein, arranged by Virgil Thomson; original narration used in previews at the White House spoken by Orson Welles.

Filmed March-May 1937 in the village of Fuentedueña and Madrid, Spain; also on the Jarama and Morata de Tajuña fighting fronts. National Board of Review of Motion Pictures, one of Top Ten of 1937.

Publications:

Script—"*Terre d'Espagne*" (includes cutting script and commentary) by Joris Ivens in *Avant-Scène du cinéma* (Paris), 15 January 1981; reviews—"*Land Without Bread* and *The Spanish Earth*" by Basil Wright in *The Documentary Tradition* edited by Lewis Jacobs, New York 1979; "La Presse" in *Avant-Scène du cinéma* (Paris), 15 January 1981; books—*The Spanish Earth* by Ernest Hemingway, Cleveland, Ohio 1938; *Joris Ivens*, edited by W. Klaue and others, Berlin 1963; *Joris Ivens* by Abraham Zalzman, Paris 1963; *Joris Ivens, Dokumentarist den Wahrheit* by Hans Wegner, Berlin 1965; *Joris Ivens* by Robert Grelier, Paris 1965; *The Camera and I* by Joris Ivens, New York 1969; *Autobiografie van een Filmer* by Joris Ivens, Amsterdam 1970; *Nonfiction Film: A Critical History* by Richard Barsam, New York 1973; *Documentary: A History of the Nonfiction Film* by Erik Barnouw, New York 1974; *The Camera and I* by Joris Ivens, Berlin 1974; *Joris Ivens, ein Filmer an den Fronten der Weltrevolution* by Klaus Kremeier, Berlin 1976; *Entretiens avec Joris Ivens* by Claire Devarrieux, Paris 1979; *Joris Ivens: 50 ans de cinéma* edited by Jean-Loup Passek, Paris 1979; *Film on the Left: American Documentary Film from 1931 to 1942* by William Alexander, Princeton, New Jersey 1981; articles—by Ernest Hemingway in *The New York Times*, 10 April 1937; "Joris Ivens: Artist in Documentary" by R. Stebbins and Jay Leyda in *Magazine of Art* (New York), July 1938; "Joris Ivens: Social Realist vs. Lyric Poet" by Cynthia Grenier in *Sight and Sound* (London), spring 1958; "*Terre d'Espagne*" by A. Cornaud in *Revue du cinéma* (Paris), October 1976; "*Terre d'Espagne*" by T. Giraud in *Cahiers du cinéma* (Paris), February 1976; "*Terre d'espagne*" by H. Oms and R. Grelier in *Cahiers de la cinémathèque* (Paris), January 1977; "Hemingway or Ivens: Spaanse aarde" by W. Verstappen in *Skoop* (Amsterdam), November 1978; "Spain and *The Spanish Earth*" by Joris Ivens in *The Documentary Tradition* edited by Lewis Jacobs, 2nd ed., New York 1979; "The Camera Reconnoiters" by Ben Belitt in *The Documentary Tradition* edited by Lewis Jacobs, 2nd ed., New York 1979; "*Terre d'espagne*" in *Avant-Scène du cinéma* (Paris), 1 January 1981.

STACHKA. Strike. La Grève. Production: Goskino; black and white, 35mm, silent; running time: 73 mins.; length: 1969 meters. Released 1924.

Produced by Boris Mikhine; screenplay by V. Pletniev, I. Kravtchunovsky, Grigori Alexandrov, and Sergei Eisenstein (called the Proletkuit Collective); directed by Sergei Eisenstein; photography by Edouard Tisse with V. Popov and V. Khvatov; production design by Vasili Rakhas; assistant directors: G. Alexandrov, A. Levshin, and I. Kravchinovski.

Cast: Maxim Straukh (*The Spy*); Grigori Alexandrov (*The Foreman*); Mikhail Gomorov (*The Worker*); I. Ivanov (*Chief of Police*); I. Klyukvine (*The Activist*); A. Antonov (*Member of the strike*); J. Glizer, B. Yourtzev, A. Kouznetzov, V. Ianoukova, V. Ouralsky, M. Mamine, and members of the Proletariat Troup.

Publications:

Books—*Film Sense* by Sergei Eisenstein, edited and translated by Jay Leyda, New York 1942; *Eisenstein, 1898-1948* by Paul Rotha, Ivor Montagu and John Grierson, London 1948; *Film Form* by Sergei Eisenstein, edited and translated by Jay Leyda, New York 1949; *Sergei Eisenstein—Künstler der Revolution*, Berlin 1960; *Kino: A History of the Russian and Soviet Film* by Jay Leyda, London 1960; *S.M. Eisenstein* by Jean Mitry, Paris 1961; *Sergej Michailowitsch Eisenstein*, edited by Konlecher and Kubelka, Vienna 1964; *Sergei Eisenstein* by Léon Moussinac, translated by Sandy Petrey, New York 1970; *Eisenstein* by Yon Barna, Bloomington, Indiana 1973; *The Complete Films of Eisenstein*, translated by John Hetherington, New York 1974; *Eisenstein* by Dominique Fernandez, Paris 1975; *Sergei M. Eisenstein: Materialien zu Leben und Werk* by W. Sudendorf and others, Munich 1975; *Sergei M. Eisenstein in Selbstzeugrissen und Bilddokumenten*, edited by E. Weise, Reinbek bei Hamburg 1975; *Cinema, The Magic Vehicle: A Guide to Its Achievement: Journey One: The Cinema Through 1949* edited by Jacek Klinowski and Adam Garbicz, Metuchen, New Jersey 1975; *Sergei M. Eisenstein* by Marie Seton, London 1978; *S.M. Eisenstein* by Jean Mitry, Paris 1978; *Montage Eisenstein* by Jacques Aumont, Paris 1979; *Eisenstein at Work* by Jay Leyda and Zina Voynow, New York 1982; articles—"Sergei Eisenstein" by Ivor Montagu in *Penguin Film Review* (London), September 1948; "Rediscovery: *Strike*" by Ivor Montagu in *Sight and Sound* (London), autumn 1956; "Eisenstein and the Mass Epic" by Arthur Knight in *The Liveliest Art*, New York 1957; "*Strike*" by John Cutts in *Films and Filming* (London), March 1961; "Cinematic Expression: A Look at Eisenstein's Silent Montage" by John Kuiper in *Art Journal*, fall 1962; "Eisenstein's *Strike*: A Study of Cinematic Allegory" by John Kuiper in *Journal of Society of Cinematologists*, no.3, 1963; "Eisenstein" by Rostislav Yourenev in *Anthologie du cinéma*, Paris 1966; "*La Grève*" (synopsis and press reaction) in *Avant-Scène du cinéma* (Paris), October 1967; "Masquage, an Extrapolation of Eisenstein's Theory of Montage-as-Conflict to the Multi-image Film" by R. Siegler in *Film Quarterly* (Berkeley), spring 1968; "Eisenstein, Pudovkin and Others" by Dwight Macdonald in *The Emergence of Film Art*, edited by Lewis Jacobs, New York 1969; "Kuleshov, Eisenstein, and the Others: Part II, Kuleshov on Eisenstein" by Lev Kuleshov in *Film Journal* (New York), fall/winter 1972; "Over het vraagstuk van een materialistiese benadering van de vrorm" by Sergei Eisenstein in *Skrien* (Amsterdam), May/June 1973; "Eisensteins Weg zum Streik" by V. Sklovskij in *Filmwissenschaftliche Beiträge* (East Berlin), no.15, 1974.

* * *

Envisioning a film which would both reflect and embody the essence of Russia's 1917 revolution, the 26-year-old Sergei Eisenstein directed his first feature film, *Strike*, in 1924. *Strike* was to have been one of eight projects in a state-sponsored series entitled *Towards Dictatorship*, with reference to the dictatorship of the proletariat. The focus of the series was intended to be the struggles of the working class which preceded and paved the way for the revolution. Eisenstein's *Strike* was the only film of this group to be realized.

At that time Eisenstein's central aesthetic concerns were the practice of montage and the concept of the mass hero. It is not his political or social intent but, rather, his methods which continue to be of interest. As propaganda the film cannot be termed an unqualified success; it does not arouse passion or provoke protest today as does Leni Riefenstahl's *Triumph of the Will*, for example. But the impact of *Strike*'s aesthetic boldness remains undiminished.

It is an impact which can be explained in terms of mechanical energy, on both formal and material levels. One function of art is to subordinate man's environment to man, to bring the technical landscape into the realm of human affairs rather than allow it to dominate or intimidate its creators.

Eisenstein, in accepting this challenge, depicts the environment of the workers in *Strike* as part of their lives. The film's opening shot of factory smokestacks sets the tone. Shots of written communications which urge, "Workers of the world, unite," are intercut with shots of machinery in motion. The workers look healthy and at home in the factory amid shining, powerful machines and moving parts; and Edouard Tisse's camera embraces factory as readily as it embraces worker. The human is not oppressed by machinery. On the contrary, the workers enlist the machinery in their struggle against the representatives of capitalism. The machines become weapons. On another level, the machinery serves a musical function; the very conscious internal rhythm of the film is often determined by spinning flywheels or other moving mechanical parts.

This Constructivist approach is less notable in the long run than is the more personal aspect of Eisenstein's work in *Strike*—his use of montage. He described his conception of montage as collision, and it is important to note that the collision of elements in his work never results in a loss of energy. The film as a whole is something of a perpetual motion machine, with each action or movement yeilding its force to a subsequent action or movement. One of the most pleasing examples of this principle is contained in the following sequence: a large crowd is seen in long shot making its way through the village; at the instant the crowd passes a liquor store, an explosion occurs and the crowd as a whole turns and veers slightly toward the explosion in a movement as graceful and precise as the movement of the arm of a conductor bringing an orchestra to a sudden halt. The pause is but momentary, and the movement continues in a new direction as the crowd flows toward the camera in the next shot.

Most of the forms of montage which Eisenstein elaborated in his books *Film Form* and *The Film Sense* can be found in *Strike*. For example, association montage compares a hand-operated citrus fruit crusher used by the dining businessmen to the rearing horses of the mounted police as they harrass a peaceful crowd of strikers. Eisenstein believed that the meaning of a film should arise from the juxtaposition of its elements rather than be contained within those elements. Although the official purpose of his government-sponsored film was to inform the masses. Eisenstein believed that films should not merely carry information but impart sensation and impression.

For this reason *Strike* is meant to inspire action, not reflection. The film never bogs down in its theoretical base. It is perhaps for these reasons that *Strike* can be distinguished from so-called "bourgeois" films. Not even when a worker commits suicide after being falsely accused of theft does the film pause for any emotion to be displayed. Rather, the worker's suicide note—"Goodbye, remember, I am not guilty"—initiates the strike. It also anticipates the film's conclusion after the slaughter of the strikers—a close shot of a pair of staring, admonishing eyes and the caption "Remember—Proletarians!"

—Barbara Salvage

STAGECOACH. Production: Walter Wanger Prod., 1939; black and white, 35mm; running time: 105 mins. Released March 1939 through United Artists.

Produced by Walter Wanger and John Ford; screenplay by Dudley Nichols from the story "Stage to Lordsburg" by Ernest Haycox; directed by John Ford; photography by Bert Glennon; edited by Dorothey Spencer and Walter Reynolds; sets by Wiard B. Ihnen; art direction by Alexander Toluboff; music by Richard Hageman, W. Franke Harling, John Leipold, Leo Shuken, and Louis Gruenberg (adapted from 17 American folk tunes of the early 1880s); musical direction by Boris Morros; special effects by Ray Binger; costumes designed by Walter Plunkett; second unit direction (stunts) by Yakima Canutt.

Filmed in Kernville, Dry Lake, Victorville, Fremont Pass, Calabasas, Chatsworth, Kayenta, Mesa, and Monument Valley. Cost: $220,000. Academy Awards for Best Supporting Actor (Mitchell) and Music Score, 1939; New York Film Critics Award, Best Direction, 1939.

Cast: John Wayne (*The Ringo Kid*); Andy Devine (*Buck*); Thomas Mitchell (*Doc Boone*); Claire Trevor (*Dallas*); Berton Churchill (*Gatewood*); Chris Martin (*Chris*); Cornelius Keefe (*Captain Whitney*); Francis Ford (*Billy Pickett*); Kent Odell (*Billy, Jr.*); Walter McGril (*Captain Sickell*); George Bancroft (*Curly Wilcox*); Berendo Fowler (*Mrs. Gatewood*); Lou Mason (*Sheriff*); John Carradine (*Hatfield*); Louise Platt (*Lucy Mallory*); Tim Holt (*Lieutenant Blanchard*); Chief Big Tree (*Indian scout*); Elvira Rios (*Chris's wife*); Florence Lake (*Mrs. Whitney*); Marga Daighton (*Mrs. Pickett*); Yakima Canutt (*Cavalry scout*); Harry Tenbrook (*Telegrapher*); Paul McVey (*Express agent*); Jack Pennick (*Bartender*); Buddy Roosevelt and Bill Cody (*Cowboys*); Chief White Horse (*Geronimo*); Duke Lee (*Sheriff of Lordsburg*); Donald Meek (*Peacock*); Tom Tyler (*Luke Plummer*): Cornelius Keefe (*Capt. Whitney*); Florence Lake (*Mrs. Nancy Whitney*); Joseph Rickson (*Hank Plummer*); Vester Pegg (*Ike Plummer*); William Hoffer (*Sergeant*); Bryant Washburn (*Capt. Simmons*); Nora Cecil (*Doc's landlady*); Helen Gibson and Dorothy Anleby (*Dancing girls*); Mary Kathleen Walker (*Lucy's baby*).

Publications:

Scripts—*20 Best Film Plays* edited by John Gassner and Dudley Nichols, New York 1943; *Great Film Plays* edited by Dudley Nichols, New York 1959; "La Chevauchée fantastique" in *Avant-Scène du cinéma* (Paris), no.22, 1963; *Stagecoach: A Film by John Ford and Dudley Nichols* (includes original short story) edited by Nicola Hayden, New York 1971; reviews—in

Film Daily (Hollywood), 15 February 1939; "Ford vs. *Stagecoach*" by Bosley Crowther in *The New York Times*, 29 January 1939; "Boys Who Made *The Informer* Untie Another Shoestring" by Michael Mok in the *New York Post*, 24 January 1939; books—*An Index to the Films of John Ford* edited by W.P. Wootten for the British Film Institute Index Series, London 1948; *Le Western* by Jean-Louis Rieupeyrout, Paris 1953; *John Ford* by Peter Bogdanovich, Berkeley 1968; *The Films of John Wayne* by Mark Ricci, Boris Zmijewsky, and Steve Zmijewsky, New York 1970; *The Cinema of John Ford* by John Baxter, New York 1971; *What is Cinema?, Vol. II* by André Bazin, translated by Hugh Gray, Berkeley 1971; *The Six-Gun Mystique* by John Cawelti, Bowling Green, Ohio 1971; *The Western Films of John Ford* by Janey Place, Secaucus, New Jersey 1973; *The Structure of John Ford's Stagecoach* by Nancy Warfield, New York 1974; *American Film Genres* by Stuart Kaminsky, Dayton, Ohio 1974; *John Wayne* by Alan Barbour, New York 1974; *John Ford's Stagecoach Starring John Wayne* edited by Richard J. Anobile, with a forward by John Ford, New York 1975; *John Ford* by Jim McBride and Michael Wilmington, New York 1975; *Six Guns and Society: A Structural Study of the Western* by Will Wright, Berkeley 1975; *Masters of the American Cinema* by Louis Giannetti, New York 1981; articles—"Reel News from Hollywood" by Elizabeth Copeland in *Richmond News Leader* (Richmond, Virginia), 14 March 1939; article by Dudley Nichols in *Magazine of the National Board of Review* (New York), March 1939; "Bert Glennon Introducing New Method of Interior Photography" by John Castle in *American Cinematographer* (Hollywood), February 1939; "John Ford" in *Films in Review* (New York), February 1951; "John Ford" by Jean Mitry in *Films in Review* (New York), August/September 1955; *Press Conference" by John Cutts in *Sight and Sound* (London), spring 1956; "Ripensando o omber rosse" by M. Quarngnolo in *Bianco e nero* (Rome), November 1957; "The Five Worlds of John Ford" by George Mitchell in *Films in Review* (New York), March 1963; "La Chevauchée de Siganarelle" by B. Tavernier in *Presence du cinéma* (Paris), March 1965; "Our Way West" by Burt Kennedy in *Films and Filming* (London), October 1969; special issue on *Stagecoach* of *Action* (Los Angeles), September/October 1971; "The American West of John Ford" by M. Zolotov in *TV Guide*, 4 December 1971; "John Ford's Stock Company" by W. E. Büler in *Filmkritik* (Munich), January 1972; "Dudley Nichols" by Paul Jensen in *The Hollywood Screenwriter* edited by Richard Corliss, New York 1972; "Fordissimo" in *Ecran* (Paris), November 1973; "Ford Forever" by C. Beylie in *Ecran* (Paris), November 1973; "Un Baromètre de l'idéologie dominante" by M. Martin in *Ecran*, November 1973; "*Stagecoach*" by John Frayne in *Journal of Aesthetic Education* (Urbana, Illinois), April 1975; "The Spectator in the Text: The Rhetoric of *Stagecoach*" by Nick Browne in *Film Quarterly* (Berkeley), winter 1975-76; "The Onomastic Code of *Stagecoach*" by D. Clandfield in *Literature/Film Quarterly* (Salisbury, Maryland), spring 1977; "*Stagecoach*" by A.L. Miller in *Film News* (New York), September/October 1979; "*Stagecoach*" by Ed Lowry in *Cinema Texas Program Notes* (Austin), 23 January 1979; "*John Fords Diligensen*" by B. Ehlers Anderson in *Filmrutan* (Stockholm), no.4, 1981.

* * *

Stagecoach is widely recognized as the hallmark of the classic western, the film that brought the genre out of its "B" movie status into the ranks of respectability. Its fame, however, extends beyond the genre: Orson Welles was once asked how he learned about filmmaking. His response was, "From the old masters—John Ford, John Ford, and John Ford." Apocryphal though the tale may be, Welles claims to have learned how to edit films by running a print of *Stagecoach* 45 times at the Museum of Modern Art.

Audiences today often find it difficult to understand the classic status of *Stagecoach*. But critic John Frayne points out, it "...was a leap forward in comparison to the simplistic westerns that preceeded *Stagecoach* within its genre." The film features complexity of characterization, a clash of social class and values, and demonstrates some depth of insight regarding the historical forces that motivate the action of the film.

Unlike other characteristic westerns, *Stagecoach*'s hero—the young John Wayne in his first truly *major* role—is not a lonely, alienated fighter. In fact, this is true of many of Ford's westerns; critic Robert Warshow eliminated Ford's films from his important essay on the characteristics of the genre. (Warshow's scheme includes the notion that the western hero is always the quintessentially alienated man.) As Frayne points out, "The Ringo Kid (Wayne) recognizes Doc Boone as someone who set his brother's arm years before." There is an extended family, a warmth of loyalty and personal indebtedness, a sense of moral, personal honor, unlike other films of the genre.

Stagecoach helped to determine the various classic western stereotypes: the hero, Ringo Kid; the "tart with a heart," Dallas; the mysterious, shady Gambler, a "gentleman/remnant" of the Confederacy, Hatfield; the snooty lady from the East, Mrs. Mallory; and perhaps most famous of all, the drunken-yet-noble Doc Boone. The actors playing these western archetypes became their best representatives: for example, of Thomas Mitchell's numerous, fine roles in 1939, he is perhaps most justifiably famous as the drunken "doc." John Carradine made an appropriately dark and brooding Hatfield; and, of course, "star iconography" as a critical term is best exemplified by John Wayne as the fair-minded outlaw, the Ringo Kid. Typical for the western hero, his actions stem from revenge (for the deaths of his father and brother) and the honorable love of a fine woman (Dallas, even though he knows of her sordid past).

Stagecoach features and foreshadows themes that would become part and parcel of later westerns. *Stagecoach* presents, if mildly, a look into social stigma, stereotyping, and class distinction through the relationship of Dallas and the Kid to society. (Ford would treat the theme in its darkest and most racist form in *The Searchers*.) Through the motivations of the Ringo Kid, the film treats the classic western theme of revenge, the need for a "man to do what he's got to do." Women are peripheral in terms of action. And, as in most Ford films, self-sacrifice for the community—Ringo's gallantry during the chase scene, for example—marks the greatest and most noble form of heroism.

Stagecoach also demonstrates Ford's unique style, which set a standard for many westerns after 1939, through the use of his characteristic "door frame" shots, chiaroscuro lighting, and his mastery of the epic long shot, particularly of Utah's Monument Valley. As Louis Giannetti notes, " Ford considered this locale 'the most complete, beautiful, and peaceful place on earth,' and...industry regulars referred to it as Ford Country." The chase scenes and stuntwork were coordinated by master stuntman Yakima Canutt, who subbed for Wayne during the chase sequence and also played the Indian who attacks him. Perhaps less impressive today, the chase sequence, innovative in 1939, still sustains audience interest.

In spite of its themes involving class structure, *Stagecoach* is still representative of Ford's conservative viewpoints. One sees the standard, "racist view" of the West; the Indians are the villains, and Hispanics decorate the film as comic relief.

Like any film that presents a director's personal view of the American West and its past, *Stagecoach* has some universal applications. Through his vendetta, the Ringo Kid "symbolically assures the continuance of the forces of order, by saving the cavalryman's wife and child, and the destruction of the forces of anarchy, by outlasting the Indians and killing the corrupt Plummer family" (McBride and Wilmington). The group in *Stagecoach*, a microcosm of life, may also be read as an inversion of a stable community. Therefore, the most disreputable characters (the prostitute, doctor, and convict) perform best in the major crises of the film (the chase/attack, and the birth of Mrs. Mallory's child). Dallas and the Kid take on a greater dignity in comparison with the more corrupt members of the group, such as Gatewood, the embezzling banker.

As the Ringo Kid and Dallas ride away from Lordsburg, Doc Boone says, "well, they're free from the blessings of civilization"—from social dogma, prejudice, and oppression. Yet Ford's vision is an idealized view of the American dream, of the "new beginning." As one critic asserts, it is a "dream whose beauty lies in its contrivance and improbability."

—Deborah H. Holdstein

A STAR IS BORN. Production: Transcona Enterprises; 1954; Technicolor, 35mm, CinemaScope; running time: 154 mins., originally 182 mins. Released 1954 by Warner Bros. Re-released 1983 with original 47 minutes restored.

Produced by Sidney Luft with Vern Alves; screenplay by Moss Hart; from the screenplay for the 1937 version (Wellman) based, in turn, on the film *What Price Hollywood?* (Cukor); directed by George Cukor; photography by Sam Leavitt; edited by Folmar Blangsted; production design by Gene Alen, set decoration by George James Hopkins; art direction by Malcolm Bert; music by Harold Arlen and Ira Gershwin, and Leonard Gershe; costumes designed by Jean Louis and Mary Ann Nyberg, *Born in a Trunk* number by Irene Sharaff; color consultant: George Hoyningen-Huene; choreography by Richard Barstow.

Cast: Judy Garland (*Esther Blodgett/Vicki Lester*); James Mason (*Norman Maine*); Jack Carson (*Matt Libby*); Charles Bickford (*Oliver Niles*); Tommy Noonan (*Danny McGuire*); Lucy Marlow (*Lola Lavery*); Amanda Blake (*Susan Ettinger*); Irving Bacon (*Graves*); Hazel Shermet (*Libby's secretary*); James Brown (*Glenn Williams*); Lotus Robb (*Miss Markham*); Joan Shawlee (*Announcer*); Dub Taylor (*Driver*); Louis Jean Heydt (*Director*); Bob Jellison (*Eddie*); Chick Chandler (*Man in car*); Leonard Penn (*Director*); Blythe Daly (*Miss Fusselow*); Mae Marsh (*Party guest*); Frank Ferguson (*Judge*); Nadene Ashdown (*Esther, age 6*); Heidi Meadows (*Esther, age 3*); Henry Kulky (*Cuddles*); Jack Harmon (*1st dancer*); Don McCabe (*2nd dancer*); Eric Wilton (*Valet*); Grady Sutton (*Carver*); Henry Russell (*Orchestra leader*); Robert Dumas (*Drummer*); Laurindo Almeida (*Guitarist*); Bobby Sailes (*Dancer*); Percy Helton (*Drunk*); Charles Watts (*Harrison*); Pat O'Malley and Samuel Barrymore Colt (*2 Men at the race track*); Charles Halton and Joseph Mell (*Studio employees*); Stuart Holmes (*Spectator*); Grandon Rhodes (*Producer*); Frank Puglia (*Bruno*); Wilton Graff (*Master of Ceremonies-last scene*); Phil Arnold; Rudolph Anders; Bess Flowers; Allen Kramer.

Publications:

Review—"Naissance du cinemascope" by Charles Bitsch in *Cah-*

iers du cinéma (Paris), June 1955; books—*Hommage à George Cukor* by Henri Langlois and others, Paris 1963; *George Cukor* by Jean Domarchi, Paris 1965; *The Musical Film* by Douglas McVay, London 1967; *Judy—The Films of Judy Garland* by Joe Morella and Edward Epstein, New York 1969; *Judy Garland* by Brad Steiger, New York 1969; *Cukor and Co.: The Films of George Cukor* by Gary Carey, New York 1971; *On Cukor* by Gavin Lambert, New York 1972; *George Cukor* by Carlos Clarens, London 1976; *Hollywood on Hollywood* by James R. Parish and Michael R. Pitts, with Gregory Munk, Metuchen, New Jersey 1978; *The Hollywood Professionals*, Cukor entry by Allen Estrin, New York 1980; *George Cukor* by Gene Phillips, Boston 1982; articles—"The Great Come-Back" by Peter Brinson in *Films and Filming* (London), December 1954; "George Cukor: His Success Directing Women Has Obscured His Other Directorial Virtues" by Romano Tozzi in *Films in Review* (New York), February 1958; "George Cukor" by Romano Tozzi in *Films in Review* (New York), February 1958; article on Cukor's work in 2 parts by John Howard Reid in *Films and Filming* (London), August and September 1960; "Connaissance de George Cukor" by Alain Jomy in *Cinéma 63* (Paris), June 1963; "Retrospective Cukor" in *Cahiers du cinéma* (Paris), February 1964; "Interview with George Cukor" by Richard Overstreet in *Film Culture* (New York), no.34, 1964; "Une Etoile est née" by Claude Beylie in *Ecran* (Paris), January 1974; "D'Entre les ombres" by M. Legrand in *Positif* (Paris), February 1974; "Cukor" by Andrew Sarris in *Film Comment* (New York), March/April 1978; "Nova: Garland in *A Star is Born*" by W. Jennings in *Quarterly Review of Film Studies* (Pleasantville, New York), no.3, 1979; "*A Star is Born*" by Robert Mitchell in *Magill's Survey of Cinema, Vol. IV* edited by Frank N. Magill, Englewood Cliffs, New Jersey 1980; "George Cukor" by DeWitt Bodeen in *Films in Review* (New York), November 1981; "Missing *Star* is Found in Warner Bros. Vaults" by Aljean Harmetz in *The New York Times*, 15 April 1983.

*   *   *

The "birth of a star" has proved to be a durable cinematic conceit. The story of the fading, alcoholic male actor who discovers a talented young woman, fosters her career, marries her, and finally commits suicide was first made in 1937, directed by William Wellman, with Janet Gaynor and Fredric March. The 1954 George Cukor version represents the basic outline of the original scenario while transforming the woman into a singer. And in 1976, the situation serves rock stardom as well, with Barbra Steisand and Kris Kristofferson. The germ for this theme and its variations is the 1932 *What Price Hollywood?*, also directed by George Cukor, starring Constance Bennett, Lowell Sherman and Neil Hamilton. There, the male figure is divided in two—a drunken director and a society husband—and the film reunites husband and wife in a happy ending. But it is the 1954 *Star* that is most often revived and best remembered.

Hollywood has made many reflexive films in which it examines its own procedures, manners, and mythology. The trenchant reflexivity of *Sunset Boulevard, The Bad and the Beautiful* and *A Star is Born* (products of those difficult Hollywood years, 1950-54) is in the intimate exposure of the performer's craft, a particularly painful exposure when we learn that craft and life are so intimately connected. It is impossible to separate Gloria Swanson and Lana Turner from the fictions they incarnate. The connections are most troubling in the case of Judy Garland, the star who is presumably born, but who, in fact, is nearly at the end of her musical career. The only other film in which her singing is prominently featured is her last effort, made in England, *I Could Go on Singing*, with its sickeningly ironic title. *A Star is Born* was meant to be the vehicle that re-established her as a viable movie star, after her humiliating dismissal from MGM in 1950. The public was aware of her personal problems, her fluctuating weight, and her suicide attempt. Now, with our knowledge of Judy Garland's difficulties in Hollywood, of her missed concert dates, her failed TV program and her tragic, drug-related death, it is impossible not to see the film's ultimate reflexivity in the way the figure of the unreliable star, the husband, is a surrogate for Garland herself. Each time Vicki Lester "bails out" Norman Maine and "understands" his problems, it is Garland looking at Garland, not James Mason—Garland exposing her own fears and weaknesses through the male character.

Made at great expense, over a long shooting schedule, the production of *A Star is Born* was fraught with difficulties that seemed to echo those of Garland. After director George Cukor finished his work, it was decided the film wasn't musical enough. Cuts were made (and deplored by Cukor) to permit the inclusion of a long sequence, "Born in a Trunk," a musical biography of a performer reminiscent of the "Broadway Melody" number in *Singin' in the Rain*. Still nervous about the film's length, the studio, several days after its release (to excellent reviews), cut it from 182 minutes to 154 minutes, hoping it would fit into a more conventional exihibition program. The film was further cut to 135 minutes.

The film's appeal survived its radical surgery. And that appeal is not limited to Garland. Rather, she is not put in relief by the elegant mise-en-scène that exploits with great care the compositional elements mandated by the CinemaScope format, by the lighting and set direction that keep in balance both the film's intimacy and its grand proportions, by the Harold Arlen score that provided Garland and all subsequent torch singers with the classic "The Man That Got Away," and by the performance of James Mason, supportive yet stellar in its own right.

A Star Is Born is, in fact, a celebration of a dual register of performance—performance as a function of artifice, technique, audience and as the revelation of personal intimacy captured by the movie camera. The stage that opens and closes the film is the gigantic Shrine Auditorium. It first exposes Norman Maine's drunken disruption of a charity show. In the final shot, it is the frame for Vicki Lester's return to her public, performing self, when she receives an ovation for presenting herself as "Mrs. Norman Maine." The performer's identity shifts through a series of qualifying frames. Norman falls in love with Vicki (still called Esther Blodgett) when he hears her sing "The Man That Got Away" with and for a small group of musicians. The song is sustained in a camera movement that accommodates her own position as well as her connection to the instrumentalists, the privileged witnesses/collaborators. Norman's witnessing is, like our own, full of wonder at the talent generated by personality and technique. Norman exhibits *his* talent at the end of the film, when he "acts" happy and cured just before going out to drown himself.

Vicki's progress to stardom is the occasion for satirical views of the movie industry, episodes familiar from other films but done here with exceptional care and wit. The starlet is literally given the run-around during her first day at the studio, as unceremoniously pushed through a series of departments and doors, only to exit where she entered. No one has really taken the time to find out who she is. That process of Hollywood de-identification is made graphic when the makeup artists examine Vicki's face, declare it is all wrong, and transform her into a caricatural idea of beauty. During her first screen appearance,

the director wants only to see her arm, waving a handerchief from a departing train. When she finally does become a star she performs her big production number all by herself in her living room, turning the furniture into the "sets" for exotic locales.

The varied scope of the star's identity is most emphatically emblemized in the scene where Vicki Lester receives an Academy Award. Norman drunkenly interrupts the ceremony and accidently slaps his wife. This private gesture is exposed before three audiences—the spectators within the fiction, those implied by the presence of the gigantic television screen within the shot, and ourselves. Yet another painful irony of this painful moment is the fact that Judy Garland, expected to win an Oscar for her performance in *A Star is Born*, lost to Grace Kelly.

—Charles Affron

STAR WARS TRILOGY

STAR WARS. Star Wars: A New Hope. Production: Lucasfilm Productions; 1977; Technicolor, 35mm; running time: 121 mins. Released spring 1977 by 20th Century Fox.

Produced by Gary Kurtz; screenplay by George Lucas; d.rected by George Lucas; photography by Gilbert Taylor; edited by Paul Hirsch, Marcia Lucas, and Richard Chew; sound by Derek Ball, Don MacDougall, Bob Minkler, and Ray West, sound effects edited by Benjamin Burtt, Jr.; art direction by John Barry, Norman Reynolds, and Leslie Dilley, set decorated by Roger Christian; music by John Williams; special effects by John Dykstra, John Stears, Richard Edlund, Grant McCune, and Robert Blalack; costumes designed by John Mollo.

Academy Awards for Art Direction/Set Direction, Sound, Best Original Score, Film Editing, Costume Design, and Visual Effects, 1977; Special Academy Award to Ben Burtt, Jr. for sound effects, 1977.

Cast: Mark Hamill (*Luke Skywalker*); Harrison Ford (*Han Solo*); Carrie Fisher (*Princess Leia Ograna*); Alec Guiness (*Ben "Obi-wan" Kenobi*); Peter Cushing (*Grand Moff Tarkin*); David Prowse (*Lord Darth Vader*, voice by James Earl Jones); Kenny Baker (*R2-D2*); Anthony Daniels (*C-3PO*); Peter Mayhew (*Chewbacca*).

Publications:

Reviews—"L'Amérique sans peur et sans reproche" by S. Le Péron in *Cahiers du cinéma* (Paris), December 1977; "*Star Wars*" in *Filmfacts* (Los Angeles), no.5, 1977; "The *Star Wars*: II Star Drek" by T.C. Fok in *Film Comment* (New York), July/August 1977; "*Star Wars* by Gordon Gow in *Films and Filming* (London), December 1977; "George Lucas' *Star Wars*" by G. Morris in *Take One* (Montreal), July/August 1977; "*Star Wars*" by A.D. Murphy in *Variety* (New York), 25 May 1977; "The Solitary Pleasures of *Star Wars*" by Jonathan Rosenbaum in *Sight and Sound* (London), autumn 1977; "*Star Wars—Krieg gegen Kinder*" by P. Ulbrich in *Film und Fernsehen* (Berlin), August 1978; "*Star Wars*" by F. Mathers in *Cinema Papers* (Melbourne, Australia), January 1978; book—*Storytelling and Mythmaking: Images in Film and Literature* by Frank McConnell, New York 1979; articles—"Star Tracks" by P. Strick in *Sight and Sound* (London), summer 1976; "L'Horizon retrouve (*La guerre des etoiles*)" by R. Benayoun in *Positif* (Paris), September 1977; "Special Effects in *Star Wars*" by D.W. Nicholson in *Cinema Papers* (Melbourne, Australia), October 1977; special issue of *American Cinematographer* (Los Angeles), July 1977; "L'Horizon retrouvé" by M. Ciment and R. Benayoun in *Posirif* (Paris), September 1977; "*Star Wars* Special Effects" by J. Canemaker in *Millimeter* (London), July/August 1977; "Le Matin du magicien, George Lucas et *Star Wars*" by C. Clouzot in *Ecran* (Paris), September 1977; "*Star Wars*" by I. Lindberg in *Kosmorama* (Copenhagen), autumn 1977; "A Space *Iliad*" by A. Lubow in *Film Comment* (New York), July/August 1977; "George Lucas Goes Far Out" by S. Zito in *American Film* (Washington, D.C.), April 1977; "*Star Wars*: The Pastiche of Myth and the Yearning for a Past Future" by Robert Collins in *Journal of Popular Culture* (Bowling Green, Ohio), summer 1977; "Not So Far Away" by D. Rubey in *Jump Cut* (Chicago), August 1978; "The Stars in our Hearts—A Critical Commentary on George Lucas' *Star Wars*" by D. Wood in *Journal of Popular Film* (Bowling Green, Ohio), no.3, 1978; "Laserstragler og romjagere" by N.K. Aas in *Film & kino* (Oslo), November 1979; "Bergsonian Comedy and the Human Machines in *Star Wars*" by L. Roth in *Film Criticism* (Edinboro, Pennsylvania), winter 1979; "*La Guerre de las galaxies*" by D. Capriles in *Cine al dia* (Caracas, Venezuela), April 1979; "Special Effects in *Star Wars*: The Difference Between Fighting a Battle and a War" by P. Lehman and D. Daso in *Wide Angle* (Athens, Ohio); "*Star Wars* Return Pacing New Pix: Beats Aug. Blahs" in *Variety* (New York), 22 August 1979; "Fox's Fear of 16mm Piracy Bars *Star Wars* from Global GI Sites" by H. Guild in *Variety* (New York), 24 January 1979; "Cashing in on *Star Wars*" by M. Pye and L. Miles in *Atlantic Monthly* (Greenwich, Connecticut), March 1979; "The Man Who Made *Star Wars*" by M. Pye and L. Miles in *Atlantic Monthly* (Greenwich, Connecticut), March 1979; "*Star Wars* Set for Radio" in *The New York Times*, 30 April 1979; "*Star Wars* (*Guerre stellari*)" by V. Tosi in *Bianco e nero* (Rome), January/February 1979; "*Star Wars*" by Ruth L. Hirayama in *Magill's Survey of Cinema, Vol. IV* edited by Frank N. Magill, Englewood Cliffs, New Jersey 1980; "The Empire's New Clothes" by D. Wood in *Film Quarterly* (Berkeley), spring 1981.

*   *   *

THE EMPIRE STRIKES BACK. Production: Lucasfilm; Rank Film Color, 35mm, Panavision, Dolby sound; visual effects shot in Panavision; running time: 124 mins. Released 14 June 1980 by 20th Century Fox.

Produced by Gary Kurtz, executive producer: George Lucas; screenplay by Leigh Brackett and Lawrence Kasdan; from an original story written for the screen by George Lucas; directed by Irvin Kershner; photography by Peter Suschitzy; edited by Paul Hirsch, visual effects edited by Conrad Buff; sound by Peter Sutton; special sound effects designed and edited by Ben Burtt; production design by Norman Reynolds, set decoration by Michael Ford; art direction by Leslie Dilley, Harry Lange, and Alan Tomkins, visual effects art direction by Joe Johnston; music by John Williams; special effects by Brian Johnson and Richard Edlund, mechanical effects supervised by Nick Adler, effects photography by Dennis Muren, optical photography by Bruce Nicholson; stop motion animation by Jon Berg and Phil

Tippet, matte painting by Harrison Ellenshaw, models made by Lorne Peterson, and ani-rotoscope by Peter Kuran; costumes designed by John Mollo; design consultant: Ralph McQuarrie; make-up for creature designed by Stuart Freeborn.

Filmed in Elstree Studios, England, and on location in Finse, Norway; special effects shot at Industrial Light and Magic, California. Academy Award, Sound, 1980; Special Achievement Academy Award for Visual Effects, 1980.

Cast: Mark Hamill (*Luke Skywalker*); Harrison Ford (*Han Solo*); Carrie Fisher (*Princess Leia*); David Prowse (*Darth Vadar*): Anthony Daniels (*C-3PO*); Peter Mayhew (*Chewbacca*); Kenny Baker (*R2-D2*); Frank Oz (*Voice and mechanical workings of Yoda*); Billy Dee Williams (*Lando Calrissian*); Alec Guiness (*Ben "Obi-wan" Kenobi*); Jeremy Bulloch; John Hollis; Jack Purvis; Des Webb; Kathryn Mullen; Clive Revill; Kenneth Colley; Julian Glover; Michael Sheard; Michael Culver; John Dicks; Milton Johns; Mark Jones; Oliver Maguire; Robin Scobey; Bruce Boaj; Christopher Malcom; Dennis Lawson; Richard Oldfield; John Morton; Ian Liston; John Retzenberger; Jack McKenzie; Jerry Harte; Norman Chancer; Norwich Duff; Ray Hassett; Brigitte Kahn; Burnell Tucker.

Publications:

Reviews—"*The Empire Strikes Back*" by R. Combs in *Monthly Film Bulletin* (London), July 1980; "*El imperio contraataca*" by J.L. Téllez in *Contracampo* (Madrid), December 1980; "*The Empire Strikes Back*" by J. Harwood in *Variety* (New Yrok), 14 May 1980; "*The Empire Strikes Back*" by T. Rogers in *Films in Review* (New York), August/September 1980; "*L'Empire contre-attaque*" by M. Tessier in *Image et son* (Paris), September 1980; "*The Empire Strikes Back*" by E. de Kuyper in *Skrien* (Amsterdam), March 1981; book—*Once Upon a Galaxy: A Journal of the Making of The Empire Strikes Back* by Alan Arnold, New York 1980; articles—special issue of *American Cinematographer* (Los Angeles), June 1980; "*The Empire Strikes Back*" in *Films and Filming* (London), April 1980; "Un Cosmos très universel" plus "Entretien avec Irvin Kershner" by M. Ciment and A. Garsault in *Positif* (Paris), September 1980; "Regijsseur Kershner gelooft in sprookjes" by P. Lierop in *Skoop* (Amsterdam), November 1980; "*Star Wars* Strikes Again" by R. McGee in *American Film* (Washington, D.C.), May 1980; "*The Empire Strikes Back*" by D. Reiss in *Filmmakers Newsletter* (Ward Hill, Massachusetts), June 1980; "John Williams et *The Empire Strikes Back*" by F. Vallerand in *Séquences* (Montreal), July 1980; "*The Empire Strikes Back*: Monsters from the Id" by Andrew Gordon in *Science Fiction Studies*, November 1980; "The Empire's New Clothes" by D. Wood in *Film Quarterly* (Berkeley), spring 1981; "Complex Design in *The Empire Strikes Back*" by A. Lancashire in *Film Criticism* (Edinboro, Pennsylvania), spring 1981; "Burden of Dreams: George Lucas" by Aljean Harmetz in *American Film* (Washington, D.C.), June 1983.

*   *   *

THE RETURN OF THE JEDI. Production: Lucasfilm Ltd.; color, 35mm, Dolby sound; running time: about 120 mins. Released spring 1983 by 20th Century Fox.

Produced by Howard Kazanjian, executive producer: George Lucas; screenplay by Lawrence Kasdan and George Lucas; from an original story for the screen by George Lucas; directed by Richard Marquand; photography by Alan Hume; edited by Sean Barton, Marcia Lucas, and Duwayne Dunham; sound designed by Ben Burtt; production design by Norman Reynolds; music by John Williams; special effects by Richard Edlund, Dennis Muren and Ken Ralston; mechanical effects supervision by Kit West; make-up and creature design by Stuart Freeborn and Phil Tippett; costumes designed by Aggie Guerard Rodgers and Nilo Rodis-Jamero.

Filmed Elstree Studios, England, and on location in Yuma, Arizona and Crescent City, California; special effects shot at Industrial Light and Magic, California.

Cast: Mark Hamill (*Luke Skywalker*); Harrison Ford (*Han Solo*); Carrie Fisher (*Princess Leia*); Billy Dee Williams (*Lando Calrissian*); Anthony Daniels (*C-3P0*); Kenny Baker (*R2-D2 and Paploo*); Peter Mayhew (*Chewbacca*); Ian McDiarmid (*The Emperor*); David Prowse (*Darth Vader, voice by James Earl Jones*); Sebastian Shaw (*Anakin Skywalker*); Warwick Davis (*Wicket*); Michael Carter (*Bib Fortuna*); Denis Lawson (*Wedge*); Alec Guinness (*Ben "Obi-wan" Kenobi*).

Publications:

Articles—"*Return of the Jedi*: Behind the Scenes with Director Richard Marquand" by Steranko in *Prevue*, July 1983; "Burden of Dreams: George Lucas" by Aljean Harmetz in *American Film* (Washington, D.C.), June 1983; "*Jedi's* Extra Special Effects" by Adam Eisenberg in *American Film* (Washington, D.C.), June 1983.

*　　*　　*

In terms of scope, the three *Star Wars* films are a modern equivalent to *The Illiad* or *The Odyssey*. Not only do they depict a mythic history in the form of an epic narrative, they also tell a personal tale of courage and cowardice, adventure and romance. Supported by a dazzling display of special effects and cinematic technology, the films are set in a vivid fantasy world, "a long time ago in a galaxy far, far away." The series is so popular that each new film has joined the ranks of the top moneymakers of all time. More importantly, the films have generated a major trend in big budget science fiction and fantasy films, a trend that has continued well into the 1980s.

The Disneyesque creator behind these films is George Lucas, who used the success of *American Graffiti* as a springboard for the production of the first *Star Wars* film, subtitled *A New Hope*. Lucas retained the rights to future *Star Wars* films and has since produced two sequels, subtitled *The Empire Strikes Back* and *Return of the Jedi*. These three films are the middle trilogy of a tentatively planned nine film opus.

The middle trilogy relates the adventures of Luke Skywalker as he and his companions battle the evil Empire, led by Luke's arch nemesis, Lord Darth Vader, who is actually the tool of the Emperor, a far more malevolent being. As they're now planned, the first trilogy will relate how the Emperor took power and will end with Luke as a young boy, while the third trilogy will begin years after Luke and his rebel allies have defeated the Emperor in *Return of the Jedi*.

The films are full of youthful energy, from the exuberance of the performers to the powerful but subtle strains of John Williams's Academy Award-winning score. Lucas may be the genius behind these films, but the contributions of others involved in the films should not be overlooked.

Although the trilogy can be seen as a simple tale of good versus evil, this doesn't do justice to its moral complexity, especially concerning the character of Luke. Luke's story is not only a fight against the evil Empire, it is also a fight against the evil within himself. His moral dilemma is complicated by the fact, as revealed in *The Empire Strikes Back*, that the villainous Darth Vader is Luke's father.

Luke's confrontation with his dark father is part of his initiation as a Jedi Knight, an initiation which involves training in the ways of the "the Force," the mysterious power that exists in everything and "binds the universe together." An important theme in the films is how the Force can be used to control technology, for good or evil ends. Luke's initiation into this mysterious Force is a rite of passage. As such, aspects of his story conform to the classic structure of separation, transition and incorporation described by anthropologist Arnold van Gennep in his 1909 book *Rites of Passage*.

For example, in *The Empire Strikes Back* Luke's right hand is cut off by his father during a fight and is later replaced with a mechanical hand. Despite this symbolic castration, Luke still sees goodness in his father, and in *Return of the Jedi* he spares his father's life when he sees that his father, who has become more machine than man, also has a mechanical hand. This device of the hands signifies a permanent separation that leads to a permanent incorporation—it is a symbol of union with the father and a mark of membership in the knighthood of the Jedi. As a result, Luke becomes a Jedi Knight and his father is again incorporated into the good side of the Force.

The duplication and inversion which exists in the confrontation between Luke and his father is reflected throughout the *Star Wars* films. For instance, the rebels must destroy two Death Stars, Luke has a twin sister, the two robots are a comical inversion of the courage and cowardice of the other main characters, and Obi-wan Kenobi is a benevolent double of the Emperor. Most importantly, the furry Ewoks of *Return of the Jedi* are an inverted duplication of the small, nasty Jawas of *A New Hope*. The primitive techology of the Ewoks is the crucial factor that defeats the more advanced technology of the Empire. The Ewoks thus demonstrate how the Emperor's inflated sense of power has caused him to minimize the powers of others resulting in the Emperor's own downfall.

In this respect, the communal celebration of all of the heroes at the forest home of the Ewoks in the final scene of *Return of the Jedi* represents an interesting development of the theme of duplication and inversion because it demonstrates the process whereby two can become one. Ultimately, the trilogy not only proclaims the unity of Luke with his father or Luke with his sister, it also proclaims the unity of the Many with the One. The spirit of togetherness at the end illustrates the essential oneness of the individual and the group.

The Emperor loses because he ignores the symbiotic nature of all such dualities; he fails to realize that the existence of the master depends on the existnce of his servant. And the power of Luke as a mythic hero is his ability to transcent the distinctions between good and evil, to see the good within the bad and the human being behind the mechanical mask.

In the final analysis, the *Star Wars* trilogy can be enjoyed as entertainment or a meaningful work of art that demonstrates how films can uplift our spirits and enrich our lives. It is no wonder that these films have captured the imagination of a generation of filmgoers.

—Thomas Snyder

STARÉ POVESTI CESKÉ. Old Czech Legends. Production: Puppet Film Prague; color, animated puppets, 35mm; length: 2480 meters. Released September 1953, Prague.

Produced by Vladimír Janovský, Vojen Masník, and Jaroslav Možiš; story by Jiří Trnka and Miloš Kratochvíl; screenplay by Jiří Trnka and Jiří Brdečka; from the book by Alois Jirásek; directed by Jiří Trnka; photography by Ludvík Hájek and Emanuel Franek; edited by Helena Lebdušková; sound by Emanuel Formánek, Emil Poledník and Josef Zavadil; music by Václav Trojan; consultants: Rudolf Turek and Albert Pek; animation by Břetislav Pojar, Bohuslav Srámek, Zdeněk Hrabě, Stanislav Látal, Jan Karpaš, Josef Kluge, and František Braun.

Filmed 1953. Venice Film Festival, Silver Medal from the president of the Festival, Lion of St. Mark, and Honorable Mention for Short Films, 1953; Locarno Festival, Prize of the Swiss Film Press, 1953.

Cast: *Voices:* Ružena Nasková; Václav Vydra, Sr.; Karel Höger; Zdeněk Stěpánek; Eduard Kohout.

Publications:

Books—*Jiří Trnka, Artist and Puppet Master* by Jaroslav Boček, Prague 1963; *Jiří Trnka*, brochure, by Marie Benešová, Prague 1970; *The Most Important Art: East European Film After 1945* by Mira Liehm and Antonín Liehm, Berkeley 1977; articles—"The Puppet Film as Art" (interview with Trnka) by J. Brož in *Film Culture* (New York), no.5-6, 1955; "An Interview with the Puppet-Film Director, Jirí Trnka" by Jaroslav Brož in *Film* (London), January/February 1956; "Trnka's Little Men" by Bernard Orna in *Films and Filming* (London), November 1956; "The Czechoslovak Animated Film" by Harriet Polt in *Film Quarterly* (Berkeley), spring 1964; article by Jaroslav Boček in *Film a doba* (Prague), no.5, 1965; "Trnkaland" in *Newsweek* (New York), March 1966; "O Jirím Trnkovi se Stanislavem Látalem a Břetislavem Pojarem" by Miloš Fiala in *Film a doba* (Prague), no.4, 1970; "Hevding Tjekke & En skaesdommernats drøm" by P. Schepelern in *Kosmorama* (Copenhagen), summer 1978.

*   *   *

After exhausting work on a long puppet film, *Bajaja*, Trnka gathered his creative strength for another ambitious enterprise, to transpose into the form of a puppet movie the "Legends of Old Bohemia," a collection of narratives about the oldest period of Czech history, in which history is mixed with mythology. It was not a simple task and doubts appeared from the very beginning. However, Trnka was convinced that puppets were most suitable for expressing the magic as well as the solemnity of old stories and myths. From the book of by Alois Jirásek, who had shaped these legends according to old chronicles and records (the book was published in 1894), he selected six stories: the arrival of First Father (Patriarch) Czech in the territory of contemporary Bohemia; the legend about the strong Bivoj; the legend of Prłemysl the Ploughman, founder of the royal dynasty of Prłemyslites reigning in Bohemia until the 15th century; the story of the Young Womens' War; about Horymír who stood up to defend the farmers' labor; and the legend of the Lucko War which is won by Cestmír, a hero of the people. Trnka did not restrict himself exclusively to Jirásek's conception; while planning the screen play, he took into consideration the most recent archaeological research which helped him interpret the probable material and cultural conditions of life in those days. However, Jirásek's text, together with the archeological research, was, for Trnka, merely a foundation on which he built a structure according to his own imagination and invention.

From the point of view of Trnka's creative career, *Old Czech Legends* represents a fundamental metamorphosis in his work. This change was manifested most expressively in the puppets themselves. In comparison with *Spalíček*, *The Emperor's Nightingale*, and *Bajaja*, whose common trait was fragility and charm, the puppets in the *Legends* are monumentally dramatic and tragic, more individualized; their countenance expresses their character, the inner essence of the represented person. Another radical innovation was the breaking of unity between the music and the picture because, in this film, Trnka's puppets speak for the first time. Václav Trojan's music does not lose its importance but it is incorporated into the overall sound design including dialogue and sound effects.

The stories in *Old Czech Legends* combine to form a total composition. The magestic arrival of Patriarch Czech is followed by the struggle of Bivoj with a wild boar; the epic about Prłemysl has lyrical passages, the Young Women's War a capricious, almost erotic mood. The dramatic narrative about Horymir is remarkable for its crowd scenes and its conclusion in which Horymír jumps over the Moldau River. The most remarkable is probably the last episode of the Legends, the narrative about the cowardly Duke Neklan who must be replaced in the war by a people's hero, Cestmír. The characterization of Neklan pushes the puppet movie to its farthest limits in expressing psychological attitudes. In his monograph about Trnka, Jaroslav Bocłek describes it as an extraordinary study of cowardice which we can only rarely find even in a movie with human actors. The second part of the story—Cestmír's battle with the Lukanians—is remarkable from another point of view. Trnka used from 70 to 100 puppets in battle scenes. Control of such a multitude of inanimate actors was, from the artistic and technical standpoint, an unusually demanding task, unthinkable in a puppet movie until then. Moreover, Trnka found, jointly with his animators, the precise shade of dramatic mood and rhythm, so that the movements of the crowd were harmonious.

The *Legends* occupy an important place in Trnka's extensive work. Trnka discovered here a new style of puppet movie, characterized by a transition from lyricism to drama and by the depiction of an individualized, psychologically conditioned hero. That this new style had the potential for further development was demonstrated by Trnka's subsequent puppet movies *The Good Soldier Svejk* and *The Dream of the Night of St. John*.

—Mrs. B. Urgosíková

STEAMBOAT WILLIE. Production: Walt Disney Productions; 1928; black and white, 35mm, animation; length: 500 feet.

Released 18 November 1928 in New York.

Produced by Roy and Walt Disney; scenario by by Walt Disney and Ub Iwerks; directed by Walt Disney; sound recording by P.A. Powers, Cinephone; music composed by Carl Stalling, music conducted by Carl Edourde; animation supervised by Ub Iwerks; animation by Wilfred Jackson, Les Clark, and Johnny Cannon.

Filmed in California.

Cast: Character voices by Walt Disney.

Publications:

Books—*The Art of Walt Disney* by Robert D. Field, New York 1942; *The Technique of Film Music* by Roger Manvell and J. Huntley, New York 1957; *Animation in the Cinema* by Ralph Stephenson, New York 1967; *The Disney Version: The Life, Times, Art and Commerce of Walt Disney* by Richard Schickel, New York 1968; *Walt Disney* by Maurice Bessy, Paris 1970; *Walt Disney: the Master of Animation* by Gerald Kurl, edited by Steve D. Rahmas, Charlottesville, New York 1971; *The Art of Walt Disney* by Christopher Finch, New York 1975; *Movie Made America: A Social History of American Movies* by Robert Sklar, New York 1975; *Walt Disney: An American Original* by Bob Thomas, New York 1976; *Walt Disney: A Guide to References and Resources* by Elizabeth Leebron and Lynn Gartley, Boston 1979; *Of Mice and Magic* by Leonard Maltin, New York 1980; *Disney Animation: The Illusion of Life* by Frank Thomas and Ollie Johnston, New York 1982; articles—"Making of a Sound Fable" in *Popular Mechanics*, summer 1930; "Mickey Mouse's Miraculous Movie Monkeyshines" in *Literary Digest*, 9 August 1930; "The Only Unpaid Movie Star" by Harry Carr in *American*, March 1931; "Walt Disney" by Gilbert Seldes in the *New Yorker*, 19 December 1931; "Profound Mouse" in *Time* (New York), 15 May 1933; "Mickey Mouse's Financial Career" by Arthur Mann in *Harper's* (New York), March 1931; "Walt Disney: Genius at Work" by P. Hollister in *Atlantic* (Boston), December 1940; "Walt Disney" by Peter Ericsson in *Sequence* (London), no.10, 1950; "A Silver Anniversary for Walt and Mickey" in *Life* (New York), 2 November 1953; "Father Goose" in *Time* (New York), 27 December 1954; "Giving Life to the Fantastic: A History of the Cartoon Film" by Roger Manvell in *Films and Filming* (London), November 1956; "Disney and Animation" in *Film and Reality* by Roy Armes, Baltimore 1974; "Disney Animation: History and Technique" by J. Canemaker in *Film News* (New York), January/February 1979; "'Building a Better Mouse': 50 Years of Disney Animation" by M. Barrier in *Funnyworld* (New York), summer 1979.

*   *   *

Steamboat Willie—starring the most famous of cartoon mouses, Mickey—has the distinction of being the very first sound cartoon. While that feat may not seem so remarkable in the context of modern sound technology, by 1928 standards it was a bold and potentially disasterous step on the part of Walt Disney. Not only was early equipment difficult and cumbersome to use, but Disney had to decide what cartoons should sound like. Since cartoons are totally fabricated, it was feared that sound might bring too much reality into play and shatter the illusion of make-believe. Luckily, Disney took a very logical (and correct) approach by using silly and bizarre sounds to match the characters and situations in his cartoons.

Up to this point Walt Disney's career was fairly active, but not secure. His *Alice* series had not been a profitable venture, and he lost the rights to the Oswald Rabbit character to his former partner Charles Mintz. In 1928 Disney and his chief animator Ub Iwerks developed a new character named Mickey Mouse. They made two cartoons with Mickey, *Plane Crazy* and *Gallopin' Gaucho*, but Disney was unable to find a distributor for the films. At this point Disney knew he had to find something unique to make his films stand out from all the others. He decided to take a risk by adding a musical soundtrack to his cartoon.

The most difficult aspect of making *Steamboat Willie* was the synchronization of picture and sound. For this reason, dialogue was kept to a bare minimum (with Walt Disney himself supplying the voices of his characters). The music for the cartoon was planned, although not scored, before any of the animation was begun. Since music can be broken down mathematically, the animation was drawn to follow a musical pattern. For example, if the music had two beats per second, the animation would hit a beat every 12 frames (besed on 24 frames per second).

The last half of *Steamboat Willie* contains several excellent examples of the synchronization of action to music. In this sequence Mickey and Minnie play a version of "Turkey in the Straw" using barnyard animals as instruments. The early Mickey Mouse was a bit more crude than the sweet and lovable creature he eventually became. In this cartoon he pulls on a cow's udders, stretches a cat's tail, throws a mother pig and her babies across the room, and plays a cow's teeth like a xylophone. All of these actions fit into the beat of the music.

Because the synchronization between picture and sound was so important, Disney knew that his recording should use the sound-on-film method rather than disc. In 1928 sound equipment was at a premium in Los Angeles, so Disney took his film to New York. The first attempt to record the soundtrack was not to his satisfaction, and Disney sold his car to finance a second attempt. His confidence in the project paid off. *Steamboat Willie* was a tremendous success and received terrific reviews. What started out as a novelty—the first sound-on-film cartoon—became the standard of cartoons to follow.

—Linda J. Obalil

———————

STERNE. Stars. Zvezdi. Production: DEFA (Berlin) and Studiya za igralni filmi (Sofia); 1959; black and white, 35mm; running time: 93 mins.; length: 2513 meters. Released March 1959, Berlin and Sofia.

Screenplay by Anzhel Wagenstein; directed by Konrad Wolf with Rangel Vulchanov; photography by Werner Bergmann; edited by Christina Wernicke; sound by Erich Schmidt; production design by Jose Sancha, set decoration by Maria Ivanova and Alfred Drosdek; music by Simeon Pironkov, Jewish folk songs sung by Jerry Wolf; costumes designed by Albert Seidner.

Filmed 1958 in Bulgaria. Cannes Film Festival, Special Jury Prize, 1959; Edinburgh Film Festival, First Prize and Honorary Diploma, 1959; 7th World Youth and Students Film Festival, Vienna, Gold Medal, 1959.

Cast: Sasha Krusharska (*Ruth*); Jürgen Frohriep (*Walter*); Erik S. Klein (*Kurt*); Stefan Peichev (*Uncle Petko*); Georgi Naumov (*Blazhe*); Ivan Kondov (*Ruth's father*); Milka Tuikova (*Police officer*); Stiliyan Kanev (*The "doctor"*); *Naicho Petrov (Police officer*); Elena Hranova (*Old Jewish woman*); Albert Zahn (*Soldier on duty*); Hannjo Hasse (*Captain*); Hans Fiebrandt (*Soldier*); Tsonka Miteva (*Mutsi*); Waltraut Kramm (*Mutsi's girlfriend*); Trifon Dzhonev (*Schmied*); Leo Konforti (*The nervous Jew*); Gani Staikov (*Feverish person*); Avram Pinkas (*Water carrier*); Luna Davidova (*Pregnant Jew*); Petar Vasilev (*Jewish merchant*); Milka Mandil (*Jewish merchant*); Marin Toshev (*Jew with cigarettes*); Bella Eschkenazy (*Jew with girl*); Kancho Boshnakov (*Greedy Jew*); Georgi Banchev (*Woodcutter*); Yuri Yakovlev (*Soldier at the station*).

Publications:

Books—*Les Ecrans de Sofia* by Albert Cervoni, Paris 1976; *The Most Important Art: East European Film After 1945* by Mira Liehm and Antonín Liehm, Berkeley 1977; *Geschichte des Films ab 1960* by Ulrich Gregor, Frankfurt 1978; article—"Konrad Wolf" by Hans-Dieter Tok in *Regiestühle*, Berlin 1972.

*   *   *

The lights and shadows of the Nazi night understandably dominated the cinemas of the East European socialist countries for almost two decades after the end of World War II before melting away, slowly and painfully, from memory into history. *Sterne* was made at that particular point when the schematic black and white "bad German" mode of depiction had already been recognised as artistically insufficient, but the new perception of human conflicts and contradictions in a complicated world, sparked by the Italian neorealism, had yet to gain prominence.

Though both Bulgaria and the German Democratic Republic had produced their own films on similar themes and of equal quality (*On The Little Island*—1958, *Lesson One*—1960, and *And We Were Young*—1961, in Bulgaria; and *Stronger Than the Night*—1954, *Betrayed Until the Last Day*—1957, *They Called Him Amigo*—1959, and *Naked Among Wolves*—1962, in the GDR), it was *Sterne* that introduced the cinemas of the two countries to the international film scene, where the Polish school and the Soviet "thaw" in the mid-fifties had already stirred the attention and dispersed the bias towards the cinema of the socialist countries. Much later Albert Cervoni in his *Les Ecrans de Sofia* (Paris, 1976) called the film "a masterpiece or a little less than that, but certainly a moving work where—rather uncustomarily—the formula of the co-production was justified on all levels, political, esthetic and also that of the screenplay itself." He stated this in part to cast a passing remark at the Quai d'Orsay, the French ministry of external affairs, for which the GDR did not exist in 1959. For this reason *Sterne* was shown at Cannes only as a Bulgarian entry.

There was a shared tragic national experience behind the co-production; the Kingdom of Bulgaria was an ally of the Third Reich from 1940 to 1944, yet managed through firm resistance to save its Jews from extermination. A personal friendship was also involved as screenwriter Anzhel Wagenstein, a Bulgarian Jew and a member of a resistance unit, and director Konrad Wolf, son of exiled Communist writer Friedrich Wolf and an officer in the Red army, studied together at Moscow's VGIK in the early fifties.

The story of the disillusioned Aryan *Unteroffizier* who falls in love with the girl from the doomed transport of Greek Jews and tries to save her could have easily turned into melodrama but for its authenticity and sharpness, imbued with elegiac overtones. Starting with its title (the stars are twinkling witnesses of the lovers, and also humiliating yellow signs of racial *Minderwertigkeit*), the film attempts to blend poetic dreams with grim reality. The poetic side is less successful partly because of the somewhat oldfashioned and artificial cinematographic means that are applied, but mostly because of the inherent intellectual approach seeking—unlike *Hiroshima, mon amour* which is structured as an emotional, unpredictable and uncontrollable response to war traumas—a rational explanation for what seems an absurd and inevitable one-way situation. Highly realistic in its sight and sound, the film's images remain in one's mind: the small and quiet Bulgarian town, the yard of the school turned temporarily into a camp, the people behind the barbed wire and their eyes that keep looking out. Eyes that bring to mind the final sequence of Mikhail Romm's *Ordinary Fascism*; eyes that seem to have seen death at the end of the tunnel and are trying, hopelessly, to hide it.

—Dimitar Bardarsky

LA STRADA. The Road. Production: Ponti-De Laurentiis (Rome); black and white, 35mm; running time: 102 mins., some sources state 107 mins. or 94 mins.; length: about 2800 meters. Released 1954, Venice Film Festival.

Produced by Carlo Ponti and Dino De Larentiis; screenplay by Federico Fellini and Tullio Pinelli with Ennio Flaiano; directed by Federico Fellini; photography by Otello Martelli; edited by Léo Catozzo; sound engineered by A. Calpini; production design by M. Ravesco, with artistic collaboration by Brunello Rondi, assited by Paolo Nuzzi; music by Nino Rota, music directed by Franco Ferrara; special effects by E. Trani; costumes designed by M. Marinari.

Filmed December 1953-May 1954 in Ponti-De Larentiis studios in Rome; also on location in Viterbo, Ovindoli, Bagnoregio, and in various small towns in Central and Southern Italy. Venice Film Festival, Silver Prize, 1954; New York Critics Award, Best Foreign Film, 1956; Academy Award, Best Foreign Film, 1956.

Cast: Giulietta Masina (*Gelsomina*); Anthony Quinn (*Zampano*); Richard Basehart (*Il matto, 'the fool'*); Aldo Silvani (*Monsieur Giraffa*); Marcella Rovere (*The widow*); Lina Venturini (*The sister*).

Publications:

Scripts—"10,000 lire per una moglie" (dialogue from opening sequence) by Federico Fellini and Tullio Pinelli in *Cinema nuovo* (Turin), 15 July 1954; "*La Strada*" by Federico Fellini and Tullio Pinelli in *Cinema nuovo* (Turin), September/October 1954; *La Strada* edited by François-Régis Bastide, Juliette Caputo, and Chris Marker, Paris 1955; "Ce que disait 'le fou'" (partial dialogue) by Tullio Penelli in *Cahiers du cinéma* (Paris), March 1955; "*La Strada*" by Federico Fellini and Tullio Pinelli with Ennio Flaiano in *Avant-Scène du cinéma* (Paris), April

1970; reviews—"*La Strada*" by Edoardo Bruno in *Filmcritica* (Rome), August/September 1954; review by Dominique Aubier in *Cahiers du cinéma* (Paris), July 1955; review by André Bazin in *Esprit* (Paris), May 1955; review by Robert Benayoun in *Positif* (Paris), no.1, 1955; "Propos un peu libres" by Bernard Chardère in *Positif* (Paris), November 1955; "The Strong Grow Weak" in *Newsweek* (New York), 16 July 1956; "The Beauty and the Beast" by James Reichley in the *New Republic* (New York), 31 December 1956; "*La Strada*" by A.H. Weiler in *The New York Times*, 17 July 1956; books—*Federico Fellini* by Renzo Renzi, Parma 1956; *Panorama del cinema contemporareo* by Luigi Chiarini, Rome 1957; *Fellini* by Suzanne Budgen, London 1966; *Federico Fellini: An Invetigation into his Films and Philosophy* by Gilbert Salachas, translated by Rosalie Siegal, New York 1969; *Federico Fellini: Discussion* by James R. Silke, Beverly Hills (American Film Institute), 1970; *Encountering Directors* by Charles Thomas Samuels, New York 1972; *Federico Fellini* by Franco Pecori, Florence 1974; *Federico Fellini: The Search for a New Mythology* by Charles B. Ketcham, New York 1976; *Fellini* by Liliana Betti, Zurich 1976; *Fellini the Artist* by Edward Murray, New York 1976; *The Cinema of Federico Fellini* by Stuart Rosenthal, London 1976; *Fellini on Fellini* edited by Christian Strich, New York 1976; *Federico Fellini: A Guide to References and Resources* by John C. Stubbs, Boston 1978; articles—"Gelsomina e Zampano sulla strada di Fellini" by Stelio Martini in *Cinema Nuovo* (Turin), 1 November 1953; "*La Strada*" by Guido Aristarco in *Cinema nuovo* (Turin), 10 November 1954; "Venice 1954" by Francis Koval in *Films in Review* (New York), October 1954; issue on *La Strada* of *Cinema* (Rome), 10 August 1954; "New Names" in *Sight and Sound* (London), winter 1955; "Cinéma italien" by Guido Aristarco in *Cinéma 55* (Paris), January 1955; "Mythologie de *La Strada*" by Dominique Aubier in *Cahiers du cinéma* (Paris), July 1955; "The Signs of Predicament" by Gavin Lambert in *Sight and Sound* (London), January/March 1955; "*La Strada*" by Yves L'Her in *Téléciné* (Paris), May/June 1955; "Le Cas Fellini" by Cecilia Mangini in *Cinéma 55* (Paris), January 1955; "*La Strada—A Poem on Saintly Folly*" by Edouard de Laurot in *Film Culture* (New York), no.1, 1956; "Peut-on parler du néo-surréealisme de Fellini?" by Raymond Lefèvre in *Image et son* (Paris), January 1956; "*La Strada*" Cinematic Intersections" by Vernon Young in *Hudson Review* (Nutley, New Jersey), autumn 1956; "An Interview with Federico Fellini" by George Bluestone in *Film Culture* (New York), October 1957; "A proposito di Fellini" by Lino Del Fra in *Bianco e nero* (Rome), June 1957; "No Road Back" by John Francis Lane in *Films and Filming* (London), October 1957; article by Guido Aristarco in *Cinema nuovo* (Turin), December 1959; "*La Strada*" by Guy Gautier in *Image et son* (Paris), summer 1962; "Federico Fellini" in *Cinema Eye, Cinema Ear* by John Russell Taylor, New York 1964; "La splendida automaniera di Fellini" by Franco Boffa in *Cineforum* (Bergamo, Italy), April 1966; "The Secret Life of Federico Fellini" by Peter Harcourt in *Film Quarterly* (Berkeley), spring 1966; "Notes on Double Structure and the Films of Fellini" by Patricia Eason in *Cinema* (London), March 1969; "*La Strada*" by Gordon Gow in *Films and Filming* (London), October 1969; "*La Strada*" in *The Great Movies* by William Bayer, New York 1973; "Fellini's Musical Alter Ego, Nino Rota: How They Work" by Eugene Rizzo in *Variety* (New York), 21 May 1975; "Les Grandes Reprises: *La Strada*/*Rencontre avec Giulietta Masina*" by C. Taconet in *Cinéma* (Paris), February 1981; "*La Strada*" by J.A. Gili in *Image et son* (Paris), January 1981; "*La Strada*" by J.M. Guajardo in *Contracampo* (Madrid), February 1981.

* * *

La strada, one of the true masterpieces of modern cinema, is the film which brought international acclaim to director Federico Fellini. It is also an important transitional work in Italian cinema because its poetic and lyrical qualities set it apart from the literalness of the neorealism school which had dominated post-World War II Italy.

Fellini is an exponent of neorealism, having apprenticed with Roberto Rossellini as a writer and assistant director on *Open City* and *Paisan*. However, when he began directing on his own, preceding *La strada* with *The White Sheik* and *I vitelloni*, he opted for a subjectivity which, while evidencing the influences of neorealism, resulted in an interior and personalized cinema second only to Buñuel.

One of the recurring motifs in Fellini's films is the circus. As a youth, Fellini had spent a number of years with an itinerant circus troupe and came to admire their simplicity and their affinity with nature. Other motifs center on his Franciscan-like religious beliefs of which he stated: "If one is to understand Christianity as an attitude of love towards another human being, then all my films revolve around it. I show a world without love inhabited by people who exploit other people, but there is always among them some significant person who wants to give love and to live for the sake of love." Both elements can be found in *La Strada*, where a simple story involving the theme of redemption is set among itinerant circus folk.

Fellini wrote *La strada* (with Tullio Pinelli and Ennio Flaiano) for his actress-wife Giulietta Masina. When he presented the project to producers Dino De Laurentiis and Carlo Ponti, they rejected it as uncommercial, then suggested filming it with Silvano Mangano (Mrs. De Laurentiis) and Burt Lancaster as the stars. Fellini insisted that only his wife would play Gelsomina, and was finally able to convince Anthony Quinn, then in Italy making *Attila, the Hun*, to accept the role of Zampano. His producers acquiesced and the project was underway.

La strada is a serio-comic tragedy in which Fellini presents many levels of emotion and contrasting images. Its abiding message is that everyone has a purpose in life, a philosophy manifested through the lives of the three leading characters. Gelsomina is the self-sacrificing, doe-eyed simpleton (love) who becomes the chattel of Zampano, the animalistic circus strongman (brutality). The catalyst in their fatal relationship is Il Matto, the Fool, whose prescience helps the ignorant Gelsomina to see her own value as a human being (imagination). On one level the story is a fable, a variation on Beauty and the Beast, with Gelsomina, whose beauty is within, loving the beast. On another level it is a religious allegory in which the Fool, says Fellini, represents Christ. It is also an unprepossessing story of life's rejects, for whom Fellini has always shown compassion, struggling with their own solitude. This juxtaposition of realism, fantasy and spirituality makes Fellini's *La strada* unique.

As defined by the title, *La strada*, or *The Road*, is an episodic journey in the lives of these three outcasts. Zampano travels from village to village with his motorcycle and three-wheeled trailer performing a strongman's feat of breaking an iron chain by expanding his muscular chest. His act requires a helpmate so he purchases Gelsomina from her destitute mother for 10,000 lire. (Zampano's former helpmate had been Gelsomina's sister who had died on the road.) Gelsomina becomes Zampano's slave. With much difficulty she learns to beat a drum, announce his act—"Zam-pan-o is here"—, play the trumpet, and fulfill his sexual needs. Zampano lives in a world of physical appetites, while Gelsomina communicates with the sea, the birds, the flowers. For a while they join a travelling circus where Il Matto, the equilibrist, taunts the brutish Zampano, and counsels Gelsomina in the spiritual.

After leaving the circus, their paths once again cross with that of Il Matto. This time when the Fool derides the strongman, Zampano accidently kills him. The Fool's death sends Gelsomina into a state of depression and Zampano selfishly deserts her. Five years later he learns that she had died and only then, through her loss, is he able to recognize his remorse and the magnitude of his own solitude. Fellini closes his film with a chilling scene by the sea where Gelsomina had always felt at home.

The impact of the film is the result of Fellini's poetic imagery and not any cinematic tricks. The most apparent cinematic device is the moving camera and beautiful photography of Otello Martelli. Nino Rota's enchanting musical score has since become an international classic. Most important to the effectiveness of the film is the acting. Quinn's performance as Zampano is superb and brought him long overdue acclaim as an actor of stature, and Basehart is a commendable and mischievous Il Matto. Most outstanding of all is the wonderful face and pantomime of Guilietta Masina whose comedic abilities were compared to those of Chaplin and Harry Langdon.

The majority of reviews were overwhelmingly positive with the Catholic press describing it as a "parable of charity, love, grace, and salvation." There were, however, dissenting votes. The Italian leftists felt Fellini had betrayed neorealism, and some government factions protested the film's exportation to other countries claiming it presented a sordid and immoral view of ordinary Italians.

The film is the first of what is often described as Fellini's trilogy of solitude—*Il bidone* and *The Nights of Cabiria* completing the trilogy. *La strada* won over 50 international awards including the Grand Prize at the Venice Festival, The New York Film Critics Award, and the Academy Award as Best Foreign Language Film.

—Ronald Bowers

Publications:

Reviews—review by Henry Hart in *Films in Review* (New York), June/July 1951; review by Richard Winnington in *Sight and Sound* (London), August/September 1951; books—*Hitchcock* by Eric Rohmer and Claude Chabrol, Paris 1957; *Hitchcock* by Barthélemy Amengual, Paris 1960; *The Cinema of Alfred Hitchcock* by Peter Bogdanovich, New York 1962; *Alfred Hitchcock* by Hans-Peter Manz, Zurich 1962; *Hitchcock's Films* by Robin Wood, London 1965; *The Films of Alfred Hitchcock* by George Perry, London 1965; *Le Cinéma selon Hitchcock* by François Truffaut, Paris 1966; *Alfred Hitchcock* by Jean Douchet, Paris 1967; *Interviews with Film Directors* edited by Andrew Sarris, New Yrok 1967; *Alfred Hitchcock* by Noel Simsolo, Paris 1969; *Focus on Hitchcock* edited by Albert J. LaValley, Englewood Cliffs, New Jersey 1972; *The Strange Case of Alfred Hitchcock* by Raymond Durgnat, Cambridge, Massachusetts 1974; *Hitch* by John Russell Taylor, New York 1978; *Film Noir* edited by Alain Silver and Elizabeth Ward, Woodstock, New York 1979; articles—issue devoted to Hitchcock in *Cahiers du cinéma* (Paris), October 1953; "Figurant et grand metteur en scène..." by Pierre Feuga in *Arts* (Paris), 26 May 1954; "Hitchcock aime l'invraiseblance" by Claude Chabrol in *Arts* (Paris), 28 December 1955; "Recontre avec Hitchcock" by François Truffaut and Claude Chabrol in *Arts* (Paris), February 1955; "Petit bilan pour Alfred Hitchcock" by Louis Seguin in *Positif* (Paris), November 1955; issue devoted to Hitchcock in *Cahiers du cinéma* (Paris), August/September 1956; "Hitchcock's World" by Charles Higham in *Film Quarterly* (Berkeley), winter 1962-63; article by Warren Sonbert in *Film Culture* (New York), summer 1966; "Robert Walker" by Phyllis Zucker in *Films in Review* (New York), March 1970; "*L'inconnu du nord-express*" by M. Humbert and D. Delosne in *Image et son* (Paris), no.286, 1974; "*Strangers on a Train*" by Ann Laemmle in *Cinema Texas Program Notes* (Austin), 14 September 1978; "L'inconnu du Nord-Express et le Maccarthisme" by A. Marty in *Image et son* (Paris), July-August 1980.

*   *   *

STRANGERS ON A TRAIN. Production: Warner Bros. Pictures, Inc.; 1951; black and white, 35mm; running time: 101 mins. Released June 1951.

Produced by Alfred Hitchcock; screenplay by Raymond Chandler and Czendi Ormonde, adapted by Whitfield Cook; from the novel by Patricia Highsmith; directed by Alfred Hitchcock; photography by Robert Burks; edited by W.H. Ziegler; sound by Dolph Thomas; production design by Ted Haworth and George James-Hopkins; music by Dimitri Tiomkin, musical direction by Ray Heindorf; special effects by H.F. Koenekamp; costumes designed by Leah Rodes.

Filmed fall 1950 in New York City, Washington, D.C., and Darien, Connecticut, and at an amusement park constructed on Rowland V. Lee's ranch in Los Angeles.

Cast: Farley Granger (*Guy Haines*); Ruth Roman (*Ann Morton*); Robert Walker (*Bruno Anthony*); Leo G. Carroll (*Senator Morton*); Patricia Hitchcock (*Barbara Morton*); Laura Elliot (*Miriam Haines*); Marion Lorne (*Mrs. Anthony*); Jonathan Hale (*Mr. Anthony*); Howard St. John (*Capt. Turley*); John Brown (*Professor Collins*); Norma Varden (*Mrs. Cunningham*); Robert Gist (*Hennessey*); John Doucette (*Hammond*); Charles Meredith (*Judge Dolan*); Murray Alper (*Boatman*).

Alfred Hitchcock's films are now as generally appreciated for their wit as much as for their handling of suspense, and *Strangers on a Train* is a particularly fine example of his quizzical style. It should be stressed that the wit lies not so much in the script nor even in all aspects of the acting, but rather in the quality of the direction. Although Raymond Chandler was partly responsible for the screenplay, his partnership with Hitchcock was not a successful one in this film and neither were happy with it. Essentially the appeal of *Strangers on a Train* lies in the purely filmic qualities of imagery and cross-cutting, which are cleverly organized to develop the coincidences upon which the somewhat implausible plot is based, in ways not indicated in the original novel by Patricia Highsmith.

Guy Haines, a successful tennis player, and Bruno Anthony meet by accident on a train. The accidental element is emphasized by the famous opening sequence which focuses on feet going one way and then another, with the flashier and more vulgar shoes (Bruno's) boarding the train first. Before we see the face of either main character, the camera dwells on the complex crisscrossing of the railway tracks as the train leaves the station: a key image in the film which reflects the criss-crossing of lives, desires, and ambitions. Bruno is a mixture of smartness, nastiness, humor, and presumption who intrudes into Guy's life. Our initial sympathy with Guy, however is quickly blunted both by his own stolid demeanor and by our recognition of a certain "edge" and perverse vitality in Bruno. Soon Bruno is proposing his scheme whereby each "stranger" will exchange murders: he will kill Guy's wife, Miriam, who stands in the way of both true love and a future political career; in return, Guy is to kill Bruno's father.

As important as the surface plot, in which the two main characters are seen as doubles of each other, is the deliberate emphasis on otherwise trivial physical objects such as Miriam's spectacles, which link her as a parallel or double with Barbara Morton. More important is the cigarette lighter which Guy accidentally leaves in Bruno's compartment in the beginning of the film. This lighter, with its crossed tennis racquet motif, relates Guy and Bruno in several ways; and the motif reinforces the criss-cross effect of the train lines as well as the tennis match later in the film (holding the lighter at the end of the opening scene, Bruno softly repeats one word to himself: "criss-cross"). This lighter is also the focus of the suspense at the climax of the film, as well as being the material clue to "guilt" and "innocence." Thus, much of the wit and intelligence of *Strangers on a Train* centers around the lighter.

That the film is to be viewed as a comedy is further reinforced by the final scene in which Guy and Ann Morton stiffly turn away from the clergyman who recognizes him with the question Bruno had asked at the beginning: "Aren't you Guy Haines?" With light humor Hitchcock here underlines the tone of the film, but Robert Walter's skillful portrayal of Bruno has ensured that the comedy earlier had a darker and perverse edge, and the power to unsettle and disturb.

—Tony Slade

A STREETCAR NAMED DESIRE. Production: Warner Bros. Pictures Inc.; 1951; black and white, 35mm; running time: 125 mins. Released 1951.

Produced by Charles K. Feldman; screenplay by Tennessee Williams; from Oscar Saul's adaptation of the play by Williams; directed by Elia Kazan; photography by Harry Stradling; edited by David Weisbart; art direction by Richard Day, set decorated by George James Hopkins; music by Alex North.

Academy Awards for Best Actress (Leigh), Best Supporting Actor (Malden), Best Supporting Actress (Hunter), and Art Direction/Set Direction—Black and White, 1951; Venice Film Festival, Best Actress (Leigh) and Special Jury Prize, 1951; New York Film Critics Awards for Best Motion Picture, Best Actress (Leigh), and Best Direction, 1951.

Cast: Vivien Leigh (*Blanche DuBois*); Marlon Brando (*Stanley Kowalski*); Kim Hunter (*Stella Kowalski*); Karl Malden (*Mitch*).

Publications:

Scripts—extract in *Sight and Sound* (London), spring 1952; "*A Streetcar Named Desire*" by Tennessee Williams in *Film Scripts One* edited by George P. Garrett, O.B. Hardison Jr. and Jane R. Gelfman, New York 1971; reviews—by Hermine Isaacs, Eleanor Nash, and Francis Patterson in *Films in Review* (New York), December 1951; review by Karel Reisz in *Sight and Sound* (London), spring 1952; books—*Film in the Battle of Ideas* by John Howard Lawson, New York 1953; *Light of a Star: The Career of Vivien Leigh* by Gwen Robyns, New York 1970; *Elia Kazan on What Makes a Director* by Elia Kazan, New York 1973; *Working with Kazan*, edited by Jeanine Basinger, Middletown, Connecticut 1973; *The Films of Marlon Brando* by Tony Thomas, Secaucus, New Jersey 1973; *Marlon: Portrait of the Rebel as an Artist* by Bob Thomas, New York 1973; *Kazan on Kazan* by Michel Ciment, New York 1974; *Brando* by David Shipman, London 1974; *Tennessee Williams and Film* by Maurice Yacowar, New York 1977; *Vivien Leigh: A Biography* by Anne Edwards, New York 1977; articles—"Uninhibited Camera" by Herb A. Lightman in *American Cinematographer* (Hollywood), October 1951; "The Brooder" by Peter Brinson in *Films and Filming* (London), October 1954; "Elia Kazan—The Genesis of a Style" by Eugene Archer in *Film Culture* (New York), vol.2, no.2, 1956; "A Quiz for Kazan" in *Theatre Arts* (New York), November 1956; "Vivien Leigh" by Ronald Bowers in *Films in Review* (New York), August/September 1965; "A Natural Phenomenon: Interview with Elia Kazan" by Michel Delahaye in *Cahiers du Cinema in English* (New York), March 1967; article by Richard Corliss in *Film Comment* (New York), summer 1968; special Kazan issue of *Movie* (London), winter 1971-72; "Elia Kazan: a Structural Analysis" by Jim Kitses in *Cinema* (Beverly Hills), winter 1972-73; "*A Streetcar Named Desire*" by Kenneth T. Burles in *Magill's Survey of Cinema, Vol. IV* edited by Frank N. Magill, Englewood Cliffs, New Jersey 1980.

*   *   *

A Streetcar Named Desire is a landmark in American film history: the film made Marlon Brando a star, it introduced Method acting to a mass audience, its musical score represented one of the earliest uses of jazz in a major film, and it forced censors to broaden their interpretation of the Production Code, thus paving the way for more serious, mature filmmaking.

The film version of *A Streetcar Named Desire* grew out of the Tennessee Williams play, which opened on Broadway in December, 1947, and ran for two years under the direction of Elia Kazan. Kazan was hired to direct the film, and he made sure that most of the Broadway cast—including Marlon Brando, Kim Hunter, and Karl Malden—were retained for the film. The role of Blanche DuBois went to Vivien Leigh, who had played Blanche in the London production of the play.

Kazan, Brando, and the other members of the Broadway production brought to *Streetcar* a new approach to acting, the Stanislavsky Method, which differed sharply from the classical acting style employed by Vivien Leigh. The classical style involves acting from the outside in: the actor remains separated from the character and bases his performance on the observation of other people or on theatrical conventions—e.g., conventions for anger. The Method involves acting from the inside out: the actor identifies with the character and bases his performance on his inner feelings—e.g., his own feelings of anger. Because the Method actor merges with his character, Method acting frequently seems more naturalistic than classical acting.

There were problems in adapting *Streetcar* for the screen: the play dealt with homosexuality, nymphomania, and rape, topics that were strictly prohibited by the Hollywood Production Code. Kazan and Williams completely eliminated the homosexuality from the screenplay, and they changed Blanche's nymphomania into a search for love and security, but they refused to sacrifice Stanley Kowalski's rape of Blanche, which was central to the story. Eventually, a compromise was worked out between the filmmakers and the Production Code censors, whereby the rape would be implied, but not shown, and Stanley would be punished by the loss of his wife's love.

When *Streetcar* was released in 1951, it became a popular and critical success, winning five Academy Awards. Although Marlon Brando did not win the award for best actor (Humphrey Bogart won for *The African Queen.*), his electrifying portrayal of the barbaric Stanley Kowalski helped to make *Streetcar* a success and Brando a star.

Today, *Streetcar* is still regarded for its fine acting, and its handling of mature themes at a time when most Hollywood films were uncontroversial family entertainment.

—Clyde Kelly Dunagan

* * *

DER STUDENT VON PRAG. The Student of Prag. Production: Deutsche Bioscop GmbH (Berlin); black and white, 35mm, silent; running time: about 60 mins.; length: 5 to 6 reels, 5046 feet, later cut to 4817 feet. Released 1913.

Screenplay by Hanns Heinz Ewers with Paul Wegener, epigraphs from Alfred de Musset's poem "The December Night"; directed by Stellan Rye; photography by Guido Seeber; art direction by Klaus Ruchter and Robert A. Dietrich.

Filmed at Belvedere Castle and Alchemists Streets in Prague and Fürstenburg, and at Lobkowitz Palaces. Cost: 30,000 marks.

Cast: Paul Wegener (*Balduin*); Fritz Weidemann (*Baron Schwarzenberg*); John Gottowt (*Scapinelli*); Lida Salmonova (*Lyduschka, country girl*); Greta Berger (*Margit, Countess Waldis-Schwarzenberg*); Lothar Körner (*Count Waldis-Schwarzenberg*).

Publications:

Books—*Der Student von Prag: Eine Idee von Hanns Heinz Ewers* by Hanns Heinz Ewers, Dr. Langheinrich-Anthos, and Heinrich Noeren, Berlin 1930; *Histoire générale du cinéma* by Georges Sadoul, Paris 1946; *From Caligari to Hitler: A Psychological History of the German Film* by Siegfried Kracauer, Princeton 1947; *Germany* by Felix Bucher, London and New York 1970; *The Haunted Screen* by Lotte Eisner, Berkeley 1973; *Cinema, The Magic Vehicle: A Guide to Its Achievement: Journey One: The Cinema Through 1949* edited by Jacek Klinowski and Adam Garbicz, Metuchen, New Jersey 1975.

* * *

Stellan Rye's version of *The Student of Prague* has been unjustly neglected in the 70 years since its production—a situation compounded by the existence of two remakes (1926, 1936) and the general unavailablity of the original until the 1960s. Seen today, the film's technical facility, though not innovative in illustrating the *Doppelgänger* motif, is nevertheless particularly adroit, serving its subject with taste, restraint and subdued visual elegance. As a tale of the fantastic, the film looks both backward to similar thematic treatments in the Germanic legend of Faust

and the tales of E.T.A. Hoffman (as well as Poe's William Wilson and Wilde's Dorian Gray) and forward to the overtly Expressionist treatment of alter egos in the great films of the 1920s (Caligari and his somnambulist-slave Cesare, Maria and her robot double in *Metropolis*.) Expressionism as an art form was flourishing by 1910, but it had not yet taken hold in film by 1913 because the cinema was still held in contempt by most "serious" artists. *The Student of Prague* is a story of the fantastic told in a naturalistic manner, photographed against picturesque backdrops of the castles and streets of Prague's old city.

All three major talents behind the film came from the theater. Director Stellan Rye was a Danish expatriate who had staged plays and scripted films in Copenhagen. Novelist Hanns Heinz Ewers was already celebrated for his supernatural tales tinged with elements of eroticism and sadism; most critics view his work in light of his subsequent infamous notoriety as official chronicler in prose and film of Nazi hero Horst Wessel. Paul Wegener, already one of the most famous actors of Max Reinhardt's Deutches Theater, had long been fascinated by the artistic potential of film, and he found the inspiration for his cinematic debut in a series of comic photographs of a man fencing and playing cards with himself. Together with Ewers, Wegener concocted the story of Balduin, a student who sells his mirror reflection to the gnomish eccentric Scapinelli in exchange for fortune and the woman of his dreams. The reflection begins to haunt Balduin, appearing with greater frequency until the desperate student shoots it, and in the process, kills himself.

To effect the multiple exposure technique necessary to make Wegener's dual roles convincing, Rye enlisted the talents of cinematographer Guido Seeber, who was already considered a master. From a photographic standpoint, Seeber's work is an unusual mixture of the archaic and the innovative. Interiors are shot in a flat, uninteresting manner, but the exteriors feature exquisitely composed vistas of Prague's castles and courtyards, leading more than one critic of the time to compare the images to paintings by the 17th-century Spanish painter Jose Ribera. The scenes in which Balduin flees from his double through the deserted streets of Prague only to encounter him at every juncture are worthy of the nightmare images of films to follow in the wake of *The Cabinet of Dr. Caligari*. Though no stylization is evident in the set design, Seeber's lighting technique becomes quite striking—indeed almost expressionist—in the gambling scene. Perhaps inspired by Reinhardt's productions, a simple overhead light illuminates Balduin's gaming table as, one by one, his card-playing adversaries lose, disappearing into darkness. Balduin remains alone for a few seconds until he is joined by his double who asks "Dare you to play with me?"

The Student of Prague was the most expensive film produced in Germany up to that time, and it was an enormous success both with the critics and audiences. Although Rye and Wegener were to work together on several more projects, the collaboration was cut short by Rye's untimely death in a French war hospital in 1914. The subsequent remakes of the film have their individual merits: Henrik Galeen's 1926 version reteams Conrad Veidt and Werner Krauss (Cesare and Caligari) and is extolled by Paul Rotha for its exceptional pictorial qualities; the 1936 Arthur Robison version with Anton Walbrook gives human motivation to the demonic pact by making Scapinelli (Theodor Loos) a jealous rival of Balduin's. The original, however, remains most important to film history. *The Student of Prague*'s marriage of naturalism to the first glimmers of Expressionism in German film provides an eloquent signpost to the dark visions to come.

—Lee Tsiantis

SULLIVAN'S TRAVELS. Production: Paramount Pictures; 1942; black and white, 35mm; running time: 90 mins. Released 1941.

Produced by Paul Jones; original story and screenplay by Preston Sturges; directed by Preston Sturges; photography by John Seitz; edited by Stuart Gilmore; art direction by Hans Dreier and Earl Hedrick; music by Leo Shuken and Charles Bradshaw, musical direction by Sigmund Krumgold; special effects by Farciot Edouart.

Cast: Joel McCrea (*John L. Sullivan*); Veronica Lake (*The Girl*); Robert Warwick (*Mr. Le Brand*); William Demarest (*Mr. Jones*); Franklin Pangborn (*Mr. Casalsis*); Porter Hall (*Mr. Hadrian*); Byron Foulger (*Mr. Vadelle*); Margaret Hayes (*Secretary*); Torben Meyer (*Doctor*); Robert Greig (*Sullivan's butler*); Eric Blore (*Sullivan's valet*); Al Bridge (*Sheriff*); Esther Howard (*Miz Zeffie*); Almira Sessions (*Ursula*); Frank Moran (*Chauffeur*); George Renavent (*Old tramp*); Victor Potel (*Cameraman*); Richard Webb (*Radio man*); Harry Rosenthal (*The trombenick*); Jimmy Conlin (*The trusty*); Jan Buckingham (*Mrs. Sullivan*); Robert Winkler (*Bud*); Chick Collins (*Capital*); Jimmie Dundee (*Labor*); Charles Moore (*Black chef*); Al Bridge (*The mister*); Harry Hayden (*Mr. Carson*); Willard Robertson (*Judge*); Pat West (*Counterman—roadside lunch wagon*); J. Farrell MacDonald (*Desk sergeant*); Edward Hearn (*Cop—Beverly Hills station*); Roscoe Ates (*Counterman—Owl Wagon*); Paul Newlan (*Truck driver*); Arthur Hoyt (*Preacher*): Gus Reed (*Mission cook*); Robert Dudley (*One-legged man*); George Anderson (*Sullivan's ex-manager*); Monte Blue (*Cop in slums*); Harry Tyler (*R.R. information clerk*): Dewey Robinson (*Sheriff*); Madame Sul-te-wan (*Harmonium player*); Jess Lee Brooks (*Black preacher*); Perc Launders (*Yard Man*); Emory Parnell (*Man at R.R. shack*): Julius Tannen (*Public defender*); Edgar Dearing (*Cop—Mud Gag*); Howard Mitchell (*Railroad clerk*); Harry Seymour (*Entertainer in air-raid shelter*); Billy Bletcher (*Entertainer in hospital*); Chester Conklin (*Old man*): Frank Mills (*Drunk in theater*).

Publications:

Books—*Agee on Film: Volume I* by James Agee, New York 1958; *Interviews with Film Directors* by Andrew Sarris, New York 1967; *Veronica: The Autobiography of Veronica Lake* by Veronica Lake with Donald Bain, London 1969; *Negative Space* by Manny Farber, New York 1971; *Film Criticism of Otis Ferguson* by Otis Ferguson, Philadelphia 1971; *Preston Sturges: An American Dreamer* by James Ursini, New York 1973; *Talking Pictures* by Richard Corliss, 1973; *The Comic Mind* by Gerald Mast, New York 1973; *Movie Comedy* edited by Stuart Byron, New York 1977; *Hollywood on Hollywood* by James R. Parish and Michael Pitts with Gregory Munk, Metuchen, New Jersey 1978; articles—biography of Preston Sturges in *Current Biography Yearbook*, New York 1941; "Where Satire and Slapstick Meet" by Bosley Crowther in *The New York Times Magazine*, 27 August 1944; "Preston Sturges" by Peter Ericsson in *Sequence* (London), summer 1948; "Preston Sturges or Laughter Betrayed" by Siegfried Kracauer in *Films in Review* (New York), February 1950; "Preston Sturges" by Penelope Houston in *Sight and Sound* (London), summer 1965; "Notes on Preston Sturges and America" by Michael Budd in *Film Society Review* (New York), January 1968; "*Sullivan's Travels*" by Eileen Bowser in *Film Notes* edited by Eileen Bowser, New York 1969; "List of Screenplays" by P. Zucker in *Films in Review* (New York), March 1971; "Preston Sturges in the 30s" by Andrew Sarris in *Film Comment* (New York), winter 1970-71; "Preston Sturges" by Richard Corliss in *Cinema* (Beverly Hills), spring 1972; "*Les Voyages de Sullivan*" by Claude Beylie in *Ecran* (Paris), April 1973; "*Les Voyages de Sullivan*: Un Divertissement non confortable" by C.M. Cluny in *Cinéma* (Paris), February 1973; "*Les Voyages de Sullivan*" by J.J. Dupuich in *Image et son* (Paris), March 1973; "*Sullivan's Travels*" by Hollis Chacona in *Cinema Texas Program Notes* (Austin), v.11, no.2, fall 1976; "Hollywood Travels: Sturges and Sullivan" by R. Rubinstein in *Sight and Sound* (London), winter 1977-78; "*Sullivan's Travels*" by James Ursini in *Magill's Survey of Cinema, Vol. IV* edited by Frank N. Magill, Englewood Cliffs, New Jersey 1980.

*   *   *

Sullivan's Travels is writer-director Preston Sturges's version of "the clown who wants to play Hamlet" in which he proves that the world needs a clown more than it needs a Hamlet. Sturges was a director of such skill and cunning that he could both destroy and elevate an institution simultaneously. *Sullivan's Travels*, one of his best films and certainly one of his most personal (as it is about a Hollywood director), both attacks and celebrates Hollywood with such balance and panache that fans and detractors are equally satisfied with the results. This ambivalence characterizes the work of Sturges, whose career has undergone a recent critical re-evaluation. One of the most successful and respected writer-directors of the 1940s, his career fell apart after a decade of critical and commercial success. He died an out-of-fashion, nearly forgotten man in 1959. Throughout the sixties and into the seventies, his work was largely unknown. Now that his career is being favorably re-assessed, his comedies of American life, manners and mores are being restored to their rightful position as first-rate examples of Hollywood filmmaking and humor.

Sullivan's Travels undertakes a bold assignment. Its narrative shifts from comedy to tragedy and back to comedy, something seldom successfully accomplished in film. Those who criticize the film do so on the basis of its serious scenes when the hero, Joel McCrea, is arrested and sent to a prison chain gang where the only thing the convicts have to look foward to is the cartoon they share with a black church group on special occasions. The film's structure, however, is skillfully executed, and the hero's descent into a social hell uncushioned by money and power is presented largely through an effective montage, followed by the prison sequence. The ultimate return to comedy is indeed abrupt, but it demonstrates the theme of the film. The structure is attune to the basic universe of the Sturges world, which is a schizophrenic one, part sophistication and part slapstick, a world of contradiction and conflict. Sturges's technical presentation carries out this confusion and chaos, by frequently disintegrating into rapid montage. Although he was a master of writing witty repartee, Sturges also loved visual gags and the sort of pratfalls associated with silent film comedy. He wove these two seemingly contradictory traditions—dialogue comedy and physical comedy—together into films like *Sullivan's Travels* which fans call "free-wheeling" and critics call "frenzied." The slambang quality of the Sturges films, coupled with the basic violence of his comedy, contributed to the eventual disfavor of his work.

Today Sturges may be seen as a great American satirist, and *Sullivan's Travels* is often called "Swiftian." It ably demonstrates the Sturges brand of comedy. The script is dense with hilarious dialogue, and the characterizations demonstrate his incredible attention to detail that makes a real human being out of the smallest, most outrageous part. The most successful portions of the film are those in which he satirizes Hollywood with an insider's advantage. As always, Sturges was adept at pointing out the absurdity and essential phonies of a world which, rotten to the core and corrupted by the desires for money and success, maintains an outward sheen of respectability and good manners.

—Jeanine Basinger

SULT. Hunger. Svält. Production: Henning Carlsen (Denmark), ABC FIlm, Sandrews (Norway), and Svensk Filmindustri (Sweden); black and white, 35mm, widescreen; running time: 111 mins.; length: 3055 meters. Released 19 August 1966, Oslo, Copenhagen, and Stockholm.

Produced by Bertil Ohlsson; screenplay by Henning Carlsen and Peter Seeberg; from the book by Knut Hamsun; directed by Henning Carlsen; photography by Henning Kristiansen; edited by Henning Carlsen; sound by Erik Jensen; art direction by Erik Aaes and Walther Dannerford; music by Krzysztof Komeda; costumes designed by Ada Skolmen.

Cast: Per Oscarsson (*The Writer*); Gunnel Lindblom (*Ylajali*); Sigrid Horne-Rasmussen (*Landlady*); Osvald Helmuth (*Pawnbroker*); Birgitte Federspiel (*Ylajali's sister*); Henki Kolstad (*Editor*); Sverre Hansen (*Beggar*); Egil Hjort Jensen (*Man in the park*); Per Theodor Haugen (*Shop assistant*); Lars Nordrum (*The Count*); Roy Björnstad (*Painter*).

Publications:

Review—by Henry Hart in *Films in Review* (New York), October 1968; books—*Figures of Light* by Stanley Kauffmann, New York 1971; *The Novel and the Cinema* by Geoffrey Wagner, Rutherford, New Jersey 1975; articles—"Biographical Note on Henning Carlsen" in *International Film Guide*, London 1968; article by Elizabeth Sussez in *Sight and Sound* (London), winter 1967-68; "Bedroom Philosophers" by Denis Duperley in *Films and Filming* (London), May 1968; article by Kingsley Canham in *Films and Filming* (London), February 1969; "Deux moments du cinéma danois" by F. Devaux in *Cinéma* (Paris), January 1980; "Le Cinéma danois + entretien avec Henning Carlsen" by E. Decaux in *Cinématographe* (Paris), January 1980.

*   *   *

All through his career Henning Carlsen has been concerned about the relationship between literature and film. Many of his films are based on important novels, but Carlsen has never been satisfied when his films were characterized as adaptations. He wanted to use literary sources as inspirations for works in another medium, works in their own right. Maybe the greatest challenge of his career was his film based on Knut Hamsun's famous, semi-autobiographical novel *Hunger*, published in 1890. The novel is about a young man, coming from the country to Kristiania, the capital of Norway. He wants to be a writer, but he is suffering from both physical and mental hunger in a hostile city. His sufferings and humiliations lead to hallucinations, and his permanent condition of starvation brings him to the brink of insanity. But his urge to express himself also results in moments of euphoria. The novel is primarily a study about the state of mind of an artistic genius. The transformation of this story, told by the main character in many inner monologues, into film presented intricate problems, which eventually were solved by Carlsen and Peter Seeberg, a highly original Danish author.

The two main characters of the book and film are the starving young man, and the city. Carlsen, his cameraman Henning Kristiansen, and the set designer Erik Aaes have authentically recreated the cityscape of Kristiania of the 1890s. The establishment of the surroundings, where the young man faces his humiliations, shows Carlsen's experience as a documentary filmmaker. It is a very impressive presentation of the place and the time. Less satisfying is the manner in which the young man is integrated into the surroundings. Part of the problem concerns the character's view of the city as a prison. The sense of claustrophobia in the film is communicated to us by the use of many close-ups or medium shots, but only results in a confusing orientation of the city.

Sult, of course, is Per Oscarsson's film. His portrait of the budding artist, split between moments of ludicity and moments of darkest despair, is film acting of the highest order. Oscarsson has occupied the mind and the body of his character to such a degree that there is an absolute congruence between the actor and the role, in the physical manifestations and in the inner mental state. It is to Carlsen's credit that he has coached Oscarsson's unique talent and Carlsen also shows his abilty as an actors' director in the way he has handled the other actors in the film. As a director he hides behind his actors, though still maintaining control. For example, one of the most magic moments in the film, the love scene between the young man and the girl Ylajali, is a complex mixture of the tragic and the comic, which could only be created by a true artist.

—Ib Monty

SUNA NO ONNA. Woman of the Dunes. Production: Teshigahara Production; black and white, 35mm; running time: 127 mins., some versions are 115 mins.; length: 4021 meters. Released 1963.

Produced by Kiichi Ichikawa and Tadashi Ohno; screenplay by Kobo Abe; from a novel by Kobo Abe; directed by Hiroshi Teshigahara; photography by Hiroshi Segawa; edited by Masako Shuzui; art direction by Totetsu Hirakawa and Masao Yamazaki; music by Toru Takemitsu.

Cannes Film Festival, Special Jury Prize, 1964.

Cast: Eiji Okada (*Jumpei Niki*); Kyoko Kishida (*Widow*); Koji Mitsui; Sen Yano; Hiroko Ito.

Publications:

Reviews—by Robert Benayoun in *Le Nouvel Observateur* (Paris), 19 November 1964; review by Jean Louis Bory in *Arts* (Paris), 18 November 1964; "Le Trou" by Michel Flacon in *Cinéma 64* (Paris), June 1964; review by Georges Sadoul in *Les*

Lettres françaises (Paris), 7 May 1964; book—*La Femme des sables* by Kobo Abe, Paris 1967; articles—"Cannes 1964" by Raymond Borde in *Positif* (Paris), no.64-65, 1964; article by Georges Sadoul in *Les Lettres françaises* (Paris), 19 November 1964; "Introducing Teshigahara" by Fabienne Cousin in *Cinéma 65* (Paris), February 1965; article by Guy Gauthier in *Image et son* (Paris), March 1965; "Un Beckett nippon" by Gilles Jacob in *Cinéma 65* (Paris), January 1965; "Comte de la dune vague" by Jean Narboni in *Cahiers du cinéma* (Paris), February 1965; articles in *Avant-Scène du cinéma* (Paris), January 1965; "*Woman in the Dunes*" by Adrienne Mancia in *Film Comment* (New York) winter 1965; "A Conversation with 2 Japanese Film Stars" in *Film Comment* (New York), winter 1965; "The Tao in *Woman in the Dunes*" by Dennis Giles in *Film Heritage* (New York), spring 1966; "Akira Kurosawa—Hiroshi Teshigahara" by Felix Bucher in *Camera*, September 1966.

*   *   *

Hiroshi Teshigahara, born in 1927 in Tokyo, is a graduate of the Tokyo Art Institute. The formal beauty of *Woman in the Dunes* reflects this artistic background. In 1961 he organized his own production company and produced his first feature film, *Pitfall*, which established him as an avant-garde director. Based on a novel by Kobo Abe, one of Japan's most respected novelists, *Pitfall* is a documentary fantasy, according to Teshigahara. *Woman in the Dunes*, also based on an Abe novel and scripted by him, was Teshigahara's second feature. The film received much attention outside of Japan. It was awarded the Special Jury Award at Cannes in 1964 and was nominated for an Academy Award.

The story of *Woman in the Dunes* is simple. While on a scientific exploration in the dessert, Jumpei Niki, an entomologist from Tokyo, misses the last bus back to the city. He is given accomodations for the night at the home of a widow at the bottom of a sand pit. Next morning when he is prepared to leave, he discovers that the rope ladder, which is the only means of exit, has been removed by the villagers up above who intend to keep him in the sand pit. The remainder of the film involves Niki's struggle for freedom, his evolving relationships with the widow, and his final resolution concerning his destiny.

As in other films with similiar plot situations (Jean Paul Sartre's *No Exit* and Luis Buñuel's *Exterminating Angel*), *Woman in the Dunes* is an allegory. Basically the film deals with man's confrontation with life and the nature of freedom. Coming out of the tradition of oriental philosophy, the film is more affirmative than either of the works by Sartre or Buñuel.

Although Niki is representative of all men in general and modern man in particular, he also serves as a specific representative of Japan who has adopted the ways of the Occident. The conflict between Eastern and Western traditions is a recurrent theme in modern Japanese literature. Niki is not only dressed in modern European clothing, but he is infused with the spirit of the West. The opening scenes reveal his obsession with material possesions, with documents and schedules, with the value of a scientific approach to life, and with ambitious desires to get ahead—all antithetical to the notions found in traditional Japanese philosophy and religion. Devoid of any human involvement, Niki exists in a spiritual wasteland as dry and arid as the desert of the opening scenes.

Although we are never shown the city, modern man's environment, Teshigahara skillfully evokes its presence. The opening credits are accompanied by the sounds and noises of the city while images of official stamp marks and fingerprints, an ever-present factor in modern life, are seen on the screen.

Niki's examination of the sand and insects through his magnifying glass typify his distance from an emotional involvement with life itself. He is little more than a microscopic organism, living out his existence as one of the millions who inhabit cities like Tokyo. Yet his arrogance belies his understanding of the true nature of his existence.

During the long months which Niki spends in the sand pit, he moves from rebellion against his fate, to accommodation, and ultimately to active affirmation. His progress can be gauged by what he gives up—his flask, his camera, his watch, his insect collection, his western clothing, and finally his desire to leave. His gains are emotional involvment, social commitment, and spiritual freedom—for true freedom is an internal state not determined by physical limitations. In order to move forward, it was necessary for Niki to have first taken several steps backward—backward to a more primitive state of existence, backward to the values of an earlier era. In order to reach salvation, he has had to return to nature, to find a means to live in harmony with nature, and lastly to accept his position in the true order of the universe.

Niki's acceptance of life in the sand pit is not to be seen as resignation, but rather as a form of enlightenment. Dennis Giles explains in his article on the influence of Taoist philosophy on *Woman in the Dunes* how the film demonstrates Niki's acceptance of the Tao:

> The Tao can be called the path of least resistance. To be in harmony with, not in rebellion against, the fundamental laws of the universe is the first step on the road to Tao. Tao, like water, takes the low-ground. Water has become, perhaps, the most popular taoist symbol. The symbolic value of water is also one of the most striking elements in *Woman of the Dunes*.... Only by remaining passive, receptive, and yielding can the Tao assert itself in the mind

Giles further points out that "the yielding nature of water is a feminine characteristic, and concave surfaces are also female in nature. Thus the valley, the pit, and the tao are all feminine." Teshigahara's camera style is perfectly suited to the allegorical nature of the film. His propensity for close-ups reflects his documentary interests and serves to distance the viewer from the characters and to allow the audience to objectively contemplate the universal meanings implicit in the story. At the same time Teshigahara creates images of rare abstract beauty which reflect the serenity and harmony implied by the Tao.

—Patricia Erens

SUNRISE. Sunrise: A Song of Two Humans. Production: Fox Film Corporation; black and white, 35mm, silent; running time: 117 mins.; length: 2792 meters. Released 29 November 1927, with music by Carli Elinor.

Scenario by Carl Mayer; from the novel *The Journey to Tilsit* by Hermann Sudermann; sub-titles by Katherine Hilliker and H.H. Caldwell; directed by Friedrich Wilhelm Murnau (F.W. Murnau); photography by Charles Rosher and Karl Struss; production design by Rochus Gliese, assisted by Edgar Ulmer and Alfred Metscher; music by Dr. Hugo Riesenfeld.

Filmed in Fox studios and backlots. Academy Awards for Best Actress (Gaynor, in conjunction with her roles in *7th Heaven* and *Street Angel*), Cinematography, and Artistic Quality of Production, 1927-28.

Cast: George O'Brien (*The Man—Ansass*); Janet Gaynor (*The Woman—Indre*); Bodil Rosing (*The Maid*); Margaret Livingstone (*The Vamp*); J. Farrell Macdonald (*The Photographer*); Ralph Sipperly (*The Hairdresser*); Jane Winton (*The Manicurist*); Arthur Houseman (*The Rude Gentleman*); Eddie Boland (*The Kind Gentleman*); Gina Corrado; Barry Norton; Sally Eilers.

Publications:

Scripts—*'Sonnenaufgang', Ein Drehbuch von Carl Mayer mit hanschriftlichen Bemerkungen von F.W. Murnau* from the Deutsches Institut für Filmkunde, Wiesbaden, Germany 1971; "*L'Aurore*" by Carl Mayer in *Avant-Scène du cinéma* (Paris), June 1974; books—*An Index to the Films of F.W. Murnau* by Theodore Huff, supplement to *Sight and Sound*, index series, London 1948; *Introduction to the Art of the Movies: An Anthology of Ideas on the Nature of Movie Art* edited by Lewis Jacobs, New York 1960; *Murnau* by Charles Jameux, Paris 1965; *Anthologie du cinéma*, vol.1, Paris 1966; *The Parade's Gone By* by Kevin Brownlow, New York 1968; *Murnau* by Lotte Eisner, translated ed., Berkeley 1973; *Cinema, the Magic Vehicle: A Guide to Its Achievement: Journey One: The Cinema Through 1949* edited by Jacek Klinowksi and Adam Garbicz, Metuchen, New Jersey 1975; articles—"The Ideal Picture Needs No Titles" by F.W. Murnau in *Theatre Magazine* (New York), January 1928; "Murnau-Ses Films" by Roger Blin in *La Revue du cinéma* (Paris), July 1931; "F.W. Murnau" by Kenneth White in *Hound and Horn* (New York), July/September 1931; "*Sunrise*—A Murnau Masterpiece" by Dorothy Jones in *Quarterly of Film, Radio, and Television* (Berkeley), spring 1955; "Janet Gaynor" by Chauncey Carr in *Films in Review* (New York), October 1959; article by Raymond Durgnat in *Films and Filming* (London), May 1962; "George O'Brien" by David Martin in *Films in Review* (New York), November 1962; "Venise 1962" by Jean Douchet in *Cahiers du cinéma* (Paris), November 1962; "Murnau et les courants d'air glacés. Études sur 6 chefs-d'oeuvres " by René Gilson in *Cinéma 63*, May 1963; article by Raymond Lefevre in *La Revue du cinéma* (Paris), no.233, 1969; "*Sunrise*" by Molly Haskell in *Film Comment* (New York), summer 1971; article by Robin Wood in *Film Comment* (New York), summer 1971; "Une Des Plus Hautes Oeuvres de l'histoire du cinéma" by Henri Agel in *Avant-Scène du cinéma* (Paris), June 1974; "Quelques Opinions sur *L'Aurore*" in *Avant-Scène du cinéma* (Paris), June 1974; "Nota su *Aurora*" by E. Bruno in *Filmcritica* (Rome), July 1974; "*Sunrise*—A Song of Two Humans" by T. Rayns in *Monthly Film Bulletin* (London), April 1975; "Karl Strauss: Man with a Camera" by Karl Strauss in *American Cinematographer* (Los Angeles), March 1977.

*   *   *

The plot of *Sunrise* was adapted to Hollywood conventions from a naturalistic novella by Hermann Sudermann. It is wrong, however, to assume the changes were all for the bad, as so many critics have done. The film's plot is neither hopelessly sentimental nor melodramatic. It is true that Carl Mayer and F.W. Murnau, with a free hand from the studio, changed the tragic ending of the novella to a happy one for the film. This change can be viewed as an improvement upon Sudermann's gratuitously ironic ending of having the young husband's death occur after the couple's reconciliation. If not viewed as an improvement, the popular-art convention of the happy ending is certainly no worse than the naturalistic one of culminating a work with a tragic twist whether it is apt or not. Also the third party of the love triangle was, in the novella, a servant girl and, in the film, is a vamp from the city. On the basis of this change, all too many critics have accused Mayer and Murnau of setting up a simplistic "good-country" and "evil-city" polarity; however, they forget that the couple's experiences in the city, with all its modern delights, bring the husband and wife back together – or perhaps together for the first time. The plot allowed Murnau to draw upon his background in art history and literature, and above all it offered the basis for a cinematic narrative *par excellence*. This plot was made for the camera, especially in motion, and for the radical oscillations of lighting and mood that are so conducive to a temporal art like film. In such fertile soil, the talents of cameramen Rosher and Struss flourished.

Human characters, in *Sunrise*, are secondary to the true protagonist – the camera. The scenes in this film are neither conceived as a staged work, like so many silent films, nor as slices of actuality on which the camera allows us to spy. The premise of the film is that the camera will move; and that it will have any excuse to move. Plots and characters seem pretenses for movement and light; boats, dance halls, trolley cars, and other city traffic – not intrigue and love – are the true forces of motion in *Sunrise*. Akin to the ballets created by the avant-garde in the Paris of the 1910s and 1920s, patterns of movement seek their *raison d'etre* in the slimmest thread of plot. In addition, the camera (and the cameramen) have been allowed so much freedom that the camera soon takes on a life of its own. Even when the camera is at rest or pauses within a shot, the effect is electric.

According to the testimony of Rosher, Murnau was obsessed with capturing the play of light, especially as it occurred on the surface of the lake – either in nature or in the studio. Water, boats, moonlight, and reeds are pretenses for capturing the fleeting effects of light, much in the same way that clouds and waterlillies are used in Claude Monet's last paintings. Indeed, the film's frequent use of mist, dim lighting, and blurred exposures reminds one of Monet's work. This impressionistic concentration on light is not just limited to the scenes of the lake; in the city, glass replaces water. In the famous restaurant scene, lighted figures are seen dancing behind a glass window; people move in front fo the window and reflected in it; and the camera moves to catch the reflected light from different angles. The effect is shimmering.

A frequent complaint concerning *Sunrise* is that the film is divided into disjointed parts and stylized scenes often clash with more naturalistic ones. Murnau compared his own narrative structure to that used by James Joyce. Just as in *Ulysses*, there is a radical shift of style to match the spirit of different episodes; so too, in *Sunrise*, is there a fluctuation between the actual and the artificial. Murnau may have had another source for his scene-structuring in the German Expressionist theatre – especially in the works of Ernst Toller, where naturalistic scenes alternate with expressionistic ones. There are few films that depict such an astute sense of the spirit of place and the events that occur there, as, for example, where the husband secretly meets the vamp, and passes through a studio-set marsh with a broodingly low horizon lit by a moon shining through the haze. Also, the trolley ride taken by the husband and wife gives the sense of a location shot made in daylight; the joyful effect is complete down to the bouncing of the trolley car. The trolley soon moves into the city, actually a studio backlot construction, that is scaled larger than life in order to convey the awe of the country couple who are seeing the city for the first time. The actual only seems to be so. Acting, like the lighting and the sets, is conceived of scene by scene. Murnau took great pains in making the actors' gestures and facial expressions fit the moment; therefore, the styles of acting fluctuate between the naturalistic and the expressionistic. And over all there is the ever-moving mercurial camera. In every way, each scene is contrived to have its own particular mood, and each fits with another like pieces of Byzantine mosaic.

Hollywood fell under the spell of *Sunrise,* and under its influence the camera took wings, only to have them clipped by the limitations of primitive sound equipment. In the long run, however, the lessons of *Sunrise* resurfaced in such films as John Ford's *The Informer* and Orson Welles's *Citizen Kane.* The camera searching through the night and fog for a reflected gleam of light was a thematic and formalistic motif in these films. On the one hand, *Sunrise* culminated film's silent experience; but, on the other, it foreshadowed the first maturity of sound.

—Rodney Farnsworth

SUNSET BOULEVARD. Production: Paramount Pictures; 1949; black and white, 35mm; running time: 110 mins. Released 1950.

Produced by Charles Brackett, associate producer: Maurice Schorr, though uncredited; screenplay by Charles Brackett, Billy Wilder, and D.M. Marshman, Jr.; from the story "A Can of Beans" by Brackett and Wilder; directed by Billy Wilder; photography by John F. Seitz; edited by Arthur Schmidt, editing supervised by Doane Harrison; sound by Harry Lindgren and John Cope; art direction by Hans Dreier and John Meehan, set decoration by Sam Comer and Ray Moyer; music by Franz Waxman, songs by Jay Livingston and Ray Evans; special effects by Gordon Jennings, process photography by Farciot Edouart; costumes designed by Edith Head.

Filming completed 18 June 1949 on location in Los Angeles. Academy Awards for Best Screenplay and Best Score for a Dramatic or Comedy Picture, 1950.

Cast: William Holden (*Joe Gillis*); Gloria Swanson (*Norma Desmond*); Erich von Stroheim (*Max von Mayerling*); Nancy Olson (*Betty Schaefer*); Fred Clark (*Sheldrake*); Lloyd Gough (*Morino*); Jack Webb (*Artie Green*); Franklyn Barnum (*Undertaker*); Larry Blake (*1st finance man*); Charles Dayton (*2nd finance man*); Cecil B. De Mille, Hedda Hopper, Buster Keaton, Anna Q. Nilsson, H.B. Warner, Ray Evans, Sidney Skolsky, and Jay Livingston play themselves.

Publications:

Reviews—by James Agee in *Films in Review* (New York), May/-June 1950; review by Penelope Houston in *Sight and Sound* (London), January 1951; books—*Billy Wilder* by Oreste del Buono, Parma 1958; *The Great Films: 50 Years of Motion Pictures* by Bosley Crowther, New York 1967; *Billy Wilder* by Axel Madsen, Bloomington, Indiana 1969; *The Bright Side of Billy Wilder, Primarily* by Tom Wood, New York 1970; *Billy Wilder in Hollywood* by Maurice Zolotow, New York 1977; *The Film Career of Billy Wilder* by Steve Seidman, Boston 1977; *Hollywood on Hollywood* by James R. Parish and Michael Pitts, with Gregory Munk, Metuchen, New Jersey 1978; *Film Noir* edited by Alain Silver and Elizabeth Ward, Woodstock, New York 1979; articles—by James Agee in *Sight and Sound* (London), November 1950; "Old Master, New Tricks" by Herb

Lightman in *American Cinematographer* (Hollywood), September 1950; "Forever Gloria" in *Life* (New York), 5 June 1950; "*Sunset Boulevard*: Hollywood Tale That Gloria Swanson Makes Great" in *Newsweek* (New York), 26 June 1950; article by Andrew Sarris in *The Village Voice* (New York), 18 August 1960; "Cast a Cold Eye: The Films of Billy Wilder" by Charles Higham in *Sight and Sound* (London), spring 1963; "The Films of Billy Wilder" in *Film Comment* (New York), summer 1965; "Gloria Swanson" by DeWitt Bodeen in *Films in Review* (New York), April 1965; "Meet Whiplash Wilder" by Charles Higham in *Sight and Sound* (London), winter 1967-68; "I Am Not Going to Write My Memoirs" by Rui Nogueira in *Sight and Sound* (London), winter 1967-68; "The Tiger" (poem) by Ray Bradbury in *Producers Guild of America Journal* (Los Angeles), no.3, 1976; "*Sunset Boulevard*" by G. Colpart in *Téléciné* (Paris), December 1976; "*Boulevard du crépuscule*" by P. Mérigeau in *Image et son* (Paris), December 1980.

* * *

Between 1950 and 1952, Hollywood produced a cycle of classic films that looked at the business of making movies: *Singin' in the Rain*, *The Bad and the Beautiful*, and *Sunset Boulevard*. Of the three, the latter gives the darkest view of the motion picture industry.

The first two films chronicle success and failure, while *Sunset Boulevard* deals only with decline. It is, in fact, a sort of mirror image of *Singin' in the Rain*, a film which was concerned with the problems caused by the coming of sound to the movies. In *Singin'* one star deservedly falls from grace with the public, another has his career transformed for the better, while a sweet-faced ingenue becomes a box-office sensation because of her singing. *Sunset Boulevard*, however, which takes place 25 years after the coming of sound, shows us a silent film star scorned by the changes brought on by the new technology, and a modern-day screenwriter whose dialogue is not good enough to get him work.

One cannot ignore the film's autobiographical aspects. Gloria Swanson plays Norma Desmond, the aging silent film star, and like Norma, Swanson's career declined shortly after the advent of sound. Also, Max, Norma's chauffeur, had been one of her greatest directors. Erich von Stroheim plays the role and, like Max, he had been one of the more talented directors of the 1920s whose career ended abruptly during the next decade. Completing the mixture of film history and fiction, Norma watches one of her films from 30 years previous; it is *Queen Kelly*, one of Swanson's movies that had been directed by von Stroheim.

Aside from holding a reflecting glass to the industry, the film itself has something of a mirror construction. After Joe, the screenwriter, meets Norma, she convinces him to work on her comeback project, a ponderous *Salome* screenplay. Joe agrees because times are hard, and as an added convenience he becomes Norma's lover. During the second half of the film, Joe meets Betty, and they too begin working on a script as the conventional counterpart to Joe's involvement with Norma. While Joe knows that Norma's script is unfilmable, both he and Betty are excited about the script they write together, and shape it to the demands of the industry. Joe and Betty also form the normal, attractive movie couple, but Joe and Norma's relationship stands out as anomalous, at least for films of the period. Norma is much older than Joe, who plays the role of a "kept man," accepting money, gifts, and a place to live from a woman protector.

In the end, jealous of Betty, Norma kills Joe. However, this is known from the beginning, for *Sunset Boulevard* is a tale told by a dead man. After the opening credits, we see Joe lying face down in Norma's swimming pool, with detectives trying to fish him out of the water. Joe then begins to narrate the events that led up to the murder. But neither this posthumous narration, nor its baroque *film noir* style, nor the bitterness with which the film examines Hollywood, made the movie unpalatable to critics of the period. At its release, it was considered a major work, and today *Sunset Boulevard* remains one of the most highly respected films from the post-World War II period.

—Eric Smoodin

THE SWEET SMELL OF SUCCESS. Production: Norma-Curtleigh Production; 1957; black and white, 35mm; running time: 96 mins., press screening was 103 mins. Released 27 June 1957 by United Artists.

Produced by James Hill, a Hecht-Hill-Lancaster presentation; screenplay by Clifford Odets, adapted by Ernest Lehman; from the short story "Tell Me About It Tomorrow" by Ernest Lehman; directed by Alexander MacKendrick; photography by James Wong Howe; edited by Alan Crosland, Jr.; sound by Jack Solomon; art direction by Edward Carrere; music by Elmer Bernstein.

Filmed spring 1957 in New York City.

Cast: Burt Lancaster (*J.J. Hunsecker*); Tony Curtis (*Sidney Falco*); Susan Harrison (*Susan Hunsecker*); Sam Levene (*Frank D'Angelo*); Barbara Nicholls (*Rita*); Martin Milner (*Steve Dallas*); Jeff Donnell (*Sally*); Joseph Leon (*Robard*); Edith Atwater (*Mary*); Emile Meyer (*Harry Kello*); Joe Frisco (*Herbie Temple*); David White (*Otis Elwell*); Lawrence Dobkin (*Leo Bartha*); Lurene Tuttle (*Mrs. Bartha*); Queenie Smith (*Mildred Tam*); Autumn Russell (*Linda*); Jay Adler (*Manny Davis*); Lewis Charles (*Al Evans*).

Publications:

Reviews—by E.F. in *Films in Review* (New York), August/September 1957; review by Derek Prouse in *Sight and Sound* (London), autumn 1957; review by Carol Rittgers in *Film Culture* (New York), October 1957; review by Jerry Tallmer in *The Village Voice* (New York), 28 August 1957; review by A.H. Weiler in *The New York Times*, 27 June 1957; book—*Film Noir* edited by Alain Silver and Elizabeth Ward, Woodstock, New York 1979; articles—"Mackendrick Finds the Sweet Smell of Success" by John Cutts in *Films and Filming* (London), June 1957; "Alexander Mackendrick" in *Films and Filming* (London), January 1963; "Oddities and One-Shots" by Andrew Sarris in *Film Culture* (New York), spring 1963; "Burt Lancaster" by Mel Schuster in *Films in Review* (New York), August/September 1969; issue on Mackendrick of *Dialogue on Film* (Washington, D.C.), no.2, 1972; "Bullies of Broadway" by Richard Blackburn in *American Film* (Washington, D.C.), December 1983.

*   *   *

One of the most original and off-beat films to be labelled *film noir*, *The Sweet Smell of Success* takes a cynical bite at the underbelly of the New York publicity game. As Sidney Falco, a thoroughly ruthless and utterly amoral press agent scrambling for his place in the sun, Tony Curtis gives the performance of his career—charming yet sleazy, ingratiating yet duplicitous. Falco aspires to a position of influence in the orbit of J.J. Hunsecker, king of the gossip pen. As impeccably played by Burt Lancaster, Hunsecker is a smooth, cold-blooded mudslinger; crewcut, single and implicitly gay; more ruthless than Falco, yet completely unsullied. The bittersweet irony of the film is that, for all of Falco's slimy dealings, it is he (and his type) who ends up doing Hunsecker's dirty work.

To curry Hunsecker's favor, Falco sets out to break up the relationship between the columnist's sister (to whom Hunsecker has more than a brotherly attachment) and a young jazz musician by circulating accusations that the musician is a Communist and a drug addict. It is a premise which provides screenwriter Clifford Odets the perfect opportunity to mount a scathing exposé of the lying, blackmailing, pimping and full-fledged witchhunting involved in the daily abuse of media power. It also provides the material from which British director Alexander Mackendrick is able to render a taut, suspenseful film in which the violence is more psychological than physical; and to create the ambience of a glamorous nocturnal world which is rotting at the core. These elements alone are enough to make *The Sweet Smell of Sucess* one of the most cynical *film noirs* of the fifties; but it is the superb black-and-white cinematography of James Wong Howe which earns the film its place among the classics of the genre. Shooting much of the film at night on the streets of New York, Howe manages to combine expressive lighting with a kind of verité realism, anticipating by several years the cystalline location cinematography of Henri Decae and Raoul Coutard in the early films of the French New Wave. If the subject of *The Sweet Smell of Success* seems unusual for *film noir*, its biting tone and duplicitous characters represent the form at its most scathing, and its visual style points ahead from forties expressionism toward the direction of *Alphaville*.

—Ed Lowery

TABU. Tabu: A Story of the South Seas. Tabou. Production: Murnau-Flaherty Production; 1941; black and white, 35mm; music track only; running time: 82 mins.; length: 2311 meters. Released 18 March 1931, distributed by Paramount Pictures, Inc.

Produced by F.W. Murnau and Robert Flaherty with David Flaherty (note: Robert Flaherty left the project in mid-production after differences of opinion with Murnau); screenplay by F.W. Murnau and Robert Flaherty; directed by F.W. Murnau, David Flaherty is sometimes listed as assistant director; photography by Floyd Crosby and Robert Flaherty; music by Hugo Riesenfeld; rushes from *Tabu* were integrated into the Italian documentary *Battuta Nel Mare Del Sud* and an extract from *Tabu* appears in *La Marie du Port* (Carné).

Filmed summer-fall 1929 in Tahiti.

Cast: Anna Chevalier (*Reri, the young girl*); Matahi (*The young man*); Hitu (*Chief*); Jean (*Police agent*); Jules (*Captain*); Kong Ah (*Chinese tradesman*).

Publications:

Scripts—"*Tabu, A Story of the South Seas*"(in story form) by F.W. Murnau and Robert Flaherty in *Film Culture* (New York), no.20, 1959; "*Turia*: Eine Originaligeschichte" by F.W. Murnau and R. Flaherty (original story on which *Tabu* was based and its relation to the film) in *Filmkritik* (Munich), May 1977; review— "*Tabu*" by Malcolm Cowley in the *New Republic* (New York), 1 April 1931; books—*Robert Flaherty: Nota biografica, filmografica e bibliografica...* by Mario Gromo, Parma 1952; *The Odyssey of a Film-Maker: Robert Flaherty's Story* by Frances Flaherty, Urbana, Illinois 1960; *Robert Flaherty et le Documentaire Poétique: Etudes cinématographique no.5* by Fuad Quintar, Paris 1960; *Robert Flaherty* by Jose Clemente, Madrid 1963; *Robert Flaherty* by Carlos Fernandez Cuenca, Madrid 1963; *Robert Flaherty* compiled by Wolfgang Klaue, Berlin (East) 1964; *Robert J. Flaherty* by Henri Agel, Paris 1965; *Murnau* by Charles Jameux, Paris 1965; *Anthologie du cinéma*, vol.1, Paris 1966; *The World of Robert Flaherty* by Richard Griffith, reprinted New York 1970; *The Innocent Eye: The Life of Robert Flaherty* by Arthur Calder-Marshall, London 1970; *Murnau* by Lotte Eisner, Berkeley 1973; *Cinema, The Magic Vehicle: A Guide to Its Achievement: Journey One: The Cinema Through 1949* edited by Adam Garbicz and Jacek Klinowski, Metuchen, New Jersey 1975; *Robert Flaherty: A Guide to References and Resources* by William Murphy, Boston 1978; articles—"*Tabu*" by Emilio Cecchi in *Sequenze* (Rome), May 1950; "Le Cinéma de la decouverte: Robert Flaherty" in *L'Amour du cinéma* by Claude Mauriac, Paris 1954; "A Few Reminiscences" by David Flaherty in *Film Culture* (New York), no.2, 1959; "Flaherty and *Tabu*" by Richard Griffith in *Film Culture* (New York), no.20, 1959; "*Tabu*" by Gary Davis in *Film Heritage* (Dayton, Ohio), spring 1960; "*Tabu*: mito e trasgressione" by F. Pecori in *Filmcritica* (Rome), July 1974; "*Tabu*" by K. Keller in *Variety* (New York), v.3, no.23, 1977; "Audiovisual Notes" by J.W. Adams in *American Anthropologist* (Washington, D.C.), no.3, 1979; "Dossier: Cu muet au parlant: l'ombre du son" by L. Audibert in *Cinématographe* (Paris), June 1979.

*   *   *

A simple basic plot structure recurs throughout F.W. Murnau's work (it is certainly by no means exclusive to it, being one of the fundamental narrative patterns of our culture, yet the recurrence is obstinate enough for one to attach a particular significance to it here): the couple threatened by a monstrous, disruptive and destructive figure. Wherever it begins (so much of Murnau's early work is lost), the structure is firmly established in *Nosferatu*, and is variously repeated in *Tartuffe*, *Faust*, *Sunrise*, *City Girl* and *Tabu*, confirming its strength by its crossing of national/cultural boundaries. The repetition, however, is far from simple: the richness of Murnau's work, considered *in toto*, resides partly in the complex permutations, and the ultimate transformation, this structure undergoes. Those permutations depend upon the way the couple is defined from film to film, the way the threat is defined, and the shifting relationship between the two; the overall development also corresponds to Murnau's increasing disengagement from German Expressionism and its ethos.

Moving directly from *Nosferatu* to *Tabu*, one finds the structure repeated but its significance totally reversed. The opening of both films evoke the Garden of Eden but in strongly contrasting embodiments. In the earlier film it is a cultivated garden in whch the man gathers a bouquet to present to the woman: the sense of an artificial, socially constructed innocence is very strong. *Tabu* gives us a natural paradise, in which flowers evoke a true innocence, characterized by an untrammelled sensuality. The eroticism that is repressed by the innocence of the couple in *Nosferatu* returns in the terrible shape of the vampire, clearly a "monster from the Id," rendered monstrous through repression. The threat in *Tabu* is the exact opposite, though it finds at times remarkably similar expression—the shadow cast over the body of the woman. Hitu, the High Priest of the island, who demands the preservation of the virginity of the young girl chosen as the elect of the gods, and punishes transgression by death, represents the threat. In Freudian terms, the dread of the Id has transformed itself into dread of the punishing Superego, the "Law of the Father," the bearer of guilt.

Two factors need to be considered in order to account for this development, one environmental, one personal. Geographically (Germany, Hollywood, Polynesia) and stylistically, Murnau moved further and further away from the dominance of German Expressionism, with its pervasive sense of doom, its characteristic dread of the release of repressed energies. In *Tabu*, of course, the "doom" is still there, but it takes on a diametrically opposed form. There was also the burden of Murnau's homosexuality: a burden, because he lived and worked when there was no gay consciousness, no gay culture, no "gay liberation." If one accepts that the source of creativity is in sexuality, then Murnau's creativity was consistently deprived of its central impulse, except in the most heavily disguised and circuitous forms: from this viewpoint, *Sunrise*, with its well celebration of the family and its systematic degradation of the erotic, is one of the cinema's most extreme acts of self-oppression.

That Murnau found a new spiritual freedom in the South Seas is obvious from *Tabu* (the spiritual being intimately connected with the erotic). The freedom expresses itself stylistically: of all Murnau's films, this is the most fluent, spontaneous, dynamic, its new-found energy embodied in the mobilty of the camera, the rhythms of movement. Indeed, style and theme become magnificently united, the freedom of movement repeatedly interrupted, at key moments, by the terrible stasis produced first by the prohibitive decrees of Hitu, later by the unnatural demands of Western capitalism/colonization. The energy and freedom intensify the tragedy of the film's ending: after the long succession of impotent male protagonists in the preceding films, here the hero fight and struggles, only to be defeated, in the final moments, by a cold and inexorable hand cutting through a rope.

—Robin Wood

TAXI DRIVER. Production: Bill/Phillips Production, an Italo-Judeo Production; 1976; Metrocolor, 35mm; running time: 113 mins. Released 1976 by Columbia Pictures.

Produced by Michael and Julia Phillips with Phillip M. Goldfarb; screenplay by Paul Schrader; title design by Dan Perri; directed by Martin Scorsese; photography by Michael Chapman; edited by Tom Rolf and Melvin Shapiro, editing supervised by Marcia Lucas; sound by Roger Pietschman and Tex Rudloff, sound effects by Frank E. Warner; art direction by Charles Rosen, set decoration by Herbert Mulligan, scenic artistry by Cosmo Sorice; music by Bernard Herrmann; special effects by Tony Parmelee; costumes designed by Ruth Morley; visual consultant: David Nichols, creative consultant: Sandra Weintraub.

Filmed 1975 in New York City. New York Film Critics Award, Best Actor (De Niro), 1976; Palme d'Or, Cannes Film Festival, 1976.

Cast: Robert De Niro (*Travis Bickle*); Cybill Shepard (*Betsy*); Jodie Foster (*Iris*); Harvey Keitel (*Sport*); Leonard Harris (*Charles Palantine*); Peter Boyle (*Wizard*); Albert Brooks (*Tom*); Murray Mosten (*Timekeeper*); Richard Higgs (*Secret Service Agent*); Vic Argo (*Melio, deli owner*); Steven Prince (*Gun salesman*); Martin Scorsese (*Taxi passenger*); Dianne Abbot (*Concession girl*).

Publications:

Reviews—"*Taxi Driver*" by B. Chavardes in *Téléciné* (Paris), July/August 1976; "*Taxi Driver*" by Peter Cowie in *Focus on Film* (London), summer/autumn 1976; "*Taxi Driver*" by H. Desrues in *Revue du cinéma* (Paris), October 1976; "*Taxi Driver*" by G. Giuricin in *Cinema nuovo* (Turin), November/-December 1976; "Day of Wrath: *Taxi Driver*" by R. Greenspun in *Penthouse* (New York), May 1976; "*Taxi Driver, Un Apres-midi de chien*" by P. Kane in *Cahiers du cinéma* (Paris), July/August 1976; "Movies" by Rex Reed in *Vogue* (New York), April 1976; "*Taxi Driver*" by T. Renaud in *Cinéma 76* (Paris), July 1976; "*Taxi Driver*" by L. Rubinstein in *Cineaste* (New York), fall 1976; book—*Film Noir* edited by Alain Silver and Elizabeth Ward, Woodstock, New York 1979; articles—"Scorsese on *Taxi Driver*" by C. Amata in *Focus on Film* (London), summer/autumn 1976; "Mindless Audience Reaction" by D. Beard in *Cinema Canada* (Montreal), October 1976; "Gunning It" by J. Coleman in *New Statesman* (London), 20 August 1976; "Rebel Heroes der 70er Jahre: Kontaktlos und gewalttaetig: zu zwei Filmen von Martin Scorsese" by K. Eder in *Medium* (Frankfurt), July 1976; "Paul Schrader" by F. Golchan in *Cinematographe* (Paris), June 1976; "Moviegoers with the Yen Eager for *Taxi Driver*" in *Boxoffice* (Kansas City, Missouri), 11 October 1976; "*Taxi Driver*: Gespraech mit Drehbuchautor Paul Schrader" by M. Racheva and K. Eder in *Medium* (Frankfurt), July 1976; "*Taxi* Takes Off in Rome" in *Boxoffice* (Kansas City, Missouri), 11 October 1976; "Screenwriter: *Taxi Driver's* Paul Schrader" by R. Thompson in *Fernseh-und-kino-Technik* (West Berlin), October 1976; "*Taxi Driver*" in *Filmfacts* (Los Angeles), no.1, 1976; "Transcendental Pornography and *Taxi Driver*" by J.C. Rice in *Journal of Popular Film* (Bowling Green, Ohio), no.2, 1976; "Prisoner of the Night" by D. Boyd in *Film Heritage* (Dayton, Ohio), winter 1976-77; "Een eindeloos verhaal zonder punten en komma's: de films van Martin Scorsese" by H. Hosman in *Skoop* (Amsterdam), February/March 1977; "Dossier: Hollywood 79: Scorsese" by F. Cuel in *Cinématographe* (Paris), March 1979; "The Italian Connection in the American Film: Coppola, Cimino, Scorsese" by P. Rule in *America* (New York), 17 November 1979; "*Taxi Driver*" by Robert Mitchell in *Magill's Survey of Cinema, Vol. IV* edited by Frank N. Magill, Englewood Cliffs, New Jersey 1980; "The Incoherent Text: Narrative Texts in the 70's" by Robin Wood in *Movie* (London), winter/spring 1980-81.

*   *   *

It was during the 1970s—the period of Vietnam and Watergate—that American society appeared in imminent danger of collapse, the crisis in ideological confidence being (quite logi-

cally) complemented by the growth of the major radical movements of contemporary culture: feminism, black militancy, gay activism. The confusions and hysteria of the social climate (the historical moment when the dominant ideology of bourgeois patriarchal capitalism and reinforcement under Carter and Reagan) were reflected in the products of Hollywood: one might say that the most interesting and distinguished films of the period were also the most incoherent, centered in the experience of contradiction, disillusionment and desperation. Their failure to develop beyond confusion and contradiction must be attributed to the continuing prohibition (within the American cultural establishment) on imagining any alternative form of cultural organization to patriarchal capitalism.

Taxi Driver is an outstanding product of this cultural situation. Its rich and fascinating incoherence has a number of sources. The collaboration of Scorsese and Schrader involved its own immediate problems. Scorsese's ideological/political position is very difficult to define (perhaps an example of the ability of art to transcend such definitions): he has consistently refused to commit himself to any definable radical position, yet, in their systematic analysis of the untenability of all our social institutions, his films clearly earn the term "radical." Schrader, on the other hand, seems plainly (and quite unashamedly) neo-Fascist: his films (as writer and director) amount to a systematic repudiation of all minority groups and any possible social alternative, in order to re-assert a quasi-mystical sense of male supremacy, heterosexual superiority, and a totally spurious "transcendence" (which amounts to little more than one person's right to slaughter other people, on the basis of some supposed achievement of spiritual transfiguration, with no foundation in material reality). One must see the curious paralysis of the film's closing sequence—clearly, on some level, ironic, but with the irony quite unfocused—as the result of this collaboraction of partial incompatibles, a view confirmed by Scorsese's *King of Comedy* (made without Schrader), with its closely parallel but precisely focused ending.

A more profitable tension arises from the film's fascinating fusion of genres: film noir, the western, the horror film. Travis Bickle (Robert De Niro)—who has swiftly become established as a significant figure in American cultural mythology—is on one level the western hero transplanted into the modern urban wilderness: he derives particularly from Ethan Edwards (John Wayne) of *The Searchers*, and Scorsese and Schrader have made it clear that Ford's film was a conscious influence. But he is also the psychopath/monster of the contemporary horror film: it is perhaps the chief distinction of *Taxi Driver* to suggest the relationship between these two apparent opposed archetypes and its significance in relation to American ideology. In fact, the film's interest is inseparable from its sense of confusion, its failure to define a coherent attitude towards its protagonist. That confusion must be seen, not merely as the result of a clash of artistic personalities, but as the reflection of a national ideological dilemma.

—Robin Wood

TENI ZABYTYKH PREDKOV. Shadows of Forgotten Ancestors. Wild Horses of Fire. Production: Dovzhenko Studios (Kiev); Magicolor, 35mm; running time: variously noted as 100 mins., 98 mins., and 95 mins. Released 1964, USSR.

Screenplay by Sergei Paradzhanov (Paradjanov) and Ivan

Chendei; inspired by the novelette *Wild Horses of Fire* by M. Kotsiubinsky, and by western Ukrainian folklore; directed by Sergei Paradzhanov; photography by Yuri Ilyenko; edited by M. Ponomarenko; sound by S. Sergienko; art direction by M. Rakovsky and G. Yakutovich; music by M. Skorik.

Filmed on location among the Gutsuls in the Carpathians. Mar del Plata Festival, Best Production, 1965.

Cast: Ivan Nikolaichuk (*Ivan*); Larissa Kadochnikova (*Marichka*); Tatiana Bestaeva (*Palanga*); Spartak Bagashvili (*Yurko the Sorcerer*); several Gutsul natives.

Publications:

Reviews—"5 From the East" by John Seeyle in *Film Quarterly* (Berkeley), summer 1966; review in *Filmfacts* (New York), no.10, 1967; review in *International Film Guide* (London), 1967; review by Gordon Gow in *Films and Filming* (London), June 1969; books—*The Most Important Art: East European Film After 1945* by Mira Liehm and Antonín Liehm, Berkeley 1977; *Serge Paradjanov* by H. Gaby, et al., Lausanne 1977; articles—"Notes on *Shadows of Our Forgotten Ancestors*" by S. Paradjanov in *Film Comment* (New York), fall 1968; "Az érzelmek, a képek, a szinek erejével" by K. Nemes in *Filmkultura* (Budapest), September/October 1974; "*Les Chevaux de feu*" by J. Delmas in *Jeune Cinéma* (Paris), September/October 1975; "*Les Chevaux de feu*" by M.C. Treilhou in *Cinéma* (Paris), September/October 1975; "The Case of Sergei Paradjanov" by Herbert Marshall in *Sight and Sound* (London), no.1, 1975; "A Certain Cowardice" by Antonin Liehm in *Film Comment* (New York), July/August 1975; "*Les Chevaux de feu*" by M.L. Potrel-Dorget in *Image et son* (Paris), May 1978.

*   *   *

Sergei Paradzhanov's *Shadows of Forgotten Ancestors* first appeared in the West in 1965; it was immediately recognized that the Soviet cinema had acquired a new genius on the order of Eisenstein and Dovzhenko. The film won 16 foreign festival awards and was theatrically released in the United States and Europe to critical acclaim. Not since the triumph of *Potemkin*, in fact, had a Soviet motion picture enjoyed such international esteem. At home, *Shadows of Forgotten Ancestors* was variously accused of "formalism" and "Ukrainian nationalism," and it was deliberately underbooked in domestic theaters by Sovkino officials. Paradzhanov found himself personally attacked by the Party Secretary for Ideological Problems, and he was consistently denied permission to travel aboard in response to the invitations that began to pour in as the film's reputation spread. During the next ten years, Paradzhanov went on to write ten complete scenarios based on classical Russian literature and folk epics, all of which were refused by Soviet authorities, and to make one more film—*Sayat Nova (The Color of Pomegranates)*—which was banned on its release in 1969 and finally given limited distribution in a version "re-edited" by Sergei Yutkevitch in the early 1970's (first seen in the United States at the 1980 New York Film Festival). Another project, *Kievskie Freski (Kiev Frescoes)*, was approved but aborted after the first edited rushes were screened—the same kind of ritual humiliation accorded Eisenstein by the Stalinists during the production of *Bezhin Meadows (Bezhin lug*, 1935). At last, while he was working on an adaption of some fairy tales of Hans Christian Andersen for Soviet television in January 1974, Paradzhanov was arrested and charged with a variety of offenses, including homosexual rape, the spreading of venereal disease, and the illegal sale of icons. Although only the charges trafficking in art objects stuck, the trial (held in secret) was patently political, and Paradzhanov was sentenced to six years at hard labor in the Gulag. An international petition campaign forced the Soviets to release him in late 1977, but he has not been allowed to work in the film industry since then and probably never will again. Recently, Paradzhanov told a friend: "I am already a dead man. I can no longer live without creating. In prison my life had direction; there was a reality to surmount. My present life is worse than death." The question poses itself: What was *Shadows of Forgotten Ancestors* to have provoked such admiration, controversy and, finally, misery for its maker? How could the unique sensibility mirrored in this richly poetic film have been perceived by the Soviet bureaucracy as a political threat at all?

Adapted by Paradzhanov and Ivan Chendei from a pre-Revolutionary novelette by the distinguished Ukrainian writer M. Kotsiubinsky to celebrate the centennial of his birth, *Shadows of Forgotten Ancestors* retells an ancient Carpathian folk legend of universal resonance. Like the legends of Tristan and Isolde and Romeo and Juliet, it is the story of a love which transcends death, and, as in those other stories, the plot is relatively simple.

Deep in the Carpathian mountains, at the farthest western reach of the Ukraine, live the Gutsuls, a proud peasant race cut off from the rest of the world by natural boundaries. They are impulsive, fierce, and—though nominally Christian—deeply superstitious and tied to pagan ways. The story begins in the childhood of the two future lovers, when the boy Ivan's father is killed in a fit of anger by the girl Marichka's father, initiating a blood-feud between the two families. But even as children Ivan and Marichka are drawn to each other by strong spiritual attraction. Later, when they are youths, the attraction becomes physical as well, and Ivan impregnates Marichka shortly before he must leave to work as a bondsman for a group of shepherds on the opposite mountain. (Ivan is the sole support of his aged and impoverished mother; Marichka's family is relatively wealthy—the source of the original dispute between the fathers.) As they part, the two lovers agree that every night before Ivan returns they will gaze at the north star to commemorate their love. One night Marichka is drawn out by the star, through the woods, to a bluff above the river. There, attempting to rescue a lost lamb (which is symbolically linked to her love for Ivan), she plunges into the river and drowns. Instinctively realizing that something is wrong, Ivan rushes to the river gorge and floats downstream on a logging barge to discover her body washed up on the shore.

After Marichka's death, Ivan goes through a long period of numbing grief and desolate wandering which leads his neighbors to conclude that he's been "ruined by love." Finally, however, he returns to the world of the living and is able to experience love for another woman, Palagna, who eventually becomes his wife. But their marriage proves joyless and barren, for Ivan finds Palagna's carnality degrading compared to the purity of his lost love. More and more, he can think only of the dead Marichka, and finally he begins to look toward death himself. Palagna, scorned, contracts an affair with the local sorcerer who promises to make her fertile with his magic. One night, the sorcerer goads Ivan into a fight in the local tavern and cleaves his skull with an ax (the same mode of death as Ivan's father). Ivan stumbles deliriously through the woods to the river where Marichka drowned, and in a vision she appears to him. They embrace and Ivan dies. Then, like his father before him, his corpse is laid out, and the men, women, and children of the village observe their ancient ritual of death.

At the level of plot, then, *Shadows of Forgotten Ancestors* offers a relatively familiar tale of undying love which has variants in cultures all over the world. But in the telling of that tale, Paradzhanov has created a vision of human experience so radical and unique as to subvert all authority. To say that *Shadows of Forgotten Ancestors* violates every narrative code and representational system known to the cinema is an understatement—at times, in fact, the film seems intent upon deconstructing the very process of representation itself. The relationship between narrative logic and cinematic space—between point of view inside and outside the frame—is so consistently undermined that most critics on first viewing literally cannot describe what they've seen. Adjectives frequently used to characterize *Shadows of Forgotten Ancestors* are "hallucinatory," "intoxicating," and "delirious"—terms that imply, however positively, confusion and incoherence. But the camera and editing techniques which elicit such comments are all part of Paradzhanov's deliberate aesthetic strategy to interrogate a whole set of historically evolved assumptions about the nature of cinematic space and the relationship which exists between the spectator and the screen.

Paradzhanov proceeds by means of perceptual dislocation, so that it becomes impossible at any given moment to image a stable time-space continuum for the dramatic action. Often, for example, the viewer will be invited by conventional stylistic means to share a point of view which is suddenly ruptured by camera movement or some other disjunction in spatial logic; spaces which appear to be contiguous in one shot sequence are revealed to be miles apart in the next; surfaces which seem to be assumes perspectives and executes manoeuvres which appear to be *physically*, as well as dramatically, impossible: the camera begin with a camera angle that encourages the viewer to misconstrue narrative space, as when a wall is momentarily made to resemble the surface of a roof. At other times, the camera assumes perspectives and executes manuoevres which appear to be *physically*, as well as dramatically, impossible: the camera looks down from the top of a falling tree perhaps 100 feet tall; it looks up through a pool, with no optical distortion, as Ivan drinks from its surface; it whirls 360 degrees on its axis for nearly a full minute, dissolving focus and color to abstraction; it turns corners and swoops down embankments with inhuman celerity. Finally, Paradzhanov and his cinematographer, Yuri Ilyenko, use a variety of lenses, including telephoto zoom and 180-degree wide-angle, or "fish-eye," to wrap the film's scenographic space to the outer limits of narrative comprehension—but never quite beyond it. The point of these techniques is not to confuse the spectator but to prevent him from constructing in his head the kind of comfortable, familiar, and logically continuous representational space associated with traditional narrative form. The reason is simply that the film posits a world which is neither comfortable, familiar, nor logically continuous, for *Shadows of Forgotten Ancestors* exists most fully not in the realm of narrative but of myth and the unconscious. It is above all else a deeply psychological film, the sophistication of which puts the Pavlovian tactics of Eisensteinian montage to shame.

Shadows of Forgotten Ancestors is rich in both Freudian and Jungian imagery. The very title, changed by Paradzhanov and Chendei from Kotsiubinsky's original *Wild Horses of Fire*, resonates with "archetypes of the collective unconscious," and the film is on one level *about* those experiences that have been common to all humanity since the race evolved—love, despair, solitude, death. Ivan's yearning after the dead Marichka is imaged in many ways as a positive desire to merge with the anima and become psychologically whole. But it is also imaged darkly as a plunging descent into a Hades-like chasm containing the river where Marichka drowned, as a terrible, desperate craving to return to womb of the mother with whom Ivan has lived in a figurally Oedipal relationship since his father's death as a child—that mother who disappears from the film inexplicably and without

comment at the very moment that Marichka drowns.

Shadows of Forgotten Ancestors's psychological subtlety extends to its use of sound and color. It has been frequently noted that the film has an operatic, pageant-like quality; and Paradjanov uses a complex variety of music—from atonal electronics, to lush orchestral romanticism, to hieratic religious chants, to vocal and instrumental folk music—to create leitmotifs for the various psychological elements in his film. For example, the dark side of the Ivan-Marichka union is first announced at their moment of sexual awakening as children (after they have just bathed in the river where Marichka will drown) by a disturbingly atonal violin piece which rises to a crescendo as the intensity of their longing mounts. This theme appears on the soundtrack whenever Paradzhanov wishes to summon forth the psychologically disruptive linkage between sex and death which underlies their relationship (as it underlies the human psyche)—when they finally consummate their love as youths, when Ivan plunges down into the river gorge in search of the drowned Marichka, whenever he yearns for her after his marriage to Palagna, and at last at his death and the lovers' spiritual reunion. Similarly, the bright, innocent, psychologically integral side of their love is celebrated by a joyful folk song, sung both by and about them, not only while Marichka lives, but also, for example, at that moment later in the film when Ivan casts down his grief and becomes, for a while at least, reconciled to her death. For the most part, however, Paradzhanov's use of sound is as anti-traditional as his use of cinematography and editing. Characteristically, Ivan's grief-stricken wanderings after Marichka's death are accompanied not by music but by the off-screen gossip of neighbors commenting on his decline. And Paradjanov manipulates his sound track in other ways—exaggerating, for example, certain naturalistic sounds for symbolic effect (as when Ivan slaps Marichka resoundingly after his father has been killed by hers) and creating certain effects for symbolic purposes (e.g., the sound of the "invisible ax" hacking away off-screen which appears at fateful cruxes in Ivan's life).

Paradzhanov spoke of having created for *Shadows of Forgotten Ancestors* a "dramaturgy of color," and this element of film composition too is used in a psychologically provocative way. When Ivan and Marichka are first drawn together by their father's violence, the prevailing color of the film is the white of the snow, corresponding to their innocence (although its opposite is prefigured by the blood of Ivan's father running down the lens at the moment of his death); the green of spring dominates their young love; monochrome and sepia tones are used to drain the world of color during the period of Ivan's grieving; but color returns riotously, if briefly, after he meets Palagna; as that relationship turns barren, the film is dominated by autumnal hues; monchrome returns during Ivan's death delirium; and at the moment of his death the natural universe is painted in surreal shades of red and blue. Less noticed are the nearly subliminal fades to white and red which connect all the major sequences and the use of fades generally to isolate symbolic detail or create symbolic association.

The effect of both the soundtrack and the color system, like that of the film's optical distortions and dislocations, is to destabilize the spectator perceptually, and therefore psychologically, in order to present a tale that operates not at the level of narrative but of myth, a tale is an archetype of life itself: youth passes from innocence to experience to solitude and death in a recurring cycle, eons upon eons. This is the "shadow" of "forgotten ancestors," the archetypal pattern that outlasts and transcends all individual identity. Now the disconcerting violations of point of view through dizzying camera movement and impossible camera angles acquire new significance. For to annihilate individual point of view is to suggest a collective one, and the "impossible" perspectives of the film are only so to humans. From the beginning of *Shadows of Forgotten Ancestors* through its final frames, Paradzhanov has forced the viewer to ask himself at every turn a single question: Through whose eyes do I see? From the top of a tree, from the bottom of a pond, from the center of a violent 360-degree rotation—through whose eyes? There can only be one answer: We see this film through the eyes of something that is greater and older than all of humankind, that is every-where at once, that discerns pattern in the midst of detail, depth in flatness and flatness in depth, what things are and simultaneously what they are not. Paradzhanov may have dabbled in political dissent and been too outspoken in his criticism of officialdom, but the Soviet bureaucrats silenced him because *Shadows of Forgotten Ancestors* is an extraordinary testament to the powers of film as religious art, and its maker was a poet of God.

—David Cook

LA TERRA TREMA. Episodio del mare (sub-title). Production: Universalia; black and white, 35mm; running time: about 160 mins. Released 1947.

Produced by Salvo d'Angelo; screenplay by Luchino Visconti; from the 19th century novel *I Malavoglia* by Giovanni Verga; directed by Luchino Visconti; photography by G.R. Aldo; edited by Mario Serandrei; sound by Vittorio Trentino; music by Willi Ferrero with Luchino Visconti; assistant directors: Francesco Rosi and Franco Zeffirelli.

Filmed 1947 in Aci-Trezza, a small fishing village in Sicily. Cost: about several million lire.

Cast: The cast is composed of the people of a small fishing village in Sicily.

Publications:

Script—*Luchino Visconti: 2 Screenplays* translated by Judith Green, New York 1970; books—*Cinema italiano* by Mario Gromo, Milan 1954; *Le Cinéma italien* by Carlo Lizzani, Paris 1955; *Luchino Visconti* by Lorenzo Pellezzari, Milan 1960; *I film di Luchino Visconti* by Pio Baldelli, Manduria, Italy 1965; *Visconti* by Yves Guillaume, Paris 1966; *Le Cinéma italien, d'Antonioni à Rosi* by Freddy Bauche, Yverdon, Switzerland 1969; *Visconti* by Guiseppe Ferrar, translated by Jean-Pierre Pinaud, 2nd ed., Paris 1970; *The Italian Cinema* by Pierre Leprohon, New York 1972; *Patterns of Realism* by Roy Armes, New York 1972; *Luchino Visconti* by Pio Baldelli, Milan 1973; *Visconti* by Geoffrey Nowell-Smith, 2nd ed., New York 1973; *Visconti: il cinema* edited by Adelio Ferrera, Milan 1977; *Album Visconti* edited by Lietta Tornabuoni, foreword by Michelangelo Antonioni, Milan 1978; *Il mio teatro*, Vols. I and II, by Luchino Visconti, Bologna, Italy 1979; *A Screen of Time* by Monica Stirling, New York 1979; *Luchino Visconti* by Gaia Servadio, New York 1983; articles—"Mitologia e contemplasione in Visconti, Ford, ed Eisenstein" by Renzo Renzi in *Bianco e nero* (Rome), February 1949; "*La terra trema*" in *Bianco e nero* (Rome), March 1951; "*La Terra tremble*" in *L'Ecran français* (Paris), January 1952; "Verismo litterario e neorealismo" by

Pietro Speri in *Cinema* (Rome), 15 March 1954; "Luchino Visconti" by G.C. Castello in *Sight and Sound* (London), spring 1956; article by Andrew Sarris in *The Village Voice* (New York), 14 October 1965; "The Vision of Visconti" by Peter Dyer in *Film* (London), March/April 1957; interview with Visconti by Jean Domarchi and Doniol-Valcroze in *Sight and Sound* (London), summer/autumn 1959; "Luchino Visconti and melodramma" by Luigi Pestalozza in *Cinema nuovo* (Turin), January/February 1959; "Luchino Visconti and the Italian Cinema" by G. Poggin in *Film Quarterly* (Berkeley), spring 1960; article by Eric Rhode in *Sight and Sound* (London), winter 1960/61; issue on Visconti of *Premier Plan* (Paris), May 1961; "The Earth Still Trembles" by Guido Aristarco in *Films and Filming* (London), January 1961; "New Old Master" by L. Minoff in *Saturday Review* (New York), 29 December 1962; issue on Visconti of *Etudes cinématographiques* (Paris), no.26-27, 1963; articles in *Cinéma 63* (Paris), September/October 1963; "Luchino Visconti" by T. Elsaesser in *Brighton* (London), February 1970; issue on Visconti of *Cinema* (Rome), April 1970; article by Walter Korte in *Cinema Journal* (Evanston, Illinois), fall 1971; article in *The New York Times*, 7 January 1979; "En travaillant avec Visconti: sur le tournage de *La Terra trema*" by F. Rosi in *Positif* (Paris), February 1979; "Visconti's Magnificent Obsessions" by D. Lyons in *Film Comment* (New York), March/April 1979.

* * *

1948, the year of *La terra trema*, is also the year of the crucial postwar Italian elections. As neorealism often has it, political history and film history coincide. Italians went to the polls for the vote that was to determine the course of Italian political life for many decades: the election of a Christian Democrat legislative majority. *La terra trema* owes its genesis in part to that coincidence.

In 1947 the director Luchino Visconti went to Sicily with two young and promising assistant directors—Francesco Rosi and Franco Zeffirelli—and two reported intentions: to record in a short documentary the historic moment of political and social renewal that was expected to result from the collective action of workers and peasants and to realize the old ambition of adapting Verga (here specifically *I Malavoglia*) to the screen. Visconti stayed for seven months. During that time the original projects underwent radical transformation: the film that finally resulted reflects an amalgam of the stylistic and ideological directions of the two. Confonted by the structures and spirit of Aci Trezza (the village on the eastern coast of Sicily that had served as setting for Verga's novel), Visconti fashioned a film honest to the reality he found rather than to the dictates of current political theory interpreted by Northern political logic. The conditions for revolution were not present; the Sicilian proletariat was in no sense prepared to rise against exploitation and oppression. Whatever few attempts there might be were doomed to failure. Nor could a version faithful to Verga bear witness to the struggle of contemporary fishermen. A powerful, essentially hostile universe, against which man is locked in the eternal drama of hopeless battle, would no longer satisfy the exigencies of the new *verismo*. The enemy needed to be identified unmistakeably as capitalism—its closed system, its greed.

The developing narrative intention demanded a form consonant with its ambition. The epic portrait of the fishermen of the Sicilian village would, it was projected, be followed by two other films of equal scope to complete a trilogy on the "southern question"—the first on the struggles of Sicilian mine workers, the second on that of peasants. But finances determined that only "the episode of the sea," the story of the Valastros, be told.

Young 'Ntoni, enraged by the crooked dealings of the fish wholesalers, exhilarated by a first expresion of revolt, in love and eager to marry, realizes that as long as he, his grandfather and brothers fish from a boat that belongs to others, they will remain in the relative poverty they have always known, cheated of the just rewards of their labor. Counter to the ways of generations of his family and neighbors, 'Ntoni mortgages the family home in order to buy a boat. After an initial moment of promise, the family fortunes begin to decline. The boat is lost in a storm, and then, because of the hostility of the wholesalers and boat owners, the family falls into debt and then abject poverty. The bank appropriates the house, the grandfather dies, one brother flees with a shadowy stranger, a sister is disgraced, another loses her chance of happiness. In the end, 'Ntoni and his younger brothers return to the sea as hired hands on another's boat. 'Ntoni realizes that individual action can only lead to failure, that in collective action alone is there any hope for success.

Like the story, the actors of *La terra trema* were found in the place of the action. The Valastros, their friends and neighbors, are played by fishermen, bricklayers, wives and daughters of Aci Trazza. The language they speak is the dialect of their village, hardly more comprehensible to the speaker of standard Italian than to any other foreigner. A narrator advances the plot through overvoice, comments, and above all through translations from the dialect of Aci Trezza into the national tongue of that part of Italy the Sicilian calls "the continent."

In the approximately 160 minutes of *La terra trema*, the camera remains confined to Aci Trezza, to the horizon accessible to it from the fixed position of the church square. The world of the camera is enclosed towards the sea by the two rocks that form a gate for the harbor, and towards land by the fields beyond the cluster of houses that constitute the village. This is the world of the inhabitants of Aci Trezza. Beyond it lie danger and death. Within the space, Aldo, Visconti's cinematographer (for whom *La terra trema* represented a remarkable first experience with moving pictures), integrated characters, decor and landscape into a startling cogent whole. Through a mise-en-scène which, as Bazin points out, for the first time demonstrated the possibilities of depth of field to exterior as well as interior locations, Aldo achieved that which Visconti had perceived as necessary to an understanding of the Valastros: their intergrity with the village and the sea, their dependency on both.

—Mirella Affron

THÉRÈSE DESQUEYROUX. Thérèse Desquerouz. Thérèse. Production: Filmel; black and white, 35mm; running time: 109 mins., English version is 107 mins. Released September 1962, Paris.

Produced by Eugène Lépicier; screenplay by François Mauriac, Claude Mauriac, and Georges Franju, dialogue by François Mauriac; from the book by François Mauriac; directed by Georges Franju; photography by Christian Matras; edited by Gilbert Natot; sound by Jean Labussière; art direction by Jacques Chalvet; music by Maurice Jarre; costumes designed by Lola Prussac.

Filmed at Franstudio, Paris Studio Cinéma, and in Bazas, Villandraut, and Uzeste. Venice Film Festival, Best Actress (Riva), 1962.

Cast: Emmanuele Riva (*Thérèse*); Philippe Noiret (*Bernard*); Edith Scob (*Anne de la Trave*); Sami Frey (*Jean Azévédo*); Jeanne Perez (*Baslionte*); Renée Devillers (*Madame Victor de la Trave*); Richard Saint-Bris (*Hector de la Trave*); Lucien Nat (*Jérôme Larroque*); Hélène Dieudonné (*Aunt Clara*); Jacques Monod (*Duros*); Jean-Jacques Rémy (*Specialist*).

Publications:

Review—by Andrew Sarris in *The Village Voice* (New York), 28 November 1963; books—*Thérèse, A Portrait in Four Parts* by François Mauriac, translated by Gerard Hopkins, New York 1947; *Anarchist Cinema* by Alan Lovell, London 1962; *French Cinema Since 1946: The Personal Style*, Vol. II, by Roy Armes, New York 1966; *Franju* by Raymond Durgnat, Berkeley 1968; *Georges Franju* by Gabriel Vialle, Paris 1968; articles—"Les Paradoxes de la fidélité" by Claude Beylie in *Cahiers de cinéma* (Paris), January 1963; "Nouvel Entretien avec Georges Franju" by Jean-Louis Fieschi and André Labarthe in *Cahiers du cinéma* (Paris), November 1963; "Undertones" by James Price in *London Magazine*, April 1965; "Therese Desqueroux" by Tom Milne in *Sight and Sound* (London), spring 1965; article by James Leahy in *Movie* (New York), summer 1965; article by Gordon Gow in *Films and Filming* (London), March 1965; article by Bernard Desch in *Film Society Review* (New York), February 1966; issue on Franju of *Image et son* (Paris), March 1966; "Franju" by G. Gow in *Films and Filming* (London), August 1971; "The Films of Luis Buñuel and Georges Franju" by A. MacLochlainn in *Film Journal* (New York), summer 1971; "*Therese Desqueroux* and *Le Sang des bêtes*" by Nick Barbaro in *Cinema Texas Program Notes* (Austin), 27 April 1978.

*   *   *

The fiercely anarchic and irreligious Georges Franju might seem an improbable choice to film a novel of sin and expiation by France's leading Catholic novelist—unless in a spirit of mocking parody. Yet *Thérèse Desqueyroux* succeeds in being both an exceptionally faithful version of François Mauriac's novel and at the same time fully consistent with Franju's own attitudes and beliefs. Mauriac himself (who co-scripted together with Franju and Mauriac's son Claude, film critic of *Le Figaro littéraire*) was delighted with the final film. With good reason: *Thérèse Desqueyroux* can be well considered one of the most successful fusions of cinema and literature ever produced.

Aided by Christian Matras's sombrely beautiful monochrome photography, Franju superbly captures the stifling claustrophobia that permeates the novel. Even before she is literally imprisoned by her relatives, Thérèse is trapped: by the narrow confines of her class and provincial society, by the oppressive monotony of the pine forests of the Landes, and by her own inability to communicate the confused, passionate emotions that torment her. Her only release lies in destruction. She disrupts the relationship between her sister-in-law Anne and a young Jewish intellectual, spurred by the ambiguous jealousy which she feels for each of them. And she tries to poison Bernard, her husband (a masterly portrayal of bovine complacency from Philippe Noiret), simply in order "to see in his eyes a momentary flicker of uncertainty."

Events are presented entirely through Thérèse's eyes; it is her interior monologue we hear on the soundtrack during the complex sequence of flashbacks that occupies the greater part of the film. Yet Franju, despite evident sympathy for his heroine, never palliates her stubborn self-absorption, the source of much of her suffering. As Thérèse, Emmanuele Riva gives a flawless performance as a woman destroyed by her own agonised sensibility, pacing restlessly about her house, snatching at the umteenth cigarette, or glaring in mute fury at the back of Bernard's impassive head. Images of fire pervade the film: the conflagrations that threaten Bernard's beloved pines, the basis of his wealth; the fire that burns constantly, an ironic symbol of cosy domesticity, in the hearth of the Desqueyroux household; Thérèse's endless succession of cigarettes with which, in her captivity, she leaves burn on her bed-sheets.

Where Franju diverges from Mauriac is in the implications he draws from the events of the story—a subtle, but crucial difference. Mauriac's Thérèse must work out, through imprisonment and suffering, expiation for her sin—which is not so much attempted murder as spiritual pride. For Franju though, Thérèse is a victim, one of the outsiders whom society cannot accommodate and therefore persecutes or destroys—the fate of many of his protagonists, from *La Tête contre les Murs* to *La Faute de l'Abbé Mouret*. Building on Mauriac's austere parable, Franju constructs his own humane vision: a lucid, grave and compassionate study of isolation, rich in visual metaphor, which vividly conveys the emotional turbulence beneath its cool surface. In Franju's intense, idiosyncratic, and often uneven output, *Thérèse Desqueyroux* stands as perhaps his finest, most fully achieved film.

—Philip Kemp

THE THIN MAN. Production: Metro-Goldwyn-Mayer Picture Corp.; 1934; black and white, 35mm; running time: 91 mins. Released June 1934.

Produced by Hunt Stromberg; screenplay by Albert Hackett and Frances Goodrich; from the novel by Dashiell Hammett; directed by W.S. Van Dyke; photography by James Wong Howe; edited by Robert J. Kern; sound recorded by Douglas Shearer; art direction by Cedric Gibbons; music by Dr. William Axt; costumes designed by Dolly Tree.

Filmed during 16 days (some sources list 12 days) of 1934 in MGM studios.

Cast: William Powell (*Nick Charles*); Myrna Loy (*Nora Charles*); Maureen O'Sullivan (*Dorothy Wynant*); Nat Pendleton (*John Guild*); Minna Gombell (*Mira Wynant Jorgensen*); Porter Hall (*MacCauley*); Cesar Romero (*Chris Jorgensen*); Henry Wadsworth (*Tommy*); William Henry (*Gilbert*); Harold Huber (*Nunheim*); Natalie Moorhead (*Julia*); Edward Brophy (*Morelli*); Edward Elis (*Clyde Wynant*); Cyril Thornton (*Tanner*); Edward Ellis (*Clyde Wynant*); Thomas Jackson (*Reporter*); Ruth Channing (*Mrs. Jorgensen*); Gertrude Short (*Gloria*); Walter Long (*Study Burke*); Clay Clement (*Quinn*); Rolfe Sedan (*Kellner*); Bert Roach (*Foster*); Creighton Hale (*Reporter*).

Publications:

Books—*Van Dyke and the Mythical City of Hollywood* by Robert Cannom, Culver City, California 1948; *Hollywood in the Thirties* by John Baxter, New York 1968; *Dashiell Hammett, A Casebook* by William Nolan, Santa Barbara 1969; *Hollywood Cameramen* by Charles Higham, Bloomington, Indiana 1970; *The Detective in Film* by William K. Everson, Secaucus, New Jersey 1972; *Adventure, Mystery, Romance* by John Cawelti, Chicago 1976; *Encyclopedia of Mystery and Detection* by Chris Steinbrunner and Otto Penzler, New York 1976; articles—"Rx for a Thin Man" in *Stage* (New York), January 1937; "William Powell" by Jack Jacobs in *Films in Review* (New York), November 1958; "Myrna Loy" by Gene Ringgold in *Films in Review* (New York), February 1963; "Woody S. Van Dyke et l'âge d'or d'Hollywood" by Hervé Dumont in *Travelling* (Lausanne), no.37, 1973; "*The Thin Man*" by Gregory Sanders in *Cinema Texas Program Notes* (Austin), v.9, no.1, 1975; "W.S. Van Dyke (1889-1943)" by H. Dumont in *Anthologie du cinéma* (Paris), July/September 1975; "*The Thin Man* and *Another Thin Man*" by Louis Black in *Cinema Texas Program Notes* (Austin), 18 January 1978; "*The Thin Man*" by Nick Roddick in *Magill's Survey of Cinema, Vol. IV* edited by Frank N. Magill, Englewood Cliffs, New Jersey 1980.

*   *   *

The Thin Man is one of the brightest and most sophisticated comedy/mysteries of the 1930's. Based on Dashiell Hammett's novel of the same name, the film combines the elements of a classic detective story with overtones of the screwball comedies that had their heyday during the Depression. The result is a lighthearted murder mystery featuring perhaps the most engaging married couple in Hollywood history: Nick and Nora Charles.

Screenwriters Frances Goodrich and Albert Hackett capture both the wit and the style of Hammett's original story. As is true of all good mysteries, strong character development is central to *The Thin Man*'s success. In the wealthy, fun-loving Charleses, film-going audiences soon discovered something that was quite new by Hollywood standards—a husband and wife who throroughly enjoyed their marriage. The reverent tones with which the film industry had previously addressed the institution of matrimony had left little room for the playfulness and high spirits that mark Nick and Nora's relationship. For them, marriage is clearly an extended love affair, and the film conveys the enviable combination of companionship and romance that sets the pair apart from their staid counterparts in other films.

Dashiell Hammett is said to have modeled the Charleses on his own long-standing relationship with playwright Lillian Hellman, but for film enthusiasts the characters have become inextricably tied to the performers who brought them life. For both William Powell and Myrna Loy, *The Thin Man* represented a critical career milestone. Each had worked extensively in silent films, Powell playing dapper villains and Loy finding herself cast repeatedly as exotic vamps. The film's popular success, however, established Powell as a wise-cracking, debonair leading man, while Loy's delightful portrayal of Nora was the beginning of her reign as Hollywood's "ideal wife." Over the next decade, the two would recreate their roles in five "Thin Man" sequels, and although none of the subsequent films ever quite equaled the effortless charm of the original, Powell and Loy remained perfectly paired throughout the series.

Goodrich and Hackett's script must share credit for *The Thin Man*'s breezy style and rapid pacing with the direction of W.S. "Woody" Van Dyke. Although Van Dyke's work has not won him a place alongside the John Fords and Howard Hawkses of the American cinema, he enjoyed a reputation during the 1930's as a highly professional director whose films generally proved popular at the boxoffice. His efficient, no-nonsense working earned him the nickname "One-Take Woody," and he completed *The Thin Man* in a remarkable 12 days. Given its tight shooting schedule, it is no surprise that the finished film reflects a heady sense of energy and elan.

In the years since its release, *The Thin Man* has spawned a number of imitators, including several successful television series. Connoisseurs of the genre, however, return again and again to Nick and Nora—and their faithful Airedale, Asta—drawn by the appeal of a film that remains fresh and original after 50 years.

—Janet E. Lorenz

THINGS TO COME. Production: London Film Productions; black and white, 35mm; running time: 130 mins., a shorter version of 96 mins. also exists. Released 1936 by United Artists.

Produced by Alexander Korda; screenplay by H.G. Wells and Lajos Biro; from the novel *The Shape of Things to Come* by H.G. Wells; directed by William Cameron Menzies; photography by George Perinal; edited by Charles Crichton; art direction by Vincent Korda; music by Arthur Bliss; special effects by Ned Mann; special camera effects by Edward Cohen and Harry Zech; costumes designed by John Armstrong, René Hubert and the Marchioness of Queensberry.

Cost: budgeted at $1,000,000.

Cast: Raymond Massey (*John Cabal/Oswald Cabal*); Ralph Richardson (*The Boss*); Edward Chapman (*Pippa Passworthy/- Raymond Passworthy*); Margaretta Scott (*Roxana Black*); Sir Cedric Hardwicke (*Theotocopulos*); Maurice Barddell (*Dr. Harding*); Sophie Stewart (*Mrs. Cabal*); Derrick de Marney (*Richard Gordon*); Ann Todd (*Mary Gordon*); Pearl Argyle (*Katherine Cabal*); Kenneth Villiers (*Maurice Passworthy*); Ivan Brandt (*Mitani*); Anthony Holles (*Simon Burton*); Allan Jeayes (*Mr. Cabal*); John Clements (*Airman*); Pickles Livingston (*Horrie Passworthy*); Patricia Hilliard (*Janet Gordon*); George Sanders (*Pilot*).

Publications:

Books—*20 Years of British Films, 1925-45* by Michael Balcon and others, London 1947; *Alexander Korda* by Paul Tabori, New York 1966; *Focus on Science Fiction* edited by William Johnson, Englewood Cliffs, New Jersey 1972; *Alexander Korda: The Man Who Could Work Miracles* by Karol Kulik, London 1975; *Caligari's Cabinet and Other Grand Illusions: A History of Film Design* by Léon Barsacq, New York 1976; *The Science Fiction Pictures* by James Robert Parish, Metuchen, New Jersey 1977; articles—"The Producer: Sir Alexander Korda" by Colin Campbell in *Sight and Sound* (London), summer 1951; "Sir Alexander Korda" by Sidney Gilliat, Graham Greene, and Ralph Richardson in *Sight and Sound* (London), 1956; "Raymond Massey" by Jeanne Stein in *Films in Review* (New York), August/September 1963; "Korda" by Peter Cowie in *Anthologie du cinéma*, vol. 6, Paris 1965; "Cedric Hardwicke" by Robert Roman in *Films in Review* (New York), January 1965; "Ralph Richardson by Alan Coulson in *Films in Review* (New York),

October 1969; "*Things to Come*" by Connie McFeeley in *Magill's Survey of Cinema, Vol. IV* edited by Frank N. Magill, Englewood Cliffs, New Jersey 1980.

*   *   *

One of the most characteristic aspects of science fiction in the thirties is its being influenced by another fantastic genre— horror—so intensively that in many cases it is hardly possible to establish a dividing line between these two categories of fantastic creation. There are very few movies which are exclusively devoted to considering scientific and societal evolution in terms of an extrapolation into the future. An exception is the English film of 1936, *Things to Come*. The book on which the film is based, *The Shape of Things to Come*, is a speculative continuation of H.G. Wells's *The Outline of History* and is, according to the author, "basically an imaginative discussion about social and political forces and possibilities." The story of the movie covers a period of a hundred years of civilization. It begins in 1940, in a time permeated by fear of an imminent war which finally explodes and lasts 25 years. During that period, the entire globe is devastated and almost all of mankind exterminated. However, the human will and spirit remain active, and so at the end of the book, in 2040, a completely different world is depicted, in which human hardships have been eliminated and man is assured of all his material as well as mental needs. Progress is unrelenting as mankind plans to leave Mother Earth and take over the universe.

Wells's work fascinated and still fascinates readers by its original images of the future. Wells himself, however, valued more highly his scientific studies than his fiction, and so the speculative aspect of *Things to Come* receives more attention than the story. The plot of the film proceeds from Wells's assumption that a war will mean the end of the Western civilization. The structure of the story is based on a conflict of two forces always present in humanity's evolution. One of them represents chaos and regression and encourages man's barbaric nature; and the other represents order, healthy reasoning, scientific progress. When these forces collide, science and intellect win although this victory will always be threatened by other pressures, due to our imperfect understanding of how best to invest our human resources.

Wells, who wrote the screenplay, was not able to transfer his ideas, opinions, or doubts into a form which would utilize all the components of the psychic process involved during the perception of a movie. Only the spectator's intellect and reason are called upon, his emotions remain untouched. In the film, the characters are not people of flesh and blood; they are merely symbols of various ideological convictions. They do not furnish the spectator with an opportunity to penetrate into the soul and mind in order to identify with them. Director William Cameron Menzies, who was working with actors for the first time, was unable, because of his lack of experience, to influence the movie's screenplay as much as the production design. He concentrates fully on the visual aspect of the movie, its structuralizations, sets, and special effects. From this point of view, the film attracted well-merited attention and, till the present time, has kept its place in film history precisely for its remarkable formal design. Cameron Menzies thoughtfully composed the movie's space; his plastic fantasy triumphs especially in his presentation of a city of the future where he exhibits a sense of balance and visual contrast. The sets dominate the action as well as the characters who, deprived of their psychological hinterland, become the composition's style-creating element. The refined sophistication of Ned Mann's special effects and his extraordinary miniature models and buildings give the impression of a "life size" dimension, and create a sense of unity of space and man. Some objects look real and concrete although they are a product of more fantasy, such as the machine by which the new city is built, or the attack of delta-winged airplanes which he used despite the protests of contemporary experts. Wells in his screenplay revealed a spirit of vision not only in details but also in basic principle—he announced the coming of the Second World War. The English public received the idea of an air attack on London with laughter; after a few years, however, this fiction became reality.

The filming of this ambitious movie devoured a significant sum of money. The producer never recovered his investment, but *Things to Come* remains a testament to its creators thoughtful examination of mankind's path into the future, and it occupies an important place in the history of the science fiction genre.

—Mrs. B. Urgošíkova

THE THIRD MAN. Production: British Lion Films; 1949; black and white, 35mm; running time: 93 mins., another version exists at 104 mins. Released 1949.

Produced by Carol Reed with Hugh Perceval; screenplay by Graham Greene; from the novel by Greene; directed by Carol Reed; photography by Robert Krasker; edited by Oswald Hafenrichter; art direction by Vincent Korda, sets by Dario Simoni; music by Anton Karas.

Filmed on location in Vienna. Best Film, Cannes Film Festival, 1949; Academy Award, Best Cinemetography (Black and White), 1950.

Cast: Joseph Cotten (*Holly Martins*); Alida Valli (*Anna Schmidt*); Trevor Howard (*Major Colloway*); Orson Welles (*Harry Lime*); Bernard Lee (*Sergeant Paine*); Ernst Deutsch (*Baron Kurtz*); Erich Ponto (*Dr. Winkel*); Wilfrid Hyde-White (*Crabbin*); Siegfried Breuer (*Popesco*); Paul Hoerbiger (*Harry's porter*); Hedwig Bleibtreu (*Anna's old woman*); Frederick Schreicker (*Hansel's father*); Herbert Halbik (*Hansel*); Jenny Werner (*Winkel's maid*); Nelly Arno (*Kurtz's mother*); Alexis Chesnakov (*Brodsky*); Leo Bieber (*Barman*); Paul Smith (*M.P.*).

Publications:

Script—*The Third Man*, New York 1968; books—*The Films of Orson Welles* by Charles Higham, Berkeley 1971; *Graham Greene: The Films of His Fiction* by Gene D. Phillips, New York 1974; *The Great Gangster Pictures* by James R. Parish and Michael R. Pitts, Metuchen, New Jersey 1976; *Orson Welles: Actor and Director* by J. McBride, New York 1977; articles—"I Give the Public What I Like" by Harvey Breit in the *New York Times Magazine*, 15 January 1950; "A Man with No Message" by Catherine De La Roche in *Films and Filming* (London), December 1954; "Carol Reed in the Context of His Time" by Andrew Sarris in *Film Culture* (New York), no.10, 1956; "First of the Realists" by Andrew Sarris in *Films and Filming* (London), September 1957; "The Stylist Goes to Hollywood" by Andrew Sarris in *Films and Filming* (London), October 1957; "Sir Carol Reed" by Marion Fawcett in *Films in Review* (New York), March 1959; "*The Third Man*: Capturing the Visual

Essence of Literary Conception" by J.A. Gomez in *Literature/-Film Quarterly* (Salisbury, Maryland), fall 1974; "Narrative Structure in *The Third Man*" by W.F. Van Wert in *Literature/-Film Quarterly* (Salisbury, Maryland), fall 1974; "I Never Knew the Old Vienna: Cold War Politics and *The Third Man*" by Lynette Carpenter in *Film Criticism* (Edinboro, Pennsylvania), 1978; "The Great Ones: *The Third Man*" in *Classic Film Collector* (Indiana, Pennsylvania), July 1979; "*The Third Man*" by Daniel D. Fineman in *Magill's Survey of Cinema, Vol. IV* edited by Frank N. Magill, Englewood Cliffs, New Jersey 1980; "The Lone Rider in Vienna: Myth and Meaning in *The Third Man*" by J.W. Palmer and M.M. Riley in *Literature/Film Quarterly* (Salisbury, Maryland), no.1, 1980.

* * *

Carol Reed's *The Third Man* is a remarkably enigmatic film in many respects, drawing in the range of talents and traditions so broad as to raise the question of authorship in a particularly acute form. The film owes debts to the Grierson/Rotha tradition of British documentary film, as well as to the post-war neorealism of Rossellini's *Roma Cittá Aperta* and DeSica's *Ladri di Bicilette*; likes its Italian predecessors, *The Third Man* studies the effects of post-war economic and social corruption within the context of a once grand though now rubble-strewn European capital (Rome for the neo-realists, Vienna for Reed). And debts are also owed to the moralistic detective fiction of Graham Greene (who wrote the original screenplay) as well as to the similarly Catholic tradition of Hitchcock's pre-war British thrillers (e.g., *The 39 Steps*). But overshadowing all of these influences is the presence of Orson Welles in the role of Harry Lime. Welles wrote much of his own dialogue; as in *Citizen Kane* he is once again paired with Joseph Cotten, who plays his boyhood friend Holly Martins; even the film's overtly stylized use of camera angles, of expressionist lighting, of stairways, owes much to the Wellesian style. Indeed, *The Third Man* is very much a film *about* authorship, or about art more generally, and the issue raised is very much one of artistic ethics. Thus the film's three major characters are all artists of one sort or another—and the range of their actions and motives helps to define our sense of the film's theme.

Holly Martins, for instance, is a western novelist (when asked about artistic influences he cites Zane Grey) whose initial interest in the investigation of the "death" of Harry Lime involves his conviction that Harry was a victim of "the sheriff" (i.e., the British military police) whose death Holly ("the lone rider") must avenge. Later he even says he is planning a new novel, based on fact, to be called "The Third Man." Likewise Anna—Harry's girl friend (whom he betrays to the Russian)—is an actress; and her willingness to betray Harry involves both ignorance (she doesn't know he betrayed her) and a melodramatic sense of her role as the doomed man's mistress (she even sleeps in Harry's pajamas).

But clearly the films central figure, its central artist, is Harry Lime himself. The complex relationship of money and art is a primary theme of the Wellesian cinema—and in *The Third Man* it finds vivid expression in the *use* Lime makes of art, to throw the occupation authorities off his trail and to further his traffic in black market drugs (diluted penicillin especially). Hence Lime plans and stage-manages his own death, even playing a part as "the third man" who helps carry the body (actually, that of an implicated associate) from the street where it was run down by a truck; and he calls his boyhood friend, Holly Martins, to Vienna to serve as his stand in. The connection of art and corruption is confirmed in Harry's famous "cuckoo clock" speech wherein the political intrigues of the Borgias are correlated with the aesthetic triumphs of Michelangelo and da Vinci. There is something remarkably childish and self-indulgent about Lime's perspective—as evidenced by the fact that he utters the line at an amusement park. But Holly gets another view of childhood, when Major Calloway (Trevor Howard) takes him to the hospital ward populated by Lime's victims, all children; and "The Third Man," as Holly eventually "rewrites" the story, becomes a parable of social responsibilty. It is Holly who finally pulls the trigger and puts the wounded Lime out of his cynical misery.

—Leland Poague

THE 39 STEPS. Production: Gaumont-British; 1935; black and white, 35mm; running time: 81 mins. Released June 1935.

Produced by Michael Balcon with Ivor Montagu; screenplay by Charles Bennett and Alma Reville, additional dialogue by Ian Hay; from the novel by John Buchan; directed by Alfred Hitchcock; photography by Bernard Knowles; edited by Derek Twist; sound by A. Birch; production design by Otto Wendorff and Albert Jullion; music by Louis Levy; costumes designed by J. Strassner.

Filmed in Lime-Grove studios.

Cast: Madeleine Carroll (*Pamela*); Robert Donat (*Richard Hannay*); Lucie Mannheim (*Miss Smith/Annabella*); Godfrey Tearle (*Professor Jordan*); Peggy Ashcroft (*Margaret*); John Laurie (*John*); Helen Haye (*Mrs. Jordan*); Wylie Watson (*Mister Memory*); Frank Cellier (*Sheriff Watson*); Peggy Simpson (*Young girl*); Gus McNaughton and Jerry Vernon (*2 Voyagers*); Miles Malleson (*Director of the Palladium*).

Publications:

Scripts—"*Les 39 Marches*" by Charles Bennett and Alma Reville in *Avant-Scène du cinéma* (Paris), 1 June 1980; reviews—"La Presse" in *Avant-Scène du cinéma* (Paris), 1 June 1980; books—*Hitchcock* by Eric Rohmer and Claude Chabrol, Paris 1957; *Hitchcock's Films* by Robin Wood, London 1965; *Hitchcock* by François Truffaut, New York 1967; *Kiss Kiss Bang Bang* by Pauline Kael, Boston 1970; *Focus on Hitchcock* edited by Albert J. LaValley, Englewood Cliffs, New Jersey 1972; *The Great Spy Pictures* by James R. Parish and Michael Pitts, Metuchen, New Jersey 1974; *The Art of Alfred Hitchcock: 50 Years of His Motion Pictures* by Donald Spoto, New York 1976; *Hitchcock's Films* by Robin Wood, New York 1977; *A Short History of the Movies* by Gerald Mast, New York 1981; *Hitchcock* by J.-A. Fieschi and others, Paris 1981; *Hitchcock— The Murderous Gaze* by William Rothman, Cambridge, Massachusetts, 1982; *A Narrative History of Film* by David Cook, New York 1982; *The Dark Side of Genius: The Life of Alfred Hitchcock* by Donald Spoto, New York, 1982; articles—"My Own Methods" in *Sight and Sound* (London), summer 1937; "Alfred Hitchcock" by Lindsay Anderson in *Sequence* (London), autumn 1949; "*Stage Fright* and Hitchcock" by Simon Harcourt-Smith in *Sight and Sound* (London), July 1950; "Hitchcock Anglais in *Cahiers du cinéma* (Paris), September 1956; article by John Pett on Hitchcock in *Films and Filming*

(London), November 1959 and continued in December 1959; "Hitchcock's World" by Charles Higham in *Film Quarterly* (Berkeley), winter 1962-63; "The Strange Case of Alfred Hitchcock" by Raymond Durgnat in *Films and Filming* (London), study of his films in 10 issues from February 1970 through November 1970; "*Les 39 marches* et *Une Femme disparait*" by Claude Beylie in *Ecran* (Paris), September/October 1973; "In Broad Daylight" by Richard Roud in *Film Comment* (New York), July/August 1974; "Mirth, Sexuality, and Suspense: Alfred Hitchcock's Adaptation of *The 39 Steps*" by S.Y. McDougal in *Literature/Film Quarterly* (Salisbury, Maryland), summer 1975; "*The 39 Steps*" by R.M. Goldstein in *Film News* (New York), January/February 1979; "*The Thirty-Nine Steps*" by Olive Graham in *Cinema Texas Program Notes* (Austin), 5 February 1979; "*The 39 Steps*" by Anthony Slide in *Magill's Survey of Cinema, Vol. IV* edited by Frank N. Magill, Englewood Cliffs, New Jersey 1980; "Une Allégorie policière" by Eric Rohmer and Claude Chabrol in *Avant-Scène du cinéma* (Paris), 1 June 1980.

*   *   *

When he completed *The 39 Steps*, director Alfred Hitchcock explained his reasons for doing the film: "I am out to give the public good, healthy, mental shake-ups. Civilization has become so screening and sheltering that we cannot experience sufficient thrills at first-hand. Therefore, to prevent our becoming sluggish and jellified, we have to experience them artificially." The film first brought Hitchcock to the attention of United States filmgoers and initiated reference to the director as "the master " in his native England. The pairing of Robert Donat and Madeleine Carroll—the suave, clever, attractive man and the cool, intelligent blonde—helped to reinforce the pattern of Hitchcockian protagonists that would recur in many of his later films.

Many critics and viewers alike feel that *The 39 Steps* is one of Hitchcock's finest films; in fact, viewer response to the film today is often as enthusiastic as during the time of its release. Adapted from a novel by John Buchan, the movie gave Hitchcock the opportunity to display his finest non-stop action sequences. Most notably, it combines what would become Hitchcock's most often-treated themes with imaginative sound and visual techniques.

Numerous scenes in *The 39 Steps* have become cinema classics, particularly those merging suspense with surprise, humor with anxiety: the murdered, mysterious spy who, after warning him that "they'll get you too," slumps over Donat's bed revealing the knife in her back; the surprise when master-spy Geoffrey Searle shows Donat his "half-pinkie," the top-joint of his finger missing; the funny and ironic sexual implications of adversaries Carroll and Donat handcuffed together, pretending to be newlyweds, "forced" to spend the night together. (As she removes her stockings, his hand must coast along with hers down her legs— "May I be of assistance?" he asks.)

And Hitchcock's technical virtuosity highlights what is perhaps his most famous scene transition, used first in *Blackmail*: the chambermaid finds the spy's body and shrieks, her cries blended to the screaming whistle of a train as the plot "relentlessly moves foward." Hitchcock's use of sound and careful lighting heighten the suspense—and humor—of the film. Throughout the melee in the music hall during the first sequence, persistent members of the audience ask, "What causes Pip in poultry?," and "How old is Mae West?" as the crowded mise-en-scene and the fast-paced editing reinforce the confusion.

The 39 Steps also featured one of Hitchcock's favorite themes:

the innocent caught in bizarre circumstances that he or she doesn't understand. The plot and its loopholes, however, provide the forum for the hero to do his or her "stuff," to demonstrate a charm and cleverness in getting out of tight spots. As the confusing plot plays itself out, however, audiences are far more interested in the characters' relationships than in the overall impetus for the narrative. In fact, the original point of the title was forgotten, and a line had to be added to the script at the end by way of explanation. *The 39 Steps* then, also illustrates the celebrated Hitchcockian "McGuffin"—"what everybody on the screen is looking for, but the audience don't care."

Particularly effective in the film are rapid changes of situation and Hitchcock's obvious contention that nothing is sacred, especially if a location or situation can be used to demonstrate the cleverness of his protagonist. Even patriotic parades and political lectures aren't safe from the thrilling chase: Donat escapes from a police station, ducks into a public hall where he is mistaken for a guest speaker, then gives an impromptu, rousing political address to a responsive audience. All of these events foreshadow Cary Grant's escape from killers at an auction and his flight from the same murderers around the Mount Rushmore National Monument in *North by Northwest* (1959); with Hitchcock, traditional connotations of safety and danger often reverse.

Visually, *The 39 Steps* enabled Hitchcock to transfer some of his skills as a director of silent films: the camera at long-shot lingers on an open window, curtains blowing in and around its frame on a stormy London night. This effective bit of "moodsetting" precedes revelation of the woman spy's murder. Later on in the film we look through the window of a farmer's cottage from his point of view; within that tight frame, we witness the conspirat, silent "dialogue" between Donat and Peggy Ashcroft, the farmer's kind wife. As with his use of sound, these sequences illustrate Hitchcock's mastery of a medium in which absence of dialogue or music can be strikingly effective.

Sydney Carroll, writing in the London *Sunday Times*, said: "In *The 39 Steps* the identity and mind of Alfred Hitchcock are continuously discernible, in fact supreme. There is no doubt that Hitchcock is a genius. He is the real star of the film." And interestingly, two "modern" remakes of the film pale miserably in comparison with the original.

—Deborah Holdstein

THIS SPORTING LIFE. Production: Independent Artists, A Julian Wintle-Leslie Parkyn Production; black and white, 35mm; running time: 134 mins., American version is 129 mins. Released January 1963, England.

Produced by Karel Reisz with Albert Fennell; screenplay by David Storey; from the novel by David Storey; directed by Lindsay Anderson; photography by Denys Coop; edited by Peter Taylor; sound recorded by John W. Mitchell and Gordon McCallum; art direction by Alan Withy, set dressed by Peter Lamont, scenic artistry by E. Brister; music composed by Roberto Gerhard, music conducted by Jacques-Louis Monod; costumes designed by Sophie Devine.

Cannes Film Festival, Best Actor (Harris) and International Critics Prize, 1963; British Academy Award, Best British Actress (Roberts), 1963.

Cast: Richard Harris (*Frank Machin*); Rachel Roberts (*Mrs. Hammond*); Alan Badel (*Weaver*); William Hartnell (*Johnson*); Colin Blakely (*Maurice Braithwaite*); Vanda Godsell (*Mrs. Weaver*); Arthur Lowe (*Slomer*); Anne Cunningham (*Judith*); Jack Watson (*Len Miller*); Harry Markham (*Wade*); George Sewell (*Jeff*); Leonard Rossiter (*Phillips*); Frank Windsor (*Dentist*); Peter Duguid (*Doctor*); Wallas Eaton (*Waiter*); Anthony Woodruff (*Head waiter*); Katherine Parr (*Mrs. Farrer*); Bernadette Benson (*Lynda*); Andrew Nolan (*Ian*); Michael Logan (*Riley*); Murray Evans (*Hooker*); Tom Clegg (*Gower*); John Gill (*Cameron*); Ken Traill (*Trainer*).

Publications:

Reviews—"*This Sporting Life*" by Tom Milne in *Sight and Sound* (London), summer 1962; review by Peter Baker in *Films and Filming* (London), March 1963; review by Ivor Howard in *Films in Review* (New York), August/September 1963; review by Gavin Miller in *Movie* (London), February/March 1963; review by Andrew Sarris in *The Village Voice* (New York), 25 July 1963; "Slummox" by Jay Cocks in *Time* (New York), 19 July 1963; books—*New Cinema in Britain* by Roger Manvell, New York 1969; *Lindsay Anderson* by Elizabeth Sussex, New York 1970; *A Mirror for England, British Movies from Austerity to Affluence* by Raymond Durgnat, New York 1971; *Directing Motion Pictures* edited by Terence St. John Marner, New York 1972; *The Long View* by Basil Wright, London 1974; *Lindsay Anderson: A Guide to References and Resources* by Charles L.P. Silet, Boston 1979; *Lindsay Anderson* by Allison Graham, Boston 198!; articles—"Sport, Life and Art" in *Films and Filming* (London), February 1963; "*This Sporting Life*: Bigger Than Life" by Brian St. Pierre in *Seventh Art* (New York), fall 1963; "Arrival and Departure" by Robert Vas in *Sight and Sound* (London), spring 1963; "Desert Island Films" in *Films and Filming* (London), August 1963; article in *Cinema* (Beverly Hills), November/December 1963; article by Paul O'Dell in *Movie* (London), July/August 1963; "An Interview with Lindsay Anderson" by Peter Cowie in *Film Quarterly* (Berkeley), summer 1964; article by Ernest Callenbach in *Film Quarterly* (Berkeley), summer 1964; interview with Anderson in *Cinema International* (Montier, Switzerland), no.16, 1967; "Biofilmographie—Lindsay Anderson" in *Avant-Scène du cinéma* (Paris), November 1971; "Lindsay Anderson—romantisk ironiker" by N. Jensen in *Kosmorama* (Copenhagen), November 1973; "Britannia Waives the Rules" by Raymond Durgnat in *Film Comment* (New York), July/August 1976.

*   *   *

At the time of its release *The Sporting Life* was considered the best of the England's "Angry Young Man" school of films—which also included *Room at the Top* (1959), *Saturday Night and Sunday Morning* (1960), and *Billy Liar* (1963). Today the film fails to hold up under critical scrutiny: now it seems little more than an artifact, important only as Lindsay Anderson's first feature film and impressive only for the intensity of the acting of Richard Harris and Rachel Roberts.

Anderson is the most talented of the filmmakers of England's Free Cinema Movement (Karl Reiz, Tony Richardson, Gavin Lambert) and one of the few British filmmakers who can be described as an *auteur*. The Free Cinema Movement promoted the social documentary and led the way to feature films with controversial subjects not considered appropriate to the middle-class-bound British cinema. Anderson's first films were such documentaries, the most famous one being the Academy Award-winning *Thursday's Child* (1954), a purposely unsentimental, almost Buñuel-esque work about teaching children at the Royal School for the Deaf in Margate, Kent. After working in this documentary tradition, Anderson collaborated with author David Storey in bringing to the screen Storey's grim but popular and prize-winning novel about a tough, young miner who becomes a successful rugby player in Northern England. The theme of the novel and the film is the exploitation of the working-class man by the industrialists, and Storey's rugby field is his microcosm of England's inequitable caste system.

The story is a very familiar one in both the theater and in films; Clifford Odets's *Golden Boy* is its foremost example. Anderson brings to the film his idiosyncratic touch—but partly because he was working from a screenplay written by the novelist and partly because Richard Harris insisted that the film closely follow the book, it is the least personal of Anderson's films.

Harris plays Frank Machin, a brawny, boorish coal miner who seeks to better himself by joining the local professional rugby team. His fierce competitiveness and brutality make him a hero to the fans, but his lack of self-awareness leads to his destroying all he touches. Machin curiously avoids all his young, adoring female fans and sets out to seduce his middle-aged landlady, Mrs Hammond (Rachel Roberts), a sexually repressed widow with a small son. He buys her a fur coat and takes her and the boy for rides in his white roadster, and finally she reluctantly submits to a physical relationship with him, refusing to offer her him love. Unable to come to terms with their innermost feelings, they allow their relationship to become one of violent arguments and mental torture. After one final corrosive argument, he leaves and later learns she had suffered a brain hemorrhage; he arrives at the hospital just in time to be with her as she dies. He then returns to his brutal sport, a man defeated, without purpose and possibly on his way back to the mines.

Anderson tells the first part of his story through flashbacks in the form of Machin's hallucinations as he sits in a dentist's chair having his teeth repaired after a particularly violent rugby match. Critic Dwight MacDonald found this device an example of "*nouvelle-vague* smartness," and today the flashbacks do seem contrived and clichéd. More importantly, the script never really integrates what are two storylines absolutely separate from each other dramatically—Machin's rugby career and his being exploited, and his affair with the widow. There is also an unresolved homosexual implication involving the old scout who helps Machin get hired by the owner of the rugby team, and the justification for what is supposed to be Machin's exploitation by the team owner is never explicated.

What does hold the film together are the first-rate performances by Harris and Roberts. This film made Harris's reputation and earned him an Oscar nomination and the Best Actor Prize at the Cannes Film Festival. Roberts was also nominated for an Oscar, and she did receive the British Academy Award as Best Actress.

Although the film was a major step away from the restrained, tight-upper-lip tradition of filmmaking in England, it did not achieve its goal of conveying what Anderson himself described as the film's subject: "...a fatal attraction between two temperaments that could never understand or accommodate each other. Neither of them is sufficiently understanding or mature enough to make allowances for the difference in the other. So they are doomed to destroy each other."

—Ronald Bowers

LA TIERRA PROMETIDA. The Promised Land. Production: Cinematografica Tercer Mondo and Instituto Cubano del Arte el Industria Cinematograficos (ICAIC); Eastmancolor, 35mm; running time: 120 mins. Released 1973.

Screenplay by Miguel Littin; based on Chilean folk tales; directed by Miguel Littin; photography by Alfonso Beato; edited by Nelson Rodriques; music by Luis Advis and the Init-Illimani Group.

Cast: Nelson Villagra (*Jose Duran*); Marcelo Gaete (*Traje Cruzado*); Rafael Benavente (*Don Fernando*); Mireya Kulchewsky (*The Virgin*); Anibal Reyna; Carmen Bueno; Pedro Alvarez; and the residents of Santa Cruz and Colchagna.

Publications:

Script—*Cine chileno: La tierra prometida* by Miguel Littin, (notes and narrative on which film was based), Caracas, Venezuela 1974; reviews—by C.M. Cluny in *Cinéma* (Paris), September/October 1974; "*La Terre promise...refusée*" by J. Delmas in *Jeune Cinéma* (Paris), June 1974; review in *Films in Review* (New York), December 1974; review by A. Head in *Image et son* (Paris), September 1974; "Chile, terre promise" by J. Magny in *Téléciné* (Paris), July/August 1974; "*The Promised Land*" by James Monaco in *Take One* (Montreal), May 1974; "Un Démenti flagrant des histoires officielles" by P.L. Thirard in *Positif* (Paris), December 1974; "*La tierra prometida*" by A. Marrosu in *Cine al Día* (Caracas, Venzuela), March 1975; books—*Chilean Cinema* by Michael Chanan, London 1976; "El Chacal de Nahueltoro: *La tierra prometida*" by Miguel Littin, Textos de cine, 5, Serie de guiones, 1, Mexico 1977; articles—"La Voix veille" by P. Bonitzer in *Cahiers du cinéma* (Paris), October/November 1974; "New Directors/New Films" by Roger Greenspun in *Film Comment* (New York), September/October 1974; "*La Terre promise*" by G. Hennebelle and M. Martin in *Ecran* (Paris), November 1974; "Culture populaire...." by J.R. Huleu, P. Kané, and I. Ramonet in *Cahiers du cinéma* (Paris), July/August 1974; "Journal de tournage" by M. Littin in *Jeune Cinéma* (Paris), June 1974; "Le Pouvoir parlé" by S. Toubiana in *Cahiers du cinéma* (Paris)., October/November 1974; "*La tierra prometida*" by S. Zambetti in *Cineforum* (Bergamo, Italy), December 1975; "*The Promised Land*" by Julianne Burton in *Film Quarterly* (Berkeley), autumn 1975; "*La tierra prometida*" by G. Cremonini in *Cinema nuovo* (Turin), September/October 1976; "The Arrival of the Instrument in Flesh and Blood: Deconstruction in Littin's *Promised Land*" by R. Scott in *Ciné-Tracts* (Montreal), spring/summer 1978; "Miguel Littin's *Recurso del metodo*: The Aftermath of Allende" by Katherine Kovacs in *Film Quarterly* (Berkeley), spring 1980.

*   *   *

La tierra prometida (*The Promised Land*) is a folk epic telling of the wandering of a homeless people, their founding of a rural community, the army's destruction of that community and people, and the symbolic rebirth of the people's revolutionary spirit. Though many historical motifs tie the narrative to the events in Chile in the early 1930's, the film is notable as a creative experiment in blending history and legend, realism and symbolism, to tell such a story. Religious and historical figures are creatively used in a symbolic way, as when Arturo Prat, the great Chilean hero of the War of the Pacific, passes his sword of resistence on to future generations. Other symbolic-allegorical motifs: the landing of the red airplane and the proclamation of Chile's new socialist government; the stopped train, a motif suggesting that the Chilean bourgeoisie has reached the end of the line literally and figuratively.

Miguel Littin has innovatively structured his folk epic. The words of an old narrator (a former participant in events) provide a commentary on the visual narrative and also give the film the tone of a popular legend. Folk ballads too are successfully used to advance the epic narrative. Critics have identified the most striking structural feature of the film as its self-critical and "dialectical" style. The film, through its use of powerful music and appealing characters, stimulates the spectator's emotional involvement. But the film also fosters a critical perspective in viewers through the use of distancing or self-critical devices that serve to comment on the film's form, content, and function. For instance, the linearity of several narrative sequences is disrupted by a deconstruction of the usual codes relating to sound, space, and perspective.

La tierra prometida has immense cultural and ideological significance. While the film clearly displays a deep appreciation for Chilean popular culture, it also offers criticism of certain aspects of that culture. For instance, the Virgen del Carmen, the patron saint of Chile, appears as a woman several times in the film. At times she appears as a supporter of the popular classes; other times she is aligned with powerful forces opposing the poor people. The suggestion is that religious symbols can be appropriated and manipulated by any class in support of vested interests.

Ideologically, *La tierra prometida* favors Marxist revolution while nevertheless describing the shortcomings of the revolutionary leaders and the revolutionary process. The popular classes demonstrate that they can organize and manage a rural community if given sufficient land, but they also show an inability—owing to a lack of knowledge and preparation—to successfully extend the revolutionary process to the regional and national levels. José Durán, the revolutionary leader, has both strengths (he grows in his political understanding) and weaknesses (he vacillates at a decisive moment in the revolutionary process).

This film has not been shown in Chile, but elsewhere critics have considered it to be of great importance in terms of innovative structural techniques and narrative strategies. The politics of the film, which are not always clear, have sparked debate among critics and the general film-going public. Some politically aware viewers have seen *La tierra prometida* as an allegory of Marxist-socialist Salvador Allende's Popular Unity coalition government (1970-73), because the film deals with issues that were also crucial for Popular Unity: the role of the army, the need to arm the people, the role of the Catholic Church, the need to educate and politicize the people, and the necessity of expropriating powerful landowning and business interests.

—Dennis West

TIRE DIÉ. Toss Me a Dime. Production: Instituto de Cinematografía de la Universidad Nacional del Litoral; black and white, 16mm blown up to 35mm; running time: 33 mins. Released 1960.

Scripted, directed, and photographed by Fernando Birri and the students at the Instituto de Cinematografía of the Universidad Nacional de Litoral, Santa Fe, Argentina; edited by Antonio Ripoll; sound by by Mario Fezia; assistant director: Manuel Horacio Gimenez.

Filmed 1958-1960 in Santa Fe, Argentina.

Cast: Guillermo Cervantes Luro (*Narrator*); Voices of Francisco Petrone and Maria Rosa Gallo.

Publications:

Books—*Breve historia del cine argentino* by Jose Agustin Mahieu, Buenos Aires 1966; *Fernando Birri e la Escuela Documental de Santa Fe* edited by Lino Micciche, Pesaro, Italy 1981; articles—"Breve historia del documental en la Argentina" by Dolly Pussi in *Cine Cubano* (Havana), October 1973; "The Connection: 3 Essays on the Treatment of History in the Early Argentine Cinema" by Jorge Miguel Couselo, introduced and translated by E. Bradford Burns in *Journal of Latin American Lore*, vol.1, no.2, 1975; interview by Julianne Burton in *Fernando Birri e la Escuela Documental de Santa Fe* edited by Lino Micciche, Pesaro, Italy 1981; "Carta a Fernando Birri" by Manuel Pereira and "Pequena critica agradecida a *Tire die*" by Rigoberto Lopez in *Cine Cubano* (Havana), no.100, 1981.

*   *   *

Though seldom seen, even in Latin American, *Tire Dié*, a 33-minute documentary, is the most revered and influential of the hundreds of documentary shorts produced throughout the continent during the quarter century of the New Latin American Cinema movement. Most viewers know only the fragment presented in Fernando Solanas' and Octavio Getino's three-part feature documentary on Argentine politics, *The Hour of the Furnaces* (1969), but the example of director Fernando Birri's approach and philosophy can be detected in dozens of other films. In its genesis, mode of production and distribution, in its style and subject matter, in its successes and in its shortcomings, *Tire Dié* blazed a trail that the entire New Latin American Cinema movement would continue to explore.

The film begins with an aerial shot of the provincial city of Santa Fe, Argentina. A voice-of-God narrator (anonymous, omniscient) intones over these perspective-of-God images in a style reminiscent of traditional, authoritarian documentary. As conventional descriptive data (founding dates, population) give way to the less conventional (statistics concerning the number of streetlamps and hair-dressers), the parodistic intent becomes clear. The neat grid of organized neighborhoods gives way to random shanties, as the narrator declares, "Upon reaching the edge of the city, statistics become uncertain.... This is where, between four and five in the afternoon...during 1956, 1957, and 1958, the first Latin American social survey film was shot."

The railroad bridge which the aerial camera surveys just prior to the credits is the site of the first post-credit sequence. From-God's vantage point, the camera has descended to the eye-level of the children who congregate there every afternoon. A little boy in a closeup stares directly at the camera, then turns and runs out of the frame. Other children appear in closeup, looking and speaking at the camera in direct address. Their barely audible voices are overlaid with the studied dramatic diction of two adult narrators, male and female, who repeat what the children are saying. This initial sequence ends as the camera follows one of the boys home and "introduces" his mother and then other members of the community.

The primary expectation deferred and eventually fulfilled by the film's intricate structuration is the arrival of the long and anxiously awaited train to Buenos Aires. The interviews in which local residents discuss their economic plight are repeatedly intercut with shots back to the tracks and the growing number of children keeping their restless vigil there. The eventual climax of expectation (subjects' and viewers') has the bravest and fleetest of the children running alongside the passing train. As they balance precariously on the narrow, elevated bridge, their hands straining upward to catch any coin the passengers might toss in their direction, children's voices on the soundtrack chant hoarsely,- "Tire dié! Tire dié!" ("Toss me a dime!") The final shot holds on the solemn, soulful face of the three-year old, protected by his mother's embrace and her assertion that "he is too young to participate in the *tire dié.*"

The first product of the first Latin American documentary film school, the Escuela Documental de Santa Fe founded by Birri in 1956, *Tire Dié* was a collaborative effort the evolution and ethos of which recall the Italian neorealism of the post-war years and anticipate certain aspects of the direct cinema of the 1960's. After selecting theme and locale from preliminary photo-reportages, Birri divided 60 students into various groups, each of which was to concentrate on a particular inhabitant of the riverside squatters' community under study. With their single camera and cumbersome tape recorder, the group made daily visits during a two-year period to the marginal community where the film was set. All the residents of the riverside squatters' camp attended the film's premiere along with municipal and universitaly dignitaries. In response to consultations with the film's subjects and general audience questionnaires, the original 59-minute version was edited down to 33. A primitive mobile cinema kept the film circulating throughout the region.

Tire Dié exemplifies the attempt to democratize the documentary form by giving voice and image to sectors of a culture which had previously been ignored and suppressed. Given the film's obvious commitment to direct visual and verbal address, the intervention of the anonymous male and female mediator/narrators is unexpected and disconcerting. Investigation into the film's mode of production reveals that this expedient derives not from prior design but from deficiencies in the original sound recording. *Tire Dié* sought to give the effect of synchronous sound without the technical facilities to do so. The over-dubbing of social actors by professional actors is the central—but not the sole—contradiction of this social document: it brands a seminal attempt to democratize documentary discouse with the unwanted but unavoidable stamp of residual authoritarian anonymity, just as the intricate patterns of editing call assumptions of transparent realism into question. In its contradictions, as well as in its achievements, *Tie Dié* stands as a landmark of Latin American social documentary.

—Julianne Burton

TIREZ SUR LE PIANISTE. Shoot the Piano Player. Production: Films de la Pléiade; black and white, 35mm, in Dyaliscope; running time: 80 mins., English versions variously noted at 84 and 92 mins. Released 22 August 1960, Paris.

Produced by Pierre Braunberger; screenplay by François Truffaut and Marcel Moussy; from the novel *Down There* by David Goodis; English titles by Noelle Gillmor; directed by François Truffaut; photography by Raoul Coutard; edited by Claudine Bouché and Cécile Decugis; sound by Jacques Gallois; art direction by Jacques Mely; music by Georges Delerue, song "Dialogues d'amoureux" by Félix Leclerc and sung by Félix Leclerc and Lucienne Vernay, song "Vanille et framboise composed and sung by Bobby Lapointe; production supervised by Serge Komor.

Filmed 1 December 1959—15 January 1960, additional shooting in March 1960. Filmed in Paris at a café and at Rue Mussard, also in Levallois and Le Sappey, France.

Cast: Charles Aznavour (*Charlie Kohler/Edouard Saroyan*); Marie Dubois (*Lèna*); Nicole Berger (*Michèle Mercier*); Serge Devri (*Plyne*); Claude Mansard (*Momo*); Richard Kanayan (*Fido*); Albert Rémy (*Chico*); Jacques Aslanian (*Richard*); Daniel Boulanger (*Ernest*); Claude Heymann (*Lars Schmeel*); Alex Joffé (*Passerby who helps Chico*); Bobby Lapointe (*Singer in café*); Catherine Lutz (*Mammy*).

Publications:

Reviews—"Uncommitted Artist?" by Penelope Houston in *Sight and Sound* (London), spring 1961; review by Raymond Durgnat in *Films and Filming* (London), February 1961; "Scrambled Satire" by Bosley Crowther in *The New York Times*, 24 July 1962; review by Stanley Kauffmann in the *New Republic* (New York), 9 July 1962; review by Andrew Sarris in *The Village Voice* (New York), 26 July 1962; books—*Cinema Eye, Cinema Ear* by John Russell Taylor, New York 1964; *French Cinema Since 1946, Vol. II: The Personal Style* by Roy Armes, Cranbury, New Jersey 1966; *The Cinema of François Truffaut* by Graham Petrie, Cranbury, New Jersey 1970; *François Truffaut* by C.G. Crisp and Michael Walker, New York 1971; *L'Univers de François Truffaut* by Dominique Fanne, Paris 1972; *Focus on Shoot the Piano Player* edited by Leo Braudy, Englewood Cliffs, New Jersey 1972; *François Truffaut* by C.G. Crisp, London 1972; *Truffaut* by Don Allen, New York 1974; *The New Wave* by James Monaco, New York 1976; *Le Cinéma de François Truffaut* by Jean Collet, Paris 1977; *François Truffaut* Annette Insdorf, Boston 1978; articles—"J'ai voulu traiter *Tirez sur le pianiste* à la manière d'un conte de Perrault" by Yvonne Baby in *Le Monde* (Paris), 24 November 1960; "L'Âme du canon" by Pierre Kas in *Cahiers du cinéma* (Paris), January 1961; "Le Pianiste de Truffaut" by Marcel Martin in *Cinéma 61* (Paris), January 1961; "Cinema of Appearance" by Gabriel and Eric Rhode in *Sight and Sound* (London), autumn 1961; "The Point Sensible" by Jean-Paul Török in *Positif* (Paris), March 1961; "Entretien avec François Truffaut" by Jean Collet, Michel Delahaye, Jean-André Fieschi, Andre S. Labarthe, and Bertrand Tavernier in *Cahiers du cinéma* (Paris), December 1962; "Entretien avec François Truffaut" by Dan A. Cukier and Jo Gryn in *Script* (Paris), April 1962; "Cinéma 1967" by Jo Gryn in *Script* (Paris), April 1962; "François Truffaut: An Interview" by Paul Ronder in *Film Quarterly* (Berkeley), fall 1963; "François Truffaut: The Anarchist Imagination" by Judith Shatnoff in *Film Quarterly* (Berkeley), spring 1963; article by Pauline Kael in *Film Culture* (New York), winter 1962-63; "The Literary Sophistication of François Trufffaut" by Michael Klein in *Film Comment* (New York), summer 1965; "Au Coeur des paradoxes" by Jean-Louis Comolli in *Cahiers du cinéma* (Paris), May 1967; "Entretien avec François Truffaut" by Jean-Louis Comolli and Jean Narboni in

Cahiers du cinéma (Paris), May 1967; "Hommage à Truffaut à Annency" in *Cinéma 1967* (Paris), January 1967; "Chabrol and Truffaut" by Robin Wood in *Movie* (London), winter 1969-70; "A Man Can Serve 2 Masters" by David Bordwell in *Film Comment* (New York), spring 1971; "*Tirez sur le pianiste*" by N. Simsolo in *Image et son* (Paris), March 1972; "The Existential Play in Truffaut's Early Films" by A. Thiher in *Literature/Film Quarterly* (Salisbury, Maryland), summer 1977;. "*Tirez sur le pianiste*" by Don Dudley in *Cinema Texas Program Notes* (Austin), 2 March 1978.

* * *

François Truffaut's astonishing success in his debut, *The 400 Blows*, was unpredictable, but that film does follow in the tradition of autobiographical first works by young and terribly sincere artists. As Truffaut himself recognized, the second work is the real test, and for his test he chose a subject and a style utterly opposed to that of *400 Blows*. *Shoot the Piano Player* is distant from Truffaut's personal life, distant some would say from life in general; it is as much as possible a filmmaker's film. Drawn from a standard detective novel called *Down There* by David Goodis, the film played with the conventions of the genre and with the stylistic possibilities of the medium. Thought to be too recherché, it received no American distribution until after the success of *Jules and Jim* (1961), but since then it has become prized by many people as Truffaut's most inventive work.

It was Truffaut's plan to inject life into contemporary French cinema first by emulating the American cinema (hence, the gangster genre) and then by gleefully upsetting the conventions and good taste that in his view had rigidified the movies in his country.

He began with casting, purposefully giving the central role to the timid and introspective Charles Aznavour. Aznavour, already a successful singer, was not without screen experience: Truffaut had admired him in Franju's *Tête Contre les Murs*. No one would have suspected that he could play Charlie Kohler, alias Edouard Saroyan, a concert pianist turned honky-tonk loser, especially when cast alongside typical tough guy characters. Truffaut exploited the contradictions by making the subject of timidity central to the film and treating it as it had never been treated in the movies before.

His chief gangsters came right out of the cartoon strips. Their tight-lipped argot is interrupted by long disquisitions about female sexuality and the unforgettable throwaway anecdote about a steel-fabric necktie. Truffaut embedded countless jokes and citations within his tale. Lars Schmeel. the lecherous impresario, is named for Lars Schmidt, the man who took Ingrid Bergman away from Rossellini, one of Truffaut's friends and heroes. Chico, Charlie's older brother, is named after Chico Marx. But far more than placing disruptive elements within a conventional story, Traffaut went out of his way to find a new way to tell such a story, to tell in fact a new kind of story.

In its first sequence *Shoot the Piano Player* announces the indirection of its method. Chico, chased down a dark street by an unseen car, runs into a lightpost and is knocked out. The first incongruity (crashing into the only bright object around) is replaced by a second as he is helped to his feet by a passerby. The chase is forgotten in a lengthy conversation about sexual fidelity and the joys of marriage. We will never see this "extra" again, but he has set the film on its way, interrupting its suspense with a tale about tenderness and love. The film as a whole proceeds in just this way: overly serious speeches (and even voice-overs) are cut short by ridiculous sub-actions (Clarisse tempting a client; the

poor mug who owns the bar getting chummy with Charlie as he tries to choke him to death).

Visually, as Roger Greenspun has noted, the film alternates blacks and whites like the keyboard which is its central image. Gangsters are funny, the heroine tells dirty jokes, milk poured on the car obscures the vision of the driver, snow on the windshield is alternately black or white depending on the sun's position.

The changes of mood that punctuate the story are actually central to its structure, for in the middle of this comic melodrama, an interior flashback gives us the tragic tale of Edouard's rise to fame and the suicide of his wife. Life itself is shown to be full of impossible shifts in fortune and feeling. It is all one big joke.

By the film's end Truffaut succeeds in bringing poignancy to the most trite of love stories through the incongruous juxtapositions of his style. Fame, obscurity, suicide, love, murder, robbery, and a whole family saga are woven together in 85 minutes under the routine theme song Charlie plays in the bar. Life is seen to be bigger than any of its events, bigger than the bitter end to which it leads all of us. Truffaut doesn't believe in his tale, but he does believe in the emotions it brings up in the powers of cinema to evoke those emotions. In mixing genres and moods and in vigorously exploring powers of elliptical editing, fluid cinemascope, and lyrical music, *Shoot the Piano Player* exalts such power and remains a delight to watch. Beyond parody, its sincerity is the love Truffaut feels for the movies. That sincerity is infectious.

—Dudley Andrew

TO BE OR NOT TO BE. Production: Alexander Korda Productions; 1942; black and white, 35mm; running time: 100 mins. Released March 1942 by United Artists.

Produced by Ernst Lubitsch, presented by Alexander Korda; screenplay by Edwin Justus Mayer; from a screen story by Ernst Lubitsch and Melchior Lengyel (uncredited); directed by Ernst Lubitsch; photography by Rudolph Maté; edited by Dorothy Spencer; sound by Frank Maher; production design by Vincent Korda, associate art direction by J. MacMillan Johnson, interior decoration by Julia Heron; music score by Werner Heyman; special effects by Lawrence Butler; Miss Lombard's costumes designed by Irene; technical supervision by Richard Ordynski; make-up by Gordan Bau.

Cast: Carole Lombard (*Maria Tura*); Jack Benny (*Josef Tura*); Robert Stack (*Lieutenant Stanislav Sobinski*); Felix Bressart (*Greenberg*); Lionel Atwill (*Rawitch*); Stanley Ridges (*Professor Alexander Siletsky*); Sig Rumann (*Colonel Ehrhardt*); Tom Dugan (*Bronski*); Charles Halton (*Dobosh*); Peter Caldwell (*Wilhelm*). Helmut Dantine and Otto Reichow (*Co-pilots*); Miles Mander (*Major Cunningham*); George Lynn (*Actor-adjutant*); Henry Victor (*Captain Schultz*); Maude Eburne (*Anna the maid*); Armand Wright (*Make-up man*); Erno Verebes (*Stage manager*); Halliwell Hobbes (*General Armstrong*); Leslie Dennison (*Captain*); Frank Reicher (*Polish official*); Wolfgang Zilzer (*Man in bookstore*); Olaf Hytten (*Polonius—in Warsaw*); Charles Irwin and Leyland Hodgson (*Reporters*); Alec Craig and James Finlayson (*Scottish farmers*); Edgar Licho (*Prompter*); Robert O. David (*Gestapo Sergeant*); Roland Varno (*Pilot*); Maurice Murphy, Gene Rizzi, Paul Barrett, and John Kellogg (*R.A.F. Flyers*); Sven-Hugo Borg (*German soldier*).

Publications:

Review—by James Shelley Hamilton in *National Board of Review* magazine (New York), March 1942; books—*An Index to the Films of Ernst Lubitsch* by Theodore Huff, index series, British Film Institute 1947; *Ernst Lubitsch* by Mario Verdone, Lyon 1964; *The Comic Mind* by Gerald Mast, New York 1973; *From Reverence to Rape* by Molly Haskell, New York 1974; *The Great Spy Pictures* by James Robert Parish and Michael Pitts, Metuchen, New Jersey 1974; *The Hollywood Exiles* by John Baxter, New York 1976; *The Cinema of Ernst Lubitsch: The Hollywood Films* by Leland Poague, London 1977; *The Lubitsch Touch: A Critical Study* by Herman Weinberg, 3rd revised edition, New York 1977; *Ernst Lubitsch: A Guide to References and Resources* by R. Carringer and B. Sabath, Boston 1978; *The Cinema of Ernst Lubitsch* by Leland Poague, South Brunswick, New Jersey 1978; articles—in *The New York Times*, 29 March 1942; special Lubitsch section in *La Revue du cinéma* (Paris), September 1948; "A Tribute to Ernst Lubitsch" by Herman Weinberg in *Films in Review* (New York), August/-September 1951; "The Films of Ernst Lubitsch", special issue of *Film Journal* (New York), June 1959; "Carole Lombard" by Homer Dickens in *Films in Review* (New York), February 1961; special Lubitsch feature in *Cahiers du cinéma* (Paris), February 1968; "Theater Film Life" by G. Petrie in *Film Comment* (New York), May/June 1974; "*To Be Or Not To Be*" by Courtenay Beinhorn in *Cinema Texas Program Notes* (Austin), 5 December 1977; "Deux Fictions de la haine" by J.L. Comolli in *Cahiers du cinéma* (Paris), July/August 1978; "De Führer ('Heil Myself') op de hak genomen door Ernst Lubitsch: *To Be or Not To Be*" by C. Boost in *Skoop* (Amsterdam), December/January 1978; "Take Two: *To Be Or Not To Be*" by A. Insdorf in *American Film* (Washington, D.C.), November 1979; "*To Be Or Not To Be*" by John Cocchi in *Magill's Survey of Cinema, Vol. IV* edited by Frank N. Magill, Englewood Cliffs, New Jersey 1980.

*   *   *

To Be or Not to Be came late in Ernst Lubitsch's successful Hollywood career, but by the very nature of its subject it caused him considerable trouble. It must be remembered that Lubitsch was Jewish and would in any case have been under heavy pressure to leave Germany after January 1933 had he not already done so ten years earlier, and in *To Be or Not to Be* he and his Hungarian-Jewish producer, Alexander Korda of Britain, were very conscious of what they were doing. In advocating that Chaplin seek to debunk Hitler through satiric impersonation Korda had originally inspired him to make *The Great Dictator* (1940); now as produecr of *To Be or Not to Be* he backed Lubitsch's idea (scripted by Edwin Justus Mayer) to render the Nazi image ludicrous in a story set in German-occupied Warsaw.

Since by the time of the film's release the dire sufferings of the Polish people under occupation were well known, it was widely felt that to make their situation the setting for a farcical comedy felt that to make their situation the setting for a farcial comedy (however sophisticated in concept) was a grave lack of taste, especially as some of the key comic characters involved were rather sentimentalized Polish-Jewish types, members of a celebrated theatrical company headed by the Turas, Maria (Carole Lombard) and her husband Joseph (Jack Benny), an actor of inordinate vanity. However, this company turn themselves into a centre for Polish resistance against the Nazis and, using their talents for disguise and impersonation, not only penetrate the Gestapo's stronghold (commanded by the ridiculous Colonel Ehrhardt, played by the German emigré comedian, Sig Rumann) but also manoeuvre their group escape from Poland by the daring device of impersonating Hitler himself and his entourage on an official visit to Warsaw—they have an actor who, given the necessary moustache and hairstyle, closely resembles the Führer.

The film in fact rapidly alternates between sheer farce and a comedy of intrigue in which the Turas are to the fore in their dealings with the Germans, Maria through deception, exploiting her sophisticated charm, Joseph through his (Jack Benny's) remarkable talent for caricature and deadpan humor. In *To Be or Not to Be* (the title comes from Joseph Tura's obsession with playing Hamlet) the Nazis are not only throughly taken in but also represented as being totally absurd, though the early scenes of the destruction of Warsaw and the occupation by the German army are presented quite straight, as in any serious war film.

When the inevitable critical attack came, Lubitsch replied on 29 March 1942 in the *New York Times*, defending himself against the accusation of lack of taste:

> Fortunately, I am not the only one accused of that crime. My co-defendant is the American motion picture audience.... Why...do audiences laugh during *To Be or Not to Be*, and at times very heartily? Aren't they aware of what happened to Poland? Did I try to make them look at the Polish background through those rose-colored glasses.? Nothing of the kind. I went out of my way to remind them of the destruction of the Nazi conquest, of the terror regime of the Gestapo.... Do I minimize their danger because I refrained from the most obvious methods in their characterization? Is whipping and flogging the only way of expressing terrorism? No, the American audiences don't laugh at those Nazis because they underestimate their menace, but they are happy to see this new order and its ideology being ridiculed.

The film's reception was also inevitably darkened by the death of Carole Lombard in a plane crash early in 1942.

—Roger Manvell

TO HAVE AND HAVE NOT. Production: Warner Bros. Pictures Corp.; 1944; black and white, 35mm; running time: 100 mins. Released October 1944.

Produced by Howard Hawks; screenplay by Jules Furthman and William Faulkner; from the novel by Ernest Hemingway; directed by Howard Hawks; photography by Sid Hickox; edited by Christian Nyby; sound by Oliver S. Garretson; art direction by Charles Novi, set decorations by Casey Roberts; music by Franz Waxman (non-credited), music direction by Leo F. Forbstein; song "Am I Blue" by Harry Akst with lyrics by Grant Drake; song "How Little We Know" by Hoagy Carmichael with lyrics by Johnny Mercer; song "Hong Kong Blues" by Hoagy Carmichael; special effects by Roy Davidson and Rex Wimpy; costumes designed by Milo Anderson; technical consultant: Louis Comien.

Cast: Humphrey Bogart (*Harry Morgan*); Walter Brennan (*Eddy*); Lauren Bacall (*Marie Browning*); Dolores Moran (*Helene de Bursac*); Hoagy Carmichael (*Cricket*); Walter Molnar (*Paul de Bursac*); Sheldon Leonard (*Lieutenant Coyo*); Marcel Dalio (*Frenchy, or Gerard*); Walter Sande (*Johnson*); Dan Seymour (*Captain Reynard*); Aldo Nadi (*Renard's bodyguard); Paul Marion (*Beauclerc*); Pat West (*Bartender*); Emmet Smith (*Emil*); Sir Lancelot (*Horatio*); Janette Grae (*Rosalie*); Eugene Borden (*Quartermaster*); Elzie Emanuel and Harold Garrison (*Negro children*); Pedro Regas (*Civilian*); Major Fred Farrell (*Headwaiter*); Adrienne d'Ambricourt (*Cashier*); Maurice Marsac, Fred Dosch, George Suzanne, Louis Mercier, and Crane Whitley (*De Gaullists*).

Publications:

Script—*To Have and Have Not* by Jules Furthman and William Faulkner, edited with an introduction by Bruce F. Kawin, Madison, Wisconsin; review—"*Le Port de l'Angoisse*: La presse" in *Avant-Scène du cinéma* (Paris), January 1973; books—*The Cinema of Howard Hawks* by Peter Bogdanovich, New York 1962; *Bogey: The Films of Humphrey Bogart* by Clifford McCarty, New York 1965; *Humphrey Bogart: The Man and His Films* by Paul Michael, Indianapolis, Indiana 1965; *Howard Hawks* by Jean-Claude Missiaen, Paris 1966; *Howard Hawks* by Robin Wood, London 1968, revised 1977; *Howard Hawks* by Jean A. Gili, Paris 1971; *Humphrey Bogart* by Alan G. Barbour, New York 1973; *Bogart and Bacall* by Joe Hyams, New York 1975; *Howard Hawks, Storyteller* by Gerald Mast, New York 1982; articles—"Howard Hawks" by Jacques Rivette and François Truffaut in *Films in Review* (New York), November 1956; "Humphrey Bogart" by Clifford McCarty in *Films in Review* (New York), May 1957; "The World of Howard Hawks" (in 2 parts) by Andrew Sarris in *Films and Filming* (London), July 1962 and August 1962; "Howard Hawks" by Peter Bogdanovich, Jacques Rivette, Mark Shivas, V.F. Perkins, and Robin Wood in *Movie* (London), December 1962; issue on Hawks of *Cahiers du cinéma* (Paris), January 1963; article by Harris Dienstfry in *Film Culture* (New York), fall 1964; "Hawks at Warner Brothers" by G. Peary and S. Groark in the *Velvet Light Trap* (Madison, Wisconsin), June 1971; "*Le Port de l'Angoisse*" (includes synopsis, about the script, shooting, etc.) in *Avant-Scène du cinéma* (Paris), January 1973; "To Have Written and Have Not Directed" by Robin Wood in *Film Comment* (New York), May/June 1973; "People Who Need People" by R.T. Jameson in *Movietone News* (Seattle), April 1975; "*Le Port de l'angoisse*" by C. Bosseno in *Revue du cinéma* (Paris), series 23, 1979; "Hawks' sorg vour Lauren Bacall" (with shot analysis) by W. Verstappen in *Skoop* (Wageningen, Netherlands), August 1979; "Review Essay" by T. E. Scheurer in *Journal of Popular Film* (Bowling Green, Ohio), summer 1981.

*   *   *

According to Howard Hawks, the genesis of *To Have and Have Not* occurred when he was on a fishing trip with Ernest Hemingway: Hawks told the author that he could make a good movie out of even his worst novel. When asked which that was, Hawks replied without hesitation. Whether *To Have and Have Not* is Hemingway's worst novel is open to debate (the competition is formidable); it certainly provided the starting-point for one of Hawks's finest films.

Scarcely more than a starting-point, however: Hawks virtually abandons the novel after the film's first ten minutes. His Harry and Marie bear only minimal resemblance to Hemingway's (indeed, Marie none at all), and it is significant that even their names are dropped (in their celebrated duologues) in favour of "Steve" and "Slim." There are, in fact, a number of more impor-

tant determinants at work on the film than Hemingway's novel, and by no means all these are directly related to Hawks. The film is influenced, for example, by the "house style" developed by Warners in the 1930's and 40's, a style that contrasts markedly with those encouraged by, say, MGM or Paramount: a preference for toughness over glamour, an emphasis on topicality and a form of "social realism," low-key, film noir-ish lighting. Its date is important: it is one of a large number of "commitment" films in which the defiantly uncommitted hero (sometimes heroine) learns to join the fight against Fascism. One of the most spectacularly successful of these "commitment" films had been *Casablanca* (also Warners, also starring Bogart), and the scenario of *To Have and Have Not* certainly owes far more, in its main lines, to Curtiz's film than to the Hemingway novel. The presence of Jules Furthman as screenwriter also has its significance. Hawks himself said in interviews that the film was related to von Sternberg's *Morocco* (especially through the characters played by Marlene Dietrich and Lauren Bacall respectively); it also relates (more obviously and more closely) to Hawks's own *Only Angels Have Wings*. Both films were scripted by Furthman.

Yet *To Have and Have Not* belongs firmly in the Hawks canon: its particularities of tone, acting, plot development, ideological position, are unthinkable without his presence. It would be extremely interesting to compare at length the films Furthman wrote for von Sternberg with the films he wrote for Hawks: there are undeniable resemblances, in the action, dialogue and characterization, yet the personal inflections the two directors brought to Furthman's material are sufficiently marked and decisive to justify one of the primary tenets of auteur theory, that the director is the real author of the film. Under Hawks, in fact, all the complex determinants are assimilated and transformed. The gross sexism of Hemingway's novel (in which Marie's sole function is to adore Harry Morgan's potency) is transformed, in the inexhaustibly engaging, semi-improvised Bogart/Bacall "duets," into one of the Hollywood cinema's most provocative male-female relationships. The Warners lighting is subsumed into Hawk's characteristic image, the little circle of light amid the surrounding darkness. The patriotic theme is re-thought in strikingly personal terms: Harry Morgan joins the war effort because "I like you and I don't like them." The idealized romantic uplift of *Casablanca*, with its emphasis on sacrifice and renunciation, is transformed into the resilience and pragmatism of Hawksian relationships ("Maybe it's just for a day," as the Bacall/Hoagy Carmichael song puts it). It is the kind of film that triumphantly resolves the common auteurist quandary in the most positive way: *To Have and Have Not* is at once totally Hollywood and totally Hawks.

—Robin Wood

TOKYO MONOGATARI. Tokyo Story. Production: Shochiku/Ofuna; color, 35mm; running time: 136 mins.; length: 12,509 feet. Released 3 November 1953, Tokyo.

Produced by Takeshi Yamamoto; screenplay by Yasujiro Ozu and Kogo Nada; directed by Yasujiro Ozu; photography by Yuhara Atsuta. edited by Yoshiyasu Hamamura; sound by Yoshisaburo Sueo; production design by Tatsuo Hamada with Itsuo Takahashi; music by Takanori Saito, (some sources list Takanobu Saito); costumes designed by Taizo Saito.

Cast: Chishu Ryu (*Father*); Chieko Higashiyama (*Mother*); So Yamamura (*Koichi*); Haruko Sugimura (*Shige Kaneko*); Setsuko Hara (*Noriko*); Kyoko Kagawa (*Kyoko*); Shiro Osaka (*Keizo*); Eijiro Tono (*Sanpei Numata*); Kuniko Miyake (*Fumiko*); Nobuo Nakamura (*Kurazo Kaneko*); Teruko Nagaoka (*Yone Hattori*); Zen Murase (*Minoru*); Mitsuhiro Mori (*Isamu*); Hisao Toake (*Osamu Hattori*); Toyoko Takahashi (*Shukichi Hirayama's neighbor*); Mutsuko Sakura (*Patron of the Oden restaurant*); Toru Abe (*Railroad employee*); Sachiko Mitani (*Noriko's neighbor*); Junko Anan (*Assistant in beauty salon*); Yoshiko Togawa and Ryoko Mizuki (*Clients in the beauty salon*).

Publications:

Scripts—*Tokyo Story* translated and edited by Donald Richie and Eric Klestadt in *Contemporary Japanese Literature* edited by Howard Hibbett, New York 1977; "*Voyage a Tokyo*" by Kogo Noda and Yasujiro Ozu in *Avant-Scène du cinéma* (Paris), 15 March 1978; review—"La Presse" in *Avant-Scène du cinéma* (Paris), 15 March 1978; books—*The Japanese Film: Art and Industry* by Donald Richie and Joseph Anderson, New York 1960; *5 Pictures of Yasujiro Ozu* by Donald Richie, Tokyo 1962; *The Japanese Movie: An Illustrated History* by Donald Richie, Palo Alto, California 1966; *Japanese Cinema: Film Style and National Character* by Donald Richie, New York 1971; *Ozu-Hito to Shigoto* (*Ozu-The Man and His Work*) edited by Jun Satomi, Tomo Shimogawara, and Shizuo Yamauchi, Tokyo 1972; *Transcendental Style in Film* by Paul Schrader, Berkeley 1972; *Masters of Japanese Cinema* edited by Leonard Schrader and Haruji Nakamura, New York 1974-75; *Ozu* by Donald Richie, Berkeley 1974; *Japanese Film Directors* by Audie Bock, New York 1978; *Cinema, The Magic Vehicle: A Guide to Its Achievement: Journey Two* edited by Jacek Klinwoski and Adam Garbicz, Metuchen, New Jersey 1979; articles—by Earl Miner in *Quarterly of Film, Radio, and Television* (Berkeley), summer 1956; article by Lindsay Anderson in *Sight and Sound* (London), winter 1957-58; "The Family of Ozu" by Robert Hatch in *The Nation* (New York), 22 June 1964; "Yasujiro Ozu" by Chishu Ryu in *Sight and Sound* (London), spring 1964; article by Gordon Gow in *Films and Filming* (London), July 1965; article by Robin Wood in *Movie* (London), summer 1965; "Ozu on Ozu" in *Cinéma* (Paris), summer 1970; "Ozu Spectrum" in *Cinéma* (Paris), summer 1970; "Ozu" by Manny Farber in *Artforum* (New York), June 1970; "Ozu on Ozu" in *Cinéma* (Paris), summer 1971; "Yasujiro Ozu: A Biographical Filmography" by Donald Richie in *Film Comment* (New York), spring 1971; article by N.S. Memon in *Take One* (Montreal), May/June 1971; "Yasujiro Ozu" by Max Tessier in *Anthologie du cinéma* (Paris), July/October 1971; "A Masterpiece" by Stanley Kauffmann in the *New Republic* (New York), 18 March 1972; "*Tokyo Story*" by N.S. Memon in *Take One* (Montreal), July 1972; "Ozu on Ozu" in *Cinéma* (Paris), winter 1972-73; "Le Temps s'est arrêté" by Max Tessier in *Avant-Scène du cinéma* (Paris), 15 March 1978; "A la découverte d'Ozu" by J. Bonnet in *Cinématographe* (Paris), February 1978; "Voyage à Tokyo" by G. Gauthier in *Image et son* (Paris), April 1978; "*Voyage à Tokyo*" by M. Martin in *Ecran* (Paris), February 1978; "*Voyage à Tokyo*" by Robin Wood in *Positif* (Paris), February 1978; "Space and Narrative in *Tokyo Story*" by D. J. Konshak in *Film Criticism* (Edinboro, Pennsylvania), spring 1980; "*Tokyo Story*" by H. Hosman in *Skoop* (Amsterdam), September 1980; "Yasujiro Ozu" by Donald Richie in *Cinema, A Critical Dictionary* edited by Richard Roud, London 1980.

TOL'ABLE DAVID. Production: Inspiration Pictures for First National; 1921; black and white, 35mm, silent; running time: about 80 mins. at 24 fps. Released 1921.

Screenplay by Henry King and Edmund Goulding; from the novel by Joseph Hergesheimer; directed by Henry King; photography by Henry Cronjager.

Cast: Richard Barthelmess (*David Kinemon*); Gladys Hulette (*Esther Hatburn*); Walter P. Lewis (*Iscah Hatburn*); Ernest Torrence (*Luke Hatburn*); Ralph Blausfield (*Luke's brother*); Forrest Robinson (*Grandpa Hatburn*); Laurence Eddinger (*Senator Gault*); Edmund Gurney (*David's father*); Warner Richmond (*Allen, David's brother*); Marion Abbot (*David's mother*); Harry Hallam (*Doctor*).

Publications:

Books—*Film Technique* by V.I. Pudovkin, London 1933; *Gentlemen to the Rescue: The Heroes of the Silent Screen* by Kalton C. Lahue, New York 1972; *The Hollywood Professionals—Vol. 2: Henry King, Lewis Milestone, Sam Wood* by Clive Denton, Kingsley Canham, and Tony Thomas, New York 1974; *American Silent Film* by William K. Everson, New York 1978; articles—interview with Henry King by M. Cheatham in *Motion Picture Classic* (Brooklyn), March 1921; "Richard Barthelmess" by Jack Jacobs in *Films in Review* (New York), January 1958; "The Life and Films of Henry King" by Charles Shibuk and Christopher North in *Films in Review* (New York), October 1958; "Henry King" by G.J. Mitchell in *Films in Review* (New York), June/July 1964; "*Tol'able David*" by Eileen Bowser and Arthur Knight in *Film Notes* edited by Eileen Bowser, New York 1969; "The Tough Race" by Roy Pickard in *Films and Filming* (London), September 1971; "*Tol'able David*" by Tom Milne in *Monthly Film Bulletin* (London), March 1975.

* * *

Tol'able David could have been a D.W. Griffith production, with Charles Ray in the lead. Its setting and storyline mirror the kind of films Griffith was making in 1921; the hero is a boyish country lad, a characterization that Ray had then mastered. However, director Henry King and star Richard Barthelmess acquit themselves most auspiciously. Barthelmess' presence here is magical; King will never be labelled a great director, but the film is one of his few enduring efforts.

Tol'able David is a timeless slice of Americana, precisely reflecting the era in which it was made in that it celebrates a pre-urbanized America, a young and thriving nation, the cornerstone of which was honesty, religion, the work ethic, and family unity. The characters are unsophisticated mountain folk, with modest values, goals and triumphs. The hero is the youngest son in a large family whose one wish is, simply, to "drive the mail." His older brother has been entrusted with the responsibility. But, when a trio of savage outlaws cripple the brother for life and shoot the father, our hero must take on a man's obligations. He is allowed to carry mail just once, and completes the task despite the harassment of the heavies.

The film is simply, poignantly constructed by its maker. *Tol'able David* is leisurely paced, with lovely cinematography and panoramic shots of the countryside. King, born in the aptly-named town of Christianburg, Virginia, was reared in an environment similar to the film's setting, and utilized his childhood memories to instill a fresh, realistic atmosphere.

D.W. Griffith initially owned the property rights to *Tol'able David*, and supposedly even prepared a scenario. But he might have decided that the story was too similar to his *Way Down East*, made a year before *Tol'able David* and also starring Barthelmess. The actor, in the process of establishing his own production company, acquired it from Griffith. With King, he formed Inspiration Pictures, and *Tol'able David* was their first production. Like *Way Down East*, it was remade as a talkie in the 1930's. Neither clicked at the box office as they had earlier: even provincial audiences were by then demanding far more sophisticated fare.

The film is easily the most successful incarnation of Henry King's most characteristic theme: life in rural America and specifically, young boys coming of age amid Main Streets and swimming holes. A representative number of King's credits are set in country locales, including *State Fair* (with Will Rogers), the remake of *Way Down East*, *Chad Hanna*, *I'd Climb the Highest Mountain* and *Wait Till the Sun Shines Nellie*. And, with *Way Down East* and *Broken Blossoms*, the film is Richard Barthelmess's best-loved credit. In all three, the actor offers quietly poignant characterizations that enthralled critics and audiences. In each, his presence seems almost spiritual.

Tol'able David is a uniquely American movie, and a depiction of a place and time that is now forever a part of history.

—Rob Edelman

TOP HAT. Production: RKO Radio Pictures, Inc.; 1935; black and white, 35mm; running time: 105 mins. Released 6 September 1935.

Produced by Pandro Berman; screenplay by Dwight Taylor and Allan Scott, adapted by Karl Noti; from a play by Alexander Farago and Aladar Laszlo; directed by Mark Sandrich. photography by David Abel and Vernon Walker; edited by William Hamilton; art direction by Van Nest Polglase, sets designed and decorated by Carrol Clark; music and lyrics by Irving Berlin; costumes designed by Bernard Newman; choreographed by Fred Astaire with Hermes Pan.

Filmed in RKO studios.

Cast: Fred Astaire (*Jerry Travers*); Ginger Rogers (*Dale Tremont*); Edward Everett Horton (*Horace Hardwick*); Helen Broderick (*Madge Hardwick*); Erik Rhodes (*Alberto*); Eric Blore (*Bates*); Donald Meek (*Curate*); Florence Roberts (*Curate's wife*); Gino Corrado (*Hotel manager*); Peter Hobbs (*Call boy*).

Publications:

Review—by Andre Sennwald in *The New York Times*, 30 August 1935; books—*Steps in Time* by Fred Astaire, New York 1959; *All Talking! All Singing! All Dancing! A Pictorial History of the Movie Musical* by John Springer, New York 1966; *Hollywood in the Thirties* by John Baxter, New York 1968; *Fred Astaire: A Pictorial Treasury of His Films* by Howard Thompson, New York 1970; *Fred Astaire and His Work* by Alfons Hackl, Vienna 1970; *The Hollywood Musical* by John Russell Taylor and Arthur Jackson, New York 1971; *We're in the Money: Depression America and Its Films* by Andrew Bergman, New York 1971; *The Fred Astaire and Ginger Rogers Book* by Arlene Croce, New York 1972; *Starring Fred Astaire* by Stanley Green and Burt Goldblatt, New York 1973; *Fred Astaire* by Benny Green, London 1979; *Fred Astaire* by Gilles Cebe, Paris 1981; *The Hollywood Musical* by Ted Sennett, New York 1981; articles—"Actor-Dancer Attacks His Part: Fred Astaire" by M. Eustis in *Theater Arts* (New York), May 1937; "Fred Astaire's Film Career" by Gerald Pratley in *Films in Review* (New York), January 1957; "Two Feet in the Air" by Derek Conrad in *Films and Filming* (London), December 1959; "*Top Hat*" by Jefferson Grieves in *Films and Filming* (London), October 1962; "Ginger Rogers" by Homer Dickens in *Films in Review* (New York), March 1966; "*Top Hat*" by Julia Johnson in *Magill's Survey of Cinema, Vol. IV* edited by Frank N. Magill, Englewood Cliffs, New Jersey 1980; "The Filmed Dances of Fred Astaire" by J. Mueller in *Quarterly Review of Film Studies*, spring 1981.

*   *   *

Top Hat was the fourth film made by Fred Astaire and Ginger Rogers for RKO/Radio and the first film written especially to showcase their own unique talents on the screen. In *Flying Down to Rio* (1933) their first film together, Astaire and Rogers were the second leads to Dolores Del Rio and Gene Raymond, but the screen chemistry created when they danced together made them the ultimate "stars" of that film. Their next two films, *The Gay Divorce* (1934) and *Roberta* (1935), were adapted from successful stage plays with some alteration to suit the Astaire-Rogers combination. By 1935, when *Top Hat* was released, they were such established stars that RKO hired no less a figure than Irving Berlin to write a new score to accompany the Dwight Taylor and Allan Scott screenplay. Although the plot is run of the mill and displays the usual "boy meets girl" twists of most of the Astaire-Rogers films, the score is one of the best they ever worked with. It includes such now standard songs as "Isn't It a Lovely Day (To Be Caught in the Rain)?", "Cheek to Cheek," and the title song, "Top Hat," which has become synonymous with the image of Fred Astaire.

As with all of their films together, *Top Hat* is both musical and a story with music. A pure musical has only musical numbers that somehow advance or explicate the plot; the story with music has songs that may be interpolated to entertain the audience yet do not affect the story at all. The title number for *Top Hat* is an interpolation: Astaire, as Jerry Travers, is a musical star, so the audience sees him performing on stage, and although it is a magnificent example of the inimitable Astaire style, the "Top Hat" number does not give any information about the character or the plot. As Astaire and/or Rogers frequently played characters who are entertainers, their audience was given ample opportunity to see the stars dancing without the necessity of tying the number to the storyline.

In *Top Hat* the memorable of the musical numbers that advances the plot is "Cheek to Cheek," perhaps the single most beautiful popular dance for two performers ever filmed. Astaire and Rogers were always cool, perfectly groomed and the essence of 1930's sophistication. The grace and symmetry of their bodies, set against the sleek black-and-white Art Deco set created by Carrol Clark (under the titular direction of Van Nest Polglase), were perfect expressions of the music. In the sequence Travers entices Dale Tremont (Ginger Rogers) into the dance to win her love. Dale, who thinks that Jerry is married to her best friend Madge Hardwick (Helen Broderick), is at first reluctant. Eventually, though, the romance of the dance and her attraction to Jerry cannot be overcome, and by the midpoint she participates fully. The refrain of the song, "Heaven, I'm in Heaven" is illuminated not only by the dance and the set, but also by the graceful beauty of Rogers' ostrich feather dress. Although there have been many published reports of fights on the set over the unwieldiness of the dress, it is definitely an asset.

There are other important dances in the film, the most memorable of which is the casual, yet sophisticated, tap dance "Isn't It a Lovely Day (To Be Caught in the Rain)." The style of this dance is happy, flippant, and fun—the complete opposite of the more involved "Cheek to Cheek" dance in which the principals are troubled by their love. In this number, even the rain is a joke, and the stars are all smiles after a brief hesitancy on the part of Rogers. In "Cheek to Cheek" even the beauty of the dance cannot make Rogers smile, and the conclusion seems bittersweet.

Fred Astaire and Ginger Rogers went on to make five more successful films for RKO in the late 1930's and one more, less successful, film in 1948, *The Barkleys of Broadway*, for MGM. (Ironically, although their last film was the only one to be produced in color, in terms of style it is the most colorless.) Their populariy was a mainstay for RKO in the 1930's, and their reception by both critics and the public alike have barely diminished over the decades.

—Patricia King Hanson

TOUCH OF EVIL. Production: Universal-International; 1958; black and white, 35mm; running time: 95 mins., also variously noted at 105 and 115 mins. Released 21 May 1958.

Produced by Albert Zugsmith; screenplay by Orson Welles; from the novel *Badge of Evil* by Whitt Masterson; directed by Orson Welles, additional scenes by Harry Keller; photography by Russell Metty; edited by Virgil M. Vogel and Aaron Stell; sound by Leslie I. Carey and Frank Wilkinson; art direction by Alexander Golitzen and Robert Clatworthy, set decoration by Russell A. Gausman and John P. Austin; music by Henry Mancini, music directed by Joseph Gershenson; costumes designed by Bill Thomas.

Filmed spring 1957 in Venice, California.

Cast: Charlton Heston (*Ramon Miguel "Mike" Vargas*); Janet Leigh (*Susan Vargas*); Orson Welles (*Hank Quinlan*); Joseph Calleia (*Pete Menzies*); Akim Tamiroff (*Uncle Joe Grandi*); Joanna Moore (*Marcia Linnekar*); Marlene Dietrich (*Tanya*); Ray Collins (*Adair*); Dennis Weaver (*Motel manager*); Victor Millan (*Manolo Sanchez*); Lalo Rios (*Rio*); Valentin de Vargas (*Pancho*); Mort Mills (*Schwartz*); Mercedes McCambridge (*Hoodlum*); Wayne Taylor, Ken Miller, Raymond Rodriguez (*Gang members*); Michael Sargent (*Pretty Boy*); Zsa Zsa Gabor (*Owner of nightclub*); Keenan Wynn (*Man*); Joseph Cotten (*Detective*); Phil Harvey (*Blaine*); Joi Lansing (*Blonde*); Harry Shannon (*Gould*); Rusty Wescoatt (*Casey*); Arlene McQuade (*Ginnie*); Domenick Delgarde (*Lackey*); Joe Basulto (*Hoodlum*); Jennie Dias (*Jackie*); Yolanda Bojorquez (*Bobbie*); Eleanor Corado (*Lia*).

Publications:

Reviews—by Jean Domarchi in *Cahiers du cinéma* (Paris), July 1958; review by Georges Sadoul in *Les Lettres françaises* (Paris), 12 June 1958; review by François Truffaut in *Arts* (Paris), 4 June 1958; review by Arthur Knight in *Saturday Review* (New York), 7 June 1958; books—*The Cinema of Orson Welles* by Peter Bogdanovich, New York 1961; *Orson Welles* by Maurice Bessy, *Cinéma d'aujourd'hui* series, Paris 1963; *The Cinema of Orson Welles* by Peter Cowie, London 1965; *The Films of Orson Welles* by Charles Higham, Berkeley 1971; *Orson Welles* by Maurice Bessy, New York 1971; *Interviews with Film Directors* edited by Andrew Sarris, New York 1971; *Orson Welles* by Joseph McBride, London 1972; *A Ribbon of Dreams* by Peter Cowie, New York 1973; *American Film Genres* by Stuart Kaminsky, Dayton, Ohio 1974; *Kings of the Bs: Working Within the Hollywood System* edited by Todd McCarthy and Charles Flynn, New York 1975; *Orson Welles: Actor and Director* by J. McBride, New York 1977; *Orson Welles: A Critical View* by André Bazin, translated by Jonathan Rosenbaum, New York 1978; *The Magic World of Orson Welles* by J. Naremore, New York 1978; *Film Noir* edited by Alain Silver and Elizabeth Ward, Woodstock, New York 1979; *Questions of Cinema* by Stephen Heath, Bloomington, Indiana 1981; articles—"L'Oeuvre d'Orson Welles" in *Cahiers du cinéma* (Paris), September 1958; interview with Welles in *Cahiers du cinéma* (Paris), June 1958; interview with Welles in *Les Lettres françaises* (Paris), 20 May 1958; "The Heroes of Welles" by Alan Stanbrook" in *Film* (London), no.28, 1961; article by Jean-Claude Allais in *Premier Plan* (Lyon, France), March 1961; "Orson Welles: Of Time and Loss" by William Johnson in *Film Quarterly* (Berkeley), fall 1967; "*Touch of Evil*" by Terry Comito in *Film Comment* (New York), summer 1971; "Heston on Welles" by James Delson in *Take One* (Montreal), July/August 1971; "Orson Welles: An Introduction" by Mike Prokosch in *Film Comment* (New York), summer 1971; "*Touch of Evil*: Style Expressing Content" by E.M. Krueger in *Cinema Journal* (Iowa City), fall 1972; "*La Soif du mal*" in *Ecran* (Paris), 7bis, July 1972; "Notes on Film Noir" by Paul Schrader in *Film Comment* (New York), spring 1972; "Welles and the Logic of Death" by N. Hale in *Film Heritage* (Dayton, Ohio), fall 1974; "Film and System: Terms of an Analysis" by Stephen Heath in *Screen* (London), spring 1975; "*La Soif du mal*" by A. Lacombe in *Ecran* (Paris), January 1975; "Prime Cut" by Jonathan Rosenbaum in *Sight and Sound* (London), autumn 1975; "Welles, Shakespeare, and Webster" by Robin Wood in *Positif* (Paris), March 1975; "Politiets blinde øje" by P. Nørgarrd in *Kosmorama* (Copenhagen), summer 1977; "*Touch of Evil*" by John Henley in *Cinema Texas Program Notes* (Austin), 19 April 1978; "Subject Position" by W. Bywater in *Film Criticism* (Edinboro, Pennsylvania), no.1, 1979.

*   *   *

After *Citizen Kane*, *Touch of Evil* is the high point in Orson Welles's career. Inspired by Whitt Masterson's novel *Badge of Evil*, the film deals with an erstwhile narcotic agent's attempt to foil a crime committed on the Mexican border which he crosses to celebrate his honeymoon with his new wife (Janet Leigh). Multiple frame-ups occur as the agent, Vargas (Charlton Heston), finds himself in the middle of a tawdry band of outlaws who are under the control of the local chief of police—the grotesque, obese, squalid figure of Hank Quinlan (played by Orson Welles).

The plot leads the viewer through the sleaze of a minor Tijuana, onto dusty vistas of desolate roads, into junky brothels, decrepit motels inhabited by sexed-up punks reeking of drugs and booze, and through a miasma of oil derricks and sewer-like rivers in which float all kinds of human rubbish. One has the impression that Welles was aiming at a portrayal of an excess that knows no limits.

The result is that the film touches on border issues of the film noir at a time when that genre was reputedly dead and, as well, on the dialectic of framing, editing and lurid desire at the basis of spectatorship in cinema in general. Because the film includes much allusion to former moments in Welles's oeuvre, it avers to be both cinematic autobiography and a subtle collage of common obsessions. (In fact, the plot hinges on the moment when Quinlan loses his cane—or his former name—that functions as a rebus of *Kane* in this film.) A Shakespearean influence is evident. The film essays American decadence in a fashion reminiscent of the Bard's rendering of a tired, disgusting and cowardly Falstaff of the second part of *Henry the Fourth*. Dennis Weaver plays the role of a dumb but impish trickster in the manner of the character well known from *Macbeth*.

But Welles is decidedly at the center of the film. He uses a wide-angle lens to record the baroque immensity of his fat body from numerous angles. Rarely does the camera ever remain in a protracted *plan américain*. When it does establish narrative sequence, the camera usually pans quickly or dollies forth in order to allow for spherical aberration to distort the edges of the composition and give to it an urgent curvilinearity. This technique, of course, extends the caricatural aspect of Welles's body *all over* the frame. Elsewhere, the wide angle lens heightens the immediacy of the narrative by making all movement accelerate, invade foreground and background, and turn with such velocity that all perspectival order appears to go awry. The opening crane shot is well known: it envelops the credits, engages the narrative and, in a great coup of symbolic blockage, explodes the composition as the insipid hero and heroine kiss for the first time. Elsewhere the camera exploits the optical range of the wide-angle lens by simulating high speed driving through the dilapidated quarters of the border town. We listen to Welles and Heston speak *on* as they drive at breakneck clip through an unreal landscape of empty carlots, shacks and run-down facades.

Welles also amplifies the soundtrack. Voice and noises are reported more percussively and cacaphonously than what we would expect from the events in frame. As if the excess of audio were not enough, Welles doubles the stakes in a remarkable final chase in the sequence of retribution. Vargas follows Quinlan through a maze of iron girders, under a bridge and through all sorts of clutter. Because Vargas has planted a microphone in the cop's pocket, we hear the heave and the slur of Welles's breathing and slimy mutterings as he loses reason with the onslaught of delirium (Quinlan has just attempted to cover up his past with the ruthless murder of one of his cohorts, strangling him in a hotel room and leaving the corpse suspended over Janet Leigh who is recovering from the effects of drugs and rape): the film plays back its immediate past, doubling the lurid dialogue; the threats of murder and gunshots redound in the claustrophobic immensity of the decor. The amplification leads us from one excess to another. Blood dripping from Quinlan's last victim, in a heap on a bridge above, falls onto his chubby hand below, thus bringing the outrageous play of sounds and visuals back into a contemporary version of Elizabethan tragedy. Quinlan is soon cornered, bullets are exchanged, he is shot and falls with a immense splash into a pool of flotsam. "Too bad. He was a great detective but a lousy cop," is the first eulogy spoken over him; to which Tanya (Marlene Dietrich) responds in her characteristically thick German accent, topping the entire film with a last word, "He was

some kind of a man."

Dietrich's presence is manifold in *Touch of Evil*, despite the fact that she plays no narrative role in the story. A former lover of Quinlan, now a dried-up madame overlaid with cheap makeup who smokes cigarettes in a frontal pose reminiscent of Lang's portrayal of her aging beauty in *Rancho Notorious* six years before, Dietrich casts the spell of fate on Quinlan. "Your time is all used up, Hank," she repeats in closeup. Remarkable in the two sequences is the momentary calm her presence brings to the riotous violence of the sounds and images. For brief moments Quinlan need not cover up the mistakes he committed in his desperate will to wipe the origins of evils from his past. In looking directly at the camera, Dietrich reminds him (and us) of the past, as if suggesting that it was contained in the great period of expressionism—inspiring Welles—in which she played a significant role in the work of Von Sternberg in the 1930's. That their time "is all played out" is doubly ironic: the wry presence of a portable television set, a sort of Cyclops in the menagerie of junk decorating her apartment, presages the end of studio cinema. Furthermore, their banter is laced with reference to Hank's passion for candy bars. She attributes his obesity to his excessive ingestion of chocolate, as if, on another allegorical surface, Welles's whole career were one of some wasted expression of potentiation or of plenitude simulated only by overdriven ambition to mark an exemplary failure of genius. Her Tarot reading seals Quinlan's fate and forces him to return outdoors, where once more the baroque distortions and endless chases lead him to his demise.

Touch of Evil stages perversions of sexuality—of rape and violation that were everywhere only intimated in Hollywood before 1957—in a sequence set at the dingy "Mirador" motel. Having left his wife behind in a bedroom while he continues to chase his suspects, Vargas retrieves her through repeated telephone calls. Supine, heaving, self-fetishizing in the bondage of her corset, Suzy's pose epitomizes Hollywood's confabulation of desire, before the camera tears it to shreds through daring innuendo in the editing and framing. She is seen sliced up (across Venetian blinds), is then subjected to a simulated gang-rape that combines the rhetoric torture Rossellini had used in the antechambers of *Open City* with the drolleries of *Reefer Madness*. Leather-jacketed punks and dikes cloy over and leave the innocent soul virtually in pieces. As in Welles's strangling of his henchman (Akim Tamiroff) in another tawdry hotel room, the director insists time and again that violence is a product of optics. The anamorphic effects created by the wide-angle lens— where long shots and closeup lead from one to another in the same shot—produce and theorize the drives of Death and Eros at the bottom of the lugubrious comedy.

As in all of Welles's better films, the combination of sound and image, the editing, and the hieroglyphic conception of the shot (owing much to Eisenstein's teachings in *Film Form*) render a cinema of grotesque redundancy. The notion of "symbolic blockage"—pioneered by the formalism of Raymond Bellour— is useful for its suggestion that the Hollywood studio film is the background for Welles's experimentation with the dialectic of images and narrative. Most work in the American tradition involves film scripts that instantly overdetermine both their storylines and the contradictions generating them. This occurs, on the one hand, between a shot and relations of agents and objects within it while, at the same time and on the other hand, the shot reproduces those contradictions in the rapport between itself and the proceeding and preceeding shots. Hollywood generally created an unconscious dimension by carefully staging tensions overdetermining an entire film within a frame and, too, in its play of sequences moving both backward and forward. Clearly, Welles is sensitive to the fashion by which the industry produced American ideologies.

In *Touch of Evil* he makes this method the real preoccupation of the film, for its visual and aural excess are so great that they play out the studio editing to a grotesquely logical conclusion. Here the virtual political drive of Welles's work can be situated: no studio version of a film noir is possible after *Touch of Evil*. Its life is indeed its formal virtue, which with rigorously comic discipline, mixes lenticular experiment with a standard genre, producing a joyous, Rabelaisian critique of a tradition reaching back to the origins of all narrative film.

Recently *Touch of Evil* has been subject of a competent reading (though somewhat derivative of French formalisms) by Stephen Heath in *Questions of Cinema*. The renascence of *Touch of Evil* owes much to the complexities Heath unearths through his alert and detailed reading, one inspired by a blend of psychoanalysis and politics.

—Tom Conley

TOUT VA BIEN. Production: Lido Films/Empire Films; color, 35mm; running time: 95 mins. Released 1972.

Produced by Jean-Pierre Rassam; screenplay by Jean-Luc Godard and Jean-Pierre Gorin; directed by Jean-Luc Godard and Jean-Pierre Gorin; photography by Armand Marco; edited by Kenout Peltier.

Filmed in Paris.

Cast: Yves Montand (*Jacques*); Jane Fonda (*Susan*); Vittorio Caprioli (*Factory manager*); Jean Pignol (*The CGT delegate*); Pierre Ondry (*Frederic*); Elizabeth Chauvin (*Genevieve*); Eric Chartier (*Lucien*); Yves Gebrielli (*Leon*).

Publications:

Reviews—by S. Kovacs in *Take One* (Montreal), June 1972; "Paris Journal" by J. Rosenbaum in *Film Comment* (New York), September/October 1972; "*Tout Va Bien*" by Roger Greenspun in *The New York Times*, 11 October 1972; "*Tout va bien*" by S. James in *Films and Filming* (London), December 1973; "*Tout va vien*" by G. Klein in *Film Quarterly* (Berkeley), summer 1973; books—*Le Cinéma française depuis la nouvelle vague* by Claire Clouzot, Paris 1972; *Godard on Godard* edited and translated by Tom Milne, London 1972; *Jean-Luc Godard* by Alberto Farassino, Florence 1974; articles—"Godard Back to Commercial Pix with *All is Well*" in *Variety* (New York), 26 April 1972; "Jean-Luc Godard Wants to Live for the Revolution, Not Die for It" by James Conway in *The New York Times*, 24 December 1972; issue on Godard of *Filmcritica* (Rome), September 1972; "La Critique et *Tout va bien*" by P. Baudry in *Cahiers du cinéma* (Paris), July/August 1972; "*Tout va bien*" by J. Delmas in *Jeune Cinema* (Paris), July/August 1972; article by M. Goodwin and N. Wise in *Take One* (Montreal), October 1972; "*Tout va bien* and *Coup pour coup*: Radical French Cinema in Context" by Julia Lesage in *Cinéaste* (Paris), summer 1972; "Les Luttes de class en France..." in *Cahiers du cinéma* (Paris), May/June 1972; "Godard is Dead: Long Live Godard/-Gorin" by R. Roud in *Sight and Sound* (London), summer 1972; "Tout ne va pas bien" by Colin Westerbeck, Jr. in *Commonweal*

(New York), 5 January 1973; "Methoden & technieken van Brechts epies theater" by A. Apon in *Skrien* (Amsterdam), November/December 1973; "Godard's Molotov Cocktail" by M. Boujut in *Lumiere* (Melbourne), May 1973; "Angle and Reality: Godard and Gorin in America" by R.P. Kolker in *Sight and Sound* (London), summer 1973; "Befragung eines Bildes" by J.-L. Godard and J.-P. Gorin in *Filmkritik* (Munich), July 1974; "*Tout va bien*" by S. Simmons in *Film Comment* (New York), May/June 1974; "*Tout va bien*" in *Skrien* (Amsterdam), January/February 1974.

*   *   *

Although it is credited jointly to Godard and Gorin, and despite their own testimonies that Gorin organized most of the filming (Godard being ill much of the time), *Tout va bien* is commonly attributed to Godard. If one thinks of "Godard" as a corpus of films rather than as an individual human being, the attribution seems correct. This is not to belittle Gorin's contribution to the film (its *difference* from other Godard works may well be due to him). But the essential question of authorship is not "Who did the work?" but "To what *oeuvre* does this belong?" To give another, more clearcut example: Ernest Lehmann has insisted that the screenplay of *North by Northwest* is entirely his, and there is no reason to doubt him. Yet if one places that screenplay beside Lehmann's other work it has no meaning beyond itself, whereas if one places it beside Hitchcock's it immediately produces resonances with 20 films. Similarly, *Tout va bien* belongs within the *oeuvre* of Godard rather than to that of the author of *Poto and Cabengo*.

The film marks Godard's first attempt to return to commercial film-making and regain a wider audience after the four years of deliberately hermetic aesthetic/political experimentation of the "Dziga Vertov Group." It confronts questions that were urgent in 1972 and are no less urgent now: How does a committed radical make films for bourgeois audiences within a capitalist industry? How does a radical sustain a revolutionary impulse in a period of reaction and recuperation? What role can bourgeios intellectuals play in revolutionary theory and practice? How does a radical make sense of the daily business of living within a capitalist culture? The film's strength lies in the complex formal/stylistic strategies it develops to render such questions accessible, rather than in its treatment of revolutionary politics *per se*. Although Peter Wollen sees it as a retrograde step from the "Dziga Vertov" films, the distinction of *Tout va bien* lies partly in its success in solving the problem Wollen himself raises in his indispensable article "*Vent d'est*: Counter Cinema" (now easily available in his book *Readings and Writings*), the problem of reconciling revolutionary art with the pleasure principle.

Exemplary here is the use of stars. Fonda and Montand are introduced quite explicity *as* stars in the opening segment, which foregrounds the conditions of commercial film-making (to get finance you need stars, to get status you need a story, etc.). They are then pushed into the background throughout most of the first half of the film (often literally, placed in long shot while the foreground is occupied by unknown non-professionals playing the strikers). They are used as audience identification-figures because of their familiarity as stars, rather than in terms of the psychological/emotional identification to which Hollywood has accustomed us: spectators and listeners, they become our means of learning. The culmination of this part of the film abruptly transports them into the position of the factory-workers whose dehumanizing work-conditions they/we have been invited to imagine.

The second (and more interesting) part of the film brings them back to the foreground but employs them in a very complex way: they are Jacques and Susan, defined fictional characters in a specific diegetic situation; they are Montand and Fonda, stars known for their efforts to maintain a radical image and position within the industry; and they relate to the film-makers themselves, the question of "how to go on working within capitalism" merging into that of "how to make this film." The film's treatment here of the problems of connecting political positions, professional needs and personal relationships is at once intellectually stimulating and very moving. More than other Godard films, *Tout va bien* succeeds in achieving "alienation" in the true Brechtian sense without sacrificing involvement and pleasure.

—Robin Wood

THE TREASURE OF THE SIERRA MADRE. Production: Warner Bros. Pictures, Inc.; 1947; black and white, 35mm; running time: 126 mins. Released January 1948.

Produced by Henry Blanke; screenplay by John Huston; from the novel by B. Traven; directed by John Huston; photography by Ted McCord; edited by Owen Marks; sound recorded by Robert B. Lee; art direction by John Hughes, sets decorated by Fred M. MacLean; music by Max Steiner, musical direction by Leo F. Forbstein, orchestration by Murray Cutter; special effects by William McGann and H.F. Koenekamp; technical advisers: Ernesto A. Romero and Antonio Arriaga.

Filmed spring through summer 1947 in Tampico, Mexico and in the mountains near San José de Purua, Mexico. Cost: $3,000,000. New York Film Critics Awards for Best Picture and Best Direction, 1948; Academy Awards for Best Direction and Best Supporting Actor (Walter Huston), 1948; Venice Film Festival, Best Music (Steiner), 1948.

Cast: Humphrey Bogart (*Fred. C. Dobbs*); Walter Huston (*Howard*); Tim Holt (*Curtin*); Bruce Bennett (*Cody*); Alfonso Bedoya (*Gold Hat*); Barton MacLane (*McCormick*); A. Soto Rangel (*Presidente*); Manuel Donde (*El Jefe*); José Torvay (*Pablo*); Margarito Luna (*Pancho*); Jacqueline Dalya (*Flashy girl*); Robert (Bobby) Blake (*Mexican boy*); John Huston (*Man in white suit*); Jack Holt (*Flophouse bum*); Ann Sheridan (*Streetwalker*).

Publications:

Script—*The Treasure of the Sierra Madre* by John Huston, edited by James Naremore, Madison, Wisconsin 1979; reviews—"*Le Tresor de la Sierra Madre*" by Robert Pilati in *L'Ecran français* (Paris), 15 February 1950; review by Jean Desternes in *La Revue du cinéma* (Paris), no.18, 1950; review by Michel Subiéla in *Positif* (Paris), no.3, 1950; books—*John Huston* by Paul Davay, Paris 1957; *John Huston* by Jean-Claude Allais, Paris 1960; *John Huston, King Rebel* by William Nolan, New York 1965; *Bogey, The Man, the Actor, the Legend* by Jonathan Hill and Jonah Ruddy, London 1965; *John Huston* by Robert Benayoun, Paris 1966; *Bogie* by Joe Hyams, New York 1966; *The Great Films: 50 Golden Years of Motion Pictures* by Bosley Crowther, New York 1967; *John Huston* by Riccardo

Cecchini, 1969; *John Huston, A Picture Treasury of his Films* by Romano Tozzi, New York 1971; *The Great Western Pictures* by James Robert Parish and Michael Pitts, Metuchen, New Jersey 1976; *John Huston* by Axel Madsen, New York 1978; *John Huston: Maker of Magic* by Stuart Kaminsky, London 1978; articles—"On the set with John Huston" by L. Allen in *Cinema* (Hollywood), July 1947; article by Lawrence Morton in *Hollywood Quarterly*, spring 1948; "Walter Huston's Bad Boy John" by Dan Fowler in *Look* (New York), 10 May 1949; "Humphrey Bogart" by Clifford McCarty in *Films in Review* (New York), May 1957; article by Eugene Archer in *Film Culture* (New York), no.19, 1959; article on John Huston in *Films and Filming* (London), September 1959 and October 1959; "Walter Huston" by Jerry Vermilye in *Films in Review* (New York), February 1960; "How I Make Films: An Interview with John Huston" by Gideon Bachmann in *Film Quarterly* (Berkeley), fall 1965; "Viewing Report: *Treasure of the Sierra Madre*" by Fred Majdalany in *Screen Education* (London), March/April 1965; "Beating the Devil: 30 Years of John Huston" by Dupre Jones in *Films and Filming* (London), January 1973; "*Treasure of the Sierra Madre*" by Olive Graham in *Cinema Texas Program Notes* (Austin), 3 May 1979.

*   *   *

The Treasure of the Sierra Madre has become the archetypal John Huston film. One reason is that it is a clear examination of the exploration or the quest. As in many of his films to come (and *The Maltese Falcon*, to some extent, before it), Huston here examines a small group of people on a quest for wealth. Generally, in his films with this theme the members of the group accomplish their initial goal: they obtain the money or the treasure. Once having attained it, however, they often find the potential power it brings too much to handle. Human greed, weakness, or obsession destroys their victory.

This is remarkably true of *Treasure*, *The Asphalt Jungle*, *Beat the Devil*, *The Kremlin Letter*, and *The Man Who Would Be King*. In all these films, however, Huston does not simply examine greed and present a moral statement about it. He examines the disintegration or change within the individual who has to learn to cope with the specter of wealth of power and the erosion of the fragile group or couple when chance, greed, envy, or obsession intrudes on their existence. *Treasure* is not a moral statement by Huston but an examination of characters under pressure, who fall apart when least expected to and rise to noble reactions when no reason is given to believe they will.

In order to make *The Treasure of the Sierra Madre* Huston convinced Warner Brothers to let him shoot on location for ten weeks in Mexico. In documentaries in the army, he had grown accustomed to location work and now felt comfortable with it. "Locationing? Nothing to it," he said. "The only time it's tough to make pictures on location is when someone is shooting at you." In his search for the concrete in making the film, Huston went to the extreme of shooting exteriors in San Jose de Purua, an isolated village 140 miles north of Mexico city. Humphrey Bogart, who played Dobbs, recalled: "John wanted everything perfect. If he saw a nearby mountain that would serve for photographic purposes, that mountain was not good; too easy to reach. If we could go to a location site without fording a couple of streams and walking through snake-infested areas in the scorching sun, then it wasn't quite right."

Huston's other stars included his father, Walter Huston, as Howard, and cowboy actor Tim Holt as Curtin. Dobbs is frequently described as a moral brute and a madman, but clearly he is a highly contradictory character until his crack-up. He is initially generous and willing to share his cash, and he rather nobly throws away the gold that Curtin offers him to pay back the extra money he has put to finance the trip. Later, it is Dobbs who agrees to help Howard rebuild the "wounded" mountain. Howard, the doctor/father, constantly warns that gold is a potential disease. He is aware of the danger and protects himself, and Curtin also learns to do so, but even Curtin has a moment of hesitation when he almost leaves Dobbs in the mine after a collapse. It is Dobbs who succumbs to the disease, but he is not viewed as evil by Huston or, for that matter, by Howard.

Time called the film "one of the best things Hollywood has done since it learned to talk.... Walter Huston's performance is his best job in a lifetime of acting." Bosley Crowther in the *New York Times* wrote that "Huston has shaped a searching drama of the collision of civilization's vicious greeds with the instinct for self-preservation in an environment where all the barriers are down." James Agee and *Newsweek* also praised the film, but there was some antagonism. John McCarten in *The New Yorker* said the film could be reduced to the idea that greed does not pay. He went on to say that "even if the premise is granted, the film's methods of elaborating on it are certainly something less than beguiling."

While the mixed reviews filtered in, Huston plunged into his next project, but his work was disrupted when the Academy Awards for 1948 were announced. For the first time, a father-and-son team won the awards, John as best director, Walter as best supporting actor.

—Stuart M. Kaminsky

TRIUMPH DES WILLENS. Triumph of the Will. Production: Universum Film Aktiengesellschaft (Ufa); black and white, 35mm; running time: 120 mins. Released March 1935.

Produced, directed, and edited by Leni Riefenstahl; the few subtitles in the beginning are credited to Walter Ruttmann; photography by Sepp Allgeier, Karl Attenberger, and Werner Bohne, plus several assistants; architectural designs by Albert Speer; music by Herbert Windt.

Filmed 4-10 September 1934 in Nuremburg at the Nazi Party congress. National Film Prize of Germany, 1935; Venice Biennale, Gold Medal, 1936 (most sources do not list this award for *Triumph*, though David Gunston in *Current Biography* states that *Triumph* did receive this award); Exposition Internationale des Arts et des Techniques (Paris), Grand Prize, 1937.

Publications:

Books—*From Caligari to Hitler* by Siegfried Kracauer, Princeton, New Jersey 1947; *Film in the Third Reich* by David Stewart Hull, Berkeley 1969; *Histoire du cinéma Nazi* by Pierre Cadars and Francis Courtade, Paris 1972; *Nonfiction Film: A Critical History* by Richard Barsam, New York 1973; *Documentary: A History of the Nonfiction Film* by Erik Barnouw, New York 1974; *Filmguide to Triumph of the Will* by Richard Barsam, Bloomington, Indiana 1975; *Propaganda, the Art of Persuasion: World War II* by Anthony Rhodes, New York 1976; *Swastika: The Cinema of Oppression* by Baxter Phillips, New

York 1976; *Leni Riefenstahl: Fallen Film Goddess* by Glenn Infield, New York 1976; *Leni Riefenstahl* by Charles Ford, Paris 1978; *The Films of Leni Riefenstahl* by David Hinton, Metuchen, New Jersey 1978; *Leni Riefenstahl et le 3e Reich* by G.B. Infield, Paris 1978; *Leni Riefenstahl* by Renada Berg-Pan, edited by Warren French, Boston 1980; articles—"Leni Riefenstahl" by D. Gunston in *Film Quarterly* (Berkeley), fall 1960; "*Triumph of the Will*" by Marshall Lewis in *New York Film Bulletin*, nos.12-14, 1960; "Romantic Miss Riefenstahl" by Robert Muller in *Spectator* (London), 10 February 1961; issue on Riefenstahl of *Film Comment* (New York), winter 1965; "The Truth About Leni" by Arnold Berson in *Films and Filming* (London), April 1965; "Leni and the Wolf: Interview with Leni Riefenstahl" by Michel Delahaye in *Cahiers du Cinema in English* (New York), June 1966; "Leni Riefenstahl: A Bibliography" by Richard Corliss in *Film Heritage* (Dayton, Ohio), fall 1969; "Leni Riefenstahl: Style and Structure" by Jeffrey Richards in *Silent Picture* (London), autumn 1970; "Leni Riefenstahl: Artifice and Truth in a World Apart" by R.M. Barsam in *Film Comment* (New York), November/December 1973; "Propaganda as Vision—*Triumph of the Will*" by K. Kelman in *Film Culture* (New York), spring 1973; "*Triumph of the Will*: Document or Artifice?" by David Hinton in *Cinema Journal* (Evanston, Illinois), fall 1975; "Leni Riefenstahl" by David Gunston in *Current Biography* (New York), May 1975; "*The Triumph of the Will*" by William K. Everson in *The Documentary Tradition* edited by Lewis Jacobs, 2nd ed., New York 1979; "*Triumph of the Will*: Notes on Documentary and Spectacle" by S. Neale in *Screen* (London), no.1, 1979; "Was Hitler There? Reconsidering *Triumph des willens*" by B. Winston in *Sight and Sound* (London), spring 1981.

*   *   *

Triumph of the Will, the official Nazi record of the 1934 Nuremburg Party rally, commissioned by Hitler and directed by Leni Riefenstahl, is one of the most controversial contributions to film history because its subject matter—Hitler and the carefully planned spectacle of 1934 party Congress; Riefenstahl's attitude towards the subject matter—her insistence that the film is soley a work of art and not propaganda; and the presentation of the subject matter—the manipulation of reality in this "documentary" record. The contributions to the art of film this work had to offer are closely tied to the controversies. *Triumph of the Will* is a masterpiece of style and editing, which in turn are the very techniques used to manipulate reality and create emotionally effective propaganda.

Riefenstahl maintains continuity and rhythm throughout the film with several different editing techniques. The most notable include the lending of movement to otherwise static images, the use of contrasting light and dark sequences, and the use of the symbols of National Socialism (eagle, swastika, flags and banners) as controlling images. In addition, her poetic style of disorientation and her disturbing depiction of people as architecture contribute to both the art and ideology of the film.

Several scenes that have potential for tedium are saved by the addition of cinematic movement. Riefenstahl takes the visually uneventful speeches of Reich leaders and the visually monotonous images of a lengthy military parade and makes them interesting by providing them with motion. One such scene is the official opening of the 1934 Party Congress. This scene slows the pace of the film considerably, but it does have rhythmic movement of its own because of Riefenstahl's editing. Rudolf Hess's introductory speech is intercut with shots of the listening crowd, individual's faces, the swastika, and the eagle. The images on the screen continue to change, adding a steady motion to this otherwise static situation. (This technique of intercutting is applied to the lengthier speeches in this scene as well as to other speeches throughout the film.) In addition, the manner in which each of the ten speakers is introduced contributes to the slow but steady pacing of this scene. Each speaker is introduced by a blurred title which then fades into focus to reveal his name. This title is then followed by a medium or close-up shot of the speaker. The repetition of this effect throughout the scene lends both rhythm and unity to this section of the film.

Hitler's speech at the closing Party Congress, the final and longest speech of the film, is not only made more visually interesting through the added movement of intercutting, but is also made more effective emotionally. The speech is animated by Hitler himself seen in close-up waving his arms, pounding his fists, and staring off-screen at some secret vision in the distance. To give addition movement to the speech, Riefenstahl intercuts images that emphasize Hitler's words. For example, when Hitler refers to the "old fighters" of the National Socialist party, close-ups of Goebbels, Todt, and Hess appear on the screen. Later in the speech Hitler states that the Nazi party "in its entity...will be like a religious order." At these words the camera focuses on the eagle with the swastika, the symbol of the party made up of "faithful followers" that Hitler descended from the sky to lead in the opening sequence of the film.

Although not a static image, a lengthy military parade can easily become a monotonous one. The parade of German military groups, labor groups, and service forces here lasts approximately 18 minutes. During this scene the camera is always moving; the parade is viewed from the air, open windows, bridges, and moving vehicles. The image of the marching troops is intercut with close-ups of party leaders and the crowd viewing the parade. Riefenstahl provides many and varied perspectives of this event. The scene impresses the viewer with the massed, marching columns at Hitler's comand.

The use of alternating light and dark sequences throughout *Triumph of the Will* also contributes to the film's movement. The transition from light to dark is sometimes gradual, as in the first few scenes of the film. The film moves from Hitler's plane descending upon the city of Nuremburg amid bright clouds and sunlight to a band concert at the hotel Deutscher Hof in the dim light of early evening, which turns into night, to the buildings of Nuremburg in the early light of what appears to be the next morning. This succession of scenes moves smoothly from day to night to day again.

In other sequences the contrast between light and dark is far more dramatic. The film very appropriately plunges into darkness during the storm troopers' night rally. The scene is torchlit and smokey; it has a mysterious, unsettling atmosphere. The screen is then suddenly filled with sunlight and young boys drumming happily as the film progresses to the next scene, the Hitler Youth rally. This use of contrasting visual images is yet another means by which Riefenstahl avoids the static newsreel style she so abhorred.

In addition to rhythmic movement, Riefenstahl also edited for continuity. The recurring images of the eagle, the swastika, and the flags and banners of National Socialism lend unity to the film as a whole and sometimes aid in the transition between scenes. *Triumph of the Will* consists of many varied scenes. In addition to common themes uniting these scenes there are common visual elements—the symbols of the Nazi party which are present in practically every scene of the film.

Riefenstahl uses this kind of visual link very effectively in the transition between the scenes of the speeches of the sixth Party Congress and the Labor Service rally. According to the sequence of the film, the final speech of the Congress is given by Konstantin Hierl, the leader of the Reich Labor Service. The excerpt of the speech that is included in the film is very brief, but what is said provides the viewer with a feel for the manner in which the Labor Service will be represented. This last speech has a strong enough thematic link to the following scene that Riefenstahl might have simply edited the two together; however, in addition to the thematic connection Riefenstahl adds a visual one. Hierl's speech ends with a close-up of the Labor Front flag; the continued close-up of this flag carries the viewer into the next scene of the Labor Service rally, making for a very smooth transition and strengthening the bond between the two scenes.

As the film progresses, the visual presence of the symbols representing National Socialism take on increasing thematic importance. In the beginning of the film the flags and banners flutter from the buildings of Nuremburg, and the eagles and swastika decorate the meeting hall of the sixth Party Congress. The flags, standards, and swastikas are then seen in the hands of soldiers and workers in various scenes. Finally, only the symbols are seen; the people carrying the flags and insignia become part of the symbol itself and can no longer be recognized as individual human beings. In a 1973 *Film Culture* article Ken Kelman calls this visual effect "disorientation" and suggests that it is achieved by omitting an important part of "reality" from the film frame. This technique is used throughout *Triumph of the Will*.

The "Twilight Parade of Flag Bearers" and the "Consecration of the Flags Ceremony" are two sections of the film in which many flag bearers are in a single shot. These scenes are photographed in such a way that the men holding the flags are barely visible, or not visible at all. Richard Barsam has referred to the "forest of flags" in these scenes, a very good description of the visual image created by this technique of disorientation. Similarly, when Hitler reviews a parade of storm troopers carrying flags and standards, the men are barely visible; the viewer is presented with a sea of marching banners bearing the insignia of the Reich.

Hitler's Messianic image in the film's opening is continued throughout the work, often through the use of disorientation. During the motorcade from the airport to the hotel Deutscher Hof, Hitler is standing in an open touring car. The camera follows the progress of the motorcade at an angle such that Hitler's vehicle is not visible in the frame; he appears to float through rows of cheering supporters, having no connection whatsoever to the ground. This image of Hitler floating through the streets of Nuremburg recurs at other points in the film where he is seen traveling in an open touring car.

Related to this use of people as symbols is the use of people as architecture, a stylistic characteristic that many critics find the most disturbing aspect of *Triumph of the Will*. In contrast to disorientation, people are not made to appear invisible in the scene but become part of the scenery itself. The most striking example of this occurs in the scene in which Hitler lays a wreath at a war memorial. The screen is filled with row upon row of SS and SA men "placed" in a neat geometrical squares on either side of a wide aisle. At first the men are not discernible; it is not clear what is forming these countless rows. Even after the viewer realizes the situation, it is impossible to look upon these men as individual human beings. As Hitler, Lutze, and Himmler walk up the aisle to approach the war memorial, they are truly the only distinguishable figures on the screen. The German people become faceless, dehumanized mass, while Hitler emerges as the only distinguishable individual in the film.

The film was a great success with Hitler upon its premiere in March of 1935. Even Goebbels, who harbored ill feelings toward Riefenstahl, praised the film and awarded it Germany's National Film Prize on May 1, 1935. Other Nazi officials, however, were not pleased; they thought that the film was too artistic for general propaganda purposes. This was perhaps an accurate judgement of the film's practical value. According to Richard Barsam, the film was not a success with the general public and did well only in larger cities of Germany.

Triumph of the Will also received recognition from France. In 1937 the film was awarded the Grand Prize at the *Exposition Internationale des Arts et des Techniques* in Paris. But Riefenstahl's appearance to receive the award was protested by French workers, a reaction that has been repeated many times since then. Critics acknowledge the film's exceptional cinematic achievements, but find it difficult to praise the film because of its disturbing ideological content.

—Marie Saeli

TURKSIB. Production: Vostok Film (USSR); black and white, 35mm; running time: 85 mins. Released 1929.

Produced by Victor Turin; screenplay by Victor Turin with Alexander Macheret, Victor Shklovsky, and Efim Aron; English titles by John Grierson; directed by Victor Turin; photography by Yevgeni Slavinski and Boris Frantzisson; English version edited by John Grierson; assistant director: Efim Aron.

Filmed in Turkestan and Siberia.

Publications:

Books—*Kino: A History of Russian and Soviet Film* by Jay Leyda, London 1960; *Nonfiction Film: A Critical History* by Richard Barsam, New York 1973; *Documentary: A History of the Nonfiction Film* by Erik Barnouw, New York 1974; articles—"*Turksib*: Building a Railroad" by K.J. Coldicutt in *The Documentary Tradition* edited by Lewis Jacobs, 2nd ed., New York 1979.

*   *   *

Turksib is a world-famous documentary that depicts the building of a railway linking Turkestan with Siberia, to carry cotton from the former in exchange for cereals and vegetables from the latter: one of its very first large-scale construction projects in the Soviet Union. Victor Turin, its director, had spent his formative years in the United States—from 1912 when he was 17 until he returned to Russia in 1922—having attended Massachusetts Institute of Technology and worked as an actor and scenarist at the Vitagraph Studios in Hollywood. He had also, of course, missed both the First World War and the Russian Revolution, which, together with his rich, middle-class background, may have adversely affected his later career.

Before *Turksib* Turin had already made three Soviet films, one of which was a feature about the class struggle in the capitalist world—*Borba Gigantov* (Battle of Giants). It was considered too "abstract" (i.e., bad). It was all the more surprising, therefore, that Turin broke away from the very romantic style then becoming popular, full of dingleberry (an old Hollywood term for foliage introduced into the top of the frame), diffusion, back-

lighting, noble close-ups and a general obsession with beautiful photography. In stark contrast, *Turksib* was a clear, direct and realistic statement, which was also gripping, touched with humor and humanity and edited with verve and a sure sense of rhythm. It was also said by Soviet critics to be "lyrical" (i.e., good). Perhaps (as frequently happens in cinema history) it was even helped by a relatively small budget and tight schedule to achieve its clarity, economy and unity—and to escape too much interference from "above." But it was Turin himself who had carefully and deliberately planned the style and content of his film. It was received abroad with even more acclaim than it won at home, and it certainly helped to put the documentary tradition back on the rails of realism.

Turksib is still enjoyable to watch and deserves the permanent place it has won in the canon of Russian classical movies, along with the works of Pudovkin, Eisenstein, Dovzhenko and Dziga Vertov. Why did its director fail to make further masterpieces? It is difficult to determine whether Turin was rewarded—or merely "kicked upstairs"—by being given an executive post at the very moment he seemed to have "arrived." He was not to direct another film until 1938—*Bakintsy*, a feature about the 1905 revolution, made at the Azerbaijani studios in Baku. *Turksib* undoubtedly proved Turin's abilities as an organizer, but it seems tragic that his other, rarer talents were not given a chance for further documentaries in his fresh, purposeful style.

—Robert Dunbar

2001: A SPACE ODYSSEY. Production: Metro-Goldwyn-Mayer Pictures Corp.; 1968; Technicolor and Metrocolor, 35mm, Super Panavision; running time: 141 mins., premiere versions were 160 mins. Released 3 April 1968, New York.

Produced by Stanley Kubrick with Victor Lyndon; screenplay by Stanley Kubrick and Arthur C. Clarke; from "The Sentinel" in *Expedition to Earth* by Arthur C. Clarke, London 1968; directed by Stanley Kubrick; photography by Geoffrey Unsworth, additional photography by John Alcott; edited by Ray Lovejoy; sound supervised by by A.W. Watkins, sound mixed by H.L. Bird, sound edited by Winston Ryder; production design by Tony Masters, Harry Lange, and Ernest Archer; art direction by John Hoesli; music from works by Khatchaturian, Ligeti, Johann Strauss and Richard Strauss; special effects directed by Stanley Kubrick and supervised by Wally Veevers, Douglas Trumbull, Con Pederson and Tom Howard; costumes designed by Hardy Amies; scientific consultant: Frederick Ordway III.

Filmed beginning 29 December 1965 in MGM's Shepperton and Boreham Wood Studios, England. Cost: $10,500,000. Academy Award, Special Visual Effects, 1968.

Cast: Keir Dullea (*Dave Bowman*); Gary Lockwood (*Frank Poole*); William Sylvester (*Dr. Heywood Floyd*); Daniel Richter (*Moon-Watcher*); Leonard Rossiter (*Smyslov*); Margaret Tyzack (*Elena*); Robert Beatty (*Halvorsen*); Sean Sullivan (*Michaels*); Douglas Rain (*HAL's voice*); Frank Miller (*Mission Control*); Penny Brahms (*Stewardess*); Alan Gifford (*Poole's Father*).

Publications:

Scripts—*2001: A Space Odyssey* by Arthur C. Clarke, New York 1968; "*2000: L'Odyssée de l'espace*" by Stanley Kubrick and Arthur C. Clarke in *Avant-Scène du cinéma* (Paris), 15 July 1979; reviews—"The Screen: '2001' is Up, Up, and Away" by Renata Adler in *The New York Times*, 4 April 1968; "Stanley Kubrick, Please Come Down" by Judith Crist in *New York*, 22 April 1968; "Trash, Art, and the Movies" collected in *Going Steady* by Pauline Kael, Boston 1970; "*2001*" collected in *Figures of Light* by Stanley Kauffmann, New York 1971; "Le Dossier: *2001*, Stanley Kubrick" in *Avant-Scène du cinéma* (Paris), 15 July 1979; books—*2001: A Space Odyssey* (novel) by Arthur C. Clarke, New York 1968; *La Foetus Astral* by Jean Paul Dumont and Jean Monod, Paris 1970; *The Making of Kubrick's 2001* edited by Jerome Agel, New York 1970; *Le Cinéma fantastique* by René Prédal, Paris 1970; *Stanley Kubrick Directs* by Alexander Walker, New York 1971; *The Lost Worlds of 2001* by Arthur C. Clarke, New York 1972; *Report on Planet 3: And Other Speculations* by Arthur C. Clarke, New York 1972; *The Cinema of Stanley Kubrick* by Norman Kagan, New York 1972; *Filmguide to 2001: A Space Odyssey* by Carolyn Geduld, Bloomington, Indiana 1973; *The Films of Stanley Kubrick* by Daniel De Vries, Grand Rapids, Michigan 1973; *Stanley Kubrick: A Film Odyssey* by Gene D. Phillips, New York 1975; *Kubrick* by Michel Ciment, Paris 1981; articles—"The Sentinel" in *Expedition to Earth* by Arthur C. Clarke, New York 1953; "Beyond the Stars" in the *New Yorker*, 24 April 1965; "Offbeat Director in Outer Space" by Hollis Alpert in the *New York Times Magazine*, 16 January 1966; "Profiles: How About a Little Game?" by Jeremy Bernstein in *The New Yorker*, 12 November 1966; "Two for the Sci-Fi" by David Robinson in *Sight and Sound* (London), spring 1966; "Kubrick, Farther Out" in *Newsweek* (New York), 12 September 1966; "Stanley Kubrick in the 21st Century" by Norman Spinrad in *Cinema* (Beverly Hills), December 1966; "*2001*: Backstage Magic for a Trip to Saturn" by R.F. Dempewolff in *Popular Mechanics* (New York), April 1967; "L'Odyséé de Stanley Kubrick: Part III: Vers l'Infini—*2001*" by Michel Ciment in *Positif* (Paris), October 1968; "*2001*: A New Myth" by Don Daniels in *Film Heritage* (Dayton, Ohio), summer 1968; "*2001: A Space Odyssey*" compiled by Tim Hunter and others in *Film Heritage* (Dayton, Ohio), summer 1968; "Playboy Interview: Stanley Kubrick" by Eric Norden in *Playboy* (Chicago), September 1968; "Stanley Kubrick" in *The American Cinema* by Andrew Sarris, New York 1968; "Creating Special Effects for *2001*" by Douglas Trumbull in *American Cinematographer* (Los Angeles), June 1968; "*2001: A Space Odyssey*" by David Austen in *Films and Filming* (London), July 1968; "Entretien avec Stanley Kubrick" by Renaud Walter in *Positif* (Paris), December 1968; "Des Tourbillons, des mondes, des années" by Michel Capdenac in *Les Lettres françaises* (Paris), October 1968; "Londres a l'heure de Stanley Kubrick" by Bertrand Tavernier in *Les Lettres françaises* (Paris), 21 August 1968; "Inside *2001*" in *Take One* (Montreal), no.11, 1968; "How They Filmed *2001*" by Herbert Shuldiner in *Popular Science* (New York), June 1968; "*2001: A Space Odyssey*" by Mark Gasser in *Cinéaste* (New York), summer 1968; "A Tentative for the Viewing of *2001*" by Gary Crowdus in *Cinéaste* (New York), summer 1968; "Is *2001* Worth Seeing Twice" by Cliff Barker in *Cineaste* (New York), summer 1968; "La Marge" by Bernard Eisenschitz in *Cahiers du cinéma* (Paris), February 1969; "*2001: A Space Odyssey*" by Hollis Alpert in *Film 68/69* edited by Alpert and Andrew Sarris, New York 1969; "*2001*: Out of the Silent Planet" by Mel McKee in *Sight and Sound* (London), autumn 1969; "Bodies in Space: Film as Carnal Knowledge" by Annette Michelson in *Artforum* (New York), February 1969; "A Talk with Stanley Kubrick" by Maurice Rapf in *Action* (Los Angeles), January/February 1969; "Echecs et maths" by Michel Sineux in *Positif* (Paris), April 1969; "Kubrick Vs. Clark" by Clive James in *Cinema* (London), March 1969; "Spaced Out By Stanley" by Vincent Canby in *The New York Times*, 3 May 1970; "Stanley Kubrick" in *The Film Director as Superstar* by Joseph Gelmis, New York 1970; "*2001*" by Max Kozloff in *Film Culture* (New York), winter/spring 1970; "*2001*: A Second Look" by Frederik Pohl in *Film Society Review* (New York), February 1970; "The New Nostalgia" by Gene Youngblood in *Expanded Cinema*, New York 1970; "*2001: A Space Odyssey*" by Michael Sragow in *Film Society Review* (New York), January 1970; "*2001*" by Gene Phillips in *Film Comment* (New York), winter 1971-72; "A Skeleton Key to *2001*" by Don Daniels in *Sight and Sound* (London), winter 1970-71; issue on *2001* of *Cahiers du cinéma* (Paris), summer 1972; "Too Bad Lois Lane: The End of Sex in *2001*" by J. Fisher in *Film Journal* (New York), September 1972; "Mode and Meaning in *2001*" by D. Boyd in *Journal of Popular Film* (Bowling Green, Ohio), no.3, 1978; "Une Odyssée formelle" by Jacques Goimard in *Avant-Scène du cinéma* (Paris), 15 July 1979; "A kozmikus ember: Kubrick: *2001: Odisszea az urben*" by P. Kuczka in *Filmkultura* (Budapest), March/April 1979; "Resor i mánniskan" by N. Hibbin in *Chaplin* (Stockholm), no.6(177), 1981.

*   *   *

In *2001: A Space Odyssey* Stanley Kubrick further explored his dark vision of man in a materialistic, mechanistic age depicted in *Dr. Strangelove* four years earlier. In explaining how the original idea for this landmark science-fiction film came to him, he says, "Most astronomers and other scientists interested in the whole question are strongly convinced that the universe is crawling with life; much of it, since the numbers are so staggering, (is) equal to us in intelligence, or superior, simply because human intelligence has exsisted for so relatively short a period." He approached Arthur C. Clarke, whose science fiction short story, "The Sentinel," would eventually become the basis for the film. They first expanded the short story into a novel, in order to completely develop the story's potential, and then turned that into a screenplay.

MGM bought their package and financed the film for six million dollars, a budget that after four years of work on the film eventually rose to ten million. Though *2001* opened to indifferent and even hostile reviews, subsequent critical opinion has completely reversed itself. As the film is often revived, it has earned back its original cost several times over.

2001 begins with the dawn of civilization in which an ape-man learns to use a bone as a weapon in order to destroy a rival, ironically taking a step further toward humanity. As the victorious ape-man throws his weapon spiralling into the air, there is a dissolve to a space ship from the year 2001. "It's simply an observable fact," Kubrick comments, "that all of man's technology grew out of the discovery of the tool-weapon. There's no doubt that there's a deep emotional relationship between man and his machine-weapons, which are his children. The machine is beginning to assert itself in a very profound way, even attracting affection and obsession."

This concept is dramatized in the film when astronauts Dave Bowman and Frank Poole find themselves at the mercy of the computer HAL 9000, which controls their space ship. (There are repeated juxtapositions of man with his human failings and fallibility immersed in machinery: beautiful, functional, but cold and heartless.) When Hal the computer makes a mistake, he refuses to admit the evidence of his own capacity for error, and proceeds to destroy the occupants of the space ship to cover it up.

Kubrick indicates here as in *Dr. Strangelove* that human fallibility is less likely to destroy man than the abdication of his moral responsibilities to presumably infallible machines.

Kubrick believes man must also strive to gain mastery over himself and not just over his machines, "Somebody said man is the missing link between primitive apes and civilized human beings. You might say that that is inherent in the story of *2001* too. We are semi-civilized, capable of cooperation and affection, but needing some sort of transfiguration into a higher form of life. Since the means to obliterate life on earth exist, it will take more than just careful planning and reasonable cooperation to avoid some eventual catastrophic event. The problem exists as long as the potential exists; and the problem is essentially a moral one and a spiritual one."

These sentiments are very close to those which Charlie Chaplin expressed in his closing speech in *The Great Dictator*: "We think too much and feel too little. More than machinery we need humanity. More than cleverness we need kindness and gentleness. Without these qualities, life will be violent and all will be lost."

The overall implications of the film suggest a more optimistic aspect to Kubrick's view of life than had been previously detected in his work. Here he presents man's creative encounters with the universe and his unfathomed potential for the future in more hopeful terms than he did, for example, in *Dr. Strangelove*.

The film ends with Bowman, the only survivor of the mission, being reborn as "an enhanced being, a star child, an angel, a superman, if you like," Kubrick explains, "returning to earth prepared for the next leap forward of man's evolutionary destiny."

Kubrick feels that "the God concept is at the heart of the film" since, if any extraterrestrial superior being were to manifest itself to man, the latter would immediately assume it was God or an emissary of God. When an artifact of these beings does appear in the film, it is represented as a black monolithic slab. Kubrick thought it better not try to be too specific in depicting these beings, "You have to leave something to the audience's imagination," he concludes.

In summary, *2001* by neither showing nor explaining too much, enables the viewer to experience the film as a whole. As Kubrick comments, "The feel of the experience is the important thing, not the ability to verbalize it. I tried to create a visual experience which directly penetrates the subconscious content of the material." The movie consequently becomes for the viewer an intensely subjective experience which reaches his inner consciousness in the same manner that music does, leaving him free to speculate about thematic content. As one critic put in, *2001* successfully brings the techniques and appeal of the experimental film into the studio feature-length film, "making it the world's most expensive underground movie." It is this phenomenon, in the final analysis, which has made *2001: A Space Odyssey* so perennially popular with audiences.

It is significant that Kubrick set the film in the year 2001, because Fritz Lang's groundbreaking silent film *Metropolis* takes place in the year 2000. This reference to Lang's film is an homage to the earlier master's accomplishment in science fiction—an achievement which Kubrick's film has successfully built on and surpassed.

—Gene D. Phillips

TYSTNADEN. The Silence. Le Silence. Production: Svensk Filmindustri; black and white, 35mm; running time: 95 mins.; length: 2623 meters. Released 23 September 1963, Stockholm.

Produced by Allan Ekelund; screenplay by Ingmar Bergman; directed by Ingmar Bergman; photography by Sven Nykvist; edited by Ulla Ryghe; sound engineered by Stig Flodin; production design by P.A. Lundgren; music by Bach; special effects Evald Anderson; costumes designed by Marik Vos.

Filmed sporadically from summer 1962-summer 1963 in Sweden.

Cast: Gunnel Lindblom (*Anna*); Ingrid Thulin (*Ester*); Jörgen Lindström (*Johan*); Haakan Jahnberg (*Hotel manager*); Lissi Alandh (*Woman in the cinema*); Leif Forstenberg (*Man in the cinema*); Nils Waldt (*Cashier at the cinema*); Birgir Lesander; Eduardo Gutierrez.

Publications:

Scripts— "*Le Silence*" (screenplay) by Ingmar Bergman in *Avant-Scène du cinéma* (Paris), May 1964; *Three Films by Ingmar Bergman*, New York 1970; reviews—by Pierre Billard in *Cinéma 64* (Paris), April 1964; review by Ado Kyrou in *Positif* (Paris), summer 1964; review by Georges Sadoul in *Les Lettres françaises* (Paris), 26 March 1964; review by Jean-Louis Bory in *Arts* (Paris), March 1964; review by Jean Collet in *Télérama* (Paris), 18 March 1964; books—*The Personal Vision of Ingmar Bergman* by Jorn Donner, Bloomington, Indiana 1964; *Ingmar Bergman* by Tommaso Chiaretti, Rome 1964; *Ingmar Bergman* by Jean Béranger and François Guyon, Lyon 1964; *Ingmar Bergman: The Search for God* by David Nelson, Boston 1964; *La Solitudine di Ingmar Bergman* by Guido Oldrini, Parma 1965; *Ingmar Bergman på teatern* by Henrik Sjögren, Stockholm 1968; *Ingmar Bergman* by Birgitta Steene, New York 1968; *The Silence of God: Creative Response to the Films of Ingmar Bergman* by Arthur Gibson, New York 1969; *Ingmar Bergman* by Robin Wood, New York 1969; *Bergman on Bergman* by Stig Björkman, Torsten Manns, and Jonas Sima, translated by Paul Britten Austin, London 1970; *Cinema Borealis: Ingmar Bergman and the Swedish Ethos* by Vernon Young, New York 1971; *Ingmar Bergman Directs* by John Simon, New York 1972; *Ingmar Bergman* by Tino Ranieri, Florence 1974; *Ingmar Bergman: Essays in Criticism* edited by Stuart Kaminsky, New York 1975; *Ingmar Bergman and Society* by Maria Bergom-Larsson, San Diego 1978; *Mindscreen: Bergman, Godard and the First-Person Film* by Bruce Kawin, Princeton 1978; *Ingmar Bergman* by Denis Marion, Paris 1979; *Ingmar Bergman: An Appreciation* by Roger Manvell, New York 1980; *My Story* by Ingrid Bergman with Alan Burgess, New York 1980; *Ingmar Bergman: The Cinema as Mistress* by Philip Mosley, Boston 1981; *Film and Dreams: An Approach to Bergman* edited by Vlada Petrić, South Salem, New York 1981; *Ingmar Bergman: A Critical Biography* by Peter Cowie, New York 1982; *A Reference Guide to Ingmar Bergman* by Birgitta Steene, Boston 1982; articles—"Le Sommet d'une trilogie esemplaire" by Jean Béranger in *Avant-Scène du cinéma* (Paris), May 1964; interview with Bergman on *Tystnaden* in *Sunday Times* (London), 15 March 1964; "Interview: Ingmar Bergman" in *Playboy* (Chicago), June 1964; "The Achievement of Ingmar Bergman" by James Scott in *Journal of Aesthetics and Art Criticism* (Cleveland), winter 1965; "Ingmar Bergman on the Silence of God" by William Hamilton in *Motive*, November 1966; "Ingmar Bergman" by Raymond Lefevre in *Image et son* (Paris), March 1969;

"Cinema Borealis" by Vernon Young in *Hudson Review* (Nutley, New Jersey), summer 1970; "Images and Words in Ingmar Bergman's Films" by Birgitta Steene in *Cinema Journal* (Evanston), fall 1970; "Devils in the Cathedral: Bergman's Triology" by W. Alexander in *Cinema Journal* (Iowa City), spring 1974; "*Le Silence*" in *Amis du Film et de la Television* (Brussels), February 1976; "Bergmans trilogi" by A. Troelsen in *Kosmorama* (Copenhagen), spring 1978.

* * *

The Silence: there are alternative or multiple significances to that title by Ingmar Bergman. The most commonly understood is an illusion (yet again: as in *The Seventh Seal*, *Winter Light*, and *Through a Glass Darkly*) to the utter unresponsiveness of God to the tribulations of humankind, but another potential implication is the silence that follows upon non-communication, misunderstanding, and the lack of sympathy between human beings. The protagonists in this film are two sisters in their thirties—Anna, the younger (Gunnel Lindblom), with her small son Johan (Jörgen Lindström), and Ester (Ingrid Thulin), who are travelling by train (the published script emphasizing its stench) to an unspecified central European country where the language is utterly unknown to them and is, indeed, an invention by Bergman. They end up in what is to be the main setting for the film—a suite of two rooms in a vast, almost unoccupied hotel in a city full of people with whom they cannot communicate and which is strangely, eerily silent. As in *Persona* (Bergman's film to be released some three years later) the two women are involved in a form of love/hate intimacy which some have tried to interpret as lesbian. While Anna is full of a lust for life and sex (which she seeks out promiscuously in this strange city), Ester (forever jealous of her younger sister) is suffering from what appears to be a terminal sickness, her only faithful attendant becoming an elderly and cadaverous floor waiter who seems to resemble Death himself.

The essence of this film lies in the failing relationship of the two sisters, who represent a polarity of opposites in temperament. Ingrid Thulin once told the writer that Bergman had considered inviting her to play both parts, thus emphasizing this polarity as dual aspects of a single person, but that the logistics of production with a single actress proved too daunting. Anna is sensual in all her contacts, even with her small son. The scenes between her and her eager lover (a man she picks up during an evening's solitary outing) caused the censors of the early 1960s some considerable concern, though they would cause little stir today. Anna's carnality contrasts with Ester's lonely austerity, and her demanding rationality. She is, according to the script, a translator, and she shows throughout the film her curiosity about certain words in the country's language, as conveyed to her by the waiter. As the elder, she attempts to dominate her sister (who is deeply resentful) and to adopt a guardian-like attitude to the boy, which makes Anna jealous. The boy himself wanders off to explore the hotel, large and empty like a mausoleum, and finds a kind of momentary, sick companionship with a party of dwarfs, creatures of his own size who are evidently a company of entertainers and virtually the only other inhabitants in the hotel. The effect of this perverse contact is somehow surreal. As for the country itself, Bergman says (*Bergman on Bergman*), "It's a country perparing for war, where war can break out any day...; all the time one feels it is something perverse and terrifying," Every so often tanks roll through the city streets, and the sinister wail of air-raid sirens can be heard.

Bergman has said much from time to time about this daunting film. In a press interview for the London *Sunday Times* (March 15, 1964) he said, "Ester loves her sister; she finds her beautiful and feels a tremendous responsibility for her, but she would be the first to be horrified if it were pointed out that her feelings were incestuous. Her mistake lies in the fact that she wants to control her sister—as her father had controlled her by his love. Love must be open. Otherwise Love is the beginning of Death. That is what I am trying to say." Some years later in *Bergman on Bergman* he added, "The crux of the matter is that Ester—even though she is ill and inwardly decaying—is struggling against the decay within her. She feels a sort of disgust for Anna's corporeality.... But Anna is uninhibitedly physical. She holds her little boy within the magic circle of her own animality, controls him."

There is, however, at least the suggestion of hope at the close of the film. Anna leaves her sister to return home, taking the child with her. But the boy carries a secret message with him from his aunt in a strange language which has excited her curiosity. Ester entertains maternal feelings towards him; the message excites him as he struggles to spell it out. As Bergman puts it (*Bergman on Bergman*), "To me Ester in all her misery represents a distillation of something indestructibly human, which the boy inherits from her.... Out of all man's misery and conflicts and his insufferable condition is crystaliized this clear little drop of something different—this sudden impulse to understand a few words in another language." The boy acts as a catalyst between the two sisters; both women, adds Bergman "turn their best sides towards the kid.... He escapes from the film almost unscathed." Nevertheless, he carries a toy gun and has a child-like vision of flight and the space age.

On its release, the film excited much hostile criticism—as anti-woman, anti-sex, as near-pornographic (partly because of Ester's moment of masturbation). The explosive, sometimes sick erotic suggestions and action in the film are thematic, not in any way pornographic. Bergman claims to have received after the film's release threatening or otherwise vicious letters and phonecalls, but in *Bergman on Bergman* he categorically rejects any of these hostile implications. The film, he says, "tells its story by simple means, not by symbols or such antics... The people in my films are exactly like myself—creatures of instinct, of rather poor intellectual capacity, who at best only think while they're talking.... My films draw on my own experience, however inadequately based logically and intellectually."

—Roger Manvell

UCCELLACCI E UCCELLINI. The Hawks and the Sparrows. Production: Arco Film; black and white, 35mm; running time: 100 mins., English version is 91 mins. Released May 1966, Rome.

Produced by Alfredo Bini; screenplay by Pier Paolo Pasolini; English sub-titles by Gideon Bachmann and Herman Weinberg; directed by Pier Paolo Pasolini; photography by Mario Bernardo and Tonino Delli Colli; edited by Nino Baragli; sound by Pietro Orotolani, sound mixed by Emilio Rosa; art direction by Luigi Scaccianoce, set decorated by Vittorio Biseo, scenic design by Angelo Rancati; music and adaptation by Ennio Morricone, song by Amedo Cassola; costumes designed by Danilo Donato; plant specialist: Pino Serpe, plants and flowers by Adriano Ceccotti, and ornithologist: Domenico Rossi. Filmed in Tuscania, near Fiumicino, and around Rome.

Cast: Toto (*Innocenti Toto/Brother Ciccillo*); Ninetto Davoli

(*Innocenti Ninetto/Brother Ninetto*); Femi Benussi (*Luna*); Rossana Di Rocco (*Friend of Ninetto*); Lena Lin Solaro (*Urganda La Sconosciuta*); Rosina Moroni (*Peasant woman*); Renato Capogna and Pietro Davoli (*Medieval louts*); Gabriele Baldini (*Dante's dentist*); Riccardo Redi (*Civil engineer*); Francesco Leonetti (*Crow's voice*).

Publications:

Script—*Uccellacci e uccellini*, Milan 1965; books—*Pier Paolo Pasolini* by Marc Gervais, Paris 1973; *Vita di Pasolini* by Enzo Siciliano, Milan 1978; *Teoria e tecnica del film in Pasolini* by Antonio Bertini, Rome 1979; *Pier Paolo Pasolini* by Stephen Snyder, Boston 1980; articles—"Pasolini—A Conversation in Rome" by John Bragin in *Film Culture* (New York), fall 1966; article by John Bragin in *Film Culture* (New York), fall 1966; article by Patrick MacFadden in *Take One* (Montreal), September/October 1966; "Pasolini: Rebellion, Art, and a New Society" by Susan MacDonald in *Screen* (London), May/June 1969; "Pier Paolo Pasolini" by John Bragin in *Film Society Review* (New York), article in 3 parts, nos.5, 6, and 7, 1969; "Pasolini: The Film of Alienation" by Noel Purdon in *Cinema* (London), August 1970; "Pasolini" by Roy Armes in *Films and Filming* (London), June 1971; "Quand le Christ, Marx et Freud se rencontrent..." by P. Sery in *Cinéma* (Paris), March 1972; "La Crise de l'idéologie dans *Uccellacci e uccellini*" by G. Fink in *Etudes cinématographiques* (Paris), no.109, 1976; issue on Pasolini of *Cinema* (Zurich), no.2, 1976; "Pier Paolo Pasolini," special issues of *Etudes cinématographique* (Paris), no.109-111, 1976, and no.112-114, 1977; "*Pajaritos y Pajarracos*" by I. Escudero in *Cinema 2002* (Madrid), October 1979.

*   *   *

Pier Paolo Pasolini's last black and white feature is an allegory of the passing of neorealism both as a cinematic style and as a response to Italian social and political conditions. The comedian Toto, the protagonist's amateur discovery, Ninetto Davoli, and a talking cow represent an ironical version of the Holy Trinity in this film of picaresque episodes. Birds and flight provide a central metaphor for the whole work, especially for the long middle episode, a gentle parody of Roberto Rossellini's *Francesco—Giulare di Dio*, in which Toto and Ninetto, as medieval monks, learn the languages of hawks and sparrows, catechise them, but fail to transform their instinctual violence to each other.

The preaching bird in the film represents a Marxist ideologue of the era of neorealism. In the end, the bird's companions dialectically sublate his message by seizing and eating him. That occurs shortly after a moving interlude in which the three travellers suddenly find themselves facing the massive public funeral of Palmiro Togliatti, the long-time head of the Italian Communist Party. According to the allegory of this film, the period of neorealism passed with the death of Togliatti. Yet the issue is not all that simple, and there are episodes to indicate that the iconographical validity of neorealism has also been diminished by the shift of Marxist energy from Moscow to the Third World, the accessibility of airplane travel to the poor, the impact of the idea of space travel, the shift of the Roman Catholic Church toward concerns of social justice during the Papacy of John XXIII, and the triumph of yellow journalism in Italy.

The welter of allusions to other films by Rossellini, Fellini, and Pasolini himself play an important role. The practice of dubbing which persists in Italy makes invention of a talking crow (or in reverse, an actor who can emit perfect bird sounds) a natural extension of the technical separation of image and picture in Italian filmmaking. In short, the film reflects on the historical and technical conditions of filmmaking in Italy. Its release corresponded to the point of maximal intensity in the filmmaker's work as a theoretician. The publication of the script was accompanied by four theoretical texts, including "The Cinema of Poetry," in which the filmmaker attempted a semiological analysis of the historical and technical issues of his film.

—P. Adams Sitney

UGETSU MONOGATARI. Production: Daiei studios; black and white, 35mm; running time: 96 mins.; length: 8622 feet. Released 1953.

Produced by Masaichi Nagata; screenplay by Matsutaro Kawaguchi; from Yoshikata Yoda's adaptation of two stories, "Asaji ga yado" (The Inn at Asaji) and "Jasei-no in" (Serpent of Desire), from the collection of stories *Ugetsu Monogatari* by Akinari Ueda (1768); directed by Kenji Mizoguchi; photography by Kazuo Miyagawa; edited by Mitsuji Miyata; sound by Iwao Otani; production design by Kisaku Ito; music by Fumio Hayasaka and Ichiro Saito; documentation of the costumes by Kusune Kainosho; pottery consultant: Zengoro Eiraku; choreography by Kinshichi Kodera.

Filmed 26 January-13 March 1953. Venice Film Festival, Silver Prize Winner and Italian Critics Award, 1953; Edinburgh Film Festival, Gold Medal Winner, 1955.

Cast: Machiko Kyo (*Wakasa*); Kinuyo Tanaka (*Miyagi*); Mitsuki Mito (*Ohama*); Masayuki Mori (*Genjuro*); Sakae Ozawa (*Tobe*); Sugisaku Aoyama (*Old priest*); Kikue Nori (*Ukon*); Mitsusaburo Ramon (*Commander of the clan NIWA*); Ryosuke Kagawa (*Village chief*); Kichijiro Tsuchida (*Silk merchant*); Syozo Nanbu (*Shinto priest*); Ichiisaburo Sawamura (*Genichi*).

Publications:

Script—"*Les Contes de la lune vague après la pluie*" in *Avant-Scène du cinéma* (Paris), 1 January 1977; reviews—by Eric Rohmer in *Cahiers du cinéma* (Paris), March 1958; "La Presse" in *Avant-Scène du cinéma* (Paris), 1 January 1977; books—*Auteurs of the Japanese Cinema* (in Japanese) by Akira Iwasaki, Japan 1958; *A Certain Mizoguchi Kenji* (in Japanese) by Hideo Tsumura, Japan 1958; *Mizoguchi Kenji* by Ve-Ho, Paris 1964; *Mizoguchi Kenji* by Michel Mesnil, revised ed., Paris 1971; *Kenji Mizoguchi* by Max Tessier, Paris 1971; *The Waves at Genji's Door* by Joan Mellen, New York 1976; *Japanese Film Directors* by Audie Bock, New York 1978; *Cinema, The Magic Vehicle: A Guide to Its Achievement: Journey Two* edited by Adam Garbicz and Jacek Klinowksi, Metuchen, New Jersey 1979; *To the Distant Observer: Form and Meaning in the Japanese Cinema* by Noël Burch, London 1979; *Il cinema di Kenji Mizoguchi*, Venice 1980; *The Japanese Film: Art and Industry* by Joseph Anderson and Donald Richie, expanded edition, Princeton 1982; articles—"Kenji Mizoguchi" by Donald Richie and Joseph I. Anderson in *Sight and Sound* (London), autumn 1955;

"Mizoguchi fut le plus grand cinéaste japonais" by Jean-Luc Godard in *Arts* (Paris), February 1958; issue on Mizoguchi of *Cahiers du cinéma* (Paris), May 1959; "*Les Contes de la lune vague après la pluie*" by René Gilson in *Cinéma 59* (Paris), May 1959; "Diableries et misères de la guerre" by Georges Sadoul in *Les Lettres françaises* (Paris), 26 April 1959; article by Alexandre Astruc in *Films and Filming* (London), summer 1961; article by Eric Rhode in *Sight and Sound* (London), spring 1962; article by Paul Rotha in *Films and Filming* (London), May 1962; issue on Mizoguchi of *Cahiers du cinéma* (Paris), August/September 1964; "Souvenirs sur Mizoguchi" by Yoshikata Yoda in *Cahiers du cinéma* (Paris), no.174, 1966; "Kenji Mizoguchi" by Akira Iwasaki in *Anthologie du cinéma* (Paris), November 1967; "The Density of Mizoguchi's Scripts", interview with Yoshikata Yoda, in *Cinema* (Los Angeles), spring 1971; "Mizoguchi: The Ghost Princess and the Seaweed Gatherer" by Robin Wood in *Film Comment* (New York), March/April 1973; "Mizoguchi" by Jean-Paul Le Pape in *Avant-Scène du cinéma* (Paris), 1 January 1977; "Contes de la lune vague après la pluie" by J.C. Godefroy in *Cinématographe* (Paris), November 1978; "Revers de la quiétude" by A. Masson in *Positif* (Paris), November 1978; "Mizoguchi and Modernism" by R. Cohen in *Sight and Sound* (London), spring 1978; "Kenji Mizoguchi" by Donald Richie in *Cinema, A Critical Dictionary* edited by Richard Roud, London 1980; "Mizoguchi: un art sans artifice" by H. Niogret in *Positif* (Paris), December 1980; "On Kenji Mizoguchi" by Tadao Sato and Dudley Andrew in *Film Criticism* (Edinboro, Pennsylvania), spring 1980.

*   *   *

Ugetsu monogatari was not the first Kenji Mizoguchi film to be shown in the West, but it was the first to reveal him to the West as a major artist. Swiftly establishing itself (especially in France) on many critics' "Ten Best" lists, the film opened the way for the acclamation of the work of Mizoguchi's final period. For some, he became the supreme filmmaker, the cinematic Shakespeare, realizing to the fullest the potential of film as an art form. That was at the time when the "potential of film" was generally felt to have been identified and adequately expounded by André Bazin; an assessment which can still be accepted if we add the proviso that Bazin accounted for only one of film's many potentials.

However, the supremacy of his "late" period and the *kind* of achievement that it represents, has been increasingly challenged since the 1960s. Two factors help account for this: one is the discovery of Mizoguchi's earlier films, previously almost unknown; the other is the politicization of film criticism and the growth, within it, of an ideological awareness. In recent years, Nöel Burch's *To The Distant Observer*, Joan Mellen's *The Waves at Genji's Door*, and Frieda Frieberg's useful pamphlet *Women in Mizoguchi's Films*—three books written from quite distinct critical positions, with quite distinct estimates of Mizoguchi's work—have agreed on one point, the application (in a derogatory sense) of the term "aestheticism" to Mizogushi's late work. Films previously hailed as the greatest ever made— *Ugetsu, Sansho dayu, The Life of Oharu*—are suddenly perceived as evidence of Mizoguchi's withdrawal from the radicalism of his work in the 1930s and 1940s, and a retreat from a social/political viewpoint into the realm of aesthetic contemplation.

The relationship between aesthetics and politics is incredibly complex: the critical problems it generates have never been successfully resolved. It is true that *Ugetsu monogatari* is ideologically more conservative than, say, *Sisters of Gion* or *My Love Has Been Burning*. The crux lies in the treatment of women. From the radical feminist protest of his earlier films to the celebration of woman as self-sacrificer, redeemer and mother in *Ugetsu* is certainly a large and disconcerting jump. (Mizoguchi's conversion to Buddhism in the early 1950s is doubtlessly a related factor.) Further, *Ugetsu* can be read as advocating the resignation to and the acceptance of one's lot. This withdrawl from the active struggle in favor of a spiritual transcendence makes the hardships of the material world not so much endurable as irrelevant. The film encourages such a reading, yet cannot be reduced to it.

Ugetsu contains within itself an answer to the charge of aestheticism. The story of Genjuro the potter can be taken as Mizoguchi's artistic testament. At the beginning of the film Genjuro is a materialistic artisan, mass-producing pots as a commodity. His encounter with the Lady Wakasa introduces him to the world of the aesthetic. She shows him fragile and exquisite vessels which she presents, and he accepts, as his creations, but which are totally unlike the crude, functional wares we have seen him almost brutally shape earlier. The complexity of response that this whole central segment evokes is sufficient in itself to call into question the reduction of the film to a single clear-cut statement. The Lady Wakasa is both evil spirit and a pathetic, victimized woman; the world of the aesthetic (which is also the world of the erotic) has a fascination and authentic beauty that make it far from easily dismissible. That alluring world, however, has three negative connotations. First, it is presented as a possible option only if one turns one's back on reality. It is a world of fantasy and illusion where the suffering of human beings in a material world of oppression, cruelty, greed, and human exploitation cannot be permitted to intrude. (One of the most expressive cuts in the history of the cinema is that from the exquisite scene of lovemaking on the cultivated lawn beside the lake to Miyagi, fearfully peering out from her hiding-place, a woman vulnerable to attack from all sides of a society created by men.) Second, Wakasa herself is not presented as an autonomous character, even in her appreciation of beauty. Everything she knows, her father had taught her. Her father (long since dead) appears in the film as a hideous, emaciated skull-like mask speaking in a disturbingly strange subterranean voice. The aesthetic, whatever else it may be, is clearly defined as a patriarchal imposition: "taste" is what women are taught by men. Finally, the father is linked to war, domination, and imperialism. Wakasa's father had the misfortune to lose, and have his clan exterminated, but the film makes clear that he would have inflicted precisely the same fate on his enemies, had the outcome been reversed.

The overall effect of the film is to suggest, not that the aesthetic is invalid in itself, but that it cannot validly exist in this world. (The film's contemporary relevance is by no means compromised by its setting in the sixteenth century.) The plot Genjuro is making at the end of the film, under Miyagi's spiritual supervision, is significantly different from the two previous kinds of work: it is made with loving care, but also the product of experience; it is a work of art yet made to be used by Genjuro's peers rather than admired by a cultivated elite. The great beauty of the film is of an order altogether different from the aestheticism of the Wakasa world. Mizoguchi never aestheticizes pain and suffering (in the manner of, say, David Lean in *Dr. Zhivago*). The extraordinary sequence-shot showing the mortal wounding of Miyagi is a case in point: the aesthetic strategies (long take, distance, complex camera movement, depth of field showing simultaneous actions in foreground and background) serve to sustain the characteristic Mizoguchian tension between involvement and contemplation, but do not in any way mitigate the horror of the scene.

If on one level *Ugetsu* tends to reinforce traditional myths of woman, on another it remains true to the radical spirit of Mizoguchi's earlier Marxist-feminist principles. The actions of both Genjuro and Tobei are motivated by the values forced upon them by patriarchal capitalism. They both seek success (Genjuro through the acquisition of wealth, Tobei through the prestige of becoming a Samurai) in order to impress their wives, neither of whom shows the smallest interest in such ambitions. The film is a systematic critique of the kind of male egoism (expressing itself in greed and violence and the destruction of human relationships, always at the expense of women) that a patriarchal capitalist civilization promotes.

—Robin Wood

UKIGUSA. Floating Weeds. Drifting Weeds. Production: Daiei (Tokyo); color, 35mm; running time: 119 mins. Released 17 November 1959, Japan.

Produced by Masaichi Nagata; screenplay by Yasujiro Ozu and Kogo Noda; from Ozu's script of his 1934 film version of this story; directed by Yasujiro Ozu; photography by Kazuo Miyagawa; art direction by Tomo Hirogawara; music by Takanori Saito.

Cast: Ganjiro Nakamura; Machiko Kyo; Ayako Wakao; Hiroshi Kawaguchi; Haruko Sugimura; Hitomi Nozoe; Chishu Ryu; Hirotsugu Mitsui; Yataro Kurokawa; Kataro Bando.

Publications:

Books—*Ozu Yasujiro no Geijutsu* [The Art of Yasujiro Ozu] by Tadao Sato, Tokyo 1971; *Ozu Yasujiro—Hito to Shigoto* [Yasujiro Ozu: The Man and His Work] edited by Jun Satomi and others, Tokyo 1972; *Transcendental Style in Film: Ozu, Bresson, Dreyer* by Paul Schrader, Berkeley 1972; *Ozu* by Donald Richie, Berkeley 1974; *Yasujiro Ozu: A Critical Anthology* edited by John Gillett, London 1976; *Japanese Film Directors* by Audie Bock, New York 1978; *The Japanese Film: Art and Industry* by Joseph Anderson and Donald Richie, expanded edition, Princeton 1982; articles—"The Later Films of Yasujiro Ozu" by Donald Richie in *Film Quarterly* (Berkeley), fall 1959; "Yasujiro Ozu" by Chishu Ryu in *Sight and Sound* (London), spring 1964; issue on Ozu of *Kinema Jumpo* (Tokyo), February 1964; "Ozu" by Akira Iwasaki in *Film* (London), summer 1965; "Ozu" by Manny Farber in *Art Forum* (New York), June 1970; "Yasujiro Ozu" by Jean-Claude Philippe in *Dossiers du cinéma: Cinéastes* no.1, Paris 1971; "Yasujiro Ozu" by Max Tessier in *Anthologie du cinéma* (Paris), July/October 1971; "Ozu" by Jonathan Rosenbaum in *Film Comment* (New York), summer 1972; "Space and Narrative in the Films of Ozu" by Kristin Thompson and David Bordwell in *Screen* (London), summer 1976; "Yasujiro Ozu" by Donald Richie in *Cinema, A Critical Dictionary* edited by Richard Roud, London 1980.

*　　　*　　　*

During his long career that lasted from the 1920's into the 1960's, Japanese director Yasujiro Ozu made a number of films with similar plots. Occasionally he remade one of his own films. *Ukigusa* is not only his best remake but also one of his best films. He first made *Ukigusa* in 1934 as a silent film. Though no major changes in the basic plot and structure were incorporated into the remake, some minor alterations and the exquisite visual style characteristic of his later years improved upon the 1934 version.

Ozu is known for his quiet films about middle class family life, but *Ukigusa* is a departure for him because the "family" in this film consists of an itinerant actor, a woman whom he is visiting for the first time in 12 years, and their teen-aged son, who does not know who his father is. *Ukigusa* is also a departure in that it contains a number of melodramatic events, such as the boy's discovery of the identity of his father. Despite these differences, *Ukigusa* represents Ozu at the height of his powers as he develops the plot with a leisurely pace, using many shots of long duration to carefully establish the setting and themes, and to develop the relationships among the characters.

Throughout the film the viewer is aware of the painterly qualities of the images. The opening scene, for example, consists of a series of shots of the seacoast with a lighthouse visible in each shot. Any one of those images could stand as a painting, but Ozu uses them to contribute to the tone of the film as a whole. Ozu gave much of the credit for the superb visual style of *Ukigusa* to Kazuo Miyagawa, the cinematographer, but if one compares *Ukigusa* with other Ozu films that Miyagawa did not photograph, it is obvious that credit should also go to the director. Particularly notable in the films of Ozu is camera placement. It is usually only three feet above the ground, eye-level for a person sitting on the traditional Japanese *tatami*.

One of the most significant themes of *Ukigusa*, typical in the work of Ozu, is that things do not change. For a short time the mother hopes that the actor will quit traveling and join her and their son in a true family, but when he leaves, she will not let the son try to stop him. It is this theme that illuminates the powerful final sequence of the film. Because the acting troupe is unsuccessful and has disbanded, the old actor goes to the railway station to make his way alone. He is determined that he will not go back to his long-time mistress, who was also a member of the troupe. At the station, the mistress finds him and makes overtures to him, but he ignores her. When she tries to light his cigarette, he ignores her as the match burns out. She strikes another match, and, finally, he allows her to light his cigarette. Not a word is spoken during this exchange. The film ends, much as it had started, with the two travelling together.

Ukigusa stands as a masterpiece for its exquisite cinematography, its restrained style, and its sensitive exploration of human feelings.

—Timothy Johnson

UMBERTO D. Production: Rizzoli-De Sica-Amato and Dear Films; black and white, 35mm; running time: 90 mins., some sources state 80 mins. Released 1952.

Director of production: Nino Misiano; screenplay by Cesare Zavattini with Vittorio De Sica; directed by Vittorio De Sica; photography by Aldo Graziati (a.k.a. G.R. Aldo); edited by Eraldo di Roma; sound engineered by Ennio Sensi; production design by Virgilio Marchi; music by Alessandro Cigognini; the opening credits begin with the dedication, "This film is dedicated to my father. Signed: Vittorio De Sica." Filmed 1951 in Cinecittà studios, and in and around Rome. Cost: about 140 million lire.

New York Film Critics Award, Best Foreign Film (shared with *Diabolique*), 1955.

Cast: Carlo Battisti (*Umberto*); Maria-Pia Casilio (*Maria*); Lina Gennari (*Landlord*); Alberto Albani Barbieri (*The fiancé*); Elena Rea (*Sister at the hospital*); Memo Carotenuto (*Voice of light for Umberto in the hospital*); Ileana Simova (*Surprised woman in the bedroom*); plus many non-professional actors.

Publications:

Scripts—*Umberto D* by De Sica and Zavattini and others, 1954; "*Umberto D*" by Cesare Zavattini with Vittorio De Sica in *Avant-Scène du cinéma* (Paris), 15 April 1980; reviews—in *Films in Review* (New York), November 1952; "*Umberto D*" by Georges Sadoul in *Les Lettres françaises* (Paris), October 1952; review by Karel Reisz in *Sight and Sound* (London), October/-December 1953; "La Presse" in *Avant-Scène du cinéma* (Paris), 15 April 1980; books—*Il cinema neorealistico italiano* by G.C. Castello, Turin, 1956; *Il neorealismo italiano* by Brunello Rondi, Parma, Italy 1956; *Le Néo-réalisme italien et ses créateurs* by Patrice Howald, Paris 1959; *Vittorio De Sica* by Henri Agel, 2nd ed., Paris 1964; *Vittorio De Sica* by Pierre Leprohon, Paris 1966; *What is Cinema?*, Vols. I and II, by André Bazin, translated by Hugh Gray, Berkeley 1967; *Encountering Directors* by Charles Thomas Samuels, New York 1972; *Patterns of Realism* by Roy Armes, New York 1972; *La mia vita con Vittorio De Sica* by Maria Mercader, Milan 1978; articles—by Catherine de la Roche in *Films and Filming* (London), December 1954; article by George Fenin in *Film Culture* (New York), winter 1955; "Italian Notes" by Gavin Lambert in *Sight and Sound* (London), January 1955; "Money, the Public, and *Umberto D*" by Vittorio De Sica in *Films and Filming* (London), January 1956; article in *The Village Voice* (New York), 8 February 1956; "Bread, Love, and Neo-Realism" by W. Sargeant in the *New Yorker*, 29 June 1957 and 6 July 1957; article by Eric Rhode in *Sight and Sound* (London), winter 1960-61; "Why Neo-Realism Failed" by Eric Rhode in *Sight and Sound* (London), winter 1960-61; "Poet of Poverty" by D. McVay in *Films and Filming* (London), October and November 1964; entire issue of articles by De Sica in *Bianco e nero* (Rome), fall 1975; "La città e lo spazio" by F. La Polla in *Bianco e nero* (Rome), September/December 1975; "La città e lo spazio" by F. La Polla in *Bianco e nero* (Rome), September/December 1976; "Vittorio de Sica 1902-1974" by Henri Agel, special issue of *Avant-Scène du cinéma* (Paris), 15 October 1978; "Vittorio de Sica" by J. Passalacqua in *Films in Review* (New York), April 1978; "Vittorio De Sica, 1902-1974" by Henri Agel in *Anthologie du cinéma*, Vol. 10, Paris 1979; "*Umberto D*" by Henri Agel in *Avant-Scène du cinéma* (Paris), 15 April 1980; "La Politesse du désespoir" by Henri Agel in *Avant-Scène du cinéma* (Paris), 15 April 1980; "Entretien avec Carlo Battisti" by Marie-Luce Thomas in *Avant-Scène du cinéma* (Paris), 15 April 1980.

*   *   *

Umberto D. is often considered Vittorio De Sica's masterpiece, the purest example of Cesare Zavattini's aesthetic, and most highly developed expression of this historic collaboration of director and screenwriter. In may also be the most relentlessly bleak of the great works of neorealism.

De Sica was aware from the start that *Umberto D.* might be susceptible to the same charge of subversion that had greeted *Miracle in Milan*. On the other hand, he had hoped, as he pointed out in a later comment, that "the story of that old retired office worker, his tragic solitude, his boundless sadness and his pathetic, awkward attempts at warming his heart (would have) a kind of universality that would be understood by everyone." This was not to be the case. De Sica was accused by many, including the then junior minister Giulio Andreotti, of washing Italy's dirty laundry in public, of irresponsibilty in projecting a negative view of the country. Against *Umberto D.* were mobilized forces strongly opposed to exporting images of an Italy depressed and without justice; following *Umberto D.*, the foreign distribution of films that were declared unflattering to Italian society was banned. The authorities feared, and with good reason, what the critic Georges Sadoul and a few others most admired. At the time of its first showing, Sadoul noted that *Umberto D.* (along with *Sciuscia*, *Bicycle Thief*, and *Miracle in Milan*, constituted an extraordinary "act of accusation" against contemporary Italy. Official hostility was followed by critical indifference, and to complete the disastrous reception, *Umberto D.* failed miserably at the box office. The story of old age, loneliness, and spiritual and material poverty was not likely to appeal to audiences who, in 1952, were eager to forget the past and to embrace the economic miracle which they thought—correctly as it turned out—was just around the corner.

Critical debate since the release of the film has focused on what is generally understood to be its central aesthetic question, the question of duration. Jean Collet was among the first to underscore that through the restitution to film of real time, De Sica had succeeded in giving the most banal of situations remarkable depth. But it is André Bazin's essay, "De Sica: Metteur en Scène," that most completely delimits and defines the issue. Bazin is specifically interested in those privileged moments in *Umberto D.* that afford a glimpse of what "a truly realist cinema of the time could be, a cinema of 'duration'." Two scenes particularly—Umberto going to bed and the awakening of the servant girl—exemplify those perfect instances in which duration determined by character creates a mise-en-scène which replaces drama with gesture, narrative with act. For Bazin, in these sequences "it is a matter of making 'life time'—the continuing to be a person to whom nothing in particular happens—(that) takes on the quality of spectacle...." Zavattini's lengthy descriptions of the most minute though absolutely necessary movements and expressions, scrupulously performed under De Sica's direction and photographed in revealing long takes by G.R. Aldo, exhibit, for Bazin, "complete fidelity to the aesthetic of neorealism." A conflicting position is taken some years later by Jean Mitry whose objection is not to the concept of duration, but to what is, in his view, a duration without significance. Duration in *Umberto D.*, according to Mitry, "is nothing more than banality and is charged very simply with prolonging, beyond the tolerable, events whose sense is clear from the very first images."

These events are as follows: Umberto D., a retired civil servant is among the aging demonstrators at a rally in support of increased pensions. (Umberto is played by a Carlo Battisti, a university professor De Sica pressed into service after a chance meeting on the streets of Rome.) Impoverished but genteel, about to be dispossessed, completely alone except for the company of his dog, Flike, and the occasional companionship of a young servant girl, Umberto determines to take his own life. His only concern is for Flike whom he attempts to find a home before doing away with himself. Failing in the first attempt, Umberto determines to kill himself *and* Flike, and failing again, has no recourse but to take up once more an entirely hopeless existence. Were it not for his indifference hostility, Umberto's confrontation with cold, often hostile persons and institutions would earn him the sympathy of the viewers, and the viewers the pleasure of the well-earned sentimental response. But De Sica, Zavattini and Aldo take the necessary measures of script, direction and camera that distance the viewer and deny easy sympathy. The cruelty of society's neglect of Umberto (which so offended the authorities), and lack of compassion of peers and institutions (which no doubt offended the charitable), and Umberto's grievous self-centeredness finally elicit, through the manipulations of style, the detachment of the viewer (and his or her attendant dissatisfaction) from Umberto's dispair. The rigor of *Umberto D.* explains both its initial failure and its subsequent reputation. Bazin's prediction was borne out; *Umberto D.* would prove "a masterpiece to which film history is certainly going to grant a place of honor...."

—Mirella Jona Affron

UNDERWORLD. Production: Paramount Famous Players Lasky; 1928; black and white, 35mm, silent; running time: 85 mins. Released 21 August 1927.

Produced by Hector Turnbull, presented by Adolph Zukor and Jesse L. Lasky; screenplay by Robert N. Lee, adapted by Charles Furthman; titles by Ben Hecht; from an original story by George Marion, Jr.; directed by Josef von Sternberg; photography by Bert Glennon; art direction by Hans Dreier.

Academy Award, Writing-Original Story, 1927-28.

Cast: George Bancroft (*Bull Weed*); Evelyn Brent (*Feathers McCoy*); Clive Brook ("*Rolls Royce*"); Larry Semon (*Slippy Lewis*); Fred Kohler (*Buck Mulligan*); Helen Lynch (*Mulligan's girl*); Jerry Mandy (*Paloma*); Karl Morse (*High Collar Sam*).

Publications:

Books—*An Index to the Films of Josef von Sternberg* by Curtis Harrington, London 1949; *Fun in a Chinese Laundry*, New York 1965, published in France as *Souvenirs d'un montreur d'ombres*, Paris 1966; *The Films of Josef von Sternberg* by Andrew Sarris, New York 1966; *Josef von Sternberg, Dokumentation, Eine Darstellung*, Mannheim, Germany 1966; *Josef von Sternberg* by Herman G. Weinberg, Paris 1966; *Josef von Sternberg: A Critical Study* by Herman G. Weinberg, New York 1967; *The Cinema of Josef von Sternberg* by John Baxter, New York 1971; *Film Noir* edited by Alain Silver and Elizabeth Ward, Woodstock, New York 1979; articles—issue on von Sternberg in *Filmcritic* (Tokyo), 1928; "Josef von Sternberg" by Jim Tully in *Vanity Fair* (New York), July 1928; "Josef von Sternberg" by Curtis Harrington in *Cahiers du cinéma* (Paris), October/November 1951; "Sternberg, le donne e i gansters" by Giovanni Scognamillo in *Bianco e nero* (Rome), November/December 1954; "Un-American Activities" by V.F. Perkins in *Movie* (London), December 1962; "Josef von Sternberg" by Herman G. Weinberg in *Film Heritage* (Dayton, Ohio), winter 1965; "L'Oeuvre de Josef von Sternberg" by Bernard Eisenschitz in *Avant-Scène du cinéma* (Paris), March 1966; "*Underworld*" by Eileen Bowser in *Film Notes* edited by Eileen Bowser, New York 1969; "*Les Nuits de Chicago*" by Claude Beylie in *Ecran* (Paris), January 1975.

* * *

Underworld, Josef von Sternberg's fourth film, was the first of his features to be both a popular and critical success. It utilized the personalized approach which von Sternberg had displayed in his earlier films: a heavy reliance on artificial studio sets rather than realistic location, subtle lighting, and the manipulation of his actors as if they were little more than puppets. *Underworld* boasted something more, a plot line involving gangsters which could easily appeal to a general audience. The plot also makes *Underworld* the first in a new line of gangster pictures, culminating in the early thirties with *Little Caesar* and *Scarface*, a genre to which von Sternberg himself added *The Dragnet* and *Thunderbolt*. (However, Andrew Sarris has argued that *Underworld* is a "pre-gangster film," with George Bancroft's "Bull" Weed "preceeding later gangsters more in the manner of poetic prophecy than of journalistic observation.")

Ben Hecht supplied the story—his first screen credit—and received the first Academy Award for Best Writing (Original Story). Presumably set in Chicago, *Underworld* is a love triangle/gangster melodrama involving Bull Weed, king of the underworld, Rolls Royce, a gentleman gangster who is the brains behind Weed's operation, and Feathers, Weed's girlfriend. On another level it is simply a human drama involving love and honor. George Bancroft is admirable as Bull Weed, and, as a result of his performance, was re-signed to a new Paramount contract. Clive Brook is perhaps a little too dapper as Rolls Royce, but Evelyn Brent is devastatingly cool, beautiful and economical in her performance as Feathers. The feathers that she wears, and that give her the nickname, are as light and sensual as Evelyn Brent's performance, which is almost a rehearsal for the roles that Marlene Dietrich was to play for von Sternberg in the thirties.

Perhaps *Underworld* is most remarkable for its curious mixture of poetic and realistic cinema. Through subtitles and sets, it attempts to bring the reality of the underworld of the gangster to its audience, but, at the same time, it can never escape the poetic qualities found in all of von Sternberg's films. In its final moments, as Bull Weed realizes the strength of the love between Rolls Royce and Feathers, he helps them escape from the police through a secret passageway. It is a sequence which could easily have lapsed into cheap melodrama, but succeeds due to von Sternberg's lighting effects and resulting atmosphere. Thanks to the director's images, a final title as clichéd as "There was something I had to find out—and that hour was worth more to me than my whole life" takes on a personal, warm meaning. Only during the gangster's ball, when Feathers is given her coronation, does the film take on a Hollywood-like flair. Perhaps, as has been suggested, *Underworld* marked von Sternberg's realization that if he was to succeed as a commercial filmmaker, a certain compromise was necessary.

—Anthony Slide

UNSERE AFRIKAREISE. Our Trip to Africa. Color, 16mm; running time: 12 1/2 mins. Released 1966.

Photographed, directed, and edited by Peter Kubelka; sound recorded and edited by Peter Kubelka.

Filmed 1961 in Africa.

Publications:

Review—by Jonas Mekas in *The Village Voice* (New York), 13 October 1966; book—*Visionary Film: The American Avant-Garde* by P. Adams Sitney, New York 1979; articles—"Kubelka Concrete (Our Trip to Vienna)" by P. Adams Sitney in *Film Culture* (New York), fall 1964; interview by Jonas Mekas in *Film Culture* (New York), spring 1967; "The Films of Peter Kubelka" by Earl Bodien in *Film Quarterly* (Berkeley), winter 1966-67; article by P. Adams Sitney in *New Cinema Bulletin*, May 1967; article in *Téléciné* (Paris), June 1973; reference in *British National Film Catalogue*, vol. 14, 1976; article in *Wide Angle* (Athens, Ohio), no.3, 1978.

* * *

In 1961, Peter Kubelka was asked to make a documentary about a group of Europeans on an African hunting trip. He accompanied them, recorded many hours of film and sound, and then spent five years editing this material into a most unconventional film. The result, *Unsere Afrikareise*, is one of the most densely-packed 13 minutes in film history, and makes truly extraordinary use of the creative possibilities of sound.

Kubelka bases his use of sound on the notion that accompanying an image with its own synchronous sound adds little, and merely imitates nature; rather, he weds an image to a sound recorded elsewhere. These combinations, which he calls "sync events," are often matched quite precisely in timing and rhythm, as when a gunshot appears to shoot a hat off a man's head; or when white and black men shake hands to the sound of thunder. By combining disparate elements, Kubelka makes "articulations" (his words), which fuse separate pieces both rhythmically and thematically is a manner possible only in film.

Kubelka's juxtaposition of images in *Unsere Afrikareise* follows similar lines. Images taken at different times and places are cut together, often on matched movements, to create momentary illusions of continuity. The images are disparate enough, however, so that the viewer is never fooled. A hunter shakes an African's hand and we cut to a zebra's leg, shaking similarly, as if the hunter were shaking *it*, but the hunter is nowhere in the shot. When the next shot reveals that the zebra is being skinned, we understand that while the hunter was not literally causing the zebra's leg to move, there was a deeper causal connection between the two shakes. Kubelka's juxtapositions are anything but arbitrary; they reveal truths inherent in his material.

The intensely concentrated quality of *Unsere Afrikareise* stems in part from the multitude of connections between image and image, sound and sound, and image and sound, that Kubelka orchestrated into a unified whole. There is often a temptation to read direct thematic statements in many of the film's articulations. Editing connections are continually made on the white hunters' gazes, hand gestures, and gun-pointing, linking those actions to suggest the Europeans' aggression toward their surroundings. Kubelka's cuts often suggest that a European has just "shot" an African, or the forest itself. The Africans, by contrast, appear as part of nature, rather than separate from it.

It would be a serious mistake, however, to limit one's perception of the film to such themes. What is most extraordinary about Kubelka's achievement is not the specific connections he establishes between elements, but rather the system that the entire network of connections form. Repeated viewings of the film reveal it as too multiple in its implications to be resolvable into a single interpretation. Thematic results of specific articulations are merely a few aspects of many in the film. Kubelka's almost-musical form establishes a grand relation between virtually every image and sound and every other across the entire film.

The resulting multitude of connections is expressive of many, rather than a few, possibilities. The viewer is ultimately led out of time, to contemplate these connections in memory, and to regard the film as if it were a monument erected as a record of civilization, not as a statement on it but as a kind of totem for it.

—Fred Camper

LES VACANCES DE MONSIEUR HULOT. Mr. Hulot's Vacation. Mr. Hulot's Holiday. Production: Cady Films/Discina; black and white, 35mm; running time: 93 mins. Released 1951.

Screenplay by Jacques Tati and Henri Marquet; directed by Jacques Tati; photography by J. Mercanton and J. Mouselle; production design by Henri Schmitt; music by Alain Romans.

Cast: Jacques Tati (*Mon. Hulot*); Nathalie Pascaud (*Martine*); Michele Rolla (*Aunt*); Valentine Camay (*Old maid*); Louis Perrault (*Boatman*); André Dubois (*Colonel*); Lucien Frégis (*Hotel proprietor*); Raymond Carl (*Waiter*).

Publications:

Books—*Monsieur Hulot's Holiday* by Jeane-Claude Carriere, New York 1959; *Jacques Tati* by Armand Cauliez, Paris 1968; *French Cinema Since 1946*, Vol.I, by Roy Armes, Cranbury, New Jersey 1970; *French Film* by Roy Armes, New York 1970; *The Comic Mind* by Gerald Mast, New York 1973; *Jacques Tati* by Penelope Gilliatt, London 1976; *The Films of Jacques Tati* by Brent Maddock, Metuchen, New Jersey 1977; articles— "Imports" in *Time* (New York), 31 March 1952; article by A.H. Weiler in *The New York Times*, 20 February 1952; "Mr. Hulot" in the *New Yorker*, 17 July 1954; "The Art of Jacques Tati" by A.C. Mayer in *Quarterly of Film, Radio, and Television* (Berkeley), fall 1955; "Jacques Tati" in *Film* (London), September/October 1958; "Hulot: Or the Common Man as Observer and Critic" by John Simon in the *Yale French Review* (New Haven), no.23, 1959; "The Comic Art of Jacques Tati" by Roy Armes in *Screen* (London), February 1970; "*Les Vacances de M. Hulot*" by F. Chevassu in *Image et son* (Paris), May 1977; "*Les Vacances de M. Hulot*" by E. Decaux in *Cinématographe* (Paris), May 1977; "Parameters of the Open Film: *Les Vacances de Monsieur Hulot*" by K. Thompson in *Wide Angle* (Athens, Ohio), no.4, 1977; "*Riemuloma Rivieralla, Enoni on toista maata, Traffic—Liikenne*" by T. Tuominen in *Filmihullu* (Helsinki, Finland), no.5, 1978; "*Die Ferien des Monsieur Hulot*" by C. Prochnow in *Film und Fernsehen* (East Berlin), vol.7, no.9, 1979; issue on Tati of *Cahiers du cinéma* (Paris), September 1979.

* * *

Les Vacances de M. Hulot is one of the most radical films ever made—the *Sacre du printemps* of the movies. If its radicalism has never been fully perceived—it has entertained audiences around the world, rather than scandalizing them—it is because *Les Vacances* is a comedy, and everyone knows that comedies aren't to be taken seriously. But without *Les Vacances*, there would be no Jean-Luc Godard, no Jean-Marie Straub, no Marguerite Duras—no modern cinema. With his 1953 film, Jacques Tati drove the first decisive wedge between cinema and classical narration. To do so, Tati had to return to the prehistory of movies—the age of Lumière, Méliès, Porter, and their anonymous predecessors, before the story-telling priority was firmly encoded in the way films were shot and edited—in order to find a non-narrative way of seeing. The gaze of Tati's camera is, as in the earliest films, almost entirely innocent: it does not make the value judgements, the selections of one element over another, that force a story out of an undifferentiated world. Tati shoots without prejudice, without priorities; he sees (or attempts to see, within the limits of the frame) everything.

Tati pretends that Griffith never existed. He holds his shots where the classical, story-telling grammar would demand that he cut away to another; he prefers long shots over close-ups, the embracing overview to the significant detail. One of the opening gags in Les Vacances involves a group of passengers running back and forth from one train platform to another, misled by the unintelligible announcements on the P.A. system as to which track their train will arrive on. A Griffith would film the scene with insert shots of passenger's panicked faces, and perhaps cut back and forth between the two tracks to emphasize the suspense—will the passengers make their train or not? But Tati simply mounts his camera on the roof of the station, where he has a clear, downward overview of the whole scene, and films the action in a single, continuous shot. As the group of travellers dashes from the far track to the near, from background to foreground, the shot becomes a kind of warm-up exercise for the film that is to follow: the viewer is led to explore the entire field of the shot, from near to far and from side to side, top to bottom. The viewer learns to direct his attentions for himself; Tati will not make the choice for him.

The English version of Les Vacances is preceded by a warning: "Don't look for a plot, for a holiday is meant purely for fun." The disingenuous wording disguises a serious challenge to the audience—what regular filmgoer would agree that "plot" and "fun" were contradictory terms? For Tati, the renunciation of narrative is a liberating act; M. Hulot's holiday will also be a vacation for the viewer, 93 minutes in which we are free to follow our own impulses, and not submit to the boss's orders. The story-teller is no longer in charge; there's no one hurrying us from one event to another, telling us where to look, when to laugh, what to feel. Tati's film is the exact opposite of "escapist" entertainment, in the sense that it doesn't relieve us of our own emotions and perceptions. It offers another kind of escape, perhaps a more profound one—an escape from domination, from regimentation—a cinematic flight to freedom.

Les Vacances has no plot, but it does have a structure. The film begins and ends with images of waves washing on to an empty beach—images of permanence, steadiness, rhythmic motion. The steady, natural rhythm embodied by the waves is echoed in the film's pronounced alteration of day and night; the film thus acquires a powerful and unique sense of real time marked by natural events. This rhythm is never monotonous—there is also a strong sense of an ebb and flow of energy, of movement giving way to inertia and then regenerating itself. The day belongs to the outdoors—the open spaces of the beach, the sea, the countryside. Morning is announced by the beautiful blonde girl, Martine, standing on her balcony and looking down at the world below. She confers a sort of blessing, and the world comes into motion, energized by the lovely saxophone line with Alain Romans's theme music. Night belongs to the hotel, with the guests crowded into the tiny lobby, silently reading, playing cards, or listening to the radio. Overlaid on this natural rhythm is the human rhythm of habit—exemplified by the ringing of the noontime dinner bell,

but reflected in a dozen specific ways in the behavior of the minor characters—the businessman continually called away to the phone, the English couple out for their promenade, the student lecturing on radical politics. Repetition is a traditional comic device, but in Les Vacances, it acquires a transcendent, poetic quality; Tati seems to have captured the heartbeat of the world.

The film's other structuring principle is psychological. The early sequences are concentrated on the beach and the hotel, but as these locations lose their novelty for the guests, they wander further and further afield—to the tennis courts, to a picnic, even (accidently) to a funeral. Sheer boredom—the chief danger that a plotless film invites—is thus incorporated into the film; it becomes a kind of ally, pointing the movie in new directions. Both of these forward impulses—repetition and boredom—are exceedingly subtle; because they operate both on the level of subject (the repetition and possible boredom of a resort vacation) and of style (traditional comic techniques, the need to move to a new situation when the first has been exhausted), they are almost imperceptible.

Tati's own character, the tall, angular, perpetually astonished M. Hulot, is as often a straight-man to the other characters as he is a comedian. Tati doesn't want to foreground himself as a star or as the center of the humor, because doing so would mean intruding too much on the spectator's freedom of choice (by the time of the 1967 Playtime, Hulot has almost disappeared). Hulot does not embody the freedom of perception that the film strives for as much as he points the way to it, through his own spectacular failures of perception. Hulot does not see (or hear—many of the film's most imaginative gags involve sound) the same way the other characters do; his curse is to constantly perceive either too little (as when he lights a match in a storeroom full of fireworks) or too much (as when he's paralyzed by the fear that a wad of taffy will drop too low on its pulling hook). Hulot is unable to control this attention—to focus his look. But in this context, where the other characters have learned to focus their attentions so tightly and narrowly that they are no longer able to see and enjoy the world around them, Hulot's handicap is a privileged gift; in the land of the one-eyed, Tati suggests the blind man is king. Hulot's under-and over-perceptions pose a threat to the established social order, which depends on a cramped restricted way of seeing. His misadventures attract those few among the guests—a young boy, an elderly gentleman, and briefly, the blonde girl—who aren't part of that order, who haven't yet lost their innocence of vision or who have been able to regain it. With Les Vacances de M. Hulot, Tati tells us how we can join them.

—Dave Kehr

VALAHOL EUROPABAN. Production: Mafirt, Radványi produkió; black and white, 35mm; length: 2812 meters. Released 1947, Hungary.

Screenplay by Béla Belázs, Géza Radványi, Judit Fejér, and Felix Mariássy; directed by Géza Radványi; photography by Barnabás Hegyi; music by Dénes Buday.

Cast: Arthur Somlay (Péter Simon); Miklós Gábor (Boy); Zsuzsa Bánki (Girl); Györgi Bárdi; László Kemény; Leci Horváth; István Rozsos; Endre Hakányi; Károly Bicskèy; András Tollas.

Publications:

Books—*Paimann's Filmlisten*, Vienna 1949; *Geschicht des modernen Films* by W. Gregor and E. Patalas, Gütersloh 1965; *Das Buch vom Film* by R. Waldekranz and V. Arpe, Berlin 1967; *Filmdokumentationen*, Osterreichisches Filmarchiv, 1975; articles—"Egy évforduló fényei" by I. Eörsi in *Filmkultura* (Budapest), January/February 1977; "Quelque part en Europe" by M. Dura in *Jeune Cinéma* (Paris), December/January 1979-80; article by Ollivier Gillisen in *Image et son* (Paris), November 1979.

*   *   *

Somewhere in the remote region, the war ends. In the midst of ruined cities and houses in the streets, in rural hamlets, everywhere where people still live, are children who have lost their homes and parents. Abandoned, hungry, and in rags, defenseless and humiliated, they wander through the world. Hunger drives them. Little streams of orphans merge into a river which rushes forward and submerges everything in its path. The children do not know any feeling; they know only the world of their enemies. They fight, steal, struggle for a mouthful of food, and violence is merely a means to get it. A gang led by Cahoun finds a refuge in an abandoned castle and encounters an old composer who has voluntarily retired into solitude from a world of hatred, treason, and crime. How can they find a common ground, how can they become mutual friends? The castle becomes their hiding place but possibly it will also be their first home which they may organize and must defend. But even for this, the price will be very high.

To this simple story, the journalist, writer, poet, scriptwriter, movie director and film theoretician Béla Balázs applied many years of experience. He and the director Géza Radványi created a work which opened a new postwar chapter in Hungarian film. Surprisingly, this film has not lost any of its impact over the years, especially on a profound philosophical level. That is to say, it is not merely a movie about war; it is not important in what location and in what period of time it takes place. It is a story outside of time about the joyless fate of children who pay dearly for the cruel war games of adults.

At the time it was premiered, the movie was enthusiastically received by the critics. The main roles were taken by streetwise boys of a children's group who created their roles improvisationally in close contact with a few professional actors, and in the children's acting their own fresh experience of war's turmoil appears to be reflected. At the same time, their performance fits admirably into the mosaic of a very complex movie language. Balázs's influence revealed itself, above all, in the introductory sequences: an air raid on an amusement park, seen in a montage of dramatic situations evoking the last spasms of war, where, undoubtedly, we discern the influence of classical Soviet cinematography. Shooting, the boy's escape, the locomotive's wheels, the shadows of soldiers with submachine guns, the sound of a whistle—the images are linked together in abrupt sequences in which varying shots and expressive sharp sounds are emphasized. A perfectly planned screenplay avoided all elements of sentimentality, time-worn stereotypes of wronged children, romanticism and cheap simplification. The authors succeeded in bridging the perilous dramatic abyss of the metamorphosis of a children's community. Their telling of the story (the scene of pillaging, the assault on the castle, etc.) independently introduced some neorealist elements which, at that time, were being propagated in Italy by De Sica, Rossellini and other film artists. The rebukes of contemporary critics, who called attention to "formalism for its own sake" have been forgotten. The masterly art of cameraman Barnabas Hegyi gave vitality to the poetic images. His angle shots of the children, his composition of scenes in the castle interior, are a living document of the times, and underline the atmosphere and the characters of the protagonists. The success of the picture was also enhanced by the musical art of composer Dénes Buday who, in tense situations, inserted the theme of the Marseillaise into the movie's structure, as a motive of community unification, as an expression of friendship and the possibility of understanding.

Valahol Europaban is the first significant postwar Hungarian film. It originated in a relaxed atmosphere, replete with joy and euphoria, and it includes these elements in order to demonstrate the strength of humanism, tolerance, and friendship. It represents a general condemnation of war anywhere in the world, in any form.

—G. Merhaut

LES VAMPIRES. No.I, La Tête coupée. (English version: The Detective's Head). Production: Film Gaumont (Paris); black and white, 35mm, silent; running time: roughly 40 mins. Released November 1915.

Scripted and directed by Louis Feuillade; photography by Manichoux.

Cast: Edouard Mathé (*Philippe Guerande, reporter*); Delphine Renot (*His mother*); Louis Lagrange (*Jane Bremontier, his fiancée*); Jeanne-Marie Laurent (*Jane's mother*); Marcel Levesque (*Oscar Mazamette*); Jean Ayme (*The First Grand Vampire, alias Doctor Nox/Count of Noirmoutier*); Stacia Naperkowska (*Marfa Koutiloff, the dancer*); Bout de Zan (*Himself*).

*   *   *

No. II, La Bacque qui Tue. Production: Film Gaumont (Paris); black and white, 35mm, silent; running time: roughly 40 mins. Released winter 1915.

Scripted and directed by Louis Feuillade; photography by Manichoux.

Cast: Edouard Mathé (*Philippe Guerande, reporter*); Delphine Renot (*His mother*); Louise Lagrange (*Jane Bremontier, his fiancée*); Jeanne-Marie Laurent (*Jane's mother*); Marcel Levesque (*Oscar Mazamette*); Jean Ayme (*The First Grand Vampire, alias Doctor Nox/Count of Noirmoutier*); Stacia Naperkowska (*Marfa Koutiloff, the dancer*); Bout de Zan (*Himself*).

*   *   *

No. III, Le Cryptogramme rouge. Production: Film Gaumont (Paris); black and white, 35mm, silent; running time: roughly 40 mins. Released 1915-16.

Scripted and directed by Louis Feuillade; photography by Manichoux.

Cast: Edouard Mathé (*Philippe Guerande, reporter*); Delphine Renot (*His mother*); Louise Lagrange (*Jane Bremontier, his fiancée*); Jeanne-Marie Laurent (*Jane's mother*); Marcel Levesque (*Oscar Mazamette*); Musidora (*Irma Vep, alias Anne-Marie Le Goff*); Stacia Naperkowska (*Marfa Koutiloff, the dancer*); Bout de Zan (*Himself*).

*   *   *

No. IV, Le Spectre. Production: Film Gaumont (Paris); black and white, 35mm, silent; running time: roughly 40 mins. Released 1915-16.

Scripted and directed by Louis Feuillade; photography by Manichoux.

Cast: Edouard Mathé (*Philippe Guerande, reporter*); Delphine Renot (*His mother*); Louise Lagrange (*Jane Bremontier, his fiancée*); Jeanne-Marie Laurent (*Jane's mother*); Marcel Levesque (*Oscar Mazamette*); Musidora (*Juliette Berteaux, typist at the Renoux-Duval bank*); Jean Ayme (*Big Jules/Monsieur Treps the real estate agent*); Stacia Naperkowska (*Marfa Koutiloff, the dancer*); Bout de Zan (*Himself*).

*   *   *

No. V, L'Evasion du mort. Production: Film Gaumont (Paris); black and white, 35mm, silent; running time: roughly 40 mins. Released 1915-16.

Scripted and directed by Louis Feuillade; photography by Manichoux.

Cast: Edouard Mathé (*Philippe Guerande, reporter*); Delphine Renot (*His mother*); Louise Lagrange (*Jean Bremontier, his fiancée*); Jeanne-Marie Laurent (*Jane's mother*); Marcel Levesque (*Oscar Mazamette*); Musidora (*Mlle. de Mortesaigues*); Jean Ayme (*Baron de Mortesaigues*); Stacia Naperkowska (*Marfa Koutiloff, the dancer*); Bout de Zan (*Himself*).

*   *   *

No. VI, Les Yeux qui fascinent. Production: Film Gaumont (Paris); black and white, 35mm; running time: roughly 40 mins. Released 1916.

Scripted and directed by Louis Feuillade; photography by Manichoux.

Cast: Edouard Mathé (*Philippe Guerande, reporter*); Delphine Renot (*His mother*); Louise Lagrange (*Jane Bremontier, his fiancée*); Jeanne-Marie Laurent (*Jane's mother*); Marcel Levesque (*Oscar Mazamette*); Musidora (*The Viscount Guy de Kerlor*); Jean Ayme (*Colonel Count de Derlor*); Stacia Naperkowska (*Marfa Koutiloff, the dancer*); Renee Carl (*The Andalusian lady*); Fernand Hermann (*Juan-Jose Moreno the burglar, alias Brichonnet/Manuel Arriga*); Bout de Zan (*Himself*).

*   *   *

No. VII, Satanas. Production: Film Gaumont (Paris); black and white, 35mm, silent; running time: roughly 40 mins. Released 1916.

Scripted and directed by Louis Feuillade; photography by Manichoux.

Cast: Edouard Mathé (*Philippe Guerande, reporter*); Delphine Renot (*His mother*); Louise Lagrange (*Jane Bremontier, his fiancée*); Jeanne-Marie Laurent (*Jane's mother*); Marcel Levesque (*Oscar Mazamette*); Musidora (*Marie Boissier of the Clock Company*); Stacia Naperkowska (*Marfa Koutiloff, the dancer*); Bout de Zan (*Himself*).

*   *   *

No. VIII, Le Maitre de la foudre. Production: Film Gaumont (Paris); black and white, 35mm, silent; running time: roughly 40 mins. Released 1916.

Scripted and directed by Louis Feuillade; photography by Manichoux.

Cast: Edouard Mathé (*Philippe Guernade, reporter*); Delphine Renot (*His mother*); Louise Lagrange (*Jane Bremontier, his fiancée*); Jeanne-Marie Laurent (*Jane's mother*); Marcel Levesque (*Oscar Mazamette*); Louis Leubas (*Satanas, the Second Grand Vampire, alias The Bishop*); Stacia Naperkowska (*Marfa Koutiloff, the dancer*); Bout de Zan (*Himself*).

*   *   *

No. IX, L'Homme des poisons. Production: Film Gaumont (Paris); black and white, 35mm, silent; running time: roughly 40 mins. Released spring 1916.

Scripted and directed by Louis Feuillade; photography by Manichoux.

Cast: Edouard Mathé (*Philippe Guerande, reporter*); Delphine Renot (*His mother*); Louise Lagrange (*Jane Bremontier, his fiancée*); Jeanne-Marie Laurent (*Jane's mother*); Marcel Levesque (*Oscar Mazamette*); Musidora (*Aurelie Plateau*); Stacia Naperkowska (*Marfa Koutiloff, the dancer*); Bout de Zan (*Himself*).

*   *   *

No. X, Les Noces sanglantes. Production: Film Gaumont (Paris); black and white, 35mm, silent; running time: roughly 40 mins. Released June, 1916.

Scripted and directed by Louis Feuillade; photography by Manichoux.

Cast: Edouard Mathé (*Philippe Guerande, reporter*); Delphine Renot (*His mother*); Louise Lagrange (*Jane Bremontier, his fiancée*); Jeanne-Marie Laurent (*Jane's mother*); Marcel Levesque (*Oscar Mazamette*); Stacia Naperkowksa (*Marfa Koutiloff, the dancer*); Bout de Zan (*Himself*).

Publications:

Script—*Les Vampires*, with Georges Meirs, Paris 1916; books—*Images du cinéma français* by Nicole Védrès, Paris 1945; *Louis Feuillade* by Francis Lacassin, Paris 1964; *French Film* by Georges Sadoul, New York 1972, originally published in 1953; articles—"Synopsis: *The Vampires*: Episode One", from Harry King Tootle (publicity manager), Gaumont Publishing, Flushing, New York 1916 (copy available in Museum of Modern Art film files); "Louis Feuillade" by Pierre Leprohon in *Radio-Cinéma-Télévision* (Paris), 27 July 1958; "Louis Feuillade" by Claude Beylie in *Ecrans de France* (Paris), 15 May 1959; "Feuillade (l'homme aimanté)" by Jean-André Fieschi in *Cahiers du cinéma* (Paris), November 1964; "Louis Feuillade" by Francis Lacassin in *Sight and Sound* (London), winter 1964/65; "Feuillade" in *Anthologie du cinéma* vol.2, Paris 1967; "Memories of Resnais" by Richard Roud in *Sight and Sound* (London), summer 1969; "Louis Feuillade, poète de la réalité" by J. Champreux in *Avant-Scène du cinéma* (Paris), 1 July 1981.

*   *   *

For French cinema, the years 1915-1922 constituted a period of renewal. A considerable number of young filmmakers emerged with their first works, and the basis of a highly important avant-garde movement was created. But the bulk of commercial production continued in a solid and unadventurous way, as if France were still the world's leading film nation. This time of transition is symbolized by the situation at the Gaumont studios in Paris in 1919, where 46-year-old veteran director and head of production, Louis Feuillade, dressed in his grey "chemist's overalls," directed alongside a 29-year-old beginner, the ex-*littérateur* Marcel L'Herbier, resplendent in his monocle and white gloves. Within this temporary co-habitation of opposites there was, of course, only one direction in which the cinema was moving. But if the early 1920s are aptly represented by L'Herbier's *L'Homme du large* or Abel Gance's *La Roue*, Feuillade's *Les Vampires* can stand for much that was the best in French cinema in 1915-16.

Feuillade had resumed his role as artistic director at Gaumont after his release from army service in 1915. In addition to making the obligatory patriotic films and the occasional meditation on the horrors of war, Feuillade plunged his energies into the crime series, echoing the success of his own *Fantômas* and facing up to the new United States competition, spear-headed by *The Perils of Pauline* and *The Exploits of Elaine*, which was on the brink of dominating the French market. The years 1915-20 saw the appearance of five successive series, of which the first and greatest was *Les Vampires*, which appeared at irregular intervals in ten parts, each constituting a self-contained story, between 13th November 1915 and 30th June 1916.

Les Vampires is strongly conditioned by the circumstances of its shooting. Forced to work quickly and without a smoothly operating studio machine behind him, and confronted with such strong American competition, Feuillade had no time to polish his scenarios or even establish a conventional script. The stories pitted an intrepid reporter and his comic side-kick against ever more bizarre and audacious exploits perpetrated by a gang of criminals led by the ruthless killer who was a master of disguise. In contrast to the American serials, *Les Vampires* had a dark-haired villainess, Irma Vep (an anagram of "vampire") played with great relish by Musidora, in place of the innocent blonde heroine. Many of the stories, increasingly improvised on the streets around the studio, give the impression of having been started without any clear idea of how they will end. In addition,

the pressures brought on by the changing cast of players meant that occasionally even the seemingly indestructible villain had to be suddenly and inexplicably killed off.

It is the improvisation and incoherence which give *Les Vampires* its power. Continually we are confronted with moments of total incongruity—a huge cannon is wheeled from nowhere, a whole party of socialities is gassed, an actress killed on stage, and a character is kidnapped by being lured to the window and lassoed from below. Unexpected deaths and resurrections, sudden car chases or rooftop pursuits, secret panels and spooky catacombs follow in a vivid pattern which has clearly been orchestrated by a director who, in continuing in the traditional style, still organizes his action in depth, with the players facing the audience in theatrical style. It is the anarchistic view of society, the supreme disregard of logic—so appropriate when the old social order of Europe was crumbling under the impact of World War I—which led André Breton and Louis Aragon to see in *Les Vampires* "the reality of this century. Beyond fashion. Beyond taste."

—Roy Armes

VAMPYR. Der Traum Des David Gray. Vampyr, ou l'etrange aventure de David Gray. Not Against the Flesh. Production: Carl Th. Dreyer Filmproduktion Paris-Berlin; black and white, 35mm; running time: originally 83 mins., currently 70 mins., also some copies exist at 65 mins. 11 seconds; length: 2271 meters originally. Released 6 May 1932 in Berlin, also released in French and English versions.

Produced by Baron Nicolas de Gunzberg; screenplay by Carl Theodor Dreyer in collaboration with Christen Jul; from the novel *In a Glass Darkly* by Joseph Sheridan Le Fanu; directed by Carl Theodor Dreyer; photography by Rudolph Maté and Louis Née; sound by Dr. Hans Bittmann, synchronized by Paul Falkenberg; art direction by Hermann Warm; music by Wolfgang Zeller; dialogue directed by Paul Falkenberg, assistants: Ralph Holm and Elaine Tabard.

Filmed summer 1930 in Senlis, Montargis, and surrounding areas.

Cast: Julian West, or Baron Nicolas de Gunzburg (*David Gray*); Henriette Gérard (*Marguerite Chopin*); Jan Hieronimko (*Doctor*); Maurice Schutz (*Lord of the Manor*); Rena Mandel (*His daughter Gisèle*); Sibylle Schmitz (*His daughter Léone*); Albert Bras (*Servant*); N. Babanini (*The girl*); Jane Mora (*The religious woman*).

Publications:

Scripts—"*Vampyr*" by Carl Theodor Dreyer in *Carl Theodor Dreyer: Four Screenplays* translated by Oliver Stallybrass, London 1970; reviews—"La Presse" in *Avant-Scène du cinéma* (Paris), 15 May 1979; books—*Carl Theodor Dreyer: A Film Director's Work* by Ebbe Neergaard, London 1950; *The Art of Carl Dreyer: An Analysis* by Børge Trolle, Copenhagen 1955; *Om Filmen* by Carl Theodor Dreyer, Copenhagen 1964; *The Films of Carl Dreyer* by Eileen Bowser, New York 1964; *Portrait of Carl Th. Dreyer* by Ib Monty, Copenhagen 1965; *Carl Th.*

Dreyer, Danish Film Director, edited by Soren Dyssegaard, Copenhagen 1968; *Carl Th. Dreyer* by Claude Perrin, Paris 1969; *Carl Theodor Dreyer*, Amsterdam 1970; *Carl Th. Dreyer* by Jean Sémolué, Paris 1970; *The Cinema of Carl Dreyer* by Tom Milne, New York 1971; *Dreyer: Carl Th. Dreyer—en dansk filmskaber* by Helge Ernst, Copenhagen 1972; *Transcendental Style in Film: Ozu, Bresson, Dreyer* by Paul Schrader, Los Angeles 1972; *Dreyer in Double Reflection*, edited by Donald Skoller, New York 1973; *Dreyer*, edited by Mark Nash, London 1977; *Carl Theodor Dreyer* by Pier Giorgio Tone, Florence 1978; *The Films of Carl-Theodor Dreyer* by David Bordwell, Berkeley 1981; articles—"The Strange Adventure of David Gray" in *Close-Up* (London), no.1, 1931; "*Vampyr*" by Glauco Viazzi in *Bianco e nero* (Rome), no.10, 1940; special issue of *Écran Français* (Paris), 11 November 1947; "Ghosties and Ghoulies" by Curtis Harrington in *Sight and Sound* (London), no.4, 1952; "The World of Carl Dreyer" by Børge Trolle in *Sight and Sound* (London), winter 1955/56; "*Vampyr*" by William K. Everson in *Cinemages* (New York), no.4, 1955; "*Vampyr*" by Ebbe Neegaard in *Cinemages* (New York), no.4, 1955; "*Vampyr* di Carl Th. Dreyer*" by Alberto Longatti in *Bianco e nero* (Rome), no.5, 1958; "*Vampyr*" by John Cutts in *Films and Filming* (London), no.3, 1960; "*Vampyr*—An Interview with Baron de Gunzburg" by Herman and Gretchen Weinberg in *Film Culture* (New York), no.32, 1964; "The World of Carl Dreyer" by Kirk Bond in *Film Quarterly* (Berkeley), fall 1965; "Dreyer" by Ken Kelman in *Film Culture* (New York), no.35, 1965; "Darkness and Light: Carl Theodor Dreyer" by Tom Milne in *Sight and Sound* (London), autumn 1965; special issue on Dreyer, *Cahiers du cinéma* (Paris), December 1968; special issue of *Kosmorama* (Copenhagen), June 1968; "*Vampyr*" by Jacques Chevallier in *Image et son* (Paris), no.221, 1968; "Uhyggen i os selv" by Poul Malmkjaer in *Kosmorama* (Copenhagen), no.102, 1971; "Carl Dreyer and the Theme of Choice" by Dai Vaughan in *Sight and Sound* (London), summer 1974; "Dreyer's Concept of Abstraction" by Vlada Petric in *Sight and Sound* (London), spring 1975; "*Vampyr* and the Fantastic" by M. Nash in *Screen* (London), no.3, 1976; "*Vampyr* and the Fantastic" by Mark Nash in *Screen* (London), no.17, 1976; "*Vampyr* et 'le complexe de la momie'" by Charles Tesson in *Avant-Scène du cinéma* (Paris), 15 May 1979; "Bram Stoker and Joseph Sheridan Le Fanu" by Roland Stragliati in *Avant-Scène du cinéma* (Paris), 15 May 1979.

*   *   *

In Carl Th. Dreyer's *oeuvre*, *Vampyr* is a unique film. "I wanted to create the daydream on film and wanted to show that horror is not a part of the things around us, but of our own subconscious mind." he said. In his later years, when Dreyer was striving for clarity and simplicity, he understandably dissociated himself from the film and its *clair obscur* of content and form. This is the only film in his career that uses ambiguity as an artistic principle, and also belongs to the horror film genre, though it is a highly unorthodox example.

The story was said to be inspired by Sheridan Le Fanu's *In a Glass Darkly*, but Dreyer wrote the script himself and took only some details from two of the stories in le Fanu's collection, "Dragon volant" and "Carmilla."

The main character is the young David Gray (played by Baron Nicolas de Gunzburg, who also financed the film). He is an almost somnambulistic dreamer, who on one of his nocturnal lonely wanderings arrives at an inn in the village of Courtempierre. David Gray is slowly involved in a series of mystifications, and tempted out into the night. In a castle nearby a young woman is in bed, sick after the bite of a vampire. David is eventually led on to the path of the vampire and its assistants.

Vampyr is a film about the good and the evil forces in life, but it is obvious that the distinction between good and evil is slowly dissolved. From a thematic point of view, *Vampyr* is a crucial film in Dreyer's career. The young woman, who in the beginning is a victim of the vampire, is towards the end transformed into one herself. In the relationship between the two sisters, lesbian undertones are suggested, while the young man is, in some scenes, split into two persons.

Vampyr's composition is based on complementary elements. It moves from reality into unreality, from the actual world into a dream world. The point of view is switched from subjective to objective camera. Doors play an important role as connections between the known and the unknown. The overall white look of the images is an important element in the film's dissolution of reality. The soundtrack (it was Dreyer's first sound film), with the inexplicable noises of a ringing bell, a crying child, and mumbling voices, adds to the surrealism and mysticism. The actors move like shadows, followed in slow travelling shots by the probing camera. All this makes *Vampyr* one of the most poetically haunting films, full of strange and subtle eroticism.

It was shot in France in the summer of 1930 in French, German and English versions. Since its first showing the film has been re-issued several times.

—Ib Monty

IL VANGELO SECONDO MATTEO. The Gospel According to St. Matthew. L'évangile selon saint-Matthieu. (Note: the word "Saint" was used in English version against Pasolini's wishes). Production: Arco Film (Italy) and C.C.F. Lux (Paris); black and white, 35mm; running time: 142 mins., English version is 136 mins. and French version is 130 mins. Released 1964, Italy.

Produced by Alfredo Bini, executive producer: Manolo Bolognini; screenplay by Pier Paolo Pasolini; from "The Gospel According to St. Matthew" in the *New Testament*; directed by Pier Paolo Pasolini; photography by Tonino Delli Colli; edited by Nino Baragli; sound by Mario Del Pezzo; art direction by Luigi Scaccianoce; music score (original music) by Luis Enriquez Bacalov, other music included selections by Johann Sebastian Bach, Sergei Sergeevich Prokofiev, Wolfgang Mozart, and Anton Webern, "Sometimes I Feel Like a Motherless Child" sung by Odetta; special effects directed by Ettore Catallucci; costumes designed by Danilo Donati; the film is dedicated to the memory of Pope John XXIII.

Filmed in Calabria, Lucania, and Puglia (southern Italy). Venice Film Festival, Special Jury Prize and Catholic Film Office award, 1964.

Cast: Enrique Irazoqui (*Jesus Christ*); Margherita Caruso (*Mary, as a girl*); Susanna Pasolini (*Mary, as a woman*); Marcello Morante (*Joseph*); Mario Socrate (*John the Baptist*); Settimo Di Porto (*Peter*); Otello Sestili (*Judas*); Ferruccio Nuzzo (*Matthew*); Giacomo Morante (*John*); Alfonso Gatto (*Andrew*); Enzo Siciliano (*Simon*); Giorgio Agamben (*Philip*); Guido Cerretani (*Bartholomew*); Luigi Barbini (*James, son of Alpheus*);

Marcello Galdini (*James, son of Zebedec*); Elio Spaziani (*Thaddeus*); Rosario Migale (*Thomas*); Rodolfo Wilcock (*Caiaphas*); Alessandro Tasca (*Pontius Pilate*); Amerigo Becilacqua (*Herod*); Francesco Leonetti (*Herod Antipas*); Franca Cupane (*Herodias*); Paola Tedesco (*Salome*); Rossana Di Rocco (*Angel*); Eliseo Boschi (*Joseph of Arimathea*); Natalia Ginzburg (*Mary of Bethany*); Renato Terra (*A Pharisee*); Enrico Maria Salerno (*Voice of Jesus*).

Publications:

Script—*Il Vangelo secondo Matteo*, Milan 1964; reviews—by Elizabeth Sussex in *Sight and Sound* (London), winter 1964-65; "Pasolini's Passion" by Stanley Kauffmann in the *New Republic* (New York), 22 March 1966; review by Rene Jordan in *Films in Review* (New York), January 1966; review by Richard Whitehall in *Cinema* (Beverly Hills), July 1966; books—*Pasolini on Pasolini*, interviews by Oswald Stack, London 1969; *Pier Paolo Pasolini* by Marc Gervais, Paris 1973; *Vita di Pasolini* by Enzo Siciliano, Milan 1978; *Teoria e tecnica del film in Pasolini* by Antonio Bertini, Rome 1979; *Pier Paolo Pasolini* by Stephen Snyder, Boston 1980; articles—"Pier Paolo Pasolini: An Epical-Religious View of the World" in *Film Quarterly* (Berkeley), summer 1965; "Pier Paolo Pasolini" by James Blue in *Film Comment* (New York), fall 1965; "Greatest Story Ever Told...By a Communist" by Maryanne Butcher in *Film Comment* (New York), fall 1965; "Pier Paolo Pasolini and the Art of Directing" by Gordon Hitchens in *Film Comment*, fall 1965; "Marxist's Christ" by G.D. Kumlien in *Commonweal* (New York), 2 July 1965; "*The Gospel According to St. Matthew*" by M. Walsh in *America* (New York), 26 February 1966; "A Conversation in Rome" by J. Bragin in *Film Culture* (New York), fall 1966; article by John Thomas in *Film Society Review* (New York), December 1966; article by Raymond Durgnat in *Films and Filming* (London), June 1967; article by F.R. Feringer in *Film Society Review* (New York), April 1967; "Pasolini face au sacre ou l'exorciste possede" by E. Maakaroun in *Etudes cinématographiques* (Paris), no.109-111, 1976; "Eretnek gondolatok egy hivo filmroi: Pasolini's *Mate Evangeliuma*" by I. Hahn in *Filmkultura* (Budapest), November/December 1979.

* * *

Pier Paolo Pasolini was one of the most controversial and fascinating of modern Italian filmmakers, and his films covered a wide variety of subjects and cinematic styles. He once described himself appropriately as a *pasticheur*, one who selected "items, objects and even styles from here and there." A writer, poet, critic and filmmaker; an avowed Marxist, atheist and homosexual, it is ironic that Pasolini made what many hailed as "the best life of Jesus Christ ever placed on film." *The Gospel According to St. Matthew* is the exact antithesis of Hollywood-produced biblical spectacles: a stark, austere, realistic, almost documentary re-enactment of the story of Christ.

Pasolini was drawn to St. Matthew's Gospel because he found it "rigorous, demanding and absolute" as opposed to Mark's version which was "too obviously written for people of little education"; or Luke who was "too literary and mellifluous"; or John who was "too much a mystic to be transmitted visually." Pasolini chose to use the dialogue intact from Matthew, using a "standard Catholic translation to avoid polemics," with two exceptions from Isaiah: one where Christ is walking with the

Apostles in Calabria prior to the investiture of Peter, and the other where Christ dies. Pasolini was quick to point out that "the whole of Matthew is full of quotes from Isaiah, so I felt that was fair enough."

This is not to say that Pasolini simply presented a literal translation of Matthew's text. His interpretation is a molding of that narrative with changes in chronology, some omissions, and some inventions, such as his version of Salome's dance. When he first began to shoot the film, Pasolini used the same "reverential" camera technique he had used with *Accatone*, but suddenly realized that approach was "gilding the lily." After just two days, he thought of abandoning the project, then opted for a technique comparable to *cinéma vérité*, using a hand-held camera and zoom shots to create a documentary-like realism.

For the physical background of the film, Pasolini used the impoverished landscape and villages of southern Italy, which he found to be analogous to those of Palestine where he had visited prior to making the film. For the background music, he chose an electric combination which complimented his unorthodox approach to the film as a whole.

The major contribution to the successful sense of realism was his use of non-professionals as actors. On many occasions Pasolini had said, "I choose actors because of what they are as human beings, not because of what they can do.... I steal from them; I use their reality." He particularly wanted no recognizable stars doing cameo turns in this interpretation of Christ's story, so his actors came from various walks of life. "Judas is a Roman truck driver," he said. "The Virgin Mary is my mother. Joseph is a lawyer and John the Baptist is a poet. I pick them for what they are; I ask them to play themselves." Likewise, for the pivotal role of Jesus Christ, Pasolini selected Enrique Irazoqui. a student from Barcelona who was visiting Rome. His voice was then dubbed in Italian by Enrico Maria Salerno.

Pasolini set out to create a "purely poetical and natural, non-denominational" version of the life of Christ and, despite his reputation as a Marxist and atheist, the critical reception was highly favorable, with some claiming it to be the finest biblical film ever made. Especially cited were with wonderful faces of the non-actors and Pasolini's pictorial recreation of tableaux inspired by the works of such painters as Botticelli, Rouault, Masaccio and Piero della Francesca.

As a self-proclaimed non-believer, Pasolini had castigated the dying Pope Pius XII, and stated later that had Pius lived three or four more years he would never have been allowed to make this film. In gratitude for the new climate brought about by the new pope, *The Gospel According to St. Matthew* is dedicated to "the dear, familiar memory of John XXIII."

The film received a Special Jury Prize at the 1964 Venice Film Festival, a citation from the International Catholic Film Office, and Academy Award nominations for Black-and-White Art Direction, Adapted Score and Black-and-White Costume Design.

—Ronald Bowers

VARIÉTÉ. Variety. Vaudeville. Production: Universum-Film-Aktiengesellschaft (Ufa); black and white, 35mm, silent; length: 2844 meters.

Produced by Erich Pommer; screenplay by Leo Birinski and E.A. Dupont; from the novel *Der Eid des Stefan Huller* by Felix Holländer; directed by E.A. Dupont; photography by Karl Freund; production design by Oscar F. Werndorff; music by Ernö Rappdée.

Cast: Emil Jannings (*Boss Huller*); Lya de Putti (*Berthe-Marie*); Warwick Ward (*Artinelli*); Maly Delschaft (*Boss's wife*); Georg John (*Sailor*); Kurt Gerron (*Docker*); Paul Rehkopf; Charles Lincoln (*Actor*); The Codonas double for Jannings, de Putti, and Ward on the trapeze.

Publications:

Books—*Panoramique du cinéma* by Léon Moussinac, Paris 1929; *The Rise of the American Film* by Lewis Jacobs, New York 1939; *From Caligari to Hitler: A Psychological History of the German Film* by Siegfried Kracauer, Princeton 1947; *Film as Art* by Rudolf Arnheim, Berkeley 1957; *The Haunted Screen* by Lotte Eisner, Berkeley 1969; *The German Cinema* by Roger Manvell and Heinrich Fraenkel, New York 1971; *Cinema, the Magic Vehicle: A Guide to Its Achievement: Journey One: The Cinema Through 1949* edited by Jacek Klinowski and Adam Garbicz, Metuchen, New Jersey 1975; *Cinema and Society: France and Germany during the Twenties* by Paul Monaco, New York 1976; articles—"Le Cinéma allemand" by Pierre Leprohon in *Le Rouge et le noir*, (Paris), July 1928; "The Rise and Fall of the German Film" by Harry Potamkin in *Cinema*, April 1930; "The Friendly Mr. Freund" by B.C. Crisler in *The New York Times*, 21 November 1937; "Karl Freund" by Herbert Luft in *Films in Review* (New York), February 1963; "Karl Freund" by Donald Deschner in *Cinema* (Beverly Hills), no.4, 1969; "Emil Jannings—A Personal View" by Harold Truscott in *Silent Picture* (London), autumn 1970; "E.A. Dupont, 1891-1956" by Herbert G. Luft in *Anthologie du cinéma, Vol. VI*, Paris 1971; "*Variete*" by R. Combs in *Monthly Film Bulletin* (London), July 1979.

*   *   *

Variety is one of the most significant films of the silent era, a work of technical expertise that liberated the stationary camera. It is a stunning example of montage, with overlapping dissolves perfectly executed—prior to the invention of the optical printing process.

The storyline of *Variety* is standard: on one level, the film is just a predictable melodrama, with characters who are more types than three-dimensional personalities. Middle-aged trapeze artist Emil Jannings leaves wife and child for a younger woman. He is cuckolded and later jailed for murdering her lover. The scenario unravels in flashback, as Jannings tells the warden his tragedy. (This character is a sexual victim, a fate shared by Professor Unrath in *The Blue Angel* and August Schiller in *The Way of All Flesh*—roles also played by Jannings.)

In *Variety*, the ordinary becomes the extraordinary in that the film is a technical tour de force, highlighted by exceptional editing and unusually striking camera movements and angles. Cinematographer Karl Freund's camera is flexible. He even sets it on a trapeze, photographing from a swinging position the actors' expressions of feelings. The camera becomes the conscience of the characters, who exist in a world of phoney glamor, two-bit circuses and decadent music halls and, finally, in the case of Jannings, a cheerless prison. As the scenario unravels, the cutting from shot to shot suggests the changes in their points of view.

There is also a superior use of subjective camera, allowing the audience to be involved in the action. As an acrobat plunges to his death, the camera drops from a high wire directly into the faces of the collectively frightened members of the audience. Dramatic tension is enhanced by low-angle shots, and multiple exposures.

While directing a season of vaudeville in Mannheim, E.A. Dupont was summoned by Erich Pommer to the UFA studio to direct *Variety*. Originally, F.W. Murnau was set to make the film but, according to Freund, Pommer felt he lacked the appropriate passion for the project. Dupont had originally wanted to shoot the film utilizing mostly compositional shots; it was Freund's input that convinced the filmmaker to perfect the method that made *Variety* so extraordinary. In this regard, *Variety* is as much a work of art by Karl Freund as E.A. Dupont. The cinematographer was a master of lighting and movement: he had also shot *The Last Laugh* for Murnau (also starring Jannings), *Metropolis* for Fritz Lang, and later such Hollywood classics as *Dracula*, *Camille*, *The Good Earth*, *Pride and Prejudice*, and *Key Largo*.

Variety breaks away from the Expressionist cinema then popular in Germany, and can be seen as the official starting point of an era that became increasingly characterized by realism. But the characters still exist in a quite unreal environment. The film is a psychological drama, with action based not on externals but thoughts and feelings.

Variety was an international hit; particularly in the United States, the film was both a critical and commercial smash. Most significant of all, it served as a model for an entire generation of filmmakers.

—Rob Edelman

————————

EL VERDUGO. Not on Your Life. La ballata del boia. Production: Naga Films (Italy) and Zebra Films (Spain); black and white, 35mm; running time: 110 mins., English version is 90 mins. Released February 1964, Madrid.

Screenplay by Luis Garcia Berlanga, Rafael Azcona, and Ennio Flajano; directed by Luis Garcia Berlanga; photography by Tonino Delli Conti; edited by Alfonso Santacana; art direction by José Antonio de la Guerra; music by Miguel Asins-Arbo.

Cast: Nino Manfredi (*José Luis*); Emma Penella (*Carmen*); José Luis López Vásquez (*Antonio*); Angel Alvarez (*Alvarez*); José Isbert (*Amedeo*); Maria Luisa Ponte (*Stefania*); Guido Alberti (*Governor of Prison*); Maruja Isbert (*Ignazia*); Félix Fernández (*1st Sacristan*); Alfredo Landa (*2nd Sacristan*); José Luis Coll (*Organist*).

Publications:

Books—*Carta abierta a Berlanga* by Diego Galan, Huelva 1978; *Luis G. Berlanga* by Ernesto Santolaya, Victoria 1979; *Sobre Luis G. Berlanga* by Julio Pérez Perucha, Valencia 1980, 1981; articles—"The Face of '63—Spain" by J. Cobos in *Films and Filming* (London), October 1963; article by Raymond Durgnat in *Films and Filming* (London), November 1965; article by Harvey Deneroff in *Film Society Review* (New York), April 1966; "Luis Berlanga aujourd'hui et hier" by J. Hernandez Les in *Jeune Cinéma* (Paris), April/May 1979; "Luis G. Berlanga" by José Luis Guarner in *International Film Guide 1981*, London 1982.

*   *   *

El Verdugo was the eighth feature film written and directed by Luis García Berlanga in collaboration with his long-time associate, Rafael Azcona. The story pivots upon the fate of a pleasant, if somewhat timid, young undertaker whose dream is to go to Germany and become a mechanic. This dream is thwarted when he happens to meet the executioner in a prison where both of them are plying their trade. In spite of the aversion that the young man (and everyone else) feels for the executioner, he not only ends up marrying the executioner's daughter, but even takes over his father-in-law's business.

El Verdugo is a farce or domestic comedy filled with macabre touches and scenes of black humor in which the taboos associated with death are transgressed. Even the actual mode of execution is the subject of morbid jokes as the executioner, who garrots his victims, measures the neck size of his future son-in-law. The film is punctuated with these bits of gallows humor as well as with comic reversals that take the audience by surprise. A particularly fine example occurs at the end of the movie when the young executioner is carried kicking and screaming like the victim into the prison where he will perform his first execution. *El Verdugo* shows that the biting black humor that we have come to associate with Buñuel is, in more general terms, a Spanish characteristic.

Berlanga's irreverent treatment of death is symptomatic of a tendency found in all of his movies—to poke fun at pomposity and pretensions, and to deflate generally accepted values and beliefs. At the same time that *El Verdugo* is highly entertaining, it also has a message that was vaguely subversive in Franco's Spain in the early 1960s. In one sense, the movie is about two outcasts, the undertaker and the executioner's daughter, both of whom are avoided by everyone. When they join together, it is with the hope of having a better life. But as Berlanga demonstrates, these hopes cannot be realized. Like other Berlanga protagonists, the undertaker becomes caught up in a destiny which he did not choose. He is a victim of innocent concessions made along the way that ultimately lead him to be sentenced to his fate of becoming the executioner. He is the true victim, the one who is strangled in a web of circumstances beyond his control, caught up in the system of justice and retribution that is all encompassing. In the context of Franco's Spain, the ideological dimensions of this message are clear. As the executioner tells his son-in-law, where there's a law, someone has to enforce it; someone has to do the dirty work. Perhaps that was Berlanga's way of saying that in a dictatorial regime, whether they are willing or not, men are coerced into aiding and abetting the *status quo*.

—Katherine Singer Kóvacs

DIE VERLORENE EHRE DER KATHARINA BLUM. The Lost Honor of Katharina Blum. Production: Bioskop-Film and Paramount-Orion; color and black and white, 35mm; running time: 106 mins. Released 1975;

Screenplay by Volker Schlöndorff and Margarethe von Trotta; from the novel by Henrich Böll; directed by Volker Schlöndorff and Margarethe von Trotta; photographed by Jost Vacano.

Filmed 1975 in Germany.

Cast: Angela Winkler (*Katharina Blum*); Mario Adorf (*Beizmenne*); Dieter Laser (*Werner Toetgen*); Heinz Bennett (*Dr. Blorna*); Hannelore Hoger (*Trude Blorna*); Harald Kuhlmann (*Moeding*); Karl Heinz Vosgerau (*Alois Straubleder*); Jürgen Prochnow (*Ludwig Goetten*); Rolf Becker (*Hach*); Regine Lutz (*Else Woltersheim*); Werner Eichhorn (*Konrad Beiters*).

Publications:

Reviews—"*Die verlorene Ehre der Katharina Blum*" by R.F. Hawkins in *Variety* (New York), 1 October 1975; "*L'Honneur perdu de Katharina Blum*" by J.C. Bonnet in *Cinématographer* (Paris), June 1976; "*L'Honneur perdu de Katharina Blum*" by B. Chavardes in *Téléciné* (Paris), July/August 1976; "*L'Honneur perdu de Katharina Blum*" by J. Chevallier in *Revue du cinéma* (Paris), October 1976; "*Die verlorene Ehre der Katharina Blum*" by H. Dekeyser in *Film en Televisie* (Brussels), July/August 1976; "*L'Honneur perdu de Katharina Blum*" by P. Kane in *Cahiers du cinéma* (Paris), May 1976; "*L'Honneur perdu de Katharina Blum*" by J.L. Passek in *Cinéma 76* (Paris), April 1976; "*Die verlorene Ehre der Katharina Blum*" by D. Wilson in *Monthly Film Bulletin* (London), May 1977; "*The Lost Honour of Katharina Blum*" by D. Elley in *Films and Filming* (London), September 1977; book—*The New German Cinema* by John Sandford, Totowa, New Jersey 1980; articles—"Indiansommar i Milano" by W. Andersson in *Filmrutan* (Tyreso, Sweden), no.1, 1976; "Boell-Verfilmung als politisches Tageskino: *Die verlorene Ehre der Katharina Blum*" by W. Gersch in *Film und Fernsehen* (East Berlin), no.10, 1976; "Volker Schloendorff e Margarethe von Trotta: *Il caso Katharina Blum*" by L. Pellizzari in *Cineforum* (Bergamo, Italy), July/August 1976; "*Die verlorene Ehre der Katharina Blum*" by M. von Trotta and others in *Film und Fernsehen* (East Berlin), no.8, 1976; "*Die verlorene Ehre der Katharina Blum*" by U. Schirmeyer-Klein in *Film und Ton Magazine* (Munich), January 1976; "*L'Honneur perdu de Katharina Blum*" by B. Chavardès in *Téléciné* (Paris), July/August 1976; "Cinematic Techniques in *The Lost Honor of Katharina Blum*" by L.D. Friedman in *Literature/Film Quarterly* (Salisbury, Maryland), no.3, 1979; "Volker Schlöndorff" by Ronald Holloway in *International Film Guide 1982*, London 1981.

* * *

The Lost Honor of Katharina Blum, co-directed by Volker Schlöndorff and Margarethe von Trotta, is based on the novel of the same name by Henrich Böll, who worked closely with the directors in the transformation of his novel into film. Schlöndorff and von Trotta had worked together on several films prior to this one. Schlöndorff had directed von Trotta as an actress and she had also served as his scriptwriter. This was their first co-directed film, a credit which von Trotta had to demand. Their differences in style became obvious in this film as Schlöndorff concentrated on the action sequences, while Trotta worked with the actors to bring out the power of their emotions. After this film they separated. Von Trotta went on to direct her own films, but occasionally helps on the scripts of Schlöndorff's films (*Circle of Deceit*). *Katharina Blum* was the most popularly successful of all their films.

Katharina Blum brought to the public's attention the extent of the political turmoil in West Germany. It followed closely on the heels of the murder of Hanns Martin Schleyer, a West German corporate leader and the prison deaths of three Baader-Meinhof terrorists. The film came at a time when the West German oppression of the left was quite harsh. The new Germany of the

1970s is shown in the film to be similar to Nazi Germany. In both the new and the old, the press, the church and the state work closely togther to smash any opposition to the policies of the government. Böll himself had been accused of harboring terrorists in his home and it is from this experience that the novel sprang. Although the film does not follow the exact pattern of the book, it carries the main theme as prescribed in the subtitle of the novel, "How Violence Develops and Where it can Lead."

The main image of the film is one of spying. The opening sequence sets the tone for the whole film as the audience is introduced to Ludwig through the spying lens of the police camera. The film boldly switches from color to black-and-white images to make the audience aware of the sequences being observed by police. This subtle (there is no break in the action) yet startling technique dramatizes the unsuspected ubiquity of the police.

Characters are constantly looking at each other through glass partitions and other barriers that separate people but allow for no privacy. For privacy in this state is an illusion, both visually and literally, as exemplified by the invasion and distortion of Katharina's privacy by the press and the police.

The plethora of mirror and glass images, in which the characters are invited to look in and through in search of a clearer perception of themselves and those around them, is reminiscent of Lotte Eisner's comments concerning German Expressionists. In her book *The Haunted Screen*, she notes that such images suggest "visions nourished by moods of vague and troubled yearnings." Troubled yearnings are present in the film but they are anything but vague. The stereotyping of the characters into such categories as "bullying police chief," "wealthy clergyman" and "insensitive journalist" make it very clear to the audience exactly who the villains are and who the heroine is. Vincent Canby of *The New York Times* writes, "The corruption portrayed by the film is so pervasive that one expects it to challenge more. But it doesn't. Instead it has the effect of numbing us. Its single minded intensity nails the imagination to the floor."

Although the film is relatively undistinguished in technical and artistic terms, it does retain interest as a social document. The film managed to set before the German public a clear (albeit stereotyped and singlemindedly distorted) picture of present day Germany.

—Gretchen Elsner-Sommer

VERTIGO. Production: Paramount Pictures; 1958; Technicolor, 35mm; running time: 127 mins. Released May 1958. Re-released 1983.

Produced by Alfred Hitchcock; screenplay by Alec Coppel and Samuel Taylor; from the novel *D'Entre les morts* by Pierre Boileau and Thomas Narcejac; directed by Alfred Hitchcock; photography by Robert Burks; edited by George Tomasini; art direction by Hal Pereira and Henry Bumstead; music by Bernard Herrmann.

Filmed in part in San Francisco.

Cast: James Stewart (*John Ferguson*); Kim Novak (*Madeleine/Judy*); Barbara Bel Geddes (*Midge*); Tom Helmore (*Galvin Eister*); Henry Jones.

Publications:

Reviews—"*Vertigo*" by Bosley Crowther in *The New York Times*, 29 May 1958; books—*Hitchcock* by Barthélemy Amengual, Paris 1960; *The Cinema of Alfred Hitchcock* by Peter Bogdanovich, New York 1962; *Alfred Hitchcock* by Hans Peter Manz, Zurich 1962; *Hitchcock's Films* by Robin Wood, London 1965; *The Films of Alfred Hitchcock* by George Perry, London 1965; *Le Cinéma selon Hitchcock* by François Truffaut, Paris 1966; *Alfred Hitchcock* by Jean Douchet, Paris 1967; *Alfred Hitchcock* by Noel Simsolo, Paris 1969; *Hitch* by John Russell Taylor, New York 1978; *L'Analyse du film* by Raymond Bellour, Paris 1979; *Hitchcock—The Murderous Gaze* by William Rothman, Cambridge, Massachusetts, 1982; *The Dark Side of Genius: The Life of Alfred Hitchcock* by Donald Spoto, New York 1983; articles—"A Master of Suspence" by John Pett in *Films and Filming* (London), November 1959, and "Improving the Formula" in *Films and Filming*, December 1959; "Alfred Hitchcock" by Henri Agel in *New York Film Bulletin*, no.15, 1961; "Hitchcock's World" by Charles Higham in *Film Quarterly* (Berkeley), December 1962/January 1963; "James Stewart" by William R. Sweigert in *Films in Review* (New York), December 1964; "Alfred Hitchcock: Master of Morality" by Warren Sonbert in *Film Culture* (New York), summer 1966; "Bernard Herrmann" by Page Cook in *Films in Review* (New York), August/September 1967; "*Vertigo* Re-viewed" by Francis M. Nevins Jr. in *Journal of Popular Culture* (Bowling Green, Ohio), fall 1968; "The Strange Case of Alfred Hitchcock" by Raymond Durgnat in 10 issue of *Films and Filming* (London), February through November 1970; "Hitchcock" by Charles T. Samuels in *American Scholar* (Washington, D.C.), spring 1970; "Aspects of Cinematic Consciousness" by D. Skoller in *Film Comment* (New York), September/October 1972; "Fragments of a Mirror: Uses of Landscape in Hitchcock" by A.J. Silver in *Wide Angle* (Athens, Ohio), no.3, 1976; "25 Years of Film Interviews: Hitchcock and the Dying Art" by P. Joyce in *Film* (London), November 1979; "*Vertigo*: The Secret of the Tower" by J. Ebert in *Framework* (Norwich, England), autumn 1980; special issue of *Camera/Stylo* on Hitchcock (Paris), November 1981; "Reissued Hitchcock Classics Reflect Obsessions of Genius" by Roger Ebert in *Sun-Times* (Chicago), 2 October 1983; "Fear of Spying" by Robin Wood in *American Film* (Washington, D.C.), November 1983.

*   *   *

Not particularly successful at the time of its release, *Vertigo* has come to be recognized as one of Alfred Hitchcock's greatest films where his profounder obsessions are reinforced by his technical inventiveness. It can be argued that Hitchcock's "greatness" comes only from the accident that his recurring obsession with voyeurism is the topic which best meshes with the ontology of the filmgoing experience. In any case, the longstanding argument over the superiority of his British vs. American periods looks to have been settled in favor of the latter. The less savory aspects of Hitchcock's life revealed since his death come as little surprise if *Rear Window*, *Vertigo*, and *Psycho* are seen as a supreme voyeuristic trilogy.

The peeping Toms in these films progress through ever-greater distress—from the ostensibly healthy (if significantly broken-legged) James Stewart with his telephoto lens in *Rear Window* through the psychotic Anthony Perkins with his motel peephole in *Psycho*. If Stewart's Scotty Ferguson, the private eye in *Vertigo*, is more fascinating than either, it's because he's so precariously balanced between their psychic states. A former police detective who's developed a pathological fear of heights since being responsible for the fatal fall of a fellow officer, Scotty is institutionalized for a year in the middle of the film after assuming (wrongly) that his "weakness" (as the coroner puts it) prevented him from stopping the suicidal leap of the woman he was hired to protect and with whom he's fallen in love. The film ends at the moment of her "second" death. It's as bleak a conclusion as in any American film of its decade; *Psycho* is a rich comedy in comparison.

The voyeuristic impulse behind Hitchcock's style is most immediately evident in the tourist sensibility that pervades his American films—a tourist will keep his careful distance from the grit of the world. Here, the Golden Gate Bridge, the Palace of the Legion of Honor, Podesta's flowershop, Ernie's restaurant, Coit Tower, Fort Point, the Palace of Fine Arts make up San Francisco's slick surface through Robert Burks's sharp-edged Technicolor. Hitchcock's silent film mastery pays off in the scenes involving Scotty's extended tailing of Madeleine, accompanied by Bernard Herrmann's haunting score.

Vertigo extends this passive, tourist's world into more intimate levels. The film's plotline is the hokiest of ghost stories ("Do you believe that someone out of the past, someone dead, can take possession of a living being?"), but it soon moves into tragedy through flaws wrought by sexual obsession. The highly-charged, pivotal scene comes quite late: Scotty has met a woman who reminds him of his dead love (in fact, she is the same woman—her fabricated "death" having been the cover for a man's murder of his wife.) They return to his bachelor apartment after an increasingly uncomfortable afternoon of buying clothes to make the woman resemble her previous incarnation. Judy's plea, spoken almost to herself, is: "Couldn't you like *me*, just me, the way I am?" What looks for an instant like Scotty's gaze of reciprocated love is instead his revelation of the key for her complete transformation: "The color of your hair!" The scene lurches forward into an ultimate degradation, as Judy agrees to remake her brunette-shopgirl self into the (Hitchcockian) blond ice-goddess, with tailored grey suit and tightly-bound hair. The scene, and the whole film, is the essence of the Hitchcockian sexuality—that is, sexuality only exists as obsession, one that degrades women and literally deranges men. In *Vertigo*, Hitchcock does manage to be pointed about the ironies of this quest: Scotty looks longingly at other blondes in harsh grey suits even while dining with a vibrant incarnation of the woman he "loves". In a sense, he gets just what he deserves.

The film's genius is depicting such perversity as merely circumstance-crossed love. In other words, its genius is in revealing the perversity behind accepted "normal" practices. What's so odd about men redressing their women? or in women remaking themselves in the adored image? Judy's plea puts it embarrassingly straight: "If I let you change me, will that do it? Will you love me?" Traditional sexual politics swells into a grand grotesque, a Chinese-box melodrama of tricks and betrayals. The scenario itself is complicated and inconsistent, but the repeated motifs in the dialogue ("please try!" "It's too late") tie the disconnected love-parings into the tighest of nets. Hitchcock is typically cruel to plain Midge, with her patient, enduring love for Scotty. Her explanation of cantilevered brassieres is a woman's anti-mystery, pathetically commonplace next to Madeleine's apparent possession by the dead. Madeleine's feigned obsession presages Scotty's genuine necrophilia. (And, as in *Psycho*, the psychiatrist can't strip away the necessary layers—the problem is more than the "acute melancholia, complicated by a guilt complex" offered as a diagnosis or explanation of the problem.)

It's easy enough to appreciate the best of Hitchcock's films, and to be jolted by them, but *Vertigo* stands alone in its ability to move audiences emotionally. Perhaps the events are uncharacteristically heartbreaking because both Scotty and Madeleine/Judy are caught in another, grander (and almost unseen) male power-play: Gavin's murder of his wife, his betrayal of his friend Scotty, and his abandonment of his accomplice Judy. A bookseller, echoing Gavin's words (and his actions) tells the tale of the original Carlotta being "thrown away" by her husband: "A man could do that in those days. He had the power and the freedom." On its visceral level, *Vertigo* succeeds because of James Stewart's explosive fury in the climax in the belltower, a betrayed idealist's fury practiced in his Frank Capra films and mastered through his Anthony Mann westerns.

It's remarkable that, considering all its plot twists, *Vertigo* should work even better after a first viewing. Once the secret's out, it's a completely different film, and a better one—no longer a harrowing ghost story, it is a profound study of sexual obsession, tied together by the city which best displays the essential acrophobic metaphor.

—Scott Simmon

VIRIDIANA. Production: Uninci S.A. and Films 59 (Spain) and Gustavo Alatriste (Mexico); black and white, 35mm; running time: 90 mins. Released 17 May 1961, Cannes Film Festival.

Produced by R. Muñoz Suay; screenplay by Luis Buñuel and Julio Alejandro; from a story by Luis Buñuel; directed by Luis Buñuel; photography by José F. Aguayo; edited by Pedro del Rey; art direction by Francisco Canet; music by Handel and Mozart, arranged by Gustavo Pittaluga.

Filmed in Spain, near Madrid and Toledo. Cannes Film Festival, Best Film, 1961.

Cast: Silvia Pinal (*Viridiana*); Francisco Rabal (*Jorge*); Fernando Rey (*Don Jaime*); Margarita Lozano (*Ramona*); Victoria Zinny (*Lucia*); Teresa Rabal (*Rita*); José Calvo, Joaquín Roa, Luis Heredia, Jośe Manuel Martin, Lola Gaos, Juan Garcia Tienda, Maruda Isbert (*Beggars*); Joaquín Mayol, Palmira Guerra, Sergio Mendizábal, Milagros Tomás, and Alicia Jorge Barriga (*Beggars*).

Publications:

Scripts—*Viridiana* by Luis Buñuel, Paris 1962; *Viridiana* by Luis Buñuel, prologue by Georges Sadoul, Mexico 1963; *3 Screenplays* by Luis Buñuel, New York 1969; reviews—by Elaine Rothschild in *Films in review* (New York), February 1962; review by Andrew Sarris in *The Village Voice* (New York), 22 March 1962; books—*Le Surréalisme au cinéma* by Ado Kyrou, Paris 1963; *Luis Buñuel* by Raymond Durgnat, Berkeley 1968; "*Viridiana*" by Ian McD. Rowe in *Screen Education Yearbook, 1968* edited by Roger Mainds, London 1968; *Luis Buñuel: Biografía crítica* by J. Francisco Aranda, Barcelona 1969; *Confessions of a Cultist: On the Cinema 1955-69* by Andrew Sarris, New York 1970; *Buñuel (Cine e ideologia)* by Manuel Alcalá, Madrid 1973; *The Cinema of Luis Buñuel* by Freddy Bauche, translated by Peter Graham, New York 1973; "Luis Buñuel and the Death of God" in *3 European Directors* by

Peter Schillaci, Grand Rapids, Michigan 1973; *Luis Buñuel: A Critical Biography* by José Francisco, translated by David Robinson, New York 1975; *Le cinéma de la cruauté: de Buñuel à Hitchcock* by André Bazin, Paris 1975; *The World of Luis Buñuel: Essays in Criticism* edited by Joan Mellen, New York 1978; *Luis Buñuel* by Virginia Higginbotham, Boston 1979; articles— by Luis Buñuel in *Film Culture* (New York), spring 1962; article by David Hull in *Film Quarterly* (Berkeley), winter 1961-62; article by Emilio Riera in *Film Culture* (New York), spring 1962; article by David Robinson in *Sight and Sound* (London), summer 1962; article by Paul Rotha in *Films and Filming* (London), June 1962; article by Andrew Sarris in *Movie* (London), June 1962; "*Viridiana*" in *Cahiers du cinéma* (Paris), January 1962; "*Viridiana*" by Marcel Martin in *Cinéma 62* (Paris), April 1962; "*Viridiana* ou les infortunes de la chiarité" by Raymond Lefevre in *Image et Son* (Paris), summer 1962; "*Viridiana*" by Robert Benayoun in *Positif* (Paris), March 1962; "*Viridiana* et les critiques" by Louis Seguin in *Positif* (Paris), March 1962; "*Viridiana*" by Robert Vas in *Monthly Film Bulletin* (London), October 1963; "The Mexican Buñuel" by Tom Milne in *Sight and Sound* (London), winter 1965-66; article by Kenji Kanesaka in *Film Culture* (New York), summer 1966; "L'envers des Fiorettis" by Michel Mardore in *Cahiers du cinéma* (Paris), March 1966; "The Devil and the Nun: *Viridiana*" by Andrew Sarris in *Renaissance of the Film*, edited by Julius Bellone, London 1970; issue on Buñuel, with interviews, *Image et son* (Paris), May 1971; Buñuel issue of *Cine Cubano*, no.78-80, 1973; "*Viridiana*" by P. Hogue in *Movietone News* (Seattle), February 1975; Buñuel issue of *Contracampo* (Madrid), October/November 1980.

*   *   *

Viridiana is the most atypical of Luis Buñuel's films. If he had set out deliberately to antagonize and shock a whole school of faith, he certainly did it in this film, which, while it was his undoubted masterpiece, concealed a bomb that made it impossible for him to ever return to his native land, Spain.

Not that he wanted to. *Viridiana* was a film he had to make in order to free himself, to let the world know that he was not in idle jest when he broke away from his Roman Catholic faith. The score he had to settle with the Church must have been building for a long, long time. It took over 60 years for him to declare himself utterly free. He was always regarded as the great iconoclast of his time; no director was as unpredictable; but few would have guessed how deep was his hatred for Roman Catholicism.

When the Spanish Civil War was concluded and Spain had settled down to a forgiving and let-it-be-forgotten peace, he as Spain's greatest film director, was invited by Franco's minister of culture to return to his native country and make whatever film he chose with the blessing of Franco. Nobody, even his co-workers, knew that he was planning so defiantly an anti-Catholic film as *Viridiana*. He always worked rapidly once he had begun and, in no time, he had finished shooting his picture and was safely across the Pyrenees, with the whole of his film smuggled out ahead of him. Franco raged, destroying the out-take films deliberately and tantalizingly left behind; he dismissed his minister of culture, and cursed the day he had ever trusted a faithless Spaniard who knew too much for Franco's good. It was not long before Spain acknowledged that it had been betrayed by its priesthood during the Civil War, and put its trust in its young, who had not seen their country go to the devil in the name of God and Franco.

Viridiana is basically the story of innocence betrayed and lost.

The heroine, Viridiana, has completed her novitiate and is about to enter the Church forever, when her Mother Superior persuades her to pay a farewell visit to Don Jaime, her uncle, who had paid for her education and entry into the service of God. Although Viridiana consents to the visit, she had always loathed her uncle because he has never shown her the slightest affection. He is very rich, however, and she is pursuaded that she must see him one last time before she takes her farewell of the world and its ways.

Don Jaime, to her surprise, is affectionate and charming, and lets her know that she is the very image of his dead wife, for whom he still maintains a kind of necrophiliac passion. He has a handsome illegitimate son named Jorge, who is attracted to the young and innocent Viridiana, but is willing to bide his time. Besides, he has brought a mistress of his own to his uncle's estate.

Don Jaime is able to drug Viridiana's wine, and later steals into her bedroom to look upon her as she lies happily unconscious. She is so devoted to Jesus that she wears a crown of thorns and a huge wooden crucifix. She is clothed only in a simple shift. Don Jaime, in a trance, utters his wife's name, removes the crown and crucifix which the girl wears, and brutally rapes her while she lies senseless before him. Consumed by guilt, he then hangs himself.

Viridiana, recovering consciousness, realizes sadly that she is not without guilt herself, for she has blinded herself to the realities of the world; she formally rejects the vows she had made, and returns to the estate she has inherited with Jorge, hoping to make her peace with God. Still imbued with a crippled kind of faith, she takes it upon herself to rescue a band of castaway and diseased gypsy beggars, inviting them to become workers on the land she inherited with Jorge.

They work the land lazily, and at night they indulge themselves in one of the most defiant orgies ever filmed. It is sacrilegious if one is a Christian, which Buñuel was pleased to say he was not. The drunken, diseased beggars stage a supper scene that is a deliberate parody of the grouping in Da Vinci's painting of "The Last Supper." They dance grotesquely, entertaining themselves lewdly to the thunder of the "Hallelujah Chorus."

The picture Buñuel made of his country's plight is replete with symbolism of what Spain had become, a warning of what it might be in a world gone mad. The only mortal salvation the film hints at it is a hope that in a reformed Viridiana and a wiser, less destructive Jorge there may be the seed for a new generation of Spain, cut clean away from the ancient hypocrisies bred in the Church. His heroine comes of age, and realizing the falseness of her onetime faith, pledges herself to a new life that may embrace complete freedom.

Viridiana may be a compelling shocker, but it is also a beautifully made picture with wonderful visuals, and the shock it gives may be virtually necessary to its meaning. Buñuel himself expressed it well when he said, "The sense of film is this: that we do not live in the best of all possible worlds."

He was never afraid to show people how vicious and contemptible they are. When it is all over, Viridiana sits playing cards, listening to rock-and-roll music with her uncle's aggressive illegitimate son. But after the cardplaying and the record has come to an end, what then?

—DeWitt Bodeen

I VITELLONI. The Young and the Passionate. The Wastrels. Production: Peg Films (Paris) and Cité Films (Rome); black and white, 35mm; running time: 104 mins. Released 1953, Venice Film Festival.

Produced by Lorenzo Pegoraro; screenplay by Federico Fellini, Tullio Pinelli, and Ennio Flaiano; from a screen story by Federico Fellini, Ennio Flaiano, and Tullio Penelli; directed by Federico Fellini; photography by Otello Martelli, Luciano Trasatti, and Carlo Carlini; edited by Rolando Benedetti; art direction by Mario Chiari; music by Nino Rota, conducted by Franco Ferrara.

Filmed December 1952-spring 1953 in Viterbo, Ostia, and Florence.

Cast: Franco Interlenghi (*Moraldo*); Alberto Sordi (*Alberto*); Franco Fabrizi (*Fausto*); Leopoldo Trieste (*Leopoldo*); Riccardo Fellini (*Riccardo*); Elenora Ruffo (*Sandra*); Jean Brochard (*Fausto's father*); Claude Farell (*Alberto's sister*); Carlo Romano (*Michele*); Enrico Viarisio (*Sandra's father*); Paola Borboni (*Sandra's mother*); Lida Baarova (*Michele's wife*); Arlette Sauvage (*Lady in the movie theater*); Vira Silenti (*Chinese maiden*); Maja Nipora (*Chanteuse*); Achille Majeroni; Guido Martufi; Silvio Bagolini; Milvia Chianelli.

Publications:

Scripts—"*I vitelloni*" (story treatment) in *Cinema* (Rome), December 1952; *Il primo Fellini. Lo sceicco bianco, I vitelloni, La strada, Il bidone* by F. Fellini, edited by Renzo Renzi, Bologna 1969; "*I vitelloni*" in *Fellini: Three Screenplays*, translated by Judith Green, New York 1970; *Quattro film: I vitelloni, La dolce vita, 8 ½, Giulietta degli spiriti* by F. Fellini, Turin 1974; reviews— "*I vitelloni*" by Rudi Berger in *Filmcritica* (Rome), September 1953; "Ce que tous fils à papa doit savoir" by André Martin in *Cahiers du cinéma* (Paris), May 1954; "*Les Vitelloni*" by Roger Tailleur and Bernard Chardère in *Positif* (Paris), September/October 1954; "*Marty*—Italian-Style" in *Newsweek* (New York), 12 November 1956; "*Vitelloni*" by Eugene Archer in *Film Culture* (New York), no.4, 1956; "*I vitelloni*" by Bosley Crowther in *The New York Times*, 24 October 1956; books— *Federico Fellini* by Renzo Renzi, Parma 1956; *Cinema Eye, Cinema Ear* by John Russell Taylor, New York 1964; *Italian Cinema Today* by Gian Luigi Rondi, New York 1965; *Fellini* by Suzanne Budgen, London 1966; *Federico Fellini* by Gilbert Salachas, New York 1969; *Federico Fellini: An Investigation into his Films and Philosophy* by Gilbert Salachas, translated by Rosalie Siegal, New York 1969; *Fellini on Fellini*, New York 1976; *The Cinema of Federico Fellini* by Stuart Rosenthal, Cranbury, New Jersey 1976; *Fellini* by Liliana Betti, Zurich 1976; *Federico Fellini: The Search for a New Mythology* by Charles B. Ketcham, New York 1976; *Federico Fellini: A Guide to References and Resources* by John C. Stubbs, Boston 1978; articles—"Troppi leoni al lido" by Giulio Cesare Castello in *Cinema* (Rome), 31 August 1953; "Strada sabarrata: via libera ai vitelloni" by Federico Fellini in *Cinema nuovo* (Turin), 1 January 1953; "Venezia 53" by Nino Ghelli in *Bianco e nero* (Rome), October 1953; "Venice 1953" by Francis Koval in *Films in Review* (New York), October 1953; "Moraldo in città incontra se stesso" by B. Benedetti in *Cinema Nuovo* (Rome), 15 August 1954; "New Names" in *Sight and Sound* (London), winter 1955; "The Signs of Predicament" by Gavin Lambert in *Sight and Sound* (London), January/March 1955; "Le Cas Fellini" by Cecilia Mangini in *Cinéma 55* (Paris), January 1955; "*Les Vitelloni*" by Gilbert Salachas in *Téléciné* (Paris), October/No-

vember 1955; "*La Strada*: Cinematic Intersections" by Vernon Young in *Hudson Review* (Nutley, New Jersey), autumn 1956; "Le Doight de Dieu est dans le champ" by Pierre Philippe in *Cinéma 58* (Paris), February 1958; "Italian Film: Failure and Emergence" by Joseph Bennett in *Kenyon Review* (Gambier, Ohio), autumn 1964; "*I vitelloni*" by Mark Sufrin in *Film Society Review* (New York), May 1970; "Fellini" by Raymond Lefevre in *Image et son* (Paris), January 1971; "Reason and Unreason in Federico Fellini's *I vitelloni*" by F.M. Burke in *Literature/Film Quarterly* (Salisbury, Maryland), no.2, 1980.

* * *

After *Lo sceicco bianco*, which despite its formal brilliance was a critical and financial failure, Fellini found himself unable to obtain backing for *La Strada*, already in scenario form. Together with scenarists Ennio Flaiano and Tullio Pinelli, he devised the story of the prankish middle-class youths—or *vitelloni* (meaning literally "big slabs of veal")—that he remembered from his Romagnan boyhood. Having high opinions of their limited talents, these aging provincial good-for-nothings prefer banding together to amuse themselves at the expense of their neighbors in lieu of settling down into responsible lifestyles and the work they consider demeaning.

The film focuses on the lives of five buddies, drawn with the profound social observation of a great satirist. Each must come to terms with the inevitable alienation that they face when confronted with their worthlessness and with the bleakness of their futures. Alberto, the saddest of the group, lives with his mother and is supported by his sister. He tries desperately to remain an adolescent for everyone except his sister to whom he acts the commanding brother and man of the family. Against his will, his sister elopes, leaving him to become the breadwinner. Fausto, the handsome Don Juan of the group, is coerced into marrying Moraldo's sister whom he has gotten pregnant; however, he doesn't hesitate to abandon his new wife at the movies to pursue the woman in the seat next to him. Fausto loses his job in a religious statuary shop (a typical Fellini touch of uncommon satirical depth) after trying to seduce the owner's wife. Through Alberto and Fausto, Fellini comments on the predatory nature of that society, and of the middle-class in particular. Leopoldo, a romantic dreamer, plays the tortured dramatist to the maid across the courtyard. His hopes shatter when he petitions a fustian travelling actor for help. Pretending to be interested in Leopoldo's play, the actor makes homosexual advances toward him. Riccardo is the least clearly characterized of the group, perhaps only used to make the group a more convenient size. Moraldo represents an ethical center in the film; while he contributes to the group's sport, he clearly does not have the avocation. In moments signalled by camera placement, editing, and music, Moraldo merges with the subjective authorial consciousness that will become more direct and forceful in the later Fellini films. He is the only one with any curiosity about life and any courage to break away for good. Moraldo is undoubtedly Fellini. His story was to have been continued in the scripted, but never filmed, *Moraldo in città*. A similar character gets off the train at the beginning of *Roma*.

Much of the wistfully tragic cadence of the film derives from a despair behind the merry masks of the *vitelloni*, a rhetorical figuration actualized in the town's frenzied carnival celebration. This Dionysian event is the perfect visual and rhythmic representation of misdirected energy, leading to a critique of the grotesque, inebriated alienation and neurotic sexual frustration at the base of the Italian society in the 1950s. The mask motif points to the director's skill in utilizing Pirandellian themes with pointedness and originality. Alberto's drag costume and enormous mask, with its features set into a grotesque, scream-like demeanor, are indications that farcical anarchy and psychological anguish are never too distant from each other.

Like Gramsci, Fellini attributes Italian fascism to these inseperable adolescent qualities, and continues to explore this problem in different contexts in his later work. Specifically, *Il bidone*, a work of less technical polish, stands out as a transmutation of these provincial *vitelloni* from harmless, middle-class parasites into hostile, ruthless con-men and thieves.

I vitelloni was enormously successful, even among critics of the left, and became the director's first film distributed internationally.

—Joel Kanoff

VIVRE SA VIE. My Life to Live. Production: Films de la Pléiade; black and white, 35mm; running time: 85 mins. Released September 1962, Paris.

Produced by Pierre Braumberger; screenplay by Jean-Luc Godard with additional narrative from Judge Marcel Sacotte's *Où en est la prostitution* and Edgar Allen Poe's "The Oval Portrait"; titles by Ursule Monlinaro; directed by Jean-Luc Godard; photography by Raoul Coutard; edited by Agnès Guillemot and Lila Lakshmanan; sound by Guy Vilette and Jacques Maumont, sound cut by Lila Lakshmanan; music by Michel Legrand, song "Ma môme, elle joue pas les starletts" by Jean Ferrat and Pierre Frachet; costumes designed by Christiane Fage; assistant directors: Bernard Toublanc-Michel and Jean-Paul Savignac.

Filmed 1966 in Paris. Venice Film Festival, Special Jury Prize and the Italian Critics Prize, 1962.

Cast: Anna Karina (*Nana*); Sady Rebbot (*Raoul*); André S. Labarthe (*Paul*); Guylaine Schlumberger (*Yvette*); Gérard Hoffmann (*The cook*); Monique Messine (*Elizabeth*); Paul Pavel (*Journalist*); Dimitri Dineff (*Dimitri*); Peter Kassowitz (*Young man*); Eric Schlumberger (*Luigi*); Brice Parain (*The philosopher*); Henri Attal (*Arthur*); Gilles Quéant (*A man*); Odile Geoffrey (*Barmaid*); Marcel Charton (*Policeman*); Jack Florency (*Bystander*); Gisèele Hauchecorne (*Concierge*); Jean-Luc Godard (*Voice*); Jean Ferrat (*Man at jukebox who watches Nana*); Jean-Paul Savignac (*Young soldier at bar*); Mario Botti (*Italian*); Laszlo Szabo (*Wounded man who enters bar*).

Publications:

Scripts—"*Vivre sa vie*" in *Avant-Scène du cinéma* (Paris), October 1962; "Scenario" (*Vivre sa vie*), translated by Louis Brigante, in *Film Culture* (New York), winter 1962; reviews—by Mark Shivas in *Movie* (London), October 1962; review by Peter Baker in *Films and Filming* (London), Januray 1963; review by Jonas Mekas in *The Village Voice* (New York), 26 September 1963; review by Andrew Sarris in *The Village Voice* (New York), 26 September 1963; books—*Jean-Luc Godard* by Jean Collet, Paris 1963; *Cinema Eye, Cinema Ear: Some Key Filmmakers of the 60's* by John Russell Taylor, New York 1964; *Jean-Luc*

Godard by Richard Roud, New York 1967; *Jean-Luc Godard: A Critical Anthology* edited by Tony Mussman, New York 1968; *The Films of Jean-Luc Godard* edited by Ian Cameron, London 1969; *Godard* by Michele Mancini, Rome 1969; *Jean-Luc Godard* edited by Jean Collet, translated by Ciba Vaughan, New York 1970; *Godard* by Richard Roud, Bloomington, Indiana 1970; *Focus on Godard* edited by Royal Brown, Englewood Cliffs, New Jersey 1972; *Godard on Godard* edited and translated by Tom Milne, London 1972; *Jean-Luc Godard* by Alberto Farassino, Florence 1974; *The New Wave* by James Monaco, New York 1976; articles—"Godard's *Vivre sa vie*" by Susan Sontag in *Against Interpretation*, New York 1961; "Entretien avec Jean-Luc Godard" by Jean Collet, et al. in *Cahiers du cinéma* (Paris), December 1962; "Jean-Luc Godard and *Vivre sa vie*" by Tom Milne in *Sight and Sound* (London), winter 1962; "Que chacun vivre sa vie" by François Truffaut in *Avant-Scène du cinéma* (Paris), October 1962; "An Interview" in the *New York Film Bulletin*, no.5, 1962; "A Movie is a Movie is a Movie is a..." by Andrew Sarris in the *New York Film Bulletin*, no.5, 1962; article in *Films and Filming* (London), December 1962; "Anna et les paradoxes" in *Cinéma 63* (Paris), July/August 1963; "Godard: Cut-Sequence: *Vivre sa vie*" by Jean-André Fieschi, translated by Gary Broughton, in *Movie* (London), January 1963; "*My Life to Live*: Portrait of a Lady" by Gary Carey and Marilyn Goldin *Seventh Art* (New York), winter 1963; "Conventional/Unconventional" by Colin Young in *Film Quarterly* (Berkeley), fall 1963; "On Godard's *Vivre sa vie*" by Susan Sontag in *Movie Goer*, summer/autumn 1964; "Godard" by Susan Sontag in the *Partisan Review* (New Brunswick, New Jersey), spring 1968; "The Films of Jean-Luc Godard" by Stephen Crofts in *Cinema* (London), June 1969; "Nana af de realiteit in een klein frans tehuis" by T. de Graff in *Skrien* (Amsterdam), spring 1972; "*Vivre sa vie*" by Siew Hwa Beh in *Women & Film*, no.1, 1972; "Life Itself: *Vivre sa vie* and the Language of Film" by M. Campbell in *Wide Angle* (Athens, Ohio), no.3, 1976; "*Vivre sa vie*" by Marjorie Baumgarten in *Cinema Texas Program Notes* (Austin), 20 November 1977; "Portrayals of Painting: Translations of *Vivre sa vie*" by T. Conley in *Film Reader* (Evanston, Illinois), no.3, 1978; "Nana of de realiteit van een klein frans tehuis" by T. de Graaff in *Skrien* (Amsterdam, Netherlands), winter 1978-79; "Music and *Vivre sa vie*" by R.S. Brown in *Quarterly Review f of Film Studies* (Pleasantville, New York), summer 1980; "The Erratic Alphabet" by Marie-Claire Ropars in *Enclitic*, no.10-11, 1981.

*   *   *

Jean-Luc Godard's fourth feature-length film, *Vivre sa vie*, forms the second shutter of a dyptych with *À bout de souffle*. Where the latter had divested the film noir of its notion of reality, the former went in the same direction but with greater consequence. Its composition externalizes to an extreme point many obsessions common to all Godard's work. Prostitution is the theme binding a number of formal experiments that touch on a variety of ideas including: the relation of art and lithography to cinema; the depressing squalor of an all-encompassing *zone* of tastelessness comprising modern life (hence the film's allegiance to Baudelaire); the breakdown of intimacy and experience as valid measures of morality; the interfilmic mix of allusions that saturate single shots and sequences; and the break-up of the illusion of perspective by which words and images form an immense hieroglyph of trash culled from such sources as advertising and the major media.

No film of Godard's attains the same rigor of rhythm in its play of sound and image, or of formal camera movement. Raoul Coutard, Godard's favorite cameraman, insists on a medium distance between the objective and Anna Karina, who plays the role of an exemplary—but very common—female who, because of the pressures of daily life, is forced into prostitution and martydom for no cause. In the first sequence, he shoots the backsides of Karina and her husband as they sit apart on barroom stools and face a mirror on the wall of the café before them. The camera pans indifferently to the left and right as the futility of their words reflects the breakdown of their marriage. If the dissolution of relationships which begins the film is conveyed by a camera that cannot reach an intimate rapport with the character's faces, then the ensuing tableaux—where the camera stands fixed for long periods of time (following Nana's pen in extreme closeup as she scripts a marginally literate letter of application for employment), or where it traces a dolly of 180 degrees from profile to the front of Nana's face as she stares at her pimp from a wall-papered vista of Paris in the Impressionist style—mark its will to distance itself more than it ever had in Godard's *oeuvre*. Seberg and Belmondo were caressed by the camera in *À bout de souffle*. This is hardly the case in *Vivre sa vie*. In the same way, sequences filmed in silence (in Parisian streets or about local monuments), or with on-location noise (in record shops or in cafés), or with ruptures of music and silence, or with speech by figures on screen (the jukebox and famous mating dance in the pool hall) make the film resemble a composition of tonal music or plastic collage.

Citing Montaigne on the need to experience (that is, to draw death from life) at the outset of the film, Godard cuts the story of Nana's life into twelve segments or stations of sainthood. Nana's death, shot in front of a "Café des Studios" along a tasteless suburban street, casually depicts the heroine falling adjacent to two cars. But it also tells of the urgent metaphysical preoccupations at the bottom of Godard's films. *Vivre sa vie* underscores an obsession with representation defined (in strict accord with the etymology of *prostatuere*, which is "to stand foward") in terms of prostitution. To reveal oneself to others, "to stand foward" in a crowd, in a contemporary and cinematic *ecce homo*, invites murder. Godard attains both deeply religious and Marxian undertones throughout the film. This is confirmed all the more in a remarkable moment just prior to the last tableau, when Nana's new lover, a young man (who is as banal as all the men who appear in his work) reads excerpts from Baudelaire's translation of Poe's "Oval Portrait" dealing with the idea of doubling a picture with words, and of a narrative finished at the price of death for the figure who is being portrayed. Godard is actually the voice reading Poe through Baudelaire; there is also no lip-synch of the voice with the young man's face (covered up to eye level by the book). We can no longer discern who, or what, is speaking to, or for, whom. Quotations abound, and suddenly the basic ventriloquism of cinema is revealed trenchantly and with abrupt conceptual force. In this fashion the film attains what the words of the text do not; the relation of words to image is complicated by having the subtitles become, like a medieval phylactery, the sacred text breaking the illusion of the spectator's association with the voice or image.

The film is a venturous mix of allusive—and haunting—references. Godard refilms Dreyer's closeups of the martyrdom of Falconetti in the excruciating sequences of *The Passion of Joan of Arc*. At one point Nana see Dreyer's film in a Left Bank theater and cries in sympathy for Joan/Falconetti. That Falconetti became a prostitute after undergoing a nervous breakdown was well known; that Godard uses Dreyer to "script" the end of Godard's marriage to Karina complicates the film and makes the adoring, yet murderous closeups of Anna Karina all the more powerful in their ambivalence.

—Tom Conley

VOINA I MIR. War and Peace. Production: Mosfilm; Sovcolor, 35mm, scope; running time: originally 373 mins. (some sources list 507 mins.), and released in two parts, later cut to 170 mins. Released 1967.

Screenplay by Sergei Bondarchuk and Vasily Solovyov; directed by Sergei Bondarchuk; photography by Anatoly Petritsky, Dmitri Korzhikin and A. Zenyan; production design by Mikhail Bogdanov and Gennady Myasnikov; music by Vyacheslav Ovchinnikov.

Cost: rumored to have been anywhere between 40 and 100 million dollars. Academy Award, Best Foreign Film, 1968; New York Film Critics Award, Best Foreign Film, 1968.

Cast: Ludmilla Savelyeva (*Natasha*); Sergei Bondarchuk (*Pierre*); Vyacheslav Tikhonov (*Andrei*); Anastasia Vertinskaya (*Princess Liza*); Vasily Lanovoi (*Kuragin*); Irina Skobotseva (*Hélène*); Boris Zakhava (*Kutuzov*); Vladislav Strzhelchik (*Napoleon*).

Publications:

Book—*A Year in the Dark: Journal of a Film Critic 1968-1969* by Renata Adler, New York 1969; articles—"A Budding Ballet Dancer Becomes the Greatest Heroine of All Russia" by Edwin Miller in *Seventeen*, August 1968; "*War and Peace*: A Soviet View" by Igor Zolotussky in *London Magazine*, March 1969; "Tolstoy Betrayed" by Alan Napier in *Film Heritage* (Dayton, Ohio), spring 1969; "Vast as an Ocean" by Vran Guralnik in *Films and Filming* (London), May 1969; "Director of the Year" in *International Film Guide*, London 1969; "Thinking Big" by J. Gillett in *Sight and Sound* (London), summer 1970; "The Road to *Waterloo*" by John Lind in *Focus on Film* (London), September/October 1970; "The Coming of the Russians" in *Action* (Los Angeles), June 1971; "Dolg i pravo hudožnika" in *Iskusstvo kino* (Moscow), August 1973; interview by S. Tschertok in *Film und Fernsehen* (Berlin), April 1975; "Soviet Cinema: Films, Personalities, Problems" by S. Gerasimov in *Soviet Film* (Moscow), no.271, 1979.

*   *   *

Sergei Bondarchuk's *War and Peace*, budgeted at over $100-million, is easily the definitive version of Tolstoy's masterpiece. In *War and Peace*, the world's greatest historical novel, Tolstoy created a panorama of vivid characters who are so realistic they breathe life before the reader's eyes. "We strove," Bondarchuk explained, "with the aid of modern cinematic means, to reproduce Tolstoy's thoughts, emotions, philosophy, and ideals." As Penelope Gilliatt wrote in the *New Yorker*, "Not the smallest blunder of style or proportion was made...."

Bondarchuk was not the first filmmaker to attempt to translate Tolstoy's narrative to the screen. In 1915, Vladimir Gardin and Yakov Protazanov directed a ten-reel *War and Peace*; 41 years later King Vidor made a static, overly-simplified Italian-American version with Henry Fonda, Audrey Hepburn and Mel Ferrer. Bondarchuk's film is easily the most ambitious. It is uncannily faithful to Tolstoy's characterizations, and the most spectacular feature ever made in Russia—perhaps also the most successful at the box office. The filmmaker labored on the project for over half a decade. His original cut, released in Russia in four parts, features battle scenes as grand as any ever put on the screen. Cannons were reproduced exactly as they were at the time of the story; paintings and props were borrowed from museums; 158 separate scenes were filmed, utilizing a similar number of locations all over the USSR. There were 272 sets, 6,000 military costumes, 2,000 civilian costumes, 30 starring roles and 120,000 soldier-extras. Not unexpectedly, the most memorable sequences are the spectacles: the ball at which Natasha and Andrei are introduced; the burning of Moscow; and specifically, the Battle of Borodino. Ballerina Ludmila Savelyeva is ravishing as Natasha; Bondarchuk himself appears as Pierre.

An hour was cut for the American print, which runs 373 minutes. It was also dubbed (unnecessarily) and released in two parts—one would be presented in the afternoon, the other in the evening. Later, it was further cut to 170 minutes. Still *War and Peace* is enormous in scope. Bondarchuk, a post-war Russian actor whose career behind the camera began during the late 1950s, specialized in epic productions. *Waterloo*, the follow-up to *War and Peace*, could almost be considered a sequel.

Bondarchuk has recently made a yet-to-be-released three-part epic, a Soviet-Italian-Mexican co-production about John Reed and Louise Bryant that perhaps reinterprets the material covered in Warren Beatty's *Reds*. In its day, *War and Peace* was the most expensive motion picture of all time. This new venture could surpass it in scope and cost.

—Rob Edelman

LE VOYAGE DANS LA LUNE. A Trip to the Moon. Production: Star Film Studios (Montreuil, France); black and white, 35mm, silent; running time: 14 mins., but varying lengths exist; length: about 825 feet. Released 1902, at Méliès' Théâtre Robert Houdin in Paris.

Scenario by Georges Méliès; inspired, at least in part, by the novel *First Men in the Moon* by H.G. Wells; directed by George Méliès; photography possibly by one or more of Méliès' regular cameramen who included Leclerc, Michaut, Lallemand, and Astaix.

Filmed 1902 in Méliès' Star Film Studios at Montreuil. Cost: 10,000 francs.

Cast: George Méliès (*Barbenfouillis, President of the Astronomer's Club*); Bluette Bernon (*Phoebe on the crescent moon*); Acrobats from the Folies-Bergère (*Members of the Selenite Army*).

Publications:

Books—*An Index to the Creative Work of Georges Méliès* by

Georges Sadoul, supplement to *Sight and Sound* (London), index series, 1947; *French Film* by Georges Sadoul, Paris 1953; *Georges Méliès* by Charles Ford, Brussels 1959; *Georges Méliès, Mage* by Maurice Bessy and Lo Duca, Paris 1961; *Georges Méliès* by Georges Sadoul, Paris 1961; *Le Boulevard du cinéma à l'époque de Georges Méliès* by Jacques Deslandes, Paris 1963; *De Méliès à l'expressionisme, le Surréalisme au Cinéma* by Ado Kyrou, Paris 1963; *Archaeology of the Cinema* by C.W. Ceram, New York 1965; *Cinéma 1900* by René Jeanne, Paris 1965; *Méliès, l'enchanteur* by Madeleine Malthête-Méliès, Paris 1973; *The Early Development of the Motion Picture* by Joseph North, New York 1973; *Marvellous Méliès* by Paul Hammond, New York 1975; *Artificially Arranged Scenes: The Films of Georges Méliès* by John Frazer, Boston 1979; *A History of Film* by Jack C. Ellis, Englewood Cliffs, New Jersey 1979; articles—"Histoire d'un film, *Le Voyage dans la lune*" by Marcel Lapierre in *Ce Soir* (Paris), December 1937; "Father of the Fantasy Film" by Alberto Cavalcanti in *The Listener* (London), 2 June 1938; "Méliès père du cinéma, fils de Jules Verne" in *Cahiers du cinéma* (Paris), no.10, 1952; "Méliès" by Maurice Bessy in *Anthologie du cinéma, Vol.II*, Paris 1967; "George Méliès" by Stan Brakhage in *Caterpillar* (New York), spring 1970; "Georges Méliès, magicien du cinéma" by Henri Langlois in *Cinéma 71* (Paris), January 1971; "Georges Méliès albo zaklinanie wulgarnej materii" by A. Helmani in *Kino* (Warsaw), January 1974; "The Magician and the Movies" by Eric Barnouw in *American Film* (Washington, D.C.), April 1978 and May 1978; "Point d'histoire: Méliès: la fin d'un mythe?" by G. Courant in *Cinéma* (Paris), May 1979; "L'Idéologie de Méliès et son epoque" by M.A.M. Quevrain in *Cinéma* (Paris), September 1979; "Portrait de l'artiste en magicien" by O.-R. Veillon in *Cinématographe* (Paris), January 1981.

*   *   *

During his years as a filmmaker (from 1896-1913), Georges Méliès produced literally hundreds of short films. Perhaps the best known and most often seen is *A Trip to the Moon*. The film is very representative of Méliès work and contains many examples of his unique style of filmmaking.

Before he began making films, Méliès was a professional stage illusionist and magician. He thought of motion pictures mainly as a way of expanding his act. As a result, his films have a rather stagey look, as though they were photographed from a perfect front-row center seat. Méliès also discovered the "magic" of filmmaking and soon became a master of special effects photography. By using dissolves, fades, mattes, double-exposures, and other filmic techniques, Méliès was able to create tricks that could never be done on the stage.

As with all of Méliès films, *A Trip to the Moon* was entirely staged for the camera. This in itself was rather innovative for the time. Most early motion picture films were a single shot of scenes from everyday life: a train pulling into a railway station, a burning building or a busy city street, for example. *Trip* was comprised of 30 separate scenes, each of which were acted out on a specially built stage. The film ran 825 feet and helped to establish the one-reeler as the new standard film length.

Trip also helped to develop the narrative film form. Each of the 30 scenes leads into the next, telling a complete story without the use of title cards. Though *Trip* is one of the very first science fiction films, it is also a comedy. It lampoons the idea of science and turns it into more of a fantasy. The humor in the film still holds up fairly well today.

The photographic tricks used were all done in-the-camera.

This was before the invention of the optical printer or process photography, and each trick had to be carefully planned. One trick which Méliès frequently used was to make a substitution with a cut in the middle of a scene. In this way he could make objects appear or disappear as if by magic. For example, in *Trip*, the Selenites are destroyed in a puff of smoke using this technique. Méliès would also use dissolves to make an object transform into something else, as in the scene where the stars change into women. In each of these examples the camera would have to be locked into position so that the substitution could be made without disturbing the rest of the scene.

Trip (as well as other of Méliès films) most certainly had an influence on later avant-garde films. The picture had a very surreal look to it with the painted backdrops and forced perspectives. For example, the surface of the moon appears to be made of different levels of painted cut-outs. Méliès never attempted to capture a "realistic" look in his films, but used the fantasy elements to his advantage.

A Trip to the Moon was an extremely popular film and helped to establish Méliès on the American and international markets. Unfortunately for Méliès, his films were often pirated and this loss of revenue eventually forced him out of business. However, his films did influence the next wave of filmmakers and helped to develop a more complex form of storytelling.

—Linda J. Obalil

VREDENS DAG. Day of Wrath. Dies Irae—Jour de Colère. Production: Palladium Copenhagen-Tage Nielson; black and white, 35mm; running time: 92 mins., some sources state 98 mins.; length: about 2675 meters, some sources state 2790 meters. Released 13 November 1943, Copenhagen.

Screenplay by Carl Theodor Dreyer, Mogens Skot-Hansen, and Poul Knudsen; from the play *Anne Pedersdotter* by Hans Wiers-Jenssen; directed by Carl Theodor Dreyer; photography by Karl Andersson; edited by Edith Schlüssel and Anne Marie Petersen; sound by Erik Rasmussen; art direction by Erik Aaes; music by Poul Schierbeck; costumes designed by K. Sandt Jensen and Olga Thomsen, from designs by Lis Fribert; historical consultant: Kaj Uldall.

Cast: Thorkild Roose (*Absalon*); Lisbeth Movin (*Anne, his wife*); Sigrid Neiiendam (*Merete, his mother*); Preben Lerdorff Rye (*Martin, his son*); Anne Svierkier (*Herlof's Marte*); Olaf Ussing (*Laurentius*); Albert Høeber (*The Bishop*); Emilie Nielsen; Kirsten Andreasen; Sophie Knudsen; Harald Holst; Preben Neergaard; Emanuel Jørgensen; Hans Christian Sørgensen; Dagmar Wildenbrück.

Publications:

Scripts—"*Vredens Dag*" by Carl Theodor Dreyer, Poul Knudsen, and M. Skot-Hansen in *Carl Theodor Dreyer: Four Screenplays* translated by Oliver Stallybrass, London 1970; "*Dies Irae*" by Carl Theodor Dreyer in *Avant-Scène du cinéma* (Paris), February 1970; review— "*Dies Irae*: la critique" in *Avant-Scène du cinéma* (Paris), February 1970; books—*Carl Theodor Dreyer: A Film Director's Work* by Ebbe Neergaard, London 1950; *The Art of Carl Dreyer: An Analysis* by Børge

Trolle, Copenhagen 1955; *Om Filmen* by Carl Theodor Dreyer, Copenhagen 1964; *The Films of Carl Dreyer* by Eileen Bowser, New York 1964; *Portrait of Carl Th. Dreyer* by Ib Monty, Copenhagen 1965; *Carl Th. Dreyer, Danish Film Director*, edited by Soren Dyssegaard, Copenhagen 1968; *Carl Th. Dreyer* by Claude Perrin, Paris 1969; *Carl Th. Dreyer* by Jean Sémolué, Paris 1970; *Transcendental Style in Film: Ozu, Bresson, Dreyer* by Paul Schrader, Los Angeles 1972; *Dreyer in Double Reflection*, edited by Donald Skoller, New York 1973; *Dreyer*, edited by Mark Nash, London 1977; *Carl Theodor Dreyer* by Pier Giorgio Tone, Florence 1978; *The Films of Carl-Theodor Dreyer* by David Bordwell, Berkeley 1981; articles—special issue of *Écran français* (Paris), 11 November 1947; "Dreyer à son sommet" by Lo Duca in *La Revue du cinéma* (Paris), no.4, 1946-47; "Continental Films of the Quarter" by Roger Manvell in *Sight and Sound* (London), no.60, 1947; "Carl Dreyer's World" by Richard Rowland in *Hollywood Quarterly*, fall 1950; "Film Style" by Carl Th. Dreyer in *Films in Review* (New York), January 1952; "Film Style" by Carl Theodor Dreyer in *Films in Review* (New York), January 1952; "Jour de colère" by Frédéric Laurent in *Image et son* (Paris), no.67, 1953; "The World of Carl Dreyer" by Børge Trolle in *Sight and Sound* (London), winter 1955/56; "Jour de colère" in *Cinéma 58* (Paris), no.32, 1958; "Dreyer" by Herbert Luft in *Films and Filming* (London), June 1961; "Dies Irae de Carl Th. Dreyer" in *Image et son* (Paris), no.65, 1963; "Tag der Rache" in *Filmkritik* (Munich), no.2, 1963; "The World of Carl Dreyer" by Kirk Bond in *Film Quarterly* (Berkeley), fall 1965; issue on Dreyer, *Cahiers du cinéma* (Paris), December 1968; special issue of *Kosmorama* (Copenhagen), June 1968; "Dreyer: De Jeanne d'Arc a dies irae" by Jean Sémolué in *Avant-Scène du cinéma* (Paris), February 1970; "Carl Dreyer and the Theme of Choice" by Dai Vaughan in *Sight and Sound* (London), summer 1974; "Dreyer's Concept of Abstraction" by Vlada Petric in *Sight and Sound* (London), spring 1975; "*Day of Wrath*" by Gordon Gow in *Films and Filming* (London), no.8, 1977.

*　　*　　*

Eleven years passed between Carl Th. Dreyer's first sound film, *Vampyr*, and his second, *Vredens Dag*, his first Danish film in 18 years. Dreyer saw *Anne Pedersdotter*, the Norwegian play by Hans Wiers-Jenssen on which the film was based, in Copenhagen in 1909, and had always wanted to film this story of a young woman burned as a witch. However, he altered the original drama in various ways.

The film takes place in a pastor's house in the country in 1623. The 21-year-old Anne, the second wife of the elderly vicar, is suffocating in the stern atmosphere of the house and suffering from the tyranny of her mother-in-law. When the pastor's young son returns, Anne falls in love with him, finally setting free her suppressed feelings. But society strikes back. Anne, whose mother was accused of being a witch, begins to fear that she too is a witch after the pastor dies. Typical of a Dreyer film, *Vredens Dag* is also about the struggle between good and evil. Anne is not only a victim of a hostile and intolerant society, she must also endure the struggle within herself.

Vredens Dag is an erotic drama about a love triangle played against a background of superstition and Christian mercilessness. In the characters Dreyer has mixed the individual with the universal, showing the strong impact of society on the formation of the individual. Whether the reactions of the main characters are based on individual, personal and egotistical motives or are the results of ideas and prejudices of the time is deliberately difficult to ascertain.

In this way, *Vredens Dag* is a historical film, trying to capture the spirit of the past. But it is also obvious now what was not clear at the time of the film's release; the film was also commenting on another dark period of Danish history—the German occupation, the time in which *Vredens Dag* was produced. In addition, the film can also be considered a timeless drama about a human being fighting for her right to self-realization.

The film is remarkable for its intense, but quiet acting and its austere visual style, which grew out of the theme. The slow camera movements, the long travelling shots, the close-ups and medium close-ups, and the beautiful compositions, inspired by 17th century paintings, serve as a means for Dreyer to recreate the slow pulse of the time.The formal beauty, the contrasts between black and white, the use of horizontal and vertical camera movements, and particularly the rhythm caused the Danish critics to call it formalistic. The film was negatively received in 1943, although there were those who defended it. Similarly, when the film was shown in New York in 1948, it got very mixed reviews. In England, however, where it was shown in 1946, it was praised by the press. Since then, *Vredens Dag* has grown in critical reputation and is now considered one of Dreyer's masterpieces.

—Ib Monty

WALKABOUT. Production: Twentieth Century-Fox; Eastmancolor, 35mm; running time: 95 mins. Released 1 July 1971, New York.

Produced by Si Litvinoff, executive producer: Max L. Raab, associate producer: Anthony Hope; screenplay by Edward Bond; from the novel by James Vance Marshall; directed by Nicolas Roeg; photography by Nicolas Roeg; edited by Anthony Gibbs and Alan Patillo; production design by Brian Eatwell; music by John Barry.

Filmed in Australia.

Cast: Jenny Agutter (*Girl*); Lucien John (*Brother*): David Gumpilil (*Aborigine*); John Mellon (*Father*); Peter Carver (*No Hoper*); John Illingsworth (*Husband*).

Publications:

Reviews—in *Filmfacts* (New York), no.14, 1971; review in *Variety* (New York), 19 May 1971; "*Walkabout*: A Tribal Study in Survival" by Vincent Canby in *The New York Times*, 2 July 1971; "*Walkabout*" by Bill Nichols in *Cinema 7*, fall 1971; "*Walkabout*" by Gavin Millar in *Sight and Sound* (London), winter 1971-72; review by Peter Cowie in *International Film Guide* (London), no.9, 1972; book—*Nicolas Roeg* by Neil Feineman, Boston 1978; articles—"*Walkabout*: Beautiful but Fake?" by Craig McGregor in *The New York Times*, 18 July 1971; "Identity: An Interview with Nicolas Roeg" by Gordon Gow in *Films and Filming* (London), January 1972; article in *Film Quarterly* (Berkeley), summer 1973; "Interview with Nicolas Roeg" by Tom Milne and Penelope Houston in *Sight and Sound* (London), winter 1973-74; "*Performance, Walkabout, Don't Look Now*, Nicolas Roeg—Permutations without Profundity" by Chuck Kleinhans in *Jump Cut* (Chicago), September/October 1974; "Film: No Sex, No Bushman"by J. Greenway in *National Review* (New York), October 1975; "Nicolas Roeg—A Sense of Wonder" by N. Waller in *Film Criticism* (Edinboro, Pennsylvania), no.1, 1976; "A Roeg's Gallery of Imagistic Motion Pictures" by Charles Champlin in *Los Angeles Times Sunday Calendar*, 12 September 1976; "The Open Texts of Nicolas Roeg" by Robert Philip Kolker in *Sight and Sound* (London), spring 1977; "Two Images of the Aboriginal: *Walkabout*, the Novel and Film" by A. Boyle in *Literature/Film Quarterly* (Salisbury, Maryland), vol.7, no.1, 1979; "Film: Sweep Week" by T. Allen in *The Village Voice* (New York), 10 December 1979; "Screen: *Aces High* and Berri's *Papa*" by Janet Maslin in *The New York Times*, 7 December 1979; "*Walkabout*: Wasted Journey" by J. Izod in *Sight and Sound* (London), spring 1980; "Another Look at Nicolas Roeg" by Joseph Gomez in *Film Criticism* (Edinboro, Pennsylvania), no.6, 1981; "*Walkabout*" by Timothy Johnson in *Magill's Survey of Cinema: English Language Films*, edited by Frank N. Magill, 2nd series, vol.6, Englewood Cliffs, New Jersey 1981.

*   *   *

Walkabout was Nicolas Roeg's first solo directorial effort. It is a stunningly beautiful and simple film shot on location in the outback of the Australian bush and, in many ways, can be seen as the first of the Australian New Wave films to receive widespread distribution in Europe and America. In spite of its seeming simplicity, the film is an intricately structured and sophisticated statement about the effects of modern civilization. It is also a film which has aroused considerable critical argument.

Walkabout's uncomplicated, straightforward plot belies the film's larger, mythic overtones. It is not just a story about the rescue by an aborigine of two white children, lost in the desert, but a comment on the clash between two mutually exclusive cultures, or rather the boundary which separates them. Further, it is a movie about lost innocence, missed opportunities and unrecoverable moments, and the regret associated with the memory of such losses. These elaborations are created by framing the simple "walkabout" adventure with complicated and suggestive shots of contemporary, urban Australia that represent modernism is general. These shots throw the child-like, elemental experiences of the youngsters in the outback into relief. Roeg intercuts the rather straightforward narrative with intrusions from the modern world reminding the audience that this is a circular journey leading from the modern world into the wilderness, back into time and toward innocence, only to return to contemporary civilization. The film also provides an unsentimentalized view of primitivism, no romantic dreams about the joys of the life of nature, no noble savages. We may come to understand that life is more elemental "out there," and recognize the superiority of the values which evolve from a harmony between man and nature that the aborigine reflects, but at no time are we led to believe that such a life is even remotely possible for the girl and her brother. It is only in retrospect that the girl, years older and married, can envision the Eden-like possibilities of her experience. Her memory, slightly distorted, echoed the lament from Houseman's *A Shropshire Lad* for a lost state of grace:

> That is the land of lost content,
> I see it shining plain,
> The happy highways where I went
> And cannot come again.

Given the relatively simple statement of the film, especially on the surface, it is curious how much negative comment it has received from the critics. Some of Roeg's detractors find the film too straightforward, reflecting a simple-minded message about escaping the evils of the contemporary world by fleeing to a edenic world of primitivism. Several commentators have harshly criticized the girl for her crass inability to respond to the aboriginal boy and the possibilities of a return to a less complex life. They also accuse her of representing the worst sort of Empire mentality by dealing with the Black only in terms of his servant-like usefulness. The girl has received the strongest condemnation for her prudish inability to enter into the less structured, and more liberating, world of the walkabout. Roeg has been condemned for his intrusive use of the camera and the intercutting of the narrative, distancing the viewer and withdrawing him from any emotional commitment.

Other reviewers have described the movie as brilliant, evocative and startling in its rendering of a complex statement in a simple, elemental story. Others have found Roeg's camera work and the structure of the film exciting and vital. The critical opinion about the effectiveness of the movie spans a wide spectrum. What the critics do uniformly agree on is the film's remarkable photography, not surprising as Roeg spent a number of years as a cameraman and cinematographer on other directors' projects. Aside from other considerations, the photography alone elevates the experience of *Walkabout* beyond mere moviegoing. The visual images are mesmerizing. Roeg through the evocation of the landscape touches something atavistic and plunges us into the core of human experience. For this reason alone *Walkabout* is an extraordinary film.

—Charles L.P. Silet

WAVELENGTH. Color, 16mm; running time: 45 mins. Released January 1968.

Produced, scripted, directed, photographed, edited, and sound recorded by Michael Snow; music by Tom Wolff.

Filmed one week of December in 1966 in a loft in New York City. 4th International Experimental Film Competition (Knokke, Belgium), Grand Prize, 1967.

Cast: Hollis Frampton (*Man who dies*); Joyce Wieland (*Woman with bookcase/Woman listening to radio*); Amy Taubin (*Woman on telephone/Woman listening to radio*).

Publications:

Books—*History of the American Avant-Garde Cinema* edited by The American Federation of Arts, New York 1976; *Abstract Film and Beyond* by Malcolm Le Grice, Cambridge, Massachusetts 1977; *Visionary Film: The American Avant-Garde* by P. Adams Sitney, New York 1979; articles—"Conversation with Michael Snow" by Jonas Mekas and P. Adams Sitney in *Film Culture* (New York), autumn 1967; "Letter from Michael Snow" in *Film Culture* (New York), no.46, 1967; "Letter" by Michael Snow in *Film Culture* (New York), October 1968; article by Bob Lamberton in *Film Culture* (New York), October 1968; articles by James Stoller in *The Village Voice* (New York), 11 January

and 11 April 1968; article by Jud Yalkut in *Film Quarterly* (Berkeley), summer 1968; "Avant-Garde Film" by P. Adams Sitney in *Afterimage* (Rochester, New York), autumn 1970; "The Life and Times by Michael Snow" by Joe Medjuck in *Take One* (Montreal), January/February 1971; "Toward Snow" by Annette Michaelson in *Artforum* (New York), June 1971; "Aspects of Cinematic Consciousness: Suspense and Presence/-Disillusion/Unified Perceptual Response" by Donald Skoller in *Film Comment* (New York), September/October 1972; "*Wavelength*" by J. Rosenbaum in *Monthly Film Bulletin* (London), February 1975; "Narrative Space" by S. Heath in *Screen* (London), no.3, 1976; "About Snow" by A. Michelson in *October* (Cambridge, Mass.), spring 1979.

* * *

Michael Snow's *Wavelength* established his reputation as a filmmaker and, with the prestige of the winning prize at the 4th International Experimental Film Competition (Knokke, Belgium, 1968), it quickly became the showpiece of a movement toward monomorphic, minimalist films (often called "structural films.") The decisiveness with which Snow staked out a territory for investigation, the simplicity and clarity of the film's overall gesture, and the intricacy of its details, were factors in the immediate and continuing attention this film has claimed.

Wavelength describes a single zoom movement for three quarters of an hour across an almost empty New York loft, resting eventually within the frame of a black-and-white photograph of waves pinned to the wall of the room. Within this pseudo-continuity there are innumerable changes of color filters, sudden shifts into negative, changes from day to night, occasional superimpositions, and a series of human events of increasing dramatic significance. The events include moving in a bookcase, listening to a song on the radio, a tramp breaking in and collapsing on the floor, and finally a woman enters, sees the body, and telephones for help because she thinks he is dead.

The human events are filmed with the direct sound which interrupts the steadily increasing sine wave of piercing electronic sound which contributes largely to the uncanniness of the film. The filmmaker dissects the illusion of continuity imposed by zoom, evoking an impressive series of metaphors for memory and death in the process. The opening installation of the bookcase, with its live, unmuffled sound of footsteps mingled with the noises of the street and its commercial traffic, sets the tone of a casual documentary. As we wait for something to happen, that casualness is cancelled by the non-realistic visual and auditory events arranged to emphasize the autonomy of the camera and sound recorder of audio-visual stimuli. Gradually we come to realize that even such conventional tools as the radio and the telephone are machines for translating sound waves into electronic traces and back into audible sound.

The zoom is a particulary appropriate tool for Snow's critique, because its movement is virtual, in actuality a relationship between two lenses, the image of an image. In the film's temporal scheme, that inner mechanism of the lens is echoed by the frame-to-frame relationship that suggests either movement or stasis depending upon the nature of the still images. The end of the film dramatizes this when Snow dissolves from one image of the photograph of the wave framed on the wall to a closer shot wholly within the photograph. The dissolve cannot be distinguished from the act of zooming. Finally, he declares the fragility of the image itself by simply changing focus on the photograph so radically that the screen goes white: the very threshold of visibility is inscribed within the lens.

Other avant-garde films had dwelled upon the uniquenesses of the cinematic images, but none so systematically as *Wavelength*.

—P. Adams Sitney

WAY DOWN EAST. Production: D.W. Griffith, Inc.; 1920; black and white, 35mm, silent; running time: 150 mins., music re-issue is 110 mins.; length: about 9000 feet, re-issue is 7200 feet. Released 1920. Re-released 1931 with musical sound track.

Produced by D.W. Griffith; screenplay by Anthony Paul Kelly; from the play by Lottie Blair Parker and Joseph Grismer; directed by D.W. Griffith; photography by G.W. Bitzer and Hendrick Sartov; edited by James and Rose Smith; art direction by Charles O. Seessel and Clifford Pember; music which accompanied film by Louis Silvers and William F. Peters; costumes designed by Lady Duff Gordon and O'Kane Cromwell.

Filmed March through August, 1920, (some sources state filming began in January), in D.W. Griffith Studios in Mamaroneck, New York, and on location in White River Junction, Vermont, and Farmington, Connecticut. Cost: $702,000.

Cast: Lillian Gish (*Anna Moore*); Mrs. David Landau (*Mrs. Moore, her mother*); Josephine Bernard (*Mrs. Tremont*); Josephine Bernard (*Diana Tremont*); Patricia Fruen (*Anna Moore's sister*); Florence Short (*Eccentric aunt*); Lowell Sherman (*Lennox Sanderson*); Burr McIntosh (*Squire Bartlett*); Kate Bruce (*Mrs. Bartlett*); Richard Barthelmess (*David Bartlett*); Vivia Ogden (*Martha Perkins*); Porter Strong (*Seth Holcomb*); George Neville (*Reuben Whipple*); Edgar Nelson (*Hi Holler*); Mary Hay (*Kate Brewster*); Creighton Hale (*Professor Sterling*); Emily Fitzroy (*Maria Poole*).

Publications:

Books—*Life and Lillian Gish* by Albert Bigelow Paine, New York 1932; *An Index to the Creative Work of D.W. Griffith* by Seymour Stern, supplement to *Sight and Sound*, index series, London 1946-47; *Movies in the Age of Innocence* by Edward Wagenknecht, Norman, Oklahoma 1962; *D.W. Griffith: American Film Master* by Iris Barry and Eileen Bowser, New York 1965; *Lillian Gish: The Movies, Mr. Griffith, and Me* by Lillian Gish with Ann Pinchot, Englewood Cliffs, New Jersey 1969; *The Silent Voice: A Text* by Arthur Lenning, New York 1969; *Griffith and the Rise of Hollywood* by Paul O'Dell, New York 1970; *The Man Who Invented Hollywood: The Autobiography of D.W. Griffith* edited by James Hart, Louisville, Kentucky 1972; *D.W. Griffith: His Life and Work* by Robert Henderson, New York 1972; *Billy Bitzer: His Story* by G.W. Bitzer, New York 1973; *Adventures with D.W. Griffith* by Karl Brown, New York 1973; *The Griffith Actresses* by Anthony Slide, New York 1973; *Dorothy and Lillian Gish* by Lillian Gish, New York 1973; *Spellbound in Darkness* by George C. Pratt, Connecticut 1973; *The Films of D.W. Griffith* by Edward Wagenknecht and Antony Slide, New York 1975; *Cinema, The Magic Vehicle: A Guide to Its Achievement: Journey One: The Cinema Through 1949* edited by Jacek Klinowski and Adam Garbicz, Metuchen, New Jersey 1975; *Star Acting: Gish, Garbo, Davis* by Charles Affron, New York 1977; *Griffith: 1st Artist of the Movies* by

Martin Williams, New York 1980; articles—"Dickens, Griffith, and the Film Today" in *Film Form* by Sergei Eisenstein, New York 1949; "Conversation with Lillian Gish" in *Sight and Sound* (London), winter 1957-58; "The Origins of United Artists" by A.L. Mayer in *Films in Review* (New York), August/September 1959; "Lillian Gish" by Romano Tozzi in *Films in Review* (New York), December 1962; issue on Griffith of *Film Culture* (New York), spring/summer 1965; "David Wark Griffith: In Retrospect, 1965" by G. Charles Niemeyer in *Film Heritage* (Dayton, Ohio), fall 1965; "Billy Bitzer—Pioneer and Innovator" by George J. Mitchell in *American Cinematographer* (Hollywood), December 1964 and January 1965; "The Films of David Wark Griffith: The Development of Themes and Techniques in 42 of His Films" by Richard Meyer in *Film Comment* (New York), fall/winter 1967; "*Way Down East*" by Iris Barry in *Film Notes* edited by Eileen Bowser, New York 1969; "The Film Artistry of D.W. Griffith and Billy Bitzer" by Herb Lightman in *American Cinematographer* (Los Angeles), January 1969; "The Films of D.W. Griffith" by Alan Casty in *Journal of Popular Film* (Bowling Green, Ohio), spring 1972; "*Way Down East*" by Stanley Kauffmann in *Horizon* (Los Angeles), spring 1972; "David Wark Griffith albo kunszt narracji" by A. Helman in *Kino* (Warsaw), February 1974; "Shooting *Way Down East*" by G.W. Bitzer in *Films in Review* (New York), October 1975; "*Way Down East*" by G. Brown in *Monthly Film Bulletin* (London), May 1979; "The Birth of *Way Down East*" by A Lennig in *Quarterly Review of Film Studies* (Pleasantville, New York), winter 1981.

*   *   *

Although *Way Down East* was the second-most expensive epic in D.W.Griffith's career (only *Orphans of the Storm* cost more to produce), it is a spectacle unlike any of his others. For once, he chose a subject unconnected with history, war, or nationalism, without crowd scenes, devoid of references to social issues, and stripped of visual and literary quotations from famous paintings or great books. This move towards a big-budget picture lacking the scope, complexity, and lofty purpose of his earlier war epics has been interpreted as a retreat into more conventional forms of narrative film. Yet, in his move away from the omniscient perspective of *The Birth of a Nation*, *Intolerance*, and *Hearts of the World*, Griffith moved towards experiments with perspective and subjective point of view more intricate than any he had tried before. In *Way Down East*, the culmination of two year's work with low-budget pastoral films, Griffith became actively involved with presentations of nature, and virtuoso acting displays that were widely studied, particularly by the Soviets.

Way Down East is generally ranked as the best of Griffith's later films, despite frequent criticisms concerning its comic scenes and Victorian sentimentality. Characteristically, scholars have studied it for its portrait of Anna Moore, the long-suffering but resilient Griffith heroine, and for its fusing of nineteenth century stage melodrama with twentieth century cinematic technique.

Way Down East was made from a highly successful play of the same name written in the 1890s by Lottie Blair Parker and revised by Joseph R. Grismer. In the hands of producer William A. Brady, it was a great success, performed around the United States for more than 20 years. Like *East Lynne* and *The Count of Monte Cristo*, it became an American perennial; so great was it popularity that Griffith paid an unprecedented $175,000—more than the entire cost of *The Birth of a Nation*—for the screen rights. (Such was the success of Griffith's films that had Brady accepted a percentage he would have earned considerably more.)

The film flaunts its melodramatic origins, rewarding the viewer's familiarity with classical dramatic formulas. The saga of Anna Moore, the innocent country girl tricked into a false marriage and then driven out into the storm, manages to combine extreme fantasy with absolute cliché. The film plays off a background of assorted texts, assimilating their most famous images and motifs. The most notable include: Eliza's flight from her pursuers across the ice in *Uncle Tom's Cabin*; Tess of the d'Ubervilles' baptism of her dead baby; and Cinderella outshining her selfish stepsisters at the regal ball.

Way Down East proved the most popular Griffith film after *The Birth of a Nation*. According to the publicity, it grossed over $4.5 million during the 1920s. In 1931, a shortened version was reissued with a sound track.

—Russell Merritt

LE WEEK-END. Weekend. Production: Films Copernic, Comacico, and Lira Films (France) and Ascot-Cineraïd (Rome); Eastmancolor, 35mm; running time: 95 mins., English version is 103 mins. Released September 1967, Venice Film Festival.

Screenplay by Jean-Luc Godard; English subtitles by Sonja Mays Friedman; directed by Jean-Luc Godard; photography by Raoul Coutard; edited by Agnès Guillemot; sound by René Levert; music by Antoine Duhamel from Mozart, Piano Sonata, K. 576, song "Alloc, allô, tu m'entends?" by Guy Béart; assistant director: Claude Miler.

Filmed September-October 1967 around Paris.

Cast: Mireille Darc (*Corinne*); Jean Yanne (*Roland*); Jean-Pierre Kalfon (*F.L.S.O. Leader*); Valérie Lagrange (*His companion*); Jean-Pierre Léaud (*Saint-Just/Man in phone booth*); Yves Beneyton (*F.L.S.O. member*); Paul Gégauff (*Pianist*); Daniel Pommereulle (*Joseph Balsamo*); Virginie Vignon (*Marie-Madeleine*); Yves Alfonso (*Tom Thumb*); Blandine Jeanson (*Emily Bronte/Young woman in farmyard*); Ernest Menzer (*Cook*); Georges Staquet (*Tractor driver*); Juliet Berto (*Woman in car crash/F.L.S.O. member*); Anne Wiazemsky (*Woman in farmyard/F.L.S.O. member*); Jean Eustache (*Hitchhiker*); J.C. Guilbert (*Tramp*); Monsieur Jojot; Isabelle Pons; Michael Cournot (*Man from farmyard*); Laszlo Szabo (*The Arab speaking for his Black brother*).

Publications:

Scripts—*Weekend* (includes themes, intent, details of characterization, alternate ending not in film) by Jean-Luc Godard, Paris 1968; *Weekend and Wind from the East* edited by Nicholas Fry, translated by Marianne Sinclair and Danielle Adkinson, New York 1972; reviews—"New Movies: Society as a Slaughterhouse" in *Time* (New York), November 1968; "Weekend in Hell" by Pauline Kael in the *New Yorker*, 5 October 1968; "*Week-End*" by Raymond Lefèvre in *Image et son* (Paris), February 1968; review by Gavin Millar in *Monthly Film Bulletin* (London), August 1968; "*Le Weekend*" by Gene Moskowitz in *Variety* (New York), 10 January 1968; review by Gilbert Salachas in *Téléciné* (Paris), February 1968; review by Robin Wood in

Movie (London), winter 1968; review by Nazareno Taddei in *Bianco e nero* (Rome), May/June 1968; books—*Jean-Luc Godard* edited by Tony Mussman, New York 1968; *Film 68/69: An Anthology by the National Society of Film Critics* edited by Andrew Sarris and Hollis Alpert, New York 1968; *Jean-Luc Godard* by Richard Roud, Bloomington, Indiana 1970; *Cinéma et société moderne: le cinéma de 1968 à 1968: Godard, Antonioni, Resnais, Robbe-Grillet* by Annie Goldmann, Paris 1971; *Godard on Godard* by Jean-Luc Godard, New York 1972; *Film and Revolution* by James Roy MacBean, Bloomington, Indiana 1975; *The New Wave* by James Monaco, New York 1976; *The World in a Frame* by Leo Braudy, Garden City, New York 1977; articles—"Adler Loves Godard—Sort Of" by Renata Adler in *The New York Times*, 27 October 1968; "Film Festival: Weekend: Godard Film Captures Despair and Violence" by Renata Adler in *The New York Times* (28 September 1968); "Directors: Infuriating Magician" in *Time* (New York), 16 February 1968; "Petit lexique pour *Weekend*" by Michel Capdenac in *Les Lettres françaises* (Paris), 9 January 1968; "*Weekend*" by Jean Collet in *Etudes* (Paris), April 1968; "Le Dur Silence des galaxies—*Weekend*" by Jean Collet and Jacques Aumont in *Cahiers du cinéma* (Paris), March 1968; "*Weekend*" by Jan Dawson in *Sight and Sound* (London), summer 1968; "*Le Weekend*: un utile exercise qui s'appelle: chine" by Jean Delmas in *Cinéma 68* (Paris), May 1968; "Putting Out Its Tongue" by Harold Hobson in *Christian Science Monitor* (Boston), 29 July 1968; "Godard's *Weekend*, or the Self-Critical Cinema of Cruelty" by James Roy McBean in *Film Quarterly* (Berkeley), winter 1968; "*Weekend*" by Joe Medjuck in *Take One* (Montreal), no.11, 1968; "The Manic Side of Godard" by Dilys Powell in *London Sunday Times*, 7 July 1968; "Le Cru et le cuit" by Wuilleumier Ropars in *Esprit* (Paris), March 1968; "*Weekend*" by Peter Whitehead in *Films and Filming* (London), February 1969; "*Weekend*" by R. Lefèvre in *Image et son* (Paris), 308bis, 1976; "Toward a Non-Bourgeois Camera Style" by Brian Henderson in *Movies and Methods* edited by Bill Nichols, Berkeley 1976; "*Weekend*" by Glen Dolfi in *Cinema Texas Program Noes* (Austin), 2 May 1978; "*Weekend* Cinematographer Discusses His Style" by R. Fisher in *Millimeter* (New York), April 1979; "Godard's *Week-end*: Totem, Taboo, and the Fifth Republic" by D. Nicholls in *Sight and Sound* (London), winter 1979-80.

*   *   *

Weekend is perhaps the most problematic film of the modern cinema's most problematic (if arguably most important) filmmaker. The problem lies partly in the complexity of the issues involved. There are the difficulties of the film itself (difficulties of obscurity in meaning, but also those arising from the nature of its radicalism, plus the wider difficulties concerning the whole twentieth century political and aesthetic debate centered on "realism" vs. "modernism."

most favorable account of the film can be offered. The dominant tradition of cinema. since its inception (the Lumière films of 1895), has been "realist" (a better word might be "illusionist"), based on deceiving the audience into believing they are seeing reality instead of an artificial construct. Even documentary and the newsreel are based on principles of selection and juxtaposition; reality in art can never be unmediated. This illusion of reality can easily become (and without awareness, inevitably becomes) a disguise under cover of which the dominant ideology (i.e. bourgeois, patriarchal capitalism) reproduces and reinforces itself: the representation of physical reality becomes the guarantee of a "truth" that is in fact ideological. Hence the first duty of the radical filmmaker is to shatter the dominant modes of representation—to destroy the illusion, to overthrow the tyranny of narrative. In our century, the cinema (with "reality" apparently guaranteed by the camera, "the truth 24 times a second", as Godard remarked in his earlier days, or "lies 24 times a second" as he subsequently reformulated it) has been the last stronghold of traditional realist art, a tradition long since challenged in literature and painting. Godard's work has been central to the emergence and development of a modernist cinema, and *Weekend* is one of the key texts in that development.

The fundamental rule of classical cinema is that everything serves the narrative: settings, characterization, realistic detail, style, presentation, etc. The narrative of *Weekend* might be linked to a clothes-line: it is necessary to hang the washing on, but what is interesting and important are the garments, linen, etc. that it sustains. The rejection of realism/illusionism and narrative dominance is at once achieved by and makes possible (it is difficult here to distinguish cause and effect) a number of strategies. For example, there are: references to the film as a film (introductory captions tell us it is "a film found on the scrapheap" and "film astray in the cosmos." and the male protagonist complains about the craziness of the movie he's in); references to other films (Buñuel's *The Exterminating Angel*, *Johnny Guitar—Saga of Gosta Berling*, and *Battleship Potemkin—The Searchers* are code names on the walkie-talkies while the Renoir and Truffaut references are telescoped in the caption "Arizona Jules"); printed captions throughout the film are used as interruptions which are frequently more enigmatic than explanatory; and, finally, *Weekend* is largely composed of digressions, its plot being capable of summation in a couple of sentences. Other strategies include: the use of direct address to the camera, monologue, and interview (*Weekend* contains an interesting—and exceptionally distancing—variation on this in the "Third World" section where the black African and Algerian garbage-collectors speak for each other, one staring insolently into camera while the other, off-screen, speaks his thoughts); the foregrounding of camera-technique, as in the celebrated tracking shot along the seemingly interminable traffic-jam where that camera moves steadily and imperturbably, refusing to privilege any incident or detail by lingering, as well as the three 360° circular tracks around the farmyard during the lecture on a Mozart piano sonata; and, finally, the intrusion into the film of a number of characters superfluous to the narrative, some historical, some fictitious, and in certain cases played by the same actor (St. Just and the young man in the phone-booth, Emily Bronte—dressed as Alice-in-Wonderland—and the pianist/lecturer's assistant.)

Instead of the closed text of classical narrative, in which an omniscient author (the connection of the term to "authority" is important) leads the reader/viewer step by step towards a position of "knowledge" (which corresponds to the imposition of a value-system), we have the open text of modernism. The author ("enunciator" has become the preferred term) foregrounds himself, and in a sense discredits himself. The lack of coherent narrative frees the viewer, making him the active explorer of an open-ended network of data, references, statements, and positions. The voices that speak within the film are not structured or "placed" in relation to a dominant discourse; we are not told how we must listen to them. So, at least, runs the argument. One can accept it up to a point; certainly, as a challenge to dominant forms and dominant norms, Godard has been salutary and indispensable.

Nevertheless, *Weekend* is a film towards which, as time passes, one feels increasingly less indulgent. When it appeared (after the events of May '68, but made before them), it seemed uncannily prescient, its formal, aesthetic, and political anarchism exhilarating and liberating. Yet there were always doubts—an uneasiness, a *squeamishness*, which the film itself seemed to define as "bourgeois," and scoff at one for feeling. Clearly in intention it is a film about the brutalization of contemporary capitalist society, but it is also in effect a brutalizing film. This becomes explicit in one of its final statements, where we are told that the horror of the bourgeoisie must be countered with even greater horror. In practice, the results of the theoretical argument I have outlined became increasingly ambiguous. The abdication from "authority" can be read as Godard's somewhat disingenuous denial of responsibility, ("*I* am not making these statements, voices in the film are making them"—voices which Godard has chosen and permitted to speak). The overthrow of "realism" (the blood is obviously red paint, the film is a film) becomes a means of allowing us to find degradation (especially of women), slaughter and cannibalism *funny*. One cannot resist the suggestion that Godard is using revolutionary politics as an excuse for indulging a number of very unpleasant fantasies of sexuality and violence.

The film constructs a position for the viewer just as surely as any classical narrative (true, that position contains a certain ambivalence, but that is a phenomenon scarcely alien to classical cinema). The presentation, in the final third of the film, of the band of revolutionary guerillas is crucial to this. Godard is careful not to endorse them in any obvious, unequivocal way. Their activities are made to appear largely ridiculous and pointless, unsupported by any coherent body of revolutionary theory. Yet he is plainly fascinated by them; their very emptiness and dehumanization provide the necessary conditions for the fantasies of violence that a *constructive* radical position could only impede. The attitude found in the later *Vent d'Est* that could explicitly encourage the placing of bombs in supermarkets and label "bourgeois" any scruples we might feel about this is already fully present in *Weekend*. Foregrounding the mechanics of cinema and the process of narration by no means guarantees ideological awareness (on the part of either the filmmaker or the spectator): that is just as pernicious a myth as its corollary, that all realist art necessarily reinforces the dominant ideology.

—Robin Wood

WHITE HEAT. Production: Warner Bros. Pictures, Inc.; 1949; black and white, 35mm; running time: 114 mins. Released 2 September 1949.

Produced by Louis F. Edelman; screenplay by Ivan Goff and Ben Roberts; from a story by Virginia Kellogg; directed by Raoul Walsh; photography by Sid Hickox; edited by Owen Marks; sound by Leslie G. Hewitt; art direction by Edward Carrere, set decoration by Fred M. MacLean; music by Max Steiner, orchestration by Murray Cutter; special effects by Roy Davidson and H.F. Koenekamp; costumes designed by Leah Rhodes.

Filmed in Warner Bros. studios, final episode filmed in Torrence, California.

Cast: James Cagney (*Cody Jarrett*); Virginia Mayo (*Verna Jarrett*); Edmond O'Brien (*Hank Fallon/Vic Pardo*); Margaret Wycherly (*Ma Jarrett*); Steve Cochran (*Big Ed Somers*); John Archer (*Phillip Evans*); Wally Cassell (*Cotton Valetti*); Fred Clark (*Trader*); Ford Rainey (*Zuckie Hommell*); Fred Coby (*Happy Taylor*); G. Pat Collins (*Reader*)l; Mickey Knox (*Het Kohler*); Paul Guilfoyle (*Roy Parker*); Robert Osterloh (*Tommy*

Ryley); Ian MacDonald (*Bo Creel*); Ray Montgomery (*Trent*); Marshall Bradford (*Chief of Police*).

Publications:

Books—*Raoul Walsh* by Michel Marmin, Paris 1970; *The Films of James Cagney* by Homer Dickens, Secaucus, New Jersey 1972; *The Hollywood Professionals* by Kingsley Canham, New York 1973; *James Cagney* by Andrew Bergman, New York 1973; *Raoul Walsh* edited by Phil Hardy, Colchester, England 1974; *Each Man in His Time* by Raoul Walsh, New York 1974; *Film Noir* edited by Alain Silver and Elizabeth Ward, Woodstock, New York 1979; articles—"James Cagney" by Don Miller in *Films in Review* (New York), August/September 1958; issue on Walsh in *Présence du cinéma* (Paris), May 1962; "Entretien avec Raoul Walsh" by Jean-Louis Noames in *Cahiers du cinéma* (Paris), April 1964; "*L'Enfer est à lui*" in *Ecran* (Paris), 7 bis, July 1972; "William Keighley, Raoul Walsh et le style Warner" by J.-P. Bleys in *Cahiers de la cinématheque* (Paris), spring/-summer 1978; "*L'Enfer est a lui*" by Robert Benayoun in *Avant-Scène du cinéma* (Paris), 1 October 1979; "*White Heat*: The Old and the New" by T. Clark in *Wide Angle* (Athens, Ohio), no.1, 1979; "*White Heat*" by Gregory William Mank in *Magill's Survey of Cinema, Vol. IV* edited by Frank N. Magill, Englewood Cliffs, New Jersey 1980; short article in *Casablanca* (Madrid), February 1981.

*   *   *

One of the toughest, most hard-bitten crime films of the forties, *White Heat* stands at the crux between the thirties gangster movie and the post-war film noir. At the center of the film is gang leader Cody Jarrett, a cold-blooded killer who runs his band of theives with an iron fist and a blazing pistol. As Jarrett, James Cagney gives one of the most maniacal, yet complex performances of his masterful career, harking back to the tragically ambitious mobster he played in *Public Enemy*, yet adding the noir-ish twist of psychopathy to the character. The white heat of the title refers in part to the debilitating headaches Cody suffers; he describes them as feeling like a buzzsaw in his brain. Jarrett's migraine attacks and insane rages clearly equate his mental condition and his sociopathic profession; yet the film plays out Cody's psychosis quite astutely in the determinant relationship of the film—his preversely oedipal attachment to his mother. Although accompanied by his voluptuous, and ultimately duplicitous, bride, Cody ignores her in favor of Ma Jarrett, a hard-nosed old woman who is mentor, advisor and comforter to her only son, and who never leaves his side until he is taken to prison. Significantly, only she seems capable of seeing Cody migraines.

Ostensibly, it is Edmund O'Brien, as police agent Hank Fallon, who plays the hero of the film, going undercover in prison to gain Jarrett's confidence and lead him to the gas chamber. Exploiting Jarrett's psychological weaknesses, Fallon manages to partially fill the emotional void left when Cody finds out his mother has been killed (a scene which provides the film's emotional peak, when, upon hearing the news, Jarrett wreaks havoc in a tour-de-force mad scene in the prison mess hall). Curiously, the vulnerability displayed by Jarrett—psychopathic and cold-blooded as he may be—makes the betrayal of his friendship by the bland, emotionless Fallon seem utterly reprehensible, no matter what side of the law he represents.

As directed by Raoul Walsh, the most accomplished craftsman working at Warner Brothers, *White Heat* never succumbs to heavy psychologism, but remains a lean and powerful, unrelenting fast-paced action film—the epitome of classical Hollywood filmmaking. Characteristic of Walsh, the film's mise-en-scene is filled with flourishes of camera movement, cutting and composition seamlessly constructed so as to avoid the "artiness" of more expressionistic films noir. Such classicism at the service of metaphor is nowhere better demonstrated than in the intercutting of the churning machinery of the prison workshop with closeups of Jarrett suffering one of his disabling headaches. The sense of locale evoked by Walsh, as atmospheric in this film as in his renowned *High Sierra*, is impeccable and quite contemporary, making imaginative use of such settings as tourist courts and drive-in movie theaters. The signs of modernity are everywhere (most obviously in the "scientific" surveillance techniques by the police to track Jarrett in his final caper), and add to the sense that the tragic figure of the gangster has outlived his day.

It is this sense of a modern world no longer concerned with the individual which finally lends *White Heat* its most biting, film noir edge, and adds a thoroughly chilling level to Jarrett's self-immolation in the film's final moments. Perched atop a refinery oil drum, engaged in a hopeless gun battle with the police, and realizing his betrayal by Fallon, Jarrett fires his pistol into the drum, shouting, "Top of the world, Ma!" The white hot explosion which follows not only marks Jarrett's ascension to the tragic, but equates his madness with the end of the world, announcing the definitive entry of the crime film into the atomic age.

—Ed Lowry

WHY WE FIGHT: PRELUDE TO WAR. Part 1. Production: Special Services, U.S. Army; 1942; black and white, 35mm; running time: 53 mins. Released 1943.

Produced by Frank Capra; screenplay by Anthony Veiller and Eric Knight; directed by Frank Capra; edited by William Hornbeck; music by Alfred Newman. Compiled 1942, in the 834th Signal Service Photograph Detachment, Dept. of the Interior Building, Washington, D.C.

Cast: Walter Huston (*Narrator*).

*   *   *

THE NAZIS STRIKE. Part 2 of *Why We Fight* series. Production: Special Services, U.S. Army; 1943; black and white, 35mm; running time: 42 mins. Released 1943.

Produced by Frank Capra; screenplay by Eric Knight, Anthony Veiler, and Robert Heller; directed by Frank Capra and Anatole Litvak; edited by William Hornbeck; music by Dimitri Tiomkin. Compiled 1943 in 20th Century Studio facilities, Hollywood.

Cast: Walter Huston and Anthony Veiler (*Narrators*).

*   *   *

DIVIDE AND CONQUER. Part 3 of *Why We Fight*. Production: Special Services, U.S. Army; 1943; black and white, 35mm;

running time: 58 mins. Released 1943.

Produced by Frank Capra; screenplay by Anthony Veiller and Robert Heller; directed by Frank Capra and Anatole Litvak; edited by William Hornbeck; music by Dimitri Tiomkin. Compiled 1943 in 20th Century Studio facilities.

*   *   *

THE BATTLE OF BRITAIN. Part 4 of *Why We Fight*. Production: Special Services, U.S. Army; 1943; black and white, 35mm; running time: 54 mins. Released 1943.

Produced by Frank Capra; screenplay by Anthony Veiler; directed by Anthony Veiler; edited by William Hornbeck; music by Dimitri Tiomkin. Compiled 1943 in 20th Century Studio facilities.

Cast: Walter Huston and Anthony Veiler (*Narrators*).

*   *   *

THE BATTLE OF RUSSIA. Part 5 of *Why We Fight*. Production: Signal Corps Army Pictorial Service; black and white, 35mm; running time: 80 mins. Released 1944.

Produced by Frank Capra; screenplay by Anatole Litvak, Anthony Veiller, and Robert Heller; directed by Anatole Litvak; edited by William Hornbeck; music arranged by Dimitri Tiomkin and selected from Tchaikovsky, Stravinsky, Prokofiev, Shostakovich, Rachmaninoff, and Rimski-Korsakov. Compiled 1944 in 20th Century Studio facilities.

Cast: Walter Huston and Anthony Veiler (*Narrators*).

*   *   *

THE BATTLE OF CHINA. Part 6 of *Why We Fight*. Production: Signal Corps Army Pictorial Service; 1944; black and white, 35mm; running time: 64 mins. Released 1944.

Produced by Frank Capra; screenplay by Anthony Veiler and Robert Heller; directed by Frank Capra and Anatole Litvak; edited by William Hornbeck; music by Dimitri Tiomkin. Compiled 1944 in 20th Century Studio facilities.

Cast: Walter Huston and Anthony Veiler (*Narrators*).

*   *   *

WAR COMES TO AMERICA. Part 7 of *Why We Fight*. Production: Signal Corps Army Pictorial Service; black and white, 35mm; running time: 70 mins. Released 1945.

Produced by Frank Capra; screenplay by Anatole Litvak and Anthony Veiler; directed by Anatole Litvak; edited by William Hornbeck; music by Dimitri Tiomkin. Compiled in 20th Century Studio facilities.

Cast: Walter Huston and Anthony Veiler (*Narrators*).

Publications:

Books—*The Signal Corps: The Test* by George Raynor Thompson et al., Washington, D.C. 1957; *Films Beget Films* by Jay Leyda, New York 1964; *The Signal Corps: The Outcome* by George Raynor Thompson, Frank Capra, et al., Washington, D.C. 1966; *Name Above the Title* by Frank Capra, New York 1971; *Non-fiction Film* by Richard Barsam, New York 1973; *The People's Art* by Richard Dyer MacCann, New York 1977; *Documentary* by Erik Barnouw, New York 1974; *The Films of Frank Capra* by Donald Willis, Metuchen, New Jersey 1974; *Frank Capra: The Man and his Films* edited by Richard Glatzer and John Raeburn, Ann Arbor, Michigan 1975; *The Cinema of Frank Capra* by Leland Poague, New York 1975; *An Historical and Descriptive Analysis of the 'Why We Fight' Series* by Thomas Bohn, New York 1977; *Frank Capra Study Guide*, edited by Dennis Bohnenkamp and Sam Grogg, Washington, D.C. 1979; *Frank Capra* by Charles Maland, Boston 1980; articles— "Memorandum to the Makers of Documentary War Movies" by Manny Farber in the *New Republic* (New York), 5 October 1942; "*Battle of Britain*" by Harold Nicolson in *Spectator* (London), 8 October 1943; "News Reels and War-Record Films" by James Agee in the *Nation* (New York), 24 June 1944; "War and Love" by Hermine Isaacs in *Theatre Arts* (New York), May 1945; "Hollywood War Films" by Dorothy B. Jones in *Hollywood Quarterly*, October 1945; "Documentary in Transition, Part I: The United States" by Robert and Nancy Katz in *Hollywood Quarterly*, no.4, summer 1948-summer 1949; "Patterns in Wartime Documentaries" by Douglas W. Gallaz in *Quarterly of Films, Radio and TV* (Berkeley), winter 1955; "Anatole Litvak" by Jack Edmund Nolan in *Films in Review* (New York), November 1967; "The Method of *Why We Fight*" by William Murphy in *Journal of Popular Culture* (Bowling Green, Ohio), summer 1972; "Why We (Should Not) Fight", interview by G. Bailey, in *Take One* (Montreal), September 1975; issue on Capra of *Film Criticism* (Edinboro, Pennsylvania), winter 1981.

*   *   *

The *Why We Fight* series was a massive effort on the part of the United States government to indoctrinate the millions of young men inducted into military service following our entry into World War II. The making of this series and other large-scale information and education films, as they were called, was planned and supervised by Frank Capra. One of the most popular Hollywood filmmakers of the late 1930s, he had no prior documentary experience.

Why We Fight was based on the assumption that servicemen would be more willing and able fighters if they knew the events that led up to, and the reasons for, our participation in the war. It had to counteract the spirit of isolationism still strong in this country up to the Japanese attack on Pearl Harbor. In this attempt it offered a gigantic historical treatise from a particular, "liberal" point of view—that is to say the New Deal view point of the Democratic administration, prevalent in the country at the time. (There is an irony here in that Capra's personal politics have always seemed to be conservative Republican, but they rested on a kind of populism that united him with the common effort led by President Franklin Roosevelt). The historical approach was a frequent one in American documentaries, going back to *The Plow that Broke the Plains* (1936) and *The River* (1937). It was scarcely used by the wartime filmmakers of other governments, such as Great Britain or Canada, Germany or the Soviet Union.

The series is perhaps most impressive in the scale of its conception and in the skill of its execution. Almost entirely compiled from existing footage including newsreels, Allied and captured enemy records of battle, bits from Hollywood features, and Nazi propaganda films—it presents a vast and coherent panorama through editing and commentary.

The first three films—*Prelude to War*, *The Nazis Strike*, and *Divide and Conquer*—cover the period 1918 to 1941. They document the rise of Japanese aggression in the Orient, the growing menace of Hitler in Europe, and—above all—the changing American foreign policy and public opinion throughout these years. *The Battle of Britain*, *The Battle of Russia*, and *The Battle of China* cover the efforts of our allies, who were in the war before we were and continued to fight alongside us. *War Comes to America* offered a recapitulation and an even more detailed examination of the tremendous changes in American opinions and attitudes, as well as the conflicting impulses and ideologies that shaped them. Picking up and consolidating the themes of the first three films, it was the last one made but intended to be shown first. Though the seven films were designed for military personnel, their excellence and dramatic power were recognized by the War Department, and some of them were made available for civilian audiences through theatrical exhibition. They were shown to all servicemen; viewing all seven was compulsory before embarkment for overseas duty.

The chief artistic problem for the makers of the films was one of giving structure to vast amounts of unstructured history. In this respect their work was like the work of Shakespeare in his chronicle plays. Dramatic form was given to each of the seven films, with exposition, mounting action, climax, denouement. They can be broken down into acts, in fact. *Divide and Conquer*, for example, has five acts, like the classical tragedy. Act I contains exposition: Germany has overrun Poland; Britain was now the goal; German strategy is outlined, and the theme of Hitler's lying treachery sounded. The content of Act II is the successful German campaign against Denmark and Norway. Act III deals with the position of France, the Maginot Line, and French weakness. Act IV comprises the German conquest of Holland and Belgium. Act V is the fall of France. The various participant countries are given character; they become characters, like dramatis personae. In this respect, rather than the Shakespeanian histories, this film bears a curious resemblance to *Hamlet*, with Germany as Claudius, the murderous villain, France as Hamlet, DeGaulle and French North Africa as Horatio, and England as Fortinbras. Here, as in *Hamlet*, things are not what they seem, with the villain protesting friendship and the tragic hero constricted by an incapacity for action.

A considerable variety of visual and audio resources are used in these compiled documentaries—very nearly the full range conceivable. Visuals in *The Nazis Strike*, for instance, include, in addition to newsreel footage, excerpts from the Nazi *Triumph of the Will*, *Hitlerjunge Quex*, and *Baptism of Fire*, bits of staged action (the victims of firing squads), still photos, drawings and maps, animated diagrams (animation by the Walt Disney Studio), and printed titles (Hitler's pronouncements). The sound track includes two narrators (Veiller for the factual, Huston for the emotional), quoted dialogue (Churchill, and an impersonation of Hitler), music (by one of Hollywood's best), and sound effects.

Dramatic conflict is obtained by painstaking manipulation of the combat footage. The editing conventions of matched action and screen direction are observed. The German attackers always move from right to left. A synthetic assemblage of diverse material is edited into a cause-effect order: German bombers in formation, bombs dropping from planes, explosions in villages, rubble. The result is almost as if all of this footage had been shot for these films—under Capra's direction.

The maps and animated diagrams give scope to the live-action sequences, clarify and relate random material to formalized patterns, consistent with the actual movement involved. In *Divide and Conquer* the sequence of refugees on the roads being strafed is especially striking; one reads into the actual what has just been seen in animated representation. In another instance from the same film, the animated arrows representing the armored Panzer divisions thrust into an outlined Ardennes forest with speed and power. The animation by itself takes on symbolic and rhetorical meaning; again in *Divide and Conquer*, swastika termites infest the base of a castle, and python-like arrows lock around the British Isles.

It must be admitted, that though the *Why We Fight* series may be greatly admired on technical and aesthetic grounds, there is some convincing evidence (see *Experiments on Mass Communication* among the publications) that it was not as effective indoctrination as hoped for and even thought to be. The problem, the social scientists inferred from their testings, was with the historical approach. It seemed to have the desired effects only on those with the equivalent of some college education; it seemed to be too intellectual, over the heads, of a majority of soldiers tested. As films, though, *Why We Fight* offers incontrovertible evidence of a very great filmmaking skill and a remarkably full and varied use of film technique.

—Jack C. Ellis

THE WILD BUNCH. Production: Warner Bros. and Seven Arts, Inc.; 1969; Technicolor, 35mm, Panavision 70 (U.S.), 70mm, CinemaScope (Europe); running time: 143 mins. (after release, the studio cut 4 scenes reducing running time to 135 mins.). Released 18 June 1969, Los Angeles.

Produced by Phil Feldman with Roy N. Sickner; screenplay by Walon Green and Sam Peckinpah; from an original story by Walon Green and Roy N. Sickner; directed by Sam Peckinpah; photography by Lucien Ballard; edited by Louis Lombardo; sound by Robert Miller; art direction by Edward Carrere; music by Jerry Fielding, music supervised by Sonny Burke; special effects by Bud Hulburd; costumes designed by Gordon Dawson.

Filmed in Torréan, El Rincon del Montero, and El Romeral, Mexico.

Cast: William Holden (*Pike Bishop*); Ernest Borgnine (*Dutch Engstrom*); Robert Ryan (*Deke Thornton*); Edmond O'Brien (*Sykes*); Warren Oates (*Lyle Gorch*); Jaime Sanchez (*Angel*); Ben Johnson (*Tector Gorch*); Emilio Fernandez (*Mapache*); Strother Martin (*Coffer*); L.Q. Jones (*T.C.*); Albert Dekker (*Pat Harrigan*); Bo Hopkins (*Crazy Lee*); Dub Taylor (*Major Wainscoat*); Jorge Russek (*Lieutenant Zamorra*); Alfonso Arau (*Herrera*); Chano Urueta (*Don José*); Sonia Amelio (*Teresa*); Aurora Clavel (*Aurora*); Elsa Cardenas (*Elsa*); Fernando Wagner (*German army officer*); Paul Harper; Constance White; Lilia Richards.

Publications:

Reviews—by David Austen in *Films and Filming* (London), October 1969; review by Arthur Clark in *Films in Review* (New York), August/September 1969; review by Andrew Sarris in *The*

Village Voice (New York), 31 July 1969; review by Penelope Gilliatt in the *New Yorker*, 5 July 1969; review by Stanley Kauffmann in the *New Republic* (New York), 19 July 1969; books—*Horizons West* by Jim Kitses, Bloomington, Indiana 1970; *Sam Peckinpah: Master of Violence* by Max Evans, Vermilion, South Dakota 1972; *Peckinpah* by Valerio Caprara, Bologna 1976; *The Great Western Pictures* by James Robert Parish and Michael Pitts, Metuchen, New Jersey 1976; *Sam Peckinpah* by Doug McKinney, Boston 1979; *Peckinpah: The Western Films* by Paul Seydor, Urbana, Illinois 1980; *Peckinpah: A Portrait in Montage* by Garner Simmons, Austin 1982; articles—"Talking with Peckinpah" by Richard Whitehall in *Sight and Sound* (London), autumn 1969; "Sam Peckinpah Lets It All Hang Out" in *Take One* (Montreal), January/February 1969; "Peckinpah's Return", interview by Stephen Farber, in *Film Quarterly* (Berkeley), fall 1969; "Shoot!", interview by John Cutts in *Films and Filming* (London), October 1969; "Sam Peckinpah Going to Mexico" by Paul Schrader in *Cinema* (Beverly Hills), no.3, 1969; "Man and Myth" in *Time* (New York), 20 June 1969; "What Directors Are Saying" in *Action* (Los Angeles), September/October 1969; article by Tom Milne in *Sight and Sound* (London), autumn 1969; article by Michael Sragow in *Film Society Review* (New York), November 1969; "*The Wild Bunch*" by William Pechter in *Film Comment* (New York), fall 1970; article by Kenneth Brown in *Cineaste* (New York), winter 1969-70; "*La Horde sauvage*: Un film de Sam Peckinpah" in *Avant-Scène du cinéma* (Paris), May 1970; "Violent Idyll" by John Simon in *Film 69/70* edited by Hollis Alpert and Andrew Sarris, New York 1970; "Sam Peckinpah and *The Wild Bunch*" by John McCarty in *Film Heritage* (Dayton, Ohio), winter 1969-70; "*The Wild Bunch* versus *Straw Dogs*" by Lawrence Shaffer in *Sight and Sound* (London), summer 1972; interview with Peckinpah in *Playboy* (Chicago), August 1972; "Towards a Cinema of Cruelty" by William Blum in *Cinema Journal* (Evanston, Illinois), spring 1972; "*The Wild Bunch* and the Problem of Idealist Aesthetics..." by Cordell Strug in *Film Heritage* (New York), winter 1974/75; Peckinpah issue edited by Anthony Macklin of *Film Heritage* (New York), winter 1974/75; "Nightmare and Nostalgia": The Cinema West of Sam Peckinpah" by Arthur Pettit in *Western Humanities Review* (Salt Lake City), spring 1975; "*The Wild Bunch*" by Nick Barbaro in *Cinema Texas Program Notes* (Austin), 8 September 1975, reprinted 17 January 1978; article by M. Pearson in *Jump Cut* (Chicago), August 1978; "*The Wild Bunch*" by Harold Meyerson in *Magill's Survey of Cinema, Vol. IV* edited by Frank N. Magill, Englewood Cliffs, New Jersey 1980.

* * *

When it was first released, *The Wild Bunch* became the subject of heated controversy among critics and the public alike due to its extraordinary level of violence. Following close on the heels of *Bonnie and Clyde*, *The Wild Bunch* surpassed the slow-motion death balletics of that film by quantum leaps, shocking and/or revolting large numbers of viewers. (At the Kansas City test screening of the 190-minute rough cut, over 30 members of the audience walked out in disgust, some reportedly throwing up in the alley behind the theater.) Fifteen years later, in an age inured to graphic screen violence and gore, the violence of *The Wild Bunch* is still remarkably provocative and disturbing. This is partially because the violence is *not* gratuitous, as some have claimed, but central to the film's vision of human experience: it posits a world in which degrees of violence provide the only standards, and violent death the only liberation. If it is a world

not predicated entirely on human evil, it is one at least in which there is very little good or hope for change. It seems clear today what many people object to in Peckinpah's extravagant depiction of violence in *The Wild Bunch* is actually his dark view of human nature.

Another reason why the film's violence still shocks and scintillates is its rendition by Peckinpah's stylized, optically jolting montage. Not since Eisenstein has a filmmaker so radically explored the conventions of traditional editing form. Much of the action in *The Wild Bunch* was filmed by as many as six Panavision, Mitchell, and Arriflex cameras running simultaneously at different speeds, each equipped with different lenses, including wide-angle, telephoto, and zoom. Peckinpah and his editor Louis Lombardo then created elaborate montage sequences by cutting footage shot in "real time" together with footage shot at varying decelerated speeds—all shot through a variety of lenses, some of which created a unique optical tension by zooming in and out nervously (and, amazingly, without calling attention to themselves) at appropriate moments. The perceptual impact of rapidly intercutting violent action shot at standard speed with slow-motion footage and a variety of telephoto zooms, in sequences that last as long as seven minutes, is both exhilarating and exhausting. *The Wild Bunch* is the most *optically* violent film ever made, one which assults the senses of its audience relentlessly with a torrent of violent images to rival and finally exceed Eisenstein's achievement in "The Odessa Steps" sequence of *Potemkin*. (In fact, *The Wild Bunch* contains more individualized cuts than any color film ever made—3,642, in a decade when 600 was standard for the average dramatic feature.)

The narrative of *The Wild Bunch* takes the form of a chase, the very stuff of the primordial cinema; but the film is at all points richly textured in style and theme, as an analysis of the opening sequence demonstrates. Pike Bishop, played by William Holden in the most brilliantly sustained performance of his career, is the aging leader of an outlaw band in the closing days of the American frontier, *c.* 1913. His close friend and lieutenant is Dutch, only slightly younger, played by Ernest Borgnine in another of the film's many virtuoso performances. Before the film begins, we learn from subsequent dialogue, that Pike has set up an elaborate scheme to rob the payroll office of a railway company in the Texas border town of Starbuck. Disguised as American army troops, complete with stolen service uniforms, horses, and weapons, Pike and his gang ride into the town as the film opens. Since *The Wild Bunch* begins as it does *in medias res*, the audience on first viewing assumes that the outlaws *are* regular army troops, underscoring the film's ambiguous moral perspective at the very outset. The credits are fully integrated into the narrative at this point, as high-contrast freeze frames stop the riders at various points in their progress to print the titles while Jerry Fielding's ominous paramilitary score seems to etch them into the screen.

Two groups of townspeople passed by the riders during this sequence come to assume key roles later in the film—one symbolic and one narrative. By the train tracks outside of town, a number of giggling Mexican and American children are circled about a pit in which two large scorpions are being overrun by an army of ants. This image becomes a metaphor for the situation of the Wild Bunch: like the scorpions, they find themselves trapped in a man-made cage of modernization and social change, and, like the scorpions, they will be pursued throughout the film and finally destroyed by hoards of inferior beings—railway men, bounty-hunters, green U.S. Army recruits, brutish Mexican federal troops—while children look on and mock them. Most generally, the image suggests that the heroic violence of the frontier has given way to the organized, institutionalized violence of the 20th century and its politics, a fact demonstrated in *The Wild*

Bunch time and time again.

Next the gang rides past a large outdoor meeting of the temperance union, composed principally of women, as they are being addressed by the mayor. Minutes later, these people will march in a parade down the town's main street singing "Shall We Gather at the River" and be caught in the murderous crossfire between the Bunch and the bounty-hunters waiting for them on the roof of the building opposite the railway office. When these bounty-hunters are first revealed in shots looking down on the street from their point of view, the ambiguity of the opening sequence deepens: they initially seem to be outlaws lying in ambush for the army detail below.

When Pike and his men reach the end of their ride and dismount at the railway office, we see what had appeared to be a dusty frontier village, is in fact a modern 20th century town with sidewalks, street lamps, and a public park. As he marches with his men towards the office after hitching his horse, Bishop bumps into a middle-aged matron and causes her to drop her parcels. These he retrieves with courtly deference and politely offers the woman his arm. This same woman will minutes later be trampled to death by Pike's horse as the gang makes its bloody escape. (Just as Eisenstein does in the prelude to "the Odessa Steps" sequence, Peckinpah in this opening sequence shows us many of the innocent people who will die in the coming massacre in the context of their daily lives. This technique creates a degree of audience identification with the victims, but it mainly serves to underscore the placid normality of the little town and therefore heighten the impact of the horrendous violence about to erupt upon it.) Like the Wild Bunch in their army uniforms, like the bounty-hunters concealed on the roof, and like Starbuck itself, nothing in this film is quite what it seems.

At this point, Pike, Dutch and their comrades enter the railway office, posting guards outside—as the temperance union prepares for its march to the center of town, attended by a brass band and crowds of children—and things crystalize in an instant. Guns drawn, they force the office personnel brutally to the wall, and Pike in a huge widescreen close-up gives his now famous command: "If they move, kill 'em!" inverting the moral perspective established so far. The frame freezes, and we read the credit "Directed by Sam Peckinpah."

Now the tension built by Peckinpah's cross-cutting between the temperance marchers approaching the railway office, the bounty-hunters on the roof, and the outlaws inside and outside of the office becomes nearly unbearable. Suddenly one of them catches a glimpse of a rifle barrel behind the parapet of the opposite roof, and quickly realizes that they're trapped and must fight their way out, using the parade as a cover. The signal to begin comes when the bound office-manager is kicked out the front door and "blasted!" Then begins one of the great montage sequences in film history—the virtual destruction of Starbuck and its citizens in a war between a gang of outlaws and an army of mercenaries hired to kill them.

"War" is not too strong a term here, and the only battle sequence in American cinema to rival its destructiveness in scale (exclusive of the film's own conclusion) is the helicopter attack on the Vietnamese village staged by Francis Ford Coppola in *Apocalypse Now*. Peckinpah's is infinitely more exposive and kinetic in its montage: we seem to see the town blown apart from literally hundreds of individual perspectives—those of the bounty-hunters, gang members, massacred citizens. The assaultive power of the sequence is such that it leaves its audiences physically exhausted: it releases the energy accumulated during the tense opening sequence in a rush of violent images, many of them quite sensuously beautiful, in the same way the concluding massacre will release the energy accumulated during the entire 143-minute course of this edgy, brooding, and dangerously volatile film.

The rest of *The Wild Bunch* takes the form of a classically structured chase, but its entire texture is like that of the opening sequence—a richly interwoven blend of hair-trigger editing and camera work, superb dialogue and sound, brilliant acting, and Fielding's dynamic, electrifying score. (Peckinpah totally redubbed the effects track after the Kansas City preview and brought it up to the level of quality that won the film the SMPTE sound effects award for 1969. These effects provide an important and distinctive complement to Peckinpah's assaultive montage.) The massacre ends, and what's left of the Bunch rides hell-bent-for-leather out of town, past the children at the pit where the scorpions have finally been overcome by the ants and burned alive. Reduced to six in number—Pike, Dutch, the brothers Tector and Lee Gorch, the Mexican national Angel, and old Sykes—the outlaws realize that they're being pursued by a posse of bounty-hunters led by Deke Thornton, a former member of the Bunch and once Pike's closest friend. Thornton works for the railroad, not by choice but because he was released from federal prison to do so, where he had been sent because of some carelessness by Pike. (Shortly after release, the producers cut 8 minutes of flashbacks which explained the relationship of Pike and Deke and the sense of mutual betrayal hanging over them both. Only Twyman Film's 16mm anamorphic print restores this footage, making it the sole version of *The Wild Bunch* available in the United States in the form originally conceived by its director.) Compounding this ambiguity is the fact that the bounty-hunters Thornton leads are the worst sort of human refuse, and he openly respects the men he's being forced to hunt down.

When the Bunch realize that they've been duped and that the payroll bags they've just blown Starbuck to pieces to obtain contain not coins but washers, they decide to move deeper into Mexico in hopes of eluding the posse and finding greener pastures. What they find instead is the Mexican Revolution in full swing.

First they visit Angel's village and are greated as liberators by the townspeople who have just been plundered by the brutal federal general Mapache (marvelously played by the Mexican director Emilio Fernandez), who commands a regiment for Huerta in the fight against Pancho Villa and the rebels. Mapache is a sadisic thug who murders and tortures indiscriminately, and his military base in the nearby town of Agua Verde is a corrupt, barely competent dictatorship propped by the powerful foreign governments (in this case Germany and her allies) and their sophisticated weapons technology. Somehow, during the raid in the village, Mapache has convinced Angel's girlfriend Teresa to come with him and the *federales*.

After something very close to a pastoral idyll in the beautiful village, the Bunch leave for Agua Verde to look for some action—all save Angel are politically neutral. Almost immediately on their arrival in the town, Angel spots Teresa with Mapache and shoots her to death, nearly plunging the Bunch into a suicidal conflict with Mapache's troops. Balanced on a hair, the situation nervously resolves itself, and the outlaws fall in with the general, agreeing to rob an American munitions train for him near the border. One night before the robbery, Angel secretly arranges to give up his share to the others in exchange for a case of rifles and ammunition with which to arm his insurgent countrymen.

In the film's second great montage sequence, the Bunch successfully robs the train in broad daylight in a thorough vindication of their professionalism, only to discover that they've been set up again: Thornton and the bounty-hunters are aboard, complete with U.S. cavalry detail. The pursuit begins, with the Bunch dynamiting a bridge across the Rio Grande in a spectacular (and, apparently, quite dangerous) special effects sequence.

This stops the Army, but not Deke Thornton, and for the rest of the film the distance between the bounty-hunters and the Wild Bunch grows progessively shorter.

As the gang moves the wagon-load of weapons (including a brand new machine gun—one of the many material tokens of changing times that populate this film) down toward Agua Verde, it is waylaid by a contingent of Mapache's troops, who attempt to seize the shipment by force. The Bunch faces them down with a harrowing threat to blow-up both the munitions and themselves with dynamite, and finally delivers the goods to Mapache as contracted, including the machine gun but minus Angel's case of rifles.

Mapache tipped off to this transaction by the murdered girl-friend's mother, captures Angel in Agua Verde with the intention of torturing him to death. In the meantime, old Sykes has been wounded by the bounty-hunters and left to die in the dessert.

Much of the film's plot and dialogue up to this point is concerned with questions of honor and loyalty among other members of the group. Early in the film, Pike asserts his authority over the gang with this statement: "We're gonna stick together just like it used to be; when you side with a man you stay with him, and if you can't do that, you're like some animal; you're finished—we're finished—*all* of us!" Later, Pike defends Deke's position in leading the posse to Dutch by saying that "he gave his word." But Dutch replies hotly that "he gave it to the railroad!" When Pike insists, "It's his *word*!" Dutch replies, "That ain't what counts—it's who you give it *to*!" With the capture of Angel, the question of ethical commitment assumes grim and disturbing new proportions, impelling the film toward its apocalyptic climax.

By common consent, Pike, Dutch, Tector, and Lee return to Agua Verde, ostensibly to do a little drinking and whoring. The first thing they encounter is Angel being dragged behind Mapache's roadster as children shower him with popping fire-crackers. Disgusted, Pike approaches Mapache and offers to "buy" Angel back for half his share of the gold. Mapache refused and, in a thinly veiled threat, suggests that they mind their own business and enjoy themselves. They retreat temporarily to a bordello, where after visiting a young prostitute, Pike has a moment of vision. He approaches the brothers in the next room with his final "Let's go"—the phrase which has been Pike's summons to action throughout the film—and Lyle responds with his final "Why not?" Collecting Dutch outside, the four remaining members of the Wild Bunch prepare to will themselves out of history and into legend.

They begin their march through the crowded streets of Agua Verde in shimmering sunlight etched by a nervous, optically hovering zoom lens, initially accompanied by the song of some drunken soldiers. But as they move toward the general's head-quarters to reclaim Angel, the ominous martial music of the opening sequence rises on the track again, bringing the film to full circle, as the final montage sequence will seem actually to project the film beyond itself into the realm of myth.

The four heavily armed men finally come face to face with Mapache and his staff—and with the martyred, half-conscious Angel. The general lurches drunkenly forward offering Angel to them and simultaneously cutting his throat on screen. It is a shocking and repellent act quickly answered by the Bunch, who blast the general repeatedly with their guns.

Then, an odd *caesura*, an electric silence, as no one moves or speaks, tension bristling in the air, the situation—for the last time in this turbulent film—balanced by a hair. The Bunch is home free, no one will retaliate. Dutch and then Tector chuckle and break the silence. One of Mapache's German military advisors glances at Pike, who levels his pistol with a grimace of moral loathing and begins firing.

It has been written that the ending of *The Wild Bunch* stands alone as "the unparalleled montage event of cinema history." It does and is, and any attempt to describe it more specifically brings a painful reminder of how insufficient a vehicle language is in the description of filmic art. The spectacular gun battle which blasts Agua Verde to pieces, both killing and mythologizing the Wild Bunch in the process, is a mad, orgasmic frenzy, as the slaughter grows more and more intense until it reaches first Eisensteinian, then Buñuelian, and finally Wagnerian proportions—Wagnerian because those proportions are epic (and the members of the Bunch are in many ways epic warriors whose doom is fated from the story's outset); Wagnerian in its dark, rhapsodic ecstasy. In that concluding massacre, an exultant Wild Bunch figuratively destroys everyone and everything (5,000 extras were 'killed" in the filming, according to wardrobe head Gordon Dawson). It is at once an apocalypse, a *Liebestod*, and a *Gotterdämmerung*—the negation of a brutal, dispirited world in one last grand, heroically destructive act.

By the time Deke Thornton and his group enter Agua Verde, the Wild Bunch has already assumed mythic stature. The bounty-hunters are in awe of the corpses, weapons, and accou-trements of these famous, infamous men. Thornton will now leave these jackels to ride with old Sykes and the insurgent Mexicans. As Thornton waits outside the gates of Agua Verde in the dust storm (an allusion both to *Rashomon* and *The Treasure of the Sierra Madre*), the bounty-hunters strip the corpses and the refugees stream forth from the destroyed town, as if some ancient ritual were being re-enacted for the millionth time. After a while, Sykes rides up from nowhere and invites Thornton to join him and the revolutionaries. "It ain't like it used to be," he cracks, "but it'll do." The two laugh, and their laughter dissolves into that of the other members of the Bunch in individual close-shots from earlier portions of the film, which in turn dissolves into the song the peasants sang, "Las Golondrinas," when the Bunch left their village as heroes, and the exit itself is reprised in the film's concluding images. As Paul Seydor has written so perceptively of this conclusion: "The Bunch's villainy is left to perish in the dusky and lurid glow of the windswept desert when Pike, Dutch, and the Gorch brothers are carried off face down over a saddle as society's outlaws. When they are next seen, it is as heros of some legendary adventure, illumined by a radiance if not celestial then at least transcendent, emanating from the faithful if fictitious folk imagination represented here by the people of Angel's village...." The Bunch has "played its string out to end," in the rhetoric of Dutch, and beyond: what began in blood ends in myth.

It seems ironic and not a little crazy today that a film so clearly focussed on themes of loyalty, honor, integrity, and heroism could have been reviled in its time for what one major critic called, "moral idiocy." But that was the late sixties, when the issue of violence in American society and American foreign policy had become central to virtually every national forum of public opinion. We stood at the end of a decade of political assassinations whose magnitude was unprecedented in our history, and we were deeply mired in a genocidal war in Vietnam. The My Lai massacre was revealed less than a year after the release of *The Wild Bunch*, but many Americans already knew what that revelation confirmed: that to fight a war against a popular insurrection is to fight a war against the populace. For many critics, positive and negative, *The Wild Bunch* seemed to be an allegory of our involvement in Vietnam, where outlaws, mercenaries, and federal troops fought to produce the largest civilian "body count" since World War II: Others saw the film more generally as a comment on the level and nature of violence in American life. But nearly everyone saw that it bore some relationship to the major social issues of the times, and, depending on how one felt about *those*, one's reaction to the film was enthusiastically positive or vehemently negative—both mistaken responses to a work whose prevailing tenor is moral ambiguity from start to finish. Today it is possible to find a middle ground; for whatever else *The Wild Bunch* may be (as it is, for example, the greatest western ever made), it is clearly a major work of American art which changed forever the way in which violence would be depicted in American films, as well as permanently restructuring the conventions of its genre. That Peckinpah has been unable to equal it since—as with Welles and *Citizen Kane*—is not testimony to his insufficiency as a film artist but to the extraordinary achievement of *The Wild Bunch* itself. It is, as Robert Culp remarked on its release, a film "more quintessentially and bitterly American than any since World War II." Like *Kane*, *The Wild Bunch* will remain an enduring work of American art—vast and explosive, vital and violent, with something both very dark and very noble at its soul.

—David Cook

THE WIND. Production: Metro-Goldwyn-Mayer Picture Corp.; black and white, 35mm, silent; running time: 73 mins.; length: 6721 feet. Released 1927. Re-released 1928 in a sound version, according to some sources.

Screenplay by Frances Marion; from the novel by Dorothy Scarborough; titles written by John Colton; directed by Victor Sjöström (Seastrom); photography by John Arnold; edited by Conrad Nevrig; production design by Cedric Gibbons and Edward Withers; theme song by Herman Ruby, William Axt, Dave Dreyer, and David Mendoza; costumes designed by Andre-ani; assistant director: Harold S. Bucquet.

Cast: Lillian Gish (*Letty*); Lars Hanson (*Lige*); Montagu Love (*Roddy*); Dorothy Cummings (*Cora*); Edward Earle (*Beverly*); William Orlamond (*Sourdough*); Laon Ramon (*Leon Janney*); Carmencita Johnson and Billy Kent Schaefer (*Cora's children*).

Publications:

Review—in *Kino Weekly*, 10 November 1927; books—*Life and Lillian Gish* by Albert Bigelow Paine, New York 1932; *Seastrom and Stiller in Hollywood* by Hans Pensel, New York 1969; *Dorothy and Lillian Gish* by Lillian Gish, New York 1973; *The Great Western Pictures* by James Robert Parish and Michael Pitts, Metuchen, New Jersey 1976; articles—in *Photoplay* (New York), November 1927; article in *Film Spectator*, no.13, 1 June 1929; "Victor Sjöström and D.W. Griffith" by D. Vaughn in *Film* (London), January/February 1958; "Victor Seastrom" by Charles L. Turner in *Films in Review* (New York), May 1960 and June 1960; "Lillian Gish" by Romano Tozzi in *Films in Review* (New York), December 1962; "Victor Sjostrom (Seastrom)" in *Anthologie du cinéma*, Vol. I, Paris 1966; "Vital Geography: Victor Seastrom's *The Wind*" by J.C. Tibbetts in *Literature/Film Quarterly* (Salisbury, Maryland), summer 1973; "Sjöström, Stiller et l'Amérique" by Claude Beylie and M. Martin in *Ecran* (Paris), September 1978; "Victor Sjöström" in *Films and Filming* (London), no.9, 1979; "Seastrom: The Hollywood Years" by Herman Weinberg in *American Classic Screen* (Shawnee Mission, Kansas), fall 1979.

*   *   *

The Wind represents a turning point in two of the most important careers in film history, those of Victor Seastrom (the anglicized version of Sjöström that appeared in the credits of his American films) and Lillian Gish. *The Wind* was the last silent film either of them made, and it virtually marked the end of their star status in Hollywood. Seastrom directed one talkie before returning to Sweden; Gish's first leading lady vehicle of the sound era, *One Romantic Night*, was also her last.

The Wind belongs to that moment of precious finality when the stylistics and the techniques of cinema, developed to serve narrative without speech, were being discarded because of the exigencies of sound recording. After the success of Warner Brothers, in the late 1920s the major studios rushed to integrate the new technology. *The Wind* suffered the fate of many of the most important non-sound films made during the period of transition. It was released without the care required by a film of such unusual qualities. It is perhaps a miracle that the film survives at all when we remember that two other MGM films made by Gish at this period and the single film directed by Seastrom, *The Divine Woman*, are lost.

Gish and Seastrom had already collaborated with success on *The Scarlet Letter*. *The Wind* is another story of a woman at odds with the community in which she lives. Letty, the genteel Easterner, is alien to the rough manners of a prairie village and a prairie husband. The film expresses this directly, in the dramatization of her disgust when her sister-in-law butchers a side of beef, when her husband tries to kiss her, and when she tries in vain, to prettify their cabin. *The Wind* also depicts the disintegration of Letty's mind and spirit in this hostile world. Letty not only acts; she is acted upon by the elements, and particularly by the sand, incessantly blown in the wind. It comes in through the cracks in the door. She is as helpless to stop its invasion of the physical space as she is helpless to prevent it from driving her mad. *The Wind* repeatedly tests the body of the actress against the presence of nature. Even in the tacked-on happy ending mandated by the studio—Gish stretching in the doorway, defying the wind and embracing her husband—the cinematic body becomes a measure of nature.

Left alone during a particularly severe storm, Letty's anxiety mounts. She is raped by a travelling man and then manages to shoot him. After burying him, she stares through the window, in mounting hysteria, as the sand uncovers his body. This sequence is suggestive of the degree to which director and actress conspire in the creation of images that contain both the exterior world and the interpretation of those images. The camera records nature (abetted, it must be admitted, by wind machines). It also frames Gish and her eyes in the window, an interior frame. These framings, without and within, hold characters and place in precise narrative equilibrium.

—Charles Affron

THE WIZARD OF OZ. Production: Metro-Goldwyn-Mayer Pictures Corp.; 1939; Technicolor, 35mm, opening and closing sequences in black and white; running time: 101 mins. Released 25 August 1939. Re-released 1948.

Produced by Mervyn LeRoy; screenplay by Noel Langley, Florence Ryerson, and Edgar Allen Woolf; from the novel by L. Frank Baum; directed by Victor Fleming (uncredited direction by King Vidor); photography by Harold Rosson; edited by Blanche Sewell; sound recording directed by Douglas Shearer;

production design by (set directions) Edwin B. Willis; art direction by Cedric Gibbons; music by Harold Arlen, lyrics by E.Y. Harburg, music adapted by Herbert Stothart, and numbers staged by Bobby Connolly; special effects by Arnold Gillespie; costumes designed by Adrian; assistant to Mervyn LeRoy: Arthur Freed; make-up by Jack Dawn and the MGM make-up department.

Filmed 1938-39, in MGM studios, Culver City, California. Cost: cost of production and distribution estimated at $2.5 million. Academy Awards for Best Song ("Over the Rainbow"), Best Original Score, and Special Award for Judy Garland for her "outstanding performance as a screen juvenile," 1939.

Cast: Judy Garland (*Dorothy*); Ray Bolger (*Hunk, the Scarecrow*); Bert Lahr (*Zeke, the Cowardly Lion*); Jack Haley (*Hickory, the Tin Woodsman*); Billie Burke (*Glinda*); Margaret Hamilton (*Miss Gulch, the Wicked Witch*); Charles Grapewin (*Uncle Henry*); Clara Blandick (*Auntie Em*); Pat Walsh (*Nikko*); Frank Morgan (*Professor Marvel, the Wizard*); the Singer Midgets (*Munchkins*).

Publications:

Review—by Frank S. Nugent in *The New York Times*, 18 August 1939; books—*The Child Stars* by Norman Zierold, New York 1965; *Hollywood in the Thirties* by John Baxter, New York 1968; *Judy: The Films and Career of Judy Garland* by Joe Morella and Edward Epstein, New York 1969; *The Hollywood Musical* by John Russell Taylor and Arthur Jackson, New York 1971; *Judy Garland* by James Juneau, New York 1974; *Rainbow: The Stormy Life of Judy Garland* by Christopher Finch, New York 1975; articles—"*The Wizard of Oz*" edited by Ward H. Green in *Photoplay Studies* (New York), no.12, 1939; "*Wizard of Oz*" by J. Hall in *Good Housekeeping* (New York), August 1939; "Judy Garland" by Robert Rosterman in *Films in Review* (New York), April 1952; "Judy Garland" by Douglas McVay in *Films and Filming* (London), October 1961; "Likable but Elusive" by Andrew Sarris in *Film Culture* (New York), spring 1963; "The Man Who Made *G.W.T.W.*" by John Howard Reid in *Films and Filming* (London), no.3, 1967; "Fleming: The Apprentice Years" by John Howard Reid in *Films and Filming* (London), January 1968; "*Le Magicien d'Oz*" by R. Lefèvre in *Cinéma* (Paris), February 1972; article by M. Tessier in *Ecran* (Paris), February 1972; "*The Wizard of Oz* and the Golden Era of the American Musical Film" by R. Bolger in *American Cinematographer* (Los Angeles), February 1978; "Following the Yellow Brick Road from *The Wonderful Wizard of Oz* to *The Wiz*" in *American Cinematographer* (Los Angeles), November 1978; "Nuove retrospettive: due film di Judy Garland" by O. De Fornari in *Filmcritica* (Rome), February 1979; "*The Wizard of Oz*" by Irene Kahn Atkins in *Magill's Survey of Cinema, Vol. IV* edited by Frank N. Magill, Englewood Cliffs, New Jersey 1980.

*   *   *

"By courtesy of the wizards of Hollywood *The Wizard of Oz* reached...the screen yesterday as a delightful piece of wonderworking which had the youngsters' eyes shining and brought a quietly amused gleam to the wiser ones," begins Frank Nugent's review of *The Wizard of Oz* in *The New York Times*. Produced and distributed by MGM at a cost of $2.5 million, the film is a

tribute to the Hollywood style and system of filmmaking. It was a bit of "wonderworking" indeed, as this fantasy film would forever alter the course of the Hollywood film musical.

Begun in 1938, *The Wizard of Oz* was produced at the apex of the classic Hollywood era, when MGM had at its disposal the foremost technical experts available in Hollywood at that time. It was this standby of talent that made the production of a film like *Wizard* feasible. Some feel that to mount such a project today would cost perhaps over $50 million. Ray Bolger (the Scarecrow), then a contract player at MGM, explains, "Working at MGM during that period was the ultimate in motion picture making, musical or otherwise."

Wizard was photographed in a little used three-strip technicolor process. In this process, three separate strips of black-and-white film were exposed through a prism which segregated the three primary colors. It was an extremely intricate process to handle and required enormous amounts of light to properly expose. While it was the most expensive process available to Hollywood at the time, it yielded an unequaled color quality. The studio chose the three-strip process because it worked out well with black-and-white stock. The framing of Dorothy's fantasy was processed in black-and-white, heightening the effect of the technicolor journey to Oz. The fact that the three-strip process originated in a black-and-white stock made this easier.

For these reasons the production of *Wizard* occurred entirely indoors on the sound stages of MGM. Because the film was studio-bound, a lot of responsibility fell on the special effects department. Mattes were used extensively to give depth to the Kansas landscape, and a sense of distance to the Land of Oz. Intricate trick photography was employed to allow a bicyclist and a man rowing a boat to float helplessly in a tornado.

No less important was the MGM art department. It was headed in 1938-39 by Cedric Gibbons whose career garnered 11 Academy Awards while at MGM. Elaborate sets were conceived and constructed in full scale to create Oz, the Wicked Witch's sanctuary, and the throne room of the Wizard of Oz. Working within the limitations imposed by the tri-color film process, Gibbon's department had to create a color scheme that the film stock could exploit. The result was a beautiful, color-conscious mise-en-scene.

Perhaps most miraculous was the role played by Jack Dawn and the MGM make-up department. It was Dawn's task to take three non-humans—a scarecrow, a tin man, and a lion—and bring them to life. He had to give them humanity, personality, and human-like qualities amidst the costumes dictated by their roles. This was done convincingly, resulting in three of the most elaborate make-up/costume designs to date in Hollywood. These costumes posed certain critical problems to production. Bert Lahr's costume for the Cowardly Lion, for instance, weighed nearly 100 pounds. This, coupled with the intense heat caused by the lighting needed to shoot, made filming for long durations impossible. The film had to be shot in segments with a day's shooting often ending before a scene was complete. As a result, before the next day's shooting could begin, make-up had to be meticulously matched and perfectly recreated to retain consistency. Daily rushes were used to aid this process. While this precision slowed the production down, the commitment to perfection became a trademark of MGM.

For their efforts both Jack Dawn and Cedric Gibbons received Academy Award nominations (though Gibbon's contract insured that his name would appear in the credits of *all* MGM films regardless of his involvement). This recognition, while falling on individuals, was no less a tribute to the system. It was a recognition of the elaborate collaborative nature of Hollywood filmmaking.

Though *Wizard* remains an elaborate technical achievement

for its time, the technology involved has since become obsolete. Perhaps the longterm contribution of the film is the precedent it set for the type of Hollywood musical identified with MGM. *Wizard* was perhaps the earliest example of what came to be called the "integrated musical." Traditionally, music in films had been in a performance setting, establishing logical moments in which to include musical numbers, such as the review films of the thirties—*Golddiggers*, and *Forty-Second Street*. In *The Wizard of Oz* the music became another dimension of the characters' language, an extension of their personalities and feelings. There is no intrinsic logic in Dorothy's singing "Somewhere Over The Rainbow," but it is understood as a viable expression of some inner longing. The film narrative is advanced by musical numbers. Songs often replace dialogue as when the Munchkins pay tribute to Dorothy for killing their nemesis, the Wicked Witch of the East. In *Wizard* music isn't a disgression, but instead a fundamental part of the narrative structure.

The Wizard of Oz has enjoyed over 20 years of revival on both television and in theaters, remaining widely popular. Internationally, the film has enjoyed wider distribution than other American film in history—fantasy, musical or otherwise. It would seem that the directness of its message—"There's no place like home"—and the sincerity of its presentation is the key. However, beneath the fantasy is one of the most polished and elaborate productions ever mounted in Hollywood. It remains a reminder of that as well.

—Robert Winning

W.R.—MYSTERIJE ORGANIZMA. W.R.—Mysteries of the Organism. Production: Neoplanta Film and Telepool; color, 35mm. Released 1971.

Scripted and directed by Dusan Makavejev; photography by Pega Popovic and Aleksander Perkovíc. Cannes Film Festival, Louis Buñuel Prize, 1971.

Cast: Milena Dravíc (*Milena*); Jagoder Kaloper (*Jagoder*); Zoran Radmilovic (*Radmilovíc*); Vica Vidovic (*Vladimir Ilyich*); Miodrag Andríc (*Soldier*); Tuli Kuperferberg (*Guerilla soldier in New York City*); Jackie Curtis; Betty Dodson; Nancy Godfrey.

Publications:

Script—*WR: Mysteries of the Organism*, New York 1972; reviews—by Andrew Sarris in *The Village Voice* (New York), 11 November 1971; "A Minor Masterpiece: Dusan Makavejev's *WR: Mysteries of the Organism*" by L. Becker in *Film Journal* (New York), September 1972; "*WR, les mystères de l'organisme*" by P. Bonitzer in *Cahiers du cinéma* (Paris), July/August 1972; "*WR—Mysteries of the Organism*" by Gordon Gow in *Films and Filming* (London), May 1972; review by Joan Mellen in *Cineaste* (New York), winter 1971-72; "*WR: Mysteries of the Organism*" by B. Weiner in *Take One* (Montreal), June 1972; "*WR: Mysteries of the Organism*" by M. Walsh in *Monogram* (London), no.5, 1974; books — *Directors and Directions* by John Taylor, New York 1975; articles—"Why Did He Do That to Wm. Reich?" by David Bienstock in *The New York Times*, 7 November 1971; "Entretien avec Dusan Makavejev" by G. Braucourt in *Ecran* (Paris), September/October 1972; "Entretien avec Dusan Makavejev" by A. Cervoni in *Cinéma* (Paris), September/October 1972; "Une Affaire de coeur" by R. Lefevre in *Cinéma* (Paris), September/October 1972; "Sex and Politics: Wilhelm Reich, World Revolution, and Makavejev's *WR*" by J.R. MacBean in *Film Quarterly* (Berkeley), spring 1972; "Fight Power with Spontaneity and Humor: An Interview with Dusan Makaveyev" by J.R. MacBean in *Film Quarterly* (Berkeley), winter 1971-72; "Dogmatizem in jpapirnati tiger" by B. Tirnanić in *Ekran* (Ljubljana, Yugoslavia), no.92-93, 1972; "Deux cinéastes yougoslaves" by A. Tournès in *Jeune Cinéma* (Paris), September/October 1972; "Pota spolnosti na filmu" by J. Weightman in *Ekran* (Ljubljana, Yugoslavia), no.94-95, 1972; "*WR—Kroppens mysterier*" by H. Schiller in *Filmrutan* (Tyresö, Sweden), no.3, 1973; "Toward the Edge of the Real...and Over" by A. Vogel in *Film Comment* (New York), November/December 1973; "The Success and Failure of *WR*" by O. Webster in *Lumiere* (Melbourne, Australia), May 1973; "Let's Put Life Back in Political Life": An Interview with Dusan Makavejev" by C.B. Thomsen in *Cineaste* (New York), no.2, 1974; "Dusan Makavejev" in *50 Major Filmmakers* edited by Peter Cowie, South Brunswick, New Jersey 1974; "*Los misterios del organismo*" by J.V.G. Santamaría in *Contracampo* (Madrid), June/July 1981.

*   *   *

Dusan Makavejev's *WR: Mysteries of the Organism* opens with the statement: "This film is in part a personal response to the life and teachings of Dr. Wilhelm Reich (1897-1957)." Part documentary, part narrative fiction, part examination of contemporary American sexual mores, and part condemnation of the legacy of Stalin in the Eastern Block, *WR* uses the career of Wilhelm Reich as a springboard from which to tackle the still burning issue of the relationship of political oppression to sexual repression.

Both a colleague of Sigmund Freud and a member of the German Communist Party in the 1920s, Reich was one of the first psychoanalysts to attempt to show the importance of the relationship between the individual psyche and the material relations of production. For Reich, sexual repression was one of the by-products of class oppression, sexual liberation one of the goals of a revolutionary struggle. After organizing a group called SEXPOL to further develop his ideas of radical psychotherapy, Reich was thrown out of the Communist Party for advocating the ideas of Freud and kicked out of German psychoanalytic circles for being a Marxist. Fleeing Hitler, Reich immigrated to the United States in 1934; he set up a clinic in a small town in Maine. In 1956, he was arrested for quackery, his books burned; he died in a federal prison in 1957.

After moving to the United States, Reich renounced his earlier Marxist theories and often boasted of voting for Eisenhower. Interestingly, in *WR*, Makavejev focuses on this Reich—the later, American Reich—and on the development of his therapy techniques in the United States and Britain (outside a socialist context). Most of the first part of the film examines this Reich—through interviews with his relatives, his American neighbors, his students, even his barber—and the state of American sexual mores after Reich, but before the Revolution. An editor of *Screw* magazine conducts business in the buff and then has his penis plaster-casted. Jackie Curtis discusses her sex change and the romantic difficulties it created as Pepsi ads blare over the radio. Tuli Kupferberg engages in guerilla street theater—roaming New York, fondling his toy M-16 like giant phallus. New York shows signs of sexual emancipation, but it is commercialized. It supports rather than contradicts American capitalism and militarism; it bears no resemblance to Reich's notion of "worker democracy."

The last half of *WR*, a fictional allegory, takes place in Yugoslavia—a country which is presented as a land caught between Stalin and the U.S. dollar, where "Marx Factor" rules. A young worker, Milena, calls for the end of sexual repression in post-revolutionary Yugoslav society. However, after breaking off her relationship with the worker next door, Milena can only make up sermons on the value of free love, while her roommate puts the theory into practice by exuberantly screwing a member of the army home on leave. At a performance of the Soviet Ice Capades, Milena sees and falls in love with Vladimir Ilyich, a handsome young skating star. (Of course, this is a self-conscious reference to Lenin, whose real name was Vladimir Ilyich Ulyanov. In the film, Vladimir Ilyich even recites a number of Lenin's more famous sayings verbatim.) Milena seduces Vladimir Ilyich. Unable to deal with the liberating force of his orgasm, however, Vladimir Ilyich goes mad and decapitates Milena with his iceskate. In the morgue, Milena's severed head analyzes the problem: "Vladimir is a man of noble impetuousness, a man of high ambition, of immense energy. He's romantic, ascetic, a genuine Red Fascist...Comrades! Even now I'm not ashamed of my Communist past!" The film ends with a photograph of Reich's smiling face.

WR was the last film Makavejev made in Yugoslavia. After the film was banned there, Makavejev was effectively excluded from the Yugoslav film industry. Also, although *WR* won the Louis Buñuel prize at Cannes in 1971, the film never received a large theatrical release in the U.S.—its distribution limited in some areas to pornography cinemas where it was billed as a "sex film."

—Gina Marchetti

WRITTEN ON THE WIND. Production: Universal Pictures; 1956; Technicolor, 35mm; running time: 99 mins. Released 1956.

Produced by Albert Zugsmith; screenplay by George Zuckerman; from the novel by Robert Wilder; directed by Douglas Sirk; photography by Russell Metty; edited by Russell Schoengarth; art direction by Alexander Golitzen, Robert Clatworthy, Russell A. Gausman, and Julia Heron; music by Frank Skinner and Joseph Gershenson, song "Written on the Wind" by Victor Young and Sammy Cahn and sung by the Four Aces; special effects by Clifford Stine; costumes designed by Bill Thomas; color consultant: William Fritzsche.

Filmed November 1955-January 1956. Academy Award, Best Supporting Actress (Malone), 1956.

Cast: Rock Hudson (*Mitch Wayne*); Lauren Bacall (*Lucy Moore Hadley*); Robert Stack (*Kyle Hadley*); Dorothy Malone (*Marylee Hadley*); Robert Keith (*Jasper Hadley*); Grant Williams (*Biff Miley*); Harry Shannon (*Hoak Wayne*); Robert J. Wilke (*Dan Willis*); Edward Platt (*Dr. Cochran*); John Latch (*Roy Carter*); Joseph Cranby (*R.J. Courtney*); Roy Glenn (*Sam*); Maide Norman (*Bertha*).

Publications:

Book—*Sirk on Sirk*, with Jon Halliday, New York 1972; articles—"Le Film gratuit" by Louis Marcorelles in *Cahiers du cinéma* (Paris), March 1957; "Lauren Bacall" by Ray Hagen in *Films in Review* (New York), April 1964; "Biofilmographie de Douglas Sirk" by Patrick Brion and Dominique Rabourdin in *Cahiers du cinéma* (Paris), April 1967; "L'Aveugle et le miroir oui l'imposible cinéma de Douglas Sirk" by Jean-Louis Comolli in *Cahiers du cinéma* (Paris), April 1967; "Entretien avec Douglas Sirk" by Serge Daney and Jean Louis Noames in *Cahiers du cinéma* (Paris), April 1967; "Sirk on Sirk" by Jon Halliday in *Cinema One*, no.18, London 1971; issue on Sirk of *Screen* (London), summer 1971; "Towards an Analysis of the Sirkian System" by P. Willemen in *Screen* (London), winter 1972/73; "Sur Douglas Sirk", in 3 parts, by E. Bourget and J.-L. Bourget in *Positif* (Paris), April and September 1972; "Patterns of Power and Potency, Repression and Violence" by M. Stern in *Velvet Light Trap* (Madison), fall 1976; "Douglas Sirk and Melodrama" by L. Mulvey in *Australian Journal of Screen Theory* (Kensington N.S.W.), no.3, 1977; "Notes on Sirk and Melodrama" by L. Mulvey in *Movie* (London), winter 1977-78; "Idol der Münchner Filmstudenten: Douglas Sirk wieder in der HFF" by T. Honickel in *Film und Ton* (Munich), February 1979; "*Written on the Wind*" by Janey Place in *Magill's Survey of Cinema, Vol. IV* edited by Frank N. Magill, Englewood Cliffs, New Jersey 1980.

*   *   *

At the end of *Written on the Wind*, Merrylee Hadley is left alone caressing a statue of an oil well. With her father dead of a heart attack induced by disgust for his two reckless offspring, her brother accidentally killed while inebriated, and the object of her affection lost to her sister-in-law, Merrylee is forced to confront emotional bankruptcy while clutching this symbol of financial security.

In this, the best of Douglas Sirks' melodramas of American life and family, money is shown as a force whose misuse creates indulgence of the most destructive kind. The case in point involves Kyle and Merrylee, the children of oil magnate Jasper Hadley, characters whose success is in wallowing in a wide range of psychological complexities, among them alcoholism, latent homosexuality, promiscuity, Oedipal guilt, wanton violence and arrested adolescence. In detailing these foibles Sirk renders this his most complex study of human failure.

While Rock Hudson and Lauren Bacall received star billing, Sirk focuses on the characters played by Robert Stack and Dorothy Malone. As the spoiled offspring of a wealthy American, they masochistically dwell on their failures, knowing they are bringing others down to their level of depravity. Graphically depicting the vertigo of these characters lives through their shared obsession with alcohol, the speed and violence of Stack's temper, and the frantic kinesis of Malone's sexual arousal, Sirk turns physical beauty into degenerate decrepitude.

Constantly depicted in her red sports car, surrounded by her red phone and vases of roses which decorate her room, or displaying the red of her toenails, lips and lingerie, Merrylee epitomizes both beauty and vulgarity, her steamy sensuality offset by a lack of dignity. Like her brother she is trapped in adolescence, unable to overcome an emotional childhood attachment to Mitch, the man who achieved rather than inherited his success. In an aural flashback Merrylee relives a romantic incident at the lake; in a booze-induced dream, Kyle recounts an exciting adventure. Brother and sister share the same romantic fixation, the difference being that Merrylee's is hysterically externalized,

Kyle's is hysterically repressed. Where booze magnifies the self-destructive tendencies of both characters by inviting public disgrace, it heightens her sexual passions while encouraging his paranoia. When his masculinity seems at stake, he encourages punishment by indulging in fisticuffs, wreckless driving and an obsessive amount of guilt; her desirability questioned, she engages in flirtations with men considered below her social status.

Having contributed to both his father's death and his wife's miscarriage, thereby negating both past and future generations of the Hadley empire, Kyle effectively self destructs, leaving his financial holdings to the unstable, unmarried sister, and his wife to his best friend.

The hope for the American family of the future is thus situated with Mitch and Lucy, the characters who opted for decency over currency. At the film's end, they seemingly are rescued from the morass.

—Doug Tomlinson

XALA. Production: Domirev; 35mm; running time: 90 mins. Released 1975.

Director of production: Paulin Soumanou Vieyra; screenplay by Ousmane Sembène; directed by Ousmane Sembène; photography by Georges Caristan; edited by Florence Eymon; sound by El Hadji Mbow; music (traditional) by El Hadji Mbow.

Filmed in Africa.

Cast: Tierno Seye; Donta Seck; Younouss Seye; Senn Samb; Fatim Diange; Myriam Niang; Markhouredia Seck; Babou Faye.

Publications:

Script—*Xala*, Paris 1973; *Xala*, translated by C. Wake, Westport, Connecticut 1976; reviews—"*Xala*" by C. Bosseno in *Revue du cinéma* (Paris), October 1976; "*Xala*" by L. Dewey in *Film* (London), December 1976; "*Xala*" by J. Forbes in *Monthly Film Bulletin* (London), December 1976; "*Xala*" by P. Jouvet in *Cinématographe* (Paris), April/May 1976; "Molier Czarnej Afryki" by B. Mruklik in *Kino* (Warsaw), February 1976; "*A gyik dala*" by K. Csala in *Filmkultura* (Budapest), July/August 1977; articles—"Problématique du cinéaste africain: l'artiste et la révolution" by T. Cheriaa in *Cinéma Québec* (Montreal), August 1974; "Coached" by J. Coleman in *New Statesman* (London), 5 November 1976; "Exhibition (*Xala*)" by D. Dubroux in *Cahiers du cinéma* (Paris), May 1976; "Ousmane Sembene" by N. Ghali in *Cinéma 76* (Paris), April 1976; "African Comedy" by B. Kumm in *Harper's Magazine* (New York), December 1976; "*Xala*" by G. Dagneau in *Image et son* (Paris), April 1976; "Ousmane Sembene" by N. Ghali in *Cinématographe* (Paris), April 1976; "Ousmane Sembene" in *Avant-Scène du cinéma* (Paris), 1 June 1979; "Ideology in the Third World Cinema: A Study of Sembene Ousmane and Glauber Rocha" by William Van Wert in *Quarterly Review of Film Studies* (Pleasantville, New York), spring 1979; "3 Faces of Africa: Women in *Xala*" by Francoise Pfaff in *Jump Cut* (Chicago), no.27, n.d.

*   *   *

Ousmane Sembene's *Xala* is the fourth major film by one of black Africa's most important directors. Based on Sembene's novel of the same title, *Xala* demonstrates his ongoing social, political and cultural concerns. Sembene had previously attacked the relatively easy targets of European racism (*Black Girl*), African bureaucracy (*The Money Order*), and past colonialism (*Lords of the Sky*), but here he denounces the neo-colonial deformities resulting from the collaboration of European businessmen and African elite.

Sembene structures his film around the concept of *xala*—in Wolof, a state of temporary sexual impotence. The protagonist, El Hadji, is a polygamous Senegalese businessman who becomes afflicted with *xala* on the occasion of taking his third wife. In search of a cure, he visits various witchdoctors, who take his money but fail to cure him. At the same time, he suffers reverses in business, is accused of embezzlement and ejected from the Chamber of Commerce. In the end, he discovers that the *xala* resulted from a curse sent by a Dakar beggar whose land El Hadji had expropriated. The protagonist finally recovers his manhood by submitting to the beggar's demands that he strip and be spat upon; the film ends with a freeze-frame of his spittle-covered body.

On a psychological level, *xala* functions as a truth-teller. El Hadji has taken a third wife purely for reasons of sexism and conspicuous consumption. "Every polygamous man," his daughter tells him, "is a liar," and although his mouth can lie, his penis cannot. The *xala*, on one level, constitutes the revenge of the women in the film; on another, it is the revenge of the oppressed classes of Senegal, represented by the beggars who have been defrauded by the new African bourgeoisie. On still another level, the *xala* symbolizes the political and economic impotence of the many newly established independent countries. El Hadji, with his Europeanized habits and tastes, encapsulates the conditions of neo-colonialism, in which an African elite takes over the positions formerly occupied by the colonizers.

Sembene portrays this elite as a kind of caricature of the European bourgeoisie. In the pre-credit sequence, we see them throw out the Europeans and take over the Chamber of Commerce. While their public speeches are in Wolof and their dress African, they speak French among themselves and reveal European suits underneath their African garb. (Continuing indirect European domination is underlined by the immediate return of the same Europeans as "advisors".) The Senegalese businessmen slavishly adore all that is European. They pour imported mineral water into the radiators of the Mercedes, and one complains that he no longer visits Spain because there are "too many blacks." The elite, in other words, have absorbed European racism and paradoxically turned it against themselves. At the same time, the film reminds us of the presence of the uncorrupted poor who look in on the ostentatious wedding celebration, and linger in the streets outside El Hadji's office. By spitting on El Hadji, they express the anger of the oppressed against the leaders who have betrayed their hopes. Yet the symbolic purging of the spittle will lead, it is implied, to the end of impotence and a kind of rebirth, for El Hadji and for his country.

Sembene masterfully deploys a diversity of narrative and aesthetic strategies in *Xala*. At times, his approach is allegorical, as in the satirical scene involving the African take-over of the Chamber of Commerce, a moment clearly evoking the historical juncture of formal independence. Each of the key women in the film has an allegorical dimension in that each represents a different stage of African history. Awa, with her traditional clothes and manners, represents the pre-colonial African woman. Omui, with her wigs, sunglasses and low-cut dress, represents the colonized woman who imitates European fashions. El Hadji's daughter Rama, finally, represents an ideal synthesis of Africa and

Europe. She speaks Wolof but studies French; she rides a moped, practical and inexpensive. She is culturally proud and politically aware, but she can also appreciate Charlie Chaplin, whose poster decorates her wall.

Sembene's achievement is that he has made an accessible political film, which speaks honestly to the problems of post-inpendent Africa, while skillfully orchestrating realism, humor, satire, and allegory.

—Ella Shochat

YANKEE DOODLE DANDY. Production: Warner Bros. Pictures Inc.; 1942; black and white, 35mm; running time: 126 mins. Released 1942.

Produced by Jack L. Warner and Hal B. Wallis with William Cagney; screenplay by Robert Buckner and Edmund Joseph; from a story by Robert Buckner; directed by Michael Curtiz; photography by James Wong Howe; edited by George Amy; sound by Nathan Levinson and Warner Bros. Studio Sound Department; music by Heinz Roemheld, musical direction by Ray Heindorf and Heinz Roemheld, songs by George M. Cohan.

Academy Awards for Best Actor (Cagney), Best Sound Recording, and Best Score of a Musical Picture, 1942; New York Critics Award, Best Actor (Cagney), 1942.

Cast: James Cagney (*George M. Cohan*); Joan Leslie (*Mary*); Walter Huston (*Jerry Cohan*); Richard Whorf (*Sam Harris*); Captain Jack Young (*The President*); S.Z. Sakall (*Schwab*); Jeanne Cagney (*Josie Cohan*); Irene Manning (*Fay Templeton*).

Publications:

Books—*Hollywood in the Forties* by Charles Higham and Joel Greenberg, New York 1968; *Cagney* by Ron Offen, Chicago 1972; *Cagney* by Andrew Bergman, New York 1973; *Cagney by Cagney*, Garden City, New York 1976; *James Cagney* by Michael Freedland, London 1982; *Cagney, The Actor as Auteur* by Patrick McGilligan, San Diego 1982; articles—"James Cagney" by Don Miller in *Films in Review* (New York), August/September 1958; "Walter Huston" by Jerry Vermilye in *Films in Review* (New York), February 1960; "Hitch Your Genre to a Star" by Harris Dienstfrey in *Film Culture* (New York), fall 1964; "Michael Curtiz" by Jack Edmund Nolan in *Films in Review* (New York), no.9, 1970; "Michael Curtiz" by Kingsley Canham in *The Hollywood Professionals, Vol. 1*, London 1973; "*Yankee Doodle Dandy*" by James J. Desmarais in *Magill's Survey of Cinema, Vol. IV* edited by Frank N. Magill, Englewood Cliffs, New Jersey 1980.

*   *   *

Yankee Doodle Dandy, the film biography of George M. Cohan, epitomizes the Hollywood studio product of the 1930s and 1940s. Though perhaps not a classic, it is an immensely entertaining film, a vehicle to display the talents of its star, James Cagney. Made at Warner Brothers, it exemplifies a brand of film

for which that studio became famous. Along with such movies as *Juarez*, *The Life of Emile Zola*, and *The Story of Louis Pasteur*, it is part of Warner's cycle of motion picture biographies. Like other Warner's films of the period, such as *The Strawberry Blonde*, and *Gentleman Jim*, it is a nostalgic return to a simpler time.

Curtiz's film, made during World War II, served a wartime purpose other than escapism. It stands out as perhaps the most enjoyable propaganda picture ever made (indeed, at the time of its release, it received outstanding reviews and did exceptionally well at the box office). It shamelessly extols the patriotic virtues, delights in showing holiday parades, and has as its centerpiece an elaborate production of "She's a Grand Old Flag."

But this is not an unsophisticated work from an era when patriotism was easier to preach. It also works in subtle ways. The film imbues Cagney-as-Cohan with a paternal strength that renders his fervent Americanism completely acceptable. As a voice-over narrator, George recounts the events of his life. This storyteller's role grants him a special status. As narrator, Cohan seemingly controls what we find out and how we find out about it. Before George begins narrating, the film's first shots show him backstage, after a performance as Franklin Roosevelt in Kaufman and Hart's *I'd Rather br Right*. Our first view of Cohan is as a supreme father figure, a third term president during wartime. Once Cohan begins reminiscing, we see him as a young boy in vaudeville, dressed in the same costume that his father had worn during an earlier number, and singing the same song. George has gone from playing the country's father figure (Roosevelt) at the film's beginning, to play an actual father (Jerry Cohan) at the start of George's narration. Later, acting with his family, George plays the part of his mother's father, thereby underscoring the mixed-up hierarchy among the Cohans. It is George who thanks the audience after each of the Cohans' performances, and it is he who decides to break up the act, and later to bring it back together. Then, when Jerry Cohan retires, it is not the father who passes on the business to the son, but just the opposite. As a birthday present, George gives his father a half-interest in all of his theaters and plays. Because he makes the familial and financial decisions, George, of all the Cohans, is the one with the controlling, paternal voice.

The film does such an expert job at presenting Cohan as a model of authority and wisdom that the spectator cannot question George's brand of enthusiastic patriotism. While he sings "Over There," George looks directly into the camera during a closeup, and shouts, "Everybody together!" But this brazen appeal to the film audience seems completely natural since the film works so subtly to underscore George's patriarchal strength. *Yankee Doodle Dandy* stands out as a remarkable blend of the obvious and the artful.

—Eric Smoodin

YAWAR MALLKU. Blood of the Condor. Production: Grupo Ukamau (Bolivia); black and white, 35mm; running time: 74 mins. Released 1969.

Produced by Ricardo Rada; screenplay by Oscar Soria and Jorge Sanjinés; directed by Jorge Sanjinés; photography by Antonio Eguino; music by Alberto Villalpando, Alfredo Dominquez, Gregorio Yana, and Ignacio Quispo.

Cast: Marcelino Yanahuaya (*Ignacio*); Benedicta Mendoza Huanca (*Paulina*); Vicente Salinas (*Sixto*); also featuring the people of the Kanta rural community.

Publications:

Reviews—"*Yawar Mallku*" by A. Apon in *Skrien* (Amsterdam), November 1972; "*Blood of the Condor*" by M. Tarratt in *Films and Filming* (London), June 1973; book—*Cine boliviano: Del realizador al critico* by Carlos D. Mesa, Beatriz Palacios, Jorge Sanjines, and Arturo Von Vacano, La Paz 1979; articles— "*Ukamau* and *Yawar Mallku*: An Interview with Jorge Sanjines" in *Afterimage* (London), summer 1971; "A Talk with Jorge Sanjines" and *Blood of the Condor* and the Rats" in *Cinéaste* (New York), winter 1970-71; "Aspects of Latin American Political Cinema" by David Wilson in *Sight and Sound* (London), summer 1972; "*Sangue di condor*" by A. Ferrero in *Cineforum* (Bergamo, Italy), December 1973; "Film as a Revolutionary Weapon: A Jorge Sanjines Retrospective" by Leon G. Campbell and Carlos Cortes in *The History Teacher*, May 1979.

* * *

The Bolivian fiction feature *Yawar Mallku* is one of the most famous examples of Latin American militant cinema. Like most Latin American militant films, this one was made on a modest budget in spite of major obstacles. Bolivia has no significant filmmaking traditions or facilities. Mules had to be used to transport the filmmakers and their equipment to a high and remote Indian community where parts of the film were shot. The Quechua-speaking Indians of this Andean community were initially hostile to the filmmakers until a coca-leaf divination ritual confirmed the filmmakers' good intentions.

It is in cultural and ideological terms that *Yawar Mallku* is most important. This controversial film is a powerful and thorough attack on United States imperialism. In the film, members of a Progress Corps (read Peace Corps) working, ironically, in an obstetric clinic, surgically sterilize unsuspecting Indian women. Jorge Sanjinés, aware of Bolivia's historic underpopulation and high infant mortality rate, had been deeply disturbed by media reports that the U.S. Peace Corps operated in such a fashion in his country. Though U.S. officials denied such activities, the film created a furor and, in the opinion of Sanjinés, was a major factor in the expulsion of the Peace Corps from Bolivia in 1971.

In *Yawar Mallku*, U.S. imperialism is not depicted solely as an attempt to biologically eliminate an "inferior" race, but also as a more subtle yet all-pervasive force. The theme of cultural imperialism is amply illustrated: the rock music played in the clinic (in contrast to the indigenous flute music), the American-style clothes donated to the Indians (in contrast to the traditional, hand-woven garb), the pinups in the house of the Indian who has migrated to La Paz. Linguistic imperialism is exemplified in a sequence in which an upper-class Bolivian mother addresses her children in English, a language commonly used by the upper classes but generally not available for study by the Indians. Sanjinés emphasizes the ties of Bolivia's ruling classes to U.S. imperialism in a banquet sequence where leading Bolivian doctors and their U.S. counterparts fail to supply the blood that a wounded Indian needs to survive. For Sanjinés, U.S. imperialism is literally and figuratively robbing Bolivian Indians of their blood—their right to life according to their own traditions and customs.

Yawar Mallku also paints an unforgettable portrait of a common figure in modern Bolivia—the rural Indian migrant (Sixto) who seeks his fortune in the metropolis, La Paz. Sixto attempts to change his cultural identity by speaking Spanish, wearing Western-style clothes, and denying his Indian roots. Nevertheless, he remains a member of a subordinant class and as such he is

"kept in his place"—begging for blood for his brother, waiting outside the club, riding in the back of the truck. At the end of the film, Sixto has adopted Indian clothing and is returning to his rural community. The final freeze-frame of upraised rifles suggests that the Indians of the traditional rural communities must unite in the armed defense of their lives and culture.

The Bolivian government, allegedly at the insistence of U.S. officials, initially banned *Yawar Mallku*. After 24 hours, however, the ban was lifted due to public pressure generated by widespread protests and demonstrations. Because of its socially significant national themes and its controversial nature, *Yawar Mallku* became immensely popular with Bolivians. Critics continue to regard the film as a leading example of Latin American militant cinema.

—Dennis West

———

YOU ONLY LIVE ONCE. Production: Wanger Productions; black and white, 35mm; running time: 87 mins. Released 29 January 1937 by United Artists.

Produced by Walter Wanger; screenplay by Gene Towne and Graham Baker; from a story by Gene Towne; directed by Fritz Lang; photography by Leon Shamroy; edited by Daniel Mandell; art direction by Alexander Toluboff; music by Alfred Newman, song "A Thousand Dreams of You" by Louis Alter and Paul Francis Webster.

Filmed in 46 days of 1936 in Wanger-United Artists studios in Hollywood.

Cast: Sylvia Sydney (*Joan Graham*); Henry Fonda (*Eddie Taylor*); Barton MacLane (*Stephen Whitney*); Jean Dixon (*Bonnie Graham*); William Gargan (*Father Dolan*); Warren Hymer (*Muggsy*); Charles "Chic" Sale (*Ethan*); Margaret Hamilton (*Hester*); Guinn Williams (*Rogers*); Jerome Cowan (*Dr. Hill*); John Wray (*Warden*); Jonathan Hale (*District attorney*); Ward Bond (*Guard*); Wade Boteler (*Policeman*); Henry Taylor (*Kozderonas*); Jean Stoddard (*Stenographer*); Ben Hal (*Messenger*); Walter De Palma.

Publications:

Reviews—in the *Monthly Film Bulletin* (London), no.4 1937; review by Frank Nugent in *The New York Times*, 1 February 1937; review in *Sight and Sound* (London), summer 1937; books—*An Index to the Creative Work of Fritz Lang* by Herman Weinberg, supplement to *Sight and Sound* (London), index series, 1946; *The Film Till Now* by Paul Rotha, New York 1949; *Fritz Lang* by Francis Courtade, Paris 1963; *Fritz Lang* by Luc Moullet, Paris 1963; *Fritz Lang* edited by Alfred Eibel, Paris 1964; *The Cinema of Fritz Lang* by Paul M. Jensen, New York 1969; *Fritz Lang* by Claire Johnston, London 1969; *Fritz Lang in America* by Peter Bogdanovich, London 1969; *Fritz Lang* by Frieda Grafe, Enno Patalas, and Hans Helmut Prinzler, Munich 1976; *Fritz Lang* by Lotte Eisner, London 1977; *Fritz Lang* by Robert Armour, Boston 1978; *The Films of My Life* by François Truffaut, translated by Leonard Mayhew, New York 1978; *The Films of Fritz Lang* by Frederick W. Ott, Secaucus, New Jersey 1979; *Fritz Lang* edited by Stephen Jenkins, London 1979; *Film*

Noir edited by Alain Silver and Elizabeth Ward, Woodstock, New York 1979; *Fritz Lang: A Guide to References and Resources* by E. Ann Kaplan, Boston 1981; articles—"Fritz Lang, Director of *Fury*, Discusses His Film *You Only Live Once*" by Eileen Creelman in the *Sun* (New York), 28 January 1937; "Fritz Lang, Master of Mood" by Ram Bagai in *Cinema Progress* (Los Angeles), May/June 1938; "Gehetzt" by Klaus Brüne in *Film-Dienst* (Dusseldorf), 9 February 1951; "Fritz Lang's America" by Gavin Lambert in *Sight and Sound* (London), summer 1955 and autumn 1955; "L'Amour Revolte: *You Only Live Once* and *Gun Crazy*" by Ado Kyrou in *Amour-erotisme et cinéma*, Paris 1957; "*You Only Live Once*" by Jean Douchet in *Cahiers du cinéma* (Paris), March 1958; "The Hautaine Dialectique de Fritz Lang" by Phillipe Demonsablon in *Cahiers du cinéma* (Paris), September 1959; "L'Erreur judiciaire: Fritz Lang" by Gilles Jacob in *Le Cinéma moderne*, Paris 1964; article in *Positif* (Paris), January 1965; "Fritz Lang" in *Les Grands Cinéastes que je propose* by Henri Agel, Paris 1967; "Interview with Henry Fonda" by Roberta Ostroff in *Take One* (Montreal), March/April 1972; "Why Hollywood?" by Thomas Elsaesser in *Monogram* (Hollywood), no.3, 1973; "Le Regard froid" by Gérard Legrand in *Positif* (Paris), January 1975; "*You Only Live Once*: The Doubled Feature" by George Wilson in *Sight and Sound* (London), autumn 1977; "American Nightmare: The Underworld in Film" by Mark Hennelly, Jr. in *Journal of Popular Film* (Bowling Green, Ohio), no.3, 1978; "*You Only Live Once*" by Alain Silver in *Magill's Survey of Cinema, Vol. IV* edited by Frank N. Magill, Englewood Cliffs, New Jersey 1980; "Fritz Lang: Only Melodrama" by Don Willis in *Film Quarterly* (Berkeley), winter 1979-80.

*   *   *

In 1934 Fritz Lang came to America at the invitation of David O. Selznick of MGM, after having escaped to France from his native Germany. He saw America, like so many refugees of the time, as a land of hope to which he intended to commit himself entirely. As he has explained to Peter Bagdanovich, he began to study the American scene and character. He travelled, read and cut newspapers, talked with everyone he could. "It is impossible to learn all this out of experience," he said, "but the next best thing is to read newspapers."

As soon as he was assigned the four-page story for his first American film, *Fury*, Lang sensed its potential as a social drama of the kind the American press was apt to handle as well as its propaganda value as an exposé. He treated *Fury* and its immediate successor, *You Only Live Once*, as social documents. He insisted on "newsreel photography," unlike the dramatic chiaroscuro associated with his expressionist German thrillers of the 1920s.

His second American film, *You Only Live Once*, was similar to *Fury* in terms of its social stance. A former criminal, supported by his newlywedded wife, attempts to go straight, but finds his past is against him. As a result of purely circumstantial evidence, he is unjustly accused and convicted of a murder committed during a bank robbery. Just before information is revealed that will clear him, he kills a prison chaplain while making a desperate escape from the death cell itself, though the chaplain was trying to convince him his pardon has come through. The film has an inevitable tragic end—the man and his wife are shot as they reach the border. The film has a grim power for which Lang's earlier experience in fantasy-melodrama had well prepared him, but his technical skill is used here for realistic effect in a situation which seems only too true to life.

William Farr, one of Britain's most perceptive critics of the period, described *You Only Live Once* as "a damning indictment of the injustice, prejudice and brutality that can be directed, in the name of justice, against an ex-criminal." He comments that the acting of Henry Fonda and Sylvia Sidney as well as Lang's style of direction are starkly naturalist, but that the action itself is obviously devised to achieve the maximum suspense, thus sliding into melodrama. "Henry Fonda," writes Farr, "who might so easily have been allowed to play for sympathy, maintains to the end his contempt and defiance for the people and the system that, by condemning him for a crime he did not commit, force him to kill the one man he had always trusted." However, he adds that "the film is never as moving as *Fury*," because the story is somewhat "manoeuvred." Lang himself, looking back on the film almost 30 years later, seems to agree, "It's a little constructed, isn't it?" For him the film, like *Fury*, had the broader implication of a man's "fight against destiny, against fate—the main theme that runs through all my pictures." Hence the shot at the end of the film where Fonda is seen through the scope of a gun. "You feel," said Lang, "will he shoot? Will he not shoot?"

—Roger Manvell

_____

YOUNG MR. LINCOLN. Production: Twentieth Century-Fox; 1939; black and white, 35mm; running time: 100 mins. Released 1939.

Produced by Darryl F. Zanuck with Kenneth MacGowan; screenplay by Lamar Trotti; from a story by Lamar Trotti; directed by John Ford; photography by Arthur Miller; edited by Walter Thompson; sound by Eugene Grossman and Roger Heman; art direction by Richard Day and Mark-Lee Kirk, set decorations by Thomas Little; music score by Alfred Newman, music direction by Louis Silvers; costumes designed by Royer.

Filmed in Fox studios.

Cast: Henry Fonda (*Abraham Lincoln*); Alice Brady (*Abagail Clay*); Marjorie Weaver (*Mary Todd*); Arleen Whelan (*Hannah Clay*); Eddie Collins (*Efe*); Pauline Moore (*Ann Rutledge*); Richard Cromwell (*Matt Clay*); Donald Meek (*John Felder*); Judith Dickens (*Carrie Sue*); Eddie Quillan (*Adam Clay*); Spencer Charters (*Judge Herbert A. Bell*); Ward Bond (*Palmer Cass*); Milburn Stone (*Stephen A. Douglas*); Cliff Clark (*Sheriff Billings*); Steven Randall (*Juror*); Charles Tannen (*Ninian Edwards*); Francis Ford (*Frank Ford*); Fred Kohler Jr. (*Scrub White*); Kay Linaker (*Mrs. Edwards*); Russell Simpson (*Woolridge*); Clarence Hummel Wilson (*Dr. Mason*); Edwin Maxwell (*John T. Stuart*); Robert Homans (*Mr. Clay*); Charles Halton (*Hawthorne*); Jack Kelly (*Matt Clay, as a boy*); Dickie Jones (*Adam Clay, as a boy*); Harry Tyler (*Barber*).

Publications:

Books—*An Index to the Films of John Ford* by W.P. Wooten, supplement to *Sight and Sound* Index series, London 1948; *John Ford* by Jean Mitry, Paris 1954; *John Ford* by Philippe Haudiquet, Paris 1966; *The Fondas: The Films and Careers of Henry, Jane, and Peter Fonda* by John Springer, New York 1970; *The Cinema of John Ford* by John Baxter, New York

1971; *John Ford* by Joseph McBride and Michael Wilmington, London 1975; *Anthologie du Cinéma*, Paris 1976; *John Ford* by Peter Bogdanovich, Berkeley 1978; *John Ford* by Andrew Sinclair, New York 1979; *Pappy: The Life of John Ford* by Dan Ford, Englewood Cliffs, New Jersey 1979; articles—"A Guide to the Study of the Historical Photoplay *Young Mr. Lincoln*" edited by Max J. Herzberg in *Photoplay Studies* (New York), no.9, 1939; "The 10th Muse in San Francisco" by Albert Johnson in *Sight and Sound* (London), spring 1955; "Press Conference" by Derek Hill in *Sight and Sound* (London), summer 1957; "Lamar Trotti" by Maynard T. Smith in *Films in Review* (New York), August/September 1958; "Henry Fonda" by John Springer in *Films in Review* (New York), November 1960; "The 5 Worlds of John Ford" by Douglas McVay in *Films and Filming* (London), June 1962; issue on Ford, *Focus on Film* (London), spring 1971; issue on Ford, *Velvet Light Trap* (Madison, Wisconsin), August 1971; "*Young Mr. Lincoln*" by Joseph McBride and Michael Wilmington in *Film Heritage* (Dayton, Ohio), summer 1971; issue on "Ford's Stock Company" in *Filmkritik* (Munich), January 1972; "Der Mister Lincoln des Mister Ford" by Sergei Eisenstein in *Filmkritik* (Munich), May 1972; "Une 'Reprise' ciné-club: *Young Mr. Lincoln* de John Ford" by R. Gieure in *Cinéma* (Paris), March 1972; "John Ford's *Young Mr. Lincoln*: A Collective Text by the Editors of *Cahiers du cinéma*" in *Screen* (London), autumn 1972; "Afterword" by Peter Wollen in *Screen* (London), autumn 1972; "How Green Was Your Valley Then, John Ford" by Ken Mate in *Velvet Light Trap* (Madison, Wisconsin), vol.8, 1973; "Notes on the Text, John Ford's *Young Mr. Lincoln* by the Editors of *Cahiers du cinéma*" by B. Brewster in *Screen* (London), autumn 1973; "Notes sur deux films Hollywoodiens" by J.C. Mairal in *Image et son* (Paris), no.269 (fiche), 1973; issue on *Young Mr. Lincoln* in *Filmkritik* (Munich), February 1974; "Critique of Cine-Structuralism" by Brian Henderson in *Film Quarterly* (Berkeley), winter 1973-74; "Paradigmatic Structures in *Young Mr. Lincoln*" by R. Abel in *Wide Angle* (Athens, Ohio), no.4, 1978; "*Young Mr. Lincoln* Reconsidered: An Essay on the Theory and Practice of Film Criticism" by R. Abramson and R. Thompson in *Ciné-Tracts* (Montreal), fall 1978; "*Young Mr. Lincoln*" by J.A. Place in *Wide Angle* (Athens, Ohio), no.4, 1978; "*Young Mr. Lincoln* de John Ford" in *Skrien* (Amsterdam), winter 1978-79; "The Spectator of American Symbolic Forms: Re-Reading John Ford's *Young Mr. Lincoln*" by Nick Browne in *Film Reader* (Evanston, Illinois), no.4, 1979; "*Young Mr. Lincoln*" by Janey Place in *Magill's Survey of Cinema, Vol. IV* edited by Frank N. Magill, Englewood Cliffs, New Jersey 1980.

*   *   *

Young Mr. Lincoln was one of three films, all among John Ford's finest, to be released in 1939. Each was noteworthy for a number of reasons, and each introduced to the director's work a particular aspect that would become identified with the thematic concerns of the rest of his career. *Stagecoach*, for example, was his first film with John Wayne and his first use of Arizona's spectacular Monument Valley as a locale. Both would become Ford institutions in succeeding years. *Drums Along the Mohawk*, the earliest of his histories, in terms of its internal chronology, also marked the beginning of an examination of the American past that would occupy much of the rest of his life.

Young Mr. Lincoln was Ford's first film with Henry Fonda, another actor with a very definite function within the director's films. Through careful crafting of Fonda's character and the

script, Ford created for the actor a persona that embodied the traditional qualities of American idealism, and a liberal attitude toward the development of the absolutes of civilization. Though this persona was continued in other Ford-Fonda collaborations until 1948 when the actor returned to the New York stage, it was initially employed to elevate the story of Lincoln's early years to the level of a national myth, a myth consistent with the director's own philosophy.

In *Drums Across the Mohawk*, the Fonda persona's aspirations toward civilization are inherent in his yearning for land and a home. When he loses his home, much of his personal stability and self-reliance vanishes with it, and the structure of his family life hovers near fragmentation. In *Young Mr. Lincoln*, however, the idea of civilization is represented by the broadest concept of the law—one that is indicated by Lincoln's statement in the trial scene. His profession that "I may not know much about the law, but I know what is right!" has less to do with a court of justice than it does to Ford's idea of a higher law. The future president is presented by the film as a proponent of God's law, which Ford relates, through a number of scenes, as being intertwined with concepts of family, the future and nature itself. One scene, in which Lincoln is sitting by a river studying Blackstone's *Commentaries* and is interrupted by Ann Rutledge to talk about the future, ties all of these ideas together as does his monologue at her grave when he invokes her memory (as well as that of his deceased mother's) to aid in his decision to become a lawyer. The entire trial sequence, in fact, casts Lincoln in the role of a defender of the American family, attemptng to keep it intact.

The use of the poem, "Nancy Hanks," at the beginning of the film establishes for the viewer a consciousness of the historical Lincoln while, at the same time, serving notice that the function of art is not simply a retelling of history but a rewriting as well. Therefore, the story that follows utilizes the audience's already mythical assumptions concerning the historical personage as one element in Ford's creation of the new myth. The character is removed from its historical context, its useful qualities extracted and merged with those of the carefully constructed Fonda persona to be employed for Ford's own purposes. So striking was the merger of the Fonda and Lincoln qualities that, for many years, the film was heralded solely for the youthful exuberance of Fonda's performance. Now, however, the film is appreciated for its classic craftsmanship, and as an exposition of the mythmaking process in America.

—Stephen L. Hanson

Z. Production: Reggane Films (Algeria) and O.N.C.I.C. (France); EastmanColor (print by Technicolor), 35mm; running time: 123 mins., American version: 127 mins., Canadian version: 152 mins., and West German version: 145 mins.; length: 3472 meters. Released February 1969, Paris.

Produced by Jacques Perrin and Hamed Rachedi with Eric Schlumberger and Philippe d'Argila; screenplay by Constantin Costa-Gavras and Jorge Semprun; from the novel by Vassilis Vassilikos; directed by Constantin Costa-Gavras; photography by Raoul Coutard; edited by François Bonnot; sound by Michèle Boehm; art direction by Jacques d'Ovidio; music by Mikis Theodorakis, music arranged and conducted by Bernard Gérard.

Filmed in Algiers. Cannes Film Festival, Best Actor (Trintignant), 1969; Academy Awards for Best Foreign Film and Film Editing, 1969; New York Film Critics Awards, Best Motion Picture and Best Direction, 1969.

Cast: Yves Montand (*The Deputy Z*); Jean-Louis Trintignant (*The Magistrate*); Jacques Perrin (*The Journalist*); François Pértier (*The Public Prosecutor*); Irene Papas (*Hélène*); Georges Géret (*Nick*); Charles Denner (*Manuel*); Bernard Fresson (*Matt*); Jean Bouise (*Pirou*); Jean-Pierre Miquel (*Pierre*); Renato Salvatori (*Yago*); Marcel Bozzufi (*Vago*); Julien Guiomar (*Colonel*); Pierre Dux (*General*); Guy Mairess (*Dumas*); Magail Noël (*Nick's sister*); Clotilde Joano (*Shoula*); Maurice Baquet (*Bald man*); Jean Dasté (*Coste*); Gérard Darrieu (*Baron*); José Artur (*Newspaper editor*); Van Doude (*Hospital director*); Eva Simonet (*Niki*); Hassan Hassani (*General's chauffeur*); Gabriel Jabbour (*Bozzini*); Jean-François Gobbi (*Jimmy the boxer*); Andrée Tainsy (*Nick's mother*); Steve Gadler (*English photographer*); Bob de Bragelonne (*Undersecretary of State*); Sid Ahmed Agoumi; Allel El Mouhib; Habib Reda; Georges Rouquier.

Publications:

Script—"*Z*" in *Avant-Scène du cinéma* (Paris), October 1969; reviews—by Pauline Kael in the *New Yorker*, 13 December 1969; review by Gordon Gow in *Films and Filming* (London), December 1969; review by Andrew Sarris in *The Village Voice* (New York), 11 December 1969; review by Aline Derain in *Films in Review* (New York), January 1970; review in *Film Society Review* (New York), January 1970; review by Lawrence Loewinger in *Film Quarterly* (Berkeley), winter 1969-70; articles—by Dan Georgakas in *Film Society Review* (New York), December 1969; article by Joseph Kostolefsky in *Take One* (Montreal), March/April 1969; "Cinéma et politique" by Philippe Esnault in *Avant-Scène du cinéma* (Paris), October 1969; "Costa-Gavras Talks" by Dan Georgakas and Gary Crowdus in *Take One* (Montreal), July/August 1969; "Pointing Out the Problems" by Costa-Gavras in *Films and Filming* (London), June 1970; "Costa-Gavras Talks About *Z*" by Dan Georgakas and Gary Crowdus in *Cineaste* (New York), winter 1969-70; "On the Scene: Costa-Gavras" in *Playboy* (Chicago), November 1970; "Jean-Louis Trintignant" by Molly Haskell in *Show* (Los Angeles), 20 August 1970; "Fascism in the Contemporary Cinema" by Joan Mellen in *Film Quarterly* (Berkeley), summer 1971; "An Interview with Costa-Gavras and Jorge Semprun" in *Film Society Review* (New York), January 1971; "*Z* Movies or What Hath Costa-Gavaras Wrought" by G. Hennebelle in *Cineaste* (New York), no.2, 1974; "In Contresens idéologique sur l'oeuvre de Costa-Gavras" by A. Marty in *Image et son* (Paris), December 1977.

ZEMLYA. Earth. Production: VUFKU (Kiev); black and white, 35mm, silent; length: 1704 meters, 6 reels. Released 8 April 1930, Kiev.

Scripted and directed by Alexander Dovzhenko; photography by Danilo Demutsky; art direction by Vasily Krichevsky; music for performance by Leonid Revutsky; assistant directors: Julia (Ioulya) Solnteseva and Lazar Bodyk.

Filmed April-November 1929 in Poltava.

Cast: Stepon Shkurat (*Opanas Trubenko*); Semen Svashenko (*Vasil, the son*); Nikola Nademsky (*Grandfather Semen*); Yelena Maximova (*Natalka, Vasil's fiancée*); I. Franko (*Arkhip Belokon, a Kulak*); P. Masokha (*Khoma*); V. Mikhailov (*Father Gerasim, the priest*); P. Petrik (*Kravchina-Chuprina, the Komsomol Secretary*); Ioulya Sointseva (*Vasil's sister*).

Publications:

Scripts—*La Terre* (scenario in Russian, English, and French), Moscow 1965; *Mother: A Film by V.I. Pudovkin and Earth: A Film by Alexander Dovzhenko*, New York 1973; books—*Kino, A History of the Russian and Soviet Film* by Jay Leyda, New York 1942; *An Index to the Creative Work of Alexander Dovjenko* by Jay Leyda, supplement to *Sight and Sound* (London), index series, 1947; *Alexander Dovzhenko* by R. Yourenev, Moscow 1958 (name transliterated as R. Jurenew in German translation, 1964); *Panorama du cinéma soviétique* by Marcel Martin, Paris 1960; *20 ans de cinéma soviétique* by Luda et Jean Schnitzer, Paris 1963; *Poetika Dovzhenko* by Igor Rachuk, Moscow 1964; *Dovjenko* by Luda and Jean Schnitzer, Paris 1966; *Alexandre Dovjenko* by Marcel Oms, Lyon 1968; *Dovjenko* by Alexandr Mariamov, Moscow 1968; *Alexandre Dovjenko* by Barthélemy Amengual, Paris 1970; *Alexander Dovzhenko: The Poet as Filmmaker*, edited by Marco Carynnyk, Cambridge, Massachusetts 1973; *Cinema, The Magic Vehicle: A Guide to Its Achievement: Journey One: The Cinema Through 1949* edited by Adam Garbicz and Jacek Klinowski, Metuchen, New Jersey 1975; articles—"Interview with Dovjenko" in *Close-Up* (London), no.4, 1930; "Interview de A. Dovjenko" by Georges Sadoul in *Les Lettres françaises* (Paris), 1956; "Dovzhenko—Poet of Eternal Life" by Ivor Montagu in *Sight and Sound* (London), 1957; special issue, *Film* (Venice), August 1957; "Autobiography" by Alexander Dovzhenko in *Iskousstvo Kino* (Moscow), no.5, 1958; "The Films of Alexander Dovzhenko" by Charles Shibuk in *New York Film Bulletin*, no.11-14, 1961; "Julia Solntséva et la terre ukrainienne" by Michel Capdenac in *Les Lettres françaises* (Paris), 25 May 1961; article by Ken Kelman in *Film Culture* (New York), winter 1963-64; "Alexander Dovzhenko" in *Anthologie du cinéma*, Vol. I, Paris 1966; special issue devoted to Dovzhenko of *Iskusstvo kino* (Moscow), September 1974; "Ein Epos unserer Epoche" by S. Frejlih in *Film und Fernsehen* (Berlin), August 1974; "*Zemlya*" by J. Pym in *Monthly Film Bulletin* (London), February 1980.

*   *   *

Earth is a tribute to life in the Ukraine, the birthplace of its creator, Alexander Dovzhenko. The film's star is essentially the Ukrainian village in which the story is set: it is not necessarily a tale of Russian farmers and kulaks but a visual poem about life, and the calm acceptance of death.

Earth's scenario is virtually lacking in plot: in fact, one of its themes—the triumph of modern farm equipment over a primitive methodology—is similiar to that of Sergei Eisenstein's *Old and New*. Youthful peasants in the community join together to purchase a tractor, to efficiently operate their farms. Vassily, head of the village committee, reaps corn with the assistance of the machine: women fasten together the cut stalks from the earth, a threshing machine toils in the fields, and the peasants produce an abundant harvest. The town's kulaks (or, well-to-do landowners who profited from the sweat of the poorer farmers; as a class they opposed Soviet politics and collectivization of the land) are intimidated by this show of unity. At the end of a workday, young lovers stare at the sunset and animals peacefully graze in the meadows. Vassily, who had earlier plowed beyond the boundaries of a kulak's farm, strolls home in the moonlight and is shot by a kulak. His father grieves over the corpse, but will not allow a traditional Christian burial. Instead, the villagers carry Vassily in an open bier, through the fields. His murderer runs into the cemetery, blurts out that he is the peasant's killer, and dances amid the graves in a weak imitation of Vassily's movements before the moment of his death. But the killer is ignored. A rain—tears from the sky—falls, and shines on the crops. The clouds disappear, and the sun glistens and dries the earth.

This short synopsis does not effectively describe the film's content and effect on the viewer. Dovzhenko lyrically captures what the earth—the soil, and the life-sustaining crops it produces—means to human beings. The earth must be lovingly nurtured, so that corn and wheat may be reaped and mouths may be fed. (Dovzhenko shot the film on the rich terrain of his beloved Ukraine.) Most significantly, the film is at once a celebration of life, and an acknowledgement of the inevitability of life's end. Dovzhenko's images, all in meticulously composed shots, are unforgettable: in the film's prologue a dying man (the grandfather of Vassily, a character patterned after the filmmaker's grandfather), serene as he approaches his end, happily pierces an apple with his teeth; Vassily ecstatically dances in the summer moonlight, kicking up dust and feeling every moment of his life before it is abruptly ended by a bullet; apple tree branches brush over the face of Vassily's corpse in the funeral caravan. In sequence after sequence, Dovzhenko brings together the two ultimate but contrasting realities: life and death. Death is not a gloomy, depressing finality, but a necessary and logical occurrence. If babies are to be born and the world replenished with the hopes, desires and energy of youth, some must vacate the earth and allow them time and space. Similarly, the earth must yield its crops so that it may again commence the cycle necessary to feed and nourish the hungry.

Earth is clearly not apolitical. Lewis Jacobs described it as a "rhapsody of victory for a new society." Dovzhenko himself explained, "I conceived *Earth* as a film that would herald the beginning of a new life in the villages." But, in its day, the film was quite controversial. Some Soviet critics were quick to condemn it as politically incorrect because the lyricism overrides the storyline. In addition, it focuses on a universal, philosophical theme; it does not just merely detail specific events and struggles relating to the Revolution. A particularly pointed article in *Izvestia* entitled "The Philosophers" by Demyan Bedny (the pseudonym for Yefim Pridvorov, considered a major proletarain poet of the 1920s), resulted in the editing of several sequences, including the scene where the tractor's radiator boils over and is cooled by the collective urine of the peasants, and another depicting Vassily's betrothed, naked and crazed with grief, mourning his death. "I was so stunned by (Bedny's) attack," Dovzhenko wrote, "so ashamed to be seen in public, that I literally aged and turned gray overnight. It was a real emotional trauma for me. At first I wanted to die."

After *Earth* premiered in Russia, Dovzhenko brought the film to Paris and Berlin, and under the title *Soil*, it opened in New York during the fall of 1930. The negative of *Earth* was destroyed by the Germans during World War II, but a copy of the original release print fortunately survived.

Earth created a sensation outside the Soviet Union. Its simple imagery influenced other directors, particularly documentary filmmakers in England and the United States. Today, it is Dovzhenko's most famous film, and one of the great achievements of world cinema.

—Rob Edelman

ZÉRO DE CONDUITE. Jeunes Diable au College. Zero for Conduct. Production: Argui-Film; black and white, 35mm; running time: 44 mins., some sources list 47 mins.; length: 1200 meters. Released 1946 (banned by the censors in August 1933 until 15 February 1946).

Production supervised by Henri Storck; scripted, directed, and edited by Jean Vigo; photography by Boris Kaufman; sound engineered by Royne and Bocquel; music by Maurice Jaubert; assistant directors: Albert Riera, Henri Storck, and Pierre Merle.

Filmed 24 December 1932-22 January 1933 in Gaumont studios.

Cast: Jean Daste (*Superintendent Huguet*); Robert Le Flon (*Superintendent Parrain, called "Pète-Sec"*); Delphin (*Principal*); Blanchar (*Superintendent Général, called "Bec de gaz"*); Larive (*Chemistry professor*); Mme. Emile (*Madame Colin, called "Mère Haricot"*); Louis de Gonzague-Frick (*Le Préfet*); Rafa (Raphael) Diligent (*Fireman*); Felix Labisse (*Fireman*); Georges Vakalo (*Fireman*); Georges Patin (*Fireman*); Henri Storck (*Le Curé*); Michele Fayard (*Correspondent's girl*); Georges Berger (*Correspondent*); Louis Lefebvre (*Caussat*); Gilbert Pruchon (*Colin*); Coco Golstein (*Bruel*); Gerard de Bedarieux (*Tabard*).

Publications:

Script—"*Zéro de Conduite*" in *Avant-Scène du cinéma* (Paris), 15 December 1962; books—*Jean Vigo* by Joseph and Harry Feldman, new index series, no.4, British Film Institute, London 1951; *Le Surréalisme au cinéma* by Ado Kyrou, Paris 1953; *Jean Vigo* by Paul Emilio Salès Gomès, Paris 1957; *Hommage à Jean Vigo* by Freddy Bauche, Paris 1962; *Jean Vigo* by Michèle Estève, monograph published by *Etudes cinématographiques*, Paris 1966; *Jean Vigo* by Pierre Lherminier, Paris 1967; *Anarchist Cinema* by Alan Lovell, London 1967; *Jean Vigo* by John M. Smith, London 1972; *Jean Vigo* by Luis Filipe Rocha, Porto Portugal 1982; articles—on the shooting of *Zéro de conduite* in *Cinémonde* (Paris), 2 February 1933; "Zero de conduite and L'Atalante" by James Agee in the *Nation* (New York), 12 July 1947; "Remembrance of Jean Vigo" by Gyula Zilzer in *Hollywood Quarterly*, winter 1947-48; "The Films of Jean Vigo" by H.G. Weinberg in *Cinema* (Beverly Hills), July 1947; issue on Vigo of *Ciné-Club* (Paris), no.5, 1949; "The Work of Jean Vigo" by George Barbarow in *Politics*, winter 1948; article on *Zéro de conduite* in *Positif* (Paris), no.7, 1953; "An Interview with Boris Kaufman" by Jonas Mekas in *Film Culture* (New York), no.4, 1955; "Portrait of Vigo" by Dudley Shaw Ashton in *Film* (London), December 1955; issue on Vigo of *Premier Plan* (Lyon), no.19, 1961; "Vigo: Ce que nous avons de meilleur en nous" by François Chevassu in *Avant-Scène du cinéma* (Paris), 15 December 1962; "Anarchy, Surrealism, and Optimism in *Zéro*

de conduite by B. Mills in *Cinema* (London), no.8, 1971;
"Anarki, surrealism och optimism i *C i uppförande*" by B. Mills
in *Filmrutan* (Stockholm), no.1, 1972; "The Playground for
Jean Vigo" by B. Teush in *Film Heritage* (Dayton, Ohio), fall
1973; "The Playground of Jean Vigo" by B. Teush in *Film
Heritage* (New York), fall 1973; "Vigo/Laubert" by C. Gorbman
in *Ciné-Tracts* (Montreal), summer 1977.

* * *

Zéro de conduite is one of only four films made by Jean Vigo
during his brief but notable career in film. (He died in 1934 at the
age of 29 just before the release of his final film, *L'Atalante*.)
Zéro de conduite is a short feature concerning life in a boy's
boarding school, focusing on four of the students. The title refers
to the frequent "zeroes" they receive when they fail to conform to
the standards of behavior imposed on them by their teachers.
The film culminates with a student rebellion launched during a
school assembly in the presence of local dignitaries.

Before it received general distribution, the film was banned by
the French Board of Censorship, presumably for its harsh, derogatory portrayal of French bourgeois institutions, and was not
commercially released in France until after World War II. (In his
biography of Vigo, P.E. Salès Gomès claims there is reason to
believe the order to ban the film originated from a higher
government ministry.) *Zéro de conduite* is often cited as the
precursor of François Truffaut's *Les 400 Coups* and Lindsay
Anderson's *If....* The comparisons are based on the film's sympathetic attitude towards the position of the children, culminating
in the rallying cry for liberty, and its corresponding condemnation of the rigid policies and hypocritical posture adopted by the
adults who control the children's lives. But in other ways the film
is very different from its so-called successors.

Vigo's films are admired for, among other things, their blend
of realistic detail and a poetic-surrealist sensibility. This quality
pervades *Zéro de conduite*. The opening sequence of the film is
exemplary in this respect. As the film begins, two of the school-
boys share a train compartment on the way back to school after
vacation. They play with various toys they have recently
acquired, transforming them in the process: balloons become
breasts, a small flute is played through the nose, and, using
feathers, they dress themselves as chickens. Finally they light
cigars, filling the compartment with smoke, creating a hazy
dream-like image. In this atmosphere, the one adult in the compartment, who is sleeping and limp, is declared dead. If the scene
opens with "realistic," concrete details (of decor and costume), it
shifts in the course of the children's play effecting an alteration in
the tone and perception of the space. Similar transformations
occur throughout the film. In the middle class a new teacher, and
the only sympathetic one, performs balancing tricks on his desk,
and sketches a cartoon figure which suddenly becomes animated. In the world of childhood and imagination, magical
metamorphosis can occur at any time.

The behavior and appearance of the authority figures are held
up for ridicule. The school principal is a midget who sports a
large top hat; in his office he keeps the hat like a relic under a
glass dome on the mantlepiece which he can barely reach. The
science teacher is an obese, overbearing man who almost walks
into a skeleton dangling in the classroom. During the commemoration day ceremony, the public audience is comprised of dignitaries in full-dress uniforms and life-size, costumed dummies. (If
this was in part due to financial restraints on the production, it is
fully in line with the film's representation of adults and ceremon-
ious activity.) These characterizing details not only condemn the
adult world to absurdity, but also contribute to the bizarre visual
texture of the film and its partially dream-like world.

The most extreme excursion into fantasy occurs the night
before the commemoration day assembly. In the dormitory, the
rebellion is launched. All of the objects in the room are thrown
around as the children express their disdain for authority. Part
way through the scene there is a shift to slow motion as pillows
and feathers fly, and the children parade through the room. The
teacher in charge in unable to constrain them and falls asleep. In
the morning he is tied to his bed and set upright in a gesture of
mock crucifixion. The four leaders of the rebellion carry their
flag to the roof and hurl various objects at the dignitaries
assembled in the courtyard. The film concludes with the four
boys marching up the rooftops towards the sky.

Vigo's depiction of school life in *Zéro de conduite* is often
described in biographical terms. In particular it is seen as
expressing the misery he experienced as a child in boarding
school and the subversive tendencies of his father, a militant
anarchist who died (reportedly murdered) in prison when Vigo
was 12 years old. While his personal circumstances certainly
influenced his attitudes and ideas, the emphasis on the film as an
autobiography obscures the degree to which the film transforms
the world. In this regard it should be recalled that Vigo's career
was closely affiliated with French avant-garde film activity in the
late 1920s.

Vigo did experience difficulties in the production of the film,
notably in the area of finance. But he was aided by a group of
committed assistants. Foremost among those in Boris Kaufman,
director of photography on all Vigo's films. They had worked
closely on *À propos de Nice*, Vigo's first film, establishing the
basis for future collaboration. This film revealed Vigo's interest
in combining an avant-garde use of the medium with aggressive
social critique. The music for *Zéro de conduite* was composed by
Maurice Jaubert, and contributes to the overall tone of the film.
He worked particularly hard on the music for the nighttime
revolt to achieve a dream-like effect; after writing the basic score
it was rescored and recorded in reverse, and then re-recorded
backwards to restore the original.

—M.B. White

NOTES ON ADVISERS
AND CONTRIBUTORS

AFFRON, Charles. Essayist. Professor of French, New York University, since 1965. Author of *Star Acting: Gish, Garbo, Davis*, 1977, and *Cinema and Sentiment*, 1982. **Essays:** All About Eve; The Best Years of Our Lives; It's a Wonderful Life; The Little Foxes; Mr. Smith Goes to Washington; Ninotchka; A Place in the Sun; Le quai des brumes; A Star Is Born; The Wind.

AFFRON, Mirella Jona. Essayist. Associate Professor, Program in Cinema Studies since 1973, and Chairperson, Department of Performing and Creative Arts since 1977, College of Staten Island, City University of New York. Member of the Executive Council, Society for Cinema Studies, since 1981. **Essays:** The Southerner; La terra trema; Umberto D.

ANDERSON, Joseph. Adviser. Manager for Operations, WGBH, Boston, President, Mass Comm/Masu Komi media consultants. Author, with Donald Richie, of *Japanese Film: Art and Industry*, 1959, 1982.

ANDREW, Dudley. Adviser and Essayist. Professor since 1981 and Head of the Film Division, University of Iowa (joined faculty, 1969). Author of *Major Film Theories*, 1976; *André Bazin*, 1978; *Kenji Mizoguchi: A Guide to References and Resources* (co-author), 1981; *Concepts in Film Theory*, 1984; and *Film in the Aura of Art*, 1984. **Essays:** À propos de Nice; Les Amants; La Bataille du rail; Chikamatsu monogatari; Les Dames du Bois de Boulogne; Le Diable au corps; Gion no shimai; Les Jeux interdits; Journal d'un curé de campagne; Jules et Jim; Le Million; Pépé-le Moko; Saikaku ichidai onna; Tirez sur le pianiste.

ARMES, Roy. Essayist. Reader in Film and Television at the Middlesex Polytechnic, London. Author of *French Cinema since 1946*, 1966, 1970; *The Cinema of Alain Resnais*, 1968; *French Film*, 1970; *Patterns of Realism*, 1972; 1983; *Film and Reality*, 1974; *The Ambiguous Image*, 1976; *A Critical History of British Cinema*, 1978; *The Films of Alain Robbe-Grillet*, 1981; and *A History of French Cinema*, 1984. **Essays:** L'Argent; La Belle et la bête; Le Chagrin et la Pitié; Charulata; Chronique des anneés de braise; Les Diaboliques; Fantômas; Farrebique; La Femme du Boulanger; Feu Mathias Pascal; Napoléon; Le Sang d'un poète; Les Vampires.

BARDARSKY, Dimitar. Adviser and Essayist. With the Short Films Department, Bulgarian Cinematography, Sofia, since 1982. With the Programming and Publications Department, Bulgarian National Film Archive, Sofia, 1978-81. Contributor to and editor of the biographical section, *In the World of Cinema*, 3 volumes, 1982-83. **Essays:** Koziyat rog; Sterne.

BARNOUW, Erik. Adviser and Essayist. Professor Emeritus of Dramatic Arts, Columbia University, New York City, since 1973 (joined faculty, 1946); organized and chaired the film division of the School of the Arts). Head, Writers Guild of America, 1957-59. Film and Television Specialist, 1977, and Chief of the Motion Picture, Broadcasting and Recorded Sound Division, 1978-81, Library of Congress, Washington, D.C. Author of *Indian Film*, with S. Krishnaswamy, 1963, 1980; *Documentary: A History of the Nonfiction Film*, 1974, 1983; *Tube of Plenty: The Evolution of American Television*, 1975; *The Sponsor: Notes on a Modern Potentate*, 1978; and *The Magician and the Cinema*, 1981. **Essay:** Hiroshima-Nagasaki.

BASINGER, Jeanine. Essayist. Professor of Film, Wesleyan University, Middletown, Connecticut, since 1969. Trustee, American Film Institute; Member of the Advisory Board, Foun-

dation for Independent Video and Film and Association of Independent Video and Filmmakers Inc. Author of *Working with Kazan*, 1973; *Shirley Temple*, 1975; *Gene Kelly*, 1976; *Lana Turner*, 1977; *Anthony Mann: A Critical Analysis*, 1979. **Essays:** An American in Paris; The Devil Is a Woman; Johnny Guitar; The Miracle of Morgan's Creek; Shock Corridor; Sullivan's Travels.

BAXTER, John. Essayist. Novelist, screenwriter, and film historian. Visiting Lecturer, Hollins College, Virginia, 1974-75; programmed seasons at the National Film Theatre, London, and worked as broadcaster with B.B.C. Radio and Television, 1976-81. Author of six novels, two anthologies of science fiction (editor), various screenplays for documentary films and features, and works of film criticism: *Hollywood in the Thirties*, 1968; *The Australian Cinema*, 1970; *Science Fiction in the Cinema*, 1970; *The Gangster Film*, 1970; *The Cinema of Josef von Sternberg*, 1971; *The Cinema of John Ford*, 1971; *Hollywood in the Sixties*, 1972; *Sixty Years of Hollywood*, 1973; *An Appalling Talent: Ken Russell*, 1973; *Stunt*, 1974; *The Hollywood Exiles*, 1976; *King Vidor*, 1976; and, with Brian Norris, *The Video Handbook*, 1982. **Essays:** Accattone; The Big Parade; Der blaue Engel; Casablanca; Chronique d'un été; The Crowd; Et...Dieu créa la femme; The Grapes of Wrath; The Last Wave.

BECK, Sandra L. Essayist. Technical Assistant, Museum of Modern Art Film Study Center and Film Circulation Department, New York City. **Essays:** Fröken Julie; Körkarlen; Pickpocket.

BOCK, Audie. Essayist. Freelance author and lecturer; visiting lecturer posts held at Harvard, Yale, University of California, etc., 1975-83; Assistant Producer of the International version of Kurosawa's *Kagemusha*, 1980. Author of *Japanese Film Directors*, 1978, and *Mikio Naruse: un maitre du cinema japonais*, 1983; translator of *Something Like an Autobiography* by Kurosawa, 1982. **Essay:** Ai no corrida.

BODEEN, DeWitt. Adviser and Essayist. Screenwriter and film critic. Author of: screenplays—*Cat People*, 1942; *Seventh Victim*, 1943; *Curse of the Cat People*, 1944; *The Yellow Canary*, 1944; *The Enchanted Cottage*, 1945; *Night Song*, 1947; *I Remember Mama*, 1948; *Mrs. Mike*, 1949; *Billy Budd*, 1962; also numerous teleplays, 1950-68; film criticism/history—*Ladies of the Footlights*; *The Films of Cecil B. DeMille*; *Chevalier*; *From Hollywood*; *More from Hollywood*; *13 Castle Walk* (novel); editor—*Who Wrote the Movie and What Else Did He Write?* *Essays:* Camille; City Lights; Les Enfants du paradis; Greed; Henry V; The Merry Widow; Viridiana.

BOWERS, Ronald. Essayist. Financial Editor, E.F. Hutton and Company, since 1982. Editor, *Films in Review*, 1979-81. Author of *The MGM Stock Company*, with James Robert Parish, 1973; and *The Selznick Players*, 1976. **Essays:** La caduta degli dei; Le Carrosse d'or; Le Crime de Monsieur Lange; Gösta Berlings Saga; Great Expectations; Little Caesar; Lola; Look Back in Anger; The Magnificent Ambersons; Miracolo a Milano; 1900; Los Olvidados; Orphée; Sciuscia; La strada; This Sporting Life; Il vangelo secondo Matteo.

BOWLES, Stephen E. Essayist. Associate Professor of Film, University of Miami, since 1976. Author of *An Approach to Film Study*, 1974; *Index to Critical Film Reviews from British and American Film Periodicals 1930-1971*, 3 volumes, 1974-75; *Sidney Lumet: References and Resources*, 1979; and *Index to*

Critical Film Reviews: Supplement I, 1971-1976, 1983; associate editor of *The Film Book Bibliography 1940-1975*, 1979. **Essays:** Blow-Up; On the Waterfront; Shane.

BOYAJIAN, Marco Starr. Essayist. Cable/Film Critic for *Manhattan East*, since 1981. Staff Member/Editor, *John Willis' Screen World*, volumes 31-33, 1980-82. **Essay:** Blade Runner.

BRITO, Rui Santana. Adviser. Film Historian, Cinemateca Portuguesa, Lisbon.

BURGOYNE, Robert. Adviser. Lecturer in Film Theory, New York University. Editor, *Enclitic*. Author of *Film Semiotics: A Lexicon of Terms*, 1983.

BURTON, Julianne. Essayist. Associate Professor, Merrill College and the Board of Studies in Literature, University of California at Santa Cruz, since 1982 (Assistant Professor, 1974-82). Author of more than 40 publications on the Latin American cinema. **Essay:** Tire die.

CAMPER, Fred. Essayist. Independent filmmaker and writer on film, since 1965. Assistant Professor, 1976-83, and Chairperson of the Filmmaking Department, 1977-81, School of the Art Institute of Chicago. **Essay:** Unsere Afrikareise.

CIMENT, Michel. Adviser. Associate Professor in American Studies, University of Paris (7). Member of the Editorial Board, *Positif*, Paris. Author of *Erich von Stroheim*, 1967; *Kazan by Kazan*, 1973; *Le Dossier Rosi*, 1976; *Le Livre de Losey*, 1979; *Kubrick*, 1980; *Les Conquerants d'un Nouveau Monde* (collected essays), 1981; *Schatzberg, de la Photo au Cinema*, 1982; co-author, with Annie Tresgot, *Portrait of a 60% Perfect Man: Billy Wilder*, 1980; *Elia Kazan, An Outsider*, 1982; *All about Mankiewicz*, 1983.

CLEMENTS, William M. Essayist. Professor of English, Arkansas State University. Author, with Frances M. Malpezzi, *Native American Folklore 1879-1979: An Annotated Bibliography*, 1983. **Essay:** Kagemusha.

CONLEY, Tom. Essayist. Professor and Chairman, Department of French and Italian, University of Minnesota, Minneapolis. Editor, *Enclitic*, since 1977. Author of *Cesures, estudios cinematographicos*, 1984. **Essays:** The Lady from Shanghai; Touch of Evil; Vivre sa vie.

COOK, David A. Adviser and Essayist. Associate Professor, Emory University, Atlanta, since 1977 (Assistant Professor, 1973-77). Author of *A History of Narrative Film*, 1981. **Essays:** Teni zabytykh predkov; The Wild Bunch.

CRIPPS, Thomas. Essayist. Professor of History and Coordinator of the Graduate Program in Popular Culture, Morgan State University, Baltimore, since 1961. Producer-Writing, Westinghouse Broadcasting, 1968-72. Author of *Slow Fade to Black: The Negro in American Film 1900-1942*, 1977, and *Black Film as Genre*, 1978; editor of *The Green Pastures*, 1979. **Essay:** Der ewige Jude.

DERRY, Charles. Essayist. Head of Motion Pictures Studies, Wright State University, Dayton, Ohio, since 1978. Author of *Dark Dreams: A Psychological History of the Modern Horror Film*, 1978, and *The Film Book Bibliography 1940-1975*, with Jack Ellis and Sharon Kern, 1980. **Essays:** The Birds; La Femme infidèle; The Go-Between.

DUNAGAN, Clyde Kelly. Essayist. Instructor in Mathematics, University of Wisconsin Center, Sheboygan. **Essays:** Apocalypse Now; Bronenosets Potemkin; Gone With the Wind; M*A*S*H; Once Upon a Time in the West; A Streetcar Named Desire.

DUNBAR, Robert. Adviser and Essayist. Freelance film critic and historian; has held various visiting professorships and lectureships since 1975. Worked for Gainsborough and Gaumont-British Studios, 1933-38, 1948-49; Director of Public and Cultural Relations, British Embassy, Moscow, 1944-47; General Manager, Imperadio Pictures, 1949-51; independent producer of feature films and documentaries, 1952-63; Chairman, London School of Film Technique, 1963-74. **Essays:** Chapayev; The Maxim Trilogy; Putyovka v zhizn; Shchors; Turksib.

EDELMAN, Rob. Essayist. Editor, reporter and freelance writer, specializing in the arts, New York City. Associate Editor of *Leonard Maltin's TV Movies*. **Essays:** The Covered Wagon; Die Dreigroschenoper; Il giardino di Finzi-Contini; Husbands; J'Accuse; Johnny Got His Gun; Last Tango in Paris; Letyet zhuravli; The Mark of Zorro; Mat; Medium Cool; The Naked City; On the Town; Tol'able David; Underworld; Variété; Voina i mir; Zemlya.

ELLIS, Jack C. Adviser and Essayist. Professor of Film since 1956, and Chairman of the Department of Radio, Television and Film since 1980, Northwestern University, Evanston, Illinois. President, Chairman of the Board of Directors, and Newsletter Editor, American Federation of Film Societies, 1955-75; President, Treasurer, and Council Member, Society for Cinema Studies, 1959-82; Editor, *Cinema Journal*, 1976-82. Author of *A History of Film*, 1979; compiler, with Charles Derry and Sharon Kern, *The Film Book Bibliography 1940-1975*, 1979; editor, with Richard Dyer MacCann, *Cinema Examined*, 1982. **Essays:** Drifters; Fires Were Started; Listen to Britain; The March of Time; Night Mail; Primary; Rien que les heures; Why We Fight.

ELSNER-SOMMER, Gretchen. Essayist. Freelance film critic. Associate Editor of *Jump Cut* magazine. **Essays:** Die Ehe der Maria Braun; Mädchen in Uniform; Die verlorene Ehre der Katharina Blum.

ERENS, Patricia. Associate Professor, Rosary College, River Forest, Illinois, since 1977. Author of *Akira Kurosawa: A Guide to References and Resources*, 1979, and *The Jew in American Cinema*, 1984; editor of *Sexual Stratagems: The World of Women in Film*, 1979. **Essays:** Biruma no tategoto; Film d'amore e d'anarchia; Hadaka no shima; O slavnosti a hostech; Suna no onna.

EVERSON, William K. Adviser. Film critic/historian: teaches at New York University, the New School for Social Research, and the School of Visual Arts, New York City. Author of *The Art of W.C. Fields*; *Classics of the Horror Film*; *The Western*: etc.

FALLER, G.S. Essayist. Instructor at Northwestern University, Evanston, Illinois. Editor/Production Manager, Filmmakers of Philadelphia, 1977-78. Assistant Editor, *Film Reader 5*, 1982. **Essays:** Cabaret; 42nd Street; The Gold Diggers of 1933; If...; The Love Parade; Singin in the Rain.

FARNSWORTH, Rodney. Member of the Associate Faculty,

English and Linguistics, Indiana University-Purdue University, Fort Wayne, Indiana (member, visiting faculty, comparative literature and film studies, 1981-82). **Essays:** India Song; Ivan Groznyi; Sunrise.

FEINSTEIN, Howard. Essayist. Researcher and Archivist, Department of Film, Museum of Modern Art, New York, since 1979; Instructor, New York University Department of Cinema Studies, and University of Bridgeport, Connecticut, since 1983. **Essays:** Konyets Sankt-Peterburga; Lucia.

FERN, Annette. Essayist. Freelance arts critic, and researcher. **Essay:** A Night at the Opera.

FITZGERALD, Theresa. Adviser. Managing Director and Writer-Producer-Director, Camden Productions Ltd., London, since 1982. Secretary, London Screenwriters Workshop, since 1983. Researcher, Academic Information Retrieval, London, 1974-82; Part-time Administrator, Association of Independent Producers, London, 1982. Lecturer in Film and Television, Barking College of Technology, Romford, Essex, 1978-80. Co-author of the forthcoming (1986) *International Film Index*.

FULKS, Barry A. Essayist. Assistant Professor of History, University of Pittsburgh, since 1983. Author of various articles on the German cinema. **Essay:** Berlin: die Sinfonie der Grossstadt.

GIANNETTI, Louis D. Adviser. Member of the faculty, Case-Western Reserve University, Cleveland. Author of books and articles on the cinema.

GOMERY, Douglas. Adviser and Essayist. Associate Professor of Radio-TV-Film, University of Maryland, College Park. Author of *High Sierra*, 1979, and the forthcoming books, *Film History*, with Robert Allen, and *Hollywood Studio System*. **Essays:** Jaws; The Man Who Shot Liberty Valance; My Darling Clementine.

GOMEZ, Joseph. Essayist. Member of the faculty, Wayne State University, Detroit. **Essay:** Meg ker a nep.

HANSON, Patricia King. Essayist. Associate Editor, Salem Press, Fort Lee, New Jersey, since 1978. Bibliographer for History and Romance Languages, University of Southern California, 1971-78. Associated Editor, with Stephen L. Hanson, *Magill's Bibliography of Literary Criticism*, 4 volumes, 1979; *Magill's Survey of Cinema, series I*, 4 volumes, 1980, *series II*, 6 volumes, 1981; *Silent Films*, 3 volumes, 1982; *Foreign Language Films*, 6 volumes, 1984; also, *Magill's Annual Survey of Cinema*, 1982; and 1983; editor of the *American Film Institute Catalogue of Films 1911-1920*. **Essays:** All the King's Men; Lost Horizon; The Roaring Twenties; Rocky; Top Hat.

HANSON, Steve. Essayist. Humanities Bibliographer, University of Southern California, Los Angeles, since 1969. Associate Editor, with Patricia King Hanson, *Magill's Bibliography of Literary Criticism*, 4 volumes, 1979; *Magill's Survey of Cinema*, series I, 4 volumes, 1980, *series II*, 6 volumes 1981; *Silent Films*, 3 volumes, 1981; *Magill's Annual Survey of Cinema*, 1982; *Foreign Language Films*, 6 volumes, 1984. **Essays:** Arsenal; East of Eden; Freaks; Madame de...; The Man in the White Suit; Neobychanye priklyucheniya Mistera Vesta v strane bolsheviko; 8½; Patton; The Public Enemy; Roma, città aperta; Young Mr. Lincoln.

HARRIS, Ann. Essayist. Doctoral student in cinema studies, New York University. **Essays:** Im Lauf der Zeit; Die Mörder sind unter uns; Salvatore Giuliano.

HECK-RABI, Louise. Essayist. Freelance writer. Public and special librarian, 1955-70. Author of *Women Filmmakers: A Critical Reception*, 1983. **Essays:** Cléo de cinq à sept; La Coquille et le clergyman; Olympia.

HENRY, Catherine. Essayist. Director of College Publications, University of Chicago, since 1980. **Essays:** The African Queen; Laura; M; The Night of the Hunter; Orfeu Negro.

HIRANO, Kyoko. Essayist. Doctoral student in cinema studies, New York University, since 1982. Editor of *Cinema Gras*, Tokyo, 1977-79. **Essays:** Entotsu no mieru basho; Jujiro; Koshikei, Nobe; Samma no aji; Shonen.

HOLDSTEIN, Deborah H. Essayist. Assistant Professor of English, Illinois Institute of Technology, Chicago, since 1980. **Essays:** Blackmail; Dracula; Duck Soup; Easy Rider; The Godfather; North by Northwest; Stagecoach; The 39 Steps.

JOHNSON, Timothy. Essayist. Freelance writer, Los Angeles, since 1978. Editor and Co-Compiler, *Crime Fiction Criticism: An Annotated Bibliography*, 1981; author of *Celluloid Egghead: Hollywood's Portrayal of the Intellectual*, 1984. **Essays:** Jigokumon; Ukigusa.

KAMINSKY, Stuart M. Essayist. Professor and Head of the Division of Film, Northwestern University, Evanston, Illinois. Author of *Don Siegel, Director*, 1973; *Clint Eastwood*, 1974; *American Film Genres*, 1977; *John Huston: Maker of Magic*, 1978; *Coop: The Life and Legend of Gary Cooper*, 1980; and, with Dana Hodgdon, *Basic Filmmaking*, 1981; editor of *Ingmar Bergman: Essays in Criticism*, 1975. Also, a novelist; works include: *Bullet for a Star*, 1977; *Murder on the Yellow Brick Road*, 1978; *You Bet Your Life*, 1980; *The Howard Hughes Affair*, 1980; *Never Cross a Vampire*, 1980; *Death of a Dissident*, 1981; *High Midnight*, 1981; *Catch a Falling Crown*, 1982; and *He Done Her Wrong*, 1983. **Essays:** The Good, the Bad, and the Ugly; High Noon; Invasion of the Body Snatchers; The Maltese Falcon; Safety Last; The Treasure of the Sierra Madre.

KANOFF, Joel. Essayist. Lecturer in the Visual Arts, Princeton University, New Jersey, since 1983. **Essays:** Ladri di biciclette; Ossessione; I vitelloni.

KAPLAN, E. Ann. Adviser. Teacher of Film and Literature, Rutgers University, New Brunswick, New Jersey. Author of *Women in Film Noir*; *Fritz Lang: A Guide to References and Resources*; *Women in Film: Both Sides of the Camera*; *Regarding Television*; etc.

KATZ, Ephraim. Adviser. Filmmaker, writer and critic. Has written, directed and produced documentary, educational and industrial films. Author of *The Film Encyclopaedia*, 1979.

KEHR, Dave. Adviser and Essayist. Film Critic, *The Reader*, Chicago, since 1974, and *Chicago* magazine, since 1979. **Essays:** Playtime; Shichinin no samurai; Les Vacances de Monsieur Hulot.

KEMP, Philip. Adviser and Essayist. Freelance writer and screenwriter, London. **Essays:** Body Heat; Casque d'Or; Du Rififi chez les hommes; Le Jour se lève; Karol Lir; Kind Hearts and Coronets; Kwaidan; La Ronde; Seppuku; Sommarnattans leende; Souffle au coeur; Thérèse Desqueroux.

KHANNA, Satti. Adviser and Essayist. Research Associate, Center for South and Southeast Asia Studies, University of California, Berkeley, since 1976. Author of *Indian Cinema and Indian Life*, 1980. **Essays:** The Apu Trilogy; Do Bigha Zamin.

KOVÁCS, Katherine Singer. Essayist. Assistant Professor, Department of Comparative Literature, University of Southern California, Los Angeles. Editor, *Humanities in Society*; Member of the Executive Committee, *The Quarterly Review of Film Studies*. Author of *Le Reve et la Vie: A Theatrical Experiment* by Gustave Flaubert, 1981. **Essays:** Muerte de un ciclista; El verdugo.

LEAB, Daniel. Essayist. Film critic and historian, New York City. **Essays:** The Bandwagon; Crossfire; I Am a Fugitive from a Chain Gang.

LEE, Sharon. Essayist. Formerly, Public Information Director, Wisconsin Arts Board, Madison. **Essays:** Chelovek s kino apparatom; La Joli Mai; Kino-pravda.

LIMBACHER, James L. Essayist. Audio-Visual Librarian, Dearborn, Michigan Department of Libraries, 1955-83. National President, American Federation of Film Societies, 1962-65, and Educational Film Library Association, 1966-70; host of the television series *Shadows on the Wall* and *The Screening Room*. Author of *Using Films*, 1967; *Four Aspects of the Film*, 1968; *Film Music: From Violins to Video*, 1974; *Haven't I Seen You Somewhere Before?*, 1979; *Keeping Score*, 1981; *Sexuality in World Cinema*, 1983; and *Feature Films on 8mm, 16mm, and Video*, 7 editions. **Essays:** The Informer; The Ox-Bow Incident.

LOCKHART, Kimball. Essayist. Member of the faculty, Department of Romance Studies, Cornell University, Ithaca, New York. Founding Editor, *Enclitic*, 1977-80. Member, Editorial Board, *Diacritics*, Cornell University, since 1978. **Essay:** Professione: Reporter.

LORENZ, Janet E. Essayist. Contributing Writer, *Magill's Survey of the Cinema*, since 1980, and *SelecTV Programming Guide*, since 1981. Assistant Supervisor, Cinema Library, University of Southern California, Los Angeles, 1979-82. **Essays:** La battaglia di Algeri; The Last Picture Show; Morte a Venezia; The Thin Man.

LOWRY, Ed. Essayist. Assistant Professor of Film Studies, Southern Illinois University, Carbondale, since 1983. Contributor to various film periodicals. **Essays:** Angst essen Seele auf; The Chelsea Girls; Scorpio Rising; The Searchers; The Sweet Smell of Success; White Heat.

MacCANN, Richard Dyer. Adviser and Essayist. Professor of Film, University of Iowa, Iowa City, since 1970. Editor, Cinema Journal, 1967-76. Author of *Hollywood in Transition*, 1962, and *The People's Films: A Political History of U.S. Government Motion Pictures*, 1973; editor of *Film and Society*, 1964; *Film: A Montage of Theories*, 1966; *The New Film Index*, 1975; and *Cinema Examined*, 1982. **Essay:** The City.

MALPEZZI, Frances M. Essayist. Associate Professor of English, Arkansas State Universtiy. Author, with William M. Clements, *Native American Folklore 1879-1979: An Annotated Bibliography*, 1983. **Essay:** Kagemusha.

MANCINI, Elaine. Essayist. Teacher of film at the College of Staten Island, New York, and film history and art history at St. John's University, New York. Author of the forthcoming books, *The Films of Luchino Visconti: A Reference Guide*; *D. W. Griffith at Biograph*; and *The Struggles of the Italian Film Industry During Fascism*. **Essays:** L'albero degli zoccoli; I pugni in tasca; Rocco e i suoi fratelli.

MANVELL, Roger. Essayist. University Professor and Professor of Film, Boston University. Director, British Film Academy, London, 1947-59, and a Governor and Head of the Department of Film History, London Film School, until 1974; Bingham Professor of the Humanities, University of Louisville, 1973. Editor, *Penguin Film Review*, 1946-49, and the Pelican annual *The Cinema*, 1950-52; Associate Editor, *New Humanist*, 1968-75, and Member of the Board of Directors, Rationalist Press, London, since 1966; Editor-in-Chief, *International Encyclopedia of Film*, 1972. Vice-Chairman, National Panel of Film Festivals, British Council, London, 1976-78. Author of *Film*, 1944; *The Animated Film*, 1954; *The Film and the Public*, 1955 *On the Air*, 1955 *The Technique of Film Music*, 1957, 1976; *The Technique of Film Animation*, with John Halas, 1959; *The Living Screen*, 1961; *Design in Motion*, with John Halas, 1962; *What is a Film?*, 1965; *New Cinema in Europe*, 1966; *This Age of Communication*, 1967; *New Cinema in U.S.A.*, 1968; *New Cinema in Britain*, 1969; *Art Movement*, 1970; *The German Cinema*, with Heinrich Fraenkel, 1971; *Shakespeare and the Film*, 1971; *Films and the Second World War*, 1975; *Love Goddesses of the Movies*, 1975; *Theatre and Film*, 1979; *Art and Animation: Halas and Batchelor 1940-1980*, 1980; *Ingmar Bergman*, 1980; also novels, biographies of theatrical personalities and of personalities of the Third Reich. **Essays:** Dr. Mabuse films; Sjunde inseglet; Smultronstället; To Be or Not to Be; Tystnaden; ;You Only Live Once.

MARCHETTI, Gina. Essayist. Researcher in film theory in Paris, on government grant, 1982-83; Instructor, University of North Carolina, Chapel Hill, 1983-84. Editor of *Film Reader 5*, 1982. **Essays:** The Rocky Horror Picture Show; W.R.—Mysterije organizma.

MAST, Gerald. Adviser and Essayist. Professor of English and General Studies in the Humanities, University of Chicago, since 1978. Member of the faculty, Richmond College, New York, 1967-78. Author of *A Short History of the Movies*, 1971, 3rd edition 1981; *The Comic Mind: Comedy and the Movies*, 1974, 1979; *Film/Cinema/Movie: A Theory of Experience*, 1977, 1982; and *Howard Hawks, Storyteller*, 1982; editor, with Marshall Cohen, of *Film Theory and Criticism: Introductory Readings*, 1974, 1979; editor of *The Movies in Our Midst: Documents in the Cultural History of Film in America*, 1982. **Essays:** The Fisherman; The Gold Rush; The Great Dictator; The Kid; Limelight; Red River; Scarface.

McELHANEY, Joe. Essayist. Graduate student, Department of Cinema Studies, New York University. **Essay:** Mean Streets.

MERHAUT, G. Essayist. Film historian. Member of staff, Film Archives of Czechoslovakia, Prague. Author of *Actors and Actresses of the Italian Cinema*. **Essays:** Noz w wodzie, Valahol Europaban.

MERRITT, Russell. Essayist. Professor, University of Wisconsin, Madison. **Essays:** The Birth of a Nation; Broken Blossoms; Intolerance; Way Down East.

MICHAELS, Lloyd. Essayist. Associate Professor of English, Allegheny College, Meadville, Pennsylvania. Editor, *Film Criticism*, since 1977. Author of the forthcoming book *Elia Kazan*. **Essay:** La Dentellière.

MILICIA, Joe. Essayist. Has taught at Colgate University, Stevens Institute, Northwestern University, and the University of Wisconsin at Sheboygan. Author of *The Fiction of H.D.* **Essays:** L'Année dernière à Marienbad; The General.

MONTY, Ib. Adviser and Essayist. Director of Det Danske Filmmuseum, Copenhagen, since 1960. Literary and Film Critic for the newspaper *Morgenavisen Jyllands-Posten*, since 1958. Editor-in-Chief of the film periodical *Kosmorama*, 1960-67; Member, Danish Film Council, 1965-69. Author of *Leonardo da Vinci*, 1953; editor, with Morten Piil, *Se- det er film I-iii* (anthology of articles on film), 1964-66, and *TV-Broadcasts on Films and Filmmakers*, 1972. **Essays:** Der var engang en krig; Gertrud; Häxan; Ordet; La Passion de Jeanne d'Arc; Sult; Vampyr; Vredens dag.

MRAZ, John. Essayist. Coordinator of Graphic History, center for the Historical Study of the Mexican Labor Movement (CEHSMO), since 1982. Lecturer in Film Studies, University of California at Santa Cruz, 1978-79; Video Coordinator, Multi-Ethnic School Environments, National Institute of Education (U.S.), 1980-81; Lecturer in Communications and History, Universidad Nacional Autonoma de Mexico, 1981-82. **Essays:** De cierta manera; La hora de las hornos; Maria Candelaria; Memorias del subdesarollo; La primera carga al machete; Los redes; Retrato de Teresa.

MURPHY, William T. Essayist. Chief, Motion Picture, Sound and Video Branch, National Archives, Washington, D.C., since 1976. Author of *Robert Flaherty: A Guide to References and Resources*, 1978. **Essays:** Louisiana Story; Man of Aran; Moana; Nanook of the North.

NARDUCY, Ray. Essayist. Film critic and historian, Chicago. **Essays:** The Adventures of Robin Hood; The Big Heat; From Here to Eternity; A Hard Day's Night; The Killers; Rosemary's Baby.

NASTAV, Dennis. Essayist. Documentary filmmaker, 1976-79. **Essays:** Lola Montès; Les Parapluies de Cherbourg.

OBALIL, Linda J. Essayist. Assistant (Special Visual Effects Unit), Dreamscape, Bruce Cohn Curtis Productions/Bella Productions, since 1983. Associate Editor, *Film Reader 4*, 1979. **Essays:** A Clockwork Orange; Dr. No; Frankenstein; The Great Train Robbery; Gycklarnas afton; King Kong; Snow White; Steamboat Willie; Le Voyage dans la lune.

O'LEARY, Liam. Adviser and Essayist. Film Viewer, Radio Telefis Eireann, Dublin, since 1966; Director, Liam O'Leary Film Archives, Dublin, since 1976. Producer, Abbey Theatre, Dublin, 1944; Director of the Film History Cycle at the National Film Theatre, London, and Acquisitions Officer, National Film Archive, London, 1953-66. Co-Founder, 1936, and Honorary Secretary, 1936-44, Irish Film Society. Director of the films, *Our Country*, 1948; *Mr. Careless*, 1950; and *Portrait of Dublin*, 1951. Author of *Invitation to the Film*, 1945; *The Silent Cinema*, 1965; *Rex Ingram, A Master of the Silent Cinema*, 1980. **Essays:** À nous la liberté; Brief Encounter; Cabiria; Erotikon; The Four Horsemen of the Apocalypse; Kameradschaft; La Kermesse héroïque; Die Nibelungen; Schatten.

PALMER, R. Barton. Essayist. Associate Professor of English and Adjunct Professor of Theatre, Georgia State University, since 1973. **Essay:** Der letzte Mann.

PĚNA, Richard. Adviser and Essayist. Director, Film Center, Art Institute of Chicago. **Essays:** Como era gostoso o meu frances; Fukushu suru wa ware ni ari.

PHILLIPS, Gene D., S.J. Essayist. Professor of English, Loyola University, Chicago (joined faculty, 1970). Contributing Editor, *Literature/Film Quarterly*, since 1977, and *American Classic Screen*, since 1979. Author of *The Movie Makers: Artists in an Industry*, 1973; *Graham Greene: The Films of His Fiction*, 1974; *Stanley Kubrick: A Film Odyssey*, 1975; *Evelyn Waugh's Officers, Gentlemen, and Rogues*, 1977; *Ken Russell*, 1979; *The Films of Tennessee Williams*, 1980; *Hemingway and Film*, 1980; *John Schlesinger*, 1981; *George Cukor*, 1982. **Essays:** Dr. Strangelove; Giant; Rear Window; 2001: A Space Odyssey.

POAGUE, Leland. Essayist. Associate Professor of English, Iowa State University, Ames (joined faculty, 1978). Author of *The Cinema of Frank Capra: An Approach to Film Comedy*, 1975; *The Cinema of Ernst Lubitsch: The Hollywood Films*, 1978; *The Hollywood Professionals*, volume 7: *Wilder and McCarey*, 1980; *Howard Hawks*, 1982; and, with William Cadbury, *Film Criticism: A Counter Theory*, 1982. **Essays:** Bonnie and Clyde; Chimes at Midnight; Citizen Kane; Psyche; Les Quatre Cents Coups; The Third Man.

POLAN, Dana B. Essayist. Film critic and historian, Pittsburgh. **Essays:** The Cat People; The Nutty Professor.

PORTON, Richard. Essayist. Graduate student in film studies, New York University. **Essays:** Jonas qui aura 25 ans en l'an 2000; La Salamandre.

RABINOVITZ, Lauren. Adviser and Essayist. Assistant Professor, Department of History of Architecture and Art, University of Illinois at Chicago, since 1980. **Essays:** Adam's Rib; Bringing Up Baby; Gertie the Dinosaur; His Girl Friday; It Happened One Night; Meshes of the Afternoon; Nashville; Now Voyager; The Philadelphia Story; Le Retour à la raison.

RACHEVA, Maria. Adviser and Essayist. Selector of films for the International Film Festival, Munich, since 1983. Teacher of Film History, High School for Cinema, Sofia, Bulgaria, 1974-81; Editor of the cultural review *Westermanns Monatshefte*, Munich, 1981-82. Author of *Presentday Bulgarian Cinema*, 1970; *Nowa fala i nowa powiesc*, 1974; *Der bulgarische Film*, with Klaus Eder, 1977; *Andrzej Wajda*, with Klaus Eder, 1980; *Neostariavashti filmi*, 1981. **Essays:** Der amerikanische Freund; Czlowiek z marmuru; Jeder für sich und Gott gegen alle; Matka Joanna od aniolow.

REYNOLDS, Herbert. Essayist. Historian and Project Co-ordinator, Museum of Modern Art Department of Art, New York City, since 1981; Consultant, American Federation of Arts Film Program, since 1982. Member, Curatorial Staff of Film Archive, George Eastman House, Rochester, New York, 1976-81. **Essay:** Mephisto.

ROBSON, Arthur G. Essayist. Professor and Chairman, Department of Classics, and Professor of Comparative Literature, Beloit College, Wisconsin, since 1966. Editor of *Latin: Our Living Heritage, Book III*, 1964; author of *Euripides'"Electra": An Interpretive Commentary*, 1983; and author, with Rodney Farnsworth, of *Alexandre Alexeieff and Claire Parker: The Artistry of Animation* (forthcoming). **Essay:** Une Nuit sur le mont chauve.

RUBINSTEIN, E. Essayist. Coordinator of the Program in Cinema Studies, College of Staten Island, City University of New York (joined faculty, 1968). Author of *Filmguide to "The General"*, 1973. **Essays:** Shanghai Express; She Done Him Wrong.

SAELI, Marie. Essayist. Tutor in Developmental Education, Triton College, River Grove, Illinois, since 1982. **Essays:** Aleksandr Nevskii; Oktiabr; Triumph des Willens.

SALVAGE, Barbara. Essayist. Researcher, Circulating Film Catalogue Project, Museum of Modern Art, New York City, since 1982. **Essays:** Die Büchse der Pandora; Stachka.

SCHADE, W. Curtis. Essayist. Associate Director of Admissions, Beloit College, Wisconsin, since 1980. **Essay:** La Noire de....

SEITER, Ellen E. Essayist. Assistant Professor, Telecommunications and Film Studies, University of Oregon, Eugene, since 1981. Contributor to various film journals. **Essay:** Saturday Night and Sunday Morning.

SELIG, Michael. Essayist. Assistant Professor, University of Vermont, since 1983. Contributor to *Film Reader*, *Jump-Cut*, and *Journal of Popular Film and Television*. **Essay:** Salt of the Earth.

SHOCHAT, Ella. Essayist. Doctoral student, Department of Cinema Studies, New York University. **Essay:** Xala.

SILET, Charles L.P. Essayist. Associate Professor of English, Iowa State University, Ames, since 1979. Co-author of *The Literary Manuscripts of Upton Sinclair*, 1972; author of *Hamlin Garland and Henry Blake Fuller: A Reference Guide*, 1977; *Lindsay Anderson: A Guide to References and Resources*, 1979; and *Paul Rosenfeld: An Annotated Bibliography*, 1981; co-editor of *The Worlds Between Two Rivers: Perspectives on American Indians in Iowa*, 1978; and *The Pretend Indians: Images of the Native Americans in the Movies*, 1980. **Essays:** Csillagosok, katonák; Paisà; Une Partie de campagne; Le Procès; Walkabout.

SIMMON, Scott. Essayist. Film Programmer, Mary Pickford Theatre, Library of Congress, Washington, D.C., since 1983. Contributor to *Film Comment*, *Journal of Popular Film and Television*, and *Literature/Film Quarterly*. **Essays:** Hallelujah; Vertigo.

SITNEY, P. Adams. Adviser and Essayist. Director of Library and Publications at Anthology Film Archives; teacher at Princeton University, New Jersey. Author of *Film Culture Reader*; *Essential Cinema*; *The Avant-Garde Film*; *Visionary Film*; etc. **Essays:** Amor de perdicão; Anemic Cinema; Il deserto rosso; Dog Star Man; La dolce vita; L'eclises; Etoile de mer; Heaven and Earth Magic; Las hurdes; Menilmontant; La notte; Persona; Uccellacci e uccellini; Wavelength.

SLADE, Tony. Essayist. Senior Lecturer in English, University of Adelaide, South Australia, since 1966. Joint Editor, *Southern Review* (Australia), 1967-68; Member of the Council, Adelaide Film Festival, 1976-77. Author of *D.H. Lawrence*,

1969. **Essays:** Chinatown; Strangers on a Train.

SLIDE, Anthony. Adviser and Essayist. Freelance writer. Associate Film Archivist, American Film Institute, 1972-75; Resident Film Historian, Academy of Motion Picture Arts and Sciences, 1975-80. Author of *Early American Cinema*, 1970; *The Griffith Actresses*, 1973; *the Films of D.W. Griffith*, with Edward Wagenknecht, 1975; *The Idols of Silence*, 1976; *The Big V: A History of the Vitagraph Company*, 1976; *Early Women Directors*, 1977; *Aspects of American Film History Prior to 1920*, 1978; *Films on Film History*, 1979; *The Kindergarten of the Movies: A History of the Fine Arts Company*, 1980; *Fifty Great American Silent Films 1912-1920*, with Edward Wagenknecht, 1980; *The Vaudevillians*, 1981; and *Great Radio Personalities*, 1982; editor of the five-volume series, *Selected Film Criticism 1896-1950*. **Essays:** All Quiet on the Western Front; Civilization; In Which We Serve; The Jazz Singer; The Old Dark House; The Phantom of the Opera; The Private Life of Henry VIII; 7th Heaven.

SMALL, Edward S. Essayist. Associate Professor of Radio-TV-Film since 1979, and Chairman of the Interdisciplinary Program in Film Studies since 1983, University of Missouri, Columbia (joined faculty, 1972). Associate Editor, *Journal of the University Film and Video Association*. **Essay:** Le Ballet mécanique.

SMOODIN, Eric. Essayist. Doctoral candidate, film studies, University of California at Los Angeles. Contributor to *Film Studies Annual* and *Journal of the University Film and Video Association*. **Essays:** Double Indemnity; The Iron Horse; Sherlock Junior; Sunset Boulevard; Yankee Doodle Dandy.

SNYDER, Thomas. Freelance writer, Chicago. Reviewer for *Video Movie Magazine*, Chicago. **Essays:** Close Encounters of the Third Kind; Raiders of the Lost Ark; Star Wars Trilogy.

STARR, Cecile. Adviser and Essayist. Freelance writer, lecturer, and filmmaker. Film Reviewer, *The Saturday Review*, New York, 1949-59. Author of *Discovering the Movies*, 1972, and, with Robert Russett, *Experimental Animation*, 1976. **Essays:** The Adventures of Prince Achmed; The Land; Song of Ceylon.

THOMPSON, Frank. Essayist. Member of staff, Films Inc., Atlanta, since 1981. Co-Founder and formerly Editor, *Motif* magazine. Author of *William A. Wellman*, 1983. **Essay:** Christopher Strong.

THORPE, Frances. Adviser. Librarian, British Film Institute, London. Formerly, Editor, *International Index to Film Periodicals*.

TOMLINSON, Doug. Essayist. Assistant Professor of Film Studies, Montclair State College, and Lecturer, Princeton University, New Jersey, since 1983. Lecturer, New York University, 1979-82. Principal Researcher for *Voices of Film Experience*, edited by Jay Leyda, 1977. **Essays:** American Graffiti; Annie Hall; The Big Sleep; Un Condamne à mort s'est échappé; Entr'acte; Gimme Shelter; Manhattan; Modern Times; Rebel Without a Cause; Room at the Top; Some Like It Hot; Written on the Wind.

TSIANTIS, Lee. Essayist. Member of staff, Films Inc., Atlanta. Taught film at the University of South Carolina,

1976-78; Research Assistant, PBS series *Cinematic Eye*, 1977-78. **Essay:** Der Student von Prag.

TUDOR, Andrew. Essayist. Sociologist: has lectured on sociology at the University of York. Contributor to various film journals. Author of *Theories of Film*. **Essays:** L'avventura; Peeping Tom.

URGOŠIKOVÁ, Mrs. B. Essayist. Film Historian, Czechoslovakian Film Archives, Prague. Author of *History of Science Fiction Films*. **Essays:** Alphaville; Eroica; Kanal; Lásky jedné plavovlásky; Metropolis; Obchod na korze; Ostře sledované vlaky; Popiól i diament; Staré pověsti české; Things to Come.

WELSH, James M. Essayist. Teacher at Salisbury State College, Maryland; Arts Editor and Reviewer, television station WBOC; Co-Editor, *Literature/Film Quarterly*. Co-author of *His Majesty the American: The Cinema of Douglas Fairbanks Sr.*, 1977, and *Abel Gance*, 1978. **Essay:** Fantasia.

WEST, Dennis. Essayist. Associate Professor, University of Idaho, Moscow, since 1981. Director, Indiana University Film Studies Program, 1976-77. Contributor on Latin American and Spanish cinema to such journals as *Latin American Research Review*, *Cineaste*, *New Scholar*, etc. **Essays:** Antônio das Mortes; La batalla de Chile; El espiritu de la colmina; Os fuzis; El otro Francisco; La tierra prometida; Yawar mallku.

WHITE, M.B. Essayist. Assistant Professor, Department of Radio-TV-Film, Northwestern University, Evanston, Illinois, since 1982. Contributor to *Enclitic*, *Purdue Film Studies Annual*, etc. **Essays:** À bout de souffle; Aguirre, der Zorn Gottes; Das Cabinet des Dr. Caligari; Un Chien andalou; Chronik der Anna Magdalena Bach; Hiroshima mon Amour; Pirosmani; Zéro de conduite.

WINNING, Robert. Essayist. Doctoral candidate in speech, Northwestern University, Evanston, Illinois. **Essays:** Dr. Jekyll and Mr. Hyde; The Wizard of Oz.

WOOD, Robin. Adviser and Essayist. Professor of Film Study, Department of Fine Arts, Atkinson College, York University, Toronto, since 1977. Member of the film studies department, Queen's University, Kingston, Ontario, 1969-72, and University of Warwick, Coventry, England, 1973-77. Author of *Hitchcock's Films*, 1965; *Howard Hawks*, 1967; *Arthur Penn*, 1968; *Ingmar Bergman*, 1969; *Antonioni*, with Ian Cameron, 1970; *Claude Chabrol*, with Michael Walker, 1971; *Apu Trilogy of Satyajit Ray*, 1971; *Personal Views: Explorations in Film*, 1976; *The American Nightmare: Essays on the Horror Film*, with Richard Lippe, Andrew Britton and Tony Williams, 1979. **Essays:** L'Atalante; Boudu sauve des Eaux; Le Charme discrèt de la bourgeoisie; Il conformista; Days of Heaven; E.T.—The Extraterrestrial; La Grande Illusion; Ikiru; Meet Me in St. Louis; Naniwa creji; Nosferatu; Nuit et brouillard; Rashomon; La Régle du Jeu; Rio Bravo; Le Sang des bêtes; Sansho dayu; The Scarlet Empress; She Wore a Yellow Ribbon; Tabu; Taxi Driver; To Have and Have Not; Tout va bien; Ugetsu monogatari; Weekend.